1 MONTH OF
FREE
READING

at

www.ForgottenBooks.com

By purchasing this book you are eligible for one month membership to ForgottenBooks.com, giving you unlimited access to our entire collection of over 1,000,000 titles via our web site and mobile apps.

To claim your free month visit: www.forgottenbooks.com/free728308

ISBN 978-0-266-70825-4
PIBN 10728308

Scanned from the collections of
The Library of Congress

Packard Campus
for Audio Visual Conservation
www.loc.gov/avconservation

otion Picture and Television Reading Room
www.loc.gov/rr/mopic

Recorded Sound Reference Center
www.loc.gov/rr/record

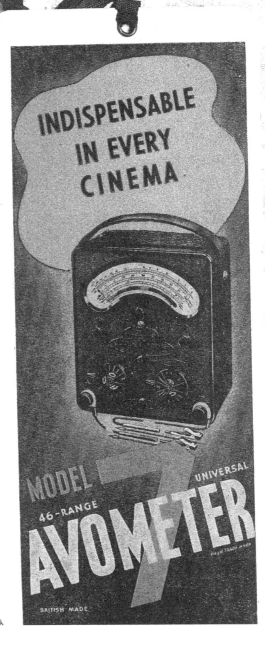

A

Premier Cinematograph Apparatus is used in all the Best Cinemas

KINEMATOGRAPH
YEAR BOOK
1 9 3 7

TWENTY-FOURTH YEAR

LONDON
KINEMATOGRAPH PUBLICATIONS LTD.
93 Long Acre W.C.2

Telephone . . . Temple Bar 2468
(60 lines)
Telegraphic Address . Southernwood, Rand,
London

CONTENTS

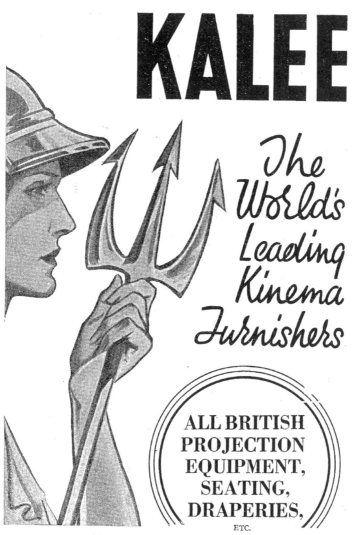

TAKING STOCK
FOR THE TRADE OF 1937.

By S. G. RAYMENT,

Editor of *The Kinematograph Weekly.*

A T the close of an eventful and even exciting year like 1936 there is a natural tendency to anticipate a comparatively peaceful period in which we can consolidate our victories or lick our wounds, as the case may be. But this time, whether the dawning year brings good or evil to the trade, it certainly shows few signs of that placid calm which might be welcomed in less volatile spheres, and the outlook, although bright, is very far from cloudless.

While I believe in keeping in close contact with the definite and material developments of the business, I know only too well that the great underlying movements—dismissed by some as mere politics—are eventually to dominate our well-being. And that is why I am anxious to make it clear that the report of Lord Moyne's Committee—and all that report stands for—is at the time of writing the supreme question. There is little of the heart-burning which preceded the passing of the 1927 Act ; in those days we were embarking on a voyage to an objective that was well understood, but by a course which was only problematically safe. Now, after nine years' experience of an enactment which, in the main, has justified itself, we have to consider the next step—a scientifically and commercially sound policy capable of encouraging, co-ordinating and controlling the complex organisms which, properly amalgamated, represent the film industry.

I do not need to emphasise that the first aim of this legislation—either past or to come—is to ensure a reasonable opportunity for British production. The statesman knows its value at last—abroad they have always understood what it meant as national propaganda in the widest sense—and we are vitally concerned in high politics and business life alike to ensure an adequate quantity and quality of British films.

H OW has this worked out in the past few months ? I am afraid it would take a super patriot to feel satisfied. We have produced 220 pictures, but the percentage of these that are able to stand comparison with the average of Hollywood is not flattering to our studios. We are still in the stage when we can make reasonably successful commercial films, and extremely fine prestige pictures. But where are those good enough to inspire the intelligent patron and ensure at the same time the support of the mass ? There is something still to be learnt in our studios, and until we master the secret Hollywood will have little to fear.

That we have tried is certain. Following upon our intensive studio-building campaign with enormous new centres at Denham, Iver, and Elstree, and great developments at Shepperton and Teddington, we have been spending out lavishly upon acting and directorial talent with a considerable increase in the technical branches which are rendered necessary. By the time all the new floors are in operation I estimate we ought to be turning out films at the rate of nearly one a day if our resources are to be kept fully occupied.

ASSUMING all these pictures are made we should be well on the way to such an output as would make the 50 per cent. quota of British pictures—a suggestion which raised many smiles when it was made—by no means impossible of achievement. To make anything like a success on such a scale, however, we have to imagine one or two more assets than we are able to count on to-day.

I have always held that our greatest lack is personnel. Stars, directors, cameramen, artists, writers, all these can be secured if we have the money—and although at the time of writing there is an outcry about the market for finance I do not believe genuine businesslike prospects will fail to find financial backing. What money cannot buy is the higher direction ; the big organising and co-ordinating brain which America has evolved but we have not.

A peculiar assembly of qualities in one man—vision, courage, power, probity, infinite patience, fierce drive, commercial shrewdness, artistic perception and sensitiveness, with a flair for showmanship over all—it is not difficult to tabulate the list of needed virtues—men with these qualifications are not to be sought for, they have to occur. But such geniuses will arise, and when they do we are going to see that move in British production we have all been waiting for. Until they do we must go on doing our best. Nobody but a flatterer will pretend that our best is good enough—yet. The hour has not produced the man.

I SHOULD be sorry to be classed with those who cry out for quality in British pictures as though this were all that mattered. If we achieved quality—of the kind indicated by many of our mentors—we should achieve suicide. Of all bad guides the intellectual snob is the worst, and we must never forget that our job is to provide entertainment by the masses for the masses. Our origins and our destiny are democratic and we have in our time suffered enough disservice at the hands of the highbrows.

There is no need to play down to the unintelligent, all we have to do is to avoid treating the millions with contempt, and leaving their entertainment to others who have a better conception of their opportunities. To give the most helpful encouragement to the coming British film, critics will have to remind themselves that the West End is not England.

If the path before the production end of the business is not exactly clear-cut, we can at least see the theatre interests in a fairly obvious course. Not too satisfactory, I am afraid, for the smaller man, but if we take the kinema owners as a class they have a record of prosperity that says much for their business abilities, as well as for the quality of the goods they have had to offer and the growth —natural and induced—of the picturegoing habit.

NOTHING in the story of the exhibitor's year is as important as the question of redundancy. Imagine the shock of a man who has spent years in building up a comfortable little clientele for his modest hall when he sees a big, smart, up-to-date house in course of erection. Of course he feels his territory is being invaded, and, knowing that it has never been more than enough for one he very naturally complains of redundancy to his C.E.A. branch and to his local authority.

Very often he is justified, but there are plenty of examples which show the intruder has a case too. His point of view is that there is more business to be done than is being done, and he is prepared to back his opinion by investing in the construction of a new hall. Of course, the place he puts up will be of the very latest design, and if he is associated with one of the circuits he is all the better able to secure product.

A PARTICULARLY unhappy position for the older established business, and it is small wonder that we hear demands for assistance. Such calls have come from all over the country during the past year or more, and many efforts have been made to help. But if there is a way out it has certainly not been discovered yet. Local authorities have obviously no excuse for banning a proposed new venture because it will be in competition with an old one. Quite opposite is their attitude as a rule, for they can see more rates and more local employment, both in building and in running the new show. In fact, although members of the trade have asked for it, any municipal action in the direction of limiting new activities would undoubtedly be strongly resisted. The only possible parallel that will stand intelligent comparison is the licensed victuallers' trade, where of course, there is direct and rigid restriction. People who call for legislative control of the redundancy position will have to think very carefully before they embark upon a policy which must, if it is to be effective, regulate competition to such an extent that new schemes will be extremely rare. We have plenty of difficulties in our path already, without adding those attached to monopoly values and vested interests. All our sympathies are with the small independent owner, but the whole trend of the businesslike minds of to-day is in favour of the big battalions.

British production itself has hardly swept ahead with the force that some of its most eager advocates had predicted. There has been quite a decent harvest it is true, but the trade has an uncomfortable feeling at the moment that business re-organisation of several of the companies must be a necessary prelude to a really practical and commercially sound advance. There is a feeling that the low rates of interest which have been ruling for so long in the City have led to an unduly easy influx of money into film production, which is at the best more speculative than most investment channels. If a rather strict supervision of expenditure in this direction comes it will be by no means to the disadvantage of the Industry in the long run. In fact, though unpleasant a purge is likely to prove extremely salutary.

We have still to face that eternal riddle—to square the circle and to make art and business run side by side. We shall never solve it, but we can confidently look forward to a practical compromise.

ONE of the chief difficulties which have always hampered quota suggestions has been the quality of the British pictures offered for public entertainment. This is what has aroused the spirit of the independent man, who knew that an opposition circuit house had the first claim on the best of the available output. Ideas in plenty have been put forward which would give the Government department charged with the drafting of a Bill something to go upon. One was the appointing of a committee which could say that such and such a film was or was not of a high enough quality to be given a quota ticket. The constitution of such a committee was not easy to envisage, but one proposal was to make it a responsibility of the British Board of Film Censors, who should be in a position to say whether a given picture was a serious attempt to satisfy the entertainment demands of an exhibitor, or was merely a get-out for the distributor, who was obliged to carry on his books a certain percentage of British production.

Another proposal was that every non-British picture should pay a tax of so much a reel for every exhibition, thus enabling the showman to run as big a proportion of foreign pictures as he liked, knowing that he could afford to pay this tax if he preferred to book good attractive films and thereby assured himself of popular support.

A CORRESPONDING suggestion, but working in the opposite direction, was that there should be a new line drawn by which British pictures should not count for quota unless the renters had successfully booked them to a certain figure. This would mean that the worthless films, made only to be nominal concessions to the law and doomed from the first to be relegated to the shelves of the renter, would no longer suffice to keep him clear of his legal obligations. Their value as practicable propositions was therefore to be estimated according to their power to justify themselves in the market.

The establishment of an entirely separate board, the sole function of which would be to adjudicate on the quality of British pictures, is also a proposal to be dealt with ; as to this I believe there is a certain sympathy in legislative circles, but I am confident the feeling in the trade would be definitely hostile. We have little faith in the understanding of such a body, however sympathetic it may be. " Better the devil we know than the devil we don't know" is the feeling of people in the trade, and, after all, they are the men whose profession it is to interpret public tastes. By putting the onus upon a body of laymen of deciding whether a given production was worthy or otherwise, we might, it is true, ensure an unbiased verdict, but one may well doubt whether this would outweigh the disadvantages—the unpractical and possibly unsympathetic reading of public reactions, as well as the failure to appreciate that what is meat in the West End of London might be poison in industrial Lancashire or Glasgow, and *vice versa*.

MANY other important questions are in the air as the year closes. One of the most interesting is the future of the Gaumont-British Corporation. A suggestion was made that the important American firms of Twentieth Century-Fox and Metro-Goldwyn-Mayer should secure controlling interest, and this aroused a great deal of excitement in the country. There is an undertaking that control should not pass out of British hands, but some arrange-ment was imperative on financial grounds, and the Ostrer brothers spent at least half the year in seeking a way out.

At one period it was stated that John Maxwell, head of the great British International Pictures and Associated British Cinemas organisation, had acquired predominating interest in Gaumont-British, but the transfer of the voting shares was dependent upon the acquiescence of the American holders, and this was not vouch-safed. Isidore and Maurice Ostrer spent several weeks in the States at the end of the year, interviewing Sidney R. Kent, J. M. Schenck and Nicholas Schenck, but no way out of the deadlock was found. The matter obviously cannot be allowed to rest where it is, because the financial position of G.-B. as discussed by the share-holders at the last general meeting, demands active overhaul.

Meantime John Maxwell is on the G.-B. board and attention is focused upon his influence. His standing in financial circles in the City is very high, and even at the shareholders' meeting, when he had only just been made a director, there was an obvious respect paid to his ability although he had to point out that he could have had no opportunity of action by that time.

ANOTHER task that the trade as a whole has failed to tackle is the establishment of a scientifically organised information bureau. In many trades far less complex than ours, data have been collected, and a library of all ascertainable facts have been codified, but although a certain fund of information exists at the head offices of the C.E.A. and the K.R.S., there is still need for something conceived on wider lines, accessible whenever the occasion demands.

Members of the trade themselves are greatly to blame for this ; when the successful effort was made a couple of years ago to secure a reduction of the Entertainment Tax on the cheaper seats, endeavour to tabulate returns on which to base the appeal had to overcome passive resistance in places where it ought to have met with enthusiastic co-operation. This, I suppose is largely a matter of psychology, for members of this Industry are individualists to a man—it is part of the mental make-up of a showman—and any idea of communal action on a wide front is foreign to their nature.

Colour, too, is still coming, and some extremely effective work has been seen during the year. It would be wrong, however, to say it has arrived. What we have seen entitles us to say it *can* arrive, and the public is having tastes whetted ; that it has shown a quick reaction only a colour-optimist would claim.

A change of outlook, however, will have to be effected somehow ; sooner or later the realisation that the whole body is greater than any of its parts will come to us. When it does we shall be more qualified to take that position which our destiny clearly decrees for the greatest power in the world of public relations.

WE are at the beginning of a new era in another field, that of television. What this has before it in the widest sense we have still to discover. Technically it has proved itself as a practicable form of entertainment ; we already knew that it would open new possibilities in the direction of discriminating living records of scenes enacted at a distance, but now we have seen it in practical operation in an important London kinema. At the Dominion, Tottenham Court Road, a regular and systematic show is given on the screen ; it remains to be seen in what direction this will grow. Kinema men are alive to it, and I believe about ten halls are already equipped, so that advantage can be taken of whatever public favour it may meet.

It is only by scanning over the events of 1936 with an eye to their effects upon 1937 that we realise the very wonderful and exciting conditions in which the trade—and art—of kinematography is being carried on. It is the story of movement, and that we are still moving is heartening and reassuring to every man in the Industry.

EVENTS OF THE YEAR.

JANUARY.

Sir Connop Guthrie honoured with baronetcy.

New Era National Pictures, Ltd., winding-up.

Ben Goetz arrives to survey possibilities of M-G-M British Production.

Clarence Elder appointed B.I.P. studio director.

Confusion has arisen in Largs over interpretation of Ribbon Development Act.

Theatre Royal, Sheffield, gutted by fire.

Odeon Circuit, Bernstein Theatres and Union Cinemas lead building boom. Capital investment involved estimated at £4,600,000.

Statistics reveal only 4 per cent. increase in British Production during 1935.

Wider distribution of B.I.P. product in America announced by Arthur Dent.

New Standard Contract draft submitted to C.E.A. delegates.

Guild of Projectionists is to institute scheme for educaton and certification of projectionists.

Oscar Deutsch announces tie-up with United Artists Corp.

£3,677,440 fresh capital attributed to kinema Industry during 1935. 338 new companies were formed.

Standard Capital Corp., relinquish option to acquire Universal Pictures Corp.

William McGaw resigns joint general managership of A.B.C.

Worton Hall Studios acquired by new company, Worton Hall Studios, Ltd.

C. E. A. General Council discusses television.

Alhambra, Carlisle, gutted by fire.

Sheffield C.E.A. criticise Standard Contract draft.

Record attendance at Sheffield C.E.A. Dinner.

B.B.C. film unit formed as first step towards establishment of a Television Service.

Francis L. Harley appointed managing director, 20th Century-Fox.

OBITUARY : J. V. Bryson ; L. A. Glasspoole, Sheffield ; A. W. Haggar, Pembroke ; S. Johnston, Rotherham ; G. Livesley, Harrogate; Miss P. Beresford, Norfolk; S. L. Rothafel.

OPENINGS : Ritz, Harringay, (A.B.C.) ; Tower, Lee-on-Solent (Lee Tower Kinema Co.) ; Carlton, Edinburgh (A. Ellis, Dr. Melville, and R. M'Laughlin) ; St. Stephen's Green Kinema, Dublin ; Royal, Bray, I.F.S. ; Royal, Limerick

(Irish Cinemas, Ltd.) ; Magnet, Cavan, I.F.S. (A. W. Gordon) ; Dorchester, Hull (Associated Hull Cinemas, Ltd.) ; State, Dartford (Medway Cinemas, Ltd.) ; New Palace, Conway (H. Christmas Jones) ; Lyric, Heaton (John Thompson and MacHarg circuit) ; Mayfair, Manchester (Essrow Cinemas, Ltd.) ; Dominion, Harrow (Dominion (Harrow), Ltd) ; Langham, Pinner (Pinner Cinema Co., Ltd.) ; Bijou, Bournemouth (R. E. Bath) ; Ritz, Maidenhead (Oxford and Berkshire Cinema Co.) ; Havana, Romford (New Victory Super Cinema Co. (Romford), Ltd.) ; Mayfair, Brick Lane, E. (D. J. James circuit).

TRANSFERS : Hippodrome, Hull, Ard Junction Kinema, Grand, Normanton, to Harry Buxton ; Princes Super, Wallgate, to George Wilson Bell ; Victoria, Kettering, to Oscar Deutsch ; Picture House, Pavilion, and Palace kinemas, Rawtenstall, to Rawtenstall Cinemas, Ltd. ; Palace, Bawtry, to John W. Simpkin ; Theatre Royal, Churchgate, Bolton, to Bolton Theatre and Entertainments Co., Ltd. ; Theatre Royal, Oldham, to Frank E. Spring ; A. H. Reed circuit to Union Cinemas Ltd ; Scala Picture House, Bath, to Harris Kinemas, Ltd. ; Princess, Millfield, Peterborough, to Oscar Deutsch ; Alexandra, Pontefract, to Pontefract Cinemas, Ltd ; Empire, Carmarthen to Capitol Cinema Co. ; Regal, Attercliffe, Sheffield, to J. F. Emery circuit ; Lido, Islington, Avenue and Walpole Kinemas, Ealing, to Oscar Deutsch ; Empire, Gateshead, and Grand, Byker, Newcastle, to E. J. Hinge ; Prince of Wales, Liverpool, to Stanley Grimshaw.

FEBRUARY.

London exhibitors are perturbed by the L.C.C.'s endeavours to restrict use of coloured neon lighting for publicity purposes.

Sussex C.E.A. protests against General Council's attitude in connection with Excise demands.

Manchester C.E.A. supports Standard Contract.

The "electron multiplier," the invention of Dr. V. K. Zworykin, R.C.A. research scientist, promises to revolutionise sound film reproduction.

Arthur Clavering resigns joint managing directorship of Twickenham Film Distributors.

£400,000 damage caused by fire at B.I.P., and B. and D. Elstree Studios.

A.B.P.C. £1,000,000 issue.

Oldbury states its case for S.O.

The Redundancy Fight has invaded London where Stoke Newington exhibitors are making strong opposition against a new A.B.C. theatre.

Featurettes, Ltd., reply to C.E.A. recommendation to members to restrict their booking of "Specials" to regular newsreel companies.

British film quality criticised by C.E.A. Northern Branch.

N. Western C.E.A: demands card vote on film rentals

Rugby loses S.O. battle.

Free Public House film shows cause anxiety in South Yorkshire and North Derbyshire.

R. Sutton Dawes appointed director of 20th Century-Fox in Great Britain.

Western Electric announces important concessions, including free repairs and replacements, to users of W.E. equipment.

Bradford electricity breakdown causes losses of over £2,500 to exhibitors.

A " black list " of kinemas has been drawn up by the Lanark County Council.

Draft Contract and Rules delay criticised at Scots C.E.A. meeting.

M. Lumière honoured by British film Trade.

Home Office demands report on kinema fires.

OBITUARY : A. L. Ward, Manchester ; W. Engelke, Cinema Traders Ltd ; F. Downey, South Shields ; J. Lynn, Willington, Co. Durham ; H. Taylor, Sheffield; A. E. Claughton Horsforth ; J. Walls, Edinburgh.

OPENINGS : Vogue, Rutherglen (Vogue Cinemas, Ltd.) ; Embassy, Glasgow (Harry Winocour) ; Odeon, Rickmansworth (Oscar Deutsch) ; Argosy, Sheerness (East Kent Cinemas, Ltd.) ; Ritz, Huddersfield (Union Cinemas, Ltd.) ; Rio, Edinburgh (Mrs. M. E. Broadhurst) ; Ritz, Ayr, (Newton-on-Ayr Picture House, Ltd.) ; Regal, Ormskirk (Regal (Ormskirk) Ltd.) ; Paramount, Tottenham Court Road, W.C. (Paramount Theatres, Ltd.) ; Arts Theatre, Cambridge (J Maynard Keynes) ; Ambassador, Slough (London and Southern Super Cinemas) ; Odeon, Newton Abbot (Oscar Deutsch) ; Regal, Coatbridge (A.B.C.).

TRANSFERS : Queen's, Stonehaven, to J. F. Donald (Aberdeen Cinemas), Ltd. ; Theatre de Luxe, Halifax, to Harry Buxton ; Pavilion, Wombwell, to Wombwell Entertainments, Ltd. ; Regent, Harpenden, to J. C. Southgate ; Pavilion Matlock, to Matlock Cinema Co., Ltd. ; Seacombe Hippodrome, Wallasey, to Miles Jervis ; Dominion, Southall, Savoy, St. Helens, and Reo, Fazakerley, Liverpool, to A.B.C. ; Scala, Liverpool, to Coun. A. Levy ; Electra, Nottingham, to Tom Wright ; Empire, Windsor, to Enterprises (Windsor), Ltd. ; Mancunian circuit to Union Cinemas, Ltd.

MARCH.

Radio Pictures to distribute Walt Disney product.

Sussex C.E.A. excise demands successful.

C.E.A. annual report issued.

S.O. defeated at Mansfield.

J. H. Iles announces building of £500,000 Rock studios at Elstree.

Brighton S.O. tax protest fails.

Lord Monsell guest of honour at C.E.A. annual dinner.

Rental penalties rejected by C.E.A. general meeting.

" Objectionable films," subject of question in the House.

Oldbury S.O. refused.

KINE inquiry reveals that colour films are to play an important part in film entertainment.

C. M. Woolf's group tie-up with Universal Pictures Corp.

Technicolor, Ltd., acquires Great West Road site for £250,000 colour film laboratory.

Serious studio blaze holds up production at Denham studios.

Carl Laemmle retires from Universal Pictures Corpn.

C.E.A. General Council warns exhibitors on violation of the Quota Act.

Hastings surfeit protest fails.

Gaumont-British rejoins the Kinematograph Renters' Society.

A number of London and Home Counties exhibitors met to consider possibilities of purchasing kinema accessories on a co-operative basis.

A company is being formed for the purpose of producing a news magazine in colour.

G.C.F. Corporation Ltd., registered to acquire 90 per cent. of issued share capital of General Film Distributors, Ltd.

British Paramount News celebrates fifth anniversary.

OBITUARY : Michael Lauer, Carlisle ; John Pennycook, Dundee ; Major Gerald Jacques, secretary, W.E. ; D. A. Strickland, St. Helens ; H. V. Gully, Bristol ; J. G. M'Callum, Edinburgh ; Alec. J. Braid, Gaumont-British Distributors, Ltd. ; Herman Fellner, Gaumont-British.

OPENINGS : Playhouse, Dundee, (George Green, Ltd.) ; Savoy, Croydon (A.B.C.) ; Odeon, Faversham (Oscar Deutsch) ; Regal, Hackney (A.B.C.) ; Odeon, Corby (Oscar Deutsch) ; Embassy, Maldon (Shipman and King circuit) ; Savoy, Reading (Savoy (Reading), Ltd.).

TRANSFERS : Dominion, Harrow, and His Majesty's Theatre, Grand Theatre, Imperial Picture House, and Palace Picture House, Walsall, to A.B.C. ; Clock Tower Kinema, Wandsworth, to Bernstein Theatres ; Trocadero, and Forum kinemas, Southport, to Coliseum (Southport), Ltd. ; Empire and Hippodrome kinemas, Chorley, to Arthur Hall ; Electric, Chirk, to W. K. Jones ; Palace, Buckley, to T. Jarvis; Deansgate Picture House, Manchester, to S. Halpern and H. King.

APRIL.

MG-M announces British production plans.

Government film, "One Family" loses £13,000.

N.A.T.E. to press for continuance of, but drastic amendments to, the Quota Act.

S. F. Doyle, Australia, talks to British producers concerning the films Dominion audiences desire.

Films Act Committee, under the chairmanship of Lord Moyne, formed to investigate position of British films.

Portsmouth C.E.A. to fight against redundancy.

Better summer film releases advocated by executive committee of L. & H. C. Branch,C.E.A.

Notts and Derby C.E.A. attack card vote system.

Ormiston shield, for largest relative contribution to S.C.T.B.F., presented to Louis Dickson, Bo'ness.

Hagen deal with P.D.C. completed.

Selo win KINE. Football Cup at Wealdstone.

Middlesex C.C. refuses Good Friday opening.

N. Ireland Government decides to take no action as regards the extension of film censorship.

Belfast building embargo declared illegal.

B.P. Fineman appointed a joint producer for Capitol Films.

Abrahams to form new Scottish circuit.

Aldgate Trustees, Ltd., financing British pictures.

T. Ormiston takes part in radio debate " Does the Public Get the Films it Wants ? "

Price cutting criticised at Sussex C.E.A.

R. C. Bromhead, F.C.A., appointed chairman of County Cinemas, Ltd.

Independent Film Distributors, Ltd., formed.

J. U. Finney, of Banbridge, protests against N. Ireland revaluation.

Major C. H. Bell's investigations in the U.S.A. prove that Britain leads in television.

E. D. Leishman's resignation as chairman of Radio Pictures and chairman and managing director of Radio Pictures International, Ltd.

General Council of the C.E.A., reject standard contract.

Expansion of Korda group proposed.

Detailed questionnaire for Quota evidence to be issued to each member of L. & H. C. branch.

E. Turnbull forms £4,000,000 group to market British films in the Dominions.

Leeds, Scotland, Leicester, S. Wales and Sheffield branches submit proposals for revision of Quota Act.

Portsmouth Town Council ignores surfeit protest.

W. B. Levy appointed U.K. and Continent representative for Walt Disney.

Majestic, Wembley, win Donada shield.

Two new stereoscopy processes discovered.

Receiver appointed for City Films.

County Cinemas' flotation withdrawn.

G.-B. interim dividend postponed.

Paragon Productions, Ltd., in liquidation.

OBITUARY : W. C. Fletcher, Sheffield ; Eric Skillman ; J. M. Beck ; William Thomas Gent, Sheffield ; Lieut-Col. V. B. Ramsden, D.S.O., M.C., Ilford, Ltd. ; A. H. Stanley Davies, Bristol ; T. Ashworth, Torquay ; Sidney Stamford Wright, Blackpool ; Thomas Piggott, Leytonstone ; Andrew M'Creadie, Girvan ; Albert Wakinshaw, Bebington ; Arthur Hill, Christchurch ; George Henry Martin, Glasgow.

OPENINGS : Odeon, Scarborough (Oscar Deutsch) ; Strand News Theatre, Strand (Associated News Theatres) (re-opening) ; Plaza, Grimsby (Reg. Kemp) ; Cinema House, Harmsworth (Reg. Kemp) ; Carlton, Bexhill ; Radio Centre Theatre, East Grinstead (Letheby & Christopher, Ltd.) ; Studio Kinema, Elstree (Fletcher-Barnet Syndicate) ; Alexandra, Pontefract (Pontefract Cinema, Ltd.) ; Ritz, Oxford (Union) ; Odeons Wimbledon, Sutton Coldfield and Colwyn Bay (Oscar Deutsch) ; Embassy, Wallasey (Harry Buxton) (re-opening) ; Magnet, Dundalk (Rev. Father Stokes) ; Kingsway, Hadleigh (Mr. and Mrs. F. A. Rolls) ; Medina, Newport.

TRANSFERS : Forum, Wythenshawe, Manchester; Electra, Cheadle; Prince of Wales, Tivoli and Strand, Grimsby ; Her Majesty's, Grand, Imperial and Palace, Walsall, to A.B.C. ; Wicker Picture House, Sheffield, to J. F. Emery; Astoria,Aberdeen, to James F. Donald (Aberdeen Cinemas, Ltd.); Rota, Denton, to Union Cinemas ; Adelphi, Liverpool, to Stanley Grimshaw ; New Coronet, Didcot, and the Welwyn Garden Theatre to Shipman and King ; Arcade, Camberley, to C. J. Donada ; Capitol, Broughty Ferry, to Lyall and Bryce ; Queens, Stonehaven, to Donald Circuit ; Princes, Wigan, to G. W. Bell.

MAY.

Deal for control of G.-B. denied by 20th Century-Fox.

Chief Constable of Liverpool takes exception to the Blackpool "Queen of Beauty" Competition in A.B.C. theatres.

Sussex support Quota abolition.

Ralph Hanbury appointed chairman and managing director of Radio.

Duke of Kent visits Strand Electric lighting demonstration.

A.C.T. prepare Quota case for B.O.T.

Co-operative booking scheme proposed by Devon.

£90,000 issue made by Nuro (Biggleswade), Ltd.

L.M.B. films wound up.

Irish Free State propose a reciprocal quota.

Free State announces reduction in entertainment tax.

Highbury Studios, Ltd., open new studios at Highbury New Park.

A.C.T. advocate increase of Quota percentage.

B.F.I. appoint Oliver Bell as general manager.

A.C.T. hold third annual conference to request new wage schedule.

Lanarkshire authorities withdraw licences for the Victoria Hall, Forth, the Picture House, Old Brae, Lesmahagow, the Picture House, Main Street, Kirkmuirhill, and the Picture House, Glenboig.

Bournemouth justices turn down licence application for new Odeon.

Five Dublin kinemas merge.

Ulster justices' veto on Sunday entertainments to be challenged.

British Equity sign Agreement with U.S. Guild.

Oscar Deutsch forms Decorative Crafts, Ltd.

U.S. adopts 2,000 ft. reel.

West Lancs C.E.A. suggests a test case should be taken up regarding block bookings.

Results of "London" questionnaire received.

Negotiations with the N.A.T.E. and the C.E.A., at Aberdeen, broken off.

Four new stages for Sound City.

Temperance Hall, Arva, Co. Cavan, gutted by fire.

Exhibitors appeal against Newry (N. Ireland) valuations.

A.C.T. want protection against foreign technicians.

"Big Stick" film booking methods alleged at Northern C.E.A.

B.O.T. footage figures show decrease in British films.

L.C.C. insists on kinema car parks.

Percy N. Furber of Trans-Lux Movies Cꞏrpn. of America visits England.

B. & D. become part owners of Pinewood Studios.

N. Wales propose independent association to tackle redundancy.

Electrical Equipment and Carbon Co., Ltd., goes into voluntary liquidation.

OBITUARY: Thomas Iseten, Co. Durham; August Burmester, Germany (Gasparcolor); Sir Philip Nash, London; Henry A. Sanders, London; Mrs. Jane Revill, Stockport; Frank Montrose, Manchester.

OPENINGS: Savoy, Northampton (A.B.C.); Cameo News Theatre, Cliftonville; Odeon, Well Hall (Oscar Deutsch); Regal, Cromer (Mr. and Mrs. V. E. Harrison) (re-opening); Odeon, Littlehampton (Oscar Deutsch); Plaza, Dudley (Ben Kennedy) (re-opening).

TRANSFERS: King's, Heswall, to Stanley Grimshaw; Regal, Cupar, to O. M. Craig; Jubilee, Golborne, Lancs, to W. J. Speakman and G. C. Doyle; Theatre Royal, Manchester, to H. D. Moorhouse; Theatre Royal, Lincoln, to F. J. Butterworth and Mrs. M. T. Butterworth; Brettel Circuit to A.B.C.; Langham, Pinner, and Embassy, Harrow, to A.B.C.; Winter Gardens, New Brighton, to Cheshire Picture Halls, Ltd.; Cosy, Porthcawl, to Ernest Joseph; Roxy, Bournemouth, to A. H. P. Mears; Savoy, Llandudno, to Llandudno Cinema Syndicate; Verona, Guide Bridge, to Oscar Deutsch; Rio, Conniesburn, Toll and Rio, Rutherglen, to Peter Crerar.

JUNE.

RCA announces new service policy.

H.M. King Edward VIII grants his patronage to the C.T.B.F.

Ernest Turnbull announces long-term contract effected by Dominion Film Distributors with G.-B., Twickenham and British Lion for marketing of these companies' product in Australia.

Firm action threatened by K.R.S. on the subject of illicit crossovers and the misuse of films booked for three-day showing.

Devon and Cornwall C.E.A. complain against municipal Sunday entertainments.

New studios opened at Bushey.

Kinema Trade Board proposal refused in Northern Ireland.

Middlesex C.C. withdraw S.O. permit for Carlton, Harrow.

The perfection of television receiving apparatus capable of giving a large-size screen picture is claimed by Scophony, Ltd.

P.E.P.M.A. to fight against overbuilding.

French studios reported at a standstill.

Joint committee of exhibitors and licensing authorities wanted in Warwickshire.

Lanark C.C. issue temporary licences to three kinemas after having refused renewal of licences.

Queen's, Aberdeen, severely damaged by fire.

Odeon chain and Donada circuit invade Scotland.

N.A.T.E. threaten to boycott certain Swansea exhibitors.

Price bars rouse N. Western C.E.A.

Merseyside · Film Society protest against double feature shows.

Sound City Studios, Shepperton, reopen.

Ministry of Health inquire into refusal of Wolverhampton B.C. to permit erection of new kinema.

G.-B. Managers' Showmanship Challenge Shield and a cheque for £50 presented to G. H. E. Selway, of the Trocadero, Liverpool.

C.E.A. Conference and Exhibition opens at Eastbourne.

Trade gives evidence on Quota to Lord Moyne's committee.

L.C.C. to inquire into outside shows.

Ministry of Health overrules Coulsdon and Purley Council's opposition to new kinema.

OBITUARY : George Henderson (Teddy Le Rone), Scotland ; Frank Nolan, Liverpool ; Ernest Vincent Dolden, Farnworth, Lancs ; Wm. Brown, Dundee ; Alexander D. Hay, Aberdeen ; Victor Tropnell, Aberdeen

OPENINGS : Majestic, Belfast (Union) ; Plaza, Dudley (Ben. Kennedy) (reopening) ; Odeon, Clacton (Oscar Deutsch) ; Luxor, Llanfairfechan (Llanrwst Cinema Co.) ; Tivoli, New Brighton, Wallasey (International Entertainments, Ltd.) (reopening) ; West's Pictures, Bournemouth (T. Jackson) (reopening) ; Ritz, Horsham (Union) ; Norwood, Glasgow (A. E. Pickard).

TRANSFERS : Tivoli, New Brighton, Wallasey, to International Entertainments, Ltd. ; Moderne, Bournemouth ; Palladium, Southbourne, Bournemouth ; Regent, Christchurch ; Swanage Cinema, Swanage ; and the Grand, Swanage, to Bournemouth Town Cinemas ; Matlock Bath Pavilion to Matlock Cinemas ; Savoy, Llandudno, to Llandudno Palladium, Ltd.; Atlas, Liverpool, to Byrom Picture Houses, Ltd. ; Casino, Fleetwood, to C. Miller ; County, Warwick, to A.B.C. ; Palace, Chatham, to G-B. ; Verona, Guide Bridge, to Oscar Deutsch ; Empress, Urmston, to Union ; Regent, Burnt Oak, to Oscar Deutsch ; Poole's Palace and Regent, Aberdeen, to County Cinemas .

JULY.

Lord Luke joins board of G.C.F. Corp., Ltd.

Western Electric announces cut in recording rates.

An attempt to obtain standardisation of electricity charges is suggested in C.E.A. Committee on Electrical Distribution's report.

Midnight Trade shows condemned at Bristol C.E.A. meeting.

Stallholders report big business at Trade exhibition.

Liverpool exhibitors complain of free film shows given by stores.

Slough wins S.O. Poll.

£1.500,000 offer by Schencks mentioned in G-B., and American deal rumours.

Barney Balaban appointed president of Paramount Pictures, Inc. Adolph Zukor re-elected chairman.

John Maxwell resigns from Film Group of F.B.I.

A striking lead to the C.E.A. Redundancy campaign was given by London and Home Counties branch, which debated subject for over two hours.

N.A.T.E. to fight for recognition in Trade.

Simon Rowson explains his scheme for all-in advertising campaign.

Lord Mayor of London officiates at brilliant opening of " Glebelands," C.T.B.F.'s rest and convalescent home.

Agreement was reached in New York regarding the Gaumont-British-M-G-M-20th Century-Fox deal.

Laemmles announce intention to produce independent films.

Manchester C.E.A. have decided to make a test case of their opposition to a new kinema at Accrington.

OBITUARY : J. H. Bocca, Newcastle ; Harry Sanderson, Rotherham ; Will Day, London ; Lionel Ewart (Leo) Poole, Gloucester ; Albert E. Wall, Whitley Bay ; Percy Ballington, Sheffield ; T. J. Everton, Stafford ; Alderman Robert Halpin, Coventry.

OPENINGS : Plaza, Southfields, S.W. (re-opened) (S.A.G. Cinemas, Ltd.) ; Odeon, Guide Bridge, Manchester (Oscar Deutsch) ; Strand, Port Erin, I.O.M. (Strand Cinema Theatre, Co.) ; Avenue, Onchan, I.O.M. (Onchan Cinema, Ltd.) ; Savoy, Cobham (Savoy (Cobham), Ltd.) ; Ritz, Burnham ; Odeon, Bridgwater (Oscar Deutsch) ; Odeon, St. Austell (Oscar Deutsch); Tonic, Bangor (J. O'Neill) ; Ritz, Seaford (Seaford Empire Co., Ltd.) ; Ritz, Penzance (Union Cinemas, Ltd.) ; Majestic, West Hartlepool (Majestic (West Hartlepool), Ltd.) ; Gaiety, Plymouth (reopened as Carlton) (E. J. and W. E. Pope) ; Century, Clacton (Twentieth Century Cinemas, Ltd.), Odeon, Deal (Oscar Deutsch) ; Majestic; Ashton-under-Lyne (reopening) (G-B.).

TRANSFERS : Circuit Kinemas, Ltd., to Union Cinemas, Ltd. ; Rialto, Bermondsey, to Mrs. Walker : Queen's, South Shields, to Sol Sheckman ; Plaza, Cardiff ; Plaza, Swansea ; Forum Bath ; and Embassy, Bristol, to Barton Cinema Co., Ltd. ; Picture House, Paisley, to Harry Winocour ; Royal, Wallasey, to D. Forrester ; New Empire (Burnley), Ltd., circuit to Associated British Properties, Ltd., and the Langworthy Picturedrome, Ltd.

AUGUST.

A.B.P.C. reports record year's trading with £926,042 gross earnings.

Statistics given in House of Commons reveal £7,337 profits on Government film production.

The possibility of the Trade being brought within the scope of new Factory Bill is adumbrated by certain questions in Parliament.

H. P. Haggar wins KINE Company of Showmen Championship Shield.

S. Sagall of Scophony ventures prophecy that Television in kinemas will be accomplished fact next year.

R.C.A. demonstrate Ultra-Violet sound recording.

Paragon, Grimsby, gutted by fire. £15,000 damages caused.

Contrasts in U.S. and U.K. film hire percentages disclosed by C.E.A. visitors to America.

Quota film clause insisting upon a minimum cost of 15s. per foot for feature films urged by T.U.C.

OBITUARY : James Tilney, London ; T. H. Groves, Stoll circuit ; William H. Bell, Aston Cross.

OPENINGS : Curzon, Brighton (Ken Nyman) ; Pavilion, East Dulwich (Carlton Cinemas, Ltd.) ; Heathway, Dagenham (Kay's Theatres, Ltd.) ; Troxy, Portsmouth (Tivoli, Portsmouth, Ltd.) ; Commodore, Ryde, I.O.W. (Ryde Cinema Co.) ; Roxy, Leicester (Westleigh Kinemas, Ltd.) ; Empire, Havant, Hants (Southern Entertainments, Ltd.) ; Picture House, Stonehaven (Messrs. Donald) ; Plaza, Sunderland (Plaza (Sunderland), Cinema, Ltd.) ; Apollo, Southsea (reopened) (F. B. B. Blake) ; Odeon, Southall (Oscar Deutsch) ; Rex, Motherwell (A.B.C.) ; Gaiety, Eastbourne (reopened) (Amusements, Eastbourne, Ltd.) ; Tivoli, Wimborne (Tivoli (Wimborne), Ltd.) ; Odeon, Ramsgate, (Oscar Deutsch) ; Majestic, Sevenoaks (Majestic (Sevenoaks), Ltd.).

TRANSFERS : Theatre Royal, Sunderland, to Black's Northern Theatres, Ltd. ; Plaza, Batley, Yorks, to David Forrester Theatres, Ltd.; Plaza, Watford, to Oscar Deutsch ; Savoy, Mottram, Cheshire, to Charles Seymour ; Reo, Liverpool, to A.B.C. ; Princes, Portsmouth, to Councillor Joe Davidson ; Carlton, Norwich, to County circuit.

SEPTEMBER.

Captain A. C. N. Dixey outlines Exhibitor-Distributor formation proposals.

Sussex C.E.A., urges immediate redundancy action.

J. Arthur Rank is mentioned in proposed formation of new kinema group.

Sam Morns, Warner vice-president, arrives.

Three hundred Trade employees visit " Glebelands."

W. A. Bach announces drastic reductions in Western Electric recording royalties.

Arrangements have been completed between Paramount Theatres and Union Cinema Co., by which the management control of the two concerns is being handled by Paramount Theatre executives.

T.U.C. resolves to boycott anti-union employers.

Henley Town Council is taking action to prevent overbuilding.

The T.U.C. demand for a 40-hour week is to be followed up by the N.A.T.E. and E.T.U.

Joseph M. Schenck reveals details of G.-B.-Metro-20th Century-Fox negotiations.

The C.E.A. has decided to endeavour to seek within the Trade a solution to the redundancy problem.

Two hundred exhibitors approve general principle of proposed Exhibitor-Distributor scheme.

G.-B. win KINE Cricket Cup.

Negotiations between G.-B., 20th Century-Fox and M-G-M have broken down.

OBITUARY : Irving Thalberg ; Georges Ercole, British Paramount News ; A. E. Vaughan, Bath; Edmund Barnes, Astley, Lancs.

OPENINGS : Regal, Lanark (Alex King) ; Palace, Freshwater, I.O.W. (Isle of Wight Theatres, Ltd.) ; Odeon, Ashford (Oscar Deutsch) ; Odeon, Ipswich (Oscar Deutsch) ; Ambassador, Hounslow (London and Southern Super Cinemas) ; Topical, Aberdeen (E. A. Bromberg) ; Chorlton Kinema, New Keynsham, Bristol (Keynsham Picture House, Ltd.) ; Haymarket, Newcastle (reopened) (A.B.C.) ; Cinenews, Portsmouth (Capital and Provincial News Theatres) ; Regal, Hammersmith (A.B.C.) ; Odeon, Muswell Hill, N.10 (Oscar Deutsch) ; Odeon, Cardiff, (Oscar Deutsch) ; Odeon, Bromley (Oscar Deutsch) ; Rex, Leytonstone (A.B.C.) ; Vogue, Dundee (G. Singleton).

TRANSFERS : Palace, Bilston, to Oscar Deutsch ; Theatre Royal, Savoy and Queens, Bilston, to Astel Pictures, Ltd. ; Lansdowne House News Theatre, Berkeley Square, London, to County Cinemas ; Ritz, Barrow, to Union Cinemas ; Britannia, Small's Wynd, Dundee, to J. B. Milne ; Palais de Danse, Ashton-under-Lyne, to G. W. Bell ; Ritz, Farnworth, to Union Cinemas ; Singleton Circuit to Oscar Deutsch ; Oddfellows Hall Cinema, Sutton Bridge, Lincs, to Albert Groves ; Rialto and Picture Palace, Londonderry, and Picture Palace, Newtownards, to Union Cinemas ; Coliseum, Leigh-on-Sea, to Cohen and Rafer ; Strand, Bootle, to G. Prince ; Giralda, Brockley, to Alfred Barnett ; Savoy, Hippodrome, and King's, Colne, Lancs, to Harry Buxton.

OCTOBER.

Captain Dixey opens provincial campaign for the formation of an independent exhibitors' distributing company.

Shareholders oppose G.T.C. adoption of accounts at the annual general meeting.

Wellington, Dundee, extensively damaged by fire.

Pinewood Studios, Iver Heath, Bucks, officially opened.

Alhambra, Leicester Square, to be replaced by modern Odeon.

Mayor of Merthyr presents KINE Showmanship Shield to H. P. Haggar, Castle, Merthyr.

Film Institute publishes annual report.

Negotiations advanced for acquisition by the G.C.F. Corporation, Ltd., of West of England circuits involving £500,000.

Jesse Lasky predicts British film boom.

Chairman of G.-B. announces no change will take place in the control of the Corporation.

Surrey C.C. proposes building time limit for new kinemas.

Union Cinemas plan £6,000,000 combine of kinemas.

Statistical bureau plan shelved.

OBITUARY: James Ritson, North Shields; William Gibson, Whitehaven and Ascot; Ald. Hewitson, Smethwick; Arthur H. Needham, Blackpool.

OPENINGS: Rex, Haslemere (Haslemere Cinema Co., Ltd.); Odeon, Harrogate (Oscar Deutsch); Odeon, Chester (Oscar Deutsch); Odeon, Stafford (Oscar Deutsch); Odeon, Horsham (Oscar Deutsch); Embassy, Gillingham (Fred White); Fosse, Leicester (Super Cinemas (Leicester), Ltd.); Scala, Coventry (Chas. Orr) (re-opening); Ritz, Bull Farm, Mansfield (J. E. Barnes, J. A. Tankard and Guy Nicholson); Eastville Hippodrome, Bristol (re-opening); Ellesmere, Manchester (Alfred Snape, Robert Taylor, Harold Ward, J.H. Fenton, J. Howard and A. Marsh); Grenada, Vauxhall (Bernstein); Regal, Chesterfield (A.B.C.); Embassy, Petts Wood (Shipman & King); Longford, Stretford (Jackson & Newport); Forum, Leeds (Central Picture Theatres, Ltd.); Plaza, Neyland (re-opening); Regal, Broughty Ferry (W. Bryce and J. Lyall); Grosvenor, Rayners Lane, Harrow (Hammond-Dawes); Lyceum, Dumfries (Dumfries Theatre Co., Ltd.); Rex, Wilmslow, Cheshire (W. W. Stansby); Cinenews, Portsmouth (Capital and Provincial News Theatres); Palace, Cricklewood (re-opening); Albion, Birmingham (Albion Picture Theatres, Ltd.) (re-opening); New Palace, Burslem (Wm. Hitchin); Odeon, Newport, I.O.W. (Oscar Deutsch); New Cinema, Stranraer (re-opening); Capitol, Nottingham (Invincible Cinemas, Ltd.); Savoy, Stoke Newington (A.B.C.); Regent, Port Talbot (Port Talbot Cinemas, Ltd.); Troxy, Belfast (Strand Cinemas, Ltd.); Scala, Runcorn (Cheshire County Cinemas, Ltd.) (re-opening).

TRANSFERS: Embassy, Wallasey, to J. R. Dovener; Palladium, Bolton, to A. Hall; Olympia Cardiff, to A.B.C.; Alhambra, Leicester Square, W.C.2, to Oscar Deutsch; Scala, Bishopston, and Plaza, Bristol, to Atkinson's Pictures, Ltd.; Palace, Dalton Brook, Rotherham, to J. Winstanley; Star, Belgrave Gate and Imperial, Leicester, to Mere Road Cinema Co., Ltd; Empire, Sutton, St. Helens, to B. Franks; Empire, Westhoughton, to J. F. Emery; Palace, County, Grand and Kingsway, Lancaster, to James Brennan; Verona, Fleetwood, to James Brennan; Winter Gardens, Llandudno, to Brooklyn Trust, Ltd.; Ritz, Shotton, to David Forrester; Palladium, Bolton, to A. Hall.

NOVEMBER.

Exhibitor-directors to the board of Independent Exhibitors' Distributing Co., nominated.

Ninth Annual General Meeting of G.-B. Corporation adjourned for presentation of consolidated statement.

Metropolitan Film Studios at Southall destroyed by fire.

L.C.C. ban children under 16 years from seeing films classed as "horrific."

Lord Selsdon opens B.B.C. television service.

Twentieth Century-Fox and C. Donada deal rumours denied.

R.P.S. and B.K.S. to merge.

Manchester C.E.A. recommends clause in Quota Act to stop free shows.

Sussex starts voluntary penny-a-week scheme for "Glebelands."

At the request of the L.C.C., the B.B.F.C. decide to delete the clause in agreement with film producers that no film shall be exhibited which had not been passed by the Board.

Union Cinema Co., Ltd., National Provincial Cinemas, Ltd. and Oxford and Berkshire Cinemas, Ltd., to be merged into a £6,500,000 company.

Birmingham C.E.A. opposes application for licence for a new kinema proposed by Captain S. W. Clift (chairman).

Union Cinemas pay 22 per cent. dividend.

Annual report of Middlesex County Council reveals increase of 19,000 seats in the district during the year.

A.C.T. compiles draft agreement for working conditions of technicians.

Percy B. Broadhead, of Manchester, elected P.E.P.M.A. president.

Dundee corporation drop proposed standing-in-kinemas ban.

B.F.I. proposes central distribution unit for films exclusively for children.

OBITUARY: Jonathan Bell, Royston, Barnsley; R. L. Roberts, Prestatyn; Sam Livesey, South Yorkshire; George Salmon, Edinburgh; H. Armstrong, Stowmarket.

OPENINGS: New Palladium, Brockley (re-opening) (A. Barnett); Regal, Cranleigh (Cranleigh (Regal) Cinema, Ltd.); Odeon, Herne Bay (Oscar Deutsch); Clifton, Leominster (Captain S. W. Clift and Leon Salberg); Ritz, Belfast (Union Cinemas); Ritz, Forest Hall, Newcastle-on-Tyne (E. J. Hinge); Odeon, Lancaster (Oscar Deutsch); Regal, Monkseaton; Picture House, Dalbeattie, Leinster, Dublin (Daniel MacAlister); Rialto, Dublin (Dublin Kinemas, Ltd.); Regal, Leicester (Regal Cinemas (Leicester), Ltd.); Odeon, Bury (Oscar Deutsch); Gaumont, Chippenham (G.-B.); New Empire, Neath (reopening); Majestic, Orrell (Robert Woods); Regal, Leeds; Gaumont,

Bromley (G.-B.) ; Savoy, Exeter (A.B.C.)`; Empire, Normanton (re-opening) (London and Southern Super Cinemas) ; Odeon, Loughborough (Oscar Deutsch).

TRANSFERS : Palladium, Hockley ; Piccadilly, Birmingham ; Imperial, Sparbrook ; Tower, West Bromwich, County, Warwick, to A.B.C.; St James', Northampton, to S. Graham ; Winter Gardens, Llandudno, to Oscar Deutsch ; Palace, County, Grand, and Kingsway, Lancaster, to James Brennan ; Regal, Bath, Scala and Regent kinemas, Leamington, to Salberg and Clift ; Alhambra, Shotton, and Tivoli, Buckley, to S. Grimshaw ; Picture House, Chesterfield, to Oscar Deutsch ; Princess, Peterborough, to J. F. Emery ; Tonic, Bangor, to Curran and Sons ; Arcade, Bridgwater, to G. Rees.

DECEMBER.

House of Commons discuss removal of ban preventing children from appearing in British films.

Sussex C.E.A. quotes apology from B.B.C. for Alistair Cook's film criticism.

Notts and Derby reveal proposed scheme for protection of exhibitors showing films inviting libel actions.

S.O. rejected in Newcastle.

Moyne report presented.

Road show activities of Western Electric, Ltd., transferred to Sound Services, Ltd.

Ritz, Ayr, burnt down.

Sir Samuel Hoare warns Trade to keep clear of Government control at annual dinner of L. & N.C. branch C.E.A.

Caterham, Surrey, turns down S.O.

John Maxwell forms Associated British Properties, Ltd.

John Logie Baird demonstrates large-screen television at the Dominion, Tottenham Court Road.

H.M. the King raises ban on plays and films of the life of Queen Victoria.

Chancellor of the Exchequer announces 6o per cent. of the total revenue from the Entertainment Tax is derived from kinemas.

L. C. J. acquits films as inciters to crime at annual B.K.S. dinner.

Cinema Theatres (G. C. F.), Ltd., formed to control a major circuit.

I.F.S. exhibitors resent British invasion.

John Maxwell and Julius Hagen complete deal for distribution of Twickenham product through Wardour.

Sam Eckman, Jun., announces M-G-M's British production plans.

Yarmouth Watch Committee approves C.E.A. letter on redundancy.

The Picture House, Peterhead, Aberdeenshire destroyed by fire.

Five-day-week inaugurated in Wardour Street.

King George VI Patron of the C.T.B.F.

Sheffield authorities introduce new standing regulations.

Chairman of Birmingham Public Entertainment Committee attacks non-flam shows in annual report.

Dominion, Tottenham Court Road, introduces regular television programmes.

L.C.C. issues order that signs must not resemble traffic lights.

Government control of kinematograph industry suggested in I.F.S.

OBITUARY : George Howard Cricks, Wallington ; Charles Sanders, Birmingham ; Will White, Belfast ; Philip Sheridan, London ; R. Gerald Balls, Chelmsford ; I. P. Sample, Durham.

TRANSFERS : Scala, Ashton-in-Makerfield, to Doman Enterprises, Ltd. ; Carnoustie Pavilion Picture House to Angus Cinema Co. ; Palace, County, Grand and Kingsway kinemas, Lancaster, to Union ; Tivoli, Wimborne, to Portsmouth Town Cinemas ; Globe, Portsmouth, to F. J. Spickernell ; Picture House, Chesterfield, and Barnet Cinema, Barnet, to Oscar Deutsch ; Morgan Street Kinema, Dundee, to Pennycock Bros.; Regent, Bolton, to Bolton Theatre and Entertainments Co., Ltd. ; Empire and Palace Kinemas, Heywood, to Frank Spring ; Palace Newcastle, to E. J. H. Theatres, Ltd. ; Gem, Peterborough, to W. Harris ; Central, South Norwood, to proprietors of Grand, Bermondsey.

OPENINGS : Palace, Chatham (Kent Proprietary Holdings, Ltd.) ; Rivoli, Charlton (Ben Kanter) ; Ambassador, Bristol ; Cameo, Victoria (C. and R. (Victoria), Ltd.) ; New Palace, Broughton, Plaza, Queen's Ferry, Flintshire (Deeside Enterprise Cinemas, Ltd.) ; Picture House, Turriff, Aberdeenshire (Turriff Cinema Co.) (re-opening) ; Tudor, Giffnock (Bernard Frutin) ; Odeon, Portsmouth (Oscar Deutsch) ; Savoy, Lincoln (A.B.C.) ; Regal, Eastleigh (Ald. G.Wright) (re-opening) ; Odeon, Falmouth (Oscar Deutsch) ; Lyric, Wellingborough ; Majestic, Aberdeen (Caledonian Theatres, Ltd.) ; Regal, West Hartlepool (C. P. & N.P. Metcalfe) ; Rex, North Shields, Palace, Tetbury, Broadway, Belfast (Curran Circuit) ; Park, Belfast (Supreme Kinemas) ; Ormeau Road Curzon, Belfast (John Caston) ; Plaza, Chichester (County Cinemas) ; Danilo, Brierley Hill (Mortimer Dent) ; News Theatre, Oxford Street, Manchester (Jacey Cinemas, Ltd.) ; Ambassador, Belfast, (D. D. Young) ; Plaza, Govan (A.B.C.) ; Ritz, Muswell Hill (A.B.C.) ; Ritz, Ipswich (Union Cinemas) ; Regal, Kettering (Cohen and Rafer) ; Coliseum, Leigh-on-Sea (Cohen and Rafer) ; Plaza, Blaydon-on-Tyne ; Rex, Northwood Hills (Shipman and King) ; Ritz, Newcastle, North Ireland (McMurray of Lurgan) ; Palladium, Coleraine (J. Menary).

1937
BELONGS
TO
METRO
GOLDWYN
MAYER

ARS GRATIA ARTIS

OVERSEAS DIRECTORY

TRADE SHOWN FILMS

RENTER OFFERS

FILMS REGISTERED

TRADE ORGANISATIO.

FILMS PERSONNEL

STUDIOS AND PERSONNEL

PERSONNEL— EQUIPMENT TRADE

GENERAL DIRECTOR, PERSONNEL TRADE

THEATRE CIRCUITS

Metro-Goldwyn-Mayer from its very beginning has been the leader in that delightful habit of making BIG BUDGET PICTURES. Each year Leo has made more and more of them. And so in 1937 we'll raise our proud standard to even greater heights in our ever present task of Glorifying the Screens of the World!

The Year Abroad

Special Reviews of Conditions in:

America
Europe
Australia
Canada
India, &c.

Overseas Trade Directory :—

Australia	Italy
Austria	Jugoslavia
Belgium	New Zealand
Canada	Norway
Czechoslovakia	Poland
Denmark	Roumania
France	Sweden
Germany	Switzerland
Greece	Turkey
Holland	Union of South Africa
Hungary	U.S. of America
India.	

THE YEAR IN AMERICA.

By Red Kann.

R EVIVAL signs which began to stir new hope in 1935 became definite beacons pointing to a new period of prosperity before 1936 had passed the mid-year. Opening of the autumn exhibition season in September sent grosses to a new four-year high in spite of a lower general scale of admissions. Optimism prevailed in all branches of the industry at the year end.

Film securities were advancing. Paramount had solved the financial problems which beset the company for the first six months, Warners' were on the road to a resumption of dividends, Twentieth Century-Fox was paying on all classes of securities, the outlook for Universal, under new management, was bright. Only R.K.O. remained in the hands of a trustee, and an early reorganisation was looked for. Loew's, Inc., was, as usual, on a firm profit basis.

PROSPERITY.—The year began with more real indications of returning prosperity than had been evident for four years and production budgets were increased generally. The mid-year reports of all producers showed marked gains. The dramatic highlight of the pickup came the second week in September—Labour Day week—when first run grosses in 29 key cities reached $2,090,144, a four-year high.

The theatre intake fell off slightly a few weeks later, after the first effects of the big autumn releases had worn off, but the recession was slight in comparison with recent years. It was generally admitted that the average weekly theatre attendance of 80,000,000 in September was from 20 to 50 per cent. higher in all sections of the country. The average for the previous years had been 65,000,000 weekly.

THEATRES.—In January, 15,278 theatres out of a total of 18,508, were open, a gain of 5 per cent. over the previous year. Openings continued during the early months of the year. New buildings were started in many sections, and during the second half of the year redecorating, installation of new sound and other improvements became general, Circuit expansion was resumed.

COMPANY REORGANISATIONS.—The year was marked by a general revamping of corporate structures and the elimination of many subsidiaries. This was due to a new law taxing corporate surpluses and barring consolidated income tax returns. First National was one of the companies to be dissolved, although the trade name was retained for pictures. All M-G-M units were merged into Loew's, Inc., but the trade names will be continued, as in the case of First National.

Paramount ended its first year out of bankruptcy in June by reverting to the theory that film men could run a film company with better financial results than bankers could achieve.

Warners, one of the three major companies which went into the depression with a capitalisation piled up during the expansion prior to 1929, advanced on the road to prosperity.

R.K.O. showed marked gains for each quarter of 1936. At the end of 1935 it had reported a net of $665,297, the first since 1930. These figures were surpassed as 1936 advanced, but the company continued in the control of a trustee throughout the year. This was due to inability to reach a compromise on a claim for $9,100,000 held by the Rockefeller interests. A settlement of this problem is predicted for the early months of 1937.

Twentieth Century-Fox paid its first dividend on the common stock in the second quarter, and at the end of the third quarter announced a net of $4,451,851; more than double the net for the same period in 1935. Joseph M. Schenck predicted a profit of over $7,000,000 for the fiscal year.

Loew's, Inc., which suffered least during the depression, continued to gain. Its 40-week net was $7,390,495, which was $1,550,144 above the 1935 net for the same period. Columbia and United Artists shared in the general gains.

Universal underwent a complete shift in control. Standard Capital Corp., headed by J. Cheever Cowdin, Charles R. Rogers, who was backed by Adolph Ramish, and C. M. Woolf and associates in Great Britain, acquired Carl Laemmle's stock, and Laemmle and his son retired from the company.

Pathé withdrew from financing independent productions and also retired from the distribution field by selling its interest in First Division to the newly-formed Grand National.

PRODUCTION.—No outstanding production innovations were introduced during the year. Colour films gained, but the big box-office successes were in black and white.

In September all major companies began to release prints on 2,000-foot reels.

SOUND.—For a short time it appeared that the two principal sound apparatus manufacturers would observe the tenth anniversary of sound by conducting a price war, but price cuts made by RCA were met by Western Electric. Each began advertising campaigns, the former on its new High Fidelity, and the latter on its Mirrophonic. At the end of the year all the major studios were using both firms' recorders for the first time. Loew's circuit was splitting its business between them for reproducers.

PERSONALITIES.—Several outstanding industry figures passed away during the year—John Gilbert, S. L. (Roxy) Rothafel, Felix F. Feist, Irving Thalberg, and Thomas Meighan.

Carl Laemmle retired from the business. Dr. A. H. Giannini dropped his rôle as industry banker and adviser to become active head of United Artists. George J. Schaefer resigned as Paramount general manager and became vice-president in charge of sales for United Artists. He was joined by A. W. Smith, Jr., who had been with Warners for years. Emanuel Cohen formed his own producing company to release through Paramount. M. H. Aylesworth resigned from N.B.C. to devote all his time to R.K.O. B. B. Kahane quit R.K.O. to join Columbia. William F. Rodgers became M-G-M sales head after the death of Felix F. Feist.

GAUMONT BRITISH-TWENTIETH CENTURY-FOX-LOEW NEGOTIATIONS.— In the spring reports were current that the Ostrers might sell their control of Gaumont British.

This excitement had hardly subsided in November when British interests acquired 35,000 shares of Loew's stock held by Irving Thalberg's estate This did not affect control of the company, but it did help keep speculation alive.

COPYRIGHTS.—During the early part of the year the American Society of Composers, Authors and Publishers was under continuous fire from exhibitors. A Government anti-trust suit is still pending. Warners withdrew its subsidiaries from the organisation, but later returned them.

There also was considerable agitation over charges in Canada. A Dominion commission investigated the Canadian Performing Rights Society, and fixed a schedule of fees early in November. In the meantime, E. C. Mills, representing Ascap, and Leslie Boosey, representing the British Performing Rights Society, reached an agreement with principal Canadian exhibitors to avoid the possibility of forcing them to make individual agreements for music licences. When the Government rates were announced, it was found they were the same as those reached in the joint negotiations.

SURVEY OF EUROPE.

By KINE. *Correspondents in European Capitals.*

AUSTRIA.

GENERAL LEGISLATION.—The standard renting contract abolishes the showing of double-feature programmes.

CENSORSHIP AND TAXATION.—Film censorship is still handled in a very different manner by each of the 26 Federal States comprising the country, so much so that films admitted unrestrictedly in some States are banned by others. The situation has become so precarious that an amendment to the Constitution providing for centralisation of censorship is contemplated by the Federal Council. Taxation remains unchanged.

IMPORTANT REGULATIONS.—No change in the complicated system of " vormerkscheine " referred to in the 1936 issue of the YEAR BOOK, beyond a 50 per cent. increase in the number needed for the import of a foreign film ; at the present situation of the market this would mainly affect British and American films, the latter of which amount to about 45 per cent. of all films imported.

Distributors importing more than 10 feature films per year are compelled to buy a certain number of shorts produced under a Government monopoly and priced at 4,000 shillings (each about 9d.) per short ; exhibitors must show these, also the official Austrian newsreels. This excludes practically the importation of foreign topicals.

The amended trade agreement with Germany for the exchange of films produced in the two countries free of " vormerkscheine " or import permits, runs until June 30, 1939, and provides for the yearly import into Germany of 14 Austrian feature films and 140 vice-versa. Germany's right of refusing films employing " non-Aryans " and her slackness in discharging her obligations to transfer 20 per cent. of the royalties belonging to the Austrians (the remaining 80 per cent. plus the " frozen " Austrian credits are compensated with the royalties for German films imported into Austria) caused a severe crisis in the Austrian film production at the end of 1936.

CZECHOSLOVAKIA.

GENERAL LEGISLATION.—For the 1936/37 season the Advisory Film Committee has granted the compulsory annual registration as distributor-importer to not more than 26 out of 51 applicants. The system of awarding producers direct subsidies out of the Film Fund was abolished in favour of State guarantees of 50 per cent. of production costs, for 20 per cent. of which, *i e.,* 40 per cent. of the guaranteed amount, the Film Fund serves as reinsurance ; the producer must deposit the remaining 50 per cent. of production costs at the bank giving the guaranteed credit, pledge to that bank the negative and all returns accruing to him, also from foreign-language versions, and assign to the Ministry of Finance a part of his profits, in case they exceed 40 per cent. of the production costs.

Single feature programmes have become customary, excepting in small-town halls. Distributors have resolved not to supply booking combines.

CENSORSHIP AND TAXATION.—No change, excepting a reduction to 10 per cent. of the entertainments tax on tickets costing one crown (slightly less than 1¾d.)

IMPORT REGULATIONS.—As reported in the 1936 issue of the YEAR BOOK. An agreement with Germany provides for a film clearing on a financial reciprocity basis, to avoid the difficulty of money transfers. Negotiations are pending for an exchange of films free of important permits.

FRANCE.

The year 1936 has been, for the film industry in France, a year full of evolutions and transformations. The first point to be noted is a very important improvement in the production, both in quantity and in quality. Nearly 150 feature films have been made, and at least 50 of them were films of high standard.

Results would have been still better if the kinema industry had not suffered, as all French industries, the consequences of a real social revolution caused by the advent of the Popular Front Government. This caused a heavy handicap for the producers.

The former big companies, such as Pathé and Gaumont, now under receivership, do nothing in the way of production, but rent their studios to independent producers and exhibit in their circuits of theatres.

Of the 150 films which have been produced, 75 to 100 are films only suitable for markets of French language as France, North Africa, Belgium, and Switzerland. French production has also turned out in 1936 about fifty important films which have penetrated the international markets with great success.

At the end of 1936 about a dozen French pictures were in production and about thirty ready for release.

There is no production of short subjects except a few sketches or very beautiful documentaries, as "Terre d'Amour," "Provincia," etc., which have a very restricted run.

DISTRIBUTION AND EXHIBITION.—It is difficult to separate these two branches of the Trade which are so close together.

In addition to French films, French distributing companies also hire American and German films which, after dubbed-in French, are booked as supporting pictures for the first part of the programmes accompanying a big French picture.

The quota law to which are submitted all foreign films introduced in France has limited to 15 theatres (different for each film if one wants) the exhibition of foreign talkies spoken in foreign languages.

These films have to be shown with French sub-titles.

For general release, these foreign films have to be dubbed in French, and they are allowed at the rate of 94 per half-year—i.e., 188 per year.

Generally speaking, the distribution and the exhibition of foreign films in France is as follows :—

(1) First run exhibition in the original version, with French sub-titles, in a specialising kinema of the Champs Elysées, or of the so-called "Grands Boulevards," Paris.

Sometimes a second run in other kinemas in Paris showing equally original versions, at the rate of two a programme.

(2) Afterwards the general release in all kind of kinemas as "dubbed" version. With the exception of the first run theatres, all the kinemas in Paris, suburbs, and provinces are now showing regularly two films per programme. The second film—feature film—is nearly always a French one.

Foreign dubbed films, no matter how important (with a few exceptions, as "The Bengal Lancers" or "Mutiny on the Bounty"), are used as supporting pictures.

Some kinemas (which are unable to book enough French films because of the circuits competition) are sometimes obliged to show two dubbed pictures per programme, which affects really their receipts.

British films are rarely shown in France with much success, with the exception of a few outstanding films, such as "Private Life of Henry VIII," "I Was a Spy," and, more recently, "Thirty-Nine Steps" and "The Ghost Goes West."

French exhibitors have per year at their disposition roughly 125 French films and 190 dubbed pictures, that is, say, about 315 films in all.

The exhibitor associations continue to fight against excessive taxes and the depreciation made by some exhibitors of the admission rates.

The problem of redundancy is unknown in France, where only about fifty new kinemas open each year, but are balanced by the closing of old-fashioned ones.

ORGANIZATION OF THE INDUSTRY.—The strikes, threats of nationalization of the kinema by the Government, and the fight with the Trade Unions, have obliged the Industry to be reorganized and the employers to unite.

The disunited employers have at last been able to form the Confederation Générale of the Cinema Industry, grouping together producers, distributors, exhibitors, and the technical sections such as laboratories, studios, etc.

On the other hand, many employees have refused to join the Trade Unions which had a political aspect, connected with the Socialist and Communist Parties, and have formed non-political syndicates, taking care only of corporative matters.

At the present time it is difficult to say what 1937 will bring to the French film industry. Everything depends on the political and economical conditions of the country itself.

GERMANY.

GENERAL LEGISLATION.—A number of new decrees were imposed during the year upon the German film industry by the Propaganda Ministry and its subordinate, the National Film Chamber—viz., exhibitors are compelled to possess not only a licence, but also a projectionist's certificate, so as to be able to judge the technical qualities of performances ; theatre tickets must be uniform in size, printed text and method of numeration ; in production, directors, cameramen and leading artistes must put a period of two weeks between contracts, etc., but the most remarkable measure is that issued personally by the Propaganda Minister, Dr. Goebbels, banning all journalistic criticism of works of literature and art, including films, and permitting analysis and description only by writers of at least 30 years of age and possessing certificates showing that they are versed sufficiently in their subjects.

With the exception of Ufa, all German producers are now depending on the Film Credit Bank for the financing of their films. The adverse situation of the German film production caused by rising production costs and losses of foreign markets (careful estimates speak of yearly losses of 6 to 10 million marks) had caused the bank, in August/September, 1936, to safeguard their interests by restricting credits. This policy had, however, to be abandoned by order of the Propaganda Ministry.

CENSORSHIP AND TAXATION.—No changes in regulations. All censorship certificates issued prior to the beginning of the Nazi regime, are cancelled and the respective films subjected to re-examination. Because of the banning of a comparatively large number of American super films which threatens the profitableness of their German distribution enterprises, and the impossibility of transferring funds to America, American firms still maintaining offices in Berlin (M.-G.-M., Fox and Paramount) are said to contemplate the liquidation of the latter.

IMPORT REGULATIONS.—Only slight changes of the Quota Act prolonged for an unlimited period, and fixing the number of regular import permits again at 175 per year, but without differentiating between soundfilms (previously 105) and silent films (previously 70, hardly any of which were used during the last years) so that their total number is now available for the former. To the facts given in the 1936 issue of the YEAR BOOK regarding the import permits allotted to distributors and exporters may be added that the former are non-transferable, whereas the latter can be transferred a single time at a price of 10,000 marks, which is subject to a reduction of 1,000 marks each for the first amount of 20,000 marks and any additional sum of 5,000 marks expended for dubbing the respective film in Germany.

The Quota Act stipulates that a film is to be recognised as a German one if (1) produced by Germans or a company founded according to German law and residing in Germany ; (2) studio shots and as far as possible location shots are taken in Germany ; (3) the idea, scenario and music originate from, and are made by, a German ; (4) production managers, directors and all collaborators are Germans. " Aryan " foreigners can be treated as though they were Germans, if they have resided in Germany uninterruptedly since January 1, 1923 ; otherwise they can be employed up to 25 per cent., within each group of film workers. For cultural or artistic reasons the Propaganda

Minister can permit the employment of a foreigner (whether " Aryan " or not) applied for by a producer, permission to be given for each special case only.

Trade agreements exist with France, Austria and Czechoslovakia.

HOLLAND.

GENERAL LEGISLATION.—The protective measures against redundancy and excessive competition among distributors adopted by the Nederlandsche Bioscoop Bond, as referred to in the 1936 issue of the YEAR BOOK, were extended for another year in a slightly alleviated form. The Bond forbids distributors to rent films to non-members, with the exception of documentaries, and compels them to also acquire the sub-standard rights of the films distributed by them.

CENSORSHIP AND TAXATION.—Generally unchanged. Notwithstanding the strict censoring of films, particularly regarding the admittance of juveniles below an age of 18, some municipalities are barring children below 14 years of age from attending all kinema performances.

IMPORT REGULATIONS.—No changes.

HUNGARY.

GENERAL LEGISLATION.—Since August 20, 1936, programmes are not allowed to contain more than one feature film of a length exceeding 1,200 metres, the total length of a programme having been fixed at not more than 3,400 metres for first-run theatres and 3,800 metres for other halls ; kinema performances, the number of which is restricted to three on weekdays and four on Saturdays, Sundays and holidays, must end before midnight ; no free tickets are issued and reduced prices may only be issued to Government officials, the press and members of the National Students' Association.—

Pending a general regulation of admission fees contemplated by the Home Office, the exhibitors of the capital, Budapest, have already taken the initiative by classifying their theatres into five categories with prices ranging from 0.80 to 3.50 pengoe for the first and 0.20 to 0.80 pengoe for the last class (one pengoe equal to 1s. 2½d. at the official rate and 9d. at the commercial rate of exchange).

CENSORSHIP AND TAXATION.—No changes. The regular censorship fee amounts to 0.04 pengoe per metre on domestic and 0.10 pengoe per metre on foreign films.

IMPORT REGULATIONS.—The exhibitors' quota of Hungarian-speaking films, original or dubbed within the country, is increased to 20 per cent. of programmes shown from August 1, 1936, till July 31, 1937. Import certificates, a certain number of which are needed for the import of a foreign film according to footage (which also applies to documentaries), are granted as follows: 8 for a domestic feature film (exceeding in length 1,200 metres), 3 for a domestically dubbed foreign feature film, 5 to 20 for a domestic documentary suited for public performances.

The Film Fund formed by the charges made by the Board of Censors for examining films regarding their suitability for the exhibitors' quota (0.06 pengoe per metre with an extra charge on dubbed films of 0.20 pengoe per metre), and by the special tax on imported films screened in a foreign language (0.20 pengoe per metre if sub-titled in Hungary and 1 pengoe per metre if sub-titled abroad) subsidises the domestic production, mainly by maintaining the State-owned Hunnia Studios, where producers are allotted space and facilities free of charge.

ITALY.

GENERAL LEGISLATION.—The regulations reported in the 1936 issue of the YEAR BOOK are to be supplemented by the following : Where the Propaganda Ministry has not granted to a producer a credit free of interest out of the Film Fund which has been endowed by the Finance Ministry with 6 million lire (100 li. about £1 1s. 6d.) per year for the next five years, he can receive it up to 60 per cent. of the production cost at a cheap rate of interest from the Autonomous Film Credit Section of the Banca del Lavoro, which has a capital of 40 million li. provided by the State and the bank in equal shares ; of a film thus subsidised the scenario must be approved of by the General Direction of Cinematography and the release effected by one of the 13 distributing firms especially authorised.

Single-feature programmes are obligatory, unless the balance of programme is replaced by a second-feature film already released in a previous season. A standard renting contract discriminating against blind-booking of foreign films by first-run theatres in large towns, is compulsory.

CENSORSHIP AND TAXATION.—No changes.

IMPORT REGULATIONS.—The synchronisation tax for the compulsory dubbing of a foreign-language film is fixed at 10 per cent. of its distribution return, with a minimum of 15,000 li. for a film exceeding in length 1,000 metres ; the collection of the tax, two-thirds of which go to the Film Fund, is entrusted to the Italian Authors' Association.

The import reductions imposed during the Abyssinian war were replaced on June 30, 1936, by an *ad valorem* quota allowing importers the annual transfer of the same amount of 13 million li., as payment in full for 82 films to be imported, which they had been permitted to transfer, according to the valuta restrictions, as part payment for 200 films imported by them in 1935.

An annual import quota of 3 million li. is allotted to Italian producers, and any additional number of films can be imported, provided the proceeds are utilised in Italy, preferably for film production. Since the Italian branches of American distributors are faring worst under the above regulations, they have remonstrated with the result that they were promised an additional quota said to amount to 8 million li. per year.

POLAND.

GENERAL LEGISLATION.—No change.

CENSORSHIP AND TAXATION.—Censorship is unchanged. Under the regulation issued by the Home Office in September, 1936, the entertainments tax is fixed at not more than four per cent. of box-office receipts in all villages and in towns up to 10,000 inhabitants, 15 per cent. in towns up to 100,000 inhabitants, 35 per cent. in larger towns, and at 65 per cent. of the takings of the first-run theatres in the capital, Warsaw, but kinemas showing at least 10 per cent. per year of " Polish " films (*i.e.* domestic productions or foreign films dealing with a Polish subject matter) of not less than 5,000 ft. per film, are granted a reduction of 25 per cent. on foreign films screened in a foreign language, and 50 per cent. on same dubbed in Poland in the Polish language. Additional reductions of 15 per cent. are granted for the screening of " Polish " shorts.

New theatres opened in communities where no kinema has been in existence, are exempt from the entertainments tax for five years. Each kinema is compelled to show two domestic feature films annually.

IMPORT REGULATIONS.—The import duty on sound-films amounts to 80 zloty (each about 9d.) per kg. on negatives and 110 zloty per kg. on positives, plus 10 per cent. for customs expenses.

SPAIN.

Owing to the conditions created by the civil war in Spain, the film industry is at a standstill and no reliable particulars are available.

SWEDEN.

Particulars of censorship and taxation, and import regulations remain as set out in the 1936 YEAR BOOK.

From July, 1935, to June 30, 1936, 293 feature films and 70 short subjects were released in Sweden. Native features numbered 22, French and German 23 each, English 14 and American 192.

THE EMPIRE - OVERSEAS.

AUSTRALIA.

Of the 481 feature films imported into Australia last year 353 came from the United States, 123 from the United Kingdom and 5 from other countries. This represents a decrease of 2.4 per cent. of British films over the previous year.

Feature films were dealt with by the Australian Censor in the past four years as under :—

	1932	%	1933	%	1934	%	1935	%
Passed without eliminations	253	51.1	212	45.8	257	53.99	335	69.7
Passed with eliminations	192	38.8	207	44.7	183	38.45	115	23.9
Rejected in first instance	50	10.1	44	9.5	36	7.56	31	6.4
Totals	495		463		476		481	
Absolute rejections ...	20	4.0	12	2.5	16	3.3	21	4.3

The Censor's comments on British films show that : Of the 123 British feature films imported, 8 were finally rejected, or 6.5 per cent., as against 3.1 per cent. American films, provoking the Censor to the tart remark that " British films are going back to the unenviable position of 1931, when the percentage of such films finally rejected was about twice as great as those of American origin. English companies are still under the impression that no film is worth production unless it drags in a shower bath or bathtub scene. The indulgence of this childish obsession involves the risk of losing important and essential dialogue.

For the information of British producers it might be as well to repeat that the decisions of the Australian Censorship are governed by the terms of Regulation 14 (Imported Films), which provides that no film shall be registered which, in the opinion of the Censorship Board, or on appeal in the opinion of the Appeal Censor—

(a) is blasphemous, indecent, or obscene ;

(b) is likely to be injurious to morality, or to encourage or incite to crime ;

(c) is likely to be offensive to the people of any friendly nation ;

(d) is likely to be offensive to the people of the British Empire ; or

(e) depicts any matter, the exhibition of which is undesirable in the public interest.

The New South Wales Film Quota Act, which came into force on October 1st, 1935, imposes on renters the obligation to acquire 5 per cent. and on exhibitors the obligation to show 4 per cent. of Australian pictures in the year ending January and July, 1937, respectively ; this represents approximately 20 Australian pictures in 1936, 30 in 1937, 40 in 1938, 50 in 1939, and 60 in 1940. It is yet too soon to estimate whether the legislation will have the intended effect of encouraging Australian film production of high quality ; four out of six of the films submitted to the Australian Films Advisory Committee have, so far, been refused registration as Quota films.

The Victorian Quota Act, with the same purpose but differing in details, comes into effect nearly six months later ; the exhibitor in this State is not required to provide Australian Quota against British films, but only against foreign films.

By the setting up of a Trade Board consisting of representatives of the distributing and exhibiting sides of the industry, it is hoped to solve the twin problem of over-seating and price-regulation. Meanwhile the Motion Picture Exhibitors' Association have resolved to introduce a sixpenny minimum admission price.

In the death of Frank Thring (head of Efftee Pictures), which occurred in Melbourne last July, the Australian film trade lost an outstanding person- ality. Mr. Thring was a pioneer of the picture business in Australia ; he rose from the position of operator to be one of the biggest figures in the Australian amusement world. He was one of the founders of Hoyts, and sold his holdings to Fox, which enabled them to secure control of Hoyts. Since then he had interested himself in production and operated a circuit of legi- timate theatres.

Ernest Turnbull, head of British Dominions (Australia), and Stuart Doyle, head of Greater Union Theatres, Cinesound Productions, British Empire Films, Associated Distributors, as well as General Theatres Corporation, visited England during 1936. Subsequently Mr. Doyle visited the United States in his capacity of head of Cinesound Productions for the purpose of engaging American stars to appear in forthcoming productions.

A colony of 400 to 500 actors exists in Sydney and Melbourne, actors who came there in the days when the stage was flourishing, and preferred to settle. They constitute a nucleus for pictures ; stages and laboratories are available and more will be built ; and with the importation of stars from Hollywood and Britain, it is hoped to capitalise Australia's famous sunshine, her miles of sandy beaches, and the wide open spaces of her vast interior.

Columbia has already extended its production field to Australia, the first subject (made at the National Studio) being an adaptation of the Zane Grey story "Rangle River," with Victor Jory in the leading rôle and Clarence Badger directing. National Productions have secured Charles Farrell for their next picture, which will be made at their Pagewood studio, eight miles out of Sydney. This studio is equipped with British Acoustic recording apparatus, which, by the way, was used over a distance of 5,000 miles in filming " The Flying Doctor,"

Among the Australian artistes at present working in English film studios may be mentioned Judy Kelly, Nancy Burne and Coral Brown ; and with the shrinking of the physical distance that separates England and Australia— strikingly indicated in such films as Roy Tuckett's " Britannia Rules the Air " —a further exchange of talent and ideas between the two countries is antici- pated.

Actually Australian kinemas already show on an average about 20 per cent. British pictures purely on merit alone and without the application of any compulsory measures.

NEW ZEALAND.

During the year 483 feature films were examined by the New Zealand Film Censors. Of these 104 came from Great Britain, 1 from Australia, 2 from New Zealand, 373 from the United States, 1 from Germany, 1 from Spain, and 1 from Italy. Five feature films were rejected, one of these being of British origin, one Spanish and three American.

An Advisory Committee has been appointed to discuss what amendments, if any, are necessary, to the Board of Trade Kinematograph Films Regula- tions, 1935 ; its members are Messrs. W. F. Stilwell, S.M., Chairman ; S. H. Craig and R. M. Stewart, representing the renters ; E. J. Righton and J. Robertson, M.P., representing the exhibitors ; R. Girling Butcher, chief inspector under the Kinematograph Films Act, and F. Johnston, of the Depart- ment of Industries and Commerce.

The New Zealand production " Primitive Passions," founded on a Maori legend and played by native actors, was given a West End release in London recently by Wardour. The New Zealand Government Tourist Bureau has leased the Wellington premises of Filmcraft with a view to increasing production of sound films of New Zealand life and interest for distribution overseas.

CANADA.

General conditions, both within and outside the motion picture entertainment field, became so definitely improved in Canada during 1936 that amusement operators ceased to talk depression and began to organise themselves for substantially increased activity. The immediate result was that the 12 months' period goes into the books as the " rebuilding year." All across the country, cinemas that had become antiquated and time-worn were reconstructed, re-equipped and generally brightened. Further, a considerable number of new theatres sprang up in long ignored locations, a sign of the times being that practically all the units were of medium size, largely serving neighbourhood requirements. The number of theatres operating increased by 12 per cent. during 1936, according to a trade survey.

Much progress was obtained by British films. The number of available British features did not increase to any great extent, but a much greater demand on the part of exhibitors and patrons was evident for the pictures that were released in the Dominion. It was pointed out late in the year that many additional theatres were showing British features where they had previously been unknown. Excellent engagements were enjoyed in large first-run theatres by a large percentage of the British pictures, and they were also shown in a rapidly increasing number of theatres in the suburbs and in small towns. The year saw the permanent reopening of the famous His Majesty's Theatre, Montreal, with an all-British policy, and a number of attractions were held over here for a second week.

Wide interest was aroused in British pictures through the making of " The Great Barrier," dealing with pioneer railway building days in the mountainous sections of British Columbia and Alberta, by Gaumont-British Picture Corporation. Production activities, covering a period of more than four months, by the largest and most comprehensive unit ever to operate in Canada, had the effect of securing a considerable amount of favourable publicity not only for the Canadian epic film, but for British pictures generally.

The question of fees to be imposed for musical presentation royalties by the Canadian Performing Right Society was an issue which occupied attention throughout the greater portion of the year, and it was not until November that the subject was settled by agreement between representatives of varied interests with the tacit concurrence of the Dominion Government. A graduated scale of performing right rates based on the seating capacities of theatres was adopted, although the Federal Government created a Copyright Appeal Board for the hearing of complaints.

Further Amusements Tax concessions were granted by the Ontario Government, but these were of minor importance in so far as the theatres were concerned. One step was the granting of exemption to attractions at exhibitions and agricultural shows. Pressure continues to be applied by theatre organisations for further relief from the heavy impost. The Dominion Government made an important pronouncement in the decision not to grant duty-free entry into Canada of equipment for the producing of motion pictures on a permanent basis.

A flare-up occurred in Ontario when the Provincial censor board chairman took issue with the Roman Catholic Legion of Decency over the classification of film features which did not coincide with the official rulings of the board. The censor chairman announced that official lists would be published for the guidance of all persons ; but Hon. M. F. Hepburn, Premier of Ontario, publicly took the censor official to task and ruled that the recommendations of the censor board would not be classified for adult or family consumption.

The Dominion Government granted a concession to film distributing interests in Canada by reducing the special tax on rental revenue sent out of the country on imported films from 5 to 2 per cent., a reduction of 60 per cent.

The most important trade change during 1936 affected the distribution of British pictures. Empire Films, Ltd., Toronto, secured the Canadian franchise for Gaumont-British Pictures, which had previously been held for years by Regal Films, Ltd., Toronto. The latter company continued to hold important British connections, however, by securing 16 features, the list including London Film Productions. Empire Films, Ltd., enjoyed further expansion by organising distribution arrangements in the Colony of Newfoundland. A highlight development was the signing of a five years' contract between N. L. Nathanson and Paramount interests for his continuance as operating head of Famous Players Canadian Corp., Canada's big theatre chain. Oscar R. Hanson, president of Empire Films, Ltd., gained further prestige and power by organising Hanson Theatres Corp. to operate a chain of theatres throughout Ontario.

INDIA.

The satisfactory position of general commerce during the year 1936 has its counterpart in a further development in most branches of the film industry. The official statistics show very little difference in import figures as compared with the year 1935, but a truer picture is obtained by regarding the purely visual evidence of progress within the film industry.

News is received of more first-class theatres either built or building. The new Metro-Goldwyn-Mayer theatre in Calcutta, opened during the last 12 months, has more than justified its existence and has been followed by the modernisation of the Empire Theatre, which is now controlled by Humayan Properties, Ltd., from whom increased activity is to be looked for in the theatre branch during the year to come. Yet another opening in Calcutta in the field of theatres catering primarily for European patronage is predicted for 1937. Another Calcutta opening of interest is the Paradise Theatre at the North end of Chowringhee Road, dedicated to a policy of exclusively Indian films.

In Bombay, Metro-Goldwyn-Mayer are busy with the preparation of a new theatre whose lines will undoubtedly follow their eminently successful venture in Calcutta. Yet another new theatre is building in a residential quarter of this city which, when completed, will include restaurant, dance lounge and apartment flats.

There are now two trade associations in India whose activities are of great interest. One is the Kinematograph Renters' Society of India, Burma and Ceylon, whose membership consists entirely of American and European interests, while the other is the Motion Picture Society of India, which draws its adherents from the indigenous side of the film industry.

The interests of European or Indian firms are clearly divided by the natural segregation of film patronage in India. There are three categories of patrons, consisting of Europeans, Anglo-Indians and Indians. The first and last-named patronise exclusively the theatres exhibiting their respective product, while the Anglo-Indians patronise both with a leaning towards the European type of programme. Any movement towards diminishing the number of films available in India, either for Europeans or Indians, is definitely retrograde and has no advantage to offset the deprivation of one section of its preferred amusement.

The Motion Picture Society of India has petitioned the Government during 1936 to increase the valuation for duty purposes on imported exposed film from 7 annas to Rs.2.8 per foot. The 7 annas basis already represents duty on a positive print of 250 per cent. *ad valorem*; the proposed new basis would become approximately 1,500 per cent. *ad valorem*.

The Kinematograph Renters' Society of India have petitioned the Government for a reduction of the 7 annas per foot basis and in support of their claim they presented an extremely well-reasoned petition.

Native production still thrives and news is received of several big successes. Low production costs and a tremendous number of potential native patrons make the Indian film producer's position a very interesting one despite the obvious complications of language.

1936 is a satisfactory year and gives ground for belief that 1937 may be regarded with optimism.

FOREIGN AND COLONIAL TRADE DIRECTORY.

Australia.

PRODUCERS, DISTRIBUTORS, SUPPLIES, ETC., NEW SOUTH WALES.

Associated Distributors, Ltd., 251A, Pitt Street.
Automatic Film Laboratories, Dowling Street, Surry Hills.
British Dominion Films, Ltd. (Sydney Branch), 300, Pitt Street
British Empire Films, Ltd., 251A, Pitt Street.
Cinesound Productions, Ltd., 2, Ebley Street, Waverley.
Columbia Pictures, Ltd., 251A, Pitt Street, Sydney.
Commonwealth Film Censorship, Watson House, Bligh Street, Sydney.
Commonwealth Film Laboratories, Wilton Street, Sydney.
Cummings and Wilson, Cinématograph Manufacturers, 29, Alberta Street, Sydney.
Expeditionary Films (1933), Ltd., 12, O'Connell Street, Sydney.
Filmcraft Laboratories, Missenden Road, Camperdown.
Film Distributors, Ltd., 251A, Pitt Street.
Fox Film Corpn. (Australasia), Ltd., 97, Goulburn Street, Sydney.
Fox Movietone News, 43, Missenden Road, Camperdown.
Hamilton and Baker, 327, Pitt Street, Sydney.
Hardman Research Laboratory, 103, Bourke Street, Waterloo.

Harringtons, Ltd., 388, George Street, Sydney.
Hawkins Film Productions, 160, Castlereagh Street, Sydney.
Metro-Goldwyn-Mayer, Ltd., 20, Chalmers Street, Sydney.
Motion Picture Dis. Assn. of Aust., Cathcart House, 11C, Castlereagh Street, Sydney.
National Productions, Ltd., 296, Pitt Street, Sydney.
National Studios, 369, George Street, Sydney.
National Theatre Supply Co., 251A, Pitt Street, Sydney.
Percival Film Laboratories, 1, Bridge Street, Petersham.
Raycophone, Ltd., 62, Booth Street, Annandale.
Paramount Film Service, Ltd., 66, Reservoir Street, Sydney.
RKO Radio Pictures (Australasia), Ltd., 300, Pitt Street.
Scott Films, 198, Pitt Street, Sydney.
United Artists (Australasia), Ltd., 221-5, Elizabeth Street, Sydney.
Universal Film Mfg. Co. (Australasia), Ltd., 280, Pitt Street, Sydney.
Warner Bros. First Natl. Pictures (Australasia), Ltd., 221-5, Elizabeth Street, Sydney.
Western Electric Co. (Aus.), Ltd., 250, Pitt Street, Sydney.

VICTORIA.

Archibald Equipment Co., 13, Finsbury Way, East Camberwell, E.6.
Associated Distributors, Ltd., 429, Bourke Street, Melbourne, C.1.
British Dominions Films, Ltd. (of Aust.), 164, Flinders Street, Melbourne, C.1.
British Empire Films, Ltd., 178A, Flinders Street, Melbourne, C.1.
Cinesound Productions, Ltd., Office, 178A, Flinders Street, Melbourne, C.1. Studio: 145, Fitzroy Street, St. Kilda, S.2.
Colombia Pictures Pty., Ltd., 234, Swanston Street, Melbourne, C.1.
Commerce Department, 419, Collins Street, Melbourne, C.1 ; Cinema and Photo Branch, Victoria Barracks, St. Kilda Road, Melbourne, C.1.
Efftee Film Productions, Princess Theatre, Melbourne, C.1.
Filmads Pty., Ltd., 201, Collins Street, Melbourne, C.1.
Film Renters Association of Australia, Ltd., 248, Swanston Street, Melbourne, C.1.
Film Tests, 2, Causeway, Melbourne, C.1.
Fox Film Corpn. (A/sia), Ltd., Lonsdale Street, Melbourne, C.1.
Gaumont British Picture Corpn., 365, Lonsdale Street, Melbourne, C.1.
General Theatres Corpn. of A/sia, Ltd., Hoyts Div., 191, Collins Street, Melbourne, C.1.

Union Div., 178A, Flinders Street, Melbourne. C.1.
Greater Australasian Films, Ltd., 234, Swanston Street, Melbourne, C.1.
Hardy, J. R., 145, Russell Street, Melbourne, C.1.
Harrington, Ltd., 266, Collins Street, Melbourne, C.1.
Herschells Pty., Ltd., 31, Agnes Street, Jolimont, C.2.
Kodak (Australasia), Pictures, Ltd., 284, Collins Street, Melbourne, C.1. (Laboratories, Southampton Crescent, Abbotsford, N.9.)
Metro-Goldwyn-Mayer, Ltd., 266, Queen Street, Melbourne, C.1.
Paramount Film Service, Ltd., 256-260, King Street, Melbourne, C.1.
RKO Radio Pictures (Australasia), Ltd., 164, Flinders Street, Melbourne, C.1.
Small, Herbert, Pty., Ltd., 308, Collins Street, Melbourne, C.1.
United Artists (Australasia), Ltd., Latham House, 234, Swanston Street, Melbourne, C.1.
Universal Film Manufacturing Co. (A/sia), Ltd., 572-574, Lonsdale Street, Melbourne, C.1.
Warner Bros. First National Pictures, Ltd., 260, Queen Street, Melbourne, C.1.
Wenzel Pty., Ltd., 313, Flinders Lane, Melbourne, C.1.

TRADE PUBLICATIONS.

Everyones, 102, Sussex Street, Sydney, and Bourke House, Bourke and Russell Streets, Melbourne.

Exhibitor's Monthly, 251A, Pitt Street, Sydney.
The Film Weekly, 136, Liverpool Street, Sydney

B

Austria.

FILM PRODUCERS.

Atlantis-Film G.m.b.H., Neubaugasse 12, Vienna
Cine Central, G.m.b.H., Marialferstr. 1c, Vienna, VI.
Donau-Film, Ges.m.b.H., Marc d'Avianogasse 1. Vienna, V.
Forst-Film Prod., G.m.b.H., Neuer Markt. 5, Vienna.
Gloria-Film, G.m.b.H., Kohlmarkt. 8, Vienna, I.
Hade-Film, G.m.b.H., Koestlerg. 5, Vienna, VI.
Horusfilm, G.m.b.H., Johannesg. 1, Vienna, I.
Kongress-Film, G.m.b.H., Trattnerhof 1, Vienna.
Luxor-Film, G.m.b.H., Kohlmarkt. 8, Vienna.
Mondial-Film A. G., Neubaugasse 2, Vienna.
Panta-Film, G.m.b.H., Johannesg. 1, Vienna, I

Patria-Film, Ges.m.b.H., Amerlingstr. 17, Vienna.
Projectograph-Film, Oskar Glück, Neubaugasse 25, Vienna.
Selenophon, Licht-u-Tonbild, G.m.b.H., Neubaugasse 8, VII, Vienna.
Schonbrunn-Film, Ges.m.b.H., Maxingstr. 13a, Vienna, XIII.
Standard-Film, G.m.b.H., Getreidemarkt. 1, Vienna, I.
Styria, Film-Ges.m.b.H., Koestlerg. 5, Vienna.
Vienna-Film, G.m.b.H., Kohlmarkt. 8, Vienna, Vienna, I.
Walter Reisch-Film, G.m.b.H., Kohlmarkt. 8. Vienna, I.

RENTERS, DISTRIBUTORS AND AGENTS.

Dr. Leo Berg, Filmvertrieb, Siebensterng. 39, Vienna, VII.
Dr. Hans L. Bohm, Filmvertr., VII., Neubaug. 25, Vienna.
Engel Hugo, Ges.m.b.H., Filmleihanstalt, Neubaugasse 28, Vienna.
Europa-Film, G.m.b.H., Neubaugasse 11, VII, Vienna.
Excelsior-Lemberger and Komp, Filmvertrieb und Verleih, Siebensterngasse 39, Vienna.
Fox-Film Corporation, Ges.m.b.H., Mariahilferstrasse 47, Vienna.
Freiwirth Paul, Filmverleih, Neubaug. 23, Vienna, VII.
Gaumont-Ges.m.b.H., Mariahilferstrasse 57/59, Vienna.
Dr. Hauser & Co., G.m.b.H., Neubaug. 38, Vienna, VII.
Huschak & Co., Film-Verleih u. Vertrieb, Neubaug. 25, Vienna.
Kiba, G.m.b.H., Filmverleih, Neubaugasse 2, Vienna.
Lux-Film-Vertriebs-u. Verleih-Ges.m.b.H., VII, Neubaugasse 25, Vienna.
Metro-Goldwyn-Mayer, Ges.m.b.H., VII, Neubaug. 1, Vienna.
R. Muller, Ges.m.b.H., VII, Neubaugasse 25, Vienna.
" Mondial " Internationale Filmindustrie, A.G., Neubaugasse 2, VII, Vienna.
Oebut, Oesterreich in Bild und Ton, Neubaugasse 8, Vienna.

Orbis-Filmverleih, Ges.m.b.H., Neubaug. 38 Vienna.
Paramount-Film, Ges.m.b.H., VII, Neubaug. 1, Vienna.
Karl Philipp, Siebensterng. 39, Vienna, VII.
Primax-Film, Ges.m.b.H., Filmvertrieb, Neubaugasse 31, Vienna.
R.K.O. Radio Films, G.m.b.H., Neubaug. 1 Vienna.
Rex Film, Ges.m.b.H., Kohlmarkt. 8. Vienna.
Rosenfeld Herm., Siebensterng 39, Vienna.
Solar-Film, P.H., Koenigfest, Neubaug. 3, Vienna.
Terra-Filmverleih-u.-Vertriebs-Ges.m.b.H., Neubaugasse 12, Vienna.
Tobis-Sascha-Filmverleih-u.Vertriebs,Ges.m.b.H., Siebensterngasse 31, Vienna.
Ufa-Film, Ges.m.b.H., Neubaugasse 1, Vienna.
Universal Pictures, Ges.m.b.H., Neubaugasse 1, Vienna.
Volksbildunghaus Wiener Urania, I, Uraniastrasse 1, Vienna.
Warner Bros. First National Films, G.m.b.H., Mariahilferstr. 71, Vienna, VII.
Weil & Co., Eduard, Filmverleih und Vertrieb, Neubaugasse 25, Vienna.
Wiener Volksbildungsverein, Stöberg, 11-15, Vienna, V.
Wirtschafter Adolf, Film-Verleih u-Vertr., Neubaugasse 36, Vienna.

MANUFACTURERS AND AGENTS OF KINEMA ACCESSORIES.

Agfa-Photo, Ges.m.b.H., III., Rennweg 52, Vienna.
Aktiengesellschaft fur elektrischen Bedarf, Neubaugasse 15, Vienna, A.E.G.
A.E.G. Union-Elektrizitats-Ges., XXI., Pirquetstr. 114, Vienna.
Bauer-Kinomaschinen, Gen.-Vertretg : Ing H. Günsburg, Neubaug. 2, Vienna.
Berka Oskar, Kopieranstalt, Braunschweiggasse 17, Vienna, XIII.
Castagna & Sohn, L. (Marconiphone Co., Ltd., London u. R.C.A., New York), Schwarzspanier str. 17, Vienna, IX.
Elin, A. G. fur elektr. Industrie, Volksgartenstr. 1-5, Vienna, I.
Friedl Gust.-Karl Chaloupka, Fein-u. Elektromechanik, Zieglerg, 29, Vienna, VII.
Gevaert-Rohfilms, Mariahilferstr. 88a, bei Kred.-Instit. d. Kinobes. Oesterr. Vienna, VII.
Herlango Photoges.m.b.H., Mariahilferstr. 51, Vienna.
Ilford, Limited, London, Repraes. f. Oesterr, Ernoe Morvay, Siebenstreng. 39, Vienna.

Illustrierter Film-Kurier, Neubaug. 251, Vienna.
Klangfilm, G.m.b.H., Vertr, Siemens & Halske, Apostelg. 12, Vienna.
Kodak, G.m.b.H., Beatrixg. 25, Vienna.
Dr. E. Kraus, Johannesg. 1, Vienna.
Oest. Siemens-Schuckert-Werke, I, Nibelungengasse 15, Vienna.
Philips, G.m.b.H., Radiorohren, Mariahilferstr. 70, VII., Vienna.
Photoges, m.b.H., Mariahilferstr, 51.
Selenophon, Licht-u.-Tonbild, Ges.m.b.H., Neubaugasse 8, Vienna, VII.
Alexander Schey, Generalvertr. fur Oest. der Ernemann und Hahn-Goerz Maschinen der Zeiss-Ikon A.G., Dresden, VII., Stiftgasse 21, Vienna.
Schmiedl Hans Film-Ausstattung, Gumpendorferstr. 132, Vienna, VI.
Schrack, E., Radiowerk A.G., Flötzersteig - Vienna, XIII.
Schwarz & Maros (Kohlenstifte Plania), Hamburgerstr. 12, Vienna, V.

Special-Film, Ges.m.b.H., Kopieranstalt, XXI, Jedleseerstr. 62, Vienna.
Tobis-Sascha-Filmindustrie A.G., Siebensterngasse 31, Vienna, (Ateliers, Kopieranstalt, Laboratorium, Mauer, Wienerstr. 100, und XIX, Sieveringerstr. 135, Vienna).

Varta, Accumulatorenfabrik A.G., Hamburgerstr. 9, Vienna, V.
Ing. H. Vavrina, Kircheng. 33, Vienna, VII.
Wacht, Siegfried, Photo-Kino-und Projektion apparate, Neubaugasse 34, Vienna.
Western Electric, G.m.b.H., Dreihufeisengasse 1, Vienna.

KINEMA TRADE PUBLICATIONS.

Oesterr. Filmzeitung, Das Organ der Oesterr Filmindustrie, Neubaugasse 25, Vienna.
Der Wiener Film, Zentralorgan der oesterr. Filmproduktion, Neustiftg. 107, Vienna.

Das Kino Journal, Officiell. Organ des Gremium der Lichtspiel unternehmer Osterreichs und samtl. Sektionen, Neubaug. 25, Vienna.

TRADE SOCIETIES AND ASSOCIATIONS.

Bund der Filmindustriellen in Oesterreich, Neubaugasse 25, Vienna.
Gremium der Lichtspielunternehmer Osterreichs, Lindengasse 38, Vienna.
Gewerkschaft der Filmschaffenden Oesterreichs VII., Neubaug. 36, Vienna.

Oesterr. Filmkonferenz, Hana, u, Gewerbekammer, Wien I.
Sektion Wien, Bund der Wiener Lichtspieltheater, Lindeng. 38, Vienna.
Verband der Klein-u. Mittelkinos, Lindeng. 38, Vienna, VI.

Belgium.

PRODUCERS, RENTERS, ETC.

A.B.C., 296, rue Royale, Brussels.
Actualites Agence, 124a, rue Royale, Brussels.
Agence Centrale Cinematographique, 19, rue du Pont-Neuf, Brussels.
Agence Generale du Film, 3, rue des Oeillets, Brussels.
Alliance Cinematographique Europeenne, 10, place de l'Yser, Brussels.
Artistes Associes, 33, bld. du Jardin Botanique, Brussels.
Atlanta Films, 12, bld. Baudouin, Brussels.
Auror Film, 118 rue des Plantes, Brussels.
Bosman & Bourland, 62, rue St. Lazare, Brussels.
Century Film, 118a, rue Neuve, Brussels.
Cineco, 17, rue du Chemin de Fer, Brussels.
Cinefilms, 26, quai aux Pierres de Taille, Brussels.
Cinelocation " Charnault," 55, rue Verte, Brussels.
C.C.B. (Cie. Cinématographique Belge), 32, Bld. du Jardin Botanique, Brussels.
Cobelcine, 10, rue Dupont, Brussels.
Crosly-Films, 74, rue Verte, Brussels.
Dardenne & Cie, 30, rue Dupont, Brussels.
D.S.D. Films, 75, rue des Plantes, Brussels.
Equitable Films, 9, rue des Hirondelles, Brussels.
Excelsior Films, 115, rue Verte, Brussels.
Exploitants Reunis, 29, rue des Plantes, Brussels.
Fama Film, 76, rue Verte, Brussels.
Films Bonamar, 42-44, rue de la Source.
Filma, 38, rue des Plantes, Brussels.
Filmavox, 26, rue Dupont, Brussels.
Films Alpha, 2, rue des Roses, Brussels.
Films Atos, 65, Montagne aux Herbes Potagères, Brussels.
Films Elde, 14, rue du Pont-Neuf, Brussels.
Films Internationaux, 28, rue Linné, Brussels.
Films Osso, 23, rue des Augustins, Brussels.
Fox Films, 16, Place des Martyrs, Brussels.
Frank Films, 100, rue du Marais, Brussels.
Gaumont Franco Films Aubert, 11, quai au Bois de Construction, Brussels.
Gilbertson Films, 124, boulevard Em. Jacqmain, Brussels.

Grandes Exclusivites Europeennes, 36, rue des Plantes, Brussels.
Handel en Export (Ideal Films), 40, rue des Plantes, Brussels.
Hendrickx Films, 67, rue des Plantes, Brussels.
I.F.D. (International Films Distributors) 117, rue Linnée, Brussels.
Kraus Films, 75, rue Verte, Brussels.
Lengnick Charles, 25, rue Philippe de Champagne, Brussels.
Luna Films, 58, rue Verte, Brussels.
Lux Film, 14, rue Locquenghien, Brussels.
Mayfair Films, 15, rue des Plantes, Brussels.
Metro Goldwyn Mayer, 4, rue des Plantes, Brussels.
Meynckens, 115, rue des Plantes, Brussels.
Monopol Film, 2, rue des Oeillets, Brussels.
Nova Films, 109, rue Verte, Brussels.
N.Y.F.A., 69, rue des Plantes, Brussels.
Paramount, 31, chaussée de Haecht, Brussels.
Pathe Consortium Cinema, 12, rue Dupont, Brussels.
P.D.C. (Producers Distributing Corp.), 19, place des Martyrs, Brussels.
Phonora Film, 43, rue des Croisades, Brussels.
Praesens Film, 1, Bld. Jardin Botanique, Brussels.
Princeps Film, 137, rue Verte, Brussels.
Publi-Cine, 13, rue du Canal, Brussels.
Royal Film, 3, rue des Hirondelles, Brussels.
Select Film, 5, rue des Hirondelles, Brussels.
S.F.E.C. (Sté Française d'Exploitation Cinématographique), 68, rue Neuve, Brussels.
Succes Films, 89, rue des Plantes, Brussels.
Union Film, 46, rue des Plantes.
Union Films Internationaux, 51, rue St. Lazare, Brussels.
Universal Films, 20, place des Martyrs, Brussels.
Tobis (Films Sonores), 18, rue Dupont, Brussels
Van Goitsenhoven, 97, rue de Laeken, Brussels.
Warner Bros. First National, 24, rue Dupont, Brussels.

MANUFACTURERS AND AGENTS OF KINEMA ACCESSORIES.

Agfa Film S.A., 79, rue Joseph II, Brussels.
Auriema Radio Corp., S.A., 32a, avenue Louise, Brussels.
Baillet, Is., 77, rue du Moulin, Brussels.
Boulanger, 137, rue Verte, Brussels.
Belot, C., 26, rue du Poincon, Brussels.
Casier, E., 7, rue de l'Ourthe, Brussels.
Cie Lorraine de Charbons pour l'Electricité, 74, rue Ant. Dansaert, Brussels.
Cinetechnique, 54, rue des Plantes, Brussels.
Cine Materiel Hanlet, 106, rue Linnée, Brussels.
Cinetone (S.A. Fichet Belge), 21, rue Fossé aux Loups, Brussels.
Columbia, 149, rue du Midi, Brussels.
Crosly Film S.A., représentant la marque " KALEE," 74, rue Verte, Brussels.
Daf-Arasalva, 64, Bld. Em. Jacqmain, Brussels.
Dubick, L., 10, rue des Plantes, Brussels.
Elecson (Ag. Maison Dardenne), 76, rue des Plantes, Brussels.
Electromagnetique, 64, Bld. Em. Jacqmain, Brussels.
Erneman (C. Rombouts), 142, rue Verte, Brussels.
Fibrocit (Fauteuils), 26, rue Masui, Brussels.
Gaumont, 11, quai au Bois de Construction, Brussels.
Gesco Belge, 36, rue Philippe de Champagne, Brussels.

Gevaert (Photo-Produits), Vieux-Dieu lez Anvers.
Guilleaume, C., 64, Bld. Em. Jacquain, Brussels.
Hardy, 33, rue des Plantes, Brussels.
Kalee (Ag. Crosly Film), 74, rue Verte, Brussels.
Kinoton (Arnold Stern), 67, rue de Locht, Brussels.
Kodak, Ltd., 43, rue de Stassart, Brussels.
Lorraine (see **Cie Lorraine**).
Lumina, 22, rue Froissart, Brussels.
Metzker, H., 120, Av. E. Demolder, Brussels.
N.Y.F.A., 69, rue des Plantes, Brussels.
Philisonor (Philips Radio), 37-39, rue d'Anderlecht, Brussels.
Projectophone Jupiter, 31, rue des Prairies, Brussels.
R.C.A. Pathe, 104, Bld. Ad. Max, Brussels.
Routiaux, J., 16, rue des Plantes, Brussels.
S.E.M. (Soc. d'Electricité & Mécanique), 54, chaussée de Charleroi, Brussels.
Siemens (G. Weinstein), 32, rue Rubens, Brussels.
Thielemans-Boogaerdt, L., 339, rue des Palais Brussels.
Tobler, W. P., Waterloo-Chenois.
Anc. Maison Van Haelewyck, C. (Oscar Lengelle succ.), 31, rue des Prairies, Brussels.
Van Reet, G., 52, Chaussée de Haecht, Brussels.
Western Electric, 9, place des Martyrs, Brussels.

KINEMA TRADE PUBLICATIONS.

Cineo Julien Flament, 14, quai aux Pierres de Taille, Brussels.

Revue Belge Du Cinema, 64, Boulevard Emi) Jacqmain, Brussels.

LABORATORIES.

Cine Service, 69, rue Botanique, Brussels.
Cine Studios (Belgian Sound Studios), 466, Chaussee de Waterloo, Brussels.
Dassonville & Co., 135-137, rue [Berthelot, Brussels.
Hackin, E., 19, rue du Marché aux Peaux, Brussels.

Meuter & Co, 69, rue Verte, Brussels.
Film Edition (Is. Moray), 37, rue des Plantes Brussels.
Studios Belges, 6, rue des Champs, Etterbeek.
Studios Sacal British, 12/16, rue des Champs, Etterbeek.

CONTROL COMMITTEE.

Commission de Controle, 95, rue Pachéco, Brussels.

TRADE ASSOCIATION.

Alliance Belge Du Film, 10 place de l'Yser, Brussels.

STUDIOS.

Belgian Sound Studios, 466, chaussée de Waterloo, Brussels.

Studios Belges de Cinématographie Sonore, 6, rue des Champs, Etterbeck, Brussels.

Canada.

FILM PRODUCERS.

Associated Screen News Limited, 5271, Western Avenue, Montreal, Quebec.

Booth-Dominion Productions, Limited, Ravina Rink, Toronto, Ontario.

Central Films Limited, Victoria, B.C. Kenneth J. Bishop, President.
Dominion of Canada Motion Picture Bureau, Department of Trade and Commerce, Ottawa, Ontario.

FILM DISTRIBUTORS AND AGENTS.

Canadian Universal Film Company, Limited, Head Office, 277, Victoria Street, Toronto, Ontario. Clair Hague, General Manager.
Columbia Pic ures of Canada, Limtied. Head Office, 21, Dundas Square, Toronto, Ontario. Louis Rosenfeld, General Manager.
Cosmopolitan Films Limited. Head Office, 277, Victoria Street, Toronto, Ontario. L. Clavir, Manager. Amkino Pictures and Vostock Films.

Empire Films, Limited. Head Office, 277, Victoria Street, Toronto, Ontario. A. W. Perry, General Manager. Canadian distributor Gaumont British, B.I.P., Twickenham, Associated Radio, Republic and Educational Pictures.

Fox Film Corporation of Canada, Limited. Head Office, 110, Bond Street, Toronto, Ontario. J. P. O'Loghlin, General Manager.

Grand National Pictures. Office, 21, Dundas Square, Toronto, Ontario. Canadian agent, Harry Allen.

La Compagnie Cinematographique Canadienne. Head Office, 1135, Beaver Hall Hill, Montreal, Quebec, Robert Hurd, President. France film.

Maritime Film Company, Head Office, 87, Union Street, St. John, N.B. Jos. Lieberman, President. Independent releases.

Paramount Film Service, Limited. Head Office, 111, Bond Street, Toronto, Ontario. M. A. Milligan, General Manager.

Peerless Films, Limited. Office : 277, Victoria Street, Toronto, Ontario. Independent features.

Regal Films, Limited. Head Office, 306, Royal Bank Building, Toronto, Ontario. Henry L. Nathanson, General Manager. Distributor of Metro-Goldwyn-Mayer, London Film. Productions, British Lion and other British releases.

R.K.O. Distributing Corporation of Canada, Limited. Head Office, 277, Victoria Street, Toronto, Ontario. L. M. Devaney, General Manager. Distributor of Radio Pictures.

Superior Films, Limited. Head Office, 287, Victoria Street, Toronto, Ontario. D. Cooper, General Manager. Independent releases.

United Artists Corporation, Limited. Head Office, 277, Victoria Street, Toronto, Ontario. H. M. Masters, General Manager.

Vitagraph Limited. Head Office, 21, Dundas Square, Toronto, Ontario. H. O. Paynter, General Manager. Distributor of Warner, Bros., First National and Vitaphone releases.

FILM LABORATORIES AND EQUIPMENT.

Associated Screen News, Limited, 5271, Western Avenue, Montreal, Quebec. B. E. Norrish, General Manager.

Canadian Theatre and Electrical Supplies, Limited, 61, Albert Street, Toronto, Ontario.

Canadian Theatre Supply Company, 366, Mayor Street, Montreal, Quebec.

Coleman Electric Company, Limited, 258, Victoria Street, Toronto, Ontario.

Dominion Sound Equipments, Limited. Post Office Box 1080, Montreal, Quebec.

Dominion Theatre Equipment Company, Limited, 60, Dundas Street East, Toronto, Ontario.

Empire Agencies, Limited, 543, Granville Street, Vancouver, B.C.

Film Laboratories of Canada, Limited, 362, Adelaide Street West, Toronto, Ontario.

J. H. Rice & Company. Canada Building, Winnipeg, Manitoba.

La Salle Recreations, Limited, 945, Granville Street, Vancouver, B.C.

Perkins Electric Company, Limited, 277, Victoria Street, Toronto.

Theatre Operating Service, Limited. 277, Victoria Street, Toronto, Ontario.

EXHIBITOR ASSOCIATIONS.

Allied Exhibitors Association of Nova Scotia. Head Office, Halifax, N.S. A. J. Mason, President, Springhill, N.S. ; T. J. Courney, Halifax, N.S.

Allied Exhibitors of Ontario. Head Office, 277, Victoria Street, Toronto, Ontario. G. J. Filman, President ; Oscar R. Hanson, General Manager, 277, Victoria Street, Toronto.

Canadian Independent Theatres Association. Head Office, 21, Dundas Square, Toronto, Ontario. H. Freedman, President ; N. Taylor, Manager, 21, Dundas Square, Toronto, Ontario.

Independent Theatre Owners of Alberta. W. J. Long, President, Rialto Theatre, Edmonton, Alberta.

Independent Theatre Owners of British Columbia. Head Office, Vancouver, B.C. R. J. Dawson, President, Maple Leaf Theatre, Vancouver ; Lawrence Butler, Secretary, Stanley Theatre, Vancouver.

Manitoba Theatre Owners Association. Head Office, Winnipeg, Manitoba. Henry Morton Garrick Theatre, Winnipeg, President ; Frank H. Kershaw, Winnipeg, Secretary.

Quebec Allied Theatrical Industries. Head Office, 660, St. Catherine Street West, Montreal. B. E. Norrish, President ; D. A. Burpee, Secretary.

Saskatchewan Motion Picture Exhibitors Association. P. W. Mahon, President, Strand Theatre, Prince Albert, Saskatchewan.

Western Associated Theatres, Limited. Head Office, Winnipeg, Manitoba. R. S. Bell, General Manager, Film Exchange Building, Winnipeg.

FILM DISTRIBUTOR ASSOCIATION.

Motion Picture Distributors and Exhibitors of Canada. Head office, Metropolitan Building, Toronto, Ontario. Col. John A. Cooper, President and Secretary. Branch Film Boards of Trade in Montreal, St. John, Winnipeg, Calgary and Vancouver.

KINEMA TRADE PUBLICATIONS.

British Film News Office, 306, Royal Bank Building, Toronto, Ontario. B. Harris, Manager.

Canadian Motion Picture Digest. Office, 259, Spadina Avenue, Toronto, Ontario. Ray Lewis, Publisher and Editor.

Czechoslovakia.

FILM PRODUCERS.

A.B. akc. Film. tovarny, Barrandov, Prague.
Czechosl. Filmwoche, Narodni 26, Prague.
Elekta-Film a.s., Närodni tr. 26, Prague.
Host A.G., Vodickova 32, Prague, Ateliers Hostivar.

Host A.G., Vodickova 32, Ateliers Hostivar. Prague,
Lloyd-Film, akc. spol., Anton Dvorakg 10, Brno.
Meissner-Film, s.sr.o., Václavské nám. 30, Prague, II.

RENTERS, DISTRIBUTORS AND AGENTS.

A.B. Pujcovna Filmu, Stepanská 57, Prague, II.
Arco-Film, Stepanská 28, Prague, II.
Beda Heller Film, Stepanská 55, Prague, II.
Brunafilm, Méninská 7, Brno.
Cinefilm, Vodicková 20, Prague, II.
Cechosl, Metro-Goldwyn-Mayer, A.G., Václavské nám, 60, Prague, II.
Dafa-Film, Dr. Feist & Co., Václavské nám. 51, Prague.
Degl a spol., Tyrsuvdum, Prague, III.
Elekta-Film a.s., Narodni tr. 26, Prague II.
Espo-Film, Václavské 23, Prague, II.
Europa-Film, Melantrichova 1, Prague, I.
Fox-Film-Corporation, spol.s.r.o., Poric 15, Prague, II.
Futurum-Film Comp., Na piskách 18, Brno.
Globusfilm, u Pujcovny 4, Prague, II.
Gloria-Film, Barthouova 20, Prague, XII.
Grand-Film, Václavské nám, 47, Prague II.
Koruna-Film, s.sr.o., Václavské nám. 1, Prague.
Lepka, Franz, Filmverlein, Václavské nám. 60, Prague II.
Lloyd Film, akc. spol., Ant. Dvorakg 10, Brno.
Lyrafilm, s.sr.o., Lützowowa 8, Prague, II.
Meissner-Film, Václavské nám. 30, Prague, II.
Merkur-Film, Vodicková 34, Prague, II.
Meteor-Film, Josefska 23, Brno.

Metropolitanfilm Comp., s.sr.o. (R.K.O.), Palac Avion, Prague, II.
Moldavia-Film, s.sr.o., Vaclavské nam. 49, Prague II.
Monopol-Film, inz. K. Waldmann, Jakubska 1, Brunn.
National-Film, spol s.r.o., Václavské nám. 51, Prague II.
Paramount Film, Stepanská 35 (Palais Habich), Prague II.
Pan-Film, Kom.sp., Václavské nám. 30, Prague II.
P.D.C., s.sr.o., Havlickovo nám. 24, Prague, II.,
Praha-Paris, s.sr.o., Václavské nám. 62, Prague.
Ringler-Film, Václavské nám. 60, Prague II.
Julius Schmitt, Václavské nám. 49, Prague.
Slavia-Film, a.s., Václavské nám. 51, Prague.
Terra-Film, Dr. Roman Miszkiewycz, Vnahradbach 8, Brno.
Ufa-Film, spol.s.r.o., Václavské nám. 49, Prague.
United Artists, Václavské nám. 49, Prague II.
Universal-Film, s.sr.o., Vodicková 20, Prague.
Vancura Rud. (Fortunafilm), Václavské nám. 30, Prague 30.
Wolfram-Film, Nachfolger E. Kobosil, Lindenst. 5, Aussig.

MANUFACTURERS AND AGENTS OF KINEMA ACCESSORIES.

A. B. akc. spol., Barrandov, Prague.
A.E.G., elektr. akc., spol. (Klangfilm), Zlatnická 10, Prague.
Agfa-Foto, Hybernská 4, Prague II.
Bioreklama-Slavia, sp.s.r.o., Národnitr. 21, Prague, I.
Favoritfilm, Vlas a sp., Veletrzní 200, Praglie, VII.
Grafofilm (Leop. Vyhnánok), Jáma 1, Prague, II.
Hanzxlik Anton, Zitná 35, Prague II.
Hera-Film, Plzenská tr. 2024, Prague-Smichov.
Kinotechnika, Ing. Jindrich Vavrina, Barthouová 70, Prague XII. (Kinovox).
Kleinhampl a spol. (Foneta, Prometa), Královská 234, Prague, VIII.
Kodak, sp.s.r.o., Biskupsky dvur 8, Prague, II.
Kostyma, Puijcovna, Klárov, Chotková 2, Prague, III.
Ing. J. Lorenc & J. Sabath, Trebizskéro 3-9, Prague VII.

Philips, A.G., Tonfilmanlagen, Karlovo nám. 8, Prague II.
Recono Ing. K. J. Zentner, Palais Fenix, Prague II.
Recordfilm, inz. Mikulas a spol., (titulky) Vaclavské nam., 62, Prague, II.
Reimann-Arnoldfilm, Vyprava, Prague-Barrdndov.
Foto Stroeminger, Francouská 17, Prague, XII.
Rudolf Stuchlik (Zeiss-Jkon, Kinoton), U Pujcovny 4, Prague II.
Sufra-Film, Pariszká 15, Prague, V.
Siemens Elektrizitats-A.G., Havlickovo nám. 15, Prague II.
Ultraphon a.s. (Telefunken), Klimentská 32, Prague, II.
Varrina Jindr. (Kinovox), Barthouová 70, Prague, XII.
Wachtl, Emil, Senovazná 8, Prague, II.
Western Electric, sp.s.r.o., Ve Smeckách 21, Prague.

KINE TRADE PUBLICATIONS.

Filmwoche, Zentral-Organ d. Fachverb. d. deutsch Kinotheater in C.S.R., Aussig. a de Elbe.
"Film," Luetzowowá 36, Prague II.
"Filmovy kuryr," Jáma 5, "U. Novaku," Prague.

Filmovy Zpravodaj, Palac Maceska, Prague XII,
"Internationale Filmschau," Stepanska 57. Prague II.
Prager Filmkurier, Palais "U Nováku," Prague II.

TRADE SOCIETIES AND ASSOCIATIONS.

Fachverband der deutschen Kinotheater in der C.S.R., Aussig a.d. Elbe, Lindenstr. 5.
Filmovy Klub, Václavské 33, Prague II.
Svaz filmoveho prumyslu a obchodu v C.S.R. Lützowowá, 36, Prague II.
Ceskosl. Filmová Unie, Národni 25, Prague.

Svaz filmovych vyrobcu ceskoslovenskych, Rasinovo nábr. 60, Prague.
Ustr. svaz. Kinematografu v C.S.R., Palais U Novaku, Prague II.
Zemsky svaz Kinematografu v Cechach, Palais "U Novaku," Prague II.

Denmark (Copenhagen).

FILM PRODUCERS.

A.S.A., Lyngby, Denmark.
Dir. Henning Karmark, Vesterport Værelse 195, Copenhagen V.
Nordisk Films Kompagni A/S., Redhavnsvej Frihavnen, Copenhagen.

Palladium A/S., Axelborg, Copenhagen V.

Teatrenes Films-Kontor A/S., Jernbanegade Copenhagen V. (John Olsen).

FILM RENTERS, etc.

Columbia Film A/S., Vestre Boulevard 2A, Copenhagen V.
First National-Warner Bros. Films A/S., Rich Bygningen, Raadhuspladsen, Copenhagen K.
Nordlys Filmaktieselskab, Vesterport, Copenhagen V.
Paramount A/S., Vestre Boulevard 29, Copenhagen V.
Fotorama Film-Bureau A/S., Nygade 3, Copenhagen K.
Fox Film, Rich Bygningen, Raadhuspladsen, Copenhagen K.
Gefion Film, Vesterport, Copenhagen V.
Gloria Film A/S., Frederiksberggade 16, Copenhagen K.

A/S., Constantin-Films, Smallegade 2B, Copenhagen F.

Nordisk Films Ko., Frederiksberggade 25, Copenhagen K.
Kosmo-Film A/S., Lovstræde 9, Copenhagen K.
Metro-Goldwyn-Mayer A/S., Vestre Boulevard 27, Copenhagen V.
Vald, Skaarup Film, Vester Voldgade 21, Copenhagen V.
Skandinavisk Film, Kobmagergade 67-69, Copenhagen K.
Teatrenes Films-Kontor A/S., Jernbanegade 4, Copenhagen V.
United Artists A/S., Vestre Boulevard 2A, Copenhagen V.

AGENTS.

Gregory, Arthur G., Kobmagergade 67, Copenhagen K.
Stark, Lothar, Kobmagergade 67, Copenhagen K.

PRINTING LABORATORIES.

A/S., Johan Ankerstjerne, Lygten 49, Copenhagen N.

Nordisk Films-Kompagni A/S., Redhavnsvej 1, Frihavnen, Copenhagen O.

TRADE PAPER.

Biografbladet, Hulgaardsvej 55, Copenhagen F. (The Cinema Owners and the Film Renters' Trade Paper).

France (Paris).

PRODUCING FIRMS, DISTRIBUTORS, AND AGENTS.

Agatos Société, 50, Quai du Point du Jour, Billancourt, Seine.
A.L.B., 65, Rue d'Amsterdam.
Albatros (Société des Films), 7, Avenue Vion-Whitcomb.
Alliance Cinématographique Européenne (subsidiary of U.F.A.), 11 bis, Rue Volney.
Arci Film, 1, Rue Lincoln.
Argus Film Production, 44, Champs Elysées.
Atlantic Film, 36, Avenue Hoche.
Auteurs Associes, 13, Rue Fortuny.
Bianco Productions, 40, Rue du Colisée.
Calamy Productions, 49, Avenue Bosquet.
Cesar Film, 44, Champs Elysées.
Cine-Arys Productions, 78, Champs Elysées.
Cineas, 92, Champs Elysées.
Cinephonic (Marcel L'herbier), 14, Rue de Marignan.
Cineprodex (André Hugon), 61, Rue du Mont-Cenis.
Compagnie Francaise Cinématographique, 40, Rue François Ier.
Compagnie Generale Cinématographique, 15, Rue Lord Byron.
Compagnie Generale de Production Cinématographique, 26, Rue Marbeuf.

Compagnie Universelle Cinematographique, 40, Rue Vignon.
Consortium Cinématographique Continental, 97, Champs Elysées.
Consortium Cinématographique Francais, 5, Rue Cardinal Mercier.
Consortium Continental Cinématographique, 10, Rue Auber.
Daven (André) Productions, 21, Rue de Berri.
Eclair Productions, 12, Rue Gaillon.
Eclair Journal, 9, Rue Lincoln.
Eden Productions, 45, Rue Vauvenargues.
Europa Film, 6, Rue Copernic.
F.C.L. Société des Productions, 44, Champs Elysées.
Fiat Film (Catholic pictures), 15, Rue Villeneuve Clichy, Seine.
Films Alfred Rode, 116, bis, Champs Elysées.
Films Epoc, 5, Rue Lincoln.
Films Fernand Rivers, 26, Rue de Bassano.
Films Hakin, 79, Champs Elysées.
Films Jacques Deval, 122, Champs Elysées.
Films J. C. Bernard, 16B, Boulevard Gouvion St. Cyr.
Films Marquis, 43, Avenue de l'Opéra.
Films R.F. (Roger Ferdinand), 2, Bld. Latour Maubourg.

Flag Film, 120, Champs Elysées.
Flora Film, 95, Champs Elysées.
Flores Film, 7, Avenue Jean Jaurès, Joinville, Seine.
Forrester Parant, 156, Champs Elysées.
France Europe Film, 120, Rue La Boétie.
France Univers Film, 68, Champs Elysées.
Franco-London Film, 55, Champs Elysées.
F.U.D., 14 bis, Avenue Rachel.
Gallic Film, 27, Rue Marignan.
Gandera (Felix) Productions, 175, Rue de Courcelles.
General Film, 15, Blvd de la Madeleine.
G.G. Films, 36, Avenue Hoche.
Gras Marcel Productions, 4, Rue de Marignan.
Gray Film, 5, Rue d'Aumale.
Hugon, André, 61, Rue du Mont Cenis.
Imperial Film, 1, Rue Lincoln.
Lauzin (Albert), Films, 61, Rue de Chabrol.
Lutece Film, 49, Avenue Montaigne.
Lux, 26, Rue de la Bienfaisance.
Maurice Cammage, 18, Rue du Bois Clichy, Seine.
Mega Film, 44, Champs Elysées.

Milo Film, 67, Champs Elysées.
Natan, Bernard et Émile, Palais du Bois de Boulogne, Route de Madrid.
Nero Film, 44, Champs Elysées.
Pagnol, Marcel, Films, 13, Rue Fortuny.
Paris Cine. Film, 172, Avenue de Neuilly, Neuilly sur Seine.
Paris Films Productions, 79, Champs Elysées.
Paris France Productions, 68, Champs Elysées.
Pathé Cinema, 6, Rue Francoeur.
Pellegrin Cinema, 4, Rue de Puteaux, Paris.
Prima Film, 97, Rue de Rome.
Realisations d'Art Cinématographique, 146, Faubourg Poissonnière.
Richebe (Société des Films Roger), 15, Avenue Victor Emmanuel III.
S.E.D.I.F., 1, Rue Lincoln.
Sigma Productions, 14 bis, Avenue Rachel.
S.N.C. (Société Nouvelle de Cinématographie), 5, Rue Lincoln.
Solar Film, 78, Champs Elysées.
Synchro Cine, 63, Champs Elysées.
Tobis Films Sonores, 44, Champs Elysées.
Trocadero Films, 44, Champs Elysées.

DISTRIBUTING COMPANIES (PARIS).

Aguiar, A. d' (Gray Film), 5, Rue d'Aumale.
Alliance Cinématographique Européenne (A.C.E.), 11 bis, Rue Volney.
Artistes Associes, 27, Rue d'Astorg.
Astra Paris Film, 3, Rue Troyon.
Atlantic Film, 36, Avenue Hoche.
Cine. Selection, 27, Rue de Turin.
Columbia Pictures, 7 bis, Rue de Téhéran.
Compagnie Commerciale Francaise Cinématographique, 99, Champs Elysées.
Compagnie Francaise Cinématographique (C.F.C.) 40, Rue François Ier.
Compagnie Parisienne de Location de Films (C.P.L.F.), 49, Avenue de Villiers.
Compagnie Francaise de Distribution de Films (C.F.D.F.), 40, Rue du Colisée.
Compagnie Universelle Cinématographique (C.U.C.), 40, Rue Vignon.
Consortium Continental Cinématographique, 10, Rue Auber.
Consortium Cinématographique Francais, 5, Rue du Cardinal Mercier.
Cristal Films, 63, Champs Elysées.
Distributeurs Associes, 95, Rue Caulaincourt.
Distributeurs Francais, 122, Champs Elysées.
Distribution Universelle Cinématographique (D.U.C.), 26, Rue Bassano.
Eclair Journal, 9, Rue Lincoln.
Fiat Film, 15, Rue Villeneuve, Clichy, Seine (Catholic Films).
Forrester Parant Productions, 150, Champs Elysées.
France Actualites Gaumont, 17, Rue Carducci.
Franco London Film, 41, Bld. Haussmann.
Gaumont Franco Film Aubert (G.F.F.A.), 35, Rue du Plateau.
G.E.C.E., 116 bis, Champs Elysées.

Grands Spectacles Cinématographiques, 5, Rue du Cardinal Mercier.
Gray Film, 5, Rue d'Aumale.
Hakim Films, 79, Champs Elysées.
Lauzin, Albert, Films, 61, Rue de Chabrol.
Lux (Cie. Cinématographique de France), 26, Rue de la Bienfaisance.
Meric Films, 17, Rue Bleue.
Metro-Goldwyn-Mayer, 37, Rue Condorcet.
Office Cinématographique International (Soviet Pictures), 6, Rond Point des Champs Elysées.
Osso, Sté des Films, 7 bis, Rue de Téhéran.
Paramount Films, 1, Rue Meyerbeer.
Paris Cinema Location, 15, Avenue Victor Emmanuel III.
Pathé Consortium Cinema, 67, Faubourg St. Martin.
Pellegrin Cinema, 4, Rue de Puteaux.
Radio Cinema, 79, Bld. Haussmann.
R.K.O. Radio Pictures, 52, Champs Elysées.
Rouhier, Séléctions Maurice, 14, Rue Grange Batelière.
Roussillon Films, 5, Rue Lincoln.
S.E.D.I.F., 52, Avenue des Ternes.
S.E.L.F., 48, Rue de Bassano.
Sefert Films, 31, Blvd. Bonne Nouvelle.
Select Film, 29, Rue de Berri.
Synchro Cine., 63, Champs Elysées.
20th Century-Fox, 33, Champs Elysées.
Tobis Films Sonores, 44, Champs Elysées.
Union des Distributeurs Independants de Films, 99, Champs Elysées.
United Artists : See **Artistes Associes.**
Universal Film, 52, Rue des Martyrs.
Venloo, P. J. de, 12, Rue Gaillon.
Warner Bros. First National, 25, Rue de Courcelles.

FILM IMPORTERS AND EXPORTERS.

Acropolis Film, 78, Champs Elysées (Belgium, Switzerland).
Ades, Maurice, 6, Rue du Helder (Near East).
Agrest, Roman, 59, Avenue des Ternes (all countries).
Aguiar, A. d', 5, Rue d'Aumale (Spain, Portugal).
Albeck, 17, Rue Hégisippe Moreau (Scandinavia).

Ameranglo Films, 55, Rue d'Amsterdam (all countries).
Arditti, 10, Rue Rodier (all countries).
Barbaza, 71, Champs Elysées (Germany, Austria).
Barki, Raymond, 16, Avenue Hoche (Egypt).
Bates, Frank, 8, Place de la Porte Champerret (U.S.A.).

Bau Bonapiata, 29, Rue du Mont Cenis (Spain, Portugal).
Bazzarello, P., 32, Bld. Exelmans (Italy).
Beaujon, Felix, 122, Champs Elysées (Switzerland).
Cavaignac, Jean de, 92, Champs Elysées (U.S.A.).
Chassaing, 40, Rue de Bruxelles (Near Orient and Balkans).
Chavez Hermanos, 79, Champs Elysées (South America).
Cine. Royal Film, 18, Rue de Marignan (all countries).
Cine. Theatres de l'Indo-Chine, 122, Champs Elysées.
Cohen, Leo B., 37, Champs Elysées (Near East).
Compagnie Cinématographique Canadienne, 92, Rue de Courcelles.
Costa, B. de, 359, Rue St. Martin (Portugal).
Delac et Vandal, 63, Champs Elysées.
Ellegard, Leo, 19, Rue Mirabeau (Great Britain, Spain, Portugal, Balkans, Egypt, Near East).
Equitable Film, 416, Rue St. Honoré Ier (all countries).
F.I.C. (Gaumont-British rights for France and Colonies), 8, Rue Catulle Mendès.
Film Export, 116 bis, Champs Elysées (all countries).
France Europe Film, 120, Rue La Boétié (all countries).
Franco London Film, 41, Bld. Haussmann (England).
Gaumont Franco Film, Aubert, 35, Rue du Plateau (all countries).
Grenier, Henri, 30, Champs Elysées (South America).

Hainsselin, Paul, 36, Rue du Colisée (all countries).
Holmberg, Folke, 38, Rue des Mathurnsi (Scandinavia).
I.F.A. (International Film Artistique), 3, Rue du Colisée (Central Europe).
Inter-Continental Film, 61, Avenue Victor Emmanuel III. (all countries).
International Film Export, 44, Champs Elysées (all countries).
Jacquemin, 6, Rue Francoeur.
Kappetanovitch, Guy, 11, Place de la Porte Champerret (Yugoslavia).
Laemmle, Max, 1, Rue Pauquet (Holland and other countries).
Leo Film, 3, Rue du Colisée (all countries).
Mackiels (Robert D.), 6, Rue Vezelay (all countries).
Majestic Film, 36, Avenue Hoche (Central Europe).
Paris Export Film Co. (Paul Graetz), 36, Avenue Hoche (all countries).
Pathé Nord, 11, Boulevard de la Madeleine (Eastern Europe).
Pathé Orient, 10, Rue Pergolèse (China and Indo-China).
Representation Commerciale de L'U.R.S.S. En France, 25, Rue de la Ville l'Evèque (Soviet Pictures).
Soriano, Maurice, 5, Rue Alexandre Cabanel (Spain and South America).
Targa, Sté, 36, Rue du Colisée (all countries).
Transat Film, 35, Champs Elysées.
Wettstein, Ernest, 116 bis, Champs Elysées.
Sindex, 44, Champs Elysées (all countries).
Solar Film, 78, Champs Elysées (all countries).

ACCESSORIES AND MATERIALS.

Agfa, 12, Rue Gaillon.
Als-Thom (Société Electrique et Mecanique), 38, Avenue Kleber.
Baird, Television Continentale, 60, Rue de la Victoire.
Bell and Howell, 2, Rue de la Paix.
Boudereau, 262, Rue de Belleville.
Boyer, 25, Boulevard Arago.
Brockliss et Cie., 6, Rue Guillaume Tell.
Camereclair, 12, Rue Gaillon.
Continsouza et Barre, 29, Rue des Panoyaux.
Debrie, André, 111, Rue Saint-Maur.
Demaria (Lapierre et Mollier), 21, Rue de Paradis.
Eclair Tirage, 12, Rue Gaillon.
Electric Research Productions (see Western Electric).
Ernemann, 20, Rue du Faubourg du Temple.
Hermagis, 38, Rue Etienne Marcel.
Jacopozzi, 44, Rue de Bondy.
Juliat Robert, 24, Rue de Trevise.
Keller Dorian (Colour Films), 157, Rue du Temple.
Kodak-Pathé (Société), 39, Avenue Montaigne.

Lorraine (Société) (Carbons), 173, Boulevard Haussmann.
Melodium (Société), 296, Rue Lecourbe.
Mecanique Industrielle de Précision, 29, Rue des Panoyeaux.
Ozaphane, 7, Avenue Percier.
Paz et Silva, 55, Rue Sainte Anne.
Rapid Films (Adverts), 6, Rue Francoeur.
R.C.A. (Photophone), 5, Faubourg Poissonniére.
Rhone Poulenc, 86, Rue Vieille du Temple.
Rombouts, L., 18, Rue Choron.
S.A.D.E. (Electric Signs), 79, Rue de Miromesnil.
Simplex (Brockliss & Co.), 6, Rue Guillaume Tell.
Thomson-Houston, 173, Boulevard Haussmann.
Tiranty, P., 103, Rue La Fayette.
Tobis, Cie. (Sound Apparatus), 39, Boulevard Haussmann.
Visatone, 11, Rue Tronchet.
Western Electric, 1, Boulevard Haussmann.
Zeiss, Carl, Société Ikonta, 18, Faubourg du Temple.

TRADE ASSOCIATIONS AND ORGANISATIONS.

Alliance Cinématographique Catholic, 38, Boulevard St. Germain.
Anciens du Cinema Francais, Oeuvre de la Maison de Retraite d'Orly, 14, Rue Turbigo.
Association des Auteurs de Film (Authors), 11 bis, Rue Balln (President : Charles Burguet).
Association des Directeurs de Publicite de Cinema, 27, Avenue de Villiers 17.
Chamber of Commerce, British, 6, Rue Halevy.
Chamber of Commerce, International, 38, Cours Albert I.
Chambre Syndicale de Photographie, 15, Rue de Clichy.

Confederation Generale de l'Industrie Cinématographique, 23, Avenue de Messine (President : Mr. Chollat).
Federation des Chambres Syndicales de la Cinématographie Francaise, 63, Champs Elysées (President : Marcel Vandal).
Federation Generale du Spectacles (Bourse de Travail), 3, Rue du Chateau d'Eau.
Federation des Syndicats de l'Industrie Cinema Francaise, 63, Avenue des Champs Elysées.
Film Exporters' Association, 38, Rue du Colisée (President : Mr. Hainsselin).

Motion Picture Producers and Distributors of America (Wm. Hays) : Paris Office, H. L. Smith, 21, Rue de Berri.
Mutuelle du Cinema (Relief Fund of the Cinema Industry), 29, Rue de Chateaudun (President : Fernand Morel).
Société des Auteurs, Compositeurs et Editeurs de Musique, 10, Rue Chaptal, Paris.
Société des Auteurs et Compositeurs Dramatiques, 9, Rue Ballu.
Société des Gens de Lettres, 38, Rue du Faubourg, St. Jacques.

Syndicat des Cinegraphistes Francais (Cameramen), 85, Rue de Vaugirard.
Syndicat Francais des Directeurs de Cinema (Exhibitors'. Association), 18, Bld. Montmartre (President : Raymond Lussiez).
Syndicat Francais des Directeurs de Cinematographes (Raymond Lussiez, president), 18, Boulevard Montmartre.
Syndicat des Operateurs de Prises de Vues, 18, Bould-Montmartre.
Union des Artistes (Chas.Martinelli, president), 7, Rue Monsigny.

TRADE PUBLICATIONS.

(a) **Weekly.**
" **Cinaedia,**" 21, Bld. des Bagaudes, St. Maur des Fosses, Seine.
" **La Cinématographie Francaise,**" 29, Rue Marsoulan.
" **Ecran** " (organ of the Exhibitors' Association), 18, Bld. Montmartre.
" **Agence d'Information Cinégraphique,**" 51, Rue St. Georges (Editor : Jean Pascal).
(b) **Fortnightly.**
" **Cine-Journal,**" 3, Rue Caulaincourt (Editor : Maurice Bex).
" **La Critique Cinématographique,**" 7, Avenue Frochot.
" **L'Action Cinématographique,**" 11, Avenue Hoche.
(c) **Monthly.**
" **Le Cineopse** " (technical and educational), 73, Blvd. de Grenelle.
" **Courrier Cinématographique,**" 39, Bld. de Magenta.

" **Filma,**" 11, Rue Montmartre, 1er.
" **Semaine Cinématograpnique,**" 40, Rue du Colisée.
(d) **Technical Reviews.**
" **La Technique Cinématographique** "(monthly), 34, Rue de Londres (Editor : Igor Landau).
" **Technique et Materiel** " (monthly supplement to " La Cinématographie Francaise "), 29, Rue Marsoulan.
(e) **Fan Publications.**
" **Cine. France** " (fortnightly), 13, Rue Beudant.
" **Cine. Miroir** " (weekly), 18, Rue d'Enghien.
" **Cinemonde** " (weekly), 1 bis, Rue Washington.
" **Mon Cine.**" (monthly), 3, Rue de Rocroy.
" **Mon Film** " (weekly), 142, Rue Montmartre.
" **Pour Vous** " (weekly), 100, Rue Réaumur.
(f) **Year Book.**
" **Le Tout Cinema,**" 19, Rue des Petits Champs, 1er.

AMATEUR CINEMA SOCIETIES.

Central Cinema, 158, Rue de Vaugirard.
Cinemat Club Francais, 126, Faubourg Poissonnière.
Club des Amateurs Cineastes en France, 35, Boulevard Richard Lenoir.
Federation Francaise des Clubs de Cinema d'Amateurs, 215, Avenue Daumesnil.

" **Le Cinaly** " (Cineastes amateurs Lyonnais), 26, Rue de la Republique, Lyon, France.
Section de Cinema d'Amateurs de la Société Francaise de Photographie, 51, Rue de Clichy.
Société de Cinema d'Amateurs, 94, Rue St. Lazare.

Germany.

FILM PRODUCERS.

Allgem. Filmaufnahme u Vertriebs, G.m.b.H. (Algefa), Admiral v. Koester Ufer 83, Berlin.
A.B.C. Film, G.m.b.H., Unt. d. Linden 18, Berlin.
Aco-Film, G.m.b.H., Friedrichstr. 8, Berlin.
Arnold & Richter, G.m.b.H., Türkenstr. 89, Muenchen.
Astra-Film, G.m.b.H.,Schmargendorf, Sulzaerstr. 4, Berlin.
Atalanta Film, G.m.b.H., Charlottenburg, Carmerstr. 7, Berlin.
Badal-Filmfabrikation, Dr. V., Kochstr. 18, Berlin.
Bavaria-Film A.G., Munchen, Sonnenstr. 15.
Bavaria-Tonwoche, Mauerstr. 43, Berlin.
Boener-Film, Friedrichstr. 13, Berlin.
Bunderfilm, A.G., Bismarkstr. 79, Berlin.
Centrofilm, G.m.b.H., Friedrichstr. 224, Berlin.
Cine-Allianz Tonfilm, G.m.b.H., Kochstr. 18 Berlin.
Comedia-Tonfilm, G.m.b.H., Unt. d. Linden 39, Berlin.
Commerz-Film, A.G., Woyrschstr. 37, Berlin.

Deutsche Tonfilm Produkt, G.m.b.H., Friedrichstr. 22, Berlin.
Delta-Film, G.m.b.H., Kurfuerstendamm 206, Berlin.
Doering-Filmwerke, G.m.b.H.,Schlieffen Ufer 42, Berlin.
Eichberg-Film, G.m.b.H., Charlottenburg, Giesebrechstr. 10, Berlin.
Euphono-Film, Ges.m.b.H., Friedrichstr. 224, Berlin.
Fanal-Film, G.m.b.H., Kurfuerstendamm 226, Berlin.
F.D.F. Fabrikation deutscher Filme, G.m.b.H., Friedrichstr. 8, Berlin.
Olaf Fjord Film Prod., G.m.b.H., Halensee, Cicerostr. 216, Berlin.
Froelich-Produktion, G.m.b.H., Tempelhof, Borussiastr. 45/9, Berlin.
Fox, toenende Wochenschau, A.G., Friedrichstr. 13, Berlin.
R. Fritsch Tonfilm, G.m.b.H.,Halensee, Cicerostr. 63, Berlin.
Institut fur Kulturforschung, Kochstr. 6, Berlin.

Itala Film, G.m.b.H., Hedemannstr. 14, Berlin
K.M.R. Tonfilm, G.m.b.H., Friedrichstr. 207., Berlin.
Klagemann-Film, G.m.b.H., Friedrichstr. 225, Berlin.
Klein-Film, G.m.b.H., Yiktor, Sybelstr. 6, Berlin-Charlottenburg.
Lola Kreutzberg Film, G.m.b.H., Passauerstr. 17, Berlin.
Lamprecht · Film, G.m.b.H., Gerhard, Friedrichstr. 224, Berlin.
Lignose-Hörfilm, G.m.b.H., Lindenstr. 32, Berlin.
Lloyd-Film, G.m.b.H., Mauerstr. 43, Berlin.
Majestic-Film, G.m.b.H., Kürfürstendamm 225, Berlin.
Maxim-Film, G.m.b.H., Friedrichstr. 19, Berlin,
Minerva-Tonfilm, G.m.b.H., Friedrichstr. 224, Berlin.
Naturfilm Hubert Schonger, Anhaltstr. 7, Berlin.
Nerthus-Film, Unter den Linden 51, Berlin, W.8.
N.E.K., Neue Filmkommand, Ges. Erich Engels, Kurfuerstendamm 32, Berlin.
Nordland Film, A.G., Friedrichstr. 20, Berlin.
Olympia-Film, G.m.b.H., Harzerstr. 39, Berlin.
Ondra Lamac Film, G.m.b.H., Friedrichstr. 12, Berlin.

Patria-Film, G.m.b.H., Friedrichstr. 19, Berlin.
Harry Piel-Ariel-Filmproduktion, Unter den Linden 64, Berlin.
R.N. Filmproduktion, G.m.b.H., Budapesterstr. 34; Berlin.
Rolf-Randolf-Film, G.m.b.H., Friedrichstr. 19, Berlin.
Schulz & Wuellner, G.m.b.H., Friedrichstr. 224, Berlin.
Lothar-Stark, G.m.b.H., Kulmbacherstr. 14, Berlin.
Suevia-Film, G.m.b.H., Jägerstr. 13, Berlin.
Terra-Film, Akt. Ges., Kochstrasse 73, Berlin.
Tobis-Magna Filmprod., G.m.b.H., Friedrichstr. 224, Berlin.
Tobis-Melofilm, G.m.b.H., Mauerstr. 43, Berlin.
Tobis-Rota Film, A.G., Mauerstr. 83/84, Berlin.
Tolirag A.G., Kurfuerstendamm 236, Berlin.
Tonbild Syndikat A.G., Mauerstr. 43. Berlin.
Tonlicht-Film G.m.b.H., Ostermayr, Wittenbergplatz. 1, Berlin.
Trenker-Film, Luis, Mauerstr. 43, Berlin.
Universum-Film Aktiengesellschaft (Ufa), Krausenstr. 38/39, Berlin.
Witt-Film, G.m.b.H., Georg, Hedemannstr. 14, Berlin.

RENTERS.

Alboe-film, G.m.b.H. (Althoff-Boecker), Friedstr. 8, Berlin.
Algi-Film-Verleih, G.m.b.H., Hedemannstr. 14, Berlin.
Atlasfilm Comp., Kopenhagen, Generalvertretung Berlin, Hedemannstr. 25, Berlin.
Bavaria-Tonwoche, Mauerstr. 43, Berlin.
Bayerische Filmgesellsch, m.b.H., Friedrichstr. 210, Berlin.
Benda & Co., Hedemannstr. 14, Berlin.
Cando-Film-Verleih, Friedrichstr. 22, Berlin.
Centro-Film, G.m.b.H., Friedrichstr. 224, Berlin.
Cine-Allianz-Tonfilm, G.m.b.H., Kochstr. 18, Berlin.
Deutsche Filmexport, G.m.b.H., Friedrichstr. 25, Berlin.
Deutsche Fox-Film, A.G., Friedrichstr. 225, Berlin.
Defira-Tonfilm- Vertrieb, G.m.b.H., Friedrichstr. 23, Berlin.
Deutsche Universal-Film, A.G., Mauerstrasse, 83/84, Berlin.
Edda-Film, G.m.b.H., Koeniggraetzerstr. 75a, Berlin.
Fritzsche, K. J., Friedrichstr. 224, Berlin.
Fundus, G.m.b.H., Friedrichstr. 13, Berlin.
Herzog & Co., Richard, Filmverleih, Friedrichstr. 13, Berlin.
Hisa-Film, G.m.b.H., Kochstr. 18, Berlin.
H.T. Filmverleih, G.m.b.H., Friedrichstr. 25/26, Berlin.
Imperiali Leop (Cines Pittaluga), Friedrichstr. 10, Berlin.
Itala-Film, G.m.H., Hedemannstr. 14, Berlin.
Knevels Filmverleih, G.m.b.H., Fritz, Friedrichstr. 224. Berlin.
Lagopoulo & Comp., Hedemannstr. 14, Berlin.
Metro-Goldwyn-Mayer Film, A.G., Friedrichstr. 225, Berlin.
Markische Film, G.m.b.H., Zimmerstr. 79/80, Berlin.

Metropol-Filmverleih, A.G., Friedrichstr. 19, Berlin.
N.A.G. Filmverleih, m.b.H., Fredrichstr. 8, Berlin.
Nitzsche A.G. Kinemategraphen & Films, Gohlis, Eisenacherstr. 72, Leipzig.
Normaton-Film, G.m.b.H., Königgrätzer-Str. 72, Berlin.
Oebels-Oebstroem-Film, G.m.b.H., Wilhelmstr. 145, Berlin.
Omnia-Film, G.m.b.H., Wilhelmstr. 122, Berlin.
Paul Oppen, Friedrichstr. 238, Berlin.
Optima-Film, G.m.b.H., Friedrichstr. 208, Berlin.
Orbis-Film, G.m.b.H., Friedrichstr. 236, Berlin.
Otzoup-Film, Friedrichstr. 22, Berlin.
Pagels, Filmvertrieb, Erich, Wilhelmstr. 7, Berlin.
Panorama-Film, G.m.b.H., Kochstr. 6-7, Berlin.
Paramount-Film, A.G., Friedrichstr. 50-51, Berlin.
Siegel-Monopol-Film, G.m.b.H., Friedrichstr. 19, Berlin.
Stark Lothar, G.m.b.H. Kulmbacherstr. 14, Berlin.
Stein Filmverleih, G.m.b.H., Friedrichstr. 13, Berlin.
Syndikat-Film, G.m.b.H., Hedemannstr. 21. Berlin, S.W.
Terra-Film-Verleih, G.m.b.H., Kochstr. 73, Berlin.
Tobis-Europa-Filmverleih, G.m.b.H., Friedrichstr. 207, Berlin.
Tobis-Melofilm, G.m.b.H., Mauerstr. 43, Berlin.
Tobis-Cinema-Film, A.G., Mauerstr. 43, Berlin.
Tobis-Rota-Film, A.G., Mauerstr. 83/84, Berlin.
Tolirag, A.G., Kurfürstendamm 236, Berlin.
Tonbild-Syndicat, A.G. (Tobis), Tonfilm—Aufnahime—und Wiedergabe—Apparaturen, Mauerstrasse 43, Berlin W.8.
Transocean-Film, G.m.b.H., Friedrichstr. 224 Berlin.
Ufa-Filmverleih-Ges.m.b.H., Krausenstr. 38-39, Berlin.
Urban Conrad, Friedrichstr. 238, Berlin.
Vitagraph-Filmges, m.b.H., Friedrichstr. 225 Berlin.

ACCESSORIES AND MATERIALS.

Akt. Ges. fur \Filmfabrikation "Afifa," Victoriastr. 13/18, Berlin.

Allgemeine Elektricitats-Ges., Friedrich Karl-Ufer 2, Berlin.

Alrobi-Musikverlag., G.m.b.H., Rankestr. 25, Berlin.

Amigo, Gustav, Fürstenstr. 3, Berlin.

Askania-Werke, A.G., Kaiserallee, 87/88, Berlin.

Bauer, G.m.b.H., Eugen, Unterturkheim, Stuttgart.

Beboton-Verlag, G.m.b.H., Nürnbergerstr. 9, Berlin.

Becker & Co., Kostum-Verleih, G.m.b.H., i.L. Rungestr. 25/27, Berlin.

Blum & Co., G.m.b.H. (Patent Holding, Syst. Phonorythmie), Friedrichstr. 23, Berlin.

Breusing-Tonsystem, G.m.b.H., Potsdamerstr. 38, Berlin.

Busch, Emil, A.G., Optische Industrie, Rathenow b, Berlin.

Conradty C., Kinokohlen, Spittlertorgraben 9, Nurnberg.

Deutschmann, G.m.b.H., Friedrichstr. 23, Berlin.

Duoskop, G.m.b.H., Bernburgerstr. 29, Berlin

Efa Gesellschaft fur Kino-Foto und Elektro-Technik, Hollmannstr. 16, Berlin.

Elektrola, G.m.b.H., Kaiser Wilhelmstr. 1, Nowawes bei Potsdam.

Erko. Maschinenbau-Ges.m.b.H., Kinotechn. u. Projekt.-Fabr., Strelitzerstr. 58, Berlin.

Eruka, Photo-u. Filmdienst, G.m.b.H., Markgrafenstrasse 77, Berlin.

Europaische Film-Allianz (E.F.A.), G.m.b.H., Cicerostr. 2/6, Berlin-Halensee.

Film-Kopieranstalt Droge & Siebert, G.m.b.H., Grosse Seestr. 4, Berlin Weissensee.

Filmkredit-Bank, G.m.b.H., Bendlerstr. 33a, Berlin.

Fikopa, Filmkopieranst, G.m.b.H., Blucherstr.12, Berlin, S.W.

Filmtitel u Kopier-G.m.b.H., i.L., Gitschinerstr. 44, Berlin.

Froehlich-Tonfilmstudio, Tempelhof, Borussiastr. 45-47, Berlin.

Geyer-Werke, A.G., Harzerstr. 39, Berlin.

Gleichrichter Ges.m.b.H., Quecksilberdampf-Umforner u electr. App., Elisabethufer 44, Berlin.

Grass & Worff, Inh. Walter Vollmann, Markgrafenstr. 18, Berlin.

Jenne, Fritz Generalvetr. der Lytaxwerke G.m.b.H., Blücherstr. 12, Berlin.

Jupiterlicht, A. G., Kersten & Brasch, Gneise-naustr. 27, Berlin.

"Kandem," Korting & Matthiesen, A.G., Wilhelmstr. 10, Berlin.

Kersten-Jaeger F. (Filmentregnung) Kochstr. 18, Berlin.

Kinobild Lechner, Ritterstr. 11, Berlin.

Kino-Foto, G.m.b.H., Wilhelmstr. 37/38, Berlin.

Kino-Schuch Inh., L. Schuch, Friedrichstr. 31, Berlin.

Kinoton, A.G., Friedrichstr. 224, Berlin.

Klangfilm, G.m.b.H., Saarlandstr. 19, Berlin.

Kosmos, Berl. Filmkopieranst, Emil Schonberg, Lindenstr. 74, Berlin.

Levy, Dr. Max. G.m.b.H., Fabr. elektr. Masch u. App., Mullerstr. 30, Berlin.

Lignose Sprengstoffwerke, G.m.b.H., Moltke-strasse 1, Berlin.

Lignose-Hörfilm, System Breusing, G.m.b.H., i.L., Lindenstr. 32/34, Berlin.

C. Lorenz, A.G., Tempelhof, Lorenzweg 1, Berlin.

Minimax, A.G., Feuerloscher fur die Filmindustrie-Schiffbauer-Damm 20, Berlin.

Minuth & Co., Emil (Filmausstattung), Luetzow-str. 95, Berlin.

Muss & Rathgeb, Kino-Apparate, Kochstr. 62, Berlin.

Nehring, W., Projektions-u. Tonfilmgeräte, Frankfurter Allee 317, Berlin.

Neldner, Elektriz, G.m.b.H., Verleih von Licht-wagen, Fontanestr. 4a, Berlin-Lichterfelde-West.

Nitsche, Akt. Ges., Gohlis, Eisenacherstr. 72, Leipzig.

Osram, G.m.b.H., Ehrenbergstr. 14, Berlin.

Projektions-Maschinenbau, G.m.b.H., Urbanstr. 70A, Berlin.

Rapid-Kopier Ges.m.b.H., Alexandrinenstr. 137 Berlin, S.W.

Recono, Komm.-Ges. Stock & Co. (Filmbear-beitung), Tempelhof, Germaniastr. 18, Berlin.

Rhythmographie, G.m.b.H., Alte Jakobstr. 133, Berlin.

Rutgerswerke, A.G., Lützowstr. 33/36, Berlin.

Schatzow, Ja., Generalvertr. d. Fa. Andre Debrie, Paris, Kurfürstendamm, 179, Berlin.

Siemens Planiawerke, A.G., fur Kohlefabrikate Lichtenberg, Herzbergstr. 128/37, Berlin.

Stachow & Co., Wilmersdorf, Landauerstr. 2, Berlin.

Telegraphon, A.G., Mauerstr. 43, Berlin.

Terra-Atelier, Wilhelm v. Siemens-str., Berlin-Marienfelde.

Tesch, Paul Filmfabrik, G.m.b.H., Bergmanstr. 68, Berlin.

Theaterkunst, G.m.b.H., Schwedterstr. 9. Berlin.

Tobis Industrieges. m.b.H., Mauerstr, 43, Berlin.

Tobis-Atelier, G.m.b.H., Grunewald, Koenigsweg 148, Berlin.

Tobis-Atelier Ges. m.b.H. (Jofa) Johannisthal. Flugplatz 6a, Berlin.

Ufa, Betrieb Neubabelsberg b. Potsdam, Stahns. dorferstr. 99/105.

Ufa, Betrieb-Tempelhof, Oberlandstr. 27, Berlin-Tempelhof.

Ufa, Handels-Ges.m.b.H., Krausenstr. 38/39, Berlin.

Ufaton-Verlags.-G.m.b.H., Krausenstr. 38/39, Berlin.

Union Tonfilm maschinenbau, G.m.b.H., Kochstr. 6, Berlin.

Universal, Filmkopieranstalt, Friedrichstr. 233, Berlin.

Universum Film, A.G. Fabr., Verleih, Vertr.,, Krausenstr. 38/39, Berlin.

Verch, G.m.b.H., Kostueme für Theater u. Film. Leibnizstr. 104, Berlin.

Voigtlander & Sohn, Opt. Werke, Zimmerstr. 79/80, Berlin.

Weinert, K., Elektrotechnische u. Bogenlampen-fabrik, Muskauerstr. 24, Berlin.

Wurlitzer-Studio (Kino-Orgeln), Unt. den Linden 14, Berlin.

Zeiss, Carl, Optische Werke, Jena.

Zeiss-ikon, A.G. (Goerz-Werk, Berlin-Zehlendorf), Dresden. Verkaufsstelle, Berlin: Friedenau, Rheinstr. 45/46.

TRADE SOCIETIES AND ASSOCIATIONS.

Degeto, Deutsche Ges. für Ton u. Bild, E.V. Bendlerstr. 10, Berlin.
Deutscher Presseklub E.V. (Haus d. Deutschen Presse), Tiergartenstr. 16, Berlin.
Filmnachweis, Friedrichstr. 210, Berlin.
Filmtechnischer Ausschuss der deutsch-Kinotechn. Ges., Bendlerstr. 32a/b, Berlin.
Film-und Bildamt der Stadt, (Berlin), Levetzowstr. 1/2, Berlin.
Filmprufstelle, Berlin (Reichsfilmzensur), Königsplatz 6, Berlin.
Filmklub, Geselliger Verein der deutschen Filmindustrie, E.V., Friedrichstr. 227. Berlin.
Kontingentstelle, Friedrichstr. 210, Berlin.
Reichsfachschaft Film, Friedrichstr. 210, Berlin.

Reichsfilmkammer : Berlin.

Fachgruppe Filmproduktion, Bendlerstr. 10, (inkt. Ein-u. Ausfuhr, Atelier).

Fachgruppe Film-u. Kinotechnik, Bendlerstr 32 a/b.
Fachgruppe Filmtheater, Bendlerstr. 32 a/b.
Gesamtverband der Filmherstellung und Filmverwertung e.V., Bendlerstr. 10.
Abt. Inl. Filmvertrieb, Bendlerstr. 33.
Fachgruppe der Kultur-u. Werbefilmhersteller, Bendlerstr. 10.
Presse und Propaganda :
   1. Inlandspresse, Bendlerstr. 32 a/b.
   2. Auslandspresse, Bendlerstr, 10.
Reichsfilmarchiv, Friedrichstr. 12.
Sonderreferat :
   Devisenangelegenheiten, Bendlerstr. 10.
Stagma, Staatlichgenehmigte Ges. zur Verwertung musikal, Urheberrechte, Adolf Hitlerplatz 7/9/11, Berlin.
Allgemeine Versicherungs - Vermittlungs, G.m.b.H., Unter d. Linden 66, Berlin.

RAW STOCK.

Gevaert-Werke G.m.b.H., Friedrichstr. 16, Berlin.
Goerz Photochemische Werke, G.m.b.H., Wannseebahn Goerzallee, Berlin.
J. G. Farbenindustrie, A.G., "Agfa," Lohmuhlenstr. 65/67, Berlin.
Kodak, A.G., Lindenstr. 27, Berlin.
Kundt Max, General-Vertr. d. Zeiss-Ikon Kinerolfilm, Friedrichstr. 25, Berlin.

Lignose-Film, A.G., Lohmühlenstr. 65, S.O. 16, Berlin.
Nobel-Film, G.m.b.H., Juelich im Rheinland.
Strehle Walter, G.m.b.H., Generalvertrieb der "Agfa" Kinefilms und Farben, Friedrichstr 8, Berlin.
Franz Vogel, Vertrieb von Gevaert Rohfilmmaterial, Friedrichstr. 224, Berlin.
Zeiss-Ikon A.G., Goerzallee, Berlin-Zehlendorf.

TRADE PUBLICATIONS.

Das Film-Magazin, Zimmerstr. 35, Berlin.
"Die Filmwoche," Dessauerstr. 7, Berlin.
Deutsche Film-Zeitung, G.m.b.H., Pestalozzistr. 1, Munich.
Film, Der, Verlag, Friedrichstr. 25/26, Berlin.
Film-Echo, Zimmerstr. 35, Berlin.
Film-Kurier (daily), Stülerstr. 2, Berlin.
Filmtechnik-Filmkunst, Friedrichstr. 204, Berlin.

Filmwelt, Zimmerstr. 35, Berlin.
Kinotechnik, Die, Stallschreiberstr. 33, Berlin.
"Lichtbildbuhne," G.m.b.H., Verlag (Zeitung) Rauchstr. 4, Berlin.
Rheinisch Westfal-Filmzeitung, Oststr. 128/32, Duesseldorf.

Greece.

FILM PRODUCERS.

Dag-Film, Ltd., Odos Metropoleos 1a, Athens.
C. & M. Gaziades, Rue Stadiou 48, Athens.

RENTERS, DISTRIBUTORS AND AGENTS.

Acropolis-Film, Rue Socratous 43, Athens.
American-Film Co., Alc. Tryandafilou, Athens.
Amolochitis & Voulgaridis, Rue Patission 32, Athens.
Athena-Film Egon Kraemer, Rue Lycourgon 18, Athens.
E. L. Caloghiros, 18, Rue Spiromiliou, Athens.
Ciné Alliance Hellénique, Rue Omirou 2, Athens
Chr. Galanis, Rue Lycourgou 18, Athens.
Fox-Film, S. A., Rue Enn-Benaki 6, Athens.
Maison Arghyris, A.E.K.E., Rue Patission 32, Athens.

Maison Anton Zervos, A.E.K.E., Rue Academias 51, Athens.
Margulies Jean, Odos Beranerou 14, Athens.
Mavrodimakis & Cie, E., Rue Scoratous 43, Athens.
Metro-Goldwyn-Mayer-Films, Ltd., Odos Themistokles 1, Athens.
Pax-Film, Rue Phidiou 11, Athens.
Soc. Anon. Cinematogr., Rue de Bucarest, Athens.
Spyridis Tel., Bld. Panepistimiou 83, Athens.
Warner Bros. First National Film, S.A., Rue Patission 32, Athens.
Zino Laoutaris, Rue Socrates 43, Athens.

KINEMA ACCESSORIES.

Charalambides & Carafakis (Nitzsche), Rue Patission 29, Athens.
Jng. Wilh. Grimm (Klang-Film), rue Omirou 2, Athens.
G. Papastofas, Rue Solomou 62, Athens.

J. Margulies (Bauer) Odos Berangerou 14, Athens.
Joannou & Mallis, Rue Patission 99, Athens.
Zinon Laoutaris, Rue Socrates 43, Athens.

TRADE ASSOCIATION.
P.E.K., Rue Panepistimiou 83, Athens.

TRADE PUBLICATION.
Kinimatografikos Astir, Odos Sokrates 43, Athens.

Holland.

FILM PRODUCERS.

AMSTERDAM.

Amstelfilm, Koningsplein 1.
Cineac, Reguliersbreestraat (newsreels).
Cinetone-Film, Keizersgracht 255.
Filmex-Film, Keizersgracht 794.
Habe-Film, Hemonylaan.
Victoria-Film, Damrak 60
Westeuropa-Film, Koningsplein 1.

ROTTERDAM.

Monopole-Film, Coolsingel 51.

HAARLEM.

Actueel-Films, Duivenvoordestraat 94.
N.V. Filmfabriek Multifilm, Kenaupark 8.
Polygoon Filmfabrick, Koudehorn 8 (newsreels).

THE HAGUE.

Loet C. Barnstijn, Benoordenhoutscheweg 2.
Haghefilms, Waldorpstraat 8.
Profilti-Nieuws, Boschlaan 3 (newsreels).

FILM STUDIOS.

Cinetone Studio's, Amsterdam (Klangfilm system).
Philips Filmstudios, Eindhoven (own system).

Loet C. Barnstyn Filmstad, The Hague (Klang film system).

KINEMA SOUND INSTALLATIONS AND ACCESSORIES.

N.V. Kinotechniek, Prinsengracht 530, Amsterdam.
N.V. Loetafoon en Philips, Eindhoven.

Nederlandsche Siemens My., Huygenspark, The Hague.
J. W. Maas, Molenlaan 132, Rotterdam.

RENTERS, DISTRIBUTORS AND AGENTS.

AMSTERDAM.

Bergfilm Comp., Hemonylaan 21.
Croeze en Bosman N.V. (Columbia and Universal), Nw. Doelenstraat 8.
Cultuurfilm-Exploitatie, Dintelstraat 29.
N.V. Filma, Prinsengracht 530.
Filmverhuur R. Minden, Haarlemmerdyk 82.
Fim-Film, Singel 469.
Fox Film, Rokin 38.
Internationaal Film Agentuur, Westermarkt 21.
Lumina Film, Nes. 23–25.
My. voor Cinematografie, Prinsengracht 452.
Meteor Films, Keizersgracht 794.
Metro-Goldwyn-Mayer, Damrak 49.
Munt Film, Hemonylaan 27.
Nova Film, Dam 2.
Nederland Film (Gaumont-British), Dam 2.
Paramount, Keizersgracht 399.
Tobis, Jan Luykenstraat 2.
Ufa, Heerengracht 590–592.
Universal Film Agency, Damrak 53.
Victoria Film, Damrak 60.
Warner Bros.-First National, Keizersgracht 778.

AMSTELVEEN.

Express-Film, Heemraadschapslaan 13.

DORDRECHT.

Centra-Film, Groote Kerksbuurt 39.

THE HAGUE.

Loet C. Barnstyn Standaard Films, Benoordenhoutscheweg 2.
City Film, Nieuwstraat 24.
Europa-Film, Nieuwstraat 24.

ROTTERDAM.

D.L.S. Film, Coolsingel 51.
Monopole-Film, Coolsingel 51.

ZANDVOORT.

Filmverhuur F.A.N.

KINEMA TRADE PUBLICATIONS.

Het Weekblad, Editor, Erik Winter, Galgewater 22, Leiden.
Nieuw Weekblad voor de Cinematografie, Editor, Pier Westerbaan, Vaillantlaan 523–529, The Hague.

Wekelyksche Mededeelingen van den Nederlandschen Bioscoop-Bond, Achtergracht 19, Amsterdam.

TRADE ASSOCIATION.

Nederlandsche Bioscoop-Bond. Director, A. de Hoop, Achtergracht 19, Amsterdam.

Hungary

FILM PRODUCERS.

City-Film, A.G., Erzsébet-körút 8, Budapest, VII.
Hunnia Film, A.G., Gyarmat ut, 35/41, Budapest, VII.
Kovacs és Faludi, Gyarmat ut. 35, Budapest.
Kruppka-Filmfabrik, Jozsef-körut 71, Budapest, VIII.

Patria-Film, Erzsébet-körut 8, Budapest, VII
Star-Filmfabrik A.G., Pasareti-ut. 122, Budapest, I.
Ungarisches Filmburo, A.G., Hungária, also Körut 15, Budapest, IX.

RENTERS, DISTRIBUTORS AND AGENTS.

Allianz-Film Kft., Rôkk-Szilárd út. 20, Budapest, VII.
Bioscop-Film, Erzsébet-Körut 9, Budapest, VII.
Cinema-Film, Erzsébet-körut, 8, Budapest, VII.
City-Film A.G., Erzsébet-körút, 8, Budapest, VII.
Danubius Kinoindustrie A.G., Erzsébet-körút 8, Budapest, VII.
Eco-Film A.G., Rákoczi-út. 14, Budapest, VII.
Fox-Film A.G., Rákoczi-út. 9, Budapest.
Harmonia-Film, Akácfa út., 7, Budapest.
Hermes-Film-Handelsges, Rákóczi-út. 36, Budapest.
Hirsoh és Tsuk, Filmges, Rákóczi-út. 14, Budapest, VII.
Kovacs Emil & Co., Erzsébet-körút 8, Budapest, VII.
Metro-Goldwyn-Mayer Corp., A.G., Főherceg Sándor-tér 3, Budapest, VIII.
Muvészfilm, Dr. Ernos Horowitz & Co., Rákoczi utca 40, Budapest.

Paramount Filmvertriebs A.G., Rákoczi út. 59 Budapest, VIII.
Patria-Filmhandelsges., Erzsébet-körut 8, Budapest, VII.
Phoebus-Film A.G. VII., Erzsébet-körút 8 Budapest, VII.
Projectograph, A.G., Rákóczi-ter 11, Budapest.
Schuchmann-Anton, Rôkk-Szilárd-út. 20, Budapest, VIII.
Stylus Filmind A.G., Erzsébet-körut 8, Budapest, VII.
Thalia-Filmprod G.m.b.H., Rôkk Szillard út. 20. Budapest, VIII
Turul-Film, Miksa-út. 7, Budapest, VII.
Ufa-Film A.G., Kossuth Lajos-út. 13, Budapest.
Ungar Sandor & Co., Rôkk-Szillárd-út.20, Budapest, VIII.
Universal-Film A.G., Népszinház út. 21, Budapest, VIII.
Warner Bros. First National Inc., Jószef-körút 30/32, Budapest, VIII.

MANUFACTURERS AND AGENTS OF KINEMA ACCESSORIES.

Agfa Rohfilmvertretung, Thököly-út. 75, Budapest, VII.
Danubius Kinoindustrie A.G., Erzsébet-körút 44, Budapest, VII.
Gamma Fabrik fur feinmechanische Maschinen und Apparate A.G., Fehervari út. 81, Budapest.
Jbusz-Filmtransport, Bálvány-ut. 2, Budapest.
Kodak, Rohfilmer-Vertr., Bécsi-út. 5, Budapest.
Kruppka-Filmkopieranstatt, József-körut 71, Budapest, VIII.

Kovács és Faludi, Filmlaboratorium, Gyarmat-út. 35, Budapest.
Meitner Mor, József-körut 21, Budapest, VIII.
Seidl & Veres, Filmlaboratorium, Thokoly-út. 61, Budapest.
Ung-Siemens-Schuckert-Werke, Elektr. A.G., Vertr. d Klangfilm, Teres körut 36, Budapest.
Wanaus Karoly (Gevaert-Rohfilm), Deák Ferencz tér 3, Budapest.
Western Electric, Korall-út 33, Budapest.

KINEMA TRADE PUBLICATIONS.

Filmkultura, Thököly-út. 75, Budapest, VII.
Mozivilag, Erzsébet-Körut 26, Budapest, VII.
Filmujság, Bérkocsis-út. 16, Budapest.

Magyar Filmkurir, Bérkocsis-út. 17, Budapest, VIII.
Magyar Mozi es Film, Miksa-út. 3, Budapest,VII.
Pesti Mozi, Bezerédy-út. 5, Budapest, VIII.

TRADE SOCIETIES.

M.M.O.E., Csokonay út. 10, Budapest, VIII.
Magyar Filmklub, Erzsébet-Körút 11, Budapest.

Országos Magyar Mozgóképipari Egyesület, Csokonay-út. 10, Budapest, VIII.

India

FILM BUYERS AND RENTERS.

Columbia Pictures, Ltd., 170, Dharamtala Street, Calcutta.
Empire Talkie Distributors, Elphinstone Street, Capitol Theatre, Building, Karachi.
Humayan Properties, Ltd., Bandmann Varieties, New Empire Theatre, 1, Humayan Place, Calcutta.
Jeena & Co., Esplanade Road, Bombay.
Madan Theatres, Ltd., 5, Dharamtala Street, Calcutta.
Metro-Goldwyn-Mayer India, Ltd., P.O. Pox No. 837, Bombay.
Oriental Film Service, 3, Siganna Naick Street, Madras.
Paramount Films of India, Ltd., 170 Dharamtala Street, Calcutta.
Pathe India, Ltd., Hague Building, Balladı Estate, Bombay, 1.

R.K.O. Radio Pictures, Ltd., Tower House Calcutta.
United Artists Corp., Ltd., Marshall Building. Ballard Road, Bombay.
Universal Pict. Corp. of India, Ltd., Film House, Lamington Road, Bombay.
Warner First National Pict., Inc., Pathe Building, Ballard Estate, Bombay.

TRADE ASSOCIATIONS.

Kinematograph Renters' Society of India, Burma & Ceylon, Forbes Building, Home Street, Bombay.
Motion Picture Society of India, Mherwan Building, Sir Phirozshaw Mehta Road, Bombay, 1.

Italy.

Direzione Generale, per la Cinematografia (Ministero Stampa e Propaganda), Via Vittorio Veneto 56, Rome.

PRINCIPAL FILM PRODUCERS.

MILAN.
Novella Film, Piazza Carlo Erba 6.
Film Italia, Via Napo Torriani 19.
Ente Nazionale Industrie Cinematografiche (Enic), Via Soperga 35.

ROME.
A.L.A. Soc. Prod. Cinematografica, Via XX Settembre 58.
Capitani Film S.A., Via XX Settembre 3.
Consorzio Cinematografico E.I.A., Via Varese 16b.
Consorzio "VIS" (Prod. Forzano), Via Maria Adelaide 7.
Industrie Cinematografiche Italiane (I.C.I.), Via del Tritone 87.
Europa Films, Salita S. Nicola da Tolentino 1b.
Minerva Films, Piazza Cavour 10.
Mondial Films, Piazza di Pietra 26.
Manenti Giulio, Via Uffici del Vicario 24a.

Cæsar Film, Circonvallazione Appia 110.
C.A.I.R. (cartoni animati Italiani Roma), Via F. Crispi 58.
Roma Film, Via Varese 16a.
Sagai (Prod. Amato), Circonvallazione Appia 110.
Tiberia Films, salita S. Nicola da Tolentino 1 bis.
Colosseum Films, Via XX Settembre 58.
Ventura (Prod. Ventura), Via Torino 149.
Stabilimenti Cines. S.A., Via Veio 51.
Titanus Film, Largo Goldoni 44.
Soc. An. It. Cinematografica, Walter Wanger, Via XX Settembre 11.

TURIN.
Est Film, Via Botero 17.

GENOA.
Ligure Film, Corso, Buenos Ayres 7.

RENTERS AND MONOPOLISTS.

BOLOGNA.
Milesi Films, Via Milazzo 8.
Borelli Alfredo, Via Pietramellara 45.
Centrale Grandi Film, Via Milazzo 8a.
Film Emilia, Via Rizzoli 3.
Lanzarini Film, Via Galliera 18.
Pegan Enrico, Via Galliera 55.
Rari Film, Via Galliera 62.
Sala, G. B., Via Galliera 93.

FLORENCE.
Compagnia Generale Cinematografica, Via dei Pecori 3.
Cine. Fono Film, Via dei Pecori 1.
E.F.A., Via Vigna Nova 26.
G.E.F.I., Piazza S. Maria Novella 5.
Rari Film, Via Brunelleschi 4.
Sala, G.B., Via Brunelleschi 4.

GENOA.
Angelini, A., Corso, B. Ayres 7-I.
Baracchini Films, Via Malta 22-R.
Culumbus Films, Via Malta 73-R.
E.I.N. Film, Corso Podesta 5-B.
Filmitalia, Via Fiasella 12.
Genova Films, Via Ugo Foscolo.
Melani, E., Via XX Settembre 2.
Pittaluga Adalgisa, Via Pozzo 6-2.
S.A.I.C., Via Frugoni 5-I.

MILAN.
Aurora Films, Via Parini 10.
Brovelli Films, Corso Venezia 13.
Brundus Films, Via Senato 8.
C.C.E. (Cons. Cin. Educativo), Via Fatebene-fratelli 21.
Filmitalia, Via N. Torriani 19.
Soc. Ambrosiana Cinematografica, Piazza Cincinnato 6.
Vittoria Film, Via Settembrini 60.
Regina Film, Via Montenapoleone 26.
Selecta Film, Via V. Pisani 12.
Italo Suisse Film, Piazzale Fiume 22.
O.M.N.I.S. Film, Via Camperio 9.
Novella Films, Piazza Carlo Erba 6.

NAPLES.
Aquila Film, Via Medina 47.
Astrea Film, Via Cesare Battisti 53.
Cirstallo G., Galleria Umberto I. 27.
S.A.S.F.I., Via Medina 67.
Titanus, Via Roma 228.
Vigor Film, Calata San Marco 24.

PADUA.
Helios Film (E. Purgatori), Via Trieste 23.
Industria Film, Via U. Foscolo 8.
Sala G.B., Corso del Popolo 16.
Veneta Films, Via Trieste 31-B.

PALERMO.
D'Alessandro & Napoli, Via N. Garzilli 24.
Vigor Film, Piazza Marina 46.

ROME.
Aquila Film, Via Gaeta 10.
Atlas Film, Via Lucrezio Caro 12.
Barbieri C.O., Via Aurelliana 53.
Effebi (F. Bonotti), Via Curtatone 8.
Capitolium Film, Via dei Mille 5.
Compagnia Generale Cinematografica, Galleria Margherita 12.
Fracassini R., Via de Mille 1.
Ricci Films, Via Palestro 63.
S.E.C.I., Via Solferino 9.
Scalzaferri, S.A., Via Marghera 13.
Titanus, Largo Goldoni 44.
Urbis Film, Via Nazionale 51.

TURIN.
Augusta Film, Via M. Gioda 19.
F.I.D.E.S. (R. Scotti), Via A. Doria 19.
Filmitalia, Piazza Bodoni 5.
Gefa, Via Doria 12.
Rex Film, Piazza Bodoni 3.
Savoia Film, Via A. Doria 19.
Taurinia Film, Via Bogino 12.

TRIESTE.

Agenzia Noleggio Film, Via Giotto 3.
Francescono dott. G., Via Timeus 8.
Helios Film, Via Giotto 3.
Kump & Rosselli, Via Zonta 8.
Moro rag. V., Via Cassa di Risparmio 11.
San Guisto Film, Via Coroneo 6.

VENICE.

Agenzia Cinematografica Veneta, San Benedetto 3938.
Bernasconi cav. G., San Luca-Calle Loredan 4147.

ACCESSORIES AND MATERIALS.

Cinelettromeccanica, Via Parmigianino 12, Milan.
Cinemeccanica, Viale Campania 25, Milan.
Fedi Ing. Angiolo, Via Quadronno 4, Milan.
Microtecnica, Via Saffi 4-6, Turin.

Officine A. Prevost & C. Apparecchi Cinematografici, Via Forcella 9-A, Milan.
Pion (Officine Pio Pion), Via Rovereto 3, Milan.
Siemens, Via Lazzaretto 3, Milan.
Sorani Vittoriano, Via Carlo Tenca 22, Milan.

FILM PRINTERS (Picture and Sound).

Cinematografica, Via Fiamma 12, Rome.
Fotocinema (F. Boschi), Via Saluzzo 10, Rome.
Fototecnica (Borsari), Via La Spezia 82, Rome.
La Fonostampa, Via Camozzi 1, Rome.
S.A.C.I. (L. Cufaro), Via Vejo 48, Rome.

Perfecta (E. Catalucci), Via Campo Boario 56, Rome.
Tecnostampa (Vinc. Genesi), Via Albalonga 38, Rome.
Positiva, Via Luisa del Carretto 187, Turin.

PRODUCTION ESTABLISHMENTS.

Milano Film, Via Baldinucci 60 (Bovisa), Milan.
Cæsar Film, Circonvallazione Appia 110, Rome.
Cines, Via Vejo 51, Rome.

Farnesina, Vicolo Farnesina, Rome.
F.E.R.T., Corso Lombardia 104, Turin.

DUBBING.

Auditorium, Via Torino 149, Rome.
Cæsar Film, Circonvallazione Appia 110, Rome.
Fono Film, Via Tommassetti 1, Rome.
Fono Roma, Via Maria Adelaide 7, Rome.
Fotovox, Via G. Camozzi, Rome.
Itala Acoustica S.A., Via XX Settembre 5, Rome.

Istituto Luce, Via Cernaia 1, Rome.
Metro-Goldwyn, Via Maria Adelaide 7, Rome.
Palatino Film, Piazza S.S. Giovanni e Paolo 8, Rome.
S.A.F.A., Via Mondovi 33, Rome.
Titanus, Via Margutta 54, Rome.

REPRESENTATIVES OF FOREIGN COMPANIES.

Artisti Associati, Via XX Settembre 11, Rome.
Columbia Pictures, Via Varese 16-B, Rome.
Films Paramount, S.A.I., Via Magenta 8, Rome.
Fox Film Corp., S.A.I., Via Vicenza 5, Rome.
Metro-Goldwyn Mayer, Via Maria Cristina 5, Rome.

Paramount New, Via Magenta 10, Rome.
Universal Film Corp., Via del Tritone 87, Rome.
Warner Bros. First National Films, S.A.I., Via Palestro 68, Rome.

TRADE PAPERS.

Cinelenco (in preparazione) Guida Annuario della Cinematografia Italiana, Via Donizzetti 16, Milan.
Cinegiornale, Via Casilina 49, Rome.
Cinema Illustrazione, Piazza Carlo Erba 6, Milan.
Cinema, Via Lazzaro Spallanzani 1-A, Rome.
Cinematografia, Via Pier Lombardo 1, Milan.
Cinemundus, Via del Babuino 169, Rome.
Corriere Cinematografico, Via Bertholet 20, Turin.

Eco del Cinema, Via Emanuele Filiberto 191, Rome.
Intercine (Rivista dell' I.C.E.), Via Spallanzani 1, Rome.
Kinema, Via Passeroni 4-6, Milan.
La Rivista Cinematografica, Via Mario Gioda 4-bis, Turin.
Le Notizie Cinematografiche, Via Lazzaro Spallanzani 1-A, Rome.

FILM TRANSPORT.

Gabella Arnaldo-Uffici : R. Dogana, Centrale-Rome, Via Genova 30, Rome.

Cipolli & Zanetti, S.A., Via Varese 16-A, Rome.

ASSOCIATIONS.

Istituto Internazionale per la Cinematografia Educativa (I.C.E.), Via Spallanzani 1, Rome.
Istituto Nazionale Luce, Via di S. Susanna 17, Rome.

Federazione Nazionale Fascista Industriali dello Spettacolo, Via Sistina 95, Rome.
Societa Italiana degli Autori ed Editori-Direzione Generale, Via Valadier 37, Rome.

Jugoslavia.

FILM PRODUCERS.

Artistic-Film, Kr. Aleksandra 93, Belgrade.
Bosna Film d.d., Jelacicev trg 1, Agram.

Jugosl, prosjetni-film, Kralja Milana 17, Belgrade.
Svetio-tonfilm, Zrinjevac 19, Zagreb.

RENTERS, DISTRIBUTORS AND AGENTS.

Adria-Film, Amruseva 1, Zagreb.
Armida-Film, Vinogradska cesta, Zagreb.
Atlantis-Film, Varsavska 8, Zagreb.
Aurora-Film, Palmoticeva 53, Zagreb.
Avala-Film, Gunduliceva 3, Zagreb.
Bosna Film d.d., Jelacicev trg 1, Zagreb.
Emco Film, ul. Kraljice Marije 30, Zagreb.
Eros Film, Strahinica Bana 80, Beograd.
Fox-Film, C. Jelacicev trg. 1, Zagreb.
Haas & Kleinlein, Berislaviceva 11, Zagreb.
Jadran-Film, Trg. Kr. Tomislava 17, Agram.
Jugo-Film, Varsavska 2, Zagreb.
Jugosl Drustvo-za promet Paramount filmova, Frankopanska ul. 5A, Zagreb.

Kosmos-Film, Bosanska ul, 17, Zagreb.
Merkurfilm, Gunduliceva 3, Zagreb.
Metro-Goldwyn-Mayer Films, Pejacevicev trg. 17. Zagreb.
Mosinger R., Monopol-Film, Pejacevicev trg. 17, Zagreb.
Pan-Film, A.G., Svacicev trg. 11, Zagreb.
Rosa-Film, Drinciceva 18, Belgrade.
Starfilm, Samostanska 11, Zagreb.
Thalia-Film, Erankopanska, 7a, Zagreb.
Union-Film, Varsavska 11, Zagreb.
Warner First National Films, Jlica 34, Zagreb.

MANUFACTURERS AND AGENTS OF KINEMA ACCESSORIES.

Agfa, Palata Riunione, Belgrade.
Artistic Film, Kr. Aleksandra 33, Belgrade.
Bosna Film d.d. Kopieranstalt Jelacicev trg. 1, Zagreb.
Kinetik, radiona za elektokino, Jlica 31, Zagreb.
Kodak-Film, Praska 2, Zagreb.

Philipps jugosl., trg. a.d., Mariceva ul., Zagreb.
Rybak-Film, Dezeliceva 17, Zagreb.
Jugosl, Siemens, A.G. (Klangfilm), Zagreb, Ratkajev prolaz 7.
Western Electric, Gunduliceva ul. 8, Zagreb.

TRADE SOCIETIES.

Savez bioskopa Kraljevine Jugoslavije, Varsavska 3, Zagreb.
Savez filmski h Produzeca, Kraljevine Jagoslavije, Zrinjskitrg. 15, Zagreb.

KINEMA TRADE PUBLICATIONS.

Jugosl-Filmski Kurir, Berislaviceva 10, Zagreb ,
Film, Baruna Jelacica 7, Zagreb.
Filmska Revija, Varsavska 3, Zagreb.

New Zealand.

PRODUCERS, DISTRIBUTORS, ETC.

British Empire Films, Courtenay Chambers, 15, Courtenay Place, Wellington, C.3.
De Forest Phonofilms, N.Z., Ltd., 45, Courtenay Place, also A.M.P. Building, Custom House Quay C.1, Wellington, C3.
Filmcraft, Ltd., Miramar, Wellington, E.4.
Film Exchanges Association (N.Z.), Inc., 87, Cuba Street, Wellington, C.2.
Fox Film Corpn. (Australia), Ltd., 55, Courtenay Place, Wellington, C.3 ; also at Guthrie Bowron Bldg., Albert Street, Auckland.
Columbia Pictures Proprietary, Ltd., Levy Bldg., Manners Street, Wellington, C.5.
Metro-Goldwyn Film (N.Z.), Ltd., Hope Gibbons Building, D:xon Street, Wellington, C.1.

N.Z. Motion Pictures Exhibitors' Assn., Inc., 29A, Courtenay Place, Wellington, C.3.
Paramount Film Service (N.Z.), Ltd., 87, Cuba Street, Wellington, C.2 ; also at Civic House Queen Street, Auckland.
R.K.O. Radio, "Evening Post" Building, Willis, Street, Wellington C.1.
United Artists Films, 55, Courtenay Place, Wellington, C.3.
Universal Pictures Corpn., Film Distributors, Nimmo's Building, Willis Street, Wellington.
Warner Bros. First National Pictures, Ltd., Plumbers' Building, Wakefield Street, Wellington.
Williamson (J.C.) Picture Corpn. Ltd., Dominion Building, Mercer Street, Wellington, C.1.

Norway.

FILM RENTERS.

A/S Fotorama, Stortingsgaten 16, Oslo.
A/S Kinografens Filmbureau, Stortingsgaten 16, Oslo.
Europafilm, Stortingsgaten 30, Oslo.
Filmaktieselskapet Paramount, Stortingsgaten 12, Oslo.
Filmhuset A/S, Bergen.
Fox A/S, Odd Fellow-Huset, Oslo.
Kamerafilm, Odd Fellow-Huset, 4, Oslo.
Kommunenes Filmcentral A/S., Tollbodgaten 35, Oslo.

Metro-Goldwyn-Mayer, Horngaarden, Oslo.
Triangel Film, Klingenberggaten 2, Oslo.
Universal-Film A/S, Klingenberggaten 2, Oslo.
Warner Bros. (First National Vitaphone Pictures A/S), Stortingsgaten 30, Oslo.

MATERIAL AND ACCESSORIES.

Elektricitets-Aktieselskapet A.E.G., Ovre Vollgt 11, Oslo.
J. L. Nerlien A/S, N. Slottsgaten 13, Oslo.
Magnus Boysen & Co. A/S, Tordenskjoldsgaten 3, Oslo.

Poland (Warsaw).

FILM PRODUCERS.

Agefilm, Marszalkowska 113, Warszawa.
Feniksfilm, Zielna 15, Warszawa.
Leo-Film, Zlotá 6.
Libkowfilm, Marszalkowska 94, Warszawa.
Muzafilm, Widok 23.

Patria-Film, Moniuszki 4.
Sfinks, Biuro Kinematogr., Wolska 42.
Szafirfilm, Marszalkowska 116, Warszawa.
Union film, Marszalkowska 113, Warszawa.

RENTERS, DISTRIBUTORS AND AGENTS.

Agefilm, Marszalkowska 113.
Austria-Film, Sp.z.o.o., Chmielna 32.
Enhafilm, sp.z.ogr.odp., Marszalkowska 125.
Erfilm, Al Jerozolimska 36.
Feniksfilm, Zielna 15.
Fortuna-Film, Marszalkowska 95.
Fox-Film, Towarzystwo, sp.z.ogr.odp., ul. Sw. Krzyska 25.
Gloria-Film, sp.z.ogr.odp., Marszalkowska 119.
Green-Film, Jasna 24.
Jarfilm, Nowy-Swiat 19.
Emil Katz, Zielna 16.
Kolos-Film, sp.z.ogr.odp., Al Jerozolimska 41, Warszawa.
Komis-Film, Jasna 24.
Lechfilma, sp.z.ogr.odp., Hoza 23.
Leo-Film, Zlota 6.

Metro-Goldwyn-Mayer, Marszalkowska 96.
Muzafilm, Widok 23.
National Film Corp., Al. Jerozolimska 15.
Paramount-Film, sp.z.ogr.odp., Sienna 4.
Polonjafilm, Jerozolimská 41.
Polski Tobis, Pl. Napoleona 9.
R.K.O. Radio Films, Marzalkowska 130.
Sfinks, Biuro, Kinematograficzne Marszalkowska 153.
Starfilm, sp.z.ogr.odp., Prózna 2.
Szafir-film, Marszalkowska 116.
Union-Film, Marszalkowska 113.
Universal Pictures Corp., Al Jerozolimska 35.
Warner Bros. Films, Jerozolimska 51.
Warsz. Kinem. sp. Akc., Zorawia 22.
Wszechfilm, Zielna 6.
Wyte Jornia Doswiadozalna, Jerozolimska 43. Warszawa.

MANUFACTURERS OF ACCESSORIES.

Agfa-Foto, Zorawia 23.
Falanga, Kopieranstalt, Trebacka 11.
Film-Foto, N. Swiat 27.
Kodak, Plac Napoleona 5.
Jarosz Teofil, Hoza 35.
Syrena, Rekord, sp.akc. fabr. plyt. gramofonowi, Chmielna 66.

Powsz. Towarz. Elektr. A.E.G., sp.z.o.o., Mazowiecka 7.

Polzkie Zaklady Siemens, S.A., Krolewska 23.

Western Electric, sp.z.ogr.odp., Glowny Rynek 5. Krakow.

KINEMA TRADE PUBLICATIONS.

Film, Marzowiecka 11.
Kino dla wszystkich, Zlota 65.

Swiat Filmu, Wierzbowa 6.
Wiadomosci filmowe, Al. Jerozolimska 43.

TRADE ASSOCIATIONS.

Zwiazek Przemyslowoow Filmowych, Widok 22.
Polski Zwiazck Producentow Krotkometr, Wilcza 19.
Zwiazek Wlascicieli Kinematograf. w Warszawie, Widok 9.

Rada Naczelna Filmowa, Widok 22.
Polski Zwiazek Producentow, Chmielna 22.
Zwaizek Zawodowy Pracownikow Branzy Kinematograficzneij, Chmielna 12.

Roumania.

FILM PRODUCERS.

Soremar-Film, Cal Victoriei 89, Bucarest.

RENTERS, DISTRIBUTORS AND AGENTS.

Arta Film, Str. Oteteleseanu 5, Bucarest.
Astoria-Film, Str. Brezoianu 9, Bucarest.
Britanic Film, B-dul. Elisabeta 3a, Bucarest.
Columbia-Film, S.A., Cal. Mósilor 88, Bucarest.
Concordia-Film, Strada Jorgu 24, Brasov.
Eforia-Film, Str. Doamnei 3, Bucarest.
Fox-Film Corp., Bd. Elisabeta 10, Bucarest.
Gaumont-Film, B-dul. Elisabeta 36, Bucarest.
Gloria-Film, Bd. Carol 22, Bucarest.
Gondola-Film, Calea Victoriei 2, Bucarest.
"Jstal," S. A. R., Str. Coltei 25, Bucarest.
Matador-Film, Str. Magureanu 7, Bucarest.
Mercur-Film, Str. Sfintilor 13, Bucarest.

Metropol-Film, Str. Coltei 1, Bucarest.
Metro-Goldwyn, S. A. R., Str. Sf. Constantin 29, Bucarest.
Nissim & Merö, Str. Stelea 3, Bucarest.
Oer-Film, M. Segall, Bulevardul Elisabeta 51, Bucarest.
Paramount Film, Str. Baratiei 2, Bucarest.
Rex-Film, Str. Spiru Haret 4, Bucarest.
Ricoli-Film, Str. Lipscani 91A, Bucarest.
Romania-Film, Str. Bucovinei 13, Bucarest.
S.A.F.J.S., Bd. Domnitei 7 Bucarest.
Soremar-Film, Cal. Viktoriei 89, Bucarest.
Sonor-Film, Bd. Elisabeta 15, Bucarest.
Sylvia-film, Strada Carol 88, Bucarest.
United Artists Film, Str. Doamnei 12, Bucarest.
Vesca-Film, Str. Cobalcescu 41, Bucarest.
Warner Bros. First National S.A.R., Str. Doamnei 12, Bucarest.

MANUFACTURERS AND AGENTS OF KINEMA ACCESSORIES.

Agfa-Foto, S.A., Str. Teilor 24, Bucarest.
Elin, S.A., Bd. Domnitei 3, Bucarest.
Gibson B. James, Str. Gl. Lahovary 86, Bucarest.
Philips, S.A., Str. Luterana 6, Bucarest.
Proector, Consortium, Stefan L. Scherer, Strada Raureanu 5, Bucarest.

Siemens Schuckert, S.A. (Klangfilm), Str. C. A. Rosetti 21, Bucarest.
"Walpeco," Cas. post. 69, Bucarest.
Western Electric, Bd. Elisabeta 12, Bucarest.

KINEMA TRADE PUBLICATION :—Cinema, Str. Const. Mille 7-11, Bucarest.

TRADE SOCIETIES AND ASSOCIATIONS.

Uniunea Caselor de Filme, Str. Brezoianu 21, Bucarest.

Uniunea Cinematografistilor din Romania. Str. Brezoianu 21, Bucarest.

Sweden.

FILM RENTERS.

Ailfilm A.-B., Drottninggatan 10, Stockholm.
Anglo Film A.-B., Kungsgatan 8, Stockholm.
Biografernas Film Depot, Drottninggatan 10, Stockholm.
Columbia Film A.-B., Sveavägen 21-23, Stockholm.
Cromo-Film A.-B., Sveavagen 21-23, Stockholm.
Europa Film A.-B., Kungsgatan 10, Stockholm.
Filmdepoten, Drottninggatan 10, Stockholm.
Film-Victoria, Vasagatan 9, Stockholm.
Fox Film, A.-B., Kungsgatan, 12-14, Stockholm.
Fribergs Filmbyra A.-B., Malmskillnadsgatan 39, Stockholm.
International Film, Kungsgatan 33, Stockholm.
Irefilm A.-B., Kungsgatan 8, Stockholm.
Le Mat-Metro-Goldwyn Film A.-B., Kungsgatan 65, Stockholm.
Lobo Film, Mastersamuelsgatan 71, Stockholm.
M.-Film, Norr-Malmsturg 1, Stockholm.
Mondialfilm, S. Kungstomet, Stockholm.
Nationalfilm Aktiebolag, Vasagatan 16, Stockholm.
Nordisk Tonefilm, Svenska A.-B., Kungsgatan 33, Stockholm.
Nordlys, Film A.-B., Kungsgatan 7, Stockholm.

Paramount Filmaktiebolaget, Hamngatan 22, Stockholm.
R.K.O. Radio Films A.-B., Vasgatan 16, Stockholm.
Rosenbergs Filmbyra, Oscar, Kungsgatan 27, Stockholm.
S.B.D., Kungsgatan 29, Stockholm. Tel. : 200577, 114778.
Stockholms Filmcentral, Kungsgatan 33, Stockholm.
Svea Film, A.-B., Kungsgatan 29, Stockholm.
Svensk Filmindustri A.-B., Filmuthyrningen, Kungsgatan 36, Stockholm.
Svensk Talfilms Distributionsbyra A.-B., Drottninggatan 47, Stockholm.
Sveriges Biografagares Distributionsbyra, A.-B. (S.B.D.), Kungsgatan 29, Stockholm.
Tullbergs Film, Kungsbroplan 3, Stockholm.
United Artists, A.-B., Kungsgatan 13, Stockholm.
Universal Film, Aktiebolag, Kungsgatan 73, Stockholm.
Warner Bros.-First National Film A.-B., Kungsgatan 30, Stockholm.
Wivefilm, A.-B., Drottninggatan 47, Stockholm.

MACHINERY AND SOUND FILM INSTALLATIONS.

A.E.G., Ljudfilmsavden, Iveavagen 21-23, Stockholm.
Aga-Baltic, Kungsgatan 13, Stockholm.
Biografagarnas Inkopsforening, Kungsgatan 13, Stockholm.
Ernst Dittmer, A.-B., Kungsgatan 10, Stockholm.
Fototon, Hornsgatan 65, Stockholm.
Erik Johanssons El Mek. versted, Kungsgatan 84, Stockholm.

Kinoton, Ostra Forstadsgatan 48, Malmo.
Klangfilm, Sveavagen 21-23, Stockholm.
Maskinfirman Frigus, Goteborg, "Holmia," Lilla Bommenstorg 2.
Phillips, Kinoavdelningen, Gavlegatan 18, Stockholm.
Skandinavisk Biografservice, Malmo.
Weichert & Carls, Kungsgatan 65, Stockholm.
Axel Ohlander, Drottninggatan 50, Stockholm.

STUDIOS AND LABORATORIES.

A.-B., Film Labor, Regeringsgatan 109, Stockholm.
A.-B. Filmtext, Bryggargatan 18, Stockholm.
Aktiebolager Kinocentralen, Drottinggatan 47, Stockholm.
Cromo Film A.-B., Djurgardsslatten, Stockholm.
Hasselblads Fotografiska, Aktiebolag, Goteborg.

Ideal Filmlaboratorier, A.-B., Keniska filmtexter, Hamngatan 22, Stockholm.
Irefilm, A.-B., Kungsgatan 8, Stockholm.
Nordiskt Filmlaboratorium, A.-B., Kunsgatan 8, Stockholm.
Svensk Filmindustri, Filmstaden, Rasunda, Stockholm.

TRADE SOCIETIES.

Filmagarnas Kontrollforening u.p.a., Drottninggatan 80A, Stockholm.
Foreningen Svenska Filmtekniker, Stockholm.
Svenska Filmlubben.
Svenska Filmsamfundet, Vasagatan 9, Stockholm.

Svenska Film-Hoch Biografmannasall skapet, Vallingatan 44, Stockholm.
Sveriges Biografagareforbund, Sveavagen 29 Stockholm.
Sveriges Filmuthyrareforening, Hamngatan 22, Stockholm.

TRADE PAPERS.

Biografagaren, paper for Sveriges Biografagaren-forbund. Editor's office and expedition— Sveavagen 29, Stockholm.

Biografbladet, Editor Knut Karlaplan 11, Stockholm.

Switzerland.

FILM PRODUCING COMPANIES.

Alpina Film-Genossenschaft, Schipfe 57, Zurich.
Arophon-Film, A.G., Nuschelerstrasse 30, Zurich.
Befa-Film, A.G., Kreuzstrasse 31, (bei J. B. Baumann), Zurich.
Berna Film, A.G., Bundesplatz 2, Berne.
Central Film, A.G., Weinbergstrasse 11, Zurich.
Cinegram, S.A., 3, rue de Beau-Site, Geneva.
Cinemas Populaires Romands, Jean Brocher, 10, avenue de la Gare des Eaux-Vives, Geneva.
Film Finanzierungs, A.G., Bahnhofstrasse 20, Zurich.
Graf & Menzi (Filmexpedition), Einsiedlerstrasse, Horgen.
Heros Film, S.A., La Pineta, Lugano-Bissone.
Ilo-Filmproduktion, Limmatquai 1, Zurich.
Kataster-Compagnie (formerly **Karin Film-Compagnie**) Kanzleistrasse 200, Zurich.
Lemania Film, S.A., Lausanne.
Meyer, R. H., Tempofilm, Freudenbergstrasse 132, Zurich.
Peka Film, Paul Karg, Theaterplatz 6, Berne.
Pinschewer Film-Atelier, Kollerweg 9, Berne.
Praesens Film, A.G., Lowenstrasse 3, Zurich.
Progress Film, A.G., Gurtengasse 6, Berne.

Schmalfilm, A.G., Falkenstrasse 14, Zurich.
Schweizerische Filmzentrale, Bahnhofstrasse 20, Zurich. (Centrale Suisse du Film, Swiss Film Central Office).
Schweizer Schul-und Volkskino, Erlachstrasse 21, Berne, Schipfe 77, Zurich.
Tonfilm, A.G., Schutzenweg, Neu-Allschwil b/Basle.
Tonfilm Frobenius, A.G., Freie Strasse 107, Basle.
Tramontana Film, A.G., Chur.
Turicia-Film, A.G., Stampfenbachstrasse 57, Zurich.

PRODUCERS.

Dahinden, Joseph, Waserstrasse 63, Zurich.
Duvanel, C. G., 3, Plateau de Champel, Geneva.
Egli, H., Germaniastrasse 5, Zurich.
Schmid, Paul, Filmpropaganda, Neufeldstrasse 7, Berne.

STUDIOS.

Basle Studio Mustermessegebaude (Tonfilm Frobenius, A.G.)
Munchenstein : Studio (Tonfilm, A.G., Neu-Allschwil).
Zurich : Studio (Praesens Film, A.G., Zurich).

FILM PRINTERS.

***Cinegram, S.A.,** Geneva.
Eoscop, A.G., Reichensteinerstrasse 14, Basle.
***Peka Film,** Berne.
Preiss, Gustave, Tonfilm-Kopier-Anstalt, Talacker 7, Zurich.

***Tempo-Film** (R. H. Meyer), Zurich.
***Turicia-Film, A.G.,** Zurich.

  * Addresses as under Film Producers.

FILM RENTERS AND AGENTS.

Aciem, via Cattedrale 16, Lugano.
Agence Cinematographique, 24, avenue de la Gare Eaux-Vives, Geneva.
Alfa-Films (Paul Beck), Schauplatzgasse 26, Berne.
Artistic-Films, S.A., 59, rue du Stand, Geneva.
Burckhardt-Film, Grabenhof 4-6, Lucerne.
Central-Film, A.G., Weinbergstrasse 11, Zurich.
Charriere-Bourquin Films, 6, Passage de Lions, Geneva.
Cinevox, S.A., Haus Capitol, Kramgasse, Berne.
Columbus-Film, A.G., Talstrasse 9, Zurich.
Comptoir Cinematographique, A.G., 4, rue Pradier, Geneva.
Coram-Film, A.-G., Limmatquai 94, Zurich.
Distributeurs de Films Ind., 26, Chaussee mon Repos, Lausanne.
Distributeurs de Films, S.A., 10, rue de la Confederation, Geneva.
Elite-Films, S.A., 10, rue Bonivard, Geneva.
Emelka-Filmgesellschaft, Lowenstrasse 55, Zurich.
Eos-Film, A.-G., Reichensteinerstrasse 14, Basle. (Ufa und Paramount).
Etna-Film Co., A.-G., Moosstrasse 4, Lucerne.
Europa Films, A.-G., Glarus.
Filmhandelsgesellschaft, Gurtengasse 3, Berne.
Film-Holding, A.-G., Lowenstrasse 55, Zurich.
Films Parlants, S.A., 59, rue du Stand, Geneva.
First-National-Films, 4, rue du Rhone, Geneva.
Fox-Film, S.A., 12 rue de la Croix d'Or, Geneva.
Fuchs-Films, 8, Quai Gustave Ador, Geneva.

Gerval Ch., Films, 2, avenue Dumas, Geneva.
Grande Production Sonores, S.A., 4, rue John Rebfous, Geneva.
Jacques-Haik-Films, S.A., 14, rue de Hollande, Geneva.
Ideal-Film, S.A., 15, rue Levrier, Geneva.
Impexfilm, A.-G., Kino Kapital Bahnhofstrasse, Arbon.
Majestic-Films, S.A., 5, Place Fusterie, Geneva.
Metro-Goldwyn-Mayer, A.-G., Sihlporteplatz 3, Zurich.
Monogram-Pictures, W. A. Ramseyer, Alfa-Films, Schauplatzgasse 26, Berne.
Monopol-Film, A.-G., Todistrasse 61, Zurich.
Monopole Pathe Films, S.A., 4, rue de la Rotisserie, Geneva.
Montana-Film, A.-G., Gerbergasse 8, Zurich.
Negoce-Films, 15, rue de l'industrie, Geneva.
Neue Interna-Tonfilm-Vertriebs, A.-G., Stauffacherstr. 41, Zurich.
Nordisk Films Co., A.G., Waisenhausstrasse 2, Zurich.
Osso-Films, 6, Passage des Lions, Geneva.
Office Cinematographique, S.A., 4, rue Lions d'or, Lausanne.
P.P.D.-Films, S.A., 10, rue Mauborget, Lausanne.
Pandora Film, A.-G., Sihlstrasse 37, Zurich.
Paramount (see Eos-Film, Basle).
Pathe (See Monopole Pathe Films, Geneva.)
Praesens-Film, A.-G., Lowenstrasse 3, Zurich.
Radio-Cine, A.-G., Gurtei gasse 6 (A. Mooser), Berne.

Resta-Film, R. E. Stamm, Zahringerstrasse 20, Zurich.
Rex-Film-Verleih, A.-G., Weinbergstrasse 17, Zurich. (Dr. Schuppli).
Schweizer Schul- & Volkskino, Erlachstrasse 21, Berne.
Selection Film, S.A., Basle.
S.F.E.C. Films, 14, rue de Hollande, Geneva.
Surber, A., Filmverleih, Stampfenbachstrasse 69, Zurich.

Tobis-Filmverleih, A.-G., Talstrasse 14, Zurich.
Trevis Film, Kapellenstrasse 28, Berne.
Ufa (see Eos-Film, Basle).
Unartisco, S.A., 3, rue de la Confédération, Geneva.
Uty, S.A., 12, rue du Marché, Geneva.
Warner-Bros. First National, 4, rue du Rhone, Geneva.

APPARATUS (STANDARD FILMS).

A.E.G., Stampfenbachstrasse 12-14, Zurich. 3, rue Neuve, Lausanne.
A.-G. fur Schwachstrom-Apparate, Scheuchzerstrasse 105, Zurich.
Alpine-Western-Electric Co., Viaductstr. 16, Basle.
Klangfilm (see A.E.G.).
Swissaphon Fr. Zaugg, Cinéma Palace, Solothurn.

APPARATUS (SUB-STANDARD).

Cine-Engros Falkenstrasse 14, Zurich. (Siemens- Apparate),

Filmo A.-G., (for Central Europe) Talackerstr. 45, Zurich. (Bell & Howell-Apparate),
Ganz & Co. (Bahnhofstrasse 40, Zurich.
Gimmi & Co., Stadelhoferplatz, Zurich.
Hausamamm & Co., A.-G., Bahnhofstrasse 91, Zurich.
Hohl, R., & Sohn, Lyss.
F. Hort, Rotes Schloss, Zurich.
Karg, P., Theaterplatz 6, Berne.
E. Paillard & Co., S.A., St. Croix (Vaud), (Eigene Fabrikation).

KINEMA ACCESSORIES.

Bachtold, Alb., Zurich-Zollikon.
Baumann & Koelliker & Co., Sihlstrasse 37, Zurich.
Cine-Philips-Sonore, Manessestrasse 192, Zurich.

Lampes Philips, S.A., route de Lyon, 109, Geneva.
Theodore Wolf, Lausanne. Agence Lumiere.

FILM PUBLICATIONS.

Cineca Verlag W. Preiss, Stussistrasse 66, Zurich.
Film-Presse-Dienst, 6, Place Cornavin, Geneva.

Schweizer Film Suisse, 27, Terreaux, Lausanne (Official organ Schweiz. Lichtspielth. Verbandes).

TRADE ASSOCIATIONS.

Verband Schweizerischer Filmproduzenten, Association des producteurs suisses du film, Hauptgasse 18, Solothurn.
Gesellschaft Schweizerischer Filmschaffender, (kein frz. Titel) Geschaftsstelle : R. Miville, Wartstr 3, Zurich.
Association des Loueurs de film en Suisse, Marktgasse 37, Berne.
Schweizerischer Lichtspiel theater-Verband, deutsche & Ital. Schweiz, Association cinematographique suisse allemande et italienne, Theaterstrass 3, Zurich, Bellinzona, Super-Cinéma.
Association cinematographique Suisse romande, 20, Chemin des Fleurettes, Lausanne.
Zurcher Lichtspieltheater-Verband, Theaterstrasse 3, Zurich.

Basler Lichtspieltheater-Verband, Munzgasse 3, Basle.
Association des representants de films, 5, rue St. Léger, Geneva.
Filmkammer Basle-Stadt, Munsterplatz 19, Basel.
Schweizerische Lehrfilmkammer, Munsterplatz 19, Basel.
Schweizerische Arbeitsgemeinschaft fur Unterrichtskinematographie, Prof. Dr. Rust, E.T.H., Soneggstr. 5, Zurich.
Bund Schweizerischer Kulturfilmgemeinden, Erlachstrasse 21, Berne.
Institut de l'enseignement par l'image lumineuse, M. E. Duvillard, Geneva.

Turkey.

FILM PRODUCERS.

Sine Melek, Jpekci Kardaslar, Beyoglu Yesil sokak 15, Istanbul.

Halil Kjamii Film, Taksim, Sine Turc, Istanbul.

RENTERS, DISTRIBUTORS AND AGENTS.

Oezenfilm, Beyoglu, Yesil Sokak 23, Istanbul.
"Disque-Film," Adalet Han, Galata, Istanbul.
Elektra-Film, Vüksekkaldirim Izmiroglu Han 2/12, Istanbul.
Fox-Film Corp., Istiklal Caddesi 193, Istanbul.
A. de Hubsch, Cinil Rihtim Han, Galata, Istanbul.
Jpekci Kardaslar, Tsokak, Beyoglu, Yesi Caddesi 15, Istanbul.
"Komal-Film," Istiklal Caddesi 373, Istanbul.

Halil Kiamil Film, Beyoglu, B.P. 2163, Istanbul.
Metro-Goldwyn-Mayer Missir Han, Ipekci Kardaslar Sine Melek, Beyoglu, Istanbul.
Mondial-Film, Beyoglu Hava sokak, Hava Apartiman 1, Istanbul.
Paramount-Film, Ipekci Kardaslar, Sine "Melek," Beyoglu, Istanbul.
"United Artists," Emin Enis & Co., Imam Sok., Beyoglu, Istanbul.

MANUFACTURERS AND AGENTS OF KINEMA ACCESSORIES.

A. E. G. Turk. A. Elektrik S. Umumiyesi, Galata, Voyvoda Cad. Eski Posta bin, Istanbul.
Ahmet Necip (Bauer), Sesli Han, Galata, Istanbul.
Filips Radyolari, Galata, Voyvada Cads 7, Istanbul.

Magasin "Lumiere," Tünel Meydun 519, Beyoglu, Istanbul.
Jack Rottenberg, Beyoglu Jstiklal Caddesi, Eski Derkos Han, Istanbul.

KINEMA TRADE PUBLICATIONS.

"Cine Turc," P. K. 2136, Istanbul.

"Hollywood," Vakit Kitap Subesi, Istanbul.

TRADE SOCIETY.

Turk Sinema ve Filmiciler Birligi, Beyoglu 373, Banka Han, Istanbul.

Union of South Africa.

African Film Productions, Ltd., Box 2787, Johannesburg
African Consolidated Films, Ltd., Box 4552, Johannesburg.
African Consolidated Films, Ltd., Box 701, Cape Town.

Independent Film Distributors, South Africa (Pty.) Ltd., Box 806, Johannesburg.
Metro-Goldwyn-Mayer Films, South Africa (Pty.), Ltd., Box 5493, Johannesburg.
Rhodesian Film Productions, Ltd., Bulawayo.

KINEMA THEATRE COMPANIES.

African Consolidated Theatres, Ltd., Johannesburg.
Independent Picture Palaces, Ltd., Johannesburg and Durban.

Metro (M-G-M), Johannesburg.
Union Theatres (Pty.), Ltd., Box 4919, Johannesburg. Also Durban, Cape Town.

United States of America.

FILM COMPANIES (NEW YORK).

Academy Pictures Distributing Corp., 1501, Broadway.
Advance Trailer Service Corp., 630, Ninth Avenue.
Ameranglo Corp., 226, West 42nd Street.
American Display Co., 521, West 57th Street.
Amity Picture Corp., Ltd., 729 Seventh Avenue.
Amkino Corp., 723, Seventh Avenue.
Amusement Securities Corp., 729, Seventh Avenue.
Amusement Supply Co., 341, West 44th Street.
Astor Pictures Corp., 1501, Broadway.
Audio Productions, Inc., 250, West 57th Street.
Beacon Films, Inc., 729, Seventh Avenue.
Biograph Studios, Inc., 807, East 175th Street.
Bray Pictures Corp., 729, Seventh Avenue.
British & Continental Trading Co., Inc., 1270, Sixth Avenue.
J. E. Brulatour, Films, 1540, Broadway.
J. E. Brulatour, Inc., 154, Crescent Street, Long Island City, N.Y.
Burroughs Tarzan Enterprises, Inc., 1270, Sixth Avenue.
Capitol Film Exchange, 630, Ninth Avenue.
Casey, Pat, Enterprises, 1600, Broadway
Castle Films, 30, Rockefeller Plaza.
Celebrated Pictures, Inc., 1560, Broadway.
Celebrity Productions, Inc., 723, Seventh Avenue.

Chesterfield Motion Pictures, Corp., 1540, Broadway.
Cinema Patents Co.; Inc., 1776, Broadway.
Columbia Pictures Corp., 729, Seventh Avenue.
Commodore Pictures Corp., 1501, Broadway.
Consolidated Film Industries, Inc., 1776, Broadway.
Copyright Protection Bureau, 1270, Sixth Avenue.
Cosmopolitan Productions, Inc., 1540, Broadway
Cosmopolitan Studio, 145, West 45th Street.
Disney, Walt, Enterprises, 727, Seventh Avenue.
Du Art Film Laboratory, 245, West 55th Street.
DuPont Film Mfg. Corp., 35, West 45th Street.
DuWorld Pictures, Inc., 729, Seventh Avenue.
Eastman Kodak Co., 356, Madison Avenue and 83, Montgomery Street, Jersey City.
Economic Films, Inc., 729, Seventh Avenue.
Educational Films Corp. of America, 1501, Broadway.
Educational Productions, Inc., 1501, Broadway.
Electrical Research Products, Inc., 250, West 57th Street.
Empire Film Distributors, Inc., 723, Seventh Avenue.
Fanchon & Marco, 30, Rockefeller Plaza.
FitzPatrick Pictures, Inc., 729, Seventh Avenue.
Fox Movietone News, 460, West 54th Street.
Gaumont British Picture Corp. of America, 1600, Broadway.

General Service Studios, Astoria, Long Island.
General Talking Pictures, 218, West 42nd Street.
Grand National Films, Inc., 1270, Sixth Avenue.
Hearst Metrotone News, 450, West 56th Street.
Hoffberg, J. H., Co., Inc., 729, Seventh Avenue
Hollywood Pictures Corp., 630, Ninth Avenue.
Ideal Pictures Corp., 729, Seventh Avenue.
Imperial Distributing Corp., 729, Seventh Avenue.
Integrity Film Corp., 220, West 42nd Street.
International Newsreel Corp., 1540, Broadway.
International Projector Corp., 88-96, Gold Street
Invincible Pictures Corp., 1540, Broadway.
Keith, B. F., Corp., 1270, Sixth Avenue.
Keith-Albee-Orpheum Corp., 1270, Sixth Avenue.
Kinematrade, Inc., 723, Seventh Avenue.
Liberty Pictures Corp., 1776, Broadway.
Loew's, Inc., 1540, Broadway.
March of Time, 135, East 42nd Street.
Mascot Pictures Corp., 1776, Broadway.
Master Art Productions, Inc., 630, Ninth Avenue.
Mentone Productions, Inc., 1270, Sixth Avenue.
Metropolis Pictures Corp., 260, Fifth Avenue.
Metro-Goldwyn-Mayer Corp., 1540, Broadway.
National Screen Service, 630, Ninth Avenue.
National Theatre Supply Co., 88-96, Gold Street.
Nuovo Mundo Motion Pictures, Inc., 1270, Sixth Avenue.
Paramount News, Inc., 544, West 43rd Street
Paramount Pictures, Inc., 1501, Broadway.
Pathe Film Corp., 1270, Sixth Avenue.
Pathe News, 35, West 45th Street.
Principal Distributing Corp., 1501, Broadway.

Prudential Film Distributors Corp., 630, Ninth Avenue.
Puritan Pictures Corp., 723, Seventh Avenue.
Raspin Productions, Inc., 1270, Sixth Avenue.
RCA Mfg. Co., Inc., Camden, N.J.
Radio-Keith-Orpheum Corp., 1270, Sixth Avenue.
RKO Radio Pictures, Inc., 1270, Sixth Avenue.
Regal Distributing Corp., 729, Seventh Avenue.
Reliance Pictures, Inc., 1501, Broadway.
Republic Pictures Corp., 1776, Broadway.
Rex Film Corp., 1270, Sixth Avenue.
Ross Federal Service, Inc., 6, East 45th Street.
Select Productions, Inc., 1776, Broadway.
Stage and Screen Productions, Inc., 729, Seventh Avenue.
Syndicate Features Corp., 341, Madison Avenue.
Technicolor, Inc., 15, Broad Street.
Times Pictures, Inc., 630, Ninth Avenue.
Trans-Lux Movies Corp., 1270, Sixth Avenue.
Twentieth Century-Fox Film Corp., 444, West 56th Street.
Ufa Films Co., 729, Seventh Avenue.
United Artists Distributing Corp., 729, Seventh Avenue.
Universal News, 1250, Sixth Avenue.
Universal Pictures, 1250, Sixth Avenue.
Van Beuren Corp., 1270, Sixth Avenue.
Variety Film Distributors, 489, Fifth Avenue.
Vitaphone Studios, 1277, East 14th Street, Brooklyn.
Warner Bros. Pictures, Inc., 321, West 44th Street.
Western Electric Co., 195, Broadway.

FILM COMPANIES (HOLLYWOOD).

Ambassador Pictures, Inc., 4516, Sunset Blvd. Hollywood.
Atherton Productions, Inc., RKO-Pathe Studios, Culver City, Cal.
C. C. Burr Productions, 506, Beechwood Drive, Hollywood.
Burroughs-Tarzan Enterprises, Inc., 8476, Hollywood Blvd., Hollywood.
Cameo Pictures Corp., 4516, Sunset Blvd., Hollywood.
Charles Chaplin Film Corp., 1416, North La Brea Avenue, Hollywood.
Columbia Pictures Corp., Ltd., 1438, North Gower Street, Hollywood.
Darmour Studios, 5823, Santa Monica Blvd., Hollywood.
Walt Disney Productions, 2719, Hyperion Ave., Hollywood.
Diversion Pictures, Inc., 1436, North Hollywood Drive, Hollywood.
Educational Studios, 7250, Santa Monica Blvd., Los Angeles.
Fanchon & Marco, Inc., 5600, Sunset Blvd., Hollywood.
First Division Productions, Inc., 4024, Radford Avenue, North Hollywood, Cal.
Futter Corporation, Ltd., 1426, North Beechwood Drive, Hollywood.
General Service Studios, Inc., 6625, Romaine Street, Hollywood.
Samuel Goldwyn, Inc., Ltd., 7210. Santa Monica Blvd., Hollywood.
Hollywood Film Enterprises, Inc., 6060, Sunset Blvd., Hollywood.
Craig Hutchinson Pictures, Inc., 7671, Fountain Avenue, Hollywood.
Liberty Pictures Corp. (RKO-Pathe Studios), Culver City, Cal.

Metro-Goldwyn-Mayer Studios, Culver City, Cal.
Paramount Productions, Inc., 5154, Marathon Street, Hollywood.
Principal Distributing Corp., 1680, North Vine Street, Hollywood.
Prudential Studios Corp., Melrose at Bronson, Hollywood.
Ramsey Pictures Corp., 1220, West Main, Oklahoma City, Okla.
Republic Productions, Inc., 4024, Radford Avenue, North Hollywood.
Resolute Picture Corp., 999, Lillian Way, Hollywood.
RKO Studios, Inc., 780, Gower Street, Hollywood.
Hal Roach Studios, Inc., Culver City, Cal.
Charles R, Rogers Talking Pictures Corp., Universal City, Cal.
Leon Schlesinger Productions, Warners Sunse Studios, Hollywood.
Selznick International Pictures, Inc., 9336, Washington Blvd., Culver City.
Sentinel Productions, Inc., 723, Guaranty Bldg., Hollywood.
Harry Sherman Productions, Inc., 650, No. Bronson Ave., Hollywood.
Twentieth Century-Fox Film Corp., Beverly Hills, Cal.
United Artists Studio Corp., 1041, North Formosa Avenue, Hollywood.
Universal Pictures Corp., Universal City, Cal.
Wafilms, Inc., 1426, North Beechwood Drive, Hollywood.
Warner Brothers Pictures, Inc., Burbank, Cal.
B. F. Zeidman Productions, Inc., 1509, North Vine Street, Hollywood

TRADE JOURNALS.

American Cinematographer, The, 6331, Hollywood Blvd., Hollywood, Cal.
Associated Publications, Inc. (Box-Office), 551, Fifth Avenue, N.Y.
Better Theatres (Quigley Publications), 1270, Sixth Avenue, N.Y.
Billboard, The, 1564, Broadway, New York.
Cinelandia (Spanish-American Publishing Co.), 1031, So. B'way, Los Angeles.
Cinema Hallmarks, P.O. Box 1911, Hollywood, Cal.
Cine-Mundial (Chalmers Publishing Co.), 516, Fifth Avenue, N.Y.
Distributor, The, 1540, Broadway, N.Y.
Fame (Quigley Publications), 1270, Sixth Avenue, N.Y.
Film Curb, 1270, Sixth Avenue, N.Y.
Film Daily, The, 1650, Broadway, N.Y.
Film Mercury, 7556, Melrose, Hollywood, Cal.
Greater Amusements, 425, Hennepin Avenue, Minneapolis, Minn.
Harrison's Reports, 1440, Broadway, N.Y.
Hollywood Filmograph, 1606, Cahuenga, Hollywood, Cal.
Hollywood Reporter, 229, West 42nd Street, N.Y.; 6717, Sunset Blvd., Hollywood, Cal.
Hollywood Variety, 1710, North Vine Street, Hollywood, Cal.
Hollywood Screen World, 859, North Vine Street, Hollywood, Cal.
Hollywood Spectator, 6513, Hollywood Blvd., Hollywood, Cal.
International Photographer, 1605, North Cahuenga Avenue, Hollywood, Cal.
International Projectionist, 580, Fifth Avenue, N.Y.
Jay Emanuel Publications, 219, North Broad Street, Philadelphia, Pa.
Morning Telegraph, 343, West 26th Street, N.Y.
Motion Picture Almanac (Quigley Publications), 1270, Sixth Avenue, N.Y.
Motion Picture Daily, 1270, Sixth Avenue, N.Y.
Motion Picture Herald, 1270, Sixth Avenue, N.Y.
National Exhibitor, The, 219, North Broad Street, Philadelphia, Pa.
New York Exhibitor, The, 219, North Broad Street, Philadelphia, Pa.
Philadelphia Exhibitor, The, 219, North Broad Street, Philadelphia, Pa.
Showmen's Trade Review, Inc., 155, West 56th Street, New York.
Studio News, The, 624, Guaranty Bldg., Hollywood, Cal.
Teatro Al Dia (Quigley Publications), 1270, Sixth Avenue, N.Y.
Variety, 154, West 46th Street, N.Y.
Zit's Weekly, 254, West 54th Street N.Y.

TRADE ORGANISATIONS.

Academy of Motion Picture Arts and Sciences, Taft Bldg., Hollywood.
Actors' Equity Association, 45, West 47th Street, New York..
Amateur Cinema League, Inc., 420, Lexington Avenue, New York.
American Dramatists, 9, East 38th Street, New York.
American Society of Cinematographers, Guaranty Bldg., Hollywood.
American Society of Composers, Authors and Publishers, 30, Rockefeller Plaza, New York.
Associated M.P. Advertisers, Inc., New York City.
Association of Motion Picture Producers, 5504, Hollywood Blvd., Hollywood.
Authors' Guild of the Authors' League of America, 9, East 38th Street, New York.
Authors' League of America, The, 9, East 38th Street, New York.
Catholic Actors' Guild of America, Hotel Astor, New York.
Catholic Writers' Guild, 128, West 71st Street, New York.
Central Casting Corporation, 5504, Hollywood Blvd., Hollywood.
Cinema Club, 65, West 44th Street, New York.
Hollywood Studio Club, 1251, Lodi Place, Hollywood.
International Alliance of Theatrical Stage Employes and M.P. Machine Operators of the U.S. and Canada, 1450, Broadway, New York.
Internationsl Federation of Catholic Alumnae Motion Picture Bureau, 294, Clinton Avenue, Brooklyn.
Masquers, The, 1765, North Sycamore Avenue, Hollywood.
Motion Picture Makeup Artists' Ass'n., 1627, No. Cahuenga Avenue, Hollywood.
Motion Picture Producers and Distributors of America, 28, West 44th Street, New York.
National Board of Review of Motion Pictures, 70, Fifth Avenue, New York.
Screen Actors' Guild, Inc., 1655 No Cherokee Avenue, Hollywood.
Screen Writers' Guild of the Authors' League of America, 1655 No. Cherokee Avenue, Hollywood.
Society of Motion Picture Engineers, 33, West 42nd Street, New York.
Variety Club, The, 617, William Penn Way, Pittsburgh.
Writers' Club, The, 6760, Sunset Blvd., Hollywood.

The
Olympic Kinematograph
Laboratories Limited

Specialists in
all kinds of
Commercial
Film Printing
& Developing

SCHOOL ROAD,
LONDON, N.W.10

Telegrams :
'OHKAYLAB,
HARLES, LONDON'

Telephone :
WILLESDEN
7233-4-5

Trade Shown Films of 1936

British films and films made in British Colonies denoted by an asterisk (*).
Trade show date in brackets. The KINE. *date given is that of the issue*
in which the review appeared. The length and release are as supplied by the
renters. List covers all films reviewed in KINEMATOGRAPH WEEKLY *up to*
November 26, 1936.

Absolute Quiet. (April 27.) Lionel Atwill, Irene Hervey, Raymond Walburn. 6,269 ft. **A.** " Kine." April 30, 1936. Rel. July 13, 1936. M-G-M.

Accusing Finger, The. (Nov. 24.) Paul Kelly, Marsha Hunt, Kent Taylor. 4,577 ft. **A.** " Kine." Nov. 26, 1936. Rel. May 3, 1937. PARAMOUNT.

*Accused. (July 27.) Douglas Fairbanks, Jnr., Dolores Del Rio, Florence Desmond. 7,600 ft. **A.** " Kine." July 30, 1936. Rel. Feb. 22, 1937. UNITED ARTISTS.

Ace Drummond. (Oct. 23.) John King, Jean Rogers, Noah Beery, Jnr. 13 eps. **A.** " Kine." Oct. 29, 1936. Rel. Jan. 25, 1937. GEN. F.D.

The Adventures of Frank Merriwell. (Jan. 16.) Donald Briggs, John King, Jean Rogers. 12 eps. **U.** " Kine." Jan. 23, 1936. Rel. Apl. 20, 1936. GEN. F.D.

Adventures of Rex and Rinty, The. (July 10.) Rex, Rin-Tin-Tin, Jnr. 12 eps. **U.** " Kine." July 16, 1936. Rel. date not fixed. A.B.F.D.

Ah, Wilderness. (Feb. 3.) Wallace Beery, Lionel Barrymore, Eric Linden. 8,485 ft. **A.** " Kine." Feb. 6, 1936. Rel. May 4, 1936. M-G-M.

Alibi for Murder. (Nov. 16.) William Gargan, Marguerite Churchill, Gene Morgan. 5,275 ft. **A.** " Kine." Nov. 19, 1936. Rel. March 8, 1937. COLUMBIA.

*All In. (Oct. 29.) Ralph Lynn, Claude Dampier, Gina Malo. 6,438 ft. **A.** " Kine." Nov. 5, 1936. Rel. Dec. 21, 1936. G.-B.D.

All One Night. (Sept. 8.) Hugh Herbert, Dorothy Vaughan, Patricia Ellis. 5,375 ft. **A.** " Kine." Sept. 10, 1936. Rel. Feb. 15, 1937. FIRST NATIONAL*

Along Came Love. (Nov. 17.) Irene Hervey, Charles Starrett, H. B. Warner. 5,959 ft. **U.** " Kine." Nov. 19, 1936. Rel. May 24, 1937. PARAMOUNT.

*The Amateur Gentleman. (Jan. 20.) Douglas Fairbanks, Jnr., Elissa Landi, Gordon Harker. 9,118 ft. **A.** " Kine." Jan. 23, 1936. Rel. Aug. 17, 1936. UNITED ARTISTS.

*Amazing Quest, The. (July 28.) Cary Grant, Mary Brian, Peter Gawthorne. 7,272 ft. **U.** " Kine." Aug. 6, 1936. Rel. Feb. 1, 1937. UNITED ARTISTS.

And So They Were Married. (June 17.) Melvyn Douglas, Mary Astor, Edith Fellows. 6,656 ft. **U.** " Kine." June 25, 1936. Rel. Sept. 28, 1936. COLUMBIA.

And Sudden Death. (July 24.) Randolph Scott, Frances Drake, Tom Brown. 5,873 ft. **A.** " Kine." July 30, 1936. Rel. Dec. 14, 1936. PARAMOUNT.

Anne Marie. (April 21.) Annabella, Pierre Richard Willm. 9,100 ft. **U.** " Kine." April 23, 1936. Rel. date not fixed. MAJESTIC.

Annie Doesn't Live Here. (Mar. 27.) Tom Brown, Marion Nixon, Lucien Littlefield. 6,621 ft. **U.** " Kine." April 2, 1936. Rel. July 13, 1936. A.B.F.D.

*Annie Laurie. (July 8.) Will Fyffe, Polly Ward, Bruce Seton. 7,444 ft. **U.** " Kine." July 16, 1936. Rel. Dec. 7, 1936. BUTCHER.

Annie Oakley. (Jan. 8.) Barbara Stanwyck, Preston Foster, Melvyn Douglas. 7,600 ft. **A.** "Kine." Jan. 16, 1936. Rel. May 25, 1936. RADIO.

Anthony Adverse. (May 19.) Fredric March, Olivia de Haviland, Claude Rains. 12,800 ft. **A.** "Kine." May 28, 1936. Rel. Jan. 11, 1937. WARNER.

Anything Goes (Feb. 14.) Bing Crosby, Ethel Merman, Charlie Ruggles. 8,246 ft. **U.** "Kine." Feb. 20, 1936. Rel. May 18, 1936. PARAMOUNT.

Arizona Raiders. (Sept. 11.) Larry Crabbe, Marsha Hunt, Raymond Hutton. 5,165 ft. **U.** "Kine." Sept. 17, 1936. Rel. Mar. 15, 1937. PARAMOUNT.

Arizona Trails. (Oct. 27.) Bill Paton, Edna Aslin, Ed. Carey. 4,430 ft. **U.** "Kine." Oct. 29, 1936. Rel. date not fixed. EQUITY.

*As You Like It. (Sept. 4.) Elizabeth Bergner, Laurence Olivier, Sophie Stewart. 8,674 ft. **U.** "Kine." Sept. 10, 1936. Rel. Feb. 22, 1937. Fox.

*Avenging Hand, The. (April 16.) Noah Beery, Kathleen Kelly, Louis Borelli. 5,850 ft. **A.** "Kine." April 23, 1936. Rel. Sept. 28, 1936. RADIO.

Back to Nature. (Oct. 15.) Jed Prouty, Spring Byington, Shirley Deane. 5,072 ft. **U.** "Kine." Oct. 22, 1936. Rel. Apl. 5, 1937. Fox.

*Ball at Savoy. (Jan. 9.) Conrad Nigel, Marta Labarr, Lu Anne Meredith. 6,750 ft. **U.** "Kine." Jan. 16, 1936. Rel. June 15, 1936. RADIO.

Bars of Hate. (Feb. 28.) Regis Toomey, Sheila Terry, Snub Pollard. 5,400 ft. **A.** "Kine." Mar. 5, 1936. Rel. Mar. 30, 1936. PATHE.

Bar 20 Rides Again. (April 27.) William Boyd, Jimmy Ellison, Jean Rouveral. 5,659 ft. **U.** "Kine." April 30, 1936. Rel. Aug. 31, 1936. PARAMOUNT.

*The Belles of St. Clements. (Jan. 29.) Evelyn Foster, Meriel Forbes. 6,170 ft. **A.** "Kine." Feb. 6, 1936. Rel. May 4, 1936. PARAMOUNT.

*Beloved Imposter, The. (Feb. 28.) Rene Ray, Fred Conyngham. 7,769 ft. **A.** "Kine." Mar. 5, 1936. Rel. July 20, 1936. RATIO.

*Beloved Vagabond, The. (Aug. 25.) Maurice Chevalier, Margaret Lockwood, Betty Stockfeld. 7,006 ft. **A.** "Kine." Sept. 3, 1936. Rel. Mar. 22, 1937. A.B.F.D.

Bengal Tiger. (Sept. 3.) Barton Maclane, June Travis, Warren Hull. 5,235 ft. **A.** "Kine." Sept. 10, 1936. Rel. Mar. 8, 1937. WARNER.

Big Broadcast of 1937, The. (Nov. 2.) Jack Benny, Gracie Allen, George Burns, Ray Millard. 8,698 ft. **U.** "Kine." Oct. 29, 1936. Rel. Mar. 29, 1937. PARAMOUNT.

Big Brown Eyes. (May 25.) Cary Grant, Joan Bennett, Walter Pidgeon. 6,860 ft. **A.** "Kine." May 7, 1936. Rel. Sept. 7, 1936. PARAMOUNT.

Big Game, The. (Nov. 10.) Philip Huston, Bruce Cabot, June Travis. 6,800 ft. **U.** "Kine." Nov. 12, 1936. Rel. Mar. 8, 1937. RADIO.

*Big Noise, The. (Mar. 24.) Alastair Sim, Norah Howard. 5,855 ft. **U.** "Kine." Mar. 26, 1936. Rel. Sept. 7, 1936. Fox.

Blackmailer. (Aug. 17.) William Gargan, Florence Rice, Paul Hurst. 5,897 ft. **A.** "Kine." Aug. 20, 1936. Rel. Nov. 16, 1936. COLUMBIA.

Black Gold. (Oct. 2.) Frankie Darro, Gloria Shea, Roy Mason. 5,416 ft. **U.** "Kine." Oct. 8, 1936. Rel. Mar., 1937. INDEPENDENT F.D.

Black Journey. (June 4.) 3,410 ft. **U.** "Kine." June 11, 1936. Rel. Sept. 21, 1936. ACE.

*Black Mask. (Dec. 11.) Wylie Watson, Aileen Marson, Ellis Irving. 6,066 ft. **A.** "Kine." Dec. 19, 1935. Rel. Feb. 10. 1936. WARNER.

*Blindman's Buff. (Mar. 25.) Basil Sydney, Enid Stamp Taylor. 6,429 ft. **A.** "Kine." April 2, 1936. Rel. Aug. 24, 1936. Fox.

*Blow Bugles Blow. (April 14.) 6,721 ft. " Kine." April 16, 1936. Rel. date not fixed. PROGRESSIVE.

*Blue Smoke. (Dec. 17.) Tamara Desni, Ralph Ince. 6,791 ft. U. " Kine." Dec. 19, 1935. Rel. May 25, 1936. Fox.

Bohemian Girl, The. (Mar. 16.) Oliver Hardy, Stan Laurel, Mae Busch. 6,374 ft. A. " Kine." Mar. 19, 1936. Rel. May 18, 1936. M-G-M.

Bonne Chance. (Feb. 14.) Sacha Guitry, Jacqueline Delubac. 7,000 ft. — " Kine." Feb. 6, 1936. Rel. date not fixed. G.-B.D.

Border Caballero. (Aug. 21.) Tim McCoy, Lois January, 5,100 ft. U. " Kine." Aug. 27, 1936. Rel. date not fixed. EQUITY.

Border Flight. (July 15.) Frances Farmer, John Howard, Grant Withers. 5,306 ft. U. " Kine." July 23, 1936. Rel. Dec. 21, 1936. PARAMOUNT.

*Born That Way. (July 29.) Elliott Mason, Kathleen Gibson, Ian Colin. 5,804 ft. U. " Kine." Aug. 6, 1936. Rel. Jan. 4, 1937. RADIO.

Born to Fight. (July 27.) Frankie Darro, Kane Richmond, Frances Grant. 6,500 ft. U. " Kine." July 30, 1936. Rel. Oct., 1937. INDEPENDENT F.D.

Born to Gamble. (Sept. 22.) H. B. Warner, Onslow Stevens, Lois Wilson. 5,870 ft. U. " Kine." Sept. 24, 1936. Rel. Dec. 14, 1936. A.B.F.D.

Boss Rider of Gun Creek. (Aug. 24.) Buck Jones, Muriel Evans, Harvey Clark. 5,190 ft. U. " Kine." Aug. 27, 1936. Rel. Dec. 21, 1936. GEN. F.D.

*Bottle Party. (Nov. 9.) Meggie Eaton, Gus Chevalier, Eric Woodburn, Windmill Girls. 4,156 ft. U. " Kine." Nov. 12, 1936. Rel. Feb. 8, 1937. ACE FILMS.

Boulder Dam. (Mar. 6.) Ross Alexander, Patricia Ellis, Lyle Talbot. 6,361 ft. U. " Kine." Mar. 12, 1936. Rel. Oct. 19, 1936. WARNER.

The Bride Comes Home. (Jan. 7.) Claudette Colbert, Fred McMurray, Robert Young. 7,430 ft. U. Kine." Jan. 9, 1936. Rel. April 27, 1936. PARAMOUNT.

Bride Walks Out, The. (July 29.) Barbara Stanwyck, Gene Raymond, Robert Young. 7,280 ft. A. " Kine." Aug. 6, 1936. Rel. Dec. 14, 1936. RADIO.

Brides are Like That. (April 7.) Ross Alexander, Anita Louise, Joseph Cawthorne. 6,429 ft. A. " Kine." April 9, 1936. Rel. Oct. 5, 1936. FIRST NATIONAL.

Bridge of Sighs. (Sept. 8.) Onslow Stevens, Dorothy Tree, Walter Byron. 5,930 ft. A. " Kine." Sept. 10, 1936. Rel. Mar. 8, 1937. WARDOUR.

Broadway Hostess. (Feb. 5.) Wini Shaw, Genevieve Tobin, Lyle Talbot. 6,342 ft. U. " Kine." Feb. 13, 1936. Rel. July 6, 1936. FIRST NATIONAL.

*Broken Blossoms. (May 20.) Dolly Haas, Arthur Margetson, Emlyn Williams. 7,000 ft. A. " Kine." May 28, 1936. Rel. Jan. 18, 1937. WARDOUR.

Broken Coin, The. (Mar. 10.) Earle Douglas, William Desmond. 5,000 ft. A. " Kine." Mar. 12, 1935. Rel. July 20, 1936. INTER CINE.

*The Brown Wallet. (Feb. 25.) Patric Knowles, Nancy O'Neil. 6,086 ft. A. " Kine." Feb. 27, 1936. Rel. July 20, 1936. FIRST NATIONAL.

Bullets or Ballots. (Aug. 18.) Edward G. Robinson, Joan Blondell, Barton Maclane. 7,446 ft. A. " Kine." Aug. 27, 1936. Rel. Jan. 18, 1937. FIRST NATIONAL.

Bulldog Courage. (Aug. 28.) Tim McCoy, Joan Woodbury, William K. Hackett. 5,750 ft. U. " Kine." Sept. 3, 1936. Rel. date not fixed. EQUITY.

Burning Gold. (Mar. 25.) Bill Boyd, Judith Allen, Lloyd Ingraham. 5,284 ft. A. " Kine." April 2, 1936. Rel. July 6, 1936. BRITISH LION.

*Busman's Holiday. (Nov. 9.) Wally Patch, Gus McNaughton, Muriel George. 5,850 ft. **U.** "KINE," Nov. 12, 1936. Rel. Mar. 15, 1937. RADIO.

The Cactus Kid. (Jan. 24.) Jack Perrin. 5,125 ft. **U.** "Kine." Jan. 30, 1936. Rel. date not fixed. EQUITY BRITISH.

*Cafe Mascot. (July 10.) Geraldine Fitzgerald, Derrick de Marney. 6,910 ft. **U.** "Kine," July 16. 1936. Rel. Dec. 21, 1936. PARAMOUNT.

Cain and Mabel. (Nov. 5.) Marion Davies, Clark Gable, Allen Jenkins. 8,167 ft. **U.** "Kine." Nov. 12, 1936. Rel. May 17, 1937. WARNER.

The Calling of Dan Matthews. (Feb. 20.) Richard Arlen, Charlotte Wynters, Donald Cook. 5,821 ft. **A.** "Kine." Feb. 27, 1936. Rel. May 25, 1936. COLUMBIA.

*Calling the Tune. (July 7.) Sam Livesey, Sally Gray, Clifford Evans. 6,467 ft. **U.** "Kine." July 9, 1936. Rel. Jan. 18, 1937. A.B.F.D.

Call of the Prairie. (July 17.) William Boyd, Jimmy Ellison, Muriel Evans. 5,994 ft. **U.** "Kine." July 23. 1936. Rel. Dec. 28, 1936. PARAMOUNT.

*Can You Hear Me, Mother? (Dec. 2.) Sandy Powell, Mary Lawson, Baby Ann Ibbitson. 7,000 ft. **U.** "Kine." Dec. 5, 1935. Rel. July 27, 1936. WARDOUR.

Captain January. (May 22.) Shirley Temple, Guy Kibbee, Slim Summerville. 6,950 ft. **U.** "Kine." May 14, 1936. Rel. Oct. 19, 1936. FOX.

Captain Blood. (Feb. 4.) Errol Flynn, Olivia de Havilland, Lionel Atwill. 10,829 ft. **U.** "Kine." Feb. 6, 1936. Rel. May 4, 1936. FIRST NATIONAL.

Captain's Kid, The. (Nov. 3.) Sybil Jason, Guy Kibbee, May Robson. 6,588 ft. **U.** "Kine." Nov. 12, 1936. Rel. Apl. 26, 1937. FIRST NATIONAL.

*Captain's Table, The. (Nov. 23.) Percy Marmont, Daphne Courtney, Louis Goodrich. 4,962 ft. **A.** "Kine." Nov. 26, 1936. Rel. Apl. 5, 1937. M-G-M.

Captured in Chinatown. (April 17.) Charles Delaney, Marion Shilling. 4,712 ft. **U.** "Kine." April 23, 1936. Rel. May 11, 1936. GEN. F.D.

*Cardinal, The. (Mar. 26.) Matheson Lang, Robert Atkins, June Duprez. 6,750 ft. **A.** "Kine." April 2, 1936. Rel. July 27, 1936. PATHE.

Case Against Mrs. Ames, The. (June 9.) Madeleine Carroll, George Brent, Alan Mowbray. 7,756 ft. **A.** "Kine." June 11, 1936. Rel. Oct. 26, 1936. PARAMOUNT.

Case of Mrs. Pembrook, The. (July 14.) Humphrey Bogart, Beverley Roberts, Helen MacKellar. 5,179 ft. **A.** "Kine." July 16, 1936. Rel. Jan. 11, 1937. FIRST NATIONAL.

Case of the Black Cat, The. (Nov. 24.) Ricardo Cortez, June Travis, Harry Davenport. 6,010 ft. **A.** "Kine." Nov. 26, 1936. Rel. May 10, 1937. FIRST NATIONAL.

Case of the Missing Man. (Dec. 16.) Roger Pryor, Joan Perry, Arthur Hohl. 5,240 ft. **U.** "Kine." Dec. 19, 1935. Rel. Apl. 13, 1936. COLUMBIA.

Case of the Velvet Claws, The. (July 3.) Warren William, Claire Dodd, Wini Shaw. 5,775 ft. **A.** "Kine." July 9, 1936. Rel. Jan. 4, 1937. WARNER.

Caught by Television. (Aug. 21.) Mary Astor, Lyle Talbot, Nat Pendleton. 5,729 ft. **U.** "Kine." Aug. 27, 1936. Rel. Jan. 11, 1937. COLUMBIA.

Cavalcade of the West. (Nov. 17.) Hoot Gibson, Rex Lease, Marlon Shilling. 5,627 ft. **U.** "Kine." Nov. 19, 1936. Rel. date not fixed. NATIONAL PROV.

Ceiling Zero. (Mar. 3.) James Cagney, Pat O'Brien, June Travis. 8,681 ft. **A.** " Kine." Mar. 12, 1936. Rel. Oct. 26, 1936. WARNER.

Champagne Charlie. (June 16.) Paul Cavanagh, Helen Wood, Herbert Mundin. 5,341 ft. **A.** " Kine." June 18, 1936. Rel. Sept. 14, 1936. Fox.

Champagne for Breakfast. (Mar. 27.) Hardie Albright, Joan Mars, Mary Carlisle. 6,069 ft. **U.** " Kine." Mar. 5, 1936. Rel. June 8, 1936. COLUMBIA.

Charlie Chan at the Circus. (April 20.) Warner Oland, Keye Luke, George and Olive Brasno. 6,476 ft. **A.** " Kine." April- 23, 1936. Rel. July 27, 1936. Fox.

Charlie Chan at the Race Track. (Sept. 22.) Warner Oland, Helen Wood, Alan Dinehart. 6,307 ft. **U.** " Kine." Sept. 24, 1936. Rel. Feb. 1, 1937. Fox.

Charlie Chan's Secret. (Jan. 15.) Warner Oland, Henrietta Crosman, Edward Trevor. 6,511 ft. **A.** " Kine." Jan. 23, 1936. Rel. May 25, 1936. Fox.

The Charm School. (Feb. 4.), Jack Oakie, Frances Langford. 7,299 ft. **U.** " Kine." Feb. 6, 1936. Rel. June 22, 1936. PARAMOUNT.

Chatterbox. (Mar. 17.) Anne Shirley, Phillips Holmes, Edward Ellis. 6,512 ft. **U.** " Kine." Mar. 19, 1936. Rel. Aug. 17, 1936. RADIO.

*Cheer Up. (Jan. 24.) Stanley Lupino, Sally Gray, Roddy Hughes. 6,570 ft. **U.** " Kine." Jan. 30, 1936. Rel. June 1, 1936. A.B.F.D.

*Chick. (Sept. 21.) Sydney Howard, Aubrey Mather, Betty Ann Davis. 6,400 ft. **U.** " Kine." Sept. 24, 1936. Rel. Mar. 22, 1937. UNITED ARTISTS.

Children of Divorce. (Oct. 19.) Joan Marsh, Robert Fraser, Natalie Moorhead. 5,872 ft. **A.** " Kine." Oct. 22, 1936. Rel. date not fixed. WARDOUR.

China Clipper. (Sept. 10.) Pat. O'Brien, Beverley Roberts, Ross Alexander. 8,073 ft. **U.** " Kine." Sept. 17, 1936. Rel. April 12, 1937. WARNER.

*Chinese Cabaret. (Mar. 16.) Lai Foun, Robert Hobbs, Lilian Graham. 4,000 ft. **U.** " Kine." Mar. 19, 1936. Rel. date not fixed. COLUMBIA.

*Christopher Wren Comes to Life. (Mar. 3.) Thomas Pauncefoot, Wilson Coleman. 3,487 ft. **A.** " Kine." July 16, 1936. Rel. July 20, 1936. M.-G.-M.

Circus Love. (Oct. 23.) Harry Peel, Susi Lanner, Hilde Brandt. 5,866 ft. **U.** " Kine." Oct. 29, 1936. Rel. Jan. 4, 1937. BUTCHER.

Clutching Hand, The. (Oct. 19.) Jack Mulhall, William Farnum, Ruth Mix. 15 eps. **U.** " Kine." Oct. 22, 1936. Rel. date not fixed. A.B.F.D.

Code of the Mounted. (April 1.) Kermit Maynard, Lilian Miles, Syd Saylor. 4,900 ft. **A.** " Kine." April 9, 1936. Rel. Oct. 5, 1936. BUTCHER.

Colleen. (April 16.) Dick Powell, Ruby Keeler, Jack Oakie. 8,000 ft. **A.** " Kine." April 23, 1936. Rel. Sept. 28, 1936. WARNER.

Come and Get It. (Nov. 20.) Edward Arnold, Frances Farmer, Joel McCrea. 9,145 ft. **A.** " Kine." Nov. 26, 1936. Rel. May 3, 1937. UNITED ARTISTS.

Comin' Round the Mountain. (Oct. 6.) Gene Autry, Ann Rutherford, Roy Mason. 5,190 ft. **U.** " Kine." Oct. 8, 1936. Rel. date not fixed. BRITISH LION.

Condemned to Live. (Nov. 29.) Ralph Morgan, Maxine Doyle, Russell Gleason. 5,469 ft. **A.** " Kine." Dec. 5, 1935. Rel. April 6, 1936. WARDOUR.

Coronado. (Dec. 17.) Johnny Downs, Betty Burgess. 6,869 ft. **U.** " Kine." Dec. 19, 1935. Rel. April 13, 1936. PARAMOUNT.

Counterfeit. (Aug. 11.) Chester Morris, Margot Graham, Lloyd Nolan. 6,607 ft. **A.** " Kine." Aug. 20, 1936. Rel. Jan. 11, 1937. COLUMBIA.

Country Beyond, The. (May 7.) Rochelle Hudson, Paul Kelly, Robert Kent. 6,170 ft. **U.** " Kine." May 14, 1936. Rel. Sept. 28, 1936. Fox.

Country Bumpkin. The. (Oct. 21.) Stuart Erwin, Edmund Gwenn, Betty Furness. 5,688 ft. **A.** " Kine." Oct. 29, 1936. Rel. April 5, 1937. M-G-M.

Country Doctor, The. (April 1.) Jean Hersholt, Dionne Quintuplets. Dorothy Peterson. 8,480 ft. **A.** " Kine." April 9, 1936. Rel. Oct. 5, 1936. Fox.

Cowboy and the Kid, The. (June 9.) Buck Jones. 4,864 ft. **U.** " Kine." June 11, 1936. Rel. Oct. 12, 1936. GENERAL F.D.

Craig's Wife. (Oct. 20.) Rosalind Russell, John Boles, Billie Burke. 6,691 ft. **A.** " Kine." Oct. 29, 1936. Rel. Mar. 8, 1937. COLUMBIA.

Crash Donovan. (Sept. 9.) Jack Holt, John King, Nan Grey. 5,052 ft. **U.** " Kine." Sept. 17, 1936. Rel. Feb. 1, 1937. GENERAL F.D.

Crashing Through Danger. (April 17.) Ray Walker, Sally Blane, Guinn Williams. 6,300 ft. **U.** " Kine." April 23, 1936. Rel. Aug. 20, 1936. A.P. & D.

Crime and Punishment. (Dec. 19.) Peter Lorre, Edward Arnold, Marian Marsh. 7,896 ft. **A.** " Kine." Dec. 26, 1935. Rel. May 11, 1936. COLUMBIA.

Crime et Chatiment. (Mar. 17.) Harry Baur, Pierre Blanchar. 8,820ft. **A.** " Kine." Mar. 19, 1936. Rel. date not fixed. FILM SOCIETY.

Crime of Dr. Forbes, The. (Aug. 18.) Gloria Stuart, Robert Kent, Sarah Haden. 6,901 ft. **A.** " Kine." Aug. 20, 1936. Rel. date not fixed. Fox.

*****Crime Over London.** (Oct. 22.) Joseph Cawthorne, Margot Grahame, Paul Cavanagh. 7,200 ft. **A.** " Kine." Oct. 29, 1936. Rel. May 24, 1937. UNITED ARTISTS.

*****Crimes of Stephen Hawke, The.** (May 13.) Tod Slaughter, Marjorie Taylor, Eric Portman. 6,203 ft. **A.** " Kine." May 21, 1936. Rel. Sept 28, 1936. M-G-M.

*****Crimson Circle, The.** (Mar. 26.) Hugh Wakefield, Alfred Drayton, June Duprez. 6,881 ft. **A.** " Kine." April 2, 1936. Rel. Aug. 10, 1936. GENERAL F.D.

*****Crown v. Stevens.** (Mar. 26.) Beatrix Thomson, Patric Knowles. 5,997 ft. **A.** " Kine." April 2, 1936. Rel. Aug. 3, 1936. WARNER.

Custer's Last Stand. (July 6.) Rex Lease, William Farnum, Dorothy Gulliver. 16 eps. **U.** " Kine." July 9, 1936. Rel. WARDOUR.

Dancing Feet. (Mar. 30.) Ben Lyon, Joan Marsh, Eddie Nugent. 6,612 ft. **U1** " Kine." April 2, 1936. Rel. Aug. 12, 1936. BRITISH LION.

Dancing Pirate. (July 2.) Charles Collins, Frank Morgan, Steffi Duna. 7,658 ft. **U.** " Kine." July 9, 1936. Rel. Nov. 30, 1936. RADIO.

Dangerous. (Feb. 11.) Bette Davis, Franchot Tone, Alison Skipworth. 7,150 ft. **A.** " Kine." Feb. 13, 1936. Rel. July 13, 1936. FIRST NATIONAL

Dangerous Intrigue. (Mar. 16.) Ralph Bellamy, Gloria Shea. 5,089 ft. **A.** " Kine." Mar, 26, 1936. Rel. Aug. 24, 1936. COLUMBIA.

Dangerous Waters. (Feb. 26.) Jack Holt, Robert Armstrong, Grace Bradley. 5,984 ft. **A.** " Kine." Mar, 5, 1936. Rel. July 20, 1926. GENERAL F.D.

Daniel Boone. (Nov. 12.) George O'Brien, Ralph Forbes, Heather Angel. 6,935 ft. **U.** " Kine." Nov. 19, 1936. Rel. Apl. 12, 1937. RADIO.

*****Dark World.** (Dec. 12.) Tamari Desni, Leon Quartermaine, Olga Lindo. 6,620 ft. **A.** " Kine." Dec. 19, 1935. Rel. May 18, 1936. Fox.

*****David Livingstone.** (Nov. 5.) Percy Marmont, Marion Spencer, Hugh McDermott. 6,570 ft. **U.** " Kine." Nov. 12, 1936. Rel. Mar. 15, 1937. M-G-M.

*Days of Destiny. (Mar. 16.) Moore Marriott. 3,150 ft. **U.** " Kine." Mar. 19, 1936. Rel. date not fixed. COLUMBIA.

*Debt of Honour. (Mar. 27.) Leslie Banks, Geraldine Fitzgerald, Niall MacGinnis. 7,465 ft. **A.** " Kine." April 2, 1936. Rel. Nov. 2, 1936. GEN.F.D.

De Kribbebijter (The Crosspatch). (Aug. 17.) Cor Ruys, Fritz van Dongen, Dolly Mollinger. 7,920 ft. **U.** " Kine." Aug. 20, 1936. Rel. date not fixed. G.-B.-D.

Desert Gold. (May 1.) Buster Crabbe, Tom Keene, Marsha Hunt. 5,266 ft. **U.** " Kine." May 7, 1936. Rel. Aug. 3, 1936. PARAMOUNT.

Desert Mesa. (Oct. 30.) Tom Wynn, Tonya Beauford, Franklyn Farnum. 4,400 ft. **U.** " Kine." Nov. 5, 1936. Rel. date not fixed. EQUITY BRITISH.

Desire. (April 1.) Marlene Dietrich, Gary Cooper, John Halliday. 8,754 ft. **A.** " Kine." April 2, 1936. Rel. Aug. 3, 1936. PARAMOUNT.

Devil Doll, The. (Aug. 19.) Lionel Barrymore, Maureen O'Sullivan, Frank Lawton. 7,032 ft. **A.** " Kine." Aug. 27, 1936. Rel. Dec. 7, 1936. M-G-M.

Devil's Squadron. (June 13.) Richard Dix, Karen Morley, Henry Mollison. 7,100 ft. **A.** " Kine." June 18, 1936. Rel. Nov. 2, 1936. COLUMBIA.

Devil Takes the Count. (Oct. 7.) Freddie Bartholomew, Jackie Cooper, Mickie Rooney. 8,220 ft. **A.** " Kine." Oct. 15, 1936. Rel. Feb. 22, 1937. M-G-M.

Die Ewige Maske. (May 25.) Mathies Wieman, Peter Petersen, Olga Tschechowa. 7,110 ft. **A.** " Kine." May 28, 1936. Rel. date not fixed. TOBIS.

*Digging for Gold. (Sept. 28.) Eric Woodburn, Edna Thompson, Afrique. 4,066 ft. **U.** " Kine." Oct. 1, 1936. Rel. Dec. 21, 1936. ACE.

Dimples. (Nov. 6.) Shirley Temple, Frank Morgan, Helen Westley. 7,056 ft. **U.** " Kine," Nov. 12, 1936. Rel. Mar. 29, 1937. Fox.

Dirigible. (Mar. 20.) Jack Holt, Fay Wray. 8,947 ft. **A.** " Kine." Mar. 26, 1936. Rel. Aug. 17, 1936. COLUMBIA.

*Dishonour Bright. (Sept. 22.) Tom Walls, Eugene Pallette, Betty Stockfeld. 7,394 ft. **A.** " Kine." Oct. 1, 1936· Rel. April 5, 1937. GEN. F.D.

Dizzy Dames. (Sept. 23.) Marjorie Rambeau, Florine McKinney, Lawrence Gray. 6,310 ft. **U.** " Kine." Oct. 1, 1936. Rel. Mar. 22, 1937. A.B.F.D.

*Dodging the Dole. (June 29.) Roy Barbour, Jenny Howard. 8,500 ft. **U.** " Kine." July 2, 1936. Rel. date not fixed. MANCUNIAN.

Dodsworth. (Oct. 21.) Walter Huston, Ruth Chatterton, Mary Astor. 9,290 ft. **A.** " Kine." Oct. 29, 1936. Rel. Feb. 15, 1937. UNITED ARTISTS.

Don't Gamble With Love. (Mar. 25.) Ann Sothern, Bruce Cabot. Irving Pichel. 5,749 ft. **A.** " Kine." April 2, 1936. Rel. Sept. 7, 1936, COLUMBIA.

Don't Get Personal. (April 8.) Sally Eilers, James Dunn, Pinky Tomlin. 5,814 ft. **U.** " Kine." April 16, 1936. Rel. July 13, 1936. GEN. F.D.

*Don't Rush Me. (Jan. 3.) Robb Wilton, Muriel Aked, Peter Haddon. 6,404 ft. **U.** " Kine." Jan. 9, 1936. Rel. June 29, 1936. WARDOUR.

Don't Turn 'Em Loose. (Sept. 24.) Bruce Cabot, Lewis Stone, James Gleason. 5,893 ft. **A.** " Kine." Oct. 1, 1936. Rel. Dec. 21, 1936. RADIO.

Down the Stretch. (Sept. 16.) Mickey Rooney, Patricia Ellis, Dennis Moore. 5,989 ft. **U.** " Kine." Sept. 24, 1936. Rel. Feb. 22, 1937. FIRST NATIONAL.

Dracula's Daughter. (June 29.) Otto Kruger, Gloria Holden, Marguerite Churchill. 6,470 ft. **A.** " Kine." July 2, 1936. Rel. Jan. 11, 1937. GEN. F.D.

Drag Net, The. (June 9.) Rod La Rocque. 6,000 ft. **A.** " Kine." June 11, 1936. Rel. Oct. 19, 1936. PATHE.

***Dreams Come True.** (Oct. 19.) Frances Day, Nelson Keys, Hugh Wakefield. 7,011 ft. **A.** " Kine." Oct. 22, 1936. Rel. Apl. 26, 1937. REUNION.

***Dream Doctor, The.** (Sept. 29.) Julie Suedo, Sydney Monckton, Yvonne Murray. 3,871 ft. **A.** " Kine." Oct. 1, 1936. Rel. Jan. 4, 1937. M-G-M.

Dressed to Thrill. (Dec. 5.) Tutta Rolf, Clive Brook, Nydia Westman. 6,192 ft. **U.** " Kine." Dec. 12, 1935. Rel. Mar. 30, 1936. Fox.

Drift Fence. (Mar. 27.) Tom Keene, Katharine de Mille, Buster Crabbe. 5,048 ft. **U.** Kine." April 2, 1936. Rel. July 27, 1936. PARAMOUNT.

Drunkard, The. (July 15.) James Murray, Janet Chandler, Theodore Lorch. 3,700 ft. **A.** " Kine." July 23, 1936. Rel. July, 1936. REUNION.

***Dusty Ermine.** (Sept. 10.) Ronald Squire, Anthony Bushell, Jane Baxter. 7,666 ft. **A.** " Kine." Sept. 17, 1936. Rel. Feb. 27, 1937. WARDOUR.

The Eagle's Brood. (Jan. 24.) William Boyd, Addison Richards, John Woodbury. 5,389 ft. **U.** " Kine." Jan, 30, 1936. Rel. July 13, 1936. PARAMOUNT.

***Early Bird, The.** (Aug. 14.) Richard Hayward, Jimmy Mageen, Charlotte Tedlie. 6,287 ft. **U.** " Kine." Aug. 30, 1936. Rel. Jan. 25, 1937. PARAMOUNT.

Early to Bed. (June 30.) Charles Ruggles, Mary Boland. 6,561 ft. **U.** " Kine." July 2, 1936. Rel. Nov. 23, 1936. PARAMOUNT.

East Meets West. (Feb. 5.) —— 5,806 ft. **U.** " Kine." Feb. 13, 1936. Rel. June 8, 1936. ACE FILMS.

***East Meets West.** (Aug. 25.) George Arliss, Lucie Mannheim, Godfrey Tearle. 6,607 ft. **A.** " Kine." Aug. 27, 1936. Rel. Oct. 26, 1936. G.-B.D.

***Educated Evans.** (Aug. 31.) Max Miller, Nancy O'Neal, Hal Walters. 7,789 ft. **U.** " Kine." Sept. 3, 1936. Rel. Mar. 1, 1937. FIRST NATIONAL.

Educating Father. (July 23.) Jed Prouty, Kenneth Howell, Shirley Deane. 5,213 ft. **U.** " Kine." July 30, 1936. Rel. Jan. 18, 1937. Fox.

***Eliza Comes to Stay.** (April 8.) Betty Balfour, Seymour Hicks, Nelson Keys. 6,300 ft. **A.** Kine." April 16, 1936. Rel. Oct. 19, 1936. WARDOUR.

Emperor's Candlesticks, The. (May 12.) Sybille Schnita, Karl Diehl. 8,200 ft. **U.** " Kine." May 14, 1936. Rel. date not fixed. G.-B.-D.

***End of the Road.** (Oct. 27.) Harry Lauder, Ruth Haven, Bruce Seton. 6,424 ft. **U.** " Kine." Nov. 5, 1936. Rel. Mar. 8, 1937. Fox

Escape from Devil's Island. (Feb. 17.) Victor Jory, Florence Rice, Norman Foster. 5,659 ft. **A.** " Kine." Feb. 20, 1936. Rel. July 13, 1936. COLUMBIA.

Eventful Journey. (Jan. 27.) Alison Skipworth, Mae Clark, Arthur Treacher. 6,930 ft. **U.** " Kine." Jan. 30, 1936. Rel. June 29, 1937. A.B.F.D.

***Everybody Dance.** (Oct. 14.) Cicely Courtneidge, Ernest Truex, Villie de la Volta. 6,793 ft. **A.** " Kine." Oct. 8, 1936. Rel. Dec. 7, 1936. G.-B.D.

Everybody's Old Man. (May 5.) Irvin S. Cobb, Richelle Hudson, Norman Foster. 7,621 ft. **U.** " Kine." May 7, 1936. Rel. Dec. 21, 1936. Fox.

Every Saturday Night. (Mar. 10.) Jed Prouty, Spring Byington, Florence Roberts. 5,546 ft. **U.** " Kine." Mar. 12, 1936. Rel. June 29, 1936. Fox.

*Everything in Life. (Nov. 17.) Gitta Alpar, Neil Hamilton, Lawrence Grossmith. 6,376 ft. **U.** " Kine." Nov. 26, 1936. Rel. date not fixed. COLUMBIA.

*Everything is Rhythm. (June 11.) Harry Roy, Princess Pearl, Agnes Brantford, 6,607 ft. **U.** " Kine." June 18, 1936. Rel. Jan. 11, 1937. A.B.F.D.

*Everything is Thunder. (July 21.) Constance Bennett, Douglas Montgomery, Oscar Homolka. 6.938 ft. **A.** " Kine." July 30, 1936. Rel. Nov. 23, 1936. G.-B.D.

Exclusive Story. (Feb. 17.) Franchot Tone, Madge Evans, Stuart Erwin. 6,676 ft. **A.** " Kine." Feb. 20, 1936. Rel. June 1, 1936. M-G-M.

*Excuse My Glove. (Jan. 29.) Len Harvey, Archie Pitt, Olive Blakeney. 6,815 ft. **A.** " Kine." Feb. 6, 1936. Rel. July 20, 1936. A.B.F.D.

Ex-Mrs. Bradford, The. (May 21.) William Powell, Jean Arthur. 7,351 ft. **A.** " Kine." May 28, 1936. Rel. Nov. 2, 1936. RADIO.

Face in the Fog, A. (April 22.) June Collyer, Lloyd Hughes, Lawrence Grey. 5,500 ft. **A.** " Kine." April 30, 1936. Rel. July 13, 1936. PATHE.

*Fair Exchange. (July 1.) Patric Knowles, Roscoe Ates, Isla Bevan. 5,710 ft. **U.** " Kine." July 9, 1936. Rel. Sept. 14, 1936. WARNER.

*Faithful. (Mar. 5.) Jean Muir, Hans Sonker, Gene Gerrard. 7.067 ft. **U.** " Kine." Mar. 12, 1936. Rel. Aug. 17, 1936. WARNER.

False Pretences. (May 25.) Irene Ware, Sidney Blackmer, Betty Compson. 6,132 ft. **U.** " Kine." May 28, 1936. Rel. Sept. 21, 1936. WARDOUR.

*Fame. (Mar. 12.) Sydney Howard, Muriel Aked, Arthur Finn. 6,120 ft. **U.** " Kine." Mar. 19, 1936. Rel. Nov. 2, 1936. GEN. F.D.

Fang and Claw. (July 28.) Frank Buck. 5,705 ft. **U.** " Kine." Aug. 6, 1936. Rel. Dec. 21, 1936. RADIO.

Farmer in the Dell, The. (April 16.) Fred Stone, Jean Parker, Frank Albertson. 6,105 ft. **U.** " Kine." April 23, 1936. Rel. Sept. 28, 1936. RADIO.

Fatal Lady. (June 23.) Mary Ellis, Walter Pidgeon, John Halliday. 6,836 ft. **A.** " Kine." June 25, 1936. Rel. Nov. 2, 1936. PARAMOUNT.

*Faust. (Feb. 10.) Webster Booth, Anne Ziegler, Dennis Hoey. 4,083 ft. **A.** " Kine." Feb. 13, 1936. Rel. Feb. 10, 1936. REUNION.

Federal Agent. (Aug. 18.) Bill Boyd, Irene Ware, Don Alvarado. 5,608 ft. **A.** " Kine." Aug. 20, 1936. Rel. date not fixed. BRITISH LION.

15, Maiden Lane. (Nov. 19.) Claire Trevor, Cesar Romero, Lloyd Nolan. 5,807 ft. **A.** " Kine." Nov. 26, 1936. Rel. Apl. 26, 1937. Fox.

Fighting Shadows. (Jan. 30.) Tim McCoy, Ward Bond. 5,228 ft. **U.** " Kine." Feb. 6, 1936. Rel. May 25, 1936. COLUMBIA.

Final Hour, The. (Aug. 13.) Ralph Bellamy, Marguerite Churchill, Marc Lawrence. 5,169 ft. **A.** " Kine." Aug. 20, 1936. Rel. Dec. 28, 1936. COLUMBIA.

*Find the Lady. (Mar. 26.) Jack Melford, Althea Henley, George Sanders. 6,363 ft. **A.** " Kine." April 2, 1936. Rel. Sept. 28, 1936. Fox.

Fire Trap, The. (April 3.) Norman Foster, Evalyn Knapp, Sidney Blackmer. 5,700 ft. **U.** " Kine." April 9, 1936. Rel. July 20, 1936. PATHE.

First Baby, The. (June 18.) Johnny Downs, Shirley Deane, Jane Darwell. 6,696 ft. **A.** " Kine." June 25, 1936. Rel. Oct. 26, 1936. Fox.

First Offence. (Feb. 21.) John Mills, Lilli Palmer, Bernard Nedell. 5,994 ft. **A.** " Kine." Feb. 27, 1936. Rel. April 6, 1936. G.-B.D.

Flash Gordon. (June 15.) Buster Crabbe, Jean Rogers, Charles Middleton. 13 eps. " Kine." June 18, 1936. Rel. June 13, 1936. GEN. F.D.

Florida Special. (June 21.) Jack Oakie, Sally Eilers, Kent Taylor. 5,997 ft. **U.** " Kine." June 4, 1936. Rel. Oct. 5, 1936. PARAMOUNT,

" F " Man. (Mar. 24.) Jack Haley, Adrienne Marden. 5,634 ft. **U.** " Kine.'" Mar. 26, 1936. Rel. June 8, 1936. PARAMOUNT.

Follow the Fleet. (Mar. 19.) Fred Astaire, Ginger Rogers. 9,900 ft. **U.** " Kine." Mar. 26, 1936. Rel. June 1, 1936. RADIO.

Follow Your Heart. (Oct. 5.) Marion Talley, Michael Bartlett. 6,891 ft. **U.** " Kine." Oct. 8, 1936. Rel. Mar. 22, 1937. BRITISH LION.

Footlights and Shadows. (May 26.) Henrietta Crosman, Russell Gleason. 5,955 ft. **A.** " Kine." May 28, 1936. Rel. Nov. 30, 1936. WARDOUR.

Forced Landing. (Jan. 14.) Onslow Stevens, Esther Ralston, Sidney Blackman. 6,120 ft. **A.** " Kine." Jan. 16, 1936. Rel. June 15, 1936. BRITISH LION.

*Forget Me Not. (Mar. 30.) Beniamino Gigli, Joan Gardner. 6,555 ft. **U.** " Kine." April 2, 1936. Rel. Dec. 21, 1936. UNITED ARTISTS.

Forgotten Faces. (May 26.) Herbert Marshall, Gertrude Michael. 6,429 ft. **A.** " Kine," May 28, 1936. Rel. Oct. 19, 1936. PARAMOUNT.

Forgotten Women. (July 6.) Evelyn Brent, June Clyde, Irene Rich. 5,295 ft. **A.** " Kine." July 9, 1936. Rel. Dec. 7, 1936. WARDOUR.

For the Service. (May 15.) Buck Jones, Clifford Jones, Beth Marion. 5,034 ft. **U.** " Kine." May 21, 1936. Rel. Sept. 7, 1936. GEN. F.D.

Framed. (June 23.) Eddie Nugent, Maxine Doyle, Fuzzy Knight. 6,160 ft. **A.** " Kine." June 25, 1936. Rel. Sept. 28, 1936. PATHE.

Frankie and Johnnie. (May 25.) Helen Morgan, Chester Morris. 6,073 ft. **A.** " Kine." May 28, 1936. Rel. Sept. 21, 1936. BRITISH LION.

Fredlos. (Nov. 2.) John Ekman, Sten Lindgren, Gul-maj. Norin. 8,156 ft. **A.** " Kine." Nov. 5, 1936. Rel. date not fixed. REUNION.

Frisco Kid. (Dec. 9.) James Cagney, Margaret Lindsay, Ricardo Cortez. 5,941 ft. **A.** " Kine." Dec. 12, 1935. Rel. Aug. 31, 1936. WARNER.

*From Nine to Nine. (Mar. 30.) Ruth Roland, Roland Drew, Kenneth Duncan. 6,677 ft. **A.** " Kine." April 2, 1936. Rel. Aug. 17, 1936. GEN. F.D.

Frontier Justice. (May 11.) Hoot Gibson, Janet Barnes. 5,500 ft. **U.** " Kine." May 14, 1936. Rel. date not fixed. INDEPENDENT F.D.

*Full Speed Ahead. (Nov. 20.) Moira Lynd, Richard Norris, Paul Neville. 6,377 ft. **U.** " Kine." Nov. 26, 1936. Rel. April 26, 1937. PARAMOUNT.

*Full Steam. (Oct. 19.) Edna Thompson, Maggie Eaton, Warden and West, Ken Douglas. 4,266 ft. **U.** " Kine." Oct. 22, 1936. Rel. Jan. 25, 1937. ACE.

Fury. (June 17.) Spencer Tracy, Sylvia Sidney, Bruce Cabot. 8.292 ft. **A.** " Kine." June 25, 1936. Rel. Nov. 16. 1936. M-G-M.

Gallant Defender. (Feb. 14.) Charles Starrett, Joan Perry. 5,001 ft. **U.** " Kine." Feb. 20, 1936. Rel. July 13, 1936. COLUMBIA.

*Gaolbreak. (Mar. 3.) Ralph Ince. 5,797 ft. **A.** " Kine." Mar. 5, 1936. Rel. Aug. 31, 1936. FIRST NATIONAL.

Garden Murder Case, The. (Mar. 9.) Edmund Lowe, Virginia Bruce, H. B. Warner. 5,466 ft. **A.** " Kine." Mar. 12, 1936. Rel. June 8, 1936. M-G-M.

Garden of Allah, The. (Nov. 23.) Marlene Dietrich, Charles Boyer, Basil Rathbone. 7,020 ft. **A.** " Kine." Nov. 26, 1936. Rel. Apl. 12, 1937. UNITED ARTISTS.

*Gay Adventure, The. (July 20.) Yvonne Arnaud, Nora Swinburne, Barry Jones. 6,600 ft. **A.** " Kine." July 23, 1936. Rel. Nov. 16, 1936. PATHE.

Gay Desperado, The. (Oct. 27.) Nino Martini, Leo Carrillo, Ida Lupino. 7,944 ft. **A.** " Kine." Oct. 29, 1936. Re.l May 17, 1937. UNITED ARTISTS.

Gay King, The. (July 30.) Armando Falcone, Luisa Ferida. 8.350 ft. **U.** " Kine." Aug. 6, 1936. Rel. Apl. 10, 1937. TOEPLITZ.

*Gay Old Dog. (Nov. 28.) Edward Rigby, Moore Marriott, Marguerite Allan. 5,670 ft. **A.** " Kine." Dec. 5, 1935. Rel. April 27, 1936. RADIO.

General Died at Dawn, The. (Oct. 13.) Gary Cooper, Madeleine Carroll, Akim Tamiroff. 8,791 ft. **A.** " Kine." Oct. 15, 1936. Rel. April 19, 1937. PARAMOUNT.

Gentleman from Louisiana, The. (Oct. 9.) Eddie Quillan, Chic Sale, Charlotte Henry. 6,423 ft. **U.** " Kine." Oct. 15, 1936. Rel. Apl. 5, 1937. BRITISH LION.

Get That Girl. (Nov. 6.) Rin Tin Tin, jun., Francis X. Bushman, jun., Lois Wild. 5,480 ft. **U.** " Kine." Nov. 12, 1936. Rel. Mar. 1, 1937. PATHE.

Get That Man. (May 27.) Wallace Ford, Finis Barton, E. Alyn Warren 5,643 ft. **A.** " Kine." June 4, 1936. Rel. Aug. 14, 1936. FIDELITY.

The Ghost Goes West. (Dec. 17.) Robert Donat, Jean Parker, Eugene Pallette. 8,200 ft. **A.** " Kine." Dec. 19, 1935. Rel. Mar. 9, 1936. UNITED ARTISTS.

Girl from Mandalay, The. (Oct. 6.) Conrad Nagel, Kay Linaker, Donald Cook. 6,296 ft. **A.** " Kine." Oct. 8, 1936. Rel. Mar. 29, 1937. A.B.F.D.

Girl of the Ozarks. (July 22.) Virginia Weidler, Henrietta Crosman, Leid Erickson. 6,121 ft. **A.** " LKine." July 30, 1936. Rel. Feb. 1, 1937. PARAMOUNT.

Girl on the Front Page, The. (Nov. 9.) Edmund Lowe, Gloria Stuart, Reginald Owen. 6,518 ft. **U.** " Kine." Nov. 12, 1936. Rel. Aug. 2, 1937. GEN. F.D.

Girls' Dormitory. (Aug. 25.) Herbert Marshall, Ruth Chatterton, Simone Simon. 5,964 ft. **A.** " Kine." Sept. 3, 1936. Rel. Jan. 25, 1937. FOX.

Give Us This Night. (April 8.) Jan Kiepura, Gladys Swarthout, Alan Mowbray. 6,263 tt. **U.** " Kine." April 16, 1936. Rel. July 13, 1936. PARAMOUNT.

G-Man's Wife. (Sept. 3.) Pat O'Brien, Margaret Lindsay, Cesar Romero. 6,324 ft. **A.** " Kine." Sept. 10, 1936. Rel. Mar. 1, 1937. WARNER.

Golden Arrow, The. (Aug. 27.) Bette Davis, George Brent, Eugene Pallette. 6,259 ft. **U.** " Kine." Sept. 3, 1936. Rel. Jan. 25, 1937. FIRST NATIONAL.

Gorgeous Hussy, The. (Sept. 23.) Joan Crawford, Robert Taylor, Lionel Barrymore. 9,263 ft. **A.** " Kine." Oct. 1, 1936. Rel. Feb. 1, 1937. M-G-M.

*Grand Finale. (Sept. 25.) Guy Newall, Mary Glynne, Eric Cowley. 6,443 ft. **A.** " Kine." Oct. 1, 1936. Rel. Feb. 1, 1937. PARAMOUNT.

Grand Jury. (Sept. 22.) Fred Stone, Louise Latimer. 5,512 ft. **A.** " Kine." Sept. 24, 1936. Rel. Jan. 25, 1937. RADIO.

The Great Impersonation. (Jan. 17.) Edmund Lowe, Valerie Robson, Wera Engels. 6,100 ft. **A.** " Kine." Jan. 23, 1936. Rel. June 22, 1936. GEN. F.D.

Great Ziegfeld, The. (Sept. 1.) William Powell, Louise Rainer, Myrna Loy. 15,660 ft. **U.** " Kine." Sept. 3, 1936. Rel. Mar. 7, 1931 M-G-M.

*Guilty Melody. (July 22.) Gitta Alpar, Nils Asther, John Loder. 6,857 ft. **A.** " Kine." July 30, 1936. Rel. date not fixed. A.B.F.D.

Gun Law. (Mar. 19.) Jack Hoxle, Nita Hammond. 5,450 ft. U. " Kine." Mar. 26, 1936. Rel. date not fixed. EQUITY.

Guns of the Pecos. (Sept. 2.) Dick Foran, Anne Nagel, Robert Middlemass. 5,110 ft. U. " Kine." Sept. 10, 1936. Rel. Dec. 28, 1936. WARNER.

*Gypsy Melody. (July 27.) Lupe Velez, Alfred Rode. 6,925 ft. A. " Kine." July 30, 1936. Rel. Dec. 14, 1936. WARDOUR.

*Hail and Farewell. (Sept. 30.) Claude Hulbert, Reginald Purdell, Joyce Kennedy. 6,612 ft. A. " Kine." Oct. 8, 1936. Rel. Mar. 29, 1937. FIRST NATIONAL.

Half Angel. (June 24.) Frances Dee, Brian Donlevy, Charles Butterworth. 5,763 ft. A. " Kine." July 2, 1936. Rel. Nov. 9, 1936. Fox.

*Happy Days are Here Again. (Mar. 2.) Houston Sisters, Syd Seymour, and his Mad Hatters. 7,650 ft. U. " Kine." Mar. 5, 1936. Rel. Aug. 10, 1936. A.P.D.

*Happy Family, The. (Aug. 19.) Hugh Williams, Leonora Corbett, Muriel George. 6,074 ft. A. " Kine." Aug. 27, 1936. Rel. Mar. 1, 1937. BRITISH LION.

Hard Rock Harrigan. (July 22.) George O'Brien, Irene Hervey, Fred Kolker. 5,500 ft. U. " Kine." July 30, 1936. Rel. Nov. 23, 1936. A.B.F.D.

Harvester, The. (June 8.) Alice Brady, Russell Hardie, Ann Rutherford. 6,900 ft. U. " Kine." June 11, 1936. Rel. Nov. 23, 1936. BRITISH LION.

*Hayseeds, The. (Feb. 19.) Cecil Kellaway, Shirley Dale, Arthur Clarke. 8,027 ft. U. " Kine." Feb. 27, 1936. Rel. Sept. 21, 1936. WARNER.

*Head Office. (Nov. 4.) Owen Nares, Nancy O'Neill, Arthur Margetson. 8,070 ft. A. " Kine," Nov. 12, 1936. Rel. May 3, 1937. WARNER.

Heart of the West. (Oct. 2.) William Boyd, Lyn Gabriel. 5,380 ft. U. " Kine." Oct. 8, 1936. Rel. April 5, 1937. PARAMOUNT.

Hearts Divided. (July 14.) Marion Davies, Dick Powell, Claude Rains. 6,906 ft. U. " Kine." July 23, 1936. Rel. Feb. 26, 1937. WARNER.

Hearts in Bondage. (Aug. 20.) James Dunn, Mae Clark, David Manners. 6,689 ft. U. " Kine." Aug. 27, 1936. Rel. Feb. 1, 1937. BRITISH LION.

*Hearts of Humanity. (Nov. 6.) Eric Portman, Pamela Randle, Hay Petrie. 6,700 ft. U. " Kine." Nov. 12, 1936. Rel. May 24, 1937. A.P. & D.

*Heirloom Mystery, The. (Nov. 13.) Edward Rigby, John Robinson, Marjorie Taylor. 6,500 ft. A. " Kine." Nov. 19, 1936. Rel. April 5, 1937. RADIO.

Heir to Trouble. (Dec. 3.) Ken Maynard, Joan Perry, Harry Woods. 5,273 ft. U. " Kine." Dec. 5, 1935. Rel. April 6, 1936. COLUMBIA.

Hell Ship Morgan. (Mar. 23.) George Bancroft, Ann Sothern. 5,839 ft. A. " Kine." Mar. 26, 1936. Rel. Aug. 31, 1936. COLUMBIA.

Here Comes Trouble. (Mar. 20.) Paul Kelly, Arline Judge. 5,611 ft. A. " Kine." Mar. 26, 1936. Rel. July 6, 1936. Fox.

*Heritage. (Mar. 19.) Frank Harvey, Margot Rhys. 8,690 ft. U. " Kine." Mar. 26, 1936. Rel. Aug. 31, 1936. COLUMBIA.

Her Master's Voice. (Jan. 31.) Edward E. Horton, Peggy Conklin. 6,823 ft. U. " Kine." Feb. 6, 1936. Rel. May 25, 1936. PARAMOUNT.

Hidden City, The (Darkest Africa). (June 12.) Clyde Beatty, Manuel King, Elaine Shepard. U. 6,591 ft. " Kine." June 18, 1936. Rel. Dec. 17, 1936. BRITISH LION.

*Highland Fling. (June 17.) Naughton and Gold, Eve Foster. 5,960 ft. U. " Kine." June 25, 1936. Rel. Oct. 12, 1936. Fox.

High Tension. (Aug. 25.) Brian Donlevy, Glenda Farrell, Norman Foster. 6,585 ft. U. " Kine." Aug. 27, 1936. Rel. Jan. 11, 1937. Fox.

His Best Man. (May 12.) Warren William, June Travis, Gene Lockhart. 5,628 ft. **A.** " Kine." May 14, 1936. Rel. Nov. 2, 1936. FIRST NATIONAL.

His Brother's Wife. (Aug. 27.) Barbara Stanwyck, Robert Taylor, Jean Hersholt. 8,005 ft. **U.** " Kine." Sept. 3, 1936. Rel. Jan. 25, 1937. M-G-M.

*His Lordship. (Nov. 5.) George Arliss, Romilly Lunge, Renee Ray. 6,445 ft. **U.** " Kine." Nov. 12, 1936. Rel. Feb. 22, 1937. G.-B.-D.

His Majesty Bunker Bean. (July 1.) Owen Davis, Junr., Louise Latimer, Hedda Hopper. 6,022 ft. **U.** " Kine." July 9, 1936. Rel. Nov. 13, 1936. RADIO.

Hohe Schule. (Feb. 10.) Rudolf Forster, Angela Salloker. 8,100 ft. **U.** " Kine." Feb. 13, 1936. Rel. Mar. 30, 1936. REUNION.

Hollywood Boulevard. (Sept. 1.) John Halliday, Marsha Hunt, Robert Cummings. 6,746 ft. **A.** " Kine." Sept. 3, 1936. Rel. Feb. 8, 1937. PARAMOUNT.

Hot Money. (July 15.) Ross Alexander, Beverley Roberts, Joseph Cawthorne. 6,260 ft. **U.** " Kine." July 23, 1936. Rel. Dec. 21, 1936. WARNER.

*Hot News. (Mar. 16.) Lupino Lane, Phyllis Clare, Ben Welden. 6,950 ft. **U.** " Kine." Mar. 19, 1936. Rel. Aug. 10, 1936. COLUMBIA.

*House Broken. (June 26.) Mary Lawson, Jack Lambert, Louis Borell. 6,627 ft. **A.** " Kine." July 2, 1936. Rel. Nov. 30, 1936. PARAMOUNT.

House of a Thousand Candles. (June 3.) Phillips Holmes, Mae Clarke, Irving Pichel. 6,479 ft. **U.** " Kine." June 11, 1936. Rel. Aug. 24, 1936. BRITISH LION.

*House of the Spaniard, The. (Oct. 28.) Brigitte Horney, Peter Haddon, Jean Galland. 6,264 ft. **U.** " Kine." Nov. 5, 1936. Rel. date not fixed. A.B.F.D.

*Howard Case, The. (Mar. 12.) Arthur Seaton, Jack Livesey, Olive Melville. 5,700 ft. **U.** " Kine." Mar. 19, 1936. Rel. Aug. 10, 1936. GEN. F.D.

Human Cargo. (June 25.) Claire Trevor, Brian Donlevy, Morgan Wallace. 5,795 ft. **A.** " Kine." July 2, 1936. Rel. Nov. 23, 1936. Fox.

I Conquer the Sea. (Mar. 10.) Seffi Duna, Stanley Morner, Douglas Walton. 6,011 ft. **A.** " Kine." Mar. 12, 1936. Rel. July 6, 1936. PATHE.

I'd Give My Life. (Sept. 18.) Guy Standing, Frances Drake, Tom Brown. 6,411 ft. **A.** " Kine." Sept. 24, 1936. Rel. Mar. 15, 1937. PARAMOUNT.

I Dream Too Much. (Jan. 11.) Lily Pons, Henry Fonda, Eric Blore. 8,500 ft. **U.** " Kine." Jan. 16, 1936. Rel. May 4, 1936. RADIO.

*If I Were Rich. (May 21.) Jack Melford, Kay Walsh, Henry Carlisle. 5,300 ft. **U.** " Kine." May 28, 1936. Rel. Oct. 5, 1936. RADIO.

I Found Stella Parish. (Dec. 16.) Kay Francis, Ian Hunter, Sybil Jason. 7,712 ft. **U.** " Kine." Dec. 19. 1935. Rel. June 15, 1936. WARNER.

If You Could Only Cook. (Dec. 17.) Herbert Marshall, Jean Arthur. 6,432 ft. **A.** " Kine." Dec. 26, 1935. Rel. May 18, 1936. COLUMBIA.

I Live My Life. (Nov. 27.) Joan Crawford, Brian Aherne, Frank Morgan. 8,756 ft. **U.** " Kine." Dec. 5, 1935. Rel. Mar. 30, 1936. M-G-M.

I'll Name the Murderer. (June 24.) Ralph Forbes, Marion Schilling. 5,800 ft. **A.** " Kine." July 2, 1936. Rel. Oct. 26, 1936. PATHE.

I Married a Doctor. (May 18.) Pat O'Brien, Josephine Hutchinson. 7,579 ft. **A.** " Kine." May 21, 1936. Rel. Nov. 9, 1936. WARNER.

*Immortal Swan. (Sept. 7.) Anna Pavlova. 3,414 ft. **U.** " Kine." Sept. 10, 1936. Rel. Dec. 28, 1936. ACE FILMS.

*Immortal Swan, The. (Jan. 21.) Anna Pavlova. 5,000 ft. U. " Kine."
Jan. 23, 1936. Rel. Dec. 28, 1936. THE IMMORTAL SWAN PROD.

Imperfect Lady, The. (Dec. 11.) Cicely Courtneidge, Frank Morgan,
Heather Angel. 6,400 ft. U. "Kine." Dec.19, 1935. Rel. April 16, 1936. M-G-M.

*Improper Duchess, The. (Jan. 17.) Yvonne Arnaud, Hugh Wakefield.
7,103 ft. A. "Kine." Jan. 23, 1936. Rel. June 1, 1936. GENERAL F.D.

In His Steps. (Nov. 13.) Eric Linden, Cecilia Parker, Harry Beresford.
7,153 ft. A. ' Kine." Nov. 10, 1936. Rel. May 24, 1937. A.B.F.D.

Injustice. (April 21.) Donald Woods, Kay Linaker, Joseph King.
5,863 ft. A. " Kine." April 23, 1936. Rel. Oct. 19, 1936. FIRST NATIONAL.

In Old Kentucky. (Nov. 27.). Will Rogers, Dorothy Wilson, Charles
Sellon. 7,690 ft. U. " Kine." Dec. 5, 1935. Rel. June 1, 1936. Fox.

In Person. (Nov. 29.) Ginger Rogers, George Brent, Alan Mowbray.
7,650 ft. U: " Kine." Dec. 5, 1935. Rel. April 13, 1936. RADIO.

*International Revue. (Nov. 3.) Ronald Frankau, Lai Foun and His
Chinese Wonders, Fred Duprez. 3,600 ft. U. " Kine." Nov. 5, 1936.
Rel. date not fixed. NATIONAL PROVINCIAL.

*Interrupted Honeymoon, The. (June 4.) Claude Hulbert, Jane Carr,
Francis L. Sullivan. 6,602 ft. A. " Kine." June 11, 1936. Rel. Dec. 21,
1936. BRITISH LION.

*In the Soup. (April 7.) Ralph Lynn, Judy Gunn, Morton Selten.
6,480 ft. U. " Kine." April 16, 1936. Rel. Nov. 2, 1936. WARDOUR.

*Invader, The. (Jan. 11.) Buster Keaton, Lupita Tower, Esme Percy.
5,500 ft. U. " Kine." Jan. 16, 1936. Rel. April 27, 1936. M-G-M.

Invisible Ray, The. (Feb. 10.) Boris Karloff, Bela Lugosi, 7,134
ft. A. " Kine." Feb. 13, 1936. Rel. July 13, 1936. GENERAL F.D.

*Irish and Proud of It. (Oct. 30.) Richard Hayward, Dina Sheridan,
George Pembroke. 6,585 ft. U. " Kine." Nov. 5, 1936. Rel. Mar. 8,
1937. PARAMOUNT.

Isle of Fury. (Oct. 13.) Humphrey Bogart, Margaret Lindsay. 5,484
ft. A. " Kine." Oct. 15, 1936. Rel. April 12, 1937. FIRST NATIONAL.

It Had to Happen. (Mar. 12.) George Raft, Rosalind Russell, Leo
Carrillo. 7,170 ft. A. " Kine." Mar. 19, 1936. Rel. July 13, 1936. Fox.

It Happened in Hollywood. (Jan. 7.) Wallace Ford, Molly Lamont.
6,300 ft. A. " Kine." Jan. 9, 1936. Rel. May 11, 1936. RADIO.

It Happened One Night. (Feb. 21.) Clark Gable, Claudette Colbert,
Walter Connolly. 9,451 ft. A. " Kine." Feb. 27, 1936. Rel. June 29,
1936. COLUMBIA. (Re-issue.)

It's a Great Life. (Mar. 31.) Joe Morrison, Paul Kelly, Rosalind Keith.
5,300 ft. U. " Kine." April 2, 1936. Rel. July 27, 1936. PARAMOUNT.

*It's in the Bag. (Sept. 2.) Jimmy Nervo, Teddy Knox, Ursula Hirst.
7,256 ft. U. " Kine." Sept. 10, 1936. Rel. April 5, 1937. WARNER.

*It's Love Again. (May 6.) Jessie Matthews, Robert Young, Sonnie
Hale. 7,599 ft. U. " Kine." May 14, 1936. Rel. Nov. 12, 1936. G.-B.D.

*It's You I Want. (Oct. 7.) Seymour Hicks, Marie Lohr, Hugh Wake-
field. 6,625 ft. A. " Kine." Oct. 15, 1936. Rel. April 12, 1937. BRITISH
LION.

Ivory Handled Gun, The. (April 16.) Buck Jones, Charlotte Wynters.
5,327 ft. U. " Kine." April 23, 1936. Rel. April 20, 1936. GENERAL F.D.

*Jack of All Trades. (Feb. 17.) Jack Hulbert, Gina Malo, Robertson Hare. 6,868 ft. **U.** " Kine." Feb. 20, 1936. Rel. April 13, 1936. G.-B.D.

Janosik. (June 22.) Palo Bislik. 6,570 ft. **A.** " Kine." June 25, 1936. Rel. Aug. 17, 1936. REUNION.

Java Seas. (Jan. 6.) Charles Bickford, Elizabeth Young, Frank Albertson. 6,341 ft. **A.** " Kine." Jan. 9, 1936. Rel. June 1, 1936. GENERAL F.D.

*Juggernaut. (Sept. 8.) Boris Karloff, Joan Wyndham, Arthur Margetson. 6,668 ft. **A.** " Kine." Sept. 17, 1936. Rel. Mar. 15, 1937. WARDOUR.

Jury's Evidence. (Jan. 7.) Hartley Power, Betty Stanton. 6,656 ft. **A.** " Kine." Jan. 9, 1936. Rel. June 29, 1936. BRITISH LION.

Kazan the Fearless. (Aug. 12.) Kazan, John King, Del Morgan. 5,100 ft. **U.** " Kine." Aug. 20, 1936. Rel. date not fixed. EQUITY.

*Keep Your Seats, Please. (Aug. 26.) George Formby, Florence Desmond, Gus McNaughton. 7,480 ft. **U.** " Kine." Sept. 3, 1936. Rel. Mar. 15, 1937. A.B.F.D.

Kelly of the Secret Service. (Sept. 11.) Lloyd Hughes, Sheila Manors, Forrest Taylor. 5,700 ft. **U.** " Kine." Sept. 17, 1936. Rel. Nov. 23, 1936. PATHE.

Kelly the Second. (July 8.) Patsy Kelly, Charley Chase, Guinn Williams. 6,320 ft. **U.** " Kine." July 16, 1936. Rel. Nov. 23, 1936. M-G-M.

Kind Lady. (Feb. 4.) Aline MacMahon, Basil Rathbone, Dudley Digges. 6,834 ft. **A.** " Kine." Feb. 13, 1936. Rel. June 29, 1936. M-G-M.

King of Burlesque. (Jan. 24.) Warner Baxter, Alice Faye, Jack Oakie. 8,142 ft. **U.** " Kine." Jan. 30, 1936. Rel. May 25, 1936. Fox.

*King of Hearts. (Mar. 3.) Will Fyffe, Gwen Gill, Richard Dolman. 7,452 ft. **U.** " Kine." Mat. 5, 1936. Rel. July 20, 1936. BUTCHER.

*King of the Castle. (Feb. 3.) June Clyde, Billy Milton, Claude Dampier. 6.270 ft. **U.** " Kine." Feb. 6, 1936. Rel. July 20, 1936. GENERAL F.D.

*King of the Damned. (Dec. 24.) Conrad Veidt, Noah Beery, Helen Vinson. 7,211 ft. **A.** " Kine." Jan. 2, 1936. Rel. Mar. 30, 1936. G.-B.D.

*King's Plate, The. (Jan. 20.) Toby Wing, Kenneth Duncan, Wheeler Oakman. 5,695 ft. **U.** " Kine." Jan. 23, 1936. Rel. May 11, 1936. M-G-M.

King Steps Out, The. (June 2.) Grace Moore, Franchot Tone, Walter Connolly. 7,597 ft. **U.** " Kine." June 11, 1936. Rel. Nov. 23, 1936. COLUMBIA.

Kliou the Tiger. (April 8.) 4,459 ft. **U.** " Kine." April 16, 1936. Rel. Aug. 10, 1936. WARDOUR.

Klondyke Annie. (April 7.) Mae West, Victor McLaglen, Phillip Reed. 7,026 ft. **A.** " Kine." April 9, 1936. Rel. June 15, 1936. PARAMOUNT.

Koenigsmark. (Jan. 16.) Elissa Landi, John Lodge, Pierre Fresnay. 8,620 ft. **A.** " Kine." Jan. 23, 1936. Rel. Aug. 24, 1936. GENERAL F.D.

*Laburnum Grove. (May 1.) Edmund Gwenn, Cedric Hardwicke, Victoria Hopper. 6,622 ft. **A.** " Kine." May 7, 1936. Rel. Nov. 16, 1936. A.B.F.D.

Ladies in Love. (Nov. 4.) Janet Gaynor, Loretta Young, Constance Bennett, Simone Simon. 8,752 ft. **A.** " Kine." Nov. 12, 1936. Rel. date not fixed. Fox.

Lady Be Careful. (Sept. 22.) Lew Ayres, Mary Carlisle, Larry Crabbe. 6,422 ft. **U.** " Kine." Sept. 24, 1936. Rel. April 5, 1937. PARAMOUNT.

Lady Consents, The. (Mar. 18.) Ann Harding, Herbert Marshall. 6,886 ft. **A.** " Kine." Mar. 26, 1936. Rel. Sept. 7, 1936. RADIO.

Lady of Secrets. (Feb. 19.) Ruth Chatterton, Otto Kruger, Marion Marsh. 6,569 ft. **A.** " Kine." Feb. 27, 1936. Rel. July 20, 1936. COLUMBIA.

La Kermesse Heroique. (Oct. 14.), Francoise Rosay, Alerme, Jean Murat. 8,000 ft. **A.** " Kine." Oct. 22, 1936. Rel. date not fixed. G.-B.D.

*Land Without Music. (Oct. 8.) Richard Tauber, Diana Napier, Jimmy Durante. 7,250 tt. **U.** " Kine." Oct. 15, 1936. Rel. April 12, 1937. GEN. F.D.

Last Assignment, The. (April 15.) Ray Walker, Joan Woodbury, William Farnum. 5,350 ft. **A.** " Kine." April 23, 1936. Rel. Aug. 17, 1936. PATHE.

Last of the Mohicans, The. (Sept. 3.) Randolph Scott, Binnie Barnes, Henry Wilcoxon. 8,312 ft. **U.** " Kine." Sept. 10, 1936. Rel. Mar. 15, 1937. UNITED ARTISTS.

Last of the Pagans, The. (Jan. 15.) Mala and Lotus. 6,342 ft. **A.** " Kine." Jan. 23, 1936. Rel. May 11, 1936. M-G-M.

Last Outlaw, The. (July 1.) Harry Carey, Hoot Gibson, Margaret Callahan. 6,342 ft. **U.** " Kine." July 9, 1936. Rel. Dec. 14, 1936. RADIO.

Last Rose, The. (June 9.) Carla Spletter, Helge Rosweange. 8,250 ft. **U.** " Kine." June 11, 1936. Rel. date not fixed. TOBIS CINEMA.

Last Waltz, The. (July 21.) Jamilla Novotna, Josephine, H. Wright, Harry Welchman. 6,500 ft. **U.** " Kine." July 23, 1936. Rel. Jan. 18, 1937. A.P. & D.

Laughing Irish Eyes. (Mar. 26.) Phil Regan, Walter C. Kelly. Evalyn Knapp. 6,315 ft. **U.** " Kine." April 2, 1936. Rel. June. 29, 1936. A.B.F.D.

Law in Her Hands, The. (June 30.) Margaret Lindsay, Glenda Farrell, Warren Hull, Lyle Talbot. 5,299 ft. **A.** " Kine." July 2, 1936. Rel. Dec. 28, 1936. FIRST NATIONAL.

Lawless Nineties, The. (Aug. 21.) John Wayne, Ann Rutherford, Harry Woods. 5,161 ft. **U.** " Kine." Aug. 27, 1936. Rel. date not fixed. BRITISH LION.

Law of the Jungle. (Dec. 16.) 4,088 ft. **U.** " Kine." Dec. 19, 1935. Rel. June 8, 1936. WARDOUR.

Law of the Lawless. (Mar. 20.) Jack Hoxie, Hilda Moreno. 5,420 ft. **U.** "Kine." Mar. 26, 1936. Rel. date not fixed. EQUITY BRITISH.

Let's Sing Again. (July 7.) Bobby Breen, George Houston, Vivienne Osborne. 5,550 ft. **U.** " Kine." July 9, 1936. Rel. Dec. 7, 1936. RADIO.

Libelled Lady. (Oct. 28.) Jean Harlow, William Powell, Myrna Loy, Spencer Tracy. 8,834 ft. **A.** " Kine." Nov. 5, 1936. Rel. April 12, 1937. M-G-M.

Liebesmelodie. (Mar. 30.) Marta Eggerth, Rolf Wanka. 8,280 ft. **A.** " Kine." April 2, 1936. Rel. date not fixed. REUNION.

Lightnin' Bill Carson. (Aug. 19.) Tim McCoy, Harry Worth, Lois January. 6,000 ft. **U.** " Kine." Aug. 27, 1936. Rel. date not fixed. EQUITY.

*Limelight. (Jan. 13.) Arthur Tracy, Anna Neagle, Tilly Losch. 7,200 ft. **U.** " Kine." Jan. 16, 1936. Rel. Sept. 28, 1936. GEN. F.D.

*Limping Man, The. (Oct. 30.) Francis L. Sullivan, Patricia Hilliard, Robert Cochran. 6,557 ft. **A.** " Kine." Nov. 5, 1936. Rel. April 19, 1937. PATHE.

Little Lord Fauntleroy. (April 28.) Freddie Bartholomew, Dolores Costello, Barrymore, C. Aubrey Smith. 9,361 ft. **U.** " Kine." April 30, 1936. Rel. Nov. 9, 1936. UNITED ARTISTS.

Little Miss Nobody. (July 2.) Jane Withers, Jane Darwell, Ralph Morgan. 6,547 ft. **U.** " Kine." July 9, 1936. Rel. Dec. 7, 1936. Fox.

Littlest Rebel, The. (Jan. 14.) Shirley Temple, John Boles, Jack Holt. 6,614 ft. **U.** " Kine." Jan. 23, 1936. Rel. Aug. 3, 1936. Fox.

*Live Again. (Nov. 3.) Noah Beery, Bessie Love, John Garrick. 6,750 ft. A. " Kine." Nov. 5, 1936. Rel. April 26, 1937. NATIONAL PROV.

Live Wire, The. (July 8.) Richard Talmadge, Alberta Vaughan. 5,250 ft. U. ",Kine." July 16, 1936. Rel. date not fixed. EQUITY.

*Living Dangerously. (Mar. 9.) Otto Kruger, Leonora Corbett, Francis Lister. 6,570 ft. A. " Kine." Mar. 12, 1936. Rel. Aug. 24, 1936. WARDOUR.

*Lonely Road, The. (Aug. 24.) Clive Brook, Victoria Hopper, Cecil Ramage. 7,212 ft. A. " Kine." Aug. 27, 1936. Rel. Mar. 29, 1937. A.B.F.D.

Lone Wolf Returns, The. (Feb. 26.) Melvyn Douglas, Gail Patrick, Tala Birell. 6,167 ft. A. " Kine." Mar. 5, 1936. Rel. July 6, 1936. COLUMBIA.

Longest Night, The. (Oct. 15.) Robert Young, Florence Rice, Ted Healy. 4,453 ft. A. " Kine." Oct. 22, 1936. Rel. Mar. 15, 1937. M-G-M.

Loser's End, The. (Jan. 29.) Jack Perrin, Tina Menard. 5,250 ft. U. " Kine." Feb. 6, 1936. Rel. date not fixed. EQUITY.

*Love at Sea. (April 17.) Rosalyn Boulter, Carl Harbord, 6,362 ft. U. " Kine." April 23, 1936. Rel. Aug. 24, 1936. PARAMOUNT.

Love Before Breakfast. (April 15.) Carole Lombard, Preston Foster, Cesar Romero. 6,298 ft. U. " Kine." April 23, 1936. Rel. Aug. 17, 1936. GEN. F.D.

*Love in Exile. (May 13.) Clive Brook, Helen Vinson, Will Fyffe. 7,023 ft. A. " Kine." May 21, 1936. Rel. Nov. 16, 1936. Dec. 7, 1936. GEN. F.D.

Love on a Bet. (Mar. 17.) Gene Raymond, Wendy Barrie. 6,937 ft. U. " Kine." Mar. 26, 1936. Rel. Aug. 17, 1936. RADIO.

*Love Up the Pole. (Sept. 15.) Ernie Lotinga, Jack Frost, Vivienne Chatterton. 7,450 ft. A. " Kine." Sept. 24, 1936. Rel. Feb. 8, 1937. BUTCHER.

Luck of the Irish, The. (Dec. 10.) Richard Hayward, Kay Walsh, Nan Cullen. 7,330 ft. U. " Kine." Dec. 12, 1935. Rel. April 6, 1936. PARA-MOUNT.

*Luck of the Turf. (Sept. 25.) Jack Melford, Moira Lynd. 5.755 ft. A. " Kine." Oct. 1, 1936. Rel. Jan. 11, 1937. RADIO.

Lucky Corrigan. (Oct. 21.) William Gargan, Molly Lamont, J. P. McGowan. 5,942 ft. U. " Kine." Oct. 29, 1936. Rel. Feb. 22, 1937. COLUMBIA.

*Lucky Fugitives. (Mar. 20.) David Manners, Maxine Doyle. 6,118 ft. A. " Kine." Mar. 26, 1936. Rel. July 27, 1936. COLUMBIA.

Madcap. (June 16.) Rod la Rocque, Maxine Doyle, Bryant Washburn. 5,142 ft. A. " Kine." June 18, 1936. Rel. Sept. 21, 1936. PATHE.

Magnificent Brute, The. (Nov. 10.) Victor McLaglen, Binnie Barnes, William Hall. 6,994 ft. U. " Kine." Nov. 19, 1936. Rel. July 26, 1937. GENERAL F.D.

Magnificent Obsession. (Feb. 11.) Irene Dunne, Robert Taylor, Charles Butterworth. 10,184 ft. U. " Kine." Feb. 20, 1936. Rel. Sept. 14, 1936. UNIVERSAL.

*Man Behind the Mask, The. (Mar. 24.) Hugh Williams, Jane Baxter. 7,131 ft. A. . " Kine." Mar. 26, 1936. Rel. Aug. 26, 1936. M-G-M.

Man from Guntown, The. (Aug. 26.) Tim McCoy, Billy Seward, Wheller Oakman. 5,500 ft. U. " Kine." Sept. 17, 1936. Rel. date not fixed. EQUITY.

Manhattan Madness. (Oct. 21.) Jean Arthur, Joel McCrea, Reginald Owen. 6,557 ft. U. " Kine." Oct. 29, 1936. Rel. Mar. 22, 1937. COL-UMBIA.

Man Hunt. (April 2.) Ricardo Cortez, Margaret Churchill, William Gargan. 5,535 ft. **A.** " Kine." April 9, 1936. Rel. Sept. 14, 1936. Rel. Aug. 24, 1936. FIRST NATIONAL.

*Man in the Mirror, The. (Oct. 15.) Edward Everett Horton, Genevieve Tobin, Ursula Jeans. 7,470 ft. **A.** " Kine." Oct. 22, 1936. Rel. Mar. 29, 1937. WARDOUR.

Man of Iron. (Dec. 17.) Barton MacLane, Mary Astor, John Eldredge. 5,614 ft. **U.** " Kine." Dec. 19, 1935. Rel. July 6, 1936. WARNER.

Man's Best Friend. (June 11.) Lightning, Douglas Haig, Frank Brownlee. 5,400 ft. **U.** " Kine." June 18, 1936. Rel. date not fixed. EQUITY.

*Man They Could Not Hang. (Nov. 29.) Ronald Roberts, Patricia Minchin, Clair Baines. 6,643 ft. **A.** " Kine." Dec. 5, 1935. Rel. April 20, 1936. GEN. F.D.

Man Who Broke the Bank at Monte Carlo, The. (Dec. 30.) Ronald Colman, Joan Bennett, Nigel Bruce. 6,104 ft. **U.** " Kine." Jan. 2, 1936. Rel. April 27, 1936. FOX.

*Man Who Changed His Mind, The. (Sept. 11.) Boris Karloff, Anna Lee, Frank Cellier. 5,914 ft. **A.** " Kine." Sept. 17, 1936. Rel. Nov. 9, 1936 ; Nov. 8, 1936. G.-B.D.

*Man Who Could Work Miracles, The. (July 23.) Roland Young, Ralph Richardson, Joan Gardner. 7.300 ft. **U.** " Kine." July 30, 1936. Rel. Feb. 8, 1937. UNITED ARTISTS.

Man Who Lived Twice, The. (Oct. 23.) Ralph Bellamy, Marion Marsh, Thurston Hall. 6,564 ft. **A.** " Kine." Oct. 29, 1936. Rel. Mar. 1, 1937. COLUMBIA.

The Man Who Pawned His Soul. (Nov. 27.) Edward Arnold. 6,137 ft. **A.** " Kine." Dec. 5, 1935. Rel. July 20, 1936. WARDOUR.

Marchant d'Amour. (Sept. 1.) Jean Galland, Rosia Derean. 7,453 ft. **A.** " Kine." Sept. 3, 1936. Rel. Oct. 1, 1936. DENNING FILMS.

Maria Bashkirtseff. (Sept. 23.) Lili Darvas, Hans Jaray. 6,837 ft. **A.** " Kine." Oct. 1, 1936. Rel. Sept. 25, 1936. WARDOUR.

Marines Have Landed, The. (May 14.) Lew Ayres, Isabel Jewell, J. Carroll Naish. 6,135 ft. **A.** " Kine." May 21, 1936. Rel. Nov. 9, 1936. A.B.F.D.

*Marriage of Corbal, The. (May 27.) Nils Asther, Hazel Terry, Hugh Sinclair. 8,100 ft. **U.** " Kine." June 4, 1936. Rel. Dec. 14, 1936. GEN. F.D.

Mary Burns Fugitive. (Dec. 6.) Sylvia Sidney, Melvyn Douglas, Alan Baxter. 7,400 ft. **A.** " Kine." Dec. 12, 1935. Rel. Mar. 2, 1936. PARAMOUNT.

Mary of Scotland. (July 30.) Katherine Hepburn, Fredric March, Florence Eldridge. 10,980 ft. **U.** " Kine." Aug. 6, 1936. Rel. Nov. 9, 1936. RADIO.

Mayerling. (Oct. 20.) Charles Boyer, Danielle Darrieux. 8,200 ft. **A.** " Kine." Oct. 22, 1936. Rel. date not fixed. G.-B.D.

Meet Nero Wolfe. (Aug. 14.) Edward Arnold, Lionel Stander, Dennis Moore. 6,447 ft. **A.** " Kine." Aug. 20, 1936. Rel. Dec. 28, 1936. COLUMBIA.

The Melody Lingers On. (Dec. 3.) Josephine Hutchinson, George Houstan, John Halliday. 7,789 ft. **A.** " Kine." Dec. 12, 1935. Rel. June 8, 1936. UNITED ARTISTS.

*Melody of My Heart. (April 21.) Derek Oldham, Lorraine La Fosse, Bruce Seton. 7,402 ft. **A.** " Kine." April 9, 1936. Rel. Oct. 5, 1936. BUTCHER.

Melody Trail. (Jan. 14.) Gene Autry, Ann Rutherford. 5,845 ft. **U.** " Kine." Jan. 16, 1936. Rel. date not fixed. BRITISH LION.

*Memory Lane. (June 24.) 4,005 ft. **U.** " Kine." July 9, 1936. Rel. Nov. 11, 1936. FIRST NATIONAL.

Men of Action. (April 7.) Frankie Darro, Barbara Worth, Ray Mason. 5,670 ft. **U.** " Kine." April 9, 1936. Rel. date not fixed. INDEPENDENT. FILM DIS.

*Men of Yesterday. (May 22.) Stewart Rome, Barbara Everest, Will Fyffe. 7,350 ft. **U.** " Kine." May 28, 1936. Rel. date not fixed. A.P. & D.

Merlusse. (Mar. 18.) Henri Poupon. 6,000 ft. — " Kine," Mar. 26, 1936. Rel. date not fixed. G.-B.D.

Message to Garcia, A. (May 14.) Wallace Beery, Barbara Stanwyck, John Boles. 7,298 ft. **A.** " Kine." May 21, 1936. Rel. Sept. 21, 1936. Fox.

Midnight Phantom. (July 7.) Reginald Denny, Lloyd Hughes, Claudia Dell. 5,006 ft. " Kine." July 9, 1936. Rel. Dec. 7, 1936. BUTCHER.

Mighty Tundra, The. (Nov. 17.) Del Crambe. 6,400 ft. **U.** " Kine." Nov. 19, 1936. Rel. May 31, 1937. WARDOUR.

Milky Way, The. (Mar. 27.) Harold Lloyd, Adolphe Menjou, Helen Mack. 7,885 ft. **U.** " Kine." Mar. 5, 1936. Rel. May 11, 1936. PARAMOUNT.

Millionaire Kid. (Oct. 29.) Betty Compson, Bryant Washburn, Charles Delaney. 5,283 ft. **A.** " Kine." Nov. 5, 1936. Rel. March 8, 1937. WARDOUR.

*Millions. (Sept. 21.) Gordon Harker, Richard Hearne, Jane Carr. 6,319 ft. **U.** " Kine." Sept. 24, 1936. Rel. Mar. 22, 1937. GENERAL F.D.

Millions in the Air. (Jan. 14.) John Howard, Wendy Barrie, Robert Cummings. 6,449 ft. **U.** " Kine." Jan. 16, 1936. Rel. April 6, 1936. PARAMOUNT.

Mine With the Iron Door, The. (July 17.) Richard Arlen, Cecilia Parker, Henry B. Walthall. 5,862 ft. " Kine." July 23, 1936. Rel. Oct. 5, 1936. COLUMBIA.

Miss Pacific Fleet. (Jan. 16.) Joan Blondell, Glenda Farrell, Allen Jenkins. 6,083 ft. **A.** " Kine." Jan. 23, 1936. Rel. June 22, 1936. F.N.

Mister Cinderella. (Sept. 30.) Jack Haley, Betty Furness, Arthur Treacher. 6,746 ft. **U.** " Kine." Oct. 8, 1936. Rel. Dec. 28, 1936. M-G-M.

M'Liss. (July 28.) Anne Shirley, John Beale, Guy Kibbee. 5,850 ft. **A.** " Kine." July 30, 1936. Rel. Dec. 28, 1936. RADIO.

Modern Madness. July 16.) Guy Kibbee, Warren Hull, Alma Lloyd. 5,193 ft. **A.** " Kine." July 23, 1936. Rel. Feb. 8, 1937. WARNER.

Modern Times. (Feb. 11.) Charles Chaplin, Pauline Goddard, Chester Conklin. 8,018 ft. **U.** " Kine." Feb. 13, 1936. Rel. Oct. 19, 1936. UNITED ARTISTS.

Moonlight Murder. (April 17.) Chester Morris, Madge Evans. Grant Mitchell. 5,973 ft. **A.** " Kine." April 23, 1936. Rel. Aug. 3, 1936. M-G-M.

Moon's Our Home, The. (May 12.) Margaret Sullavan, Henry Fonda, Charles Butterworth. 7,413 ft. **U.** " Kine." May 14, 1936. Rel. Sept. 21, 1936. PARAMOUNT.

*Mr. Cohen Takes a Walk. (Dec. 13.) Paul Graetz, Chili Bouchier, Mickey Brantford. 7,461 ft. **U.** " Kine." Dec. 19, 1935. Rel. July 6, 1936. WARNER. ...

Mr. Deeds Goes to Town. (April 29.) Gary Cooper, Jean Arthur. 10,390 ft. **U.** " Kine." May 7, 1936. Rel. Oct. 12, 1936. COLUMBIA.

Mummy's Boys. (Nov. 11.) Bert Wheeler, Robert Woolsey, Barbara Pepper. 6,128 ft. **A.** " Kine." Nov. 19, 1936. Rel. Mar. 22, 1937. RADIO.

Murder at Glen Athol. (May 27.) John Miljan, Irene Ware, Noel Madison. 6,265 ft. **A.** " Kine." June 4, 1936. Rel. Sept. 28, 1936. WARDOUR.

Murder by an Aristocrat. (May 19.) Lyle Talbot, Marguerite Churchill. Claire Dodd. 5,455 ft. **A.** " Kine." May 21, 1936. Rel. Nov. 23, 1936. WARNER.

*Murder by Rope. (Aug. 25.) D. A. Clarke-Smith, Sunday Wilshin, W. Hyde-White. 5,872 ft. **A.** " Kine." Aug. 27, 1936. Rel. Jan. 4, 1937. PARAMOUNT.

Murder in the Big House. (July 2.) Craig Reynolds, June Travis, Barton MacLane. 5,454 ft. **A.** " Kine." July 9 1936. Rel. Dec. 7, 1936. WARNER.

Murder on a Bridle Path. (April 14.) James Gleason, Helen Broderick, Christian Rub. 5,760 ft. **A.** " Kine." April 16, 1936. Rel. Sept. 14, 1936. RADIO.

Murder With Pictures. (Oct. 23.) Lew Ayres, Gail Patrick, Onslow Stevens. 6,348 ft. **A.** " Kine." Oct. 29, 1936. Rel. April 26, 1937. PARAMOUNT.

Music Goes Round, The. (Mar. 24.) Harry Richman, Rochelle Hudson, Walter Connolly. 7,737 ft. **U.** " Kine." April 2, 1936. Rel. July 6, 1936. COLUMBIA.

Music is Magic. (Dec. 10.) Alice Fay, Ray Walker, Bebe Daniels. 5,850 ft. **U.** " Kine." Dec. 12, 1936. Rel. May 11, 1936. Fox.

*Music Maker, The. (Mar. 20.) Arthur Young, Violet Loxley. 4,840 ft. **U.** " Kine." Mar. 26, 1936. Rel. Oct. 19, 1936. M-G-M.

Mutiny on the Bounty. (Dec. 23.) Charles Laughton, Clark Gable, Franchot Tone. 11,933 ft. **A.** " Kine." Jan. 2, 1936. Rel. Sept. 21, 1936. M-G-M.

My American Wife. (Aug. 24.) Francis Lederer, Ann Sothern, Fred Stone. 6,595 ft. **U.** " Kine." Aug. 27, 1936. Rel. Jan. 11, 1937. PARAMOUNT.

My Man Godfrey. (Sept. 8.) William Powell, Carole Lombard, Alice Brady. 8,422 ft. **A.** " Kine." Sept. 17, 1936. Rel. Feb. 15, 1937. GENERAL F.D.

My Marriage. (Feb. 25.) Claire Trevor, Kent Taylor, Pauline. Frederick. 6,215 ft. **A.** " Kine." Feb. 27, 1936. Rel. June 22, 1936 Fox.

My Old Man's a Fireman. (Dec. 23.) Ed. Wynn. 5,500 ft. **U.** " Kine." Jan. 2, 1936. Rel. June 22, 1936. WARDOUR.

Mysterious Avenger. (Oct. 20.) Charles Starrett, Joan Perry, Wheeler Oakman. 4,802 ft. **U.** " Kine." Oct. 22, 1936. Rel. Feb. 8, 1937. COLUMBIA.

Mystery Mountain. (April 29.) Ken Maynard, Verna Hillie, Ed. Cobb. 12 eps. **U.** " Kine." May 7, 1936. Rel. date not fixed. A.B.F.D.

Mystery Ship, The. (Sept. 2.) Phillips H. Lord, Alice Wessler. 5,900 ft. **A.** " Kine." Sept. 10, 1936. Rel. Feb. 1937. INTER CINE.

Natural Born Salesman, A. (Sept. 17.) Joe E. Brown, June Travis, Guy Kibbee. 6,257 ft. **U.** " Kine." Sept. 24, 1936. Rel. Mar. 8, 1937. FIRST NATIONAL.

Navy Born. (Nov. 9.) William Gargan, Claire Dodd, George Irving. 6,130 ft. **U.** " Kine." Nov. 12, 1936. Rel. May 3, 1937. A.B.F.D.

Navy Wife. (Dec. 19.) Claire Trevor, Ralph Bellamy, Kathleen Burke. 6,675 ft. **A.** " Kine." Dec. 26, 1935. Rel. May 18, 1936. Fox.

Nevada. (Feb. 7.) Buster Crabbe, Kathleen Burke, Monte Blue. 5,282 ft. **U.** " Kine." Feb. 13, 1936. Rel. Aug. 17, 1936. PARAMOUNT.

Never Too Late. (Aug. 12.) Richard Talmadge, Thelma White, Mildred Harris. 5,250 ft. **A.** " Kine." Aug. 20, 1936. Rel. date not fixed. EQUITY.

New Frontier, The. (Mar. 24.) John Wayne, Muriel Evans. 5,056 ft. **A.** " Kine." Mar. 26, 1936. Rel. date not fixed. BRITISH LION.

Next Time We Live. (Mar. 19.) Margaret Sullavan, James Stewart. 7,180 ft. **A.** " Kine." Mar. 26, 1936. Rel. June 29, 1936. GENERAL F.D.

Night at the Opera, A. (Jan. 31.) Groucho, Chico and Harpo Marx. 8,438 ft. **U.** Kine." Feb. 6, 1936. Rel. Sept. 7, 1936. M-G-M.

Night Cargo. (Mar. 11.) Jacqueline Wells, Lloyd Hughes, Walter Miller. 5,892 ft. **A.** " Kine." Mar. 19, 1936. Rel. Aug. 17, 1936. WARDOUR.

Nobody's Fool. (July 1.) Edward Everett Horton, Glenda Farrell, Cesar Romero. 5,700 ft. **U.** " Kine." July 9, 1936. Rel. Jan. 18, 1937. GENERAL F.D.

*Nothing Like Publicity. (Sept. 21.) Billy Hartnell, Marjorie Taylor, Moira Lynd. 5,848 ft. **U.** " Kine." Sept. 24, 1936. Rel. date not fixed. RADIO.

*Not So Dusty. (May 20.) Wally Patch, Gus McNaughton, Phil Ray. 6,300 ft. **U.** " Kine." May 28, 1936. Rel. Nov. 2, 1936. RADIO.

North of Arizona. (Oct. 21.) Jack Perrin, Blanche Mehaffey, Al Bridge. 5,340 ft. **U.** " Kine." Oct. 29, 1936. Rel. date not fixed. EQUITY.

Oil Raider, The. (Jan. 17.) Buster Crabbe, Gloria Shea. 5,536 ft. **U.** " Kine." Jan. 23, 1936. Rel. July 6, 1936. INTER. CINE.

Old Homestead, The. (Mar. 23.) Mary Carlisle, Lawrence Gray. 6,363 ft. **U.** " Kine." Mar. 26, 1936. Rel. Aug. 17, 1936. A.B.F.D.

Old Hutch. (Oct. 8.) Wallace Beery, Eric Linden, Cecilia Parker. 7,154 ft. — " Kine." Oct. 15, 1936. Rel. Feb. 15, 1937. M-G-M.

Old School Tie, The. (July 22.) Charles Butterworth, Hugh Herbert, Una Merkel. 6,137 ft. **A.** " Kine." July 30, 1936. Rel. Nov. 9, 1936. M-G-M.

O'Malley of the Mounted. (Nov. 10.) George O'Brien, Irene Ware, Stanley Fields. 6,360 ft. **U.** " Kine." Nov. 12, 1936. Rel. May 10, 1937. A.B.F.D.

*Once in a Million. (Mar. 13.) Buddy Rogers, Mary Brian, W. H. Berry. 6,900 ft. **U.** " Kine." Mar. 19, 1936. Rel. Aug. 3, 1936. WARDOUR.

*One Good Turn. (June 5.) Leslie Fuller, George Harris, Molly Fisher. 6,545 ft. **U.** " Kine." June 11, 1936. Rel. Oct. 12, 1936. A.B.F.D.

One Rainy Afternoon. (June 27.) Francis Lederer, Ida Lupino, Hugh Herbert. 7,280 ft. **U.** " Kine." June 4, 1936. Rel. Dec. 7, 1936. UNITED ARTISTS.

One Way Ticket. (Dec. 20.) Lloyd Nolan, Peggy Conklin, Walter Connolly. 6,421 ft. **A.** " Kine." Dec. 26, 1935. Rel. April 20, 1936. COLUMBIA.

On Probation. (April 16.) Monte Blue, Lucille Brown, William Bakewell. 5,766 ft. **U.** " Kine." April 23, 1936. Rel. April 27, 1936. GEN. F.D.

On Secret Service. (Sept. 10.) Dick Foran, Paula Stone, Gordon Elliott. 5,110 ft. **U.** " Kine." Sept. 17, 1936. Rel. Jan. 25, 1937. FIRST NATIONAL.

*On Top of the World. (Jan. 27.) Betty Fields, Frank Pettingell, Billy Bray. 7,150 ft. **U.** " Kine." Jan. 30, 1936. Rel. July 27, 1936. A.P. & D.

Oregon Trail, The. (Mar. 27.) John Wayne, Ann Rutherford. 5,131 ft. **U.** " Kine." April 2, 1936. Rel. date not fixed. BRITISH LION.

O'Riley's Luck. (Nov. 10.) Eleanore Whitney, William Frawley, Tom Brown. 6,869 ft. **U.** " Kine." Nov. 12, 1936. Rel. May 3, 1937. PARAMOUNT.

Our Relations. (Sept. 15.) Stan Laurel, Oliver Hardy, Daphne Pollard. 6,563 ft. **U.** " Kine." Sept. 24, 1936. Rel. Dec. 28, 1936. M-G-M.

*Ourselves Alone. (April 27.) John Loder, Antoinette Cellier, John Lodge. 6,200 ft. **A.** " Kine." April 30, 1936. Rel. Sept. 21, 1936. WARDOUR.

Outlaw Deputy, The. (Sept. 4.) Tim McCoy. 5,250 ft. **U.** " Kine."
Sept. 10, 1936. Rel. date not fixed. EQUITY.

Outlaw Justice. (Mar. 13.) Jack Hoxie, Dorothy Gulliver, Jack Trent.
5,250 ft. **U.** " Kine." Mar. 19, 1936. Rel. date not fixed. EQUITY BRITISH

Paddy O'Day. (Jan. 17.) Jane Withers, Pinky Tomlin, Rita Cansino.
6,874 ft. **U.** " Kine." Jan. 23, 1936. Rel. June 8, 1936. Fox.

Palm Springs Affair. (July 14.) Frances Langford, Guy Standing,
Smith Bellew. 6,478 ft. **U.** " Kine." July 16, 1936. Rel. Dec. 28, 1936.
PARAMOUNT.

*****Pal o' Mine.** (Mar. 16.) Charles Paton, Herbert Langley, 3,800 ft.
U. " Kine." Mar. 19, 1936. Rel. Aug. 3, 1936. RADIO.

Panic on the Air. (Feb. 24.) Ann Sothern, Lloyd Nolan, Douglas
Dumbrille. 5,974 ft. **A.** " Kine." Feb. 27, 1936. Rel. Aug. 3, 1936.
COLUMBIA.

Parisienne Life. (Mar. 23.) Max Dearly, Conchita Montenegro.
7,200 ft. **A.** " Kine." Mar. 26, 1936. Rel. Aug. 24, 1936. UNITED
ARTISTS.

Parole. (Oct. 25.) Henry Hunter, Ann Preston, Alan Dinehart.
5,590 ft. **A.** " Kine." Oct. 1, 1936. Rel. May 17, 1937. GEN. F.D.

*****Pathetone Parade.** (Jan. 24.) Ten well-known Variety Artistes. 3,300
ft. **U.** " Kine." Jan. 30, 1936. Rel. June 15, 1936. PATHE.

Pay Box Adventure. (June 12.) Syd Crossley, Billy Watts, Marjorie
Corbett. 6,148 ft. **U.** " Kine." June 18, 1936. Rel. Oct. 12, 1936.
PARAMOUNT.

Pecos Dandy. (Oct. 29.) George Lewis, Dorothy Gulliver, Betty Lee.
4,120 ft. **U.** " Kine." Nov. 5, 1936. Rel. date not fixed. EQUITY.

Pepper. (Oct. 6.) Jane Withers, Irvin S. Cobb, Slim Summerville.
5,777 ft. **U.** " Kine." Oct. 8, 1936. Rel. April 12, 1937. Fox.

Peter Ibbetson. (Dec. 3.) Gary Cooper, Ann Harding, John Halliday.
7,433 ft. **A.** " Kine." Dec. 5, 1935. Rel. Mar. 16, 1936. PARAMOUNT.

Petrified Forest, The. (Mar. 6.) Leslie Howard, Bette Davis, Humphrey
Bogart. 7,490 ft. **A.** " Kine." Mar. 12, 1936. Rel. Sept. 14, 1936.
WARNER.

Petticoat Fever. (April 15.) Robert Montgomery, Myrna Loy, Reginald
Owen. 7,190 ft. **A.** " Kine." April 23, 1936. Rel. Sept. 28, 1936. M-G-M.

The Phantom Empire. (Jan. 3.) Gene Autry, Frankie Darro, Betsy
King Ross. 12 eps. **U.** " Kine." Jan. 9, 1936. Rel. date not fixed.
A.B.F.D.

Phantom Gondola, The. (June 16.) Marcelle Chantal, Roger Karl.
7,400 ft. **A.** " Kine." June 25, 1936. Rel. date not fixed. G.-B. CURZON.

Phantom Rider, The. (Sept. 3.) Buck Jones, Maria Gibson, Harry
Woods. 15 eps. **U.** " Kine." Sept. 10, 1936. Rel. Oct. 12, 1936. GEN.
F.D.

Piccadilly Jim. (Sept. 9.) Robert Montgomery, Madge Evans, Frank
Morgan. 8,567 ft. **U.** " Kine." Sept. 17, 1936. Rel. Feb. 8, 1937. M-G-M.

*****Pictorial Review.** (Mar. 17.) Ronald Frankau, Robb Wilton, Geraldo
and Orchestra. 3,663 ft. " Kine." Mar. 19, 1936. Rel. Aug. 17, 1936.
PATHE.

Poor Little Rich Girl, The. (Aug. 13.) Shirley Temple, Alice Faye,
Claude Gillingwater. 7,144 ft. **U.** " Kine." Aug. 20, 1936. Rel. Dec. 28,
1936. Fox.

Poppy. (July 10.) W. C. Fields, Rochelle Hudson, Richard Cromwell.
6,305 ft. **U.** " Kine." July 16, 1936. Rel. Nov. 9, 1936. PARAMOUNT.

Postal Inspector. (Sept. 30.) Ricardo Cortez, Patricia Ellis, Bela
Lugosi. 5,266 ft. **U.** " Kine." Oct. 8, 1936. Rel. June 7, 1937.

*****Pot Luck.** (April 1.) Tom Walls, Ralph Lynn, Robertson Hare.
6,468 ft. **A.** " Kine." April 9, 1936. Rel. May 11, 1936. G.-B.D.

Preview Murder Mystery, The. (Mar. 10.) Ian Keith, Gail Patrick, Reginald Denny. 5,454 ft. **A.** " Kine." Mar. 12, 1936. Rel. Aug. 10, 1936. PARAMOUNT.

Princess Comes Across, The. (July 7.) Carole Lombard, Fred MacMurray. 6,791 ft. **A.** " Kine." July 9, 1936. Rel. Nov. 16, 1936. PARAMOUNT.

*Prison Breaker. (Feb. 14.) James Mason, Marguerite Allan, Andrews Engelman. 6,286 ft. **A.** " Kine." Feb. 20, 1936. Rel. June 15, 1936. COLUMBIA.

Prisoner of Shark Island, The. (April 2.) Warner Baxter, Gloria Stuart, Claude Gillingwater. 8,560 ft. **A.** " Kine." April 9, 1936. Rel. Aug. 31, 1936. Fox.

Prison Shadows. (Sept. 9.) Eddie Nugent, Lucille Lund, Syd Saylor. 6,200 ft. **A.** " Kine." Sept. 17, 1936. Rel. Dec. 14, 1936. PATHE.

Professional Soldier. (Feb. 6.) Victor McLaglen, Freddie Bartholomew, Gloria Stuart. 6,982 ft. **A.** " Kine." Feb. 13, 1936. Rel. Aug. 17, 1936. Fox.

*Public Nuisance No. 1. (Mar. 5.) Frances Day, Arthur Riscoe. 7,087 ft. **A.** " Kine." Feb. 27, 1936. Rel. May 25, 1936. GEN. F.D.

*Queen of Hearts. (Feb. 13.) Gracie Fields, John Loder, Fred Duprez. 7,200 ft. **U.** " Kine." Feb. 20, 1936. Rel. Oct. 5, 1936. A.B.F.D.

Racing Luck. (Jan. 10.) Bill Boyd, Barbara Worth, George Ernest. 5,310 ft. **U.** " Kine." Jan. 16, 1936. Rel. June 1, 1936. BRITISH LION.

*Radio Lover. (Oct. 27.) Wylie Watson, Betty Ann Davies, Jack Melford. 5,773 ft. **U.** " Kine." Oct. 2, 1936. Rel. April 5, 1937. A.B.F.D.

*Railroad Rhythm. (Mar. 27.) Vilma Vanne, Jack Browning. 4,000 ft. **U.** " Kine." April 2, 1936. Rel. June 15, 1936. ' EXCLUSIVE.

The Rainmakers. (Nov. 27.) Bert Wheeler, Robert Woolsey, Dorothy Lee. 6,500 ft. **U.** " Kine." Dec. 5, 1935. Rel. April 27, 1936. RADIO.

Ramona. (Oct. 16.) Loretta Young, Don Ameche, Kent Taylor. 7,572 ft. **A.** " Kine." Oct. 22, 1936. Rel. Mar. 1, 1937. Fox.

The Rawhide Mail. (Jan. 22.) Jack Perrin, Lillian Gilmore, Nelson McDowell. 5,150 ft. **U.** " Kine." Jan. 30, 1936. Rel. date not fixed. EQUITY.

Rawhide Terror, The. (Oct. 22.) Art Mix, Edmund Cobb, Francis Morris. 4,640 ft. **U.** " Kine." Oct. 20, 1936. Rel. date not fixed. EQUITY.

Reckless Way, The. (June 19.) Marion Nixon, Kane Richmond, Inez Courtney. 5,895 ft. **A.** " Kine." June 25, 1936. Rel. Oct. 5, 1936. PATHE.

Red Blood of Courage. (Sept. 14.) Kermit Maynard, Ann Sheridan, Reginald Barlow. 5,067 ft. **U.** " Kine." Sept. 17, 1936. Rel. Feb. 8, 1937. BUTCHER.

Red River Valley. (June 10.) Gene Autry, Francis Grant, Smiley Burnette. 5,165 ft. **U.** " Kine." June 18, 1936. Rel. date not fixed. BRITISH LION.

*Rembrandt. (Nov. 9.) Charles Laughton, Gertrude Lawrence, Elsa Lanchester. 7,650 ft. **A.** " Kine." Nov. 12, 1936. Rel. April 26, 1937. UNITED ARTISTS.

Remember Last Night. (Nov. 26.) Edward Arnold, Constance Cummings, Robert Young. 7,009 ft. **A.** " Kine." Dec. 5, 1935. Rel. May 18, 1936. UNIVERSAL.

Return of Jimmy Valentine, The. (Mar. 31.) Roger Pryor, Charlotte Henry, Robert Warwick. 6,570 ft. **U.** " Kine." April 2, 1936. Rel. July 27, 1936. BRITISH LION.

Return of Sophie Lang, The. (July 28.) Gertrude Michael, Guy Standing, Elizabeth Paterson. 5,755 ft. **A.** " Kine." July 30, 1936. Rel. Jan. 25, 1937. PARAMOUNT.

Revenge Rider. (June 10.) Tim McCoy, Billie Seward, Edward Earle. 5,040 ft. **U.** " Kine." June 18, 1936. Rel. Nov. 30, 1936. COLUMBIA.

Revolt of the Zombies. (June 18.) Dorothy Stone, Dean Jagger, Robert Noland. 6,111 ft. **A.** " Kine." June 25, 1936. Rel. Nov. 9, 1936. PATHE.

*Rhodes of Africa. (Mar. 16.) Walter Huston, Oscar Homolka, Peggy Ashcroft. 8,268 ft. **U.** " Kine." Mar. 19, 1936. Rel. Sept. 7, 1936. G.-B.D.

*Rhythm in the Air. (Sept. 1.) Jack Donohue, Tutta Rolf, Kitty Kelly. 6,438 ft. **U.** " Kine." Sept. 10, 1936. Rel. Feb. 8, 1937. Fox.

Rhythm on the Range. (Aug. 11.) Bing Crosby, Frances Farmer, Bob Burns. 7,670 ft. **U.** " Kine." Aug. 13, 1936. Rel. Jan. 18, 1937. PARA-MOUNT.

Rhythm on the River. (Feb. 12.) Frank McHugh, Patricia Ellis, Warren Hull. 6,136 ft. **U.** " Kine." Feb. 20, 1936. Rel. Aug. 17, 1936. FIRST NATIONAL.

Ride 'em Cowboy. (Aug. 4.) Buck Jones, Luana Walters, George Cooper. 5,144 ft. **U.** " Kine." Aug. 6, 1936. Rel. Oct. 26, 1936. GEN. F.D.

Riffraff. (Jan. 29.) Jean Harlow, Spencer Tracy, Una Merkel. 8,460 ft. **A.** " Kine." Feb. 6, 1936. Rel. April 6, 1936. M-G-M.

Ring Around the Moon. (Sept. 10.) Donald Cook, Erin O'Brien Moore, Ann Doran. 6,272 ft. **A.** " Kine." Sept. 17, 1936. Rel. Feb. 15, 1937. WARDOUR.

Rio Rattler. (May 14.) Tom Tyler, Marion Shilling, Charles Whittaker. 4,860 ft. **U.** " Kine." May 21, 1936. Rel. Aug. 17, 1936. GEN. F.D.

Road to Glory. (Oct. 1.) Fredric March, Warner Baxter, June Lang. 9,203 ft. **A.** " Kine."Oct. 8, 1936. Rel. Feb. 8, 1937. Fox.

Roaming Lady. (June 12.) Ralph Bellamy, Fay Wray. 6,187 ft. **U.** " Kine." June 18, 1936. Rel. Nov. 23, 1936. COLUMBIA.

Roaring Guns. (Sept. 2.) Tim McCoy, Rosalind Price, Wheeler Oakman. 5,750 ft. **U.** " Kine." Sept. 10, 1936. Rel. date not fixed. EQUITY.

*Robber Symphony, The. (April 16.) Hans Feher, Magda Sonja, Webster Booth. 12,600 ft. **U.** " Kine." April 23, 1936. Rel. date not fixed. CONCORDIA.

*Robber Symphony, The. (Nov. 6.) Hans Feher, Magda Sonja. 8,150 ft. **U.** " Kine." Nov. 12, 1936. Rel. date not fixed. CONCORDIA.

Robin Hood of El Dorado. (Mar. 18.) Warner Baxter, Ann Loring. 7,480 ft. **A.** " Kine." Mar. 26. 1936. Rel. July 27, 1936. M-G-M.

Rogues' Tavern, The. (June 10.) Wallace Ford, Marjorie Burns. 6,200 ft. **A.** " Kine." June 18, 1936. Rel. Sept. 14, 1936. PATHE.

Romeo and Juliet. (Nov. 16.) Norma Shearer, Leslie Howard, John Barrymore. 11,000 ft. **U.** " Kine." Oct. 15, 1936. Rel. Mar. 29, 1937. M-G-M.

Rose Marie. (Feb. 26.) Jeanette Macdonald, Nelson Eddy, Reginald Owen. 9,900 ft. **U.** " Kine." Mar. 5, 1936. Rel. Nov. 2, 1936. M.G-M.

Rose of the Rancho. (Jan. 30.) Gladys Swarthout, John Boles, Charles Bickford. 7,359 ft. **U.** " Kine." Feb. 6, 1936. Rel. April 20, 1936. PARAMOUNT.

*Royal Eagle. (June 5.) Nancy Burne, John Garrick, Edmund Willard. 6,212 ft. **A.** " Kine." June 11, 1936. Rel. Sept. 21, 1936. COLUMBIA.

*Ruling the Roost. (Dec. 2.) Bert Bailey. 8,411 ft. **U.** " Kine." Dec. 5, 1935. Rel. May 4, 1936. GEN. F.D.

*Sabotage. (Feb. 6.) Victor Varconi, Joan Maude, D. A. Clarke Smith. 6,300 ft. **A.** " Kine." Feb. 13, 1936. Rel. June 1, 1936. REUNION.

Sagebrush Troubadour, The. (Mar. 26.) Gene Autry, Smiley Burnette. 5,403 ft. **U.** " Kine." April 2, 1936. Rel. date not fixed. BRITISH LION.

San Francisco. (July 15.) Clark Gable, Jeanette Macdonald, Spencer Tracy. 10,380 ft. **A.** " Kine." July 23, 1936. Rel. Jan. 11, 1937. M-G-M.

Sans Famille. (Jan. 9.) Robert Lynen. 8,370 ft. **U.** " Kine." Jan. 9, 1936. Rel. Mar. 16, 1936. REUNION.

Satan Met a Lady. (Oct. 8.) Bette Davis, Warren William, Alison Skipworth. 6,768 ft. **A.** " Kine." Oct. 15, 1936. Rel. Mar. 22, 1937. FIRST NATIONAL.

Savoy Hotel 217. (Sept. 22.) Hans Albers, Brigitte Horney. 8,200 ft. **A.** " Kine." Oct. 1, 1936. Rel. date not fixed. G.-B.D.

Sea Spoilers. (Nov. 11.) John Wayne, Nan Grey, Russell Hicks. 5,664 ft. **U.** " Kine." Nov. 19, 1936. Rel. July 12, 1937. GENERAL F.D.

Second Bureau. (Jan. 7.) Jean Murat, Vera Korene. 9,000 ft. **A.** " Kine." Jan. 9, 1936. Rel. date not fixed. G.-B.D.

Second Wife. (Sept. 23.) Gertrude Michael, Walter Abel, Eric Rhodes. 5,363 ft. **A.** " Kine." Oct. 1, 1936. Rel. Jan. 11, 1937. RADIO.

***Secret Agent.** (May 5.) Madeleine Carroll, Peter Lorre, John Gielgud. 7,816 ft. **A.** " Kine." May 14, 1936. Rel. June 29, 1936. G.-B.D.

Secret Interlude. (July 1.) Robert Taylor, Loretta Young. 7,154 ft. **A.** " Kine." July 9, 1936. Rel. Nov. 16, 1936. Fox.

***Secret of Stamboul, The.** (Oct. 6.) Frank Vosper, Valerie Hobson, James Mason. 8,375 ft. **A.** " Kine." Oct. 15, 1936. Rel. April 19, 1937. GENERAL F.D.

***The Secret Voice.** (Feb. 18.) John Stuart, Diana Beaumont. 6,005 ft. **A.** " Kine." Feb. 20, 1936. Rel. June 29, 1936. PARAMOUNT.

***Servants All.** (April 14.) Robb Wilton, Ian Colin, Eve Lister. 3,053 ft. **U.** " Kine." April 16, 1936. Rel. July 20, 1936. Fox.

Seven Keys to Baldpate. (Jan. 8.) Gene Raymond, Margaret Callahan, Eric Blore. 6,120 ft. **U.** " Kine." Jan. 16, 1936. Rel. June 8, 1936. RADIO.

***Seven Sinners.** (June 24.) Edmund Lowe, Constance Cummings, Thomy Bourdelle. 6,286 ft. **A.** " Kine." July 2, 1936. Rel. Nov. 30, 1936. G.-B.D.

Shadows of the Orient. (April 8.) Regis Toomey, Esther Ralston, Sidney Blackmer. 6,267 ft. **A.** " Kine." April 16, 1936. Rel. June 29, 1936. PATHE.

Shadow of Silk Lennox, The. (June 12.) Lon Chaney, Jun., Jack Mulhall. 5,740 ft. **A.** " Kine." June 18, 1936. Rel. Sept. 7, 1936. VIKING.

Shakedown. (Sept. 21.) Lew Ayres, Joan Perry, Thurston Hall. 5,021 ft. **A.** " Kine." Sept. 24, 1936. Rel. Dec. 21, 1936. COLUMBIA.

***She Knew What She Wanted.** (May 11.) Betty Ann Davies, Fred Conyngham, Claude Dampier. 6,750 ft. **U.** " Kine." May 14, 1936. Rel. July 27, 1936. WARDOUR.

***She Shall Have Music.** (Nov. 28.) Jack Hylton and his Band, June Clyde, Claude Dampier. 6,310 ft. **U.** " Kine." Dec. 5, 1935. Rel. April 20, 1936. WARDOUR.

***Shipmates o' Mine.** (May 18.) John Garrick, Cynthia Stock, Mark Daly. 7,850 ft. **U.** " Kine." May 21, 1936. Rel. Oct. 26, 1936. BUTCHERS.

Show Boat. (June 12.) Irene Dunne, Paul Robeson, Allan James. 10,315 ft. **U.** " Kine." June 18, 1936. Rel. Jan. 25, 1937. GEN. F.D.

***Show Flat.** (Oct. 9.) Clifford Heatherley, Polly Ward, Anthony Hankey. 6,387 ft. **U.** " Kine." Oct. 15, 1936. Rel. Feb. 15, 1937. PARAMOUNT.

Silly Billies. (April 15.) Bert Wheeler, Robert Woolsey, Dorothy Lee. 5,763 ft. **U.** " Kine." April 23, 1936. Rel. Sept. 21, 1936. RADIO.

Silver Spurs. (April 17.) Buck Jones. 5,147 ft. **U.** " Kine." April 23, 1936. Rel. date not fixed. GEN. F.D.

Sing, Baby, Sing. (Oct. 13.) Alice Faye, Adolphe Menjou, Gregory Ratoff. 7,868 ft. **A.** "Kine." Oct. 22, 1936. Rel. Feb. 22, 1937. Fox.

Singende Jugende. (Oct. 5.) Martin Lojda, Julia Janssen. 7,830 ft. **U.** "Kine." Oct. 8, 1936. Rel. date not fixed. ACE.

Singing Kid, The. (May 12.) Al Jolson, Sybil Jason, Edward E. Horton. 7,714 ft. **U.** "Kine." May 21, 1936. Rel. Nov. 30, 1936. FIRST NATIONAL.

Singing Vagabond, The. (Mar. 23.) Gene Autry, Ann Rutherford. 5,184 ft. **U.** "Kine." Mar. 26, 1936. Rel. date not fixed. BRITISH LION.

Sinister House. (Mar. 18.) Preston Foster, Margaret Callahan. 6,249 ft. **A.** "Kine." Mar. 26, 1936. Rel. Aug. 24, 1936. RADIO.

Sins of Man. (June 11.) Jean Hersholt, Don Ameche, Allan Jenkins. 7,050 ft. **U.** "Kine." June 18, 1936. Rel. Dec. 14, 1936. Fox.

Skull and Crown. (Oct. 27.) Rin Tin Tin, Jun., Regis Toomey, Molly O Day. 5,280 ft. **U.** "Kine." Oct. 29, 1936. Rel. date not fixed. PATHE.

Sky Parade, The. (May 19.) William Gargan, Katherine de Mille, Kent Taylor. 6,288 ft. **U.** "Kine." May 21, 1936. Rel. Sept. 14, 1936. PARAMOUNT.

Small Town Girl. (May 6.) Janet Gaynor, Robert Young, Winnie Barnes. 9,474 ft. **A.** "Kine." May 14, 1936. Rel. Oct. 12, 1936. M-G-M.

Snowed Under. (May 26.) George Brent, Genevieve Tobin, Glenda Farrell. 5,714 ft. **A.** "Kine." June 4, 1936. Rel. Dec. 14, 1936. FIRST NATIONAL.

Soak the Rich. (Feb. 25.) Walter Connolly, John Howard. 6,695 ft. **A.** "Kine." Feb. 27, 1936. Rel. June 29, 1936. PARAMOUNT.

*Soft Lights and Sweet Music. (Feb. 12.) Ambrose and his Orchestra and a galaxy of radio stars. 7,782 ft. **U.** "Kine." Feb. 20, 1936. Rel. July 20, 1936. BRITISH LION.

*Someone at the Door. (May 4.) Aileen Marson, Billy Milton, Noah Beery. 6,737 ft. **A.** "Kine." May 7, 1936. Rel. Sept. 28, 1936. WARDOUR.

Son Comes Home, A. (Sept. 8.) Mary Boland, Julie Haydon, Donald Woods. 6,732 ft. **A.** "Kine." Sept. 10, 1936. Rel. Feb. 15, 1937. PARAMOUNT.

Song and Dance Man. (May 6.) Claire Trevor, Paul Kelly, Michael Whalen. 6,547 ft. **U.** "Kine." May 14, 1936. Rel. Aug. 10, 1936. Fox.

*Song of Freedom, The. (Aug. 17.) Paul Robeson, Elizabeth Welch, Esme Percy. 7,225 ft. **U.** "Kine." Aug. 20, 1936. Rel. date not fixed. BRITISH LION.

Song of the Saddle. (Jan. 31.) Dick Foran, Alma Lloyd. 5,266 ft. **U.** "Kine." Feb. 6, 1936. Rel. May 4, 1936. FIRST NATIONAL.

Sons o' Guns. (July 7.) Joe E. Brown, Joan Blondell, Eric Blore. 7,937 ft. **U.** "Kine." July 9, 1936. Rel. Dec. 21, 1936. FIRST NATIONAL.

So Red the Rose. (Dec. 4.) Margaret Sullavan, Walter Connolly, Randolph Scott. 7,440 ft. **U.** "Kine." Dec. 12, 1935. Rel. Mar. 2, 1936. PARAMOUNT.

*Southern Roses. (Sept. 29.) George Robey, Neil Hamilton, Gina Malo. 7,093 ft. **U.** "Kine." Oct. 8, 1936. Rel. May 10, 1937. GEN. F.N.

The Spanish Cape Mystery. (Jan. 9.) Donald Cook, Helen Twelvetrees. Frank Sheridan. 6,570 ft. **A.** "Kine." Jan. 16, 1936. Rel. May 25, 1936, BRITISH LION.

Special Investigator. (May 19.) Richard Dix, Margaret Callahan. 5,521 ft. **A.** "Kine." May 28, 1936. Rel. Oct. 12, 1936. RADIO.

Speed. (May 21.) James Stewart, Wendy Barrie, Ted Healy. 6,366 ft. **U.** "Kine." May 28, 1936. Rel. Aug. 31, 1936. M-G-M.

Spendthrift. (July 31.) Henry Fonda, Pat Paterson, Edward Brophy. 001 ft. **A.** "Kine." Aug. 6, 1936. Rel. Jan. 4, 1937. PARAMOUNT.

Splendour. (Jan. 7.) Miriam Hopkins, Joel McCrea, Helen Westley. 6,971 ft. **A.** " Kine." Jan. 2, 1936. Rel. Aug. 31, 1936. UNITED ARTISTS.

*Spy of Napoleon. (Sept. 9.) Richard Barthelmess, Dolly Haas, Francis L. Sullivan, Frank Vosper. 9,048 ft. **U.** " Kine." Sept. 17, 1936. Rel. Mar. 1, 1937. WARDOUR.

Stage Struck. (Nov. 4.) Dick Powell, Joan Blondell, Jeanne Madden. 8,415 ft. **U.** " Kine." Nov. 12, 1936. Rel. May 3, 1937. WARNER.

*Star Fell from Heaven, A. (June 9.) Joseph Schmidt, Florine McKinney, 6,383 ft. **U.** " Kine." June 18, 1936. Rel. Nov. 30, 1936. WARDOUR.

Star for a Night. (Oct. 7.) Claire Trevor, Jane Darwell. 6,884 ft. **U.** " Kine." Oct. 15, 1936. Rel. Mar. 22, 1937. FOX.

*Stars on Parade. (Jan. 2.) Debroy Somers and Band, Lucan and McShane, Robb Wilton. 7,360 ft. **U.** " Kine." Jan. 9, 1936. Rel. Sept. 7, 1936. BUTCHERS.

Stars Over Broadway. (Dec. 17.) James Melton, Pat O'Brien, Jean Muir. 8,145 ft. **U.** " Kine." Dec. 26, 1935. Rel. July 20, 1936. WARNER.

Stepping in Society. (July 2.) Louise Fazenda, Maude Eburne. 6,504 ft. **U.** " Kine." July 9, 1936. Rel. Nov. 9, 1936. A.B.F.D.

*Story of Captain Scott, The. (Sept. 2.) 5,400 ft. **U.** " Kine." Sept. 10, 1936. Rel. date not fixed. INTER CINE.

Story of Louis Pasteur. The, (Mar. 4.) Paul Muni, Josephine Hutchinson. 7,856 ft. **A.** " Kine." Mar. 12, 1936. Rel. Oct. 12, 1936. WARNER.

Straight from the Shoulder. (Sept. 15.) David Holt, Ralph Bellamy, Katherine Locke. 6,064 ft. **A.** " Kine." Sept. 17, 1936. Rel. Mar. 8, 1937. PARAMOUNT.

*Strange Cargo. (Mar. 6.) Moore Marriott, Kathleen Kelly. 6,131 ft. **A.** " Kine." Mar. 12, 1936. Rel. July 20, 1936. PARAMOUNT.

*Strangers on Honeymoon. (Nov. 16.) Constance Cummings, Noah Beery. 6,233 ft. **A.** " Kine." Nov. 19, 1936. Rel. Jan. 18, 1937. G.-B.D.

Streamline Express. (May 27.) Victor Jory, Evalyn Venable. 6,460 ft. **A.** " Kine." June 4, 1936. Rel. Aug. 31, 1936. A.B.F.D.

*Strike Me Lucky. (Jan. 20.) Roy Rene. 6,002 ft. **U.** " Kine." Jan. 23, 1936. Rel. May 18, 1936. GEN. F.D.

Strike Me Pink. (Feb. 17.) Eddie Cantor, Sally Eilers. 9,050 ft. **U.** " Kine." Feb. 20, 1936. Rel. Sept. 28, 1936. UNITED ARTISTS.

Student of Prague, The. (April 20.) Dorothea Wieck. 7,781 ft. **A.** " Kine." April 23, 1936. Rel. Sept. 1, 1936. DENNING FILMS.

*Such Is Life. (Oct. 30.) Gene Gerrard, Claude Dampier. 7,200 ft. **A.** " Kine." Nov. 5, 1936. Rel. April 5, 1937. NATIONAL PROV.

Suicide Club, The. (July 1.) Robert Montgomery, Rosalind Russell, 6,675 ft. **A.** " Kine." July 9, 1936. Rel. Oct. 26, 1936. M-G-M.

Suicide Squad. (April 17.) Norman Foster, Joyce Compton. 5,356 ft. **U.** " Kine." April 23, 1936. Rel. Aug. 10, 1936. PATHE.

Sunset of Power. (May 14.) Buck Jones, Dorothy Dix, C. B. Middleton. 5,196 ft. **U.** " Kine." May 21, 1936. Rel. Aug. 3, 1936. GEN. F.D.

Sunset Range. (April 28.) Hoot Gibson. 4,730 ft. **U.** " Kine." April 30, 1936. Rel. date not fixed. A.B.F.D.

*Sunshine Ahead. (Jan. 16.) Jack Payne and band, and other well-known Radio Stars. 5,859 ft. **U.** " Kine." Jan. 23, 1936. Rel. July 6, 1936. UNIVERSAL.

Sutter's Gold. (June 18,) Edward Arnold, Binnie Barnes, Lee Tracy. 8,554 ft. **A.** " Kine." June 25, 1936. Rel. Nov. 2, 1936. GEN. F.D.

Suzy. (Aug. 12.) Jean Harlow, Franchot Tone, Cary Grant. 8,390 ft. **A.** " Kine." Aug. 20, 1936. Rel. Jan. 18, 1937. M-G-M.

Sweeney Todd, The Demon Barber of Fleet Street. (Mar. 2.) Tod Slaughter, Eve Lister, Bruce Seton. 6,111 ft. **A.** " Kine." Mar. 5, 1936. Rel. June 29, 1936. M-G-M.

Sweet Aloes. (Sept. 8.) Kay Francis, George Brent, Roland Young. 7,913 ft. **A.** "Kine." Sept. 17, 1936. Rel. Mar. 22, 1937. WARNER.

Sweet Surrender. (Dec. 5.) Frank Parker, Tamara, Helen Lynd. 7,131 ft. **U.** "Kine." Dec. 12, 1935. Rel. May 25, 1936. GEN. F. D.

Swell Head. (Mar. 20.) Wallace Ford, Dickie Moore. 5,354 ft. **U.** "Kine." Mar. 26, 1936. Rel. July 27, 1936. COLUMBIA.

Swifty. (Sept. 4.) Hoot Gibson, George F. Hayes, June Gala. 5,600 ft. **A.** "Kine." Sept. 10, 1936. Rel. date not fixed. INDEPENDENT F.D.

Swing Time. (Sept. 24.) Fred Astaire, Ginger Rogers, Helen Broderick. 8,550 ft. **U.** "Kine." Oct. 1, 1936. Rel. Dec. 28, 1936. RADIO.

*Sword to Sword. (Mar. 13.) 7,740 ft. **A.** "Kine." Mar. 19, 1936. Rel. Aug. 10, 1936. FIRST NATIONAL.

Sworn Enemy. (Aug. 5.) Robert Young, Florence Rice, Joseph Calleia. 6,454 ft. **A.** "Kine." Aug. 13, 1936. Rel. Nov. 30, 1936. M-G-M.

Sylvia Scarlett. (Feb. 25.) Katherine Hepburn, Cary Grant, Edmund Gwenn. 8,100 ft. **A.** "Kine." Mar. 5, 1936. Rel. June 8, 1936. RADIO.

Sylvia und ihr Chauffeur. (Sept. 7.) Olga Tschechowa, Wolf Albach Betty. 7,340 ft. **U.** "Kine." Sept. 10, 1936. Rel. date not fixed. G.-B.D.

A Tale of Two Cities. (Jan. 30.) Ronald Colman, Elizabeth Allan, 11,351 ft. **A.** "Kine." Feb. 6, 1936. Rel. Oct. 5, 1936. M-G-M.

Tango. (Sept. 9.) Marion Nixon, Chick Chandler, Matty Kemp. 6,340 ft. **A.** "Kine." Sept. 17, 1936. Rel. Feb. 8, 1937. WARDOUR.

*Tenth Man, The. (Aug. 12.) John Lodge, Antoinette Cellier. 6,037 ft. **A.** "Kine." Aug. 20, 1936. Rel. Jan. 25, 1937. WARDOUR.

Texas Jack. (Oct. 23.) Jack Perrin, Jayne Regan, Nelson McDowell. 5,160 ft. **U.** "Kine." Oct. 29, 1936. Rel. date not fixed. EQUITY.

Texas Rangers, The (Oct. 1.) Jack Oakie, Fred MacMurray, Jean Parker. 8,813 ft. **A.** "Kine." Oct. 8, 1936. Rel. Feb. 15, 1937. PARAMOUNT.

Thank You, Jeeves. (Oct. 21.) Arthur Treacher, Virginia Field, David Niven. 5,135 ft. **U.** "Kine." Oct. 20, 1936. Rel. Feb. 15, 1937. FOX.

These Three. (April 22.) Miriam Hopkins, Merle Oberon, Joel McCrea. 8,466 ft. **A.** "Kine." April 30, 1936. Rel. Oct. 26, 1936. UNITED ARTISTS.

*They Didn't Know. (April 24.) Eve Grey, Leslie Perrins, Maidie Hope. 6,082 ft. **A.** "Kine." April 30, 1936. Rel. July 20, 1936. M-G-M.

They Met in a Taxi. (Oct. 22.) Chester Norris, Fay Wray. 6,166 ft. **U.** "Kine." Oct. 29, 1936. Rel. April 12, 1937. COLUMBIA.

*Things to Come. (Feb. 20.) Raymond Massey, Ralph Richardson, Margaretta Scott. 10,000 ft. **U.** "Kine." Feb. 27, 1936. Rel. Sept. 14, 1936. UNITED ARTISTS.

Thirteen Hours by Air. (April 21.) Fred MacMurray, Joan Bennett, Zasu Pitts. 6,971 ft. **U.** "Kine." April 23, 1936. Rel. July 6, 1936. PARAMOUNT.

36 Hours to Kill. (Sept. 24.) Biran Donlevy, Gloria Stuart, Douglas Fowley. 5,908 ft. **A.** "Kine." Oct. 1, 1936. Rel. Mar. 8, 1937. FOX.

*This Green Hell. (Mar. 20.) Edward Rigby, Sybil Grove. 6,450 ft. **A.** "Kine." Mar. 26, 1936. Rel. Aug. 31, 1936. RADIO.

This'll Make You Whistle. (Nov. 12.) Jack Buchanan, Elsie Randolph. 7,000 ft. **A.** "Kine." Nov. 19, 1936. Rel. April 19, 1937. GEN. F.D.

*This Motoring. (Mar. 17.) Sir Stenson Cooke. 4,014 ft. **U.** "Kine." Mar. 19, 1936. Rel. June 8, 1936. ACE.

This is the Land. (Mar. 5.) 6,092 ft. **U.** "Kine." Mar. 12, 1936. Rel. date not fixed. BRITISH LION.

*Thoroughbred. (July 15.) Helen Twelvetrees, Frank Leighton. 6,122 ft. **U.** "Kine." July 23, 1936. Rel. Dec. 7, 1936. WARDOUR.

Thousand Dollars a Minute. (Jan. 1.) Roger Pryor, Leila Hyams. 6,300 ft. **U.** "Kine." Jan. 9, 1936. Rel. June 8, 1936. A.B.F.D,

Three Cheers for Love. (July 21.) Eleanore Whitney, Robert Cummings, William Frawley. 5,453 ft. **U.** " Kine." July 23, 1936. Rel. Nov. 30, 1936. PARAMOUNT.

Three Godfathers, The. (Mar. 19.) Chester Morris, Lewis Stone. 7,279 ft. **A.** " Kine." Mar. 26, 1936. Rel. June 22, 1936. M-G-M.

Three Live Ghosts. (Feb. 5.) Richard Arlen, Claude Allister. 5,477 ft. **A.** " Kine." Feb. 13, 1936. Rel. April 20, 1936. M-G-M.

Three Married Men. (Sept. 29.) Roscoe Karns, Mary Brian, William Frawley. 5,497 ft. **A.** " Kine." Oct. 1, 1936. Rel. Mar. 1, 1937. PARAMOUNT.

*Three Maxims, The. (June 30.) Anna Neagle, Tullio Carminati, Leslie Banks. 7,800 ft. **U.** " Kine." July 2, 1936. Rel. Feb. 1, 1937. GEN. F.D

The Three Musketeers. (Dec. 2.) Walter Abel, Paul Lukas, Margot Grahame. 8,370 ft. **U.** " Kine." Dec. 5, 1935. Rel. April 20, 1936. RADIO.

Three on the Trail. (Sept. 4.) William Boyd, Muriel Evans. 6,015 ft. **U.** " Kine." Sept. 10, 1936. Rel. Feb. 8, 1937. PARAMOUNT.

Three Wise Guys. (June 3.) Robert Young, Betty Furness. 6,654 ft. **A.** " Kine." June 11, 1936. Rel. Oct. 19, 1936. M-G-M.

*Ticket of Leave. (Jan. 3.) Dorothy Boyd, John Clements. 6,295 ft. **A.** " Kine." Jan. 9, 1936. Rel. May 25, 1936. PARAMOUNT.

Ticket to Paradise. (Nov. 12.) Roger Pryor, Wendy Barrie, Claude Gillingwater. 6,053 ft. **U.** " Kine." Nov. 19, 1936. Rel. Jan. 11, 1937. A.B.F.D.

Till We Meet Again. (June 16.) Herbert Marshall, Gertrude Michael. 6,432 ft. **U.** " Kine." June 18, 1936. Rel. Oct. 12, 1936. PARAMOUNT.

Timber War. (May 20.) Kermit Maynard, Lucille Lund, Wheeler Oakman. 4,600 ft. **U.** " Kine." May 28, 1936. Rel. Oct. 26, 1936. BUTCHER'S.

Timothy's Quest. (Feb. 21.) Elizabeth Patterson, Eleanore Whitney. 5,815 ft. **U.** " Kine." Feb. 27, 1936. Rel. May 4, 1936. PARAMOUNT.

To Beat the Band. (Feb. 19.) Helen Broderick, Hugh Herbert, Roger Pryor. 6,000 ft. **A.** " Kine." Feb. 27, 1936. Rel. June 29, 1936. RADIO.

To Mary—With Love. (Aug. 26.) Warner Baxter, Myrna Loy, Ian Hunter. 8,267 ft. **A.** " Kine." Sept. 3, 1936. Rel. Jan. 4, 1937. Fox.

*To-morrow We Live. (Oct. 7.) Godfrey Tearle, Haidee Wright, Renee Gadd. 6,491 ft. **A.** " Kine." Oct. 15, 1936. Rel. April 12, 1937. A.B.F.D.

Tonto Kid, The. (April 17.) Rex Bell, Ruth Mix, Theodore Lorch. 5,300 ft. **U.** " Kine." April 23, 1936. Rel. June 1, 1936. EXCLUSIVE.

*To Catch a Thief. (June 29.) John Garrick, Mary Lawson. 6,000 ft. **U.** " Kine." July 2, 1936. Rel. Nov. 16, 1936. RADIO.

Too Many Parents. (April 28.) Frances Farmer, George Ernest. 6,598 ft. **U.** " Kine." April 30, 1936. Rel. Aug. 31, 1936. PARAMOUNT.

Too Tough to Kill. (Dec. 13.) Victory Jory, Sally O'Neill, Robert Gleckler. 5,174 ft. **U.** " Kine." Dec. 19, 1935. Rel. April 27, 1936. COLUMBIA.

*A Touch of the Moon. (Feb. 19.) John Garrick, Dorothy Boyd, David Horne. 6,024 ft. **U.** Kine." Feb. 27, 1936. Rel. July 27, 1936. RADIO.

Tough Guy. (Feb. 18.) Jackie Cooper, Joseph Calleia, Rin-Tin-Tin, Jr. 6,816 ft. **A.** " Kine." Feb. 20, 1936. Rel. May 25, 1936. M-G-M.

Trail of the Lonesome Pine, The. (April 16.) Sylvia Sidney, Henry Fonda, Fred MacMurray. 8,876 ft. **U.** " Kine." April 23, 1936. Rel. Sept. 28, 1936. PARAMOUNT.

Trapped. (Nov. 3.) Rin-Tin-Tin, Jun., Grant Withers, Monte Blue. 4,900 ft. **U.** " Kine." Nov. 5, 1936. Rel. Feb. 8, 1937. PATHE.

Trapped by Wireless. (June 9.) Lew Ayres, Florence Rice, Murray Alper. 4,980 ft. **A.** "Kine." June 11, 1936. Rel. Oct. 5, 1936. COLUMBIA.

Treachery Rides the Range. (April 16.) Dick Foran. 5,129 ft. **U.** " Kine." April 23, 1936. Rel. Aug. 10, 1936. WARNER.

*Tropical Trouble. (Oct. 7.) Douglass Montgomery, Betty Ann Davies, 6,325 ft. **A.** " Kine." Oct. 15, 1936. Rel. May 31, 1937. GEN. F.D.

Trouble Busters. (Mar. 18.) Jack Hoxie, Kaye Edwards. 4,900 ft. **U.** " Kine." Mar. 26, 1936. Rel. date not fixed. EQUITY.

*Troubled Waters. (Feb. 4.) Virginia Cherrill, Alastair Sim, James Mason. 6,396 ft. **A.** " Kine." Feb. 6, 1936. Rel. June 22, 1936. Fox.

Trust the Navy. (Dec. 17.) Lupino Lane, Nancy Burne. 6,490 ft. **U.** " Kine." Dec. 19, 1935. Rel. May 4, 1936. COLUMBIA.

*Tudor Rose. (April 30.) Nova Pilbeam, Cedric Hardwicke, John Mills. 7,077 ft. **U.** " Kine." May 7, 1936. Rel. Aug. 24, 1936. G.-B.D.

*Tugboat Princess. (June 10.) Edith Fellows, Walter C. Kelly. 6,150 ft. **U.** " Kine." June 18, 1936. Rel. Sept. 14, 1936. COLUMBIA.

*Twelve Good Men. (Mar. 27.) Henry Kendall, Nancy O'Neill. 5,821 ft. **A.** " Kine." April 2, 1936. Rel. Aug. 17, 1936. WARNER.

*Twenty-one To-day. (Mar. 3.) Arthur Prince, Frank Titterton. 3,076 ft. **U.** " Kine." Mar. 5, 1936. Rel. date not fixed. M-G-M.

*Twice Branded. (Jan. 7.) Robert Rendel, James Mason, Lucille Lisle. 6,400 ft. **U.** " Kine." Jan. 9, 1936. Rel. May 11, 1936. RADIO.

Two-Fisted Gentleman. (Oct. 20.) James Dunn, Muriel Evans. 5,642 ft. **U.** " Kine." Oct. 22, 1936. Rel. Jan. 18, 1937. COLUMBIA.

Two in a Crowd. (Sept. 10.) Joan Bennett, Joel McCrea. 7,393 ft. **U.** " Kine." Sept. 17, 1936. Rel. Mar. 15, 1937. GEN. F.D.

Two in Revolt. (May 19.) John Arledge, Louise Latimer, Moroni Olsen. 5,812 ft. **U.** " Kine." May 21, 1936. Rel. Oct. 19, 1936. RADIO.

Two in the Dark. (Feb. 18.) Walter Abel, Margot Grahame, Wallace Ford. 6,663 ft. **A.** " Kine." Feb. 20, 1936. Rel. July 13, 1936. RADIO.

*Two on a Doorstep. (April 29.) Kay Hammond, Harold French, 6,435 it. **A.** "Kine." May 7, 1936. Sept. 14, Rel. 1936. PARAMOUNT.

*Two's Company. (April 30.) Ned Sparks, Gordon Harker, Mary Brian. 6,400 ft. **U.** " Kine." May 7, 1936. Rel. Oct. 12, 1936. UNITED ARTISTS.

*Under Cover. (Jan. 22.) Charles Starrett, Adrienne Dore, Kenneth Duncan. 5,425 ft. **A.** " Kine." Jan. 30, 1936. Rel. April 6, 1936. M-G-M.

*Under Proof. (Feb. 27.) Betty Stockfeld, Tyrrell Davis, Judy Kelly. 4,570 ft. **U.** " Kine." Mar. 5, 1936. Rel. July 20, 1936. Fox.

Undersea Kingdom. (Oct. 8.) Ray Corrigan, Lois Wilde, Monte Blue. 12 eps. **U.** " Kine." Oct. 15, 1936. Rel. date not fixed. BRITISH LION.

Under Two Flags. (May 27.) Ronald Colman, Claudette Colbert, Victor McLaglen. 9,990 ft. **A.** " Kine." June 4, 1936. Rel. Nov. 2, 1936. Fox.

Unguarded Hour. (April 29.) Loretta Young, Franchot Tone, Lewis Stone. 7,817 it. **A.** " Kine." May 7, 1936. Rel. Aug. 10, 1936. M-G-M.

*Unlucky Jim. (May 19.) Bob Stevens, Tony Jones. 4,000 ft. **U.** " Kine." May 21, 1936. Rel. Oct. 26, 1936. RADIO.

Valiant is the Word for Carrie. (Oct. 26.) Gladys George, Arline Judge, John Howard. 9,792 ft. **A.** " Kine," Oct. 22, 1936. Rel. May 17, 1937. PARAMOUNT.

Valley cf Gold, The. (Mar. 11.) Jack Hoxie, Alice Day. 4,700 ft. **U.** " Kine." Mar. 19, 1936. Rel. date not fixed. EQUITY.

*Vandergilt Diamond Mystery, The. (Jan. 8.) Elizabeth Astell, Bruce Seton, Hilary Pritchard. 5,425 ft. **A.** " Kine." Jan. 16, 1936. Rel. May 18, 1936. RADIO.

*Vanity. (Feb. 27.) Jane Cain, Percy Marmont, John Counsell. 6,942 ft. **U.** " Kine." Mar. 5, 1936. Rel. date not fixed. COLUMBIA.

*Variety Parade. (Nov. 19.) Mrs. Jack Hylton and her Boys, Noni and Partner, Teddy Brown. 7,500 ft. **U.** " Kine." Nov. 26, 1936. Rel. April 5, 1937. BUTCHER'S.

*Vasant Bengali. (Feb. 14.) 7,799 ft. **A.** " Kine." Feb. 20, 1936. Rel. July 27, 1936. FIRST NATIONAL.

Veille d'Armes. (Mar. 4.) Annabelle, Victor Francen. 8,800 ft. **A.** " Kine." Mar. 19, 1936. Rel. date not fixed. CINEMA HOUSE.

Via Pony Express. (Mar. 12.) Jack Hoxie, Marceline Day. 5,100 ft. **U.** " Kine." Mar. 19, 1936. Rel. date not fixed. EQUITY.

Voice cf Bugle Ann, The. (Mar. 13.) Lionel Barrymore, Maureen O'Sullivan, Eric Linden. 6,460 ft. **A.** " Kine." Mar. 19, 1936. Rel. June 15, 1936. M-G-M.

*Voice of Ireland. (Mar. 27.) Victor Haddick, Richard Hayward, 4,400 ft. **U.** " Kine." April 2, 1936. Rel. date not fixed. INTER. CINE.

*A Wager in Love. (Feb. 21.) 7,703 ft. **U.** " Kine." Feb. 27, 1936. Rel. Oct. 5, 1936. WARNER.

Walking Dead, The. (April 22.) Boris Karloff, Edmund Gwenn. Marguerite Churchill. 5,912 ft. **A.** " Kine." April 30, 1936. Rel. Dec. 16, 1936. FIRST NATIONAL.

Walking on Air. (Sept. 22.) Ann Sothern, Gene Raymond. 6,248 ft. **U.** " Kine." Oct. 1, 1936. Rel. Feb.´ 1, 1937. RADIO.

Wanted Men. (April 17.) Russell Hopton, Frankie Darro. 5,623 ft. **U.** " Kine." April 23, 1936. Rel. July, 1936. INDEPENDENT F.D.

Way of the West. (Oct. 28.) Wally Wales, Bobbie Parker, Myrla Bratton. 4,920 ft. " Kine." Nov. 5, 1936. Rel. date not fixed. EQUITY.

Wedding Group. (Mar. 4.) Fay Compton, Barbara Greene, Patric Knowles. 6,226 ft. **U.** " Kine." Mar. 12, 1936. Rel. Aug. 10, 1936. FOX.

Wedding Present. (Nov. 3.) Joan Bennett, Cary Grant. 7,322 ft. **U.** " Kine." Nov. 5, 1936. Rel. April 12, 1937. PARAMOUNT.

*Wednesday's Luck. (May 22.) Susan Bligh, Patrick Barr. 6,213 ft. **A.** " Kine." May 28, 1936. Rel. Sept. 7, 1936. PARAMOUNT.

We're Only Human. (Feb. 19.) Preston Foster, Jane Wyatt. 6,162 ft. **A.** " Kine." Feb. 27, 1936. Rel. July 6, 1936. RADIO.

Western Courage. (Jan. 30.) Ken Maynard, Geneva Mitchell, Tarzan. 5,189 ft. **U.** " Kine." Feb. 6, 1936. Rel. Aug. 10, 1936. COLUMBIA.

Westerner, The. (Aug. 27.) Tim McCoy, Marion Shilling. 5,077 ft. **U.** " Kine." Sept. 3, 1936. Rel. Dec. 7, 1936. COLUMBIA.

We Who are about to Die. (Nov. 12.) John Beal, Ann Dvorak. 7,292 ft. **A.** " Kine." Nov. 19, 1936. Rel. April 19, 1937. RADIO.

*What the Puppy Said. (Feb. 7.) Woggles, Moore Marriott, Dorothy Vernon. 3,568 ft. **U.** "Kine." Feb. 6, 1936. Rel. July 20, 1936. BUTCHERS.

When a Man's a Man. (Jan. 3.) George O'Brien, Dorothy Wilson, Paul Kelly. 6,300 ft. **A.** " Kine." Jan. 9, 1936. Rel. June 1, 1936. A.B.F.D.

*When Knights Were Bold. (Feb. 19.) Jack Buchanan, Fay Wray, 6,848 ft. **U.** "Kine." Feb. 27, 1936. Rel. Sept. 14, 1936. GENERAL F.D.

When Lightning Strikes. (July 8.) Lightning, Francis X. Bushman, Jun. 5,110 ft. **U.** " Kine." July 16, 1936. Rel. date not fixed. EQUITY.

*When the Kellys Rode. (Feb. 7.) Hay Simpson, John Appleton, 7,137 ft. **U.** "Kine." Feb. 13, 1936. Rel. July 13, 1936. FIRST NATIONAL.

When We Look Back. (Jan. 6.) Ben Lyon, Helen Twelvetrees, Rod la Rocque. 6,281 ft. **A.** " Kine." Jan. 9, 1936. Rel. June 8, 1936. BRITISH LION.

*Where's Sally? (April 28.) Gene Gerrard, Reginald Purdell, Claude Hulbert. 6,429 ft. **A.** " Kine." May 7, 1936. Rel. Sept. 28. 1936. FIRST NATIONAL.

*Where There's a Will. (June 16.) Will Hay, Hartley Power, Gina Malo. 7,233 ft. **A.** " Kine." June 25, 1936. Rel. Aug. 10, 1936. G.-B.D.

Whipsaw. (Jan. 1.) Myrna Loy, Spencer Tracy, Harvey Stephens. 7,245 ft. **A.** "Kine." Jan. 9, 1936. Rel. April 27, 1936. M-G-M.

White Angel, The. (July 16.) Kay Francis, Ian Hunter, Donald Crisp 8,370 ft. **A.** "Kine." July 23, 1936. Rel. Jan. 18, 1937. WARNER.

White Fang. (Aug. 20.) Michael Whalen, Jean Muir, Slim Summerville. 6,658 ft. **U.** "Kine." Aug. 27, 1936. Rel. Nov. 30, 1936. Fox.

*Whom the Gods Love. (Feb. 14.) Victoria Hopper, John Loder. 7,445 ft. **U.** "Kine." Feb. 20, 1936. Rel. Oct. 12, 1936. A.B.F.D.

Widow from Monte Carlo, The. (Mar. 24.) Warren William, Dolores del Rio, Warren Hymer. 5,426 ft. **U.** "Kine." Mar. 26, 1936. Rel. Sept. 7, 1936. FIRST NATIONAL.

A Wife or Two. (Jan. 10.) Henry Kendall, Nancy Burne. 5,795 ft. **A.** "Kine." Jan. 16, 1936. Rel. June 22, 1936. BRITISH LION.

Wife Versus Secretary. (April 8.) Clark Gable, Myrna Loy, Jean Harlow. 7,874 ft. **A.** "Kine." April 16, 1936. Rel. Sept. 14, 1936. M-G-M.

Wilderness Mail. (Dec. 16.) Kermit Maynard. 5,074 ft. **A.** "Kine." Dec. 19, 1935. Rel. Sept. 7, 1936. BUTCHER.

*Wings Over Africa. (Sept. 23.) Joan Gardner, Ian Colin. 5,700 ft. **U.** "Kine." Oct. 1, 1936. Rel. Jan. 18, 1937. RADIO.

Without Orders. (Nov. 10.) Sally Eilers, Robert Armstrong, Vinton Haworth. 5,770 ft. **A.** "Kine." Nov. 19, 1936. Rel. April 26, 1937. RADIO.

Witness Chair, The. (May 20.) Ann Harding, Walter Abel. 5,760 ft. **A.** "Kine." May 28, 1936. Rel. Oct. 26, 1936. RADIO.

Wives Never Know. (Oct. 20.) Charlie Ruggles, Mary Boland, Adolphe Menjou. 6,574 ft. **A.** "Kine." Oct. 22, 1936. Rel. Mar. 22, 1937. PARAMOUNT.

Wolf Riders, The. (Jan. 23.) Jack Perrin, Lillian Gilmore. 5,110 ft. **U.** "Kine." Jan. 30, 1936. Rel. date not fixed. EQUITY BRITISH.

*Wolf's Clothing. (Mar. 17.) Claude Hulbert, Gordon Harker, 7,267 ft. **A.** "Kine." Mar. 26, 1936. Rel. July 20, 1936. GEN. F.D.

*Woman Alone, A. (July 24.) Anna Sten, Henry Wilcoxon. 7,094 ft. **A.** "Kine." July 30, 1936. Rel. Jan. 25, 1937. UNITED ARTISTS.

Woman of Destiny. (June 11.) Lila Lee, Creighton Chaney. 5,700 ft. **A.** "Kine." June 17, 1936. Rel. date not fixed. EQUITY BRITISH.

Woman Rebels, A. (Nov. 11.) Katharine Hepburn, Herbert Marshall, Elisabeth Allan. 8,100 ft. **A.** "Kine." Nov. 19, 1936. Rel. Mar. 29, 1937. RADIO.

Woman Trap. (Mar. 3.) Gertrude Michael, George Murphy, 5,719 ft. **A.** "Kine." Mar. 5, 1936. Rel. June 1, 1936. PARAMOUNT.

*Women are Dangerous. (May 28.) Rochelle Hudson, John Warburton. 6,122 ft. **A.** "Kine." June 4, 1936. Rel. Nov. 23, 1936. WARDOUR.

Women are Trouble. (July 9.) Stuart Erwin, Paul Kelly, Florence Rice. 5,250 ft. **A.** "Kine." July 16, 1936. Rel. Mar. 18, 1937. M-G-M.

Yellow Dust. (Mar. 19.) Richard Dix, Leila Hyams. 6,100 ft. **U.** "Kine." Mar. 26, 1936. Rel. Aug. 3, 1936. RADIO.

Yellcwstone. (Oct. 9.) Henry Hunter, Judith Barrett, Alan Hale. 5,692 ft. **A.** "Kine." Oct. 15, 1936. Rel. June 28, 1937. GEN. F.D.

You Must Get Married. (Nov. 13.) Frances Day, Robertson Hare, Neil Hamilton. 6,100 ft. **A.** "Kine." Nov. 19, 1936. Rel. June 14, 1937. GEN. F.D.

Yours for the Asking. (Aug. 28.) George Raft, Dolores Costello Barrymore, Ida Lupino. 6,325 ft. **A.** "Kine." Sept. 3, 1936. Rel. Dec. 7, 1936. PARAMOUNT.

Your Uncle Dudley. (Jan. 16.) Edward Everett Horton, Lois Wilson, Alan Dinehart. 6,165 ft. **U.** "Kine." Jan. 23, 1936. Rel. June 8, 1936. Fox.

KAY
LABORATORIES

SPECIAL
ANNOUNCEMENT
P.T.O.

(K)

OXFORD ROAD
FINSBURY PARK
N. 4
TELEPHONE: ARC 3050

KAY
(WEST END)
LABORATORIES

22, SOHO SQUARE
W.I
TELEPHONE: GER   5092

OPENING EARLY 1937

RENTERS' OFFERS OF THE YEAR.

Subjects Trade shown by Renting Houses from December 1935 to November 1936,
For Release Dates and other details see Trade Shown Films of 1936, on page 59 and
following.

Films under the heading of UNIVERSAL were trade shown by that company, but
have since been taken over for release by GENERAL FILM DISTRIBUTORS

Films under the heading of TWICKENHAM FILM DISTRIBUTORS were trade
shown by that company, but have since been taken over for release by WARDOUR.

A.B.F.D.

Jan.	1.	Thousand Dollars a Minute, A.
,,	3.	Phantom Empire, The.
,,	3.	When a Man's a Man.
,,	24.	Cheer Up.
,,	27.	Eventful Journey.
,,	29.	Excuse My Glove.
Feb.	13.	Queen of Hearts.
,,	14.	Whom the Gods Love.
Mar.	23.	Old Homestead, The.
,,	26.	Laughing Irish Eyes.
,,	27.	Annie Doesn't Live Here.
April	28.	Sunset Range.
,,	29.	Mystery Mountain.
May	1.	Laburnum Grove.
,,	14.	Marines Have Landed, The.
,,	28.	Streamline Express.
June	5.	One Good Turn.
,,	11.	Everything is Rhythm.
July	2.	Stepping in Society.
,,	7.	Calling the Tune.
,,	10.	Adventures of Rex and Rinty.
Aug	24.	Lonely Road.
,,	25.	Beloved Vagabond, The.
,,	26.	Keep Your Seats, Please.
Sept.	22.	Born to Gamble.
,,	23.	Dizzy Dames.
Oct.	6.	Girl from Mandalay, The.
,,	7.	To-morrow We Live.
,,	19.	The Clutching Hand.
,,	27.	Radio Lover.
,,	28.	House of the Spaniard, The
Nov.	9.	Navy Born.
,,	10.	O'Malley of the Mounted.
,,	12.	Ticket to Paradise.
,,	13.	In His Steps.

Ace.

Feb.	5.	East is West.
Mar.	17.	This Motoring.
June	4.	Black Journey.
Sept.	7.	Immortal Swan, The.
,,	28.	Digging for Gold.
Oct.	5.	Singende Jugende.
,,	19.	Full Steam.
Nov.	9.	Bottle Party.

A.P.D.

Jan.	27.	On Top of the World.
Feb.	17.	Pals of the Prairie.
Mar.	2.	Happy Days are Here Again.
April	17.	Crashing Through Danger.
May	22.	Men of Yesterday.
July	21.	Last Waltz, The.
Nov.	6.	Hearts of Humanity.

British Lion.

Jan.	6.	When We Look Back.
,,	7.	Jury's Evidence.
,,	9.	Spanish Cape Mystery, The.
,,	10.	Racing Luck.
,,	10.	Wife or Two, A.

Jan.	14.	Melody Trail.
,,	14.	Forced Landing.
Feb.	12.	Soft Lights and Sweet Music.
Mar.	5.	This is the Land.
,,	23.	Singing Vagabond, The.
,,	24.	New Frontier, The.
,,	25.	Burning Gold.
,,	26.	Sagebrush Troubadour, The.
,,	27.	Oregon Trail, The.
,,	30.	Dancing Feet.
,,	31.	Return of Jimmy Valentine, The.
May	25.	Frankie and Johnnie.
June	3.	House of a Thousand Candles, The.
,,	4.	Interrupted Honeymoon.
,,	8.	Harvester, The.
,,	10.	Red River Valley.
,,	12.	Darkest Africa.
Aug.	17.	Song of Freedom.
,,	18.	Federal Agent.
,,	19.	Happy Family, The.
,,	20.	Hearts in Bondage.
,,	21.	Lawless Nineties, The.
Oct.	5.	Follow Your Heart.
,,	6.	Comin' Round the Mountain.
,,	7.	It's You I Want.
,,	8.	Undersea Kingdom, The.
,,	9.	Gentleman from Louisiana, The.
Nov.	24.	Sporting Love.
,,	25.	One For All.
,,	26.	Oh, Susanna.
,,	26.	Sitting on the Moon.
,,	27.	Lady Reporter.

Butcher.

Dec.	16.	Wilderness Mail.
Jan.	2.	Stars on Parade.
Feb.	7.	What the Puppy Said.
Mar.	3.	King of Hearts.
April	1.	Code of the Mounted.
,,	21.	Melody of My Heart.
May	18.	Shipmates of Mine.
,,	20.	Timber War.
July	7.	Midnight Phantom.
,,	8.	Annie Laurie.
Sept.	14.	Red Blood of Courage.
,,	15.	Love Up the Pole.
Oct.	23.	Circus Love.
Nov.	19.	Variety Parade.

Columbia.

Dec.	3.	Heir to Trouble.
,,	13.	Too Tough to Kill.
,,	16.	Case of the Missing Man, The.
,,	17.	Trust the Navy.
,,	17.	If you Could Only Cook.
,,	19.	Crime and Punishment.
,,	20.	One Way Ticket.
Jan.	30.	Fighting Shadows.
,,	30.	Western Courage.
Feb.	14.	Prison Breaker.
,,	14.	Gallant Defender.

Feb.	17.	Escape from Devil's Island.
,,	19.	Lady of Secrets.
,,	20.	Calling of Dan Matthews, The.
,,	21.	It Happened One Night. (Reissue).
,,	24.	Panic on the Air.
,,	26.	Lone Wolf Returns, The.
,,	27.	Vanity.
,,	27.	Champagne for Breakfast.
Mar.	16.	Chinese Cabaret.
,,	16.	Days of Destiny.
,,	16.	Hot News.
,,	18.	Dangerous Intrigue.
,,	19.	Heritage.
,,	20.	Swell Head.
,,	20.	Lucky Fugitives.
,,	20.	Dirigible.
,,	23.	Hell Ship Morgan.
,,	24.	Music Goes Round, The.
,,	25.	Don't Gamble with Love.
April	29.	Mr. Deeds Goes to Town.
June	2.	King Steps Out, The.
,,	5.	Royal Eagle.
,,	9.	Trapped by Wireless.
,,	10.	Tugboat Princess.
,,	10.	Revenge Rider.
,,	12.	Roaming Lady.
,,	13.	Devil's Squadron, The.
,,	17.	And so They Were Married.
,,	17.	Mine With the Iron Door, The.
July	22.	Hard Rock Harrigan.
,,	22.	Guilty Melody.
Aug.	11.	Counterfeit.
,,	13.	Final Hour, The.
,,	14.	Meet Nero Wolfe.
,,	17.	Blackmailer.
,,	21.	Caught by Television.
,,	27.	Westerner, The.
Sept.	21.	Shakedown.
Oct.	20.	Craig's Wife.
,,	20.	Two Fisted Gentleman, The.
,,	20.	Mysterious Avenger, The.
,,	21.	Lucky Corrigan.
,,	21.	Manhattan Madness.
,,	22.	They Met in a Taxi.
,,	23.	Man Who Lived Twice, The.
Nov.	16.	Alibi for Murder.
,,	17.	Everything in Life.

Concordia.

| April | 16. | Robber Symphony, The. |
| Nov. | 6. | Robber Symphony. |

Denning Films.

| April | 20. | Student of Prague, The. |
| Sept. | 1. | Marchand D'Amour. |

Equity.

Jan.	22.	Rawhide Mail, The.
,,	23.	Wolf Rides, The.
,,	24.	Cactus Kid, The.
,,	29.	Loser's End, The.
Mar.	11.	Valley of Gold, The.
,,	12.	Via Pony Express.
,,	13.	Outlaw Justice.
,,	18.	Trouble Busters.
,,	19.	Gun Law.
,,	20.	Law of the Lawless.
June	11.	Woman of Destiny.
,,	11.	Man's Best Friend.
July	8.	Live Wire, The.
,,	8.	When Lightning Strikes..
Aug.	12.	Kazan the Fearless.
,,	12.	Never Too Late.
,,	19.	Lightning Bill Carson.
,,	21.	Border Caballero.
,,	26.	Man from Guntown, The.
,,	28.	Bulldog Courage.

Sept.	2.	Roarin' Guns.
,,	4.	Outlaw Deputy.
Oct.	21.	North of Arizona.
,,	22.	Rawhide Terror.
,,	23.	Texas Jack.
,,	27.	Arizona Trails.
,,	28.	Way of the West.
,,	29.	Pecos Dandy.
,,	30.	Desert Mesa.

Exclusive.

| Mar. | 27. | Railroad Rhythm. |
| April | 17. | Tonto Kid, The. |

Fidelity.

| Mar. | 27. | Get That Man. |

Film Society.

| Mar. | 17. | Crime et Chatiment. |

First National.

Jan.	16.	Miss Pacific Fleet.
,,	31.	Song of the Saddle.
Feb.	4.	Captain Blood.
,,	5.	Broadway Hostess.
,,	7.	When the Kellys Rode.
,,	11.	Dangerous.
,,	12.	Rhythm on the River.
,,	14.	Vasant Bengali
,,	25.	Brown Wallet.
Mar.	3.	Goalbreak.
,,	13.	Sword to Sword.
,,	24.	Widow from Monte Carlo, The.
April	2.	Man Hunt.
,,	7.	Brides are Like That.
,,	21.	Injustice.
,,	22.	Walking Dead, The.
,,	28.	Where's Sally.
May	12.	Singing Kid, The.
,,	12.	His Best Man.
,,	26.	Snowed Under.
June	24.	Memory Lane.
,,	30.	Law in Her Hands, The.
July	7.	Sons o' Guns.
,,	14.	Case of Mrs. Pembrook, The.
Aug.	18.	Bullets or Ballots.
,,	27.	Golden Arrow.
,,	31.	Educated Evans.
Sept.	8.	All One Night.
,,	10.	On Secret Service.
,,	16.	Down The Stretch.
,,	17.	Natural Born Salesman, A.
,,	30.	Hail and Farewell.
Oct.	8.	Satan Met a Lady.
,,	13.	Isle of Fury.
Nov.	3.	Captain's Kid, The.
,,	24.	Case of the Black Cat, The.

Fox.

Dec.	5.	Dressed to Thrill.
,,	10.	Music is Magic.
,,	12.	Dark World.
,,	17.	Blue Smoke.
,,	19.	Navy Wife.
,,	30.	Man Who Broke the Bank at Monte
		Carlo, The
Jan.	14.	Littlest Rebel, The.
,,	15.	Charlie Chan's Secret.
,,	16.	Your Uncle Dudley.
,,	17.	Paddy O'Day.
,,	24.	King of Burlesque.
Feb.	4.	Troubled Waters.
,,	6.	Professional Soldier.
,,	25.	My Marriage.
,,	27.	Under Proof.
Mar.	4.	Wedding Group.
,,	10.	Every Saturday Night.
,,	12.	It Had to Happen.
,,	20.	Here Comes Trouble.

Mar.	24.	Big Noise, The.
,,	25.	Blind Man's Buff.
,,	26.	Find the Lady.
April	1.	Country Doctor, The.
,,	2.	Prisoner of Shark Island, The.
,,	14.	Servants all.
,,	20.	Charlie Chan at the Circus.
May	5.	Everybody's Old Man.
,,	6.	Song and Dance Man.
,,	7.	Country Beyond, The.
,,	14.	Message to Garcia, A.
,,	22.	Captain January.
,,	27.	Under Two Flags.
June	11.	Sins of Man.
,,	16.	Champagne Charlie.
,,	17.	Highland Fling.
,,	18.	First Baby, The.
,,	24.	Half Angel.
,,	25.	Human Cargo.
July	2.	Little Miss Nobody.
,,	6.	Secret Interlude.
,,	25.	Educating Father.
Aug.	13.	Poor Little Rich Girl, The.
,,	18.	Crime of Doctor Forbes, The.
,,	20.	White Fang.
,,	25.	High Tension.
,,	25.	Girls' Dormitory.
,,	26.	To Mary, With Love.
Sept.	1.	Rhythm in the Air.
,,	4.	As You Like It.
,,	22.	Charlie Chan at the Race Track.
,,	24.	36 Hours to Kill.
Oct.	1.	Road to Glory, The.
,,	6.	Pepper.
,,	7.	Star for a Night.
,,	13.	Sing, Baby, Sing.
,,	15.	Back to Nature.
,,	16.	Ramona.
,,	21.	Thank You, Jeeves.
,,	27.	End of the Road, The.
Nov.	4.	Ladies in Love.
,,	6.	Dimples.
,,	19.	15, Maiden Lane.

G.-B.-D.

Dec.	24.	King of the Damned.
Jan.	7.	Second Bureau.
Feb.	4.	Bonne Chance.
,,	17.	Jack of All Trades.
,,	21.	First Offence.
Mar.	16.	Rhodes of Africa.
,,	18.	Merlusse.
April	1.	Pot Luck.
,,	30.	Tudor Rose.
May	6.	It's Love Again.
,,	12.	Emperor's Candlesticks, The.
June	16.	Where There's a Will.
,,	24.	Seven Sinners.
July	21.	Everything is Thunder.
Aug.	17.	De Kribbebijter.
,,	25.	East Meets West.
Sept.	7.	Sylvia and the Chauffeur.
,,	11.	Man Who Changed His Mind.
,,	22.	Savoy Hotel 217.
Oct.	14.	Everybody Dance.
,,	14.	La Kermesse Heroique.
,,	20.	Mayerling.
,,	29.	All In.
Nov.	5.	His Lordship.
,,	16.	Strangers on Honeymoon.

General F.-D.

Jan.	13.	Limelight.
,,	16.	Koenigsmark.
,,	17.	Improper Duchess, The.
Feb.	3.	King of the Castle.
,,	19.	When Knights Were Bold.

Mar.	5.	Public Nuisance No. 1.
,,	12.	Fame.
,,	27.	Debt of Honour.
May	13.	Love in Exile.
,,	14.	Rio Rattler.
,,	14.	Sunset of Power.
,,	15.	For the Service.
,,	28.	Marriage of Corbal, The.
June	9.	Cowboy and the Kid.
,,	10.	Show Boat.
,,	15.	Flash Gordon.
,,	18.	Sutter's Gold.
,,	29.	Dracula's Daughter.
,,	30.	Three Maxims, The.
July	1.	Nobody's Fool.
,,	31.	Ride 'Em Cowboy.
Aug.	4.	Ride 'Em, Cowboy.
,,	24.	Boss Rider of Dun Creek, The.
Sept.	3.	Phantom Rider, The.
,,	8.	My Man Godfrey.
,,	9.	Crash Donovan.
,,	10.	Two in a Crowd.
,,	21.	Millions.
,,	22.	Dishonour Bright.
,,	25.	Parole.
,,	29.	Southern Roses.
,,	30.	Postal Inspector.
Oct.	6.	Secret of Stamboul, The.
,,	7.	Tropical Trouble.
,,	8.	Land Without Music.
,,	9.	Yellowstone.
,,	23.	Ace Drummond.
Nov.	9.	Girl on the Front Page, The.
,,	10.	Magnificent Brute, The.
,,	11.	Sea Spoilers.
,,	12.	This'll Make You Whistle.
,,	13.	You Must Get Married.

Independent Film Dis.

April	7.	Men of Action.
,,	17.	Wanted Men.
May	11.	Frontier Justice.
July	27.	Born to Fight.
Sept.	4.	Swifty.
Oct.	2.	Black Gold.

Immortal Swan Productions.

Jan.	21.	The Immortal Swan.

Inter. Cine.

Jan.	17.	Oil Raider, The.
Mar.	10.	Broken Coin, The.
,,	27.	Voice of Ireland, The.
Sept.	2.	Mystery Ship, The.
,,	2.	Story of Captain Scott, The.

Majestic.

Apl.	21.	Anne Marie.

Mancunian.

June	29.	Dodging the Dole.

M.-G.-M.

June	17.	Fury.
July	1.	Suicide Club.
,,	8.	Kelly the Second.
,,	9.	Women are Trouble.
,,	15.	San Francisco.
,,	22.	Old School Tie, The.
Dec.	11.	Imperfect Lady, The.
,,	23.	Mutiny on the Bounty.
Jan.	1.	Whipsaw.
,,	11.	Invader, The.
,,	15.	Last of the Pagans, The.
,,	20.	King's Plate, The.
,,	22.	Under Cover.
,,	27.	Riff Raff.
,,	30.	Tale of Two Cities, A.
,,	31.	Night at the Opera, A.

Feb.	3.	Ah! Wilderness.
,,	4.	Kind Lady.
,,	5.	Three Live Ghosts.
,,	17.	Exclusive Story.
,,	18.	Tough Guy.
,,	26.	Rose Marie.
Mar.	2.	Sweeney Tod.
,,	3.	Wren Comes to Life.
,,	3.	Twenty One To-day.
,,	9.	Garden-Murder Case, The.
,,	13.	Voice of Bugle Ann, The.
,,	16.	Bohemian Girl, The.
,,	18.	Robin Hood of Eldorado, The.
,,	19.	Three Godfathers, The.
,,	20.	Music Maker, The
,,	24.	Man Behind the Mask, The.
April	8.	Wife versus Secretary.
,,	15.	Petticoat Fever.
,,	17.	Moonlight Murder.
,,	24.	They Didn't Know.
,,	27.	Absolute Quiet.
,,	29.	Unguarded Hour, The.
May	6.	Small Town Girl.
,,	13.	Crimes of Stephen Hawke, The
,.	21.	Speed.
June	3.	Three Wise Guys.
Aug.	5.	Sworn Enemy.
,,	12.	Suzy.
,,	19.	Devil Doll.
,,	27.	His Brother's Wife.
Sept.	1.	Great Ziegfeld, The.
,,	9.	Piccadilly Jim.
,,	15.	Our Relations.
,,	23.	Gorgeous Hussy, The.
,,	29.	Dream Doctor, The.
,,	30.	Mister Cinderella.
Oct.	7.	Devil Takes the Count, The.
,,	8.	Old Hutch.
,,	15.	Longest Night, The.
,,	21.	Country Bumpkin, The.
,,	28.	Libelled Lady.
Nov.	5.	David Livingstone.
,,	16.	Romeo and Juliet.
,,	23.	Captain's Table, The.
,,	25.	Mad Holiday.

National Provincial.

Oct.	30.	Such is Life.
Nov.	3.	Live Again.
,,	3.	International Revue.
,,	17.	Cavalcade of the West.

Paramount

Dec.	3.	Peter Ibbetson.
,,	4.	So Red the Rose.
,,	6.	Mary Burns, Fugitive.
,,	10.	Luck of the Irish.
,,	17.	Coronado.
Jan.	3.	Ticket of Leave.
,,	7.	Bride Comes Home, The.

Jan.	14.	Millions in the Air.
,,	24.	Eagles' Brood, The.
,,	29.	Bells of St. Clements, The.
,,	30.	Rose of the Rancho.
,,	31.	Her Master's Voice.
Feb.	4.	Charm School, The.
,,	7.	Nevada.
,,	14.	Anything Goes.
,,	18.	Secret Voice, The.
,,	21.	Timothy's Quest, The.
,,	25.	Soak the Rich.
,,	27.	Milky Way, The.
Mar.	3.	Woman Trap.
,,	6.	Strange Cargo.
,,	10.	Preview Mystery, The.
,,	24.	" F " Man.
,,	27.	Drift Fence.
,,	31.	It's a Great Life.
Apl.	1.	Desire.
,,	7.	Klondike Annie.
,,--	8.	Give Us This Night.
,,	16.	Trail of the Lonesome Pine, The.
,,	17.	Love at Sea.
,,	21.	Thirteen Hours by Air.
,,	24.	Bar 20 Rides Again.
,,	28.	Too Many Parents.
,,	29.	Two on a Doorstep.
May	1.	Desert Gold.
,,	12.	Moon's Our Home, The.
,,	19.	Sky Parade, The.
,,	22.	Wednesday's Luck.
,,	25.	Big Brown Eyes.
,,	26.	Forgotten Faces.
June	2.	Florida Special.
,,	9.	Case Against Mrs. Ames, The.
,,	12.	Pay Box Adventure.
,,	16.	Till We Meet Again.
,,	23.	Fatal Lady.
,,	26.	House Broken.
,,	30.	Early to Bed.
July	7.	Princess Comes Home, The.
,,	10.	Café Mascot.
,,	10.	Poppy.
,,	14.	Palm Springs Affair.
,,	15.	Border Flight.
,,	17.	Call of the Prairie, The.
,,	21.	Three Cheers for Love.
,,	22.	Girl of the Ozarks.
,,	24.	And Sudden Death.
,,	28.	Return of Sophie Lang, The.
,,	31.	Spendthrift.
Aug.	11.	Rhythm on the Range.
,,	14.	Early Bird, The.
,,	24.	My American Wife.
,,	25.	Murder by Rope.
,,	28.	Yours for the Asking.
Sept.	1.	Hollywood Boulevard.
,,	4.	Three on the Trail.
,,	8.	Son Comes Home, A.
,,	11.	Arizona Raiders.
,,	15.	Straight from the Shoulder.
,,	18.	I'd Give My Life.
,,	22.	Lady, be Careful.
,,	25.	Grand Finale.
,,	29.	Three Married Men.

Oct.	1.	Texas Rangers.
,,	2.	Heart of the West.
,,	9.	Show Flat.
,,	13.	General Died at Dawn, The.
,,	20.	Wives Never Know.
,,	23.	Murder with Pictures.
,,	26.	Valiant is the Word for Carrie.
,,	30.	Irish and Proud of It.
Nov.	2.	Big Broadcast of 1937, The.
,,	3.	Wedding Present.
,,	10.	O' Riley's Luck.
,,	17.	Along Came Love.
,,	20.	Full Speed Ahead.
,,	24.	Accusing Finger, The.
,,	27.	Scarab Murder Case, The.

Pathe.

Jan.	24.	Pathetone Parade of '36.
Feb.	28.	Bars of Hate.
Mar.	10.	I Conquer the Sea.
,,	17.	Pictorial Review.
,,	26.	Cardinal, The.
Apl.	3.	Fire Trap, The.
,,	8.	Shadows of the Orient.
,,	15.	Last Assignment, The.
,,	17.	Suicide Squad, The.
,,	22.	Face in the Fog, A.
June	9.	Drag Net, The.
,,	10.	Rogues' Tavern, The.
,,	16.	Madcap.
,,	18.	Revolt of the Zombies.
,,	19.	Reckless Way.
,,	23.	Framed.
,,	24.	I'll Name the Murderer.
July	20.	Gay Adventure, The.
Sept.	9.	Prison Shadows.
,,	11.	Kelly of the Secret Service.
Oct.	27.	Skull and Crown.
,,	30.	Limping Man, The.
Nov.	3.	Trapped.
,,	6.	Get That Girl.
,,	27.	No Escape.
,,	30.	Murder in the Air.

Progressive Film Institute.

| Apl. | 14. | Blow Bugles Blow. |

Radio.

Dec.	2.	Three Musketeers, The.
Jan.	7.	Twice Branded.
,,	7.	It Happened in Hollywood.
,,	8.	Annie Oakley.
,,	8.	Vandergilt Diamond Mystery, The
,,	8.	Seven Keys to Baldpate.
,,	9.	Ballat Savoy.
,,	11.	I Dream Too Much.
Feb.	18.	Two in the Dark.
,,	19.	We're Only Human.
,,	19.	To Beat the Band.
,,	19.	Touch of the Moon, A.
,,	25.	Sylvia Scarlett.
,,	28.	Beloved Imposter, The.
Mar.	16.	Pal o' Mine.
,,	17.	Chatterbox.
,,	17.	Love on a Bet.
,,	18.	Sinister House.
,,	18.	Lady Consents, The.
,,	19.	Fellow Dust.
,,	19.	Follow the Fleet.
,,	20.	This Green Hell.

Apl.	14.	Murder on the Bridle Path.
,,	15.	Silly Billies.
,,	16.	Avenging Hand, The.
,,	16.	Farmer in the Dell, The.
May	19.	Unlucky Jim.
,,	19.	Two in Revolt.
,,	19.	Special Investigator.
,,	20.	Not So Dusty.
,,	20.	Witness Chair, The.
,,	21.	If I were Rich.
,,	21.	Ex Mrs. Bradford, The.
June	29.	To Catch a Thief.
July	1.	Last Outlaw, The.
,,	1.	His Majesty, Bunker Bean
,,	2.	Apron Fools.
,,	2.	Dancing Pirate.
,,	7.	Let's Sing Again.
,,	28.	In Liss.
,,	28.	Fang and Claw.
,,	29.	Born that Way.
,,	29.	Bride Walks Out, The.
,,	30.	Mary of Scotland.
Sept.	21.	Nothing Like Publicity.
,,	22.	Grand Jury.
,,	22.	Walking on Air.
,,	23.	Second Wife.
,,	23.	Wings Over Africa.
,,	24.	Don't Turn 'Em Loose.
,,	24.	Swing Time.
,,	25.	Luck of the Turf.
Nov.	9.	Busman's Holiday.
,,	10.	Big Game, The.
,,	10.	Without Orders.
,,	11.	Mummy's Boys.
,,	11.	Woman Rebels, A.
,,	12.	Daniel Boone.
,,	12.	We Who are About to Die.
,,	13.	Heirloom Mystery, The.

Reunion.

Jan.	9.	Sans Famille.
Feb.	6.	Sabotage.
,,	10.	Faust.
,,	10.	Hohe Schule.
,,	22.	Janosik.
,,	15.	Drunkard, The.
Mar.	30.	Liebesmelodie.
Oct.	19.	Dreams Come True.
Nov.	2.	Fredlos.

Tobis.

| May | 25. | Die Ewige Maske. |
| June | 9. | Last Rose, The. |

Toeplitz.

| July | 30. | Re Burlone. |

Twickenham Film Dis.

April	7.	In the Soup.
,,	8.	Eliza Comes to Stay.
May	20.	Broken Blossoms.
,,	25.	False Pretences.
,,	26.	Footlights and Shadows.
,,	27.	Murder at Glen Athol.
,,	28.	Women are Dangerous.
Sept.	8.	Bridge of Sighs.
,,	8.	Juggernaut.
,,	9.	Tango.
,,	9.	Spy of Napoleon.
,,	10.	Ring Around the Moon.
,,	10.	Dusty Ermine.

Oot. 15. Man in the Mirror, The.
Sept. 23. Maria Bashkirtseff.

United Artists.

Dec. 3. Melody Lingers On, The.
,, 17. Ghost Goes West, The.
Jan. 7. Splendour.
,, 20. Amateur Gentleman, The.
Feb. 11. Modern Times.
,, 17. Strike Me Pink.
,, 20. Things to Come.
Mar. 23. Parisienne Life.
,, 30. Forget Me Not.
April 22. These Three.
,, 28. Little Lord Fauntleroy.
,, 30. Two's Company.
May 29. One Rainy Afternoon.
July 23. Man Who Could Work Miracles, The.
,, 24. Woman Alone, A.
,, 27. Accused.
,, 28. Amazing Quest, The.
Sept. 3. Last of the Mohicans, The.
,, 21. Chick.
Oct. 21. Dodsworth.
,, 22. Crime over London.
,, 27. Gay Desperado, The.
Nov. 9. Rembrandt.
,, 20. Come and Get It.
,, 23. Garden of Allah, The
,, 26. Men Are Not Gods.

Universal.

Dec. 3. Ruling the Roost.
,, 5. Sweet Surrender.
Jan. 6. Java Seas.
,, 16. Sunshine Ahead.
,, 16. Adventures of Frank Merriwell, The
,, 17. Great Impersonation, The.
,, 20. Strike Me Lucky.
Feb. 10. Invisible Ray, The.
,, 11. Magnificent Obsession, The
,, 26. Dangerous Waters.
Mar. 12. Howard Case, The.
,, 17. Wolf's Clothing.
,, 19. Next Time We Live.
,, 26. Crimson Circle, The.
,, 30. From Nine to Nine.
April 8. Don't Get Personal.
,, 15. Love Before Breakfast.
,, 16. Ivory Handled Gun, The.
,, 16. On Probation.
,, 17. Silver Spurs.
,, 17. Captured in Chinatown.

Viking Films.

June 12. Shadow of Silk Lennox, The.

Wardour.

Dec. 16. Law of the Jungle.
,, 23. My Old Man's a Fireman.
Mar. 9. Living Dangerously.
,, 11. Night Cargo.
,, 13. Once in a Million.
April 8. Kliou.
,, 27. Ourselves Alone.
May 4. Someone at the Door.
,, 11. She Knew What She Wanted.
June 9. Star Fell from Heaven, A.
July 6. Custer's Last Stand.
,, 6. Forgotten Women.
,, 15. Thoroughbred.
,, 30. Stars of To-morrow.
Aug. 12. Tenth Man, The.
Oct. 19. Children of Divorce.
,, 29. Millionaire Kid.
Nov. 17. Mighty Tundra, The

Warner.

Dec. 9. 'Frisco Kid.
,, 11. Black Mask.
,, 13. Mr. Cohen Takes a Walk.
,, 16. I Found Stella Parish.
,, 17. Man of Iron.
,, 17. Stars Over Broadway.
Feb. 19. Hayseeds, The.
,, 21. Wages in Love.
Mar. 3. Ceiling Zero.
,, 4. Story of Louis Pasteur, The.
,, 5. Faithful.
,, 6. Petrified Forest, The.
,, 6. Boulder Dam.
,, 26. Crown V. Stevens.
,, 27. Twelve Good Men.
April 16. Colleen.
,, 16. Treachery Rides the Range.
May 18. I Married a Doctor.
,, 19. Murder by an Aristocrat.
,, 19. Anthony Adverse.
July 1. Fair Exchange.
,, 2. Murder in the Big House.
,, 3. Case of the Velvet Claws, The.
,, 14. Heart's Divided.
,, 15. Hot Money.
,, 16. Modern Madness.
,, 16. White Angel.
Sept. 2. Guns of the Pecos.
,, 2. It's in the Bag.
,, 3. Bengal Tiger.
,, 3. G. Man's Wife.
,, 8. Sweet Aloes.
,, 10. China Clipper.
Nov. 4. Head Office.
,, 4. Stage Struck.
,, 5. Cain and Mabel.
Nov. 25. Green Pastures.

LONDON TRADE SHOW THEATRES.

The following list of Kinemas and Theatres in the West End of London which specifically cater for the Trade show requirements of renters, has been compiled from data supplied by the managements concerned. Facilities are also available at other houses when they are not open for public performances, but these are generally governed by special arrangements with the proprietors.

ADELPHI THEATRE.

STRAND, W.C.
Telephone: Tem. 7611.
Capacity: 1,500.

Sound System: Western Electric Wide Range.
Available by arrangement on application to F. Carter, His Majesty's Theatre, Haymarket, S.W.1. Tel.: Whi. 7241.

BAUER.

137, WARDOUR STREET, W.1.
Telephone: Gerrard 1242.
Capacity: 30.
Sound System: Bauer.

Available at any time on application to Bauer, Ltd.

BRITISH SCREEN SERVICE.

54–8, WARDOUR STREET, LONDON, W.1.
Telephone: Gerrard 6543–4.
Capacity: 30 seats.
Sound System: B.T.H.
Available all day by arrangement with K. Rick.
Rental Charges: By arrangement.

CAMBRIDGE THEATRE.

SEVEN DIALS, W.C.
Telephone: Tem. 6056.
Capacity: 1,220.

Available by arrangement on application to F. Carter, His Majesty's Theatre, Haymarket, S.W.1. Whi. 724 .1

CROWN THEATRE.

86, WARDOUR STREET.
Telephone: Gerrard 5223.
Capacity: 80 seats.

Sound System: British Acoustic (full range).
Available all day and week-ends by arrangement.

Rental Charges: Morning, 25s. per hour; Afternoon, 25s. per hour; Evening, 30s. per hour; Two double-head projectors for unmarried prints; two sound-heads for mixing tracks before re-recording. Charge for double-head screening, 6s. per reel.

GAUMONT-BRITISH PRIVATE THEATRES.

FILM HOUSE, WARDOUR STREET, W.1.
Telephone: Gerrard 9292 (Ext. 78).
Capacity: No. 1, 210 seats; No. 2, 68 seats.
Sound System: British Acoustic.

Available by arrangement with J. S. Abbott.
Rental Charges: Morning and afternoon, 10s. per reel, sound; 5s. per reel, silent. Evening, quotation on application.

LONDON HIPPODROME.

CRANBOURN STREET, W.C.2.
Telephone: Gerrard 3238.
Capacity: 1,348 seats.
Sound System: Western Electric.

Available, morning and afternoon. by arrangement with Frank Boor, Manager.

NEW GALLERY KINEMA.

123, REGENT STREET, LONDON, W.1.

Telephone : Regent 2255.

Telephone No. of Letting Office : Regent 8080.

Capacity : 1374.

Sound System : Western Electric.

Available : Morning. Must be cleared by 11.40 a.m.

Rental Charges : Morning, £25.

Application should be addressed to A. W. Jarratt, Esq., New Gallery House., 123 Regent Street, W.1.

PALACE THEATRE.

SHAFTESBURY AVENUE, W.1.

Telephone : Gerrard 4144 and 6834/5.

Capacity : 1,350.

Sound System : Western Electric.

Rental Charges : Morning 20 guineas ; Afternoon 30 guineas ; Evening 40 guineas.

Available by arrangement on application to F. H. Short.

PHŒNIX THEATRE.

CHARING CROSS ROAD, W.C.2.

Telephone : Temple Bar 7431.

(*Box Office :* Temple Bar 8611).

Capacity : 1,050.

Sound System : Western Electric.

Available by arrangements with Victor Luxemburg, Managing Director, Phoenix Theatre.

Rental Charges : Morning 10 guineas ; Afternoon, £31 10s. ; Evening, £45.

PICCADILLY THEATRE.

PICCADILLY CIRCUS, W.1.

Telephone : Gerrard 2397.

Capacity : 1182.

Sound System : Western Electric Wide Range.

Available all day.

Rental Charges and other information : Apply to Pinero Buckwell, Piccadilly Theatre.—Gerrard 2397.

RCA. PHOTOPHONE PRIVATE THEATRE.

ELECTRA HOUSE, VICTORIA EMBANKMENT, W.C.2

Telephone : Temple Bar 2971.

Capacity : 25.

Sound System :—RCA Photophone "High Fidelity."

Available on application to Sales Dept., RCA.

Rental Charges : Morning, 25s. per hour or 5s. per 1,000 ft. reel ; Afternoon, 25s. per hour or 5s. per 1,600 ft. reel ; Evening, Extra charge of 50 per cent. on time basis only.

RIALTO.

COVENTRY STREET, W.1.

Telephone : Gerrard 3488.

Capacity : 694.

Sound System : Western Electric.

Available : Morning.

Rental Charges : £12 12s., one feature and shorts ; £15 15s., two features.

Applications should be addressed to Trade Shows Dept., A.B.C. Ltd., 30, Golden Square, W.1. Gerrard 7887.

ROYAL ADELPHI.

STRAND, W.C.

Capacity : 1,509.

Sound System : Western Electric (wide range).

Available subject to theatrical productions permitting.

Letting and Rental Charges : By arrangement with F. Carter, His Majesty's Theatre, S.W.1. Whi. 7241.

STUDIO ONE AND STUDIO TWO.

225, OXFORD STREET, W.1.

Telephone : Gerrard 3300.

Capacity : Studio One, 630 ; Studio Two, 356.

Sound System : Western Electric.

Available : Morning.

Rental Charges : £10 10s. each theatre.

Applications should be addressed to Amalgamated Picture Theatres, Ltd., 225, Oxford Street, W.1.

(UNITED KINEMA SUPPLIES, LTD.).
U.K.S. (Formerly Bawer, Ltd.).

137, WARDOUR STREET, W.1.

Telephone : Gerrard 1242.

Capacity : 20.

Sound System : Parmeko.

Available, morning, afternoon and evening.

Rental Charges : Morning, 4s. per reel (1,000 ft.) ; Afternoon, 4s. per reel ; Evening, 4s. 6d. per reel.

Application should be addressed to Mr. Farmer.

WESTERN ELECTRIC PRIVATE THEATRE.

BUSH HOUSE, ALDWYCH, W.C.2.

Telephone : Temple Bar 1000.

Capacity : 100.

Sound System : Western Electric Wide Range Interlocked Projectors for 35 mm. mute and sound, and 35 mm. mute and 17.5 mm. sound. 16 mm. sound-on-disc. 33⅓ r.p.m. reproduction from vertical or lateral cut discs. Announcing system. Picture size 10 ft. by 8 ft. Screen illumination 15 ft. candles.

Available morning, afternoon and evening by arrangements with F. G. Humberstone.

Rental Charges : Morning, 30s. per hour minimum ½ hour ; Afternoon, 30s. per hour minimum ½ hour ; Evening, £3 per hour, minimum after 7 p.m. 1½ hours. Buffet facilities available.

RENTING COMPANIES' PERSONNEL

ASSOCIATED BRITISH FILM DISTRIBUTORS, A. T. P. House, 169-171, Oxford Street, W.1.
BOARD OF DIRECTORS ... Basil Dean (Chairman and Joint Managing Director), Reginald P. Baker, F.C.A. (Joint Managing Director), Stephen L. Courtauld, Major J. S. Courtauld, .A.C., M.P.
SECRETARY ... ... G. W. G. Rayner.
GENERAL MANAGER ... B. Henry.
BRANCH MANAGERS :
  \ London ... ... A. de Solla.
  Birmingham ... R. Solomon.
  Cardiff ... ... L. Jacobs.
  Dublin ... ... L. M. Elliman.
  Glasgow ... ... E. Pyser.
  Leeds ... ... C. Willis.
  Liverpool ... ... H. Bushell.
  Manchester ... E. Hardman.
  Newcastle ... ... S. H. Partridge.
PUBLICITY DIRECTOR ... Horace Judge.

ASSOCIATED PRODUCING AND DISTRIBUTION CO.
BOARD OF DIRECTORS ... N. G. W. Loudon (Chairman), L. Grandfield Hill, W. L. Garton.
GENERAL MANAGER ... Sam Phillips.
COMPANY SECRETARY ... L. Grandfield Hill.
BRANCH MANAGERS :
  Birmingham ... W. H. Smith (Sovereign Exclusives)..
  Cardiff ... ... F. Taylor.
  Dublin N. Ormsby Scott (Irish Distributing Agency).
  Glasgow ... ... J. B. Campbell (Horace S. Coxall. Ltd).
  Leeds ... ... Booth Grainge, (County Films).
  Liverpool ... ... S. Darlington.
  Manchester ... C. H. Yonwin.
  Newcastle-on-Tyne G. Cowan, (Central AgeLcy Films).
  Nottingham ... F. Gill (Famous Films (Midlands), Ltd.).
PUBLICITY MANAGER ... A. S. Whittaker.

BRITISH LION FILM CORPORATION, LTD., 76-78, Wardour Street, W.1.
BOARD OF DIRECTORS ... S. W. Smith (Chairman and Managing Director), N. L. Nathanson, Andrew Holt, I. Charles Flower, Sir Robert John Lynn, M.P.
GENERAL MANAGER ... S. A. Myers.
SECRETARY ... ... H. Franklin.

BRANCH MANAGERS :
  Birmingham ... M. Myers.
  Cardiff ... ... H. Owen.
  Dublin ... ... L. Elliman.
  Glasgow ... ... P. Gordon.
  Leeds ... ... H. Mitchell.
  Liverpool ... ... T. Charles.
  Manchester ... A. Jackson.
  Newcastle ... ... T. Henderson.
PUBLICITY MANAGER ... F. G. Kay.

BUTCHER'S FILM SERVICE, LTD., 175, Wardour Street, W.1.
MANAGING DIRECTOR ... F. W. Baker.
GENERAL SALES MANAGER ... ... D. Smalley.
COMPANY SECRETARY... Chas. E. Houghton.
BRANCH MANAGERS :
  Belfast ... ... W. Barry.
  Birmingham ... J. E. Fishley.
  Cardiff ... ... A. G. Burn.
  Dublin ... ... L. Atkin.
  Glasgow ... ... M. L. Reid.
  Leeds ... ... B. Grainge.
  Manchester ... S. Pink.
  Newcastle ... ... J. Henderson.
  Nottingham ... E. Durand.
PUBLICITY DIRECTORS... F. Pullen, Archibald Haddon, F. W. Minde.

COLUMBIA PICTURES, LTD., 139, Wardour Street, W.1.
BOARD OF DIRECTORS : Harry Cohn, Jack Cohn, H. Sydney Wright, A. Schneider, M. Thorpe, G. R. Webb, Jos. Friedman (Managing Director).
GENERAL SALES MANAGER ... ... Max Thorpe.
COMPANY SECRETARY ... George J. Maidment.
BRANCH MANAGERS :
  London ... ... A. Kutner.
  Birmingham ... W. Smith.
  Cardiff ... ... W. E. Dovey.
  Dublin ... ... C. E. McGuinness
  Glasgow ... ... R. Booth
  Leeds ... ... G. Jay.
  Liverpool ... ... L. Faber.
  Manchester ... L. Deal.
  Newcastle ... ... B. Fields.
PUBLICITY DIRECTOR ... H. F. Kessler-Howes.

FIRST NATIONAL FILM DISTRIBUTORS, LTD.,
135, Wardour Street, W.1.
BOARD OF DIRECTORS : D. E. Griffiths (Managing Director), Max Milder, Sam E. Morris, E. G. M. Fletcher.
GENERAL SALES MANAGER ... ... D. C. Dobie.
COMPANY SECRETARY ... D. A. Harber.
BRANCH MANAGERS :
Birmingham	...	L. Mangan.
Cardiff	...	R. Brewer.
Dublin	...	J. Kerr.
Glasgow	...	W. Arthur.
Leeds	...	J. Evans.
Liverpool ...	...	L. Marshall.
Manchester	...	C. S. McGregor.
Newcastle ...	...	W. H. Lindon Travers.
PUBLICITY DIRECTOR ... Frederick J. Allen.

FOX FILM Co., LTD.,
13, Berners Street, W.1.
BOARD OF DIRECTORS : S. R. Kent (Chairman), F. L. Harley (Managing Director), W. J. Hutchinson, W. C. Michel, R. Sutton Dawes.
DIRECTOR OF SALES ... R. Sutton Dawes.
COMPANY SECRETARY ... K. N. Hargreaves.
BRANCH MANAGERS :
London	...	A. Wesson.
Birmingham	...	J. Pattinson.
Cardiff	...	G. Dartnall.
Dublin	...	V. R. Jones.
Glasgow	...	W. Carruthers.
Leeds	...	M. Lawrence.
Liverpool ...	...	J. Todd.
Manchester	...	H. G. Newman.
Newcastle ...	...	H. T. Holdstock.
PUBLICITY DIRECTOR ... Roy Simmonds.

GAUMONT-BRITISH DISTRIBUTORS, LTD.,
Film House, Wardour Street, W.1.
BOARD OF DIRECTORS : Isidore Ostrer (Chairman), Mark Ostrer (Managing Director), Maurice Ostrer, Jeffrey Bernerd (General Manager), David Ostrer, Leon Gaumont (French), John Maxwell.
GENERAL SALES MANAGER ... ... Syd. Taylor.
COMPANY SECRETARY ... E. Russell.
BRANCH MANAGERS :
Belfast	...	H. Wilton
Birmingham	...	P. C. Balcon.
Cardiff	...	W. Phillips.
Dublin	...	W. A. Green.
Glasgow	...	A. E. Barnett.
Leeds	...	A. Bass.
Liverpool ...	...	D. Freedman.
Manchester	...	A. Jacobs.
Newcastle ...	...	H. Boodson.
DIRECTOR OF PUBLICITY Francis Meynell (for all G.-B. and associated companies).
PUBLICITY MANAGER ... L. A. Lewis.

GENERAL FILM DISTRIBUTORS, LTD.,
127-133, Wardour Street, W.1.
BOARD OF DIRECTORS : Lord Portal (Chairman), C. M. Woolf (Managing Director), P. Lindenberg (British, German Origin), J. Arthur Rank, D.L., J.P., L. W. Farrow, M. Woolf, L. A. Neel, S. F. Ditcham.
GENERAL SALES MANAGER ... ... John Woolf.
COMPANY SECRETARY ... H. Rogers.
BRANCH MANAGERS :
Belfast	...	C. P. Roberts.
Birmingham	...	B. Rose.
Cardiff	...	D. Thomas.

Dublin	...	B. Cowan
		R. C. McKew
Glasgow	...	R. Ancill.
Leeds	...	S. Caverson.
Liverpool ...		L. Blond.
Manchester	...	D. Carr.
Newcastle-on-Tyne		C. Graves.
PUBLICITY MANAGER ... Leila Stewart.

INTERNATIONAL CINE. COMPANY, LTD.,
101, Wardour Street, W.1.
BOARD OF DIRECTORS : Graham S. Hewett, D.S.C., Major Gilbert E. Cohen, A. Zatouroff (Russian), Reginald W. West, F.C.A.
GENERAL MANAGER ... Richard L. Sheridan.
SECRETARY ... ... H. L. Newton.

METRO-GOLDWYN-MAYER PICTURES, LTD.
19, Tower Street, W.C.2.
BOARD OF DIRECTORS : S. Eckman, Jun. (Managing Director), A. M. Loew, James C. Squier, J. R. Rubin, H. Sydney Wright.
GENERAL SALES MANAGER ... ... J. C. Squier.
ASSISTANT SALES MANAGER ... ... F. E. Hutchinson.
COMPANY SECRETARY ... G. R. Webb.
CHIEF ACCOUNTANT ... Matthew Raymond.
BRANCH MANAGERS :
London	...	J. Goldman.
Birmingham	...	B. Cresswell
Cardiff	...	D. King.
Dublin	...	Alfred Neville.
Glasgow	...	A. F. Gibson.
Leeds	...	L. Hutchinson
Liverpool ...	...	A. J. Whetter.
Manchester	...	T. Connor
Newcastle-on-Tyne		E. Hancock.
PUBLICITY DIRECTOR ... Selby S. Howe.

NATIONAL PROVINCIAL FILM DISTRIBUTORS, LTD.,
32, St. James's Street, S.W.1.
BOARD OF DIRECTORS : G. B. Morgan, W. H. W. Gossage, P. S. Planden, T. S. Wallace, C. N. Wilkinson.
COMPANY SECRETARY ... R. F. Sheppard, F.C.A. A.S.A.A.
SALES DIRECTOR ... C. N. Wilkinson.
PUBLICITY MANAGER ... Mrs. E. Bateman.

PATHE PICTURES, LTD.,
84, Wardour Street, W.1.
BOARD OF DIRECTORS : John Maxwell (Chairman), W. J. Gell (Managing Director) William Douglas Scrimgeour.
GENERAL SALES MANAGER ... ... A. E. Andrews.
COMPANY SECRETARY ... Edward Mann.
BRANCH MANAGERS :
London	...	T. Ebeling.
Birmingham	...	R. Davis.
Cardiff	...	A. Verran.
Dublin	...	J. Gordon Lewis.
Glasgow	...	W. A. Mann.
Leeds	...	F. Barker.
Liverpool ...	...	J. W. Edwards.
Manchester	...	E. L. Jennings.
Newcastle ...	...	E. White.
PUBLICITY DIRECTOR ... G. T. Mowforth.

PARAMOUNT FILM SERVICE, LTD.,
102-170, Wardour Street, W.I.

BOARD OF DIRECTORS : J. C. Graham (Managing Director), C. S. Karuth, E. Ayres.

GENERAL SALES MAN-
AGER ... ... M. Goldman.
COMPANY SECRETARY ... E. Ayres.
DISTRICT MANAGERS :
Newcastle, Glasgow Leeds : I. Collins.
Liverpool, Manchester, Dublin: B.Simmons.
BRANCH MANAGERS :
London ... ... D. Abbey.
Birmingham ... J. Corper.
Cardiff ... ... C. Coles.
Dublin ... ... J. M. Ritchie.
Glasgow ... ... J. Hamson.
Leeds ... ... J. Goldman.
Liverpool ... ... H. Nisbet
Manchester ...... D. Gilpin.
Newcastle ... ... T. Ledger.
ADVERTISING AND
PUBLICITY DIRECTOR F. L. C. Thomas.

RADIO PICTURES, LTD.
2-3-4, Dean Street, W.1.

BOARD OF DIRECTORS : Ralph J. Hanbury (Chairman and Managing Director), Merlin H. Aylesworth, Alfred Clark, Randle F. Holme, G. W. Dawson.

SECRETARY ... ... G. W. Dawson.
GENERAL SALES MAN-
AGER ... ... W. W. Jay.
BRANCH MANAGERS :
London ... ... Harold Possener.
Birmingham ... Norman Smith.
Cardiff ... ... J. Simons.
Glasgow ... ... E. D. Burns.
Leeds ... ... A. Bayley.
Liverpool ... ... C. Beveridge.
Manchester ... W. S. Browning.
Newcastle ... ... G. Chester.
Ireland ... ... Walter McNally.
PUBLICITY DIRECTOR ... Harry Burgess.

REUNION FILMS, LTD.,
Regency House, 1-4, Warwick Street, W.1.

BOARD OF DIRECTORS : John W. Gossage (Chairman), Lt.-Col. H. A. Browne, A. McAuslane, C.A.
COMPANY SECRETARY ... A. McAuslane, C.A.
GENERAL SALES MAN-
AGER ... ... H. Rose.
BRANCH MANAGERS :
Birmingham ... W. H. Smith (Sovereign Exclusives), 97, John Bright Street).
Cardiff ... ... F. Taylor.
Dublin ... ... N. Ormsby-Scott.
Glasgow ... ... S. Bendon (Bendon Trading Co),H.S.Coxall
Leeds ... ... C. Last (Progress Films, Ltd.).
Manchester ... Carr & Rigg (Progress Films, Ltd.).
Newcastle ... ... G. Cowan (Central Agency Films), 11, Bath Lane.
Nottingham ... W. & A. Film Distributors.
PUBLICITY MANAGER Paul Boyle.

UNITED ARTISTS CORPORATION. LTD.,
Film House, Wardour Street, W.1.

BOARD OF DIRECTORS : M. Silverstone (Chairman and Managing Director), Mary Pickford, Charles Schwartz, Arthur W. Kelly, James A. Mulvey, F. M. Guedalla, E. T. Carr, G. Archibald, J.P., Sir Connop Guthrie, K.B.E.

GENERAL SALES MAN-
AGER ... ... E. T. Carr.
SECRETARY & TREASURER G. Archibald.
ASSISTANT GENERAL
SALES MANAGER ... A. Silverstone.
BRANCH SUPERVISOR ... E. Isaacs.
BRANCH MANAGERS :
London ... ... W. Walsh.
Birmingham ... L. Edgar.
Cardiff ... ... H. J. Williamson.
Dublin ... ... J. J. Martin.
Glasgow ... ... W. Bendon.
Leeds ... ... J. Baker
Liverpool ... ... S. Dubow.
Manchester ... E. G. Milloy.
Newcastle ... ... A. C. Henderson.
PUBLICITY DIRECTOR ... Edmund Quarry.
ADVERTISINGMANAGER B. W. Dudman.

WARDOUR FILMS, LTD.,
Film House, Wardour Street, W.1.

BOARD OF DIRECTORS : John Maxwell (Chairman), Maurice Arthur Dent (Managing Director), W. D. Scrimgeour, George H. Gaunt.
COMPANY SECRETARY ... George H. Gaunt.
GENERAL MANAGER ... W. A. Fielder.
SALES MANAGER ... Arthur W. Greenspan.
BRANCH MANAGERS :
London ... ... C. Westcott.
Birmingham ... C. Solomon.
Cardiff ... ... J. Lindsay.
Belfast & Dublin ... R. O'Flanagan.
Glasgow ... ... J. McPhie.
Leeds ... ... B. Schofield.
Liverpool ... ... A. Sydney.
Manchester ... H. Crossley.
Newcastle ... ... C. West.
PUBLICITY MANAGER ... Horace Williams.

WARNER BROS PICTURES, LTD.,
Warner House, Wardour Street, W.1.

BOARD OF DIRECTORS : Max Milder, D. E. Griffiths, Dr. G. E. M. Fletcher, S. E. Morris.
GENERAL SALES MAN-
AGER ... ... J. Walton Brown.
COMPANY SECRETARY ... W. Turner.
BRANCH MANAGERS :
London ... ... Mark Grotsky.
Birmingham ... M. E. Jones.
Cardiff ... ... R. Francis Wilkinson
Dublin ... ... J. Kerr.
Glasgow ... ... George Lee.
Leeds ... ... Laurie Pickard.
Liverpool ... ... T. P. Nicol.
Manchester ... F. W. Stanbury.
Newcastle ... ... G. T. Turnbull.
PUBLICITY MANAGER ... Gayne Dexter.

CONSULTANTS FOR THE COMPLETE EQUIPPING OF CINEMAS
PROJECTION, SOUND EQUIPMENT, FURNISHING, CARPETS,
DRAPERIES, SEATS, WIRING, ILLUMINATING, ETC., ETC.

The Compton Electrone

The Compton 1937 Electrone is the most sensational and revolutionary achievement ever attained in the field of music for the Theatre. Its beautiful and arresting new tonal effects give it an outstanding value in popular appeal.

THE JOHN COMPTON ORGAN CO. LTD.
CHASE ROAD, WILLESDEN, N.W.10

TELEPHONE: WILLESDEN 6666.

FILMS REGISTERED UNDER THE ACT.

Official Board of Trade List.

UNDER the new Films Act, Section 6, the Board of Trade must keep a register of films to which the Act applies. By the courtesy of the Editor of the *Board of Trade Journal*, we are enabled to present a list covering the period from December 1, 1935, to November 29, 1936.

Films, the names of which appear in italics, are parts of series (or serials).

The figures under the heading "Length (feet)" have, in several cases, been altered since the original registration and the corrected figures now appear. Other corrections as notified by the Board of Trade have been made : Br. before the Registered No. indicates a British Film ; F., a Foreign Film ; and E. is British, but not available for British quota.

BRITISH

Title of Film.	Registered by.	Maker's name.	Length (feet).	No.
DECEMBER 2, 1935.				
She Shall Have Music	Twickenham Film Dis.	Twickenham Film Studios	8,310	Br. 12433
DECEMBER 3.				
Music Masters—No. 1	Butcher's	Inspiration Films	931	E. 12436
Music Masters—No. 2	,,	,,	840	E. 12437
Music Masters—No. 3	,,	,,	900	E. 12438
The Man They Could Not Hang	Universal	Invicta Productions	6,643	Br. 12439
Two Hearts in Harmony	Wardour	Time Pictures	6,816	Br. 12440
DECEMBER 4.				
His Apologies	Westanmor, Ltd., trading as Famous Films (London).	Westanmor, Ltd., trading as Famous Films (London).	1,785	Br. 12441
DECEMBER 5.				
Ruling the Roost	Universal	Cinesound Prod.	8,411	Br. 12447
DECEMBER 6.				
Vanity	Columbia	George Smith Prod.	6,942	Br. 12450
DECEMBER 10.				
Can You Hear Me, Mother ?	P.D.C.	New Ideal Pictures.	6,924	Br. 12457
Langford Reed's Limericks.	Equity	A. F. C. Barrington.	580	Br. 12458
Gold	International Prod.	African Film Prod.	3,606	E. 12460
DECEMBER 11.				
Foreign Affairs	G.-B.D.	Gainsborough	6,492	Br. 12461
Facts and Figures	Zenifilms	Central Film Prod.	1,723	Br. 12462
The Luck of the Irish	Paramount	Crusade Films	7,330	Br. 12463
DECEMBER 12.				
Pied Piper's Country	Kinograph Dist.	C. E. Hodges Prod.	1,650	E. 12468
Moscow Nights	General F.D.	London Film Prod. and Capitol Film Corp.	6,746	Br. 12471
DECEMBER 14.				
Dark World	Fox	Fox British Pict.	6,620	Br. 12473

Title of Film.	Registered by.	Maker's name.	Length (feet).	No.
DECEMBER 17.				
Mr. Cohen Takes a Walk	Warner	Warner First Nat.	7,300	Br. 12481
DECEMBER 18.				
Romance of England—No. 1	Columbia	Inspiration Films	932	Br. 12487
Nature's Little Jokes	Universal	Australian Educational Films Pty.	567	E. 12493
Catching Crocodiles	,,	,,	710	E. 12494
People of the Ponds	,,	,,	1,026	E. 12495
Cliff Dwellers	,,	,,	828	E. 12496
The Winged Empress	,,	,,	917	E. 12497
You'd Never Guess	,,		809	E. 12498
DECEMBER 20.				
Blue Smoke	Fox	Fox British Pictures.	6,791	Br. 12509
For All Eternity	M-G-M	New Era Prod.	1,463	Br. 12510
DECEMBER 23.				
Black Mask	Warner	Warner - First National.	6,066	Br. 12514
Trust the Navy	Columbia	St. George's Pictures.	6,490	Br. 12515
Romance of England—No. 2.	,,	Inspiration Films	902	Br. 12516
DECEMBER 30.				
In Search of Gold	Rhodesian Film Prod.	Rhodesian Film Prod.	966	E. 12521
JANUARY 1, 1936.				
Heart of an Empire	M-G-M	Travel and Industrial Development Association of Great Britain and Ireland.	694	Br. 12525
JANUARY 6.				
Stars on Parade	Butcher's	Butcher's	7,360	Br. 12535
Don't Rush Me	P.D.C.	Fred Karno Film Co.	6,404	Br. 12536
JANUARY 8.				
Twice Branded	Radio	G.S. Enterprises, Ltd.	6,142	Br. 12553
JANUARY 9.				
Vandergilt Diamond Mystery.	,,	Randall Faye	5,284	Br. 12558
Jury's Evidence	British Lion	British Lion	6,656	Br. 12559
JANUARY 10.				
Ball at Savoy	Radio]	John Stafford Prod.	6553	Br. 12566
JANUARY 11.				
Ticket of Leave	Paramount	B. & D.	6,295	Br. 12569
JANUARY 13.				
The Invader	M-G-M	British & Continental Film Productions, Ltd.	5,500	Br. 12570
A Wife or Two	British Lion	British Lion	5,795	Br. 12571
Polly's Two Fathers	Exclusive Films.	W. H. Prod.	2,100	Br. 12580
JANUARY 15.				
King of the Damned	G.-B.D.	G.-B. Picture Corp.	6,835	Br. 12581
JANUARY 17.				
Limelight	General F.D.	Herbert Wilcox Productions.	7,041	Br. 12589
The Ghost Goes West	United Artists	London Film Prod.	7,400	Br. 12590
JANUARY 20.				
The Dragon of Wales	W. B. Pollard, Jr.	W. B. Pollard, Jr.	1,501	E. 12597
Sunshine Ahead	Universal	John Baxter and John Barter.	5,859	Br. 12600
JANUARY 21.				
The Improper Duchess	General F.D.	City Film Corp.	7,013	Br. 12607
The King's Plate	M-G-M	Booth Dominion Prod.	5,695	Br. 12608

Title of Film.	Registered by.	Maker's name.	Length (feet).	No.
JANUARY 22.				
Under Cover	M-G-M	Booth Dominion Productions.	5,425	Br. 12614
Strike Me Lucky ..	Universal ..	Cinesound Productions.	6,002	Br. 12615
JANUARY 23.				
The Amateur Gentleman	United Artists ..	Criterion Film Productions.	9,118	Br. 12617
JANUARY 29.				
On Top of the World..	A.P. & D. ..	City Film Corp.	7,150	Br. 12632
JANUARY 30.				
The Belles of St. Clements	Paramount ..	B. & D. ..	6,170	Br. 12635
FEBRUARY 4.				
King of the Castle ..	General F. D. ..	City Film Corp. ...	6,270	Br. 12646
FEBRUARY 6.				
Excuse My Glove ..	A.B.F.D... ..	Alexander Film Productions.	6,815	Br. 12653
What the Puppy Said	Butcher's ..	Widgey R. Newman.	3,568	Br. 12657
FEBRUARY 7.				
Troubled Waters ...	Fox	Fox British Pict.	6,396	Br. 12658
FEBRUARY 11.				
Sabotage	Reunion	Sound City ..	5,889	Br. 12668
Keyboard Talks ..	G.B. Equipments	G.B. Instructional	990	E. 12669
FEBRUARY 12.				
Old Timers	First National ..	Warner - First National.	2,206	Br. 12670
FEBRUARY 14.				
Faust	Reunion	Publicity Picture Productions.	4,063	Br. 12679
Cheer Up	A.B.F.D... ..	Stanley Lupino Productions.	6,174	Br. 12680
Pathetone Parade of '36	Pathe	Pathe	3,168	Br. 12681
FEBRUARY 15.				
Queen of Hearts ..	A.B.F.D... ..	A.T.P.	7,165	Br. 12683
FEBRUARY 18.				
Whom the Gods Love	A.B.F.D... ..	A.T.P.	7,445	Br. 12684
The Prison Breaker ..	Columbia ..	George Smith Prod.	6,286	Br. 12685
FEBRUARY 19.				
Romance of England, No. 3.	Columbia ..	Inspiration Films	1,029	Br. 12692
The Secret Voice ..	Paramount ..	B. and D. ..	6,005	Br. 12699
FEBRUARY 20.				
When Knights were Bold	General F.D. ..	Capitol	6,848	Br. 12708
FEBRUARY 21.				
Soft Lights and Sweet Music.	British Lion ..	British Lion ..	7,988	Br. 12709
A Touch of the Moon	Radio	G.S. Enterprises	6,024	Br. 12710
FEBRUARY 22.				
The Eildons	Universal ..	Viking Pictures ..	851	Br. 12712
Land o' the Leal ..	,, ...	,, ...	787	Br. 12713
Wee Hoose	,, ...	,, ...	895	Br. 12714
Highland Mary ..	,, ...	,, ...	885	Br. 12715
Flora Macdonald's Lament.	,, ...	,, ...	868	Br. 12716
Robin Adair	,, ...	,, ...	825	Br. 12717

Title of Film.	Registered by.	Maker's name.	Length (feet).	No.
FEBRUARY 24.				
Jack of all Trades	G.-B.D.	Gainsborough	6,868	Br. 12720
Things to Come	United Artists	London Film Prod.	8,830	Br. 12721
FEBRUARY 25 .				
The Hayseeds	Warner	J. C. Williamson Pict. Synd.	8,037	Br. 12722
Romance of England, No. 4.	Columbia	Inspiration Films	941	Br. 12723
Romance of England, No. 5.	,,	,,	938	Br. 12724
FEBRUARY 26.				
Wager in Love (*Silent*)	Warner	Imperial Film Co.	8,044	Br.12726
FEBRUARY 28.				
Under Proof	Fox	Fox British	4,570	Br. 12738
FEBRUARY 29.				
Romance of England, No. 6.	Columbia	Inspiration Films	889	Br. 12739
Romance of England, No. 7.	,,	,,	943	Br. 12740
MARCH 2.				
Public Nuisance No. 1	G.F.D.	Cecil Film, Ltd.	7,087	Br. 12745
Beloved Imposter	Radio	John Stafford Prod.	7,769	Br. 12746
The Loopytone News, No. 1.	International Prod.	International Pod.	583	Br. 12747
MARCH 3.				
Sweeney Todd, the Demon Barber of Fleet Street.	M-G-M	F. George King	6,111	Br. 12749
Vasant Bengali	First National	Imperial Film Co.	8,214*	Br. 12750
MARCH 4.				
Christopher Wren Comes to Life	M-G-M.	Ratcliffe Holmes Prod.	3,487	Br. 12751
Twenty-One To-day	,,	Albany Studios	3,076	Br. 12752
The Great Crusade	Pathé	Pathé	1,540	E. 12757
MARCH 5.				
The Brown Wallet	First National	Warner First Nat. Prod.	6,086	Br. 12758
Sardinia	Kinograph Dis.	Hanover Prod.	1,750	E. 12759
Sicily	,,	,,	1,593	E. 12760
MARCH 6.				
Wedding Group	Fox	Fox British Pict.	6,226	Br. 12764
King of Hearts	Butcher's	Butcher's	7,452	Br. 12765
First Offence	G.-B. D.	Gainsborough	5,994	Br. 12766
MARCH 9.				
Strange Cargo	Paramount	B. & D.	6,131	Br. 12770
MARCH 10.				
Faithful	Warner	Warner First Nat. Prod.	7,067	Br. 12777
MARCH 11.				
Gaolbreak	First National	Warner First National.	5,797	Br. 12781
Happy Days are Here Again.	A.P. & D.	Argyle Talking Pictures.	7,950	Br. 12782
MARCH 14.				
Fame	General F.D.	Herbert Wilcox Productions.	6,373	Br. 12792
MARCH 16.				
The Howard Case	Universal	Sovereign Films	5,881	Br. 12793
The Key to Scotland	Strand Film Co.	The Travel and Industrial Development Association of Gt. Britain and Ireland.	1,244	E. 12797

Title of Film.	Registered by.	Maker's name.	Length (feet).	No.
MARCH 17.				
When the Kellys Rode	First National ..	Imperial Feature Films.	7,137	Br. 12798
Sword to Sword	,, ...	Imperial Film Co.	7,710*	Br. 12799
Nursery Island ..	G.-B.D. ..	G.B. Instructional Ltd.	1,642	E. 12801
London Visitors ..	,, ...	,, ..	985	E. 12802
Pal O'Mine ..	Radio ..	Film Sales ..	3,864	Br. 12803
MARCH 18.				
Rhodes of Africa ..	G.-B.D. ..	G.-B. Pic. Corp...	8,175	Br. 12805
MARCH 20.				
Once in a Million ..	Wardour ..	B.I.P.	6,900	Br. 12817
Living Dangerously ..	,, ..	..	6,446	Br. 12818
Wolf's Clothing ..	Universal ..	J. G. and R. B. Wainwright.	7,267	Br. 12833
MARCH 21.				
This Green Hell ..	Radio ..	Randall Faye ..	6,610	Br. 12836
MARCH 23.				
Pictorial Revue ..	Pathé ..	Pathé	3,663	Br. 12838
MARCH 24.				
Talking Hands ..	Harmonicolor Films.	Harmonicolor Films.	1,968	Br. 12839
MARCH 25.				
The Music Maker ..	M-G-M ..	Inspiration Films	4,840	Br. 12841
British Lion Varieties —No. 1.	,, ..	British Lion ..	978	Br. 12842
British Lion Varieties —No. 2.	,, ..	,, ...	1,000	Br. 12843
British Lion Varieties —No. 3.	,, ..	,, ...	987	Br. 12344
British Lion Varieties —No. 4.	,, ..	,, ...	1,011	Br. 12845
British Lion Varieties —No. 5.	,, ..	,, ...	1,011	Br. 12846
British Lion Varieties —No. 6.	,, ..	,, ...	1,040	Br. 12847
Cabaret Nights—No. 1	,, ..	Highbury Studios	947	Br. 12848
Cabaret Nights—No. 2	,, ..	,, ..	959	Br. 12849
Cabaret Nights—No. 3	,, ..	,, ..	902	Br. 12850
Cabaret Nights—No. 4	,, ..	,, ..	979	Br. 12851
MARCH 26.				
The Big Noise ..	Fox ..	Fox British ..	5,855	Br. 12856
Blind Man's Bluff ..	,, ..	,, ..	6,429	Br. 12857
The Man Behind the Mask.	M-G-M ..	Joe Rock ..	7,131	Br. 12864
MARCH 27.				
Find the Lady ..	Fox ..	Fox British ..	6,363	Br. 12865
Crown V. Stevens ..	Warner ..	Warner - First National.	5,997	Br. 12866
Love Me, Love My Dog	,, ..	,, ..	1,878	Br. 12867
MARCH 28.				
Twelve Good Men ..	Warner ..	Warner - First National.	5,821	Br. 12870
The Cardinal	Pathe ..	Grosvenor Sound Films.	6,800	Br. 12871
MARCH 30.				
Hot News	Columbia ..	St. George's Pictures.	6,950	Br. 12872
Days of Destiny ..	,, ..	Bernard Smith ..	3,150	Br. 12873
Heritage	,, ..	Expeditionary Films.	8,690	Br. 12874
Lucky Fugitives ..	,, ..	Central Films ..	6,118	Br. 12875
Chinese Cabaret ..	,, ..	Bijou Film Co. ..	3,872	Br. 12876
Romance of England— No. 8.	,, ..	Inspiration Films	1,040	Br. 12877
Romance of England— No. 9.	,, ..	,, ...	908	Br. 12878

British Lion's " Calling All Stars "—Davy Burnaby & Billy Bennett

Title of Film.	Registered by.	Maker's name.	Length (feet).	No.
MARCH 30.—contd.				
Romance of England— No. 10.	Columbia	Inspiration Films	911	Br. 12879
The Crimson Circle ..	Universal	J. G. and R. B. Wainwright.	6,881	Br. 12896
Debt of Honour ..	General F.D. ..	British National	6,550	Br. 12897
Women Are That Way	Warner ..	Warner - First National.	2,001	Br. 12898
MARCH 31.				
From Nine to Nine ..	Universal	Coronet Pictures	6,677	Br. 12901
Railroad Rhythm ..	Exclusive Films	Carnival Films ..	3,788	Br. 12903
Here and There ..	Universal	John Baxter and John Barter.	1,363	Br. 12904
The Voice of Ireland ..	International Cine.	Victor Haddick..	4,457	Br. 12907
APRIL 3.				
Hard Labour ..	Columbia	Bertram Hyman Hyams.	1,444	Br. 12934
Sign Please ..	,,	,,	1,426	Br. 12935
Romance of England, No. 11.	,,	Inspiration Films, Ltd.	979	Br. 12936
APRIL 6.				
Cabaret Nights, No. 5	M-G-M ..	Highbury Studios, Ltd.	932	Br. 12942
Cabaret Nights, No. 6	,,	,,	945	Br. 12943
APRIL 9.				
In the Soup ..	Twickenham Film Dis.	Twickenham Film Studios.	6,600	Br. 12951
Pathé Pictorial (series) :—				
Pathe Pictorial No. 1	Pathe	Pathe	999	Br. 12959
Pathe Pictorial No. 2	,,	,,	1,022	Br. 12960
APRIL 14.				
The Beauty Doctor ..	Viking Films ..	L. C. Beaumont..	1,500	Br. 12961
Eliza Comes to Stay ..	Twickenham Film Dis.	Twickenham Film Studios.	6,500	Br. 12963
APRIL 15.				
Pot Luck ..	G.-B.D. ..	Gainsborough ..	6,460	Br. 12964
Pathe Pictorial (series) :—				
Pathe Pictorial No. 3	Pathe	Pathe	1,020	Br. 12965
APRIL 16				
Servants All ..	Fox	Fox British Pict.	3,053	Br. 12974
APRIL 17.				
City of Towers	British Lion	Assoc. Screen News	931	Br. 12975
Westminster of the West	,,	,,	1,016	Br. 12976
The Return of the Buffalo.	,,	,,	920	E. 12977
Sky Fishing ..	,,	,,	904	E. 12978
The Avenging Hand ..	Radio ..	John Stafford Prod.	5,974	Br. 12979
Love at Sea ..	Paramount	B. and D. ..	6,362	Br. 12990
APRIL 23.				
Pathé Pictorial (series)—				
Pathe Pictorial No. 4	Pathé	Pathé	849	Br. 13004
APRIL 24.				
Men Against the Sea ..	Frank Bowden and William Haddock Farr	Frank Bowden and William Haddock Farr	1,800	E. 13005
Melody of My Heart ..	Butcher's	Butcher's and Incorporated Talking Films.	7,456	Br. 13006
Blow Bugles Blow ..	Progressive Film Institute	Rudolph Messel	6,721	Br. 13007
The Game Is Up ..	British Lion	Associated Screen News	936	E. 13008
APRIL 25.				
They Didn't Know ..	M-G-M ..	British Lion ..	6,082	Br. 13012
APRIL 28.			(feet).	
Pathé Pictorial (series)—				
Pathe Pictorial No. 5	Pathé ..	Pathé ..	947	Br. 13024
Carmen.. ..	Reunion ..	Anglia Films ..	850	Br. 13025
Alt ! Oo Goes Theer ..	,,	,,	868	Br. 13026
Low Water ..	Turner-Robertson Films.	Turner-Robertson Films.	1,730	E. 13027

Title of Film.	Registered by.	Maker's name.	Length	No.
APRIL 29.				
Birthplace Of America	M-G-M ..	A. Moncrieff Davidson	858	Br. 13029
Milestones	M-G-M ..	A. Moncrieff Davidson	598	Br. 13030
MAY 1.				
Where's Sally	First National ..	Warner Bros. First Nat.	6,429	Br. 13057
Two On A Doorstep ..	Paramount	B. & D. Film Corp.	6,435	Br. 13058
Little Paper People ..	A.B.F.D...	Cyril Jenkins ..	800	Br. 13060
Bassetsbury Manor ..	A.B.F.D...	Cyril Jenkins ..	1,589	Br. 13061
MAY 4.				
Tudor Rose	G.-B.D. ..	Gainsborough Pic.	7,077	Br. 13077
Laburnum Grove ..	A.B.F.D...	A.T.P.	6,622	Br. 13080
MAY 5.				
Propellers	G.-B.D. ..	G.B.I.	738	E. 13086
Shipcraft	G.-B.D. ..	G.B.I.	748	E. 13087
PowerInThe Highlands	G.-B.D. ..	G.B.I.	870	E. 13088
Streamline	G.-B.D. ..	G.B.I.	1,005	E. 13089
Pathé Pictorial (series) :—				
Pathe Pictorial No. 6	Pathé ..	Pathé Pict., Ltd.	975	Br. 13090
MAY 6.				
Two's Company ..	United Artists ..	Soskin Productions and B. and D.	6,616	Br. 13094
The Story of Papworth	General F.D. ..	British Pictorial Productions	1,697	E. 13095
MAY 7.				
Death on the Road ..	G.B. Equipments	G.B. Instructional	1,500	E. 13106
MAY 11.				
Pathe Pictorial (series) :—				
Pathe Pictorial No. 7 ..	Pathe	Pathe	930	Br. 13113
MAY 12.				
Bob Bowman Calling	Ace Films ..	Ace Fims ..	1,646	Br. 13116
MAY 14.				
The Crimes of Stephen Hawke.	M-G-M ..	George King. ..	6,203	Br. 13118
MAY 15.				
It's Love Again ..	G.-B. D. ..	G.-B. Pict. Corp.	7,395	Br. 13126
Secret Agent	,, ..	,, ...	7,809	Br. 13127
MAY 16.				
Love in Exile	General F.D. ..	Capitol	7,023	Br. 13128
MAY 19.				
Pathé Pictorial (series) —				
Pathe Pictorial No. 8	Pathé	Pathé	962	Br. 13135
Northward Ho ! ..	C. E. Hodges' Productions.	C. E. Hodges' Productions.	1,580	E. 13136
Someone at the Door	Wardour ..	B.I.P.	6,737	Br. 13139
Ourselves Alone ..	,, ...	,, ...	6,285	Br. 13140
MAY 20.				
Unlucky Jim	Radio ..	Master Prod. ..	3,125	Br. 13141
MAY 21.				
Shipmates o' Mine ..	Butcher's ..	Butcher's and T. A. Welsh Prod.	7,850	Br. 13150
Not So Dusty	Radio ..	G.S. Enterprises	6,407	Br. 13152
The Green Plover ..	G.-B.D. ..	G.-B. Instructional	851	E. 13155
Dry Dock	,, ..	,, ..	969	E. 13156

Title of Film.	Registered by.	Maker's Name.	Length (feet).	No.
MAY 22.				
If I Were Rich ..	Radio ..	Randall Faye ..	5,367	Br. 13166
MAY 25.				
Night Mail	A.B.F.D... ..	H.M. Postmaster-General.	2,115	E. 13171
Men of Yesterday ..	A.P. & D. ..	U.K. Films, Ltd.	7,350	Br. 13173
Wednesday's Luck ..	Paramount ..	B. & D.	6,213	Br. 13174
Pathe Pictorial (series) :—				
Pathe Pictorial No. 9	Pathe	Pathe	962	Br. 13181
MAY 27.				
Cabaret Nights No. 7	M-G-M	Highbury Studios	988	Br. 13184
British Lion Varieties, No. 7.	,, ...	British Lion ..	997	Br. 13185
British Lion Varieties, No. 8.	,, ...	,, ...	1,012	Br. 13186
British Lion Varieties, No. 9.	,, ...	, ...	1,006	Br. 13187
MAY 28.				
Broken Blossoms ..	Twickenham F.D.	Twickenham Film Studios.	7,725	Br. 13191
JUNE 2.				
Pathé Pictorial (series) :—				
Pathe Pictorial No. 10	Pathe	Pathé	939	Br. 13202
JUNE 8.				
One Good Turn ...	A.B.F.D.... ...	Leslie Fuller Pict.	6,545	Br. 13213
Pathé Pictorial (series)—				
Pathe Pictorial No. 11	Pathé	Pathé	876	Br. 13214
Royal Eagle	Columbia ...	Quality Films ...	6,212	Br. 13215
JUNE 9.				
The Marriage of Corbal	General F.D.	Capitol	8,329	Br. 13221
The Interrupted Honeymoon.	British Lion ...	British Lion ...	6,607	Br. 13222
She Knew What She Wanted	Wardour ...	Rialto Prod. ...	6,910	Br. 13223
JUNE 12.				
A Star fell from Heaven	Wardour ...	B.I.P.	6,383	Br. 13238
JUNE 15.				
Pathé Pictorial (series) :				
Pathe Pictorial No. 12	Pathé	Pathé	941	Br. 13242
Pay-Box Adventure ...	Paramount ...	B. and D. ...	6,148	Br. 13243
JUNE 16.				
Tugboat Princess ...	Columbia ...	Central Films ...	6,150	Br. 13252
JUNE 18.				
Everything is Rhythm	A.B.F.D.... ...	Joe Rock Prod.	6,607	Br. 13255
Highland Fling ...	Fox	Fox British ...	5,960	Br. 13258
JUNE 20.				
The Robber Symphony	Concordia ...	Concordia ...	8,000	Br. 13262
JUNE 22.				
Pathé Pictorial (series) :—				
Pathe Pictorial No. 13	Pathé	Pathé	941	Br. 13265
Zambesia	Rhodesian Film Prod.	Rhodesian Film Prod.	1,426	E. 13266
JUNE 25.				
All Is Safely Gathered In.	Exclusive Films	Gordon Donkin...	714	E. 13279
Golden Fleece... ...	,, ...	,, ...	977	E. 13280

Title of Film.	Registered by.	Maker's name.	Length (feet).	No.
JUNE 29.				
House Broken... ...	Paramount ...	British and Dominions Film Corp.	6,627	Br. 13282
Pathe Pictorial (series) :—				
Pathe Pictorial No. 14	Pathe	Pathe Pictures ...	1,031	Br. 13286
JUNE 30.				
Where There's a Will...	G.-B.D.	Gainsborough Pictures.	7,233	Br. 13290
To Catch a Thief ...	Radio	G.S. Enterprises, Ltd.	5,793	Br. 13291
JULY 1.				
Seven Sinners... ...	G.-B.D.	G.-B. Pic. Corp.	6,286	Br. 13294
JULY 2.				
Memory Lane... ...	First National ...	National Talkies, Ltd.	4,005	Br. 13304
JULY 3.				
Fair Exchange ...	Warner Bros. ...	Warner Bros.First Nat. Prod.,Ltd.	5,710	Br. 13307
Apron Fools	Radio	Marks Pict. Corp., Ltd.	3,102	Br. 13308
JULY 7.				
Pathe Pictorial (series) :—				
Pathe Pictorial No. 15	Pathe	Pathe Pict., Ltd.	1,081	Br. 13322
JULY 9.				
Dodging the Dole ...	Mancunian Film Corp.	Mancunian Film	8,128	Br. 13329
Annie Laurie	Butcher's ...	Butcher's and Mondover Film Productions.	7,444	Br. 13330
JULY 11.				
Calling the Tune ...	A.B.F.D.... ...	I.F.P. Limited, Proprietors of Phœnix Films.	6,141	Br. 13344
JULY 13.				
Café Mascot	Paramount ...	Pascal Film Productions.	6,910	Br. 13345
JULY 14.				
Pathe Pictorial (series) :—				
Pathe Pictorial No. 16	Pathe	Pathe ...	1,049	Br. 13359
JULY 17.				
Pathe Pictorial (Nos. 27 to 52) series :—				
Pathe Pictorial No. 27	Pathe	Pathe	1,031	Br. 13370
Pathe Pictorial No. 28	,, ...	,, ...	999	Br. 13371
Pathe Pictorial No. 29	,, ...	, ...	965	Br. 13372
JULY 20.				
Pathe Pictorial (series) :—				
Pathe Pictorial No. 17	,, ...	,, ...	1,017	Br. 13375
JULY 21.				
Thoroughbred ...	Wardour ...	Cinesound Prod.	6,122	Br. 13382
JULY 22.				
The Gay Adventure ...	Pathé	Grosvenor Sound Films.	6,710	Br. 13391
JULY 27.				
Romance of England No. 12.	Columbia ...	Inspiration Films, Ltd.	952	Br. 13414
The Man Who could Work Miracles.	United Artists ...	London Film Prod.	7,384	Br. 13418
JULY 28.				
Pathé Pictorial (series) :—				
Pathe Pictorial No. 18	Pathé	Pathé	930	Br. 13426
JULY 30.				
Born that Way ...	Radio	Randall Faye ...	5,804	Br. 13433

Title of Film.	Registered by.	Maker's name.	Length (feet).	No.
JULY 31.				
Below Rio	Kinograph Dist.	G. K. Aldersley & S. C. W. Turner, trading as Kookaburra Films.	1,550	Br. 13437
AUGUST 1.				
Home in the Valley ...	G.-B. D.	G.B. Instructional	1,031	E. 13438
Ravenous Roger ...	,, ...	,, ...	883	E. 13439
Community Life ...	,, ...	,, ...	1,086	E. 13440
The New Generation ...	,, ...	,, ...	964	E. 13441
Safety First	,, ...	,, ...	916	E. 13442
The Saw Fly ...	,, ...	,, ...	826	E. 13443
Life in the Balance ...	,, ...	,, ...	847	E. 13444
AUGUST 4.				
Accused	United Artists ...	Criterion Film Productions.	7,866	Br. 13446
AUGUST 5.				
Everything is Thunder	G.-B.D.	G.-B. Picture Corp.	6,938	Br. 13452
AUGUST 6.				
Fire Fighters	Kinograph Dist.	W. B. Pollard, Jr., and Peter Collin.	1,402	E. 13459
AUGUST 7.				
Pathe Pictorial (series) :—				
Pathe Pictorial No. 19	Pathe	Pathe	953	Br. 13460
The Tawny Owl ...	G.-B.D.	G.B. Instructional	900	E. 13466
AUGUST 10.				
Guilty Melody ...	A.B.F.D.... ...	Franco London Film.	6,211	Br. 13469
AUGUST 12.				
The Highway Code ...	National Progress Film Co.	National Progress Film Co.	980	E. 13473
AUGUST 13.				
Ebb Tide	G.-B.D. ...	G.B. Instructional	787	E. 13474
Fish Face	,, ...	,, ,, ...	964	E. 13475
AUGUST 14.				
Analysis of Exercises	,, ...	,, ,, ...	952	E. 13476
Physical Training— Carriage.	,, ...	,, ,, ...	1,071	E. 13477
Ball Handling ...	,, ...	,, ,, ...	1,104	E. 13478
Boys' Summer Games	,, ...	,, ,, ...	1,096	E. 13479
Physical Training—.				
Infants, Pt. 1. ...	,, ...	,, ,, ...	1,234	E. 13480
Infants, Pt. 2 ...	,, ...	,, ,, ...	1,127	E. 13481
Rural School	,, ...	,, ,, ...	1,075	E. 13482
Boys' Winter Games ...	,, ...	,, ,, ...	1,029	E. 13483
Rock Pools	,, ...	,, ,, ...	866	E. 13486
Pathe Pictorial (Series) :—				
Pathe Pictorial No. 20	Pathe	Pathe	985	Br. 13488
AUGUST 17.				
The Early Bird ...	Paramount ...	Crusade Films ...	6,287	Br. 13490
AUGUST 18.				
Pathe Pictorial No. 21	Pathe ...	Pathe ...	940	Br. 13501
AUGUST 24.				
Murder by Rope ...	Paramount ...	British and Dominions Film Corp., Ltd.	5,862	Br. 13512
AUGUST 25.				
Pathe Pictorial (series) :—				
Pathe Pictorial No. 22	Pathe	Pathe	873	Br. 13521
AUGUST 31.				
The Happy Family ...	British Lion ...	British Lion ...	6,076	Br. 13538

Title of Film.	Registered by.	Maker's name.	Length (feet).	No.
SEPTEMBER 1.				
Lonely Road	A.B.F.D.... ...	A.T.P.	6,517	Br. 13540
Pathé Pictorial (series) :—				
Pathé Pictorial No. 23	Pathé	Pathé	1,000	Br. 13541
SEPTEMBER 2.				
Educated Evans ...	First National ...	Warner - First National.	7,736	Br. 13542
SEPTEMBER 3.				
Rhythm in the Air ...	Fox	Fox British ...	6,438	Br. 13547
Song of Freedom ...	British Lion ...	Hammer Productions.	7,225	Br. 13550
SEPTEMBER 4.				
It's in the Bag ...	Warner	Warner - First National.	6,531	Br. 13551
SEPTEMBER 5.				
Secrets of the Grand National.	Ace Films ...	Ace Films ...	1,604	Br. 13573
Derby Secrets, 1936 (series) :—				
On the Derby in General.	,, ...	,, ...	814	Br. 13574
Wiltshire Winners ...	,, ...	,, ...	776	Br. 13575
Gordon Richards and the Derby.	,, ...	,, ...	784	Br. 13576
Round and About Newmarket.	,, ...	,, ...	798	Br. 13577
Possible Acceptors ...	,, ...	,, ...	809	Br. 13578
As Usual the Winner	,, ...	,, ...	778	Br. 13579
Nautical Nonsense ..	Columbia ..	Cinesound Productions, Ltd...	1,795	Br. 13580
Evolution of the Waltz	,, ..	,, ..	682	Br. 13581
(The registration of the film entitled " South Sea Varieties " (Br. 11426) has been amended and is now registered as above (Br. 13580 and 1).				
SEPTEMBER 8.				
East Meets West ...	G.-B.D.	G.-B. Picture Corp.	6,695	Br. 13590
Pathe Pictorial (series) :—				
Pathe Pictorial No. 24	Pathe	Pathe	943	Br. 13591
SEPTEMBER 9.				
Gypsy Melody ...	Wardour ...	British Artistic Films.	6,925	Br. 13592
Great Gable	Ace Films ...	Ace Films ...	1,589	Br. 13593
The Mine	G.-B.D.	G.B Instructional	1,612	E. 13597
SEPTEMBER 10.				
Keep Your Seats, Please	A.B.F.D.... ...	A.T.P. ...	7,670	Br. 13598
SEPTEMBER 11.				
Tenth Man	Wardour ...	B.I.P.	6,098	Br. 13605
SEPTEMBER 12.				
As You Like It ...	Fox	Interallied Film Producers.	8,674	Br. 13612
SEPTEMBER 14.				
The Beloved Vagabond	A.B.F.D.... ...	Toeplitz Prod. ...	6,803	Br. 13613
The Man Who Changed His Mind.	G.-B.D.	Gainsborough ...	5,914	Br. 13614
SEPTEMBER 16.				
Pathe Pictorial (series) :—				
Pathe Pictorial No. 25	Pathe	Pathe	993	Br. 13628
SEPTEMBER 17.				
Love Up the Pole ...	Butcher's ...	Butcher's Film Service, Ltd., Hope-Bell Productions, Ltd., and British Comedies, Ltd.	7,450	Br. 13635

Title of Film.	Registered by.	Maker's name.	Length (feet).	No.
SEPTEMBER 21.				
The Kingdom of Kerry	Viking Pictures ...	Viking Pictures ...	1,200	E 13640
Sweet Vale of Avoca ...	,, ...	,, ...	947	E 13641
Isle of a Million Gems	,, ...	,, ...	963	E 13642
Silent O'Moyle ...	,, ...	,, ...	856	E 13643
Cover to Cover ...	A.B.F.D.... ...	Strand Film Co,	1,855	E 13648
You Ought to Know ...	British Lion ...	Associated Screen News	946	E 13649
SEPTEMBER 22.				
Spy of Napoleon ...	Twickenham Film Dis.	J. H. Productions, Ltd.	9,048	Br. 13652
Dusty Ermine ...	,, ...	,, ...	7,666	Br. 13653
Nothing Like Publicity	Radio	G.S. Enterprises	5,848	Br. 13654
SEPTEMBER 23.				
Juggernaut	Twickenham F.D.	J.H. Prod., Ltd.	6,518	Br. 13661
Pathe Pictorial (series) :—				
Pathe Pictorial No.26	Pathe	Pathe	925	Br. 13662
SEPTEMBER 24.				
Chick	United Artists ...	B. & D.	6,446	Br. 13670
Wings Over Africa ...	Radio	Premier Stafford Productions.	5,658	Br. 13674
SEPTEMBER 25.				
Dishonour Bright ...	General F.D. ...	Cecil Films ...	7,394	Br. 13679
SEPTEMBER 28.				
Luck of the Turf ...	Radio	Randall Faye ...	5,755	Br. 13694
SEPTEMBER 29.				
Grand Finale	Paramount ...	B. & D.	6,443	Br. 13702
Millions	General F.D. ...	Herbert Wilcox Productions.	6,340	Br. 13703
SEPTEMBER 30.				
Southern Roses ...	General F.D. ...	Grafton Films ...	6,815	Br. 13704
London after Midnight	M-G-M	B.S. Productions	1,732	Br. 13705
The Dream Doctor ...	,, ...	Bernard Smith & Widgey R.Newman	3,671	Br. 13706
Romantic England No. 1	,, ...	Inspiration Films	1,021	Br. 13707
Romantic England No. 2	,, ...	,, ...	1,031	Br. 13708
OCTOBER 8.				
Tropical Trouble ...	General F.D. ...	City Film Corp., Ltd.	6,325	Br. 13722
The Secret of Stambou	,, ...	J. G. and R. B. Wainwright, Ltd.	7,853	Br. 13723
Secret Hiding Places ...	Kinograph Distributors.	J. Granville Squiers	1,568	Br. 13724
OCTOBER 12.				
Africa Looks Up ...	Joseph Best ...	Joseph Best	5,011	E. 13737
Land Without Music ...	General F.D. ...	Capitol	7,289	Br. 13738
Show Flat	Paramount ...	B. and D. ...	6,387	Br. 13740
Hail and Farewell ...	First National ...	Warner - First National.	6,612	Br. 13742
OCTOBER 13.				
Everybody Dance ...	G.-B.D.	Gainsborough ...	6,793	Br. 13747
OCTOBER 20.				
Pathé Pictorial (Nos. 27 to 52) (series) :—				
Pathe Pictorial No.30	Pathé	Pathé	917	Br. 13769
Modernising Madame	Viking	Viking	1,550	Br. 13770
OCTOBER 21				
It's You I Want ...	British Lion ...	British Lion ...	6,625	Br. 13771
OCTOBER 23				
Lobsters	Bury Productions	Bury Productions	1,448	E. 13775

Title of Film.	Registered by.	Maker's name.	Length (feet).	No.
OCTOBER 27				
Pathé Pictorial (Nos 27 to 52) series :—				
Pathe Pictorial No 31	Pathé	Pathe	1 041	Br. 13801
OCTOBER 28.				
The Fox Hunt	Denning Films	London Film Productions	716	Br. 13807
Let Dogs Delight	National Canine Defence League	National Canine Defence League	1,315	E. 13808
Digging For Gold	Ace Films	Ace Films	4,066	Br. 13810
OCTOBER 29.				
The Man in the Mirror	Twickenham F.D.	J. H. Productions	7,362	Br. 13811
The End of the Road	Fox	Fox British Pictures.	6,472	Br. 13812
Crime Over London	United Artists	Criterion Film Productions.	7 143	Br. 13813
OCTOBER 30.				
And So to Work	Kinograph Distributors.	Richard Massingham.	1,654	Br. 13818
NOVEMBER 2.				
Such Is Life	National Provincial F.D.	Incorporated Talking Films.	7,465	Br. 13822
Full Steam	Ace Films	Ace Films	4,266	Br. 13823
Radio Lover	A.B.F.D...	City Film Corp.	5,773	Br. 13824
House of the Spaniard	,,	I.F.P. Limited, Proprietors of Phœnix Films.	6,264	Br. 13825
The Limping Man	Pathe	Welwyn Studios	6,550	Br. 13842
NOVEMBER 3.				
Irish and Proud of It	Paramount	Crusade Films	6,585	Br. 13843
NOVEMBER 4.				
Pathé Pictorial (Nos. 27 to 52) series :—				
Pathe Pictorial No. 32	Pathé	Pathé	1,041	Br. 13844
Lucky Corrigan	Columbia	Central Films	5,679	Br. 13845
NOVEMBER 6.				
Head Office	Warner	Warner First National.	6,070	Br. 13848
NOVEMBER 7.				
To-morrow We Live	A.B.F.D...	Conquest Prod...	6,491	Br. 13861
David Livingstone	M-G-M	Fitzpatrick Pict.	6,570	Br. 13862
NOVEMBER 9.				
Beat the Retreat	A.P. and D.	Anglia Films	810	Br. 13863
Sam's Medal	,,	,,	835	Br. 13864
Hearts of Humanity	,,	U.K. Films	6,750	Br. 13865
Dreams Come True	Reunion	London and Continental Pictures.	6,939	Br. 13873
NOVEMBER 10.				
Busman's Holiday	Radio	G.S. Enterprises	6,122	Br. 13874
NOVEMBER 11.				
His Lordship	G.-B.D.	G.-B. Picture Corp.	6,445	Br. 13877
All In	,,	Gainsborough Pictures (1928), Ltd.	6,438	Br. 13878
NOVEMBER 12.				
Pathé Pictorial (Nos. 27 to 52) series :—				
Pathe Pictorial No. 33	Pathe	Pathe	930	Br. 13884
Bottle Party	Ace Films	Ace Films	4,156	Br. 13892

Title of Film.	Registered by.	Maker's name.	Length (feet).	No.
NOVEMBER 13.				
Analysis of Agility Exercises.	G.-B.D. ..	G.B. Instructional	991	E. 13894
NOVEMBER 14.				
Live Again	National Provincial. F.D.	Morgan Productions.	7,666	Br. 13898
NOVEMBER 16.				
This'll Make You Whistle.	General F.D. ..	Herbert Wilcox Productions.	6,750	Br. 13899
The Heirloom Mystery	Radio ..	G.S. Enterprises..	6,181	Br. 13900
The Farm Factory ..	G.-B.D. ..	G.B. Instructional	1,961	E. 13904
Expansion of Germany	,, ...	,, ...	1,003	E. 13905
Mediæval Village ..	,, ...	,, ...	1,703	E. 13906
Development of English Railways.	,, ...	,, ...	754	E. 13907
NOVEMBER 18.				
Pathe Pictorial (Nos. 27 to 52) series :—				
Pathe Pictorial No. 34	Pathe ..	Pathe	879	Br. 13912
NOVEMBER 19.				
Everything in Life ..	Columbia ..	Tudor Films ..	6,376	Br. 13919
NOVEMBER 20.				
Rembrandt	United Artists	London Film Productions.	7,913	Br. 13923
NOVEMBER 23.				
Variety Parade ..	Butcher's ..	Butcher's and Malcolm Picture Productions.	7,500	Br. 13925
Full Speed Ahead ..	Paramount ..	Lawrence Huntington.	6,377	Br. 13926
Roof Tops of London..	M-G-M ..	Strand Film Co.	1,254	Br. 13929
NOVEMBER 24.				
Strangers on Honeymoon.	G.-B.D. ..	G.-B. Picture Corp.	6,233	Br. 13934
The Captain's Table ..	M-G-M ..	Fitzpatrick Picures.	4,962	Br. 13935
Beauty Under Canvas	Viking Films ..	Viking Films ..	1,550	Br. 13936
NOVEMBER 25.				
Pathe Pictorial (Nos. 27 to 52) series :—				
Pathe Pictorial No. 35	Pathe ..	Pathe	1,043	Br. 13938
NOVEMBER 26.				
Scenes in Harmony	Fidelity ..	Kingdon-Ward Productions.	824	E. 13942
Ocean Tempest ..	,,	,, ..	908	E. 13943
A Cornish Idyll ..	,,	,, ..	930	E. 13944
NOVEMBER 27.				
Taking to the Water	,,	Pennine Films ..	750	E. 13949
NOVEMBER 30.				
Men are Not Gods ..	United Artists ..	London Film Productions.	8,105	Br. 13955
The Scarab Murder Case.	Paramount ..	B. and D. ..	6,152	Br. 13956
Happy Hampstead !	Denning Films ..	Denning Films ..	966	E. 13958

FOREIGN.

Title of Film.	Registered by.	Maker's Name.	Length (feet).	No.
DECEMBER 2, 1935.				
In Person	Radio	R.K.O. Corp.	7,844	F. 12428
The Perfect Clue	P.D.C.	Majestic Corp.	5,728	F. 12429
Honeymoon Bridge	Columbia	Columbia	1,608	F. 12430
Oh! My Nerves	,,	,,	1,708	F. 12431
Calling All Cars	Inter. Cine.	Empire Film Dis.	5,597	E. 12432
DECEMBER 3.				
The Three Musketeers	Radio	R.K.O. Corp.	8,603	F. 12434
Heir to Trouble	Columbia	Columbia	5,273	F. 12435
DECEMBER 4.				
Peter Ibbetson	Paramount	Paramount Inter.	7,433	F. 12442
Jungle Waters	,,	,,	693	F. 12443
Condemned to Live	P.D.C.	Invincible Corp.	5,469	F. 12444
DECEMBER 5.				
So Red the Rose	Paramount	Paramount Inter.	7,440	F. 12445
Shorty Goes South— V5-3.	,,		862	F. 12446
Three Orphan Kittens	United Artists	Walt Disney Prod.	813	F. 12448
The Melody Lingers On	,,	Reliance Pictures	7,789	F. 12449
DECEMBER 6.				
Tailspin Tommy in the Great Air Mystery (serial):—				
Episode 6	Universal	Universal	1,811	F. 12451
Episode 7	,,	,,	1,838	F. 12452
DECEMBER 9.				
Dajos Bela and His Band—No. 1.	Zenifilms	Willy Goldberger	700	F. 12453
Mary Burns, Fugitive	Paramount	Paramount Inter.	7,400	F. 12454
King of the Mardi Gras	,,	,,	748	F. 12455
Dressed to Thrill	Fox	Fox	6,192	F. 12456
DECEMBER 10.				
Sweet Surrender	Universal	Broadway Prod.	7,131	F. 12459
DECEMBER 11.				
Follow the Leader	Paramount	Paramount Inter.	888	F. 12464
Frisco Kid	Warner	Warner	6,941	F. 12465
By Request	,,	,,	993	F. 12466
Lonesome Trailer	,,	,,	1,609	F. 12467
DECEMBER 12.				
Surprise	Warner	Warner	1,956	F. 12469
Music is Magic	Fox	Fox	6,062	F. 12470
DECEMBER 13.				
The Imperfect Lady	M-G-M	M-G-M	6,373	F. 12472
DECEMBER 14.				
Betty Boop and Grampy	Paramount	Paramount Inter.	647	F. 12474
Broadway Highlights— No. 3, V5-1.	,,	,,	858	F. 12475
Cavalcade of Music	,,	,,	772	F. 12476
Hooked Lightning	,,	,,	895	F. 12477
I Wished on the Moon	,,	,,	676	F. 12478
Movie Milestones—V4-27	,,	,,	840	F. 12479
Sirens of Syncopation	,,	,,	816	F. 12480
DECEMBER 17.				
Wee Men	Warner	Warner	957	F. 12482
Gold Diggers of '49	,,	,,	754	F. 12483
Tailspan Tommy in the Great Air Mystery (serial):—				
Episode 8	Universal	Universal	1,635	F. 12484
Episode 9			1,771	F. 12485
Episode 10			1,710	F. 12486

Title of Film.	Registered by.	Maker's Name.	Length (feet).	No.
DECEMBER 18.				
The Case of the Missing Man.	Columbia	Columbia	5,132	F. 12488
Yoo Hoo Hollywood..	,,	,,	1,579	F. 12489
Too Tough to Kill ..	,,	,,	5,174	F. 12490
Trouble in Toyland ..	First National	Vitaphone Corp.	1,076	F. 12491
Wilderness Mail	Butcher's	Guaranteed Pictures Co.	5,075	F. 12492
DECEMBER 19.				
Coronado	Paramount	Paramount Inter.	6,869	F. 12499
Making Manhandlers ..	,,	,,	890	F. 12500
Take a Letter..	Wardour..	Master Art Prod.	724	F. 12501
I Found Stella Parish	Warner	Warner	7,712	F. 12502
Check Your Sombrero	,,	,,	1,728	F. 12503
Man of Iron ..	,,	,,	5,614	F. 12504
The Fire Alarm	,,	,,	618	F. 12505
Stars Over Broadway	,,	,,	8,145	F. 12506
Hollywood Capers	,,	,,	610	F. 12507
Keystone Hotel	,,	,,	1,391	F. 12508
DECEMBER 21.				
New Babylon ..	Progressive Film Institute.	Leningrad Goskino	7,010	F. 12511
Tailspin Tommy in the Great Air Mystery (serial) :—				
Episode 11 ..	Universal	Universal	1,742	F. 12512
Navy Wife	Fox	Fox	6,675	F. 12513
DECEMBER 23.				
Crime and Punishment	Columbia	Columbia	7,896	F. 12517
One Way Ticket	,,	,,	6,346	F. 12518
Let's Ring Doorbells	,,	,,	654	F. 12519
If You Could Only Cook	,,	,,	6,432	F. 12520
DECEMBER 30.				
Mutiny on the Bounty	M-G-M	M-G-M	11,933	F. 12522
Tailspin Tommy in the Great Air Mystery (serial) :—				
Episode 12 ...	Universal	Universal	1,730	F. 12523
Alias St. Nick ...	M-G-M	M-G-M	905	F. 12524
JANUARY 1, 1936.				
The Pie Man ...	M-G-M...	M-G-M	951	F. 12526
Gymnastics	,,	,,	835	F. 12527
Barnyard Babies	,,	,,	876	F. 12528
The Old Plantation ...	,,	,,	931	F. 12529
The Man Who Broke the Bank at Monte Carlo.	Fox	Twentieth Century Fox	6,014	F. 12530
JANUARY 2.				
Splendour	United Artists	Samuel Goldwyn	6,971	12531
My Old Man's a Fireman.	Wardour	M-G-M	5,500	F. 12532
JANUARY 3.				
Whipsaw	M-G-M	M-G-M	7,345	F. 12533
Thousand Dollars a Minute.	A.B.F.D...	Mascot Corp.	6,288	F. 12534
JANUARY 6.				
Reifende Jugend	G.-B.D.	Froelich Film G.m.b.H.	8,158	F. 12537
The Bride Comes Home	Paramount	Paramount Inter.	7,425	F. 12538
Judge for a Day	,,	,,	694	F. 12539
When a Man's a Man	A.B.F.D...	British and Continental Trading Co., Inc.	6,030	F. 12540
The Singing Cowboy ..	,,	Mascot Corp.	2,953	F. 12541
The Phantom Empire (serial) :—				
The Thunder Riders	,,	,, ,,	1,804	F. 12542
The Lightning Chamber	,,	,, ,,	1,908	F. 12543

Title of Film.	Registered by.	Maker's name.	Length (feet).	No.
JANUARY 6—contd.				
Phantom Broadcast..	A.B.F.D...	Mascot Corp. ..	1,716	F. 12544
Beneath the Earth ...	,, ...	,, ,, ..	1,940	F. 12545
Disaster from the Skies	,, ...	,, ,, ..	1,740	F. 12546
From Death to Life	,, ...	,, ,, ..	1,867	F. 12547
Jaws of Jeopardy ..	,, ...	,, ,, ..	1,918	F. 12548
Prisoners of the Ray	,, ...	,, ,, ..	1,650	F. 12549
The Rebellion ..	,, ...	,, ,, ..	1,744	F. 12550
A Queen in Chains	,, ...	,, ,, ..	1,685	F. 12551
The End of Murania	,, ...	,, ,, ..	1,798	F. 12552
JANUARY 8.				
Tuned Out	Radio ..	.. R.K.O. Corp.	1,845	F. 12554
It Happened in Holly-wood.	,, ...	,, ...	6,223	F. 12555
Happy Tho' Married ..	,, ...	,, ...	1,644	F. 12556
The Timid Young Man	G.-B.D. ..	Educational Film Corp. of America.	1,787	F. 12557
JANUARY 9.				
When We Look Back	British Lion	.. Republic Corp. ...	6,281	F. 12560
Comi-Colour Cartoon Nursery Rhymes (serial):—				
Old Mother Hubbard Part 1.	,, ..	.. Celebrity Prod. ...	732	F. 12561
Sinbad the Sailor Part 2.	,, ..	,, ...	683	F. 12562
Homework	Radio ..	.. R.K.O. Corp. ..	1,758	F. 12563
Annie Oakley	,, ..	,, ...	8,154	F. 12564
Java Seas	Universal	.. Universal ..	6,341	F. 12565
JANUARY 10.				
Seven Keys to Baldpate	Radio ..	.. R.K.O. Corp. ..	6,216	F. 12567
Sans Famille	Reunion ..	.. La Société Agatos	8,573	F. 12568
JANUARY 13.				
Racing Luck	British Lion	.. Republic Pictures Corp.	5,207	F. 12572
Comi-Colour Cartoon Nursery Rhymes (Serial):—				
The Three Bears Part 3.	,, ..	.. Celebrity Prod. ...	716	F. 12573
2nd Bureau	G.-B.D. ..	.. La Compagnie Francaise Cine-magraphique.	9,641	F. 12574
I Dream Too Much ..	Radio ..	.. R.K.O. Corp. ..	8,739	F. 12575
Molly Moo-Cow and the Butterflies.	,, ..	.. Amedee J. Van Beuren.	722	F. 12576
Monkey Love	Columbia	.. Columbia ..	597	F. 12577
Tetched in the Head ..	,, ..	,, ...	648	F. 12578
Bon Bon Parade ..	,, ..	,, ...	797	F. 12579
JANUARY 15.				
The Spanish Cape Mystery.	British Lion	.. Republic Pictures Corp.	6,570	F. 12582
Broadway Highlights, No. 4—V. 5-4.	Paramount	.. Paramount Inter.	890	F. 12583
Millions in the Air ..	,, ..	,, ...	6,449	F. 12584
JANUARY 16.				
Forced Landing ..	British Lion	.. Republic Pictures Corp.	6,214	F. 12585
Melody Trail	,, ..	,, ...	5,345	F. 12586
Charlie Chan's Secret	Fox ..	.. Fox ..	6,511	F. 12587
The Littlest Rebel ..	,, ..	,, ...	6,614	F. 12588
JANUARY 17.				
Last of the Pagans ..	M-G-M ..	.. M-G-M ..	6,342	F. 12591
Gus Van's Music Shoppe	Universal	.. Mentone Prod. ..	1,767	F. 12592
Clubhouse Party ..	Universal..	.. Mentone Prod. ..	1,810	F. 12593
Monkey Wretches ..	,, ..	. Universal ..	652	F. 12594

Title of Film.	Registered by.	Maker's Name.	Length (feet).	No.
JANUARY 18.				
Broken Toys	United Artists ..	Walt Disney Prod.	722	F. 12595
Koenigsmark	General F.D. ..	Société Des Films Roger Richebe S.A. and Capital Film Corp.,Ltd.	8,620	F. 12596
JANUARY 20.				
Your Uncle Dudley ..	Fox	Fox	6,165	F. 12598
Paddy O'Day ..	,, ..	,, ..	6,874	F. 12599
Doctor Oswald ..	Universal ..	Universal ..	683	F. 12601
Case of the Lost Sheep	,, ...	,, ...	634	F. 12602
The Adventures of Frank Merriwell (serial) :—				
Episode 1	,, ...	,, ...	1,675	F. 12603
Episode 2	,, ...	,, ...	1,859	F. 12604
Episode 3	,, ...	,, ...	1,702	F. 12605
Miss Pacific Fleet ..	First National ..	Warner ..	6,083	F. 12606
JANUARY 21.				
Manhattan Monkey Business.	M-G-M	Hal E. Roach ..	1,837	F. 12609
The Oil Raider ..	Inter. Cine. ..	Empire Film Dis.	5,536	F. 12610
The Great Impersonation.	Universal ..	Universal ..	6,129	F. 12611
JANUARY 22.				
Jack Denny's Orchestra (1888).	First National ..	Vitaphone Corp.	974	F. 12612
Hot Money	M-G-M	Hal E. Roach ..	1,566	F. 12613
The Loser's End ..	Equity	Reliable Picture Corp.	5,250	F. 12616
JANUARY 23.				
The Rawhide Mail ..	Equity	Reliable Picture Corp.	5,150	F. 12618
Hot Paprika	,, ..	Columbia ..	1,553	F. 12620
Three Little Beers ..	,, ..	,, ..	1,485	F. 12621
His Marriage Mix Up..	,, ..	,, ..	1,344	F. 12622
JANUARY 24.				
The Wolf Riders ..	Equity	Reliable Picture Corp.	5,100	F. 12623
JANUARY 27.				
Public Ghost No. 1 ..	M-G-M	Hal E. Roach ..	1,819	F. 12624
Our Gang Follies of 1936	,, ..	,, ..	1,593	F. 12625
Top Flat	,, ..	,, ..	1,739	F. 12626
Life Hesitates at 40 ..	,, ..	,, ..	1,353	F. 12627
Football Teamwork ..	,, ..	M-G-M ..	721	F. 12628
Honeyland	,, ..	,, ..	908	F. 12629
The Eagle's Brood ..	Paramount ..	Paramount Inter.	5,389	F. 12630
Symphony in Black ..	,, ..	,, ..	864	F. 12631
JANUARY 29.				
The Cactus Kid ..	Equity ..	Reliable Picture.. Corp.	5,125	F. 12633
King of Burlesque ..	Fox	Twentieth Cen-.. tury Fox.	8,142	F. 12634
JANUARY 30.				
Babes in Hollywood ..	Paramount ..	Paramount Inter.	902	F. 12636
Eventful Journey ..	A.B.F.D. ..	Republic Corp. ..	6,900	F. 12637
JANUARY 31.				
Riff Raff	M-G-M	M-G-M	8,460	F. 12638
Rose of the Rancho	Paramount ..	Paramount Inter.	7,359	F. 12639
Jumping Champions	,, ..	,, ..	866	F. 12640
FEBRUARY 3.				
A Tale of Two Cities ..	M-G-M ..	M-G-M	11,351	F. 12641
A Night at the Opera	,, ..	,, ...	8,438	F. 12642
Her Master's Voice ..	Paramount ..	Paramount Inter.	6,832	F. 12643
Cock of the Walk ..	United Artists ..	Walt. Disney Prod.	765	F. 12644
Song of the Saddle ..	First National ..	Warner ..	5,266	F. 12645

Title of Film.	Registered by.	Maker's name.	Length (feet).	No.
FEBRUARY 4.				
Fighting Shadows ..	Columbia ..	Columbia ..	5,228	F. 12647
Western Courage ..	,, ..	,, ...	5,189	F. 12648
FEBRUARY 5.				
Ah, Wilderness ! ..	M-G-M	M-G-M	8,458	F. 12649
Musical Memories ..	Paramount ..	Paramount Inter.	638	F. 12650
Adventures of Popeye ..	,, ...	,, ...	715	F. 12651
The Charm School ..	,, ...	,, ...	7,299	F. 12652
FEBRUARY 6.				
Kind Lady	M-G-M	M-G-M	6,843	F. 12654
Captain Blood ..	First National ..	Warner	10,829	F. 12655
Billboard Frolics ..	,, ...	Vitaphone Corp.	608	F. 12656
FEBRUARY 7.				
Desert Death	M-G-M	M-G-M	1,893	F. 12659
Three Live Ghosts. ..	,, ...	,, ...	5,477	F. 12660
Der Kleine Schornstein-feger.	Film Society ..	Charlotte Koch-Reiniger.	1,416	F. 12661
Broadway Hostess ..	First National ..	Warner	6,342	F. 12662
Okay Jose	,, ...	Vitaphone Corp.	1,588	F. 12663
FEBRUARY 10.				
Nevada..	Paramount ..	Paramount Inter.	5,282	F. 12664
Making Stars	,, ...	,, ...	603	F. 12665
Professional Soldier ..	Fox	Twentieth Century Fox.	6,982	F. 12666
On Ice	United Artists ..	Walt. Disney Prod.	736	F. 12667
FEBRUARY 12.				
Comi-Colour Cartoon Nursery Rhymes (series) :—				
Mary's Little Lamb	British Lion ..	Celebrity Prod.	673	F. 12671
FEBRUARY 13.				
Modern Times.. ..	United Artists ..	Charles Chaplin Film Corp.	8,018	F. 12672
Mickey's Polo Team	,, ..	Walt. Disney Productions.	800	F. 12673
Dangerous	First National ..	Warner	7,150	F. 12674
The Invisible Ray ..	Universal ..	Universal ..	7,134	F. 12675
FEBRUARY 14.				
Magnificent Obsession	Universal ..	Universal ..	10,184	F. 12676
Rhythm on the River..	First National ..	Warner	6,136	F. 12677
Hohe Schule	Reunion ..	A.B.C. Film G.m.b.H.	8,139	F. 12678
FEBRUARY 15.				
Anything Goes ..	Paramount ..	Paramount Inter.	8,246	F. 12682
FEBRUARY 18.				
Gallant Defender ..	Columbia ..	Columbia ..	5,001	F. 12686
Exclusive Story ..	M-G-M	M-G-M	6,676	F. 12687
An All American Toothache.	,, ..	Hal. E. Roach ..	1,768	F. 12688
Pals of the Prairie ..	A.P. and D. ..	Imperial Distributing Corp.	2,750	F. 12689
Major Bowes Amateur Night, No. 4.	Radio ..	Biograph Pictures	1,691	F. 12690
Scotty Finds a Home	,, ..	Amedee J. Van Beuren.	719	F. 12691
FEBRUARY 19.				
Escape from Devil's Island	Columbia ..	Columbia ..	5,659	F. 12693
Tough Guy	M-G-M	M-G-M	6,816	F. 12694
The Count Takes the Count.	,, ..	Hal E. Roach ..	1,747	F. 12695
Two in the Dark ..	Radio ..	R.K.O. Corp. ..	6,663	F. 12696
Bird Scouts	,, ..	Amedee J. Van Beuren.	689	F. 12697

Title of Film.	Registered by.	Maker's name	Length (feet).	No.
FEBRUARY 19—contd.				
Flowers for Madame ..	First National ..	Vitaphone Corp.	676	F. 12698
It's Easy to Remember	Paramount ..	Paramount Inter.	878	F. 12700
Strike Me Pink ..	United Artists	Samuel Goldwyn Productions.	9,106	F. 12701
The Immortal Swan ..	Immortal Swan Productions.	Immortal Swan Productions.	3,414	F. 12702
FEBRUARY 20.				
We're Only Human ..	Radio ..	R.K.O. Corp. ..	6,212	F. 12703
Major Bowes' Amateur Night, No. 6.	,, ...	Biograph Pictures	1,564	F. 12704
To Beat the Band ..	,, ...	R.K.O. Corp. ..	6,053	F. 12705
Lady of Secrets ..	Columbia ..	Columbia ..	6,569	F. 12706
Patch Mah Britches ..	,, ...	, ...	623	F. 12707
FEBRUARY 21.				
Parrotville Post Office	Radio	Amedee J. Van Beuren.	701	F. 12711
FEBRUARY 22.				
Timothy's Quest ..	Paramount ..	Paramount Inter.	5,815	F. 12718
Sport on the Range ..	,, ...	,, ...	660	F. 12719
FEBRUARY 25.				
The Calling of Dan Matthews	Columbia ..	Columbia ..	5,821	F. 12725
FEBRUARY 26.				
Battleship Potemkin .. (*Silent*)	Progressive Film Institute.	Len Films ..	4,446	F. 12727
Sylvia Scarlett ..	Radio	R.K.O. Corp. ...	8,151	F. 12728
Soak the Rich ..	Paramount ..	Paramount Inter.	6,695	F. 12729
Betty Boop with Henry	,, ...	,, ..	629	F. 12730
FEBRUARY 27.				
My Marriage	Fox	Fox	6,215	F. 12731
FEBRUARY 28.				
Rose Marie	M-G-M	M-G-M	9,990	F. 12732
Vitaphone Casino ..	First National ..	Vitaphone Corp.	991	F. 12733
Dangerous Waters ..	Universal ..	Universal ..	5,984	F. 12734
The Milky Way ..	Paramount ..	Paramount Inter.	7,885	F. 12735
What's the Answer ..	,, ...	,, ..	802	F. 12736
The Spinach Overture	,, ...	,, ..	737	F. 12737
FEBRUARY 29.				
Panic on the Air ..	Columbia ..	Columbia ..	5,974	F. 12741
Kannibal Kapers ..	,, ...	,, ..	603	F. 12742
Champagne for Breakfast.	,, ...	,, ..	6,069	F. 12743
The Lone Wolf Returns	,, ...	,, ..	6,167	F. 12744
MARCH 2.				
Alibi Racket	M-G-M	M-G-M	1,628	F. 12748
MARCH 4.				
Major Bowes' Amateur Night No. 5.	Radio	Biograph Pict. ...	1,603	F. 12753
Woman Trap	Paramount ..	Paramount Inter.	5,719	F. 12754
Parade of the Maestros	,, ...	,, ...	932	F. 12755
Bars of Hate	Pathé	Victory Corp. ..	5,400	F. 12756
MARCH 5.				
Ceiling Zero	Warner	Warner	8,681	F. 12761
P's and Cues	,, ...	,, ...	844	F. 12762
Plane Dippy	,, ...	,, ...	775	F. 12763
MARCH 6.				
The Story of Louis Pasteur.	,, ...	,, ...	7,856	F. 12767
Double Exposure ..	,, ...	,, ...	1,911	F. 12768
Alpine Antics	, ...	,, ...	635	F. 12769

Title of Film	Registered by	Maker's name	Length (feet)	No.
MARCH 9.				
Radio Rhapsody ..	Paramount ..	Paramount Inter.	898	F. 12771
Rooftops of Manhattan	Warner	Warner	1,961	F. 12772
Some Class	,, ...	,, ...	1,001	F. 12773
The Petrified Forest ..	,, ...	,, ...	7,490	F. 12774
Wild Wings	,, ...	,, ...	885	F. 12775
Carnival Day	,, ...	,, ...	1,441	F. 12776
MARCH 10.				
The Garden Murder Case	M-G-M ..	M-G-M	5,466	F. 12778
La Veille D'Armes ..	G.-B. D. ..	Imperial Films ..	8,850	F. 12779
Vamp Till Ready ..	M-G-M ..	Hal E. Roach ..	1,772	F. 12780
MARCH 11.				
The Broken Coin ..	Inter. Cine.	Guaranteed Pict. Co.	3,913	F. 12783
Preview Murder Mystery	Paramount	Paramount Inter.	5,454	F. 12784
MARCH 12·				
The Valley of Gold ..	Equity ..	Majestic Corp. ..	4,700	F. 12785
Crime et Châtiment ..	Film Society	General Product.	8,820	F. 12786
Every Saturday Night	Fox ..	Fox	5,599	F. 12787
MARCH 13.				
It Had to Happen ..	,, ..	Twentieth Century Fox	7,170	F. 12788
I Conquer the Sea ..	Pathé ..	Academy Pictures Dis. Corp.	6,011	F. 12789
MARCH 14.				
The Voice of Bugle Ann	M-G-M ..	M-G-M	6,460	F. 12790
Orphan's Picnic ..	United Artists ..	Walt Disney Prod.	724	F. 12791
MARCH 16.				
Night Cargo	Wardour ..	Peerless Corp. ..	5,892	F. 12794
Via Pony Express ..	Equity ..	Majestic Corp. ..	5,100	F. 12795
Outlaw Justice ..	,, ..	,, ..	5,250	F. 12796
MARCH 17.				
Papageno	Film Society ..	Charlotte Koch-Reiniger.	992	F. 12800
Bonne Chance ..	G.-B.D. ..	Les Distributeurs Francais	6,500	F. 12804
MARCH 18.				
The Bohemian Girl ..	M-G-M ..	M-G-M	6,374	F. 12806
Chatterbox	Radio ..	R.K.O. Corp. ..	6,152	F. 12807
A Returned Engagement	,,	,,	1,921	F. 12808
Love on a Bet ..	,,	,, ..	6,937	F. 12809
Molly Moo-Cow and Rip Van Winkle.	,,	Amedee J. Van Beuren.	713	F. 12810
MARCH 19.				
Trouble Busters ..	Equity ..	Majestic Corp. ..	4,900	F. 12811
House of Fate ..	Radio ..	R.K.O. Corp. ..	6,249	F. 12812
The Lady Consents ..	,,	,, ..	6,886	F. 12813
Molly Moo-Cow and the Indians.	,,	Amedee J. Van Beuren.	728	F. 12814
Counselitis	,,	R.K.O. Corp. ..	1,641	F. 12815
Comi-Color Cartoon Nursery Rhymes (series):—				
Balloonland	British Lion	Celebrity Productions.	639	F. 12816
MARCH 20.				
Gun Law	Equity ..	Majestic Corp. ..	5,450	F. 12819
Robin Hood of Eldorado	M-G-M ..	M-G-M	7,465	F. 12820
Three Godfathers ..	,,	,, ..	7,279	F. 12821
Yellow Dust ..	Radio ..	R.K.O. Corp. ..	6,103	F. 12822
Follow the Fleet ..	,,	,, ..	9,896	F. 12823
Toonerville Trolley ..	,,	Amedee J. Van Beuren.	667	F. 12824
20 Ace Comedies (series) :—				
Blue Blackbirds ..	Ace Films	Educational Film Corp. of America.	1,811	F. 12825

Title of Film.	Registered by.	Maker's name.	Length (feet).	No.
MARCH 20—contd.				
The Inventors	Ace Films	Educational Film Corp. of America	1,789	F. 12826
Hail Brother..	,,	,,	1,753	F. 12827
The Farmer's Fatal Folly.	,,		1,731	F. 12828
He's a Prince	,,	,,	1,600	F. 12829
Way up Thar	,,		1,645	F. 12830
Rural Romeos	,,	,,	1,825	F. 12831
Domestic Bliss-ters	,,	,,	1,717	F. 12832
Boulder Dam ..	Warner ..	Warner ..	6,331	F. 12834
While the Cat's Away	,,	,,	1,991	F. 12835
MARCH 21.				
Law and Lawless	Equity ..	Majestic Corp. ..	5,594	F. 12837
MARCH 24.				
Merlusse	G.-B.D. ..	Film Marcel Pagnol	6,694	F. 12840
MARCH 25.				
Divot Diggers ..	M-G-M ..	Hal E. Roach ..	1,316	F. 12852
The Lucky Corner	,,	,,	1,452	F. 12853
The Pinch Singer	,,	,,	1,553	F. 12854
The Singing Vagabond	British Lion	Republic Pictures Corp.	5,173	F. 12855
Widow from Monte Carlo	First National ..	Warner Bros. Pictures, Inc.	5,426	F. 12858
MARCH 26.				
Vitaphone Headliners	First National ..	Vitaphone Corp.	972	F. 12859
Burning Gold ..	British Lion	Republic Corp.	5,284	F. 12860
The New Frontier	,,	,,	5,056	F. 12861
October	Progressive Film Institute, Ltd.	Mosfilms	10,440*	F. 12862
Parisienne Life	United Artists ..	Nero Film S.a.r.l.	7,130	F. 12863
The Oregon Trail	British Lion	Republic Corp. ..	5,131	F. 12868
MARCH 28.				
The Sagebrush Troubadour.	British Lion	Republic Corp. ..	5,380	F. 12869
Swell Head ..	Columbia	Columbia	5,354	F. 12880
MARCH 30.				
Dangerous Intrigue ..	Columbia	Columbia	5,089	F. 12881
Ants in the Pantry ..	,,	,,	1,596	F. 12882
I Don't Remember ..	,,		1,653	F. 12883
Unrelated Relations ..	,,		1,662	F. 12884
Scrappy's Boy Scouts	,,		675	F. 12885
20 Ace Comedies (series)—				
Love a la Mode	Ace Films	Educational Film Corp. of America.	1,837	F. 12886
Racket Cheers	,,	,,	1,967	F. 12887
Big Business	,,		1,575	F. 12888
A Good Scout	,,		1,588	F. 12889
An Ear for Music	,,		1,663	F. 12890
Educating Papa	,,	,,	1,478	F. 12891
Divorce Sweets	,,		1,636	F. 12892
Annie Doesn't Live Here	A.B.F.D.	Liberty Corp.	6,621	F. 12893
The Old Homestead ..	,,	,,	6,363	F. 12894
Laughing Irish Eyes ..	,,	Republic Corp. ..	6,315	F. 12895
MARCH 31.				
Next Time we Live ..	Universal	Universal Corp...	7,810	F. 12899
The Mother ..	A.B.F.D...	Joe Rock ..	1,053	F. 12900
The Adventures of Frank Merriwell (serial)—				
Episode 4 ..	Universal	Universal	1,721	F. 12902
Dancing Feet ..	British Lion	Republic Corp. ..	6,612	F. 12905
The Return of Jimmy Valentine.	,,	,,	6,507	F. 12906
APRIL 1.				
Shadows of the Orient	Pathe	Larry Darmour ..	6,267	F. 12908
Vim, Vigor and Vitality	Paramount	Paramount Inter.	598	F. 12909
The Collie	,,	,,	899	F. 12910
" F " Man	,,	,,	5,634	F. 12911

Title of Film.	Registered by.	Maker's name.	Length (feet).	No.
APRIL 1—cont.				
Broadway Highlights, No. 5, V5-7.	Paramount ..	Paramount Inter.	905	F. 12912
Desire	,, ...	,, ...	8,574	F. 12913
Somewhere in Dream-land.	,, ...	,, ...	798	F. 12914
Drift Fence	,, ...	Paramount ..	5,048	F. 12915
Little Nobody ..	,, ...	,, ...	591	F. 12916
Sporting Network ..	,, ...	,, ...	874	F. 12917
It's a Great Life ..	,, ...	,, ...	5,300	F. 12918
APRIL 2.				
Here Comes Trouble ..	Fox	Fox	5,611	F. 12919
The Adventures of Frank Merriwell (serial) :—				
Episode 5 ..	Universal ..	Universal ..	1,855	F. 12920
Episode 6 ..	,, ...	,, ...	1,698	F. 12921
Episode 7 ..	,, ...	,, ...	1,928	F. 12922
Episode 8 ..	,, ...	,, ...	1,673	F. 12923
Episode 9 ..	,, ...	,, ...	1,754	F. 12924
Episode 10 ..	,, ...	,, ...	1,718	F. 12925
Episode 11 ..	,, ...	,, ...	1,844	F. 12926
Episode 12 ..	,, ...	,, ...	1,783	F. 12927
APRIL 3.				
Dont' Gamble with Love	Columbia ..	Columbia ..	5,749	F. 12928
Movie Maniacs ..	,, ...	,, ...	1,551	F. 12929
Hell Ship Morgan ..	,, ...	,, ...	5,839	F. 12930
Dr. Bluebird ..	,, ...	,, ...	725	F. 12931
The Music Goes 'Round	,, ...	,, ...	7,737	F. 12932
The Bird Stuffer ..	,, ...	,, ...	572	F. 12933
Important News ..	M-G-M	M-G-M	897	F. 12937
Let's Dance ..	,, ...	,, ...	728	F. 12938
Audioscopiks	,, ...	,, ...	741	F. 12939
The Country Doctor ..	Fox	Fox	8,440	F. 12940
Grand Opera	United Artists ..	Walt Disney Prod.	696	F. 12941
APRIL 6.				
The Prisoner of Shark Island.	Fox	Twentieth Century Fox.	8,560	F. 12944
Code of the Mounted	Butcher's Film Service.	Guaranteed Pictures.	4,990	F. 12945
Liebesmelodie ..	Reunion Films, Ltd.	Standard-Film Gesellschaft.	8,154	F. 12946
Man Hunt	First National ..	Warner	5,535	F. 12947
Double or Nothing ..	,, ..	Vitaphone Corp.	1,937	F. 12948
APRIL 8.				
The Fire Trap ..	Pathe ..	Larry Darmour	5,700	F. 12949
Klondike Annie ..	Paramount ..	Paramount ..	7,026	F. 12950
APRIL 9.				
Brides are Like That	First National ..	Warner	6,090	F. 12952
I Wanna Play House ..	,, ...	Vitaphone Corp.	656	F. 12953
Shorty at Coney Island	Paramount ..	Paramount ..	881	F. 12954
Give Us this Night ..	,, ..	,, ..	6,263	F. 12955
Don't Get Personal ..	Universal ..	Universal ..	5,814	F. 12956
You Can be Had ..	,, ...	,, ...	1,255	F. 12957
Carnival Time ..	,, ...	Mentone Prod. ..	1,652	F. 12958
APRIL 14.				
Wife Vs. Secretary ..	M-G-M	M-G-M	7,874	F. 12962
APRIL 15.				
Murder on a Bridle Path	Radio ..	R.K.O. Corp. ..	5,988	F. 12966
Alladin from Manhattan	,, ...	,, ...	1,582	F. 12967
APRIL 16.				
Comi-Colour Cartoon Nursery Rhymes (series) :—	,, ...	,, ...		
Summertime ..	British Lion ..	Celebrity Prod. Inc.	727	F. 12968
Silly Billies ..	Radio ..	R.K.O. Corp. ..	5,763	F. 12969
Uppercutlets ..	,, ...	,, ...	1,682	F. 12970
Winged Champions ..	Paramount ..	Paramount ..	885	F. 12971
The Little Stranger ..	,, ...	,, ...	712	F. 12972
The Last Assignment ..	Pathe ..	Victory Pictures	5,349	F. 12973

Title of Film.	Registered by.	Maker's name.	Length (feet).	No.
APRIL 17				
The Farmer in the Dell	Radio	R.K.O.	6,105	F. 12980
Camera Cranks	,,	,,	1,726	F. 12981
Petticoat Fever	M-G-M	M-G-M	7,190	F. 12982
The Trail of the Lonesome Pine.	Paramount	Paramount	8,876	F. 12983
A Clean Shaven Man	,,		551	F. 12984
APRIL 18.				
Treachery Rides the Range.	Warner	Warner	5,129	F. 12985
Katz Pajamas	,,	,,	2,006	F. 12986
Phantom Ship	,,	,,	694	F. 12987
Crashing through Danger	A.P. & D.	Sig. Neufeld and Leslie Smmonds.	6,300	F. 12988
APRIL 20.				
Moonlight Murder	M-G-M	M-G-M	5,973	F. 12989
APRIL 21.				
Lucky Stars V5-9	Paramount	Paramount	919	F. 12991
Suicide Squad	Pathe	Puritan Pictures	5,356	F. 12992
Colleen	Warner	Warner	8,147	F. 12993
Boom Boom	,,	,,	692	F. 12994
Steel and Stone	,,	,,	900	F. 12995
Men of Action	Independent Film Distributors.	Conn Picture Corp.	5,670	F. 12996
Kliou the Killer	Wardour	Bennett Pictures Corp.	4,459	F. 12997
Tonto Kid	Exclusive Films	Resolute Prod.	5,300	F. 12998
APRIL 22.				
Charlie Chan at the Circus.	Fox	Fox	6,476	F. 12999
Thirteen Hours by Air	Paramount	Paramount	6,971	F. 13000
Accent on Girls	,,	,,	797	F. 13001
APRIL 23.				
Injustice	First National	Warner	5,863	F. 13002
Vitaphone Celebrities	,,	Vitaphone Corp.	1,007	F. 13003
APRIL 24.				
The Walking Dead	First National	Warner	5,890	F. 13009
Broadway Ballyhoo	,,	Vitaphone Corp.	1,908	F. 13010
A Face in the Fog	Pathé	Victory Pictures Corp.	5,500	F. 13011
APRIL 25.				
Anne-Marie	G.-B. D.	Majestic Film S.A.	10,168	F. 13013
APRIL 27.				
Forget Me Not	United Artists	London Film Productions, and Itala Film G.m.b.H.	6,555	F. 13014
The Student of Prague	G.-B. D.	Cine-Allianz Tonfilm.	7,781	F. 13015
They're Off	First National	Vitaphone Corp.	1,919	F. 13016
Shop Talk	,,	,,	1,999	F. 13017
The Half Witness	,,	,,	1,002	F. 13018
The Lucky Swede	,,	,,	1,515	F. 13019
Officer's Mess	,,	,,	1,958	F. 13020
Can it be Done ?	,,	,,	997	F. 13021
Bar 20 Rides Again	Paramount	Paramount	5,659	F. 13022
Betty Boop and the Little King.	,,	,,	574	F. 13023
APRIL 28.				
These Three	United Artists	Samuel Goldwyn, Inc.	8,466	F. 13028
APRIL 29.				
Absolute Quiet	M-G-M	M-G-M	6,269	F. 13031
Hit And Run Driver	M-G-M	M-G-M	1,765	F. 13032
A Thrill For Thelma	M-G-M	M-G-M	1,615	F. 13033
Two Hearts In Wax Time	M-G-M	M-G-M	1,362	F. 13034
Starlit Days At The Lido	M-G-M	M-G-M	1,730	F. 13035

Title of Film.	Registered by.	Maker's name.	Length (feet).	No.
APRIL 29—cont.				
Pirate PartyAt Catalina Isle	M-G-M	M-G-M	1,649	F. 13036
Vitaphone Troupers ..	Warner Bros. Pic.	Warner Bros.Pic.	1,014	F. 13037
Red Nichols And His WorldFamousPennies	Warner Bros.Pic.	Warner Bros.Pic.	958	F. 13038
Jolly Coburn and His Orchestra.	Warner	Warner	871	F. 13039
Slide Nellie, Slide	,,	,,	1,723	F. 13040
Between the Lines	,,	,,	1,914	F. 13041
Study and Understudy	,,	,,	1,977	F. 13042
Too Many Parents	Paramount	Paramount	6,589	F. 13043
No Other One	,,	,,	631	F. 13044
Wanted Men ..	Independent Film Distributors	Conn Pictures Corp.	5,625	F. 13045
APRIL 30.				
Love Before Breakfast	General F.D.	Universal	6,298	F. 13046
Soft Ball Game	,,	,,	655	F. 13047
On Probation ..	,,	Peerless Pictures	5,766	F. 13048
Alaska Sweepstakes ..	,,	Universal	703	F. 13049
The Ivory Handled Gun	,,	,,	5,327	F. 13050
Captured in Chinatown	,,	Consolidated Pictures Corp.	4,712	F. 13051
Signing Off	,,	Mentone Productions	1,703	F. 13052
Skits " N " Sketches..	,,	Universal	902	F. 13053
Silver Spurs	,,	,,	5,147	F. 13054
The Vaud-O-Mat	,,	Mentone Productions	1,723	F. 13055
Slumberland Express..	,,	Universal	635	F. 13056
MAY 1.				
Movie Milestones No. 2, V. 5–11	Paramount	Paramount	860	F. 13059
Mystery Mountain — The Battler	A.B.F.D...	Republic Picture Corp.	2,756	F. 13062
Mystery Mountain (serial) :—				
Mystery Mountain— The Man Nobody Knows	A.B.F.D...	Republic	1,792	F. 13063
Mystery Mountain— The Eye That Never Sleeps	,,	,,	1,711	F. 13064
Mystery Mountain— The Human Target	.,	,,	1,638	F. 13065
Mystery Mountain— The Phantom Outlaw	,,	,,	1,506	F. 13066
Mystery Mountain— The Perfect Crime.	,,	,,	1,684	F. 13067
Mystery Mountain— Tarzan the Cunning	,,	,,	1,578	F. 13068
Mystery Mountain— The Enemy's Stronghold	,,	,,	1,913	F. 13069
Mystery Mountain— The Fatal Warning	,,	,,	1,618	F. 13070
Mystery Mountain— The Secret of the Mountain	,,	,,	1,763	F. 13071
Mystery Mountain— Behind the Mask	,,	,,	1,684	F. 13072
Mystery Mountain— The Judgment of Tarzan	.,	,,	1,869	F. 13073
Sunset Range	A.B.F.D...	First Division Exchanges	4,730	F. 13074
MAY 2.				
Little Lord Fauntleroy	United Artists	Selznick International Pictures	9,361	F. 13075
The Unguarded Hour..	M-G-M	M-G-M	7,817	F. 13076

Title of Film.	Registered by.	Maker's name.	Length (feet).	No.
MAY 4.				
Choose Your Partners	G.-B.D. ..	Educational Film Corp. of America	1,756	F. 13078
Stage Door Romance	.. ..	,, ...	1,910	F. 13079
Ali Baba and the Forty Thieves	A.B.F.D...	Gasparcolor ..	1,025	F. 13081
Desert Gold	Paramount	Paramount ..	5,266	F. 13082
Moscow Moods	,, ...	,, ...	923	F. 13083
Elmer Elephant	United Artists ..	Walt Disney Prod.	775	F. 13084
MAY 5.				
Mr. Deeds Goes to Town	Columbia	Columbia ..	10,391	F. 13085
Wild Waters	Wardour	Imperial Corp. ..	1,675	F. 13091
Death Fangs	,, ..	,, ...	1,400	F. 13092
Crack-Up	,, ..	,, ...	1,762	F. 13093
MAY 6.				
Three on a Limb ..	G.B.D. ..	Educational Film Corp. of America	1,707	F. 13096
Perfect Thirty-Sixes ..	,, ..	,, ,,	1,652	F. 13097
Ladies Love Hats ..	,, ..	,, ,,	1,771	F. 13098
Movie Melodies on Parade	Paramount	Paramount ..	941	F. 13099
Big Brown Eyes ..	,, ..	,, ..	6,860	F. 13100
MAY 7.				
Beware of Blondes ..	G.-B.D. ..	Educational Film Corp. of America	1,833	F. 13101
Thanks, Mr. Cupid ..	,, ..	,, ,,	1,596	F. 13102
The Brain Busters ..	,, ..	,, ,,	1,580	F. 13103
Everybody's Old Man	Fox ..	Fox	7,621	F. 13104
Song and Dance Man	,, ..	,, ...	6,547	F. 13105
MAY 8.				
Small Town Girl ..	M-G-M ..	M-G-M	9,474	F. 13107
The Jonker Diamond	,, ..	,, ...	885	F. 13108
Grand Slam Opera ..	G.-B.D. ..	Educational Film Corp. of America	1,860	F. 13109
Love in September ..	,, ..	,, ,,	1,843	F. 13110
Mixed Policies ..	,, ..	,, ,,	1,786	F. 13111
Iski Loveski Youski ..	Paramount	Paramount ..	568	F. 13112
MAY 11.				
The Country Beyond ..	Fox ..	Fox	6,170	F. 13114
La Belle Au Bois Dormant	G.-B.D. ..	Carnel Sarbo ..	530	F. 13115
MAY 12.				
Run Sheep, Run ..	M-G-M ..	M-G-M	929	F. 13117
MAY 14.				
Arbor Day	M-G-M ..	Hal E. Roach ..	1,569	F. 13119
The Moon's Our Home	Paramount	Paramount ..	7,413	F. 13120
Finer Points	,, ..	,, ..	642	F. 13121
His Best Man	First Nationa	Warner	5,628	F. 13122
Singing Kid	,, ..	,, ...	7,714	F. 13123
The Cat Came Back ..	,, ..	Vitaphone Corp.	741	F. 13124
Wash Your Step ..	,, ..	,, ...	1,977	F. 13125
MAY 18.				
I'm a Big Shot Now ..	,, ..	,, ...	658	F. 13129
Marines Have Landed	A.B.F.D...	Republic Corp. ..	6,135	F. 13130
Rio Rattler	General F.D.	Reliable Corp. ..	4,860	F. 13131
Beauty Shoppe ..	,, ..	Universal ..	612	F. 13132
Sunset of Power ..	,, ..	,, ...	5,196	F. 13133
The Barnyard Five ..	,, ..	,, ...	452	F. 13134
MAY 19.				
Sun Chaser	Paramount	Paramount ..	854	F. 13137
A Message to Garcia ..	Fox ..	Twentieth-Century Fox.	7,298	F. 13138
MAY 20.				
Special Investigator ..	Radio ..	R.K.O. Corp. ..	5,521	F. 13142
Foolish Hearts ..	,, ..	,, ...	1,672	F. 13143

Title of Film.	Registered by.	Maker's name.	Length (feet).	No.
MAY 20—cont.				
Two in Revolt..	Radio ..	R.K.O. Corp. ..	5,812	F. 13144
The Worm Burns	,, ..	,, ..	1,547	F. 13145
For the Service	General F.D. ..	Universal ..	5,034	F. 13146
Playing for Fun	,, ..	Mentone Prod. ..	1,214	F. 13147
The Sky Parade	Paramount	Paramount ..	6,288	F. 13148
Not Now	,, ..	,, ..	596	F. 13149
MAY 21.				
Timber War ..	Butcher's	Guaranteed Pict.	4,600	F. 13151
The Witness Chair	Radio ..	R.K.O. Corp. ..	5,766	F. 13153
Too Many Surprises ..	,, ..	,, ..	**1,900**	**F. 13154**
MAY 22.				
I Married a Doctor ..	Warner ..	Warner ..	7,579	F. 13157
Ramon Ramos and his Orchestra.	,, ..	,, ..	874	F. 13158
Murder by an Aristocrat	,, ..	,, ..	5,455	F. 13159
Blow Out ..	,, ..	,, ..	691	F. 13160
Paris in New York ..	,, ..	,, ..	2,001	F. 13161
Anthony Adverse ..	,, ..	,, ..	12,800	F. 13162
Beneath the Sea ..	,, ..	,, ..	755	F. 13163
Frontier Justice ..	Ind. F. Dis.	Diversion Pict.,Inc.	5,500	F. 13164
The Emperor's Candle-sticks.	G.-B.D. ..	Gloria Film ..	8,257	F. 13165
The Ex Mrs. Bradford	Radio ..	R.K.O. Corp. ..	7,351	F. 13167
The Goose that Laid the Golden Egg.	,, ..	Amedee J. Van Beuren.	699	F. 13168
Down the Ribber ..	,, ..	R.K.O. Corp. ..	1,916	F. 13169
MAY 23.				
Speed	M-G-M ..	M-G-M ..	6,366	F. 13170
MAY 25.				
Comi-Colour Cartoon Nursery Rhymes (series) :—				
Simple Simon ..	British Lion	Celebrity Prod. ..	610	F. 13172
Star Reporter	Paramount	Paramount ..	827	F. 13175
20 Ace Comedies (series) :—				
Going Spanish ..	Ace Films	Educational Film Corp. of America.	1,882	F. 13176
Static	,, ..	,,	1,857	F. 13177
That Rascal ..	,, ..	,,	1,914	F. 13178
Er Sweeties ..	,, ..	,,	1,902	F. 13179
Bride and Gloomy ..	,, ..	,,	1,865	F. 13180
MAY 26.				
Captain January ..	Fox ..	Fox ..	6,959	F. 13182
MAY 27.				
Frankie and Johnnie	British Lion ..	Republic Picture Corp.	6,075	F. 13183
Second Childhood ..	M-G-M ..	Hal E. Roach ..	1,708	F. 13188
Table Tennis ..	,, ..	M-G-M ..	862	F. 13189
Bottles	,, ..	,, ..	919	F. 13190
MAY 28.				
Footlights and Shadows	Twickenham F.D.	Invincible Corp.	5,955	F. 13192
False Pretences ..	,, ..	Chesterfield Corp.	6,132	F. 13193
Forgotten Faces ..	Paramount	Paramount ..	6,429	F. 13194
Brotherly Love ..	,, ..	,, ..	582	F. 13195
Comi-Colour Cartoon Nursery Rhymes (series) :—				
Humpty Dumpty ..	British Lion ..	Celebrity Produc-tions, Inc.	605	F. 13196
White Lights on Sport —Boxing.	Kinograph Dis...	Invicta Film Pro-ductions.	1,739	F. 13197
Murder at Glen Athol..	Twickenham F.D.	Invincible Corp.	6,280	F. 13198
Snowed Under ..	First National ..	Warner	5,714	F. 13199
Little Jack Little's Orchestra.	,, ...	Vitaphone Corp.	991	F. 13200
MAY 29.				
Dei Ewige Maske ..	Film Society ..	Progress-Film A.G.	7,110	F. 13201

Title of Film.	Registered by.	Maker's name.	Length (feet).	No.
JUNE 2.				
Women are Dangerous	Twickenham F.D.	Chesterfield Corp.	6,122	F. 13203
Under Two Flags ..	Fox	Twentieth Century Fox.	9,990	F. 13204
One Rainy Afternoon..	United Artists ..	Pickford-Lasky Productions.	7,280	F. 13205
Three Little Wolves ..	,, ...	Walt Disney Productions.	851	F. 13206
Marine Follies.. ..	General F.D. ..	Mentone Productions.	1,571	F. 13207
JUNE 4.				
The Three Wise Guys	M-G-M	M-G-M	6,654	F. 13208
Streamline Express ...	A.B.F.D.... ...	Republic Corp. ...	6,460	F. 13209
Florida Special ...	Paramount ...	Paramount ...	5,997	F. 13210
Betty Boop and Little Jimmy	,, ...	,, ...	526	F. 13211
JUNE 5.				
House of a Thousand Candles.	British Lion ...	Republic Corp. ...	6,479	F. 13212
JUNE 8.				
Caught in the Act ...	Columbia ...	Columbia ...	1,628	F. 13216
Lil' Ainjil	,, ...	,, ...	543	F. 13217
The King Steps Out ...	,, ...	,, ...	7,597	F. 13218
Catching Trouble ...	Paramount ...	Paramount ...	760	F. 13219
Get that Man	Fidelity Dist. ...	Empire Film Dis.	5,643	F. 13220
JUNE 10.				
King of the Islands ...	First National ...	Vitaphone Corp.	1,596	F. 13224
The Harvester... ...	British Lion ...	Republic Corp. ...	6,308	F. 13225
The Drag Net	Pathé ...	William N. Selig	6,000	F. 13226
The Case against Mrs. Ames.	Paramount ...	Paramount ...	7,756	F. 13227
Breezy Rhythm ...	,, ...	,, ...	930	F. 13228
The Cowboy and the Kid.	General F.D. ...	Universal ...	4,864	F. 13229
Fun House	,,	.. ...	607	F. 13230
JUNE 11.				
Trapped by Wireless ...	Columbia ...	Columbia ...	4,980	F. 13231
Midnight Blunders ...	,, .	,, ...	1,534	F. 13232
Scrappy's Pony ...	,,	.. ...	576	F. 13233
JUNE 12.				
Man's Best Friend ...	Equity British ...	Regal	5,400	F. 13234
Woman of Destiny ...	,, ...	Showman Productions.	5,700	F. 13235 .
Red River Valley ...	British Lion ...	Republic Corp. ...	5,165	F. 13236
Rogues' Tavern ...	Pathé	Puritan Corp. ...	6,000	F. 13237
JUNE 13.				
Darkest Africa ...	British Lion ...	Republic Corp. ...	6,591	F. 13239
The Cobweb Hotel ...	Paramount ...	Paramount ...	703	F. 13240
JUNE 15.				
Show Boat	General F.D. ...	Universal ...	10,315	F. 13241
Midnight Melodies ...	Paramount ...	Paramount ...	930	F. 13244
Sins of Man	Fox	Twentieth Century Fox	7,050	F. 13245
JUNE 16.				
Flash Gordon (serial):				
Episode 1	General F.D. ...	Universal Corp. ...	1,772	F. 13246
Episode 2	,, - ...	,, ...	1,722	F. 13247
Episode 3	,, ...	,, ...	1,805	F. 13248
Revenge Rider ...	Columbia ...	Columbia ...	5,040	F. 13249
Share the Wealth ...	,, ...	,, ...	1,610	F. 13250
Roaming Lady ...	,,	,, ...	6,187	F. 13251
JUNE 17.				
Madcap	Pathé ...	Victory Corp. ...	5,142	F. 13253
Till We Meet Again ...	Paramount ...	Paramount ...	6,432	F. 13254

Title of Film.	Registered by.	Maker's name.	Length (feet).	No.
JUNE 18.				
The Devil's Squadron	Columbia ...	Columbia ...	7,100	F. 13256
Champagne Charlie ...	Fox	Fox	5,341	F. 13257
The First Baby ...	,, ...	,, ...	6,696	F. 13259
JUNE 19.				
Sutter's Gold	Gen. F.D. ...	Universal ...	8,554	F. 13260
Fury	M-G-M ...	M-G-M	8,292	F. 13261
JUNE 20.				
And So They Were Married.	Columbia ...	Columbia ...	6,656	F. 13263
Spark Plug	,, ...	,, ...	708	F. 13264
JUNE 22.				
The Reckless Way ...	Pathé	Puritan P. Prod.	5,895	F. 13267
Revolt of the Zombies	,, ...	Academy P. Corp.	6,100	F. 13268
Bed and Sofa	Progressive Film Institute.	Len Films ...	6,316*	F. 13269
JUNE 23.				
Romance in the Air ...	First National ...	Vitaphone Corp.	1,778	F. 13270
JUNE 25.				
The Last Rose (Letzte Rose).	G.-B.D. ...	Lloyd Film G.m.b.H.	7,971	F. 13271
The Phantom Gondola	G.-B.D. ...	Film Export ...	7,388	F. 13272
Broadway Highlights, No. 6, V.5-14.	Paramount ...	Paramount Pictures, Inc.	754	F. 13273
Fatal Lady	,, ...	,, ...	6,836	F. 13274
Reg'lar Kids	Warner Bros. ...	Warner Bros. Pictures, Inc.	1,584	F. 13275
The Shadow of Silk Lennox.	Viking Films ...	Commodore Film Productions	5,740	F. 13276
Half Angel	Fox	Twentieth Century Fox.	5,763	F. 13277
Framed...	Pathe	Victory Pictures Corp.	6,160	F. 13278
JUNE 26.				
I'll Name the Murderer	Pathe ...	Puritan Pictures Corp.	6,200	F. 13281
JUNE 29.				
La Fiesta De Santa Barbara	M-G-M ...	M-G-M	1,679	F. 13283
Polo	,, ...	,, ...	697	F. 13284
Janosik...	Reunion Films ...	Lloyd Films ...	6,750	F. 13285
Human Cargo... ...	Fox	Fox Film Corp., Inc.	5,795	F. 13287
Flash Gordon (serial):—				
Episode 4	General Film Distributors.	Universal Pictures Corp.	1,551	F. 13288
Episode 5	,, ...	,, ...	1,548	F. 13289
JUNE 30.				
Melody in May ...	Radio	R.K.O. Corp. ...	1,787	F. 13292
Dracula's Daughter ...	General Film Distributors.	Universal Pictures, Corp.	6,470	F. 13293
JULY 1.				
Early to Bed	Paramount ...	Paramount Pict., Inc.	6,561	F. 13295
JULY 2.				
His Majesty Bunker Bean.	Radio ...	R.K.O. Corp. ...	6,022	F. 13296
The Last Outlaw ...	Radio ...	R.K.O. Corp. ...	6,342	F. 13297
Gasoloons	,, ...	,, ...	1,430	F. 13298
Go West	Viking Films ...	Padman Red Star Prod.	740	F. 13299
The Man Pays... ...	,, ...	,, ...	780	F. 13300
Nobody's Fool ...	Gen. Film Dis. ...	Universal Pic.Corp.	5,700	F. 13301
International Broadcast	,, ...	Mentone Prod.,Inc.	1,858	F. 13302
Farming Fools ...	,, ...	Universal Pict. Corp.	619	F. 13303
Black Network ...	Warner Bros. ...	Warner Bros., Pict., Inc.	1,922	F. 13305
The Law in Her Hands	First National ...	,, ...	5,299	F. 13306

Title of Film.	Registered by.	Maker's name.	Length (feet).	No.
JULY 3.				
Radiobarred	Radio	R.K.O. Corp. ...	1,432	F. 13309
Dancing Pirate ...	,, ...	Pioneer Pict., Inc.	7,658	F. 13310
The Old Mill Pond ...	M-G-M	M-G-M	728	F. 13311
The Suicide Club ...	,, ...	,, ...	6,675	F. 13312
JULY 6.				
Stepping in Society ...	A.B.F.D.... ...	*Republic Film Corp.	6,504	F. 13313
Murder in the Big House	Warner Bros. ...	Warner Bros. Pict. Inc.	5,454	F. 13314
For the Love of Pete	,, ...	,, ...	1,986	F. 13315
Vitaphone Billboard	,, ...	,, ...	929	F. 13316
The Case of the Velvet Claws.	,, ...	,, ...	5,775	F. 13317
The City Slicker ...	,, ...	,, ...	1,966	F. 13318
Little Miss Nobody ...	Fox	FoxFilmCorp.,Inc.	6,574	F. 13319
Let's Sing Again ...	Radio	PrincipalPic.,Inc.	6,172	F. 13320
Thru' the Mirror ...	U.A.	Walt Disney Prod., Inc.	803	F. 13321
JULY 7.				
Forgotten Women ...	Wardour ...	Guaranteed Pict. Corp., Inc.	5,296	F. 13323
JULY 8.				
Midnight Phantom ...	Butcher's ...	Reliable Corpn....	5,086	F. 13324
Neptune Nonsense ...	Radio	Amedee J. Van Beuren.	691	F. 13325
Secret Interlude ...	Fox	Fox	7,154	F. 13326
The Princess Comes Across.	Paramount ..	Paramount ...	6,791	F. 13327
I Feel Like a Feather in the Breeze.	Butcher's ...	Reliable Corpn. ...	676	F. 13328
JULY 9.				
When Lightning Strikes	Equity	Regal Corp. ...	5,110	F. 13331
The-Live Wire ...	,, ...	Reliable Picture Corp.	5,250	F. 13332
JULY 10.				
Perils of the Plains ...	Wardour · ...	Weiss Productions	2,250	F. 13333
Custer's Last Stand (serial) :—				
Custer Comes to For Henry.	Wardour ...	,, ...	1,890	F. 13334
Thundering Hoofs ...	,, ...	,, ...	1,940	F. 13335
Red Vengeance ...	,, ...	,, ...	1,926	F. 13336
Sons o' Guns	First National ...	Warner	7,204	F. 13337
Maid for a Day ...	,, ...	Vitaphone Corp.	1,937	F. 13338
Kelly the Second ...	M-G-M	Hal E. Roach ...	6,320	F. 13339
JULY 11.				
Women Are Trouble...	M-G-M	M-G-M	5,250	F. 13340
Poppy	Paramount ...	Paramount ...	6,305	F. 13341
Dangerous Jobs V.5-16	,, ...	,, ...	810	F. 13342
Bridge Ahoy	,, ...	,, ...	619	F 13343
JULY 13.				
We Did It	Paramount ...	Paramount ...	541	F. 13346
The Adventures of Rex and Rinty—The God Horse of Sujan.	A.B.F.D.... ...	Mascot P. Corp.	2,597	F. 13347
The Adventures of Rex and Rinty (serial) :—				
The Adventures of Rex and Rinty—Sport of Kings.	,, ...	,, ...	1,852	F. 13348
The Adventures of Rex and Rinty—Fangs of Flame.	,, ...	,, ...	1,690	F. 13349
The Adventures of Rex and Rinty—Homeward Bound.	,, ...	,, ...	1,607	F. 13350
The Adventures of Rex and Rinty—Babes in the Wood.	,, ...	,, ...	1,670	F. 13351

Title of Film.	Registered by.	Maker's name.	Length (feet).	No.
JULY 13—cont.				
The Adventures of Rex and Rinty — Dead Man's Tale.	A.B.F.D....	Mascot P. Corp.	1,546	F. 13352
The Adventures of Rex and Rinty—End of the Road.	,,	,,	1,515	F. 13353
The Adventures of Rex and Rinty—A Dog's Devotion.	,,	,,	1,659	F. 13354
The Adventures of Rex and Rinty — The Stranger's Recall.	,,	,,	1,672	F. 13355
The Adventures of Rex and Rinty — The Siren of Death.	,,	,,	1,644	F. 13356
The Adventures of Rex and Rinty — New Gods for Old.	,,	,,	1,601	F. 13357
The Adventures of Rex and Rinty—Primitive Justice.	,,	,,	1,761	F. 13358
JULY 14.				
Men and Jobs	Progressive Film Institute.	Len Films	6,664	F. 13360
JULY 15.				
Palm Springs Affair	Paramount	Paramount	6,478	F. 13361
The Rookie Fireman V5–16	,,	,,	810	F. 13362
JULY 16.				
Hearts Divided	Warner	Warner	6,906	F. 13363
Hot Money	,,	,,	6,220	F. 13364
Vitaphone Varieties	,,	,,	1,007	F. 13365
Westward Whoa	,,	,,	671	F. 13366
Border Flight	Paramount	Paramount	5,307	F. 13367
Case of Mrs. Pembrook	First National	Warner	5,179	F. 13368
Let It Be Me	,,	Vitaphone Corp.	719	F. 13369
JULY 17.				
San Francisco	M-G-M	M-G-M	10,380	F. 13373
JULY 18.				
The Three Maxims	General F.D.	Herbert Wilcox Prod., Ltd., and Cie Pathé Consortium.	7,736	F. 13374
JULY 20.				
Modern Madness	Warner	Warner	5,193	F. 13376
Vitaphone Highlights	,,	,,	1,002	F. 13377
Vincent Lopez and Orchestra.	,,	,,	991	F. 13378
The White Angel	,,	,,	8,370	F. 13379
Changing of the Guard (Technicolor).	,,	,,	1,766	F. 13380
Call of the Prairie	Paramount	Paramount	5,994	F. 13381
JULY 22.				
Flash Gordon (serial) :—				
Episode 6	General F.D.	Universal	1,401	F. 13383
Episode 7	,,	,,	1,490	F. 13384
Episode 8	,,	,,	1,311	F. 13385
Episode 9	,,	,,	1,651	F. 13386
Episode 10	,,	,,	1,701	F. 13387
Episode 11	,,	,,	1,641	F. 13388
Episode 12	,,	,,	1,581	F. 13389
Episode 13	,,	,,	1,815	F. 13390
Three Cheers for Love	Paramount	Paramount	5,509	F. 13392
The Last Waltz	A.P. & D.	Gina Carton Prod.	6,300	F. 13393
The Tomb of the Unknown Warrior.	,,	Mars Film Prod.	2,030	F. 13394
JULY 23.				
The Mine with the Iron Door.	Columbia	Columbia	5,862	F. 13395

Title of Film.	Registered by.	Maker's name.	Length (feet).
JULY 23—cont.			
Half Shot Shooters ...	Columbia... ...	Columbia... ...	1,659
Major Google	,, ...	,, ...	760
Girl of the Ozarks ...	Paramount ...	Paramount ...	6,121
JULY 24.			
Custer's Last Stand (serial) :—			
The Ghost Dancers ...	Wardour ...	Weiss Productions	1,916
Trapped	,, ...	,, ...	1,835
Human Wolves ...	,, ...	,, ...	1,701
Demons of the Desert	,, ...	,, ...	1,890
White Treachery ...	,, ...	,, ...	1,904
The Circle of Death	,, ...	,, ...	1,897
Flaring Arrows ...	,, ...	,, ...	1,805
Warpath	,, ...	,, ...	1,792
Firing Squad ...	,, ...	,, ...	1,893
Red Panthers ...	,, ...	,, ...	1,790
Custer's Last Ride ...	,, ...	,, ...	1,893
Custer's Last Stand...	,, ...	,, ...	1,798
JULY 27.			
The Old School Tie ...	M-G-M	M-G-M	6,137
The Early Bird and the Worm.	,, ...	,, ...	828
Peppery Salt ...	Columbia ...	Columbia ...	1,584
Scrappy's Camera Troubles.	,, ...	,, ...	619
Just Speeding	,, ...	,, ...	1,562
A Woman Alone ...	United Artists ...	Garrett Klement Pictures.	7,094
Moving Day	,, ...	Walt Disney Prod.	855
And Sudden Death ...	Paramount ...	Paramount ...	5,873
Educating Father ...	Fox	Twentieth Century-Fox.	5,213
JULY 28.			
Pan Handlers	M-G-M	Hal E. Roach ...	1,824
The Perfect Set-up ...	,, ...	M-G-M	1,825
On the Wrong Trek ...	,, ...	Hal E. Roach ...	1,658
Hill-Tillies	,, ...	,, ...	1,611
JULY 29.			
M'liss	Radio	R.K.O. Corp. ...	5,969
Will Power	,, ...	,, ...	1,450
Bold King Cole ...	,, ...	Amedee J. Van Beuren.	708
Mickey's Rival ...	United Artists ...	Walt Disney Prod.	757
The Return of Sophie Lang.	Paramount ...	Paramount ...	5,755
Born to Fight ...	Independent Film Distributors.	Conn Pict. Corp.	6,500
JULY 30.			
The Bride Walks Out	Radio	R.K.O. Corp. ...	7,280
A Wedtime Story ...	,, ...	,, ...	1,906
JULY 31.			
The Amazing Quest of Ernest Bliss.	United Artists ...	Garrett Klement Pictures, Ltd.	7,188
AUGUST 1.			
Mary of Scotland ...	Radio	R.K.O. Corp. ...	11,090
AUGUST 4.			
Spendthrift	Paramount ...	Paramount ...	7,001
Yankee Doodle Rhapsody	,, ...	,, ...	847
The Poodle V 5-7 ...	,, ...	,, ...	830
AUGUST 5.			
Hard Rock Harrigan	A.B.F.D.... ...	Principal Prod. ...	5,500
Re Burlone	,, ...	Capilani Film Co.	8,565
AUGUST 6.			
Stars of To-morrow No. 1	Wardour ...	Columbia ...	834
Stars of To-morrow No. 2	,, ...	,, ...	954

Title of Film.	Registered by.	Maker's name.	Length (feet).	No.
AUGUST 6—cont.				
Stars of To-morrow No. 3	Wardour ...	Columbia ...	936	F. 13455
Stars of To-morrow No. 4	,, ...	,, ...	747	F. 13456
Stars of To-morrow No. 5	,, ...	,, ...	1,000	F. 13457
Stars of To-morrow No. 6	,, ...	,, ...	968	F. 13458
AUGUST 7.				
Sworn Enemy ...	M-G-M	M-G-M	6,454	F. 13461
Rhythm on the Range	Paramount ...	Paramount ...	7,670	F. 13462
Ride 'em Cowboy ...	General F.D. ...	Universal ...	5,144	F. 13463
Flippen's Frolics	,, ...	Mentone Prod. ...	1,632	F. 13464
Battle Royal	,, ...	Universal ...	632	F. 13465
AUGUST 8.				
River of Thrills ...	Paramount ...	Paramount ...	852	F. 13467
What, No Spinach ...	,, ...	,, ...	585	F. 13468
AUGUST 11.				
Disorder in Court ...	Columbia ...	Columbia ...	1,494	F. 13470
Pain in the Pullman ...	,, ...	,, ...	1,738	F. 13471
The Champ's a Chump	,, ...	,, ...	1,653	F. 13472
AUGUST 14.				
Never Too Late ...	Equity British ...	Reliable Picture Corporation.	5,100	F. 13484
Kazan, the Fearless ...	,,	Regal Film Corporation.	5,250	F. 13485
Suzy	M-G-M	M-G-M	8,390	F. 13487
AUGUST 15.				
The Drunkard ...	Reunion	Stage and Screen Plays.	3,750	F. 13489
AUGUST 17.				
Lucky Starlets... ...	Paramount ...	Paramount Pictures.	804	F. 13491
Poor Little Rich Girl	Fox	Twentieth Century Fox.	7,144	F. 13492
AUGUST 18.				
Untrained Seal ...	Columbia ...	Columbia ...	680	F. 13493
Meet Nero Wolfe ...	,, ...	,, ...	6,447	F. 13494
Football Bugs ...	,, ...	,, ...	692	F. 13495
The Final Hour ...	,, ...	,, ...	5,169	F. 13496
Glee Worms	,, ...	,, ...	667	F. 13497
Counterfeit	,, ...	,, ...	6,544	F. 13498
How to Behave ...	M-G-M	M-G-M	893	F. 13499
Comi-Colour Cartoon—				
Nursery Rhymes (series) :—				
Tom Thumb... ...	British Lion ...	Celebrity Productions.	635	F. 13500
AUGUST 19.				
Gold Bricks	G.-B.D.	Educational Film Corp. of America.	1,821	F. 13502
Give 'Im Air	,, ...	,, ...	1,660	F. 13503
Fresh from the Fleet ...	,, ...	,, ...	1,617	F. 13504
AUGUST 20.				
Blackmailer	Columbia ...	Columbia ...	5,897	F. 13505
Mister Smarty ...	,, ...	,, ...	1,609	F. 13506
The Crime of Dr. Forbes	Fox	Twentieth Century Fox.	6,901	F. 13507
Bullets or Ballots ...	First National ...	Warner Bros. Pictures, Inc.	7,446	F. 13508
AUGUST 21.				
Lightnin' Bill Carson	Equity British ...	Puritan Pictures, Inc.	6,000	F. 13509
The Devil Doll ...	M-G-M	M-G-M	7,032	F. 13510
White Fang	Fox	Twentieth Century Fox	6,658	F. 13511

Title of Film.	Registered by.	Maker's name.	Length (feet).	No.
AUGUST 24.				
My American Wife ...	Paramount ...	Paramount ...	6,595	F. 13513
The Lawless Nineties...	British Lion ...	Republic Picture Corp.	5,161	F. 13514
Hearts in Bondage ...	,, ...	,, ...	6,689	F. 13515
Federal Agent ...	,, ...	,, ...	5,608	F. 13516
Border Caballero ...	Equity British ...	Puritan Pictures, Inc.	5,100	F. 13517
Calling all Tars ...	First National ...	Vitaphone Corp.	1,942	F. 13518
Caught by Television...	Columbia ...	Columbia ...	5,729	F. 13519
Playing Politics ...	,, .	,, ...	579	F. 13520
AUGUST 25.				
The Boss Rider of Gun Creek.	General Film Dist.	Universal ...	5,190	F. 13522
Music Hath Charms ...	,,	,, ...	719	F. 13523
Kiddie Revue	,,	...	652	F. 13524
Going Places with Lowell Thomas—No. 24.	,,	,, ...	846	F. 13525
AUGUST 26.				
De Kribbebijter (The Cross-Patch).	G.-B. D.	Holfi-Film ...	7,920	F. 13526
AUGUST 27.				
Man from Guntown ...	Equity	Puritan Pict.Corp.	5,500	F. 13527
Girls' Dormitory ...	Fox	Twentieth Century Fox.	5,946	F. 13528
High Tension ...	,, ...	,, ...	5,685	F. 13529
AUGUST 28.				
To Mary—With Love	,, ...	,, ...	8,267	F. 13530
The Westerner ...	Columbia ...	Columbia ...	5,077	F. 13531
AUGUST 31.				
His Brother's Wife ...	M-G-M ...	M-G-M	8,005	F. 13532
Yours for the Asking	Paramount ...	Paramount ...	6,425	F. 13533
Bulldog Courage ...	Equity	Puritan Pict.Corp.	5,750	F. 13534
Golden Arrow ...	First National ...	Warner	6,259	F. 13535
Medium Well Done ...	,, ...	Vitaphone Corp.	1,006	F. 13536
I'd Love to Take Orders from You.	,, ...	,, ...	720	F. 13537
SEPTEMBER 1.				
Alpine Climbers ...	United Artists ...	Walt Disney Prod.	870	F. 13539
SEPTEMBER 2.				
I Don't Want to Make History.	Paramount ...	Paramount ...	692	F. 13543
Hollywood Boulevard	,, ...	,, ...	6,746	F. 13544
I'm Much Obliged ...	First National ...	Vitaphone Corp.	2,005	F. 13545
Love to Singa ...	,, ...	,, ...	752	F. 13546
SEPTEMBER 3.				
Roaring Guns	Equity	Puritan Pictures	5,750	F. 13548
The Great Ziegfeld ...	M-G-M	M-G-M	15,901	F. 13549
SEPTEMBER 4.				
Bengal Tiger	Warner	Warner	5,235	F. 13552
Guns of the Pecos ...	,, ...	,, ...	5,110	F. 13553
Rhythmitis	,, ...	,, ...	1,784	F. 13554
When You're Single ...	,, ...	,, ...	1,909	F. 13555
Shanghaied Shipmates	,, ...	,, ...	642	F. 13556
Here's Howe	,, ...	,, ...	1,956	F. 13557
Fish Tales	,, ...	,, ...	622	F. 13558

Title of Film.	Registered by.	Maker's name.	Length (feet).	No.
SEPTEMBER 5.				
Gus Van's Garden Party	General F.D. ...	Mentone Productions.	959	F. 13559
Musical Airways ...	,, ...	,, ...	975	F. 13560
The Phantom Rider (serial):—				
Episode 1	General F.D.	Universal ...	1,787	F. 13561
Episode 2	,, ...	,, ...	1,832	F. 13562
Episode 3	,, ...	,, ...	1,679	F. 13563
Episode 4	,, ...	,, ...	1,685	F. 13564
Episode 5	,, ...	,, ...	1,781	F. 13565
Episode 6	,, ...	,, ...	1,597	F. 13566
Episode 7	,, ...	,, ...	1,671	F. 13567
Episode 8	,, ...	,, ...	1,598	F. 13568
Episode 9	,, ...	,, ...	1,725	F. 13569
Episode 10	,, ...	,, ...	1,675	F. 13570
Episode 11	,, ...	,, ...	1,757	F. 13571
Episode 12	,, ...	,, ...	1,830	F. 13572
SEPTEMBER 7.				
The Last of the Mohicans.	United Artists ...	Reliance Pictures	8,312	F. 13582
G-Man's Wife ...	Warner	Warner	6,234	F. 13583
Porky's Pet	,, ...	,, ...	601	F. 13584
Nick Lucas and his Troubadours.	,, ...	,, ...	963	F. 13585
The Rhythm Party ...	Paramount ...	Paramount ...	735	F. 13586
Three on the Trail ...	,, ...	,, ...	6,015	F. 13587
Marchand D'Amour ...	Twickenham Film Dis.	Alliance Cinematographique Europeenne.	7,453	F. 13588
Outlaw Deputy ...	Equity	Puritan Pictures	5,250	F. 13589
SEPTEMBER 9.				
My Man, Godfrey ...	General F.D. ...	Universal ...	8,421	F. 13594
A Son Comes Home ...	Paramount ...	Paramount ...	6,732	F. 13595
Shorty at the Seashore V5–19.	,, ...	,, ...	735	F. 13596
SEPTEMBER 10.				
Crash Donovan ...	General F.D. ...	Universal ...	5,052	F. 13599
All One Night ...	First National ...	Warner	5,275	F. 13600
College Dads	,, ...	Vitaphone Corp.	1,957	F. 13601
Vitaphone Hippodrome	,, ...	,, ...	1,002	F. 13602
Sweet Aloes	Warner	Warner	7,913	F. 13603
Can You Imagine ...	,, ...	,, ...	897	F. 13604
SEPTEMBER 11.				
Harnessed Rhythm ...	M-G-M	M-G-M	870	F. 13606
Piccadilly Jim ...	,, ...	,, ...	8,567	F. 13607
The Phantom Rider (serial) :				
Episode 13	General F.D. ...	Universal ...	1,641	F. 13608
Two in a Crowd ...	,, ...	,, ...	7,393	F. 13609
Worn Out	British Lion ...	Imperial Dist. Cp.	787	F. 13610
Prison Shadows ...	Pathe	Puritan Corp. ...	6,000	F. 13611
SEPTEMBER 14.				
Neighbourhood House	M-G-M	Hal E. Roach ...	1,780	F. 13615
China Clipper	Warner	Warner	8,073	F. 13616
Porky the Rain Maker	,, ...	,, ...	696	F. 13617
On Secret Service ...	First National ...	,, ...	5,110	F. 13618
Stars Can't Be Wrong	,, ...	Vitaphone Corp.	1,850	F. 13619
Page Miss Glory ...	,, ...	,, ...	703	F. 13620
Bridge of Sighs ...	Twickenham F.D.	Invincible Corp.	5,930	F. 13621
Ring Around the Moon	,, ...	Chesterfield Corp.	6,272	F. 13622
Tango	,, ...	Invincible Corp.	6,340	F. 13623
Swifty	...Independent F.D.	Diversion Pictures	5,569	F. 13624
SEPTEMBER 15.				
Mickey's Circus ...	United Artists ...	Walt Disney Prod.	736	F. 13625

Title of Film.	Registered by.	Maker's name.	Length (feet).	No.
SEPTEMBER 15—cont.				
Arizona Raiders ...	Paramount ...	Paramount ...	5,165	F.13626
Music in the Morgan Manner.	,, .	,, ...	927	F.13627
SEPTEMBER 16.				
Straight from the Shoulder	Paramount ...	Paramoun ...	6,064	F.13629
You're Not Built that Way	,, ...	. ,, ...	645	F.13630
Sylvia Und Ihr Chauffeur	G.-B.D. ...	Ernst Neubach ...	7,340	F.13631
SEPTEMBER 17.				
Our Relations... ...	M-G-M ...	Hal E. Roach ...	6,563	F.13632
Sunkist Stars at Palm Springs	,, ...	M-G-M ...	1,789	F.13633
Kelly of the Secret Service	Pathe ...	Victory Pictures Corp.	5,869	F.13634
Red Blood of Courage	Butcher's ...	Guaranteed Pictures Corp.	5,067	F.13636
SEPTEMBER 18.				
Down the Stretch ...	First National ...	Warner ...	5,918	F.13637
Meet the Kernel	,, ...	Vitaphone Corp.	942	F.13638
When I Yoo Hoo- ...	,, ...	,, ...	656	F.13639
SEPTEMBER 21.				
A Natural Born Salesman	First National ...	Warner	6,257	F.13644
Bingo Crosbyana ...	,, ...	Vitaphone Corp.	719	F.13645
I'd Give My Life ...	Paramount ...	Paramount ...	6,411	F.13646
Musical Fashions ...	,, ...	,, ...	926	F.13647
Aquatic Artistry ...	M-G-M ...	M-G-M ...	763	F.13650
SEPTEMBER 22.				
All Business	Radio ...	R.K.O. Corp. ...	1,694	F.13651
A Waif's Welcome ...	,, ...	Amedee J. Van Beuren	693	F.13655
Trolley Ahoy	,, ...	,, ...	725	F.13656
Framing Father ...	,, ...	R.K.O. ...	1,514	F.13657
Fight is Right ...	,, ...	,, ...	1,574	F.13658
High Beer Pressure ...	,, ...	,, ...	1,644	F.13659
SEPTEMBER 23.				
Two Little Pups ...	M-G-M ...	M-G-M ...	706	F.13660
Grand Jury	Radio ...	R.K.O. Corp. ...	5,512	F.13663
Sleepy Time	,, .	,, ...	1,839	F.13664
Molly Moo-Cow and Robinson Crusoe.	,, ...	Amedee J. Van Beuren.	704	F.13665
Walking On Air ...	,, ...	R.K.O. Corp.	6,248	F.13666
Dummy Ache	,, ...	,, ...	1,701	F.13667
Highway Snobbery ...	Columbia ...	Columbia ...	609	F.13668
Shakedown	,, ...	,, ...	5,021	F.13669
SEPTEMBER 24.				
Toby Tortoise Returns	United Artists ...	Walt Disney Prod.	684	F.13671
Lady Be Careful ...	Paramount ...	Paramount ...	6,422	F.13672
Sporting Comparisons	,, ...	,, ...	894	F.13673
Second Wife	Radio ...	R.K.O. Corp. ...	5,363	F.13675
Swing It	,, ...	,, ...	1,483	F.13676
Born to Gamble ...	A.B.F.D....	Liberty Pict. Corp.	5,875	F.13677
Dizzy Dames	,, ...	,, ...	6,310	F.13678
SEPTEMBER 25.				
Slum Fun	Warner ...	Warner	1,976	F.13680
Vitaphone Topnochers	,, ...	,, ...	1,007	F.13681
A Day's Journey ...	,, ...	,, ...	918	F.13682
Vitaphone Stage Show	,, ...	,, ...	944	F.13683
Good Old Plumbertime	,, ...	,, ...	1,839	F.13684
Shake Mr. Shakespeare	,, ...	,, ...	1,673	F.13685
Swing Time	Radio ...	R.K.O. Corp.	9,323	F.13686
Don't Turn 'Em Loose	,, ...	,, ...	5,893	F.13687

Title of Film.	Registered by.	Maker's name.	Length (feet).	No.
SEPTEMBER 25—cont.				
Major Bowes' Amateur Parade No. 1.	Radio	Biograph Pictures	863	F. 13688
The Gorgeous Hussy ...	M-G-M	M-G-M	9,263	F. 13689
How to Train a Dog ...	M-G-M	M-G-M	707	F. 13690
I Wanna be a Lifeguard	Paramount ...	Paramount ...	586	F. 13691
SEPTEMBER 26.				
Charlie Chan at the Race Track.	Fox	Twentieth Century Fox.	6,307	F. 13692
36 Hours to Kill ...	,, ...	,, ...	5,908	F. 13693
SEPTEMBER 28.				
Wholesailing Along ...	Radio	R.K.O. Corp. ...	1,620	F. 13695
Parole	General F.D. ...	Universal ...	5,590	F. 13696
The Phantom Rider (serial) :—				
Episode 14	,, ...	,, ...	1,664	F. 13697
Episode 15	,, ...	,, ...	1,663	F. 13698
Maria Bashkirtseff ...	Twickenham F.D.	Panta Film ...	6,837	F. 13699
More Pep	Paramount ...	Paramount ...	518	F. 13700
New Shoes	M-G-M	M-G-M	932	F. 13701
SEPTEMBER 30.				
Three Married Men ...	Paramount ...	Paramount Pict., Inc.	5,494	F. 13709
OCTOBER 1.				
Savoy-Hotel 217 ...	G.-B.D.	Universum-Film A.G.	8,631	F. 13710
Mr. Cinderella ...	M-G-M	Hal E. Roach ...	6,746	F. 13711
Little Boy Blue ...	,, ...	M-G-M	932	F. 13712
Postal Inspector ...	General F.D. ...	Universal ...	5,266	F. 13713
The Mystery Ship ...	Inter. Cine. Co. ... Ltd.	Arcturus Films, Inc.	5,850	F. 13714
OCTOBER 2.				
Comi-Color Cartoon Nursery Rhymes (series) :—				
Dick Whittington's Cat	British Lion ...	Celebrity Prod. ...	683	F. 13715
Ali Baba	,, ...	,, ...	631	F. 13716
Texas Rangers ...	Paramount ...	Paramount ...	8,813	F. 13717
OCTOBER 5.				
Heart of the West ...	Paramount ...	Paramount ...	5,380	F. 13718
A Song a Day ...	,, ...	,, ...	642	F. 13719
The Road to Glory ...	Fox	Twentieth Cent. Fox	9,203	F. 13720
OCTOBER 7.				
Wedad the Slave ...	A.P. and D. ...	M.I.S.R. Films (Cairo).	5,770	F. 13721
OCTOBER 8.				
Pepper	Fox	Twentieth-Century Fox.	5,777	F. 13725
Star for a Night ...	,, ...	,, ...	6,884	F. 13726
The Devil Takes the Count.	M-G-M ...	M-G-M	8,220	F. 13727
Singende Jugend ...	Ace Films ...	Meteor-Film C.A.	7,830	F. 1 728
OCTOBER 9.				
Old Hutch	M-G-M	M-G-M	7,154	F. 29
OCTOBER 10.				
Gentleman from Louisiana.	British Lion ...	Republic Productions.	6,423	F. 13730
Comin' Round the Mountain.	,, ...	,, ...	5,190	F. 13731
Follow Your Heart ...	,, ...	,, ...	6,863	F. 13732
Undersea Kingdom— Beneath the Ocean Floor.	,, ...	,, ...	2,849	F. 13733

TRADE

Title of Film.	Registered by.	Maker's name.	Length (feet).	No.
OCTOBER 10—cont.				
Undersea Kingdom (serial):—				
The Undersea City ...	British Lion ...	Republic Productions	1,782	F. 13734
Arena of Death ...	,, ...	,, ,, ...	1,761	F. 13735
Revenge of the Volkites	,, ...	,, ...	1,683	F. 13736
OCTOBER 12.				
Yellowstone	General F.D. ...	Universal ...	5,692	F. 13739
Hills of Old Wyomin'...	Paramount ...	Paramount ...	868	F. 13741
Satan Met a Lady ...	First National ...	Warner	6,768	F. 13743
Double Crossky ...	,, ...	Vitaphone Corp.	1,870	F. 13744
Bored of Education ...	M-G-M	Hal E. Roach ...	912	F. 13745
The Old House ...	,, ...	M-G-M	894	F. 13746
OCTOBER 13.				
Girl from Mandalay	A.B.F.D.... ...	Republic Picture Corp.	6,296	F. 13748
OCTOBER 15.				
Isle of Fury	First National ...	Warner	5,484	F. 13749
Vitaphone Spotlight ...	,, ...	Vitaphone Corp.	933	F. 13750
Undersea Kingdom (serial):—				
Prisoners of Atlantis	British Lion ...	Republic Prod. ...	1,632	F. 13751
The Juggernaut Strikes	,, ...	,, ...	1,555	F. 13752
The Submarine Trap	,, ...	,, ...	1,635	F. 13753
Into the Metal Tower	,, ...	,, ...	1,566	F. 13754
Death in the Air ...	,, ...	,, ...	1,569	F. 13755
Atlantis Destroyed ...	,, ...	,, ...	1,626	F. 13756
Flaming Death ...	,, ...	,, ...	1,802	F. 13757
Ascent to the Upperworld.	,, ...	,, ...	1,695	F. 13758
Romeo and Juliet ...	M-G-M	M-G-M	11,201	F. 13759
OCTOBER 16.				
The Longest Night ...	,, ...	,, ...	4,543	F. 13760
The General Died at Dawn.	Paramount ...	Paramount ...	8,791	F. 13761
Neptune's Scholars ...	,, ...	,, ...	854	F. 13762
Greedy Humpty Dumpty	,, ...	,, ...	696	F. 13763
Black Gold	Independent Film Distributors	Conn Pictures Corp.	5,416	F. 13764
Sing Baby Sing ...	Fox	Twentieth-Century Fox.	7,868	F. 13765
Back to Nature ...	... ...	,, ...	5,072	F. 13766
OCTOBER 19.				
La Kermesse Heroique	G.-B. D.... ...	Films Sonores Tobis	8,009	F. 13767
OCTOBER 20.				
Ramona	Fox	Twentieth Century Fox	7,572	F. 13768
OCTOBER 21				
Wives Never Know ..	Paramount ..	Paramount ..	6,574	F. 13772
Lucky Spills ..	,, ..	,, ..	855	F. 13773
OCTOBER 22				
North of Arizona ..	Equity	Reliable Corp. ...	5,240	F. 13774
OCTOBER 23				
It's a Bird ..	Independence Films	J H Hoffberg Co.	1,600	F. 13776
Mysterious Avenger ..	Columbia ..	Columbia ..	4,802	F. 13777
Craig's Wife	,, ..	,, ..	6,691	F. 13778
Novelty Shop ..	,,	,, ..	604	F. 13779
Two Fisted Gentleman	,,	..	5,642	F. 13780
Manhattan Madness ..	,, ..	..	6,557	F. 13781
False Alarms	,, ..	,, ..	1,504	F. 13782
Country Bumpkin ..	M-G-M	M-G-M ..	5,688	F. 13783
Dodsworth	United Artists ..	Samuel Goldwyn	9,290	F. 13784
Donald and Pluto ..	,, ..	Walt. Disney Prod.	763	F. 13785
OCTOBER 26.				
Ace Drummond (serial):—				
Episode 1	General F.D. ..	Universal ..	1,854	F. 13786

Title of Film.	Registered by.	Maker's name.	Length (feet).	No.
OCTOBER 26—*cont.*				
Episode 2	General F.D. ..	Universal ..	1,740	F. 13787
Episode 3	,,	,,	1,720	F. 13788
Beachcomber	,,		772	F. 13789
Night Life of the Bugs	,,	,,	681	F. 13790
Valiant is the Word for Carrie	Paramount ..	Paramount ..	9,792	F. 13791
Happy You and Merry Me	,,	,,	620	F. 13792
Murder with Pictures	,,	,,	6,348	F. 13793
Thank You Jeeves ..	Fox ..	Twentieth Century Fox.	5,135	F. 13794
Circus Love	Butcher's ..	Ariel Film G.m.b.H.	5,866	F. 13795
They Met in a Taxi ..	Columbia ..	Columbia ..	6,166	F. 13796
The Man who Lived Twice	,,	,,	6,564	F 13797
Rawhide Terror ..	Equity ..	Security Corp. ..	4,640	F. 13798
Texas Jack	,,	Reliable Corp. ..	5,100	F. 13799
Mayerling	G.-B.D. ..	Nero Film ..	8,393	F. 13800
OCTOBER 27.				
The Clutching Hand— Who is the Clutching Hand ?	A.B.F.D... ..	Weiss Productions.	2,750	F. 13802
The Clutching Hand (serial) :—				
Shadows	,,	,,	1,880	F. 13803
House of Mystery ..	,,	,,	1,830	F. 13804
The Phantom Car ..	,,	,,	1,730	F. 13805
The Double Trap ..	,,	,,	1,820	F. 13806
OCTOBER 28.				
Arizona Trials ..	Equity ..	Superior Talking Pictures.	4,400	F. 13809
OCTOBER 29.				
The Gay Desperado ..	United Artists ..	Pickford - Lasky Productions.	7,944	F. 13814
Fun in a Fire House ..	General F.D. ..	Mentone Productions.	914	F. 13815
Skull and Crown ..	Pathe ..	Reliable Picture Corp.	5,250	F. 13816
Way of the West ..	Equity ..	Superior Talking Pictures.	4,900	F. 13817
OCTOBER 30.				
Libelled Lady.. ..	M-G-M ..	M-G-M	8,834	F. 13819
Children of Divorce ..	Wardour ..	Sentinel Productions.	5,872	F. 13820
The Pecos Dandy ..	Equity ..	Security Picture Corp.	4,110	F. 13821
NOVEMBER 2.				
Master Will Shakespeare.	M-G-M ..	M-G-M	946	F. 13826
The Pups' Picnic ..	,,	,,	743	F. 13827
Desert Mesa	Equity ..	Security Picture Corp.	4,400	F. 13828
Big Broadcast of 1937	Paramount ..	Paramount ..	9,407	F. 13829
Play Don	,,	,,	911	F. 13830
Millionaire Kid ..	Wardour ..	Reliable Corp. ..	5,268	F. 13831
The Clutching Hand (serial) :—				
Steps of Doom ..	A.B.F.D... ..	Weiss Productions	1,780	F. 13832
Invisible Enemy ..	,,	,,	1,824	F. 13833
A Cry in the Night ..	,,	,,	1,718	F. 13834
Evil Eyes	,,	,,	1,888	F. 13835
A Desperate Chance..	,,	,,	1,838	F. 13836
The Ship of Peril ..	,,	,,	1,785	F. 13837

Title of Film.	Registered by.	Maker's name.	Length (feet).	No.
NOVEMBER 2—cont.				
Hidden Danger ..	A.B.F.D... ..	Weiss Productions	1,740	F. 13838
Mystic Menace ..	,, ...	,, ...	1,755	F. 13839
The Silent Spectre ..	,, ...	,, ...	1,735	F .13840
The Lone Hand ..	,, ...	,, ...	1,750	F. 13841
NOVEMBER 4.				
Let's Get Movin' ..	Paramount ..	Paramount ..	560	F. 13846
Wedding Present ..	,, ...	,, ...	7,322	F. 13847
NOVEMBER 6.				
Rush Hour Rhapsody	Warner	Warner	1,789	F. 13849
Stage Struck	,, ...	,, ...	8,415	F. 13850
Vacation Spots ..	,, ...	,, ...	933	F. 13851
Porky's Moving Day ..	,, ...	,, ...	631	F. 13852
The Captain's Kid ..	First National ..	,, ...	6,588	F. 13853
Carl Hoff and His Orchestra.	,, ...	Vitaphone Corp.	954	F. 13854
Vitaphone Entertainers	,, ...	,, ...	994	F. 13855
Ladies in Love ..	Fox	Twentieth Century Fox.	8,752	F. 13856
Trapped	Pathé	Reliable Pic.Corp.	5,038	F. 13857
Ace Drummond (serial) :—				
Episode 4	General F.D. ..	Universal ..	1,868	F. 13858
Episode 5	,, ...	,, ...	1,710	F. 13859
Episode 6	,, ...	,, ...	1,855	F. 13860
NOVEMBER 9.				
Cain and Mabel ..	Warner	Warner	8,167	F. 13866
Logging Along ..	,, ...	,, ...	907	F. 13867
Porky's Poultry Plant	,, ...	,, ...	732	F. 13868
Get that Girl	Pathé	Reliable Pic.Corp.	5.480	F. 13869
Mickey's Elephant ..	United Artists ..	Walt Disney Prod.	782	F. 13870
Trouble for Three ..	G.-B.D.	Educational Film Corp.of America.	1,452	F. 13871
Where is Wall Street ?	,, ...	,, ...	1,712	F. 13872
NOVEMBER 10.				
Dimples	Fox	Twentieth Cent. Fox.	7,056	F. 13875
Bad Medicine	Radio	R.K.O. Corp. ..	1,431	F. 13876
NOVEMBER 11.				
Echo Mountain ..	Warner	Warner Bros. Pictures, Inc.	1,593	F. 13879
Without Orders ..	Radio	R.K.O. Corp. ..	5,776	F. 13880
And So to Wed ..	,, ...	,, ...	1,746	F. 13881
The Big Game ..	,, ...	,, ...	6,714	F. 13882
The Girl on the Front Page.	General F.D. ..	Universal ..	6,518	F. 13883
NOVEMBER 12.				
A Woman Rebels ..	Radio	R.K.O. Corp. ..	7,967	F. 13885
Major Bowes' Amateur Parade No. 2.	,, ...	Biograph Pictures	900	F. 13886
Mummy's Boys ..	,, ...	R.K.O. Corp. ..	6,123	F. 13887
The Magnificent Brute	General F.D. ..	Universal ..	6,994	F. 13888
Sea Spoilers	,, ...	,, ...	5,664	F. 13889
O'Riley's Luck ..	Paramount ..	Paramount ..	6,869	F. 13890
Never Kick a Woman	,, ...	,, ...	591	F. 13891
Three Blind Mouseketeers.	United Artists ..	Walt Disney Prod.	796	F. 13893
NOVEMBER 13.				
We Who Are About to Die.	Radio	R.K.O. Corp. ..	7,285	F. 13895

Title of Film.	Registered by.	Maker's name.	Length (feet).	No.
NOVEMBER 13—cont.				
Daniel Boone	Radio	R.K.O. Corp. ..	6,935	F.13896
Listen to Freezin ..	,, ...	,, ...	1,398	F.13897
NOVEMBER 16.				
Dog Blight	Radio	R.K.O. Corp. ..	1,535	F.13901
Fredlos	Reunion Films ..	Nordiskfilm ..	8,180	F.13902
Dare Devilty	M-G-M	M-G-M	788	F.13903
NOVEMBER 17.				
Ticket to Paradise ..	A.B.F.D... ..	Republic Pictures, Inc.	6,053	F.13908
O'Malley of the Mounted	,, ..	Atherton Productions, Inc.	5,360	F.13909
Navy Born	,, ..	Republic Pictures, Inc.	6,130	F.13910
Comi-Color Cartoon Nursery Rhymes (series):—				
Little Boy Blue ..	British Lion ..	Celebrity Productions, Inc.	642	F.13911
NOVEMBER 18.				
Punch and Beauty ..	First National ..	Vitaphone Corp.	1,995	F.13913
The Oily Bird	,, ,, ..	,, ..	1,772	F.13914
Wife of the Party ..	,, ...	,, ..	1,983	F.13915
Vitaphone Review ..	,, ...	,, ..	770	F.13916
Along Came Love ..	Paramount ..	Paramount ..	5,959	F.13917
Training Pigeons ..	,, ...	,, ..	601	F.13918
NOVEMBER 19.				
Alibi for Murder ..	Columbia ..	Columbia ..	5,275	F.13920
Am I Having Fun ..	,, ..	,, ..	1,672	F.13921
Cavalcade of the West	National Provincial.	Diversion Pictures.	5,627	F.13922
NOVEMBER 20.				
The Mighty Tundra ..	Wardour ..	Burroughs-Tarzan Pictures.	6,400	F.13924
NOVEMBER 23.				
Gipsy Revels	Paramount ..	Paramount ..	937	F.13927
In His Steps	A.B.F.D... ..	Grand National Films.	7,153	F.13928
Whoops I'm an Indian	Columbia ..	Columbia ..	1,562	F.13930
Loony Balloonists ..	,, ...	,, ...	612	F.13931
Ace Drummond (serial):—				
Episode 7	General F.D. ..	Universal ..	1,799	F.13932
NOVEMBER 24.				
15, Maiden Lane ..	Fox	Twentieth Century Fox.	5,807	F.13933
Come and Get It ..	United Artists ..	Samuel Goldwyn	9,145	F.13937
NOVEMBER 25.				
The Accusing Finger	Paramount ..	Paramount ..	4,577	F.13939
Music Over Broadway	,, ..	,, ..	855	F.13940
The Garden of Allah	United Artists ..	Selznick International Pictures.	7,213	F.13941
NOVEMBER 26.				
Mad Holiday ..	M-G-M	M-G-M	6,424	F.13945
Case of the Black Cat	First National ..	Warner	6,010	F.13946
Harry Reser and His Eskimos.	,, ..	Vitaphone Corp. ..	844	F.13947
Vitaphone Gayeties	,, ..	,, ..	1,006	F.13948

Title of Film.	Registered by.	Maker's name.	Length (feet).	No.
NOVEMBER 27.				
Emil Coleman and Orchestra.	Warner	Warner	938	F. 13950
Sitting on the Moon	British Lion ..	Republic Prod. ...	6,323	F. 13951
NOVEMBER 28.				
One for All	,,	,,	.. 7,462	F. 13952
Oh, Susanna ! ..	,,	,,	.. 5,589	F. 13953
Lady Reporter ..	,, ...	,,	.. 5,249	F. 13954
NOVEMBER 30.				
Broadway Highlights V6-2	Paramount ..	Paramount ..	891	F. 13957

LATE ADJUSTMENTS.

In the course of the year certain corrections have been published concerning details in the length, title or description of films registered. Where these alterations affect films in the 1936 list, the necessary corrections have been made ; appended we give notification of alterations which affect films registered on earlier dates.

ALTERATION OF LENGTH.

Title of Film.	Registration No.	Original length. (feet).	Length as altered (feet).
Twenty Dollars a Week (Zenifilms)... ...	F. 11833	5,618	5,508
When the Cat's Away (Zenifilms)	Br. 12020	3,150	2,000
Arms and the Girl (United)	F. 12251	6,554	6,291
Cheerio (Fidelity)	Br. 12412	1,612	1,561

*** The Inter-Cine film entitled "90° South," registered length 6,699 feet (E. 8834), has been altered to "The Story of Captain Scott," registered length 5,403 feet.

*** The registration of the A. P. & D. film entitled "Cavalcade of the Movies" (F. 9937), has been amended, and now includes six short films as under : —
Cavalcade of the Movies—Part 1—888 feet.
Cavalcade of the Movies—Part 2—978 feet.
Cavalcade of the Movies—Part 3—1,024 feet.
Cavalcade of the Movies—Part 4—998 feet.
Cavalcade of the Movies—Part 5—837 feet.
Cavalcade of the Movies—Part 6—715 feet.

*** The registration of the Columbia film entitled "Opening Night" (Br. 11271) has been amended and now includes two short films entitled "Dress Rehearsal," registered length 1,989 feet, and "Rhythm and Song," registered length 1,699 feet.

*** The length of the United Artists film "Escape Me Never" (Br. 11,481) has been altered to 8,584 feet.

*** The length of the film "Off the Dole" (Br. 11625) has been altered to 7,793 feet.

*** The length of the Film Society film "La Dame Aux Camelias" (F. 11765) has been altered to 7,500 ft.

*** The title of the United Artists film "Where's George" (Br. 12017) has been altered to "The Hope of His Side."

*** The length of the Reunion film "Jazz Comedy" (F. 12171) has been altered to 6,702 feet.

*** The length of the Warner film "A Midsummer Night's Dream" (F. 12216) has been altered to 10,653 feet.

*** The title of the Universal film "Three Kids and a Queen" (F. 12397) has been altered to "The Baxter Millions."

LONDON

FILMS

Present **FIVE MORE GREAT FILMS**

● Read about them overleaf

Charles Laughton
IN
REMBRANDT
WITH
GERTRUDE LAWRENCE
ELSA LANCHESTER
DIRECTED BY
ALEXANDER KORDA

FIRE OVER ENGLAND
PRODUCED BY
ERICH POMMER
A thrilling, romantic drama
DIRECTED BY
WILLIAM K. HOWARD

DARK JOURNEY
PRODUCED BY
VICTOR SAVILLE
STARRING
Conrad Veidt
AND
Vivien Leigh

MEN ARE NOT GODS
STARRING
Miriam Hopkins
A fast-moving comedy drama
DIRECTED BY
WALTER REISCH

ELEPHANT BOY
Based on Rudyard Kipling's famous story "Toomai of the Elephants," directed in India by
ROBERT FLAHERTY

Presented by
LONDON FILM PRODUCTIONS
Distributed by UNITED ARTISTS

TRADE

ORGANISATIONS

(ASSOCIATIONS, SOCIETIES, UNIONS, ETC.)

INDEX

Trade Organisations.

The Cinematograph Exhibitors' Association of Great Britain and Ireland.

Reg. No. 1622T.

Registered under Trade Union Acts.

Offices : Broadmead House, 21, Panton Street, Haymarket, S.W.1.
Phone : Whitehall 0191–4.
Telegraphic Address : Ceabilrex 'Phone London.

GENERAL COUNCIL.

President :
THEO. H. FLIGELSTONE, 11, Berkeley Court, Baker Street, N.W.1.

Vice-President :
CHAS. P. METCALFE, 54, Merrion Street, Leeds.

Hon. Treasurer :
THOS. ORMISTON, C.B.E., 6, Brandon Street, Motherwell.

General Secretary :
W. R. FULLER, " Broadmead House," 21, Panton Street, London, S.W.1.
('Phone : Whitehall 0191-2-3-4.)

Ex-Officio :
RICHARD DOONER, 2, Office Road, Maesteg.

Solicitor :
NORMAN HART, B.A., "Broadmead House," 21, Panton Street, London, S.W.1.

DELEGATES.
(*Elected* 10*th March,* 1936.)

Birmingham and Midlands Branch.—S. W. Clift, 5, Union Street, Birmingham ; H. B. Lane, 106, Linden Road, Bourneville, Birmingham ; A. W. Rogers, Victoria Playhouse, Aston, Birmingham ; Sydney K. Lewis, Empire Cinema, Loughborough, Leics. *Bradford and District Branch.*—J. E Anderton, Ivy House, Russell Street, Bradford ; P. Goodall, Savoy Cinema, Albion Street, Cleckheaton ; T. Lund, 44, Parkfield Avenue, Silverhills Road, Bradford. *Bristol and West of England Branch.*—A. B. Atkinson, 32, Salisbury Road, Redland, Bristol, 1 ; F. G. W. Chamberlain, Gaiety Cinema, Knowle, Bristol ; G. Rees, 112, Brynland Avenue, Bristol, 7. *Devon and Cornwall Branch.*—Major A. O. Ellis, "Homeside," Higher Warberry Road, Torquay ; W. Pickles, J.P., Picture House, Buckfastleigh, South Devon. *Eastern Counties Branch.*—Douglas F. Bostock, 54, Chevallier Street, Ipswich ; V. E. Harrison, The Lido, Aylsham Road, Norwich. *Hants and Isle of Wight Branch.*—Councillor G. W. A. Wright, Regal Cinema, Eastleigh, Hants ; H. P. E. Mears, Plaza Cinema, Winton Road, Bournemouth. *Hull and District Branch.*—T. Fawley Judge, A.C.A., Hull Picture Playhouses, Ltd., Parliament Street, Hull ; Brinley Evans, Cecil Theatre, Paragon Square, Hull. *Kent Branch.*—Morris M. Levy, Westminster Lodge, 34, Highfield Gardens, N.W.11 ; Major C. H. Bell, O.B.E., National House, 60/66, Wardour Street, W.1. *Leeds and District Branch.*—Charles P. Metcalfe, 54, Merrion Street, Leeds ; A. Cunningham, Tower Crest, Heysham, Morecambe ; J. Claughton, Crescent Picture House, Dewsbury Road, Leeds ; J Prendergast, New Rialto Cinema, Fulford Road, York. *Leicestershire Branch.*—G. H. Scarborough, " Ashfield," Elmfield Avenue, Leicester. *London and Home Counties Branch.*—K. A. Nyman, B.Sc., Pollen House, 10-12, Cork Street, W.1 ; Capt. Alfred Davis, Davis Theatre, Croydon ; Major A. J. Gale, O.B.E., J.P., Pollen House, 10-12, Cork Street. W.1 ; J. Alexander, 9, St. Mary's Mansions, Paddington, W.2 ; Ralph S. Bromhead, A.C.A., Dean House, Dean St., W.1 ; Thomas France, 108, Great Russell St., W.C.1 ; A. Freedman, 62, Oxford St., W.1 ; Alderman T. L. Harrold, Yelverton, Fordington Rd., N.6 ; Councillor E. A. Huddleston, Peoples Palace, Witney, Oxon ; C. A. Mathes, St. Giles, Vallance Road, Alexandra Park, N.22 ; A. S. Moss, 30-31, Golden Square, W.1 ; Ernest W. P. Peall, New Gallery House, 123, Regent Street, W.1. *Manchester Branch.*—T. H. Hartley, " Burcot," 421, Rossendale Road, Burnley ; A. Peel, 239, Manchester Road, Nelson ; Capt. G. B. Row, 6, Sefton Road, Smithills, Bolton ; Chas. Littler, 32,

Cromford House, Cromford Court, Market Street, Manchester, 4 ; J. Mather, La Scala Cinema, Bury *Northern Branch.*—W. Carr, Queen's Hall, Seaton Delaval ; W. S. Gibson, 4, Palladium Buildings, Eastbourne Road, Middlesbrough. ; E. J. Hinge, 72, Grey Street, Newcastle-on-Tyne ; F. W. Morrison, Greenbank, Dunston Hill, Dunston-on-Tyne ; J. S. Snell, 72, Grey Street, Newcastle-on-Tyne ; Thos. Thompson, 4, Palladium Buildings, Eastbourne Road, Middlesbrough. *North Staffordshire Branch.*—L. A. V. Plumpton, Royal-Picture House, Anchor Road, Longton, Stoke-on-Trent ; M. A. Vachon, Plaza Theatre, Newcastle, Staffs. *North Western Branch.*—Philip M. Hanmer, 51, North John Street, Liverpool ; Alderman E. Trounson, J.P., 1, Park Road, Southport ; J. R. Dovener, 18, Union Street, Liverpool ; R. P. Rutherford, Queen's Picture House, Poulton Road, Wallasey ; W. J. Speakman, Capitol Cinema, Overton Street, Edge Hill, Liverpool ; S. Grimshaw, Carlton Villa, Dee Banks, Chester. *Notts and Derby Branch.*—Councillor J. Pollard, J.P., 27, Atkins Lane, Mansfield ; Fred. A. Prior, F.S.A.A., General Buildings, Bridlesmith Gate, Nottingham ; J. Drew, Scala Theatre, Long Eaton. *Portsmouth Branch.*—Councillor F. J. Spickernell, Tivoli Cinema, Copnor Road, Portsmouth ; *Scottish Branch.*—Alex. B. King, J.P., 167, Bath Street, Glasgow ; Thos. Ormiston, C.B.E., 6, Brandon Street, Motherwell ; James Welsh, J.P., 1, Endfield Avenue, Glasgow, W.2 ; D. A. Stewart, J.P., 105, St. Vincent Street, Glasgow ; Provost Timmons, Cinema-de-Luxe, Lochgelly ; R. McLaughlin, C.A., Caley Picture House, Lothian Road, Edinburgh ; L. D. Dickson, Hippodrome, Bo'ness ; H. J. Green, 182, Trongate, Glasgow ; G. Singleton, 39, Kirkpatrick Street, Glasgow, E. ; G. U. Scott, 154, West Regent Street, Glasgow. *Sheffield and District Branch.*—A. R. Favell, "Sunningdale," Dobcroft Road, Ecclesall Road South, Sheffield ; T. F. McDonald, 352, Sharrow Lane, Sheffield. *Southern Midlands Branch.*—C. C. Day, 145, Orford Road, Hoe Street, Walthamstow, E. ; R. Chetham, The Plaza, Bedford ; Councillor L. Salmons, J.P., Electric Theatre, Newport Pagnell. *South Wales and Mon. Branch.*—H. Victor Davis, "Elvaston," Newbridge, Mon. ; S. Attwood, " Rosslyn," Glassllwch, Newport, Mon. ; A. B. Watts, F.S.A.A., 14, St. Andrews Crescent, Cardiff ; F. Phillips, 3, Greenland Road, Brynmawr. *Sussex Branch.*—Randolph E. Richards, Picturedrome, Eastbourne ; H. Shanly, 7, King's Bench Walk, Temple, E.C.4. *Wes Lancashire Branch.*—Harry Hargreaves, "Cedir," South Avenue, South Road, Morecambe ; Henry Simpson, Palladium, Victoria Road, Ulverston.

OBJECTS.

The objects of the Association are :—

(a) To promote good will and a good understanding between all Proprietors of Kinemas and other places of entertainment, and between them and such persons as work for them, and between them and the Manufacturers and Renters of Films.

(b) To provide a fund for the protection of the interests of the Members of the Association and to protect them from oppression.

(c) To secure unity of action among Proprietors of cinemas and other places of entertainment and in particular to secure that film rentals paid or payable by Members of the Association shall not exceed the maximum sums fixed from time to time by the Council of the Association in accordance with these Rules.

(d) To promote by all lawful means the adoption of fair working rules and customs of the trade.

(e) To organise means to secure and if at any time considered necessary themselves supply means whereby a free and unrestricted circulation of films and other trade requisites may be secured for Members of the Association.

(f) To resist by all lawful means the imposition by public authorities or other persons of terms and conditions upon the trade which are unreasonable or unnecessary.

(g) To secure legislation for the protection of the interests of Members, and to promote or oppose and join in promoting or opposing Bills in Parliament.

(h) To adopt such means of making known the operations of the Association as may seem to the Council expedient.

(i) To promote a good understanding between all local authorities and the Members of the Association, and to take any steps in furtherance thereof in matters which are the subject of local government, and which in the opinion of the Council may be in the interests of, or for the protection of the Members.

(j) To adopt any means which in the opinion of the Council may be incidental or conducive to the above objects.

British Lion's "Calling All Stars"—More Lavish than "Soft Lights & Sweet Music"

BRANCHES.

BIRMINGHAM AND MIDLANDS BRANCH.—Central House, 75, New Street, Birmingham. *Chairman*, S. W. Clift, 5, Union Street, Birmingham. *Vice-Chairman*, Councillor W. T. Hodge, Northfield Cinema, Bristol Road South, Birmingham. *Treasurer*, William Astley, "Ivybank," Cartland Road, Stirchley, Birmingham. *Secretary*, B. C. Muggleton, C.A., 75, New Street, Birmingham. *Trustees*, William Astley, H. B. Lane. *Committee*, S. W. Clift; Councillor W. T. Hodge ; William Astley ; Oscar Deutsch, 63, Temple Row, Birmingham ; I. L. Lyons, 115, Colmore Row, Birmingham ; A. W. Rogers, Victoria Playhouse, Aston, Birmingham ; H. B. Lane, 106, Linden Road, Bournville, Birmingham ; A. G. May, Victoria Playhouse, Aston, Birmingham ; F. P. Cozens, Saltley Grand Picture House, Alum Rock Road, Birmingham ; C. H. Russ, West End Cinema, Suffolk Street, Birmingham ; W. H. Bull, 43, Franklin Road, Bournville, Birmingham ; V. I. Oliver, Piccadilly, Stratford Road, Sparkhill ; F. Hardy, West End Cinema, Suffolk Street, Birmingham ; Sydney K. Lewis, Empire Cinema, Loughborough, Leicestershire ; H. F. Cornforth, Scala Cinema, Smallbrook Street, Birmingham ; T. Hellet, Alhambra Theatre, Moseley Road, Birmingham. *Delegates*, S. W. Clift ; H. B. Lane ; A. W. Rogers ; Sydney K. Lewis.

BRADFORD AND DISTRICT BRANCH.—Lion Chambers, 29, Kirkgate, Bradford. *Chairman*, P. Goodall, Savoy Cinema, Albion Street, Cleckheaton. *Vice-Chairman*, J. E. Anderton, Ivy House, Russell Street, Bradford. *Treasurer*, J. E. Rouse, Travellers Rest Hotel, 49, Duckworth Lane, Bradford. *Secretary*, Councillor H. Goldsbrough, F.C.R.A., 29, Kirkgate, Bradford. *Trustees*, J. E. Anderton ; A. Cansfield, Woodlawn, 179, Fagley Road, Bradford ; P. Goodall. *Committee*, P. Goodall ; J. E. Anderton ; A. Cansfield ; J. E. Rouse ; T. Lund, 44, Parkfield Avenue, Silverhills Road, Bradford. *Delegates*, J. E. Anderton ; P. Goodall ; T. Lund.

BRISTOL AND WEST OF ENGLAND BRANCH.—14, Colston Street, Bristol, 1. *Chairman*, A. B. Atkinson, 32, Salisbury Road, Redland, Bristol, 6. *Vice-Chairman*, F. G. W. Chamberlain, Gaiety Cinema, Knowle, Bristol, 4. *Treasurer*, G. H. Blackburn, New Palace Theatre, Baldwin Street, Bristol, 1. *Secretary*, S. W. Savery, A.I.S.A., 14, Colston Street, Bristol, 1. *Committee*, A. B. Atkinson ; F. G. W. Chamberlain ; G. H. Blackburn ; W. S. Chamberlain, "Cerne Abbas," Down Road, Portishead ; Councillor E. S. L. Collins, Palace Theatre, Priory Road, Wells, Som. ; V. E. Cox, The Picture House, Clevedon, Som. ; O. J. Pugsley, 206, Cranbrook Road, Bristol ; G. Rees, 112, Brynland Avenue, Bristol, 7 ; Councillor H. F. Wren, J.P., Regal Picture House, Staple Hill, Bristol ; J. D. Saunders, 15, Middle Street, Yeovil, Som. ; J. E. Williams, Embassy Cinema, Clifton, Bristol, 8. *Delegates*, A. B. Atkinson, F. G. W. Chamberlain, G. Rees.

DEVON AND CORNWALL BRANCH.—49, North Street, Plymouth. *Chairman*, Major A.O. Ellis, "Homeside," Higher Warberry Road, Torquay. *Vice-Chairman*, Harry J. Watkins, Capitol Cinema, St. Austell. *Treasurer-Secretary*, C. H. Rundle, 49, North Street, Plymouth. *Trustees*, Major A. O. Ellis ; W. Pickles, J.P., Picture House, Buckfastleigh, S. Devon. *Committee*, Major A. O. Ellis ; Harry J. Watkins ; C. H. Rundle ; W. Pickles, J.P. ; E. B. Hoyle, Belgrave Theatre, Mutley, Plymouth ; H. B. Mather, Ford Palladium, Devonport ; A. Bedford, Hippodrome, Devonport ; H. Gilley, Regent Cinema, Plymouth ; W. J. Bayley, Lounge Cinema, Fore Street, Exeter ; W. F. Gilley, Regent Cinema, Paignton ; F. E. Bowen, Plaza Cinema, Exeter. *Delegates*, Major A. O. Ellis, W. Pickles, J.P.

EASTERN COUNTIES BRANCH.—"Carmel," Hadley Road, Sheringham. *Chairman*, Councillor Ernest V. Barr, 11, Trafalgar Road, Great Yarmouth. *Vice-Chairman*, Douglas F. Bostock, 54, Chevallier Street, Ipswich. *Treasurer*, E. H. Field, 16a, South Quay, Great Yarmouth. *Secretary*, W. Waters, "Carmel," Hadley Road, Sheringham. *Trustess*, Councillor E. V. Barr ; Douglas F. Bostock ; V. E. Harrison, The Lido, Aylsham Road, Norwich. *Committee*, Councillor Ernest V. Barr ; Douglas F. Bostock ; E. H. Field ; W. Waters ; George F. Allen, 87, Northdenes Road, Gt. Yarmouth ; Douglas M. Attree, The Coliseum, Gorleston-on-Sea ; F. G. Graves, The Playhouse, Buttermarket, Bury St. Edmunds ; V. E. Harrison ; Reginald Pareezer, Theatre de Luxe, St. Andrews Street, Norwich ; H. W. Pinchon, 54, Chevallier Street, Ipswich ; R. G. Rogers, Pooles Picture Palace, Ipswich ; J. H. Troughton, J.P., "Cardigan," Newmarket. *Delegates*, Douglas F. Bostock, V. E. Harrison.

HANTS AND ISLE OF WIGHT BRANCH.—11, Portland Street, Southampton. *Chairman*, Major A. W. Banner, O.B.E., The Picture House, Above Bar, Southampton. *Vice-Chairman*, Councillor G. W. A. Wright, Regal Theatre, Eastleigh, Hants. *Treasurer*, Councillor W. D. Buck, Atherley House, Shirley, Southampton. *Secretary*, H. H. C. Mitchener, F.L.A.A., 11, Portland Street, Southampton. *Trustees*, Major A. W. Banner, O.B.E. ; Councillor W. D. Buck. *Committee*, Major A. W. Banner, O.B.E. ; Capt. A. N. Kendall, 73, North Walls, Winchester ; Councillor W. D. Buck ; H. H. C. Mitchener, F.L.A.A. ; Councillor G. W. A. Wright ; H. P. E. Mears, Plaza Theatre, Winton Road, Bournemouth ; Capt. G. H. Clement, The Regent Cinema, Shirley, Southampton ; J. W. Parker, Standard Cinema, East Street, Southampton. *Delegates*, Councillor G. W. A. Wright, H. P. E. Mears.

HULL AND DISTRICT BRANCH.—Friary Chambers, Whitefriargate, Hull. *Chairman*, T. Fawley Judge, A.C.A., Hull Picture Playhouses, Ltd., Parliament Street, Hull. *Vice-Chairman*, Brinley Evans, Cecil Theatre, Paragon Square, Hull. *Treasurer*, D. Desmond, Paragon Buildings, Paragon Square, Hull. *Secretary*, Councillor Wallace Rockett, Friary Chambers, Whitefriargate, Hull. *Trustees*, T. Fawley Judge, A.C.A. Alderman R. W. Wheeldon, J.P., "Hillcrest," 95, Swanland Road, Hessle, E.Y. ; H. Vaughan Evans, F.A.I., County Buildings, Land of Green Ginger, Hull. *Committee*, T. Fawley Judge, A.C.A. ; Alderman R. W. Wheeldon, J.P. ; D. Desmond ; Councillor Wallace Rockett, Cinema Palace, Boothferry Road, Goole ; A. Spinks, 6, Spring Street, Hull ; Brinley Evans ; J. Wheeldon, 545, Anlaby Road, Hull ; E. Lamb, Waterloo Picture House, Waterloo Street, Hull ; E. F. Symons, Picture Playhouse, Beverley ; H. Vaughan Evans. *Delegates*, T. Fawley Judge, A.C.A., Brinley Evans.

KENT BRANCH.—Gloucester House, Warren Road, Bexley Heath. *Chairman*, Major C. H. Bell, O.B.E., National House, 60, Wardour Street, W.1. *Vice-Chairman*, Morris Levy, Westminster Lodge, 34, Highfield Gardens, N.W.11. *Treasurer*, Reginald V. Crow, 11, Avenue Lodge, Avenue Road, N.W.8. *Secretary*, Harry Quinton, The Palace, Bexley Heath. *Trustees*, Reginald V. Crow ; C. G.

Manning, Great Hall Cinema, Tunbridge Wells; Morris M. Levy, Westminster Lodge, 34, Highfield Gardens, N.W.11. *Committee*, Officers and Immediate Past Chairman, Chas. Collins, Royal Cinema, Deal. *Delegates*, Morris M. Levy Major C. H. Bell, O.B.E.

LEEDS AND DISTRICT BRANCH.—7, Headingley Crescent, Leeds, 6. *Chairman*, Charles P. Metcalfe, Russell Chambers, 54, Merrion Street, Leeds, 1. *Vice Chaorman*, J. Claughton, Crescent Picture House,, Dewsbury Road, Leeds. *Treasurer*, C. H. Whincup, Tower Picture House, Briggate, Leeds. 1. *Secretary*, E. M. Rush, 7, Headingley Crescent, Leeds, 6. *Trustees*, A. Cunningham, Tower Crest, Heysham, Morecambe; J. Claughton; E. M. Rush. *Committee*, J. Jesson, Town Hall, Penistone; Mrs. Gaines, Haddon Hall, Kirkstall Road, Leeds; E. Friedman, Savoy Picture House, Marsh, Huddersfield; C. T. Shayler, Picture House, Church Lane, Pudsey; H. Hopkins, Palace Cinema, Meadow Road, Leeds; Charles P. Metcalfe; J. Claughton; C. H. Whincup; A. Cunningham; J. Prendergast, New Rialto Cinema, Fulford Road, York. *Delegates*, J. Claughton, A. Cunningham, Chas. P. Metcalfe, J. Prendergast.

LEICESTER BRANCH.—7, St. Martin's East, Leicester. *Chairman*, G. H. Scarborough, "Ashfield," Elmfield Avenue, Leicester. *Vice-Chairman*, A. W. Black, Belgrave Cinema, Belgrave Road, Leicester. *Treasurer*, A. W. Black. *Secretary*, C. F. Bailey, 7, St. Martin's East, Leicester. *Trustees*, Fred Stafford, Jnr., Aylestone Cinema, Grace Road, Leicester; Councillor G. Smith, Picture House, South Wigston, Nr. Leicester; A. W. Black. *Committee*, G. H. Scarborough; A. W. Black; C. F. Bailey; Fred. Stafford, Jnr.; Edward G. Bigney, Floral Hall, Leicester; F. T. Towers, Olympia Theatre, Leicester; W. S. Hudson, Princes Theatre, Leicester; P. Gorton, City Cinema, Market Place, Leicester. *Delegate*, G. H. Scarborough.

LONDON AND HOME COUNTIES BRANCH.—Broadmead House, Panton Street, S.W.1. *Chairman*, K. A. Nyman, B.Sc., Pollen House, 10-12, Cork St., W.1. *Vice-Chairman*, Capt. Alfred Davis, Davis Theatre, Croydon. *Treasurer*, Major A. J. Gale, O.B.E., J.P., Pollen House, 10-12, Cork Street, W.1. *Secretary*, Arthur Taylor, Broadmead House, Panton Street, S.W.1. *Trustees*, Reginald V. Crow, 11, Avenue Lodge, Avenue Rd., N.W.8; Thomas France, 108, Great Russell St., W.C.1; Major A. J. Gale, O.B.E., J.P. *Committee*, K. A. Nyman, B.Sc.; Capt. Alfred Davis; Major A. J. Gale, O.B.E., J.P.; Reginald V. Crow; Thomas France; J. Alexander, 9, St. Mary's Mansions, Paddington, W.2; Ralph S. Bromhead, A.C.A., Dean House, Dean St., W.1; J. W. Davies, 23, Meard St., W.1; J. Davis, 147, Wardour Street, W.1; S. Dorin, 35, Gloucester Road, Regent's Park, N.W.1; Arthur Ferriss, 14, Deansway, East Finchley, N.2; Theo. H. Fligelstone, 11, Berkeley Court, Baker Street, N.W.1; A. Freedman, 62, Oxford Street, W.1; L. Freeman, Plaza Cinema, Tottenham Lane, Crouch End, N.8; Alderman T. L. Harrold, Yelverton, Fordington Road, Highgate, N.6; Councillor E. A. Huddleston, People's Palace, Witney, Oxon; S. Hyams, 90, Regent Street, W.1; D. J. James, Cinema House, 225, Oxford Street, W.1; Ben Jay, 145, Wardour Street, W.1; H. Lennox, Coronation House, 4, Lloyds Avenue, E.C.3; Morris M. Levy, 34, Highfield Gardens, Golders Green, N.W.; H. A. McCullie, Picardy Cinema, High Street, Harlesden, N.W.10; C. A. Mathes, St. Giles, Vallance Road, Alexandra Park, N.22; Louis Morris, 52, Shaftesbury Avenue, W.1; A. S. Moss, 30-31, Golden Square, W.1; Ernest W. P. Peall, New Gallery House, 123, Regent Street, W.1; H. Pesaresi, Kapunda, Woodland Rise, Muswell Hill, N.; H. P. Selwyn, 26, Albert Court, Kensington, S.W.7. *Delegates*, K. A. Nyman, B.Sc., Capt. Alfred Davis, Major A. J. Gale, O.B.E., J.P., J. Alexander, Ralph S. Bromhead, Thomas France, A. Freedman, Alderman T. L. Harrold, Councillor E. A. Huddleston, C. A. Mathes, A. S. Moss, Ernest W. P. Peall, H.P. Selwyn.

MANCHESTER AND DISTRICT BRANCH.—32, Cromford House, Cromford Court, Market Street, Manchester, 4. *Chairman*, T. H. Hartley, "Burcot," 421, Rossendale Road, Burnley. *Vice-Chairman*, A. Peel, 239, Manchester Road, Nelson. *Treasurer*, H. Lyons, 84, Walton Lane, Nelson. *Secretary*, Charles Littler, 32, Cromford House, Cromford Court, Market Street, Manchester, 4. *Trustees*, T. H. Hartley; H. Lyons; W. L. Johnson, Boro Cinema, Halliwell Street, Salford. *Committee*, T. H. Hartley; Charles Littler; A. Peel; H. Lyons; W. L. Johnson; Capt. G. B. Row, 6, Sefton Road, Smithills, Bolton; E. Wardle, 10, Orthes Grove, Heaton Chapel, Stockport; J. Holden, Pavilion Cinema, Rawtenstall; W. E. Woolstencroft, 35, Church Street, Leigh; Taylor Barnes, Palace Cinema, Manchester Old Road, Middleton; L. G. Bailey, 118, Hill Lane, Blackley, Manchester; E. Woodall, Ideal Cinema, Castleton; J. Mather, La Scala Cinema, Bury; A. Ingham, New Empire (Burnley), Ltd.; 3, Grimshaw Street, Burnley; H. Hoyle, Empire Cinema, Haslingden; C. Dowding, Deansgate Picture House, Deansgate, Manchester. *Delegates*, T. H. Hartley, A. Peel, Capt. G. B. Row, Chas. Littler, J. Mather.

NORTHERN BRANCH.—Grainger Chambers, 104, Grainger Street, Newcastle-on-Tyne. *Chairman*, T. H. Scott, Queen's Hall, Hexham-on-Tyne. *Vice-Chairman*, F. W. Morrison, Greenbank, Dunston Hill, Dunston-on-Tyne. *Treasurer*, S. Bamford, Grainger Chambers, 104, Grainger Street, Newcastle-on-Tyne. *Secretary*, Alfred Smith, F.I.S.A., Grainger Chambers, 104, Grainger Street, Newcastle-on-Tyne. *Trustees*, S. Bamford; J. MacHarg, Central Buildings, Station Road, Wallsend-on-Tyne; W. S. Gibson, 4, Palladium Buildings, Eastbourne Road, Middlesbrough. *Committee*, T. H. Scott; F. W. Morrison; S. Bamford; W. Carr, Queen's Hall, Seaton Delaval, Northumberland; W. S. Gibson; E. J. Hinge, 72, Grey Street, Newcastle-on-Tyne; J. S. Snell, 72, Grey Street, Newcastle-on-Tyne; T. Thompson, 4, Palladium Buildings, Eastbourne Road, Middlesbrough; A. V. Adams, Olympia, Blackhill, Co. Durham; J. C. Bell, Brighton Electric Theatre, Newcastle-on-Tyne; C. Crowe, 52, Stowell Street, Newcastle-on-Tyne; S. Dawe, Messrs. Dawe Bros., Gibb Chambers, Westgate Road, Newcastle; E. R. Eadie, Apollo Cinema, Birtley, Co. Durham; F. M. Horsfall, Havelock Cinema, Sunderland; A. C. Harris, Stoll Theatre, Westgate Road, Newcastle-on-Tyne; T. F. Massicks, Plaza Theatre, West Road, Newcastle-on-Tyne; J. MacHarg; G. W. Oliver, Shadwell Towers, East Boldon, Co. Durham; B. Renwick, Bamboro' Electric Cinema, Byker, Newcastle-on-Tyne; C. Wood, Norton Cinema, The Avenue, Norton-on-Tees. *Delegates*, W. Carr, W. S. Gibson, E. J. Hinge, F. W. Morrison, J. S. Snell, T. Thompson.

NORTH STAFFORDSHIRE BRANCH.—17, Albion Street, Hanley, Stoke-on-Trent. *Chairman*, Alderman R. Beresford, Pavilion, Newcastle-under-Lyme. *Vice-Chairman*, J. Barrington, Victoria Street

Hartshill, Stoke-on-Trent. *Treasurer,* L. Myatt, Alhambra, Normacot, Longton. *Secretary,* T. A. Grant,A.C.A., 17, Albion Street, Hanley, Stoke-on-Trent. *Trustees,* Alderman R. Beresford, L. Myatt, T. A. Grant, A.C.A. *Committee,* M. A. Vachon, Plaza Theatre, Newcastle, Staffs. ; G. Edney, c/o Ald. G. H. Barber, The Palace, Tunstall, Stoke-on-Trent ; N. Dean, The Regal Theatre, Newcastle, Staffs. ; Capt. B. Hughes, O.B.E., The New Plaza Picture Playhouse, Fenton, Stoke-on-Trent ; T. J. Dyson, Hippodrome, Kingsway, Stoke-on-Trent ; L. A. V. Plumpton, Royal Picture House, Anchor Road, Longton, Stoke-on-Trent ; C. A. J. Plant, The Palace Cinema, Albion Square, Hanley, Stoke-on-Trent ; F. V. Chambers, The New Roxy, Glass Street, Hanley, Stoke-on-Trent ; P. J. Thornton, Electric Palace, Burton-on-Trent. *Delegates,* M. A. Vachon, L. A. V. Plumpton.

NORTH WESTERN BRANCH.—Lloyds Bank Buildings, 11-13, Victoria Street, Liverpool, 2. *Chairman,* Alderman E. Trounson, J.P., 1, Park Road, Southport. *Vice-Chairman,* S. Grimshaw, Carlton Villa, Dee Banks, Chester. *Treasurer-Secretary,* G. Dudley West, F.C.A., Lloyds Bank Buildings, 11-13, Victoria Street, Liverpool,2. *Trustees,* Alderman E. Trounson,J.P. ; S. Grimshaw ; J. R. Dovener, 18, Union Street, Liverpool. *Committee,* C. Adams, The Palace, Sea View Road, Wallasey, Cheshire ; B. Allman, 7, Thornton Road, Wallasey, Cheshire ; F. J. Beardsworth, 7, Heydale Road, Mossley Hill, Liverpool ; P. Brimelow, 40, Sandrock Road, Wallasey, Cheshire ; J. R. Dovener ; Councillor R. Duncan French, North House, North John Street, Liverpool ; W. J. Grace, "Trefula," Calder Drive, Mossley Hill, Liverpool ; S. Grimshaw ; J. H. Haigh, 10, Commutation Row, Liverpool ; Philip M. Hanmer, 51, North John Street, Liverpool ; W. H. Lennon, St. James' Picturedrome, St. James' Street, Liverpool ; F. W. Locke, "Sunnyside," Judges Drive, Newsham Park, Liverpool ; S. Menin, "Sandford," Chiltern Drive, Hale, Cheshire ; R. P. Rutherford, Queens Picture House, Poulton Road, Wallasey ; J. R. Saronie, Saxone Buildings, Church Street, Liverpool ; W. J. Speakman, Capitol Cinema, Overton Street, Edge Hill, Liverpool ; E. B. Thompson, Liverpool Picturedrome, Kensington, Liverpool ; Alderman E. Trounson, J.P. *Delegates,* Alderman E. Trounson, J.P., S. Grimshaw, Philip M. Hanmer, J. R. Dovener, R. P. Rutherford, W. J. Speakman.

NOTTS AND DERBY BRANCH.—General Buildings, Bridlesmith Gate, Nottingham. *Chairman,* E. A. Wilcock, 8, Carlton Road, Nottingham. *Vice-Chairman,* H. Elton, Commerce Chambers, Elite Buildings, Parliament Street, Nottingham. *Treasurer,* E. A. Wilcock. *Secretary,* Fred. A. Prior, F.S.A.A., General Buildings, Bridlesmith Gate, Nottingham. *Trustees,* Councillor J. Pollard, J.P., 27, Atkins Lane, Mansfield ; E. A. Wilcock ; Fred. A. Prior, F.S.A.A. *Committee,* NOTTINGHAM.— E. B. Day, Vernon Road Picture House, Basford, Nottingham ; S. Graham, 154, Gordon Road, West Bridgford, Notts. ; E. C. Morris, Scala Theatre, Market Street, Nottingham ; C. Woodward, Kinema, Haydn Road, Sherwood, Nottingham ; H. J. Widdowson, Bulwell, Nottingham. NOTTS.—Councillor J. Pollard, J.P. ; J. White, Empire Hucknall, Notts. ; R. Kemp, 3, Newcastle Chambers, Nottingham. DERBYSHIRE.—J. Langham Brown, Empire Cinema, Long Eaton ; J. Drew, Scala Theatre, Long Eaton ; G. Beastall, Premier Electric Theatre, Somercotes ; F. J. Harris, The Picture House, Holywell Street, Chesterfield ; T. W. Swift, Allenton Picture House, Osmaston Road, Derby ; E. Rudge, Victoria Picture House, Knifesmith Gate, Chesterfield. LINCOLN.—H. B. Harris, 241, Monks Road, Lincoln. *Delegates,* Councillor J. Pollard, J.P. ; Fred. A. Prior, F.S.A.A. ; J. Drew.

PORTSMOUTH BRANCH.—Bank Chambers, 57, Palmerston Road, Southsea. *Chairman,* F. B. B. Blake, Apollo Cinema, Albert Road, Southsea. *Vice-Chairman,* Capt. J. Smithson, Troxy Cinema, Portsmouth. *Treasurer,* J. W. Mills, Arcade Cinema, Commercial Road, Portsmouth. *Secretary,* A. Daniels, F.S.A.A., Bank Chambers, 57, Palmerston Road, Southsea. *Trustees,* J. W. Mills; V. Pannell, Globe Cinema, Fratton Road, Portsmouth. *Committee,* H. J. Cook, "Oakcroft," Fareham ; J. W. Mills ; J. G. Woods, Palace Theatre, Commercial Road, Portsmouth ; E. A. Barry, Regent Theatre, North End, Portsmouth ; J. Holland, Carlton Theatre, High Street, Cosham ; A. Levison, Empire Cinema, North End, Portsmouth ; F. B. B. Blake ; Capt. J. Smithson ; V. Pannell. *Delegate,* Councillor F. J. Spickernell, Tivoli Cinema, Copnor Road, Portsmouth.

SCOTTISH BRANCH.—Gordon Chambers, 90, Mitchell Street, Glasgow, C.1. *Chairman,* new appointment to be made. *Vice-Chairman,* George Singleton, 39, Kirkpatrick Street, Glasgow, E.1. *Treasurer,* H. J. Green, 182, Trongate, Glasgow. *Secretary,* John A. Houston, C.A., J.P., 90, Mitchell Street, Glasgow. *Hon. Solicitor,* new appointment· to· be made. *Trustees,* Thos. Ormiston, C.B.E., 6, Brandon Street, Motherwell ; A. S. Albin, Rosevilla, Viewforth, Edinburgh ; H. J. Green. *Committee,* GLASGOW AND WEST OF SCOTLAND.—A. A. Goldberg, 7, Broomhill Gardens, Glasgow ; Thos. Anderson, 4, Kingsford Avenue, Muirend ; R. Bennell, New Savoy, Hope Street, Glasgow ; H. W. Morton, Braemar, Glaisnock Street, Old Cumnock ; George Taylor, Partick Picture House, Vine Street, Partick. EDINBURGH.—J. S. Dunbar, Capitol, Manderston Street, Leith ; W. H. Albin, Pavilion, Dalkeith ; W. Macguire, C.A., Palace, Edinburgh. ABERDEEN.—James A. Jeffrey, C.A., 9, Golden Square, Aberdeen ; Miss Minnie M. McIntosh, Princess Cinema, Hawkhill, Dundee. DUMFRIES.—John Darlison, Regal, Dumfries. *Delegates,* Alex. B. King, J.P., 167, Bath Street, Glasgow ; Thos. Ormiston, C.B.E. ; George Singleton ; James Welsh, J.P., 1, Endfield Avenue, Glasgow, W.2 ; D. A. Stewart, J.P., 105, St. Vincent Street, Glasgow ; Provost Timmons, Cinema-de-Luxe, Lochgelly ; R. McLaughlin, C.A., Caley Picture House, Lothian Road, Edinburgh ; L. D. Dickson, Hippodrome, Bo'ness ; H. J. Green ; G. Urie Scott, 154, West Regent Street, Glasgow.

SHEFFIELD AND DISTRICT BRANCH.—Hoole's Chambers, 47, Bank Street, Sheffield, 1. *Chairman* T. F. McDonald, 352, Sharrow Lane, Sheffield. *Vice-Chairman,* A. R. Walker, Palace Theatre, Attercliffe, Sheffield. *Treasurer,* G. H. Newton, 46, Hallowmoor Road, Wisewood, Sheffield. *Secretary,* Arnold R. Favell, A.S.A.A., 47, Bank Street, Sheffield, 1. *Trustess,* I. Graham, 37, Collegiate Crescent, Sheffield ; S. Kirkham, The Tivoli, Norfolk Street, Sheffield. *Committee,* T. F. McDonald ; S. Kirkham ; G. H. Newton ; A. R. Walker ; I. Graham ; A. R. Favell "Sunningdale," Dobcroft Road, Ecclesall Road South, Sheffield ; J. Harrison, Unity Picture Palace, Langsett Road, Sheffield ; H. W. Silvey, Star Picture House, Eccleshall Road, Sheffield ; J. W. Keeton, 529, City Road, Sheffield ; Councillor H. S. Gent, 12, Kenbourne Road, Sheffield ; H. Popplewell, Don Picture Palace, West Bar, Sheffield ; C. Vessey, 322, Heavygate Road, Sheffield ; W. F. Sykes, Regent Varieties, Howard Street, Rotherham. *Delegates,* A. R. Favell, T. F. McDonald.

SOUTHERN MIDLANDS BRANCH.—Central Cinema, Cheshunt, Herts. *Chairman*, Councillor L. Salmons, J.P., Electric Theatre, Newport Pagnell. *Vice-Chairman*, Theo. H. Fligelstone, 11, Berkeley Court, Baker Street, N.W.1. *Treasurer*, R. Chetham, The Plaza, Bedford. *Secretary*, Ernest J. Carpenter, Central Cinema, Cheshunt, Herts. *Trustees :* W. F. J. Hewitt, The Palace, Wellingborough ; C. C. Day, 145, Orford Road, Hoe Street, Walthamstow, E. ; W. Southan Morris, 68, Wyckham Road, Golders Green, N.W. *Committee*, N. A. Ayres—Baldock Cinema, White Horse Street, Baldock ; J. W. Davies, New Coliseum, St. Albans Road, Watford ; E. E. Smith, Regent Cinema, Bishops Stortford, Herts ; W. D. Murkett, Grand Palace, Huntingdon ; A. J. Pointer, New Victoria Cinema, Cambridge ; Councillor L. Salmons, J.P. ; Councillor H. Bancroft, The Hippodrome, Wisbech ; E. W. Cheesman, Princess Theatre, Hemel Hempstead ; R. Chetham ; A. W. Green, Regal Cinema, Lytton Road, New Barnet ; Theo. H. Fligelstone ; H. D. Pascoe, Cinema de Luxe, Campbell Street, Northampton. *Delegates*, R. Chetham, C. C. Day, Councillor L. Salmons, J.P.

SOUTH WALES AND MON. BRANCH.—3, Park Place, Cardiff. *Chairman*, H. Victor Davis, "Elvaston," Newbridge, Mon. *Vice-Chairman*, W. Berriman, Great Western Workmen's Hall, hopkinstown, Pontypridd. *Treasurer*, A. B. Watts, F.S.A.A., 14, St. Andrews Crescent, Cardiff. *Secretary*, W. J. Fooks, F.S.A.A., 3, Park Place, Cardiff. *Trustees*, A. B. Watts, H. Victor Davis, W. J. Fooks. *Committee*, A. B. Watts ; Richard Dooner, 2, Office Road, Maesteg ; A. Jones, "The Firs," Abercarn, Mon. ; H. V. Davis ; F. Phillips, 3, Greenland Road, Brynmawr ; W. Hyman, 43, Eaton Crescent, Swansea ; W. L. Smith, Workmen's Hall, Mountain Ash ; W. Berriman ; J. E. Sprague, Palladium Buildings, Pontypridd ; S. Attwood, "Rosslyn," Glassllwch, Newport, Mon. ; F. Norman Wright Lyceum, Newport, Mon. ; A. Morgan, Workmen's Hall, Blaenavon ; W. J. Vaughan, Albert Hall, Swansea ; F. Thomas, 71, Greenfield, Newbridge, Mon. ; David Thomas, "Brookville," Clydach Vale, Rhondda. *Delegates*, H. Victor Davis, S. Attwood, A. B. Watts, F.S.A.A., F. Phillips.

SUSSEX BRANCH.—Bank Chambers, 57, Palmerston Road, Southsea. *Chairman*, P. G. Lundy, Savoy Cinema, East Street, Brighton. *Vice-Chairman*, Dan Benjamin, Princes Cinema, North Street, Brighton. *Treasurer*, R. Briggs, Cinema-de-Luxe, St. Mary's, Station Street, Lewes. *Secretary*, A. Daniels, F.S.A.A., Bank Chambers, 57, Palmerston Road, Southsea. *Trustees*, R. Briggs, C. A. Seebold, Rivoli Cinema, Worthing ; R. E. Richards, Picturedrome, Langney Road, Eastbourne. *Committee*, J. Van Koert, Arcadia Cinema, 16, Lewes Road, Brighton ; C. A. Seebold ; R. H. Ainsworth, Regent Cinema, Brighton ; R. Briggs ; C. A. Maguire, Lido Cinema, Hove ; D. Benjamin, Princess Theatre, Brighton ; P. G. Lundy ; R. E. Richards ; H. Shanly, 7, King's Bench Walk, Temple, E.C.4. *Delegates*, R. E. Richards, H. Shanly.

WEST LANCASHIRE BRANCH.—"Ceair," South Avenue, South Road, Morecambe. *Chairman*, James Atroy, The Picturedrome, Church Street, Lancaster. *Vice-Chairman*, Henry Simpson, Palladium Cinema, Victoria Road, Ulverston. *Treasurer and Secretary*, Harry Hargreaves, "Ceair," South Avenue, South Road, Morecambe. *Committee*, No Committee appointed—all members invited to meetings. *Delegates*, Harry Hargreaves, Henry Simpson.

The Kinematograph Renters' Society of Great Britain and Ireland, Ltd.

General Offices : 30, OLD COMPTON STREET, W.!.

Telephone : Gerrard 4262-6.

OFFICERS.

D. E. GRIFFITHS (President), First National Film Distributors Ltd., Warner House, Wardour Street, W.1.

F. W. BAKER (Hon. Treasurer), Butcher's Film Service, Ltd., 175, Wardour Street, W.1.

FRANK HILL, F.C.I.S. (Secretary), 30, Old Compton Street, W.1.

COUNCIL.

ASSOCIATED BRITISH FILM DISTRIBUTORS, LTD., 169, Oxford Street, W.1.
BENDON, S. (Bendon Trading Co.), 132, West Nile Street, Glasgow.
BRITISH LION FILM CORPORATION, LTD., 76, Wardour Street, W.1.
BUTCHER'S FILM SERVICE, LTD., 175, Wardour Street, W.1.
COLUMBIA PICTURES CORPORATION, LTD., 139, Wardour Street, W.1.
FIRST NATIONAL FILM DISTRIBUTORS, LTD., 135/141, Wardour Street, W.1.
GAUMONT BRITISH DISTRIBUTORS LTD., Film House, Wardour Street, W.1.
GENERAL FILM DISTRIBUTORS, LTD., 127/133, Wardour Street, W.1.
METRO-GOLDWYN-MAYER PICTURES, LTD., 19, Tower Street, W.C.2.

British Lion's Outstanding Triumph—"Calling All Stars"

PARAMOUNT FILM SERVICE, LTD., 166, Wardour Street, W.1.
PATHE PICTURES, LTD., 103, Wardour Street, W.1.
RADIO PICTURES, LTD., 2-4, Dean Street, W.1.
UNITED ARTISTS CORPORATION, LTD., Film House, Wardour Street, W.1
UNIVERSAL PICTURES, LTD., Film House, Wardour Street, W.1.
WARDOUR FILMS, LTD., Film House, Wardour Street, W.1.
WARNER BROS., PICTURES, LTD., 135-141, Wardour Street, W.1

SOLICITOR.

HUGH V. HARRAWAY, 2, Field Court, Gray's Inn, W.C.1.

LIST OF MEMBERS.

LONDON.

Associated British Film Distributors, Ltd.
Associated Producing and Distribution Co.
British Lion Film Corporation, Ltd.
Butcher's Film Service, Ltd.
Columbia Pictures Corporation, Ltd.
First National Film Distributors, Ltd.
Gaumont British Distributors, Ltd.
General Film Distributors, Ltd.
Metro-Goldwyn-Mayer Pictures, Ltd.
National Screen Service, Ltd.
Paramount Film Service, Ltd.

Pathé Pictures, Ltd.
Radio Pictures, Ltd.
Reunion Films, Ltd.
Sherwood Exclusive Films., Ltd.
Twickenham Film Distributors, Ltd
United Artists Corporation, Ltd.
Universal Pictures, Ltd.
Wardour Films, Ltd.
Warner Bros. Pictures, Ltd.
Winads, Ltd.

MANCHESTER.	NEWCASTLE.	GLASGOW.	DUBLIN.
Blakeleys Productions, Ltd.	John Henderson & Son.	Bendon Trading Co.	W. McNally.

PROVINCIAL CENTRES.

GLASGOW.—Centred at 227, West George Street. (Secretary, A. Levy.)
DUBLIN.—Centred at 7, St. Andrew Street. (Secretaries, Taylor, Son and Robinson.)

OBJECTS.

To promote and protect in every possible legal manner the interests, financial welfare and success of the kinematograph film-renting trade, and to devise means to promote co-operation amongst those engaged in the kinematograph industry for the protection of their mutual interests.

To watch and keep records for reference and comparison of all matters, in any way affecting the kinematograph industry and of all developments thereof, and by the united opinion and experiences of the members of the Society to decide upon and initiate and support proper methods for dealing with any contingency affecting the kinematograph trade or the members of the Society that may arise.

To procure information for members of the Society as to the standing and responsibility of parties with whom they propose to transact business.

To give legal advice to members of the Society.

To promote, organise and carry on such charitable institution work of funds and for such purposes as shall be thought fit.

The Incorporated Association of Kinematograph Manufacturers, Ltd.

Offices : Carlisle House (Circa 1670), Soho, London, W.1.
Phone : Gerrard 1946.

OFFICERS.

Chairman :	... ...	Tom E. Davies, J.P.
Treasurer :	... ...	C. G. Fox.
Secretary :	... ...	J. Brooke Wilkinson.

COUNCIL.

E. E. Blake, c/o Kodak, Ltd., Kingsway, W.C.2.
A. S. Newman, Newman & Sinclair, Ltd., 2, Salisbury Road, Highgate, N.
J. Skittrell, Olympic Kine Laboratories, Ltd., School Road, Victoria Road, N.W.
W. Vinten, 89, Wardour Street, W.1.

OBJECTS.

. To promote the consideration and discussion of all questions affecting and generally to watch over, protect, and advance the interests of the trade of manufacturers and/or publishers and/or sellers of kinematograph films (in this memorandum called the "said trade," which expression shall include all ancillary and allied trades and every branch of such trade and whether such trade or trades shall be carried cn in England or elsewhere), to promote economy, efficiency and excellence in the said trade, and to facilitate the operations thereof, and to co-operate with members of the Association of the various branches of the said trade for the promotion of mutual interests.

THE CINEMATOGRAPH TRADE BENEVOLENT FUND.

Patron : His Majesty the King.

President : Sir William F. Jury.

Trustees :
Sir William F. Jury ; Lt.-Col. A. C. Bromhead, C.B.E. ; John Maxwell.

Council : ·
Reginald C. Bromhead, *Chairman.*

E. Ayres.	D. E. Griffiths.
F. W. Baker.	F. T. Harvey.
R. S. Bromhead.	Arthur W. Jarratt.
Arthur Cunningham.	C. Littler.
S. F. Ditcham.	F. W. Morrison.
R. Dooner.	Randolph E.Richards.
S. Eckman, Jun.	Arthur Watts.
T. Fligelstone.	G. Dudley West.
E. W. Fredman.	J. Brooke Wilkinson.
W. J. Gell.	H. T. S. Young.

Hon. Treasurer : J. Brooke Wilkinson, "Glebelands," Wokingham.
Convalescent and Rest Home of the Fund.
Suptdt. : O. Diver. *Matron :* Mrs. O. Diver.
Medical Officer : Dr. H. F. Curl.
Secretary and Offices :
Reginald C. O. Viveash, 52, Shaftesbury Avenue, London, W.1.
Telephone : Gerrard 4104.

THE CINEMATOGRAPH TRADE PROVIDENT INSTITUTION.

President : Sir William F. Jury.

Registered under the Friendly Societies Act, 1896. (Registered No. 1667.) Affiliated to The Cinematograph Trade Benevolent Fund.

Trustees :
Sir William F. Jury ; Lt.-Col. A. C. Bromhead, C.B.E. ; John Maxwell.

Committee :
Reginald C. Bromhead, *Chairman.*

E. Ayres.	E. W. Fredman.
F. W. Baker.	W. J. Gell.
R. S. Bromhead.	F. T. Harvey.
Arthur Cunningham.	J. Brooke Wilkinson.
T. Fligelstone.	H. T. S. Young.

Hon. Treasurer : J. Brooke Wilkinson.

Secretary and Offices :
Reginald C. O. Viveash, 52, Shaftesbury Avenue, London, W.1.

Telephone : Gerrard 4104.

Full particulars of membership of this Trade Friendly Society can be obtained on application to the Secretary.

GUILD OF BRITISH KINEMA PROJECTIONISTS AND TECHNICIANS, LTD.

Registered Office: 40, RUSSELL SQUARE, LONDON, W.C.1.

General Office: 20, VILLIERS STREET, LONDON, W.C.2.

Founded to uphold the status of Projectionists through efficiency and good service.

President:
S . T. PERRY, Empire Theatre, Leicester Square, London, W.C.2.

Vice-President:
H. B. SMITH, Trocadero Cinema, Liverpool.

General Secretary:
F. H. WOODS, " Forum," Villiers Street, London, W.C.2.

Joint General Treasurers:
G. E. LANSDOWN, Ship Carbon Co. of Gt. Britain, Ltd., National House, Wardour Street, London, W.1.

W. A. WARD, Ship Carbon Co. of Gt. Britain, National House, Wardour Street, London, W.1.

Hon. Solicitor:
J. H. JOHN, 40, Russell Square, London, W.C.1.

Branches: Birmingham, Bradford, Cardiff, Leeds, Nottingham, Huddersfield, Middlesbrough, Liverpool, Manchester, London, Sheffield, Southampton, Portsmouth, Newcastle, Preston, Stoke and Bristol.

The government of the organisation is by the Officers and a Council of members elected annually by the General Members.

BRITISH BOARD OF FILM CENSORS.

Offices:
Carlisle House (*circa* 1670), Soho, London, W.1.

Telephone: GERRARD 1946.

President:
The Rt. Hon. Lord TYRRELL OF AVON, G.C.B., G.C.M.G., K.C.V.O.

Consultative Committee:
J. BROOKE WILKINSON. M. H. DAVIS, J.P.
Lieut.-Colonel Sir CECIL LEVITA, K.C.V.O., C.B.E., D.L., J.P.
H. W. SKINNER. H. S. BUTTON.
H. ROWLAND. T. SKURRAY.
S. A. HECTOR. J. MAXWELL.
Alderman Lieut.-Colonel G. WESTCOTT, O.B.E., J.P. Alderman WYLES, J.P.
GEORGE A. BRYSON, J.P.
RICHARD RUTHERFORD, J.P.
Miss ROSAMUND SMITH.

THE PERFORMING RIGHT SOCIETY LIMITED.

COPYRIGHT HOUSE, 33, MARGARET STREET. LONDON, W.1.

Telephone: Langham 3864 (four lines).

Telegrams: PERFORIGHT, WESDO, LONDON.

An Association of Composers, Authors, Publishers and Proprietors of Copyright musical works, established to issue licences for the public performance of such works. The Society is not concerned with plays, sketches or other works of a non-musical character, nor with operas, musical plays or other dramatico-musical works performed in their entirety, but it is concerned, *inter alia,* with performances of music in conjunction with cinematograph films.

The Copyright Act of 1911 prohibits any public performance without the written permission of the Copyright Owners, and the Society's licence gives the permission required by the Act for about two million works in its repertoire, including those of the affiliated Societies of France, U.S.A., Italy, Germany, Austria, Spain, and many others.

Licences are required for any public performance, whether given by mechanical means or otherwise, and are granted not to musical directors, vocalists or musicians as such, but to proprietors of premises at which music is publicly performed or to the promoters of musical entertainments.

ADVISORY COMMITTEE TO THE BOARD OF TRADE ON THE CINEMATOGRAPH FILMS ACT.

Lt.-Col. Sir ARNOLD WILSON, K.C.I.E., C.S.I., C.M.G., D.S.O., M.P.—*Chairman.*

F. W. BAKER.	A. B. KING, J.P.
G. R. HALL CAINE, C.B.E., M.P.	JOHN MAXWELL. C. P. METCALFE.
Hon. ELEANOR PLUMER.	S. W. SMITH.
P. GUEDALLA.	E. TROUNSON, J.P.
J. HALLSWORTH.	C. M. WOOLF.
T. H. FLIGELSTONE.	

Secretary: L. T. MOORBY.

ASSOCIATION OF CINE-TECHNICIANS.

Address: 30, PICCADILLY MANSIONS, LONDON, W.1.

Telephone: GERRARD 2366.

Vice-Presidents:
DESMOND DICKINSON, THOROLD DICKINSON, J. C. GEMMELL, KENNETH GORDON, IVOR MONTAGU.

Secretary:
GEORGE H. ELVIN, A.C.I.S.

Catering for film technicians of all departments and grades, including the following :— Camera, Allied Camera, Sound, Allied Sound, Editing and Cutting, Art, Still, Floor Staff, Production Staff, Scenario, Laboratory, Television.

Objects and Activities:

Examination of Conditions of Employment and consideration of suggested improvements to mutual benefit of employers and employed.

Establishment and maintenance of Professional Status.

Runs Employment Bureau, licenced annually by L.C.C., with accurate records of disengaged technicians of all departments and grades.

Health and Hospital Benefits.

Consultation with Authorities on employment of foreign technicians.

Quarterly Journal.

Educational Facilities, including Lectures and Film Shows.

ELECTRICAL TRADES UNION.

Affiliated to the Trades Union Congress and the Labour Party.

Registered Office: 11, Macaulay Road, Clapham, London, S.W.4. *London District Office:* Rugby Chambers, 2, Chapel Street, W.C.1.

General Secretary: J. ROWAN, J.P., 11, Macaulay Road, Clapham, London, S.W.4.

Branches confined solely to Kinema Operators :—

London, Aberdeen, Belfast, Birmingham, Brighton, Dundee, Edinburgh, Glasgow, Leeds, Liverpool, Manchester, Newcastle, Sheffield, Bolton, Bradford, Bristol, Cardiff, Hull, Leicester, Northampton, Nottingham, Oldham, Portsmouth, Southampton.

London Cinema Operators Branch meets every Sunday morning at 11.30 a.m. at "The Blue Post," Edward Street, Wardour Street, W.1.

FEDERATION OF BRITISH INDUSTRIES
(*Film Group*).

Incorporated by Royal Charter.

Offices:

21, TOTHILL STREET, WESTMINSTER, S.W.1.

Telephone: WHITEHALL 6711.

Director: GUY LOCOCK, C.M.G.

General Secretary: D. L. WALKER.

Objects:

The F.B.I. exists to encourage and develop British manufactures, and to safeguard the interests of British manufacturers both at home and abroad. Nothing that concerns the welfare of British industry falls outside its scope.

Special attention is given to the encouragement of British Film production, having regard to the recognised value of the film as a medium for national and industrial publicity. The Federation, through its Film Producers' Group, acts as the official organisation of all the principal film producers in Great Britain ; it assists in the furtherance of all the objects of the industry and endeavours to secure the widest possible distribution of British films throughout the world.

BRITISH KINEMATOGRAPH SOCIETY.

President: S. ROWSON, M.Sc., F.S.S.,

32, SHAFTESBURY AVENUE, LONDON, W.C.,

Telephone: Gerrard 2318.

Vice-President: ARTHUR S. NEWMAN, F.R.P.S. 25, HORNSEY LANE, N.6.

Hon. Secretary: E. ORAM, 314, Regent St., W.1.

Hon. Treasurer: PAUL KIMBERLEY, O.B.E.

BROADWICK HOUSE, BROAD STREET, W.1.

Executive:

Capt. A. G. D. WEST, M.A., B.Sc.
D. WRATTEN.
LESLIE EVELEIGH, F.R.P.S.
F. WATTS.
W. VINTEN.
P. BASTIE.

The Scientific and Technical Society of the Industry whose meetings are held in the Gaumont British Theatre, Film House, Wardour Street, on the second Monday of each of the Winter months. The Society exists for the dissemination of knowledge and the elucidation of technical problems within the Industry.

INCORPORATED SOCIETY OF MUSICIANS

(Representative of the Musical Profession.)

ESTABLISHED 1882. INCORPORATED 1892.
(RECONSTITUTED 1928.)

General Office: 19, BERNERS STREET, LONDON,
W.1.

Telegrams: Scherzo, Rath, London.
Telephone: Museum 7876-7.

General Secretary: FRANK EAMES.

Officers: 1937.
President: Sir PERCY C. BUCK, M.A., D.Mus.
Oxon.

Past-President: STANLEY MARCHANT, C.V.O.,
D.Mus.Oxon., F.R.A.M., F.R.C.O.

President-Elect: ROBERT J. FORBES, F.R.M.C.M·
F.R.C.M.

Treasurer: FREDERICK G. SHINN, D.Mus. Dunelm,
F.R.C.O., A.R.C.M., Hon. R.A.M.

CINEMA ORGANISTS' SECTION.

Officers and Committee, 1936 :
Warden: EDGAR PETO, A.R.C.O.
Past-Warden: THOMAS W. GROSCH, B.A.London.
Treasurer: ARTHUR W. OWEN.

Committee:
HUBERT E. COOTER, A.R.C.O.; GERALD J.
DINGLEY, A.R.C.M.; REGINALD FOXWELL,
A.R.C.O.; ALLENDER FRYER, A.R.C.M.; GUY
HINDELL; REGINALD NEW; GEORGE T.
PATTMAN, F.R.C.O.; ERIC SPRUCE, A.R.C.M.

Objects:
To improve the professional status of Cinema
Organists; to further their particular interests;
the improvement of facilities and conditions
incidental to their calling, by all or any of the
following :—

(*a*) To admit to membership professional
Cinema Organists.

(*b*) To afford mutual help (particularly to the
provincial members) by exchange of ideas
through the medium of the Society's monthly
journal; and by periodical meetings both in
London and the provinces.

(*c*) To maintain a Register of vacant and new
appointments; to circulate the Register
periodically to members and to supply on request
the list of members available to employers and
organ builders.

(*d*) To act as an advisory body with regard to
improvements in the designing and construction
of Cinema Organs.

and by all other convenient means which will be
of assistance to members in their professional
work.

Condition of Membership:
"That the member's primary professional
practice is or has been that of a Cinema
Organist."

Applicants must have held a post (or posts)
as Cinema Organist for a minimum period of
twelve months.

ROYAL PHOTOGRAPHIC SOCIETY.

(KINE GROUP.)

Offices:
35, RUSSELL SQUARE, LONDON, W.C.1.

CENTRAL INFORMATION BUREAU FOR EDUCATIONAL FILMS, LTD.

Address:
KINGSWAY HOUSE, 103, KINGSWAY, LONDON,
W.C.2.

Telephone: Holborn 3163.
Telegrams: Holborn 3163, London.

Officers:
J. RUSSELL ORR (late Director of Education,
Colony and Protectorate of Kenya), Managing
Director.
Major H. M. C. ORR.

Objects:

(*a*) Active encouragement of the use of the
Cinematograph for Educational purposes;
Scientific and Industrial Research, etc.

(*b*) Advising and supplying Cinematographic
apparatus of every kind.

(*c*) Compilation of Film programmes for
special purposes.

(*d*) Exchange of information with Foreign
Countries.

(*e*) Distributors of "Film Flex" film
preservative.

(*f*) News Distribution Service.

CINEMA VETERANS, 1903.

President: W. C. JEAPES.
Vice-President: H. S. CHAMBERS.

Hon. Secretary: THOMAS FRANCE, 108, Great
Russell Street, London, W.C.1 (Museum 5221).

Hon. Treasurer: R. W. PAUL.

Committee.

F. W. BAKER.	R. DOONER.
W. BARKER.	A. J. GALE.
E. E. BLAKE.	E. GRAY.
I. BOSCO.	W. C. JEAPES.
COL. A. C. BROMHEAD.	R. W. PAUL.
S. H. CARTER.	SIR WILLIAM JURY.
H. S. CHAMBERS.	M. RAYMOND.
A. CHEETHAM.	E. H. ROCKETT.
A. P. CROSS.	C. URBAN.
A. CUNNINGHAM.	W. VINTEN.
G. A. CHEETHAM.	T. A. WELSH.

And the *Hon. Secretary:* THOMAS FRANCE.

"A Cinema Veteran is one who was actively
employed in the Cinema Industry in (or before)
1903 and remained therein for a reasonable
period."

There is no entrance fee or subscription, but
all applicants must submit their records of
service, before acceptance, to the Committee and
only those whose records are approved and
confirmed are entitled to wear the Association's
Badge.

An Annual Re-Union Dinner is held on first
Monday in December.

VARIETY ARTISTES' FEDERATION.

FOUNDED 1906.

Offices: 18, CHARING CROSS ROAD, W.C.2

Hon. Chairman: HARRY CLAFF.
General Secretary: A. V. DREWE.
Telephone: TEMPLE BAR 6950.
Telegraphic Address: "ARTIFEDERA,
LESQUARE."

THE BRITISH ACTORS' EQUITY ASSOCIATION.

(Incorporating THE STAGE GUILD.)

Office: 24, THAVIES INN, HOLBORN, E.C.I.

Telephone: Central 5622.

President: GODFREY TEARLE. *Vice-Presidents:* LEWIS CASSON AND MAY WHITTY.

Treasurer: ARTHUR WONTNER.

Hon. General Secretary: ALFRED M. WALL.

Assistant Secretary: GEOFFREY ROBINSON.

Trustees:

LEWIS CASSON, LESLIE HENSON, GODFREY TEARLE, J. FISHER WHITE.

Trustees Equity-Benevolent Fund:

MARIE BURKE.   MARGARET SCUDAMORE.
FRANK COCHRANE.   BEN WEBSTER.

Solicitors: Pattinson & Brewer.
Chartered Accountants and Auditors: Watson, Collin & Co.

Council:

GEORGE ARLISS.	GORDON HARKER.
YVONNE ARNAUD.	*LESLIE HENSON.
*FELIX AYLMER.	*MARIE LOHR.
REGINALD BACH.	RAYMOND MASSEY.
LESLIE BANKS.	CLIFFORD MOLLISON.
W. GRAHAM BROWNE.	MARIE NEY.
JACK BUCHANAN.	*LAURENCE OLIVIER.
*MARIE BURKE.	CECIL PARKER.
JEAN CADELL.	FLORA ROBSON.
LEWIS CASSON.	*ATHENE SEYLER.
FRANK CELLIER.	*BARRY SHERWOOD.
O. B. CLARENCE.	GODFREY TEARLE.
ROBERT DONAT.	*SYBIL THORNDIKE.
FRANKLYN DYALL.	*AUSTIN TREVOR.
*EDITH EVANS.	FRANK VOSPER.
GWEN FFRANGCON-DAVIES.	BEN WEBSTER.
JOHN GIELGUD.	*MARGARET WEBSTER.
*ELEANOR HALLAM.	*J. FISHER WHITE.
*NICHOLAS HANNEN.	MAY WHITTY.
SirCEDRIC HARDWICKE.	*ARTHUR WONTNER.

*Members of Executive Committee.

SOCIETY OF ENTERTAINMENT MANAGERS AND MUSICAL DIRECTORS

(*Affiliated with the Association of Touring and Producing Managers.*)

Offices: 10, KING STREET, COVENT GARDEN' W.C.2.

Telegrams: LUICASON RAND, LONDON.

Telephone: Temple Bar 1606.

President: OSCAR BARRETT, JNR.

Secretary: LOUIS CASSON.

Officers for Year 1935-36.

Chairman: A. GIFFORD STACEY.

Vice-Chairman: S. H. LAYCOCK.

Deputy-Chairman: A. C. TOONE.

HARRY F. ASHTON; C. B. BENJAMIN; A. C. BROCKLEBANK; MAT. C. BYRNE; JOHN COMMINS; NORMAN CRAIG; WALLACE DAVIDSON; LIONEL FALCK; TREVOR JONES; J. LANGDON LEE; HERBERT J. MALDEN; CLIVE McKEE; SAMUEL NEWBERRY; EDWARD OUSTON; PERCY RENDELL; F. ROTHERY-ELLIS; C. W. SCOTT-BUCCLEUCH; GORDON SMYTHE; ALBERT B. VASCO.

THE BRITISH FILM INSTITUTE.

President: His Grace the Duke of Sutherland, K.T.

Vice-President: The Right Hon. Lord Tweedsmuir, C.H.

Governors: Sir Charles Cleland, K.B.E. (Chairman), F. W. Baker, Professor W. Lyon Blease, LL.M., Sir William Brass, M.P., A. C. Cameron, M.C., M.A., W. R. Fuller, R. S. Lambert, M.A., The Hon. Eleanor Plumer, Dr. Percival Sharp, LL.D., B.Sc., and C. M. Woolf.

Offices:

4, GREAT RUSSELL STREET, LONDON, W.C.I.

General Manager: OLIVER BELL.

Secretary: Miss Olwen Vaughan.

Telephone: Museum 0607-8.

The main object of the British Film Institute will be to encourage the use and development of the cinematograph as a means of entertainment and instruction and to this end it will undertake:—

(*a*) To act as a clearing house for information on all matters affecting films at home and abroad.

(*b*) To influence public opinion to appreciate value of films as entertainment and instruction.

(*c*) To advise educational and other institutions on the supply, use and exhibition of films.

(*d*) To act as a means of liaison between the trade and cultural and educational interests.

(*e*) To undertake research into the various uses of the film and of allied visual and auditory apparatus.

(*f*) To maintain a national repository of films of permanent value.

(*g*) To catalogue educational and cultural films.

(*h*) To give advice to Government Departments concerned with films.

(*i*) To certify films as educational, cultura or scientific.

(*j*) To undertake, if required, similar duties in relation to the Empire.

(*k*) To establish branches and local associations to promote the objects of the Institute.

INSTITUTE OF AMATEUR CINEMATOGRAPHERS, LTD.

Offices:

BURLEY HOUSE, 5-11, THEOBALD'S ROAD, LONDON, W.C.I.

Telephone: Chancery 8338.

President: HIS GRACE THE DUKE OF SUTHERLAND, K.T.

Secretary: WM. E. CHADWICK, F.A.C.I.

Objects:

To promote the general advance of Amateur Cinematography, moving pictures, sound on film, sound records and their applications, and secure for such amateurs a recognised amateur status and to raise the standard of cinematic art generally.

The Institute, in pursuing the attainment of its general objects, encourages research in cinematography, sound on film, sound records, makes investigations from time to time into particular conditions or problems affecting the amateur, and provides general and special information for the use of its Fellows, Members, Affiliated Societies and Associates.

F

BRITISH SUB-STANDARD CINEMATOGRAPH ASSOCIATION.

Office : 12, HOLBORN, LONDON, E.C.1.

Telephone : HOLBORN 6621.

Chairman : H. BRUCE WOOLFE.

Secretary : E. GALE HARDY, J.P.

Objects :

To represent and promote the interests of the British Sub-Standard Cinematograph Industry.

This will include such action as is necessary :

(*a*) To secure and extend the use of British Sub-Standard Sound Films and Equipment throughout the British Empire.

(*b*) To extend by all proper means the use of Sub-Standard Sound Films and Equipment for educational and general purposes.

(*c*) To direct public attention to the educational, commercial, industrial, and general value of Sub-Standard Sound Films and Equipment by organising exhibitions, demonstrations, competitions, etc.

(*d*) To watch over the interests of British manufacturers and users of Sub-Standard Sound Fil '' quipment with a view to the improvement v. _anufacturing and general trading conditions, the obtaining of increased facilities for the use of these films and equipment, and the prevention of unnecessary limitations of the same.

(*e*) To co-operate and render mutual assistance when and where possible.

PROVINCIAL ENTERTAINMENTS PROPRIETORS' AND MANAGERS' ASSOCIATION, LTD.

Offices : 73, BRIDGE STREET, MANCHESTER 3.

President : PERCY B. BROADHEAD (Manchester).

Vice-Presidents : MATTHEW MONTGOMERY (Liverpool) ; E. P. LAWTON (Sheffield); H. D. MOORHOUSE (Manchester) ; NORMAN R. BOOTH (Halifax).

Executive Committee : W. R. BLEAKLEY (Bolton) ; J. BREARLEY (Manchester) ; J. H. CLEGG (Blackpool) ; F. HARGREAVES (Altrincham) ; C. F. HARRISON (Manchester) ; JESSE HEWITT (Manchester) ; J. LEVER (Manchester) ; ROBERT PARKER (Blackpool) ; J. CHRISTIE (Stoll Offices, London) ; C. SHAYLER (Wakefield) ; W. STANSFIELD (Hyde) ; FRED WORSWICK (Wigan).

Secretary : P. PERCIVAL.

Telephone : Blackfriars 8365.

London Office : 174, St. STEPHEN'S HOUSE, WESTMINSTER BRIDGE, S.W.1.

Objects : To protect and advance the interests of all proprietors and managers of places of public Entertainments including Theatres, Cinemas, Circuses, Pier Pavilions, Concert Halls, Ball Rooms and Pleasure Gardens. The Association was founded in the year 1913 and has proved itself a powerful means of bringing the needs and grievances of the entertainment industry before Parliament and local governing authorities. It has at all times when necessary defended to the best of its ability its own members from arbitrary and unjust action emanating from any source,

PHONOGRAPHIC PERFORMANCE, LIMITED.

Office :

144, WIGMORE STREET, LONDON. W.1.

Telephone : Welbeck 7306 and 3096.

Telegrams : Perphono, Wesdo, London.

Directors :

LOUIS STERLING (U.S.A. Origin) ; JAMES GRAY ; HOWARD FLYNN ; WILLIAM DAVID STERNBERG (U.S.A.) ; E. R. LEWIS ; D. WARNFORD-DAVIS.

General Manager : H. M. LEMOINE.

Secretary : J. P. CARRIGAN.

A Company founded by the British phonographic industry to control the rights of the leading manufacturers of gramophone records and to issue Licences for the public performance of all records bearing the following names and marks :

Ariel, Beltona, Broadcast, Brunswick, Columbia, Crown, Crystalate, Decca, Edison Bell, Eclipse, Electron, Forum, Fourtune, 4-in-1, H.M.V., His Master's Voice, Homochord, Imperial, Imperial-Broadcast, Kid-Kord, Odeon, Panachord, Parlophone, Parlophone-Odeon, Peacock, Plaza, Polydor, Regal, Regal-Zono, Rex, Solex, Sterno, Vocalion, Winner, Zonophone.

The Catalogues controlled by Phonographic Performance, Ltd., contain about 100,000 different records of all classes of music by world-famous Artistes ; and about 200 new records are published every month.

ADVERTISING AND INDUSTRIAL FILMS ASSOCIATION

Office : 5–6, WEST STREET, W.C.2.

Telephone : Temple Bar 6484.

Executive Committee :

G. E. TURNER ,Publicity Films, Ltd. (*Chairman*) ; HARRY ADLEY, National Film Corporation, Ltd., and Younger Publicity Service, Ltd., E. P. L. PELLY, Western Electric Co., Ltd. (*Vice Chairman*) ; S. PRESBURY (S. Presbury & Co., Ltd.), (*Vice Chairman*) ; T. F. AVELING GINEVER, Gee-Films, Ltd., (*Treasurer*) ; W. DEVONPORT HACKNEY, Garrick Film Company ; H. HALES DUTTON, G. B. Equipments, Ltd.

Objects :

To promote confidence in the Advertising and Industrial Film Industry and the prestige of its members.

To establish that membership of the Association is recognised throughout the business world, and itself gives a status in the Industry.

MISSIONARY FILM COMMITTEE.

(Under the Auspices of the following Missionary Societies : B.M.S., C.E.Z.M.S., Ch. of Scotland, C.M.S., L.M.S., M.M.S., and S.P.G.)

Office :

104, HIGH HOLBORN, LONDON, W.C.1.

Telephone : Holborn 2197.

Telegrams : Missiofilm, Westcent, London.

Presidents : Right Rev. THE LORD BISHOP OF GUILDFORD; REV. J. SCOTT LIDGETT, D.D.

Chairman : W. E. LAXON SWEET, M.B.E.

Secretary : T. H. BAXTER, F.R.G.S.

Hon. Treasurer : R. ROSEVEARE.

SOUND FILM MUSIC BUREAU LIMITED

Office: 9A, SACKVILLE STREET, PICCADILLY, LONDON, W.I.

Telephone: Regent 4381.

Telegrams: ' Dixerat, Phone, London."

Manager: CHARLES J. DIXEY.

Secretary: JOYCE M. DIXEY.

Council:

LESLIE A. BOOSEY, FREDERICK DAY, T. J. WATKINS, F. SLEVIN, HERBERT SMITH, T. H. WATSON and M, DE WOLFE.

The Sound Film Music Bureau, Ltd., a company limited by guarantee, was formed in August, 1934, to take over the work hitherto carried on by the Talking Film Department of the Music Publishers' Association, Ltd., regarding the use of copyright music in sound films. All enquiries regarding such use of music should now be addressed to the Bureau. The Bureau is not a profit-making concern, and it is intended to develop it with the object of making it increasingly useful to Film Producers, Musical Directors, and others using music in sound films.

NATIONAL ASSOCIATION OF THEATRICAL AND KINE EMPLOYEES.

Offices:

34, LITTLE NEWPORT STREET, LONDON, W.C.2.

Telegraphic Address:

STAGELAND, LESQUARE, LONDON.

Telephone: GERRARD 5214.

General Secretary:

T. O'BRIEN.

Affiliated to the Trade Union Congress, London, and Provincial Trades Councils.

MUSICIANS' UNION.

General and Registered Offices: 7, SICILIAN AVENUE, SOUTHAMPTON ROW, LONDON, W.C.I.

Telephone: HOLBORN 1238.

Telegrams: Amuse, Phone, London.

General Secretary: F. DAMBMAN.

London District Branch Office: 7, SICILIAN AVENUE, SOUTHAMPTON ROW, LONDON, W.C.I.

Telephone: HOLBORN 2218.

Secretaries: W. BATTEN, F. GREENWOOD.

Branches in most of the important towns. This organisation is a Trade Union composed mainly of members of Symphony, Theatre Kinema and Music Hall Orchestra.

THE LONDON POSTER ADVERTISING ASSOCIATION LIMITED.

THE BRITISH POSTER ADVERTISING ASSOCIATION.

Offices:

48, RUSSELL SQUARE, W.C.I.

Telephone: MUSEUM 1485.

Telegrams: DISTHENE, WESTCENT, LONDON

Consulting Secretary: GEO. F. SMITH.

Secretary: FREDERICK WILLS, LL.B.

ASSOCIATED REALIST FILM PRODUCERS LIMITED.

Registered Offices: 33, SOHO SQUARE, LONDON, W.I.

Members:

EDGAR ANSTEY, WILLIAM COLDSTREAM, *ARTHUR ELTON, *MARION GRIERSON, *J. B. HOLMES, *STUART LEGG, PAUL ROTHA, ALEX SHAW, EVELYN SPICE, DONALD TAYLOR, HARRY WATT, BASIL WRIGHT.

* Executive Director.

Consultants:

ANDREW BUCHANAN, ALB. CAVALCANTI, JOHN GRIERSON, PROF. J. B. S. HALDANE, F.R.S., PROF. LANCELOT HOGBEN, F.R.S., JULIAN S. HUXLEY, E. McKNIGHT KAUFFER, WALTER LEIGH, BASIL WARD, A.R.I.B.A.

Associated Realist Film Producers is a group of film directors formed to encourage the development of the realist film in every possible way. As a group, A.R.F.P. acts as a consultante and loans out directors to those who requirt them. It does not enter into either the production or distribution field directly, but works through the established trade organisations.

MOTION PICTURE PRODUCERS AND DISTRIBUTORS OF AMERICA, INC.

Offices:

28, WEST 44TH STREET, NEW YORK CITY, U.S.A.

Cable Address: WILLHAYS, NEW YORK.

President: WILL H. HAYS.

Secretary: CARL E. MILLIKEN.

Treasurer: F. L. HERRON.

British Representative: JAMES MONTGOMERY BECK. *Temporary Address:* 106, Piccadilly, London, W.I.

(Grosvenor 3155.)

The Board of Directors is mostly composed of the Presidents of the major American producing Companies.

The objects of the Association are similar to those of any trade association either here or in America.

INCORPORATED SOCIETY OF AUTHORS, PLAYWRIGHTS AND COMPOSERS.

Offices:

II, GOWER STREET, W.C.I.

Secretary: D. KILHAM ROBERTS.

Kinema Committee:

Chairman: EDGAR JEPSON.

ARTHUR APPLIN.   DOUGLAS FURBER.
VICTOR BRIDGES.   RAFAEL SABATINI.

THE AMUSEMENT CATERERS' ASSOCIATION (NORTHERN IRELAND).

WHITE CINEMA CLUB, BELFAST.

President: D. D. YOUNG, Lyric Cinema, Belfast.

Treasurer: Councillor GEORGE GRAY, J.P. Fort Garry, Cregagh, Belfast.

Hon. Secretary: J. H. CRAIG, Midland Picture House, 7-9, Canning Street, Belfast.

Formed for safeguarding trades interests in Northern Ireland, and also for social purposes.

ASSOCIATED FILM CARRIERS OF GREAT BRITAIN, LTD.

26, CHARING CROSS ROAD, LONDON, W.C.2.
Telephone : TEMPLE BAR 1623.
Officers :
Chairman : A. G. DOLPHIN.
Vice-Chairman : E. W. MORRIS.
Joint Hon. Secretaries : J. VERNON GREEN and
H. W. RICHARDS.
Hon. Treasurer : F. H. RICHARDS.
Objects :
To promote, protect and develop the general interests of the film transport industry and persons and bodies engaged in, or concerned with the supply and transport of cinematograph films and accessories by road.

LANCASHIRE CINEMA "OLD BOYS."

Past Presidents :
1925—L. G. BAILEY.
1926—Coun. J. H. STANSFIELD.
1927—H. D. MOORHOUSE, J.P.
1928—J. HARRISON. (Deceased.)
1929—JAMES MARKS. (Deceased.)
1930—JOHN WALTERS. (Deceased.)
1931—A. CAPLAN.
1932—F. H. HOUGH.
1933—C. W. BOWMER. (Deceased.)
1934—T. H. HARTLEY.
1935—B. C. GIBBS.
1936—J. BREARLEY.
President Elect : CHAS. H. YONWIN
Secretary :
CHAS. H. YONWIN, 3, The Parsonage, Manchester.
Telephone : Blackfriars 3946.
Treasurer :
E. L. JENNINGS, 30, Victoria Street, Manchester.
Qualification : Service in the Cinema trade prior to March 10th, 1913.
Annual Re-union generally held in March.

CINEMA CLUB, GLASGOW.

INSTITUTED 1919.

Hon. President : PRINCE BENDON.

President : J. R. McPHIE, 39, Bath Street, Glasgow. (Douglas 40).

Vice-President : WM. CARRUTHERS, J. P., 142A, St. Vincent Street, Glasgow. (Central 1056.)

Hon. Treasurer : S. BENDON, 132, West Nile Street, Glasgow. C.1. (Douglas 579).

Hon. Secretary : WM. KEMPSELL, 163, Hope Street, Glasgow. (Central 3114-5).

Established for the
(1) Promotion of social intercourse among its members. Meets once Monthly, 2nd Friday, for Luncheon.
(2) To co-operate with and assist all schemes which have for their aim the advancement, welfare and success of the Cinematograph Trade in all its branches.

FEDERATION OF BRITISH FILM SOCIETIES.

56, MANCHESTER STREET, LONDON, W.1.
Telephone : Welbeck 2171.
Objects :
To collect information for mutual assistance and for the advice of new Film Societies ; to organise representation to authority of the needs of the Film Societies, and to organise the collective booking of films.

AMATEUR FILM CLUBS, etc.

Abbreviations.
M.P.C. = Motion Picture Club.
A.C.P. = Amateur Cine Players.
A.C.S. = Amateur Cine Society.
A.C.A. = Amateur Cinematographers' Association.
A.C.C. = Amateur Cine Club.
A.F.S. = Amateur Film Society.
C.C. = Camera Club.
F.P.S. = Film Producing Society.
F.S. = Film Society.

London :

Amateur Cinematographers' Association, Mrs. S. W. Bowler, 4, Majestic Mansions, 36A, Tottenham Court Road, W.1. (Museum 6483).
Barton-Gore Studios, Colin B. Gower, 9, Howard Road, Walthamstow, E.17.
Blackheath Film Club, Mrs. D. A. Vale, 72, Harvey Road, Blackheath, S.E.3.
Brondesbury C.S., B. Ludin, 134, High Street, Notting Hill Gate, W.11. (Park 0163). Studio : 100, Chamberlayne Road, N.W.10.
Catford Film Players, Mrs. V. W. Payne, 7. Station Buildings.
Catholic Film Society, Miss John O'Sullivan, 34, Great Smith Street, Westminster, S.W.1.
Children's F.S., Miss C. Winifred Harley, Everyman Cinema Theatre, Hampstead, N.W.3.
Cyclops A.F.S., J. O. Trilling, 3, Nutley Terrace, N.W.3.
Eltham Film Society, F. Rainbow, 7, Spearman Street, Woolwich, S.E.18.
Finchley A.C.S., Miss T. Burrough, 64, Avondale Avenue, Woodside Park, N.12. Studio, Dollis Mews, Church End, Finchley, N.3.
Hampstead F.S., J. S. Fairfax-Jones, 10, Golden Square, London, W.1. (Gerrard 7271)
Institute of Amateur Cinematographers (Incorporated under the Companies' Act, 1929, as a Company limited by guarantee). President, His Grace the Duke of Sutherland, K.T. Chairman, Lt.-Col. J. T. C. Moore-Brabazon, M.C., M.P. Secretary, W. E. Chadwick, F.A.C.I., Burley House, 5-11, Theobalds Road, W.C.1.
London A.F.C., Miss May Jasper, 99, Cambridge Street, S.W.1.
London F.S., 56, Manchester Street, W.1. (Welbeck 2171.)
Palmers Green Cine Society, A. D. G. Garner, 716, Lordship Lane, Wood Green, N.22.
Planet Amateur Film Society, Hugh Baddeley, 84, Powys Lane, Palmers Green, N.13.
South London Photographic Society (Cine group), L. A. Warburton, 78, Danby Street, S.E.15.
St. Benedict's F.S., F. X. Newton, 8, Montpelier Road, Ealing, W.5.
Whitehall C.S., Harry Walden, "Heatherbell," 3, Copse Avenue, West Wickham, Kent. (Meetings, Somerset House, W.C.2.)
Wimbledon Cine Club, C. W. Watkins, 79, Mostyn Road, Merton Park, S.W.19.

Provincial and Country :

Ace Movies, J. B. Fisher, 5, Crescent Way, Streatham, S.W.16. Studios : 90, High Street Mews, Wimbledon, S.W.19.
Attleborough A.C.C., T. N. Eastland, Chemist, Attleborough, Norfolk. Phone : 12.
Balham Amateur Cine Society, A. F. Durell, 52, Melrose Avenue, Mitcham, Surrey.

Beckenham C.S., J. W. Mantle, 36, Croydon Road, Beckenham, Kent.

Billingham F.S., H. S. Coles, 3, Cambridge Terrace, Norton-on-Tees, co. Durham.

Bournemouth Crystal Pictures, R. G. Torrens, 85, Wimborne Road, Bournemouth. (Winton 486.)

Bury Film Society, Miss B. H. Roberts, 267, Walmersley Road, Bury, Lancs.

Cambridge P.C. Cine Group, Eric J. Twinn, Tennis Courts, Burrell's Walk, Cambridge.

Croydon F.S., R. H. Muxlow, 16, Northampton Road, Croydon.

Devonia A.C.C., J. W. Lowe, 92, Sidwell Street, Exeter.

Eton College F.S., Charterhouse Film Society, Charterhouse School. George Snow, Sutton Cottage, Charterhouse, Godalming.

Grimsby Photographic Society, L. Sleight, 21, Mirfield Road, Grimsby.

Harrow and Pinner Cine Society, J. Stone, 97, Headstone Lane, Harrow.

Heston Cine Club, H. Edwards, 84, Greencroft Road, Heston.

Ilford Amateur Cine Society, A. D. Taylor, 9, Middleton Gardens, Ilford, Essex.

Kingston Cine Club, W. J. Kelsey, 24, Market Place, Kingston.

Ledbury Amateur Cine Society, D. Higginbotham, "Stratheam" Newbury Park, Ledbury.

Leeds Film Institute Society, S. G. Crawford. B.Sc., 3, Hare's Mount, Shepherd's Lane, Leeds.

Leicester F.S., E. Irving Richards, Vaughan College, Leicester.

Manchester and District Film Institute Society, J. D. Sinclair, 716, Chester Road, Old Trafford, Manchester.

Manchester Film Society, Peter le Neve Foster, 1, Raynham Avenue, Didsbury, Manchester. (Didsbury 2104.)

Manchester and Salford Workers' F.S., 69, Liverpool Street, Salford. T. Cavanagh, 86, Hulton Street, Salford, 5.

Merseyside Film Institute S. (Branch of the British Film Institute), J. Alex. Parker, 5 & 6, Bluecoat Chambers, School Lane, Liverpool 1.

Metropolitan-Vickers Electrical Co., Ltd., A.C.S., Trafford Park, Manchester 17.

Minehead A.C.P., J. H. Martin Cross, 23, The Avenue, Minehead, Somerset.

Newcastle A.C.A., (Newcastle & District), 24, Leazes Terrace, Newcastle-on-Tyne.

Northwich F.S., W.R.D. Manning, I.C.I. (Alkali), Ltd., Northwich, Cheshire.

Nottingham A.C.S., Albert E. Hammond. junr., "Malvern," Sandfield Road, Arnot Hill, Arnold, Notts.

O.K. Film Club, M. Overmass, Beckett House, East Street, Andover, Hants.

Oldham Film Society, W. Rothwell Heywood, 73, Queens Road, Oldham, Lancs.

Oxford F.S., 105, Victoria Road, Oxford.

Salford A.C.S., K. W. Kenyon, 9, Westfield, Chaseley Road, Salford 6, Lancs.

Scienthian Film Society, A. H. Bayliss, 16, Stoneygate Road, Leicester.

Seeall F.S., John Gordon, "Bordersmead," Loughton, Essex.

Southampton F.S., J. S. Fairfax-Jones, 10, Golden Square, London, W.1 (Gerrard 7271). D. A. Yeoman, 16, Ascupart House, Portswood, Southampton. Miss R. Keyser, 12, St. Swithin Street, Winchester.

Southborne Seaside Scenarios, G. W. O. Saul, 7, St. Catherine's Road, Southborne, Hants.

South Manchester Amateur Cine Society, Basil H. Reynolds, Milton House, Springfield Road, Sale, Manchester.

Stockport F.S., H.W. Greenwood, Lyndhurst, Broadoak Road, Smallshaw, Ashton-under-Lyne, and J. Hidderley, The Croft, Mile End Lane, Stockport.

Sub Standard Film Productions. J. H. Spencer, 68, Portland Terrace, Southampton.

Synchrolux Sound Films, R. F. Hasdell 8, St. Michael's Mount, Northampton.

Tyneside F.S., M. C. Pottinger, c/o. Literary and Philosophical Society, Newcastle-on-Tyne, 1.

Warrington Cine Society, P. Hughes, 9, Alexandria Street, Warrington.

Warrington F.S., Edward Steel, Mill Street Chambers, Warrington.

West Essex F.S., E. J. Philpott, 7, Wellington Road, East Ham, E.9.

West Middlesex A.C.C., Graham Howard Allen, 110, Argyle Road, Ealing, W.13.

Wirral Film and Dramatic Society, John Wills-Browne, 30, Glenavon Road, Prenton, Birkenhead.

York A.F.S.: President, Henry Foster, Hon. Sec., W. Holden, 3, Acomb Road, York.

Welsh Clubs :

Rhos A. F. Prods., B. M. Clementson, 54, Church Walks, Llandudno, N. Wales.

Scottish Clubs :

Dennistoun C.C. (Cine section), John Macdonald, 27, Aberfeldy Street, Glasgow, E.1.

Dundee C.S., J. Clifford Todd, Grange, Erroll, Perthshire.

Edinburgh Film Guild, J. C. H. Dunlop, 4a, St. Andrew Square, Edinburgh, 2.

Glasgow F.S., D. Paterson Walker, 127, St. Vincent Street, Glasgow, C.2.

Meteor F.P.S. : Ian S. Ross, 80, Buchanan Street, Glasgow, C.1.

Scottish Educational Film Association, Andrew Ingli, 25, Tynwald Avenue, Burnside, Rutherglen Glasgow.

OFFICIAL DATA

GOVERNMENT DEPARTMENTS DEALING WITH THE FILM INDUSTRY

THE FILMS OFFICER, H.M. CUSTOMS AND EXCISE, STRAND 5th STATION (FILMS), MILL HOUSE, (SECOND FLOOR), 87 SHAFTESBURY AVENUE, LONDON, W.1.
Telephone: Gerrard 2189.

All information regarding the importation and exportation of films, as well as the special facilities accorded to. British films, may be obtained on application to the above officer.

IMPORT DUTY ON FILMS.

Blank film, one third of a penny per ft.
Printed Positive, 1d. per ft.
Exposed Negative, 5d. per ft.
Film negative taken abroad by a British Company can be imported at one-third of a penny per ft. on obtaining, before departure abroad, a certificate of approval from H.M. Customs, under Section 12 of the Finance Act, 1922; or a Board of Trade Certificate that the film is British within the meaning of the Cinematograph Films Act, 1927.

BONDED FILM STORES, LTD.,
33-35, ENDELL STREET, W.C.2.
Telephone: Temple Bar 3887.

INDUSTRY AND MANUFACTORY BRANCH, HORSEFERRY HOUSE, HORSEFERRY ROAD, LONDON, S.W.1.
Telephone: Victoria 8740.
Issue of certificates that films are British.
Board of Trade.

GOVERNMENT CINEMATOGRAPH ADVISER.

The Government Cinematograph Adviser and Custodian of Official Films of the Great War
G. HUGHES-ROBERTS, M.V.O.,
H.M. STATIONERY OFFICE, PRINCES STREET S.W.1.

Telephone: Whitehall 4343.

(And ROOM 0028, THE WAR OFFICE, WHITEHALL, S.W.1.)

Telephone: Whitehall 9400.

SCIENTIFIC FILMS.

Under Section 8 of the Finance Act, 1928, Scientific films manufactured in foreign countries can be imported duty free, subject to a Certificate being obtained from the Royal Society.

EDUCATIONAL FILMS.

Under Section 7 of the Finance Act, 1935. No customs duty shall be charged on the importation into the United Kingdom of any Cinematograph film which is certified by the Board of Education. Notice issued by the Commissioners of Customs and Excise. No. 59.

L E G A L

SECTION

The Legal Survey

By NORMAN HART, B.A.

(Solicitor to the Cinematograph Exhibitors' Association.)

I HOPE that this article will prove of interest to the readers of the "Kinematograph Year Book" for 1937. I have dealt shortly with matters which, in my opinion, seemed to have concerned the Industry the most during the past year. There are, of course, numerous other matters which one could include in this article, but space does not permit.

The first one I propose to deal with is that of redundancy. I have already dealt with this matter in my article in the "Year Book" for 1935, but there still appears some doubt as to whether or not Licensing Justices are acting *intra vires* when they take into consideration the question of redundancy when a licence is being applied for, and also in considering any objections to any application for a licence on those grounds. Personally, I think that the question of redundancy is one that should be considered by the Licensing Authorities when an application is made to them for the approval of plans for the erection of a new theatre. I think they should consider the interest of the public and the facilities in force for the enjoyment of that public, and if they think that in that particular neighbourhood the facilities for public enjoyment are ample, then I think they would be entitled to refuse an application for approval of plans for a new cinema or a provisional licence as the case may be, on such grounds. It must, however, be borne in mind that the Cinematograph Act, 1909, says nothing at all about "objections."

The second with regard to provisional licences and approval of plans. In some towns the Licensing Authorities grant a provisional licence, and in others they merely approve the plans, in some cases adding a recommendation that if the building is erected in accordance with the plans produced a licence will follow, and on such a recommendation I think one could quite safely commence the erection of his theatre, though, of course, an approval of plans does not necessarily mean a licence will follow. Previous to the passing of the Town and Country Planning Act, 1932, and the Restriction of Ribbon Development Act, 1935, if one's plans were approved by the surveyor for the Council, all was well, but to-day plans before they finally reach the Licensing Authorities have to be approved by the Committees appointed under the Town and Country Planning Act, 1932, and also probably under the Restriction of Ribbon Development Act, 1935.

Under the Town and Country Planning Act, the authorities have power to make schemes relating to the development and planning of land, whether urban or rural, and in that connection can repeal and re-enact with amendments the enactments relating to town planning ; to provide for the protection of rural amenities, and the preservation of buildings and other objects of interest or beauty, to facilitate the acquisition of land for garden cities, and to make other provisions in connection with these matters ; they can provide provisions setting out the space about buildings, limiting the number of buildings, regulating the size, height, design and external appearance of buildings ; impose restrictions upon the user of any such buildings and prohibiting building operations or regulating such operations, subject to certain exceptions. It will be seen, therefore, that there are a good many things to be complied with under this Act by a person wishing to erect a theatre, but when he has been able to satisfy the Town and Country Planning Act Committee as to his plans, he may then have to adopt a similar procedure under the Restriction of Ribbon Development Act, 1935, and under this Act he may find his plans materially altered and a good deal of ground which he has purchased taken away before he will be allowed to put up his theatre.

Under this Act, the authorities can provide for the imposition of restrictions upon development along the frontages of roads to enable Highway

Authorities to acquire land for the reconstruction or improvement of roads or for preserving amenities or controlling development in the neighbourhood of roads. It also gives power to the Local Authorities relating to accommodation for the parking of vehicles. The authorities have power under this Act to acquire any land within 220 yards from the middle of any road, the acquisition of which is, in their opinion, necessary for the purposes of reconstruction or improvement of the road or of preventing the erection of buildings detrimental to the view on the road. It will be seen from this Act that a person proposing to erect a cinema may find that a good deal of his frontage has been taken away or other part of the land thereby reducing the seating capacity of his theatre, or, may be, altering its original construction very much. Of course, when he has had his plans approved under the Town Planning Scheme and under the Ribbon Development Act, he has then to submit his plans to the Licensing Authority for their final approval which, if there is no opposition, go through as a matter of course.

I have only dealt shortly with the position, but would advise any person contemplating erecting a theatre to carefully consider the plans, as, in my experience, I have found that by the time your plans have gone through and satisfied the various Committees, you have got a very different building to what you thought you were going to have. Any person buying a piece of land for the purpose of erecting a theatre, should be very careful to see that any contract entered into should be subject to his approval of the amended plans, and to the plans being approved or a provisional licence granted as the case may be.

The third, with regard to the quota under the Cinematograph Films Act, 1927, and the position of an exhibitor under the Act, who has failed to comply with his quota. In the year 1936 there have been several summonses issued by the Board of Trade for failure to comply with the quota for the year 1935, which was 15 per cent., and from the evidence given in cases I have had I am afraid it is going to be quite impossible to comply with the quota for 1936, which will be increased to 20 per cent., at any rate, so far as the smaller or independent exhibitor is concerned. I am sure the Act was never brought in to inflict, nor did it mean to inflict, hardship on an exhibitor. In the event of an exhibitor being summoned for shortage in his quota, he should rely on Section 23 (2) and Section 32 (2), especially of the Act. Section 23, sub-section (2) says, "where on submission by the renter or exhibitor or otherwise it appears to the Board of Trade, after consultation with the advisory committee hereinafter mentioned, in any case where the Board of Trade contemplate the refusal of a certificate, that though the requirements of this Part of this Act with respect to the renters' quota or the exhibitors' quota, as the case may be, have not been complied with, the reasons for non-compliance were reasons beyond the control of the renter or exhibitor, they shall issue a certificate to that effect." And Section 32, sub-section (2) says, "Where compliance on the part of a renter or exhibitor with the provisions of this Act as to quota was not commercially practicable by reason of the character of the British films available or the excessive cost of such film non-compliance with those provisions on that ground shall, for the purpose of this Act, be treated as due to reasons beyond his control."

Whilst one is aware that under the Act the Board of Trade, if satisfied on the facts before them as to why such a person was short in his quota, can issue a certificate of exemption, but from my experience this does not appear to have been very often done, and when once a summons has been issued, it is almost impossible to get it withdrawn.   There have been several summonses issued this year for breaches of the quota in 1935, and whilst one has been successful in several cases in getting some of them dismissed, yet, on the other hand, there have been convictions, and, of course, exhibitors should bear in mind that if there are three convictions they are liable to lose their licence altogether.   I can only advise that if an exhibitor finds himself unable to comply with the quota or unlikely to be able to comply with it by the end of the quota year, that he should, at once, communicate with the Board of Trade, setting out the facts fully, asking them under such circumstances to grant him a certificate of exemption.   On the other hand, if he is not successful, and is summoned, then his strong point of defence should be under the Sections of the Act before referred to.   It is up to the exhibitor to show that he has complied with the Cinematograph Films Act, 1927, as far as he possibly could, but that he has found it commercially impracticable and commercially impossible for him to do so.

I think it can quite fairly be contended that if there are several theatres in a particular neighbourhood, forming part of a group of other theatres, that they necessarily are in a better position to obtain sufficient good British films to enable them to comply with the quota, whereas the exhibitor with, say, only one or two halls will have to take what he can get (and to-day, unfortunately, many British films are not at all good), and run the risk of offending his patrons simply in order to comply with the quota, because to-day the public know what films they want, and if they cannot get them will go elsewhere or not at all.   I think that, at any rate, is one very good point to show that on such grounds as these it is commercially impossible to comply with the quota.   If, on the other hand, he can only obtain such British films, but at a price which it is impossible for him to pay I think he should be able to successfully contend that it is also commercially impracticable and that in such case he will be able to satisfy the Court that he has done all he can, and that it was commercially impracticable and impossible for him to comply with the Act, and the summons will be dismissed.

In a case in which I was instructed just lately before a London stipendiary magistrate, where the summons against the exhibitor was dismissed, the learned magistrate gave a very excellent decision, in which he said :—

" These matters really are extremely difficult to determine, because one has to be very much on one's guard and particularly in determining whether the exhibition of films up to the quota is commercially practicable or not.   It clearly cannot be the intention that the exhibitor should be driven to a point at which he has to face ruin solely for the purpose of exhibiting the prescribed quota."

And he ended up his decision by stating :—

" Shortly stated, I have come to the conclusion that in this particular year, having regard to the special circumstances relating to competition, it would not be commercially practicable to exhibit the full amount, and I am therefore dismissing the summonses."

Lastly, the position of the employment of children in cinemas.   The Shops Act, 1934, does not apply to cases where they are employed amongst other employments in selling chocolates, and those sort of things ; nor does the Employment of Women and Young Persons Act, 1936.   At the same time, of course, an exhibitor should bear in mind that if an " A " film is being shown any attendant under the age laid down under their licence should not be in the theatre during the exhibition of that particular film otherwise he may find himself open to proceedings being taken against him even although he may be selling chocolates, sweets, etc.

The Acts of Parliament and local bye-laws which relate to or affect the exhibition, storage or transit of kinematograph films are of paramount importance to the trade, and should be closely studied by all engaged in it. Below will be ound a condensed digest of the principal regulations governing this industry. This has been prepared by a leading solicitor, who has explained the most essential points in a manner which will be readily understood by readers.

(We accept no liability for any inaccuracy which may appear in the following summary.)

REVISED BY NORMAN HART, SOLICITOR, ASSOCIATION.

CINEMATOGRAPH ACT, 1909.

All kinematograph exhibitions must be held at premises which are icensed (s. 1).

This Act was passed for making better provision for securing safety at kinematograph and other exhibitions.

Under Clause 1, provided premises comply with the regulations laid down by the Secretary of State, which are regulations dealing with the question of safety, nothing more is required.

All premises must hold a licence where inflammable films are used. The Act contains no definition of the word " inflammable."

Exceptions.—A licence is not necessary in the following cases :—

(a) Where non-inflammable films are used (as to whether a film is non-flammable or flammable is one of fact for the Justices to decide). (*See Victoria Pier, Ltd.* v. *Reeves*, 1912, 28 T.L.R. 443 ; also see *re* Dickman and Moore, *Times* Newspaper, December 17, 1912.) (*Note.*—If an exhibitor holds a licence for premises upon which he originally used inflammable films and decides in future to use non-flammable films only, he is still bound by the conditions on the licence granted although otherwise no licence would be necessary.)

(b) For exhibitions in private dwelling-houses where the general public are not admitted whether on payment or otherwise. (*Note.*—A hospital has been held not to be a private house under Section 7 of the Act, for which a licence is required—National Hospital for Paralysed and Epileptic Persons, *Times*, October 11, 1913.)

(c) Where premises are only used occasionally and not more than six days in any one year. But in this case the occupier must—

i. Give seven days' notice in writing to the Licensing Authority and the chief officer of police of the police area ;

ii. Comply with the regulations as to safety ;

iii. Comply with any conditions imposed in writing by the Licensing Authority.

(d) On premises used for the purpose of exhibiting films to *bonâ-fide* purchasers—*Att.-Gen.* v. *Vitagraph Co.*, 1915, C.H. 206,

MOVABLE BUILDINGS OR STRUCTURES, provided the owner

(a) .Has a licence in respect of the building or structure from the Licensing Authority for the district where he ordinarily resides.

(b) Has given two days' notice in writing to the Licensing Authority for the district where the exhibition is to take place, and to the chief officer of police of the police area.

(c) Complies with any conditions imposed in writing by the Licensing Authority.

REGULATIONS AS TO SAFETY.

These are made by the Home Secretary (Act s. 1) except in Scotland and Ireland, where the Secretaries for Scotland and Ireland respectively exercise this power (Act ss. 8 and 9). They are known as the Cinematograph Regulations, 1910 (Statutory Rules and Orders [1910] No. 189) and 1913 (St. R. & O. [1913] No. 566). Every owner and manager of a kinema must make himself familiar with these regulations, which are binding, even if the conditions of the licence happen to be inconsistent with them.

LICENSING AUTHORITY.

(1) ENGLAND.—The Council of the County or County Borough, but as a rule these powers are, in the first instance at least, exercised by a committee. Where the place is licensed by the Lord Chamberlain for stage plays, that official also grants kinematograph licences.

The County or County Borough Council may delegate these powers to the local justices (Act s. 5). Licensing Justices sit as an administrative body, not as a Court of Summary Jurisdiction—*Huish* v. *Liverpool Justices*, [1914] 1 K.B. 109. Therefore they have no power to state a case. Doubtful if any appeal of licensing authorities where a licence is refused without any reason.

If reasons are stated and not been satisfactory or a proper hearing has not been given, proceedings by way of mandamus should be taken to the Court of Appeal. A further appeal in such a case can be taken to the House of Lords, or proceedings might be taken in the King's Bench Division for a declaration that proposed conditions which the Licensing Authorities have decided to put upon licences are *ultra vires* and an injunction asked for to restrain the authorities from enforcing same. In cases before the Court of Summary Jurisdiction where the procedure is by way of case stated to the Divisional Court no further appeal is allowed.

(2) SCOTLAND.—The Council of the County or the magistrates of a royal parliamentary or police burgh. There is nop ower of delegation (Act s. 8).

(3) IRELAND.—The Council of the County or County Borough or Urban District or the Commissioners of the Town. There is no power of delegation, but a County Council may, in writing, authorise any officer of the Council to exercise any of the powers of the Act (Act s. 9).

GRANT, RENEWAL AND TRANSFER OF LICENCES.

Licences are normally for one year, but may be for shorter periods (Act s. 2 (2)). The Act makes no provision for granting provisional licences.

For new grants or transfers seven days' notice in writing must be given to the Licensing Authority and to the chief officer of police of the police area, but no notice need be given in the case of a renewal (Act s. 2 (4).

FEES PAYABLE.—One year's licence (grant or renewal), £1. Shorter periods, 5s. a month (but not to exceed £1 for every year). Transfers, 5s. (Act s. 2 (5)).

LICENSEES.—The Licensing Authority has a discretion (Act s. 2 (1) (3)). Where the refusal was based on the ground that several of the directors and the majority of the shareholders of the company in question were alien enemies, the refusal was upheld by the Court (*Rex* v. *L.C.C. ex parte London and Provincial Electric Theatres*, [1915] 2 K.B. 466).

CONDITIONS.—Under Clause 2, Section 1, Licensing Authorities have much further powers than those given under Clause 1, as they can grant licences subject to such conditions as they may think fit in addition to the regulations of the Secretary of State as regards safety. The condition must be reasonable—*L.C.C.* v. *Bermondsey Bioscope*, 80 L.J.K. 1314. It has been argued on the words of the Act that these must be decided upon when the application for each licence is made, and not determined beforehand (*e.g.*, most of the authorities issue a list of conditions which licensees must submit to), but this argument has not met with favour (see *Rex* v. *Burnley Justices* (1916), 32 T.L.R. at p. 696).

Conditions or undertakings which have been upheld in the Courts include

Against opening on Sundays and Holy Days, even where non-inflammable films used (*L.C.C.* v. *Bermondsey Bioscope Co.*, [1911] 1 K.B. 445; *Ellis* v. *North Metropolitan Theatres*, [1915] 2 K.B. 61).

Against showing any film to which the Authority objects (*ex p Stott*, [1916] 1 K.B. 7) ;

As to hours of opening and closing (*Rex* v. *Burnley Justices, supra*). Against showing any licentious or indecent film (*Rex* v. *Burnley Justices, supra*).

There is a distinction between conditions and undertakings and a condition as to the admission of children has been held bad (*Halifax Theatre de Luxe* v. *Gledhill*, [1915] 2 K.B. 49), but an undertaking of not so widespread a character relating to the same matter has been upheld (*Rex* v. *Burnley Justices, supra*).

Breach of a condition is an offence for which the licensee may be fined, and at once lose his licence ; breach of an undertaking may lead to refusal of renewal.

A condition that no film can be shown if a specified number of justices object is void, as different groups may think differently (*Rex* v. *Burnley Justices, supra*).

Where the Licensing Authority enforce a condition that no film to which the Authority objects may be shown, the owner of the film is apparently without any adequate remedy (*ex p. Stott*, [1916] 1 K.B. 7 ; *Stott* v. *Gamble*, [1916] 2 K.B. 504).

A condition that no film be shown which has not been certified for public exhibition by the British Board of Film Censors is *ultra vires*, as it sets up in place of the Licensing Committee another Body whose *ipse dixit* should be a test of what might be exhibited. (*Ellis* v. *Dubouski*, [1921] 3 K.B.D.)

As to whether, therefore, the above conditions are *intra vires* is somewhat doubtful, and it might be argued that even if a film had not been censored and no notice given to the Local Licensing Authority, the only legal ground for proceeding against an exhibitor for showing the picture would be that of indecency.

The argument was upheld in a summons brought against an exhibitor in the Midlands, by the Licensing Authority, on the condition that if it was desired to show a film that had not been passed by the Censor, three clear days' notice must be sent to the Licensing Authority.

POLICE SUPERVISION.—Any police officer and any person authorised by the Licensing Authority may enter any premises (whether licensed or not) where he has reason to believe that a kinematograph exhibition is being or is about to be given. A police officer needs no authority, and while there may pay attention to any other breaches of the law that he may suspect (*McVittie* v. *Turner*, [1916] 85 L.J.K.B. 23). If anyone prevents or obstructs him, the offender is liable to be fined up to £20 (Act s. 4).

A Constable without consent s not entitled to take away a piece of a film for the purpose of testing whether it is inflammable or non-flammable.

PENALTIES.

Besides the offence just mentioned, the *owner* of a kinematograph or other apparatus who uses it or allows it to be used in contravention of the Act or the Regulations or the conditions of the licence, and the *occupier* of premises who allows them to be used in contravention of the same, may be fined up to £20, and in the case of a continuing offence £5 a day, and the licence may be revoked on conviction (Act s. 3). The manager of a kinema owned by a company is not an occupier, and cannot be summoned as such (*Bruce* v. *McMaines*, [1915] 3 K.B. 1).

A kinematograph licence does not authorise musical accompaniments. A music licence is not necessary where music is subsidiary to the picture.— See Hallinan, 73 J.P.N. 458.

THEATRE AND MUSIC AND DANCING LICENCES may also be necessary. Theatre Licences for Stage Plays are obtained from the Lord Chamberlain in London, and from the justices elsewhere. Music and Dancing Licences, are granted by the County and County Borough Councils, who can delegate this power to the local justices.

Music and Dancing Licences in London are governed by the Music Hall Act, 1751. In Middlesex by the Music and Dancing Middlesex Act, 1894. In other areas beyond 20 miles from the Cities of London and Westminster under the Public Health Acts (Amendment Act), 1890, Sec. 4. Music Licences are renewable only once each year. They may contain conditions (in view of the section of the Public Health Act) different to the conditions of a kinematograph licence, as that act does not apply to Music and Dancing Licences. A Music and Dancing Licence does not authorise stage plays, nor does a Theatre Licence, under the Theatre Act, 1843, include Music and Dancing.

CHILDREN.

Where an entertainment is given for children (*i.e.*, under fourteen), or the majority of persons present are children, and their number exceeds one hundred, and access to any part of the building is by stairs, then it is the duty of the occupier (if he is paid) and of the person giving the entertainment (in any case) to see that an adequate number of adult attendants are present to prevent overcrowding in any part, to control the movements of the audience when entering and leaving, and also to take all reasonable precautions for safety. Police officers have the right of entry. The penalty for a first offence is up to £50, for a second or subsequent offence up to £100, and any licence held in respect of the building may be revoked (Children Act, 1908, s. 121). The kinematograph licence is not mentioned, as it had not come into existence at that date.

The Employment of Children Act, 1903, s. 1, enables local authorities to make bye-laws relating to the employment of children (*i.e.*, under fourteen), and many of them have exercised this power. A licensee should enquire at the council offices whether the local authority of his district has made any bye-law affecting him (*e.g.*, as to programme, sweet, or cigarette sellers, etc.).

No child (under sixteen) employed half-time in a factory or workshop may be employed elsewhere (Act 1903, s. 3 (3)), nor may any child be employed before six a.m. or after nine p.m., unless the local bye-laws allow it (Act 1903, s. 3 (1)). The fine is up to 40s. for a first offence, and £5 afterwards (Act 1903, s.5 (1)).

Under the Children and Young Persons Act, 1933, where there is provided in any building an entertainment for children or an entertainment at which the majority of the persons attending are children, then, if the number of children attending the entertainment exceeds one hundred the person providing the entertainment must station and keep stationed wherever necessary a sufficient number of adult attendants, properly instructed as to their duties, to prevent more children or other persons being admitted to the building, and to control the movement of the children and other persons admitted while entering and leaving the building or any part thereof, and to take all other reasonable precautions for the safety of the children.

Under Section 4 of this Act a constable may enter the building at any time with a view to seeing whether the provisions of the Act are being properly carried out.

By the Royal assent having been given to the Shops Hours of Closing Act, 1928, patrons can buy tobacco, matches, table waters, sweets, chocolates or other sugar confectionery or ice-cream at any time during performances in any Theatre, Kinema, Music Hall or other similar place of entertainment so long as the sale is to bona-fide members of the audience and not on a part of the building to which other members of the public have access.

This does away with the ban put upon Kinemas by D.O.R.A. some years ago.

ENTERTAINMENTS TAX.

For tax purposes an " entertainment " includes any exhibition, performance, amusement, game, or sport to which persons are admitted for payment. Admission to the place where the entertainment is held is sufficient, otherwise tax could be evaded by charging admission and giving a free show. If there is an additional charge to go to another part of the premises, tax is levied on both charges. The proprietor for this purpose includes the person responsible for the management. The rates as now altered by the Finance (No. 2) Act, 1931, are as follows :

RATE OF ENTERTAINMENTS DUTY.

Amount of payment.	*Duty.*
Where the amount of payment for admission, excluding the amount of the duty—	
Does not exceed 6d.	No tax.
Exceeds 6d. and does not exceed 7½d. ...	Three halfpence.
Exceeds 7½d. and does not exceed 10d. ...	Two pence.
Exceeds 10d. and does not exceed 1s. 0½d. ...	Two pence halfpenny.
Exceeds 1s. 0½d. and does not exceed 1s. 3d.	Three pence.
Exceeds 1s. 3d.	Three pence for the first 1s. 3d. and one penny for every 5d. or part of 5d. over 1s. 3d.

The rate of duty in the above scale appropriate to any price of admission exclusive of the duty and exceeding 1s. 3d. may be calculated by dividing the price by 5 and by mounting up the result to the next whole penny in cases where the result includes a fraction of a penny.

Admission can only be given by ticket stamped with a mark denoting that duty has been paid, or in special cases, if the Commissioners approve, through a barrier which automatically registers the numbers admitted. But the proprietor can make arrangements with the Commissioners dispensing with these conditions on the terms of furnishing certified returns at stated

times and giving security for due payment of the duty.   Penalty for breach :
Proprietor, £50 and duty ; Person admitted, £5.   Special provision is made
for lump sum payments in the case of clubs or societies, or in the case of season
tickets or tickets for a series of entertainments.

Duty is not payable where the Commissioners are satisfied :

(a) That the proceeds are devoted to philanthropic or charitable
purposes *without deduction of expenses,* or

(b) That the entertainment is wholly educational (in case of difference
the Board of Education decides) ; or

(c) That the entertainment is for children only, and the charge is
not more than one penny per person ; or

(d) That the entertainment is provided for partly educational or
partly scientific purposes by a society, and not run for profit ; or

(e) That it is provided by or on behalf of a school or educational
institution if the school or institution is not run for profit, and the
entertainment is provided solely for promoting some object of the
school or institution, and that all the persons who are performers
are under sixteen and are scholars or ex-scholars of the school
or institution.

In the case of a charity performance where the whole of the expenses ·
are deducted, but do not exceed 20 per cent. of the receipts, the duty is
repaid to the proprietor.

Any officer of excise authorised to do so may enter a place of entertainment and any person who prevents or obstructs him is liable to a fine up to
£20.

The Commissioners can make regulations, any breach of which entails
an excise penalty of £50, and they may make arrangements whereby the
local authority (county, borough, or urban district council), or the police
may exercise all or any of the powers of the Commissioners as to this duty.
The law is contained in the Finance (New Duties) Act, 1916, ss. 1 and 2, and
the Finance Act, 1916, s. 12.

IMPORTS AND EXPORTS.

There is no restriction on the export of celluloid substances, but as regard-
the import of Films it is subject to the owner's right of copyright, and to the
payment of the Import Duties imposed by the Finance Acts, 1925–1928.

(2) IMPORTS.—The import of films is affected in three ways :

(a) *Copyright.*

(b) *Customs Duty.*

(c) *Restriction of Imports.*

(a) The owner of British copyright may notify the Customs that he
objects to copies made out of the United Kingdom of his work
which would be an infringement if made here, being imported.
The Customs make regulations dealing with this matter, and
breach of the prohibition leads to forfeiture and destruction of
the offending copies.

(b) The duty on imported films is as follows : Rate per foot of the
standard width, 1⅜ inches : Blank film (also called raw film or
stock), ⅓d. ; positives, *i.e.,* films ready for exhibition, 1d. ; negatives, *i.e.,* films containing a photograph from which positives
may be prepared, 5d.   They can be placed in bond.

(c) Imported films must comply with the regulations for railway
transit.

TRANSIT BY RAIL.

RAILWAY REGULATIONS IN REGARD TO FILM BOXES.—The specification of the Railway Clearing House of the type of metal boxes required by the Railway Companies to be used for the transit of films is as follows :

Boxes must be rectangular, wood-lined cases, to hold not more than six films and measure not more than $14\frac{1}{2}$ inches outside either way. They must be made of galvanised iron of not less thickness than .022 of an inch (No. 25 B.G.) for the small one and two film cases, and not less than .028 of an inch (No. 23 B.G.) for the larger sizes (three to six film cases).

All the corners of the sides and bottom must be strengthened by folding seams, the top of the body having wired edges turned inwards. The hinge lid must be turned down all round for a depth of one and a quarter inches. It must fit over the body of the case and have wired edges turned outwards. It must be attached to the body by two strong hinges, firmly riveted to both body and lid, and fastened by stout wire hasps fitting over iron staples riveted to the front of the case. Each hasp and staple must be locked, either by padlock or by a spring safety hook, permanently to the staple by a short length of stout chain. Cases for one and two films need only have one clasp and staple fastening ; other sizes must have two.

Other conditions are that a thin metal label frame, open at the top, must be riveted to the case in such a position that the top edge of the label frame is covered by the lid when closed ; all the boxes must be completely lined with plain wood of half-inch thickness fastened by rivets to the lid and body of the case ; the following words must be painted in black on the lid : " Cinema Films," in one-inch block letters, and " Keep in a cool place," in letters five-eighths of an inch depth. No other lettering must appear on the lid. The name and address of the owners may be painted on the sides or ends, and the cases must be unpainted.

OTHER LEGISLATION.

HOUSES (ADDITIONAL POWERS) ACT, 1919.

Gives powers to Councils to make orders prohibiting the construction of works or theatres on grounds that the production of dwelling accommodation is likely to be delayed by a deficiency of labour or materials arising out of the employment of labour, or material in the construction of such works or buildings. Any person aggrieved by such an order of prohibition can appeal, subject to the rules of procedure set down by the Ministry. A Tribunal of Appeal can be set up under this Act to hear appeals against any such Order.

LICENSING (CONSOLIDATION) ACT, 1910.

Where it is desired to sell intoxicating liquors by retail on the premises a Licence must be obtained.

REFRESHMENT HOUSES ACT, 1860.

Any House, Room or Building can be opened for Public resort and entertainment between 10 p.m., and 5 a.m., but if not being licensed for beer, wine and spirits must take out a Refreshment House Excise Licence.

SUNDAY OBSERVANCE ACT, 1781.

Any house opened for Public amusement or debate on a Sunday to which persons shall be admitted by payment of money shall be deemed a Disorderly House—Penalty £200 for every Sunday opened. (Note)—If a reasonable number of persons are admitted free there is no offence under the Act in making a charge for a reserved seat ; it will be noted that the Act speaks of admission, not to a seat, but to the entertainment.

FINANCE ACT, 1920.

This was an Act passed to grant certain duties to Customs and Inland Revenue, to alter other duties, and to amend the law relating to Customs and Inland Revenue and the National Debt and to make further provision in connection with finance.

HOME COUNTIES, MUSIC AND DANCING LICENCES ACT, 1926.

This was an Act passed to amend the law as regards Music and Dancing Licences in parts of certain Home Counties and in certain County Boroughs adjacent thereto. It gave powers to the Council to grant Licences for any period not exceeding 13 months to such persons as they thought fit.

Under this Act the Council can delegate all or any of its powers to a Committee consisting wholly or partly of members of the Council.

UNEMPLOYMENT INSURANCE ACT, 1920,

was an act passed to amend the Law in respect of Insurance against Unemployment. All persons of the age of 16 and upwards who are engaged in employment as specified by the Act shall be insured against unemployment in manner provided by the Act.

TRADE UNIONS AND TRADE DISPUTES ACT, 1927,

amends the law relating to Trade Disputes and Trade Unions and regulates the position of Civil Servants and persons employed by public authorities in respect of membership of trade unions and similar organisations and to extend section 5 of the Conspiracy and Protection of Property Act, 1875.

1923. NEW REGULATION UNDER CINEMATOGRAPH ACT, 1909.

Exhibitors should always keep a copy of these regulations by them as they take the place of the previous regulations dated 18th February, 1910, and 20th May, 1913.

1921. THE ENTERTAINMENTS DUTY REGULATIONS.

are regulations made by the Commissioners of Customs and Excise under Section 2 of the Finance New Duties Act, 1916, for securing the payment of Entertainments Duty.

The points to be noted are that the price of admission must be printed on the tickets. Adhesive stamps are not to be issued except upon the tickets. No tickets other than stamped tickets to be issued on payment made for admission. Tickets and stamps to be issued undefaced and defaced subsequently. No Government ticket is to be used for admitting more than one person. (Note : Arrangements approved by the Commissioners can be made for providing returns of payments for admission to an entertainment.)

THE EMPLOYMENT OF CHILDREN

in entertainments, Statutory Rules and Orders 1920, No. 21.

An application for a licence to enable a child to take part in an entertainment or series of entertainments must be made in writing to the Local Educational Authority signed by the parent and the employer of the child in the form contained in the first schedule thereto, together with the necessary documents.

Under this rule the term " parent " includes guardian and every person who is liable to maintain or has actual custody of the child.

THE FACTORIES BILL, 1920.

This Bill abolishes the distinction between factories and workshops and between textile and non-textile factories, and employs only the one word " Factory."

LANDLORD AND TENANT ACT, 1927.

This Act came into force on the 25th March of this year. It provides (*inter alia*) for compensation for improvements and compensation for loss of goodwill.

CINEMATOGRAPH FILMS ACT, 1927,

being an Act to restrict blind booking and advance booking of Cinematograph films, and to secure the renting and exhibition of a certain proportion of

British films and for purposes connected therewith. *The Act is printed* in extenso *at the end of this section.*

THE FACTORY AND WORKSHOP ACT, 1901.

Under Section 20 of this Act electrical stations are defined as any premises or that part of any premises in which electrical energy is generated or transformed for the purpose of supply by way of trade or for the lighting of any street, &c.

This section therefore brings a cinema which generates its own energy under the above Act, and therefore the requirements of the above Act must be complied with.

THE RATING AND VALUATION ACT, 1925,

was passed (*inter alia*) to define what machinery and plant was deemed to be part of the hereditament for rating purposes.

THE RATING AND VALUATION ACT, 1928,

was an Act passed to extend to the Administrative County of London the provisions of the Rating and Valuation Act, 1925, with respect to the valuation of hereditaments containing machinery and plant and to make temporary provision with respect to the deduction to be made in ascertaining the rateable value—to amend Sections 11 and 37 and the 4th and 5th Schedules of the 1925 Act and to provide for the tenant decisions on points of law with a view to securing uniformity in valuation.

THE RATING AND VALUATION (APPORTIONMENT) ACT, 1928,

was an Act passed to make provision with a view to granting of relief from rates in respect of certain classes of hereditaments to be affected and the apportionment in Valuation Lists of the net annual value of such hereditaments according to the extent and user thereof for various purposes.

Section 3, sub-section 1 of this Act contains provisions as to " Industrial Hereditaments." " Industrial Hereditament " has been defined to mean a hereditament occupied and used as a mine or mineral railway or as a factory or workshop. A hereditament though part of it may be in law a " factory " or " workshop " is not to be treated as an Industrial hereditament if the premises as a whole are not primarily used for the purposes of a factory or workshop.

With regard to the position of a Kinematograph Theatre, in view of the fact that the premises are not used primarily for the purposes of a factory or workshop I do not consider it comes under the heading of " Industrial Hereditament " and therefore does not appear to be entitled to " relief " as an " Industrial hereditament."

The Rating and Valuation (Apportionment) Act Rules, 1928, made by the Minister of Health under section 58 of the Rating and Valuation Act, 1925, and of the Rating and Valuation (Apportionment) Act, 1928, prescribes the forms of notices, claims and lists to be used for the purposes of the first Schedule to the last mentioned Act and the dates to be observed in connection with the preparation and approval of lists under that Schedule.

The list of valuations is deposited by the Rating Authorities at the office of the Authority and any person aggrieved can object to the assessment within 25 days of the deposit of the Valuation List. Forms of objection can be obtained from the Rating Authorities, and the forms should contain every possible ground for complaint. One person can object to another person's assessment on the ground that it is too low, and in such a case the occupier is entitled to receive notice from the Assessment Committee of the objection.

Administrative County of London

PLACES OF PUBLIC ENTERTAINMENT

Revised Rules of Management which came into Operation on 1st January, 1935.

CENSORSHIP OF " NEWS-REELS."

8.   (b) No cinematograph film which has not been passed for " universal " exhibition or for " public exhibition to adult audiences " by the British Board of Film Censors shall be exhibited unless the licensee obtains the express consent of the Council in writing, provided that such consent shall not be necessary in respect of any exhibition of films (known in the trade as " Topical " or " Locals ") of actual events, recorded in the press at or about the time of the exhibition, whether exhibited, with or without sound-effects or commentary.

8.   (d) Unless the licensee obtains the express consent of the Council in writing no cinematograph film—other than the films described in the proviso to clause (b) of this rule—which has not been passed for " universal " exhibition by the British Board of Film Censors shall be exhibited at the premises during the time that any child under or appearing to be under the age of 16 years is therein, provided that this rule shall not apply in the case of any child who is accompanied by a parent or bona fide adult guardian of such child.

Clauses (a), (c), (e), (f) and (g) of rule 8 have not been altered.

STANDING IN GANGWAYS, ETC.

18.   (a) In no circumstances shall persons be permitted to—
(i) Sit in any gangway.
(ii) Stand in any gangway which intersects the seating.

(b) Standing may be permitted inside and rear gangways provided that clauses (c) and (d) of this rule be strictly complied with and that the number of persons permitted to stand be limited as follows :—

(i) In a side gangway.—One row of persons against the wall provided that the number does not exceed the number prescribed in writing by the Council.
(ii) In a rear gangway.—One row of persons against the barrier at the rear of the seating.   For each complete foot of width of the gangway over 3 feet 6 inches, one additional row of persons may be permitted to stand not exceeding (i) three rows in all and (ii) the number prescribed in writing by the Council. Provided that, in that portion of a rear gangway which connects an intersecting gangway or side gangway with the nearest exit, a clear space at least 3 feet 6 inches in width shall be maintained between the persons standing and the wall.

(c) Standing shall not in any circumstances be permitted in front of exits or in front of entrances to sanitary conveniences.

(d) Notices shall be exhibited on the walls in conspicuous positions in each side and rear gangways indicating in block letters not less than $1\frac{1}{2}$ inches in height, the number of persons permitted to stand as limited by clause (b) of this rule.   Such notices shall be adequately illuminated.

14.   The following notice shall be printed for the information of the public on the programme of the performance on the same page as the cast or other particulars of the entertainment and in similar type to that used below—
In accordance with the requirements of the London County Council :—
(i) The public may leave at the end of the performance or exhibition by all exit doors and such doors must at that time be open.
(ii) All gangways, corridors, staircases, and external passageways intended for exit shall be kept entirely free from obstruction, whether permanent or temporary.
(iii) Persons shall not be permitted to stand or sit in any of the gangways intersecting the seating, or to sit in any of the other gangways.   If standing be permitted in the gangways at the sides and rear of the seating, it shall be limited to the numbers indicated in the notices exhibited in those positions.
If a safety curtain is provided, the following additional notice shall be printed on the programme :—
(iv) The safety curtain must be lowered and raised in the presence of each audience.

FIRE APPLIANCES.

33. (a) Fire appliances and equipment as approved by the Council shall be efficiently maintained. They shall be in charge of the fireman, or, if a fireman is not employed, of some other suitable person specially nominated for the purpose, who shall see that they are always available for use.

(b) Each length of hose provided at the premises shall, at the cost of the licensee, be tested annually by an engineer, recognised by the Council for the purpose, to 75 lb. water pressure or to the pressure of the mains supplying the fire hydrants at the premises, whichever is the greater, and a certificate to the effect that the hose is in satisfactory condition shall be submitted to the Council. An efficient length of hose shall be substituted for each length removed for testing.

(c) Each chemical extinguisher provided at the premises shall be discharged in the presence of the Council's inspecting officer at least once in three years. When an extinguisher is discharged for any purpose, the date of discharge shall be painted on the extinguisher. On the occasion of the annual survey of the fire appliance by the Council's officers all chemical extinguishers shall, at the licensee's option either be fully opened up for inspection or tested by discharge.

Alternatively, the licensee shall submit to the Council an annual certificate by a fire engineer or other competent person to the effect that each extinguisher provided at the premises is in efficient working order and is mechanically sound, giving, where appropriate, the date of discharge and recharging.

Whichever procedure is adopted, each extinguisher shall be tested by discharge at least once in three years.

(d) Hand pumps shall be tested annually in the presence of the Council's inspecting officer.

(e) If a fireman is employed at the premises the tests, examinations, etc., carried out in accordance with clauses (b), (c) and (d) of this rule, and also any other tests or repairs of appliances or equipment, shall be recorded in his logbook.

CANDLES, ETC., ON THE STAGE.

109. (a) Real flame shall not be employed on the stage unless, in the opinion of the Council, it is essential to the action as distinct from the atmosphere of a play and the consent of the Council is obtained in writing. In no circumstances will such consent be granted in respect of premises where a safety curtain, maintained in efficient working order, is not provided to the proscenium opening.

(b) In order to ascertain whether the Council's consent can be obtained in accordance with clause (a) of this rule, the licensee shall, at least seven days before the first performance of the play, submit an application in writing (i) stating fully the reasons why electric substitutes cannot be used, (ii) containing an assurance that rough action will not take place at any time while the lighted candles or effects are in use, and (iii) giving particulars of any rehearsal or rehearsals in order that an officer of the Council may, if possible, attend.

SUNDAY CINEMATOGRAPH ENTERTAINMENTS.

At the annual licensing meeting to be held on 9th November, 1934, consideration will be given to the question of attaching to all Sunday opening cinematograph permissions granted on that date a condition requiring, during the year 1935, licensees opening their premises for cinematograph entertainments on Sundays, to pay to charity 14 per cent. of the certified net Sunday admission takings, i.e., certified gross Sunday admission takings, less Entertainments Duty. The amount payable to the Council for transmission to the Privy Council for the Cinematograph Fund will, as at present, be one-nineteenth of the sum payable to charity.

SUNDAY ENTERTAINMENTS ACT, 1932.

An Act to permit and regulate the opening and use of places on Sundays for certain entertainments and for debates, and for purposes connected with the matters aforesaid. 						[13th July, 1932.]

Be it enacted by the King's most Excellent Majesty, by and with the advice and consent of the Lords Spiritual and Temporal, and Commons, in this present Parliament assembled, and by the authority of the same, as follows :—

1.—(1) The authority having power, in any area to which this section extends, to grant licences under the Cinematograph Act, 1909, may, notwithstanding anything in any enactment relating to Sunday observance, allow places in that area licensed under the said Act to be opened and used on Sundays for the purpose of cinematograph entertainments, subject to such conditions as the authority think fit to impose :

Provided that no place shall be allowed to be so opened and used unless among the conditions subject to which it is allowed to be so opened and used there are included conditions for securing—

(A) that no person will be employed by any employer on any Sunday in connection with a cinematograph entertainment or any other entertainment or exhibition given therewith who has been employed on each of the six previous days either by that employer in any occupation or by any other employer in connection with similar entertainments or exhibitions ; and

(B) that such sums as may be specified by the authority not exceeding the amount estimated by the authority as the amount of the profits which will be received from cinematograph entertainments given while the place is open on Sundays, and from any other entertainment or exhibition given therewith, and calculated by reference to such estimated profits or to such proportion of them as the authority think fit, will be paid as to the prescribed percentage thereof, if any, to the authority for the purpose of being transmitted to the Cinematograph Fund constituted in accordance with the provisions of this Act, and as to the remainder thereof to such persons as may be specified by the authority for the purpose of being applied to charitable objects ;

and for the purpose of any conditions imposed by an authority as to the payment of sums calculated by reference to such estimated profits as aforesaid, the profits shall be computed in such manner as the authority may direct

(2) For the purposes of section four of the Cinematograph Act, 1909 which contains provisions as to the enforcement of the conditions of licences) any conditions subject to which a place is allowed under this section to be opened and used on Sundays shall be deemed to be conditions of the licence granted under that Act in respect of the place.

(3) If, in any place allowed under this section to be opened and used on Sundays for the purpose of cinematograph entertainments, any person is employed on any Sunday contrary to the conditions subject to which the place was allowed to be so opened and used, and either—

(A) it is proved—

(i) that the employment was solely due to an emergency caused by a mechanical breakdown, or to the unavoidable absence of a skilled worker due to attend on that Sunday for whom no substitute could readily have been obtained ; and

(ii) that the emergency was notified, within twenty-four hours after it occurred, to the authority by whom the place is licensed under the Cinematograph Act, 1909 ; and

(iii) that the person employed on that Sunday contrary to the said conditions received a day's rest in lieu of that Sunday ; or

(B) it is proved—

(i) that the person was employed contrary to the said conditions only by reason of his having been employed on each of the six days previous to that Sunday in connection with similar entertainments or exhibitions by an employer other than the employer who employed him on that Sunday : and

(ii) that the last-mentioned employer had, after making due inquiry, reasonable ground for believing that he had not been so employed as aforesaid ;

that employment shall be deemed not to have been a contravention of the conditions subject to which the place was allowed to be so opened and used as aforesaid.

(4) In the event of a contravention of any conditions subject to which a place was allowed under this section to be opened and used on Sundays for the purpose of cinematograph entertainments, the person who held the licence for that place granted under the Cinematograph Act, 1909, shall be liable on summary conviction to a fine not exceeding twenty pounds, and shall, in the case of a contravention consisting of a failure to pay in accordance with the condition any sum thereby required to be paid to any authority or person, be liable to pay that sum as a debt due to that authority or person, as the case may be.

Any sum recoverable under this subsection may, if it does not exceed fifty pounds, be recovered summarily as a civil debt.

(5) This section extends to every area in which places licensed by the authority having power in that area to grant licences under the Cinematograph Act, 1909 were, within the period of twelve months ending on the sixth day of October, nineteen hundred and thirty-one, opened and used on Sundays for the purpose of cinemato-

graph entertainments, in pursuance of arrangements purported to have been made with the authority, and shall also extend to any borough or county district to which it may be extended by an order laid before Parliament in accordance with the provisions of the Schedule to this Act, and approved by a resolution passed by each House of Parliament :

Provided that, if in any area the arrangements in pursuance of which places were so opened and used as aforesaid related only to specific occasional entertainments, then, unless and until it is extended to that area by such an order as aforesaid, this section shall extend to that area subject to the modification that the powers thereby conferred shall not be exercised with respect to more than two Sundays in any year.

2.—(1) There shall be established under th dire ction and control of the Privy Council a fund, to be called the "Cinematograph Fund," and all sums paid to an authority in accordance with conditions imposed by them under the last foregoing section for the purpose of being transmitted to that fund shall be so transmitted at such times and in such manner as may be prescribed by regulations made by a Secretary of State and laid before Parliament.

(2) The moneys from time to time standing to the credit of the Cinematograph Fund shall, subject as hereinafter provided, be applied in such manner as may be directed by the Privy Council for the purpose of encouraging the use and development of the cinematograph as a means of entertainment and instruction :

Provided that a sum equal to the amount certified by the Treasury as the amount of the expenses incurred by the Privy Council in the administration of the said Fund shall be deducted annually from the Fund and applied in accordance with directions given by the Treasury as an appropriation in aid of the moneys provided by Parliament for the purposes of the Privy Council.

(3) The accounts of the Cinematograph Fund shall be kept in such form as may be directed by the Treasury, and an account showing the revenue and expenditure of the Fund shall be transmitted annually to the Comptroller and Auditor General, who shall certify and report upon the account, and the account and report shall be laid before Parliament.

3. The power of any authority in any area to grant licences under any enactment for the regulation of places kept or ordinarily used for public dancing, singing, music, or other public entertainment of the like kind, shall include power to grant such licences in respect only of musical entertainments on Sundays, and the power to attach conditions to any such licence shall include power to attach special conditions in respect of such entertainments on Sundays.

4. No person shall be guilty of an offence or subject to any penalty under the Sunday Observance Acts, 1625 to 1780, by reason of his having managed, conducted, assisted at, or otherwise taken part in or attended or advertised—

(A) any cinematograph entertainment at any place allowed under this Act to be opened and used on Sundays for that purpose ;

(B) any musical entertainment at any place licensed to be opened and used on Sundays for that purpose or at any place authorised by virtue of letters patent or royal charter to be kept or used for entertainments ;

(C) any museum, picture gallery, zoological or botanical garden or aquarium ;

(D) any lecture or debate ;

or by reason of his being the keeper of any place opened and used on Sundays for the purpose of any cinematograph entertainment or musical entertainment for which it is allowed under this Act or licensed to be so opened and used, or of any museum, picture gallery, zoological or botanical garden or aquarium, or of any place at which a lecture or debate is held on Sunday.

5. In this Act, unless the context otherwise requires, the following expressions have the meanings hereby respectively assigned to them, that is to say :—

"Cinematograph entertainment" means the exhibition of pictures or other optical effects by means of a cinematograph or other similar apparatus with or without the mechanical reproduction of sound :

"Contravention" in relation to any condition, includes a failure to comply with that condition :

"Musical entertainment" means a concert or similar entertainment consisting of the performance of music, with or without singing or recitation :

"Museum" includes any place permanently used for the exhibition of sculpture, casts, models, or other similar objects :

"Prescribed percentage" means such percentage, not exceeding five per cent., as a Secretary of State may, if he thinks fit, prescribe by regulations made by him and laid before Parliament :

"Sunday Observance Acts, 1625 to 1780," means the Sunday Observance Act, 1625, the Sunday Observance Act, 1677, and the Sunday Observance Act, 1780.

6.—(1) This Act may be cited as the Sunday Entertainments Act, 1932.

(2) The Sunday Performances (Temporary Regulation) Act, 1931, is hereby repealed, as from the thirtieth day of September, nineteen hundred and thirty-two.

(3) This Act shall not extend to Scotland or to Northern Ireland.

SCHEDULE.

Extension of Powers to allow Cinematograph Entertainments.

Power to submit Draft Orders to Secretary of State.

1. Subject to the provisions of this Schedule the council of any borough or county district may submit to the Secretary of State a draft order in the terms following, that is to say :—

"In accordance with the provisions of the Sunday Entertainments Act, 1932, I, . , one of His Majesty's Principal Secretaries of State, hereby order that as from the date on which this order has been approved by resolutions passed by both Houses of Parliament, section one of the said Act shall extend to the borough [or urban district or rural district] of ."

Provided that, before so submitting any such draft order, the council shall publish by means of placards and by advertisement in at least one newspaper circulated in the borough or district in two successive weeks a notice stating—

(A) the terms of the draft order ; and

(B) that the council propose to submit the draft order to the Secretary of State.

Procedure in the case of Boroughs and Urban Districts.

2. The notice of a proposal to submit a draft order under this Schedule published by the council of any borough or urban district shall state that a public meeting of local government electors for the borough or urban district will be held on a day named, not being less than fourteen nor more than twenty-eight days after the first advertisement of the notice, for the purpose of considering the question of the submission of the draft order to the Secretary of State.

3. A public meeting of such electors as aforesaid shall be held in accordance with the notice, and in relation to the meeting and to any poll and other proceedings subsequent thereto, the provisions of paragraphs 3 to 16 of the First Schedule to the Borough Funds Act, 1903, shall apply as if for references therein to " the Bill " and to " the promotion of the Bill " there were substituted, respectively, references to " the draft order " and " the submission of the draft order," and as if for references to " the Minister of Health " there were substituted references to " the Secretary of State," so, however, that so much of the said paragraphs as relates to separate resolutions in favour of the promotion of any part or parts or clause or clauses of the Bill shall not apply.

Procedure in the case of Rural Districts.

4. The notice of a proposal to submit a draft order under this Schedule published by the council of any rural district shall state that an objection to the submission of the draft order may be made to them in writing by any local government elector for the district within a period specified in the notice, not being less than fourteen nor more than twenty-eight days after the first advertisement of the notice, and that if at the expiration of that period objections have been duly made and not withdrawn by at least one hundred such electors or one-twentieth in number of such electors, whichever may be the less, then the council will cause to be held a local inquiry into the question of the submission of the draft order to the Secretary of State upon such date, not being less than seven days after the expiration of the period aforesaid, and at such time and place as may be specified in the notice.

5. Any such inquiry as aforesaid shall, in accordance with the notice, be help in public by a person appointed by the Secretary of State, and any local government elector for the district shall, subject as hereinafter provided, be entitled to appear personally and be heard thereat, and the person holding the inquiry shall, after the conclusion thereof, report in writing to the council whether public opinion in the district appears to him to be in favour of or against the extension of section one of this Act to the district :

Provided shat the person holding the inquiry shall have power to conclude the inquiry when, in his opinion, he has received sufficient evidence to enable him to make the report aforesaid.

Submission of Draft Order to and by the Secretary of State.

6. No draft order shall be submitted to the Secretary of State under the provisions of this Schedule by the council of a borough or urban district unless the result of a poll under this Act, or the decision of a meeting of local government electors when final, is in favour of the submission thereof ; and, except where by reason of there being no objection or an insufficient number of objections to the submission of the draft order an inquiry is not required under the foregoing provisions of this Schedule, no such draft order shall be so submitted by the council of a rural district unless the person by whom the inquiry was held has reported that public opinion in the district appears to him to be in favour of the extension of section one of this Act to the district.

Any such draft order submitted to the Secretary of State shall be accompanied, as the case may be, by a statement of the result of the poll or the decision of the meeting of local government electors, if final, certified by the mayor or chairman, or (except where an inquiry is not so required as aforesaid) by the report of the person by whom the inquiry was held, certified by him.

7. A draft order duly submitted to the Secretary of State in accordance with the foregoing provisions of this Schedule shall be laid by him before Parliament,

together with a copy of the certified statement or report (if any) submitted to him therewith.

Supplementary.

8, Section five of the Borough Funds Act, 1903 (which relates to offences in relation to polls), shall apply in relation to polls held under this Schedule as it applies in relation to polls held under that Act.

9, Any expenses incurred by a council in connection with the holding of any meeting, poll, inquiry or other proceeding under this Schedule (including such fee to the person holding any such inquiry as may be determined by the Secretary of State) shall be defrayed by the council out of the general rate.

COPYRIGHT.

Under the Copyright Act, 1911, the owner of a literary or dramatic work has the sole right to make a kinematograph film or other contrivance by which the same may be mechanically performed, and to authorise such acts. Before the Act it was held that there was no such right (*Karno* v. *Pathé Frères*, 100 L.T. 260).

Infringement is doing without the owner's consent anything which conflicts with the owner's rights. It includes selling, or letting for hire, or by way of trade exposing or offering for sale or hire, or by way of trade exhibiting in public or importing for sale or hire any work which infringes copyright or would do so if the work had been made in the country where infringement takes place. It also includes the case of a person who, for his private profit, permits a theatre or place of entertainment to be used for the public performance of a work without the owner's consent unless the person so doing was not aware *and had no reasonable ground for suspecting* that it was an infringement.

Copyright lasts during the life of the *author* and fifty years after his death. In the case of photographs, it is fifty years from the making of the original negative. All transfers or licences must be in writing and signed by the owner or his agent. The author cannot assign his copyright for longer than twenty-five years after his death.

A compulsory licence can be obtained twenty-five or thirty years after the author's death, but this provision cannot apply before 1936 at the earliest. The Privy Council has the power to grant a compulsory licence at any time after the author's death if it is proved that the work has been published or performed in public, and the present owner of the copyright has refused to allow republication, etc., so that the work is in effect withheld from the public.

An employee or apprentice does not acquire the copyright in work he does for his employer. Where a photograph is taken at the order of the sitter, who pays for it, he, and not the photographer, is the owner. It is a criminal offence to infringe copyright *knowingly*, and the offender is liable to a fine up to 40s. for every copy, but not more than £50 for any one transaction. In the case of second or subsequent offences, the justices can send the offender to prison for two months without the option of a fine, and in all cases may order the copies to be destroyed. No criminal charge under the Act can be brought more than six months after the act complained of. In civil proceedings the usual remedy is an injunction, but the defendant is also liable for damages unless he proves not merely that he did not know of the copyright, but also that he had no reasonable grounds for suspecting its existence. For example, if a kinema proprietor hires a film to show at one hall, he is liable for damages if he shows it at any other place (*Fenning Film Service* v. *Wolverhampton, etc., Cinemas* [1914] 3 K.B. 1171). Where the alleged infringement is such that the Court would not protect it as an original work (*e.g.*, on the ground of indecency), the owner of the copyright cannot sue under the Act, but can claim damages for defamatory representation of his work (*Glyn* v. *Western Feature Film Co.* [1916] 1 Ch. 261). The proper way to prove a film is to call someone who has seen it shown and not to produce the film unless some point turns on the film itself.

LOCAL GOVERNMENT BOARD REGULATIONS.

The Local Government Board have power under Section 130 of Public Health Act, 1875, and amendments to issue regulations with a view to preventing the spread of any epidemic or infectious disease. Regulations known as the Public Health (Influenza) Regulations, 1918, were issued by the Local Government Board under general orders dated November 18 and 22, 1918 :—

1. Limiting the time of entertainment to not more than 4 hours consecutively.

2. An interval of not less than 30 minutes between any two entertainments.

3. During such interval the place to be effectually and thoroughly ventilated, the penalty for breach not exceeding £100, and in case of a continuing offence to a further penalty not exceeding £50 for every day which the offence continues.

4. No children to be admitted to exhibitions where public elementary schools in the district have been temporarily closed. Notice must be given to the proprietor, otherwise regulation not effective.

These restrictions can be relaxed by any local authority upon such conditions as they may determine on the advice of their Medical Officer for Health. They do not concern the Licensing Authorities, who have no power to deal with such restrictions.

For removal of regulations application should be made to the District or Urban Council of the place where the theatre is situated.

[*These regulations have been rescinded. Attempts are being made to make them conditions on kinematograph licences, but it is doubtful whether such conditions are " intra vires."*]

THE CELLULOID ACT.

An Act known as " The Celluloid and Cinematograph Film Act of 1922 " has been passed to make better provision for the prevention of fire in premises where raw celluloid or kinematograph films are stored or used. The purposes to which this Act applies are :—

(1) The keeping or storing of raw celluloid—
    (*a*) In quantities exceeding at any one time one hundredweight ; or
    (*b*) In smaller quantities unless kept (except when required to be exposed for the purpose of the work carried on in the premises) in a properly closed metal box or case ; and

(2) The keeping or storing of kinematograph film—
    (*a*) In quantities exceeding at any one time twenty reels or eighty pounds in weight, or
    (*b*) In smaller quantities unless each reel is kept (except when required to be exposed for the purpose of the work carried on in the premises) in a separate and properly closed metal box or case :—

Provided that :—
    (i.) For the purpose of this Act, kinematograph film shall be deemed to be kept in any premises where it is temporarily deposited for the purpose of examination, cleaning, packing, re-winding or repair, but celluloid or kinematograph film shall not be deemed to be kept or stored in any premises where it is temporarily deposited whilst in the course of delivery, conveyance or transport ; and
    (ii.) The provisions of this Act shall not, except in the cases referred to in paragraphs (*c*), (*d*) and (*e*) of Sub-section (1) of Section 1 thereof, apply to premises to which the

Factory and Workshop Acts, 1901 to 1920 apply. Nor do the provisions of this Act apply to premises licensed under the Cinematograph Act, 1909. It should be pointed out, however, that under this Act any Officer duly authorised by a local authority may at any time take for analysis sufficient samples of any material which he suspects to be or to contain Celluloid.

HOME OFFICE REGULATIONS, 1923.

The 1923 Regulations under the Cinematograph Act. 1909, are somewhat important, and have been somewhat amended from their original form, owing to various meetings that took place between the Sub-Committee of the C.E.A. and the Home Office.

The Regulations took the place of previous Regulations of February 18, 1910 and May 20, 1913. The Regulations must be exhibited in the enclosure and easily accessible to operators. They are dated July 30, 1923, and operate from that date, but they would not affect any licence for the period for which it was granted, though, of course, when the same is renewed the new conditions will appear.

As regards clause 4, " Fire Appliances " footnote should be noticed, as it lays down that a fireman need not be employed exclusively in taking charge of the fire appliances. He must not, however, be given other work during an exhibition which would take him away from the building or otherwise prevent him from being immediately available in case of danger or alarm of fire.

As regards No. 5, " Smoking," it should be observed that notices stating that smoking is prohibited shall be kept posted in the enclosure and film room or anywhere where films are stored, wound or repaired.

As regards No. 7, relating to enclosure, fire-resisting material now includes teak or oak not less than two inches thick.

With regard to clause 7," Enclosures," Sec. 8, it will be noticed that in case of need the enclosure may be left for a short period in charge of a competent assistant over 16 years of age.

As to what is the exact definition of a " competent operator," one does not know, but apparently it can be taken to mean that an operator who can satisfactorily operate would come within the definition of a " competent operator."

With regard to clause 13, " Lighting,' it should be pointed out that if the general lighting is by electricity the safety lighting shall be by (a) electricity from another source (b) gas or (c) oil or candles.

One does not take this to mean that the safety lighting, if electricity, shall be taken from an entirely different supply, but merely that there shall be primary and secondary lighting installed in the building, the intention, of course, being that should the electric light supply be temporarily interrupted, the theatre will not be put into darkness

Clause 14, on " Electrical Installation,' it should be noticed that the Wiring Rules of the Institution of Electrical Engineers apply, a copy of which can always be obtained from Odhams Press Ltd., Technical Book Dept., 85, Long Acre, London, W.C.2. Price 1/2 post free.

It should be observed that Sections A, E, F and G of these Regulations do not apply to wiring in existence before July 30, 1923, except in the event of such wiring being altered or renewed.

With regard to clause 15, it should be noticed that the requirements in paragraphs C, D M and N shall not apply to apparatus in use before the date of these Regulations, and the requirements in paragraphs E, G, I, J and K do not apply until July 29, 1925, except in the event of the apparatus being renewed or materially altered.

STATUTORY RULES AND ORDERS, 1923, No. 983.

REGULATIONS, DATED JULY 30, 1923, MADE BY THE SECRETARY OF STATE
UNDER THE CINEMATOGRAPH ACT, 1909 (9 EDW 7, C. 30).]

PART I.—GENERAL.

DEFINITIONS.

1.—In these Regulations—

(*a*) The word "*building*" shall be deemed to include any booth, tent or similar structure.
(*b*) The expression "*new building*" means a building newly erected or adapted after the date on which these regulations come into force for the purpose of cinematograph exhibitions.
(*c*) The expression "cinematograph exhibition" includes any exhibition to which the Act applies.

SEATING AND EXITS.

2.—(*a*) No building shall be used for cinematograph exhibitions unless it be provided with an adequate number of exits clearly indicated and so placed and maintained as readily to afford the audience ample means of safe egress.

(*b*) The doors of all exits shall be so constructed and maintained as easily to open outwards on being pressed from within.

(*c*) The seating in the building shall be so arranged as not to interfere with free access to the exits.

(*d*) The gangways, the staircases, and the passages leading to the exits shall, during the presence of the public in the building, be kept clear of obstructions. No person shall be allowed to stand or sit in any of the gangways intersecting the rows of seats, or in the space between the front row of seats and the screen ; and if standing be permitted by the licensing authority in any other gangway or portion of the auditorium, sufficient room shall be left to allow persons to pass easily to and fro.

STAFF.

3.—(*a*) The licensee or some responsible person nominated by him in writing for the purpose shall be in charge during the whole time of any exhibition and there shall also be during that time a sufficient staff of attendants in the building for the purpose of securing safety.

(*b*) All persons responsible for or employed in or in connection with the exhibition shall take all due precautions for the prevention of accidents, and shall abstain from any act whatever which tends to cause fire and is not reasonably necessary for the purpose of the exhibition.
(This paragraph of the Regulations has now been revised.)

FIRE APPLIANCES.

4.—(*a*) Fire appliances suitable to the character of the building and adequate to deal with an outbreak of fire shall be provided and maintained in good working order. During the exhibition such appliances shall be in the charge of some person (A) specially nominated for that purpose who shall see that they are kept constantly available for use.

(*b*) There shall always be within the enclosure sufficient means of dealing with fire readily available for use, and these shall include the following, namely, a thick woollen blanket, two buckets of water, and a bucket of dry sand. Before the commencement of each exhibition the operator shall satisfy himself that the fire appliances within the enclosure are ready for use.

(A) It is not required that the person specially nominated should *necessarily* be employed exclusively in taking charge of the fire appliances, but he must not be given other work during an exhibition which would take him away from the building or otherwise prevent him from being immediately available in case of danger or alarm of fire.

SMOKING.

5.—No smoking shall at any time be permitted within the barrier or enclosure, nor in the film room nor in any part of the premises in which films are stored, wound, or repaired. Notices stating that smoking is prohibited shall be kept posted in the enclosure and film room and any such part of the premises as aforesaid.

INFLAMMABLE ARTICLES.

6.—No inflammable article shall unnecessarily be taken into, or allowed to remain in, the enclosure, the film room, or any part of the premises in which films are stored, wound, or repaired.

ENCLOSURES.

Regulations applying to all classes of buildings.

7.—(1) (a) The projecting apparatus shall be placed in an enclosure of substantial construction made of or lined internally with fire-resisting material and of sufficient dimensions to allow the operator to work freely.

(b) All fittings and fixtures within the enclosure other than the frames of outside windows shall be constructed of or covered with fire-resisting material.

The entrance to the enclosure shall be suitably placed and fitted with a self-closing close-fitting door which shall be kept closed during the exhibition.

For the purpose of this Regulation the expression " fire resisting material " includes teak or oak not less than two inches thick.

(c) The openings through which the necessary pipes and cables pass into the enclosure shall be efficiently sealed or bushed, as the case may be.

(d) The openings in the front face of the enclosure shall be covered with glass and shall not be larger than is necessary for effective projection and observation.

Each such opening shall be fitted with a screen of fire-resisting material, which can be released from both the inside and the outside of the enclosure so that it automatically closes with a close-fitting joint. The screens shall be so constructed and arranged that they can all be released simultaneously from the operating position near any of the projectors.

The openings shall not exceed two for each projecting apparatus and not more than two of the openings shall be left unscreened at any one time notwithstanding that there be two or more lanterns in the enclosure unless a control is provided by which all the screens can be released simultaneously from both the inside and the outside of the enclosure.

(e) The door of the enclosure and all openings, bushes, and joints shall be so constructed and maintained as to prevent, so far as possible, the escape of any smoke into the auditorium or any part of the building to which the public are admitted.

(f) Adequate means of ventilation shall be provided with sufficient inlets and outlets so as to ensure a constant supply of fresh air. The inlets and outlets shall communicate directly with the outside of the building, and shall be so arranged as not to expose the operator to a direct draught.

(g) If the enclosure is inside the auditorium, either a suitable barrier shall be placed round the enclosure at a distance of not less than two feet from it, or other effectual means shall be taken to prevent the public from coming into contact with the enclosure.

Provided that this requirement shall not apply where the enclosure is of permanent construction and is not entered from the auditorium.

(h) The enclosure shall be in charge of a competent operator over eighteen years of age, who shall be present in the enclosure during the whole time that the apparatus is in use. This shall not prevent the operator leaving the enclosure for a short period in case of need provided that a competent assistant, over sixteen years of age, is left in charge and the operator remains within immediate call.

(i) No unauthorised person shall go into the enclosure or be allowed to be within the barrier.

Regulations applying only to specified classes of buildings.

(2) In the case of buildings used habitually for cinematograph exhibitions the enclosure shall be outside the auditorium ; and in the case of permanent buildings used habitually as aforesaid the enclosure shall also be permanent.

Provided that if the licensing authority is of opinion that, in the case of an existing building, compliance with either or both of the requirements in the preceding paragraph is impracticable or in the circumstances unnecessary for securing safety, the requirement or requirements shall not apply.

In any new building where the enclosure is permanent, the enclosure shall also comply with the following requirements :—

(a) a window or skylight shall be provided.
(b) the entrance shall be from the open air.
(c) alternative means of egress shall be provided unless the licensing authority is satisfied that compliance with this requirement is impracticable.

PROJECTING APPARATUS AND FILMS.

8.—(a) The projecting apparatus shall be placed on firm supports constructed of fire-resisting material.

(b) Every lantern shall be fitted with a metal shutter which can readily be inserted by hand between the source of light and the film-gate, and every projector shall be fitted with a metal shutter so arranged as automatically to cut off the film-gate from the source of light when the projector stops.

(c) The construction of the film-gate shall be substantial and such as to afford ample heat-radiating surface. The passage for the film shall be sufficiently narrow to prevent flames travelling upwards or downwards from the light-opening.

9.—(a) Projectors shall be fitted with two metal boxes of substantial construction to and from which the film shall be made to travel, unless both the film spools are contained in a metal chamber of substantial construction *below* the projector. There shall not be more than 2,000 feet of film in either of the two metal boxes.

(b) The film boxes or chamber shall be made to close in such a manner, and shall be fitted with film slots so constructed, as to prevent the passage of flame to the interior of the box or chamber, and they shall remain so closed during the whole time that projection is taking place.

10.—Take-up spools shall be mechanically driven and films shall be wound upon spools so that the wound film shall not at any time reach or project beyond the edges of the flanges of the spool.

11.—(a) During the exhibition all films when not in use shall be kept in closed metal boxes of substantial construction. When in the enclosure not more than six spools shall be kept in one box at the same time.

(b) Not more than 12 spools or 20,000 feet of film altogether shall be kept in the enclosure and the rewinding room at the same time.

REWINDING ROOM.

12.—(a) A separate room shall be provided for the rewinding and repairing of films, which shall be constructed throughout of, or lined internally with, fire-resisting material.

(b) All fittings and fixtures within the rewinding room shall be constructed of, or covered with, fire-resisting material, and the entrance shall be provided with a self-closing close-fitting door of fire-resisting material which shall not communicate directly with the auditorium or any part of the building to which the public are admitted. If there is any communicating doorway or other opening between the enclosure and the rewinding room it shall also be provided with a door or shutter of fire-resisting material

For the purposes of this Regulation the expression " fire-resisting material " includes teak or oak not less than 2 inches thick.

(c) The rewinding room shall be provided with adequate means of ventilation, with sufficient inlets and outlets so as to ensure a constant supply of fresh air. The inlets and outlets shall communicate directly with the outside of the building.

(*d*) Alternative means of egress shall be provided other than through the enclosure.

Provided that if the licensing authority is of opinion that compliance with any of the requirements of this regulation is impracticable or, in the case of any of the requirements in paragraphs (*a*), (*b*) and (*d*), that it is in the circumstances unnecessary for securing safety, the requirement or requirements shall not apply.

LIGHTING AND ELECTRICAL INSTALLATION.

13.—(*a*) Where the general lighting of the premises can be controlled from within the enclosure, there shall also be separate and independent means of control outside of and away from the enclosure.

(*b*) The auditorium and exits therefrom to the outside of the building and all parts of the building to which the public are admitted shall throughout be adequately illuminated (A) during the whole time the public is present. The lighting for this purpose (hereinafter referred to as safety lighting) shall be supplied from a separate source from that of the general lighting of the premises and shall not be controllable from the enclosure (B). Where oil amps ar e provided colza oil shall be used.

14.—Where electrical energy is used for lighting or other purposes within the building the following requirements shall be observed :—

(*a*) Except as otherwise provided in these Regulations, the installation generally shall be in accordance with the Wiring Rules of the Institution of Electrical Engineers.
(*b*) The main supply fuses and switches shall not be accessible to the public. They shall be located where there is ample space and head room and where there is no risk of fire resulting therefrom.
(*c*) A separate circuit shall be taken from the source of supply for the projector circuit so that no accident to this circuit can affect the general lighting.
(*d*) Each of the main circuits shall be separately protected by an efficient linked switch and by a fuse on each pole.
(*e*) The general wiring of the building shall be protected by metal conduit mechanically and electrically continuous or by hard wood casings, except as regards any necessary flexible conductors such as may be required for pendant lamps or movable fittings.
(*f*) All fuses and distribution boards shall be of a completely protected type so constructed that the fuse holders can be handled for renewal of the fuse wires without risk of touching live metal.
(*g*) Portable lamps for the orchestra or similar lighting shall be connected to a separate circuit or circuits from the distribution fuse boards.
(*h*) The electrical installation shall be in charge of a competent person, whether the operator or another, who shall have received an adequate electrical training for his duties.
(*i*) The competent person shall satisfy himself before the commencement of each performance that the electrical apparatus, including the projector circuits, is in proper working order
Provided that paragraphs (*a*),(*e*),(*f*),(*g*) of this Regulation shall not apply to such parts of the electrical installation as were in use before the date of these Regulations, except in the event of such parts being altered or renewed.

15.—No illuminant other than electric light, limelight, or acetylene shall be used within the lantern and the following conditions shall be observed :

(1) *Electric Light.*—(a) All cables and wires for the projector circuits within and without the enclosure shall be heavily insulated and any necessary slack cable within the enclosure shall be heavily covered with asbestos.

For permanent enclosures installed after the date of these Regulations the cables and wires except as regards any necessary slack cable shall, unless armoured, be further protected by heavy gauge screwed metal conduit efficiently earthed. The conduit and fittings shall be bushed where necessary to prevent abrasion of the insulating material.

For temporary enclosures the cables and wires shall be secured by insulating cleats. Within the enclosure they shall be heavily protected by asbestos and without the enclosure they shall be protected by casings in all positions where they are liable to damage.

(*b*) An efficient double-pole main switch shall be fixed within the enclosure whereby all pressure may be cut off from the projector circuit or circuits within the enclosure, and where the lantern is earthed an additional double-

(A) By adequate illumination it is meant that there should be such a degree of light as to enable the spectators to see their way out.
(B) *e.g.*, if the general lighting is by electricity, the safety lighting shall be by (*a*) electricity from another source, (*b*) gas, or (*c*) oil or candles.

pole switch shall be fixed for each arc lamp so that the pressure may be cut off whilst recarboning is taking place.

(*c*) Where two or more projectors are installed and a change-over switch is required, it shall, unless it be a double-pole switch having a secure " off " position, be in addition to and not in substitution for the above main switch.

(*d*) All live parts of apparatus within five feet of the projector shall be shielded so that they cannot be accidentally touched. The covers of enclosed switches shall be of metal and, with the exception of change-over switches shall be so constructed that the switch handle does not work through an open slot. Where live metal is exposed so that it may be touched the floor within a radius of three feet from a point immediately below the live metal shall be covered with insulating material.

(*e*) Within the enclosure the pressure of the supply between any two conductors or between any conductor and earth shall not at any time exceed 250 volts direct or 125 volts alternating for the projector circuit.

Where the supply of alternating current is at a higher pressure, the pressure shall be reduced by means of a double-wound transformer.

In the case of a stand-by or temporary supply from across the outer conductors of a direct-current 3-wire system exceeding 250 volts, the projector circuit shall be taken as a shunt across part of a resistance connected across the outer conductors of the supply, so that the pressure within the enclosure shall not at any time exceed 250 volts.

(*f*) The projector motor circuit shall be controlled by a double-pole switch or hand-shield plug. The motor starter and its resistance may be within the enclosure, but these and all other parts of the circuit shall be protected so that no live metal can be inadvertently touched.

(*g*) Fuses shall be protected by enclosure in covers or cabinets against scattering of hot metal and shall be mounted in carriers or holders, so constructed that the hand cannot inadvertently touch live metal and that the hand is protected from the flash should a fuse blow on the insertion of the carrier in the contacts.

(*h*) The lamp or lamps for lighting the enclosure and the rewinding room shall not be connected to the safety lighting.

(*i*) All metal work liable to become accidentally charged, including the projecting apparatus, shall be efficiently earthed. The size of the earth wires shall be in accordance with the requirements of the Wiring Rules of the Institution of Electrical Engineers.

(*j*) The arc lamp adjusting handles shall be made of insulating material and shall be so constructed and arranged that the hand cannot inadvertently touch live metal.

(*k*) An ammeter shall be provided in the projector circuit within the enclosure.

(*l*) Resistances shall be so constructed and maintained that no coil or other part shall at any time become unduly heated. (A)

The framework, supports and enclosures of resistances shall be made entirely of fire-resisting material.

Resistances shall not be attached to wood work and shall, as far as possible, be kept away from any wood work. All wood work shall, where necessary, be effectively protected against overheating.

The terminals of the resistances and the connecting cables shall not be placed above the resistance elements.

Resistances placed where they are liable to be accidentally touched shall be efficiently guarded.

(*m*) Resistances, in which more than two kilowatts are dissipated, shall be placed outside the enclosure and in a room or place other than the r winding room accessible only to the technical staff. Adequate precautions shall be taken against fire resulting therefrom. If within the building, the room or place shall not communicate directly with the auditorium. It shall be well

(A) *e.g.*, they should not become so heated that a piece of newspaper placed in contact with any part of the resistance would readily ignite.

ventilated by ample inlets and outlets connecting directly with the outside air.

Switches suitably placed shall be provided by means of which the pressure may be cut off from the resistances.

(*n*) The motor generators or the electrical generating plant, as the case may be, and the main switchgear shall be in a fire-resisting room or rooms which may also contain the main resistances and the main supply fuses and switches. This room shall be well ventilated and shall not communicate directly with the auditorium or any part of the building to which the public are admitted.

Provided that the requirements in paragraphs (*c*), (*d*), (*m*), (*n*) shall not apply to apparatus in use before the date of these Regulations and the requirements in paragraphs (*e*), (*g*), (*i*), (*j*), (*k*) shall not apply, as regards such apparatus, until two years from the said date, except in the event of the apparatus being renewed or materially altered.

(2) *Limelight.*—The tubing shall be of sufficient strength to resist pressure from without and shall be properly connected up.

Cylinders containing gas under pressure other than acetylene gas shall be constructed, tested and filled in conformity with the recommendations either of the Committee on the manufacture of Compressed Gas Cylinders appointed by the Home Office in 1895 or of the Committee on Compressed Gas Cylinders appointed by the Department of Scientific and Industrial Research in 1918.

(3) *Acetylene.*—Acetylene, whether or not in conjunction with oxygen shall be used only when supplied :—

> (*a*) direct from cylinders or other vessels containing a homogeneous porous substance with or without acetone, which in regard to their contents and the degree of compression, comply with the requirements of the Secretary of State's order (A) regulating the compression of acetylene gas into cylinders containing a porous substance, and in force for the time being ; or (B) from a generator which shall be situated outside the building in a place approved by the licensing authority, the gas being supplied to the operator's box, so far as practicable, by pipes of metal other than unalloyed copper, and such flexible tubing as is necessarily employed being of sufficient strength to resist pressure from without and being properly connected up.

Provided that acetylene supplied direct from a generator shall not be employed as an illuminant in wooden buildings or in tents, or other movable or temporary structures.

EXHIBITION OF REGULATIONS.

16.—The licensee shall see that a copy of these Regulations is exhibited in the enclosure and is easily accessible to the operators.

BUILDINGS OCCASIONALLY USED.

17.—Where a building is used only occasionally for the purposes of a cinematograph exhibition, the provisions of the following Regulations shall not apply unless specially imposed and notified as conditions by the licensing authority in pursuance of Section 7 of the Act in cases of exceptional danger, viz. :—

Regulations 2(*b*), 11(*b*), and 14 (excepting paragraphs (*c*) (*h*) and (*i*) in so far as they relate to the projector circuits), but the following requirements shall be complied with, viz. :—

> (*a*) The doors of all exits shall be arranged to meet any requirements of the licensing authority
> (*b*) The film-boxes fitted to the projector shall not exceed 14 inches in diameter, inside measurement.
> Not more than 3 spools altogether shall be kept in the enclosure at any one time.

PART II.—PORTABLE PROJECTORS.

18.—Where a portable self-contained projector is used, regulations 2(*b*), 4(*a*), 5 to 12 inclusive and 14 to 17 (*except* 17(*a*)) inclusive shall not apply provided that regulations 1, 2(*a*), (*c*), (*d*), 3, 4(*b*) (with the substitution of the words " reserved space " for the word " enclosure "), 13 (with the substitution

(A) The Order at present in force is that dated the 23rd June, 1919 (Statutory Rules and Orders 1919, No. 809).

G

of the words " reserved space " for the word " enclosure "), 17(a) (whether or not the building is only occasionally used) and 19 to 26 inclusive are complied with

RESERVED SPACE.

19.—(a) If the projector is erected in any part of the auditorium or any place to which the public have access, effectual means shall be taken, whether by the erection of a suitable barrier or otherwise, to maintain round the projector a clear space of at least 3 feet, hereinafter referred to as " the reserved space."

(b) No unauthorised person shall be allowed within the reserved space.

(c) No smoking shall at any time be permitted within the reserved space.

(d) No inflammable article shall unnecessarily be taken into or allowed to remain in the reserved space.

PROJECTORS AND FILMS.

20.—The projector shall be placed on a firm support and shall be kept clear of the access to any exit.

21.—(a) The projector and the illuminant shall be entirely enclosed in a casing of fire-resisting material except for such openings as are necessary for effective manipulation and ventilation.

(b) Any electric wiring or terminals fitted within the casing shall be so placed that it shall be impossible for films in use in the projector to come in contact with them.

(c) Each electric circuit on the projector shall be fitted with a separate switch controlled from outside the casing, and so placed as to be within reach of the operator when standing at the projector.

(d) No illuminant other than electric light in hermetically sealed lamps shall be used within the projector, and the illuminant shall be separately encased in such a way as to prevent contact with the film.

(e) The heat of the illuminant, and its position in relation to the optical system, shall be such that it is impossible for the rays of light to ignite a stationary film. (A)

22.—(a) The projector shall be fitted with film-boxes of fire-resisting material, which shall be made to close in such a manner, and (where ribbon film is employed) shall be fitted with film-slots so constructed as to prevent the passage of flame to the interior of the box.

(b) The film-boxes shall not be capable of carrying films of more than 10 inches in diameter, and shall be so constructed as to be easily detachable from the apparatus.

(c) All films shall be contained in film-boxes, which shall be attached to or removed from the projector without being opened, so that at no time shall a film be exposed except the portion necessary for threading up.

(d) During an exhibition not more than three film-boxes (including the two actually attached to the projector) shall be in the auditorium at any one time. If further film-boxes are required, they shall be kept in closed metal boxes outside the auditorium, and, if in the building, in a place approved by the licensing authority.

ELECTRIC CIRCUITS FOR THE PROJECTOR.

23.—(a) All electric conductors shall be of adequate size for the current they have to carry and shall be efficiently covered with insulating material and shall be either (i) placed out of reach of persons in the anditorium and where they are not liable to damage, or (ii) protected against injury by suitable casings.

(b) Resistances shall be made entirely of fire resisting material, and shall be so constructed and maintained that no coil or other part at any time shall become unduly heated. (A) If inside the auditorium, they shall be adequately protected by a wire guard or other efficient means of preventing

(A) This requirement will be considered as met if a film stationary in the film-gate fails to ignite within a period of three minutes.

accidental contact, and shall not be placed within reach of persons in the audience.

(c) The operator shall satisfy himself before the commencement of each performance that all cables, leads, connections, resistances, and fuses are in proper working order. The resistances, if not under constant observation, shall be inspected at least once during each performance. If any fault is detected, current shall be immediately switched off, and shall remain switched off until the fault has been remedied.

(d) The projector circuit shall be independently protected by a double pole switch and fuses properly enclosed and placed near the source of supply or the point of connection with the general lighting supply, as the case may be. Provided that, where the current does not exceed five amperes and the connection of the projector circuit to the general lighting supply is made by means of a connector as described in paragraph (e) below, such a connector may be used in substitution for a double-pole switch.

(e) Where the projector circuit is connected to the general lighting supply it shall be connected only at a point where the wires of the general lighting supply are of ample size for the current they may have to carry, and the connection shall be either by (a) securely made joints or connections, or (b) a properly constructed wall type connector of hand shield type. It shall not be connected to any lighting fitting, or by means of an " adaptor " to a lamp-holder.

EXHIBITION OF REGULATIONS.

24.—A copy of so much of these Regulations as applies when a portable projector is used shall be exhibited in any room or place in which a portable projector is used for the purposes of an exhibition.

PART III.—LICENCES.

25.—Subject to the provisions of No. 26 of these Regulations, every licence granted under the Act shall contain a clause providing for its suspension by the licensing authority in the event of any failure on the part of the licensee to carry out these Regulations, or of the building becoming otherwise unsafe, or of any material alteration being made in the building or enclosure without the consent of the licensing authority.

26.—Where a licence has been granted under the Act in respect of a movable building, a plan and description of the building, certified with the approval of the licensing authority, shall be attached to the licence. Such a licence may provide that any of the conditions or restrictions contained therein may be modified either by the licensing authority, or by the licensing authority for the district where an exhibition is about to be given. The licence and plan and description or any of them shall be produced on demand to any police constable or to any person authorised by the licensing authority, or by the authority in whose district the building is being, or is about to be, used for the purpose of an exhibition.

PART IV.—REPEAL.

27.—The Regulations dated February 18th, 1910 (B), and May 20th, 1913 (C) made under the Cinematograph Act, 1909, are hereby repealed, provided, nevertheless that any licence granted prior to such repeal shall remain valid for the period for which it was granted without the imposition of any more stringent condition than may have been imposed at the time of the grant.

The most important Statutes affecting the Industry generally speaking are the Disorderly Houses Act, 1751 ; Theatres Act, 1843 ; Public Health Acts (Amendment) Act, 1890 ; and the Cinematograph Act, 1909.

In the Home Counties the Home Counties Music and Dancing Act, 1926.

In Middlesex the Music and Dancing (Middlesex) Act, 1894.

In London, the Metropolis Management and Building Acts. Amendment Act, 1878 ; and the London County Council (General Powers) Act, 1924.

(A) *e.g.*, they should not become so heated that a piece of newspaper placed in contact with any part of the resistance would readily ignite.

(B) S.R. & O., 1910, No. 189.　　　　　(C) S.R. & O., 1913, No, 566.

Cinematograph Films Act, 1927.

An Act to restrict blind booking and advance booking of cinematograph films, and to secure the renting and exhibition of a certain proportion of British films, and for purposes connected therewith.

Be it enacted by the King's most Excellent Majesty, by and with the advice and consent of the Lords Spiritual and Temporal, and Commons, in this present Parliament assembled, and by the authority of the same, as follows :—

PART I.

RESTRICTIONS ON BLIND BOOKING AND ADVANCE BOOKING OF FILMS.

1.—(Restriction on Blind Booking of Films).—(1) As from the commencement of this Act no agreement shall be entered into to rent or imposing an obligation when called on to rent for public exhibition in Great Britain any film to which this Act applies unless every such film to which the agreement relates has been registered under this Act or a valid application for the registration thereof has been made :

Provided that—

(*a*) this provision shall not apply to a film which has been exhibited to exhibitors or to the public in Great Britain before the commencement of this Act ; and

(*b*) in the case of a serial film or a series of films within the meaning of this Act, it shall be sufficient if any three parts thereof have been registered or a valid application for the registration of three parts thereof has been made.

(2) In the case of a film which has not been previously exhibited to exhibitors or to the public in Great Britain, this section shall not operate so as to prohibit the making prior to the registration or application for registration thereof of an agreement for the exhibition of the film in one theatre only on a number of consecutive days.

2.—(Restriction on Advance Booking.)—(1) As from the commencement of this Act, no agreement shall be entered into for the exhibition to the public in Great Britain a date later than the expiration of the authorised period from the date of the agreement of any film to which this Act applies :

Provided that in the case of a serial film or a series of films within the meaning of this Act, the authorised period shall apply only in respect of the date of exhibition of the first three parts.

Provided that in the case of a serial film or a series of films within the meaning of this Act the authorised period shall apply only in respect of the date of exhibition of the first three parts.

(2) For the purposes of this section the authorised period shall—

(*a*) in the case of an agreement made before the first day of October, nineteen hundred and twenty-eight, be twelve months ;

(*b*) in the case of an agreement made on or after the first day of October, nineteen hundred and twenty-eight, and before the first day of October, nineteen hundred and thirty, be nine months;

(*c*) in the case of an agreement made on or after the first day of October, nineteen hundred and thirty, be six months.

3.—(Penalty on Contraventions.)—If any person enters into an agreement in contravention of this Part of this Act, or if any person exhibits to the public in Great Britain a film the right to exhibit which has been acquired by him under any such agreement, he shall be guilty of an offence and liable on summary conviction to a fine not exceeding fifty pounds, and any agreement in contravention of this part of the Act, wherever made, shall be invalid.

4.—(Provision as to Existing Agreements.)—Any agreement entered into after the twenty-fifth day of September, nineteen hundred and twenty-six, and before the commencement of this Act which if entered into after the commencement of this Act would be an invalid Agreement under the foregoing provisions of this Part of this Act shall, if and so far as it affects any films to which this Act applies to be delivered for public exhibition in Great Britain after the thirty-first day of December, nineteen hundred and twenty-eight, cease to have effect on that day.

PART II.

REGISTRATION OF FILMS.

5.—(Prohibition Against Exhibition of Unregistered Films.)—(1) On and after the first day of April, nineteen hundred and twenty-eight, no film to which this Act applies, or, in the case of a serial film or a series of films, no part thereof, shall be exhibited to the public in Great Britain unless the film or the part thereof exhibited has been registered in accordance with this Part of this Act

Provided that—

(*a*) a film in respect of which a provisional application for registration has been made may, before registration, be exhibited in Great Britain at a series of public exhibitions held at one theatre only on consecutive days.

(*b*) the prohibition contained in this section shall not apply to a film which has been exhibited before the commencement of this Act.

(2) If any person exhibits a film, or, in the case of a serial film or a series of films, any part thereof, in contravention of this section he shall be guilty of an offence and liable on summary conviction to a fine not exceeding twenty pounds for each day on which the film or part has been so exhibited.

6.—(Registration of Films.)—(1) The Board of Trade shall keep a register of films to which this Act applies, and shall enter therein such particulars as may be prescribed ; and the register shall specify whether the film is registered as a British film or a foreign film.

Provided that a film which has been exhibited to exhibitors or to the public before the first day of October, nineteen hundred and twenty-seven shall not be registered unless the Board of Trade, after consultation with the Advisory Committee hereinafter mentioned, determine that the registration of the film shall be allowed.

(2) The Board of Trade shall publish weekly in the " Board of Trade Journal " lists of the film registered in accordance with the provisions of this Act.

(3) An application to register a film shall be made by or on behalf of the maker or renter of the film, and shall be accompanied by the prescribed fee, and by such information as the Board of Trade may require, and in particular, where the application is for the registration of the film as a British film, such information as may be necessary to determine whether the film is a British film.

(4) An application shall not be a valid application unless the film has been trade shown, nor if more than fourteen days have elapsed since it was trade shown :

Provided that—

(a) a provisional application may be made before a film has been trade shown, and in such case on the film being trade shown within six weeks after the lodging of the provisional application, the provisional application shall as from the date of the trade show become a valid application.

(b) an application made more than fourteen days after the film was trade shown may be accepted by the Board as a valid application if satisfied that the delay was due to special circumstances and was not intentional.

(5) On the registration of a film, the Board shall issue to the applicant a certificate of registration, and the certificate shall state the length of the film and whether the film is registered as a British film or a foreign film.

7.—(Inspection of Register, etc.)—(1) The register of films kept under this Act shall at all reasonable times be open to inspection by any person on payment of the prescribed fee, and any person inspecting the register may make copies or extracts from the register.

(2) Any person may on payment of the prescribed fee require to be furnished with a copy of any entry in the register certified to be a true copy by an officer of the Board of Trade appointed to keep the register.

(3) The registration of a film may be proved by the production of a copy of the Board of Trade Journal, containing a notification of the registration of the film or, of a certificate of registration, or of a certified copy of the entry in the register relating to the film, and a certificate purporting to be a certificate of registration or a copy of any entry purporting to be certified as a true copy by such officer as aforesaid shall in all legal proceedings be evidence of the matters stated therein without proof of the signature or authority of the person signing it.

8.—(Correction of Register.)—(1) If the Board of Trade at any time have reason to believe that the length of a film has been or has become incorrectly registered, or that a film has been incorrectly registered as a British film, they may call for such evidence as they think fit as to the correctness or otherwise of the registration, and if satisfied that the film has been or is incorrectly registered, they shall correct the register and issue an amended certificate of registration.

(2) On the issue of an amended certificate, the former certificate shall cease to have effect except that the Board of Trade may in any particular case allow the film to be counted for the purposes of the provisions of Part III. of this Act relating to renters' and exhibitors' quotas as being of the length originally registered, or as a British film, as the case may be.

9.—Power to Require Reference to High Court.)—(1) If any person is aggrieved by the refusal of the Board of Trade to register a film, or to register a film as a British film, or by a decision of the Board to correct the registration of a film, the matter shall, subject to rules of court, be referred by the Board of Trade to the High Court for determination, and the decision of the Court on any such reference shall be final and no appeal shall lie therefrom to any other court.

(2) When the person aggrieved is a person whose principal place of business is in Scotland this section shall apply as if the reference to the High Court were a reference to the Court of Session.

10.—(Provisions as to Alterations of the Length of Films.)—(1) If the length of a film is altered to the extent of more than ten per cent. thereof after an application for registration thereof has been lodged or after the registration thereof, it shall be the duty of the maker of the film or, if at the time of alteration the film has been acquired by a renter, the renter, to send to the Board of Trade notice of the alteration, and if he fails to do so, he shall be guilty of an offence, and shall be liable on summary conviction to a fine not exceeding twenty pounds.

11.—(Marking of Registered Films.)—(1) On every copy of a registered film there shall be marked in the prescribed manner :—

(a) the registered number of the film ;

(b) the person in whose name the film is registered;

(c) the registered length of the film ;

(d) the words " registered as a British film " or " registered as a foreign film," as the case may be.

Provided that it shall not be necessary to comply with the above requirements in respect of any film if, whenever a copy thereof is issued to an exhibitor for exhibition to the public in Great Britain, an invoice containing such particulars as aforesaid is sent by the renter to the exhibitor.

(2)   If after copies of a film have been so marked or invoices have been so sent the registration of the film is corrected in manner provided by this part of the Act, then—

(*a*) in the former case a corresponding alteration shall be made in all copies of the film ; and

(*b*) in the latter case, new invoices containing the correct particulars shall be sent.

(3)   If any person fails to comply with any of the provisions of this section, or issues a copy of any registered film incorrectly marked or any invoice containing incorrect particulars, he shall be guilty of an offence, and shall be liable on summary conviction to a fine not exceeding twenty pounds in respect of each copy.

12.—(Special Provisions as   Serial Films, etc.)—In the case of a serial film or a series of films the provisions of this Part of this Act shall apply subject to the following modifications :—

(1)   The separate parts of the film or series of films shall be separately registered and each part shall be treated as a separate film ;

(2)   Where three parts of the film or series have been trade shown, any other part may be registered without having been trade shown and notwithstanding that more than fourteen days have elapsed since the said three parts were trade shown.

Provided that if the Board are at any time of opinion that it is no longer desirable to dispense with a trade show in the case of the remaining parts of serial films and series of films, they may make an order to that effect, and on the making of the order this paragraph shall cease to apply.

PART III.
PROVISIONS FOR SECURING QUOTA OF BRITISH FILMS.
By the Renters.

13.—(Provisions as to Renters' Quota)—(1)   In the year commencing on the first day of April nineteen hundred and twenty-eight, and ending on the thirty-first day of March, nineteen hundred and twenty-nine, and in each of the nine succeeding years, any person engaged in the business of renting registered films to exhibitors for the purpose of public exhibition in Great Britain (hereinafter referred to as a renter) shall acquire for the purposes of such renting a total length of registered British films representing at least such proportion of the total length of all registered films so acquired by him in the year as is specified as respects the year in Part I. of the Schedule to this Act, and such proportion as hereinafter referred to as the renters' quota, and if the films so acquired include both long films (that is to say, films the registered length of which is three thousand feet or upwards) of short films (that is to say, films the registered length of which is less than three thousand feet), the requirements of this section must be satisfied as respects the long films so acquired as well as respects all films so required.

(2)   If any such year a renter fails to comply with the requirements of this Part of the Act as to the renters' quota he shall be guilty of an offence, unless such a certificate as is hereinafter mentioned has been issued by the Board of Trade, or unless he proves to the satisfaction of the court that the reasons for non-compliance were reasons beyond his control.

(3)   In this section, "registered British film" means a British film which either at the time of its acquisition by the renter is, or later within the same year becomes, a registered British film "registered film" means a film which either at the date of its acquisition by the renters is, or later within the same year becomes a registered film.

(4)   If a film is not registered at the time of its acquisition by a renter, and is registered after the expiration of the year in which it is so acquired, the film shall, for the purposes of this part of the Act, be treated as if it had been acquired by the renter in the year in which it is registered.

(5)   Where a renter has in any such year acquired any registered films and subsequently in the same year his business as a renter by assignment or will or on intestacy or by operation of law, becomes vested in some other licensed renter, that other renter and not the first-mentioned renter shall for the purposes of the provisions of this Part of this Act as to the renters' quota be deemed to have acquired the films.

14.—(Power of Small Renters to Combine).—Any number of renters none of whom, or of whom not more than one, during any such year acquires for the purposes of renting to exhibitors more than six long registered films, as hereinbefore defined, may, if the Board of Trade consent, combine for the purposes of the provisions of this Part of this Act relating to the renters' quota the total length of registered British films so acquired by them in that year and the total length of all registered films so acquired by them in that year, and in such case if the total length of such registered British films bears the proper proportion to the total length of all such registered films, and the total length of all such long registered British films bears the proper proportion to the total length of all such long registered films, each renter shall as respects that year be deemed to have satisfied the provisions of this Part of this Act as to the renters' quota.

15.—(Provisions Applicable Where Same Film Rented by Different Persons for Different Areas.) —Any renter whose business is limited to the renting of films for exhibition exclusively in a limited geographical area within Great Britain may for the purposes of his renters' quota count any registered British film for the renting of which in that area he has acquired the exclusive right and which has not been previously exhibited to the public in that area, notwithstanding that the film has been already counted for the purposes of the renters' quota by some other renter, being a renter who has acquired the exclusive right to rent it for exhibition in some other limited area, or in Great Britain exclusive of the first-mentioned area.

16.—(Prohibition of Counting Film More than Once for Quota Purposes.)—No British film shall be counted more than once for the purposes of the provisions of this Part of this Act with respect to the renters' quota, nor, save as hereinbefore expressly provided, shall any British film be counted for the purposes aforesaid by more than one renter.

Provided that, if a renter in any year acquires old British films and also acquires old foreign films, he shall be entitled to count the old British films for the purposes of the renter's quota—

(a) if the only films acquired by him during the year are old films ; or

(b) if he has acquired films other than old films during the year and the requirements of this part of this Act as to renter's quota would have been satisfied as respects those other films had they been the only films acquired by him during the year.

For the purposes of this proviso the expression "old" in relation to a film means acquired by a renter not less than one year after the close of the year in which it was acquired by another renter.

17.—(Prohibition Against Carrying on Business of Renter Unless Licensed).—(1) On and after the first day of April, nineteen hundred and twenty-eight, and until the thirty-first day of March, nineteen hundred and thirty-eight, no person shall carry on the business of renting registered films for exhibition to the public in Great Britain unless he holds a licence for the purpose from the Board of Trade

Provided that where an application for such a licence has been made, it shall be lawful for the applicant to carry on such business as aforesaid pending the determination of the application.

(2) No films to which this Act applies shall during the period aforesaid be exhibited to the public in Great Britain unless—

(a) the film has been acquired by the exhibitor from a person entitled to carry on such business as aforesaid ; or

(b) the exhibitor is himself a person who is entitled to carry on such business as aforesaid and has acquired the film for the purpose of renting it for public exhibition in Great Britain.

(3) If any person carries on such business as aforesaid or exhibits any film in contravention of this section, he shall be guilty of an offence and liable on summary conviction to a fine not exceeding twenty pounds for each day during which he so carries on the business or exhibits the film as the case may be

18.—(Returns and Records.)—(1) Every person who at any time during any year ending on the thirty-first day of March was a licensed renter shall furnish to the Board of Trade before the first day of the following May or such later date as in any particular case the Board of Trade may allow a return giving such particulars as may be prescribed with respect to the registered films acquired by him during the year in question in order to enable the Board of Trade to ascertain whether the requirements of this Part of this Act with respect to the renters' quota have been satisfied by him during the year to which the return relates.

Provided that if any licensed renter in the course of any such year ceases to carry on business as a renter, the return shall be made within one month from the time when he so ceases to carry on the business, unless previously and in the same year his business as a renter has become vested in some other licensed renter.

(2) Every person required to make a return under the last foregoing sub-section shall, before the first day of May in the year following the year in which the return was made, furnish to the Board of Trade a supplementary return relative to the year to which the original return related, giving such particulars as could not have been given in the original return owing to bookings for exhibitions not having been completed.

(3) Any such return as aforesaid may be used for the purpose of ascertaining whether the films entered in the return as having been acquired by the renter making the return were in fact acquired by him for the purpose of renting them to exhibitors for exhibition to the public in Great Britain.

(4) Every licensed renter shall also keep a book and shall as soon as practicable record therein the title, registered number, and registered length of every film acquired by him (distinguishing between British and foreign films), the theatres at which each film has been booked for exhibition and the dates for which such bookings are made, and shall when so required produce the book for inspection by any person authorised in that behalf by the Board of Trade.

Exhibitors' Quota.

19.—(Provisions as to Exhibitors' Quota.)—(1) In the year commencing on the first day of October, nineteen hundred and twenty-eight, and ending on the thirtieth day of September, nineteen hundred and twenty-nine, and in each of the nine succeeding years, every person who carries on the business of exhibiting registered films to the public in Great Britain shall exhibit at each theatre during the period in any year during which he so exhibits films at that theatre at least such proportion of registered British films as is mentioned with respect to the year in question in Part II. of the Schedule to this Act, and such proportion is hereinafter referred to as the exhibitor's quota, and if the films so exhibited include both long and short films as hereinbefore defined the requirements of this section must be satisfied as respects the long films so exhibited as well as repects all the films so exhibited.

(2) The proportion of British registered films exhibited during such period as aforesaid at any theatre shall be ascertained by comparing—

(a) the aggregate arrived at by adding together the products of the total number of feet of each registered British film which has been exhibited during the normal hours in the ordinary programme multiplied by the number of times the film has been so exhibited during the said period ; and

(b) the aggregate arrived at by adding together the products of the total number of feet of each registered film which has been so exhibited multiplied by the number of times the film nas been so exhibited during the said period.

(3) If in any year an exhibitor fails to comply with the requirements of this Part of this Act n respect of any theatre he shall be guilty of an offence unless such a certificate as is hereinafter mentioned has been issued by the Board of Trade, or unless he proves to the satisfaction of the court that the reasons for non-compliance were reasons beyond his control.

20.—(Prohibition Against Carrying on Business of Exhibitor Unless Licensed.)—(1) On and after the first day of October, nineteen hundred and twenty-eight, and until the thirtieth day of September, nineteen hundred and thirty-eight, no person shall carry on the business of exhibiting registered films to the public in any theatre unless ue hold a licence for the purpose in respect of that theatre from the Board of Trade :

Provided that where an application for such a licence has been made, it shall be lawful for the applicant to carry on the business in any theatre to which the application relates pending the determination of the application.

(2)   If any person carries on such business as aforesaid in contravention of this section, he shall be guilty of an offence, and shall be liable on summary conviction to a fine not exceeding ten pounds for each day on which he so carries on the business.

21.—(Returns and Records.)—(1)   Every person who at any time during any year ending on the thirtieth day of September was a licensed exhibitor shall furnish to the Board of Trade before the first day of the following November a return giving such particulars as may be prescribed with respect to the registered films exhibited by him in each theatre during the year in question, and the dates and number of times on which they were exhibited in order to enable the Board of Trade to ascertain whether the requirements of this Part of this Act with respect to the exhibitors' quota have been satisfied by him in respect of the theatre during the year to which the return relates.

Provided that if any licensed exhibitor in the course of any such year ceases to exhibit at any theatre, the return with respect to that theatre shall be made within one month from the time when he so ceases to exhibit thereat.

(2)   Every licensed exhibitor shall also keep in respect of each theatre at which he exhibits films a book and shall as soon as practicable record therein the tit le, registered number, and registered length of each film exhibited by him at the theatre to the publ ic (distinguishing between British and foreign registered films), the dates of all exhibitions of each film, and the number of times the exhibition of each film each day during the normal hours in the ordinaryprogramme, and every such book shall be open to inspection by any person authorised in that behalf by the Board of Trade.   The book relating to any theatre shall be kept at that theatre so long as the exhibitor continues to exhibit thereat.

22.—(Provisions as to Itinerant Exhibitors.)—In the case of any exhibitor who in any such year as aforesaid does not exhibit in any one theatre on more than six days nor in more than one theatre at the same time, the provisions of this Part of this Act shall apply subject to the following modifications :—

(a) it shall not be necessary for any such exhibitor to comply with the provisions as to the exhibitors' quota as respects any particular theatre if, had all the exhibitions given by him in the year been exhibitions at the same theatre, those provisions would have been complied with ;

(b) it shall not be necessary for the exhibitor to make a return to the Board of Trade after ceasing to exhibit at any particular theatre, or to keep a separate record book in respect of each theatre at which he exhibits ;

(c) a licence to carry on the business of exhibiting films to the public shall suffice, and it shall not be necessary for the exhibitor to obtain a licence in respect of each theatre at which he exhibits.

General.

23.—(Examination of Returns.)—(1)   The Board of Trade shall examine every return furnished to them under this Part of this Act, and for the purpose of such examination may call on the renter or exhibitor making the return for such information and explanations as they may think necessary; and may authorise any person appointed by them for the purpose to examine the record books kept by the renter or exhibitor.

(2)   Where on submission by the renter or exhibitor or otherwise it appears to the Board of Trade after consultation with the Advisory Committee hereinafter mentioned in any case where the Board of Trade contemplate the refusal of a certificate that though the requirements of this Part of this Act with respect to the renters' quota or the exhibitors' quota, as the case may be. have not been complied with, the reasons for non-compliance were reasons beyond the control of the renter or exhibitor, they shall issue a certificate to that effect.

24.—(Proceedings for Failure to Comply with Provisions as to Quota.)—(1)   Any offence to failing to comply with the provisions of this Part of this Act as to the renters' quota or exhibitor's quota may be prosecuted summarily or on indictment, and—

(a) if the accused is proceeded against summarily, he shall on conviction if a renter be liable to a fine not exceeding one hundred pounds ; and if an exhibitor to a fine not exceeding fifty pounds ; and

(b) if the accused is proceeded against on indictment he shall on conviction be liable to a fine not exceeding five hundred pounds.

(2)   In the case of a conviction on indictment, the court, in addition to imposing any such fine as aforesaid—

(a) where the offender is a renter, may, if of opinion that the offence was deliberate, and if the offence is a third offence, order that his licence be revoked and may order that no licence shall be issued to him, or to any person with whom he is financially associated, or to any person who acquires his business, or to any person who took part in the management of his business and was knowingly a party to the offence. for such period in each case as may be specified in the order ;

Provided that where any such order is made the order shall not operate so as to prevent the renter carrying out for a period not exceeding six months any obligations under any contract entered into by him before the institution of the proceedings ;

(b) where the offender is an exhibitor, may, if of opinion that the offence is deliberate, and if the offence is a third offence order his licence under this act in respect of the theatre with respect to which the offence, was committed to be revoked, and may order that for such period in each case as may be specified in the order no licence in respect of that theatre shall be issued to him or to any person with whom he is financially associated or to any person who took part in the management of his business and was knowingly a party of the offence, or to any person whose licence in respect of any theatre has been revoked during the twelve months previous to the date of the conviction.

(3) Summary proceedings for the offence of not complying with the requirements of this Part of this Act as to the renters' quota or as to the exhibitors' quota may, notwithstanding anything in the Summary Jurisdiction Acts, be instituted at any time within two years after the commission of the offence in the case of a renter, and one year after the commission of the offence in the case of an exhibitor.

25.—(Provisions as to Licences.)—(1) A licence under this Act shall be granted by the Board of Trade to any person applying for the licence if the applicant is not disqualified for holding the licence applied for, and if the application is accompanied by such information verified in such manner as the Board may reasonably require in order to satisfy themselves that the applicant is not disqualified for holding the licence applied for and by the prescribed fee.

(2) A person shall not be qualified to hold a licence under this Part of the Act unless he has a place of business within Great Britain and has sent notice thereof and of any charge therein to the Board of Trade.

(3) A licence granted under this section shall remain in force until the expiration of the year ending on the thirty-first day of March or the thirtieth day of September, as the case may be, in respect of which it is granted, unless previous to that date the holder thereof to be qualified for holding the licence.

26.—(Penalties for Failure to Make Returns and Keep Record Books.)—(1) If any person required to make a return under this Part of this Act fails to make the return within the time within which he is required to make the return, or on being so required fails to give any information or explanation respecting the return which it is in his power to give, he shall be guilty of an offence, and shall be liable on summary conviction to a fine not exceeding five pounds for every day during which the default continues.

(2) If any person who is required to keep a book and record therein such particulars as are mentioned in this Part of this Act fails to do so, or when required by a person authorised in that behalf by the Board of Trade to produce the book for inspection at any reasonable time fails to do so, he shall be guilty of an offence and shall be liable on summary conviction to a fine not exceeding twenty pounds.

PART IV.

GENERAL.

27.—(Films to which Act applies.)—(1) The films to which this Act applies are all cinematograph films other than :—

(a) films depicting wholly or mainly news and current events ;

(b) films depicting wholly or mainly natural scenery ;

(c) films being wholly or mainly commercial advertisements ;

(d) films used wholly or mainly by educational institutions for educational purposes ;

(e) films depicting wholly or mainly industrial or manufacturing processes ;

(f) scientific films, including natural history films.

Provided that—(i) if it appears to the Board of Trade, on application by the maker or renter that, having regard to the special exhibition value of the film, any film of any such class as aforesaid should be allowed to be registered and to count for the purposes of the renters' quota and exhibitors' quota, they may allow the film to be registered and so counted ; and (ii) any film being a British film and a film of class (b), (d), (e), or (f) of the classes above mentioned shall *without* being made trade shown be registerable as if it were a film to which this Act applies, and if so registered, shall be deemed to be a registered film for the purposes of the provisions of this Act other than those relating to the renters' quota.

(2) For the purposes of this Act, " serial film or series of films " means a serial film or series of films comprising a number of parts not exceeding twenty-six, each part not exceeding two thousand feet in length, intended to be exhibited at successive dates at intervals not exceeding fourteen days.

(3) For the purposes of this Act a film shall be deemed to be a British film if, but not unless, it complies with all the following requirements :—

(i) It must have been made by a person who was at the time the film was made a British subject, or by two or more persons each of whom was a British subject, or by a British company ;

(ii) After the first day of December, nineteen hundred and twenty-eight, the studio scenes must have been photographed in a studio in the British Empire.

(iii) The author of the scenario must have been a British subject ;

(iv) Not less than seventy-five per cent. of the salaries, wages and payments specifically paid for labour and services in the making of the film (exclusive of payments in respect of copyright and of the salary or payments to one foreign actor or actress or producer, but inclusive of the payments to the author of the scenario) has been paid to British subjects or persons domiciled in the British Empire but it shall be lawful for the Board of Trade to relax this requirement in any case where they are satisfied that the maker had taken all reasonable steps to secure compliance with the requirement, and that his failure to comply therewith was occasioned by exceptional circumstances beyond his control, but so that such power of relaxation shall not permit of the percentage aforesaid being less than seventy per cent.

(4) Every film which is not a British film shall for the purposes of this Act be deemed to be a foreign film.

(5) For the purposes of this section :—

The expression " British company " means a company constituted under the laws of any part of the British Empire, the majority of the directors of which are British subjects.

The expression "British Empire " includes territories under His Majesty's protection and such (if any) of the territories in respect of which a mandate on behalf of the League of National has been accepted by His Majesty, as His Majesty may from time to time by Order in Council direct shall be treated as if they were included in His Majesty's Dominions for the purposes of this Act.

28.—(Penalties for misrepresentation.)—If any person :—

(a) in connection with an application for registration of any film under this Act ; or

(b) for the purpose of obtaining a licence under this Act for himself or any other persons ; or

(c) in or in connection with any return required by this Act, or in the record book kept in pursuance of this Act :

knowingly makes any statement or gives any information which is false in any material particular, he shall be guilty of an offence under this Act and shall be liable on summary conviction to imprisonment for a term not exceeding three months or to a fine not exceeding fifty pounds.

29.—(Power of Board of Trade to make régulations.)—The Board of Trade may make regulations for prescribing anything which under this Act is to be prescribed, and generally for carrying this Act into effect, and in particular may, subject to the consent of the Treasury so far as they relate to fees, by regulations prescribe :—

(a) the particulars to be entered in the register ;

(b) the form of applications for registration ;

(c) the particulars and evidence necessary for establishing the British nature of a film ;

(d) the fees to be paid on an application for registration, for an inspection of the registers and for certified copies of the register ;

(e) the form of the returns to be made, and of the records to be kept under this Act ;

(f) the fees to be paid on applications for licences under this Act ;

(2) Fees shall be so fixed, and from time to time if necessary be so readjusted, that the aggregate amount produced thereby as from the commencement of this Act up to any date would be approximately equal to the expenses incidental to the carrying out of the Act up to the same date, and the fees payable on application for registration and licences shall not exceed those specified in the Second Schedule to this Act.

(3) Regulations under paragraph (d) shall provide that the particulars required as to salaries wages and payments shall be certified by an accountant being a member of an incorporated society of accountants.

30.—(Advisory Committee.)—Until the expiration of the quota period for the purpose of advising them on the administration of the provisions of this Act, the Board of Trade shall constitute an advisory committee consisting of—

(a) two representatives of film makers ;

(b) two representatives of film renters ;

(c) four representatives of film exhibitors ;

(d) five members, of whom one shall be chairman, and including a woman, being persons having no pecuniary interest in any branch of the film industry.

The time of office of a person appointed to be a member of the Advisory Committee shall be such period not exceeding three years, as may be fixed at the time of his appointment, but a retiring member shall be eligible for reappointment.

31.—(Institution of Proceedings.)—(1) Proceedings for any offence under this Act may, in England and Wales, be instituted by or on behalf of the Board of Trade, but not otherwise.

(2) Any process or notice required to be served on any person for the purposes of this Act, shall that person is out of Great Britain but has a place of business in Great Britain, be sufficiently served addressed to that person and left at or sent by post to such place of business as aforesaid.

32.—Interpretation.—(1) For the purposes of this Act, unless the context otherwise requires :—

The expression " trade shown " in relation to a film means either—

(a) displayed within the administrative county of London to exhibitors of films or their agents in a building and under conditions allowing for the satisfactory viewing of the film after announcement to such persons at least seven days before the display, the display not being open to any member of the public on payment ; or

(b) displayed to the general public in one theatre only on the first occasion on which the film is displayed in Great Britain either to exhibitors or to the public, and being the first of a series of public exhibitions of the film held on a number of consecutive days :

The expression " maker " in relation to any film means the person by whom the arrangement necessary for the production of the film are undertaken:

The expression "producer" in relation to any film means the person responsible for the organisation and direction of the scenes to be depicted on the film :

The expression "renting" in relation to films means renting or otherwise issuing films or exhibitors at a rent or for other consideration, or making other arrangements with exhibitors for the exhibition thereof :

The expression "acquire" in relation to a renter includes the making or obtaining possession of films for the purpose of renting them :

The expression "length" in relation to a film means the total length of film as offered for projection at public exhibitions thereof :

The expression "theatre" includes any premises in respect of which a licence is required to be issued under the Cinematograph Act, 1909, or would be so required if the film were an inflammable film, except that it does not include—

(a) Any church, chapel or other place of religious worship, or any hall or other premises used in connection with and for the purposes of any such church, chapel, or place of religious worship, unless the number of preformances (exclusive of religious services) at any church, chapel, place, or premises, which consist of or comprise the exhibition of registered films exceed six in any year ending on the thirtieth day of September, or

(b) Any premises performance at which consist partly of the exhibitions of films, but so that at no one performance in the year does the total length of the registered film or films exhibited exceed two thousand feet.

(2) Where compliance on the part of a renter or exhibitor with the provisions of this Act as to quota was not commercially practicable by reason of the character of the British films available or the excessive cost of such films, non-compliance with those provisions on that ground shall for the purposes of this Act be treated as due to reasons beyond his control.

(3) Anything required or authorised under this Act to be done by or to the Board of Trade may be done by or to the President or secretary or assistant secretary of the Board, or any person authorised in that behalf by the President of the Board.

33.—Short title, extent and commencement. (1) This Act may be cited as the Cinematograph Films Act, 1927.

(2) This Act shall not extend to Northern Ireland, and for the purposes of the Government of Ireland Act, 1920, the enactment of legislation for purposes similar to the purposes of this Act shall not be deemed to be beyond the powers of the Parliament of Northern Ireland by reason only that such legislation may affect trade with places outside Northern Ireland.

(3) This Act shall come into operation on the first day of January, nineteen hundred and twenty eight.

(4) Part I. and Part II. of this Act shall continue in force until the thirtieth day of September, nineteen hundred and thirty-eight, and no longer.

SCHEDULE I.

	Maximum Fee. £ s.
On an application for the registration of a film	1 1
On an application for a renter's licence	5 5
On an application for an exhibitor's licence	1 1

For each theatre in respect of which a licence is applied for.

SCHEDULE II.

Renters' Quota.		Per cent.	Exhibitors' Quota.		Per cent
Year ending March 31, 1929	...	7½	Year ending Sept. 30, 1929	...	5
,, ,, 1930–31	...	10	,, ,, 1930–31	...	7½
,, ,, 1932	...	12½	,, ,, 1932	...	10
,, ,, 1933	...	15	,, 1933	...	12½
,, ,, 1934–35	...	17½	,, 1934–35	...	15
,, ,, 1936–38	...	20	, 1936–38	...	20

THE FINEST WORKS ON
inematography

Here is a list of the finest books yet written on Kinematography in all of its many aspects. No theatre projectionist or sound engineer should be without them.

●

Modern Minature Cameras. By Robert M. Fanstone, A.R.P.S. Contains everything that the amateur or professional photographer will want to know. Well illustrated. (1934.) **3/10.**

Kinematograph Trade Accounts. Book 1, Exhibitors' Accounts. By Charles H. Travis, F.C.A. Essential to the successful running of a kinema. (1928. **5/4.**

The Complete Projectionist. By R. Howard Cricks, A.R.P.S. A guide to kinema operating. A book that every projectionist and kinema engineer needs daily. Fully illustrated. Second Edition. (1937). **5/4.**

Kinematograph Trade Accounts. Book 2, Renters' Accounts. By Charles H. Travis, F.C.A. Deals with the subject in a comprehensive manner. **7/10.**

Kinematograph Trade Accounts. Book 3, Producers' Accounts and Organisation. By Charles H. Travis, F.C.A. An invaluable book. **7/10.**

Commercial Cinematography. By George H. Sewell, F.A.C.I. Describes the elementary principles of successful film making of business undertakings. (1934.) **7/10.**

Stage Lighting; Principles and Practice. By C. H. Ridge and F. S. Alfred, with an Introduction by Herbert M. Prentice. The treatment of stage lighting in this book is essentially practical, but the artistic side is always prominent. For both professional and amateur electricians the book is an invaluable guide. **7/10.**

Sound-Film Reproduction. By G. F. Jones, (Consulting Sound Engineer). This hand-book is intended to appeal to cinema managers and operators, and to others who are interested in the technique of the subject. Contents : General Survey, Details of Apparatus ; Operation and Maintenance ; Early Systems and Modern Installations ; Some Points in Design ; Future Prospects. (1931.) **3/9.**

Talking Pictures and Acoustics. By C. M. R. Balbi, A.M.I.E.E., A.C.G.I., with a foreword By Sir Oliver Lodge. An exhaustive study of the history of the whole subject, with chapters on Modern Commercial Recording Apparatus ; Talking Picture Systems ; Acoustics ; Cinema Power Plant, etc. (1931,) **7/10.**

Talking Pictures. By Bernard Brown, B.Sc. Contains full details of production and projection of talking films and the installation of plant ; expert advice for the operator and manager, and authoritative information of studio and theatre acoustics. Second Edition. (1932,) **13/-.**

Servicing Sound Motion Picture Equipment. By James R. Cameron. The Projectionist's up-to-date pocket guide. Third Edition, enlarged and revised. (1936.) **18/6.**

Sound Motion Pictures From the Laboratory to the Presentation. By Harold B. Franklin. (1929.) **18/6.**

Cameron's '' Encyclopaedia on Sound Motion Pictures.'' 336 pages crammed full of Motion picture facts. What you want to know in this book. (1930). **18/6.**

Richardson's Bluebook of Projection. A complete guide and textbook on motion picture projection and sound reproduction. Sixth Edition. (1935). Illustrated. **23/-.**

Sound Equipment, Motion Picture Projection— Public Address Systems. By James R. Cameron. Claimed to be the standard authority on the subject. Sixth Edition. (1936.) **25/6.**

Motion Pictures with Sound. By James R. Cameron, with Introduction by William Fox (President of Fox Film Corporation). Contains nothing but '' Sound Picture '' information. 400 pages. Over 150 illustrations. (1929.) **25/6.**

Motion Picture Photography. By Carl L. Gregory, F.R.P.S. Second Edition. (1927). **30/9.**

Prices quoted include postage.

IN THE COURTS

COURTS

A Summary of Leading Cases of the Year

INDEX

NOTE—Only cases of general interest, involving a principle of wide application or establishing precedents likely to affect the whole Trade, have been included in the following pages.

In the Courts

BREACH OF REGULATIONS.

Padlocked Exit.—Changes in the staff personnel of the Supershow, Wandsworth, shortly after a second summons had been served for a breach of conditions attached to kinema licence were told at South Western Police Court. Mr. Platts Mills (defending) admitted that Supershows, Ltd., only a short time previously had been fined for a similar offence. As soon as the second summons was served on the company, the manager immediately resigned and the employee who had been responsible for locking the door while a show was in progress had been dismissed. Since then the entire staff of the kinema has been changed. For the L.C.C. it was said that the door was found locked 20 minutes before the show was due to end. It was stated that the clock in the hall of the kinema had been 20 minutes fast, and the door was locked in error. The company were fined £7 and ordered to pay £3 3s. 6d. costs.

No B.O.T. Licence.—Joseph Petters was fined £5 and five guineas costs on January 16 at Portsmouth for exhibiting registered films at the Queen's, Portsmouth, without the Board of Trade licence on December 3, at which date, it was alleged, he was the proprietor of the kinema. F. E. Blagg, who prosecuted, said that Petters had never held a Board of Trade licence, which was necessary under the Kinematograph Act, 1927. The previous licence in respect of the kinema was held by Lilian Sarah Scott, whom Petters married, but Mrs. Petters died last May. W.A. Way, who defended, argued that defendant was not the proprietor of the kinema, although he had been left an interest in it under his wife's will. Only the proprietor of the kinema could hold the Board of Trade licence, and Mr. Way's contention was that Petters did not carry on the business.

" A " Film Prosecution.—For showing an " A " film to children under the age of sixteen without the consent of the Watch Committee, the Ecclesall and Endcliffe Picture Palace Co., Ltd., and William Henry Rodgers, their manager at the Greystones Picture Palace, Sheffield, were each fined £2 10s. and costs at the Sheffield City Police Court. The film in question was Tom Walls in " Fighting Stock." Two girls (one aged 13 and the other 14) were challenged. When one of the girls replied 14, she was told, " You had better go in with somebody else." A man who was standing by said, " You can go in with me," and they went in together. For the defence it was suggested that the two girls got in by a trick, persuading someone to take them in.

Unlicensed Child Act.—H. Winocour and Graham Young, manager of the Embassy, Shawlands, were fined £3 and £2 at the Glasgow Central Police Court for having had a four-year-old girl impersonating Shirley Temple without a theatre licence. It was stated that it never occurred to Mr. Winocour that a music-hall licence would be required for this special occasion.

Studio Safety Regulations.—At Feltham court Warner Brothers-First National Film Productions, Ltd., were fined £10 for a breach of the film safety regulations—allowing waste and completed film to be stored in a room not set apart for that purpose.

Mr. C. P. Gourley, for the Home Office, said that after a fire at the studios a quantity of film in excess of that allowed by the regulations had been left in the cutting-room instead of being put away in the store-room. Mr. Vernon Gattie expressed the company's regret and said : " The fact that the regulations were not observed did not cause the fire. On the day of the fire, a new film had been shot, and it was waiting inspection by the managing director before being put away."

The scrap film was not transferred to the store-room because it was being sorted for a film library.

Smoking in Projection Room.—Although warning notices were exhibited forbidding smoking in the vicinity of the operating-room, neglect by an assistant operator to obey the instruction led to his employer, Harry Willoughby, licensee and manager of the Victory Kinema, Miles Platting, Manchester, being fined £10 at the Manchester City Police Court on April 8 for a breach of the Cinematograph Act. William Sullivan, the assistant operator, was summoned for " aiding and abetting." This latter summons was dismissed, the magistrate holding that the assistant operator could not be held to have aided and abetted in an offence which the occupier was charged with permitting, notwithstanding that Sullivan was the person who smoked. The regulations made only the occupier responsible for any breach of them.

QUOTA PROSECUTIONS.

Quota Charge Dismissed.—That his company would always like to show British pictures, but that they had a difficulty in getting enough of a high standard, was stated by a witness called by the defence in a prosecution brought by the Board of Trade at North London Police Court. The Board has summoned Kingsland Pictures, Ltd., of 31-4, Stoke Newington Road, N.16, for failing to show the stipulated quota of British films at the Plaza Theatre, Kingsland Road, Dalston. Norman Hart, solicitor, who appeared for the company, pleaded not guilty and said that his defence rested on Section 32, Sub-section 2 of the Act, which laid it down that where compliance with the regulations was not commercially practicable by reason of the character of the British films available or the excessive cost of such films non-compliance was, for the purpose of this Act, to be treated as due to reasons beyond his control. In this case the defendants had shown over 14 per cent. and hardly anything below the 15 per cent. The position here was that there were nine other kinemas in this district and they "barred" each other. The magistrate said that he did not think the prosecution had made out their case, and dismissed the summons.

Quota Oversight.—J. Wellesley Orr, the Manchester stipendiary magistrate, on September 30, imposed a fine of £50 on Associated British Cinemas, Ltd., of London, for not showing a sufficient quota of British films at the New Royal Kinema, Openshaw, Manchester, in the year ended September 30, 1935. Eight guineas costs were also allowed. It was stated that the "long" British films shown totalled 13.48 per cent., and the quota of "all" British films used was 11.52 per cent. On behalf of the defendant company, it was pleaded the mistake arose through the manager of the theatre leaving before he sent his quarterly returns to head office. The new manager did not know that the returns had not been made and the head office overlooked the fact, not finding out the error until the end of the year.

£200 Quota Fine.—For failing to furnish the Board of Trade with the required particulars under the Cinematograph Films Act, 1927, in respect of the Empire Theatre, Heywood, Lancs, William Constantine, proprietor, and his son Kenneth William Constantine, manager, were each fined £100 and £5 5s. costs by Mr. Dummett at Bow Street. There were several convictions for similar offences against both defendants, it was stated, and the magistrate said it was one of the worst cases he had ever heard. The defendants he added, had paid no regard to the requirements of the law.

BREACH OF CONTRACT.

Actress's Contract.—The hearing was concluded on October 19 in the King's Bench Division before Mr. Justice Branson, after a hearing over several days, of an action by Warner Bros. Pictures, Inc., against Miss Bette Davis, for an injunction to restrain her from appearing in any stage or motion picture productions without their consent during the currency of her contract with them. It was suggested by the plaintiffs that Miss Davis had no legal ground for repudiating her contract and that she desired to do so merely because another producer, Mr. Toeplitz, had offered her a larger salary. Miss Davis said that the plaintiffs had broken their contract, that they wished her to play more than six hours a day, and that they either gave her too many films or too few, and that they required her to do unreasonable things. She also contended that the Court could not enforce a prohibitive clause to a contract of this description.

Mr. Justice Branson, giving judgment, said no authority had been cited in support of the contention that the contract was unlawful, as being in restraint of trade. With regard to the question of whether the Courts would enforce specific performance of contracts containing negative covenants, his lordship said the conclusion to be drawn from the authorities was that where the provisions of the negative covenants would not amount to a decree of specific performance of the positive covenants, or a decree under which the defendant must either remain idle or perform the services,

the Court would enforce these covenants. The period of the injunction should give reasonable protection and no more, to the plaintiffs. If the injunction were in force during the continuance of the contract, or for three years, whichever was the shorter, that would substantially meet the case. Judgment was accordingly entered for Warner Brothers, with costs.

Damages for Producers.—Frances Day was ordered to pay £1,530 damages to Gaumont-British, and costs of arbitration, in her contract dispute with the company. This was the decision following a special case which was stated by Walter Monckton as arbitrator before Mr. Justice Porter in the King's Bench Division. For Miss Day it was submitted that the contract was unenforceable because it imposed no obligation on Gaumont-British to provide the artiste with any work at all and it contained what a judge had called "servile" incidents. F. Van den Berg, for G.-B., argued that no one could really say this contract was void for want of mutuality, and the arbitrator had found that it was not unreasonable. Nor could it be said to be void as against public policy. Mr. Justice Porter, giving judgment, said he could not regard the contract as void for want of mutuality. Nor could he say it was void as against public policy. He held it was a valid contract. They were entitled to put the lady "off salary" until the completion of "Jack of All Trades," in which she had failed to make ready to perform. It would be extending the law to hold that Gaumont-British were not entitled to claim damages as well.

Script Writers' Claim.—Judgment for the plaintiffs was entered by Mr. Justice Goddard for £541 9s. damages and costs in the action brought against Criterion Film Productions, Ltd., by Akos Tolnay and James Bailiff Williams in respect of a contract by which plaintiffs were to write the scenario, synopsis, treatment and shooting script of "The Amateur Gentleman." Plaintiffs alleged that after they had done a considerable amount of work the defendants wrongfully repudiated the contract, with the result that the plaintiffs lost screen publicity and the balance of £350 which was to have been paid to them under the agreement. Defendants alleged breaches of contract by the plaintiffs in not delivering material according to time, and they counter claimed damages in respect of the additional expense to which they had been put. Plaintiffs denied that they had broken the contract. Mr. Justice Goddard found that defendants had undoubtedly committed a breach of the contract, in respect of which the plaintiffs were entitled to recover the balance of £350 less £8 11s. which the defendants paid for the services of a typist. Dealing with the question of damages for the loss of screen publicity, he observed : " I don't doubt that loss of publicity to an author is serious. One way in which the plaintiffs can expect employment is by getting their names before the public." The damage in this respect was assessed at £100 for each of the plaintiffs.

Furnishing Contract.—An action brought by Bulman Jupiter Screen Co., Ltd., Shaftesbury Avenue, W., in the King's Bench Division on January 27 against Associated British Cinemas, Ltd., Golden Square, and Theatre Equipment, Ltd., of Wardour Street, for alleged breach of contract, was dismissed. The defence was that there was no binding agreement such as the plaintiffs set up. The action arose out of an arrangement said to have been made in 1932 when Bulman Jupiter Screen Co., Ltd., bought all the shares in Carpets and Curtains, Ltd. They alleged that they did so on the faith of an undertaking that the defendants would continue to give their work to Carpets and Curtains, Ltd., as they had done before, and that, in fact, they continued to do so for twenty months. Mr. Justice Lewis held that there was no binding contract of the kind alleged by the plaintiffs. It was unfortunate for Mr. Bundy, but there was no agreement binding either Associated British Cinemas, Ltd., or Theatre Equipment, Ltd., to give further work to Carpets and Curtains, Ltd.

Kinema Share Action.—In the High Court on November 9, judgment was delivered by S. R. C. Bosanquet, K.C., Official Referee, on a claim by Carol Adolf Seebold, of Bedford Row, Worthing, for damages estimated at £7,600 for a breach of a contract entered into in 1934 with Mr. and Mrs. Louis Morris, of Forty Lane, Wembley, for the purchase of the whole of the share capital in Plaza (Worthing), Ltd. According to the plaintiff, he agreed to pay £20,000 for the shares, 16,000 at £1 each. He paid a deposit of £2,000, but the defendants refused to complete the transaction and transferred the shares to a Mr. Weston. Plaintiff pleaded that had he obtained the control of the Plaza he would have been able to hire films for his three other kinemas on far more favourable terms than with the Plaza as a rival enterprise. Plaintiff had already obtained judgment in the King's Bench Division on the question of liability for breach of contract, and the Official Referee now gave judgment on the question of damages.

The Official Referee said that taking into account all the circumstances, he (the Official Referee) assessed the damages at £3,000, with costs.

ADVERTISING.

Publicity Prosecution.—A publicity stunt in connection with a film resulted in a prosecution at Clerkenwell Police Court. Bertie Horace Berners Upcher, of Hopton Road, Streatham, was summoned for using a motor car for the purpose of advertisement in Tottenham Court Road on November 28. Rex Publicity Service, Ltd., of Golden Square, Westminster, were summoned for causing the motor-car to be so used. Charles Henry Johnson, of Arlington Road, Camden Town, was summoned for unlawfully wearing a fancy dress within a scheduled street mainly for the purpose of advertisement. Rex Publicity Service, Ltd., were summoned for causing the dress or costume to be worn. The summonses were taken out under provisions of the London Traffic Regulations. All the defendants tendered a plea of guilty.

P.C. Ledger said the motor-car, driven by Upcher, was draped with a white sheet on which were the words, "The New Adventures of Tarzan, now at the Rialto, Coventry Street." Sitting on the car was the defendant Johnson, dressed in a skin, to represent an ape. Upcher said, "I am delivering these envelopes to different kinemas." Counsel said Rex Publicity

Service, Ltd., took full responsibility. The magistrate said he would not inflict a penalty on the other defendants, these summonses being dismissed under the Probation of Offenders Act. The company would be fined 40s. on the summons relating to fancy dress.

TRADE DISPUTES.

Claim Against Laboratory.—A claim in respect of part of a film negative which was alleged to have been spoiled during development was made in an action heard by Mr. Justice du Parcq in the King's Bench Division on March 3. The plaintiffs were Carnival Films, Ltd., Shaftesbury Avenue, W., and the defendants Standard Kine Laboratories, Ltd., Mortimer Street, London. The defendants were not represented. Valentine Holmes, for the plaintiffs, said Carnival Films, Ltd., produced a colour film "Railroad Rhythm" and employed the defendants to develop and print the negative. It was alleged that the work was done negligently and part of the negative was spoiled. Three scenes had to be retaken, and the cost, including development and printing, was £952 5s. 11d. There was a counterclaim by the defendants for £190 16s. 1d. for work done, and the plaintiffs had agreed to give credit for that amount. Mr. Justice du Parcq entered judgment for the plaintiffs for £761 9s. 10d. with costs.

An Author's Rights.—Before Mr. Justice Greaves-Lord in the King's Bench Division, Garry Allighan sued Producers' Distributing Co. (U.K.), Ltd., of Great Newport Street, Westminster, claiming £400 as money due under an agreement with defendants or as damages. Defendants contended that under the terms of the agreement, the rights of the story had reverted to Mr. Allighan, and they were accordingly not liable to pay. Mr. Justice Greaves-Lord gave judgment for defendants with costs.

CONTEMPT OF COURT.

Newsreel Contempt of Court.—Rules *nisi* of attachment for contempt of court, which had been granted in respect of newspaper reports and a newsreel account of the incident at Constitution Hill on July 16 were argued on July 29 before a King's Bench Divisional Court, composed of Justices Swift, Humphreys and Goddard. The respondents, who appeared to show cause against the rules being made absolute, were the editors and proprietors of the "Evening News" and "Daily Express"; J. H. Hutchison, manager of Hendon Central Cinema, Ltd. (proprietors of the Ambassador Cinema, Hendon Central), and Hendon Central Cinema, Ltd.; and Gaumont-British Distributors, Ltd. The facts, as set out in an affidavit by Mr. Kerstein, solicitor to McMahon, were that in the newsreel of the Gaumont-British News, exhibited at the Ambassador on July 18, there was a caption containing the words, "Attempt on the King's Life," and, in the commentary there were words to the effect that a revolver had been aimed by a man at His Majesty and that the revolver had been knocked out of the man's hand. Outside the kinema was a poster containing the words : "Assassination Attempt."

Mr. Beyfus read an affidavit by Mark Ostrer, chairman of the directors of the Gaumont-British Company, expressing profound regret for what had been done, and the company's sincere apologies. Mr. Hutchison was a layman who, on the Thursday evening, received a poster precisely similar to the posters in the street in which his kinema was situated. It was in those circumstances that Mr. Hutchinson put the poster out, and the Court was asked to say that, while it did not excuse him, it did palliate his conduct. Mr. Van den Berg, K.C., for Gaumont-British Distributors, Ltd., expressed the sincere apology of his clients for what had happened. Giving judgment, Mr. Justice Swift remarked : "The film is no more immune from the rules which deal with contempt of Court than is a newspaper. The proprietors of kinemas and distributors of films must realise that they must take care, when they want to produce these sensational films, to use language in describing them which is not likely to bring about any derangement in the carriage of justice. He took the view that Mr. Hutchison and the Hendon Central Cinema, Ltd., may be dealt with, after the warning which has been given, very leniently, and no more will be required of them except that they pay the costs. So far as Gaumont-British Distributors, Ltd., are concerned, the case is more serious. They distributed this film—or, rather, they distributed this caption and poster —not only to Mr. Hutchison and his kinemas, but to 262 other kinemas throughout the country, They will be fined £50 and will pay the costs."

COPYRIGHT.

Title Dispute.—An *ex parte* motion by Frederick Roy Tuckett for an interim injunction to restrain Radio Pictures, Ltd., from showing their film, " Wings Over Africa," was granted by Mr. Justice Lewis in the Vacation Court.

F. Ashe Lincoln, for plaintiff, said the action was for damages for breach of copyright ; alternatively, it was in respect of " passing-off," and there was a claim for an injunction.

Plaintiff in an affidavit stated in 1933 he made a film of the first regular mail flight undertaken by Imperial Airways from Croydon to Cape Town and called it " Wings Over Africa." The defendants had produced a film with the same title which they intended to show on Wednesday, September 23.

GENERAL.

Engine Noise.—In the action of interdict and damages raised by Miss Janet Forbes (Inverurie) against the Inverurie Picture House, Ltd., Sheriff Laing awarded damages of £150, but in the matter of interdict allows the defenders an opportunity of taking steps to meet the complaint of the pursuer in regard to the noise caused by an engine in the kinema. The main points in plaintiff's case were that the defenders had encroached on a mutual lane between their ground and hers ; that the proximity of the kinema restricted her light and air space ; and that the noise of the engine constituted a nuisance to herself and her tenants. The Sheriff found that defenders had encroached on Miss Forbes' property. Regarding the noise of the engine, there is no doubt that it constituted a nuisance, but, he pointed out, the kinema is a place of public entertainment, and he was therefore reluctant to take a course which would interfere with the pleasure and enjoyment of the public. He therefore allowed a period of 40 days to permit the defenders to carry out certain suggestions for reducing the noise.

The question of expenses was reserved.

Kinema Lease Claim.—The Court of Appeal (Lords Justices Slesser, Romer and Greene), on March 6, dismissed the appeal of the Union Cinemas Co., Ltd., and Oxford and Berkshire Cinemas, Ltd., from the judgment of Mr. Justice Farwell on November 21 last on a summons taken out by Plaza Theatre (Maidenhead), Ltd., to determine the rent due to them from the appellants for the Plaza, Rialto and Picture Theatre, Maidenhead. At the hearing it was explained that the question turned on the construction of a lease by respondents to the Union Co. The second appellants were the assignees of the lease and controlled the three theatres. By the lease, the rent payable was £216 13s. 4d. per calendar month, with an addition of 2½ per cent. of the nett takings over £700 a week. If the Rialto or Picture theatres were sold while the lease was running the rent was to be increased to £238 6s. 8d., but the additional rent would not be payable. A proviso said that the lessee should have the right to close the Picture Theatre as a kinema, and during the closure the increased rent should not be payable on the remaining theatres, but the 2½ per cent. would be payable if the Plaza and Rialto takings exceeded £700 a week. The Rialto and Picture theatres were sold to Oxford and Berks Cinemas on October 1, 1934, and the respondents claimed that the rent of £238 6s. 8d. became payable from that date. Mr. Justice Farwell admitted the claim and held that a further proviso was meaningless and could be disregarded. Mr. Lionel Cohen, K.C., for the appellants submitted that as there was no sale that severed the ownership of the three theatres the additional rent did not become payable. Lord Justice Slesser said the proviso did not apply and the appeal must be dismissed. Lords Justices Romer and Greene agreed.

K.R.S. Withdraws Charges.—Clifford Kemp, of Leeds, appeared at Marlborough Street Police Court on October 14, to answer a summons for having received certain money for and on account of divers limited companies he unlawfully and fraudulently converted the money to his own use and benefit at Wardour Street, W. G. D. Roberts, on behalf of the prosecutors, the Kinematograph Renters' Society of Great Britain and Ireland, 30, Old Compton Street, W., applied for the summons to be withdrawn. He said that since process was applied for further information had been given to the prosecutors which was not available when process was granted. They now recognised that no suggestion could be made against the defendant, and desired to express profound regret for the trouble that he had been caused.

Ceiling Collapse.—E. Haigh and Son, owners of the Tatler News Theatre, Church Street, Liverpool, at Liverpool Assizes claimed £3,161 18s. 7d. expenses and loss (including £547 2s. 8d. paid in settlement of injury claims arising out of the accident), against Honeywill and Stein, Ltd., engineers and theatre acoustic specialists, of New London Street, London, and John Rimmer, building contractor, of Low Hill, Liverpool. Third parties to the action were A. R. Ball and Co., Ltd., plasterers, of Oil Street, Liverpool. The action was the sequel to the collapse of a part of the ceiling during a performance, resulting in the injury of six people. The defendants said the responsibility rested with the plasterers. No evidence was called, as a settlement was reached on terms which were not disclosed in court.

Exhibitor's Technical Offence.—Benjamin Kaye (41), kinema proprietor, of Stamford Hill, London, was sentenced at the Central Criminal Court on October 26 to fourteen days' imprisonment and immediately released. Kaye was found guilty of applying to his own use the lease of the Globe, Plumstead, with intent to defraud, and obtaining by false pretences £500 from George Ravenshere. During the hearing the judge directed the jury that there was no evidence on a further charge of applying to his own use £3,798 belonging to Kaye's Cinemas, Ltd., of which he was a director. Kaye was said to be a man of good character. The Common Serjeant said he considered the conversion of the lease was merely a technical offence. With regard to the charge of obtaining money by false pretences, "it is clear," he said, "that all you have done was to exaggerate the profits, and I propose to pass a sentence of 14 days' imprisonment, dating from the beginning of the sessions, which will mean your immediate discharge."

Patron's Accident.—Judge Clarke Williams, K.C., at Bridgend County Court, awarded £100 damages and costs against the Bridgend Cinemas, Ltd., in an action arising from an accident alleged to have happened at the Pavilion Cinema, Bridgend, to Ethel Browning, the claimant, of the Petrol Filling Station, Laleston. It was alleged that when plaintiff visited the Pavilion the kinema was in darkness, and when ascending some steps the floor gave way beneath her. Plaintiff fell with great violence to the floor, and but for the prompt action of her companion would have fallen through the hole. Counsel said the defence denied responsibility, but plaintiff contended that Manager Isaacs told her he would accept complete responsibility.

George Rufus Isaacs, the manager, said the alleged large hole was only 9 in. deep. She might have slipped on the step and hit her side against a seat.

Injured Artiste.—Judgment for Miss Peggy Crawford, film actress, for £126 19s. against Criterion Film Productions, Ltd., was given by Mr. Justice Porter in the King's Bench Division on November 16. Miss Crawford appeared in the film "The Amateur Gentleman." She sued the company and Gunther Krampf, the cameraman, claiming damages in respect of injury to her eyes by the studio lights. Mr. Justice Porter found that the lighting was not of supra-normal power or intensity. The defendant company knew the dangers of the lighting, and were prepared to risk temporary damage to the performers' eyes to obtain a good picture. He also found that the danger of "Kleig eye" was not generally known. There was no negligence by Mr. Krampf. Judgment was entered for Miss Crawford against the film company, and also for Mr. Krampf, with costs.

Employee's Injury.—At Sheffield County Court, May 7, Douglas William Barton sued Associated British Cinemas, Ltd., for compensation arising out of an accident. It was stated that the applicant went to the L.M.S. railway station on instructions to collect a film which had come by train. As he was leaving the station he slipped on the edge of the pavement and broke his thigh. He was in hospital for a time. Defence suggested that plaintiff suffered from a lack of muscular control. Compensation at the rate of 16s. 10d. a week was awarded.

Licensee's Responsibility.—At the Widnes Police Court, on March 5, T. Swale, solicitor, asked for the music and dancing licence of the Regal, Widnes, to be transferred to Robert Wilkinson and that he be given the renewal of the kinema licence. The hearing had been adjourned as a result of H. Reeves, a former manager of the kinema, raising an objection to the transfer. Mr. Reeves told the court that he was dismissed from the managership without due cause or reason, and that he was entitled to £26 from the owners. He also objected to the theatre licence being in his name after he had been discharged, and that on the Saturday there was no one in the kinema with power from that court to carry on. He would have been responsible had anything happened. Mr. Swale said that the owner or occupier would have been responsible if there had been any infringements of the kinema licence. So far as the music and dancing licence was concerned, the holder would have been responsible. The transfer of the licence was approved.

Film Smuggling.—Mrs. Rose Barone, whose address was given at Mullagh, Co. Cavan, was fined £100 at Dundalk District Court before District Justice Curry with the attempted evasion of Customs duty on six rolls of kinematograph film. J. B. Hamill, State solicitor, prosecuting, said that the defendant was a passenger in a mail train from Northern Ireland. On arrival at Dundalk, which was in the Free State, in a parcel behind her, a Customs officer found a roll of film, and on examining her coat, two rolls of film sewn in the lining. In the office three further rolls were produced.

D. O'Hagan, for the defence, said that the defendant and her husband ran a travelling kinematograph show, and she was offered the films at a cheap rate and bought them. Then she foolishly yielded to the temptation to save the duty. Mr. Hamill said the duty was at the rate of 1d. per foot, and as there were about 5,300 ft. of film, it would mean about £22 had it been declared.

Judge on Film Contracts.—In the King's Bench Division, on December 16, before Mr. Justice Greaves-Lord, Mrs. Betty Balfour Campbell Tyrie (professionally known as Betty Balfour), of West Heath Road, Hampstead, sued Twickenham Film Studios, Ltd., of Wardour Street, W.1, in respect of payments due to her for her part in the film "Squibs." The main question was whether, in arriving at the sum due, the defendants were entitled to deduct the cost of all copies of the film, or only the copies made for sale abroad. For the plaintiff, Mr. John W. Morris, K.C., said she was to receive £1,000 in five instalments of £200 each, during production, plus five per cent. of the gross bookings from theatres and foreign sales abroad, less the cost of copies and agents' commission on sales abroad of 15 per cent. The film was distributed through Gaumont-British, and was generally released in September, 1935.

Giving judgment, Mr. Justice Greaves-Lord said that his view of the construction of the contract was that "cost of copies" meant the cost of all copies which were necessary for the purpose of producing the "gross bookings" and for the purpose of making particular sales. But that cost must be limited to the actual cost of copies actually made, in connection with the sales and bookings, and no more. So far as the rest was concerned, his Lordship directed that interest be paid at 4 per cent. per annum on amounts the payment of which had been delayed.

FINANCIAL SECTION

New Companies Registered during the Year.

DECEMBER, 1935.

Name.	Capital.	Nature of Business.	Registered Office.
Associated Cinema Holdings, Ltd.	£160,000 in £1 shares ...	Kinema Proprietors ...	66, Coleman Street, E.C.2.
Associated Realist Film Producers, Ltd.	£100 in £1 shares.........	Film Producers	33, Soho Square, W.1.
David A. Bader, Ltd. ...	£1,000 in £1 shares	Film Producers and Agents.	—
Educational and General Services for Cinema and Radio Supplies, Ltd.	Limited by guarantee...	To promote the exhibition of films in schools, etc.	Solicitors: Richards, Butler, Stokes and Woodham Smith, 88, Leadenhall Street, E.C.
Faraday Film Studios, Ltd.	£100 in £1 shares.........	Builders and Lessors of Studios.	Solicitors: L. Bingham & Co., 3, Crown Court, E.C.2.
Film Transport Services (North Western) Ltd.	£5,000 in £1 shares	Public Carriers	Park Street, Motherwell.
Rex Gerard Productions, Ltd.	£100 in £1 shares.........	Kinema Proprietors ...	586, Barton Arcade Chambers, Deansgate, Manchester.
Gordon Theatres, Ltd. ...	£2,000 in 2,250 "A" ord. shares of 2s. each, 700 "B" ord. shares of £1 each, and 1075 6 p.c. cum. pref. shares of £1 each.	Kinema Proprietors ...	Regal Chambers, Ferensway, Hull.
Horsham Theatres, Ltd.	£1,000 in £1 shares	Kinema Proprietors ...	Solicitors: Bulcraig & Davis, Amberley House, Norfolk St., W.C.2.
Isis Cinemas, Ltd.	£1,000 in £1 shares	Kinema Proprietors ...	Solicitors: Bulcraig & Davis, Amberley House, Norfolk St., W.C.2.
Jameswood Press, Ltd. ...	£500 in £1 shares	Printers and Advertising Contractors.	—
London Opera Films, Ltd.	£5,000 in £1 shares	Film Producers	Solicitors: Allen & Overy, 3, Finch Lane, E.C.
Palace Cinema (Bawtry), Ltd.	£500 in £1 shares.........	To acquire a Kinema.	4, Tickhill Street, Balby, Doncaster.
Perranporth Pavilion, Ltd.	£20,000 in £1 shares (5,000 5% cum. pref.).	To acquire a Kinema.	70a, Basinghall Street, E.C.
Queen's Cinema (Nottingham), Ltd.	£2,000 in £1 shares	Kinema Proprietors ...	26, Park Row, Nottingham.
Rawtenstall Cinemas, Ltd.	£100 in £1 shares.........	Kinema Proprietors ...	Picture House, Bacup Road, Rawtenstall.
Regal Pictures (Lanark) Ltd.	£15,000 in £1 shares ...	Kinema Proprietors ...	156, St. Vincent Street, Glasgow, C.2.
Rosumcliff Cinemas, Ltd.	£10,000 in £1 shares, (4,000 ord. and 6,000 6% accum. pref.).	To erect a Kinema	Rosumcourt, Bloxwich Road, Leamore, Walsall.
Sirec Films (Britain, Ltd.)	£150 in £1 shares.........	Film Agents	Kent House, 87, Regent Street, W.1.
Sloane Productions, Ltd.	£500 in 10s. shares (500 ord. and 500 "A" ord.)	—	Solicitors: J. D. Langton & Passmore, 8, Bolton Street, W.1.
Solar Cinemas, Ltd.	£2,000	Kinema Proprietors ...	44, Corporation Street, Belfast.
Somlo Films, Ltd.	£1,000 in £1 shares	Film Renters	—

Name.	Capital.	Nature of Business.	Registered Office.
South Downs Cinemas, Ltd.	£5,000 in £1 shares (1,000 5% cum. pref. 3,900 6% cum. pref. ord. and 100 def. ord.)	To acquire Kinemas ...	Solicitors: F. G. Allen & Sons, 15, Landport Terrace, Portsmouth.
Stanmore Productions, Ltd.	£100 in £1 shares	Film Producers	—
Twentieth Century Cinemas, Ltd.	£240,000 in 240,000 6% cum. par pref. shares of 10s. and 480,000 shares of 5s. each.	To acquire Kinemas ...	14-15, Lancaster Place, Strand, W.C.2.
Vicky Publications, Ltd.	£200 in £1 shares	Cartoon Producers	91, Regent Street, W.1
Welwyn Studios, Ltd. ...	£1,000 in £1 shares	Film Studios	—

JANUARY, 1936.

Name.	Capital.	Nature of Business.	Registered Office.
Ace Studios Ltd.	£5,000 in 4,500 6% non-cum. par. pref. shares of £1 and 10,000 ord. shares of 1s.	Film Producers and Renters.	60–66, Wardour Street, W.1.
Alliance Cinemas, Ltd. ...	£100 in £1 shares	Kinema Proprietors ...	Solicitors: Bulcraig & Davies, Amberley House, Norfolk Street, W.C.2.
Avalon, Ltd.	£100 in £1 shares	Kinema Proprietors ...	—
Ayrshire Property Co., Ltd.	£1,000 in £1 shares	To erect kinemas	Royal Bank Buildings, Prestwick.
Berkley Film Productions, Ltd.	£100 in £1 shares	Film Producers	17, St. Swithin's Lane, E.C.4.
Bermingham, Burke & Coates, Ltd.	£100 in £1 shares	Kinema Proprietors ...	Solicitors: Godfrey Warr & Co., 19, Fenchurch Street, E.C.3.
Bi-Vision, Ltd.	£1,000 in 10,000 7% pref. and 10,000 def. shares of 1s.	Manufacturers of scientific apparatus.	Solicitors: Mead & Dennis, 8, Adam Street, W.C.2.
Broadway Cinema (Stoke) Ltd.	£3,000 in £1 shares	Kinema Proprietors ...	Heath Street, Hanley, Stoke on Trent.
Carlton (Harrow), Ltd. ...	£100 in £1 shares	Kinema Proprietors ...	Carlton Cinema, Harrow on the Hill.
Chiswick Productions (Cinema), Ltd	£100 in £1 shares	Kinema Proprietors ...	Solicitor: A. Robson, 1, Chiswick Common Road, Chiswick.
Cinema Development, Ltd.	£5,000 in £1 shares	Kinema Builders	Solicitors: Bulcraig & Davis, Amberley House, Norfolk Street, W.C.2.
Neville Clark Productions, Ltd.	£1,100 in 1,000 5% pref. shares of £1 each and 2,000 ord. shares of 1s. each.	Film Producers	12, Park Place, S.W.1.
C.M. Cinemas, Ltd.	£1,000 in £1 shares	Kinema Proprietors ...	Solicitors: M. A. Jacobs & Sons, 73-74, Jermyn Street, S.W.1.
Consett Cinemas, Ltd. ...	£50,000 in £1 shares (20,000 red. 6% cum. pref. and 30,000 ord.).	To acquire a kinema ...	Plaza Buildings, Consett, Durham.
Denham Laboratories, Ltd.	£100,000 in £1 shares (50,000 6% cum. par. pref. and 50,000 ord.).	Indicated by the title...	Solicitors: Slaughter & May, 18, Austin Friars, E.C
Denham Securities Ltd.	£52,500 in 45,000 6% cum. red. pref. shares of £1 and 150,000 ord. shares of 1s.	To finance Fim Production.	Solicitors: Kirklater & Paines, 2, Bond Court Walbrook, E.C.
Dofil, Ltd.	£5,000 in 4,750 5% cum. pref. shares of £1 each and 5,000 ord. shares of 1s. each.	Film Producers	5 & 6, Bucklersbury, E.C.4.
Dufay-Chromex, Ltd. ...	£750,000 in £1 shares (150,000 6% red. non-cum. second pref. and 500,000 ord.).	To amalgamate Dufay and Chromex	Solicitors: Stephenson, Harwood & Tatham, 16, Old Broad Street, E.C.4.
Essolds Theatre (Newcastle), Ltd.	£10,000 in £1 shares ...	Kinema Proprietors ...	Solicitors: Hannay & Hannay, South Shields.

Name.	Capital.	Nature of Business.	Registered Office.
Excelsior Productions, Ltd.	£500 in £1 shares	Film Producers	Solicitors: Ponsford & Devenish, 13–14, Walbrook, E.C.4.
Farnham Royal Super Cinemas, Ltd.	£7,000 in £1 shares	Kinema Proprietors	Solicitors: J. D. Langton & Passmore, 16, Tokenhouse Yard, E.C.
Harrison Film Productions, Ltd.	£100 in £1 shares	Film Producers	41, Moorfields, E.C.
Henley Cinematograph Co., Ltd.	£500 in 10,000 pref. and 10,000 ord. shares of 6d. each.	Film Exhibitors	17, Shaftesbury Avenue, Piccadilly, W.1.
Hinge's Cinemas, Ltd.	£5,000 in 5s. shares	Kinema Proprietors	Solicitors: Smirke & Thompson, Newcastle on Tyne.
Hope Bell Film Productions, Ltd.	£1,000 in £1 shares	Kinema Lessees	Solicitors: Amery Parkes & Co., 1, Arundel Street, W.C.2.
Hounslow West Super Cinemas, Ltd.	£7,500 in £1 shares	Kinema Proprietors	Solicitors: J. D. Langton & Passmore, 16, Tokenhouse Yard, E.C.2.
Industrial & Equitable Advertising Films, Ltd.	£100 in £1 shares	Film Producers	Secretary: H. J. M. Gregory, 20, Essex Street, W.C.2.
Invergordon Picture House, Ltd.	£1,200 in £1 shares (600 7% non-cum par. pref. and 600 ord.).	Kinema Proprietors	Royal Bank Buildings, Inverness.
Invincible Cinemas, Ltd.	£10,000 in £1 shares	Kinema Proprietors	—
Jacobean Productions Ltd.	£20,000 in 19,000 6% cum. pref. shares of £1 each and 20,000 founders shares of 1s. each.	Film Producers	—
Lamaright, Ltd.	£200 in 2s. shares	To erect kinemas	The Palace, Pilsley, Nr. Chesterfield.
La Scala Cinema (Dundee) Ltd.	£400 in £1 shares	To lease a kinema	
Montague Lyon, Ltd.	£500 in £1 shares	Variety Agents	York House, Lower Regent Street, S.W.1.
Majestic Cinema (Dundee) Ltd.	£400 in £1 shares	To lease a kinema	108, West Regent Street, Glasgow.
Max Factor, Hollywood & London (Sales), Ltd.	£10,000 in £1 shares	Manufacturers of cosmetics.	49, Old Bond Street, W.1.
McGookin Brothers, Ltd.	£1,500 in £1 shares	Kinema Proprietors	Irish Quarter, South Carrickfergus.
Odeon (Ashford), Ltd.	£10,000 in £1 shares (5,000 ord. and 5,000 6% cum. pref.).	Kinema Proprietors	39, Temple Row, Birmingham.
Odeon (Islington), Ltd.	£5,000 in £1 shares (2,500 ord. and 2,500 7% cum pref.).	Kinema Proprietors	39, Temple Row, Birmingham.
Palace (Chatham), Ltd.	£16,000 in 15,500 8% cum. pref. shares of £1 and 10,000 ord. shares of 1s.	Kinema Proprietors	Solicitors: Basset & Boucher, 156, High Street, Rochester.
Picture House (Goldthorpe), Ltd.	£1,000 in £1 shares	To aquire a kinema	4, Tickhill Road, Doncaster.
Picture Theatre Publicity, Ltd.	£1,000 in £1 shares	Advertising Specialists	—
Phoenix Theatre (Salisbury), Ltd.	£45,000 in £1 shares	Kinema Proprietors	Solicitors; Whitehead, Vizard & Venn, 35, The Canal, Salisbury.
Reunion Productions Distributions, Ltd.	£27,000 in 15,000 7% pref. and 10,000 ord. shares of £1 and 80,000 founders shares of 6d.	Film Producers and Distributors.	Solicitors: G. B. Morgan, 32, St. James's Street, S.W.1.
Savoy (Reading), Ltd.	£1,200 in £1 shares	Kinema Proprietors	Regency House, Room 21, Warwick Street, W.1.
St. Ives Cinemas (Cornwall), Ltd.	£100 in £1 shares	Kinema Proprietors	Scala High Street, St. Ives.
School Cine Equipments, Ltd.	£325 in £1 shares	Producers and dealers in Equipment.	7–9, James Street, Liverpool.

GOOD NEWS? BEST EVER—BRITISH PARAMOUNT !

Name.	Capital.	Nature of Business.	Registered Office.
Screen Services, Ltd. ...	£500 in £1 shares.........	Casting Agents............	———
Stedmans Cinematograph Laboratory, Ltd.	£1,200 in £1 shares	Film Manufacturers ...	———
Stella Pictures, Ltd........	£100 in £1 shares.........	Film Producers ...	58a Grays Inn Road, W.C.
Strand Cinema, Ltd. ...	£10,000 in £1 shares ...	Kinema Proprietors ...	———
Swansea Cinemas, Ltd. ...	£3,500 in £1 shares	Kinema Proprietors ...	Regal Cinema Woodfield Street, Morriston, Swansea.
Trafalgar Film Productions, Ltd.	25,000 in £1 shares	Film Producers	Marcol House, 289, Regent Street, W.1.
Viking Films, Ltd.........	£1,000 in 970 7½% red. pref. of 1s. each.	Film Producers	107, Shaftesbury Avenue, W.1.
Wombwell Entertainments, Ltd.	£3,200 in £1 shares	Kinema Proprietors ...	Stancliffe Grimethorpe, Barnsley, Yorks.
Worton Hall Studios, Ltd.	£10,000 in £1 shares ...	To acquire studios	Solicitors: F. M. Guedalla & Co., Grand Buildings, W.C.2.

FEBRUARY.

Name.	Capital.	Nature of Business.	Registered Office.
Amalgamated Productions, Ltd.	£1,000 in £1 shares ...	Film Agents	———
Blackfen Theatre Co., Ltd.	£5,000 in £1 shares ...	Kinema Proprietors ...	Solicitors: Kenneth Brown, Baker, Baker, Essex House, W.C.2.
Broadspread, Ltd.	£100 in 2,000 shares of 1s. each.	Film Producers	Solicitors: Montague & Cox & Cardale, 86, Queen Victoria Street, E.C.4.
Buckingham Film Productions, Ltd.	£25,000 in £1 shares ...	Film Producers	289, Regent Street, W.1
Cinema, Totnes, Ltd.	£100 in £1 shares.........	Kinema Proprietors ...	Solicitors: Shelly & Johns, Princess House, Plymouth.
Eastbourne Theatre, Ltd.	£4,000 in £1 shares ...	Kinema Proprietors ...	Solicitors: Davenport, Jones & Glenister, Eastbourne.
Enterprises (Windsor), Ltd.	£1,000 in 980 8 % cum. pref. shares of £1 and 400 ord. shares of 1s. each.	Kinema Proprietors ...	Solicitor: A. Blackmore, 37, Bedford Row, W.C.1.
Exhibitions, Ltd.	£100,000 in £1 shares ...	Exhibition Promoters...	Solicitors: Simmons & Simmons, 1, Threadneedle Street, E.C.2.
Film Transporters Association of Great Britain.	Limited Company by guarantee.	———	26, Charing Cross Road, W.C.2.
Finance & Development Trust Ltd.	£1,000 in £1 shares ...	———	17, Shaftesbury Avenue, W.1.
Flag Films, Ltd.	£75,000 in 60,000 6% pref. ord. shares of £1 each and 300,000 def. ord. shares of 1s. each.	Film Producers	Solicitors: Albert Fletcher & Kaufman, 23, College Hill, E.C.
Fletcher-Barnett Syndicate, Ltd.	£1,000 in £1 shares......	Kinema Proprietors ...	9, Clements Lane, E.C.4
Granada (Woolwich), Ltd.	£5,000 in 20,000 6% cum. pref. and 30,000 ord. shares of £1.	To construct a kinema	Solicitors: Culross & Co., 65, Duke Street, W.1.
Hollywood Cosmetic Co., Ltd.	£1,000 in £1 shares ...	Cosmetic Manufacturers	26, D'Arblay Street, W.1.
Independent Film Distributors, Ltd.	£5,000 in £1 shares 1,000 6% cum. par. pref. and 4,000 ord.).	Film Producers	Danes Inn House, 265, Strand, W.C.2.
International Film Recording Co., Ltd.	£1,000 in 5s. shares ...	Indicated by the title ...	22, Grosvenor Street, W.1.
Ker Lindsay, Ltd.	£500 in £1 shares.........	Theatre Decorators ...	10, George Street, Hanover Square, W.1.
London & Continental Pictures, Ltd.	£1,000 in 500 ord. shares of £1, and 10,000 founders shares of £1 each.	Film Producers	———

Name.	Capital.	Nature of Business.	Registered Office.
Majestic (Sevenoaks), Ltd.	£10,000 in £1 shares ...	Kinema Proprietors ...	60–66, Wardour Street, W.1.
M. & J. Cinemas, Ltd.	£100 in £1 shares	Kinema Proprietors ...	
Monarch Productions, Ltd.	£11,000 in 10,000 6% cum. red. pref. shares £1 each and 20,000 ord. shares of 1s.	——	Solicitors : Linklaters & Paines, 2, Bond Court, Walbrook.
New Style Films, Ltd.	£100 in £1 shares	——	46–47, London Wall, E.C.
Opticolor, Ltd.	£30,000 in 20,000 7% non-cum. par. pref. shares of £1 each and 100,000 ord. shares of 2s. each.	Film Producers, etc. ...	Solicitors : Ashurst, Morris, Crisp & Co., 17, Throgmorton Avenue, E.C.
Pacific Film Corporation, Ltd.	£1,000 in £1 shares (500 5% cum. pref. and 500 ord.).	Publicity Agents ...	172, Romford Road, E.7.
Pathé Radio & Television Co., Ltd.	£100 in £1 shares	Television Instrument Dealers.	95, Bath Street, Glasgow.
Picture Plays, Ltd.	£100 in £1 shares	Scenario Writers ...	Canada House, Norfolk Street, W.C.2.
Premier Cinemas, Ltd.	£100 in £1 shares	Kinema Proprietors ...	Solicitors : Bulcraig & Davies, Amberley House, Norfolk Street W.C.2.
Regent Theatre (Wisbech), Ltd.	£500 in £1 shares	Kinema Proprietors ...	Regent Theatre, Wisbech.
Ritz (Chesterfield), Ltd.	£5,000 in £1 shares	Kinema Proprietors ...	Solicitors : Billingshurst, Wood & Pope 7, Bucklersbury, E.C.4.
Rivoli Estates, Ltd.	£5,000 in £1 shares	Kinema Proprietors ...	Solicitor : J. G. Mahaffy, 29, Blacfriars Street, Manchester 3.
Strand Electric Holdings	£115,000 in 5s. shares	Manufacturers of electrical apparatus.	Solicitors : Ashurst, Morris, Crisp & Co., 17, Throgmorton Avenue, E.C.2.
Unifilm Co., Ltd.	£500 in £1 shares	Producers and Distributors.	——
United Entertainments, Ltd.	£120,000 in £1 shares	Film Producers ...	——

MARCH.

Name.	Capital.	Nature of Business.	Registered Office.
Ashley Securities, Ltd.	£100 in £1 shares	To acquire and hold property, etc., as investments.	Furnival House, 14–18, High Holborn, W.C.
Associated and Reading Cinemas, Ltd.	£1,000 in £1 shares	Kinema Proprietors ...	Solicitors : Forsyte, Kerman and Phillips, 9, Carlos Place, W.
Birman Properties, Ltd.	£100 in £1 shares	Kinema Proprietors...	3, Stanley Street, Liverpool.
Bitterne Picture Theatre, Ltd.	£10,000 in £1 shares	Kinema Proprietors...	Solicitors : A. Bickmore, 37, Bedford Row, W.C.
British Ozaphane, Ltd.	£15,000 in £1 shares	Manufacturers of sound reproducing apparatus.	72A, Carlton Hill, Maida Vale, W.
Central Club and Agency (Screen and Stage), Ltd.	£100 in 1s. shares	Indicated by title ...	14–15, Ham Yard, W.1.
Cope and Ashley, Ltd.	£100 in £1 shares	To acquire and hold property, etc., as investments.	Furnival House, 14–18, High Holborn, W.C.1.
Cope Trust, Ltd.	£100 in £1 shares	To acquire and hold property, etc., as investments.	Furnival House, 14–18, High Holborn, W.C.1.
Cosy Cinemas (Dolgelly), Ltd.	£500 in £1 shares	Kinema Proprietors...	Solicitors : Guthrie, Jones & Jones, Bank Chambers Dolgelly.

Name.	Capital.	Nature of Business.	Registered Office.
Crescent Cinema Co., Ltd.	£25,700 in 25,000 ord. shares of £1 each and 14,000 def. shares of 1s.	To erect a kinema	21, Blythswood Square, Glasgow.
Dorian Film Productions, Ltd.	£100 in £1 shares	Film Producers	—
Francis Henry Securities, Ltd.	£100 in £1 shares	To acquire and hold property, etc., as investments.	Furnival House, 14–18, High Holborn, W.C.1.
G.C.F. Corporation, Ltd.	£1,225,000 in 1,175,000 8 p.c. cum. pref. ord. shares of £1 each and 1,000,000 def. ord. shares of 1s. each.	Film Producers and Distributors.	Solicitors : Richards, Butler, Stoke and Woodham Smith, Cunard House, Leadenhall Street, E.C.
Grasmere Trust, Ltd.	£1,000 in £1 shares	Amusement Caterers	8, Britannia Buildings, Huddersfield.
Horsfield, Daunt and Chart, Ltd.	£100 in £1 shares	Kinema Proprietors	40, Shaftesbury Avenue, W.1.
Ideal Cinema (Lowestoft), Ltd.	£2,000 in £1 shares	To acquire a kinema	Golden Lion Chambers, Whitby.
Ilkeston Scala and Globe Picture Houses, Ltd.	£8,000 in £1 shares	To acquire a kinema	—
I.M.P.A., Ltd.	£1,000 in £1 shares	Film Producers	181, Wardour Street, W.1.
International Entertainments, Ltd.	£2,000 in £1 shares	Kinema Proprietors	27, Brazennose Street, Manchester.
J. H. Productions Social and Sports Club, Ltd.	£5	Indicated by title	Solicitors : Travers, Smith, Braithwaite & Co., 4, Throgmorton Avenue, E.C.4.
Karno Komedy Ko., Ltd.	£100 in £1 shares	Film Producers	—
Kinetours, Ltd.	£500 in 400 7 p.c. cum. pref. shares of £1 and 2,000 ord. shares of 1s. each.	Kinema Proprietors	Solicitors : Cockburn, Gosling and Co., Hove.
L.A.N. Securities, Ltd.	£100 in £1 shares	To acquire and hold property as investments	Furnival House, 14–18, High Holborn, W.C.1.
Mallin Securities, Ltd.	£100 in £1 shares	To acquire and hold property as investments.	Furnival House, 14–18, High Holborn, W.C.1.
National Provincial Film Distributors, Ltd.	£11,000 in 10,000 ord. shares of £1 and 40,000 founders' shares of 6d. each.	Film Distributors	Solicitors : R. F. Sheppard, 12, Holborn Viaduct, E.C.1.
New Scala (Stourbridge), Ltd.	£2,000 in £1 shares	Kinema Proprietors	Lombard House, Great Charles Street, Birmingham.
Northumbrian Entertainments, Ltd.	£500 in £1 shares	Kinema Proprietors	Solicitors : Newlands, Newlands and Patterson, South Shields.
North Britain Theatres, Ltd.	£100 in £1 shares	—	Solicitors : R. Hamilton Twyford & Co., 12, Soho Square, W.1.
Ocean Films, Ltd.	£10,000 in 9,000 6 p.c. pref. shares of £1 and 20,000 ord. shares of 1s.	Film Producers	Solicitors : Dod, Longstaffe and Fenwick, 16, Berners Street, W.1.
Pall Mall Productions, Ltd.	£10,000 in £1 shares	Film Producers	Solicitors : Walter Burgis and Co., 4 and 5, Bond Court, Walbrook, E.C.4.
Pendennis Pictures Corporation, Ltd.	£10,000 in £1 shares	Film Producers	Solicitor : Gerald D. Spyer, 21, Pine Grove, Totteridge.
Pendleton Estates, Ltd.	£6,000 in £1 shares	Kinema Builders and Contractors.	40, Hoghton Street, Southport.
Plaza Cinema (Hastings), Ltd.	£3,000 in £1 shares	Kinema Proprietors	Plaza Cinema Robertson Street, Hastings.
Princes Theatre (Manchester), Ltd.	£5,000 in £1 shares	Kinema Proprietors	Prince's Theatre, Oxford Street, Manchester.
Regal (Beverley), Ltd.	£10,000 in £1 shares	To acquire kinemas	Regal Chambers, Ferensway, Hull.
Regal (Kettering), Ltd.	£12,500 in £1 shares	Kinema Proprietors	National House, Wardour Street, W.1.

Name.	Capital.	Nature of Business.	Registered Office.
Regal Cinema (Leicester), Ltd.	£10,000 in £1 shares	Kinema Proprietors ...	—
Regent (Sunderland), Ltd.	£1,200 in £1 shares	Kinema Proprietors ...	4, Palladium Buildings, Eastbourne Road, Middlesborough.
Regal (Tring), Ltd..........	£6,000 in £1 shares	Kinema Proprietors ...	1, Friar Street, Reading.
Regal (W. Hartlepool), Ltd.	£15,000 in 12,000 pref. ord. shares of £1 each and 12,000 def. ord. of 5s. each.	To erect a kinema	Solicitors: Smith, Graham and Wilson, 10a, Tower Street, W. Hartlepool.
Roscrea and Athy Picture Co., Ltd.	£5,000 in £1 shares	Kinema Proprietors ...	
Sandmount Film Corporation, Ltd.	£100 in £1 shares	Film Producers	27, Leadenhall Street, E.C.3.
Sokal Film Productions, Ltd.	£100 in £1 shares.........	Film Producers	Solicitors: Kenneth Brown, Baker Baker, Essex House, Essex Street, W.C.2.
Stanway Productions, Ltd.	£100 in £1 shares.........	Theatrical Agents	20, Sackville Street, W.1.
Stott and Barrow, Ltd....	£2,000 in £1 shares	Film Producers and Distributors.	64, Victoria Street Manchester.
Thurso Picture House Co., Ltd.	£2,500 in £1 shares	To acquire a kinema ...	25, Olrig Street, Thurso.
U.K. Screen Publicity Service, Ltd.	£1,000 in £1 shares	Producers of Advertising Films.	Queen's Chambers, 5, John Dalton Street, Manchester.
Universal - Wainwright Studios, Ltd.	£500 in £1 shares.........	Film Producers	62, Shaftesbury Avenue, W.1.

APRIL.

Name.	Capital.	Nature of Business.	Registered Office.
Anglo Scottish Theatres, Ltd.	£1,000 in £1 shares	Kinema Proprietors ...	Solicitors: Kenneth Brown, Baker Baker, Essex House, W.C.2.
Ambassador Cinema (Bristol), Ltd.	£100 in £1 shares.........	Kinema Proprietors ...	45, Newhall Street Birmingham.
Associated Picture Houses Ltd.	£85,000 in £1 shares ...	Kinema Proprietors ...	—
Astel Pictures, Ltd.	£100 in £1 shares.........	Kinema Proprietors ...	45, Newhall Street, Birmingham.
Alfred Brookes Theatrical Supplies, Ltd.	£1,000 in £1 shares	Theatre Equipment Dealers.	2, Ashmead Street South Lambeth.
C. & H. Productions, Ltd.	£1,000 in £1 shares	Film producers	27, Golden Square, W.1.
C. & R. (Victoria), Ltd....	£20,000 in £1 shares ...	Kinema Proprietors ...	199, Piccadilly, W.1.
Carlton Film Productions, Ltd.	£1,000 in £1 shares	Producers and Distributors.	Solicitors: Justice and Pattenden, 12, Bernard Street, W.C.1.
Charing Cross News Theatre, Ltd.	£2,000 in £1 shares	Kinema Proprietors	Solicitors: H. S. Wright & Webb, 18, Bloomsbury Square, W.C.1.
Corporate Films, Ltd. ...	£100 in £1 shares.........	Film Producers	Solicitors: T. and N. Blanco White, 10, Bedford Row, W.C.1.
Deansgate Picture House (1936), Ltd.	£6,000 in £1 shares	Kinema Proprietors ...	Solicitors: Skelton & Co., Manchester.
Dominion (Acton), Ltd....	£1,000 in £1 shares	Kinema Proprietors ...	37, Golden Square, W.1.
Donalds' Cinemas (Holdings), Ltd.	£20,000 in 16,000 5% cum. pref. and 4,000 ord. shares of £1 each.	Kinema Proprietors ...	19, North Silver Street, Aberdeen.
Ealing & District Property Co.	£30,000 in £1 shares (10,000 6% cum. pref. and 20,000 ord.)	To construct kinemas...	Maxwell House, Arundel Street, W.C.2.
Embassy (Wallasey), Ltd.	£100 in £1 shares.........	Kinema Proprietors ...	Law Association Buildings, 14, Cook Street, Liverpool.
Excelsior Film Productions, Ltd.	£1,000 in £1 shares	Producers and Distributors.	Solicitors: Justice & Pattenden, 12, Bernard Street, W.C.1.
Grand Theatre (Oldham), Ltd.	£6,000 in £1 shares	Kinema Proprietors ...	Solicitors: Billinghurst, Wood & Pope, & Bucklersbury, E.C.

Name.	Capital.	Nature of Business.	Registered Office.
Keystone Cinemas, Ltd....	£10,000 in 9,000 6% non-cum. pref. shares of £1 each and 20,000 def. shares of 1s. each.	Kinema Proprietors ...	Solicitors : Kenneth Brown, Baker and Baker, Essex House, W.C.2.
Leevers, Rich & Co., Ltd.	£2,400 in £1 shares	Kinematograph dealers	37, Walbrook, E.C.4.
London Theatre Studios, Ltd.	£5,000 in 4,995 ord. shares of £1 each and 100 def. ord. shares of 1s. each.	Film Producers	Solicitors : J. D. Langton and Passmore, 16, Tokenhouse Yard, E.C.
Michan, Ltd.	£20 in 1s. shares	Kinema Proprietors ...	Solicitors : Lipton and Jefferies, 36, Duke Street, St. James's S.W.1.
M o l e - R i c h a r d s o n (England), Ltd.	£15,000 in £1 shares ...	Photographic Dealers...	Solicitors : Mayo, Elder and Rutherfords, 10, Drapers' Gardens, E.C.
Moortown Cinema Co., Ltd.	£10,000 in £1 shares (1,000 pref. ord. and 9,000 ord.).	Kinema Proprietors ...	Solicitors : Thomas Lister Croft & Co., 19, King Street, Wakefield.
North British Film Corporation, Ltd.	£100 in £1 shares.........	Film Producers	37, Clifton Street, Blackpool.
N.T.P., Ltd. ....:	£1,000 in £1 shares	To acquire kinemas......	17, North John Street, Liverpool.
Nuro (Biggleswade), Ltd.	£175,000 in 5s. shares...	Manufacturers of photographic materials.	Nuro Works, Biggleswade, Beds.
Odeon (Bolton), Ltd. ...	£15,500 in 15,000 7% cum. pref. shares of £1 and 10,000 ord. shares of 1s.	Kinema Proprietors ...	39, Temple Row, Birmingham.
Odeon (Burnley), Ltd. ...	£12,500 in 12,000 7% cum. pref. shares of £1 and 10,000 ord. shares of 1s.	Kinema Proprietors ...	39, Temple Row Birmingham.
Odeon (Chorley), Ltd.......	£12,500 in 12,000 7% cum. pref.shares of £1 and 10,000 ord. shares of 1s.	Kinema Proprietors ...	39, Temple Row, Birmingham.
Odeon (Dudley), Ltd. ...	£15,500 in 15,000 7% cum. pref. shares of £1 and 10,000 ord.shares of 1s.	Kinema Proprietors ...	39, Temple Row, Birmingham.
Odeon (Hanley), Ltd. ...	£15,500 in 15,000 7% cum. pref. shares of £1 and 10,000 ord. shares of 1s.	Kinema Proprietors ...	39, Temple Row, Birmingham.
Odeon (Horsham), Ltd....	£12,500 in 12,000 7% cum. pref. shares of £1 and 10,000 ord. shares of 1s. each.	Kinema Proprietors ...	39, Temple Row, Birmingham.
Odeon (Lancaster), Ltd...	£12,500 in 12,000 7% pref shares of £1 and 10,000 ord. shares of 1s. each.	Kinema Proprietors ...	39, Temple Row, Birmingham.
Odeon (Loughborough), Ltd.	£12,500 in 12,000 7% cum. pref.shares of £1 and 10,000 ord. shares of 1s.	Kinema Proprietors ...	39, Temple Row, Birmingham.
Odeon (Peterborough), Ltd.	£12,500 in 12,000 7% cum. pref. shares of £1 and 10,000 ord. shares of 1s.	Kinema Proprietors ...	39, Temple Row , Birmingham.
Odeon (Rhyl), Ltd.	£20,500 in 20,000 7% cum. pref. shares of £1 and 10,000 ord. shares of 1s.	Kinema Proprietors ...	39, Temple Row, Birmingham.
Odeon (West Bromwich), Ltd.	£15,500 in 15,000 7% cum. pref. shares of £1 each and 10,000 ord. shares of 1s.	Kinema Proprietors ...	39, Temple Row, Birmingham.
Odeon (Wolverhampton), Ltd.	£20,500 in 20,000 7% cum. pref. shares of £1 and 10,000 ord. shares of 1s.	Kinema Proprietors ...	39, Temple Row, Birmingham.

Name	Capital.	Nature of Business.	Registered Office.
Odeon (Wrexham), Ltd....	£12,500 in 12,000 7% cum. pref. shares of £1 and 10,000 ord. shares of 1s.	Kinema Proprietors ...	39, Temple Row, Birmingham.
Oxford Films, Ltd..........	£1,000 in £1 shares	Film Producers	Solicitors: W. A. Crump & Son, 27, Leadenhall Street, E.C.3.
Paxon & Chambers, Ltd.	£400 in £1 shares.........	To acquire a kinema ...	New Roxy Cinema, Glass Street, Hanley, Stoke-on-Trent.
Personality Pictures, Ltd.	£100 in £1 shares.........	Film Producers	Solicitors: Bartlett and Gluckstein, 199, Piccadilly, W.1.
R.E.F., Ltd.	£500 in 2,000 shares of 5s. each.	Kinema Proprietors ...	Solicitors: J. D. Langton and Passmore, 8, Bolton Street, Piccadilly, W.1.
Victor Saville Productions, Ltd.	£10,000 in £1 shares ...	Film Producers	Solicitors: Kenneth Brown, Baker Baker, Essex House. W.C.2.
Al Schulberg, Ltd.	£1,000 in £1s hares	Employment Agents ...	12, Henrietta Street, W.C.2.
Swaledale Entertainments Ltd.	£7,000 in £1 shares (3,500 ord. and 3,500 5% pref.)	Kinema Proprietors ...	Solicitor: J. W. Hunton, Richmond, Yorks.
Trading Corporation for Educational General Services, Ltd.	£20,000 in £1 shares ...	Producers of Religious and educational films.	Solicitors: Richard Butler, Stokes and, Woodham Smith, 88, Leadenhall Street, E.C.3.
United Compass Cameras, Ltd.	£56,000 in 50,000 8% red. pref. shares of £1 and 120,000 ord. shares of 1s.	Manufacturers and dealers in photographic apparatus.	4, St. Mary Axe, E.C.3.

MAY.

Name.	Capital.	Nature of Business.	Registered Office.
Anglo Scottish Cinema Trust, Ltd.	£100 in 1s. shares.........	Kinema Proprietors ...	Solicitors: Kenneth Brown, Baker, Baker, Essex House, W.C.2.
Animated Waxworks, Ltd.	£11,000 in £10,000 7½% cum. pref. shares of £1 and 20,000 ord. shares of 1s. each.	Kinema Proprietors ...	87a, Guildford Street, W.C.1.
Bazell Ltd....................	£500 in £1 shares	Kinema Proprietors ...	Solicitors: Maxwell, Brownjohn, Clarke & Co., 5, Raymond Buildings, W.C.2.
Rudolf Becker & Co. Ltd.	£5,000 in £1 shares	Film Producers	7-8, Great Winchester Street, E.C.2
Brighouse Picture House, Ltd.	£15,000 in £1 shares......	To acquire a kinema ...	5, Rawson Street Halifax.
Britannic Cinemas, Ltd....	£100 in £1 shares.........	Kinema Proprietors.	Solicitors: Bulcraig & Davis, Amberley House, Norfolk Street, W.C.2.
British Playhouses & Film Studios (Parent) Co. Ltd.	£2,000 in 1,500 7% non-cum. pref shares of £1 each and 10,000 ord. shares of 1s.	Film Producers.	24, New Bond Street, W.1.
British Regional Cinemas, Ltd.	£100 in £1 shares	Kinema Proprietors ...	Solicitors: Bulcraig & Davis, Amberley House, W.C.2.
Century Developments, Ltd.	£150,000 in £1 shares ...	Kinema Financiers......	Solicitors: Culross & Co., 65, Duke Street, Grosvenor Square, W.1.
Cinema Holdings (Kirkcaldy) Ltd.	£10,000 in £1 shares......	Kinema Proprietors ...	—
Clifton Cinema (Lye) Ltd.	£8,000 in £1 shares (4,000 ord. and 4,000 6% accum. pref.	To erect a kinema	25, Bennetts Hill, Birmingham

Name.	Capital.	Nature of Business.	Registered Office.
Clifton Cinema (Sedgley) Ltd.	£8,000 in £1 shares (4,000 ord. and 4,000 6% accum. pref.)	To erect a kinema	25, Bennetts Hill, Birmingham
Comar Cinemas, Ltd	£2,000 in £1 shares	To acquire a kinema ...	The Hippodrome Moses Gate, Nr. Bolton.
Cumulus Pictures, Ltd....	£10,000 in £1 shares......	Film Producers............	Solicitors: Clarke, Square & Co., 28, Bolton Street, W.1.
Decorative Crafts, Ltd....	£5,000 in 4,000 6% cum. pref. shares of £1 each and 4,000 ord. shares of 5s. each.	Kinema Decorators and furnishers	39, Temple Row, Birmingham.
Dela Films British Productions Co., Ltd.	£5,000 in 4,000 7% cum. par. pref. shares of £1 each and 10,000 ord. shares of 2s. each.	Film Producers	19, Grosvenor Place, S.W.1.
Doman Enterprises, Ltd.	£1,000 in £1 shares.	Kinema Proprietors ...	15, Victoria Street, Liverpool.
Grayfoss, Ltd	£100 in £1 shares	Film Producers	5, Hampstead Square, N.W.3.
H.D.M. (Cinema), Ltd....	£1,000 in £1 shares ...	Kinema Proprietors ...	Imperial Buildings, Oxford Road, Manchester.
Holbrook Theatres, Ltd.	£1,000 in £1 shares	To acquire a kinema ...	Brookville Theatre, Holbrook Lane, Coventry
International Religious Films, Ltd.	£100 in £1 shares	Film Producers	——
Irish Provincial Cinemas, Ltd.	£20,000 in £1 shares......	Kinema Proprietors ...	——
Kinematographic Instruments, Ltd.	£2,000 in £1 shares	Manufacturers and Dealers of Kinematographic Apparatus.	Clarke's Factory, Egerton Street, Nottingham.
McAndrew & Co., (Cinema Proprietors), Ltd.	£5,000 in 2,000 ord. and 3,000 5½% cum. pref. shares of £1.	Kinema Proprietors ...	Picture House, 23, Castlegate, Lanark.
National Sound-on-Film Library, Ltd.	£1,500 in £1 shares	To establish a Film Library.	
North of Scotland News Theatres (Aberdeen) Ltd.	£2,000 in £1 shares	Kinema Proprietors ...	222, Union Street, Aberdeen.
Odeon (Bury St. Edmunds) Ltd.	£10,500 in 10,000 7% cum. non-par. pref. shares of £1 and 10,000 ord. shares of 1s.	Kinema Proprietors ...	39, Temple Row, Birmingham.
Odeon (Lowestoft), Ltd.	£15,500 in 15,000 7% cum. pref. shares of £1 and 10,000 ord. shares of 1s. each.	Kinema Proprietors ...	39, Temple Row, Birmingham.
Paisley Entertainments, Ltd.	£400 in £1 shares.........	Kinema Proprietors ...	108, West Regent Street, Glasgow.
Penn Cinema Co., Ltd. ...	£12,000 in £1 shares ...	Kinema Proprietors ...	Lombard House, Great Charles Street, Birmingham.
Polyfoto (U.S.A.), Ltd. ...	£300 in £1 shares.........	Dealers in Photographic Apparatus.	Solicitors: Denton, Hall & Burgin, 3, Grays Place, W.C.
Popular Film Enterprises, Ltd.	£1,100 in 1,000 6% nonpar. pref. and 100 ord. shares of £1 each.	Film Producers	53, Berners Street, W.1.
Premier Stafford Productions, Ltd.	£100 in £1 shares.........	Film Producers	Solicitors: M.A. Jacobs & Sons, 73, Jermyn Street, S.W.1.
Q.P. & H. Proprietors, Ltd.	£4,000 in £1 shares	To acquire a kinema ...	27, Hardy's Buildings, 3, Cateaton Street, Manchester.
Regal Cinema (Crossgates) Ltd.	£15,000 in £1 shares......	Kinema Proprietors ...	Regal Cinema, Crossgates, Leeds.
Ritz Pictures (Mansfield), Ltd.	£6,090 in 90 def. and 6,000 ord. shares of £1.	Kinema Proprietors ...	
Ritz, (Wokingham), Ltd.	£8,100 in £1 shares (8,000 10% cum. pref. and 100 ord.).	Kinema Proprietors ...	Solicitors: Bulcraig & Davis Amberley House, Norfolk Street W.C.2.

Name.	Capital.	Nature of Business.	Registered Office.
St. Martin's Picture Corporation, Ltd.	£100 in £1 shares	Film Producers	Leicester House, 5, Green Street, W.1.
Sheridan Studios, Ltd. ...	£100 in £1 shares.........	Film Producers	75-77 Shaftesbury Avenue, W.1.
S. R. Films, Ltd.	£3,000 in £1 shares......	Film Producers	Solicitors: Herbert Smith & Co., 62, London Wall, E.C.
S. R. G. Cinemas, Ltd. ...	£5,000 in £1 shares......	Kinema Proprietors ...	Wimbledon Park Road, S.W.
Talbach and Port Talbot Cinema Co., Ltd.	£5,000 in £1 shares......	Kinema Proprietors ...	——
Union Exhibitors, Ltd. ...	£100 in £1 shares.........	Kinema Proprietors ...	Solicitors: Bulcraig & Davis, Amberley House, Norfolk Street, W.C.2.
Unital Talking Pictures, Ltd.	£100 in £1 shares.........	Film Producers	7, Park Lane, W.1.
Wickford Cinemas, Ltd....	£5,000 in 4,500 10% cum. pref. ord. shares of £1 and 5,000 def. ord. shares of 2s. each.	Kinema Proprietors ...	——

JUNE

Name.	Capital.	Nature of Business.	Registered Office.
Allied (Times) Theatres, Ltd.	£15,000 in 14,995 shares of £1 and 100 founders shares of 1s. each.	Kinema Proprietors ...	3, Stanley Street, Liverpool.
Anglo American Theatrical Corporation, Ltd.	£1,200 in £1 shares	Kinema Proprietors ...	18, Charing Cross Road, W.C.2.
Banking Accomodation Trust, Ltd.	£1,000 in £1 shares	Merchant bankers	Solicitors: W. H. Sanders, 7, Bloomsbury Square, W.C.1.
Barton Cinema Co., Ltd.	£8,000 in 7,000 6½% pref. shares of £1 and 20,000 ord. shares of 1s. each.	Kinema Proprietors ...	10, Windsor Place, Cardiff.
Birstall Cinema Co., Ltd.	£2,500 in £1 shares	Kinema Proprietors ...	——
Blaydon Cinema, Ltd. ...	£10,000 in £1 shares......	To erect a kinema	Solicitors: Longden, Mann & Hodinett, Newcastle-on-Tyne.
British Alliance Pictures, Ltd.	£100 in £1 shares.........	Film Producers	Solicitors: Halliday Clarke & Co., 39, Albemarle Street, W.1.
British Ondiacolor, Ltd....	£12,500 in 1s. shares ...	Colour processors.........	110, Cannon Street, E.C.4.
Broughton Palace Picture Co., Ltd.	£2,000 in £1 shares	Kinema Proprietors ...	——
Carlton Cinema (Salford), Ltd.	£1,000 in £1 shares	Kinema Proprietors ...	1, Princess Street, Manchester.
Carshalton Regional Theatre, Ltd.	£35,000 in 30,000 6% cum. par. pref. shares of £1 and 100,000 ord. shares of 1s.	Kinema Proprietors ...	142, Wardour Street, W.1.
Cheam Cinemas, Ltd.......	£5,000 in 15,000 "A" ord. and 5,000 "B" ord. shares of 5s.	Kinema Proprietors ...	Solicitors: Culross & Co., 65, Duke Street, W.1.
Chemical & Carson Products, Ltd.	£1,000 in £1 shares	Importers and dealers in carbon products.	91, Moorgate, E.C.2.
Chinese White Productions, Ltd.	£500 in 475 par pref. shares of £1 each and 500 ord. shares of 1s. each.	——	11, Waterloo Place, S.W.1.
Cinegram, Ltd.	£1,000 in £1 shares	To acquire patent relating to sound apparatus.	50, Pall Mall, S.W.1.
Cinematograph Finance and Discount Co., Ltd.	£100 in 95 "A" shares of £1 and 100 "B" shares of 1s. each.	Financiers.................	King William Street, E.C.4.
Cinema Utilities, Ltd.......	£1,000 in £1 shares......	Film Producers	——
Cinetitles, Ltd.	£100 in £1 shares.........	Film Producers	1, Golden Square, W.1.
Clifton Cinema (Leominster), Ltd.	£6,000 in £1 shares (3,000 ord. and 3,000 6% cum. pref.)	To erect a kinema	25, Bennetts Hill, Birmingham.

Name.	Capital.	Nature of Business.
Concordia Distributors, Ltd.	£100 in £1 shares	Film Distributors ......
Darwen Estates, Ltd. ...	£1,000 in £1 shares	Kinema Proprietors ...
Dodds & Heppard, Ltd....	£2,000 in £1 shares	Commercial film producers.
Dominion (Bakers Arms), Ltd.	£5,000 in £1 shares	Theatre Proprietors......
Embassy Picture House (Troon), Ltd.	£10,000 in £1 shares (5,000 pref. 5,000 ord.)	Kinema Proprietors ...
Greenwick Properties, Ltd.	£5,000 in 5s. shares (15,000 "A" and 5,000 "B.")	——
Haltemprice Cinemas, Ltd.	£12,000 in £1 shares ...	To erect a kinema ......
Hollywood Studios, Ltd...	£500 in £1 shares.........	Magazine Publishers ...
Holt Cinema, Ltd.	£3,000 in £1 shares	To acquire kinemas......
George Humphries & Co., Ltd.	£100,000 in £1 shares ...	Film processors and dealers in kinema apparatus.
International Trust of Pictures Corporation, Ltd.	£300 in £1 shares.........	Film Producers ...,......
L. & S. Cinemas, Ltd.......	£1,000 in £1 shares	Kinema Proprietors ...
Lustrocolour, Ltd.	£100 in £1 shares.........	Film Producers ....
Mancunian Circuit (1936), Ltd.	£100 in 1s. shares	Kinema Proprietors ...
Odeon, Ltd....................	£10,500 in 10,000 7% cum. pref. shares of £1 each and 10,000 ord. shares of 1s. each.	——
Odeon (Burnt Oak), Ltd.	£10,500 in 10,000 6% cum. pref. shares of £1 each and 10,000 ord. shares of 1s. each.	Kinema Proprietors ...
Odeon (Forest Gate), Ltd.	£10,500 in 10,000 7% cum. pref. shares of £1 and 10,000 ord. shares of 1s. each.	Kinema Proprietors ...
Odeon (Guide Bridge), Ltd.	£2,100 in 2,000 7% cum. pref. shares of £1 and 2,000 ord. shares of 1s.	Kinema Proprietors ...
Odeon (Newport, Mon.), Ltd.	£15,000 in 15,000 7% pref. shares of £1 each and 10,000 ord. shares of 1s. each.	Kinema Proprietors ...
Odeon (Yeovil), Ltd.	£15,000 7% cum. pref. shares of £1 each and 10,000 ord. shares of 1s. each.	Kinema Proprietors ...
Offerton Cinemas, Ltd. ...	£5,000 in £1 shares	Kinema Proprietors ...
Ritz Picture House (Sheffield), Ltd.	£15,000 in £1 shares ...	Kinema Proprietors ...
Ritz (Warrington), Ltd....	£10,000 in £1 shares ...	Kinema Proprietors ...
Standard International Pictures, Ltd.	£6,000 in 5,000 7% cum. par. pref. shares of £1 and 20,000 ord. shares of 1s. each.	Film Producers ....
Sutton Grand Cinema, Ltd.	£7,500 in £1 shares......	Kinema Proprietors ...

Name.	Capital.	Nature of Business.	Registered Office.
Tiger Cinemas, Ltd.	£3,000 in £1 shares	Kinema Proprietors ...	60 Bridge Street, Bolton.
Tivoli (Wimborne), Ltd....	£100 in £1 shares.........	Kinema Proprietors ...	Allen House, Newarke Street, Leicester.
Tudor Cinema (Caversham), Ltd.	£7,000 in 5s. shares (2,000 7% cum. pref.)	Kinema Proprietors ...	Hermitage Cinema, Hitchin.
Victoria Investment (Cambridge), Ltd.	£750 in 30,000 shares of 6d. each.	—	Sussex House, Hobson Street, Cambridge.
Ward Wing Films, Ltd....	£100 in £1 shares.........	Film Producers	—
Windsor Productions, Ltd.	£100 in £1 shares.........	Film Producers	17, Berkeley Square, W.
World Window, Ltd.	£100 in £1 shares.........	Film Producers	Imperial House, 80–86, Regent Street, W.1.

JULY.

Name.	Capital.	Nature of Business.	Registered Office.
Argyle British Productions, Ltd.	£10,000 in £1 shares ...	Film Producers	Solicitors: Argyle & Sons, Tamworth, Staffs.
Ashton Entertainments, Ltd.	£6,100 in £1 shares	Kinema Proprietors ...	Solicitors: Wilson, Wright Earle & Co., Manchester.
Associated Artists, Ltd.	£1,000 in 500 shares of £1 each and 10,000 shares of 1s. each.	Producers and Distributors.	—
Associated Film Carriers of Great Britain, Ltd.	—	To promote the interests of the film transport industry.	Solicitors: Mawby, Barrie & Letts, 55, Moorgate, E.C.
Baileys Estates, Ltd. ...	£100 in £1 shares.........	—	2, Cathedral House, Manchester.
George Banyai Plays, Ltd.	£100 in £1 shares.........	Theatre Proprietors ...	17, Berkeley Square, W.1.
Basford Cinemas, Ltd. ...	£5,000 in £1 shares	Kinema Proprietors ...	Solicitors: Allcock, Allcock & Cousin, 32, Bridlesmith Gate, Nottingham.
Beaumont Films Productions, Ltd.	£100 in £1 shares.........	Film Producers	58, Haymarket, S.W.1.
Brinsdale Cinema, Ltd....	£1,000 in £1 shares	Kinema Proprietors ...	14, Sunbeam Road, N.W.10.
Broadcast Enterprises, Ltd.	£1,000 in £1 shares......	Broadcasting, Theatrical and Kinema Agents.	503, Abbey House, Victoria Street, S.W.1.
Broadway Cinemas (Accrington), Ltd.	£10,000 in £1 shares ...	Kinema Proprietors ...	The Hippodrome, Ellison Street, Accrington.
Bulman Jupiter Screen Co. (1936), Ltd.	£1,000 in £1 shares	Screen Manufacturers...	Solicitors: Harold Button, 76, Shaftesbury Avenue, W.1.
Capitol Theatre (Gateshead) Ltd.	£20,000 in £1 shares ...	To acquire a Kinema ...	Solicitors: Thomas Hall & Betts 37, Groat Market Newcastle-on-Tyne.
Celluloid Despatch Services.	£100 in £1 shares.	Film cleaners and repairers.	167, Wardour St., W.1
Chelten Cinema Co., Ltd.	£2,000 in £1 shares	Kinema Proprietors ...	10, Windsor Place, Cardiff.
Clarkson (Wardour Street) Ltd.	£8,000 in £1 shares (4,000 ord. and 4,000 6% cum. pref.)	Theatrical Costumiers...	—
John Clein Pictures, Ltd.	£100 in 1s. shares	Film Producers	Solicitors: John Lyons & Co., 121, Cannon Street, E.C.
Clifton Picture House (York), Ltd.	£10,000 in £1 shares (6,000 6% cum. pref. 2,000 "A" ord. and 2,000 "B" ord.)	To erect a kinema	48, Stonegate, York.
Coliseum Cinema (Northampton), Ltd.	£500 in £1 shares.........	To acquire a kinema ...	Coliseum Buildings, Kingsthorpe Hollow, Northampton.
C.R.P. Productions, Ltd.	£100 in £1 shares.........	Film Producers	5, Budge Row, E.C.
Deo Securities, Ltd.	£1,000 in £1 shares	Film Producers	Canada House, Norfolk Street, W.C.2.
Dillon Damen Productions Corporation.	£1,000 in £1 shares	Film Producers	—
Dublin Cinemas, Ltd.......	£20,000 in £1 shares	Kinema Proprietors ...	—

Name.	Capital.	Nature of Business.	Registered Office.
Elephant Film Studios, Ltd.	£1,000 in 500 7½% cum. pref. shares of £1 each and 10,000 ord. shares of 1s. each.	Film Producers	341A, Walworth Road, S.E.17.
Empire (Bollington), Ltd.	£1,000 in £1 shares	Kinema Proprietors ...	Palmerston Street, Bollington, near Macclesfield.
Essoldo (SouthShields), Ltd.	£1,000 in £1 shares	Kinema Proprietors ...	Solicitors : Grunhut, Grunhut and Makepeace, South Shields.
Facts & Fantasies, Ltd.	£100 in £1 shares.........	Dealers in kinemagraphfilms, etc.	24, Old Broad Street, E.C.2.
F.T.S. (Great Britain), Ltd.	£100,000 in 80,000 ord. shares of £1 and 80,000 def. shares of 5s.	To acquire film transport services.	Fairfield House, Broxburn, West Lothian.
Gaiety (Brighton), Ltd.	£100 in £1 shares.........	Kinema Proprietors ...	Solicitors : C. Burt Brill & Edwards, 46, Old Steine, Brighton.
Glebe Cinema Co., Ltd.	£5,000 in £1 shares	Kinema Proprietors ...	Langdykeside, Lesmahagow.
Robert Hale & Co.	——	Film stripping............	Great Tarpots, South Benfleet, Essex.
Harefield Investment Trust, Ltd.	£1,000 in £1 shares	——	Solicitors : Allen & Overy, 3, Finch Lane, E.C.3.
Iver Heath Clubs, Ltd.	£1,000 in £1 shares	——	Pinewood Studios, Iver Heath, Bucks.
Lido Cinema (Bolton) Ltd.	£1,000 in £1 shares.	Kinema Proprietors ...	1, Princess Street, Manchester.
London Theatre Centre, Ltd.	£5,000 in 2s. shares	Kinema Proprietors ...	1 & 2, Finsbury Square, E.C.2.
Magnet Productions, Ltd.	£1,000 in £1 shares	Film Producers	7, Suffolk Street, Pall Mall, S.W.1.
Malcolm Picture Productions, Ltd.	£1,000 in £1 shares	Film Producers	145, Wardour Street, W.1.
Marine Co., Ltd.	£1,000 in £1 shares	To erect a kinema........	——
Milford Haven Cinemas, Ltd.	£1,000 in £1 shares......	Kinema Proprietors...	Empire, Milford Haven.
Norwich Cinemas, Ltd.	£5,000 in £1 shares......	Kinema Proprietors ...	Solicitors : Stephenson, Harwood & Tatham, 16, Old Broad Street, E.C.
Picture House (Battle) Ltd.	£13,700 in 13,000 6% non-cum. pref. shares of £1 and 4,000 ord. shares of 1s. each.	Kinema Proprietors ...	Solicitors : John B. Purchase & Clark, 50, Pall Mall, S.W.1.
H. V. Polley, Ltd.	£500 in £1 shares.........	Dealers in kinema equipment.	Solicitors : J. H. John & Co., 40, Russell Square, W.C.1.
Provincial Developments (Stourbridge), Ltd.	£100 in £1 shares.........	Kinema Proprietors ...	Solicitors : W. A. & H. M. Foster & Co., 31, Queen Street, Wolverhampton.
Arthur Riscoe & Clifford Whitley, Ltd.	£100 in 1s. shares	——	Solicitors : Simmons & Simmons, 1, Threadneedle Street, E.C.
Roseland Halls, Ltd.......	£1,000 in £1 shares	Kinema Proprietors ...	Roseland Hall, Bohella, St. Mawes, Cornwall.
William Rowland Pictures Ltd.	£100 in 1s. shares	Film Producers	Solicitors : John Lyons & Co., 121, Cannon Street, E.C.
Regal (Barnstaple), Ltd.	£15,000 in 10,000 6% cum. red. pref. and 5,000 ord. shares of £1.	Kinema Proprietors ...	5–6, Broad Street Reading.
Rembrandt Film Productions, Ltd.	£100 in £1 shares.........	Film Producers	7, Poultry, E.C.2.
Ritz (Sheerness), Ltd. ...	£4,000 in £1 shares	Kinema Proprietors ...	Solicitors : Billinghurst, Wood & Pope, 7, Bucklersbury, E.C.4.
Rock Studios, Ltd.........	£200,000 in 175,000 10% cum. pref. shares of £1 each and 500,000 ord. shares of 1s. each.	Film Producers	Solicitors : Gadsden & Co., 28, Bedford Row, W.C.1.

Name.	Capital.	Nature of Business.	Registered Office.
Roxy Cinema (Notting-ham), Ltd.	£8,000	Kinema Proprietors ...	———
Savoy Kinema (Syston), Ltd.	£5,000 in £1 shares (4,000 5% non-cum. ref. pref. and 1,000 ord.)	Kinema Proprietors ...	Solicitors: Whetstone & Frost, 8, Bishop Street, Leicester.
Shemilt Bros., Ltd.	£1,000 in £1 shares	To acquire a kinema ...	———
Stanley Scott Productions, Ltd.	£1,000 in 5s. shares......	Kinema Proprietors ...	2, Broad Street Place, E.C.2.
Star Theatre (Bo'ness), Ltd.	£8,000 in £1 shares	To acquire a kinema ...	Bloomfield House, Bath-gate.
Strong Electric Distribu-tors, Ltd.	£1,500 in £1 shares	Dealers in kinema equip-ment.	132, Wardour Street, W.1.
Sunbury Park Studios, Ltd.	£100 in 2,000 def. shares of 1s. each.	To build film studios ...	26, D'Arblay Street, Wardour Street, W.1.
Supa Films, Ltd.............	£100 in £1 shares.........	Film Producers	Solicitors: Abbott, Hudson & Anderson, 3–4, Clement's Inn, W.C.2.
Sutton-on-Sea Cinemas, Ltd.	£1,000 in £1 shares	Kinema Proprietors ...	Solicitor: W. Warwick James, Welling-borough.
Syston Cinema Co., Ltd.	£2,500 in £1 shares	Kinema Proprietors ...	———
T.A.C. Developments, Ltd.	£1,000 in £1 shares......	Producers, repairers, etc. of sound and silent films.	99, Charlotte Street, W.1.
U. B. Film Co., Ltd.......	£100 in £1 shares.........	Film Producers.	Solicitors: Godden, Holme & Ward, 34, Old Jewry, E.C.
World's Band Centre (Midlands), Ltd.	£300 in £1 shares.........	To organise kinema orchestras, etc.	5, Dean Street, W.1.
World Copyrights, Ltd....	£500 in £1 shares.........	Literary Agents	21, Denmark Street, W.C.2.

AUGUST.

Name.	Capital.	Nature of Business.	Registered Office.
A. & G. Studio Lighting & Equipment Co., Ltd.	£5,000 in £1 shares	Indicated by title	Ergon Works, Worton Road, Isleworth.
Arderne Cinema, Ltd. ...	£25,000 in 21,000 7% cum. pref. and 31,000 ord. shares of 10s.	To erect a kinema	Solicitors: James Gass, 85A, Wellington Road South, Stockport.
Beaumont Films Produc-tions, Ltd.	£100 in £1 shares	Film Producers	58, Haymarket, S.W.1.
British Realita Syndicate, Ltd.	£20,000 in £1 shares ...	Producers and Distri-butors.	Solicitors: Thomas Eggar & Son, 18, Dartmouth Street, S.W.1.
Carlton Cinema (Bexhill), Ltd.	£100 in £1 shares	Kinema Proprietors ...	Solicitor: M. Norman Freedman, Shell Mex House, W.C.2.
Clifton Cinema (Welling-ton), Ltd.	£7,000 in £1 shares (3,500 ord. and 3,500 6% cum. pref.)	To erect a kinema	25, Bennett's Hill, Bir-mingham.
Cosham Super Cinemas, Ltd.	£7,500 in £1 shares	Kinema Proprietors ...	Solicitors: J. D. Lang-ton & Passmore, 16, Tokenhouse Yard, E.C.2.
Direct Recorders, Ltd. ...	£100 in £1 shares	Manufacturers of record-ing apparatus ...	56, Bank Chambers, 329, High Holborn, W.C.
Display Construction Co., Ltd.	£1,000 in £1 shares	Kinema Display De-signers.	Nelson Street Works, Camden Town, N.W.1.
Emelco, Ltd.	£4,000 in £1 shares	Film Distributors	Solicitors: Slaughter & May, 18, Austin Friars, E.C.
Fanfare Pictures, Ltd. ...	£2,000 in £1 shares	—	Canada House, Norfolk Street, W.C.2.
General Film Finance, Ltd.	£2,000 in £1 shares	Film Producers	Solicitors: Walter Burgis & Co., 4 & 5, Bond Court, E.C.4.
Harrow Holdings, Ltd. ...	£4,000 in £1 shares	Kinema Proprietors ...	Solicitors: Billing-hurst, Wood & Pope, 7, Bucklersbury, E.C.4

Name.	Capital.	Nature of Business.	Registered Office.
Kay (West End) Laboratories, Ltd.	£20,000 in £1 shares	Kinematograph Film Printers.	49A, Oxford Road, Finsbury Park, N.4.
Kessex Cinemas, Ltd.	£190,000 in £1 shares (160,000 "A" ord. and 30,000 "B" ord.).	Kinema Proprietors	Solicitors: Richards, Butler, Stokes & Woodham Smith, 88, Leadenhall Street, E.C.3.
Malcolm Picture Productions, Ltd.	£1,000 in £1 shares	Film Producers	145, Wardour Street W.I.
March of Time, Ltd.	£5,000 in £1 shares	Film Producers	Solicitors: Slaughter & May, 18, Austin Friars, E.C.2.
North British Film Corporation, Ltd.	£3,000 in 2,500 ord. shares of £1 and 4,000 def. shares of 2s. 6d. each.	Film Producers	11, Norfolk Street, Manchester.
Odeon (Aylesbury), Ltd.	£12,500 in 12,000 7% cum. pref. shares of £ and 10,000 ord. shares of 1s· each.	Kinema Proprietors	39, Temple Row, Birmingham.
Odeon (Harlesden), Ltd.	£12,500 in 12,000 7% cum. pref. shares of £1 and 10,000 ord. shares of 1s. each.	Kinema Proprietors	39, Temple Row, Birmingham.
Odeon (Sittingbourne), Ltd.	£5,250 in 5,000 7% cum. pref. shares of £1 and 5,000 ord. shares of 1s. each.	Kinema Proprietors	39, Temple Row, Birmingham.
Odeon (Watford), Ltd.	£48,000 in 46,000 7% cum. pref. shares of £1 and 50,000 ord. shares of 1s. each.	Kinema Proprietors	39, Temple Row, Birmingham.
Pinnacle Pictures Productions, Ltd.	£100 in £1 shares	Film Producers	7, Poultry, E.C.2.
Arthur Riscoe & Clifford Whitney, Ltd.	£100 in 1s. shares	—	Solicitors: Simmons & Simmons, 1, Threadneedle Street, E.C.
Ritz (Harrow), Ltd.	£2,000 in £1 shares	Kinema Proprietors	Solicitors: Billinghurst, Wood & Pope, 7, Bucklersbury, E.C.4.
Ritz (Watford), Ltd.	£10,000 in £1 shares	Kinema Proprietors	Solicitors: Billinghurst, Wood & Pope, 7, Bucklersbury, E.C.4.
Savoy Cinema (Netherton), Ltd.	£1,000 in £1 shares	Kinema Proprietors	Northfield House, Netherton, nr. Dudley.
S. S. Productions, Ltd.	£4,000 in £1 shares	Film Producers	Solicitors: Sanders & Co., 32, Savile Row, W.I
Supa Films, Ltd.	£100 in £1 shares	Film Producers	Solicitors: Abbott, Hudson & Anderson, 3-4, Clements Inn, W.C.2.
United Kingdom Theatres Ltd.	£1,000 in 1s. shares	Kinema Proprietors	Solicitors: Kenneth Brown, Baker, Baker, Essex House, Essex Street, W.C.2.
Vineburgh Pictures (Irvine), Ltd.	£7,000 in £1 shares	Kinema Proprietors	—
Whitehall Film Corporation, Ltd.	£100 in £1 shares	—	Solicitors: Gordon, Gardener, Carpenter & Co., 7, Serjeant's Inn, E.C.4.
Winwood Pictures, Ltd.	£1,000 in £1 shares	Film Producers	—

SEPTEMBER.

Name.	Capital.	Nature of Business.	Registered Office.
Adelphi Film Productions, Ltd.	£100 in £1 shares	Film Producers	—
Harry S. Anderson, Ltd.	£100 in £1 shares	Film Producers	19, Garrick Street. W.1.
Beeston Picture House, (Leeds), Ltd.	£1,000 in £1 shares	To erect a kinema	—

Name.	Capital.	Nature of Business.	Registered Office.
Carlton Cinema (Westgate), Ltd.	£100 in £1 shares.........	Kinema Proprietors ...	Shell Mex House, W.C.2.
Chichester Regional Theatre, Ltd.	£18,000 in 13,000 6% cum. par. pref. shares of £1 each and 100,000 ord. shares of 1s. each.	Kinema Proprietors ...	142, Wardour Street, W.1.
Cinema Accessories, Ltd.	£1,000 in 1,000 ord. shares of £1 each.	Dealers in Kinema Accessories.	25, Bennetts Hill, Birmingham.
Clifton Cinema (Fallings Park), Ltd.	£8,000 (4,000 ord. £1 shares and 4,000 6% cum. pref.)	To erect a kinema	25, Bennetts Hill, Birmingham.
Coliseum (Leigh-on-Sea), Ltd.	£4,000 in £1 shares	Kinema Proprietors ...	37, Golden Square, S.W.1.
Colosseum Film Productions, Ltd.	£100 in £1 shares.........	Film Producers	317, High Holborn, W.C.1.
Cosy Cinema (Colwyn Bay), Ltd.	£2,000 in 2,000 shares of £1.	To acquire a kinema ...	—
Charles Farrell Productions, Ltd.	£3,000 in 1,500 ord. and 1,500 7% par. pref. shares of £1 each.	Film Producers	Manchester House, 164, Aldersgate Street, E.C.
Glenroyal Cinema Company, Ltd.	£6,000 in 2,000 6% pref. and 4,000 ord. shares of £1.	Kinema Proprietors ...	—
New Era Cinema Company, Ltd.	£3,000 in 1s. shares ...	Kinema Proprietors ...	Soicitors : Brandon and Nicholscn, Suffolk House, Pall Mall, S.W.1.
Odeon (Boston), Ltd.......	£10,500 in 10,000 7% cum. pref. shares of £1 each and 10,000 ord. shares of 1s. each.	Kinema Proprietors ...	39, Temple Row, Birmingham.
Odeon (Crewe), Ltd.	£10,500 in 10,000 ord. shares of 1s. each and 10,000 7% cum. pref. shares of £1 each.	Kinema Proprietors ...	39, Temple Row, Birmingham.
Odeon (Epsom), Ltd. ...	£10,500 in 10,000 7% cum.	Kinema Proprietors	— 39, Temple Row, Birmingham.
Odeon (Exeter), Ltd. ...	£20,500 in 10,000 ord. shares of 1s. each and 20,000 7% cum. pref. shares of £1 each.	Kinema Proprietors ...	39, Temple Row, Birmingham.
Odeon (Morecambe), Ltd.	£15,500 in 10,000 ord. shares of 1s. each and 15,000 7% cum. pref. shares of £1 each.	Kinema Proprietors ...	39, Temple Row, Birmingham.
Odeon (Peckham), Ltd.	£10,500 in 10,000 7% non-par. cum. pref. shares of £1 each and 10,000 ord. shares of 1s. each.	Kinema Proprietors	39, Temple Row, Birmingham.
Odeon (Penge), Ltd.	£5,250 in 5,000 ord. shares 7% cum. pref. shares of £1 each.	Kinema Proprietors ...	39, Temple Row, Birmingham.
Odeon (Skipton), Ltd. ...	£1,100 in 1,000 7 % cum. pref. shares of £1 each and 2,000 ord. shares of 1s. each.	Kinema Proprietors ...	39, Temple Row, Birmingham.
Plaza (Oldham), Ltd.......	£100 in £1 shares.........	Kinema Proprietors ...	70, Norman Road, Manchester, 14.
Rosslyn Productions Ltd.	£100 in 100 shares of £1 each.	Kinema Proprietors ...	11, Waterloo Place, S.W.1.
Strand Cinemas (Leeds), Ltd.	£20,000 in £1 shares ...	Kinema Proprietors ...	Solicitors : L. Altman, 4, Park Square, Leeds.
Theatre Variety Circuit, Ltd.	£1,500 in £1 shares ...	Kinema Proprietors ...	—
Townhill Cinemas, Ltd....	£10,000 in £1 shares ...	Kinema Proprietors ...	Solicitor : L. Benjamin, 13, Albemarle Street. W.1.
Twentieth Century Music Corporation, Ltd.	£1,000 in £1 shares	To acquire musical copyrights in films, etc.	Solicitors : Joynson-Hicks & Co., Lennox House, Norfolk St., W.C.2.
United British Cinemas (London), Ltd.	£2,000 in £1 shares	Kinema Proprietors ...	Solicitors : David Morris & Co., 1-3, St. Paul's Churchyard, E.C.4.

Name.	Capital.	Nature of Business.	Registered Office.
Western Film Corpora-tion, Ltd.	£1,200 in 1,000 shares of £1 each and 4,000 shares of 1s. each.	Film Producers	2, Clements Inn, W.C.2.

OCTOBER

Name.	Capital.	Nature of Business.	Registered Office.
Arcadian Film Produc-tions, Ltd.	£100 in 100 shares of £1 each.	Film Producers	7, Poultry, E.C.
Askews Pleasure Co., Ltd.	£100 in 100 shares of £1 each.	Kinema Proprietors ...	——
Atkinson's Pictures, Ltd.	£10,000 in 10,000 shares of £1 each.	Kinema Proprietors ...	Solicitors: D. G. Cooke, 28, Broad Street, Bristol.
Attree and Barr, Ltd. ...	£10,000 in 10,000 shares of £1.	Kinema Proprietors ...	——
British Unity Pictures, Ltd.	£10,000 ord. shares of £1 each.	Film Producers	Solicitors: William A. Crump and Son, 27, Leadenhall Street, E.C.3.
Cranbourn Theatres, Ltd.	£1,000 in 1,000 shares of £1 each.	Kinema Proprietors ...	Cathedral House, 8, Pater-noster Row, E.C.4.
Dayray Films, Ltd.	£500 in 500 shares of £1 each.	Film Producers	27, High Street, Croydon.
D.C.P. Durochrome, Ltd.	£1,000 in 20,000 shares of 1s. each.	Film Producers	Solicitors: Ernest Bevir and Son, 4. York Build-ings, Adelphi, W.C.2.
Eagle Film Productions, Ltd.	£100 in 100 shares	Film Producers	Imperial House, Regent Street, W.1.
Entertainment Caterers, Ltd.	£100 in 100 shares of £1 each.	Kinema Proprietors	28b, Albemarle Street, W.1.
Envoy Cinemas and Tele-vision Co., Ltd.	£2,500 in 2,500 shares of £1 each.	Kinema Proprietors	Solicitors: Stanley Robinson and Commin, 53, Shorts Gardens, Drury Lane, W.C.2.
Grahams Cinemas, Ltd.	£100 in 100 shares of £1 each.	Kinema Proprietors ...	Corridor Chambers, Mar-ket Place, Leicester.
Granton Cinema Co.	£15,000 in £1 shares ...	Kinema Proprietors ...	——
Hallking Cinema Co., Ltd.	£1,000 in 1,000 shares of £1 each.	Kinema Proprietors ...	10, Windsor Place, Car-diff.
Hillside Ridgeway, Ltd.	£1,000 in 1,000 shares of £1 each (500 5 p.c. cum. pref.)	Film Producers	746, High Road, Totten-ham, N. 17.
Hippodrome (Dover), Ltd.	£100 in 100 shares of £1 each.	Kinema Proprietors ...	Solicitors: R. Hamilton Twyford and Co., 72, Soho Square, W.1.
International Talking Pictures, Ltd.	£100 in 100 shares of £1 each.	Film Producers	Trafalgar House, 11, Waterloo Place, S.W.1.
Inveresk Cinema Co.,Ltd.	£15,000 in £1 shares ...	Kinema Proprietors ...	——
Kine-Ads., Ltd.	£100 in 100 shares of £1	Film Producers and Publicity Agents.	——
London and District Cinemas, Ltd.	£100 in 400 shares of 5s. each.	Kinema Proprietors ...	Solicitors: Herbert Oppenheimer, Nathan Vandyk and Mackay, 1-2, Finsbury Square, E.C.2.
Marconnel Productions, Ltd.	£100 in 400 shares of 5s. each.	Proprietors of Theatres	Solicitors: J. D. Lang-ton and Passmore, 8, Bolton Street, W.1.
Maypole Cinema, Ltd. ...	£2,000 in 1,000 5 p.c. pref. and 1,000 ord. shares each.	Kinema Proprietors ...	Shore Street, Holywood, Co. Down.
Maypole Cinema, Ltd. ...	£10,000 in 10,000 shares of £1 each (2,000 ord. and 8,000 6 p.c. accum. pref.)	Kinema Proprietors ...	25, Bennetts Hill, Bir-mingham.
MobileEntertainmentLtd.	£100 in £1 shares.........	Indicated by the title	——
New-Era Cinema (Lowes-toft), Ltd.	£100 in 100 ord. shares of £1 each.	Kinema Proprietors ...	Solicitors: Brandon and Nicholson, Suffolk Place, S.W.1.

Name.	Capital.	Nature of Business.	Registered Office.
New Plaza (Prestwich), Ltd.	£5,000 in 5,000 shares of £1 each.	Kinema Proprietors ...	Bury New Road, Prestwich, Manchester.
Odeon (Llandudno), Ltd.	£10,500 in 10,000 6 p.c. cum. pref. shares of £1 and 10,000 ord. shares of 1s.	Kinema Proprietors ...	39, Temple Row, Birmingham.
Odeon (Radcliffe), Ltd.	£5,250 in 5,000 6 p.c. cum. pref, shares of £1 and 5,000 ord. shares of 1s.	Kinema Proprietors ...	39, Temple Row, Birmingham.
Paladium Cinemas (Burslem) Ltd.	£1,000 in £1 shares ...	Kinema Proprietors ...	Palladium Cinema, Burslem, Stoke-on-Trent.
Paramount Theatre Corporation (Great Britain) Ltd.	£100 in 2,000 shares of 1s. each.	Kinema Proprietors ...	Solicitors: Kenneth Brown Baker, Baker, Essex House, Essex Street, W.C.2.
Pembroke Productions Ltd.	£100 in 100 shares of £1 each.	Kinema Proprietors ...	Solicitors: Knapp-Fisher and Wartnaby, Chapter Clerk's Office, Westminster Abbey, S.W.1. and 27, Bolton Street, W.1
Photographic Murals Ltd.	£1,300 in £1 shares. ...	... Photographers manufacturers of film photographic backings.	
Portavon Cinema Co., Ltd.	£5,000 in £1 shares ...	Kinema Proprietors ...	10, Windsor Place, Cardiff.
Priority Productions Ltd.	£2,000 in 2,000 shares of £1.	Film Producers	Solicitors: Farman, Daniell and Co., 259, High Holborn, W.C.1.
Riddrie Picture House, Ltd.	£15,000 in £1 shares ...	Kinema Proprietors ...	105, St. Vincent Street, Glasgow, C.2.
Savoy Cinema (Kilkenny) Ltd.	£10,000 in £1 shares ...	Kinema Proprietors ...	——
Screnus Manufacturing Co., Ltd.	£100 in 100 shares of £1 each.	Manufacturers of kinematographic apparatus.	——
Stoke Entertainments, Ltd.	£6,000 in 6,000 shares of £1 each.	Kinema Proprietors ...	Lloyds House, Albert Square, Manchester.
St. James's Films, Ltd.	£10,000 in 1s. shares ...	Film Producers	Cunard House, 88, Leadenhall Street, E.C.3.
Warrington Holdings, Ltd.	£9,000 in 9,000 shares of £1 each.	Kinema Proprietors ...	Solicitors: Billinghurst, Wood and Pope, 7, Bucklersbury, E.C.

NOVEMBER

Name.	Capital.	Nature of Business.	Registered Office.
Ajax Film Corporation, Ltd.	£1,000 in 2,000 ord. and 2,000 6 p.c. par. pref. shares of 5s. each.	Film Producers	125, New Bond Street, W.1.
Associated British Freehold and Leaseholds, Ltd.	£100 in 100 ord. shares of £1 each.	Kinema Proprietors ...	Solicitors: Clifford Turner and Co., 11, Old Jewry, E.C.2.
Associated British Properties, Ltd.	£100 in 100 ord. shares of £1 each.	Kinema Proprietors ...	Solicitors: Clifford Turner and Co., 11, Old Jewry, E.C.2.
Adelphi Cinema (Burry Port), Ltd.	£6,000 in 6,000 shares of £1 each.	Kinema Proprietors ...	16, Northampton Place, Swansea.
British Animated Films, Ltd.	£2,000 in 1,000 5 p.c. cum. pref. shares of £1 and 14,950 "A" ord. and 5,050 "B" ord. shares of 1s.	Film Producers	Solicitors: Sutton, Ommanney and Oliver, 7-8, Great Winchester Street, E.C.2.
Bulwell Adelphi, Ltd. ...	£10,000 in 10,000 shares of £1 each.	Kinema Proprietors ...	——
Bushey Film Corporation Ltd.	£1,000 in 1,000 shares of £1 each.	Film Producers	——
Cinema Ground Rents and Properties, Ltd.	£5,000,000 in 5,000,000 shares of £1 each.	Kinema Proprietors ...	Solicitors: Simmons and Simmons, 1, Threadneedle Street, E.C.2.
Fortune Films, Ltd. ...	£100 in £1 shares.........	Film Producers	177, Regent Street, W.1.

Name.	Capital.	Nature of Business.	Registered Office.
Galaxy Production Corporation, Ltd.	£15,000 in 1,400 6 p.c. par. pref. shares of £10 each and 20,000 ord. shares of 1s. each.	Kinema Proprietors ...	——
G. L. Cinema, Ltd.	£12,000 in 12,000 shares of £1 each.	Kinema Proprietors ...	Lombard House, Gt. Charles Street, Birmingham.
Haven Pictures, Ltd. ...	£500 in 500 shares of £1 each.	Kinema Proprietors ...	45, Newhall Street, Birmingham.
Horizon Pictures Corporation, Ltd.	£500 in 1,000 shares of 10s. each.	Kinema Proprietors ...	Solicitors: J. D. Langton and Passmore, 2, Bolton Street, W.
Improved Cinema Equipment, Ltd.	£3,500 in 6 p.c. cum. pref. shares of £1 each and 10,000 ord. shares of 1s. each.	——	Salisbury Square House, Fleet Street, E.C.4.
Irving Harris, Ltd. ...	£1,000 in 1,000 shares of £1 each.	Kinema Proprietors ...	171, Wardour Street, W.1
Latin America Film Film Distributors, Ltd.	£10,500 in 10,000 10 p.c. cum. pref. shares of £1 and 10,000 shares of 1s. each.	Film Dealers	Solicitors: McKenna and Co., 31, Basinghall Street, E.C.
Marquis Productions, Ltd.	£100 in 100 shares of £1 each.	Film Producers	60-66, Wardour Street, W.1.
Messulam Picture Corporation, Ltd.	£100 shares of £1 each...	Film Producers	86, Queen Victoria Street, E.C.4.
Metro Goldwyn Mayer British Studios, Ltd.	£25,000 in £1 shares ...	Film Producers	18, Bloomsbury Square, W.C.1.
Metropolis Films, Ltd.	£500 in 500 ord. shares of £1 each.	Film Producers	16, Albemarle Street, W.1
Odeon (Bristol) Ltd.	£10,500 in 10,000 6 p.c. cum. pref. shares of £1 and 10,000 ord. shares of 1s.	Kinema Proprietors ...	39, Temple Row, Birmingham.
Odeon (High Barnet) Ltd.	£5,000 in 5,000 6 p.c. cum. pref. shares of £1 and 2,000 ord. shares of 1s.	Kinema Proprietors ...	39, Temple Row, Birmingham.
Odeon (Southsea) Ltd. ...	£10,500 in 10,000 6 p.c. cum. pref. shares of £1 and 10,000 ord. shares of 1s. each.	Kinema Proprietors ...	39, Temple Row, Birmingham.
Odeon (Swiss Cottage) Ltd.	£10,500 in 6 p.c. cum. pref. shares of £1 and 10,000 ord. shares of 1s. each.	Kinema Proprietors ...	39, Temple Row, Birmingham.
Regal Cinemas, Ltd. ...	£3,000 in £1 shares ...	To acquire a kinema ...	——
Regal Cinema (Tadcaster), Ltd.	£6,000 in £1 shares ...	Kinema Proprietors ...	——
Ritz Cinema Co. (Pilsley), Ltd.	£2,000 shares of £1 each.	Kinema Proprietors ...	Solicitors: Harrop White Gamble and Vallace, Mansfield.
School Films, Ltd.	£9,000 in 9,000 shares of £1 each.	Film Producers and Distributors.	3, Denmark Street, Holborn, W.C.
Shannon Cinemas, Ltd.	£20,000 in £1 shares ...	Kinema Proprietors ...	Solicitors: Garton and Co., 9, Cavendish Sq., W.1.
Sheffield News Theatres, Ltd.	£2,000 in 2,000 shares of £1 each.	Kinema Proprietors ...	18, Devonshire Street, Bishopsgate, E.C.2.
Sound Services, Ltd. ...	£120,000 in £1 shares (20,000 6 p.c. cum. pref. and 100,000 rd.)	Distributors of educational and propaganda films.	Bush House, Aldwych, W.C.2.
Sydney Wake, Ltd.	£5,000 in £1 shares	Film Printers	Kent House, 87, Regent Street, W.1.
Trade Colour Films, Ltd.	£1,000 in £1 shares	Film Producers	10, Sussex Place, S.W.7.
Triangle Film Productions, Ltd.	£100 in £1 shares.........	Film Producers	Solicitors: Kerly, Sons and Karuth, 10 and 11, Austin Friars, E.C.2.
Universal Royalties, Ltd.	£15,000 in £1 shares ...	Manufacturers and Distributors of Kinematographic Apparatus.	12, Norfolk Street, W.C.2.
Ward's Theatres, Ltd.	£100 in 100 shares of £1 each.	Kinema Proprietors ...	Kent House, 87, Regent Street, W.1.

Bankruptcies, Liquidations, etc.

No attempt has been made, under this heading, to cover all the minor instances of failure in the^e Industry, only cases likely to have a general interest being included.

RECEIVERSHIPS, APPOINTMENTS, AND RELEASES.

A. and C. Theatres, Ltd., 30, Gerrard Street, W.1.—Henry H. Franklin, of 30, Gerrard Street, W.1, was appointed Receiver and Manager on November 5, 1936, under powers contained in debenture dated April 30, 1936.

A.C. 1923, Ltd.—S. A. Letts, of 5, Arundel Street, W.C.2, ceased to act as Receiver and Manager on March 26, 1936.

Albany Studios, Ltd.—Fdk. F. Sharles, of 63, Coleman Street, E.C., was appointed Receiver on January 22, 1936, under powers contained in debenture dated April 1, 1935.

Associated Theatre (Margate), Ltd.—W. T. S. Thorn, accountant, of 5, Cecil Square, Margate, was appointed Receiver and Manager on July 4, 1936, under powers contained in mortgage dated February 28, 1935.

Astoria (Purley), Ltd.—F. V. Arnold, of Midland Bank Chambers, 153, North Street, Brighton, ceased to act as Receiver on May 13, 1936.

Authentic Intelligence Depot, Ltd. (art directors, publicity agents, caterers for the manufacture of films, photo and other plays, etc., 12, Whitehall, S.W.1).—E. O. Simpson, of Eagle house, Jermyn Street, S.W.1, was appointed Receiver and Manager on September 12, 1936, under powers contained in debenture dated August 28, 1936.

Automatic Electrical and Mechanical Controls, Ltd.—G. F. Salas, of 19, Hanover Buildings, Thomas Street, W.1, was appointed Receiver and/or Manager on March 30, 1936, under powers contained in debentures dated March 6 and 17, 1936.

British Publicity Talking Films, Ltd.—J. Gough, of 267-8, Castle Street, Dudley, ceased to act as Receiver and/or Manager on April 24, 1936.

British Utility Films, Ltd., 10, Regent Square, W.C.1.—M. J. Wilson, of 54-8, Wardour Street, W.1, was appointed Receiver on June 12, 1936, under powers contained in debenture dated May 9, 1935.

Bulman Jupiter Screen Co., Ltd.—H. W. Maguire, commercial accountant, of 195, Croxted Road, West Dulwich, S.E.21, was appointed Receiver and/or Manager on May 5, 1936, under powers contained in debenture dated February 12, 1934.

Capitol (Winchmore Hill), Ltd., 30-31, Golden Square, W.1.—J. H. MacDonald, of 14, Heddon Street, W., was appointed Receiver on August 28, 1936, under powers contained in second debenture dated March 16, 1932.

Capitol (Winchmore Hill), Ltd., 30-31, Golden Square W.1.—Two notices of the appointment (1) of F. H. Parrott, C.A., of 4, Southampton Row, W.C.1, and (2) J. R. Easton, of Mayes Road, Wood Green, N.22, as Receivers and Managers on July 23, 1936, under powers contained in debentures dated March 16, 1932.

Capitol (Winchmore Hill), Ltd., 30-31, Golden Square, W.1.—F. H. Parrott, of 4, Southampton Row, W.C.1, ceased to act as Receiver and Manager on August 12, 1936.

Chopwell Cinema Co., Ltd.—J. S. Armstrong and H. J. Armstrong, both of 2, Collingwood Street, Newcastle-upon-Tyne, were appointed Receivers on January 1, 1936, under powers contained in mortgage dated August 6, 1921, and further charge dated August 29, 1921, and debenture dated March 21, 1922, in place of J. W. Armstrong, deceased.

Cinema and Interior Decorations, Ltd.—H. G. W. Gibson C.A., of Aldwych House, Aldwych, W.C.2, was appointed Receiver on May 8, 1936, under powers contained in debenture dated May 10, 1934.

City Film Corporation, Ltd.—S. B. Smith, of 4 and 6, Throgmorton Avenue, E.C., was appointed Receiver and Manager on April 9, 1936, under powers contained in instruments dated March 14, 19 and 23, and April 2, 1936. (See also "Mortgages and Charges.")

Dayzite, Ltd.—W. A. J. Osborne, of Balfour House, Finsbury Pavement, E.C., was appointed Receiver and Manager on January 31, 1936, under powers contained in trust deed dated April 30, 1934.

Dennis Connelly, Ltd.—R. M. Honeybone, of 110, Cannon Street, E.C., was appointed Receiver and Manager on January 3, 1936, under powers contained in debenture dated November 1, 1934.

Elite Picture Theatre (Middlesbrough), Ltd., 30-31, Golden Square, W.1.—J. H. McDonald, of 14, Heddon Street, W.1, was appointed Receiver on November 10, 1936, under powers contained in third mortgage debentures dated July 27, 1923.

Film Dubbing Corporation, Ltd. 179, Wardour Street, W.1).—R. O. Young, of 30, Upper Berkeley Street, W., was appointed Receiver on September 9, 1936, under powers contained in debentures dated April 29, 1936.

Film Dubbing Corporation, Ltd., 179, Wardour Street, W.—Richard O. Young, of 30, Upper Berkeley Street, W.1, ceased to act as Receiver and/or Manager on October 13, 1936.

Film Services, Ltd.—W. F. Grimwood, solicitor's managing clerk, of "Upwey," Downsview Road, Beulah Hill, S.W., was appointed Receiver and Manager on January 16, 1936, under powers contained in debenture dated October 1, 1935.

Finchley Theatre Co., Ltd., Effingham House, Arundel Street, W.C.2.—Percy F. Hedges, of The Briars, Southend Road, Hockley, Essex, ceased to act as Receiver and/or Manager on October 10, 1936.

Fotex Works (Biggleswade), Ltd.—Bernardo T. Crew, of 4, Dove Court, Old Jewry, E.C.2, ceased to act as Receiver and Manager on April 20, 1936.

International Kinograph, Ltd.—Fdk. F. Sharles, of 63, Coleman Street, E.C.2, was appointed Receiver on January 22, 1936, under powers contained in debenture dated April 1, 1935.

Jesba Films, Ltd.—W. B. Cullen, of Granby Chambers, 44, Friar Lane, Nottingham, was appointed Receiver on February 18, 1936, under powers contained in second debentures created July 29, 1935.

Lewisham Theatres, Ltd., 36, Golden Square, W.1.—Alfred Laban, of 25-27, Oxford Street, W.1., ceased to act as Receiver on June 9, 1936.

Manchester Theatre Royal Cinema (1923), Ltd., Peter Street, Manchester.—W. G. Lithgow, of 413, Lord Street, Southport, ceased to act as Receiver and/or Manager on July 2, 1936. Notice filed September 4, 1936.

Milheath Studios, Ltd., 89-91, Wardour Street, W.1.—R. L. Tillett, C.A., of 16, John Street, Adelphi, W.C.2, was appointed Receiver and Manager on June 25, 1936, under powers contained in instrument dated April 17, 1936.

New Ideal Pictures, Ltd.—H. G. Judd, of 8, Frederick's Place, E.C.2, was appointed Receiver and Manager on January 30, 1936, under powers contained in charge dated December 3, 1935.

Omnicolor, Ltd., 220, Fulham Palace Road, W.6. —Two notices of the appointment of R. T. Cuff, of 17, Bedford Row, W.C., as Receiver on July 20, 1936, under powers contained in debentures dated (1) March 20, 1936, and (2) second debenture dated April 3 and 17, May 15, June 5 and 26, and July 10, 1936.

Producers Distributing Co. (U.K.), Ltd. (formerly P.D.C., Ltd.).—H. G. Judd, of 8, Frederick's Place, E.C.2, was appointed Receiver and Manager on January 30, 1936, under powers contained in debenture or charge dated November 23, 1935.

"Q" Film Studios, Ltd.—M. J. Wilson, of 54-8, Wardour Street, W., ceased to act as Receiver and Manager on March 6, 1936.

R.I. Films, Ltd., 20, Fawcett Street, Sunderland.—P. W. Strauss, of 3, Great Winchester. Street, E.C., was appointed Receiver and Manager on September 1, 1936, under powers contained in debenture dated April 29, 1935.

Rivoli Estates, Ltd.—Mortgage and charge on properties in Chorlton-on-Medlock, Manchester, and the company's undertaking and other property, present and future, including uncalled capital, dated March 2, 1936, to secure all moneys due or to become due from the company to the Midland Bank, Ltd.

Geoffrey Rowson, Ltd.—Charles E. M. Emmerson, of 28, King Street, Cheapside, E.C., ceased to act as Receiver and/or Manager.

Scenario Productions, Ltd., 12, D'Arblay Street, W.1.—H. G. N. Lee, of 24, John Street, Bedford Row, W.C.1, ceased to act as Receiver and Manager on July 7, 1936.

Standard Kine Laboratories, Ltd. (formerly Standard Kinematograph Co., Ltd.).—C. M. Duncan, C.A., of 19a, Coleman Street, E.C., was appointed Receiver on February 19, 1936, under powers contained in first and second debentures dated July 23, 1926, November 15, 1934, and October 15, 1935.

Stereotone, Ltd., cameras, kinema screens, etc., 72a, Osborne Road, Acton, W.—(1) R. Y. Lowe, of 91, Shaftesbury Avenue, W.1, ceased to act as Receiver on August 7, 1936, and (2) C. L. Walker, of the above address, was appointed Receiver and Manager on same date, under powers contained in debentures dated November 4, 1935, and March 7, 1936.

Stereotone, Ltd., manufacturers of cameras, kinema screens, etc., 72a, Osborne Road, Acton, W.—Russell Yorke Lowe, of 91, Shaftesbury Avenue, W.1, was appointed Receiver and Manager on July 28, 1936, under powers contained in debentures dated November 4, 1935, and March 7, 1936.

T.A.C. Developments, Ltd., producers of colour films, etc., 99, Charlotte Street, W.1.—John F. Duff, of 20, Beechcroft Avenue, Golders Green, N.W.11, was appointed Receiver on November 5, 1936, under powers contained in debenture dated July 30, 1936.

United Kingdom Photoplays, Ltd., 4, Park Place, Cardiff.—P. H. Walker, of 4, Park Place, Cardiff, ceased to act as Receiver and Manager on August 31, 1936.

United Picture Theatres, Ltd., 123, Regent Street, W.—N. W. Wild, of Orient House, 42-5, New Broad Street, E.C., ceased to act as Receiver and Manager on September 3. 1936.

COMPANIES WINDING UP.

VOLUNTARY AND COMPULSORY LIQUIDATIONS.

Authentic Intelligence Depot.—The statutory meeting of creditors of Authentic Intelligence Depot, Ltd., Whitehall, London, S.W., was held on September 16 at Eagle House, 110, Jermyn Street, London, S.W.1, when Ulric C. de Burgh, chairman of the company, presided, and said that the shareholders had passed a resolution for the appointment of S.F. Aspell as liquidator.

According to a statement of affairs, the liabilities amounted to £477 0s. 3d., and the assets after deducting £12 for preferential claims were estimated to realise £123 6s. 11d., thus disclosing a deficiency of £353 13s. 4d. The issued capital of the company was £1,850, divided into 2,000 ordinary shares of 1s. each, fully paid, and 1,750 preference shares of £1 each, fully paid.

The chairman said that with regard to the assets, the ultimate dividend for creditors would depend to a very large extent on the amount received for a film called "Captain Scott at the South Pole." The company were entitled to receive a commission on all the bookings of this film.

A resolution was passed confirming the appointment of Mr. Aspell as liquidator.

British and Far East Pictures in Liquidation.— In the compulsory liquidation of British and Far East Pictures Corporation, Ltd., film exhibitors and distributors, High Holborn House, High Holborn, London, W.C.1, the Official Receiver, who is also liquidator, has issued a summary of the company's statement of affairs which discloses gross liabilities £5,394, of which £1,101 are unsecured and with regard to creditors an estimated surplus in assets of £2,855. With reference to the shareholders, a deficiency of £11,371 is shown.

The Official Receiver reports in his accompanying observations that the company was registered as a private company on February 27, 1935, with a nominal capital of £25,000, of which £14,227 was issued, and was formed by Shripaul Chandera Jaina, who came to England from India in May, 1934. His scheme was to distribute British films of a good moral class in India. Various titled people, some of whom had important associations with India, expressed willingness to use their influence to support the venture and to become shareholders in the proposed company.

Film rights, prints and publicity matter were acquired by the company for a total of approximately £15,650, and in respect of substantially the whole of these purchases Jaina is recorded as the vendor. All films purchased by the company have been sent to India.

It appears that all the company's films are claimed by creditors as security for the payment of their accounts, and that no films are available for realisation as free assets in the liquidation. The Official Receiver, however, is in negotiation with the parties who have the custody of the films and with the late managing agents, with the object of arranging if possible for the late managing agents to take over all films lying in bond in India on terms which would provide a cash payment for the benefit of the liquidation. Unless these negotiations can be concluded successfully, there would appear to be no prospect of any funds becoming available for unsecured creditors.

According to Jaina, the failure of the company is due entirely to the very serious adverse effect upon the company's business of an article published in a weekly periodical dated April 22, 1935. Jaina states that this article was brought to the notice of the company's managing agents in India, and, in consequence, financial support promised by them to the extent of Rs. 50,000 (£3,750), and more as and when required, was not forthcoming. Jaina and the company commenced proceedings for libel, but the action was dismissed as neither Jaina nor the company complied with an Order of the Court to provide security for costs.

Lombard Finance Corporation Meeting.—The statutory meetings of the creditors and of the shareholders under the compulsory liquidation of Lombard Finance Corporation, Ltd., 69, Basinghall Street, London, E.C.2, were held on August 28 at 33, Carey Street, Lincoln's Inn, London W.C.2.

According to the statement of affairs filed there were liabilities amounting to £3,129 against assets of £4. The issued capital of the company was £10 only.

The Assistant Official Receiver reported that A. McNicol Turner (a director) was formerly associated with the Women's International Film Association (Wifa), a body of women's opinion designed to better the quality of kinematograph films shown in this country.

The Lombard Finance Corporation was formed in April, 1934, to effect the conversion of "Wifa" into a limited company and induce the "Wifa" members to become shareholders, but the response was so poor that few shares were sold. The company was to receive £15,000 for promoting Wifa films, but the arrangements fell through owing to the failure to attract capital.

The liquidation was left in the hands of the Official Receiver.

New Ideal Pictures, Ltd., Hammersmith.—In this compulsory liquidation the Official Receiver, who is also liquidator, has issued a summary of the company's statement of affairs showing the position at January 30 last, when a receiver was appointed on behalf of the debenture-holder.

Gross liabilities are estimated at £54,556, of which £18,505 are expected to rank, there being 202 unsecured creditors for £15,375, and the assets are valued at £6,534, but are subject to the payment of preferential claims amounting to £20 and also that of the debenture-holder, which is scheduled at £5,250. A deficiency of £17,241 is accordingly disclosed regarding the creditors.

The Official Receiver reports that the company was formed by Simon Rowson and was registered as a private company on October 18, 1933, with a nominal capital of £100 divided into shares of £1 each. The nominal capital was increased to £10,000 on July 26, 1935. The issued capital is £100, subscribed for cash.

The failure of the company is attributed by the directors to the lack of money to pay pressing creditors who were not willing to wait until the revenues from the films were received; to

inability to raise money on contracts more than six months ahead; and to the fact that the costs of the films exceeded the estimates.

The Official Receiver alleges that this amounts to an admission of mismanagement on the part of the directors in seriously underestimating the financial requirements of the company and failing to make adequate provision to meet them, or alternatively to keep expenditure within the limits of the financial resources of the company, charging the entire assets of the company.

The receiver for the debenture-holder, Mr. H. G. Judd, C.A., of 8, Frederick's Place, E.C., recently sold the company's principal assets and he has informed the Official Receiver that he cannot see that there is likely to be any sum available for the unsecured creditors.

Producers Distributing Co. (U.K.), Ltd.—In this compulsory liquidation the Official Receiver, who is also liquidator, has issued a summary of the company's statement of affairs showing the position at January 30 last, when a receiver was appointed on behalf of the debenture holder.

The gross liabilities are returned at £81,962, of which £28,335 are expected to rank, there being 217 unsecured creditors with claims totalling £25,677. The assets are estimated at £55,449, and after payment of the preferential claims, which are returned at £2,544, and that of the debenture holder of £10,500, show an estimated surplus of £14,270 regarding creditors. In relation to the shareholders there is, however, disclosed a deficiency of £5,729.

The Official Receiver reports that the company was formed by Reginald Cyril Smith and was registered as a private company on April 10, 1931, under the name of P.D.C., Ltd. On June 29, 1935, the name was changed to Producers Distributing Co. (U.K.), Ltd.

The failure of the company is attributed by Simon Rowson to inadequate capital and heavy overhead expenses. He states that the overheads were not excessive for a business of this kind and could not be materially reduced. The policy of the company was directed to increasing the volume of business without increasing the overheads.

Mr. Smith attributes the failure to the fact that the company was unable to acquire and distribute sufficient British pictures, for which there was a greater demand than for American of the class for which the company acquired distribution rights. He stated that the policy was to distribute 12 English and 30 American pictures, but only three of the former were obtained. In the opinion of the Official Receiver the failure was due to excessive overhead charges attributable to mismanagement (so he alleges) on the part of the directors.

The Receiver (H. G. Judd) has sold the company's principal assets, and he has informed the Official Receiver that it is unlikely that any surplus will become available for the unsecured creditors.

BANKRUPTCIES.

Frederick William Ratcliffe-Holmes, film producer and agent, 53-54, Haymarket, London, S.W.1.

In this bankruptcy the Official Receiver has issued a summary of the debtor's statement of affairs showing gross liabilities £3,049, of which £1,507 are unsecured, and estimated assets £818.

The Official Receiver reports that the debtor has failed on two previous occasions, and it appears from his statements that, following his previous bankruptcy in June, 1932 (from which he has obtained his discharge), he was employed in making films.

On February 26, 1934, he formed " Reality Films, Ltd.," for the purpose of producing and distributing films at 42, Copthall Avenue, London, E.C.2, and later at 53-4. Haymarket, W., and his wife became its first and only directors without remuneration. The company, which had an issued capital of £2 only, obtained on March 2, 1934, a loan of £500, in respect of which a debenture was issued on its undertaking. One picture was produced, and after six months' trading, during which period he. drew about £250 for his services, the. company became dormant until its recent revival.

A completed film (length about 3,490 ft.) was ultimately delivered in February, when the advance by bankers of £1,700 was repaid and the guarantor released the assignment mentioned, but on March 24, 1936, judgment was obtained against him by another firm which had advanced money, and these proceedings ensued.

Benjamin Hyman Zimmerman, kinema proprietor, 52, Sydner Road, Stoke Newington, London, formerly associated with the Empire, Windsor.

The Official Receiver has issued a summary of the debtor's statement of affairs showing liabilities £2,177, of which £560 are unsecured, and net assets £273,. apart from a reversionary interest and shares, the realisable value of which is given as uncertain.

CREDITORS' MEETINGS.

Film Services, Ltd., Statement of Affairs.—The adjourned first meetings of the creditors and shareholders of **Film Services, Ltd.,** 29, Gt. Pulteney Street, London, W.1, were held at the offices of the Board of Trade, Carey Street, W.C.

The Official Receiver reported that the company was registered in September, 1934, with a nominal capital of £1,000. About June, 1935, it appeared that the company was seriously handicapped by lack of cash capital, and Joseph Wm. Dude, a director, acting for himself and under a power of attorney for his co-director, a German national, and being interested only in. the technical side of the business, sold to the Safare (Africa), Ltd., the vendors' respective shareholdings in Film Services, Ltd., for £750, to be paid by the purchasers out of the net profits of the business. Under the management of the Safare (Africa), Ltd., the activities of Film Services, Ltd., were considerably stimulated and the company showed signs of a profitable undertaking. In September, 1935. however, it became necessary for Safare (Africa), Ltd., to curtail its film productions, and it was obvious that unless the company could obtain productions from other sources it could not meet its obligations. The failure was attributed to the lack of cash working capital.

M. J. Wilton, certified accountant, of 58 Wardour Street, was nominated for the position of liquidator by resolution of the creditors and shareholders. The statement of affairs shows liabilities £767. of which £178 is unsecured, no assets and a total deficiency as regards shareholders of £1,178.

Delayed Exhibition of Picture.—Under a receiving order against Frederick William Ratcliffe-Holmes, film producer, 53-54, Haymarket, London, S.W.1, made on June 4 on a creditor's petition, the first meeting of creditors was held in Bankruptcy Buildings, Carey Street, W.C.

It appears that after May, 1932, Mr. Ratcliffe-Holmes was engaged as a journalist and in making films for other persons. In or about February, 1934, a company was formed and of this he became the governing director. He was interested in a proposed expedition to make a film of wild life in Africa, but it did not go.

Mr. Holmes estimates his liabilities at £2,300, and attributes his failure to the technical difficulties and details which arose in the production of a certain film which resulted in the costs of production far exceeding the original estimate and delayed its exhibition, thus losing revenue. The precise value of the assets had apparently not yet been ascertained.

A resolution was passed for the appointment of F. S. Salaman, C.A., 1 and 2, Bucklersbury, E.C., to act as trustee of the debtor's estate, the fidelity bond being recommended at £200, but it was agreed that the usual application for adjudication should be delayed for 14 days.

Losses Attributed to Fire.—The statutory first meeting of creditors was held on Wednesday, September 2, at London Bridge Buildings under the failure of Joseph Maxwell Signy, kinema proprietor, of 211, Hendon Way, and lately of Woodstock Avenue, Golders Green.

According to the. debtor's statement, a previous failure was recorded against him in July, 1931, from which proceedings he has not applied to be discharged. After the failure he was employed by various kinema companies, and in January, 1935, in partnership with one Albert Jacobs, he secured a 21 years' lease of the Princes Cinema at The Broadway, Wimbledon. They redecorated the theatre, and installed new seating accommodation and talkie apparatus at a cost of about £1,400.

The improvements were effected on hire-purchase terms, and under the conditions of the lease everything put into the kinema. became landlord's fittings.

After two months they formed Princes Cinema (Wimbledon), Ltd., which acquired their interest in the concern of a number of shares. A fire occurred in July, 1935, and although the property was insured for only £1,500 they claimed £1,900 for loss of profits. That claim is still pending.

In November, 1935, the landlords obtained judgment for arrears of rent, and an order for possession. The lease was cancelled and the company became more or less moribund.

The debtor estimates his liabilities at £700 and the only assets are shares in Princes Cinema (Wimbledon), Ltd., of doubtful value. He attributes his insolvency to the cessation of the business of Princes Cinema (Wimbledon), Ltd., owing to the fire and to guarantees given on behalf of the company.

A resolution was passed for Percy Phillips, accountant, 118-122, Gt. Portland Street, W., to act as trustee and administer the estate. in bankruptcy, with the assistance of a committee of inspection, consisting of representatives of Gaumont-British Picture Corporation, Ltd., Fox Film Co., Ltd., and Mills Conduit Investments, Ltd.

APPLICATIONS FOR DISCHARGE.

J. Redfern Collins Applies for Discharge.—On January 29, John Redfern Collins, film distributor, 24, Denmark Street, London, W.C.1, applied at the London Bankruptcy Court for a discharge.

Mr. Collins failed in July last year with liabilities of £7,052 and assets which realised £10.

It appeared that applicant for a time traded in partnership with another as the Commercial Film Service, and during 1929 commenced to supply films and apparatus to the Royal Navy. After the introduction of sound films in 1930 considerable sums were spent in experimenting for apparatus suitable for use on ships at sea, and after 1930 he also exhibited films at Malta.

His insolvency was attributed to the advent of sound films, which necessitated considerable expenditure in experiments; to law costs in connection with the venture at Malta; and to loss of the shipping contracts.

On statutory grounds the discharge was suspended for nine months.

Lena Maud Purcell, lately carrying on business at the Chingford Kinema, who was adjudged a bankrupt on October 12 last, applied in the London Bankruptcy Court for her discharge.

Mr. C. Bruce Park, Official Receiver, said that the ranking liabilities were estimated at £7,319, and, according to the report of the trustee in bankruptcy, the total probable realisation would be £112, the whole of which, would, however, be absorbed by fees, costs, charges and preferential claims.

After hearing Mr. Raeburn on behalf of the trustee in bankruptcy and Mr. Aronson for the debtor, his Honour suspended the discharge for six months.

GENERAL FINANCIAL CASES.

B. and N. Films.—A declaration of solvency was filed on July 15 relating to B. and N. Films, Ltd., which was registered as a "private" company on February 15, 1933, to carry on the business cf producers of kinematograph plays and films, etc. The authorised capital is £1,000 in £1 shares, of which, to December 26, 1935, 504 shares (including one forfeited) had been issued and fully paid up in cash. The shareholders at the date named were :—Patrick O. Brunner, Baron Nahum and Geo. M. Lloyd. At the date of the return there were mortgages and charges for £9,000 outstanding, but these were fully paid off on July 1, 1936. The directors are Patrick O. Brunner and Arthur P. Richards. The registered office is at 193, Wardour Street, W.1.

Astoria (Southend).—A declaration of solvency was filed on July 13 relating to the Astoria (Southend), Ltd., which was registered as a "private" company on April 21, 1934.

The authorised capital was originally £100, but it was increased in June, 1934, and is now £45,500 in 40,000 7 per cent, cumulative redeemable preference shares of £1 each and 110,000 ordinary shares of 1s. each. To December 31, 1935, 28,250 preference and 86,500 ordinary shares had been issued and fully paid up in cash.

The shareholders at the date named were :—

	Ord.	Pref.
Wm. J. Griggs	10,000	5,000
Wm. L. Stephenson ...	1	5,000
Chas. Hugh Bell	1	2,000
Stanley L. Groom	10,000	5,000
Edward A. Stone	1	5,000
Wm. W. Turner	5,000	2,500
Cecil F. Karuth and Hugh V. Harraway	59,997	—
John J. Broad	—	500
Drake and Gorham, Ltd. ...	—	1,500
John Compton Organ Co., Ltd.	—	1,000
Wm. Ward	1,500	750
	86,500	28,250

At the date of the return there were mortgages and charges for £75,500 outstanding, but these were fully paid off on June 15, 1936.

The directors are Edward Albert Stone, Chas. H. Bell, O.B.E., and Hugh Harraway.

Thos. W. Bowyer is the secretary and the registered office is at 20, Berkeley Street, Piccadilly, W.1.

Petition Adjourned.—In the Companies Court on Monday, June 15, a petition by Maison Arthur, Ltd., for the compulsory winding-up of City Film Corporation, Ltd., was mentioned to Mr. Justice Bennett.

Mr. Wolfe, for the petitioners, stated that the petition came before Mr. Justice Clauson on May 13 and was adjourned until June 15 for the film company to formulate a scheme. The negotiations had apparently broken down, and the company now wanted a further adjournment on some other grounds.

Mr. P. J. Sykes, for the film company, said that further negotiations were on foot for the sale of the assets and asked for one week's adjournment. If a winding-up order was made there was not the slightest possibility of the unsecured creditors getting anything.

His lordship granted an adjournment.

Fulham Picture Palace.—A declaration of solvency was filed on July 20 relating to Fulham Picture Palace, Ltd., which was registered as a "private" company on January 3, 1911. The authorised capital is £5,000 in £1 shares, of which, to August 6, 1935, 3,272 shares had been issued and fully paid up. The shareholders at the date named included :—Hilda E. Seel, Wm. F. Reeve, Tom E. Davies, Mrs. Minnie M. Grant, Geo. F. Green, Edwin Middleton, and Mrs. Keturah Philpot. There were no mortgages or charges outstanding at the date of the return. The directors are Tom E. Davies (directors of Broadway Gardens, Ltd.), Stephen R. Philpot, Edwin Middleton and Percy W. Summers. H. A. Mabbott is the secretary and the registered office is at 260, North End Road, Fulham, S.W.6.

Achievement!

Move forward or fall back
that's the law of the entertainment world
It's also the reason
why shrewd producers and exhibitors choose
Sound by Western Electric
They've watched its swift climb from
achievement to achievement—
shared the benefits of each new advance.
They know
that it will go on climbing,
that in 1937 as in 1927
Sound by Western Electric
will still be the world's most perfect
Sound System

WESTERN ELECTRIC CO. LTD., BUSH HOUSE, ALDWYCH, LONDON, W.C.2

EQUIPMENT
AND
TECHNICAL
SECTION

INDEX

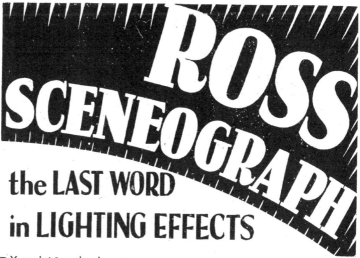

the LAST WORD in LIGHTING EFFECTS

COUNTER-WEIGHTING

THE KINEMATOGRAPH THEATRE

Equipment and Technique in 1936

By A. L. Carter.

THE prosperity of the Kinema industry during 1936 reflected the improved economic position in the country generally. Money continued to be plentiful for theatre expansion and film production, and it is a tribute to the stability of the British Trade that the orthodox financier has at length been persuaded of the general soundness of British film business.

The number of new kinemas built during the year was greater than ever and in the provision of studio facilities activity has been unprecedented, while the quality of the British product has enhanced the reputation of our producers, particularly in the Overseas markets.

Television has come a stage nearer serious consideration as an entertainment factor. New advances have occurred in technical equipment, particularly in the sound recording and reproduction fields. The increasing use of colour, attended with its own peculiar problems, has affected the technique of production, processing and projection. Other phases of studio operation have also witnessed developments, particularly illumination. Otherwise current tendencies have been towards the improvement and refinement of existing equipment.

The amazing increase in the theatre field has been the most interesting feature of the past year. Although much of the new construction work has been undertaken by circuits, the independent exhibitor has by no means been lacking in enterprise. The full effect of the reduction of the Entertainment Tax on the cheaper seats has now been felt and the contention of the C.E.A. that it would aid the exhibitor in carrying out long-delayed schemes of expansion or modernisation has been more than justified. In addition to the 200 new buildings erected during 1936, at least treble that number of reconstructions or re-equippings have been undertaken. Indeed it may fairly be contended that kinema building has played its share in the industrial recovery.

According to a reliable survey the number of places in Great Britain and Ireland wired for public entertainment, excluding church halls, clubs, etc., amounts to 5,016, as follows :—

		Wired.	Dark.
England	...	3,774	183
Wales ...	...	343	52
Scotland	...	534	79
Ireland ...	...	365	52
Total	...	5,016	366

The number of " dark " halls includes kinemas which are now permanently closed, the majority of which will be converted to other commercial uses. Nearly all are of small capacity ; their present derelict condition is due partly to the recent depression and partly also to the effects of the competition from newly built kinemas, the number of which in 1936 exceeded 200. While it is obvious that a proportion of these new theatres possibly come within the official designation of " redundant," the fact that increased patronage and improved financial returns are everywhere reported affords a measure of justification to their sponsors.

A record of kinemas opened during 1936 shows that the medium size theatre seating from 1,500 to 2,000 persons is considered the most suitable for convenience and economy of operation. This capacity is generally adopted in normal situations by the major circuits. Exceptions are found, however, among the building programmes of the Odeon and Union chains which, in addition to catering for populous areas, also erect kinemas adequate for the needs of districts of lesser densities of population.

Interest attaches to the growth of the newsreel theatre movement. The popularity of this class of entertainment in London and other big centres as led to the establishment up and down the country of similar enterprises. The average capacity ranges from 300 to 450, although the most recent example in London holds over 600 patrons. There is great danger of this sort of entertainment being over-done even in Central London. Dearth of attractive shorts and unsuitable situations are factors militating against the success of the newsreel theatres, several of which in the provinces have had to close down or, adopting the ordinary programme methods, have made a further contribution to the local "redundancy" problem. On the other hand, the adoption of television to commercial kinema requirements is indicated as a fruitful field for activity of the news theatre.

Although the independent exhibitor is still numerically important, there are signs that he is unable to resist the example of the larger circuits and engage in a form of voluntary rationalisation. Men who have previously owned one, two or three halls, are gradually extending their activities, which eventually becomes the nucleus of another circuit of anything up to 20 halls. There are many of these small enterprises in being to-day, despite the fact that already some of these groupings have already been absorbed by the big chains.

GROWTH OF THE CIRCUITS.

The circuit system of kinema operation has taken on a new significance during the past year. After many years' ascendancy, the supremacy of the two major groups, Gaumont-British and A.B.C., is being challenged by newcomers. Oscar Deutsch's Odeon circuit, which became associated with United Artists early in 1936, has since then built or acquired some fifty theatres and now numbers over 150 halls. Another hundred kinemas are projected during 1937 including a super Odeon now in course of erection on the Alhambra site in Leicester Square, London. The progress of Union Cinemas, which has a tie-up with the Paramount Theatres, has also been rapid ; Fred Bernhard is said to control nearly 200 kinemas and his plans this year reveal considerable activity in Northern Ireland. Plans are also in preparation by C. J. Donada for the expansion of County kinemas. The Emery and the Hinge organisations are also busy in the North of England.

To these established groups must be added another which is associated with General Films Distributors, and the board of which includes Lord Portal, A. J. Rank and C. M. Woolf. A circuit of 100 kinemas is planned and they already control a number of West of England kinemas and have acquired two circuits of important halls in the Home Counties besides other properties.

The circuit situation is further complicated by the negotiations now proceeding between John Maxwell and the Ostrers, which, if finalised, will represent a booking block of 600 kinemas.

MAKE A *PERFECT* PICTURE
OF YOUR CINEMA

INCREASE — THE PLEASURE OF YOUR PATRONS.

INCREASE — YOUR BOX OFFICE RETURNS BY USING

HOLOPHANE FREE ADVISORY SERVICE OF EXPERTS

The HOLOPHANE Service of Artists and Engineers are available for the preparation of Lighting Schemes for all classes of Cinemas. The HOLOPHANE demonstration theatre shown above is open daily for the purpose of showing the various new and original lighting effects designed by our experts. Write for Colour. Lighting Book.

REGULATIONS.

There is evidence of a general tightening up of local regulations. . Much of this attitude is directly traceable to the publication last year by the Home Office of the " Manual of Safety Requirements," many of the provisions of which have already been adopted by licensing authorities without giving the opportunity to the Trade of examination or amendment. C.E.A. executives have discussed this subject with the Home Office but their representations so far have not succeeded in favourably influencing the attitude of the various councils concerned. At the same time practical experience of the functioning of some clauses in the Manual has suggested to the Home Office that some sort of revision is necessary and it is probable that its more impracticable requirements will be modified in a subsequent edition.

In the London area particularly, concern has been expressed at some of the requirements demanded of exhibitors by the London, Surrey and Middlesex County Councils and the West Ham Borough Council. There is observable in at least two of the areas a tendency towards the institution of minimum standard of structure, the enforcement of which will entail severe financial strain upon owners of some of the older premises. Instances have already occurred in the Middlesex area where exhibitors have been unable to afford to modernise their premises to the extent demanded and perforce have had to close down. Particular attention is also being paid to this matter in the provinces. In Lancashire, following inspections and a report by the county architect which stressed the danger of fire and the unhygienic nature of certain kinemas, a black list was compiled and a closure order was issued to four kinemas. This significant sentence from the report justifies the Council's action : " a number of these buildings are of composite or timber construction, and in the event of an outbreak of fire, complete ignition would only be a matter of minutes." Similar action is reported from Blackpool and in other districts.

In the *Ideal Kinema*, George Coles, F.R.I.B.A., referred to the effects of the Restriction of Ribbon Development Act and the Town and Country Planning Act which are far-reaching in that they frequently not only render land useless for a kinema site but they also cause delays in obtaining site approvals. With regard to the former the architect is faced with the problem of being unable to determine (a) the building line ; (b) whether a service roadway will be insisted upon, and (c) the extent of car parking accommodation that may be insisted upon. In the London County area the insistence on the private runway operated as from November 1st, and in more than one instance the building of a new super kinema has been prevented by the requirement under the London Building Act that garage facilities shall be provided for new kinemas over a certain capacity erected in a congested traffic area.

No further statement has been forthcoming as to the intentions of the Government with regard to the proposal to amend the Cinematograph Act of 1909. At the moment attention has been focused on the deliberations of the Lord Moyne Committee on the working of the Films Act of 1927, the findings of which are discussed at length elsewhere in this publication. It is not anticipated, however, that there will be any progress in regard to the former until decisive action is taken in the implementing or otherwise of the recommendations of the departmental committee. It is patent that the appointment of the suggested Film Commission would infer the establishment of an authority whose views would be essential in the revising of the 1909 Act. Meanwhile there is a growing body of opinion even among exhibitors which would welcome official action in the direction of co-ordination of the basic regulations under which kinema exhibitions function.

NON-FLAM.

And in this connection exhibitors would applaud more stringent action in regard to the showing of non-flam films and the inclusion of a Government regulation bringing all types of entertainment buildings into line with the safety requirements demanded of the kinema. Hitherto exhibitions of films on non-flam stock have been outside the scope of the 1909 Act or where action has been taken it has proved abortive failing an agreed definition of the term "non-inflammable." Attempts to control non-flam screenings have been vigorously contested by various amateur associations and those interested in educational and propaganda screenings. The situation is still far from satisfactory and the Trade would welcome the announcement of a solution to the problem.

The decision of the Surrey County Council to institute a form of control of the showing over so-called non-flam film exhibitions has been followed by other districts. The Council decided to grant licences at a cost of 5s. to premises (subject to the condition that only non-flam films are used) which satisfy its minimum requirements. This enables schools to employ kinema projectors. Similar action has been taken at Birmingham which also insists upon the observance of special safety requirements on the lines of those operating in the commercial kinemas of the district.

In the case of Birmingham the Council insists that the films shown shall bear the certificate of the British Board of Film Censors, a significant proviso which indicates upon which lines, failing the intervention of the Government, the future control of " non-flam " exhibitions, will be based.

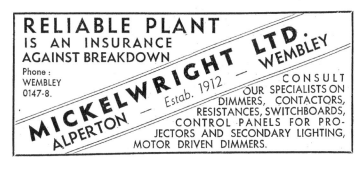

COMPETITION OF FREE SHOWS.

The number of free entertainments and shows in unlicensed premises is assuming such proportions that the General Council has been urged to take prompt action in a situation that has become fraught with danger to the livilihood of the legitimate film exhibitor. Reports from all over the country emphasise the continued growth of this form of competition. Free entertainments are given regularly in churches, religious institutes, public-houses and political and social clubs, and in addition various public utility companies have adapted the kinema to publicity uses. Remarkable facts respecting the circulation of advertising and propaganda films were revealed by Western Electric which has now formed a subsidiary to deal exclusively with these types of screenings. During $2\frac{1}{2}$ years W.E. road show programmes have been screened to 30,000 different audiences. One film alone had grossed 8,000 bookings. In addition to the advertising film show the provision of film entertainment by religious bodies is another menace. Practically every new church hall and many chapels are " wired for sound." Many of them possess all the equipment and the amenities of a first-class kinema and as nearly all comply with the necessary safety regulations, the exhibitor cannot combat this competition with a weapon which has proved successful in the case of some school halls which do not conform to safety requirements. It has been suggested that where such church exhibitions cannot be attacked on the grounds of public safety, it should be possible to approach the rating authority with a hint that the premises are not being employed for a purpose wholly religious. The former argument has been successfully represented to the London County Council which, in June, was stated to be inquiring into the film shows run by departmental stores, and the Home Secretary promised, if information were forthcoming of similar practices in the provinces, to communicate with the local authorities concerned.

The attitude of the renting firms in connection with the free show problem has been criticised by exhibitors who contend that too much complacency is shown in their policy of securing revenue alike from legitimate exhibitors and of organisers of free shows. It is urged that the letting of all entertainment films of whatever age should be refused by the renters.

Another form of competition which has increased considerably of late years is the sub-standard exhibition. In Yorkshire there are several halls which attract large audiences by this type of programme which, as it is projected on " non-flam " stock is not amenable to local safety regulations. Many of these shows are described as educational and cultural, yet so great a proportion of the programme comprises 35 mm. features that they provide competition to be reckoned with.

KINE.-VARIETY.

The number of kinemas playing vaudeville has shown a considerable increase during the year among the circuits and the larger independent houses. Union Cinemas have adopted the kine.-variety policy in its chief houses, and have established the touring system in conjunction with Paramount Astorias, whose spectacular shows have been a feature in the entertainment of picturegoers in suburban London and the more important provincial cities. Gaumont-British use variety in the majority of their London houses, and in the provinces continue the stage traditions previously established.

In Lancashire and other industrial areas there is a distinct trend towards this form of mixed programme, and there are many small exhibitors who have endeavoured, within their obvious limitations, to participate in this tendency.

Circuit chiefs are by no means convinced of the desirability of the extension of kine.-variety to all classes of kinemas. They consider that it is suitable only in selected situations where local circumstances demand a certain standard of entertainment. The fact that such an important circuit as County Cinemas plays variety at but one or two theatres goes to prove that, at its best, it is but a contribution to the general standard of entertainment. At the same time there has been a growth in the employment of guest orchestras which present what practically amounts to an all-in vaudeville programme.

The value of the modern unit organ is now widely recognised by exhibitors. The popularity of the descriptive organ-interlude is now so widespread that it has become an integral part of the entertainment. The use of a little ingenuity with the assistance of a capable slide maker enables a first-class show to be put over by any competent organist. Specimens of organ interludes are published each week in the *Kinematograph Weekly.*

It is impossible for the smaller exhibitor, already operating on the smallest margin of profit, to incur the increased overheads necessitated by kine.-variety. The great majority, indeed, have no desire to compete with the larger circuits, and, wisely enough, depend wholly upon the attractiveness of their film programme ; but even in these cases it has been found that patrons welcome the modicum of variety introduced by economically planned presentations and prologues which afford just that measure of programme strength that is needed to put over an occasional indifferent picture. A modest stage lighting installation scientifically applied, a little ingenuity and a measure of common-sense employed in operating the non-sync., the small man has at his finger-tips all the elements of a successful stage show.

Many exhibitors have found that kine.-variety demands the installation of stage amplification equipment ; indeed it has been found essential wherever stage acts are put on in any of our larger auditoria or where it is desired to increase the volume of a small organ. There are many types of installations, such as the " Ardente," which are entirely independent of the sound equipment. It all depends on the acoustic properties of the theatre. One kinema may utilise three footlight microphones, one stand microphone and two loudspeakers ; another may need four footlight and two stand microphones, with four loudspeakers, to give even distribution over the whole of the auditorium. In the case of the Rio, Barking, the six microphones on the stage can be individually controlled from the back of the circle. Loudspeakers are concealed in the decorations. It is, of course, necessary to give amplification without any directional effect from the loudspeakers. Other well-known sets are Western Electric, R.C.A., B.T.-H., Gaumont-British, Strong Electric Distributors, which have all been specially designed for this type of kinema amplification.

STAGE LIGHTING.—Whatever may be the future of the kine-variety policy, exhibitors have always inclined to the very sound view that a stage is an essential in the modern kinema. In most kinemas, irrespective of size, a stage and some lighting equipment will usually be found. In its simplest form the latter may consist of a single batten and a footlight which if handled with any degree of expertness and appreciation of colour values, is capable of some extremely effective results. The addition of a front of the house combined spot and effects lantern provides for most of the requirements of the average kinema presentation. In those larger kinemas where stage shows verge on the spectacular, the equipment is correspondingly elaborate and, indeed, surpasses that of many legitimate theatres.

One of the developments of interest in stage lighting is the new Strand " mirror spot " which employs novel optical principles. An 8-in. diameter silvered glass mirror projects an intense beam of light on a variable gate.

This is focused by a 6-in. diameter step lens. By this means rectangular spots of various sizes can be projected with an intensity of over double that obtained from a standard spotlight of the same size and wattage. Masking, to spot irregular objects on the stage hitherto impossible, can now be easily accomplished. This lantern is particularly suitable for circle front or batten spotting in the legitimate theatre. Another interesting feature is the more widespread use of low voltage spots. A good deal of progress has been made in new types of gaseous conductor lamps, and it is upon these lines, according to illumination experts, that further progress may be expected. The present great objection to the mercury vapour kind of lamp, apart from its retention of its usual blue-green properties, is the impossibility of employing a dimmer. Noticeable advances have also been made in regard to mobile units and control.

There have been few other developments in ordinary stage equipments, although many of the manufacturers, such as Holophane, Beard, G.E.C., D. Walter & Co., have introduced several refinements which add to the concentration of illumination and facilitate operation. Strand has recently perfected an automatic colour-illumination control, the light console, specially designed for the stage show and for cyclorama operation.

THE KINEMA ORGAN.

The kinema organ is as strongly entrenched as ever in the affections of the picture patron, and the fact that over 40 installations were made during the year indicates that the progressive showman is under no illusions as to its box-office value; indeed, theatre organ music has become one of the most popular items of modern entertainment. Recent developments have added so greatly to the musicianly attributes of this instrument, and its flexibility has so widely extended its original uses as a solo instrument that it is generally employed to provide the accompanimental work either with or without orchestra for the Variety turns of the mixed programme.

Although more attention is being paid by the architect to the requirements of the organ builder, there is still room for a great deal of improvement. It is now generally recognised that, given the inclusion in the original design of the theatre of a roomy chamber in the correct position with grille openings directing the sound to the screen instead of into the auditorium, the organ gives out 100 per cent. of its capacity with natural voicing and correct tonal imitation in solo orchestral stops. Co-operation between organist and architect has been achieved in many instances with ultimate results that are highly satisfactory to exhibitor, patron and the Variety artist.

The size of organ to be installed is governed by a number of circumstances, and in the opinion of A. W. Owen, musical critic of the *Kine.*, a house with 2,500–3,000 seating capacity in which an orchestra is deemed necessary, demands an organ of at least nine ranks, fully extended, as a minimum and 12 to 15 units a sounder proposition. The installation of any organ for solo work of less than five fully extended units is not recommended. These units should include at least a diapason or similar basis and a fine quality reed unit. In the small organ the quality of tone-colour must show a definite contrast, and the blending together of each and all units is the secret of the small instrument's utility. A defect which must be avoided in the employment of the small organ is over-amplification, which results in the distortion of its tone-colours to such an extent that it becomes merely a " blasted " form of a well-worn gramophone disc.

If general calibre of organ playing has improved enormously, the standard of requirements is also considerably higher than hitherto. The organist of to-day is regarded as more of a Variety artist than as a straight instrumentalist, and he depends to a far greater extent upon personality and his capabilities as an entertainer and showman. It is probably this development that has caused the introduction in many circuits of the touring system which, providing as it does a constant change of player and methods, has proved highly popular.

Improvement is noted generally in the status of the organist, due in no small measure to the efforts of the kinema organists section of the Incorporated Society of Musicians.

Exhibitors who have not already considered the desirability of installing organs have a wide field from which to select. The John Compton Organ Company and Wurlitzer are well known in this field, which they have made particularly their own ; the Christie, made by Hill, Norman and Beard, and the Conacher, are others that have also found favour.

COMPTON.—The year has seen numerous developments in the British-made Compton theatre organ, both tonally and mechanically. The electrone is now so firmly established that it is installed in almost every Compton organ. Detail improvements have been embodied in the action which are at once noticeable to the modern organist virtuoso.

Amongst the many important installations during 1936 are the large four-manual organ for the Dutch (AVRO) Radio Station at Hilversum ; the magnificent twin-consoled four-manual organ for the Southampton Civic Centre ; the new Paramount in Tottenham Court Road, and a vast number of fine instruments for regular Compton users, such as the Union Cinema Company, Ltd.; the Gaumont-British Picture Corporation, Ltd.; Associated British Cinemas, Ltd.; the Odeon Circuit, Louis Morris ; and, finally their greatest achievement—the new four-manual instrument for the B.B.C. in St. George's Hall, London, one of the most modern and complete theatre organs in the country.

WURLITZER.—Every indication points to the fact that 1937 will be a " bumper " year for Wurlitzer. The most enterprising circuits have decided that kine.-variety and unit organs have come to stay and are an important part of a satisfying picture entertainment. Bernstein Theatres, for instance, feature Reginald Dixon by arrangement with Blackpool Tower Co. whenever he is available. These circuits are providing accommodation for unit organs in all their new theatres.

The Wurlitzer is regarded as an ideal instrument for showmanlike organ interludes and for accompanying variety acts ; and to meet the demand for their organs Wurlitzer has had to enlarge its London factory and instal new machinery to enable more of the instruments to be manufactured in this country, and so further reduce their selling price. Wurlitzer's prospective installations for 1937 have already reached over thirty.

PIPELESS ORGAN.—Interest was exhibited in a model of the electric pipeless organ demonstrated in London during September. The instrument, of American make, comprises a two-manual console with pedal board and row of drawbars above the top keyboard controlling the harmonics, giving variety to the tone-colour which can be set in nine different positions. Tone is produced, varied, swelled and modified, electrically ; and, it is claimed, is entirely unaffected by temperature or humidity.

SCREENS AND SCREEN BRIGHTNESS.

Valuable research work on the subject of screen illumination is being undertaken by the Projection Screen Brightness Committee of the S.M.P.E. of America, in the August transactions of which appears a résumé of the data considered and of an interim report of the conclusions arrived at. The suggestion is put forward that a temporary screen brightness standard would be adopted with benefit to the Industry. Logical limits for such a standard are put forward as being 7 foot-lamberts* for the low value and 14 for the high. The value 7 is based upon the value attainable from a diffusing screen about 30 ft. wide with an efficient optical system in good adjustment. The value 14 is the limiting value beyond which point contrast of print image adjusted for the mean level of 10 foot-lamberts would appear too great. The values should be determined at the centre of the screen with the projector running with no film in the gate.

Of the important factors in screen brightness, that of the illumination characteristics of the screen itself and its sound transmission qualities are continuing to engage the close attention of the S.M.P.E. Committee. Actually, however, there have been few developments in screens, although minor technical improvements are constantly being incorporated in the products of Andrews, Smith and Harkness, who make the famous Westone screen which enjoys wide-world popularity, and E. G. Turner, whose wide range of sound screens is also well known.

The new Westone beaded screen is commended for its highly reflecting surface and its sound efficiency. In this type of screen it is claimed that by a choice of suitable beads, the directivity of the screen can be varied to suit the plan of the auditorium.

Screens are also being made of perforated metal, and E. J. Turner reports several installations made at the expense of fabric screens, which have proved entirely satisfactory. It is argued that a better reflecting surface is obtained with the metal screen, which needs only 14 perforations to the square inch as compared with 46 of the fabric screen. Other advantages claimed are better sound characteristics owing to its being non-absorbent, improved screen illumination, and an installation that is wholly fireproof.

A new firm, H. V. Polley, Ltd., besides marketing a perforated screen, are shortly introducing a woven asbestos screen, while J. Hibbert Diggle has demonstrated a new translucent rear projection screen. The principle of the concave screen, which it is claimed imparts a stereoscopic depth to the picture, has been tried out in full scale at the Pavilion, East Dulwich, but proved to result in an intolerable distortion of the picture.

A point concerning which there appears to be a diversity of opinion is the actual size of the screen. The small hall may use a screen 18 ft. or less, while the largest standard size of screen is about 24 ft. to 28 ft. in width, the height being three-quarters of the width. Of course, the area is considerably extended, sometimes up to 75 per cent., when the " magnascope " lens is employed.

The use of the dark screen border is queried in a paper issued by the Eastman Kodak Laboratory, in which it is stated that " nearly everyone who has worked upon the physiology of vision will condemn this practice upon the basis of eye fatigue or even injury. We must be prepared for changes in projection practice that may involve a border brightness that is low, but not negligible, as compared with the brightness of the screen."

PICTURE THEATRE DESIGN.

Owing to its complexity, the planning of a kinema has become, perhaps more than any department of architecture, the business of a specialist. The exhibitor, therefore, who is contemplating the erection of a new hall would be wise to entrust it to an architect who has some knowledge of the peculiar problems involved. Such factors as the relation between cost, capacity and equipment and the possible return can only be arrived at by experience of the trade : the interpretation of the local regulations is another matter to which attention must be given with a view to possible future adjustments of the requirements of the local authority.

---

*A foot-lambert is a unit of brightness and is concerned with the quantity of light **leaving** the surface. A foot-candle is a unit of illumination and is concerned with the quantity of light **striking** a surface.

Under the circumstances, the ideal policy is to give the architect full control not only to the planning of the building but also, in a large measure, of its equipment. There are cases when the granting of such wide responsibility is neither practicable nor desirable, but so far as possible the whole construction and its technical installation should be regarded as part of a co-ordinated whole.

An important influence in building costs is the site, a subject which has been fully discussed in the *Ideal Kinema* by George Coles, the Architectural Editor. He has pointed out that consideration must be given to the bearing quality of the soil, the pressure of water near the subsoil and the levels are all matters which have a direct bearing on the ultimate costs. It is also his experience that economies in construction permitted by differing interpretation of building by-laws of local authorities may affect the building costs to the extent of 5 per cent. There are a few examples where expert knowledge has been known to restrict the price of kinema construction.

The enterprise associated with the extension of the Odeon circuit of which some 30 houses were opened last year is seen in the architectural policy followed by Oscar Deutch. The strikingly imaginative treatment of many of these kinemas present an admirable blend of the aesthetic and the utilitarian. This trend which is also disclosed in the design of other important picture theatres, represents an artistic and functional development of the more conventional forms which formerly characterised the planning of places of entertainment. The Continental influence continues to be apparent but modifications arising from insular and functional circumstances and, to a certain extent, from the use of new materials, have been introduced without disturbing the tendency towards simplicity and good taste. It is to the credit of the specialised architect that there exist so many kinemas where these desiderations have been successfully achieved without involving the proprietor in other than economic outlay.

An interesting contribution to the kinema planning problem was made in the *S.M.P.E. Journal* by Ben Schlanger, the American architect, who is one of the keenest advocates of the reversed floor. He considers that if " the usual acuity, apparent screen size and distortion are properly considered in design, the seating capacity should not greatly exceed 2,000 persons."

The importance of avoiding pronounced and unbroken surfaces, such as domes, recessed walls and vaulted ceilings is emphasised in another paper from E.R.P.I. Non-parallelism of surfaces is an important consideration, particularly in the design of small theatres. In the design of a stage, it is suggested that if the space behind the screen exceeds 10 ft., it is frequently desirable to provide a drop of heavy-weight velour suspended behind the sound horns, of an area at least approximating to that of the screen. The most desirable locations for acoustic material are generally the rear wall surface and the side walls extending forward from the rear wall. In theatres having balconies it is considered not generally necessary to treat the rear and side walls beneath the balcony unless the depth is less than approximately twice the height.

A new survey of theatre planning by the Italian architect Morette discloses that the fan shape is by far the most widely adopted design, and is also one that permits of innumerable variations in design.

In some modern theatres too much emphasis is laid upon the advertisement facilities offered by the façade and it happens that an otherwise satisfactory design is spoiled by the introduction of an incongruous feature. However, authorities nowadays pay more attention to the perspective of their streets and criticisms are frequently levelled at the realisation of an exhibitor's bright idea for attracting attention to his theatre. Sometimes such opposition has led to the rejection of the licence, in other instances the Town Surveyor has been unable to intervene but generally speaking the policy that alienates public sympathy is an ill advised one.

Construction Materials.—Another feature of contemporary kinema construction is the growing acceptance of the American view that an entertainment building becomes obsolete within a very few years. The large number of reconstructions, sometimes of comparatively modern buildings, that has taken place during the past year is an expression of the exhibitor's own view of the impermanency of the modern theatre. Possibly this accounts for the lighter touch observable in exterior design. Heavy façades are being regarded with less favour, and the use of glass bricks and large illuminated glass surfaces in various forms and sometimes of metallic sheathing have provided façades with the necessary " arresting " qualities. For suburban and provincial kinemas, however, brick with faience entrance, trim and plinth is largely employed with excellent effect particularly as these materials need never be out of harmony with the adjacent buildings. There is also great scope for façade treatment with coloured cements.

Decorative glass is widely used for interior decoration, although its use in the auditorium must necessarily be limited owing to its reflective properties in regard to light and also to sound. In the foyer, cafés and circulating spaces, however, many decorative purposes have been found for glass in various colours and in sand-blast designs and it has also been used extensively in kinemas for special features such as glass columns with vertical coloured illumination strips. There has been considerable development in the application of art metal and in woods and veneers, which affords the decorative artist a wealth of attractive surfaces, some of which are easily applied to plaster walls. For the minor internal furnishings as barriers, stair handrails, counters and display cases, hardwood and metal is usually insisted upon by the regulations. Wood handrails are usually of oak and the metal handrails can be of iron, brass, bronze, stainless steel, chromium-plated, or aluminium. Very decorative effects can be obtained by the use of hardwood and chromium plate with stainless steel. Any particular colour scheme can be matched with cellulose enamel.

DECORATION.

Although the kinema presents a wide variety of interior decoration, it is largely governed by structural and acoustic requirements. Modern decorative treatment is unassuming and depends upon the employment of surface designs on textured plaster finishes, aided by general trough illumination designed to emphasise the screen as the focal point of the interior. The moulded contour system introduced by Holophane employs curvatures and bold decorative features which are flooded with reflected and coloured light from different directions. Cornices brilliantly illuminated on the three-colour system form the dominant note in other popular decorative schemes.

The so-called " atmospheric " type of interior has lost its fascination for both exhibitor and patron—it was at no time popular with the architect and it has passed away to join those highly ornamental interiors which was formerly a tradition of theatrical architecture. There has, however, been a revival of interest in the mural painting and in sculptural decorations. One or two recently opened houses exhibit pleasing examples of this type of treatment which provide the patron with a degree of pictorial expression which is well in keeping with the imaginative form of entertainment presented by the kinema.

In planning the decorative scheme each ancillary contribution to the pleasure and comfort of the patron should be considered. Everything, the wall treatment, decorative motifs, doors, carpets, furnishings and upholstery should play its part towards an harmonious whole. There is little difficulty in achieving this in a new construction but in the case of modernisation, the work should be handled by a specialist, even in a small job.

The main feature to be considered is the general soft furnishings of the house and on this subject the aid of one of the many specialist seating firms should be enlisted in providing drapes and upholsteries. It is not only a matter of decorative harmonies which have to be considered but also the quality of the material and, as regards seating, the design of the chair and the wearing qualities of the upholstery. The luxuriousness of the kinema seat has been one of the main features of the success of the film as an entertainment, it is the prime factor in providing that luxury and comfort which is the hallmark of the picture theatre. Chairs are designed on anatomical principles and standards, frames, tip-up devices are constantly being improved upon by manufacturers in their efforts to achieve that standard of comfort and durability which is now generally expected. In this connection there has been a widespread adoption by chair makers of Dunlopillo cushioning for seats, backs and arm pads, and its use has proved a profitable investment as has been proved by the repeated applications from patrons for seats in rows where Dunlopillo is exclusively used. Even where Dunlopillo is employed to a limited extent as an arm rest its popularity is such that there are nearly a million of them in use. Another advantage of this material is that it affords the highest acoustic absorption yet reached in kinema seating.

FURNISHINGS.

The kinema seating business is not free from price cutting, but the exhibitor would be ill-advised to purchase solely on price without inquiring into the merits of the article upon which so much of his goodwill depends, as delay in delivery, cheap upholstering and bad workmanship will soon involve him in expenditure far exceeding any saving arising from the first cost. To obviate this he should deal only with reputable firms, names of which appear in the columns of the *Kinematograph Weekly* or the *Ideal Kinema*.

Carpets are nowadays the most popular floor covering for lounges and auditorium, even in working class districts. A closely-woven fabric, will, if properly looked after, give satisfaction alike to the exhibitor and his patron.

A yet more luxurious tread is given to carpets where a Dunlopillo underlay is used. It eliminates noise and its softness reduces wear. In the vestibule and foyers, however, rubber, cork or a combination material are recommended. They can be supplied in a variety of colours and are laid in attractive designs and are reccommended for their hygienic, wear-resisting qualities and for economy of maintenance. They are also extensively used for stairways and other parts of the theatre.

GENERAL EQUIPMENT.

Cleanliness should be regarded as a prime consideration and although the vacuum cleaning plant is a commonplace in a new theatre, there are older halls in which the use of these labour saving and hygienic devices are not made fully available. The durability of all soft furnishings is immeasurably increased if they are regularly cleansed and repaired.

Where electricity can be obtained at a low price per unit it may be advisable for the small kinema owner to consider the practicability of using electrical heating, which has the advantage of absolute cleanliness and the absence of labour costs. The amount of heating needed, and consequently its cost, depends materially upon the construction of the building and the insulating properties of walls and roof.

Another matter of which complaint is made by patrons of small halls is the ventilation. Competition with newly erected kinemas is so intense that no exhibitor can afford to overlook a factor which contributes so largely to his patron's comfort. It may not be possible to instal an elaborate heating and ventilating plant but a local architect should be able to evolve an economical and effective system which would bring the older house into line with its competitors.

The exhibitor who neglects to incorporate these and other modern refinements, who fails to bring his decorative scheme into line with up-to-date

PERSONNEL—

practice and who is content to carry on his business along lines that were regarded as old-fashioned a decade ago, is inviting competition and no repetition of the blessed word "redundancy" will remove the responsibility from his own shoulders.

The distribution of admission tickets is carried out in some halls in the same inefficient and haphazard fashion as was common in pre-war days. An automatic ticket issuing machine is an essential to any kinema with pre-tensions to modernity, not only because it hastens the incoming patronage but also because it enables a check to be kept on the cashier and facilitates the Inland Revenue Commitments of the exhibitor. There are many types of these machines available. There is the high speed issuer of the "Automaticket" Model "K" or Model "H" type, or the "Accurate" Silent-Electric type, and a hand-operated ticket machine of the "Automaticket" Model "C" type, or the "Accurate" Model "AC" type, and a change-giving machine, either keyboard at £15 or "Automaticket Coinometer" type at £9 10s. In new constructions architects are making provision in the box office for this equipment. Automaticket, Ltd., have made no new departures from their standard machines. The Model "K" is favoured in urban kinemas, whereas the Model "H" is usually specified for rural areas. The "Accurate" Model "S" Silent-Electric multiple-issue ticket machine issues adult and half-price tickets, etc. Simultaneously, Accurate Check, Ltd., has brought out the "Handy Thousands" cartons, which are sealed and have a delivery device and contain 1,000 tickets. They retain the unissued tickets intact. The company also offers an inexpensive change-giving machine. Another machine available is the "Alpha" which offers complete protection to the proprietor and is accurate and simple in operation.

Another method of improving business which the exhibitor would do well to develop is the installation of deaf aid apparatus on a certain number of seats in each grade of accommodation. The sound film has deprived a huge number of kinema goers of their only source of recreation, so that the intro-

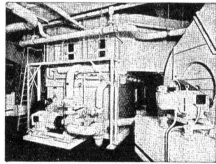

duction of these seats will result in the accession to the theatre of a regular and appreciative clientele. Consideration, however, must be given to the placing of these installations. There should be no attempt to segregate the deaf patrons and every regard should be paid by the exhibitor to the innate sensitiveness of deaf patrons regarding their affliction. Among the firms who specialise in this equipment are "Ardente," who provide an attractive walnut framed announcement concerning its installation, a trailer and, in addition, regularly circularise many thousands of deaf people respecting the forthcoming attractions at their house. Earphone equipment is also handled by most of the manufacturers of sound equipment, including Western Electric, R.C.A., B.T-H., B.T.P., etc.

KINEMA CATERING.

The possession of a café is now generally regarded as an integral part of the kinema business. It is not merely a question of service to the customer but has become a definite financial asset. It is true that local economic conditions may not be suitable for an elaborate restaurant type of café but there are few situations where facilities for a light snack and tea and coffee will not become of financial benefit to the exhibitor. The real problem which faces the exhibitor is not whether he should dispense altogether with feeding arrangements but what type of facilities he can afford. As a general rule it may be accepted that an efficiently managed café in a suitable neighbourhood is invariably a successful revenue producing department.

The question of direction must also be carefully considered. Sometimes the theatre management is able satisfactorily to perform the catering arrangements with consequent financial benefit : in others it has been found desirable to sub-let the whole catering facilities, with or without theatre sales, to a contractor who will pay an agreed commission which will generally be found

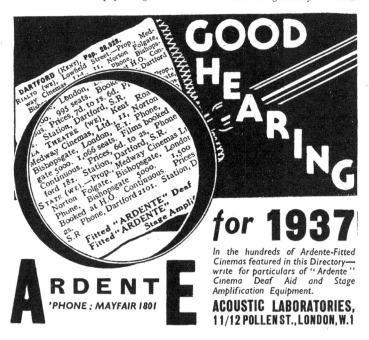

to provide a handsome yearly profit on the exhibitor's original capital outlay. The addition of a dance floor is a frequent feature of the kinema amenities, particularly in provincial and suburban districts, and the value of the café-ballroom policy is considerably enhanced by the presence of a car park, the whole, with the kinema, making a local centre of entertainment and good cheer of a type which is becoming increasingly popular in its appeal.

KINEMA LIGHTING.

The improved architectural characteristics of the modern kinema and particularly the treatment of the façade has led to the adoption of a new note in exterior lighting for which neon is now largely employed. There is evidence of careful collaboration between architect and the engineer, which is as it should be, as the one has a very close relationship with the other. In lighting a kinema it should be remembered that two contrasting requirements have to be considered. The building itself must compete successfully with the illuminated announcements of adjoining premises and the entrance and foyer must be prominently emphasised in comparison with surrounding shops and windows. Proper regard for these requirements will achieve the desired publicity end-and, if carried out with due appreciation of the aesthetic factors of the structure, will not offend the artistic sensibilities of the beholder.

Another development is the increasing use of glass as a building material, the consequence of which is the adoption for right effect of methods of interior illumimation.

Electric discharge tube lighting continues to be the most popular form of exterior illumination and has practically displaced the old running sign system. Indeed, night architecture is now synonymous with neon tubes which, outlining the contour of the building frequently becomes the only embellishment to a dull façade. It is employed in a number of arresting colours and in some situations, owing to the kinema neon of red, amber and green, conflicting with adjacent traffic lights, Councils have indicated that the use of these colours is undesirable. Floodlighting by high-pressure gas and electric light units, although not so extensively used as formerly, is employed to a considerable degree where proprietors consider the elevation is of sufficient architectural worth to warrant its employment or where the use of cut-outs and similar advertising matter renders it a necessity. Flood-lighting narrow angle lens, giving a beam of high intensity over a restricted area, will be found most suitable in these circumstances.

As I have indicated earlier in this article, lighting enters prominently into all the decorative schemes of the kinema. In some kinemas, auditoria are decorated solely by multi-coloured lighting effects from concealed trough-ing in plaster cones which are sited according to the decorative requirements. Indeed colour lighting has almost superseded the use of white-light owing to the wider range of artistic effects available which if white-light were being used would merely be ugly. In the case of indirect and concealed lighting by cornice and trough form, the engineer demands co-operation from the architect, particularly in the case of the former where sufficient room is neces-sary to throw the light up and over the whole ceiling. Here the exhibitor should be reminded that matt surfaces are better for interior illumination as streaky illumination will result if a glossy finish is employed.

In vestibules and foyers, indirect lighting is also used as a complement to the ordinary lighting unit which has undergone remarkable improvement

during the past year. F. H. Pride gives his view that the alliance ot art with utility in units in decorative metal and glass work affords an effect of gaiety and cheerfulness so necessary to the kinema. Similar experience is reported by other firms as Falk, Stadelmann, G.E.C., Strand Electric, Holophane and D. Walter & Co., to mention a few who. have specialised in the application of light in all entertainment forms.

The outstanding development in recent years is the use of tube lighting for interior illumination. The advantages in kinemas of light spaces spread over large areas, of low surface brightness, of warmth of tone, vitality and flexibility are fully appreciated by the architect and engineer. This system of lighting offers all these advantages combined with an efficiency in terms of light output for current consumption that can only be described as remarkable. Research work carried out by the G.E.C. has resulted in the production of electric discharge tubes of high illuminating efficiency and in an ever increasing variety of colours, the use of which enhances mural decoration, fabrics, carpets, etc. The tubes will only operate off A.C. supplies, and as they are of the high tension type, it is necessary to have suitable space available as near the tubes as possible to accommodate the requisite transformers.

The policy of co-ordinating auditorium and stage illumination is being increasingly adopted, thanks to the automatic control systems developed by the Holophane, Strand Electric, and other firms, to facilitate the functioning even by unskilled operatives.

Any reputable lighting firm will aid exhibitors who wish to bring their present lighting installations into line with modern requirements. Designs of equipment and plans of installations will be supplied to meet any particular requirement.

INDEPENDENT PLANT ADVANTAGES.

The use of the independent plant for the generation of electricity is growing among exhibitors, who are beginning to realise that the possession of a private lighting and power installation is the only possible alternative in towns where local charges for mains supplies are considered exorbitant. This attitude has been stressed on more than one occasion where branches of the C.E.A. have approached local supply companies with a view to reductions in their tariffs. A dispassionate investigation of the subject, moreover, has convinced many exhibitors that its adoption would be attended by increased economy and improved service.

An exhibitor demands that his electrical supply shall be reliable and as free from interruption as possible ; factors which are not invariably associated with the functioning of the grid system. Breakdowns during a performance entail considerable financial loss and lessening of prestige. A notable instance of the loss occasioned by these disturbances occurred early in the year at Bradford, where no fewer than 39 kinemas were put out of action throughout the whole of one evening.

Several firms have made a special study of the exhibitor's requirements as regards the independent prime mover. The Natural Gas & Oil Engine Co. recommends one of its series of " B " engines, which is available in a range of sizes from 10 to 100 b.h.p. ; these are silent, vibrationless, and exceedingly economical. The fuel cost, even on the small sizes, is less than $\frac{1}{2}$d. a unit.

According. to figures supplied by Petter's, of Yeovil, it has been found where Diesel engine sets are employed, that the all-in costs, including capital, interest, depreciation, maintenance, fuel and lubricant expenses, per electric unit generated is about three farthings, a figure which increases slightly as the capacity of the plant diminishes. The modern Diesel engine generating set has been brought to such a high state of efficiency that very exact figures can be supplied to any exhibitor contemplating a new installation, and it can be proved that these are not always in favour of the grid even in the most favourable circumstances.

An important point is emphasised by Blackstone's, who lay stress on the fact that the lower cost of electrical energy encourages greater use of lighting for advertising and publicity purposes. Thus the employment of an independent plant is not only a direct contributory factor of increased box-office receipts, but it may be used in the secure knowledge that the longer hours and the nearer full load the plant is worked, the lower will be the cost per unit.

The economical functioning of these plants is provided by two kinemas in Stamford. One has an 8½ kw. oil engine generator plant and the *all-in cost* of running is 14s. per week ; while a second one has a 10 kw. installation and the all-in cost is £1 per week. The latter includes very extensive outside lighting and power for ventilating fans. As public supply is dear in Stamford, each kinema makes an actual saving of £250 to £300 per annum for a first cost not much in excess of the annual saving.

In an interesting brochure issued by Ruston & Hornsby, it is suggested that absolute security from breakdown and greater economy in working can be obtained by installing two sets of such capacity that the full winter evening load can be carried by both working together, and the morning and other slack period load can be taken by one set working alone. When Ruston oil engines are used, either the vertical or the horizontal types, current can be taken direct from the generator both for sound reproduction and for lighting. Two examples are furnished : one kinema possessing two 17½ kw. generators each independently driven, uses 67,600 units per annum at an average unit cost of .85d. ; and another where one 59 kw. generator is driven by a 90 h.p. oil engine, generates 81,000 units per annum at a cost of 1.04d. per unit.

A large number of Crossley's independent Diesel plants have also been installed with beneficial results. The reliability of this equipment, coupled with absence of noise, smell or vibration, with clean running and steady voltage, makes them particularly successful in kinema work. The whole of the electrical and mechanical services of the Regent, South Shields, a 1,850 capacity house, demanding 130 kw. for lighting and power on full load are catered for by two 3-cylinder Crossley Scavenge pump engines, each of 82 b.h.p., and directly coupled to 40 kw. 220-volt D.C. generator. There is also a Crossley single-cylinder vertical 2-stroke, 23 b.h.p. Diesel directly coupled to a kw. 220-volt D.C. dynamo and used during the morning for lighting and cleaning work. A Crossley equipment at the Regent, Kimberley Notts, is computed to generate current at a cost not exceeding ½d. per unit.

Another firm which proposes to specialise in plant for independent generation is the Kohler Co., Ltd., which already has installed many emergency lighting equipments comprising a 2,000-watt automatic electric set, working on gas fuel at £128 nett. This firm has under development a range of Diesel plants which will be available some time this year.

The above survey of possibilities of the independent generating equipment indicates the means by which a cheap, reliable supply can be assured not only for general illumination, projection and sound, but also for outside lighting and other advertising effects.

NOISE INSULATION.

One matter to be considered in the installation of these plants is that of sound insulation. Cases have occurred where owners of adjoining properties have successfully alleged that the functioning of an independent prime mover

has created a nuisance. Such complaints may be obviated by the adoption in the first instance of methods for the isolation of noise and vibration. Considerable success has attended the system used by W. Christie & Grey, Ltd., in treating theatres. This comprises the scientific treatment with cork of the engine foundations or the use of spring anti-vibrators on which the plant is mounted. This system of isolation proved effective at the Scala, Dublin, where the plant was installed on the roof. A particularly interesting job carried out recently by the firm was the isolation of the television studios at Alexandra Palace.

ELECTRICITY CHARGES.

The high cost of electricity supplies and the wide variation in schedules of the supply undertakings throughout the country have continued to exercise the minds of kinema proprietors, whose hopes of any benefit arising from the general application of the grid system throughout the country have been far from realised.

Representations on behalf of the exhibitors were made in 1935 by the C.E.A. to the Government Committee of Enquiry into electrical charges, but although the report of the committee, published in July, acknowledges that kinemas and the photographic industries are entitled to special consideration, there is little indication that any real benefit will accrue to the Industry.

This and subsequent paragraphs of the report were received by the C.E.A. with approval, particularly the clause which proposed that there should be greater uniformity in the methods of charge offered by the various authorities.

Clause 342 of the report states : Where, however, throughout the country there are special classes having similar technical characteristics, and in respect of which, therefore, it should be possible to devise a uniform basis of charge, the associations representative of the supply authorities could with advantage confer with the associations representing such special classes of user. Such consultation should go a long way towards securing greater uniformity in the basis of charge applied by the different authorities.

343. We note that this course has already been adopted with considerable success in the case of supplies of electricity for industrial purposes, and that, as a result of conferences between the Federation of British Industries and the supply associations, a considerable measure of agreement has been reached as to what can be regarded as a reasonable and appropriate basis of tariff.

344. Apart from any action which the associations representing the supply authorities may be able to take, we are of opinion that a considerable measure of uniformity could be obtained by local consultations between the undertakers themselves in various areas. The Advisory Committee representative of authorised undertakings in each reorganised area would be a valuable medium, not only for discussion between the undertakers themselves, but also between the undertakers and representative groups of consumers.

345. The relation of a flat rate charge to a two-part tariff is another matter which has been brought prominently to our notice. It would seem that in some cases it is the policy to reduce the lighting flat rate to a low level in preference to making reductions in the alternative two-part tariff. We are informed that in some cases the lighting flat rate is as low as 1½d. per unit, which, unless confined to exceptional cases of long hour users, appears to be an uneconomic rate. In other cases it appears to be the policy to keep the lighting flat rate at a higher level and to concentrate on reducing as much as possible the charges under a two-part tariff.

346. Certain consumers' organisations whom we have heard attach great importance to the reduction of the lighting flat rate, and it would seem that it is the difference between the lighting flat rates of different areas which is one of the principal grounds of complaint to-day. We feel that the importance of such differences can be over-emphasised, and it may well be that in certain areas the present lighting flat rate is, in fact, too low.

347. We have received a considerable amount of evidence to the effect that an attractive two-part tariff is, particularly in the case of domestic supplies, the most effective means of bringing about a substantially extended use of the supply, and is, therefore, one of the principal factors in reducing distribution costs, and in facilitating further reductions in charges to all classes.

The C.E.A. particularly commended perusal of this section of the report to those particularly interested, and the Technical Committee of the Association recommended the General Council to call representatives of a number of selected trades (with similar interests in electrical consumption) to consider ways and means of achieving representation on Electrical Advisory Committees.

More satisfactory results, however, have followed from the inauguration of an Electricity Department within the C.E.A. organisation, to which some 540 kinema undertakings subscribed in the first instance. The services of L. Knopp, the Gaumont British expert, were retained in a consultative capacity. It is, however, emphasised that the cost of such specialised work should be a charge upon the member, notwithstanding the contention submitted by some branches, that such work should be regarded as part of the normal service of the C.E.A. The services of the Electrical Department have been largely utilised by members of the Association and an extension of the facilities offered may well be anticipated.

PROJECTION PRACTICE AND ACCESSORIES.

Higher intensities of illumination are demanded both by exhibitors and by the kinema patron, a tendency in projection practice which has been adequately met by the technicians. Recent developments have placed high intensity projection within economic reach of even the smaller exhibitor. The Peerless Magnarc, introduced by Brockliss last year, has seemingly justified the original high opinions expressed by its users. The future Brockliss range of illuminants also includes Hall and Connolly Stelmar, H.I. Arcs and the Stelmar A.C. Lamp, which will be available for exhibitors this year.

ASHCRAFT SUPREX.—The Ashcraft Suprex arc, to which I referred last year, is handled by Jack Roe, and combines easy accessibility and screen brilliance. It is a sound optical and mechanical job. Even for its 14 in. mirror, the lamphouse is extremely spacious : there are two doors at the rear, one providing access to the negative carbon for recarboning, and the other carrying the mirror, the whole of the negative carbon feed, and the motor drive. The positive carbon is fed by a chain, the travel taking a full 12 in. turn. Motor feed provides separate adjustment for negative and positive feeds. Lateral and vertical adjustments are provided in a conveniently accessible position for the negative carbon. Double dowsers are provided. A test which conveys some idea of the unusual consistency of illumination across the screen provided the following photometer readings : 8, 8.9, 9.4, 9.3, 7.9, an average of 8.7 foot candles, obtained on only 50 amps. on a 22 ft. screen. An Ashcraft Type " E " lamp is also available, and is electrically identical with the former, except that it is built into a lamphouse, only three-quarters the size.

THE STRONG ARC LAMP.—Although introduced only a year ago, the " Strong " range of arc lamps already has a formidable list of installations to its credit. There are several models for A.C. or D.C., high intensity or low, but the most popular is the " Utility " model for D.C. or A.C. H.I.

The design of the " Utility " lamp is on simple lines, yet has a remarkable number of very useful features. It is fitted with a 10¼ in. heat and draught-resisting elliptical reflector of such efficiency that it functions successfully and throws up to 140 ft. and screens up to 26 ft. in width, at a current consumption of no more than 45/50 amperes. Great economy is claimed as the arc wattage is low, and with the modern low-line-volt rectifier, it represents a great economy.

By means of the automatic control the Strong " Utility " can be relied upon to operate at 100 per cent. light brilliancy for the entire twenty minute period of a 2,000-ft. reel without calling for any manual adjustment. The Strong arc utilises the small Suprex type of copper coated carbons, 7 mm. positives, with 6 mm. negatives, being suitable for 40/45 amperes and 6 mm. positives with 5 mm. negatives for 25/35 amperes. Greater illumination can be obtained if conditions require, as the Strong arc will accommodate carbon combinations suitable for operation up to or even over 70 amperes.

WALTURDAW.—Admirable results are also reported from the use of the latest Zeiss Ikon H.I. lamps, for which a special mirror of heat-resisting Ignal glass is employed, the rear surface of which is covered with a heat-resisting silvering, the whole being remarkably free from the effects of " pitting."

GAS DISCHARGE LAMPS.—The announcement made last year of the successful experiment with the high-pressure mercury-vapour lamp led to many inquiries concerning the feasibility of its use for projection purposes. Inquiry, however, reveals that the lamp is not on the market, and there is no information as to when it will be available. This lamp is similar to the amazing stroboscopic lamp demonstrated by B.T.H. at the British Kinematograph Society this year, which is operated from an A.C. supply, and at the peak of the positive half-cycle is flashed by a condenser discharge of 1,000 amps., lasting for only ten-millionths of a second. Both lamps possess the feature of low thermal inertia, which means that the moment the current is cut off, the light is extinguished. This property suggests potential employment in non-intermittent projection, where a lamp of this type, energised from a simple discharge circuit, might conceivably replace the complicated optical systems which are the basic methods of non-intermittent projectors.

An interesting development of projection practice is reported from Germany, where A.E.G. have constructed a special projection mechanism for open-air performances, with throw of 220 ft. This is efficiently negotiated by the employment of a H.I. parabolic mirror arc lamp and a particularly luminous projector lens of 150 mm. diameter, which, together, have a useful capacity of 250 lumens, a figure hitherto unapproachable in the projection of films. Cooling is effected by constructing the whole of the back part of the lamp casing as a ventilator.

Projection light economy is claimed for the invention of J. Gardner, a Liverpool chief projectionist, by which a make-and-break switch, operated from a synchronised part of the apparatus, such as the film feed or shutter, interrupts the electrical current to the illuminant, the load being increased during the projection period so that the average watt consumption remains the same. A device is included to divert the current to a second light source in order to maintain the screen illumination during the obliteration periods.

The problem of the A.C. arc was referred to by R. H. Cricks in the *Ideal Kinema*, who suggests that its adaptation to projection is purely an optical job, the devising of some means of collecting light for both craters. He describes a method employed by Frank Durban, of J. Frank Brockliss & Co., Ltd., who seems to have overcome this problem by means of the Stelmar optical system, the principle adopted being that of placing a spherical mirror behind the crater and a Stelmar unit in front of it. The rays from the front crater are reflected by the mirror back into the unit, which picks up the rays of the rear crater and focuses both on the gate.   It is claimed that the only difference in the light from that of a D.C. arc was that, presumably owing to the lower crater temperature, it is slightly less blue.

REAR PROJECTION.—An installation of the Translux rear-projection principle was made early this year in a medium-size kinema.   A special prism and lens system takes the place of the normal projection lens.   Inside it the picture image undergoes a double reflection, in order to reverse the image ; the rays emerge at an angle of 45 deg. to the projector centre line, so that the two projectors are aligned at angles either side of the centre line of the screen, lens centres being less than 12 in. apart.   The screen width in this particular installation is 21 ft. ; the Translux lens has such an equivalent focus that the projectors are placed 1 ft. from the screen for every foot of screen width, consequently the throw is only 21 ft., yet, the short throw notwithstanding, no supplementary lens behind the gate is needed.   The illuminant is the Stelmar running at 90 amps., rather higher than recommended, but presumably satisfactory provided the reflectors are cleaned several times a day.   The special translucent screen in this particular installation appears to be exceptionally efficient and almost entirely free from à flare spot.

. Although there has been a considerable lessening of interest shown by exhibitors in rear projection, the quality of the picture screened by the Translux system is a big advance upon ordinary forms of rear projection, and its possibilities will doubtless be explored by exhibitors in cases where the elimination of the projection room would be advantageous for structural reasons.   It seems likely that the method will be commonly adopted for the news-reel type of theatre.

ARC MIRRORS.—The life of the mirror in these days of increased illumination presents a problem to most projectionists, who have found economies can be made with Epalite type of metal mirror, which does not radiate any more heat than glass and does not pit.   The Effulgent water-cooled arc mirror has also proved effective.   The mirrors are installed in the ordinary mirror frame and small pipes carry the supply to the water jacket. The actual mirror surface is highly polished metal and, in one situation after two years' service, is to all appearances equal to that of a glass mirror after a few days' use.   Zeiss Ikon supply a special mirror of Ignal heat-resisting glass, which is not only unbreakable but resists " pitting " to a remarkable degree.   A new Bosch mirror, based on the " paralyptic "—the Zonolyptic—has been introduced, which has the advantage of a more durable glass and coincides almost exactly with the average coefficient of expansion of the silver and the silver-protecting coats preventing any tendency to peel under the tremendous heat of modern projection conditions.

THE 2,000-FT. SPOOL.—The discussions taking place in America concerning the 2,000-ft. reel are being closely followed by British projectionists. Although American distributors decided to institute the new length reel last August, that decision has by no means proved unanimous, at least one local authority having declared against the proposals on the grounds of non-compliance with the safety regulations.   No definite action has been decided upon in this country, but it is considered that if the double reel is no longer than 1,500 ft. (many American reels at present are not more than 800 ft. in length) no difficulty will occur other than those arising from the decision to employ a larger core. Although the elimination of cutting and joining should appeal to both renters and projectionists, there seems little hope of unanimous support over here for the 2,000-ft. reel. It must, however, be remembered that Gaumont British has for years fixed a maximum reel length of 1,500 ft., which experience has shown to be most suitable from the various points of view of handling, spool size, gate heat, and emulsion pick-up. A similar length has also been adopted by Wardour Films.

Specifications of leaders and cues for 35 mm. release prints were printed in the *Kine. Weekly* in October. These are briefly :—Protective leader, 8 ft. ; 24 frames identification leader (type of print, reel number, picture title), synchronising leader, 20 frames ahead of start mark ; then after 12 ft. opaque, figures 6 and 9 are to be in words as well as figures on every foot, footage in numerals. Motor cues are to be circular opaque holes reproduced from a punched hole in the negative. Following these, 10 ft. 12 frames before the beginning of the change-over cue, which has marks similar to the motor cue. Thence, follow 18 frames to the run-out trailer, 3 ft. in length, and the identification and protective trailer. The dimensions of the actual spool given in the *Kine. Weekly* of January 16 have been reduced to 14½ in. diameter with a 4-in. hub.

PROJECTION LENS.

Makers of projection lenses are adequately aware of the increasing preference both of exhibitor and patron for improved screen brilliance, and the design of the modern optical system is directed towards the provision of uniform screen illumination, utilising to the fullest degree the light from the efficient modern arc. The density of release prints, of which many complaints have been registered, and the availability of a greater number of colour pictures, are two factors which have not been disregarded by the makers, who have not been slow to appreciate that the accuracy of control of projector illumination is almost of equal importance to the quality of the light.

The "Ultimum" lenses manufactured by Taylor, Taylor & Hobson, Ltd., have been specially designed to cope effectively with these problems. With their large apertures they are particularly suitable for the projection of colour film. As pioneers of the short back-focus projection lenses, Taylor & Hobson point out that the back component of their lenses is designed to correct coma and astigmatism of the front element and at the same time to exert a condensing action on the oblique light.

The "Truvex" lenses have been designed by the British Optical Lens Co. to replace the ordinary plano convex condenser system for any purpose where an accurate beam of high intensity and uniformity is required with economy of light.

The latest application of the "Truvex" type is in heat-resisting glass, and it is claimed that where a 5-in. lens is situate at 4 in. from a 10-kw. arc lamp it gives an increase of about 25 per cent. in screen brightness.

This lens is now being produced in smaller sizes for 9 mm. and 16 mm. machines, the increased intensity of the screen illumination for which is said to exceed 30 per cent.

The "Neokino" lenses have again been recalculated by the Emil Busch Optical Co., and now employ slightly different glasses, which pass even more light than the 1935 models. Lens jackets of duralumin have replaced brass to lighten the lenses. Considerable saving of light is claimed from the use, where the mechanism permits, of the super size lens with diameter of 82.5 mm.

The "Polykino" variable focus lens, priced at 25 guineas, also maintains its popularity.

Current economy and increased illumination are also claimed for the Kershaw "Super C" and "Super B" lens. The constant F/value and "short back focus" features are the secret of the efficiency of the "Super C"

range, which provides sharp critical definition over the whole of the screen. Its further property of converting the light beam into useful image-forming light results in brilliant, contrasting pictures and even screen brilliance. The " Super B " is an inexpensive high efficiency lens and an entirely new optical system, the design of which permits the rear component to collect a far greater amount of light than a lens of the set zone construction ensures even distribution.

A full range of projection lenses is manufactured by Ross, characteristics of whose products are freedom from chromatic aberration and coma. The popular D.P.L. extra large aperture lens (any focus) is standard on Ross projectors. Their diameter is 52.6 mm. with range of foci from 2½ in. to 8 in. in ¼-in. steps. A ¼-in. intermediate foci may be made to special order. The new variable focus model specially designed for " magnascopic " effects increases the dimensions of the image from normality by 30 per cent. This lens may be procured in three varieties, and is only made to order and specification of throw and sizes of images desired.

Walturdaws are handling a new Zeiss Ikon lens, the " Almar," for the foci 4 to 10 cm.; lenses of the Petzval type generally used show at these foci a marginal fuzziness which, as the focus is shortened, becomes the more pronounced. The marginal sharpness is only maintained by reducing the aperture proportion, which means, however, a diminution of the brightness of the image. The " Alinar " surmounts these difficulties and with an unchanged aperture proportion of 1 : 1.9 this lens offers down to the shortest foci a uniform sharpness over the whole field of image.

THE FIRE HAZARD

Although there has been no loss of life and personal injury so rare as to be negligible, evidence exists that the Home Office is not oblivious to the implication of even the smallest outbreak of fire in a place of public entertainment. At Croydon, for instance, an outbreak of fire arising at the projection gate resulted in a Home Office request that a special report of the circumstances should be forwarded to Whitehall.

Four kinemas were destroyed by fire during the year, but in no case was the outbreak due to any mechanical defect of the projection apparatus. There were, however, several occurrences similar to that already referred to at Croydon. A Bradford incident of this nature caused the local fire officer to recommend to the Home Office that future regulations should specify that " fire extinguishers having automatic means of operation should be fitted to all projectors."

This procedure is generally followed by all the larger kinemas, where reliance is placed upon the Pyrene automatic extinguisher. This ingenious appliance is fitted to the projector and not only puts out the fire with CO_2 gas the instant it occurs, but simultaneously stops the motor and cuts the arc. It is therefore impossible for film to be fed into the gate when fire occurs or for the arc to cause re-ignition of film. The fire itself operates the mechanism, but the CO_2 gas is so rapidly distributed that the outbreak is extinguished within two or three seconds. Only a frame or so of film is actually affected by the flame ; therefore the performance may be continued just as if an ordinary break had occurred.

Two other methods of preventing the spread of a fire at the projector gate have been reported. The one relies upon the use of a paper fuse more inflammable than celluloid, which when ignited releases a knife which cuts the film and leaves a blank screen, the light from which tends to prevent panic by reducing the risk of reflecting any flames. The other is the invention of P. McGregor, an Edinburgh projectionist, and consists of a feeler member actuating a shutter controlling the aperture, when the tension on the film is interrupted.

FOR CINEMAS

Complete fire protection throughout Cinema Theatres is provided by the range of "PYRENE" Fire appliances.

"PYRENE" Fire Protection Service includes both installation *and* erection. General fire risks are covered by "CONQUEST" Soda-Acid Fire Extinguishers, — "PYRENE" Everyway, Hose Reels, "PYRENE" Hose, Hose Cradles, Hydrants, Branchpipes, etc., and Fire Buckets.

"PYRENE" Extinguishers deal with electrical plant. The "PYRENE" Automatic Fire Extinguisher for Cinema projectors puts out film fires instantly with CO_2 gas. It simultaneously cuts off the arc and stops the motor. This Automatic Safeguard is so rapid that only a frame or so of film is burnt. No panic—no mess—no damage—no delay !

Pyrene FIRE APPLIANCES

PYRENE 'EVERYWAY' HOSE REEL

"CONQUEST," Soda-Acid Fire Extinguisher

PROJECTOR CARBONS.

The chief developments in projector illuminants have mainly been in the popularisation among the smaller capacity kinemas of high intensity projection. Numerous lamps, both British and foreign, have been introduced, having as the basic feature the employment of H.I. carbons with chemically impregnated cores in diameters of 6, 7 or 8 mm., working at currents of from 30 to 60 amps. These are gradually replacing the low intensity reflector arc. The Ship Suprex No. 91 Carbons are a direct development of the Hilo Carbon introduced in 1931. The high luminous output of the Suprex No. 91 carbon, and the equally high utilisation factor of most of the modern lamps in which they are used,—undoubtedly supplies the exhibitor with a light projector of high efficiency and reasonable economy.

At the same time, experience is showing that it is unwise to over-rate the capabilities of these lamps by installing them in theatres where the screen illumination requirements are such as continuously to demand utmost performance with no reserve margin to counteract fog, dense film or natural depreciation in lamp efficiency. Developments have recently taken place in more than one make of rotating—13.6 mm.—positive lamp, whereby considerable advances have been made in the matter of utilisation efficiency, and it would seem that we may confidently expect to hear more in this direction during the coming year.

Incidentally, it should be mentioned that the agreement entered into last year between the C.E.A. and Chas. H. Champion, Ltd., manufacturers of Ship carbons, has been found to be of considerable benefit to members, and is still functioning very successfully. The latest product of this firm is the " Suprex A " carbon, which, it is claimed, gives greater efficiency and easier control on arcs employing the miniature H.I. type of carbon.

The G.E.C. position in the projector carbon market has been still further strengthened during the past year. A new type of coppered high intensity carbons recently introduced has been very favourably received and has been particularly successful in the modern arc lamps that make use of small diameter coppered carbons.

A new testing laboratory has been opened at the Witton Carbon Works of the Company at Birmingham, incorporating new equipment of the highest standard of accuracy and efficiency, and the full resources of the G.E.C. research organisation, both at Wembley and Birmingham, are employed continuously in development work and ensuring an output of the highest quality and reliability.

Owing to the growth of the demand for Morganite Carbons, additional works extensions have had to be embarked upon. No new grades have been put on the market, but all the established grades continue to be improved.

The demand for the smaller copper-coated " Suprex " type of carbon has again brought Siemens to the fore, despite the duty which was imposed on imported goods of this type. The original Siemens high brilliancy brand is now called the " Koh-i-noor," and has a specially heavy copper coating for use in the new " Suprex " high intensity arc lamps. Standard diameters and lengths are all available for amperages from 25 up to 75. The " Koh-i-Noor " carbons are available for use in all low intensity arc lamps for giving high intensity effect. Since the passing of the original Siemens House, Strong Electric Distributors, Ltd., are handling this product.

B.T.-H.—The B.T.-H. range of equipment handled by Sound and Cinema Equipment, Ltd., comprises the B.T.-H. silent rear shutter projector with high intensity mirror-arc and a junior model, also rear shutter type designed for use with a low intensity mirror arc. Two types of stand are provided, one a universal base, and the other a more compact job, expressly designed for use with B.T.-H. projector mechanism and lantern. All controls are mounted on the lantern table, and all drives are fully enclosed. The motor is accommodated in the stand trunnion, thus reducing the width to a minimum.

Distinctive features of the projector mechanism include intermittent sprocket driven by maltese cross and roller mechanism operating in an oil bath. Parallel opening type gate with shutter immediately behind. Totally enclosed take-up drive. Fixed optical centre. Static gate cooling which obviates the disadvantages of air blast or water cooling.

The operating cost of Type C projector lantern is no higher than that of many low intensity installations. The feed mechanism is fully automatic and easy to operate by simply turning an adjusting knob. The hand feed gives independent feed to either carbon or simultaneous feed to both. Controls are provided for adjusting the mirror of the negative carbon in the vertical and horizontal planes. There is no mechanism in the lantern body which is easily accessible. The low intensity arc is designed for small and medium sized kinemas. It is designed to operate at current values between 20 and 50 amps. at 80 and 110 volts D.C., and is suitable for throws up to 100 ft.

In addition B.T.-H. company market a spot and slide projector designed to operate between 20 and 50 amps. at 80-110 line volts. Low intensity carbons are employed. The lantern table is affixed to the stand by a hinged and swivelling joint operating in vertical or horizontal planes. Other kinema equipment comprises mercury arc rectifiers and hot cathode rectifiers in suitable sizes for kinema use, together with arc control panels, unbreakable grid arc resistances and fire shutters.

There are also many forms of B.T.-H. stage amplification equipment either for operating in conjunction with the reproducer or for independent operation as direct stage amplification or for deaf aid.

ERNEMANN.—The Ernemann VIIB projector, handled by the Walturdaw Cinema Supply Co., Ltd., is a machine which combines projector and sound unit in one mechanism. The sound unit is provided with a rotary reproducing drum. The coupling of the flywheel of the projector mechanism with the sound track provides for an absolutely uniform run. The preparatory smoothing of the film is obtained in a very effective manner by means of a roller loop filter which can be lifted off, and there is no necessity to employ brake-shoes which always lead to the formation of film deposits. Between the bottom sprocket and rotary sound drum a damping eliminator device with resilient double rollers and air damping is situated. This arrangement enables an elastic and absolutely reliable compensation to be obtained thus eliminating all irregularities from the sound track and has the advantage of cutting down oscillation to a minimum. The photo-cell is of a new half-moon shape, built into the rotary sound track. This makes it possible to keep to the direct radiation of the light upon the photo-electric cell which means that the maximum volume of light flux passing through the sound strip is brought to the photo-cell.

The projector is driven by a flanged motor. To the front end of the motor axis a hand-starting knob is fixed, which while allowing a very exact adjustment of the transport mechanism, eliminates the necessity of the hand crank on the operating side of the projector. The combined sound-picture projector is also provided with a built-in change-over device allowing an automatic change-over with picture and sound by simply turning down a lever.

Walturdaw's are also handling a new sound-head, "Ernophone," which as with the combined sound-picture projector Ernemann VIIb, is provided with rotary sound track, damping eliminator device, roller loop filter and direct radiation of the light flux upon the photo-electric cell.

Among this firm's other projectors, manufactured by Zeiss Ikon-Ernemann, the cold-projector Ernemann V. has maintained its predominating position. Since the projector types Ernemann IV., Ernemann II. and Ernon IV, are also continued, Walturdaw offer just as in former years, a large assortment of projectors.

A new equipment, the Chromotrope front of the house projector has recently been added to the Walturdaw range. The structure—pedestal stand, lamp-house, arc lamp "Panzer"—is similar to the double dia-projector.

The Zeiss Ikon mirrors, made of heat-resisting Ignal glass are particularly adapted for use with high intensity lamps; where, however, the throw is at an abnormal angle, the Zeiss Ikon metal reflector is commended.

FILM INDUSTRIES.—The combined projector mechanism and sound reproducing equipment are described on page 284.

G.-B. EQUIPMENTS.—Following the same basic principles which proved so successful in the Eclipse projector, the "Magnus II" is an entirely new projector designed to meet the full requirements of the present exacting theatre conditions, and further embracing many features incorporated to meet the ultimate common place projection of colour films, has been added to the three recent G.-B. Equipment projectors, "Magnus," "Magnette," and the "N" type portable reproducer. Practically every modern refinement is to be found in these four machines.

"Magnus," which is adaptable to all types of sound equipment, is claimed to be an ideal machine for any hall. Every projectionist will appreciate the simplicity of its design, which does not prevent its containing every refinement necessary in the projection room of to-day. In particular, the substitution of vertical racking for the rotary method often adopted to-day enables a number of gears to be eliminated, while every modern improvement is embodied, such as front-opening gate, rear shutter, large diameter rigid lens mount, detachable oil-bath, and pump lubrication. The machine requires appreciably less power than usual to drive it, because of its simplicity, thus imposing less strain upon motor and sound-unit drive.

The "Magnette" is a replica in miniature for use in smaller halls.

The "N" type portable reproducer, recently produced to Royal Navy specifications for special use on shipboard, weighs roughly one cwt. All working parts have been designed on a generous scale hitherto unknown. It includes many of the improvements incorporated in the "Magnus," and if necessary can be used in the largest halls.

IMPERIAL.—Numerous special features have been incorporated in the design of the latest Imperial projector. The projector can be supplied with or without speed counter or front cover. The main drive spindle is a separate unit and is interchangeable for the different methods of drive and gear ratios, which gives ease with less cost for adaptation to any make of sound system. A drum shutter is incorporated with a novel gear arrangement controlling the shutter phasing when masking. The Maltese cross box is a separate unit

and is easily removable should occasion arise. The mechanism is lubricated by means of a pump which has a removable oil filter protecting the mechanism against any foreign matter.

Price of mechanism only £70, plus top spool box and arm £5, bottom spool box with take-up mechanism, £7, speed counter £5, front cover with plate-glass door £8, main drive with reduction gear for driving the bottom spool box £3, pedestal stand for mechanism £15. Hire-purchase terms :—25 per cent. deposit, plus 6 per cent. charges on the balance, payment spread over one or two years.

An arc lamp embodying the latest features in arc lamp construction will shortly be available.

The design of the whole equipment is such as will allow any addition or adaptations to be fitted by the purchaser himself should he so desire. All parts have been standardised, and any spares that may be required can be supplied from stock. There exists a considerable foreign demand for the Imperial projector.

KALEE MODEL ELEVEN.—Designed for sound, but equally for silent projection, the Kalee Eleven embodies all the following desirable features :— Silence in action, ease of manipulation, simplicity and reliability, precision workmanship, automatic lubrication by pump to all bearings, gears and intermittent motion, masking by revolving intermittent sprocket, combined flicker and safety shutter, film speed indicator.

The price of the Kalee Eleven varies according to the sound system or purpose for which it is required, but models are available from £99. Special terms of 2½ per cent. for cash or deferred payment are available.

A welcome addition to the latest type of arcs using the small diameter high intensity carbons is the Kalee " Regal " N.L. type arc costing £97 10s., which incorporates many special features. It is built on massive, sturdy lines, and all parts are easily accessible, although once the carbons have been inserted there is no need to open doors on the back of the lamp house, for adjusting the negative carbon. This can be done by a special device situated at the rear, and the movement at the same time removes any carbon deposit.

There are also many other types of Kalee arcs including the Kalee H.M.L. costing £50 ; it can be operated on low or high intensity, the running costs are economical, and highly efficient screen illumination is obtainable on 60–75 amperes. There is also a powerful type of arc in the Kalee H.L. Sperry pattern, suitable for use by kinemas with very long throws and operated on 125–150 amperes. The cost is £95, with arc voltmeter at an extra £4.

The Kalee type T.L. is for use on any current up to 100 amperes. This right-angle arc incorporates 6 in. by 9 in. heat-resisting condensers, and is designed for exhibitors requiring an inexpensive form of high intensity arc lamp, without automatic feed, which can be purchased at the very moderate cost of £39. The lamp, incorporating automatic carbon control, can be purchased for £56 complete.

For this latter type of arc there is an increasing demand, as it over-comes the difficulty experienced in so many kinemas with steep angles, of the frequent breakages of mirrors. One of the features of the type T.L. arc is that there are no mirrors employed, thus enabling kinemas to obtain a type of arc lamp which gives very efficient illumination at a very low cost and without the cost of the upkeep of mirrors.

Kalee also handle a 16 mm. silent projector, which gives a screen picture of 12 ft. by 9 ft. up to 50 ft. throw, rectifiers and complete talking picture equipment.

KAMM.—Kamm Projectors manufactured at their London works are still recognised for their fundamental soundness in design, although additions have been made from time to time which further improve their efficient qualities. Two models are at present in production—the open type " Junior " model, and the " Wembley " totally enclosed machine, which are both well tried and proved.

In the early part of 1937, it is intended to produce a larger model to conform to the requirements of " Western " Soundhead adaptation, primarily with the object of supplying for use in " super " cinemas and for large halls, where its capacity would be equal to the tasks imposed upon it. Totally enclosed, it will incorporate several new features which the exhibitor will find of special interest when considering the installation of new equipment in his theatre.

KAPLAN PROJECTOR.—The sole agency for the American-made Kaplan projector, a machine widely used in the States, has been acquired by Jack Roe. Its adaptation to the leading sound systems is easy, as only the simplest mechanical parts are involved. The whole of the mechanism and film track is enclosed. Centralised lubrication is provided. The method of manufacture of the Maltese cross and intermittent sprocket ensures a rock-steady picture. The film trap is of the parallel opening type and can be easily examined and cleaned. Provision is made for the use of any special shape of aperture plate. An important feature of the Kaplan projector is the generous heat shield in which the safety shutter slides and, forming the rear wall of the casing, protects the gate from the heat of the arc. The gate is further protected by a rear shutter. The lens mount is provided with sensitive focussing and will accommodate most types of lenses. The stand with a five-point support is of a very substantial type with easy adjustment. Not the least valuable feature of the machine is the fact that all parts are strictly interchangeable and are supplied in sealed cartons. Practically all the " sure-fit " parts can be fitted with the aid only of a screw-driver.

. **ROSS.**—The Ross F.C. projector, which has been expressly designed to withstand the rigour of continuous service prevailing under modern conditions, remains substantially the same as last year. The more practical system of fixed optical centreing employed has at once simplified and rendered working efficient and effective in action. The radical change made in the system of transmission has proved successful, the new train of gearing of the special type has practically achieved inaudibility in the running of the mechanism. The automatic shutter controlled by a sensitive centrifugal governor is instantaneous in action whenever the margin of safety is inadequate. The light cone is in direct contact with the gate aperture which, with its ribbed and flanged inner conical lining, achieves a remarkable degree of heat insulation. The flicker shutter, located at the rear, also reduces gate temperature. The front shutter model offers every facility for conversion to the latest type rear-shutter model. A feature of the Ross is the ease with which adjustments in setting may be undertaken with the machine in actual operation. A robust stand with tripod base is easily controlled as regards projection angle.

Two searchlight arc lamps are available, Types B and C. These are fitted with 8-in. and 10-in. ellipsoidal mirror in a sheet steel lamp-house. The arc is entirely enclosed and well ventilated, and automatic arc control fitted externally to the rear compartment of the lamp-house is available.

The Type C lamp, which has recently been introduced, embraces the general characteristics of the B type apart from a somewhat lower current carrying capacity. The new design permits the use of super carbons, thus bringing its performance into line with well-known American products. The average load is approximately 70 amps., which renders it particularly suitable to medium-sized halls.

The Ross " Sceneograph " Effects machine is a simple combination of appliances that affords a high degree of efficiency in the production of theatrical effects from the operating box. In brief, this appliance consists of a double optical lantern comprising two Ross vertical arc lamps, with very many refinements directed towards a three-fold instead of a single purpose. Its triple functions are those of spot and flood lighting with dynamic and combined colours, scenic effect projector and lantern slide projector.

The lamps are mounted above each other, each with its own controls, their movement being governed on the rack and pinion principle. There are two sets of four projection lenses of foci ranging from $7\frac{1}{2}$ in. to 28 in., mounted in rotary turrets for rapid location. For use on either unit there are two pre-set framing shutters, two dissolving iris shutters with lens control, pre-set and adjustable iris star shutter, motor-driven colour wheel, slide carriers with swivel adjustments, coloured gelatines, and 10 design effect plates.

The Ross spotlight for front of the house spotting comprises Ross searchlight arc lamp with 8-in. ellipsoidal mirror, automatic control, air blower, iris diaphragm and set of tinters. It is mounted on strong pedestal stand with swivel adjustment.

SIMPLEX EQUIPMENT.—It is claimed that one of the features of the Simplex Projector throughout the last 21 years has been that the basic construction of the mechanism has remained materially the same ; in other words the mechanism from its earliest days up to the present moment has been continuously improved without having to introduce an entirely re-designed model. This has been one of the great factors in the successful selling of this projector, the possession of which enables the exhibitor to bring it right up to modern day standard, by adding the improvements which have been introduced by the manufacturers. Consequently the exhibitor has not been forced to the expense of scrapping existing equipment in order to take advantage of the new models taking their place.

Improvements have taken place during the past year, adding to the high state of efficiency hitherto reached by the Super Simplex. Extremely close tolerances have been worked to in the intermittent movement, and the film trap has been made extra heavy, a fact which assures absolute alignment of the film at all times. The rear-shutter model has now become practically universal, and actually in America the standard front-shutter model has now become obsolete, although it will still be available to European exhibitors who desire same.

In the range of illuminants, the Hall and Connolly High Intensity Arc Lamp, the Peerless Magnarc Reflector Arc, and the Stelmar Arc Lamp are still strongly in favour, and sales of the Peerless Magnarc Arc Lamp, particularly have been very large during 1936. Messrs. Brockliss have still new arcs to, put on the market—namely, the Hall and Connolly Stelmar High Intensity Arc Lamp and the Stelmar Alternating Current Arc Lamp. Both these arcs have passed the experimental stage, and have been tested out with gratifying results, and are ready for marketing in 1937.

THE PROJECTIONISTS GUILD.

After five years' existence, the Guild of British Kinema Projectionists and Technicians continues to justify the aspirations of its founders whose goal was proficiency in every department of projection. The insistence upon a standard of technical efficiency has created a craft organisation which, without Trade Union organisation or affiliation, has steadily raised the status and, incidentally, the remuneration of each member. The value to the trade of the Guild lecture system and other educative propaganda is becoming increasingly appreciated by exhibitors who recognise the increasing demands the theatre operation makes upon their technicians whose normal duties touch upon such a wide variety of scientific knowledge. The success of the Guild in England has resulted in enquiries concerning the possibility of the establishment of a similar organisation in other parts of the Empire. In northern Ireland a Guild is already functioning with success both technically and socially.

One important phase of the Guild work is the educational lectures held under its auspices In London the Gaumont-British organisation co-operated in a series of lectures and in other areas the local C.E.A. have afforded practical aid to similar efforts sponsored by the guild. Various local authorities have included extension classes for projectionists in their curriculum. In Scotland, the Glasgow Council and the Ayrshire County Council have insti-tuted similar classes, the fees for which are fixed at about 5s. per pupil for the

course.   The value of these classes was pointed out at the Scots C.E.A. annual meeting, when it was stated that owing to the tremendous technical developments that had taken place in a very short time, it was not possible for projectionists to acquire thorough theoretical knowledge necessary without attendance at such classes.

Another attempt was made by exhibitors during the year to institute a scheme for purchasing accessories, from carpets to furnishings, on a co-operative basis. The scheme was explained to members of the London and Home Counties branch in March and it was decided to form a society, open only to C.E.A. members, for the purpose indicated provided a minimum membership of 100 was obtained. No further information has since been forthcoming concerning the proposal.

An interesting outcome of the C.E.A. conversations with the Home Office on the manual of safety requirements was the formation of an advisory panel of experts which members might refer when questions arise in respect of new electrical equipment. The following names were put forward to the Home Office in March as constituting the proposed panel : T. J. Digby, M.I.E.E. ; Basil Davis, A.M.I.E.E. ; John Hall, B.Sc., A.M.I.E.E. (of the firm of Troughton and Young, Ltd.) ; S. Hart, M.I.E.E. (chief engineer, Gaumont-British Picture Corporation, Ltd.) ; G. H. Buckle (of the firm of E. Wingfield-Bowles and Partners) ; S. B. Donkin, M.I.C.E., M.I.E.E. ; H. M. Winstanley, M.I.E.E. (of the firm of Handcock and Dykes) ; L. Knopp (Gaumont-British Picture Corporation, Ltd.).

RECTIFIERS.

Since the introduction of the rectifier into the kinema a few years ago some remarkable developments and improvements have been made which enable current rectification to be effected without trouble or anxiety. Among the newcomers to this field is the Westinghouse, which uses the same principle as is employed in the widely used Westinghouse dry-plate rectifiers for amplifiers, battery chargers and other equipment. At present it is being made in three sizes—a twin 30-ampere, twin 35-ampere and twin 80-ampere. A unique method of control cutting out resistance losses and minimising reactive losses assures a very high efficiency. The overall efficiency averages from 65 per cent. to 70 per cent. at a power factor of about 0.85.

A full range of mercury and hot-cathode rectifiers is now being manufactured by British Thomson-Houston Co. The mercury type is made in the following ratings : 75-ampere continuous rating for two 60-ampere arcs; 100-ampere continuous rating for two 70-ampere arcs, and 150-ampere continuous rating for two 120-ampere arcs. A feature of the hot-cathode model ir that the same size of bulb is used for all ratings, each giving full wave sectification, the ratings being 100-amperes for two 75-ampere arcs, 75-amperes for two 60-ampere arcs, 60 amperes for two 50-ampere arcs, 42-amperes for two 35-ampere arcs, all at 110 volts.

The equipment manufactured by the Electric Construction Co. of Wolverhampton, comprises a mercury rectifier and is listed in numerous sizes from 100 to 1,000 amperes. The efficiency is unusually high, ranging in the case of the smallest type from 87 per cent. with a power factor of 0.9 to a maximum for the largest sizes of 93.5 per cent. with a power factor of 0.94. The principle of grid control has also been developed.

There is a Davenset rectifier to suit every requirement, and the equipment has the advantage of extremely small size compared with wattage output. The installation requires the minimum wiring with no external switchgear. The characteristics of the Hewittic mercury rectifier, the efficiency of which is recognised by its numerous installations, the Elin, the Metrum and the Morrison have been described in previous years.

An important feature of either mercury or oxide-cathode rectifiers is that they require practically no maintenance other than, in the former case, the usual attention to the fan motor. Another advantage is that they can be operated by remote control from the projection chamber.

The features of the Newton and Crypto hot cathode rectifiers are now combined in the Crypton, handled by Walturdaw ; its high-grade performance has commended this equipment to a large number of exhibitors. They are made in a range of sizes and outputs from 18 amperes to 180 amperes, suitable respectively for two 15-ampere arcs and two 150-ampere arcs. still larger outputs, of course, can be obtained by paralleling cubicles together. A very high efficiency is maintained through those sizes ranging in all but the very smallest, from 81 per cent. to 85 per cent., with a power factor of 0.9.

EMERGENCY LIGHTING EQUIPMENT.

Although batteries are now largely superseded in sound equipment, a much wider scope for their use in kinemas has been found as a stand-by source of current in the event of failure of the supply mains. Where power is taken off the grid most authorities insist that there should be available two independent sources of supply to places of entertainment, so that complete failure of one source will not affect the means of secondary lighting. Circumstances, however, have been frequent where interference with the one source has caused failure in the other. Consequently the exhibitor who desires immunity from such troubles has little hesitation in adopting the storage battery as a convenient and an efficient source of emergency lighting. The requirements of the exhibitor have been very fully considered by the leading battery manufacturers and there is no difficulty in selecting a system which meets the most exigent demands of the local authorities from the products of such firms as Alklum Storage Batteries, Ltd., Chloride Electrical Storage Co., Ltd., D.P. Battery Co., Ltd., and the Tungstone Accumulator Co., Ltd.

Batteries, Ltd., handle the " 'Nife ' Neverfayle " equipment, which conforms to the regulations in force both in England and Scotland. Both installations incorporate " Nife " nickel cadmium alkaline batteries, which occupy a very small space and owing to the absence of corrosive fumes do not require a separate battery room. Moreover, the steel plates never require renewing. Two distinct systems are handled by Chloride Co.: (1) The Keepalite, and (2) the floating battery. In the former the battery is maintained fully charged by a continuous trickle charge current and is brought automatically on to the safety lights in the event of any interruption in the normal supply. In the floating battery system, which is also employed by other makers, the battery floats constantly across the D.C. output of a motor generator or rectifier and takes up the load on an emergency. In a method devised by the D.P. Battery Co., the main lighting circuits are supplied from outside, but the safety lighting is connected to a motor generator running off the mains with a battery " floating." This permits the use of a battery of smaller capacity, equal to, say, three hours' supply in case of emergency. The Tungstone Accumulator Co. also manufactures a complete range of lead-acid accumulators meeting all requirements. The well-known Tungstone plant type plate with its additional weight and strength can be relied upon to give many years of care free service.

BRITISH TALKING PICTURES.—The B.T.P. Sound Reproducing Apparatus remains substantially as at the last review except for certain detail improvements designed to improve reproduced sound. The Minor Reproducer sold at £375 for halls seating up to 500 persons still has adherents on account of its attractive selling price and exceptional reproduction, whilst

the type PN.T. reproducers for Wide Range, High Fidelity, Natural Tone, and other systems of extended frequency range recordings are being installed and, on account of its level acoustic output over a frequency range from 30 to 10,000 cycles, is giving reproduction which is receiving very favourable comment.

A new departure is the V series of equipment. The VN.T. Reproducer for kinemas up to 800 persons sells at £525, and provides the same high quality as the PN.T. series at less cost. It is marketed to meet the requirements of those exhibitors who are primarily concerned with the quality of reproduction at competitive prices.

Type PN.T. Reproducers are available for 700 seater kinemas at £680 to 3,000 seats at £1,310, which prices include projector adaptation parts, screen, screen framework, masking, felting and loudspeaker tower and non-synchronous attachment, material which is usually charged as extra by competitive manufacturers.

Arrangements are available whereby payment may be made over three years and an additional incentive to purchase is provided by the ability to purchase the equipment outright for cash and to hire purchase in addition to the more usual ten-year lease.

Service charges vary with the type of apparatus, but are definitely the most favourable available because as the designation service implies this department is regarded by the company as an organisation, maintained by the exhibitor for service.

B.T.-H.—The B.T.-H. Extended Frequency Range Reproducer is all-mains driven. The frequency range covered is from approximately 30 cycles to 10,000 cycles, and the optical system and amplifier chain have been completely redesigned to cover this range.

The extended frequency range amplifier is 4-stage and in two types, a small one for 11 watts undistorted output, and the larger one 22 watts. For theatres seating up to approximately 1,000 a single 11-watt amplifier is utilised ; for theatres seating up to 2,000, 22 watt ; for theatres seating over 2,000, two 22-watt amplifiers would be utilised. Naturally, duplication of either 11 or 22 watt can be made in any case where a theatre requires same.

In common with all other B.T.-H. reproducers, there are no head amplifiers as the optical system, together with the Mazda PE7B photocell is efficient enough to give a large signal.

The number of speakers utilised in a theatre depends on the size and shape of the auditorium. The average number for the small theatres is two, and for the larger theatres is four.

In addition to the extended frequency range reproducer there is another type of normal range essentially for the very small theatre. This is known as the XM, and is priced at £350, including installation and wiring.

Standard prices are as follows :—Type J/A, 11 watts, suitable for up to 1,000 seats, A.C. supply, £565, installed and wired. (D.C. supply, £50 extra.)

Type K/A, suitable for up to 2,000 seats, A.C. supply, £745, installed and wired. (D.C. supply, £20 extra.) Larger equipments are subject to special quotations.

Service maintenance of all types of equipment, 37s. 6d. per week with full maintenance, including supply of valves, exciter lamps, photocells, soundhead repairs, etc., at no additional charge. Full emergency service free and regular monthly inspections.

G.-B. EQUIPMENTS.—Early in 1937 G.-B. E, promise the introduction of the "DUOSONIC" Sound System, which is claimed to apply to sound, a measure of stereophony. There are three main British Acoustic sound-film equipments—the "N" Type Portable, the "Q" and "QX."

The "N" type, full size equipment possesses 2,000 ft. spoolboxes, and was designed mainly for use on board warships. Results are claimed to be comparable in every respect with those obtainable from full-size equipment in theatres seating up to 800, the undistorted output from amplifier being 12 watts. The illuminant is normally a 1,000 watt biplane projector lamp, but, alternatively, an arc lamp is fitted capable of operating on amperages up to 30. The arc lamp has several particularly novel features, and is designed to be operated by absolutely unskilled persons and, therefore, is fitted with a special one-knob control.

The "Q" type, introduced towards the end of 1935, has proved so successful that apart from detail refinement no changes have been made. This type of equipment is ideal for theatres seating up to 1,000 ; it has an undistorted output of 12 watts, all-mains operated, and fitted with "Full Range" speaker assembly. Maintenance costs are exceptionally low.

The "QX" type equipment is built very much on the lines of the "Q" type, and is suitable for halls seating 1,000 to 2,500. The number of speakers is varied according to the size and shape of each individual theatre. This equipment can be supplied either with the PU3 soundhead or the type PU high precision universal soundhead. The amplifier has an undistorted output of 30 watts.

A feature of both the "Q" and "QX" equipments is the rapid manner in which the various units can be supplied either as a single or duplicated channel equipment, and provision is made for the addition on the actual racks of such accessories as managers' announcement system, organ repeater, deaf aid, etc. Volume control, a particularly ingenious device, is used for remote operation of the fader from both projectors, and also, in many instances, from the auditorium. This unit also permits the operator, on the projector remote from the volume control, not only to adjust the volume, but also to change over sound simultaneously with the picture. Both the PU and PU3 type soundheads can be adapted to any well-known make of projector.

Service is compulsory during the period of Hire Purchase Agreement only, at the following rates :—

"Q" type equipments—monthly visits, £1 1s. per week ; fortnightly visits, £1 10s. per week. All emergency calls free of charge.

"QX" type equipments—weekly visits, £3 per week ; fortnightly visits, £2 per week.

FILM INDUSTRIES.—Both Senior Model, type A, for kinemas seating up to 3,000, and the Junior Model, type B, for seating capacity up to 1,000, are still being offered, but with certain alterations to bring the equipment in accord with modern requirements. The amplifier consists of two special neon-voltage-controlled H.T. supply units for the photo-electric cell, single or double amplifier channel and rectifying and smoothing equipment for the exciter lamps using Westinghouse metal rectifiers. In case of any failure, either H.T. unit or either rectifier unit may supply both machines. The whole is of rack and panel construction with detachable units. A new cone-type

loudspeaker is added with special wooden horn baffle. This has a very wide frequency response to meet the requirements of present-day recording.

In addition to the two equipments mentioned above, there is also the F.I. portable type C 35 mm. apparatus, which, together with the amplifier and loudspeaker, is contained in three portable cases.

A special feature of this equipment is the absence of fire danger. It conforms strictly to the regulations of the British Home Office for Portable Projectors, and permission (subject to review after a period) has also been obtained from the British Board of Trade allowing its use between decks without the necessity of enclosing the apparatus in a fireproof cabinet. Two further important and unique features of this machine are that films may be stopped during showing to expose a still picture for special study, and that by the use of special filter glass, eye strain is obviated.

SOUND REPRODUCING APPARATUS.

IMPERIAL.—The Imperial Sound System is largely known to the small exhibitor. Simplicity of driving the sound sprocket shaft without gearing is a special feature. The ease of removal of the optical unit and gate parts will be appreciated by the operator. The head amplifier is incorporated in the soundhead. The optical unit is of a special design for reproducing the higher frequencies on present day recorded films.

Although the Imperial Soundhead has been designed for use with the Imperial Projector, it can easily be installed on any other make of projector. The soundhead is complete on pedestal stand with bottom spool-box drive, motor, silent chain drive, head amplifier, photo cell and exciter lamp. A special design of main amplifier and speaker with horn is supplied with the complete equipment.

Price of complete equipment installed £360. Soundhead, amplifier and speaker can be supplied separately if desired. Hire purchase terms : 25 per cent. deposit plus 6 per cent. charges on the balance ; payment spread over one or two years.

KALEE UNIVERSAL SOUND SYSTEM is extremely solid, and includes a heavy cast-iron pedestal stand with built-in soundhead of the fully mechanically driven type, with filter flywheel feeding, a special contraphase amplifier, which by eliminating all phase lag ensures unusually brilliant attack and reproduction of transients, with straight line response through the frequency range. This amplifier forms a particularly neat unit, entirely enclosed in a steel cabinet with Monitor speaker mounted on top, and the high quality chain is completed by the use of twin-diaphragm Voigt speakers at the stage end.

The whole apparatus, is, of course, entirely all-mains driven, and can be fitted to any current model of Kalee projector.

A further Kalee product is a semi-professional model complete sound-film reproducer, based on the new Kalee " Invicta " model projector. It has been designed for non-professional use such as churches, clubs, institutions, schools, hospitals, etc. This equipment, in spite of its moderate price, £270 single and £440 double, embodies the latest practice throughout, the projector being of the rear drum shutter type with central oiling, micrometer focussing, framing lamp, and practically all the refinements of its older brothers. It is

fitted with a 10-inch mirror arc lamp with automatic arc striking and differential carbon feed of an unusually clever and simple design.

The soundhead is again the fully mechanically driven type with filter flywheel, and the amplifying equipment follows the same lines as the Universal, including special contraphase amplifier and the Voigt stage speakers.

KAMM.—Simplicity and ease of operation is the keynote of design of the " Kamm " Sound Reproducing Equipment. The amplifier is all-mains, providing for complete reproduction of all range frequencies, and meeting the requirements of the most advanced recording technique. It is available in two types with undistorted output of 12 and 24 watts respectively.

The Soundhead is of the totally enclosed type and visual observation of the sound track is made possible as the film runs through the machine. The design of the " B " type machine reduces vibration to a minimum, the whole of the weight being loaded through the centre of gravity of the machine. The totally enclosed " Wembley " model reduces the risk of fire to a minimum, is extremely solid in design and for this class of machine is competitive in price and outstanding in performance.

An important addition to the range will be a larger machine of the totally enclosed type embodying adaptation to " Western " soundheads. This machine will be specially suitable for use in " Super " halls.

Price range of Kamm equipment commences at £250 and upward according to requirements. Inquiries are cordially invited for all types of installation.

MIHALY.—Several improvements have been effected which may be attached or added to existing installations of the Mihaly Sound equipment. All mains are now used throughout, and existing amplifiers have been modified to permit of a greater range of frequencies being effectively reproduced. There have been several conversions made from battery to all mains sets, and in this and other directions a large number of old equipments have been brought up to date during the last year, all with good results. In the case of certain types of projectors, a more efficient form of motor drive has been fitted. Owing to their simplicity of operation the Mihaly equipment is claimed to be eminently suitable for use not only in the commercial cinema but also in schools, institutes and church houses. Mihaly also service installations.

MORRISON-ELECTRIC Sound apparatus remains as last year, wide range, push pull output, fitted with frequency compensators, and double-diaphragm speakers.

The prices remain at £220 for the small equipment up to 350 seating ; £260 for the 1,000 seater, and £500 for the 2,000 seater.

PHILIPS CINE SONOR.—The latest development of the Philips type 3834 Soundhead is a greatly improved gear system using helically cut worm gearing. This soundhead is notable for its compactness and the fact that it is driven by means of a single-phase synchronous motor.

A number of new amplifiers have also been introduced. The Philips type 3745 microphone amplifier is all mains operated and of extremely compact construction. This amplifier may be used with dynamic ribbon or crystal microphone, since the inherent hum level has been reduced to zero. The Philips type 3758 all mains operated amplifier is of the push-pull type throughout and provides an undistorted output of 20 watts.

A most useful addition to the Philips amplifying equipment is the type 3762 A.C./D.C. Universal amplifier. It is suitable for operation from either A.C./D.C. mains and alternatively provision is made so that the filaments may be operated from 12 volt accumulators, whilst high tension is furnished by a rotary converter or some other supply. This amplifier is also push-pull throughout and provides an undistorted output of 10 watts. The amplifier is fitted in a strong metal case with carrying handle.

RCA. PHOTOPHONE.—Four types of RCA. photophone theatre equipment are marketed in this country : (1) Small (up to 1,000 seats), £495 ; (2) Medium (up to 1,500 seats), £750, De Luxe model, £825 ; (3) Large (up to 2,500 seats), £1,155, De Luxe model, £1,197 10s. ; (4) Super De Luxe (over 2,500 seats), £1,610. Deferred terms are available over one, two or three years.

These equipments constitute a considerable advance on earlier models. The new type PS.24 " Rotary Stabiliser " Soundhead, which is standard, entirely eliminates the use of the usual sound gate which is replaced by a rotating sound take-off drum. By means of a " fluid fly-wheel " drive, constant speed is ensured regardless of all external variables, such as the accuracy of driving gears and the eccentricity of sprockets or the condition of the film.

All equipments are designed to operate from an A.C. power supply of 110 volts, 50 cycles. The difference between the standard equipment and De Luxe equipment consists mainly in the type of speaker system supplied. The latest type " High Fidelity " 6-inch electro-dynamic speaker units with directional baffles are supplied with the standard equipment, while the De Luxe equipment incorporates the new RCA. Multi-Cellular High Frequency speaker unit, which embodies the very latest advances made in loudspeaker design.

A novel type of soundhead shortly being introduced to the market embodies an ingenious system capable of running either standard or push-pull tracks.

The latest model RCA. 35 mm. portable sound reproducer is available for sound-on-films use only. All RCA. Photophone High Fidelity reproducers operate from A.C. 110 volts, 50 cycles supply. These portables are available in single and double projectors. The price of the single is £350 and the double unit £550. The R.C.A. portable can be set up ready for projection in 15 minutes.

R.C.A. Photophone now undertake to service and fully maintain all new theatre equipments under their latest All-in Maintenance policy at no increased cost beyond the normal service rate. Maintenance includes the supply of all so-called consumable parts, such as photo-electric cells, valves, exciter lamps, etc., in addition to non-consumable items.

WESTERN ELECTRIC.—A comprehensive range of sound reproduction equipment is handled by Western Electric. There is a series of five com-

ponents to cover the requirements of all sizes and types of theatres at prices ranging from £525 upwards. Modern installations,. practically without exception, are of the wide range equipment, and there is a large demand for the conversion of the older equipment to embody the wider range of frequencies. For an expenditure varying from £100 to £275 the original Western Electric System may be converted so as to give results comparable to those obtained from the latest installations. For 1937 Western Electric announce a further development which has already proved immensely satisfactory in America. Although details are not available at the time of writing the new Mirrophonic system is understood to embody the application of stereoscopic principles to sound production

A highly efficient service organisation is maintained throughout the British Isles (each engineer covering a limited number of theatres), providing regular routine overhauls and emergency service, and is always available during all the hours theatres are operating. Approximately 200 engineers residing within easy reach of the theatres under their control are permanently in the field.

Apart from the principal towns such as London, Manchester, Birmingham, Leeds, Newcastle, Glasgow, Cardiff and Dublin, where branch offices exist and major stocks are maintained, there are in addition 28 emergency stock centres from which field engineers may draw. Thus every part of the country is provided for in the event of emergencies arising calling for the replacement of defective equipment at short notice. The system of routine inspection has been brought to such a state of perfection, however, that emergencies of this nature seldom arise, and possible faults are discovered and rectified before a loss of sound is incurred.

BRITISH PRODUCTION.

The progress recorded last year of British production has been fully maintained in 1936. Concomitant with the numerical increase in product has been a general improvement in its entertainment and technical qualities, but whether in sufficient degree to justify the amount of money sunk in local production, is open to question.

During the past year 222 British features and 196 short subjects were registered with the Board of Trade, an increase over the previous year of 24 long and 54 short films respectively. These figures of British production represent 27.9 per cent. of the whole footage registered and is considerably in excess of either the exhibitors' or renters' quota which now stands at 20 per cent. Too great a significance, however, is not attached to these figures by the average exhibitor, particularly by the independent man who is severely critical of the quality of the product available. He complains that so many pictures of little entertainment merit are acquired by renters merely for quota purposes, and so high a proportion is economically un-obtainable in competition with the circuits and super halls, that it is im-possible to satisfy his own quota requirements except at a financial sacrifice. The scandal of the "quota question" has been one of the major topics of discussion by the C.E.A., which was particularly outspoken in regard to the worthless Empire product, such as Indian pictures, which, bought solely for quota, was frankly recognised as unemployable and shelved by their owners.

The seriousness of the plight in this respect of the independent exhibitor led to strong representations being made to the Advisory Committee under the 1927 Films Act. Following a detailed examination of the exhibitors' case and in view of the expiry in 1938 of the Act, the Government set up the Departmental Committee on the working of the Act over which Lord Moyne presided. After an exhaustive investigation, which covered every phase of trade activity from redundancy to studio operation, a report was issued in November making, among other recommendations, proposals for the financing of the Trade, its supervision by a Government Commission and the institution of a quota with a quality stipulation rising to 50 per cent. An analysis of the trade reactions to the Committee's report does not come within the province of this article, but it is obvious, that whatever effect it may have upon the general structure of the trade and the relationship of its component sections, it will undoubtedly stimulate worth-while British production. For the moment, however, it is unlikely there will be any legislation based upon the report for another year or two.

Meanwhile, there has been an unprecedented boom in British production. Money has been plentiful and the hazardous nature of the investment has not deterred insurance companies, banks and prominent private industrialists from providing generous subsidies to British and foreign producers. One of the results of this financial support has been the multiplication of studio facilities; another, but less satisfactory effect, has been the extravagant and uneconomic spending upon quite unworthy subjects. Nor, in the majority of instances has it contributed to the entertainment value of the pictures concerned, for although the general level of presentation has certainly been raised and certain pictures have obtained U.S. release, the number of box-office successes is quite disproportionate to the production costings. It has been estimated that nearly £4,000,000 has been sunk in British production during 1936. Unfortunately, however, the financial situation of some production concerns at the end of the year appears to have jeopardised the confidence of certain financial circles in some aspects of British production.

STUDIO SPACE INCREASES. —The development of our studio resources has been the most remarkable feature of the past year. It is estimated early in 1937 that approximately there were some 23 studios of varying capacities available, comprising 75 floors of a total area of 774,588 square feet. During the year 30 up-to-date floors were made available. The most spectacular contribution was the opening in April of Alexander Korda's London Films studio at Denham, where a completely self-contained production centre with five huge stages, each measuring 250 ft. by 120 ft., have been established, in addition to the Denham Laboratories, the most modern producing plant in the world. No less important were the Pinewood Studios at Iver Heath, which when its eight floors are completed will have cost over £1,000,000. Five new floors and various technical facilities, including what is claimed to be the largest sound stage in Europe, make Sound City at Shepperton a studio much favoured by producers, the amenities of its exterior lot being greatly in demand. Construction work at Elstree indicates that this corner of Hertfordshire retains its pre-eminence as a production centre—a position which will be unassailable when the promised railway facilities mature. The defection of British and Dominion Films, which now operates Pinewood,

K

has been more than made good by the expansion policy initiated by the Joe Rock studios, where four large stages, complete with ancillary departments, are being erected. There is also the ambitious scheme of the Amalgamated Studios with its six stages and every technical and production convenience, which enable them to rank with the finest service studios in the world. The former Independent studios, near Elstree station, were thoroughly reconditioned on acquisition by Julius Hagen. The Highbury studios, with two modern equipped floors, were also opened during the year, and another stage was added to the Fox British studios at Wembley. Expansions were also made at Worton Hall, Isleworth, now operated by Criterion Films.

Removal of the B. and D. activities from Elstree to Iver followed upon a disastrous fire which completely destroyed six floors of the B. and D. and associated British studios, and occasioned £400,000 damage. At Denham much damage was also caused early in the year by a fire which destroyed one of the large stages and delayed the start of productions. More recently the small studio at Southall owned by Fidelity films was completely destroyed.

The number of studio fires that have occurred has directed attention to various types of extinguisher apparatus, and the sprinkler system is in common use in all modern erections. Among the experts who cater for every conceivable form of fire risk is the Pyrene Co., who will give details of insurance rebates, methods of extinction and details of all approved extinguishing media.

ELECTRICAL SUPPLIES.—Many of the newly built studios have installed independent generating plant, owing to the cheaper cost of generation as compared with the two-part tariff of a public supply undertaking and what is more important in studio operation, to the absence of restrictions on the free use of electricity. Where Diesel engine plants have been installed, it has been found of greater general benefit to the undertaking. It is asserted, of course, that immunity from noise and vibration should be achieved in connection with this plant, and other moving machinery of the studio, and this is best obtained by the cork insulation methods, in which the firm of W. Christie and Grey, Ltd., have long specialised.

RECORDING PROCESS.—Equipment factors have benefited by the increase in studio facilities, and technical development has kept abreast of requirements. In the direction of sound recording, the chief achievement has been RCA ultra violet recording, for which high quality reproduction with clean sharp frequencies, owing to the elimination of scatter effects, is claimed. The first installation was made at the Rock Studios. In order to obtain the maximum benefits of the innovation, modification of the printer is recommended. The RCA push-pull track is likely to be increasingly used; a principle upon which Western Electric has also been working. The latter's wide range recording is universally employed by all W.E. licensees. Improvements include lower mechanical flutter in recorders, in the wide range loud speaker monitor system, and in the introduction of the Q.B. type mains operated portable equipment. An improved system of Visatone noiseless recording employs the Round track, known as the eel track, which embodies a novel method of noise reduction. British Acoustic has introduced a new six-peak track and other manufacturers, such as " Capco," made by the

Caplin Engineering Co., have also brought their equipment into line with the most modern requirements. Klangfilm has changed from a variable density track to a bilateral track. The Phillips-Miller mechano-graphical system has been installed by the B.B.C. in their Maida Vale studios.

There have been many advances in studio process work. Back projection is commonly used, special projectors for which have been marketed by the Simplex concern, and RCA is exploring the suggestion that a continuous projector should be employed for such work. Multiple effects produced by mirrors have been exploited by Winads under the name of the Multiscene process. Facilities for optical printing are available in all laboraties.

In film printing, mention has been made of the RCA non-slip ultra-violet printer. In combined picture and sound printer, the Vinten in this country, and Bell and Howell in America are increasingly popular. The Vinten standard rotary printer is in much demand, and the 16 mm. built on similar lines is getting into this difficult market. Indeed the reduction to sub-standard has received considerable attention, machines having been produced by Vinten, Debrie, RCA (who formerly favoured re-recording), and Eastman. Various types of optical printers are also made by Lawley, and Kamm, for reduction from 35 mm. to 16 mm., both of picture and sound and for 35 mm. track work. Several new processing machines have appeared on the market, including the Vinten high-speed equipment, which runs up to 150 ft. per minute. George Humphries and Co. have installed high-speed machines of their own design and an original design has been adopted by Debrie in the Multiplex high-speed developing machine having a frictional drive and working in daylight, which is installed at Denham.

SOUND RECORDING APPARATUS.

CANTOPHONE.—A most ingenious principle is incorporated in the Cantophone recording camera. The modulator unit embodies no oscillo-graph, light valve, or other magnetic device ; instead, it has a V-shaped shutter, which is moved vertically over the slit, and vibrated solely by electrostatic means.

Advantages claimed for this principle are the fact that virtually no current is needed for operating it, and consequently distortion cannot be caused by overloading of the amplifier output valves, and that the track is of the bi-lateral type, or could, if preferred, be of the variable density type.

" CAPCO."—The Capco recorder, built by the Caplin Engineering Co., Ltd., is virtually identical with the Ambiphone equipment used at the Elstree and Welwyn studios and also, under the name of " Capco," by two newsreel companies, Pathe and Universal, in addition to overseas installations.

The recording camera embodies the finest of mechanical precision, and is completely self-contained ; it carries standard camera magazines. The film is recorded upon a rotating drum, positioned in front of the optical slit, the film being subjected to no friction whatever. The drum has an adjustable flange for maintaining the film in lateral adjustment, and effectually prevents " weave." The film is fed by three sprockets, the sound sprocket being driven through an efficiently loaded filter, which eliminates any possibility of flutter or speed variation.

The whole of the optical and modulation system is supported upon a compound slide, which provides adjustment in three directions. Lateral alignment of the track is controlled by a differential screw, fitted with a pointer reading to thousandths of an inch. The recording lamp has longitudinal, tangential, transverse, vertical and radial adjustments. The oscillograph also has its separate adjusting device ; it is of the strung mirror type, tuned to 10,000 cycles per second.

The amplifier consists of three panels. The first is the microphone control panel, providing for the inputs from three microphones, and fitted with faders calibrated in decibels. The main feeder panel has, in addition, a modulation meter, H.T., L.T., and anode feed meters. A modern refinement, which may be added if desired, is a monitoring system embodying a cathode-ray tube, which enables the actual wave-form of the recorded sound to be watched. The third panel provides for a monitoring speaker with its own volume.

Practical features of the " Capco ' equipment are that standard Osram or Marconi valves are used, replacements for which can be obtained throughout the world ; and the amplifier response is flat to within 2db. from 50 to 10,000 c.p.s.

An additional panel can be provided, chiefly for location work, housing the necessary switches, resistances, and cable terminations.

A particularly ingenious vehicle has recently been brought into use by Pathe Pictures, Ltd. It consists of a private saloon car, to all appearances an ordinary passenger vehicle, but actually containing a " Capco " recording outfit, motor-alternator, batteries, and cable drums.

The advantage of a vehicle of this nature is that it can be used without attracting the attention of a crowd.

FIDELITY.—There have been no alterations in the technical design of the complete studio or mobile equipments manufactured by Fidelity Films, Ltd., of the Metropolitan Studios, Southall. This system is claimed to combine the advantages of both the variable area and variable density methods of recording, while at the same time possessing the disadvantages of neither.

The recording is made quite independently of any mechanical movement and is obtained from the image of a gas discharge tube. The system incorporates the use of the company's recording device which possesses no inertia, and another unique feature is that background noise has been abolished by the employment of purely electrical methods.

The purity of recording, the achievement of maximum and perfect range have commended Fidelity to a wide circle of users. The Company has sold 24 channels to India in addition to other important foreign deals, including Spain and the Irish Free State. A studio set is in operation at the Metropolitan Studios, Southall.

Mobile recording equipments installed in a two-ton van are available at a cost of £1,750 ex works, and studio equipments from £1,400 ex works.

Fidelity also manufacture re-recorders, and have developed 16 mm. recording, either by direct recording or by reduction from existing 35 mm. track.

FILM RECORDERS.—A straightforward type of recording camera is that made by Film Recorders, Ltd., and used by a number of Wardour Street studios and laboratories. The camera is of conventional design, and employs a Cambridge oscillograph. A particularly efficient smoothing system is incorporated.

For monitoring purposes, the back-swing of the beam is focused upon a ground-glass screen, and adjustment is especially simple. A feature of the amplifier is the provision made for frequency tests. The track produced is of the standard variable area type.

GAUMONT-BRITISH EQUIPMENTS.—The proven quality, advanced design and economy of both installation and maintenance commend the British Acoustic Full-Range System of sound film recording to the producer. A new B.A.F. Recording Van, incorporating the most modern facilities and lay-out, has now been made available to producers at low daily and weekly hire rates. The highest and most modern sound quality is assured by means of new "Double-Hump Biased Track," which is fully covered by B.A.F. patents.

Re-recording equipment has been further improved, resulting in the production of the type P.D. re-recording head, fitted with pattern A.Z. optics and the P.E.D. re-recording head amplifier.

In cases where adaptability and weight reduction are of importance, but quality has still to be considered, British Acoustic recommend the L.P.3 S. equipment, which operates from batteries and employs the unit principle of inter-connection and assembly. It may be rapidly erected in either a studio or a truck, and no permanent wiring arrangements are necessary.

Equipment for recording, re-recording and sound reproduction, using split 35 mm. film, i.e. 17.5 film for sound tracks only, has also been developed upon parallel lines with those of the normal 35 mm. apparatus. It is suitable for broadcast advertising programmes, and is extremely economical.

The world-wide distribution of B.A. equipment is a fitting testimony to its high quality. There are B.A. licensees in a dozen or more different countries. B.A. have an extremely strong patent position throughout the world, resulting in the ability to provide producers with the "Double-Hump Biased" sound track, while a recent development is the triple or "six-hump" track, assuring certain important advantages in processing and reproduction.

Importation of films into Germany from England is assured by reason of the B.A. agreement with the German monopoly holders. B.A. British licensees are assured of excellent service at all times, the B.A. works and laboratories being situated in London—but a few miles distant from any of the British studios.

LEEVERS, RICH.—Recent developments of the Leevers, Rich equipment have been towards enabling the reliability and quality of modern studio recording to be extended to location work under the most difficult conditions. This has involved the adoption of the transportable unit system of construction for all amplifiers, etc.

The main control unit comprises a two- or three-way mixer, frequency correcting circuits, recording amplifier and volume indicator, built in the form of a compact portable unit. Microphone battery feeds are included and easy access to all components for servicing is a feature. A valuable refinement is the provision of facilities for play-backs.

It has been found possible to match the response characteristics of the sound on film and sound on disc recording machines very closely, so that the standard mixer-amplifier unit is equally suitable for feeding either machine.

Radial type pressure crystal microphones of an improved design are used exclusively and have been found to give consistently good results over wide variations of temperature and humidity. Wind and background noises have been reduced to a very low level.

The complete film or disc equipment is available in mobile truck form, with its own power supplies and charging arrangements.

PHILIPS-MILLER.—The Philips-Miller system of electro-mechanical recording of sound-on-film has been perfected and is now widely used.

Briefly, the recording is carried out by a jewel cutter applied to a special film. The sound track is of the variable area symmetrical type. The linear frequency response available is beyond that of ordinary film. The sound may be reproduced on the same machine on which it is recorded, as, due to the great speed of rewinding, an immediate play-back of the finished recording is available in a very few minutes.

The tape requires no treatment or processing of any description and may be reproduced any number of times without affecting the quality of the sound. It is non-light sensitive, chemicallly inactive, and non-inflammable.

From the technician's standpoint there is a great advantage in the fact that monitoring is taken direct from the finished soundtrack, which not only checks the quality of the sound, but also permits immediate detection of speed variation.

The simplicity and speed of operation of this equipment is unexcelled ; whilst the fact that the film requires no processing is a leading advantage both from an operational and economical standpoint.

RCA. PHOTOPHONE.—During the past year RCA. Photophone has continued to apply the full resources of its research staff to the improvement of the quality of sound recording. The recording developments have proceeded along the lines of improved pick-up devices, constant speed mechanisms for recording and scanning, improved optical systems and light modulating units, extension of frequency range, more elaborate and exact monitoring devices, a further reduction of ground noise, improved resolution of film emulsions, and the elimination of distortions emanating from developments and printing.

The Uni-directional Microphone has been developed as a sequel to the bi-directional ribbon, and as a practical answer to the request for a device which would permit sound waves to be collected from the required direction only.

The Neon Volume Indicator has been designed to provide a means of giving an accurate indication of the amplitude of modulated light reaching the film when sound is being monitored at a remote position from the recorder.

The New Non-Slip Printer is now being introduced, which it is anticipated will eliminate the cause of distortions in printing work amd ensure that films whether for daily rushes, re-recording or release are a close replica of the original negative.

The new system of recording by means of the Ultra-Violet portion of the spectrum has been developed and is already being introduced into the leading studios. both in America and this country.

There has also been a development of a novel type of sound track which allows an extension of the track volume range, while at the same time, without the assistance of amplifiers requiring careful adjustment, it automatically reduces ground noise to a very low level. This is known as the push-pull type of track.

TANAR PORTABLE.—The Tanar Portable Recording Equipment (Single System) has been developed during the year, and is recognised as being ideally suitable for the recording of speech and sound effects on location. In order to supply the requirements of those people preferring to record the sound on separate film to the picture, the Tanar (British) Corporation have been developing a Sound Recording Camera. This has recently been completed, and even from preliminary results it more than exceeds expectations. The camera is to form part of a Double System Equipment, complete with interlock motors, and while of necessity this will be larger than the Single System, it will still retain the maximum portability, which characterises this firm's products.

The salient features in the design of this camera are simplicity of construction resulting in easy loading, minimum number of working parts, combined speed and footage counter. The Tanar adjustable optical unit, which is used so successfully for matching sound track with picture on the Single System will be used with this new equipment in order to provide for any adjustment to suit various makes of film stock. This optical unit is ideal for location equipment since it is very rigid in construction and is not affected by temperature changes.

The Tanar portable recording equipment (Single System) has been used by many of the major production companies during the year, and it is interesting to note that a third equipment was supplied to the U.S.S.R. again fitted to the Debrie Parvo ".L.S." Camera.

A complete outfit fitted to a Bell and Howell camera is available for hire at very reasonable cost. This equipment includes everything ready for " shooting."

VISATONE.—The latest development of the Visatone system is the provision of an exceedingly ingenious system of providing a noiseless track, due to the appearance of which it has been christened the " eel-track."

The one essential, if ground-noise is to be obviated in reproduction, is that the transparent portion of the positive track shall be reduced to a minimum. Capt. Round's method of achieving this is to add what are in effect two additional tracks to the original modulation ; the sinuous nature of these tracks is the origin of the name given to the system.

These additional tracks follow the modulation of the main track, during silent passages or passages of low modulation, and serve to fill in the greater proportion of the track. When the volume of sound reaches 5 per cent. modulation the outer track vanishes, and at 20 per cent. modulation the same thing happens to the second track, so that above this amplitude the track is of the ordinary width type. The method of achieving this is quite simple. In front of the recording lamp is a transparent window, mounted on a galvanometer which is fed with rectified speech current and is damped to give a low rate of movement ; this window carries two vertical lines, one slightly shorter than the other, and, as the window lifts, first one, then the other, is withdrawn from the light beam. Since the beam is modulated after passing through this window, the lines naturally form modulated tracks identical with the original track; as the window lifts the lines gradually vanish from the track.

For monitoring purposes the back-swing of the beam is reflected, much magnified by means of a mirror system, upon a screen. The galvanometer or oscillograph movement is of a type specially evolved by Capt. H. J. Round, M.I.E.E., employing cork damping, which is claimed to be practically unaffected by atmospheric conditions. The microphone used in conjunction with this system is of the carbon type, and has proved so satisfactory in working conditions that it is being used with competing recording systems.

VINTEN.—Vinten variable density system is used with Vinten H mute cameras. The condenser microphones and cameras can be operated up to 200 ft. from the truck. The Vinten A.C.-D.C. Interlock system ensures perfect synchronisation and running of the camera motors. There is no royalty charge. Mobile equipment intended for hiring for either complete production work or sound only, including post-synchronisation, comprises a recording camera using independent film and the same glow tube complete with amplifier, microphones, cables, all installed in a Bedford 12-cwt. van, complete with picture camera outfit, 48-cycle interlocking electric drive for batteries that are automatically charged off the van engine. This van outfit sells at £1,400 ex works.

WESTERN ELECTRIC.—Western Electric Wide Range permits the frequency range capable of being recorded on films to be extended a further two octaves, and this, when reproduced over wide range reproducing equipment, produces sound ranging from 30-8,000 cycles with fidelity and realism. Added improvements in sound recording quality are being introduced. A new permanent magnet light valve has been developed, combining the advantages of portability and adaptability of the flashing lamp with the advantages inherent to the light valve principle. Motor distribution, speed control systems have been made more portable.

Outstanding improvements include lower mechanical flutter in re-recorders as evidenced by the " Q " re-recorders; improvements in Wide Range loudspeaker monitor systems and review rooms ; operation from the mains of all portable equipment when operating in the studio; a microphone, the properties of which can be varied to a considerable extent.

The Western Electric variable density system provides for recording both sound-on-film and sound-on-disc. The main features of the equipment are moving-coil microphones, high quality amplifiers, mixing equipment, and horns arranged for either direct or photo-cell monitoring, recorders equipped with noise reduction equipment, etc., each item having a linearity of response which permits a flexibility of arrangements to suit the specific requirements of individual producers. High quality re-recording or dubbing and scoring equipment is available, and is also complete transmission testing apparatus for checking the frequency response characteristic of the entire system or its component units. All driving motors are electrically interlocked through the medium of a distributor system which holds the speed constant to the equivalent of 90 feet of film per minute and, in the permanent studio installations a complete interphone and visual signalling system are connected between all operating points in the studio.

Film testing equipment, comprising sensitometer and dessitometer and film cutting and editing machines, are also available for studios and film laboratories.

A complete recording installation usually includes a review room equipped with electrically or mechanically interlocked projectors or double film attachments, permitting separate sound and picture films to be projected synchronously.

AIDING THE ART DIRECTOR.—The sprayed-on painted background is no longer used in our studios, having been superseded by photographic backgrounds of the type supplied by Autotype Co., Ltd. Art directors are employing these giant photographs for all purposes. Where exact reproductions of friezes, tapestries and other decorations are required they are indistinguishable from the original. For tracking shots a photographic background of unlimited length can be made, which is so convincing that action can be immediately photographed without need of elaborate sets. Another service of the company is an up-to-date print library from which the art director can choose his subject. Backings of any size can be made from the smallest negatives from paper prints or process reproductions.

Another firm specialising in photographic backings is International Art Services, controlled by Richard Gerrard, formerly chief still cameraman for B.I.P. In addition, a special international department can obtain photographs of all subjects and authentic backgrounds from all parts of the world.

Most of our leading producers have availed themselves of the organisation of the Historical Research Society, of which F. W. Kelly is principal. The Society designs and supervises the dressing of period and historical subjects, supplying a full range of colourful designs of undisputable authenticity. The service not only includes instructions to costumiers and dressers, but also tells the artiste how to wear them.

MODERN LABORATORIES.—The laboratory facilities of the industry have been added to by the erection of the Denham Laboratories, where, under the direction of Garé Schwartz, are operated two distinct plants—one for release prints, and the other for negative developing, daily prints, master positives, and duplicate negatives, etc. Still departments, cutting and editing rooms, and review theatres, added to chemical and electrical research, provide for every production requirement: Another new laboratory has been opened by Technicolor, which deals with the peculiar demands of the colour lenses, and will obviate the sending to America for processing of Technicolor production. Our well-established laboratories, such as George Humphries, Olympic, Strange and others are also fully equipped with technical facilities to undertake every department of modern film processing.

EDITING AND EQUIPMENT.—Wide variety is offered in editing equipment. Modifications have been made to the Marriola (National Progress Films) and the Cantophone, while the Editola is a very compact editing head, sponsored by Photographic Electrical Co.

Another equipment is the triple play-off, manufactured by Films and Equipment, Ltd., which is of use either for editing or re-recording and mixing sound tracks. This firm also handles a complete range of joining, synchronising and storage equipment which is in use at Pinewood. The Caplin Engineering Co. has perfected a new horizontal winder of improved design and an automatic joining machine. A new Vinten cutting track will also shortly be in production.

Among testing instruments should be mentioned the Vinten perforation gauge, the Kodak densitometer, invaluable in these days of sensitometric methods of laboratory control, and, of course, the Avometer, probably the most widely used electrical testing instrument. It covers a range of recordings, making it suitable for any type of test, and combines the functions of an A.C. and D.C. ammeter (0.1 ma. to 12 amps.); voltmeter (1 m.v. to 1,200 v.) ; and D.C. ohmmeter (0.1 ohm to 1 megohm). The wide range of Weston testing instruments is marketed by Films and Equipment, another of whose specialities are the making of microphone booms. Vintens and E. F. Moy also make similar equipment.

STUDIO LIGHTING.—Continued progress has been made in studio lighting equipment. It is pointed out by G.E.C. that a vast number of units employing different optical systems are often used to do two diametrically opposed things. The fact that studio requirements demand powerful directional floodlighting of even illumination, and also high intensity spots supplies the argument for the listing together of units employed for a particular purpose. G.E.C. has standardised fittings under four heads—overheads, broadsides, illuminators and spotlights. G.E.C. has produced a new range of incandescents, and is engaging upon research in regard to new mirrors of the lens type of special contour and affording higher illuminating values.

Quite a large proportion of the lighting units employed in our studios consists of Mole-Richardson 14.9 arc units and solar incandescents, spots of a type which have won an assured popularity in the States. All of this equipment, however, is being manufactured in this country. A stepped lens of a varying focal length across its diameter, culminating in a very acute angle at the edges, is employed and attains a remarkable evenness of illumination. Several types of arcs are made with the same optical system, the more popular employing a 120-amp. or 150-amp. H.I. arc, fitted with rotating-positive motor feeds. These lamps are specially adapted to colour work. Mole Richardson (England), Ltd., is establishing a complete studio and location lighting service.

Units manufactured by R. R. Beard, Ltd., are to be found in every studio. Among their specialities are 150-amp, sun arcs fitted with facet mirrors, for which parabolic mirrors can be also supplied. Various incandescent illuminators of various sizes of 5.2 and 1 kw. and the 1 and 1½ kw.

mounted rifle floods are also available. Kandem studio units include every size of light source from the 500 watt photoflood to 5 kw. incandescent and 300 amp. arcs. "Britelite" studio equipment is handled by D. Walter & Co., who provide a full range of lighting for studio purposes, the latest model being a concentrating H.I. 2,000 watt flood.

CAMERAS.—The Vinten range of cameras is firmly established both in this country and overseas. This equipment, the motor of which is specially designed to ensure silent and accurate running, is used exclusively by A.B.P. at Elstree and Welwyn. A small type of gyroscopic tripod, half the weight of the standard model, is the latest product of this firm, which has also designed a new run-truck. Both Vinten and Films and Equipment specialise in all types of microphone booms.

In America a new camera for the three-colour Technicolor process is reported and various improvements have been made to the Mitchell. Progress to the absolutely silent camera is claimed for apparatus made by 20th Century Fox in association with Debrie.

Vintens have produced a camera capable of reaching the extreme speed of 3,000 pictures per second, while Zeiss Ikon have made a high frequency camera with a maximum rate of picture shift of 1,500 pictures a second.

COLOUR.

Although there have been three or four much heralded colour films shown this year, box office results have not been so overwhelming as to suggest that colour in itself is a prime attraction. The tones of the recent examples of Technicolor have been highly satisfying artistically but lacking the prime factor of a good actionful story, have not impressed the patron to the extent it was hoped. The programmes announced for 1937 include a dozen or so colour subjects from America, and an increasing number of cartoons to which the colour medium is admirably adaptable. In England the excellent reports attending the New World Company's experiment, "Wings of the Morning," and the processing facilities afforded by the establishment of the Technicolor laboratories at Harmondsworth, have attracted the attention of our producers. The only other English colour effort was its use in certain fantasy sequences by Capitol Films in "Pagliacci."

Theoretical interest in colour shows no diminution. A number of other systems have been demonstrated during the year—Dunningcolor, Harmonicolor, Ondiacolor and Francita Realita (formerly Opticolor) the only additive process, and in the sub-standard field, Kodachrome. Two systems now, in the opinion of R. H. Cricks, F.R.P.S., which have shown the greatest improvements are Dufaycolor, for which a negative-positive process has been adopted, and Gasparcolor.

On the Continent experimental work is proceeding on the Opticolor lenticular process, while in America the possibilities of the Keller-Dorian process are being actively explored and, it is said, will be seen this year in feature subjects. European financial interests are concerned.

TELEVISION.

In future years, 1936 may very well be remembered as the year of Television. Television, concerning which so much has been written of recent years, actually became an accomplished fact, and the sale of home television receivers, a commercial proposition. The completion in September of the B.B.C. television station at the Alexandra Palace, provided the necessary impetus and at the Radio Exhibition in that month, television sets provided one of the outstanding attractions. Before this date experimental transmission by Baird E.M.I. and Scophony had demonstrated that there were few technical difficulties to be overcome by large screen television.

The industry has arrived at the conclusion that the new development cannot be ignored and very sensibly are endeavouring to employ it to their own benefit. Many kinemas now being erected have been planned, so far as present knowledge of television requirements permit, with a view to the fullest possible advantage of the newest force in entertainment. It may be that novelty value will be the prime factor in the early success of television, but this argument was also true of the early animated pictures. The fact that it has been found practicable to present television regularly as an item of entertainment is of deep significance to the trade.

Monday, January 4, may conceivably be an historic date in the history of the trade, for it was then that the Dominion, Tottenham Court Road, presented the first televised programme. Reproduction was by means of a single channel, the screen size being 8 ft. by 6 ft. 6 in.

There is no technical reason why similar installations in other kinemas in the London area should not present simultaneously the identical programme shown. Mr. Cricks points out, however, that this apparatus is not capable of reproducing B.B.C. programmes.

An earlier experimental demonstration of large screen television was given in August by Scophony on a 4 ft. 6 in. screen, and it was anticipated that within a few months a 12-ft. picture would be available.

One phase of television that has exercised the minds of exhibitors is the use of films. While there seems little likelihood of renters supplying either entertainment films or news reels for private or public reproduction, concern has been expressed at the possibility of the B.B.C. establishing its own film production centre and making news reels and entertainment films for transmissions. A C.E.A. Committee was set up to consider the implication of such a policy and to make contact with the K.R.S., the Manufacturers' Association and the B.B.C., to urge the regulation of television so as not to compete with the Industry.

Suggestions have been made that the opportunity afforded for popularising home television by the Coronation celebrations this year will not be ignored by the B.B.C. It is obvious, indeed, that this national occasion will be utilised to give a much needed impetus to the sales of domestic television sets. Once installed, such sets will provide the kinema with competition of formidable proportions. Fortunately, however, the entertainment seeker is a gregarious person and would rather seek amusement in company with his fellows than remain at home in a condition of strained intensity witnessing an indifferent televised programme.

This view is endorsed by the opinion of Merlin H. Aylesworth, vice-chairman of the N. B. Co. of America, and chairman of R.K.O.–Radio, who believes that the home will be the limit of television entertainment capacity for four or five years. The mass of kinema-goers, he thought, were satisfied to enjoy the screen fare provided by the sound film of the day.

On the Continent various public television services have been instituted. Attention was directed to the German experiment of televising the Olympic games, but generally speaking, observers consider these less favourably technically than the B.B.C. transmissions.

In America there exists an association of interests in the television field between Western Electric and RCA. E.R.P.I. has been conducting experiments over a period of years and RCA. is known to have made exceptional scientific advances which are claimed to exceed what has been done elsewhere.

STEREOSCOPY.

No advance has been reported towards the stereoscopic picture during the year, the anaglyph principle has been revived in the " audioscopics" shorts handled by M-G-M and in the system perfected by Louis Lumiere, but R.H. Cricks has referred to the good work done in Germany and in America on the substitution of the red and green gelatines by polarising screens, which, it is claimed, gives better definition and less eye strain. These, however, for the moment remain but novelties, and meanwhile neither Ives nor Zafirapulo has reported any progress on their previous researches into this subject. A system of stereoscopy described by A. Martin, a Frenchman, involves taking a number of exposures with a very wide aperture lens focussed upon different planes and arranging the subsequent transparencies at corresponding planes inside a tunnel illuminated from the rear. Experiments have been made in Germany by Zeiss Ikon. By means of a polarisation filter placed before a normal camera loaded with ordinary raw stock, a film is made bearing two partial pictures that are situated alongside each other and have very light differences regarding the outlines of the subject photographed. The projected pictures are viewed through special binocular spectacles. Similar viewing apparatus is necessary with the American Polaroid process, in which two films are simultaneously shot eye-width apart.

TRADE ASSOCIATIONS.

Associations concerned with various trade activities have been busy during the year, particularly in respect to the representations made to the Moyne Committee on the working of the 1927 Film Acts. Apart from this aspect, a great deal of work of benefit to the technicians and other workers has been accomplished. Although the C.E.A. redundancy campaign has not been attended with the degree of success anticipated, at least it has emphatically drawn attention of local authorities to the potential dangers of surfeit. The campaign to obtain more equitable electricity charges for the exhibitor is bearing successful fruit and benefits have been derived from the establishment of the expert panel in connection with the " Manual of Safety Requirements." The British Kinematograph Society has made valuable contributions to the technical problems of all trade departments, and the interests of the Royal Photographic Society's kinematograph section have been widened to embrace the entertainment field. During the year the advantages of a fusion of interests of the R.P.S. and the B. K. S. have been explored and proposals to this effect are being considered by the executives of both these technical societies. The British Film Institute has passed its initial stages of development and has concerned itself with the non-theatrical film particularly as regards medical and educational product and the provision of suitable films for children. A statement in the House of Commons revealed that the work of the Film Institute generally was under consideration. The grant now received from the Sunday opening percentage was increased by £1,000 to £7,000. The Association of Cine-Technicians has made considerable progress, and has successfully intervened in many subjects affecting the welfare of its members. Special attention is paid to the question of the employment of foreign technicians in studios.

OBITUARY.

The technical side of the Industry lost many notable personalities in 1936. The deaths have occurred of Will Day, pioneer exhibitor and technician, and latterly world famous as the historian of the kinema. His collection of relics and old machinery was unique ; H. A. Sanders, formerly editor of the Pathé Gazette, one of the earliest producers and actors and for a quarter of a century with Pathé ; Lieut.-Col. V. B. Ramsden, production manager of Ilford ; W. Engelke, managing director of Cinema Traders ; Major Gerald Jacques, secretary of Western Electric ; S. L. Rothafel (Roxy), America's best-known showman and exhibitor ; A. Burnester, sales manager of Gasparcolor ; Charles Roe, of Western Electric Service Engineering Dept. ; Georges Ercole, cameraman, Paramount News ; J. Walls, kinema engineer and Scots pioneer ; George H. Cricks, early technician and producer, one of the small group who formed the K.M.A.

Data for Kinematograph Technicians.

CARBONS FOR PROJECTION ARCS.

MIRROR CARBONS. (Low Intensity.)			INTERMEDIATE TYPE. (Hilo, High Brilliancy, etc.).		
Current in amps.	Positive cored.	Negative cop. cored.	Current in amps.	Positive.	Negative.
7 /10	8 mm.	6 mm.	25 /30	6 mm.	5 mm.
10 /15	9 mm.	7 mm.	35 /45	7 mm.	6 mm.
15 /20	10 mm.	7 mm.	45 /55	8 mm.	7 mm.
18 /22	11 mm.	7 mm.	55 /65	9 mm.	7·5 mm.
20 /25	12 mm.	8 mm.			
25 /30	12 mm.	9 mm.			
30 /35	13 mm.	9 mm.			
35 /40	14 mm.	10 mm.			

These carbons when burnt in an obtuse-angled arc require a magnetic flame control.

HIGH-INTENSITY, UNCOPPERED POSITIVES.			HIGH INTENSITY, COPPERED.		
Current in amps.	Positive.	Negative.	Current in amps.	Positive.	Negative.
90 /100	11 mm.	9 mm.	65 /75	9 mm.	7.5 mm.
105 /115	12 mm.	10 mm.	75 /85	10 mm.	8 mm.
115 /125	13·6 mm.	10 mm.	85 /95	11 mm.	8 mm.
125 /145	13·6 mm.	11 mm.	100 /110	12 mm.	9 mm.
150 /170	16 mm.	12 mm.			

The rating of High-Intensity Carbons depends largely upon the type of arc. In arcs with front contact of unsatisfactory design, the use of copper-coated positive is recommended. When H.I. carbons are used a flue is required to carry the fumes direct to the open air. -

STRAIGHT ARCS.

CONTINUOUS CURRENT.				ALTERNATING CURRENT.	
Current in amps.	Positive cored.	Negative. Coppered.	Solid.	Current in amps.	Both carbons (cored).
10 /20	16 mm.	8 mm.	11 mm.	15 /25	10 mm.
20 /30	18 mm.	9 mm.	12 mm.	25 /35	13 mm.
30 /40	20 mm.	10 mm.	14 mm.	30 /40	16 mm.
40 /60	22 mm.	11 mm.	—	40 /50	18 mm.
60 /80	25 mm.	12 mm.	—	50 /65	20 mm.

V.I.R. CABLES.

Standard.	Superseded S.W.G.	I.E.E. rating amps.
1 /.044	1 /18	6.1
3 /.029	3 /22	7.8
3 /.036	3 /20	12
7 /.029	7 /22	18.2
7 /.036	7 /20	24
7 /.044	7 /18	31
7 /.064	7 /16	46
19 /.044	19 /18	53
19 /.064	19 /16	83
19 /.083	19 /14	118
37 /.064	37 /16	130
37 /.083	37 /14	184

All cables in kinema work are required to be run in screwed conduit. For other requirements as to electrical installation see Legal Section, (Digest of Acts) *supra.*

TABLE OF WIRE FUSES.

Approximate Fusing Current in Amps.	APPROXIMATE STANDARD WIRE GAUGE.		
	Tin.	Lead.	Copper.
5	25	23	38
10	21	20	33
15	19	18	30
20	17	17	28
25	16	15	26
30	15	14	25
35	14	13	24
40	14	13	23
45	13	12	22
50	13	12	21
60	12		21
70			20
80	Strip fuses above this gauge.	Strip fuses above this gauge.	19
90			18
100			18
120			17

The full normal load on a fuse should be two-thirds of its fusing load. For arcs, use copper fuses rated at double normal current to allow for striking. On motor circuits the allowance will depend upon the starting current. Allow 50 to 100 per cent. for D.C. motors or A.C. repulsion-induction motors, four times for wound induction motors, six to eight times for squirrel-cage. On 3-phase motor circuits always fuse heavily.

STANDARD 3:4 APERTURES

The following standardised aperture sizes are so computed as to maintain the 3 : 4 proportion in the projected picture while leaving space for the sound track.

Camera : 0·631 in. by 0·868 in., the centre line to be 0·7445 in. from guiding edge of the film.

Projector : 0·600 by 0·825 in., the centre line to be 0·738 in. from the guiding edge.

ACOUSTICS

The acoustic properties of a theatre have a direct bearing upon the quality of reproduction and the audibility of speech.

An echo is a reflection from some definite surface ; the cure is to cover the offending surface with sound-absorbent material, or to break it up into smaller surfaces.

The period of reverberation is defined as the time which a sound of standard intensity takes to die away. It can be calculated by Sabine's formula—

$$t = \frac{.05\,V}{a}$$

This formula should be used in conjunction with the following table, the areas of the various materials (in square feet) being multiplied by their respective co-efficients and added together giving factor *a*. *V* is the volume of the hall in cubic feet. Experience shows that the most satisfactory period of reverberation is from 1 second for a small hall to 1.3 seconds for a hall seating 2,000.

Table of Sound Absorption Co-efficients

Open window	...	... 1.00	Linoleum	...	... ...	.03
Plaster	...	.025–.034	Carpets	...	...	.15–.29
Concrete	...	... .015	Cretonne cloth	...	...	.15
Brick ...	...	... .025	Heavy curtains	...	.5 to 1.0	
Marble...	...	... .01	1 in. hairfelt	...	...	.45
Glass ...	...	... .027	Audience, per person	...	4.7	
Wood, plain ...	...	... .061	Wood seats, each	...	...	.1
Wood, varnished	...	... .03	Upholstered seats, each	1.0 to 2.0		
Cork ...	...	... .03				

CALCULATING ARC RESISTANCES

The value of a resistance R to pass a given current C at voltage V is expressed, according to Ohm's law, by the formula—

$$R = \frac{V}{C}$$

In calculating arc resistances, however, the value of the back voltage A of the arc must be considered. This may be reckoned as 45 volts for low-intensity arcs, and for high-intensity from 25 volts for a horizontal-negative mirror arc or 45 for an inclined-negative mirror arc, up to 65 or 70 volts for rotating-positive arc. The formula then becomes—

$$R = \frac{V - A}{C}$$

The earlier studs of a resistance should be so computed as to allow the arc to be struck on not more than one-third of its full current.

ORDINARY FILM CEMENT.

Amyl Acetate 4 *oz., Acetone* 6 *oz.*

This may either be used as it is, in which case the cement will be a thin fluid with not much more body in it than water, or it may be thickened to any desired extent by dissolving it in celluloid chips. Celluloid film base from which the gelatine coating has been cleaned off will serve.

For non-flam. film add glacial acetic acid, the proportion depending upon the type of base ; thicken only with the same type of film base for which the cement is required.

PROJECTION CHART (for 35mm. STANDARD FILM).

SHOWING WIDTH OF SCREEN PICTURE.

Distance lens to screen in feet	FOCUS OF LENS IN INCHES															Distance lens to screen in feet
	3 in. Ft. In.	3¼ in. Ft. In.	3½ in. Ft. In.	3¾ in. Ft. In.	4 in. Ft. In.	4¼ in. Ft. In.	4½ in. Ft. In.	4¾ in. Ft. In.	5 in. Ft. In.	5¼ in. Ft. In.	5½ in. Ft. In.	5¾ in. Ft. In.	6 in. Ft. In.	6¼ in. Ft. In.	6½ in. Ft. In.	
20-ft.	5 6	5 1	4 9	4 5	4 1	3 11	3 8	3 6	3 4	3 2	3 0	—	—	—	—	20-ft.
25-ft.	6 10	6 4	5 11	5 6	5 2	4 10	4 7	4 4	4 1	3 11	3 9	3 7	3 5	3 4	3 2	25-ft.
30-ft.	8 3	7 7	7 1	6 7	6 2	5 10	5 6	5 3	4 11	4 9	4 6	4 4	4 1	4 0	3 10	30-ft.
35-ft.	9 7	8 11	8 3	7 8	7 3	6 10	6 5	6 1	5 9	5 6	5 3	5 0	4 10	4 7	4 5	35-ft.
40-ft.	11 0	10 2	9 5	8 10	8 3	7 9	7 4	6 11	6 7	6 3	6 0	5 9	5 6	5 3	5 1	40-ft.
45-ft.	12 4	11 5	10 7	9 11	9 3	8 9	8 3	7 10	7 5	7 1	6 9	6 5	6 2	5 11	5 9	45-ft.
50-ft.	13 9	12 8	11 9	11 0	10 4	9 8	9 2	8 8	8 3	7 10	7 6	7 2	6 10	6 7	6 4	50-ft.
55-ft.	15 1	14 0	13 0	12 1	11 4	10 8	10 1	9 7	9 1	8 8	8 3	7 11	7 7	7 3	7 0	55-ft.
60-ft.	16 6	15 3	14 2	13 2	12 4	11 8	11 0	10 5	9 11	9 5	9 0	8 7	8 3	7 11	7 7	60-ft.
65-ft.	17 10	16 6	15 4	14 4	13 5	12 7	11 11	11 3	10 9	10 3	9 9	9 4	8 11	8 7	8 3	65-ft.
70-ft.	19 3	17 9	16 6	15 5	14 5	13 7	12 10	12 2	11 7	11 0	10 6	10 1	9 7	9 3	8 11	70-ft.
75-ft.	20 7	19 0	17 8	16 6	15 6	14 7	13 9	13 0	12 4	11 9	11 3	10 9	10 4	9 11	9 6	75-ft.
80-ft.	22 0	20 4	18 10	17 7	16 6	15 6	14 8	13 11	13 2	12 7	12 0	11 6	11 0	10 7	10 2	80-ft.
85-ft.	23 4	21 7	20 0	18 8	17 6	16 6	15 7	14 9	14 0	13 4	12 9	12 2	11 8	11 3	10 9	85-ft.
90-ft.	24 9	22 10	21 3	19 10	18 7	17 6	16 6	15 8	14 10	14 2	13 6	12 11	12 4	11 11	11 5	90-ft.
95-ft.	26 1	24 1	22 5	20 11	19 7	18 5	17 5	16 6	15 8	14 11	14 3	13 8	13 1	12 6	12 1	95-ft.
100-ft.	27 6	25 5	23 7	22 0	20 7	19 5	18 4	17 4	16 6	15 9	15 0	14 4	13 9	13 2	12 8	100-ft.
105-ft.	28 10	26 8	24 9	23 1	21 8	20 5	19 3	18 3	17 4	16 6	15 9	15 1	14 5	13 10	13 4	105-ft.
110-ft.	30 3	27 11	25 11	24 2	22 8	21 4	20 2	19 1	18 2	17 3	16 6	15 9	15 1	14 6	14 0	110-ft.
115-ft.	31 7	29 2	27 1	25 4	23 9	22 4	21 1	20 0	19 0	18 1	17 3	16 6	15 10	15 2	14 7	115-ft.
120-ft.	33 0	30 6	28 3	26 5	24 9	23 4	22 0	20 10	19 10	18 10	18 0	17 3	16 6	15 10	15 3	120-ft.
125-ft.	34 4	31 9	29 6	27 6	25 9	24 3	22 11	21 9	20 7	19 8	18 9	17 11	17 2	16 6	15 10	125-ft.
130-ft.	35 9	33 0	30 8	28 7	26 10	25 3	23 10	22 7	21 5	20 5	19 6	18 8	17 10	17 2	16 6	130-ft.
135-ft.	37 1	34 3	31 10	29 8	27 10	26 2	24 9	23 5	22 3	21 3	20 3	19 4	18 7	17 10	17 2	135-ft.
140-ft.	38 6	35 6	33 0	30 10	28 10	27 2	25 8	24 4	23 1	22 0	21 0	20 1	19 3	18 6	17 9	140-ft.
145-ft.	39 10	36 10	34 2	31 11	29 11	28 2	26 7	25 2	23 11	22 9	21 9	20 10	19 11	19 2	18 5	145-ft.
150-ft.	41 3	38 1	35 4	33 0	30 11	29 1	27 6	26 1	24 9	23 7	22 6	21 6	20 7	19 10	19 0	150-ft.

Standard aperture .825″ × .600″   The height of picture is approximately ¾ of the width.

Reproduced by permission of Taylor, Taylor and Hobson, Ltd.

WHO'S WHAT

And Where In the Trade

The following details have been supplied by the persons concerned, and though every effort has been made to keep them up to date we cannot accept responsibility . . for omissions or errors . .

Who's What in the Trade.

Harry Adley.

Born 1902. Entered Industry in 1924 as producer of advertising films and formed, in 1925, Younger Publicity Service, Ltd., to replace slide and curtain advertising by the more modern method of films. Two years later Younger Film Prod., Ltd., was formed as the production unit. Their Studios are now in Gt. Windmill Street, where they are the largest producers in this country of cartoon films. National Film Corp., Ltd., was formed in 1930 as producers of advertising and propaganda films. Managing director of the three above-mentioned companies. Director of several kinema companies. Chairman of the Publicity Committee of the Advertising and Industrial Film Association *Addresses :* 34/36, Oxford Street, W.1, and Harman Lodge, Harman Drive, N.W.2. *Phone :* Museum 4816 and Gladstone 3193.

Arthur S. Albin.

Born 1875. Early in his career was a solo pianist at a kinema. In 1913 opened a picture house of his own at Shettleston, and later purchased another at Hawick, both of which he disposed of. Is an ex-Chairman of C.E.A. Scottish Branch and on the Benevolent Fund Committee, and has been chairman of the East of Scotland section of the C.E.A. for the past eleven years. Until recently proprietor of Tollcross Cinema, now General Manager, New Tivoli, Edinburgh. *Clubs :* Cinema and Drapers' Athletic Assoc *Private Address :*—Rose Villa, Viewforth, Edinburgh.

J. Alexander.

Born 1886. Educated Marylebone Grammar School. Entered the Industry as Manager of the Trafalgar Cinema, Greenwich, in 1912. Joined renting side of the business in 1919 as general manager of a company now out of existence, and transferred to Universal Film Co. in 1921. Took over Trafalgar Cinema in 1924. Elected to Executive Committee of London and Home Counties Branch of the C.E.A. in 1928. Delegate to General Council since 1930. Chairman of London and Home Counties Branch in 1933, *Addresses:* 82, Trafalgar Road, Greenwich, S.E.10, and 9, St. Mary's Mansions, W.2. *Phone :* Greenwich 0179.

Frederick J. Allen.

Entered Industry 1908. Two years in Canada and United States as representative for Lux Film, Paris, Ambrosio, Turin, and Cines of Rome. Has acted as Publicity Manager of Eclair Film Company and Film Booking Offices. Now publicity manager of First National Film Distributors, Ltd.—*Addresses :*—54, Hamilton Road, N.5, and 135, Wardour Street, W.1. *Phones :* Canonbury 2771 and Gerrard 5600.

F. Alven.

Born 1886. Educated Greys College, Port Elizabeth, S.A. Came to Europe 1908 to study languages. Employed in agricultural machine business for 10 years in Russia and Siberia. Commercial adviser on Military Governor's staff, Cologne, 1919. Represented British manufacturers in Germany and in 1926 joined executive of Fanamet Films, Berlin, organising branch houses and sales in Western Europe. In December, 1928, joined B.I.P. Ltd. *Address :* Film House, Wardour Street, W.1.

L. G. Applebee.

Born 1889. First entered the Entertainment Industry in 1906, being engaged in the electrical installations of the Putney Hippodrome and the Globe Theatre, London. Also joined producing staff of the late George Edwardes, and was actively engaged in lighting all the Gaiety Theatre, London, productions from 1907 to 1910. Joined the London and General Theatres, Ltd., as Assistant Consulting Engineer in 1910. After demobilisation joined Grossmith and Laurillard at the Winter Garden, and then transferred to C. B. Cochran at the Princes Theatre and London Pavilion. Finally joined the Strand Electric and Engineering Co., Ltd., in 1922, as special designer of stage switchboards and lighting apparatus. Member Illuminating Engineering Society and B.K.S. Now Manager, Theatre Lighting Department, the Strand Electrical and Engineering Co., Ltd. *Address :* 24, Floral Street, W.C.2. *Phone :* Temple Bar 7464.

George Archibald, J.P.

Has been Kinema Manager, Film Traveller, Director of several kinemas and associate editor of the *Cinematograph Times.* Member of Glasgow Town Council, 1920-28. Magistrate, 1925-28. Now Director of United Artists Corporation, Ltd., and United Artists (Export), Ltd. *Address :* 35, Downshire Hill, N.W.3. *Phone :* Hampstead 6506.

Albert Bacal.

Born 1904. Managing director, Dominions, Hounslow, Acton, and Baker's Arms ; director, Manor and Empire, Hounslow. Member Vaudeville Golfing Society and Screen Golfing Society. *Addresses :* 37/8, Golden Square, W.1, and Chalgrove Gardens, Finchley, N.W. *Phones :* Gerr. 7138 and 6464, and Finchley 1798.

William Alfred Bach.

Born in Canada, 1891. Managing director, Western Electric Co. Ltd. Educated Toronto Technical School and University of Toronto. Formerly mining engineering, advertising agency. Started with Universal Pictures Corporation, Canada, next with M. H. Hoffman, New York, then with W. W. Hotchkiss Corpn. Joined

Paramount and remained until 1925. Joined First National in Canada and was transferred in 1926 as managing director of First National, England. 1928 with Electrical Research Products. Became president of Audio Productions upon its formation, 1933. Appointed managing director of Western Electric Company, July 1936. *Address :* Bush House, Aldwych, W.C.2. *Phone :* Temple Bar 1001.

David A. Bader.

Born 1900. Entered Universal 14 years ago. First publicity job was to put "Baby Peggy" on the map. Prepared data of Carl Laemmle's career for biography written by John Drinkwater. On succession of S. F. Ditcham to managing directorship of Universal Pictures, Ltd., in England, was appointed to control special exploitations and department for closer co-operation with exhibitors as Carl Laemmle's personal representative in U.K. Later edited *Universal Weekly* with J. L. Williams. *Address :* 10, Haymarket, S.W.1. *Phone :* Whitehall 2875.

T. Thorne Baker, F.Inst.P., A.M.I.E.E., F.R.P.S.

Was associated with Spicers, Ltd., in the manufacture of film base and in the production of Dufaycolor kinematograph film. Now in New York as technical advisory consultant to Dufaycolor, Inc., of America. *Address :*—Dufaycolor, Inc., 30, Rockefeller Plaza, New York.

Francis William Baker.

Butcher's Film Service, Ltd.

F. W. Baker was born at Hollesley, Suffolk, on November 25, 1877. Forsook dentistry and entered the Industry in 1897, joining British Muto. and Biograph Syndicate. Overseas service in R.A.F., 1916-1919. Managing Director, Butcher's Film Service, Ltd. Ex-President and present Treasurer, K.R.S. ; Ex-Treasurer, I.A.K.M. Appointed by Board of Trade Member of Advisory Committee ; Member Council C. T. Benevolent Fund. Member Consultative Committee, B.B.F.C. Governor, British Film Institute. Founder Anima Lodge, 3634. *Address :*— 175, Wardour Street, W.1, and Hollesley, London Road, Sutton, Surrey. *Phones :* Gerrard 7282 and Sutton 5024.

Michael Balcon.

Born 1896, Birmingham. Entered films as Director of Victory M.P. Co., a small Midlands renting concern. Subsequently became associated with Gainsborough Pictures, now a subsidiary of G-B. At the Islington Studios he produced many early British successes, and when talkies arrived, followed up with such pictures as "Journey's End," "The Ghost Train," "Hindle Wakes," "Sunshine Susie," and others. With the opening of the new G-B. Studios at Shepherd's Bush, was appointed Director of Production. Outstanding successes include "Rome Express," "Good Companions," "I Was a Spy," "Evergreen," "The Thirty-nine Steps," "The Guv'nor," "Tudor Rose," "Rhodes," "First a Girl," "It's Love Again," "O.H.M.S.", "King Solomon's Mines," etc.,

etc., etc. *Address :* Lansdowne House, W.1. *Phones :* Shepherd's Bush 1210. From January 1, 1937, Chief producer M-G-M British.

Ald. George Herbert Barber, J.P.,
Ex-Chairman, North Staffs. C.E.A. Branch.

One of the old exhibitors in the country, G. H. Barber was born at Congleton, in 1860, and has been connected with the kinematograph business from its earliest days. Before the passing of the Kinematograph Act he ran a travelling motion picture show, and did his own operating. He built the first kinematograph hall in Tunstall, erecting and opening a total of eight kinemas in four years. He has been a member of the General Council and of the North Staffordshire Branch of the C.E.A. for 17 years, and also sits on the National Industrial Conciliation Committee. Ex-Lord Mayor, Stoke-on-Trent, 1929-1930 ; member of the Stoke-on-Trent Town Council since the Federation of the Potteries in 1910 ; Ex-Chairman of Guardian Relief Committee, Chairman of the Old Age Pension Committee, Member of City Water Board Committee for the Borough of Stoke-on-Trent. Of late years travelled by air over Europe, Palestine, Egypt and Russia. Member of National Flying Service Club, Stoke. *Address :* —Coronation House, Victoria Road, Tunstall, Stoke-on-Trent.

James William Barber, C.B.E.

Born in 1884, and was educated at the secondary school and University College, Cardiff. He afterwards received training in marine and electrical engineering, and was for many years connected with the technical side of the Trade. In 1917 he was retained as technical adviser on kinematograph matters to the Department of Information, and was afterwards appointed to Director of Kinematography to the National War Aims Committee, Downing Street. He was also responsible for the touring kinema propaganda work carried out by the Government departments throughout the country. He is a consulting engineer ; managing director of the Church Pictorial Movement, Ltd. ; honorary technical adviser to the C.E.A., member of the General Council of the C.E.A., and past chairman of the London branch. *Address :*—1, Portland Court, W.1.

Percy H. Bastie.

Born 1871. Served apprenticeship in mechanical engineering. Engaged for several years on theatre lighting. Joined the late Ernest F. Moy as one of the original directors of Ernest F. Moy, Ltd., and became managing director at his death. Joint patentee in 1907 of the automatic shutter for projectors. Joint patentee in 1908 of the Moy Camera. Life hon, member of the London Association of Engineers. Member of the executive of the B.K.S. *Addresses :* 4, Greenland Place, N.W.1 and 6, Beech Drive, Fortis Green, N.2. *Phones :* Gulliver 5451 and Tudor 4031.

James Montgomery Beck.

Born in Philadelphia, U.S.A., 1892, and has lived in England continuously since 1919. Was 1st Lieutenant in the American Forces in France. A member of the Executive Committee of the Gramophone Co. (His Master's Voice) until 1926 ; Western Electric 1927/8 ; appointed British Representative of the Hays Organisation in 1929 with which he is now associated. *Clubs :* —St. Jame.'s, Garrick, Pilgrims, American, in London ; Knickerbocker and Metropolitan, in New York ; Travellers, in Paris. *Address :—* 106, Piccadilly, W.1. *Phone :* Grosvenor 3155.

Major C. H. Bell, O.B.E.

Born 1890. Consulting Engineer. Specialist in electrical and mechanical installations for theatres. Managing Director, Astorias, Folkestone and Southend. *Addresses :—*National House, 60/66, Wardour Street, W.1 ; 6, Spaniards Close, N.W.11. *Phones :* Gerrard 2822 ; Speedwell 6249.

Oliver Bell.

Born 1898. Left school to join R.F.C., served overseas. Returned to Oxford University. Secretary of the O.U.D.S. 1921-22. Joined League of Nations Union staff 1923. Became a member of its Films Committee and general editor of its publications. Joined Conservative Central Office staff 1934. Keenly interested in films for political propaganda. *Addresses :—* 2a, Aylward Road, Merton Park, S.W.20, and 4, Great Russell Street, W.1. *Phones :* Liberty 3042 and Museum 0607.

Prince Beadon.

Partner, Bendon Trading Co.

One of the pioneers of the Industry, both on the exhibiting and renting sides, having produced and exhibited pictures over thirty years ago. In addition to being the proprietor of the Bendon Trading Co., he founded and is now hon. president of the Glasgow Cinema Club and ex-president of the Royal Clyde Motor Yacht Club. For six years president of Scottish K.R.S. Twenty years member A.A.A. and member Scottish Motor-Boat Racing Club. Has installed speed boat for taking pictures on Loch Lomond. *Addresses :—*8, Maxwell Road, Glasgow, S.1, and 1, Battlefield Crescent, Langside, Glasgow. *Phone :* Douglas 579.

Ritson Bennell.

Commercial training in office organisation and equipment business with Kenrick & Jefferson, Ltd. Joined Trade in 1912 as buyer for B.B. Pictures. subsequently took charge of B.B. Picture Renting interests. After leaving the Army had renting experience with Goldwyn and Gaumont Co., and rejoined B.B. Pictures in 1926 as managing director. Joined Gaumont-British 1929 and became supervisor of the Corporation's interests in Scotland. *Address :—* New Savoy, Hope Street, Glasgow.

D. Benjamin.

Born 1884. Originally interested in decorating business in England, New York, and South Africa. Joined Kinema Industry in 1916 as manager of the Haymarket Picture House and Theatre de Luxe, Norwich. In 1930 took over Maidstone Cinemas, Ltd., as Joint Director and Managing Director, controlling the Central Picture Playhouse, Maidstone, the Pavilion Cinema, Maidstone, and the Palace Theatre Maidstone. In 1935 acquired Princes Cinema, Brighton, taking over personal management. *Addresses :—*Princes, North Street, Brighton, and 30, Brunswick Square, Hove. *Phones :* Brighton 3563 and Hove 3818.

Jeffrey Bernerd.

Director and General Manager, Gaumont British Distributors, Ltd. ; Director, General Theatre Corporation, Ltd.

Entering the industry through the M.P. Sales Agency Jeffrey Bernerd was appointed Manager of Film Booking Offices upon the formation of that company ; resigned 1918 to become Managing Director of the Stoll Film Co. In 1925 registered his own company while acting as special representative for Harold Lloyd. A year later was appointed Joint General Manager of W. & F. Film Service, Ltd., and then director and general manager of Gaumont British Distributors, Ltd. In April, 1935, was appointed in charge of distribution of films in the U.K. In 1931 was appointed a director of the General Theatre Corporation, Ltd. Particularly active as Chairman of the House Committee of the Screen Golfing Society, of which he was founder. *Address :—*Film House, Wardour Street, W.1. *Phone :* Gerrard 9292.

C. F. Bernhard

Entered the Industry in 1919 with British Exhibitors' Films Ltd.; producing a series of twenty British pictures. Became Managing Director of Tiffany Productions Ltd., in 1925. In 1928 formed and became Managing Director of Union Cinema Company Ltd. Towards the end of 1936 amalgamated various Associated Companies and formed a new Company called Union Cinemas Ltd., with a capital of £6,500,000, the third largest circuit in the country, controlling over 200 theatres. Managing Director of : Union Cinemas Ltd., Alliance Cinemas Ltd., Benwell Theatre Co. Ltd., British Exhibitors' Films Ltd., Cambridge Cinemas Ltd., Cambridge Holdings Ltd., Cinema Development Ltd., Circuit Cinemas Ltd., Folkestone Amalgamated Cinemas Ltd., Gravesend Majestic Theatres Co. Ltd., Hastings Amalgamated Cinemas Ltd., Kemble Theatre Ltd., Luxor Eastbourne Ltd., Majestic Belfast Ltd., Majestic Cinema (Oxford) Ltd., New Theatre Cambridge Ltd., Plaza Gravesend Ltd., Pointer & Co. Ltd., Premier Cinemas Ltd., Provincial & Urban Cinemas Ltd., Regal (Hastings) Ltd., Regal (Newbury) Ltd., Ritz (Belfast) Ltd., Ritz Wokingham Ltd., Slough Playhouse Ltd., Southan Morris Circuit Ltd., S. & U. Cinemas Ltd., Super Cinemas (Maidstone) Ltd., Theatre Cinema Cambridge Ltd., Tunbridge Wells Entertainments Ltd., Tunbridge Wells Victory Theatre Ltd., Florida Restaurants Ltd., Uxbridge Entertainments Ltd, Uxbridge Picture Playhouse Ltd., Windsor Playhouse Ltd., Yiewsley Playhouse Ltd., Montague Lyon Ltd., Midland Entertainments Ltd. *Address :—*Union House, 15, Regent Street, S.W.1. *Phone :* Whitehall 8484.

Sidney L. Bernstein.

Chairman, Granada Theatres, Ltd., Bernstein Theatres and Denman London Cinemas, Ltd., and Kinematograph Equipment Co., Ltd. One of the founders of the Film Society. *Address :—* 36, Golden Square, W.1. *Phone :* Gerrard 3554.

G. H. Blackburn.

Licensee and Manager of the New Palace Theatre, Bristol, for Gaumont-British Circuit. One of the members of the "old brigade " and been in the business from near the beginning. Formerly with Biocolor at the "Old Brit." and "Sadler's Wells." Later at Derby, Watford, and now in twelfth year in the Metropolis of the West.

Ernest E. Blake.

Born 1879. Trained as professional photographer, and in 1897 entered the kinematograph industry, using machines by Lumiere, Paul, Wrench and others, and touring a show with his brother, the late W. N. Blake. Joined Kodak in 1902 and is now managing director of this and its subsidiary companies. One of the founders of the Veterans. *Address:*—Kodak, Ltd., Kingsway, W.C.2. *Phone:* Holborn 7841.

Clement D. Bond.

Born 1899. Apprenticed to electrical and mechanical engineering. After discharge from army joined W. J. Furse & Co., Ltd., of Nottingham, London and Manchester. Now kinema engineering expert to this firm, specialising in complete electrical installations. Associate of Institute of Electrical Engineers. *Addresses:*—W. J. Furse & Co., Ltd., Traffic Street, Notting. ham, and Rowan Dene, Burton Joyce, Notts- *Phones:* Nottingham 8213 and Burton Joyce 57.

Charles Boot, J.P.

Director, Pinewood Studios, Ltd.

Son of Henry Boot, of Broomhall Park, Sheffield. Born 1874. Director of Henry Boot & Sons Ltd., Welwyn Garden City, Ltd., and 24 other companies. Justice of Peace for City of Sheffield. *Clubs:* Carlton, Constitutional, City Livery, Royal Automobile. *Address:* —Thornbridge Hall, Ashford-in-the-Water, near Bakewell, Derbyshire.

H. Granville Boxall.

Joined Paramount Islington Studios 1919, later Assistant Studio Manager until 1925, Studio and Production Manager for Gainsborough 1925-1929. Appointed General Manager, Gainsborough Pictures (1928), Ltd., April, 1929, and also Assistant to General Manager of Production, Shepherd's Bush. *Phone:* Shepherd's Bush 1210.

Billie Bristow

Served in advertising agency, on editorial and advertising staffs of Sunday and daily national newspapers. Became assistant studio and publicity manager for Broadwest. Publicity Manager for Fox and P.D.C. Started independent press agency in 1919. Has organised and controlled press and advertising campaigns for productions and renting organisations; openings of the Astorias, the Hyams Theatres, the Curzon, etc. Organiser of charity and commercial film presentations including several Royal matinées, also of Health and Beauty. Exhibition, 1935, and has conducted numerous commercial publicity campaigns. Director of independent film production company. Author or part author and scenarist for "Leave it to Me"; "Deadlock"; "Self Made Lady"; "Men of Steel"; "Tiger Bay"; "Shepherd's Warning"; "House of Trent"; "Night Mail"; "Warn London"; "Gay Love." *Address:*—10-12, Cork Street, W.1. *Phone:* Regent 6862.

J. Frank Brockliss.

Founder of J. Frank Brockliss, Ltd.

Born 1879, at Kensington. Educated Kensington Gardens Preparatory School, St. Charles College, Kensington, and the Polytechnic. Entered trade in 1909. Director and owner of several companies connected with the industry, and Managing Director of his own firm, J. Frank Brockliss, Ltd. For several years chairman of the I.A.K.M., and chairman of the Committee of B.B.F.C. During the War in charge of British Military Kinemas. 1921 to 1925 established the Paris office and Continental organisation of

the Soc. Anon. des Films Loew-Metro, being managing director of that company, and 1925 to 1927 was managing director of First National Pictures, Ltd., England, 1928-29, organised Continental business J. Frank Brockliss, under title Sociata Anonyme Francaise Brockless et Cie., Head Office, 6, Rue Guillaume Tell, Paris (17e) and continues to take an active part in the affairs of both companies. *Clubs:*—R.A.C., Eccentric (London), St. Cloud Golf Club (Paris) and Screen (New York). *Address:* 14, Lovelace Road, Surbiton-on-Thames, Surrey.

Lt.-Col. A. C. Bromhead, C.B.E.

Director, Moss Empires, Ltd., and Denman Street Trust, Ltd.

Colonel Bromhead founded the original Gaumont business in London in 1898 in the form of an agency for Leon Gaumont of Paris. Opened one of the first film studios in this country, and one of the first kinematograph theatres. He was one of the pioneers of the film hire service, and the originator of the "exclusive" film and "booking by contract." With M. Gaumont exhibited "Chronochrome" in 1913. In 1914 the Gaumont Co. constructed and equipped the first large modern film studios in London. In 1922 the Gaumont Company came entirely under British control, the majority proprietary interest being acquired by Col. Bromhead and his British associates. In 1922 the Company installed a large plant of the most modern automatic machinery for developing at their laboratory at Shepherd's Bush, and considerable extensions were completed early in 1927. In the same year a large new studio was built and in 1929 the first sound-proof studio in England was constructed for the production of "Talkies" by the British Acoustic process. The Gaumont-British Picture Corporation was formed in 1927 to acquire "The Gaumont Co., Ltd." The Ideal Film Renting Co. and the W. & F. Film Service, Ltd., together with a group of 22 theatres, subsequently acquired the ordinary share capital of Denman Picture Houses, Ltd., General Theatre Corporation, Ltd. and P.C.T., and other companies, thereby achieving control of more than 300 theatres and becoming, under the Chairmanship of Col. Bromhead, the most important concern of its kind in Europe. Col. Bromhead withdrew from the Chairmanship and severed his connection with the Gaumont British Corporation and its Associated and subsidiary companies in August, 1929. *Club:* Royal Societies. *Address:*—Douglas House, Petersham, Surrey. *Phone:*—Richmond 0240.

Ralph Sidney Bromhead, A.C.A.

Qualified as chartered accountant 1928. Theatre controller, Gaumont British and P.C.T. 1927-29. Later assistant general manager, A.B.C., Ltd., then managing director Regent Circuit, Ltd., now General Manager County Cinemas, Ltd.; Chairman, L. & H.C. Branch of the C.E.A. 1935. Delegate to C.E.A. General Council, and member of Councils of C.T.B.F. and Provident Institutions. *Club:*—Badminton. *Addresses:*—7, Highview Avenue, Edgware, Middlesex, and Dean House, Dean Street, W. *Phone:*—Gerrard 4543.

Reginald C. Bromhead, F.C.A.

Associated with the Gaumont Company since 1903, Mr. Bromhead was appointed secretary in 1915, becoming Joint Managing Director in 1921. Managing Director Gaumont British Picture Corporation, Ltd., and subsidiary companies, 1927. Vice-Chairman, Denman Picture Houses, Ltd.; Vice-Chairman, General Theatres Corporation, Ltd. January, 1929; Joint Man. Dir. and Vice-Chairman P.C,T. and subsidiary companies. Resigned August, 1929. Director, Moss Empires, Ltd. Fellow Institute of Chartered Accountants, Past-President K.R.S , Chairman Executive Committee, Kinematograph Sports Associatio , Cinematograph Trade Provident Institution and Benevolent Fund Committees. _Clubs_:—Royal Societies, St. James's. _Private Address_:—9, Cavendish Road, St. John's Wood, N.W.8.

E. Oswald Brooks.

Twenty years in film business. Successively with Gaumont Company of America, Mutual Film Corporation (U.S.A.), Pathé Exchange, Inc., and Paramount News, in New York up to 1931, holding positions as serial sales manager, general sales manager, and serial production manager. Transferred from the New York office of Paramount News when the British Paramount News was inaugurated in 1931. Executive Assistant British Paramount News, 1931-36. _Address_:—44, Ealing Village, W.5. _Phone_: Perivale 4665.

Henry Anthony Browne.

Born in 1875 in Warwickshire. Educated at Cheltenham and Birmingham University. After some years on the renting side is now chiefly interested as an exhibitor. _Clubs_:—Ranelagh, Union. Thatched House.

Shiavax Cawasjee Cambata, J.P.

Justice of Peace, and Honorary Presidency Magistrate for the City of Bombay. Member of the Bombay Municipal Corporation and other public bodies and commercial associations. Managing Director of Shiavax C. Cambata & Co., Ltd., Bombay. Director of the Hirdagarh Collieries, Ltd. Director of several other commercial firms. A pioneer in the Central Provinces coal industry. Promoted in September, 1936, important Bombay super Kinema. _Address_:—Cook's Building, 324, Hornby Road, Fort, Bombay. _Tel. address:_ "Coalpits," Bombay.

Samuel Robert Caplin.

Born 1890 at Leeds. Served apprenticeship at mechanical engineering. Founded Caplin Engineering Co., precision engineers, 1918, which later became limited company. Entered film trade in 1929 experimenting, designing and manufacturing kinematograph apparatus (Capco Sound on film Recording Equipment),Member B.K.S., M.J.Inst.E. _Address_:—32, Geary Road, N.W.10. _Phone_:—Willesden 0692.

Sydney H. Carter.

Started as New Century Pictures in Bradford. Birmingham, Leeds and Sunderland in 1902, At present director of Queen's Theatre, Holbeck, Ltd.; Londesborough and Capitol (Scarborough), Ltd.; and Prince's Hall, Shipley, Ltd. _Address:_ —26, Park Row, Leeds.

Cecil L. O. Cattermoul.

Managing Director, Cecil Cattermoul, Ltd., and Strand Film Co., Ltd.

Born 1890. Joined Industry 1912. Is a specialist in overseas markets and an authority on film export. Was London buyer for Scandinavian Film Trust for some years, then formed own company. Operates in most countries of the world, and is British Representative for a large number of the foremost foreign Distributors and Theatre Owners. Amongst others, is resident British Representative of Svensk Filmindustri of Sweden. _Address:_ 184, Wardour Street, W.1. _Phone_:—Gerrard 2903.

Charles H. Champion.

Born 1885. M.I.Mech.E., M.A.S.M.E., M.A.I.E.E., A.M.I.E.E., F.R.S.A., F.R.P.S., M.I.E.S., B.K.S., _Hon._ M.G.B.K.P.T. After several years with New British Engineering Co., Langdon Davies Motor Co., Harper Bros. and Co., Consulting Engineers; and Union Electric Co., in 1912 went to U.S.A. as technical manager of American branch of last-named company Founded Charles H. Champion & Co., Ltd., in 1921. Director of Charles H. Champion & Co., Ltd., Ship Carbon Company of Great Britain, Ltd. _Clubs_:—R.A.C. and Richmond Golf. _Address_:—National House, 60-66, Wardour Street, W.1; and "Inwood," Westmead, Roehampton, S.W.15. _Phones_:—Gerrard 2744 and Putney 2764.

T. A. Charlesworth.

Born 1896. Educated Dartford Grammar School and Imperial College Science and Technology, London University. Previously associated with engineering concerns until entering the industry in 1931. Managing Director: British Publicity Talking Films, Ltd. and British Colour Films, Ltd. _Addresses_:—75, Holland Road, Kensington, W. and 99, Charlotte Street, W.1. _Phones_:—Western 3489 and Museum 4426.

Thomas Chilton.

Educated Durham University. Entered industry 1912 with Thos. Thompson Film Hire Service; subsequently held appointments as supervising branch manager (with headquarters at Manchester) of Thompson-Thanhouser Films, Ltd., Imperial Film Co.; Ltd., and Hepworth Film Service, Ltd. Joined J. Frank Brockliss in 1924 as general manager; made director in 1928. Also director Powers Distributing Corporation, Ltd. Member Projection Advisory Council, U.S.A. Member B.K.S. _Address_:— 58, Gt. Marlborough Street, W.1. _Phone_:— Gerrard 2911.

Gilbert Church.

Born London 1899. Educated Tottenham County School. Director of Gilbert Films, Ltd., and Famous Films (Midlands), Ltd. Was responsible for the first talking films in the Midlands (Phonofilms). In conjunction with Fred White presented the first German dialogue film "Vienna Waltzes," at the Rialto Theatre, W. _Clubs_:—R.A.C. _Address_:—65, Albion Gate. Hyde Park, W.2. _Phone_:—Paddington 5233

Elisha Montague Charles Clayton.

Associated with pictures since the early days, E. M. C. Clayton was born in 1882, and educated at the Central Secondary School, Sheffield. The proprietor of Clayton's Bioscope, Sheffield, he is also Managing Director of the Oxford Picture House, Heeley Electric Palace, Pavilion, Attercliffe, Lyric Picture House, Darnall, all Sheffield halls, Hoyland Cinema, near Barnsley, the Electric Palace, Parkgate, Rotherham, and Picture House, Chesterfield. He has done much to popularise pictures in the Isle of Man, where he is an active director of the Strand Cinema. Douglas Pavilion, Peel, and the Picture House, Douglas. Also a director of Heeley and Amalgamated Cinemas, Ltd., Sheffield, managing director of the Palace, Woodseats, Sheffield, and Goldthorpe Hippodrome, Ltd., near Barnsley. _Addresses_:— Bank Chambers, 70, The Moor, and 535, Fulwood Road, Sheffield.

Isaac Collins.
Northern Branch, Paramount Film Service.
Isaac Collins was born in Newcastle-on-Tyne where he is now engaged in practically the only business he has known—the kinematograph industry. For several years he was associated with the Trade in America, and eighteen years ago commenced in the renting business at Newcastle, where he also had interests as an exhibitor. His elder brother, J. R. Collins, founded the Newcastle Film Supply Company, and when he died the business was taken over by Isaac Collins and A. Collins, and it was later merged into the business of the Famous-Lasky Corporation, now Paramount, for whom Isaac Collins operates in the four northern counties, also district manager for Scotland. He and his brother formerly controlled a large northern circuit, which is now sold to Denman Pict. Corp., Ltd. *Addresses :* —Paramount House, Bath Lane, Newcastle ; Burnside, Moor Crescent, Gosforth, Newcastle.

Frank Collinson.
Born in Bradford, Yorks, in 1875, and educated at Cambridge. For two years despatch manager for the B.B. Film Hiring Service, Glasgow, and was afterwards General Manager of the Palatine Film Co. for six years. He was also with Hibbert's Mutual Film Services as Lancs. manager. He is now Joint Secretary of the Lancs. Emergency Transport Committee of the C.E.A. and K.R.S. Was the first and only secretary of the Lancashire K.R.S. *Address :* —Barcol, Poynton Cheshire.

Marcus F. Cooper.
Entered industry in 1929 as sound engineer to Gainsborough. With British Lion Film Corporation until 1931 but left to take charge of Sound department of A.R.P. Studios. Now directing shorts and industrials for Publicity Films, Ltd. *Address :*—269, Kingston Road, Merton Park, S.W.19.

Hugh M. Cotterill
Born 1909. Educated at Winchester and Magdalene College, Cambridge, where he first took an interest in theatre lighting. After a period of training in the G.E.C. research laboratories at Wembley, joined Major Equipment Co. in 1931, subsequently becoming a director in 1936 of Strand Electric Holdings, Ltd.; Strand Electric & Engineering Co., Ltd., Strand and Interchangeable Signs, Ltd. Member Arts Theatre Club, and Illuminating Engineering Society. *Addresses :*—19-28, Floral Street, W.C.2, and 5, Imperial House, Grosvenor Road, S.W.1. *Phones :* Temple Bar 7464, and Vic. 2180.

Sir Gordon Craig.
Born 1891. Knighted 1929. Liveryman Gold and Silver Wyre Drawers Company, Vice-president "Old Contemptibles" Association. President Hackney Branch British Legion. General manager, British Movietonews, Ltd. *Clubs :*—Royal Thames Yacht and Sunningdale. *Address :*—13, Berners Street, W.1. *Phone :* Museum 5113.

Ian Cremieu-Javal.
Born 1900. Educated at Trent and Marlborough. Flying Officer, R.A.F., 1918. Entered film business with Stoll in 1919 on production work. Joined H.M.V. 1924, as artiste and recording manager. Toured America for H.M.V. as liaison of artistes. On his return promoted film activities for H.M.V., which embraced such talking films as "Splinters" and "Rookery Nook." Joined R.C.A., 1930 as General Manager, leaving January 1933 to join British

Acoustic Films, Ltd. Now director of G.-B. Equipments, Ltd. ; British Acoustic Films, Ltd ; G.-B. Instructional, Ltd.; G.-B. Screen Services, Ltd. ; Itala Acoustica, S.A.I. (Rome), British Film Producers, Bush Radio, Ltd. ; Baird Television, Ltd. ; *Clubs.*—Savage, Aldwych. *Addresses :*—Film House, Wardour Street, W.1. ; 17a, Davies Street, Berkeley Street, W.1 ; White Cottage, Gracious Pond, Chobham, Surrey. *Phone :*—Gerrard 9292.

Reginald Howard Cricks, F.R.P.S.
Son of George H.Cricks. Has specialised in the technical branch of the trade, having been for 10 years with W. Vinten, and, since 1926, in business as kinematograph engineer and consultant. Has designed much apparatus for studio, dark-room, and kinema, and is a regular contributor to the technical pages of the *Kine Weekly*. Fellow of the Royal Photographic Society, technical editor *Ideal Kinema*. *Addresses :* 159, Wardour Street, W.1, and 6, Dulverton Road, Selsdon, South Croydon. *Phone :* Gerrard 6889.

Reginald V. Crow.
Ex-President, C.E.A.
One of the leading figures in Kentish Trade circles, Mr. Crow is managing director and secretary of the Ramsgate and District Popular Amusements Co., Ltd., managing director and secretary of the Kent Films Motor Transport Co., Ltd. Director and secretary Balexcro Theatres, Ltd., an ex-Councillor of the Borough of Ramsgate, Treasurer and Ex-Chairman of the Kent C.E.A. Chairman, 1929, and Trustee, London and Home Counties branch. President C.E.A., 1931. *Address :*—11, Avenue Lodge, Avenue Road, N.W.8. *Phone :* Primrose 0340.

Arthur Cunningham.
Formerly in business in Leeds as tip-up chairs and furniture manufacturer and specialist in the fitting up of theatres. Equipped some of the first picture houses in this country, in about 1897, and has been interested in pictures ever since. Joined up with Sydney Carter and formed New Century Pictures, Ltd., about 1905. In 1919 he was elected a member of the Leeds C.C. One of the first members of the Council (Cinema Defence) about 1908. Now the C.E.A. first vice-president, in 1917. When New Century Pictures was sold to Denman Picture Houses, Ltd., was retained as managing director. Director at present time of Londesborough and Capitol, Scarborough, and Queens Theatre, Leeds. Ex-president 1902 Cinema Veterans, on the Council of the C.T.B.F., delegate Leeds Branch C.E.A. Has a national reputation as an organiser for charity. *Addresses :*—26, Park Row, Leeds, and Tower Crest, Heysham, Morecambe. *Phones :* Leeds 27318 and Heysham 17.

L. W. Dalton.
Pioneer film publicity man. Joined M.P. Sales in 1910 to edit the *Pictures*, first fan paper, and take charge of advertising for Biograph. Kalem, Lubin, etc., and later Famous Players, Journalistic experience includes editing magazines for Pearsons and Amalgamated Press. Founded Star Illustration Works, Ltd. on discharge from Army in 1918. *Address :*—Star, D'Arblay Street, W.1. *Phone :* Gerrard 3033.

Dillon Damen.
First General Manager and in charge of Publicity "The Book Society," after several years freelance film and general Advertising and Publicity. Joined Fox Film Company as assistant publicity manager, thence to

Universal in similar capacity. Until November 1935 was advertising and publicity manager Warner Bros., Pictures, Ltd. *Address :*—Dillon House, Hayland Close, Kingsbury, N.W.9. *Phone :* Colindale 8436.

C. H. Dand.
Born 1902. Educated Glasgow University. Several years in Provincial and London journalism. Entered industry as literary adviser and publicity director to Associated Sound Film Industries, Ltd. Now engaged in production and direction of colour films. *Addresses :*—6, Cannon Place, London, N.W.3, and Gasparcolor Ltd., 3, St. James's Square, S.W.1. *Phones :* Hampstead 3632 and Whitehall 8701.

Demetre L. Daponte.
Born 1896. D.Sc., L.Sc. (Antwerp). Mechanical, optical and illuminant research work. In charge of the study of " Persistence of vision," at the Sorbonne, Paris. Study of stereoscopic projection which established the Pulsograph system. Gave lectures and demonstration on stereoscopy at the British Association. Financed many mechanical, chemical and optical inventions. Managing Director of Dufay-Chromex, Ltd.; vice-president of Dufaycolor Corporation, U.S.A.; managing director of Cinecolor, Ltd., and of British Industrial Laboratories ; director of Dufaycolor, Ltd. *Club :*—R.A.C. *Addresses :*—52, Barn Hill, Wembley Park, and 89, Long Acre, W.C.2. *Phones :* Arnold 1077 and Temple Bar 3221

Tom E Davies, J.P.
Born in 1868, and was educated at Shrewsbury. Left the banking business in 1911 to enter the film Trade, joining the Western Import Co., Ltd. He is a J.P. for Hertfordshire, and has occupied several prominent positions in Film Trade organisations. Chairman of Incorporated Association of Kinematograph Manufacturers, Ltd. Director of Shrewsbury Empires Ltd., Broadway Gardens, Ltd., Walham Green ; Fulham Picture Palace, Fulham *Address :*—19, Dryburgh Road, Putney, S.W.15. *Phone :* Putney 5281.

Alfred Davis.
Deputy Managing Director of Davis' Theatre (Croydon) Ltd.
Born 1899. Joined the Army at the age of 15, served throughout the war, at the age of 18 being made a Captain in the M.G.C. After the War joined the Davis' Pavilion Circuit, being made a director and controlling the film booking and publicity departments. Joined Board of Gaumont-British on its formation in April, 1927, and was appointed Film Booking Manager. Retired end of 1928 to take control of Davis' Theatre, Croydon. Director of New Era National Pictures, Ltd., until July 1932. Vice-Chairman, London & H.C. Branch C.E.A. *Addresses :*—12, Hyde Park Place, and Marble Arch Pavilion. *Phone :*—Mayfair 1811.

Basil Davis, A.M.I.E.E.
Consulting Electrical Engineer to Kinemas and Theatres.
Born August 1892. Responsible for design of over 100 of the largest installations, including new stage lighting at Royal Opera House, Covent Garden, Regal Cinema, Edmonton ; Trocadero, Elephant and Castle ; Garrick, Southport ; Davis, Croydon ; Curzon, Mayfair ; also many Donada and G.-B. houses. Grown up in trade with the original Davis Pavilion Circuit ; three years chief engineer to G.-B.,

four years consulting engineer to G.E.C. *Address :*—Elettra, Brockley Hill, Stanmore, Middlesex. *Phone :* Edgware 1944.

H. Victor Davis.
Ex-President, C.E.A.
Entered the Industry in 1911. After fourteen years' service in the C.E.A. and at least three previous invitations to stand for the office, which he declined, Mr. Davis was in 1927 elected Vice-President of the Association and President for 1928-9. Endowed with the eloquence of the Welsh, he has always been called upon when missionary work was to be done, one of the most notable of which efforts was in connection with British Film Week in 1924. He served on the Joint Committee for British films in 1925-6. He represents the South Wales Branch (which he founded) on the General Council of the C.E.A. Chairman and co-managing director Abertillery Theatres, Ltd. ; managing director Ebbw Vale Theatres, Ltd. ; proprietor, Public Hall, Newbridge. *Phone :*—Newbridge 32.

G. Dawson.
Secretary of Radio Pictures Ltd., since the beginning of the Company. Formerly with Ideal Films, Ltd. *Address :*—Dean House, Dean Street, W.1. *Phone :*—Gerrard 3201.

G. W. Dawson.
Director and secretary of Radio Pictures, Ltd. Director of March of Time, Ltd. Entered film business in 1921 with Ideal Films, Ltd. Joined Radio Pictures, Ltd., as secretary, 1930. Appointed director of Radio Pictures, Ltd., and March of Time, Ltd., in 1936. *Address :*—Dean House, Dean Street, W.1. *Phone :* Gerrard 3201.

John Richard Dearn.
Born in Sheffield, 1870. Accountant by profession, being a Fellow of the London Association of Accountants from its inception in 1905. Also Fellow National Association of Auctioneers. Has holdings in several Sheffield Picture Companies. Formerly Managing Director, Victory Palaces (Sheffield), Ltd. *Address :*—55, Vivian Road, Firth Park, Sheffield.

H. R. A. de Jonge.
Born 1901. Educated at Bedford College Entered film business in 1927 as supervisor for the Gaumont Company on French production. Later became Berlin and Central Europe, representative of the Gaumont Co. until 1930 being transferred in that year to Copenhagen. Became assistant to managing director of British Acoustic Films in 1931. Appointed director of British Acoustic films and the following subsidiary companies in 1933: G.-B. Equipments, Ltd., Electrical Fono-films Co. ; A/s (Copenhagen) ; Nordisk Films Kompagni (Copenhagen). *Addresses :*—Film House, Wardour Street, London, W.1 ; 41, Arthur Court, Queen's Road, London, W.2. *Phone :*—Gerrard 9292.

Maurice Arthur Dent.
Originally associated with the stage, Mr. Dent entered the film side of the entertainment industry under J. D. Walker, and was responsible for the Scottish distribution of Lasky pictures. Later became managing director of Waverley Films, Ltd. In November, 1927, this company became part of British International Pictures. Ltd., the board of which Mr. Dent joined. Director Associated British Picture Corp., Ltd. Managing Director, B.I.P. (Export), Ltd., and Wardour Films, Ltd. When

in Glasgow was one of the founders of the Scottish Trade Benevolent Fund, the Cinema Club, and was a founder member of the Lodge Anima (1223) Glasgow. *Address :*—Film House, Wardour Street, W.1. *Phone :*—Gerrard 4314.

Oscar Deutsch.

Born 1893 at Birmingham. Chairman and Governing Director of the prominent and rapidly growing Odeon Circuit. Entered the Industry on the renting side, being Chairman of W. & F. Film Service (Midlands) Ltd., for several years. Entered exhibiting side in 1925, but it was not until 1933 that he commenced the building up of the Odeon chain. Also Chairman of the Odeon Trust, Ltd., Sound & Cinema Equipment Ltd., the marketing Company of the B.T.H. Sound Reproducer, Scophony, Ltd., Deutsch & Brenner, Ltd., and of Cinema Service Ltd. His other interests are very numerous and cover a wide field. Chairman of the Birmingham C.E.A. Branch, 1931-1932. *Addresses :*—5, Augustus Road, Birmingham. *Phone :* Edgbaston 0738. *Office :* —22, Bennett's Hill, Birmingham, 2. *Phone :* Midland 2781. 49, Park Lane, London, W.1. *Phone :* Mayfair 7811.

Mrs. Oscar Deutsch.

Wife of Governing Director of Odeon Theatres, Ltd., is responsible for the colour schemes and interior decorations in all Odeon Theatres already built and now in course of construction ; director of Decorative Crafts, Ltd., Broad Street, Birmingham (a subsidiary company of Odeon Theatres, Ltd.). *Address :*—5, Augustus Road, Edgbaston, Birmingham. *Phone :* Edgbaston 0738.

Louis D. Dickson.

Born in 1880, Mr. Dickson after training as an electrical engineer entered trade in 1899. Appointed kinematographer to Scottish National Exhibition, Edinburgh, 1908. Proprietor and manager. Hippodrome. Bo'ness, which he built in 1912. Vice-Chairman Scottish Branch C.E.A., 1926, Chairman 1927, delegate to C.E.A. General Council. Director, Astoria, Corstorphine. *Address :*—" Mora," Bo'ness.

S. F. Ditcham.

Managing Director Universal Pictures, Ltd. Director General Film Distributors, Ltd.

Joined Ruffell's Bioscope in the early days. Then several years with Gaumont. Opened up with Universal, 1922-1936, when that company was taken over by General F.D. *Address :* 127, Wardour Street, W.1. *Phone :* Gerrard. 7311.

Arthur Carlyne Niven Dixey.

Born 1889 Started as solicitor in Manchester Entered Parliament 1923, and has held the seat for nine consecutive years, successfully contesting four elections. Managing Director of the Berkley Property and Investment Company. Managing Director of the Bruton Trust Company. *Address :*—22, Grosvenor Street, W.1. *Phone :* Mayfair 4371.

D. C. Dobie.

Born 1899. Connected with the motor business until 1920, when joined Pathé in Liverpool under Charlie Graham. Six months later took charge of their sub-office in Manchester until 1924. Joined Famous Lasky Film Service. After one year resigned to become connected again with Pathé 1925, with whom he remained until the merger with First National, when he was transferred to the London Office and operated the South Coast. After eighteen months in that

territory was transferred to Liverpool as Branch Manager, where he remained until returning to Head Office in 1931, when the demerger of First National and Pathé took place, and First National Film Distributors came into being, to take position of General Sales Manager. *Address :* 135-141, Wardour Street, W.1. *Phone :*— Gerrard 5600.

C. J. Donada.

Founder of County Cinemas, Ltd., and associated companies. Born 1895. Educated in Switzerland, France and University in Germany. Entered the industry in 1913, joining Famous Players Film Co., Ltd. (now Paramount), as Foreign Correspondent. Remained with this organisation for nearly 19 years, during which he filled many important posts. In 1932, owing to the extension of his exhibiting interests, he was compelled to sever his connection with Paramount. His organisation now controls over 50 kinemas. *Address :*—Dean House, Dean Street, W.1. *Phone :* Gerrard 4543.

Richard Dooner.

President C.E.A., 1935-6.

Pioneer of the kinema movement in Wales, was born in 1872, at Eastwood, Nottingham. Became chairman South Wales and Monmouth branch of the Cinematograph Exhibitors' Association, and owner of the Plaza and New Theatre (Maesteg), Coliseum and Pavilion (Abergavenny) and Olympia, Ogmore Vale. *Address :*—2, Llwynvi Road, Maesteg.

Anson Dyer.

Born at Brighton. Started as landscape artist, then entered stained glass studios and concentrated on Ecclesiastical Art. Entered Film World and made first cartoons in 1918 " John Bull's Animated Sketch Book," " Brer Rabbit," etc. Joined Hepworths 1922, then followed some films of diagrammatic Cartoon work. In 1930 directed Port of London Film, and several big industrial films ; made 6-reel cartoon. "Story of the Flag," for Archibald Nettlefold Productions. At present managing director of Anglia Films Ltd. Started in March, 1935, making British colour and sound cartoons "Sam and his Musket," etc. (Stanley Holloway Series), "Carmen." *Addresses :*—109, Jermyn Street, S.W.1, and 28, Coval Gardens, Temple Sheen, S.W.14. *'Phones :* Whitehall 7585 and Prospect 3556.

Sam. Eckman, Jnr.

Managing Director M-G-M and Past President, K.R.S.

Entered Industry as an exhibitor and was an early member of organisation formed to protect the exhibiting side of the trade. President of the New York Exhibitors' Leagues. In 1914 became New York manager of the Mutual Film Corp., later, with the formation of the Triangle Film Corporation assumed the management of its New York Branch. In 1917, took charge of the New York office of the newly formed Goldwyn Pict. Corp. In 1922, elected vice-president of the Goldwyn Distributing Corp. With the amalgamation of M-G-M in 1924 took over the management of the entire Eastern Division. One of the former presidents of the New York Film Board of Trade, and is still an honorary member of that body. In September, 1927, appointed managing director of J.-M.-G. (now M-G-M Pict., Ltd.). President of the K.R.S., 1931-2, 1932-3 and 1933-4. *Clubs :*—Army and Navy, New York ; Sojourners, New York ; Motion Picture New

York; Two Thirty Three, Los Angeles, Calif.; Army Athletic Association, West Point, New York; and American Club, London; American Chamber of Commerce in London; American Society, London; The English Speaking Union of the British Empire; Reserve Officers' Association of the United States; The Jewish Theatrical Guild of America. *Masonic Bodies:* —Pacific Lodge No. 233, New York (Past Master); Constitution Chapter No. 230, Royal Arch Masons; Scottish Rite Consistory; Mecca *Temple:* Anima Lodge, London. *Addresses:*— 73, Devonshire House, W.1, and 19, Tower Street, W.C.2. *Phone:*—Temple Bar 8444.

Major A. O. Ellis.

Born 1877. Trained as a surveyor and became a member of the Surveyors' Institution. Entered the film Industry as exhibitor in 1910. From 1907 to 1913 member of Devonport Borough Council, and for two years chairman of the finance committee. Served throughout the Great War and was wounded at Ypres in 1917. Now owns kinemas in Plymouth, Torquay, Paignton, Brixham and Tiverton. Chairman and delegate of the Devon and Cornwall Branch of the C.E.A. *Address:*—Homeside, Higher Warberry Road, Torquay.

Arthur Elton.

Born February 1906. Educated at Marlborough and Cambridge. Joined Scenario Department of Gainsborough Pictures, 1927. Joined E.M.B. Film Unit in 1930; G.P.O. Film Unit in 1934. Producers to the Ministry of Labour 1934-5. Since then, free lance producer to various industries. Helped to found Associated Realist Film Producer, Ltd., in 1936. Specialist in documentary and realist films, which include: "Upstream," "Aero Engine," "Workers and Jobs," "Housing Problems," and others. Editor of the March of Time Series of books for Longmans, Green. *Address:* 33, Soho Square, W.1. *Phone:* Gerrard 2484.

Herbert Elton.

Born 1894. Entered the industry in 1920 as salesman at Cardiff branch of Ideal Films, promoted to management of Nottingham branch in 1922. Resigned from this position in 1930 to control exhibiting interests. Managing Director, Eskay, Ltd., Aleph Entertainments, Ltd., and Midland Empire Theatres, Ltd., Abbey Theatres, Ltd. *Address:*—Commerce Chambers, Elite Buildings, Nottingham. *Phone:* Nottingham 42364.

J. F. Emery, M.P., J.P.

A principal of Mancunian Circuit Ltd., a £300,000 Company formed in April, 1935, controlling the Capitol, Didsbury; the Pyramid, Sale; the Lido, Burnage; the Broadway, Eccles, and the Riviera, Cheetham Hill. He is also the proprietor of the Emery Film Circuit. A native of Wigan, he started in business as a telegraphist at Gathurst Station under the old Lancashire and Yorkshire Railway Company. He left the railway service in 1919 and started business on his own account in Salford, where he quickly made his mark in kinema trade affairs. In November, 1921, was elected to the Salford City Council, subsequently becoming alderman, and in 1932-33, at the age of 45, was made Mayor. Returned to Parliament for Salford West, November, 1935. *Address:* Midland Bank House, 26, Cross Street, Manchester. *Phones:* Blackfriars 5618 and Pendleton 2611.

S. Taylor Farrell.

Resident manager, Abbeydale Picture House, Sheffield. *Address:*—34, Sheldon Road, Nether Edge, Sheffield, 7. *Phone (Theatre):*—50540.

W. G. Faulkner.

Born 1864 in the Midlands. Began life as a teacher. Left the profession in 1888 to become a journalist, reaching the editorial chair of a well-known weekly dealing with London government. Left that work for the editorial staff of the London *Evening News* as an authority on all matters relating to London government. Vice-chairman Ilford School Board, 1896-1902. Began study of moving-picture production and exhibition in 1909; wrote first regular criticisms of films in any British newspaper in the *Evening News*, in 1910, and became film editor of that journal. Spent three months in the United States in 1920 investigating the moving-picture Industry there, both in the East and in California. Resigned the film editorship of the *Evening News* in October, 1921, and established his own Film Review. Founded the British Association of Film Directors. *Addresses:*—32, Shaftesbury Avenue, W.1, and 53, London Road, S.E.23. *Phones:* Gerrard 5514 and Forest Hill 1954.

Ivor E. Faull.

Born 1891. Served apprenticeship at Electrical and Mechanical Engineering. Joined Columbia Pictures in 1912, later, Royal Canadian Pictures. Ran Coliseum, Tylerstown, pictures and variety. After discharge from army in 1915 joined Walturdaw in 1921 as Technical Representative; appointed sales manager and director. Later resigned and joined as technical representative Kalee, Ltd. Director of Plaza, Exeter, and managing director of New Theatre, Northampton. Acted as consulting engineer to large number of kinemas, including Embassy, Bristol; Regent, Leamington; Forum, Bath; Savoy, Fareham; Plaza, Gloucester, etc. *Address:*—60, Wardour Street, London, W.1. *Phone:* Gerrard 5137.

Arnold Rowland Favell.

Born 1903. Incorporated accountant. Secretary Sheffield Branch C.E.A., Walkley Palladium, Ltd.; Ecclesall and Endcliffe Picture Palace, Ltd.; Sheffield Amusements Co., Ltd.; Director Grosvenor Hall & Estate Co., Ltd. Son of Sheffield branch delegate. Acquired in 1928 the practice of the late G. E. Wright. *Address:* 47, Bank Street, Sheffield.

Arthur Rowland Favell.

A. R. Favell, born in 1869, is a Fellow of the London Association of Accountants. He is director, general manager and secretary of Grosvenor Hall and Estate Co., Ltd., which owns the Kinema House, Hillsborough, managing director of the Walkley Palladium, Sheffield, and director of Adelphi Picture House, Attercliffe. *Address:*—Sunningdale, Dobcroft Road, Ecclesall Road South, Sheffield 11. *Phone:* 70748.

A. Mary Field.

Born 1896. Trained in Historical Research, Holds degree of M.A. (London) with distinction. Education department, British Instructional Films, 1927-1929; Continuity for B.I.F., 1929-1930; Editor and director, 1931-1933. Director G.B. Instructional, and also on Board of the company, 1933. *Club:*—Forum. *Address:* 12, D'Arblay Street, W.1. *Phone:* Gerrard 7386.

W. A. Fielder.

Originally connected with the grain trade as a member of the Baltic. Entered Film Industry in 1919 in Sales Dept. of Wardour Films, Ltd. pro noted to London branch manager ; later to assistant sales manager, and is now general manager. *Addresses :*—Film House, Wardour Street, and 70, Ealing Village, Hanger Lane, W.5. *Phones :* Gerrard 4314 and Perivale 5311.

Norman File.

Born 1893. Entered Film business 1913, as representative for Fox Film Co., held executive position with Goldwyn Ltd. F.B.O., Ltd., United Artists, then became general manager, Reunion Films. Now personal representative for J. Henry Iles, chairman of Rock Studios, Ltd. *Address :* Astor House, Aldwych, W.C.2. *Phone :* Holborn 3360.

Hugh Findlay.

Studio Publicity Manager, Gaumont British Picture Corporation, Ltd.

Brief commercial experience before joining Army in September, 1914. In 1919 entered Civil Service, Medical Division, Ministry of Pensions ; joined publicity department of Pathé Frères, having previously essayed free-lance journalism. Subsequently took up an appointment in the Gaumont Company's Publicity Department, of which he took charge in 1929. In 1931 appointed studio publicity manager, Gaumont British Picture Corporation, Ltd., becoming responsible for publicising production activities at the Shepherd's Bush and Islington Studios and elsewhere. *Address :*—Lime Grove, Shepherd's Bush, W.12. *Phone :*—Shepherd's Bush 1210.

Theo. H. Fligelstone.

President, C.E.A., 1936-7.

Born in 1895 at Cardiff, enlisted 1914, gained M.C. Joined Servalls' Exclusives, Ltd., as managing director. South Wales delegate to K.R.S. 1928-1930, took over control of Lewisham Hippodrome. Managing director of T.H.F. Theatres Ltd., and Watford Amusements, Ltd. *Club :*—R.A.C. *Address :*—11, Berkeley Court, Baker Street, N.W.1. *Phone :*—Welbeck 2301.

Victor A. Foot, F.I.P.I.

Born 1897. Managing Director of Ossicaide, Ltd., deaf specialists. Instrumental in equipping a large number of kinemas throughout the country with deaf sets so that deaf and hard of hearing people may enjoy sound films. Entered the public address field in 1932 with Ossicaide amplifiers and "Foot" microphones. Has a large number of patents to his credit in connection with sound. Fellow of the Institute of Patentees Incorporated. *Address :*—447, Oxford Street, London, W.1. *Phone :* Mayfair 1528-9.

Chas. G. Fox, F.C.I.S.

Born 1872. Educated at Owen's School, Islington. Started manufacturing kinematograph apparatus in conjunction with the late Ernest F. Moy at end of 1895. Formed the Cinematograph Co., Ltd., in 1898. Is now chairman of Ernest.F. Moy, Ltd.; treasurer and member of the Standards Committee of the I.A.K.M.; and Fellow of the Chartered Institute of Secretaries. *Club :*—Rotary. *Address :*— 76, West Hill, Highgate, N.6.

Thomas Nicholson France.

Born 1885. Joined the late Sidney Bacon in 1896, and was associated with him in all branches of the Entertainment world. Managing Director

of Sidney Bacon's Pictures, Ltd., which controls a circuit of kinemas. Represents Northern Branch as Delegate to the General Council of the C.E.A. Trustee of London Branch. Member of The Kinema Veterans. *Addresses :* 59, Wood land Rise, Muswell Hill, London, N., and 108 Great Russell Street, W.C.1. *'Phone :* Museum 5221.

R. Duncan French, J.P.

Born at Kendal in 1872, Mr. French went to Liverpool in 1893, where he qualified as an Incorporated Accountant. In 1912 became interested in the flotation of Picturedrome Companies. Now secretary of twelve such companies and his firm are auditors of others. Director of Tunnel Road Picturedrome Co., Ltd. Member of the Committee of the North-Western Branch of the C.E.A. Member of the Liverpool City Council for the past 14 years, and is Chairman of the Housing Committee, and member of the Finance, Co-ordination and Parliamentary Committees of that Corporation. *Club :*—Liverpool Constitutional Club. *Addresses :*—Arran, Dowhills Road, Blundellsands, Liverpool ; and 17, North John Street, Liverpool.

Joseph Friedman.

Managing director, Columbia Pictures Corporation, Ltd., director of Columbia Pictures (Export), Ltd., director of Columbia (British) Productions, Ltd., director of Capitol Film A.G., Berlin, director of Columbia Film A.B., Stockholm, director of Columbia Films S.A., Paris, director of Columbia Films S.A., Spain, and director of Columbia Films A/S, Copenhagen. *Addresses :*—9, Berkeley Court, Baker Street, N.W.1, and 139, Wardour Street, W.1. *Phones :* Welbeck 5809 and Gerrard 4321.

W. R. Fuller.

General Secretary, C.E.A.

Since succeeding W. Gavazzi King as General Secretary of the C.E.A. in 1925-26, Mr. Fuller, has contributed valuable aid to the Industry in several directions, notably in regard to the strengthening of the Association's power in the course of the long negotiations preparatory to the drafting of the Cinematograph Films Bill and the organisation of the policy put forward to the Government during its consideration of the measure. As a Barrister-at-Law his qualifications have been important factors in the work of the C.E.A. *Address :*—Broadmead House, Panton Street, S.W.1. *Phone :* Whitehall 0191-4.

B. T. S. Gamble.

Apprenticed to electrical engineering with B.T.-H. at Rugby ; served successively with the English Electric Company and with Courtalds, Ltd., Coventry. In January 1927 joined Micklewright, Ltd., as manager, and in July 1935 became associated with F. H. Pride, the well known lighting specialist, as manager of switchgear department. Member of the Society of Illuminating Engineers and of the B.K.S. *Address :*—69-81, High Street, Clapham, S.W.4. *Phone :* Macaulay 2281.

Bernhard Gardner.

Managing Director, RCA Photophone, Ltd.

Born 1874. Canadian subject. For many years president of the RCA Victor Co., of Canada, a subsidiary of the Radio Corporation of America. In 1927 went to Japan and China to establish plants for the RCA Victor Co., in Yokohama and Shanghai. Returned to the U.S.A., and became export manager of the International Division of the RCA Victor Co. Inc. In January, 1936, came to London to take up the position of European manager of the Radio Corporation of America, and the RCA Manufacturing Co., Inc., (which include? the Photophone activities) and managing director of their British subsidiary, RCA Photophone, Ltd. *Addresses :*—Electra House, Victoria Embankment, W.C.2, and 48, Elsworthy Road, N.W.3. *Phone :* Temple Bar 2976.

Robert Garrett.

Born 1910, at Tadworth, Surrey, and educated at Cambridge, Universities of Munich and Bonn and the Sorbonne, Paris. Joint managing director Garrett Klement Pictures, Ltd., and Garrett and Klement, Ltd. Studied for the Diplomatic Service before entering film industry. Co-producer of "A Woman Alone," and "The Amazing Quest of Ernest Bliss." *Address :*—32, St. James's Street, S.W.1. *Phone :* Whitehall 4296.

W. J. Gell.

Managing Director, Pathe Pictures, Ltd.

First joined the Gaumont Company in 1910, in which Company he occupied various positions until appointed Joint General Manager in 1922. In March, 1928, elected to the Board of Directors, to the Gaumont Company as Joint Managing Director, becoming sole Managing Director in March, 1929. In September, 1933, he resigned his position with the Gaumont Company and also the seat he held on the boards of the following companies :—British Acoustic Films, Ltd. ; International Acoustic Films, Ltd.; Gainsborough Pictures (1928), Ltd.; Film Clearing Houses, Ltd. ; and Denman Picture Houses, Ltd. On November 1, 1933, he was appointed Managing Director of Pathe Pictures, Ltd., and to the Board of British Instructional Films, Ltd., and Pathé Equipment, Ltd. *Clubs:*—R.A.C. and City Livery. *Addresses :*—103-109, Wardour Street, W.1 ; and Scarlet Oaks, Camberley, Surrey. *Phone :* Gerrard 5701.

Aveling Ginever.

Born 1898. Educated at Harrow. Formerly Journalist. Entered Industry 1928, with British Talking Pictures, Ltd. Founded own production company, Gee Films, Ltd., 1931. Writer, director, producer. Managing director Pearl Productions, Ltd., and Gee Films, Ltd. Liveryman, Stationer's Company. *Club :*—Junior Constitutional. *Address :*—32, Shaftesbury Avenue, W.1. *Phone :* Gerrard 6403 and 6325.

John Winwood Gossage.

Born 1905. Educated Uppingham. Formerly Recording Manager to Decca Gramophones, and later to Peter Maurice Publishing Company. Joined Board of Reunion Films as Director in July 1935. Now Managing Director of that firm. Founder and managing director London & Continental Pictures, Ltd.; last production "Dreams Come True." *Club :* Savage. *Addresses :*—68, Gloucester Terrace, W.2, and Regency House, 1-4, Warwick Street, W.1. *Phone :* Gerrard 5391.

Isaac Graham.

Central Picture House, Sheffield

Born at Hull in 1877, receiving his education in that city. A business man with many interests in the commercial life of Sheffield, he at first took up "Movies" as a hobby, but since those days has greatly increased his interests in the Trade. In 1914 he became an active director of Premier Pictures, Ltd., Sheffield, and more recently of the Abbeydale Picture House Co., Ltd., and Central Picture House

Co. (Sheffield), Ltd. He is also Managing Director of the Palace Picture Theatre, Newark, and the Newark Kinema. *Address :*—37, Collegiate Crescent, Broomhall Park, Sheffield.

John Cecil Graham.

Became identified with the film business in its early days and has continued in the Industry since, with the following concerns : Western Film Co., St. Louis, Mo. ; Swanson Crawford Film Co. ; Reliance Motion Picture Co., New York ; Universal Film Manufacturing Co., New York ; Mutual Film Corp., New York. Director of the following companies : Paramount Film Service, Ltd., London ; Plaza Theatre Company, Ltd., London ; Carlton Theatre Company, Ltd., London ; Paramount (Manchester) Theatre, Ltd.; Paramount-Astoria-Theatres, Ltd.; Paramount-Newcastle-Theatre, Ltd.; Paramount-Leeds-Theatre, Ltd. ; Olympic Kinematograph Laboratories, Ltd., London ; Paramount Film Service, Ltd., Sydney, Australia. *Address :*—Paramount House, 166-170 Wardour Street, W.1. *Phone :* Gerrard 7700.

Walter Grant.

Born in 1879, educated at Mill Hill House and University of Birmingham. Qualified in Medicine and Dental Surgery. Entered the Industry in 1909. Founded P.C.T. with the late Dr. Jupp, and became one of the first Directors. Now with Gaumont British Corporation, P.C.T. and associated companies. *Club :* Royal Automobile. *Address :*—13, Norland Square, Holland Park, W.11.

Frank Davis Gray.

Ex-Chairman, Leicester Branch, C.E.A.

Mr. Gray filled the office of Chairman of the Leicester branch of the C.E.A. for a period of three years, during which the branch passed through a very strenuous time. Was manager of the Olympia Picture Theatre, Leicester, but after 22 years' service retired Easter 1935. *Address :*—220, London Road, Leicester.

Frank Green.

Man. Dir. Ace Films, Ltd. *Address :*—National House, Wardour Street, W.1. *Phone :* Gerrard 3291.

H. J. Green.

Ex-Chairman, Scottish Branch of the C.E.A.

Son of the late George Green and a principal of the well-known Green's circuit of halls. Treasurer of the Scottish Branch since 1930, and Vice-Chairman of the Scottish C.T.B.F. His recent presidency of the Scottish branch was a popular one, and since then the large amount of hard work put in by him in the interests of exhibitors and the trade generally has been recognised on all sides. The Green circuit, in which he and his brother are associated, includes the Playhouse, Renfield Street, Glasgow, the largest kinema in Europe. *Address :*—Avonton, Bellahouston, Glasgow.

J. Leslie Greene.

Born in 1875, at Liverpool, Leslie Greene has become one of the leading figures in Liverpool film circles. He was educated privately, and entered the journalistic profession, becoming finally managing director of the Liverpool City Press, Ltd. He afterwards entered the film business, and is now chairman of the Hope Hall, Cinema, Liverpool, the Kingsway, Hoylake, and Walton Vale P.H., managing director, Metropole Theatre, Bootle, and Queen's, Hoylake, Chairman, Enterprises (Liverpool), Ltd., Booking Agent for the Victoria Cinema, Liverpool. Chairman and managing director.

New Carlton Rooms, and was in 1920 made the first president of the Liverpool Kinema Exchange. *Club :*—Liverpool Press Club. *Office Address :*—7. Elliott Street. Liverpool. W. *Phone :*—Royal 538. *London Offices :*—78, Shaftesbury Avenue, W.1, and 128, Nightingale Lane, S.W.12. *Phones :* Gerrard 7301 and Battersea 2647.

John Grierson.

Born Deanstown, N.B., 1898. Educated Glasgow University. Rockefeller Research Fellowship in Social Science 1924-27 and during that time worked at American Universities. Surveyed educational and propaganda film methods in different countries for the Empire Marketing Board and formed E.M.B. Film Unit. Film Officer E.M.B., 1928. Film Officer G.P.O. 1933. *Address :*—21, Soho Square, W.1. *Phone :* Gerrard 2666.

D. E. Griffiths.

General Sales Manager First National-Pathé Ltd. Born at Barry Dock, Glam., 1895. Several years' experience in the United States on the renting side of the industry with Fox and Famous Players. Joined First National in 1926 as Branch Manager, Cardiff. Later appointed London Branch Manager, and then became General Sales Manager. Now Managing Director First National Film Distributors, Ltd., and Director Warner Bros., Ltd. *Addresses :*—Argyll, 54, Gunnersbury Avenue, Ealing, W.5, and Warner House, Wardour Street, W.1. *Phones :* Acorn 3012 and Gerrard 5600.

Stanley Grimshaw.

Born 1898. Joined Army at age of 18. On return from service Palestine and Syria, founded Westminster Advertising Co., handling slides, films, curtains, etc. Still chairman of this and Westminster Screen Rights, Ltd. Joined kinema trade proper in 1931 taking over control of Carlton, Liverpool. Now controlling circuit of 12 Halls, and adding more, all in Liverpool and district. Vice-chairman of N.W. Branch C.E.A. Elected to General Council this year. *Addresses :*—Carlton Villa, Dee Banks, Chester, and Prince of Wales, Clayton Square, Liverpool. *Phones :* Chester 883 and Liverpool Royal 6290-1.

I. R. Grove, J.P.

Born 1892. Left electrical business in 1911, to enter film trade. Joined Navy at outbreak of war, and served until 1919, assisting the Fleet Cinema Commission and being responsible for the film and theatrical shows aboard ship. Conducted kinematograph performances for the Allied Fleet Commission of Kiel, *H.M.S. Hercules*, in 1918. Became proprietor of Kinema House, Uphall, in 1920. Formed first specialised Film Transport Company in Scotland in 1921, and now Managing Director of Film Transport Services (Broxburn) Ltd., Film Transport Services (Cardiff), Ltd., Film Transport Services (North Western), Ltd., Film Transport Services (North and South), Ltd.,, and F.T.S. (Great Britain), Ltd., handling transport of films for over 2,000 theatres, with depots covering the country from Aberdeen to Exeter. Managing Director of Star Theatre (Armadale), Ltd., Star Theatre (Bathgate), Ltd., Star Theatre (Lochore), Ltd., and Star Theatre, Bo'ness. Director of the Grand Picture House, Cambridge Theatre, Uphall, and Astoria Cinema, Glasgow, and Director of Picture House, Arbroath. J.P. for West Lothian 1930. Appointed to Conciliation Board for the Road Transport Industry for Scotland, August 1934. *Address :*—Kilpunt House, Broxburn. *Phone :* Broxburn 42.

William Arthur Guy.

Director Cinema Traders, Ltd.

Born 1890. Entered business life with a firm of brewers 1904-14, then educated by H.M.S. to War conditions 1914-1919, 1919 engaged by Cinema Traders, Ltd., as book-keeper. 1921, became Secretary of the Company. 1926, joined Board of Directors. On death of W. Engelke, in 1936, appointed managing director with sole control of company. *Addresses :*—86, Surbiton Road, Kingston-on-Thames, and 26, Church Street, W.1. *Phones :*—Kingston 4408, and Gerrard 5287-8.

Julius Hagen.

Born 1884. At the age of eighteen went into partnership with Leon M. Lion in various plays. Afterwards joined Fred Terry and Julia Neilson. He left the stage to enter the film business, joining Ruffells'. From there he was engaged by Essanay Company to break down the boycott which existed all over the United Kingdom on the Chaplin Films. From this company he joined Stoll's and afterwards left to join Universal as London manager. He was instrumental with J. B. Williams in forming the W.P. Film Company and in 1928 formed the Strand Film Co., Ltd. Chairman and managing director, Twickenham Film Studios, Ltd., and J. H. Productions, Ltd. *Address :* 111, Wardour Street, W.1. *Phone :* Gerrard 3421.

Alderman Edwin Haigh, J.P.

(*Ex-Chairman, Liverpool Branch, C.E.A.*).

Born in 1864, at Liverpool. Proprietor, director or managing director of many of the leading kinemas in the Merseyside area, including Tatler News Theatre; new Hope Hall Cinema, Ltd.; Futurist (Liverpool), Ltd.; Wallasey Cinema, Ltd. Also connected with many Billiard Halls and Roller Skating Rinks. Original founder and first Chairman of the C.E.A. in Liverpool, and is also an Alderman of the Liverpool City Council and a magistrate of the City of Liverpool. His son (Captain J. H. Haigh, M.C.) is the other partner in the firm of E. Haigh & Son. *Club :*—Liverpool Senior Conservative. *Address :*—"San Roque," Calderstones Park, and 30, Tarleton Street, Liverpool, 1. *Phone :*—Royal 1170.

H. Hales Dutton

Appointed publicity executive to Gaumont-British technical and educational subsidiaries July, 1933. Activities now embrace G.-B. Equipments, Ltd. ; G. B. Instructional, Ltd. ; British Acoustic Films, Ltd. ; "Gebescope" (sub-standard Films and projectors) section ; Baird Television, Ltd. *Club :*—Aldwych. *Addresses :*—Film House, Wardour Street, W.1, and 3, Donovan Court, S.W.10. *Phones :*—Regent 8080 and Kensington 8487.

Ralph Hanbury.

Ten years with the Stoll Film Company, rising from branch manager to general manager, holding latter position for five years and making several trips to the States for the Company. Joined the Welsh-Pearson Company on its inception as general manager, and after three years in this position, went to M-G-M for a short while as branch supervisor, leaving there to join Radio Pictures when that concern was inaugurated. Now chairman and managing director. *Address :*—Dean House, Dean Street, W.1. *Phones :* Gerrard 3201 and Perivale 4726:

Harry Hargreaves.

Born in 1865 at Clitheroe, Lancashire. Took over the management of the Albert Hall and Queen's Market, Morecambe, 1895, converted the Market into a kinema 1920, now called the Palladium. Ran his first picture 1900. Secretary and Treasurer, West Lancashire Branch, C.E.A., and delegate to the General Council. Hon. Secretary and Treasurer Morecambe Entertainment Proprietors and Managers Association. A well-known character in the kinema world. *Address :* —Ceair, South Avenue, South Road, Morecambe, Lancs. *Phone :* Morecambe 43.

Francis L. Harley.

Born 1895, at North Wales, Pennsylvania. Managing director, Fox Film Co., Ltd. Took B.A. degree at University of Pennsylvania and graduated in 1916. Entered United States Army; ambulance driver for two years on the French front. Spent a year in Poland with American Red Cross. From 1920 to 1925 Mediterranean manager of Washburn Crosby, flour millers, with offices in Constantinople, Athens and Alexandria. In 1926 entered the service of Fox Films and came to England. In 1927 was appointed assistant to the Fox Managing Director in Paris. In 1929 was appointed Near-Eastern manager with offices in Athens. In December, 1930, appointed managing director of Fox, in Brazil, at Rio de Janeiro. Returned to Paris as managing director of the French company in April, 1935. Appointed managing director of Fox Films, London, February, 1936. *Clubs :* American, Screen Golfing. Member of American Society. *Addresses :* 13, Berners Street, W.1 and 3, Hollycroft Avenue, N.W.3. *Phones :* Museum 5113 and Hampstead 2197.

Hugh V. Harraway.

Solicitor, K.R.S.

Admitted a solicitor of the Supreme Court in 1906, Mr. Harraway has always been closely identified with the film renting industry. He was instrumental in forming the Kinematograph Renters' Society of Great Britain and Ireland. Limited, and has since acted as its solicitor ; as also its predecessor, the Cinematograph Trade Protection Society. *Address :*—2, Field Court, Gray's Inn, W.C.1. *Phone :*—Chancery 8981.

Samuel Harris, F.A.I.

Born 1873. Educated Brighton College. Senior partner of Harris & Gillow. Fellow of the Auctioneers' Institute. Expert valuer and adviser in regard to kinema and theatrical properties for all the prominent firms in the industry since establishment of the business. Appointed valuer to various County Councils. *Clubs :*—Constitutional, Royal Motor Yacht and Royal Aero. *Address :*—80 & 82, Wardour Street, W.1. *Phone :*—Gerrard 2504.

Norman Hart.

Solicitor, C.E.A.

Norman Hart was born in Bradford and educated at the Grammar School and Denstone College. For some years he was connected with the manufacturing and merchandise of the Bradford trade, but eventually gave this up and went to Cambridge, where he represented his college at tennis, cricket and football during the three years he was residing there. Then taking a Law Degree he was articled in London, where he has since been in practice. Since being appointed solicitor to the C.E.A., he has dealt with a number of Trade cases. *Addresses :* —37, Pembroke Square, S.W.1, and Broadmead House, Panton Street, S.W.1. *Phone :*—Whitehall 6814.

Victor Hayes-Jones.

Born 1896. Started business career with Chappell and Co., Ltd. Entered the profession as a tenor vocalist in 1919, giving recitals at Steinway Hall and leading London and Provincial concerts. After one year in business in West Africa was appointed and held the position for five years as assistant to the Director of Music for P.C.T. Associated with the Christie Unit Organ as Sales Manager until November, 1935, when he joined Wurlitzer. Also Director of Wardour Musical and Variety Bureau, Ltd. *Address :*—52, Kings End, Ruislip. *Phone :* Ruislip 2702.

H. E. Hayward.

Joined the exhibiting side in 1920. Managing Director of the New Royalty Kinema, Brixton ; and later Managing Director of the Rivoli, Southend. In 1924 commenced film renting, produced a number of educational and interest films. Many years member of Executive Committee C.E.A., London Branch, and on the Technical Committee. *Address :*—106, King's Avenue, S.W.4. *Phone :*—Tulse Hill 3904.

Charles F. T. Heath.

Left Fleet Street 1913 to join B. and C. as publicity chief. Then with Pathé's camera staff 1917-1918. Official kinematographer to the American Red Cross in England during the War. Nine years News Editor *Topical Budget,* then managing director of Studio Sound Service, Ltd., 89, Wardour Street ; photographed and directed the series " The Nation's Heritage " in collaboration with the National Trust. Managing Director of Barnes-Heath & Co., Ltd., 89, Wardour Street (sound equipment). *Address :* —89-91, Wardour Street, W.1. *Phone :* Gerrard 6747.

Edward Thomas Heron, J.P.

Founder and Secretary, Anima Lodge.

E. T. Heron has been responsible for the founding of eight Freemasons' Lodges, including the Anima Lodge, of which he was the first Worshipful Master. Born in 1867, he was educated at the Haberdashers' School. He is an ex-alderman of the Borough of St. Pancras, and was mayor in 1908-9. He is the founder of the *Kinematograph Weekly* and other Trade journals, and of E. T. Heron and Co., Ltd., printers and publishers, of Silver End and London, managing director Maxclif Publishing Co., Ltd. Chairman South Coast Properties (Hastings and St. Leonards), Ltd., Chairman Melina Estates, Ltd. Proprietor of St. Leonards golf course and tennis courts. *Address :*—" Silver End," St. Leonards-on-Sea.

Graham Scott Hewett, D.S.C.

Born 1889. International Cinematograph Corporation, 1912. International Productions, 1930. Three years' naval service. Awarded D.S.C. in *Vindictive* at Zeebrugge. On Council of K.R.S. Has distributed nearly 2,000 British and foreign films in the United Kingdom, and supervised many notable productions, including " Tommy Atkins " (in 1914), " When Fleet Meets Fleet," " Interviewing Wild Animals," " Twenty Years After " (The British Legion film, with H.R.H. the Prince of Wales), etc. Arranged first public demonstration Television, Coliseum, London. *Clubs :* Royal Corinthian Yacht, and The Ice. *Addresses :* " Westover," Derby Road, Sutton, Surrey ; and 101, Wardour Street, W.1. *Phone :* Gerrard 3131, and Sutton 1109.

Frank Hill, F.O.I.S.
Secretary, K.R.S.

Born 1887. In 1912 elected an Associate of the Chartered Institute of Secretaries and Fellow in 1928. In 1913 he became Secretary of the Telephone Development Company (1912), Ltd.; and had charge of the affairs of the Constantinople Telephone Company. During this period also a large proportion of the work in liquidating the National Telephone Company, Ltd., devolved upon him. From 1915 to 1918 he was general manager and secretary of the Performing Right Society, Ltd. He was appointed secretary of the K.R.S. in January, 1919. *Address :—* "Heathcote," Pangbourne.

Edward J. Hinge.

Born 1888, Faversham, Kent. Intended for scholastic profession. Became a concert artist in 1907, and also toured for several years in repertory. Joined the late Stanley Rogers as manager in 1913, appointed general manager of Stanley Rogers Cinemas in 1922, and on its conversion to a limited company in 1931 was appointed managing director. Also is managing director of Hinge's Cinemas, Ltd., and other companies. Now controls the largest independant circuit of kinemas in the North East. Has held office of chairman of the Northern Branch of the C.E.A. for two periods. Member of the General Council. *Address :—*72 Grey Street, Newcastle-upon-Tyne, 1. *Phone :* Newcastle 20317-8. *'Grams :* Hinge, Newcastle-upon-Tyne.

Abe Hollander.

Born at Leicester in 1883, Abe Hollander was educated at the Nottingham University. He has been Managing Director of Special Productions, Ltd.; the Futurist, Manchester ; the Whitehall, Derby ; the Globe, Cheetham ; the Queen's, Hollinwood ; the Scala, Hyde ; the Alexandra, Hyde ; and at the same time was a Director of the Scala Middlesbrough, and Futurist and Scala, Birmingham. He was owner of the Scala, Brighton, and Chairman of Keycities, Ltd., controlling a number of films, and the Gaiety Theatre, Manchester. In 1913 he was partner with Sol Levy in Midland Film Co., together with Sol Levy and Alfred Leslie built the Scala and Futurist, Birmingham. In 1914 head traveller for Sun exclusives, later becoming manager for eight counties. Specialises in launching gigantic supers, and put out, in England originally, "Birth of a Nation," "Hearts of the World," and "Intolerance." *Clubs :—*Central Birmingham, Derby County, Manchester Kinema Club and the Stadium, London. *Address :—*"St. Malo," Queenscourt, Wembley, Middx. *Phone :—*Wembley 2746.

C. E. Hodges.

Managing director, Community Service, Ltd., 1921-1934. From 1925-1929 "Uncle Peter" of B.B.C. Director of C. E. Hodges Productions for writing, directing and, supplying commentaries for travel and technical films. *Address :—* Bedford Row Chambers, 42, Theobalds Road, W.C.1. *Phone :* Holborn 7738.

S. H. Hope.

General Manager, Rex Publicity Service, Ltd. Born 1898. Educated King Edward VI's School, Birmingham. Stage and screen career commenced after the War. Later general manager, Futurist, Liverpool. Joined Savoy Cinemas, Ltd., subsequently appointed publicity manager A.B.C., Ltd. Transferred to Rex Publicity Service, Ltd., as general manager, in 1919 ; director Associated Studios, Ltd. *Club :—* Publicity Club of London. *Addresses :—*31, Golden Square, W.1, and Woodlands, Bourne Road, Bushey, Herts. *Phones :* Gerrard 3445 and Bushey Heath 179.

John A. Houston, J.P.
[Secretary Scottish Branch of the C.E.A.]

Besides being the very active Secretary of the Scottish Branch of the C.E.A., he is also Secretary for a few picture houses in Scotland. A partner of the well-known chartered accountancy firm of Turner and Houston, he has done much to further the interests of the kinema Trade in Scotland. Has done good work for the Benevolent Fund in the capacity of secretary of that organisation. Justice of the Peace for the City of Glasgow. *Address :—*90, Mitchell Street, Glasgow, C.1.

Alex. Howie.

Born in Lanarkshire. Entered film business as an exhibitor in 1919. Past member of executive committee of Scottish Branch and General Council C.E.A. Past president Cinema Club (Glasgow). Managing director of Rex Publicity Service, Ltd., 31, Golden Square, London, W., and 95, Renfield Street, Glasgow, and Associated Studios Ltd. (Art Display Service), London, Birmingham and Manchester. *Clubs :—*Royal Scottish Automobile, Aldwych, Coombe Hill Golf Club, Screen Golfing Society. *Address :—* 92, Lancaster Gate, London, W. *Phone :* Paddington 2251.

A. Hubrich.

Born 1886. Educated in Austria and Hungary. Joined the Trade in 1919 with the former Decla Company (Foreign Department) in Berlin. Represented Decla and later Ufa for several years in Holland. Represented Ufa in the United Kingdom from November, 1925, until December, 1927. Now associated with British International Pictures, Ltd. *Address :—*Film House, Wardour Street, W.1.

J. G. Hughes-Roberts, M.V.O.

Born 1894. Entered H.M. Stationery Office 1913. War service 1917-1919. Government Kinematograph Adviser since May, 1934. *Address :—* H.M. Stationery Office, S.W.1. *Phone :* Whitehall 4343.

Norman J. Hulbert, M.P.

Born 1903. Managing Director and Chairman of Capital and Provincial News Theatres, Ltd. Member of the London County Council (East Islington). National Conservative Member of Parliament for Stockport. *Clubs :—*Junior Carlton, Brooklands Automobile Racing. *Addresses :* —17, Victoria Square, S.W.1, and 172, Buckingham Palace Road, S.W.1. *Phone :* Sloane 6424.

W. J. Hutchinson.

Born in 1892. Mr. Hutchinson entered the kinematograph industry fourteen years ago. In the course of his experience he has carried on Fox business in many countries. Appointed General Foreign Manager 20th Century-Fox in December, 1935.

Frederick William Ingram.

Entered the Trade in 1910 as manager of Selig Polyscope, after spending about two years in Canada, ranching, and four in the United States in the lumber industry. After demobilisation joined Ideal, appointed branch manager 1921, sales manager 1925, and later general sales manager of Gaumont Ideal, Ltd. Resigned from G.-B. Distributors July 1936 to become managing director of Liberty Films, Ltd. *Addresses :* 4, Golden Square, W.1 and 7, The Highway, Sutton, Surrey. *Phones :* Gerrard 1204 and Sutton 2371.

Sam Jay.

Born 1888, Birmingham. Educated Saltley College ; and first business experience gained in the engineering profession ; is still director of Holyoake & Co., Ltd., Birmingham. First came into the industry as director of Broadmead Cinemas, Ltd., and is now also director of Minehead Entertainments, Ltd. *Address :* —62, Oxford Street, W.1. *Phone :*—Museum 5189.

W. W. Jay.

Born 1892. Entered Film business in 1910 with African Films Trust, Ltd., Johannesburg. Returned to this country after the war. Yorkshire representative for Phillips Films Co., Ltd. From 1921 to 1926 branch manager, Fox Film Co., Leeds. 1926-1930 branch manager, Film Booking Offices, Ltd., Liverpool. Joined Radio Pictures as Liverpool branch manager, August 1930. Appointed assistant sales manager, head office, Radio Pictures, 1931. Appointed general sales manager, November 1935. *Addresses :* 11, Georgian Court, Hendon, N.W.4, and Dean House, Dean Street, W.1. *Phones :* Hendon 6058 and Gerrard 3201.

Stuart M. Johnston.

Joined Cinema House, Ltd., in 1911 as manager of Burslem Cinema, Staffs. Served in P.C.T. under F. E. Adams. Joined R.C.A. Photophone, Ltd., as district manager for Scotland in 1930. Now Sales Manager of the organisation. *Addresses :*—32, Egerton Gardens, West Ealing, W.13, and Electra House, Victoria Embankment, W.C.2. *Phone :*—Temple Bar 2971.

Horace Judge, B.A., Int. B.Sc. (Lond.).

Manager in U.S.A. for Charles Dillingham and George C. Tyler with George Arliss, Elsie Janis and Fritzi Scheff, and other leading stars. Assistant advertising manager Universal (U.S.A.) and First National Pictures, Inc. (U.S.A.), Manager of Publicity and Advertising First National Pictures, Ltd., 1923-1928. Member of the Board of Directors, 1924-1929 ; general manager in France for French Phototone, Ltd., 1929 ; Director, Fulvue Film, Ltd., 1930-32. In 1933 appointed publicity manager, A.B.F.D., Ltd. *Address :*—Park Cottage, Manor Way, Beckenham, Kent. *Phone :*—Beckenham 0244.

Sir William Jury.

Born in 1870. Sir William Jury is one of the oldest members of the Trade, with widespread interests in every branch. He was prominently identified with the Trade Ambulance Fund and is also keenly interested in the Trade Benevolent Fund. During the war Sir William was the organiser of the supply of films to the Western Front, Italy, Salonica, Mesopotamia, Egypt and Palestine, whilst he also rendered considerable help in connection with the War Loan and in organising war charities. These various services were recognised in 1918, when he was created a knight. Managing Director of Jury-Metro-Goldwyn, Ltd., 1924 to 1927. Presented "Glebelands," as convalescent home to the Cinematograph Trade Benevolent Fund, November, 1935. *Address :*—Sherwood House, Reading.

Theodore Kanssen.

Born 1898. Came to London in 1934 and joined the Trade after having been interested in the trade abroad. Promoter of Twentieth Century Cinemas, Ltd., which was formed in December 1935, with a share capital of £240,000. Managing director of Twentieth Century Cinemas, Ltd.; Metropolitan and Provincial Cinematograph Theatres, Ltd.'; and Eldorado Cinemas, Ltd. Chairman of Eldorado Cinema (Clacton-on-Sea), Ltd., and Anglo-Continental Picture Playhouses, Ltd. *Addresses :*—7, Park Mansions, Knightsbridge, S.W.1, and Brettenham House, Lancaster Place, W.C.2. *Phones :* Kensington 7344 and Temple Bar 1144.

Michael Neville Kearney.

Head of the Film Industries Department of the F.B.I. and Secretary of the Film Producers' Group.

Born in Co. Durham, 1885. Educated in England and on the Continent. After a brief commercial career, was employed on H.M.'s Consulate-General at Antwerp, transferred to the Foreign Office in April, 1915, and later appointed Commercial Secretary at Brussels. Was secretary of the Inter-Allied Commission for the Economic Reconstruction of Belgium and director of that Commission in Brussels from the Armistice until its work was completed. On retiring from the Government Service in 1920 controlled a financial corporation in the City and later acted as financial adviser to certain industrial firms. Joined the Federation of British Industries in 1929, and was in charge of the Contracts, Company Law and Film Industries Departments. Represented the interests of the British Film Production Industry at Ottawa during the Imperial Economic Conference, 1932, and on other occasions. Member of jury, International Film Festival, Venice, 1936. *Address :* —21, Tothill Street, S.W.1. *Phone :* Whitehall 6711.

Clifford Kemp.

Commenced in exhibiting side, at Hippodrome, Wakefield, with Bennett & Tolfree, 1911. Entered renting with Chas. P. Metcalfe, 1916. Joined Paramount 1919, resigned appointment 1928. During that time held leading sales position for U.K. on more than one occasion. Joined Universal, in London. Later relinquished that position to open up Tiffany Productions for the North from Leeds and Newcastle centre. Has been independent renter since 1931. *Address :*—91, The Headrow, Leeds. *Phone :*—27702.

Cecil Kershaw, F.Inst.P.

Born 1884. Man. Dir. of Soho, Ltd., formerly Amalgamated Photographic Manufacturers, Ltd., 3, Soho Square, London, W.1. Proprietors of A. Kershaw and Son, Leeds. Manufacturers of Kalee Projectors and Accessories, and other scientific, optical and precision engineering work. *Addresses :*—3, Soho Square, W.1 ; 200, Harehills Lane, Leeds, and "Glenroyd," Park Lane, Roundhay, Leeds.

H. F. Kessler-Howes.

Born Stockton-on-Tees. Joined Industry through Jasper Redfern, 1904, migrated in 1906 to Albany Ward for 16 years. Afterwards ran own circuit. In recent years with Goldwyn, First National, F.B.O., Ltd., and personal representative for Eric Hakim. In 1933 joined the newly formed Columbia Pictures Corporation, Ltd., as director of publicity and advertising. *Address :*—139, Wardour Street, W.1. *Phone :*—Gerrard 4321.

Paul Kimberley, O.B.E., A.R.P.S.

Born Langley, near Birmingham. Assistant Manager to Church Army Lantern Dept., 1905; joined Frank Brockliss 1909; founded Imperial Film Co., June, 1913; supervised production of "Ivanhoe," the biggest British production of that time. Became associated with Hepworth Picture Plays, 1917; appointed director, sales and distribution manager. Managing director, Hepworth Film Service, Ltd., until 1924. Now managing director National Screen Service, Ltd. Hon. Treasurer B.K.S. In 1916 founded scheme for training disabled ex-Service men as operators, afterwards taken over by the National Kinema Trades Advisory Committee; appointed technical adviser to Committee. *Address:*— 1, Pierrepoint Road, Acton, W., and Broadwick House, Broad Street, Wardour Street, W.1. *Phone:*—Gerrard 4851.

Alex B. King.

Born 1888. Has been in the business since the age of 12. Member C.E.A. General Council and Cinematograph Films Advisory Committee. As chairman of the Entertainment Tax Committee of the C.E.A. was instrumental in securing remission in seats up to 6d. in the 1935 Budget. *Clubs:*—Gleneagles, Turnberry, Western Gailes Screen Golfing Society. *Addresses:*—167, Bath Street, Glasgow, C.2., and "Coniston," 6, Carlaverock Road, Newlands, Glasgow. *Phones:* Glasgow, Douglas 1195, and Langside 366.

J. Scott Knight.

Chairman, Knight and Co. (Engineers), Ltd.

Born 1878. Educated Liverpool Institute. Technical training, Experimental Workshops, Liverpool University. Kinephotographic experience in development in crossed hayrake days. Accidentally entered theatre engineering in 1920. Thought there was a field for first-class engineering on original lines and has found a sufficient number of progressive owners, prominent architects and enlightened consulting engineers to have changed thinking into conviction. Responsible for the largest orchestra lift, the first revolving console lift, the first electrically hauled and hydraulically lowered fire curtain and first completely mechanised stage in this country. *Address:*—Winchmore Works, Chase Road, Southgate, London, N.14.

Alexander Korda.

Before entering the industry was a European journalist. His first films were made for Continental companies, including Ufa. He then went to Hollywood and made numerous successful films, including the witty "Private Life of Helen of Troy." On his return to Europe he made pictures for Paramount French organisation and then came to England and made his first British film, "Service for Ladies," followed by "Wedding Rehearsal," "The Girl from Maxim's," "The Private Life of Henry VIII," "Catherine the Great," "Don Juan," "Scarlet Pimpernel," "Sanders of the River," "The Ghost Goes West," "The Shape of Things to Come," and "The Man who could work Miracles." He is Managing Director of London Film Productions, Ltd. *Address:*—Denham Studios, Uxbridge, Middlesex. *Phone:* Denham 2345.

John Lambert.

First entered the business in association with the late Henry Hibbert at Bradford. Founded the Wellington Film Service at Leeds. Now is managing director of the Central Cinema, Harrogate; Regal, Shipton, Ltd.; New Gallery, Ltd., Leeds; Regal, Ecclesbill, Bradford; Modern Theatres, Ltd., Leeds; Cinemas, Leeds and Bolton, Ltd., etc. Deputy Lord Mayor Leeds, 1927-8. He was the founder and first chairman of directors, Yorkshire Kinema Exchange. *Clubs:*—Leeds and County and Yorkshire Cinema. *Address:*—Lynwood, Park Villas, Roundhay, Leeds. *Phone:* Leeds 61238.

Frank Lane.

Actively associated with the industry for over 17 years, covering import, export, production, editing, renting and exhibiting. Formerly director and secretary of Screen-Art, Ltd; Federated Film Enterprises, Ltd; director of Folkestone Amalgamated Cinemas, Ltd., controlling the Central and Playhouse Picture Theatres, Folkestone; is joint managing director of Renters, Ltd.; L. & B. Cinemas, Ltd.; managing director of Wallis Products, Ltd; Cinema Theatre Exhibitor, etc. *Addresses* —6, Denman Street, W.1, and 8, Hayes Crescent, Golders Green, N.W.11. *Phones:* Gerrard 6777, Speedwell 6949, and Sevenoaks 1303.

Henry B. Lane.

Was for 39 years in the printing trade in Birmingham, became director of Stirchley Empire in 1914, later director of Dudley Road Picture House and the Heath Picture House, becoming managing director of the latter in 1919; director of the Coronet Cinema (Small Heath) Ltd., which company owns the Coronet, Grange and Kingston Kinemas; assisted in promotion and building of the Beaufort, Washwood Heath, in 1929, of which company is now chairman of directors; director of the Regalia Cinema Co., which owns the Rock Cinema, Saltley. Past Chairman of the Birmingham Branch of the C.E.A. and delegate to the General Council. *Address:*—106, Linden Road, Bournville, Birmingham. *Phone:*—King's Norton 1706.

W. L. de S. Lennox.

Clement Blake and Day.

Founded, and now the sole proprietor of the business of Clement Blake and Day, one of the oldest established firms engaged in the sale of kinemas and theatres; authority on kinema values; and the purchasing agent of many of the leading circuits. *Address:*—Lennox House, 22, Wardour Street, W.1.

Charles Leven, M.I.E.E., F.R.S.A.

Born 1864. Has had a unique experience in the electrical trade both in England and the U.S.A., extending over a period of 50 years. Connected with the industry since its infancy. *Clubs:*—Devonshire and R.A.C. *Address:*— 6, Abbey Road Mansions, N.W.8. *Phone:* Maida Vale 3139.

Ernest Levy.

Entered the Trade in Glasgow in 1912, and has been associated with P. Levy and Co. since 1914. He covers the whole of Ireland on behalf of the firm. *Private Address:*—314, Antrim Road, Belfast.

Henry Levy.

Entered the Trade in 1914 in conjunction with Sol Exclusives, Birmingham. Opened offices in Belfast and Dublin. Now acting as sole Irish Agent for the leading independent renters, in conjunction with his son, Ernest Levy. Brother of the late Sol Levy, Birmingham, and Alf Levy, Liverpool. Vice President of Belfast Chess Club. *Private Address:*—314, Antrim Road, Belfast.

L. A. Lewis.
Publicity Manager, Gaumont-British Distributors, Ltd.
After a specialised training in advertising, joined the old Gaumont Co. Following the 1914-1918 "interruption," became first assistant in the Gaumont Publicity Department. Appointed publicity manager in May, 1931, and subsequently occupied the same position with the Gaumont-Ideal Co., March, 1932. Remained until merger into Gaumont-British Distributors, Ltd. Appointed to present position September, 1935. *Address :*—5–6, Cork Street, W.1. *Phone:* Regent 8080.

Norman Loudon.
Born Campbeltown, Scotland, 1902. Started business as an accountant; was independent merchant in Germany 1922-24; managing director, Camerascopes, Ltd., 1925; rotary printing, 1927; managing director Flicker Productions, Ltd., 1930; entered film industry 1932. Purchased Littleton Park, Shepperton. Chairman and Managing Director Littleton Park (Holdings) Ltd.; Sound City (Films) Ltd. *Address :*—Littleton Park, Shepperton, Middlesex. *Phone :*—Chertsey 290.

Edward F. Lyons.
Born 1895. In 1915 founded E. A. Langrish & Co., which in conjunction with Kershaws, formed Kalee, Ltd. in 1934. Is managing director of this company. *Addresses :*—Seadown, Hove, Sussex, and National House. Wardour Street, W.1. *Phone :*—Gerrard 5137.

I. I. Lyons.
Born in 1874, Mr. Lyons entered the Trade in 1912, and has taken an important part in its development in the Birmingham area. He has been chairman of the Birmingham and Midland branch of the C.E.A., 1926 and 1927. *Address :*—21, Calthorpe Road, Edgbaston, Birmingham.

F. G. H. MacRae.
Educated at Beccles College and Polytechnic School of Engineering. After four years in electrical generating stations entered entertainment world, becoming chief engineer of the Stoll Empires. After 5 years as engineer in Indian Ordnance Dept. returned in 1924 and was appointed technical adviser to Stoll P.T., Kingsway, where he demonstrated application of colour lighting in relation to stage presentation. Recognised as authority and writer on the subject of light and colour. Now at Theatre Royal, Drury Lane. *Phone :*—Temple Bar 8182.

Moss Mansell.
Born London 1883. Apprenticed to electrical engineering 1898. Started in business on own account 1903. Proprietor of one of the first kinemas in West London 1909. One of the earliest makers of Arc Lamp Resistances and Dimmers for kinemas. Inventor of several useful electrical devices, the latest being for the control of dimmers by magnetic clutches as installed at Royal Opera House, Covent Garden, which has made possible the Console and Chromolux Controls marketed by the Strand Electric and Engineering Co., Ltd. Director of that Company, Strand and Interchangeable Signs, Ltd., and Mansell and Ogan, Ltd. from 1918-1936. Now acting as consultant only. *Address :*—"Selworthy," Strawberry Vale, Twickenham. *Phone :*—Popesgrove 2424.

J. B. McDowell, O.B.E., M.C.
Apprenticed to the engineering trade in 1893. In 1898 joined the British Mutoscope and Biograph Syndicate from 1906-9; chief cameraman to Walturdaw and W. G. Barker

Warwick Trading Company, founded the British & Colonial Kinematograph Co., 1909, in conjunction with the late A. H. Bloomfield. Managing Director 1909-1918. In 1916 appointed official War Office Kinematographer on the Western Front. With Agfa Kine Film Department 1926-1936. *Address :*—Bonne Esperance Gordon Avenue, Pitsea, Essex.

Robert McLaughlin.
Born 1898 Qualified Chartered Accountant in 1923, and joined Caley Picture House Company as Secretary same year. Now a Director as well as General Manager and Booking Manager for that company. Director, Cinema Properties, Ltd., and Cinema Holdings (Kirkcaldy), Ltd. President of the Scottish Branch of the C.E.A., 1934. *Address :*—8, Abercorn Crescent, and 7, North St. Andrew Street, Edinburgh. *Phone :* 27361.

Margaret Marshall.
After editorial experience joined the publicity department of W. & F. in 1924. Press manager for some years, appointed press manager for Gaumont British Distribution, Ltd., October 1933; in 1934 joined Twickenham Film Studios in similar capacity. *Addresses :*—111, Wardour Street, W.1, and 31, Compayne Gardens, N.W.6. *Phone :* Gerrard 3421.

John Maxwell.
President, K.R.S.
Entered the film business in 1912 as an exhibitor. Was formerly a solicitor in Scotland. Later he became actively interested in Wardour Films, Ltd., and as Chairman of that company did much to make it the foremost independent renting house in the trade. Next he turned his attention to film production and was the moving light in the creation of British International Pictures, Ltd., Chairman and Managing Director, Associated British Picture Corporation, Ltd., and Chairman, Madame Tussauds, Ltd. *Address :*—Film House, Wardour Street, W.1. *Phone :*—Regent 3272.

Charles P. Metcalfe.
Vice-President, C.E.A.
Born at West Hartlepool in 1883, C. P Metcalfe first entered the exhibiting business in 1909, and opened the first twice nightly picture hall in Leeds. He is Managing Director of the Mid. Yorkshire Entertainments, Ltd., North Eastern Entertainments, Ltd., the Harrogate Theatre Co., Ltd., and a director of Tees Entertainments, Ltd. and European Theatres, Ltd. Chairman Leeds C.E.A. branch and General Councillor; member Board of Trade Advisory Committee. *Addresses :*—16, Lidget Park Road, Roundhay, Leeds, and 54, Merrion Street, Leeds. *Phone :* 61631, and 25008 Leeds.

Francis Meynell.
Born 1891. News Editor and director *Daily Herald* 1922. Founded Nonesuch Press (of which still a director) 1923. Associated with London Press Exchange 1932-3. Feature writer *News Chronicle* 1934. Director of Publicity, United Artists 1935. Chief of Publicity and Advertising Gaumont-British Corporation, and all associated companies, 1936. Author of book and many articles on theory and practice of advertising. Contributor to *Times* Encyclopaedia Britannica, etc. Editor "The Week-End Book" and other less popular works. *Clubs :*—Sainstsbury and Savile. *Addresses :*—5, Cork Street, W.1 ; 39, Woburn Square, W.C.1 and Toppesfield, Essex. *Phones :*—Regent 8080, Museum 0695 and Great Yeldham 28.

Max Milder.

Managing Director Warner Bros. Pictures, Ltd.
Twenty-six years in the trade, now nearly five in England. *Addresses :*—52, Berkeley Court, Baker Street, N.W.1., and Warner House, Wardour Street, W.1. *Phone:*—Gerrard 5600.

Harold B. Millar.

Born 1902, marine engineer, orchestral management for 10 years, late proprietor of Princes Cinema, Brighton. Pioneer exhibitor of Continental and unusual films. Past vice-chairman, C.E.A. (Sussex Branch). Managing director of Rallim Theatres, Ltd., Phono-disc, Ltd. and The World Window, Ltd. *Address :* 79, Dyke Road, Brighton.

George Bernard Morgan.

Born 1894. Educated Ellesmere. Studied Birmingham Law Society. Admitted Solicitor 1922, with Honours and Birmingham Law Society's Medal. Captain, R.F.A. Served France and Belgium from January 1915 until Armistice. Practising solicitor at 32, St. James's Street, S.W.1. Previously chairman of Reunion Films, Ltd., now chairman and managing director National Provincial Film Distributors, Ltd. and Morgan Productions, Ltd. and also a director of other production units. Recent productions : "Live Again," "Such is Life," "The Mill on the Floss," etc. *Club :*—Junior United Service Club. *Addresses :*—"Ashleigh Grange," Haywards Heath, Sussex, and 32, St. James's Street, S.W.1. *Phone :* Whitehall 8501.

William M. Morgan.

Born 1878. Has operated lanterns since 15 years old and entered the kinema business in 1903 as one of the early operators. Joined London Cinematograph Co., Ltd. in 1908 and afterwards with the Co-operative Film Co., Ltd. ; Butchers Film Service as assistant manager. Joined Jury's Pictures, Ltd., as manager of B Department in 1910 and in 1913 entered partnership with A. E. Major and was known as the Excelsior Motion Picture Co. until the death of his partner Mr. Major. Commenced business as the proprietor of Cine Requirements in 1922. Served in R.A.S.C. 1915-1919. Prominent in hospital charity work. Councillor, Lambeth 1916-19 and Holborn since 1931. *Clubs :*—Holborn Stadium and Bartholomew Club, City of London. *Address :*—203, Shaftesbury Avenue, W.C. *Phone :* Temple Bar 4292.

E. C. Morris.

Entered Industry 1909. Many years' experience of renting and exhibiting. Patentee of the Morris Dividing Kinema screen. General Manager, Scala, Nottingham. *Club :*—Constitutional. *Address :*—Manor House, Gregory Street, Lenton, Nottingham, and Scala, Market Street, Nottingham. *Phones :*—75727 and 3633.

W. Southan Morris.

Born 1897. Joined trade 1913. Served, throughout War 1914-19. Managing Director. Super Cinemas (Maidstone), Ltd. ; Joint Managing Director, Uxbridge Entertainments, Ltd.; Director, Slough Playhouse, Ltd., and Windsor Playhouse, Ltd., Yiewsley Playhouse, Ltd., Southan Morris Circuit, Ltd., Empire (Wolverton). Ltd. *Address :*—68, Wykeham Road, Hendon, N.W.4. *Phone :*—Hendon 6602.

Fred W. Morrison.

Delegate, Northern Branch, C.E.A.
Trustee to the C.E.A. and member of the General Council, F. W. Morrison is one of the six delegates of the Northern Branch. He was one of the original founders of an association of kinema exhibitors which was formed in Newcastle in the infancy days of the Industry, and he represented that district at the Birmingham Conference which gave birth to the C.E.A. Owns the Imperial Hall at Dunston-on-Tyne. Born in 1873, he began life as a newspaper boy in his native city, Newcastle-on-Tyne. *Club :*—Newcastle Rotary. *Address :*—"Greenbank," Dunston Hill, Dunston-on-Tyne. *Phone :* Dunston 84320.

M. C. Morton.

Born in London, 1900. Entered film trade January 1919, on leaving Army, with Ruffells Bioscope, as salesman at Cardiff branch. Opened Cardiff branch for Universal Pictures. Associated six years with Graham-Wilcox Productions. Formed his own independent renting company, Morton Lever & Co., Ltd. Was five years London branch manager of Radio Pictures, joining them at their inception and leaving to become general sales manager of Twickenham Film Distributors, Ltd. *Address :* 409 Endsleigh Court, W.C.1. *Phone :*—Euston 4994.

A. S. Moss.

Born 1893. Was manager, supervisor, area superintendent, assistant theatre controller for Gaumont-British and P.C.T. Kinema theatre controller for Moss Empires, eventually chief supervisor and general manager to A.B.C. Member of the executive committee of the London and Home Counties branch of the C.E.A., and delegate to the general council. *Addresses :* 30-31, Golden Square, W.1 and 3, Randolph Court, Maida Vale, W.9. *Phones :* Gerrard 7887 and Maida Vale 5455.

Archibald Nettlefold.

Head of Nettlefold Productions. *Address :*—Comedy Theatre, S.W.1.

Alfred Ernest Newbould.

Ex-President, C.E.A.
Born in 1873, and educated at Burton Grammar School. He is a director of Associated Provincial Picture Houses, Ltd., Albany Ward Theatres, Ltd., and chairman and managing director of Palmer Newbould & Co., Ltd. From 1914 until March of 1920 he was President of the C.E.A. and many useful Trade movements were initiated during his term of office. In March, 1919, he was elected M.P. for the West Leyton division of Essex by a very large majority, but lost his seat at the General Election in November, 1922. *Address :*—8, Selwood Place, S.W.7. *Club :*—Reform.

Kenneth A. Nyman, B.Sc.

Born 1899. Entered industry in 1924. Chairman of London and Home Counties C.E.A. branch. Director of kinema-owning companies, member of entertainment and scientific research panels of British Film Institute. *Address :*—10, Cork Street, W.1. *Phone :* Regent 4794.

Edwin Oram.

London Manager of Taylor, Taylor & Hobson, Ltd.
Trained as engineer and for some time taught machine drawing and design. Commenced with Taylor, Taylor & Hobson, Ltd., in 1918 after service in the army. Was made Sales Manager about 1925 and handled the distribution of their projection and photographic lenses and other optical equipment for the trade. Hon. Secretary of the B.K.S. and Member of the Society of Motion Picture Engineers. *Addresses :*—314, Regent Street, W.1, and 51, Lawrence Gardens, Mill Hill, N.W.7. *Phones :*—Langham 1260 and Mill Hill 2265.

Isidore Ostrer.

President, Gaumont-British Picture Corporation. Ltd., Chairman, Gaumont - British Distributors Ltd.
Was a member of the London Stock Exchange, afterwards a merchant banker; style of firm Ostrer Bros., 25-31, Moorgate, E.C.2. A prime factor in the creation of the Gaumont-British Picture Corporation, Ltd., and the development of Baird Television, Ltd. As president of the Corporation, Mr. Ostrer was determined from its inception to afford British production the finest possible facilities and this was realised when the Shepherd's Bush Studios were opened in June, 1932. *Address :*—Film House, Wardour Street, W.1. *Phone :*—Gerrard 9292.

Mark Ostrer.

Chairman and Managing Director, Gaumont British Picture Corporation, Ltd., and Gaumont British Distributors, Ltd.
Originally a merchant banker. With his brothers, Isidore and Maurice, took a financial interest in the Gaumont Co., Ltd., in 1922, and was active in the formation of the Gaumont-British Picture Corporation, Ltd., of which he is Chairman and Managing Director. He is also Chairman of P.C.T., Ltd. ; Denman Picture Houses, Ltd., and General Theatre Corporation, Ltd., Managing Director of Gaumont-British Distributors, Ltd., and a Director of Denman Street Trust Co., Ltd. and Moss Empire, Ltd. *Address :*—80, Portland Place, W.1.

Maurice Ostrer.

Born 1896. Was a merchant banker, style of firm, Ostrer Bros., 25-31, Moorgate E.C.2. With his brothers, Isidore and Mark became financially identified with the Gaumont Co., Ltd., in 1922. Subsequently became Chairman of International Acoustic Films, Ltd., British Acoustic Films, Ltd., and Referee (1931) Ltd. Is Assistant Managing Director of Gaumont-British Picture Corporation, Ltd.; Gaumont-British Distributors, Ltd.; P.C.T., Ltd.; General Theatre Corporation, Ltd.; Denman Picture Houses, Ltd. *Club :*—Sunningdale Golf. *Address :*—Film House, Wardour Street, W.1. *Phone :* Gerrard 9292.

Ambrose Palmer.

Experienced kinema decorator. Art student trained as decorator. Travelled a great deal throughout thirty years of experience, inventor of several new decoration effects and illuminations for kinemas and theatres. Well known in Cumberland public life as a town councillor and justice of the peace for the County. Assisted by his son, also a decorator. *Address :*—Pow Street, Workington. *'Phone:*—224.

R. Norman Parkinson.

Born Victoria, Australia. Has been associated with the carbon side of the industry since his arrival in England in 1928, when he joined Henrion Carbons, Ltd., as manager of the kinema carbon department. In 1935 was made manager and director of the above company, and in February, 1935, was also appointed to a directorship in Heath & Serena, Ltd. *Addresses :*—Dean House, Dean Street, London, W.1, and 44, Vicarage Court, Kensington, W.8. *Phones :*—Gerrard 5748-9 and Western 1856.

Gordon Parry.

Born Liverpool, July 1908. Educated in Scotland. Entered industry as assistant director. In 1932 joined Gaumont-British. Worked on 'I was a Spy,' "Jack Ahoy!" '' "Evergreen,"

"King of the Damned," all for G.-B. In 1935 joined Soskin Productions, Ltd., as production manager. *Address :*—Sackville House, 40, Piccadilly, W.1. *Phone :* Regent 2616.

E. W. Pashley Peall.

Born 1876. Mr. Peall was educated at Dulwich College. After a commercial career entered the Industry on the exhibiting side, and was one of the first members of the C.E.A. General Council. Was hon. sec. and later chairman of the London Branch. One of the three founders of the C.T.B.F. and is chairman of the Goodwin Memorial Fund. Now with Gaumont-British Picture Corpn., the Provincial Cinematograph Theatres and associated companies. *Club :*—Royal Automobile. *Private Address :*—9, Princes Square, Hove, Sussex.

John Pearson.

Entered the industry in 1913. General manager of the Vitagraph Co., Ltd., in 1914, and joined the executive of Warner Bros. Pictures Ltd., when that firm purchased Vitagraph in 1925. Vice-president K.R.S. in 1924 and 1925. *Address :*—11, Salisbury Road, Wimbledon, S.W.

Arthur Pereira, F.R.P.S., F.R.G.S.

Entered industry in 1908 inventing machinery and processes for Kinora Co. Later joined filming expeditions in Africa and India as photographer (West Africa, Timbuktu and Everest Expeditions, (1924). Was technical adviser to British Talking Pictures, Wembley, from commencement. Recently in India and the Far East, filming travel subjects, now with Dufaycolour, Ltd. *Address :*—Royal Photographic Society, 35, Russell Square, W.C.1.

Sam Phillips.

Born at Newport, Mon., entered the industry over 20 years ago, being first identified with the Gerrard Film Co. Leaving that concern, he became the London manager of the Clarion Film Co. which at that time was handling the World Films in this country. Subsequently London manager of the Fox Film Co., a post which he held for four years, and which he vacated to become a director and general manager of the W. & F. Film Service. Resigned these positions on the absorption of W. & F. by the Gaumont-British Corporation and was appointed general sales manager. Resigned this post and was appointed general manager of the Associated Producing and Distribution Co. in December 1936. *Club :*—Screen Golfing. *Addresses :*—"Omrah," Dunstan Road, Golders Green, N.W., and 193, Wardour Street, W.1. *Phone :*—Gerrard 4962.

Percy Phillipson.

Born in 1879. Before joining the Trade some 20 years ago was a Dramatic Elocutionist (Gold Medallist). Entered the Trade in 1909 on the exhibiting side in the capacity of manager. Early in 1914 joined Pathé Frères in charge of Exclusive Dept. 1919, transferred to Leeds as Yorkshire Branch manager. Early 1920, promoted to sales manager, resigned from that position in April of 1921 to take up the position of general sales manager with Associated First National Pictures, Ltd., and in 1923 was made a director of the Company. Managing director, Automaticket, Ltd., since September, 1926. *Addresses :*—"Bide-a-Wee," Cornwall Road, Cheam, and 197 Wardour Street, W.1. *Phone :* Gerrard 3483.

Joseph Pollard, J.P.
Ex-President C.E.A.

Born at Bradford, Yorks, in 1882. Resigned municipal appointment in 1907 to enter the kinema industry ; managing director kinema and variety theatres in Notts, Derby, and Yorks. He is delegate to C.E.A. General Council for Notts and Derby ; member of Mansfield Town Council and President of Mansfield Branch of Toc H. Member of Mansfield Town Council and Mayor, 1931-2. *Addresses :*—Bentinck Chambers, Market Place, Mansfield, and Oak Lea, Atkins Lane, Mansfield. *Phones :*— 760 and 422.

S. Presbury.

Born 1872. Commenced career with David Allen & Sons, Ltd. First established as the South West Billposting Co., and was a member of the early Billposters' Association. Was chairman of the first film advertising association, the Screen Advertising Association of G.B. & I. Pioneered in this field. Vice-Chairman Advertising and Industrial Film Association. Was on the first Council of the Advertising Association, and is still a member, also member of the London Chamber of Commerce and the F.B.I. Fellow of the Royal Economic Society. Member of the Metropolitan Water Board and London Old Age Pension Committee. Vice-president of the Lion Hospital Aid Society, and life governor of the Women's Hospital, South London. Now governing director of S. Presbury & Co., Ltd., with which is incorporated the Theatres Advertising Co., and governing director of Presbury (Printers) Ltd. and Presbury Properties, Ltd. *Clubs :*—National Liberal and Croham Hurst Golf. *Addresses :*—36, Thornton Avenue, S.W.2, and 87, Charing Cross Road, W.C.2. *Phone :* Gerrard 1347.

Herbert Charles Pride, M.B.E.

Corporate Member of the Institute of Illuminating Engineers, and Member of the London Chamber of Commerce, proprietor of the firm of F. H. Pride, 81, High Street, Clapham, S.W.4. Leading specialist in kinema lighting fitments. Joined the firm in 1897, which was founded by his father in 1878. Has been concentrating on kinema lighting for 28 years, commencing in the days of the Pyke Circuit, since when he has been associated with the decorative lighting of most of the principal kinemas in this country. Had the honour of carrying out important contracts in Marlborough House and Buckingham Palace. Has invented many useful patents connected with lighting fitments, his latest being combined lighting and heating electrolier, in the modern style. *Address :*— 67-81, High Street, Clapham, S.W.4. *Phone :* Macaulay 2281.

Fred. A. Prior.

Born 1888. Incorporated accountant and secretary of the Notts and Derby Branch of the C.E.A. since 1918. A member of the General Council of the C.E.A., 1924 and 1925. *Private Address :*—"Ralmar,"Melton Road, West Bridgford, Notts.

Maj. Henry Adam Procter, M.A., LL.B., M.P.
Chairman of Capitol Film Corporation, Ltd.

Born Liverpool, 1883. Left school at 12, served apprenticeship to engineering ; worked passage to U.S.A., and while employed as engineer continued college and university studies. Gained B.A. at Bethany College and won prize for oratory. Went to Australia, entered Melbourne University, and graduated M.A. 1914-1918 served in France with Aus-

tralian forces. Afterwards pursued research work Edinburgh University, graduating LL.B,. and passing into Ph.D. in political science. In 1920 was commissioned in 18th Brigade and was later attached to Royal Scots Regiment. Retired 1923 with rank of Major. Has since specialised in hydrogenation of coal and has invented several new coal processes. Elected M.P. for Accrington in 1931 and re-elected 1935. Became keenly interested in film production two years ago. Is now chairman of Capitol and also of Cecil Films, Ltd. President of the Film Artistes Association. *Address :*— 293, Regent Street, W.1. *Phone :*—Langham 1851.

Edmund Quarry.

Born 1895. Editorial staff, *Times* 1913, *Financial Times* 1916. Since war editor of trade journals ; publicity officer Advertising Association. Joined United Artists as Press publicity manager, January, 1935. Now publicity director United Artists. Author of "Dictionary of Musical Compositions" and much thriller fiction ; also of film scenarios. *Address :*—The Croft, Whitehall Lane, Egham, and Film House, Wardour Street, W.1. *Phone :* Gerrard 6301.

C. W. Rabbetts
Assistant Manager, Berkeley Electrical Engineering Co., Ltd.

Experience of kinema and theatre installation work dates from 1908, then lapse to gain practical electrical experience in various other branches of electrical industry. Joined Tredegars in 1911, when was associated with installations in several of the smaller halls up to outbreak of war. Re-entered the business after the war, joined Berkeley Electrical Engineering Co., Ltd., and one of the first jobs was the Tivoli, London. Since then has installed complete installations in upwards of 30 theatres, as chief engineer and assistant manager to his present firm. Responsible for the design and development of the Pre-set switchboard in this country. *Address :* Vincent House, Vincent Square, S.W.1. *Phone :*—Victoria 8986.

J. Arthur Rank, D.L., J.P.

Born 1889. Served in the R.A. from 1914-1918 returning with rank of Major. Managing Director, Joseph Rank, Ltd.; Chairman, British National Films, Ltd. ; Director, Pinewood Studios, Ltd.; and General Film Distributors, Ltd. *Clubs :*—Bath and Walton Heath. *Addresses :*—Heathfield, Reigate Heath, Surrey and Sutton Manor, Sutton Scotney, Hampshire.

Matt Raymond.

Matt Raymond, kinema pioneer of 1895, was born in 1874, and was educated at the Regent Street Polytechnic. He was appointed electrical engineer for the exhibition of the Lumiere Cinematograph, the first moving picture shown in London as a commercial proposition. Founder of the Raymond Animated Picture Co. (1905 to 1925). Ex-Treasurer of the C.E.A. *Private Address :*—Fig Tree House, Callis Court Road, Broadstairs.

George Rees.

Born in 1885. Educated for commercial career. Commenced in the kinematograph Industry in the early days. Some years with the " Tyler Apparatus Co., Ltd." Afterwards managing director of the Bristol Eureka Cinematograph Co., Ltd. Has had studio experience with Turner Films, Ltd., played with the late Albert Chevalier in " My Old Dutch."

One of the first members of the Bristol Branch of the C.E.A., and Secretary 1913 to 1915. Early in 1920 joined the head office staff of Albany Ward Theatres, Ltd., 1923. Now proprietor Regent Theatre, Truro, Regent Picture House, Highbridge; Partner Regent Picture House, Kingswood, Bristol, and director Keynsham Cinema Co., Ltd. Ex-Chairman of the Bristol and West of England Branch of the C.E.A. *Address :*—112, Brynland Avenue, Bishopston, Bristol.

F. F. Renwick, F.C.G.I., F.I.C. Hon. F.R.P.S.
Born 1877. Research director, Ilford, Ltd. *Address :*—Lone Oak, Gidea Park, Essex.

H. E. Reynolds.
Managing Director of Beacon Film Distributing Co., Ltd. Born 1894. Entered industry with Pathé Frères in Liverpool in 1913, occupying important positions at the various branches and resigned from position of London Branch Manager in 1928 to become General Sales Manager to British and Foreign Films, Ltd. Formed own company in July, 1932. *Address :* —12, D'Arblay Street, W.1. *Phone :*—Gerrard 2931.

Randolph E. Richards.
Ex-President, C.E.A.
Born 1885, and joined the entertainment industry at Cardiff in 1904, first at the Empire, later at Olympia. Later managed the Stoll Picture Theatre, Kingsway, and Stoll P.T., Newcastle. Now managing director Picturedrome, Eastbourne, Amusements (Eastbourne), Ltd. ; Gaiety (Hastings), Ltd. ; Gaiety, Bexhill, Ltd., Kinema Playhouses, Ltd., and Gaiety (Brighton), Ltd. Ex-chairman Sussex Branch C.E.A., and president C.E.A., 1931-2. *Address :*—Windermere, Seaside Road, Eastbourne. *Club:*—R.A.C.

H. Rogers.
Became assistant secretary to Film Booking Offices upon the conclusion of the war, after four-and-a-half years' service. Joined W. and F. as secretary in 1923, and became director in 1928. Was appointed secretary to Gainsborough Pictures in 1928, and in August, 1929, became secretary to the Gaumont Co. Resigned May, 1936, to become secretary, General Film Distributors, Ltd., Herbert Wilcox Productions, Ltd., and secretary and director, Universal Pictures, Ltd. *Address :*—127-133, Wardour Street, W.1. *Phone :* Gerrard 7311.

Paul Rotha.
Born 1907. Educated at London University (Slade School of Art). Painter and designer. Exhibited pictures in London and International Exhibitions on the Continent. Art director and literary critic to *Connoisseur.* Entered film industry in art department in 1928. Wrote "The Film Till Now" (Jonathan Cape) 1929, accepted universally as standard text book on subject. In 1930 worked at Empire Marketing Board in conjunction with John Grierson. Wrote "Celluloid—The Film To-day" (Longmans) 1931 ; produced first feature documentary film "Contact" for British Instructional Films, 1932. Produced "Rising Tide," "Shipyard," "Face of Britain," and "Death on the Road," 1933-1935—all documentaries, in association with Gaumont-British Instructional, Ltd. (Awards at Brussels and Venice Film festivals.) Wrote "Documentary Film" (Faber & Faber), 1936. Director of productions for the Strand Film Company, and has produced—"Cover to Cover," "Chapter and Verse," "The Way to the Sea," etc. Wrote pictorial survey of the

kinema, "Movie Parade" (Studio Ltd.). *Address :*—c/o Strand Film Co., Ltd., 37-39, Oxford Street, W.1. *Phone :* Gerrard 3122.

S. Rowson.
Born in Manchester 1877. Graduate M.Sc. in Physics and Mathematics (Honours), Guy Medallist in Silver of the Royal Statistical Society for contributions to Statistical Science. Formerly Statistician to Tariff Commission, and Economic Adviser to Unionist Party. First interested in Trade about 1910. Joint managing director Ideal Films, Ltd. ; director Gaumont-British Picture Corporation, Ltd., director Denman Picture Houses, Ltd., until 1933. President 1926-27, K.R.S., and member of Joint Trade Committee on British Films. Member of Board of Trade Advisory Committee under the Films Act 1927-1933. President British Kinematograph Society, Became joint-managing director Grosvenor Films, December, 1936. *Club :*— Constitutional. *Addresses :*—1, Fawley Road, N.W.6, and 87, Regent Street, W.1. *Phones :* Hampstead 3338 and Regent 3764.

Chas. Halderson Rundle.
Past Chairman, Devon and Cornwall Branch C.E.A.
An enthusiastic advocate of the organisation of the Industry and one of the best known figures in kinema circles of the South-West, C.H. Rundle was born in 1871 at Ridgway, Plympton, and educated at Plympton Grammar School and in Plymouth. He was instrumental in the formation of the Plymouth and District Entertainment Managers' Association. Out of this developed a Plymouth section of the Bristol Branch of the C.E.A., which his energy subsequently converted into an independent branch covering the whole of Devon and Cornwall. *Address :*—49, North Street, Plymouth.

J. Rowland Sales.
Entered amusement business by running concert parties and theatrical touring companies. Then joined George Foster's Theatrical and Variety Agency as booking representative. Founded J. Rowland Sales & Co., Theatrical, Variety and Concert Agency in King William Street, Strand. After naval service during the War founded The London Booking Office (Theatrical, Variety, Concert and Circus Agents). Managed the theatrical agency of Reeve & Russell, Ltd., and later controlled several theatres up and down the country and also managed West End theatres. Entered the kinema business and formed a circuit of halls. In 1932 created and managed the Cinema and Theatre Estates Department for Hampton & Sons, Ltd., and acted as Estates manager for Union Cinema Co., Ltd. Now personally directing the Cinema and Theatre Estates Department of Maple & Co., Ltd., *Addresses :*— 5, Grafton Street, Bond Street, W.1, and The Fernery, The Hythe, Staines, Middlesex. *Phones :*—Regent 4685 and Staines 197.

Lewin P. Samuel.
Born 1857. Set up in business for himself at Tunstall at the age of 19, afterwards taking up interests in the jewellery and pawnbroking trade. Foundation member and life member of the Council of the National Pawnbrokers' Association. In the kinema world he has long been a director of the Greater Scala, Birmingham, and has given many years' service to the local C.E.A. branch and the General Council. Untiring worker in the cause of charity and closely

associated with the kinema Hospital Sunday movement in Birmingham. Director, James Collins, Ltd., Brights (Aston) Ltd. *Address :—* 272; Pershore Road, Edgbaston. *Phone :* Calthorpe 0563.

Gerald Fountaine Sanger.
Producer of British Movietone News.
Born 1898. Educated Shrewsbury ; Royal Marines (1917-1919) and Keble College, Oxford. Secretary to Hon. Esmond Harmsworth (1922-1929). *Clubs :*—Windham ; *Address :*—13, Gerald Road, London, S.W.1. *Phone :* Sloane 6551.

Max Schach.
Director of Productions, Capitol Film Cor. Ltd., and associated companies.
Born 1890. Educated in Vienna, studied at Berlin University. Theatrical critic and editor of important Berlin dailies, head of scenario department of Ufa, started film production in 1922, became General Continental Manager for Universal. New York, later general manager of Emelka, Munich. Came to United Kingdom in 1934 and founded Capitol Film Productions, Ltd. *Address:*—293, Regent Street, W.1. *Phone:* Langham 1851.

Garé Schwartz.
Born 1891. Experience with motion picture laboratory in all its phases since 1905. General manager, Denham Laboratories Ltd., previously, Paramount Laboratories. Educated Morriss High School, Cooper Union Technical Institute and Technical High School, New York. *Address:* —Denham Laboratories, Denham, Middlesex, and Sheepcote Cottage, Denham, Bucks. *Phones :* Denham 214 and 2121.

Dixon Scott.
Born 1883. Commenced Trade career 1908 at Jarrow-on-Tyne with "The Kino." Owner Electric Theatre, Prudhoe-on-Tyne. Managing Director, Haymarket Theatre (Newcastle), Ltd.; managing director, News Theatre, Newcastle. *Clubs :*—English Speaking Union, Berkeley Square, W. *Private Address :*—39, Percy Gardens, Tynemouth.

George Urie Scott.
Recognised as one of the pioneers of the Industry. Began in 1908 as an exhibitor, and gradually acquired a circuit of seven theatres in Scotland. He disposed of these a few years ago, but still retains an active interest in the Industry, and is director of some halls. Managing Director Scott Theatres, Ltd ; managing director Anderston Pictures and Variety Theatres, Ltd. ; director West End Playhouse, Ltd. In addition to being past-president of the Cinema Club, Glasgow, he is past-president of the Scottish Branch of the C.E.A. *Address :*—154, West Regent Street, Glasgow.

Walter Scott.
Born 1879. First connected with sanitary engineering and building trade ; for six years a licensed victualler, and then director of Jas. Scott, Ltd., electrical engineers. Later became managing director of Gainsborough (Bootle), Ltd. ; ex-Chairman N.W. Branch of C.E.A. Licensed Victuallers Fed., and President Bootle F. League. Delegate C.E.A. General Council ; Chairman Governors, Secondary and Technical Schools, Bootle ; Vice-Chairman Education Committee. Member Bootle Council and Bootle Constitutional Association and Conservative Club. *Address :*—Belmont Cinema, Liverpool.

Frank Shaw.
Publicity manager Capitol Film Corporation Ltd. and associated companies.
Born 1904 near Lancaster and educated there ; gold medallist higher mathematics, so joined a bank ; obtained bankers' degree, then left to find excitement in Fleet Street. Varied experience free-lance journalism, including film reviewing, advertising agency, and editorial publicity, from boxing and greyhounds to glass bottles and fine books. Joined United Artists 1931 ; did exploitation, dealt with Continental publicity, and was press contact until resignation 1935 to join Capitol. *Address :*—293, Regent Street, W. *Phone :* Langham 1851.

Harold R. Shilling.
Born 1894. Served for 20 years in various branches of the trade, commencing with the management of Pathé Frères Projector Machinery Department, leaving to take up a special appointment in Boltons Mutual Films, Ltd. Later reopened the bioscope and machinery department of Jury's Imperial Pictures, filling the position of Sales Manager for a number of years. Opened and took over the full management for three years of the Grand Palace, St. Albans, finally leaving to resume activities on the projector machinery side of the business, being appointed sales manager to the Kershaw Projector Company, and upon this company's amalgamation with F. A. Langrish & Co., Ltd., was appointed to the board as sales manager and director of the new combine now called Kalee, Ltd. *Addresses :*—Rayfield, Oakleigh Park South, N.20, and 3, Soho Square, W.1. *'Phones :*—Hillside 2170 and Gerrard 2184.

Maurice Silverstone.
Managing Director of United Artists Corp., Ltd.
Educated New York University, of which he holds the LL.B. degree. Began career as Member of Crown Prosecutor's Staff, New York. Entered Film business 1918, and became general manager of Cosmopolitan Productions. Subsequently represented United Artists in Central America, Australasia and other countries. *Address :*—142, Wardour Street, W.1. *Phone:*—Regent 2242.

Roy Simmonds, O.B.E.
Publicity Director, Fox Film Co., Ltd.
Born Edinburgh. Trained as art student ; entered journalism and spent three years in India. Author of "Humours of India." Enlisted as dispatch rider in Indian Cavalry and served in France during the War. Gazetted out in 1920 with rank of Major. Travelled round the world. On editorial staff of London *Evening News* for three years. Assistant Advertising and Publicity Manager of J. Lyons and Company Limited for five years. Took up present position with Fox, in 1930. *Club :* Press. *Address :* 13, Berners Street, W.1. *Phone:*—Museum 5113.

Shirley R. Simpson.
Born 1893. Before war was with Miss Horniman's Company at the Gaiety Theatre. Joined up August, 1914, commissioned 1915 and served in R.F.A. in France. Joined Indian Army and served Afghanistan Campaign 1919. Joined P.C.T. 1922, subsequently General Manager Midland Counties Circuit, Ltd. Was General Manager of Regal, Marble Arch from opening November 1928 until appointed London Supervisor for A.B.C. Chairman C.E.A. Leicester Branch 1924. *Addresses :*—7, Gloucester Court, N.W.11 ; and 30, Golden Square, W.1. *Phone :* Gerrard 7887.

James B. Sloan.

In 1919 joined Famous-Players Lasky and was promoted to assistant production manager, 1921-22 ; 1923 ; studio production manager in Paris for Gloria Swanson's "Sans Gene"; 1924; directed series of Walter Forde British comedies and was production manager for various independent units ; 1926, production manager, Pathé, London ; 1927, production manager for First National, London, and then held same position successively with Blattner, London and Berlin, ATP for RKO, London ; Rex Ingram, at Nice, France ; Cinema House Productions, London ; and in 1934 at Sound City with Fox British Wainwright Productions ; 1935, production manager, British National, London; 1936, general manager, Pinewood Studios, Iver Heath, Bucks. *Address :*—42, Wimborne Gardens, Ealing, W.13.

Alfred Smith, F.C.I.S.

Secretary, Northern Branch C.E.A.

Born at Burnley, Lancs. Engaged in commercial administration Burnley, Manchester, and Newcastle-on-Tyne, previous to 1917, when he entered the industry as assistant manager at the Brighton Electric Theatre, Newcastle-on-Tyne. In 1918 was appointed secretary of the Northern Branch of the C.E.A. Is a Chartered Secretary with many and varied interests. Managing Director, Provincial Advertisements, Ltd. Member of the Newcastle Rotary Club. *Address :* Walden, Wingrove Road, Newcastle-on-Tyne.

Capt. Jack Smith.

Born August 24, 1878. Thirty-eight years in kinematograph business. Joined Williamsons 1921. Past-President Veterans' Society. Started in business on his own account, September, 1933 as Trade expert all branches, plant, projection, sound, photographic, and enquiry agent. *Address :*—277, Main Road, Sidcup, Kent. *Phone :* Sidcup 179.

S. W. Smith.

Born 1889. Entered trade in Canada, 1910. Returned to England in 1913 and established business as film exporter, renter, and producer. Since responsible for many British productions. Managing director of British Lion Film Corpn., Ltd.; pioneer of exploitation of British films in Canada ; managing director of Anglo-Canadian Distributors, Ltd., who control distribution throughout Dominion of Canada and Newfoundland of all principal British producing companies, including London. Capitol, Gaumont-British, British Lion, British and Dominions, and Herbert Wilcox Productions, Ltd. Appointed member of the Films Advisory Committee to the Board of Trade, 1934. (*Club :*—R.A.C.— *Addresses :*—76-8, Wardour Street, and 57, Berkeley Court, Baker Street, W.1. *Phones :* Gerrard 2882 and Welbeck 8965.

Cecil R. Snape.

Born 1888. Joined the Trade in 1911, becoming General Manager and Secretary of the Kinematograph Trading Co., Ltd., and its associated concerns. After the war (during which served as photographer in the R.F.C. and R.A.F.), spent much time in America in connection with some of the biggest productions of those days. Editor of "Empire News Bulletin" and later of "Universal Talking News" since No. 1. *Addresses :*—6, Troy Court, Kensington, W.8 and 90, Wardour Street, W.1. *Phones :*—Western 2802 and Gerrard 3265.

J. S. Snell.

A native of Tynemouth and has been in industry 25 years. Three times chairman of Northern C.E.A. Branch, and for several years member of General Council. General manager of Shipcote Co., Ltd. ; past-president Gateshead Rotary Club. *Club :*—Gateshead Constitutional. *Addresses :*—Shipcote Hall, Gateshead, and Kenmore, Dryden Road North, Low Fell. *Phone :*—Gateshead 72019.

Paul Soskin.

Born 1905. Managing director and executive producer, Soskin Productions, Ltd., London. Qualified architect, travelled Continent studying styles in European cities. Entered film industry as art director ; in 1931 became a director of British European Film Corporation, Ltd., London ; in 1934 formed own company, Soskin Productions, Ltd., and produced film versions of : "Ten Minute Alibi" and "While Parents Sleep" ; then "Two's Company" for United Artists. *Address :*—Sackville House, 40, Piccadilly, W.1. *Phone :* Regent 2616.

Coun. F. J. Spickernell.

Lord Mayor of Portsmouth.

Born 1871. After period in army started furniture business, stood for City Council unsuccessfully and turned to film exhibiting. Built Regent, and later Plaza, Portsmouth. The latter was the first house outside London to instal W.E. equipment, which gave him nine months' start, without opposition. Defying official ban, opened Plaza on Sunday evenings, was prosecuted, but remains strong advocate of Sunday opening. Opened third hall, Tivoli and projecting new one at Southampton. Recently returned unopposed to Portsmouth City Council. *Address :*—Tivoli, Copnor Road, Portsmouth. *Phone :*—6347.

J. C. Squier.

Born in 1880, his trade career has included associations with W. Butcher and Son, Ltd. ; Walter Tyler ; Globe Film Co., Ltd. : General manager and director of Jury's Imperial Pictures, Ltd., general sales manager and director of Metro-Goldwyn-Mayer, Ltd. *Addresses :*—19-21, Tower Street, W.C.2, and Jesver, The Drive, Rickmansworth, He ts · *Phone :* Temple Bar 8444.

W. Stanley-Aldrich.

Managing Director, Strong Electric Distributors Ltd.

Born 1899. After war service overseas, joined industry. After years with Gaumont and sales manager to the Sentry Safety Control Corpn., Ltd., was representative for Siemens carbons, founded Strong Electric Distributors Ltd., in 1936 as sole concessionaire for the Strong Electric Corpn. of America. Member S.M.P.E. and Guild of British Projectionists. *Address :*—132, Wardour Street, W.1. *Phones :* Gerrard 6246 and Liberty 1865.

R. S. Steuart.

Born 1902. Producer and Director. Scientific and industrial training at Imperial College of Science and London University. Manager of works. Formed Steuart Films 1932. *Address :* The Old Rectory, North Farnbridge, Chelmsford, Essex.

David A. Stewart, J.P.

Entered the picture industry in 1907. In 1913 joined Scottish Cinema and Variety Theatres Limited, when it was the proud possessor of three halls. Now General Manager and Director of the Company, which, in conjunction with A.B.C., controls the largest circuit in Scotland. Justice of the Peace of the City of Glasgow. *Club :*—Glasgow Rotary. *Address :*—105, St. Vincent Street, Glasgow. *Phone :*—Central 2830.

Leila Stewart.

Entered film business in 1916, after editorial, advertising and agency experience in Fleet Street, as publicity manager Bolton's Mutual Films, then became publicity and Press agent Stoll Picture Theatre. Inaugurated Stoll Picture Theatre Club. Publicity manager Allied Artists. W. and F. and Warner Brothers Pictures. Casting director Gaumont-British and Gainsborough productions. Afterwards publicity manager, Gaumont-British Distributors, Ltd., now publicity manager General Film Distributors Ltd. *Address :*—7, Suffolk Street, Pall Mall, S.W. *Phone :* Whitehall 9332.

Will Stone.

One of the best known of the Welsh exhibitors, Will Stone is a pioneer of kinematography. Born in 1882, and educated in London, he is proprietor of a circuit of halls at Tonypandy, Dowlais, Blackwood, Pontycymmer, Rhymney and Midsomer Norton. He is an ex-chairman of the South Wales branch of the C.E.A. *Address :* The Firs, Weston-super-Mare.

Eric P. Strelitz.

European Representative of the following Australian companies : British Empire Films, Ltd. ; Greater Union Theatres, Ltd. ; Cinesound Productions, Ltd. ; General Theatres Supplies, Ltd. Since establishing himself in London, he has been responsible for the negotiating of many important deals in connection with the placing of British product in the Commonwealth. Entered industry in 1923 as assistant booking manager for Union Theatre Circuit ; later filled the post of vaudeville booking manager for the same company. Travelled to America in 1928 ; remained for 18 months, filling the post of New York Manager for Australasian Films, Ltd. *Addresses :*—Dorland House, 14-16, Regent Street, S.W.1, and Carrington House, Hertford Street, Mayfair, W.1. *Phones :* Whitehall 5897 and Mayfair 0670.

Ronald Strode.

Publicist, Ronald Strode and Associates, London. Born 1903. Educated, New College, Worthing. Was motor engineer, then copy writer and general manager of advertising agency. Exploiteer for United Artists, responsible for road shows : "City Lights," "Palmy Days," and others. In charge of publicity, Dominion Theatre for United Artists. Two years publicity director, British Lion. Now handling publicity for Garrett-Klement Pictures, Soskin Productions, Hammer Productions, British Empire Films, Strand Films and a number of other independent production companies. *Address :* —74a, Regent Street, W.1. *Phones :* Regent 5945 and 3462.

Sally Sutherland.

Free-lance journalist. Joined the trade as assistant to Billie Bristow, publicity manager to New Era Films, in 1928. Accompanied Miss Bristow when she established her independent organisation in 1929. Left to become assistant in publicity department, Wardour Films, and in 1930 was appointed publicity manager, British International Pictures at Elstree. In 1936 was appointed publicity manager, British and Dominions Film Corporation, Pinewood Studios. *Club :*—Pinewood Country Club. *Address :*—39, Albany Street, N.W.1. *Phone :* Museum 2772.

Miss M. Swift.

Educated at the Central Foundation School, City of London. Entered the Film trade in 1911, commencing with J. Frank Brockliss. Joined Pathé Freres and was on Gazette Department for two War years and then twelve months with Sidney Bernstein, after which she represented the Apollo Films, Ltd., and many other American and Continental agencies. Sole representative for Guaranteed Pictures Co., Inc. of America. *Clubs :*—Seaford Head and Mersea Island Golf Clubs. *Addresses :*—130, Wardour Street, W.1. and 17, Craven Terrace, Lancaster Gate, W. *Cables :* Swiftfilms, London. *Phone :* Whitehall 7958.

Lauri Lawlor Tavelli.

Director of Bocchi Ricci Films, Rome, 1919. publicity and later first assistant to management during production of " Ben Hur " for Metro Goldwyn Mayer. With Universal in publicity; with Case Hoagland at Allied Artists ; publicity manager for Consolidated Films Studios; publicity manager for International Player Pictures. For several years special representative for the *Kinematograph Weekly* in Italy.

Victor F. Taylor.

Born 1894. Managing Director, Screen Services, Ltd. Formerly Director of Publicity, British Lion Film Corporation, 1930-1933. Previously Publicity Manager, British Filmcratf, Patrick K. Heale Prod., and John Harvel Prod. Joined trade in 1912, later appointed Publicity Manager of Selig Polyscope Company. Went to Jury-Metro-Goldwyn and was appointed film editor by Sir William Jury. Responsible for English versions of "Four Horsemen," " Prisoner of Zenda," etc. Then put over publicity at the Palace Theatre and Philharmonic Hall, where he secured a Royal Command at Windsor Castle for the presentation of " The Light of Asia." Additionally has been responsible for the editing of over one thousand films. *Addresses :*—21, Netherfield Road, Tooting Bec Common, S.W.17, and Imperial House, 80-86, Regent Street, W.1. *Phone :* Regent 4826-7

Charles Bruce Locker Tennyson, C.M.G.

Chairman, Film Manufacturers' Group of the Federation of British Industries ; Assistant Legal Adviser to the Colonial Office, 1911-19, Born, 1879. Educated Eton College (King's Scholar) and King's College, Cambridge. Called to Bar 1905. Secretary, Dunlop Rubber Co., Ltd. *Address :*—3, Onslow Square, S.W. *Phone :* Kennington 0731.

Frederick L. Thomas.

Director of Advertising & Publicity, Paramount. First connection with film trade through Western Electric. First in charge of personnel, later handled all publicity and advertising. Previously connected with production side of legitimate stage and one time marine broker at Lloyd's. *Addresses :*—21A, Upper Addison Gardens, W.14, and 162-170, Wardour Street, W.1. *Phone :* Gerrard 7700.

Thomas Thornton.

Entered the Industry in 1913. Chairman of Oxford P.H. and Birch Lane Cinema, Bradford, and Proprietor of the Picture House, Idle, and the Savoy P.H., Brighouse. Chairman Bradford Branch C.E.A., 1925. Proprietor, Thorntons, Cinema. Member Bradford City Council since 1922. Member of the Watch, Licensing and Assessment Committees, and chairman of the Markets and Fairs Committee. For five years president Undercliffe Cricket Club, and member Bradford Moor Golf Club. *Address :*—83, Pollard Lane, Bradford.

J. C. A. Thorpe.

Entered the film trade in 1910, when he joined the Film Service, then operating from Rupert Street ; became exclusive manager for Pathé Frères, and in 1913 opened the Cardiff branch for that firm. In 1916 returned to Wardour Street, and took over the management of Pathé's serial department. In November, 1918, joined Bolton's Mutual Films, which subsequently became Wardour Films, Ltd., with which company he remained general manager until March, 1927, when he became general manager of B.I.P. Resigned in June, 1931, to form Associated Metropolitan Pictures, Ltd., from which company he resigned in July, 1932, to join Gaumont-British Picture Corporation, Ltd., as foreign manager. Resigned in June, 1933, to establish and control British and Overseas Film Sales, Ltd. *Addresses :*—169, Oxford Street, W.1. and 93, Uphill Road, Mill Hill, N.W.7. *Phone :*—Gerrard 3991.

Max Thorpe.

Born 1897. Hails from Yorkshire. Cardiff manager, then Manchester manager and afterwards London sales manager, Universal, for period of four years. Relinquished same to become general sales manager, Warner Bros. Pictures, Ltd. In 1933 joined in similar capacity Columbia Pictures Corporation, Ltd., and is now a director of that company. *Address :*— 139, Wardour Street, W.1. *Phone :*—Gerrard 4321.

John F. Tidswell.

One of the best known and most popular men in the business on the exhibiting side in Yorkshire. Formerly in business as an auctioneer and valuer in Hull, he turned his attention to the kinematograph in 1913-14, and built and floated the Tower, Hull ; Strand; Hull ; the Tower, York ; Tower, Grimsby ; Majestic, Malton, and many other companies, including the Tower, Leeds; Tower, Goole; Catlins, Scarborough Entertainments, Ltd. ; Victory, Sheffield ; Carlton, Leeds. Director of the Playhouse and Grand, Wakefield. Managing director Princess, Hoyland, and owner of the Victory, Leeds, and Electra lounge, Leeds, Also interested in and booking director for Capitol and Londesborough, Scaroorough ; Queen's, Leeds ; Princess, Shipley ; Grand, Majestic, Princess, Hull ; St. James, Harrogate ; Victoria, Halifax ; and Winter Gardens, Bridlington. Director and booking director Ritz, Doncaster. *Clubs :*— Yorks, Cinema Exchange, *Private Address :*— "Woodville," Newton Park, Leeds. Phone :— Chapeltown, Leeds 41417.

Frank Tilley.

Born 1889. Early education on drapery leather, mining and financial weeklies. Later short story writing, book reviews, etc., on Chesterton's *New Witness*. Edited the late Cecil Chesterton's "Short History of the United States." Edited *Encore*, later *Performer*, and joined *Kine. Weekly*, 1918. Press agent with Paramount 1919, rejoined *Kine.* and remained as editor till end 1924. Film production and free-lancing, also British film representative of *Variety*. In July 1930 joined Radio Pictures, Ltd., as General Manager of Publicity and Advertising. Was first film critic of *Evening Standard* and has contributed articles on motion pictures, especially in relation to economics, to most of the leading newspapers of the world. Appointed to Committee of Management, Radio Pictures, in November 1934. *Address :*— 2, 3 & 4' Dean Street, W.1. *Phone :*—Gerrard 3201.

Michael Charles Toner.

Born Belfast. Served apprenticeship as electrical engineer. Had 3 years' experience in South Africa as sales representative for Austin Motors, travelling throughout the Union territory and Rhodesia. Joined Holophane Ltd. Expert on colour lighting installations before becoming publicity manager of that firm. Journalistic experience as free-lance and on staff of several national dailies. Member of Advertising Managers' Association, London. *Clubs :* Publicity, Right Advertising, and Arts Theatre. *Addresses :*—5, Gatestone Road, Upper Norwood, S.E.19, and Elverton Street, Vincent Square, S.W.1. *Phone :* Victoria 8062.

Angus N. Trimmer.

Born 1896. Military service from 1914. Demobilised in 1921 and was given an appointment at the War Office. Left there in 1924 to become personal assistant and secretary to James V. Bryson. Held this position for seven and a half years. Joined Columbia Pictures Corporation, Ltd., four years ago as personal assistant to Joseph Friedman, managing director. Subsequently service manager Columbia Pictures (Export), Ltd. Now British Production contact. *Address :*—139, Wardour Street, W.1. *Phone :*—Gerrard 4321.

Alderman E. Trounson.
Ex-President, C.E.A.

A Justice of the Peace and a former Mayor of Southport. Director of the Coliseum, Palace and Scala, Southport, and Plaza, Ainsdale. Member Advisory Committee Board of Trade ; Ex-chairman of the North-Western Branch of the C.E.A. ; member of the General Council, C.E.A. ; served as representative of the C.E.A. on the Industrial Council ; ex-chairman of Tax Abolition Committee ; chairman of Southport, Birkdale and West Lancashire Water Board ; ex-chairman of Southport Corporation Gas Committee ; chairman Parks Committee, Southport Corporation. He was first chairman of the Southport Football Club, a pioneer of aviation meetings (in the early days of flying) and motor trials. *Address :*—Hesketh Park, Southport.

Edward George Turner.

One of the early pioneers of the kinematograph trade, E. G. Turner commenced business as a film renter in 1896. He is a director of several companies. He was one of the pioneers of film producing in Great Britain, with a studio at Wembley Park. He was also a pioneer, with J. D. Walker, of the film renting system, and the originator of release dates on films. In conjunction with the late W. Holmes, he was the inventor of the fireproof gate, automatic shutter and spool boxes. He was the maker and user of the first iron operating box with automatic shutters. Has been chairman of the K.M.A. and the K.R.S. In an official capacity E. G. Turner had 33 continuous years' service with the Walturdaw Co., Ltd., and the

Walturdaw Cinema Supply Co., Ltd. Now managing director Patent Fireproof Rear Projection Screen, Ltd., and of Perforated Front Projection Screen Co., Ltd. *Clubs :*—Hickling Gun. *Addresses :*—72, Minchenden Crescent, Southgate, N.14 ; 43-49, Higham Street, E.17. *Phone :* Larkswood 1061.

P. Tussaud-Birt.
Direct descendant of Madame Tussaud. Trained as a journalist, became scientific correspondent for *Science and Invention,* New York. Later joined G.-B. and held various appointments at their theatres, including the Palace, Luton, and New Victoria, Preston, from 1929-34. Was responsible, in collaboration with George Searle, for the sound reproduction at the Royal National Eisteddfod of Wales, 1934, for B.T.-H. Afterwards became general manager for the Snape-Ward Circuit, at the Kingsway, Manchester ; the controlling interest in this theatre was sold in July 1935, and he became manager and licensee at the Empire, Sutton, St. Helens, for R. E. Dockerty, who also controls the Empire, Eccles, Lancs ; appointed general manager, Trocadero, Leicester, 1936. *Addresses :*—32, Humberstone Drive, Leicester, and 2, Meadway, Barnet, Herts.

Archibald F. Twaddle.
Active member of the C.E.A. Scottish Branch Executive, for many years Treasurer, member of the Arbitration Panel. Has also been connected with the Scottish Cinema Trade Benevolent Fund since its inception. Was for many years Treasurer of the Cinema Club (Glasgow) and President for one year. *Address :*—149, Great Western Road, Glasgow.

R. J. Vivian Parsons.
Born 1898 ; joined the Kinema business at fourteen ; 22 years' experience, incorporating the following branches, Exhibiting, Accessories and Mechanical side, Free lance cameraman. Renting, Trailer Services. Invalided out in 1917, went on the exhibiting side, then joined Fleet Photoplays ; later appointed New Era representative for Wales, opened Cardiff branch, and also controlled West of England ; promoted to Supervisor at the London Office. Then general manager Winads, Ltd., until the interest was sold, when he reverted to New Era Films, Ltd. ; after seven years with this company he joined P.D.C., in March, 1930, until this company closed in 1933, when he took over management of Fox Cardiff branch. Promoted, June, 1936, to circuits manager for 20th Century Fox. *Club :*— Whitchurch Golf. *Addresses :*—Shakespeare house, 20, Amity Grove, Wimbledon, S.W.20, and 13 Berners Street, W.1. *Phone :* Museum 5113.

Vivian Van Damm.
Born in 1889 and early trained as an engineer, he became in 1915 assistant manager at the Pavilion, Marble Arch ; 1916 was nominated general manager of the Scala, Liverpool ; in March, 1918, opened and ran the Polytechnic Cinema, Regent Street, until May, 1921. August, 1922, took over the general management of the Palace Theatre. September, 1923, opened the Tivoli Theatre, Strand, and the new Empire, November, 1924. General manager of De Forest Phonofilms, Ltd., 1926 to 1928. International Speedways to 1929, Syntok Talking Films Ltd., 1929-1930.

Sir Edward Villiers, Bt.
Born 1889. Educated Harrow and Christ Church, Oxford. Served R.F.C. and R.A.F. in European War and in R.A.F. in 1919 Afghan War. Member Bengal Legislative Council 1924 to 1926. President, European Association of India 1931 and 1932 ; vice-chairman Union of Britain and India 1933-4-5. Joined London Film Productions, June 1936. Joined board of New World Films, November 1936. *Address:*— c/o J. W. Villiers, 49, Hans Place, S.W.1. *Phone :*—Kensington 0142.

Reginald G. O. Viveash.
Joined the industry in 1910 on the exhibiting side ; transferred to the renting side in 1913 with the Gaumont Co., Ltd., until 1924, when he was appointed secretary of the Cinematograph Trade Benevolent Fund and Provident Institution. *Address :*—52, Shaftesbury Avenue, London, W.1. *Phone :*—Gerrard 4104.

William C. Vinten.
One of the veterans of the Trade, has designed and manufactured trade machinery from an early age, working for A. S. Newman, R. W. Paul and then Charles Urban (Kinemacolour) before forming own business which became limited company in 1928. Keenly interested in the internationalisation of standard dimensions appertaining to the industry. Member B.K.S., R.P.S. and K.M.A. *Club :*—Eccentric. *Addresses:* —106, Wardour Street, and North Circular Road, Cricklewood, N.W.2. *Phones :*—Gerrard 4792 and Gladstone 6373-4.

Helen Wagstaff.
Publicist, Ronald Strode and Associates; London
Born 1906. Educated private schools, England and Paris. Was copy-writer, Derrick's Advertising Agency. Publicity manager, Pathe Pictures, 1932-1933. In 1933 set up free-lance publicity agency. Wagstaff Press Service formed in 1934, becoming Ronald Strode and Associates in 1936. *Address :*—74a, Regent Street, W.1. *Phone :* Regent 5945.

John George Wainwright.
Director J. G. & R. B. Wainwright, Ltd.
Well known in the industry as an importer and exporter, J. G. Wainwright is a director of J. G. and R. B. Wainwright, Ltd. (sole U.K. representatives of U.F.A., Berlin), B.A.T. Films, Ltd., Pavilion (Aylesbury), Ltd., Exchange Theatre, Ltd., Picture House (Leatherhead), Ltd Plaza (New Malden), Ltd., Market Theatre, (Aylesbury), Hermitage Cinema (Hitchin), Hertford County Cinema, Ltd., and Capitol (Epsom) Ltd. British representative Jean de Merly, and Paris International Films. *Club :*— Royal Automobile. *Address :*—Moorside, West Hill. S.W.15.

Richard Butler Wainwright, A.F.C.
Director of J. G. & R. B. Wainwright, Ltd. (sole U. K. representatives of U. F. A. Berlin), Managing Director of Pavilion (Aylesbury), Ltd., (controlling Pavilion Theatre and Market Theatre, Aylesbury), Exchange Theatre, Ltd., Plaza (New Malden), Ltd., The Capitol (Epsom), Ltd., and Picture House (Leatherhead), Ltd. *Clubs :*—R.A.F., R.A.C., International Sportsmen's Club. *Address :*—Kingsmead, Elsworthy Road, N.W.3.

Sydney Wake.
Born 1883. Entered the industry in 1910 with Crystal Film Mfg. Co. Later with Excel Kinematograph Co. ; managing director Regal Films, Ltd. In 1921 established Standard Kine Laboratories, of which he is life chairman and managing director. Chairman of British Synchronised Productions, Ltd., and director of Walton Photographic Ltd. *Address :*—Rythe Works, Portsmouth Road, Thames Ditton, Surrey.

S. Waller.

Born 1891. Educated King's College, London. Vice-President Valuers, Surveyors and Estate Agents Association of Great Britain. Head of the firm of Way and Waller, Estate Agents and Surveyors, Specialists in the sale and valuation of Kinemas. 7, Hanover Square, W.1. *Phone:* Mayfair 8022. (10 lines).

Albany Ward.

One of the pioneers of the Trade, he was born in London in 1879, and educated at Christ's Hospital. He commenced his career in 1895, and was one of the first to tour the provinces with pictures. Established his first permanent theatre at Weymouth, in 1906. He sold his circuit to the Albany Ward Theatres, Ltd. (a subsidiary company of the G.B.-P.C.T. group). Managing Director of the following companies: Award Theatres, Ltd.; Salisbury Press, Ltd.; Salisbury Billposting Co., Ltd.; Salisbury Poster Advertising Service, Ltd.; Swindon Poster Advertising Co., Ltd.; Cotswold Poster Advertising Co., Ltd.; Hereford and Mon. Advertising Co., Ltd.; Abergavenny and Dist. Billposting Co., Ltd.; Western Publicity Co., Ltd.; and is also a director of Albany Ward Theatres, Ltd. *Address:*—3-5, Wilton Road, Salisbury.

A. B. Watts, F.S.A.A.

Born in 1886, and was educated at Long Ashton School, Bristol, and Cardiff Higher Grade School. He is a director of Utility Patents, Ltd.; Splott Construction Co., Ltd.; Luxury Cinemas, Ltd. etc. Chairman and treasurer and formerly secretary of South Wales Branch of the C.E.A. Delegate to the General Council C.E.A. Joint managing director Splott (Cardiff) Cinema Co., Ltd. *Address:*—14, St. Andrew's Crescent, Cardiff.

Frederick Watts.

Started with the old Pathé company in Liverpool on the sales side 22 years ago. After the war came south and took over the preparation and editing of Pathé Periodicals. Created "Eve's Film Review," discovered "Felix the Cat," started "Pathétone." Produced various novelty features and interest films, such as "Speed" (in conjunction with the late Sir Henry Segrave), Wembly Official Films, "Lure of the East," "Pathétone Parade," etc. Production supervisor "Meet My Sister" etc. (Pathé). Now production manager, Pathé Pictures, Ltd., and general manager, British Instructional Films, Ltd. *Addresses:*—84, Wardour Street, W.1, and "The Shadows," Bonnersfield Lane, Harrow. *Phones:* Gerrard 5701 and Harrow 1065.

James Welsh.

Ex-President, C.E.A.

Born 1881. Ex M.P. for Paisley. J.P. for the City of Glasgow. Long experience of Local Government work. Entered the Industry in 1910 as exhibitor. Managing director Mecca P.H. and director of Kingsway Cinema, Glasgow. Active in C.E.A. since its formation. Two years secretary of the Scottish Branch. Past-President of the C.E.A. *Club:*—National Labour. *Address:* — 1, Endfield Avenue, Glasgow, W.2. *Phone:*—West 5447.

T. A. Welsh.

Joined Colonel A. C. Bromhead as junior clerk at the Gaumont Co., in the early days and later became general manager and secretary of the company. In 1916 was appointed a member of the Government Cinema Committee and organised the distribution of the Official British War Films throughout France. In 1918 founded Welsh Pearson & Co., Ltd., and, in association with George Pearson, produced many notable film successes including "The Better 'Ole," the "Squibs" series, "Love, Life and Laughter," "Nothing Else Matters," etc., etc. Introduced Betty Balfour to the screen. Has always been foremost in any movement to better the British Film Production Industry. His scheme to provide studios and production facilities in England equal to the best to be found in America, backed by an International Sales Organisation for the exploitation of British films all over the world, was originally propounded at the Glasgow conference of the C.E.A. in 1925 and resulted in the passing of the Films "Quota" Act and the building of the Elstree studios. In association with Michael E. Balcon produced "Journey's End," by R. C. Sheriff, and "The Good Companions," by J. B. Priestley. Chairman and managing director of T. A. Welsh Productions, Ltd., 25-27, Oxford Street, London, W.1. *Phone:* Gerrard 5426. *Address:* 6, Seaforth Gardens, Winchmore Hill, London, N.21. *Phone:* Palmers Green 0824.

G. Dudley West, F.C.A.

Senior Partner, Simon Jude and West, Chartered Accountants, Liverpool.

Born 1882. Secretary and auditor of a number of kinematograph, theatrical and music-hall companies. Secretary and treasurer of N.W. Branch of the C.E.A. Member of the Council of the Cinematograph Trade Benevolent Fund. Fellow of the Institute of Chartered Accountants. Chairman, Stockport Hippodrome, Ltd., Winter Gardens (Hoylake), Ltd.; Life Governor Stanley Hospital, Liverpool. *Clubs:* Chartered Accountants' Golfing Society, Leasowe Golf Club (Captain 1925-6 and 1934-5), Heswall Golf Club (Honorary Life Member). *Private Address:*—"Cranford," Spital, Cheshire.

Ald. R. W. Wheeldon, J.P.

Born 1867. Lord Mayor 1932, Sheriff 1931, Member of the City Council for Kingston-upon-Hill. Managing director of the following companies: Eureka Picture Hall, Ltd., Hull; Sherburn Picture Hall, Ltd., Hull (controlling Sherburn and Ritz Halls); Marble Arch Picture Palace Co. (Beverley), Ltd., Beverley, East Yorkshire. First entered business along with the late William Henry Maggs, in 1911, being vice-chairman of the companies with him until his death in 1924, when he succeeded to the position of managing director; vice-president, Hull C.E.A. Branch; president of the above, and representative on the C.E.A. General Council in 1925-6, prior to which vice-president of the Hull branch for many years. *Private Address:*—"Broxholme," 392, Anlaby Road, Hull, Yorkshire. *Phone:*—15299

A. S. Whittaker.

Born Durham. Entered the business with Moss Empires over 20 years ago. Held many important managerial posts in the business including Capitol, Cardiff, City, Leicester and the Dominion Theatre, London. Exploitation manager and theatre controller for the late James V. Bryson. Publicity manager, the London Division Gaumont British. Now, publicity director A.P.D. also Sound City and personal assistant to the general manager of A.P.D. *Address:* 193, Wardour Street, W.1. *Phone:*—Gerrard 4962.

Olga A. Wieland.

Joint managing director Wieland's Agency, daughter of H. W. Wieland, who founded the bureau in 1870. The Agency has world wide reputation, having successfully transacted business with most of the leading Stars of the Profession. *Address :*—Piccadilly House, 16-17, Jermyn Street, S.W.1. *Phone :* Regent 1141.

Herbert Wilcox.
Managing Director Herbert Wilcox Productions, Ltd.
Director of British and Dominions Film Corporation, Ltd.
Born in Cork, 1891. Officer in the Royal Flying Corps during the war 1914-1918. Entered the film industry in 1919 on demobilisation. After making many successful silent films, has been producer or director of the following recent films : "Peg of Old Drury." Now engaged in line up of Herbert Wilcox Productions : "Fame," "The Three Maxims," "Millions," "This'll Make you Whistle," "London Melody," "Splinters in the Air," "The Navy Eternal." *Address :*—Pinewood Studios, Iver Heath, Bucks. *Phone :* Iver 460.

R. Gillespie Williams.
Born 1902. Invented and developed Inter-zone system of lighting and supervised electrical contracts of every description. Specialised in scientific lighting for nearly seventeen years. Invented and developed the Holophane colour lighting system for Holophane, Ltd., and put in a great amount of propaganda work for improving the general technique of kinema showmanship. Now chief colour engineer for Holophane, Ltd. Member of Junior Institute ot Engineers ; Guild of British Projectionists and Technicians ; and B.K.S. *Addresses :*—16, Cumberland Drive, Esher, Surrey, and Elverton Street, Vincent Square, S.W.1. *Phone :* Victoria 8062.

Horace Williams.
Originally connected with shipping. Entered film industry at inception of First-National Pictures in England, in charge of publicity sales and exploitation. Joined Wardour Films Ltd. in 1928 as press and exploitation representative. Publicity manager, Wardour Films Ltd., from 1933. *Address :*—Film House, Wardour Street W.1. *Phones :* Terminus 3966 and Gerrard 4314.

J. Leslie Williams.
After nine years' Fleet Street experience with *Daily Sketch, Sunday Graphic,* United Newspapers, Allied Newspapers, and as joint London Editor *New York Herald-Tribune* Syndicate, became Press manager to European M.P. Co., then publicity director Universal Pictures, Ltd and associated theatre enterprises. Now independent publicist and personal representative, specialising in films, stage and radio. *Address :*—Empire House, 117-9, Regent Street, W.1. *Phone:* Regent 4220.

Harold Wood.
Born Windsor, 1884. Educated Taplow Grammar School. Entered the industry by joining Kodak, Ltd., in 1915 and after the war was transferred to the Motion Picture Film Sales Department under E. E. Blake. Member of the B.K.S. *Addresses :*—"Applegarth," Beaufort Road, Kingston-on-Thames, and Kingsway, W.C.2. *Phone :*—Holborn 7841.

Charles M. Woolf.
Entered the Industry in 1919 as one of the partners in W. and F. ; came into great prominence by his immensely successful exploitation of Harold Lloyd comedies. For years has persistently and courageously encouraged the production of British pictures, contributing in a high degree to the advancement of British production. As chairman of Gainsborough

Pictures was responsible for a steadily increasing output of excellent British pictures and, through W. and F. releases, for the many productions of the British and Dominions Studios. His consistent advocacy of, and work for, British pictures is fitly crowned not only by the completion of the Gaumont-British Studios at Shepherd's Bush, but by the standard reached by its initial productions. Was president of the K.R.S. in 1927. Was deputy chairman and joint managing director of Gaumont-British Corporation, Ltd., and director of Associated Companies ; now managing director General Film Distributors, Ltd., and British and Dominion Film Corporation. Ltd. *Address :*—Film House, Wardour Street, W.1. *Phone :*—Gerrard 9292.

John Woolf.
Born 1912. Went through all departments in W. & F. Became General Sales Manager on amalgamation with Gaumont-British. Now General Sales Manager, General Film Distributors, Ltd. *Addresses :*—1, Templewood Avenue, Hampstead, and Pollen House, 11-12, Cork Street, W.1. *Phone :* Hampstead 4365, and Regent 5354.

H. Bruce Woolfe.
Started in film business, 1910. Formed Eclipse Exclusives, 1914. War service, 1915-1919. Formed British Instructional Films, Ltd., 1919. Represented producers Board of Trade Advisory Committee. Member Colonial Office Films Committee. Represented F.B.I. on Educational and Cultural Films Commission. Director, G.B. Instructional, Ltd., 1933. *Address :*—66, Cholmley Gardens, N.W.6.

S. J. Wright.
Born 1876. Represents, in partnership with Walter Pearce, the Wurlitzer Kinema Organ and the Wurlitzer Radio, conducting the sales in Great Britain. Commanded Brigade of Artillery in the war, retiring with the rank of Major. *Club :* M.M. *Address :*—Leicester Square Chambers, Leicester Square, W.C.2. *Phone :*—Whitehall 6864.

Thomas Wright.
Born 1885. Up to commencement of war, auctioneer and valuer. Joined Forces, August, 1914, and served until January, 1918, then joined H. B. Stone in his numerous Midland ventures. On retirement of H. B. Stone carried on ; managing director Nottingham Cinemas, Ltd. ; Lenton Pictures, Ltd.; Globe, Nottingham, Ltd.; Meadows Cinemas, Ltd. Director Notts County Football Club, Member Nottingham City Council. *Private Address :*—St. Ives, Westdale Lane, Mapperley, Nottingham. *Phone:*—65157.

Herbert A. Yapp.
Promoter of Wandsworth P.T., Putney Palace, Royalty, North Kensington. Forum Theatres at S. Kensington, Ealing, and Kentish Town, Morden Cinema, and is managing director of other businesses. *Address:*—Uplands, Wimbledon Common, S.W.19. *Phone :* Wimbledon 5852.

H. T. S. Young.
Hon. Sec. Screen Golfing Society.
Joined the Gaumont Co., Ltd., in 1909 and was placed in charge of the branches. In 1914 went to Dublin as manager for Ireland. Returned in 1923 and was made export manager. Became assistant to the managing director in 1929. Now film manager G.B. Equipments, Ltd. Hon. sec., Screen Golfing Society. *Address :*—55, Glenthorne Avenue, Addiscombe, Surrey. *Phone :*—Addiscombe 2901.

BRITISH STUDIOS

Personnel and Equipment

The following details have been supplied
by the persons concerned, and though
every effort has been made to keep them
up to date we cannot accept responsibility
. . for omissions or errors . .

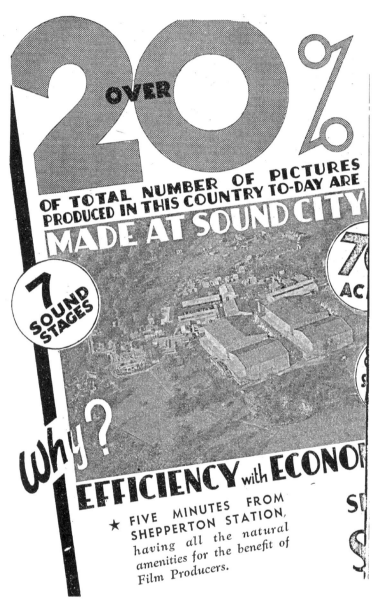

OVER 20%

OF TOTAL NUMBER OF PICTURES PRODUCED IN THIS COUNTRY TO-DAY ARE

MADE AT SOUND CITY

7 SOUND STAGES

Why?

EFFICIENCY with ECONO

★ FIVE MINUTES FROM SHEPPERTON STATION, having all the natural amenities for the benefit of Film Producers.

- THE BRITISH STUDIOS WHICH OFFER EVERY TYPE OF "SHOT" FROM BOND STREET TO THE JUNGLE.
- Sound City offers the Largest Sound Stages in Europe 268 feet by 120 feet.
- Large Stocks of Existing Sets give Producers Real Opportunities for Economical Production.
- Street and Village Sets already built stand on the "lot." There is Sound City River on which such magnificent pictures as "SANDERS OF THE RIVER," etc., were shot.
- 17,000 square feet Concrete Pool provided for Special Exterior Work and Trick Shots.
- Sound City is built on the principle of unit production with their own Dressing Rooms, Property Rooms, Theatres, etc.
- R. C. A. High Fidelity, Ultra Violet Ray recording, and Marconi Visatone, 5 mobile recording trucks and the latest back projection and cranes.
- The Mansion provides Office and Living Accommodation for Artists and Production Staff.

BRITISH STUDIOS.
Personnel and Equipment of our Producing Units.

ACE STUDIOS, LTD.
73-75, ALBANY STREET, REGENT'S PARK, N.W.1
Telephone : Euston 3622.
Managing Director : JOHN H. TAYLOR.
Two floors, 3,900 sq. ft.
Registered Offices : National House, Wardour Street, W.1.
Telephone: Gerrard 3336, 3337, 3338.
Telegrams and Cables : Acefilmz, Rath. London.
Directors : R. A. Hopwood, D. R. Frazer, B. Cazenove, Frank Green.

Secretary	M. Holman.
Chief Cameraman	Ken Perry.
Assistant	Gordon Peace.
Recording Engineers	V. C. Sawyer,
	T. Crowther.
Studio Manager	D. R. Frazer.

Vinten Sound Camera Studio Unit.
Visatone Recording Unit, Noiseless and Open Track. Triple-headed dubbing and re-recording. Full post synchronising facilities. Two stages. Pre-view theatre. Cutting room.

AMALGAMATED STUDIOS, LTD.
60, WARDOUR STREET,
Telephone : Gerrard 2822.
Directorate : S. H. Soskin, C. H. Bell, O.B.E., E. A. Stone.
Eight stages and administrative buildings in course of erection at Elstree.

ANGLIA FILMS, LTD.
EAGLE STREET, 109, JERMYN STREET, S.W.1.
Telephone : Whitehall 7585.

Directorate	A. Nettlefold and
	E. Anson-Dyer.
Secretary	G. D. Midgley.
Production Manager ...	Anson-Dyer.
Studio Manager	S. Griffiths.
Cameraman	H. C. Stobbart.

PRODUCTIONS, 1936 : "Sam" series of colour cartoons (Stanley Holloway).

ASSOCIATED TALKING PICTURES, LTD.
A.T.P. STUDIOS, EALING GREEN, W.5.
Telephone : Ealing 6761 (9 lines).
Directorate : Basil Dean, R. P. Baker, F.C.A.
Joint Managing Directors : S. L. Courtauld, Major J. S. Courtauld, M.C.,M.P., R. F. Ould.
Three floors—one 135 ft. by 85 ft., two 85 ft. by 73 ft.

Studio Manager	W. A. Lott.
Publicity Manager ...	Horace Judge.
Chief Engineer	S. G. Double.
Floor Electrician	Jack Ford.

Cameraman ...	...	...	Jan Stallich.
Sound Engineer	...	...	Paul F. Wiser.
Chief Recordist	...	...	E. Williams.
Make-up ...	...	...	Robert Wilton.
Film Editor	...	...	C.D. Milner
			Kitchen.
Film Editing Dept. Manager			E. Aldridge.
Master Carpenter ...	...		E. Marlow.

Recording System :—R.C.A. High Fidelity.
Electrical Equipment :—Own generating plant, Arc and incandescent lighting.
PRODUCTIONS, 1936 : "Queen of Hearts," "Lonely Road," "Keep Your Seats, Please," "The Show Goes On" and a George Formby subject not yet titled.

ASSOCIATED SOUND FILM INDUSTRIES, LTD.
WEMBLEY PARK.

Telephone : Wembley 3041.
Directorate : F. W. E. Morgan (*Chairman*); M. R. Cahill, W. M. Campbell, B. A. A. Thomas, J. W. Vincent.

BRITISH INTERNATIONAL PICTURES, LTD.
BOREHAM WOOD, ELSTREE, HERTS.
WELWYN STUDIOS, WELWYN, HERTS.
Telephone : 541/3.
Telephone : Elstree 1600.

Total acreage : 40 acres. Floor stages : 9 sound stages, 3 water tanks.

Chairman	...		John Maxwell.
Director of Productions	...		W. Mycroft.
Studios Director	...	...	Clarence Elder.
Studio Manager	...	...	J. Grossman.
Chief Engineer Sound		...	A. S. Attkins.
Film Editing Department	...		A. C. Hammond.
Laboratory :			
Business Manager		...	C. Parfrey.
Technical Manager		...	G. Alderson.
Chief Cameramen : ...		...	Otto Kanturek.
			Claude Friese-Green.
			James Harvey.
Musical Director	...		Harry Acres.
Recording System :			—Ambiphone—B.I.P.'s

own patent.

PRODUCTIONS, 1936 : "Living Dangerously" (Herbert Brenon), "Someone at the Door" (Herbert Brenon), "Ourselves Alone" (Brian Hurst), "Star Falls From Heaven" (Paul Mersabch), "The Tenth Man" (Brian Hurst). "Aren't Men Beasts."

BRITISH LION FILM CORPORATION, LTD.

STUDIO : BEACONSFIELD, BUCKS.

Telephone : Beaconsfield 555-8.

Registered Office : 76/78, Wardour Street, W.1:

Telephone : Gerrard 2882–5.

Managing Director : S. W. SMITH.　*Secretary*
H. W. FRANKLIN.

One floor ; area, 115 ft. by 55 ft.

General Manager	... ...	S. A. Myers.
General Manager (Studio)	...	A. W. Osborne.
Production Supervisor	...	Herbert Smith.
Art Director	... ...	Norman G. Arnold.
Casting	... ...	Herbert Smith.
Film Directors	...	Herbert Smith
		MacLean Rogers.
		Ralph Ince.
		Leslie Hiscott.
Assistant Director	...	Arthur Alcott.
Scenarists	... ...	Maclean Rogers.
		Michael Barringer.
Press Representative (Studio)	Kenneth Green.
Publicity Manager (H.O.)	...	F. G. Kay.
Cameramen	... ...	Harry Rose.
		G. D. Stretton
Recordists	... ...	H. V. King.
		J. J. Y. Scarlett.
Film Editors	...	Arthur Tavares.
		Brereton Portar.
Chief Engineer	...	W. A. Bigsworth.
Still Photographer	...	F. G. Johnson.
Make-up	...	Gerald Fairbank.
Publicity Manager	...	G. F. Kay.
Properties	...	J. Ramsay.
Lab. Superintendent	...	W. Crisp.
Lighting	... ...	H. Strickland.
Chief Carpenter	...	W. R. Teall.

Recording System :—RCA High Fidelity.

PRODUCTIONS, 1936: " They Didn't Know,"
" The Interrupted Honeymoon," " The Song of
Freedom," " Sporting Love," " It's You I
Want," " Fine Feathers," " Murder in the
Stalls," " Playing the Game," " Musical Shorts."

BRITISH MOVIETONEWS, LTD.

13, NEWMAN STREET, W.1.

Telephone : Museum 6176-1893-8241-8242.

Three floors ; area, 6,000 sq. ft.

Editor	... ...	Sir Malcolm
		Campbell, M.B.E
Producer	... ...	G. F. Sanger.
General Manager	...	Sir Gordon Craig.
Assistant Editor	...	T. F. Scales.
News Editor	...	B. B. Saveall.
Production Manager	...	J. W. Cotter.

Recording System :—Western Electric.

BRITISH PARAMOUNT NEWS.

10, SCHOOL ROAD, NORTH ACTON, N.W.10.

Telephone : Willesden 5511 (6 lines).

Editor & Gen. Manager	...	G. T. Cummins.
Editorial Secretary	...	F. W. Bayliss.
Assignment Editor	...	E. J. H. Wright.
Make-Up Editor	...	W. Mellor.
Technical Supervisor	...	K. F. Hanson.
Asst. Technical Supervisor	C. W. Green.
Accounts Dept.	... ...	E. L. Cohen.

Recording System :—Western Electric.

BRITISH PICTORIAL PRODUCTIONS, LTD.

Registered Offices : 90, WARDOUR STREET,
LONDON, W.1.

Telephone : Gerrard 3265-6.

Managing Director : WILLIAM C. JEAPES.
Studios : (Under direction of Clifford W,
Jeapes)—90, WARDOUR STREET, LONDON.
W.1.

Producing newsreels, Universal Talking News
and Empire News Bulletin.

Editor ... ... Cecil R. Snape.

BRITISH SCREEN SERVICE,

54–58, WARDOUR STREET.

Telephone : Gerrard 6543–4.

Directorate : M. J. WILSON, G. WILSON.
STUDIOS : One floor with Film Recorders recording system. Other facilities include : Re-
recording, Interlock, Projection Theatre, Cutting
Rooms, Disc Recording.

Studio Manager	...	G. Hobbs.
Film Editors	...	K. Rick, C. Leeds.
Chief Sound Engineer	...	N. Leevers.

BUSHEY FILM CORP., LTD.

MELBOURNE ROAD, BUSHEY.

Telephone : Bushey Heath 1341.
Directors : Walter West and Henry J. Cook.

CRITERION FILM PRODUCTIONS, LTD.

WORTON HALL STUDIOS, ISLEWORTH, MIDDX.

Telephone : Hounslow 2323.

Directorate : DOUGLAS FAIRBANKS, JR., GEORGE
SMITH, H. A. HAWES, F.C.A., CAPT. A. CUNNING-
HAM-REID, D.F.C., M.P., MARCEL HELLMAN.
Floors : Three sound stages, dubbing stage,
and very large silent stage, cutting rooms
theatres, etc.

Recording System : Western Electric (Wide
Range).

Electrical Equipment :—Diesel engines supply
8,000 amps.

Producer	... ...	Marcel Hellman.
Production Manager	...	Louis London.
Studio Manager	...	Desmond Tew.
Film Directors	...	Thornton Freeland.
		Tay Garnett.
		Raoul Walsh.

DENHAM

LABORATORIES

CUTTING **AND**
EDITING
ROOMS

☆

REVIEW
THEATRES

☆

CHEMICAL AND
ELECTRICAL
RESEARCH

☆

Telephone: DENHAM 2323

LTD.

QUALITY

SERVICE

Scenarists	...	John Meehan.
		John Balderston,
		Clemence Dane.
		Adela Rogers
		St. Johns, etc.
Dialogue Supervisor	...	Harold French.
Film Editor ...	...	Conrad von Molo.
Art Director ...	...	Edward Carrick
Chief Sound Engineer	...	D. Scanlan.
Floor Electrician ...	...	Reg. Wilson.
Chief Camera and Lighting		Victor Armenise
Assistant	...	Denis Williams.
Assistant Director ...	...	William Boyle
Publicity Director ...	...	David L. Blumen-
		feld.

PRODUCTIONS, 1936 :—"Accused." "Crime over London,"—"Thief in the Night."

FOX BRITISH PICTURES LTD.

FOX STUDIO, EMPIRE WAY, WEMBLEY PARK, MIDDLESEX.
Telephone : Wembley 3000.
Directorate : E. Gartside (*Managing Director*), F. L. Harley, R. Simmonds, W. J. Hutchinson, A. Bryce, N. H. Nesse (*Secretary*).
Two floors : 12,252 sq. ft.
Recording Systems :—Visatone and Asfi-Tobis Electrical Equipment : Arc and Incandescent. Other Facilities : Tank, Laboratory and Lot.

Studio Manager ...	...	A. T. Jones.
Film Directors ...	...	A. Bryce.
		A. Parker.
Film Editors ...	...	R. Beck.
		R. E. Tanner.
Art Director ...	...	W. Hemsley.
Recording Engineers		J. Cox.
		C. Mason.
		D. Wright.
Cameramen	...	A. Bryce (Chief).
		R. Kellino.
		S. Grant.
		R. Neame.
Publicity Manager ...	...	R. Simmonds.
Asst. Publicity Manager	...	G. Davies.

PRODUCTIONS, 1936 : "Wedding Group," "Big Noise," "Blind Man's Bluff," "Find the Lady," "Highland Fling," "Ryhthm in the Air," "Café Colette," "Café Mascot," "The End of the Road," "Black Tulip," "Strange Experiment," "Full Steam Ahead," "Toilers of the Sea," "Double Alibi."

GAUMONT BRITISH PICTURE CORPORATION LTD.

REGISTERED OFFICES : 142/150, WARDOUR STREET, W.I.
Telephone : GERrard 9292.
GAUMONT BRITISH STUDIOS : LIME GROVE, SHEPHERD'S BUSH, W.12.
Telephone : Shepherd's Bush 1210.
GAINSBOROUGH STUDIOS : POOLE STREET, ISLINGTON, N.I.
Telephone : CLErkenwell 9100.

Director of Production	...	Mark Ostrer.
Production Manager	...	Victor Peers.
Literary Editor ...	...	H. E. Alexander.
Film Editor	...	Otto Ludwig.

Director of Music ...	...	Louis Levy.
Publicity Manager	...	Hugh Findlay.
Recording Supervisor	...	George Gunn.
Dress Supervisor ...	...	Mrs. Horn.
Casting Manager ...	...	Pat Morton.
Film Directors ...	...	Geoffrey Barkas.
		Sonnie Hale.
		Alfred Hitchcock.
		Herbert Mason.
		Robert Stevenson.
Cameramen	...	Mutz Greenbaum.
		Bernard Knowles.
		Glen MacWilliams.
		Derek Williams.
Stills	...	Otto Dyar.
Make-up	...	H. Heigseldt.

SHEPHERD'S BUSH.

Studio Manager ...	...	J. Croydon.
Chief Engineer ...	...	S. Templeman.
Art Directors ...	...	W. A. Murton.
		Erno Metzner.
		A. Junge.

Six stages, area 90,000 sq. ft., largest 136 ft. by 85 ft. containing water tank 48 ft. by 20 ft. deep (capacity 270 tons). Fitted with British Acoustic (full range) recording. Available for letting, details on application.
Lighting : fresh air supply (per hour) 14 tons. Fire prevention : 4,000 sprinkler heads, piping 10 miles. Separate water mains : 2. Light and power generators (weight, 8 tons each) : 6. Capacity at normal rating : 1,000 kilowatts. Capacity at half hour rating : 1,500 kilowatts. 1,500 K.V.A Transformers serving above : two. 250 K.V.A. transformers for house lighting : one. Weight of armoured cable feeding stage lighting switchboard : 15 tons. Stage lighting central switchboard : 16 tons. Studio floor lighting units : 662. Ordinary lighting of building and offices : cables, 20 miles, steel conduits, 5 miles.
Restaurant seating 600. Dressing room accommodation for 500/600, three viewing theatres, one orchestration theatre, 15 cutting rooms, 62 film vaults, carpenters', plasterers' and modelling shops. Cameras : Cinephon, Debrie, Eclair, Newman, Sinclair, Mitchell and a Bell Howell.
Equipment :—Aerograph plant. Two recording trucks for location work, each equipped with British Acoustic full range recording equipment and all necessary power supplies for recording and camera gear. Camera accessories : Mitchell tripods, Cineplion tripods, Debrie tripods and Fearless Velocitators, two Gabler dollies, three camera cranes, four other camera dollies (various makes). Tubular scaffolding : 100,000 ft. tubular scaffolding, 10,000 couplers, 5,000 base plates, 200 wheels (various).
PRODUCTIONS, 1936 : "Sabotage," "East Meets West, "His Lordship," "O.H.M.S.," "Head Over Heels," "It's Love Again," "The Great Barrier," "King Solomon's Mines," "Take My Tip."

British Studios.

FOX BRITISH PICTURES LTD.

GAUMONT BRITISH PICTURE CORPORATION LTD.

ISLINGTON.

Director of Production and Administration	... ...	Maurice Ostrer.
General Manager of Production	... ...	Edward Black.
Production Manager	...	Fred Gunn.
Film Directors	... ...	Marcel Varnel.
		William Beaudine.
		R. W. Neal.
Scenario Editor	... ...	Frank Launder.
Film Editor	... ...	R. E. Dearing.
Director of Music	...	Louis Levy.
Dress Supervisor	...	Paula Newman.
Casting Manager	...	Betty White.
Publicity Manager	...	MacMurray.
Studio Manager	...	F. Coven.
Chief Electrician	...	S. Sargent.
Art Director	...	A. Vetchinsky.
Cameramen	... ...	Jack Cox.
		Arthur Crabtree.
		Jack Parry.

PRODUCTIONS, 1936 : "Tudor Rose," ' Pot Luck," " Where There's a Will," "The Man Who Changed His Mind," " All In," " Everybody Dances," " Windbag the Sailor," " Good Morning Boys," "O.K. for Sound."

GAUMONT BRITISH NEWS.

STUDIOS : LIME GROVE, SHEPHERD'S BUSH.

Editor	... ...	R. S. Howard.
Production Manager	...	H. W. Bishop.
Contact	... ...	H. Bromige.
Cameramen	... ...	P. Cannon.
		A. Edmonds.
		G. Golding.
		J. Humphries.
		H. Morley.
		E. Owen.
Recorders	... ...	H. Abbott.
		A. Prentice.
		W. Hooker.
		E. Runkel.
		H. Fraser.
Cutters	... ...	R. Drew.
		W. Rowe.
Commentator	... ...	E. V. H. Emmett.
Sound Equipment : B.A.F.		

G. B. INSTRUCTIONAL, LTD.

CLEVELAND HALL STUDIOS, 54, CLEVELAND STREET, W.

Telephone : Museum 4353.

Directors : MAURICE OSTRER (Chairman), HARRY CLAYTON, MARY FIELD, M.A., IAN CREMIEU JAVAL, H. BRUCE WOOLFE.

Scenario Editor : MARY FIELD.

Production Manager	...	F. N. Bush.
Film Editor	... ...	B. G. Salt.
Engineer	... ...	M. Reynolds.
Cameramen	... ...	George Pocknaell.
		Frank Bundy.
		Jack Rose.
		Harry Rignold.
Recordists	... ...	J. Douglas.
		F. Jay.
Publicity Manager	...	H. Hales Dutton.

Facilities : Studio and Recording Room with B.A. Equipment and special sound-mixing apparatus and sound recording van.

PRODUCTIONS IN 1935 :—"Face of Britain," "This was England," "Great Cargoes," "Shipyard," "Citizens of the Future," "Progress," and many cultural and educational films dealing with Geography, Hygiene, History, Physical Training, Sport, and various Class-room Subjects.

G.P.O. FILM DEPT. (Late E.M.B.).

Office : 21, SOHO SQUARE, LONDON, W.1.
Telephone : Gerrard 2666-8.
Studio : Bennet Park, Blackheath.
Telephone : Lee Green 3363-4.
Film Library : Imperial Institute, South Kensington, London, S.W.7.
Telephone : Kensington 3264.
Film Officer and Producer : JOHN GRIERSON.

Office Manager	... ...	S. J. Fletcher.
Production Manager	...	J. P. R. Golightly
Film Directors	... ...	Basil Wright.
		A. Cavalcanti.
		Evelyn Spice.
		R. H. Watt.
Music Composers	...	Walter Leigh
		Benjamin Britten
First Camera	... ...	F. H. Jones.
Recordist	... ...	E. K. Webster.
Recording System : Visatone.		

The Department produces and distributes films dealing with communications. Distribution through Associated British Film Distributors.

HIGHBURY STUDIOS LTD.

96a, HIGHBURY NEW PARK, HIGHBURY, N.5.
Telephone :—Clissold 3003-3004.
Directorate : M. J. WILSON, F. KINGDON-WARD.
Floors : No. 1. 113ft. by 60 ft. No. 2. 60ft. by 30 ft.
Recording System : R.C.A. and Film Recorders ; three Channel re-recording.
Electrical Equipment :—B.T.H., Mole Richardson Kandem.

Production Manager	...	Gerald Hobbs.
Studio Manager	...	Charles Leeds.
Chief Sound Engineer	...	A. D. Valentine.
Electrician	...	Geoffrey Witts.
Cameramen	... ...	Germain Burger.
		Lou Burger.

PRODUCTIONS, 1936 :— " Hard Labour." "Sign Please," " Early Bird," " Cabaret Nights," " Everything in Life," " Midnight at Madame Tussaud's," " Ghosts Alive,"

J.H. PRODUCTIONS, LTD.

(In Liquidation.)
STATION ROAD, BOREHAM WOOD, ELSTREE.
Telephone : Elstree 1341.
Managing Director and Producer : Julius Hagen.
Head Office : 111, Wardour Street, W. 1.
One Floor : 1st Floor, 125 ft. by 86 ft.
Recording System : R C A.
Complete electrical equipment and all other production facilities.

Director of Productions : MAURICE ELVEY.
PRODUCTIONS, 1936: "Dusty Ermine,"
"Spy of Napoleon," "Juggernaut," "Man
in the Mirror."

JACKATOON FILM CO. LTD.

17, DALTON SQUARE, LANCASTER.
Telephone : Lancaster 716.
Telegrams, Cables : Jackatoon Films, Lancaster.
Director of Production ... Travis Jackson.
Publicity Film Dept. ... J. V. Clarke.
Editing ... ... Teresa Honour.
Own studios. Extra floor space available as
required.
PRODUCTIONS :—Interest, Scientific, Enter-
tainment and Publicity Films.

LEEVERS-RICH SOUND FILM UNIT.

LEEVERS RICH & CO., LTD.,
47-48, BERNERS STREET, W.1.
Telephone : Museum 4141.
Directorate : NORMAN LEEVERS, B.Sc., A.C.G.I.
ROY RICH.
Secretary ... ... R. E. Cooban.
Cameraman ... ... Billie Williams.
Self-contained mobile unit for studio or
location use. Recording on film or disc. Play-
back and public address equipment.
PRODUCTIONS, 1936 :—"Vacation Rhythm,"
"Cabaret," "Safety First," "Road to the
South," etc.

LONDON FILM PRODUCTIONS LTD.

DENHAM, UXBRIDGE, MIDDLESEX.
Telephone : Denham 2345.
Floor Space : Three sound stages with floor
space of 30,000 sq. ft. each. One silent stage with
floor space of 30,000 sq. ft.
Directorate : ALEXANDER KORDA (*Chairman and
Managing Director*), SIR CONNOP GUTHRIE, BT.,
K.B.E., H. A. HOLMES, EDWARD STEVINSON,
J. R. SUTRO.
Denham Studios : *Tel :* Denham 2345.
Number of floors: 7. Western Electric Recording.
Production Manager ... ... David Cunyng-
hame.
Studio Manager ... ... Jack Okey.
Directors on Contract : ... W. C. Menzies.
Rene Clair.
Zoltan Korda.
Walter Reisch.
Jaques Feyder
Robert Flaherty.
Scenarists ... ... Lajos Biro.
Arthur Wimperis.
H. G. Wells.
Film Editor ... ... William Hornbeck
Art Director ... ... Vincent Korda
Cameramen ... ... Georges Perinal.
Hans Schnee-
berger.
Osmond Borro-
daile.
Henry Stradling.
Special Effects ... ... Ned Man.
Publicity Manager ... ... John B. Myers.
Studio Publicity ... ... Geoffrey Carter.
PRODUCTIONS 1936: "Rembrandt," "Ele-
phant Boy," "Triangle," "Knight Without
Armour," "Fire Over England," etc.
All Western Electric Sound Recording appar-
atus. Four Western Electric mobile sound
recording trucks. Five Way Western Electric
dubbing channel. Equipped with latest models
Mitchell and Debrie sound, silent and high speed
cameras. Latest model camera cranes, rotam-
bulators and Velocitators, etc.
165 acres of grounds with spacious gardens,
lawns, woods, meadows, river and trout stream,
etc.

Power Station equipped with six Diesel
electric generators, each capable of developing
750 KW continuously, and 25 per cent. overload
for two hours, capable of delivering over 50,000
ampères at 110 volts for all purposes, or 40,000
ampères at 110 volts can be delivered for two
hours to the four Stages.
Shops, etc. : Carpenters and Wood Machinists
shops (floor space 35,000 sq. ft.), Metal and
Engineers' shops, Foundry and Blacksmith's
shop, Plaster and Modeller's shops, Paint shop,
Electrical Repair shop, Wardrobe workshop,
Wig-making Workshop, Scenic Studio, Drapery
Workshop, Prop and Model Making shop, Prop
Rooms with 31,000 sq. ft. floor space. 14 self-
contained Cutting Rooms, fully equipped, with
latest equipment. Stills Developing, Retouch-
ing and Printing Laboratories, Optical Printing
and Experimental Laboratories, Scoring Studio
with 4,000 sq. ft. floor space. Restaurant with
seating capacity for 1,000 persons.

MARYLEBONE STUDIOS, LTD.

245, MARYLEBONE ROAD, N.W.1.
Telephone : Paddington 2444/5.
Directorate : IAN D. SCOTT (Managing Director)
and H. G. Halsted.
Two stages, comprising 3,600 sq. ft.
Recording system :—Piezo Electric Sound.
Electrical Equipment :—One generating plant
2,500 amp. D.C., 110 volts.
Production Manager ... F. C. Faithfull.
Studio Manager ... ... H. G. Halsted.
Chief Engineer ... ... G. E. Manning.
Floor Electrician ... ... G. Yeardye.
Cameraman ... ... W. Wilbur.
Publicity Manager ... ... Ian D. Scott.
PRODUCTIONS, 1936 :—"Toilers of the Sea,"
"Dangerous Venture," "The Dentist Chair,"
"Love Thy Dog," "Cover to Cover," "The
Dream Doctor," etc., etc.

METROPOLITAN FILM STUDIOS, LTD.

GLADSTONE ROAD, SOUTHALL, MIDDLESEX.
Telephone : Southall 2238/9.
Directorate : D. S. MacDONALD and C. R.
FOGWELL.
Director of Production : REGINALD FOGWELL.
Two floors, 90 ft. by 50 ft. and 60 ft. by 40 ft.
Recording System : New Fidelity Noiseless
Recording.
Electrical Equipment : 4,000 amps., A.C. and
D.C.
Large exterior lot adjoining studio, two
complete Vinton Sound camera outfits, mobile
sound track for exteriors.
Film Director ... ... Reginald Fogwell.
Chief Sound Engineer ... S. Crowther, B.Sc.
Chief Engineer ... ... W. Tagg.
Floor Electrician ... ... H. Rosenthal.
Cameraman ... ... Roy Fogwell.
Recorder ... ... W. Bulkley.
Publicity Manager ... ... Christopher Mann.

NETTLEFOLD STUDIOS.

HURST GROVE, WALTON-ON-THAMES.
Telephone : Walton 1460.
Proprietor :—ARCHIBALD NETTLEFOLD.
One floor, 100 ft. by 70 ft.
Studio Manager and
Secretary ... ... M. C. Nicholson.
Art Director ... ... D. Russell.
Sound ... ... H. Fuller.
Camera ... ... Geoffrey Faithfull.
Chief Electrician ... ... W. Bowden.
Recording System :—RCA High Fidelity
Process (Mobile for exterior work).

Electrical Equipment :—Two Metropolitan Vickers rotary converters capable of output of 6,000 amps; arcs and incandescent lighting.
PRODUCTIONS, 1936 : "Tropical Trouble," "You Must Get Married," "This Green Hell," "Not So Dusty."

PATHETONE STUDIO.

103/9, WARDOUR STREET, W.I.
Telephone : Gerrard 5701'
One floor, approximately 50 ft. by 50 ft.
Studio Manager	...	F. Watts.
Sound Recordist		George Newberry
Art Director	...	W. S. MacPherson.
Chief Electrician	...	J. Williamson.
Chief Carpenter	...	J. Brewster.
Cameramen	...	M. Redknap.
		K. Gordon.
		C. R. Martin.
		A. Farmer.

Recording Systems:—RCA and Ambiphone.
Lighting Equipment :—Three banks of 24 500 watt lamps on runners suspended from roof. Eleven filament spots from 2,000 to 5,000 watts on wheels and telescopic stands. Six filament broadsides, etc. Arc spots, 1 100 amp. choked arc on travelling cradle; two 50 amp. choked arcs; two 150 amp. sunlight arcs; two 100 amp. floods; two 35 automatic broadsides, etc. Max. amp. available over 1,000 amp. at 110 volts. One 220 volt line to carry 100 amps.

PINEWOOD STUDIOS, LTD.

PINEWOOD, IVER HEATH, BUCKS.
Telephone : Iver 460.
Registered Office : PINEWOOD STUDIOS.
Telegrams : Pinestudio, Iver Heath.
Cables : Pinestudio, London.
Directorate : J. ARTHUR RANK (*Chairman*); E. RONALD CRAMMOND, C. M. WOOLF, The Hon. R. NORTON (*Managing Director*), CHARLES BOOT, HERBERT WILCOX, JOHN CORFIELD, SPENCER M. REIS, W. H. COCKBURN, H. G. JUDD, C.B.E., A. L. DUGON (*General Secretary*), M. L. AXWORTHY (*Studio Secretary*).
General Manager	...	J. B. Sloan.
Studio Manager	...	H. G. Coward.
Consulting Art Director	...	L. P. Williams.
Chief Sound Engineer		L. Murray.
Chief Electrical Engineer	...	F. V. Hauser.
Maintenance Engineer	...	T. Knight.
Chief Accountant	...	W. H. V. Able.
Floor Manager	...	W. Gerhold.
Chief Carpenter	...	F. Holt.
Laboratory Contact	...	B. Sewell.

Five stages: 3—165 by 110ft., 2—110 by 82ft. Exterior lots : 48 acres.
Recording System : Western Electric Wide Range all mains.
Lighting : Direct current supply at 230 and 110 volts from own Diesel driven power station of 2,500 kw., 22,700 amperes at 110 volts. Incandescent lighting chiefly latest Mole-Richardson types; including 80 5-kw. and 450 2-kw. units.
Arc equipment comprises 10—1,000 m/m and 24—700 m/m illuminators, together with a large number of high intensity automatic arcs and smaller illuminators and spot lamps.
Resident Production Companies : British & Dominions Film Corporation, Ltd.; Herbert Wilcox Productions; British National Films, Ltd.; British Paramount Pictures.
Adjoining Pinewood Country Club; private suites, 80 bedrooms, first-class cuisine (fully licensed), swimming pool, squash and tennis courts, 16 acres of ornamental gardens.

PUBLICITY FILMS, LTD.

FILMICITY HOUSE, UPPER ST. MARTIN'S LANE, LONDON, W.C.2.
Telephone : Temple Bar 6482·4.
STUDIO : 269, KINGSTON ROAD, MERTON PARK, S.W.19.
Telephone : Liberty 4291.
Directorate : J. A. M. BOND, G. HARRISON S. C.LESLIE, G. E. TURNER.
Sound Equipment : RCA.
PRODUCTION, 1935 : "Sweets to the Sweet."

RIVERSIDE STUDIOS.

CRISP ROAD, HAMMERSMITH, W.6.
(*In Liquidation*).
Telephone : Riverside 5012 (6 lines).
Studios comprise two floors equipped with British Acoustic Full Range recording.
See Twickenham Film Studios.

JOE ROCK PRODUCTIONS.

ROCK STUDIOS, BOREHAM WOOD, ELSTREE.
Telephone : Elstree 1644.
Registered Offices :—ASTOR HOUSE, ALDWYCH, W.C.2.
Directorate : JoeRock (*Managing Director*), J. H. Iles (*Chairman*), H. F. B. Iles, H. L. Goldby.
Two sound stages and spacious exterior lot.
Studio Manager	...	Gerry Blattner.
Scenario Supervisor	...	Syd Courtenay.
Film Directors	...	Michael Powell.
		Bernard Vorhaus.
		Redd Davis.
Scenarists	... ...	Scott Pembroke.
		Jack Byrd.
		Barry Peak.
		Georgie Harris.
		E. P. Thorne.
		Lester E. Powell.
Art Director	...	George Provis.
Buyer for Productions		George Battershall.
Chief Cameraman	...	Ernie Palmer.
Assistant Cameraman		Erwin Hiller
Recording Chief	...	W. H. O. Sweeny
Film Editor	...	Sam Simmonds.
Musical Director	...	Cyril Ray.
Publicity Manager	...	G. R. M. Mutter.
Production Manager	...	Frank Mills.
Assistants	... ...	Dicky Leeman.
Stills	... ...	H. W. Devereux.
Costumes	... ...	Renee Granville.
Wardrobe	... ...	Jack Rayner.
Distribution	... ...	Norman File.

Recording System :—"Visatone" and R.C.A. ultra violet.
PRODUCTIONS, 1936 :—"The Man Behind the Mask," "Big Hearted Bill," "Cotton Queen," "Edge of The World," "Calling All Stars."

SOUND CITY (FILMS), LTD.

STUDIOS AND ADMINISTRATIVE OFFICES : SOUND CITY, SHEPPERTON, MIDDLESEX.
Telephone :
Chertsey 2211/4. Artistes Chertsey 3288.
London Office : 193, WARDOUR STREET, W.I.
Telephone : Gerrard 4962-4.
Chairman and Managing Director: NORMAN G. W. LOUDON.
Secretary and General Manager	... ...	L. Grandfield Hill.
Asst. General Manager and export manager	...	W. L. Garton.
Studio Manager	...	P. Bell.

Sound Recordists	...	... J. K. Byers.
		C. Pryke.
Cameraman ...	...	... H. M. Glendinning.
		J. Parker.
Chief Engineer	...	... R. J. Duxon.

Studio space : 7 stages—2 size 150ft. by 120 ft.; 2 size 120 ft. by 100 ft. ; 1 size 100 ft. by 80 ft., and 2 size 70 ft. by 40 ft. Stages can be utilised to give a total length shot of 268 ft., are air-conditioned and four are fitted with tanks. 60 acres of grounds, including river, gardens, woodland, park and ornamental lake.

Recording Systems : Two Mobile Channels RCA and two Mobile Channels Visatone with silent track. Equipment includes latest model De Brie cameras, camera crane, modern lighting, tubular scaffolding, back-projection, play-back, wind machine, 12 cutting rooms, 3 viewing theatres, vaults, post-recording theatre, RCA and Visatone dubbing equipment.

Power supply from 5 Ruston Hornsby Diesel engines and electric generators with reserve battery set giving an output of 17,000 amps. at 110 volts.

Scenic docks with large stocks of sets available for use by tenants.

Workshops are fully equipped with the most modern machinery and equipment for facilitating the work of carpenters, plasterers, painters and electricians.

Hotel and restaurant accommodation in mansion.

Studios and exteriors are available to independent producers.

Productions for which stages and exteriors have been used during 1936 include :—" On Top of the World," (A.P.D. & City Films) ; " Happy Days are Here Again " (A.P.D. & Argyle Talking Pictures) ; " Wolf's Clothing ' (Wainwright Prod.) ; "Sweeney Todd" (George King Prod.) ; " Crimson Circle " (Wainwright Prod) ; "Stephen Hawke " (George King Prod.); "Men of Yesterday" (A.P.D. & U.K. Films) ; "You Must Get Married " (City Films) ; "Sporting Love " (Hammer Prod.) ; " Hearts of Humanity " (A.P.D. & U.K. Films) ; "Secret of Stamboul" (Wainwright Prod.) ; 'Murder by Rope " (B. & D.) ; "Show Flat " (B. & D.) ; "Wings Over Africa" (Stafford Prod.) ; "Second Bureau " (Stafford Prod.) ; " Captain's Table " (Fitzpatrick Pic.) ; " Such is Life " (Incorporated Talking Films) ; "Song of the Road " (A.P.D. & U.K. Films) ; " Mill On the Floss " (Clein Prod.) ; " Thunder in the City " (Atlantic Films) ; "Wake Up Famous " (Stafford Prod.) ; "Reasonable Doubt " (Pascal Prod.).

STOLL PICTURE PRODUCTIONS, LTD.

Temple Road, Cricklewood. N.W.2.
Registered Office : Stoll Offices, Coliseum Buildings, W.C.2.
Telephone : Temple Bar 1500.

Production Office : Stoll Studios, Temple Road, N.W.2.
Telephone : Gladstone 2261.
Chairman and Managing Director :
Sir Oswald Stoll.
Secretary : A. P. Bartlett.

Two large sound stages, 125 ft. by 65 ft., 100 ft. by 50 ft.

Recording System : Visatone, sound-on-film, working under patent licence from Marconi's Wireless Telegraph Co., Ltd.

Electrical Equipment : Rotary Converter Plant, 800 kilowatts. Fully equipped with arcs and incandescents.

The policy of the Studio is to let floor space and portable sound truck.

Studio Manager : W. C. Green.		
Production Manager: Oswald A. Mitchell.		
Film Editing Dept.		... Miss Dooley.
Chief Engineer ...		... S. E. Course.
Sound Engineer		... Archie Langridge.
Recordist	...	... Chas. E. Knott.
Cameramen	...	... Desmond Dickinson..
		Gerald Gibbs.
Still Cameraman		... Cedric Haine.
Chief Carpenter		... Eric Smith.

Productions, 1936 :—" King of Hearts," " Melody of My Heart," "Shipmates o' Mine," " Annie Laurie," " Love Up the Pole," " Variety Parade," " Well Done Henry ! "

STUDIO SOUND SERVICE, LTD.

Studio : 89, Wardour Street, W.1.
Telephone : Gerrard 6747-8.
Directorate : C. F. T. Heath, J. Aspinal, D. G. Carr, D. Diamond.

Studio fully equipped for film production, post synchronising, and sound on film and sound on disc recording.

TWICKENHAM FILM STUDIOS, LTD.

(In Liquidation.)
St. Margaret's, Middlesex.
(See also J. H. Productions, Ltd.).
Telephone : Popesgrove 4444 (10 lines).
Managing Director : Julius Hagen.

One sound floor, 130 ft. long by 80 ft. wide.

Studio Manager	...	... W. P. R. Rowley.
Casting Manager	...	... Ronnie Philip.
Scenarist	...	... H. Fowler Mear.
Assistant	...	... John Soutar.
Scenario Editor	...	... Gerald Malvern.
Chief Editor...		... Jack Harris.
Publicity Manager	...	... Enid Jones.
Art Director	...	... James Carter.
Film Directors	...	... Henry Edwards.
		Bernard Vorhaus.
Assistant Directors		... Arthur Barnes.
		James Davidson.
Camera	...	... Sydney Blythe.
		William Luff.
Still Camera	...	... Cyril Stanborough.
		Laurie Turner.
Recordists	...	... Baynham Honri.
		Carlisle Mountenay

Properties ... ... Charles Hasler.
Chief Electrician ... ... William Cavender
Recording Systems : RCA and Visatone.
The studios are completely independent of outside electric plants through the installation of a B.T.-H. Rectifier, which supplies electrical power. This equipment is the only one of its kind fitted in any British studio.
PRODUCTIONS, 1936: "In the Soup," "Eliza Comes to Stay," "Juggernaut," "Underneath the Arches," "Silver Blaze," "Beauty and the Barge."

WARNER BROS. FIRST NATIONAL PRODUCTIONS, LTD.

BROOM ROAD, TEDDINGTON, MIDDLESEX.
Telephone : Kingston 2181-2189.
Chairman and Managing Director : IRVING ASHER.
Associate Producer ... ... Jerome J. Jackson.
Secretary ... ... F. V. Royce,F.C.A.
Studio Manager ... ... A. M. Salomon.
Scenario Editor ... ... Russell Medcraft.
Assistant Directors ... ... Martin Sandy
　　　　　　　　　　　　　Tod Sloan
　　　　　　　　　　　　　Kenneth Horne.
Cameras ... ... Basil Emmot.
　　　　　　　　　　　　　R. Laprelle.
Film Editors ... ... A. Bates.
　　　　　　　　　　　　　L. Norman.
Art Directors ... ... P. Proud.
　　　　　　　　　　　　　G. H. Ward.
Sound Supervisor ... ... H. C. Pearson.
Recording Engineers ... A. Straughan.
　　　　　　　　　　　　　H. Nunn.
Stills ... ... Russell Westwood.
Recording System : Western Electric.
PRODUCTIONS, 1936: "Murder at Monte Carlo," "Mr. What's His Name," "Hello, Sweetheart," "Get Off My Foot," "Someday," "Man of the Moment," "So You Won't Talk," "Crime Unlimited," "Mr. Cohen Takes a Walk," "Brown Wallet," "Black Mask," "Faithful," "Crown v. Stevens," "Gaol Break," "Where's Sally," "Twelve Good Men," "Fair Exchange."

WELWYN STUDIOS, LTD.

REGENT STUDIO, WELWYN GARDEN CITY.
Telephone : Welwyn Garden 541/5.
Directorate : J. NORMAN PARKER, J. H. MAC-DONALD, FRANK BROWETT.
Three stages: 100 ft. by 80 ft., 90 ft. by 60 ft. and 60 ft. by 40 ft. Complete dubbing and back projection equipment. No Royalty charge. A large outside lot is also available.
Recording System : Ambiphone.
General Manager : FRANK BROWETT.
Chief Engineer ... ... P. Abbott.
Sound Recordist ... ... F. Midgley.
PRODUCTIONS, 1936: "Beloved Impostor," "Paradise Hotel" (John Stafford Prod.), "Crimson Circle" (Exteriors) (Wainwright), "The Gay Adventure" (Grosvenor), "You Must Get Married" (Exteriors) (City), "Knights for a Day" (Pearl), "Price of Folly," "The Limping Man" and "No Escape" (Pathé), "Kathleen Mavourneen" (Argyle British).

WORTON HALL STUDIOS, LTD.

ISLEWORTH, MIDDLESEX.
Telephone : Hounslow 1131.
Head Office : 28, Brook Street, W.1.
Directorate : DOUGLAS FAIRBANKS, JNR., CAPT. A. S. CUNNINGHAM-REID, M.P., MARCUS HELLMAN, PAUL CZINNER.
Studio Director : Edward R. Gourdeau.
Three soundproof stages : 130 ft. by 86 ft., 130 ft. by 45 ft., 100 ft. by 45 ft., seven-acre exterior lot. Proposed new sound stage, 120 ft. by 250 ft.
Latest Western Electric wide range and phase shift equipment. Two channels including van hydraulic camera crane. Two diesel engines supplying 8,000 amps. battery supply of 2,000 volts. Two review theatres, etc.

YOUNGER FILM PRODUCTIONS, LTD.

CENTRAL HOUSE, 34-36, OXFORD STREET, W.1.
Telephone : 4816.
Directors : H. ADLEY (*Managing Director*), I. ISAACS, J. D. MARKS, S. H. BELL, F. N. BLOOMFIELD.
STUDIOS GREAT WINDMILL STREET, W.1.
Advertising Films.

BRITISH PRODUCTION UNITS.

(Other than those possessing their own Studios.)

ALEXANDER FILM PRODUCTIONS, LTD.

26/27, D'ARBLAY STREET, WARDOUR STREET, W.1.
Telephone : Gerrard 3772, 1206.
Directorate : R. HOWARD ALEXANDER (*Managing Director*), J. R. BENSON, B. LEE-SMITH (*Secretary*).

AMALGAMATED FILMS ASSOCIATION, LTD.

Directors : F. T SWANN, MAJOR R. C. G. MIDDLETON.

ARGYLE TALKING PICTURES, LTD.

REGISTERED OFFICE : 4, GUNGATE, TAMWORTH STAFFS.
Telephone : Tamworth 57.
Directorate : JOHN F. ARGYLE, F. H. ARGYLE and C. P. V. COLLIN.
STUDIOS : STOLL, CRICKLEWOOD AND SOUND CITY.
Managing Director : JOHN F. ARGYLE.
Director of Productions : JOHN F. ARGYLE.
PRODUCTIONS, 1935: "Variety" and "Happy Days are Here Again."

BAXTER AND BARTER PRODUCTIONS.

91, REGENT STREET, LONDON, W.1.
Telephone : Regent 7560-2533.
See U.K. Films, Ltd.

BIJOU FILM CO., LTD.

245, OXFORD STREET, W.1.
Telephone : Regent 3031.
Directorate : BUDDY HARRIS (*Man. Director*), MOY LONG, RAE SALOMON, J. ENGELS (*Secretary*).
PRODUCTION, 1935 :—"Chinese Cabaret," directed by Buddy Harris.

BRITISH AND DOMINIONS FILM CORPORATION, LTD.

STUDIOS : PINEWOOD STUDIOS, IVER HEATH BUCKS.
Telephone : Iver 460.
LONDON OFFICE : FILM HOUSE, 142, WARDOUR STREET, W.1.
Telephone : Gerrard 7855.
Executive Director ... ... The Hon. R. Norton.
Studio Manager ... ... H. G. Coward.

Asst. Studio Manager	...	E. Holding
Publicity Manager ...	...	Sally Sutherland.
Chief Art Director ...	...	L. P. Williams.
Asst. Director	...	W. Bangs.
Camera	...	Francis Carver.

Recording System - Western Electric Noiseless Recording.

BRITISH NATIONAL FILMS, LTD.

HEAD 'OFFICE : PINEWOOD STUDIOS, IVER
HEATH, IVER, BUCKS.
Telephone.: Iver 460.
Directorate: LADY YULE, J.ARTHUR RANK, D.L.
J.P. (*Chairman*), JOHN CORFIELD.
Secretary ; H. E. S. BAYLIS.
PRODUCTION; 1936 : "Debt of Honour."

BUCKINGHAM FILM PRODUCTIONS, LTD.

293, REGENT STREET, LONDON, W.I.
Telephone: Langham 1851.
Directorate: ARTHUR BEVERLEY BAXTER, M.P. (*Chairman*), LOUIS ANTHOINE NEEL. MAX SCHACH (*Joint Managing Directors*), HENRY ADAM PROCTER, M.A., LL.D., M.P., S. BAYLISS SMITH, F.C.A.

BUTCHER'S FILM SERVICE, LTD.

HEAD OFFICE : 175, WARDOUR STREET
LONDON, W.I.
PRODUCTION OFFICE : 175, WARDOUR STREET,
LONDON, W.I.
Telephone: Gerrard 7282 (3 lines).
Managing Director: F. W. BAKER.
STUDIOS USED : CRICKLEWOOD, ISLEWORTH, EALING, ETC.
PRODUCTIONS, 1936 : "Cock o' the North," "Lt. Daring, R.N.," "Father o' Flynn," "What the Parrot Saw " "King of Hearts," "Stars on Parade," "Shipmates o' Mine," "Melody of My Heart," "Annie Laurie," "Love Up the Pole," "Variety Parade."

CAPITOL FILM CORPORATION LIMITED.

293, REGENT STREET, W.I.
Telephone: Langham 1851.
Directorate: MAJOR H. A. PROCTER, M.A., LL.B., M.P. (*Chairman*), L. A. NEEL AND MAX SCHACH (*Joint Managing Directors*), A. BEVERLEY BAXTER, M.P., D. R. A. JONES (*Secretary*)
STUDIOS : B.I.P. AND B. & D., BOREHAM WOOD, ELSTREE.

Gen. Manager of Studios	...	P. C. Stapleton.
Publicity Manager ...	...	Frank Shaw.
Casting Director	...	Lionel Barton.
Film Directors	...	Karl Grune.
		Walter Forde.
		Anthony Asquith.
		Paul Stein.
		Thornton Freeland.
Assistant Directors ...	...	F. Brunn.
		Donald Wilson.
		Roy Goddard.
		Peter Bolton.
Cameramen ...	...	Alfred Black.
		Phil Tannura.
		John Boyle.
Still Photographer ...	...	L. Beattie.
Musical Director	...	Boyd Neel.
Editors ...	...	E. Stokvis.
		E. B. Jarvis.
Recordist ...	...	A. R. Ross.
Recording System	...	Western Electric.

PRODUCTIONS, 1936 : "Land Without Music," "Dishonour Bright" (Capitol-Cecil), "Love in Exile."

CARNIVAL FILMS, LTD.

95/99, SHAFTESBURY AVENUE, LONDON, W.I.
Telephone: Gerrard 6528/9.
Directorate: SIR HAROLD V. MACKINTOSH, BART.,
ERIC D. MACKINTOSH, W. DEVENPORT
HACKNEY.
PRODUCTION, 1935 : "Railroad Rhythm."

CECIL FILMS LIMITED.

293, REGENT STREET, W.I.
Telephone: Langham 1851.
Directorate: Major H. A. PROCTER (*Chairman*),
L. A. NEEL, MAX SCHACH, A. BEVERLEY
BAXTER, M.P.
PRODUCTIONS, 1936 : "Dishonour Bright "
(Capitol-Cecil).

COLUMBIA (BRITISH) PRODUCTIONS, LTD.

REGISTERED OFFICE : 18, BLOOMSBURY SQUARE,
LONDON, W.C.
Telephone: Museum 9744.
PRODUCTION OFFICE : 139, WARDOUR ST., W.I
Telephone: Gerrard 4321.
Managing Director: JOSEPH FRIEDMAN.
Secretary and Production Contact:
Geo. J. Maidment.
Publicity Manager ... ... H. F. Kessler-Howes.

CONCORDIA FILMS, LTD.

80-86, REGENT STREET, LONDON, W.I.
Telephone: Regent 5348.
Directorate: J. B. ELLISON, FRIEDRICH FEHER.
HAROLD B. MILLAR (*Managing Director*).

DENHAM FILM CORPORATION, LTD.

DENHAM, UXBRIDGE, MIDDLESEX.
Telephone: Denham 2345.

EMBASSY PICTURES (ASSOCIATED), LIMITED

39, HILL STREET, W.I.
Telephone: Grosvenor 1907.
Directorate: G. KING, O. KING.
STUDIOS : WALTON-ON-THAMES, SOUND CITY.

Production Manager	...	Billy Phelps.
Studio Manager	...	Desmond Tew.
Film Directors	...	George King,
		Milton Rosmer.
		Redd Davis.
Scenarists ...	...	H. F. Maltby.
		Jack Celestian.
Film Editors	...	John Seabourne.
		C. Saunders.
Art Directors	...	Don Russell.
		C. Daniels.
Chief Engineer	...	William Bowden.
Floor Electrician	...	George Luker.
Cameramen ...	...	Jeoffrey Faithfull.
		George Stretton.
		Arthur Grant.
		Allan White.
		Ronnie Neame.
		Maurice Ford.
Publicity Manager ...	...	Christopher Mann.

PRODUCTIONS, 1936 : "Sweeney Todd the Demon Barber of Fleet Street," "The Crimes of Stephen Hawke,' "Reasonable Doubt," "Silvertop," "Wanted," "House of Red Lanterns."

FANFARE PICTURES, LTD.

Canada House, Norfolk Street, Strand, W.C.2
Telephone : Temple Bar 1104.
Directorate: GORDON WELLESLEY, JOHN G.
SAUNDERS.
Studios Used : A. T. P. Studios, Ealing, W.5.
Producer ... ... Gordon Wellesley

Production Manager	...	Cecil Dixon.
Personal Assistant to Producer	...	John Seago.
Film Director	...	Thorold Dickinson.
Scenarist	...	Katherine Strueby
Film Editor	...	Sidney Cole.
Art Director	...	R. Holmes Paul.
Cameraman	...	Otto Heller.

PRODUCTIONS, 1936 : "The General Goes too Far."

FRANCO-LONDON FILM, LTD.
PANTON HOUSE, 25, HAYMARKET.
Telephone : Whitehall 5358, 6985.
Directorate : F. DEUTSCHMEISTER (*Managing Director*), R. S. FREEMAN, M. T. HARRAWAY.
STUDIOS USED : RIVERSIDE STUDIO, HAMMERSMITH.
PRODUCTION, 1936 : "Widow's Island."

GAIETY FILMS, LTD.
SUITE 65, IMPERIAL HOUSE, 80, REGENT STREET, W.1.
Telephone : Regent 4826.
Directorate : STANLEY LUPINO, J. W. O. HAMILTON, V. F. A. TAYLOR, W. FLOWER (*Secretary.*)

GARRETT, KLEMENT PICTURES, LTD.
32, ST. JAMES STREET, LONDON, S.W.1.
Telephone : Whitehall 4296.
Directorate : ROBERT GARRETT, OTTO KLEMENT.
MORGAN R. DAVIES (*Secretary.*)
| Publicity Manager ... | ... | Ronald Strode. |
| | | Jock McGregor. |

GARRICK FILM CO., LTD.
PRINCES HOUSE, PRINCES ARCADE, PICCADILLY, W.1.
Telephone : Regent 2103/4.
Directorate : W. Devenport Hackney, Frank Hall, John Weatherhead, John Bill.
PRODUCTIONS, 1936 : "Cafe Colette," and Commercial Films.

GEORGE SMITH'S PRODUCTIONS, LTD.
91, SHAFTESBURY AVENUE, W.1.
Telephone : Gerrard 6881.
Director : A. GEORGE SMITH.
Film Directors	...	...	Maclean Rogers, Adrian Brunel.
Film Editor		...	Dan Birt.
Camerman	...	...	Geoffrey Faithful.

G. S. ENTERPRISE, LTD.
91, SHAFTESBURY AVENUE, W.1.
Telephone : Gerrard 6881.
Directorate : GEORGE SMITH, L. W. PAUL.
| Film Director | ... | ... | P. Maclean Rogers, Adrian Brunel. |
| Film Editor | ... | ... | Dan Birt. |
PRODUCTIONS, 1936 : "Touch of the Moon," "To Catch a Thief," "Not so Dusty," "Busman's Holiday," "Nothing Like Publicity," "Craftsman."

GROSVENOR SOUNDFILMS LIMITED.
KENT HOUSE, 87, REGENT STREET, W.1.
Directorate : G. A. L. SINCLAIR HILL, HARCOURT TEMPLEMAN, CLARENCE WILENKIN, CHARLES J. BLACK.
Studios used : Ealing (A.T.P.), Ealing Green.
Telephone : Ealing 6761.
General Manager of Production.		Harcourt Templeman.
Film Director	...	...	Sinclair Hill.
Scenarists	...	...	B. D. Wyndham Lewis.

Film Editor	...	...	Michael Hankinson.
Art Director	...	...	Aubrey Hammond.
Cameraman	...	...	Cyril Bristow.
Publicity Manager...	...	Dennison Thornton.
PRODUCTIONS 1936 :—"The Gay Adventure," "Take a Chance."

HAMMER PRODUCTIONS, LTD.
PRODUCTION OFFICES : IMPERIAL HOUSE, 80-86, REGENT STREET, W.1.
Telephone : Regent 7461-2.
Directorate : GEORGE A. GILLINGS, H. FRASER PASSMORE (*Joint Managing Directors*), W. HAMMER (*Chairman*), GEORGE MOZART, J. ELDER WILLS.
STUDIOS USED : A. T. P. EALING—NETTLEFOLDS.
PRODUCTIONS, 1935 :—"Mystery of the Marie Celeste."

HERBERT WILCOX PRODUCTIONS, LTD.
PINEWOOD STUDIOS, IVER HEATH, BUCKS.
Telephone : Iver 460.
Directorate : HERBERT WILCOX (*Managing Director*), C. M. WOOLF (*Chairman*), J. R. STEPHENS, MAURICE WOOLF, JOHN WOOLF, A. HYMAN.
Production Manager	...	Tom White.
Art Director	...	...	L. P. Williams.
Cameraman	...	...	F. A. Young.
Publicity Manager ...	...	Tom Burdon.
PRODUCTIONS, 1936 : "Fame," "The Three Maxims," "Millions," "This'll Make You Whistle," "London Melody," "Splinters in the Air," "The Navy Eternal."

I.F.P. LTD.
Proprietors of PHŒNIX FILMS.
28, MORTIMER STREET, W.1.
Telephone : Museum 1922/5.
Directorate : JAMES GRAY, HUGH PERCEVAL, REGINALD DENHAM, BASIL MASON.
STUDIOS : A.T.P. STUDIOS, EALING.
Production Manager	...	Hugh Perceval.
Studio Manager	...	...	W. Lott.
Film Directors on Contract		Reginald Denham. Edmund Greville.
Scenarist	...	...	Basil Mason.
Film Editor...	...	...	Thorold Dickinson.
Art Director	...	...	R. Holmes Paul.
Chief Engineer	...	...	S. Double.
Floor Electrician	...	...	H. Spurgeon.
Cameramen ...	...	...	Franz Wiehmayr. Otto Heller.
PRODUCTIONS, 1936 : "Calling the Tune," "The House of the Spaniard," "No Escape."

IMMORTAL SWAN PRODUCTIONS, LTD.
30, CRAVEN STREET, W.C.2.
Telephone : Whitehall 0195.
Directorate : V. DANDRE (*Chairman*), L. NAKHIMOFF, EDWARD NAKHIMOFF.
Secretary, MADGE LYNCH.

INTERALLIED FILM PRODUCERS, LTD.
4, ST. JAMES STREET, S.W.1.
Telephone : Whitehall 4686.
Directorate : JOSEPH M. SCHENCK (U.S.A.), DIXON BOARDMAN (U.S.A.), PAUL CZINNER (Austrian), F. J. CHART, C. B. COCHRAN, F. M. GUEDALLA.
Production Manager	...	Robert J. Cullen.
Film Director	...	...	Paul Czinner.
Literary Editor	...	...	Carl Mayer.
PRODUCTIONS, 1936 :—"As You Like It" (Elisabeth Bergner).

INTERNATIONAL PLAYER PICTURES.
9, CAVENDISH SQUARE, W.1.
Telephone: Welbeck 7166.
Directorate: M. HAWORTH-BOOTH, CARR DE RIED.

JOHN CLEIN PICTURES, LTD.
SOUND CITY, SHEPPERTON.
PRODUCTION, 1936: " The Mill on the Floss."

LESLIE FULLER PICTURES, LTD.
REGISTERED OFFICES : ASTOR HOUSE, ALDWYCH W.C.2.
Telephone: Holborn 3360.
Directorate: JOE ROCK (*Managing Director*)
J. H. ILES (*Chairman*) ; H. F. B. ILES, H. L. GOLDBY.
STUDIOS USED : ROCK STUDIOS, BOREHAM, WOOD, ELSTREE.
Telephone: Elstree 1644.

LIBERTY FILMS, LTD.
4, GOLDEN SQUARE, W.1.
Telephone: Gerrard 1204.
Directorate: LEONARD-W. FINCH (Chairman) ;
F. W. INGRAM (Managing Director) ; IVAR CAMPBELL (Director of Production) ; H. E. G. PIPER ; W. G. DUNCALF ; JOHN PAYNE.

LONDON & CONTINENTAL PICTURES, LTD.
REGENCY HOUSE, 1-4, WARWICK STREET, W.1.
Telephone: Gerrard 5391.
Directorate: JOHN W. GOSSAGE H. A. BROWNE,
A. MCAUSLANE, ILIA SALKIND.
STUDIO · EALING.
Production Manager ... Frank Cadman.
Film Director ... ... Reginald Denham.
Film Editor ... ... Ray Pitt.
Art Director ... ... D. W. L. Daniels.
Cameramen ... ... Otto Heller
Publicity Manager ... Alexander Kahn.
PRODUCTIONS, 1936 :—" Dreams Come True."

MALCOLM PICTURE PRODUCTIONS, LTD.
145, WARDOUR STREET, W.1.
Telephone: Gerrard 1895/6.
Directorate: IAN SUTHERLAND, REGINALD LONG, JOHN HAMILTON.

THE MARCH OF TIME, LTD.
ADDRESS: DEAN HOUSE, 2-4, DEAN STREET, W.1.
Telephone: Gerrard 6335/7.
Board of Directors—*Chairman :* ROY E. LARSEN ;
Managing Director : RICHARD DE ROCHEMONT;
Directors : RALPH J. HANBURY, J. R. WOOD, Jr.,
G. W. DAWSON, D. W. BRUMBAUGH, CHARLES L. STILLMAN.
PRODUCTION UNIT.
Director ... ... Edgar Anstey.
Camera ... ... James S. Hodgson, F.R.P.S.
Sound ... ... Dennis F. Scanlan.
Research ... ... Maurice Lancaster.
Promotion ... ... Bernard Green.

MORGAN PRODUCTIONS, LTD.
32, ST. JAMES'S STREET, LONDON, S.W.1.
Telephone: WHITEHALL 8501.
Directorate: G. B. MORGAN, C. A. MORGAN.
R. F. SHEPPARD.

NEW WORLD PICTURES, LTD.
3, ST. JAMES' SQUARE, S.W.1.
Telephone: Whitehall 8396.
Directorate: ROBERT T. KANE, E. H. GEORGE, EDWARD F. STOREY.
STUDIOS USED : DENHAM, MIDDLESEX.
Telephone: Denham 2345.
Production Manager ... W. H. Levita.

Film Directors on Contract Harold Schuster.
 Victor Seastrom.
 Harry D'Arrast.
Scenarist ... ... Tom Gerachty.
Film Editor ... ... James B. Clark.
Art Director ... ... Ralph Brinton.
Publicity Manager ... ... John Downing.
PRODUCTIONS, 1936 : " Wings of the Morning," " Under the Red Robe."

PALL MALL PRODUCTIONS. LTD.
3/5, BURLINGTON GARDENS, LONDON, W.1.
Telephone: Regent 2776-7.
Directorate: LOTHAR MENDES, RT. HON. LORD PONSONBY, HARRY B. HAM, AUBREY H. SMITH, THOMAS KILBEY.
Secretary, H. ALAN HAWES.
STUDIOS USED : DENHAM STUDIOS, DENHAM, BUCKS.
Telephone: Denham 2345.
Production Manager ... P. C. Samuel.
Film Director on Contract ... Lothar Mendes.
Film Editor ... ... Philip Charlot.
Art Director ... ... Laurence Irving.
Cameraman ... ... Jans Stallich.
Publicity Manager ... ... Frederick Brisson.
PRODUCTION, 1936 : " Moonlight Sonata."

PANTHER PICTURE CO., LTD.
REGISTERED OFFICE : 22, CHANCERY LANE, W.C
Studios : TEMPLE ROAD, CRICKLEWOOD, N.W.2
Telephone: Gladstone 2261 (5 lines).
Managing Director : OSWALD A. MITCHELL.
Secretary ... ... A. P. Bartlett.
Production Manager ... Morris Johns.
Cameraman ... ... Desmond Dickinson.
Recording System : Visatone.
PRODUCTION, 1935 : " Cock o' The North " (Oswald Mitchell and Challis Sanderson).

PARAMOUNT BRITISH PRODUCTIONS, LIMITED.
162-170, WARDOUR STREET, LONDON, W.1.
Telephone: Gerrard 7700.
Directorate: J. C. GRAHAM (*Managing Director*),
E. AYRES, C. F. KARUTH, MRS. L. V. K.
COHEN (*Secretary*).
Publicity Manager ... F. W. Thomas.
Scenario Dept. ... ... D. B. Mayne.
PRODUCTIONS, 1936 : " Expert's Opinion."
" Ticket of Leave," " The Secret Voice,"
" Wednesday's Luck," " Two on a Doorstep,"
" Strange Cargo," " House Broken," " Grand Finale," " Cafe Mascot," " Murder by Rope,"
" Early Bird," " Show Flat."

PENNINE FILMS, LTD.
TONTINE STREET, BLACKBURN.
Telephone: Blackburn 7691.
Directorate: C. J. CAYLEY (Managing), G. R. WHITESIDE, E. A. POLLARD.
Floor Area : About 2,000 sq. 1t.
Recording Equipment : " Syncrotone " Sound-on-Film Recording.
PRODUCTIONS, 1936 : " Where Kingdoms Meet," " Taking to the Water," " By Dove and Derwent," " This Other Eden," " Lancashire Lakes."

PHŒNIX FILMS.
REGISTERED OFFICE :
28, MORTIMER STREET, W.1.
Telephone: Museum 1922/5.
See I.F.P., Ltd.

PREMIER STAFFORD PRODUCTIONS, LTD.
SOUND CITY, SHEPPERTON, MIDDLESEX.
Telephone: Chertsey 2291-2-3.
Directorate: JOHN STAFFORD, HARWOOD L. M. COTTER, W. VICTOR HANBURY.
Secretary, M. KNOPMUSS.

STUDIOS USED: STAFFORD STUDIOS, SOUND
CITY, SHEPPERTON, MIDDLESEX.
Telephone: Chertsey 2291–2–3.

Production Manager	... Jack Martin.
Film Directors on Contract	W. V. Hanbury.
	L. Vajda.
Scenarist	Akos Tolnay.
Film Editors	Julian Wintle.
	Ralph Thomas.
Art Director	Jack Hallwood.
Chief Engineer	G. R. Duxon.
Floor Electrician ...	Ernest Sullivan.
Cameraman	James Wilson.
Publicity Manager	John Montgomery.

PRODUCTIONS, 1936: "Wings Over Africa,"
"Second Bureau," "Wake Up Famous" and
(in preparation) "The Wife of General Ling."

QUALITY FILMS, LTD.
67 AND 68, JERMYN STREET, S.W.1.
Telephone: Whitehall 6804, 6805.
Directorate: LT.-COMDR. C. LOEHNIS, A.M.I.E.E.
(Man. Dir.), ARNOLD RIDLEY, JAMES DOOTSON,
R. W. J. GIBBON, M.C., (Secretary) W. BARRIE,
C.A.

Production Supervisor	... Lt.-Cdr. C. Loehnis.
Film Director and Author	... Arnold Ridley.
Publicity Director ...	... Peter Burnup.

PRODUCTIONS, 1936 :— "Royal Eagle,"
"Zander."

RADIUS FILMS, LTD.
199, WARDOUR STREET, W.1.
Telephone: Gerrard 7172.
Directorate: J. HAIMANN, J. H. McDONALD, G.
GRAY.
STUDIOS USED: B. and D.

SOSKIN PRODUCTIONS, LTD.
SACKVILLE HOUSE, 40, PICCADILLY, W.1.
Telephone: Regent 2616.
STUDIOS: AMALGAMATED STUDIOS, BOREHAM
WOOD, HERTS.
Directorate: S. SOSKIN (Chairman), PAUL
SOSKIN (*Managing Director*), Major C. H.
BELL, O.B.E.
PRODUCTION, 1936: "Two's Company."

STANDARD INTERNATIONAL PICTURES, LTD.
199, PICCADILLY, W.1.
Telephone: Regent 3811 (2 Lines).
Directorate: ROBERT B. SOLOMON (Chairman),
E. V. FALK, C. M. ORIGO, K.C. ALEXANDER,
E. J. B. ROSE.
Studios Used: Sound City, Shepperton.

Production Manager	... Mickey Delamar.
Film Director	Alfred Zeisler.
Scenarists	Jeffrey Dell.
Film Editors	George Grace.
Art Director	David Rawnsley.
Cameraman	Eric Cross.
Publicity Manager	Ronald Strode

PRODUCTIONS, 1936: "Make-Up."

STRAND FILM CO., LTD.
REGISTERED OFFICE: 37/39, OXFORD STREET,
W.1.
Telephone: Gerrard 1605 and 6537.
Directorate: DONALD F. TAYLOR, RALPH KEENE,
C. L. HESELTINE, C. H. CLARKE.

Director of Productions	... Paul Rotha.
Film Directors	Alexander Shaw.
	J. B. Holmes.
	Stanley Hawes.
Cameramen	George Noble.
	Paul Burnford.
Scenarist	R. I. Grierson.

ST. GEORGE'S PICTURES, LTD.
145, WARDOUR STREET, LONDON, W.1
Telephone: Gerrard 1895–6.
Directorate: IAN SUTHERLAND, CECIL GOODWIN,
C. H. THOMPSON.

Director of Productions	... Lupino Lane.
Production Manager	... Cecil Goodwin.
Film Director on Contract	... Henry W. George.
Scenarist	... Reginald Long.

PRODUCTIONS, 1935: "Who's Your Father,"
"Deputy Drummer," "Trust the Navy."

STANLEY LUPINO PRODUCTIONS, LTD.
(See Gaiety Films, Ltd.)

TOEPLITZ PRODUCTIONS, LTD.
REGISTERED OFFICES: 15, HANOVER SQUARE,
W.1.
Telephone: Mayfair 3614.
Telegrams and Cables: Toeplitz. London.
Directorate: SIR HARRY CASSIE HOLDEN, BT.
(Chairman), GIUSEPPE TOEPLITZ, LUDOVICO
TOEPLITZ DE GRAND RY (Managing Director),
MAJOR WALTER d'E WILLIAMS, SIR CHARLES
PETRIE, BT.
Studios used for first production A.T.P., Ealing.

Secretary	... A. L. Roper.
Publicity Manager ...	... T. Lageard.
Film Director	... Kurt Bernhardt.
Photography ...	... Franz Planer.
Art Director ...	... André Andreiev.
Cameramen on first production	Walter Blakely.
	P. Cooney.
Film Editor ,,	... Paul Weatherwax.
Make-up ,,	... Len Garde.
	K. Herlinger.

Recording System: R.C.A. High Fidelity.

TRAFALGAR FILM PRODUCTIONS, LTD.
293, REGENT STREET, W.1.
Telephone: Langham 1851.
Directorate: LOUIS ANTHOINE NEEL (*Chairman
and Joint Managing Director*), MAX SCHACH
(*Joint Managing Director*), ARTHUR BEVERLEY-
BAXTER, M.P., HENRY ADAM PROCTER, M.A.,
LL.D., M.P.
Secretary, D. R. A. JONES.

Publicity Manager ... ... Frank Shaw.
Casting Manager ... ... Lionel Barton.
Film Directors ... ... Karl Grune.
Rowland V. Lee.
Cameramen ... ... Otto Kanturek,.
A.C.T.
Phil Tannura.
John Boyle.
Alfred Black.
PRODUCTION, 1936 : " Love from a Stranger.'

U.K. FILMS, LTD.

Incorporating :— Baxter and Barter Productions.
91, REGENT STREET, LONDON, W.I.
Telephone : Regent 7560 and 2533.
STUDIOS USED : SOUND CITY.
Directorate : SIR HARRY BRITTAIN, K.B.E.,
C.M.G., LL.D. (*Chairman*), JOHN BAXTER,
JOHN BARTER (*Managing Directors*), L.
GRANDFIELD HILL, N. G. W. LOUDON,
FREDERICK WHITE.
Secretary, ALBERT G. AUKETT.
Production Manager ... Wallace Orton.
Casting Director ... ... Archie Woof.
Film Directors ... ... John Baxter.
Wallace Orton.
Assistant Directors ... ... Robert Jones.
Michael Trueman.
Musical Director ... ... Kennedy Russell.
Publicity Manager ... ... John Montgomery.
Art Director ... ... John Bryan.
Technical Supervision ... Lance Comfort.
Continuity ... ... Phyllis Ross.
Buyer for Productions ... Jack Edmonds.
Film Editor ... ... Sidney Stone.
PRODUCTIONS, 1936 : "Men of Yesterday,"
"Hearts of Humanity," "Song of the Road."

VIKING FILMS, LTD.

107, SHAFTESBURY AVENUE.
Telephone : Gerrard 5004.
Directorate: ERIC HUMPHRISS, P. R. T. GARNETT,
B. P. HOWELL, C. A. BRAMALL.
Production Manager : ERIC HUMPHRIES.
PRODUCTIONS, 1936 : "Beauty Under Canvas,"
"Modernising Madam," "Frosty Frolics."

VISUAL EDUCATION, LTD.

TEMPLE ROAD, CRICKLEWOOD, N.W.2.
Telephone : Gladstone 2261 (5 lines).
Production Office : TEMPLE ROAD, CRICKLEWOOD,
N.W.2.
Chairman : SIR JAMES MARCHANT, K.B.E.,
LL.D.
Manager : C. A. Radley, F.R.G.S., Geo.D.
Technical Assistant ... G. A. F. King.
Studios used : Stoll Studios.
PRODUCTIONS, 1936 : "Fighting Ships,"
"Pilots of the Port of London," "Flying
Instructors."

VOGUE FILM PRODUCTIONS, LTD.

7, PARK LANE, W.I.
Telephone : Grosvenor 3044.

J. G. & R. B. WAINWRIGHT, LTD.

ASTORIA HOUSE, 62, SHAFTESBURY AVENUE,
LONDON, W.I.
Telephone : Gerrard 4948 (3 lines).
Directorate : J. G. WAINWRIGHT, R. B. WAIN-
WRIGHT.
STUDIOS USED : UNIVERSAL-WAINWRIGHT
STUDIOS, SOUND CITY, SHEPPERTON.
Telephone : Chertsey 2281.
Recording System : R.C.A. High Fidelity.
Film Directors on Contract... Andrew Marton.
Reginald Denham.
Scenarists ... ... Howard Irving
Young.
L. Benedek.
R. Beltinson.
L. du Garde Peach.
Art Director ... ... D. W. L. Daniels.
Chief Engineer ... ... J. Duxon.
Floor Electrician ... ... J. E. Sullivan.
Cameramen ... ... Phillip Tannura.
Henry Harris.
PRODUCTIONS, 1936 : " Wolf's Clothing,"
" Crimson Circle," "Secret of Stamboul."

WESTMINSTER FILMS, LTD.

London Office : 186, Wardour Street.
Telephone : Gerrard 4592.
Managing Director ... Jerome Jackson
Film Director ... ... Michael Powell.

WIDGEY R. NEWMAN PRODUCTIONS.

NATIONAL HOUSE, 60/66, WARDOUR STREET,
W.I.
Telephone : Gerrard 3827.
Gerrard 3359 (night line).
Director : Widgey R. Newman.
Secretary : J. HARKER.
STUDIOS USED : MARYLEBONE AND BUSHEY.
Production Manager ... John Miller.
Film Directors ... ... Widgey R. New-
man.
R. W. Lotinga.
Cameramen .,. ... ... Keith Wilbur.
Frank Parnell.
Roy Fogwell.
Musical Director ... ... John Reynders.
Art Director... ... ... Roy Plaskitt.
Assistant Director ... ... Roy Boulting.
Recording System : Peizo-Electric, Studio Sound
Service, Visatone.
Foreign Sales : A. Fried.
PRODUCTIONS, 1936 : "What the Puppy
Said," "The Dream Doctor," "Pal O' Mine,"
"Apron Fools," "Derby Secrets," "His
Apologies," "Broad Waters," "Our Royal
Heritage "—a National film produced for the
King George Memorial Fund.

WINWOOD PICTURES, LTD.

32, ST. JAMES'S STREET, LONDON, S.W.I.
Telephone : Whitehall 8501.
Directorate : W. H. W. GOSSAGE, R. F.
SHEPPARD.

WYNDHAM FILMS, LTD.
NATIONAL HOUSE, 60-66, WARDOUR STREET, W.I.
Telephone : Gerrard 6826-7.
Chairman : MAJOR K. HORAN.
Managing Director : J. B. WYNDHAM.
Secretary : H. B. SLAUGHTER.
STUDIOS USED : A.T.P. STUDIOS, EALING GREEN.

PRODUCERS OF ADVERTISING PROPAGANDA & SUB-STANDARD FILMS, ETC.

ANGLIA FILMS, LTD.
EAGLE HOUSE, 108-111, Jermyn St., S.W.I.
Telephone : Whitehall 7585.
Directorate : A. Nettlefold, E. Anson Dyer.
Secretary ... . G. D. Midgley.
PRODUCTIONS, 1936: Advertising Cartoons in Monochrome and Colour.

BRITISH COMMERCIAL FILMS (DODDS & HEPPARD, LTD.).
50, BRYANSTON STREET, PORTMAN SQUARE, W.I.
Telephone : Paddington 4060.
Directorate : A. W. DODDS (Managing Director), A. G. DODDS.
Production Manager ... Gustav Pauli.
Scenarists ... ... Margaret Cross.
Vernon G. Clancey.
PRODUCTIONS, 1936 :—Commercial films.

BRITISH UTILITY FILMS, LTD.
OFFICES AND STUDIOS : 10, REGENT SQUARE, W.C.I.
Telephone : Terminus 6660 and 5000
Directorate : JOHN E. ALDERSON, J. C. EMERSON (Joint Managing Directors), MRS. F. KINGDON-WARD.
Secretary ... ... J. C. Emerson.
Film Director and Scenario John E. Alderson.
Editor
Cameraman ... ... James G. Berger.
Advertising, Industrial and Educational Films—35 mm. and 16 mm.
PRODUCTIONS 1935 : "A Plane Tale" "Winning Spirit" "Silver Lining," and "Stand Up and Breathe."

BRUCE'S, LTD.
28A, BROADWAY, EALING, W.5.
Telephone : Ealing 1033.

COMMERCIAL AND EDUCATIONAL FILMS.
10 & 11, RED LION COURT, FLEET STREET, E.C.4.
Directorate : J. B. HELSBY (Chairman and Managing Director), E. J. J. MALLISON, V. M. PALMER, A. S. PARKES, H. STOWELL. J. OLIVER.
STUDIOS : RED LION COURT, FLEET STREET, E.C.4.
Manager and Film
Director ... ... J. Oliver.
Cameramen ... ... V. St. Locke.
E. Coble.
L. Clifford.

PRODUCTIONS, 1936 : "Engine on the Shed," "Events Station Working," "Anytown," "The Royal Scot," Topical and Magazine Items.

DORLAND ADVERTISING, LTD.
DORLAND HOUSE, 14-20, REGENT STREET, S.W.I.
Telephone : Whitehall 0112 (11 lines).
STUDIOS USED : PATHE PICTURES, LTD.
Film Director : C. R. Stilwell.

GARRICK FILM CO., LTD.
PRINCESS ARCADE, PICCADILLY, W.I.
Telephone: Regent 2103-4.

G.-B. SCREEN SERVICES, LTD.
FILM HOUSE, 142-150, WARDOUR STREET, W.I.
Telephone : Gerrard 9292.
Directorate : MARK OSTRER (Chairman), MAURICE OSTRER, MICHAEL E. BALCON, ARTHUR W. JARRATT, IAN CREMIEU-JAVAL, BASIL DAVIES.
Manager : BASIL DAVIES.
Asst. Manager : A. C. SNOWDEN.
Secretary : W. B. ROBINSON.
Studios Used : GAUMONT-BRITISH PICTURE CORPORATION.
Scenario Editor : H. B. GOODWIN.
Production Manager : A. G. JACKSON.
Distribution Manager : A. ARBLASTER.
Publicity and Advertising Manager : H. HALES, DUTTON.
Recording System : British Acoustic.

GRAPHIC FILMS.
THAMES HOUSE, MILLBANK, LONDON, S.W.I.
Telephone : Victoria 9696.
Directorate : H. ROYDS TIDSWELL.
PRODUCTIONS, 1936 : Experimental work.

C. E. HODGES' PRODUCTIONS.
C. E. HODGES and C. L. GALLAVAN.
BEDFORD ROW CHAMBERS, 42, THEOBALD'S RD., W.C.I.
Telephone : Holborn 7738.
Producers of dramatic, interest and industrial films, scenarios and commentaries.

McCONNELL-HARTLEY, LTD.
10, PEARSE STREET, DUBLIN.
Telephone : Dublin 43227.
London Office : 30, BOUVERIE STREET, E.C.4.
Telephone : Central 1240.
Directorate : C. E. McCONNELL (Man. Dir.) COL. C. F. RUSSELL.

NATIONAL FILM CORPORATION, LIMITED
34-36, OXFORD STREET, W.I.
Telephone : Museum 4816.
Directorate : H. ADLEY, A. E. LEYWOOD, J. D. MARKS, S. H. BELL, I. ISAACS.
Production Manager : R. H. KEMP.
PRODUCTIONS, 1935 : Commercial Advertising and Propaganda Films.

NATIONAL PROGRESS FILM CO., LTD.

REGISTERED OFFICE: NATIONAL HOUSE
WARDOUR STREET, W.I.
Telephone: Gerrard 3913 (3 lines).
Telegrams: Profilmads.
Studios Used: Nettlefold, Walton-on-Thames
Chairman: EDWARD WYNER.
Managing Director: PHILIP L. WEINER.
Secretary: B. WEINER.

Sales Director	...	... J. A. Jacobs.
Director of Productions		... Charles Barnett.
Studio Manager	...	... P. L. Weiner.
Chief Engineer	...	... Charles Taylor.
Music Direction	...	... De Wolfe.
Cameramen ...	...	... C. Barnett.
		D. P. Cooper.
		Roy Fogwell.
		Wm. Shenton.

Recording Systems: R.C.A. and Visatone.

S. PRESBURY & CO., LTD.

87, CHARING CROSS ROAD, W.C.2.
Directors: S. PRESBURY (Governing Director)
P. S. PRESBURY, J. G. PRESBURY, R
SALISBURY.
Studio Manager ... ... G. Mitchell.
Scenario Editor ... ... J. G. Presbury.
Advertising Films and Slides.

PUBLICITY FILMS, LTD.

FILMICITY HOUSE, UPPER ST. MARTIN'S LANE,
LONDON, W.C.2.
Telephone: Temple Bar 6482-4.
Directorate: J. A. M. BOND, G. HARRISON,
G. E. TURNER.
STUDIO: 269, KINGSTON ROAD, MERTON PARK,
S.W.19.
Telephone: Liberty 4291.
Recording System: RCA.
Scenarist ... ... Sydney Fox.
Studio Manager ... G. Wynn.
Producers of Advertising Films.

PUBLICITY PICTURE PRODUCTIONS, LTD.

93. WARDOUR STREET, W.I.
Telephone: Gerrard 5843-4.
Directorate: ALL HOPKINS, R. H. WYER, M. J.
SAMUEL.
Cartoon Producing Studio.

Production Manager	...	E. M. Pye.
Studio Manager	...	J. Silk.
Film Directors	...	A. E. C. Hopkins.
		R. H. Wyer.
Scenarists ...	...	L. W. Price.
		C. Millet.
Film Editor	...	M. Samuel.
Art Director	...	I. A. Mathieson.
Cameraman	...	G. Capper.

PRODUCTIONS, 1936:—"Fashion Sketches"
(colour), "Sweets o Victory" (colour), "Magic
Letters" (colour), "Film Fake," "Hoarse
Sense" (colour), "The Cup Final," "Petersen *v.*
Harvey," "Proportional Representation," etc.

RCA PHOTOPHONE, LTD.

ELECTRA HOUSE, VICTORIA EMBANKMENT, W.C.2.
Telephone: Temple Bar 2971-2975.
Telegrams: Ircapp. Estrand.

REVELATION FILMS, LTD.

BUSH HOUSE, LONDON, W.C.2.
Telephone: Temple Bar 5109, 5100
(Booking Dept. 3870).
Directorate: CHARLES A. COCHRANE, RICHARD
A. NEWTON.
STUDIOS USED: SOUND CITY, MARYLEBONE;
STOLL, etc.
PRODUCTIONS, 1936: Educational and Commercial Films and Colour Cartoons.

SCIENCE FILMS, LTD.

27, CLAREVILLE GROVE, LONDON, S.W.7.
Telephone: Kensington 7663.
Directorate: W. B. A. Woolfe, F. A. Goodliffe,
W. E. Woolfe.
Cartoon and animation, trick photography,
optical printing.
Cameramen ... ... Frank A. Goodliffe.
A. E. Jeakins.
Norman Macqueen.

STEUART FILMS.

CHELMSFORD STUDIOS, NORTH FAMBRIDGE.
CHELMSFORD, ESSEX.
Telephone: Latchingdon 317.
Joint Managing Directors:
R. S. STEUART and I. STEUART.
OWN STUDIOS AND CARTOON STUDIOS.
Chief Cameraman ... ... D. J. Beck.
PRODUCTIONS, 1936: Documentary, Publicity
and Educational Films.

TRAVIS JACKSON PRODUCTIONS.

HEAD OFFICE: 79, SOUTH ROAD, MORECAMBE.
Telephone: Morecambe 525.
One sound floor, two unwired. Facilities
include electric cartooning racks, electric effects,
micro-photography, mirror reflex animation.
Production Manager: Travis Jackson, Dpl. Arts
Lond., Assoc. B. & A.F.A.
Scenarist ... ... Theresa Honour.
Film Editor ... ... V. NORDELLA.
PRODUCTIONS, 1936:—Trade contracts and
shorts. Technical and scientific camera work.

YOUNGER PUBLICITY SERVICE, LTD.

CENTRAL HOUSE, 34-36, OXFORD STREET, W.I
Telephone: Museum 4816.
Directors: I. ISAACS, H. ADLEY Managing
Director), J. D. MARKS, S. H. BELL, F. M.
BLOOMFIELD.
Studios at Great Windmill Street, W.
Associated Companies are National Film
Corporation, Ltd., and Younger Film Productions, Ltd.

F. G. WARNE, LTD.

30, BALDWIN STREET, BRISTOL, I.
Telephone: Bristol 24920.
Directorate: F. G. WARNE (Managing), R. F.
WARNE, M. L. HANSFORD.
16 mm. Commercial and Documentary Films,
Local Topicals, etc.

Who's What and Where in the Studio

Aherne, Brian.—Born 1902. Educated Malvern College. Successful West End actor. "The Squire of Long Hadley," "King of the Castle," "Safety First," "A Woman Redeemed," "Shooting Stars," "Underground," "The W. Plan," "Song of Songs," "Constant Nymph." *Club* : Connaught.

Aherne, Pat.—Born 1901, Ireland. Starred in "Blinkeyes," "Virginia's Husband," "Silver Lining," "Carry On," "The Game Chicken," "Huntingtower," "Auld Lang Syne," "City of Play."

Ainley, Henry.—Famous stage actor, appeared in films from 1915 onwards for Hepworth, Ideal, Stoll, etc. "Inscrutable Drew" series, "First Miss Fraser," "As You Like It," "Fire Over England."

Aked Muriel.—Character actress, in several silent films, "Rome Express," "Evensong," etc.

Allen Adrienne (Mrs. Raymond Massey).—Leading lady, "Loose Ends," "The Stronger Sex," "Conflict," "Black Coffee."

Alleyn, Muriel.—Born 1875 ; on stage since 1895. Screen authoress for 20 years. *Address :* —Monks Barn, Amhurst Road, Telscombe Cliffs, Sussex.

Allgood, Sara.—Famous Irish Player. "Blackmail," "Juno and the Paycock."

Arliss, George.—Born 1868. London stage career, 1886 onwards. Films in Hollywood from 1920 ; "The Devil," "Disraeli," "The Green Goddess," "Old English," etc. 1934, made first British film, "The Iron Duke," "The Guv'nor," "East is West," "His Lordship," for Gaumont-British. *Clubs* : Garrick, Green Room.

Arnaud, Yvonne.—Anglo-French farce comedienne. "Canaries Sometimes Sing," "On Approval," "Cuckoo In the Nest," "Princess Charming," "Lady in Danger," "Improper Duchess," "Gay Adventure," etc.

Arnold, Charles W.—Art director, B. & D. "The Outsider," "Rich and Strange," "Money for Nothing," "Tin Gods," "No. 17," "Dick Turpin," "Sorell and Son," "Escape me Never," "When Knights were Bold," "Where's George ?" *Address :* 5, West Drive, Harrow Weald. *Phone :* Stanmore 320.

Arnold, N. Gregory.— Technical direction Famous Players-Lasky British Producers, Ltd., and Grham Wilcox, Ltd. *Address :* "Brookside," Chiltern Avenue, Bushey.

Asher, Billy.—Born 1879 ; formerly Hunt Jockey and in vaudeville ; assistant to Shaw and other London Film directors ; floor manager Alliance Studios, latterly with Herbert Wilcox.

Asher, Irving.—Production Chief, Warner. First National Studios, Teddington, from 1931.

Asquith, Anthony.—Studied film making in Hollywood and assisted in "Boadicea " ; wrote and produced "Shooting Stars," directed by A. V. Bramble. Directed "Underground," "A Runaway Princess," "A Cottage on Dartmoor," "Tell England," "Dance, Little Lady," "Five and Six," "Lucky Number," "Moscow Nights."

Astell, Betty.—Ingenue in British Lion subjects 1932-3.

Ault, Marie.—Whole life on stage. Principal character part in "East of Suez," at His Majesty's Theatre. Took up film work in S. Africa.—"Wee Macgregor's Sweetheart," "Paddy the Next Best Thing," "Woman to Woman," "Monkey's Paw," "Starlit Garden," "Every Mother's Son," "The Rat," "Roses of Picardy," "The Lodger," "Silver Lining." "Kitty," "Life," "Return of the Rat." "Third Time Lucky."

Ayrton, Randle.—Educated King's School, Chester, and Geneva University. Many years on the stage in London and U.S.A. Produced Shakespeare Festivals in England. Played lead at the Stratford-on-Avon Theatre and in own companies. Started filming in 1913 with the London Film Co. Produced for Harma and National Film Co., Boston, U.S.A. Played in "Chu Chin Chow," "Southern Love," "Decameron Nights," "Nell Gwyn," "The Little People," "Passion Island," "One of the Best." 1927, directed "His House in Order." 1928, played in "Eileen," "The Manxman," "High Seas," "Two Worlds." "The Great Game," "Iron Duke," "The Man Who Could Not Forget."

Baddeley, Angela.—"Speckled Band," "The Ghost Train."

Baddeley, Hermione. — Brilliant young stage comedienne ; played for Nettlefold and in "Guns of Loos."

Balcon, S. Chandos.— b. 1891. Production manager, Gaumont-British Pictures. 1928 ; formerly assistant to Hitchcock, Cutts, Brunel.

Balfour, Betty.—Famous British screen comedienne. "Nothing Else Matters," "Mary Find-the-Gold," "Squibs," "Mord Em'ly," "Wee Macgregor's Sweetheart," "Squibs Wins the Calcutta Sweep," "Love, Life and Laughter," "Squibs, M.P." "Squibs' Honeymoon," "Reveille," "Satan's Sister" (all directed by George Pearson), "Monte Carlo," "Somebody's Darling," "The Sea Urchin," "Blinkeyes," "Cinders," "A Sister of Six," "A Little Bit of Fluff." 1927, on contract to British International. "Champagne," "Paradise," "Daughter of the Regiment," "Vagabond Queen," "Raise the Roof," "The Brat," "Evergreen," "My Old Dutch," "Brown On Resolution," "Squibs," "Eliza Comes to Stay."

Banfield, George J.—Managing director, British Filmcraft in 1926. In industry since 1908 on all sides. Directed two-reelers, also "Burgomaster of Stilemonde," "Spangles," "Power Over Men."

Banks, Leslie.—Much American and London stage work in leading roles. British films : "The Fire Raisers," "Man Who Knew Too Much," "Sanders of the River," "The Tunnel." "Fire Over England."

Banks, Monty.—Italian-American comedian and director of many B.I.P. comedy features. "Eighteen Minutes," "So You Won't Talk." etc.

Baring, Norah.—Leading roles in "Underground," "Celestial City," "At the Villa Rose," "Two Worlds," "Murder," "Dance of Witches."

Barkas, Geoffrey.—Many years cameraman Directed "Palaver," "Q-Ships."

Barnes, Arthur.—Experienced assistant director with Wilcox, Cutts, etc. Co-directed "White Cargo."

Barnes, Binnie.—Stage and variety soubrette in B.I.P. films, including "The Last Coupon," "Counsel's Opinion," Katherine Howard in "Private Life of Henry VIII," "Heads We Go," "Private Life of Don Juan," "No Escape," "Forbidden Territory," etc.

Barnes-Heath, Reginald.—Radio and landline work with Fultograph : also editing, Director, Barnes-Heath & Co. (sound equipment), Assistant studio manager and technical adviser Milheath studios. *Phone :* Bushey Heath 1183.

Barrie, Wendy.—First films 1932. "Wedding Rehearsal," "Men of To-morrow," "Private Life of HenryVIII,""Cash,""Digging Deep,"etc.

Barringer, Michael.—Joint director with Geoffrey Barkas of "Q-Ships" and his own story "The Infamous Lady."

Bartlam, Dorothy.—"The Ringer," "Stranglehold," "Tin Gods," "Fascination," "Up for the Derby."

Barry, Joan.—Many silent films; talkies; "The Outsider," "Rich and Strange," "Man of Mayfair," "First Mrs. Fraser," "Rome Express."

Bayley, Hilda.—Stage and screen actress of repute. Chief pictures :—"Under Suspicion," "Carnival," "The Scandal," "The Woman Who Obeyed."

Beaudine, William.— Hollywood director. British films : "Boys will be Boys," "Educated Evans," etc.

Bellamy, George.—b. Bristol. On stage since 1887. Commenced screen career 1905. "Called Back," "The Mother of Dartmoor," "Houp La," "Red Aces." *Club :*—The Green Room.

Belmore, Bertha.—Robust comedienne of musical comedy. Films : "Please Teacher ! " etc.

Benson, Annette.—Leading roles in British and French subjects since 1921.

Bentley, Thomas.—Began screen career 1910. Producer of "Oliver Twist," "David Copperfield," "The Chimes," "Hard Times," "Barnaby Rudge," "Beau Brocade," "Milestones," "The Labour Leader," "Daddy," "Les Cloches de Corneville," "Once upon a Time," "The Divine Gift," "General Post," "Beyond the Dreams of Avarice," "A Master of Craft," "Adventures of Mr. Pickwick," "Old Curiosity Shop," "Through Fire and Water," "White Heat," "The Silver Lining," "Not Quite a Lady," "Young Woodley," "The American Prisoner," "Harmony Heaven," "Compromising Daphne," "Keepers of Youth," "Hobson's Choice," "After Office Hours," "Last Coupon," "Sleepless Nights," "Third Degree," "Those Were the Days," "Silver Blaze."

Bergner, Elisabeth.—Famous German actress : married Dr. Paul Czinner, her director. British pictures : "Catherine the Great," "Escape Me Never," "As You Like It," "Dreaming Lips."

Berry, W. H.—Musical comedy star. Films : "Dominant Sex," etc.

Best, Edna (Mrs. Herbert Marshall).—Several silent films. Talkies "Loose Ends," "Sleeping Partners," "Calendar," "Michael and Mary," "Faithful Heart," "Man Who Knew Too Much."

Best, Joseph (B.Sc. Lond.).—25 years in film industry as author, editor, cameraman and producer. Educational editor to Methuens, Heinemanns ; entered industry with Pathé Frères (to 1914), produced for Gaumont, Universal and others ; also Government and well-known, Societies. Filmed in U.K., Europe, Asia, Canada and Africa. Producer, "Africa Looks Up ; " "Epic of Modern India." Accepts film commissions in any part of the world. *Office :* 176 Wardour Street, W.1. *Address :*—58, Menelik Road, N.W.2.

Betts, John.—Director. Made many short sporting subjects.

Bevan, Isla.—Ingenue heroine of "Nine Till Six," "Sign of Four," etc.

Beville, Richard.—Experienced assistant director of many films ; made "Radio Revue" (B.I.P.) with Archie de Bear.

Bird, Richard.—Stage actor of repute. Leading film roles include "Scotland Yard Mystery," "Great Defender," "What Happened Then ?" "Sensation."

Biro, Lajos.—Hungarian-born author. From Hollywood joined Alexander Korda on formation of London Films ; wrote and collaborated on nearly every Korda story since. *Address :*— Denham studios.

Bishop, H. W.—Joined Trade 1910. Specialised on technical and production side. First in processing in Laboratories then 10 years cameraman, Newsreel, Scientific and Studio Production. Technical Adviser Gaumont Co., now Production Manager Gaumont British News. *Address :* 29, Baronsmede, Gunnersbury Park, Ealing, W.5.

Blackwell, Carlyle.—Famed American screen idol for many years; in British pictures since 1922, "The Virgin Queen," "Beloved Vagabond," "She." Director of Gainsborough Pictures, Ltd. Starred in "The Rolling Road," "One of the Best," "The Wrecker," "The Crooked Billet."

Blake Gerald.—b. 1896. Started in E. F. Moy's workshops; actor, toured own shows; 1934, joined Alba Films as director of shorts, including "The Land They Knew" series. *Address:* Colnbrook, Oak Avenue, Shirley, Surrey. *Phone:* Spring Park 2286.

Bland, Joyce.—Stage leading roles at Embassy and West-end. Films, "Good-night, Vienna," "Crime at Blossoms." "Spy of Napoleon."

Bland R. Henderson.—Actor and poet. With Alexander, Tree, Waller. Films : "From Manger to Cross," "General Post," "Gwyneth of the Welsh Hills," etc. *Clubs:*—Green Room, Lotus, N.Y.

Boothby, Geoffrey.—Son of famous author of thrillers ; assistant director for Gaumont, etc.

Bosco, Wallace.—"Prisoner of Zenda," "Arsene Lupin," "Middleman," "Two Roads," "Lion's Cubs," "Snow in the Desert," "Turf Conspiracy," "Quinneys," "Sailors Don't Care," etc.

Bouchier, Dorothy (formerly Chili).—Graduated from mannequin : silent film successes and "Carnival," "Ebb Tide," "Purse Strings," etc.

Bowden, William.—Directed "The Blue Lagoon" for I.V.T.A. ; 1927, assistant director on Elstree subjects with Bentley and Syd Chaplin.

Bowler, Stanley, W., A.R.P.S.—Industrial and scientific production, standard and sub-standard; diagrammatic and technical cartoons. *Address:* —4, Majestic Mansions, Tottenham Court Road. *Phone:* Museum 6483.

Boxall, H. Granville.—Entered industry 1919. Actively connected with adaptation and installation as well as their conversion to sound stages of the Islington Studios. From 1929 Director of administration, Gaumont-British studios, Shepherd's Bush. *Phone:* Shepherd's Bush 1210.

Boyd, Dorothy.—Phonofilms, 1926. "Easy Virtue," "Constant Nymph," "Toni," and ingenue lead in "Somehow Good," "Love's Option," "Auld Lang Syne," "Birds of Prey." "Girl in the Night," "Iron Stair." *Recreation:*— Tennis, swimming.

Braddell, Maurice.—Juvenile lead: "Dawn," "Men of To-morrow," etc.

Bramble, A. V.—b. Portsmouth. Started acting for the screen in 1914. Since produced many films, including "A Girl of London," "Zeebrugge," for New Era, jointly with H. Bruce Woolf; King Henry, in "Becket" (Stoll) : "Chick"; "The Man Who Changed His Name." Directed "Shooting Stars" for Anthony Asquith. 1933, "Mrs. Dane's Defence."

Braniford, Aggie.—b. 1915. Juvenile roles of many British films, also "Mare Nostrum." *Address:*—20, Wakeman's Hill Avenue, Colindale, N.W.9. *Phone:*—Colindale 6497.

Brantford, Mickey,—b. 1912. Juvenile roles "Carry On !" "Dawn," "Sexton Blake" "The Burgomaster of Stilemonde," "Mr. Cohen Takes a Walk," "My Old Dutch," etc. *Address:*—102, Ealing Village, W.5. *Phone:* Perivale 3612.

Brenon, Herbert.—b. Dublin. Started as West End call-boy ; actor, author, directed many big Hollywood films, including "Beau Geste." Returned 1934 for B.I.P. "Living Dangerously," "Someone at the Door," "The Dominant Sex."

Breon, Edmond.—Stage light comedian in leading British talkie parts.

Brisson, Carl.—b. Copenhagen. Was amateur boxing champion of Scandinavia and Central Europe at the age of fifteen. One of England's leading musical comedy favourites. Starred in "The Ring," "The Manxman," "The American Prisoner," "Song of Soho," "Knowing Men," "Prince of Arcadia," "Two Hearts in Waltz Time." Paramount Hollywood contract, 1934.

Brittain, H. Leslie.—b. Birmingham. Film editor.

Brouett, Albert.—b. France. Comedian and producer. Many years in film industry, with Eclair and P.F. Played in Alhambra revues, produced "A Rogue in Love," and three comedies based on Fred Karno's sketches.

Brunel, Adrian, F.R.G.S.—Director and Scenarist. Author of "Filmcraft," "Only Yesterday," and "Film Production." Joined Moss Empires Bioscope in 1915. 1917, Manager of Productions and Scenario Departments of the Ministry of Information. Joined British Actors' Film Company 1919 as Scenario-Editor ; 1920, directed A. A. Milne comedies for Minerva Films. In 1922 directed Ivor Novello and Nina Vanna in "The Man Without Desire." Later joined Gainsborough, directing "Blighty," "The Constant Nymph," "A Light Woman," "The Vortex," and "The Crooked Billet." Has since made "A Taxi to Paradise," "I'm an Explosive," "Badger's Green," "Variety," "City of Beautiful Nonsense," "Menace," "Important People," "Little Napoleon," and "While Parents Sleep." *Address:*—28, Park Mansions, Knightsbridge, W.2. *Phone:* Kensington 9383.

Buchanan, Andrew.—b. 1897. Dramatist, novelist and film director. Lecturer on film production. Originator of the Cinemagazine, now Gaumont-British Magazine, in 1926. Author of "Films—The Way of the Cinema," "He Died Again." "Art of Film Production" (1936). *Address:*—G.-B. Distributors, Ltd., Film House, Wardour Street, W.1. *Phone:*—Gerrard 9292.

Buchanan, Jack.—Revue and musical comedy star. "The Happy Ending," "Bulldog Drummond's Third Round," "Toni," "Settled Out of Court," "Man of Mayfair," "Good-Night, Vienna," "Yes, Mr. Brown" (directed and acted), "That's a Good Girl," "Brewster's Millions," "Come Out of the Pantry," "When Knights were Bold," "This'll Make You Whistle."

Burdon, Albert.—Revue comedian, in "Maid of the Mountains," "Letting in the Sunshine," "It's a Boy."

Burnaby, Davy.—Comedian, former Co-optimist. Films, "Three Men In a Boat," "Cleaning Up," "Keep it Quiet," "Radio Parade of 1934," "Song of the Road," etc.

Busholl, Anthony. First films in Hollywood; including "Journey's End." British pictures, "The Ghoul," "Soldiers of the King," "Channel Crossing," "Red Wagon," etc.

Butt, Lawson.—Brother of Dame Clara. Stage and screen experience of twenty years. Returned from Hollywood, 1927. "Toni," "The Ringer," "Lady of the Lake," "City of P.ay "; directed "Afterwards."

But'er, Alexander.—Directed several features for G. B. Samuelson.

"Cable, Boyd" (Col. E. A. Ewart).—b. 1873 India. Writer of film stories, scenarios, dialogue. Has published many books and stories and articles in almost every magazine and newspaper of standing in the country. Travelled Africa, Australia, New Zealand, and the East (sometimes as passenger, sometimes as a "hand" in sail or steam). Student and writer military and nautical history. Member, Society Nautical Research, Army Historical Research Society. *Address:* 9, Stone Buildings, Lincolns Inn, W.C.2. *Phone :* Chancery 8039.

Cadman, T. E. F.—In films since 1916; cameraman to several companies; assistant director with Gainsborough ; joined B.I.P. 1933 ; directed shorts. *Address :* Red Gable Oldfield Lane, Greenford. *Phone :* Perivale 1731.

Calthrop, Donald.—Prominent juvenile and stage comedian who resumed film work, after broadcasting fame, with "Shooting Stars," and at Beaconsfield, first talkie : "Blackmail," then "Atlantic," "Song of Soho," "Elstree Calling," "Two Worlds," "Loose Ends,'" "Cock-·ney War Stories," "Almost a Honeymoon," "The Bells," "Ghost Train," "No. 17," "Rome Express," "F.P. One," "Sorrell and Son," "Scrooge," "Thunder in the Air," "Love From a Stranger."

Calvert, C. C.—Producer : "Silent Evidence," "A Prince of Lovers," "Lights of London," "Bonnie Prince Charlie," and Cosmopolitan shorts, 1925.

Carew, James.—Began screen career 1915. "Twelve-Ten," "The Nature of the Beast," "Sunken Rocks," "The Forest on the Hill" "Alf's Button," "Narrow Valley," "Wild Heather," "Mr. Justice Raffles," "Tansy," "Mist in the Valley," "Strangling Threads," "As He Was Born" (all Hepworth), "Love Story of Aliette Brunton," "A Colombo Night" "Love's Option," "Lady of the Lake," "High Seas," "Guilt," "To Oblige a Lady," "Brother Alfred," "Mischief," "It's a Lion," "You Made Me Love You," "Mayfair Girl," "S.O.S. Iceberg," "Too Many Millions," "Freedom of the Seas," "Dictator," "All at Sea," "Come Out of the Pantry," "Mary Celeste," "The Tunnel," "The Improper Duchess," "Spy of Napoleon," "Livingstone," "Thunder in the City," "Wings Over Africa." *Club :*—Green Room. *Address :*—15, Burleigh Mansions, W.C.2. *Phone :* Temple Bar 6156.

Carlisle, Peggy.—Many leads for Stoll; also in "Hindle Wakes," "The Ring," etc.

Carr, Cameron. — b. Kingston-on-Thames. Commenced screen career, 1909. "A Fortune at Stake," "A Turf Conspiracy," "A Soul's Crucifixion," "In the Gloaming," "Under Suspicion," "A Gentleman Rider," "A Daughter of Eve," "A Dead Certainty," "Her Son," "Trents Last Case," "A Rank Outsider," "Out to Win," "Silver Lining," "The Ware

Case," "Poppies of Flanders," "The Blue Peter," "The Third Eye," "The W. Plan." *Address :* —3, Minerva Road, Kingston-on-Thames.

Carr, Jane.—Formerly cabaret and revue. B.I.P.films, also "Dick Turpin,""Keep it Quiet."

Carroll, Madeleine.—Leading lady, "Guns of Loos," "The Firstborn," "The Crooked Billet," "American Prisoner," "Atlantic," "School for Scandal," "French Leave," "Kissing Cup's Race," "Young Woodley," "The W Plan," "Escape," "Madame Guillotine," "Fascination," G.-B. contract 1932. "Sleeping Car," "I Was a Spy," "Thirty-nine Steps," "The Secret Agent." Made "The World Moves On," in Hollywood, 1934.

Carter, Geoffrey.—Studio press officer, London Films, Denham.

Carter, James.—Formerly art director, Stolls etc., joined Twickenham Studios 1929, late studio manager and on board of directors. *Address :* Twickenham Film Studios.

Casson, Ann.—Daughter of Dame Sybil Thorndike. "Escape," "Dance, Little Lady," "No. 17."

Cellier, Frank.—Prominent Stage actor. Films : "Colonel Blood" (title role) "Passing of the Third Floor Back," "Man Who Changed His Name," "Rhodes," etc.

Chapman, Edward.—Young character actor talkie successes in "Juno and the Paycock," "Murder," "The Skin Game," "Things to Come," "Rembrandt," etc.

Chrystall, Belle.—Leading rôles : "Hindle Wakes," "Friday the 13th," "Third Degree," etc.

Churchill, Diana.—Stage actress. Films : "Dishonour Bright," "Sensation," "The Dominant Sex."

Clarke-Smith, D. A.—Leading West End actor. "The Ghoul," "Turkey Time," etc.

Clarbour, Percy.—Twenty years on stage. Started in 1912 as an artist ; in 1919 became casting agent. *Address :*—Palace House, Shaftesbury Avenue. *Phone :*—Regent 2716.

Cliff, Laddie.—Comedian, former Co-optimist. Silent film lead in "The Card." Talkies : "Sleeping Car," "Happy," "Sporting Love," etc.

Clive, Colin.—"Journey's End" (in Hollywood) ; "Stronger Sex," "Spring Cleaning."

Coffin, Mrs. C. Hayden.—"Kissing Cup's Race," "Christie Johnstone," "The Bonnie Brier Bush," "This Freedom," "Bonnie Prince Charlie," "Haunted Houses," "The Burgomaster of Stilemonde." *Address :*—55, Campden Street, Kensington, W.8. *Phone :*—Park 3623.

Collins, Edwin J.—Commenced screen career with Messrs. Cricks and Martin. Then followed engagements with the Clarendon and Ideal. "God and the Man," "The Starting Point," "Foul Play," "The Channings," "Hard Cash," "Miss Charity," "The God in the Garden."

Collins, José.—Musical comedy star. Silent films 1920–23. Talkies : "Facing the Music."

Compton, Fay.—b. 1894. Famous stage star First film, "One Summer's Day," then "A Woman of No Importance," "A Bill of Divorcement," "This Freedom," "Mary Queen of Scots," "Claude Duval," "Eleventh Commandment," "The Happy Ending," "Settled Out of Court," "London Love," "Somehow

Good," "Zero," "Fashions in Love," "Tell England," "Cape Forlorn," "The Happy Husband," "Waltzes From Vienna," "Autumn Crocus," "Blossom Time," "Song at Eventide."

Cooper, Frederick.—Notable London stage successes include dipsomaniac in "Outward Bound." Films include "Every Mother's Son," "The Only Way."

Cooper, George A.—Film editor of British and Italian pictures for many years. 1922–23, directed brilliant series of two-reel Quality Plays, which established him as a coming director; directed "Claude Duval," "The Eleventh Commandment," "The Happy Ending," "Settled Out of Court," "Somebody's Darling." 1927, Phonofilms. 1928. "Master and Man." 1932, "Face at the Window," "Puppets of Fate." Twickenham quota subjects, 1933, 1935, "Royal Eagle."

Cooper, Richard.—"Sillyass" talkie roles in "At the Villa Rose," "House of the Arrow," "Bed and Breakfast," "The Last Hour," "Lord Richard in the Pantry," "Kissing Cup's Race," "Enter the Queen."

Corbett, Leonora.—West End stage actress. Films: "Love on Wheels," "Constant Nymph," "Warn London," "Heart's Desire," "Living Dangerously," "The Tenth Man."

Courtneidge, Cicely (Mrs. Jack Hulbert).—Comedienne. "Elstree Calling," "Jack's the Boy," "Soldiers of the King," "Aunt Sally," "Me and Marlborough." "Everybody Dance," "Take My Tip."

Croise, Hugh.—b. Cornwall. "The Game of Liberty," "Dop Doctor" (Samuelson). Produced "Four Men in a Van" (Direct), "Three Men in a Boat" (Artistic). In 1923, writing and producing in Germany; 1924, "The Old Man in the Corner" (Stoll); 1928, British Talking Pictures, Wembley Park. *Address :*—c/o *Kinematograph Weekly.*

Cullen, R. J.—Assistant director to many prominent British and American directors. "Reveille," "Squibs, M.P.," "Satan's Sister," "Squibs' Honeymoon," "Mumsee." "Dawn." Production manager, British and Dominions.

Cunningham, Robert.—Veteran stage actor and vocalist; the Admiral in "The Luck of the Navy." *Address :*—Stage Guild.

Currie, Finlay.—American character expert. "Rome Express," "Princess Charming," etc.

Curzon, George.—Son of Ellis Jeffreys, formerly in Navy; actor since 1924. Films since 1931, "After the Ball," "Things to Come, ' etc. *Phone :*—Kensington 8302.

Cutts, J. H. Graham.—b. in 1885. Has been associated with the Industry for many years. First production, "The Wonderful Story." "Flames of Passion," "Paddy the Next Best Thing," "Woman to Woman," "The White Shadow," "The Passionate Adventure," "The Blackguard," "The Prude's Fall," "The Rat," "The Sea Urchin," "The Rolling Road" "Confetti," "Triumph of the Rat," "Chance the Idol," "Return of the Rat," "Three Men in a Boat." Unit manager and co-director, Gaumont-British; joined O'Bryen, Linnit and Dunfee, 1936. "Aren't Men Beasts," for B.I.P.

D'Aragon, Lionel.—Actor of thirty years' experience. "Guy Fawkes" (Earl Salisbury) "Mary Queen of Scots," "Mist in the Valley," "Balaclava," "High Treason." *Address :*— 12, Alexandra Road, Upper Norwood.

Dane, Frank.—Former West-End actor; films under George Loane Tucker onwards. In U.S.A. 1924–6; parts in "Pagliacci," "Flag Lieutenant," "Lloyd of the C.I.D." "The Ringer," "Down Stream." *Address :*—c/o Gorringe's, 9a, Green Street, Leicester Square, and Radnor Hall County Club, Elstree.

Dare, Phyllis.—Former musical comedy star. Talkies : "The Crime at Blossoms," "Man Who Couldn't Forget."

Davenport, A. Bromley.—b. Warwickshire. Educated at Eton. "The Persistent Lovers " "The Great Gay Road," "The Bigamist," "Fox Farm," "Starlit Garden," "Bonnie Prince Charlie," "Physician," "Captivation," "Mischief," "Self-Made Lady," "Return of Raffles," "Lord Camber's Ladies," "Face at the Window," "Lily of Killarney," "Iron Stair," "Lost in the Legion," "Vintage Wine," "Scarlet Pimpernel," "So You Won't Talk, " "Crouching Beast," "London Melody." etc. *Clubs :*—Garrick, Green Room. *Address :*— 24, Pelham Street, S.W.7. *Phone :*—Kensington 2583.

Day, Frances.—American musical star, leading lady of "Girl from Maxims," "Two Hearts in Waltz Time," "Oh, Daddy !" "Public Nuisance No. 1."

Dean, Basil.—Famous theatrical producer, impresario and dramatist, of Reandean repute. Produced (with Adrian Brunel) "The Constant Nymph " (Gainsborough), and for Paramount in New York. Founded Associated British Producers, 1929. Directed "Escape," "Birds of Prey," "Sally in Our Alley," "Nine till Six," "Loyalties," "Constant Nymph," "Autumn Crocus," "Sing as We Go," "Lorna Doone," "Look Up And Laugh," "Whom The Gods, Love," "Queen Of Hearts."

De Casalis, Jeanne.—b. Africa, 1896. Paris New York and London stage star. "Settled Out of Court," "Glad Eye," "Arcadians," "Knowing Men," "Nine Till Six," "Mrs. Feather," "Mixed Doubles," "Nell Gwyn " *Address :*—105, Hallam Street, W.1.

De Courville, Albert.—Revue producer. Directed talkies, "The Wolves," "77 Park Lane," "There Goes the Bride," "Midshipmaid," "This is the Life," "Wild Boy," "Seven Sinners," "She Got What She Wanted."

Denham, Reginald.—Actor under Benson Tree ; directed over 100 plays on London and New York stage. Joined Paramount-British, 1931, as dialogue director ; director 1933 onwards : "Death at Broadcasting House," "The Silent Passenger," "Crimson Circle," "Dreams Come True," etc. Director of I.F.P., Ltd., proprietors of Phœnix Films, 28, Mortimer Street, W.1. *Phone :* Museum 1922.

Desmond, Florence.—Revue star and mimic ; films, "Accused," etc.

Dewhurst, George.—Actor with Liverpool Repertory and in West End. Entered film world as actor, script-writer, and producer. With Broadwest produced "A Great Coup." With Hepworth appeared in "The Narrow Valley," his own story ,"Wild Heather," etc. Directed "What the Butler Saw," Harry Tate in "Motoring," and "A Sister to Assist 'Er " (three versions).

Dixon, Cecil.—Assistant director and production manager with leading studios. *Address :* 32, Loxley Road, S.W.18. *Phone :* Battersea 5239.

Dodds, J. W.—Assistant director from 1928. Gainsborough and Gaumont-British pictures.

Dolman, Richard.—Young actor who started in revue. Films, " Love on the Spot," " Looking on the Bright Side."

Donaldson, C.—Ex-naval officer : assistant director on " Middle Watch," " Dick Turpin," etc., founded City Films, 1935.

Donat, Robert.—West End stage juvenile. Film debut, " Men of To-morrow," " Bright Lights of London," " Cash," " Private Life of Henry VIII," " 39 Steps," " Ghost Goes West," " Knight Without Armour," etc.

Dormand, Francis W.—Production manager and producer, Dorland Advertising, Ltd. Now producer, Fidelity Films. *Address :*—Heatherlea, Kingston Road, West Ewell, Surrey. *Phone :* Derwent 1918.

Double, Stanley G.—Born 1895. Studio and consulting engineer. Completed equipment installation at Islington studios, 1920 ; chief engineer there four years. 1926, completed whole electrical scheme at Elstree (British National) supervising since foundations. Chief engineer, British International, 1927-1930, Equipped Warner's Teddington Studios, 1931. chief engineer, A.T.P. studios, Ealing. *Address :* 71, Park Side Drive, Cassiobury Park, Watford. *Phone :*—Watford 3490 and Ealing 6761.

Downing, John.—Press studio representative, British and Dominions Films, Herbert Wilcox Productions. Formerly on staff, "Daily Express," " Film Weekly," " Daily Film Renter."

Drayton, Alfred.—Character stage actor. Many old silent pictures ; Edgar Wallace talkies : " The Squeaker," " Jack Ahoy," " Aren't Men Beasts ? " etc.

Duke, Ivy.—b. South Kensington. " The Garden of Resurrection," " The Lure of Crooning Water," " Duke's Son," " Testimony," " The Persistent Lovers," " Starlit Garden " (all George Clark productions), " The Great Prince Shan," " Decameron Nights," " A Knight in London."

Dupont, A. E.—German director. At Elstree supervised " Madame Pompadour." Directed " Moulin Rouge," " Piccadilly," " Atlantic," " Two Worlds," " Cape Forlorn."

Dyall, Franklin.—Celebrated stage villain ; appeared in " Easy Virtue " for Gainsborough and his first talkie, " Atlantic," " Limping Man," " Night in Montmartre."

Edwards, Henry.—b. Somerset. Spent life on stage, producing, playing leads, play-writing including " Doorsteps," " Man Who Took a Chance." Played in West End, also in America with Ethel Barrymore. Commenced screen career 1915. Produced and played in " A Welsh Singer," and " East is East." Wrote, produced and played in " Broken Threads," " Towards the Light," " Merely Mrs. Stubbs," " The City of Beautiful Nonsense," " His Dearest Possession," " A Temporary Vagabond," " The Amazing Quest of Ernest Bliss," " John Forrest Finds Himself," " Aylwin," " A Lunatic at Large," " Hanging Judge," " The Bargain," " Tit for Tat," " Lily of the Alley," (a six-reel no title picture), " The World of Wonderful Reality," " Boden's Boy." " The Naked Man." All these for Edwards' series of Hepworth picture plays. " Owd Bob," " Flag Lieutenant, " The Fake," " The Joker,"

" Further Adventures of the Flag Lieutenant," " Fear," " Three Kings," Talkies : " Call of the Sea," " Girl in the Night," " Stranglehold," " Brother Alfred," directed " Flag Lieutenant," " Barton Mystery," " Discord," " Lord of the Manor," " Purse Strings," " Anne One Hundred," " General John Regan," " Man Who Changed His Name," " The Lad," " Lord Edgware Dies," " Are You a Mason ? " " Rocks of Valpre," " D'ye Ken John Peel." " Squibs," " Vintage Wine," " Private Secretary," " Scrooge," " Eliza Comes to Stay," " In the Soup," " Juggernaut," " Beauty and the Barge," " Vicar of Bray." *Club :*—Savage. *Address :*—Gracious Pond, Chobham, Surrey. *Phone :*—Long Cross 33.

Elsom, Isobel.—Many silent films for most studios. Talkies : " Thirteenth Candle."

Elvey Maurice.—Former stage producer, director of over 100 films since 1913. " Mr. Wu," " Fruitful Vine," " Sally Bishop " ; many Matheson Lang subjects for Stoll ; Gaumont, 1926, " Mdlle. from Armentieres," " Hindle Wakes," " Roses of Picardy," " Flag Lieutenant," " Quinneys," " Balaclava," " High Treason," " School for Scandal," " Sally in Our Alley," " The Lodger," " Soldiers of the King." " Lily of Killarney," " Wandering Jew," " Princess Charming," " This Week of Grace." " The Code," " Road House," " The Clairvoyant," " The Tunnel." " Spy of Napoleon," " Man in the Mirror," " Widow's Island." Has directed in Germany, also in Hollywood for Fox and Metro. *Club :*—Savage.

Elvin, George H., A.C.I.S.—Secretary, Association of Cine-Technicians, 30, Piccadilly Mansions, Shaftesbury Avenue, W.1. *Phone :* Gerrard 2366.

Emery, Pollie.—b. 1875. First stage appearance under father's (Frank Emery's) management, Liverpool. Toured the world. Films : " Perpetua," " A Sister to Assist 'Er," " Nell Gwyn," " Peg of Old Drury," " While Parents Sleep," " The Wedding Group." *Club :*—Arts Theatre. *Address :*—7, Kenyon Mansions, Queen's Club Gardens, W.14. *Phone :*—Fulham 055.

English, Lt.-Col. Robert, D.S.O.—Player of many distinctive and military roles since 1920. Recently, " Love in Exile," " Guilty Melody," " Secret of Stamboul," " Educated Evans," " Everything is Rhythm." *Address :*—291, Brompton Road, S.W.3. and Garrick Club. *Phone :*—Kensington 2634.

Esmond, Annie.—Actress of extensive West End and touring experience. " Lily of the Alley," " Love, Life and Laughter," " Young Lochinvar," " City of Youth," " Prince of Arcadia," " This Week of Grace," etc.

Evans, Maurice.—Stage juvenile of " Journey's End " fame. Films, " White Cargo," " Raise the Roof," " Should a Doctor Tell ?" " Chinese Bungalow," " Marry Me," " Scrooge," etc.

Eveleigh, Leslie, F.R.P.S.—Cinematographer director, production manager, since 1910. Visited Hollywood, 1925. On executive, British Kinematograph Society. Production manager, National Screen Service. *Address :*—Gaisford House, Gaisford Street, Kentish Town, N.W.5. *Phone :*—Gulliver 1957.

Fairbank, Jerry.—Make-up expert : Rex Ingram, Paramount, B.I.P., Beaconsfield

Fairbrother, Sydney.—b. London. " The Temporary Gentleman " (Samuelson), " The Children of Gibeon " (Master), " Laddie "

(Progress), "Married Love," "The Beloved Vagabond," "Confetti," "Third String," "Murder on the Second Floor."

Field, Alexander.—Cockney specialist. "Tin Gods," "Crooked Billet," "Ebb Tide," "Dick Turpin," "Sally in Our Alley," "Red Wagon," "Limelight," etc.

Field, Ben.—Well-kn wn West End character actor; "South Sea Bubble " "Man Who Changed His Name," "Sally in Our Alley," etc.

Fields, Gracie.—Comedienne. b. Rochdale. Touring revue with husband (Archie Pitt) for eight years before appearing in London. Films: "Sally in Our Alley," "Looking on the Bright Side," "This Week of Grace," "Sing as We Go," "Look Up and Laugh," "Queen of Hearts."

Findlay, Hugh.—Entered Industry with Pathé Joined Gaumont publicity staff, became studio publicity manager Gaumont-British, 1931. *Address :*—G. B. Studios, Shepherd's Bush.

Fitzgerald, Geraldine.—Irish ingenue. Leading lady, "Turn of the Tide," "Man Who Could Not Forget," etc.

Flaherty, Robert. — Irish-American director of "Nanook," "Moana," etc. 1933-4, made "Man of Aran." 1935, "Elephant Boy."

Fogwell, R. G.—Fox London p blicity manager 1921; 1926, returned from Hollywood, wrote many stories and scripts. Directed "Consequences," "Introspection," "Guilt." Formed production unit, 1930. Wrote and directed "Madame Guillotine." 1932, "Wonderful Story."

Forde, Walter.—b. Bradford. Screen comedian who has directed himself in many "shorts," U.S.A., 1923-25. Director of "Wait and See," "What Next," "The Silent House," "Would You Believe It," "You'd be Surprised," "Red Pearls," "Lord Richard in the Pantry," "Third Time Lucky," "Ghost Train," "Splinters in the Navy," "Jack's the Boy," "Rome Express." "Orders Is Orders," "Jack Ahoy," "Chu Chin Chow," "Brown On Resolution," "Bulldog Jack," "King of the Damned," "Land Without Music."

Formby, George.—Comedian. Films: "Off the Dole," "No Limit."

Fox, Reginald.—Recent leads: "Palaver," "Under Arabian Skies."

French, Harold.—Juvenile lead in many silent and talking subjects.

Freshman, William.— Juvenile, b. Australia; films: "Luck of the Navy," "Guns of Loos," "Rising Generation," "Glorious Youth," "Widdicombe Fair," "They Had to Love," "Bachelor's Baby." "Street Singer's Serenade." *Phone :*—Hampstead 7310.

Fuller, Leslie.—Comedian of the Margate Pedlers, and in B.I.P. broad comedy talkies notably "The Last Coupon." Formed own unit, 1934. "Big Hearted Bill."

Fyffe, Will.—Famous Scots comedian. "Elstree Calling," "Happy," "Man Who Could Not Forget."

Gaffney, Marjorie.—Assistant director of "Atlantic," "W. Plan," "Middle Watch," "Conflict." *Address :*—The Timber House, Deacons Hill, Elstree. *Phone:*—Elstree 267.

Garrick, John.—Juvenile lead, Hollywood and London. British films: "Turn of the Tide," etc.

Gawthorne, Peter.—Formerly musical comedy hero; in Hollywood 1925-31. "Flag Lieutenant," "Jack's the Boy," "Prince of Arcadia," etc.

Gay, Maisie.—Broad comedienne, "To Oblige a Lady," "The Old Man."

Gee, George.—Musical comedy star. "Cleaning Up," etc.

Gee, Hugh.—Art Director: "Tesha," "Kitty," "Vagabond Queen," "To-morrow We Live," etc.

Gerrard, Gene.—Musical and revue comedian. Talkies: "Bridegroom's Widow," "Out of the Blue," "Brother Alfred," "Lucky Girl," "Let Me Explain, Dear," "The Guv'nor," "No Monkey Business," "Such is Life," etc.

Gielgud, John.—Famous young classic stage actor. Films: "Insult," "Good Companions," "The Secret Agent."

Gill, Basil.—Stage actor with Tree, etc. Films in 1918-20. Talkies: "High Treason," "Should a Doctor Tell ?" etc.

Glyn, Elinor.—Famous authoress and discoverer of "It." Directed personally "Knowing Men," at Elstree, 1929.

Goddard, Alf.—Born 1897 London. "Mademoiselle from Armentieres," "Every Mother's Son," "Remembrance," "Sailors Don't Care," "Verdun," "Balaclava," "Alf's Button." "Pride of the Force," "Lost in the Legion," "It's a Bet," "First a Girl," "No Limit." *Address :*—373, Corfield Street, E.2.

Godfrey, Peter.—Actor-producer, of Gate Theatre celebrity. Directed Gaumont talkies 1930: "Thread o' Scarlet," "Down River."

Goodner, Carol.—American actress. Silent films at B.I.P. Talkies, "Just Smith," "Fire Raisers."

Gordon, Hal.—Variety comedian, in many B.I.P. comedies.

Gott, Barbara.—Sound stage and screen artist in mature strong rôles. "Not Quite a Lady," "A Sister to Assist 'Er," "At the Villa Rose."

Graham, Margot.—B.I.P. contract 1930, after stage success, "The Love Habit," "Happy Husband," "Stamboul," "Easy Money," "Prince of Arcadia," "Sorrell and Son," etc.

Gray, Eve.—Born Birmingham, 1904. Much Australian stage experience. Leading film roles in "Silver Lining," "Poppies of Flanders," "One of the Best," "Moulin Rouge," "Smashing Through," "Sweet Pepper," "Loves of Robert Burns," "Night Birds," "At Midnight."

Gray, Hugh.—Scenario writer, London Film Productions, b. 1900. Educated, Louvain University and Oxford. F.R.G.S. Army 1918-1919. Merchant Service. Author, journalist and lecturer. Organiser and head of Gaumont-British Research Dept., 1932-1935. Collaborator on script of "Conquest of the Air " for London Film Productions. *Address :*—Denham Studio.

Greenwood, Edwin.—b. 1895. Educated St. Paul's and Sorbonne. Stage director and actor. 1912-1918. Liverpool Repertory, J. B. Fagan, 1922, June, produced "Romance of History," "Gems of Literature," and "Wonder Women of History" series for B. & C. 1922, stage director for Maurice Moscovitch. "The Fair Maid of Perth," "A Woman in Pawn," "What Money Can Buy," British Acoustic subjects, "To What Red Hell." On scripts for B.I.P., 1931.

Grey, Ann.—Leading lady; "Guilt," "Man at Six," "Calendar," "No. 17," "Leap Year," "Lady in Danger," etc.

Grossman, Joe.—b. London 1888. Educated B.B.S., Brentford, Dover Higher Grade. Has been through every branch of the variety business; with David Devant five years. Left the stage on the outbreak of war; served five years. Mentioned three times in dispatches, awarded the M.S.M., and also granted the special Diploma of the Grand Order of St. John of Jerusalem for services in connection with the transport of sick and wounded. In June, 1924, was personally invested with the Order of St. John by H.M. the King at Buckingham Palace. In June, 1931, again personally decorated with the Conspicuous Service Medal of the Order of St. John of Jerusalem. Decorated with Order of Mercy by H.R.H. Prince of Wales, 1932. Also possessor of the Gold Badge of the Royal National Life-Boat Institution, presented by the Lord Mayor of London in May, 1933. Upon demobilisation joined Violet Melnotte, acting manager of the Duke of York's Theatre, and at the same time acting manager of the Kingsway Theatre. Joined Stoll as studio manager at Surbiton, June, 1920; transferred to Cricklewood, 1921. Studio manager for British International Pictures, July, 1927.

Groves, Fred.—b. London. Commenced film work 1912. "The Manxman," "The Labour Leader," "Squibs," "Out of the Blue," "Suspense." *Club:*—Green Room.

Grune, Karl.—b. 1892 in Vienna, studied at Viennese Conservatory for Dramatic Art, stage experience as actor on Austrian and German provincial stages, then as actor and director on Volksbühne, Vienna, and Reinhardt's Deutsches Theatre, Berlin. Film career since 1922 directed for Ufa and other Berlin companies "Night Without Dawn," "Count of Charolais," "The Street," "Explosion," "Jealous," etc. Director of productions for Emelka, Munich. Started directing in England in 1934 with "Abdul Hamid" for B.I.P., Capitol.

Gullan, Campbell.—Stage director and actor. Directed talkie of "Caste," 1930. Dialogue director, "Iron Duke."

Gundrey, V. Gareth.—In Industry since 1920, film and scenario editor, productions manager. Directed "The Devil's Maze," "Just for a Song," "Symphony in Two Flats," "Stronger Sex," "Hound of the Baskervilles." Proprietor, The Book Mart. *Address:*—12, Sunbury Avenue, East Sheen, S.W.14. *Phone:*—Prospect 4111.

Gunn, Judy.—Ingenue; "Lilies of the Field," "Vintage Wine," etc., on Twickenham contract.

Gwenn, Edmund.—Prominent West End character actor. Played Hornblower in silent film, 1920, and in Hitchcock's talkie version, 1930 of "The Skin Game," "Love on Wheels," Oakroyd in "Good Companions," "Channel Crossing," "Friday the 13th," "Spring in the Air," "Laburnum Grove."

Hale, Binnie.—Musical comedy star. "Road House," "Hyde Park Corner," "Take a Chance."

Hale, Sonnie.—Light comedian; married Jessie Matthews. Talkies: "Happy Ever After," "Friday the 13th," "Wild Boy," "Evergreen," "My Song for You," "Just a Girl." Directed "Head Over Heels."

Hamer, Gladys.—Quaint comedy roles for Stoll, Pathé, Gaumont. etc. *Address:*—6, Kilburn Priory, N.W.6. *Phone:*—Maida Vale 1086

Hamilton, John.—On stage at age of six. "Mountain Eagle," "Mdlle. from Armentieres" "Last Witness," "Shadow of Egypt," "Silver Lining," "South Sea Bubble," "Three Kings," "To What Red Hell."

Hammond, Kay.—Comedienne, member of the Standing family. Films from 1930. "Nine Till Six," "Britannia of Billingsgate," "Sleeping Car," etc.

Harcourt, William.—Formerly cameraman on remote trips, including Tibet, South Seas, Africa, also Paramount, Long Island. Became make-up editor, Paramount News; assistant general manager, Denham laboratories. *Address:*—Lal-Koti, Latchmoor Avenue, Gerrards Cross.

Harding, Jack.—Formerly with "Lieut. Daring"; production manager to Elinor Glyn, and (1930) to Famous Players Guild for William Hutter on "77, Park Lane."

Harding, Lyn.—Very famous stage actor. "When Knighthood was in Flower," "Further Adventures of Flag Lieutenant," "Land of Hope and Glory," "The Speckled Band," "Wild Boy," "The Barton Mystery," "Constant Nymph," "Bachelor Husband," "Man Who Changed His Name," "The Lash," "Escape Me Never," etc. *Address:*—"The Dutch Cottage," Furze Hill. Boreham Wood, Herts., and Garrick Club. *Phone:* Elstree 1060.

Hardwicke, Sir Cedric.—Leading actor of much versatility. Films, "Nelson," "Dreyfus" (both title roles), "Rome Express," "The Ghoul," (Jew Suss," "King of Paris," "Nell Gwynn," "Peg of Old Drury," "Tudor Rose," "Laburnum Grove," "King Solomon's Mines."

Hare, J. Robertson.—For ten years in Aldwych farces, and in all of them in screen form, for B. and D. and Gaumont-British.

Harker, Gordon. — Well-known West End actor; film debut in "The Ring," followed by "The Farmer's Wife," "Champagne," "The Crooked Billet," "Return of the Rat," "Taxi for Two," "The W. Plan," "Escape," "Sport of Kings," "Michael and Mary," "Frightened Lady," "Love on Wheels," "Rome Express." "This Is the Life," "Britannia of Billingsgate." "Road House," "My Old Dutch," "Phantom Light," "Dirty Work," "Boys Will Be Boys," "Hyde Park Corner," "Millions."

Harlow, John.—Actor, then stage manager, "Kingsway Theatre. Assistant director to Jack Raymond, A. E. Dupont, etc., 1931, studio and production manager, A.R.P. Studios, Ealing and B. & D., Elstree.

Harrison, Jack.—With Samuelson, 1913–21; responsible positions with Graham-Wilcox (supervised Albert Hall presentations): B.I.P., F.-N. Pathe, production manager, British Sound Films, Wembley. On directorate, Fidelity Film, Worton Hall, Isleworth. 1934, London Films.

Harvel, John.—Director of "Captivation," "The Beggar Student."

Harvey, Morris.—Comedian. " Princess Charming," etc.

Hawthorne, David.—b. Kettering, Northamptonshire. Educated Kenbolton College, Hants. Commenced screen career 1913, with London Film Co. " Testimony," " Sword of Fate," " His House in Order," " Birds of Prey," " Woman Between," " Money for Nothing."

Hay, Will.—British variety comedian. Films : " Those Were the Days," " Dandy Dick," " Radio Parade of 1934," " Boys Will be Boys," " Good Morning, Boys."

Haynes, H. Manning.—b. Lyminster, Sussex. Stage career began 1906 ; took up production in 1921, after acting. Part-author and co-director of " Monty Works the Wires." Director of " A Will and a Way," " Sam's Boy," " The Monkey's Paw," " The Convert," " The Constable's Move," " Lawyer Quince," and other Jacobs releases by Artistic. " London Love," " Passion Island," " The Ware Case." " They Had to Love," " Should a Doctor Tell ? " " To Oblige a Lady," " The Old Man," " To-morrow We Live."

Hayward, Lydia.—b. Isle of Wight. Scenarist. Educated France. Commenced screen career 1916. Part author of " Monty Works the Wires." Adapted many W. W. Jacobs' stories. Recently, " The Ware Case," " Peep Behind the Scenes," " Mary Was Love," " Somehow Good," " Zero," " Mary Was Gold," etc.

Heale, Pat. K.—Scenarist, composer ; founded own unit, 1930, making musical talkies. *Address :*—93, Churchill Road, N.W.10.

Heatherley, Clifford.—b. 1888. Stage career with Tree, Bourchier, Cochran, Basil Dean, etc. Countless films, including " Bleak House," " Roses of Picardy," " Sea Urchin," " Rolling Road," " Boadicea," " King's Highway," " After the Ball," " Discord," " Bitter Sweet," " Catherine the Great." etc. Club :—Stratford, Stratford Place. *Address :*—11, Rookfield Avenue, N.10. *Telephone :*—Mountview 6526

Henson, Leslie.—Musical comedy star. Silent film triumph, 1920, in " Alf's Button." 1930, invaded talkies ; " A Warm Corner," " Sport of Kings," " Girl from Maxim's," " It's a Boy," " Oh, Daddy ! "

Hepworth, Cecil M.—One of the pioneers of kinematography and inventor of many things appertaining. Started producing films in 1896. " Alf's Button," " Helen of Four Gates," " Mrs. Erricker's Reputation," " Wild Heather," " Tansy," " Through Three Reigns," " The Pipes of Pan," " Mist in the Valley," " Strangling Threads," " Comin' Thro' the Rye." Perfected " stretched film " process ; managing director Walter Photographic Co., Ltd. ; director of Standard Kine Laboratories.

Hewland, Philip.—Stage actor since 1900. Commenced screen career 1913. *Address :*—97, Princes Avenue, W.3.

Hicks, Sir Seymour.—Prominent stage actor; talkies : " Sleeping Partners," " The Love Habit," " Glamour," " Money for Nothing," " Mr. What's His Name," " Vintage Wine," " Scrooge," " Dirty Ermine," " Eliza Comes to Stay."

Hill, Sinclair.—b. Surbiton, 1896. Educated St. Paul's; entered film industry, 1912, with the Tyler Film Co. Pre-war experience in Continental firms. After the War, wrote scenarios for Stoll, Ideal, and other British firms. First British production for Stoll, " The Tidal Wave," followed by " The Place of Honour," " Expiation," " Indian Love Lyrics," " White Slippers," " The Squire of Long Hadley," " The Secret Kingdom," " The Qualified Adventurer." Managing director at Cricklewood. " A Woman Redeemed," " King's Highway," " Guns of Loos," " The Price of Divorce." Sound films : " Mr. Smith Wakes Up," " Unwritten Law," " Dark Red Roses," " Greek Street," " Such is the Law," " Great Gay Road," " Gentleman of Paris," " First Mrs. Fraser," " Man from Toronto," " Britannia of Billingsgate," " My Old Dutch." Chairman and director, Grosvenor Sound Films, Ltd., 1935, " Hyde Park Corner," " The Cardinal," " Take a Chance." *Address :*—106, Hallam Street, W.1.

Hiscott, Leslie S.—Assistant producer, Famous Players-Lasky British productions ; Maurice Tourneur, George Pearson, George Fitzmaurice J. Parker Read. Producer of " Mrs. May " (two reelers), " Passing of Mr. Quin," " S.O.S." " At the Villa Rose," " House of the Arrow," " Call of the Sea," " Brown Sugar," " Sleeping Cardinal," " Alibi," " Black Coffee," " The Iron Stair," " She Shall Have Music," etc.

Hitchcock, A. J.—In editorial department of F.P.-L. British productions ; assistant and scenarist to Graham Cutts in " Woman to Woman," " Passionate Adventure," " Blackguard." Director for Gainsborough, 1925 ; " The Pleasure Garden," " The Lodger," " Easy Virtue." Joined British International ; " The Ring," " The Farmers' Wife," " Champagne," " The Manxman," " Blackmail," " Juno and the Paycock," " Murder," " The Skin Game," " Rich and Strange," " No. 17," " Waltzes from Vienna," " Man Who Knew Too Much," " Thirty-Nine Steps," " Secret Agent," " Sabotage." *Address :*—153, Cromwell Road, S.W.

Hobbs, Hayford.—Formerly juvenile lead with London Film Co.; four years in Hollywood ; returned 1926. " The Luck of the Navy," " Toni," " Devil's Maze," etc.

Hobbs, Jack.—" Tom Brown's Schooldays," " Inheritance," " The Shuttle of Life," " The Call of Youth," " The Eleventh Commandment," " The Happy Ending," " All of a Tremble." *Address :*—Green Room Club.

Hogan, Michael.—Stage and radio actor. Leading film roles in " Windjammers," " Mayor's Nest," " My Old Dutch."

Holles, Anthony.—Born 1901 ; stage since 1916. Films : " Watch Beverley," " Easy Money," " Limelight," " Sensation," etc. *Phone :* Abercorn 2604.

Hopper, Victoria.—Stage ingenue ; first film part, 1933, " Tessa," in " The Constant Nymph " ; " Lorna Doone," " Whom the Gods Love." Married Basil Dean, 1933. " Mill on the Floss," " Lonely Road."

Hopson, Violet.—b. San Francisco, California, Former star of Hepworth and Broadwest silent films. " A Gamble for Love," " The Ragged Messenger," " A Turf Conspiracy," " A Fortune at Stake," " A Soul's Crucifixion," " Snow in the Desert," " Her Son," " The Case of Lady Camber," " The Lady Owner," " The Great Turf Mystery," " A Daughter of Love," " Widdicombe Fair."

Howard, Sydney.—Comedian, " French Leave," " Tilly of Bloomsbury," " Up for the Cup," " Splinters in the Navy," " The Mayor's

Nest," "Up for the Derby," "Night of the Garter," "Girls, Please," "Where's George?" "Chick," "Splinters in the Air."

Howes, Bobbie.—Comedian, "Guns of Loos." Talkies: "Third Time Lucky," "Lord Babs," "For the Love of Mike." "Over the Garden Wall," "Please Teacher."

Hughes, Harry.—Editor and cutter for years; directed "A Daughter in Revolt," "Virginia's Husband," "Troublesome Wives," "Hell-cat," "Little Miss London," "The Man at Six," "Bachelor's Baby," "His Night Out," "Improper Duchess," etc.

Hulbert, Claude.—Light comedian, in B.I.P. and B. & D. comedies, etc.

Hulbert, Jack.—Light comedian, "Elstree Calling," "Ghost Train," "Sunshine Susie," "Jack's the Boy," "Love on Wheels," "Happy Ever After," "Jack Ahoy!" "Camels are Coming," "Bulldog Jack," "Jack of All Trades," "Take My Tip."

Hume, Benita.—Young stage actress, starred in "A Light Woman," "Balaclava," Clue of the New Pin," "High Treason," "House of the Arrow," "Escape," "Service for Ladies," "Happy Ending," "Help Yourself," "Jew Suss," "Eighteen Minutes."

Hume, Marjorie.—b. Yarmouth. Commenced screen work 1917. "The Swindler," "Scarlet Kiss," "Kitty Tailleur," "Bluff," "Afterwards," "Triumph of Scarlet Pimpernel." "Lord Richard in the Pantry," "Deadlock."

Humphreys, Cecil.—Commenced screen work 1916. "The Prodigate," "The Amateur Gentleman," "The Tavern Knight," "Four Just Men," "Woman in White," "The Old Man," "It's a King," "77, Park Lane," "Dick Turpin," "Gay Lord Strathpeffer," "Unfinished Symphony," "Koenigsmark," "Accused," "Chick," etc. *Club :*—Green Room.

Hunter, Ian.—West End actor. Film leads for Stoll, also "Downhill," "Easy Virtue," "The Ring," "His House in Order," "Cape Forlorn," "Sally in Our Alley," "Man from Toronto," "Marry Me," "Water Gipsies," etc. Warner Hollywood contract, 1934.

Hunter, T. Hayes.—Director of "Earthbound," "Desert Gold," etc. Gainsborough, 1927; directed "One of the Best," "South Sea Bubble," "Triumph of Scarlet Pimpernel," "The Silver King," "Man They Couldn't Arrest," "The Calendar," "Frightened Lady," "Whiteface," "The Ghoul."

Hurst, Brian Desmond.—Director, b. Ireland. Films: "Ourselves Alone," "Sensation," "Glamorous Night," etc.

Huth, Harold.—Character actor, entered films 1927 in "One of the Best," "Guilt," "Leave It to Me," "Down River," "The Outsider," "First Mrs. Fraser," "Discord," "Rome Express," "The Ghoul." 1934, general manager Toeplitz Productions. 1935-6, casting director, Gaumont-British.

Hyson, Dorothy.—Daughter of Dorothy Dickson. "Soldiers of the King," "The Ghoul," "Turkey Time," etc.

Imeson, A. B.—Started career as actor with Ben Greet, Tree, Alexander, H. B. Irving, Harvey, Benson. Films include "The Breed of the Treshams," "The House of Peril," "The Monkey's Paw," "Burgomaster of Stilemonde,"

"After the Verdict," "Spangles." *Address :*—63, Old Compton Street, W.1. *Phone :*—Gerrard 1808. *Clubs :*—Stage, Golfing.

Ince, Ralph.—Actor and director. 20 years in Hollywood. Made and acted in British pictures from 1933.

Irving, Stanley.—Assistant director, Paramount British, Stolls, London Films since 1927. "Private Life of Henry VIII," "Sanders of the River," "Conquest of the Air," etc. *Address :* c/o London Films, Denham, Bucks.

Isham, Gyles.—Oxford Shakespearean actor. Films: "Purse Strings," "Ann One Hundred," "Iron Duke."

Jay, Jean.—Films since 1923; "Every Mothers' Son," "Afterwards," leading lady "The Silver King." Married John Longden.

Jay, Sidney.—Went on the music halls and toured the world with a juggling act. Film artists' agent. *Address :*—Palace House, Shaftesbury Avenue, W.1.

Jeans, Isabel.—Stage star. Film leads includ "The Triumph of the Rat," "Downhill," "Easy Virtue," "Further Adventures of Flag Lieutenant," "Return of the Rat," "Power Over Men."

Jeans, Ursula.—Many films, latterly "I Lived With You."

Jennings, Gladys.—b. Oxford, 1902; screen career, 1919. "The Lady Clare," "The Lamp in the Desert," "Should a Doctor Tell?" "To Oblige a Lady."

Jones, Enid.—Press representative, Twickenham Studios and J. H. Studios, Elstree. Popesgrove 4444.

Keats, Viola.—R.A.D.A. medallist. Film debut 1933 in Twickenham subjects.

Keen, Malcolm.— Stage actor. Talkies: "Wolves," "77, Park Lane," etc.

Kellino, W. P.—b. London. Ecko Film Co., 1910; joined Cricks and Martin. From 1913-1915 produced comedies and "The Fall of a Saint," "The Fordington Twins," "Saved From the Sea." For Stolls: "Young Lochinvar," "Colleen Bawn," "His Grace Gives Notice," "We Women," "Money Isn't Everything," "Not for Sale," "The Gold Cure," "Confessions," Lupino Lane comedies in Hollywood, 1926. Returned 1927. "Further Adventures of Flag Lieutenant," "Sailors Don't Care." "Smashing Through," "Alf's Carpet," "Alf's Button." Gainsborough burlesques.

Kenyon, Neil.—Scots comedian. Talkies: "Robert Burns," "The Great Game."

Kelly, Judy.—Australian girl put on B.P.I. contract 1932. "Money Talks," "His Night Out."

Kendall, Henry.—Stage actor: "Flying Fool," "Bill the Conqueror," "Timbuctoo," "Rich and Strange," "Gay Lord Strathpeffer," "Counsel's Opinion," "Girl in Possession," "Digging Deep," etc.

Kennedy, Joyce.—Stage actress, Film leads, "Bracelets," "Man from Chicago," "Say It With Music," "Return of Bulldog Drummond." "Black Mask," "Seven Sinners," "Twelve Good Men," "Hail and Farewell." *Address :*—100, Gt. Russell Street, W.C.1. *Phone:* Museum 6341.

Keys, Nelson.—Leading light stage comedian; Films : "Tiptoes," "Pompadour," "Mumsie," "Triumph of the Scarlet Pimpernel," "When Knights Were Bold," "Splinters," "Last Journey," " In the Soup," " Knight for a Day." *Address :*—17, Stratton Street, W.1.

King, George.—Exploitation expert who became agent and then director ; "Deadlock," "Too Many Cooks," "Two-Way Street," "Men of Steel," etc.

Kitchen, Fred.—Veteran variety star. Film, "Wild Boy."

Knight, Esmond.—Romantic juvenile lead, "77, Park Lane," "Waltzes from Vienna," "Dandy Dick," etc.

Knight, James.—Actor. b. 1891, Canterbury. "Romany Lass,"" Brenda of the Barge," "The Education of Nicky," "Love in the Hills," "Trainer and Temptress," "Maria Marten." Now assistant director.

Korda, Alexander.—Austro-Hollywood director, maker of "Service for Ladies," "Wedding Rehearsal," "Girl from Maxim's." Production chief, London Film Productions. "Private Life of Henry VIII," "Private Life of Don Juan," "Scarlet Pimpernel," "Things to Come," "Rembrandt."

Korda, Vincent.—Art director, London Film Productions.

Korda, Zoltan.—Director for London films. Experienced in Berlin, Vienna and Hollywood. "Sanders of the River." *Address :*—81, Avenue Road, N.W.

Konstam, Phyllis.—Stage actress ; talkie debut " Murder," then "Compromising Daphne," Chloe in " The Skin Game," " Tilly of Bloomsbury."

Kove, Kenneth.—" Silly-ass " comedian. First talkie, " The Great Game," " Greek Street," " Two White Arms," etc.

Kraemer, F. W.—Berlin director. Directed at Elstree " Dreyfus," " Tin Gods," " Daughters of To-day."

Lanchester, Elsa (Mrs. Charles Laughton).—Ann of Cleves in " Private Life of Henry VIII," " Rembrandt."

Lane, Lupino.—Famous comedian in Hollywood comedies for seven years; returned to act for B.I.P. in " The Yellow Mask," etc., and became director of " Maid of the Mountains," etc.

Lang, Matheson.—West End actor-manager ; star of many silent Stoll films ; Talkies : " The Chinese Bungalow," " Carnival," " Channel Crossing," " Great Defender," " Drake of England."

La Plante, Laura (Mrs. Irving Asher) — Hollywood star, 1920-31 ; British films, "The Church Mouse," " Water Nymph," etc.

Latimer, Henry.—Stage since 1897, varied experience all over the country. Films : " Under Suspicion," "Glorious Adventure," "King's Highway," " Motoring," " Crooked Billet," etc.

Lawrence, Gertrude.—Revue and musical comedy star. Films, " Aren't We All ? " " Lord Camber's Ladies," "No Funny Business," "Men Are Not Gods " " Rembrandt."

Lauder, Sir Harry.—Famed Scots comedian. "Huntingtower," 1925 ; " Auld Lang Syne," 1928. Song shorts, 1930. "End of the Road."

Laughton, Charles.—Character actor. Hollywood contracts, 1931-2. British talkies : " Private Life of Henry VIII," "Rembrandt," etc.

Laurier, Jay.—Variety comedian. Films ; " Waltz Time," " I'll Stick to You," etc.

Lawton, Frank.—Son of Frank Lawton, comedian. Stage debut 1925. Films include "Michael and Mary," "After Office Hours," "Heads We Go," etc. "David Copperfield" (in Hollywood), 1934.

Laye, Evelyn.—Musical comedy star. Silent film, "Luck of the Navy." In Hollywood, "One Heavenly Night," Gaumont, "Waltz Time," "Princess Charming," "Evensong."

Lee, Anna.—Blonde ingenue ; Gaumont contract, 1934. "Camels are Coming," "The Code." "Passing of the Third Floor Back," "Just a Girl," "O.H.M.S.," "King Solomon's Mines." Married Robert Stevenson.

Lee, Norman.—Revue author and producer, made comedy features for B.I.P. from 1931.

Leigh, Vivien.—From stage ingenue to studios, signed by Korda, 1935. "Fire Over England," "Dark Journey," "Storm in a Teacup."

Levey, Ethel.—American revue star. Film debut, " Call Me Mame."

Levy, Benn.—Dramatist. Directed "Lord Camber's Ladies " for B.I.P.

Lewis, Cecil.—Formerly B.B.C. "Uncle," directed first Shaw talkie, "How He Lied to Her Husband," "Carmen," "Indiscretions of Eve" (own story), "Arms and the Man."

Lind, Gillian.—"Man Outside," "Dick Turpin," etc.

Lipscomb, W. P.—Author ; formerly actor. Scripts of "Splinters," "French Leave," "Plunder," "Canaries Sometimes Sing," "On Approval," "The Speckled Band," "Jack's the Boy," "Faithful Heart," "There Goes the Bride," "Good Companions," "Loyalties." "Man from Toronto," "Soldiers of the King," "The Bracelet," "Channel Crossing," "I Was a Spy," "Me and Marlborough," "Clive of India" part author, "Camels are Coming." Wrote and directed "Colonel Blood." Hollywood 1934, "Les Miserables," "Richelieu," "Under Two Flags," "Message to Garcia."

Llewellyn, Fewlass.—b. Hull, 1866. Nearly forty years successful stage acting ; of vast experience. Films : "A Bill of Divorcement," "This Freedom," "The Flag Lieutenant" (and sequel), "Virginia's Husband," "Officer's Mess," "Outsider," "Those Charming People," "Red Ensign," "Ask Beccles," "Phantom Light," "Stormy Weather," "Jack of All Trades," "Lazybones," "Scrooge," "Excuse My Glove," "Tudor Rose," "All In," "Second Bureau," etc. *Address :*—15, Atney Road, Putney, S.W.15. *Phone :* Putney 0664.

Loder, John.—Prisoner of War in Germany. Began in Berlin studios, then to Elstree and Hollywood. Returned for "Wedding Rehearsal," "Sing as We Go," "Lorna Doone," "Warn London," "Eighteen Minutes," "Sabotage," "King Solomon's Mines " etc.

Lodge, John.—Formerly New York manager ; Hollywood leads. British films, " Ourselves Alone," " Sensation."

Longden, John.—Liverpool Repertory actor ; films for Nettlefold, etc. ; Joe Quinney in " Quinneys," " Palais de Danse," " The Last Post," " Flying Squad," " Blackmail," " Atlantic," " Flame of Love," " Two Worlds," " Skin Game."

Loraine, Violet.—Revue star. Film : " Britannia of Billingsgate," " Road House."

Lotinga, Ernie.—Variety comedian. Talkies " Josser, P.C.," " House Full."

Lott, W. A.—Production manager, Nettlefold studios, Walton ; joined Ealing studios in same capacity 1932.

Lupino, Stanley.—Comedian, " Love Lies," " Love Race," " King of the Ritz," " Happy," " Honeymoon for Three," " Sporting Love," etc.

Lynn, Ralph.—Aldwych comedian. Talkie debut, " Rookery Nook," " Plunder," " Tons of Money," " Mischief," " Chance of a Night Time," " A Night Like This," " Thark," " Just My Luck," " A Cup of Kindness," " Turkey Time," " Dirty Work," " Fighting Stock," " All In," " In the Soup."

Macardle, Donald.—b. 1900, Dundalk. Stage since 1920. Films : " Wee McGregor's Sweet heart," " Mary Queen of Scots," " Mumsie," " Guns of Loos." 1931, scenario editor, B. & D., Elstree ; adapted " Carnival." *Address :—* 35a, Gloucester Road, S.W.7.

Mackay, Barry.—Juvenile lead, " Evergreen," " Forbidden Territory," " Great Barrier," etc.

MacPhail, Angus.—b. 1903. Educated, Westminster and Cambridge. Entered film industry in 1925 ; joined Gainsborough 1927 as scenario editor. At Gaumont-British studios with Michael Balcon in various capacities, including associate producer, story supervisor and personal assistant. *Address :—*1, St. James Street, S.W.1.

Malins, G. H.—b. Boston, 1887. *Produced:* " Hearts of Gold," " The Castaways," " Abide with Me," " On the Banks of Allan Water," " The Golden Web,"" Patricia Brent, Spinster,' Directed 28 films for War Office, " Bluff,"" The Recoil," " The Scourge," " Wonderful Wooing." W. W. Jacobs shorts, 1928.

Maio, Gina.—b. Cincinnati 1909. Musical comedy star. Films : " Goodnight Vienna," " Jack of All Trades," etc.

Mander, Miles.—b. Wolverhampton, 1888 Educated at Harrow and MacGill Univ., Montreal. Exhibitor in 1913-14. Commenced film acting and production, 1920. Is F.R.G.S., Fabian Society. " The Pleasure Garden," " The Fake," " The Physician," " The First-born," " Conflict," " Matinee Idol," " Private Life of Henry VIII," " Loyalties." Directed " Fascination," " Morals of Marcus," " Youthful Folly." *Club :*—Bath.

Mannock, Patrick L.—Scenario editor, Broadwest, 1918-21, with Hepworth's 1922-23 ; Editor Picturegoer 1927-30 ; film and theatre critic, Daily Herald, 1930 ; wrote the scenarios of " The Wonderful Story " " Trent's Last Case," " A Dead Certainty," " The Imperfect Lover," " The Happy Ending " " The Crimson Circle," " A Rank Outsider," " The Flag Lieutenant," " One of the Best," " His House

in Order," " Auld Lang Syne " (original Lauder story), and many two-reelers. *Address :* —19, Brunswick Gardens, W.8. *Phone :—* Bayswater 2801.

Margetson, Arthur.—b. 1897. Films : " Other People's Sins," " Many Waters," " Broken Blossoms," etc.

Marmont, Percy.—b. London, began films 1918 in S. Africa ; in Hollywood till 1927 ; many successes culminating in " If Winter Comes." Since returning to London, " Lady of the Lake," " The Silver King," " The Squeaker, " Rich and Strange," " Say it with Music," " Secret Agent." *Address :*—5, Westbourne Terrace, W2.

Marriott, Moore.—First theatre part, aged 7. Starred in " Monkey's Paw," and several W. W. Jacobs' comedies. Also " London Love," " Victory," " Flying Scotsman," " Goodwin Sands," " Bill the Conqueror," " Turn of the Tide," " Accused," etc.

March, Garry.—Juvenile " heavy " leads in " Night Birds,"" Third Time Lucky," " Keepers of Youth," " After Office Hours," " Warn London," " Fires of Fate," " Mr. What's His Name," etc.

Marshall, Margaret.—Publicity expert with W. & F. and Gaumont ; Twickenham Film Distributors, Ltd. *Phone :*—Gerrard 3421.

Marson, Aileen.—Ingenue heroine of " My Song for You," " Road House," " Green Park," " Ten Minute Alibi," " Someone at the Door."

Mason, Basil.—Author and Adapter: " Death at Broadcasting House," " Silent Passenger," etc. *Address :*—Phoenix Films, 28, Mortimer Street, W.1.

Mason, Haddon.—b. 1898. Lead, " Palaver " " God's Clay," " The Woman in White," Tallien in " Triumph of the Scarlet Pimpernel," juvenile lead " Lady of the Lake," " A Peep Behind the Scenes."

Mason, Herbert.—Actor-producer since 1909, stage-manager, etc., with Gaumont from 1928 as assistant director. 1935, directed "Bad Blood." " East Meets West," " His Lordship," " Take My Tip."

Massey, Raymond.—Leading stage actor. Films : " Speckled Band," " Dreaming Lips."

Matthews, Jessie.—Musical and revue actress, began with Charlot and Cochran. Filming first at B.I.P., 1931. Star of " There Goes the Bride," " Man from Toronto," " Midshipmaid." Gaumont contract, 1932 ; " Good Companions," " Friday the 13th," " Evergreen," " First a Girl," " Head Over Heels."

Matthews, Lester.—B.I.P. films 1930 and onwards.

Maude, Arthur.—Played in American films, " The Vision," in Technicolour, awarded gold medal. Returned to England, 1927 ; directed " Poppies of Flanders," " Toni," " The Ringer," " The Flying Squad," " Clue of the New Pin."

Maude, Cyril.—Veteran actor-manager. Silent film " The Headmaster." Talkies: " Counsel's Opinion," " Orders Is Orders," " The Code."

Mazzei, Andrew L.—Art director with, Paramount, Gaumont and Continental firms ; on " Mlle. from Armentières," " Flag Lieutenant," " Hindle Wakes " (both versions) ; " High Treason," " Happy Ending," " Rome Express," " Blarney Stone," " Prince of Arcadia," " Night of the Garter," " Two Hearts in Waltz-Time,"

"Ten Minute Alibi," "In Town To-Night," "Gabriel Perry," "Monkey Business," "A Woman Alone," "Turn of the Tide," "Dusty Ermine," "Man in the Mirror," "Spy of Napoleon," etc. *Address :—*"Woodside," 52, Hertford Avenue, East Sheen, S.W.14. *Phone :* Prospect 3606.

McLaglen, Cyril. — Experienced in many British pictures, "Hindle Wakes," "The Flight Commander," "Quinneys," "Underground," "Balaclava." Went to Hollywood, 1933.

McLaglen, Kenneth. — Youngest of seven brothers; appeared in "Land of Hope and Glory " and "Dick Turpin," shorts.

McLaughlin, Gibb.—b. Sunderland, 1885, Much stage experience, provincial and West End. First film, 1919. "The Road to London." "Bohemian Girl," "Carnival," Barsad in "The Only Way," Duke of York in "Nell Gwyn " (Wilcox), "Poppies of Flanders," "The Silent House," "Power Over Men," "Congress Dances," "King of the Ritz," "Jew Suss," etc.

McNaughton, Gus.—Variety comedian, in many B.I.P. comedies.

Millar, Adelqui.—b. 1890 in Chile. Educated in Italy and France, played for the screen since 1910 in America, Italy, France, England and Holland, "The Arab," "The Apache." Production manager and director, Whitehall Films, 1927. Directed "The Inseparables " and "Life."

Miller, Frank.—With London Film Co. ; many scenarios since. Director, "Cupid in Clover," "Verdict of the Sea."

Miller, Max.—Variety star. Film debut "Good Companions." G.B. contract 1933. "Channel Crossing," "Wild Boy," "Princess Charming," "Educated Evans," "Don't Get Me Wrong," "Get Off My Foot," etc.

Miller, Ruby.—Many silent films. First talkie, "Sorrell and Son."

Mills, Frank. — Experienced at Islington Studios. Assistant director to A. J. Hitchcock on "Easy Virtue," "The Ring," "The Farmer's Wife," "The Manxman," "Blackmail," etc.

Mills, John.—Juvenile lead with stage experience. Films : "Forever England," "Car of Dreams," etc.

Mitchell, Oswald.—Began with Sir Oswald Stoll in 1919, in picture-house management. Later transferred to Variety Booking Committee, Stoll Theatre Circuit. Spent several months in U.S.A., studying the production and exhibition of motion pictures. General and Production Manager of Stoll Picture Productions since 1927. Director of Visual Education, Ltd. Wrote and produced "Danny Boy " "Cock o' The North," "Stars on Parade," "Shipmates o' Mine," "King of Hearts," "Love Up the Pole," "Variety Parade," for Butcher's release. *Address :—* 7, Amersham House, Craven Road, W.2.

Morgan, Joan.—Began screen career, 1913 "World's Desire," "Lowland Cinderella," "Lilac Sunbonnet," "Lady Noggs," "A Window in Piccadilly." Now given up acting for scenario work. *Address :—*7, Buckingham Palace Gardens, S.W.1. *Phone :*—Sloane 5578.

Morgan, Sidney.—First productions : "The Brass Bottle," "Little Dorrit," "Two Little Wooden Shoes," "The Mayor of Casterbridge," "Miriam Rozella," "The Shadow of Egypt," etc. Equipped and organised Progress Daylight Studios at Shoreham-on-Sea. "Bulldog Drummond's Third Round." Hon. Sec., British Association of Film Directors.

Mollison, Clifford.—West End light comedian, talkies : "Almost a Honeymoon," "The Bridegroom's Widow," "Lucky Number," "Contraband," "Radio Parade," "Freedom of the Seas," etc.

Murray, Douglas.—Assistant director, B.I.P. "Red Wagon," etc.

Murton, Walter W.—Art director of the Stoll Picture Productions, was born at Norwich, 1892. Trained at Norwich School of Art, articled to a firm of furniture and interior designers, and held posts in leading London and Birmingham furniture and interior studios. On leaving H.M. Forces, joined Stoll Picture Productions, and designed exclusively for them. With Gainsborough, 1930. *Address :—* 110, Leeside Crescent, Golder's Green. *Phone :*— Speedwell 6605.

Mycroft, Walter C.—Film critic of *Evening Standard* until 1927, when he became literary and scenario chief at B.I.P., Elstree. Director of Productions, 1933.

Myers, John, B.—Studio Press representative, director of publicity and advertising, London Film Productions, Denham.

Napier, Diana.—Ingenue on London Films contract. Married Richard Tauber.

Nares, Owen.—b. Maiden Erleigh, Berks. Began screen career 1913. Principal screen productions : "Just a Girl," "Tinker Tailor," "Gamblers All," "The Faithful Heart," "Miriam Rozella," "This Woman Business," "Loose Ends," "Middle Watch," "Woman Between," "Frail Women," "Sunshine Susie," "Love Contract," "There Goes the Bride," "Discord," "Where is This Lady ? " "I Give My Heart." *Address :—*Bath Club, Dover Street.

Nash, Percy.—Many years stage director ; with Irving and Tree. Directed for Cines and Tiber in Rome. Producer of "Enoch Arden," "Temporal Power," "Disraeli," "Rodney Stone." Started London Films Co. ; built first Elstree studios ; F.B.I. producer, 1924 ; first President, British Association of Film Directors. (*Club :*—Green Room. *Address :*—144, Mill Lane, N.W.6.

Neagle, Anna (formerly Marjorie Robertson).— Ingenue in "Chinese Bungalow," "Should a Doctor Tell ? " "Good Night, Vienna," "Little Damozel," "Flag Lieutenant," "Bitter Sweet," "The Queen," "Nell Gwyn," "Peg of Old Drury," "Limelight," "Three Maxims," "London Melody,"

Nedell, Bernard J.—American actor who scored in London in "Broadway." British films : "A Knight in London," "The Return of the Rat," "The Silver King." Talkies : "Call of the Sea," "Man from Chicago," "Flying Fool," "The Code," "Lazybones," "Heat Wave," "Bad Blood," "First Offence," "The Shadow Man." *Address :—*"Grey Thatch," Ruxley, Claygate. *Phone :*—Esher 658.

Nettlefold, Archibald.—Head of Archibald Nettlefold Productions. *Address :—*Comedy Theatre.

Nowell, Guy. b. in Hove. Commenced screen career with London Film Co. in 1911. After the war joined George Clark as George Clark Productions. "The Garden of Resurrection," "The Lure of Crooning Water," "Duke's Son," "Persistent Lovers." Producer of "Testimony" and "Persistent Lovers," "The Bigamist," "Boy Woodburn," "Fox Farm," "Maid of the Silver Sea," "The Ghost Train." Talkies: "Potiphar's Wife," "Rodney Steps In."

Newland, Mary (formerly Lillian Oldland).—b. 1905. Screen debut "The Secret Kingdom," "Bindle," "The Flag Lieutenant," "A Daughter in Revolt," "Passion Island," "Virginia's Husband," "To Oblige a Lady."

Newman, Widgey R.—Born at Bedford, 1900. Started with Gaumont, and then with de Forest Phonofilms. Organised introduction of talkies in Middle Europe for Astra. Productions include the famous "Derby Secrets" every year. Chosen to Direct "Our Royal Heritage" for King George Memorial Fund. *Address :*—National House, Wardour Street, W.1. *Phone :* Gerrard 3827.

Ney, Marie.—Stage actress of note. Films : "Home Sweet Home," "Wandering Jew,"

Nolbandov, Sergei (British.)—Production management, editing and scenario writing. London Film Productions ; Associated Sound Film Industries, Ltd. ; and British Sound Film Productions, Wembley Park ; Gloria Swanson British Productions ; Warner Bros., Teddington ; Criterion Films. Graduate in Law, Moscow University. Languages : German, French, Russian. Production manager, "Amateur Gentleman" ; co-author of Pommer production. "Fire Over England." *Address :*—55, Swan Court, Chelsea. *Phone :* Flaxman 4941.

Norris, Herbert.—Author, costume architect, settings expert. Lecturer on historical costume, 22 years' stage and pageantry experience, supervised historical details in "Mary Queen of Scots," "Claude Duval," "Triumph of the Scarlet Pimpernel," "When Knights Were Bold." Period adviser, "Bitter Sweet," "Jew Süss." "Iron Duke." c/o Aubrey Blackburn, Christopher Mann, Ltd., 14, Waterloo Place, S.W.1.

Novello Ivor,—Actor-author-composer, born, Cardiff, 1893. Films : "The Call of the Blood," "Carnival," "The Bohemian Girl" "The Man Without Desire," "The White Rose" (D. W. Griffith), "Bonnie Prince Charlie" "The Rat" (Gainsborough), his own story, "Triumph of the Rat," "The Lodger," "Constant Nymph," "Return of the Rat," "Symphony in Two Flats." On M-G-M contract, 1931-2 : then "The Lodger," "Sleeping Car," "I Lived with You," "Autumn Crocus." *Address :*—11, Aldwych, W.C.

Noy, Wilfred.—Director since 1918 ; Hollywood 1925-31. Recently, "Land of Hope and Glory," and other Cricklewood subjects.

Oberon, Merle.—Young actress on London Films contract. Anne Boleyn in "Private Life of Henry VIII," etc.

O'Bryen, W. J.–Publicity and casting manager, Gainsborough Pictures, 1926-29. Much experience in handling screen rights with Curtis Brown, visited Hollywood, 1924. Founded Albemarle Press Service, 1929. Artistes' business manager —*Phone :* Mayfair 0111.

Olivier, Lawrence. Born 1907. Married Jill Esmond. On stage since 1922. Hollywood film career, 1930. British pictures : "Potiphar's Wife," "Yellow Passport," "Perfect Understanding,' "Moscow Nights," "Things to Come," etc.

Orton, John.—Formerly with Adrian Brunel. Assistant to Brunel, Walter Summers, and in Sweden. 1928 with British Instructional, directed "The Celestial City," "The Windjammer," "I imping Man," "Bad Companions."

Osborne, A. W.—b. 1882. Formerly Accountant and Secretary to companies. Entered industry, 1922, as Director and Secretary of George Clark Pictures, Ltd. Sold the studio at Beaconsfield on behalf of George Clark to British Lion Film Corporation, Ltd., in 1927 and carried on with the latter company as Studio Manager.

Parker, Albert.—Hollywood director till 1928, then series of British Films for Fox at Wembley.

Patch, Walter.—Character actor. "Turf Authority," "Don Quixote," "Good Companions," "Orders Is Orders," "Sorrell and Son," "Sport of Kings," "Man Who Worked Miracles," "Where's George ?" "Trouble," etc. - *Address :*—20, Ashworth Mansions, W.9.

Paul, Fred.—Experienced director of countless films with London, Ideal, Stoll, etc. "The Last Witness," "The Broken Melody" and "The Luck of the Navy."

Payne, Douglas.—On stage since 1901 Played the original "Knight" in "The Miracle" Olympia. Films since 1912. *Address :*—38, Seymour House, Compton Street, W.C.1 *Telephone :*—Terminus 3719.

Payne, John.—Former actor, producer and agent, founded Bramlins. *Address:*—Piccadilly Mansions, 17, Shaftesbury Avenue.

Pearson, George.—b. London. Educated Culham College, and began life as a schoolmaster. Scenarist, producer, studio manager. "The Better 'Ole," "Garryowen," "Nothing Else Matters," "Mary Find-the-Gold," "Squibs," "Mord Em'ly," "Wee Macgregor's Sweetheart," "Squibs Wins the Calcutta Sweep," "Love, Life, and Laughter," "Squibs, M.P.," "Squibs' Honeymoon," "Reveille," "Satan's Sister," "Blinkeyes," "Huntingtower," "Love's Option," "Auld Lang Syne," "East Lynne on the Western Front," "Third String." Supervised "Journey's End" in Hollywood. Twickenham subjects, 1933.

Peers, Victor.—Assistant producer to Sinclair Hill in "Indian Love Lyrics" and many other Stoll successes. Gaumont production executive, 1932. Directed for Dinah Shurey, 1927. Co-director, "Shiraz."

Pember, Clifford.—Stage director in New York ; art director to D. W. Griffith, Alfred Hitchcock, Adrian Brunel, Herbert Wilcox, Hayes Hunter, Jack Raymond, Tom Walls, Basil Dean. *Clubs :*—United University, Savage.

Percival, Hugh.—Publicity, casting and production manager to Paramount-British, Fox and manager to Paramount-British, Fox and Columbia. Formed Phœnix Films, 28, Mortimer Street, W.1. *Phone :* Museum 3209.

Pettingell, Frank.—Character comedian. Films, "Hobson's Choice," "Good Companions." Twickenham subjects: "Red Wagon," "Keep It Quiet," etc.

Phillips, Bertram. — Responsible for many productions at Thornton House, Clapham ; with de Forest Phonofilms, 1927.

Pilbeam, Nova.—Juvenile actress ; leading role in "Little Friend," "The Man Who Knew Too Much," "Tudor Rose."

Poulton, A. G.—Robust character actor of long experience on stage and screen.

Poulton, Mabel.—"Heart of an Actress," "A Daughter in Revolt," "The Glad Eye," etc. Tessa in "The Constant Nymph" (Gainsborough). "Hell Cat," "The Silent House," "Alley Cat," "Return of the Rat," "Not Quite a Lady," "Taxi for Two," "Escape," "Children of Chance." *Address :*—19, Cumberland Terrace Mews *Phone :*—Museum 0940.

Powell, Michael.—Started in Nice with Rex Ingram ; then on Elstree camera work. Directed "Caste," "Two Crowded Hours," "Rynox," "To Meet the King," "Fire Raisers," etc.

Power, Hartley.—American actor who came to London in "Broadway." Films, "Just Smith," "Good-night, Vienna," "Camels are Coming," "Road House," etc.

Pressburger, Arnold.—b. 1885. Entered film business 1909 in Austria. Founder of Sascha Film A.G. and Sascha Studios, Vienna. Transferred activities to Berlin in 1925 and started Cine-Allianz Film Co. Produced the first large-scale British sound film, "City of Song," starring Jan Kiepura, at Asfi Studios, Wembley, in 1930 and, later on, for G.-B. English versions of "Tell me To-night," "Unfinished Symphony;" "My Heart is Calling," etc. Founded British Cine-Alliance, Ltd., in 1934. *Address:*—6-8, Old Bond Street, London, W.1. *Phone :*—Regent 3465/66.

Price, Nancy.—Stage character actress First film, "The Lyons Mail," with H. B. Irving ; more recently "Huntingtower," "His House in Order," "American Prisoner," "Down Our Street." *Address :*—5 Gordon Place, W.C.1. Museum 6050.

Pusey, Arthur. — Much stage experience. Films include "The Blue Lagoon," "Bachelor's Club," "Land of Hope and Glory," "To What Red Hell."

Rains, Fred.—b. 1875, and on the stage since ten years old, playing for the screen since 1906. Produced Lupino Lane comedies.

Randolph, Elsie.—Musical comedy star. "Night of the Garter," "Yes, Mr. Brown," "That's a Good Girl," "This'll Make You Whistle."

Rawlinson, Gerald.—Young light comedian who scored in "The Rising Generation," "Young Woodley," "The Devil's Maze," etc.

Ray, Rene.—In films since 1925. Leading roles : "Passing of the Third Floor Back," "Accused," etc.

Raymond, Jack.—Assistant director for many years ; directed "Second to None," "Somehow Good," "Zero," "A Peep Behind the Scenes," "Splinters," "French Leave," "Speckled Band," "Tilly of Bloomsbury," "Mischief," "Say it With Music," "Just My Luck," "Sorrell and Son," "King of Paris," "Girls Please," "Where's George ? " "Come Out of the Pantry," "When Knights were Bold."

Rayner, Minnie.—Character comedienne, long on stage. "I Lived With You," "Song at Eventide " etc.

Raynham, Fred.—b. 1880. Well-known player of many parts ; "Sign of Four," "Indian Love Lyrics," "Somebody's Darling," "Flag Lieutenant" (and sequel), "Boadicea," author of "Spangles." *Phone :*—Chiswick 0817.

Reardon, James.—Comedy character actor of long experience and assistant to George Pearson; director many comedies. Now with G.-B. Studios, Shepherd's Bush. *Address :*—5, Shottfield Avenue, East Sheen, S.W.14. *Phone :*—Prospect 3729.

Reed, Carol.—b. 1907. Actor till 1928 ; stage producer for Edgar Wallace ; joined Basil Dean at Ealing. Directed "Midshipman Easy." "Laburnum Grove," "A Man With Your Voice."

Reville, Alma (Mrs. A. J. Hitchcock).—Expert cutter ; began with London Film Co.; the first British lady assistant director; scenarist did script of "The Constant Nymph" for Basil Dean, etc.

Rich, Thomas Lionel.—b. 1893. Educated at Aldenham. Unit production manager, Gaumont-British.

Richards, Lloyd.—Assistant director, B. & D. and Herbert Wilcox Productions.

Richardson, Ralph.—West End actor. Films : "The Ghoul," "Return of Bulldog Drummond," "Man Who Worked Miracles."

Riscoe, Arthur.—Comedian, born 1899 ; first appearance in Australia, 1914. Musical comedy star in West End. Films : "Publici Nusance No. 1," etc.

Ritchard, Cyril.—Musical comedy hero who scored in "Blackmail," "Just for a Song," "Symphony in Two Flats."

Robertshaw, Jerrold.—Actor for many years Played Othello, Hamlet, Macbeth and most great parts. Films include "Beside the Bonnie Brier Bush," Talleyrand in "A Royal Divorce," title-rôle in "Don Quixote," "Bolibar," "The Inseparables." *Club :*—Royal Automobile. *Address :*—"The Barn Cottage," Merstham, Surrey. *Phone :*—Merstham 204.

Robeson, Paul.—Negro actor and singer. British films : "Sanders of the River," "Song of Freedom," "King Solomon's Mines," "Big Fella."

Robey, George.—Leading variety comedian since 1896. Several silent Stoll films. Talkies: "Bindle," "Marry Me," "Don Quixote" (with Chaliapin).

Robson, Flora.—b. 1902. On stage 1921. Films : "Dance, Pretty Lady," "Fire Over England."

Rogers, P. Maclean.—Formerly publicity expert and editor, First National. Directed "The Third Eye " for Graham Wilcox, 1928. Joined B. & D. as editor ; directed "The Mayor's Nest," "Up for the Derby," "Bluff," etc.

Rome, Stewart.—b. Newbury, Berkshire Jan. 30, 1886. Studied civil engineering, but gave it up for the stage. Joined Hepworth 1912 ; Broadwest, 1919. "Coming Thro' the Rye," "Iris," "The Touch of a Child," "Sweet Lavender," "Trelawny of the Wells," "The White Hope," "A Daughter of Eve," "A Gentleman Rider," "Her Son," "Snow in the Desert," "A Great Coup," "The Great Gay Road," "Prodigal Son," "The Eleventh

Commandment," "The Stirrup Cup Sensation," 1924–6, "Somehow Good," "The Ware Case," "Zero," "Man Who Changed His Name," "Dark Red Roses," "The Last Hour," "Kissing Cup's Race," "Deadlock," "Reunion." "Temptation," "Man who Could Not Forget." "Men of Yesterday," "Wings of the Morning." *Address :*—10, Chisholm Road, Richmond.

Rooke, Arthur.—Producer "Mirage" (George Clark); "A Sporting Dorble," "The Scandal," "Weavers of Fortune," "Sport of Kings," "A Bachelor's Baby," "M'Lord of the White Road," "Eugene Aram," "The Diamond Man," "The Salving of a Derelict," "The Gay Corinthian," "The Blue Peter."

Rooke, Irene.—(Mrs. Milton Rosmer).— Took up films during war. "Lady Winder-mere's Fan," "The Fruitful Vine," "Half a Truth," "Westward Ho!" "The Rosary," "Hindle Wakes," "The Woman in White." *Address :*—16, Weymouth Street, W.1. *Phone :*—Welbeck 5094.

Roscoe, Basil.—b. 1897. Three years secretary to British National Film League. Assistant director, Gaumonts, 1926, with four directors. Then with Burlington.

Rosmer, Milton.—First film for Ideal in 1913. "Wuthering Heights," "Torn Sails," "Dia-mond Necklace," "The Will," "Belphegor," and "The Passionate Friends." Directed "Dreyfus" (with F. W. Kraemer), "The Perfect Lady," "Many Waters." "After the Ball," "Channel Crossing," "The Guv'nor." "Everything is Thunder." *Address :*—16, Wey-mouth Street, W.1.

St. Helier, Ivy. — Stage comedienne. First film, "Bitter Sweet."

Samuel, P. C.—Joined industry 1925. Collabor-ated with F.B.I. on sound track duty question and on juvenile employment. Introduced tubular studio scaffolding. Studio manager. Gaumont-British studios, Shepherd's Bush, 1933-5. *Address :*—6A, Wychcombe Studios, England's Lane, N.W.3.

Samuelson, G. B.—Pioneer producer. "The Game of Life" his most ambitious of countless efforts. Many excellent productions from Isle-worth, 1914, and onwards. Made three films in California, 1920.

Sanderson, Challis N.—In production since 1918; Stoll, Ideal, A.S.F.I., Blackton, Warners; adaptor and director. *Address :*—1, Fernhill Court, Richmond Road, Kingston.

Saunders, W. G.—Formerly character actor and assistant director at Cricklewood. Studio manager, Nettlefold Studios, Hurst Grove, Walton-on-Thames.

Saville, Victor.—b. 1897. Associated with Cutts on "Woman to Woman"; directed jointly "Mademoiselle from Armentieres," which he wrote, "Hindle Wakes," "Roses of Picardy," "Glad Eye." Directed "The Arca-dians." Managing director, Burlington films; directed "Tesha," "Kitty," "Woman to Woman" (in U.S.A.), "The W. Plan." "A Warm Corner," "Sport of Kings," "Michael and Mary," "Sunshine Susie," "Faithful Heart," "Love on Wheels," "Good Com-

panions," "Friday the 13th," "I Was a Spy," "Evergreen," "The Iron Duke," "The Dictator," "Me and Marlborough," "Just a Girl," "Dark Journey," "Storm in a Teacup."

Scott, Margaretta.—Born 1912, on stage 1928 onwards; Ophelia at 19. Films: "Two Hearts in Waltz Time," "Things to Come," etc. *Club :*— Arts Theatre.

Seacombe, Dorothy.—"The Flag Lieutenant," "The Third Eye," "Loves of Robert Burns." "The Yellow Mask."

Selten, Morton.—Born 1860, on stage since 1878. Films: "Service for Ladies," "The Shadow Between," "Moscow Nights," etc. *Phone :*—Primrose 0495.

Shotter, Winifred.—For seven years at Ald-wych Theatre and in film versions of the comedies. "Love Contract," "Jack's the Boy," "Mis-chief," "Just My Luck," "Lilies of the Field," etc.

Shurey, Dinah.—Responsible for Britannia Films subjects: "Afraid of Love," "Every Mother's Son," "Carry On."

Sloan, James B.—Assistant studio manager F.P.-L. studios, Islington, 1919–22; studio production manager to Gloria Swanson "Sans Gene" unit in France, 1923; assistant director to Cutts, Niebuhr, Manning Haynes; directed Walter Forde comedies, 1926; appointed pro-duction manager, Pathé, 1926 and Blattner Pictures, 1928–9. Basil Dean productions, 1930. With Rex Ingram, 1931, Erick Hakim, 1932, and British National, 1935. Studio manager, Pine-wood, Bucks. *Address :*—42, Wimborne Gardens, W.5. *Phone :*—Perivale 5103.

Smith, Cyril.—Formerly assistant director; character comedian and actor. "Orders Is Orders," "I Was a Spy," "Waltzes from Vienna," etc.

Smith, Herbert.—b. 1901. Supervisor of production and director, British Lion, Beacons-field. "On the Air," "Night Mail," "In Town To-night," "Soft Lights and Sweet Music," "Calling all Stars."

Smith, Percy.—b. 1880. 1896–1910, Board of Education. Producer of scientific nature films for British Instructional, and later for Gaumont-British Instructional. *Address :*—King's Villas, Chase Road, Southgate, N.14.

Spark, Connie.—Formerly with Sidney Jay, now controlling Connie's Agency.

Squire, Ronald.—Born 1886. Actor since 1909. Films: "Unfinished Symphony," "Come Out of the Pantry," "Love in Exile," etc.

Stafford, John.—Director. "No Funny Busi-ness," "Dick Turpin," "Ball at the Savoy," etc.

Standing, Percy.—Stage and screen actor of long English and American experience; brother of Wyndham and Sir Guy Standing.

Stanley, S. Victor.—Comedian. Talkie debut, 1933.

Stanmore, Frank.—Formerly medical student, then actor under Tree. Commenced screen career 1912 with London Film Company, playing comedy rôles for George Loane Tucker, Harold

Shaw, and Frank Miller for five years
" Satan's Sister," " Blinkeyes," " Wait and See,"
" House Opposite," " Great Gay Road, " Lucky
Girl," " Don Quixote," " That's a Good Girl,"
" The Love Wager," " Jew Suss." *Address :—*
53, Chandos Street, Trafalgar Square, W.C.2.

Stannard, Eliot.—Scenarist ; son of " John
Strange Winter."

Stapleton, P. C.—General manager, B.I.P.
studios, Elstree, 1930-35.

Steerman, A. Harding.—Before taking up film
work (and since) has played hundreds of parts
on the stage. Screen parts in " Love, Life and
Laughter," " Lights of London." A worker for
his fellow professionals ; vice-chairman, Actors'
Association for ten years. *Address :—*79D,
Holland Road, W.14. *Phone :* Western 3015.

Stein, Paul.—German-Hollywood director
British films, " Lily Christine," " Red Wagon,"
.' Blossom Time," " Heart's Desire."

Sterroll, Gertrude.—b. Weybridge. "The Grass
Orphan," " The Hypocrites," " A Daughter in
Revolt," " Not Quite a Lady." *Clubs :—*New
Century, Interval, Arts Theatre. *Address :—*
54, St. John's Wood Road, N.W.8. Phone,
Cunningham 2379.

Stevenson, Robert.—Born 1905. President
Cambridge Union, 1928. Scenarios and dialogue
for Gainsborough Pictures ; adapted " Sunshine
Susie " and " Faithful Heart," besides many
with Angus McPhail. With Ufa 1932 in Berlin.
Director of " Falling For You," " Jack of All
Trades," " Man Who Changed His Mind,"
" King Solomon's Mines " ; wrote and directed
" Tudor Rose." Married Anna Lee. *Address :*
—Cardinal's Wharf, Bankside, Southwark.

Stockfeld, Betty.—b. Australia. West End
stage actress. Films : " City of Song," " 77, Park
Lane," " Maid of the Mountains," " Ann One
Hundred," " Lord of the Manor," " King of the
Ritz," etc.

Stuart, John.—b. 1898. Educated Eastbourne
College. Began screen career, June, 1920, as
juvenile lead in " Her Son," " The Great Gay
Road," " The Lights of Home," " Land of M.
Fathers," " Sinister Street," " Hindle Wakes,"
" No Exit," " Kissing Cup's Race," " Hound
of the Baskervilles," " Verdict of the Sea."
" No. 17," " In a Monastery Garden," " Men of
Steel," " Abdul Hamid," " Show Flat."

Stuart, Madge.—Commenced screen career
1916. " Flames," " Gay Lord Quex," " Amateur
Gentleman," " The Iron Stair," " A Question of
Trust," " The Tavern Knight," " The Pointing
Finger," " General John Regan," " The Be-
loved Vagabond," " The Only Way."

Suedo, Julia.—Played in " The Rat," " One
of The Best," " The Vortex," " The Dictator,"
" Brewster's Millions," " McGlusky the Sea
Rover," " Whom the Gods Love," " Queen of
Hearts," " Accused," "Sharps & Flats." *Address :*
—64, Orchard Gate, Sudbury Town. *Phone :*
Wembley 4340.

Sullivan, Francis L.—Character actor. " Fire
Raisers," " Wandering Jew," " Princess
Charming," etc. Went to Hollywood, 1934.

Summers, Walter G.—With Hepworth
several years ; directed for Samuelson 1922-4 ;
also " Ypres," " Mons," " The Falklands and
Coronel Battles," " Chamber of Horrors,"
Betty Balfour in " Raise the Roof," " Suspense,"

" The Man from Chicago," " The Flying Fool,"
" Men Like These," " The House Opposite,"
" Timbuctoo," " McGlusky the Sea Rover," "The
Limping Man," etc.

Swinburne, Nora.—b. Bath, July 24, 1902.
" Hornet's Nest," " His Grace Gives Notice,"
" Alf's Button," " Caste," " Potiphar's Wife,"
" These Charming People," " Man of Mayfair,"
" Bill the Conqueror," " Perfect Understanding."
"Lonely Road," etc. *Address :—*11, Gloucester
Place, W.1. *Phone :—*Welbeck 3515.

Sydney, Basil.—Many years famous stage
actor here and in the U.S. Films : " Accused,"
" A Man With Your Voice."

Tate, Harry.—Veteran variety comedian.
Silent film comedian, 1924. Talkies, " Her
First Affaire," " Happy," " Look Up and
Laugh."

Tauber, Richard.—Austrian tenor and operatic
star. British films : " Blossom Time," " Heart's
Desire," " Land Without Music."

Taylor, Alma.—b. 1895, London. Commenced
screen work 1907. First big roles : " Oliver
Twist " and " The Heart of Midlothian." Lead-
ing roles in " Helen of Four Gates," " Mrs.
Erricker's Reputation," " Tansy," " Pipes of
Pan," " Mist in the Valley," " Strangling
Threads," " Comin' Thro' the Rye," " The
Shadow of Egypt," " Quinneys."

Tearle, Godfrey.—Noted stage actor. Silent
films, also : " These Charming People," " Shadow
Between," " Puppets of Fate," " 39 Steps,"
.' To-morrow We Live," etc.

Templeman, Harcourt.—Joined industry 1919 ;
associate producer Stolls, A.S.F.I. On " City
of Song," " The Bells " ; B. & D. production
manager, 1931. 1935, managing director,
Grosvenor Sound Films.

Tennyson, Walter.—Juvenile lead in " Tell
your Children," " Call of the East," " The
Virgin Queen," " The Bells," " School for
Scandal " " Eugene Aram," " The Infamous
Lady," " The Price of Things."

Terriss, Eilaline.—Celebrated stage actress
daughter of a famous tragedian. " Blighty,"
" Land of Hope and Glory," " Atlantic,"
" Iron Duke."

Thomas, Queenie.—Screen heroine of many
Bertram Phillips' pictures, also " The Temple
of Shadows," " Warned Off."

Thomas, Yvonne.—" Land of My Fathers,"
"Squibs, M.P.," " Owd Bob," Kate in " Con-
stant Nymph." *Address :—*19, Rupert Street,
W.1.

Thompson, Noel.—b. 1904. Formerly in Fleet
Street, joined Gaumont with Beverley Baxter.
1934, Director of publicity, A.T.P., A.B.F.D.
*Address :—*3, St. Mark's House, Regents Park
Road, N.W.1.

Thorndike, Dame Sybil.—Leading actress
Films : " Dawn," " Hindle Wakes," " Lady
Jane Grey," etc.

Tod, Malcom.—Juvenile lead, " The Romany,"
" Corinthian Jack," " Dick Turpin's Ride to
York," " Expiation," " A Bachelor's Baby,"
" The Thief," " The Audacious Mr. Squire."
Also in France, Germany, Italy and Austria.
*Address :—*17c, Redcliffe Square, S.W.10.
Phone :—Flaxman 9514.

Todd, Ann.—West End stage ingenue. "Keepers of Youth," "Water Gipsies."

Toeplitz, Ludovici de Grand Ry.—Italian banker and financier : joined London Films. 1932. Formed Toeplitz Productions, 1934. "The Dictator," "The Beloved Vagabond."

Travers, Ben.—Author of Aldwych farce successes for 10 years ; active collaborator on their production, at B. and D. and Gaumont, with Tom Walls, Ralph Lynn, etc.

Travers, Roy.—Twenty years on stage, countless films since 1911. Actor, stage manager, studio manager and assistant director. "Q Ships," "Down Channel," "Middle Watch," etc. *Address :*—32, Abercorn Place, N.W.8. *Phone :* Maida Vale 3113.

Tripod, Irene.—b. London. "The Impossible Woman," "The Feather," "At the Villa Rose," "School for Scandal," etc. *Address :*— 53, Chandos Street, W.C.2.

Vanbrugh, Irene.—Famous stage actress. Films : "Head of the Family," "Catherine the Great," "Escape Me Never."

Vanbrugh, Violet.—Famous stage actress Films at Teddington and "Catherine the Great."

Veidt, Conrad.—German-Hollywood star. British films : "Rome Express," "Wandering Jew," "Jew Suss," "Bella Donna," "Passing of the Third Floor Back," "King of the Damned," "Dark Journey," "Under the Red Robe."

Verno, Jerry.—Musical comedy comedian Films : "Taxi for Two," "There Goes the Bride," "To Meet the King," "Thirty-Nine Steps," "Land Without Music," "Pagliacci," etc.

Vibart, Henry.—Born 1863 ; commenced stage career, 1886. Started film work with Hepworth, 1913. "The Bondman," "High Treason." *Club :*—The Green Room. *Address :*—24, Cleveland Road, Barnes, S.W.13. *Phone :*— Putney 1926.

Viertel, Berthold.—Director, formerly Hollywood and Continent. "Little Friend," "Passing of the Third Floor Back," "Rhodes."

Vorhaus, Bernard.—Director. "The Last Journey," "Dusty Ermine," "Cotton Queen," etc.

Vosper, Frank.—b. London, 1899. Actor and dramatist. Film roles : "Rome Express," "Jew Suss." *Address :*—55c, Greencoat Place, S.W.1. *Phone :*—Victoria 7102.

Wakefield, Hugh.—Light comedy actor, in "City of Song," "Sport of Kings," "King of the Ritz," "Crime at Blossoms," "Improper Duchess," "Limping Man," etc.

Walker, Norman.—Director of Tommy Atkins," "Widdicombe Fair," "Hate Ship," "Loose Ends," "Middle Watch," "Uneasy Virtue," "Shadow Between," "Bill the Conqueror," "Fires of Fate," "Lilies of the Fields." "Turn of the Tide," "The Man Who Could Not Forget," "The Navy Eternal." *Address :*— Hedgeside, Moor Park, Northwood.

Walls, Tom. — Noted stage comedian; "Rookery Nook," "On Approval," "Plunder," "Tons of Money," "Canaries Sometimes Sing," "A Night Like This," "Thark," "Leap Year," "Turkey Time," "Blarney Stone," "A Cup of Kindness," "Just Smith," "Cuckoo In the Nest," "Turkey Time," "Lady in Danger," "Fighting Stock," "Stormy Weather," "Dishonour Bright." Directs himself.

Ward, Poille—Revue soubrette. "This Marriage Business." leading roles, "Harmony Heaven," "Alf's Button."

Ward, Warwick.—Several years on stage Films : "Wuthering Heights." Played for nearly every British and Continental Company, opposite Gloria Swanson in "Looping the Loop," "Sans Gene," "Variety" (opposite Jannings), "The Wonderful Lie," "Informer," "Yellow Mask," "Birds of Prey," "To Oblige a Lady," "Stamboul."

Wareing, Lesley.—Ingenue actress, formerly on the B.I.P. contract. 1934, "The Iron Duke."

Watts, Dodo.—b. 1910. Stage and screen ingenue; in W. W. Jacobs' shorts and "Auld Lang Syne." Elstree contract, 1930, "Middle Watch," "Almost a Honeymoon," "Man From Chicago," "The Happy Husband."

Watson, Wylie.—Broad comedian of musical comedy fame. Films : "Thirty-Nine Steps," "Please, Teacher."

West, Walter.—b. London. Joined Broadwest 1914. Producer of "A Bold Adventuress," "The Case of Lady Camber," "The Great Gay Road." Started Walter West Productions 1921. "When Greek Meets Greek," "Son of Kissing Cup," "Scarlet Lady," "Hornet's Nest," "The Lady Owner," "Vi of Smith's Alley," "The Great Turf Mystery," "In the Blood," "Trainer and Temptress." Steve Donoghue subjects. "Maria Marten," "Sweeney Todd," "Warned Off."

Wetherell, M.A., F.R.G.S., F.Z.S.—b. 1884. Stage career from 1902, largely in Africa. Leading man in African films and in London, 1923, formed company and made and played "Livingstone," then "Robinson Crusoe." Directed "The Somme," "Victory," "Life of Stanley," "Wanderlust," "Hearts of Oak." *Club :*— Sports.

Whelan, Albert.—Australian entertainer. Successful talkie debut in "Man from Chicago."

White, Chrissie.—b. 1895, London. "Barnaby Rudge," "Towards the Light," "John Forrest Finds Himself," "A Lunatic at Large," "Wild Heather," and "The Bargain," "Tit for Tat," "World of Wonderful Reality," "Lily of the Alley," "Boden's Boy." Married Henry Edwards.

White, J. Fisher.—b. 1865. Famed stage actor since 1892. Films include : "Owd Bob," "The Only Way," "Great Defender," "Old Curiosity Shop," "City of Beautiful Nonsense," "Turn of the Tide," "Tudor Rose," "As You Like It," "Dreaming Lips," "Moonlight Sonata."—*Club* :—Green Room. *Address* :—13, Ladbroke Road, W.11. *Phone* :Park 5506.

White, Tom.—Assistant director, Hepworth Twickenham, etc. with Henry Edwards. 1935 production manager, Herbert Wilcox Productions.

Wilcox, Herbert.—Director. First production "Chu Chin Chow," made in Germany with British artistes, 1923, "Southern Love," "Decameron Nights," "The Only Way," "Nell Gwyn," "Madame Pompadour," "Mumsie," "Dawn," "The Woman in White," "The Bondman," "Loves of Robert Burns," "Blue Danube," "Carnival," "Good Night, Vienna." "Little Damozel," "Bitter Sweet," "The Queen's Affair," "Peg of Old Drury." Formed Herbert Wilcox Productions, 1935. "Limelight," "The Three Maxims," "London Melody."

Williams, Eric Bransby.—b. 1900. Son of famed father. "His Grace Gives Notice," "Jungle Woman," "Wonderful Wooing," "Easy Virtue," "Troublesome Wives," "When Knights Were Bold," "Wonderful Story."

Williams, Emlyn.—Actor and dramatist. Films : "Frightened Lady," "City of Youth," "Friday the 13th," "Iron Duke," "The Dictator," "Road House," "City of Beautiful Nonsense," "Broken Blossoms."

Williams, Hugh.—Stage actor. Films, "Insult," "After Dark," "Rome Express." On Fox-Hollywood contract, 1933-4.

Williams, L. P., A.R.I.B.A.—b. 1905. Aldenham School and Architectural Association prizeman. Joined B. & D., 1928. Art director on many pictures, recently "Nell Gwyn," "Peg of Old Drury," "Limelight," "Millions," "Three Maxims," "London Melody," "Navy Eternal."

Wills, J. Elder.—Formerly Scenic Artist under McLeary at Drury Lane. Forsook advertising 1927, to become Art Director for British International Pictures. Was responsible for the art direction of 15 pictures in two years. Joined British Sound Film Productions, Ltd., 1929. Director and art director for A.S.F.I., Wembley. Directed "Tiger Bay " for Wyndham Films, "Song of Freedom," "Big Fella," etc.

Wontner, Arthur.—Stage actor of repute. Silent films include "Eugene Aram." First talkie role, Sherlock Holmes in "The Sleeping Cardinal," "Missing Rembrandt," "Gentleman of Paris," "Sign of Four," "Return of Sherlock Holmes." "Silver Blaze."

Woods, Arthur.—Studio expert, director 1933 for B.I.P. "Secret Agent," "Radio Parade of 1935," "Rhythm in the Air."

Wright, Haidee.—Born 1868. Member of famous stage family. Many recent films, including "To-morrow We Live." *Phone* :—Temple Bar 9348.

Wright, Humberston.—Over thirty years stage and screen. "Roses of Picardy," "Mademoiselle from Armentières." "Garden of Allah," "High Treason," "Alf's Button."

Wright, Hugh E.—"The Better 'Ole," "Kiddie in the Ruin," "Victory Derby," "Garryowen," "Nothing Else Matters" (collaborated with George Pearson on the story and scenario) and all the "Squibs" series. "Auld Lang Syne," "The Silver King," "Brother Alfred," "Royal Eagle."

Wyer, Reginald.—Joint managing director Publicity Productions, 93, Wardour Street, W.1. Speciality : advertising talkie cartoons.

Wyndham, Joan.—Leading lady. "Loyalties," "Love's Old Sweet Song," "Lucky Number," "Loyalties," etc.

Wynne, Bert.—Director. "Tom Jones," "My Sweetheart," "The Game of Liberty," "Jeff's," "God and the Man," "Remembrance."

Zelnik, Fredrick.—Berlin director. "Happy" (B.I.P.).

CAMERAMEN.

Anscombe, R. G.—Entered Trade 1922, assistant cameraman B.I.P., etc. Now on colour research.

Anthony, P. B.—Long experience in Trade. "The School for Scandal," "Why?" "The Gayest of the Gay."

Austin, A. A.—Formerly on portraiture. Sound City, Shepperton and Twickenham subjects. *Address:*—31, Queens Court, Queens Road, W.2. *Phone:*—Bayswater 0240.

Bassill, F. A.—Pathé Gazette. Joined Warwick Trading Co. 1908. Served in all departments of the Trade, projection, dark-room, studio and topical. Was official kinematographer to British armies in France. *Address:*—Pathe Freres, 103–109, Wardour Street, London, W.1.

Bawcombe, Philip.—Art director with G.B., B.I.P., A.T.P., Stafford, City Films, etc.

Birch, Albert F.—Recordist, G.B.

Blakeley, Walter.—Many years first-class experience, England and U.S.

Blythe, Sydney.—In 1910 took charge of Barker's laboratory. With British Super Films, Samuelson, Napoleon, Universal, New Era, Twickenham Studios. "The Somme," "Q Ships," "At the Villa Rose," "Wandering Jew," "Vintage Wine," "Scrooge," "She Shall Have Music," "Underneath the Arches," "Widow's Island." *Address:*—Twickenham Studios, St. Margarets.

Bonnet, S. R.—On Colburn films and staff of Gaumont. Everest Expedition, 1933.

Borrodaile, O.—Cameraman on recent B. & D. subjects.

Bovill, F. Oscar.—Joined Gaumont 1908 ; with Barker's three years ; 1933 in Vienna ; many British subjects since. *Address:*—c.o. A.C.T., 30, Piccadilly Mansions, W.1.

Boyle, John W.—Chief cameraman, A.T.P., Ealing. Vice-President, A.S.C., Hollywood.

Bristow, Cyril.—Cameraman on B. & D. and A.R.P. subjects.

Brocklebank, R.—Supervisor, camera dept., G.B. studios, W.12.

Bryce, Alex.—Chief cameraman, Fox-British Pictures, Wembley.

Bryce, Charles.—Started as Press photographer and served with Williamson's. B. and C., Trans-Atlantic, London, and Hepworth.

Burgess, George E.—Sound recorder, Gainsborough Studios.

Burger, J. G.—Turned for London Stoll, Phonofilms, Astra-National. Colour research, Jofa, Polychromide. *Address:*—143, St. Margaret's Road, Twickenham. *Phone:*—Popesgrove 2583.

Carter, Frederick W.—Chief still photographer, Gainsborough Pictures.

Cameron, Alex.—G.B. recordist.

Carrington, William G.—Started in Gaumont's dark room in 1905, after taking juvenile parts in their first productions, 1903-1904. Later became cameraman for same company. Since 1914 has been chief photographer for Vickers,

Ltd., engaged on producing films for propaganda and technical purposes.

Chorlton, M. C.—Film editor to Twickenham Film Studios.

Christian, Jack.—Twenty years at still photography. Joined Chas. Urban as kinematographer in 1908, and many years' studio work. *Address:*—3, Melbourne Road, Bushey, Herts.

Cooper, D. P.—Worked for most companies, seven years with Stoll ; "Prodigal Son," "Great Prince Shan," "King of the Castle," "Call of the Road," "Woman Redeemed," "Last Post," "King s Highway," "Guns of Loos." *Address:*—151, Kew Road, Richmond.

Cornwell, Arthur R.—Art director, London Films, Denham.

Cotter, Jack.—Production manager, British Movietone News. Formerly for many years with Pathé.

Cox, John Jaffray.—b. London. Commenced career with L. Fitzhamon, 1910, and with him worked for B. and C. Co., Martin's Films, Charles Urban Trading Co., Gaumont, etc. Was cameraman to Maurice Elvey on all pictures for four years. Shot "The Ring," "The Farmer's Wife," "Champagne," "The Manxman," "Blackmail," "Juno and the Paycock," "Murder," "How He Lied to Her Husband," "The Skin Game," "Rich and Strange," "No. 17," "Red Wagon," etc.

Cross, Eric.—Chief cameraman, A.S.F.I. Studios, Wembley, etc.

Daley, George.—Still photographer, B.I.P., Elstree.

Dorto, Philip.—Recordist, G.B. Studios.

Dennis, P.—Laboratory technician ; Barkers' Chromatic Film Printers. Photographer since 1900. Now specialist in enlargements from film negatives for reproduction, inserts, slides, stills, etc. Direct colour work on glass and still enlargements from films. *Address:*—38, Mortlake Road, Kew.

Dickenson, Desmond.—Chief cameraman, Stolls, Cricklewood. "City of Beautiful Nonsense," "Stars on Parade," "A Real Bloke," "Variety," etc. *Address:*—47, Beaumont Court, Sutton Lane, W.4.

Dines, G. P.—Lighting expert and first operator, A.T.P., Ealing.

Dudgeon-Stretton, G.—Chief cameraman, British Lion. Recently : "Jury's Evidence," "Fine Feathers," "It's You I Want." *Address:*—88, Ralph Court, Queen's Road, W.2.

Dykes, Robert, F.R.P.S.—"Potter's Clay," "Treasureland," "Britain's Birthright," "World Cruise of H.M.S. Hood," "The Congo," "The Tallyman," etc. Author of "Night Photography," "Tropical Photography," etc. and camera expert on Gold Coast, Ashanti, Nigerian, and other expeditions. Research chemist and geologist. Chief assistant with the late Sir John Murray, explorer. 1930, experimental research, British Raycol. 38, Gledstanes Road, W.14.

Eaton, Sydney.—Long studio and topical experience. Hepworth, London, Pathé, etc.

Edmonds, A. R.—Cameraman, G.-B. News.

Egrot, Lucien G.—Technician of long and varied experience. With Pathé Freres of Paris in 1904. Later joined up with Gaumont's, then Pathé Lux. Started the study of electrical lighting while with Gaumont's in 1905. Took " The Better 'Ole," " Her Benny," " Wonderful Story," " Rogue in Love," etc. Worked for Griffith, Ingram, Pearson, Wilcox ; associate member S.M.P.E.

Emmott, Basil W. G.—" Rob Roy," " Prince of Lovers," " Silent Evidence," " Young Lochinvar," " Colleen Bawn," " Eleventh Commandment," etc. Started in laboratory with Gaumont. Accompanied Cobham and shot " With Cobham to the Cape."

Faithfull, Geoffrey —Many years with Hepworth, latterly with Nettlefold, at Walton Studios.

Farmer, Arthur.—Pathétone cameraman. Topical and interest cameraman. In topical business since 1921.

Fisher, Arthur L.—Formerly Pathé expert, etc., travelling all over the world, 1932-3 Everest expedition.

Fogwell, Roy. — Free-lance, own outfit. *Phone :*—Tulse Hill 4532.

Ford, Bert.—Formerly cameraman to Warwick, Windsor, Welsh Pearson, British Lion, British and Dominions, G. Clark, etc. Photographed " Duke's Son," " Owd Bob," " Huntingtower," " Hobson's Choice," etc. *Address :*— 9, Erlesmere Gardens, Ealing, W.13. *Phone :*— Ealing 4948.

Ford, F. B.—Cameraman, London Films.

Ford, Maurice.—Gaumont-British, Twickenham, Wilcox, British Lion, Fox ; now with Paramount Sound News. Address :— 10, Windmill Court, Ealing, W.5.

Frend, Charles H.—Film editor, Gaumont-British Studios, W 12.

Friese-Greene, Claude H.—Started camera work in 1905. On the camera staff of the *Eclair Journal,* 1911. Originated the kinema section of the R.F.C. in 1915. After demobilisation specialising in aerial kinematography. Demonstrated new colour process, and established company for production, 1924. Shot " Widdicombe Fair," " Tommy Atkins," " Cape Forlorn," " Middle Watch," " Happy Husband," " Shadow Between," " Bill the Conqueror."

Garmes, Lee.—Hollywood camera expert, with London Films, Denham.

Gemmell, J. C.—Gained experience in darkrooms and laboratory with Warwick Trading Co. and Barker's Motion Photography during 1910-11-12. Joined " Pathé Gazette,' April, 1912. Opened and managed Liverpool Laboratory for Pathé. Photographic officer in R.A.F. during war, discharged May, 1919. Joined "Topical Budget," May, 1919. Rejoined "Pathé Gazette," June, 1920.

Gibbs, G. E.—Cameraman B.I.P. and Stoll subjects. *Address :*—30, Queen's Gate Terrace, S.W.7.

Gillain, Henry.—First camera operator, B.I.P., Elstree.

Goldman, J. M.—Assistant associate producer, G.-B. Studios.

Goodwin, Cecil.—Production manager, St. George's Pictures, Ltd.

Gordon, Kenneth R. L.—Topical and slow motion expert. Filmed the Delhi Durbar and the Balkan War, 1912. Official photographer to the North Russian Relief Force, 1919-20. Served in the war, 1914-1919. Now with " Pathé Pictorial" Pathetone, topical and Wardour Street studio. Vice-president, Association of Cine-technicians.

Graham, E. A. — Studio Freelance, own outfit. *Phone :*—Gerrard 2366.

Grainger, Frank.—Started in the optical lantern business with the late Walter Tyler. Manager of the Tyler Film Co., Ltd., from its start, and later general manager of the Cosmopolitan Film Co , Ltd. *Address :* — 3, Claygate Road, West Ealing, W.13.

Grant, Stanley.—Cameraman, Fox-British.

Greenbaum, Mutz.—Berlin expert of long experience ; G.-B. contract, 1931. "The Ghoul," " Princess Charming," etc. *Address :*— 11, Parkway, N.W.11. *Phone :*—Speedwell 5230.

Haggett, William.—Expert since 1919 ; patentee of apparatus ; trick work. Chief camera and laboratory engineer, B.I.P., Elstree. *Address :*—131, Uphill Grove, Mill Hill, N.W.7.

Harris, Dick. — Cameraman, Warwick Chronicle, 1908 ; B. & C. ; R.F.C. in war ; Topical Budget ; 1931 ; British Movietone. *Address :*—17, The Priory, St. Mark's Hill, Surbiton. *Phone :*—Elmbridge 1025.

Harris, Henry.—Continental experience with Adrian Brunel, etc. " Claude Duval " (Gaumont) and Phonofilms. " Shiraz " in India. " Come Out of the Pantry," " Street Singer's Serenade," etc. *Phone :*—Pollard 1342.

Harrison, Harvey.—Cameraman of long experience, on political subjects, 1935.

Harvey, W.—First cameraman, lighting expert, B.I.P., etc. Phone :—Edgware 2033.

Hawkins, Edward H.—Topical and commercial cameraman. Started in Kenito's dark-room in 1911. Paramount News and G.-B. News. *Address :*—36, Hartington Road, Chiswick.

Heath, Charles F. T.—Left Fleet Street in 1913 to become B. and C.'s publicity chief. Later joined Pathé's camera staff. During the war was official photographer to the American Red Cross in England. Later with Gaumont, and Topical. *Address :*—Milheath Studios, Bushey.

Hesse, Cecil M.—Sound engineer, Western Electric.

Hodgson, James S.—b. 1891. Started twenty years ago in Barker's dark-rooms, Pathé's, Gaumont, Williamson, M.P. Sales, etc. Expedition through Togoland. 1913, filming native life and producing " Odd Man Out," " White Goddess," etc. Antarctic and Whaling Expedition for Lever Bros., " March of Time," 1936. *Address :*—37, Woodbastwick Road, S.E.26. *Phone :*—Sydenham 5323.

Hopkins, Bert.—Joint managing director, Publicity Picture Productions, 89, Wardour Street. Creator of publicity talking cartoons ; studio expert.

Howell, Sydney.—Supervisor, camera department, A.T.P. Studios, Ealing.

W. & F. Films, New Era, British and Dominion, Burlington, W. & P. Productions, British Lion, Strand Films, etc. Now chief still cameraman, Twickenham, J. H. of Riverside Studios. Address :—603, Upper Richmond Road, Richmond. Phone :—Prospect 2570.

Stewart, Hugh S.—Recordist, British Lion, Beaconsfield.

Stein, David.—Editor, National Film Agency, Manchester.

Starmer, Harry.—Formerly Big Ben Productions, 1913. With "Pathé Gazette" for many years. Free-lance. *Phone :*—Beckenham 1831.

Strong, Percy.—Experienced chief cameraman on Betty Balfour silent films ; latterly on important Gaumont-British Talkies. *Phone :*—Ruislip 338.

Sutherland, Duncan M.—Art director, free lance.

Talbot, Geoffrey.—First operative cameraman, Dufay, Swanson, A.S.F.I., research, etc.

Tannura, Phil.—Edison's laboratory ; cameraman to various Hollywood studios ; with Paramount at Joinville and Elstree. London film productions, Gaumont : "Channel Crossing," "Princess Charming."

Terraneau, Randel.—Long experience with practically every firm. Partner in George Humphries' Laboratories.

Thomas, Ralph.—Film editor, British Lion, Beaconsfield.

Thumwood, Theodore R.—b. 1891. Joined the Clarendon Film Co., 1905. In 1912, joined Messrs. J. H. Martin and concentrated on photography in trick comedy films. Publicity films for London Press Exchange.

Tobin, P.—Many years in industry. Perilous news-reel work in Ireland, 1918. Fox News, Bonzo Cartoons, British Instructional work in Greece ; B.I.P., 1929, on "The Flying Scotsman"; and Topical Budget. *Address :*—324, Streatham High Road, S.W.16.

Tunwell, Alfred A.—Since 1911 turned for most firms, especially Samuelson and British Lion. 1929, with British Movietone News. *Address :*—67, Kenilworth Road, Putney, S.W.15. *Phone :*—Putney 1784.

Van Enger, C.—Teddington talkies ; G.B., contract. "Turkey Time," etc. Extensive Hollywood experience since 1910 ; turned on over 60 subjects, many of them famous.

Vetchinsky, Alex.—Art director, Gainsborough Studios.

Waller, H. N.—Chief art draughtsman, London Films, Denham.

Warneforde, E.—British Instructional's expert on nature subjects, responsible for countless examples of brilliant work.

Wells, Ralph.—Former script author, now unit production manager. Address :—Rembrandt Productions, 128, Shaftesbury Avenue, W.1.

Westwood, Russell.—Still cameraman, Warner Studios, Teddington.

Williams, Derick.—Born 1906 ; Cameraman, 1927, on "Blackmail," "Ghost Train," wrote and directed shorts ; 1933, head of Islington studios cameras and lighting expert. On G.-B. Australian picture "Flying Doctor," 1936. *Address :*—11A, Montpelier Street, S.W.7.

Wilson, Fred L.—Kinemacolour and Kineto in 1911. Official kinematographer throughout the war ; later with "Topical Budget." Accompanied the late Lord Leverhulme on his 17,000 miles expedition in West Africa, 1924-5. Empire and News Bulletin, Paramount Sound News, Universal Sound News. *Phone :*—Gladstone 4812.

Wilson, James.—Long experience with Broadwest, Gainsborough and B.I.P. "One of the Best," "Just for a Song," "Symphony in Two Flats," "Man from Chicago," etc.

Woods-Taylor, George.—Started 1911 as editor, Topical Film Co., then with Cinechrome, Ltd., experimenting in colour and ultra-rapid kinematography. Took first slow-motion in news film. Official photographer, Prince of Wales' Indian tour. British Filmcraft Productions, Ltd. "Burgomaster of Stilemonde" and "Spangles." Technical manager, Blunt & McCormack, Ltd. Official kinematographer, War Office Experimental Dept., Shoeburyness. *Address :*—26, Barnstaple Road, Thorpe Bay, Essex. *Phone :*—Thorpe Bay 8506.

Wratten Jan, D.—Research with Kodak, N.Y. 1923 at Hollywood. *Address :*—Mansfield, Malpas Drive, Pinner, and Kodak, Kingsway.

Wyand, Paul.—Movietone News cameraman; motor-racing expert.

Wyand, Leslie.—Gaumont Graphic, 1910. Pathé in U.S.A., now "Pathé Gazette." Premier Akley panoramic camera expert. Representing Hearst News with Gaumont Sound News.

Wynn, Reginald.—Joint managing director Publicity Productions, 89, Wardour Street. Speciality : advertising talkie cartoons.

Wyser, Paul F.—Chief sound engineer, A.T.P., Ealing.

Young, Hal.—Associate cameraman, Twickenham Studios.

Young, Fred·A.—Turned on many Gaumont pictures, Gainsborough, New Era, and B. & D. "The W Plan," "A Warm Corner," "Good-Night, Vienna," "Bitter Sweet," "That's a Good Girl," "Queen's Affair," "Nell Gwyn," "King of Paris," "When Knights were Bold," "This'll Make You Whistle," "Three Maxims," "Two's Company," etc. Address:—The Timber House, Deacon's Hill, Elstree.

PLACE YOUR NEXT
ORDER WITH PATHE

*S*O great has been the demand for Pathe theatre chairs during the past twelve months that we have found it necessary to open an extensive new factory and warehouse at Mitcham. We actually supplied during 1936 seventy-five thousand seats to Exhibitors all over the country.

173 Wardour St., London, W.1.
'Phones: GERrard 1544-5-6.

Grams:
Theatequip, Rath,
London.

SEATING &
FURNISHING
SPECIALISTS

SOLE SELLING AGENTS for famous

ROSS PROJECTORS
Unrivalled for efficiency and extra long service

GENERAL
AND
CLASSIFIED
TRADE
DIRECTORY

General Trade Directory

For Classification according to Trades, see pages 425 to 448.

Will foreign readers note that in order to economise space, the word London is omitted from all London addresses. These can be identified by the district numbers—W.1, etc.

A.W.H. Engineering Co., Ltd., Moreton-in-Marsh, Gloucester..... Moreton-in-Marsh 79——Sofilmko
A.W.H. Sound Reproducing Co., Ltd., Camden Works, King's
   Road, St. Pancras, N.W.1 .... North 2173-4—Sofilmko, Norwest.
Abertillery Theatres, Ltd., New Hall, Bargoed....................... Abertillery 3.
Abrahams, A. E., 25, Shaftesbury Avenue, W.1 .... Gerrard 2756 —— Abrahmend
   Lesquare.

Academy Cinema Co., 266, High Street North, E. Ham, E.12 ... Grangewood 1059.
Accumulator Makers' Association, 66, Victoria Street, S.W.1 ... Victoria 2853.
Accurate Check, Ltd., 94, Wardour Street, W.1 .... Gerrard 1703——Unreserved,
   Rath.
Ace Films, National House, Wardour Street, W.1.................... Gerrard 3336-8——Acefilmz, Rath
Ace Films, Ltd., 3, The Parsonage, Manchester .... Blackfriars 3062.
Ace Films, Ltd., 182, Trongate, Glasgow. .... Bell 1077——Films, Glasgow.
Ace Films, Ltd., Film House, Mill Hill, Leeds, 1. ....
Ace Films, Ltd., 17, Somerton Buildings, John Bright Street, Midland 2015.
   Birmingham.
Ace Films, 11, Bath Lane, Newcastle-on-Tyne .... Newcastle 24885.
Ace Films, Ltd., 23, Charles Street, Cardiff........................... Cardiff 1024.
Ace Studios, 73–75, Albany Street, Regent's Park, N.W.2......... Euston 3622.
Ackers, 3, Burton Street, Collyhurst, Manchester....................
Ad-Visers, Ltd., Panton House, 25, Haymarket, S.W.1 .... Whitehall 3332.
Aerofilms, Ltd., Bush House, Aldwych, W.C.2 .... Temple Bar 2164-5—Aerofilms,
   Bush, London.
Aero Pictorial, 136, Regent Street, W.1................................ Regent 4340.
African Consolidated Films, Ltd., 31/33, Lisle Street, W.C.2 ... Gerrard 1951-6.
Ager Circuit, 10, Church Street, Colchester .... Colchester 3681.
Agfa-Photo Ltd., 1-4, Lawrence Street, W.C.2 .... Temple Bar 6101 —— Agfafoto,
   Westcent.

Aish, Clifford, F.S.I., L.R.I.B.A., 22, Bedford Street, W.C.2 ..... Temple Bar 2061.
Alba Films, Denmark House, 25, Denmark Street, W.C.2 .... Temple Bar 2992.
Albany Ward Theatres, Ltd., New Gallery House, 123, Regent
   Street, W.1... Regent 8080——Procinthe, Piccy.
Alexander Film Productions, Ltd., 26-7, D'Arblay Street, W.1 ... Gerrard 3772.
Alpha Ticket Issuing Co., Kingsland Works, St. Peter's Road, W.1
Allen Construction Co., Ltd., 235, Bath Street, Glasgow, C.2 ... Douglas 1243——Allen, Douglas
   1243 Glasgow.
Allen, David, & Sons, Ltd., 23, Buckingham Gate, S.W.1 .... Victoria 8482——Advancement.
Alliata, P., 75 Chandos Court Mansions, Buckingham Gate,S.W.1 Victoria 9782.
Allied Arts Ltd., 192, Albany Street, N.W.1 .... Museum 6517-8.
Allied Guilds, Ltd., Guild House, Tyburn Road, Erdington,
   Birmingham .... Erdington 1616——Beautify, Bir-
   mingham.
Allighan, Garry, 9, Cavendish Street, W.1............................. Langham 1085.
Amalgamated Films Assoc., Ltd., 25, Haymarket, S.W.1 .... Whitehall 3332.
Amalgamated Picture Theatres, Ltd., Cinema House, Oxford
   Street, W.1 .... Gerrard 4242 and 3300.
Amalgamated Studios, Ltd., Elstree Way, Boreham Wood, Herts Elstree 1678.
Amalgamated Studios, Ltd., 60, Wardour Street, W.1............... Gerrard 2822-3.
Amusement Caterers' Association (Northern Ireland), White
   Cinema Club, Lyric Cinema, Belfast.
Andrew, Smith, Harkness, Ltd., 17, Lexington Street, W.1...... Gerrard 5295-6.
Angel Morris & Son, Ltd., 117-119, Shaftesbury Avenue, W.C.2... Temple Bar 5181—— Theatridio,
   Westcent, London.

Anglia Films, Ltd., 108-111, Jermyn Street, S.W.1 .... Whitehall 7585.

Anglo-Canadian Distributors, Ltd., 76-78, Wardour Street ,W.1 Gerrard 2882-5——Micofilm.

Anima Film Co. Ltd., 76, Wardour Street, W.1 .... Gerrard 2882.

Anselm Odling & Sons, Ltd., 132, New North Road, N.1 .... Clerkenwell 8740.

Anson, C .R. (P.A. & D. ,Ltd.), 36, Wilton Place, Knightsbridge Sloane 5151.

Apex Film Co., Ltd., 193, Wardour Street, W.1 .... Gerrard 1736.

Ardente Acoustic Laboratories (R. H. Dent, Ltd.), 11-12, Pollen
Street, W.1.. Mayfair 1801 and 1718—Acoucies,
Wes do. Holborn 9200.

Argonaut Film Co., Sentinel House, Southampton Row, W.C.1

Argyle Talking Pictures, Ltd., 4, Greengate, Tamworth,
Birmingham .... Tamworth 37.

Armin Trading Co., 32, Artillery Lane, Bishopsgate, E.1. .... Avenue 8883.

Army and Navy Supply Stores, 118-120, Praed Street, Padding-
ton, W.2 .... Paddington 2066-7—— Cash, Paddington 2066.

Arrow Achievements Co., 141, Duke Street, Liverpool .... Royal 3771.

Artads Service, Waterloo Road, Cricklewood, N.W.2............... Gladstone 5433——Nuadz, Gold.

Artons, Ltd., 6, Clark's Mews, High Street, London, W.C.2 ...... Museum 9989 & Temple Bar 7028.

Ascherberg, Hopwood & Crew, Ltd., 16, Mortimer Street, W.1... Museum 1671 —— Ascherberg.
Wesdo.

Associated British Cinemas, Ltd., 30-31, Golden Square, W.1. ... Gerrard 7887——Britcin, Piccy

Associated British Film Distributors (Dominion and Foreign),
Ltd., 169-171, Oxford Street , ... Gerrard 2644 (five lines).

Associated British Film Distributors, Ltd.,169-171, Oxford Street,
W.1 .... Gerrard 2644 (seven lines).

Associated British Film Distributors, Ltd., 114, Union Street,
Glasgow .... Central 1436.

Associated British Film Distributors, Ltd., 88, John Bright
Street, Birmingham .... Midland 3653-4

Associated British Film Distributors, Ltd., 11, Commutation
Row, Liverpool... North 366.

Associated British Film Distributors, Ltd., 70, Middle Abbey
Street, Dublin .... Dublin 43450.

Associated British Film Distributors, Ltd., 87, Westgate Road,
Newcastle .... Newcastle 23920.

Associated British Film Distributors, Ltd., 58, Wellington Street,
Leeds .... Leeds 20364.

Associated British Film Distributors, Ltd., Orme's Building, 14,
the Parsonage, Manchester .... Blackfriars 0911.

Associated British Film Distributors, Ltd. Dominions
Arcade, Queen Street, Cardiff .... Cardiff 7696.

Associated British Picture Corporation, Ltd., Film House,
Wardour Street, W.1 .... Gerrard 4314 (eight lines)——
Natpicture, Rath.

Associated Film Carriers of Great Britain, Ltd., 26, Charing Cross
Road, W.C.2 .... Temple Bar 1623.

Associated Metropolitan Productions, Ltd., Film House, Wardour
Street, W.1 .... Gerrard 4314.

Associated News Theatres, Ltd., 147, Wardour Street, W.1 ...... Gerrard 1416.

Associated Provincial Picture Houses, Ltd., New Gallery House,
123, Regent Street, W.1... Regent 8080——Procinthe, Piccy

Associated Realist Film Producers, Ltd., 33, Soho Square, W.1 Gerrard 2484.

Associated Sound-Film Industries, Ltd., Wembley Park .... Wembley 3041.

Associated Talking Pictures Ltd., A.T.P. Studios, Ltd., Ealing
Green, W.5 .... Ealing 6761——Emptalpic, Ealux,
London.

Associated Theatres (P. A. & D.), Ltd., Dean House, Dean Street,
W.1.. Gerrard 4543.

Association of Cine-Technicians, 30, Piccadilly Mansions, W.1..... Gerrard 2366.

Atkinson, Robert, F.R.I.B.A., and A. F. B. Anderson, F.R.I.B.A.,
13, Manchester Square, W.1... Welbeck 4147.

Atkinson's Pictures, Ltd., 9, North Road, St. Andrews, Bristol, 6 Bristol 44190.

Atlantic Film Productions, Ltd., 37, Maddox Street, W.1. ...... Mayfair 4752.

Augener, Ltd., 18, Gt. Marlborough Street, W.1 .... Gerrard 6706——Augener, Wesdo.

Automatic (Barnes, 1932), Ltd., National House, Wardour Street,
W.1 .... Gerrard 5535-6.

Automatic (Barnes, 1932), Ltd. (Laboratory), Charles Street,
Barnes, S.W.13 .... Prospect 1073-4.

Automaticket, Ltd., 197, Wardour Street, W.1. .... Gerrard 3482-3—Tradrego, Rath,
London.

Automaticket, Ltd., First Floor, Suffolk House, Suffolk Street,
Birmingham .... Midlands 4915.

Automaticket, Ltd., 47/9, Roscoe Street, Liverpool .... Royal 3463.

Automaticket, Ltd., 96, Renfield Street, Glasgow................. Douglas 1362.

Automaticket, Ltd., 34, Wellington Road, Leeds.................... Leeds 25001.

Automaticket, Ltd. (Crowe & Co., 52, Stowell Street, Newcastle) Newcastle 25539.

Automaticket, Ltd. (L. Elliman, 70 Middle Abbey Street, Dublin)	Dublin 43450.
Automaticket, Ltd. (H. Murphy, New Lodge, Muckamore, Co. Antrim)	Antrim 6.
Autotype Co., Ltd., 59, New Oxford Street, W.C.1	Temple Bar 9331——Autotype London.
Award Theatres, Ltd., Weymouth House, Wilton Road, Salisbury	Salisbury 2396.
B. & A. Productions, Ltd., 143, Wardour Street	
Bacal, Albert, 37-38, Golden Square, W.1	Gerrard 7138 & 6464.
Bacon's Pictures, Ltd., Sidney, 108, Great Russell Street, Bloomsbury, W.C.1	Museum 5221-2 ——Nocabdis, Westcent.
Bader, D. A., Ltd., 10, Haymarket, S.W.1	Whitehall 2875.
Baer, M. (Continental Film Exchange), 176, Wardour Street, W.1	Gerrard 5719 —Biophone, London.
Bagenal, Hope, A.R.I.B.A., 36, Bedford Square, W.C.	Museum 0974.
Baggott's Bros. Cinema Transport, 66, Willenhall Road, Wolverhampton	Wolverhampton 1894.
Baird Television, Ltd., 66, Haymarket, S.W.1	Whitehall 5454——Televisor, Lesquare.
Baker, Harry, 202, Hope Street, Glasgow, C.4	Douglas 5105.
Baker, H., Water Lane, Thaxted, Essex	
Baldwin Cinema Service, 22, Parsonage, Manchester	Blackfriars 7769 & Sale 1967.
Baldwin Cinema Service, 10 Commutation Row, Liverpool	North 370.
Balleny, H. T., 404, Warwick Road, Solihull, Birmingham	
Bamford, Sidney, 28, Grainger Street, Newcastle-on-Tyne	Central 25614.
Bancroft, H., Hippdrome, Wisbech	Wisbech 116.
Barber, Geo. H., Palace, Tunstall, Staffs.	Hanley 7453——Palace.
Barker, John, Palace, Lancaster.	
Barnett, C., 4, Sidmouth Road, Brondesbury Park	Willesden 1328.
Batteries, Ltd., Hunt End Works, Redditch, Worcestershire	Astwood Bank 4 —— Batteries, Redditch.
Bauer, Ltd., 137, Wardour Street, W.1	Gerrard 1242——Cinesound, London.
Bausch & Lomb, 67, Hatton Garden, E.C.	Holborn 2640.
B.B. Cinema Circuit, West Down, nr. Ilfracombe	Ilfracombe 7.
Baxter & Barter, 91, Regent Street, W.1	Regent 7560 & 2533
Beacon Carbons, Ltd., Albion Works, Bingley	Bingley 113——Electricos.
Beale, Arthur, 194, Shaftesbury Avenue, W.C.2	Temple Bar 2960.
Beard, J. Stanley, F.R.I.B.A., and Bennett, 101, Baker Street, W.1	Welbeck 2858-9.
Beard, R. R., Ltd., 10, Trafalgar Road, S.E.15	Rodney 3136——Biojector Peck.
Beaver Electrical Supply Co., 5, Gt. Chapel Street, W.1	Gerrard 3335.
Beck, J. M. (Hays Organisation) 106, Piccadilly, W.1.	Grosvenor 3155.
Beck, R. & J., Ltd., Head office : 69, Mortimer Street, W.1	Museum 3608 —— Objective, Wesdo.
Beck, R. & J., Ltd., Factories, Kentish Town, N.W.	Gulliver 2281.
Beck & Windibank, Ltd., Clement Street, Birmingham	Central 3834——Carpets.
Bedford Cinemas (1928) Ltd., 19, Castle Street, Liverpool, 2	Central 1544.
Beever's, 26, Aldermanbury, London, E.C.2	Metropolitan 3272—Beevonaire, Phone, London.
Bell, C. H., & Co., Ltd., 60, Wardour Street, W.1	Gerrard 2822.
Bell & Howell Co., Ltd., 320, Regent Street, W.1	Langham 3988 —— Belanhowe, Wesdo.
Bell Punch Co., Ltd., 39, St. James's Street, S.W.1	Regent 1532——Belpunch Piccy.
Bendon Trading Co., 132, West Nile Street, Glasgow, C.1	Douglas 579——Bendon.
Benham & Sons, Ltd., 66, Wigmore Street, W.1	Welbeck 9253——Benham, Wesdo.
Benjamin Electric, Ltd., Brantwood Works, Tariff Road, N.17	Tottenham 1500.
Bennie, John, Ltd., 149, Moncur Street, Glasgow, S.2	Bell 3116.
Benslyn, W. T., A.R.C.A., F.R.I.B.A., 17, Easy Row, Birmingham	Central 5979.
Bentley's (Walter) Agency, 40, Shaftesbury Avenue, W.1	Gerrard 6606-7——Yeltneb, Lesquare.
Berger, Lewis & Sons, Ltd., Homerton, E.9	Amherst 3321—Lewberg, Telex.
Berkeley Electrical Engineering Co., Ltd., Vincent House, Vincent Square, S.W.1.	Victoria 8051 (4 lines)—Berkelon, Sowest.
Berman, M., Ltd., 18, Green Street, Leicester Square, W.C.2	Whitehall 5726-8.
Bernstein, Sidney L., 36, Golden Square, W.1	Gerrard 3554——Berdarold, Piccy.
Berry, W. E., Ltd., Nesfield Printing Works, Nesfield Street, Bradford	Bradford 1291——Posters
Bersel Manfg. Co., Lawrence Works, Tottenham, N.15	
Betterways, Ltd., 33, Great Queen Street, W.C.1	Holborn 3213.
Beverley, Samuel, F.R.I.B.A. (Verity & Beverley) 32, Old Burlington Street, W.1	Regent 2117
Bijou Film Co., Ltd., 245, Oxford Street, W.1	Regent 3031.

Binns, J. J., Fitton & Haley, Ltd., Bramley Organ Works, Leeds　Stanningley 71028.

B I.P. (Export) Ltd., Film House, Wardour Street, W.1 .... Gerrard 4314 ——— Natpicture, Rath.

Birchenough, J., 10, Portland Place, Stalybridge.....................

Birmingham Sound Reproducers, Ltd., Claremont Works, Old Hill, Staffs. .... Cradley Heath 6212-3—Electronic, Old Hill.

Blackmore & Sykes (Blackmore, A.C., L.R.I.B.A., P.A.S.I. & W. E. Sykes, F.S.I.), Ruskin Chambers, Scale Lane, Hull　... Central 35369.

Black's Enterprises, Ltd., Suite 9, 115, Shaftesbury Avenue, London, W.C.2 .... Temple Bar 9324.

Blackstone & Co., Ltd., Stamford, Lincs. .... Stamford 107-8——Blackstone.

Blackstone & Co., Ltd., Imperial House, 15-19, Kingsway, W.C.2　Temple Bar 9681——Enginmanu, Estrand.

Blackstone & Co., Ltd., Baltic Chambers, Wellington Street, Glasgow. Central 7604-5——Blackstone.

Blackstone & Co., Ltd., 2, Lon Dan-y-Coed, Sketty, Swansea ... Swansea 7363——Blackstone, Sketty.

Blackstone & Co., Ltd., 40, Victoria Square, Belfast .... Belfast 24145——Blackstone.

Blackstone & Co., Ltd., 44, South Dock Street, Dublin............ Dublin 62204——Ralister.

Blackwell & Co., Ltd., 7, Dyers Buildings, Holborn, E.C.1 .... Holborn 5486-7——Wellblack.

Blackpool Film Transport, " Sunny Bank," Brown Lane, Heald Green, Cheshire .... Gatley 2526.

Blake, W. H., & Co., Ltd., Victoria Works, Queens Road, Sheffield　Sheffield 20154.

Blue Halls, Ltd., Coronation House, 4, Lloyd's Avenue, London, E.C.3.. Royal 6158-9

Blue Light, Ltd., 80, Wardour Street, W.1 .... Gerrard 2271.

Blyth, S. S. Kinemas Ltd., Waterloo Chambers, Bath Lane, Newcastle-on-Tyne.. Newcastle 27864.

Board of Trade (Films Dept.), Horseferry House, Horseferry Road, S.W.1.. Victoria 8740.

Bonded Film Stores, Ltd., 33-35, Endell Street, W.C.2. .... Temple Bar 3887.

Boosey & Hawkes, Ltd., 295, Regent Street, W.1 .... Langham 2741——Sonorous.

Booth, Henry (Hull), Ltd., Nautch Printing Works, Park Avenue, Hull .... Central 7491 & 7267—Numerical.

Boreham & Co., 20, Buckingham Street, Adelphi, W.C.2. .... Temple Bar 6123.

BORO' BILLPOSTING CO., Ranelagh Road, Grosvenor Road, London, S.W.1.. Victoria 8131.——Borobilpo, Sowest.

Boro' Electric Signs, Ranelagh Road, S.W.1 .... Victoria 7722—Boroelsign, Sowest London.

Boro' Electric Signs, Pollard Street, Manchester .... Central 1160 ——— Boroelsign Manchester.

Boro' Electric Signs, A. B. Row, Birmingham 4 .... Aston Cross 1661.

Boro' Electric Signs, 14, Blenheim Terrace, Woodhouse Lane, Leeds 2.. Leeds 24582.

Boro' Electric Signs, 30 Gordon Street, Glasgow, C 1 .... Central 1079.

Bosworth & Co., Ltd., 8, Heddon Street, Regent Street, W.1 ... Regent 4961.

Braham Products (London) Ltd., 75, Sancroft Street, S.E.11...... Reliance 3395-6.

Bowman, Fredk., H. V., 141, Duke Street, Liverpool .... Royal 3771.

Bramlin's Film Agency, Ltd., 17, Shaftesbury Avenue, W.1 ...... Gerrard 4407—Bramlifilm, Piccy.

Brandt Automatic Cashier Co., Ltd., 40-41, Conduit Street, W.1 .... Regent 5429.

Branford, V., Gaiety Cinema, Whitehaven .... Whitehaven 124.

Brearley, J., 21, Bridge Street, Manchester .... Blackfriars 9892.

Brennan's (Jas.) Cinemas, 107, Duke Street, Barrow-in-Furness... Barrow 990——Brennan, Barrow.

Brent Laboratories (Topical Film Co., Ltd.) North Circular Road, Cricklewood, N.W.2 .... Gladstone 4271. —Tophilma Gold.

Brilliant Neon, Ltd., Paragon Works, Uxbridge Road, W.12　... Shepherd's Bush 2281——Signboards, London.

Bristow, Billie, 10-12, Cork Street, W.1 .... Regent 6862.

Britannia Batteries, Ltd., Union Street, Redditch .... Redditch 155.

British Actors' Equity Association, 24, Thavies Inn, Holborn, E.C.1 .... Central 5622.

British Acoustic Films, Ltd., 14, Dover Street, W.1 .... Regent 1160.

British Board of Film Censors, Carlisle House, Carlisle Street, Soho, W.1. .... Gerrard 1946 ——— Censofilm, Phone, London.

British Chemicolour Process, Ltd., Walmer House, 296, Regent Street, W.1.. Langham 3858.

British Cinematograph Theatres, Ltd., 199, Piccadilly, W.1 ...... Regent 1227.

British & Continental Film Productions, 14-16, Regent Street, S.W.1.. Whitehall 1657.

British and Continental Trading Co., Inc., Regency House, Warwick Street, W.1 .... Gerrard 3884—Cables, Barnsfilm.

British and Dominions Film Corporation, Ltd., 142, Wardour Street, W.1. .... Gerrard 7855——Bridofilms, Rath

British and Dominions Film Corporation, Ltd., Imperial Studios, Boreham Wood, Elstree, Herts .... Elstree 1616——Bridofilms.
British Dominions Films, Ltd., Sentinel House, Southampton Row, W.C.1 .... Holborn 9200.
British Electrical Installations Co., 8, Parton Street, W.C.1 ...... Holborn 1571.
British Empire Films, Ltd., Dorland House, Regent St., S.W.1 Whitehall 5897.
British European Film Corporation, Ltd., 117, Regent Street, W. Regent 2616.
British Exhibitors' Films, Ltd., 15, Regent Street, S.W.1......... Whitehall 8484.
British Film Institute, 4, Gt. Russell Street, W.C.1 .... Museum 0607-8.
British Furtex, Ltd., Luddenden Foot, Yorks ....
British Industrial Laboratories, Ltd., 8-9, Long Acre, W.C.1 ... Temple Bar 3221.
British Institute of Cinematography, 5-11, Theobalds Road, W.C.1 Chancery 8338.
British Instructional Films, Ltd., 84, Wardour Street, W.1 ...... Gerrard 4360——Pathirema,Rath.
British International Pictures, Ltd., Boreham Wood, Elstree, Herts .... Elstree 1600—Natstudios, Phone Boreham Wood.

British International Pictures, Ltd., Film House, Wardour Street, W.1 .... Gerrard 4314 (8 lines) —Natpicture, Rath, London.

British Kinematograph Society, (E. E. Oram, Hon. Sec.), 314, Regent Street, W.1. .... Langham 1262.
British Lion Film Corporation, Ltd., 76-78, Wardour Street, W.1 Gerrard 2882-5——Brilionfil, Rath.
British Lion Film Corporation, Ltd., Lion Studios, Beaconsfield, Bucks .... Beaconsfield 555.
British Majestic Productions, Ltd., 25, Haymarket, S.W.........
British Movietonews, Ltd., 22, Soho Square, W.1.................... Museum 8241-2 —— Movietone, Rath.

British National Films, Ltd., Pinewood Studios, Iver Heath, Bucks .... Iver 460——Brincorfilm, Iver.
British Needle Co., Ltd., Argosy Works, Redditch .... Redditch 119——Argosy,Redditch,
British Ondiacolor, Ltd., 167-169, Wardour Street, W.1............ Gerrard 2579.
British and Overseas Film Sales, Ltd., 169-171, Oxford Street...... Gerrard 3991——Bofilms, Rath·
British Optical Lens Co., Ltd., Victoria Works, 315, Summer Lane, Birmingham ·.. Aston Cross 1156-8——Galalith, Birmingham.
British Paramount News, 10, School Road, North Acton, N.W.10 Willesden 5511——Nuparamo. Phone.

British Pictorial Productions, Ltd. (Empire News Bulletin, and Universal Talking News) 90, Wardour Street, W.1 ...... Gerrard 3265—Filmolitan, Rath.
British Poster Advertising Assocn., 48, Russell Square, W.C.1 ... Museum 1485 —— Disthene, Westcent.
British Publicity Talking Films, Ltd., 99, Charlotte Street, W.1 Museum 4426-7 —— Talkiads Phone, London.

British Publicity Pictures, 1, Edward Terrace, Queen Street, Cardiff .... Cardiff 141-2.
British Radio Corporation, Ltd, 46, Grosvenor Gardens, S.W.1. Sloane 0071.
British Schufftan Process, Ltd., Elstree, Herts .... Elstree 181.
British Screen Service, 54-58, Wardour Street, W.1................ Gerrard 6543-4 —— Winadfilm Rath.
British Sound Film Productions, Ltd., Wembley Park, Middlesex Wembley 3041.
British Sound Studio, Gladstone Road, Southall, Middlesex ...... Southall 1907.
British Sub-Standard Cinematograph Association, 12, Holborn, E.C.1. ....
British Talking Pictures, Ltd., Exhibition Grounds, Wembley Park, Middlesex .... Wembley 3738-9——Musvoxfilm, Wembley.

British Thomson-Houston Co., Ltd., Crown House, Aldwych, W.C.2 (Head Office, Rugby)...................................... Temple Bar 8040.
British Trane Co., Ltd., 5, Newcastle Place, E.C.1 .... Clerkenwell 6864.
British Unity Pictures, Ltd., Pollen House, 10-12, Cork Street, W.1 Regent 5372-3.
British United Film Producers, Film House, Wardour Street, W.1
British Utility Films, Ltd., 10, Regent Square, W.C.1.............. Terminus 6660.
British Vacuum Cleaner and Engineering Co., Ltd., Parson's Green Lane, London, S.W.6 .... Fulham 5566-9——Vacuumiser, Phone.

Brockliss, J. Frank, Ltd., 58, Great Marlborough Street, W.1 ... Gerrard 2911-3—Stafilm, Wesdo.
Brockliss, J. Frank, Ltd., 181, Howard Street, Glasgow .... Bell 1156.
Brockliss, J. Frank, Ltd., 67, Britannia House, Wellington Street, Leeds .... Leeds 24509.
Brockliss, J. Frank, Ltd., 3, The Parsonage, Manchester .... Blackfriars 5974.
Brockliss, J. Frank, Ltd., 110, John Bright Street, Birmingham Midland 3491.
Brooks, José, 20, Poland Street, W.1 .... Gerrard 3460—Showorld, Rath.
Brooks, J. B., & Co., Ltd., Great Charles Street, Birmingham ... Central 3670——Brooks.
Brown, F., Ltd., Langley Works, Long Acre, W.C.2 ·.............. Temple Bar 7222.
Brown, J. & Co., 228, Fulwood Road, Sheffield .... Sheffield 61126.
Browne & Son, Percy L., Pearl Buildings, Northumberland Street, Newcastle-on-Tyne .... Newcastle 23215——Details, Newcastle.

Bruce's, Ltd., Broadway 16mm. Commercial Film Service, 28-28A, Broadway, Ealing, W.5 .... Ealing 1033

Bruce, Peebles & Co., Ltd., Edinburgh 5 .... Edinburgh (Granton) 83261-4.
Bruce, Peebles & Co., Ltd., Hastings House, 10, Norfolk Street,
Strand, W.C.2 .... Temple Bar 6591-2.
Budd, S. W., Chartered Civil Engineers, 64, Victoria Street, S.W. Victoria 4943-4.
Bull, J. F., 1a, Ladas Road, West Norwood, S.E.27 ....
Bulman-Jupiter Screen Co. (1936). Ltd., 94, Wardour Street, W.1
and Stanley Works, Gonsalva Road, S.W.8 .... Gerrard 3591——Curtacarp,
Wesdo.
Buoyant Upholstery Co., Ltd., Sandiacre, Nottingham .... Sandiacre 13 and 14.
Burkitt, Frank, Ltd., 8a and 10, Lant Street, Borough, S.E.1 ... Hop 0865——Burkiproof, Sedist.
Burt Bros. (Bow) Ltd., Stoneleigh Works, Stonefield Road, Bow,
E.3. .... Advance 1675——Burtflora.
Bury & District Film Transport Co., Weybourne, Holt, Norfolk
Bury St. Edmunds Cinemas, Ltd., 54, Chevalier Street, Ipswich ... Ipswich 4036——Lekas, Ipswich
Busch, Emil, Optical Co., Ltd., 36-38, Dean Street, W.1. .... Gerrard 7194-5 —— Buschoptil .
Rath.
Butcher's Film Service, Ltd., 175, Wardour Street, W.1 .... Gerrard 7282——Butchilms, Rath .
Butcher's Film Service, Ltd., 1-5, Hill Street, Birmingham ...... Midland 0047——Butchilms.
Butcher's Film Service, Ltd., Dominion House, Queen Street,
Cardiff .... Cardiff 3182——Butchilms.
Butcher's Film Service, Ltd., 81, Dunlop Street, Glasgow ...... Central 1034.
Butcher's Film Service, Ltd., 41, Albion Street, Leeds.............. Leeds 26339——Butchilms.
Butcher's Film Service, Ltd., 3, The Parsonage, Manchester ... Blackfriars 1433.——Butchilms.
Butcher's Film Service, Ltd., 11, Bath Lane, Newcastle-on-Tyne. Newcastle 23136.——Films
Butcher's Film Service, Ltd. (E. Durand), 9, Birkland Avenue,
Peel Street, Nottingham .... Nottingham 2011.
Butcher's Film Service, Ltd. (W. Barry) 87, Donegal Street,
Belfast .... Belfast 26443.
Butcher's Film Service, Ltd. (L. Atkin, Agent for Irish Free
State) 52, Middle Abbey Street, Dublin .... Dublin 45359.
Buxton, Joseph and Harry, 4, Grange View, Leeds .... Leeds 41594——Buxton, Leeds.
Callender's Cable & Construction Co., Ltd., Hamilton House,
E.C.4 .... Central 5241——Callender, Fleet.
Callow Rock Lime Co., Ltd., Shipham, Winscombe, Somerset ... Cheddar 21.
Callow Rock Lime Co., Ltd., 4, Lloyds Avenue, E.C.3 .... Royal 6995——Calhydra, Fen.
Cambridge and District Film Transport Co., 17, Chase Avenue,
King's Lynn, Norfolk, ... King's Lynn 2335.
Cambridge Union Cinema Society, 33, Bridge Street, Cambridge...
Campbell Bros., Ltd., 28, Albert Embankment, S.E.11 .... Reliance 2217.
Cantophone, 187 Wardour Street, W.1. ....
Capital and Provincial News Theatres, Ltd., 172, Buckingham
Palace Road, S.W.1 .... Sloane 9132
Capitol Film Corporation Ltd., 293, Regent Street, W.1............ Langham 1851—Cables: Capifilm.
Caplin Engineering Co., Ltd., Beaconsfield Road, Willesden,
N.W.10 .... Willesden 0692.——Caplinko.
Cardiff Cinema Corporation Ltd., 7, St. Andrew's Crescent, Cardiff Cardiff 7279.
Carnival Films, Ltd., Princes House, Princes Arcade, Piccadilly,
W.1... Regent 2103.
Carpenter, F. H., & Co., Ltd., 1, Stanhope Street, London,
N.W.1 .... Museum 9730.
Carpets & Curtains, Ltd., 17, Mortimer Street, W.1, and Stanby
Works, Gonsalva Road, S.W.8.. Museum 1278—Curtacarp., Wesdo.
Macaulay, 3371
Carrier Engineering Co. Ltd., 24, Buckingham Gate, West-
minster, S.W.1 .... Victoria 6712.
Carter, Percival J., Palace, Blandford .... Blandford 12—— Palace, Bland-
ford.
Cary & Co., 13-15, Mortimer Street, W.1 .... Museum 1772 —— Muscaryoel,
Wesdo.
Castle & Central Cinemas, Ltd., 3, 5 and 7, The Hayes, Cardiff Cardiff 2982 —— Omnibus.
Cathode Corporation, Ltd., Meadow Works, Gt. North Road,
Barnet .... Barnet 217.
Cattermoul, Cecil, Ltd., 184, Wardour Street, W.1 .... Gerrard 2903-4 —— Scanofil,
Westcent.
Cavendish Pictures, Ltd., 26, St. Anne's Court, W.1 .... Gerrard 2208-9 —— Highflier,
Rath.
Cawthra, N., 11, St. Margarets Terrace, Bradford ....
Cecil Films, Ltd., 6, Old Bond Street, W.1 .... Regent 3465.
Celluloid Dispatch Services, Ltd., 167-9, Wardour Street, W.1...... Gerrard 5906-7.
Celluloid Products, Ltd., Fresh Wharf, Highbridge Road,
Barking .... Grangewood 3525.
Celotex Co. of Gt. Britain, 324, Australia House, W.C.2............
Cement Marketing Co., Ltd., Portland House, Tothill Street,
S.W.1 .... Whitehall 2323——Portland, Pal.
Central Agency Films, 11, Bath Lane, Newcastle, 4................. Newcastle 24885 & Gosforth 51846
Central Information Bureau for Educational Films, Ltd.,
Kingsway House, 103, Kingsway, W.C.2 .... Holborn 3163.
Central Printing Co. (C. Sowden, Ltd.) Rosendale Road, Burnley Burnley 4030.

Chalmers, John, 213, Buchanan Street, Glasgow, C.1 .... Douglas 3132.
Champion, Chas. H., & Co., Ltd., National House, 60-66, Wardour
    Street, W.1 .... Gerrard 2744-5-6——Karbonimpo,
                                                           Rath.
Champion, Chas. H., & Co., Ltd., Grove Road, Chadwell Heath,
    Essex .... Seven Kings 2421.
Champion, J. B., & Sons (Dursley), Ltd., Reliance Works, Dursley,
    Glos. .... Dursley 5——Champion.
Chappell Piano Co., Ltd. (Mustel Organs), 50, New Bond Street,
    W.1 .... Mayfair 7600.
Chemical Air Cleaning Co., 62, Brewery Road, N.7 .... North 1644——Lamparex, London.
Chemical Cleaning & Dyeing Co., Argyll Street, W.1. .... Gerrard 1911.
Cheshire County Cinemas Ltd., Empress Theatre, Runcorn ...... Runcorn 199.
Cheshire Picture Halls, Ltd., Park Road North, Birkenhead ... Birkenhead 3524.
Chester, J. & W., Ltd., 11, Great Marlborough Street, W.1. ...... Gerrard 4041—Guarnerius, Wesdo.
Chloride Electrical Storage Co., Ltd., Head office : Exide Works,
    Clifton Junction, Nr. Manchester .... Swinton 2011 —— Chloridic,
                                            Pendlebury.
Chloride Electrical Storage Co., Ltd. (Exide), 205, Shaftesbury
    Avenue, W.C.2 .... Temple Bar 5454.
Chloride Electrical Storage Co., Ltd. (Exide), 18-22, Bridge Street,
    Manchester .... Blackfriars 1158/9.
Chloride Electrical Storage Co., Ltd. (Exide), 57/58, Dale End,
    Birmingham .... Central 7629.
Chloride Electrical Storage Co., Ltd. (Exide) 15/18, Broadmead,
    Bristol .... Bristol 22461.
Chloride Electrical Storage Co., Ltd. (Exide), 40/44 Tureen Street,
    Glasgow .... Bridgeton 985.
Chloride Electrical Storage Co., Ltd., 137, Victoria Street, S.W.1 Victoria 6308—Chloridic, Sowest.
Christie Unit Organs, 372, York Road, N.7 .... North 1137-9 —— Bassoonist,
                                           Kentish.
Christie, W., & Grey, Ltd., 4, Lloyd's Avenue, E.C.3............... Royal 7371-2—Typhagitor, Fen.
Cinechrome, 8-9, Long Acre, W.C.2 .... Temple Bar 3221.
Cine Requirements, 203, Shaftesbury Avenue, W.C.2............... Temple Bar 4292.
Cinema Advertising Service, Ltd., 12, Manette Street, W.1 ...... Gerrard 1921.
Cinema Building Co., 182, Trongate, Glasgow .... Bell 1660-2——Carnival.
Cinema Christian Council, Gwydyr Chambers, 104, High Holborn,
    W.C.1. .... Holborn 2197.
Cinema Contact, Ltd., Oxford House, Oxford Street, W. 1......... Gerrard 6080.
Cinema Construction Co., Ltd., 154, West Regent Street, Glasgow Douglas 5071-2.
Cinema Employment and Sale Bureau, 18, Cecil Court, W.C.2 ... Temple Bar 1414.
Cinema Equipments, 47, Gerrard Street, W.1 and 98, Hackford
    Road, Brixton, S.W.9 .... Gerrard 5760 and Reliance 2792.
Cinema House, Ltd., 225, Oxford Street, W.1 .... Gerrard 3814-8——Screenopic,
                                           Wesdo.
Cinema & Interior Decorations, Ltd. 12, Regent Street, S.W.1... Whitehall 2858.
Cinema News, 80-82, Wardour Street, W.1 .... Gerrard 2504——Faddist, Rath.
Cinema Publicity Supply Co., 60, Lime Street, Liverpool .... Royal 102.
Cinema (Rotherham) and Electra, Ltd., Regent Theatre, Howard
    Street, Rotherham. .... Rotherham 291 —— Regent,
                                           Rotherham.
Cinema Screen Servicing Co., 339, Chingford Road, E.17 .... Larkswood 1808.
Cinema Service, Ltd., Cornhill House, Bennetts Hill, Birmingham Midland 2781.
Cinema Signs, Ltd. (Studios), King's Place, King Street, Camden
    Town, N.W.1 .... Euston 1416.
Cinema Signs, Ltd., 147, Wardour Street, W.1 .... Gerrard 1416.
Cinema & Theatre Construction, 52, Fetter Lane, E.C.4 .... Central 9914.
Cinema Traders, Ltd., 26, Church Street, W.1. .... Gerrard 5287—— Biocinema,
                                           Rath.
Cinema Veterans, 1903, 108, Great Russell Street, London, W.C.1 Museum 5221.
Cinematograph Exhibitors' Association of Gt. Britain and Ireland,
    Broadmead House, Panton Street, S.W.1 .... Whitehall 0191-4—Ceabilrex,
                                           Phone, London.
Cinematograph Times, Broadmead House, Panton Street, S.W.1 Whitehall 3940.
Cinematograph Trade Benevolent Fund, 52, Shaftesbury Avenue,
    W.1 .... Gerrard 4104.
Cinematograph Trade Provident Institution, 52, Shaftesbury
    Avenue, London, W.1.. Gerrard 4104.
Cinemise Film Advertising Service, Elstree .... Elstree 296.
Cinepro, Ltd., 1, New Burlington Street, W.1 .... Regent 2085——Cinepro, Piccy.
Cinesales, Ltd., 20, Old Compton Street, W.1........................ Gerrard 5457.
Cinesound Productions, Ltd., Dorland House, Regent Street,
    S.W.1 .... Whitehall 5897.
Clage's Baltic Yard, Hoe Street, Walthamstow, E.17 .... Walthamstow 1628.
Clarbour's (Percy) Cinema and Theatrical Agency, Palace House,
    128-132, Shaftesbury Avenue, W.1 .... Gerrard 6156

Clark & Fenn, Ltd., Charlotte Studios, Charlotte Place, North Street, Clapham, S.W.4 .... Macaulay 2455——
Plasdecor, Clapcom.
James Clark & Sons, Ltd., Scoresby House, Hill Street, Blackfriars Road, S.E.1 .... Waterloo 4611.
Clark's Cinemachinery, 101, Wardour Street, W.1 .... Gerrard 3957.
Clarke & Vigilant, Ltd., Atkinson Street, Deansgate, Manchester
Claude-General Neon Lights, Ltd., Pitman House, Parker Street, Kingsway, W.C.2 .... Holborn 7294.
Clavering & Rose, 199, Piccadilly, London, W.1 .... Regent 1146.
Clayton, E. C., Bank Chambers, 70, The Moor, Sheffield .... Sheffield 24673.
Clement Blake and Day, 22, Wardour Street, W.1 .... Gerrard 1192——Lennocks.
Cleveleys Advertising Co., Ltd., Electric House, Topping Street, Blackpool.. Blackpool 430——Wallaby.
Clifford Kemp, 15, Cavendish Chambers, 91, The Headrow, Leeds Leeds 27702.
Clifton-Hurst Productions, Ltd., 56, Whitcomb Street, W.C.2 ... Whitehall 8943.
Coates & Co., Ltd., Balhousie Works, Perth .... Perth 63——Coates, Perth.
Cochran, Chas. B., 49, Old Bond Street, W.1 .... Regent 1241.
Coles, George, F.R.I.B.A., 40, Craven Street, W.C.2 .... Whitehall 7756-8.
Coliseum Cinema (Southport) Ltd., 3, Tulketh Road, Southport...
Collins, J., & Son, Ltd., 17-19, Quaker Street, E.1 .... Bishopsgate 2498 and 5203.
Collins, Pat., Gondola Works, Shaw Street, Walsall, Staffs. ...... Walsall 3175——Gondola.
Coltman, A. & Co., Ltd., Fairfield Works, Hounslow, Mdsx. ... Hounslow 3265-6——Fairfield, Hounslow.
Coltman Displays, Ltd., 92, Wardour Street, W.1 .... Gerrard 6690 and 1396.
Columbia (British) Productions, Ltd., 139, Wardour Street, W.1 Gerrard 4321.
Columbia Graphophone Co., Ltd., 98 to 108, Clerkenwell Road, E.C.1.. Clerkenwell 7620——Talkingdom, Phone.
Columbia Graphophone Co., Ltd. (Recording Studios), 3, Abbey Road, N.W.8 .... Maida Vale 7386.
Columbia Pictures, 139, Wardour Street, W.1 .... Gerrard 4321.
Columbia Pictures, Columbia House, 90-92, John Bright Street, Birmingham .... Midland 3373.
Columbia Pictures, Dominion Arcade, Queen Street, Cardiff ... Cardiff 4275.
Columbia Pictures, 1-2, Eden Quay, Dublin .... Dublin 43343.
Columbia Pictures, 164, Buchanan Street, Glasgow .... Douglas 306.
Columbia Pictures, 9, Mill Hill, Leeds .... Leeds 30274.
Columbia Pictures, 14A, Norton Street, Liverpool .... North 284.
Columbia Pictures, 42, Deansgate, Manchester .... Blackfriars 5624.
Columbia Pictures, 87, Westgate Road, Newcastle .... Newcastle 21104.
Columbia Pictures, 14, Donegal Street, Belfast .... Belfast 23338.
Commercial & Educational Films, 10-11, Red Lion Court, E.C.4
Commercial Films, Furze Hill Road, Elstree .... Elstree 1296.
Commercial Film, 98, Gt. Russell Street, W.C.1.................. Museum 2073.
Community Service, Ltd., Bedford Row Chambers, 42, Theobalds Road, W.C.1 .... Holborn 7738.
Compton Organ Co., Ltd., John, Chase Road, Willesden, N.W.10 Willesden 6666-8——Willesden.
Conacher, P., & Co., Springwood, Huddersfield................... Huddersfield 53.
Concordia Distributors, Ltd., 95/99, Shaftesbury Avenue, W.1... Gerrard 5020.
Concordia Films, Ltd., 27, Old Bond Street, W.1................. Regent 5348.
Connies, Ltd., 92, Regent Street, W.1 .... Regent 2531.
Conquest Pictures, 72, Wardour Street, W.1. .... Gerrard 2231.
Conradty Products, Ltd., 101, Wardour Street, W.1 .... Gerrard 3888—Conradty, Rath.
Constructors, Ltd., Nickel Works, Tyburn Road, Erdington Road, Birmingham.. Erdington 1616——Equipstors.
Continuous Projectors, Ltd., 51, Ladbroke Grove, W.11 .... Park 1587.
Cook, E. W., A.M.I.C.E., M.I.S.E. (Structural), 16, Caxton Street, S.W.1.. Victoria 4669.
Cook, Gordon & Co., Cintra House, Hornsey, 8.................... Mountview 3932——Cintravert, Crouchway.
Cook, Gordon & Co., Peebles Works, Palmerston Road, Kilburn, N.W...
Cooke, F., 160, Brunshaw Road, Burnley, Lancs.
Cook's Publicity Service, Ltd., 40, Maida Vale, W.9 .... Maida Vale 1566 and 1781——Inducement, Padd.
Co-operative Cinematograph Co., Ltd., 225, Oxford Street, W.1 ... Gerrard 1871—Screenopic, Wesdo.
Cooper & Smith, 94, Charlotte Street, W.1 .... Museum 9994.
Co-ordinations, Ltd., 32, Shaftesbury Avenue, W.1 .... Gerrard 3697.
Cotter, A. V. W., International Photographic Art Services, Ltd., Boreham Wood, Elstree, Herts ....
Cotton, A., Cromwell House, Fulwood Place, High Holborn, W.C.1 Chancery 7054.
County Cinemas, Ltd., Dean House, Dean Street, W.1 .... Gerrard 4543-4-5——Cinecounty. Rath.
County Equipments, Ltd., Dean House, Dean Street, W.1 ...... Gerrard 2971.
County Films (I. M. Grainge), 41, Albion Street, Leeds............ Leeds 26946.
County Publicity, Ltd., 45, High Street, Aldershot .... Aldershot 987.
Cowan Mirror Protector Co., Ltd., Darby Gardens, Sunbury-on-Thames .... Sunbury 107.

Cowan Mirror Protector Co., Ltd., 30, Duke Street, Piccadilly, S.W.1 ....

Cox & Co., 135, Lower Richmond Road Putney, S.W.15 ....

Coxall, Horace S., Ltd., 182, Trongate, Glasgow ....
Cramer & Co , P. A., 41, Old Compton Street, W.1.................
Crampton, W., 104, Bolton Road, Pendleton ....
Crawford, W. S., Ltd., 233, High Holborn, W.C.1 ....
Crest Films, 22, Denman Street, W.1 ....
Cricks, R. Howard, F.R.P.S., 159, Wardour Street, W.1 ....
Criterion Films, Worton Hall Studios, Worton Road, Isleworth...
Criterion Plates, Paper Films, Ltd., Criterion Works, Stechford, Birmingham ....

Cromie, Robert, F.R.I.B.A., 6, Cavendish Square, W.1 ....
Crompton Parkinson, Ltd., Bush House, Aldwych, W.C.2 (Works: Guiseley, Leeds) ....

Crossley Brothers, Ltd., Openshaw, Manchester ....

Crow, Reg. V., 11, Avenue Lodge, Avenue Road, N.W.8 ....
Crowe & Co. (Kinematograph Engineers) Ltd., 52, Stowell Street, Newcastle-on-Tyne ....

Crown Theatre, 86, Wardour Street, W.1 ....
Cullum & Co., Horace W., Ltd., 57-63, Wharfedale Road, King's Cross, N.1 ....

Cummings, Peter, F.R.I.B.A., 31, King Street, West Manchester
Curtis Brown, Ltd., 6, Henrietta Street, W.C.2 ......,............

Curtis Manufacturing Co., Ltd. (Reg. Office), 26-28, Paddenswick Road, W.6 ....
Customs & Excise (Films Office) 87-89, Shaftesbury Avenue, W.1

Daily Film Renter, 127-133, Wardour Street, W.1 ......:.........
Dairy Supply Co., Ltd., Cumberland Avenue, Park Royal, N.W.10

Dallis Film Corporation, Midland Bank Chambers, High Street, Walton-on-Thames ....
Dallmeyer, J. H., Ltd., 31, Mortimer Street, W.1, and Church End Works, High Road, Willesden, N.W.10 ....

Danilo Companies, 3, New Street, Birmingham ....
Daponte, Demetre L., 8-9, Long Acre, W.C.2 ....
Davidson, A., Spreadeagle Hotel, Hillgate, Stockport.............
Davis, Basil, A.M.I.E.E., Elettra, Stanmore, Middlesex.........
Davis Bros., Illuminating Engineers, Ltd. (Office and Showroom), 22, Buckingham Street, Strand, W.C.2............................
Davis Bros., Illuminating Engineers, Ltd. (Works), 5, Bryan Street, N.1 ....
Davis (J.) Circuit, 147, Wardour Street, London, W.1 ....
Davis Poster Service, Ltd., High Street, Newcastle, Staffs ......
Day, Will, Ltd., 19, Lisle Street, W.C.2 ....
Day, E. J., & Co., Ltd., 10-16, Rathbone Street, W.1..................
Dean, Basil, A.T.P. Studios, Ealing Green, W.5.....................
Decra, Ltd., Hanbury Road, Acton, W.3 ....

Deeming (Chas. K.) Circuit, Grand Cinema, Coalville ....
De Jong, F. & Co., Ltd., 84, Albert Street, N.W.1 ....
Demolition & Construction Co., 74, Victoria Street, S.W.1.........
Denham Film Corporation, Ltd., Denham, Bucks.....................
Denham Laboratories, Ltd., Denham, Bucks. ....
Denman Picture Houses, Ltd., Film House, 142, Wardour Street, W.1 ....
Denman (London) Cinemas, Ltd., 36, Golden Square, W.1 ......
Denman Press Agency, 22, Denman Street, W.1 ....
Denning Films, Ltd., 10, Golden Square, W.1 ....
Dennison, Kett & Co., Ltd., Kenoval House, 226-230, Farmer's Road, S.E.5 ....
Detroit Engine Co., Market Place, Brentford, Middlesex ....
Diamond Tread Co., Ltd., 28, Victoria Street, S.W.1 ....
Dicken, W. Trueman, " Majestic," Burnham-on-Sea, Somerset ...
Dickinson & Sayle, 7, Newport Street, Lambeth, S.E.11 ....
Digbys, 39, Gerrard Street, W.1 ....
Dofil, Ltd., 5, Bucklersbury, E.C. ....
Dofil, Ltd. (Distribution), 37-39 Oxford Street, W.1 ....
Donaldson, F. G., 14, The Parsonage, Manchester ....

Dorland Advertising, Ltd., Dorland House, 14-20, Regent Street, S.W.1...

Doyle, Henry, 175, Kingsway, Burnage, Manchester	Rusholme 2341
D.P. Battery Co. Ltd., The, 50, Grosvenor Gardens, S.W.1	Sloane 6255-6——Cumulose, Sowest.
D.P. Battery Co. Ltd., The, Bakewell, Derbyshire	Bakewell 81-2——Battery, Bakewell.
Draper, W. & Co. (Electrical Installations), Ltd., 234, St. Vincent Street .Glasgow	Central 2179——Fuite, Glasgow.
Draper, W. & Co. (Electrical Installations), Ltd., 121, Victoria Street, Westminster, S.W.1	Victoria 3561——Fulitelec, Sowest, London.
Drem Products, Ltd., 37, Bedford Street, Strand, W.C.2	Temple Bar 2430.
Drew, Clark & Co., Diamond Patent Ladder Works, Leyton,E.10	Leytonstone 2246——Druanklark London.
Dublin Theatre Co., Ltd., 32, Shaftesbury Avenue, W.1............	Gerrard 3306.
Dufaycolor, see Ilford Cine (Sales Dept)................................	
Duncan Watson Electrical Engineers, Ltd., 61-62, Berners Street, W.1	Museum 2860,'(Night Pinner 3581) ——Kathode.
Dundealgan Electric Theatre Co., Ltd., St. Helena, Dundalk	Dundalk 116.
Dunlop Rubber Co., Ltd., Rubber House, Brookes Market, Holborn, E.C.1	Holborn 8571——Lark, Smith.
Dunlop Rubber Co., Ltd., Cambridge Street, Manchester	Central 7147——Rubber, Manchester.
Dunning Process (England), Ltd., 71-73, Whitfield Street, and 10, North Court,Chitty Street, Tottenham Court Road,W.1	Museum 0302——Bestlab,Eusroad.
Dyson, J., & Co., Ltd., Godwin Street, Bradford	Bradford 6037-9——Equipment.
Eagle Picturedromes, Ltd., County Playhouse, King Street, Wigan	Wigan 3476
East & Kent Co., Ltd., Canada House, Norfolk Street, W.C.2......	Temple Bar 1104——Kismet, Londo ♯.
East Ham Amusements, Ltd., 75-77, Shaftesbury Avenue, W.1	Gerrard 4973-4.
East London (Film) Motor Service, 73, Blake Hall Road, Wanstead, E.11	Wanstead 2721, and Maryland 1091.
Eastern Counties Cinemas, Ltd., Regent Theatre, Moulsham Street, Chelmsford	Chelmsford 2094—Regent Theatre.
Eaton, Parr & Gibson (Glass Merchants), Ltd., 41-53, Kingsland Road, E.2	Clerkenwell 3525—Measurement, Beth.
Edison, Thomas A, Ltd. Edison Storage Battery Division, Victoria House, Southampton Row, W.C.1	Holborn 6673——Accedison, Westcent.
Edison Swan Electric Co., Ltd., 155, Charing Cross Road, W.C.2	Gerrard 8660.
Educational Film Review, 8-11 Southampton Street, Strand......	Temple Bar 7760.
Educational Films Bureau, 101, Wardour Street, W.1	Gerrard 2344.
Educational Films Co., Ltd., Film House, Wardour Street, W.1	Gerrard 9292—Edrusfilms, Rath.
Effectograph Co., 8, Noel Street, W.1....................................	Gerrard 5171.
Electa Films, Ltd., 185a, Wardour Street, W.1	Gerrard 2332.
Electric (Cinema) Printing Co., Ltd., Waterloo Road, Manchester, 8..	
Electric Construction, Ltd. (Shell-Mex House)	Temple Bar 8306.
Electrical Equipment & Carbon Co., Ltd. (Siemens-Plania Carbons), 107-111, New Oxford Street, W.C.1	Temple Bar 7058-9——Thermotype, Westcent.
Electrical Installations, Ltd., 65, Vincent Square, S.W.1............	Victoria 5915 —— Stanlorio, Sowest.
Electric Lamp Manufacturers' Association, 25, Bedford Square, W.C.1	Museum 0766——Britelma, Westcent.
Electric Lamp Manufacturers' Association of Great Britain Ltd., 2, Savoy Hill, W.C.2..	Temple Bar 7337.
Electrical Trades Union, 1-7, Rugby Chambers, 2, Chapel Street, W.C.1	Holborn 6046-7.
Electro-control, Riotes Place, Barkergate, Nottingham	Nottingham 41184.
Electrocord, Ltd., 17, Wellington Street, Leeds	Leeds 26692——Elecord, Leeds.
Elite Entertainments Syndicate, East Church Street, Buckie ...	Buckie 106
Elite Picture House, Ltd., Elite Picture House, Toller Lane, Bradford	Bradford 3576.
Elliman, Louis, Ltd., 73, Middle Abbey Street, Dublin	Dublin 43371——Elliman, Dublin.
Ellis's Cinematograph Theatres, " Homeside," Higher Warberry, Torquay	Torquay 2895.
Elstree Film Laboratories, Ltd., B.I.P. Studios, Shenley Road, Boreham Wood, Elstree	Elstree 1600——Natstudios, Boreham Wood.
Elton, Herbert, Commerce Chambers, Elite Buildings, Nottingham	Nottingham 42364
Elvins, T. & Sons, Ltd., Naden Works, Soho Hill, Birmingham 19	North 2217-8.
Elvy, J. C., 32, Shaftesbury Avenue, W.1	Gerrard 2694.
Embassy Pictures (Associated), Ltd., 39, Hill Street, W.1	Grosvenor 1907.

Emerton, A. R., 46, Earlham Grove, Forest Gate, E.7 .... Maryland 2345.
Emery, J. F., J.P., M.P., Midland Bank House, 26, Cross Street,
 Manchester .... Blackfriars 0472 and Pendleton
 2611.
Empire Marketing Board (see G.P.O.) ....
Empire News Bulletin (*See* British Pictorial Productions).
English Electric Co., Ltd., 28, Kingsway, W.C.2 .... Holborn 6966.
Empire Seating Co., 49, Greek Street, W.1 .... Gerrard 4774.
Ensign, Ltd., 88-89, High Holborn, W.C.1 .... Holborn 6900.
Epalite Mirrors, Ltd., 2, Hall Street, Birmingham, 18............... Central 5252.
Eppel, Dr. I. J., 1, Walton Place, Knightsbridge, S.W.3 .... Kensington 2860.
Equity British Films, Ltd., 26, St. Anne's Court, W.1.......... Gerrard 2208-9 —Highflier, Rath.
Esspell Cinema, Ltd., 361, City Road, E.C.1............................ Clerkenwell 5126.
Etna Lighting and Heating Co., Ltd., Etna Chambers, 293-5, Midland 3071-2——Etna, Bir-
 Broad Street, Birmingham, 1. mingham.
Evans, Chas. J. & Co., 58a-70, Mountgrove Road, Blackstock
 Road, Highbury, N.5... Canonbury 1135.
Everett, Edgcumbe & Co., Ltd., Colindale Works, Hendon, N.W.9. Colindale 6045——Evergendos.
Exclusive Films, Ltd., National House, 60-66, Wardour Street W.1 Gerrard 2309.
Exide Battery Co. (See Chloride Electrical) ....
Express Lift Co., Ltd. (Incorporating Smith, Major & Stevens,
 Ltd.), Greycoat Street Works, S.W.1 ....:.......... Victoria 8830.

Fairfax, Ltd., 72 .Borough High Street, S.E.1..........................
Fairweather, John & Son, F.A.R.I.B.A., 182, Trongate, Glasgow Bell 1660. .
Falk, Stadelmann & Co., Ltd., 83-93, Farringdon Road, E.C.1 Holborn 7654——Lamps,London
Famous Films (London), Ltd., 174, Wardour Street, W.1. .... Gerrard 5830 & 4732.
Famous Films (Midlands), Ltd., 17, Forman Street, Nottingham Nottingham 43828——Familion
Farm Ice Creamery, Ltd., Chase Estate, Acton Lane, N.W.10 ... Willesden 2767-9.
Farquharson, John F., M.I.Struct.E., High Holborn House, W.C.1 Chancery 7255.
Faulkner, W. G.. & Co., Ltd., 32, Shaftesbury Avenue, W.1 ... Gerrard 5514.
Federation of British Film Societies, 56, Manchester Street, W.1... Welbeck 2171.
Federation of British Industries (F.B.I.), 21, Tothill Street, S.W.1. Whitehall 6711 and 6995 (late).
Feltons Advertising Agency (1924), Ltd., 58, Dean Street, W.1 Gerrard 5515——Stranded, Rath.
Fenton Circuit, 16, Central Buildings, Darlington .... Darlington 2496.
Ferodo, Ltd., Chapel-en-le-Frith, Stockport .... Chapel 19——Friction.
Ferrar, G., & Sons, 35, Claremont Road, Irlam o' th' Heights,
 Pendleton
Ferris Arthur, 14, Deansgate, N.2 .... Tudor 4314.
Ferry Engine Co., Ltd., Woolston, Southampton .... Woolston 88256——Cylinder
 Southampton.
Fidelity Distributors, 167, Wardour Street, W.1 .... Gerrard 5906-7.
Fidelity Films, Ltd. (Works), 103, Pears Road, Hounslow, Mdx. Hounslow 3177.
Fidelity Films, Ltd., Metropolitan Studios, Gladstone Road,
 Southall, Mddx. .... Southall 2238.
Fieldson & Co., 71, High Street, Rushden, Northants .... Rushden 4312.
Fifeshire Cinema Co., Ltd., Leven, Fifeshire .... Leven 147.
Film Alliance, 199, Wardour Street, W.1. .... Gerrard 3929.
Film Booking Offices, Ltd., 22, Soho Square, W.1 .... Gerrard 3912.
Film Clearing Houses, Ltd., 142-150, Wardour Street, London,
 W.1. .... Gerrard 9292.
Film Editorial Service, 94, Wardour Street, W.1 .... Gerrard 3856.
Film Enterprises (Ireland), National House, 60-66, Wardour
 Street, W.1... Gerrard 2309.
Film Industries, Ltd., (Reg. Office), 73, Gower Street, W.C.1 ... Welbeck 2293-4.——Troosound
 Wesdo.
Film Industries, Ltd., Head Office, 60, Paddington Street, W.1 Welbeck 2293-4 and 2385-6 ——
 Troosound, Wesdo.
Film Industries (Ltd.), 229, St. Vincent Street, Glasgow C.1....... Central 127.
Film Institute (see British Film Institute).
Film Laboratories, Ltd., 90, Wardour Street, W.1 .... Gerrard 3265 —— Filmolitan,
 Westcent.
Film Library, Ltd., 16, Great Chapel Street, W.1 .... Gerrard 1572——Librafilms, Rath,
 London.
Film Music Service, 16, Panton Street, S.W.1 .... Whitehall 0197.
Filmophone Renters, Ltd., National House, 60-66, Wardour
 Street, W.1 .... Gerrard 5745——Albritalki.
Film Publicity Service (Fred Pullin), 94, Wardour Street, W.1 Gerrard 3856.
Film Rights, Ltd., 24, Whitcomb Street, W.C.2....................... Whitehall 8896-7——Cables:
 Hayeshunt, London.
Films & Equipments, Ltd., 145, Wardour Street, W.1.............. Gerrard 671: -2—Katja, London.
Film Sales, Ltd., 191, Wardour Street, W.1 .... Gerrard 1464 —— Garanfieed,
 Rath.
Film Society, 56, Manchester Street, W.1 (Miss Barbara Frey,
 Secy.) .... Welbeck 2171.
F.T.S. (Great Britain) Ltd., 6, Union Glen, Aberdeen.............. Aberdeen 4575.
F.T.S. (Great Britain), Ltd. Fairfield House, Barr Street, Hockley,
 Birmingham .... Northern 0928.

F.T.S. (Great Britain), Ltd., Central Garage, Kingswood, Bristol ... Bristol 73357.
F.T.S. (Great Britain), Ltd., Fairfield House, Broxburn .... Broxburn 42.
F.T.S. (Great Britain), Ltd., Fairfield House, 449-453, Newport Road, Cardiff .... Cardiff 3612.
F.T.S. (Great Britain), Ltd., Coldside Road, Dundee .... Dundee 3772.
F.T.S. (Great Britain), Ltd., Woodmill Street, Dunfermline ...... Dunfermline 692.
F.T.S. (Great Britain), Ltd., Landscore Road, St. Thomas. Exeter .... Exeter 3398.
F.T.S. (Great Britain), Ltd., Fairfield House, Arcadia Street, Bridgeton, Glasgow .... Bridgeton 1350-1.
F.T.S. (Great Britain), Ltd., Fairfield House, Clarence Road, Hunslett, Leeds .... Leeds 31227-8.
F.T.S. (Great Britain), Ltd., Drummond Road, Belgrave, Leicester .... Leicester 61494.
F.T.S. (Great Britain), Ltd., 10-12, Beech Street, Liverpool ..... Anfield 1710.
F.T.S. (Great Britain), Ltd., Fairfield House, Glebe Road, Willesden, London .... Willesden 7181-2.
F.T.S. (Great Britain), Ltd., Fairfield House, Bamford Street, Clayton, Manchester .... East 1237.
F.T.S. (Great Britain), Ltd., 10, Back Goldspink Lane, Newcastle Newcastle 23596.
F.T.S. (Great Britain), Ltd., Cloister Square, Old Lenton, Nottingham..................... Nottingham 7147.
F.T.S. (Great Britain), Ltd., Thomson's Garage, Queen's Road, Sheffield .... Sharrow 50837.
Film Transport Co., Ltd., 26, Charing Cross Road, W.C.2......... Temple Bar 1623.
Films Office, H. M. Customs, 87-89, Shaftesbury Avenue, W.1.., Gerrard 2189.
Film Weekly, Martlett House, Martlett Court, Bow Street, W.C.2 Temple Bar 2468.
First National Film Distributors, Ltd., Warner House, 135-141, Wardour Street, W.1 .... Gerrard 5600——Firnatex, Rath.
First National Film Distributors, Ltd., 87, Station Street, Birmingham .... Midland 3083——Firnatex.
First National Film Distributors, Ltd., Dominions House, Queen Street, Cardiff. .... Cardiff 4509——Firnatex.
First National Film Distributors, Ltd., 62, Middle Abbey Street, Dublin .... Dublin 43941-2——Firnatex.
First National Film Distributors, Ltd., 81, Dunlop Street, Glasgow .... Central 6333-4——Firnatex.
First National Film Distributors, Ltd., 3, Alfred Street, Boar Lane, Leeds .... Leeds 21564-5——Firnatex.
First National Film Distributors, Ltd., 5-9, Slater Street, Liverpool .... Royal 4806-7——Firnatex.
First National Film Distributors, Ltd., Cromford House, Cromford Court, Manchester .... Blackfriars 4201-2——Firnatex.
First National Film Distributors, Ltd., Jayson Buildings, 47, Pink Lane, Newcastle-on-Tyne .... Newcastle 22405-6——Firnatex.
Fligelstone T. H., 11, Berkeley Court, Baker Street, N.W.1 ...... Welbeck 2301-2.
Fontagene Soda Fountains, Ltd., De Laune Street, New Street, Kennington, S.E.17 .... Reliance 1347.
Forbes, S., Palace Theatre, Glasgow, SS. .... South 270 and Western 4100.
Foster's Agency, Piccadilly House, Piccadilly Circus, W.1 ...... Regent 5367-8——Confirmation
Foster, Fred A. (Nottingham), Ltd., 94, Westdale Lane, Mapperley, Nottingham..................... Nottingham 6047.
Fox British Pictures, Ltd., 15-16, Newman Street, W.1............ Museum 5113.
Fox British Pictures, Ltd., Fox Studio, Empire Way, Wembley... Wembley 3000.
Fox Film Co., Ltd., 13, Berners Street, Oxford Street, W.1 ..... Museum 5113-4——Effoxifil,Rath.
Fox Film Co., Ltd., 51, John Bright Street, Birmingham .... Midland 4755—Effoxifil.
Fox Film Co., Ltd., Dominions Arcade, Cardiff .... Cardiff 1744——Effoxifil.
Fox Film Co., Ltd., 9B, Lower Abbey Street, Dublin, C.8......... Dublin 43068——Effoxifil.
Fox Film Co., Ltd., 142A, St. Vincent Street, Glasgow C.2 ...... Central 1056——Effoxifil.
Fox Film Co., Ltd., 54, Aire Street, Leeds .... Leeds 29651——Effoxifil.
Fox Film Co., Ltd., 31, Norton Street, Liverpool .... North 435-6—Effoxifil.
Fox Film Co., Ltd., 38, King Street West, Manchester .... Blackfriars 7634——Effoxifil.
Fox Film Co., Ltd., 180, Westgate Road, Newcastle-on-Tyne ... Newcastle 21641——Effoxifil.
Fox, C. G., & Co., Ltd., 61, St. Mary Axe, E.C.3..................... Avenue 1869-70——Pinerous.
Foxwell, Daniel & Son, Ltd. (Vacuum Cleaners), Cheadle, Cheshire Gatley 2141.
Foyle, W. & G., Ltd., 119-125, Charing Cross Road, W.C.2 ...... Gerrard 5660.
Francis, Day & Hunter, Ltd., 138-140, Charing Cross Road, W.C.2 Temple Bar 9351.
Franco-British Electrical Co., Ltd. (Franco Signs), 25, Oxford Street, W.1 .... Gerrard 6671——Crystalry.
Franco-London Film, Ltd., Panton House, Haymarket, S.W. ... Whitehall 5358.
Freeman, Son and Gaskell, 11, Carr Lane, Hull .... Hull 35502——Gaskell, Architect.
French, R. Duncan, J.P., C.C., 17, North John Street, Liverpool... Bank 5836.
Friern Manor Caterers, Ltd., Hankey Place, S.E.1..................... Hop 0686——Kinecator, Phone.
Friese-Greene, Nicholson & Co., Ltd., 109, Queen Street, Sheffield Sheffield 25613.
Friese-Greene, Kenneth, Campo Chambers, Campo Lane, Sheffield Sheffield 26027.
Fuller Accumulator Co. (1926), Ltd., Woodland Works, Chadwell Heath, Essex .... Seven Kings 1200——Fuller.
Fuller Accumulator Co. (1926), Ltd., 48, Gt. Charles Street, Birmingham .... Central 1989.

Fuller Accumulator Co. (1926), Ltd., 53, Back George Street,
Princess Street, Manchester .... Central 6356.
Fulvue-Film, Ltd., 8, Laurence Pountney Hill, E.C.4 .... Mansion House 4958.
Furse, W. J. & Co., Ltd., 9, Carteret Street, S.W.1 .... Whitehall 3938.
Furse, W. J., & Co., Ltd., Traffic Street, Nottingham............... Nottingham 8213-5——Furse.
Fyfe, Wilson & Co., Ltd., 30, Budge Row, E.C.4 .... City 2602——Ductility.
Fyfe & Fyfe, Ltd., 55, Bath Street, Glasgow .... Douglas 706——Douglas 706.
G. & A. Signs, Ltd. (See Modern Poster Service) ....
Gaiety Films, Ltd., Suite D, Victory House, 99-100, Regent
Street, W.1. .... Regent 4826.
Gainsborough Pictures (1928), Ltd., Film House, Wardour Street,
W.1 .... Gerrard 9292
Gainsborough Pictures (1928), Ltd. (Studios), Poole Street, New
North Road, Islington, N.1 .... Clerkenwell 9100 and 9271 ——
Gainspic, Mordo.
Gardiner, Sons & Co., Ltd., Midland Iron Works, Willway Street,
St. Philip's, Bristol .... Bristol 25541——Gardsons.
Gardner, Albert V., 11, Bath Street, Glasgow ....
Gardner, J. Starkie, Ltd., Merton Road, Southfields, S.W.18 ... Putney 5721.
Garrett Klement Pictures, Ltd., 32, St. James' Street, S.W.1...... Whitehall 4296-8.
Garrick Film Co., Ltd., Princes House, Princes Arcade, Picca-
dilly, W.1... Regent 2103.
Gasparcolor, Ltd., 3, St. James's Square, S.W.1 .... Whitehall 8701-2.
G.-B. Instructional, Ltd., 12, D'Arblay Street, W.1 .... Gerrard 7386—Gebestruct, Rath.
G.B. Instructional, Ltd., Cleveland Hall Studios, 54, Cleveland
Street, W. .... Museum 4353.
Gaumont British Distributors, Film House, Wardour Street, W.1 Gerrard 9292——Okaphilms.
Gaumont British Distributors, 1, Broad Street Chambers,
Birmingham .... Midlands 2351-4——Okaphilms.
Gaumont British Distributors, 46, Charles Street, Cardiff........... Cardiff 2733-4——Okaphilms.
Gaumont British Distributors, 77, Mitchell Street, Glasgow......... Central 2786——Okaphilms.
Gaumont British Distributors, 12, Lands Lane, Leeds............... Leeds 29745-8.——Okaphilms.
Gaumont British Distributors, 15, Renshaw Street, Liverpool... Royal 5657-8.—— Okaphilms.
Gaumont British Distributors, 3, The Parsonage, Manchester...... Blackfriars 7454-5.——Okaphilms.
Gaumont British Distributors, Film House, Westgate Road,
Newcastle-on-Tyne.. Central 26681-3——Okaphilms.
G.-B. Equipments, Ltd., Film House, Wardour Street, W.1 .... Gerrard 9292——Gebequip, Rath.
Gaumont British Instructional, Ltd., Film House, Wardour
Street, W.1 .... Gerrard 9292——Gebestruct,Rath.
Gaumont-British Picture Corporation, Ltd., Film House, 142/150,
Wardour House, Regent Street, ... Gerrard 9292——Gaupicor, West-
cent.
Gaumont British Picture Corporation (Theatres), New Gallery
House, Regent Street, ... Regent 8080.
Gaumont British Picture Corporation, Ltd. (Publicity) 5 & 6,
Cork Street .... Regent 8080.
Gaumont-British Picture Corporation, Ltd., The Studio, Lime
Grove, Shepherd's Bush, W.12.................................... Shepherd's Bush 1210 and 2300.
G.-B. Screen Services, Ltd., Film House, Wardour Street, W.1... Gerrard 9292——Gebescreen,Rath
Gaumont Super-Cinemas, Ltd., Pollen House, 10-12, Cork Street,
W.1 .... Regent 4794-5.
Gaze, H. E., Ltd., Euston Buildings, London, N.W.1.............. Museum 0222——Gaze, Euston
Buildings, London.
Gee Films, Ltd., 32, Shaftesbury Avenue, W.C.2 .... Gerrard 6403 and 6325.
Geipel, Wm., Ltd., 156-170, Bermondsey Street, S.E.1 .... Hop 0594.
General Acoustics, Ltd., 77, Wigmore Street, W.1 .... Welbeck 7223 —— Acousticon
Wesdo.
General Cinema Theatres, Ltd., 19, Albemarle Street, W.1 ...... Regent 4419.
General Electric Co., Ltd., The Magnet House, Kingsway, W.C.2
(Branches throughout Great Britain) .... Temple Bar 8000——Electricity
Wescent.
General Film Distributors, Ltd., 127/133, Wardour Street, W.1 Gerrard 7311——Genfidis, Rath.
General Film Distributors, Ltd., 3, The Parsonage, Manchester... Blackfriars 3686.
General Film Distributors, Ltd., 9, Camden Street, Liverpool...... North 535.
General Film Distributors, Ltd., 42/42A/43, Horsefair, Bir-
mingham .... Midland 4361.

General Film Distributors, Ltd., 15A, Wellington Street, Leeds ... Leeds 28578.
General Film Distributors, Ltd., Dominions Arcade, Queen Street, Cardiff .... Cardiff 6101.
General Film Distributors, Ltd., 134, Westgate Road, Newcastle Newcastle 27248.
General Film Distributors, Ltd., 97, Bath Street, Glasgow, C.2 Douglas 4944.
General Film Distributors, Ltd., 17, King's Crescent, Knock, Belfast .... Belfast 5415.
General Film Distributors, Ltd., 93, Middle Abbey Street, Dublin Dublin 44936.
General Theatre Corporation, Ltd., Film House, 142, Wardour Street, W.1 .... Gerrard 9292——Genthecorp.
George Smith Productions Ltd., 91, Shaftesbury Avenue, W.1... Gerrard 6881.
German Railways Information Bureau, 9, Queen's Gardens, Lancaster Gate, W.2 .... Paddington 2826—Eisenbahn.
Gerrard Advertising, 145, Wardour Street, W.1 .... Gerrard 4732.
Gevaert Ltd., 115, Walmer Road—North Kensington, W.10 ... Park 4333——Artoveg, Nottarch.
Gibbons A. O., Ltd., 16, Carlisle Street, W.1. .... Gerrard 2128.
Gibbs, Ben. C., Ltd., 3, The Parsonage, Manchester .... Blackfriars 3062.
Gibson; A. L. & Co., Ltd., Radnor Works, Strawberry Vale, Twickenham, Middlesex .... Popesgrove 2276—Shannies, Twickenham.
Gimson & Co. (Leicester), Ltd., Vulcan Road, Leicester .... Leicester 60272——Gimson.
Girosign, Ltd., 90, Wardour Street, W.1 .... Gerrard 3526-7.
Girosign, Ltd. (Factory), Rifle Court, Kennington, S.E.11 .... Reliance 3527.
Girosign Ltd. (Studios), 86-88, Wardour Street, W.1 ....
Glen, W. R., F.R.I.A.S., 30–31, Golden Square, W.1 .... Gerrard 7887.
Glover, C. W., & Partners (Acoustic), Shell-Mex House, W.C.1.. Temple Bar 4053.
Goldstones (Cinemas), Ltd., 9, Wetherby Road, Leeds .... Oakwood 66788.
Goodall's Pictures (1931), Ltd., Albion Street, Cleckheaton ..... Cleckheaton 224——Savoy
Goodlass, Wall & Co., Ltd., 42, Seel Street, Liverpool, and 30/34, Royal 2973 (L'pool.)
    Langham Street, W.1 .... Langham 3303.
Goodman (*see* Leon Goodman Displays)............................... Archway 2606.
Gordon Cook & Co., Cintra House, Priory Road, Hornsey, N.8, and Peebles Works, Palmerston Road, Kilburn .... Mountview 3932——Cintravert Crouchways.
Gordon's Sales and Advertising Service, Ltd., Imperial Buildings, Oxford Road, Manchester .... Ardwick 1461.
Gotch, J. H. (Circuit), Regal, Soham, Ely, Cambs................... Soham 72.
Gourdeau, E. R., 80–82, Wardour Street, W.1 .... Gerrard 6691.
G.P.O. Film Dept., 21, Soho Square, W.1 .... Gerrard 2666–8.
G.P.O. Film Dept. (Studio), Blackheath .... Lee Green 3363.
G.P.O. Film Dept. (Library), Imperial Institute, S.W.7 .... Kensington 3264.
Gradley Electrical Co., Ltd., 1, Castle Street, City Road, E.C.2 Clerkenwell 7218–9 ——Slickserv Finsquare.
Grafton Films, Ltd., 74A, Regent Street, W.1 .... Gerrard 5084.
Graham, J., 17, Blythswood Square, Glasgow .... Western 2305.
Graham, S., Park House, Friar Lane, Nottingham .... Nottingham 2552.
Gramophone Co. Ltd. (Factories), Hayes, Middlesex .... Southall 2468.
Gramophone Co., Ltd., Recording Studios, 3, Abbey Road, St. John's Wood, N.W.8 .... Maida Vale 7386
Gramophone Co., Ltd., 98-108, Clerkenwell Road, E.C.1 .... Clerkenwell 3426.
Gramo-Radio, Ltd., Church, Nr. Accrington .... Accrington 2576.
Grand Theatre Circuit, Dean House, Dean Street, London, W.1 Gerrard 5551–2–3.
Granger, W. F., F.R.I.B.A., 9, Savile Row, W.1 .... Regent 5539.
Granville-Procter Film Co., Ltd., 4, Broad Street Place, E.C.2..
Gratton, S. A., and Son, 9, Macfarlane Street, Glasgow, E.......... Bell 2215.
Graves Cinemas, Ltd., Athenæum Buildings, Maryport .... Maryport 16.
Gray & Davison, Ltd., 1–3, Cumming Street, N.1 .... Terminus 6508 —— Cantabile, Moordo.
Gray, Evans & Crossley, 51, North John Street, Liverpool........ Bank 1446.
Gray, Eric, 16a, John Street Adelphi .... Temple Bar 7423.
Gray, J. W., & Son, Ltd., 50–51, High Holborn, W.C.1 .... Chancery 7425.
Great Metropolitan Flooring Co., Ltd., 75, Kinnerton St., Wilton Place, Knightsbridge, S.W.1 .... Sloane 7005, 3276 and 2103—— Greatmet, London.

Green, Geo., Ltd., 182, Trongate, Glasgow .... Bell 1660-1-2.
Green G. J., & Sons, Wicklow Street, Britannia Street, Gray's
Inn Road, W.C.1 .... Terminus 6033.
Greene, Leslie, 7, Elliot Street, Liverpool .... Royal 538——Royal 538.
Greene, Leslie, 128 Nightingale Lane, S.W.12 .... Whitehall 5504 and Battersea 2647
——Battersea 2647.
Gregory Ratoff Films, 62, Shaftesbury Avenue, W.C.2 ....
Gregory & McCarthy, 32, Shaftesbury Avenue, W.1 .... Gerrard 6456.
Grimshaw, Stanley, Prince of Wales, Clayton Square, Liverpool... Royal 6290-1.
Grove, I. R., Fairfield House, Broxburn .... Broxburn 42——Grove, Broxburn
Grosvenor Sound Films, Ltd., Kent House, Regent Street, W.1... Regent 4354.
G. S. Enterprises, Ltd., 91, Shaftesbury Avenue, W.1 .... Gerrard 6881.
Guaranteed Pictures Co., Inc., of New York (Rep. : Miss Swift Whitehall 7938.
130, Wardour Street)
Guild of British Kinema Projectionists and Technicians, Ltd.,
40, Russell Square, W.C.1..
Guilds of Light (See Religious Film Society)...........................
Guiterman, S., & Co., Ltd., 35–36, Aldermanbury, E.C.2. .... Metropolitan 8074——Guiterman.
Guys of Cardiff, 54–6, Portmanmoor Road, Cardiff .... Cardiff 663——Guys, Printers.
Haden, G. N., & Sons, Ltd., Lincoln House, 60, Kingsway, W.C.2 Holborn 7800——Warmth, West
cent.
Haigh, E., & Son, 30, Tarleton Street, Liverpool.................... Royal 1170.
Hailwood & Ackroyd, Ltd., 71, New Oxford Street, W.C.1 ...... Temple Bar 6594 & 7358 ——
Hailwarox, Westcent.
Hakim, Eric, Flat 47, Grosvenor House, Park Lane, W. ....
Haling, S., 12, Moreton Street, Gt. Ducie Street, Manchester 3... Blackfriars 4198——Featufilm.
Halder Laboratories, 252, Green Lanes, N.4 .... Stamford Hill 3667.
Hall and Dixon, Ltd., 19, Garrick Street, W.C.2 .... Temple Bar 1930 & 8331——Hal-
dixon, Lesquare.
Hall & Kay, Ltd., Engineers, Ashton-under-Lyne, Lancs. ...... Ashton-under-Lyne 2281-2.
Hall & Kay, Ltd., 25, Haymarket, S.W.1 .... Whitehall 9150.
Hall's, 12, City Road, E.C.1 .... National 1788.
Hallett, G., 6, Victoria Avenue, Penarth (Agent for Beck and
Windibank) .... Penarth 438.
Hall Manufacturing and Supply Co., Ltd., Stafford Road, Brixton,
S.W.9 .... Brixton 2008——Haulix.
Hampshire Transport Co.,Ltd. 66 Onslow Road, and Rockstone
Lane, Bevois Valley, Southampton .... Southampton 2348.
Hammer Productions, Ltd., Imperial House, 80-86, Regent Street,
W.1 .... Regent 7461-2.
Hampton & Sons, Ltd. (Estate Dept.), 6, Arlington Street, St.
James's, S.W.1 .... Regent 8282.
Hampton & Sons, Ltd., Pall Mall East, S.W.1 .... Whitehall 1020——Hamit : London.
Hanmer, Philip M., 51, North John Street, Liverpool .... Bank 610.
Hanau, J., Unafilm S.A., 7, Park Lane................................. Mayfair 7082.
Hardiker's Cinecraft Publicity Services, Ltd., Alexandra Studio,
Theatre Street, Preston.. Preston 3936.
Harmonicolor Films, Ltd., Piccadilly House, Jermyn Street, W.1
Harold (Uniforms), Ltd., Alfred, 86-88 Wardour Street, W.1 ... Gerrard 6311.——Uniforms Rath.
Harper Piano Co., Ltd., 258-262, Holloway Road, N.7 .... North 4822——Pertaining.
Harris & Gillow, 80 & 82, Wardour Street, W.1 .... Gerrard 2504——Faddist, Rath,
London.
Harris, M., & Sons, 44-52, New Oxford Street, W.C.1 .... Museum 2121-2——Artisonne,
Westcent.
Harrison, C. R., & Sons, Ltd., Newton-le-Willows, Lancs......... Newton-le-Willows 100.
Harrods, Ltd., Knightsbridge, S.W.1 .... Sloane 1234——Everything,
Harrods, London.
Harry Hughes Productions, Ltd., 75-77, Shaftesbury Avenue, W.1 Gerrard 3086.
Hart Accumulator Co., Ltd., Stratford, E.15 .... Maryland 1361-3——Hartmossel,
Strat.
Hart Accumulator Co., Ltd., 50, Grosvenor Gardens, London,
S.W. 1 .... Sloane 7933.
Hart Accumulator Co., Ltd., 90, Victoria Street, Bristol .... Bristol 2319.
Hart Accumulator Co., Ltd., Abbey House, 63, Hockley Hill,
Birmingham 18 .... Northern 1266.
Hart Accumulator Co., Ltd., 50, Charles Street, Cardiff .... Cardiff 5500.
Hart Accumulator Co., Ltd., Dagenite House, Bridge Street, Cork Cork 1581-2.
Hart Accumulator Co., Ltd., 93, Dunlop Street, Glasgow C.2...... Central 3428.
Hart Accumulator Co., Ltd., 64, Worsley Road, Manchester...... Swinton 324.
Hart Accumulator Co., Ltd., 2, Devonshire Road, Nottingham... Nottingham 65770.
Hart & Co., Buckton's Mills, Meadow Road, Leeds......................Leeds 28295.
Hart, Norman (B.A., Cantab), Broadmead House, 21, Panton
Street, S.W.1 .... Whitehall 6814.
Hawkins, L. G. & Co., Ltd., 30–35, Drury Lane, W.C.2 .... Temple Bar 5811——Elemechex.
Hathernware, Ltd., Loughborough .... Hathern 261——Bricks, Lough-
borough.
Haworth & Son (Southport), Ltd., 34-36, East Bank Street,
Southport .... Southport 2728.

Headway (London) Advertising Ltd., 3-4, King Street, Covent Garden, W.C.2 .... Temple Bar 2597.

Heathman, J. H., Ltd., 10, Parson's Green, S.W.6 .... Fulham 0150.

Heatly-Gresham Engineering Co., 40, Wood Street, S.W.1 ...... Victoria 9770-1——Excluding Parl.

Heatly-Gresham Engineering Co., Ltd., Craven Ironworks, Ordsall Lane, Salford ....

Heaton Tabb & Co., Ltd., Adelphi Works, Cobbold Road, N.W.10 ... Willesden 1816——Hetontabb, Willroad.

Heaton Tabb & Co., Ltd., 1, Adam Street, W.C. .... Temple Bar 3280.

Heaton Tabb & Co., Ltd., 55, Bold Street, Liverpool .... Royal 3457-8——Hetontabb, Liverpool.

Heeley, A. & M. San Remo, Lancaster Road, Pendleton .... Eccles 109.

Hellenbrand, J. H., 66A, Bournemouth Park Road, Southend-on-Sea ....

Henderson's Film Laboratories, 18, St. Johns Road, S.E.25 ...... Livingstone 2255-6

Henderson, John, Waterloo Chambers, 11, Bath Lane, Newcastle-on-Tyne .... Newcastle 23136——Films.

Hendry, J., 114, Union Street, Glasgow. .... Central 2012.

Henley's (W.T.) Telegraph Works Co., Ltd., Holborn Viaduct, E.C.1 .... City 3210——Henletel, Cent.

Henly. A. T., A.M.I.H.V.E., A.F.A.S., 6, Park Place, S.E.9 ...... Eltham 2481.

Henrion Carbons, Ltd., Dean House, Dean Street, W.1............ Gerrard 5748-9——Carboneros.

Hepworth, Cecil M., Coombs Moss, Sidney Road, Walton-on-Thames .... Walton-on-Thames 1206.

Herbert Wilcox Productions, Ltd., Pinewood Studios, Iver Heath, Bucks .... Iver 460.

Herts & Beds Film Transport, 30, Stotfold Road, Arlsey, Beds. ... Arlsey 50.

Hewitsons, Ltd., Windsor Theatre, Smethwick, Staffs .... Bearwood, Birmingham 2244.

Hewittic Electric Company, Ltd., Hersham, Walton-on-Thames, Surrey .... Walton-on-Thames 762-4——Hewittic, Walton-on-Thames.

Heywood, John, Ltd., 121, Deansgate, Manchester .... Blackfriars 8161——Books, Manchester.

Hibbert-Diggle, A., 186, Peel Green Road, Patricroft, Lancs. ... Museum 8016.

Hickman, Ltd., 10-11, Gt. Russell Street, W.C.1 ....

Hill, Mrs. G. (Isle of Wight Theatres), Theatre Royal, Ryde, I.O.W. .... Ryde 2387.

Hill, W., & Son, & Norman & Beard, Ltd., 372, York Road, N.7 ... North 3001-3——Bassoonist, Kentish.

Hinchliffe, P. A., F.R.I.B.A., 40, Victoria Road, Barnsley........

Hinge, E. J., 72, Grey Street, Newcastle-on-Tyne, 1 .... Newcastle 20317. —— Hinge, Newcastle

Historical Research Society, Hoylake Crescent, Ickenham, Mddx. Elstree 1710.

Hodges, C. E., Productions, Bedford Row Chambers, 42, Theobalds, Road, W.C.1.. Holborn 7788.

Hodgson, F., 12, Eldon Terrace, Leeds, 2 .... Leeds 22609——Kinads, Leeds.

Holiday & Hemmerdinger, Holmer Works, Dolefield, Bridge Street, Manchester 3 .... Blackfriars 4096.

Holophane, Ltd., 41, Elverton Street, Vincent Square, S.W.1...... Victoria 8062 —— Holophane, Sowest.

Hollywood Reporter, Grosvenor House, Park Lane, W. .... Grosvenor 6363.

Home Counties Theatres, Ltd., Athenæum, Muswell Hill, N.10 ... Tudor 5848-9.

Honeywill & Stein, Ltd., 15, Regent Street, S.W.1.................. Whitehall 8021.——Tyche, Piccy.

Hoyle, R., 259, Ainsworth Road, Elton, Bury, Lancs. ....

H. S. B. Advertising Specialists, Ltd., Suite 92, Imperial House, 80-86, Regent Street, W.1 .... Regent 6466.

Hull Cinemas, Ltd., Cecil Theatre, Anlaby Road, Hull.............. Hull 15315.

Hummel Optical Co., Ltd., 94, Hatton Garden, E.C.1 .... Holborn 1752——Bycorner, London

Humphries, George, and Co. (Laboratories), 71-77, Whitfield Street, and 10, Northcourt, Chitty Street, Tottenham Court Road, W.1 .... Museum 0302 —— Bestlab, Eusroad, London.

Hunt, J. A. H., Ltd., 233, Bradford Street, Birmingham .... Victoria 1993-4——Lighting, Birmingham.

Hyman, Sydney M., Ltd., 8, St. Martin's Place, W.C.2 .... Temple Bar 3696——Domesday, London.

IDEAL KINEMA AND STUDIO, 85, Long Acre, W.C.2......... **Temple Bar 2468.**

I.F.P. Films (See Phoenix Films)

Igranic Electric Co., Ltd., 149, Queen Victoria Street, E.C.4...... Central 7123——Igranic, London.

Ilford Cine (Sales Dept.), National House, 60-66, Wardour Street, W.1 .... Gerrard 2763——Seloservo, Rath. Gerrard 6889.

Illustra Enterprises, 159, Wardour Street, W.1 ....

Ilkeston Cinema Co., Ltd., King's Picture House, Bath Street, Ilkeston .... Ilkeston 17.

Immortal Swan Productions, Ltd., 30, Craven Street, W.C.2...... Whitehall 0195.

Impartial Film Agency, 10-12, Hanway Street, W.1 .... Museum 2872.

Imperial Lighting Co., 2, 4, & 6, Pocock Street, Blackfriars Road, S.E.1.. Hop 3931 and 7040 ——Implitico.

Imperial Sound Studios, 84, Wardour Street, W.1......................	Gerrard 1963.
Imperial Sound System, 71, St. Barnabas Road, Leicester.........	Leicester 27396.
Imperial Sound System, 145, Wardour Street, W.C.	Gerrard 6394.
Incorporated Association of Kinematograph Manufacturers, Ltd., Carlisle House, Carlisle Street, Soho	Gerrard 1946—Kinnefilm, Rath.
Incorporated British Renters, Ltd., 6, Denman Street, W.1......	Gerrard 6777.
Incorporated Society of Authors, Playwrights and Composers, 11, Gower Street, W.C.1	Museum 1664 —— Autoridad, Westcent.
Incorporated Society of Musicians, 19, Berners Street. W.1	Museum 7876-7—Scherzo, Rath.
Independence Films, Ltd., 58-59, Shaftesbury Avenue, W.1	Gerrard 4145-6.
Independent Film Distributors, 130, Wardour Street, W.1	Whitehall 7938.
Independent Sprinklers, Ltd., Sardinia House, Kingsway, W.C.2	Holborn 2402——Indsprink, Holb.
Institute of Amateur Cinematographers, Burley House, 5-11, Theobalds Road, W.C.	Chancery 8338. ——Iacfilm s.
Interallied Film Producers, Ltd., 4, St. James Street, S.W.1	Whitehall 4686.
International Acoustic Films, Ltd., 142-150, Wardour Street, W.1	Gerrard 9292.
International Cinematograph Co., Ltd., 101, Wardour St., W.1	Gerrard 3131——Filmrenta.
International Council of Music Users, Ltd., 23, Bedford Row, W.C.1	Chancery 7516.
International Film Advisers, Ltd., 10, Stanhope Terrace, Hyde Park, W.2	Paddington 9683.
International Film Distributors, Ltd., Piccadilly House, Piccadilly Circus, W.1......	
International Photographic Art Services, Ltd., Boreham Wood, Elstree	Elstree 1710.
International Player Pictures, 96, Portland Place, W.1............	Welbeck 7166.
International Productions, Ltd., 101, Wardour Street, W.1	Gerrard 3131——Filmrenta.
International Talking Films, 53, Haymarket, S.W.1	Whitehall 2662.
International Variety and Theatrical Agency, Ltd., Daly's Theatre Buildings, 31-33, Lisle Street, W.C.2	Gerrard 1951-55—Affiltrus, West rand.
Interworld Films, Ltd., 80-82, Wardour Street, W..................	Gerrard 6691.
Ionlite, 89, Scrub's Lane, N.W.10	Willesden 2241—Ionlite, Harles.
Irish Cinemas, Ltd., 32, Shaftesbury Avenue, W.1..................	Gerrard 3306.
Irish Cinemas, Ltd. (Reg. Office), 19, Upper Connell Street, Dublin	Dublin 44788.
Irish Electric Palaces, Ltd., 79, Donegal Street, Belfast	Belfast 5800.
Irish Film Renters, Ltd., 204, Pearse Street, Dublin	Dublin 44829——Lens .
Isle of Wight Theatres, Ltd., Theatre Royal, Ryde, I.W.	Ryde 2387.
Jackatoon Film Co., Ltd., 17, Dalton Square, Lancaster	Lancaster 716.
Jacksons' Amusements, Ltd., Hippodrome, Rochdale...............	Rochdale 3212——Hippodrome, Rochdale
Jaeger, A. C., 26, Dulley's Sheep Street, Wellingborough	Wellingborough 517.
James, E. H. 4, Cae Llan, Llanwrst, N. Wales	
James (D. J.) Circuit, Cinema House, 225. Oxford Street, London, W.1.	Gerrard 4242-3 and 3300.
Jameswood Press, Ltd., 165, Grays Inn Road, W.C.1	
Jamilly, D., 10, D'Arblay Street, W.1	Gerrard 2826——Bismillah.
Jardine & Co., Ltd., Elsinore Road, Old Trafford, Manchester, 16	Trafford Park 1306.
Jarrold & Sons, Ltd., London Street, Norwich........................	Norwich 1480.
Jay, Ben, 145, Wardour Street, W.1.	Gerrard 2239.
Jay, Sidney, 128, Shaftesbury Avenue, W.1	Gerrard 7351-2——Jay. Gerrard.
Jay's Film Service, Ltd., 17, Blythswood Square, Glasgow, C.2	Central 132—Jayfilms, Glasgow.
J.D.F. Studios, Ltd., 2-3, Union Mews, Wells Street, Oxford Street, W.1	Museum 3826.
Jeapes, W. C., 90, Wardour Street, London, W.1	Gerrard 2418.
Jefton Entertainments, Ltd., 26, Cross Street, Manchester.........	Blackfriars 0752.
Jeffreys, J. & Co., Ltd., Barrons Place, S.E.1	Hop 1534.
Jensen, G. K. & Co., Ltd., 38, Harlesden Road, Willesden, N.W.10	Willesden 2156.
Jensen, G. K. & Co., Ltd., 15, Dartmouth Street, S.W.1	Whitehall 8044.
Jersey and Guernsey Amusements Co., Ltd., New Gallery House, 123, Regent Street, W.1	Regent 8080——Procinthe. Piccy.
J. H. Productions, Ltd., 111, Wardour Street, W.1..................	Gerrard 3421——Hagenfil, Rath
J.H. Productions, Ltd. (Studio), Station Road, Boreham Wood...	Elstree 1341.
Johns-Manville Co., Ltd., Horseferry House, Horseferry Road, S.W.1	Victoria 0157——Johnmanville Phone.
Johnson & Sons, Manufacturing Chemists, Ltd., Hendon Way, N.W.4	Hendon 8051.
Jordison & Co., Ltd., National House, 60-66, Wardour Street, W.1	Gerrard 6129——Jordison, Gerr. 6129 London.
Jukes Coulson, Stokes & Co., Howards Road Ironworks, Plaistow, E.13...	Albert Dock 1283 ——Kolsonsto, Strat., London.
Kafa Table Co., 66-70, Great Eastern Street, E.C.2.................	Bishopsgate 1739.
Kalee, Ltd., National House, 60-66, Wardour Street, W.1	Gerrard 5137-9.
Kalee, Ltd., 49, Donegal Street, Belfast................................	Belfast 7065.

Kalee, Ltd., 32, John Bright Street, Birmingham	Midland 3619.
Kalee, Ltd., 9, Park Lane, Cardiff	Cardiff 7676.
Kalee, Ltd., 34, Lower Abbey Street	Dublin 45059.
Kalee, Ltd., 211, Hope Street, Glasgow	Douglas 1305——Langrish.
Kalee, Ltd., 17, Wellington Street, Leeds.............................	Leeds 28259.
Kalee, Ltd., Parsonage Chambers, 3, The Parsonage, Manchester	Blackfriars 8317.
Kalee, Ltd., 17, Fenkle Street, Newcastle-on-Tyne	Newcastle 23038.
Kamm & Co., Ltd., 27, Powell Street, Goswell Road, E.C.1	Clerkenwell 6595——Zerograph, Barb.
Kandem Electrical, Ltd., 769, Fulham Road, S.W.6	Fulham 2387-9——Kortmath, Walgreen.
Kay (West End) Laboratories, Ltd., 22, Soho Square, W.1........	Gerrard 4092.
Kay Film Printing Co., Ltd. (Laboratories & Offices), 49A, Oxford Road, Finsbury Park, N.4	Archway 3050.
Kean & Scott, Ltd., 110, Corporation Street, Birmingham........	Central 5900-1—Kean-Scott, Birmingham.
Kean & Scott, Ltd., Lower Priory, Birmingham	Central 8361-2——Canvas.
Keepalite (see Chloride Electrical Storage Co., Ltd.)	
Keith, Prowse & Co., Ltd., 38, Berners Street, W.1	Museum 0096.
Kemble Theatre, Ltd., 167-9, Wardour Street, W.1................	Gerrard 6363-6.
Kempsell's Advertising Service, 163, Hope Street, .Glasgow, C.2	Central 3114-5.
Kendal, A. N., Ltd., Hippodrome, Tidworth	Winchester 1364.
Kent Film Motor Transport Co., Ltd., King's Theatre Bldgs., Market Place, Ramsgate	Ramsgate 209.
Ker Lindsay, Ltd., 10, George Street, Hanover Square, W.3......	Mayfair 5641-2.
Kershaw Projector Co., The (See also Kalee, Ltd.), Albion Walk, Albion Street, Leeds..	Leeds 22237——Projector.
Kessex Cinemas, Ltd., 197, Wardour Street, London, W.1........	Gerrard 2835.
K. F. M. Signs, 186-188, Shaftesbury Avenue, W. C.2.	Temple Bar 5154—— Kayefem, Phone, London.
Kine-Ads, Ltd., Imperial Buildings, Oxford Road, Manchester...	Ardwick 1461.
Kinematograph Equipment Co., Ltd., 177, Wardour Street, W.1	Gerrard 5102—Experience, Rath.
Kinematograph International Exhibitions, Ltd., 5, Devonshire Street, W.1	Welbeck 8291.
Kinematograph Manufacturers' Association (see Incorporated Association of Kinematograph Manufacturers, Ltd.)	
KINEMATOGRAPH PUBLICATIONS, LTD., 85, Long Acre, W.C.2	**Temple Bar 2468 —— Southern-wood, Rand.**
Kinematograph Renters' Society of Great Britain and Ireland, Ltd., 30, Old Compton Street,W.1..............................	Gerrard 4262-6 (5 lines)
" KINEMATOGRAPH WEEKLY," 85, Long Acre, W.C.2......	**Temple Bar 2468 —— Southern-wood, Ran'l.**
" KINEMATOGRAPH WEEKLY," 163, Hope Street, Glasgow	**Central 3114-5**
" KINEMATOGRAPH WEEKLY," 2, Chester Street, Oxford Street, Manchester	**Central 4660.**
" KINEMATOGRAPH YEAR BOOK," 85, Long Acre, W.C.2	**Temple Bar 2468.**
Kine-Technic Services, Ltd., 60, Aylward Road, S.W.20	Liberty 2426.
King, A. B., 167, Bath Street, Glasgow	Douglas 1195-6——Kenifilm.
King & Newman, 1067A, Finchley Road, N.W.11................	Speedwell 4114.
King, W. J., F.R.I.B.A., Piccadilly House, 16-17, Jermyn Street, S.W.1	Regent 4329.
King's Patent Agency, Ltd., 146A, Queen Victoria Street, E.C.4	Central 0682.
Kino Films (1935), Ltd., 84, Gray's Inn Road, W.C.1	Holborn 1760.
Kinograph Distributors, Ltd., 191, Wardour Street................	Gerrard 4148——Sherfilclu, Rath.
Kirwan Publicity Film Services, (M. B. Kirwan, props.), Kirwan House, Birley Street, Blackpool	Blackpool 2224——Films.
Knight & Co. (Engineers), Ltd., Winchmore Works, Chase Road, N.14	Palmers Green 0536.
Knight, John, F.R.I.B.A., 5, Cross Street, Manchester...........	Blackfriars 2215.
Knock Out Fire Extinguishers, Ltd., 16-18, Bardwell Street, North Road, Holloway, N.7..	North 3747.
Kodak, Ltd., Cine Dept., Kingsway, W.C.2	Holborn 7841——Kodak.
Korkoid Decorative Floors, 90, Regent Street, W.1..............	Regent 0171-2
Korkoid Decorative Floors, 95, Bothwell Street, and 813, Summerfield Street, Bridgeton, Glasgow.	Central 4910 & Bridgeton 1850.
Korkoid Decorative Floors, 320, Royal Liver Buildings, Liverpool	
Korkoid Decorative Floors, The Manor, Newcastle.................	
Lakes Variety Agency, Ltd., 142, High Holborn, W.C.1...........	Holborn 7941——Moccadora.
Lambert, G. H. (Suburban Cinema News Service), 39 Wood Lane, W.12..	Shepherds Bush 4279.
Lamson Pneumatic Tube Co., Ltd., 132, Cheapside, E.C.2........	National 0202—Kelywil, Cent.
Lancashire Dynamo & Crypto, Ltd., Acton Lane, N.W.10........	Willesden 6363-8——Commutator, Phone, London.
Lancashire Entertainments, Ltd., Regent P.H., Eccles, Manchester	Eccles 3843.
Lawisto Advertising Co., 87, Horton Grange Road, Bradford......	Bradford 4728——Lawisto 4728.

Lawley Apparatus Co., Ltd., 26, Church Street, Charing Cross Road, W.1 .... Gerrard 3022.

Lawrence Wright Music Co., Ltd., 19, Denmark Street, Charing Cross Road, W.C.2 .... Temple Bar 2141-5——Vocable, Westcent.

Lazarus, H., & Son. Ltd., 10A, Great Eastern Street, E.C.2...... Bishopsgate 7538-9 ——Malleable, Finsquare.

L.C.V. Circuit, 34, St. Enoch Square, Glasgow .... Central 4465.

Lea & Son, Oxygen Works, Runcorn, Cheshire........................ Runcorn 1——Lea, Oxygen.

Leach, S. G. & Co., Ltd., 26-30, Artillery Lane, E.1.................. London Wall 3840——Adnil, Ald.

Leadlay News Service, Ltd., Racquet Court, 114, Fleet Street, E.C.4... Central 7134.

League of British Dramatists, 11, Gower Street, W.C.1 .... Museum 1664—Autoridad, Westcent.

Leathart, J., F.R.I.B.A., 39, Gordon Square, W.C.1............... Museum 8884.

Leeds & District Picture Houses, Ltd., The Lounge, North Lane, Headingley, Leeds 6. .... Headingley 52419.

Leevers, Rich & Co., Ltd., 47-48, Berners Street, W.1 .... Museum 4141.

Lennox. Ltd., Cecil, 134, Charing Cross Road, W.C.2............... Temple Bar 9456-7.

Leon Goodman Displays, Ltd., 139-147, Fonthill Road, Finsbury Park, N.4.. Archway 2606

Leslie Fuller Pictures, Ltd., Rock Studios, Boreham Wood ...... Elstree 1644.

Le Personne, L., & Co., Ltd., 7-8, Old Bailey, E.C.4 .... City 3852——Lepersonne, London.

Letchworth Palace, Ltd., Broadway, Letchworth .... Letchworth 721.

Levy Circuit, 9, Ranelagh Street, Liverpool .... Royal 5675.

Levy, P., & Co., 110A, North Street, Belfast........................... Belfast 1877 & (Night) Fortwilliam 243——Butchilms.

Lewis & Tylor, Ltd., 9, St. Thomas Street, S.E.1..................... Hop 3623——Upshot Phone Ltd.

Lewsley, J. W., Ltd., 97, Derby Road, Nottingham.................. Nottingham 43820.

Leyland & B'ham Rubber Co., Ltd., The, Leyland, Lancs. ...... Leyland 81434——Rubber, Leyland.

Leyland Paint & Varnish Co., Ltd., Leyland, Lancs............... Leyland 81481—Quality, Leyland

Liberty Films, Ltd., 4, Golden Square, W.1........................... Gerrard 1204.

Liddon, J., 8, Gray's Inn Passage, W.C.1............................... Chancery 8120.

Lift & Engineering, Ltd., 622, Wandsworth Road, S.W.8 ...... Macaulay 4112

Lincoln & District Film Transport Co., Ramseyville, Frieston Road, Boston, Lincs...

Lindsay, Thomas, Dundee Court, Falkirk............................... Falkirk 181.

Line, John & Sons, Ltd., 213-6, Tottenham Court Road, W.1 Museum 3300——Linealis, Phone.

Lion Cinematograph Co., Ltd., 43, Whitcomb Street, Leicester Square, London, W.C.2 .... Streatham 3688 and Whitehall 4088.

Lion Cinematograph Co., Ltd.(West End Office), 43, Whitcomb Street, W.C.2 .... Whitehall 4088.

Lippold, A., Kennington Works, Montford Place, S.E.11........... Reliance 1523.

Lipton's Spray Products, Ltd., 150, Southampton Row, W.C.1... Terminus 4922.

Lister & Co., Ltd., Manningham Mills, Bradford .... Bradford 3850——Lister.

Lithalun Products, Ltd., Pontalun Works, Bridgend............... Bridgend 213——Lithalun, Bridgend.

Lizars, J., 6, Shandwick Place, Edinburgh.............................. Edinburgh 22272——Optical.

L.M.B. Films, Ltd., 25, Denmark Street, W.C.2...................... Temple Bar 1926 and 6015.

Lockwood, L. B., & Co., 4, Newall Street, Bradford................ Bradford 2980—Seating, Bradford

London Advertising Service, Ltd., 3-5, High Street, Islington, N.1 Terminus 4473-4

London and Coastal Advertising Services, 40, Shaftesbury Avenue, W.1 .... Gerrard 7494.

London and Continental Pictures, Ltd., Regency House, Warwick Street, W.1 .... Gerrard 5391——Loconti, Piccy,

London and East Anglian Film Services, 149, Norwich Road, Ipswich, Suffolk. .... Ipswich 2019.

London & Midland Steel Scaffolding Co., Ltd., Iddesleigh House, Caxton Street, S.W.1 (Works, Old Hill, Staffs.) .... Victoria 6483-4——Dubelgrip, Sowest.

London & Provincial Advertising Agency, Ltd., 104, High Holborn, W.C.1 .... Chancery 8374.

London & Provincial Films Motor Transport Co., Ltd., 3 Dansey Place, and 7, Wardour Street, W.1 .... Gerrard 2181.

London & Southern SuperCinemas, Ltd., 32, Shaftesbury Avenue, W.1 .... Whitehall 0183.
London Electric Firm, The, Brighton Road, South Croydon ... Uplands 4871——Electric, Croydon.
London Film Institute Society, 4, Gt. Russell Street, W.C.1.......
London Film Productions, Ltd., Denham Studios, Denham, Bucks. ....
London Paramount Advertising Co., Ltd., 52, Shaftesbury Avenue .... Gerrard 3897.
London Play Co., Ltd., 51, Piccadilly, W.1............................. Regent 4989 & 2463.
London Poster Advertising Association, Ltd., 48, Russell Square, W.C.1 .... Museum 1485—Disthene Westcent.
London Screen Plays, Ltd., 65-67, Imperial House, 80-86, Regent Street, W.1 .... Regent 4144-5.
London, Slough and District Film Transport, 3, Dansey Place, Wardour Street, London, W.1, and 3, Alexandra Gardens, Hounslow................................. Gerrard 2181 and Hounslow 0869.
Luke, E. S., Kenton House, 19, Upper Shirley Road, Croydon ... Addiscombe 1507.
Lumley, L. & Co. (Props. Geo. Adlam & Sons, Ltd.), The Minories, E.C.3 .... Royal 1807.
Lusty, W. & Sons, Ltd., Lloyd Loom Furniture, Bromley by Bow, E.3.................... East 5020 & 7521——Comparison. Bochurch.
Luton, J. T. & Son, Ltd., Maryland Works, 14, Forest Lane, E.15 Maryland 3844.
Luxury Cinema Theatres, Ltd., 14, St. Andrew's Crescent, Cardiff Cardiff 2901-2.
Lynes, B. J., Ltd., 9a, Diana Place, Euston Road, N.W.1............ Euston 4082-3.
Lyon, Montague, Ltd., Union House, 15, Regent Street, S.W.1 Whitehall 8484—Playlet, Phone.
Lyon, J. S., Ltd., 112, High Holborn, W.C.1 .... Holborn 1152 and 3674-5——Proscenium.
MacDonald, Alister, 14, John Street, Adelphi, W.C. .... Temple Bar 6192.
Mac's Poster Service, 22, Jamaica Street, Glasgow, C.1 .... Central 1030.
McConnell, Hartley, Ltd., Publicity House, 10. Pearse Street, Dublin .... Dublin 43227——Adcraft Dublin.
McFarlane, Walter & Co., Ltd., Saracen Foundry, Possilpark, Glasgow .... Douglas 1070.
McFarlane, Walter & Co., Ltd., 47, Victoria Street, Westminster, S.W.1 .... Victoria 3520.
McKaig, W. H., Friar Street, Hereford.................... McKaig Meters, Hereford...
McKibbins Circuit 108, Shankhill Road, Belfast .... Belfast 4422.
McLaren, J. & H., Ltd., Midland Engine Works, Leeds, 10 ...... Leeds 29091-2 —— Maclaren Leeds.
McPherson, Mervyn, Empire Theatre Chambers, W.1 .... Gerrard 7173 and 1234.
Magnet Advertising Co., Ltd., 91, Church Street, Stoke Newington, N.16................... Clissold 6992-3 —— Magadvert, Finspark.
Majestic Enterprises, 197, Wardour Street, W.1 .... Gerrard 1422.
Majestic Theatres Corporation, 11, Ironmonger Lane, E.C.2 ......
Major Equipment Co., Ltd., 162, Millbank, S.W.1 .... Victoria 3148 —— Majorlon, Sowest.
Mallin, John, & Co., Sandwell Works, Roebuck Lane, West Bromwich .... West Bromwich 0269.
Manchester Film Producing Co., 64, Victoria Street, Manchester Blackfriars 3989.——Animated.
Mancunian Film Corporation, Ltd., 3, The Parsonage, Manchester................... Blackfriars 1023.
Mann, Christopher, Ltd., Sackville House, Piccadilly, W.1......... Regent 6941.
Mansell & Ogan, Ltd., Power Road, Gunnersbury, W.4 .... Chiswick 6385.
M. & P. Enterprises, Ltd., 2, Victoria Colonnade, Southampton Row, W.C.1................... Holborn 0497——Everseal, Westcent.
Maple & Co., Ltd., Tottenham Court Road, W.1.................... Museum 7000.
Maple & Co., Ltd., Estate Department, 5, Grafton Street, Bond Street, W.1 .... Regent 4685-6——Maple London.
Marc, Henri, & Laverdet, Regent House, Fitzroy Square, W.1.... Museum 3719.
Marels & Co., Ltd., Swinton Works, Swinton Street, Gray's Inn Road, W.C.1 .... Terminus 3868.
March of Time, Ltd., 2-4, Dean Street, W.1........................ Gerrard 6336.
Markham, T. E., Ye Olde Wyche Theatre, Nantwich............... Nantwich 5338.
Marks, B. Martin., 12, Lower Regent Street, S.W.1................ Whitehall 6839.
Marks Circuit Cinemas, Exchange Buildings, 6, St. Mary's Gate, Manchester, 1................... Blackfriars 4078.
Marryat & Scott, Ltd., 75, Clerkenwell Road, E.C.1 .... Holborn 5686 & 8181——Marryat.
Marshall, W. R., 178, Westgate Road, Newcastle-on-Tyne......... Newcastle 27451.
Marshall Sound System, Ltd., 12, Low Pavement, Nottingham.... Nottingham 40065-6.
Martin, J. H., Ltd., 176, Wardour Street, W.1..................... Gerrard 6861.
Martin, J. H., Ltd. (Labs.), Quinton Avenue, Merton Park, S.W. 19 .... Liberty 1726.
Marylebone Studios, Ltd., 245, Marylebone Road, N.W.1 .... Paddington 2444-5.
Masey, Cecil, F.R.I.B.A., 15, Caroline Street, W.C.1.............. Museum 3896
Masters, D. J., Ltd., 52, Gray's Inn Road, W.C.1.................. Holborn 1204——Optimastex.
Matcham, Frank & Co., 62, Oxford Street, W.1...................... Museum 2357.

Matlock Cinemas, Ltd., Cinema House, Matlock	Matlock 12.
Matthews, A. G., 8, Overwood Drive, Glasgow, S.4	Merrilee 2317
Matthews & Yates, Ltd., 20, Bedford Row, W.C.1	Chancery 7823——Ventilo, London.
Matthews & Yates, Ltd., 144, St. Vincent Street, Glasgow	Central 33.——Cyclone, Glasgow.
Matthews & Yates, Ltd., Swinton, Manchester	Swinton 2273——Cyclone, Swinton, Lancs.
May & Baker, Ltd., Dagenham	Ilford 3060.
May & Sons, Ltd., 9, Great Western Road, Paddington, W.9	Abercorn 1050.
Mears (Joseph) Theatres, Ltd., 5, Hill Street, Richmond, Surrey	Richmond 2900.
Medway Cinemas, Ltd., Walmar House, 288, Regent Street, W.1	Langham 2677.
Medway Film Studios, 89, Wardour Street, W.1	
Meiklejohn Circuit, 22, Jamaica Street, Glasgow	Central 7180.
Metal Reflectors, Ltd., 68, Victoria Street, S.W.1	Victoria 3921.
Metcalfe, Chas., P., 54, Merrion Street, Leeds 2	Leeds 25008
Meteor Film Producing Society, 234, Sauchiehall Street, Glasgow	
Metro-Goldwyn-Mayer Pictures, Ltd., 19-21, Tower Street W.C.2	Temple Bar 8444——Metrofilms, Telex, London.
Metro-Goldwyn-Mayer Pictures, Ltd. Publicity	Temple Bar 5658.
Metro-Goldwyn-Mayer Pictures, Ltd., 21, Smallbrook Street, Birmingham	Midland 3937——Metrofilms.
Metro-Goldwyn- Mayer Pictures, Ltd., Dominions House, Queen Street, Cardiff	Cardiff 1203-4——Metrofilms.
Metro-Goldwyn-Mayer Pictures, Ltd., 9A, Lower Abbey Street, Dublin	Dublin 44853——Metrofilms.
Metro-Goldwyn-Mayer Pictures, Ltd., 10, Dixon Street, Glasgow	Central 2955——Metrofilms.
Metro-Goldwyn-Mayer Pictures, Ltd., 34, Wellington Street, Leeds	Leeds 20885——Metrofilms.
Metro-Goldwyn-Mayer Pictures, Ltd., 2, Wood Street, Liverpool	Royal 4720——Metrofilms.
Metro-Goldwyn-Mayer Pictures, Ltd., Arkwright House, Parsonage Gardens, Manchester	Blackfriars 4208——Metrofilms
Metro-Goldwyn-Mayer Pictures, Ltd., 210, Westgate Road, Newcastle-on-Tyne	Central 27656——Metrofilms.
Metropole Film Distributors, 95, Shaftesbury Avenue, W.1	Gerrard 2077——Metropoic Lesquare.
Metropolitan Advertising Co., Ltd., 58, Dean Street, W.1	Gerrard 4466——Atractad, Rath.
Metropolitan Film Studios, Ltd., Gladstone Road, Southall	Southall 2238.
Metropolitan & Provincial Cinematograph Theatres, Ltd., Brettenham House, 14-15, Lancaster Place, W.C.2	Temple Bar 4758-9.
Metropolitan Sound Equipment, 228, Fulwood Road, Sheffield	Sheffield 61126.
Metropolitan-Vickers Electrical Co., Ltd., 1, Kingsway, W.C.2	Temple Bar 4422——Multiphase, Estrand.
Metropolitan-Vickers Electrical Co., Ltd., Trafford Park, Manchester, 17	Trafford Park 2431——Metrovick, Manchester.
Metzler & Co., (1920), Ltd., 139 New Bond Street, W.1	Mayfair 4672——Lermetz.
Mexborough Theatres, Ltd., Empire, Swinton Road, Mexborough	Mexborough 108.
Meyrowitz, E B., Ltd., 157, Regent Street, W.1	Regent 2370.
Mickey Mouse Weekly, 93-95, Wardour Street, W.1	
Mickelwright, Ltd., Electrical Engineers, Alperton, Wembley, Middlesex	Wembley 0147-8.
Middleton Fireclay Co., St. Pancras Goods Station, Kings Road, N.W.1	Euston 2309.
Middleton Fireclay Co., Middleton, Leeds	Hunslet 75761.
Mihaly Service, Ltd., 193, Wardour Street, W.1	Gerrard 3882.
Milgate, V., 3, Parsonage, Manchester	Blackfriars 9901——Walturdaw.
Milheath Studios, Melbourne End, Bushey, Herts	Bushey 1183-4
Miller, J., 35, Bathurst Mews, Paddington, W.2	
Mills, Winter, Ltd., Carlton House, Regent Street, S.W.1	Whitehall 1371.
Milne's (J.B.) Enterprises, Victoria Theatre, Dundee	Dundee 4793.
Minter, F. G., Ltd., Ferry Works, S.W.15	Putney 7401.
Missionary Film Committee, 104, High Holborn, W.C.	Holborn 2197.
Mitchell, Russell & Co., Chattan Foundry, Bonnybridge, Scotland	Bonnybridge 40-1——Chattan, Bonnybridge.
Mobile Talkies & Sound Equipment Ltd., 16, Linden Road, Redland, Bristol	Bayswater 4149.
Modern Cinemas, Ltd., Queen's Cinema, Bayswater, W.2	
Modern Poster Service (props., G. & A. Signs, Ltd.), 13-15, Seven Sisters Road, N.7.	
Mole-Richardson (England), Ltd., St. Leonards Road, Acton, W.3	Willesden 6834.
Mollo & Egan, 15, Elizabeth Street, S.W.1	Sloane 5211.
Mondover Film Productions, 11, Waterloo Place, S.W.1	Whitehall 6331.
Moon, Henry, & Sons, Ltd., 10/12, Holloway Head. Birmingham	Midland 2298——Moonograph, Birmingham.
Moorhouse, H. D., J.P., Imperial Buildings, 7, Oxford Road, Manchester	Ardwick 2226-8——Cinemoor, Manchester.
Moorhouse, Sidney & Co. (1935), Ltd., Victoria Works, Stalybridge, Ches.	Stalybridge 2551 —— Moorhouse, Stalybridge.
Mordecai, J., 12B, Manor Road, Stoke Newington, N.16	Clissold 0546.

Morgan Crucible Co., Ltd., Battersea Works, Church Road, S.W.11

Morgan Productions, Ltd., 32, St. James's Street, S.W. 1 .... Whitehall 2474.

Morgans Projected Publicity, 3, Princeton Street, Holborn, W.C.1 .... Holborn 8970.

Morison & Co., 56, Shandwick Place, Edinburgh..................... Edinburgh 20386.

Morison, Ian K., 34, Newrow, Perth .... Perth 1380.

Morris, Louis, 52 Shaftesbury Avenue, W.1 .... Gerrard 1668-9,——Kendermor, Lesquare.

Morrison, James, A.R.I.B.A.,Cecil Chambers, 76-86, Strand, W.C.2 Temple Bar 6307.

Morrison, A. E., & Sons, Ltd., Gartree Street, Leicester............ Leicester 5171——Mortric.

Morton Circuit, Picture House, Old Cumnock, Ayrshire .... Cumnock 11——Pictures, Cumnock.

Moss & Sons, Ltd., Wm., North Circular Road, Cricklewood, N.W.2 .... Gladstone 4248——Granicrete Crickle, London.

Moss Empires, Ltd., Cranbourn Mansions, Cranbourn Street, London, W.C.2 .... Gerrard 2274.

Moss Pym, Ltd., 53, Berners Street, W.1 .... Museum 0278.

Motion Picture Herald, 4, Golden Square, W.1....................... Whitehall 7541.

Motion Picture Daily as *Motion Picture Herald* ....

Motion Picture Export Corpn., 63-69, New Oxford Street, W.1

Motion Picture Producers and Distributors of America, Inc., 106, Piccadilly, London, W.1 .... Grosvenor 3155.

Mott-Cowan, M., Film Renter, Elm Hall Drive, Mossley Hill, Liverpool.. Mossley Hill 406——Emsee.

Movie-Signs, Ltd., Salisbury House, E.C.2 ...., Metropolitan 1083.

Moy, Ernest F., Ltd., Greenland Place, Camden Town, N.W.1 Gulliver 5451-3——Móvedor, Norwest.

Mulchinock, L. H., 15-17, City Road, E.C.1........................... Metropolitan 2267.

Mulliner, S., Ltd., 11, Westover Road, Wandsworth, S.W.18 ...

Multiple Photo Printers, 341, London Road, Mitcham, W.2 ...... Mitcham 2208.

Musicians' Union, 7, Sicilian Avenue, Southampton Row, W.C.1 Holborn 1238.

Müller, W. H., & Co. (London), Ltd., Lincoln House, 60, Greek Street, W.1 .... Gerrard 5524-6——Auricle, Rath.

Music Publishers Association, *see* Sound Film Bureau.

Musikon, Ltd., 17, Lisle Street, W.C.2 .... Gerrard 4476——Titles, Lesquare.

Musgrave & Co., Ltd., 112, Sardinia House, Sardinia Street, W.C.2 Holborn 0886.

M.W.T., Ltd., Central House, 75, New Street, Birmingham ...... Midland 5251.

Nalder Bros., & Thompson, 97a, Dalston Lane, E.8 .... Clissold 2365.

Napoleon Films, Ltd., 76-78, Wardour Street, W.1 .... Gerrard 2882-5——Smicofilm.

Nash & Hull, Ltd., 22, High Street, Bloomsbury, W.C.2 .... Temple Bar 3711——Invincibly. Westcent.

Nash & Hull, Ltd., 65, Harmood Street, N.W.1 .... Gulliver 3363.

National Advertising Corporation, 5-8, Regal Cinema, Marble Arch, W.1 .... Paddington 6011.

National Association of Theatrical and Kine Employees, 34, Little Newport Street, W.C.2 .... Gerrard 5214-Stageland, Lesquare.

National Cinema Inquiry Committee, Victory House, Leicester Square, W.C.2· .... Gerrard 2774.

National Distributors, Ltd., 225, Oxford Street, W.1 .... Gerrard 3814.

National Electric Theatres, Ltd., Film House, Wardour Street, W.1 .... Gerrard 9292.

National Film Agency, 64, Victoria Street, Manchester .... Blackfriars 3989——Animated.

National Film Corporation, Ltd., Central House, 34-36, Oxford Street, W.1 .... Museum 4816——Wypeeyes, Rath.

National Film & Theatrical Service, 60, Wardour Street, W.1 ...

National Gas and Oil Engine Co., Ltd., 117, Queen Victoria Street, E.C.4 .... Central 7084.——Forgerons, Cent.

National Gas and Oil Engine Co., Ltd., Ashton-u-Lyne.............. Ashton 1861——National A-u-l.

National Progress Film Co., Ltd., 60-66, Wardour Street, W.1 Gerrard 3913——Profilmads Rath.

National Provincial Film Distributors, Ltd., 97-99, Dean Street, W.1... Gerrard 2771-3——Natprofilm, Rath.

National Provincial Picture Houses, Ltd., 62, Shaftesbury Avenue, W.1 .... Gerrard 3224—— Cinebrit, Piccy.

National Publicity Co., Oldbourne Hall, 43-44, Shoe Lane, E.C.4 Central 7871——Unitrader.

National Screen Service, Ltd., Broadwick House, Broad Street, Wardour Street, W.1 .... Gerrard 4851-5—— Nascreno, Piccy.

National Talkies, Ltd., Gloucester Mansions, Cambridge Circus, W.2.. Temple Bar 4045.

National Vaudeville Corpn., Suite 26-8, Faraday House, Charing Cross Road, W.1.. Temple Bar 5677——Natvaude, Lesquare.

Nelson Art Signs, Ltd., 30, Seaford Road, Enfield, Mdx. .... Enfield 2388.

Neon Manufacturers, Ltd., Regent House, Kingsway, W.C.......... Holborn 9811.

Nettlefold Productions (see Archibald Nettlefold Productions)	
Nettlefold Studios, Hurst Grove, Walton-on-Thames	Walton 1460-3.
Neuman & Co., Ltd., 156-164, Trongate, Glasgow	Bell 1480——Favorable, Glasgow.
Nevelin Electric Co., Ltd., 107-111, New Oxford Street, W.C.1...	Temple Bar 2578.
Neville & Churchill, 22, Manor Drive, Wembley Park.	Wembley 1832.
New Agency Film Co., 115A, Ebury Street, S.W.1	Sloane 4141.
Newalls Insulation Co., Washington Station, co. Durham	Lowfell 76035.
Newalls Insulation Co., Asbestos House, Southwark Street, S.E.1	Hop 1941, Newcoustic, Boro h.
Newalls Insulation Co., 70, Wellington Street, Glasgow	Central 1364—Newsulate.
Newalls Insulation Co., Bank Chambers, 24, Grainger Street West, Newcastle-on-Tyne	Newcastle 26757——Newsulate.
Newalls Insulation Co., Stock Exchange Buildings, Great Charles Street, Birmingham 3	Central 0702——Newsulate.
Newalls Insulation Co., 10, Parsonage Gardens, Manchester	Blackfriars 7441-2. [B'ham.
New Empire (Burnley), Ltd., Empire Theatre, Burnley	Burnley 2453——Empire Theatre, Burnley.
New Era National Pictures, Ltd., 26-27, D'Arblay Street, W.1	Gerrard 6635——Nürafilm, Rath.
New Ideal Pictures, Ltd., Riverside Studios, Crisp Road, Hammersmith, W.6	Riverside 5012.
Newman, Widgey R., National House, Wardour Street, W.1	Gerrard 3827.
Newman & Sinclair, Ltd., 2, Salisbury Road, N.19	Archway 1013.
Newman & Guardia, 63, Newman Street, W.1	Museum 1081.
New Pelapone Engine Co., Ltd., 45, Baker Street, W.1	Welbeck 2519——Newpela.
Newton, John M., & Sons, Ltd., 20-23, Charles Street, Hatton Garden, E.C.1	Holborn 2651.
New World Pictures, Denham Studios, Denham, Mdx.	Denham 140.——Neworlfilm, Denham.
New World Pictures, Ltd., Denham Studios, Bucks.	Denham 2345.
Nicolette, Ltd., 7-8, Idol Lane, E.C.3	
Nobel Chemical Finishes, Ltd., Nobel House, Buckingham Gate, S.W.1	Victoria 8432.
No-fume Patents, Ltd., 180, Fleet Street, E.C.4	Holborn 9409——Nonfumo Fleet.
Non-Flam Film Hiring Co. (Artons, Ltd.), 6, Clark's Mews, High Street, London, W.C.2	Museum 9989 and Temple Bar 7028
Nordella Educational (see Jackatoon).	
Norfolk & District Films Transport, Mountergate, Norwich	Norwich 2818 (day) 2210 (night)
Norman's Film Library, 86-88, Wardour Street, W.1	Gerrard 7481 and 6413.
Norris Henty & Gardners, Ltd., 115, Queen Victoria Street, E.C.4, Works (Patricroft, Lancs)	Central 1451——Nornodeste, Cent.
North British Film Corpn., 37, Clifton Street, Blackpool	Blackpool 2080.
North British Rubber Co., 204, Tottenham Ct. Rd. W.1.	Museum 5460.
Northcourt Film Services, Ltd., North Court, Chitty Street, W.1	Museum 6372.
North East Coast Cinemas, Ltd., 11, Bath Lane, Newcastle-on-Tyne	Newcastle 27864.
Northern Theatres Co., Ltd., Nothcoli House, Clare Road, Halifax	Halifax 2512.
Northern Transport Agency (London), Ltd., 7, Gerrard Street, W.1	Gerrard 3011 (6 lines)—— Orthertrag-Lesquare, London.
North Western Film Booking Agency, 70, Lime Street, Liverpool	Royal 4911——Palais de Luxe.
Nuway Publicity Service, 22, Church Street, W.1	Gerrard 3316.
O'Brien, Chas., National House, Wardour Street	Gerrard 2708.
O'Bryen, Linnit & Dunfee, 28, Brook Street, W.1	Mayfair 0111.
Odeon Theatres, Ltd. (Oscar Deutsch), 49, Park Lane, W.1	Mayfair 7811——Odeons, Audley.
Odeon Theatres, Ltd. (Oscar Deutsch), Cornhill House, Bennetts Hill, Birmingham	Midland 2781-2792——Odeons, Birmingham.
Odeon Trust, Ltd., 49, Park Lane, W.1	Mayfair 7811-9.
ODHAMS PRESS BOOK DEPARTMENT, 85, Long Acre, W.C.2.	**Temple Bar 2468.**
ODHAMS PRESS LTD., 85-94, Long Acre, W.C.2.	**Temple Bar 2468 — Southernwood, Rand.**
Oetzmann & Co., Ltd., 67-87, Hampstead Road, N.W.1	Euston 5000—Oetzmann.
Ollerton Pictures, Ltd., Empire, Somercotes, Derbyshire	Leabrooks 148.
Olympic Kinematograph Laboratories, Ltd., School Road, N.W.10	Willesden 7233 and 5182—— Ohkaylab, Harles.
Olympodromes, Ltd., 30-31, Golden Square, W.1	Gerrard 7887.
Opperman, O. R., 3, Albemarle Street, E.C.1	Clerkenwell 2465.
Opticolour, Ltd., 11, Hamilton Place, W.1	Grosvenor 4161.
Orr Circuit, 92, Barkers Butts Lane, Coventry	Coventry 2112-4.
Ossicaide, Ltd. (V. A. Foot), 356-366, Oxford Street, W.1	Mayfair 1528-9——Ossicaide, Wesdo.
Ossicaide Ltd. (V. A. Foot), 62 Market Street, Manchester	Deansgate 3065.
Overhead, Ltd., 74, Victoria Street, S.W.	Victoria 1031.
Oxford Film Transport Service, Clarks Garage, Rose Hill, Iffley	Cowley 7029.
Oxon & Bucks Film Transport Co., Tower Hill Garage, Witney	Witney 100.
P.A. and D., Ltd. (See Anson)	
Pacey's Agency, Imperial House, Regent Street, W.1	Regent 2264. ——Paceys

P.C.S., Ltd., 74, Victoria Street, S.W.1 .... Victoria 1031   Hydroloar,
                                                                      Sowest.
Pall Mall Productions, Ltd., 3-5, Burlington Gardens, W.1 .... Regent 2776.
Palmer Ambrose. 22, Pow Street, Workington, Cumberland ......
Palmer, George (Universal Cinema Supplies), Ltd., 13, Gerrard
    Street, W.1 .... Gerrard 5476——Geremlapsi
                                                                      Lesquare.
Palmer Newbould & Co., Ltd., 5 and 6, Cork Street, W.1 .... Regent 4306.
Panther Picture Co., Ltd., Temple Road, Cricklewood, N.W.2 ... Gladstone 2261.
Paramount-Astoria-Theatres, Ltd. (Administration), 104–8,
    Oxford Street, W.1 .... Museum 4721——Theapara, Rath.
Paramount-Astoria-Theatres, Ltd., Reg. Offices, 162-170,
    Wardour Street, W.1 .... Gerrard 7700.
Paramount British Productions, Ltd., Reg. Office, 162-170,
    Wardour Street, W.1.. Gerrard 7700.
Paramount Film Service, Ltd. 162-170, Wardour Street, London,
    W.1 .... Gerrard 7700——Paraserv, Rath.
Paramount Film Service, Ltd., 10-12, John Bright Street,
    Birmingham .... Midland 3781-2——Paraserv.
Paramount Film Service, Ltd., 14-18, The Friary, Cardiff ...... Cardiff 7673-4——Paraserv.
Paramount Film Service, Ltd., Paramount House, 11, Pearse
    Street, Dublin .... Dublin 44267——Paraserv.
Paramount Film Service, Ltd., 184, St. Vincent Street, Glasgow... Central 4420-1——Famlaserv.
Paramount Film Service, Ltd., 48, Wellington Street, Leeds ...... Leeds 20471——Paraserv.
Paramount Film Service, Ltd., Paramount House, Fraser Street,
    Liverpool .... North 741——Paraserv.
Paramount Film Service, Ltd., 22 and 24, Dickinson Street,
    Manchester .... Central 4793——Paraserv.
Paramount Film Service, Ltd., Paramount House, Bath Lane,
    Newcastle-on-Tyne.. Newcastle 21564-5——Paraserv.
Paramount-Newcastle-Theatre, Ltd. (Administration), 104,
    Oxford Street, W.1 .... Museum 4721.
Paramount-Newcastle Theatre Ltd. (Reg. Office), 162-170
    Wardour Street, W.1 .... Gerrard 7700.
Paramount Sound News, School Road, Acton .... Willesden 5511.
Park Royal Engineering Co., Ltd., Bush House (West Wing),
    Aldwych, W.C.2 .... Temple Bar 0037.
Parkes and Mainwarings, Ltd., Coleshill Street, Birmingham...... Aston Cross 1164-5——Posters.
Parkes, H. T., 22, Jesmond Crescent, Crewe .... Crewe 2549.
Parkin-Shelley, Ltd., 60, Cregoe Street, Birmingham .... Cal. 3800.
Parnell, F., Gloucester Mansions, 140A, Shaftesbury Avenue,
    W.C.2 .... Temple Bar 5972.
Parsons & Stewart, 5, Charing Cross Road, W.C.................. Temple Bar 4219
Partridge & Mee, Ltd., Parmeko Works, Aylestone Park, Leicester Aylestone 487——Parmeko.
Partridge, Wilson & Co., Ltd., Davenset Works, Evington Valley
    Road, Leicester .... Leicester 24612——Davenset,
                                                                      Leicester.
Partridge, Wilson and Co., Ltd., 21, Douglas Street, Glasgow ...
Pascall, James, Ltd., Furzedown Works, Mitcham, Surrey .... Mitcham 2162.
Patent Fireproof Rear Projection Screen Co. (E. G. Turner),
    43-49, Higham Street, Walthamstow, E.17 .... Larkswood 1061-2.
Paterson (Glasgow), Ltd., 79, Howard Street, Glasgow .... Central 5289.
Pathé Equipment, Ltd., 173, Wardour Street, W.1 .... Gerrard 1544-6——Theatequip
                                                                      Rath.
Pathé Equipment, Ltd., 75, Station Street, Birmingham .... Midland 0742——Pathire.
Pathé Equipment, Ltd., Dominions House, Queen Street, Cardiff Cardiff 7803-4——Pathire.
Pathé Equipment, Ltd., 96, Lower Abbey Street, Dublin.......... Dublin 43221——Pathire.
Pathé Equipment, Ltd., 114, Union Street, Glasgow .... Central 1965-6——Pathire.
Pathé Equipment, Ltd., 10, Millhill, Leeds .... Leeds 2 7814——Pathire.
Pathé Equipment, Ltd., 208, Westgate Road, Newcastle-on-
    Tyne .... Newcastle 28474——Pathire.
Pathé Equipment, Ltd., 23, Islington, Liverpool .... North 268——Pathire.
Pathé Equipment, Ltd., 19-20, Hardy's Buildings, Victoria Street,
    Manchester .... Blackfriars 7699——Pathire.
Pathé Pictures, Ltd., 84, Wardour Street, W.1 .... Gerrard 4360——Patherima, Rath
Pathé Pictures, Ltd., 114, Union Street, Glasgow, C.1 .... Central 1965-6——Pathire.
Pathé Pictures, Ltd., 208, Westgate Rd., Newcastle-on-Tyne 4 ... Newcastle 28474——Pathire.
Pathé Pictures, Ltd., 10, Millhill, Leeds, 1 .... Leeds 27814——Pathire.
Pathé Pictures, Ltd., 23, Islington, Liverpool 3 .... North 268.
Pathé Pictures, Ltd., 8-9, Hardy's Building, 30, Victoria Street,
    Manchester 3 .... Blackfriars 7699——Pathire.
Pathé Pictures, Ltd., 75, Station Street, Birmingham, 5 ...... Midland 0742——Pathire.
Pathé Pictures, Ltd., Dominions House, Queen Street, Cardiff... Cardiff 7803-4——Pathire.
Pathé Pictures, Ltd., 66, Middle Abbey Street, Dublin .... Dublin 43226——Pathire.
Pathescope, Ltd., 10, Great Marlborough Street, W.1.......... Gerrard 5736.
Pathéscope, Ltd., North Circular Road, Cricklewood, N.W.2 ... Gladstone 6544——Gold.
Pathetone Studio, 103-9, Wardour Street, W.1 .... Gerrard 5701.

Pearson, J. R. (Birmingham), Ltd., Porchester Street, Aston, Birmingham .... Aston Cross 2617.
Peacock, G. W. (Wales), Ltd., 16–20, Swansea Arcade, Goal Street, Swansea .... Swansea 7471.
Pearl Productions (*see* Gee Films)..
Pearl Alexander, 178, Walm Lane, N.W.2.............................. Gladstone 5567.
Pearson, J. R. (Birmingham), Ltd., 8, Buckingham Street, W.C.2 Temple Bar 3676.
Peeling & Van Neck, Ltd., 4, Holborn Circus, E.C.1 .... Central 9196.
Pennine Films, Ltd., Tontine Street, Blackburn .... Blackburn 7691.
Penzance Cinema, Ltd., Regent Hotel, Penzance..................... Penzance 146 and 330——Cinema Penzance.
Peradin Rubber Sales, Ltd., Carlton House, Lower Regent Street, S.W.1 .... Whitehall 8661—Peradin, Piccy.
"Perfect" Opaque Lantern Plates, Imperial Works, Shankiin Road, N.8 .... Mountview 7187.
Perforated Front Projection Screen Co., Ltd. (E. G. Turner), 43-49, Higham Street, Walthamstow, E.17. .... Larkswood 1061-2.
Performing Right Society, Ltd., Copyright House, 33, Margaret Street, W.1 .... Langham 3864—Perforight, Wesdo. .
Periodical, Trade Press and Weekly Newspaper Proprietors' Association, Ltd., 6, Bouverie Street, E.C.4 .... Central 2441——Weneppa, Fleet.
Petters, Ltd., Bush House, Aldwych, W.C.2 .... Temple Bar 0167.
Petters, Ltd., Westland Works, Yeovil .... Yeovil 141——Petters, Yeovil.
Philips Industrial, 145, Charing Cross Road, W.C.2.................. Gerrard 7777——Phildustry, Westcent.
Philips Cine-Sonor, 147, Wardour Street, W.1 ....:.. Gerrard 6732-3—Cinesonor, Rath.
Philpot Circuit, 116, Much Park Street, Coventry .... Coventry 2366.
Phœnix Films, 28, Mortimer Street, W.1. .... Museum 1922-5.
Phœnix Film Service, Ltd., 23, Charles Street, Cardiff .... Green 1024 Cardiff.
Phonographic Performance, Ltd., 144, Wigmore Street, W. ...... Welbeck 7306 and 3096—— Perfono, Wesdo.
Photo Electrograph Co., Ltd., Norway House, Cockspur Street, S.W.1 .... Whitehall 6596.
Photographic Electrical Co., Ltd., 80–82, Wardour Street, W.1... Gerrard 1365.
Photoplays, Ltd., 71, Howard Street. North Shields .... North Shields 219.
Pickard, A. E., Norwood Cinema, St. George's Road, Glasgow...... Douglas 690 and 330.
Pickard, T., Ltd., 4, Church Vale, East Finchley, N.2 .... Tudor 2525. .
PICTUREGOER, 93, Long Acre, W.C.2 .... **Temple Bar 2468—Southernwood, Rand.** ˙
Piena Music Co. (W. & G. Foyle, Ltd.), Trefoile-House, Manette Street, W.1 .... Gerrard 5660——Foylibra, Westcent.
Pilkington's (A. Austin) Theatres, 20, London Road, Salisbury...
Pinewood Studios, Ltd., Iver Heath, Bucks..........................
Pin-o-lite Screen Co., Ltd., Arch Works, Temperance Street, Ardwick, Manchester 1 .... Ardwick 2093——Pinolite.
Pirelli Ltd., 343, Euston Road, N.W.1 .... Museum 9802——Pircllicon,Telex.
Pitchford, R. Watkins, 34, High Holborn, W.C.1.................... Chancery 8724.
Pitman, Sir Isaac & Sons, Ltd., 39-41, Parker Street, Kingsway, W.C.2............... .... Holborn 3558.
Pixtons, Ltd. (Chair Factory), Queens Factory, High Wycombe, Bucks. .... High Wycombe 160.
Pixtons, Ltd., 47, Berners Street, W.1 .... Museum 6172-3—Pixtonar, Rath.
Platt, George & Sons, Ltd., Oakes Street, Liverpool.................. Central 1867.
Platt, T., 56, Farrow Street, Shaw ....
Players' Club, The, 12, Denman Street, Piccadilly Circus, W.1 ... Gerrard 2143.
Plaza Cinema Circuit, Hay, Hereford .... Hay 4——Plaza, Hay.
Plaza Theatre (Rugby) Ltd., Crown House, Rugby................... Rugby 2244.
Polley, H. V., Ltd., 32, Shaftesbury Avenue, W.1 .... Gerrard 1480.
Poole, C. W. & J. R. Entertainments, 31, Eastgate, Gloucester ... Gloucester 2127——Dates.
Pooles Theatres, Ltd. (See Poole's C.W. Entertainments)
Pooley & Austin, 34, Broadway, Westminster, S.W.1 .... Victoria 2913 and 3373.
Popular Cinemas, Ltd., Phœnix House, 19, Oxford Street, W.1 Gerrard 1405.
Portsmouth Film Service, 88, Clarendon Road, Southsea .... Portsmouth 5748——Films,
Portsmouth Town Cinemas, Ltd., Shaftesbury Cinema, Kingston Road, Portsmouth .... Portsmouth 4976.
Potter, Fredk., E., Ltd., Aldwych House, Aldwych, W.C.2 ...... Holborn 5992——Exultation, Estrand.
Potteries and Cinema Supply Co., The, 13, Leek Road, Smallthorne, Stoke-on-Trent .... Hanley 7658.
Potteries Transport & Cinema Supply Co., 13, Leek Road, Smallthorne, Stoke-on-Trent ....
Powers & Privileges, Ltd., 5, Tavern Street, Ipswich .... Ipswich 2654 and 2249.
Pratt, H., Ltd., High Street, Aston, Birmingham .... East 1416-7— Saniventi.
Premier Stafford Prodns., Ltd., Sound City, Shepperton, Mdx.... Chertsey 2291-3.
Presbury, S. & Co., Ltd., 87, Charing Cross Road, W.C.2 .... Gerrard 1347-8——Adpuprin. Lesquare.
Preston Film Service, Picturedrome, Brackenbury Place, Preston Preston 5465. .

Pride, F. H., 69-81, High Street, Clapham, S.W.4...................... Macaulay 2281-4——Pridelite, Clapcom.
Prism Manufacturing Co., California Works, Brighton Road, Belmont, Surrey .... Sutton 5361-2.
Pritlove, S. B., 6, Denman Street, W.1 .... Gerrard 4098.
Producers Distributing Corporation Ltd., 111, Wardour Street, W.1 .... Gerrard 4222——Pedecelim, Ratn
Producers Distributing Corporation Ltd., Borough Buildings, 72, John Bright Street, Birmingham .... Midland 5281.
Producers Distributing Corporation Ltd., 20, The Friary, Cardiff Cardiff 4309.
Producers Distributing Corporation Ltd., 114, Union Street, Glasgow, C.1 .... Central 3131.
Producers Distributing Corporation Ltd., 71, Albion Street, Leeds Leeds 24876.
Producers Distributing Corporation Ltd., 10, Commutation Row, Liverpool .... North 19.
Producers Distributing Corporation Ltd., 15, Cromford House, Cromford Court, Manchester .... Blackfriars 9263.
Producers Distributing Corporation Ltd., Clayton Chambers, 61, Westgate Road, Newcastle .... Newcastle 22332.
Producers Distributing Corporation Ltd. Louis Elliman, Ltd. , 70, Middle Abbey Street, Dublin.................................. Dublin 43450——Elliman, Dublin.
Progressive Film Institute Ltd., 80, Wardour Street, W.1 ......
Progressive Publicity, Albion Works, Albion Street, King's Cross, N.1 .... Terminus 3260.
Provincial Cinematograph Theatres, Ltd., New Gallery House, 123, Regent Street, W.1 .... Regent 8080—— Procinthe, Piccy.
Provincial Cinematograph Trading Co., 17, Wellington Street, Leeds 1... Leeds 26692——Elecord, Leeds.
Publicity Films, Ltd., Filmicity House, Upper St. Martin's Lane, W.C.2, and Merton Park Studios, S.W. .... Temple Bar 6482——Filmicity.
Publicity Picture Productions, 93, Wardour Street, W.1 .... Gerrard 5843.
Pugh Bros., Ltd., 54-6, Compton Street, Goswell Street, E.C.1 ... Clerkenwell 3211.
Pullin, Fred, 94, Wardour Street, W.1 .... Gerrard 3856.
Pyrene Co., Ltd., Great West Road, Brentford, Middlesex ...... Ealing 3444——Pyrene, Brentford.
Quality Films, 67-68, Jermyn Street, S.W.1......................... Whitehall 6804-5.
Quigley Publications, 4, Golden Square, W.1 .... Whitehall 7541.
Radro Development Co. (props., Epoch Reproducers, Ltd. , Aldwych House, Aldwych, W.C.2) ....
Radio International Pictures, Ltd., 2, 3 & 4, Dean Street, W.1 Gerrard 3201.
Radio Pictures, Ltd., 2; 3 and 4, Dean Street, W.1 .... Gerrard 3201-5——Arkopict
Radio Pictures, Ltd., City Chambers, John Bright Street, Birmingham .... Midland 4101-2——Arkopict.
Radio Pictures, Ltd., Dominion House, Queen Street, Cardiff Cardiff 3319——Arkopict.
Radio Pictures, Ltd., 10a, Bothwell Street, Glasgow .... Central 4032——Arkopict.
Radio Pictures, Ltd., 1, Wellington Chambers, City Square, Leeds Leeds 30048-9——Arkopict.
Radio Pictures, Ltd., 60, Lime Street, Liverpool .... Royal 5754——Arkopict.
Radio Pictures, Ltd., 3, The Parsonage, Manchester 3.............. Blackfriars 4224-5——Arkopict.
Radio Pictures, Ltd., 19, Bath Lane, Newcastle-on-Tyne .... Newcastle 22810——Arkopict.
Radius Films, Ltd., 199, Wardour Street, W.1. .... Gerrard 7172.
"Rainbow," 23, Clarence Terrace, Hounslow ....
Rallim Theatres, Ltd., Imperial House, 80-86, Regent Street, W.1 Regent 3712.
Ratcliff (R.E.) Circuit, "Raheny," Roby, Lancs. .... Huyton 382
Ratcliffe Tool Co., Ltd., 83, Denzil Road, N.W.10 .... Willesden 5780.
Ratner Safe Co., Ltd., 48, Bread Street, E.C.4 .... City 2309——Thiefproof, Centra .
Raycol British Corporation, Ltd., Canada House, 4-5, Norfolk Street, W.C. ....
Rayne, H. & M., Ltd., 15, Rupert Street, W.1 .... Gerrard 5336.
Rayner & Co., 5, Chancery Lane, W.C.2............................. Holborn 0738
RCA Photophone, Ltd., Electra House, Victoria Embankment, W.C.2 .... Temple Bar 2971-5
RCA Photophone, Ltd., 110, John Bright Street, Birmingham... Midland 5708.
RCA Photophone, Ltd., 57-59, Charles Street, Cardiff............. Cardiff 3594.
RCA Photophone, Ltd., 19, Blythwood Square, Glasgow .... Central 3685.
RCA Photophone, Ltd., 26, Cloth Market, Newcastle .... Newcastle 27771
RCA Photophone, Ltd. (Representative, 34, Lower Abbey Street, Dublin).. Dublin 43842.
RCA Photophone, Ltd., 274, Deansgate, Manchester .... Blackfriars 7092.
RCA Photophone, Ltd., 118, Royal Avenue, Belfast .... Belfast 25829.
Regent Enterprises, Ltd., 51, North John Street, Liverpool ...... Bank 610.
Reid's Film Service, 81, Dunlop Street, Glasgow .... Central 1034
Reliance Film Co., 193, Wardour Street........................... Gerrard 1333.
Religious Film Society, 104, High Holborn, W.C.1 .... Holborn 2241.
Renters, Ltd., 6, Denman Street, W.1 .... Gerrard 6777.
Republic Pictures Corporation, 76, Wardour Street, W.1 .... Gerrard 6555.
Reubenson, Reginald, 193, Wardour Street, W.1 .... Gerrard 1333— Reubenson.
Reunion Films, Ltd., Regency House, 1-4, Warwick St., W.1 ... Gerrard 5391.
Revelation Films, Ltd., Bush House, Aldwych, W.C.2 .... Temple Bar 5109 & 3870——Rev films.

Rex Publicity Service, Ltd., 31, Golden Square, W.1 .... Gerrard 3445-8——Rexervis,Piccy
Rex Publicity Service, Ltd., 95, Renfield Street, Glasgow, C.2...... Douglas 4545-6——Reservis, Glasgow.
Rex Ta'kie Entertainments, 203, Shaftesbury Avenue, W.C.2 ... Temple Bar 4292.
Richards, Randolph E., Picturedrome, Eastbourne.................. Eastbourne 1441.
Richsyn Equipments (I. & A. Rich), 42, Market Street, Longton, Stoke-on-Trent .... Longton 3811.
Rigby, Robert, Ltd., Little James Street, London, W.C.1 ...... Holborn 2944-5. —— Precinemat.
Rigby Taylor, Ltd., Victoria Works, Bolton .... Bolton 2752-3——Chemical.
Robinsons Home Cinema Service, Manchester House, Lowestoft (South) .... Lowestoft 500.
Rock Studios, Boreham Wood, Elstree, Herts........................ Elstree 1644.
Roe, Jack, 8, Noel Street, Wardour Street, W.C. .... Gerrard 5171.
Roe, Jack, 59, Canterbury Road, N.1 .... Clissold 2614.
Rogerson, Robert, 39-41, Blythswood Street, Glasgow, C.2 ...... Central 4209.
Rolls & Co. 489a, Oxford Street, W.1.................................. Mayfair 1470.
Romney Brit'sh (see Jackatoon)...
Ross, Ltd., 3, North Side, Clapham Common, S.W.4 .... Macaulay 2472——Rossicaste, Phone.
Ross, Ltd., 26, Conduit Street, W.1 .... Mayfair 4316——Rossano, Wesdo.
Ross Ltd. (for provincial addresses see Pathé Equipment).
Rotax, Ltd., Willesden Junction, N.W.10 .... Willesden 2480——Rodynalite, Phone.
Rothermel, R. A., Ltd., Rothermel House, Canterbury Road, Kilburn, N.W.6 .... Maida Vale 6066——Rothermel, London.
Rowson, Simon, Kent House, 87, Regent Street, W.1............. Regent 3764.
Rowe, Victor W., East End Way, Pinner, Middlesex .... Pinner 831.
Royal Photographic Society of Great Britain, 35, Russell Square, W.C.1 .... Museum 0411.
R.oyston Soaps, Ltd., 51, Biggar Street, Glasgow. .... Bridgeton 1274.
R R. Films, Ltd., 193, Wardour Street, W.1 .... Gerrard 5830.
Rubber Flooring Manufacturers, Ltd., 108-9, Fore Street, E.C.1 Metropolitan 2249.
Rubber-Tar, Ltd., 51, Biggar Street, Glasgow .... Bridgeton 1274.
Runnymede Rubber Co., Ltd., 6, Old Bailey, E.C.4 .... City 2471——Rubberflor, Cent.
Ruston & Hornsby, Ltd., Engineers, Lincoln .... Lincoln 580——Ruston, Lincoln.
Ruston & Hornsby, Ltd., 15, Kingsway, W.C. .... Temple Bar 5865.
Rutt, R. Spurden & Co., Ltd., 490, High Road, Leyton, E.10 ... Leytonstone 3249.
St. Albans Rubber Co., Ltd., The Camp, St. Albans .... St. Albans 451-2——Saltire.
St. George's Pictures, Ltd., 145, Wardour Street, W.1 .... Gerrard 1895.
St. Helens Cable & Rubber Co., Ltd., Slough .... Slough 333——St. Helens, Slough
St. Ives Cinemas (Cornwall) Ltd., Scala, High Street, St. Ives, Cornwall .... St. Ives 143.
Salisbury Photo Press, Queens Road Station, S.E.15 .... New Cross 4920.
Sandbach Cinemas, Ltd., Palace, Sandbach .... Sandbach 103.
Saronies Enterprises, 7-8, Saxone Buildings, Church Street, Liverpool .... Royal 2013.
Satchwell, Roland, L.R.I.B.A., 6, New Street, Birmingham ...... Midland 5561.
Saville, W. J., & Co., "Savko" House, Eagle Wharf Road, N.1... Clerkenwell 3491-5.
Schulberg, Ad., 7, Park Lane, W.1 .... Grosvenor 3095-6.
Science Films, Ltd., 27, Clareville Grove, S.W.7 .... Kensington 7663.
Scientific Sound Systems, Ltd., 10, Featherstone Buildings, High Holborn, W.C.1 .... Chancery 7010.
Scophony, Ltd., Thornwood Lodge, Campden Hill, W.8........... Park 8181.
Scopes & Co., Ltd., Princes Street, Ipswich ....
Scott, Dixon, Haymarket House, Newcastle-on-Tyne .... Newcastle 23347.
Scott, H. S., A.R.I.B.A., Kings Court, 115-17, Colmore Row, Birmingham ....
Scott, R., Haymarket House, Newcastle .... Newcastle 23347.
Scottish Cinema & Variety Theatres, Ltd., 105, St. Vincent Street, Glasgow .... Central 2830——Cinesup.
Scottish Films Productions (1928), Ltd., 26, India Street, Glasgow, C.2...
Scott Theatres, Ltd., 56, Brandon Street, Motherwell.............. Motherwell 601.
Scott's Empires, Ltd., Cinema, Dunbar ....

Scott Russell, J., 6 7, Great Castle Street, W.1 .... Langham 4304.
Screen Services, Ltd., Suite D, Victoria House, 99-101, Regent
Street, W.1. .... Regent 4826—Filmstarz, Piccy.
Seamless Sound Screen Co., Ltd., 89, Tetley Road, Hall Green,
Birmingham .... Acocks Green 514.
Seander Publishing Co., Caxton Press, Hyde .... Hyde 115——Seander.
Seapak Insulators Co., 72, Oxford Street, W.1...................... Museum 5974——Proceed, Rath.
Selo Cine Service (Ilford, Ltd.), National House, 60–66,
Wardour Street, W.1 .... Gerrard 2763.——Selo Servs
                                                                                        Rath.
Sentry Safety Control, 52a, Bow Lane, E.C.4.......................... City 2959.
Shaw, Son & Co., J., Holmfirth, Huddersfield .... Holmfirth 124.
Shaw's Glazed Brick Co., Ltd., 170, Strand, W.C.2 .... Temple Bar 1612.
Shaw's Glazed Brick, Co., Ltd., Whitebrik, Darwen, Lancs.......... Darwen 654.
Sheffield & District Cinematograph Theatres, Ltd., 3, Hartshead,
Sheffield .... Central 20888—Cinema.
Sheffield Photo Co., Ltd., 6, Norfolk Row, Fargate, Sheffield ... Central 23891——Photo, Sheffield.
Shennan, A. E., F.R.I.B.A., 14, North John Street, Liverpool ...
Sheridan, Victor, 75, Shaftesbury Avenue, W.1 .... Gerrard 4973.
Sherville & Co., 193, Regent Street, W.1 .... Regent 5192.
Sherwood Films, Ltd., 191, Wardour Street, W.1.................... Gerrard 4148——Sheralclu, Rath.
Ship Carbon Co. of Great Britain, Ltd., National House, 60-66,
Wardour Street, W.1 .... Gerrard 2744-6——Karbonimpo,
                                                                                        Rath.
Ship Carbon Co. of Great Britain, Ltd., Grove Road, Chadwell
Heath, Essex .... Seven Kings 2421-2.
Shipman & King, M.84, Shell-Mex House, Strand, W.C.2............ Temple Bar 5077-8.
Short Film Productions, 67, Abbey Road, N.W.8....................
Siemens Electric Lamps and Supplies, Ltd., 38-39, Upper Thames
Street, E.C.4 .... Central 2332——Siemotor, Cent.
Siemens Plania Carbons, Agents, Electrical Equipment and Car-
bon Co., Ltd., 107-111, New Oxford Street, W.C.1 .... Temple Bar 7058-9——Thermopl-
                                                                                        type, Westcent.

Sight and Sound (*see* British Film Institute) ....
Sika Francois, Ltd., 39, Victoria Street, S.W.1.......................
Simons, M., 8, Union Road, S.E.16.................................... Bermondsey 2065.
Sinclair & Co., James A., Ltd., 3, Whitehall, S.W.1 .... Whitehall 1788——Oraculum,
                                                                                        Parl.
Slide House, Ltd., 52, Queen Victoria Street, E.C.4 .... City 2505.
Small Electric Motors, Ltd., Eagle Works, Church Fields Road,
Beckenham .... Beckenham 0066.
Small Tone Films, 3, Meard Street, W.1 .... Gerrard 2379—Smatfilms, Rath.
Smith & Hardcastle, Ltd., 49-53, Godwin Street, Bradford ...... Bradford 6326-7
Smith, A., Film Transporter, 29a, Range Road, Manchester 16... Moss Side 1771.
Smith, A. George, 91, Shaftesbury Avenue, W.1 .... Gerrard 6881.
Smith, Bernard, 26, St. Anne's Court, Wardour Street, W.1 ... Gerrard 2208-9 —— Highflier,
                                                                                        Rath.
Smith, P., Imperial Works, Shanklin Road, Crouch End, N.8 ... Mountview 7187.
Smith, S. W., 76-78, Wardour Street, W.C.2.......................... Gerrard 2882-5——Smicofilm.
Smith-Walker, Ltd., 16, Caxton Street, Westminster, S.W.1 ... Victoria 2123——Formation,
                                                                                        Sowest, London.
Snape & Ward, 13 St. Ann Street, Manchester .... Blackfriars 3731.
Soho, Ltd., 3, Soho Square, W.1 .... Gerrard 2184.
Soho, Ltd., 16, Potters Road, New Barnet .... Barnet 3087.
Sol Exclusives, Ltd., 21, Bennetts Hill, Birmingham 2.............. Midland 0347.
Soskin Productions, Ltd., Sackville House, 40, Piccadilly, W.1... Regent 2616—Soskins, Piccy.
Sound City (Films), Ltd., Sound City, Shepperton, Middx. ... Chertsey 2211-7——Souncity,
                                                                                        Shepperton.
Sound City (Films), Ltd., 193, Wardour Street, W.1.................. Gerrard 4962-4——Souncity,Rath
Sound City Distributors Ltd., 193, Wardour Street, W.1. .... Gerrard 4962-4——Souncity, Rath
Sound and Cinema Equipment, Ltd., 20, Gerrard Street, W.1 ... Gerrard 7211-3——Soundequi,
                                                                                        Lesquare.
Sound Film Music Bureau, Ltd., 9a, Sackville Street, Piccadilly,
W.1 .... Regent 4381——Dixerat, Phone
Sound, Ltd., New Hall, Bargoed, Glam. .... Bargoed 72——Newhall, Bargoed.
Sound Services, Ltd., Bush House, Aldwych, W.C.2 .... Temple Bar 9621.

o

South Downs Cinemas, Ltd., 2, Rugby Road, Southsea .... Portsmouth 3456.

Southern and Suburban Film Transport Co., Ltd., 41, Mitcham Lane, Streatham, S.W.16 .... Streatham 5262.

South Wales Cinemas, Ltd., Albert Hall, De La Beche, Swansea ... Swansea 4597 and 4576.

Sovereign Exclusives, 97, John Bright Street, Birmingham ... Midland 0601——Sovereign.

Specterman, Ralph, Dorland House, 18-20, Regent Street, W.1 Whitehall 9313.

Speechly, Henry, & Sons, Camden Organ Works, St. Mark's Road, E.8 .... Clissold 2916.

Spicer-Dufay (British), National House, 60-66, Wardour Street, W.1. .... Gerrard 2763.

Splott (Cardiff) Cinema Co.,Ltd.,14, St. Andrews Crescent, Cardiff Cardiff 2901-2.

Spotlight Casting Directory, 43, Cranbourn Street, W.C.2 ...... Gerrard 3002-3.

Sponsored Film Productions, Ltd., National House, 60, Wardour Street, W.1 .... Gerrard 2522.

Spring's (Frank E.) Circuit, Parsonage Chambers, 3, The Parsonage, Manchester .... Blackfriars 7905.

Springvale Electrical Co., Masbro Road, Kensington, W.14. ...... Shepherds Bush 4321.

Stafford & Co., Ltd., 50, Berners Street, W.1........................... Museum 6245-6.

Stafford & Co., Ltd., Netherfield, Nottingham........................ Nottingham 58214-5.

Stafford Entertainments Ltd., Picture House, Stafford .... Stafford 291.

Stafford Studios, Ltd., Sound City, Shepperton .... Chertsey 2291-3.

Stahl Pyramid Films, Ltd., 130, Wardour Street, W.1 Gerrard 3400.

Standard Film Agency, 26, St. Anne's Court, W.1 .... Gerrard 2208——Highflier, Rath.

Standard Kine Laboratories, Ltd., 87, Wardour Street, W.1 ... Gerrard 1330.

Standard Kine Laboratories, Ltd., Portsmouth Road, Thames Ditton .... Emberbrook 2350-1——Standard.

Standard Telephones & Cables, Ltd., Connaught House, Aldwych, W.C. .... Holborn 8765.

Stanley Lupino Prods., Ltd. (see Gaiety Films, Ltd.) ....

Stanley Rogers Cinemas, Ltd., 72, Grey Street, Newcastle-on-Tyne .... Newcastle 20317-8——Hinge, Newcastle.

Star Cinemas, Ltd., 5, Manchester Avenue, E.C.1..................... Metropolitan 4292.

Star Illustration Works, Ltd., 5, 6 & 7, D'Arblay Street, W.1..... Gerrard 3033——Twinkle, Rath

Stereotone, Ltd., 72A, Osborne Road, Acton Town, W.3 .... Acorn 2125.

Steuart Films, Chelmsford Studios, N. Fambridge, Essex ...... Latchingdon 317.

Stevenson, V. & J., 315, Manchester New Road, Middleton, Manchester ....Middleton 2370.

Stilwell, Darby & Co., Ltd., 29A, Charing Cross Road, W.C.......... Whitehall 4768.

Stitson, White & Co., Ltd., 102, Victoria Street, Westminster, S.W.1 .... Victoria 8071-2

Stoll Picture Productions, Ltd., Temple Road, N.W.2 .... Gladstone 2261.

Stoll Picture Productions, Ltd. (Regd. Office and Foreign Sales Dept.), Stoll Offices, Coliseum Buildings, W.C.2............... Temple Bar 1500——Oswastoll, Lesquare.

Stone, E. A., F.S.I., M.Inst.R.A., 20, Berkeley Street, W.1,........ Mayfair 6363.

Stone's (Will) Circuit, New Hippodrome, Tonypandy, S. Wales... Tonypandy 54——Stone.

Strand and Interchangeable Signs, Ltd., 24-28, Floral Street, W.C.2 .... Temple Bar 3168-9——Sineerecta, Rand.

Strand Cinema Theatre Co. (1920), Ltd., The, 39, Strand Street, Douglas, I.O.M. .... Douglas 14——Strand Cinema.

Strand Electric & Engineering Co., Ltd., 19-24 and 28, Floral Street, W.C.2 .... Temple Bar 7464 (6 lines)——Spotlite, Rand.

Strand Electric & Engineering Co., Ltd. (Works), Power Road, Gunnersbury, W.4 ....

Strand Film Co., Ltd., 37-39, Oxford Street, W.1 .... Gerrard 3122.

Strange, R. E., & Co., Ltd., 12, Little Denmark Street, W.C.2 ... Temple Bar 1728-9——Printafilm Westcent.

Streatly House Group, Furnivalls, Amersham, Bucks.............. Holmer Green 48.

Strelitz, Eric P., 14-16, Regent Street, W.1 .... Whitehall 5897.

Strode, Ronald and Associates, Callard House, 74A, Regent Street, W.1 .... Regent 5945 and 3462.

Strong Electric Distributors, Ltd., 132, Wardour Street, W.1 ... Gerrard 6246——Carbonark.

Stubbs, N. H. (Dist. Dupont Stock), 26, Attimore Road, Welwyn Garden City.. Welwyn Garden 699.

Studio Film Laboratories, Ltd., 80, Wardour Street, W.1 .... Gerrard 1365-6.

Studio Sound Service Ltd., 89-91, Wardour Street, W.1............ Gerrard 6747.

Sturtevant Engineering Co., Ltd., 147, Queen Victoria Street, E.C.4 .... Central·7121——Sturtevant.

Sulzer Bros. (London), Ltd., 31, Bedford Square, W.C.1 .... Museum 0702-6——Gebsulzer, Westcent.

Sumerling & Co., Ltd., (Works) 63 to 66, Bunhill Row ; (Showrooms) 145, Old Street, E.C.1... Clerkenwell 0381——Sumerling Finsquare. London.

Sunderland Amusements Ltd. 37, King Street, South Shields ... South Shields 6.

Super Cinemas, Ltd., 36-37, Queen Street, E.C.4 .... Central 9156—Atwonce, London.

Suprema Publicity Service, Ltd., 9, 10, 11, Carlow Street, Camden Town, N.W.1	Euston 3711-3.
Superlite Cinema Screen Co., Ltd., 49, Higham Street, Walthamstow, E.17	Larkswood 1061 and Palmers Green 3614.
Superlite Cinema Screen Co., Ltd., 94, Wardour Street, W.1	Gerrard 3591.
Sussex Film Transport, 3 and 4, Ham Yard, W.1	Gerrard 6431.
Swanser & Son, Ltd., 52, Blackstock Road, N.4	Canonbury 2043.
Swift, Miss M. (U.K. rep. for Guaranteed Pictures, N.Y.), 130, Wardour Street, W.1	Whitehall 7938——Swiftfilms——Cables, Swiftfilms.
Sydney Wake, 22, Frith Street, W.1	Gerrard 2781-2.
Sydney Wake, Rythe Works, Portsmouth Road, Thames Ditton	Emberbrook 2350-1——Night Line : Emberbrook 1087.
Synclocks, Ltd., Colindale Works, Hendon, N.W.4	Colindale 6045.
Synchrophone, 1936 Co., Mead Works, Hertford	Hertford 156-7——Syncro-Phone.
Tait, J. & N., Panton House, 25, Haymarket, S.W.1	Whitehall 1981.
T. & M. Electrical Co., Ltd., 157, Wardour Street, W.1	Gerrard 6521.
Talking Picture News, 141, Duke Street, Liverpool	Royal 3771.
Tanar (British) Corporation, Ltd., 145, Wardour Street, W.1	Gerrard 1412——Tanarlight, Rath. London.
Tann, John, Ltd., 117, Newgate Street, E.C.1	National 2267——Safejotann.
Tate Bros., Garage, Old Shoreham Road, Portslade, Brighton	
Tay Garnett Productions, 24, Whiteant Street, S.W.	
Taylor Circuit, George, 27, Merkland Street, Partick, Glasgow, W.1	Western 2766.
Taylor, Taylor & Hobson, Ltd., 314, Regent Street, W.1 (and Stoughton Street Works, Leicester)	Langham 4287——Illiquo.
Technicolor, Ltd., Bath Road, Harmondsworth, Middlesex	West Drayton 2211.
T. D. S. Advertising, Ltd., Dilke House, Malet Street, W.C.1	Museum 6858-9——Sykes, Museum.
Technical & Research Products, Ltd., 6, Aldwych, W.C.2	Temple Bar 4001.
Technique Films, 93, Wardour Street, W.1	Gerrard 3376.
Thawpit (Proprietary), Ltd. Woodstock Road, Shepherd's Bush, W.12	Shepherd's Bush 4124.
Theatres Advertising Co., 87, Charing Cross Road, W.C.2	Gerrard 1347-8———Adpuprin, Lesquare.
Theatre & Cinema Caterers, Ltd., Dean House, Dean Street, W.1	Gerrard 4711-3.
Theatrical Artists Film Society (T.A.F.S.), 16, York Street, Covent Garden, W.C.2	
Thompson, Charles, Weetwood Chambers, Albion Street, Leeds, 1	Leeds 25859——Ceetee, Leeds.
Thompson & Dean, Ltd., Phoenix Works, 38, Hurst Street, Birmingham	Midland 0094——Cineseats.
Thompson's Enterprises, Ltd., 4, Palladium Buildings, Eastbourne Road, Middlesbrough	Linthorpe 88156.
Thraves, Alfred J., F.R.I.B.A., Whitefriars House, Friar Lane, Nottingham	Nottingham 42687.
Tidswell, J. F., 26, Park Row, Leeds	Leeds 28775.
Tilling, Thos., Ltd., 71, High Street, Peckham, S.E.15.	Rodney 2272——Tilling, Peck, London.
Tillotson & Firth, Ltd., Printers and Poster Writers, Morley, Leeds	Morley 231———T. & F.
Timadays, Ltd., 364, Hoe Street, Walthamstow, E.17	Walthamstow 1781.
Tobis Film Distribution, Ltd., 53–54, Haymarket, S.W.1	Whitehall 7409.
Tobis (Gt. Britain), Ltd., 53–54, Haymarket, S.W.1	Whitehall 7409.
Toeplitz Productions, 15, Hanover Square, W.1	Mayfair 3614.
Topical Productions, 411, St. Vincent Street, Glasgow, C.3	Central 82——Incidents.
Touring Talking Picture Co., Chase Ave., King's Lynn, Norfolk	King's Lynn 2335.
Tower Film Productions, Ltd., National House, Wardour Street, W.1	Gerrard 2708.
Trade, Board of, Great George Street, S.W.1	Whitehall 5140.
Trafalgar Film & Productions, Ltd., 293, Regent Street, W.1	Langham 1851.
Trafalgar Film Corporation, Ltd., Suite 62, Imperial House, Regent Street, W.1 Reg. Office, Friars House, New Broad Street, E.C.2	Regent 7126.
Transoceanic Forwarding Co. (successors to) (See Müller, W. H.)	
Transreceivers, Ltd., 444, Ewell Road, Surbiton, Surrey	Elmbridge 2960.

Trent, W. E., F.R.I.B.A., F.S.I., G-B Picture Corpn., 123 Regent Street, W.1 .... Regent 8080.
Trespeuh, A. L., 40, Gerrard Street, W.1 .... Gerrard 1272—Filmger, Lesquare.
Trinity Chair Works, Ltd., Scarborough .... Scarboro 345.
Trinity Chair Works, Ltd. (United Kinema Supplies), 137, Wardour Street, W.1.. Gerrard 1242.
Trinity Chair Works, Ltd., Cathedral House, Manchester .... Blackfriars 8587.
Trinity Chair Works, Ltd. (J. O. Wyndham, Ltd.), 46, Charles Street, Cardiff .... Cardiff 3397.
Trinity Chair Works, Ltd., 202, Hope Street, Glasgow. .... Douglas 5705.
Trix Electrical Co., Ltd., 8-9, Clerkenwell Green, E.C.1 .... Clerkenwell 3014-5——Trixadio Smith.
Troughton & Young, Ltd., 143, Knightsbridge, S.W.1 .... Kensington 8881——Teanwye, Knights.
Truecolour Film, Ltd., 54, Sussex Place, S.W.2 .... Kensington 8834——Trucol.
Trutone Talking Picture Service (K.N. Farmon), 136, Wicklow Drive, Leicester.
Tucker, J. H. & Co., Ltd., Kings Road, Tyseley, Birmingham ... Acocks Green 0616-7—Switches, Phone, Haymills.
Tudor Accumulator Co., Ltd., 50, Grosvenor Gardens, S.W.1 ... Sloane 0168-9 —— Subconical, Sowest.
Tudor Films, Ltd., 60, Wardour Street, W.1 .... Gerrard 6826.
Tungstone Accumulator Co., Ltd., 11, Salisbury Square, E.C.4... Central 8156——Typify, Fleet.
Turnbull, W. W., Greenside, Durham Road, Coxhoe, Ferryhill, Co. Durham.. Coxhoe 5.
Turner, C. A., 68, Dorothy Road, Leicester .... Leicester 24380.
Turner Lord, W. and Co., 20, Mount Street, W.1 .... Grosvenor 3161.
Turner (W. W.) & Co., Ltd., Station Road, Northfield, Birmingham Priory 1171-2——Cinechair.
Turner (W. W.) & Co. Ltd., 28, Newman Street, W.1 .... Museum 3606.
Tussauds, Ltd., Madame, Baker Street Station, N.W.1 .... Welbeck 8661.——Tussauds.
Twentieth Century Cinemas, Ltd., 14-15, Lancaster Place, W.C.2 Temple Bar 1144.
Twickenham Film Distributors, Ltd. (Head Office), 111, Wardour Street, W.1 .... Gerrard 3421.——Hagenfil, Rath.
Twickenham Film Studios, Ltd., St. Margarets, Middlesex ...... Popesgrove 4444. ——Twickfilm, Twickenham.
Tyne Picture Houses, Ltd., Station Road, Wallsend-on-Tyne Wallsend 63566.

U.K. Films, Ltd., 91, Regent Street, W.1 .... Regent 7560 and 2533.
Unafilm (*See* Hanau.)
Uniform Clothing & Equipment Co., Ltd., 10 and 11, Clerkenwell Green, E.C.1 .... Clerkenwell 5551-3 —— Uniquip.
Uniform Supply Co., Ltd., 136, Wardour Street, W.1 .... Gerrard 4402.
Union Cinemas, Ltd., Union House, 15, Regent Street, S.W.1 ... Whitehall 8484.
Unique Pictures, 5 Lisle Street, W.C.2 .... Gerrard 6336.
United Artists Corporation, Ltd., Film House, Wardour Street, W.1 .... Gerrard 6301-4——Unartisco.
United Artists Corporation, Ltd., 1-5, Hill Street, Birmingham Midland 3733-4——Unartisco.
United Artists Corporation, Ltd., 40, Charles Street, Cardiff ... Cardiff 5556——Unartisco.
United Artists Corporation, Ltd., 71, Middle Abbey Street, Dublin .... Dublin 44820——Unartisco.
United Artists Corporation, Ltd., 240, Clyde Street, Glasgow ... Central 8350——Unartisco.
United Artists Corporation, Ltd., 39, Albion Street, Leeds ...... Leeds 30148-9——Unartisco.
United Artists Corporation, Ltd., 12, Norton Street, Liverpool ... North 22——Unartisco.
United Artists Corporation, Ltd., 3, The Parsonage, Deansgate, Manchester .... Blackfriars 8885.——Unartisco.
United Artists Corporation, Ltd., Waterloo Chambers, 11, Bath Lane, Newcastle-on-Tyne .... Central 23804——Unartisco.
United Automobile Services, Ltd., 6, Haymarket, Newcastle ... Newcastle 24211.
  Newcastle Enquiry Office, Marlborough Crescent .... Newcastle 21469.
  Newcastle Parcels Depot, Leadyard Gallowgate .... Newcastle 26602.
  United Automobile Services, Ltd. (Depots and Offices) ... Blyth 344
    " " Alnwick 182.
    " " Ashington 52.
    " " Morpeth 254.
    " " Durham 256.
    " " Hexham 61.
    " " Rothbury 58.
    " " Whitley Bay 1068.
    " " Berwick 283.
    " " Wooler 59
    " " Carlisle 919.
United Kinema Supplies, Ltd., 137, Wardour Street, W.1......... Gerrard 1242——Cinesound.
United Kingdom Advertising Co., Ltd., 25, Shaftesbury Avenue, W.1 .... Gerrard 6041——Alsafraz, Piccy.
United Picture Theatres, Ltd., 123, Regent Street ,W.1............ Regent 8080.

Unity Heating, Ltd., Vincent House, Vincent Square, S.W.1 ...... Victoria 3118.
Unity Heating, Ltd., Broadwater Road, Welwyn Garden City — Welwyn Garden 156——Unity.
Universal Entertainments, Ltd., Dorland House, 18–20, Regent
   Street, S.W.1 .... Whitehall 9313-6.
Universal Pictures, Ltd., 127-133, Wardour Street, W.1 .... Gerrard 9020——Unfilman, Rath.
Universal Pictures, Ltd., Dominion House, Queen Street, Cardiff. Cardiff 6101——Unfilman.
Universal Pictures, Ltd., 9, Camden Street, Liverpool .... North 534-5——Unfilman.
Universal Pictures, Ltd., Parsonage Chambers, The Parsonage,
   Manchester .... Blackfriars 3686-7——Unfilman.
Universal Publicity, 12, Oval Road, N.W.1 .... Gulliver 1793.
Universal Theatre Furnishing Co., Royd Works, Keighley......... Keighley 3021.
Utility Arts ,Ltd., 8 ,Cirencester Street, W.2 .... Abercorn 4423.
Vabest Co., Ltd., Regent House, Kingsway, W.C.2 .... Holborn 9811-2.
Variety Artistes' Federation, 18, Charing Cross Road, W.C.2. ... Temple Bar 6950——Artifedera,
   Lesquare.
Varley, E. H., Pavilion, Bridge Street, Girvan .... Girvan 111.
Vaughan Edward, Ltd., 87, Wardour Street, W.1 .... Gerrard 1330.
V.E.H. Cinemas, Ltd., The Lido, Aylesham Road, Norwich ...... Norwich 894.
Venreco, Ltd., 55 & 76, Neal Street, W.C.2 .... Temple Bar 5902-3 and 8937—
   Lumenite, Westcent.
Verity, Frank T., F.R.I.B.A. (Verity and Beverley), 32, Old
   Burlington Street, W.1 .... Regent 2117.
Vevers, C. C., 3, Fryston Street, Dewsbury Road, Leeds 11. ...... ——Vevers.
Vickery, Ltd., George, Taunton .... Taunton 3184.
Victory Theatres, Ltd., Edgar Street Accrington .... Accrington 2701.
Viking Films, Ltd., 107, Shaftesbury Avenue, W.1 .... Gerrard 5004-6.
Viking Pictures, 89-91, Wardour Street, W.1 .... Gerrard 4796.
Vinten, W., Ltd., North Circular Road, London, N.W.2 .... Gladstone, 6373-4.
Vinten, W., Ltd., 106, Wardour Street, W.1 .... Gerrard 4792.
Visatone, Stoll Picture Prodns., Ltd., Coliseum Buildings, St.
   Martins Lane, W.C.2... Temple Bar 1500——Oswastoll.
Visco Engineering Co., Ltd., Stafford Road, Croydon .... Fairfield 4181-3 ——Curtmit,
   Croydon.
Visual Education Ltd., Stoll Studios, Temple Road, N.W.2 ...... Gladstone 2261.
Vogue Film Productions, Ltd., 7, Park Lane, W.1 .... Grosvenor 3044.
Voigt Patents, Ltd., The Courts, Silverdale, Sydenham, S.E.26 Sydenham 6666.
W. & A. Film Distributors, 46, High Pavement, Nottingham ... Nottingham 45217.
Waddington John, Ltd., Wakefield Road, Leeds .... Leeds 75281——Wadding.
Wagstaff Press Service, Callard House, 74A, Regent Street, W.1 Regent 5945 & 3462.
Wainwright, J. G. & R. B., Ltd., 62, Shaftesbury Avenue, W.1 ... Gerrard 4948——Eximwainri,
   Lesquare.
Wallace Heaton, Ltd., 127, New Bond Street, W.1 .... Mayfair 0924—Zodellaria, Wesdo.
Wallaw Pictures, Ltd., Wallaw Buildings, Ashington, North-
   umberland .... Ashington 31——Wallaw.
Walpamur Co., Ltd., 35-36, Rathbone Place, W.1 .... Museum 6600.
Walt Disney—Mickey Mouse, Ltd., 62, Shaftesbury Avenue ...... Gerrard 7446/7——Mickmouse.
Walter, D., & Co., Ltd., 61-63, Lant Street, Borough, S.E.1 ... Hop 3651.
Walters & Sons, Ltd., Austin, Graythorn Electric Works,
   Manchester .... Central 4109——Ohmic
Walturdaw Cinema Supply Co., Ltd., 46, Gerrard Street, W.1.... Gerrard 1067——Albertype
   Lesquare.
Walturdaw Cinema Supply Co., Ltd. (A. H. Tucker), 48, Donegal
   Street, Belfast... Belfast 20371.
Walturdaw Cinema Supply Co., Ltd. (C. W. Hutchin), 37,
   John Bright Street, Birmingham .... Midland 4092.
Walturdaw Cinema Supply Co., Ltd. (H. G. Watkins), 27, Charles
   Street, Cardiff.. Cardiff 2399.
Walturdaw Cinema Supply Co., Ltd. (F. Cremer), 112, Marlborough
   Street, Dublin, C.8... Dublin 44250.
Walturdaw Cinema Supply Co., Ltd. (H. Tommey), 60, Lime
   Street, Liverpool.. Royal 3440.
Walturdaw Cinema Supply Co., Ltd., Parsonage Chambers, 3'
   Parsonage, Manchester 3 .... Blackfriars 9901.
Walturdaw Cinema Supply Co., Ltd. (G. Baker), 130, Renfield
   Street, Glasgow .... Douglas 4767.

Wardour Cinema & Estate Agency, 7, Wardour Street, W.1	Gerrard 2181.
Wardour Films, Ltd., Film House, Wardour Street, W.1	Gerrard 4314——
Wardour Films, Ltd., Garfield Chambers, 44, Royal Avenue, Belfast	[Mutuamos, Rath Belfast 3444——Mutuamos.
Wardour Films, 53, John Bright Street, Birmingham 1	Midland 1292-3——Mutuamos.
Wardour Films, Ltd., 48, Charles Street, Cardiff	Cardiff 111——Mutuamos.
Wardour Films, Ltd., 17, Pearse Street, Dublin	Dublin 44161——Wavfilm.
Wardour Films, Ltd., 39, Bath Street, Glasgow	Douglas 40——Mutuamos.
Wardour Films, Ltd., 11, Wellington Street, Leeds 1	Leeds 22364——Mutuamos.
Wardour Films, Ltd., 9, Commutation Row, Liverpool 1	North 1324——Mutuamos.
Wardour Films, Ltd., 3, The Parsonage, Manchester 3	Blackfriars 5464——Mutuamos.
Wardour Films, Ltd., 134/6, Westgate Road, Newcastle-on-Tyne	Newcastle 27825——Mutuamos.
Waring & Gillow (1932), Ltd., 164/182, Oxford Street, W.1	Museum 5000——Warison, Rath
Warner Bros. First National Productions, Ltd., Teddington Studios	Kingston 2181 and 2189—— Firnatex, Teddington.
Warner Bros. Pictures, Ltd., Warner House, Wardour Street, W.1	Gerrard 5600——Wabropic, Rath
Warner Bros. Pictures, Ltd., Severn House, 94-95, John Bright Street, Birmingham	Midland 4821——Wabropic.
Warner Bros. Pictures, Ltd., Dominions House, Queen Street, Cardiff	Cardiff 1365——Wabropic.
Warner Bros. Pictures, Ltd., 62, Middle Abbey Street, Dublin	Dublin 43941——Wabropic.
Warner Bros. Pictures, Ltd., 81, Dunlop Street, Glasgow	Central 4468——Wabropic.
Warner Bros. Pictures, Ltd., Cabinet Chambers, Basinghall Street, Leeds	Leeds 30028-9——Wabropic.
Warner Bros. Pictures, Ltd., 6 & 8, Islington, Liverpool	North 320——Wabropic.
Warner Bros. Pictures, Ltd., Cromford House, Cromford Court, Manchester	Blackfriars 5233——Wabropic.
Warner Bros. Pictures, Ltd., Imperial Chambers, Westgate Road, Newcastle-on-Tyne	Newcastle 26627——Wabropic.
Warren & Co. (Regent Street), Ltd., 16, St. Martin's Street, Leicester Square, W.C.2	Whitehall 1832-3—Warrenoboe, Lesquare.
Warston Pictures, Ltd., 20, Brazennose Street, Manchester 2	Blackfriars 6965.
Watkins & Watson, Ltd., 17, White Lion Street, Islington, N.1	Terminus 3191.——Hydisblow, Nordo.
Watkins, W. H., F.R.I.B.A., 1, Clare Street, Bristol	Bristol 20491.
Watson, A., 57, King Street, Maidstone	
Watts Cinemas, Ltd., "Poolstock," Finedon, Northants	Finedon 9.
Way & Waller, 7, Hanover Square, W.1	Mayfair 8022——10 lines.
Way, F. C., 20, Roe Street, Macclesfield	
Weaver, George, Cinema Displays and Costumes, "Sunny Bank," Red Bank Road, Bispham, Blackpool	Blackpool 51820.
Webber & Meecham, Ltd., 38, Gt. Windmill Street, W.1	Gerrard 4076.
Webb, W. A., & Co., 192, Sherlock Street, Birmingham 5	Midland 3732——Comacite.
Weddell Bros., Ltd., 407-409, Hornsey Road, Upper Holloway, N.19	Archway 1668-9.
Weinberg, Harris, 3, Lovell Street, Leeds	
Weiner, J., Ltd., 71-75, New Oxford Street, W.C.1	Temple Bar 9393——Lithoprint
Welwyn Studios, Ltd., Welwyn Garden City	Welwyn Garden 541.
Wembley Cinemas, Ltd., 11, Norton Folgate, E.1	Bishopsgate 5000.
Western Cinemas Circuit, 2, Penybryn Villas, Penydarren, Merthyr Tydfil	
Western Electric Co., Ltd., Bush House, Aldwych, London, W.C.	Temple Bar 1001——Westelcol.
Western Electric Co., Ltd., 42A, Horsefair, Birmingham 5	Midland 6435——Westelcol.
Western Electric Co., Ltd., Dominion House, Queen Street, Cardiff	Cardiff 7234——Westelcol.
Western Electric Co., Ltd., Veritas House, 7-8, Lower Abbey Street, Dublin	Dublin 44976——Westelcol.
Western Electric Co., Ltd., 22A, West Nile Street, Glasgow.	Central 8411——Westelcol.
Western Electric Co., Ltd., 64, Britannia House, Wellington Street, Leeds, 1	Leeds 29751——Westelcol.
Western Electric Co., Ltd., Old Colony House, South King Street, Manchester, 2	Blackfriars 3652-4——Westelco .
Western Electric Co., Ltd., Imperial Buildings, Westgate Road, Newcastle-on-Tyne	Central 20619——Westelcol.
Westinghouse Brake & Signal Co., Ltd., 82, York Road, King's Cross, N.1 (Works, Chippenham, Wilts.)	Terminus 6432——Westinghouse, Nordo.
Westminster Films, Ltd., 186, Wardour Street, W.1	Gerrard 4592.
Weston, Harry, M.I.Struct.E., F.I.A.S., 81, Chester Square, S.W.1	Sloane 2178.
West Sussex Film Transport, "Shenfield," Arundel Road, Littlehampton	Littlehampton 123.
West Sussex Film Transport, 3, Dansey Yard, Wardour Street, W.1	Gerrard 2181.
Western Union Telegraph Co., 151, Wardour Street, W.1	Gerrard 7343.
Wettstein, Ernest, Ltd., 184, Wardour Street, W.1	Gerrard 2903-4——Laureatus, Leeds 23137. [Westcent.
Whincup, C. H., The Tower, Briggate, Leeds	
White & Carter, Ltd., Carlton House, 11, Regent Street, S.W.1	Whitehall 4178.

White's Film Depot, 38, Talbot Street, Southport, Lancs.........	
Wholesale Fitting Co., Ltd., 23, Commercial Street, E.1...........	Avenue 5828.
Wigan Entertainments Co., Ltd., 1, College Avenue, Wigan	Wigan 3673.
Willbank Publications, Ltd., 93-95, Wardour Street, W.1	Gerrard 7474.——Willbank.
Wilkins, Campbell & Co., Ltd., Britannia Works, West Drayton, Middlesex..	WestDrayton 324—— Kinswli, Yiewsley.
Williams Cinemas, Ltd., Hippodrome, Workington..................	Workington 194.
Williams, J. Leslie & Co., Empire House, 117, Regent Street, W.1	Regent 4244.
Williamson Manufacturing Co., Ltd., Litchfield Gardens, Willesden Green, N.W.10..	Willesden 0073——Kinetogram Willroad.
Willis, W. E., Globe Cinema, Albany Road, Penylan, Cardiff ...	Cardiff 3072.
Willsons, Gloucester Mansions, Cambridge Circus, W.C.2	Temple Bar 5326——Willprintz, Westcent.
Willsons, King Street, Leicester	Leicester 21213-4-5——Streamers.
Willsons, Mount Street, Nottingham	Nottingham 40074——Printeries.
Wilson, C. R., Allendale, Bewdley Road, Stourport, Worcs.	
Wilton, Harry, 87, Donegall Street, Belfast	Belfast 6443.
Winads, Ltd., 54/58, Wardour Street, W.1	Gerrard 6543-4.
Windermere & Ambleside Cinemas, Ltd., 33, James St., Liverpool	Bank 4000.
Windsor Films. *See* Quality Films.	
Wingfield-Bowles, E., & Partners, 28, Victoria Street, S.W.1......	Victoria 0030-1.
Wiring, Ltd., 76, Seymour Place, W.1	Paddington 9024——Bloomgar, [Wesdo
Wirral Picturedromes, Ltd., Queen's Picturedrome, Wallasey...	
Withers, A., New Hall, Bargoed, South Wales	Bargoed 72——Newhall.
Wolfe & Hollander, Ltd., 251-256, Tottenham Court Road, W.1...	Museum 6652——Wolfhol.
Wondersigns, Ranelagh Road, S.W.1.	Victoria 8131.——Wundasigns, Sowest.
Wood, James, 25, Field Street, King's Cross..........................	Terminus 4755-6.
Wood's Picture Halls, Ltd., Wood's Palace, Bilston	Bilston 41388.
World Film News and Cinema Quarterly, Oxford House, 9, Oxford Street, W.1	Gerrard 6080.
World's Film News and Cinema Quarterly 24, N.W. Thistle Street, Edinburgh	Edinburgh 20245.
World Location Co., 23, Denmark Street, W.C.2	Temple Bar 7235.
World Screen Classics, Ltd., 197, Wardour Street, W.1	Gerrard 4913.
Worton Hall Studios, Isleworth, Middlesex	Hounslow 2323.
Wright, John, & Co., Ltd., Essex Works, Aston, Birmingham	Central 2169 —— Eureka, Bir- [mingham.
Wright, Samuel, & Co., Ltd., Crossend Works, Hackney Downs, E.8	Clissold 0412.
Wright, W., 50, Chester Mews, Albany Street, N.W.1	
Wurlitzer Organs (W. Pearce), Leicester Square Chambers,W.C.2	Whitehall 6864.
Wylie & Lockhead, Ltd., 53, Kent Road, Glasgow	Central 5732.
Wyndham, J. O., 46, Charles Street, Cardiff	
Wyndham Films, Ltd., National House, Wardour Street, W.1 ...	Gerrard 6826.
Yarmouth & Lowestoft Cinemas, Ltd., 16, South Quay, Gt. Yarmouth	Yarmouth 40.
Yonwin, Chas. H., Film Agent, 3, Parsonage Chambers, Manchester...	Blackfriars 3946.
Younger Film Productions, Ltd., 34-36, Oxford Street, W.1	Museum 4816.
Younger Publicity Service, Ltd., 34-36, Oxford Street, W.1	Museum 4816-7——Wypeeyes, Rath.
Zeiss Ikon, Ltd., Mortimer House, 37-41, Mortimer Street, W.1	Museum 9031——Zeissikona.
Zwart Ltd., 14-19, Portman Mews South, Orchard Street, W.1	Mayfair 1766-7——Jaxwart, Wesdo, London.

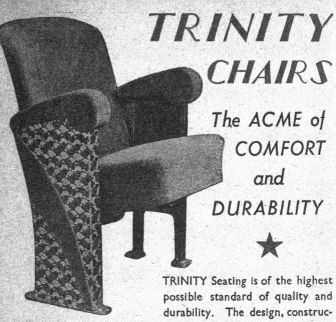

RCA
PHOTOPHONE
LIMITED

ULTRA - VIOLET
RECORDERS

HIGH FIDELITY
REPRODUCERS

THE EMBLEM OF — PERFECT SOUND

ELECTRA HOUSE,
VICTORIA EMBANKMENT, LONDON, W.C.2.
Telephone : Temple Bar 2971

CLASSIFIED TRADE DIRECTORY
For detailed addresses, etc., see pages 389-423.

ACOUSTIC ENGINEERS.
Bagenal, Hope, A.R.I.B.A.
Glover, C. W., & Partners.
Western Electric Co.

ACOUSTIC MATERIAL.
(See also Sound Insulation.)
Cullum, H. W., & Co.
Honeywill & Stein.
Johns-Manville Co., Ltd.
Lithalun Products, Ltd.
Newalls Insulation Co.
Seapak Insulation Co.

ADVERTISING. Advertising Films (see also Film Producers) ; Agents (see also Agents) ; Advertising Novelties ; Banners ; Cut-Outs ; Exploitation Accessories ; Frames (Lobby Display) ; Signs (see also Signs) ; Programme Boards ; Slides (see Slides) ; Trailers (see Trailers) ; Billposting (see next Section).

Advertising.
Ad-Visers, Ltd.
Arrow Achievements, Ltd.
Artads Service.
Betterways.
Cinema Publicity Co.
Chalmers, John.
Cleveleys Advertising.
Cinema Advertising Service, Ltd.
Cinema Publicity Supply Co.
Cinema & Theatrical Services.
Clage's.
Clayton, E. C.
County Publicity.
Davis, S., & Co. (Aldwych .
Dorland Advertising, Ltd.
Emerton, A. R.
Girosign, Ltd.
Gordon Cook & Co.
Gordon's Sales and Advertising Service
Guys of Cardiff.
Hardiker's Cinecraft Publicity.
Headway (London) Advertising, Ltd.
H.S.B. Advt. Specialists.
Jaeger, A. C.
Jerrold & Sons.
Kempsell's Advt. Service.
Kirwan Advertising Film Service.
Lawisto Advtg. Co.
Leadlay News Service, Ltd.
Leon Goodman Displays.
London Advtg. Service.
London and Coastal Advtg.
London & Provincial Advt. Co.
London Paramount Press Service.
Magnet Advtg. Co.
Metcalfe, C. P.

Metropolitan Advt. Co.
Mordecai, J.
National Advtg. Corp.
National Publicity Co.
Nuway Publicity Service.
Pickard, T., Ltd.
Potter, Fredk. E., Ltd.
Presbury, S., & Co., Ltd.
Progressive Publicity.
Pullin, Fred.
Rex Publicity Service.
Star Illustration Works (Blocks).
Stilwell, Darby & Co., Ltd.
Suburban Cinema News Service.
Theatres Advertising Co.
T.D.S. Advertising.
United Kingdom Cinema Display.
Universal Publicity.
Wagstaff Press Service.
Weaver, George.
Webb, W. A., & Co.
Willsons.
White & Carter.
Williams, J. Leslie.

Banners and Cut-outs.
Artads.
Allied Arts.
Beale, Arthur (Bunting and Ropes).
Cinema Advertising Service, Ltd.
Cinema Signs.
Coltman Displays.
Girosign, Ltd.
Gordon's Sales & Advertising.
Modern Poster Service.
Nelson Art Signs, Ltd.
Suprema Publicity.
Timadays.
Universal Publicity.
Willsons.

Bill Posting.
Allen, David.
Boro' Billposting Co.
British Poster Advt. Association.
Felton's Advertising Agency.
London Poster Advt. Association.
Nat. Advtg. Corp.

Lobby and Front of House Display.
Allied Arts, Ltd.
Artads.
Autotype Co., Ltd.
British Electrical Installations (Interchangeable Letters).
Coltman Displays.
Cinema Signs.
Coltman, A., & Co.
Cooke's Publicity Service.
Girosign, Ltd.
Gordon, Cook & Co.

Gordon's Sales & Advertising.
Lea & Son (Hydrogen for Balloons).
Leon Goodman Displays.
London Advertising Service.
Multiple Photo. Printers.
Nelson Art Signs, Ltd.
Presbury, S., & Co., Ltd. (Category
   Boards).
Moviesigns.
Nash & Hull.
Richsign Cinema Display.
Saville, W. J.
Sovereign Exclusives.
Suprema Publicity.
Theatres Advertising Co.
Timadays, Ltd.
Weaver, George.
Willsons.

Posters and Printers.
Baker, Herbert.
Berry, W. E.
Blackwell & Co.
British Poster Advertising Association.
Cawthra, N.
Central Printing Co.
Cinema Displays.
Cinema Publicity Supply.
Clage's.
Day, E. J., & Co., Ltd.
Electric (Cinema) Printing Co.
Hardiker's Cinecraft Publicity.
Jordison & Co., Ltd.
Mac's Poster Service.
Modern Poster Service.
Nelson Art Signs.
Parkes & Mainwaring.
Photo. Electrigraph, Ltd.
Seander Publishing Co.
Stafford & Co.
Suprema Publicity Service, Ltd.
Tillotson & Firth.
T D.S. Advertising, Ltd.
Timadays.
Universal Publicity.
Waddington, John.
Weddell Bros.
Weiner, J.
Willsons.
Zillwood, F., & Sons.

Programmes.
Ballman, S. V.
Balleny, H. T.
British Publicity Pictures.
Cleveley's Advertising.
Cook's Publicity Service.
County Publicity.
Cramer, P. A.
Electric (Cinema) Printing Co.
Gordon, Cook & Co.
Gordon's Sales & Advertising.
Hodgson, F.
Jameswood Press, Ltd.
London & Coastal Advertising.

London Paramount Press Service.
Magnet Advertising.
Norman's Film Library.
Parkes & Mainwarings, Ltd.
Pickard, T., Ltd.
Presbury, S., & Co., Ltd.
Theatres Advertising.
T.D.S. Advertising, Ltd.
Willsons.

Screen Publicity.
Ballman, S. V.
British Publicity Pictures.
Cleveley's Advertising.
Gordon's Sales & Advertising.
Heywood, John, Ltd.
Hodgson, F.
Kirwan Publicity Film Service.
London & Coastal Advertising.
Magnet Advertising.
Parkes and Mainwarings, Ltd.
Pickard. T.. Ltd.
Presbury, S., & Co., Ltd.
Revelation Films.
Seander Publishing Co.
Stillwell, Darby & Co.
Theatres Advertising.
T.D.S. Advertising, Ltd.
Younger Publicity Service.

Sandwich Boards (London).
Felton's Advertising Agency.
Metropolitan Advertising.
Nuway Publicity Service.
Rex Publicity.

AGENTS.
Advertising and Publicity
Ad-Visers.
Allighan, Garry.
Allison, G. F.
Arrow Achievements Co.
Balleny, H. T.
Bristow, Billie.
Cleveley's Advertising.
Crawford, W. S., Ltd.
Dorland Advertising.
Film Publicity Service
Gregory & MacCarthy.
Guys of Cardiff.
Hardikers Cinecraft Publicity.
Headway (London), Advertising, Ltd.
H.S.B. Advertising Specialists.
Kempsell's Advt. Service.
Lawisto Advt. Co.
Leadlay News Service, Ltd.
Macpherson, Mervyn.
Mann, Christopher.
Marks, B. M.
Palmer, Newbould & Co.
Pickard, T., Ltd.
Presbury, S., & Co., Ltd.
Pullin, F.
Rex Publicity.
Strode. Ronald.
Theatres Advertising Co.
T.D.S. Advertising.

Cricks, R. H., A.R.P.S. (Talkie).
Cromie, Robert, F.R.I.B.A.
Cummings, Peter, A.R.I.B.A.
Davis, Basil, A.M.I.E.E.
Elvy, J. C.
Fairweather, J., A.R.I.B.A.
Farquharson, J. F., M.I.Struct.E
Freeman, Son & Gaskell.
Gardner, A. V.
Glen, W. R., F.R.I.A.S.
Glover, C. W., & Partners.
Granger, W. F., F.R.I.B.A.
Gray & Evans.
Henly, A. T., M.I.H.V.E.
Hinchliffe, P. A., F.R.I.B.A.
King, W. J.,F.R.I.B.A.
Knight, John, F.R.I.B.A.
Leathart, F.R.I.B.A.
Luke, E. S.
Masey, Cecil, F.R.I.B.A.
Matcham, Frank, & Co.
Morrison, James, A.R.I.B.A.
Pritlove, S. B.
Satchwell, Roland, L.R.I.B.A.
Scott, H. S., A.R.I.B.A.
Shennan, A. E., F.R.I.B.A.
Thraves, A. J., F.R.I.B.A.
Trent, W. E., F.S.I.
Verity, Frank T., F.R.I.B.A.
Watkins, W. H., F.R.I.B.A.
Weston, H., M.Inst.R.A., F.I.A.S.

BATTERY MANUFACTURERS.
Batteries, Ltd.
Britannia Batteries.
Brown, J., & Co.
Chloride Electrical.
D.P. Battery Co.
Detroit Engine Co.
Fuller Accumulator Co.
General Electric Co., Ltd.
Hart Accumulator Co.
Siemens Electric Lamps.
Thomas A. Edison, Ltd.
Tudor Accumulator.
Tungstone Accumulator.

BUILDING & BUILDING MATERIALS
Allen Construction Co.
Allied Guilds (Decoration).
Anselm, Odling & Sons, Ltd.
Atkinson, Harry.
Bennie, John, Ltd.
Blake, W. H., & Co.
Callow Rock Lime.
Cement Marketing Co., Ltd.
Christie & Grey, Ltd. (Vibration Specialists).
Cinema Building Co.
Cinema Construction, Ltd.
Clark & Fenn (Plaster Work).
Cullum, H. W., & Co. (Flooring).
Decra, Ltd. (Decorations).
Dennison Kett (Roller Shutters, etc.).
Diamond Tread Co., Ltd.
Drew Clark (Scaffolding).

Elvins, T., & Sons.
Ferodo, Ltd. (Stairtreads).
Foster, Fred A. (Paint Plaster).
Friese-Greene, Nicholson (Ironwork).
Gardiner & Starkey, Ltd. (Metalwork.)
Gardiner, Sons & Co. (Canopies).
Gaze, H. E., Ltd.
Gibson, A. L. (Scene Dock Shutters).
Goodlass Wall & Co. (Paint).
Gratton, S. A., & Sons.
Gray, J. W. (Flagstaffs, etc.).
Great Metropolitan Flooring.
Green, G. J. (Plaster).
Hampton & Sons (Plasterwork).
Harrods.
Hathernware, Ltd. (Faience).
Heathman, J. H.
Honeywill & Stein (Acoustic Correction).
Johns-Manville Co., Ltd. (Asphalt Tiles).
Korkoid Decorative Floors.
Leyland Paint & Varnish Co.
Lindsay, Thomas.
London & Midland Steel Scaffolding.
Macfarlane, Walter (Art Metal).
Maple & Co.
Marels & Co. (Plaster).
Middleton Fireclay Co. (Faience).
Minter, F. G.
Moss, Wm., & Sons.
Musgrave & Co., Ltd. (Struct. Steel).
Newall's Insulation.
Nobel Chemical Finishes, Ltd. (Paint).
Pearson, J. R., Ltd. (Canopies, etc.).
Platt, Geo., & Sons.
Sankey, J. H., & Son (Fireproof Cement).
Shaw's Glazed Bricks.
Sika-Francois, Ltd. (Damp Exclusion).
Smith Walker, Ltd. (Struct. Steel).
Stacey & Co. (French Polishers).
Wylie & Lochhead.

CABLES.
Callenders.
Dyson, J.
Falk, Stadelmann.
General Electric Co., Ltd.
Hall Mfg. & Supply.
Henley's, Ltd.
Kandem Electrical.
Pirelli.
Siemens Electric Lamps.
St. Helens Cable & Rubber Co.
Standard Telephones & Cables.

CARBONS.
(*See also Equipment Supply*).
Beacon Carbons.
Brockliss, J. Frank, Ltd.
Brown, J., & Co.
Champion, Chas. H., & Co.
Conradty Products.
Dyson, J.
Elec. Equipment & Carbon Co.
Films & Equipment.
G.B. Equipment.
General Electric Co., Ltd.
Geipel, Wm.

Honrion Carbons, Ltd.
Kalee, Ltd.
Kamm, J., & Co.
Kandem Electrical.
Kinematograph Equipment.
London Electric Firm.
Milgate, V.
Morgan Crucible Co.
Morris, J. R. (Nat. Carbon Co.).
Pathe Equipment.
Ship Carbon Co.
Siemens-Plania Carbons.
Sloan Electrical Co.
Strand Electric.
Walturdaw.

CARTOONS.
(See under Producers Advertising.)

CAMERAS, etc.
Agence Debrie.
Ambassador Film Dist., Ltd.
Beck, R. & J.
Bell & Howell.
British Schufftan Process
Brockliss, J. Frank, Ltd.
Cine Art Productions.
Dallmeyer, J. H.
Drem Products.
Ensign, Ltd.
Films & Equipment.
Hummel, M. & M.
Jarrold & Sons, Ltd.
Kamm & Co.
Kershaw, A., & Son.
Lawley Apparatus Co., Ltd.
Le Personne, L., & Co.
Liddon, J.
Lizars, J.
Lynes, B. J.
McKaig, Wm.
Meyrowitz, E. B.
Moss, Pym.
Moy, Ernest F.
Newman & Sinclair.
Purser, Henry F.
Ross, Ltd.
Sheffield Photo Co., Ltd.
Sinclair, J. A., & Co.
Soho, Ltd.
Tanar (British) Corporation.
Taylor, Taylor, Hobson, Ltd.
Vinten, W.
Wheeler, J. S.
Williamson Mfg. Co., Ltd.
Zeiss-Ikon.

CATERERS.
Farm Ice Creamery.
Friern Manor Caterers.
Mulchinock, L. H. (Van Houtens).
Pascall, J.
Theatre & Cinema Caterers.
Warren & Co.

CATERING EQUIPMENT.
Armin Trading Co. (Art Flowers).
Benham & Sons.

Dairy Supply Co.
Flugel & Co.
Fontagene.
Friese-Greene, Nicholson.
Kafa Table Co.
Lumley, L., & Co.
Rich, I. and A.
Sumerling & Co.
Wright, John, & Co.

CHEMISTS (MANUFACTURING).
Johnson & Sons.
May & Baker.
Parkin-Shelley, Ltd.

CIRCUITS (see page 454 *et seq.*).

CLEANERS & DYERS.
Braham Products (London), Ltd.
Chemical Cleaning & Dyeing.
Royston Soaps, Ltd. (Cleaning Material).
Wilkins, Campbell & Co., Ltd. (Liquid Soaps).
Rubber Tar, Ltd.

COLOUR FILMS.
Brewstercolour (see Revelation Films).
British Colour Films.
British Ondiacolor, Ltd.
Cinechrome.
Daponte, Demetre (Cinecolour).
Dunning Process.
Dufay Color, Ltd.
Gasparcolor, Ltd.
Harmonicolor Films, Ltd.
Opticolor, Ltd.
Raycol British Corporation.
Spicer-Dufay.
Talkiecolor.
Technicolor, Ltd.
Zoechrome.

CONSULTING ENGINEERS.
(See Architects and Consulting Engineers.)

COSTUMES.
Angel, Morris, & Son.
Army & Navy Supply Stores.
Berman, M., Ltd.
Rayne, H. & M.Ltd.
Uniform Supply Co.
Weaver, George.

CURTAIN CONTROL.
Beck & Windibank.
Brown, J., & Co.
Bulman Jupiter Screen Co. (1936), Ltd.
Carpets & Curtains.
Cinesales.
Draper, W., & Co.
Electro-Control Co.
Etna Lightg. & Heating.
Foster, Fred. A.
Friese-Greene, Kenneth.
Furse, W. J., & Co.
Geipel, Wm., Ltd.
Hall & Dixon.
Hall Mfg. & Supply Co., Ltd.
Jensen, G. K., & Co.

Kalee, Ltd.
Kershaw, A., & Son.
Knight & Co. (Engrs.), Ltd.
Major Equipment.
Mickelwright, Ltd.
Milgate, V.
Pathe Equipment.
Sound & Cinema Equipment.
Strand Electric.
Vabest Co., Ltd.
Venreco, Ltd.
Walturdaw.
Walter, D., & Co.

DEAF APPARATUS.

Ardente.
Birmingham Sound Reproducers.
British Talking Pictures.
General Acoustics (Acousticon).
Ossicaide.
Partridge & Mee.
Philips' Industrial.
Prism Mfg. Co.
Radio Development Co. (Epoch).
Sound & Cinema Equipment.
Trix Electrical.
Western Electric.

DECORATION.

Allied Guilds.
Armin Trading Co. (Art Flowers).
Beale, Arthur (Ropes & Bunting).
Berger, Lewis & Sons (Paints).
Boro Electric Signs.
Campbell Bros., Ltd.
Carpets & Curtains, Ltd.
Cinemas & Interior Decoration.
Clark & Fenn (Fibrous Plaster).
Collins, J., & Son (Basketwork).

De Jong, F., & Co. (Fibrous Plaster).
Decra, Ltd.
Drew, Clark, & Co. (Scaffolding).
Foster, Fred. A.
Gardiner, Sons & Co. (Art metal).
Gaze, H. E. (Plaster).
Goodlass, Wall & Co. (Paint).
Great Metropolitan Flooring Co.
Greene, G. J., & Sons (Plaster).
Guys of Cardiff (Floral).
Hall & Dixon, Ltd.
Hampton & Sons, Ltd.
Harrod's.
Hart & Co.
Heathman, J. H. (Scaffolding).
Heaton, Tabb & Co., Ltd.
Honeywill & Stein.
Jackson, H., & Sons (Art metal).
Kalee, Ltd.
Ker-Lindsay, Ltd.
Kinematograph Equipment Co.
Leyland Paint & Varnish Co.
Line, John, & Sons (Paint, Wallpapers).
Marels & Co. (Plaster).
Mollo & Egan.
Nash & Hull (Art metal).
P.C.S., Ltd.
Palmer, Ambrose.
Palmer & Ashford.
Pratt, H.
Pugh Bros. (Glass).
Rainbow.
Shaw, J., Son & Co.
Sayer, F. J.
Utility Arts (Lampshades).
Walpamur (Paint, Wallpaper).
Waring & Gillow.
Walsh Glass Supply.

Williams, H. L. (Fire-resisting Paint).
Wright, Saml., & Co. (Plaster).
Wylie & Lockhead.
Zwart, Ltd.

DEODORISING EQUIPMENT & MATERIAL.

Bersel Mfg. Co.
Fox, C. G., & Co.
Hall's, Ltd.
Lipton's Spray Products.
M. & P. Enterprises.
May & Baker.
Rigby, Taylor.
Wilkins, Campbell (Disinfectants, etc.).

EDUCATIONAL FILMS.
(See Producers—Educational.)

EDITING ROOMS.

Crown Theatre.
Norman's Film Library.

ELECTRICAL CONTRACTORS.

Beard, R. R., & Co.
Benjamin Elec., Ltd.
Berkeley Electrical.
British Elec. Installations.
Brockliss, J. Frank, Ltd.
Brown, J., & Co.
Caplin Engineering Co.
Crompton Parkinson.
Crypto Electrical Co.
Curtis Manfg. Co. (Resistances).
Digby, Robert, Ltd.
Donaldson, F. G.
Draper, W., & Co.
Duncan Watson.
Electrical Installations, Ltd.
Etna Lighting & Heating Co.
Everett, Edgcumbe & Co.
Falk, Stadelmann & Co., Ltd.
Furse, W. J., & Co.
Fyfe, Wilson & Co.
Geipel, Wm.
General Electric Co., Ltd.
Gibbons, A. O.
Haden, G. N., & Sons.
Hampton & Sons.
Hawkins, L., & Co.
Hewittic Electric Co.
Holophane, Ltd.
Igranic.
Imperial Lighting Co.
Jensen, G. K., & Co., Ltd.
Kamm & Co.
Kalee, Ltd.
Kandem Electrical, Ltd.
Kinematograph Equipment.
Leach, S. G., & Co.
Lewsley, J. W.
Lippold, A.
McLaren, J., & H.
Major Equipment.
Metropolitan Sound Equipment.
Metropolitan Vickers.
Mickelwright, Ltd.

Nash & Hull
Park Royal Eng. Co., Ltd.
Partridge, Wilson & Co. (Resistances, etc.).
Pathe Equipment.
Philips' Industrial, Ltd.
Pooley & Austin.
Pratt, H.
Siemens Electric Lamps.
Sloan Electrical Co.
Small Electric Motors.
Smith & Hardcastle.
Sound & Cinema Equipment.
Standard Telephones & Cables.
Strand Elec. & Engineering.
Troughton & Young.
T. and M. Electrical (Accessories).
Tucker, J. H., & Co. (Accessories).
Venreco.
Walter, D., & Co.
Waring & Gillow.
Webb, W. A., & Co.
Webber & Meecham.
Wiring, Ltd.
Wyndham, J. O.

EQUIPMENT ENGINEERS.

Bauer, Ltd.
Beard, R. R.
Berkeley Elec.
Brown, J., & Co.
Brockliss, J. Frank, Ltd.
Burkitt, Frank, Ltd.
Caplin Engineering Co.
Clark's Cinemachinery.
Crompton Parkinson.
Donaldson, F. G.
Duncan Watson.
Draper, W., & Co.
Elec. Equipment & Carbon Co.
Electrocord, Ltd.
Etna Lighting & Heating.
Film Industries.
Films and Equipment.
Furse, W. J., & Co., Ltd.
Fyfe, Wilson & Co.
G.-B. Equipments, Ltd.
General Electric Co., Ltd.
Gimson & Co. (Leicester), Ltd.
Gradley Electrical Ltd.
Gramo-Radio, Ltd.
Hall Mfg. & Supply Co., Ltd.
Hawkins, L. G., & Co.
Heatly-Gresham.
Imperial Sound System.
Jeapes, W. C.
Kalee, Ltd.
Kamm & Co.
Kandem Electrical, Ltd.
Kinematograph Equipment, Ltd.
Knight & Co. (Engineers), Ltd.
Lawley Apparatus Co.
Lewsley, J. W.

Lippold, A.
Lynes, B. J.
McLaren, J. & H.
McKnight, Cyril.
Major Equipment.
Mansell & Ogan.
Mickelwright, Ltd.
Milgate, V.
Moy, Ernest F.
Park Royal Engineering.
Partridge & Mee.
Partridge, Wilson & Co.
Pathe Equipment.
Peacock (Wales), Ltd.
Philips' Industrial.
Provincial Cine Trading.
Rigby, Robert, Ltd.
Roe, Jack.
Ross, Ltd.
Siemens.
Scott, Richard.
Sound & Equipment, Ltd.
Strand Electric.
T. & M. Electrical Co., Ltd.
Turner, C. A.
Vabest.
Venreco, Ltd.
Vinten, W.
Walturdaw.
Wyndham, J. O.
Webb, W. A., & Co.
Williamson Manufacturing Co.
Wiring, Ltd.
Western Electric.

EQUIPMENT SUPPLY (General) AND INSTALLATION.
Arrow Achievements Co.
Baldwin Cinema Service.
Baker, Harry.
Brown, J., & Co.
Bulman Jupiter Screen Co., Ltd.
Burkitt, Frank, Ltd.
Caplin Engineering.
Cinema Building Co.
Cinema Equipments.
Cine Requirements.
Cinesales.
Cinema Traders.
Clark's Cinemachinery.
Constructors, Ltd. (Steel Storage Equipment).
Co-operative Cinematograph Co.
Curtis Mfg. Co.
Donaldson, F. G.
Edinburgh Cine Supplies.
Empire Seating Co.
Film Industries.
Films and Equipment.
Friese-Greene, Kenneth.
Gibbs, Ben. C.
Gradley Electrical Co.
Hampton & Sons, Ltd.
Kalee, Ltd.
Kinematograph Equipment.
Lewsley, J. W.
Lion Cinematograph Co., Ltd.

Manchester Film Producing.
Major Equipment.
Metropolitan Sound Equipment.
Mickelwright, Ltd.
Milgate, V.
Morison, Ian K.
National Film Agency.
No-Fume, Ltd. (Ash Receivers).
Northern Contractors.
Palmer, George (Univ. Cinema Supplies).
Pathe Equipment.
Provincial Cinematograph Trading.
Roe, Jack.
Sound & Cinema Equipment.
Thompson & Dean.
United Kinema Supplies, Ltd.
Walturdaw.
Webb, W. A., & Co.
Wyndham, J. O.

ESTATE & KINEMA AGENTS.
(*See Agents.*)

EXPORTERS.
B.I.P. (Export), Ltd.
British United Film Producers.

FILM CLEANERS.
Clark's Cinemachinery.
Daponte, Demetre.
Henderson's Film Laboratories.
Norman's Film Library.
Pall Mall Productions.
Parkin-Shelley, Ltd. (Chemicals).
Rigley, Robert, Ltd.
Thawpit (Cleaning Material).
Walturdaw.

FILM PRINTERS.
Automatic (Barnes).
Brent Laboratories.
Commercial Films.
Denham Laboratories, Ltd.
Dunning Process (England).
Elstree Film Laboratories.
Film Laboratories.
Henderson's Film Laboratories.
Humphreys, G., & Co.
Kay Film Printing Co.
Kay (West End) Laboratories.
Lynes J. B.
Olympic Kine. Laboratories.
Standard Kine. Laboratories.
Strange, R. E., & Co.
Studio Film Laboratories (also Titles).
Sydney Wake.

FILM PRINTING PLANT.
Bell & Howell.
Films and Equipment.
Lawley Apparatus Co.
Moy, Ernest F., Ltd.
Philips Cine-Sonor.
Vinten, W.

FILM STOCK.
Agfa Photo.
Criterion Plates.
Dupont (see Stubbs).

RESISTANCES

*27 YEARS' EXPERIENCE MANUFACTURING
THOUSANDS OF RESISTANCES FOR THE
LEADING FIRMS, ENSURE A RELIABLE JOB.*

Latest Practice:

PARALLEL ARC RESISTANCES

as supplied to the leading West End Cinemas, Tivoli, Carlton, Leicester
Square, Dominion, etc. Also supplied to the leading West End
Theatres, and leading distributing Companies.

RESISTANCE

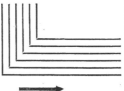

→

REMOTE CONTROL

THEATRE
CIRCUITS

Gevaert, Ltd.
Guiterman, S., & Co. (Film Base).
Ilford Cine. Service.
Kodak, Ltd.
Non-Inflammable Film Co.
Pathé of France.
Stubbs, N. H. (Dupont).
Zeiss Ikon.

FIRE APPLIANCES.
(*See Safety Devices.*)

FURNISHING, DRAPERY, CARPETS, ETC.
(*See also Equipment Supply.*)

Allied Guilds.
Beck & Windibank.
British Furtex.
Brooks, J. B. (Steel furniture).
Bulman Jupiter Screen Co. (1936), Ltd.
Carpenter, F. H., & Co., Ltd.
Carpets & Curtains, Ltd.
Champion, J.B., and Sons (Dursley), Ltd.
Cinema Building Co.
Cinema Equipments.
Coates & Co.
Cox & Co. (Steel Furniture).
Dunlop Rubber Co. (Carpet Underlay).
Dyson, J.
Edgcombe, J. H.
Emerton, A. R.
Evans, C. J., & Co.
Everett & Edgcumbe (Clocks).
Foster, Fred A.
Friese-Greene, Kenneth.
Great Metropolitan Flooring.
Hall & Dixon, Ltd.
Hampton & Sons, Ltd.
Harrison, C. R., & Sons.
Harris, M. (Period Furniture).
Harrods.
Haworth & Sons.
Heaton Tabb & Co., Ltd.
Holophane.
Kalee, Ltd.
Kean & Scott, Ltd.
Kinematograph Equipment.
Lazarus & Son.
Lindsay-Hickman, Ltd.
Lister & Co.
Lockwood, L. B., & Co.
Lusty, W., & Sons.
Maple & Co.
Oetzmann & Co., Ltd.
Paterson (Glasgow), Ltd.
Parkes, H. T.
Pathe Equipment.
Pixton, Ltd.
Sayer, F. J.
Shaw, J., Son, & Co.
Sound & Cinema Equipment, Ltd.
Thompson & Dean, Ltd.
Trinity Chair Works.
Turner, W. W., & Co.
Turner, Lord.

Walturdaw.
Waring & Gillow.
Wolfe & Hollander.
Wylie & Lockhead.

GENERATORS.
B. T.-H., Ltd.
Bruce, Peebles & Co.
Crompton Parkinson.
Crossley Bros.
Electrical Equipment & Carbon Co.
Electrocord.
Films & Equipment.
Fyfe, Wilson & Co., Ltd.
General Electric Co., Ltd.
Kandem Electrical Co., Ltd.
Lancashire Dynamo & Crypto.
Metropolitan Vickers.
McLaren, J. & H., Ltd.
Morrison, A. E., & Sons, Ltd.
National Gas & Oil Engine.
Petters, Ltd.
Provincial Cinematograph Trading.
Ruston & Hornsby.
Sound & Cinema Equipment, Ltd.
Walturdaw, Ltd.

GLASS.
Brilliant Sign Co.
Clark, James, & Sons, Ltd.
Eaton, Parr & Gibson.
Holophane.
Newton John M., & Sons.
Pugh Bros.

HEATING & VENTILATION
Benham & Sons.
British Trane Co., Ltd.
Carrier Engineering Co.
Chemical Air Cleaning.
Etna Lighting & Heating.
General Electric Co., Ltd.
Haden, G. M., & Sons.
Hall & Kay.
Jeffreys, J. & Co., Ltd.
Lamson Pneumatic.
Matthews & Yates.
Moorhouse, Sidney & Co.
Mulliner, S.
Musgrave & Co., Ltd.
Pratt, H.
Siemens Electric Lamps.
Smith & Hardcastle.
Stitson, White & Co.
Sturtevant Engineering Co.
Sulzer Bros.
Unity Heating, Ltd.
Visco Engineering Co.
Webb, W. A., & Co.
Wright, John, & Co.

HOME KINEMAS EQUIPMENT
(*See Non-Theatrical Equipment.*)

FILM JOURNALISTS

Film Critics

B.B.C. Alistair Cooke.

Bystander, 346, Strand, W.C.2. Sydney Tremayne. Temple Bar 8020.

Daily Express, 8, Shoe Lane, E.C.4. Guy Morgan. Central 8000.

Daily Herald, 16, Wilson Street, W.C.2. P. L. Mannock. Temple Bar 7788.

Daily Mail, Northcliffe House, E.C.4. Seton Margrave (W. A. Mutch). Central 6000.

Daily Mirror, Geraldine House, Fetter Lane, E.C.4. R. J. Whitley. Holborn 4321.

Daily Sketch, 200, Gray's Inn Road, W.C.1. S. H. Butt. Museum 9841.

Daily Telegraph, 135, Fleet Street, E.C.4. Campbell Dixon. Central 4242.

Evening News, Carmelite House, E.C.4. A. Jympson Harman. Central 6000.

Empire News, 200, Gray's Inn Road, W.C.1. Reg. Mortimer. Museum 9841.

Evening Standard, 47, Shoe Lane, E.C.4. Ian Coster. City 3000.

Film Pictorial, Fleetway House, E.C.4. Clarence Winchester. Central 8080.

Film Weekly, 112, Strand, W.C.2. John Gammie. Temple Bar 8171.

Morning Post, 15, Tudor Street, E.C.4. J. Whittingham. City 1500.

Motion Picture Herald (of America), 4, Golden Square, W.1. Bruce Allan. Whitehall 7541.

News Chronicle, Bouverie Street, E.C.1. A. T. Borthwick. Central 5000.

News of the World, Bouverie Street, E.C.4. Ewart Hodgson. Central 5501.

Observer, 22, Tudor Street, E.C 4. C. A. Lejeune. Central 2943.

People, 93, Long Acre, W.C.2. Hannen Swaffer. Temple Bar 2468.

Picturegoer, 93, Long Acre, W.C.2. Lionel Collier. Temple Bar 2468.

Picture Show, Fleetway House, Farringdon Street, E.C.4. Maud Hughes. City 0202.

Referee, 17, Tudor Street, E.C.4. Paul Dehn. City 0854.

Reynolds' Illustrated News, 8, Temple Avenue, E.C.4. John Ramage. City 7557.

Screen Pictorial, Henrietta Street, W.C.2. Makin.

Sketch, 346, Strand, W.C.2. Michael Orme. Temple Bar 8020.

Star, Bouverie Street, E.C.4. Richard Haestier. Central 5000.

Sunday Express, 8, Shoe Lane, E.C.4. Stephen Watts. Central 8000.

Sunday Chronicle, 200, Gray's Inn Road, W.C.1. Anthony Gibbs. Museum 9841.

Sunday Dispatch, Northcliffe House, E.C.4. Connery Chappell. Central 6000.

Sunday Graphic, 200, Gray's Inn Road, W.C.1. Harris Deans. Museum 9847.

Sunday Pictorial, Geraldine House, Fetter Lane, E.C.4. Walter Webster (W. A. Mutch). Holborn 4321.

Sunday Times, 135, Fleet Street, E.C.4. Sydney Carroll. Central 4242.

Tatler, 346, Strand, W.C.2. James Agate. Temple Bar 8020.

Times, Printing House Square, E.C.4. W. A. J. Lawrence. Central 2001.

Kinematograph Weekly Correspondents

ABERDEEN.—Alex. C. Dempster, *Aberdeen Daily Press.*

BELFAST.—David Goldstein, Cooldarrgh Park, Cavehill Road.

BIRMINGHAM.—E. Adkins, 64, Milcote Road, Smethwick.

BLACKBURN.—H. H. Green, Berwyn, Wilpshire, N. Blackburn.

BLACKPOOL.—A. Ratledge, 3, Links Road.

BRADFORD.—H. L. Overend, Wilkinson Chambers, Greengate. Idle 339.

BRIGHTON.—A. B. Hunt, 53, Stanford Road. Brighton 1756.

BRISTOL.—J. Thomas, 34, Elmgrove Road, Fishponds. Fishponds 383.

CARDIFF.—F. Hill, 27, Western Mail Chambers.

EDINBURGH.—D. Ballantine, 2, Elliott Place, Colinton, Midlothian.

GLASGOW.—W. Kempsell, 163, Hope Street.

HULL.—J. A. Goodrick, Whitefriars Carr Lane, Willerby.

LEEDS.—G. Cohen, *Yorks Evening News*, 17, Trinity Street.

LIVERPOOL.—F. Gronback, 7, Staplands Road, Broad Green. Old Swan 1873.

MANCHESTER.—F. Gronback, 7, Staplands Road, Broad Green, Liverpool.

NEWCASTLE-ON-TYNE.—T. S. Fenwick, 23, Sea View, Tynemouth.

NOTTINGHAM.—L. Richmond, 16, Teesdale Road.

PLYMOUTH.—W. T. Roberts, 94, Tavistock Road.

PORTSMOUTH.—E. J. Didymus, 120, Francis Avenue.

PRESTON.—K. Nightingale, *Lancs. Daily Press.*

ROTHERHAM.—W. Margison, "Rossendale," Wickersley Road, Wickersley. Rotherham 1

JUNK FILM DEALERS.

Artons.
British Film Cleaners.
Celluloid Products, Ltd.
Edinburgh Ciné. Supplies.
Haling, S.
Lynes, B. J., Ltd.
Manchester Film Producing Co., Ltd.

KINEMATOGRAPH ENGINEERS.

Bauer, Ltd.
Beard, R. R.
Brockliss, J. Frank, Ltd.
Brown, F., Ltd.
Brown, J., & Co.
Caplin Engineering Co.
Cinema Screen Servicing Co.
Cinesales.
Clark's Cinemachinery.
Co-operative Cinematograph Co., Ltd.
Crowe & Co.
Cricks, R. H., F.R.P.S.
Donaldson, F. G.
Dyson, J., & Co., Ltd.
Electrocord.
G.-B. Equipments.
Imperial Sound System.
Jensen, G. K., & Co.
Kamm & Co., Ltd.
Kalee, Ltd.
Knight & Co. (Engineering), Ltd.
Lancashire Dynamo & Crypto, Ltd.
Lawley Apparatus Co., Ltd.
Lippold, A.
Lynes, B. J., Ltd.
May & Baker, Ltd.
Metropolitan Sound Equipment.
Milgate, V.
Moy, Ernest F., Ltd.
Pathe Equipment.
Philips Industrial.
Provincial Cinematograph Trading.
Roe, Jack.
Rigby, Robert, Ltd.
Ross, Ltd.
Scott, R.
Sinclair, J. A., & Co.
Sound, Ltd.
Sound & Cinema Equipment, Ltd.
Vinten, W., Ltd.
Walturdaw.
Webb, W. A., Ltd.
Wheeler, J. S.
Williamson Mfg. Co.

LABORATORY EQUIPMENT.

Caplin Engineering Co.
Lawley Apparatus Co.
Moy, E. F.
Vinten, W.

LENSES.

Baldwin Cinema Services.
Bausch & Lomb.
Beck, R. & J., Ltd.

Bell & Howell.
Brockliss, J. Frank, Ltd.
Busch (Emil) Optical Co.
Cinepro.
Cotton, A.
Dallmeyer, J. H., Ltd.
Draper, W., & Co., Ltd.
Films & Equipment.
Fulvue.
Hummel Optical Co., Ltd.
L.P.D. Co
Kalee, Ltd.
Le Personne, L.
Lizars, J.
Lynes, B. J., Ltd.
Masters, D. J., Ltd.
Milgate, V.
Ross, Ltd.
Sinclair, J. A., & Co., Ltd.
Soho, Ltd.
Taylor, Taylor, Hobson, Ltd.
Walturdaw.
Zeiss-Ikon.

LIFTS (Organ & Orchestra).

Express Lift Co., Ltd. (Service, Passenger)
Furse, W. J., & Co., Ltd.
Gardiner, Sons & Co., Ltd.
General Electric Co., Ltd.
Gimson & Co. (Leicester), Ltd.
Jensen, G. K., & Co., Ltd.
Knight & Co. (Engr.), Ltd.
Lift & Engineering, Ltd.
Marryat & Scott, Ltd.

LIGHTING.
(See also Equipment Supply.)

Beard, R. R., Ltd.
Benjamin Elec., Ltd.
Berkeley Electrical.
Boro Electric Signs.
British Elec. Installation.
Brown, J., & Co.
Cooper & Smith.
Davis Bros.
Digby's.
Draper, W., & Co.
Duncan Watson (Elec. Engrs.), Ltd
Ediswan Electric.
Electrical Installation, Ltd.
Falk, Stadelmann & Co., Ltd.
Friese-Greene, Kenneth.
Furse, W. J., & Co., Ltd.
General Electric Co., Ltd.
Haden, G. N., & Sons.
Hampton & Sons, Ltd.
Harcourts, Ltd.
Hawkins, L. G., & Co.
Holophane, Ltd.
Hunt, J. A. H., Ltd.
Imperial Lighting.
Jensen, G. K., & Co.
Kalee, Ltd.
Kandem Electrical, Ltd.
Kinematograph Equipment.
Lippold, A.

London Electric Firm.
Major Equipment.
Mansell & Ogan, Ltd.
Metropolitan Vickers.
Mickelwright, Ltd.
Moon, Henry, & Sons, Ltd.
Neon Installations, Ltd.
Pathe Equipment.
Philips' Industrial.
Pride, F. H.
Siemens Electric Lamps.
Smith & Hardcastle.
Sound and Cinema Equipment.
Strand Elec. & Engineering.
Troughton & Young.
Tucker, J. H.
Utility Arts, Ltd.
Venreco, Ltd.
Walter, D., & Co.
Walturdaw, Ltd.
Webb, W. A., & Co.
Wholesale Fittings.
Wiring, Ltd.

MUSIC.

Organs.
Binns, J. J., Fitton & Haley, Ltd
Compton, John, Organ Co.
Conacher, P., & Co.
Gray & Davison.
Jardine & Co., Ltd.
Rutt, R., Spurden.
Speechley, H., & Sons.
Watkins & Watson (Organ Blowing).
Whomes, Ltd.
Wurlitzer Organs.

Instrument Dealers.
Keith Prowse.
Metzler & Co.
Piena Music Co.

Pianos.
Chappell Piano Co.
Harper Piano Co., Ltd.

Publishers.
Ascherberg, Hopwood & Crew.
Augener, Ltd.
Boosey & Hawkes, Ltd.
Bosworth & Co., Ltd.
Cary & Co.
Chester, J. & W., Ltd.
Francis, Day & Hunter.
Keith Prowse.
Lawrence Wright Music Co.
Lennox, Cecil, Ltd.
Piena Music Co.

NON-THEATRICAL EQUIPMENT.
Agfa Photo.
Artons.
Bauer Ltd.
Beard, R. R. (Studio Lighting).
Bell & Howell (Cameras).
British Needle Co., Ltd.
British Utility Films.

Brockliss, J. Frank, Ltd.
Bruce's, Ltd.
Bulman Jupiter (Screens).
Cine. Art Productions.
Cinepro.
Clark's Cinemachinery.
Community Service.
Continuous Projectors, Ltd.
Cotton, A.
Crest Films.
Dallmeyer, J. H., Ltd. (Cameras).
Day, Will (Permarec).
Electrocord.
Ensign, Ltd. (Sub-Standard Equipment
   and Library).
Film Editorial Service.
Film Industries, Ltd. (Projectors, etc.).
Films and Equipment Ltd.
Film Library, Ltd.
G.-B. Equipments.
Haling, S.
Hummel, M. & S.
Illustra Enterprises.
Kalee, Ltd.
Kamm & Co.
Kandem Electrical (Lighting).
Kodak, Ltd.
Lawley Apparatus Co.
Lizars, J.
Metropolitan Sound Equipment.
Mihaly.
Moss Pym.
Non-Flam Film Hiring Co.
Norman's Film Library.
Pathescope.
Pathe Equipment.
Portsmouth Film Service (Libraries).
RCA
Religious Film Society.
Rex Talkie Entertainments.
Robinson's Home Cinema Service.
Ross, Ltd.
Sheffield Photo Co., Ltd.
Sinclair, J. A., & Co. (Cameras).
Trix.
Soho, Ltd.
Sound Services,
Sound & Cinema Equipment, Ltd.
Stedman, R. F.
Taylor, Taylor, Hobson, Ltd.
Visual Education.
Wallace Heaton, Ltd.
Westminster Photo Ex.
Wheeler, J. S.
Wholesale Fittings Co., Ltd. (Lighting).
Zeiss-Ikon.

PLANT (Independent).
Blackstone & Co., Ltd.
British Vacuum Cleaner & Engineers.
Brown, J., & Co.
Crompton Parkinson, Ltd.
Crossley Bros., Ltd.
Duncan Watson (Elec. Engr.), Ltd.

Electrical Equipment & Carbon Co.
Ferry Engine Co., Ltd.
Fyfe, Wilson & Co., Ltd.
General Electric Co., Ltd.
Hart Accumulator Co., Ltd.
Heatly-Gresham Engineering Co.
Kamm & Co., Ltd.
Kandem Electrical, Ltd.
McLaren, J. & H., Ltd.
Metropolitan Vickers.
National Gas and Oil Eng. Co
New Pelapone Engine Co.
Norris, Henty & Gardners.
Partridge Wilson & Co.
Petters, Ltd.
Pooley & Austin.
Ruston & Hornsby, Ltd.

PRESENTATION & PRODUCTION.

Ad-Visers.
Burt Bros. (Bow), Ltd. (Artificial Flowers).
Cinema Displays.
Cinema Signs, Ltd.
Dickinson & Sayle.
Friese-Greene, K.
Harris, M. (Furniture).
Hart & Co. (Scenery).
Holophane.
Lea & Sons (Oxygen).
Leon Goodman Displays.
Progressive Publicity.
Rainbow.
Rayne, H. & W.
Strand Elec. & Eng.
Suprema Publicity.
Tilling, Thos. (Horses and Vehicles).
Weaver, George.

PRODUCERS (Entertainment).

See also Studios pp. 339-358.
Ace Films.
Amalgamated Films Assn.
Argyle Talking Pictures.
Associated British Picture Corpn.
Association Metropolitan Prods.
Associated Sound Film Industries.
Associated Talking Pictures.
Atlantic Film Productions.
British & Continental Trades, Co.
British & Dominions Film Corpn.
British Instructional Films.
British International Pictures.
British Lion Film Corporation.
British National Films.
British Screen Service.
British Sound Film Productions.
British Sound Studio.
British Utility Films.
Butcher's Film Service.
Capitol Film Corporation, Ltd.
Carnival Films.
Columbia (British) Productions.
Criterion Film Productions.
Denning Films.
Educational Films Co., Ltd.
Embassy Pictures.
Fidelity Films, Ltd.
Fox British Pictures, Ltd.
Franco-London Films.
Gainsborough Pictures (1928), Ltd.
G.-B. Instructional.
Garrett-Klement Pictures.
Gaumont-British Picture Corporation.
George Smith Productions, Ltd.
Grosvenor Sound Films, Ltd.
Hammer Productions, Ltd.
Herbert Wilcox Productions.
H. & S. Films.

Kirwan, M.B.
Lawisto Advertising.
McConnell, Hartley, Ltd.
Magnet Advertising Co.
Meteor Film Producing Society.
Metropolitan Advertising.
National Advertising Film Service
National Film Corporation.
National Progress Film Co.
New Ideal Pictures Ltd.
Non Flam Film Hiring.
Pathé Pictures.
Peerless Pictures.
Photographic Art Productions.
Pickard, T., Ltd.
Presbury, S. & Co., Ltd.
Publicity Films.
Publicity Picture Productions (and Cartoons).
Revelation Films.
Russell, J. Scott.
Scott-Russell, J.
Scottish Film Productions.
Sponsored Film Productions, Ltd.
Steuart Films.
Stanley Stock, Ltd.
Theatres Advertising Co.
Topical Productions.
U.K. Commercial Educational Films.
Visual Education.
Walton Photographic Co.
Winads.
Western Electric.
Younger Publicity Service (and Cartoons)

Educational.
Aerofilms.
Artons, Ltd.
British Instructional.
Commer. & Educ. Film Co.
Commercial Films.
Community Service.
Dorland Advertising.
Educational Films Co.
Ensign, Ltd.
G.-B. Instructional.
Gee Films.
G.P.O. Film Unit.
G. S. Enterprises.
Hodges, C. E.
Missionary Film Committee.
Non-Flam Film Hiring Co. (Artons).
Peerless Pictures.
Religious Film Society.
Revelation Films.
Sound City, Ltd.
Stanley Stock.
Visual Education.

PROJECTION EQUIPMENT.
(See also Equipment Supply.)
Agfa.
Agence Debrie (Lenses).
Bauer, Ltd.
Beard, R. R., & Co. (Spotlights).

Brockliss, J. Frank, Ltd.
Brown, J.
Cine. Requirements.
Cinema Universal Stores.
Clayton, E. C.
Continuous Projectors.
Cotton, A. (Arc Mirrors).
Cowan Mirror Protector Co.
Day, Will.
Emerton, A. R.
Ensign, Ltd.
Epalite Mirrors.
Film Industries, Ltd.
Films and Equipment, Ltd.
Fulvue Film.
G.-B. Equipment.
Hummel, M. & S.
I.P.D., Ltd.
Imperial Sound System.
Jukes, Coulson, Stokes & Co.
Kalee, Ltd.
Kamm & Co.
Kandem Electrical, Ltd.
Kershaw, A., & Son.
Kinematograph Equipment.
Lea & Son.
Lynes, B. J.
Major Equipment (Control Gear).
Metcalfe, C. P.
Metropolitan Sound Equipment.
Milgate, V.
Moy, Ernest F., Ltd.
Peeling & Vanneck (Lenses).
Philips Cine-Sonor.
Provincial Cinematograph Trading.
Rigby, Robert, Ltd.
Roe, Jack.
Ross, Ltd.
Sound and Cinema Equipment, Ltd.
Strong Electric Distributors, Ltd.
Pathé Equipment.
Vinten, W.
Walturdaw Cinema Supply.
Webb, W. A., & Co.
Western Electric.
Wheeler, J. S.
Zeiss Ikon, Ltd.

PROJECTORS.
Bauer, Ltd.
Brockliss, J. Frank, Ltd. (Simplex).
G.-B. Equipment (Gaumont).
Imperial Sound System.
Kalee, Ltd.
Kamm & Co.
Ross, Ltd.
Sound & Cinema Equipment, Ltd.
Walturdaw (Ernemann).

PUBLICATIONS.
Cinema News & Prop. Gazette.
Cinema, Theatre & General Construction.
Cinematograph Times.
Commercial Film.
Daily Film Renter.
Film Weekly.

Foyle, W. & G., Ltd.
Imperial Film Agency.
IDEAL KINEMA AND STUDIO.
KINEMATOGRAPH WEEKLY.
KINEMATOGRAPH YEAR BOOK.
Motion Picture Herald (U.S.)
Odhams Press Technical Book Dept.
Picturegoer.
Quigley Publications.
Sir Isaac Pitman & Sons.
Spotlight Casting Directory.
Talking Picture News.
Willbank Publications, Ltd.
World Film News and Cinema Quarterly.

RECTIFIERS.

Batteries, Ltd.
Brockliss, J. Frank, Ltd.
Conradty Products.
Crompton Parkinson, Ltd.
Electrical Equipment & Carbon Co.
Electrocord, Ltd.
Films & Equipment.
General Electric Co., Ltd.
Hewittic Electric Co., Ltd.
Imperial Sound System.
Lancashire Dynamo & Crypto.
Major Equipment Co., Ltd.
Metropolitan Vickers.
Morrison, A. E.
Nevelin Electric Co., Ltd.
Partridge, Wilson & Co.
Philips Industrial.
Provincial Cinematograph Trading.
Sound & Cinema Equipment, Ltd.
Walturdaw.
Westinghouse Brake & Signal Co., Ltd.

RENTERS (Entertainment).

Ace Films.
Anglo-Canadian Distribs.
Anima Film Co.
Associated British Film Distbtrs.
Bendon Trading Co.
British Empire Films.
British European Film Corpn.
British Exhibitors Films.
British Lion Film Corporation.
Butcher's Film Service.
Cavendish Pictures.
Clayton, E. C.
Clifford Kemp.
County Films (I. M. Grainge).
Collins, Pat.
Columbia Pictures.
Concordia Distributors.
Coxall, Horace.
Crest Films.
Denning Films.
Elliman, Louis.
Equity British.
Famous Films

Fidelity Films
Film Enterprises (Ireland), Ltd.
Filmophone Renters.
First National Film Distributors.
Fox Film Co.
Gaumont-British Distributors.
General Film Distributors.
Gibbs, Ben C.
H. & S. Films.
Immortal Swan Productions.
Incorporated British Renters.
Independent Film Distributors.
International Cine. Co.
International Productions.
Irish Film Renters.
Kean & Scott.
Kemp, Clifford.
Kinograph Distributors.
Levy, P.
Metropole Film Distributors.
Metro-Goldwyn-Mayer.
Mott-Cowan, M.
Napoleon Films.
National Distributors.
National Film Agency.
National Provincial Film Distributors.
New Agency Film Co.
North-Western Film Booking Agency.
Paramount Film Service.
Pathé Pictures.
Phœnix Film Service.
Photoplays, Ltd.
Portsmouth Film Service.
Producers Distributing Co. (U.K.),Ltd.
Radio Pictures, Ltd.
Reid's Film Service.
Republic Pictures Corpn.
Reliance Film Co., Ltd.
Renters, Ltd.
Reunion Films.
Sherwood Films, Ltd.
Sol Exclusives.
Sound City Distributors.
Sovereign Exclusives.
Stahl Pyramid Films.
Standard Film Agency.
Thompson, Chas.
Thompson, W. G., Productions.
United Artists Corporation.
Universal Pictures.
Viking Films, Ltd.
Warner Bros.
Wardour Films.
W. & A. Film Distributors.
White's Film Depot.
Wilton, Harry.
World's Screen Classics.

RENTERS (Commercial & Educational)

Artons, Ltd.
Bruce's, Ltd.
Cine. Art Productions.
Cinemise Film Advt. Service.
Community Film Service.
Cramer & Co.
Dorland Advertising.

Not just a rectifier but a complete mains-to-arc equipment the high overall efficiency of which will halve your power bills.

CINEMA ARC RECTIFIERS
WESTINGHOUSE BRAKE & SIGNAL CO., LTD.,
82, York Road, King's Cross, London, N.1.

Educational Films Bureau.
Ensign, Ltd.
Exclusive Films, Ltd.
Film Library, Ltd.
Foyle, W. & G.
Garrick Films.
G.P.O. Film Unit.
H. & S. Films.
Haling, S.
Jay's Film Service.
Kinograph Distributors.
Mackane, David, Productions.
Missionary Film Committee.
National Advertising Film Service.
Non-Flam. Film Hiring Co.
Norman's Film Library.
Religious Film Committee.
Russell's Animated Pictures.
Sherwood Exclusive Film Agency.
Sound Services, Ltd.
Thompson, Charles.
Visual Education.
Westminster Photo. Ex.

RUBBER FLOORING.
Dunlop Rubber Co., Ltd.
Haworth & Son.
Harrison, C. R., & Sons, Ltd.
Johns-Manville Co.
Korkoid Decorative Floors.
Leyland & Birmingham Rubber Co.
North British Rubber Co.
Oetzmann & Co., Ltd.
Peradin Rubber Sales.
Rubber Flooring Manfrs., Ltd.
Runnymede Rubber Co., Ltd.
St. Albans Rubber Co., Ltd.
St. Helen's Cable & Rubber Co.

SAFES.
Ratner Safe Co.
Tann, John, Ltd.

SAFETY DEVICES.
Brockliss, J. Frank, Ltd.
Clarke & Vigilant Sprinklers.
Dennison Kett (Iron Doors).
Furse, W. J. (Panic Bolts).
Heathman, J. H. (Fire Escapes)
Independent Sprinklers, Ltd.
Jukes, Coulson, Stokes & Co.
Kalee, Ltd.
Knight & Co. (Engrs.), Ltd.
Knock-Out Fire Extinguisher, Ltd.
Lewis & Tylor, Ltd. (Fire Hose).
Pathé Equipment.
Pyrene Co., Ltd.
Roe, Jack.
Sentry Safety Control.
Walturdaw.

SCREENS.
(See also Equipment Supply.)
Andrew, Smith, Harkness.
Baldwin Cinema Service.
Brockliss, J. Frank. Ltd.
Bull, J. F.

Bulman Jupiter Screen (1935) Co., Ltd.
Cinema Screen Servicing Co.
Cinesales, Ltd.
Hall Mfg. & Supply.
Kalee, Ltd.
Kamm & Co.
Kinematograph Equipment.
Milgate, V.
Patent Fireproof Rear Projection Screen
　　Co. (E. G. Turner).
Perforated Front Projection Screen Co.
Pin-o-lite.
Polley, H. V., Ltd.
Roe, Jack.
Sayer, F. J.
Sound & Cinema Equipment, Ltd.
Stereotone.
Superlite Screen Co., Ltd.
Walturdaw.
Webb, W. A., & Co.
Western Electric.
Westone. (See Andrew, Smith, Harkness.)

SEATING.
(See also Equipment Supply.)
Allied Guilds.
Baker, Harry.
Beck & Windibank.
Brockliss, J. Frank, Ltd.
Brooks, J. B., & Co., Ltd. (Steel).
Buoyant Upholstery.
Carpets & Curtains, Ltd.
Carpenter, F. H.
Cine. Requirements.
Collins, J., & Sons.
Cox & Co. (Steel).
Dunlop Rubber Co., Ltd.
Emerton, A. R.
Empire Seating Co., Ltd.
Evans, C. J., & Co.
Friese-Greene, Kenneth.
Haling, S.
Hall & Dixon.
Hampton & Sons.
Harrison, C. R., & Sons.
Harrods.
Haworth & Son.
Hellenbrand, J. H.
Kalee, Ltd.
Kinematograph Equipment Co.
Lazarus, H., & Son.
Lindsay-Hickman, Ltd.
Lister & Co. (Fabrics).
Lockwood, L. B., & Co.
Lusty, W., & Sons, Ltd.
Maple & Co.
Mitchell Russell (Chair Standards).
Pathé·Equipment.
Paterson (Glasgow), Ltd.
Pixton's Ltd.
Sayer, F. J.
Shaw, J., Son, & Co.
Sound & Cinema Equipment, Ltd.
Thompson & Dean, Ltd.
Trinity Chair Works.

Turner, Lord.
Turner, W. W., & Co.
United Kinema Supplies.
Universal Seating.
Walturdaw.
Waring & Gillow.
Webb, W. A., & Co.
Wolfe & Hollander.
Wylie & Lockhead.

SIGNS (Illuminated).
Accurate Check Taker.
Allied Guilds.
Boro' Electric Signs.
Brilliant Neon, Ltd.
Brilliant Sign Co.
British Electrical Installation Co
Claude-General Neon Lights Cinema Signs.
Davis Bros.
Digby's.
Etna Lighting & Heating.
Falk Stadelmann & Co., Ltd.
Fieldson & Co.
Franco-British Electrical.
General Electric Co., Ltd.
Girosign, Ltd.
Gordon Cook.
Hailwood & Ackroyd.
Holophane, Ltd.
Hunt, J. A. H.
Imperial Lighting Co.
Ionlite.
K.F.M. Engineering Co.
Major Equipment.
Moviesigns.
Nash & Hull.
Neon Manufacturers, Ltd.
Pride, F. H.
Siemens' Electric Lamps.
Strand & Interch. Signs.
Tubolume.
Venreco, Ltd.

SLIDES.
(See also Equipment Supply)
Autotype Co., Ltd.
Baker, Herbert.
Brockliss, J. Frank, Ltd.
Brown, J., & Co., Ltd.
Cawthra, N.
Chalmers, John.
Cinema Signs.
Cleveleys Advertising Co.
Community Service.
Cramer, P. A., & Co.
Girosign, Ltd.
Gordon, Cook & Co.
Heywood, John, Ltd.
Kalee, Ltd.
Kinematograph Equipment.
Kirwan, M. B., Ltd.
Lawisto Advertising Co.
Lizars, J.
Metropolitan Advertising Co.
Morgan's Projected Publicity.

Pathé Equipment.
Perfect Opaque Lantern Plates.
Presbury, S, & Co.,.Ltd.
Sinclair, J. A., & Co.
Slide House, Ltd.
Smith, P.
T. D. S. Advertising.
Theatres Advertising.
Vevers, C. C.
Willsons.
Younger Publicity Service.

SOUND INSULATION AND MATERIAL.
Christie and Grey.
Cullum, H. W., & Co., Ltd.
Honeywill & Stein, Ltd.
Lithalun Products.
Newall's Insulation Products.
Williams, H. L.

SOUND REPRODUCING EQUIPMENT.
(See also Amplifiers.)
Sound on Film.
  A.W.H. Sound Repro. Co.
  Bauer, Ltd.
  Beck, R. & J.
  Birmingham Sound Reproducers.
  British Acoustic.
  Brockliss, J. Frank, Ltd.
  B.T.-H.
  British Sound Film Productions.
  British Radio Corporation (Speakers).
  British Talking Pictures.
  Electrocord.
  Epoch (Speakers).
  Radio Development Co.
  Film Industries.
  Films & Equipment.
  G.-B. Equipments.
  Gramo-Radio (speaker).
  Imperial Sound System.
  Kamm & Co.
  Mihaly Service, Ltd.
  Morrison, E. A., & Sons, Ltd.
  Moy, Ernest F., Ltd.
  Partridge & Mee.
  Philips Cine-Sonor.
  Prism Mfg. Co. (Public Address).
  RCA Photophone.
  Rothermel (Speakers).
  Scientific Sound System,
  Sound, Ltd.
  Sound & Cinema Equipment, Ltd.
  Synchropone (Records).
  Tanar British Corporation.
  Trix Electrical Co., Ltd.
  Vinten, W.
  Voigt Patents (Speakers).
  Western Electric.

Non Sync.
  British Needle Co.
  Columbia Graphophone.
  Filmophone.
  Gramophone Co.
  Gramo-Radio.

Igranic.
Lever (Trix).
Will Day (Permarec).

SOUND RECORDING (Film.
Bauer, Ltd.
Blue-Light, Ltd.
British Acoustic.
British Talking Pictures.
Caplin Engineering.
Films & Equipment.
Gramo-Radio.
Leevers, Rich, & Co., Ltd. (Mobile).
Partridge & Mee.
Philips Cine-Sonor.
RCA Photophone.
Tanar British Corporation.
Vinten, W., Ltd.
Visatone.
Voigt Patents, Ltd.
Western Electric.

STAGE EQUIPMENT.
(See also Equipment Supply.)
Baldwin, H. G.
Beard, R. R., Ltd.
Beck & Windibank.
Berkeley Electrical.
Brockliss, J. Frank, Ltd.
Brown, J., & Co., Ltd.
Bulman Jupiter Screen Co.
Burkitt, Frank, Ltd.
Carpenter, F. H., & Co.
Carpets & Curtains, Ltd.
Curtis Manufacturing Co.
Dennison, Kett & Co., Ltd. (Fireproof
    Shutters).
Digby, Robert, Ltd.
Draper, W., & Co.
Etna Lighting & Heating.
Express Lift Co.
Furse, W. J., & Co.
General Electric Co., Ltd.
Geipel, Wm., Ltd.
Gibson, A. L. (Fireproof Shutters).
Gimson & Co. (Leicester), Ltd.
Hall Manufacturing & Supply Co., Ltd.
Hampton & Sons.
Hart & Co.
Heathman, J. H.
Heaton Tabb.
Holophane, Ltd.
Jensen, G. K., & Co.
Kandem Electrical, Ltd.
Kinematograph Equipment Co.
Knight & Co. (Engineers), Ltd.
Lippold, A.
Major Equipment.
Mallin, John, & Co.
Mansell & Ogan.
Mickelwright, Ltd.
Milgate, V.
Polley, H. V., Ltd.
Pride, F. H.
Rigby, Robert, Ltd.
Sayer, F. J.
Strand Electric & Engineering.
T.D.S. Advertising, Ltd.
Venreco, Ltd.
Walter, D., & Co.
Walturdaw.
Webb, W. A., & Co.

STILLS.
Autotype Co., Ltd. (Enlargements).
Bruce's Ltd.
Girosign, Ltd. (Illuminated)
Gray, Eric.

Kodak.
Russell's Animated Pictures.
Salisbury Photo Press.
Vevers, C. C.

STOCK SHOTS
Clark's Cinemachinery.
International Photographic.
Norman's Film Library.
Crest Films.

TELEVISION APPARATUS.
Baird Television Apparatus.
Bauer, Ltd.
General Electric Co., Ltd.
Gramophone Co., Ltd.
Moy, Ernest F., Ltd.
Scophony, Ltd.

STUDIO SUPPLIES
Autotype Co., Ltd. (Photographic Back-
    grounds).
Beard, R. R.
Bell & Howell.
Blue-Light, Ltd. (Editing Table).
British Schufftan Process.
Brockliss, J. Frank, Ltd.
Cotton, A.
Films and Equipment.
Fulvue-Film.
General Electric Co., Ltd.
Hart & Co. (Scenery).
Harris, M., & Sons (Period Furniture).
Hummel (Lenses).
International Photographic (Back-
    grounds).
Kandem Electrical.
Lynes, B. J., Ltd.
Lyon, J. S., Ltd. (Furniture Hire).
Moy, Ernest F.
Philips Cine-Sonor.
Rigby, Robert, Ltd.
Sinclair, J. A., & Co.
Venreco, Ltd.
Vinten, W.
Duncan Watson.
Walter, D., & Co.
World Location Co. (Location).

STUDIOS.
(See pages 339-358)

TICKETS & TICKET ISSUING
MACHINES.
Accurate Check.
Automaticket.
Bell Punch Co., Ltd.
Booth, Hy. (Hull).
Brandt Automatic Cashier.
Guys of Cardiff.
Kalee, Ltd.
Omnia Kine. Apparatus.
Willsons.

TITLE MAKERS.
Studio Film Laboratories.

TRADE SHOW THEATRES.
Crown Theatre.
Bauer, Ltd.
G-B. Distributors.
Western Electric.
Zenifilms.

TRAILERS.
British Screen Service.
Dorland Advertising Co.
National Screen Service.
Standard Kine Laboratories, Ltd.
Studio Film Labs.
Winads.

WESTERN ELECTRIC SOUND

will never be outmoded or

taken by surprise . . . it is

something that is and always

will be as new as tomorrow

 IT IS THE STANDARD
OF THE INDUSTRY

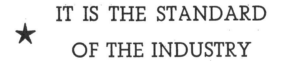

WESTERN ELECTRIC LIMITED, BUSH HOUSE, ALDWYCH, W.C.2

TRANSPORT
Ackers.
Baggott Bros.
Barlow, J.
Birchenough, J.
Blackpool Film Transport.
Brown, G.
Bury & District Film Transport.
Cambridge & District Film Transport.
Crampton, W.
Cooke, F.
Davidson, A.
Doyle, Henry.
East London Film Motor Service
Eastern Counties Film Service.
Ferrar, G., & Sons.
Film Clearing Houses.
F.T.S. (Great Britain), Ltd.
Film Transport Co., Ltd.
Greenwood, P. A.
Hampshire Transport Co.
Heeley, A. & M.
Herts & Beds.
Hoyle, R.
Kent Films Motor Transport.
Lincoln & District Film Transport.
London & East Anglian Film Transport.
London & Provincial Films Motor Trans.
London, Slough & District Transport.
May & Sons, Ltd.
Miller, J.
Muller, W. H., & Co. (London), Ltd.
Norman's Film Library.
Northcourt Film Services, Ltd.
Norfolk & District Films Transport.
Northern Transport Agency.
North Kent Film Service.
Oxford Film Transport.

Oxon & Bucks Film Transport.
Parkes, H. T.
Potteries Transport.
Powers & Privileges.
Smith Film Transporter.
Southern & Suburban.
Stevenson, V. & J.
Sussex Film Transport.
Tate Bros.
Tilling, Thomas, Ltd.
United Automobile Services.
West Sussex Film Transport.
Wilson, C. R.
Wright, W.

UNIFORMS.
Angel, Morris.
Army & Navy Supply.
Beevers.
Berman, M., Ltd.
Fairfax.
Harold (Uniforms), Ltd.
Neuman & Co., Ltd.
Parsons & Stewart.
Simons, M.
Uniform Clothing & Equipment Co.
Uniform Supply Co., Ltd.

VACUUM CLEANING.
Barr & Co.
British Vacuum Cleaner & Engineering Co.
Foxwell, Daniel, & Sons, Ltd.
General Electric Co., Ltd.
Jeffreys & Co., Ltd.
Lamson Pneumatic.
Siemens Electric Lamps.
Sturtevant Engineering Oo., Ltd.
Visco Engineering Co.

Our Leading Companies

Official Details and Personnel

Associated British Picture Corporation Ltd., formerly British International Pictures, Ltd.

Incorporated March 20, 1926.
Directorate: John Maxwell (Chairman and Managing Director), Sir Clement Kinloch-Cooke, Bart., K.B.E., Jerome Denny Bright, William Douglas Scrimgeour, Maurice Arthur Dent and Robert Gordon Simpson, M.C. Secretary, George Hind Gaunt. *Authorised Capital:* £4,000,000 divided into 2,000,000 6 per cent. first Cum. Pref. Shares of £1 each and 8,000,000 Ordinary Shares of 5s. each. *Issued Capital:* 2,000,000 6 per cent. first Cum. Pref. Shares of £1 each fully paid and 6,200,000 Ordinary Shares of 5s. each fully paid.
Film House, Wardour Street, London, W.1.

Associated Sound Film Industries Ltd.

Incorporated October 31, 1929.
Directorate: F. W. E. Morgan (Chairman), M. R. Cahill, W. M. Campbell, B. A. A. Thomas, J. W. Vincent. Secretary, G. Morgan. *Authorised Capital:* £1,000,000 divided into 1,000,000 Ordinary Shares of 10s. each and 500,000 8 per cent. Participating Preference Shares of £1 each. *Issued Capital:* £500,000 and £135,707 respectively.
Wembley Park.

British and Dominions Film Corporation, Ltd.

Incorporated February 13, 1928.
Directorate: E. Ronald Cramond (Chairman) C. M. Woolf (Managing Director), Herbert S Wilcox, Capt. the Hon. R. Norton and W. H Cockburn. Secretary, A. L. Dugon, A.C.A *Authorised Capital:* £500,000 in shares of £1 each.
Film House, 142, Wardour Street, London, W.1.

British Lion Film Corporation, Ltd.

Incorporated November 27, 1927.
Directorate: Samuel Woolf Smith, (Chairman and Man. Director), N. L. Nathanson, A. P. Holt, I. C. Flower and Sir Robert John Lynn, M.P. Secretary: H. W. Franklin, F.C.A. *Authorised Capital:* £750,000.
76-78, Wardour Street, London, W.1.

British National Films, Ltd.

Incorporated July 30, 1934.
Directorate: J. Arthur Rank (Chairman), Lady Yule and John Corfield. *Authorised Capital:* £100,000. Private Company.
Pinewood Studios, Iver Heath, Bucks.

British Talking Pictures, Ltd.

Incorporated August 3, 1928.
Directorate: F. W. E. Morgan (Chairman), M. R. Cahill, W. M. Campbell, H. Holt, Sir Nairne Sandeman, Bart., M.P., B. A. A. Thomas and J. W. Vincent. Secretary, G. Morgan. *Authorised Capital:* £500,000. *Issued Capital:* £464,452.
River Plate House, Finsbury Circus, London, E.C.2.

Columbia Pictures Corporation, Ltd.

Incorporated September 17, 1929.
Directorate: Harry Cohn, Jack Cohn, H. Sydney Wright, A. Schneider, G. R. Webb, Jos. Friedman (Managing Director) and Max Thorpe. Secretary: George Maidment. *Authorised Capital:* £25,000.
139, Wardour Street, London, W.1.

County Cinemas, Limited.

Incorporated July 20, 1927.
Directorate: J. Amery-Parkes, George Gee, W. D. Bartholomew, Commander G. P. Lewis, M. Silverstone (alternate G. Archibald), and C. J. Donada. Secretary: G. M. J. L. Whitmore, B.A. *Authorised Capital:* £125,000, divided into 10,000 7½ per cent. First Preference, 20,000 7½ per cent. Second Preference, and 95,000 Ordinary Shares of £1 each. *Issued Capital:* £108,707, divided into 10,000 7½ per cent. First Preference, 9,215 8 per cent. Second Preference, and 89,492 Ordinary Shares of £1 each fully paid.
Dean House, Dean Street, London, W.1.

Denman Picture Houses, Ltd.

Incorporated March 12, 1928.
President: Isidore Ostrer. *Directorate:* Mark Ostrer (Chairman), Col. H. A. Micklem, C.B., C.M.G., D.S.O., M. Ostrer, R. H. Gillespie, and M. E. Balcon. Secretary, W. B. Robinson. *Authorised Capital:* £1,650,000 in 3,300,000 Ordinary Shares of 10s. each. *Issued Capital:* £1,400,000 in 2,800,000 Ordinary Shares of 10s. each fully paid. *Debenture Stock Authorised.* Issued and outstanding £3,027,444, less £62,062 stock redeemed. 5 per cent. First Mortgage Debenture Stock. Registered Office: 142-150, Wardour Street, London, W.1.

First National Film Distributors, Ltd.

Incorporated October 15, 1931.
Directorate: D. E. Griffiths (Man. Director)· Sam E. Morris, Max Milder and E. G. M Fletcher, Secretary, D. A. Harber. *Authorised Capital:* £1,600.
Warner House, 135-141, Wardour Street, London, W.1.

Fox Film Co., Ltd.

Incorporated March 25, 1916.
Directorate: S. R. Kent (Chairman), F. L. Harley (Managing Director), W. J. Hutchinson, W. C. Michel and R. Sutton Dawes. Secretary, K. N. Hargreaves. *Authorised and Issued Capital:* £2,000 in shares of £1 each, fully paid.
13, Berners Street, London, W.1.

Gainsborough Pictures (1928), Ltd.

Incorporated April 27, 1928.
Directorate: Mark Ostrer (Chairman), Maurice Ostrer, and Michael Balcon (Man. Director), Secretary, W. B. Robinson. *Authorised Capital:* £262,500. *Issued Capital:* £156,250.
Film House, Wardour Street, London, W.1.

P

Gaumont-British Distributors, Ltd., formerly Gaumont-Ideal, Ltd.

Directorate : Isidore Ostrer, Mark Ostrer, Maurice Ostrer, Leon Gaumont, J. Bernerd and David Ostrer. Joint Secretaries, W. B. Robinson and E. R. Russell. *Authorised and Issued Capital :* £35,826 of £1 each. 142-150, Wardour Street, London, W.1.

Gaumont-British Picture Corporation, Ltd.

Incorporated March 24, 1927.

President : Isidore Ostrer. *Vice-President :* Viscount Lee of Fareham, P.C. *Directorate :* Mark Ostrer (Chairman and Man. Director), M. Ostrer (Assistant Man. Director), Col. H. A. Micklen, C.B., C.M.G., D.S.O., S. R. Kent, D. Boardman, O. H. C. Balfour, C.M.G., John Maxwell, C. H Dade and I. P. Little. Secretary, W. B. Robinson. *Authorised Share Capital :* 3,250,000 5½ per cent. Cum. First Préf. Shares of £1 each. 5,000,000 Ordinary Shares of 10s. each, 2,000,000 "A" Ordinary Shares of 5s. each. *Issued Share Capital :* £3,250,000 5½ per cent. Cum. First Pref. Shares of £1 each fully paid, 5,000,000 Ordinary Shares of 10s. each fully paid, 2,000,000 "A" Ordinary Shares of 5s. each fully paid. *Debenture Stock—Authorised :* £6,500,000 4½ per cent. First Mortgage Debenture Stock, *Issued and Outstanding:* £5,160,000 less £123,282 redeemed to date. 142-150, Wardour Street, London, W.1 (Registered Offices). 25-31, Moorgate Street, London, E.C.2 (Transfer Offices). 123, Regent Street, London, W.1. (Theatre Management Offices).

General Theatre Corporation, Ltd.

Incorporated February 11, 1928. *President:* Isidore Ostrer. *Directorate :* Mark Ostrer (Chairman), George Black, Maurice Ostrer and J. Bernerd. Secretary, W. B. Robinson.

Authorised Share Capital :

1,250,000 15% Participating Preferred Ordinary shares of 6s. 8d. each	416,666	13	4
1,550,883 Ordinary shares of £1 each	1,550,883	0	0
650,000 Ordinary shares of 1s. each	32,500	0	0
	£1,999,999	13	4

Issued Share Capital :

1,250,000 Participating Preferred Ordinary shares of 6s. 8d. each fully paid ...	416,666	13	4
650,000 Ordinary shares of 1s. each fully paid	32,500	0	0
	£449,166	13	4

6½ per cent. First Mortgage Debenture Stock authorised and issued £2,250,000. *Outstanding* £1,951,071.

Registered Offices : 142-150, Wardour Street, London, W.1.

Transfer Office : 25-31, Moorgate Street, London, E.C.2.

General Film Distributors, Ltd.

Incorporated May 27, 1935.

Directorate : Lord Portal of Laverstoke (Chairman), C. M. Woolf (Managing Director), P Lindenberg, J. Arthur Rank, D.L., J.P., L. W. Farrow, M. Woolf, L. A. Neel. Secretary, Harold Rogers. *Issued Capital :* £270,000. Private Company. 127-133, Wardour Street, London, W.1.

G.B. Equipments, Ltd.

Incorporated June 9, 1933. *Directorate :* Maurice Ostrer, H. Clayton, I. H. Cremieu-Javal. Secretary, H. S. White. *Authorised and Issued Capital :* £5,000 of £1 each. 142-150, Wardour Street, London, W.1.

G-B Instructional, Ltd.

Incorporated November 6, 1933. *Directorate :* Maurice Ostrer (Chairman), Harry Clayton, H. B. Woolfe, I. H. Cremieu-Javal, and Miss Mary Field, M.A. Secretary, H. S. White. *Authorised and Issued Capital :* 2,000 in £1 Shares. Private Company. 142-150, Wardour Street, London, W.1.

Ilford, Ltd.

Incorporated May 17, 1898. *Directorate :* Sir Ivor Philipps, K.C.B., D.S.O. (Chairman), Colonel F. W. Evatt, Capt. T. Midgley Illingworth, W. H. Dimsdale, R. D. Lewis, Major D. Blundell Mein, D.S.O., M.C., F. F. Renwick, and B. L. Drake. Secretary, B. L. Drake, F.C.I.S. *Authorised Capital :* £1,400,000. *Issued Capital :* £1,264,200. 23, Roden Street, Ilford Essex.

Kodak, Limited.

Incorporated, November 15th, 1898. *Directorate :*—Walter Gregory Bent, Ernest Edgar Blake, Granville Edward Bromley-Martin, Harold Stuart Carpenter, John Cuthbert Denison-Pender, Frank William Lovejoy, Ernest Augustus Wicks Maitland, Francis Charles Mattison, John Theodore Cuthbert Moore-Brabazon and William Robert Webb. Secretary, William Heatley Faulkner. *Authorised and Issued Capital :* 350,000 £1 Ordinary Shares. Kodak House, Kingsway, London, W.C.2.

London Film Productions, Ltd.

Incorporated February 13, 1932. *Directorate :* Alexander Korda (Chairman and Managing Director), J. R. Sutro, H. A. Holmes, E. Stevinson, C. Holmes Brand, and Sir Connop Guthrie, Bt., K.B.E. Secretary, E. H. George. *Authorised Capital :* £825,000 divided into 375,000 First Pref. shares of £1 each, 350,000 6 per cent. Cum. Participating Pref. Ord. Shares of £1 each and 2,000,000 Deferred Ord. shares of 1s. each. *Issued Capital :* £428,799 in 333,549 6 per cent. Cum. Participating Pref. Ord. shares of £1 each, and 1,905,000 Def. Ord. shares of 1s. each, both fully paid. Denham Studios, Denham, Bucks.

Metro-Goldwyn-Mayer Pictures, Ltd.

Incorporated August 20, 1924. *Directorate :* S. Eckman, Junr. (Man. Director), Arthur M. Loew, J. Robert Rubin, H. Sydney Wright and J. C. Squier. Secretary, G. R. Webb. *Authorised Capital :* £200,000. *Issued Capital :* 100,000 Ordinary Shares of £1 each, and 57,455 7 per cent. Preference Shares. 19-21, Tower Street, London, W.C.2.

Moss Empires, Ltd.

Incorporated December 15, 1899.

Directorate: James John Gillespie (Chairman), Richard Henry Gillespie (Man. Director), John Thompson, Walter Payne, Alfred Claude Bromhead, Reginald Charles Bromhead, Mark Ostrer and George Black. Secretary, David Simpson, S.S.C. *Authorised Capital:* £1,361,000 in 500,000 cum. 5 per cent. Pref. shares of £1 each and 861,000 Ordinary shares of £1 each. *Issued Capital:* £1,339,785 in 478,785 cum. 5 per cent. Pref. shares of £1 each, and 861,000 Ordinary shares of £1 each. *Four per cent. Debenture Stock:* Authorised £400,000, Issued and Subscribed, £370,987. 4½ per cent. Debenture Stock. *Authorised,* £400,000 ; *Issued and Subscribed,* £200,000.

4, Charlotte Square, Edinburgh.

Odeon Theatres Limited.

Incorporated October 13, 1933.

Directorate: Oscar Deutsch (Chairman and Governing Director), Frederick Stanley Bates, William George Elcock. Secretary: William George Elcock. *Authorised Capital:* £200,000 divided into 150,000 6 per cent. Preference shares of £1, and 100,000 Ordinary shares of 10s. each. *Issued Capital:* 150,000 6 per cent. Preference shares of £1 each, 100,000 Ordinary shares of 10s. each.

39, Temple Row, Birmingham.

Paramount Film Service, Ltd.

Incorporated February 8, 1915, as J. D. Walker's World's Films, Ltd. ; title changed March 19, 1919, to Famous Lasky Film Service, Ltd. ; title changed to Paramount Film Service, Ltd., June 27, 1930.

Directorate: John Cecil Graham (Chairman and Man. Director), Edward Ayres and Cecil Frank Karuth. Secretary, Edward Ayres. *Authorised and Issued Capital:* £20,000.

162-170, Wardour Street, London, W.1.

Pathe Pictures, Ltd.

Incorporated 1911.

Directorate: John Maxwell (Chairman), W. J. Gell (Man. Director), and William Douglas Scrimgeour. Secretary, E. Mann: Private company.

103, Wardour Street, London, W.1.

Pinewood Studios, Ltd.

Incorporated August 2, 1935.

Directorate: J. Arthur Rank (Chairman), E. Ronald Crammond (Vice-Chairman), Capt. The Hon. R. Norton (Managing Director), Charles Boot, Herbert Wilcox, C. M. Woolf, John Corfield, Spencer M. Reis, W. H. Cockburn, and Harold G. Judd. General Secretary, A. L. Dugon. Secretary, M. L. Axworthy. Private Company. *Authorised Capital:* £300,000. Fulmer Road, Iver Heath, Bucks.

Provincial Cinematograph Theatres, Ltd.

Incorporated November 12, 1909.

Directorate: Mark Ostrer (Chairman and Man. Director), Sir William F. Jury, Maurice Ostrer, Col. H. A. Micklem, C.B., C.M.G., D.S.O., and A. W. Jarratt. Secretary, Edmund A. Crisp. *Authorised and Issued Capital:* £3,200,000 divided into 100,000 7½ per cent. "A" Cumulative Preference Shares of £1 each ; 600,000 7½ per cent. "B" Cumulative Preference Shares of £1 each ; 2,000,000 7½ per cent. Cumulative Participating Preferred Ordinary Shares of £1 each ; and 1,000,000 Ordinary Shares of 10s. each.

New Gallery House, 123, Regent Street, London, W.1.

RCA Photophone, Ltd.

Incorporated September 10, 1929.

Directorate: B. Gardner (Managing Director), E. T. Cunningham, J. Moxon Broad, F. R. Deakins, B. E. G. Mittell, and R. H. Oxley. General Manager and Secretary, A. Collins. *Authorised and Issued Capital:* £10,000.

Electra House, Victoria Embankment, London, W.C.2.

Radio Pictures, Ltd.

Incorporated June 18, 1930.

Directorate: R. J. Hanbury (Chairman and Managing Director), A. Clark, M. H. Aylesworth, R. F. Holme and G. W. Dawson (also Secretary). *Authorised and Issued Capital:* £10,000 in 10,000 Ordinary Shares of £1 each.

2, 3 and 4, Dean Street, Soho, London, W.1

Sound City (Films), Ltd.

Incorporated July 21, 1933.

Directorate: Norman Greenlees Weir Loudon (Chairman and Managing Director), Lawrence Grandfield Hill and John Patrick Steacy. Secretary, Lawrence Grandfield Hill. *Authorised Capital:* £875,000 divided into 175,000 6 per cent. Cum. Participating Pref. shares of £1 each, and 700,000 Ordinary shares of 5s. each. *Issued Capital:* 134,800 6 per cent. Cum. Participating Pref. shares of £1 each and 624,852 Ordinary shares of 5s. each.

Registered Office, Sound City, Shepperton, Middlesex. Registrar and Transfer Office, F. R. Allen, 3 and 4, Clement's Inn, London, W.C.2.

Stoll Picture Productions, Ltd.

Incorporated May 6, 1920.

Directorate: Sir Oswald Stoll (Chairman and Man. Director), Sir James Marchant, K.B.E., LL.D., Llewellyn Johns, Oswald Leslie Stoll and Lincoln Erlanger Stoll. *Authorised and issued Capital:* £458,393 divided into 200,000 8 per cent. Cumulative Participating Preference Shares of £1 each ; 58,393 8 per cent. "B" Cumulative Preference Shares of £1 each ; and 200,000 Ordinary Shares of £1 each.

The Stoll Offices, Coliseum Buildings, London, W.C.2.

Union Cinemas, Ltd.

Incorporated December, 16, 1936.

Directorate: David Bernhard (Chairman), Charles Frederick Bernhard (Managing Director) and Lawrence Joseph Clements. Secretary, Alfred Ernest Davis. *Authorised Capital:* £6,500,000 divided into 2,000,000 Redeemable 6 per cent. Cumulative First Preference Shares of £1 each, 1,500,000 Redeemable 6 per cent. Cumulative Second Preference Shares of £1 each, 10,000,000 "A" Ordinary Shares of 5s. each, 2,000,000 Ordinary Shares of 5s. each. *Issued Share Capital:* £3,264,724 divided into: First Preference shares 657,406, £657,406 ; Second Preference shares 657,406, £657,406 ; "A" Ordinary shares 5,839,227, £1,459,806 15s. ; Ordinary shares 1,960,421, £490,105 5s.

15, Regent Street, London, S.W.1.

United Artists Corporation, Ltd.

Incorporated as The Allied Artists Corporation, Ltd., March 15, 1921. Name changed by permission of the Board of Trade March 4, 1929, to United Artists Corporation, Ltd.

Directorate: M. Silverstone (Chairman and Managing Director), Mary Pickford, Arthur W. Kelley, James A. Mulvey, F. M. Guedalla, E. T. Carr, G. Archibald, J.P. (also Secretary and Treasurer), Sir Connop Guthrie, Bt., K.B.E. *Authorised Capital:* £7,500.

Film House, Wardour Street, London, W.1.

United Picture Theatres, Ltd.

Incorporated January 12, 1928.

Directorate: Mark Ostrer (Chairman and Man. Director), A. W. Jarratt and A. E. de B. Jennings. Secretary, E. A. Crisp. *Authorised Capital:* £525,000 divided into 500,000 10 per cent. Participating Preferred Ordinary Shares of £1 each and 500,000 Deferred Shares of 1s. each. *Issued Capital:* 500,000 10 per cent. Participating Preferred Ordinary Shares of £1 each and 500,000 Deferred Shares of 1s. each.

New Gallery House, 123, Regent Street, W.1.

Universal Pictures, Ltd.

Incorporated as European Motion Picture Co., Ltd., May 11, 1922. Name changed by permission of the Board of Trade, July 2, 1929.

Directorate: M. Woolf,· S. F. Ditcham (Man. Director) and H. Rogers.

127–133, Wardour Street, London, W.1.

Walturdaw Cinema Supply Co., Ltd.

Incorporated 1896.

Directorate: Col. J. W. Abraham (Chairman), and N. R. Armitage. Secretary, A. Cecil Ayling. Private company.

46, Gerrard Street, London, W.1.

Wardour Films, Ltd.

Incorporated October 28, 1916.

Directorate: John Maxwell (Chairman), Maurice Arthur Dent, William Douglas Scrimgeour, and George Hind Gaunt (also Secretary). *Authorised and Issued Capital:* £50,000 in 50,000 Ordinary Shares of £1 each.

Film House, Wardour Street, London, W.1.

Warner Bros. Pictures, Ltd.

Incorporated June 8, 1912, as Vitagraph Co., Ltd. Title changed November 1, 1926.

Directorate: Max Milder (Man. Director), D. E. Griffith, Dr. E. G. M. Fletcher and S. E. Morris. Secretary, W. Turner. *Authorised and Issued Capital:* £5,000.

Warner House, Wardour Street, London, W.1

Western Electric Co., Ltd.

Incorporated April 15, 1929.

Directorate: W. A. Bach, Whitford Drake (U.S.A.), E. P. L. Pelly, J. A. Hall (U.S.A.), H. L: Marsterson, E. M. Hall (U.S.A.), J. H. Somake and H. C. Humphrey (U.S.A.). Secretary, J. H. Somake. *Authorised and Issued Capital:* £20,000.

Bush House, Aldwych, London, W.C.2.

WURLITZER

THE PIONEERS OF UNIT ORGANS, FAULT-LESS IN CONSTRUCTION, SUPREME IN TONAL BEAUTY.

THE ONLY ORGAN WHICH ADDS "GAIETY" TO YOUR ENTERTAINMENT.

CHOSEN BY LEADING SHOWMEN PHILIP HYAMS AND SIDNEY BERNSTEIN—A RECOGNITION OF THESE OUTSTANDING FEATURES.

SOME NOTABLE INSTALLATIONS

Bedford—Granada.
Belfast—Classic.
Blackpool—Empress Ballroom.
Blackpool—Tower Ballroom.
Bristol—Regent.
Bournemouth—Regent.
Exeter—Gaumont.
Kingston—Regal.
London — Crystalate Gramophone Studio ; Empire, Leicester Sq. ; Granada, Tooting ; Leicester Sq. Theatre ; Metropole, Victoria; New Gallery. Plaza, Piccadilly ; Tivoli, Strand ; Trocadero, Elephant ; Troxy, Stepney.
Leeds—Paramount.
Manchester—Gaumont
Manchester—Paramount.
Newcastle—Paramount.

WURLITZER
LEICESTER SQUARE CHAMBERS, LEICESTER SQUARE, W.C.2

DIRECTORY

OF

KINEMAS

IN THE

UNITED KINGDOM

AND

IRELAND

With the exception of circuit halls, which are arranged under the general heading of the proprietary company or individual, the theatres of the country are arranged ALPHABETICALLY by TOWNS under the headings of LONDON, ENGLAND, WALES, SCOTLAND, IRISH FREE STATE and NORTHERN IRELAND.

INDEX

THEATRE CIRCUITS, &c.

Registered Offices, Phones and Halls in Circuits.

ABERTILLERY THEATRES, LTD.—Booking Office : **Carlisle House, Abertillery.**
Chairman : ALFRED WITHERS.
Managing Director : ALFRED WITHERS and JACKSON WITHERS.
Secretary : RUPERT PROSSER.
Telephone : Abertillery 3.
Empress Cinema, Abertillery
Gaiety, Abertillery.
Metropole, Abertillery.
Pavilion Theatre, Abertillery.
Palace, Abertillery.

A. & C. THEATRES, LTD.—Head Office Picture House, **Station Road, Redhill.**
Managing Director : M. LEONARD ABRAHAMS.
Telephone : REDHILL 104.
Picture House, Redhill.
Pavilion, Redhill.
Pavilion, Tonbridge.
Star Cinema, Tonbridge.
Capitol, Tonbridge

ACADEMY CINEMA CO.—Head Office : **286, High Street North, East Ham, E.12.**
Proprietors : W. T. SCRIVEN and W. HUXTABLE.
General Manager : ARTHUR TENCH
Telephone : Grangewood 1059.
Academy Cinema, Leytonstone.
Picture Coliseum, Upton Park.
Coliseum Cinema, East Ham.

AD-VISERS, LTD.—Office : **Panton House, 25, Haymarket, London, S.W.1.**
Telephone : Whitehall 3332.
Malvern Theatre, Malvern.
Picture House, Malvern.
Link Picture Theatre, Malvern.

AGER-CIRCUIT.—Address : **10, Church Street, Colchester.**
Proprietor : AGER'S CINEMA CIRCUIT, LTD.
Telephone : Colchester 3681.
Woodbridge Theatre, Woodbridge.
Gainsborough Theatre, Sudbury.

AMESBURY CINEMAS.—Head Office : **Plaza, Amesbury, Wilts.**
General Manager : HUGH R. S. DUNCAN.
Telephone : Amesbury 354.
Plaza, Amesbury.
Playhouse, Moreton-in-Marsh.
Regal, Warminster.

ASSOCIATED BRITISH CINEMAS, LTD.—Office : **30-31, Golden Square, London, W.1.**
Chairman and Managing Director : JOHN MAXWELL.
General Manager : A. S. MOSS.
Telephone : Gerrard 7887.
Telegrams : Britcin, Piccy.

Savoy, Bradford.
Savoy, Chorlton-cum-Hardy
Queen's, Cardiff.
Pavilion, Cardiff.
Regal, Hammersmith.
Westover, Bournemouth.
Bordesley Palace, Birmingham
Premier, Manchester.
Claremont, Manchester.
Gaiety, Birmingham.
Adelphi, Hay Mills, Birmingham.
Aston Cross Picture House, Birmingham
Hippodrome, Nuneaton.
Olympia, Darlaston.
Plaza, West Bromwich.
Empire, Crewe.
Picture House, Edgbaston
Playhouse, Miles Platting.
Broadway, Hammersmith
Capitol, Wallasey.
King's, Bristol.
Lido, Golders Green.
Olympia, Newport.
Picture House, Doncaster.
Regent, Chatham.
Regent, Great Yarmouth.
New Coliseum, Whitley Bay.
Princes, Leicester.
Empire, Rotherham
Vandyck, Bristol.
Capitol, Barking.
Ritz, Bordesley Green.
Hippodrome, Willesden.
Grand, Mansfield.
Savoy, Brighton.
Forum, New Street, Birmingham.
Grand, Warrington.
Capitol, Winchmore Hill.
Hippodrome, Belfast.
Plaza, Dover.
Regal, Lincoln.
Majestic, Northampton.
Savoy, Northampton.
Empire, Derby.
Forum, Liverpool.
Commodore, Liverpool.
Carlton, Boscombe.
Marina, Lowestoft.
Rialto, Hull.
Hippodrome, Sheffield.
Palladium, Oldham.
Capitol, St. Helens.
Savoy, Wandsworth.
Empire, Islington.
Ritz, Edgware.
Picture House, Balham.
Bedford, Camden Town.
Palace, Camberwell.
Commodore, Southsea.

Empire, Bristol.
Playhouse, Colchester.
Hippodrome, Ipswich.
Albion, Castleford.
Melbourne, Leicester.
Savoy, Newcastle-under-Lyme.
Rialto, Broughton.
Hippodrome, Stockport.
Theatre Royal, Chorley.
La Scala, Manchester.
Queens, Openshaw.
Regal, Bolton.
Majestic, Blackburn.
Palladium, Brixton.
Coronation, Manor Park.
Queens, Forest Gate.
Lido, Ealing.
Alhambra, Moseley Road, Birmingham.
Palace, Burnley.
Casino, Rusholme.
Picture House, Ardwick.
New Royal, Openshaw.
Olympia, Liverpool.
Palace, Erdington.
Orient, Aston.
Robin Hood, Birmingham.
New Empress, Nottingham.
Theatre Royal, Wolverhampton
Majestic, Mitcham.
Regal, Purley.
Ritz, Leeds.
Ritz, Southgate.
Olympia, Shoreditch.
Hippodrome, Poplar.
Whiteladies, Bristol.
Triangle, Bristol.
Beau Nash, Bath.
Majestic, Stoke.
Capitol, Hanley.
Grainger, Newcastle.
Regal, Marble Arch.
Hippodrome, Croydon.
Dominion, Walthamstow.
Central, Reading.
Rialto, Coventry Street, W.1.
Regal, Walham Green.
Forum, Ealing.
Carlton, Essex Road.
Forum, Kentish Town.
Ritz, Neasden.
Palaseum, Commercial Road.
Rex, Stratford.
Carlton, Upton Park.
Hippodrome, Rotherhithe.
Roxy, Blackheath.
Royalty, Ladbroke Grove.
Queens, Bayswater.
Prince of Wales, Harrow Road.
Palace, Kensal Rise.
Hippodrome, Putney.
Hippodrome, Woolwich.
Majestic, Woodford.
Regent, Kings Cross.
Savoy, Teddington.
Palladium, Mile End.

Astoria, Brighton.
Granada, Hove.
Grand, Bournemouth.
Granada, Dover.
Gaiety, Southsea.
Park, Bristol.
Cabot, Filton, Bristol.
Burlington, Torquay.
Plaza, Plymouth.
Castle, Merthyr Tydfil.
Theatre Royal, Merthyr Tydfil.
Hippodrome, Norwich.
Trocadero, Tankerton.
Central, Canterbury.
Regal, Canterbury.
Forum, Southampton.
Oak, Selly Oak.
Tudor, Birmingham.
Empire, Stirchley, Birmingham.
Elite, Bordesley Green, Birmingham.
Royalty, Harborne, Birmingham.
Palace, Summerhill, Birmingham.
Metropole, Snow Hill, Birmingham.
Crown, Ladywood, Birmingham.
Regal, Handsworth, Birmingham.
Astoria, Aston.
Picture House, Erdington.
Popular, Derby.
Rialto, Wednesbury.
Regent, Tipton.
Empire, Longton.
Regent, Bradford.
Playhouse, Dewsbury.
Empire, Huddersfield.
Central, Kidderminster.
Empire, Kidderminster.
Gaiety, Manchester.
Capitol, Bolton.
Savoy, Blackburn.
Olympia, Darwen.
Palladium, Oswaldtwistle.
Carlton, Liverpool.
Granada, Liverpool.
Regent, Liverpool.
Regal, Norris Green, Liverpool.
Astoria, Walton, Liverpool.
Coliseum, Walton, Liverpool.
Victory, Walton, Liverpool.
Popular, Liverpool.
Gem, Liverpool.
New Coliseum, Paddington, Liverpool.
Regent, Tranmere.
Theatre Royal, Preston.
Haymarket, Newcastle.
Embassy, North Harrow.
Empire, Mile End Road.
Langham, Pinner.
Rex, Leytonstone.
Savoy, East Acton.
Ritz, Harringay.
Dominion, Southall.
Dominion, Harrow.
Savoy, Croydon.
Regal, Hackney.
Savoy, Enfield.

Savoy, Stoke Newington.
Ritz, Muswell Hill.
Rex, Norbury.
Regal, Old Kent Road.
Regal, Wembley.
Olympia, Cardiff.
Atherley, Southampton.
Broadway, Southampton.
Plaza, Worthing.
Savoy, Exeter.
Savoy, Swindon.
Regal, Salisbury.
Regal, Lincoln.
Regal, Wakefield.
Elite, Middlesbrough.
Scala, Middlesbrough.
Empire, Stockton-on-Tees.
Gaiety, Leeds.
Strand, Grimsby.
Tivoli, Grimsby.
Prince of Wales, Grimsby.
Regal, Cambridge.
Piccadilly, Birmingham.
New Palladium, Hockley, Birmingham.
New Imperial, Moseley Road, Birmingham.
Tower, West Bromwich.
Regal, Chesterfield.
Her Majesty's, Walsall.
Grand, Walsall.
Imperial, Walsall.
Palace, Walsall.
County Theatre, Warwick.
Forum, Wythenshawe, Manchester.
Electra, Cheadle.
Reo, Fazakerley, Liverpool.
Belmont, Liverpool.
Regent, Crosby, Liverpool.
Savoy, St. Helens.
Palace, Ashton-in-Makerfield:
Gainsborough, Bootle.

AND CONTROLLING AND ASSOCIATED WITH :—

SCOTTISH CINEMA AND VARIETY THEATRES,
LTD.—Head Office : 105, St. Vincent Street,
Glasgow.
General Manager : D. A. STEWART, J.P.
Telephone : Central 2830.
Telegrams : Cinesup, Glasgow.
King's, Charing X, Glasgow.
The Bank, Clydebank.
Palace, Clydebank.
Prince's, Springburn, Glasgow.
Portbrae Picture House, Kirkcaldy.
King's, Montrose.
Palace, Arbroath.
Govan Cinema, Govan, Glasgow.
Empire, Clydebank.
Opera House, Kirkcaldy.
Coliseum, Glasgow.
Palace, Dundee.
Regal, Kilmarnock.
Plaza, Wishaw.
La Scala, Motherwell.
Regal, Glasgow.
Arcadia, Glasgow.
Waverley, Glasgow.
Govanhill, Glasgow.
Dennistoun, Glasgow.
Phoenix, Glasgow.
Ritz, Cambuslang.
Plaza, Dundee.
Ritz, Edinburgh.
Picture House, Falkirk.
George, Kilmarnock.
Ritz, Oatlands.
Rex Picture House, Riddrie.
Regal, Greenock.
Regal, Hamilton.
Rialto, Cathcart.
Picture Palace, Parkhead.

Grosvenor, Hillhead.
Savoy, Stockbridge.
Palace, Kirkcaldy.
Rialto, Dumbarton.
Regal, Dumfries.
Regal, Stirling.
Regal, Falkirk.
Regal, Paisley.
Mayfair, Battlefield.
Toledo, Muirend.
Lyceum, Edinburgh.
Tower, Helensburg.
Regal, Coatbridge.
Playhouse, Galashiels.
Rex, Motherwell.
SCALA (BIRKENHEAD), LIMITED.
Scala, Birkenhead.
BLACKPOOL ENTERTAINMENTS (1920), LIMITED.
Hippodrome, Blackpool.
Princess, Blackpool.
ALEXANDRA PICTURE HOUSE AND THEATRE CO.,
LTD.
Regent, Norwich.
BURLINGTON PICTURE HOUSE (TORQUAY),
LIMITED.
Regal, Torquay.
ELEPHANT & CASTLE THEATRE, LIMITED.
Elephant & Castle Theatre, London, S.E.
EMPIRE THEATRE (COVENTRY), LIMITED.
Empire, Coventry.
B. H. S. SYNDICATE, LIMITED.
Mayfair, Tooting.
PRINCESS (DAGENHAM), LIMITED.
Princess, Dagenham.
PAVILION (STIRCHLEY), LIMITED.
Pavilion, Stirchley.
PAVILION (WYLDE GREEN), LIMITED.
Pavilion, Wylde Green.
LEWISHAM CINEMA, LIMITED.
Prince of Wales, Lewisham.
ATTRACTIVE CINEMA (HAMMERSMITH), LIMITED.
Commodore, Hammersmith.
ATTRACTIVE CINEMA (FOREST HILL), LIMITED.
Capitol, Forest Hill.
FORUM THEATRE, LTD.
Forum, Fulham Road.
GOLDEN DOMES (STREATHAM), LTD.
Golden Domes, Streatham.
WIMBLEDON AMUSEMENTS, LTD.
Elite, Wimbledon.
ASTORIA (CLIFTONVILLE), LTD.
Astoria, Cliftonville.
ELITE PICTURE THEATRE (NOTTINGHAM) LTD.
Elite, Nottingham.
TRAFFORD PICTURE HOUSE, LTD.
Picture House, Old Trafford.

**ATKINSON PICTURES, LTD.—Head Office :
9, North Road, St. Andrews, Bristol 6.**

Telephone : Bristol 44190.

Ashton Cinema, Bristol.
Hotwells Cinema, Bristol.
Plaza Cinema, Bristol.
Scala Cinema, Bristol.
Town Hall Cinema, Bedminster, Bristol.
Vestry Hall, Bristol.

**BAMFORD, SIDNEY.—Head Office 28,
Grainger Street, Newcastle.**

Telephone : Central 25614.

Central Cinema, Blyth.
King George Hall, Cramlington.
Shipcote Hall, Gateshead.
Howard Hall, North Shields.
Royalty Cinema, Gosforth.

**BANCROFT, (H), CIRCUIT.—Head Office :
Hippodrome, Wisbech.**
Telephone : Wisbech 116.
Hippodrome, Wisbech.
Hippodrome, Huntingdon.
New Hippodrome, March.
Hippodrome, Holbeach.
Palace, Peterborough.
Rex, Ely.
City Cinema, Peterborough.
Empire, Wisbech.
Empress, Chatteris.
Regent, March.
Public Rooms, Ely.

**BARBER, GEO. H.—Head Office : Palace,
Tunstall, Staffs.**
Prop. : ALDERMAN GEO. H. BARBER, J.P.
Gen. Manager : COUNCILLOR E. A. BARBER.
Telephone : Hanley 7453.
Telegrams : Palace, Tunstall, Staffs.
Palace, Tunstall.
Regent Hall, Tunstall.
Palace, Wolverton.
Scala, Stony Stratford.

**B.B. CINEMA CIRCUIT.—West Down, Nea
Ilfracombe.**
Proprietor : CAPTAIN J. H. BLACKHURST.
Telephone : Ilfracombe 7.
Telegrams : Blackhurst, West Down.
B.B. Cinema, Hatherleigh.
B.B. Cinema, Lynton.
B.B. Cinema, Dulverton.
B.B. Cinema, Princetown.

**BEDFORD CINEMAS (1928), LTD.—Head
Office : 19, Castle Street, Liverpool 2.**
Managing Director : JOHN F. WOOD.
Booking Manager : W. J. McAREE.
Telephone : Central 1544.
Telegrams : Logical, Liverpool.
Plaza, Birkenhead.
Rialto, Bebington, Ches.
Curzon, Old Swan, Liverpool.
Empire, Garston, Liverpool.

**BENTLEY, (WALTER), CIRCUIT.—Head Office :
40, Shaftesbury Avenue, London, W.1.**
Telephone : Gerrard 6607.
Telegrams : Yeltneb, Lesquare, London.
Regent, Totton.
Savoy, Totton.

**BERNSTEIN-THEATRES, LTD.—Address : 36,
Golden Square, London, W.1.**
Managing Director : SIDNEY L. BERNSTEIN.
Telephone : Gerrard 3554.
Telegrams : Berdarold, Piccy, London.
Granada, Tooting.
Granada, Walthamstow.
Granada, Wandsworth.
Granada, East Ham.
Granada, Bedford.
Granada, Maidstone.
Granada, Willesden.
Granada, Shrewsbury.
Kings, Shrewsbury.
Empire, Shrewsbury.
County, Shrewsbury.
Plaza, Sutton.
Plaza, Rugby.
Plaza, Mansfield.
Hippodrome, Mansfield.
Regal, Rugby.
Regent, Rugby.
Regal, Oswestry.
Cinema, Loughton.
Rialto, Leytonstone.

Rialto, Enfield.
Empire, Edmonton.
Empire, Bedford.
Electrodrome, Bow.
Kinema, Plumstead.
Kinema, West Ham.

**BLACK'S THEATRES.—Head Office :
Suite 9, 115, Shaftesbury Avenue, London,
W.C.2.**
Managing Director : ALFRED BLACK.
Telephone : Temple Bar 9324.
Black's Regal Theatre, Sunderland.
Black's Regal Theatre, Byker, Newcastle.
Coliseum, Ilford.
New Rink, Sunderland.
Black's Regal Theatre, South Shields.
Black's Theatre, Gateshead-on-Tyne
Black's Royal Theatre, Sunderland.

**BLUE HALLS, LTD.—Office : Coronation House,
4, Lloyd's Avenue, London, E.C.3.**
General Manager and Secretary : H. LENNOX.
Telephone : Royal 6158/9.
Blue Hall, Edgware Road, W.
Palladium Opera House, Brighton.
Coliseum, Harrow.
Broadway Cinema, Harrow.
State, Thornton Heath.

**S. S. BLYTH KINEMAS, LTD.—Address :
Waterloo Chambers, Newcastle-on-Tyne.**
Managing Director : SOL SHECKMAN.
Telephone : Newcastle-on-Tyne 27864.
Royal, Blyth.
Hippodrome, Blyth.
Empire, Blyth.
Royal, Middlesbrough.

**BRANFORD'S (V.) CIRCUIT.—Head Office :
Gaiety Cinema, Whitehaven.**
Telephone : Whitehaven 124.
Queen's, Whitehaven.
Gaiety, Whitehaven.
Garrison Theatre, Catterick Camp
Alhambra, Penrith.
Palace, Wigton.
Grand Theatre, Cockermouth.

**JAMES BRENNAN'S CINEMAS.—Head Office
107, Duke Street, Barrow-in-Furness.**
Proprietor : JAMES BRENNAN.
Secretary : W. H. COLMAN.
Telephone : Barrow 990.
Telegrams : Brennan, Barrow.
Empire Cinema, Dalton-in-Furness
The Kinema, Carnforth.
Verona, Knott End, near Fleetwood.

**BRITISH CINEMATOGRAPH THEATRES.
LTD.—Head Office : 199, Piccadilly, W.1**
Managing Director : A. W. BANNER, O.B.E
Telephone : Regent 1227.
Picture House, Above Bar, Southampton.
Picture House, Tavern Street, Ipswich.
Empire Cinema, Fore Street, Ipswich.
Grand Cinema, Desborough Road, High Wy_
combe.

**BROWN, J. & CO.—Office : 228, Fulwood Road,
Sheffield.**
Manager : R. O. BROWN.
Telephone : Sheffield 61126.
Town Hall, Wirksworth.
Memorial Hall, Eyam.
Memorial Hall, Bradwell.
Memorial Hall, Hathersage, Sheffield.

BURTON-ON-TRENT PICTUREDROME CO., LTD.—Head Office : 44, Victoria Crescent, Burton-on-Trent.
Booking Manager : Miss A. ORTON.
Telephone : Burton-on-Trent 3588.
Picturedrome, Burton-on-Trent.
Regent Cinema, Burton-on-Trent.
Ritz Cinema, Burton-on-Trent.

BURY ST. EDMUNDS CINEMAS, LTD.—54, Chevallier Street, Ipswich.
Telephone : Ipswich 4036.
Telegrams : Lekas, Ipswich.
Regal, Brightlingsea.
Playhouse, Bury St. Edmunds.
Central Cinema, Bury St. Edmunds.
Playhouse, Haverhill, Suffolk.
Empire, Haverhill, Suffolk.
Broadway Kinema, St. Ives, Hunts.
Empire, Dovercourt.
Regal, Dovercourt.
Regent, Dovercourt.
Palace, Harwich.
Regal Cinema, Swaffham.
Kinema, Dunmow.
Kinema, Coggeshall.
Regal, Watton.

JOSEPH AND HARRY BUXTON CIRCUIT.—Head Office. : Cinema House, 4, Grange View, Leeds.
Managing Director : HARRY BUXTON.
Telephone : Leeds 41594.
Telegrams : Buxton, Leeds.
Regent Cinema, Blackburn.
Tatler Cinema, Bradford.
Hippodrome, Colne.
King's Colne.
Savoy, Super, Colne.
Regal Super Cinema, Dewsbury.
Town Hall, Mirfield.
Majestic Cinema, Dewsbury.
Roxy, Birkenhead.
Roxy, Blackburn.
Kings, Blackburn.
Roxy, Halifax.
Hippodrome, Hulme.
Pavilion, Liverpool.
Junction Cinema, Manchester.

CAPITAL AND PROVINCIAL NEWS THEATRES, LTD.—Head Office, 172, Buckingham Palace Road, London, S.W.1.
Telephone : Sloane 9132.
Victoria Station News Theatre.
Waterloo Station News Theatre.
Eros News Theatre, Shaftesbury Avenue, W.1.
Cinenews, Tooting.
Tatler News Theatre, Liverpool.
Cinenews, Portsmouth.

CARDIFF CINEMA CORPN., LTD.—Head Office : 7, St. Andrew's Crescent, Cardiff.
Managing Director : Max Corne.
Telephone : Cardiff 7279.
Telegrams : Cardiff Cinema Corporation.
Castle Cinema, Caerphilly.
Palladium Cinema, Pontypridd.
White Palace, Pontypridd.

PERCIVAL J. CARTER.—Head Office : Palace Blandford, Dorset.
Telephone : Blandford 12.
Telegrams : Palace, Blandford.
Palace, Blandford.
Savoy, Shaftesbury.
Carlton, Sherborne.
Palace, Gillingham.
Plaza, Wincanton.

CASTLE AND CENTRAL CINEMAS, LTD.—Address : 3, 5 and 7, The Hayes, Cardiff, Directors : F. E. ANDREWS, A. ANDREWS, W. ANDREWS, P. ANDREWS.
Telephone : Cardiff 2982.
Telegrams : Omnibus, Cardiff.
Central Cinema, The Hayes, Cardiff.
Castle Cinema, Worcester Place, Swansea.
Central Cinema, Hannah Street, Porth.

CHESHIRE COUNTY CINEMAS, LTD.—Head Office : Empress Theatre, Runcorn.
Telephone : Runcorn 199.
Empress, Runcorn.
King's, Runcorn.
Scala, Runcorn.
Pavilion, Northwich.
Plaza, Northwich.
Central, Northwich.
New Theatre, Northwitch (Building).
Co-op., Widnes.

CHESHIRE PICTURE HALLS, LTD.—Head Office : Park Road North, Birkenhead.
Secretary : W. A. WALLACE.
Telephone : Birkenhead 3524.
Coliseum Picture House, Birkenhead.
Empire Cinema, Birkenhead.
Palladium, Birkenhead.
Avenue, Birkenhead.
Picture House, Moreton.
Lyceum, New Ferry.

CINEMA HOUSE, LTD.—Cinema House, 225, Oxford Street, London, W1.
Secretary : H. G. Clark.
Telephones : Gerrard 3814-3818.
Telegrams : Screenopic, Wesdo.
Hippodrome, Sheerness.
Academy, 167, Oxford Street.
Picturedrome, Gloucester.
Oxford, Sheerness.
Empire, Park End, Gloucester.
King's, Gloucester.
Chingford Cinema, Chingford.

CINEMA (ROTHERHAM) & ELECTRA, LTD.—Head Office : Regent Theatre, Howard Street, Rotherham.
General Manager : W. F. SYKES.
Telephone : Rotherham 291.
Telegrams : Regent, Rotherham.
Regent Theatre, Rotherham.
Cinema House, Rotherham.

CLAVERING & ROSE.—Head Office : 199, Piccadilly, W.1.
Telephone : Regent 1146.
Empire, Walthamstow.
Queen's, Walthamstow.
Plaza, Leyton.
King's Cinema, Leyton.
Cameo News Theatre, Charing Cross Road, W.
Piccadilly News Theatre, Gt. Windmill Street, W.
Broadway Cinema, New Cross.
Cameo News Theatre, Victoria Street, S.W.1.

CLAYTON, E. C.—Bank Chambers, 70 The Moor, Sheffield 1.
Telephone : Sheffield 24673.
Heeley Electric Theatre, Sheffield.
Oxford Picture Palace, Sheffield.
Pavilion, Attercliffe, Sheffield.
Lyric Picture House, Darnall, Sheffield.
Hoyland Cinema, near Barnsley.
Strand Cinema, Douglas, I.O.M.
Picture House, Douglas, I.O.M.
Pavilion, Peel, Isle of Man
Strand Cinema, Port Erin, I.O.M.

Palace, Woodseats, Sheffield.
Regal, Rawmarsh (near Rotherham).
Princess Theatre, Hoyland (near Barnsley).

COLISEUM CINEMA (SOUTHPORT), LTD.—Regd. Office : 3, Tulketh Street, Southport.
Coliseum, Southport.
Palace, Southport.
Scala, Southport.
Plaza, Ainsdale.

COOPER, E. OWEN.—Office : Palace Cinema, Hadleigh, Suffolk.
Phone : Hadleigh 81.
Palace, Hadleigh, Suffolk.
Regent, Hertford.
Plaza Cinema, Manningtree.

COUNTY CINEMAS, LTD.—Head Office : Dean House, Dean Street, London, W.1.
Managing Director : CHARLES J. DONADA.
Telephone : Gerrard 4543.
Telegrams : Cinecounty, Rath, London.
County, Fleet.
County, Marlow.
County, Farncombe.
County, Bletchley.
Alexandra, Aldershot.
Manor Park Pavilion, Aldershot.
County, Weybridge.
Plaza, Chichester.
Playhouse, Guildford.
Plaza, Guildford. ·
Regal, Colchester.
Headgate, Colchester.
Royal, Winchester.
COUNTY CINEMAS (WYCOMBE & STAINES) LTD.
Majestic, Staines.
Majestic, High Wycombe.
EMPIRE (ALDERSHOT) LTD.
Empire, Aldershot.
PAVILION (READING) LTD.
Pavilion, Reading.
Vaudeville, Reading.
ASSOCIATED THEATRE (WEMBLEY) LTD.
Majestic, Wembley.
Capitol, Wembley.
LIDO (HOVE) LTD.
Lido, Hove.
REGAL (HAMPSTEAD) LTD.
Regal, Golders Green.
REGAL (CAMBERLEY) LTD.
Regal, Camberley.
Arcade, Camberley.
REGAL (FARNHAM) LTD.
Regal, Farnham.
County, Farnham.
S.E. CINEMAS, LTD.
Beacon, Smethwick.
Cinema, Tyseley.
LICHFIELD CINEMA, LTD.
Regal, Lichfield.
REGAL (WIMBLEDON) LTD.
Regal, Wimbledon.
RITZ (NOTTINGHAM) LTD.
Ritz, Nottingham.
HULL CITY & SUBURBAN CINEMAS, LTD.
Regal, Hull.
Rex, Hull.
Royalty, Hull.
Regis, Hull.
Regal, Beverley.
SCALA (FARNBOROUGH) LTD.
Scala, Farnborough.
REGAL (SOUTHAMPTON) LTD.
Regal, Southampton.
Plaza, Southampton.
REGAL (MARGATE) LTD.
Regal, Margate.

ORPHEUM THEATRE (FINCHLEY) LTD.
Orpheum, Golders Green.
RITZ (SOUTHEND) LTD.
Ritz, Southend.
REGAL (GODALMING) LTD.
Regal, Godalming.
RITZ (CHELMSFORD) LTD.
Ritz, Chelmsford.
ASSOCIATED THEATRES (P. A. & D.) LTD.
Astoria, Folkestone.
Astoria, Southend.
Regent, Aberdeen.
Palace, Aberdeen.
Hippodrome, Derby.
Hippodrome, Devonport.
Regent, Plymouth.
NORWICH CINEMAS LTD.
Carlton, Norwich.

J. DAVIS CIRCUIT.—Address : 147, Wardour Street, London, W.1.
Managing Director : J. DAVIS.
Telephone : Gerrard 1416.
Boleyn Electric Theatre, East Ham.
Broadway Cinema, East Ham.
Corinth Cinema, Hayes.
Electric Palace, Deptford.
Golden Domes, Camberwell.
Monseigneur News Theatre, Piccadilly.
Sphere News Theatre, Tottenham Court Road.
Strand News Theatre, Agar Street, Strand.
Monseigneur, Strand.
Monseigneur, Edinburgh.
Monseigneur, Charing Cross.
Monseigneur, Leicester Square.
Monseigneur, Fargate, Sheffield.
Monseigneur, Leeds.
Monseigneur, Park Lane, Marble Arch.

CHARLES K. DEEMING CIRCUIT.—Address : Grand Cinema, Coalville.
Managing Director : CHARLES K. DEEMING.
Telephone : Coalville 56.
Telegrams : Deeming, Coalville.
Grand Cinema, Coalville.
Regal Cinema, Coalville.
Picture House, Cannock, Staffs.
Picture House, Rugeley, Staffs.
Victory Cinema, Loughborough.
Empire Cinema, Loughborough.
Theatre Royal, Loughborough.
Premier Dance Hall, Loughborough.

TRUEMAN DICKEN CINEMAS.—Head Office " Majestic," Burnham-on-Sea.
Prop. and Gen Man. : W. TRUEMAN DICKEN.
Telephone : Burnham-on-Sea (Som.) 107.
Majestic, Burnham-on-Sea. ·
Ritz, Burnham-on-Sea.
Arcade Cinema, Bridgwater.
Town Hall Cinema, Bridgwater.
Palladium, Midsomer Norton.
Palace, Radstock.
Victoria Hall, Newtown, N. Wales (Leased to B. C. Woods).

DUNDEALGAN ELECTRIC THEATRE CO., LTD.— Registered Offices : St. Helena, Dundalk.
Secretary : Con O'Mahony.
Telephone : Dundalk 116.
White Horse Hotel, Drogheda.
Whitworth Hall, Drogheda.
Town Hall, Enniskillen.

EAGLE PICTUREDROMES, LTD.—Registered Office : County Playhouse, King Street, Wigan.
Telephone : Wigan 3476.
County Playhouse, Wigan.
Gidlow Picture House, Wigan.

Queen's Theatre, Pemberton.
Carlton, Pemberton.
Palace, Platt Bridge.
Savoy, Atherton.
Palace, Atherton.
Majestic, Tyldesley. (*Union Playhouses, Ltd.*)
Lyme House Cinema, Prescot. (*Lyme House Cinemas, Ltd.*)
Palace, Prescot. (*Lyme House Cinemas, Ltd.*)
Rivoli, St. Helens. (*County Playhouses, Ltd.*)

EASTERN COUNTIES CINEMAS, LTD.—Head Office : Regent Theatre, Moulsham Street, Chelmsford.
General Manager : R. GERALD BALLS.
Telephone : Chelmsford 2094.
Telegrams : Regent Theatre, Chelmsford.
Electric Theatre, Norwich.
Regent Theatre, Chelmsford.
Empire Picture House, Chelmsford.
Empire Theatre, Norwich.

ELITE ENTERTAINMENTS SYNDICATE.— Address : East Church Street, Buckie.
Telephone : Buckie 106.
Palace Cinema, Buckie.
Palace Cinema, Keith.
Palace Cinema, Nairn.
Palace Cinema, Huntly.

ELITE PICTURE HOUSE, LTD.—Registered Office : Elite Picture House, Toller Lane, Bradford.
Managing Director : JOHN E. ANDERTON.
Telephone : Bradford 3576.
Elite Picture House, Bradford.
Coliseum, Bradford.
Picturedrome, Bradford.

ELLIS'S CINEMATOGRAPH THEATRES.— Head Office : Homeside, Higher Warberry, Torquay.
Sole Proprietor and Managing Director A. O. ELLIS.
Telephone : Torquay 2895.
Electric Palace, Paignton.
Electric Theatre, Brixham.
Electric Theatre, Tiverton.
Empire, Plymouth.
Tudor Theatre, Torquay.

ELTON, HERBERT.—Head Office : Commerce Chambers, Elite Buildings, Nottingham.
Telephone : Nottingham 42364.
Forum, Aspley, Nottingham.
Rialto, Sutton-in-Ashfield.
Tivoli, Sutton-in-Ashfield.
King's, Sutton-in-Ashfield.
Portland, Sutton-in-Ashfield.
Astoria, Tenton Abbey, Beeston.
Empire, Alfreton.
Empire, Heanor.
Empire, Ripley.
Empire, Somercotes.
Victory, Stapleford.

J. F. EMERY'S CIRCUIT.—Head Office : Midland Bank House, 26, Cross Street, Manchester.
Proprietor : J. F. EMERY, J.P., M.P.
Telephones : Blackfriars 0472 and Pendleton 2611.
Shakespeare, Cheetham.
New Central Hall, Collyhurst.
Empire, Broughton.
Empress Cinema, Pendleton.
Scala, Pendleton
Market Street Picture House, Manchester.
Oxford Picture House, Manchester.
Palace, Walkden.

Dominion, Salford.
Royal, Pendleton.
Adelphi, Swinton.
Plaza, Swinton.
Rex Cinema, Salford.
Weaste, Salford.
Savoy, Darwen.
Savoy, Gorton.
Royal, Rochdale Road.
Regal, Sheffield.
Star, Sheffield.
Wicker, Sheffield.

FENTON CIRCUIT.—Head Office : 16, Central Buildings, Darlington.
Telephone : Darlington 2496.
Garrison Cinema, Catterick Camp.
Central Cinema, Darlington.

FIFESHIRE CINEMA CO., LTD.—Head Office : Leven, Fifeshire.
General Manager : JAMES RODEN.
Telephone : Leven 147.
Globe, Buckhaven.
Empire, East Wemyss.
Regent, Leven.

FORBES'S.—Address : Palace Theatre, Glasgow. S.S.
Telephone : South 270 and Western 4100.
Palace Theatre, Gorbals Street, Glasgow, C5.
Olympia, Bridgeton, Glasgow.
Pavilion, Largs.

FYFE AND FYFE, LTD.—Head Office : 55, Bath Street, Glasgow.
Booking Manager : R. MAXWELL.
Telephone : Douglas 706.
Telegrams : Douglas 706.
Pavilion Theatre, Galashiels.
Pavilion Theatre, Forfar.

GAUMONT-BRITISH PICTURE CORPORA-TION, LTD., & ASSOCIATED COMPANIES, —Offices : 142/150, Wardour Street, London, W.1.
President : ISIDORE OSTRER.
Vice-President : THE RT. HON. VISCOUNT LEE OF FAREHAM, P.C.
Chairman : MARK OSTRER.
Managing Director : MARK OSTRER.
Telephone : Gerrard 9292.
Telegrams : Gaupicor, Rath, London.
Theatre Management Office : 123, Regent Street, London, W.1.
Telephone : Regent 8080.
Telegrams : Procynthe, Piccy, London.
GAUMONT-BRITISH PICTURE CORPORATION, LTD
Marble Arch Pavilion.
Shepherd's Bush Pavilion.
News Theatre, Shaftesbury Avenue.
Tatler, Charing Cross Road.
Empire, Holloway.
Gaumont Palace, Streatham.
Dalston Picture House.
Britannia, Hoxton.
Electric Pavilion, Lavender Hill.
Gaumont Palace, Camden Town.
Gaumont Palace, Lewisham.
Empire Picture House, Hanley.
Hippodrome, Stoke.
Coliseum, Burslem.
Empire, Bradford.
Savoy, Glasgow.
Academy Picture Theatre, Brighton.
Coliseum, Newport.
New Palace, Bristol.
Savoy, Plymouth.
Empire, Colchester.
Hippodrome, Colchester.

Savoy, Grimsby.
Palais de Danse, Wimbledon.
Gaumont Palace, Coventry.
Gaumont Palace, Birmingham.
Gaumont. Manchester.
Majestic, Rochester.

DENMAN PICTURE HOUSES, LTD.
Super Cinema, West Kensington.
Grand Kinema, Edgware Road.
Canterbury Music Hall, Westminster
   Bridge Road.
Ye Olde Varieties Cinema, Hoxton
Hoxton Cinema.
Imperial Playhouse, Stratford.
Ambassadors, Hendon.
Grand, Bromley.
Palais de Luxe, Bromley.
Broadway Super Cinema, Stratford.
Palmadium, Palmers Green.
Canning Town Cinema.
Grand Cinema, Canning Town.
New Cross Kinema.
Lion, Rotherhithe.
Grand Hall, North Finchley.
New Bohemia, Finchley.
Gaumont, Finchley.
Gaumont, Bromley.
Empire Kinema, Plumstead.
Kinema, West Ham.
Empire Kinema, East Ham.
Empire, Willesden.
Rialto, Enfield.
Rialto, Leytonstone.
Empire, Edmonton.
Queen's Hall, Cricklewood.
Queen's Hall, Rushey Green.
Pavilion, Balham.
King's Theatre, Sunderland.
Borough Theatre, North Shields.
Borough Theatre, Wallsend.
Grand Theatre, Byker.
Scala Theatre, Gateshead.
New Palace Theatre, Gateshead.
Parade Picture House, Dennistoun.
New Pavilion Theatre, Newcastle-on-Tyne.
New Westgate Theatre, Newcastle-on-Tyne.
Hippodrome, Middlesbrough.
Gaumont Palace, Middlesbrough.
Pavilion, Middlesbrough.
Empire, Whitley Bay.
Picture House, West Hartlepool.
Coliseum, Leeds.
Pavilion, Leeds.
Assembly Rooms, Leeds.
Scala, Leeds.
Morley Street, Bradford.
St. George's Hall, Bradford.
Scala, Harrogate.
Empire, Barnsley.
Princess, Barnsley.
Carlton, Wakefield.
Empire, Wakefield.
Picture House, Saltaire.
Corona Cinema, Gt. Crosby.
Rivoli, Aigburth.
Gaumont, Dingle.
Empress Picture House, Tue Brook.
Electric Theatre, York.
Electric Theatre, Halifax.
Grand Theatre, Nottingham.
Electra Palace, Nottingham.
Mechanics' Hall, Nottingham.
Electric Pavilion, Kettering.
King's Hall, Penge.
Princes Picture Playhouse, Kennington.
Tivoli, Partick, Glasgow.
Gaumont Palace, Redditch.
Electric Theatre, Sowerby Bridge
La Scala, Alloa.

Alhambra, Perth.
La Scala, Hamilton.
Picture Theatre, Bellshill.
Rialto, Kirkcaldy.
Palladium, Plymouth.
Hippodrome, Thornley.
Albert Hall, Sheffield.
Corona, Manchester.
Electric Theatre, Burton-on-Trent.
Magnet Cinema, Wavertree.
Grand Cinema, Liverpool.
Beresford Cinema, Liverpool.
Tower, Morecambe.
Empire Picture House, Dudley.
Haymarket Picture House, Norwich.
Empire Picture House, Mansfield.
Rock Picture House, Mansfield.
Villa Cross, Handsworth.
Picture House, Harborne.
Electric Theatre, Cape Hill, Smethwick.
Rink, Smethwick.
Electric Theatre, Chatham.
Cinema, Wishaw.
Holderness Hall, Hull.
Pavilion, Motherwell.
Pavilion, Kirkintilloch.
Pavilion, Falkirk.
Capitol, Ibrox, Glasgow.
Grand Cinema, Gainsborough.
King's, Gainsborough.
Picture House, Ayr.
B. B. Cinerama, Glasgow.
B. B. Cinerama, Perth.
B. B. Cinerama, Coatbridge.
Regent Picture House, Weston-super-Mare.

GENERAL THEATRE CORPORATION, LTD.
Capitol, Haymarket.
Astoria Cinema, Charing Cross Road.
Palladium, Argyll Street (Music Hall).
Highbury Picture Theatre.
Blue Hall, Islington.
Blue Hall Annexe, Islington.
Holborn Empire (Music Hall).
Penge Empire (Music Hall).
Palladium, Balham.
Rink Cinema, Clapton.
Imperial Picture Theatre, Highbury.
Crouch End Hippodrome.
Park, Birkenhead.
Queen's, Birkenhead.
Conway Street, Birkenhead.
Hippodrome, Birmingham (Music Hall).
Broadway Cinema and Billiard Hall, Bootle.
Strand, Bootle.
Hippodrome, Boscombe (Music Hall).
Hippodrome and Palm Court, Brighton
   (Music Hall).
Court Theatre and Billiard Room, Brigh-
   ton.
Majestic, Chester.
Glynn, Chester.
Music Hall, Chester.
St. Andrew Square, Edinburgh.
Regent, Abbeymount, Edinburgh.
Capitol, Leith.
Gaumont Palace, Egremont.
Globe, Gosforth.
Scala, Heaton.
Hippodrome, Leeds (Music Hall).
King's Hall, Little Sutton.
Hippodrome, Liverpool.
Bedford, Walton, Liverpool.
Gaumont Palace, Liverpool.
Rialto Cinema and Ballroom, Liverpool.
Savoy, Liverpool.
Casino Cinema, Ballroom and Billiard
   Hall, Liverpool.
Plaza, Liverpool.
Palace Theatre, Luton.

Trocadero, New Brighton.
Hippodrome, Wolverhampton.
Queen's Hall, Newcastle-on-Tyne.
Hippodrome, Portsmouth (Music Hall).
Marina, Seacombe.
Hippodrome, Shildon.
Hippodrome, Southampton (Music Hall).
Gaumont Palace, Southend.
Palladium, Southport.
Scala Cinema, South Shields.
Palace, Sunderland.
Rutland Picture House, Edinburgh.
Alhambra, Paris.

**GENERAL CINEMA THEATRES, LTD.—
Head Office : 19, Albemarle Street, London
W.1.**
Telephone : Regent 4419.
New Pavilion, Kensal Rise.
Gaisford Cinema, Kentish Town.
Kinema, Putney Bridge.
Britannia, Camden Town.
Court, East Molesey.
Plaza Cinema, West Wickham.
Rex, Hayes, Kent.
Plaza, Queensbury (Building.) Middlesex.
Savoy, Beckenham (Building).

**GOLDSTONES (CINEMAS), LTD.—Registered
Office : 9, Wetherby Road, Leeds.**
Managing Director : Max Goldstone.
Telephone : Oakwood 66788.
Wellington Picture House, Leeds.
Regal, Hunslet, Leeds.
Victoria Picture Hall, Leeds.
Tivoli, Middleton, Leeds.

**GOODALL'S PICTURES (1931) LTD.—Registered
Office : Albion Street, Cleckheaton.**
Secretary : PERCY GOODALL.
Telephone : Cleckheaton 224.
Telegrams : Palace, Cleckheaton.
Pavilion, Ravensthorpe, Dewsbury.
Picture Palace, Dudley Hill, Bradford.
Picture Palace, Cleckheaton.
Picture Palace, Heckmondwike.
Savoy Picture House, Cleckheaton.

**GOTCH, (J. H.) CIRCUIT : Head Office, Regal,
Soham, Ely, Cambs.**
Manager : J. H. GOTCH.
Telephone and Telegraphic Address : Soham 72
Plaza, Saffron Walden.
Regal, Soham.
Picture House, Sheringham.
Central,Soham.

**J. GRAHAM,—Head Office : 17, Blythswood
Square, Glasgow.**
Telephone : Western 2305.
Standard, Partick, Glasgow.
Palladium, Pollokshows, Glasgow.
Picture House, Possil Park, Glasgow.
Picture House, Springburn, Glasgow.
Victoria Theatre, Whiteinch, Glasgow.
Carlton, Glasgow.
Roxy Theatre, Maryhill, Glasgow.

**S. GRAHAM.—Head Office : Park House, Friar
Lane, Nottingham.**
Telephone : Nottingham 2552.
Curzon Cinema, Nottingham.
Scala Cinema, Long Eaton.
Ritz, Carlton, Nottingham.
Capitol, Nottingham.
Roxy, Nottingham.
Adelphi, Nottingham.
Roxy, Northampton.

**GRATTON, S. A., AND SON.—Address : 9,
McFarlane Street, Glasgow. E.**
Telephone : Bell 2215.
Grafton Picture House, Glasgow.
King's Theatre, Bridgeton, Glasgow.
Pavilion, Kilsyth.

**GRAVES CINEMAS, LTD.—Registered Office :
Athenaeum Buildings, Maryport, Cumber-
land.**
Joint Managing Directors : JAMES GRAVES
AND J. GRAVES.
Booking Manager : PERCY HALEY.
Telephone : Maryport 16.
Empire, Maryport.
Carlton, Maryport.
Star, Denton Holme, Carlisle.
Theatre Royal, Workington.
Oxford, Workington.
Opera House, Workington.
Carnegie, Workington.
Ritz, Workington (Building).

**GREEN, GEORGE, LTD.—Head Office : 182,
Trongate, Glasgow.**
Telephone : Bell 1660-1-2.
Playhouse, Renfield Street, Glasgow.
Cinema, Tollcross, Glasgow.
Cinema, Rutherglen.
Picturedrome, Gorbals, Glasgow.
Playhouse, Ayr.
Picturedrome, Irvine.
Pavilion, Bathgate.
Pavilion, Johnstone.
Rex Cinema, Lockerbie.
Bedford Picture House, S.S. Glasgow.
Playhouse, Dundee.

**LESLIE GREENE CIRCUIT.—Head Office : 7,
Elliot Street, Liverpool.**
Telephone : Royal 538.
Telegrams : Royal 538 Liverpool.
London Offices : West End—Gloucester House,
19, Charing Cross Road, W.C.2, and 128,
Nightingale Lane, London, S.W.12.
Telephone : Whitehall 5504, and Battersea
2647.
Telegrams : Whitehall 5504, and Battersea
2647. London.
Metropole Theatre, Bootle.
Walton Vale Picture House, Liverpool.
Carlton Rooms, Liverpool.
Hope Hall, Liverpool.

**STANLEY GRIMSHAW. —Office : Prince of
Wales Cinema, Clayton Square, Liverpool.**
Telephones :
Private : Chester 883.
Office : Central 5378.
Adelphi, Liverpool.
Atlas, Liverpool.
Burlington, Liverpool.
Carlton, Liverpool.
Derby, Liverpool.
Gaiety, Liverpool.
Prince of Wales, Liverpool.
Glynn Picture House, Wrexham.
Empire Picture House, Wrexham.
Queens Picture House, Ellesmere Port.
Grand, Frodsham.
Kings, Heswall.

**I. R. GROVE.—Head Office : Fairfield House,
Broxburn.**
General Manager : I. R. GROVE, J.P.
Telephone : Broxburn 42.
Telegrams : Grove, Broxburn.
Star Theatre, Armadale.
Star Theatre, Bathgate.
Star Theatre, Bo'ness.
Star Theatre, Lochore.

E. HAIGH AND SON.—Head Office: 30, Tarleton Street, Liverpool, 1.
Telephone: Royal 1170.
New Hope Hall Cinema, Liverpool.
Wallasey Cinema, Liverpool.
Tatler News Cinema, Liverpool.

J. HENDRY.—Head Office: 114, Union Street, Glasgow.
Telephone: Central 2012.
Central Picture House, Musselburgh.
Central Picture House, Portobello.
Central Picture House, Broxburn.
Regal, Renfrew.

HEWITSONS, LTD.—Office : Windsor Theatre, Smethwick, Staffs.
General Manager: ALAN E. HEWITSON.
Telephone: Bearwood 2244.
Telegrams: Windsor, Smethwick.
Windsor Theatre, Smethwick.
Empire Theatre, Smethwick.
Majestic Picture Theatre, Smethwick.
Princes Hall, Smethwick.

E. J. HINGE CIRCUIT.—Head Office : 72, Grey Street, Newcastle-on-Tyne.
Telephone: Newcastle-on-Tyne 20317.
Telegrams: "Hinge," Newcastle-on-Tyne.
Gaiety, Newcastle-on-Tyne.
Palladium, Newcastle-on-Tyne.
Empire, Blaydon-on-Tyne.
Corona, Felling-on-Tyne.
Hippodrome, Cleator Moor.
Hippodrome, New Silksworth.
Globe, Crawcrook.
Grand, Pelaw-on-Tyne.
Globe, Durham.
Grand, Benwell, Newcastle-on-Tyne.
Globe, Gosforth.
Empire, Shotton.
Grand, Byker.
Hippodrome, Darlington.
Rialto, Benwell.
Picture House, Whitley Bay.
Classic, Low Fell, Gateshead.
Royalty, Gosforth
Lyric, Throckley.
Regal, Fenham, Newcastle-on-Tyne.
Millfield, Sunderland.
Marina, Fulwell, Sunderland.
Regal, Durham.
Crown, Scotswood Road, Newcastle-on-Tyne.
Coliseum, Morpeth.
Ritz, Forest Hall.
Lyric, Grangetown-on-Tees.

HOME COUNTIES THEATRES, LTD.—Head Office : Athenæum, Muswell Hill, N.10.
Managing Director: ARTHUR FERRISS.
Gen. Manager and Secretary : P. A. WALLIS, M.C.
Telephone: Tudor 5848-9.
Athenaeum Picture Playhouse, Muswell Hill.
Summerland Cinema, Muswell Hill.
Coliseum Cinema, East Finchley.

HULL CINEMAS, LTD.—Head Office : Cecil Theatre, Anlaby Road, Hull.
Booking Manager: BRINLEY EVANS.
Telephone: Hull 15315.
Cinema Palace, Goole.
Tower, Goole.
Carlton, Hull.
Cecil Hull.
Central, Hull.
Cleveland, Hull.
Criterion, Hull.
Dorchester, Hull.

Langham, Hull.
Monica, Hull.
National, Hull.
Playhouse, Hull.
Savoy, Hull.
West Park, Hull.

EXORS. OF W. HUTSON, Decd., and N. H. CHAPMAN.—77, Northumberland Street, Newcastle-on-Tyne.
Manager: JAMES WADE.
Coronation Hall, Annitsford.
Grand Electric, Dudley.
Queen's Hall, Seaton Burn.

ILKESTON CINEMA CO., LTD.—Head Office : King's Picture House, Bath Street, Ilkeston.
Managing Director: H. W. BRAILSFORD.
Booking Manager: C. W. BAMBER.
Telephone: Ilkeston 17.
Telegrams: Kings, Ilkeston.
Picture House, Ashby-de-la-Zouch.
King's Picture House, Ilkeston.
New Theatre, Ilkeston.

IRISH CINEMAS, LTD.—Address : 32, Shaftesbury Avenue, London, W.1.
Managing Director: JOHN EDWARD PEARCE.
Telephone: Gerrard 3306.
Savoy Cinema and Restaurant, Dublin.
Savoy Cinema and Restaurant, Cork.

IRISH ELECTRIC PALACES, LTD.—Head Office : 79, Donegall Street, Belfast.
Telephone: Belfast 5800.
Picture Palace, Bangor, Co. Down.
Picture House, Larne.

ISLE OF WIGHT THEATRES, LTD.—Head Office : Theatre Royal, Ryde, I.O.W.
Managing Director: MRS. G. HILL.
Telephone: Ryde 2387.
Theatre Royal, Ryde.
Scala, Ryde.
Grand, Newport.
Queen's, Sandown.
Royalty, Cowes.
Gaiety, Ventnor.
Regent, Freshwater.
Kings, East Cowes.

JACKSONS' AMUSEMENTS, LTD. — Head Office : The Hippodrome, Rochdale.
Secretary and Circuit Supervisor: J. J. McCRACKEN.
Telephone: Rochdale 3212.
Telegrams: Hippodrome, Rochdale.
Hippodrome, Rochdale.
Ceylon Cinema de Luxe, Rochdale.
Coliseum, Rochdale.
Empire, Rochdale.
Empire, Bacup.
La Scala, Rochdale.
Rialto, Rochdale.

E. H. JAMES.—Office : 4, Cae Llan, Llanrwst North Wales.
Concert Hall, Llanberis.
Public Hall, Bethesda.
Town Hall Cinema, Menai Bridge.
Cinema, Llanrwst.
Town Hall Cinema, Llanfairfechan.

D. J. JAMES CIRCUIT.—Head Office : Cinema House, 225, Oxford Street, London, W.1.
Telephones: Gerrard 4242-3 and 3300.
Mayfair Cinema, Chadwell Heath.
Capitol Cinema, Upminster.

Capitol Cinema, St. Albans.
Grand Palace Cinema, St. Albans.
Museum Cinema, Bethnal Green, E.
Majestic Cinema, Stoke Newington, N.
Park Cinema, Hither Green, S.E.
Trafalgar Cinema, Greenwich, S.E.
Super Cinema, Hornchurch (Closed).
Towers Cinema, Hornchurch.
Mayfair Cinema, Stepney
Regent Cinema, Hatfield.

BEN JAY.—Head Office : 145, Wardour Street London, W.1.
Telephone: Gerrard 2239.
Astoria Cinema, Forest Hill.
Regent Cinema, Holloway.
Empire Cinema, Ilford Lane.

A. N. KENDAL, LTD.—Registered Office : Hippodrome, Tidworth.
Governing Director: A. N. KENDAL.
Telephone: Winchester 1364.
Hippodrome, Tidworth.
Garrison Theatre, Bulford.
Garrison Theatre, Larkhill.

KESSEX CINEMAS, LTD. (Controlled by Kay Bros.).—Offices : 197, Wardour Street, London, W.1.
Telephone: Gerrard 2835-6.
Rio Cinema, Barking.
Heathway Cinema, Dagenham.
Savoy Cinema, Ilford.
Regent Cinema, Becontree.
Grange Cinema, Dagenham.

KING (A. B.)—Office : 167, Bath Street, Glasgow.
Telephones: Douglas 1195 and 1196.
Telegrams: Kenaûlm, Glasgow.
La Scala, Glasgow.
Regent, Glasgow.
Bedford, Glasgow.
La Scala, Paisley.
Kelburne Cinema, Paisley.
Lyceum, Govan, Glasgow.
Elder Picture House, Govan, Glasgow
Lorne Cinema, Ibrox, Glasgow.
Hampden Picture House, Crosshill, Glasgow.
Rosevale Cinema, Partick, Glasgow.
Gaiety Theatre, Anderston, Glasgow.
Cambridge Cinema, Glasgow.
New Grand Theatre, Glasgow.
Casino, Townhead, Glasgow.
Astoria, Possilpark, Glasgow.
B.B. Cinema, Greenock.
Eclipse Pictures, Port Glasgow.
Regal Cinema, Lanark.
Strand Cinema, Alexandria.
La Scala, Helensburgh.
Countess Cinema, Saltcoats.
Empire, Kilmarnock.
Cinema, Coatbridge.
New Cinema, Airdrie.
Orient Cinema, Ayr.
Palace Cinema, Rothesay.
Gaiety Theatre, Leith.
Cinema House, St. Andrews.
Lyceum, Dumfries.
La Scala, Inverness.
Empire, Inverness.
Picture House, Elgin.
Playhouse, Elgin.
Playhouse, Peterhead.
Playhouse, Montrose.
Playhouse, Keith.
Playhouse, Peebles.
Playhouse, Perth.
Playhouse, Invergordon.

Picture House, Tain.
Victoria Hall, Kingussie.
New Pavilion, Wick.
Breadalbane Hall, Wick.
Alhambra, Dunfermline.
Picture House, Cowdenbeath.
Opera House, Lochgelly.
Palace Cinema, Methil.

L. C. V. CIRCUIT (Lessee : Mrs. H. W. Urquhart).—Head Office : 34, St. Enoch Square, Glasgow.
Booking Manager: MISS S. CALLAGHAN.
Telephone: Central 4465.
Picture House, Blantyre.
Hippodrome, Hamilton.
Playhouse, Hamilton.
Kingsway Cinema, Kilwinning.
Town Hall, Millport.

LANCASHIRE ENTERTAINMENTS, LTD.— Head Office : Regent Picture House, Eccles, Manchester.
General Manager: W. E. MARSHALL.
Telephone: Eccles 3843.
Majestic Picture House, Patricroft.
Regent Picture House, Eccles.

LEEDS AND DISTRICT PICTURE HOUSES, LTD.—Head Office : The Lounge, North Lane, Headingley, Leeds 6.
Managing Director: LEONARD DENHAM.
Telephone: Headingley 52419.
The Lounge, Headingley.
Crown Cinema, Leeds.
Regent, Burmanlofts.

LETCHWORTH PALACE, LTD.—Head Office : Palace, Letchworth.
Managing Director: J. W. E. POWELL.
Telephone: Letchworth 53.
Palace, Letchworth.
Broadway, Letchworth.
Royal Theatre, Rushden.
Silver Cinema, Wellingborough.

LEVY CIRCUIT.—Office : Liverpool Cinema Feature Film Co., Ltd., 9, Ranelagh Street, Liverpool, 1.
Managing Director: ALFRED LEVY.
Telephone: Royal 5675
Scala, Ashton-in-Makerfield.
Scala, Liverpool.
Futurist, Liverpool.
Claughton Picture House, Birkenhead.
Scala, Nuneaton.
Scala, Birmingham.
Futurist, Birmingham.
Scala, Middlesbrough.

LION CINEMATOGRAPH Co., LTD.—Office : 43, Whitcomb Street, Leicester Square, London, W.C.2.
Directors: MORRIS M. LEVY and B. HARRIS,
Telephone: Streatham 3688 and Whitehall 4088.
Central Cinema, Upper Tooting, S.W.17.
Astoria Cinema, Leyton, E.15.
Strathcona, Northfleet, Kent.
Northfleet Cinema, Kent.
Capitol, Mill Hill, N.W.7.

LONDON & DISTRICT CINEMAS, LTD.— Registered Office : Astoria House, 62, Shaftesbury Avenue, London, W.1.
Managing Director: R. B. WAINWRIGHT.
Telephone: Gerrard 7215.
Telegrams: Londicines, Lesquare, London.
Capitol, Epsom.
Picture House, Leatherhead.

Plaza, New Malden.
Pavilion, Aylesbury.
Market Theatre, Aylesbury.
Exchange Theatre, Chichester.
Hippodrome, Greenwich.
Empire Theatre, Greenwich.
Cinema, Woolwich.
Premier Electric Theatre, Woolwich.
Empire, Hounslow.
Alcazar, Hounslow.
Plaza, Plumstead.
Imperial Theatre, Clapham Junction.
Globe Theatre, Clapham.
Grand Theatre, Clapham

LONDON & SOUTHERN SUPER CINEMAS LTD.—Office : 32, Shaftesbury Avenue, London, W.1.

Managing Director : ARTHUR COHEN.
Telephone : Whitehall 0183.
Ambassador, Bedminster, Bristol.
Ambassador, Cosham, Portsmouth.
Ambassador, Farnham Royal, Slough.
Ambassador, Hounslow West.
Empire, Normanton.
Plaza, Woking.
Tredegar Hall Picture Theatre, Newport(Mon.)
Astoria Cinema, Woking.
Ambassador, Hendon.
Bloomsbury Super Cinema, Theobald's Road, W.C.
Capitol Cinema, Walton-on-Thames.
Regal, Rotherham.

MAJESTIC THEATRES CORPORATION, LTD —Registered Office : 11, Ironmonger Lane. London, E.C.2.

Chairman and Managing Director : W. E. GREENWOOD.
Majestic Theatre, Mitcham.
Majestic Theatre, Woodford.

T. E. MARKHAM.—Office : Ye Olde Wyche Theatre, Nantwich.

Telephone : Nantwich 5338.
Hippodrome, Market Drayton.
Ye Olde Wyche Theatre, Nantwich.
Palladium, Whitchurch.

MARKS CIRCUIT CINEMAS.—Head Office : Exchange Buildings, 6, St. Mary's Gate, Manchester 1.

Proprietors : M. MARKS, S. H. MARKS AND P. MARKS.
Telephone : Blackfriars 4078.
Palace, Westhoughton.
Cinema, Leigh.
Empire, Milnrow.
New Palladium, Mill Hill, Blackburn.

MARSHALL AND BROUGHTON.—Head Office : 178, Westgate Road, Newcastle.

Managing Director : W. R. MARSHALL.
Secretary : W. C. KIDD.
Telephone : Newcastle 27451.
Bromarsh, Sunderland.
Raby Grand, Newcastle.
New Picture House, Forest Hall.
Queen's Hall, Wallsend.
Crown Electric, Tyne Dock.
Imperial Picture House, Tyne Dock.

MATLOCK CINEMAS, LTD.—Head Office : Cinema House, Matlock.

Booking Manager : H. HODGKINSON.
Telephone : Matlock 121.
Telegrams : Cinema, Matlock.
Electric Theatre, Grassmoor, near Chesterfield.
Cinema House, Matlock.
Picture Palace, Dale Road, Matlock.
Grand Pavilion, Matlock Bath.

A. G. MATTHEWS.—Head Office : 8, Overwood Drive, Glasgow, S.4.

Telephone : Merrylee 2317.
Picture House, Peterhead.
Picture House, Fraserburgh.
Picture House, Banff.
Central, Greenoek.
Cinema, Lerwick.
Picture House, Thurso.
Victoria Cinema, Inverurie.
Cinema House, Motherwell.
Picture House, Forres.
Empire, Fraserburgh.
Playhouse, Fort William.
Playhouse, Stornoway.
Playhouse, Oban.

McKIBBIN'S CIRCUIT.—Head Office : West End Picture House, 108, Shankhill Road, Belfast.

Proprietors : McKIBBIN ESTATE, LIMITED.
Telephone : Belfast 24460.
Midland Picture House, Belfast
Shankhill Picturedrome, Belfast.
West End Picture House, Belfast.

JOSEPH MEARS THEATRES, LTD.—Head Office : 5, Hill Street, Richmond, Surrey

Telephone : Richmond 2900.
The Kensington, Kensington.
The Richmond Kinema, Richmond.
The Sheen Kinema, East Sheen.
The Luxor, Twickenham.
The Twickenham, Twickenham.
Royalty Kinema, Richmond.

MEDWAY CINEMAS, LTD.—Registered Office : Walmar House, 288, Regent Street, London, W.1.

General Manager : E. L. MANCHES.
Telephone : Langham 2677.
Scala, Dartford.
Rialto, Dartford.
Gem, Dartford.
State, Dartford.
Rialto, Upper Norwood.
Albany, Upper Norwood.
State, Sydenham.

MEIKLEJOHN CIRCUIT. — Address : 22, Jamaica Street, Glasgow.

Telephone : Central 7180.
Grand Central Picture House, Glasgow.
Imperial Picture House, Paisley Road, Glasgow.

MEXBOROUGH THEATRES, LTD.—Registered Office : Empire, Swinton Road, Mexborough.

Managing Director : J. J. WOFFINDEN.
Telephone : Mexborough 108.
Empire, Mexborough.
Majestic, Mexborough.
Oxford, Mexborough.
Grand Theatre, Wath-on-Dearne.
Picture House, Swinton

J. B. MILNE'S ENTERPRISES.—Head Office : Victoria Theatre, Dundee.

Booking Manager : J. B. MILNE.
Telephone : Dundee 4793.
Telegrams : Victoria, Dundee.
New Palladium, Dundee.
Picture House, Tayport, Fife.

New Britannia, Small's Wynd, Dundee.
Victoria, Dundee.

H. D. MOORHOUSE CIRCUIT.—Offices : Imperial Buildings, 7, Oxford Road, Manchester, 1.

Proprietor : H. D. MOORHOUSE.
General Manager : G. M. MONTANINI.
Telephones : Ardwick 2226–7–8.
Telegrams : Cinemoor, Manchester.
Alhambra, Openshaw.
Adelphi, Moston.
Boro, Salford.
Capitol, Congleton.
Coliseum, Leicester.
Criterion, Walkden.
Crown Theatre, Eccles.
Deansgate Manchester.
Empire, Middleton.
Empire, Oldham.
Empire, Preston.
Gem, Heywood.
Globe, Old Trafford.
Globe, Cheetham Hill.
Grand, Crewe.
Grosvenor, All Saints.
Hippodrome, Stalybridge.
Hippodrome, Hyde.
Hippodrome, Wrexham.
Hippodrome, Bolton.
King's, Longsight.
Lyceum, Hulme.
Olympia, Leicester.
Osborne, Manchester.
Palace, Droylsden.
Palace, Sale.
Palace, Levenshulme.
Palace, Farnworth.
Palace, Stalybridge.
Palace Theatre, Salford.
Palace Cinema, Salford.
Palace Cinema, Wigan.
Palatine, Withington.
Palladium, Darwen.
Pavilion, Rochdale.
Picture House, Altrincham.
Princess, Dukinfield.
Prince's, Openshaw.
Rex, Openshaw.
Seedley Cinema.
Shaftesbury, Longsight.
Shaftesbury, Leicester.
Savoy, Farnworth.
Sovereign, Leicester.
Theatre Royal, Ashton.
Theatre Royal, Bolton.
Theatre Royal, Manchester.
Tower, Broughton.
Temple, Cheetham.
Victory, Blackley.
Victory, Middleton.
Victory, Oldham.
Victory, Rochdale.
Victoria, Broughton.

L. MORRIS.—Address : 52, Shaftesbury Avenue , London, W.1.

Telephone : Gerrard 1668/9.
Telegrams : Kendermor, Lesquare, London.
Savoy, Willesden.
Astoria, Boscombe.
Savoy, Boscombe.
Regal, Bow.
Ritz, Bridgnorth.
Ritz, Chesterfield.
Ritz, Grantham.
Kingsway, Hadleigh.
Ritz, Harrow.
Ritz, Oldham.

Regal, Sheerness.
Ritz, Warrington.
Ritz, Watford.
Plaza, Sutton.

MORTON CIRCUIT.—Address : Picture House Old Cumnock, Ayrshire.

Telephone : Cumnock 11.
Telegrams : Pictures, Cumnock.
Picture House, Old Cumnock.
Picture House, Auchinleck.

MOSS EMPIRES, LTD.—Offices : Cranbourn Mansions, Cranbourn Street, London, W.C.2.

Chiarman : J. J. GILLESPIE.
Telephone : Gerrard 2274.
Of the 22 Theatres owned by the Company the following are wired for sound pictures :—
London Hippodrome.
Grand Theatre, Birmingham.
Empire Theatre, Cardiff.
Empire Theatre, Southampton.

NEW EMPIRE (BURNLEY), LTD.—Office : The Empire Theatre, Burnley.

Telephone : Burnley 2453.
Telegrams : Empire Theatre, Burnley.
Empire Theatre, Burnley.
Savoy Cinema, Burnley.
Grand Cinema, Burnley.
Empress Cinema, Burnley.
Imperial Cinema, Burnley.
Tivoli Cinema, Burnley.
Pentridge Cinema, Burnley.
Temperance Cinema, Burnley.
Royal Cinema, Burnley.
Coliseum Cinema, Radcliffe.
Picturedrome Cinema, Radcliffe.
Bridge Cinema, Radcliffe.
Grand, Padiham.
Globe, Padiham.

NORTH-EAST COAST CINEMAS, LTD.— Registered Office : 11, Bath Lane, Newcastle-on-Tyne.

Managing Director : SOL. SHECKMAN.
Telephone : Newcastle-on-Tyne 27864.
Hippodrome, Crook.
Empire Palace, Crook.
Theatre Royal, Crook.

NORTHERN THEATRES CO., LTD.—Head Office : Nothcoli House, Clare Road, Halifax.

Managing Director : NORMAN R. BOOTH.
Film Booking Manager : FRED A. KAY.
Telephone : Halifax 2512.
Theatre Royal, Halifax.
Theatre Royal, Bury.
Theatre Royal, Blackburn.
New Hippodrome, Tudor Super Cinema, Huddersfield.
Picture House, Huddersfield.
Grand Picture House, Halifax.
Palace Tudor Super Cinema, Rochdale.
Theatre Royal, Rochdale.
Tudor Theatre, Dewsbury.

NORTH-WESTERN FILM BOOKING AGENCY —Head Office, 70, Lime Street, Liverpool.

Telephone : Royal 4911.
Telegrams : Palais de Luxe, Liverpool.
Aintree Palace, Aintree.
Everton Palace, Liverpool
Palais de Luxe, Liverpool.
Liverpool Picturedrome, Kensington.
Rock Ferry Palace, Rock Ferry.

St. James' Picturedrome, Liverpool.
Palace, Liscard.
Palladium, Prestatyn.
Majestic, Wrexham.
Embassy, Wallasey.
Princess, Kirkdale, Liverpool.

ODEON THEATRES, LTD.—Head Office : Cornhill House, Bennetts Hill, Birmingham 2.
London Office : 49, Park Lane, London, W.1.

Governing Director : OSCAR DEUTSCH.
Telephones : Birmingham-Midland 2781-2792. (Private Branch Exchange) London—Mayfair 7811.
Telegrams : ODEONS, BIRMINGHAM.
Telegrams : ODEONS, AUDLEY, LONDON.

Odeon Theatre, Acton. (In course of construction.)
Odeon Theatre, Alfreton.
Odeon Theatre, Andover.
Odeon Theatre, Ashford (Kent).
Odeon Theatre, Aylesbury.
Odeon Theatre, Balham. (In course of construction.)
Odeon Theatre, Barnet.
Odeon Theatre, Bath.
Palace Theatre, Bilston.
Odeon Theatre, Blackheath, near Birmingham.
Odeon Theatre, Bloxwich.
Odeon Theatre, Bognor Regis.
Odeon Theatre, Bolton. (In course of construction.)
Odeon Theatre, Boston. (In course of construction.)
Odeon Theatre, Bournemouth. (In course of construction.)
Odeon Theatre, Brentwood. (In course of construction.)
Odeon Theatre, Bridgwater.
Odeon Theatre, Brierley Hill.
Odeon Theatre, Brighton.
Odeon Theatre, Bristol. (In course of construction.)
Royalty Theatre, Broadstairs.
Odeon Theatre, Bromley.
Odeon Theatre, Burnley. (In course of construction.)
Regent Cinema, Burnt Oak, Edgware.
Odeon Theatre, Bury.
Odeon Theatre, Bury St. Edmunds.
Friars Theatre, Canterbury.
Odeon Theatre, Cardiff.
Odeon Theatre, Chester.
Picture House, Chesterfield.
Odeon Theatre, Chingford.
Odeon Theatre, Chorley. (In course of construction.)
Odeon Theatre, Clacton-on-Sea.
Odeon Theatre, Cleveleys.
Odeon Theatre, Colindale.
Odeon Theatre, Colwyn Bay.
Odeon Theatre, Corby.
Odeon Theatre, Crewe. (In course of construction.)
Odeon Theatre, Croydon.
Odeon Theatre, Deal.
Odeon Theatre, Deptford. (In course of construction.)
Odeon Theatre, Derby.
Odeon Theatre, Dudley.
Victoria Theatre, Dursley.
Odean Theatre, Ealing.
Walpole Theatre, Ealing.
Odeon Theatre, Epsom.
Odeon Theatre, Erith. (In course of construction.)

Odeon Theatre, Exeter. (In course of construction.)
Odeon Theatre, Falmouth.
Odeon Theatre, Faversham.
Odeon Theatre, Finchley.
Odeon Theatre, Forest Gate.
Odeon Theatre, Guide Bridge.
Odeon Theatre, Guildford.
Odeon Theatre, Hanley.
Odeon Theatre, Harlesden. (In course of construction.)
Odeon Theatre, Harrogate.
Odeon Theatre, Haverstock Hill.
Odeon Theatre, Hereford.
Odeon Theatre, Herne Bay.
Odeon Theatre, Hinckley.
Regent Cinema, Hinckley.
Odeon Theatre, Horsham.
Odeon Theatre, Ipswich.
Odeon Theatre, Isleworth.
Odeon Theatre, Islington.
Odeon Theatre, Kemp Town.
Odeon Theatre, Kenton.
Odeon Theatre, Kettering.
Odeon Theatre, Kingstanding.
Odeon Theatre, Kingston-on-Thames.
Odeon Theatre, Kingsbury.
Odeon Theatre, Lancaster.
Regal Theatre, Lancing.
Odeon Theatre, Leicester. (In course of construction.)
Odeon Theatre, Leicester Square, London. (In course of construction.)
Odeon Theatre, Lewes.
Odeon Theatre, Littlehampton.
Winter Gardens, Llandudno.
Odeon Theatre, Llanelly. (In course of construction.)
Odeon Theatre, Loughborough.
Odeon Theatre, Lowestoft.
Morden Cinema, Morden.
Odeon Theatre, Morecambe. (In course of construction.)
Odeon Theatre, Muswell Hill.
Odeon Theatre, Newport, I.O.W.
Odeon Theatre, Newport, Mon. (In course of construction.)
Odeon Theatre, Newton Abbot.
Odeon Theatre, Oldham.
Odeon Theatre, Penge.
Odeon Theatre, Perry Barr, Birmingham.
Odeon Theatre, Peterborough.
Odeon Theatre, Portsmouth.
Odeon Theatre, Port Talbot. (In course of construction.)
Odeon Theatre, Radcliffe, Lancs. (In course of construction.)
Odeon Theatre, Ramsgate.
Odeon Theatre, Reading.
Odeon Theatre, Redhill.
Odeon Theatre, Rickmansworth.
Odeon Theatre, Rhyl. (In course of construction.)
Odeon Theatre, St. Austell.
Odeon Theatre, Scarborough.
Odeon Theatre, Shirley, near Birmingham.
Odeon Theatre, Sidcup.
Odeon Theatre, Sittingbourne.
Regal Cinema, Skipton.
Odeon Theatre, Southall.
Odeon Theatre, Southgate.
Odeon Theatre, South Harrow.
Odeon Theatre, South Norwood. (In course of construction.)
Odeon Theatre, Southsea. (In course of construction.)
Odeon Theatre, Spalding. (In course of construction.)

Odeon Theatre, Stafford.
Odeon Theatre, Sudbury, Middlesex.
Odeon Theatre, Surbiton.
Odeon Theatre, Sutton Coldfield.
Odeon Theatre, Swiss Cottage. (In course of construction.)
Odeon Theatre, Taunton.
Odeon Theatre, Tolworth.
Royal Theatre, Torquay.
Odeon Theatre, Wallington.
Warley Odeon, Warley, near Birmingham.
Odeon Theatre, Warrington.
Odeon Theatre, Watford.
Odeon Theatre, Wealdstone.
Odeon Theatre, Well Hall, Eltham.
Odeon Theatre, Welling.
Odeon Theatre, Weston-super-Mare.
Odeon Theatre, Weybridge.
Odeon Theatre, Weymouth.
Odeon Theatre, Wimbledon.
Odeon Theatre, Winchester.
Odeon Theatre, Wolverhampton. (In course of construction.)
Odeon Theatre, Woolwich. (In course of construction.)
Silver Cinema, Worcester.
Odeon Theatre, Worcester Park.
Odeon Theatre, Worthing.
Odeon Theatre, Wrexham.
Odeon Theatre, Uxbridge. (In course of construction.)
Odeon Theatre, Yeovil.
Odeon Theatre, York.

OLLERTON PICTURES, LTD.—Office : Empire, Somercotes, Derbyshire.

Managing Director : T. DENNIS.
Telephone : Leabrooks 148.

Ollerton Picture House, Knutsford.
Palace, Pinxton.
Palace, South Normanton.
Empire, Somercotes.

ORMISTON, THOS., F.C.I.S.—Address : 6, Brandon Street, Motherwell.

Telephones : Motherwell 381 and 382.

La Scala, Cupar.
Salon, Falkirk.
Picture House, Gourock.
Picture House, Kilbirnie.
Empire Theatre, Shotts.

ORR CIRCUIT.—Head Office : 92, Barkers Butts Lane, Coventry.

Telephone : Coventry 2112-3.
Telegrams : Orr, Coventry.

Scala Theatre, Coventry.
Globe Theatre, Coventry.
Rialto Theatre, Coventry.
Carlton Theatre, Coventry.
Regal Theatre, Coventry.
Astoria Theatre, Coventry.
Rialto Casino, Coventry.

PARAMOUNT-ASTORIA-THEATRES, LTD.—Registered Office : 162-170, Wardour Street, London, W.1. Administrative Offices: 104/8, Oxford Street, London, W.1.

Managing Director : JOHN CECIL GRAHAM.
Telephone : Museum 4721.

Astoria, Streatham.
Astoria, Brixton.
Astoria, Old Kent Road, S.E.
Astoria, Finsbury Park.

F. PARNELL.—Head Office : Gloucester Mansions, 140a, Shaftesbury Avenue, London, W.C.2.

Telephone : Temple Bar 5972.

Apollo Picture Theatre, Custom House
Electric Theatre, Custom House.

PENZANCE CINEMA, LTD.—Office : Regent Hotel, Penzance.

Managing Director : ROBERT THOMAS.
Secretary : S. H. V. OSBORNE.
Telephones : Penzance 146 and 330.
Telegrams : Cinema, Penzance.

Pavilion Theatre, Penzance.
Cinema, Penzance.
Regal, Penzance.

PHILPOT CIRCUIT.—Head Office : 116, Much Park Street, Coventry.

Managing Director : H. T. A. PHILPOT.
Telephone : Coventry 2366.

Forum, Coventry.
Plaza, Coventry.
Alexandra, Coventry.
Roxy, Coventry.
Rex, Coventry.
Rivoli, Coventry.
Palladium, Coventry.

A. AUSTIN PILKINGTON'S THEATRES.—Head Office : 20, London Road, Salisbury.

Palace, Devizes.
Regal, Ringwood.
Regal, Shepton Mallet.
Regal, Wells.

THE PLAZA CINEMA CIRCUIT.—Head Office : Hay, Hereford.

Manager : DESMOND J. MADIGAN.
Telephone : Hay 4.
Telegraphic Address : Plaza Hay.

Plaza, Llandrindod Wells.
Plaza, Hay.
Castle Cinema, Rhayader.
Plaza, Knighton.
Cinema, Presteign.

PLAZA THEATRE (RUGBY), LTD.—Registered Office : Crown House, Rugby.

Managing Director : HALFORD W. L. REDDISH, F.C.A.
Telephone : Rugby 2244.
Telegrams : Adastra, Rugby.

Plaza, Rugby.
Regal, Rugby.
Regent, Rugby.

POOLE'S THEATRES, LTD. — Head Office : Hippodrome, Gloucester.

Managing Director : JOHN R. POOLE.
General Manager : ERNEST C. ROGERS.
Telephone : Gloucester 2127.
Telegrams : Dates, Gloucester.

Hippodrome, Gloucester.
King's Hall, Stourbridge.

And in association :—
Synod Hall, Edinburgh.
Poole's Picture Palace, Ipswich.

POPULAR CINEMAS, LTD.—Head Office, Phoenix House, 19, Oxford Street, London, W.1.

Booking Director : E. W. CHEESMAN.
Telephone : Gerrard 1405.

Royal West London Theatre, Edgware Rd., W.2.
Princess Theatre, Hemel Hempstead.

**PORTSMOUTH TOWN CINEMAS, LTD.
Head Office : Shaftesbury Cinema, Kingston
Road, Portsmouth.**
Booking Manager : C. B. FOWLIE.
Telephone : Portsmouth 4976. .
Moderne, Bournemouth.
Regent, Christchurch.
Criterion, Gosport.
Gosport Theatre, Gosport.
Ritz, Gosport.
Palace, Portsmouth.
Shaftesbury, Portsmouth.
Palladium, Southbourne.
Cinema, Swanage.
Grand, Swanage.

**PROVINCIAL CINEMATOGRAPH THEATRES,
LTD.—Head Office : New Gallery House ,
123, Regent Street, London, W.1.**
Chairman and Managing Director : MARK
OSTRER.
Secretary : E. A. CRISP.
Telephone : Regent 8080.
Telegrams : Procinthe, Piccy, London.
Globe Kinema, Acton.
Majestic Picture House, Ashton-under-Lyne.
Classic, Belfast.
West End Cinema, Birmingham.
Regent, Bournemouth.
New Victoria, Bradford.
Regent, Brighton.
Regent, Bristol.
Gaumont Place, Chadwell Heath.
Gaumont Palace, Chelsea.
Gaumont Palace, Chester.
Majestic, Clapham.
Arcade Cinema, Darlington.
Court Kinema, Darlington.
Alhambra, Darlington.
Gaumont Palace, Derby.
Gaumont Palace, Doncaster.
King's Theatre, Dundee.
Hackney Pavilion.
New Picture House, Edinburgh.
New Victoria, Edinburgh.
Premier Super Cinema, East Ham.
Picture House, Glasgow.
Empire, Glossop.
Regent, Hanley.
Marlborough Theatre, Holloway.
Super Cinema, Ilford.
Regent, Ipswich.
Palace Cinema, Kentish Town.
Dominion Theatre, London.
Palace, Maida Vale.
Kilburn Grange, N.W.
Apollo, Stoke Newington.
Picture House, Chorlton-cum-Hardy.
Gaumont, Manchester.
Majestic, Leeds.
City Cinema, Leicester.
Picture House, Leicester.
Trocadero, Liverpool.
New Gallery, Regent Street, W.1.
Tivoli, Strand, W.C.
New Victoria, S.W.
Exchange Cinema, Northampton.
Prince's Theatre, North Shields.
Hippodrome, Nottingham.
Coronet, Notting Hill.
Broadway Kinema, Peterborough.
Gaumont Palace, Plymouth.
New Victoria, Preston.
Regent, Sheffield.
Regent, Stamford Hill.
Havelock Picture House, Sunderland.
Rink Cinema, Sydenham.

Palace, Tottenham.
Gaumont, Worcester.
Red Hall Cinema, Walham Green.
Picture House, York.
St. George's Hall, York.
Gaumont Palace, Peckham.
Tower Cinema, Peckham.
Tower Cinema Annexe, Peckham.
Gaumont Palace, Cheltenham.
Gaumont Palace, Exeter.
Gaumont Palace, Taunton.

Also controlling :—
ASSOCIATED PROVINCIAL PICTURE HOUSES, LTD.

Picture House, Aberdeen.
Criterion, Dudley.
Regent, Dudley.
Gaumont Palace, Wood Green.
Finsbury Park Cinema, Finsbury Park, N.
Picture House, Halifax.
Angel Cinema, Islington.
King's Cross Cinema, King's Cross.
Palace Cinema, Leigh.
Regent, Portsmouth.
Plaza, Southsea.
Surrey County Cinema, Sutton.
Picture House, Walsall.
Picture House, Wednesbury.
Picture House, Willenhall.
Queen's, Wolverhampton.
Gaumont Palace, Wolverhampton.
Scala, Wolverhampton.
Trocadero, Elephant and Castle.
Tivoli, New Brighton.
Troxy, Stepney.
Trocette, Bermondsey.
Grand Theatre, Oldham.

ALBANY WARD THEATRES, LTD.

Gaumont Palace, Barnstaple.
Palace, Bridgwater.
Gaumont, Chippenham.
Neild Hall, Chippenham.
Palace, Colne.
Palace, Chepstow.
Palace, Cinderford.
Picture House, Cirencester.
Palace, Dorchester.
Palladium, Exeter.
Palace, Frome.
Scala, Ilfracombe.
The Picture House, Lydney.
The Picture House, Monmouth.
Gaumont Palace, Salisbury.
Picture House, Salisbury.
New, Salisbury.
Gaumont Palace, Stroud.
Palace, Swindon.
Regent, Swindon.
Palace, Trowbridge.
Regent Theatre, Weymouth.
Belle Vue, Weymouth.
Gaumont Palace, Yeovil.
Palace, Easton.

THE JERSEY AND GUERNSEY AMUSEMENTS
Co., LTD.

Opera House, Jersey.
Gaumont Palace, Guernsey.
Lyric, Guernsey.

SCALA THEATRES, LTD.

Broadway Palladium, Ealing.
Grange Cinema, Kilburn.
Palace, Maida Vale.

**R. E. RATCLIFF CIRCUIT.—Office : " Raheny,"
Roby, Lancs.**
Telephone : Huyton 382.
Crescent Picture House, Douglas.
Royalty Cinema, Douglas.
Regal, Douglas.
Tunnel Road Picturedrome, Liverpool.
Cinema House, Ramsey, I.O.M.
Plaza, Ramsey, I.O.M.
Cosy, Castletown, I.O.M.
Royal Cinema, Wigan.
Pavilion, Warrington.
Avenue, Oucham, I.O.M.
Gaiety Theatre, Douglas.

**REGENT ENTERPRISES, LTD.—Office : 51
North John Street, Liverpool.**
General Manager : PHILIP M. HANMER.
Telephone : Bank 610.
Coliseum Cinema, Litherland.
Garrick Cinema, Kirkdale.
Grosvenor Cinema, Kirkdale.
Homer Cinema, Liverpool.
Mere Lane Picture House, Liverpool.
Kings Picture House, Liverpool.
Princes Picture House, Liverpool.
Regent Picture House, Warrington.
Queen's Picture House, Formby.
Swan Cinema, Liverpool.
Royal Picture House, Liverpool.
Victoria Cinema, Walton.

**RANDOLPH E. RICHARDS.—Head Office :
Picturedrome, Eastbourne.**
Telephone : Eastbourne 1441.
Gaiety, Brighton.
Picturedrome, Eastbourne.
Gaiety, Eastbourne.
Gaiety, Hastings.
Playhouse, Bexhill-on-Sea.
Gaiety, Bexhill-on-Sea.
Kinema, St. Leonards-on-Sea.

**ST. IVES CINEMAS (CORNWALL), LTD.—
Registered Office : Scala, High Street,
St. Ives, Cornwall.**
Telephone : St. Ives 143.
Royal, St. Ives. (Building).
Scala, St. Ives.

**SANDBACH CINEMAS, LTD.—Head Office :
Palace, Sandbach.**
General Manager : R. SMITH.
Telephone : Sandbach 103.
Palace, Sandbach.
Magnet, Winsford.
Alhambra. Middlewich.

**SARONIES ENTERPRISES.—Chief Office : 7-8
Saxone Buildings, Church Street, Liverpool.**
Telephone : Royal 2013.
Scala, Prestatyn.
City Picture House, Bangor.
Plaza, Bangor.

**DIXON SCOTT.—Address : Haymarket House,
Newcastle-on-Tyne.**
Telephone : Newcastle 23347.
Haymarket Theatre, Newcastle-on-Tyne.
New Theatre, Newcastle-on-Tyne.
Electric Theatre, Prudhoe-on-Tyne.

**SCOTT THEATRES, LTD.—Head Office : 56,
Brandon Street, Motherwell.**
Joint Secretaries : ROBERT WEIR, C.A., and
JAMES G. S. McLEES, B.L.
Telephone : Motherwell 601
Empire Theatre, Larkhall.
Pavilion, Barrhead.
Palaceum, Shettleston.

Premier, Shettleston.
Pavilion, Hawick.
Theatre, Hawick.

**SCOTT'S EMPIRES, LTD.—Address : Cinema,
Dunbar.**
Empire Cinema, Dunbar.
Empire Cinema, North Berwick.
Empire Cinema, Peebles.
Empire Cinema, Penicuik.
Empire Cinema, Linlithgow.
Burgh Cinema, Peebles.

**SEEMAN, S.—Address : 216, Imperial House,
Regent Street, W.1.**
Telephone : Regent 2809.
Classic, Chelsea.
Classic, Croydon.
Classic, Mile End.
Embassy, Notting Hill Gate.
Classic, Sydenham.

**SHEFFIELD AND DISTRICT CINEMATO-
GRAPH THEATRES, LTD.—Registered
Office : 3, Hartshead, Sheffield.**
Telephone : Central 20888.
Telegrams : Cinema, Sheffield.
Cinema House, Sheffield.
Electra Palace, Sheffield.
Globe Theatre, Attercliffe.
Don Picture Palace, Sheffield.

**SHIPMAN & KING.—Head Office : M 84.
Shell Mex House, Strand, London, W.C.2**
Telephone : Temple Bar 5077-8.
Embassy, Braintree.
Embassy, Chesham.
Embassy, Maldon.
Embassy, Northwood Hills.
Embassy, Petts Wood, Chislehurst.
Embassy, Tenterden.
Embassy, Fareham ⎫
Embassy, Hailsham ⎬ Building.
Embassy, Waltham Cross ⎭
Regent, Amersham.
Regent, Crowborough.
Regent, Horley.
Regent, Rye.
Regent, Waltham Cross.
Pavilion, Hoddesdon.
Electric Palace, Tenterden.
Pavilion, Hailsham.
Hippodrome, Maldon.
Central Cinema, Braintree.
Oriel Cinema, Leighton Buzzard.
Court Theatre, Berkhamsted.
Pavilion, Horley.
Exchange Theatre, Leighton Buzzard.
Hippodrome, Reigate.
Majestic, Reigate.
Savoy, Fareham.
Rivoli, Ruislip.
Astoria, Ruislip.
New Coronet, Didcot.
Welwyn Theatre, Welwyn Garden City.

**SINGLETON (GEORGE).—Head Office : 39,
Kirkpatrick Street, Glasgow.**
Telephone : Bridgeton 1111.
Pavilion Picture House, Airdrie.
Premier Pictures, Bridgeton, Glasgow.
Plaza, Burnbank, Hamilton.
Commodore, Scotstoun, Glasgow.
Empire, Coatbridge.
Cinema, Falkirk.
Paragon, Glasgow.
Empire, Dundee.
King's, Hawick.
Broadway, Shettleston, Glasgow.
Vogue, Rutherglen.
Vogue, Dundee.

SNAPE & WARD.—Office : Equitable Buildings, 13, St. Ann Street, Manchester.
Director : A. SNAPE.
Telephone : Blackfriars 3731.
Coliseum, Burnley.
Ambassador Super Cinema, Manchester.
Heaton Park Cinema, Manchester.
Carlton Super Cinema, Manchester.
New Popular Picture House, Manchester.
New Empire Cinema, Leigh.
Plaza Cinema, Stockport.
Sems Picture House, Leigh.
Pavilion Picture House, Lees, Oldham.
Ellesmere Super Cinema, Swinton.

SOUTH DOWNS CINEMAS, LTD.—Head Office : 2, Rugby Road, Southsea.
Directors : S. FILER AND L. H. FILE.
Telephone : Portsmouth 3456.
Palladium, Littlehampton.
Regent, Littlehampton.
Savoy, Petersfield.
Palace Cinema, Bordon, Hants.

SOUTH WALES CINEMAS, LTD.—Head Office : Albert Hall, De La Beche, Swansea.
General Manager : W. J. VAUGHAN.
Telephone : Swansea 4597.
Albert Hall, Swansea.
Carlton Cinema, Swansea.
Picture House, Swansea.
Gnoll Cinema, Neath.
Windsor Cinema, Neath.
Palace Cinema, Ammanford.

SPECTERMAN, RALPH.—Head Office : Dorland House, 18-20, Regent Street, London, W.1.
Telephones : Whitehall 9313.
Grand Theatre, Brighton.
Imperial Theatre, Edgware Road, W.2.
New Palladium, Shepherds Bush.
Silver Cinema, Shepherds Bush.
King's Hall, Lewisham.
Savoy Cinema, Lee Green.
Star Kinema, Wandsworth.
Polytechnic Theatre, Regent Street, W.1.

SPLOTT (CARDIFF) CINEMA CO., LTD.—Office : 14, St. Andrew's Crescent, Cardiff.
Telephone : Cardiff 2901-2.
Telegrams : Balance, Cardiff.
Splott Cinema, Cardiff.
Gaiety Cinema, Cardiff.
Canton Cinema, Cardiff.
Ninian Cinema, Cardiff.
Regent Cinema, Ely, Cardiff.

FRANK E. SPRING'S CIRCUIT.—Head Office : Parsonage Chambers, 3, The Parsonage, Manchester.
Telephone : Blackfriars 7905.
Empire, St. Annes-on-Sea.
Theatre Royal, Oldham.
Empire, Wigan.
Palladium, Blackley.
Princess, Harpurhey.

STAFFORD ENTERTAINMENTS, LTD.—Head Office : Picture House, Stafford.
Chairman and Managing Director : S. G. EVERTON.
Telephone : Stafford 291.
Albert Hall, Stafford.
Picture House, Stafford.
Sandonia Theatre, Stafford.

STAR CINEMAS, LTD.:—Office : 5, Manchester Avenue, London, E.C.1.
Managing Director : W. ECKART.
Telephone : Metropolitan 4292.
New Star, Castleford.
Regent, Huddersfield.

Majestic, Normanton.
Plaza, Fitzwilliam, near Pontefract.
Ritz, South Kirkby.
Regal, Worksop.

STOLL CIRCUIT.—Head Office : The Stoll Offices, Coliseum Buildings, London, W.C.2.
Chairman : SIR OSWALD STOLL.
Telephone : Temple Bar 1500.
Telegrams : Oswastoll, Lesquare, London.
Stoll Picture Theatre, Kingsway, London (The London Opera House).
Hackney Empire, London.
Shepherd's Bush Empire, London.
Stoll Picture Theatre, Newcastle-on-Tyne.
Floral Hall Picture Theatre, Leicester.
Hippodrome, Bristol.
Hippodrome, Bedminster.
Empire, Chatham.
Picture House, Chatham.
Palace, Leicester.
Empire, Wood Green, London.
Other Wired Theatres include —
The Coliseum, London.
Empire, Chiswick.
New Manchester Hippodrome, Ardwick.
(Films Booked by W. P. Carter at the Stoll Offices.)

WILL STONE'S CIRCUIT.—Head Office : Town Hall, Pontypridd.
Proprietor : WILL STONE.
General Manager : CECIL H. ROCHE.
General Secretary and Accountant : P. A. JAMES.
Telephone : Pontypridd 2311.
Telegrams : Stone, Pontypridd ; by phone, 2311.
Victoria Hall, Rhymney, Mon.
Public Hall, Pontycymmer, Glam.
Oddfellows' Hall, Dowlais, Glam.
Palace, Treharris.

STRAND CINEMA THEATRE CO. (1920), LTD., THE.—Head Office : 39, Strand Street, Douglas, Isle of Man.
Telephone : Douglas 14.
Telegrams : Strand Cinema, Douglas.
Picture House, Douglas.
Strand Cinema Theatre, Douglas.
Pavilion, Peel.
Strand Cinema, Port Erin.

STREATLEY HOUSE GROUP.—Head Office : "Furnivalls," Amersham, Bucks.
Managing Director and Secretary : D. R. BLAIR.
Telephone : Holmer Green 48.
Empire, Streatham High Road, S.W.
Golden Domes, Streatham High Road, S.W.
Golden Domes, Denmark Hill, S.E.
Mile End Cinema, Mile End Road.
Paisley Picture Theatre, Paisley.
Dundee Cinema Palace, Dundee.
Her Majesty's Theatre, Dundee.

GEORGE TAYLOR CIRCUIT.—Office : 27, Merkland Street, Partick, Glasgow, W.1.
General Manager : GEORGE TAYLOR.
Telephone : Western 2766.
Strand, Stockbridge, Edinburgh.
Partick Picture House, Glasgow, W.1.
West End Cinema, Paisley.
Alexandra Cinema, Paisley.
Kelvin Cinema, Finnieston, Glasgow, C.
New Star Cinema, Maryhill, Glasgow, N.W.
Picture House, Dunoon.
Orient Kinema, Glasgow, E.

CHARLES THOMPSON'S CIRCUIT. — Head Office : Weetwood Chambers, Albion Street, Leeds, 1.
Telephone : Leeds 25859.
Telegrams : Ceetee, Leeds.
Palace, Doncaster.
Grand Theatre, Doncaster.
Palace, Grimsby.

THOMPSON'S ENTERPRISES, LTD. — Head Office : 4, Palladium Buildings, Eastbourne Road, Middlesbrough.
Governing Director : THOS. THOMPSON.
Telephone : Linthorpe 88156.
Regent, Redcar.
Central, Redcar.
Empire, Loftus.
Empire, Gainsborough.
And in Association with :—
Palladium, Middlesborough.
Palladium, Hartlepool.
Palladium, Durham.
Palladium, South Shields
Regent, South Shields.
Regent, Sunderland.
Gem, North Ormesby.
Hippodrome, Shildon.
Gaiety, Ferryhill.
Royal Aquarium, Great Yarmouth.
Regent, Acomb, York.

J. F. TIDSWELL.—Office : 26, Park Row, Leeds.
Telephone : Leeds 28775.
Capitol, Scarboro'.
Londesborough, Scarboro'.
Queen's, Holbeck, Leeds.
Playhouse, Wakefield.
Strand, Hull.
Victory, Leeds.
Winter Gardens, Bridlington
Grand, Wakefield.
Victoria, Halifax.
Electra Lounge, Leeds.
Ritz, Doncaster.

TOURING TALKING PICTURE CO.—Head Office : Chase Avenue, King's Lynn, Norfolk.
Telephone : King's Lynn 2335.
Cosy Cinema, Buntingford.
Cosy Cinema, Redbourn.

W. W. TURNBULL.—Address : Greenside, Durham Road, Coxhoe, Ferryhill, Co. Durham.
Telephone : Coxhoe 5.
Unity Cinema, Sherburn Hill
Alhambra, Fishburn, Stockton-on-Tees.

TWENTIETH CENTURY CINEMAS, LTD.— Office : Brettenham House, 14-15, Lancaster Place, Strand, London, W.C.2.
Managing Director : TH. KAUSSENS.
Telephone : Temple Bar 1144 and 4758.
Empress, Hackney.
Century, Clacton.
Electric, Clacton.
Tivoli, Clacton.
METROPOLITAN AND PROVINCIAL CINEMATO-
GRAPH THEATRES, LTD. :—
Kilburn Empire.
Croydon Empire.
Ilford Hippodrome.
Hammersmith Palace.
Islington Empire.

TYNE PICTURE HOUSES, LTD.—Office : Central Buildings, Station Road, Wallsend-on-Tyne.
General Manager : W. THORBURN.
Telephone : Wallsend 63566.

Tyne Picture Theatre, Wallsend-on-Tyne.
Royal Pictures, Wallsend-on-Tyne.
Brinkburn Picture Theatre, Byker, Newcastle-on-Tyne.
Apollo Super Cinema, Byker, Newcastle-on-Tyne.

UNION CINEMAS, LTD., AND ASSOCIATED COMPANIES.—Registered Office : Union House, 15, Regent Street, London, S.W.1.
Managing Director : FRED BERNHARD.
Telephone : Whitehall 8484.
Oxford Super Cinema, Oxford.
Electra Palace, Oxford.
George Street Cinema, Oxford.
Palace, Cowley Road, Oxford.
Rialto, Maidenhead.
Plaza, Maidenhead.
St. James' Theatre, King's Lynn.
Electric Theatre, King's Lynn.
Majestic Cinema, King's Lynn.
Theatre Royal, King's Lynn.
Majestic, Benwell.
Adelaide Picture Hall, Benwell.
Grand Picture Theatre, Huddersfield.
Victoria Hall, Portsmouth.
Alexandra, Southampton.
Picture Theatre, Woolston.
Picture Theatre, Winchester.
Palace Theatre, Banbury.
Kemble Theatre, Hereford.
Garrick Theatre, Hereford.
Regal Cinema, Newbury.
Carlton Cinema, Newbury.
Super Cinema, Gravesend.
Plaza, Gravesend.
Ritz, Tunbridge Wells.
Great Hall, Tunbridge Wells.
Central Cinema, Cambridge.
Playhouse, Cambridge.
Tivoli, Cambridge.
New Cinema, Cambridge.
Empire, Ashton-under-Lyne
Regal, Dewsbury.
Victoria, Cambridge.
Regal, Uxbridge.
Adelphi, Slough.
Playhouse, Windsor.
Regal, Windsor.
Royalty, Windsor.
Empire, Wolverton.
Empire, Luton.
Palace, Dunstable.
Ritz, Maidstone.
Plaza, Luton.
Central Playhouse, Maidstone.
Picturedrome, Luton.
Palace, Maidstone.
Capitol, Horsham.
Winter Garden Theatre, Horsham.
Carfax, Horsham.
Opera House, Tunbridge Wells.
Kosmos, Tunbridge Wells.
Regal, Hastings.
Elite, Hastings.
Cinema de Luxe, Hastings.
Luxor, Eastbourne.
Ritz, Belfast.
Savoy, Uxbridge.
Ritz, Eastbourne.
Ritz, Oxford.
Regal, Cowley, Oxford.
Ritz, Ipswich.
Regal, Dunstable.
Ritz, Grimsby.
Marlborough, Yiewsley.
Ritz, Huddersfield.
Strand, Belfast.
Ritz, Luton.
Central, Maidstone.

Ritz, Hereford.
Majestic, Belfast.
Ritz, Maidenhead.
Regal, Cleethorpes.
Ritz, Banbury.
Rivoli, Southend-on-Sea.
Whitehall Theatre, Rotherham.
Ritz, Penzance.
Electric Palace, Highgate.
Ritz, Darlington.
Empire, Highgate.
Ritz, Hyde.
Regal, St. Leonards.
Ritz, West Hartlepool.
Elite, St. Leonards.
Ritz, Dukinfield.
Princess's, Crayford.
Ritz, Macclesfield.
Picture House, Erith.
Lonsdale, Carlisle.
Public Hall, Carlisle.
Olympia, Newcastle-on-Tyne.
Ritz, Horsham.
Ritz, Chatham.
Ritz, Stafford.
Regal, Bexley Heath.
City Picture House, Carlisle.
Grand Theatre, Falmouth.
St. George's Hall, Falmouth.
Casino, Herne Bay.
Red Lantern, Herne Bay.
Central, Folkestone.
Playhouse, Folkestone.
Pleasure Gardens Theatre, Folkestone.
Majestic, Darlington.
Regal, Kingston.
Regal, Beckenham.
Regal, Sidcup.
Alma, Luton.
Palace, Eltham.
Regal, Yarmouth.
Plaza, Catford.
Broadway, Eccles.
Capitol, Didsbury.
Kingsway, Levenshulme.
Regal, Altrincham.
Regal, Abingdon.
Pavilion, Abingdo .
Ritz, Aldershot.
Ritz, Bexhill.
Regal, Bicester.
Regal, Bracknell.
Ritz, Blackburn.
Ritz, blackpool.
Ritz, Burnley.
Ritz, Felixstowe.
Majestic, Gravesend.
Regal, Gravesend.
Ritz, Hastings.
Ritz, Hythe.
Ritz, Halifax.
County Cinema, Lancaster.
Palace Theatre, Lancaster.
Grand Theatre, Lancaster.
Kingsway Cinema, Lancaster
Ritz, Leek.
Ritz, Market Harboro'.
Majestic, Oxford (Botley).
Ritz, Richmond.
Ritz, Tonbridge.
Regal, Wallingford.
Ritz, Woking.
Ritz, Wokingham.
Savoy, Wokingham.
Ritz, Nuneaton.
Ritz, Bedminster.
Ritz, Newport.
Tower, Ancoats (Manchester)
Ritz, Barrow-in-Furness

Regal, Barrow-in-Furness.
Coliseum, Barrow-in-Furness.
Palace, Barrow-in-Furness.
Gaiety, Barrow-in-Furness.
Ritz, Swansea.
Cosmo., Gorton (Manchester).
Ritz, Middlesbrough.
Rota, Reddish.
Pavilion, Salthouse.
Ritz, Ripon.
Ritz, Rochdale.
Empress, Urmston.
Ritz, Stockport.
Walney Theatre, Walney Island.
Ritz, Warrington.
Ritz, Wigan.
Ritz, Barnsley.
Ritz, Wallsend-on-Tyne.
Ritz, Worksop.
Ritz, Keighley.
Ritz, Scunthorpe.
Don, Beswick (Manchester).
Ritz, Coleraine.
Ritz, Armagh.
Ritz, Ballymena.
Ritz, Larne.
Ritz, Lisburn.
Ritz, Londonderry.
Ritz, Lurgan.
Ritz, Newtownards.

UNITED PICTURE THEATRES, LTD.—
Registered Office : 123, Regent Street,
London, W.1.
Chairman and Managing Director : MARK
OSTRER.
Telephone : Regent 8080.
Hippodrome, Camden Town.
Palace, Kilburn.
Old Kent Picture House, Old Kent Road.
Rivoli, Whitechapel Road.
Shakespeare Theatre, Clapham Junction.
Palace, Southall.
Stamford Hill Cinema, Clapton Common.
Palace, Putney.
Palace, Wandsworth.
Savoy, Leyton.

E. R. VARLEY.—Office : The Pavilion, Bridge
Street, Girvan.
Telephone : Girvan 111.
Pavilion, Girvan.
Picture House, Stewarton.
Kinema, Stranraer.

V.E.H. CINEMAS, LTD.—Head Office : The
Lido, Aylsham Road, Norwich.
Managing Director : V. E. HARRISON.
Telephone : Norwich 894.
Capitol, Norwich.
Lido, Norwich.
Regal, North Walsham.
Central, Cromer.
Olympia, Cromer.
Regal, Walton-on-Naze.
Kino, Walton-on-Naze.
Regal, Stowmarket.
Plaza, Gt. Yarmouth.

GEORGE VICKERY, LTD.—Head Office :
Taunton.
Telephone : Taunton 3184.
Gaiety, Rowbarton, Taunton.
Tivoli, Weston-super-Mare.
Palace Theatre, Cheltenham.

VICTORY THEATRES, LTD.—Head Office:
Edgar Street, Accrington.
General Manager : ARTHUR PEEL.
Telephone : Accrington 2350, 2701.

Empire Picture House, Accrington.
Majestic Theatre, Nelson.
Princes Theatre, Accrington.
Palace, Accrington.

WALLAW PICTURES, LTD.—Registered Office : Wallaw Buildings, Ashington, Northumberland.
Managing Director : WALTER LAWSON.
Telephone : Ashington 31.
Pavilion Theatre, Ashington.
Buffalo Picture Palace, Ashington.
Miners' Theatre, Ashington.
Wallaw Cinema, Blyth.
Playhouse, Morpeth.
Palace Theatre, Bedlington.
Wallaw P.H., Newbiggin-by-the-Sea.

WARSTON PICTURES, LTD.—Registered Office : 20, Brazennose Street, Manchester, 2.
Telephone : Blackfriars 6965.
Palace, Urmston.
Star Kinema, Warrington.
Picturedrome, Warrington.
Also associated with :
King's Picture Playhouse, Chelsea
Imperial, Brook's Bar.
Queen's, Longsight
Coliseum, Ardwick Green.

WATTS' CINEMAS, LTD.—Registered Office : "Poolstock," Findeon, Northants.
Booking Manager : ALFRED T. WATTS.
Telephone : Finedon 9.
Cinema, Burton Latimer.
Cinema, Finedon.
Cinema, Irthlingborough.

WHINCUP, (C. H.)—Office : The Tower, Brig gate, Leeds.
Telephone : Leeds 23137.
Majestic, Driffield.
Majestic, Howden.
Tower Picture House, Leeds.
Carlton Cinema, Leeds.
Pavilion, Stanningley.
Capitol, Meanwood, Leeds.
Hyde Park Picture House, Leeds.
Majestic Cinema Pocklington.

WIGAN ENTERTAINMENTS CO., LTD.— Registered Office : 1, College Avenue, Wigan.
Booking Manager : F. WORSWICK.
Telephones : (Day) Wigan 3173 ; (Night) Wigan 2394.
Telegrams : Worswick, Wigan.
Embassy, Formby.
Palace, Hindley.
Pavilion, Wigan.

WILLIAMS CINEMAS, LTD.—Office : Hippodrome, Workington.
Telephone : Workington 194.
Stanley Hall, Carlisle.
Regal, Carlisle.
Hippodrome, Workington

WILLIS, W. E.—Head Office : Globe Cinema, Albany Road, Penylan, Cardiff.
Telephone and Telegrams : Cardiff 3072.
Grand Theatre, Swansea.
Cosy Cinema, Aberdare.
Park Cinema, Aberdare.
Palace, Cwmaman.
Royal Cinema, Tonypandy.
Picturedrome, Tonypandy.
Empire Theatre, Tonypandy.
Hippodrome, Tonypandy.
Coliseum, Cardiff.
Globe Cinema, Cardiff.
Rialto Cinema, Whitchurch.
Grand Theatre, Pentre.
New Palace Cinema, Swansea.
Empire, Torquay.
Abergorky Hall, Treorchy.

WINDERMERE AND AMBLESIDE CINEMAS LTD.—Head Office : 33, James Street, Liverpool.
Managing Director : L. H. CLEGG.
Telephone : Liverpool, Bank, 4000.
Telegrams : Praebere, Liverpool.
Royalty Theatre, Bowness on Windermere.
Cinema, Windermere.

OLD COLWYN PICTURE THEATRE, LTD. :—
Supreme Picture Theatre, Old Colwyn.

WIRRAL PICTUREDROMES, LTD. (QUEEN'S PICTURE HOUSE CIRCUIT).—Booking Office : Queen's Picturedrome, Wallasey.
Queen's, Seacombe Wallasey.
Queen's, Walton.
Queen's, Waterloo.
Queen's, Ashton-in-Makerfield.
Queen's, Warrington.

WITHERS, A.—Head Office : New Hall, Bargoed, South Wales.
General Manager : F. A. CAM.
Telephone : Bargoed 72.
Telegrams : Newhall, Bargoed.
New Hall, Bargoed.
Palace Cinema, Bargoed.
Hanbury Cinema, Bargoed.

WOOD'S PICTURE HALLS, LTD. (Owners and Lessors).—Office : Wood's Palace, Bilston.
Managing Director : THOMAS R. WOOD.
Telephone : Bilston 41388.
Savoy, Bilston.
Theatre Royal, Bilston.
Queen's, Bradley, Bilston.

YARMOUTH & LOWESTOFT CINEMAS, LTD.— Head Office : 16, South Quay, Great Yarmouth.
Managing Director : E. H. FIELD.
Telephone : Yarmouth 40.
Empire, Great Yarmouth.
Gem Picture House, Great Yarmouth.
Palace, Lowestoft.
Hippodrome, Lowestoft.

DIRECTORY OF KINEMAS

Every effort has been made to ensure accuracy in the particulars given in this Directory, but the publishers do not hold themselves responsible for any inaccuracies that may occur.

LONDON

The Sound system installed is shown after the name. (BTP)= British Talking Pictures, Ltd.; (RCA)=RCA Photophone Inc. ; (WE)=Western Electric Co., Ltd; (BA)=British Acoustic; (BTH)=British Thomson-Houston. Other systems are indicated by name.

ACTON, W.

CARLTON CINEMA (BA), Horn Lane, W.3—Prop., Carlton Cinema (Acton), Ltd. 580 seats. Continuous. Booked at Hall, Prices, 7d to 1s. 6d. Station, Acton (G.W.R.), Phone : Acorn 1544.

CROWN KINEMA (RCA), High Street, W.3—Prop., Amenik Theatres, Ltd. 600 seats. Continuous. Stage, 14 ft. deep. Prices, 7d. to 1s. 3d. Phone : Acorn 2786.

GLOBE CINEMA (WE), High Street, W.3.—Prop., Provincial Cinematograph Theatres, Ltd., New Gallery House, 123, Regent Street, London, W.1. Phone : Regent 8080. 2,406 seats. Phone : Acorn 1458.

ODEON (BTH), King Street—Props., Odeon (Acton), Ltd., Cornhill House, Bennetts Hill, Birmingham, Booked at 49, Park Lane, W.1. (In course of construction).

BAKER STREET, N.W.

CLASSIC CINEMA, 96 and 98, Baker Street, W.1.

TUSSAUD'S CINEMA (RCA)—Props., Madame. Tussaud's Ltd., Welbeck 1832. 1,714 seats. Booked at Associated British Cinemas, Ltd., Golden Square, W.1. Continuous. Prices, 1s. to 3s. 6d. Proscenium width, 43 ft. Cafe. Phone : Welbeck 8661.

WURLITZER ORGAN
Installed in this Kinema

BALHAM, S.W.

BALHAM HIPPODROME (late Duchess Cinema) (WE), Balham Hill, S.W.12.—Prop., Lucien Sammett. 1,050 seats. Prices, 4d. to 2s. 6d. Phone : Balham 1232.

BALHAM PALLADIUM (RCA), Balham High Road.—Prop., General Theatre Corporation, Ltd., 123, Regent Street, W.1. 900 seats. Booked at H.O. Continuous. Two changes weekly. Prices, 6d. to 2s. 6d. Phone: Streatham 0596.

BALHAM PICTURE HOUSE (WE).—Prop.; Associated British Cinemas, Ltd., 30-31, Golden Square, W.1. 1,300 seats. Booked at H.O. Continuous. Three changes weekly. Prices, 9d. to 1s. 6d.

ODEON THEATRE (BTH), Cr. Malwood Road and Balham Hill, S.W.12.—Prop., Odeon (Balham) Ltd., Cornhill House, Bennett's Hill, Birmingham. Phone : Midland 2781. (In course of construction).

PAVILION (WE), Balham High Road.—Prop., National Electric Theatres, Ltd. 1,037 seats. Booked at H.O. Continuous. Pictures and Variety. Two changes weekly. Prices, 6d. to 2s. Phone : Streatham 0471.

BARNES, S.W.

RANELAGH SUPER CINEMA (WE)—(Closed). 550 seats.

BATTERSEA, S.W.

GLOBE CINEMA (WE), 15-17, Northcote Road, Battersea, S.W.11. Prop., Globe Cinema, Ltd. Continuous. Booked at H.O. Pictures and occasional Variety. Prices, 6d. to 1s. 10d. Proscenium width 60 ft. Stage 16 ft. deep ; two dressing rooms. Phone : Battersea 6649. Station, Clapham Junction, S.R.

GRAND HALL (Battersea Town Hall).—Seats 1,056. Special Children's performances at 5-30—8.15. Prices, 2d. to 6d. Phone : Battersea 2200. Station, Clapham Junction.

IMPERIAL CINEMA, 9, St. John's Hill, Battersea, S.W.11.—Prop., Clapham Theatre, Ltd.

SUPER PALACE (WE), 32, York Road.—Props., Supershow (Battersea) Ltd., 60 High Holborn, W.C. 862 seats. Booked at H.O. Continuous. Two changes weekly. Prices 6d. to 1s. 6d. Phone : Battersea 1810. Station, Battersea (S.R.) and Road Transport.

BAYSWATER, W.2.
QUEENS (WE).—Props., Associated British Cinemas, Ltd., 30-31, Golden Square, London, W.I. Phone: Gerrard 7887. 1,428 seats. Pictures and Variety. Stage, 15 ft. deep. Proscenium width, 40 ft. Prices, 1s. to 3s. 6d. Phone: Bayswater 4149.
ROXY (WE), 90-92, Westbourne Grove, W.2.— Prop., Vincent W. Beecham. 360 seats. Booked at Hall. Continuous. Prices, 6d to 1s. 8d. Phone: Bayswater 4680.

BEAR STREET, W.1.
CAMEO REVUEDENEWS, (WE).—Prop., Clavering and Rose, 199, Piccadilly, W.I. Regent 1146. 500 seats. Booked at Hall. Continuous. Prices, 6d. to 2s. Proscenium width, 35 ft. Phone: Whitehall 1638.

C O M P T O N
ORGAN featured here.

BERMONDSEY, S.E.
GRAND CINEMA (Kamm), Grange Road, S.E.— Prop., Miss R. Lever. 500 seats. Booked at Hall. Continuous. Pictures and Variety. Three changes weekly. Prices, 6d. to 1s. 3d. Phone: B.rmondsey 2565. Station, Elephant and Castle (S.R.)
PALACE CINEMA (RCA), 256, Southwark Park Road.—Prop., Palace Cinema (Southwark Park Road), Ltd. Phone: Bermondsey 1404. 850 seats. Pictures and Variety. Booked at Hall. Three changes weekly. Stage, 30 ft. wide, 12 ft. deep; two dressing rooms. Prices, 4d. to 1s. 6d. Station, London Bridge (S.R.)
RIALTO CINEMA (BTH), St. James Road.—Prop., H. A. Walker. 890 seats. Booked at Hall. Continuous. Prices, 6d. to 1s. 3d. Pictures and Variety. Proscenium width, 30 ft. Phone: Bermondsey 3244.
STAR CINEMA (BA), 189, Abbey Street.—Prop., W. S. Penney and J. V. Watson. 590 seats. Continuous. Booked at Hall Proscenium width, 24 ft. Stage, 20 ft. deep, two dressing rooms. Prices, 3d. to 1s. Phone: Bermondsey 3220. Station, London Bridge.
TROC-ETTE (WE), Tower Bridge Road.—Prop., Gaumont British Super Cinemas, Ltd., 90, Regent Street, W.I. Phone: Regent 4794. 2,500 seats. Continuous. Booked at H.O. Pictures and Variety. Prices, 6d. to 1s. 6d. Proscenium width, 25 ft. Stage, 14 ft. deep; five dressing rooms. Phone, Hop 1448.

WURLITZER ORGAN
Installed in this Kinema

BETHNAL GREEN, E.
EMPIRE PICTUREDROME (BTP), 62-66, Green Street.—Prop., Charles Spencer. 750 seats. Booked at Hall. Continuous. Pictures and Variety. Three changes weekly. Prices, 3d. to 1s. Phone: Advance 3746.
EXCELSIOR KINEMA (WE), Mansford Street, E.2.—Prop., Excelsior Hall, Ltd. 840 seats. Continuous. Pictures and Variety. Stage 78 ft. deep; five dressing rooms. Three changes weekly. Prices, 6d. to 1s. 3d. Phone: Bishopsgate 5060. Station, Bethnal Green (L.N.E.R.).
FORRESTERS' CINEMA (WE), 93, Cambridge Road, E.1.—Prop., Foresters' Cinema Co., Ltd. 1,058 seats. Phone: Bishopsgate 4061.

MUSEUM CINEMA (WE), Cambridge Road.— Prop., Museum Picture Theatre, Ltd., Cinema House, 225, Oxford Street, W.I. 802 seats. Booked at H.O. Continuous. Three changes weekly. Prices, 6d. to 1s. Proscenium width, 30 ft. Station, Cambridge Heath, (L.N.E.R.).
SMART'S PICTURE PALACE (WE), 281-283, Bethnal Green Road.—Prop., H.B.N., Picture House, Ltd. 865 seats. Booked at Pollen House, 10-12, Cork Street, W.I. Continuous. Three changes weekly. Proscenium width, 24 ft. Stage, 7 ft. 6 in.; two dressing rooms. Prices, 5d. to 1s. Phone: Bishopsgate 1040. Café.

BLACKFRIARS ROAD, S.E.
GRAND CENTRAL THEATRE (WE).—Props., Ben Jones, J. E. Phillips, and Mrs. E. E. Cauvin. 600 seats. Continuous. Three changes weekly. Prices, 6d. to 9d. Phone, Waterloo 4019.

BLACKHEATH, S.E.
ODEON THEATRE.—Props., Odeon Theatres, Ltd., Cornhill House, Bennett's Hill, Birmingham, 2. Phone, Midland 4667.
ROXY (WE), Old Dover Road.—Props, Associated British Cinemas, Ltd., 30-31, Golden Square, W.I. Phone: Gerrard 7887. 1,342 seats. Booked at H.O. Continuous. Prices, 6d. to 2s. Proscenium width 40 ft. Stage 20 ft. deep; three dressing rooms. Café. Phone: Greenwich 2977. Station, Blackheath, S.R.

BLOOMSBURY, W.C.
BLOOMSBURY SUPER CINEMA (WE), Theobalds Road.—Prop., Bloomsbury Cinema, Ltd. 1,372 seats. Booked at 32, Shaftesbury Avenue, W.I. Continuous. Three changes weekly. Prices, 9d. to 1s. 10d. Proscenium width, 40 ft. Phone, Holborn 7153

BOROUGH, S.E.
TRINITY HALL CINEMA (Mihaly), Trinity Street. —Prop., R. W. Ross, Palace Cinema, Broadway, Cricklewood, N.W.2. 350 seats. Continuous. Three changes weekly. Booked at Hall. Prices, 4d. to 9d. Phone: Hop. 4455.

BOW, E.
ELECTRODROME (BA), Fair Green.—Prop., Bernstein Theatres, Ltd., 36, Golden Square, London, W.I. Phone: Gerrard 3554. Booked at H.O. Phone: Advance 3215. Station, Mile End, D.R.
REGAL (WE), 156, Bow Road, E.3.—Prop., Regal (Bow) Ltd., 52, Shaftesbury Avenue, W.I. Phone: Gerrard 1668. 940 seats. Continuous. Three changes weekly. Prices, 6d. to 1s. 6d. Proscenium width, 30 ft. Stage, 40 ft. deep; five dressing rooms. Phone: Advance 2788. Café.

BRIXTON, S.W.
BRIXTON ASTORIA (WE),—Stockwell Road, S.W.4.—Prop., Paramount Astoria Theatres, Ltd., 104-108, Oxford Street, W.I. 3,090 seats. Phone: Museum 4721. Pictures and Variety. Continuous. Prices, 6d. to 3s. 6d. Phone: Brixton 5482.

C O M P T O N
ORGAN featured here.

BRIXTON PAVILION (BTP).—Props., Brixton Pavilion Co. 800 seats. Continuous. Prices, 6d. to 2s. Phone : Brixton 1649.

EMPRESS (BTP).—Prop., Empress Theatre of Varieties, Ltd. 1,900 seats.

NEW ROYALTY KINEMA (RCA), 101-3, Brixton Hill, S.W.2.—Prop., H. E. Hayward Cinemas, Ltd. 900 seats. Continuous. Two changes weekly. Prices, 9d. to 1s. 6d. Phone : Tulse Hill 2219.

PALLADIUM CINEMA (RCA).—Prop., Associated British Cinemas, Ltd., 30-31, Golden Square, W.1. Phone : Gerrard 7887. 1,200 seats. Booked at H.O. Continuous. Prices, 5d. to 3s. Proscenium width, 30 ft. Phone : Brixton 4663. Station, Brixton S.R.

WURLITZER ORGAN
Installed in this Kinema

BROCKLEY, S.E.

NEW PALLADIUM CINEMA (BTH), Foxberry Road, S.E.4.—Prop., Alfred Barnett, 26, Park Hill, Clapham. 800 seats. Continuous. Booked at Hall. Prices, 6d. to 1s. 3d. Phone : Tideway 2054. Station, Brockley, S.R.

RIVOLI (WE), Brockley Road.—Props., F. G. Lockwood. 700 seats. Booked at Hall. Continuous. Three changes weekly. Prices, 6d. to 1s. 6d. Proscenium width, 30 ft. Phone : New Cross 2165. Station, Crofton Park.

CAMBERWELL, S.E.

CORONET CINEMA (AWH), Wells Street.—Prop. John Ashcroft. Seats 550. Booked at Hall. Continuous. Three changes weekly. Prices, 6d. to 1s. 2d. Phone : Rodney 3830. Station, Camberwell New Road (S.R.).

GOLDEN DOMES (WE), 28, Denmark Hill, S.E.5.—Props., Golden Domes (Camberwell) Ltd. 746 seats. Booked at H.O. Pictures and Variety. Continuous. Two changes weekly. Prices, 6d. to 1s. 6d. Proscenium width, 35 ft. Phone : Briston 2128.

NEW EMPIRE (RCA), Denmark Hill, S.E.5.—Prop., Camberwell Empire, Ltd. 1,000 seats. Booked at Hall. Continuous. Prices 4d. to 1s. 6d. Pictures and Variety. Stage 28 ft. deep ; three dressing rooms. Phone : Brixton 4880. Station, Denmark Hill (S.R.).

NEW GRAND HALL CINEMA (BA), Camberwell New Road.—Prop., New Grand Hall (Camberwell), Ltd. 840 seats. Booked at hall. Continuous. Two changes weekly. Prices, 6d. to 1s. 6d. Phone : Rodney 4335. Station, Denmark Hill (S.R.).

PALACE (WE), Camberwell.—Props., Associated British Cinemas, Ltd., 30-31, Golden Square, W.1. 1,396 seats. Booked at H.O. Continuous. Prices, 4d. to 1s. 6d. Phone : Rodney 4816.

PURPLE PICTURE PALACE (RCA), Camberwell Gate, S.E.17.—Prop., Purple Picture Palaces, Ltd. 900 seats. Booked at 37-38, Golden Square, W.1. Continuous. Two changes weekly. Prices, 6d. to 1s. 6d. Phone : Rodney 3527. Station, Elephant and Castle (S.R.)

SAVOY (BTH), Camberwell Road, S.E.—Props., R. W. Ross. 550 seats. Continuous. Three changes weekly. Prices, 4d. to 1s. Phone : Rodney 3142.

CAMDEN TOWN, N.W.

BEDFORD (RCA), 93 & 95, High Street.—Prop., Associated British Cinemas, Ltd, 30-31, Golden Square, W.1. 1,259 seats. Booked at H.O. Continuous. Prices 3d. to 1s. 9d. Phone : Museum 0760. Road Transport.

BRITANNIA CINEMA (WE), High Street, N.W.1.—Prop., General Cinemas, Ltd., 19, Albemarle Street, W.1. Phone : Regent 4419. 731 seats. Booked at H.O. Continuous. Two changes weekly. Prices, 9d. to 2s. 5d. Phone : Gulliver 2443,

CAMDEN HIPPODROME (BA), High Street, N.W.1, —Prop., United Picture Theatres, Ltd., 123. Regent Street, London, 101. Phone : Regent 8080. Continuous. Prices, 5d. to 3s. Three changes weekly. Phone : Euston 1616.

GAUMONT PALACE.—Prop., Gaumont British Picture Corpn., Ltd., 142-150, Wardour Street, W.1.

C O M P T O N
O R G A N f e a t u r e d h e r e .

CANNING TOWN, E.

GRAND CINEMA (WE), Barking Road.—Prop., Denman Picture Houses, Ltd., 123, Regent Street, W.1. 1359 seats. Booked at H.O. Continuous. Two changes weekly. Prices, 6d. to 1s. 2d. Phone : Albert Dock 1784. Road Transport.

CATFORD, S.E.

HIPPODROME (see Lewisham).

PLAZA (BTH).—Controlled by Union Cinemas, Ltd., 15, Regent Street, London ; S.W.1. Phone : Whitehall 8484. Continuous. Booked at H.O. Prices, 6d. to 1s. 6d. Phone, Hither Green 3306. Station, Catford Bridge (S.R.)

QUEEN'S HALL (RCA), Rushey Green.—Prop. Gaumont-British Picture Corporation, Ltd., Regent Street, W.1. 830 seats. Continuous. Three changes weekly. Prices, 6d. to 1s. 6d. Proscenium width, 16 ft. Phone : Hither Green 1711.

CHARING CROSS ROAD, W.C.2

ASTORIA (WE).—Props., General Theatres Corp. Ltd., New Gallery House, Regent Street, W.1. 1,696 seats. Booked at H.O. Pictures and Variety. Prices, 1s. to 3s. Continuous. Booked at H.O. Phone : Gerrard 5528. Stage, 14 ft. Dance hall and café.

Fitted "ARDENTE" Deaf Aids
See page 258

C O M P T O N
O R G A N f e a t u r e d h e r e .

CAMEO (see under Bear Street).

PHOENIX (WE).—Props., Charing Cross Road Theatres, Ltd. Phone : Temple Bar 7431. 1,034 seats. Booked by Bernstein Theatres Ltd., and by Manager.

TATLER THEATRE (BA).—Props., The Gaumont British Picture Corporation Ltd. New Gallery House, Regent Street, W.1. 690 seats. Continuous. Prices, 6d. and 1s. Phone Gerrard 4815.

C O M P T O N
O R G A N f e a t u r e d h e r e .

136 WARDOUR STREET, LONDON, W.1.

CHARLTON, S.E.

PLAYHOUSE (RCA), 473, Woolwich Road, S.E.—
—Prop., Sparrow & Arundel, Ltd., 400 seats.
Booked at hall. Continuous Prices, 7d. to
1s. 3d. Phone ; Greenwich 0711. Stations,
Charlton (S.R.

CHELSEA

CHELSEA PALACE, King's Road, S.W.3.—Prop.
Variety Theatre Consolidated, Ltd.
GAUMONT PALACE (BA), Kings Road and Manor
Street, Chelsea.—Props., Provincial Cine-
matograph Theatres, Ltd. 2,502 seats.
Continuous. Booked at H.O. New Gallery
House, Regent Street, W.1. Prices, 6d. to
2s. 6d. Pictures and Variety. Proscenium
width, 52 ft. Stage, 26 ft. deep. Eight
dressing rooms. Café attached.
Fitted "ARDENTE" Deaf Aids
See page 258

C O M P T O N
ORGAN featured here

KING'S PICTURE PLAYHOUSE (WE), 279, King's
Road, S.W.3.—Prop., Chelsea Picture House,
Ltd. 964 seats. Continuous. Phone : Flax-
man 3139.

CLASSIC (WE), 148, King's Road, S.W.3.—Prop.'
Classic Picture Theatres, Ltd., 201, Imperial
House, Regent Street, W.1. Booked at H.O.
386 seats. Continuous. Two changes weekly.
Prices, 6d. to 1s. Phone : Flaxman 4388.
Station, Sloane Square (District).

CHINGFORD, E.

CHINGFORD CINEMA (RCA), Station Road, E.4.—
Prop., Cinema House Ltd. 225, Oxford Street,
W.1. 600 seats. Continuous. Two changes
weekly. Prices, 7d. to 1s. 6d. Phone :
Silverthorn 1134. Station, Chingford.
ODEON THEATRE (BTH), Cherrydown Avenue.—
Prop., Odeon (Chingford), Ltd., Cornhill
House, Bennetts Hill, Birmingham. Phone:
Midland 2781. Booked at 49, Park Lane, W.1.
Prices, 6d. to 2s. Phone : Silverthorn 2210.

CHISWICK, W.

CHISWICK EMPIRE (WE).—Prop., Stoll Theatres,
Coliseum Buildings. 2,154 seats. Prices,
6d. to 2s. Phone : Chiswick 1249-1250.
Variety twice nightly. Station, Chiswick
Park (District Railway).

CLAPHAM, S.W.

MAJESTIC THEATRE (WE), High Street.—Prop.,
Provincial Cinematograph Theatres, Ltd.
1,562 seats. Continuous. Prices, 9d. to 2s.
Phone : Macaulay 4048.
Fitted "ARDENTE" Deaf Aids
See page 258

C O M P T O N
ORGAN featured here.

PAVILION (WE), 33, High Street.—Prop., J. V:
and T. A. Dobbin. 719 seats. Booked at
Hall. Continuous. Two changes weekly.
Prices, 9d. to 2s. Proscenium width, 24 ft.
Phone : Macaulay 1647. Station, Clapham
North.

CLAPHAM JUNCTION, S.W.

ELECTRIC PAVILION (WE), Lavender Hill, S.W.
—Prop., Gaumont British Picture Corpn.,
Ltd. 1,250 seats. Booked at H.O. Continuous.
Prices, 9d. to 2s. 6d. Phone : Battersea 1399.
Station, Clapham Junction (S.R.).

C O M P T O N
ORGAN featured here.

GLOBE (WE).—Prop., London & District Cinemas,
Ltd., Astoria House, 62, Shaftesbury Avenue,
W.1.

C O M P T O N
ORGAN featured here.

GRAND THEATRE (WE), St. John's Hill.—Prop.,
London & District Cinemas, Ltd., Astoria
House, 62, Shaftesbury Avenue, W.1. 1,528
seats. Continuous. Films booked at H.O.
and Variety by Montague Lyon Agency.
Stage, 26 ft. deep. Six dressing rooms. Prices,
6d. to 1s. 10d. Proscenium width, 39 ft.
Phone : Battersea 0088. Station, Clapham
Junction, (S.R.).
IMPERIAL THEATRE (WE), St. John's Hill, S.W.11.
—Prop.' London & District Cinemas, Ltd.
Astoria House 62, Shaftesbury Avenue, W.1.
720 seats. Booked at H.O. Continuous.
Prices, 6d. to 1s. 10d. Phone : Battersea 0275.
Station, Clapham Junction (S.R.).
SHAKESPERE (BA), Lavender Hill, S.W.11. --
Prop., United Picture Theatres, Ltd. 1,175
seats. Continuous. Two changes weekly.
Prices, 6d. to 2s. Phone, Battersea 1292.
Station, Clapham Junction (S.R.).

CLAPTON, E.

CLAPTON RINK CINEMA (RCA), Lower Clapton
Road.—Prop., Gaumont British Picture
Corpn., Ltd. Pictures and Variety. 2,000
seats. Booked at H.O. Continuous. Prices,
6d. to 2s. Two changes weekly. Phone :
Amherst 1061. Station, Clapton (L.N.E.R.).
KENNING HALL CINEMA (RCA), 229, Lower,
Clapton Road.—700 seats. Booked at Hall.
Continuous. Prices, 6d. to 1s. 6d. Phone:
Clissold 1314. Station, Clapton.

COLINDALE, N.W.

ODEON THEATRE (BTH), Edgware Road.—Prop.,
Odeon (Colindale), Ltd., Cornhill House,
Bennetts Hill, Birmingham. Phone : Mid-
land 2781. Booked at 49, Park Lane, W.1.
Prices, 9d. to 2s. 6d. Phone : Col. 7643.

COMMERCIAL ROAD, E.

PALASEUM (BA), 226, Commercial Road, E.—
Prop., Associated British Cinemas, Ltd.,
30-31, Golden Square, W.1. Booked at H.O.
7887. 920 seats. Booked at H.O. Continuous. Prices, 6d. to 1s. 6d. Phone : Stepney
Green 4152. Film Transport.
TROXY (WE).—Props., Gaumont Super Cinemas,
Ltd., Pollen House, Cork Street, W.1. 3,520
seats. Booked at H.O. Continuous. Pictures and Variety. Prices, 6d. to 2s. Proscenium width, 55 ft. Stage, 30 ft. deep.
Eleven dressing rooms. Cafés. Phone : East'
4216. Station, Stepney (S.R.).

WURLITZER ORGAN
Installed in this Kinema

UNIFORM SUPPLY COMPANY, LTD.,

OOVENTRY STREET, W.1.

RIALTO (WE).—Prop., Rialto Cinemas, Ltd. Booked by Associated British Cinemas, Ltd., 30-31, Golden Square, W.1. Phone: Gerrard 7887. 700 seats. Continuous. Proscenium width, 19 ft. Café. Prices, 1s. 6d. to 8s. 6d. Phone: Gerrard 3488.

CRANBOURN STREET, W.C.2.

LONDON HIPPODROME (WE).—Prop., Moss Empires, Ltd., Cranbourn Mansions, Cranbourn Street, W.C.2. Phone: Gerrard 2274. Proscenium width, 41 ft. Phone: Gerrard 3238, Station, Leicester Square (Tube).

CRICKLEWOOD, N.W.

PALACE CINEMA (Kamm), Broadway, N.W.2.— Prop., R. W. Ross. 377 seats. Booked at Hall. Continuous. Three changes weekly. Prices, 6d. to 1s. 4d. Phone: Gladstone 1943. Road Transport.

QUEEN'S HALL (WE).—Prop., Catwood Cinemas, Ltd. 2,006 seats. Continuous. Prices, 9d. to 2s. Phone: Gladstone 5,996. Café attached. Station, Willesden Green.

Fitted "ARDENTE" Deaf Aids See page 258

CROUCH END, N.

HIPPODROME (BA).—Prop., General Theatre Corp., Ltd. 1,000 seats. Booked at H.O. Continuous. Two changes weekly. Prices, 6d. to 2s. Stage. Phone: Mountview 0420.

PLAZA (WE) Tottenham Lane.—Prop., B. Sampson. 600 seats. Continuous. Two changes weekly. Prices, 6d. to 1/6. Booked at Hall. Phone: Mountview 1369. Station, Hornsey via King's Cross; and Road Transport.

CUSTOM HOUSE, E.

APOLLO PICTURE THEATRE (BTH), Freemason's Road.—Prop., F. Parnell. 800 seats. Continuous from 5.30 p.m. Mat., Mon., Thurs. and Sat. Three changes weekly. Prices, 4d. to 9d. Pictures and Variety. Proscenium width, 21 ft. Stage, 10 ft. deep. One dressing room. Phone: Albert Dock 2786. Station, Custom House (L.M.S.).

CUSTOM HOUSE, ELECTRIC THEATRE (BTH), Adamson Road.—Prop. F. Parnell. Continuous from 5.30 p.m. Mat., Sat. Prices, 2d. to 4d.

DALSTON, E.

AMHURST HALL (WE), High Street, Kingsland, —Prop., Watford Amusements Ltd., 903 seats. Continuous. Prices, 6d. to 1s. 4d. Phone: Clissold 1642. Station, Dalston Junction (L.M.S.).

KINGSLAND EMPIRE (WE), High Street, Kingsland.—Prop., Watford Amusements Ltd. 1,000 seats. Booked at H.O. Continuous. Two changes weekly. Prices, 6d. to 1s. 4d. Phone: Clissold 3484. Station, Dalston Junction (L.M.S.).

PICTURE HOUSE (WE), Dalston Lane, E.8.— Prop., Gaumont-British Picture Corporation, Ltd. 2,260 seats. Booked at H.O. Continuous. Prices, 6d. to 1s. 6d. Proscenium, width, 48 ft. Stage, 18 ft. deep; Café. Phone: Clissold 3568. Station, Dalston Junction.

COMPTON
ORGAN featured here.

PLAZA (BTH), 538-40, Kingsland Road, N.W..— Props., Kingsland Pictures, Ltd., 33, Stoke Newington Road, N.16. Phone: Clissold 1844-5. 1,000 seats. Booked at H.O. Continuous. Prices, 6d. to 1s. 6d. Phone: Clissold 1399. Road Transport.

DEPTFORD, S.E.

BROADWAY THEATRE (BA). Broadway. 1,300 seats.—(See New Cross.)

DEPTFORD ELECTRIC PALACE (BTH), High Street —Prop., Deptford Electric Palace, Ltd., 147, Wardour Street, W.1. 628 seats. Booked at H.O. Continuous. Three changes weekly Prices, 5d. to 1s. 3d. Phone: New Cross 1538. Station, Deptford High Street (S.R.).

ODEON THEATRE (BTH), Church Street.—Props., Odeon (Deptford) Ltd., Cornhill House, Bennetts Hill, Birmingham. Phone: Midland 2781. Booked at 49, Park Lane, W.1. (In course of construction).

EALING, W.

BROADWAY PALLADIUM (WE), 22, Broadway, W.5.—Prop., Scala (Ealing) Ltd. Associated with Provincial Cinematograph Theatres, Ltd. 1,260 seats. Booked at H.O. Stage, 32 ft. deep. Six dressing-rooms. Dance hall. Continuous. Two changes weekly. Prices, 6d. to 2s. 4d. Phone: Ealing 1276. Station, Ealing Broadway, G.W.R.

FORUM (WE).—Prop., Associated British Cinemas Ltd., 30-31, Golden Square, London, W.1. Phone: Gerrard 7887.

Fitted "ARDENTE" Deaf Aids See page 258

COMPTON
ORGAN featured here.

LIDO (WE), West Ealing.—Prop., Associated British Cinemas, Ltd., 30-31, Golden Square, W.1. Phone: Gerrard 7887. 1,097 seats. Continuous. Booked at H.O. Prices, 6d. to 2s. Proscenium width, 30 ft. Phone: Ealing 0934. Station, Ealing (G.W.R.).

COMPTON
ORGAN featured here.

ODEON THEATRE (WE), Northfields.—Prop., Odeon Theatres, Ltd., Cornhill House, Bennett's Hill, Birmingham. Phone: Midland 2781. Continuous. Booked at 49, Park Lane, London W.1. Prices, 6d. to 2s. Proscenium width, 45 ft. Stage 15 ft. deep ; three dressing rooms. Phone: Ealing 3939. Stations, Northfields (Underground) and West Ealing (G.W.R.). Road Transport.

COMPTON
ORGAN featured here.

WALPOLE CINEMA (WE), Bond Street, W.5.— Prop., Odeon (Ealing) Ltd., Cornhill House, Bennett's Hll, Birmingham. Midland 2781. Booked at 49, Park Lane, London, W.1. Continuous. Prices, 6d. to 1s. 6d. Proscenium width, 24 ft. Phone: Ealing 3396. Station, Ealing Broadway, G.W.R.

136 WARDOUR STREET, LONDON, W.1.

EARLSFIELD, S.W.

PREMIER ELECTRIC THEATRE (WE), 468, Garratt Lane, S.W.18.—Prop., Supershows (Earlsfield), Ltd., 61-2; Chancery Lane, W.C.2. Phone: Holborn 4731. 585 seats. Booked at H.O. Continuous. Three changes weekly. Variety, Tues. and Fri. Stage, 5 ft. deep; four dressing rooms. Prices, 6d. to 1s. 6d. Phone, Battersea 1481. Station, Earlsfield (S.R.).

EAST DULWICH, S.E.

PAVILION (BTH), Grove Vale.—Prop., Carlton Picture Houses, Ltd. 550 seats. Continuous. Phone: New Cross 2704. Station, East Dulwich (S.R.).

EAST HAM, E.

BROADWAY CINEMA (WE), High Street South.—Prop., D. and F. Properties, Ltd., 147, Wardour Street, W.1. Phone: Gerrard 1416. 735 seats. Booked at H.O. Continuous. Three changes weekly. Prices, 7d. to 1s. 6d. Proscenium width, 38 ft. Phone: Grangewood 0427. Station, East Ham (L.M.S.).

GRANADA (WE), Barking Road, E.6.—Prop., Denman London Cinemas Ltd., 36, Golden Square, W.1. Booked at H.O. Continuous. Pictures and Variety. Phone: Grangewood 0672.

WURLITZER ORGAN
Installed in this Kinema

NEW BOLEYN THEATRE (RCA), Barking Road, E.6.—Prop., Davis & Rose, 147, Wardour Street, W.1. 800 seats. Booked at H.O. Continuous. Prices, 6d. to 1s. 6d. Phone: Grangewood 0385. Station, Upton Park.

NEW REGAL PALACE (WE),—Prop., East Ham Amusements, Ltd., 75-77, Shaftesbury Avenue, W.1. Phone: Gerrard 4973. Pictures on Sunday only. 1,575 seats. Phone: Grangewood 0054.

PICTURE COLISEUM (Picturetone), High Street North.—Props., W. T. Scriven and W. J. Huxtable. 550 seats. Gen. Man., A. Tench. Booked at Hall. Continuous. Prices, 4d. to 1s. 3d. Phone: Grangewood 1059. Station, East Ham (Tube).

PREMIER SUPER CINEMA (WE), High Street North.—Prop., Provincial Cinematograph Theatres, Ltd., 123, Regent Street, W. Phone: Regent 8080. 2408 seats. Pictures and Variety. Café. Booked at H.O. Continuous, and 6 to 10 p.m. on Sundays. Two changes weekly. Prices, 7d. to 2s. Stage and three dressing rooms. Proscenium width, 42 ft. Phone: Grangewood 0227. Station, East Ham (Met.).

EAST SHEEN, S.W.

SHEEN KINEMA (WE), Sheen Lane.—Prop., Joseph Mears Theatres, Ltd., 5, Hill Street, Richmond. 1,500 seats. Booked at H.O. Continuous. Prices, 9d. to 2s. 5d. Phone: Prospect 4123. Station, Mortlake (S.R.).

EDGWARE ROAD, W.

BLUE HALL (WE).—Prop., Blue Halls, Ltd., Coronation House, 4, Lloyds Avenue, E.C. Phone: Royal 6158-6159. 1,250 seats. Booked at H.O. Continuous. Prices, 9d. to 3s. 6d. Phone: Paddington 7188. Station, Edgware Road (Tube).

CONNAUGHT CINEMA (RCA).—Prop., Connaught Kinema, Ltd. 500 seats. Booked at Hall. Continuous. Two changes weekly. Prices, 9d. to 2s. 4d. Phone: Paddington 2612.

GRAND KINEMA (BA).—Props., Gaumont-British Corporation, Ltd., and P.C.T., 123, Regent Street, London, W.1. 2,200 seats. Booked at New Gallery House, 123, Regent Street, W.1. Pictures and Variety. Continuous. Two changes weekly. Prices, 9d. to 2s. 6d. Stage. Café attached. Phone: Paddington 6313.

COMPTON

ORGAN featured here.

IMPERIAL THEATRE (RCA).—Props., Universal Entertainment, Ltd., 18-20, Regent Street, W.1. Phone: Whitehall 9313. 400 seats. Booked at H.O. Continuous. Two changes weekly. Prices, 6d. to 1s. 4d. Phone: Paddington 0136.

METROPOLITAN MUSIC HALL (BTP).—Props., Metropolitan Theatres of Varieties, Ltd., Cranbourn Street, W.C.2. 1,650 seats. Sundays only. Prices, 6d. to 3s. 6d. Booked at H.O. Phone: Ambassadors 2478-9.

ROYAL WEST LONDON THEATRE (Floydophone), 69, Church Street.—Prop., Popular Cinemas, Ltd., Phoenix House, 19, Oxford Street, W.1. Phone: Gerrard 1405. 1,000 seats. Booked at H.O. Continuous. Three changes weekly. Prices, 4d. to 1s. 3d. Café. Phone: Paddington 0864.

SELECT ELECTRIC THEATRE (BTP). 411a, Edgware Road.—Prop., A. Curzon. 600 seats. Booked at Hall. Continuous. Three changes weekly. Prices, 6d. to 2s. Proscenium width, 25 ft. Phone: Ambassadors 1905.

EDGWARE, N.W.

REGENT CINEMA (WE), Burnt Oak.—Props., —Odeon (Burnt Oak) Ltd., Cornhill House, Bennett's Hill, Birmingham. Phone: Midland 2781. Booked at 49, Park Lane, W.1. Continuous. Prices 9d. to 2s. Café attached. Phone: Edgware 0660. Station, Burnt Oak (Underground).

COMPTON

ORGAN featured here

RITZ (WE).—Props., Associated British Cinemas, Ltd., 30-31, Golden Square, W.1. Phone: Gerrard 7887. 2,190 seats. Continuous. Booked at H.O. Pictures. Variety on

Fiidays. Prices, 6d. to 2s. Proscenium width, 40 ft. Stage, 14 ft. deep; four dressing rooms. Variety booked at Paceys Agency, 80, Regent Street, W.1. Phone: Edgware 2164. Café attached. Station, Edgware, L.N.E.R.

COMPTON

ORGAN featured here.

EDMONTON, N.
ALCAZAR PICTURE THEATRE (BTH).—Prop., Alcazar Picture Theatre (Edmonton), Ltd., 5, Chancery Lane, W.C.2. Holborn 6683. 1,230 seats. Continuous. Two changes weekly. Booked at Hall. Tea Room. Prices, 6d. to 1s. 6d. Proscenium width, 32 ft. Stage, 8 ft. deep; three dressing rooms. Phone: Tottenham 2147. Station: Silver Street. L.N.E.R.
EMPIRE (WE).—Prop., Denman London Cinemas, Ltd., 36, Golden Square, W.1. Phone: Gerrard 3554. Continuous. Pictures and Variety. Booked at H.O. Phone: Tottenham 0110. Station, Lower Edmonton (L.N.E.R.).

WURLITZER ORGAN
Installed in this Kinema

HIPPODROME (WE), Angel Road.—Prop., A. Barnett, 26, Park Hill, Clapham, S.W. Phone: Macaulay 3494. 600 seats. Booked at New Palladium, Croydon. Continuous. Two changes weekly. Prices, 5d. to 1s. 6d. Proscenium width, 18 ft. Phone: Tottenham 1489. Station, Silver Street (L.N.E.R.).
REGAL (WE), Silver Street.—Prop., H. and G. (Edmonton) Ltd., Pollen House, Cork Street, W.1. Phone: 2,940 seats. Booked at H.O. Prices, 9d. to 2s. Proscenium width, 58 ft. Stage, 45 ft.; 16 dressing rooms. Café and Dance Hall attached. Phone Tottenham 3030.

ELEPHANT & CASTLE, S.E.
ELEPHANT AND CASTLE THEATRE (WE), 26-28, New Kent Road, S.E.1.—Props., Elephant and Castle Theatre, Ltd. 2,315 seats. Controlled by Associated British Cinemas, Ltd. Stage. Booked at H.O. Continuous. Pictures and Variety. Phone: Rodney 2635. Station, Elephant and Castle (S.R. and Tube).
TROCADERO (WE).—Props., Gaumont Super Cinemas, Ltd., Pollen House, Cork Street, W.1. Phone: Regent 4794. 3,500 seats. Booked at H.O. Continuous. Pictures and Variety. Stage, 28 ft. deep; eight dressing rooms. Prices, 6d. to 2s. 6d. Proscenium width, 45 ft. Café. Phone: Hop 1344-6. Café, Station, Elephant and Castle.
Fitted "ARDENTE" Deaf Aids
See page 258

WURLITZER ORGAN
Installed in this Kinema

ELTHAM, S.E.
-ELTHAM CINEMA THEATRE (BTH), High Street.— (Closed).
ODEON THEATRE (BTH), Well Hall.—Props., Odeon (Well Hall) Ltd., Cornhill House, Bennetts Hill, Birmingham. Phone: Midland 2781. Booked at 49, Park Lane, W.1. Continuous. Films and Variety. Prices, 6d. to 2s. Proscenium width, 42 ft. Stage 12 ft. deep; one dressing room. Phone: Eltham 3351. Station, Eltham (Well Hall), S.R.
PALACE (BTH), High Street, S.E.9.—Controlled by Union Cinemas, Ltd., 15, Regent Street, London, S.W.1. Phone: Whitehall 8484. Booked at H.O. Continuous. Variety and Films. Prices, 9d. to 1s. 10d. Cafe attached. Phone: Eltham 1311. Station, Well Hall, Eltham.

EUSTON ROAD, N.W.
EUSTON CINEMA (WE), 81, Euston Road.— Prop., Euston Cinema. Ltd. 1,154 seats. Booked at Hall. Continuous. Prices, 9d. to 3s. Phone: Euston 1542. Station, Euston.
REGENT THEATRE (WE).—Prop., King's Cross Cinemas, Ltd., 60-66, Wardour Street, London, W.1. 1,000 seats. Booked at Hall. Pictures and Variety. Café attached. Phone: Gerrard 4117.

FINCHLEY, N.

COLISEUM (BTP), 38, High Road, East Finchley. —Prop., Home Counties Theatres, Ltd., Athenæum Playhouse, Muswell Hill, N.10. Phone: Tudor 5848. 500 seats. Booked at H.O. Continuous. Two changes weekly. Prices, 8d. to 2s. Phone: Tudor 2463.
GAUMONT.—Prop., Gaumont British Picture Corporation, Ltd., 142-150, Wardour Street, W.1.

COMPTON

ORGAN featured here.

GRAND HALL (BA), Tally Ho! Corner, N.12.— Prop., Denman Picture Houses, Ltd., 123, Regent Street, W.1. Phone: Regent 8080. 700 seats. Booked at H.O. Continuous. Prices, 9d. to 2s. Phone: Hillside 0873. Station, Church End, Finchley, L.N.E.R.
NEW BOHEMIA CINEMA (RCA), Church End, N.3.—Prop., National Electric Theatres, Ltd., 142-150, Wardour Street, W.1. Booked at New Gallery House, W.1. 1,170 seats. Continuous. Prices, 9d. to 2s. Lounge Café. Station, Church End, L.N.E.R. Phone: Finchley 2,300.
ODEON THEATRE (BTH), High Street, N.12.— Props., Odeon (Finchley) Ltd., Cornhill House, Bennetts Hill, Birmingham. Phone: Midland 2781. Booked at 49, Park Lane, W.1. Continuous. Prices, 9d. to 2s. Phone Hillside 1698.
ORPHEUM (WE), Finchley Road, N.W.—Prop., Orpheum Theatre (Finchley) Ltd., Dea.

Q

FINCHLEY, N.—contd.

House, Dean Street, W.1. Phone: Gerrard 4543. 2,800 seats. Continuous. Pictures and Variety. Booked at H.O. Variety booked at Hall. Prices, 9d. to 2s. 6d. Proscenium width, 35 ft. Stage, 40 ft. deep. Ten dressing rooms. Café. Phone: Speedwell 7401. Station, Golders Green (Tube).

COMPTON
ORGAN featured here

FINSBURY PARK, N.

ASTORIA (WE).—Prop., Paramount-Astoria Theatres, Ltd., 104-108, Oxford Street, W.1. Phone: Museum 4721. 2,802 seats. Booked at H.O. Continuous. Pictures and Variety. Variety booked Fosters Agency, Leicester Square Theatre Chambers, W.C. Stage, 35 ft. deep ; 12 dressing rooms. Prices, 1s. to 3s. 6d. Proscenium width, 64 ft. Phone, Archway 2224. Station, Finsbury Park, L.N.E.R.

COMPTON
ORGAN featured here.

FINSBURY PARK RINK CINEMA (WE), Seven Sisters Road, N.4.—Prop., Provincial Cinematograph Theatres, Ltd. 2,212 seats. Booked at H.O. Continuous. Pictures. Cafe. Prices, 9d. to 2s. Phone: Stamford Hill 2676.
Fitted "ARDENTE" Deaf Aids See page 258

WURLITZER ORGAN Installed in this Kinema

FOREST GATE, E.

GRAND CINEMA (BTP), Woodgrange Road.— (Closed).

ODEON THEATRE (BTH), Romford Road.—Prop., Odeon (Forest Gate) Ltd., Cornhill House, Bennett's Hill, Birmingham. Phone: Midland 2781. Booked at 49, Park Lane, W.1.

QUEEN'S THEATRE (RCA), Romford Road.— Prop., Associated British Cinemas, Ltd., 30-31, Golden Square, W.1. Phone: Gerrard 7887. 1,750 seats. Booked at H.O. Continuous. Pictures and Variety. Variety booked at Universal Variety Agency, 25 Charing Cross Road. Proscenium width, 30 ft. Stage, 8 ft. deep. Three dressing rooms. Prices, 6d. to 1s. 6d. Phone: Maryland 1341. Station, Forest Gate, L.N.E.R.

REGAL (BTH), 55, Woodgrange Road, E.7.— Prop., Suburban Entertainments, Ltd., 120, High Street, N.W.10. Phone : Willesden 3206. 600 seats. Booked at H.O. Continuous. Prices, 6d. to 1s. 3d. Proscenium width, 25 ft. Phone : Maryland 1652.

SPLENDID CINEMA (WE), Forest Gate, E.7.— Props., Forest Lane Cinema, Ltd., 600 seats. Booked at Hall. Continuous. Prices, 6d. to 1s. 6d. Phone : Maryland 1820

FOREST HILL, S.E.

ASTORIA CINEMA (WE), Westdale Road, S.E.— Prop., Ben Jay. Booked at H.O., 145, Wardour Street, W.1. 772 seats. Continuous. Prices. 6d. to 1s. 3d. Phone : Sydenham 1018. Station, Forest Hill (S.R.). Films by Motor Transport.

CAPITOL CINEMA (WE).—Attractive Cinema (Forest Hill), Ltd. Controlled by Associated British Cinemas Ltd. 1,700 seats. Booked at H.O. Pictures and Variety. Continuous. Café. Prices, 6d. to 2s. Stage, 22 ft. deep. Three dressing rooms. Phone : Sydenham 2188. Station, Forest Hill, S.R.

COMPTON
ORGAN featured here.

FULHAM, S.W.

BROADWAY CINEMA (WE).—Props., Broadway Gardens, Ltd., Station Approach, Walham Green, S.W.6. Phone : Fulham 4193. 850 seats. Booked at Hall. Continuous. Prices, 6d. to 2s. Station, Walham Green (District Rly.)

FORUM THEATRE (WE), Fulham Road, S.W.10. Prop., Forum Theatre, Ltd., 30-31, Golden Square, W.1. 2,200 seats. Pictures and Variety. Continuous. Prices, 9d. to 2s. 6d. Variety booked at Hall. Proscenium width, 45 ft. Stage, 30 ft. deep. Eight dressing rooms. Café. Phone : Kensington 5234.

COMPTON
ORGAN featured here.

GRAND THEATRE (Shilling Theatre) (RCA).—Prop. London Cinemas, Ltd. 1,100 seats. Booked at Hall, Films Sundays only. Phone : Putney 2248.

STAR KINEMA (WE), Wandsworth Bridge Road. —606 seats. Booked at 46, Gerrard Street, W.1. Continuous. Two changes weekly. Prices 6d. to 1s. 4d. Proscenium width, 25 ft. Phone : Fulham 0436. Road Transport.

THE RITZ (WE), North End Road, S.W.6.— Prop., Fulham Picture Palace, Ltd. 802 seats. Booked at Broadway Gardens Cinema, Walham Green. Continuous. Two changes weekly. Prices, 7d. to 1s. Phone, Fulham 3813. Station, West Brompton (Tube).

GOLDERS GREEN, N.W.

IONIC PICTURE THEATRE (BTH), Finchley Road, N.W.11.—Prop., Ionic Theatre, Ltd., 1,000 seats. Booked at Hall. Continuous. Prices, 9d. to 2s. 6d. Phone: Speedwell 1724. Station, Golders Green (Tube).

LIDO PICTURE HOUSE (WE), Golders Green Road, N.W.11.—Props., Associated British Cinemas, Ltd., 30-31, Golden Square, W.1. Continuous. Booked at H.O. 2,000 seats. Prices, 6d. to 2s. Proscenium width, 27 ft. Stage, 12 ft. deep ; three dressing rooms. Café attached. Phone: Speedwell 6161. Station, Golders Green (Tube). Road Transport.

REGAL (WE), Prop., Regal (Hampstead), Ltd.— Booked at Dean House, Dean Street, W.1. 2,218 seats. Continuous. Prices, 9d. to 2s. 4d. Café. Ballroom. Phone: Speedwell 7001. Station, Golders Green.

WURLITZER ORGAN Installed in this Kinema

GREAT WINDMILL STREET, W.1.

PICCADILLY NEWS THEATRE (WE).—Prop.,P.C.C. Ltd., 199, Piccadilly, W. 256 seats. Booked at H.O. Continuous. Two changes weekly. Prices, 6d. and 1s. Phone: Gerrard 1653.

UNIFORM SUPPLY COMPANY, LTD.,

WINDMILL THEATRE (RCA), 17-19, Great Windmill St., W.1. Prop.; Windmill Theatre Co., Ltd. 310 seats.

GREENWICH, S.E.
EMPIRE CINEMA (WE).—Prop., London & Distrct Cinemas, Ltd., Astoria House, 62, Shaftesbury Avenue, W.1. 562 seats. Continuous. Three changes weekly. Prices, 6d. to 1s. 3d. Phone: Greenwich 1431. Station, Greenwich (S.R.).
GRANADA.

WURLITZER ORGAN
Installed in this Kinema

GREENWICH HIPPODROME (WE).—1, Stockwell Street, S.E.10.—Prop., London & District Cinemas, Ltd., Astoria House, 62, Shaftesbury Avenue, W.1. Booked at H.O. 732 seats. Continuous. Three changes weekly. Prices, 5d. to 1s. 3d. Phone: Greenwich 9425. Station, Greenwich (S.R.).
TRAFALGAR CINEMA (WE), 82, Trafalgar Road, S.E.—Props., Trafalgar Cinema (Greenwich), Ltd. Cinema House, Oxford Street, W.1. Booked at H.O. 1,400 seats. Continuous. Three changes weekly. Prices, 6d. to 1s. 6d. Stage, 20 ft. deep; two dressing rooms. Phone: Greenwich 3,000. Station, Maze Hill (S.R.).
Fitted "ARDENTE" Stage Amplification
See page 258

HACKNEY, E.
EMPIRE (WE), Mare Street, E.8.—Prop., Hackney and Shepherd's Bush Empire Palaces, Ltd. Stoll Circuit. 2,218 seats.
EMPRESS ELECTRIC THEATRE (RCA), Mare Street, E.8. 1,100 seats. Continuous. Prices, 7d. to 2s. Phone: Amherst 2351. Stage. Station, Hackney (L.N.E.R.).

COMPTON
ORGAN featured here.

GRAND CENTRAL THEATRE (WE), Hackney Road, E.2.—Prop., George Smart, 331, Mare Street, Hackney. Phone: Amherst 2911. 350 seats. Booked at H.O. Continuous. Three changes weekly. Prices, 6d. to 1s. 6d. Phone: Bishopsgate 6300.
HACKNEY PAVILION (WE), 290, Mare Street, E.8.—Prop., Provincial Cinematograph Theatres, Ltd., 123, Regent Street, W.1. 1,162 seats. Booked at H.O. Continuous, Phone: Amherst 2681.
REGAL (WE), Mare Street.—Props', Associated British Cinemas, Ltd., 30, Golden Square, W.1. Phone: Gerrard 7887. 1,846 seats. Booked at H.O. Pictures and Variety. Variety booked at H.O. Continuous. Prices, 6d. to 2s. Proscenium width, 44 ft. Stage, 24 ft. Nine dressing rooms. Phone: Amherst 3036. Film Transport.
SOUTH HACKNEY PICTURE THEATRE (WE), 133-137, Well Street, E.9.—Prop., SouthHackney Picture Theatre Co., Ltd. 1,200 seats. Pictures and Variety. Continuous. Two changes weekly. Prices, 4d. to 1s. 3d. Stage Phone: Amherst 4623.
STANDARD CINEMA (WE), 153-157, Goldsmiths' Row, Hackney, E.2.—882 seats. (See London Fields, E.)

HAMMERSMITH, W.
ACADEMY CINEMA (WE), 139, King Street, W.6.—Props., J. Dodd and W. J. Clayton. 950 seats. Booked at Hall. Continuous. Three changes weekly. Prices, 6d. to 1s. 1od. Station, Hammersmith (Tube).
BROADWAY SUPER CINEMA (RG), 8 to 14, Queen Street, W.6.—Prop., Associated British Cinemas, Ltd. 1,206 seats. Booked at H.O. Continuous. Prices, 6d. to 1s. 6d. Phone: Riverside 6120.
COMMODORE (WE), King Street (Young's Corner).—Controlled by Associated British Cinemas, Ltd. 2,964 seats. Continuous. Picture and Variety. Stage, 28 ft. deep; eight dressing rooms. Prices, 6d. to 2s. 6d. Proscenium width, 50 ft. Phone: Riverside 2896-7. Café attached. Station, Stamford Brook. Films by Transport.
GAUMONT PALACE (BA), Queen Street, W.6.—Props., Gaumont British Picture Corporation Ltd. 4,000 seats. Booked at H.O. Continuous Pictures and Variety. Prices, 9d. to 2s. 6d. Stage, 35 ft. Proscenium width, 63 ft. Café. Phone: Riverside 3029-3030. Station, Hammersmith.
Fitted "ARDENTE" Deaf Aids
See page 258

COMPTON
ORGAN featured here.

PALACE (WE).—Props., 20th Century Cinemas, Ltd., 14-15, Brettenham House, Lancaster Place, W.1. Phone; Temple Bar 4758. 1,740 seats. Continuous. Booked at H.O. Pictures and Variety. Phone: Riverside 2721.
REGAL (WE), King Street.—Prop., Associated British Cinemas, Ltd., 30-31, Golden Square, W.1. 2,277 seats. Booked at H.O. Pictures and Variety. Variety booked at Booking Dept., Forum Theatre, Fulham, S.W.10 Stage 16ft. deep; four dressing rooms. Continuous. Prices, 6d. to 2s. Proscenium width, 43 ft. Phone: Riverside 2388. Station, Ravenscourt Park (District).
Fitted "ARDENTE" Deaf Aids
See page 258

COMPTON
ORGAN featured here.

SAVOY (WE), Western Avenue, North Hammersmith, W.12. 1,650 seats. Pictures and Variety. Films booked at Hall. Continuous. Phone: Shepherd's Bush 4591. Stage. Café attached. Station, E. Acton (C.L.R.)

COMPTON
ORGAN featured here.

HAMPSTEAD, N.W.
EVERYMAN CINEMA THEATRE (WE), Holly Bush Vale, N.W.3.—Lessees, Repertory Entertainments, Ltd. 285 seats. Booked at 10, Golden Square, W.1. Phone: Gerrard 7271. Phone: Hampstead 2285.
PICTURE PLAYHOUSE (WE), Pond Street, N.W.3.—Prop., Hampstead Picture Playhouse, Ltd.,

136 WARDOUR STREET, LONDON, W.1.

Q2

HAMPSTEAD, N.W.—contd.
Pond Street, N.W.1. 1.500 seats. Booked at Hall. Continuous. Three changes weekly. Prices, 6d. to 2s. 6d. Phone : Primrose 3200. Station, Hampstead Heath, L.M.S.

HANWELL, W.
GRAND THEATRE (WE), Broadway.—Props., Progress Theatres (Robinson and Cerling). 973 seats. Continuous. Two changes weekly. Booked at H.O. Prices, 6d. to 1s. 6d. Proscenium width, 34 ft. Phone : Ealing 1106. Station, Hanwell, G.W.R.

HARLESDEN, N.W.
ODEON THEATRE (BTH), St. Albans Road and Craven Park Road.—Props., Odeon (Harlesden), Ltd., Cornhill House, Bennett's Hill, Birmingham. Phone: Midland 2781. (In course of construction)
PICARDY CINEMA (RCA), High Street, N.W.10.— Props., Suburban Entertainments, Ltd. 686 seats. Booked at Hall. Continuous. Prices 6d. to 1s. 4d. Proscenium width, 20 ft. Phone : Willesden 3206. Station, Willesden Junction, L.M.S. and Road Transport.
PICTURE COLISEUM (BA), Manor Park Road, N.W.10.—Prop., H. J. Morgenstern, 1, Wren Avenue, N.W.2. Phone : Gladstone 2812. 850 seats. Booked at Hall. Continuous. Prices, 6d. to 1s. 6d. Phone : Willesden 1350. Station, Willesden Junction.
WILLESDEN HIPPODROME (WE), High Street.— Props., Associated British Cinemas, Ltd., 30-31, Golden Square, W.1. 1,900 seats. Booked at H.O. Continuous. Two changes weekly. Occasional Variety. Variety booked by Walter Stanley, 1, Waller Road, S.E. Prices, 4d. to 1s. 6d. Proscenium width, 40 ft. Stage, 30 ft. deep. Eight dressing rooms. Phone : Willesden 6438. Station, Willesden Junction.

HARRINGAY N.
COLISEUM (RCA), Green Lanes, N.8.—Prop., W. and M. A. Jennand. 650 seats. Booking Man., Mrs. Rose Linden. Proscenium width, 29 ft. Continuous. Prices, 6d. to 1s. 6d. Phone : Stamford Hill 2664.
PREMIER ELECTRIC THEATRE (WE), Frobisher Road.—Prop., River Park Cinemas, Ltd. 730 seats. Booked at H.O. Continuous. Prices, 7d. to 1s. 6d. Phone: Mount View 1070. Station, Hornsey.
RITZ.—Green Lanes.—Props., Associated British Cinemas, Ltd., 30-31, Golden Square, W.1.

HARROW ROAD, W.9.
COLISEUM (RCA), 324, Harrow Road.—Prop., Woodfield Cinemas, Ltd., 4, Sutherland Avenue, Paddington, W9. Booked at Hall. Continuous. Three changes weekly. Prices, 7d. to 1s. 3d. 800 seats. Phone : Abercorn 1150. Station, Royal Oak (Met.).
PRINCE OF WALES' CINEMA (WE).—Prop., Associated British Cinemas, Ltd., 30-31, Golden Square, W.1. Phone : Gerrard 7887. 1,570 seats. Continuous. Pictures and Variety. Variety booked at Forum, Fulham. Films at H.O. Prices, 6d. to 2s. Phone : Abercorn 3303. Station, Westbourne Park (Met.).
Fitted "ARDENTE" Deaf Aids
See page 258
HAVERSTOCK HILL, N.W.3.
ODEON (BTH).—Prop., Odeon (Haverstock)- Ltd., Cornhill House, Bennett's Hill, Birming,

ham. Phone: Midland 2781. Booked at 49, Park Lane, London, W.1. Prices, 9d. to 2s. 6d. Phone: Primrose 6875.

C O M P T O N
ORGAN featured here.

HAYMARKET, S.W.
CAPITOL (WE).—Prop., General Theatre Corpn. Ltd., Film House, Wardour Street, W.1. Phone : Regent 4455. 1560 seats. Booked at H.O. Continuous. Prices, 2s. 6d. to 6s. Café. Phone : Whitehall 6655.
Fitted "ARDENTE" Deaf Aids
See page 258

C O M P T O N
ORGAN featured here.

CARLTON THEATRE (WE).—Props., Carlton Theatre Co., Ltd., 166, Wardour Street, W.1. 1,100 seats. Four shows daily. Two on Sundays. Prices, 2s. 6d. to 10s. 6d. Proscenium width, 37 ft. Phone : Whitehall 3711. Stage, 70 ft. deep ; 14 dressing rooms. Tea lounge.

HENDON, N.W.
AMBASSADOR (WE).—Prop., Hendon Central Cinema, Ltd., 32, Shaftesbury Avenue, London, W.1. Phone : Whitehall 0183. 2,000 seats. Booked at G.-B. H.O. Continuous. Prices, 9d. to 2s. Pictures and occasional Variety. Café. Phone : Hendon 1137. Road Transport.

C O M P T O N
ORGAN featured here.

CARLTON (WE), Belle Vue Road, Brent Street, N.W.4.—Props., Hendon Theatres (1932), Ltd. 705 seats. Booked at Hall. Continuous. Prices, 6d. to 1s. 10d. Occasional Variety. Phone: Hendon 1165. Station, Hendon, L.M.S.

HERNE HILL, S.E.
GRAND CINEMA (WE), Railton Road, S.E.— Props., J. & M. Mindel and A. Ellis. 550 seats. Booked at Hall. Continuous. Two changes weekly. Prices, 5d. to 1s. 6d. Phone : Brixton 0234. Station, Herne Hill, S.R.

HIGHAMS PARK, E.
REGAL CINEMA (WE).—Props., A. W. and R. B. Green. 615 seats. Continuous. Booked at Hall. Phone: Larkswood 1888. Prices, 6d. to 2s. Station, Highams Park, L.N.E.R.

HIGHBURY, N.
IMPERIAL PICTURE THEATRE.—Prop., General Theatres Corporation, Ltd., 142-150, Wardour Street, W.1.

HIGHGATE, N.
ELECTRIC PALACE (WE), Highgate Hill, N.19.— Controlled by Union Cinemas, Ltd., Union House, 15, Regent Street, London, S.W.1. Phone: Whitehall 8484. Booked at H.O. Continuous. Prices, 6d. to 1s. 4d. Phone Archway 1821. Station, Upper Holloway, L.M.S.

UNIFORM SUPPLY COMPANY, LTD.,

HIGHGATE EMPIRE (WE), Holloway Road.—
Controlled by Union Cinemas, Ltd., Union
House, 15, Regent Street, London, S.W.1.
Phone, Whitehall 8484. Booked at H.O.
Continuous. Prices, 6d. to 1s. 4d. Phone:
Archway 2003. Station, Upper Holloway,
L.M.S.

HITHER GREEN, S.E.

PARK CINEMA (WE).—Props., Park Picture
Theatres, Ltd., Cinema House, 225, Oxford
Street, W.1. 500 seats. Booked at H.O.
Continuous. Three changes weekly. Prices,
6d. to 1s. 6d. Phone: Lee Green 2244.
Station, Hither Green, S.R.

HOLLOWAY, N.

HIGHBURY IMPERIAL PICTURE THEATRE (RCA),
2, Holloway Road, N.7.—Prop., General
Theatre Corpn., Ltd. 1,500 seats. Con-
tinuous. Two changes weekly. Prices, 6d.
to 2s. North 2887. Road Transport.
HOLLOWAY EMPIRE (WE), Holloway Road.—
Prop., Gaumont-British Picture Corporation,
Ltd. 1,140 seats. Booked at H.O. Con-
tinuous. Prices, 6d. to 2s. Phone: Archway
1550. Station, Holloway.
MARLBOROUGH THEATRE (WE), Holloway Road,
—Props., Provincial Cinematograph Theatres,
Ltd., 123, Regent Street, W.1. 1,685 seats.
Phone: Regent 6641. Booked at H.O.
Continuous. Occasional Variety. One
change weekly. Prices, 5d. to 3s. Pros-
cenium width, 30 ft. Phone: North 1903.
Station, Holloway.

COMPTON

ORGAN   featured   here.

PALACE (WE), 69, Seven Sisters Road, N.7.—
Prop., Morris Myers. 656 seats. Booked at
Hall. Continuous. Two changes weekly.
Prices, 5d. to 1s. 6d. Phone: North 1806.
REGENT CINEMA (WE), 196, Holloway Road,
N.7.—Prop., Regent Cinema (Holloway),
Ltd., 950 seats. Booked at 145, Wardour
Street, W.1, by Ben Jay. Continuous. Three
changes weekly. Prices, 6d. to 1s. 6d. Phone:
North 1298. Station, Holloway Road (Tube).
Road Transport.

HOMERTON, E.

CASTLE CINEMA (Cinephone), 64, Brooksby's
Walk.—Prop., M. C. Properties, Ltd., 17,
Shaftesbury Avenue, W.1. Phone: Gerrard
1713. 616 seats. Booked at H.O. Continuous.
Three changes weekly. Prices, 4d. to 1s.
Phone: Amherst 2811. Station, Homerton
(L.M.S.).

HOXTON, N.

BRITANNIA THEATRE (BA), Hoxton Street, N.—
Prop., Gaumont-British Picture Corporation
Ltd. Booked at H.O. Continuous. Prices,
4d. to 1s. Phone: Clerkenwell 3963. Station,
Old Street (Underground).
EAST ROAD CINEMA (Mihaly), East Road.—
Prop., D. F. Lintine. 400 seats. Booked at
Hall. Continuous. Three changes weekly.
Prices, 3d. to 9d. Phone: Clerkenwell
7545. Station, Old Street (Tube).
HOXTON CINEMA (BA), Pitfield Street, N.1.—
Props., Denman Picture Houses, Ltd., 123,
Regent Street, London, W.1. 866 seats.
Booked at H.O. Continuous. Prices, 2d.
to 1s. Phone: Clerkenwell 5966. Road
Transport.

HOXTON CINEMA THEATRE (Ye Olde Varieties)
(B.A.). Pitfield Street, N.1. 572 seats.—Props.,
Denman Picture Houses, Ltd. Continuous.
Booked at H.O. Prices, 4d. to 1s. Phone:
Clerkenwell 5640.

ISLINGTON, N.

ANGEL CINEMA (WE), 7, High Street, N.1.—
Prop., Associated Provincial Picture Houses,
Ltd. 1,463 seats. Booked at H.O. Continuous.
Two changes weekly. Prices, 9d. to 2s.
Phone: Ter. 3738.
BLUE HALL (WE), Upper Street, N.1.—Prop.,
General Theatre Corpn., Ltd.   145-150,
Wardour Street, W.1. Seats 1,340. Booked
at H.O. Continuous. Pictures and Variety.
Price, 6d. to 1s. 6d. Proscenium width.
27 ft. Stage, 18 ft. deep; three dressing
rooms. Phone: Clerkenwell 9274. Station,
Angel.
BLUE HALL ANNEXE (BA), 46, Essex Road.—
Prop., General Theatre Corpn., Ltd., New
Gallery House, Regent Street, W.1. 599
seats. Booked at H.O. Continuous. Prices,
7d. to 1s. 6d. Proscenium width, 16 ft.
Phone: Clerkenwell 5297. Road Transport.
CARLTON CINEMA (WE).—Associated British
Cinemas, Ltd., 30-31, Golden Square, W.1.
Phone: Gerrard 7887. 2,368 seats. Continu-
ous. Booked at H.O. Pictures and Variety.
Variety booked direct. Prices, 6d. to 2s.
Stage, 26 ft. deep; four dressing rooms.
Café. Phone: Canonbury 2957. Road
Transport.

COMPTON

ORGAN   featured   here.

EMPIRE (WE).—1,596 seats. Continuous. Booked
at H.O. Pictures and Variety. Prices, 4d. to
1s. 6d. Proscenium width, 30 ft. Stage,
45 ft. deep; eight dressing rooms. Phone :
Clerkenwell 8571. Road Transport.
EMPRESS PICTURE THEATRE (WE), 83, Upper
Street, N.1.—Prop., A. Claff. 489 seats.
Booked at Hall. Continuous. Three changes
weekly. Prices, 7d. to 1s. 3d. Phone: Clerken-
well 8020.
ODEON THEATRE (WE) Upper Street, N.1.—
Prop., Odeon (Islington) Ltd., Cornhill
House, Bennett's Hill, Birmingham. Phone:
Midland 2781. Booked at 49, Park Lane, W.1.
Continuous. Prices, 9d. to 2s. Phone:
Canonbury 2442.
STAR (WE), Hornsey Road.—Lessee, E. Covan
500 seats. Prices, 4d. to 1s. 3d. Continuous.
Phone: Archway 3779. Road Transport.
VICTORIA CINEMA (WE), 272-280, New North
Road, N.1.—Prop., Clissold Cinemas, Ltd.
731 seats. Booked at Hall. Continuous.
Three changes weekly. Prices, 5d. to 1s. 6d.
Phone: Clissold 2206. Station, Essex Road
(Tube).

KENNINGTON, S.E.

KENNINGTON THEATRE (BA), Kennington Park
Road, S.E.—(Closed).
PRINCE'S PICTURE PLAYHOUSE (ECA), 2-6,
Kennington Park Road, S.E.11.—Prop., New-
ington Electric Theatre, Ltd. 1,600 seats.
Controlled by Provincial Cinematograph
Theatres, Ltd. Booked at H.O. Continuous.
Prices, 6d. to 1s. 10d.

136 WARDOUR STREET, LONDON, W.1.

KENSAL RISE, N.W.

NEW PAVILION (RCA), Chamberlayne Road.—Prop., General Cinema Theatres, Ltd., 19, Albemarle Street, W.1. Phone: Regent 4419. 1,500 seats. Booked at H.O. Continuous. Prices, 6d. to 2s. Phone: Willesden 1837. Station, Kensal Rise.

PALACE (WE), Chamberlayne Road, N.W.10.—Prop., Associated British Cinemas, Ltd., 30-31, Golden Square, W.1. Phone: Gerrard 7887. 1,600 seats. Booked at H.O. Pictures and variety. Continuous. Prices 6d. to 2s. Stage, 16ft. deep. Procenium opening 40 ft. Phone: Willesden 1913.

KENSINGTON, W.

BOLTONS CINEMA (BTH), Drayton Gardens, S.W.10.—Prop., V. W. Beecham, 65, Drayton Gardens, S.W.10. 278 seats. Booked at Hall. Continuous. Prices, 9d. to 2s. 6d. Phone: Kensington 1794. Station, Gloucester Road (District).

KENSINGTON KINEMA (WE), Kensington High Street, W.8.—Prop., Joseph Mears Theatres, Ltd., 5, Hill Street, Richmond. 2,020 seats. Booked at H.O. Continuous. Restaurant and Tea Rooms. Prices, 1s. to 3s. 6d. Phone: Western 3577.

ROYAL KINEMA, High Street.—Prop., Harris Silverman. 400 seats. Continuous. Three changes weekly. Prices, 9d. to 3s. Phone: Western 6044.

WEST KENSINGTON SUPER CINEMA (RCA), 235-7, North End Road.—Props., Denman Picture Houses, Ltd., 123, Regent Street, W.1. 1,000 seats. Continuous. Prices, 9d. to 2s. Phone: Fulham 0666. Station, West Kensington (District).

KENTISH TOWN, N.W.

COURT CINEMA (RCA), Malden Road, N.W.5.—Props., M. & J. Cinemas, Ltd. 460 seats. Booked at Hall. Continuous. Three changes weekly. Prices, 6d. to 1s. Proscenium width, 15 ft. Phone: Gulliver 2461. Station, Kentish Town (L.M.S.).

FORUM (WE).—Props., Associated British Cinemas, Ltd., 30-31, Golden Square, W.1. 2,175 seats. Booked at H.O. Prices, 6d. to 2s. Pictures and Variety. Variety booked by Cecil Braham, Charing Cross Road, W.C.2. Proscenium width, 35 ft. Stage 25 ft. deep Six dressing rooms. Café attached. Phone: Gulliver 4221. Station, Kentish Town.
Fitted "ARDENTE" Deaf Aids
Fitted "ARDENTE" Stage Amplification
See page 258

COMPTON
ORGAN featured here.

GAISFORD CINEMA (BTH), Gaisford Street.—Props., General Cinema Theatres, Ltd. 502 seats. Booked at Pavilion, Kensal Rise, N.W. Continuous. Prices, 6d. to 1s. 3d. Phone: Gulliver 1892. Station, Kentish Town.

PALACE CINEMA (WE), Kentish Town Road, N.W.5.—Prop., Provincial Cinematograph Theatres, Ltd. 1,062 seats. Continuous. Booked at H.O. Two changes weekly. Prices, 5d. to 2s. Phone: Gulliver 3943.

KILBURN, N.W.

EMPIRE (WE).—Props., Metropolitan and Provincial Cinematograph Theatres, Ltd., Brettenham House, 14/15, Lancaster Place, W.C.2. Phone: Temple Bar 1144. 1,762 seats. Pictures and Variety. Continuous. Booked at H.O. Prices, 9d. to 2s. 6d. Proscenium width, 38 ft. Stage, 40 ft. deep; 12 dressing rooms.

GRANGE CINEMA (WE), High Road, N.W.6.—Prop., Scala (Kilburn), Ltd, 6, Vigo Street, W.1. Booked by H.O. 2,000 seats. Continuous. Prices, 9d. to 2s. 6d. Pictures and Variety. Variety booked by H.O. Proscenium width, 40 ft. Stage, 10 ft. deep; six dressing rooms. Café attached. Phone: Maida Vale 1664.
Fitted "ARDENTE" Deaf Aids
See page 258

WURLITZER ORGAN
Installed in this Kinema

KILBURN PICTURE PALACE (WE), 256, Belsize Road, N.W.6.—Prop., United Picture Theatres, Ltd. 1,775 seats. Continuous. Prices, 9d. to 1s. 3d. Two changes weekly. Phone: Maida Vale 2019. Station, Kilburn, L.M.S.

TROC CINEMA (AWH), Salusbury Road.—Prop., Mundill and Janson. 450 seats. Booked at Hall. Continuous. Prices 3d. to 1s. Proscenium width, 16 ft. Phone: Maida Vale 3384. Station, Queen's Park.

KINGSBURY, N.W.

ODEON (BTH), Kingsbury Road, N.W.3.—Props., Odeon (Kingsbury), Ltd., Cornhill House, Bennetts Hill, Birmingham. Phone: Midland 2781. Continuous. Booked at 49, Park Lane, W.1. Prices, 9d. to 2s. 6d. Phone: Colindale 8237.

KING'S CROSS, N.

COPENHAGEN CINEMA (Mihaly), Copenhagen Street, N.1.—Prop., E. Cowan, 420 seats. Continuous. Three changes weekly. Prices, 3d. to 6d. Phone: Terminus 5570. Station, King's Cross.

GLOBE CINEMA (BTP), Skinner Street, Rosebery Avenue.—Prop., Frankels, Ltd. 650 seats. Booked at Hall. Continuous. Three changes weekly.—Prices, 3d. to 1s. 3d. Stage, four dressing rooms. Phone: Clerkenwell 6289. Station, King's Cross.

KING'S CROSS CINEMA (RGA), Pentonville Road, N.1.—Prop., Associated Provincial Picture Houses, Ltd., 123, Regent Street, W.1. Booked at H.O. Continuous. Prices, 9d. to 2s. Station, King's Cross. Phone: Terminus 3534.

REGENT.—Prop., Associated British Cinemas, Ltd., 30-31, Golden Square, W.1. Phone: Gerrard 7887.

KINGSWAY, W.C.

STOLL PICTURE THEATRE (WE).—Prop., Stoll Theatres Corpn., Ltd., Stoll Offices, W.C.2. Phone: Temple Bar 1500. 2,425 seats. Booked at H.O. Continuous from 12 noon to 11 p.m. Prices, 6d. to 3s. 9d., including tax. Phone: Holborn 3703.

LAMBETH, S.E.

THE IDEAL, Lambeth Road, S.E.1.—Controller, Rev. T. Tiplady. 750 seats. Continuous. Phone: Reliance 2166. Booked at Hall.

UNIFORM SUPPLY COMPANY, LTD.,

LANGHAM PLACE, W.1.
ST. GEORGE'S HALL.—Prop., British Broadcasting Corporation.

COMPTON
ORGAN featured here.

LEE, S.E.
SAVOY CINEMA (WE), Lee Green.—Prop. Attractive Cinemas (Lee Green), Ltd., 18/20, Regent Street, W.1. 900 seats. Booked at H.O. Continuous. Three changes weekly. Prices, 9d. to 1s. 6d. Phone: Lee Green 0848. Station, Lewisham Junction.

LEICESTER SQUARE, W.C.2.
ALHAMBRA (ODEON) (WE).—Prop., Odeon Theatres, Ltd., Cornhill House, Bennetts Hill, Birmingham. Phone: Midland 2781. (In course of reconstruction.)
EMPIRE THEATRE (WE), Leicester Square, W.C.2.—Props., The New Empire, Ltd., 18, Bloomsbury Square, W.C.1. 3,226 seats. Cafe. Phone: Gerrard 1234
Fitted "ARDENTE" Deaf Aids
See page 258

WURLITZER ORGAN
Installed in this Kinema

HIPPODROME.—1,713 seats.
Fitted "ARDENTE" Deaf Aids
See page 258
LEICESTER SQUARE THEATRE (WE).—Props. Leicester Square Estates, Ltd., St. Martin's Street, W.C.2. 1,900 seats. Prices, 1s. 6d. to 8s. 6d. Phone: Whitehall 5252.
Fitted "ARDENTE" Deaf Aids
See page 258

WURLITZER ORGAN
Installed in this Kinema

MONSEIGNEUR, 147, Wardour Street, W.1. Prop., J. Davis.

LEWISHAM.
GAUMONT PALACE (BA), Loampit Vale, S.E.13. —Props., Gaumont British Picture Corpn., Ltd., New Gallery House, Regent Street, W.1. Booked at H.O. Continuous. Pictures and Variety. Prices, 9d. to 2s. 6d. Proscenium width, 54 ft. Stage, 40 ft. deep.; 12 dressing rooms. Café. Phone: Lee Green 5938-5591. 5942. Station, Lewisham Junction, S.R.
Fitted "ARDENTE" Deaf Aids
See page 258

COMPTON
ORGAN featured here.

HIPPODROME (WE).—2,492 seats. Films on Sundays. Prices, 6d. to 2s.
Fitted "ARDENTE" Stage Amplification
See page 258
KING'S HALL (WE), High Street.—Props. Universal Entertainments, Ltd., 18/20, Regent Street, W.1. 925 seats. Phone: 1435. Booked at H.O. Continuous. Stage, 14 ft. deep; two dressing rooms. Prices, 6d. to 2s. Proscenium width, 30 ft. Phone: Lee Green 1202. Road Transport.
PRINCE OF WALES' PICTURE PLAYHOUSE (WE), 210, High Street.—Prop., Lewisham Cinema,

Controlled by Associated British Cinemas, Ltd. 2,000 seats. Booked at H.O. Continuous. Pictures and Variety. Variety booked at H.O. Stage, 10 ft. deep; four dressing rooms. Prices, 7d. to 2s. Cafe. Phone: Lee Green 0609. Station, Lewisham.
TOWN HALL.

COMPTON
ORGAN featured here.

LEYTON, E.
ASTORIA CINEMA (Kamm), 80, High Road, Leyton, E.15.—Prop., Lion Cinematograph Co., Ltd. 500 seats. Booked at 43, Whitcomb Street, W.C.2. Continuous. Prices, 6d. to 1s. 3d. Phone: Maryland 1941. Station, Leyton (L.N.E.R.).
KING'S CINEMA (WE), High Road.—Prop., Amusements (Leyton), Ltd., 969 seats. Booked by Clavering & Rose, at 199, Piccadilly, W.1. Phone: Regent 1146. Continuous. One change weekly. Prices, 6d. to 2s. Phone: Leytonstone 3522. Station, Hoe Street.
PICTURE HOUSE (RCA), High Road.—Prop., L. Segalov, 85, Clapton Common, E.5. 850 seats. Booked at Hall. Continuous. Two changes weekly. Prices, 6d. to 1s. 6d. Phone: Leyton 2438.
PLAZA (RCA), Hoe Street.—Props., Amusements (Leyton), Ltd., 199, Piccadilly, W.1. 820 seats. Booked at H.O. Prices, 6d. to 1s. 6d. Phone: Leytonstone 3522. Station, Hoe Street, L.N.E.R.
REGAL (WE), Lea Bridge Road, E.10.—Props. W. A. Robinson and N. Carling. 639 seats. Continuous. Three changes weekly. Prices, 6d. to 1s. 6d. Phone: Leytonstone 3462.
SAVOY (WE), Bridge Road.—Props., United Picture Theatres, Ltd. 1,779 seats. Booked at H.O. Continuous. Stage, 20 ft. deep; three dressing rooms. Prices, 6d. to 2s. Proscenium width, 46 ft. Phone: Leytonstone 3211. Station, St. James Street, L.N.E.R.

COMPTON
ORGAN featured here.

LEYTONSTONE, E.
ACADEMY CINEMA (Phillips), Harrow Green.— Props., W. T. Scriven and W. J. Huxtable. 1,100 seats. Booked by Arthur Tench at Coliseum, East Ham. Continuous. Prices, 6d. to 1s. 6d. Phone: Maryland 1817. Station, Leytonstone.
PREMIER CINEMA (RCA), High Road.—Props., Premier Electric Theatre (Leytonstone), Ltd., 750 seats. Booked at Hall. Continuous. Prices, 6d. to 1s. 6d. Phone: Leytonstone 1677. Station, Leytonstone, L.N.E.R.
REX (WE), High Road.—Props., Associated British Cinemas, Ltd., 30-31, Golden Square, London, W.1. 1,952 seats. Booked at H.O. Continuous. Pictures and Variety. Prices, 6d. to 2s. Proscenium width, 42 ft; four dressing rooms. Phone: Leytonstone 2309. Station, Leytonstone, L.N.E.R.
Fitted "ARDENTE" Deaf Aids
See page 258
RIALTO (WE), High Road and Kirkdale Road, E.—Prop., Denman London Cinemas, Ltd.,

136 WARDOUR STREET, LONDON, W.1.

LEYTONSTONE, E.—contd.

36, Golden Square, W.1. Phone : Gerrard 3554. Booked at H.O. Continuous. Pictures and Variety. Phone : Leytonstone 1425. Station, Leytonstone, L.M.S. and L.N.E.R.

COMPTON
ORGAN featured here.

LONDON FIELDS, E.

STANDARD SUPER CINEMA (WE), Goldsmith Row, E.—Prop., Executors of S. Ducker, 275, Evering Road, Clapton, E.5. 1,153 seats. Phone : Clissold 4678. Booked at Hall. Continuous. Stage, 7 ft. deep ; two dressing rooms. Prices, 5d. to 1s. 6d. Phone : Bishopsgate 2791. Station, Cambridge Heath, L.N.E.R.

MAIDA VALE, W 9.

MAIDA VALE PICTURE HOUSE (WE).—Prop., Provincial Cinematograph Theatres, Ltd. 1,001 seats. Booked at H.O. Continuous. Three changes weekly. Prices, 8d. to 3s. Phone : Maida Vale 1421.

**WURLITZER ORGAN
Installed in this Kinema**

MANOR PARK, E.

COLISEUM (WE), Romford Road, E.—Prop., Black Theatres, Ltd., 115, Shaftesbury Avenue, W.1. Phone : Temple Bar 9324. 1,197 seats. Booked at H.O. Continuous. Two changes weekly. Prices, 6d. to 2s. 5d. Phone : Ilford 0907. Station, Ilford,L.N.E.R.

CORONATION CINEMA (WE), High Street North, E.12.—Prop., Associated British Cinemas, Ltd., 30/31, Golden Square, W.1. 1,904 seats. Booked at H.O. Continuous. Prices, 6d. to 2s. Pictures and Variety. Variety booked by Pacey's Agency. Three dressing rooms. Proscenium width, 36 ft. Stage, 20 ft. deep. Cafe. Phone : Grangewood 0357. Station, Manor Park, L.N.E.R.
Fitted "ARDENTE" Deaf Aids
See page 258

COMPTON
ORGAN featured here.

MARBLE ARCH, W.

MARBLE ARCH PAVILION (WE), 505, Oxford Street, W.1.—Props., Gaumont British Picture Corporation, Ltd., New Gallery House, 123, Regent Street, W.1. Phone : Regent 8080. 1,200 seats. Continuous. Booked at New Gallery House. Prices, 1s. 4d. to 6s. Proscenium width, 36 ft. Stage, 12 ft. deep ; three dressing rooms. Cafe. Phone : Mayfair 5112.
Fitted "ARDENTE" Deaf Aids
See page 258

REGAL CINEMA (WE).—Props., Hyde Park Cinemas, Ltd. Controlled by Associated British Cinemas, Ltd., 30/31, Golden Square, W.1. 2,500 seats. Continuous. Stage. Booked at H.O. Cafe attached. Prices, 1s. 6d. to 8s. 6d. Phone : Paddington 9911.
Fitted "ARDENTE" Deaf Aids
See page 258

MAYFAIR, W.

CURZON STREET CINEMA (RCA).—Props., Curzon Cinemas, Ltd., Curzon Street, W.1. Phone :

Grosvenor 4100. 492 seats. Booked at Hall. Continuous. Prices, 2s. 6d. to 8s. 6d. Proscenium width, 33 ft.
Fitted "ARDENTE" Deaf Aids
See page 258

LANSDOWNE CINEMA.

MILE END, E.

CLASSIC (BTH), 44, Mile End Road, E.1.—Props., Davies and Hammond, 52-54, Imperial House, Regent Street, W.1. Phone : Regent 5832. 423 seats. Booked at H.O. Prices, 4d. to 6d. Phone : East 3722. Film Transport.

COLISEUM (RCA), 396-8, Mile End Road, E.—Props., L. and B. Cohen. 900 seats. Booked at Hall. Continuous. Two changes weekly. Phone : Stepney Green 1924.

MILE END EMPIRE (BA), Mile End Road, E.—Props., Associated British Cinemas, Ltd, 30-31, Golden Square, W.1. 2,000 seats. Booked at H.O. Pictures and Varieties. Proscenium width. Stage, 48 ft. ; six dressing rooms. Continuous. Prices, 4d. to 2s. Café. Phone : Stepney Green 2365.
Fitted "ARDENTE" Stage Amplification
See page 258

PALLADIUM (RCA), 370, Mile End Road, E.—Props., Associated British Cinemas, Ltd., 30/31, Golden Square, W.1. Phone : Gerrard 7887. 1,400 seats. Continuous. Two changes weekly. Phone : East 0924. Station, Stepney Green.

MILL HILL, N.W.7.

CAPITOL.—Lion Cinematograph Co., Ltd., 680 seats. Booked at 43, Whitcomb Street, W.C.2. Continuous. Prices, 6d. to 2s. Phone : Mill Hill 2549. Station, Mill Hill.

MUSWELL HILL, N.10.

ATHENÆUM PICTURE PLAYHOUSE (BTP), Fortis Green Road.—Props., Home Counties Theatres Ltd. 598 seats. Booked at Hall. Continuous. Two changes weekly. Prices, 6d. to 1s. 6d. Phone : Tudor 5848.

ODEON THEATRE (BTH), Fortis Green Road.—Props., Odeon (Muswell Hill), Ltd., Cornhill House, Bennetts Hill, Birmingham. Phone : Midland 2781. Booked at 49, Park Lane, London, W.1. Continuous. Prices, 9d. to 2s. Phone : Tudor 1001.

RITZ.—Props., Associated British Cinemas, Ltd., 30-31, Golden Square, W.1. Phone : Gerrard 7887.

SUMMERLAND CINEMA (BTP), Summerland Gds.—Props., Home Counties Theatres Ltd. 680 seats. Booked at Athenæum, Muswell Hill. Continuous. Two changes weekly. Prices, 6d. to 1s. 6d. Phone : Tudor 5849.

NEASDEN, N.W.

RITZ (WE).—Props., Associated British Cinemas, Ltd., 30/31, Golden Square, W.1. Phone : Gerrard 7887. Continuous. Prices, 6d. to 2s. Booked at H.O. Proscenium, width, 42 ft. Phone : Gladstone 1124. Cafe attached. Station, Willesden, L.M.S.

NEW CROSS, S.E.

BROADWAY THEATRE (BA), Broadway, S.E.14.—Prop., Broadway Entertainments, Ltd., 199, Piccadilly, W.1. Phone : Regent 1146. 1,300 seats. Booked at H.O. Continuous. Stage, 30 ft. ; six dressing rooms. Prices, 6d. to 2s. Phone : New Cross 0196. Station, New Cross, S.R.

UNIFORM SUPPLY COMPANY, LTD.,

NEW CROSS SUPER KINEMA (WE).—Prop., Denman Picture Houses, Ltd., New Gallery House, Regent Street, W.I. 2,089 seats. Booked at H.O. Pictures and Variety. Stage, 30 ft. deep ; three dressing rooms. Dance Hall and Cafe. Continuous. Phone : New Cross 1336, 1343, 2106. Station, New Cross.

Fitted "ARDENTE" Deaf Aids
See page 258

WURLITZER ORGAN
Installed in this Kinema

NEW SOUTHGATE, N.
CORONATION CINEMA (WE), High Road, N.II. —Props., May and Hopkinson. 800 seats. Booked at Hall. Continuous. Prices, 6d. to 1s. 6d. Phone : Enterprise 1084, Station, New Southgate, L.N.E.R.

ODEON THEATRE (BTH).—Prop., Odeon (Southgate), Ltd., Cornhill House, Bennetts Hill, Birmingham. Phone: Midland 2781. Booked at 49, Park Lane, London, W.I. Continuous. Prices, 6d. to 1s. Phone : Palmers Green 5893.

RITZ (WE), Arnos Grove. — Prop., Associated British Cinemas, Ltd., 30/31, Golden Square, London, W.I. 2,000 seats. Phone : Gerrard 7887.

NORTH KENSINGTON, W.11.
ROYALTY CINEMA (RCA), 105/9, Lancaster Road, W.II.—Props., Associated British Cinemas, Ltd., 30/31, Golden Square, W.I. Phone: Gerrard 7887. 1,288 seats. Continuous. Prices, 9d. to 2s. Pictures and Variety. Proscenium width, 44 ft. Stage, 12 ft. deep ; three dressing rooms. Phone : Park 1044.

COMPTON
ꝺRGAN f e a t u r e d h e r e.

NORBURY, S.W.16.
NORBURY CINEMA (BTH), London Road.— Props., Consolidated Entertainments, Ltd., 36-37, Queen Street, E.C.4. Phone : Central 9156. 859 seats. Booked at H.O. Continuous. Prices, 6d. to 1s. 6d. Phone : Pollards 1887. Station, Norbury, S.R.

REX.—Prop., Associated British Cinemas, Ltd., 30-31, Golden Square, W.I. Phone: Gerrard 7887.

Fitted "ARDENTE" Deaf Aids
See page 258

NORWOOD, S.E.
ALBANY CINEMA (WE), Upper Norwood.—Prop., Excelsior Super Cinemas, Ltd., Waimar House, 288, Regent Street, W.I. Phone : Langham 2677. 970 seats. Continuous. Prices, 6d. to 1s. 6d. Station, Crystal Palace, S.R.

CENTRAL HALL, PICTURE PALACE (Mills), Portland Road, South Norwood.—Prop., H. Mills. 495 seats. Booked at Hall. Continuous. Three changes weekly. Prices, 4d. to 1s. Addiscombe 2118.

NEW GAIETY CINEMA (RCA), High Street, S.E.25.—Props., J. D. Harris. 800 seats. Booked at H.O. Continuous. Two changes weekly. Prices, 6d. to 2s. Phone : Livingstone 3767. Station, Norwood Junction, S.R.

ODEON THEATRE (BTH), Station Road.—Props., Odeon (South Norwood) Ltd., Cornhill House, Bennetts Hill, Birmingham. Phone: Midland 2781. (In course of construction).

REGAL (WE).—Prop., H. & G. Kinemas, Ltd., 90, Regent Street, W.I. Phone : Regent 4794. 2,010 seats. Booked at H.O. Continuous. Pictures and Variety. Prices, 9d. to 2s. Proscenium width, 40 ft. Stage, 22 ft. deep. Five dressing rooms. Cafe and Dance Hall. Phone : Streatham 9411. Station, West Norwood, S.R.

RIALTO (WE), Upper Norwood.—Prop., Excelsior Super Cinemas, Ltd., Walmar House, 288, Regent Street, W.I. 1,393 seats. Booked at H.O. Continuous. Prices, 6d. to 1s. 10d. Phone : Livingstone 2244. Station, Crystal Palace, S.R.

ROYAL (AWH).—Props., C.M.H. Cinemas, Ltd., 76, Knight's Hill, S.E. 320 seats. Booked at Hall. Continuous. Mats., Sat. Two changes weekly. Prices, 6d. to 1s. 3d. Phone : Streatham 1891. Station, West Norwood, S.R.

NOTTING HILL GATE, W.
EMBASSY NEWS AND INTEREST THEATRE (BTH), High Street.—Prop., Embassy (Notting Hill Gate), Ltd. 314 seats. Booked at Hall. Continuous. Prices, 7d. to 9d. Phone : Park 1188.

IMPERIAL PLAYHOUSE (RCA).—Prop., Imperial Ltd., Playhouse (Notting Hill), 10-12, Cork Street, W.I. Phone : Regent 4794. 600 seats. Booked at H.O. Continuous. Three changes weekly. Prices, 5d. to 1s. Phone : Park 1625.

THE CORONET THEATRE (BA), Notting Hill Gate, W.II.—Prop., Gaumont-British Picture Corporation, Ltd., New Gallery House, 123, Regent Street, W. Phone : Regent 8080. 1,010 seats. Booked at H.O. Continuous. Prices, 6d. to 2s. Proscenium width, 35 ft. Phone : Park 6705.

OLD FORD, E.
OLD FORD PICTURE PALACE, St. Stephen's Road, E.3.—Prop., Old Ford Picture Palace Co., Ltd. 510 seats. Booked at Hall. Continuous. Two changes weekly. Prices, 4d. to 1s. Phone : Advance 1977. Station, Coborn Road.

OLD KENT ROAD, S.E.
ASTORIA (WE).—Prop., Paramount Astoria Theatres, Ltd., 104-108, Oxford Street, W.I. Phone : Museum 4721. 2,899 seats. Booked at H.O. Continuous. Pictures and Variety. Prices, 6d. to 2s. Cafe. Phone : New Cross 4716.

COMPTON
ORGAN f e a t u r e d h e r e.

GLOBE ELECTRIC THEATRE (WE).—Prop., Globe Electric Theatre, Ltd. 1,200 seats. Booked at Hall. Continuous. Two changes weekly. Pictures and Variety. Variety booked by H. Barclay, 319, Queens Road, New Cross. Stage, 16 ft. deep ; three dressing rooms. Prices, 6d. to 1s. 6d. Phone : Bermondsey 3120. Station, Elephant and Castle, S.R.

OLD KENT PICTURE HOUSE (BA), 42-44, Old Kent Road, S.E.I.—Prop., United Picture

136 WARDOUR STREET, LONDON, W.1.

OLD KENT ROAD, S.E.—contd.
Theatres, Ltd. 1,993 seats. Continuous. Prices, 6d. to 1s. 6d. Phone: Rodney 3459.
REGAL.—Prop., Associated British Cinemas Ltd., 30-31, Golden Square, W.1. Phone: Gerrard, 7887.
Fitted "ARDENTE" Deaf Aids
See page 258

COMPTON
ORGAN featured here.

OXFORD STREET, W.1.
ACADEMY CINEMA (WE), 165, Oxford Street.—Props., Cinema House, Ltd., 225, Oxford Street. Phone: Gerrard 3814. 529 seats. Booked at H.O. Continuous. Prices, 1s. 6d to 8s. 6d. Phone: Gerrard 2981.
Fitted "ARDENTE" Deaf Aids
See page 258

STUDIO ONE (WE).—Prop., Amalgamated Picture Theatres, Ltd., 225, Oxford Street, W.1. Phone: Gerrard 4242. 600 seats. Booked at H.O. Continuous. One change weekly. Prices, 1s 6d. to 8s. 6d. Phone: Gerrard 3300.
Fitted "ARDENTE" Deaf Aids
See page 258

STUDIO TWO (WE).—Props., Amalgamated Picture Theatres, Ltd., 225, Oxford Street, W.1. 350 seats. Booked at H.O. Prices, 1s. Phone: Gerrard 3300.
Fitted "ARDENTE" Deaf Aids
See page 258

PADDINGTON, W.
GRAND CINEMA (RCA), Gt. Western Road.—Prop., Grand Cinema, Paddington, Ltd. 1,200 seats. Booked by Mr. Pesaresi. Continuous. Two changes weekly. Prices, 6d. to 2s. Phone: Abercorn 1400.
WORLDS NEWS THEATRE (RCA), 5, Praed Street—Props., Harris & Elkan. 400 seats. Continuous. Prices, 1s. and 6d. Phone: Paddington 5716. Station, Paddington, G.W.R., Praed Street. Tube and Met.

PALMER'S GREEN, N.
PALMADIUM (WE), Palmer's Green, N.13.—Prop., Denman Picture Houses, Ltd. 2,188 seats. Continuous. Prices, 6d. to 2s. 6d. Phone: Palmer's Green 0700. Station, Palmer's Green, L.N.E.R.
Fitted "ARDENTE" Deaf Aids
See page 258

QUEEN'S HALL CINEMA (RCA), Green Lanes,—Prop., Moss Harris. 1,100 seats. Booked at Hall. Continuous. Prices, 6d. to 2s. Phone: Palmer's Green 0860. Station, Palmer's Green, L.N.E.R.

PARK LANE, W.
GROSVENOR HOUSE (BTP).
MONSEIGNEUR.—Prop., J. Davis, 147, Wardour Street, W.1.

PECKHAM, S.E.
GAUMONT PALACE (BA) (late Hippodrome), High Street.—Props., Provincial Cinematograph Theatres, Ltd. 2,250 seats. Pictures and Variety. Continuous. Booked at H.O. New Gallery House, Regent Street, London,

W.1. Stage, 18 ft. Proscenium opening, 35 ft. Prices, 6d. to 2s. Phone: New Cross 1302.
Fitted "ARDENTE" Deaf Aids
See page 258

COMPTON
ORGAN featured here.

IDEAL KINEMA (WE), Queen's Road, S.E.15.—600 seats. Continuous. Three changes weekly. Prices, 7d. to 1s. 3d. Phone: New Cross 0368.
QUEEN'S HALL PICTURE THEATRE (WE), High Street, S.E.15.—Prop., L. Segalov. 600 seats. Continuous. Three changes weekly. Prices, 6d. to 1s. 6d. Stage. Phone: New Cross 194. Station, Peckham Rye, S.R.
TOWER CINEMA (WE), 116, Rye Lane, S.E.15.—Prop., Provincial Cinematograph Theatres, Ltd. 1,952 seats. Booked at H.O. Continuous. Pictures and Variety. Stage, 14 ft.; four dressing rooms. Prices, Evenings, 6d. to 2s. Cafe attached. Phone: New Cross 2079.
TOWER ANNEXE CINEMA (BA), Rye Lane, S.E. 15.—Prop., P.C.T., Ltd., 123, Regent Street, W.1. Phone: Regent 6641. Booked at H.O. Continuous. Prices, 6d. to 1s. 6d. Phone: New Cross 1174. Station, Peckham Rye, S.R.

PENGE, S.E.
KING'S HALL (BA), High Street, S.E.20.—Prop., Denman Picture Houses, Ltd., New Gallery House, Regent Street, W.1. 1,200 seats. Continuous. Two changes weekly. Prices, 7d. to 2s. 6d. Phone: Sydenham 1596. Station, Penge, S.R.
ODEON THEATRE (BTH), High Street.—Props., Odeon (Penge) Ltd., Cornhill House, Bennetts Hill, Birmingham. Phone: Midland 2781. Booked at 49, Park Lane, W.1.

PICCADILLY CIRCUS, W.1.
LONDON PAVILION (WE).—Prop., Crescent Theatres, Ltd., Film House, Wardour Street, W.1. Phone: Gerrard 5084. 1,217 seats. Continuous. Prices, 1s. 6d. to 8s. 6d. Café attached. Phone: Gerrard 2982/3.
MONSEIGNEUR NEWS THEATRE (WE).—Prop., Wardour Theatres, Ltd., 18, Devonshire Street, Bishopsgate, E. Phone: Bis. 2087. 280 seats. Booked at Sphere Theatre, Tottenham Court Road. Prices, 1s. to 2s. Café attached.
PICCADILLY NEWS THEATRE (BTH). (See Great Windmill Street)
PICCADILLY THEATRE (WE).—Props., Theatrical Enterprises, Ltd, 1,182 seats.
PLAZA THEATRE (WE).—Prop., Plaza Theatre Co., Ltd., 166, Wardour Street, W.1. Phone: Gerrard 7700. 1,891 seats. Continuous. Prices, 1s. 6d. to 8s. 6d. Stage. Phone: Whitehall 8944.
Fitted "ARDENTE" Deaf Aids
See page 258
WURLITZER ORGAN
Installed in this Kinema

PLAISTOW, E.
CANNING TOWN KINEMA (BA), 317, Barking Road, Plaistow, E.13.—Prop., Denman Picture Houses, Ltd., New Gallery House, Regent Street, W.1. Phone: Regent 8080. 850 seats. Booked at H.O. Continuous.

UNIFORM SUPPLY COMPANY, LTD.,

Three changes weekly. Prices, 4d. to 9d. Phone: Albert Dock 1382. Station, Canning Town, L.N.E.R.

GREEN GATE THEATRE (RCA), Barking Road, E.13.—Prop., Greengot (Plaistow), Ltd. 600 seats. Booked at Theatre. Continuous. Three changes weekly. Prices, 6d. to 1s. 6d. Phone: Grangewood 0036. Station, Plaistow.

PLAZA CINEMA (BTH), Richmond Street, E.13. —Prop., L. A. Katz. 600 seats. Booked at Hall. Continuous. Three changes weekly. Prices, 4d. to 1s. Phone: Grangewood 0036. Station, Plaistow, L.M.S.

PLUMSTEAD, S.E.

GLOBE CINEMA (WE), Plumstead Common Road. —Prop., Chandos Cinemas, Ltd., 113, Plumstead Common Road, S.E.18. 661 seats. Booked at Hall. Continuous. Prices, 6d. to 1s. 6d. Three changes weekly. Phone: Woolwich 1556. Station, Woolwich Arsenal, S.R.

KINEMA (RCA), High Street, S.E.18.—Prop., Denman London Cinemas, Ltd., 36, Golden Square, W.1. Phone: Gerrard 3554. Booked at H.O. Continuous. Phone: Woolwich 0524. Station, Plumstead.

PLAZA (WE), High Street.—Prop., London & District Cinemas, Ltd., Astoria House, 62, Shaftesbury Avenue, W.1. 528 seats. Continuous. Prices, 6d. to 1s. 3d. Station, Plumstead. Phone: Woolwich 0521.

POPLAR, E.

GAIETY CINEMA (RCA), 73, East India Dock Road.—Prop., Poplar Cinema, Ltd. 412 seats. Booked at Hall. Continuous. Three changes weekly. Prices, 5d. to 1s. 6d. Phone: East 4038. Transport.

GRAND PALACE (RCA), Robin Hood Lane, E.14. —Prop., Geo. Smart, 331, Mare Street, Hackney, E. 850 seats. . Continuous. Two changes weekly. Prices, 7d. to 2s. 4d. Phone: East 3943.

IDEAL PICTURE PALACE (BTP), 12-13, King Street, Poplar.—Prop., M. Muriani, 22, Chessington Avenue, Finchley. 600 seats. Continuous. Pictures and Variety. Prices, 5d. to 9d. Stage, 12 ft. deep; two dressing rooms. Phone: East 4479. Station, Poplar.

KING GEORGE'S PICTURE HALL (Poplar Methodist Mission), East India Dock Road.— (Closed). 500 seats.

PALACEADIUM (WE), White Horse Street, E.1.— Prop., Palaceadium, Ltd. 564 seats. Booked at Hall. Four shows daily. Three changes weekly. Prices, 3d. to 1s. Phone: East 1145.

POPLAR HIPPODROME (RCA), East India Dock Road. –Props., Olympodromes, Ltd., 30-31, Golden Square, W.1. 2,317 seats. Booked at H.O. Continuous. Two changes weekly. Prices, 4d. to 1s. 6d. Proscenium width, 23 ft. Stage, 40 ft. deep; eight dressing rooms. Phone: East 0064. Station, Poplar.

POPLAR PAVILION (WE), East India Dock Road, E.—Prop., Geo. Smart, 331, Mare Street, Hackney, E. 1,318 seats. Booked at H.O. Continuous. Two changes weekly. Pictures and Variety. Stage, 12 ft. by 28 ft. Prices, 5d. to 1s. 6d. Phone: East 0733.

PUTNEY, S.W.

GLOBE KINEMA (WE), Upper Richmond Road.— Prop., R. T. Davies. 380 seats. Booked at Hall. Continuous. Three changes weekly. Stage. Prices, 6d. to 1s. 10d. Phone: Putney 0032. Station, Putney, S.R.

PUTNEY BRIDGE KINEMA (RCA), Putney Bridge Approach, S.W.6.—Prop., General Cinema Theatres, Ltd., 19, Albemarle Street, W.1. Phone: Regent 4419. 750 seats. Booked at H.O. Continuous. Prices, 6d. to 1s. 6d. Station, Putney Bridge, District.

PUTNEY HIPPODROME (BA), Felsham Road.— Prop., Associated British Cinemas, Ltd., 30-31, Golden Square, W.1. Phone: Gerrard 7887. 1,420 seats. Continuous. Pictures and Variety. Prices, 3d. to 2s. Proscenium width, 30 ft. Stage, 55 ft. deep; six dressing rooms. Phone: Putney 2002.

PUTNEY PALACE (BA), High Street.—Prop., United Picture Theatres, Ltd. 1,430 seats. Continuous. Two changes weekly. Prices, 9d. to 2s. Phone, Putney 4756.

COMPTON

ORGAN featured here.

REGENT STREET, W.1.

LONDON PALLADIUM, Argyll Street.—Prop, General Theatre Corporation, Ltd.

NEW GALLERY KINEMA (WE).—Props., Gaumont-British Picture Corporation, New Gallery House, 123, Regent Street, London. W.1. 1,450 seats. Phone: Regent 8080. Booked at H.O. Continuous. Prices, 1s. 6d. to 8s. 6d. Phone: Regent 2255.
Fitted "ARDENTE" Deaf Aids
See page 258

WURLITZER ORGAN
Installed in this Kinema

POLYTECHNIC THEATRE (WE), Regent Street, W.1.—Prop., Attractive Cinema (Wandsworth) Ltd., 18-20, Regent Street, W.1. 610 seats. Continuous. Booked at Hall. Not open Sundays. Special programmes. Prices, 1s. 3d. to 6s. Phone: Langham 1744.
Fitted "ARDENTE" Deaf Aids
See page 258

COMPTON

ORGAN featured here.

ROTHERHITHE, S.E.

LION CINEMA (BA), Rotherhithe New Road, S.E.—Prop., Denman Picture Houses, Ltd., 123, Regent Street, W.1. 656 seats. Booked at H.O. Continuous. Prces, 4d. to 1s. 3d. Phone: Bermondsey 2228. Station, Surrey Docks.

ROTHERHITHE HIPPODROME (RCA), Lower Road, Bermondsey, S.E.16.—Props., Associated British Cinemas, Ltd., 30-31, Golden Square, W.1. Phone: Gerrard 7887. 1,200 seats. Continuous. Pictures and Variety. Stage 30 ft.; nine dressing rooms. Prices, 4d. to 1s. 6d. Phone: Bermondsey 3609.

SEVEN DIALS, W.C.

CAMBRIDGE THEATRE (WE).—Phone: Temple Bar 6056-7. 1,191 seats.

SHAFTESBURY AVENUE, W.1.

EROS NEWS THEATRE (BTH), 7, Shaftesbury Avenue, W.1. Prop., Capital and Provincial News Theatres, Ltd., 172, Buckingham Palace Road, S.W.1. Phone: Sloane 9132. 199

136 WARDOUR STREET, LONDON, W.1.

SHAFTESBURY AVENUE, W.1.—contd.
seats. Booked at H.O. Continuous. Prices,
1s. Phone: Gerrard 3839.

G.-B. NEWS THEATRE (BA).—101, Shaftesbury
Avenue.—Prop., Gaumont-British Picture
Corporation, Ltd., 123, Regent Street, W.1.
Phone: Regent 8080. 510 seats. Continu-
ous. Prices, 6d. and 1s. Phone: Gerrard
3981. Station, Leicester Square.

PLACE THEATRE (WE).—Three shows daily,
while showing films. Phone: Gerrard 6834.
1,603 seats.

SHEPHERD'S BUSH, W.

NEW PALLADIUM (WE), Shepherd's Bush Green,
W.12.—Prop., Universal Entertainments, Ltd.
18/20, Regent Street, W.1. 763 seats. Booked
at H.O. Continuous. Prices, 6d. to 1s. 6d.
Phone: Shepherd's Bush 1646. Station,
Shepherd's Bush, Metro.

COMPTON
ORGAN featured here.

NEW PARK CINEMA (WE), Goldhawk Road.—
Prop., W. Sloman. 525 seats. Booked at
Hall. Continuous. Prices, 6d. to 1s. 6d.
Phone: Riverside 5642. Station, Goldhawk
Road, Shepherd's Bush.

**Fitted "ARDENTE" Deaf Aids
See page 258**

PAVILION (WE), Shepherd's Bush Green.—Prop.
Gaumont-British Picture Corporation, Ltd.
2767 seats. Booked at H.O. Pictures and
Variety. Stage, 20 ft. deep ; four dressing
rooms. Café. Continuous. Prices, 6d. to
2s. 6d. Phones: Shepherd's Bush 2306 and
2307. Station, Shepherd's Bush (Tube).

**Fitted "ARDENTE" Deaf Aids
See page 258**

COMPTON
ORGAN featured here.

SHEPHERD'S BUSH EMPIRE (WE).—Prop., Hack-
ney & Shepherd's Bush Empire Palaces, Ltd.,
Stoll Offices, Coliseum Buildings, W.C. Phone :
Temple Bar 1500. 1,680 seats. Booked at H.O.
Pictures, Sunday only. Booked at H.O.
Phone: Shepherd's Bush 4531.

SILVER CINEMA (WE), Uxbridge Road—Prop.
Universal Entertainments, Ltd., 18/20,
Regent Street, W.1. Phone: Gerrard 1435.
1,016 seats. Booked at H.O. Continuous.
Two changes weekly. Prices, 9d. to 2s.
Phone: Shepherd's Bush 2862.

SHOREDITCH, E.

GAIETY CINEMA (BA), 117, Kingsland Road.—
Props., C. L. Adams, 7, Eastwick Avenue,
Taunton, Som. Phone: Taunton 2586.
400 seats. Booked at Hall. Continuous.
Prices, 3d. to 9d. Proscenium width, 18 ft.
Phone: Clerkenwell 4484. Films by Trans-
port.

LUXOR (WE), Commercial Street and Quaker
Street.—Prop., Geo. Smart. 852 seats.

OLYMPIA (RCA), High Street, E.—Prop.,
Associated British Cinemas, Ltd., 30-31,
Golden Square, W.1. Phone: Gerrard 7887.
1,546 seats. Booked at H.O. Stage, 60 ft.
deep ; 12 dressing rooms. Continuous.
Prices, 4d. to 1s. 6d. Proscenium width,
38 ft. Phone: Bishopsgate 1628. Station,
Liverpool Street, L.N.E.R.

SILVERTOWN, E.

ALBERT CINEMA (AWH).—Lessee, Harry W.
Pinchon. 400 seats. Continuous. Booked
at Hall. Phone: Albert Dock 1970.

SLOANE SQUARE, S.W.

ROYAL COURT (WE).—Prop., Royal Court
Cinema, Ltd. 550 seats. Booked at Hall.
Continuous. Prices, 6d. to 5s. Proscenium
width, 22 ft. Phone: Sloane 0058.

SOUTHFIELDS, S.W.

PLAZA (RCA), Wimbledon Park Road.—Prop.,
S.R.G. Cinemas, Ltd. 1,100 seats. Prices,
6d. to 1s. 6d. Phone: Putney 3906. Station,
Southfields, S.R.

SOUTHWARK, S.E.

SOUTH LONDON PALACE, 92, London Road,
S.E.1.—Prop., Variety Theatres Consolidated
Ltd. Phone: Waterloo 4644.

ST. MARTIN'S LANE, W.C.

COLISEUM (WE).—Prop., Coliseum Synd., Ltd.
2,138 seats.

ST. PANCRAS.

TOLMER CINEMA (WE), Tolmer Square, Hampstead Road.—Prop., Cinema, Goldhawk
Street, Hackney, E.8. Phone: Amhurst
2911. 1,050 seats. Continuous. Three
changes weekly. Prices, 6d. to 1s. 6d.
Phone: Museum 8873. Station, Euston
Square (Tube).

**WURLITZER ORGAN
Installed in this Kinema**

STAMFORD HILL, N.

REGENT THEATRE (WE).—Prop., Provincial
Cinematograph Theatres, Ltd., 123, Regent
Street, London, W.1. Phone: Regent 8080.
2,182 seats. Continuous. Booked at H.O.
Prices, 9d. to 2s. 6d. Special matinee prices.
Stage, 40 ft. deep ; 10 dressing rooms. Café.
Phone: Stamford Hill 1504. Station, Stam-
ford Hill, or Manor House (Piccadilly Line).

**Fitted "ARDENTE" Deaf Aids
See page 258**

**WURLITZER ORGAN
Installed in this Kinema**

ROXY CINEMA (BTH), High Road.—Wardcott
Cinemas, Ltd. 440 seats. Continuous.
Prices, 6d. to 1s. 3d. Phone: Tottenham
2001. Station, Seven Sisters, L.N.E.R.

STAMFORD HILL CINEMA (BA).—Prop., United
Picture Theatres, Ltd., New Gallery House,
Regent Street, W.1. 1,780 seats. Booked at
H.O. Continuous. Prices, 6d. to 1s 6d.
Phone: Clissold 4332. Station, Stamford
Hill, L.N.E.R.

STEPNEY, E.

CABLE PICTURE PALACE, 103, Cable Street.—
Prop., Mrs. Yetta Wassersug. 350 seats.

LA BOHEME CINEMA (WE), 560, Mile End Road.
—Props., A. Moss and B. Zuikin. 900 seats.
Booked at Hall. Continuous. Two changes
weekly. Dance Hall. Prices, 6d. to 1s. 6d.
Phone: Advance 1504. Station, Mile End.

MAYFAIR CINEMA (WE), Brick Lane.—D. J.
James Circuit, 225, Oxford Street, London,
W.1. Phone: Gerrard 4242. 1,500 seats.
Phone, Bishopsgate 6000. Prices, 6d. to
1s. 6d.

UNIFORM SUPPLY COMPANY, LTD.,

POPULAR CINEMA (RCA), 516, Commercial Road, E.1.—Prop., H. & G. (Stepney), Ltd., Pollen House, 10/12, Cork Street, W.1. Phone: Regent 4794 Booked at H.O. 600 seats. Continuous. Three changes weekly. Prices, 5d. to 1s. Phone : East 1331.

ST. GEORGES CENTRAL HALL (BA), Cable Street, E.1.—Prop., Rev. Percy Imeson, 583, Commercial Road, E.1. Children at 5 p.m. to 7 p.m. each evening. Adults, Saty., 7.45 p.m. Booked at Central Hall, Stepney. Prices, 3d. to 6d.

STEPNEY CENTRAL HALL (Kalee), 583, Commercial Road, E.q.—Prop., Rev. Percy Ineson, East - End Mission, 583, Commercial Road, E.1. 1,000 seats. Booked at Hall. Children 5 till 7 each evening. Adults, Sats., at 7.45. Prices Children 1d., Adults 3d. and 6d. Phone : Stepney Green 3366/7.

TROXY.—Prop., Provincial Cinematograph Theatres, 123, Regent Street, W.1.

STOCKWELL, S.W.

STOCKWELL PALLADIUM (RCA), Clapham Road. —Prop, Pindar Trust, Ltd., 550 seats. Continuous. Two changes weekly. Prices, 7d. to 1s. 6d. Phone : Brixton 2513.

STOKE-NEWINGTON, N.15.

ALBION CINEMA, 4, Albion Parade.—Prop., E. W. Drice. Phone : Clissold 3833. 450 seats.

ALEXANDRA THEATRE (WE).—Prop., Alexandra Theatre (Lessees), Ltd. 1,462 seats. Booked at Hall. Sundays only. Prices, 6d. to 1s. 6d. Phone : Clissold 2345-6.

AMBASSADORS (late APOLLO), Stoke Newington Road, N.16.—Prop., Watford Amusements Ltd. 1,180 seats. Continuous. Prices, 9d. to 1s. 6d. Phone : Clissold 5251. Station, Stoke Newington, L.N.E.R.

APOLLO. — Prop., Provincial Cinematograph Theatres, Ltd., 123, Regent Street, W.1.

COLISEUM (BTH), Stoke Newington Road, N.16. —Prop., Kingsland Pictures, Ltd., Stoke Newington Road, N.16. 600 seats. Booked at Hall. Three shows daily. Prices, 6d. to 1s. 3d. Phone : Clissold 1844.

MAJESTIC CINEMA (RCA), High Street, N.16.— Prop., Palasino Picture Theatre, Ltd. Cinema House, Oxford Street, W.1. Phone : Gerrard 4242. 700 seats. Booked at H.O. Continuous. Pictures. Three changes weekly. Prices 6d. to 1s. Phone : Clissold 3322. Station, Dalston Junction.

SAVOY.—Prop., Associated British Cinemas, Ltd., 30-31, Golden Square, W.1. Phone: Gerrard 7887.
Fitted "ARDENTE" Deaf Aids
See page 258

COMPTON

ORGAN featured here.

STRAND, W.C.2.

ADELPHI (WE).
MONSEIGNEUR NEWS THEATRE (RCA).—J. Davis Circuit, 147, Wardour Street, W.1. Phone : Gerrard 1416.

STRAND NEWS CINEMA (Mihaly), 3-5, Agar Street.—Prop., Strand News Theatre, Ltd., 18, Devonshire Street, Bishopsgate, E.

500 seats. Continuous. Booked at 147, Wardour Street, W.1. Two changes weekly. Prices, 7d. and 1s. Phone : Temple Bar 5601.

TIVOLI THEATRE (WE.), Strand.—Prop., Tivoli Palace, Ltd., 123, Regent Street, London, W.1. 2,073 seats. Continuous. Prices, 1s. 6d to 8s. 6d. Phone : Temple Bar 5025. Café attached.
Fitted "ARDENTE" Deaf Aids
See page 258

WURLITZER ORGAN
Installed in this Kinema

FORUM, Villiers Street.—Prop., Original Forum Cinema Co., Ltd. Phone : Temple Bar 3931.

STRATFORD, E.

BROADWAY SUPER CINEMA (WE), Tramway Avenue.—Props., Denman Picture Houses. Ltd. 2,768 seats. Continuous. Booked at H.O. Pictures and Variety. Stage 34 ft. ; six dressing rooms. Café. Prices, 6d. to 2s. Phone : Maryland 2186. Station, Stratford Market, L.N.E.R.
Fitted "ARDENTE" Deaf Aids
See page 258

WURLITZER ORGAN
Installed in this Kinema

GROVE CINEMA (BTH), Maryland Point.—Prop., H. & M. Keff. 450 seats. Booked at H.O. Continuous. Prices, 6d. to 1s. 3d. Proscenium width, 28 ft. Phone : Maryland 3100. Station, Maryland Point, L.N.E.R. .

KINEMA (BA), West Ham Lane, E.15.—Prop., Denman London Cinemas, Ltd., 36, Golden Square, W.1. Phone : Gerrard 3554. 1,659 seats. Continuous. Booked at H.O. Prices, 7d. to 1s. Phone : Maryland 1208. Station, Stratford, L.N.E.R.

REX (RCA), High Street. Prop., Associated British Cinemas, Ltd., 30/31, Golden Square, W.1. 2,000 seats. Booked at H.O. Pictures and Variety. Continuous. Prices, 6d. to 2s. Proscenium width, 34 ft. Stage, 20 ft. deep. Four dressing rooms. Phone : Maryland 2022 Station, Stratford.
Fitted "ARDENTE" Deaf Aids
Fitted "ARDENTE" Stage Amplification
See page 258

WURLITZER ORGAN
Installed in this Kinema

TROCADERO (WE), Ward Road.—(Closed.)

STREATHAM, S.W.

ASTORIA (WE).—Prop., Paramount—Astoria Theatres, Ltd., 162/170, Wardour Street, W.1. Phone : Gerrard 7700. 2,614 seats. Continuous. Pictures and Variety. Stage. Café. Phone : Streatham 8610. Station, Streatham Hill, S.R.

COMPTON

ORGAN featured here.

GAUMONT PALACE (BA), Streatham Hill,—Props. Gaumont-British Picture Corporation, Ltd. 2,381 seats. Booked at H.O. Continuous: Pictures and Variety. Prices, 6d. to 2s. 6d. Proscenium width, 57 ft. Stage, 35 ft. deep ; .

136 WARDOUR STREET, LONDON, W.1.

STREATHAM, S.W.—contd.
six dressing rooms. Café attached. Phone : Tulse Hill 5251. Station, Streatham Hill.
Fitted "ARDENTE" Deaf Aids
See page 258

COMPTON
ORGAN featured here.

GOLDEN DOMES PICTURES THEATRE (RCA). Streatham, S.W.16.—Associated British Cinemas, Ltd., 30/31, Golden Square, W.1. 1,010 seats. Continuous. Two changes weekly. Prices, 4d. to 2s. Phone : Streatham 1470. Station, Streatham Hill, S.R.

STREATHAM HILL THEATRE, 56 to 60, Streatham Hill, S.W.2. Prop, Streatham Hill Playhouse, Ltd.

SWISS COTTAGE, N.W.
ODEON THEATRE (BTH), Finchley Road and Avenue Road.—Props., Odeon (Swiss Cottage) Ltd., Cornhill House, Bennetts Hill, Birmingham. Phone: Midland 2781, (In course of construction).

SYDENHAM, S.E.
QUEEN'S HALL KINEMA (Picturetone), Sydenham Road, S.E.26.—Prop., L. C. Bell-Cox, 57, Philbeach Gardens, S.W.5. 500 seats. Booked at Hall. Continuous. Three changes weekly. Prices, 7d. to 1s. 6d. Phone : Sydenham 8068. Station, Sydenham, S.R.

STATE CINEMA (WE), Sydenham, S.E.26.—Prop., Medway Cinemas, Ltd., Walmer House, 288, Regent Street, W.1. Phone : Langham 2677. 1,600 seats. Booked at H.O. Continuous. Prices, 6d. to 2s. Phone : Sydenham 8696. Station, Sydenham.

SYDENHAM RINK CINEMA (WE), Silverdale, S.E.26.—Props., Provincial Cinematograph Theatres, Ltd., New Gallery House, 123, Regent Street, W.1. 1,518 seats. Phone : Regent 8080. Booked at H.O. Stage, 8 ft. deep ; five dressing rooms. Continuous. Three changes weekly. Prices, 6d. to 2s. Proscenium width, 48 ft. Phone : Sydenham 7727. Station, Sydenham. S.R.

WURLITZER ORGAN
Installed in this Kinema

TOOTING, S.W.
ASTORIA (late Tooting Electric Pavilion) (WE), Mitcham Road.—Props., Davison and Singer. 950 seats. Booked at Hall. Continuous. Two changes weekly. Prices, 7d. to 2s. 9d. Phone : Streatham 2485.

BROADWAY PALACE THEATRE (Cinephone).— 24, Mitcham Road, S.W.—Prop., A. H. Batley. 900 seats. Continuous. Two changes weekly. Prices, 6d. to 2s. 6d. Stage. Phone : Streatham 1810. Station, Tooting Broadway, Tube. Road Transport.

CENTRAL CINEMA, Upper Tooting Road, S.W.17. —Prop., Lion Cinematograph Co., Ltd. Booked at 43, Whitcomb Street, W.C.2. Continuous. Three changes weekly. Prices, 6d. to 1s. 10d. Phone : Streatham 3688.

CINENEWS (BTH), High Street.—Props., Capital and Provincial News Theatres, Ltd., 172, Buckringham Palace Road, S.W. 418 seats. Continuous. Prices, 6d. and 1s. Phone : Streatham 8544.

GRANADA (WE).—Controlled by Bernstein Theatres, Ltd., 36, Golden Square, W.1.

Phone : Gerrard 3554. Booked at H.O. Continuous. Pictures and Variety. Phone . Streatham 6000.

WURLITZER ORGAN
Installed in this Kinema

MAYFAIR (WE).—Prop., B. H. S. Syndicate, Ltd., 30-31, Golden Square, W.1. 1,950 seats. Continuous. Pictures and Variety. Prices, 7d. to 2s. 6d. Proscenium width, 46 ft. Stage, 20 ft. deep ; nine dressing rooms. Café. Dance Hall. Road Transport. Phone : Srreatham 1000.

REGENT CINEMA (BTP), 183-185, High Street, S.W.17. (Closed.)

TOTTENHAM, N.
BRUCE GROVE CINEMA (WE), Bruce Grove, N.—Prop., Tottenham Cinema and Entertainment Co., Ltd. 1,789 seats. Booked at Hall. Continuous. Dance Hall. Prices, 6d. to 2s. Proscenium width, 45 ft. Phone : Tottenham 2232. Road Transport.

CORNER (WE), Seven Sisters Corner.—Prop., Davies Cinemas, Ltd. 553 seats. Booked at 23, Meard Street, W.1. Continuous. Two changes weekly. Prices, 6d. to 1s. 3d. Phone : Stamford Hill 2746. Road Transport.

IMPERIAL CINEMA (WE), West Green Road.— Prop., H. & G. Sado, 5, Dean Street, W.1. Phone : Gerrard 6483. 472 seats. Booked at H.O. Continuous. Two changes weekly. Prices, 6d. to 1s. Phone : Bowes Park 2394.

PAVILION (WE), 678, High Road, N.17.—Prop., Davies Cinemas, Ltd., 23, Meard Street, W.1. 529 seats. Booked at H.O. Continuous. Prices, 6d. to 1s. 3d. Two changes weekly. Phone : Tottenham 1724. Station, Bruce Grove, L.N.E.R.

ROXY, High Road.—See under Stamford Hill.

TOTTENHAM PALACE (RCA), High Road.— Prop., Provincial Cinematograph Theatres, Ltd., New Gallery House, Regent Street, W.1. Phone : Regent 8080. Booked at H.O. Pictures and Variety. Stage, 32 ft. 6 in. Continuous. Dance Hall and Café. Prices, 6d. to 2s. . Phone : Tottenham 2141. Station, Bruce Grove, L.N.E.R.

WURLITZER ORGAN
Installed in this Kinema

TOTTENHAM COURT ROAD, W.
CARLTON PICTURE THEATRE, (F.I.) 30, Tottenham Court Road, W.1.—Prop., A. E. Ewer. 650 seats. Continuous. Prices, 8d. to 2s. 4d. Phone : Museum 7181.

DOMINION THEATRE (WE).—Prop., Gaumont British Corporation, Ltd. Booked at H.O., New Gallery House, Regent Street, W.1. Regent 8080. Continuous. Pictures and Variety. 2,858 seats. Phone : Museum 2176-7· Prices, 1s. to 3s. 6d. Proscenium width, 54 ft. Café attached.
Fitted "ARDENTE" Deaf Aids
See page 258

COMPTON
ORGAN featured here.

MAJESTIC PICTUREDROME (WE).—Prop., A. E. Ewer. 638 seats. Continuous. Prices ,7½d. to 2s. net. Proscenium width, 20 ft. Phone : Museum 7181.

PARAMOUNT THEATRE.

C O M P T O N
ORGAN featured here.

SPHERE NEWS THEATRE (Phillips).—Props., London News Theatre, Ltd., 18, Devonshire Street, Bishopsgate, E. 300 seats. Booked at 147, Wardour Street, W.1. Continuous. Prices, 7d. and 1s. Phone: Museum 2348.

UPTON PARK, E.

PICTURE COLISEUM (Picturetone), Green Street. —Props., W. T. Scriven and W. J. Huxtable. 800 seats. Booked at H.O. by A. Tench, Gen. Manager. Continuous. Prices, 4d. to 1s. Phone: Grangewood 0381. Station, Upton Park.

THE CARLTON (WE).—Props., Associated British Cinemas, Ltd., 30-31, Golden Square, W.1. 2,177 seats. Booked at H.O. Pictures and Variety. Variety booked at Forum Theatre Fulham. Continuous. Prices 6d. to 2s. Proscenium width 44 ft. Stage, 30 ft.; six dressing rooms. Café. Phone: Grangewood 2644. Station, Upton Park.

C O M P T O N
ORGAN featured here.

VAUXHALL, S.W.

GRANADA (WE), 128-130, Wandsworth Road, S.W.8.—Prop., Vauxhall Properties, Ltd. Controlled by Bernstein Theatres, Ltd., 36, Golden Square, W.1. Phone: Regent 3554. Booked at H.O. Continuous. Phone: Macaulay 2117. Station, Vauxhall, S.R.

WURLITZER ORGAN
Installed in this Kinema

SUPER SHOW (RCA), 92-94, Wandsworth Road, S.W.8.—Prop., Super Shows, Ltd., 61-62, Chancery Lane, W.C.2. 785 seats. Pictures and Variety. Booked at H.O. Continuous. Three changes weekly. Prices, 5d. to 1s. 4d. Phone: Macaulay 2510.

VICTORIA, S.W.

BIOGRAPH CINEMA (WE), 47, Wilton Road, S.W.1.—Props., Wilton Cinema, Ltd. Astor House, Aldwych, W.C.2. Phone: Holborn 9159. 700 seats. Booked at Pallen House, Cork Street, W.1. Continuous. Three changes weekly. Prices, 9d. to 2s. Proscenium width, 32 ft. Stage, 20 ft. deep; four dressing rooms.

CAMEO NEWS, Victoria Street.—Props., Clavering & Rose, Ltd. 600 seats. Booked at Cameo, Charing Cross Road. Continuous. Prices, 6d. to 2s.

METROPOLE KINEMA (WE).—Prop., Metropolitan Cinema Investment Corporation, Ltd., Astor House, Aldwych, W.C.2. Phone: Holborn 9159. 2,000 seats. Booked at Pallen House, Cork Street, W.1. Continuous. Occasional Variety. Stage, 25 ft. deep; six dressing rooms. Prices, 1s. to 5s. 9d. Proscenium width, 37 ft. Restaurant. Phone: Victoria 4673. Station, Victoria.

Fitted "ARDENTE" Deaf Aids
See page 258

WURLITZER ORGAN
Installed in this Kinema

NEW VICTORIA (WE).—Prop., Provincial Cinematograph Theatres, Ltd., New Gallery House, Regent Street, W.1. 2,600 seats. Continuous. Booked at H.O. Pictures and Variety. Prices, 1s. 6d. to 3s. 6d. Café. Phone: Victoria 2544.

Fitted "ARDENTE" Deaf Aids
See page 258

C O M P T O N
ORGAN featured here

VICTORIA PALACE, 126, Victoria Street, S.W.1. —Prop., Victoria Palace, Ltd.

VICTORIA STATION NEWS THEATRE (BTH), Buckingham Palace Road, S.W.1.—Prop., Capital & Provincial News Theatres, Ltd. 172, Buckingham Palace Road, S.W.1. Phone: Sloane 9132. 240 seats. Booked at H.O. Continuous. Prices, 6d. to 1s. Phone: Victoria 7641.

VICTORIA PARK, E.

VICTORIA PICTURE THEATRE (BTP), Grove Road, E.—Prop., Victoria Park Picture Theatre Co., Ltd., 184-186, Grove Road, Bow, E.3. Phone: Advance 3907. 460 seats. Booked by C. A. Mathes, South Picture Theatre, Well Street, E.9. Continuous. Two changes weekly. Prices, 4d. to 9d. Phone: Advance 3907. Road Transport.

WALHAM GREEN, S.W

GRANVILLE THEATRE OF VARIETIES.—Prop., Granville Theatre of Varieties (Walham Green), Ltd., The Broadway, Walham Green, S.W.6.

RED HALL, PICTURE PALACE (RCA), Vanston Place.—Prop., Provincial Cinematograph Theatres, Ltd. 1,500 seats. Boooked at H.O. Continuous. Phone: Fulham 4181. Station, Walham Green (Tube).

REGAL (RCA).—Prop., Associated British Cinemas, Ltd., 30/31, Golden Square, London, W.1. Phone: Gerrard 7887. Booked at H.O. Continuous. 1,929 seats. Prices, 6d. to 2s. Proscenium width, 41 ft. Station, Walham Green.

C O M P T O N
ORGAN featured here.

WALTHAMSTOW, E.

CARLTON CINEMA (WE), High Street, E.17.— Prop., T. H. F. Theatres, Ltd., 11, Berkeley Court, Baker Street, N.W.1. Phone: Welbeck 2301. 1,450 seats. Continuous. Booked at Hall. Two changes weekly. Prices, 6d. to 1s. 6d. Phone: Walthamstow 0382. Station Hoe Street.

CROWN PICTURE THEATRE (RCA).—Props., Weaver Bros. 650 seats. Continuous. Booked at Hall. Prices, 5d. to 1s. 4d. Phone: Walthamstow 0667. Station, Wood Street, L.N.E.R.

DOMINION (WE), Buxton Road.—Props., Picture Theatre (Walthamstow), Ltd., 30/31, Golden Square, W.1. 1,685 seats. Continuous. Booked at H.O. Pictures and Occasional Variety. Prices, 5d. to 1s. 6d. Proscenium width, 45 ft. Stage, 16 ft. deep; two dressing

136 WARDOUR STREET, LONDON, W.1.

WALTHAMSTOW, E.—contd.
rooms. Phone: Walthamstow 1010. Station,
St. James Street, L.N.E.R.

WURLITZER ORGAN
Installed in this Kinema

EMPIRE CINEMA (RCA), Bell Corner.—Booked by
Clavering & Rose, 199, Piccadilly, W.1.
Phone: Regent 1146. 860 seats. Continu-
ous. Prices, 6d. to 2s. Phone: Walthamstow
0305.
GRANADA (WE), Hoe Street.—Props., The
Granada Theatres, Ltd. Controlled by Bern-
stein Theatres, Ltd., 36, Golden Square, W.1.
Phone: Gerrard 3554. Continuous. Pictures
and Variety. Phone: Walthamstow 3177.
Station, Hoe Street, L.N.E.R.
QUEEN'S CINEMA (RCA), Hoe Street.—Booked
by Clavering & Rose, 199, Piccadilly, W.1.
Phone: Regent 1146. 606 seats. Continu-
ous. Prices, 6d. to 1s. 3d. Phone: Walthamstow 1277.

WALWORTH ROAD, S.E
MONTPELIER CINEMA (Mihaly), Montpelier Street,
Walworth Road, S.E.—Prop., Montpelier
Cinema, Ltd., 18, Montpelier Street, Camber-
well Gate, S.E.17. Phone: Rodney 2503.
500 seats. Booked at Hall. Continuous.
Prices, 4d. and 6d. Stage, 15 ft. deep ; two
dressing rooms.
RIALTO, (RCA). 47, Walworth Road, S.E.1—
681 seats. Booked at Hall. Continuous.
Three changes weekly. Prices, 4d. to 1s. 6d.
Phone: Rodney 3641. Station, Elephant and
Castle (Tube and S.R.).

WANDSWORTH, S.W.
GRANADA (WE), 128, Wandsworth Road, S.W.8.
(See Vauxhall.)
SAVOY (WE), York Road.—Props., Associated
British Cinemas, Ltd., 30/31, Golden Square,
W.1. Phone: Gerrard 7887. 2,166 seats.
Continuous. Booked at H.O. Occasional
Variety. Prices, 6d. to 1s. 10d. Proscenium
width, 32 ft. Stage, 11 ft. deep ; two dres-
sing rooms. Phone: Battersea 2801. Station,
Wandsworth Town.

COMPTON
ORGAN featured here.

STAR (BTH).—Prop., Ralph Specterman, 18/20,
Regent Street, W.1.
SUPER SHOW, 92-94, Wandsworth Road, S.W.8.
785 seats.—(See Vauxhall.)
WANDSWORTH PALACE (BA), High Street.—
Prop., United Picture Theatres, Ltd. 1,307
seats. Continuous. Two changes weekly.
Prices, 6d. to 2s. 4d. Phone: Battersea 4507.

COMPTON
ORGAN featured here.

WANSTEAD. E.
KINEMA (WE).—Prop., S. Shinebaum, 6, Great
Alie Street, E.1. Phone: Royal 0881. 570
seats. Continuous. Two changes weekly.
Booked at H.O. Prices, 9d. to 2s. Phone:
Wanstead 3383. Station, Snaresbrook,
L.N.E.R.

WATERLOO, S.E.
NEWS THEATRE (BTH), Waterloo Station.—
Prop., Capital & Provincial News Theatres,
Ltd., 172, Buckingham Palace Road, S.W.1.
Phone: Sloane 9132. 248 seats. Booked at
H.O. Continuous. Prices, 6d. and 1s. Pros-
cenium width, 24 ft. Phone: Waterloo 4323.

WEST HAM, E.
ENDEAVOUR CINEMA, 74, Plaistow Road PhoLe:
Maryland 2238.
KINEMA.—Controlled by Bernstein Theatres.
Ltd., 36, Golden Square, W.1. Phone: Gerrard
3554.

WESTMINSTER BRIDGE ROAD, S.E.
CANTERBURY (BA).—Prop., Denman Picture
Houses, Ltd., Booked at New Gallery House,
Regent Street, W.1. 1,874 seats. Continu-
ous. Three changes weekly. Prices, 4d. to
1s. 3d. Phone: Waterloo 6809.
GATTI'S (RCA).—Prop., X.G.L., Syndicate, Ltd.
Continuous. Three changes weekly. Phone:
Hop 5418.

WHITECHAPEL, E.
RIVOLI CINEMA (BA), Whitechapel Road.—
Prop., United Picture Theatres, Ltd. 2,268
seats. Booked at H.O. Continuous. Prices,
9d. to 1s. 6d. Café. Phone: Bishopsgate
5183.

WILLESDEN, N.W.
GRANADA (WE), Church Road, N.W.—Prop.,
Denman London Cinemas, Ltd., 36, Golden
Square, W.1. Phone: Gerrard 3554. 1,778
seats. Booked at H.O. Continuous. Pictures
and Variety. Phone: Willesden 2917. Station,
Willesden Green.

HIPPODROME (see Harlesden).
SAVOY ELECTRIC THEATRE (WE), High Road.—
Prop., J. Alexander. 378 seats. Booked at
Hall. Prices, 6d. to 1s. 6d. Proscenium
width, 22 ft. Phone: Willesden 1625.

WIMBLEDON, S.W.
ELITE (WE), Merton Road, S.W.19.—Prop.,
Wimbledon Amusements, Ltd. 1,285 seats.
Continuous. Two changes weekly. Prices,
7d. to 2s. 5d. Proscenium width, 22 ft.
Phone: Liberty 2082. Station, Wimbledon,
S.R.

KING'S PALACE (RCA), The Broadway.—Prop.,
Mrs. E. Hurst. 789 seats. Booked at H.O.
Continuous. Prices, 6d. to 1s. 6d. Pros-
cenium width, 24 ft. Phone: Liberty 4711.
Café attached. Station, Wimbledon, S.R.

ODEON (BTB), Worple Road.—Props., Odeon (Wimbledon), Ltd., Cornhill House, Bennetts Hill, Birmingham. Phone : Midland 2781. Booked at 49, Park Lane, London, W.1. Continuous. Prices, 6d. to 3s. Phone : Wimbledon 4577.

PRINCES CINEMA (BTP), Broadway.—(Closed.)

REGAL (WE), Merton Road.—Prop., Regal (Wimbledon), Ltd. 2,000 seats. Booked by County Cinemas, Ltd., Dean House, Dean Street, London, W.1. Phone : Gerrard 4543. 2,000 seats. Continuous. Variety booked at Theatre. Prices, 6d. to 3s. Proscenium width, 48 ft. Stage, 25 ft. deep ; 12 dressing rooms. Café attached. Phone : Liberty 2227. Station, Wimbledon, S.R.

TOWN HALL KINEMA.—Prop., Wimbledon Borough Council. Phone : Wimbledon 6263.

COMPTON
ORGAN featured here.

WINCHMORE HILL, N.

CAPITOL (WE).—Prop., Associated British Cinemas, Ltd., 30-31, Golden Square, W.1. Phone : Gerrard 7887. 1,929 seats. Prices, 6d. to 2s. Pictures and Variety. Booked at H.O. Continuous. Proscenium width, 45 ft. Stage, 39 ft. deep ; seven dressing rooms. Phone : Palmers Green 1582. Road Transport.

COMPTON
ORGAN featured here.

WOODFORD, E.

MAJESTIC (RCA).—1,890 seats. Prop., Associated British Cinemas, Ltd., 30-31, Golden Square, W.1.
Fitted "ARDENTE" Deaf Aids
Fitted "ARDENTE" Stage Amplification
See page 258

PLAZA CINEMA (BTH), George Lane.—Props., Empire Cinemas (Epping), Ltd., 179a, High Street, Epping. 1,600 seats. Continuous. Two changes weekly. Prices, 6d. to 2s. Phone : Wanstead 0788. Station, George Lane, South Woodford, L.N.E.R.

WOOD GREEN, N.

EMPIRE (WE).—Stoll Circuit, Coliseum Buildings, London, W.C.2. 1,811 seats. Booked at H.O. Continuous. Prices, 6d. to 2s. Proscenium width, 43 ft. Stage, 37 ft. deep ; eight dressing rooms. Phone : Bowes Park 4660. Road Transport.

GAUMONT PALACE (BA).—Controlled by Provincial Cinematograph Theatres. 2,505 seats. Booked at H.O. Pictures and Variety . State, dressing rooms. Café.
Fitted "ARDENTE" Deaf Aids
See page 258

COMPTON
ORGAN featured here.

PALAIS DE LUXE (WE), Station Road.—Prop., River Park Cinema, Ltd. 796 seats. Booked at Hall. Continuous. Two changes weekly. Prices, 6d. to 1s. 6d. Phone : Bowes Park 1860.

PALLADIUM (WE).—Prop., Wood Green Picture Palladium, Ltd. Gen. Man., Dudley Wynton. 1,184 seats. Continuous. One change weekly. Booked at Hall. Prices, 6d. to 2s. Phone : Bowes Park 3333. Station, Hornsey.

WOOLWICH, S.E.

CINEMA (WE), Beresford Square.—Prop., London & District Cinemas, Ltd., Astoria House, 62, Shaftesbury Avenue, W.1. 1,000 seats. Booked at H.O. Continuous. Stage, 8 ft. deep ; four dressing rooms. Prices, 6d. to 1s. 6d. Proscenium width, 24 ft. Phone : Woolwich 0225. Station, Woolwich Arsenal.

EMPIRE (WE).—Prop., Woolwich Empire, Ltd., 19, Charing Cross Road, W.C.2. 1,313 seats. Continuous. Booked at Hall. Pictures and Variety. Variety booked by General Theatrical Agency. Prices, 6d. to 2s. Proscenium width, 25 ft. Stage, 30 ft. deep ; six dressing rooms. Phone : Woolwich 0156. Station, Woolwich Arsenal, S.R.

GRANADA.
WURLITZER ORGAN
Installed in this Kinema

ODEON THEATRE (BTH).—Props., Odeon (Woolwich), Ltd., Cornhill House, Bennett's Hill, Birmingham. Phone : Midland 2781. Booked at 49, Park Lane, London, W.1. (In course of construction.)

PALACE (BTH), New Road.—Prop., S. J. Huff. 450 seats.

PREMIER ELECTRIC THEATRE (WE), Powis Street. —Prop., London & District Cinemas, Ltd., Astoria House, 62, Shaftesbury Avenue, W.1. 900 seats. Booked at H.O. Continuous. Three changes weekly. Prices, 7d. to 1s. 10d. Proscenium width, 25 ft. Phone : Woolwich 0560. Station, Woolwich Arsenal, S.R.

WOOLWICH HIPPODROME (BA), Wellington Street.—Props., Associated British Cinemas, Ltd., 30-31, Golden Square, W.1. Phone : Gerrard 7887. Booked at H.O. 1,580 seats. Continuous. Two changes weekly. Prices, 6d. to 2s. Proscenium width, 30 ft. Phone : Woolwich 0069. Station, Woolwich Arsenal.

COMPTON
ORGAN featured here.

ENGLISH KINEMAS.

The Sound system installed is shown after the name. (BTP) = British Talking Pictures, Ltd. ; (RCA) = RCA Photophone Inc. ; (WE) = Western Electric Co., Ltd. (BA) = British Acoustic ; (BTH) = British Thomson-Houston. Other systems are indicated by name.

ABERBARGOED (Mon).—**Pop. 5,200.**
Rialto (Morrison).—Prop., W. Worlock, "Oakdene," 3,Gwenthoner Road; Hengoed. 500 seats. Booked at Hall. Continuous. Prices, 4d. to 9d. Proscenium width, 20 ft.

ABERCARN (Mon.), **Pop. 20,554.**
Victoria Hall (BA)—Props., Victoria Hall Co. (Abercarn), Ltd. 500 seats. Booked at Cardiff. One show nightly, two on Saturdays. Prices, 6d. to 9d. Proscenium width, 28 ft. Phone, Abercarn 32. Station, Abercarn. G.W.R.

ABERGAVENNY (Mon.), **Pop. 8,608.**
Coliseum (WE), Lion Street.—Prop., Abergavenny Coliseum Co., Ltd. 780 seats. Booked at 2, Office Road, Maesteg, by R. Dooner. Twice nightly. Prices 6d. to 1s. 6d. Proscenium width, 25 ft. Phone, Abergavenny 33. Stations, Abergavenny, G.W.R. and L.M.S.
Pavilion (WE).

ABERSYCHAN (Mon.), **Pop. 25,627.**
Capitol (BA) (late Empire).—Prop., Harold E. Williams, Gravel House, Blackwood, Mon. Phone, Blackwood 57. 500 seats. Booked at Hall. Continuous. Prices, 6d. to 1s. Station, Abersychan, G.W.R.

ABERTILLERY (Mon.), **Pop. 31,799.**
Empress Cinema (Sound Ltd.).—Prop., Abertillery Theatres, Ltd., Pavilion, Abertillery. 800 seats. Booked at Carlisle House, Abertillery. Continuous. Phone, Abertillery 3. Station, Abertillery, G.W.R.
Gaiety (Sound Ltd.)—Prop., Abertillery Theatres, Ltd., Pavilion, Abertillery. 1,200 seats. Booked at Carlisle House, Abertillery. Continuous. Phone, Abertillery 3. Station, Abertillery, G.W.R.
Metropole (Kamm).—Prop., Abertillery Theatres, Ltd., Pavilion, Abertillery. Booked at Carlisle House, Abertillery.
Palace (Sound Ltd.).—Prop., Abertillery Theatres, Ltd. 450 seats.
Pavilion Theatre (Sound Ltd.)—Prop., Abertillery Theatres, Ltd., Pavilion, Abertillery. 600 seats. Booked at Carlisle House, Abertillery. Continuous. Phone, Abertillery 3. Station, Abertillery, G.W.R.

ABINGDON (Berks), **Pop. 7,240.**
Kinema (BTH), Stert Street.—Prop., W. Thatcher, 63' Stert Street, Abingdon. 500 seats. Booked at Hall. Twice nightly. Two changes weekly. Prices, 6d. to 1s. 10d. Phone, Abingdon 20. Station, Abingdon, G.W.R.

The Pavilion (BTH) The Square.—Controlled by Union Cinemas, Ltd., Union House, 15, Regent Street, London, S.W.1. Phone, Whitehall 8484. Continuous. Booked at H.O. Prices, 6d. to 1s. 6d. Phone, Abingdon 322. Station, Abingdon, G.W.R.
Regal (BTP).—Controlled by Union Cinemas, Ltd., Union House, 15, Regent Street, London, S.W.1. Phone. Whitehall 8484. Continuous. Booked at H.O. Prices, 6d. to 1s. 6d. Phone Abingdon 322. Station, Abingdon, G.W.R.

ACCRINGTON (Lancs), **Pop. 42,973.**
Empire (WE), Edgar Street.—Prop., Victory Theatres, Ltd. Gen. Man. Arthur Peel. 900 seats. Three shows daily. Two changes weekly. Prices, 6d. to 1s. 3d. Phone, Accrington 2350. Station, Accrington, L.M.S.
King's Hall (Morrison), Whalley Road.—Prop., John Hamer. 450 seats. Two shows nightly. Mat., Sat. Two changes weekly. Prices 3d. to 6d. Proscenium width, 17 ft. Phone, 2431. Station, Accrington, L.M.S.
New Hippodrome (WE), Ellison Street.—Prop. Broadway Cinemas (Accrington), Ltd. 849 seats. Booked at Hall. Three shows daily. Prices 6d. to 1s. Proscenium width, 28 ft. Stage, 24 ft. deep. 6 dressing rooms. Phone, Accrington 2500. Station, Accrington, L.M.S.
Palace (WE).—Prop., Victory Theatres (Accrington), Ltd. 803 seats. Three shows daily. Prices, 6d. to 1s. 3d. Phone, Accrington 2589. Station Accrington, L.M.S.
Picture House (GB).—Prop., Wilson and Barlow. 802 seats. Booked at Hall. Twice nightly and matinee. Prices, 3d. to 6d. Proscenium width, 17 ft. Café. Phone, Accrington 2464. Station, Accrington, L.M.S.
Princes Theatre (WE), Edgar Street.—Prop., Victory Theatres, Ltd. Gen. Man., Arthur Peel. 904 seats. Three shows daily. Prices, 7d. to 1s. 3d. Phone, Accrington 2701. Station, Accrington, L.M.S.

ADDLESTONE (Surrey), **Pop. 8,098.**
Plaza (WE), Station Road.—Prop. Southern Cinemas, Ltd. 311 seats. Booked at Gem, Southall. Continuous. Two changes weekly. Prices, 7d. to 2s. Phone, Weybridge, 1373. Station, Addlestone, S.R.

ADLINGTON (Lancs), **Pop. 4,179.**
Cinema (Electrocord), Railway Road.—Prop., W. Hartley. 450 seats. Booked at Hall. One show nightly, 3 shows Saturday. Prices, 4d. to 1s. Station, Adlington, L.M.S.

ALCESTER (WARWICK), **Pop. 2,259.**
REGENT CINEMA (BA), High Street.—Props., J. and E. Bolas. 313 seats. Booked at Hall. Continuous. Prices, 6d. to 1s. Phone, Alcester 60. Station, Alcester, L.M.S. and Road Transport.

ALDEBURGH (SUFFOLK), **Pop. 2,480.**
PICTURE HOUSE, High Street.—Prop., Aldeburgh Cinema and Amusements, Ltd. 400 seats. One show nightly. Two changes weekly. Phone, Aldeburgh 37. Station, Aldeburgh, L.N.E.R.

ALDERSHOT (HANTS), **Pop. 34,281.**
ALEXANDRA CINEMA (WE).—Prop., County Cinemas, Ltd., Dean Street, London, W.1. Phone, Gerrard 4543. 710 seats. Booked at H.O. Three shows daily. Once on Sunday. Prices, 6d. to 2s. Phone Aldershot 356. Stage, 4 ft. deep, one dressing room. Station, Aldershot Town, S.R.

EMPIRE THEATRE (WE).—Prop., Empire (Aldershot), Ltd., Associated with County Cinemas, Ltd. 1,458 seats. Booked at H.O. Three shows daily. Prices, 7d. to 2s. Phone, Aldershot 760. Café attached. Station, Aldershot, S.R.

COMPTON
ORGAN featured here.

GARRISON THEATRE (WE), Queen's Avenue.—Lessee, Chas. Darby. 500 seats. Booked at Scala Theatre, Farnborough. Twice nightly. Prices, 6d. to 1s. Café attached. Phone, Aldershot 482. Station, Aldershot Town, S.R.

MANOR PARK PAVILION (WE), High Street.—Prop., County Cinemas, Ltd., Dean House, Dean Street, London, W.1. 836 seats. Booked at H.O. Continuous. Once on Sunday. Prices, 6d. to 2s. Proscenium width, 30 ft. Stage, 10 ft. deep. Two dressing rooms. Phone, Aldershot 567. Station, Aldershot, S.R.

PALACE PICTURE THEATRE (WE), Station Road.—Prop., Aldershot Picture Palace, Ltd. 708 seats. Three shows daily. once Sunday, Two changes weekly. Prices, 6d. to 2s. Phone, Aldershot 99. Station, Aldershot Town, SR.

RITZ (WE).—Controlled by Union Cinemas, Ltd., Union House, 15, Regent Street, London, S.W.1. Whitehall 8484. Booked at H.O. Station, Aldershot, S.R.

WURLITZ+R ORGAN
Installed in this Kinema
TUDOR CINEMA, Crookham.

WELLINGTON CINEMA (BTH).—Prop., Committee Royal Garrison Church Institute. 468 seats. Booked at Hall by Man. Twice nightly. Children's Mat. Sat. Prices, 6d. to 1s. 3d. Proscenium width, 28 ft. Phone, Aldershot 440. Café attached. Station, Aldershot, S.R.

ALFORD (LINCS), **Pop. 2,227.**
RITZ (Parmeko) Prop., E. Armitage. Booked at Hall. 250 seats. Once nightly. Pictures and Variety. Prices 6d. to 1s. 6d. Proscenium width, 13 ft. Phone, Alford 75. Stage, 14 ft. deep. Three dressing rooms.

ALFRETON (DERBYSHIRE), **Pop. 21,232.**
EMPIRE (WE).—700 seats. Phone, Nottingham 42364. Occasional Variety. Booked at H.O.

Continuous. Two shows Sat. Phone, Alfreton 146. Station, Alfreton.

ODEON (BTH), High Street.—Props., Picture Houses (Derbyshire), Ltd., Cornhill House, Bennetts Hill, Birmingham. Phone, Midland 2781. Booked at 49, Park Lane, London. W.1. Continuous. Prices, 6d. to 1s. 4d, Proscenium width, 40 ft. Stage, 30 ft. deep. Six dressing rooms. Phone, Alfreton 44. Station, Alfreton, L.M.S.

ALNWICK (NORTHUMBERLAND), **Pop. 6,882.**
CORN EXCHANGE (WE).—Prop. and Res. Man., J. H. Sanderson. 670 seats. Booked at Newcastle. Twice nightly. Prices, 5d. to 1s. 3d. Phone, Alnwick 51. Station, Alnwick, L.N.E.R.

PLAYHOUSE (WE).—Prop., Alnwick Playhouse Ltd. 1,000 seats. Pictures and Stage Plays. Booked at Newcastle. Prices, 6d. to 2s. Proscenium width, 22 ft. Stage, 18 ft. deep ; four dressing rooms. Continuous. Station, Alnwick, L.N.E.R.

ALSTON (CUMBERLAND), **Pop. 3,344.**
CINEMA (Electrocord).—Prop., Nelson and Nicholson. 300 seats. Booked by F. H. Nicholson at Hall. Occasional variety. One show Thurs. two on Sat. Prices, 2d. to 1s, Proscenium width, 20 ft. Stage, 12 ft. deep ; 2 dressing rooms. Dance hall attached. Station, Alston, L.N.E.R.

ALTON (HANTS), **Pop. 6,172.**
ALTON PICTURE THEATRE (RCA), Normandy Street.—Prop., B. & R. Hyman. Booked at Hall. Continuous. Two changes weekly. Prices, 6d. to 1s. 6d. 'Phone, Alton 103. Station, Alton, S.R.

PALACE (RCA).—Prop., B. and R. Hyman. 620 seats. Booked at Hall. Prices 6d. to 1s. 6d. Phone, Alton 103.

ALTRINCHAM (CHESHIRE), **Pop. 21,356.**
CINEMA HOUSE (WE), Willowtree Road.—Prop., Hale Pictures, Ltd., 4, Exchange Buildings, 6, St. Mary's Gate, Manchester. Phone, City 1968. 890 seats. Booked at Hall. Continuous. Prices, 9d. and 1s. 6d. Café attached. Phone, Altrincham 2600. Station, Hale, Cheshire Lines.

HIPPODROME (RCA).—Props., T. Hargreaves (Altrincham), Ltd. 1,000 seats. Booked at Rialto, Rochdale. Twice nightly. Prices. 6d. to 1s. Proscenium width, 27 ft. Phone No. 331. Station, Altrincham,

PICTURE HOUSE.—H. D. Moorhouse Circuit, 7, Oxford Road, Manchester. Phone, Ardwick 2226.

PICTURE THEATRE (WE), Stamford New Road.—Prop., Altrincham Picture Theatre, Ltd. 1,750 seats. Three shows daily. Two changes weekly. Prices, 5d. to 1s. 3d. Phone, Altrincham 800. Station, Altrincham, M.S. and A.R.

REGAL SUPER CINEMA (BTH).—Controlled by Union Cinemas, Ltd., 15, Regent Street, London, S.W.1. Phone, Whitehall 8484. Pictures and Variety. Films booked at H.O. Continuous. Prices, 2d. to 2s. Phone, Altrincham 2626. Café attached. Stations, Broadheath or Altrincham, L.M.S.

COMPTON
ORGAN featured here.

AMBLE (NORTHUMBERLAND), **Pop. 4,208.**
CENTRAL THEATRE.—Prop., Amble Picture Hall Co. One show nightly. Station, Amble, L.N.E.R.
COQUET HALL (WE). 769 seats.

AMBLESIDE (WESTMORLAND), **Pop. 2,343.**
CINEMA, ASSEMBLY ROOMS.—Prop. and Man., Frank Townson. 430 seats. Booked at Hall. Twice nightly. Prices, 4d. to 1s. 6d. Station, Windermere, L.M.S. Films by Film Transport Service.

AMERSHAM (nr. **Chesham**), (BUCKS), **Pop. 4,220.**
REGENT (WE).—Prop., Shipman & King, M.84, Shell Mex House, Strand, London, W.C.2. Phone, Temple Bar 5077. Pictures and occasional variety. Booked at Hall. Continuous. Mat., Wed., Thurs. and Sat. Prices, 6d. to 2s. 4d. Stage, 30 ft. deep. Proscenium width, 27 ft. Phone, Amersham 470. Station, Amersham, Met. R.

AMESBURY (WILTS), **Pop. 1,531.**
PLAZA THEATRE (AWH).—Prop., Duncan & Co. 500 seats. Booked at Hall. Continuous nightly. Mat. Sat. Occasional Variety. Prices, 6d. to 2s. Proscenium width, 24 ft. Stage, 16 ft. deep. Café. Phone, Amesbury 354. Station, Amesbury, S.R.
PLAZA.—Prop., Amesbury Cinemas. Phone, Amesbury 354. Booked at Hall.

AMPTHILL (BEDS), **Pop. 2,167.**
KINEMA (AWH).—Prop., J. F. Mongiardino, 72, Biscot Road, Luton. 300 seats. Booked by Prop. Continuous. Prices 7d. to 1s. 3d. Station, Ampthill, L.M.S.

ANDOVER (HANTS), **Pop. 9,692.**
NEW THEATRE (BTP), near Market Place.— Prop., Andover Cinema Theatre Co., Ltd. 500 seats. Booked at Hall. Continuous. Prices, 6d. to 1s. 6d. Phone, Andover 92. Station, Andover Junction, S.R.
ODEON (WE), Jackson Road.—Prop., Odeon (Winchester) Ltd., Cornhill House, Bennett's Hill, Birmingham. Phone, Midland 2781. Booked at 49, Park Lane, London. W.1. Continuous. Prices, 6d. to 2s. Phone, Andover 208. Station, Andover Junction, S.R.

ANNFIELD PLAIN (CO. DURHAM), **Pop. 15,922.**
KING'S PAVILION (BTP).—Prop., T. Cass Craven. 830 seats. Continuous. Two changes weekly. Prices, 4d. to 8d. Phone, Annfield Plain 22. Station, Annfield Plain, L.N.E.R.
PALACE THEATRE.

ANNITSFORD (NORTHUMBERLAND), **Pop. 1,200.**
CORONATION HALL (Knightfone). — Props., Exors. of W. Hutson (Deceased) and N. H. Chapman, 85, Northumberland Street, Newcastle-on-Tyne. 450 seats. Booked at Hall by R. Henderson. One show nightly. Two on Sat. Occasional Variety. Prices, 2d. to 8d. Station, Annitsford, L.N.E.R.

ANSTEY (LEICS), **Pop. 3,000.**
PICTURE HOUSE, Ellis Street.—Props., C. C. Baum and J. Fisher. Four shows weekly. Booked at Futurist, Sileby. Prices, 5d. to 1s. Station, Sileby.

APPLEBY (WESTMORLAND), **Pop. 1,618.**
KINEMA.

APPLEDORE (N. DEVON), **Pop. 4,000.**
GAIETY CINEMA (Browns).—Prop., G. Taylor. 300 seats. Booked at Hall. Pictures and occasional Variety. Continuous. Prices, 8d. to 1s. 3d. Stage, 9 ft. deep ; one dressing-room. Station, Bideford.

ARLESEY (BEDS), **Pop. 2,170.**
PREMIER CINEMA (Morrison).—Prop., A. H. Street, 4, The Gardens, Arlesey Road, Stotfold. 250 seats. Once nightly. Three shows Saturday. Prices, 6d. to 1s. 3d. Transport. Three Counties.

ARNOLD (NOTTS), **Pop. 14,470.**
BONINGTON THEATRE (BTH).—Prop., Jos. Wardle, Bentwell House, Arnold. Phone, No. 68145. 900 seats. Booked at H.O. Continuous. Prices, 7d. to 1s. 3d. Station, Daybrook, L.N.E.R.
KING'S THEATRE (BTH).—Props., Jos. Wardle, Bentwell House, Arnold, Notts. Phone, Arnold 68145. 600 seats. Continuous. Booked at H.O. Prices, 7d. to 1s. Station, Daybrook, L.N.E.R.

ASHBOURNE (DERBY), **Pop. 4,507.**
EMPIRE (BA).—Prop., Mrs. Stebbings. 550 seats. Continuous Thurs. to Sat. only. Mat. Sat. Prices, 6d. to 1s. 4d.
ELITE CINEMA (BA).—Prop., Mrs. Stebbings, Hillside, Ashbourne. 550 seats. Booked at Hall. Continuous. Mat. Mon., Thurs. and Sat. Prices, 6d. to 1s. 6d. Phone, Ashbourne 121. Station, Ashbourne, L.M.S.

ASHBY (nr. **Scunthorpe**), (LINCS), **Pop. 6,000.**
GLOBE CINEMA (BTP).—Prop., W. H. Webster, Grand Theatre, Brigg, Lincs. Tel. No., 31. 600 seats. Booked at H.O. Continuous. Two changes weekly. Prices, 4d. to 1s. Phone, Scunthorpe 248Y2. Proscenium width, 30 ft. Station, Scunthorpe, L.N.E.R.

ASHBY-DE-LA-ZOUCH (LEICS), **Pop. 5,093.**
THE PICTURE HOUSE (WE).—Prop., Ilkeston Cinema Co., Ltd., Bath Street, Ilkeston, Derbyshire. Phone, Ilkeston 17. 471 seats. Booked at King's P.H., Ilkeston. Twice nightly. Mat. Sat. Two changes weekly. Prices, 4d. to 1s. Proscenium width, 20 ft. Phone, Ashby-de-la-Zouch 111. Station, Ashby-de-la-Zouch, L.M.S.

ASHFORD (KENT), **Pop., 15,239.**
CINEMA (WE).—Prop., The Cinema (Ashford),
Ltd. 833 seats. Booked at Hall. Continu-
ous. Occasional Variety. Prices, 6d. to 1s. 6d.
Proscenium width, 35 ft. Stage, 20 ft. deep.
Three dressing-rooms. Phone, Ashford 124.
Station, Ashford, S.R.
EXCHANGE THEATRE, Bank Street.—Prop.,
Ashford Entertainments Co., Ltd. Occasional
shows. Proscenium width, 24 ft. Stage, 24 ft.
deep. Five dressing-rooms. Dance Hall.
ODEON THEATRE (BTH).—Props., Odeon (Ash-
ford), Ltd., Bennett's Hill, Birmingham.
Booked at 49, Park Lane, London, W.1.
Continuous. Prices, 6d. to 2s. Proscenium
width, 39 ft. Phone, Ashford 496. Station,
Ashford, S.R.
PALACE (WE), Tufton Street.—East Kent
Cinemas, Ltd., Plaza, East Street, Sitting-
bourne. 800 seats. Booked H. G. Carey, 3,
Hartsdown Mansions, Margate. Continuous.
Prices, 6d. to 1s. 6d. Phone, Ashford 237.
Station, Ashford Junction, S.R.

ASHFORD (MIDDX.), **Pop. 7,690.**
CLARENDON CINEMA (BA), Clarendon Road.
Prop., F. H. Barton, Johnson. 380 seats.
Continuous. Booked at Hall. Prices, 6d. to
1s. 4d. Proscenium width, 30 ft. Phone,
Ashford 2390. Ashford Transport.

ASHINGTON (NORTHUMBERLAND), **Pop. 29,418.**
BUFFALO PICTURE PALACE (BTH), Station Road.
—Prop., Wallaw Pictures, Ltd. Man. Dir.,
W. Lawson. Continuous, once on Sunday.
Prices, 6d. to 1s. Phone, Ashington 31.
Station, Ashington, L.N.E.R.
HIPPODROME (BTP).—Prop., Wm. Henderson,
7, Stavordale Terrace, Gateshead. Phone,
Gateshead 71626. 950 seats. Booked at
Hall. Continuous. Prices, 6d. and 9d.
Proscenium width, 26 ft. Phone, Ashington
122. Station, North Seaton, L.N.E.R.
MINERS' THEATRE (WE), Station Road.—
Props., Wallaw Pictures, Ltd. Man. Dir.,,
W. Lawson. 1,422 seats. Booked at H.O..
Woodhorn Road. Twice nightly, once on Sun.
Prices, 7d. to 1s. Phone, Ashington 4.
PAVILION (BTH).—Prop., Wallaw Pictures,
Ltd. Man. Dir., W. Lawson. Twice nightly.
One change weekly. Prices, 4d. to 1s. Phone,
Ashington 6. Station, Ashington, L.N.E.R.

ASHTON-IN-MAKERFIELD (LANCS), **Pop. 20,541.**
PALACE (BTP), Bryn Street.—Prop., Associated
British Cinemas, Ltd., 30/31, Golden Square,
W.1. 500 seats. Booked at H.O. Twice
nightly. Prices 4d. to 1s. Phone, Ashton-in-
Makerfield 7304. Station, Bryn, L.M.S.
QUEEN'S PICTURE HOUSE (WE).—Prop
Ashton-in-Makerfield Pciture House Co., Ltd.
868 seats. Twice nightly. Two changes weekly.
Prices, 3d. to 1s. Phone, Ashton-in-Maker-
field 7166.Station, Bryn, L.M.S.

SCALA CINEMA (WE), Heath Road.—550 seats.
Twice nightly. Mat., Mon. and Thurs. Prices
3d. to 9d. Proscenium width, 22 ft. Stage,
10 ft., three dressing rooms. Phone, Ashton
7337. Stations, Ashton - in - Makerfield,
L.N.E.R., and Bryn, L.M.S.

ASHTON-UNDER-LYNE (LANCS), **Pop. 51,573.**
EMPIRE SUPER CINEMA (BTP).—Controlled by
Union Cinemas, Ltd., Union House, 15,
Regent Street, London, S.W.1. Phone.
Whitehall 8484. Booked at H.O. Contin-
uous. Prices 3d. to 1s. 3d. Variety and
Films. Phone, Ashton-under-Lyne 2095.
Station, Charlestown, L.M.S.

COMPTON
ORGAN featured here.

MAJESTIC PICTURE HOUSE (WE), Old Street.—
Prop., Provincial Cinematograph Theatres,
Ltd. Booked at H.O. Continuous during
week; twice Sat. Daily Mat. Prices, 4d.
to 1s. 3d. Café and Dance Hall attached.
Station, Charlestown, L.M.S.

COMPTON
ORGAN featured here.

PICTURE PAVILION (WE), Old Street.—Props.,
Pavilion (Ashton-u.-Lyne), Ltd. 1,300 seats.
Booked at H.O. Continuous. Two changes
weekly. Prices, 6d. to 1s. Proscenium
width, 35 ft. Phone, Ashton 1895. Stations,
Charlestown, L.M.S., and Park Parade and
Oldham Road, L.N.E.R.
QUEEN'S ELECTRIC THEATRE (WE), Wellington
Road.—Prop., Queen's Cinema (Ashton-
under-Lyne), Ltd. 905 seats. Seventeen
shows weekly. Two changes weekly. Prices,
4d. to 1s. Phone, Ashton 2375. Station,
Charlestown, L.M.S.
STAR PICTURE THEATRE (BTH), Church Street.
644 seats. Continuous nightly. Two Mats.
weekly. Two changes weekly. Prices, 3d. to
6d. Proscenium width, 30 ft. Phone, 1124.
Station, Charlestown, L.M.S.
THEATRE ROYAL (BTP).—Lessees, Ashton New
Cinema, Ltd. 1,700 seats.

ASKERN, nr. Doncaster (YORKS), **Pop. 6,000.**
PICTURE HOUSE (Morrisons).—Prop., Askern
Dyson. 500 seats. Once nightly Mon. to
Fri., two shows Sat. Prices, 4d. to 1. Films
by Motor Transport.

ASPATRIA (CUMBERLAND), **Pop. 3,239.**
PALACE CINEMA (BA).—Props., C. H. Over and
Sons, Market Square, Aspatria. 500 seats
Booked at Newcastle. Picture and Variety,
Twice nightly. Two changes weekly. Prices.
6d. to 1s. Stage 16 ft. deep. Two dressing
rooms. Phone, Aspatria 15. Station,
Aspatria, L.M.S.

ASTLEY (Lancs), **Pop. 3,900.**
The Cinema (ba).—420 seats.

ATHERSTONE (Warwick), **Pop. 5,700.**
Picturedrome (awh).—Props., Exors. of J. W. Briggs. 375 seats. Twice nightly, three on Sat. Prices, 6d. to 1s. 3d. Proscenium width, 16ft. Phone, Atherstone 6. Station, Atherstone, L.M.S.
Victoria Cinema (btp).

ATHERTON (Lancs), **Pop. 19,985.**
Palace (btp), Market Street.—Prop., Eagle Picturedromes, Ltd. Booked by T. C. Robinson, Cromford House, Manchester, Twice nightly. Two changes weekly. Prices, 5d. to 9d. Phone, Atherton 57.
Savoy (we).—Props., Eagle Picturedromes Ltd., County Playhouse, King Street, Wigan. T. C. Robinson, Cromford House, Manchester. 814 seats. Prices, 5d. to 9d. Phone, Atherton 57. Station, Atherton.

ATTLEBOROUGH (Norfolk), **Pop. 2,513.**
Cinema (Morrison), Town Hall.—Prop., W, J. Balls, Ellingham Road. Attleborough. 250 seats. Booked at " The Laurels," Queen's Square, Attleborough. Once nightly, two shows Sat. Prices, 6d. to 1s. 3d. Station, Attleborough, L.N.E.R., and by Bury and District Road Transport.
Regal (we).—450 seats.

AUDLEY (Staffs), **Pop. 13,619.**
The Palace (Marshall), Hall Street.—Prop., E. M. Plant, " The Laurels," King's Avenue, Wolstanton. Phone, Stoke-on-Trent 67166. 525 seats. Booked at " The Laurels," Continuous. Prices 3d. to 1s. Films by Road Transport.

AVONMOUTH (Glos).
Cinema (bth), Collins Street.—Prop., W. J. Rolph. 500 seats. Booked at Hall. Continuous. Prices, 7d. to 1s. 3d. Station, Avonmouth Dock, G.W.R.

AXMINSTER (Devon), **Pop. 2,320.**
Guildhall Cinema (Gaumont-Edibell).—Prop., Axminster Guildhall Co., Ltd 566 seats. Booked at Hall. Prices 6d. to 1s. 6d. Dance Hall. Phone, Axminster, 123. Station, Axminster, S.R.

AYLESBURY (Bucks), **Pop. 13,382.**
Market Theatre (rca), Market Square.—Prop., London & District Cinemas, Ltd., 62, Shaftesbury Avenue, W.1. 691 seats. Booked at H.O. Continuous. Three mats. Two changes weekly. Prices, 6d. to 1s. 6d. Phone Aylesbury 242. Station, Aylesbury, L.N.E.R.
Odeon Theatre (bth), Cambridge Street.—Prop., Odeon (Aylesbury), Ltd., Cornhill House, Bennett's Hill, Birmingham. Phone, Midland 2781. Booked at 49, Park Lane, London, W.1.
Pavilion (rca).—Prop., London & District Cinemas, Ltd., 62, Shaftesbury Avenue, W.1. 1,300 seats. Booked at H.O. Continuous. Three mats. Two changes weekly. Prices, 6d. to 2s. 6d. Phone, Aylesbury 242. Station, Aylesbury, L.N.E.R.

AYLSHAM (Norfolk), **Pop. 2,460.**
Cinema.

BACUP (Lancs), **Pop. 20,606.**
Empire (we).—Prop., Jackson's Amusements, Ltd., Hippodrome, Rochdale. Phone, 2161. Booked at Rialto Theatre, Rochdale. 1017 seats. Continuous. Twice Sats., and holidays. Prices, 4d. to 1s. Stage and seven dressing-rooms. Phone, Bacup 159. Station, Bacup, L.M.S.
Regal Super Cinema (we) (formerly Kozy), Burnley Road.—Prop., The Valley Entertainments (Waterfoot), Ltd. 916 seats. Twice nightly. Prices, 6d. to 1s. 3d. Stage. Proscenium, 42 ft. Phone, Bacup 104. Station Bacup, L.M.S.

BACKWORTH (Northumberland), **Pop. 2,350.**
Workmen's Club.

BAGSHOT (Surrey), **Pop. 5,000.**
Princes Cinema (bth), High Street.—Prop., Princes Cinema (Bagshot), Ltd. 355 seats. Booked at Hall. Continuous. Prices, 6d. to 1s. 6d. Phone, Bagshot 195. Station, Bagshot, S.R.

BAILDON, Nr. Shipley (Yorks), **Pop. 7,794.**
Picture House (we), Northgate.—Props., H. & B. Cinema Circuit Co. 400 seats. Booked at Hall. Once nightly. Three shows Sat. Prices, 4d. to 9d. Proscenium width, 22 ft. Café and Ballroom attached. Phone, Shipley 1056. Station, Shipley, L.M.S.

BAKEWELL (Derby), **Pop. 3,012.**
Picture House (we), Haddon Road.—Prop., Holmwood Picture Palace Co., Ltd., Greyfriars, Bakewell Road, Matlock. Phone, Matlock 72. 655 seats. Booked at H.O. Continuous. Prices, 6d. to 1s. 6d. Proscenium width, 38 ft. Phone, Bakewell 144. Station, Bakewell, L.M.S.

BALDOCK (Herts), **Pop. 3,171.**
Cinema, White Horse Street.—Prop., Baldock Cinema Co., Ltd. 500 seats. Continuous. Prices, 3d. to 1s. 3d. Phone, Baldock 88. Café attached. Station, Baldock. Films by Herts and Beds Transport.

BAMBER BRIDGE (Lancs).
Empire Picture Palace (Electrooord).—400 seats.

BANBURY (Oxford), **Pop. 13,953.**
Grand Theatre (Imperial), Broad Street.—Prop., E. A. Bagley. 950 seats. Booked at Hall. Continuous. Prices, 6d. to 1s. 6d. Phone, Banbury 2159. Station, Banbury, G.W.R.
Palace Theatre (ba), Market Square.—Controlled by Union Cinemas, Ltd., Union House, 15, Regent Street, London, S.W.1. Phone, Whitehall 8484. Booked at H.O. Continuous. Prices 6d. to 1s. 6d. Phone, Banbury, 2154. Station, Banbury, G.W.R. and Film Transport.
Ritz (we).—Controlled by Union Cinemas, Ltd., Union House, 15, Regent Street, London, S.W.1. Phone, Whitehall 8484. Continuous. Booked at H.O. Station, Banbury, G.W.R.

BARKING (Essex), **Pop. 51,277.**
Broadway Theatre (bth), Broadway.—Prop., W. H. Clayton. 600 seats. Continuous. Prices, 4d. to 1s. Phone, Grangewood 0170. Station, Barking, L.M.S.

UNIFORM SUPPLY COMPANY, LTD.,

CAPITOL (WE). Props., Associated British Cinemas, Ltd. 1,266 seats. Continuous. Booked at H.O. Prices 6d. to 1s. 6d. Phone, Rippleway 2702. Station, Barking.

CENTRAL HALL MISSION.

ELECTRIC THEATRE (WE), Rippell Road.— Props., Rose and Bockner. 808 seats. Two shows nightly. Two changes weekly. Prices 4d to 1s. 3d. Phone East Ham 61. Station, Barking, L.M.S.

RIO (RCA).—Props., Kessex Cinemas, Ltd., 197, Wardour Street, W.1. Phone, Gerrard 2835. 3,000 seats. Booked at H.O. Continuous. Pictures and Variety. Prices, 6d. to 2s. 6d. Phone, Grangewood 2900.

Fitted "ARDENTE" Stage Amplification See page 258

BARLESTONE (LEICS).

CINEMA.—Thur. and Sat. only. Prices, 4d. to 1s.

BARNARD CASTLE (Co. DURHAM), Pop. 3,883.

SCALA CINEMA (WE), 13, Galgate.—Prop., M.B.C. Cinemas, Ltd. 500 seats. Booked at Hippodrome, Workington. Twice nightly. Prices, 6d. to 1s. 3d. Phone, Barnard Castle 50. Station, Barnard Castle, L.N.E.R.

WYCLIFFE CINEMA (Mihayl).—Prop., M. B. C. Cinemas. 750 seats. Booked at Newcastle or Workington. Continuous. Prices, 3d. to 1s. Station, Barnard Castle, L.N.E.R.

BARNET (HERTS), Pop. 14,721.

BARNET CINEMA (WE), High Street.—Prop. Home Counties Kinemas, Ltd. 1,066 seats, Pictures and Variety. Films booked at Hall or H.O., Walthamstow, and Variety by Harry Bennett, 12, Little Newport Street, W.C.2. Stage, 16 ft. deep; two dressing-rooms, Continuous. Two changes weekly. Prices. 6d. to 2s. 4d. Proscenium width, 33 ft. Café and Dance Hall. Phone, Barnet 0677.

ODEON (BTH), Great North Road.—Props., Odeon (Barnet) Ltd., Cornhill House, Bennetts Hill, Birmingham. Phone, Midland 2.781 Booked at 49, Park Lane, London, W.1. Prices, 6d. to 2s. Phone, Barnet 4147.

REGAL CINEMA (RCA), Lytton Road.—Props., Leebert Theatres, Ltd. 500 seats. Continuous. Booked at Hall. Prices 7d. to 1s. 6d. Proscenium width, 24 ft. Stage and two dressing-rooms. Phone, Barnet 3010. Station, New Barnet, L.N.E.R. Films by Road Transport.

BARNOLDSWICK (YORKS), Pop. 11,915.

MAJESTIC PICTURE HOUSE (Cinephone).—Prop., M. Hartley. 760 seats. One show nightly. Two changes weekly. Prices, 3d. to 8d. Station, Barnoldswick, L.M.S.

PEOPLE'S PALACE (WE).—Prop., People's Palace (Barnoldswick), Ltd., St. James Square, Barnoldswick. Phone No. 98. 700 seats. Booked at Leeds. Once nightly, twice on Sat. Mats., Wed. and Sat. Occasional Variety. Prices, 6d. to 1s. Proscenium width, 20 ft, Stage, 20 ft. deep; six dressing-rooms. Phone. Barnoldswick 98. Station, Barnoldswick.

BARNSLEY (YORKS), Pop. 71,522.

ALHAMBRA THEATRE (WE), Doncaster Road. Prop., Alhambra Theatre (Barnsley), Ltd., The Arcade, Barnsley. Phone, Barnsley 453. 2362 seats. Booked at Theatre. Continuous. Prices, 2d. to 1s. Phone, Barnsley 236. Station, Barnsley Court House, L.M.S.

ELECTRIC THEATRE (Marshall), Eastgate.— Prop., Barnsley Electric Theatre, Ltd., 16, Cambridge Street, Sheffield. Phone, No. 25350. 500 seats. Booked at H.O. Continuous. Prices, 3d. to 6d. Proscenium width, 18 ft. Phone, Barnsley 403.

EMPIRE SUPER CINEMA (BA), Eldon Street.— Prop., by Gaumont British Pictures Corpn. 1,160 seats. Booked at H.O. Continuous. Prices, 6d. to 1s. Phone, Barnsley 363.

GLOBE PICTURE HOUSE (WE), New Street.— Prop. Globe Picture House (Barnsley), Ltd. Res. Man. and Licensee, Mrs. A. Wyham. 872 seats. Booked at Hall. Continuous. Daily Mat. Prices, 4d. to 1s. 3d. Phone, Barnsley 467. Station, Barnsley Court House.

PAVILION PICTURE THEATRE (WE).—Props., Mid-Yorkshire Entertainments, Ltd., Russell Chambers, Merrion Street, Leeds. Phone, 25008. 1,452 seats. Booked at H.O. Continuous. Prices, 4d. to 1s. Phone, Barnsley 388. Station, Court House, L.M.S.

PRINCESS PICTURE PALACE (BA), Town End.— Continuous. Prop., New Century Pictures, Ltd. 850 seats. Booked by Gaumont-British Pictures Corpn. Prices, 3d. to 6d. Proscenium width, 30 ft. Phone, Barnsley 237.

PUBLIC HALL, Harvey Institute, Eldon Street.— Props., The Mayor, Aldermen and Burgesses' of the County Borough of Barnsley. Phone 470. 1,100 seats. Available for Theatrical and Kinematograph Exhibition.

RITZ (WE)—Controlled by Union Cinemas, Ltd., Union House, 15, Regent Street, London, S.W.1. Phone, Whitehall 8484. Continuous. Booked at H.O. Station, Barnsley, L.M.S.

WURLITZER ORGAN
Installed in this Kinema

SAVOY CINEMA (BTH), Lundwood.—Props., Lundwood Cinemas, Ltd. 684 seats. Booked at Hall. Prices, 4d. to 9d. Proscenium width 45 ft. Phone, Brierley 42.

STAR PICTURE HOUSE (Marshall).—Prop., Barnsley Electric Theatre, Ltd., 16, Cambridge Street, Sheffield. 500 seats. Booked at Sheffield. Continuous. Station, Barnsley.

BARNSTAPLE (DEVON), Pop. 14,693.

ALBERT HALL (BTH), Boutport Street.—Prop., Barnstaple Entertainments, Ltd. Continuous. Prices, 6d. to 1s. 10d. Phone, Barnstaple 469. Stations, Barnstaple, G.W.R., and Barnstaple Junction, S.R.

GAUMONT PALACE (BA), Boutport Street.— Prop., Gaumont-British Picture Corporation, Ltd., 123, Regent Street, W.1. 1,122 seats, Booked at H.O. Continuous from 6 p.m. Mat., Wed., Fri. and Sat. Prices, 6d. to 2s. Proscenium width, 40 ft. Phone, Barnstaple 550. Stations, Barnstaple, G.W.R., and Barnstaple Junction, S.R.

Fitted "ARDENTE" Deaf Aids See page 258

REGAL, The Strand.—Props., Regal (Barnstaple), Ltd.

BARROW-IN-FURNESS (LANCS), Pop. 66,366.

COLISEUM (WE), Abbey Road.—Controlled by Union Cinemas, Ltd., Picture House, 15. Regent Street, London, S.W.1. Phone, Whitehall 8484. Booked at H.O. Continuous. Pictures and Variety. Prices, 3d. to 1s. 3d. Phone, Barrow 28. Station, Barrow Central, L.M.S.

136 WARDOUR STREET, LONDON, W.1.

BARROW-IN-FURNESS—contd.

ELECTRIC THEATRE (BTH), Dalton Road.—Prop., Furness Electric Theatre Co., Ltd. 760 seats. Booked at Hall. Twice nightly. Mat., Mon., Thurs. and Sat. Two changes weekly. Prices, 5d. to 1s. Phone, Barrow 184. Station, Central, L.M.S.

GAIETY (WE), Abbey Road.—Controlled by Union Cinemas, Ltd., Union House, 15, Regent Street, London, S.W.1. Phone, Whitehall 8484. Separate Performances. Booked at H.O. Prices, 2d. to 1s. Phone, Barrow 375. Station, Central, L.M.S.

COMPTON

ORGAN featured here.

OSBORNE THEATRE (Morrison).—Prop., Osbornes Ltd. 531 seats. Continuous. Booked at Hall. Prices, 3d. to 9d. Phone, No. 30. Station, Barrow Central.

PALACE THEATRE (WE), Duke Street.—Controlled by Union Cinemas, Ltd. Union House, 15, Regent Street, London, S.W.1. Phone, Whitehall 8484. Booked at H.O. Continuous. Prices, 3d. to 1s. Phone, Barrow 418. Station, Barrow-in-Furness (Central) L.M.S.

PAVILION CINEMA (WE).—928 seats. Two shows daily. mat. Sat. Prices, 3d. to 1s. Phone, No. 515. Station, Central, L.M.S.

REGAL (WE), 47, Forshaw Street.—Controlled by Union Cinemas, Ltd., Union House, 15, Regent Street, London, S.W.1. Phone, Whitehall 8484. Continuous. Prices, 4d. to 1s. 2½d. Phone, Barrow 549. Station, Barrow Central.

RITZ (WE).—Controlled by Union Cinemas, Ltd., Union House, 15, Regent Street, London, S.W.1. Booked at H.O. Prices, 3d. to 2s. 1d. Phone, Barrow 999. Station, Barrow Central.

COMPTON

ORGAN featured here.

SALTHOUSE PAVILION (WE).—Controlled by Union Cinemas, Ltd., 15 Regent Street. London, S.W.1. Phone, Whitehall 8484. Continuous. Booked at H.O. Prices, 3d. to 1s. Phone, Barrow 515. Station—Central.

WALNEY THEATRE (BTH).—Controlled by Union Cinemas, Ltd., Union House, 15, Regent Street, London, S.W.1. Phone Whitehall 8484. Continuous. Price, 2d. to 6d. Phone, Barrow 422. Station, Barrow-in-Furness (Central), L.M.S.

BARTON-ON-HUMBER (LINCS), Pop. 6,330.

OXFORD PICTURE THEATRE (BTH).—Prop., Cecil Whiteley. 600 seats. Booked at Hall. Once nightly, twice Saturday. Two changes weekly. Prices, 6d. to 1s. 3d.

STAR THEATRE (AWH).—350 seats. Once nightly, twice Saturday. Booked at Hall. Stage, 12 ft. deep ; two dressing-rooms. Prices, 6d. to 1s. Phone, Barton 109. Station, Barton-on-Humber, L.N.E.R.

BARTON-UNDER-NEEDWOOD (STAFFS), Pop. 2,500.

CENTRAL HALL.—(Closed).

BARWELL (LEICS).

EMPIRE (AWH).—700 seats.

PALACE.—350 seats. Once nightly, Mon., Tues. and Thurs. Two shows Sat. Prices, 6d. to 1s.

BASINGSTOKE (HANTS), Pop. 13,862.

SAVOY ELECTRIC THEATRE (AWH), Wote Street.—Prop, Davis S. Handford, 167, Wardour Street, W.1. 358 seats. Booked at H.O. Continuous. Prices, 6d. to 1s. 10d. Phone Basingstoke 133. Station, Basingstoke, S.R.

GRAND CINEMA (WE). 598 seats.

PLAZA (WE).—700 seats.

WALDORF (WE).

BASLOW (DERBY).

STOCKWELL HALL (Metropolitan).—200 seats.

STOCKDALE HALL (Metropolitan).—200 seats.

BATH (SOMERSET), Pop. 68,801.

BEAU NASH PICTURE HOUSE (WE), Westgate Street.—Prop., Associated British Cinemas, Ltd., 30-31, Golden Square, London, W.1. Phone, Gerrard 7887. 1,089 seats. Booked at H.O. Continuous. Prices, 7d. to 2s. Proscenium width, 25½ ft. Phone, Bath 4330. Station, Bath, G.W.R. and L.M.S.

FORUM (WE), Southgate Street.—Prop., Avon Cinema Co., Ltd., 10, Windsor Place. Phone, Cardiff 225. 2,000 seats. Booked at H.O. Prices, 6d. to 2s. Proscenium width, 50 ft. Phone, Bath 4962. Cafe attached. Station, Bath, G.W.R.

Fitted "ARDENTE" Deaf Aids
See page 258

LITTLE THEATRE (WE).—Prop., Cousels de Reyes, Citizen House, Bath. Booked at Everyman Theatre, Hampstead. Continuous. 218 seats. Prices, 6d. and 1s. Proscenium width 16ft. Stage 16ft. deep. Six dressing rooms. Café attached. Station, G.W.R. and Road Transport.

ODEON THEATRE (WE), Southgate Street.—Prop., Bath Electric Cinema Co., Ltd., Cornhill House, Bennetts Hill, Birmingham. Phone, Midland 2781. Booked at 49, Park Lane, London, W.1. Continuous. Prices, 6d. to 1s. 6d. Phone, Bath 3533. Café attached. Station, Bath, G.W.R.

OLDFIELD PICTURE HOUSE (WE).—Props., Harris Cinemas, Ltd. 808 seats. Booked at Hall. Continuous. Prices, 9d. to 1s. 4d. Phone, Bath 5020. Stations, Bath, G.W.R. and L.M.S.

PALACE THEATRE.—Prop., W. S. Pearce. 1,000 seats. Variety with Cinematograph Licence. Phone, Bath 2161.

BATLEY (YORKS), Pop. 34,573.

COLLINS CINEMA (WE), Victoria Street, Batley Carr.—Prop., T. Bickler, "Roseholme," Harehills Lane, Leeds. Phone, Chapeltown 41426. Occasional Variety. Booked at Leeds. Continuous. Prices, 4d. to 1s. Phone, Dewsbury 267. Stage. Station, Batley Carr, L.M.S. and L.N.E.R.

EMPIRE CINEMA (WE), St. James Street.—Prop., Batley Theatre and Opera House, Ltd. 963 seats. Booked at Hall. Continuous. Two changes weekly. Prices 4d. to 1s. Phone, Batley 412. Station, Batley, L.N.E.R. and L.M.S.

PLAZA (WE).—Props., Jefton Entertainments, Ltd., Cross Street, Manchester. 850 seats. Continuous. Prices, 4d. to 1s. 3d. Phone, Batley 308. Station, Batley, L.M.S.

REGENT PICTURE HOUSE (WE), Bradford Road.—Props., Regent Pictures (Batley), Ltd. 823 seats. Booked at Hall. Continuous Mon. to Fri. Two shows, Sat. Mat., Tues., Wed. and Sat. Prices, 4d. to 1s. Phone, Batley 449. Station, Batley, L.N.E.R. and L.M.S.

VICTORIA HALL (RCA), Branch Road.—Props., Regent Pictures (Batley), Ltd., St. James Street, Batley. 900 seats. Films booked at Empire Cinema. Two shows nightly. Prices, 3d. to 9d. Phone, Batley 412. Station, Batley, L.M.S. and L.N.E.R.

BAWTRY (Yorks), **Pop. 1,220.**
PICTURE PALACE.—Prop., T. Frost, Wharf Street, Bawtry. Prices, 4d. to 1s. Phone, Bawtry 9. Station, Bawtry, L.N.E.R.

BEACONSFIELD (BUCKS), **Pop. 4,843.**
PICTURE HOUSE (Picturetone).—Prop., H. S. Morgan, Meadow Flat, Beaconsfield. 500 seats. Booked at Hall. Continuous. Prices 9d. to 2s. 4d. Phone, Beaconsfield 248. Station, Beaconsfield, G.W.R. and G.C. Joint R.

BEAUFORT (MON.), **Pop. 4,755.**
CINEMA.—Props., Beaufort Cinema and Billiard Hall Co., Ltd. Continuous when open. Stations, Beaufort or Ebbw Vale, L.M.S., and Ebbw Vale, G.W.R.
GAIETY (BA).—560 seats.

BEBINGTON (CHESHIRE), **Pop. 26,740.**
RIALTO (WE).—Prop., Bedford Cinemas (1928) Ltd., 19, Castle Street, Liverpool. 1,271 seats. Continuous. Prices, 6d. to 1s. 3d.

COMPTON
ORGAN featured here.

BECCLES (SUFFOLK), **Pop. 6,544.**
CINEMA.—Props., Beccles Cinema Co., Ltd. 400 seats.
REGAL THEATRE (WE), Ballygate.—Prop., Beccles Cinema Co., Ltd. 647 seats. Booked at Hall. Continuous. Twice on Sat. Mats., Wed. and Sat. Prices, 7d. to 2s. Proscenium width, 36 ft. Phone, Beccles 133. Station, Beccles, L.N.E.R.

BECKENHAM (KENT), **Pop. 43,834.**
REGAL (WE), High Street.—Controlled by Union Cinemas, Ltd., 15, Regent Street, London, S.W.1. Phone, Whitehall 8484. Continuous. Booked at H.O. Prices, 6d. to 2s. Café attached. Phone, Beckenham 1171/1172. Stations, Clock House or Beckenham Junction, S.R.

WURLITZER ORGAN
Installed in this Kinema
SAVOY (Building).—Props., General Cinema Theatres, Ltd., 19, Albemarle Street, London, W.1.

BECONTREE (ESSEX), **Pop. (including Dagenham) estimated 130,000.**
REGENT CINEMA (RCA), Green Lane, Chadwell Heath.—Prop., Kessex Cinemas, Ltd., 1,500 seats. Pictures and Variety. Booked at H.O. 197, Wardour Street, London, W.1. Phone, Gerrard 2835. Continuous. Prices, 7d. to 1s. 6d. Café attached. Stage and four dressing-rooms. Phone, Seven Kings 2302. Station, Chadwell Heath, L.N.E.R.
See also under Dagenham.

BEDALE (YORKS), **Pop. 1,400.**
ASSEMBLY ROOMS.—Occasional shows. 200 seats.

BEDFORD (BEDS), **Pop. 40,573.**
EMPIRE (WE).—Prop., Granada (Bedford) Ltd., Controlled by Bernstein Theatres, Ltd.,

36, Golden Square, W.1. Phone, Gerrard 3554. Booked at H.O. Phone, Bedford 3848. Station, Bedford, L.M.S.
GRANADA (RCA), St. Peters.—Prop., Granada (Bedford), Ltd., 36, Golden Square, W.1. Phone, Gerrard 3554. Booked at H.O. Continuous. Pictures and Variety. Phone, Bedford 3848. Café attached.

WURLITZER ORGAN
Installed in this Kinema
PICTUREDROME (WE), Duck Mill Walk.—Prop., R. Chetham. 800 seats. Continuous. Booked at Hall. Prices, 6d. to 1s. 6d. Phone, Bedford 3331. Station, Bedford, L.M.S.

PLAZA (WE).—Prop., R. Chetham. 1,052 seats. Continuous. Proscenium width, 40 ft. Phone, Bedford 2345. Station, Bedford. Midland Road, L.M.S.

BEDLINGTON (NORTHUMBERLAND), **Pop. 6,625.**
PALACE THEATRE (WE).—Prop., Wallaw Pictures, Ltd., Ashington, Northumberland. Booked at H.O. 1,356 seats. Two shows nightly. Prices, 6d. to 1s. Full stage; five dressing-rooms. Phone, Bedlington 50. Station, Bedlington.
PRINCE OF WALES (WE).—Prop., F. L. Hastwell, c/o Walton, 53, Westlands Road, Darlington. 736 seats. Twice nightly. Two changes weekly. Prices, 6d. and 9d. Station, Bedlington, L.N.E.R.

BEDWAS AND MACHEN (MONMOUTH), **Pop. 6,800.**
WORKMEN'S HALL (RCA).—Props., Bedwas Workmen Hall Institute. Booked at Hall. 850 seats. Continuous. Prices, 4d. to 1s. Proscenium width, 22 ft. Phone, Bedwas 23. Stations, Bedwas and Caerphilly, G.W.R.

BEDWORTH (WARWICK), **Pop. 12,058.**
GRAND CINEMA, Bulkington.—Prop., — Nicholls. Booked at Hall. Continuous. Two changes weekly. Station, Bedworth, L.M.S.
PALACE (BTH).—Prop., Edward W. Wallis. 850 seats. Booked at Hall. Continuous. Two changes weekly. Prices, 6d. to 1s. 3d. Proscenium width, 20 ft. Phone, Bedworth 86. Station, Bedworth, L.M.S.
STAR CINEMA (Morrison), King Street.—Prop., Edward W. Wallis, Coventry Road, Bulkington. 386 seats. Booked at Hall. Continuous. Prices, 5d. to 11d. Station, Bedworth, L.M.S.

BEESTON (NOTTS), **Pop. 16,016.**
ASTORIA, Lenton Abbey, Beeston.—Booked by Herbert Elton, Commerce Chambers, Elite Buildings, Nottingham.
PALLADIUM SUPER CINEMA (BTH), High Road.—Props., Palladium (Beeston, Notts), Ltd., Burton Bldgs., Parliament Street, Nottingham. Phone, Nottingham 42081. 750 seats. Booked at H.O. Continuous. Stage, 15 ft. deep. Prices, 6d. to 1s. 4d. Proscenium width, 25 ft. Phone, Beeston 54619. Station, Beeston, L.M.S.
PICTURE PALACE (WE), High Road.—Prop., J. H. H. Allsop. 700 seats. Booked at Hall. Continuous. Two changes weekly. Prices, 7d. to 1s. 4d. Station, Beeston, L.M.S., and Road Transport.

BEIGHTON (DERBY), **Pop. 5,500.**
CENTRAL HALL (BTH). 420 seats. Once nightly, twice Sat. Prices, 4d. to 1s.

136 WARDOUR STREET, LONDON, W.1.

BELPER (DERBY), **Pop. 13,1023.**
EXCHANGE (Electrocord).—600 seats.
PALACE (WE).—Prop., Thos. P. Moorley. 850
seats. One show nightly, twice Sat. Two
changes weekly. Prices, 7d. to 1s. Phone, 153.
Station, Belper, L.M.S.

BELTON, nr. Doncaster (LINCS), **Pop. 1,528.**
PUBLIC HALL, Grey Green.—Prop., Trustees.
Occasional shows. Prices, 6d. to 1s. 6d.
Station, Belton, Axholme Ry.

BELVEDERE (KENT), **Pop. 9,283.**
BELVEDERE CINEMA (AWH). Picardy Street.—
Prop ., J. Helsdon Borton, 4, Bloomsbury
Place, Southampton Row, W.C.1. Phone,
Museum 5853. 400 seats. Continuous.
Booked at H.O. Prices, 6d. to 1s. 6d.

BENTHAM (YORKS), **Pop. 2,430.**
PICTURE HOUSE.

BENTLEY with ARKSEY, near Doncaster
(YORKS), **Pop. 16,458.**
COLISEUM (WE).—900 seats.

BERKELEY (GLOS), **Pop. 793.**
ELECTRIC CINEMA, High Street.—Lessee, Alan
G. Cason. Booked at Hall. Once nightly,
twice on Sat. Two changes weekly. Prices,
6d. to 1s. 3d. Station, Berkeley, G.W.R.
Films by Road Transport.

BERKHAMSTED (HERTS), **Pop. 8,053.**
COURT THEATRE (WE), High Street.—Props..
Shipman and King, M.84, Shell Mex House,
Strand, London, W.C. Phone, Temple Bar
5077. Booked at H.O. Continuous. Pro-
scenium width, 34 ft. Prices, 7d. to 2s. 5d.
Phone, Berkhamsted 154. Station, Berk-
hamsted, L.M.S.

BERWICK-ON-TWEED (NORTHUMB.), **Pop.
12,299.**
BERWICK THEATRE (WE).—Props., Berwick
Theatre, Ltd., Hide Hill. 1,100 seats. Booked
in Newcastle. Twice nightly. Proscenium
width, 32 ft. Cafe and Dance Hall. Phone,
Berwick 268. Station, Berwick, L.N.E.R.
PLAYHOUSE (WE).—Props., Berwick Playhouse
Co. 992 seats. Booked at Hall. Continuous.
Prices, 6d. to 1s. 3d. Stage, four dressing-
rooms. Phone, Berwick 155. Station,
Berwick, L.N.E.R.

BEVERLEY (YORKS), **Pop. 14,011.**
MARBLE ARCH PICTURE PALACE (WE), Butcher
Row.—Props., Marble Arch Picture Palace
Co. (Beverley), Ltd. 1,042 seats. Booked
at Leeds. Continuous. Mat., Mon., Fri.,
and Sat. Two changes weekly. Occasional
Variety. Prices, 6d. to 1s. 4d. Stage, 14 ft.
deep. Phone, Beverley 168. Cafe attached.
Station, Beverley, L.N.E.R. ; and Road
Transport.
PICTURE PLAYHOUSE (Wired), Corn Exchange.—
Prop., E. F. Symmons. 480 seats. Booked at
Hall. Continuous. Two shows Sat. Mat.,
Mon. and Thurs. Prices, 6d. to 1s. 4d.
Phone, Beverley 15. Station, Beverley,
L.N.E.R.
REGAL (WE).—Props., Hull City & Suburban
Cinemas, Ltd., associated with County
Cinemas, Ltd., Dean House, Dean Street,
London, W.1. Booked at H.O. 946 seats.
6d. to 1s. 6d. Phone, 368. Station, Beverley,
L.N.E.R. ; and Road Transport.
Fitted "ARDENTE" Deaf Aids
See page 258

BEWDLEY (WORCS) **Pop. 2,868.**
GARDEN CINEMA (Classitone).—Props., B. and B.
Cinemas, Ltd., Central House, 75, New Street,
Birmingham. Phone, Midland 5251. Booked
at H.O. 500 seats. Pictures, Variety, etc.
Continuous, Mon. to Fri. Mat., Sat. Prices,
4d. to 1s. Proscenium width, 30 ft. Stage,
12 ft. deep ; two dressing-rooms. Phone,
Bewdley 26. Station, Bewdley, G.W.R.

BEXHILL-ON-SEA (SUSSEX), **Pop. 21,229.**
GAIETY (WE), London Road.—Props., Gaiety
(Bexhill), Ltd. Booked at Picturedrome,
Eastbourne. Continuous. Phone, Bexhill
680.
PLAYHOUSE (WE), Western Road.—Props.,
Kinema Playhouses, Ltd. Man. Dir.,
Randolph E. Richards. 899 seats. Booked
at Picturedrome, Eastbourne. Continuous.
Phone, Bexhill 78. Station, Bexhill, S.R.
RITZ (WE). Controlled by Union Cinemas, Ltd.,
Union House, 15, Regent Street, London,
S.W.1. Booked at H.O. Continuous. Sta-
tion, Bexhill, S.R.
CARLTON CINEMA (AWH), Town Hall Square.—
Prop., C. J. W. Raphael. 450 seats. Booked
at Hall. Continuous. Prices, 6d. to 1s. 6d.
Phone, Bexhill 423. Station, Bexhill, Central,
S.R. (from Charing Cross and Victoria).

BEXLEY AND BEXLEYHEATH (KENT)
Pop. 32,940.
BROADWAY CINEMA (WE), Broadway.—Prop.,
Harry Quinton. 734 seats. Continuous.
Booked at Hall. Proscenium width, 22 ft.
Stage, 14 ft. deep ; two dressing-rooms.
Prices, 6d. to 2s. Phone Bexleyheath 1999.
Station, Bexleyheath, S.R.
PALACE (BTP).—Prop., Harry Quinton, Glouces-
ter House, Warren Road, Bexleyheath.
Phone, 1999. 786 seats. Continuous. Booked
at Hall. Prices, 6d. to 2s. Station, Bexley-
heath, S.R.
REGAL (WE), Broadway.—Controlled by Union
Cinemas, Ltd., Union House, 15, Regent
Street, London S.W.1. Phone, Whitehall
8484. Continuous. Booked at H.O. Films
and Variety. Prices, 6d. to 2s. Phone,
Bexley 1680. Station, Bexleyheath, S.R.
Films by Road Transport.
Fitted "ARDENTE" Deaf Aids
See page 258

COMPTON
ORGAN featured here.

BICESTER (OXON), **Pop. 3,109.**
CROWN CINEMA (BTH), Sheep Street.—Prop.,
Alfred Tilt. Phone, Bicester 23. 320 seats.
Booked at Hall. Continuous. Mat., Sat.
Prices, 6d. to 1s. 6d. Proscenium width,
22 ft. Stations, Bicester, G.W.R. and L.M.S.
REGAL CINEMA (BTP), London Road.—Controlled
by Union Cinemas, Ltd., 15, Regent Street,
London, S.W.1. Phone, Whitehall 8484.
Continuous. Booked at H.O. Prices, 6d. to
1s. 6d. Phone, Bicester 169. Stations, Bi-
cester, G.W.R. and L.M.S. Motor Transport.

BIDDULPH (STAFFS), **Pop. 7,936.**
PALACE (Kamm), King Street.—Props., Crooks,
Turner and Shemilt. 500 seats. Booked at
Hall by Geo. H. Crooks. One show nightly.
Prices, 3d. to 1s. Station, Tunstall, L.M.S.

BIDEFORD (Devon), **Pop. 8,782.**
Palace Theatre (bth).—Props., Palace Theatre (Bideford), Ltd. 800 seats. Continuous. Prices, 6d. to 1s. 10d. Phone, Bideford 213. Station, Bideford, S.R.

BIGGLESWADE (Beds), **Pop. 5,844.**
Empire (awh), Hitchin Street.—Props., A. Hill & Son. 480 seats. Booked at Hall. Continuous. Prices, 6d. to 1s. 6d. Phone, Biggleswade 97. Station, Biggleswade, L.N.E.R.
Regal (bth), Station Road.—Props., A. Hill & Son. Booked at Hall. 736 seats. Continuous. Prices, 6d. to 2s. 4d. Phone, Biggleswade 236.

BILLINGBOROUGH (Lincs).
Foresters' Hall.—Once weekly, Friday. Prices, 7d. to 1s.

BILLINGHAM-ON-TEES (Durham), **Pop. 17,972.**
Picture House (we).—Props., Picture House (Billingham), Ltd. 778 seats. Booked at Newcastle. Continuous. Prices, 3d. to 1s. Phone, Norton 311. Station, Billingham, L.N.E.R.

BILLINGHAY (Lincs), **Pop. 1,500.**
Cosy Cinema (Morrison), Billinghay.—Prop., C. R. Gaskill. 290 seats. Booked at Leeds. Once nightly. Two shows Sat. Proscenium width, 12 ft. Prices, 3d. to 1s. 3d. Station, Tattershall.

BILSTON (Staffs), **Pop. 31, 248.**
Alhambra (we), High Street.—Prop., E. K. Hawtin, Allport Road, Cannock. Tel., Cannock 187. 425 seats. Continuous. Prices, 5d. to 9d. Stage, 7 ft. deep ; two dressing-rooms. Proscenium width, 22 ft. Phone, Bilston 41400. Station, Bilston, G.W.R.
Coseley Picture House (Gyrotone), near Bilston.—Prop., W. Page, "The Bungalow," Ivy House Lane, Coseley, near Bilston. Booked at Hall. Continuous nightly. Mats., Mon., Thurs., Sat. Prices, 4d. to 1s. Proscenium width, 20 ft. Station, Coseley, L.M.S.
Palace Theatre (bths),Lichfield Road.—Props., Odeon Theatres, Ltd., Cornhill House, Bennett's Hill, Birmingham. Continuous. Booked at 49, Park Lane, London, W.1. Prices, 6d. to 1s. 3d. Stage and 7 dressing-rooms. Phone, Bilston 41025. Café attached. Station, Bilston, G.W.R.
Queen's.—Props., Wood's Picture Halls, Ltd. Wood's Palace, Bilston.
Savoy (bth).—Props., Wood's Picture Halls,Ltd. 800 seats. Booked at Hall by Man. Dir. Continuous. Prices, 5d. to 9d. Phone, Bilston 41388. Station, Bilston, G.W.R.
Theatre Royal (bth).—Props., Wood's Picture Halls, Ltd. 800 seats. Pictures and Variety. Booked at H.O. Continuous. Prices, 6d. to 2s. Proscenium width, 26 ft. Stage, 25 ft. deep ; six dressing-rooms. Phone, Bilston 41388. Station, Bilston, G.W.R.

BINGLEY (Yorks), **Pop. 20,553.**
Bingley Hippodrome (we), Main Street.—Props., Bingley Hippodrome, Ltd., Old Bank Chambers, Keighley. Phone, Keighley 2264. 739 seats. Booked at Leeds. Two shows nightly. Two changes weekly. Prices, 7d. to 1s. 6d. Proscenium width, 26 ft. Phone, Bingley 174. Station, Bingley.

Myrtle Cinema (we).—Props., Bingley Cinema, Ltd., 9, Henry Street, Keighley. Phone, 204. 900 seats. Booked at H.O. Continuous. Prices, 6d. to 9d. Phone, Bingley 211. Station, Bingley, L.M.S.

BIRCHINGTON-ON-SEA (Kent), **Pop. 3,500.**
Ritz (Kalee).—Props., Birchington Picture House, Ltd. 400 seats. Continuous Sunday at 8 p.m. Prices, 6d. to 1s. 6d.

BIRKENHEAD (Cheshire), **Pop. 147,946.**
Avenue Super Theatre (bth), Bidston Avenue. Prop., Cheshire Picture Halls, Ltd., Park Road North, Birkenhead. 1,300 seats. Pictures and occasional Concerts. Booked at H.O. Continuous, Mon. to Fri. Twice on Sat. Prices, 6d. to 1s. 6d. Café. Phone, Birkenhead 3524. Stations, Liverpool Central, C.L.C., and Park. Birkenhead, Mersey R.
Claughton Picture House (bth), Claughton Road.—Prop., Claughton Picture House Co., Ltd., 8, Cook Street, Liverpool. Phone, Bank 8605. 900 seats. Booked at 9,Ranelagh Street, Liverpool, by Alfred Levy. Continuous evenings. Daily Mat. Prices, 3d. to 1s. Dance Hall attached. Phone, Birkenhead 2029. Stations,Central, Mersey R., and Woodside.
Coliseum Picture House (we), Tranmere. Prop., Cheshire Picture Halls, Ltd., Park Road North, Birkenhead. Booked at H.O. Three shows daily. Two changes weekly. Prices, 6d. to 1s. Phone, Rock Ferry 355. Station, Green Lane, Mersey R.
Empire Cinema (we), Conway Street.—Prop., Cheshire Picture Halls, Ltd. 1,021 seats. Booked at Park Road North. Pictures and Variety. Three shows daily. Prices, 9d. to 1s. 10d. Phone, Birkenhead 1815. Station, Woodside, G.W.R.
Hippodrome (we), Grange Road.—1,375 seats.
Lyric Cinema (ba), Price Street.—700 seats. Booked at Hall. Continuous. Prices, 4d. to 6d. Stations, Central, Mersey R., and Woodside, G.W.R.
Palladium (bth), Price Street.—Prop., Cheshire Picture Halls, Ltd. 800 seats. Booked by W. F. Williams at Park Road North, Birkenhead. Continuous. Prices, 4d. to 9d. Phone, Birkenhead 2093. Station, Park, Mersey, and L.M.S.
Park Cinema (ba), Park Road East.—Prop., Gaumont-British Pictures Corpn., 123, Regent Street, London, W.1. Phone, Regent 6641. 928 seats. Booked at H.O. Continuous. Daily Mat. Two changes weekly. Prices, 3d. to 1s. Proscenium width, 31 ft. Phone, Birkenhead 36. Station, Woodside, G.W.R.
Plaza Theatre (we), Borough Road.—Prop., Bedford Cinemas (1928), Ltd., 19, Castle Street, Liverpool. Phone, Central 1545. 2,560 seats. Booked by J. F. Wood, 19, Castle Street, Liverpool. Continuous. Two shows Sat. Mat. daily. Prices, 9d. to 2s. Stage 18 ft. deep ; four dressing-rooms. Cafe attached. Phone, Birkenhead 1119. Stations, Birkenhead (Woodside or Central).

COMPTON
ORGAN featured here.

Queen's Hall (ba), Claughton Road.—Prop., General Theatre Corpn., Ltd., 123, Regent

136 WARDOUR STREET, LONDON, W.1.

BIRKENHEAD—contd.

Street, London, W.I. Pictures and Variety. Booked at H.O. Continuous. Daily Mat. Prices, 4d. to 6d. Phone, Birkenhead 1498. Stations, Liverpool Termini.

REGENT PICTURE HOUSE (WE), Church Road, Tranmere.—Prop., Associated British Cinemas, Ltd., 30-31, Golden Square, London, W.I. Phone, Gerrard 7887. 1,100 seats. Booked at H.O. Continuous. Mat. daily. Prices, 7d. to 1s. Proscenium width, 28 ft. Phone, Rock Ferry 611. Station, Central, Mersey R.

RIALTO (WE), Bebington Road.—Prop., Bedford Cinemas (1928), Ltd., 19, Castle Street, Liverpool. Phone, Central 1544. Booked at H.O. Continuous. Two shows Sat. Daily Mat. Proscenium width, 40 ft. Prices, 6d. to 1s. 3d. Phone, Rock Ferry 1383. Station, Woodside, Birkenhead.

ROCK FERRY PALACE, New Chester Road.—Continuous. Twice on Sat.. Phone, 289.

ROXY (BTH), Charing Cross.—Prop., Harry Buxton, 4, Grange View, Leeds. 1,000 seats. Continuous. Prices, 6d. to 1s. 3d. Proscenium width, 22 ft. Occasional Variety. Phone, Charing Cross 1911. Station, Woodside or Central.

SCALA (RCA), Argyle Street.—Prop., Scala (Birkenhead), Ltd. Controlled by Associated British Cinemas, Ltd., 30/31, Golden Square, W.I. Phone, Gerrard 7887. 976 seats. Booked at H.O. Café. Continuous evenings, daily Mat. Prices, 5d. to 1s. Phone, Birkenhead 161. Station, Woodside, Birkenhead, Mersey R.

SUPER CINEMA (BA), Conway Street.—Prop., Gaumont British Picture Corpn., Ltd. Booked at 123, Regent Street, W.I. 750 seats. Continuous. Daily Mat. Prices, 5d. to 1s. 3d. Phone, Birkenhead 2211. Station, Central, Mersey R.

BIRMINGHAM (WARWICK), **Pop. 1,002,413.**

ADELPHI SUPER CINEMA (RCA), Hay Mills.—Prop., Associated British Cinemas, Ltd., 30/31, Golden Square, W.I. Phone, Gerrard 7887. 1,248 seats. Booked at H.O. Continuous Daily Mat. Prices, 6d. to 1s. 3d. Phone, Victoria 1208. Station, New Street, L.M.S.

ALBION PICTURE THEATRE (WE), New Inns, Handsworth. — Prop., Albion Picture Theatres, Ltd. Booked at Hall. Continuous. Two changes weekly. Prices, 6d. to 1s. 6d. Phone, Northern 0433. Station, Snow Hill.

ALHAMBRA (RCA), Moseley Road.—Props., Associated British Cinemas, Ltd., 30-31, Golden Square, London, W.I. Phone, Gerrard 7887. 1,348 seats. Booked at H.O. Continuous. Prices, 6d. to 1s. 3d. Proscenium width, 50 ft. Phone, Victoria 2826. Stations, New Street and Snow Hill.

APOLLO PICTURE PLAYHOUSE (BTH), Tyburn Road.—Prop., Apollo Picture Playhouse, Ltd., 8, Waterloo Street, Birmingham.. 1,225 seats. Booked at Hall. Prices, 6d. to 1s. 4d. Continuous nightly. Two shows Sat. Mat. Mon., Wed., Thurs., and Sat. Phone, Erdington 0834. Stations, New Street, L.M.S., and Snow Hill, G.W.R. Films by Road Transport.

C O M P T O N
ORGAN featured here

ASHTED ROW PICTURE HOUSE (WE) Highgate Picture House, Darwin Street, Birmingham. Man. Dir., A. N. Ardagh. 824 seats Booked

at H.O. Continuous. Mat., Mon., Thurs., and Sat. Prices, 4d. to 9d. Phone, Aston Cross 3432. Station, New Street, L.M.S.

ASTON CROSS PICTURE HOUSE (RCA).—Lichfield Road.—Prop., Associated British Cinemas, Ltd., 30/31, Golden Square, London, W.I. Phone, Gerrard 7887. 1,000 seats. Booked at H.O. Continuous, Mat. daily. Prices, 4d. to 9d. Phone, East 0430. Station, New Street, L.M.S., and Snow Hill, G.W.R.

ASTORIA CINEMA (BTH).—Prop., Associated British Cinemas, Ltd., 30-31, Golden Square, W.I. 1,100 seats. Booked at H.O. Continuous. Mat. daily. Prices, 3d. to 9d. Phone, Aston Cross 2384. Stations, Station Street, L.M.S., and Snow Hill, G.W.R.

BALSALL HEATH PICTUREDROME (BTH).—Balsall Heath Road.—Props., Balsall Heath Picturedrome, Ltd. 650 seats. Booked at Hall. Continuous. Mats., Mon., Wed. and Thurs. Two changes weekly. Prices, 6d. to 1s. Phone, Calthorpe 1040.

BEACON CINEMA (WE), Brasshouse Lane, Smethwick.—Prop., S.E. Cinemas, Ltd., 47, Temple Row, Birmingham. Phone, Midland 0156. Booked at Dean House, Dean Street, London, W.I. 962 seats. Continuous. Prices, 5d. to 1s. Proscenium width. 24 ft. Phone, Smethwick 1045. Station, Smethwick, L.M.S.

BEAUFORT CINEMA (WE), Coleshill Road, Ward End.—Props., Beaufort Cinema (Birmingham), Ltd. Licensee, F. J. Studd. 1,122 seats. Booked at Hall. Prices, 6d. to 1s. 3d. Proscenium width, 35 ft. Phone, Stechford 2307. Station, Stechford, L.M.S.

C O M P T O N
ORGAN featured here.

BIRCHFIELD PICTURE HOUSE (RCA), Perry Barr. Prop., Birchfield Picture House, Ltd. Booked at Hall. Continuous. Mats. daily except Fri. Prices, 6d. to 1s. 4d. Phone, Birchfields, 4333. Stations, New Street, L.M.S., and Snow Hill, G.W.R.

BORDESLEY PALACE CINEMA (RCA), High Street. Associated British Cinemas, Ltd., Golden Square, W.I. 1,360 seats. Continuous. Daily Mats. Booked at H.O. Proscenium width, 30 ft. Prices, 4d. to 1s. Phone, Victoria 1830. Film Transport.

BOURNBROOK CINEMA (BTP), Grange Road, Selly Oak.—(Closed.)

BROADWAY CINEMA (FI). Bristol Street.—Prop., Mesdames N. C. Smith and E. Booth. 985 seats. Gen. and Bkg. Man., P. D. Reeves. Booked at Warwick Cinema, Acocks Green. Continuous. Mat. daily. Prices, 6d., 9d., 1s., and 1s. 3d. Phone, Midland 1799. Stations, New Street, L.M.S., and Snow Hill.

CAPE HILL ELECTRIC THEATRE (BA), Smethwick. —Prop., Denman Picture Houses, Ltd. Booked at H.O. Continuous. Prices 5d. to 9d. Phone, Smethwick 0181. Station, Smethwick, L.M.S., and Transport.

CAPITOL CINEMA (WE), Ward End.—Prop., Capitol Cinema (Ward End), Ltd. 1,410 seats. Booked at Hall. Res. Man. and Licensee, Wm. Moseley. Continuous. Prices, 6d. to 1s. 3d. Phone, 0528. Station, Stechford, L.M.S.

CARLTON PICTURE THEATRE (WE), Taunton, Road, Sparkbrook. Prop., M. W. T., Ltd. Central House, 75, New Street, Birmingham. 1,504 seats. Continuous. Mat., Mon., Wed., Thurs., and Sat. Prices, 6d. to 1s. 3d. Phone, South 2636. Station, New Street, L.M.S.

CULISEUM THEATRE (BTH), Saltley Road.— Prop., M.W.T., Ltd., Central House, 75, New Street, Birmingham. Booked at Hall. Three shows daily. Stage, 40 ft. deep. Prices, 3d. to 1s. Phone, Aston Cross 3396. Station, New Street, L.M.S., and Snow Hill, G.W.R.

CORONET CINEMA (WE), Coventry Road, Small. Heath.—Prop., Coronet Cinema (Small. Heath), Ltd. 1,155 seats. Booked at Hall Continuous. Sat., twice nightly, 6 and 8.30 Mat. daily (except Frid.) at 2.45. Prices, 4d. to 1s. 3d. Phone, Victoria 0420. Station, New Street, L.M.S. Film Transport.

CROWN THEATRE (WE), Icknield Port Road.— Prop., Associated British Cinemas, Ltd., 30-31, Golden Square, W.1. 1,331 seats. Booked at H.O. Continuous. Mat., Mon., Wed., Thur. and Sat. Prices, 6d. to 1s. Phone, Edgbaston 1122. Stations, New Street, L.M.S., and Snow Hill, G.W.R.

DELICIA (WE), Gosta Green.—Prop., The Delicia (Birmingham), Ltd., Messrs. Gompertz Evans Co., 45, Newhall Street, Birmingham. 1,110 seats. Booked at Hall. Continuous. Prices, 4d. to 1s. Phone, Aston Cross 5951. Stations, New Street and Snow Hill.

EDGBASTON (RCA), Monument Road.—Props., Associated British Cinemas Ltd., 149-151, Regent Street, London, W.1. 1,616 seats. Booked at H.O. Continuous. Prices, 6d. to 1s. 6d. Phone, Edgbaston 2973. Stations, New Street, L.M.S.; Snow Hill.

C O M P T O N
ORGAN featured here.

ELECTRIC CINEMA, Smethwick.

ELITE THEATRE (RCA) Bordesley Green.— Prop., Associated British Cinemas, Ltd., 30-31, Golden Square, London, W.1. Phone, Gerrard 7887. 1,327 seats. Booked at H.O. Continuous. Daily Mats. Prices, 4d. to 9d. Stage, 30 ft. deep ; two dressing-rooms. Phone, Victoria 0169.

ELITE PICTURE HOUSE (BTH), Soho Road, Handsworth.—Prop., Elite (Soho Picture House, Ltd. 1,000 seats. Booked at Hall. Continuous. Mats., Mon., Wed. and Sat. Two changes weekly. Proscenium width, 30 ft. Prices, 6d. to 1s. 3d. Phone, Northern 0665. Station, New Street, L.M.S., and Snow Hill, G.W.R.

EMPIRE PAVILION (Edibell), Blackheath.

EMPIRE THEATRE (BTH), Pershore Road, Stirchley.—Prop., Associated British Pictures, Ltd., 30-31, Golden Square, W.1. Booked at H.O. Continuous. Mats., Mon., Wed., Thurs. and Sat. Two changes weekly. Prices, 6d. to 1s. Phone, King's Norton 1663, Station, Birmingham Termini.

EMPRESS CINEMA (FI), Witton.— Prop., Suburban Halls, Ltd. 500 seats. Booked at Hall. Continuous. Prices, 5d. to 1s. Phone, East 0804. Station, Witton, L.M.S.

ERA CINEMA (BTH), Bordesley Green.—Prop., J. H. Hodge, 982, Bristol Road South, Northfield, Birmingham. 653 seats. Continuous. Prices, 6d. and 9d. Proscenium width, 24 ft. Phone, Victoria 0543. Station, New Street, L.M.S.

FORUM (WE).—Prop., Associated British Cinemas, Ltd., 30/31, Golden Square, W.1. 1,226 seats. Booked at H.O. Continuous. Prices, 1s. to 3s. Phone, Midland 4549. L.M.S. and G.W.R.

C O M P T O N
ORGAN featured here.

FUTURIST THEATRE (WE), John Bright Street. —Prop., Greater Scala (Birmingham), Ltd. 1,223 seats. Continuous. Prices, 1s. 4d. to 2s. Café attached. Phone, Midland 0292.

GAIETY (WE).—Prop., Associated British Cinemas, Ltd., 30/31, Golden Square, London, W.1. Phone, Gerrard 7887. 1,400 seats. Booked at H.O. Continuous. Mat. daily. Prices, 3d. to 9d. Phone, Central 1186. Stations, New Street, L.M.S.

GAUMONT PALACE (BA), Steelhouse Lane.— Props., Gaumont British Picture Corpn., Ltd., 123, Regent Street, London, W.1. Phone, Regent 6641. 2,092 seats. Continuous. Prices, 1s. to 2s. 6d. Booked at H.O. Café attached. Stations, Snow Hill, G.W.R.

**Fitted "ARDENTE" Deaf Aids
See page 258**

C O M P T O N
ORGAN featured here.

GLOBE ELECTRIC PALACE (RCA), High Street Aston.—Prop., Lyons Estate, 117, Colmore Row, Birmingham. 700 seats. Booked at H.O. Continuous. Mat. daily. Two changes weekly. Prices, 3d. to 6d. Phone, Birmingham, Aston Cross 0652. Station, New Street, L.M.S.

GRAND PICTURE HOUSE (BTP), Alum Rock Road.—Prop., Saltley Grand Picture House Co., Ltd., 84, Colmore Row, Birmingham , Phone, Central 3343. 806 seats. Booked at Hall. Continuous. Mat., Mon., Wed., Thurs. and Sat. Two changes weekly. Prices, 4d. to 1s. Phone, East 1271. Station, New Street, L.M.S. (Parcels Office).

GRAND PICTURE PALACE (BTP), Soho Road, Handsworth.—Prop., C. G. H. S. Cinema Co., Ltd. 750 seats. Continuous, 6.30 to 10.30. Mats., Mon., Wed., and Sat. Two changes weekly. Prices, 4d. to 1s. Phone, Northern 0595. Station, Handsworth, L.M.S.

GRANGE SUPER CINEMA (WE), Coventry Road, Small Heath.—Prop., Coronet Cinema (Small Heath), Ltd. Phone, Victoria 0434. 1,471. seats. Booked at Hall. Continuous. Mat. daily, except Fri. Prices, 6d. to 1s. 3d. Station, Small Heath Film Transport.

BIRMINGHAM—contd.

GRAVELLY HILL PICTURE HOUSE (WE), Slade Road.—Prop., William Devey. 976 seats. Continuous. Mat., Mon., Wed., Thurs., and Sat. Prices, 6d. to 1s. Phone, East 0461. Station, Aston.

GREEN LANE PICTURE HOUSE (Film Industries), Green Lane, Small Heath.—Prop., Green Lane Picture House, Ltd. 772 seats. Booked at Hall. Continuous nightly. Mat. daily. Two changes weekly. Prices, 4d. and 6d. Proscenium width, 25 ft. Phone, Victoria 0504. Station, New Street, L.M.S.

GROVE CINEMA (WE), Dudley Road, Birmingham.—Prop., Grove Cinema (Birmingham), Ltd. 1,607 seats. Continuous. Matinees daily except Fri. Prices, 6d., 9d. and 1s. Phone, Smethwick 0343. Station, New Street, L.M.S., and Snow Hill, G.W.R.

HARBORNE PICTURE HOUSE (BA).—Prop., Denman Picture Houses, Ltd., 123, Regent Street, London, W.1. 700 seats. Continuous. 6 to 10.30. Mats., Mon., Thurs., and Sat., at 2. Three changes weekly. Prices, 6d. to 1s. Phone, Harborne 1281. Station, New Street, L.M.S.

HEATH CINEMA (BTH), Washwood Heath Road, Saltley.—Prop., Victoria Talkie Theatres, Ltd. Booked at Hall. 800 seats. Continuous. Mat., Mon., Thurs. and Sat. Two changes weekly. Prices, 4d. to 1s. Phone, East 0230. Stations, New Street, L.M.S., and Snow Hill, G.W.R.

HIGHGATE PICTURE THEATRE (BTH), Darwin Street.—Prop., Highgate Picture Theatre,, Ltd. 713 seats. Booked at Hall. Continuous. Prices, 5d. to 9d. Phone, Victoria 0724. Stations, New Street, L.M.S., and Snow Hill, G.W.R.

KINGS (Edibell), Blackheath.

KINGSTON CINEMA (WE), Coventry Road, Small Heath.—Props., Coronet Cinema (Small Heath), Ltd. 1,475 seats. Continuous. Prices, 6d. to 1s. 3d. Phone, Victoria 2639. Station, New Street.

KINGSWAY CINEMA (WE), King's Heath— Prop., Kingsway Cinema (King's Heath), Ltd. 1,167 seats. Booked at Hall. Continuous. Prices, 7d. to 1s. 6d. Phone, South 1352.

LOZELLS PICTURE THEATRE, Lozells Road.— Prop., Lozells Picture House, Ltd. 1,250 seats. Continuous. Two changes weekly. Cafe adjoining. Prices, 6d. to 1s. Phone, Northern 49. Station, New Street, L.M.S.

WURLITZER ORGAN
Installed in this Kinema

LYRIC PICTURE PLAYHOUSE (BTH), Edward Street Parade.—Prop., Birmingham Lyric Picture Playhouse, Ltd., Parade, Birmingham. Phone, Central 0630. 1,100 seats. Booked at Hall by Man. Continuous. Daily Mat., except Fri. Prices, 6d. to 1s. Mats., 4d, and 6d. Phone, Central 0630. Stations, New Street, L.M.S., and Snow Hill, G.W.R.

MAJESTIC PICTURE THEATRE (BTH).—Prop., Hewitsons, Ltd., Windsor Theatre, Bearwood Road, Smethwick. Phone, Bearwood 2229. 700 seats. Booked at H.O. Continuous. Mat., Wed. and Sat. Two changes weekly. Prices, 6d. to 1s., including tax. Station, Smethwick, L.M.S.

MAYFAIR CINEMA (RCA), College Road, Perry Common.—Prop., Mayfair Cinema (Birmingham), Ltd., 117, Colmore Row, Birmingham. 1,624 seats. Booked at H.O. Continuous.

Daily Mat. Prices, 6d. to 1s. Proscenium width 45 ft. Phone, Erdington 1773. Station, New Street, L.M.S., and Snow Hill, G.W.R.
Fitted "ARDENTE" Deaf Aids
See page 258

METROPOLE (RCA), Snow Hill.—Prop., Associated British Cinemas, Ltd., 30/31, Golden Square, W.1. Phone Gerrard 7887. 1,892 seats, Booked at H.O. Continuous. Daily Mat. Prices, 2d. to 6d. Phone, Central 3986. Station, Snow Hill, G.W.R.

MOSELEY PICTURE HOUSE (BTH), Moseley Road, —Licensee and Man., J. Levey. 900 seats. Booked at Hall. Continuous. Mat., Mon., Wed., Thurs. and Sat. Prices, 6d. to 1s. Phone, Calthorpe 1753. Station, Camp Hill.

NEW IMPERIAL SUPER CINEMA (WE), 516, Moseley Road.—Prop., Associated British Cinemas, Ltd., 30-31, Golden Square, London, W.1. 963 seats. Continuous. Mats. Daily except Fri. Prices, 6d. to 1s. 4d. Phone, Calthorpe 2283. Stations, New Street, L.M.S. and Snow Hill, G.W.R.

NEW OLYMPIA PICTURE HOUSE (RCA), Ladypool Road, Sparkbrook.—Props., The Triangle Co. 804 seats. Continuous from 6 p.m. Daily Mat. Prices, 4d. and 6d. Phone, Victoria 0124. Station, New Street, L.M.S.

NEW PALLADIUM (WE), Soho Hill, Hockley, Handsworth.—Prop., Associated British Cinemas, Ltd., 30-31, Golden Square, London, W.1. 926 seats. Continuous. Mat., daily, except Fri. Prices, 7d. to 1s. 4d. Phone, Northern 0380. Station, Snow Hill, G.W.R,

NEW REGENT (BTP), Ledsam Street.—Prop., Ladywood Pictures, Ltd. 700 seats. Booked at Hall. Continuous from 6 p.m. Prices, 5d. to 9d. Phone, Edgbaston 1113. Stations, New Street, L.M.S., and Snow Hill, G.W.R.

NEWS THEATRE (BTH), High Street,—Prop., Jacey Cinemas, Ltd. Continuous. Programme of News and Interest only lasting one hour. Prices, 6d. and 1s. Phone, Midland 0260. Stations, New Street, L.M.S. and Snow Hill, G.W.R.

NEWTOWN PALACE (WE), Newtown Row.— Prop., Newtown Palace, Ltd., Licensee and Man., F. M. Hood. 1,564 seats. Pictures and Variety. Full size stage ; seven dressing rooms. Continuous, 6.30 to 10.30. Mat. daily at 2 p.m. Two changes weekly. Prices 5d. to 7d. Phone Aston Cross 5379. Stations, New Street, L.M.S., and Snow Hill, G.W.R.

NORTHFIELD CINEMA (BTP), Bristol Roae South Northfield.—Prop., Northfield Pictures, Ltd. 1,178 seats. Continuous. Booked by W. H. Smith, " Lynda Vista," Barrows Road, South Yardley, Birmingham. Prices, 4d. to 1s. 3d. Proscenium width, 36 ft. Phone, Priory 1463. Station, Northfield, L.M.S.

OAK CINEMA, Selly Oak.—Props., Associated British Cinemas, Ltd., 30-31, Golden Lane, London, W.1. Phone, Gerrard 7887.

ODEON CINEMA (BTH), Stratford Road.— Props., Odeon (Shirley), Ltd., Cornhill House, Bennetts Hill, Birmingham. Phone, Midland 2781. Booked at 49, Park Lane, London, W.1- Continuous. Prices, 6d. to 1s. 6d. Phone, Shirley 1183.

ODEON THEATRE (BTH), Birchfield Road, Perry Barr.—Prop., Odeon (Perry Barr), Ltd., Cornhill House, Bennetts Hill, Birmingham. Phone, Midland 2781. Booked at 49, Park Lane, London, W.1. Continuous. Prices, 6d. to 1s. 6d. Proscenium width, 60 ft.

Phone, Birchfield, 4453. Station, Perry Barr, L.M.S.

ODEON (BTH), Long Lane, Blackheath, near Birmingham.—Props., Odeon (Blackheath), Ltd., Cornhill House, Bennetts Hill, Birmingham. Phone, Midland 2781. Booked at 49, Park Lane, London, W.1. Continuous. Twice on Sat. Prices, 6d. to 1s. 3d.

ODEON THEATRE (BTH), Kingstanding.—Prop., Odeon (Kingstanding), Ltd. Cornhill House, Bennetts Hill, Birmingham. Phone, Midland 2781. Booked at 49, Park Lane, London, W.1. Continuous. Prices, 6d. to 1s. 3d. Phone, Sutton 2551.

OLTON CINEMA (WE), Warwick Road, Olton, near Birmingham. 1418 seats.

ORIENT (WE), Six Ways, Ashton.—Prop., Associated British Cinemas, Ltd., 30-31, Golden Square, W.1. 1,540 seats. Booked at H.O. Continuous. Prices 6d. to 1s. 3d.

OXFORD (BTH), High Street.—350 seats.

PALACE (WE), High Street, Erdington. Prop., Associated British Cinemas, Ltd., 30-31, Golden Square, W.1. 1,449 seats. Booked at H.O. Continuous. Prices, 6d. to 1s. 3d. Café, Ballroom and Tennis Courts attached. Phone, Erdington 1623. Station, Erdington.

PALACE THEATRE (RCA), Summerhill Road.—Prop., Associated British Cinemas, Ltd. 30-31, Golden Square, W.1. Phone, Gerrard 7887. Booked at H.O. Continuous evenings. Mats. daily. Two changes weekly. Prices 4d. to 1s. Proscenium width, 32 ft. Phone Central 5636. Station, New Street, L.M.S. and Snow Hill, G.W.R.

PAVILION (WE), Stirchley.—Props., Pavilion (Stirchley), Ltd. Controlled by Associated British Cinemas, Ltd., 30/31, Golden Square, London, W.1. Phone, Gerrard 7887. 1,938 seats. Continuous. Booked at H.O. Prices, 6d. to 1s. 6d. Proscenium width, 53 ft. Café. Phone, King's Norton 1241.

PAVILION (WE), Wylde Green.—Props., Pavilion (Wylde Green), Ltd. Controlled by Associated British Cinemas, Ltd., 30/31, Golden Square, London, W.1. Phone, Gerrard 7887. 2,128 seats. Booked at H.O. Conti nuous. Mat. Mon., Wed., Thurs. and Sat. Prices, 6d. to 1s. 6d. Proscenium width, 47 ft. 6 in. Café. Phone, Erdington 0224. Station, Chester Road, Erdington.

PICCADILLY SUPER CINEMA (WE), Stratford Road. Prop., Associated British Cinemas, Ltd., 30-31, Golden Square, London, W.1. Phone, Gerrard 7887. 1,910 seats. Booked at Hall. Continuous. Daily Mat. Prices. 6d. to 1s. 6d. Proscenium width, 40 ft. Stage, 12 ft. deep ; three dressing-rooms. Phone, Victoria 1688. Stations, Snow Hill, G W.R., and New Street, L.M.S.

C O M P T O N
ORGAN featured here.

PICTURE HOUSE (WE), High Street, Erdington.—Prop., Associated British Cinemas, Ltd., 30-31, Golden Square, W.1. Phone, Gerrard 7887. 537 seats. Booked at H.O. Continuous nightly. Mats. daily. Prices, 6d. to 1s. Proscenium width, 20 ft. Phone, Erdington 1484. Station, Erdington, L.M.S.

PLAZA (BTH), Stockland Green.—Prop., Stockland Green Playhouse, Ltd., 43, Cannon Street, Birmingham. Phone, Midland 5221. Booked at Hall. Continuous. Mat., Mon.,

Wed., Thurs. and Sat. Two shows Sat. Prices, 6d. to 1s. 3d. Phone, Erdington 1048. Stations, New Street, L.M.S., and Snow Hill, G.W.R.

PRINCES HALL (BTH), Smethwick.—Prop, Hewitsons, Ltd. 1,590 seats. Booked at Windsor Theatre, Smethwick. Continuous. Two changes weekly. Prices, 7d. to 1s. Phone, Smethwick 0221. Stations, Smethwick, L.M.S., Smethwick Junc., G.W.R.

C O M P T O N
ORGAN featured here.

REGAL CINEMA (WE), Soho Road, Handsworth Prop., Associated British Cinemas, Ltd., 30-31 Golden Square, W.1. Phone, Gerrard 7887 2,116 seats. Booked at H.O. Continuous Mats. daily. Prices, 6d. to 1s. 6d. Phone Northern 1801. Stations, Snow Hill, G.W.R. or New Street, L.M.S.

C O M P T O N
ORGAN featured here.

RIALTO (BTH), Stratford Road, Hall Green.—Prop., Springfield Picture Playhouse, Ltd., 33, Paradise Street Birmingham. 958 seats. Booked at Hall. Continuous. Two shows Sat. Four Mats. weekly. Prices, 6d. to 1s. 6d. Phone, Springfield 1270. Station, New Street, L.M.S.

C O M P T O N
ORGAN featured here.

RINK CINEMA (BA), Windmill Lane, Smethwick, —Prop., Denman Picture Houses, Ltd., 123, Regent Street, London, W.1. Phone, Regent 6641. Booked at H.O. Continuous. Prices, 6d. to 1s. 6d. Phone, Smethwick 0950. Station, Smethwick, L.M.S.

C O M P T O N
ORGAN featured here.

RITZ CINEMA (WE), Bordesley Green East.—Prop., Associated British Cinemas, Ltd., 30-31, Golden Square, W.1. Booked at H.O. 1,450 seats. Continuous. Daily Mat. Prices, 6d. and 1s. Phone, Victoria 1070. Stations, New Street, L.M.S., or Stechford, L.M.S.

ROBIN HOOD THEATRE (WE), Stratford Road, Hall Green.—Prop., Associated British Cinemas Ltd., 30-31, Golden Square, London, W.1.. 1,517 seats. Booked at H.O. Continuous. Prices, 6d. to 1s. 6d. Phone, Springfield 2371 Stations, Snow Hill, G.W.R., and New Street.

ROCK CINEMA (WE).—Prop., Regalia Cinema Co. (Birmingham), Ltd., 25, Bennetts Hill, Birmingham. 1,600 seats. Continuous from 6 p.m. Prices, 6d. to 1s. Phone, East 0476. Films by Road Transport.

ROOKERY PICTURE HOUSE (BA), Handsworth.—Prop., C. Williams, Elmdean, Carlyle Road, Edgbaston. 650 seats. Booked at Hall. Continuous. Mat. Mon., Wed., and Sat. Two changes weekly. Prices 6d. to 1s. Proscenium width, 20 ft. Phone, Northern 0691. Station, Snow Hill, G.W.R.

136 WARDOUR STREET, LONDON, W.1.

BIRMINGHAM—contd.

ROYALTY (WE), High Street, Harborne.—Prop., Associated British Cinemas, Ltd., 30-31, Golden Square, W.1. Phone, Gerrard 7887. 1,500 seats. Booked at H.O. Continuous. Mats., Mon., Wed., Thurs. and Sat. Prices, 9d. to 1s. 6d. Phone, Harborne 1619. Stations, New Street, L.M.S., and Snow Hill.

SAVOY (BTH), King's Norton, Breedon Cross.—Prop., C. S. Dent, Bonehill, Tamworth. Booked at Hall. 989 seats. Continuous. Prices 6d. to 1s. 6d. Proscenium width, 25 ft. Stage, 15 ft. deep ; two dressing-rooms. 'Phone, King's Norton 1069. Station, Lifford, King's Norton, L.M.S.

SCALA THEATRE (WE), Smallbrook Street.—Prop., Greater Scala (Birmingham), Ltd., 21, Bennetts Hill, Birmingham. Phone, Midland 0347. 800 seats. Booked at H.O. Continuous. One change weekly. Prices, 1s. 3d. to 2s. Phone, Midland 0578. Proscenium width, 26 ft. Station, New Street, L.M.S.

SELLY OAK CINEMA (WE).

SMETHWICK EMPIRE (BTH), Smethwick.—Prop., Hewitsons, Ltd., Windsor Theatre, Bearwood Road, Smethwick. Continuous. Booked at Windsor Theatre. Phone, Bearwood 2244. Stage, 28 ft. deep ; six dressing-rooms. Prices, 6d. to 1s. including tax. Phone, Smethwick 0757. Stations, Smethwick, L.M.S., and Smethwick Junction, G.W.R.

SOLIHULL PICTURE HOUSE (BTH), High Street.—Prop., Solihull Picture House Co., Ltd., Daimler House, 33, Paradise Street, Birmingham. 600 seats. Booked at Victoria Playhouse, Aston. Prices, 7d. ro 1s. 6d. Phone, Solihull 0398. Station, Solihull. G.W.R.

SPRINGFIELD PICTURE PLAYHOUSE (BTH). Stratford Road, Sparkhill.—Prop., C. J. Pictures, Ltd., Stratford Road, Sparkhill. 600 seats. Booked at Hall. Continuous. Prices, 6d. to 1s. Proscenium width, 26 ft. Phone, Springfield 1211. Stations, New Street, L.M.S., and Snow Hill, G.W.R.

TIVOLI (WE), Yardley.—Prop., Tivoli Cinema (Yardley), Ltd., Coventry Road, South Yardley. 1,356 seats. Booked at Hall. Continuous. Prices, 6d. to 1s. 3d. Phone, Acocks Green 0808. Station, New Street, L.M.S.

TRIANGLE CINEMA (RCA), Gooch Street.—Props., Lyons Estate, King's Court, Colmore Row, Birmingham. Phone, Central 3298. 600 seats. Booked at H.O. Continuous. Prices, 4d. and 6d. Phone, Calthorpe 1060.

TUDOR THEATRE (BTH), Haunch Lane, Yardley Wood (Classitone).—Props., Associated British Cinemas, Ltd., 30-31, Golden Lane, London, W.1. Phone, Gerrard 7887. 1,500 seats. Continuous. Mats., Mon., Wed., Thurs. and Sat. Prices, 7d. to 1s. 6d. Proscenium width, 40 ft. Phone, Highbury 2861. Stations, New Street, L.M.S., and Snow Hill, G.W.

TYSELEY CINEMA (WE), Warwick Road.—Prop., S. & E. Cinemas, Ltd. 960 seats. Booked by County Cinemas, Ltd., Dean House, Dean Street, W. Mat., and Evenings. Prices, 7d. to 1s. Phone, Acocks Green 0133. Station, Tyseley, G.W.R.

VICTORIA PLAYHOUSE (BTH), Victoria Road, Aston.—Prop. and Res. Man., A. W. Rogers. 1,300 seats. Booked at Hall. Mats. daily. Prices, 2d. to 1s. Phone, East 0479. Station, Birmingham.

VILLA CROSS PICTURE HOUSE (BA), Handsworth —Prop., Denman (Midland) Picture Houses, Ltd., 123, Regent Street, London, W.1. Phone, Regent 8080. 1,500 seats. Booked at H.O. Continuous. Two changes weekly. Prices, 6d. to 1s. 3d. Phone, Northern 0607. Stations, New Street, L.M.S., and Snow Hill, G.W.R.

WALDORF PICTURE THEATRE (WE), Walford Road, Sparkbrook.—Prop., Arthur E. Parry "The Orchard," Dovehouse Lane, Solihull near Birmingham. Phone, Acocks Green 1429. 897 seats. Booked at Hall by Prop. Continuous. Prices, 6d. to 1s. 3d. Proscenium width, 30 ft. Phone, Victoria 0503. Stations, New Street, L.M.S., and Snow Hill, G.W.R.

WARLEY ODEON (BTH), Hagley Road West.—Props., The Warley Ltd., Cornhill House, Bennett's Hill, Birmingham. Phone, Midland 2781. Booked at 49, Park Lane, London, W.1. Prices, 6d. to 2s. Phone, Bearwood 1549.

WARWICK (FI), Westley Road, Acocks Green.—Props., Smith and Booth. 1,350 seats. Booked at Hall. Continuous. Mat. daily, except Fyidey. Prices, 6d. to 1s. 3d. Phone, Acocks Gyeen. 0780. Station, Acocks Greeh.

WEST END CINEMA (WE), Suffolk Street.—Prop., Gaumont-British Cpn., Ltd., 123, Regent Street, London, W.1. Phone, Regent 6641. 1,385 seats. Booked at H.O. Continuous. Occasional Variety. Café and Dance Hall attached. Prices, 1s. 3d., 2s., and 3s. Phone, Midland 0022. Stations, New Street, L.M.S.

Fitted "ARDENTE" Deaf Aids
See page 258

WURLITZER ORGAN
Installed in this Kinema.

WINDSOR THEATRE (BTH).—Prop., Hewitson's Ltd. 1,500 seats. Pictures and Occasiona Variety. Booked at Hall. Continuous Prices, 6d. to 1s. including tax. Phone Bearwood 2244. Stage 25 ft. deep ; eight dressing-rooms. Café attached. Station, Smethwick, L.M.S.

COMPTON
ORGAN featured here.

WINSON GREEN PICTURE HOUSE (WE), Winson Green Road.—Prop., Winson Green Picture Palace Co., Ltd. 1,299 seats. Continuous. Four Mats. weekly. Two changes weekly. Prices, 5d. to 9d. Phone, Northern 1790. Station, Winson Green, L.M.S.

BIRSTALL (YORKS), **Pop. 7,205.**

LOW LANE CINEMA (BA).—Prop., Varieties (Yorkshire), Ltd. 500 seats. Booked at H.O. Continuous. Phone, Batley 275. Station, Bradford, M.R., and L.N.E.R. Films collected in Leeds.

PRINCES PICTURE PALACE (WE), Market Street. —Prop., Pictures (Birstall) Ltd. 770 seats. Booked at Leeds. Continuous. Prices, 4d. to 1s. Proscenium width, 24 ft. Phone, Batley 470. Films by Road Transport.

BIRTLEY (CO. DURHAM), **Pop. 11,278.**

CO-OPERATIVE CINEMA (WE), Durham Road.—Prop., L. S. Makepeace, Front Street, Birtley. Booked at Newcastle-on-Tyne. 630 seats. Continuous. Prices, 6d. to 1s. Proscenium width, 15 ft. Phone, Birtley 77. Dance Hall attached. Station, Birtley, L.N.E.R.

UNIFORM SUPPLY COMPANY, LTD.,

NEW APOLLO (WE), Jones Street.—Prop., Eade & Faid. 900 seats. Continuous. Prices, 4d. to 9d., Proscenium width, 32 ft. Phone, Birtley 123. Station, Birtley.

THEATRE ROYAL (BTH), Orchard Street.—Prop., F. J. Russell. 750 seats. Continuous. Prices, 3d. to 9d. Stage 15 ft. deep ; three dressing-rooms. Proscenium width, 23 ft. Station, Birtley, L.N.E.R.

BISHOP AUCKLAND (Co. DURHAM), **Pop. 12,269.**

GRAND THEATRE (AWH), West Auckland.— Props., Etherington Bros. 800 seats. Once nightly including Sunday. Two shows Sat., and Children's Mat. Prices, 6d. and 8d. Proscenium width, 26 ft. Station, West Auckland, L.N.E.R.

HIPPODROME PICTURE HOUSE (AWH) Railway Street.—Props., J. G. L. and M. Drummond. 900 seats. Booked at Hall. Twice nightly. Two changes weekly and Sunday programme, Prices, 4d. to 1s. 3d. Phone, Bishop Auckland 121. Station, Bishop Auckland, L.N.E.R.

KING'S HALL (AWH).—Prop., The Hippodrome. 950 seats. Booked at Hippodrome. Twice nightly. Prices, 4d. to 1s. 3d. Phone, Bishop Auckland 121. Station, Bishop Auckland, L.N.E.R.

BISHOP'S STORTFORD (HERTS), **Pop. 9,509.**

REGENT (BA), South Street.—Prop., E. E. Smith, "Merlewood," Pine Grove Road, Bishop's Stortford. Booked at Hall by Prop. 1,200 seats. Continuous. Prices, 6d. to 2s. 6d. Phone, Bishop's Stortford 456. Station, Bishop's Stortford L.N.E.R. Films by Cambs. and District Transport.

PHŒNIX (BA), South Street.—Prop., E. E. Smith, "Merlewood," Pine Grove Road, Bishop's Stortford. 600 seats. Booked at Regent. Continuous. Pictures and Variety. Prices, 6d. to 1s. 6d. Phone, 456. Station, Bishop's Stortford, L.N.E.R.

BISHOP'S WALTHAM (HANTS), **Pop. 2,597.**

PALACE CINEMA.—Nightly in winter, one show. Thurs. to Sat., in summer. Prices, 7d. to 1s. 4d.

BLACKBURN (LANCS), **Pop. 122,695.**

ALEXANDRA PICTURE THEATRE (Gramo-Radio), Dock Street, Eanam.—Prop., Ainsworth and Hudson. 450 seats. One show nightly. Mats., Thurs. and Sat. Two changes weekly. Prices, 6d. to 9d. Phone, Blackburn 5748. Station, Blackburn, L.M.S.

CHARNLEYS PICTURES (WE), VICTORIA HALL, Eanam Bridge.—Props., Charnleys Pictures, Ltd. 1,010 seats. Gen. Man., I. Oddie. One show nightly. Three mats. weekly. Two changes weekly. Prices, 6d. to 9d. Proscenium width, 24 ft. Phone, Blackburn 5152. Station, Blackburn, L.M.S.

CO-OP CINEMA (BTH), George Street, Whalley.— 840 seats. Twice daily. Prices, 6d. and 9d. Co-op. Society, Ltd. 500 seats. Once nightly. Twice Sat. Prices, 3d. and 6d. Cafe. Phone, Whalley 91. Station, Whalley, L.M.S.

EMPIRE ELECTRIC THEATRE (WE), Aqueduct Road, Ewood.—Props., Empire Electric Theatre (Blackburn), Ltd. 900 seats. One show nightly. Mats., Sat. Two changes weekly. Prices, 5d. to 9d. Phone, Blackburn 5615. Station, Blackburn, L.M.S.

KING'S HALL (WE).—Prop., Buxton Theatre Circuit, Ltd., 4, Grange View, Leeds. 850 seats. Booked at Hall. Once nightly.

Three Mats. weekly. Prices, 5d. and 9d. Proscenium width, 24 ft. Phone, Blackburn 5552. Station, Blackburn, L.M.S.

MAJESTIC CINEMA (WE), King William Street.— Prop., Associated British Cinemas, Ltd., 30-31, Golden Square, London, W.1. Phone, Gerrard 7887. 1,573 seats. Continuous. Mat. daily. Price, 6d. to 1s. 6d. Phone, Blackburn 6433. Station, Blackburn, L.M.S.

NEW CENTRAL HALL (RCA), Mincing Lane.— Prop., Langworthy Picturedrome, Ltd., Newgate Chambers, Rochdale. 1,380 seats. Continuous evenings. Mat. daily. Prices, 6d. to 1s. Proscenium width, 20 ft. Phone, Blackburn 6357. Station, Blackburn, L.M.S.

OLYMPIA (WE), St. Peter's Street.—Prop., Langworthy Picturedrome, Ltd., Newgate Chambers, Rochdale. 1,050 seats. Twice nightly. Mat. daily. Prices, 6d. to 1s. 3d. Phone, Blackburn 6498. Station, Blackburn, L.M.S.

PALLADIUM (WE), Mill Hill, near Blackburn.— Prop., Marks Circuit Cinemas. 664 seats. One show nightly. Mat. Mon., Thurs. and Sat. Prices, 4d., 7d. and 9d. Phone, Blackburn 6240. Station, Mill Hill, L.M.S.

REGENT.—Prop., J. & H. Buxton, 4, Grange View, Leeds.

RIALTO LUXURY CINEMA AND CAFE (WE), Penny Street.—Prop., Associated British Properties, Ltd., Newgate Chambers, Rochdale, Lancs. Phone, Rochdale 3212. 1,879 seats. Continuous, Mon. to Fri. Three shows Sat. Daily Mat. Phone, Blackburn 4246. Station, Blackburn, L.M.S.

C O M P T O N
ORGAN featured here

RITZ (WE).—Controlled by Union Cinemas, Ltd., Union House, 15, Regent Street, London, S.W.1. Phone, Whitehall 8484. Continuous. Booked at H.O. Station, Blackburn, L.M.S

ROXY CINEMA (BTP), King Street.—Prop., Joseph and Harry Buxton Circuit, 4, Grange View, Leeds. Phone, Leeds 41594I. 1,200 seats. One show nightly. Two Sat. Mat. daily. Two changes weekly. Prices, 5d. and 9d. Proscenium width, 24 ft. Phone, Blackburn 6648. Station, Blackburn, L.M.S.

SAVOY PICTURE HOUSE (BTP), Bolton Road.— Prop., Associated British Cinemas, Ltd., 30-31, Golden Square, London, W.1. Phone, Gerrard 7887. 1,017 seats. Booked at H.O. Continuous evenings. Mat. daily. Two changes weekly. Prices, 3d. to 6d. Proscenium 25 ft. deep. Phone, Blackburn 5233. Station, Blackburn, L.M.S.

STAR PICTURE PALACE (WE), Plane Street.— Prop., E. Taylor, "Rosamond," Brownhill, Blackburn. Phone, Blackburn 48119. 911 seats. Booked at Hall. Once nightly, twice Sat. Prices, 6d. to 1s. Proscenium width, 29 ft. Phone, Blackburn 6249. Station, Blackburn, L.M.S.

THEATRE ROYAL (WE).—Prop., Northern Theatres Co., Ltd. 1,500 seats. Three shows daily. Phone, Blackburn 6810. Station, Blackburn, L.M.S.

BLACKDOWN CAMP (SURREY).

GARRISON THEATRE.—Prop., Navy, Army and Air Force Institutes, Imperial Court, Upper Kennington Lane, S.E.11. Phone, Hop 6060.

136 WARDOUR STREET, LONDON, W.1.

R

BLACKHALL COLLIERY (Co. Durham). Super Cinema (BTP).

BLACKHALL MILL (Co. Durham), **Pop. 5,000.**

Palace Picture House (BTP), Hamsterley Colliery.—Prop., Chopwell Cinema Co., Ltd., 1, Lesbury Terrace, Chopwell, Co. Durham. 600 seats. Booked at King's Theatre, Chopwell, by George Stoddart. One show nightly. Two on Mon. and Sat. Two changes. Occasional Variety. Stage 22 ft. deep ; three dressing rooms. Prices, 3d. to 1s. Station. High Westwood, L.N.E.R. Carrier collects in Newcastle.

BLACKHILL (Co. Durham), **Pop. 5,141.**

Olympia (BTH).—Prop., Olympia Cinema (Blackhill), Ltd. 750 seats. Mon. to Fri. once nightly. Twice Sat. Booked at Hall. Prices, 6d. to 1s. Phone, Consett 130. Station, Blackhill, L.N.E.R.

BLACKPOOL (Lancs), **Pop. 101,543.**

(Sunday evening shows at all kinemas all year round.)

Clifton Palace (BA), Church Street.—Prop., Blackpool Clifton Palace Co., Ltd. 700 seats. Continuous from 6.30 p.m. Daily Mat. Two changes weekly. Prices, 6d. to 1s. 3d. Phone, Blackpool 153. Station, Blackpool (Talbot Road).

Empire Cinema (WE), Hawes Side Lane, Marton.—Prop., A. Hall, 575, Lytham Road, Blackpool. Phone, South Shore 42164, 840 seats. Twice daily. Prices, 6d. and 9d. Proscenium width, 21 ft. Phone, South Shore 41266. Station, Blackpool South, L.M.S.

Empress Ballroom.

WURLITZER ORGAN
Installed in this Ballroom

Grand (WE), Church Street.—Prop., Blackpool Tower Co., Ltd. 1,711 seats. Twice daily. Prices, 9d. to 1s. 6d. Proscenium width, 30 ft. Twelve dressing rooms. Phone, Blackpool 1. Stations, Blackpool Central and North, L.M.S.
Fitted "ARDENTE" Deaf Aids
See page 258

Hippodrome (WE), Church Street.—Prop., Blackpool Entertainments (1920), Ltd, Controlled by Associated British Cinemas, Ltd., 30/31, Golden Square, London, W.1. Phone, Gerrard 7887. 2,820 seats. Booked at H.O. Four shows daily summer ; three shows daily in winter season. Prices, 7d. to 1s. 6d. Stage, 25 ft. deep ; eight dressing-rooms. Proscenium width, 32 ft. Phone, Blackpool 2233. Station, Blackpool, North, L.M.S.

Imperial Picture Palace (WE).—Dickson Road, North Shore.—Prop., North Shore Pictures, Ltd. 743 seats. Booked at Hall by Francis Fennell. Three shows daily. Prices, 6d. to 1s. 3d. Phone, Blackpool 270. Stations, Blackpool (Talbot Road) and Central, L.M.S.

King Edward Picture Palace (WE), Central Drive.—Prop., Blackpool Central Picture Palace Co., Ltd. 985 seats. Three shows daily in summer ; twice daily in winter season. Two changes weekly. Prices, 7d. to 1s. 3d. Phone, Blackpool 1061. Station, Blackpool, L.M.S.

Palace Picture Pavilion (WE), Promenade.—Prop., Blackpool Tower Co., Ltd. 1972 seats. Booked at Hall. Three shows daily. Prices,

9d. to 1s. 9d. Phone, Blackpool 1. Cafe and Ballroom attached. Stations, Blackpool North and Central, L.M.S.
Fitted "ARDENTE" Deaf Aids
See page 258

Palace Variety Theatre (WE), Promenade.—Prop., Blackpool Tower Co., Ltd. 2,012 seats. Booked at Hall. Variety. Twice nightly. Prices, 9d. to 1s. 6d. Stage, 37 ft. deep ; twelve dressing-rooms. Cafe and Ballroom in same building. Phone, Blackpool 1.

Palladium (WE), Waterloo Road.—Prop., South Shore Theatres, Ltd. 1,450 seats. Booked at Manchester and Liverpool. Prices, 9d. to 1s. 3d. Proscenium width, 28 ft. Cafe. Phone, South Shore 42023. Station, Blackpool, South, L.M.S.

Plaza Theatre (BTH), Manchester Square.—Prop., Central Circuits, Ltd., 15, Stanley Street, Liverpool. 700 seats. Booked at Hall. Continuous. Prices, 7d. to 1s. Four dressing-rooms. Phone, Blackpool 297. Station, Blackpool Central.

Princess Cinema, Promenade.—Prop., Blackpool Entertainments (1920), Ltd. Controlled by Associated British Cinemas, Ltd., 30-31, Golden Square, London, W.1. Phone, Gerrard 7887. Booked at H.O. Continuous winter ; four shows in summer. Prices, 6d. to 1s. 6d. Phone, Blackpool 467. Café attached, Stations, Blackpool Central and North, L.M.S.

Regent Picture House (WE), Church Street.—Prop., Regent Picture House (Blackpool), Ltd. 1,092 seats. Booked at Hall by Francis Fennell. Three shows daily. Prices, 6d. to 1s. 3d. Phone, Blackpool 1357. Stations Blackpool (Talbot Road) and Central

Rendezvous Cinema and Cafe (WE), 57, Bond Street.—Prop., Howarth and Beardshaw, Ltd. 1,200 seats. Booked at 21, Bridge Street, Manchester, by J. Brearley. Three shows daily. Prices, 7d. to 1s. 3d. Cafe attached. Phone, South 42079.

Ritz (WE).—Controlled by Union Cinemas, Ltd., Union House, 15, Regent Street, London, S.W.1. Phone, Whitehall 8484. Continuous. Booked at H.O. Station, Blackpool, L.M.S.

Tivoli Picture Theatre (WE), Talbot Square.—Prop., A. Hall. 920 seats. Booked at Palladium. Three shows daily summer, twice in winter. Two changes weekly. Prices, 6d. to 1s. 3d. Phone, Blackpool 508. Station, Blackpool (Talbot Road), L.M.S.

Tower Ballroom.

WURLITZER ORGAN
Installed in this Ballroom

Waterloo Picture House (WE), Waterloo Road.—Prop., South Shore Theatre Co., Ltd., 22, Barley Street, Blackpool. 950 seats. Booked at Palladium. Three shows daily in summer ; twice daily winter. Two changes weekly. Prices, 6d. to 1s. 3d. Phone, South Shore 41026. Station, Blackpool South.

Winter Gardens Pavilion (WE), Church Street.—Prop., Blackpool Winter Gardens and Pavilion Co., Ltd. 2,443 seats. Three shows daily. Prices, 9d. upwards. Stage, 38 ft. deep ; twenty dressing-rooms. Phone, Blackpool 1. Cafe and Ballroom attached. Station, Blackpool, L.M.S.
Fitted "ARDENTE" Deaf Aids
See page 258

BLACKWOOD (Mon.), **Pop. 6,200.**

Capitol (Sound, Ltd.), Hall Street.—Prop., Blackwood Cinemas, Ltd., Pavilion, Aber-

tillery, Mon. 900 seats. Booked at Hall. Continuous. Prices, 7d. to 1s. Phone, Blackwood 38. Station, Blackwood, L.M.S.
PALACE (BTH), High Street.—Prop., Blackwood Cinemas, Ltd., Pavilion, Abertillery. 450 seats. Booked at Hall. Continuous. Prices, 7d. to 1s. Station, Blackwood L.M.S.
OAKDALE WORKMEN'S LIBRARY AND INSTITUTE (PICTURE HOUSE) (BA).—Once nightly, Mon. to Fri. Twice on Sat. 533 seats. Booked at Institute. Prices, 6d. and 9d. Proscenium width, 26 ft. Phone, Blackwood 85. Films by Film Transport Services (Cardiff), Ltd.

BLAENAVON (MON.), Pop. 11,075.
COLISEUM (MIHALY).—Props., Attwood Theatres, Ltd. 650 seats. Booked at Cardiff. One show nightly. Two changes weekly. Phone, Blaenavon 48. Station, Blaenavon, G.W.R.
WORKMEN'S HALL (RCA).—Prop., Blaenavon Workmen. Sec., Cecil.A. S. Northcote. 940 seats. Booked at Hall. One show nightly. Occasional Variety. Stage, 17½ ft. deep Prices, 6d. to 1s. Phone, Blaenavon 24 Station, Blaenavon, G.W.R. (low level).

BLAINA (MON.).
EMPIRE.—Prop., Blaina Cinematograph Co., Ltd.
GAIETY (BTH), High Street.—Prop., Blaina Cinematograph Co., Ltd. 500 seats. Prices, 6d. to 9d. Road transport.

BLANDFORD (DORSET), Pop. 3,149.
PALACE (IMPERIAL), East Street.—Prop., Percival J. Carter. 500 seats. Booked at Hall. One show nightly. Prices, 6d. to 1s. 6d. Proscenium width, 22 ft. Stage, 20 ft. deep, Phone, Blandford 12. Station, Blandford. S.R.

BLAYDON-ON-TYNE (Co. DURHAM), Pop. 32,259.
EMPIRE (BTP), Church Street.—Props., Stanley Rogers Cinemas, Ltd., 72, Grey Street, Newcastle-on-Tyne. Phone, Newcastle, 20317. 750 seats. Booked at H..O. Two shows nightly. Occasional Variety. Prices, 4d. to 9d. Phone, Blaydon 19. Station, Blaydon-on-Tyne, L.N.E.R.
PAVILION THEATRE (BA).—Prop. and Res. Man., H. T. Smelt. 200 seats. Two shows nightly. Two changes weekly. Station, Blaydon-on-Tyne, L.N.E.R.

BLETCHLEY (BUCKS), Pop. 6,169.
COUNTY CINEMA (WE), High Street.—Prop., County Cinemas, Ltd., Dean House, Dean Street, London. 514 seats. Booked at H.O. Twice nightly. Prices, 4d. to 1s. 6d. Phone, Bletchley 165. Station, Bletchley, L.M.S.

BLIDWORTH, NR, MANSFIELD (NOTTS), Pop. 3,500.
SCALA (BTP).—Prop., Blidworth Scala, Ltd. Once nightly. Twice on Sat. Prices, 4d. to 1s. Phone, Blidworth 82. Station, Mansfield, L.M.S. Films by Road Transport.

BLOXWICH (STAFFS), Pop. 8,950.
ODEON THEATRE (WE), High Street.—Prop., Odeon (Perry Bar), Ltd., Cornhill House, Bennett's Hill, Birmingham. Phone, Midland 2781. Booked at 49, Park Lane,London, W.1. Continuous. Phone, Bloxwich 6371. Station, Bloxwich, L.M.S.

BLYTH (NORTHUMBERLAND), Pop. 31,808.
CENTRAL CINEMA (RCA), Market Place.—Prop., Central Cinemas (Blyth), Ltd. 1,300 seats. Continuous. Prices, 4d. to 1s. Phone, Blyth 189. Station, Blyth, L.N.E.R.
EMPIRE CINEMA (BTP), Beaconsfield Street,— Prop., S. S. Blyth Kinemas, Ltd., 11, Bath Lane, Newcastle. Phone, 27864. 1275 seats. Booked at H.O. Continuous. Prices, 4d. to 9d. Phone, Blyth 221. Station, Blyth, L.N.E.R.
HIPPODROME (BTP).—Prop., S.S. Blyth Kinemas, Ltd., Waterloo Chambers, 11, Bath Lane, Newcastle-on-Tyne. Phone, Newcastle 27864. 1,100 seats. Booked at H.O. Continuous. Prices, 4d. to 9d. Phone, Blyth 221. Stage, 18 ft. deep ; 2 dressing-rooms. Ballroom attached. Station, Blyth, L.N.E.R.
THEATRE ROYAL (WE).—Prop., S. S. Blyth Kinemas, Ltd., 11, Bath Lane, Newcastle-on-Tyne. Phone, Newcastle 27864. 1,800 seats. Continuous. Twice nightly Sat. Proscenium width, 30 ft. Prices, 4d. to 1s. 2d. Phone, Blyth 221. Station, Blyth, L.N.E.R.
WALLAW CINEMA.—Prop., Wallaw Pictures, Ltd., Wallaw Buildings, Ashington, Northumberland.

BODMIN (CORNWALL), Pop. 5,526.
PALACE THEATRE (BTH).—Prop., R. Hill. 500 seats. Booked at Palace, Truro. One show nightly. Prices, 6d. to 1s. 6d. Phone 132. Station, Bodmin, G.W.R.

BOGNOR REGIS (SUSSEX), Pop. 13,510.
ODEON THEATRE (BTH).—Prop., Odéon (Bognor), Ltd., Cornhill House, Bennett's Hill, Birmingham. Phone, Midland 2781. Booked at 49, Park Lane, London, W.1. Prices, 9d. to 2s. Phone, Bognor 88. Station, Bognor, S.R.
PICTUREDROME (WE), Canada Grove.—Prop., Bognor Pier Co., Ltd., 50, High Street, Bognor. Phone, Bognor 97. 662 seats. Booked at H.O. Continuous. Prices, 6d. to 1s. 6d. Phone, Bognor 138. Cafe attached.
PIER CINEMA (WE).—Prop., Bognor Pier Co., Ltd., 50, High Street, Bognor. 924 seats. Booked at H.O. Continuous. Prices, 9d. to 2s. Phone, Bognor 77. Station, Bognor, S.R.

BOLDON COLLIERY (Co. DURHAM), Pop. 8,000.
PALACE ELECTRIC (BTH), North Road.—Prop., Buldon Electric Palace, Ltd. 700 seats. Booked at Hall by Man. Once nightly, twice Mon. and Sat. Two changes weekly. Prices, 4d. to 7d. Station, Boldon Colliery, L.N.E.R.

BOLLINGTON (nr. Macclesfield) (CHESHIRE), Pop. 5,027.
EMPIRE PICTURE THEATRE, Palmerston Street. —Prop., E. and A. H. Whittaker. 500 seats. Booked at Hall. One show nightly ; three on Sat. Prices, 4d. to 1s. Phone, Bollington 52. Station, Bollington, L.N.E.R.

BOLSOVER (DERBY), Pop. 11,811.
CENTRAL HALL, Carr Vale.—Prop., J. R. Dakin. 450 seats. Nine shows weekly. Two changes weekly. Station, Bolsover, L.N.E.R.
NEW PALACE (BTH), Town End.—Prop., New Palace (Bolsover), Ltd. Gen. Man., W. A. Pitkin. 589 seats. Booked at Hall. Continuous. Prices, 6d. to 1s. Proscenium width 24 ft. Café. Stations, Bolsover, L.N.E.R. and L.M.S. Films by Road Transport.

136 WARDOUR STREET, LONDON, W.1.

R2

BOLTON (LANCS), **Pop. 1 77,253**

BELLE CINEMA (BTH), Belmont Road, Astley Bridge.—Prop. and Man., Geo. Hutchinson. 580 seats. Booked at Hall. Two shows nightly Two changes weekly. Prices, 4d. to 9d. Phone, Bolton 1199. Station, Bolton, L.M.S.

CAPITOL CINEMA (BTH), Churchgate.—Prop., Associated British Cinemas, Ltd., 30-31, Golden Square, London, W.1. Phone, Gerrard 7887. Continuous. Prices, 7d. to 1s. 6d. Proscenium width, 33 ft. Phone, Bolton 2587. Station, Trinity Street, L.M.S.

CARLTON THEATRE (BTH), Mount Street.— Prop., Bolton Cinematograph Co., Ltd. 14, Wood Street, Bolton. Phone, Bolton 1625. 1,000 seats. Booked by F. S. Hampson. Pictures and Variety. Continuous. Mats. Mon. and Sat. Variety booked by Percy Hall, Oxford Road, Manchester. Stage, 7 ft. deep ; two dressing rooms. Prices, 4d. to 1s. Proscenium width, 22 ft. Phone, Bolton 1673. Stations, Trinity Street and Gt. Moor Street, Bolton, L.M.S.

CROMPTON CINEMA (BTP), Crompton Way.— Prop., Arthur Hall, Palladium Theatre, Blackpool. 1,200 seats. Booked at Manchester. Continuous. Daily Mat. Prices, 3d. to 1s. 3d. Two dressing rooms. Café attached. Proscenium width, 46 ft. Phone, Bolton 1089. Station, Trinity Street, L.M.S.

DERBY CINEMA (BTP), Derby Street.—Prop., Derby and Empire Cinemas. 750 seats. Booked at Hall. Continuous. Prices, 4d. and 6d. Phone, Bolton 3654.

EMBASSY (WE).

EMPIRE CINEMA (BTP), Howard Street.—Prop., J. Cohen. 472 seats. Booked at Hall. Twice nightly. Prices, 3d. to 6d. Phone, Bolton 1363. Station, Bolton, L.M.S.

GEM CINEMA (BTH), Darley Street.—Prop., Gem Cinemas (Bolton), Ltd. 1,050 seats. Booked by Jas. Brearley, 21, Bridge Street, Manchester. Continuous. Prices, 4d. to 1s. Phone, Bolton 2049. Station, Trinity Street, Bolton, L.M.S.

GRAND.—1,200 seats.

HIPPODROME (BTH), Deansgate.—Prop., Bolton Theatre and Entertainments Co., Ltd., 14' Wood Street, Bolton. 1,086 seats. Booked by H. D. Moorhouse Circuit, 7, Oxford Road, Manchester. Continuous nightly. Daily Mat. Prices, 6d. to 1s. 4d. Phone, Bolton 781. Station, Trinity Street, L.M.S.

IMPERIAL (WE), Deansgate.—(Closed). 550 seats.

KING'S HALL, Farnworth.—Prop., Magee, Marshall and Co., Ltd. Continuous. Two changes weekly. Prices, 3d. to 1s. Station, Farnworth, L.M.S.

MAJESTIC CINEMA (WE), Daubhill.—Lessees, Cinemas (Leeds and Bolton), Ltd., Martin's Bank Chambers, Bradford. 1913 seats. Booked at H.O. Daily Mat. Continuous nightly. Prices, 3d. to 1s. Phone, Bolton 1716. Station, Bolton, Trinity Street, L.M.S.

ODEON THEATRE (BTH). Ash Burner Street.— Props., Odeon (Bolton), Ltd., Bennett's Hill, Birmingham. Phone, Midland 2781. (In course of construction.)

PALACE PICTURE HOUSE (WE), Bury Old Road. —Prop., Palace Picture House (Bolton), Ltd. 1,021 seats. Booked at 76, Victoria Street, Manchester, by Ogdens. Continuous. Prices, 4d. to 6d. Proscenium width, 30 ft. Stage, 9 ft. deep ; 2 dressing-rooms. Phone, Bolton 1155. Station, Trinity Street, Bolton.

PALLADIUM PICTURE HOUSE (WE), Higher Bridge Street.—Lessee, A. J. Campy, 353, Blackburn Road, Bolton. 1,250 seats. Booked at Hall. Prices, 4d. to 1s. Phone, Bolton 2024.

PLAZA (BTP), 336, Deane Road.—Prop., Bessie Nixon. 600 seats Booked at H.O. Continuous. Proscenium width, 18 ft. Prices, 3d. to 9d. Phone, Bolton 2624.

QUEEN'S PICTURE HOUSE (BTH), Bradshaw-gate.—Prop., Rialto (Bolton), Ltd., Queen's Picture House, Trinity Street, Bolton. 1,300 seats. Booked at Hall. Continuous. Prices, 6d. to 1s. 6d. Cafe attached. Phone, Bolton 1251. Station, Trinity Street, L.M.S.

REGAL (WE).—Prop., Associated British Cinemas, Ltd., 30-31, Golden Square, London, W.1. Phone, Gerrard 7887. Booked at H.O. 2,380 seats. Continuous nightly. Daily Mat. Prices, 4d. to 9d. Occasional Variety, Stage, 10 ft. ; two dressing-rooms.

REGENT (WE) Deane Road.—Prop., Bolton Moore Kinema, Ltd., Man. Dir., T. Jones. 940 seats. Booked at Hall. Continuous. Two changes weekly. Prices, 3d. to 9d. Phone, 2188. Station, Bolton, L.M.S.

RIALTO PICTURE PLAYHOUSE (WE), St. George's Road.—Prop., Rialto (Bolton), Ltd. 1,147 seats. Booked at Hall. Continuous Prices, 6d. to 1s. Phone, Bolton 137.

RITZ.—750 seats. Continuous. Prices, 3d. to 6d. Phone, Bolton 1300.

ROYAL CINEMA (BTP), St. George's Road.— Prop., R. C. Roy, 27, King Street West, Manchester. Phone, Blackfriars 4428. Booked at H.O. 761 seats. Daily Mats. Continuous nightly. Two changes weekly. Prices, 3d. to 1s. Phone, Bolton 1086.

THEATRE ROYAL (WE), Church Gate.—H. D. Moorhouse Circuit, 7, Oxford Road, Manchester. 1,700 seats. Booked at H.O. Continuous. Prices, 4d. to 2s. Café. Phone, No. 469. Station, Trinity Street, L.M.S.

BOOSBECK (YORKS), **Pop. 1,250.**

EMPIRE CINEMA (BTP), Skelton Road.—Lessee and Man., C. Bielby, 11, Park Lane, Guisborough. 1,000 seats. Booked at Hall. One show nightly, two on Sat. Prices, 5d. to 1s. Phone, Skelton 39. Proscenium width, 31 ft. Station, Boosbeck, L.N.E.R.

BOOTLE (LANCS.), **Pop. 76,799.**

BROADWAY CINEMA (RCA), Stanley Road.— Prop., Gaumont British Picture Corporation, Ltd., 123, Regent Street, London, W.1. Phone, Regent 8080. 1,400 seats. Booked at H.O. Continuous. Prices, 6d. to 1s. 3d. Phone, Bootle 125. Station, Lime Street.

GAINSBOROUGH (BTH), Knowsley Road.— Prop., Gainsborough (Bootle), Ltd. 700 seats. Continuous evening. Mat daily. Stage, 41 ft. wide. Prices, 4d. to 1s. Phone, Bootle 183.

IMPERIAL (WE), Stanley Road.—Prop.. Bootle Amusements, Ltd. Man. Dir., George Prince. 885 seats. Booked at Hall. Continuous. Mat. daily. Prices, 3d. to 1s. Phone, Bootle 722. Station, Lime Street (Parcels Office).

METROPOLE THEATRE (WE).—Leslie Greene Circuit. H.O., 7, Elliot Street, Liverpool. Phone, Royal 538. London Offices, 19, Charing Cross Road, W.C.2. Phone, Whi. 5504. 1,149 seats.

PALACE (WE), Marsh Lane.—Prop., Bootle Palace, Ltd. Man. Dir., George Prince. Booked at Hall. Continuous. Daily Mat. 722 seats. Two changes weekly. Phone, Bootle 17.

UNIFORM SUPPLY COMPANY, LTD.,

St. Andrew's Hall.
Strand Cinema (BA), Irlam Road.—Prop., General Theatre Corpn., Ltd., 123, Regent Street, London, W.1. Phone, Regent 6641. 975 seats. Booked at H.O. Continuous. Phone, Bootle 286. Station, Marsh Lane, L.M.S.

BORDON (Hants).
Palace.—Prop., South Downs Kinemas, Ltd., 2, Rugby Road, Southsea. Phone, Portsmouth 3456. 600 seats. Booked at H.O. Continuous. Two changes weekly. Prices, 6d. to 1s. 4d. Phone, Bordon 14. Station, Bordon, S.R. ; and Road Transport.

BOROUGH GREEN (Kent).
Borough Green Electric Theatre (Syntok).—300 seats. Pictures and variety. Prices, 6d. to 1s. 6d. Phone, Borough Green 109.

Palace (Morrison).—Prop., H. H. D. Sawdy. Once nightly. Twice Sat. Prices, 6d. to 1s. 6d. Phone, Borough Green 109. Station, Borough Green, S.R.

BOSTON (Lincs), Pop. 16,597.
New Theatre (WE), Market Place.—Prop., Boston Scala Theatre, Ltd. Reg. Office, 18. Low Pavement, Nottingham. 1,000 seats, Booked at Hall. Phone, 135. Two shows nightly. Prices, 6d. to 1s. 8d. Proscenium width, 27 ft. Stage, 30 ft. deep ; six dressing-rooms. Station, Boston, L.N.E.R.

Odeon Theatre (BTH), South Square.—Prop., Odeon (Boston), Ltd., Cornhill House, Bennett's Hill, Birmingham. Phone, Midland 2781. (In course of construction.)

Scala (WE).—Prop., Boston Scala Theatre, Ltd. H.O., 18, Low Pavement, Nottingham. 900 seats. Booked at New Theatre, Boston. Twice nightly. Two changes weekly. Mat., Thurs. and Sat. Prices, 3d. to 1s. 3d. Proscenium width, 22 ft. Cafe. Phone, Boston 135. Station, Boston, L.N.E.R.

BOURNE (Lincs), Pop. 4,889.
Tudor (BTH).—500 seats. Once nightly, twice Sat. Prices, 7d. to 1s. 4d.

BOURNE END (Bucks).
Royalty (BTH), Parade.—Prop., Charles F. Cheshir. 600 seats. Booked at Hall. Continuous. Prices, 6d. to 2s. Café. Phone, Bourne End 299. Station, Bourne End, G.W.R.

BOURNEMOUTH (Hants), Pop. 116,780.
Astoria (BTH), Boscombe.—Frank Okin, 31-33, Stoke Newington Road, London, N.16. Phone, Clissold 2700. 1,500 seats. Booked at H.O. Continuous. Prices, 9d. to 2s. Proscenium width, 26 ft. Phone, Southbourne 1425. Station, Boscombe, S.R.

C O M P T O N

ORGAN featured here

Carlton Super Cinema (WE), Christchurch Road.—Prop., Associated British Cinemas, Ltd., 30-31, Golden Square, London. Gerrard 7887. 1,650 seats. Booked at H.O. Prices, 6d. to 1s. 6d. Proscenium width, 30 ft. Cafe. Phone, Boscombe 455. Station, Boscombe, S.R.

Coronation Picture Palace (Edibell), Holden-hurst Road.—Prop., A. Clafton. 750 seats. Continuous. Two changes weekly. Prices, 6d. to 1s. 6d. Phone, Boscombe 2044.

Electric Theatre (WE), Commercial Road.—Prop., Capital and Counties Electric Theatres, Ltd. 1,187 seats. Booked at Regent, Poole. Prices, 9d. to 3s. Continuous. Café. Phone, Bournemouth 2165. Station, Bournemouth West.

**Fitted "ARDENTE" Deaf Aids
See page 258**

Grand Super Cinema (RCA), Westbourne.—Prop., Associated British Cinemas, Ltd., 30-31, Golden Square, W.1. Phone, Gerrard 7887. 995 seats. Booked at H.O. Continuous. Prices, 6d. to 1s. 6d. Cafe attached. Phone, Bournemouth 3118. Station, Bournemouth West, S.R.

Moderne (WE).—Props., Portsmouth Town Cinemas, Ltd., Shaftesbury Cinema, Portsmouth. 1,500 seats. Booked at H.O. Continuous. Prices, 6d. to 1s. 6d. Café. Phone, Winton 1234. Station, Bournemouth Central.

Odeon Theatre (BTH).—Props., Odeon (Bournemouth), Ltd., Cornhill House, Bennett's Hill, Birmingham. Phone, Midland 2781. (In course of construction.)

Palladium (BTH), Fisherman's Walk, Southbourne.—Prop., Portsmouth Town Cinemas, Ltd., Shaftesbury Cinema, Kingston Road, Portsmouth. 550 seats. Booked at H.O. Continuous. Prices, 7d. to 2s. Proscenium width, 19 ft. Phone, Southbourne 163 Station, Bournemouth Central.

Pavilion.

C O M P T O N

ORGAN featured here.

Plaza (Perfectatone), Wimborne Road, Winton.—Prop., H. P. E. Mears. 600 seats, Continuous. Two changes weekly. Prices. 6d. to 1s. 6d. Phone, Winton 790. Station, Bournemouth Central, S.R.

Regent (WE).—Prop., Provincial Cinematograph Theatres, Ltd., New Gallery House, 123, Regent Street, London, W. Phone, Regent 6641. 2,274 seats.
**Fitted "ARDENTE" Deaf Aids
See page 258**

**WURLITZER ORGAN
Installed in this Kinema**

Savoy (BTH), Christchurch Road.—Prop., M. & O, Theatres, Ltd., 31-33, Stoke Newington Road London, N.16. Phone, Clissold 1844. 700 seats. Booked at H.O. Continuous. Prices, 6d. to 2s. Proscenium width, 30 ft. Phone, Boscombe 1798. Station, Boscombe.

Victoria Cinema (WE), Wimborne Road, Winton.—Prop., Victoria Cinema (Winton), Ltd. 808 seats. Booked at Hall. Continuous. Mat., Wed. and Sat. Prices, 6d. to 1s. 6d. Proscenium width, 22 ft. Phone, Winton 75. Station, Bournemouth Central, S.R.

Westover Cinema (WE).—Prop., Associated British Cinemas, Ltd., Golden Square, London, W.1. Phone, Gerrard 7887. 1,830 seats. Booked at H.O. Continuous. Prices, 1s. to 3s. 6d. Phone, Bournemouth 433. Station, Bournemouth Central, S.R.

136 WARDOUR STREET, LONDON, W.1.

BOURNEMOUTH—Contd:

WEST'S SUPER CINEMA (WE), Shaftesbury Hall, Ltd. 940 seats. Booked at Hall. Continuous. Prices, 6d. to 2s. Café. Phone, Bournemouth 1191. Station, Bournemouth Central, S.R.

BRACKLEY (NORTHANTS), Pop. 2,181.
TOWN HALL.

BRACKNELL (BERKS), Pop. 4,000.
REGAL (RCA).—Controlled by Union Cinemas, Ltd., 15, Regent Street, London, S.W.1. Phone, Whitehall 8484. Continuous. Booked at H.O. Prices, 6d. to 1s. 6d. Phone, 204. Station, Bracknell.

VICTORIA CINEMA (AWH).—Prop., Border (Berks) Cinemas, Ltd., Crowthorne, Berks. Phone, Crowthorne 220. Booked at H.O. Continuous. Prices, 6d. to 1s. 6d. Station, Bracknell, S.R., and Films by London and Provincial Films Motor Transport Co., Ltd.

BRADFORD (YORKS), Pop. 298,041.
BIRCH LANE CINEMA (RCA), West Bowling.— Prop., Bowling Cinema Co. 750 seats. Booked at Hall by J. T. Wilcock. Continuous. Two changes weekly. Prices, 3d. to 9d. Phone, Bradford 4946. Station, Bradford, L.M.S.

CARLTON (WE), Manchester Road.—Prop., Marshfield Cinema Co., Ltd. 1,344 seats. Booked at Leeds. Continuous. Two changes weekly. Prices, 4d. to 1s. Phone, Bradford 6152. Station, Bradford.

COLISEUM (BTP), Toller Lane.—Prop., Elite Picture Houses, Ltd. Phone, Bradford 3576. 1,192 seats. Booked in Leeds or by appointment in Bradford by J. E. Anderton. Phone, Bradford 4598. Continuous. Mat., Sat. Prices, 4d. to 1s. Phone, Bradford 4919. Station, Bradford, L.M.S. and L.N.E.R. Films by Leeds and Bradford Transport Co.

CORONET PICTURE HOUSE (WE), Otley Road.— Prop., A. Harrison. 750 seats. Booked at Hall by Prop. Continuous. Prices, 4d. to 6d. Phone, Bradford 6829. Films by Road Transport.

COSY CINEMA (WE), Fair Road, Wibsey.—Prop., Marshfield Cinema Co., Ltd., Manchester Road. Phone, Bradford 6152. 761 seats. Booked at Leeds. Continuous. Prices, 4d. to 1s. Stage, 20 ft. deep. Two dressing-rooms. Phone, Low Moor 32. Station, Bradford.

COVENTRY HALL CINEMA (AWH), Wakefield Road.—Prop., Northern Cinema Co., 29, Kirkgate, Bradford. Phone, Bradford 4097. 450 seats. Booked at H.O. Continuous. Two changes weekly. Prices, 4d. to 9d. Phone, Bradford 3501. Stations, Bradford (Foster Square and Exchange), L.M.S.

ELITE PICTURE HOUSE (BTP), Toller Lane.— Prop., Elite Picture House, Ltd. 1,200 seats. Booked in Leeds or by appointment in Bradford by J. E. Anderton. Phone, Bradford 4598. Continuous, 6.30 to 10.15. Two changes weekly. Prices, 6d. to 1s. Phone, 3576. Station, Bradford, L.M.S. and L.N.E.R.

ELYSIAN PICTURE HOUSE, Lidget Green.— Lessee and Man., Greengates Cinema Co., Ltd. 400 seats. Booked at Leeds. Continuous. Prices, 4d. to 9d. Proscenium width, 16 ft. 6 in. Phone, Bradford 6139. Road Transport. Station, Great Horton, L.N.E.R.

EMPIRE SUPER CINEMA (WE), Horton Road.— Prop., Gaumont British Picture Corporation, Ltd., 123, Regent Street, W.1. Regent 8080. 1,288 seats. Continuous. Booked at H.O. Prices, 5d. to 1s. 3d. Proscenium width, 40 ft. Phone, Bradford 1788. Station, Bradford, L.M.S., and L.N.E.R., and Road Transport.

EMPRESS PICTURE HOUSE (WE), Legrams Lane.— Prop., Listerhills Cinema, Ltd. 584 seats. Res. and Booking Man., A. Meynell. Booked at Hall. Two shows nightly. Two changes weekly. Prices, 4d. to 1s. Phone, Bradford 4945. Station, Bradford, L.M.S. and L.N.E.R.

GRANGE PICTURE HOUSE (BTH), Great Horton Road.—Prop., Grange Picture House, Ltd. 1,088 seats. Booked at Hall. Continuous. Mats., Wed. and Sat. Prices, 6d. to 1s. Phone, Bradford 76. Stations, Bradford Exchange or Forster Square. Films by Road Transport.

GREENGATES CINEMA (BA).—Prop., Greengates Cinema Co., Ltd. 575 seats. Booked at Leeds. Continuous. Prices, 4d. to 1s. Proscenium width, 22 ft. Phone, Idle 249. Films by motor from Leeds.

HIPPODROME (WE).—Prop., Bradford Hippodrome (1929), Ltd. 1,537 seats. Booked at Leeds and London. Continuous. Price, 7d. Phone, Bradford 4207. Station, Bradford, L.M.S.

IDLE PICTURE HOUSE (BA).—Props., J. and F. Thornton. 500 seats. Booked at Leeds. Continuous. Prices, 4d. to 9d. Phone, Idle 144.

LOW MOOR PICTURE HOUSE (BTH), Huddersfield Road.—Prop. and Res. Man., John Lush. 538 seats. Once nightly. Twice Sat. Two changes weekly. Station, Low Moor, L.N.E.R.

LYCEUM CINEMA (WE), Bradford Lane, Laisterdyke.—Prop., Lyceum Cinema Co., Ltd, 1,112 seats. Booked at Leeds. Continuous. Two changes weekly. Prices, 4d. to 1s. Phone, 4987. Station, Laisterdyke, L.N.E.R.

MARLBORO CINEMA (BTH), Carlisle Road.— Prop., Marlboro Cinema, Ltd. 1,250 seats. Booked at Hall and at Leeds. Continuous. Two changes weekly. Phone, 5560. Stations, Bradford, L.M.S. and L.N.E.R., and Road Transport.

MORLEY STREET PICTURE HOUSE (BA).—Prop., Denman Picture Houses, Ltd., 148-150, Wardour Street, London, W.1. 1,200 seats. Booked at H.O. Continuous. Prices, 6d. to 1s. Phone, Bradford 2438. Station, Bradford—L.M.S. and L.N.E.R., and Road Transport.

NEW VICTORIA (BA).—Prop., Gaumont British Corporation, Ltd., 123, Regent Street, London, W.1. 3,500 seats. Booked at H.O.

Prices, 7d. to 2s. 6d. Proscenium width, 60 ft. Stage, 45 ft. deep; twelve dressing-rooms. Café. Ballroom. Phone, 9183-4. Station, Bradford, L.N.E.R. Exchange, L.M.S. Forster Square.
Fitted "ARDENTE" Deaf Aids
See page 258

WURLITZER ORGAN
Installed in this Kinema

ORIENTAL CINEMA (WE), Oak Lane, Manningham.—Prop., P. Richardson, 54, Haworth Road, Bradford. 704 seats. Booked at Hall. Continuous Mon. to Fri. Two shows Sat. Station, Bradford, L.M.S. and L.N.E.R.

OXFORD PICTURE HOUSE (WE), Undercliffe.—Prop., Undercliffe Picture House Co., Ltd., Dudley Hill Road, Underhill, Bradford. 650 seats. Booked at Leeds. Continuous. Mat., Wed, and Sat. Prices 4d. to 1s. Phone, Bradford 5785. Station, Bradford, L.M.S.

PICTUREDROME (BTP), Bridge Street.—Prop., Picturedrome (Bradford), Ltd. 800 seats. Booked at Leeds or by appointment in Brad, ford by J. E. Anderton. Phone, Bradford, 4598. Continuous. Prices, 5d. to 1s. Phone-Bradford 5348. Station, Bradford, L.N.E.R.

PICTURE PALACE (AWH), Dudley Hill.—400 seats.

PLAZA (WE), Cross Lane, Great Horton.—Prop., West Bradford Picture Theatres, Ltd., 20, Fountain Street, Bradford. Continuous nightly; Mat., Wed. and Sat. 787 seats. Proscenium width, 19 ft. Prices, 4d. to 1s. Phone, Bradford 4948. Station, Great Horton.

QUEEN'S HALL CINEMA (WE), Laisterdyke.—Prop. and Res. Man., H. Butler. 480 seats. Booked at Hall. Continuous. Two changes weekly. Phone, Dudley Hill 106. Station, Laisterdyke, L.N.E.R.

REGAL CINEMA (BTH), Five Lane Ends, Eccleshill.—Prop., Modern Theatres, Ltd., 26, Bond Street, Leeds. 861 seats. Phone, Leeds 24334. Booked at 10, Mill Hill, Leeds. Continuous. Prices, 3d. to 1s. Phone, Idle 402.

REGENT THEATRE (RCA), Manningham Lane—Prop., Associated British Cinemas, Ltd., 30-31, Golden Square, W.1. 1,384 seats. Booked at H.O. Continuous. Phone, Bradford 2898.

RIALTO (Harrison's), Station Road.—Prop., Roy Firth, 8, Rand Place, Bradford. Phone, Bradford 7458. 362 seats. Booked at Hall. Once nightly. Twice Sats. and holidays. Prices, 4d. to 9d. Proscenium width, 18 ft. Phone, Thornton 38. Station, Clayton.

ST. GEORGE'S HALL (WE), Bridge Street.—Prop., Denman Picture Houses, Ltd., 123, Regent Street, London, W.1. 2,196 seats. Booked at H.O. Continuous. Prices, 6d. to 1s. 6d. Phone, Bradford 1718. Station, Bradford (Exchange), L.N.E.R.

SAVOY CINEMA (WE), Darley Street.—Prop., Associated British Cinemas, Ltd., Golden Square. W.1. 1,508 seats. Booked at H.O. Continuous. Prices, 6d. to 1s. 6d. Café attached. Phone, Bradford 94. Stations, Forster Square, L.M.S. and Exchange, L.N.E.R.

TATLER PICTURE HOUSE (WE), 4, Thornton Road.—Prop., Regal Cinemas (Warrington), Ltd., 4, Grange View, Leeds. 650 seats. Booked at H.O. Continuous. Prices, 4d. to 1s. 6d. Proscenium width, 25 ft. Café attached. Phone, Bradford 3654.

TENNYSON CINEMA (WE), Otley Road.—Prop., Lyceum Cinema Co., Ltd., Laisterdyke, Bradford. 1,157 seats. Booked at Lyceum, Laisterdyke. Twice nightly. Prices, 4d. to 1s. Phone, Bradford 1133.

THEATRE ROYAL PICTURE HOUSE (WE), Manningham Lane.—Prop., Bradford Theatre Royal Picture House, Ltd. 1,312 seats. Booked at Hall. Continuous, Mon. to Fri. Three shows Sat. Prices, 9d. to 2s. Proscenium width, 32 ft. Phone, Bradford 3245-6.

THE CINEMA (BA).—Props., J. and F. Thornton, Booked at Leeds. Continuous. Matinee and two shows daily. Prices, 4d. to 9d. Phone Thornton 129. Station, Thornton, Bradford.

TIVOLI PICTURE HALL (BTH), Leeds Road.—Prop., Tivoli Picture Co. 500 seats. Booked at Leeds. Continuous. Two changes weekly. Prices, 3d. to 6d. Phone, Bradford 3728. Station, Bradford, L.M.S.

TOWERS HALL (BTP), Manchester Road.—Prop., Hibberts' Pictures, Ltd. 1,140 seats. Films booked at Hall. Continuous. Two changes weekly. Prices, 4d. to 1s. Phone, Bradford 4926. Station, Exchange (Bradford), L.N.E.R.

VICTORIA (WE), Thornton Road, Girlington. Prop., Victoria Palace (Girlington), Ltd. 1,000 seats. Booked at Hall by Man. Continuous. Prices, 5d. to 9d. Phone, Bradford 4920. Films by Road Transport.

WESTERN TALKIE THEATRE (WE), Park Road.—Prop., J. R. Whiteley. 675 seats. Continuous. Booked at Hall. Prices, 4d. to 9d. Phone, 6290. Station, Bradford, L.M.S.

WYKE HIPPODROME (BTH).—600 seats.

BRADFORD-ON-AVON (WILTS), Pop. 4,735.

ALEXANDER PICTURE THEATRE (BTH), 49A, St. Margaret Street.—Prop., Bradford-on-Avon Cinema Co., Ltd. 618 seats. Booked at Hall. Continuous. Pictures and Variety. Prices, 9d. to 1s. 3d. Stage and two dressing-rooms. Phone, Bradford-on-Avon 165. Station, Bradford-on-Avon, G.W.R., and Film Transport Service.

BRADLEY, nr. Bilston (STAFFS).

QUEEN'S PICTURE HOUSE (BTH).—Props., Wood's Picture Halls, Ltd., Wood's Palace, Bilston. Booked at H.O. Continuous. Prices, 4d. to 7d. Phone, 41025. Station, Bilston, G.W.R.

BRADWELL (DERBYSHIRE), Pop. 1,200.

MEMORIAL HALL (Magnatorque).—Prop., J. Brown and Co. 250 seats. All correspondence to R. O. Brown, 228, Fulwood Road, Sheffield. Tues. and Thurs. only. Prices, 2d. to 1s. Phone, Sheffield 61126.

BRAINTREE (Essex), **Pop. 8,912.**
CENTRAL CINEMA (WE), High Street.—Props.,
Shipman and King, M 84, Shell Méx .House,
Strand, London, W.C.2. Phone, Temple
Bar 5077. Booked at H.O. Continuous.
Mat., Sat. Prices, 6d. to 1s. 10d. Phone,
Braintree 78. Station, Braintree, L.N.E.R .
and Films by Essex Transport.
EMBASSY (WE), FairfieldRoad.—Props., Shipman
and King, M 84, Shell Mex House, Strand,
W.C.2. Phone, Temple Bar 5077. Booked at
H.O. Prices, 6d. to 2s. Stage and dressing-
rooms. Café. Phone, Braintree 78. Station,
Braintree, L.N.E.R.

BRAMLEY (near LEEDS) (Yorks), **Pop. 11,400.**
LIDO CINEMA (WE), Town Street.—Prop.,
Bramley Cinema, Ltd., 433, Leeds Road,
Dewsbury. Phone, Dewsbury 188. 374 seats.
Booked at Hall by Manager. Continuous.
twice Sat. Prices, 4d. to 1s. Phone, Stan-
ningley 71208. Station, Bramley, L.N.E.R.

BRANDON (Suffolk), **Pop. 2,500.**
AVENUE (BTH), London Road.—Prop., B. C.
Culey, Palace Cinema, Thetford. Phone,
Thetford 79. 495 seats. Once nightly.
Prices 6d. to 2s. Proscenium width 30 ft.
Stage, 12 ft. deep. Two dressing-rooms.
Phone, Brandon 36. Station, Brandon,
L.N.E.R.

BRAUNTON (Devon), **Pop. 3,500.**
PLAZA (BROWN), Exeter Road. Prop., G. A.
Drake, 37, North Street, Braunton. 492 seats.
Booked at H.O. Once nightly, continuous
Wed. two shows Sat., mat. Sat. Prices, 7d. to
1s. 6d. Proscenium width, 25 ft. Phone,
Braunton 53. Station, Braunton, S.R.
Films by Auto Services (Cardiff), Ltd.

BRENTFORD (Mddx.), **Pop. 17,039.**
QUEEN'S CINEMA (RCA), Half Acre.—Props.,
Watford Amusements, Ltd., River Plate
House, Finsbury Circus, E.C.2. 650 seats.
Met. 6282. Continuous. Prices, 6d. to
1s. 6d. Phone, Ealing 2274. Station, Brent-
ford, S.R.

BRENTWOOD (Essex), **Pop. 7,209.**
ODEON THEATRE (BTH), High Street.—Prop.,
Odeon (Brentwood), Ltd., Cornhill House,
Bennett's Hill, Birmingham. Phone, Midland
2781. (In course of construction.)
PALACE (BTP), High Street.—Props., S. Dorin
and Partners. 1,100 seats. Booked at Hall.
Continuous. Prices, 6d. to 2s. Proscenium
width, 32 ft. Café attached. Phone, Brent-
wood 64. Stations, Brentwood, L.N.E.R.
PARADE CINEMA (BTP).—Props., S. Dorin and
Partners. 600 seats. Continuous. Mats.
Wed. and Sat. Prices, 6d. to 1s. 6d. Phone,
Brentwood 96. Station, Brentwood, L.N.E.R.

BRIDGNORTH (Shropshire), **Pop. 5,151.**
PALACE THEATRE (WE).—Prop., B. & B. Cinemas
Ltd., 75, New Street, Birmingham. 650 seats.
Booked at Hall. Continuous. Prices, 7d. to
1s. 4d. Pictures and Variety ; three dressing
rooms. Dance Hall attached. Phone, Bridg-
north 125. Station, Bridgnorth, G.W.R.
RITZ.—Prop., L. Morris, 52, Shaftesbury Avenue,
London, W.1. 1,200 seats.

BRIDGWATER (Som.), **Pop. 17,139.**
ARCADE CINEMA (Mihaly).—Prop. W. Trueman
Dicken, Majestic, Burnham-on-Sea. 317
seats. Booked by Prop. Continuous. Three

shows Sat. Prices, 6d. to 1s. 3d. Phone, 368.
Station, Bridgwater.
ODEON THEATRE (BTH), Penel Orlieu.—Prop.,
Odeon (Bridgwater), Ltd., Cornhill House,
Bennett's Hill, Birmingham. Phone, Midland
2781. Booked at 49, Park Lane, London,
W.1. Contonuous. Prices 9d. to 2s.
PALACE THEATRE (BA).—Prop., Albany Ward
Theatres, Ltd. Continuous. Phone, Bridg-
water 159. Station, Bridgwater, G.W.R.
TOWN HALL (Morrison).—Lessee, W. Trueman
Dicken, Burnham-on-Sea. 700 seats. Twice
nightly. Prices, 7d. to 1s. 3d. Booked by
Lessee. Phone, Bridgwater 368. Stations,
Bridgwater, G.W.R., and Bridgwater, S.R.
(S. & D. Branch), and Road Transport.

BRIDLINGTON (Som.), **Pop. 3,500.**
PICTURE HOUSE.

BRIDLINGTON (Yorks), **Pop. 19,704.**
LOUNGE (WE).—Props., Esplanade Café, Ltd.
968 seats. Continuous during summer. Once
nightly winter. Prices, 1s. to 1s. 4d.
Proscenium width, 32 ft. Café. Phone,
2225. Station, Bridlington.
PALACE PICTURE HOUSE (BA), Prospect Street.
—Prop., Palace (Bridlington), Ltd., 3, Harts-
head, Sheffield. Phone, No. 20888. 724 seats.
Booked at H.O. Continuous evenings, season,
Mats., daily. Non-season, Mats., Tues., Thurs.
and Sat. Prices, 7d. to 1s. 4d. Proscenium
width, 30 ft. Phone, Brid. 3352. Stage and six
dressing rooms. Station, Bridlington,
L.N.E.R.
ROXY THEATRE (Eastern Electric), Quay Road.
400 seats. Evening continuous. Sat. Mat.
Prices, 6d. to 1s. Station, Bridlington.
WINTER GARDENS SUPER SOUND CINEMA (WE),
The Promenade.— Prop., Winter Gardens
(Bridlington), Ltd. 1,025 seats. Booked at
26, Park Row, Leeds, by J. F. Tidswell. Continuous summer 2.30 to 10.30, and winter 6.15
to 10.30. Mats., daily. Stage, 28 ft. deep ;
six dressing rooms. Prices, 9d. to 2s. Proscenium width, 29 ft. Phone, Bridlington
3012. Station, Bridlington, L.N.E.R.

BRIDPORT (Dorset), **Pop. 5,917.**
ELECTRIC PALACE (BTH).—Prop., Bridport
Electric Palace Co., Ltd. 600 seats. Booked
at Hall by Dirs. Continuous. Stage, 15 ft.
deep. Prices, 6d. to 2s. Station, Bridport,
G.W.R.
LYRIC CINEMA (AWH), Barrack Street.—Prop.,
H. & M. Cinemas, Ltd. Continuous. Prices,
5d. to 1s. 6d.

BRIERFIELD (Lancs), **Pop. 7,696.**
NEW STAR CINEMA (WE).—Prop., W. H. Smith.
650 seats. Booked at Manchester. Once
nightly. Three shows Sat. Occasional
Variety. Prices, 3d. to 9d. Proscenium
width, 24 ft. Stage, 15 ft. deep. Two dressing rooms. Phone, Nelson 910. Station,
Brierfield, L.M.S.

BRIERLEY HILL (Staffs), **Pop. 14,344.**
CORONET.
DANILO (RCA).—Prop., Danilo (Brierley Hill),
Ltd., 3, New Street, Birmingham. Phone,
Midland 0871. Occasional variety. 1,200
seats. Proscenium width, 34 ft. Prices, 5d.
to 1/3. Phone, Brierley Hill 7474.

Fitted "ARDENTE" Deaf Aids
See page 258

The BEST Is Cheapest; PATHE GAZETTE.

PALACE CINEMA.—Props., C. F. and M. Couper.
ODEON THEATRE (BTH), High Street.—Props., Odeon (Perry Bar), Ltd., Cornhill House, Bennett's Hill, Birmingham. Phone, Midland 2781. Booked at 49, Park Lane, London, W.1. Continuous. Prices, 5d. to 1s. Phone, Brierley Hill 7104. Station, Brierley Hill, G.W.R.
QUEEN'S HALL (Morrison).—Prop. and Res. Man., C. F. Couper. 800 seats. Two shows nightly except Fri. Two changes weekly. Prices, 2½d. to 9d. Phone, Brierley Hill 102

BRIGG (LINCS), **Pop. 4,019.**
ELECTRIC PLAYHOUSE (BA), Market Place.— W. H. Webster, Grand Theatre, Brigg. 650 seats. Booked at Grand. One show nightly. Two changes weekly. Prices, 6d. to 1s. 3d. Phone, Brigg 87. Station, Brigg, L.N.E.R.
GRAND THEATRE (BTP), Wrawby Street.—Prop., W. H. Webster. 750 seats. Booked at Hall. Once nightly, Mon. to Wed. Twice nightly, Thurs. to Sat. Prices, 4d. to 1s. 4d. Stage and three dressing-rooms. Phone, Brigg 31. Station, Brigg, L.N.E.R.

BRIGHOUSE (YORKS), **Pop. 19,756.**
ALBERT THEATRE (WE), Huddersfield Road.— Prop., Brighouse Picture House, Ltd., 5, Rawson Street, Halifax. Phone, 4414. 901 seats. Booked at Leeds by W. Slater Greenwood. Once nightly. Two changes weekly Prices, 4d. to 1s. Station, Brighouse, L.M.S

SAVOY (WE).—Prop., The Savoy Picture House Co. 680 seats. Booked at Hall. Twice nightly. Mats., Tues. and Sat. Two changes weekly. Prices, 5d. to 1s. 3d. Proscenium width, 16 ft. Phone 304. Station, Brighouse, L.M.S.

BRIGHTLINGSEA (ESSEX), **Pop. 4,145.**
EMPIRE THEATRE (BTP), Station Road.— Prop., Brightlingsea Electric Theatre, Ltd., Hall Cut. 400 Seats. Booked at H.O. Twice nightly. Two changes weekly. Prices, 6d. to 1s. Phone, Brightlingsea 2. Station, Brightlingsea, L.N.E.R.
REGAL.—Prop., Bury St. Edmund's Cinemas, Ltd., 54, Chevallier Street, Ipswich.

BRIGHTON (SUSSEX), **Pop. 147,427.**
ACADEMY THEATRE (BA), West Street.—Prop., Gaumont British Picture Corporation, Ltd., 123, Regent Street, London, W.1. Phone, Regent 8080. 1,000 Seats. Booked at H.O. Continuous. Prices, 6d. to 1s. 6d. Proscenium width, 30 ft. Café attached. Phone, Brighton 359511. Station, Brighton. S.R.
ARCADIA CINEMA, Lewes Road.—500 seats. Continuous. Three changes weekly. Mats. Prices, 5d. to 1s. Phone, Brighton 5197. Station, Brighton (Central), S.R.
ASTORIA (WE), Gloucester Place.—Prop., Associated British Cinemas, Ltd., 30-31, Golden Square, London, W.1. Phone, Gerrard, 7887. 2,000 seats. Films and Variety. Booked at H.O. Continuous. Prices, 1s. to 2s. 6d. Proscenium width, 42 ft. Stage, 20 ft. deep. Four dressing rooms. Café Restaurant attached. Phone, Brighton 6685. Station, Brighton, S.R.
**Fitted "ARDENTE" Deaf Aids
See page 258**

COMPTON
ORGAN featured here.

CINEMA DE LUXE (WE), 150, North Street.— Prop., T. Easten Rutherford. 529 seats. Booked at Hall. Continuous. Prices, 9d. to 2s. Phone, Brighton 3048. Station, Brighton, S.R.
COURT PICTURE THEATRE (RCA), New Road.— Prop., Majestic (Brighton), Ltd. 1,200 seats. Booked at Hall. Continuous. Prices, 6d. to 2s. Proscenium width, 34 ft. Phone, Brighton 2266. Station, Brighton (Central), S.R.
CURZON KINEMA (RCA), Western Road.—Props., Regal Cinema Co. Booked at 10-12, Cork Street, W.1. 600 seats. Prices, 9d. to 2s. Phone, Brighton 2841.
DUKE OF YORK'S THEATRE (BTH), Preston Circus.—Prop., Sussex Picturedrome Co., Ltd., 115, Western Road, Brighton. 830 seats. Gen. Man., H. E. Jordan. Sec., H. C. Evans, F.C.R.A. Continuous. Three changes weekly. Prices, 6d. to 2s. Phone, Brighton 2503. Station, Brighton (Central), S.R.
GAIETY.—Prop., R. E. Richards, Picturedrome, Eastbourne.
GRAND (WE), North Road.—Props., Universal Entertainments, Ltd., 46, Gerrard Street, London, W.1. Phone, Gerrard 1435. 1,140 seats. Booked at H.O. Continuous. Prices, 6d. to 1s. 4d. Proscenium width, 32 ft. Stage, 30 ft. deep. 8 dressing rooms. Phone 3627.
HIPPODROME.—1,500 seats.
KINGSCLIFF CINEMA, Kemp Town.—Prop., L. R. Fellows. 370 seats. Continuous. Three changes weekly. Prices, 4d. to 1s. Proscenium width, 21 ft. Phone, Brighton 1348. Station, Brighton, S.R.
ODEON THEATRE (BTH), Kemp Town.—Prop., Odeon (Kemp Town), Ltd. Cornhill House, Bennett's Hill, Birmingham. Phone, Midland 2781. Prices, 6d. to 1s. 6d. Continuous. Booked at 49, Park Lane, London, W.1. Proscenium width, 42 ft. Variety every Friday. Phone, Brighton 6792.
ODEON (WE), 85, King's Road.—Prop., Odeon (Brighton), Ltd. Cornhill House. Bennett's Hill, Birmingham. Phone, Midland 2781. Booked at 49, Park Lane, London, W.1. Continuous. Prices, 1s. to 2s. 4d. Phone, Brighton 3235. Café attached. Station, Brighton, S.R.
PRINCES CINEMA (WE), North Street.—Prop., Dan Benjamin, 30, Brunswick Square, Hove. Phone, Hove 3818. 550 seats. Booked at Hall. Continuous. Prices, 6d. to 2s. Phone, Brighton 3563. Station, Brighton (Central), S.R. and Brighton Film Transport.
PRINCES HALL (Phillips), Aquarium. Prop., Brighton Corporation. 1,520 seats. Pictures, Concerts, Dance, Lectures. Prices, 7d. to 2s. 4d. Stage, 24 ft. deep; two dressing-rooms. Phone, Brighton 2094. Proscenium width, 28 ft. Café and Bar attached.
REGENT (WE), Queen's Road.—Prop., Gaumont British Picture Corporation and Provincial Cinematograph Theatres, Ltd., New Gallery House, 123, Regent Street, London, W.1. Phone, Regent 8080. 2020 seats. Booked at H.O. Continuous. Prices, 1s. to 3s. 6d. Restaurants, Café and Dance Hall attached. Phone, Brighton 1120 and Restaurant 1140. Station, Brighton, S.R.
**Fitted "ARDENTE" Deaf Aids
See page 258**

**WURLITZER ORGAN
Installed in this Kinema**

Put Pep into Programmes With PATHE PICTORIAL.

BRIGHTON—Contd.

SAVOY (WE), East Street.—Prop., Associated British Cinemas, Ltd., 30-31, Golden Square. London, W.1. Phone, Gerrard 7887. 2630 seats. Booked at H.O. Continuous. Prices, 1s. to 2s. 6d. Proscenium width, 34 ft. Café, Restaurant and Dance Hall attached. Phone, Brighton 2156-7. Station, Brighton (Central), S.R.

COMPTON
ORGAN featured here.

TROXY CINEMA (BTP), North Road.—Prop., George Howe. 400 seats. Prices, 4d. to 1s. 6d. Phone, Brighton 4889. Station, Brighton (Central), S.R.

BRINSCALL (nr. **Chorley**) (LANCS.), **Pop. 3,500.**

BEAVER'S PICTURE HOUSE (Imperial).—Prop., M. Walsh, 63, East Park Road, Blackburn. Phone No. 4005. 275 seats. One show nightly. Two changes weekly. Prices, 6d. to. 1s. Phone No. 55. Station, Brinscall, L.M.S.

BRISTOL (GLOS.), **Pop. 396,918.**

AMBASSADOR.—Bedminster. Booked by London & Southern Super Cinemas, Ltd., 32, Shaftesbury Avenue, London, W.1

ASHTON CINEMA (Mihaly), 275, North Street, Bedminster. — Prop., Atkinson's Pictures, 9, North Road, St. Andrews, Bristol. Phone, Bristol 44190. 480 seats. Continuous. Prices, 6d. to 1s. Phone, Bristol 63018. Station, Temple Meads, G.W.R.

BATHS CINEMA (BTH).—800 seats. (Closed.)

BRISLINGTON PICTURE HOUSE (Mihaly), Sandy Park Road.—Props., G. I. and K. L. Tomkins. 434 seats. Continuous. Two changes weekly. Prices, 5d. to 1s. Phone, Bristol 76990. Station, Temple Meads, G.W.R.

CABOT (RCA), Filton.—Props., Associated British Cinemas, Ltd., 30-31 Golden Square, London, W.1. Phone, Gerrard 7887. Booked at H.O. Continuous nightly. Daily Mat. Prices, 6d. to 1s. 3d. Phone, Filton 100. Station, Filton.

CARLTON KINEMA (BA).—Prop., George Allen (Bristol), Ltd. Booked at His Majesty's, Eastville, Bristol. Continuous. Prices, 9d. to 1s. 6d. Café attached. Phone, Westbury 67021. Station, Shirehampton, G.W.R.

CHARLTON CINEMA (WE), Charlton Road, Keynsham.—Prop., Keynsham Picture House, Ltd. Phone, Keynsham 110. 880 seats. Booked at Town Hall, Bedminster. Continuous. Prices, 6d. to 1s. 6d. Proscenium width 30 ft. Stage 20 ft. deep; four dressing rooms. Station, Keynsham, G.W.R.

CINEMA (Edibell), High Street, Portishead.—Prop., S. W. Durlins. 400 seats. Once nightly. Prices, 7d. to 1s. Films by Transport Service.

CINEMA HALL, Severn Beach. (Closed.)

COLSTON HALL.—Prop., Bristol Corporation. 2,500 seats. Booked at Hall. Occasional shows. Café attached. Proscenium width, 60 ft. Stage, 30 ft. deep; six dressing rooms. Phone, Bristol 22957. Station, Temple Meads, G.W.R.

EASTVILLE HIPPODROME (BA), Stapleton Road. —Prop., Eastville Hippodrome Co., Ltd., 424, Stapleton Road. Man. Dir., George Allen. 650 seats. Booked at H.O. Con-

tinuous. Mat. daily. Three separate performances Sat. Prices, 6d. to 1s. 3d. Phone, Bristol 56738. Station, Stapleton Road, G.W.R.

EMBASSY CINEMA (WE), Queen's Avenue.—Prop., Avenue Cinema Co., Ltd., 10, Windsor Place, Cardiff. Phone, Cardiff 225. 2,100 seats. Booked at H.O. Continuous. Prices, 9d. to 2s. Café attached. Phone, Bristol 22940. Stations, Temple Meads, G.W.R., and Film Transport.

Fitted "ARDENTE" Deaf Aids
See page 258

EMPIRE (RGA).—Props., Associated British Cinemas, Ltd., 30-31, Golden Square, W.1. 1,900 seats. Booked at H.O. Continuous. Prices, 6d. to 1s. 6d. Proscenium width, 33 ft. Stage, 34 ft. deep. 12 dressing rooms. Phone, Bristol 22251. Stations, L.M.S. and G.W.R.

GAIETY (BTP), Wells Road.—Prop. and Man. F. G. W. Chamberlain. Continuous. Prices 6d. to 1s. 3d. Dance Hall attached. Station Temple Meads, G.W.R.

GLOBE PICTURE THEATRE (WE), Lawrence Hill.—Props., Exors. of late J. Pugsley. 1,128 seats. Booked at Hall. Continuous. Mat. daily. Two changes weekly. Prices, 6d. to 1s. 6d. Phone, Bristol 57017. Station, Lawrence Hill, G.W.R.

GRANADA (WE), Church Road, Redfield.—Prop., Exors. of Joseph Pugsley, Lawrence Hill, Bristol. 767 seats. Booked at Globe Picture house. Continuous. Mats daily. Prices, 6d. to 1s. 6d. Phone, Bristol 56235. Station. Lawrence Hill, G.W.R.

HIPPODROME (WE), East Street, Bedminster.— Prop., Stoll Offices, Coliseum Buildings, London, W.C.2. Phone, Temple Bar 1500. 1,887 seats. Booked at H.O. Continuous. Stage, 20 ft. deep. Proscenium width, 38 ft. Prices, 5d. to 1s. 4d. Phone, 63360. Station, Temple Meads, G.W.R. and L.M.S.

HIPPODROME (WE).—St. Augustine's Parade Hippodrome (Bristol), Ltd., Coliseum Buildings, St. Martin's Lane, W.C.2. Temple Bar 1500. 2,000 seats. Booked at H.O. Prices, 6d. to 2s. Proscenium width, 48 ft. Café. Phone, Bristol 23077 and 24342. Station, Temple Meads, G.W.R.

Fitted "ARDENTE" Deaf Aids
See page 258

HIS MAJESTY'S (WE), Stapleton Road, Eastville.—Prop., Eastville Hippodrome Co., Ltd., 424, Stapleton Road. 1,200 seats. Booked at H.O. Continuous. Prices, 6d. to 1s. 6d. Phone, Bristol 56738. Station, Stapleton Road, G.W.R.

HOTWELL'S CINEMA (Mihaly), Hotwell Road.— Prop., Atkinson Pictures, 9, North Road, St. Andrews, Bristol. 350 seats. Booked at Town Hall, Bedminster. Twice nightly. Prices, 5d. to 9d. Station, Temple Meads, G.W.R.

KING'S CINEMA (WE), Old Market Street.— Prop., Associated British Cinemas, Ltd., 30/31, Golden Square, W.1. 1,485 seats. Booked at H.O. Continuous. Prices, 7d. to 2s. Tea room attached. Station, Bristol (Temple Meads), G.W.R.

KINGSWAY KINEMA (BTP), Two Mile Hill.— Props., T. Burnham and G. H. England. 600 seats. Booked at Hall. Continuous. Nightly.

Mat., Wed. and Sat. Prices, 7d. to 1s. 4d. Phone, Kingswood 73273. Station, Lawrence Hill, G.W.R.

KNOWLE PICTURE HOUSE (Edibell).—Prop. and Res. Man., F. G. W. Chamberlain. 600 seats. Booked at Gaiety, Knowle. Continuous. Two changes weekly. Prices, 6d. to 1s. 3d. Phone, Bristol 76224. Station, Temple Meads, G.W.R.

MAGNET CINEMA THEATRE (Edibell), St. Paul's. —Prop., W. S. Chamberlain, " Cerne Abbas," Down Road, Redcliffe Bay, Portishead. 750 seats. Booked at residence by appointment. Continuous. Two changes weekly. Prices, 3d. to 1s. Station, Temple Meads, G.W.R.

MÉTROPOLE CINEMA (WE), Ashley Road.— Prop., Eastville Hippodrome Co., Ltd., 424, Stapleton Road, Eastville, Bristol. Phone, Bristol 56738. 564 seats. Booked at H.O. Continuous. Prices, 6d. to 1s. 3d. Phone, Bristol 57357. Station, Stapleton Road, G.W.R.

NEW PALACE (RCA), Baldwin Street.—Prop., Gaumont British Picture Corporation, Ltd., 123, Regent Street, London, W.1. Phone, Regent 8080. Booked at H.O. Continuous Café attached. Prices, 1s. to 2s. Phone, Bristol 25882I. Station, Temple Meads, Bristol, G.W.R.

NEWS THEATRE (BTH).—Prop., Jacey Cinemas, Ltd., 1, Waterloo Street, Birmingham. Phone, Midland 4538. 400 seats. Continuous Phone Bristol 23338.

ODEON THEATRE (WE), Cr. Union Street and Broadmead.—Prop., Odeon (Bristol) Ltd., Cornill House, Bennett's Hill, Birmingham. Phone, Midland 2781. (In course of construction).

OLYMPIA (WE), Carey's Lane.—Prop., S. H. Justin. 870 seats. Continuous. Two changes weekly. Phone, Bristol 24975. Station, Temple Meads, G.W.R.

PARK CINEMA (WE), St. George.—Prop., Associated British Cinemas, Ltd., 30/31, Golden Square, London, W.1. 1,000 seats. Booked at H.O. Continuous evenings. Daily mat. Two changes weekly. Prices, 4d. to 1s. Proscenium width, 24 ft. Phone, Bristol 57648. Station, Lawrence Hill, G.W.R.

PLAZA (WE), Cheltenham Road.—Prop., Atkinsons Pictures, Ltd., 9, North Road, St. Andrews, Bristol. 457 seats. Continuous. Two changes weekly. Prices, 7d. to 1s. Phone, Bristol 250831.

PREMIER CINEMA THEATRE (WE), Gloucester Road.—Prop., S. H. Justin. 980 seats. Continuous. Two changes weekly. Phone, Bristol 24975. Station, Montpelier, G.W.R.

REDCLIFEE CINEMA (Mihaly), Redcliffe Hill.— Prop., Harold A. Teed. 500 seats. Booked at Hall. Continuous. Prices, 4d. to 9d. Phone, Bristol 23104. Station, Bristol (Temple Meads, G.W.R.

REGAL CINEMA (BA), Staple Hill.—Prop.,Herbert Wren, Riebesk House, Staple Hill. 978 seats. Continuous. Daily mat. Booked at Hall. Prices, 6d. to 1s. 6d. Proscenium width, 29 ft. Stage, 12 ft. Café. Phone, Fishponds 215. Station, Stapleton Road, G.W.R.

REGENT (WE).—Props., Provincial Cinematograph Theatres, Ltd., New Gallery House, 123, Regent Street, London, W.1. Phone, Regent 8080. 2,050 seats. Pictures and Variety.

Booked at H.O. Continuous. Prices, 7d. to 2s. 6d. Stage, 30 ft. deep ; 5 dressing-rooms. Café attached. Phone, Bristol 20141I. Station, Temple Meads, Bristol, G.W.R. and L.M.S.

Fitted "ARDENTE" Deaf Aids
See page 258

WURLITZER ORGAN
Installed in this Kinema

REGENT PICTURE HOUSE (BTH), Kingswood.— Props., G. Rees and A. B. Atkinson. 645 seats. Booked at Hall. Continuous. Prices, 6d. to 1s. 3d. Proscenium width, 22 ft. Station, Lawrence Hill, G.W.R.

RITZ (WE).—Controlled by Union Cinemas, Ltd., Union House, 15, Regent Street, London, S.W.1. Phone, Whitehall 8484. Continuous. Booked at H.O. Station, Temple Meads. G.W. Rly.

SAVOY KINEMA (WE), Station Road, Shirehampton.—Prop., Shirehampton Cinema Co., Ltd., 5, Whiteladies Road, Bristol. Phone, Bristol 33368. 982 seats. Booked at 5, Whiteladies Road, Bristol. Continuous. Prices 6d. to 1s. 4d. Phone, Avonmouth 4. Station, Shirehampton, G.W.R.

SCALA CINEMA (WE), Zetland Road.—Prop., Atkinsons Pictures, Ltd., 9, North Road, St. Andrews, Bristol. 750 seats. Continuous. Two changes weekly. Prices, 7d. to 1s. 4d. Phone, Bristol 44190. Station, Montpelier, G.W.R.

TOWN HALL KINEMA (RCA), Bedminster.—Prop., Atkinsons Pictures, Ltd., 9, North Road, St. Andrews, Bristol. 600 seats. Three times daily. Prices, 6d. to 1s. Phone, Bristol 63018. Stations, Temple Meads, L.M.S. and G.W.R.

TRIANGLE HALL (WE), Clifton.—Props., Associated British Cinemas Ltd., 30-31, Golden Lane, London, W.1. Phone, Gerrard 7887. Booked at H.O. 1,336 seats. Continuous. Prices, 6d. to 1s. 3d. Café attached. Phone, Bristol 25012. Station, Temple Meads, Bristol, G.W.R.

VANDYCK PICTURE HOUSE (WE), Fishponds.— Prop., Associated British Cinemas, Ltd., 30-31, Golden Square, London, W.1. Phone, Gerrard 7887. Booked at H.O. 1,173 seats. Continuous. Prices, 6d. to 1s. 3d. Proscenium width, 35 ft. Phone, Fishponds 2. Station, Stapleton Road, G.W.R.

VESTRY HALL (RCA), Pennywell Road.—Prop., Atkinsons Pictures, Ltd., 9, North Road, St. Andrews, Bristol. 560 seats. Booked at Town Hall. Two shows nightly. Prices, 4d. to 9d. Phone, Bristol 5018. Station, Lawrence Hill, G.W.R.

VICTORIA ROOMS, Clifton.—Props., University of Bristol. Occasional shows. Prices, 1s. 2d. to 3s. 6d. Phone, Bristol 2560. Station, Clifton Down, G.W.R.

WHITELADIES PICTURE HOUSE (WE), Clifton.— Prop., Associated British Cinemas, Ltd., 30-31, Golden Square, W.1. Phone, Gerrard 7887. 1,320 seats. Booked at H.O. Continuous. Prices, 1s. to 1s. 6d. Proscenium width, 30 ft. Phone, Bristol 33640. Café and Ballroom attached. Station, Temple Meads, Bristol, G.W.R.

BRISTON (NORFOLK).
CINEMA.—Tuesdays and Saturdays only.

PATHETONE WEEKLY, The Super Screen Magazine !

BRIXHAM (DEVON), **Pop. 8,147.**
ELECTRIC THEATRE (Picturetone).—Prop., Electric Theatre (Brixham), Ltd. Man. Dir., A. O. Ellis. 500 seats. Booked at "Homeside," Higher Warberry, Torquay. Phone, Torquay 2895. Continuous. Prices, 6d. to 1s. 6d. Station, Brixham, G.W.R.

BROADSTAIRS (KENT), **Pop. 12,748.**
PICTURE HOUSE (BTH).—Prop., Broadstairs Picture House, Ltd. 700 seats. Booked at Hall. Continuous. Prices, 6d. to 1s. 6d. Phone, Broadstairs 86. Films by Kent Film Transport Co.
ROYALTY (WE), York Street.—Prop., Odeon (Broadstairs), Ltd., Cornhill House, Bennett's Hill, Birmingham. Midland 2781. Booked at 49, Park Lane, London, W.1. Continuous, Prices, 6d. to 2s. Phone, Broadstairs 12. Station, Broadstairs, S.R.

BROMHILL (NORTHUMBERLAND).
ELECTRIC THEATRE (AWH).—Props., T. Gibson and J. Bell. 350 seats. Prices, 6d. and 9d. Once nightly, Mon. and Fri. Twice Sat. Own Carrier.

BROMLEY (KENT), **Pop. 45,348.**
GAUMONT (BA) High Street.—Props., Gaumont British Picture Corpn., Ltd., New Gallery House, Regent Street, W.1. 2,498 seats. Continuous. Pictures and Variety. Booked at H.O. Prices, 9d. to 2s. 6d. Café. Station, Bromley South.
Fitted "ARDENTE" Deaf Aids
See page 258

COMPTON
ORGAN featured here.

GRAND THEATRE (WE), High Street.—Prop., G.-B. Picture Corporation, Ltd., New Gallery House, Regent Street, W.1. 1,095 seats. Continuous, daily 2.45 to 10.30. Two changes weekly. Pictures and Variety. Phone, Ravensbourne 3849. Station, South Bromley, S.R.
ODEON THEATRE (BTH), The Mart.—Props., Odeon (Bromley), Ltd., Bennett's Hill, Birmingham. Booked at 49, Park Lane, London, W.1. Phone, Midland 2781. Continuous. Prices, 6d. to 2s. Phone, Ravensbourne 4425. Station, Bromley North.
PALAIS DE LUXE CINEMA (WE) High Street.—Prop., Denman Picture Houses, Ltd. 881 seats. Continuous. Daily mat. Phone, Ravensbourne 1406. Station, North Bromley.
SPLENDID (BTH), Bromley Road. Prop., Super Cinemas, Ltd., 36/37, Queen Street, E.C.4. Phone, Central 9156. 2,231 seats. Occasional Variety. Booked at H.O. Prices, 6d. to 2s. Proscenium width 40 ft. Phone, Hither Green 2000. Café. Station, Grove Park (S.R.) ; Road Transport.

BROMSGROVE (WORCS), **Pop. 9,520.**
CATSHILL CINEMA, Stourbridge Road. Once nightly. Station, Bromsgrove.
PLAZA (WE), Church Street.—Prop., Thomas McDermott, Ltd. 920 seats. Booked at Hall. Continuous. Prices, 6d. to 1s. 6d. Stage, 23 ft. deep. Proscenium width, 31 ft. Phone, Bromsgrove 28. Station, Bromsgrove, L.M.S.
REGAL (BTP), Worcester Street.—Prop., T. McDermott, Ltd. 500 seats. Continuous

evening. Mats., Mon. and Thurs. Prices, 6d. to 1s. 3d. Proscenium width, 22 ft. Stage, 14 ft. deep. Phone, Bromsgrove 28. Station, Bromsgrove, L.N.E.R.

BROMYARD (HEREFORDSHIRE), **Pop. 1,571.**
PLAZA TALKIE THEATRE (AWH and Edibell), New Road.—Prop., B. Longfield. Booked at Hall. Continuous evenings. Mats., Thurs. and Sat. Prices, 7d. to 1s. 6d. Proscenium width, 17 ft. Phone 67. Station, Bromyard, G.W.R.

BROTTON (YORKS), **Pop. 4,425.**
GRAND CINEMA (AWH).—Prop., Thomas Lord. 400 seats. Pictures and occasional Variety. Booked at Hall. Once nightly ; twice Sat. Prices, 3d. to 8d. Stage, 9 ft. deep ; 2 dressing-rooms. Station, Brotton, L.N.E.R., and by Film Carrier.

BROWNHILLS (STAFFS), **Pop. 18,368.**
PALACE (Melotone).—Props., S. J. Bray and W. F. W. Davies. 550 seats. One show daily, two on Sats. Mat., Sat. Two changes weekly. Prices, 4d., 5d. and 9d. Station, Brownhills, L.M.S.
REGENT PICTURE HOUSE (Marshall).—Props., S. J. Bray and W. F. W. Davies. 700 seats. Continuous evenings, three shows on Sat. Prices, 4d. to 1s.

BUCKFASTLEIGH (DEVON), **Pop. 2,400.**
PICTURE HOUSE (Mihaly).—Prop., W. Pickles, Station Road, Buckfastleigh. 270 seats. Once nightly. Mat. Sat. Prices, 6d. to 1s. 6d. Booked at Hall. Station, Buckfastleigh, G.W.R.

BUCKINGHAM (BUCKS), **Pop. 3,082.**
CHANDOS (BTP), London Road.—Prop., W. O. Parker. 450 seats. Booked at Hall. Once nightly, Tues., Wed. and Fri. Two shows, Mon., Thurs. and Sat. Mat., Sat. Proscenium width, 26 ft. Prices, 6d. to 1s. 3d. Phone, Buckingham 196. Station, Buckingham, L.M.S.
ELECTRIC CINEMA (Morrison).—Closed.

BUDE (with Stratton), (CORNWALL), **Pop. 3,836.**
PICTURE HOUSE (BTH).—Prop., Bude Picture House, Ltd. 614 seats. Booked at Hall. Continuous. Two changes weekly. Prices, 6d. to 1s. 6d. Phone, Bude 16. Station, Bude.
Fitted "ARDENTE" Deaf Aids
See page 258

BUDLEIGH SALTERTON (DEVON), **Pop. 3,160.**
CARLTON CINEMA (WE).

BULFORD (WILTS), **Pop. 3,797.**
GARRISON THEATRE, Bulford.—Managers, A. N. Kendal, Ltd. 674 seats. Booked at 73, North Walls, Winchester. Prices, 7d. to 1s. 3d. Proscenium width, 20 ft. Station, Bulford, S.R.
GARRISON THEATRE (BTP), Larkhill.—Managers, A. N. Kendal, Ltd., Hippodrome, Tidworth, Andover. Prices 6d. to 1s. 6d.

BULWELL (NOTTS), **Pop. 18,508.**
HIGHBURY CINEMA (WE).—Prop., Highbury Cinema, Ltd. 903 seats. Booked at Hall. Continuous. Mat. Mon., Thurs. and Sat. Prices, 5d. to 1s. Phone, Bulwell 113.
OLYMPIA (Picturetone).—Prop., Bulwell Pictures and Variety Co., Ltd. Head office, Bank

Yard, Bulwell. Man. Dir., Hy. J. Widdowson. 900 seats. Booked at H.O. Continuous. Prices, 6d. to 1s. 3d. Phone Bulwell 78031.
PALACE (Picturetone), Main Street.—Prop., Bulwell Pictures and Variety Co., Ltd. Head Office, Bank Yard, Bulwell. Man. Dir., Hy. J. Widdowson. 800 seats. Booked at H.O. Two shows nightly. Two changes weekly. Prices, 6d. to 1s. Phone, Bulwell 78438. Station, Bulwell, L.M.S.

BUNGAY (SUFFOLK), **Pop. 3,098.**
NEW THEATRE (BTP).—Prop., J. C. Walton. 300 seats. Booked at Hall by Prop. One show nightly. Three Sat. Stage, 15 ft. deep. Prices, 9d. to 1s. 6d. Station, Bungay, L.N.E.R. Films by East Anglian Film Transport.

BUNTINGFORD (HERTS), **Pop. 4,927.**
COSY CINEMA (Morrison).—Prop., Touring Talking Picture Co., Chase Avenue, King's Lynn. Phone, King's Lynn 2335. Once nightly. Continuous Sat. Prices, 6d. to 1s. 6d. Proscenium width, 18 ft.

BURGESS HILL (SUSSEX), **Pop. 5,975.**
SCALA CINEMA, Cyprus Road.—Prop., P. C. Bingham. 458 seats. Pictures and Variety. Continuous. Prices, 9d. to 2s. Stage, 17 ft. deep. Two dressing rooms. Phone, Burgess Hill 137. Station, Burgess Hill, S.R., and by Transport.

BURNHAM MARKET (NORFOLK).
COSY CINEMA (Imperial).—Props., East Coast Cinemas, Ltd., Church Lane, Mildenhall, Suffolk. Phone, Mildenhall 81. 230 seats. Booked by D. F. Bostock, 54, Chevalier Street, Ipswich. Once nightly in summer. Winter, Thurs., Fri., one show; two on Sat. Prices, 9d. to 1s. 6d. Phone, Wells 33. Films by Road Transport to Wells.

BURNHAM-ON-CROUCH (ESSEX). **Pop. 3,395.**
PRINCES CINEMA (BTP), High Street.—Prop., Francis Bertram, "Rio," Canvey Island. 500 seats. Booked at H.O. Once nightly. Prices, 6d. to 1s. 6d. Proscenium width, 20 ft. Phone, Burnham-on-Crouch 97. Stage, 14 ft. deep. Station, Burnham-on-Crouch, L.N.E.R.

BURNHAM-ON-SEA (SOMERSET), **Pop. 5,120.**
MAJESTIC PICTURE HOUSE (Morrisons).—Prop., W. Trueman Dicken. 650 seats. Booked at Hall. Twice nightly. One Mat. Two changes weekly. Prices, 6d. to 1s. 3d. Phone, Burnham 107. Station, Burnham-on-Sea, Somerset, G.W.R., and S. and D.R. Films by Road Transport.

RITZ.—Prop., W. Trueman Dicken. Continuous. Prices, 5d. to 2s. Phone, Burnham 107. Station, Burnham, G.W.R.

BURNLEY (LANCS), **Pop. 98,259.**
ALHAMBRA PICTURE THEATRE (WE).—Prop., Alhambra (Burnley), Ltd. 1,300 seats. Two shows daily. Three on Sat. Booked at Hall. Prices, 4d. to 10d. Phone, Burnley, 2765. Station, Burnley Barracks, L.M.S.
ANDREWS PICTURE HOUSE (BTH), Church Institute.—Prop., J. Livesey Cook. 1,000 seats. Once nightly. Mat. Tues. and Sat. Phone Burnley 2577. Station, Burnley.

COLISEUM CINEMA (RCA).—Prop., Harold Ward, 6, Brown Street, Manchester. 850 seats. Booked at H.O. One show nightly, two Sat. Prices, 4d. to 9d. Phone, Burnley 2876. Station, Rosegrove, L.M.S.
EMPIRE THEATRE (WE), St. James Street.—Prop., New Empire (Burnley), Ltd., Newgate Chambers, Rochdale. Phone No. 3212. 1,808 seats. Three shows daily. Booked at Rochdale. Prices, 6d. to 1s. 3d. Phone, Burnley 2453. Station, Bank Top, L.M.S.
EMPRESS CINEMA (WE), Sandygate.—Prop., New Empire (Burnley), Ltd., Newgate Chambers, Rochdale. 1,376 seats. Booked at Manchester. One show nightly, two Sat. Two changes weekly. Prices, 4d. to 9d. Proscenium width, 24 ft. Phone, Burnley, 2827. Station, Burnley Barracks, L.M.S.
GRAND CINEMA (WE), St. James Street.—Props., New Empires (Burnley), Ltd., St. James Street, Burnley. 916 seats. Booked at Manchester. Three shows daily. Prices, 6d. to 1s. 3d. Proscenium width, 17¼ ft. Phone, Burnley 3632. Station, Burnley Bank Top, L.M.S.
IMPERIAL PICTURE HOUSE (BTP), Redruth Street.—Prop., New Empire (Burnley), Ltd 950 seats. Booked at Hall. Once nightly, twice Sat. Prices, 5d. to 9d. Phone, Burnley 3933. Station, Burnley Barracks, L.M.S.
MAJESTIC (BTP).—Props, Stoneyholme Picture-drome, Ltd., Brougham Street. Phone, Burnley 2777. 800 seats. Once nightly. Booked at Manchester. Prices, 4d. to 7d. Proscenium width, 27 ft. Station, Bank Top.
NEW KINGS (BTP), Thorne Street.—Prop., M. Palmer. 450 seats. Booked at Hall. Once nightly. Mats., Tues. and Thurs. Twice Sat. Prices, 3d. to 6d. Proscenium width, 21 ft. Phone, Burnley 2847. Station, Bank Top, Burnley, L.M.S.
ODEON THEATRE (BTH), Greensmith Lane.—Props., Odeon (Burnley), Ltd., Bennett's Hill, Birmingham. Phone, Midland 2781. Booked at 49, Park Lane, London, W.1. (In course of construction.)
PALACE (WE).—Prop., Associated British Cinemas, Ltd., Golden Square, W.1. Phone, Gerr. 7887. 1,600 seats. Booked at H.O. Continuous. Prices, 4d. to 1s. 3d. Stage, 32 ft. deep; 12 dressing rooms. Proscenium width, 32 ft. Station, Burnley, Bank Top, L.M.S.
PENTRIDGE CINEMA (WE), Oxford Road.—Props., New Empire (Burnley), Ltd. 1,189 seats. Three shows daily. Prices, 4d. to 1s. Phone, Burnley 3048. Stations, Bank Top or Burnley Barracks, L.M.S.
PRIMROSE BANK INSTITUTE (BTP), County Borough of Burnley. Phone, 2195. 350 seats.
RITZ (WE).—Controlled by Union Cinemas, Ltd., Union House, 15, Regent Street, London, S.W.1. Films and Variety. Prices, 6d. to 2s. Continuous. Booked at H.O. Station, Burnley, L.M.S.
ROYAL (BTP), Robinson Street.—Prop., New Empire (Burnley), Ltd. 600 seats, Two changes weekly. Popular prices.
SAVOY CINEMA (WE).—Prop., New Empire Burnley), Ltd. 1,004 seats. Three shows daily. Four on Sat. Booked at Manchester.

BURNLEY—Contd.
Prices, 6d. to 1s. 3d. ; boxes, 7s. 6d. Café attached. Phone, 2519. Station, Bank Top or Manchester Road, L.M.S.
TEMPERANCE CINEMA (BTP), Parker Lane.— Prop., New Empire (Burnley), Ltd., Empress Cinema, Sandygate, Burnley. Phone, 2453. 900 seats. Booked at Manchester. One show nightly. Mat., Tues., and Sat. Prices, 3d. to 6d. Proscenium width, 24 ft. Phone, Burnley 3655. Station, Burnley, Bank Top, L.M.S.
TIVOLI PICTURE HOUSE (WE), Colne Road.— Prop., New Empire (Burnley), Ltd. 1,097 seats. Three shows nightly. Two changes weekly. Phone, Burnley 2726. Station, Bank Top, L.M.S.

BURNOPFIELD (Co. DURHAM), Pop. 13,000.
DERWENT PAVILION (BTH).—600 seats. Twice nightly. Prices, 3d. to 9d. Phone, Burnopfield 349. Station, Rowlands Gill, L.N.E.R.
GRAND (Edibell).—550 seats. Two shows nightly. Two changes weekly. Station, Rowlands Gill, L.N.E.R.

BURSCOUGH BRIDGE (LANCS), Pop. 3,167.
CINEMA (Electrocord).—Prop., John R. Horrocks. 500 seats. Station, Burscough Junction, L.M.S.

BURSLEM (STAFFS.), Pop. 42,450.
COLISEUM (WE).—Prop., Gaumont British Picture Corporation, Ltd., 123, Regent Street, London, W.1. 1,790 seats. Booked at H.O. Continuous. Prices, 6d. to 1s. 8d. Phone, Stoke-on-Trent 11. Station, Burslem, L.M S.

C O M P T O N
ORGAN featured here.

GLOBE PICTURE PLAYHOUSE (AWH), Moorland Road.—Prop., Globe Cinemas (Burslem), Ltd., Midland Bank Chambers, Burslem. 500 seats. Booked at Birmingham. Continuous. Prices, 3d. to 1s. Proscenium width, 24 ft. Phone, Hanley 8064. Station, Burslem, L.M.S.
HIPPODROME.—Pat Collins' Circuit, Gondola Works, Shaw Street, Walsall. 1,000 seats.
PALACE (WE), Cleveland Street.—Prop., Palace (Burslem), Ltd. 1,800 seats. Pictures and Variety. Booked at Hall. Continuous. Prices, 4d. to 1s. 3d. Proscenium width, 40 ft. Stage, 28 ft. deep ; four dressing rooms. Phone, Stoke-on-Trent 7078. Station, Burslem, L.M.S.
PALLADIUM (AWH), Waterloo Road.—Prop., Huntley and Allan. 500 seats. Booked at Hall. Continuous. Two changes weekly. Prices, 4d. to 1s. Station, Burslem, L.M.S.

BURTON LATIMER (NORTHANTS), Pop. 3,358.
CINEMA.—Prop., Watts' Cinemas, Ltd., " Poolstock," Finedon, Northants. Phone, Finedon 9. Booked by A. T. Watts at H.O. One nightly. Continuous Sat. Prices 4d. to 1s. 3d. Film Transport.

BURTON-ON-TRENT (STAFFS), Pop. 49,485.
ELECTRIC THEATRE (BA), High Street.—Controlled by Gaumont British Picture Corpn., Ltd. Booked at H.O. 1,050 seats. Continuous. Prices, 6d. to 1s. 4d. Café attached.

Phone, Burton 3448. Station, Burton-on-Trent, L.M.S.
Fitted "ARDENTE" Deaf Aids
See page 258
NEW PICTUREDROME (WE), Curzon Street.— Prop., Burton-on-Trent Picturedrome Co., Ltd., 44, Victoria Crescent, Burton-on-Trent. 1,800 seats. Continuous. Prices, 6d. to 1s. 6d. Proscenium width, 48 ft. Phone, Burton 2700. Café attached. Station, Burton-on-Trent, L.M.S.
REGENT (WE).—Prop., Burton-on-Trent, Picturedrome Co., Ltd., 44, Victoria Crescent, Burton-on-Trent. 750 seats. Booked at H.O. Continuous. Prices, 4d. to 1s. 3d. Proscenium width, 30 ft. Phone, Burton-on-Trent 2475. Station, Burton-on-Trent.
RITZ, Guild Street.—Props., Burton-on-Trent Picturedrome, Ltd., 44, Victoria Crescent, Burton-on-Trent. 1,000 seats. Booked at Hall. Prices, 6d. to 2s. Proscenium width, 48 ft. Café. Station, Burton-on-Trent, L.M.S

BURWELL (CAMBS), Pop. 2,140.
CINEMA.—Mondays only.
GARDNER MEMORIAL HALL (wired), Exning Road.—Prop., Burwell Parish Council. Hired by Mr. R. Wolsey. Two shows weekly. Prices, 9d. to 1s. 6d. Station, Burwell, L.N.E.R.

BURY (LANCS), Pop. 56,186.
ART PICTURE HOUSE (WE), Knowsley Street.— Prop., Bury Cinematograph Co., Ltd. 1,136 seats. Booked at Hall. Three shows daily. Prices, 6d. to 1s. Restaurant attached. Phone, Bury 591. Station, Bury, L.M.S.

C O M P T O N
ORGAN featured here.

CASTLE PICTURE HOUSE (BTP), Bolton Street.— Prop., Bury Cinematograph Co., Ltd. Reg. Office, Art Picture House, Bury. 800 seats. Booked at H.O. Three shows daily. Two changes weekly. Prices, 6d. to 9d. Phone, Bury 516. Station, Bolton Street, L.M.S.
EMPIRE (BA), Bolton Street.—Prop., I. Jacobson. 650 seats. Booked at Hall. Continuous, except Sat. Prices, 3d. to 6d. Phone, Bury 446.
HIPPODROME (BTP).—Prop., Bury Hippodrome, Ltd. 900 seats. Booked at La Scala, Bury. Kinema and Music Hall. Twice nightly. Proscenium width, 24 ft. Stage, 25 ft. deep ; six dressing-rooms. Phone, Bury 146. Station, Bury, L.M.S.
LA SCALA (WE), Spring Street.—Prop., Scala Theadrome Co., Ltd. 1,050 seats. Gen. Man. and Sec., John Mather. Booked at Hall. Three shows daily. Prices, 6d. to 1s. 3d. Occasional Variety. Stage, 12 ft. deep. Two dressing-rooms. Phone, Bury 140. Station, Knowsley Street, Bury, L.M.S.
ODEON (BTH), The Rock.—Prop., Odeon (Bury) Ltd., Cornhill House, Bennett's Hill, Birmingham. Phone, Midland 2781. Booked at 49, Park Lane, London, W.1. Continuous. Prices 6d. to 1s. 6d. Phone, Bury 588.
STAR PICTURE HOUSE (WE).—Prop., Star Picture Hall Co. (Bury), Ltd. 490 seats. Booked at Manchester. Twice nightly. Mats., Mon.

and Tues. Two changes weekly. Prices, 3d. to 9d. Phone, Bury 634. Station, Knowsley Street, Bury, L.M.S.

THEATRE ROYAL (WE).—Prop., Northern Theatres Co., Ltd., Nothcote House, Clare Road, Halifax. Phone, Halifax 2512. 1,000 seats. Twice nightly. Daily Mat. Prices, 6d. to 1s. 3d. Proscenium width, 28 ft. Phone, Bury 133. Station, Bury (Knowsley Street), L.M.S.

BURY ST. EDMUNDS (SUFFOLK), **Pop. 16,708.**

CENTRAL CINEMA (WE), Hatter Street.—Prop., Bury St. Edmunds Cinemas, Ltd. 660 seats. Booked at 54, Chevalier Street, Ipswich. Twice nightly; Mat., Mon., Thurs. and Sat. Prices, 6d. to 2s. Phone, Bury St. Edmunds 477. Station, Bury St. Edmunds, L.N.E.R. Films by Transport.

ODEON THEATRE (BTH) Brent Ford Street, Well Street.—Props., Odeon (Bury St. Edmunds) Ltd., Cornhill House, Bennett's Hill, Birmingham. Phone, Midland 2781. Booked at 49, Park Lane, London, W.1.

PLAYHOUSE (BTP), Buttermarket.—Prop.. Playhouse Co. (Bury St. Edmunds), Ltd. 680 seats. Booked at 54, Chevalier Street, Ipswich. Twice nightly; Mat., daily. Prices,. 6d. to 2s. Stage, 28 ft. deep; seven dressing rooms. Phone, Bury St. Edmunds 296. Station, Bury St. Edmunds, L.N.E.R. Films by Transport Co.

BUTTERKNOWLE (CO. DURHAM), **Pop. 2,000.**

KINO PICTURE HOUSE (disc).—Prop., Joseph Wm. Coates, Prospect House, Butterknowle. 250 seats. Booked at Newcastle. Once nightly, two shows Sat. Prices 3d. to 9d. Station, Cockfield Fell.

BUXTON (DERBY), **Pop. 15,353.**

OPERA HOUSE (BTH).—Lessees, Buxton and High Peak Entertainments, Ltd. 1,200 seats. Continuous. Mat., Mon., Wed. and Sat. Prices, 6d. to 2s. Proscenium width, 30 ft. Phone, Buxton 819. Station, Buxton, L.M.S.

PICTURE HOUSE (BTH), Spring Gardens.—Prop., Buxton and High Peak Entertainments, Ltd. 750 seats. Continuous. Prices, 6d. to 1s. 4d. Phone, Buxton 131. Station, Buxton, L.M.S.

CAISTOR (LINCS), **Pop. 2,000.**

PUBLIC HALL CINEMA (SIS).—Prop., Kinemas of East Anglia, Ltd., 50, Market Place, Hull. One show Fri., two Sat. 300 seats. Prices, 6d. to 1s. 3d. Proscenium width, 18 ft. Station, Moortown, L.N.E.R.

CALLINGTON (CORNWALL), **Pop. 1,801.**

PUBLIC HALL (RCA).—Prop., J. H. Crick & Sons. Once weekly.

CALNE (WILTS), **Pop. 3,463.**

PALACE THEATRE (BA), Mill Street.—Prop., Albany Ward Theatres, Ltd., 123, Regent Street, London, W.1. 500 seats. Booked at Hall. One show nightly. Two shows Sat. Prices, 7d. to 1s. 6d. Phone, Calne 88. Station, Calne, G.W.R., or Transport Co.

CAMBERLEY (SURREY), **Pop. 17,000.**

ARCADE CINEMA (Edibell).—Prop., Regal (Camberley) Ltd. Booked by County Cinemas Ltd., Dean House, Dean Street, W.1. 682 seats. Continuous. Two changes weekly. Prices, 6d. to 1s. 10d. Phone No. 410. Station, Camberley, S.R.

REGAL CINEMA (WE), London Road.—Prop., Regal-(Camberley), Ltd. 1,210 seats. Booked by County Cinemas, Ltd., Dean House, Dean Street, London, W.1. Phone, Gerrard 4543. Continuous. Daily Mat. Prices, 6d. to 2s. Café attached. Phone, Camberley 909. Station, Camberley, S.R.

CAMBORNE (CORNWALL), **Pop. 14,157.**

PALACE THEATRE (Morrison).—Prop., P. R. Slater, Carthew, St. Ives, Cornwall. 350 seats. Prices, 6d. to 1s. 6d. Proscenium width, 30 ft. Phone, Camborne 192. Station, Camborne, G.W.R.

SCALA (BA), St. George's Hall.—Prop., British Riviera Cinedrome, Ltd. 950 seats. Booked at Hall by Man. One show nightly, Mon. to Fri.; three shows Sat. Prices, 6d. to 1s. 6d. Proscenium width, 30 ft. Stage 14 ft. deep; four dressing rooms. Dance Hall attached. Phone, 88. Station, Camborne, G.W.R.

CAMBRIDGE (CAMBS), **Pop. 66,803.**

ARTS THEATRE (BTP), Peas Hill.—Props., Arts Theatre of Cambridge, Ltd., 6, St. Edwards Passage, Cambridge. Phone 4099. Booked at Hall. Separate performances. 581 seats. Prices, 1s. to 3s. Phone, Cambridge 4231 Restaurant attached. Films by R.T.

CENTRAL CINEMA (WE).—Controlled by Union Cinemas, Ltd., 15, Regent Street, London, S.W.1. Phone, Whitehall 8484. Booked at H.O. Continuous. Prices, 6d. to 2s. 5d. Proscenium width 25 ft. Phone 3813. Station, Cambridge L.N.E.R., and Film Transport.

COSMOPOLITAN CINEMA (BTH), Market Passage. —Prop., Cosmopolitan Cinemas, Ltd., 14, St. John's Street, Cambridge. 296 seats. Open during University Terms only. Four shows daily. Booked at Empire, Littleport, Cambs. Prices, 1s. to 2s. Proscenium width, 24 ft. Stage, 27 ft. deep; two dressing-rooms. Phone, Cambridge 2799. Station, Cambridge, L.N.E.R. Films by Film Transport Co., Ltd., Charing Cross Road, W.C.

KINEMA (WE), Mill Road.—Prop., Pointer & Coulson. 498 seats. Booked at Victoria Cinema. Continuous from 6.30. Mat., Sat. Two changes weekly. Prices, 5d. to 1s. 3d.

NEW CINEMA (WE).—Controlled by Union Cinemas, Ltd., Union House, 15, Regent Street, London, S.W.1. Phone, Whitehall 8484. 900 seats. Booked at H.O.

PLAYHOUSE (BA), Mill Road.—Controlled by Union Cinemas, Ltd., Union House, 15, Regent Street, London, S.W.1. Phone, Whitehall 8484 Booked at H.O. Continuous. Prices 6d. to 1s. 10d. Phone, Cambridge 5151. Station, Cambridge, L.N.E.R.

REGAL.—Prop., Associated British Cinemas, Ltd., 30-31, Golden Square, London, W.1.

COMPTON
ORGAN featured here.

RENDEZVOUS CINEMA (RCA), Magrath Avenue.— Props., Rendezvous (Cambridge), Ltd., 24A, St. Andrew's Street, Cambridge. Phone, 2029. 1,100 seats. Booked at H.O. Continuous. Two changes weekly. Prices, 6d. to

CAMBRIDGE—Contd.
  2s. Proscenium width, 32 ft. Café and Ballroom attached. Phone, Cambridge 3969. Station, Cambridge.

C O M P T O N
ORGAN featured here.

THEATRE CINEMA (WE), St. Andrew's Street.— Controlled by Union Cinemas, Ltd., Union House, 15, Regent Street, London, S.W.1. Phone, Whitehall 8484. Continuous. Variety and Films. Booked at H.O. Prices, 6d. to 2s. 5d. Phone, Cambridge 3948. Station, Cambridge, L.N.E.R. and Film Transport.
TIVOLI (BA), Chesterton Road.—Controlled by Union Cinema, Ltd., Union House, 15, Regent Street, London, S.W.1. Phone, Whitehall 8484. Booked at H.O. Continuous. Prices, 6d. to 1s. 10d. Phone, Cambridge 4637. Station, Cambridge, L.N.E.R. and Film Transport.
VICTORIA CINEMA (WE), Market Hill.—Controlled by Union Cinemas, Ltd., Union House, 15, Regent Street. London, S.W.1. Phone, Whitehall 8484. Continuous. Booked at H.O. Prices, 6d. to 2s. 6d. Station, Cambridge, L.N.E.R.

CANNOCK (STAFFS), Pop. 8,400.
CANOCK PICTURE HOUSE (WE), Walsall Road.— Prop., Charles K. Deeming. 955 seats. Booked at Grand, Coalville. Continuous. Two changes weekly. Prices, 6d. to 1s. 6d. Phone, Cannock 141. Station, Cannock, L.M.S.
CENTRAL PICTURE HOUSE (BTP), Blackfords.— Props., Messrs. W. S. Roobottom, J. H. Hudson, and J. Bate. 360 seats. Booked at Hall. Continuous. Prices, 4d. to 1s.
FORUM THEATRE (RCA) (late Hippodrome).— Props., Forum Entertainments (Cannock), Ltd. 900 seats. Continuous. Variety. Booked at Hall. Prices, 6d. to 1s. Stage, 40 ft. deep ; four dressing-rooms. Phone, 187. Station, Cannock.

CANTERBURY (KENT), Pop. 24,450.
CENTRAL PICTURE THEATRE (WE).—Props., Associated British Cinemas, Ltd., 30-31, Golden Square, W.1. Phone, Gerrard 7887. 750 seats. Continuous. Phone, Canterbury 71. Stations, Canterbury (East or West), S.R. Films by Road Transport.
FRIARS THEATRE (BTH).—Prop., Odeon (Canterbury), Ltd., Cornhill House, Bennett's Hill, Birmingham. Phone, Midland 2781. Booked at 49, Park Lane, London, W.1. Continuous. Prices, 6d. to 2s. 6d. Phone, Canterbury 480. Station, Canterbury, S.R.
REGAL CINEMA (WE).—Props., Associated British Cinemas, Ltd., 30-31, Golden Square, London, W.1. Phone, Gerrard 7887. 1,058 seats. Continuous. Prices, 6d. to 2s. Proscenium width, 43 ft. 4 in. Stage, 10 ft. deep ; three dressing-rooms. Café and Ballroom attached. Phone, Canterbury 22. Stations, Canterbury (East or West), S.R.

C O M P T O N
ORGAN featured here.

CARCROFT, Nr. Doncaster (YORKS), Pop. 7,500.
PICTURE THEATRE (WE).—Prop., C. F. Ward. Phone, Adwick-le-Street 20. 867 seats. Booked by G. Brocklesby, F.I.A.A., Certified Accountant, Conisborough, near Rotherham. Phone, Conisborough 29. Continuous, Mon to Fri. Twice nightly Sat. Prices, 4d. to 9d. Stations, Adwick-le-Street and Carcroft, L.N.E.R.

CARLISLE (CUMBERLAND), Pop., 57,107.
BOTCHERGATE PICTURE HOUSE (RCA), 37, Botchergate.—Prop., Carlisle Picture House Co., Ltd., 95, Bath Street, Glasgow. Phone, Douglas 2769. 1,006 seats. Booked at H.O. by J. Matthews. Continuous. Café attached. Prices, 6d. to 1s. 6d. Phone, Carlisle 411. Station, Carlisle Citadel, L.M.S., or Motor Transport.
CINEMA (BTH) Gretna.
CITY PICTURE HOUSE (WE), English Street.— Controlled by Union Cinemas, Ltd., Union House, 15, Regent Street, London S.W.1. Phone, Whitehall 8484. Continuous. Booked at H.O. Prices, 6d. to 1s. 6d. Phone, Carlisle 540. Café attached. Station, Carlisle, L.M.S.
LONSDALE (WE), Warwick Road.—Controlled by Union Cinemas Ltd., Union House, 15, Regent Street, London, S.W.1. Phone, Whitehall 8484. Continuous. Booked at H.O. Pictures and Variety. Prices, 6d. to 2s. Phone, Carlisle 1219. Station, Citadel, L.M.S.
NEW PALACE (BTP), Botchergate.—Prop., Macnaghten Vaudeville Circuit, Ltd., Kings Chambers, Angel Street, Sheffield. Phone, 23449. 1,100 seats. Booked at H.O. by W. Bryan. Continuous from 6.15. Mats. Mon., Thurs., and Sat. Prices, 6d. to 1s. 3d. Proscenium width, 30 ft. Phone, Carlisle 144. Station, Carlisle, L.M.S.
PUBLIC HALL (WE), Chapel Street.—Controlled by Union Cinemas, Ltd., Union House, 15, Regent Street, London, S.W.1. Phone, Whitehall 8484. Booked at H.O. Continuous. Prices, 3d. to 6d. Phone, Carlisle 428. Stations, Carlisle, L.M.S. & L.N.E.R.
REGAL (WE), Caldergate.—Prop., The Williams Cinemas, Ltd. Hippodrome, Workington. Phone, Workington 194. 705 seats. Booked at H.O. Continuous. Prices, 5d. to 9d. Phone, Carlisle 932. Station, Carlisle (Citadel).
STANLEY HALL (RCA), Botchergate.—Prop., The Williams Cinemas, Ltd., Hippodrome, Workington. Phone, Workington 194. 517 seats. Booked at H.O. Continuous. Prices, 4d. to 6d. Phone, Carlisle 926. Station, Carlisle (Citadel).
STAR PICTURE THEATRE (BTH), Denton Holme.— Lessees, Graves Cinema, Ltd., Athenæum Buildings, Maryport. 550 seats. Booked at H.O. Prices, 4d. to 1s. Phone, Carlisle 458. Station, Carlisle (Citadel), L.M.S.

CARLTON (NOTTS), Pop. 22,330.
VICTORIA PALACE (BTH).—Prop., Joseph Wardle, Brentwell House, Arnold, Notts. Phone, Arnold 68145. 600 seats. Booked at H.O. Continuous. Two changes weekly. Prices 7d. to 1s. 2d. Station, Carlton and Netherfield, L.M.S.

CARNFORTH (LANCS), Pop. 3,193.
KINEMA (BTH), Market Street.—Prop., James Brennan, 107, Duke Street, Barrow-in-Furness. Phone, Barrow-in-Furness 28. 780

PATHE GAZETTE—The Most Popular of News Reels !

seats. Booked at Hall. Continuous Mon. to Fri. Twice Sat. Prices, 5d. to 1s. Phone, Carnforth 37. Station, Carnforth, L.M.S.

CARSHALTON (SURREY), **Pop. 28,769.**
PALACE THEATRE (Phillips), High Street. 486 seats. Continuous. Prices, 6d. to 2s. Dance Hall attached. Phone, Wallington 3340. Station, Carshalton, S.R. Films by Transport.

CASTLE DONINGTON (LEICS.), **Pop. 2,530.**
COUNTY CINEMA (Marshall).—Prop., J. F. S. Minton, County Cinema Enterprises. 400 seats. Booked at Market Street. Two shows Mon. and Sat. Once daily rest of week. Prices, 4d. to 1s. 3d. Station, Castle Donington, L.M.S.

CASTLEFORD (YORKS), **Pop. 24,183.**
ALBION PICTURE PALACE (WE), Albion Street. Lessees, Associated British Cinemas, Ltd., 30-31, Golden Square, W.1. 985 seats. Booked at H.O. Continuous. Two changes weekly. Prices, 4d. to 1s. Phone, Castleford 2032. Station, Castleford, L.N.E.R.
NEW STAR (WE).—Props., Star Cinemas (London), Ltd., 5, Manchester Avenue E.C.1. Booked at H.O. 850 seats. Three shows daily. Prices, 6d. to 1s. 3d. Sports Arcade. Phone, Castleford 2531. Station, Castleford, L.N.E.R.
PICTURE HOUSE (Eastern Electric), Airedale. 500 seats.
PICTURE HOUSE (WE), Station Road.—Prop., R.T.A. Pictures, Ltd. 1,100 seats. Booked at Hall. Twice nightly. Daily mat. Two changes weekly. Prices, 6d. to 1s. 3d. Phone, Castleford 2351. Café and Dance Hall attached. Station, Castleford, L.N.E.R.
QUEEN'S (Eastern Electric).—Props., Queen's Theatre Co., Ltd. 980 seats. Continuous. Booked at Hall. Prices, 4d. to 9d. Proscenium width, 24 ft. Stage, 26 ft. deep. Eight dressing rooms. Phone, 2268. Station, L.N.E.R.

CASTLETON (I.O. MAN).
COSY.—Booked by R. E. Ratcliff, "Raheny," Roby, Liverpool. Phone, Huyton 382.
PAVILION.

CASTLETON (LANCS.), **Pop. 3,918.**
IDEAL (WE).—Prop., E. Woodall. 577 seats. Phone, Castleton 3452. Booked at Hall and Manchester Twice nightly. Mat., Mon. and Thurs. Two changes weekly. Prices, 4d. to 1s. Phone, Castleton 5906. Station, Castleton, L.M.S.
PRINCESS CINEMA (BTH), Princes Street.—Prop., E. Woodall, Ideal Cinema, Castleton. 600 seats. Booked at Hall or at Manchester. Once nightly. Twice Sat. Two changes weekly. Prices, 4d. to 9d. Phone, Castleton 5906. Station, Castleton, L.M.S.

CATERHAM (SURREY), **Pop. (with Warlingham), 25,100.**
CAPITOL CINEMA (WE).—Lessee, R. J. Drew. 865 seats. Booked at Hall. Continuous. Phone, Caterham 462. Café attached. Station, Caterham, S.R.

CATTERICK (YORKS), **Pop. 565.**
CAMP CINEMA.—Prop., Catterick Cinema Co. Continuous. Three changes weekly. Prices, 6d. to 1s. 3d. Station, Catterick Bridge. L.N.E.R.
GARRISON CINEMA (BA).—Lessees. George P. Fenton and A. Branford. 1,250 seats. Pictures and Variety. Booked by G. P. Fenton, Central Buildings, Darlington. Continuous. Prices, 4d. to 1s. 3d. Four dressing-rooms. Station, Richmond, Yorks.

CAVERSHAM (near Reading) (BERKS).
ELECTRIC THEATRE (film and disc), Church Street.—Prop. and Res. Man., C. J. Stanley. 500 seats. Booked at Hall. Continuous. Prices, 6d. to 1s. 3d. Phone, Reading 71729. Station, Reading, G.W.R., or by Road Transport.

CHADDERTON (near Oldham) (LANCS), **Pop. 27,455.**
CASINO PICTURE PALACE (WE), Reville Street. Prop., Oldham Cinemas, Ltd. 982 seats. Booked at Manchester. One show nightly, two on Sat. Mat. Sat. Two changes weekly. Prices, 4d. to 9d. Phone, Oldham 1026. Two dressing rooms. Station, Oldham (Werneth), L.M.S.
FREE TRADE HALL (WE).—Prop., Alfred Wright. 550 seats. Booked at Hall. Prices, 2d. to 9d. Station Werneth.
LYRIC CINEMA (WE), Milne Street.—Prop. Alfred Wright, 140, Grange Avenue, Oldham. 500 seats. Two shows nightly. Prices, 2d. to 9d. Phone, Chadderton 2185. Station, Werneth, L.M.S.

CHADWELL HEATH (ESSEX), **Pop. 8,100.**
GAUMONT PALACE (WE).—Prop., Provincial Cinematograph Theatres, Ltd., New Gallery House, Regent Street, W.1. Booked at H.O. Pictures and Variety. 1,806 seats. Prices, 6d. to 2s. Proscenium width, 40 ft. Stage, 24 ft. Four dressing-rooms. Phone, Seven Kings 3292. Station, Chadwell Heath.

COMPTON

ORGAN featured here.

MAYFAIR CINEMA (WE).—D. J. James Circuit, Cinema House, 225, Oxford Street, London, W.1. 1,764 seats. Booked at H.O. Continuous. Variety. Prices, 6d. to 1s. 6d. Boxes 7s. 6d. Phone, Seven Kings 3,000.

Fitted "ARDENTE" Stage Amplification See page 258

CHALFONT ST. PETER (BUCKS). **Pop. 4,000.**
BROADWAY CINEMA (Picturetone), late Memorial Hall Cinema.—Prop., Broadway Cinema (Chalfonts), Ltd., Market Place. 400 seats. Booked at Hall by Man. Continuous. Prices, 6d. to 1s. 10d. Phone, Gerrards Cross 904. Station, Gerrards Cross, G.W.R.

CHAPEL-EN-LE-FRITH (DERBYSHIRE), **Pop: 5,283.**
EMPRESS CINEMA.—350 seats. Twice nightly. Prices 4d. to 1s.
REGENT (BA), late Constitutional Hall, Eccles Road.—Prop., Chapel-en-le-Frith. Constitutional Hall Co., Ltd. 450 seats. Booked at Manchester. Twice nightly, Tues., Wed., Thurs., Fri. and Sat. Prices, 3d. to 1s. Two dressing-rooms. Proscenium width, 10 ft. Phone, Chapel-en-le-Frith 32. Station, Central, L.M.S.

CHAPELTOWN (near Sheffield) (YORKS), **Pop. 8,701.**
CHAPELTOWN PICTURE PALACE (BTH), Station Road.—Prop., Chapeltown Picture Palace, Ltd. Phone, Sheffield 40145. 560 seats. Once nightly. Twice Sat. Two changes weekly. Prices, 6d. to 1s. Station, Chapeltown, L.M.S.

CHARD (SOMERSET), **Pop. 4,053.**
PICTURE HOUSE (BTH).—Prop., Rowland Reeves. 550 seats. Booked at Hall. Once nightly ; two Wed., and three on Sat Prices, 4d. to 1s. 6d. Phone, Chard 74. Station, Chard, S.R. and G.W.R.

CHASETERRACE (STAFFS).
CHASE CINEMA (BTP).—Prop., Miles Jerriss, Bridge Cross, Chaseterrace. 750 seats. Continuous Mon. and Thurs. Three shows Sat. ; one show Tues., Wed., Fri. Prices, 5d. to 1s. Phone, Burntwood 32. Station, Brownhills.

CHATHAM (KENT), **Pop. 42,996.**
EMPIRE (WE).—Props., Empire Theatre of Varieties, Ltd. Stoll Offices, Coliseum Buildings, St. Martin's Lane, W.C.—1,893 seats. Booked at H.O. Continuous. Prices, 6d. to 2s. Phone, Chatham 2757. Station, Chatham, S.R.
Fitted "ARDENTE" Deaf Aids
See page 258

INVICTA CINEMA (WE), High Street.—Prop., J. H. Canvin. 930 seats. Booked at Hall Continuous. Two changes weekly. Prices, 3d. to 1s. 3d. Proscenium width, 30 ft. Phone, Chatham 2472. Station, Chatham, S.R. Films by Kent Film Transport Co., Ltd.
NATIONAL ELECTRIC THEATRE (BA), High St.— Prop., Denman Picture Houses, Ltd., 123, Regent Street, London, W.1. 837 seats. Booked at H.O. Continuous. Prices, 5d. to 1s. 3d. Phone, Chatham 2314. Station, Chatham, S.R. Films by Motor Transport.
PALACE.

Fitted "ARDENTE" Deaf Aids
See page 258

COMPTON
ORGAN featured here.

PICTURE HOUSE (BTP).—Props., Stoll Circuit Coliseum Buildings, W.C.2. 1,120 seats. Booked at H.O. Continuous. Prices, 5d. to 1s. 6d. Phone, Chatham 2757. Station, Chatham, S.R.
REGENT (RCA).—Prop., Associated British Cinemas, Ltd., 30-31, Golden Square, London, W.1. Phone, Gerrard 7887. 1,200 seats. Booked at H.O. Continuous. Prices 6d. to 1s. 6d. Phone, Chatham 2618. Station, Chatham, S.R.
RITZ (WE).—Controlled by Union Cinemas, Ltd., Union House, 15, Regent Street, London, S.W.1. Phone, Whitehall 8484. Continuous. Booked at H.O. Station, Chatham, S.R.

WURLITZER ORGAN
Installed in this Kinema

CHATTERIS (CAMBS), **Pop. 5,153.**
EMPRESS (WE).—H. Bancroft Circuit, Hippodrome, Wisbech. Phone, Wisbech 116.
PICTURE PALACE (BTP).—Prop. and Res. Man., Russell Wright. Booked at Majestic Theatre, Ely. 500 seats. Continuous. Two changes weekly. Prices, 4d. to 1s. 3d. Station, Chatteris, L.N.E.R.

CHEADLE (CHESHIRE), **Pop.** (with **Gatley** and **Cheadle Hulme), 18,469.**
ELECTRA PICTURE HOUSE (WE).—Prop., Associated British Cinemas, Ltd, 30-31, Golden Square, W.1. Booked at Hall. Continuous.

Two changes weekly. Prices, 6d. to 1s. 3d. Phone, Gatley 2839. Station, Gatley, L.M.S.

CHEADLE (STAFFS), **Pop. 5,841.**
OSBORNE CINEMA (BTH).—Prop., Boyce Wood. 850 seats. Booked at Hall. One show nightly. Mat., Sat. Two changes weekly. Prices, 2½d. to 9d. Station, Cheadle (Staffs), L.M.S.
PALACE (BTH).—Prop. and Res. Man., J. Bibbys. 400 seats. One show nightly, two on Sat. Two changes weekly. Prices, 5d. to 9d. Station, Cheadle (Staffs), L.M.S.

CHEADLE HULME (CHES.).
ELYSIAN CINEMA (WE).—Prop., W. W. Stansby, Station Road, Cheadle Hulme. 900 seats. Booked at Manchester. Continuous, Mon. to Fri. Two shows Sat. Prices, 7d. to 1s. 4d. Phone, Cheadle Hulme 346. Café attached. Station, Cheadle Hulme, L.M.S.

CHELMSFORD (ESSEX), **Pop. 26,537.**
EMPIRE PICTURE HOUSE (WE), Springfield Rd.— Prop., Eastern Counties Cinemas, Ltd., Regent Theatre, Chelmsford. 524 seats. Booked at H.O. by Gerald Balls. Continuous. Phone, Chelmsford 2094. Station, Chelmsford, L.N.E.R.
PAVILION SUPER CINEMA (BA), Rainsford Rd.— Prop. and Man., H. Hull. 450 seats. Continuous. Two changes weekly. Station, Chelmsford.
REGENT THEATRE (WE), Moulsham Street.— Prop., Eastern Counties Cinemas, Ltd., Regent Theatre, Chelmsford. 1,000 seats. Res. and Booking Man., R. Gerald Balls. Continuous. Phone, Chelmsford 2094. Station, Chelmsford. L.N.E.R.
RITZ (WE).—Prop., Ritz (Chelmsford), Ltd. Booked at County Cinema Ltd., Dean House, Dean Street, W.1. 1,750 seats. Continuous.
SELECT KINEMA (Klangfilm), off Moulsham Street.—Prop., Select Kinema, Ltd. 600 seats. Booked at Hall. Twice nightly. Mats., Wed. and Sat. Prices, 7d. to 1s. 10d. Phone, Chelmsford 424. Station, Chelmsford, L.N.E.R.

CHELTENHAM (GLOS.), **Pop. 49,835.**
COLISEUM (BTH).—Prop., H. G. Beard. 1,000 seats. Booked at Hall. Continuous. Prices, 9d. to 1s. 6d. Stage, 30 ft. deep ; 9 dressing rooms. Proscenium width, 30 ft. Phone, Cheltenham 3715. Station, Cheltenham (St. James), G.W.R.
DAFFODIL PICTURE HOUSE (WE), Suffolk Parade.—Prop., Daffodil Picture House, Ltd. 780 seats. Booked at Hall. Continuous. Prices, 9d. to 1s. 6d. Phone, Cheltenham 3360. Station, Cheltenham (St. James), G.W.R.
GAUMONT PALACE (BA).—Prop., Gaumont British Picture Corporation Ltd., 123, Regent Street, W. Phone, Regent 8080. 1,774 seats. Booked at H.O. Continuous. Prices, 9d. to 2s. Proscenium width, 44 ft. Stage, 20 ft. deep ; five dressing rooms. Restaurant. Phone, 4081-11. Stations, Cheltenham, L.M.S. and G.W.R.
Fitted "ARDENTE" Deaf Aids
See page 258

COMPTON
ORGAN featured here.

OPERA HOUSE (WE).—Props., The Cheltenham Theatre and Opera House Co., Ltd. Phone, Cheltenham 3159. 1,000 seats. Proscenium width, 24 ft. Café. Station, G.W.R. St. James's, L.M.S., Lansdown.

PALACE PICTURE THEATRE (WE).—Prop., W. G. & E. J. Vickery, Ltd. 750 seats. Booked at Taunton. Continuous. Prices, 6d. to 1s. 6d. Phone, Cheltenham 2553. Station, Cheltenham, G.W.R. Films by Road Transport.

CHEPSTOW (MON.), Pop. 4,303.
PALACE THEATRE (Cinephone).—Prop., Albany Ward Theatres, Ltd., New Gallery House, 123, Regent Street, London, W.1. 424 seats. Booked at H.O. Twice nightly Mon., once Tues. to Fri., three shows Sat. Two changes weekly. Prices, 5d. to 1s. 6d. Proscenium width, 18 ft. Phone, Chepstow 310. Station, Chepstow, G.W.R.

CHERTSEY (SURREY), Pop. 17,130.
CONSTITUTIONAL HALL, Guildford Street.—Prices, 3d. to 1s. 3d. Open, Sat. only.

GLOBE CINEMA (BTH).—Prop., Southern Cinemas, Ltd. 375 seats. Continuous. Booked at Gem, Southall. Prices, 7d. to 2s. Proscenium width, 24 ft. Phone, Chertsey 267. Station, Chertsey, S.R.

PLAYHOUSE (BTH), Guildford Street.—Prop., Southern Cinemas, Ltd. The Gem, Southall. Booked at H.O. Continuous. Prices, 7d. to 2s. Phone, Chertsey 267. Station, Chertsey, S.R.

CHESHAM (BUCKS), Pop. 8,809.
ASTORIA (WE), Broadway.—Prop., Chesham Pictures, Ltd. 505 seats. Booked at H.O. Continuous. Prices, 6d. to 2s. Stage, 14 ft. deep; two dressing rooms. Proscenium width, 18 ft. Phone, Chesham 103. Station, Chesham.

EMBASSY.—Props., Shipman & King, M84, Shellmex House, Strand, W.C.2. Phone, Temple Bar 5077. Booked at H.O. Continuous. Prices, 6d. to 2s.

Fitted "ARDENTE" Deaf Aids
See page 258

CHESHUNT (HERTS.), Pop. 14,651. (Inc., Waltham Cross).
CENTRAL CINEMA (AWH), College Road.—Prop. E. J. Carpenter. 400 seats. Booked at Hall. Continuous Evening. Mats., Mon., Thurs. and Sat. Prices, 6d. to 1s. 6d. Proscenium width, 18 ft. Phone, Waltham Cross 250. Station, Cheshunt, L.N.E.R.

CHESTER (CHESHIRE), Pop, 41,438.
ENTERPRISE CINEMA (Morrisons), Station Road, Queensferry.—Prop., Deeside Enterprise Cinemas, Ltd., 1, Hunter Street, Chester. Phone, Chester 530. 350 seats. Booked at Bridge House, Queensferry. Phone, Connah's Quay 49. Once nightly, twice Sat. Prices, 6d. to 1s. Station, Queensferry, L.M.S.

GAUMONT PALACE (BA), Brook Street.—Prop., Provincial Cinematograph Theatres, Ltd., New Gallery House, Regent Street, London, W.1. 1,910 seats. Booked at H.O. Continuous. Prices, 9d. to 1s. 6d. Stage, 30 ft. deep; nine dressing rooms. Proscenium width, 41 ft. Café. Phone, Chester 2100. Station, Chester, L.M.S. and G.W.R.
Fitted "ARDENTE" Deaf Aids
See page 258

COMPTON
ORGAN featured here.

HIPPODROME (BA), Connah's Quay.—Deeside Enterprise Cinemas, Ltd. 700 seats.

MAJESTIC PICTURE HOUSE (BA), Brook Street.—Prop., General Theatre Corpn., Ltd., 123, Regent Street, London, W.1. Phone, Regent 6641. Booked at H.O. Continuous from 6.30. Mats., Mon., Wed. and Sat. Prices, 7d. to 1s. Phone, Chester 599. Station, Chester, L.M.S. and G.W.R.

MUSIC HALL (RCA), Northgate Street.—Prop., General Theatre Corpn., Ltd., 123, Regent Street, London, W.1. Phone, Regent 8080. Continuous nightly Mon. to Fri. Three shows Sat. Prices, 6d. to 1s. 6d. Phone, 380. Station, Chester, L.M.S. and G.W.R.

ODEON (BTH), Northgate Street.—Props., Odeon (Chester) Ltd., Cornhill House, Bennett's Hill, Birmingham. Phone, Midland 2781. Booked at 49, Park Lane, London, W.1. Continuous. Prices, 6d. to 2s. Phone, Chester 1573.

PARK CINEMA (BTP), Saltney.—Prop., Deeside Enterprise Cinemas, Ltd., Bridge House, Queensferry, Chester. Phone, Connah's Quay 49. 500 seats. Booked at H.O. Twice nightly. Prices, 6d. to 1s. Proscenium width 26 ft. Phone, Chester 1430. Station, Saltney G.W.R.

TATLER (RCA), Forgate Street.—Props., Chester (Times), Theatres, Ltd., 3 Stanley Street, Liverpool. 535 seats. Booked at Tatler, Oxford Street, Manchester. Prices, 6d. to 1s. Proscenium width, 22 ft.

CHESTERFIELD (DERBY), Pop. 64,146.
BRAMPTON COLISEUM (BTH), Chatsworth Road, —Prop., Entertainments (Chesterfield), Ltd. 450 seats. Booked by W. Wood at Hall. One show nightly. Prices, 4d. to 9d. Station, Chesterfield, L.M.S.

CORPORATION THEATRE (BTH), Corporation Street.—Lessees, Hippodrome (Chesterfield), Ltd. 772 seats. Booked at Hall. Continuous. Prices, 6d. to 1s. 3d. Proscenium width, 30 ft. Six dressing rooms. Phone, Chesterfield 2901. Station, Chesterfield, L.M.S.

LYCEUM (BTH).—Prop., Lyceum Co., Ltd. 650 seats. One show nightly, two on Sat. Two changes weekly. Prices, 4d. to 1s. Station, Whittington Moor, L.M.S.

HASLAND CINEMA.—600 seats. Once nightly, two shows Sat. Prices, 6d. to 1s.

HIPPODROME (BTH).—Prop., Hippodrome (Chesterfield), Ltd. 1,000 seats. Pictures and Variety. Booked at Hall. Twice nightly. Prices, 6d. to 1s. 10d. Proscenium width, 30 ft. Stage 28 ft. deep; 8 dressing rooms. Phone, Chesterfield 2335. Station, Chesterfield, L.M.S.

OXFORD PICTURE PALACE (BTH), New Whittington.—Prop., Oxford Palace (New Whittington), Ltd. 650 seats. Booked at Hall. Once nightly. Three Sat. Phone, Old Whittington 61. Prices, 7d. to 1s. Billiards Hall attached. Station, New Whittington, L.M.S.

Put Pep into Programmes With PATHE PICTORIAL.

CHESTERFIELD—Contd.
PALACE (BA).—Prop., Holmwood Picture Palace Co., Ltd. 600 seats.
PICTURE HOUSE (WE), Holywell Street.—Prop., Chesterfield Picture House, Ltd. Cornhill House, Bennett's Hill, Birmingham. Phone, Midland 2781. Continuous. Mats. Mon., Wed. and Sat. Café, Restaurant and Dance Hall attached. Prices, 6d. to 1s. 3d. Proscenium width, 30 ft. Phone, Chesterfield 2791. Station, Chesterfield, L.M.S.
REGAL.—Prop., Associated British Cinemas, Ltd., 30-31, Golden Square, London, W.1.

COMPTON

ORGAN featured here.

RITZ.— Prop., L. Morris, 52, Shaftesbury Avenue, London, W.1. 2,000 seats.
VICTORIA PICTURE HOUSE (WE), Knifesmith Gate.—Prop., Victoria Enterprises, Ltd. 1,190 seats. Three shows daily. Two changes weekly. Prices, 5d. to 1s. 6d. Café and Dance Hall attached. Phone, Chesterfield 2677. Station, Chesterfield, L.M.S.

CHESTER-LE-STREET (Co. DURHAM), **Pop. 16,639.**
EMPIRE THEATRE AND CINEMA (BA).—Prop., Smelt's Theatres, Ltd., 125, Westgate Road, Newcastle. Phone, 27887. 700 seats. Pictures and Variety. Films booked at Newcastle-on-Tyne. Continuous. Stage, 40 ft. deep; ten dressing rooms. Prices, 6d. to 9d. Proscenium width, 26 ft. Dance Hall attached. Phone, Central 3202. Station, Chester-le-Street, L.N.E.R.
PALACE (RCA), Low Chase.—Prop. and Man., T. H. Worley, Sea View House, Tanlobic, Newcastle. 760 seats. Booked at Hall. Two shows nightly and Mats. Prices, 6d. to 1s. Phone, Chester-le-Street 80. Station, Chester-le-Street, L.N.E.R
QUEEN'S HALL (WE), South Burns.—Prop., Cestrian Entertainments, Ltd. 1,313 seats. Booked at Newcastle. Continuous. Prices, 6d. to 1s. Proscenium width, 39 ft. Phone, Chester-le-Street 220. Station, Chester-le-Street, L.N.E.R.
SAVOY CINEMA (BA).—Props., Smelt's Theatres, Ltd., 125, Westgate Road, Newcastle. Phone, Newcastle 33341. 612 seats. Booked at H.O. Continuous. Prices, 4d. to 9d. Proscenium width, 22 ft. Phone, Chester-le-Street 3202.

CHESTERTON (STAFFS), **Pop. 5,000.**
ALEXANDRA PICTURE HOUSE (Edibell).—Prop. Shemilt Bros., Granville, High Lane, Burslem. 800 seats. Booked at H.O. Continuous. Prices 5d. to 1s. Proscenium width, 45 ft. Station, Longport, L.M.S., and by Potteries Transport.

CHICHESTER (SUSSEX), **Pop. 13,911.**
EXCHANGE THEATRE, East Street.—Props., London & District Cinemas, Ltd., Astoria House, 62, Shaftesbury Avenue, London, W.1. 800 seats. Booked at H.O. Continuous. Prices, 6d. to 2s. Phone, Chichester 407. Station, Chichester. S.R.
PLAZA (WE), South Street.—Prop., County Cinemas, Ltd., Dean House, Dean Street, London, W.1. Phone, Gerrard 4543. 1,063 seats. Booked at H.O. Continuous Two changes weekly. Prices, 6d. to 1s. 6d., Café attached. Phone, Chichester 298. Station, Chichester, S.R.

CHIPPENHAM (WILTS), **Pop. 8,493.**
GAUMONT PALACE.
Fitted "ARDENTE" Deaf Aids
See page 258
NEILD HALL.—Prop., Albany Ward Theatres, Ltd., 123, Regent Street., London, W.1.
PALACE THEATRE (Cinephone), Station Hill.— Prop., Albany Ward Theatres, Ltd., 123, Regent Street, London, W.1. 536 seats. Booked at H.O. Twice nightly. Mat., Sat. Two changes weekly. Prices, 6d. to 1s. 6d. Proscenium width, 18 ft. Phone, Chippenham 35. Station, Chippenham, G.W.R.

CHIPPING NORTON (OXON), **Pop. 3,489.**
NEW CINEMA (BTP).—Prop., New Cinema (Chipping Norton), Ltd. 506 seats. Booked at Hall. Continuous. Prices, 6d. to 1s. 6d. Phone, Chipping Norton 141.
PICTURE HOUSE (BA), London Road.— Prop., T. W. Grant, 19, Albion Street, Chipping Norton. 300 seats. Booked at Hall. Nightly. Prices, 6d. to 1s. 6d. Phone, Chipping Norton 9. Station, Chipping Norton, G.W.R.

CHIPPING SODBURY (GLOS.), **Pop. 1,000.**
PICTUREDROME (Imperial).—Prop., J. L. Mott, 10, Oxford Road, Malmesbury. Booked at H.O. One show nightly. Two changes weekly. Prices, 6d. to 1s. 4d. Phone, Chipping Sodbury 30. Station, Chipping Sodbury, G.W.R., and Film Transport.

CHISLEHURST (KENT), **Pop. 9,900.**
EMBASSY, Petts Wood.—Prop. Shipman & King, M 84, Shell Mex House, Strand, W.C.2.

CHOPPINGTON (NORTHUMBERLAND), **Pop. 5,432.**
MEMORIAL CINEMA (Electrocord), Stakeford.— 200 seats.
PICTURE HOUSE, Stakeford.

CHOPWELL (Co. DURHAM), **Pop. 10,000.**
KING'S THEATRE (BTP).—Prop., Chopwell Cinema Co., Ltd., 1, Ledbury Terrace. Phone, Chopwell 4. 900 seats. Booked at H.O. Two shows nightly. Mon. and Sat., one rest of week. Station, High Westwood, L.N.E.R.
VICTORIA CINEMA (AWH).—Props., Trotter and Murray. 450 seats. Twice nightly, Mon. and Sat. Once nightly rest of week. Prices, 2d. to 1s. Proscenium width, 36 ft. Station, Newcastle-on-Tyne.

CHORLEY (LANCS), **Pop. 30,795.**
EMPIRE (WE), Dole Lane.—Prop., Perfecto Filmograph Co., Ltd. 800 seats. Booked at Hall. Two shows nightly. Mat. Mon., Wed., and Sat. Prices, 4d. to 1s. Proscenium width, 26 ft. Phone, Chorley 247. Station, Chorley, L.M.S.
HIPPODROME (WE), Gillibrand Street. Prop., Perfecto Filmograph Co., Ltd. 900 seats. Booked at the Empire. Twice nightly. Mat., Sat. Prices, 4d. to 1s. Proscenium width, 28 ft. Phone, Chorley 247. Station, Chorley, L.M.S.
ODEON THEATRE (BTH), Market Street.— Props., Odeon (Chorley), Ltd., Bennett's Hill, Birmingham. (In course of construction).
PAVILION CINEMA (Electrocord).—Prop., A. Hooley. 950 seats. Booked at Manchester. C. T. Robinson's Circuit. Twice nightly, Mat., Sat. Prices, 4d. to 1s. Phone, Chorley 2762. Stage, 16½ ft. deep; two dressing rooms. Station, Chorley, L.M.S., or Auto Road Service.

THEATRE ROYAL (WE), Market Street.—Prop., Associated British Cinemas, Ltd., 30/31, Golden Square, W.1. 896 seats. Twice nightly. Mat. Mon., Wed. and Sat. Booked at H.O. Prices, 4d. to 1s. Phone, Chorley 2484. Station, Chorley, L.M.S.

CHRISTCHURCH (HANTS), Pop. 9,183.
REGAL (Mihaly).—646 seats.
REGENT (WE), High Street—Props., Portsmouth Town Cinemas, Ltd. Shaftesbury Cinema, Portsmouth. Booked at H.O. Continuous. Prices, 6d. to 1s. 6d. Phone, 153. Station, Christchurch, S.R.

CHURCH, Nr. ACCRINGTON (LANCS.), Pop. 6,185.
QUEEN'S HALL (BTF).—Prop., Queen's Hall (Church), Ltd. 710 seats. Booked at Hall by John Wilson. Twice nightly. Three shows Sat. Prices 3d. to 6d. Proscenium width, 27ft. Phone, Accrington 2291. Station, Church, L.M.S.

CHURCH CROOKHAM (HANTS), Pop. 1,000.
TUDOR CINEMA (Marshalls).—Crookham.—Prop., G. Scarrott, Chestnut Grove, Crookham. 220 seats. One show daily. Prices, 7d. to 1s. Station, Fleet, S.R.

CINDERFORD (GLOS.), Pop. 3,399.
PALACE (Cinephone).—Prop., Albany Ward Theatres, Ltd., 123, Regent Street, London, W.1. 450 seats. Booked at H.O. Once nightly. Three shows Sat. Prices, 6d. to 1s. 3d. Phone, Cinderford 77. Station, Cinderford, G.W.R.

CIRENCESTER (GLOS.), Pop. 7,200.
PICTURE HOUSE AND THEATRE (BA).— Props., Albany Ward Theatres, Ltd. Booked at New Gallery House, 123, Regent Street, London, W.1. Twice nightly. Stage 20 ft. deep. Prices, 6d. to 2s. 4d. Phone, Cirencester 70. Station, Cirencester, G.W.R.

CLACTON-ON-SEA (ESSEX) Pop., 15,851.
CENTURY THEATRE (WE), Pier Avenue.—Props., 20th Century Cinemas, Ltd., Brettenham House, 14-15, Lancaster Place, W.C.2. Booked at H.O. Continuous. 1,738 seats. Prices, 6d. to 2s. Phone, Clacton 899. Station, Clacton, L.N.E.R.
ELECTRIC THEATRE (Mihaly), Great Clacton.— Prop., 20th Century Cinemas, Ltd., Brettenham House, 14-15, Lancaster Place, London, W.C.2. 450 seats. Booked at H.O. Continuous. Mat. Wed. and Sat. Prices, 6d. to 1s. Phone, Clacton 228. Station, Clacton-on-Sea, L.N.E.R.
KINEMA GRAND (AWH), West Avenue.—Prop., Capt. E. R. F. Pennell, D.F.C. 700 seats. Booked at Hall. Continuous. Prices, 6d. to 2s. Phone, Clacton 81. Station, Clacton-on-Sea, L.N.E.R.
ODEON THEATRE (BTH), Station Road. —Props., Odeon (Clacton-on-Sea), Ltd., Cornhill House, Bennett's Hill, Birmingham. Phone, Midland 2781. Booked at 49, Park Lane, London, W.1. Continuous. Prices, 6d. to 2s. Phone, Clacton 1103.
PALACE.—950 seats.
TIVOLI (WE).—Prop., 20th Century Cinemas, Ltd., Brettenham House, 14-15, Lancaster Place, London, W.C.2. Booked at H.O. 750 seats. Continuous. Two Mats. Prices, 6d. to 2s. Phone, Clacton 300. Station, Clacton-on-Sea, L.N.E.R.

CLAY CROSS (DERBY), Pop. 8,493.
HIPPODROME (BTH).—Prop., Clay Cross Hippodrome, Ltd. Man. Dir., H. Minney. 800 seats. Phone, Clay Cross 20. Pictures and Variety. Films booked at Hall. Once nightly. Twice on Sat. Prices, 6d. to 1s. 2d. Proscenium width, 30 ft. Stage, 30 ft. deep; eight dressing rooms. Phone, Clay Cross 90. Station, Clay Cross, L.M.S.

CLAYTON (YORKS), Pop. 5,040.
RIALTO (Harrison), Station Road.—Prop., R. Firth, 8, Rand Place, Bradford. Phone No. 7458. 366 seats. Booked at Hall. Once nightly. Twice Sat. Prices, 4d. to 9d. Phone, 2138. Station, Clayton, L.N.E.R.

CLAYTON-LE-MOORS (LANCS.), Pop. 7,910.
EMPRESS CINEMA (BA).—Prop., Jas. Caton, Freda Villa, Offerton, nr, Stockport. 500 seats. Booked at Manchester. Twice nightly Prices, 4d. to 9d. Proscenium width, 20 ft. Station, Accrington, L.M.S.
STAR PICTURES (WE).—Prop., J. Yates. 859 seats. Once nightly, twice Sat. Station, Accrington, L.M.S.

CLEATOR MOOR (CUMBERLAND), Pop. 6,582.
HIPPODROME (BTP).—Stanley Rogers Cinemas, Ltd., 72, Grey Street, Newcastle-on-Tyne. Phone, Newcastle 20317. 550 seats. Booked at H.O. Prices, 3d. to 9d. Proscenium width, 27 ft. Stage, 18 ft. deep; three dressing rooms. Phone, Cleator Moor 30. Station, Whitehaven L.M.S. and Furness Ry.

CLECKHEATON (YORKS), Pop. 12,868.
PICTURE PALACE (AWH), Albion Street.—Prop., Goodalls Pictures (1931), Ltd. 800 seats. Twice nightly. Mat., Mon. and Thurs. Two changes weekly. Prices, 3d. to 1s. Phone, Cleckheaton 224. Station, Cleckheaton, L.M.S.
SAVOY PICTURE HOUSE (BTH), Albion Street.— Prop., Goodall's Pictures (1931), Ltd., H.O., Albion Street, Cleckheaton. 1,200 seats. Once nightly. Mat., Wed., Fri., and Sat. Two changes weekly. Prices, 6d. to 1s. 3d. Café attached. Phone, Cleckheaton 224 Station, Cleckheaton, L.M.S.

CLEETHORPES (LINCS), Pop. 28,624.
EMPIRE CINEMA (RCA), Alexandra Road.— Prop., Cleethorpes Empire, Ltd. 943 seats. Booked at Theatre Royal. Continuous. Prices, 6d. to 1s. 3d. Phone, Cleethorpes 59. Station, Cleethorpes, L.N.E.R.
REGAL.—Controlled by Union Cinemas, Ltd., 15, Regent Street, London, S.W.1. Booked at H.O.
RITZ (WE).—Controlled by Union Cinemas, Ltd., Union House, 15, Regent Street, London, S.W.1. Continuous. Booked at H.O. Station, Cleethorpes, L.N.E.R.
THEATRE ROYAL (WE).—Prop., Cleethorpes Empire, Ltd., Grant Street, Cleethorpes. Phone, 73. 1,350 seats. Booked at Hall. Twice nightly. Café and Dance Hall. Station, Cleethorpes, L.N.E.R.
Fitted "ARDENTE" Deaf Aids See page 258

CLEVEDON (SOMERSET), Pop. 7,033.
PICTURE HOUSE (Picturetone), Old Church Road.—Prop. and Man., Victor E. Cox, trading as The Clevedon Cinephone Co. 42, Old Church Road, Clevedon. 750 seats

PATHETONE WEEKLY, The Super Screen Magazine!

CLEVEDON—Contd.
Booked at Hall. Continuous. Mat., Wed.
and Sat. Two changes weekly. Prices, 6d.
to 1s. 6d. Stage, 17 ft. deep; two large
dressing-rooms. Proscenium width, 32 ft.
Café and Dance Hall attached. Phone,
Clevedon 58. Station, Clevedon, G.W.R.

CLEVELEYS (LANCS), **Pop. 5,000.**
BEANLAND'S PAVILION (WE).—Prop., W. Bean-
land. 460 seats. Booked at Hall by Prop.
Pictures and Variety. Continuous in summer
season, once nightly in winter. Prices, 7d. to
1s. 3d. Stage, 20 ft. deep; four dressing
rooms. Proscenium width, 21½ ft. Phone
Cleveleys 113. Station, Thornton (for Cleve-
leys), L.M.S.
ODEON (BTH).—Props., Odeon (Cleveleys), Ltd.,
Cornhill House, Bennett's Hill, Birmingham.
Phone, Midland 2781. Booked at 49, Park
Lane, London, W.1. Prices, 9d. to 1s. 6d.
Phone, Cleveleys 2294. Café attached.
Station, Thornton, L.M.S.
SAVOY CINEMA (WE), Victoria Road.—Prop.,
Cleveleys Entertainments, Ltd., Chairman
R. Pilling; Sec., H. Mills. 498 seats. One
show nightly. Twice nightly, Wed. and Sat.
Mat., Sat., 2.30. Prices, 7d. to 1s. Pros-
cenium, width, 22 ft. Phone, Cleveleys 46,
Station, Thornton (for Cleveleys), L.M.S.

CLEY NEXT THE SEA (NORFOLK).
TOWN HALL CINEMA (Sound).—Saturdays only.

CLIFFE-AT-HOO (KENT), **Pop. 2,250.**
GLOBE CINEMA (AWH).—Prop., R. G. Whitaker,
4, Norwood Road, Cliffe-at-Hoo. Booked at
Hall. 350 seats. Once nightly. Prices, 4d.
to 1s. Proscenium width, 15 ft. Station,
Cliffe-at-Hoo (via Gravesend), S.R.

CLITHEROE (LANCS), **Pop. 12,000.**
GRAND KINEMA (WE).
PALLADIUM PICTURE HOUSE (BTH).—Prop.,
and Man., H. Lyons. 779 seats. Booked at
Hall. Twice nightly. Prices, 6d. to 1s.
Phone, Clitheroe 147. Station, Clitheroe,
L.M.S.
PICTURE HALL (WE), King Lane.—Prop.,
Clitheroe Equitable Co-operative and Indus-
trial Society, Ltd., 2, Moor Lane, Clitheroe.
822 seats. Booked J. Brearly, Bridge Street,
Manchester. Continuous nightly. Twice on Sat.
Pictures and occasional Variety. Stage, 24 ft.
deep; two dressing-rooms. Variety booked
by Brearly, 21, Bridge Street, Manchester.
Prices, 6d. to 1s. Proscenium width, 24 ft.
Phone, Clitheroe 67. Station, Clitheroe
(Passenger), L.M.S.

CLOWNE (DERBY), **Pop. 6,037.**
PALACE (WE), Rectory Road.—Prop., Clowne
and District Cinematograph Co., Ltd. 500
seats. Booked at Hall. One show nightly.
Prices, 4d. to 1s. Station, Clowne, L.M.S.

COALVILLE (LEICESTER), **Pop. 21,886.**
GRAND CINEMA (WE).—Prop., Coalville Theatres,
Ltd. Booked at Hall by C. K. Deeming.
919 seats. One show nightly. Mat., Mon.
and Sat. Prices, 4d. to 1s. Phone, Coalville 56. Station, Coalville, L.M.S.
PALACE (Edibell).—Prop., Whitwick and District Picture House Co., Ltd., Silver Street.
600 seats. Booked at Hall. One show
nightly. Twice Sat. Prices, 4d. to 1s. 3d.
Phone, Whitwick 89. Station, Whitwick,
L.M.S.

REGAL THEATRE (WE), Marlborough Square
—Prop., Coalville Theatres, Ltd., Man. Dir
C. K. Deeming. Booked at Hall by C. K
Deeming. One show nightly, two on Sat.
Prices, 6d. to 1s. 3d. Phone, Coalville 56.
Station, Coalville, L.M.S.
RITZ (———).—Props., Ritz (Coalville) Ltd.
1,000 seats. Continuous. Booked at Grand,
Coalville. Phone No. 56. Station, Coalville.

COBHAM (SURREY).
SAVOY (BTH), Portsmouth Road.—Props.,
Savoy (Cobham) Ltd., Regency House,
Warwick Street, S.W.1. Phone, Gerrard
5520. Continuous. 895 seats. Prices 6d.
to 2s. 6d. Booked at H.O. Occasional
Variety. 45 ft. Phone, Cobham 611.
Station, Cobham, S.R.

COBRIDGE, Stoke-on-Trent (STAFFS), **Pop. 10,711.**
COBRIDGE PICTURE HALL (BA).—(Closed).

COCKERMOUTH (CUMBERLAND), **Pop. 4,789.**
GRAND THEATRE (BA), Station Road.—Prop.,
Grand Theatre and Cinema Co., Ltd. 740
seats. Booked at Hall. Once nightly, Tues.,
Wed. and Fri. Twice Mon., Tues. and Sat.
Two changes weekly. Prices, 6d. to 1s.
Stage, 25 ft. deep; four dressing-rooms.
Phone, 54. Station, Cockermouth, L.M.S.

COCKFIELD (CO. DURHAM).
CROWN CINEMA (Echo).

COGGESHALL (ESSEX), **Pop. 3,100.**
CINEMA (BTP), West Street.—Booked at 54,
Chevalier Street, Ipswich. Phone, Ipswich
4036. 400 seats. Once nightly. Mon. to Fri.
Three shows Sat. Prices, 6d. to 1s. 3d.
Proscenium width, 15 ft. Phone, Coggeshall
90. Station, Kelvedon, L.N.E.R.

COLCHESTER (ESSEX), **Pop. 48,607.**
CORN EXCHANGE CINEMA.
EMPIRE (RA), Mersea Road.—Props., Gaumont
British Picture Corporation, Ltd., 123, Regent
Street, London, W.1. Phone, Regent 6641.
Booked at H.O. Continuous. Prices, 6d. to
1s. 3d. Phone, Colchester 34611. Station,
Colchester (North), L.N.E.R.
HEADGATE THEATRE (WE).—330 seats. Booked
by County Cinemas, Ltd., Dean House, Dean
Street, W.1. Three shows daily. Prices, 6d. to
1s. 6d. Phone, Colchester 2939. Station,
Colchester, L.N.E.R.
HIPPODROME (RCA), High Street.—Prop.,
Gaumont British Picture Corporation, Ltd.,
123, Regent Street, London, W.1. Phone,
Regent 8080. 1,000 seats. Booked at H.O.
Continuous. Stage, 36 ft. deep. Café at-
tached. Prices, 5d. to 2s. Phone, Colchester
309411. Station, Colchester (North).

Fitted "ARDENTE" Deaf Aids
See page 258

PLAYHOUSE (WE).—Props., Associated British
Cinemas, Ltd., 30-31, Golden Square, W.1.
Gerrard 7887. 1,158 seats. Booked at H.O.
Continuous. Prices, 6d. to 1s. 6d. Stage and
nine dressing-rooms. Phone, Colchester 3680.
Station, Colchester, L.N.E.R.
REGAL (WE).—Booked by County Cinemas, Ltd.,
Dean House, Dean Street, W.1. 1,450 seats.
Continuous. Pictures and Variety. Prices,
6d. to 2s. 5d. Stage, 15 ft. deep; four dressing

rooms. Proscenium width, 54 ft. Café attached. Phone, Colchester 2294. Station, Colchester, L.N.E.R.

WURLITZER ORGAN
Installed in this Kinema

COLEFORD (GLOS.), **Pop. 2,777.**
CINEMA (Edibell).—Prop. and Res. Man., R, Reeves. 400 seats. Booked at Hall. One show nightly, Tues., Wed., and Fri. Two shows Mon., Thurs. and Sat. Occasional Variety. Stage, 18 ft. deep ; two dressing rooms. Prices, 6d. to 1s. 6d. Proscenium width, 25 ft. Phone, Coleford 49. Station, Lydney, G.W.R. and L.M.S. Films by Film Transport (Broxburn), Ltd.

COLESHILL (WARWICKSHIRE), **Pop. 3,200.**
COLESHILL KINEMA.
THE CINEMA (Gyrotone).—Props., John Wynn and G. French. Booked at Hall. Continuous. Prices, 6d. to 1s. 3d. Phone, Coleshill 69. Station, Coleshill, L.M.S.

COLNE (LANCS), **Pop. 23,790.**
CENTRAL HALL.—Prop., J. Ferguson. Station, Colne, L.M.S.
HIPPODROME (WE).—Prop., Victoria Picturedrome (Colne) Ltd. 980 seats. One show nightly. Two on Sat. Mats., Tues. and Sat. Two changes weekly. Prices, 5d. to 1s. 3d. Phone, Colne 108. Station, Colne, L.M.S.
KING'S THEATRE.—850 seats. One show nightly, two on Sat. Two changes weekly. Prices, 9d. to 2s. 4d. Phone, Colne 108.
MUNICIPAL HALL.—Occasional shows. 860 seats. Station, Colne, L.M.S.
SAVOY CINEMA (BTP), Market Street. 900 seats. —Props., Victoria Picturedrome (Colne) Ltd. Station, Colne, L.M.S.

COLYTON (DEVON), **Pop. 1,880.**
VILLAGE HALL.

CONGLETON (CHESHIRE), **Pop. 14,500.**
CAPITOL (BA).—Prop. Congleton Capitol Theatre, Ltd. 800 seats. Booked by H. D. Moorhouse Circuit. Pictures, Variety, etc. Prices, 3d. to 1s. Station, Congleton, L.M.S.
PREMIER (WE), High Street.—Prop., Premier Picture House (Congleton), Ltd. 823 seats. Booked at Manchester. Continuous. Prices, 3d. to 1s. Proscenium width, 22 ft. Phone, Congleton 88. Station, Congleton, L.M.S.
NEW CINEMA (BTP), Royle Street.—600 seats. Three shows daily. Pictures and Variety. Prices, 3d. to 1s. Proscenium width, 32 ft. Stage, 6 ft. deep; two dressing-rooms. Phone, Congleton 130. Station, Congleton, L.M.S.

CONISBORO' (YORKS), **Pop. 18,179.**
GLOBE PALACE (Morrison).—Lessee, J. Hall. 650 seats. One show nightly, two on Sat. Two changes weekly. Prices, 3d. to 9d. Station, Conisboro', L.N.E.R.

CONISTON (LANCS), **Pop. 1,098.**
CINEMA.—250 seats. Once or twice weekly.

CONSETT (CO. DURHAM), **Pop. 12,251.**
EMPIRE PALACE (WE), Plaza Buildings.—Props., Consett Cinemas, Ltd. Plaza Buildings, Consett. 1,160 seats. Pictures and Variety. Booked at Newcastle-on-Tyne. Variety booked by Hinges Productions and B. Knight, Newcastle. Twice nightly. Once Fri. Two changes weekly. Prices, 6d. to 1s. Proscenium width, 26 ft. Stage 20 ft. deep ; nine dressing-rooms. Phone, Consett 137. Station, Consett, L.N.E.R.
PLAZA (WE), Plaza Bldgs., Consett.—Props., Consett Cinemas, Ltd. 1,425 seats. Booked at Newcastle-on-Tyne. Twice nightly. Once Fri. Two changes weekly. Prices, 6d. to 1s. 3d. Proscenium width, 30 ft. Phone, Consett 137. Station, Consett, L.N.E.R.
TOWN HALL (BTH).—Props., Consett Cinemas, Ltd., Plaza Buildings, Consett. Phone, Consett 137. 640 seats. Booked at Newcastle-on-Tyne. Once nightly, two shows Sat. Two changes weekly. Prices, 6d. to 1s. Proscenium width, 20 ft.; five dressing-rooms. Station, Consett, L.N.E.R.

COPPULL (nr. Chorley) (LANCS), **Pop. 6,500.**
ELECTRIC PALACE (Electrocord), Mill Lane.— Prop., Electric Palace, Coppull, Ltd. 450 seats. Booked at Manchester and Liverpool. Once nightly. Twice Sat. Prices, 4d. to 9d. Station, Coppull via Wigan, L.M.S.

CORBY (NORTHANTS), **Pop. 1449.**
CORBY CINEMA (Imperial).—Lessee, B. Willson, Roselawn, Uppingham. Booked at Cosy Cinema, Uppingham. Once nightly, two shows Sat. Prices, 6d. to 1s. Phone, Uppingham 123. Station, Weldon and Corby, L.M.S.
ODEON (BTH), Rockingham Road and Stephensons Way.—Props., Odeon (Corby), Ltd., Cornhill House, Bennett's Hill, Birmingham. Phone, Midland 2781. Booked at 49, Park Lane, London, W.1. Continuous. Prices, 6d. to 1s. 6d. Phone, Corby 236. Station, Corby, L.M.S.

CORSHAM (WILTS), **Pop. 3,941.**
REGAL (Morrison).—Prop., A. J. Stratford, Corsham. 270 seats. Booked at Hall. Continuous. Prices, 6d. to 1s. 3d. Proscenium width, 20 ft. Phone, Corsham 113. Station, Corsham, G.W.R.

COTTENHAM (CAMBS.).
LORDSHIP HALL.

COUNDON (CO. DURHAM), **Pop. 6,912.**
EDEN PAVILION (AWH).—Prop., Norham Thompson. Continuous. One show Sunday evening. Occasional Variety. Two changes weekly. Prices, 5d. to 1s. 3d. Proscenium width, 24 ft. Stage, 16 ft. deep; two dressing-rooms. Phone, Bishop Auckland 205. Station, Coundon, L.N.E.R.

COVENTRY (WARWICKS.), **Pop. 167,046.**
ALEXANDRA THEATRE (WE), Ford Street.— Philpot Circuit, 116, Much Park Street, Coventry. 800 seats. Continuous. Once on Sunday, daily Mat. Prices, 7d. to 1s. 6d. Phone, Coventry 4716. Station, Coventry, L.M.S.
ASTORIA (WE) Albany Road.—Prop., Scala Entertainments Ltd., 92, Barkers Butts Lane, Coventry. Phone 2112. 1,400 seats. Booked at H.O. Continuous. Mat., daily, except Fri. ; two dressing-rooms. Prices, 6d. to 1s. Proscenium width, 33 ft. Phone, Coventry 2056. Station, Coventry, L.M.S.
BALSALL PALACE (Gyrotone), Balsall Common.— Prop., Gyrotone, Ltd., Coleshill, Warwickshire. Phone, 69. 270 seats. Booked at H.O. Three shows weekly. Prices, 6d. to 1s. 3d. Phone 78. Station, Berkswell, L.M.S.

COVENTRY—Contd.

BROOKVILLE (WE), Holbrook Lane.—Prop., Holbrook Theatres, Ltd. 965 seats. Booked at Hall. Continuous. Prices, 6d. to 1s. Proscenium width 36 ft. Stage 12 ft. deep ; two dressing rooms. Dance Hall attached. Phone, Coventry 8258. Station, Coventry, L.M.S.

CARLTON THEATRE (WE). Stoney Stanton Road.—Prop., Scala Entertainments (Coventry), Ltd., 94, Barkers Butt Lane, Coventry. Phone, No. 2113. 475 seats. Booked at H.O. Continuous. Mat., Mon., Thurs., Sat. Prices, 6d. to 1s. Proscenium width, 18 ft. Phone, Coventry 8548. Station, Coventry, L.M.S.

CROWN THEATRE (BTH), Far Gosford Street.—Prop., Crown Theatre (Coventry), Ltd. 900 seats. Continuous. Mats. daily. Two changes weekly. Prices, 4d. to 9d. Phone, Coventry 3962. Station, Coventry.

EMPIRE THEATRE (WE), Hartford Street.—Prop., Associated British Cinemas, Ltd., 30-31 Golden Square, W.1. 1,547 seats. Booked at H.O. Continuous. Prices, 6d. to 2s. Proscenium width, 42 ft. Stage, 21 ft. deep. Three dressing-rooms. Phone 3600 Station, Coventry, L.M.S.

C O M P T O N
ORGAN featured here.

FORUM (WE), Walsgrave Road, Philpot Circuit 116, Much Park Street, Coventry. Phone, Coventry 2366. 1,640 seats. Booked at H.O. Prices, 6d. to 1s. 6d. Proscenium width 45 ft. Phone, 2583. Station, Coventry. L.M.S.

GAUMONT PALACE (BA), Jordan Well.—Prop., Gaumont British Pictures Corporation. Ltd. 2,650 seats. Booked at H.O. Continuous. Daily Mat. Dance Hall and Café attached. Phone, Coventry 204211.

Fitted "ARDENTE" Deaf Aids
See page 258

C O M P T O N
ORGAN featured here.

GLOBE THEATRE (BTH), Primrose Hill Street.—Prop., Scala Entertainments (Coventry), Ltd., 92, Barkers Butts Lane, Coventry. Phone, 2113. 1,004 seats. Booked at H.O. Continuous, daily Mat. Two changes weekly. Prices, 6d. to 1s. 3d. Phone, Coventry 3813. Station, Coventry.

GRAND CINEMA (WE), Foleshill Road.—Prop., F. and S. Cinemas, Ltd. Booked at Hall. Continuous. Prices, 5d. to 1s. Proscenium width, 24 ft. Phone, Coventry 8312. Station, Coventry, L.M.S.

IMPERIAL (Gyrotone).—Prop., A. W. Pell, Ltd. 450 seats. Booked at Hall. Continuous. Two changes weekly. Prices, 6d. to 1s. Phone, Coventry 2470.

LYRIC (BTH), Holbrook Lane.—Prop., Lyric Theatre (Coventry), Ltd. Booked at Hall. 900 seats. Continuous. Prices, 6d. to 1s. Proscenium width, 34 ft. Phone, Coventry 8585. Station, Coventry, L.M.S. or F.T.S.

PALLADIUM PICTURE HOUSE (WE).—Prop., Plaza (Coventry), Ltd., 116, Much Park Street, Coventry. 763 seats. Booked at H.O. Evenings and Mats. Two changes

weekly. Prices, 7d. to 1s. Phone, Coventry 2738. Station, Coventry, L.M.S.

PLAZA CINEMA (WE).—Prop., Plaza (Coventry), Ltd., 116, Much Park Street, Coventry. Phone, 2366. 1,412 seats. Booked at H.O. Continuous. Prices, 6d. to 1s. 6d. Café attached. Phone, Coventry 4822. Station, Coventry, L.M.S.

PRINCE OF WALES THEATRE (BTH), Stoney Stanton Road.—Prop., Crown Theatre (Coventry), Ltd. 460 seats. Continuous. Mat., Mon., Thurs. and Sat. Two changes weekly. Prices, 5d. to 9d. Phone Coventry 8337. Station, Coventry, L.M.S.

REDESDALE (AWH), Tolehill Road.—Prop., W. H. Bassett Green, The Three Spires Avenue, Coventry. Booked at Hall. Continuous. Prices, 4d. to 1s. 4d. Phone 2389. Station, Coventry, L.M.S. and Film Transport.

REGAL (WE). Props., Scala Entertainments (Coventry), Ltd., 92, Barkers Butts Lane, Coventry. Phone, Coventry 2112. 800 seats.

REX.—Philpot Circuit, 116, Much Park Street, Coventry.

WURLITZER ORGAN
Installed in this Kinema

RIALTO CASINO (WE).—Prop., Scala Entertainments (Coventry), Ltd., 92, Barkers Butts Lane, Coventry. Phone, 2112. 1,300 seats. Two changes weekly. Phone, Coventry 3768.

C O M P T O N
ORGAN featured here.

RIVOLI (AWH), Longford Road.—Prop., Plaza (Coventry), Ltd., 116, Much Park Street, Coventry. Phone, Coventry 2366. 1,200 seats. Booked at H.O. Continuous. Prices, 4d. to 1s. 3d. Phone, Coventry 8325. Station, Coventry or Foleshill, L.M.S.

ROXY.—Philpot Circuit, 116, Much Park Street, Coventry. Phone, Coventry 2366. 1,575 seats. Prices, 6d. to 1s. 3d. Phone No. 2389. Station, Coventry.

SCALA (WE), Far Gosford Street.—Prop., Scala Entertainments (Coventry), Ltd., 92, Barkers Butt Lane, Coventry. Phone 2112. 1,300 seats. Booked at H.O. Continuous. Proscenium width, 35 ft. Phone, Coventry 3768. Station, Coventry. L.M.S.

COWES (I. OF W.), Pop 10,179

KINGS (BA), East Cowes.—Props., Isle of Wight Theatres, Ltd., Theatre Royal, Ryde, I.O.W. Phone, Ryde 2387. 678 seats. Booked at Theatre Royal, Ryde. Twice nightly. Mat. Wed. and Sat. Prices, 6d. to 1s. 10d. Proscenium width, 28 ft. Phone, Cowes 261. Station, Cowes, S.R.

ROYALTY THEATRE (BA), Birmingham Road. Props., Isle of Wight Theatres, Ltd. 500 seats. Booked at Theatre Royal, Ryde. Two shows nightly. Two changes weekly. Mat. Sat. Prices, 6d. to 1s. 10d. Proscenium width, 28 ft. Phone, Cowes, 2389. By S. & I.W.S.P. Co., and S.R.

COXHOE (Co. DURHAM), Pop. 4,000.

AVENUE CINEMA (WE).—Props., T. and F. Iseton. 838 seats. Booked at Hall. Once or twice nightly. Prices, 3d. to 1s. Proscenium width, 20 ft. Phone. Coxhoe 29. Station, Coxhoe Bridge, L.N.E.R.

GEM (AWH).—Props., T. and F. Iseton, Avenue Cinema, Coxhoe. 300 seats. Booked at Avenue Cinema. Once nightly. Prices, 3d. to 9d. Proscenium width, 19 ft. Station, Coxhoe Bridge, L.N.E.R.

PICTURE HOUSE (Morrison), 500 seats.

CRADLEY HEATH (STAFFS), **Pop. 10,101.**

EMPIRE THEATRE (Celebritone), High Street.— Prop., Empire Theatre (Cradley Heath), Ltd. 650 seats. Man. Dir. W. Williams, Coldingham. Belbroughton. Phone, Belbroughton 24. Two shows nightly. Two changes weekly. Prices, 3d. to 6d. Phone, Cradley 188. Station, Cradley Heath. G.W.R.

IMPERIAL CINEMA (Morrison), Netherton.— Prop., C. E. Couper. Continuous. Two changes weekly.

MAJESTIC (WE).—Five Ways.—Prop., Majestic Cinema (Cradley Heath), Ltd., Shell Bldgs., Blackheath, Birmingham. Phone, Back-1316. 1309 seats. Booked at H.O. Continuous daily Mon. to Fri. Three shows Sat. Two changes weekly. Prices, 6d. to 1s. 3d. Proscenium width, 36 ft. Phone, Cradley Heath 6150. Station, Cradley Heath, G.W.R.

ROYAL THEATRE (Classitone), Bank Street.— 750 seats. Booked at Hall. Two shows nightly. Two changes weekly. Prices, 3d. to 6d. Phone, Cradley 188. Station, Cradley, G.W.R.

WORKMEN'S INSTITUTE.

CRAMLINGTON (NORTHUMBERLAND), **Pop. 8,238.**

KING GEORGE HALL (BTP).—Prop., Northumberland Picture and Public Hall Co., Ltd. 500 seats. One show nightly ; two on Sat. Two changes weekly. Station, Cramlington L.N.E.R.

CRANBROOK (KENT), **Pop. 3,831.**

THE CINEMA.—Prop., F. W. Malpass. Booked at Hall. Two changes weekly. Prices, 5d. to 1s. 3d. Phone 57. Station, Cranbrook, S.R.

CRANLEIGH (SURREY), **Pop. 3,749.**

THE REGAL (BA), High Street.—Props., Cranleigh Cinema, Ltd., 81, Chester Square, S.W.1. Phone, Sloane 2178. Booked at Hall. Continuous nightly. Mats. Wed. and Sat. 481 seats. Prices, 6d. to 2s. Proscenium width 30 ft. Phone No. 373. Station, Cranleigh, Surrey.

CRANWELL (Near SLEAFORD, LINCS.), **Pop, 2,000.**

ROYAL AIR FORCE CINEMA (BTH). 750 seats. Booked by Cinema Committee. Twice nightly, Wed. and Sat. Once nightly, Thurs. and Sun. 750 seats. Prices, 4d. to 1s. 6d. Proscenium width, 22 ft. Phone, Sleaford 64. Ext. 134. Station, Sleaford, L.N.E.R.

CRAVEN ARMS (SALOP).

REGAL (BTP).—Craven Cinemas, Ltd., 296 seats. Once nightly. Prices, 6d. to 1s. 6d Proscenium width, 21 ft. Phone, Craven Arms 78. Station, Stokesay and Craven Arms.

CRAWCROOK (CO. DURHAM), **Pop. 4,000.**

GLOBE ELECTRIC THEATRE (BTP).—Lessees, E. J. Hinge Circuit, 72, Grey Street, Newcastle-on-Tyne. Occasional Variety. 700 seats. Booked at H.O. Prices, 4d. to 1s. Phone, Ryton 86. Station, Ryton-on-Tyne, L.N.E.R.

CRAWLEY (SUSSEX), **Pop. 4,421.**

IMPERIAL CINEMA (WE), Brighton Road.—Prop , C. Gadsdon. 506 seats. Booked at Hall. Continuous. Prices, 4d. to 2s. Proscenium width, 28 ft. Phone, Crawley 39. Station, Crawley, S.R.

CRAYFORD (KENT), **Pop. 15,887.**

PRINCESS'S THEATRE (WE).—Controlled by Union Cinemas, Ltd., Union House, 15, Regent Street, London, S.W.1. Phone, Whitehall 8484. Booked at H.O. Continuous. Prices, 6d. to 1s. 4d. Phone, Bexley Heath 336. Station, Crayford, S.R.

CREDITON (DEVON), **Pop. 3,490.**

PALACE CINEMA (BA).—Prop., Crediton Cinema Co., Ltd. 364 seats. Once nightly. Three shows Sat. Booked at Hall. Prices, 6d. to 1s. 6d. Phone, Crediton, 108. Station, Crediton.

CRESWELL (NOTTS), **Pop. 6,000.**

ELECTRIC PALACE (Regent).—Prop., Creswell Electric Palace Co., Ltd., King Street, Creswell, near Mansfield. 410 seats. Pictures and Variety. Booked at Hall. Once nightly Twice Sat. Prices, 6d. to 1s. 0d. Stage, 14 ft. deep ; three dressing-rooms. Proscenium width, 24 ft. Phone, Creswell 1. Station Elmton and Creswell, L.M.S.

CREWE (CHESHIRE), **Pop. 46,061.**

EMPIRE PICTURE HOUSE (RCA), Heath Street.— Prop., Associated British Cinemas, Ltd., 30-31, Golden Square, W.1. 938 seats. Booked at H.O. Continuous. Daily Mat. Prices, 6d. to 9d. Proscenium width, 29 ft. Phone, Crewe 2732. Station, Crewe, L.M.S.

GRAND CINEMA (BTP) West Street.—H.D. Moorhouse Circuit. 996 seats. Booked at H.O. Three times daily. Two changes weekly. Prices, 3d. to 1s. Proscenium width, 36 ft. Phone, Crewe 2861. Station, Crewe, L.M.S.

KING PICTURE HOUSE (RCA), Co-operative Street.—Prop. and Res. Man., A. Hand. 1,400 seats. Booked at Hall by Prop. Pictures and Variety. Continuous. Five Mats. Two changes weekly. Prices, 4d. to 1s. 6d. Stage 20 ft. deep ; two dressing-rooms. Proscenium width, 30 ft. Phone, Crewe 2230. Station, Crewe, L.M.S.

ODEON THEATRE (BTH), Delamere Street.— Props., Odeon (Crewe), Ltd., Bennett's Hill, Birmingham. Phone, Midland 2781. (In course of construction.)

PALACE (WE) Edleston Road.—Pictures and Variety. 974 seats. Films booked at Manchester and Liverpool ; Variety by W. Dalton at 57, Parsonage Road, Withington, Manchester. Prices, 4d. to 1s. 2d. Phone, Crewe, 65. Stage, 28 ft. deep. Station, Crewe, L.M.S.

QUEEN'S HALL (WE).—806 seats.

CREWKERNE (SOMERSET), **Pop. 3,509.**

PALACE THEATRE (BTH), West Street.—Prop., Capt. K. E. Coleberd. 600 seats. Booked at Hall. Prices, 5d. to 2s. Station, Crewkerne. S.R.

CRICH (DERBYSHIRE) **Pop. 3;500.**

PICTURE HOUSE (Marshall).—(Closed.)

The Pick Of Variety And Radio Stars In PATHETONE WEEKLY.

CROMER, (NORFOLK), **Pop. 4,177.**
REGAL CINEMA (BTH), Hans Place.—Prop.,
V. E. H. Cinemas, Ltd., The Lido, Aylsham
Road, Norwich. 500 seats. Booked at H.O.
Continuous. Prices, 7d. to 2s. Proscenium
width, 20 ft. Phone, Cromer ·257. Station,
Cromer, L.N.E.R. Films per E. R. Ives, Ltd.
Norwich.
OLYMPIA (BTH).—Prop., V. E. H. Cinemas, Ltd.
The Lido, Aylsham Road, Norwich. Open
during Summer season only.

CROOK (CO. DURHAM), **Pop. 11,690.**
EMPIRE PALACE (BTH), 12, South Street.—Prop.,
North East Coast Cinemas, Ltd., 11, Bath Lane,
Newcastle-on-Tyne. Phone, Newcastle 27864.
700 seats. Continuous. Booked at H.O.
Two changes weekly and Sunday programme.
Prices, 4d. to 1s. 4d. Station, Crook, L.N.E.R.
HIPPODROME (WE), Bankfoot Road.—Prop.,
North East Coast, Cinemas, Ltd., 11 Bath
Lane, Newcastle-on-Tyne. 950 seats. Booked
at H.O. Continuous. Prices, 4d. to 1s. 4d.
Stage, 14 ft. deep ; two dressing-rooms.
Proscenium width, 23 ft.
THEATRE ROYAL (BTH), Addison Street. 800
seats.—Closed.

CROSBY (near **Liverpool**) (LANCS), **Pop. 3,800.**
CORONA CINEMA (BA), College Road.—Prop.,
Denman Picture Houses, Ltd., 123, Regent
Street, London, W.1. 900 seats. Booked at
H.O. Continuous. Prices, 7d. to 1s. 4d.
Phone, Crosby 762. Station, Blundellsands,
L.M.S.
REGENT PICTURE HOUSE (WE).—Prop., Associ-
ated British Cinemas, Ltd., 30-31, Golden
Square, London, W.1. Continuous. Café.
Lounge attached. Prices, 6d. to 1s. 3d.
Phone Crosby 700. Stations, Waterloo and
Crosby, L.M.S.

CROSSGATES (NR. LEEDS), **Pop. 7,000.**
PICTURE HOUSE (BTP).—Prop., Crossgates
Picture House Co., Ltd., 6, Park Square,
Leeds. 500 seats. Booked at Hall. Con-
tinuous. Twice on Sat. Prices, 6d. to 1s.
Proscenium width, 18 ft. Phone. 85489.
Station, Crossgates, L.N.E.R.

CROSSHILLS (YORKS), **Pop. 5,000.**
PICTURE HOUSE (BTH), Station Road.—Prop.,
Crosshills Picture House Co. 500 seats.
Booked at Hall. One show nightly. Two on
Sats. and holidays. Prices, 3d. to 9d. Pros-
cenium width, 25 ft. Phone, Crosshills 83.
Station, Kildwick and Crosshills, L.M.S.

CROSTON (LANCS.), **Pop. 1,935.**
CINEMA (Electrocord), Station Road.—Prop.,
E. Jackson and Sons. 300 seats. Once
nightly, twice Sat. Prices, 3d. to 1s. Phone,
Croston 36. Station, Croston, L.M.S.

CROWBOROUGH (SUSSEX), **Pop. 6,500.**
REGENT (WE).—Props., Shipman and King,
M 84, Shell Mex House, Strand, W.C.2.
Phone, Temple Bar 5077. Booked at H.O.
Continuous from 6 p.m. Mat. Wed. and Sat.
at 2.30. Station, Crowborough, S.R.

CROWLAND (LINCS).
FORESTERS HALL.—Once weekly Thurs., at
7.30 p.m. Prices, 7d. to 1s.

CROWLE (LINCS), **Pop. 2,838.**
PICTURE HOUSE (Morrison).—Props., J. Spivey
and Sons. 500 seats. Once nightly. Three
shows Sat. Booked at Hall. Prices, 6d. to 1s.

Proscenium width, 16 ft. Phone No. 49.
Station, Crowle, L.N.E.R.

CROWTHORNE (BERKS), **Pop. 5,000.**
ST. GEORGE'S (AWH), High Street.—Prop.,
Border (Berks) Cinemas, Ltd. 300 seats.
Booked at H.O. Continuous. Mat., Sat.
Two changes weekly. Prices, 6d. to 1s. 6d.
Phone, Crowthorne 220. Station, Crowthorne
(late Wellington College), S.R. Films by
London and Provincial Films Motor Transport
Co., Ltd.

CROYDON (SURREY), **Pop. 233,115.**
CLASSIC (BTH), Brighton Road, S. Croydon.—
Prop., Unique Cinema (Croydon), Ltd. Booked
at Hall. Continuous. Phone, Croydon 6655.
Station, South Croydon, S.R.
CROYDON PAVILION (BTP), Broad Green—
Prop., R. Dormer, 247, Norbury Avenue.
Norbury, S.W. Phone, Pollard 4818. 302,
seats. Booked at Hall. Continuous. Prices, 6d.
to 1s. 3d. Phone, Thornton Heath 2082.
Station, West Croydon, S.R.
DAVIS THEATRE (WE).—Prop., Davis Theatre
(Croydon), Ltd. Marble Arch Pavilion,
London, W.1. 3,712 seats. Continuous.
Pictures and Variety. Prices, 7d. to 3s. 6d.
Stage, 30 ft. deep ; six dressing-rooms.
Café with dance floor. Phone, Croydon 3156.
Station, East Croydon, S.R.
Fitted "ARDENTE" Deaf Aids
See page 258

COMPTON
ORGAN featured here.
EMPIRE (WE).—Prop., Metropolitan and Pro-
vincial Cinematograph Theatres, Ltd.,
14-15, Lancaster Place, Strand, London,
W.C.2. Phone, Temple Bar 1144. 1,868 seats.
Booked at H.O. Continuous. Pictures and
Variety. Phone, Croydon 1174. ' Station,
West Croydon, S.R.
HIPPODROME (WE), Crown Hill.—Prop., Croy-
don Amusements, Ltd., 30-31, Golden Square,
W.1. 1,250 seats. Booked at H.O. Con-
tinuous. Stage, 30 ft. deep ; ten dressing-
rooms. Prices, 6d. to 1s. 6d. Proscenium
width, 32 ft. Phone, Croydon 1444. Stations,
West and East Croydon, S.R.
LUXOR (AWH), Windmill Road.—Prop., Tudor
Theatre (Selhurst), Ltd. 500 seats. Booked
at Hall. Continuous. Prices, 6d. to 1s. 3d.
Phone, Thornton Heath 3717. Station,
Selhurst, S.R.
NEW PALLADIUM (WE), Surrey Street.—Prop.,
Alfred Barnett. 760 seats. Booked at Hall.
Continuous. Prices, 6d. to 3s. 6d. Phone,
Croydon 1827. Station, East Croydon, S.R.
ODEON THEATRE (WE), 108, North Road.—
Prop., Odeon Theatres, Ltd., Cornhill House,
Bennett's Hill, Birmingham. Phone, Midland
2781. Booked at 49, Park Lane, London,
W.1 Continuous. Prices, 6d. to 1s. 6d. Tea
room attached. Phone, Croydon 0202.
Station, West Croydon, S.R.
SAVOY (RCA), Broad Green.—Props., Associated
British Cinemas, Ltd., 30-31, Golden Square,
W.1. Booked at H.O. Continuous. Prices,
tinuous. Prices, 6d. to 1s. 6d. Phone,
Croydon 0486. Station, West Croydon.
SCALA (WE), North End.—Prop., Gaiety Picture
House (Southampton), Ltd. 822 seats.
Booked at Hall. Continuous. Prices, 6d. to
1s. 6d. Phone, Croydon 1620. Station,
East Croydon, S.R.

CRUMLIN (MON.)
EMPIRE (BA).—Prop., E. Ruddick. 600 seats.
Once nightly. Continuous Sat. Prices, 3d.
to 9d. Proscenium width, 22 ft. Occasional
Variety. Stage, 18 ft. deep ; two dressing-
rooms. Station, Crumlin, G.W.R.

CUDWORTH (YORKS), Pop. 9380.
PALACE, Barnsley Road.—Prop., Palace of
Varieties, Ltd.
ROCK CINEMA (WE).

CULLOMPTON (DEVON), Pop. 2,741.
REGAL (BA).—Prop., Cullompton Cinema Co.,
Ltd. Phone 54. 350 seats. Booked at
5, High Street, Cullompton. Once nightly,
three shows Sat. Prices, 3d. to 1s. 6d. Proscenium width, 16 ft. Café attached. Station,
Cullompton, G.W.R.

CWM (MON.), Pop. 9,824.
COLISEUM (BTH).—Prop., Ebbw Vale Theatres.
Ltd., Palace, Cannon Street, Ebbw Vale,
800 seats. Booked at Palace, Ebbw Vale.
One show nightly. Two changes weekly.
Prices, 6d. to 1s. Proscenium width, 30 ft.
Phone, Cwm 11. Station, Cwm, G.W.R.
Films by Road Transport.

CWMCARN (MON.), Pop. 4,000.
PARK HALL (WE).—Prop., Park Hall Co. 860
seats. One show nightly. Two changes
weekly. Prices, 7d. to 1s. Station, Cwmcarn,
G.W.R.

CWMFELINFACH (MON), Pop. 4,000.
NINE MILE POINT COLLIERY WORKMEN'S IN-
STITUTE (RCA).—Prop., Local Workmen. 700
seats. Booked at Hall by Committee. One
show nightly, two on Sat. Prices, 3d. to 1s.
Dance Hall. Phone, Ynysddu 20. Station,
Ynysddu, L.M.S. Films by Road Transport.

DAGENHAM (ESSEX), Pop. 89,365.
GRANGE CINEMA (RCA), London Road.—Prop.,
Kessex Cinemas, Ltd. 1,280 seats. Pictures
and Variety. Booked at 197, Wardour Street,
London, W. Phone, Gerrard 2835. 1,200
seats. Continues. Prices, 6d. to 1s. 10d.
Two dressing-rooms. Phone, Rainham, Essex,
193. Stations, Dagenham Dock and Gale
Street, L.M.S. ; or Motor Transport.
HEATHWAY CINEMA.—Prop., Kessex Cinemas,
Ltd., 197, Wardour Street, London, W.1.
Phone, Gerrard 2835.
PRINCESS (WE).—Prop., Princess (Dagenham),
Ltd. Controlled by Associated British
Cinemas, Ltd. 30·31, Golden Square, W.1.
Phone, Gerrard 7887. 1,987 seats.

DALTON BROOK (near Rotherham)
(YORKS), Pop. 5,000.
PALACE (Mihaly).—Prop., Young and Prior.
300 seats. Booked at Hall. Two shows nightly.
Two changes weekly. Prices 6d. to 9d.
Station, Westgate, Rotherham, L.M.S.

DALTON-IN-FURNESS (LANCS), Pop·
10,338.
CO-OPERATIVE HALL (BTP), Chapel Street.—
Prop., Harry Simpson, New Market Street,
Ulverston. Phone, Ulverston 151. 700 seats.
Occasional Variety. Booked at H.O. Once
nightly. Two shows Sat. Prices 4d. to 1s.
Stage, 16 ft. deep ; two dressing-rooms.
Proscenium width, 20 ft. Phone No. 15.
Station, Dalton-in-Furness, L.M.S., and
Northern Film Transport Service.

EMPIRE PICTURE PALACE (BTH).—Prop., Back-
house and Drinkwater Picture Palaces, Ltd.,
28, Station Road, Dalton-in-Furness. Phone,
Dalton 66. Lessee, James Brennan, 107,
Duke Street, Barrow-in-Furness. Phone,
Barrow 990. 676 seats. Once nightly, Mon.
to Friday. Three shows Sat. Prices, 4d. to 1s.
Proscenium width, 29 ft. Stage, 14 ft. deep ;
two dressing-rooms. Phone, Dalton-in-
Furness 14. Station, Dalton-in-Furness,
L.M.S.

DARFIELD (YORKS), Pop. 5,260.
EMPIRE THEATRES (Wired).—Prop., Provincial
Empire Theatres, Ltd. 600 seats. Booked at
Home Farm, Royston, by J. Ball. One show
nightly, two on Sat. Prices, 3d to 10d. Phone,
Royston 12. Station, Darfield, L.M.S.

DARLASTON (STAFFS), Pop. 19,736.
OLYMPIA PICTURE PALACE (RCA).—969 seats.
Continuous. Two changes weekly. Prices, 5d.
to 9d. Phone, Darlaston 19. Stations,
Darlaston, L.M.S., and Wednesbury, G.W.R.
PICTUREDROME (WE), Crescent Road.—Prop.,
Brettell & Olliver. 840 seats. Continuous.
Prices, 6d. to 1s. Phone, Darlaston 6. Station,
James Bridge, Darlaston, L.M.S., or Wednes-
bury, G.W.R.

DARLINGTON (Co. DURHAM), Pop. 72,093.
ALHAMBRA (RCA), Northgate.—Prop., Provincial
Cinematograph Theatres, Ltd., New Gallery
House, Regent Street, London, W.1. Phone;
Regent 8080. 1,000 seats. Continuous.
Prices 7d. to 1s. 3d. Phone, Darlington 2108.
Station, Darlington, L.N.E.R.
ARCADE CINEMA (BA), Skinnergate.—Prop.,
Provincial Cinematograph Theatres, Ltd.
New Gallery House, 123, Regent Street,
London, W. Phone, Regent 8080. Booked
at H.O. Continuous. Prices, 5d. o 1s. Phone,
Darlington 2695. Station, Darlington.
CENTRAL CINEMA (GB), Market Square.—Prop.,
George P. Fenton. 600 seats. Booked by
P. George Fenton, 16, Central Buildings,
Darlington. Continuous. Prices, 3d. to 9d.
Phone, Darlington 2496. Station, Darlington.
COURT KINEMA (WE) Skinnergate.—Prop.,
Gaumont British Picture Corpn. Ltd., and
Provincial Cinematograph Theatres, Ltd.
123, Regent Street, London, W.1. 1,119 seats.
Booked at H.O. Continuous. Prices, 7d. to
1s. 6d. Phone, Darlington 2616. Station,
Darlington (Bank Top), L.N.E.R.
Fitted "ARDENTE" Deaf Aids
See page 258
EMPIRE (WE).—Prop., Darlington Cinemato·
graph Co., Ltd. 890 seats. Continuous.
Daily Mat. Two changes weekly. Prices,
6d. to 1s. 6d. Phone, Darlington 2156.
Station, Darlington, L.N.E.R.
HIPPODROME.—E. J. Hinge Circuit, 72, Grey
Street, Newcastle-on-Tyne.
MAJESTIC (WE), Bondgate.—Props., Majestic
(Cinema) Darlington, Ltd., High Row. Phone,
3595. Controlled by Union Cinemas, Ltd., 15,
Regent Street, London, S.W.1. 1,580 seats.
Continuous. Prices, 6d. to 1s. 6d. Proscenium
width, 45 ft. Stage, 17 ft. deep ; five dressing-
rooms. Café attached. Phone, 2879. Station,
Darlington, L.N.E.R.

C O M P T O N
ORGAN featured here.

DARLINGTON—Contd.

PLAZA CINEMA (AWH) (late Assembly Hall), High Northgate.—Prop., Darlington Cinematograph Co., Ltd., 12, Commercial Street, Darlington. 700 seats. Prices, 5d. to 9d. Phone, Darlington 2940. Station, Darlington, L.N.E.R.

RITZ (WE).—Controlled by Union Cinemas, Ltd., Union House, 15, Regent Street, London, S.W.1. Booked at Head Office. Continuous. Prices. 3d. to 1s. 6d. Station, Darlington, L.N.E.R.

SCALA CINEMA (BTP), Eldon Street.—Prop., J. Weightman, " Ennerdale," King's Road, Middlesbrough. 600 seats. Booked at Newcastle. Continuous. Children's Mat., Sat. Prices, 5d. to 1s. Proscenium width, 25 ft. Phone, Darlington 2152. Station, Darlington, L.N.E.R.

DARNALL (near Sheffield) (YORKS), Pop. 5,000.
(See Sheffield.)

DARTFORD (KENT), Pop. 28,928.

GEM.—Prop., Medway Cinemas, Ltd., Walmar House, 288, Regent Street, London, W.1.

RIALTO (WE), Lowfield Street.—Prop., Medway Cinema, Ltd., Walmar House, 288, Regent Street, W.1. Phone, Langham 2677. 995 seats. Booked at H.O. Continuous. Prices, 7d. to 1s. 6d. Phone, Dartford 372. Station, Dartford, S.R.

SCALA THEATRE (WE), Kent Road.—Prop., Medway Cinemas, Ltd., Walmar House, 288, Regent Street, W.1. Phone, Langham 2677. 1,066 seats. Films booked at H.O. Continuous. Prices, 6d. to 2s. Phone, Dartford 182. Station, Dartford, S.R.

STATE (WE).—Prop., Medway Cinemas, Ltd., Walmar House, 288, Regent Street, W.1. Phone, Langham 2677. 1,500 seats. Booked at H.O. Continuous. Prices, 6d. to 2s. Phone, Dartford 2101. Station, Dartford, S.R.

Fitted "ARDENTE" Deaf Aids
Fitted "ARDENTE" Stage Amplification
See page 258

C O M P T O N

ORGAN featured here.

DARTMOUTH (DEVON), Pop. 6,707.

CINEDROME (BTH), Mayor's Avenue.—Props., George and Northcott, 12, Hillcrest, Mannamead, Plymouth. 600 seats. Booked by Col. W. A. E. Northcott, at 6, The Octagon, Plymouth. Twice nightly. Occasional Variety. Stage, 20 ft. deep. Prices, 6d. to 1s. 6d. Station, Dartmouth, G.W.R.

DARTON (near Barnsley) (YORKS), Pop. 12,595.

EMPIRE (BTH).—Prop., Provincial Empire Theatres, Ltd. 650 seats. One show nightly. Two on Sat. Two changes nightly. Prices, 5d. to 9d. Proscenium width, 24 ft. Station, Darton, L.M.S.

DARWEN (LANCS), Pop. 36,010.

ALBERT HALL (BTP).—Duckworth Street.— Prop., A. Waddicor. 600 seats. Booked at Hall. Two shows nightly. Daily Mat. Prices, 4d. to 1s. Proscenium width, 25 ft. Phone, Darwen 214. Station, Darwen, L.M.S.

OLYMPIA THEATRE (WE), Bolton Road.—Prop., Associated British Cinemas, Ltd., 30-31, Golden Square, W.1. 1,325 seats. Booked at H.O. Two changes weekly. Proscenium width, 30 ft. Stage, 45 ft. deep. Prices, 4d. to 1s. Phone, Darwen 384. Station, Darwen, L.M.S.

PALLADIUM (WE).—Props., Palladium (Darwen), Ltd. 1,012 seats. Twice nightly. Booked by H. D. Moorhouse, Imperial Buildings, Oxford Road, Manchester. Prices, 4d. to 1s. Proscenium width, 24 ft. Phone, 480. Station, Darwen, L.M.S.

PUBLIC HALL (BTP).—Prop., George Harwood. 650 seats. Booked at Hall. Once nightly except Fri., Sats., and holidays. Prices, 3d. to 9d. Station, Darwen.

SAVOY PICTURE HOUSE (WE), Blackburn Road — Prop., W. Lloyd. 938 seats. Booked by Emery Circuit. Twice nightly. Mats. Tues., Thurs. and Sat. Two changes weekly. Prices, 5d. to 1s. Proscenium width, 21 ft. Phone, Darwen 39. Station, Darwen, L.M.S.

DAVENTRY (NORTHANTS), Pop. 3,608.

REGAL (BA).—Props., Daventry Picture Theatre Co., New Street, Daventry. 600 seats. Booked at Hall. Prices, 6d. to 1s. 3d. Proscenium width, 30 ft. Stage, 15 ft. Dance Hall attached. Transport.

DAWDON COLLIERY (Co. DURHAM), Pop. 3,000.

PRINCES (WE).—Prop., Princess Entertainments, Ltd. 1,000 seats. Booked at Hall. Two shows nightly. Two changes weekly. Occasional Variety. Prices, 4d. to 9d. Proscenium width, 40 ft. Stage, 20 ft. deep; four dressing rooms. Station, Seaham Harbour, L.N.E.R.

DAWLEY (SALOP), Pop. 5,600.

COSY. CINEMA (AWH).—550 seats.

DAWLISH (DEVON), Pop. 4,578.

SCALA (Mihaly).—Prop., A. R. Phern, Lyceum, Teignmouth. Phone, Teignmouth 163. 400 seats. Booked at Teignmouth. Continuous. Stage, 18 ft. deep ; four dressing-rooms. Proscenium width, 26 ft. Phone, Dawlish 91. Station, Dawlish, G.W.R.

DEAL (KENT), Pop. 13,680.

ODEON THEATRE (BTH), Queen Street.—Props., Odeon (Deal), Ltd., Bennett's Hill, Birmingham. Phone, Midland 2781. Booked at 49, Park Lane, London, W.1. Continuous. Prices, 6d. to 2s. Phone, Deal 866. Station, Deal, S.R.

PLAZA (WE), High Street.—Prop., H, G. Carey. Phone, Margate 1545. 305 seats. Two shows nightly. Mats. Mon., Wed., Thurs. and Sat. Prices, 6d. to 1s. Phone, Deal 585. Station, Deal, S.R.

REGENT (WE).—Prop., Regent Cinema (Deal) Ltd. 900 seats. Continuous nightly. Daily Mat. Booked at Hall. Prices, 6d. to 1s. 10d. Phone, 600. Station, Deal.

ROYAL CINEMA (WE), King Street.—Prop., Deal and Walmer Amusements, Ltd., 4 and 5, Park Street, Deal. Phone, Deal 99. 616 seats. Booking Manager, Chas. Collins. Continuous. Two changes weekly. Prices, 6d. to 1s. 6d. Phone, Deal 394. Station, Deal, S.R.

The BEST Is Cheapest; PATHE GAZETTE.

DELABOLE (CORNWALL).
PICTUREDROME (Brown).—J. H. Wills, 1, Park Place, Wadebridge. 300 seats. Booked at H.O. Once nightly. Prices, 6d. to 1s. 6d. Station, Delabole, S.R.

DENABY MAIN (near Rotherham) (YORKS), Pop. 3,000.
EMPIRE PALACE (WE), Doncaster Road.—Props., Empire Palace (Denaby), Ltd. 850 seats. Booked at Hall. Twice nightly. Prices, 4d. to 9d. Phone, Conisborough 46. Station, Conisborough, L.N.E.R.

DENHOLME (near Bradford) (YORKS), Pop. 2,662.
MECHANICS' HALL.—Props., Trustees of Denholme Mechanics' Institute. Hon. Supervisors, H. V. Bancroft and Chas. Moore. One show on Thurs., Fri. and Sat. 365 seats. Prices, 3d. to 9d. Station, Denholme, L.N.E.R.

DENTON (LANCS), Pop. 17,383.
DENTON PALACE, Ashworth Street.—Props., Denton Palace, Ltd. 650 seats. Two shows nightly. Two changes weekly. Prices, 3d. to 9d. Phone, Denton 78. Station, Denton, L.M.S.
PEOPLE'S HALL (WE).—Res. Man., Mrs. A. M. Fidler, 43, Peal Street, Denton, to whom all communications should be addressed. Twice nightly. Mats., Tues., Thurs., and Sat. Prices, 4d. to 1s. Stations, Denton, L.M.S., and Guide Bridge, L.N.E.R.
ROTA (WE).

DERBY (DERBYSHIRE), Pop, 142,406.
ALEXANDRA THEATRE (WE), Normanton Road, —Props., Alexandra Theatre (Derby), Ltd. 1,200 seats. Continuous. Two changes weekly. Prices, 6d. to 1s. 3d. Phone, Derby 429. Station, Derby, L.M.S.
ALLENTON CINEMA (Marshall), Osmaston Road. —Props., Allenton Cinema Co., Ltd. 650 seats. Booked at Hall. Continuous. Mat., Sat. Prices, 6d. to 1s. 3d. Phone, Derby 3305, extension from Alvaston P.H. Station, Derby, L.M.S.
ALVASTON PICTURE HOUSE (Marshall), London Road.—Props., T. Swift and Sons. 650 seats. Booked at Hall. Continuous. Mat., Sat. Prices, 6d. to 1s. Phone, Derby 1665. Station, Derby, L.M.S.
ART PICTURE HALL (WE), Dairyhouse Road.— Props., Art Picture Hall, Ltd. Booked at Hall. Continuous. Phone, Derby 1111. Station, Derby, L.M.S.
CENTRAL HALL CINEMA.—Promoters, Derby Co-operative Society Educational Committee. Sec., A. W. Bingham. Concerts, Lectures, etc. Phone, Derby 3151. Dance Hall attached. Station, Derby, L.M.S.
COLISEUM (WE), London Road.—Props., The Coliseum (Derby), Ltd. 1,250 seats. Booked at Hall. Continuous. Prices, 6d. to 1s. 6d. Proscenium width, 34 ft. Café attached. Phone, Derby 1214. Station, Derby, L.M.S.
COSMOPOLITAN CINEMA (BTP), Upper Boundary Road.—Prop., Miss D. France. 750 seats. Booked at Hall. Continuous. Prices, 6d. to 1s. Phone, Derby 1770. Station, Derby, L.M.S.
COSY PICTURE HOUSE (BTH).—Props., London Road Cinema, Ltd. 620 seats. Booked at Hall by Man. Dir. Continuous. Two changes

weekly. Prices, 6d. to 1s. 3d. Phone, Derby 1159. Station, Derby, L.M.S.
EMPIRE CINEMA (WE), Beckett Well Lane.— Props., Associated British Cinemas, Ltd., 30-31, Golden Square, London, W.1. 1,254 seats. Booked at H.O. Continuous. Prices, 5d. to 1s. 6d. Proscenium width, 26 ft. Phone, Derby 1382. Station, Derby, L.M.S.
GAUMONT PALACE (BA), London Road.—Props., Gaumont British Corporation, Ltd., New Gallery House, Regent Street, W.1. 2,175 seats. Booked at H.O. Continuous. Prices, 6d. to 2s. Stage and 14 dressing-rooms. Café attached. Phone, Derby 3014. Station, Derby, L.M.S.

Fitted "ARDENTE" Deaf Aids
See page 258

COMPTON
ORGAN featured here.

HIPPODROME SUPER CINEMA (WE), Green Lane.— Props., Associated Theatres (P.A. & D.), Ltd., Dean House, Dean Street, W.1. 1,901 seats. Continuous. Stage, 40 ft. deep ; 10 dressing-rooms. Proscenium width, 38 ft. Phone, Derby 196. Station, Derby, L.M.S.
NORMANTON CINEMA (WE), Dairy House Road. Props., Art Picture Hall, Ltd. 1,057 seats. Continuous. Phone, Derby 1111. Station, Derby, L.M.S.
ODEON THEATRE (BTH), St. Peter's Street.— Props., Odeon (Derby), Ltd., Cornhill House, Bennett's Hill, Birmingham. Phone, Midland 2781. Booked at 49, Park Lane, London, W.1. Continuous. Prices, 6d. to 1s. 6d. Phone, Derby 1061. Station, Derby, L.M.S.
PICTURE HOUSE (WE), Babington Lane.—Props., Midland Electric Theatres (1911), Ltd., Head Office, 36, St. Mary's Gate, Derby. Phone, Derby 1673-4. 1,150 seats. Booked at H.O. Continuous. Prices, 6d. to 1s, 6d. Café attached. Phone, Derby 708. Station, Derby, L.M.S.
POPULAR PICTURE HOUSE (WE), Mill Street.— Props., Associated British Cinemas, Ltd., 30-31, Golden Square, London, W.1. Phone, Gerrard 7887. 1,132 seats. Continuous. Prices, 6d. to 1s. Phone, Derby 1908. Station, Derby, L.M.S.

DEREHAM (NORFOLK), Pop. 5,640.
SWIMMING POOL CINEMA (BTP).—Props., Exchange Theatre Co., Phoenix House, London Road, Chelmsford. 385 seats. Booked at H.O. Continuous evenings. Prices, 6d. to 1s. Proscenium width, 24 ft. Phone, No. 76.

DESBOROUGH (NORTHANTS), Pop. 4,407.
ODDFELLOWS' HALL (wired).—Props., Oddfellows' Friendly Society. 350 seats. Booked at Hall. Prices, 2d. to 1s. Phone, Desborough 228. Station, Desborough, L.M.S.

DEVIZES (WILTS), Pop. 6,058.
CORN EXCHANGE (WE).
PALACE (WE).—Props., A. Austin Pilkington's Theatres. 900 seats. Booked at H.O., Salisbury. Once nightly, Tues. to Fri. Two shows, Mon. and Sat. Phone, Devizes 171.
Fitted "ARDENTE" Deaf Aids
See page 258

PARISH HALL, Market Lavington.
PICTURE HOUSE.

Put Pep into Programmes With PATHE PICTORIAL.

DEVONPORT (Devon). **(See PLYMOUTH).**

DEWSBURY (Yorks), **Pop. 54,303.**
Majestic Cinema (bth), Wellington Road.—
Props., Andrew's Picture Houses, Ltd. Booked
at Hall. 1,200 seats. Continuous from 5.30
p.m. Mat. daily. Two changes weekly. Prices,
3d. to 1s. 3d. Phone, Dewsbury 304. Ball-
room attached. Stations, Dewsbury, L.M.S.
and L.N.E.R.
Pavilion (awh), Ravensthorpe.—Props.,
Goodall's Pictures (1931), Ltd., The Savoy,
Cleckheaton. Phone, 224. 900 seats. Booked
at H.O. Twice nightly. Prices, 6d. to 1s.
Phone, Dewsbury 792. Stations, Ravens-
thorpe and Thornhill, L.M.S.
Pioneer Pictures (we).—Props., Dewsbury
Pioneer Industrial Society, Ltd., Union Street.
Phone, Dewsbury 1202. 1,459 seats. Booked
at Hall. Continuous. Pictures and Variety.
Prices, 5d. to 1s. 6d. Proscenium width, 31 ft.
Stage, 25 ft. deep; four dressing-rooms.
Café. Phone, Dewsbury 1206. Stations,
Dewsbury, L.M.S. and L.N.E.R.
Playhouse (we).—Props., Associated British
Cinemas, Ltd., 30-31, Golden Square, London,
W.1. Phone, Gerrard 7887. 1,850 seats.
Booked at H.O. Continuous. Occasional
Variety. Prices, 6d. to 2s. Proscenium
width, 50 ft. Six dressing-rooms. Phone,
Dewsbury 1299. Café. Stations, Dewsbury,
L.M.S. and L.N.E.R.

COMPTON
ORGAN featured here.

Regal Super Cinema (we), Market Place.—
Controlled by Union Cinemas, Ltd., Union
House, 15, Regent Street, London, S.W.1.
Phone, Whitehall 8484. Continuous. Booked
at H.O. Prices, 6d. to 2s. Phone, Dewsbury
249. Stations, Dewsbury, L.M.S. and L.N.E.R.

COMPTON
ORGAN featured here.

Tudor Theatre Super Cinema (we), Theatre
Lane.—Props., Northern Theatres Co., Ltd.,
Nothcoli House, Clare Road, Halifax.
Phone, Halifax 2512. 1,250 seats. Booked
by Fred A. Kay, at H.O. Continuous nightly.
Mat. daily. Prices, 6d. to 1s. 3d. Phone,
Dewsbury 330. Café attached. Stations,
Dewsbury, L.M.S. and L.N.E.R.

DIDCOT (Berks.), **Pop. 2,154.**
New Coronet Cinema (we).—Props., Shipman
& King, M 84, Shellmex House, Strand,
W.C.2. Phone, Temple Bar 5077. Booked
at H.O. Continuous. Prices, 6d. to 1s. 10d.
Ball-room attached. Phone, Didcot 43.
Station, Didcot, G.W.R. Films by Oxford
Film Transport Service.

DIDSBURY (Lancs), **Pop. 14,798.**
Bijou (btp).
Capitol.—Controlled by Union Cinemas, Ltd.,
15, Regent Street, London, S.W.1. Phone,
Whitehall 8484.
Didsbury Picture Theatre (btp).—Props.,
Didsbury Picture Theatre Co., Elm Grove.
Gen. Man., A. H. W. Nash. Pictures and
Variety. Booked at Trocadero, Rusholme,

Manchester. Continuous. Prices, 6d. and 1s,
Stage, 14 ft. deep; 2 dressing-rooms. Station.
Didsbury, L.M.S.

DINNINGTON (nr. Sheffield) (Yorks),
Pop. 4,900.
Palace (we).—Prop., Dinnington Palace, Ltd.
457 seats. Booked at Hall. One show
nightly Tues., Wed. and Fri. Two shows
Mon. and Thurs. Three on Sat. Prices, 6d.
to 1s. 3d. Phone, Dinnington 22. Station,
Kiveton Park, L.N.E.R. Film Transport.

DIPTON (co. Durham).
Empire Cinema (Edibell).—300 seats. Booked
at H.O. Twice nightly. Prices, 3d. to 9d.
Phone, Dipton 17.

DISS (Norfolk), **Pop. 3,422.**
New Picture House (we), Victoria Road.—
Prop., E. Stevens. 400 seats. Booked at
Hall. Twice nightly. Prices, 6d. to 1s. 6d.
Phone, Diss 154. Station, Diss, L.N.E.R. Films
by Road Transport.

DONCASTER (Yorks), **Pop. 63,308.**
Arcadia (we), Waterdale.—Prop., Arcadia
(Doncaster), Ltd. 850 seats. Booked at
Hall by Harry Russell, Man. Director. Con-
tinuous. Daily Mat. Prices, 4d. to 1s. 6d.
Phone, Doncaster 345. Station, Doncaster
(Central), L.N.E.R.
Balby Cinema (we), High Road, Balby.—
Prop., Balby Cinema, Ltd. 699 seats. Con-
tinuous. 6.30 to 10.30. Mat., Tues., Thurs.
and Sat. Two changes weekly. Prices, 6d.
to 1s. Phone, Doncaster 1605. Station,
Doncaster, L.N.E.R.
Empire (we), Moorends. — Props., Moorends
Empire, Ltd. Booked at Hall. Continuous
Mon. to Fri. Two shows and Mat. on Sat.
Prices, 6d. to 1s. Proscenium width, 30 ft.
Stage, 50 ft. deep. Phone, Thorne 108.
Stations, Moorends, North and South,
L.N.E.R.
Gaumont Palace (rca), Hallgate.—Prop.,
Doncaster Majestic Cinemas, Ltd., 6, Vigo
Street, London, W.1. Booked at H.O.
Continuous. Phone, Doncaster 1864. Café
attached. Station, Doncaster, L.N.E.R.
**Fitted "ARDENTE" Deaf Aids
See page 258**

COMPTON
ORGAN featured here.

Grand Theatre, Station Road.—Lessees
Palace Theatre (Doncaster), Ltd. 1,950 seats
Booked by Charles Thompson at Weetwood
Chambers, Albion Street, Leeds. Twice night-
ly. Prices, 6d. to 2s. Stage, 30 ft. deep;
nine dressing-rooms. Proscenium width, 30 ft.
Phone, Doncaster 417. Station, Doncaster,
L.N.E.R.
Palace Theatre (we), Silver Street.—Prop.,
Palace Theatre (Doncaster), Ltd. 2,030 seats.
Booked by Charles Thompson at Westwood
Chambers, Albion Street, Leeds. Continuous.
Prices, 6d. to 1s. 6d. Stage, 30 ft. deep;
eight dressing-rooms. Proscenium width,
30 ft. Phone, Doncaster 365. Station,
Doncaster, L.N.E.R.
Picture House (rca), High Street.—Prop.,
Associated British Cinemas, Ltd., 30-31,
Golden Square, London, W.1. Phone, Ger-
rard 7887. 1,132 seats. Booked at H.O.

PATHE GAZETTE: At All Events

Continuous. Two changes weekly. Prices, 4d. to 1s. 6d. Café attached. Proscenium width, 26 ft. Phone, Doncaster 460. Station Doncaster, Central, L.N.E.R.

REGAL (AWH), Frenchgate.—Prop., Doncaster Electric Theatre Co., Ltd. 600 seats. Booked at Hall. Continuous nightly. Three Mats. weekly. Prices, 7d. to 1s. Phone, Doncaster 1530. Station, Doncaster, L.N.E.R

RITZ SUPER CINEMA (WE), Hallgate.—Prop., Ritz (Doncaster), Ltd., 26, Park Row, Leeds. 2,500 seats. Booked at H.O. by J. F. Tidswell. Continuous. Prices, 7d. to 1s. 6d. Proscenium width, 34 ft. Stage, 36 ft. deep; nine dressing rooms. Café and Ball-room attached. Phone, Doncaster 1859. Station, Doncaster, L.N.E.R.

SAVOY CINEMA.—(Closed.)

SCALA (Marshall), Church Lane, Armthorpe.— Props., Scala (Armthorpe), Ltd. 893 seats Booked at Hall. Continuous. Prices, 4d. to 1s. Proscenium width, 20 ft. Phone, Armthorpe 37. Station, Doncaster, L.N.E.R.

DONINGTON (LINCS.)

DIAL HALL.—Three shows Sat. only. Prices 7d. to 1s. 3d.

DORCHESTER (DORSET), Pop. 10,030.

PALACE THEATRE (BA), Durngate Street. —Prop., Albany Ward Theatres, Ltd., 123, Regent Street, London, W.1. Phone, Regent 6641. Booked at H.O. by A. W. Jarrett. Stage, 20 ft. deep; three dressing-rooms. Prices, 6d. to 1s. 6d. Phone, Dorchester 155. Station, Dorchester, S.R. and G.W.R.

PLAZA (WE).—986 seats.

DORKING (SURREY), Pop. 10,109.

ELECTRIC THEATRE.—510 seats.

PAVILION CINEMA (WE), South Street.—Prop., P. Segalov, Cedar Close, Dorking. Phone, Dorking 212. 964 seats. Booked at Hall. Continuous. Prices, 9d. to 2s. 5d. Proscenium width, 27 ft. Stage, 15 ft. deep; two dressing-rooms. Phone, Dorking 3017. Station, Dorking (North), S.R., and Leyland Transport.

REGENT CINEMA (RCA), South Street.—Prop., P. Segalov, Cedar Close, Dorking. Phone, Dorking 212. 600 seats. Continuous. Booked at Pavilion. Prices, 6d. to 2s. Proscenium width, 25 ft. Phone, Dorking 3017. Station, Dorking (North), S.R.

DOUGLAS (ISLE OF MAN), Pop. (winter) 20,000. (Summer) 60,000.

CRESCENT (WE).—Prop., Palace and Derby Castle, Ltd., The Gaiety Theatre, Douglas. Booked by R. E. Ratcliff, "Raheny," Roby, Liverpool. 2,000 seats. Prices, 9d. to 2s. Phone, Douglas 387.

CUNNINGHAM HOLIDAY CAMP CINEMA (WE).— One show nightly. Price to public, 6d. Free to Residents. Proscenium width, 20 ft. Café and Dance Hall attached. Phone, Douglas 1018. Station, Douglas, I.O.M. Steam Packet Co.

GAIETY THEATRE (Fox).—Prop., Palace and Derby Castle, Ltd., The Gaiety, Douglas. Booked by R. E. Ratcliff, "Raheny," Roby, Lancs. Plays, Films every Sunday and occasionally weekdays. Phone, Douglas 191.

NEW REGAL CINEMA (WE).—Prop., Palace and Derby Castle, Ltd., The Gaiety Theatre,

Douglas. Booked by R. E. Ratcliff. "Raheny," Roby, Lancs. Continuous. Prices, 9d. to 1s. 6d. Phone, Douglas 355.

COMPTON
ORGAN featured here.

PICTURE HOUSE (WE), Strand Street.—Props., Strand Cinema Theatre Co. (1920), Ltd' Continuous. Phone, Douglas 14. Station, Douglas.

COMPTON
ORGAN featured here.

ROYALTY CINEMA (WE), Walpole Avenue.— Prop., Palace and Derby Castle, Ltd., Gaiety Theatre, Douglas. Phone 191. Booked by R. E. Ratcliff, "Raheny," Roby, Liverpool. Continuous. Prices, 6d. to 1s. 9d. Phone, Douglas 759.

STRAND CINEMA (WE), Strand Street.—Props., Strand Cinema Theatre Co. (1920), Ltd. Continuous. Phone, Douglas 14. Station, Douglas, I.O.M. Steam Packet Co.

DOVER (KENT), Pop. 41,095.

GRANADA (WE), Castle Street.—Props., Associated British Cinemas, Ltd., 30-31, Golden Square, W.1. Phone, Gerrard 7887. 1,717 seats. Booked at H.O. Prices, 4d. to 1s. 6d. Continuous. Proscenium width, 35 ft. Stage, 15 ft. deep; four dressing-rooms. Phone, Dover 750. Station, Dover Priory, S.R.

HIPPODROME.—800 seats.

KING'S HALL THEATRE (RCA).—Props., Dover Entertainments, Ltd. Booked at H.O. 1,050 seats. Continuous. Prices, 6d. to 2s. Proscenium width, 32 ft. Stage, 36 ft. deep; nine dressing-rooms. Phone, Dover 580. Station, Dover Priory, S.R.

PLAZA (WE), New Street.—Prop., Associated British Cinemas, Ltd., 30-31, Golden Square, W.1. Phone, Gerrard 7887. 1,200 seats. Booked at H.O. Continuous. Sunday from 5 p.m. Prices, 4d. to 1s. 6d. Proscenium width, 25 ft. Station, Dover Priory, S.R.

REGENT CINEMA (BTH).—Prop., Universal Cinema Theatres, Ltd. 2,000 seats. Booked at Hall. Continuous. Proscenium width, 50 ft. Station, Dover Priory, S.R.

TOWN HALL.—Non-flam films only. The Hall is not licensed for Cinematograph performances, but occasional shows are given with the special consent of the Town Council. For particulars, apply to Town Clerk, Brook House, Dover. 750 seats. Phone, Dover 90.

DOVERCOURT (ESSEX), Pop. 15,800.

EMPIRE (BA), Kingsway.—Prop., D. F. Bostock. Booked at 54, Chevallier Street, Ipswich. Phone, Ipswich 4036. Twice nightly. Mats. daily. Prices, 6d. to 1s. 4d. Proscenium width, 29 ft. Phone, Dovercourt 249. Station Dovercourt Bay, near Harwich. L.N.E.R.

REGAL.—Booked at 54, Chevallier Street, Ipswich.

REGENT (BTP), Main Road.—Prop., D. F. Bostock. Booked at 54, Chevallier Street, Ipswich. Phone, Ipswich 4036. 750 seats. Twice nightly. Mat. Mon., Wed. and Sat. Prices, 6d. to 1s. 6d. Proscenium width, 32 ft. Phone, Dovercourt 266. Station Dovercourt, L.N.E.R.

DOWNHAM MARKET (Norfolk), **Pop. 2,463.**
Regent (btp).—Prop., Provincial Amusements.
Ltd. 750 seats. Once nightly. Twice Wed,
Mat., Sat. Prices, 7d. to 1s. 6d. Phone,
Downham Market 112. Station, Downham
Market, L.N.E.R.

DRIFFIELD (Yorks), **Pop. 5,916.**
Majestic Cinema (ba).—Props., Majestic
Cinema (Pocklington), Ltd., Manor Buildings,
Pocklington, Yorks. 720 seats. Prices, 6d.
and 1s. Proscenium width, 38 ft. Twice
nightly. Mat. Sat. Phone, 79. Café attached.
Station, Driffield, L.N.E.R.
Victoria Theatre (awh), 63, Middle Street,
South.—Prop., Driffield Victoria Theatre and
Café Co., Ltd. Man. Dir., Capt. F. A. Webb.
400 seats. Booked at The Doon, Harpenden,
Herts, by Man. Dir. Continuous. Two changes
weekly. Prices, 6d. to 1s. 3d. Café attached
Station, Driffield, L.N.E.R.

DRIGHLINGTON (Yorks), **Pop. 4,064.**

DROITWICH (Worc.), **Pop. 4,553.**
New Salters Cinema (btp).—Prop., G. Dowell.
650 seats. Continuous. Mats., Wed., Thurs.
and Sat. Booked at Hall. Prices, 6d. to
1s. 6d. Phone, Droitwich 3290. Station, Droitwich, L.M.S.
Winter Gardens (rca).—350 seats.

DRONFIELD (Derby), **Pop. 4,530.**
Electra Palace (ba), Chesterfield Road.—
Prop., Dronfield Picture Palace, Ltd. 450
seats. Pictures, Variety, Revue and Drama.
Booked at Hall by W. Dodson Twigg. One
show nightly. Three on Sat. Two changes
weekly. Prices, 5d. to 1s. Stage, 14 ft.
deep, three dressing-rooms. Proscenium
width, 20 ft. Station, Dronfield, L.M.S.
Films by Broxburn Film Transport Service.

DROYLSDEN (Lancs), **Pop. 13,277.**
Electric Theatre (Gramo-Radio), Ashton
Gate.—Prop., Droylsden Electric Theatre Co.,
Ltd. 500 seats. Two shows Sat., continuous
rest of week. Four changes weekly. Prices
3d. to 9d. Phone, Openshaw 262. Station
Fairfield, L.N.E.R.
Palace Theatre, Ashton Road.—H. D. Moor-
house Circuit, 7, Oxford Road, Manchester.
Phone, Ardwick 2226.

DRYBROOK (Glos.), **Pop. 5,000.**
Cinema.—Prop., W. Gibbs, 1, James Street
Brithdir, Glam. Booked at H.O. One show
nightly. Prices, 5d. to 1s. Station, Cinderford, G.W.R.

DUDLEY (Northumberland), **Pop. 4,000.**
Grand Electric Theatre (Knighton).—Props.,
Exors. of W. Hutson (decd.) and Norman H.
Chapman. 530 seats. Booked at 85, North-
umberland Street, Newcastle-on-Tyne. One
show nightly. Two Sat. Occasional Variety.
Prices, 2d. to 8d. Station, Annitsford,
L.N.E.R.
Lyric (btp), Burradon.—Props., C. & T.
Cinemas, Ltd., 52, Stowell Street,Newcastle-on-
Tyne. Phone, No. 25539 . 362 seats. Prices,
3d. to 4d. Once daily. Sat. two shows.
Station, Killingworth, L.N.E.R.

DUDLEY (Worc.), **Pop. 59,579.**
Alexandra Hall (Imperial), Lower Gornall.—
Prop., Ernest A. Grenville Jones. Head Office,
Castle Cinema, Dudley. 500 seats. Booked at
H.O. Twice nightly Mon. and Sat., and Mats.

Once nightly rest of week. Prices, 3d. to 1s.
Phone, Dudley 2617 and 2673. Station,
Dudley, L.M.S.
Castle Cinema (ba).—Prop., Ernest A. Gren-
ville Jones. 850 seats. Booked at Hall by
Prop. Continuous. Daily Mats. Prices,
5d. to 1s. Phone, Dudley 2617. Stations,
Dudley, L.M.S. and G.W.R.
Criterion Cinema (b.a.), 42, High Street.
—Prop., Associated Provincial Picture Houses,
Ltd., 123, Regent Street, London, W.1.
Phone, Regent 8080. 1,200 seats. Booked at
H.O. Continuous. Three shows Sat. Daily
Mat. Prices, 4d. to 1s. 3d. Proscenium
width, 38 ft. Café attached. Phone, Dudley
2164-11. Stations, Dudley, L.M.S. and
G.W.R.
Empire (Cinephone), Hall Street.– Prop.,
Gaumont-British Picture Corpn., Ltd., 123,
Regent Street, London, W.1. 1,300 seats.
Booked at H.O. Continuous evenings. Two
shows Sat. Mats. daily. Two changes week-
ly. Prices 3d. to 1s. Stage, 16 ft. deep ;
Three dressing rooms. Phone, 262811.
Station, Dudley.
Hippodrome (Morrison).—Sedgley.—600 seats.
Netherton Pictureland.—Prop., H. Bishop.
Odeon Theatre (bth), Castle Hill.—Props.,
Odeon (Dudley), Ltd. Cornhill House,
Bennett's Hill, Birmingham. Phone, Midland
2781. Booked at 49, Park Lane, London, W.1.
Plaza Theatre (we).—Prop., B. Kennedy.
1,500 seats. Booked at Hall. Continuous
Prices, 6d. to 1s. 3d. Phone, Dudley 2287
Stations, Dudley, G.W.R. and L.M.S.
Regent (we), High Street.—Prop., Gaumont
British Corporation, 123, Regent Street,
London, W.1. 1,250 seats. Booked at H.O.
Continuous. Prices, 6d. to 1s. 6d. Phone,
Dudley 280111. Stations, Dudley, L.M.S.
and G.W.R.

WURLITZER ORGAN
Installed in this Kinema

DUDLEY HALL (Yorks).
Picture Palace (awh).—Prop., Goodall's
Pictures. Ltd., Albion Street, Cleckheaton.
Phone, Cleckheaton 224. Booked at H.O.
by P. Goodall. Continuous, Mon. to Fri.,
Three shows Sat. Prices, 5d. to 1s. Phone,
Dudley Hill 108. Station, Dudley Hill,
L.N.E.R.

DUDLEY PORT (Staffs), **Pop. 4,685.**
Alhambra (rca).
Victoria Cinema (Classitone).—Prop., Victoria
Talkie Theatres, Ltd., 192, Sherlock Street,
Birmingham. 300 seats. Continuous evenings.
Mats., Mon., Thurs. and Sat. Two changes
weekly. Prices, 4d. to 9d. Phone, Tip. 1072.
Station, Dudley Port, L.M.S.

DUKINFIELD (Cheshire), **Pop. 19,309.**
Oxford Super Cinema (we).—792 seats
Continuous, Mon. to Fri. Two shows Sat.
Two changes weekly. Prices, 4d. to 1s,
Phone, Ashton 1916. Station, Stalybridge.
L.M.S.
Palladium (Morrison), Crescent Road.—Prop.,
Palladium, Dukinfield. 450 seats. Booked
at Hall. Continuous. Two changes weekly.
Prices, 4d. to 6d. Phone, Ashton 1335.
Station, Dukinfield, L.M.S.
Princess Picture Theatre (btp), King Street .
—Prop., Ashton New Cinema, Ltd. Man.
Dir., H. D. Moorhouse, Imperial Buildings,

Oxford Road, Manchester. Phone, Ashton, 1769. Booked at H.O. Station, Ashton,, Charlestown, L.M.S.

RITZ.—Controlled by Union Cinemas, .Ltd., Union House, 15, Regent Street, London, S.W.I. Phone, Whitehall 8484. Booked at H.O.

DULVERTON (SOM.).
B.B. CINEMA.—Prop., B.B. Cinema Circuit, West Down, near Ilfracombe. Booked by Capt. J. H. Blackhurst at H.O. Phone, Ilfracombe 7.

DUNMOW (ESSEX), **Pop. 2,510.**
KINEMA (BA), High Street.—Prop., Bury St. Edmund's Cinema, Ltd., 54, Chevalier Street, Ipswich. Phone, Ipswich 4036. 299 seats. Booked at H.O. Continuous. Prices, 6d. to 1s. 4d. Proscenium width, 18½ ft. Phone, Dunmow 97. Station, Dunmow, L.N.E.R.

DUNSTABLE (BEDS), **Pop. 8,972.**
CINEMA (Imperial),Toddington.—Prop., J. H. W. Marsden. 200 seats. Booked at London. Once nightly. Twice Sats. Prices, 6d. to 1s. 3d. Proscenium width, 18 ft. Stage, 18 ft. deep; one dressing-room. Station, Harlington, L.M.S.

PALACE (RCA).—Controlled by Union Cinemas, Ltd., Union House, 15, Regent Street, London, S.W.I. Phone, Whitehall 8484. · Booked at H.O. Continuous. Prices, 6d. to 1s. 6d. Phone, Dunstable 268. Station, Dunstable, L.N.E.R. and Film Transport.

REGAL.—Controlled by Union Cinemas, Ltd., 15, Regent Street, London, S;W.I. Phone, Whitehall 8484. Booked at H.O.

RITZ (WE).—Controlled by Union Cinemas, Ltd., Union House, 15, Regent Street, London, S.W.I. Phone, Whitehall 8484. Booked at H.O. Continuous. Station, Dunstable, L.N.E.R., and Film Transport.

DUNSTON-ON-TYNE (Co. DURHAM), **Pop. 9,272.**.
ALBERT PICTURE PALACE (BTH), Ravensworth Road.—Prop., Dunston Picture Hall Co. Ltd., 100 seats. Station, Gateshead, L.N.E.R.

IMPERIAL HALL (RCA), Ravensworth Road.— Prop., F. W. S. J. Morrison. 520 seats. Booked at Newcastle-on-Tyne. Two shows nightly. Mats., Mon. and Sat. Two changes weekly. Prices, 4d. to 9d. Proscenium width, 22 ft. Phone, Dunston 20. Station, Gateshead, L.N.E.R.

DURHAM (Co. DURHAM), **Pop. 16,223.**
CINEMA (BTH), Craghead.—Prop., Hugh Brennan, Low Fell, Newcastle. Pictures and Variety. Booked at Newcastle. Variety by R. Grieves, at 6, Bath Lane, Newcastle. Twice nightly. Prices, 5d. to 7d. Stage, 24 ft. deep; two dressing rooms. Proscenium width, 16 ft. Station, Pelton, L.N.E.R.

CRESCENT (L. Elect.), Gilesgate Moor.—Prop. G. Lamb and Son, Gilesgate Moor, Durham. 346 seats. Sep. shows. Prices, 3d. to 6d, Proscenium width, 18 ft. Station, Durham.

GLOBE CINEMA (BTP), 51½, North Road,Durham. ——E. J. Hinge Circuit, 72, Grey Street, Newcastle-on-Tyne. Phone, 20317. 344 seats. Booked at H.O. Twice nightly. Prices, 4d. to 1s. Phone, Durham 238. Station, Durham, L.N.E.R.

MINERS' HALL (BTP), Burnhope.—Props., Joseph Briggs and Sons. 450 seats. Once nightly, Twice Mon., Sat. Prices, 4d. to 9d. Proscenium width, 28 ft. Station, Annfield Plain, L.N.E.R.

PALACE (RCA).—Prop., Rawes. Entertainments Co., Ltd. 750 seats. Twice nightly. Two changes weekly. Prices, 5d. to 1s. Phone, Durham 137. Station, Durham.

PALLADIUM (WE), Claypath, Durham City.— Prop., Palladium (Durham), Ltd., Barclays Bank Chambers, Durham. Phone 206. 1,087 seats. Three shows daily. Booked by Thompson's Enterprises, Ltd., 4, Palladium Buildings, Middlesbrough. Prices, 6d. to 1s. Proscenium width, 27 ft. Phone, Durham 365.

REGAL (WE).—E. J. Hinge Circuit, 72, Grey Street, Newcastle-on-Tyne. Phone, Newcastle-on-Tyne 20317. 1,090 seats. Booked at H.O. Twice nightly. Daily Mat. Prices 7d. to 1s. 6d. Proscenium width, 29 ft. Stage, 12 ft. deep. Four dressing rooms. Phone, Durham 184. Station, Durham, L.N.E.R.

WELFARE HALL AND INSTITUTE, East Hetton.

DURSLEY (GLOS.), **Pop. 2,601.**
VICTORIA CINEMA (BTH).—Prop., Odeon (Hinckley), Ltd., Cornhill House, Bennett's. Hill, Birmingham. Phone, Midland 2781. One show Mon. to Fri. Twice Sat. Prices, 6d. to 1s. 6d. Phone, Dursley 67. Station, Dursley, L.M.S.

E

ARBY (YORKS), **Pop. 5,522.**
EMPIRE (WE).—Prop., Earby Cinema, Ltd. 477 seats. Pictures, Variety and Revues. Booked at Hall. Once nightly. Stage and dressing rooms. Station, Earby, L.M.S.

EARLESTOWN (LANCS), **Pop. 10,500.**
CURZON.

EMPIRE PAVILION (BTH).—Prop., South Lancashire Hippodrome Co., Ltd. 475 seats. Booked by Gen. Man., Fred Harrison. Prices, 3d. to 1s. Phone, Newton-le-Willows 63. Station, Earlestown, L.M.S.

PAVILION (BTH), Market Street.—Lessees, South Lancashire Hippodrome Co., Ltd, Man. Dir. and Booking Man., Fred Harrison. 1,100 seats. Pictures and occasional Variety. Two shows nightly. Prices, 3d. to 1s. Phone, Newton-le-Willows 63. Station, Earlestown Junction, L.M.S.

EARL SHILTON (LEICESTER), **Pop. 4,435.**
PALACE (AWH).—Prop. and Man., H.S. Cooper, 14, The Hollow, Earl Shilton. 560 seats. Booked at Hall. Once nightly. Twice on Sat. Two changes weekly. Prices, 6d. to 1s. Proscenium width, 22 ft. Station, Earl Shilton 37. Station, Hinckley, L.M.S.

EASINGTON (Co. DURHAM), **Pop. 12,000.**
EMPIRE THEATRE (WE), School Street, Easington Colliery.—Prop., W. and B. Theatres, Ltd., Easington Colliery. 890 seats. Booked at Newcastle-on-Tyne. Pictures and Variety. Variety booked by North's Variety Agency, Sunderland. Twice nightly. Prices, 4d. to 9d. Proscenium width, 28 ft. Stage, 20 ft. deep; five dressing-rooms. Phone, Easington 352. Station, Easington. L.N.E.R,

EASINGTON—Contd.
HIPPODROME (WE), Seaside Lane.—Prop.,
Hippodrome (Easington), Ltd. 850 seats.
Booked at Newcastle-on-Tyne. Continuous.
Prices, 4d. to 9d. Phone, Easington 352.
Station, Easington, L.N.E.R.
RIALTO (WE).

EASINGWOLD (YORKS), **Pop. 2,084.**
CINEMA (AWH), Market Place.—Prop., E. H.,
Burton. 250 seats. Booked by Prop., at
Normandene, Easingwold. Once nightly.
Prices 7d. to 1s. Films by motor from Leeds.

EAST ARDSLEY (YORKS), **Pop. 5,000.**
EMPIRE PICTURE PALACE (Wired).—Prop. and
Res. Man., H. Dodsworth. 500 seats. One
show nightly. Two changes weekly. Prices,
4d. to 9d. Station, Ardsley, L.N.E.R.

EASTBOURNE (SUSSEX), **Pop. 57,435.**
EASTERN CINEMA (WE), Seaside.—Prop., H.
Baker. 440 seats. Continuous. Daily Mat.
Two changes weekly. Phone, Eastbourne 705.
Station, Eastbourne, S.R.
GAIETY CINEMA (BA), Seaside.—Prop., Amuse-
ments (Eastbourne), Ltd. H.O., Picture-
drome, Eastbourne. 632 seats. Continuous.
Booked by Randolph E. Richards, Man. Dir.,
at Picturedrome, Eastbourne. Prices, 6d. to
1s. 6d. Proscenium width, 30 ft. Phone,
Eastbourne 43. Station, Eastbourne, S.R.
LUXOR CINEMA (WE), Pevensey Road.—Con-
trolled by Union Cinemas, Ltd., Union House,
15, Regent Street, London, S.W.1. Phone,
Whitehall 8484. Booked at H.O. Continuous.
Prices, 9d. to 2s. 6d. Phone, Eastbourne 3612.
Station, East bourne, S.R.

Fitted "ARDENTE" Deaf Aids
See page 258

COMPTON

ORGAN featured here.

NEW CENTRAL CINEMA (WE), Seaside Road.—
Prop., Central and Eastern Cinemas, Ltd.
Res. and Bkg. Man., P. V. Lunch. 671 seats.
Continuous. Prices, 6d. to 1s. 6d. Phone,
Eastbourne 1183. Station, Eastbourne, S.R.
PICTUREDROME (WE), Langley Road.—Prop.,
Picturedrome (Eastbourne), Ltd. 1,217 seats.
Booked at Hall by Man. Dir., Randolph E.
Richards. Prices, 9d. to 2s. 6d. Continuous.
Phone, Eastbourne 1441.
RITZ (WE).—Controlled by Union Cinemas, Ltd.,
Union House, 15, Regent Street, London,
S.W.1. Phone, Whitehall 8484. Continuous.
Films and Variety. Booked at H.O. Station,
Eastbourne, S.R.
PLAZA (BTH), High Street, Old Town.—Prop.,
C. and K. Murray. 375 seats. Booked at
Hall. Continuous. Mat., Sat., and Bank
Holidays. Prices, 6d. to 1s. 3d. Proscenium
width, 16 ft. Phone, Eastbourne 1293. Road
Transport.
TIVOLI SUPER-CINEMA, Seaside Road.—Prop.,
Parton and Dearden. 650 seats. Continu-
ous. Two changes weekly. Prices, 8d. to
2s. 4d. Phone, Eastbourne 1031. Station,
Eastbourne, S.R.
WINTER GARDEN CINEMA (BTH).—Props., Jordan
and Young. Booked at Hall. Continuous.
Prices, 6d. to 1s. 10d. Phone, Eastbourne
3373. Films by Sussex Transport.

EAST DEREHAM (NORFOLK), **Pop. 5,641.**
EXCHANGE THEATRE (BTP).—Prop., Exchange
Theatre Co., R. G. Balls, 1, Phœnix House,
Chelmsford. Phone, Chelmsford 94. 754
seats. Twice nightly. Mat., Wed., Fri., and
Sat. Prices, 6d. to 1s. 6d. Phone, East
Dereham 76. Station, E. Dereham, L.N.E.R

EAST GRINSTEAD (SUSSEX), **Pop. 7,901.**
RADIO CENTRE (WE).—Prop., Letheby and
Christopher, Ltd. 1,012 seats. Continuous.
Prices, 6d. to 2s.6d. Café attached. Phone,
East Grinstead 688. Station, East Grinstead.
SOLARIUS (WE).—Prop., Letheby and Chris-
topher, Ltd. 390 seats. Continuous. Mat.
daily. Prices, 6d. to 2s. Phone, East
Grinstead 82.
WHITEHALL PALACE (WE).—Prop., Letheby and
Christopher, Ltd., Gen. Man., Fred C. Maples-
den. 576 seats. Continuous. Mat. daily. Prices,
6d. to 2s. Phone, East Grinstead 82. Res-
taurant and Dance Hall attached. Station,
East Grinstead, S.R.

EASINGTON.
RIALTO (WE).—Prop., Yoden Theatres, Ltd.
Phone, Horden 349. 1,250 seats. Twice
nightly. Prices, 4d. to 1s. Proscenium width,
38 feet. Stage, 26 feet deep. 10 dressing
rooms. Phone, Easington 224. Station,
Easington.

EAST KIRKBY (NOTTS).
REGENT (WE).—Prop., Kirkby Pictures, Ltd
Booked at Hall. Continuous. Prices, 6d. to
1s. 6d. Phone, East Kirkby 2226. Station,
East Kirkby, L.M.S.
STAR THEATRE (BTH), Kingsway, East Kirkby.
—Prop., Kirkby Pictures, Ltd., Regent
Buildings, East Kirkby. 650 seats. Pic-
tures and Variety. Booked at Regent. Con-
tinuous Mon., to Fri., two shows Sat. Prices,
6d. to 1s. Stage, 20 ft. deep; two dressing
rooms. Phone, East Kirkby 3275. Station,
Kirkby-in-Ashfield, L.M.S., L.N.E.R.

EASTLEIGH (HANTS), **Pop. 18,333.**
NEW CINEMA.—850 seats.
PICTURE HOUSE (RCA), Market Street.—Prop.
G. Wright. 650 seats. Phone, Eastleigh 29.
Booked at Hall. Prices, 6d. to 1s. 3d. Pro-
scenium width, 25½ feet. Station, East-
leigh, S.R.
REGAL THEATRE (RCA), Market Street.—Prop.,
Geo. W. A. Wright. 1,000 seats. Occasional
Variety. Booked at Hall. Continuous. Three
changes weekly. Stage, 27½ ft. deep. Prices,
6d. to 1s. 3d. Phone, Southampton 87329.
Station, Eastleigh, S.R.

EAST AND WEST MOLESEY (SURREY), **Pop. 8,460.**
COURT CINEMA (WE), Bridge Road, East Molesey.
—Prop., General Cinema Theatres, Ltd.,
19, Albemarle Street, W.1. 472 seats. Booked
at H.O. Continuous. Two changes weekly.
Prices, 7d. to 2s. Proscenium width, 22½ feet.
Station, Hampton Court, S.R.

EASTWOOD (NOTTS), **Pop. 5,360.**
EMPIRE (WE).—Prop., F. G. Stubbs and J. T.
Woods. 760 seats. Booked at Hall. Continuous. Prices, 6d. to 1s. Proscenium width,
19 feet. Phone, Langley Mill 23. Stations,
Langley Mill, L.M.S., and Eastwood, L.N.E.R.
and Film Transport.

PATHE GAZETTE—For The Exhibitor Who Thinks For Himself.

EBBW VALE (MON.), **Pop. 31,695.**
CINEMA.—(In course of construction.)
PALACE (WE), Church Street.—Prop., Ebbw Vale Theatres, Ltd. 860 seats. Booked at Pavilion, Abertillery. Continuous. Prices, 6d. and 1s. Proscenium width, 42 ft. Phone, Ebbw Vale 41. Films by Road Transport.
WHITE HOUSE (WE), Bethcar Street.—Prop., Ebbw Vale Theatres, Ltd. 734 seats. Booked at Pavilion, Abertillery. Continuous. Prices, 6d. and 1s. Proscenium width, 22 ft. Phone, Ebbw Vale 41. Films by Road Transport.

ECCLES (LANCS), **Pop. 44,415.**
BROADWAY (WE), Church Street.—Controlled by Union Cinemas, Ltd., 15, Regent Street, London, S.W.1. Phone, Whitehall 8484. Booked at Hall. Continuous. Pictures and Variety. Prices, 6d. to 2s. Phone, Eccles 3265. Café attached. Station, Eccles ; and Road Transport.
CROWN THEATRE (BTP), Church Street.—Prop., Crown Cinema (ECCLES), Ltd., Imperial Buildings, Oxford Road, Manchester. Continuous. Booked at H.O. Two shows nightly. One change weekly. Prices, 3d. to 3s. Proscenium width, 30 ft. Phone 3824. Station, Eccles, L.M.S.
EMPIRE (BTH).—Prop., Robert E. Dockerty. 400 seats. Continuous evenings. Twice Sat., Mat. Daily. Booked at Hall. Prices, 6d. to 1s. Proscenium width, 22 ft. Phone, 3321. Station, Eccles, L.M.S.
PRINCES (BTP), Monton Road.—Prop., Monton Cinemas, Ltd. 900 seats. Booked at Hall. Continuous, Mon. to Fri. Twice nightly Sat. Prices, 6d. to 1s. Proscenium width, 28 ft. Stage, 10 ft. deep ; two dressing-rooms. Phone, Eccles 3426. Station, Monton Green, L.M.S.
REGENT (WE).—Prop., Lancs. Entertainments, Ltd. Man. Dir., E. Marshall. 921 seats. Station, Eccles.

ECCLESFIELD (near Sheffield) (YORKS).
CINEMA HOUSE (Morrison), The Common.— Prop., M. J. Gleeson. 648 seats. Booked at Hall. Continuous. Mon. to Fri. Twice nightly Sat. Prices, 5d. to 9d. Proscenium width, 21 ft. Phone, Ecclesfield 40182. Road Transport.

ECCLESALL (YORKS.).
GREYSTONES CINEMA.

ECKINGTON (DERBY), **Pop. 12,164.**
ELECTRA PALACE (BA).—Props., Electra Palace (Eckington) Ltd., 73, Surrey Street, Sheffield. Phone, Sheffield 20672. 610 seats. Booked at H.O. One show nightly. Three Sat. Prices, 5d. to 9d. Phone, Eckington 138.
PICTURE HOUSE (BTH).—Lessees, Rotherham District Kinemas, Ltd., Empire, Killamarsh, near Sheffield. 600 seats. One show nightly, two on Sat. Prices, 4d. to 1s. Stage, 15 ft. deep ; three dressing-rooms. Dance Hall adjoining. Station, Eckington, L.N.E.R. and L.M.S.

EDENBRIDGE (KENT), **Pop. 2,895.**
CINEMA.—Prop., Adelphi Advertising Co., Ltd. 275 seats. Continuous. Prices, 6d. to 1s. 6d. Station, Edenbridge, S.R.

EDLINGTON (nr. Doncaster) (YORKS).
CINEMA (BTP).—Prop., Edlington Cinema, Ltd., 54, High Street, Doncaster. 750 seats. Booked by G. Brocklesby, F.L.A.A., certified accountant, Conisborough. Phone, Conis-

borough 29. Nightly. Prices, 3d. to 1s. Station, Doncaster, L.N.E.R.

EGHAM (SURREY), **Pop. 15,915.**
BOHEMIA (WE), 153, High Street.—Prop. E. H. Sneath. Booked at Hall. Nightly. Prices, 6d. to 1s. 3d. Phone, Egham 433. Station, Egham, S.R.
GEM ELECTRIC THEATRE, High Street.

EGREMONT (CHESHIRE), see **Wallasey.**

EGREMONT (CUMB.), **Pop. 8,042.**
CASTLE CINEMA (BTH).—Prop., Egremont Cinema, Ltd. 750 seats. Booked at Hall. Once nightly. Twice Mon. and Sat. Pictures, Varieties and Theatricals. Depth of stage, 14 ft. Empire Dance Hall attached. Prices, 4d. to 1s. Proscenium width, 30 ft. Phone, Egremont 35. Station, Egremont, L.M.S.
EMPIRE THEATRE.

ELDON LANE (CO. DURHAM), **Pop. 3,000.**
CLUB CINEMA (AWH).—Prop., The Eldon Lane Workmen's Club and Institute, Ltd. 900 seats. Booking Man., J. C. Harwood. Once nightly, twice Sat. Two changes weekly and Sunday programme. Prices, 2d. to 6d. Station, Bishop Auckland, L.N.E.R.

ELLAND (YORKS), **Pop. 10,327.**
CENTRAL PICTURE HOUSE (BTH).—Prop., Central Pictures (Elland), Ltd. 500 seats. Booked at Hall. Continuous. Prices, 4d. to 1s. Phone, Elland 140. Station, Elland, L.M.S.
PALLADIUM (WE), Southgate.—Prop., Central Pictures (Elland), Ltd. 700 seats. Booked at Hall. Continuous. Two changes weekly. Prices, 4d. to 1s. Phone, Elland 140. Station, Elland, L.M.S.

ELLESMERE (SALOP), **Pop. 1,872.**
CINEMA.

ELLESMERE PORT (CHESHIRE), **Pop. 18,898.**
NEW HIPPODROME (WE).—Prop., Hippodrome (Ellesmere Port), Ltd., Carnegie Street, Ellesmere Port, Wirrell. 650 seats. Booked at Hall. Continuous. Twice on Sat. Prices, 5d. to 1s. 3d. Proscenium width, 40 ft. Stage, 17½ ft. deep ; three dressing-rooms. Café and Dance Hall attached. Phone, Ellesmere Port 54. Station, Ellesmere Port, L.M.S. and G.W.R.
QUEEN'S CINEMA (BTH), Whitby Road.—Prop., St. George Cinema, Ltd., 1-3, Stanley Street, Liverpool. Phone, Bank 9236. 686 seats. Booked at Prince of Wales News Theatre, Liverpool. Continuous nightly. Mats. Mon., Wed., Thurs., Sat. Prices, 6d. to 1s. 3d. Phone, Ellesmere Port 87. Station, Ellesmere Port, G.W.R.

ELSECAR (YORKS), **Pop. 4,500.**
ELECTRA PALACE THEATRE (BTH).—Prop. Elsecar Electric Palace Theatre, Ltd. 450 seats. Booked at Hall. Continuous. Two shows Sat. Two changes weekly. Prices, 4d. to 9d. Proscenium width, 24 ft. Station, Elsecar and Hoyland, L.M.S.

ELY (CAMBS), **Pop. 8,382.**
MAJESTIC THEATRE (IMPERIAL), Newnham Street.—Props., Russell Wright and Frank H. Wright, trading as Majestic Entertainments, 26, High Street, Ely. 400 seats. Continuous. Booked at Hall by R. Wright. Prices, 6d. to 1s. 6d. Phone, Ely 230. Films by Road Transport.

ELY—Contd.
PUBLIC ROOM CINEMA (FI), Market Place.—Props., Ely Cinema Co., Ltd. 300 seats Booked at Hippodrome, Wisbech. Continuous. Prices, 3d. to 1s. 6d. Phone, Ely 115. Station, Ely, L.N.E.R., and Film Transport.

REX THEATRE (WE), Market Street.—Prop., Ely Cinema Co., Ltd. 800 seats. Pictures and Variety. Booked by Harry Bancroft, Hippodrome, Wisbech, Cambs. Continuous. Prices, 6d. to 2s. Phone, Ely 115. Stage, 35 ft. deep ; two dressing-rooms. Station, Ely, L.N.E.R. Films by Road Transport.

EMSWORTH (HANTS), **Pop. 4,337.**
PAVILION (BTH), The Square.—Prop. and Man., C. B. Fowlie. Booked at Hall. Prices, 6d. to 1s. 6d. Phone, Emsworth 214. Station, Emsworth, S.R. and Road Transport.

ENFIELD (MIDDX.), **Pop. 67,869.**
PREMIER CINEMA (WE), Enfield Wash.—Prop., Davies Cinemas, Ltd. 897 seats. Continuous. Prices, 6d. to 1s. 10d. Phone, Enfield 1237. Station, Enfield Lock, L.N.E.R. Films by Transport.

QUEEN'S HALL KINEMA (BTF).—Props., L. and A. G. Rata. 1,000 seats. Booked at Hall. Continuous. Two changes weekly. Prices, 9d. to 2s. Stage, 5 ft. deep ; two dressing-rooms. Café. Phone, Enfield 0439. Station, Enfield, L.M.S. and L.N.E.R.

RIALTO THEATRE (WE).—Props. Denman London Cinemas, Ltd., 36, Golden Square, London, W.1. Gerrard 3554. Booked at H.O. Continuous. Phone, Enfield 0711. Station, Enfield, L.M.S. and L.N.E.R.

SAVOY (WE), Southbury Road.—Props., Associated British Cinemas, Ltd., 30-31, Golden Square, London, W.1. Films and Variety. 2,246 seats. Continuous. Films and Variety booked at H.O. Prices, 6d. to 1s. 6d. Proscenium width, 60 ft. Stage, 25 ft. deep ; five dressing-rooms. Café attached. Phone, Enfield 4411. Station, Enfield Town, Films by Road Transport.

WURLITZER ORGAN
Installed in this Kinema

EPPING (ESSEX), **Pop. 4,956.**
EMPIRE CINEMA (RCA), High Street.—Props., Empire (Epping), Ltd., Westminster Bank Chambers, Epping. 405 seats. Booked at Hall. Continuous. Prices, 6d. to 2s. Phone, Epping 208. Station, Epping, L.N.E.R.

EPSOM (SURREY), **Pop. 27,089.**
CAPITOL (RCA), Church Street.—Prop., London & District Cinemas, Ltd., 62, Shaftesbury Avenue, London, W.1. 1,500 seats. Booked at H.O. Continuous. Two changes weekly. Prices, 6d. to 2s. 6d. Phone, Epsom 9876. Café attached. Station, Epsom, S.R.

CINEMA ROYAL (RCA), High Street.—Prop., Mrs. M. Thompson. 650 seats. Booked at Hall,. Continuous. Prices, 6d. to 2s. 4d. Phone, Epsom 438. Station, Epsom, S.R., and Surrey Transport Service.

ODEON THEATRE (BTH), High Street.—Prop., Odeon (Epsom), Ltd., Cornhill House, Bennett's Hill, Birmingham. Phone, Midland 2781. Booked at 49, Park Lane, London, W.1.

ERITH (KENT), **Pop. 32,780.**
ODEON THEATRE (BTH), High Street and Avenue Road. Props., Odeon (Erith), Ltd., Cornhill House, Bennett's Hill, Birmingham. Phone Midland 2781. (In course of construction.)

PICTURE HOUSE (RCA):—Controlled by Union Cinemas, Ltd., Union House, 15, Regent Street, London, S.W.1. Phone, Whitehall 8484. Booked at H.O. Continuous. Prices, 6d. to 1s. 4d. Phone, Erith 2487. Station, Erith, S.R.

RIALTO CINEMA (PICTURETONE).—Prop., C. G. Quinton. 400 seats. Booked at Hall. Continuous. Two changes weekly. Prices, 6d. to 1s. 6d. Proscenium width, 12 ft. Phone, Erith 331. Films by Motor Transport.

ESH WINNING (CO. DURHAM), **Pop. 3,080.**
MEMORIAL HALL CINEMA (Edibell), Brandon Road.—Props., Trustees, Esh Colliery Welfare. 400 seats. Booked at Newcastle. Once nightly, twice Sat. Prices, 4d. to 9d. Phone, Esh Winning 22. Station, Waterhouses, L.N.E.R.

PAVILION (AWH).—Prop., F. W. Storey, Commercial Street, Cornsay. 650 seats. Pictures and Variety. Films booked at Hall by F. W. Storey. Variety by Billy Knight at Newcastle. One show nightly, two on Sat. Prices. 4d. to 9d. Stage, 30 ft. deep ; five dressing rooms. Phone, Esh Winning 4. Station, Waterhouses, L.N.E.R.

EVENWOOD (near **Bishop Auckland**) (CO. DURHAM), **Pop. 5,000.**
EMPIRE (Morrison).—Prop., Etherington Bros. 200 seats. One show nightly. No performance Friday. Two on Sat. Prices, 6d. and 8d. Proscenium width, 26ft. Station, Evenwood, L.N.E.R.

EVESHAM (WORCS.), **Pop. 8,799.**
REGAL SUPER CINEMA (WE), 41, Port Street.—Prop., Regal Super Cinema (Evesham), Ltd. 945 seats. Booked at Hall. Continuous, evenings. Prices, 6d. to 1s. 6d. Proscenium width, 28 ft. Phone, Evesham 6002. Café attached. Station, Evesham, G.W.R. and L.M.S.

THE SCALA THEATRE (WE), High Street.—Prop., The Super Cinema and Theatre (Evesham), Ltd. 900 seats. Gen. Man., A. E. Icke. Booked at Hall. Continuous. Nightly. Mat., Mon., Thurs. and Sat. Prices, 6d. to 1s. 6d. Stage, 21 ft. deep ; five dressing-rooms. Proscenium width, 30 ft. Phone, Evesham 217. Station, Evesham, G.W.R. and L.M.S.

EXETER (DEVON), **Pop. 66,039.**
EMPIRE THEATRE (BTH), 248, High Street.—Prop., Exeter Cinematograph Co., Ltd. 314 seats. Booked at Hall. Continuous. Prices, 9d. to 1s. 6d. Phone, Exeter 2707. Stations, St. David's G.W.R. ; Queen Street, S.R.

GAUMONT PALACE (BA).—Props., Gaumont British Corporation, 123, Regent Street, W.1. 1,500 seats. Booked at H.O. Continuous Prices, 6d. to 2s. Proscenium width, 56 ft. Phone, 207311. Station, St. Davids, G.W.R. (Central), S.R.

Fitted "ARDENTE" Deaf Aids
See page 258
WURLITZER ORGAN
Installed in this Kinema

PATHE GAZETTE—The Most Popular of News Reels !

KING'S HALL PICTURE HOUSE (BTP), St. Thomas.
—Prop., King's Hall (Exeter), Ltd. 700
seats. Sec., Edgar House. Booked at Hall.
Two shows nightly. Mat. daily. Two changes
weekly. Prices, 7d. to 1s. 6d. Station,
Exeter, G.W.R.

LOUNGE (NEWS KINEMA) (BTH) Fore Street.—
Prop., City of Exeter Palaces, Ltd. 300 seats.
Booked at Hall. Continuous. Prices, 6d.
to 1s. 6d. Phone, Exeter 37511. Station,
Exeter, G.W.R. and S.R.

ODEON THEATRE (BTH), Sidwell Street.—Prop.
Odeon (Exeter), Ltd., Cornhill House, Bennett's Hill, Birmingham. Phone, Midland
2781. (In course of construction.)

PALLADIUM (RCA), Paris Street.—Prop., Provincial Cinematograph Theatres, Ltd. 800
seats. Booked at H.O. Continuous. 2 to
10.30. Prices, 6d. to 1s. 6d. Phone, Exeter
201911. Stations, St. David's, G.W.R., and
Queen Street, S.R.

PLAZA, Old London Inn Square.—1,000 seats.

Fitted "ARDENTE" Deaf Aids
See page 258

SAVOY.—Prop., Associated British Cinemas,
Ltd., 30-31, Golden Square, London, W.1.
Phone, Gerrard 7887.

Fitted "ARDENTE" Deaf Aids
See page 258

COMPTON

ORGAN featured here.

EXMOUTH (DEVON), **Pop. 14,584.**

CAPITOL CINEMA (British Cinephone).—Prop.
and Res. Man., Walter J. A. Bayley. Booked
at Hall. Continuous. Mat. daily. Two
changes weekly. Station, Exmouth, S.R.

GRAND (BTH), Exeter Road.—Props., C. H.
Palmer, " Eastnor," Rolle Road, Exmouth,
Booked at the Regal, Exmouth. Continuous.
550 seats. Prices, 6d. to 1s. 6d. Proscenium
width, 28 ft. Phone, Exmouth 96. Station,
Exmouth, S.R.

NEW PICTURE HOUSE (WE), Parade.—Prop.,
and Res. Man., L. B. Thomas. 517 seats.
Booked at Hall. Three shows daily. Prices,
6d. to 2s. 4d. Phone, Exmouth 487. Station,
Exmouth, S.R.

REGAL CINEMA (BTH), St. Andrew's Road.—
Prop., C. H. Palmer, 16, Rolle Street, Exmouth. 630 seats. Booked at Hall. Continuous. Prices 6d. to 1s. 10d. Proscenium width,
28 ft. Stage 20 ft. deep. Six dressing-rooms,
Phone, Exmouth 96. Station, Exmouth,
S.R., also by Auto Services.

SAVOY CINEMA (BTH), Rolle Street.—Prop.,
J. E. Brooks, Messrs. Crews & Son, Rolle
Street, Exmouth. 850 seats. Booked at
Hall. Continuous. Daily Mat. Prices, 6d.
to 2s. Proscenium width, 26 ft. Stage 27 ft.
deep; five dressing-rooms. Phone, Exmouth
866. Station, Exmouth, S.R.

EYAM (near Sheffield) (DERBYSHIRE), **Pop.
1,000.**

MEMORIAL HALL (Metropolitan).—Prop., J.
Brown & Co. All correspondence to R.O.
Brown, 228, Fulwood Road, Sheffield. Once
nightly, Friday. Prices, 4d. to 1s. Phone,
Sheffield 61126. Road Transport.

FACIT (LANCS.) **Pop. 2,437.**

STAR CINEMA (Gramo-Radio).—Prop., E. Hilton.
400 seats. One show nightly. Prices, 3d. to
8d. Station, Facit, L.M.S.

FAILSWORTH (LANCS) **Pop. 15,724.**

GRAND THEATRE (WE) Oldham Road.—Prop.,
Chas. Ogden, 76, Victoria Street, Manchester.
Phone, Blackfriars 7445. 1,150 seats. Booked
at H.O. Continuous. Prices, 4d. to 9d.
Proscenium width 22 ft. Stage, 12 ft. 6 in.
Three dressing-rooms. Phone, Failsworth
1075. Station, Failsworth, L.M.S.

POPULAR PALACE (BTP).—Prop. and Res. Man.
D. Turner. 950 seats. Continuous. Two
changes weekly. Phone, Failsworth 1940.
Station, Failsworth, L.M.S.

FAKENHAM (NORFOLK), **Pop. 3,181.**

CENTRAL CINEMA (BTP).—Props., Fakenham
Cinema, Ltd, Market Place, Fakenham.
Phone, No. 67. 700 seats. Booked at Hall.
Twice nightly. Prices 6d. to 1s. 6d. Phone,
Fakenham 125. Station, Fakenham, L.N.E.R.
and M. & G.N.R.

ELECTRIC PAVILION, Holt Road.

FALMOUTH (CORNWALL), **Pop. 13,492.**

GRAND THEATRE (WE), Market Street.—Controlled by Union Cinemas, Ltd., 15, Regent
Street, London, S.W.1. Phone, Whitehall
8484. Booked at H.O. Continuous. Pictures
and Variety. Prices 6d. to 1s. 9d. Phone,
Falmouth 412. Station, Falmouth, G.W.R.

ODEON THEATRE (BTH).—Props., Odeon (Falmouth), Ltd., Cornhill House, Bennett's Hill,
Birmingham. Phone, Midland 2781. Booked
at 49, Park Lane, London, W.1. Continuous.
Prices, 9d. to 2s.

POLYTECHNIC CINEMA.—Lessees, Grand Theatre
(Falmouth), Ltd., 15, Market Strand, Falmouth. Booked at H.O. Two shows nightly.
Mat. Sat. Prices, 4d. to 1s. Station, Falmouth, G.W.R. (Parcel Office).

ST. GEORGE'S HALL (WE), Church Street.—
Controlled by Union Cinemas, Ltd., 15,
Regent Street, London, S.W.1. Phone,
Whitehall 8484. Booked at H.O. Two
shows nightly. Prices, 9d. to 1s. 6d. Phone,
Falmouth 169. Station, Falmouth, G.W.R.

FAREHAM (HANTS), **Pop. 11,575.**

EMBASSY.—Props., Shipman and King, M84,
Shell Mex House, Strand, W.C.2. (Building.)

SAVOY (WE).—Prop., Shipman and King, M84,
Shell Mex House, Strand, W.C.2. Phone,
Temple Bar 5077. Booked at H.O. Continu-
ous. Prices, 6d. to 1s. 6d. Proscenium
width, 40 ft. Stage and dressing-rooms. Café.
Station, Fareham.

FARINGDON (BERKS), **Pop. 3,076.**

CINEMA (Gyrotone).—Prop., Oram Bailey.
300 seats. Booked at hall. Once nightly.
Three Shows, Sat. Prices, 7d. to 1s. 6d.
Phone, No. 78. Road Transport.

RIALTO (AWH) Closter Street.—Prop., M. C.
Elliott. Seats 450. Prices, 6d. to 1s. 10d.
Station, Faringdon.

FARNBOROUGH (HANTS), **Pop. 16,359.**

AVENUE PALACE, Camp Road.—(Closed).

SCALA (WE), Camp Road.—Prop., Scala (Farnborough), Ltd., Associated with County
Cinemas, Ltd. 716 seats. Twice nightly.
Phone, S. Farnboro' 60. Station, S. Farnborough, S.R.

For Snap And Sparkle PATHE PICTORIAL Cannot Be Beaten.

FARNCOMBE (SURREY), **Pop. 3,841.**
COUNTY (WE), Meadrow.—Prop., County Cinemas, Ltd., Dean House, Dean Street, London, W.1. Phone, Gerrard 4543. 559 seats. Booked at H.O. Continuous. Prices, 6d. to 2s. Phone, Godalming 455. Station, Farncombe, S.R.

FARNDON (CHESHIRE).
PALACE (Celebritone). 300 seats.

FARNHAM (SURREY), **Pop. 18,294.**
COUNTY CINEMA.—Prop., Regal (Farnham), Ltd. Booked at County Cinemas, Ltd., Dean House, Dean Street, London, W.1.
PALACE (WE), 8, East Street.—800 seats. Three shows daily. Two changes weekly. Prices, 7d. to 1s. 6d. Phone, Farnham 99. Station, Farnham, S.R.
REGAL (WE) Props., Regal (Farnham), Ltd. Booked at County Cinemas, Ltd., Dean House. Dean Street, London, W.1. 1.280 seats.

FARNWORTH (LANCS), **Pop. 28,711.**
EMPIRE (RCA), Albert Road, Farnworth.—Prop., Picture House Co., Ltd. Man. Dir., W. Ramsden. 1,050 seats. Continuous. 3d. to 9d. Phone, Farnworth 362. Station, Moses Gate, L.M.S.
HIPPODROME (BTH), Moses Gate.—Props., Comar Cinemas, Ltd. 1,100 seats. Booked at Hall. Continuous. Phone, Farnworth 78. Station, Moses Gate, L.M.S.
KING'S HALL.
PALACE CINEMA (BTP), King Street.—Prop., Stalybridge Enterprise, Ltd., Imperial Bldgs., Oxford Road, Manchester. Phone, Ardwick 2226. 736 seats. Booked at H.O. Continuous Mon. to Fri., two shows Sat. Prices, 3d. to 9d. Phone, Farnworth 28. Station, Moses Gate, L.M.S.
RITZ (WE), Peel Street, Farnworth Lancs.— Controlled by Union Cinemas, Ltd., Union House, 15, Regent Street, London, S.W.1. Phone, Whitehall 8484. Booked at H.O. Continuous. Prices, 3d. to 1s. Phone, Farnworth 322. Station, Farnworth and Halshaw Moor, L.M.S.
SAVOY PICTURE HOUSE (BTP), Long Causeway. —Prop., Savoy Picture House (Farnworth), Ltd. 750 seats. Booked by H. D. Moorhouse Circuit, Imperial Bldgs., Oxford Road, Manchester. Continuous Mon. to Fri., two shows Sat. Mats., Mon., Wed., Thurs. and Sat. Prices, 3d. to 1s. Phone, Farnworth 263. Station, Moses Gate, L.M.S.

FAVERSHAM (KENT), **Pop. 10,091.**
ARGOSY (BTH) Preston Street. Props., East Kent Cinemas, Ltd. 700 seats. Continuous. Prices, 6d. to 1s. 6d. Station, Faversham.
EMPIRE PICTURE HALL (BTH), Tanner Street.— (Closed).
ODEON (BTH),—Props., Odeon (Faversham), Ltd., Cornhill House, Bennett's Hill, Birmingham. Phone, Midland 2781. Booked at 49, Park Lane, London, W.1. Prices, 6d. to 1s. 6d. Phone, Faversham 56.

FEATHERSTONE (YORKS), **Pop. 14,952.**
HIPPODROME (WE).—Prop., Hippodrome, Featherstone, Ltd. 610 seats. Booked by T. C. Holden, Empire, Harrogate. One show nightly. Two changes weekly. Prices, 3d. to 1s. Phone, Featherstone 27. Station, Featherstone, L.M.S.

FELIXSTOWE (SUFFOLK), **Pop. 12,037.**
PLAYHOUSE (BTH), Hamilton Road.—Prop., Felixstowe Picture House, Ltd. 600 seats. Booked at Hall. Twice nightly. Mats., Wed. and Sat. Prices, 6d. to 1s. 10d. Phone, Felixstowe 170. Station, Felixstowe Town, L.N.E.R.
RITZ (WE).—Controlled by Union Cinemas, Ltd., Union House, 15, Regent Street, London, S.W.1. Whitehall 8484. Booked at H.O. Continuous. Station, Felixstowe, L.N.E.R.
VICTORIA CINEMA.—Under same control as Playhouse. 400 seats.

FELLING (CO. DURHAM), **Pop. 27,041.**
CORONA THEATRE (BTP), Coldwell Street.— Prop., J. Hinge Circuit, 72. Grey Steeet, Newcastle on-Tyne. 700 seats. Booked at H.O. Twice nightly. Occasional variety. Prices, 5d. to 9d. Proscenium width, 24 ft. Phone, Felling 82248. Station, Felling-on-Tyne, L.N.E.R.
NEW IMPERIA (WE), Victoria Square.—Prop., Imperia Hall Co. (Felling), Ltd. 950 seats. Booked at Hall. Two shows nightly. Two changes weekly. Prices, 6d. to 1s. Proscenium width, 30 ft. Café attached. Phone Felling 82336. Station, Felling, L.N.E.R.

FELTHAM (MIDDX.), **Pop. 16,316.**
PLAYHOUSE (WE).—Prop., Feltham Playhouse, Ltd., Gem Cinema, Southall: Phone, Southall 1735. 850 seats. Booked at H.O. Continuous. Prices, 6d. to 2s. Proscenium width, 35 ft. Phone, Feltham 300. Station, Feltham, S.R.
ROXY, New Chapel Road.—Prop., W. S. Pinney, 30, Briar Road, Pollards Hill, Norbury. 390 seats. Booked at Hall. Continuous. Prices, 6d. to 1s. 6d. Station, Feltham, S.R.

FENCEHOUSES (CO. DURHAM), **Pop. 6,000.**
PALACE (BTH).—Prop., North Eastern Cinemas de Luxe, Ltd., Carlton Cinema, Tynemouth. Phone, North Shields 1210. 530 seats. Booked at Carlton, Tynemouth. One show nightly, Tues. to Fri. Two shows Mon. and Sat. Two changes weekly. Prices, 6d. to 1s. Proscenium width, 21 ft. Phone, Fencehouses 50. Station, Fencehouses, L.N.E.R.

FENNY STRATFORD (BUCKS), **Pop. 4,310.**
ELECTRIC PALACE, High Road.

FENTON (STAFFS), **Pop. 25,620.**
NEW PLAZA PICTURE PLAYHOUSE (BTH), Market Street.—Prop., Plaza (Fenton), Ltd., 550 seats. Booked at Hall. Continuous. Prices, 3d. to 1s. Proscenium width, 35 ft. Films by Potteries Transport.
PALACE, Market Street.—Prop., Fenton Picture Palace Co., Ltd. Two shows nightly. Mat., Tues., Wed. and Sat. Three changes weekly. Prices, 5d. to 9d. Phone, Longton 3693.
ROYAL CINEMA (AWH), Manor Street.—Prop. Harper and Ashton, Ltd. 700 seats. Booked at Hall. Continuous. Prices, 5d. to 9d. Station, Fenton, L.M.S.

FERRYHILL (CO. DURHAM), **Pop. 10,133.**
GAIETY THEATRE (RCA).—Prop., Thompson's Enterprises, Ltd., Palladium Bldgs., Eastbourne Road, Middlesbrough. Phone, Linthorpe 88156. 828 seats. Booked at H.O. Once nightly. Three shows Sat. Prices, 6d. to 1s. Proscenium width, 25 ft. Variety

The BEST Is Cheapest; PATHE GAZETTE.

occasionally. Stage 22 ft. deep; three dressing-rooms. Phone, Ferryhill 55. Station, Ferryhill, L.N.E.R.

MAJESTIC THEATRE (BTP), Dean Bank.—Prop., Joseph Cadman. 750 seats. Twice nightly. Pictures, Variety. Prices, 6d. to 1s. Proscenium width, 23 ft., Stage, 21 ft. deep. 4 dressing-rooms. Station, Ferryhill, L.N.E.R.

PAVILION (WE).—Props., Wall and Thompson. Booked at Newcastle-on-Tyne. 901 seats. Once nightly. Two shows Sat. Occasional Variety. Prices, 6d. to 1s. Phone, Ferryhill 47. Station, Ferryhill, L.N.E.R.

STAR CINEMA (BTP), Durham Road, Chilton Bldgs.—Prop., Mrs. M. E. James, 18, Osborne Terrace, Deeholme, nr. Bishop Auckland. 380 seats. Booked at Newcastle. Once nightly. Two shows Sat. Prices, 3d. to 9d. Proscenium width, 18 ft. Station, Ferryhill, L.N.E.R.

FILEY (YORKS), Pop. 3,730.

GRAND THEATRE AND CINEMA (Ultramonic), Union Street.—Prop., Filey Enterprises, Ltd. 500 seats. Man. Dir., Andie Caine. Booked at Leeds and London. One show nightly. Two changes weekly. Prices, 6d. to 1s. 6d. Proscenium width, 23 ft. Station, Filey, L.N.E.R.

FINEDON (NORTHANTS), Pop. 4,100.

CINEMA.—Prop.; Watts, Cinemas, Ltd., "Poolstock," Finedon. 300 seats. Booked at H.O. by A. T. Watts. Once nightly, Mon. to Fri. Continuous Sat. Prices, 4d. to 1s. 3d. Phone, Finedon 9. Road Transport.

FISHBURN (CO. DURHAM), Pop. 4,000.

ALHAMBRA (Morrison).—Props., W. W. Turnbull. 560 seats. Booked by W. W. Turnbull at Greenside, Coxhoe. Prices, 4d. to 8d. Station, Coxhoe Bridge, L.N.E.R.

FLEET (HANTS), Pop. 4,528.

COUNTY CINEMA (WE).—Prop., County Cinemas, Ltd., Dean House, Dean Street, London, W.1. Phone, Gerrard 4543. 357 seats. Booked at H.O. Twice nightly. Mat. Wed., and Sat. Prices, 6d. to 2s. Proscenium width, 21 ft. Café attached. Phone, Fleet 200. Station, Fleet, S.R., and by Film Transport.

FLEETWOOD (LANCS), Pop. 22,933.
Sunday evening shows all the year round.

ART PICTURES (WE), Lord Street.—Prop., Blackpool Tower Co., Ltd. 900 seats. Booked at H.O. Three shows daily. One on Sun. Two changes weekly. Prices, 6d. to 1s. Proscenium width, 30 ft. Café attached. Phone, Fleetwood 429. Station, Fleetwood, L.M.S.

Fitted "ARDENTE" Deaf Aids
See page 258

REGENT CINEMA (WE), Lord Street.—Prop., North Lancashire (Fleetwood) Electric Theatres, Ltd. 720 seats. Two shows nightly. Two changes weekly. Prices, 6d. to 1s. Phone, Fleetwood 667. Station, Fleetwood, L.M.S.

PIER PAVILION (WE), Esplanade.—Prop., Fleetwood Pier, Ltd. 850 seats. Continuous nightly. Daily Mat. Two changes weekly. Prices 6d. to 1s. Café and Ballroom. Phone, 563. Station, Fleetwood, L.M.S.

VERONA, Knott End, near Fleetwood. Booked by James Brennan at 107, Duke Street, Barrow-in-Furness.

VICTORIA CINEMA (WE), Poulton Road.—Prop., Victoria Cinema (Fleetwood), Ltd. 1,124 seats. Booked at Hall. Continuous. Mat. daily. Prices, 6d. to 1s. Stage, 15 ft. deep; three dressing-rooms. Phone, Fleetwood 708. Station, Fleetwood, L.M.S.

FOLKESTONE (KENT). Pop. 35,890.

ASTORIA (WE), Props., Associated Theatres (P. A. & D.), Ltd. 1,650 seats. Continuous. Occasional variety. Prices, 9d. to 2s. 6d. Proscenium width, 38 ft. Stage, 20 ft. deep. Four dressing-rooms. Phone, Folkestone 2274. Café. Station, Folkestone Central, S.R.

C O M P T O N

ORGAN featured here.

CENTRAL CINEMA (WE), George Lane. Controlled by Union Cinemas, Ltd., 15, Regent Street, London, S.W.1. Phone, Whitehall 8484. Booked at H.O. Continuous. Prices, 6d. to 2s. 6d. Phone, Folkestone 3335. Station, Folkestone Central, S.R.

Fitted "ARDENTE" Deaf Aids
See page 258

PLAYHOUSE (WE), Guildhall Street.—Controlled by Union Cinemas, Ltd., 15, Regent Street, London, S.W.1. Phone, Whitehall 8484. Booked at H.O. Continuous. Prices, 6d. to 2s. 6d. Café attached. Phone, Folkestone 3554. Station, Folkestone Central, S.R.

Fitted "ARDENTE" Deaf Aids
See page 258

C O M P T O N

ORGAN featured here.

PLEASURE GARDENS THEATRE, Bouverie Road.—Controlled by Union Cinemas, Ltd., Union House, 15, Regent Street, London, S.W.1. Telephone, Whitehall 8484. Variety. Prices, 3d. to 5s. 9d. Telephone, Folkestone 2115. Station, Folkestone Central.

SAVOY SUPER CINEMA (WE), Grace Hill.—Prop., S. S. Cinema, Ltd. 884 seats. Continuous. Booked at Hall. Two changes weekly. Prices, 6d. to 2s. 6d. Proscenium width, 30 ft. Phone, Folkestone 208511. Station, Central. S.R.

FOREST HALL (NORTHUMBERLAND).

NEW PICTURE HOUSE (BTP).—Prop., Stanhope (Newcastle-on-Tyne) Cinema Co., Ltd., 178, Westgate Road, Newcastle-on-Tyne. Phone, Newcastle 27451. 520 seats. Booked at H.O. by W. R. Marshall. Two shows nightly, one show Sun. Mats., Mon. and Sat. Two changes weekly. Prices, 5d. to 9d. Phone, Benton 61143. Station, Forest Hall, L.N.E.R.

RITZ.—D. J. Hinge Circuit, 72, Grey Street, Newcastle-on-Tyne.

FORDINGBRIDGE (HANTS), Pop. 3,456.

REGAL.— Prop., R. N. Haggar, 38, King George Avenue, Bournemouth. Phone, Bournemouth 5711. 250 seats. Booked by Prop. One show three nights weekly. Two shows Sat. Prices, 6d. to 1s. 3d. Station, Fordingbridge, S.R.

FORMBY (LANCS), **Pop. 7,557.**
EMBASSY (WE), Freshfield.—Prop., Wigan Entertainments Co., Ltd., 1, College Avenue, Wigan. 714 seats. Booked at Liverpool. Phone, Wigan 3173. Once nightly, Mon., Tues., Thurs. and Fri., two shows Wed. and Sat. Prices, 6d. to 1s. 3d. Proscenium width, 40 ft. Phone, Formby 463. Station, Freshfield, L.M.S.
QUEEN'S PICTURE HOUSE (BTP).—Three Tuns Lane.—Prop., Coliseum (Liverpool), Ltd., 1/3, Stanley Street, Liverpool. 450 seats. Booked by Regent Enterprises, Ltd, 51, North John Street, Liverpool. Two shows Mon., Wed. and Sat. Once rest of week. Prices, 6d. to 1s. 6d. Phone, Formby 430. Station, Formby, L.M.S.

FOWEY (CORNWALL), **Pop. 2,382.**
CINEMA (BTH).—Prop., Mrs. A. Walford, 51, Esplanade. 280 seats. Booked by Prop. One show nightly. Mat. Wed. and Sat. Two changes weekly. Prices, 6d. to 1s. 6d. Proscenium width, 26 ft. Station, Fowey, G.W.

FRAMLINGHAM (SUFFOLK), **Pop. 2,100.**
ASSEMBLY HALL.—Prop., Sullings & Co., 101, Foxhall Road, Ipswich. Station, Framlingham, L.N.E.R.

FRESHWATER (ISLE OF WIGHT), **Pop. 3,440.**
PALACE THEATRE (BA).—(Closed).
REGENT.—Prop., Isle of Wight Theatres, Ltd., Theatre Royal, Ryde, I.O.W.

FRINTON-ON-SEA (ESSEX), **Pop. 2,196.**
IMPERIAL HALL.—Closed.

FRIZINGTON (CUMB.), **Pop. 3,656.**
PALACE THEATRE (Mihaly), Main Street.—Lessee, Claude D. Rhodes. 450 seats. Booked at Hall. Once or twice nightly. Prices, 4d. to 9d. Stage, 18 ft. deep ; 2 dressing-rooms. Films by Carrier from Newcastle.

FRODSHAM (near Warrington) (CHESHIRE), **Pop. 4,000.**
THE GRAND (VERIVOX), Church Street.—Lessees, Byron Picture Houses, Ltd., 1·3, Stanley Street, Liverpool Phone, Bank 9236. Booked at Princes Cinema, Liverpool. 500 seats. Once nightly. Mat. and two shows Sat. and holidays. Pictures and Variety. Stage, 10 ft. deep ; 2 dressing-rooms. Prices, 6d. to 1s. 3d. Proscenium width, 24 ft, Phone, Frodsham 100. Station, Frodsham. L.M.S. and G.W.R. joint.

FROME (SOMERSET), **Pop. 10,738.**
PALACE THEATRE (Cinephone).—Prop., Gaumont British Picture Corpn., Ltd., 123, Regent Street, London, W.1. Phone, Regent 8080. Booked at H.O. Continuous. Two changes weekly. Prices, 6d. to 1s. 6d. Phone, Frome 203. Station, Frome, G.W.R.
GRAND CINEMA (Memorial Hall) (BTH).—Prop., Somerset Theatres, Ltd. 800 seats. Continuous. Twice Sat. and 2 Mat. Prices, 6d. to 1s. 6d. Phone, 273. Station, Frome, G.W.R.

FRESHWATER (I.O.W.).
REGENT (BA).—Props., Isle of Wight Theatres, Ltd. Phone, 2387. Booked at Theatre Royal, Ryde. 518 seats. Twice nightly. Prices, 6d. to 1s. 10d. Phone, 283. Station, Freshwater, S.R.

GAINSBOROUGH (LINCS), **Pop. 18,684**

GRAND (BA), Market Place.—Prop., Denman Picture Houses, Ltd., 123, Regent Street London, W.1. Phone, Regent 8080. 1260 seats. Booked at H.O. Continuous. Prices, 7d. to 1s. 4d. Phone, Gainsborough 90. Stations, Gainsborough, Lea Road and Central, L.N.E.R.
KING'S THEATRE (BA), Trinity Street.—Prop. Denman Picture Houses, Ltd., 123, Regent Street, London, W.1. Phone, Regent 6641. 750 seats. Booked at H.O. by Props. Twice nightly. Pictures, Variety and Touring Companies. Stage, 24 ft. ; 5 dressing-rooms. Prices, 6d. to 1s. 6d. Phone, Gainsborough 95. Station, Gainsborough Lea Road, L.N.E.R.

GARFORTH (YORKS), **Pop. 3,774.**
PICTURE HOUSE (Metropolitan), Station Road.—Prop., John Lambert. 400 seats. Booked at 10, Mill Hill, Leeds. Once nightly. Twice Sat. Prices, 4d. to 1s. Station, Garforth, L.N.E.R.

GARNDIFFAITH (near Pontypool), (MON.).
GARNDIFFAITH WORKMEN'S HALL AND INSTITUTE, LTD. (BA), 5, Herbert's Road. Booked at Hall. One performance nightly. Twice Sat. Prices, 7d. and 9d. Phone, Talywain 32. Stations, Abersychan and Talywain, and Road Transport by Film Transport Services, Cardiff, Ltd.

GARSTANG (LANCS), **Pop. 832.**
CINEMA, High Street.—Prop., Westmorland Entertainments, Ltd., "Elmhurst," Ainside, Westmorland. Booked at H.O. Two shows weekly. Thurs. and Sat. Prices, 5d. to 1s. Station, Garstang, L.M.S. Films by Auto.

GATESHEAD-ON-TYNE (CO. DURHAM). **Pop. 122,379.**
ASKEW PICTURE HOUSE (BTH).—Prop., Cecil Horn. 150 seats. Booked at Newcastle-on-Tyne. Two shows nightly. Prices, 2d. to 4d. Phone, Gateshead 134. Station, Gateshead, L.N.E.R.
BENSHAM PICTURE HOUSE (RCA).—Prop., Bensham Picture House (1923), Ltd. 1,050 seats. Booked at Hall. Twice nightly. Prices, 6d. to 9d. Phone, Gateshead 72441. Proscenium width, 28 ft. Station, Gateshead-on-Tyne, L.N.E.R.
BLACK'S THEATRE.—Prop., Black's Theatres, Suite 9, 115, Shaftesbury Avenue, London, W.C.2.
CAPITOL (WE), Durham Road, Low Fell.—Prop., Smelts Theatres, Ltd., 125, Westgate Road, Newcastle-on-Tyne. Phone, Newcastle 27887. Booked at H.O. 1,449 seats. Continuous. Prices, 6d. to 1s. Proscenium width, 30 ft. Phone, Low Fell 76938. Station, Gateshead-on-Tyne.
CLASSIC PICTURE HOUSE (BA), Kell's Lane, Low Fell.—Prop., Classic (Low Fell), Ltd., 72, Grey Street, Newcastle-on-Tyne. Booked at H.O. 1,022 seats. Twice nightly. Prices, 6d. to 1s. Phone, Low Fell 76894. Station, Newcastle, Central, L.N.E.R.
COATSWORTH PICTURE HALL (WE).—Bewick Road West.—Prop., Coatsworth Picture Hall, Ltd., 1,334 seats. Two shows nightly. Two changes weekly. Prices, 6d. to 1s. Phone, Gateshead 71606.
COSY PICTURE HOUSE, Swalwell.—Prop., James Ritson, 9, Albany Park Road, Tynemouth. Booked at Newcastle-on-Tyne. Twice nightly. Two changes weekly. Prices, 2d. to 6d.

PATHE GAZETTE: At All Events

EMPRESS ELECTRIC (BTH).—Prop. and Res. Man., G. Bolam. 650 seats. Two shows daily. Two changes weekly. Station, Gateshead-on-Tyne.

PALACE THEATRE (BA), Sunderland Road.—Prop., Denman Picture Houses, Ltd., 4-6, 123, Regent Street, London, W.1. Phone, Regent 6641. 700 seats. Booked at H.O. Twice nightly. Prices, 4d. to 8d. Phone, Gateshead 14. Station, Gateshead-on-Tyne, L.N.E.R.

PALLADIUM PICTURE HOUSE (BTH), Saltwell Road, Bensham.—Prop., L. Evans, 7, Grange Road West, Jarrow. Phone 67057. 560 seats. Booked at Hall and Jarrow. Two shows nightly. Prices, 4d. to 9d. Phone, Gateshead 71423. Station, Bensham, L.N.E.R.

RAVENSWORTH PICTURE HALL (BA).—Prop., Photoplays, Ltd., 71, Howard Street, North Shields. 750 seats. Booked at Hall. Twice nightly. Two changes weekly. Phone, Gateshead-on-Tyne 72021. Station, Gateshead-on-Tyne, L.N.E.R.

REGAL
Fitted "ARDENTE" Deaf Aids
Fitted "ARDENTE" Stage Amplification
See page 258

C O M P T O N
ORGAN featured here.

SCALA THEATRE (BA), Jackson Street.—Prop., Denman Picture Houses, Ltd., 123, Regent Street, London, W.1. 1,220 seats. Booked at H.O. Twice nightly. Prices, 3d. to 9d. Phone, Gateshead 72462. Proscenium width, 28 ft. Station, Gateshead, L.N.E.R., or Newcastle-on-Tyne, L.N.E.R.

SHIPCOTE HALL (RCA), Durham Road.—Prop., Shipcote Co., Ltd. 1,200 seats. Booked at Hall. Continuous. Phone, Gateshead 72019. Station, Gateshead, L.N.E.R.

GERRARD'S CROSS (BUCKS), **Pop. 2,200.**
THE PLAYHOUSE (WE).—567 seats.

GIGGLESWICK (YORKS), **Pop. 953.**
KINEMA.

GILLINGHAM (DORSET), **Pop. 4,100.**
PALACE.—(Closed).

REGAL (BTH).—Prop., R. W. M. Robinson. 305 seats. Once nightly, Mon., Tues., Fri. Twice nightly, Wed., Thurs., and Sat. summer months. Twice nightly winter. Prices, 6d. to 1s. 6d. Phone, 125. Station, Gillingham (Dorset), S.R.

GILLINGHAM (KENT), **Pop. 60,983.**
EMBASSY.

GRAND CINEMA (WE), Skinner Street.—Prop., C. W. Raphael, 203, Regent Street, London, W.1. 700 seats. Booked at Theatre. Continuous. Prices, 5d. to 1s. 3d. Phone, Gillingham 5450. Station, Gillingham, S.R.

KING'S HALL CINEMA, King Street.—Prop., Garrett and Tyler. 450 seats. Continuous. Two changes weekly. Booked at Hall. Prices, 5d. to 1s. Phone, Gillingham 5741. Station, Gillingham, S.R.

PLAZA CINEMA (WE).—2,000 seats. Continuous Prices, 4d. to 1s. 3d. Proscenium width, 28 ft. Phone, Gillingham 5539. Station, Gillingham, S.R.

GLASTONBURY (SOMERSET), **Pop. 4,513.**
CINEMA (Morrison).—350 seats.

GLOSSOP (DERBY), **Pop. 19,510.**
EMPIRE THEATRE (BA).—Prop., Gaumont British Corporation, 123, Regent Street, London, W.1. Pictures and occasional Variety. Booked at H.O. Continuous. Twice Sat. Prices, 6d. to 1s. 3d. Stage and 4 dressing-rooms. Phone, Glossop 114. Station, Glossop, Central L.N.E.R.

GLOUCESTER (GLOS), **Pop. 52,937.**
EMPIRE (BTH), Park End Road.—Prop., Cinema House, Ltd., 225, Oxford Street, London, W.1. Phone, Gerrard 3814. 450 seats. Booked at H.O. Continuous. Prices, 6d to 1s. 6d. Proscenium width, 19 ft. Phone, Gloucester 3389. Station, Gloucester, G.W.R. and L.M.S.

HIPPODROME (WE).—Prop., Poole's Theatre, Ltd. 1,600 seats. Booked at H.O. Continuous. Prices, 9d. to 2s. Phone, Gloucester 2127. Stations, L.M.S. and G.W.R.
Fitted "ARDENTE" Deaf Aids
See page 258

KING'S THEATRE (WE), Westgate Street.—Prop., Cinema House, Ltd., 225, Oxford Street, London W.1. Phone, Gerrard 3814. 800 seats. Continuous. Prices, 6d. to 1s. 6d. Phone, Gloucester 2600. Station, Gloucester, L.M.S. and G.W.R.

PLAZA (WE).—Props., Elton Cinema Co., Ltd., 10, Windsor Place, Cardiff. Phone No. 225. 1,845 seats. Booked at H.O. Continuous. Prices, 9d. to 2s. Proscenium width, 44 ft. Phone, No. 3757. Café attached. Station, G.W.R., or L.M.S.

PICTUREDROME (WE), Barton Street.—Prop., Cinema House, Ltd., 225, Oxford Street, London, W.1. Phone, Gerrard 3814. 744 seats. Continuous. Prices, 6d. to 1s. 6d. Phone, Gloucester 2932.

THEATRE DE LUXE (WE), Northgate Street.—. 1,050 seats. Continuous. Prices, 9d. to 2s. 5d. Café attached. Phone, Gloucester 2937. Proscenium width, 25 ft. Station, Gloucester, L.M.S. and G.W.R.

WURLITZER ORGAN
Installed in this Kinema

GODALMING (SURREY) **Pop., 11,000.**
REGAL (WE) Ockford Road.—Prop., Regal (Godalming) Ltd. Booked at County Cinemas Ltd., Dean House, Dean Street, W.1. 1,200 seats. Booked at H.O. Prices, 6d. to 2s. Proscenium width, 36 ft. Phone, Godalming 933. Station, Godalming, S.R.

GOLBORNE (near Warrington) (LANCS), **Pop. 7,322.**
JUBILEE CINEMA (BTP).—Props., Doman Enterprises, Ltd., 11-13, Victoria Street, Liverpool. Phone, Bank 5504. 650 seats. Twice nightly. Mats. Mon., Sat. Prices, 4d. to 1s. Phone 111. Station, Golborne, L.M.S.

ROYAL PAVILION (BTP).—Prop., West Lancashire Cinema Co. 500 seats. Booked at Hall. One show nightly. Prices, 4d. to 9d. Phone, P.O. 1. Station, Golborne, L.M.S.

GOLCAR (YORKS), **Pop. 9,812.**
ALHAMBRA PICTURES (BTH), Leymoor Road.—Prop., Walker and Singleton, Leymoor Road, Golcar. 586 seats. Continuous nightly. Booked at Leeds. Prices, 4½d. to 11d. Proscenium width, 16 ft. Phone, Milnsbridge 153. Station, Golcar, L.M.S.

PATHETONE WEEKLY, The Super Screen Magazine!

GOLDENHILL (STAFFS), **Pop. 5,200.**
ELECTRIC THEATRE (Morrison), High Street.—
Lessee and Man., Hayward Hogton. 500 seats.
Booked at Hall. Continuous. Phone, Kids-
grove 132. Station, Tunstall, L.M.S.

GOLDTHORPE (YORKS), **Pop. 10,000.**
EMPIRE (BA), Barnsley Road.—Prop. and Res.
Man., E. H. West. Booked at Leeds and
London. Continuous. Prices, 6d. to 1s. Stage,
15 ft. deep ; 6 dressing-rooms. Proscenium
width, 34 ft. Phone, Goldthorpe 28. Station,
Wath-upon-Dearne, L.M.S. and L.N.E.R.,
or Transport.
PICTURE HOUSE (BA).—Lessee, E. H. West,
Empire, Goldthorpe. Continuous. Booked at
Leeds. Prices, 6d. to 9d. Phone, Goldthorpe
28. Station, Wath-upon-Dearne, L.M.S.

GOOLE (YORKS), **Pop. 20,238.**
CARLTON PICTURE HOUSE (WE), Boothferry
Road.—Prop., Picture Hall (Goole), Ltd.
701 seats. Booked at Hall. Continuous.
Prices, 4d. to 1s. Phone, Goole 277. Station,
Goole, L.M.S.
CINEMA PALACE (WE), Boothferry Road.—Prop.,
Savoys (Hull), Ltd., Bank Chambers, Goole.
Res. Dir., W. Rockett. 800 seats. Booked
by Brinley Evans, Cecil Theatre, Paragon
Square, Hull. Continuous. Prices, 6d. to
1s. 3d. Phone, Goole 47. Station, Goole,
L.N.E.R. and L.M.S.
TOWER CINEMA (BTP), Carlisle Street.—Props.,
Savoy (Hull), Ltd. 928 seats. Booked at
H.O. Continuous. Prices, 6d. to 1s. Pro-
scenium width, 25 ft. Stage, 21 ft. deep ;
seven dressing rooms. Phone, No. 47. Station,
Goole, L.M.S. Road Transport.

GORLESTON-ON-SEA (SUFFOLK), **Pop.
12,000.**
COLISEUM (Marshall), High Street.—Prop.,
Attree & Barr, Ltd. 1,000 seats. Booked at
Hall. Once nightly. Mat., Mon. Thurs. and
Sat. Prices, 6d. to 1s. 3d. Proscenium width,
26 ft. Dance Hall attached. Phone, Gorleston
73. Station, Gorleston, L.N.E.R. Films by
Motor Transport.

GOSFORTH (NORTHUMB), **Pop. 18,042.**
GLOBE THEATRE (BA), Salters Road.—E. J.
Hinge Circuit, 72, Grey Street, Newcastle.
Phone, Newcastle-on-Tyne 20317. 883 seats.
Booked at H.O. Continuous. Prices, 6d. to
1s. Phone, Gosforth 52271. Station, South
Gosforth, L.N.E.R.
ROYALTY CINEMA (BTP).—Prop., Royalty
Cinema (Gosforth), Ltd. 1,400 seats. Booked
by E. J. Hinge, 72, Grey Street, Newcastle-
on-Tyne. Continuous. Prices, 6d. to 1s.
Proscenium width, 40 ft. Phone, Newcastle
52324. Station, Newcastle.

GOSPORT (HANTS), **Pop. 37,928.**
CRITERION CINEMA (WE), Forton Road.—
Prop., Portsmouth Town Cinemas, Ltd.,
Shaftesbury Cinema, Kingston Road, Ports-
mouth. Phone, Portsmouth 4976. 655 seats.
Booked at H.O. Continuous. Two changes
weekly. Prices, 6d. to 1s. Phone, Gosport
8128. Station, Portsmouth Harbour, S.R.
GOSPORT THEATRE (WE), High Street.—Prop.,
Portsmouth Town Cinemas, Ltd., Shaftesbury
Cinema, Portsmouth. Phone, Portsmouth
4976. 771 seats. Booked at H.O. Continu-
ous. Prices, 7d. to 1s. 3d. Proscenium
width, 24 ft. Phone, Gosport 8401. Station,
Portsmouth Harbour, S.R.

OLYMPIA PICTURE HOUSE (BTP), Stoke Road.—
Prop., E. F. Horne. 678 seats. Booked at
Hall. Continuous. Mat., Wed. and Sat.
Prices, 6d. to 1s. 3d. Phone, Gosport 8307.
Station, Gosport, S.R.
RITZ SUPER CINEMA (WE), Walpole Road.—
Props., Portsmouth Town Cinemas, Ltd.
Phone, Portsmouth 4976. Booked at Shaftes-
bury Cinema, Portsmouth. 1,508 seats.
Continuous. Prices, 6d. to 2s. Proscenium
width, 50 ft. Phone, GosPort 8691. Café
attached. Station, Portsmouth Harbour.
**Fitted "ARDENTE" Deaf Aids
See page 258**

GOUDHURST (KENT), **Pop. 2,970.**
GOUDHURST CINEMA, Church Road.—Prop.
and Man., F. W. Malpass. One show weekly.
Prices, 5d. to 1s. 3d. Station, Goudhurst, S.R.

GRANGETOWN-ON-TEES (YORKS). **Pop.6,518·**
LYRIC.—E. J. Hinge Circuit, 72, Grey Street,
Newcastle-on-Tyne.

GRANGE-OVER-SANDS (LANCS), **Pop. 2,648·**
PALACE CINEMA (BA).—Prop., Albert Nelson.
500 seats. Booked at Hall. Once nightly.
Prices, 6d. to 1s. 6d. Phone, Grange-over-
Sands 22. Café and Ballroom attached.
Station, Grange-over-Sands, L.M.S.

GRANGE VILLA (Co. DURHAM).
PAVILION (BTH).

GRANTHAM (LINCS), **Pop. 19,709.**
CENTRAL CINEMA (BTH).—Prop., Peterborough
Picture House Co., Ltd. Man. Dir., J. A.
Campbell. 650 seats. Booked at Central
Chambers, Grantham. Continuous. Two
changes weekly. Prices, 4d. to 1s. Station,
Grantham, L.N.E.R.
PICTURE HOUSE (BTH), St. Peter's Hill.—Prop.,
St. Peter's Hill Picture House Co., Ltd. Man.
Dir., J. A. Campbell. 1,000 seats. Booked at
Central Chambers, Grantham. Continuous.
Two changes weekly. Prices, 5d. to 2s. 6d.
Phone, Grantham 245. Station, Grantham,
L.N.E.R.
RITZ.—Prop., L. Morris, 52, Shaftesbury Avenue,
London, W.1. 1,500 seats.
THEATRE ROYAL (WE).—Continuous. Mat.
Sat. 750 seats. Prices, 5d. to 2s.

GRASSMOOR (DERBY), **Pop. 2,000.**
ELECTRIC THEATRE (Metro), North Wingfield
Road.—Prop., Matlock Cinemas, Ltd.,
Cinema House, Matlock. Phone, Matlock 121.
500 seats. Booked at H.O. Once nightly.
Mon. to Fri. Three shows Sat. Pictures and
Variety. Prices, 6d. to 1s. Station, Chester-
field, L.M.S.

GRAVESEND (KENT), **Pop. 35,490.**
MAJESTIC (BTH), King Street.—Controlled by
Union Cinemas, Ltd., Union House, 15,
Regent Street, London, S.W.1. Telephone,
Whitehall 8484. Continuous. Prices, 6d.
to 2s. Booked at H.O. Films and Variety.
Station, Gravesend Central, S.R. Telephone,
Gravesend 470.

COMPTON
ORGAN featured here.

PLAZA CINEMA (RCA), Windmill Street.—
Controlled by Union Cinemas, Ltd., Union
House, 15, Regent Street, London, S.W.1.
Phone, Whitehall 8484. Booked at H.O.
Continuous. Prices, 4d. to 1s. 10d, Phone

Gravesend 163. Station, Gravesend (Central), S.R., or Motor Transport.

REGAL THEATRE (BTH), New Road.—Controlled by Union Cinemas, Ltd., Union House, 15, Regent Street, London, S.W.1. Telephone, Whitehall 8484. Continuous. Booked at H.O. Prices, 6d. to 1s. 6d. Films and Variety. Station, Gravesend, Central S.R. Phone, Gravesend 374.

SUPER CINEMA (WE), New Road.—Controlled by Union Cinema Cos., Union House, 15, Regent Street, London, S.W.1. Phone, Whitehall 8484. Pictures and Variety. Booked at H.O. Continuous. Prices, 6d. to 1s. 10d. Phone, Gravesend 753. Station, Gravesend Central, S.R., and Film Transport.

C O M P T O N
ORGAN featured here.

GRAYS (ESSEX), Pop. 18,172.

EMPIRE (BTH), High Street.—Prop., Frederick's Electric Theatres, Ltd., 25, Shaftesbury Avenue, W.1 (Gerrard 2756). 600 seats. Booked at H.O. Two shows nightly. Four Mats. weekly. Occasional Variety. Prices, 7d. to 1s. 4d. Phone, Tilbury 142. Station, Grays, L.M.S., or Motor Transport.

REGAL (WE), New Road.—Prop., Frederick's Electric Theatres, Ltd., 1,490 seats. Occasional Variety. Booked at H.O. Continuous. Mat., Mon., Thurs. and Sat. Prices, 6d. to 2s. 6d. Proscenium width, 31 ft. Stage, 20 ft. deep; six dressing-rooms. Station, Grays, L.M.S.

GREAT AYTON (YORKS), Pop. 2,320.

EMPIRE PICTURE PALACE.—Prop., Thompson and Jones. One show nightly, Mon. and Wed., two on Sat. Two changes weekly. Prices, 6d. to 9d. Station, Great Ayton, L.N.E.R.

GREAT BRIDGE (near Tipton), (STAFFS).

PALACE (BTH).—Prop., Storer Pictures, Ltd., 45, Newhall Street, Birmingham. Phone, Central 6299. 650 seats. Booked at Hall. Continuous. Evenings, Three Mats. Prices, 4d. to 9d. Phone, Tipton 1595. Station, Great Bridge, G.W.R.

GREAT HARWOOD (LANCS), Pop. 12,787.

GRAND (WE), Blackburn Road.—Prop., Gt. Harwood Pictures, Ltd. 869 seats. One show nightly, Mon. to Fri. Three shows Sat. Two changes weekly. Prices, 5d. to 9d. Phone, Gt. Harwood 148. Station, Great Harwood, L.M.S.

PALACE (WE), Rushton Street.—Prop., North Cheshire Amusements, Ltd., Parrs Bank Buildings, 3' York Street, Manchester. 986 seats. One nightly. Mat. Mon., and Tues. Three shows Sat. Prices, 4d. to 9d. Phone, Great Harwood 42. Station, Great Harwood, L.M.S.

GREAT WIGSTON (LEICS.).

MAGNA (WE).

GREAT YARMOUTH (NORFCLK), Pop. 56,769.

EMPIRE PICTURE PLAYHOUSE (BTH).—Prop., Yarmouth and Lowestoft Cinemas, Ltd., 16, South Quay. Phone 40. 932 seats. Booked at H.O. by E. H. Field. Continuous. Prices, 6d. to 1s. 6d. Proscenium width, 25 ft. Phone, Yarmouth 3147. Station, South Town, L.N.E.R. All Films by Norfolk and

District Transport, Dansey Yard, Wardour Street, London, W.

GEM THEATRE (BTH), Marine Parade.—Prop., Yarmouth and Lowestoft Cinemas, Ltd., 16, South Quay. 700 seats. Booked at H.O. Continuous. Two changes weekly. Prices, 7d. to 1s. 6d. Proscenium width, 25 ft. Phone, Great Yarmouth 727. Station, Great Yarmouth, L.N.E.R..

HIPPODROME (BA), Marine Parade.—Prop., T. C. Read. Res. and Booking Man. W. O'Brien. Booked at Hall. Circus in Summer and stage shows preceded by shorts in winter. Prices, 9d. to 3s. Phone, Gt. Yarmouth 214. Stations, Gt. Yarmouth. (Southtown, Vauxhall and Beach), L.N.E.R.

PLAZA THEATRE (BTH), Market Place.—Props., V.E.H. Cinemas, Ltd., The Lido, Aylsham Road, Norwich. Phone, Norwich 894. Sublessee, Alan Williams. 550 seats. Booked at H.O. Continuous. Prices, 4d. to 1s. 3d. Proscenium width, 26 ft. Phone 804. Films by Ives Transport, Ltd.

REGAL (WE).—Controlled by Union Cinemas, Ltd., 15, Regent Street, London, S.W.1. Phone, Whitehall 8484. Booked at H.O. Continuous. Prices, 4d. to 3s. 6d. Proscenium width, 42 ft. Phone, 1191. Station, Gt. Yarmouth.

C O M P T O N
ORGAN featured here.

REGENT (WE).—Prop., Associated British Cinemas, Ltd., 30–31, Golden Square, W.1. Phone, Gerrard 7887. 1,667 seats. Booked at H.O. Continuous. Prices, 6d. to 1s. 6d. Proscenium width, 32 ft. Stage, 30 ft. deep; four dressing-rooms. Phone, Yarmouth 554. Station, Great Yarmouth, L.N.E.R.

ROYAL AQUARIUM (WE).—Prop., Royal Aquarium, Ltd., 15, Upper King Street, Norwich. Phone, Norwich 350. 1,500 seats. Continuous.

GREENFORD (MIDDLESEX).

PLAYHOUSE (WE), Ruislip Road.—Prop., Greenford Playhouse, Ltd., Gem Cinema, The Green, Southall. 910 seats. Booked at H.O. Continuous. Mat. daily. Station, Greenford, G.W.R.

GREENHITHE (KENT).

TIVOLI, Swanscombe.

GRIFFITHSTOWN (MON.), Pop. 5,036.

PALACE (BA).—Prop., Griffithstown Palace Co., Ltd. One show nightly. Two changes weekly. Prices, 5d. to 1s. 3d. Station, Griffithstown, G.W.R.

GRIMETHORPE (near Barnsley), (YORKS), Pop. 4,000.

EMPIRE PALACE (BTH).—Prop., Grimethorpe, Empire Palace Co., Ltd. 600 seats. Booked at Stancliffe, Grimethorpe. Twice nightly. Two changes weekly. Prices, 5d. to 11d. Proscenium width, 32 ft. Phone, Brierley 42. Station, Cudworth, L.M.S.

GRIMSBY (LINCS.), Pop. 92,463.

CHANTRY CINEMA (RCA), Cartergate.—Prop., Leonard Bass, 5, Princes Avenue, Grimsby. 550 seats. Booked at Hall. Continuous. Prices, 3d. to 1s. Phone, Grimsby 3232. Station, Grimsby Town, L.N.E.R.

GRIMSBY—Contd.

GLOBE PICTURE THEATRE (WE), Victoria Street. —Prop., R. B. Jones, 29, Manor Avenue, Grimsby. 750 seats. Booked at Hall. Continuous. Prices, 4d. to 1s. Proscenium width, 30 ft. Phone, 2174. Station, Grimsby Town, L.N.E.R.

LYRIC (Morrison).—Prop., N. Blair. 350 seats. Booked at Hall. Continuous. Two changes weekly. Phone, 2958. Station, Grimsby Town, L.N.E.R.

PALACE (WE), Victoria Street.—Prop., Grimsby Palace Theatre and Buffet, Ltd. Booked by Charles Thompson, Weetwood Chambers, Albion Street, Leeds. 1,509 seats. Continuous nightly. Daily mat. Sat. continuous. Prices, 6d. to 1s. 4d. Proscenium width, 35 ft Stage, 35 ft. deep ; 10 dressing-rooms. Phone, Grimsby 2837. Station, Grimsby, L.N.E.R.

PARAGON CINEMA (WE), Corporation Road.— Props., King's (Grimsby), Ltd., 121, Corporation Road. Phone, Grimsby 3388.

PLAZA (BTH), 128, Cleethorpes Road.—Prop., K. A. & W. Enterprises, Ltd., 3, Newcastle Chambers, Nottingham. 900 seats. Booked at H.O. Continuous nightly. Daily Mat. Two changes weekly. Prices, 6d. to 1s. Station, Grimsby Docks, L.N.E.R.

PRINCE OF WALES.—Prop., Associated British Cinemas, Ltd., 30-31, Golden Square, W.1.

QUEENS HALL (BTH), Alexandra Road.—Prop., Queens Hall (Grimsby), Ltd. 1,400 seats. Booked at Hall. Continuous nightly. Daily Mat. Prices, 6d. to 1s. 4d. Phone, Grimsby 2069. Station, Grimsby Town, L.N.E.R.

COMPTON

ORGAN featured here.

RIALTO SUPER CINEMA (RCA), Roberts Street.— Prop., Harry Ellins. 1,200 seats. Booked at Hall. Continuous. Films and Variety. Prices, 4d. to 1s. Proscenium width, 30 ft. Stage, 8 ft. deep ; one dressing-room. Phone, Grimsby 3920. Station, Grimsby Town (Goods), L.N.E.R.

RITZ (WE).—Controlled by Union Cinemas, Ltd., Union House, 15, Regent Street, London, S.W.1. Telephone, Whitehall 8484. Continuous. Booked at H.O. Station, Grimsby Town, L.N.E.R.

SAVOY PICTURE HOUSE (WE), Victoria Street.— Props., Gaumont British Picture Corp., Ltd., 123, Regent Street, London, W.1. 1,430 seats. Booked at H.O. Continuous. Prices, 6d. to 2s. Cafe attached. Phone, 2576. Station, Grimsby Town, L.N.E.R.

**Fitted "ARDENTE" Deaf Aids
See page 258**

STRAND CINEMA THEATRE (WE), Park Street.— Prop., Associated British Cinemas, Ltd., 30-31, Golden Square, W.1. 1,331 seats. Booked at H.O. Two shows nightly. Two changes weekly. Prices, 6d. to 1s. 3d. Phone, Grimsby 2611. Station, Grimsby Town, L.N.E.R.

TIVOLI (WE).—Prop., Associated British Cinemas, Ltd., 30-31, Golden Square, W.1. Booked at Theatre. Continuous. 1,217 seats. Prices, 6d. to 1s. 3d. Phone, Grimsby 2135. Station, Grimsby Docks, L.N.E.R.

TOWER PICTURE THEATRE (WE), Kent Street.— Prop., Tower Picture Theatre (Grimsby), Ltd., 23, Anlaby Road, Hull. Phone, Hull 33602. 1,071 seats. Booked by Robt. Freeman, Jameson Chambers, Jameson Street, Hull. Continuous Prices, 5d. to 1s. 4d. Phone, Grimsby 2627. Station, Grimsby Docks, L.N.E.R.

GUERNSEY (CHANNEL ISLANDS), Pop. 40,121.

GAUMONT PALACE (BA).—Prop., Provincial Cinematograph Theatres, Ltd., New Gallery House, 123, Regent Street, London, W.1. Phone, Regent 8080. 758 seats. One show nightly. Mat., Thurs. and Sat. Prices, 1s. to 2s. 8d. Station, Guernsey, St. Peter Port, via Weymouth.

**Fitted "ARDENTE" Deaf Aids
See page 258**

LYRIC HALL, New Street, St. Peter Port.— 569 seats. One show nightly, Sunday at 8 p.m. Mats., Thurs. and Sat. Three changes weekly. Prices, 7d. to 1s. 6d. Stations, Weymouth, G.W.R., and Southampton, S.R.

NORTH CINEMA (Electrocord), Vale Avenue, Guernsey.—Prop., C. H. Cross, Newington Place, Guernsey. Booked at H.O. by Prop. Prices, 6d. to 1s. 7d. Proscenium width, 22 ft. Phone, Guernsey 4262. Station, Guernsey, G.W.R.

GUIDE BRIDGE (LANCS).

ODEON THEATRE (BTH), Stockport Road, Audenshaw.—Prop., Odeon (Guide Bridge) Ltd., Cornhill House, Bennett's Hill, Birmingham. Phone, Midland 2781. Booked at 49, Park Lane, London, W.1. Continuous. Prices, 6d. to 1s. 3d. Phone, Ashton 1498.

GUILDFORD (SURREY), Pop. 30,753.

CINEMA (RCA), Woodbridge Road.—Prop., Guildford Cinema, Ltd. 985 seats. Man. Dir., Frederick Renad. Booked at Hall. Continuous. Café attached. Phone, Guildford 1234. Station, Guildford, S.R., and Motor Transport Co.

ODEON (BTH), Epsom Road.—Prop., Odeon (Guildford), Ltd., Cornhill House, Bennett's Hill, Birmingham. Phone, Midland 2781. Booked at 49, Park Lane, London, W.1. Prices, 9d. to 2s. 6d. Phone, Guildford 1990. Station, Guildford, S.R.

PLAYHOUSE (WE), High Street.—Props., County Cinemas, Ltd., Dean House, Dean Street, London, W.1. 925 seats. Booked at H.O. Continuous. Café and Winter. Gardens attached. Prices, 6d. to 2s. 6d. Phone, Guildford 50. Station, Guildford, S.R. Films by Road Transport.

PLAZA (WF), Onslow Street.—Prop., County Cinemas, Ltd., Dean House, Dean Street, London, W.1. Phone, Gerrard 4543. 511 seats. Three shows daily. Prices, 6d. to 2s. Phone, Guildford 368. Station, Guildford Town, S.R.

GUISBOROUGH (YORKS), Pop. 6,306.

EMPIRE (WE).—Prop., Thompson's Enterprises, Ltd., 4, Palladium Buildings. Eastbourne Road, Middlesbrough. 581 seats. Booked at H.O. Once nightly, Mon. to Fri. ; three on Sat. Two changes weekly. Prices, 4d. to 1s. Phone, Guisborough 78. Station, Guisborough L.N.E.R.

GUISELEY (YORKS), Pop. 6,607.
PICTURE HOUSE (BTP), Otley Road.—Prop., Guiseley Picture Palace Co., Ltd. 535 seats. Booked at Leeds. Continuous nightly Mon. to Fri. Twice nightly and Mat. Sat. Prices, 2d. to 1s. Proscenium width, 22 ft. Phone, Guiseley 173. Station, Guiseley, L.M.S.

HADFIELD (DERBYSHIRE), Pop. 6,730.

PICTUREDROME (RCA), Bank Street.—Prop., Hadfield Picturedrome Co. 866 seats. Booked at Hall. by Man. Once nightly, Mon. to Fri. Three shows Sat. Prices, 6d. to 1s. 4d. Phone, Glossop 273. Station, Hadfield, L.N.E.R.

HADLEIGH (ESSEX).
KINGSWAY CINEMA.

Fitted "ARDENTE" Deaf Aids
Fitted "ARDENTE" Stage Amplification
See page 258

COMPTON
ORGAN featured here.

HADLEIGH (SUFFOLK), Pop. 2,952.
PALACE CINEMA (Marshall).—Props., E. Owen Cooper. Booked at Hall. Continuous Mon. and Sat. Once nightly Tues. to Fri. 300 seats, Proscenium width, 17 ft. Prices, 6d. to 1s. 6d. Phone, Haldeigh 81.

HAILSHAM (SUSSEX), Pop. 4,604.
EMBASSY.—Props., Shipman & King, M84, Shell Mex House, Strand, W.C.2.—(Building).
PAVILION (WE), George Street.—Props., Shipman & King, M84, Shell Mex House, Strand, London, W.C.2. Phone, Temple Bar 5077. Booked at H.O. Continuous. Prices, 6d. to 1s. 6d. Station, Hailsham, S.R.

HALESOWEN (WORCS.), Pop. 31,058.
COSY CORNER CINEMA (Marshall), Peckingham Street.—698 seats. Booked by W. Jackson, Builder, Langley Green. Twice nightly. Mats., Mon. and Thurs. Prices, 4d. to 1s. Phone, Halesowen 3623. Station, Halesowen, G.W.R.
DRILL HALL.
PICTURE HOUSE (BTP). 900 seats.

HALESWORTH (SUFFOLK), Pop. 2,024.
CINEMA.—Prop., Miss M. Hopperson. 300 seats. Booked at Cinema, Beccles, by Mrs. C. C. Hipperson. Once nightly. Prices, 5d. to 1s. 6d. Station, Halesworth, L.N.E.R.
PICTURE PALACE, Corn Hall.—Prop., C. R. Punchard, 39, London Road. 300 seats. Booked at H.O. One show nightly, two on Sat. Two changes weekly. Prices, 5d. to 1s. 3d. Phone, Halesworth 2. Station, Halesworth.

HALIFAX (YORKS), Pop. 98,122.
ALHAMBRA (RCA), St. James' Road.—Prop. Bernard Scholfield. 750 seats. Booked at Hall. Continuous nightly, Mon. to Fri. Mat., Mon., Thurs. and Sat. Twice nightly Sat. Prices, 3d. to 1s. Phone, Halifax 2021. Station, Halifax, L.M.S.
COSY CORNER CINEMA (BTH), Queen's Road.— Prop., Halifax Cosy Corner, Ltd. 698 seats. Booked at Leeds. Continuous. Prices, 3d. to 1s. Phone, Halifax 362311. Station, Halifax Old Station, L.M.S.

ELECTRIC THEATRE (BA), Commercial Street.—Prop., Gaumont-British Picture Corpn., Ltd., 123, Regent Street, London, W.1. Phone, Regent 8080. 1,728 seats. Booked at H.O. Continuous. Prices, 6d. to 1s. 3d. Phone, Halifax 382611. Station, Halifax, L.M.S. and L.N.E.R.
GRAND PICTURE HOUSE (WE).—Prop., Northern Theatres Co., Ltd. 974 seats. Booked at Nothcoli House, Clare Road, Halifax. Continuous. Prices, 3d. to 9d. Phone, Halifax 4123. Stations, Halifax, L.M.S. and L.N.E.R.
KINGSTON PICTUREDROME (BTH), Queen's Road, King's Cross.—Prop., John Woodhead. "Waldolph," 80, Crow Wood Park, Halifax. 545 seats. Booked at Leeds. Continuous. Prices, 4d. to 9d. Proscenium width, 18 ft. Dance Hall attached. Phone, Halifax 61412. Station, Old Station, Halifax, L.M.S.
PALLADIUM PICTURE HOUSE (WE), King's Cross. Prop., Palladium Pictures, Halifax, Ltd. 876 seats. Booked at Hall. Continuous. Phone, Halifax 3538. Station, Halifax, L.M.S.
PICTURE HOUSE (WE), Ward's End.—Props. Gaumont-British Picture Corpn., Ltd., 123, Regent Street, London, W.1. Phone, Regent 6641. 1,365 seats. Booked at H.O. Continuous. Prices, 6d. to 1s. 6d. Café attached. Phone, Halifax 362511. Station, Halifax, L.M.S. and L.N.E.R.

Fitted "ARDENTE" Deaf Aids
See page 258

RITZ (WE).—Controlled by Union Cinemas, Ltd., Union House, 15, Regent Street, London, S.W.1. Phone, Whitehall 8484. Continuous. Booked at H.O. Station, Halifax, L.M.S.
ROXY (BTH), Northgate.—Prop., J. & H. Buxton, 4, Grange View, Leeds. 500 seats. Booked at Hall. Continuous. Daily Mat. Two changes weekly. Phone, Halifax 4118. Station, Halifax, L.M.S. Films by Road Transport.
THEATRE ROYAL (WE).—Prop., Northern Theatre Co., Ltd., Northcote House, Clare Road, Halifax. 1,549 seats. Booked at H.O. Continuous. Prices, 4d. to 1s. 6d. Phone, Halifax 2724. Films by Road Transport.
VICTORIA HALL (RCA), Ward's End.—Prop., Halifax Concert Hall and Public Rooms Co., Ltd., 8, Ward's End, Halifax. Phone, Halifax 4034. 2150 seats. Booked at Leeds. Continuous. Prices, 6d. to 1s. Phone, Halifax 360311. Station, Halifax, L.M.S. and L.N.E.R.

HALSTEAD (ESSEX), Pop. 5,878.
COLNE VALLEY CINEMA (WE).—Prop., Ager and Thomson, 10, Church Street North, Colchester. Phone, Colchester 3681. 350 seats. Booked at H.O. Continuous. Twice on Sat. Prices, 6d. to 1s. 6d. Phone, Halstead 155. Station, Halstead, L.N.E.R.
EMPIRE (BTH), Beridge Road.—Prop., Essex Amusements, Ltd. 450 seats. Booked at Chelmsford by R. G. Balls. Continuous nightly. Mats., Wed. and Sat. Two changes weekly. Prices, 7d. to 1s. 3d. Proscenium width, 20 ft. Station, Halstead, L.N.E.R. Films by road transport.

HALTWHISTLE (NORTHUMB.), Pop. 4,510.
GEM THEATRE (Filmophone).—600 seats.

HAMPTON (MIDDLESEX), Pop. 13,053.
PALACEUM.—Continuous. Two changes weekly. Prices, 6d. to 1s. 3d. Phone, Molesey 476 Station, Hampton, S.R.

The Pick Of Variety And Radio Stars In PATHETONE WEEKLY.

HAMWORTHY (In Poole).
EMPIRE CINEMA.—Prop., Randolph Meech.
Phone, Poole 640.

HANLEY (Staffs), **Pop. 66,255.**
CAPITOL THEATRE (WE), New Street.—Props.,
Associated British Cinemas, Ltd., 30-31,
Golden Square, London, W.1. Phone, Gerrard 7887. 1,258 seats. Booked at H.O. Continuous. Stage, 18 ft. deep. Café and Lounge attached. Prices, 6d. to 1s. 6d. Phone, Stoke-on-Trent 5027. Station, Hanley, L.M.S. or Pott Transport.
EMPIRE (BA), Piccadilly.—Prop., Gaumont-British Picture Corpn., Ltd., 123, Regent Street, London, W.1. Phone, Gerrard 8080. 929 seats. Booked at H.O. Continuous. Two changes weekly. Prices, 6d. to 1s. 3d. Phone, Hanley 5170-1. Station, Hanley.
ODEON THEATRE (BTH), Trinity Street.—Props., Odeon (Hanley) Ltd., Cornhill House, Bennett's Hill, Birmingham. Phone, Midland 2781. Booked at 49, Park Lane, London, W.1. Prices, 6d. to 2s. Café attached.
PALACE CINEMA (BTP), Albion Square.—Prop., Palace Amusements, Ltd. 2,600 seats. Booked at Hall. Continuous. Prices, 6d. to 1s. 3d. Proscenium width, 36 ft. Phone, Hanley 5413. Café. Station, Hanley, L.M.S., and Potteries Transport.
REGENT (WE).—Prop., Gaumont-British Picture Corpn., Ltd., Regent Street, London, W.1. 2,500 seats. Booked at H.O. Prices, 6d. to 2s. Proscenium width, 36 ft. Stage, 30 ft. deep; 12 dressing-rooms. Café-Restaurant attached. Station, Hanley.

Fitted **"ARDENTE" Deaf Aids**
See page 258
WURLITZER ORGAN
Installed in this Kinema

ROXY (WE), Glass Street.—Lessees, Paxon and Chambers, Ltd. 1,000 seats. Booked at Hall. Continuous. Prices, 4d. to 1s. Phone, Stoke-on-Trent 5497. Station, Hanley, L.M.S.

HARBORNE (Staffs), **Pop. 14,876.**
PICTURE HOUSE (BA), Serpentine Road.—Prop., Denman Picture Houses, Ltd., 123, Regent Street, London, W.1. Booked at H.O. Continuous. Prices, 5d. to 1s. Phone, Edgbaston 1281. Station, Harborne, L.M.S.

HARLESTON (Norfolk).
CINEMA.—250 seats.

HARPENDEN (Herts), **Pop. 8,349.**
AUSTRAL.
REGENT (BTH).—Props., J. C. Southgate and O. Melhuish. Continuous. 410 seats. Prices, 9d. to 2s. Phone, No. 860. Station, Harpenden, L.M.S.

HARROGATE (Yorks), **Pop. 39,785.**
CENTRAL CINEMA (WE), Oxford Street.—Prop., Central Cinema (Harrogate), Ltd. 922 seats. Booked at 10, Mill Hill, Leeds. Continuous. Prices, 6d. to 1s. 6d. Proscenium width, 25 ft. Phone, Harrogate 2357. Station, Harrogate, L.N.E.R.
ODEON (BTH), East Parade.—Prop., Odeon (Harrogate), Ltd., Cornhill House, Bennett's Hill, Birmingham. Phone, Midland 2781. Booked at 49, Park Lane, London, W.1. Prices, 6d. to 2s. 6d. Phone, Harrogate 3626.

PALACE THEATRE (BTH), Skipton Road.—Lessee, C. D. Rhodes. 400 seats. Booked at Hall. Continuous from 6.30 p.m. Prices, 5d. to 1s. Stage, 15 ft. deep ; 8 dressing-rooms. Phone, Harrogate 2188. Station, Harrogate, L.N.E.R.
ROYAL HALL (WE).—Prop., Harrogate Corporation. 1,275 seats. Gen. Man., John E. E. Wilshere. Booked at Hall. Continuous. Prices, 6d. to 2s. 6d. Proscenium width, 33 ft. Phone, Harrogate 3649.
SCALA (WE), Cambridge Street.—Prop., Gaumont British Picture Corporation, Ltd., 123, Regent Street, London, W.1. Phone, Regent 6641. 1,366 seats. Booked at H.O. Continuous. Prices, 6d. to 2s. 6d. Private Box seats, 3s. 6d. Café attached. Phone, Harrogate 3325 11. Station, Harrogate, L.N.E.R.
Fitted **"ARDENTE" Deaf Aids**
See page

ST. JAMES PICTURE HOUSE (BTP).—Lessee, Francis D. Sunderland. 1,000 seats. Booked at Hall. Continuous. Two changes weekly. Prices, 6d. to 2s. 6d. Phone, Harrogate 2958.

HARROW (Middx), **Pop. 26,378.**
BROADWAY CINEMA (Brown), Station Road.—Controlled by Blue Halls, Ltd., Coronation House, 4, Lloyds Avenue, London, E.C.3. 494 seats. Booked at H.O. Continuous. Prices, 6d. to 1s. 3d. Proscenium width, 20 ft. Phone, Harrow 1626. Station, Harrow-on-the-Hill, Met.
COLISEUM (WE), Station Road.—Controlled by Blue Halls, Ltd., Coronation House, 4, Lloyds Avenue, London, E.C.3. Phone, Royal 6159. 1181 seats. Continuous. Booked at H.O. Two changes weekly. Prices, 9d. to 2s. 6d. Café. Phone, Harrow 0266. Station Harrow, Met. R.

COMPTON
ORGAN featured here.

COSY CINEMA (WE), High Street, Harrow-on-the-Hill.—Prop., J. Symons, 37, Teignmouth Road, Brondesbury 673 seats. Booked at Hall. Continuous. Films and Variety. Prices, 7d. to 2s. Phone Byron 2267. Station, Harrow-on- the-Hill, Met. Ry.
DOMINION (WE).—Props., Associated British Cinemas, Ltd., 30-31, Golden Square, W.1. Booked at H.O. Continuous. 2,500 seats. Pictures and Variety. Proscenium width, 61 ft. Stage, 29 ft. deep. 12 dressing rooms. Station, Harrow & Wealdstone, L.M.S.
EMBASSY (RCA), Pinner Road, North Harrow.—Prop., Associated British Cinemas, Ltd., 30-31, Golden Square, London, W.1. 1,500 seats. Booked at H.O. Continuous. Prices, 6d. to 2s. Café attached. Phone, Harrow 3463. Station, North Harrow, Met. R.
GROSVENOR, Rayners Lane
ODEON THEATRE (BTH), Northolt Road, South Harrow.—Prop., Odeon (South Harrow), Ltd., Cornhill House, Bennett's Hill, Birmingham. Phone, Midland 2781. Booked at 49, Park Lane, London, W.1. Continuous. Prices, 9d. to 2s. 6d. Proscenium width, 45 ft. Stage, 15 ft. deep. Two dressing-rooms. Phone, Byron 2711. Stations, Harrow and Wealdstone, L.M.S.
RITZ.—Prop., L. Morris, 52, Shaftesbury Avenue, London, W.1. 2,100 seats.

PATHE GAZETTE—The Most Popular of News Reels!

HARWICH (Essex), **Pop. 12,700.**
Electric Palace (we).—Lessee, D. F. Bostock. Booked at 54, Chevalier Street, Ipswich. Phone, Ipswich 4036. 310 seats. Continuous from 6 p.m. Mat., Wed., and Sat. Prices, 7d. to 1s. 6d. Phone, Harwich 228. Station, Harwich, L.N.E.R. Films by Road Transport

HARWORTH, near Doncaster (Yorks).
Cinema House (Marshall), Scrooby Road, Harworth, near Doncaster.—Prop., Cinema House (Harworth) Ltd. General Buildings, Bridlesmith Gate, Nottingham. Once nightly. Prices, 4d. to 1s. Phone, Tickhill 43, Station, Bawtry, L.N.E.R.

HASLEMERE (Surrey), **Pop. 4,340.**
Regal (we), Weyhill.—Prop., Haslemere Cinema Co., Ltd. 610 seats. Booked at 12, The Square, Petersfield. Twice nightly. Prices, 6d. to 1s. 6d. Continuous. Proscenium width, 21 ft. Phone, Haslemere 575. Station, Haslemere, S.R.
Rex.—Prop., Haslemere Cinema Co. 1,100 seats. Twice nightly. Prices, 9d. to 2s. Phone, 44. Café attached.
Fitted "ARDENTE" Deaf Aids See page 258

HASLINGDEN (Lancs), **Pop. 16,637.**
Empire Cinema (btp), Deardengate.—Prop., Palace and Empire Cinemas (Haslingden), Ltd. Man. Dir., E. A. Hoyle, Gen. Man., Bert Hoyle. 1,600 seats. One show nightly, two on Sat. Two changes weekly. Prices, 4d. to 1s. Phone, Rossendale 269. Station, Haslingden.
Palace (btp), Beaconsfield Street.—Prop., Palace and Empire Cinema (Haslingden), Ltd., Deardengate. Man. Dir., E. A. Hoyle. Gen. Man., Bert Hoyle. 700 seats. One show nightly, two on Sat. Two changes weekly. Prices, 4d. to 1s. Phone, Rossendale 269. Station, Haslingden, L.M.S.

HASSOCKS (Sussex).
Chinese Garden Cinema, Hurstpierpoint.
Elite.—Controlled by Union Cinemas, Ltd., 15, Regent Street, London, S.W.1. Phone, Whitehall 8484.

HASTINGS (Sussex), **Pop. 65,199.**
Gaiety (we), Queens Road.—Prop., Gaiety (Hastings), Ltd. 1,098 seats. Continuous. Booked by R. E. Richards, Picturedrome, Eastbourne. Phone, Hastings 517. Station, Hastings, S.R.
Plaza (bth).—Prop., Plaza Cinema (Hastings), Ltd. 535 seats. Booked at Hall. Continuous. Prices, 6d. to 2s. Phone, No. 1985. Station, Hastings, S.R.
Regal.—Controlled by Union Cinemas, Ltd., 15, Regent Street, London, S.W.1. Phone, Whitehall 8484.
Ritz (we).—Controlled by Union Cinemas, Ltd., Union House, 15, Regent Street, London, S.W.1. Phone, Whitehall 8484. Continuous. Booked at H.O. Station, Hastings, S.R.
Cinema de Luxe (we), Pelham Place.—Prop., Union Cinemas, Ltd., Union House, 15, Regent Street, London, S.W.1. Phone, Whitehall 8484. Booked at H.O. Continuous. Prices, 4d. to 2s. Phone, Hastings 903. Station, Hastings, S.R.

HASWELL (Co. Durham), **Pop. 5,860.**
Palace (bth).—Prop., Wm. Johnson, 3, Rose Mount, Haswell. 650 seats. Booked at H.O. Once nightly. Prices, 5d. and 8d. Station, Haswell, L.N.E.R.

HATFIELD (Herts), **Pop. 9,070.**
Regent (we).—Props., Capitol (St. Albans), Ltd., 225, Oxford Street, London, W.1. Phone, Gerrard 4242. Booked at H.O. Continuous. Phone, Hatfield 2001.

HATHEREIGH (Devon), **Pop. 1,200.**
B.B. Cinema.—Prop., Capt. J. H. Blackhurst, West Down, near Ilfracombe. Phone, Infracombe 7.

HAVANT (Hants), **Pop. 4,264.**
Empire (we).—Prop., Southern Entertainments, Ltd. 670 seats. Booked at Hall. Continuous. Prices, 6d. to 1s. 6d. Proscenium width, 24 ft. Phone, Havant 179. Station, Havant, S.R.

HAVERHILL (Suffolk), **Pop. 3,827.**
Empire Cinema (btp)—Props.,Bury St.Edmunds Cinemas, Ltd. 54, Chevalier Street, Ipswich. Phone, Ipswich 4036. 350 seats.
Playhouse (ba).—Prop., Bury St. Edmunds Cinemas, Ltd. 54, Chevalier Street, Ipswich. Phone, Haverhill 91. 750 seats. Station, Haverhill, L.N.E.R. Films by Road Transport.

HAVERTON HILL (Co. Durham), **Pop. 6,000.**
Cinema (bth).—Prop., Tees Entertainments Ltd. 600 seats. Continuous. Booked at Newcastle. Prices, 3d. to 1s. Station, Haverton Hill, L.N.E.R.

HAWES (Yorks), **Pop. 1,425.**
Market Hall.—Prop., W. C. Sykes. Two shows Wed. only. Prices, 7d. to 1s. 1od.

HAWKHURST (Kent), **Pop. 3,123.**
Victoria Hall.—Prop. and Man., F. W. Malpass. Occasional Shows. Station, Hawkhurst, S.R.

HAWORTH (Yorks), **Pop. 5,912.**
Bronte Cinema (bth), Victoria Road.—Prop., Bronte Cinema Co., Ltd. 778 seats. Booked at Leeds by Sec. and Man. Once nightly. Three shows Sat. Prices, 4d. to 1od. Phone, Haworth 212. Station Haworth, L.M.S.
Hippodrome (bth), Belle Isle Road.—Prop., Haworth Hippodrome, Ltd., Old Bank Chambers, Keighley. Phone, Keighley 2264. 570 seats. Booked at Leeds and Keighley. One show nightly. Two and Mat. on Sat. Prices, 2d. to 9d. Station, Haworth, L.M.S.

HAY (Hereford).
Plaza Super Sound Cinema (Morrison).—Prop., D. J. Madigan, Hill Crest, Hay. Booked at Hall. Prices, 4d. to 1s. 6d. Proscenium width, 12 ft. Phone, Hay 4. Station, Hay, L.M.S. and G.W.R. Joint. Films by Road Transport.

HAYDOCK (Lancs), **Pop. 10,352.**
Picturedrome (Gram-Radio), Clipsley Lane. —Prop., H. Bracegirdle, 235, Clipsley Lane, Haydock. 450 seats. Booked at Hall. Two shows nightly. Prices, 4d. to 1s. Phone, Haydock 2064. Stations, Haydock and St. Helens, L.N.E.R.

For Snap And Sparkle PATHE PICTORIAL Cannot Be Beaten.

HAYDON BRIDGE (NORTHUMBERLAND), **Pop. 2,445.**
TOWN HALL CINEMA.

HAYES (KENT), **Pop. 1,700.**
REX.—Prop., General Cinema Theatres, Ltd., 19, Albemarle Street, London, W.I. Phone, Regent 4419.

HAYES (with Harlington) (MIDDLESEX), **Pop. 23,646.**
CORINTH (BTH).—Prop., Corinth (Hayes), Ltd., 147, Wardour Street, London, W.I. 700 seats. Booked at hall. Continuous. Prices, 7d. to 2s. Proscenium width, 36 ft. Stage, 16 ft. deep ; two dressing-rooms. Phone, Hayes 691. Station, Hayes, G.W.R.
REGENT CINEMA (WE).—Prop., Broadmead Cinemas, Ltd. 1,100 seats. Booked at 62, Oxford Street, London, W.I. Continuous. Pictures and · Variety. Prices, 9d. to 2s. Proscenium width 27 ft. Stage, 40 ft. deep. Cafe and Dance Hall. Phone, Hayes 167. Station, Hayes, G.W.R.

HAYLE (CORNWALL), **Pop. 915.**
COPPERHOUSE CINEMA.—Prop., Wilkinson Jones. 350 seats. Booked at Gaiety de Luxe, Newlyn, by Prop. One show nightly. Prices, 4d. to 1s. Station, Hayle.
PALACE THEATRE (Morrison).—Prop., R. N. Haggar. 320 seats. Booked at Hall. Nightly. Prices, 6d. to 1s. 6d. Proscenium width, 27 ft. Station, Hayle, G.W.R.

HAYLING ISLAND (HANTS), **Pop. 1,840.**
SAVOY CINEMA (BA), Church Road.—Prop., Frank Parmiter. 400 seats. Booked at Hall. Continuous. Prices, 6d. to 1s. 6d. Phone, Hayling 77788. Station, Hayling Island, S.R.

HAYWARDS HEATH (SUSSEX), **Pop. 5,382.**
BROADWAY CINEMA (BTH), · Broadway.—Prop., Mid-Sussex Cinemas, Ltd. 850 seats. Booked at 16, Lewes Road, Brighton. Continuous. Two changes weekly. Phone, Haywards Heath 47. Station, Haywards Heath, S.R.
PERRYMOUNT (BTH).—Prop., Mid-Sussex Cinemas. Ltd. 800 seats. Booked at 16, Lewes Road, Brighton. Continuous. Phone, Haywards Heath 401.

HAZEL GROVE (CHESHIRE), **Pop. 13,300.**
GROVE CINEMA (WE), Commercial Road.—Props., P. and N. Hall. 495 seats. Booked at Manchester. Twice nightly. Children's Mat. on Sat. Two changes weekly. Prices, 5d. to 1s. Proscenium width, 16 ft. Phone, Great Moor 2732. Station, Hazel Grove, L.M.S.

HEACHAM (NORFOLK), **Pop. 2,250.**
ELECTRIC CINEMA.

HEANOR (DERBY), **Pop. 22,386.**
COSY CINEMA (BTH), Market Place.—Prop., Heanor Picture House, Ltd. 780 seats. Booked at Hall. Continuous. Two changes weekly. Prices, 6d. to 1s. 3d. Station, Heanor.
EMPIRE THEATRE (WE).—Prop., Midland Empire Theatre, Ltd., Elite Buildings, Parliament Street, Nottingham. Phone, Nottingham 42,364. 733 seats. Booked at H.O. Twice nightly. Continuous. Three shows Sat. Proscenium width, 23 ft. Prices, 6d. to 1s. 3d. Six dressing rooms. Phone, Langley Mill 169. Stations Langley Mill, L.M.S. Films by Transport Service.

HEATH (DERBY), **Pop. 2,132.**
HOLMEWOOD PICTURE PALACE (B.A).—Prop., Holmewood Picture Palace Co., Ltd. 600 seats. One show nightly, two on Sat. Prices, 4d. to 1s. Station, Heath, L.N.E.R.

HEATH HAYES (STAFFS), **Pop. 10,000.**
NEW PICTURE HOUSE, Hednesford Road.—Prop., Thos. Jervis. 475 seats. Booked at Birmingham. Continuous Mon. and Thurs., two shows Sat. evening. Prices, 3d. to 1s. Proscenium width, 16 ft. Films by Road Transport.

HEATHFIELD (SUSSEX), **Pop. 3,155.**
PLAZA (BTH), High Street.—Prop., The Cinema (Heathfield), Ltd. 468 seats. Booked at Hall by Gen. Man., H. S. Martin. Continuous. Prices, 6d. to 2s. 6d. Proscenium width, 23 ft. Phone, Heathfield Town 196. Station, Heathfield, S.R., and Sussex Film Transport.

HEBBURN (CO. DURHAM), **Pop. 24,125.**
GEN THEATRE (WE), William Street.—Prop., Gem Theatres, Ltd., 67, Ellison Street, Jarrow. Phone, Jarrow 67431. 840 seats. Booked at Newcastle-on-Tyne. Two shows nightly. Films and Variety. Prices, 4d. to 1s. Proscenium width, 29 ft.; three dressing-rooms. Phone, Hebburn 37. Station, Hebburn, L.N.E.R., and Films by own carrier.
THEATRE ROYAL (WE).—Lessees, J. H. Dawe, Ltd., Gibb Chambers, Westgate Road, Newcastle-on-Tyne. 750 seats. Two shows nightly. Phone, Hebburn 79. Station, Hebburn-on-Tyne, L.N.E.R.

HEBDEN BRIDGE (YORKS), **Pop. 6,312.**
PICTURE HOUSE (Electrocord), New Road—Prop., Thistleholme Estate Co., Ltd. 954 seats. Res. and Bkg. Man., Geo. A. Greenwood. Once nightly. Twice Sat. Prices, 6d. to 1s. Phone, Hebden Bridge 147. Station, Hebden Bridge, L.M.S.

HECKMONDWIKE (YORKS), **Pop. 8,991.**
PAVILION (BTH).—Prop., West Riding Picture Pavilion Co., Ltd. 1,000 seats. Once nightly. Twice Sat. Mats., Mon., Tues., Thurs. and Sat. Prices, 4d. to 1s. 4d. Proscenium width, 39½ ft. Stage, 11 ft. deep ; three dressing-rooms. Phone, Heckmondwike 246. Station, Heckmondwike, L.M.S.
PICTURE PALACE (AWH), Croft Street.—Prop., Goodall's Pictures (1931), Ltd., Albion Street, Cleckheaton. Phone, Cleckheaton 224. 560 seats. Booked at H.O. Once nightly. Mats , Mon., Tues. and Sat. Two changes weekly. Prices, 4d. to 1s. 3d. Phone, Heckmondwike 186. Station, Heckmondwike, L.M.S.

HEDNESFORD (STAFFS), **Pop. 5,149.**
EMPIRE (Gyrotone), Rugeley Road.—Prop., Premier Picture Theatres, Ltd. 760 seats. Booked at Hall. Continuous nightly. Mat., Sat. Prices 6d. to 9d. Phone, Hednesford 75. Station, Hednesford, L.M.S.
TIVOLI (WE).—Prop., Premier Picture Theatres, Ltd. 750 seats. Booked at Hall. Continuous nightly. Three Mats. weekly. Prices, 5d. to 1s. Phone, Hednesford 75. Station, Hednesford, L.M.S.

HELSTON (CORNWALL), **Pop. 2,544.**
EMPIRE THEATRE (BTH), Wendron Street.—Prop., R. Hill. 350 seats. Booked at Palace, Truro. One show nightly. Mat. Sat. Prices, 6d. to 1s. 6d. Phone, Helston 53. Station, Helston, G.W.R.

The BEST Is Cheapest; PATHE GAZETTE.

HEMEL HEMPSTEAD (HERTS), **Pop. 15,122.**
LUXOR THEATRE (WE), Marlowes.—Prop., Luxor Theatre (Hemel Hempstead), Ltd. 718 seats. Booked at Hall. Continuous. Stage, 16 ft. deep ; three dressing-rooms. Prices, 6d. to 2s. Phone, Boxmoor 36. Station, Boxmoor, L.M.S.

PRINCESS THEATRE (WE).—Prop., Popular Cinemas, Ltd., Phœnix House, 19, Oxford Street, W.1. Phone, Gerrard 1405. 700 seats. Booked at H.O. Continuous. Mats., Wed., Thurs. and Sat. Prices, 6d. to 2s. Phone, Boxmoor 108. Station, Boxmoor, L.M.S., and Film Transport, Ltd.

HEMSWORTH (YORKS), **Pop. 13,001.**
HIPPODROME (BTH).—Hemsworth Hippodrome Co., Ltd., Stancliffe House, Grimethorpe, Nr. Barnsley. Phone, Brierley 42. Booked at Hall. Continuous. 918 seats. Prices, 6d. to 1s. Phone, Hemsworth 11. Station, Hemsworth.

HENLEY-ON-THAMES (OXFORD), **Pop. 6,618.**
NEW PALACE CINEMA (WE), 33, Bell Street.— Prop., Consolidated Cinematograph Theatres, Ltd. 472 seats. Booked at 17, Shaftesbury Avenue, W.1. Continuous. Mat., Sat. Prices, 6d. to 2s. Large stage. Phone, Henley 244. Station, Henley-on-Thames, G.W.R. Films by Oxford Film Transport Service.

HENLOW (BEDS), **Pop. 1,200.**
R.A.F. CINEMA (AWH), Henlow Camp.—600 seats. Booked at Camp by Secretary, Cinema Committee. Once nightly, Sundays included. Prices, 6d. to 1s. Phone, Hitchin 137, Ex. 22. Films by Transport. Station, Henlow, Beds., L.M.S.

HEREFORD (HEREFORDSHIRE), **Pop. 24,159.**
GARRICK THEATRE (WE), Widemarsh Street.— Controlled by Union Cinemas, Ltd., Union House, 15, Regent Street, London, S.W.1. Phone, Whitehall 8484. Booked at H.O. Continuous. Prices, 6d. to 1s. 6d. Phone, Hereford 2186. Station, Hereford, G.W.R.

KEMBLE THEATRE (FI), Broad Street.—Controlled by Union Cinemas, Ltd., Union House, 15, Regent Street, London, S.W.1. Phone, Whitehall 8484. Booked at H.O. Continuous. Pictures and Occasional Variety. Prices, 6d. to 1s. 10d. Phone, Hereford 2665. Station, Hereford, G.W.R.

ODEON THEATRE (BTH), High Town.—Props., Odeon (Hereford), Ltd., Bennett's Hill, Birmingham. Phone, Midland 2781. Booked at 49, Park Lane, London, W.1. Prices, 6d. to 2s.

PALLADIUM (Cinephone).—Prop., Palladium (Hereford), Ltd., Southlands, Stroud Road, Gloucester. Phone, Gloucester 3112. 650 seats. Booked at Hall. Twice nightly. Mats., Mon., Wed., Thurs. and Sat. Prices, 6d. to 1s. 6d. Phone, Hereford 2492. Station, Hereford, G.W.R.

RITZ (WE).—Controlled by Union Cinemas, Ltd., Union House, 15, Regent Street, London, S.W.1. Phone, Whitehall 8484. Booked at H.O. Continuous. Station, Hereford, G.W.R.

HERNE BAY (KENT), **Pop. 11,244.**
CASINO (BTH), Promenade Central.—Controlled by Union Cinemas, Ltd., 15, Regent Street, London, S.W.1. Phone, Whitehall 8484.

Booked at H.O. Continuous. Prices, 6d. to 2s. 6d. Phone, Herne Bay 601. Station, Herne Bay, S.R.

ODEON THEATRE (BTH). Cr. High Street and Richmond Bay.—Props., Odeon (Herne Bay), Ltd., Cornhill House, Bennett's Hill, Birmingham. Phone, Midland 2781. Booked at 49, Park Lane, London, W.1. Continuous. Prices, 6d. to 2s. Phone, Herne Bay 930.

RED LANTERN (BTH), High Street.—Controlled by Union Cinemas, Ltd., 15, Regent Street, London, S.W.1. Phone, Whitehall 8484. Booked at H.O. Continuous. Prices, 6d. to 2s 6d. Phone, Herne Bay 425. Station, Herne Bay, S.R.

HERTFORD (HERTS), **Pop. 11,376.**—
CASTLE CINEMA (BTH), The Wash.—Prop., Hertford Castle Cinema, Ltd., Hermitage Cinema, Hitchin. Phone, Hitchin 525. 700 seats. Continuous. Prices, 6d. to 1s. 3d. Proscenium width, 26 ft. Phone, Hertford 141. Station, Hertford (North), L.N.E.R.

COUNTY CINEMA (BTH).—Prop., Hertford County Cinema, Ltd., Hermitage Cinema, Hitchin. Phone, Hitchin 525. 1,158 seats. Continuous. Prices, 6d. to 2s. Proscenium width, 24 ft. Stage, 20 ft. deep. Eight dressing-rooms. Phone, Hertford 390. Station, Hertford (East), L.N.E.R.

REGENT (BTH), Market Street.—Prop., E. Owen Cooper. 210 seats. Continuous. Booked at Palace, Hadleigh, Suffolk. Prices, 3d. to 1s. 6d. Proscenium width, 30 ft. Phone, Hertford 503. Station, Hertford, L.N.E.R.

HESSLE (YORKS), **Pop. 6,430.**
STAR PICTURE HOUSE (BA), Hull Road.—Prop., A. G. Parkin, Florence House, Hessle. 350 seats. Booked at Hall. Continuous. Prices, 5d. to 1s. Phone, Hessle 171. Station, Hessle, L.N.E.R. Film Transport (Broxburn), Ltd.

HESWALL (CHESHIRE).
KING'S PICTURE HOUSE (BA), Telegraph Road.— Continuous. Mon. to Fri. ; Mat., Sat. and two evening shows. Prices, 6d. to 1s. 6d. Phone, Heswall 108. Station, Heswall, L.M.S. and G.W. Joint (via Hooton or Chester).

HETTON-LE-HOLE (CO. DURHAM), **Pop. 17,672.**
IMPERIAL CINEMA (BTH), Station Road.—Prop., Hetton-le-Hole Picture House Co., Ltd. 800 seats. Booked at Newcastle. Continuous. Twice nightly Sat. Prices, 4d. to 1s. Proscenium width, 28 ft. Phone, Hetton 50. Station, Hetton L.N.E.R.

PAVILION CINEMA (BTH), Richard Street.— Prop., Hetton Pavilion Cinema, Ltd., 40, Westgate Road, Newcastle-on-Tyne. Phone, 22401. 650 seats. Booked at Newcastle-on-Tyne. Continuous Mon. and Sat. Once nightly, Tues., to Fri. Prices, 4d. to 9d. Proscenium width, 22 ft. Phone, Hetton-le-Hole 20. Station, Hetton, L.N.E.R.

HEXHAM (NORTHUMB.), **Pop. 8,888.**
GEM PALACE (WE), Market Place.—Prop., Hexham Entertainments Co., Ltd., Queen's Hall, Hexham. 1,050 seats. Booked at H.O. by Tom H. Scott. Once nightly. Twice Sat. Prices, 6d. to 1s. 3d. Occasional Variety. Stage 35 ft. deep; 10 dressing-rooms. Proscenium width, 55 ft. Phone, Hexham 213. Station, Hexham, L.N.E.R.

Put Pep into Programmes With PATHE PICTORIAL.

HEXHAM—Contd.
QUEEN'S HALL (WE), Beaumont Street.—Prop., Hexham Entertainments Co., Ltd. 750 seats. Booked at Hall by Tom H. Scott. Twice nightly. Prices, 6d. to 1s. 3d. Occasional Variety. Variety booked by Matt. Steele, Imperial Agency, Westgate Road, Newcastle-on-Tyne. Stage 16 ft. deep; 6 dressing rooms. Café and Ballroom. Proscenium width, 21 ft. Phone, Hexham 213. Station, Hexham, L.N.E.R.

HEYWOOD (LANCS), **Pop. 25,967.**
EMPIRE CINEMA (BTH), Wood Street.—Prop., F. W. Constantine. 608 seats. Booked at Hall. Continuous Mon. to Fri. Twice on Sat. Daily Mat. Prices, 3d. to 1s. Proscenium width, 24 ft. Phone, Heywood 6189. Station, Heywood, L.M.S.
GEM PICTURE HOUSE (BA), Market Street.—Prop., Gem Cinema (Heywood) Ltd. Booked by H. D. Moorhouse Circuit. 600 seats. Booked at Manchester. Twice nightly. Two changes weekly. Prices, 3d. to 9d. Proscenium width, 16 ft. Phone, Heywood 6230. Station, Heywood, L.M.S.
PALACE (WE).—Prop., F. D. Constantine, Empire, Wood Street. 900 seats. Booked at Empire. Continuous Mon. to Fri. Twice nightly Sat. Prices, 3d. to 1s.
PICTUREDROME (WE), Market Street.—Prop., Picturedrome (Heywood), Ltd. 900 seats. Continuous and Matinées. Prices, 4d. to 1s. Phone, Heywood 6580. Station, Heywood, L.M.S.

HIGHBRIDGE (SOMERSET), **Pop. 2,584.**
REGENT PICTURE HOUSE - (Edibell).—Prop., G. Rees, 112, Brynland Avenue, Bristol. Phone, Bristol 44770. 325 seats. Booked at Bristol. Continuous. Prices, 6d. to 1s. 6d. Phone, Highbridge 9. Station, Highbridge, G.W.R.

HIGH SPEN (Co. DURHAM), **Pop. 4,000.**
PALACE (BTH), Front Street.—Prop., North Eastern Theatres, Ltd., 11, Bath Lane, Newcastle-on-Tyne. Phone, Central 5104. 400 seats. Booked at H. O. by Sol Sheckman, Man. Dir. Prices, 3d. to 8d. Station, Rowlands Gill, L.N.E.R.

HIGH WYCOMBE (BUCKS), **Pop. 21,950.**
GRAND CINEMA (RCA), Desborough Road.—Prop., British Cinematograph Theatres, Ltd., 199, Piccadilly, London, W.1. Phone, Regent 1227. 519 seats. Continuous. Mat., daily. Prices, 6d. to 1s. 6d. Phone, High Wycombe 145. Station, High Wycombe, G.W.R. (Transport).
MAJESTIC THEATRE (WE), Castle Street.—Controlled by County Cinemas, Ltd., Dean House, Dean Street, London, W.1. Phone, Gerrard 4543. 1,480 seats.

COMPTON
ORGAN featured here.

PALACE CINEMA (WE), Frogmore.—Prop., High Wycombe Theatre Co., Ltd. Booked at Hall. 1,400 seats. Continuous. Prices, 6d. to 2s. Proscenium width, 40 ft. Cafe and Dance Hall. Phone, High Wycombe 341. Station High Wycombe, G.W.R. Films by Motor Transport, Dansey Yard, W.1.

HINCKLEY (LEICESTER), **Pop. 16,030,**
DANILO (RCA).—Prop., Danilo (Hinckley), Ltd., 3, New Street, Birmingham. Phone, Midland 0871. 1250 seats. Proscenium width, 46 ft. Phone, Hinckley 523.
Fitted "ARDENTE" Deaf Aids
See page 258
ODEON (BTH).—Prop., Odeon (Hinckley) Ltd., Cornhill House, Bennett's Hill, Birmingham. Phone, Midland 2781. Booked at 49, Park Lane, London, W.1. Twice nightly. Four shows Sat. Prices, 6d. to 1s. 3d. Phone, Hinckley 85. Station, hinckley.
REGENT (BTH), Rugby Road and Lancaster Road.—Prop., Odeon (Hinckley), Ltd., Cornhill House, Bennett's Hill, Birmingham. Phone, Midland 2781. Booked at 49, Park Lane, London, W.1. Prices, 6d. to 1s. 3d. Phone, Hinckley 97. Station, Hinckley, L.M.S.

HINDERWELL (YORKS), **Pop. 2,147.**
CINEMA.

HINDLEY (LANCS), **Pop. 21,629.**
CASTLE PICTURES (RCA).—Prop. and Res. Man., F. E. Thwaites. 540 seats. Booked at Manchester and Liverpool. Twice nightly Fri. and Sat. Once nightly rest of week. Prices, 4d. and 6d. Proscenium width, 24 ft. Phone, Wigan 5135. Station, Hindley, L.M.S.
PALACE (BA).—Prop., Wigan Entertainments, Ltd., 1, College Avenue, Wigan. 1,000 seats. Booked at Renters' office by P. Worswick. One show nightly. Two changes weekly. Prices, 4d. to 9d. Phone, Wigan 373. Station, Hindley, L.M.S.
VICTORIA HALL.—Prop. and Res. Man., F. E. Thwaites. 500 seats. Booked at Manchester and Liverpool. Nine shows weekly. Two changes weekly. Prices, 4d. to 6d. Station Hindley, L.M.S.

HIPSWELL (YORKS).
CAMP CINEMA (WE).—Prop., F. L. Hastwell, The Terrace, Richmond, Yorks. 600 seats. Continuous. Prices, 9d. to 1s. 6d. Station, Richmond, L.N.E.R.

HITCHIN (HERTS), **Pop. 14,382.**
HERMITAGE CINEMA (BTH).—1,400 seats. Phone, Hitchin 525.
PLAYHOUSE (BTH), Market Square.—Props. Hitchin Amusements Co. 750 seats. Continuous. Two changes weekly. Prices, 6d. to 1s. 6d. Phone, Hitchin 179.

HODDESDON (HERTS), **Pop. 6,811.**
PAVILION (WE), High Street.—Prop., Shipman and King, M84, Shell Mex House, Strand, London, W.C.2. Phone, Temple Bar 5077. Booked at H.O. Continuous. Prices, 6d. to 2s. Phone, Hoddesdon 171. Station, Broxborne L.N.E.R.

HOLBEACH (LINCS), **Pop. 6,111.**
NEW HIPPODROME (BA).—Prop., Holbeach Amusements, Ltd., 7, South Brink, Wisbech. Phone, Wisbech 53. 617 seats. Continuous. Prices, 9d. to 1s. 10d. Phone, Holbeach 130. Station, Holbeach, L.M.S.

HOLLINWOOD (LANCS), **Pop. 10,745.**
LA SCALA (WE), Gregory Street.—Prop., A. and C. Ogden, 76, Victoria Street, Manchester.

PATHE GAZETTE: At All Events

1,045 seats. Booked at H.O. Phone, Black-friars 7445. Continuous, Mon. to Fri. Twice nightly, Sat. Prices, 3d. to 9d. Phone, Oldham Main 3071. Station, Hollinwood, L.M.S.

QUEEN'S PICTURE THEATRE (BTP), Hudson Street.—Prop., Hollinwood Cinema Co., Ltd., 4, Exchange Buildings, 6, St. Mary's Gate, Manchester. Phone, City 1968. 1,200 seats. Booked at Hall. Continuous. Prices, 4d. to 9d. Phone, Failsworth 1947. Station, Hollinwood.

HOLMFIRTH (YORKS), Pop. 10,407.
VALLEY THEATRE (WE).—Prop., Valley Pic-ture Theatre Co., Ltd., Eldon Yard, Holm-firth. 779 seats. Booked at Hall. One show nightly, two on Sats. and holidays. Mat., Sat. and holidays. Prices, 6d. to 1s. 3d. Phone, Holmfirth 184. Station, Holmfirth, L.M.S.

HOLSWORTHY (DEVON), Pop. 1,403.
CINEMA (Morrison), The Square.—Prop., Bennet and Silifant. 400 seats. Booked at Hall. Daily. Prices, 7d. to 1s. 6d. Station, Hols-worthy, S.R.

HOLT (NORFOLK), Pop. 2,254.
ELECTRIC CINEMA (AWH).—450 seats.

HONITON (DEVON), Pop. 3,008.
DEVONIA CINEMA (Edibell), High Street.— Managing Director, H. Stevenson. 410 seats. Booked at Hall. Twice nightly. Prices, 7d. to 1s. 6d. Phone, Honiton 180. Station, Honiton, S.R. Films by Film Transport (Cardiff), Ltd.

HONLEY (YORKS), Pop. 4,611.
PALLADIUM (BA), Eastgate.—Prop., Honley Palladium, Ltd. 600 seats. Booked by Mr. Earnshaw, Princess, Huddersfield. One show nightly. Two Sat. Two changes weekly. Prices, 5d. to 1s. Station, Honley, L.M.S.

HOOLEY HILL, near Manchester (LANCS).
STAMFORD PICTURE HOUSE.—Prop., Merry-weather and Cramer.

HORBURY (YORKS), Pop. 7,791.
HORBURY CINEMA (BA).—Prop., Horbury Industrial Co-operative Society, Ltd. Phone, Horbury 124. 550 seats. Booked at Pioneer Pictures, Dewsbury. Twice nightly. Occa-sional variety. Prices, 4d. to 9d. Station, Ossett and Horbury, L.N.E.R.

HORDEN (CO. DURHAM), Pop. 12,000.
EMPRESS THEATRE (WE), Blackhills Road.— Prop., Horden Electric Theatre, Ltd., 40, Westgate Road, Newcastle-on-Tyne. Phone, Newcastle 22401. 960 seats. Booked at H.O. Twice nightly. Prices, 4d. to 9d. Pros-cenium width, 36 ft. Phone, Horden 326. Station, Horden L.N.E.R. Films by Road Transport.

PICTURE HOUSE (WE).—1,120 seats.

HORLEY (SURREY), Pop. 6,098.
PAVILION (WE), Massets Road.—Prop., Shipman and King, M84, Shell Mex House, Strand, London, W.C.2. Phone, Temple Bar 5077. Booked at H.O. Continuous.

REGENT (WE).—Prop., Shipman and King, M84, Shell Mex House, Strand, London, W.C.2. Phone, Temple Bar 3269. Booked at H.O. Continuous. Prices, 6d. to 2s. Proscenium width, 36 ft. Phone, Horley 537. Station, Horley, and Road Transport.

HORNCASTLE (LINCS.), Pop. 3,496.
VICTORY CINEMA (Morrison), High Street.— Prop., Horncastle Cinema Ltd., 10. Banks Street, Horncastle. Phone, Horncastle 5, 430 seats. Booked by W. K. Morton. Phone No. 19. Twice nightly Mon., Wed. and Sat. Once Tues., Thurs., Fri. Prices, 4d. to 1s. 6d. Station, Spilsby, L.N.E.R., also Boston and District Film Transport Co. Boston.

HORNCHURCH (ESSEX).
TOWERS CINEMA.—D. J. James Circuit, Cinema House, 225, Oxford Street, London, W.1. Phone, Gerrard 4242.

Fitted "ARDENTE." Deaf Aids
Fitted "ARDENTE" Stage Amplification
See page 258

HORNSEA (YORKS), Pop. 4,450.
STAR PICTURE THEATRE (BA), Newbegin.— Prop., Hornsea Amusements, Ltd. 600 seats. Continuous. Prices, 7d. to 1s. 10d. Proscenium width, 28 ft. Stage, 35 ft. deep ; six dressing-rooms. Phone, Hornsea P.O. 136. Station, Hornsea, L.N.E.R.

HORSHAM (SUSSEX), Pop. 13,579.
CAPITOL (RCA), London Road.—Controlled by Union Cinemas, Ltd., Union House, 15, Regent Street, London, S.W.1. Phone, Whitehall 8484. Booked at H.O. Continuous. Prices, 6d. to 2s. Pictures and Variety. Phone 247. Café and Dance Hall attached. Station, Horsham, S.R.

CARFAX THEATRE (BA).—Controlled by Union Cinemas, Ltd., Union House, 15, Regent Street, London, S.W.1. Phone, Whitehall 8484. Booked at H.O. Continuous. Prices, 6d. to 1s. 4d. Phone, Horsham 247. Station, Horsham, S.R.

ODEON THEATRE (BTH).—Props., Odeon (Hor-sham), Ltd., Bennett's Hill, Birmingham. Phone, Midland 2781. Booked at 49, Park Lane, London, W.1. Continuous. Prices, 6d. to 2s. 6d. Café attached. Phone, Horsham 920. Station, Horsham, S.R.

RITZ (WE).—Controlled by Union Cinemas, Ltd., Union House, 15, Regent Street, London, S.W.1. Phone, Whitehall 8484. Continuous. Booked at H.O. Prices, 6d. to 2s. 6d. Phone, Horsham 900. Station, Horsham, S.R.

COMPTON
ORGAN featured here.

WINTER GARDENS THEATRE (BA).—Controlled by Union Cinemas, Ltd., Union House, 15, Regent Street, London, S.W.1. Phone, Whitehall 8484. Booked at H.O. Con-tinuous. Prices, 6d. to 1s. 4d. Phone, Horsham 247. Station, Horsham, S.R.

HORWICH (LANCS), Pop. 15,680.
PALACE (WE), Church Street.—Prop., Horwich Picture House, Ltd., Chorley New Road. 460 seats. Booked at Picture House. Con-tinuous. Two shows Sat. Two changes weekly. Prices, 3d. to 1s. Phone, Horwich 159. Station, Horwich, L.M.S.

PICTURE HOUSE (WE), Chorley New Road.— Props., Horwich Picture House, Ltd. 722 seats. Booked at Hall by Man. Continuous. Prices, 4d. to 1s. 3d. Phone, Horwich 158. Station, Horwich, L.M.S.

HORWICH—contd.

PRINCES THEATRE AND CINEMA (WE), Lee Lane.—Lessees, Horwich Picture House, Ltd., Chorley New Road, Horwich. 680 seats. Booked at Picture House. Continuous. Two shows Sat. Prices, 3d. to 1s. Proscenium width, 21 ft. Phone, Horwich 255. Station, Horwich, L.M.S.

HOUGHTON-LE-SPRING (CO. DURHAM), **Pop. 10,492.**

COLISEUM (WE).—Props., Lishman and Robinson. 1,002 seats. Booked at Hall by J. Lishman. Twice nightly. Prices, 6d. to 1s. Phone, Houghton-le-Spring 87. Station, Fence Houses. L.N.E.R.

EMPIRE THEATRE (WE).—Prop., Houghton Empire Theatre, Ltd. 600 seats. Booked at Hall by G. Wheatley. One show nightly, two on Mon. and Sat. Prices, 3d. to 1s. Phone, Houghton 52. Station, Fence Houses, L.N.E.R.

NEW GRAND THEATRE (WE), Newbottle Street, —Prop., John Lishman. 1,077 seats. Pictures, Drama and Variety. Booked at Hall. Twice nightly. Prices, 6d. to 1s. Stage, 30 ft. deep ; six dressing-rooms. Phone, Houghton 137. Station, Fence Houses, L.N.E.R.

HOUNSLOW (MIDDLESEX), **Pop. 31,381.**

ALCAZAR (WE).—Props., London and District Cinemas, Ltd., 62, Shaftesbury Avenue, W.1. 1,141 seats. Continuous. Prices, 6d. to 1s. 6d. Phone, Hounslow 0122. Stations, Hounslow, S.R. and District.

AMBASSADORS, Hounslow West.—Prop., London and Southern Super Cinemas, Ltd., 32, Shaftesbury Avenue, London, W.1.

COMPTON
ORGAN featured here.

DOMINION CINEMA (WE), London Road.—Prop., Hounslow Cinemas, Ltd., Dean House, Dean Street, W.1. Phone, Gerrard 5551. 2,022 seats. Pictures and Variety. Films booked at H.O. and Variety by Montague Lyon's Agency, 19, Charing Cross Road, W.C. Continuous. Prices, 9d. to 2s. 4d. Stage, 24 ft. deep ; three dressing-rooms. Proscenium width, 45 ft. Phone, Hounslow 1420. Café attached. Station, Hounslow, S.R., and Hounslow, E. (Piccadilly Line).

WURLITZER ORGAN
Installed in this Kinema

EMPIRE CINEMA (WE), High Street.—Prop., London and District Cinemas, Ltd., 62, Shaftesbury Avenue, W.1. 1,020 seats. Booked at H.O. Continuous. Proscenium width, 15 ft. Prices, 6d. to 2s. Stage, 15 ft. deep ; two dressing-rooms. Phone, Hounslow 0269. Station, Hounslow, S.R.

HOVE (SUSSEX), **Pop. 54,994.**

GRANADA (WE), Portland Road.—Prop., Associated British Cinemas, Ltd., 730-31, Golden Square, W.1. Phone, Gerrard 7887. 1,638 seats. Continuous. Prices, 6d. to 2s. Proscenium width, 45 ft. Stage, 22 ft. deep ; nine dressing-rooms. Café attached. Phone, Hove 3985. Station, Hove, S.R.

LIDO (WE).—Prop., Lido (Hove), Ltd. Booked by County Cinemas, Ltd., Dean House, Dean Street, London, W.1. Phone, Gerrard 4543. **2,137** seats. Continuous (including Sundays). Prices, 6d. to 2s. Café and Dance Hall attached. Phone, Hove 1188. Stations, Hove and Brighton, S.R.

WURLITZER ORGAN
Installed in this Kinema

TIVOLI (Wired), Western Road.—Prop. and Man. D. V. L. Fellows. 500 seats. Booked at Hall by Prop. Continuous. Prices, 6d. to 1s. 6d. Proscenium width, 20 ft. Phone, Hove 5124. Station, Brighton, S.R.

HOWDEN (YORKS).

MAJESTIC.—C. H. Whisecup Circuit, The Tower, Briggate, Leeds.

HOYLAKE (CHESHIRE), **Pop. 16,628.**

KINGSWAY PICTURE HOUSE (BTH), Market Street.—Prop., K. and W. Cinemas, Ltd., Angel Row, 3, Newcastle Chambers, Nottingham. Phone, Nottingham 43276. Continuous. Daily Mat. Two changes weekly. Prices, 6d. to 1s. 3d. Proscenium width, 48 ft. Phone, Hoylake 682. Café and lounge attached. Station, Hoylake, L.M.S.

WINTER GARDENS CINEMA (BTP), Alderley Road.—Prop., Winter Gardens Cinema (BTP), 610 seats. Continuous. Booked at Hall. Prices, 6d. to 1s. 3d. Stage, 16 ft. deep ; six dressing-rooms. Proscenium width, 32 ft. Phone, Hoylake 1345. Station, Hoylake, L.M.S.

HOYLAND (NR. BARNSLEY, YORKS), **Pop. 16,008.**

CINEMA (BTH), Market Street.—Prop., Hoyland Cinema Co., Ltd. Booked by Clayton's Bioscope, Bank Chambers, 70, The Moor, Sheffield. Phone, Sharrow 50822. 704 seats. Continuous. Prices, 4d. to 1s. Proscenium width, 24 ft. Phone, Hoyland 3299. Station, Elsecar and Hoyland, L.M.S.

PRINCESS CINEMA KINO (BTH).—Prop., Hoyland Cinema Co., Ltd. 1224 seats. Booked by Clayton's Bioscope, Bank Chambers, 70, The Moor, Sheffield. Continuous. Prices, 4d. to 1s. Phone, Hoyland 3245. Films by Film Transport. Elsecar and Hoyland, L.M.S.

HUCKNALL (NOTTS), **Pop. 17,338.**

EMPIRE (Marshall), Vine Terrace.—Prop., Hucknall Empire, Ltd. 1,000 seats. Booked at 3, Newcastle Chambers, Nottingham. Continuous nightly ; two shows Sat. Mats., Tues. and Sat. Prices, 6d. to 1s. Proscenium width, 30 ft. Stage, 40 ft. deep. 4 dressing-rooms. Phone, Hucknall 72. Station, Hucknall, L.M.S., and Road Transport.

SCALA (BTH), Annesley Road.—Prop., Pilot Palace Co., Ltd., General Buildings, Bridlesmith Gate, Nottingham. Nottingham Phone, 44584. 950 seats. Booked at Newcastle Chambers, Angel Road, Nottingham. Continuous, Mon. to Fri. Twice on Sat. Prices, 6d. to 1s. Phone, Hucknall 81. Station, Hucknall.

HUDDERSFIELD (YORKS), **Pop. 113,467.**

COSY NOOK CINEMA (BTP), Salendine Nook, nr. Huddersfield.—Prop., E. & F. M. Pearson. 600 seats. Continuous. Mat. Sat. Prices, 3d. to 1s. Proscenium width, 20 ft. Phone, Huddersfield 3768.

EMPIRE PICTURE HOUSE (WE), John William Street.—Lessees, Associated British Cinemas, Ltd., 30-31, Golden Square, W.1. 840 seats. Booked at H.O. Continuous ; Prices, 6d.

to 1s. 6d. Phone, Huddersfield 1798. Station, Huddersfield, L.M.S.

EXCELDA (WE).—Prop., Lockwood Picture House, Ltd. Booked at Hall. Continuous. Prices, 5d. to 1s. Phone, Huddersfield 544. Films by Road Transport.

GRAND PICTURE THEATRE (WE), Manchester Road.—Controlled by Union Cinemas, Ltd., Union House, 15, Regent Street, London, S.W.1. Phone, Whitehall 8484. Booked at H.O. Continuous. Prices, 6d. to 1s. 6d. Phone, Huddersfield 703. Station, Huddersfield, L.M.S.

HIPPODROME (WE).—1,551 seats.

LYCEUM (BTH), Moldgreen.—Prop., Lyceum Cinema (Moldgreen), Ltd. 1,000 seats. Booked at Leeds or office. Continuous. Prices, 4d. to 1s. Proscenium width, 26 ft. Phone, Hudd. 2101. Station, Huddersfield, L.M.S.

NEW STAR CINEMA (BTH), Viaduct Street.—Prop., Huddersfield Star Cine, Ltd., 16, Wood Street, Longwood, Huddersfield. 600 seats. Man. Dir., W. Walker. Booked at Leeds. Continuous. Prices, 4d. to 1s. Station, Huddersfield, L.M.S.

PALACE (BTH), Viaduct Street, Milnsbridge.—Prop., Milnsbridge Picture Palace, Ltd. Booked at Hall. Continuous. Prices, 6d. to 1s. Phone, Milnsbridge 217. Films by Road Transport.

PALLADIUM (BTH), Birkby.—Prop., Palladium Picture Co. (Birkby), Ltd. 500 seats. Booked at Hall. Continuous. Prices, 5d. to 1s. Phone, Huddersfield 3422. Station, Huddersfield, L.M.S.

PICTUREDROME (BTP), Buxton Road.—Prop.; Hibbert's Pictures, Ltd. Bradford. 900 seats. Booked at Hall. Continuous. Prices, 5d. to 1s. 3d. Proscenium width, 24 ft. Phone, Huddersfield 610. Station, Huddersfield, L.M.S.

PICTURE HOUSE (WE), School Hill, Kirkburton.—Booked at Hall. Once nightly. Phone, Kirkburton, 115. Films by Road Transport.

PICTURE HOUSE (WE), Ramsden Street.—Prop., Northern Theatres Co., Ltd. 873 seats. Booked at Nothcoli House, Clare Road. Halifax. Continuous. Prices, 6d. to 1s. 6d. Phone, Huddersfield 874. Station, Huddersfield.

PLAZA (BTH), Thornton Lodge.—Prop., Plaza Picture Theatre Co. (Huddersfield), Ltd. 1,000 seats. Booked at Hall. Continuous. Mat., Sat. Prices, 4d. to 1s. Stage, 15 ft. deep; four dressing-rooms. Proscenium width, 30 ft. Phone, Huddersfield 3555. Station, Huddersfield, L.M.S.

PREMIER PICTURE PALACE (WE), Paddock Head.—Prop., Premier Picture Palace Co. (Paddock), Ltd. 800 seats. Booked at Hall by Man. Continuous. Mats., Sat. Prices, 4d. to 1s. Phone, Huddersfield 2133. Station, Huddersfield, L.M.S.

PRINCESS PICTURE HOUSE (WE), 3, Northumberland Street.—Prop., Princess Pictures, Ltd. 900 seats. Booked at Hall. Continuous. Prices, 6d. to 1s. 6d. Phone, Huddersfield 2235. Proscenium width, 26 ft. Café and Dance Hall attached. Station, Huddersfield, L.M.S.

REGENT CINEMA (BTH) Fartown.—Prop., W. & R. Eckart, 5, Manchester Avenue, Aldersgate Street, E.C.1. Phone, Met. 4292. 668 seats. Booked at H.O. Continuous. Prices, 6d. to

1s. 3d. Phone, Huddersfield 2849. Films by Road Transport.

RITZ.—Controlled by Union Cinemas, Ltd., Union House, 15, Regent Street, London, S.W.1. Phone, Whitehall 8484. Booked at H.O. Continuous. Variety and Films. Prices, 6d. to 2s. 4d. Phone, 4130. Café attached. Station, L.M.S.

WURLITZER ORGAN
Installed in this Kinema

SAVOY PICTURE HOUSE (BTH), Marsh.—Prop., Savoy Picture House (Huddersfield), Ltd. 900 seats. Films booked at Hall and Variety direct. Continuous. Prices, 5d. to 1s. 3d. Phone, Huddersfield 1900. Station, Huddersfield, L.M.S.

TUDOR SUPER (WE).—Prop., Northern Theatres. Ltd., Clare Road, Halifax. Booked at H.O. Continuous. Tel. No. 874.

WATERLOO PICTURES (WE).—Prop., Waterloo Pictures (Hudds.), Ltd. 1,000 seats. Booked at Hall. Prices 6d. to 1s. Phone, Huddersfield 3440. Station, Huddersfield, L.M.S.

HULL (YORKS), Pop. 313,366.

ASTORIA (WE), Holderness Road.—Props., Astoria Cinema (Hull), Ltd. 1,500 seats. Booked by J. Prendergast. Rialto, York. Continuous. Prices, 3d. to 1s. 3d. Proscenium 59 ft. Café attached. Phone, Hull 3186. Station, Paragon, L.N.E.R.

COMPTON
ORGAN featured here.

CARLTON PICTURE THEATRE (WE), Anlaby Road·—Prop., Hull Cinemas, Ltd., Cecil Theatre, Anlaby Road, Hull. Phone, Hull 15315. 1671 seats. Booked at Cecil Theatre, Hull, by Gen. Man. Continuous. Prices, 6d. to 1s. 6d. Phone, Central 32306. Station, Paragon, L.N.E.R.

CECIL THEATRE (WE), Anlaby Road.—Prop., Hull Cinemas, Ltd. 1,958 seats. Booked at Hall by Brinley Evans. Continuous. Café attached. Prices, 1s. to 2s. Proscenium width, 35 ft. Phones, Central 15315 and 15348. Station, Paragon, L.N.E.R.

CENTRAL PICTURE THEATRE (WE), Prospect Street.—Prop., Hull Cinemas, Ltd., Cecil Theatre, Hull. 910 seats. Booked at Leeds. Continuous 2 p.m. till 10.30. Prices, 1s. to 2s. Mat. prices, 6d. to 1s. Proscenium width, 25½ ft. Phone, Central 16576. Station, Paragon, L.N.E.R.

CLEVELAND PICTURE HOUSE (WE), Cleveland Street.—Prop., Cleveland (Hull) Picture House, Ltd. 830 seats. Booked at Cecil Theatre, Hull. Continuous. Mats., Sat. Prices, 3d. to 6d. Phone, Central 33625. Station, Hull, L.N.E.R.

CRITERION PICTURE THEATRE (WE), George Street.—Prop., Associated Hull Cinemas, Ltd. 1,111 seats. Booked by Brinley Evans, Cecil Theatre, Hull. Continuous. Prices, 9d. to 1s. 6d. Phone, Central 33884. Station, Paragon, L.N.E.R.

DORCHESTER THEATRE (WE).— Prop., Associated Hull Cinemas, Ltd., Parliament Street, Hull 1,300 seats. Booked by Brinley Evans, Ceci Theatre, Hull. Continuous. Prices, 1s. to 2s Proscenium width, 42½ ft. Phone, Hull 33450

PATHE PICTORIAL—Novel, Entertaining, Unique.

HULL—Contd.

EUREKA PICTURE THEATRE (WE), Hessle Road.—Prop., Eureka Picture Hall, Ltd., Paragon Buildings, Paragon Street, Hull. 1,460 seats. Booked at H.O. Continuous. Prices 4d. to 1s. Proscenium width, 30 ft. Phone, Central 38036. Station, Paragon, L.N.E.R.

HOLDERNESS HALL (BA), Holderness Road.—Prop., Gaumont British Picture Corporation. 1,850 seats. Continuous. Daily Mat. Prices, 5d. to 1s. Phone, Corporation 33878. Station, Paragon, L.N.E.R.

Fitted "ARDENTE" Deaf Aids
See page 258

LANGHAM THEATRE (WE), Hessle Road.—Prop., Hull Cinemas, Ltd. 2,600 seats. Booked at Cecil Theatre. Hull. Continuous. Two changes weekly. Prices, 6d. to 1s. 6d. Proscenium width, 45 ft. Phone, 37322. Station, Paragon, L.N.E.R.

LONDESBOROUGH CINEMA (BTH), Wenlock Street.—Prop., L. and W. Maggs. 700 seats. Booked at Hall. Continuous. Prices, 4d. to 8d. Phone, 35302. Station, Paragon, L.N.E.R.

MAYFAIR (WE), Beverley Road.—Prop., Eureka Picture Hall, Ltd., Paragon Buildings, Paragon Street, Hull. Phone, Central 35754. 1,936 seats. Pictures and occasional Variety. Booked at H.O. Continuous. Prices, 7d. to 1s. 6d. Stage, 9 ft. deep ; two dressing rooms. Proscenium width, 30 ft. Café attached. Phone, Central 8752. Station, Paragon, Hull, L.N.E.R.

MONICA PICTURE HOUSE (WE), Newland Avenue.—894 seats. Booked at Hull Cinemas, Ltd., Cecil Theatre, Hull, by Brinley Evans. Continuous. Two changes weekly. Prices, 6d. to 1s. Station, Paragon, L.N.E.R.

NATIONAL PICTURE THEATRE (WE), Beverley Road.—Prop., Hull Cinemas, Ltd. Booked at Cecil Picture Theatre, Anlaby Road, Hull. 1,050 seats. Continuous. Nightly. Daily Mat. Prices, 6d. to 1s. Proscenium width, 24 ft. Phone, Central 8392. Station, Paragon, Hull.

PALACE THEATRE, Anlaby Road.—Prop., Moss Empires, Ltd. Booked at H.O., London. Two shows nightly. One change weekly. Prices, 6d. to 2s. 6d. Station, Paragon.

PLAYHOUSE CINEMA (WE), Porter Street.—Prop., Hull Picture Playhouses, Ltd., Parliament Chambers, Quay Street, Hull. 1,173 seats. Phone, Central 36801. Booked at Cecil Theatre, Hull, by Brinley Evans. Continuous. Mat. daily. Prices, 5d. to 1s. Phone, Central 33237. Station, Paragon, L.N.E.R.

PRINCES HALL (WE), George Street.—Lessee, Tom Morton. 838 seats. Changes weekly. Prices, 4d. to 1s. Phone, Central 33320. Station, Paragon, L.N.E.R.

REGAL (WE), Ferensway.—Prop., Hull City and Suburban Cinemas, Ltd. 2,650 seats. Booked by County Cinemas, Ltd., Dean House, Dean Street, London, W1.

Fitted "ARDENTE" Deaf Aids
See page 258

REGENT PICTURE THEATRE (WE), Anlaby Road, Prop., Regent Picture Theatre (Hull), Ltd., 23, Anlaby Road, Hull. 909 seats. Booked at Leeds. Continuous. Prices, 6d. to 1s. 6d. Phone, Central 16876. Station, Hull, Paragon, L.N.E.R.

REGIS (WE), Gipsyville.—Props., Hull City an Suburban Cinemas Ltd. 1,045 seats. Booked at Dean House, Dean Street, W.1. Continuous nightly. Mats., Mon., Thurs., Sat. Prices, 6d. to 1s. Proscenium width, 45 ft. Phone, 38050. Films by Road Transport.

REX (WE).—Prop., Hull City and Suburban Cinemas, Ltd. Controlled by County Cinemas. Ltd., Dean House, Dean Street, London, W.1,

RIALTO (WE), Beverley Road.—Prop., Associated British Cinemas, Ltd., 30-31, Golden Square, London, W.1. 2,073 seats. Booked at H.O. Continuous. Mat. daily. Prices, 4d. to 6d. Proscenium width, 36 ft. Phone, Central 8236. Station, Paragon (Station Hall), L.N.E.R.

RITZ (WE), Holderness Road.—Prop., Sherburn Picture Theatre Co., Ltd. 1,640 seats. Booked at H.O. Continuous. Two changes weekly. Prices, 6d. to 1s. 3d. Café. Phone, Central 33173.

WURLITZER ORGAN
Installed in this Kinema

ROYALTY (WE), Southcoates Lane.—Props., Hull City and Suburban Cinemas, Ltd. 1,045 seats. Booked at Dean House, Dean Street, W.1. Continuous nightly. Mats., Mon., Thurs., Sat. Prices ,6d. to 1s. Proscenium width 40 ft. Phone, 34954 Station, Paragon, L.N.E.R.

SAVOY PICTURE THEATRE (WE), Holderness Road.—Prop., Savoy (Hull), Ltd. 1,330 seats. Continuous nightly. Daily Mat. Two changes weekly. Booked at Cecil Theatre. Prices, 6d. to 1s. 3d. Proscenium width, 21 ft. Occasional Variety. Stage, 6 ft. deep. One dressing room. Phone, Central 31250. Station, Paragon, L.N.E.R.

SHERBURN PICTURE HALL (WE), Sherburn Street.—Prop., Sherburn Picture Hall, Ltd., 14, Paragon Chambers, Paragon Street, Hull. Phone, Hull 35754. 1,173 seats. Booked at H.O. Continuous. Two changes weekly. Prices, 5d. 7d. and 1s. Phone, Hull 31383. Station, Paragon, L.N.E.R. Films by Road Transport.

STRAND PICTURE THEATRE (WE), Beverley Road.—Prop., Beverley Road Picture Theatre (Hull), Ltd. Booked by J. F. Tidswell, "Woodville," Newton Park, Leeds. 1,224 seats. Continuous. Mats. daily. Two changes weekly. Prices, 6d. to 1s. Phone, Central 35522. Station, Paragon, L.N.E.R.

TOWER PICTURE PALACE (WE), Anlaby Road.—Prop., The Tower Picture Palace (Hull), Ltd., Jameson Chambers, Jameson Street, Hull. Phone, Central 36351. 778 seats. Booked at H.O. by Robert Freeman. Continuous. Prices, 6d. to 2s. Phone, 36101. Station, Paragon, L.N.E.R.

WATERLOO CINEMA (Pearlamb), Waterloo Street.—Prop., E. Lamb, Hayburn, Silverdale Road, Hull. 975 seats. Booked at Leeds. Continuous. Two changes weekly. Proscenium width, 26 ft. Prices, 3d. to 9d. Phone, Central 33341. Station, Paragon, Hull, L.N.E.R.

WEST PARK PICTURE THEATRE (WE), Anlaby Road.—Prop., Hull Picture Playhouses, Ltd. Parliament Street, Hull. Phone, 35786. 773 seats. Booked by B. Evans at Cecil Theatre, Hull. Twice nightly. Two changes weekly. Prices, 7d. to 1s. Phone, Central 16855. Station, Paragon, L.N.E.R.

HUNGERFORD (BERKS), **Pop. 2,784.**
CINEMA (AWH).—Prop., F. J. Freeman. 300 seats. Three times weekly. Prices, 6d. to 1s. 3d. Station, Hungerford, G.W.R., and Western Films Motor Transport.

HUNSTANTON (NORFOLK), **Pop. 4,282.**
CAPITOL (BTH).—Prop., Hunstanton Cinemas. Ltd. Phone, Hunstanton 194. 700 seats, Continuous. Prices, 6d. to 2s. Proscenium. width, 30 ft. Station, Hunstanton, L.N.E.R,

HUNTINGDON (HUNTS), **Pop. 4,108.**
GRAND CINEMA (BTH).—Prop., Murkett Bros. 500 seats. Booked at Hall by W. D. Murkett. Continuous. Prices 6d. to 1s. 6d. Phone, Huntingdon 298. Station, Huntingdon, L.N.E.R.
HIPPODROME (WE).—Props., Huntingdon Hippodrome, Ltd., 7, South Brink, Wisbech. Phone, Wisbech 53. 813 seats. Continuous. Booked at Hippodrome, Wisbech. Prices, 5d. to 1s. 1od. Proscenium width, 25 ft. Phone, Huntingdon 32. Station, Huntingdon L.N.E.R.
MANDSVILLE HALL, Kimbolton.

HURSTMONCEUX (SUSSEX).
CASTLE PLAYHOUSE (Morrison).—Prop., E. D. Curtis, Old Brew House, Hurstmonceux. 290 seats. Booked at Hall. Continuous. Prices, 6d. to 1s. 6d. Proscenium width, 18 ft. Phone, 56. Station, Hailsham, S.R.

HUTHWAITE (NOTTS). **Pop. 5,092.**
LYRIC (FI).—650 seats. Continuous. Mat. Sat. Prices, 5d. to 11d.

HYDE (CHESHIRE), **Pop. 32,066.**
ALEXANDRA PAVILION (BA), Corporation Street. —Prop., Pictures and Varieties, Ltd., 22. Cathedral House, Manchester. 500 seats, Booked at H.O. Two shows nightly. Prices, 3d. to 1s. Phone, Hyde 193. Station, Hyde, L.N.E.R.
HIPPODROME AND OPERA HOUSE (WE).—Prop., W. Stansfield and Co. 1,513 seats. Booked by H. D. Moorhouse Circuit. Pictures and Variety. Two changes weekly. Prices, 4d. to 1s. Stage, 26 ft. deep ; 11 dressing rooms. Phone, Hyde 215. Stations, Hyde, L.N.E.R. or Denton, L.M.S.
QUEEN'S CINEMA (PTA), Manchester Road.— Prop., Northern Amusements, Ltd., Prudential Chambers, South Parade, Rochdale, Lancs. Phone, Rochdale 2072. Continuous nightly Mon. to Fri. Three shows Sat. 524 seats. Booked at Arcadia Cinema, Yew Tree Avenue, Levenshulme. Prices, 4d. to 9d. Proscenium width, 25 ft. Phone, Hyde 458. Station, Hyde, L.M.S.
RITZ (WE).—Controlled by Union Cinemas, Ltd., Union House, 15, Regent Street, London, S.W.1. Phone, Whitehall 8484. Booked at H.O. Continuous. Prices, 4d. to 2s. Station, L.N.E.R.
SCALA PICTURE HOUSE (Picturetone), Clarendon Street.—Prop., S. O'Brien and J. H. Davies. 500 seats. Booked at Hall. Two shows nightly. Two Mats. Prices 3d. to 1s. Phone, Hyde 139. Station, Hyde, L.N.E.R.
THEATRE ROYAL (WE).—Prop., G. W. Bell. 1,500 seats. Twice nightly. Mats. Mon., Tues., Thurs., Sat. Prices, 4d. to 1s. Occasional Variety. Stage, 35 ft. deep ; ten dressing rooms. Phone, Hyde 206. Station, Hyde, L.N.E.R.

HYTHE (KENT), **Pop. 8,397.**
GROVE CINEMA (WE), Prospect Road.—Prop., Hythe Picture Palace (1913), Ltd., 132, High Street, Hythe. 694 seats. Booked by J. H. Kent, Man. Dir., The Morehall, Folkestone. Continuous. Prices, 6d. to 1s. 6d. Phone, Hythe 67302. Station, Hythe, S.R.
RITZ (WE).—Controlled by Union Cinemas, Ltd., 15, Regent Street, S.W.1. Phone, Whitehall 8484. Booked at H.O. Continuous. Station, S.R.

IBSTOCK (LEICESTER), **Pop. 6,000.**
PALACE (AWH), High Street.—Prop., R. E. and M. Ball, High Street, Earl Shilton. Phone, Earl Shilton 102. 700 seats. Booked at Earl Shilton. One show nightly. Twice Sat. Prices, 6d. to 1s. Phone, Ibstock 12. Stations. Heather and Ibstock, L.M.S. Films by Road Transport.

ILFORD (ESSEX), **Pop. 131,046.**
COLISEUM.—Booked by Black's Theatres, 115, Shaftesbury Avenue, London, W.C.2.
EMPIRE CINEMA (WE), Ilford Lane.—Prop., Ben. Jay, 145, Wardour Street, W. 964 seats. Booked at H.O. Continuous. Prices, 6d. to 1s. 6d. Proscenium width, 42 ft. Stage, 38 ft. deep ; two dressing-rooms. Phone, Ilford 0280. Station, Ilford, L.N.E.R.
HIPPODROME (WE).—Prop., Metropolitan and Provincial Cinematograph Theatres, Ltd., Brettenham House, 14-15, Lancaster Place, Strand, W.C.2. Phone, Temple Bar 1144. 1,874 seats.
SAVOY CINEMA.—Prop., Kessex Cinemas, Ltd., 197, Wardour Street, London, W.1. Phone, Gerrard 2835. 2,190 seats. Booked at H.O. Continuous. Prices, 9d. to 2s. 6d. Variety. Proscenium width 38 ft. Stage 27 ft. deep ; five dressing rooms. Café. Phone, Val. 2500. Station, Ilford.

Fitted "ARDENTE" Stage Amplification See page 258
SUPER CINEMA (WE).—Prop., Provincial Cinematograph Theatres, Ltd., New Gallery House, 123, Regent Street, London, W.1. Phone, Regent 8080. 2336 seats. Booked at H.O. Continuous. Pictures and Variety. Prices, 6d. to 2s. Café attached. Station, Ilford, L.N.E.R.

COMPTON
ORGAN featured here.

ILFRACOMBE (DEVON), **Pop. 9,174.**
NEW CINEMA (Morrison).—Prop., W. L. and K. A. Barrett, 131, High Street, Ilfracombe. 309 seats. Continuous. Booked at H.O. Prices, 6d. to 1s. 6d. Proscenium width, 20 ft. Phone, Ilfracombe 53, Station, Ilfracombe.
SCALA THEATRE (BA).—Prop., Albany Ward Theatres, Ltd. Booked at H.O., New Gallery House, Regent Street, W.1. 1,000 seats. Continuous. Prices, 6d. to 2s. 4d. Phone, Ilfracombe 52. Station, Ilfracombe, S.R.

ILKESTON (DERBY), **Pop. 32,809.**
KING'S PICTURE HOUSE (WE), Bath Street.— Prop., Ilkeston Cinema Co., Ltd. Man. Dir., H. Wm. Brailsford. 1,340 seats. Booked at Hall. Twice nightly. Two changes weekly. Prices 6d. and 1s. Proscenium width, 30 ft. Phone, Ilkeston 17, Station, Ilkeston, L.M.S.

ILKESTON—Contd.

NEW SUPER THEATRE (WE), Lord Haddon Road. —Props., Ilkeston Cinema Co., Ltd., Bath Street. 750 seats. Twice nightly. Booked at King's Picture House, Bath Street. Prices, 6d. to 1s. Pictures and Variety. Stage; six dressing-rooms. Phone, Ilkeston 17.

SCALA PICTURE HOUSE (WE), Market Place.— Prop., Mr. Wilcock, 8, Carlton Road, Nottingham. Phone, Nottingham 41750. 835 seats. Booked at H.O. Continuous, Mon. to Fri. Two shows Sat. evening. Prices, 6d. and 1s. Phone, Ilkeston 241. Station, Ilkeston, L.N.E.R., and Transport.

ILKLEY (YORKS), Pop. 9,721.

GROVE PICTURE HOUSE (WE).—Prop., Picture House (Ilkley), Ltd. 728 seats. Booked at Hall. Once nightly. Two changes weekly. Prices, 6d. to 1s. 3d. Phone, Ilkley 111. Station, Ilkley, L.M.S. and L.N.E.R.

KING'S HALL, Station Road.—Ilkley Urban District Council. Phone, Ilkley 155. Station, Ilkley, L.N.E.R. and L.M.S.

NEW CINEMA (BTH), Railway Road.—Prop., The New Cinema (Ilkley), Ltd., 16, Brook Street, Ilkley. Phone, Ilkley 520. 1,070 seats. Booked at Hall, Once nightly, twice on Sat. Mats., Mon., Wed. and Sat. Prices, 6d. to 1s. 6d. Proscenium width, 36 ft. Stage. 9 ft. deep; one dressing room. Dance Hall, attached. Phone, Ilkley 275. Station, Ilkley, L.M.S. and L.N.E.R.

ILMINSTER (SOMERSET), Pop. 2,230.

PLAZA (BTH).—Prop., Rowland Reeves. 200 seats. Once nightly. Booked at Hall. Prices, 3d. to 1s. 3d. Station, Ilminster, G.W.R.

INGLETON (YORKS), Pop. 2,000.

CINEMA (Eastern), Main Street.—Prop. and Man., J. T. Marsden. 349 seats. Booked at Hall. Prices, 6d. to 1s. Phone, Ingleton 28. Proscenium width, 17 ft. Station, Ingleton, L.M.S., or Earby Film Transport.

IPSWICH (SUFFOLK), Pop. 87,557.

CENTRAL CINEMA (WE), Princes Street.—Prop., Farrer Cinemas, Ltd. 700 seats. Continuous. Prices, 6d. to 1s. 4d. Proscenium width, 30 ft. Phone, Ipswich 2732. Station, Ipswich, L.N.E.R.

EMPIRE CINEMA (Edibell), Fore Street.—Prop., British Cinematograph Theatres, Ltd., 199, Piccadilly, London, W.1. Phone, Regent 1227. 600 seats. Booked at Picture House. Continuous. Prices, 5d. to 1s. 3d. Phone, Ipswich 2654. Station, Ipswich, L.N.E.R. Films by Transport.

HIPPODROME (WE).—Lessees, Associated British Cinemas, Ltd., 30-31, Golden Square, W.1. Phone, Gerrard 7887. 1,110 seats. Booked at H.O. Continuous. Prices, 6d. to 1s. 6d. Proscenium width 30 ft. Phone, Ipswich 2447. Station, Ipswich, L.N.E.R.

ODEON THEATRE (BTH).—Props., Odeon (Ipswich), Ltd. Bennetts Hill, Birmingham. Phone, Midland 2781. Booked at 49, Park Lane, W.1. Prices, 9d. to 2s. Phone, Ipswich 2082.

PICTURE HOUSE (WE), 5, Tavern Street.—Prop., British Cinematograph Theatres, Ltd. Head Office, 199, Piccadilly, London, W. Phone, Regent 1227. 1,012 seats. Booked at H.O. by Man. Continuous. Prices, 9d. to 2s. Phone, Ipswich 2654. Station, Ipswich, L.N.E.R. Films by Transport.

POOLE'S PICTURE PALACE (Picturetone), Tower Street.—Props., Poole's Entertainments, Ltd., Hippodrome, Gloucester. 422 seats. Booked at H.O., Gloucester. Continuous. Prices, 4d. to 1s. Phone, Ipswich 2637. Station, Ipswich, L.N.E.R.

PUBLIC HALL.

REGENT CINEMA (RCA), St. Helen Street.— Prop., Gaumont British Pictures Corp., 123, Regent Street, London, W.1. Phone, Regent 6641. 2,000 seats. Booked at H.O. Occasional Variety. Continuous. Prices, 8d. to 2s. 4d.; boxes, 10s. Stage, 36 ft. deep; six dressing-rooms. Cafe attached. Phone, Ipswich 3641. Station, Ipswich.

Fitted "ARDENTE" Deaf Aids
See page 258

WURLITZER ORGAN
Installed in this Kinema

RITZ (WE).—Controlled by Union Cinemas, Ltd., 15, Regent Street, S.W.1. Phone, Whitehall 8484. Booked at H.O. Continuous. Station, L.N.E.R.

WURLITZER ORGAN
Installed in this Kinema

IRLAM (LANCS), Pop. 12,898.

PALACE CINEMA (BTH), Liverpool Road.— Licensee and Man., A. H. Lord. 800 seats. Pictures and Variety. Films booked at Hall and Variety by Sley's Agency, 140, Oxford Road, Manchester. Once nightly. Three shows Sat. Prices, 4d. to 1s. Stage, 18 ft. deep; three dressing-rooms. Phone, Irlam 49. Station, Irlam, C.L.C.R.

RIALTO CINEMA (WE), Liverpool Road.—Props., Irlam Cinemas, Ltd. 757 seats. Booked at Hall. Continuous nightly, Mon. to Fri. Twice nightly Sat. Mats., Wed. and Sat. Occasional Variety. Stage, 12 ft. deep; three dressing-rooms. Prices, 2d. to 10d. Phone, Irlam 109. Station, Irlam, C.L.C.R.

IRLAM O' THE HEIGHTS (LANCS).

OLYMPIA PICTURE HOUSE (BA), West Street.— Prop., James Caton, Freda Villa, Offerton lane, Offerton, near Stockport. 520 seats. Booked at Hall. Continuous. Two shows Sat. Prices, 4d. to 1s. Proscenium width, 20 ft. Phone, Pendleton 2020. Station, Manchester, L.M.S.

IRONBRIDGE AND BROSELEY (SALOP).

PLAZA (BA).

CENTRAL HALL.—Prop., John France, Trench, Wellington, Salop.

IRTHLINGBOROUGH (NORTHANTS), Pop. 4,715.

PICTURE HOUSE.—Prop., Watts' Cinemas, Ltd. "Poolstock," Finedon. Phone, Finedon 9. 300 seats. Bkg. Man., A. T. Watts. Booked at H.O. One show nightly. Continuous Sat. Three changes weekly. Prices, 4d. to 1s. 3d. Station, Irthlingborough, L.M.S. (via Northampton). Road Transport.

ISLEWORTH (MIDDLESEX).

ODEON THEATRE (BTH).—Props., Odeon (Isleworth), Ltd. Cornhill House, Bennetts Hill, Birmingham. Booked at 49 Park Lane, W.1. Phone, Midland 2781. Booked at H.O. Prices, 9d. to 2s. Phone, Hounslow 1000.

PATHE GAZETTE—The Most Popular of News Reels!

IVER (Bucks), **Pop. 3,100.**

PLAZA THEATRE (BTH).—Prop., Chiswick Productions Cinemas, Ltd., 1, Chiswick Common Road, W.4. Phone, Chiswick 6278. Booked at Hall. 560 seats. Continuous. Prices, 6d. to 1s. 10d. Proscenium width, 25 ft. Stage 22 ft. deep; two dressing rooms. Café. Phone, Iver 146. Station, Iver, G.W.R. or Film Transport.

C O M P T O N

ORGAN featured here.

JACKSDALE (Notts), **Pop. 6,000.**

PALACE (BTH), Selston Road.—Prop., J. Pollard, Bentick Chambers, Mansfield. Phone, 760- 470 seats. Booked at H.O. One show Monto Fri. Two shows, Sat. Prices, 6d. to 1s. Proscenium width, 23 ft. Phone, Lenbrooks 62. Stations, Codnor Park, L.M.S.; Jacksdale, L.N.E.R.

JARROW-ON-TYNE (Co. Durham), **Pop. 32,018.**

EMPIRE (WE), Union Street.—Lessees, Dawe Bros. Ltd., Gibb Chambers, Westgate Road, Newcastle-on-Tyne. 796 seats. Twice nightly Phone, Jarrow 67082. Station, Jarrow, L.N.E.R.

PICTURE HOUSE (WE), North Street.—Prop., John Weddle and Co., Ltd., 67, Ellison Street, Jarrow-on-Tyne. Phone, 67431. 1,088 seats. Two shows nightly. Two changes weekly. Prices, 4d. to 9d. Proscenium width, 40 ft. Phone, Jarrow 67283. Station, Jarrow, L.N.E.R.

REGAL THEATRE (WE), Grange Road.—Prop., Jarrow Kino, Ltd., 40, Westgate Road, Newcastle-on-Tyne. Phone, Newcastle 22401. 1,157 seats. Continuous from 6.30 p.m. Two houses Sat. Prices, 4d. to 9d. Phone, Jarrow 67,200. Station, Jarrow, L.N.E.R.

THEATRE ROYAL, Market Square.—991 seats.

JERSEY (Channel Islands), **Pop. 49,500.**

FORUM (WE), St. Helier.—Props., Forum, Ltd., 16, Hill Street, Jersey. Phone, Central 344. 1,615 seats. Booked at H.O. Proscenium width 38 ft. Prices, 7d. to 2s. 6d. Stage, 31 ft. deep; six dressing rooms. Café attached. Station, St. Helier, Jersey.

Fitted "ARDENTE" Deaf Aids
See page 258

C O M P T O N

ORGAN featured here.

OPERA HOUSE (BA).—Prop., Jersey and Guernsey Amusements Co., Ltd., New Gallery House, 123, Regent Street, London, W.1. Phone, Regent 6651. Booked at H.O. Occasional Pictures. Phone, Jersey 764. Stations, Weymouth, G.W.R.; Southampton, S.R.

Fitted "ARDENTE" Deaf Aids
See page 258

PICTURE HOUSE (Cinephone), Don Street.—Prop., Jersey and Guernsey Amusements Co., Ltd. New Gallery House, 123, Regent Street, London, W.1. Phone, Regent 6641. Booked at H.O. Continuous from 2.45. Prices, 9d. to 3s. Phone, Jersey 764. Station, Weymouth.

ROYAL HALL (BTH), Peter Street, St. Helier.— Prop., West's Pictures (Jersey), Ltd. 1,000 seats. Booked at Hall. Three shows daily. Ballroom and Café adjoining. Prices, 7d. to 2s. 6d. Phone, Central 487. Stations, Weymouth, G.W.R.; Southampton, S.R.

KEGWORTH (Leicester), **Pop. 2,225.**

COUNTY CINEMA (Marshall).—Prop., J. F. I. Minton, County Cinema Enterprises, Market Street, Castle Donington. 330 seats. Booked at H.O. Two shows Mon. and Sat. Once daily rest of week. Prices, 4d. to 1s. Station, Kegworth, L.M.S.

KEIGHLEY (Yorks), **Pop. 40,440.**

COSY CORNER PICTURE HOUSE (WE) Low Street. —Prop., M.P. Cryer, Old Bank Chambers, Keighley (Phone, Keighley 2264). 700 seats. Booked in Leeds. Continuous. Three shows Sat. Prices, 3d. to 1s. Proscenium width, 17 ft. Phone, Keighley 2526. Station, Keighley, L.M.S. and L.N.E.R.

OXFORD HALL (WE), Oakworth Road.— Prop., The Picture House, 9, Henry Street, Keighley. Phone, 2042. 560 seats. Booked at H.O. Continuous. Prices, 3d. to 6d. Proscenium width, 20 ft. Phone, Keighley 3068. Station, Keighley, L.M.S. and L.N.E.R. Films by Road Transport.

PALACE (BTH), Cavendish Street.—Prop., Keighley Palace, Ltd., Sec., M. P. Cryer. Phone, Keighley 2264. 600 seats. Booked at Leeds. Continuous. Two changes weekly. Prices, 2d. to 9d. Sats., 3d. to 1s. Phone, Keighley 2451. Station, Keighley, L.M.S. and L.N.E.R.

PICTURE HOUSE (RCA), Skipton Road.—Prop., Picture House (Keighley), Ltd., 9, Henry Street, Keighley. 1,100 seats. Booked at H.O., Keighley. Three shows daily. Two changes weekly. Prices, 6d. to 9d. Sats., 9d. to 1s. Phone, Keighley 2561. Station, Keighley.

REGENT PICTURE HOUSE (WE), North Street.— Prop., Keighley Regent Pictures, Ltd. 866 seats. Booked by M. P. Cryer, Old Bank Chambers, Keighley. Three shows daily. Prices, 6d. to 1s. 3d. Phone, Keighley 2660. Station, Keighley, L.M.S. and L.N.E.R.

RITZ (WE).—Controlled by Union Cinemas, Ltd., 15, Regent Street, S.W.1. Phone, Whitehall 8484. Booked at H.O. Prices, 6d. to 1s. 6d. Station, Worksop, L.M.S. and L.N.E.R.

KELVEDON (Essex), **Pop. 1,500.**

INSTITUTE (Chel Radio).—Lessee, P. Gilby, Homeleigh, Kelvedon. Shows three times a week. Booked at Institute. Prices, 5d. to 1s. 2d. Station, Kelvedon, L.N.E.R.

KENDAL (Westmorland), **Pop. 15,575.**

PICTURE HOUSE (BTH), Sandes Avenue.—Prop., Picture House Co. (Kendal), Ltd., 17, North John Street, Liverpool. Phone, Bank 5836. 550 seats. Booked at Hall. Twice nightly. Mat. Sat. Two changes weekly. Prices, 6d. to 1s. 6d. Phone, Kendal 411. Station, Kendal, L.M.S.

PALLADIUM (WE).—Prop., Palladium (Kendal), Ltd. 1,278 seats. Booked at Newcastle. Two shows nightly. Prices, 6d. to 1s. 6d. Proscenium width, 33 ft. Phone 152. Station, Kendal, L.M.S.

S. GEORGE's (WE).—Prop., S. George's Theatre Co., Ltd. Twice nightly. One Mat. weekly. Phone, Kendal 57. Station, Kendal, L.M.S.

KENILWORTH (WARWICK), **Pop. 7,592.**
ALEXANDRA THEATRE (WE), Station Road.—
Prop., Mrs. C. E. Strong, Alexandra Theatre,
Coventry. Phone, Coventry 4716. 396 seats.
Booked by H. Heath at Coventry. Con-
tinuous. Mats., Mon., Thurs. and Sat. Prices,
6d. to 1s. 4d. Phone, Kenilworth 200.
Station, Kenilworth, L.M.S.

KENTON (MIDDLESEX).
ODEON THEATRE (BTH).—Props., Odeon (Kenton)
Ltd., Cornhill House, Bennett's Hill, Birm-
ingham. Phone, Midland 2781. Booked at
49, Park Lane, W.1. Prices, 9d. to 2s.
Phone, Wordsworth 3192.

KESWICK (CUMB.), **Pop. 4,635.**
ALHAMBRA (BTH). St. John Street.—Prop.,
Keswick Alhambra Theatre Co., Ltd., New
Market Street, Ulverston. Phone, Ulverston
151. 600 seats. Booked at H.O. Twice
nightly and Mat. Sat., from Easter to Sept.
30th. Twice nightly, Mon., Tues., Thurs. and
Sat. Once nightly Wed. and Fri. Mat. Sat.,
winter months. Prices, 6d. to 1s. 6d. Phone,
Keswick 195. Station Keswick, L.M.S., and
by Film Transport Service.
PAVILION, Station Road.—Props., Keswick
Alhambra Theatre Co., Ltd., New Market
Street, Ulverston. Phone, 151. 1,000 seats.
Booked at H.O. Once nightly. Proscenium
width, 35 ft. Stage, 35 ft. by 23 ft. Café and
Dance Hall. Phone, Keswick 195. Station,
Keswick, L.M.S.

KETTERING (NORTHANTS), **Pop. 31,220.**
COLISEUM (BTP), Russell Street.—Prop., J.
Sherwood. 760 seats. Continuous. Two
changes weekly. Prices, 3d. to 1s. Proscen-
ium width, 26 ft. Phone, Kettering 794.
Station, Kettering, L.M.S.
ELECTRIC PAVILION (BA), High Street. Prop.,
Gaumont British Picture Corpn., Ltd. and
Provincial Cinematograph Theatres, Ltd.,
123, Regent Street, London, W.1. Phone,
Regent 6641. 800 seats. Booked at H.O.
Continuous. Daily mat. Two changes
weekly. Prices, 6d. to 1s. 3d. Phone,
Kettering 353. Station Kettering, L.M.S.
Fitted "ARDENTE" Deaf Aids
See page 258
EMPIRE CINEMA (BA). Montague Street.—Prop.,
T. H. Bamford. 475 seats. Booked at 45,
Montague Street. Continuous. Twice Sat.
Two changes weekly. Prices, 4d. to 1s. Phone.
775. Station, Kettering, L.M.S.
KETTERING WORKING MEN'S CLUB (BTP), Wel,
lington Street. Pictures and Variety. Week-
end shows only. Booked at Club by Enter-
tainment Secretary. Prices, 3d. and 4d.
Two dressing rooms. Station, Kettering,
L.M.S.
ODEON (BTH), Gold Street.—Prop., Victoria
Playhouses (Kettering), Ltd., Bennett's
Hill, Birmingham. Phone, Midland 2781.
Booked at 49, Park Lane, W.1. Continuous.
Prices, 6d. to 2s. Phone, Kettering 365.
Station, Kettering, L.M.S.

KIDDERMINSTER (WORC.), **Pop. 28,914.**
CENTRAL (WE), Oxford Street.—Prop., Associated British Cinemas, Ltd., 30-31, Golden
Square, London, W.1. Phone, Gerrard 7887.
1,271 seats. Mat. daily. Continuous from
5.45. Three shows Sat. Prices, 6d. to 1s. 3d.
Proscenium width, 40 ft. Phone, Kidderminster 612. Station, Kidderminster, G.W.R.

EMPIRE (WE).—Prop., Associated British Cine-
mas, Ltd. 30-31, Golden Square, London, W.1.
Phone, Gerrard 7887. 566 seats. Continuous.
Prices, 3d. to 1s. Proscenium width, 25 ft.
Phone, Kidderminster 612. Station, Kidder-
minster, G.W.R.
FUTURIST (WE), Vicar Street.—Prop., B. P.
Priest. 900 seats. Continuous. Mats. daily.
Booked at Grand, Old Hill. Occasional
Variety. Prices, 6d. to 1s. 3d. Proscenium
width, 39 ft. Stage, 15 ft. deep. Three
dressing rooms. Phone No. 105. Station,
Kidderminster, G.W.R.
GRAND THEATRE (WE), Mill Street.—Prop., B. P.
Priest, Forest House, Kenver. Phone No. 7.
1,010 seats. Booked at Grand Theatre, Old
Hill, by G. Smith. Continuous. Two shows
Sat. Daily Mat. Occasional variety. Prices,
6d. to 1s. 6d. Proscenium width, 25 ft.; four
dressing-rooms. Phone, Kidderminster 120.
Station, Kidderminster, G.W.R.
OPERA HOUSE CINEMA DE LUXE (BTH). Comber-
ton Hill.—Prop., John Jacques, High Street.
Broadway. Phone, Broadway 39. 900 seats,
Occasional Variety. Three
shows daily. Prices, 5d. to 1s. 3d. Proscen-
ium width, 30 ft. Stage, 30 ft. deep; five
dressing rooms. Phone, Kidderminster 255.
Station, Kidderminster, G.W.R.

KIDSGROVE (STAFFS), **Pop. 9,937.**
VALENTINE CINEMA (Edibell), Liverpool Road.—
Prop., Kidsgrove Cinema Co., Ltd. 700 seats.
Booked at Hall. Continuous. Prices, 4d.
to 1s. Station, Hare castle, L.M.S.

KILLAMARSH (DERBY), **Pop. 4,544.**
EMPIRE PICTURE HOUSE (BTH).—Lessees, Rother-
ham District Cinemas, Ltd. 600 seats.
Booked at Hall. Occasional Variety. One
show nightly, three on Sat. Prices, 6d. to 1s.
Stage, 10 ft. deep; two dressing-rooms.
Proscenium width, 28 ft. Station, Killamarsh
L.M.S. and L.N.E.R.

KIMBERLEY (NOTTS), **Pop. 5,170.**
PICTURE HOUSE, Regent Street.—Prop., W.
Wilkinson. 700 seats. One show nightly.
Two changes weekly. Prices, 5d. to 1s.
Station, Kimberley, L.N.E.R.

KINGSBRIDGE (DEVON), **Pop. 2,978.**
PALACE (Mihaly).—Prop., J. Anderton and Sons.
Once nightly. Three shows Sat. Prices, 7d.
to 1s. 3d. Station, Kingsbridge.
REGAL CINEMA (BTP), The Island.—Props.,
Moyce and Sons. 300 seats. Booked at Hall.
Twice nightly. Prices, 6d. to 1s. 6d. Pros-
cenium width, 18 ft. Phone, Kingsbridge 53.
Station, Kingsbridge, G.W.R.

KING'S LYNN (NORFOLK), **Pop. 20,580.**
ELECTRIC THEATRE (BTH), Broad Street.—
Controlled by Union Cinemas, Ltd., Union
House, 15, Regent Street, London, S.W.1.
Phone, Whitehall 8484. Booked at H.O.
Separate performances. Two changes weekly.
Prices, 6d. to 1s. 4d. Phone, King's Lynn
2056. Station, King's Lynn, L.N.E.R.
MAJESTIC CINEMA (WE), London Road.—Con-
trolled by Union Cinemas, Ltd., Union House,
15, Regent Street, London, S.W.1. Phone,
Whitehall 8484. Booked at H.O. Separate
performances. Prices 6d. to 2s. Proscenium
width, 28 ft. Café and Dance Hall attached.
Phone, King's Lynn 2603. Station, King's
Lynn, L.N.E.R.

The BEST Is Cheapest; PATHE GAZETTE.

St. James' Theatre (we), St. James' Place.— Controlled by Union Cinemas, Ltd., Union House, 15, Regent Street, London, S.W.1. Phone, Whitehall 8484. Booked at H.O. Separate performances. Prices, 5d. to 2s. 6d. Dance Hall attached. Phone, King's Lynn 2056. Station, King's Lynn, L.N.E.R.

Theatre Royal (bth).—Controlled by Union Cinemas, Ltd., Union House, 15, Regent Street, London, S.W.1. Phone, Whitehall 8484. Booked at H.O. Pictures and Variety. Prices, 5d. to 1s. 6d. Phone, King's Lynn 137. Station, King's Lynn, L.N.E.R.

KINGSTON-ON-THAMES (Surrey), **Pop. 39,052.**

Elite Picture Theatre (we), London Road.— Prop., Elite Picture Theatre (Kingston-on-Thames), Ltd. 1,300 seats. Continuous. Booked at 10, New Bond Street, W.1. Prices, 6d. to 2s. Café attached. Phone, Kingston 1860. Station, Kingston, S.R.

Kingston Kinema (we), Richmond Road.— Prop., Mrs. L. Gardner & Son. 580 seats. Booked at Hall. Continuous. Prices, 9d. to 2s. 5d. Proscenium width, 20 ft. Phone, Kingston 0207. Station, Kingston, S.R.

Odeon Theatre (bth).—Prop., Odeon (Kingston), Ltd., Cornhill House, Bennett's Hill, Birmingham. Phone, Midland 2781. Booked at 49, Park Lane, W.1. Continuous. Prices, 6d. to 2s. 6d. Proscenium width, 40 ft. Café and dance hall. Phone, Kingston 0688. Station, Kingston-on-Thames.

COMPTON

ORGAN featured here.

Regal (we), Richmond Road.—Controlled by Union Cinemas, Ltd., 15, Regent Street, London, S.W.1. Booked at H.O. Variety and Films. Continuous. Prices, 6d. to 2s. Café. Phone, Kingston 6325.

WURLITZER ORGAN
Installed in this Kinema

Super Cinema (rca), Fife Road.—Prop., Thames Theatres, Ltd. 900 seats. Continuous. Prices, 5d. to 2s. Phone, Kingston 2330. Station, Kingston, S.R.

KINGSWINFORD, near DUDLEY (Staffs), **Pop. 4,500.**

Grand Cinema (rca), Market Street.—Prop., Selected Cinemas Amalgamation, Ltd. 650 seats. Booked at "Oldstead," Moss Grove, Kingswinford. Continuous. Mat. Sat. Two changes weekly. Prices, 2d. to 1s. Proscenium width, 26 ft. Phone, 104. Station, Brettle Lane, G.W.R.

KINGTON (Hereford), **Pop. 1,742.**

Picture House (bth).—Prop., Arthur L. Dickinson. 200 seats. Booked at Hall. One show nightly. Two changes weekly. Prices, 9d. to 1s. 6d. Proscenium width, 13 ft. Phone, Kington 77. Station, Kington, G.W.R.

KIPPAX (Yorks), **Pop. 4,075.**

Alhambra Picture Palace (Electrocord), High Street.—Prop., G. Restall, 433, Leeds Road, Dewsbury. Phone 188. Booked at H.O. Once nightly. Tues., Wed. and Thurs. Continuous Mon., Fri., and Sat. Prices, 4d. to 9d. Phone, Garford 112. Station, Kippax, L.N.E.R.

KIRBYMOORSIDE (Yorks), **Pop. 1,692.**

Cinema.—450 seats.

KIRKBY-IN-ASHFIELD (Notts), **Pop. 17,798.**

King's Palace (Picturetone).—Prop., Exors. Edwin Widdowson, Bank Yard, Bulwell Nottingham. Phone, Bulwell 78438. 500 seats, Booked at H.O. Continuous. Stage, 15 ft. deep ; two dressing-rooms. Prices, 6d. to 1s. Phone, East Kirkby 33. Station, Kirkby-in-Ashfield, L.M.S. and L.N.E.R.

KIRKBY STEPHEN (Cumb.), **Pop. 1,545.**

Cinema (Morrison).—Prop., J. & H. Morland, Riverside, Kirkby Stephen. 400 seats. Booked at Manor House, Manor Drive, Doncaster. Twice nightly. Prices, 6d. to 1s. 6d. Proscenium width, 24 ft. Phone, Kirkby Stephen 55. Station, Kirkby Stephen, L.N.E.R.

KIRKHAM (Lancs), **Pop. 4,301.**

Co-operative Picture Hall.—Prop., Fylde Co-operative Society, Ltd., Poulton Street. Phone, Kirkham 22. 384 seats. Once nightly, twice Sat. Mats., Mon. and Sat. Prices, 6d. to 1s. Phone, Kirkham 56. Station, Kirkham, L.M.S.

Empire (btp), Birley Street.—Prop., Gordon C. Bishop. Booked at Hall. Nightly, Mon. to Fri. at 7.30. Two shows Sat. Once on Sunday, Mat., Mon. and Sat. Prices, 6d. to 1s. Phone No. 138. Films by Smith's Auto Transport.

KIVETON PARK (Yorks), **Pop. 2,500.**

Regal cinema (bth).—Prop., Ducal Enterprises, Ltd. 430 seats. Booked at Hall. Once nightly. Twice Sat. Price, 6d. to 1s. Stage and two dressing-rooms. Phone, Kiveton 284. Station, Kiveton Bridge, L.N.E.R.

KNARESBOROUGH (Yorks), **Pop. 5,942.**

Cinema (Electrocord), Park Parade.—Prop., Cinema (Knaresborough), Ltd. 400 seats. Booked at Hall. Continuous. Prices, 4d. to 1s. Phone, Knaresborough 192. Station, Knaresborough, L.N.E.R.

Cinema (Electrocord).—Prop., Robert Taylorson. Stockwell Grove, Knaresborough. 303 seats. Booked at Leeds. Continuous. Prices, 3d. to 1s. Station, Knaresborough, L.N.E.R.

KNOTTINGLEY (Yorks), **Pop. 6,842.**

Palace Cinema (bth).—Props., A. & H. D. Wood, Ltd., Albion Works, Savile Street, Milnsbridge, nr. Huddersfield. 500 seats. One show nightly. Twice Mon. and Sat. Booked at H.O. Prices, 3d. to 1s. Proscenium width, 20 ft. Phone, No. 56. Station Knottingley, L.M.S.

KNOWLE (Warwick), **Pop. 2,357.**

Knowle Picture Playhouse.—Prop. and Res. Man., John Chamberlain. 318 seats. Booked at Hall. Continuous. Prices, 5d. to 1s. 3d. Stations, Knowle and Dorridge, G.W.R.

KNUTSFORD (Cheshire), **Pop. 5,878.**

Marcliffe (RCA).

Ollerton Picture House.—Prop., Ollerton Pictures, Ltd., Empire, Somercotes, Derbyshire.

Picture House (we).—Booked by L. Rimmer, at Picture House, Horwich, near Bolton. 480 seats. Continuous. Phone, Knutsford 328. Station, Knutsford, Cheshire Lines.

LAINDON (Essex), **Pop. 2,000.**

LAINDON PICTURE PALACE (BA), High Road.—
Prop., Louis Silverman. 700 seats. Booked
at Hall. Continuous. Prices, 6d. to 1s. 6d.
Stage, 12 ft. deep; two dressing-rooms.
Proscenium width, 30 ft. Phone, Laindon 90.
Station, Laindon, L.N.E.R.

LANCASTER (Lancs), **Pop. 43,396.**

COUNTY CINEMA (WE), Dalton Square.—Controlled by Union Cinemas, Ltd., 15, Regent
Street, S.W.1. Phone, Whitehall 8484.
Booked at H.O. Continuous. Phone, Lancaster 810. Station, Lancaster Castle, L.M.S.

GRAND (WE). Controlled by Union Cinemas,
Ltd.—Prop., Hippodrome (Lancaster), Ltd.
Booked at H.O. Two shows daily. Mats.
Wed. and Sat. Prices, 6d. to 1s. Phone,
Lancaster 810. Station, Lancaster Castle,
L.M.S.

NEW KINGSWAY CINEMA (WE), Parliament
Street. Controlled by Union Cinemas—Prop.,
Hippodrome (Lancaster), Ltd. Continuous.
Booked at H.O. Prices, 4d. to 9d. Phone,
Lancaster 810. Station, Lancaster Castle,
L.M.S.

ODEON THEATRE (BTH), King Street.—Props.,
Odeon (Lancaster), Ltd., Cornhill House,
Bennett's Hill, Birmingham. Phone, Mid-
land 2781. Booked at 49, Park Lane, W.1.
Prices, 6d. to 1s. 6d. Phone, Lancaster 1111.

PALACE THEATRE (WE), Dalton Square.—
Controlled by Union Cinemas (Ltd.) Prop.,
Hippodrome (Lancaster) Ltd. Prices, 6d.
to 1s. 3d. Booked at H.O. Phone, Lancaster
810. Station, Lancaster Castle, L.M.S.

PALLADIUM PICTURE HOUSE AND CAFE RENDEZ-
VOUS (WE), Market Street.—Prop., Lancaster
Palladium, Ltd. 575 seats. Booked at Liver-
pool. Thrice daily. Prices, 5d. to 1s. 6d.
Proscenium width, 40 ft. Café and dance hall
attached. Phone, Lancaster 563. Station,
Lancaster Castle, L.M.S.

PICTUREDROME (BTP), Church Street.—Prop.,
and Res. Man., J. Atroy. 700 seats. Continuous. Mat., Mon., Wed. and Sat. Two
changes weekly. Prices, 3d. to 1s. 3d. Proscenium width, 24 ft. Phone, Lancaster 546.
Station, Lancaster Castle, L.M.S.

LANCHESTER (Co. DURHAM), **Pop. 5,097.**

MEMORIAL HALL (Morrison). 225 seats.

LANCING (Sussex), **Pop. 3,162.**

REGAL THEATRE (BTH), Penhill Road.—Prop.,
Odeon (Lancing), Ltd., Cornhill House,
Bennett's Hill, Birmingham. Phone, Midland
2781. Booked at 49, Park Lane, W.1. Continuous nightly. Mat. daily. Prices, 9d. to
1s. 6d. Phone, Lancing 66.

LANGLEY GREEN (Worcester).

THE REGENT (BA), Crosswell Road, Langley,
near Birmingham.—Prop., J. M. Dent, St.
Romans, Somerville Road, Sutton Coldfield.
800 seats. Booked at Hall. Continuous.
Two changes weekly. Prices, 3d. to 1s. Proscenium width, 27 ft. Café. Phone, Broadwell 1120. Station, Langley Green, G.W.R.

LANGLEY MILL (Derby), **Pop. 4,166.**

PICTURE HOUSE (BTH).—Prop., Langley Mill
Picture House Co. 400 seats. Booked at
Hall by Man. Once nightly. Two Sat.
Prices, 4d. to 9d. Station, Langley Mill,
L.M,S.

LANGLEY MOOR (Co. DURHAM), **Pop. 5,000.**

EMPIRE (BTP), High Street.—Prop., P. Wood.
900 seats. Once nightly, twice on Sat. Booked
at Newcastle. Prices, 3d. to 9d. Proscenium
width, 30 ft. Stage, 30 ft. deep; six dressing-
rooms. Station, Brandon Colliery, L.N.E.R.

HIPPODROME, (Morrison), Front Street.—Prop.,
Miss C. Cobden, "Dena House," Church Street,
Walker, Newcastle. 442 seats. Booked at
Newcastle. Once nightly, two shows Sat.
Occasional variety. Stage 15 ft.; six dressing-
rooms. Prices, 3d. to 9d. Proscenium width,
10 ft. Phone, Brandon 55. Station, Brandon
Colliery, L.N.E.R.

LANGOLDS, near Worksop (Notts.) **Pop. 4,000.**

PALACE CINEMA (WE).—Prop., Picture House,
Ltd. 785 seats. Booked at Hall. Once
nightly. Continuous. Mon., Sat. Prices,
5d. to 1s. Proscenium width, 30 ft. Phone,
North Carlton 235. Station, Worksop, L.N.E.R.

LANGWITH (Derby), **Pop. 6,000.**

REGAL (Imperial), Co-operative Hall, Main
Street.—Prop., Langwith Cinematograph Co.
Ltd. 499 seats. Booked at The Pharmacy,
Main Street, Langwith. Nightly, including
Sunday. Twice Sat. Mat., Tues. and Sat.
Prices, 6d. to 1s. Phone, Shirebrook 284.
Station, Langwith, L.M.S.

LAUNCESTON (Cornwall), **Pop. 4,071.**

PICTURE THEATRE (BTH).—Prop., Launceston
Picture Theatres, Ltd. 400 seats. Booked
at Hall. Ten shows weekly. Continuous.
Sat. Prices, 8d. to 1s. 6d. Phone, Launceston
33. Station, Launceston, G.W.R. and S.R.

LEAMINGTON SPA (Warwick), **Pop. 28,946.**

BATH CINEMA, CAFE AND RESTAURANT (WE).
Spencer Street.—Props., Bath Cinema Co.,
Ltd. 930 seats. Res. and Booking Man.,
J. H. Potter. Booked at Hall. Continuous.
Mat. daily except Mon. Prices, 6d. to 1s. 6d.
Ballroom and garage attached. Phone,
Leamington Spa 278. Station, Leamington,
G.W.R. and L.M.S.

REGAL (WE), Portland Place.—Props., Bath
Cinema Co. (Leamington) Ltd. 1,305 seats.
Continuous. Prices, 6d. to 1s. 6d. Proscenium
width, 43 ft. Phone, 1336. Stations, Leamington, G.W.R.

REGENT PICTURE HOUSE (WE), Regent Grove.—
Props., Paramount Picture Theatres, Ltd.
1,200 seats. Continuous. Pictures and Variety.
Prices, 6d. to 1s. 9d. Phone, 1628. G.W.R.
Fitted **"ARDENTE"** Deaf Aids
See page 258

COMPTON

ORGAN featured here.

SCALA (AWH), Bedford Street.—Prop., Bath
Cinema Co. (Leamington), Ltd., Spencer
Street, Leamington. 527 seats. Booked at
Bath Cinema. Continuous. Prices, 6d.
to 1s. Phone, Leamington 697.

LEATHERHEAD (Surrey), **Pop. 6,916.**

GRAND THEATRE.

PICTURE HOUSE (SIS), High Street.—Props.,
London & District Cinemas, Ltd., 62, Shaftesbury Avenue, London, W.1. 308 seats

Booked at H.O. Continuous. Mat., Wed. and Sat. Prices, 6d. to 1s. 4d. Phone, Leatherhead 425. Station, Leatherhead, S.R.

LEDBURY (HEREFORDSHIRE), **Pop. 3,283.**
CINEMA HOUSE (BTH), The Homend.—Prop. and Res. Man., L. W. Crossley. 400 seats. Twice nightly. Two changes weekly. Prices, 6d. and 1s. 6d. Phone, Ledbury 32. Station, Ledbury, G.W.R.

LEEDS (YORKS.), **Pop. 482,789.**
ABBEY PICTURE HOUSE (RCA), Abbey Road, Kirkstall.—Lessee, A Sutcliffe. 420 seats. Booked at Hall. Continuous. Two changes weekly. Prices, 4d. to 1s. Phone, Leeds 51669. Station. Kirkstall, L.M.S.

ACADEMY CINEMA (RCA), Boar Lane.—460 seats. Continuous. Prices, 6d. to 2s. Phone, Leeds 24920. Station, Leeds (Wellington), L.M.S. and L.N.E.R.

ASSEMBLY ROOMS (BA), New Briggate, Briggate.—Prop., Provincial Cinematograph Theatres, Ltd., 123, Regent Street, London, W.1. Phone, Regent 6641. 900 seats. Booked at H.O. Continuous. Phone, Leeds 26882. Station, Leeds.

BEESTON PICTURE HOUSE (WE), Town Street.—Prop., Beeston Picture House (Leeds), Ltd. 1,960 seats. Booked in Leeds. Continuous. Twice Sat. Prices, 4d. to 9d. Phone, Beeston 75120. Station, Leeds, L.M.S.

BELGRAVE CENTRAL HALL, Cross Belgrave Street.—Prop., Rev. J. G. Sutherland. 1,600 seats. Occasional kinema Shows. Prices, 6d. to 1s. Station, Leeds, L.M.S.

CAPITOL (BTP), Meanwood.—Props., Associated Tower Cinemas, Ltd, The Tower, Briggate, Leeds. 1,200 seats. Booked at H.O. Continuous. Café. Ballroom attached. Prices, 6d. to 1s. Proscenium width, 40 ft. Phone, Leeds 51801. Station, Leeds, L.M.S.

CARLTON CINEMA (WE), Carlton Hill.— Associated Tower Cinema, Ltd., The Tower, Briggate, Leeds. 927 seats. Booked at H.O. by C. H. Whincup. Continuous. Prices, 4d. to 8d. Phone, Leeds 27279. All Leeds Stations.

COLISEUM *(BA), Cookridge Street.—Prop. Gaumont British Picture Corp., Ltd., 123 Regent Street, London, W.1. 2,000 seats Booked at H.O. Continuous. Mat. daily Phone, Leeds 26898. Station, Leeds, L.M.S

COSY CINEMA (BTH), Accommodation Road.— Props., L. Cartwright and W. Lightowler. Booked at Hall. Twice nightly. Prices. 2d. to 6d. Phone, No. 23194. Station, Leeds.

CRESCENT PICTURE HOUSE, (BTP), Dewsbury Road.—Prop., Crescent Picture House, Ltd. Man. Dir., J. Claughton. 1,400 seats. Booked at Hall. Continuous. Twice nightly Sat. Two changes weekly. Prices, 4d. to 1s. Phone, 75747. Station. Leeds, L.M.S.

CROWN CINEMA (WE), Tong Road, Wortley.— Prop., Leeds and District Picture Houses, Ltd. Phone, Headingley 52419. 958 seats. Booked by L. Denham, The Lounge, Headingley. Continuous. Mon. to Fri. Twice nightly Sat. Mat. daily. Prices, 4d. to 9d. Proscenium width, 17 ft. Phone, Leeds 38253. Station, Leeds. L.M.S., c.o. Parcels Office.

DOMINION (WE), Chapel Allerton.—1,539 seats. Continuous. Mat. Wed. and Sat, Phone, Leeds 41679.

ELECTRA PICTURE LOUNGE (Eastern Electric) Jubilee Terrace.—Prop., J. F. Tidswell Woodville, Newton Park, Leeds. Phone 41417. 550 seats. Booked at Hall. Continuous. Two changes weekly. Prices, 4d, to 9d. Phone, Leeds 25398. Station, Leeds. L.N.E.R.

EMBASSY CINEMA (WE), Kirkstall Road.—Prop., Atlas Pictures, 103, Vicar Lane, Leeds. 750 seats. Booked at Hall. Twice nightly. Two changes weekly. Prices, 4d. to 1s. Proscenium width, 25 ft. Phone, Leeds 38136. Station, Leeds, L.M.S.

FORUM (WE), Chapeltown Road.—Props., Central Picture Theatre (Lincoln), Ltd., 55, Cowper Street, Leeds, 7. Phone, 41249. 1,500 seats. Continuous. Prices, 6d. to 1s. 6d. Proscenium width, 36 ft. Stage, 20 ft. 4 dressing-rooms. Café. Phone, 42755. Station, L.N.E.R. and L.M.S.

GAIETY KINEMA (WE), 91, Roundhay Road.— Prop., Associated British Cinemas, Ltd., 30-31, Golden Square, London, W.1. 950 seats. Booked at Hall. Three shows daily. Prices, 6d. to 1s. Proscenium width, 30 ft. Phone, Chapeltown 41954. Station, Leeds, L.N.E.R.

GAINSBOROUGH CINEMA (Electrocord), Domestic Street.—Props., T. Palmer & Co. 850 seats. Booked at Hall. Twice nightly. Daily Mat. Prices, 3d. to 9d. Phone, Leeds 22495. Station, Leeds, L.N.E.R.

HADDON HALL PICTURE HOUSE (Eastern Electric), Burley Hill.—Prop., Haddon Hall. Ltd. 600 seats. Booked at Hall. Continuous. Twice Sat. Prices, 4d. to 1s. Proscenium width, 13 ft. Phone, Leeds 51160. Station Leeds, L.N.E.R.

HAREHILLS PICTURE HOUSE (WE), Harehills Corner. — Prop., Harehills Amusements Co., Ltd. 780 seats. Continuous. Daily Mat. Two changes weekly. Prices, 7d. to 1s. Phone, Leeds 42227. Station, Leeds, L.M.S.

HEADINGLEY PICTURE HOUSE (WE), Cottage Road, Headingley. — Prop., Headingley Picture House, Ltd., Cottage Road, Leeds. 600 seats. Booked at Hall by Man. Continuous. Three shows Sat. Prices, 6d. to 1s. Proscenium width, 24 ft. Phone, Headingley 51606. Stations, Leeds, L.M.S.

HILLCREST PICTURE LOUNGE (WE, Harehills Lane.—Prop., Hillcrest Picture Lounge Ltd. 1,153 seats. Booked at Hall. Continuous Mon. to Fri. Twice Sats. and holidays. Prices, 6d. to 1s. Phone, National 27691. Station, Leeds, L.N.E.R.

HYDE PARK PICTURE HOUSE (WE), Brudenell Road.—Prop., Hyde Park Picture House (Leeds), Ltd. 542 seats. Booked at Tower Picture House, Leeds, by C. H. Whincup. Continuous. Twice nightly Sat. Prices, 6d. to 1s. Proscenium width 14 ft. Phone 52045. Station, Leeds, L.M.S.

IMPERIAL (WE), Horsforth.—1,000 seats.

IMPERIAL PICTURE HOUSE (BTH), Kirkstall Road.—Prop., Kirkstall Entertainments (Leeds), Ltd. 604 seats. Booked at Hall. Continuous nightly. Prices, 4d. to 11d. Phone, Leeds 26235. Station, Leeds, L.N.E.R. and L.M.S.

LOUNGE (WE), Headingley.—Prop., Leeds and District Picture Houses, Ltd. 800 seats. Booked by Leonard Denham, Man. Dir. Continuous. Sat. twice nightly. Two

PATHETONE WEEKLY, The Super Screen Magazine!

LEEDS—Contd.
changes weekly. Prices, 9d. to 1s. 3d. Café attached. Phone, Headingley 52419. Station, Leeds.

LYCEUM PICTURE HOUSE (BTP), Cardigan Road.—Props., J. B. Midgley & Sons. 850 seats. Booked at Hall. Continuous. Prices, 4d. to 1s. Phone, Leeds 51765. Station, Leeds, L.N.E.R.

LYRIC (BA), Tong Road.—Prop., West Leeds Amusements, Ltd. 950 seats. Booked at Hall. Continuous. Twice nightly Sat. Prices, 3d. to 1s. 3d. Phone, Armley 38154. Station, Leeds, L.M.S.

MAJESTIC (WE), City Square.—Prop., Gaumont British Picture Corporation, Ltd. 2,392 seats. Continuous. Prices, 1s. to 1s. 6d. Café and Dance Hall attached. Phone, Leeds 2725. Stations, Leeds (Central, New and Wellington), L.M.S. and L.N.E.R.
**Fitted "ARDENTE" Deaf Aids
See page 258**

MALVERN PICTURE PALACE (RCA), Beeston Road.—Prop., Paragon Picture Co. (1920), Ltd. 800 seats. Booked at Hall by Man. Continuous. Prices, 5d. to 9d. Phone, Leeds 75751. Station, Leeds, L.M.S.

MONSEIGNEUR.—Prop., J. Davis Circuit, 147, Wardour Street, London, W.1.

NEW MANOR CINEMA (Electrocord), Manor Road, Holbeck.—Props., T. Palmer & Co. 420 seats. Booked at Theatre de Luxe, Kirkgate. Two shows nightly. Prices, 3d. to 7d. Phone, Leeds 23279. Station, Leeds (Central), L.M.S.

NEWTOWN PICTURE PALACE (RCA), 2, Bristol Street.—Lessees, The Paladium (Ossett), Ltd. 750 seats. Booked by Mr. Friedman at Hall. Two shows nightly. Mats., Mon. and Sat. Prices, 4d. to 9d. Phone, Leeds 22462. Station, Leeds, L.M.S.

PALACE (BTH), Eyres Avenue, Armley.—Prop. Armley Rink Co., Ltd. Man. Dir., F. W. Gillard. 1,300 seats. Booked at Hall. Continuous, Mon. to Fri. Two shows Sat. Prices 4d. to 9d. Café and Skating Rink attached. Phone, Leeds 38256. Station, Armley, L.M.S.

PALLADIUM PICTURE PALACE (BA), Bridge Road, Holbeck. Prop., J. Bickler, "Roxholme," Roxholme Avenue, Harehills Lane. Phone, No. 41426. 700 seats. Booked at Hall. Two shows nightly. Prices, 3d. to 6d. Phone, Leeds 23713. Station, Leeds.

PARAMOUNT THEATRE (WE).—2,550 seats.

WURLITZER ORGAN
Installed in this Kinema

PARKFIELD PICTURE PALACE (WE), Jack Lane, Hunslet.—Prop., W. H. Burrell, 11, Barrowly Avenue, Whitkirk, Leeds. 850 seats. Booked at Hall. Two shows nightly. Prices 3d. to 7d. Phone, Leeds 22642. Station, Leeds, L.N.E.R.

PAVILION, Stanningley.—Prop., C. H. Whincup Circuit, The Tower, Briggate, Leeds. Phone, Leeds 23137.

PAVILION THEATRE (BA), Dewsbury Road.—Prop., Denman Picture Houses, Ltd., 123 Regent Street, London, W.1. 1,000 seats. Booked at H.O. Two shows nightly. Mats. Wed. and Sat. Phone, Leeds 22325. Station, Leeds.

PEOPLE'S PICTURE PALACE (BTH), Meadow Road.—Lessee, H. Hopkins, 6, Bank View, Chapel Allerton. 855 seats. Booked at Hall. Two shows nightly. Daily mat. Prices, 3d. to 1s.

PICTODROME (WE), Wortley Road, Armley.—Prop., Cansfield and Marsden. 838 seats. Continuous. Two changes weekly. Prices, 3d. to 6d. Phone, Leeds 22083. Station, Armley

PICTODROME (RCA), Waterloo Road, Hunslet.—Prop., J. G. Smart, Allerton Drive, East Keswick. Phone, Collingham Bridge 25. 500 seats. Two shows daily. Mats., Mon. and Sat. Prices, 3d. to 7d. Phone, Leeds 75134. Station, Leeds, L.N.E.R.

PICTURE HOUSE (RCA), Burley Road.—Prop. Burley Picture House Co., Ltd· Lessee and Bkg. Man., E. Armitage. 584 seats. Continuous. Prices, 4d. to 9d. Phone, Leeds 22203. Station, Leeds.

PICTURE HOUSE (RCA), Domestic Street, Holbeck.—Prop., Holbeck Picture House Co. 825 seats. Booked at Hall. Two shows nightly. Mats., and Thurs. Two changes weekly. Prices, 4d. to 9d. Phone, Leeds 22862. Station, Leeds, L.M.S.

PICTURE HOUSE (WE), Easy Road.—Prop., H. White and Sons. 750 seats. Booked at Hall by A. White. Twice nightly. Two changes weekly. Phone, Leeds 24097. Station, Leeds.

PICTURE HOUSE (BTH), Rodley.—550 seats.

PICTURE HOUSE (BTP), Woodhouse Street.—Lessee, Albert Groves. Phone, Leeds 21765. 650 seats. Gen. and Bkg. Man., Edward M. Rush. Booked at Lyceum, Cardigan Road, Leeds. Twice nightly. Prices, 3d. to 6d.

PLAZA (BA), Wellington Road, Wortley.—Prop., West Leeds Amusements, Ltd. 600 seats. Booked at Lyric, Tong Road, Leeds. Continuous. Daily Mat. Prices, 5d. to 1s. Phone, Leeds 38696.

PREMIER (Electrocord).—450 seats.

PRINCESS CINEMA (WE), Pontefract Lane.—Prop., Strand Cinemas (Leeds) Ltd., Strand Cinema, Jack Lane, Hunslet, Leeds. 893 seats. Phone, Leeds 42012. Booked at Hall. Twice nightly. Prices, 4d. to 9d. Phone, Leeds 21251. Station, Leeds.

QUEEN'S PICTURE HOUSE (WE), Meadow Road, Holbeck.—Prop., Holbeck Theatre, Ltd., 26, Park Row, Leeds. Phone, Leeds 29318. 1,409 seats. Booked at H.O. Con-

tinuous, Mon. to Fri. Twice nightly Sats. Mat. daily. Prices, 3d. to 1s. Phone, Leeds 25942. Station, Leeds, Central.

REGAL CINEMA (WE), Low Road, Hunslet.—Prop. Goldstone (Cinemas), Ltd., 9, Wetherby Road, Leeds. Phone, Oakwood 66788. 675 seats. Booked at H.O. Twice nightly. Prices, 4d. to 9d. Phone, Hunslet 75095. Station, Leeds, L.M.S.

REGENT PICTURE HOUSE (WE), Burmantofts.—Prop., Leeds and District Picture Houses, Ltd., The Lounge, Headingley. 1,012 seats. Booked at H.O. by L. Denham. Continuous. Two changes weekly. Prices, 4d. to 9d. Phone, Leeds 23350. Station, Leeds, L.M.S.

RIALTO (WE), Briggate.—Prop., Cinemas (Leeds and Bolton), Ltd. Man. Dir., John Lambert. 1,256 seats. Booked at Hall. Continuous. One change weekly. Prices, 1s. to 2s. Phone, Leeds 21357.

RITZ CINEMA (WE), Vicar Lane.—Prop., Associated British Cinemas, Ltd., 30/31, Golden Square, London, W.1. Phone, Gerrard 7887. 1,951 seats. Booked at H.O. Continuous. Prices, 6d. to 2s. 6d. Proscenium width. 36 ft. Stage, 15 ft. deep ; 6 dressing-rooms. Phone, Leeds 22665. Station, Leeds, L.M.S,

COMPTON

ORGAN featured here.

ROYAL CINEMA (WE), Meanwood Road.—Prop. Atlas Pictures, Embassy Cinema, Leeds. 908 seats. Twice nightly. Prices, 4d. to 9d. Proscenium width, 35 ft. Phone, Leeds 41197.

SCALA THEATRE (WE), Albion Place.—Prop., Gaumont British Pictures Corpn., 123, Regent Street, London, W.1. 1,794 seats. Booked at H.O. Continuous. Prices, 1s. to 2s. Stage, 6 ft. deep ; two dressing-rooms. Ballroom attached. Phone, Leeds 27057. Stations, New, L.M.S., and Central, L.N.E.R.

COMPTON

ORGAN featured here.

SHAFTESBURY (BTP), York Road.—Prop.' Shaftesbury Cinema of Leeds, Ltd. 1,250 seats. Pictures and Variety. Booked at Leeds or by appointment in Bradford by J. E. Anderton. Continuous. Prices, 7d. to 1s. Stage, 30 ft. by 24 ft.; 10 dressing rooms. Dance Hall attached. Phone, Leeds 21341. Station, Leeds, L.M.S.

STRAND (WE), Jack Lane, Hunslet.—Prop., Strand Cinemas (Leeds), Ltd. 1,110 seats. Booked at Hall. Twice nightly. Prices, 4d. to 9d. Phone, 75745. Station, Leeds.

TATLER (RCA), Boar Lane.—Props., Allied (Time) Theatres, Ltd., 3, Stanley Street, Liverpool. 300 seats. Booked at Manchester. Prices, 6d. to 1s. Proscenium width, 18 ft.

TIVOLI (WE), Middleton. Prop., Goldstones (Cinemas), Ltd., 9, Wetherby Road, Leeds. Phone, Oakwood 66788. 1,152 seats. Booked at H.O. Twice nightly. Prices, 4d. to 9d. Phone, Hunslet 75130. Station, Leeds, L.M.S. and L.N.E.R.

TOWER PICTURE HOUSE (WE), New Briggate.—Prop., Associated Tower Cinemas, Ltd. 1,125 seats. Booked at Hall by C. H. Whincup. Continuous. Prices, 6d. to 1s. 3d. Phone, Leeds 23137. All Leeds Stations.

VICTORIA PICTURE HALL (WE), York Road.—Prop., Goldstones (Cinemas), Ltd., 9, Wetherby Road, Leeds. Phone, Leeds 62988. 705 seats. Booked at Hall. Two shows nightly. Prices, 5d. to 9d. Phone, Leeds 23620. Station, Leeds L.M.S. and L.N.E.R.

VICTORY CINEMA (Eastern Elec.), Camp Road. —Prop., J. F. Tidswell. 900 seats. Booked at Leeds. Continuous. Prices, 4d. to 6d. Phone, Leeds 22185.

WELLINGTON PICTURE HOUSE (WE), Wellington Street.—Prop., Goldstones (Cinemas), Ltd., 9, Wetherby Road, Leeds. Phone, Roundhay 62988. 719 seats. Booked at H.O. Twice nightly. Prices, 4d. to 9d. Phone, Leeds 26323. Station, Leeds, L.M.S.

WESTERN TALKIE THEATRE (WE), Branch Road, Armley.—Prop., Leeds Entertainments, Ltd. Booked at Western Talkie Theatre, Florence Street. 500 seats. Continuous. Sat., twice nightly. Two changes weekly. Prices, 6d. to 7d. Phone, Leeds 38175. Station, Armley, L.N.E.R.

WESTERN TALKIE THEATRE (WE), Florence Street, Harehills, Leeds.—Prop., Leeds Entertainments, Ltd. 900 seats. Continuous. Films booked at Hall. Prices, 4d. to 6d. Phone, Leeds 42078. Station, Leeds, L.M.S.

WOODLESFORD PICTURE HOUSE (WE).—Prop., West Yorkshire Cinemas, Ltd., Aberford Road, Woodlesford, near Leeds. 550 seats Booked at Hall. Once nightly, two shows Sat. Prices, 4d. to 1s. Phone, Rothwell 96. Station, Woodlesford, L.M.S.

WORTLEY CINEMA.—Prop., Leeds and District Picture Houses, Ltd., The Lounge, North Lane, Headingley, Leeds, 6. Phone, Headingley 52419.

LEEK (STAFFS), Pop. 18,556.

MAJESTIC (WE).—Prop., The Majestic Picture House (Leek), Ltd. Reg. Office, Majestic Picture House, Union Street, Leek. 758 seats. Booked at Hall. Twice nightly. Prices, 6d. to 1s. 3d. Phone, 138. Station, Leek.

NEW GRAND (WE).—Prop., Buxton High Peak Entertainments, Ltd., 48, Bridge Street, Manchester. Phone, Manchester City 3572. 1,758 seats. Booked at 21, Bridge Street, Manchester. Continuous, Mon. to Fri. Twice nightly Sat. Pictures and Variety. Prices, 6d. to 1s. 3d. Proscenium width, 22 ft. Stage, 19 ft. deep ; 6 dressing-rooms. Station, Leek, L.M.S

PALACE (BTH).—Prop., Buxton High Peak Entertainments, Ltd. Booked at 21, Bridge Street, Manchester. Continuous. Prices, 4d. to 1s. Proscenium width, 25 ft. Stage, 15 ft. deep ; 1 dressing-room. Station, Leek.

PICTURE HOUSE (BTH), High Street.—Prop., Allan, Carlton Holm, Buxton Milton. 800 seats. Booked at 21, Bridge Street, Manchester. Twice nightly. Prices, 6d. to 1s. 2d. Stage, 15 ft. deep. ; 2 dressing-rooms.

RITZ (WE).—Controlled by Union Cinemas, Ltd., 15, Regent Street. S.W.1. Phone, Whitehall 8484. Booked at H.O. Prices, 6d. to 2s. Station, Leek, L.M.S.

LEE ON SOLENT (HANTS).

LEE TOWER CINEMA (WE).—Booked at H.O. Continuous. 845 seats. Prices, 4d. to 1s. 6d. Proscenium width, 45 ft. Stage width, 30 ft. 3 dressing-rooms. Station, Fareham or Portsmouth Harbour.

LEICESTER (LEICS), Pop. 239,111.

ARCADIA (WE), High Street.—Prop., High Street Cinema, Ltd. 780 seats. Booked by C. E. West at Evington Cinema, Leicester. Continuous. Two changes weekly. Prices, 6d. to 1s. 3d. Phone, Leicester 58783. Station, Leicester, L.M.S.

LEICESTER—Contd,

AYLESTONE CINEMA (BTH), Grace Road.—Prop., Aylestone Cinema, Ltd. 1,300 seats. Booked at Birmingham. Continuous. Mat., Mon., Thurs. and Sat. Prices, 3d. to 1s. 6d. Phone, Aylestone 266. Station, Leicester, L.M.S. and L.N.E.R.

BELGRAVE CINEMA (WE), Belgrave Road.—Prop., E. Black. 760 seats. Continuous. Booked at Hall. Mats., Mon. and Thurs. Two changes weekly. Prices, 4d. to 1s. Phone, 61460. Station, Leicester, L.M.S. and L.N.E.R.

CARLTON (WE), Gipsy Lane.—Props., Carlton Kinemas, Ltd. Booked at Evington Cinema, Ltd. Prices, 6d. to 1s. 3d.

CITY CINEMA AND CAFE (WE), Market Place.—Prop., City Cinemas, Ltd., 123 Regent Street, W.1. Regent 8080. 2,020 seats. Continuous from 2 p.m. Prices, 1s. to 2s. Phone, Leicester 60251. Café attached. Stations, Leicester, L.M.S. and L.N.E.R.
Fitted "ARDENTE" Deaf Aids
See page 258
WURLITZER ORGAN
Installed in this Kinema

CLARENDON PARK CINEMA, Welford Road.—Prop., Clarendon Park Cinema, Ltd. (In course of construction.)

COLISEUM (BTP), Melton Road.—Prop., Coliseum Cinema, Ltd. Head Office, Imperial Buildings, Oxford Road, Manchester. 1,000 seats. Continuous. Mats., Mon., Thurs. and Sat. Two changes weekly. Prices, 5d. to 1s. Phone, Leicester 61227.

EVINGTON CINEMA (WE), East Park Road.—Prop., Evington Cinema, Ltd. 978 seats. Booked at Hall by C. E. West. Continuous. Prices, 4d. to 1s. 3d. Phone, Leicester Central 24354. Station, Leicester, L.M.S. and L.N.E.R.

FLORAL HALL PICTURE THEATRE (BTP), Belgrave Gate.—Prop., Leicester Palace Theatre, Ltd. 900 seats. Booked at Stoll Offices by W. P. Carter. Continuous. Prices, 6d. to 1s. 5d. Phone, Leicester Central 58424.

HIPPODROME (BTH), Wharf Street.—Prop., R.W. Marchbanks. 850 seats. Booked at Hall. Continuous. Mats., Mon., Thurs. and Sat. Prices, 4d. to 1s. Proscenium width, 16 ft. Phone, Leicester Central 20722. Station, Leicester, L.M.S., and Broxbourne Road Transport.

IMPERIAL PICTURE HOUSE (Imperial), Green Lane Road.—Prop., A. Maynard, 256, Narboro' Road, Leicester. 700 seats. Booked at Star Picture House, Leicester. Continuous. Two changes weekly. Prices, 4d. to 1s. Phone, Leicester Central 2568. Station, Leicester, L.M.S.

KNIGHTON CINEMA (WE) Welford Road.—Props., Knighton Kinema, Ltd. 1,291 seats. Booked at Evington Cinema, Leicester. Continuous. Prices 6d. to 1s. 3d.

MELBOURNE PICTURE HOUSE (WE), Nedham Street.—Prop., Associated British Cinemas, Ltd., 30-31, Golden Square, W.1. 941 seats. Continuous. Booked at H.O. Two changes weekly. Prices, 5d. to 1s. Phone, Leicester Central 21381. Station, Leicester, L.M.S.

ODEON THEATRE (BTH), Queen Street.—Prop., Odeon Theatres, Ltd., Cornhill House, Bennett's Hill. Birmingham. Booked at 49, Park Lane, W.1. (In course of construction).

OLYMPIA (BTP), Narborough Road.—Prop., Leicester Enterprise, Ltd. Head Office, Imperial Buildings, Oxford Road, Manchester. 800 seats. Booked at H.O. Continuous. Mats., Mon., Thurs. and Sat. Prices, 6d. to 1s. Phone, Leicester 22373. Station, Leicester, L.N.E.R. and L.M.S.

PALACE THEATRE (WE), Belgrave Gate.—Prop., Stoll Circuit, Coliseum Buildings, London, W.C.2. Phone, Temple Bar 1500. 1,883 seats. Continuous. Booked at H.O. Prices, 5d. to 2s. Proscenium width, 38 ft. Phone, 58243. Station, Leicester, L.M.S. and L.N.E.R.
Fitted "ARDENTE" Deaf Aids
See page 258

PICTUREDROME (BTH), Mere Road.—Prop., High Street Cinema, Ltd. 450 seats. Continuous. Mat., Mon., and Sat. Two changes weekly. Phone, Leicester 2076c. Station, Leicester, L.M.S.

PRINCES THEATRE (WE), Granby Street. Lessees, Associated British Cinemas, Ltd., 30-31, Golden Square, W.1. Phone, Gerrard 7887. 1,170 seats. Booked at H.O. Continuous. Occasional variety. Prices, 1s. to 2s. Proscenium width, 26 ft. Occasional variety. Stage, 12 ft. 6 in. deep; 3 dressing-rooms. Phone, Leicester 20519. Station, Leicester, Midland, L.M.S., and Central, L.N.E.R.

RATBY CINEMA (Imperial).—Props., H. and G. Weston. 250 seats. Booked at Hall. Nightly. Prices, 4d. to 1s. Film by Broxburn Transport.

REGAL.—
Fitted "ARDENTE" Deaf Aids
See page 258

SHAFTESBURY PICTURE HOUSE (BTP).—Uppingham Road.—Prop., Leicester Cinemas, Ltd. Head Office, Imperial Buildings, Oxford Road, Manchester. Phone, Ardwick 2226. 800 seats. Booked at H.O. Continuous. Mats., Mon. Thurs. and Sat. Prices, 4d. to 1s. Phone, Leicester Central 27532. Station, Leicester, L.M.S.

SOVEREIGN PICTURE HOUSE (WE), Woodgate.—Prop., H. D. Moorhouse Circuit, 7, Oxford Road, Manchester. 900 seats. Booked at H.O. Continuous. Prices, 4d. to 1s. 6d. Phone, Leicester Central 2808. Station, Leicester, L.N.E.R. and L.M.S.

STAR PICTURE HOUSE (Imperial), Belgrave Gate.—Prop., Alfred Maynard, 256, Narboro' Road, Leicester. 500 seats. Booked at Hall. Continuous. Prices, 4d. to 9d. Phone, Leicester 20795. Station, Leicester, L.M.S.

THE PICTURE HOUSE (WE), Granby Street.—Prop., Provincial Cinematograph Theatres, Ltd., 123, Regent Street, London, W.1. Phone, Regent 8080. Booked at H.O. Continuous. Prices, 1s. to 2s. Phone, Leicester 602511. Cafés attached. Proscenium width, 40 ft. Station, Leicester, L.M.S. and L.N.E.R.
Fitted "ARDENTE" Deaf Aids
See page 258
ROXY——

TROCADERO (WE), Humberstone.—Prop., Trocadero Cinemas (Leicester), Ltd., 1, Berridge Street, Leicester. 2,160 seats. Booked at Birmingham. Continuous. Prices, 6d. to 2s. Proscenium width, 80 ft. Phone, Leicester 27588. Café and Ballroom attached. Station, Leicester, L.M.S.

TUDOR CINEMA (BTP), Vaughan Street.—Prop.,
Leicester Pictures, Ltd., 4, Horsefair Street,
Leicester. 1,294 seats. Continuous. Two
changes weekly. Mats., Mon., Thurs. and Sat.
Prices, 5d. to 9d. Phone, Leicester 20069.
Station, Leicester, L.N.E.R. and L.M.S.
WESTLEIGH KINEMA (WE), Fosse Road.—Con-
tinuous. Mon., Thurs. and Sat. Mat. Prices,
7d. to 1s. 3d.

LEIGH (LANCS), **Pop. 45,313.**
ASSEMBLY ROOMS.
BEDFORD PICTUREDROME (Picturetone).—Prop.,
W. T. .Kelly, 15, Ashley Cresent, Swinton,
Manchester. Phone, Swinton 1348. 640 seats.
Booked at Hall. Prices, 6d. to 1s. Phone,
Leigh 692. Station, Leigh, L.M.S.
CINEMA, Leigh Road.—Mark's Circuit Cinemas,
6, St. Mary's Gate, Manchester. Phone,
Blackfriars 4078. 715 sests. Continuous.
Phone, Leigh 257. Station, Leigh, L.M.S.
SEMS PICTURE HOUSE (WE).—Props., Snape and
Ward, 13, Ann Street, Manchester. Phone,
Leigh 153. Station, Leigh, L.M.S. 866 seats.
GRAND (WE).—753 seats.
HIPPODROME CINEMA (BTH).—Prop., Leigh
Grand Theatre and Hippodrome, Ltd.
Booked by J. Brierley, 21, Bridge Street,
Manchester. 1,700 seats. Twice nightly.
Prices, 2d. to 9d. Proscenium width, 32 ft.
Stage, 39 ft. deep ; 6 dressing-rooms. Phone,
Leigh 128. Station, Leigh, L.M.S.
NEW EMPIRE CINEMA (BTH), Bradshawgate.—
Prop., Harold Ward, 6, Brown Street,
Manchester. Phone, Deansgate 3542. 600
seats. Booked by Prop., at H.O. Con-
tinuous. Prices, 4d. to 9d. Pictures and
Variety. Stage, 10 ft. deep ; 2 dressing-rooms.
Phone, Leigh 25. Station, Leigh, L.M.S.
PALACE (BA), Railway Road.—Prop., Associated
Provincial Picture Houses, Ltd. 1,028 seats.
Continuous nightly. Two shows Sat. Mats.,
Mon., Tues., Wed., Thurs, and Sat. Two
changes weekly. Prices, 6d. to 1s. Phone,
Leigh 411. Station, Leigh, L.M.S.
**Fitted "ARDENTE" Deaf Aids
See page 258**
THEATRE ROYAL.—900 seats.

LEIGH-ON-SEA (ESSEX), **Pop. 45,000.**
COLISEUM CINEMA (WE), Elm Road.—Prop.,
Coliseum (Leigh-on-Sea), Ltd., 37-38, Golden
Square, W.1. Phone, Whitehall 6967/8.
1,200 seats. Booked at H.O. Continuous.
Prices, 6d. to 1s. 6d. Proscenium width,
26 ft. Phone, Leigh-on-Sea 7191. Station,
Leigh-on-Sea, L.M.S., or Motor Transport.
CORONA CINEMA (BTP), Leigh Road.—Prop.,
South Essex Cinema Syn., Ltd. 1,350 seats.
Booked at Hall. Continuous. Occasional
Variety. Stage, 16 ft. deep ; 2 dressing-
rooms. Café attached. Prices, 7d. to 1s. 6d.
Phone, Leigh-on-Sea 75668. Station, Leigh-
on-Sea, L.M.S., or Motor Transport.
EMPIRE PALACE (BTP), Broadway.—Prop.,
South Essex Cinema Syn., Ltd. 450 seats.
Booked at Hall. Continuous. Two changes
weekly. Prices, 7d. to 1s. 4d. Station,
Leigh-on-Sea, L.M.S., or Motor Transport.
(See also Southend-on-Sea.)

LEIGHTON BUZZARD (BEDS), **Pop. 7,031.**
EXCHANGE THEATRE.—Props., Shipman and
King, M84, Shell Mex House, Strand, London,
W.C.2. Phone, Temple Bar 5077. Booked
at H.O. Phone, Leighton Buzzard 160.
Station, Leighton Buzzard, L.M.S.
ORIEL CINEMA (WE).—Prop., Shipman and King,
M84, Shell Mex House, Strand, London,
W.C.2. Phone, Temple Bar 5077. Booked
at H.O. Continuous. Phone, Leighton
Buzzard 160. Station, Leighton Buzzard,
L.M.S.
YE OLD VIC.

LEISTON (SUFFOLK), **Pop. 4,184.**
PICTURE HOUSE (BA), High Street.—Prop.,
Leiston Picture House, Ltd. 500 seats,
Booked at Hall by W. S. Hammick. Nightly.
Mat., Sat. Prices, 6d. to 1s. 6d. Phone,
Leiston 49. Station, Leiston, L.N.E.R.
Films by Road Transport.

LEMINGTON-ON-TYNE (NORTHUMB.), **Pop.
11,000.**
PRINCE OF WALES THEATRE (Cinephone).—
Prop., J. Grantham. 950 seats. Booked at
H.O. Continuous. Twice nightly Sat. Two
changes weekly. Prices, 5d. to 9d. Phone,
Lemington 146. Station, Lemington-on-
Tyne, L.N.E.R.

LEOMINSTER (HEREFORD), **Pop. 5,707.**
CENTRAL CINEMA. 550 seats.
CLIFTON CINEMA.
PICTURE HOUSE (AWH), Corn Square.—Prop.,
Leominster Entertainments, Ltd. Man. Dir.,
J. B. Binmore, Picture House, Ludlow.
Booked at H.O. Continuous. Prices, 9d. to
1s. 6d. Phone, Leominster 200. Station,
Leominster, G.W.R.

LETCHWORTH (HERTS), **Pop. 14,454.**
BROADWAY.—Prop., Letchworth Palace, Ltd.
1,420 seats. Booked at Hall. Continuous.
Prices, 6d. to 2s. Phone, Letchworth 728.
Station, Letchworth, L.N.E.R.
PALACE (BTH), Eastcheap.—Prop., Letchworth
Palace, Ltd. 1,000 seats. Booked at Hall
by Man. Dir. Continuous. Prices, 6d. to 2s.
Phone, Letchworth 53. Station, Letchworth,
L.N.E.R.

LEWES (SUSSEX), **Pop. 10,785.**
CINEMA DE LUXE (WE), School Hill.—Prop.,
Lewes Cinema Co., Ltd., 2, Paddock Terrace,
Lewes. 620 seats. Booked at Hall. Con-
tinuous. Prices, 6d. to 2s. Phone, Lewes
196. Station, Lewes, S.R., or Southern Road
Transport.
ODEON THEATRE (BTH).—Prop., Odeon (Lewes),
Ltd., Cornhill House, Bennetts Hill, Birming-
ham. Phone, Midland 2781. Booked at 49.
Park Lane, W.1. Continuous. Prices, 6d. to
2s. Proscenium width, 44 ft. Stage, 15 ft. deep.
One dressing-room. Café attached. Phone,
Lewes 610. Station, Lewes, S.R.

LEYBURN (YORKS), **Pop. 868.**
ELITE (Morrison).—Props., L. Y. and G. E,
Dobson, Pengarth, Leyburn. 500 seats.
Booked at Hall. Once nightly, twice Sat.
Prices, 6d. to 1s. 10d. Proscenium width, 20 ft.
Stage, 12 ft. deep ; 2 dressing-rooms. Phone,
Leyburn 52. Station, Leyburn, L.N.E.R.
PAVILION (Gramo-Rauio).—Prop., W. C. Sykes,
Picture House, Middleham, Yorks. 250
seats. Booked at Hall. Once nightly.
Prices, 6d. to 1s. 10d. Station, Leyburn,
L.N.E.R.

PATHE PICTORIAL—Novel, Entertaining, Unique.

LEYLAND (LANCS), **Pop. 10,573.**

NEW PALACE CINEMA (BTH).—Prop., Regent Cinema (Leyland), Ltd., Wellfield, Leyland. 500 seats. Booked at Regent. Once nightly, Mon. to Fri. Mat. and twice nightly, Sat. Prices, 6d. to 1s. Proscenium width 20 ft. Phone, Leyland 81138. Station, Leyland, L.M.S.

REGENT SUPER CINEMA (BTH).—Prop., Regent Cinema (Leyland), Ltd. 1,000 seats. Booked at Hall. Twice nightly, Mon., Thurs. and Sat. Continuous, Tues., Wed. and Fri. Mat., Mon. and Thurs.. Prices, 6d. to 1s. 3d. Proscenium width, 30 ft. Phone, Leyland 81138. Station, Leyland, L.M.S.

LEYSDOWN (KENT).

BEACH HALL CINEMA, Leysdown.—Prop., Leysdown Hotel and Amusements, Ltd. J. D. F. Andrews. Twice weekly summer months only. Prices, 6d. to 1s. 3d. Phone, Leysdown 16. Dance Hall attached. Station, Leysdown, S.R.

LICHFIELD (STAFFS), **Pop. 8,508.**

PALLADIUM (BA). — Prop., J. M. Dent, St. Romans, Sutton Coldfield, Birmingham. Phone, Sutton 1666. 560 seats. Continuous. Booked at Birmingham. Prices, 4d. to 1s. 3d. Proscenium width, 26 ft. Stage, 22 ft.; 4 dressing-rooms. Café. Lichfield 112. Station, Lichfield, L.M.S.

REGAL (WE).—Prop., Lichfield Cinema, Ltd., 1,235 seats. Continuous. Booked by County Cinemas, Ltd., Dean House, Dean Street. W.1. Prices, 6d. to 1s. 6d. Proscenium width, 40 ft. Café. Phone, No. 247. Station, Lichfield City, L.M.S.

LINCOLN (LINCS), **Pop. 66,246.**

CENTRAL CINEMA (WE).—Prop., Central Picture Theatres (Lincoln), Ltd. 923 seats. Continuous. Prices, 7d. to 1s. 6d. Café and Dance Hall attached. Phone, Lincoln 525. Station, Lincoln, L.N.E.R. and L.M.S.

EXCHANGE KINEMA (WE).—Prop., Exchange Talkies (Lincoln), Ltd. 1,180 seats. Booked at Hall by H. B. Harris, Gen. Man. Continuous. Daily Mats., except Friday. Prices, 6d. to 1s. 4d. Phone, Lincoln 559. Stations, Lincoln, L.M.S. and L.N.E.R.

GRAND CINEMA (WE), High Street.—Prop., Central Picture Theatres (Lincoln), Ltd. 1,136 seats. Booked at H.O. Continuous. Prices, 7d. to 1s. 6d. Phone, Lincoln 533. Station, Lincoln, L.N.E.R. and L.M.S.

PLAZA (WE).—Props., Yorks and Lincs. Picture Houses, Ltd. 1,450 seats. Booked at Central Cinema. Three shows daily. Prices, 7d. to 1s. 6d. Café and Lounge. Phone, 1369. Stations, Lincoln, L.M.S. and L.N.E.R.

REGAL (WE), High Street.—Prop., Associated British Cinemas, Ltd., 30-31, Golden Square, London, W.1. Phone, Gerrard 7887. 1,130 seats. Booked at H.O. Continuous. Prices, 6d. to 1s. 3d. Proscenium width, 29 ft. Café Phone, Lincoln 251. Station, Lincoln, L.N.E.R. and L.M.S.

SAVOY.

Fitted "ARDENTE" Deaf Aids
See page 258

COMPTON

ORGAN featured here.

LISCARD (CHESHIRE). **See Wallasey.**

LISKEARD (CORNWALL), **Pop. 4,266.**

CINEDROME (Parmeko).—Props., E. J. and W. E. Pope. 700 seats. Booked at Hall. Once nightly. Mats., Wed. and Sat. Prices, 6d. to 1s. Proscenium width, 30 ft. Phone, Liskeard 32. Station, Liskeard, G.W.R.

ELECTRIC (Mihaly).—Prop., W. Pickles. 400 seats.

LISS (HANTS), **Pop. 2,320.**

SEYMOUR HALL (BA).—Prop., Church of England Soldiers and Sailors Institute, Longmoor Camp. 328 seats. Five shows weekly. Prices, 6d. to 1s. Phone, Blackmoor 27. Station, Liss, S.R.

LITTLEBOROUGH (LANCS), **Pop. 12,028.**

QUEEN'S CINEMA (AWH), Church Street.—Prop., Littleborough Picture Theatre Co., Ltd. 500 seats. Booked at Manchester. One show nightly. Twice Sat. Prices, 5d. to 1s. Phone, Littleborough 8498. Station, Littleborough.

VICTORIA PICTURE PALACE (BTH), Sale Street. —Prop., S. J. Fletcher. 700 seats. Booked at Manchester. Mon. to Fri., Continuous. Three shows Sat. Two changes weekly. Station, Littleborough, L.M.S.

LITTLEHAMPTON (SUSSEX), **Pop. 10,181.**

PALLADIUM, Church Street.—Prop., South Downs Kinemas, Ltd., 2, Rugby Road, Southsea. Phone, Portsmouth 3456. 890 seats. Booked at H.O. Continuous. Prices, 6d. to 1s. Phone, Littlehampton 44. Station, Littlehampton, S.R. Films by West Sussex Film Transport.

ODEON THEATRE (BTH).—Props., Odeon (Littlehampton), Ltd., Cornhill House, Bennetts Hill, Birmingham. Phone, Midland 2781. Booked at 49, Park Lane, W.1. Prices. 9d. to 2s. Phone, Littlehampton 254.

REGENT.—Props., South Downs Kinemas, Ltd., 2, Rugby Road, Southsea. Phone, Portsmouth 3456. 650 seats. Booked at H.O. Continuous. Prices, 6d. to 1s. 6d. Phone, Littlehampton 44. Station, Littlehampton, S.R. Films by West Sussex Film Transport.

LITTLE LEVER (LANCS), **Pop. 4,944.**

CORONA CINEMA (BTH).—Prop., Jackson and Newport, Ltd. 600 seats. Booked at Manchester. Continuous Mon. to Fri. Sat. and Holidays, twice nightly. Prices, 3d. to 9d Proscenium width, 18 ft. Phone, Farnworth 261. Station, Bradley Fold, L.M.S.

PALACE (BTH).

LITTLEPORT (CAMBS), **Pop. 4,477.**

CINEMA THEATRE (BTH).—Prop., R. Victor Watson, Victoria Street, Littleport. 500 seats. Booked at Victoria Street. Phone, Littleport 35. One show nightly. Prices, 5d. to 1s. 3d. Station, Littleport, L.N.E.R.

EMPIRE CINEMA (BTH). Props., Cosmopolitan Cinemas, Ltd., 14, St. John's Street, Cambridge. Phone, 2799. 500 seats. Booked at Hall. Prices, 6d. to 1s. 6d. Station, Littleport, L.N.E.R., and Film Transport.

LITTLE SUTTON (near Birkenhead)
(CHESHIRE), **Pop. 2,000.**

NEW KING'S PICTURE HOUSE (BA).—Prop., Hippodrome (Ellesmere Port), Ltd., Carnegie Street, Ellesmere Port. Phone, 54. 320 seats. Booked at H.O. Continuous. Prices, 6d. to 1s. 6d. Phone, Hooton 267. Station, Little Sutton (Cheshire).

LIVERPOOL (LANCS), Pop. 855,539.

ADELPHI.—Booked by S. Grimshaw at Prince of Wales Cinema, Clayton Square, Liverpool.

ASTORIA (WE), Walton Road.—Prop., Associated British Cinemas, Ltd., 30-31, Golden Square, W.1. 1,401 seats. Booked at H.O. Continuous, Mon. to Fri. Twice nightly, Sat. Prices, 6d. to 1s. 3d. Proscenium width, 35 ft. Phone, North 537. Station, Lime Street, L.M.S.

ATLAS SUPER TALKIE THEATRE (WE), Rice Lane.—Prop., Byron Picturehouses, Ltd., 1-3, Stanley Street, Liverpool. Phone, Bank 9236. Continuous. Booked at Prince of Wales Theatre, Clayton Square, Liverpool. Prices, 4d. to 1s. Proscenium width, 30 ft. Phone, Walton 145. Stations, Lime Street and Exchange.

BEDFORD HALL (BA), Bedford Road, Walton.—Prop., Gaumont British P. Corp., Ltd. 1,100 seats. Continuous evening performances. Mats., daily. Two changes weekly. Phone, Walton 298.

BELMONT ROAD PICTURE HOUSE (BTP).—Lessees, Associated British Cinemas, Ltd., 30-31, Golden Square, London, W.1. 700 seats. Continuous. Daily Mat. Two changes weekly. Prices, 3d. to 9d. Phone, Anfield 275. Station, Lime Street, L.M.S.

BERESFORD CINEMA (BA), Park Road.—Prop., Denman Picture Houses, Ltd., 123, Regent Street, London, W.1. 1,047 seats. Booked at H.O. Continuous. Twice on Sat. Prices, 5d. to 1s. Phone, Royal 4079. All Liverpool Stations.

BURLINGTON CINEMA (RCA), Vauxhall Road.—1,200 seats. Booked at Prince of Wales Theatre, Clayton Square, Liverpool. Mat. and twice nightly on Mon., Wed. and Sat. Prices, 2d. to 6d. Stations, Lime Street and Exchange, L.M.S.

CABBAGE HALL PICTURE HOUSE (BTH), Anfield. —Prop., Cabbage Hall Picture House, Ltd. 700 seats. Booked by R. J. Tatham at 20, Mayville Road, Mossley Hill, Liverpool. Continuous. Prices, 3d. to 9d. Phone, Anfield 203. Station, Lime Street, L.M.S.

CAPITOL (WE), Overton Street, Edge Hill.—Prop., Capitol (Edge Hill), Ltd., 11/13, Victoria Street, Liverpool. Phone, Bank 5504. 1,551 seats. Occasional Variety. Booked by C. J. Doyle, 15, Victoria Street, Liverpool. Three shows daily. Prices, 6d. to 1s. 3d. Stage, 6 ft. deep; 2 dressing-rooms. Proscenium width, 23 ft. Phone, Royal 5438. Stations, Lime Street or Edge Hill, L.M.S.

CARLTON THEATRE (BTP), Green Lane.—Prop., Associated British Cinemas, Ltd., 30-31, Golden Square, London, W.1. Phone, Gerrard 7887. 2,000 seats. Continuous. Daily Mat. Twice nightly Sat. Prices, 4d. to 1s. 6d. Proscenium width, 40 ft. Stage, 8 ft. deep. 3 dressing-rooms. Phone, Old Swan 921. Café attached. Stations, Lime Street and Exchange, L.M.S.

CARLTON CINEMA (WE), Moss Lane, Walton.—Prop., Orrell Park Picture House, Ltd., 1 and 3, Stanley Street, Liverpool. 1,510 seats. Booked at Prince of Wales Theatre, Liverpool. Continuous. Daily Mat. Twice nightly Sat. Prices, 6d. to 1s. Phone, Walton 579. Station, Lime Street.

CARLTON ROOMS (WE).—Leslie Greene Circuit. H.O., 7, Elliot Street, Liverpool. Phone, Royal 538.

CASINO CINEMA (WE). 6, Prescot Road.—Prop., General Theatre Corporation, Ltd., 123, Regent Street, London, W.1. Phone, Regent 6641. Booked at H.O. Continuous. Daily Mats. Prices, 4d. to 1s. 3d. Proscenium width, 60 ft. Phone, Anfield 977. Station, Lime Street, L.M.S.

CLUBMOOR P.H. (WE), Townsend Lane West, Derby, Liverpool.—Prop., Clubmoor P.H. Co., Ltd., 10, Dale Street, Liverpool. Phone. Central 4757. 904 seats. Booked by C. O, Davies at Hall. Occasional Variety. Prices, 6d. to 1s. 6d. Stage, 8 ft. deep; 2 dressing-rooms. Phone, Anfield 1280.

COLISEUM PICTURE HOUSE (WE), Linacre Road, Litherland.—Prop., Litherland Picture House, Ltd., 1,442 seats. Booked at 51, North John Street, Liverpool. Continuous. Prices, 5d. to 1s. Phone, Waterloo 75. Station, Seaforth.

COLISEUM, Walton.—Prop., Associated British Cinemas, Ltd., 30-31, Golden Square, London, W.1. Phone, Gerrard 7887.

COMMODORE PICTURE HOUSE.—Prop., Associated British Cinemas, Ltd., 30-31, Golden Square, London, W.1. Booked at H.O. 1,881 seats.

COSY PICTURE HOUSE (RCA), Boaler Street.—Prop., Cosy Picture House (Liverpool), Ltd. 630 seats. Booked at Hall. Continuous. Prices 4d. to 9d. Phone, Anfield 1513. Station, Lime Street, L.M.S,

CURZON, Prescot Road.—Prop., Bedford Cinemas (1928), Ltd., 19, Castle Street, Liverpool.

COMPTON

ORGAN featured here.

DERBY CINEMA (RCA), 318, Scotland Road.—Props., Byron Picture Houses, Ltd., 1-3, Stanley Street, Liverpool. Phone, Bank 9236. 1,100 seats. Pictures booked by Stanley Grimshaw at Prince of Wales, Clayton Square, Liverpool. Stage, 9 ft. deep; two dressing rooms. Three shows daily. Prices, 4d. to 6d. Proscenium width, 33 ft. Phone, North 949. Stations, Lime Street, Central and Exchange, L.M.S.

DORIC CINEMA (RCA), Smith Street.—Prop., H. E. Barham, 152, Princes Road. Liverpool. 650 seats. Phone, Royal 5434. Booked at Hall. Continuous evenings. Mat. daily. Prices, 3d. to 6d. Phone, North 633. Stations, Lime Street, Exchange and Central, L.M.S.

EMBASSY, Wallasey, North Western Film Booking Agency, 70, Lime Street, Liverpool.

EMPIRE (WE).—Prop., Bedford Cinemas (1928), Ltd., 19, Castle Street, Liverpool. 890 seats.

EMPIRE (WE) 890 seats.

EMPRESS PICTURE HOUSE (BA), Tuebrook.—914 seats. Booked by Prop. Continuous. Mat daily. Prices, 6d. and 1s. Phone, Old Swan 453. Station, Lime Street, L.M.S.

EVERTON ELECTRIC PALACE (BTH), Heyworth Street.—Prop., Everton Electric Palace, Ltd. 1,040 seats. Continuous 6.30 to 10.30. Mat. daily. Two changes weekly Prices, 4d. and 6d. Phone, Anfield 385.

FORUM (WE), Lime Street.—Prop., Associated British Cinemas, Ltd., 30-31, Golden Square, W.1. Phone, Gerrard 7887. 2,000 seats.

T2

LIVERPOOL—Contd.

Booked at H.O. Continuous. Prices, 1s. to 2s. 6d. Proscenium width, 37 ft. Café. Phone, Royal 6277-8. Station, Lime Street, Liverpool.

C O M P T O N
ORGAN featured here

FUTURIST (WE).—Prop., Futurist (Liverpool), Ltd. Booked by Alfred Levy, Granelagh Street, Liverpool, 1. 1,029 seats. Continuous. Occasional Variety. Proscenium width, 36 ft. Stage 10 ft. deep ; one dressing-room. Prices, 1s. 3d. and 2s. Phone, Royal 3100. Station, Lime Street, L.M.S.

GAIETY CINEMA (RCA), 41-45, Scotland Road.— Stanley Grimshaw Circuit, Prince of Wales Cinema, Clayton Square, Liverpool. 600 seats. Two shows nightly. Mat. daily. Two changes weekly. Prices, 4d. to 9d. Phone, Central 5378.

GARRICK PICTURE HOUSE (WE), Westminster Road.—Prop., Garrick (Regent), Ltd. 1,300 seats. Booked at 51, North John Street, Liverpool. Continuous. Two changes weekly Prices, 5d. to 9d. Phone, Bootle 1270. Station, Lime Street, L.M.S.

GARSTON EMPIRE (WE), James Street.—Prop., Bedford Cinemas (1928), Ltd., 19, Castle Street, Liverpool. Phone, Central 1545. Continuous Mon. to Fri., twice nightly Sats. and holidays. Films booked at H.O. by J. F. Wood. Prices, 6d. to 1s. Stage, 15 ft. deep ; 7 dressing-rooms. Phone. Garston 392. Stations, Garston, Cheshire, R.

GAUMONT, Dingle.

GAUMONT PALACE (BA), Oakfield Road, Anfield, —Prop., General Theatre Corporation, Ltd., Wardour Steeet, W.1. 2,000 seats. Booked at H.O. Continuous. Mats. daily. Prices, 6d. to 1s. 3d. Phone, Anfield 9. Station, Liverpool, L.M.S.

GEM PICTURE HOUSE (WE), Vescock Street, Liverpool.—Prop., Associated British Cinemas, Ltd., 30-31, Golden Square, W.1. 1,496 seats. Twice nightly. Mat. daily. Prices, 3d. to 9d. Phone, North 598. Station, Lime Street.

GRANADA CINEMA (BTP), Dovecot.—Prop., Associated British Cinemas, Ltd., 30-31, Golden Square, W.1. 1,800 seats. Continuous nightly Mon. to Fri. Twice nightly Sat. Daily Mat. Prices, 4d. to 1s. 3d. Proscenium width, 50 ft. Phone, Old Swan 176. Stations, Lime Street, Exchange and Central, L.M.S.

GRAND CINEMA (BA), Smithdown Road.— 824 seats. Continuous. Mat., Mon., Wed., Thurs. and Sat. Two changes weekly. Phone, Wavertree 252.

GROSVENOR PICTURE HOUSE (BTH), Stanley Road.—Prop., Grosvenor (Regent), Ltd. 1,040 seats. Booked at 51, North John Street, Liverpool. Prices, 5d. to 9d. Phone, North 680. Station, Lime Street, L.M.S.

HIPPODROME (BA).—3,200 seat s.

HOMER CINEMA (WE), Great Homer Street.— Prop., Homer (Regent), Ltd. Booked at 51, North John Street, Liverpool. 950 seats. Two shows nightly. Mat. daily. Prices, 4d. to 9d. Phone, North 1066. Stations, Lime Street and Exchange, L.M.S.

HOPE HALL CINEMA (BTP), Hope Street,— Films and Variety. Continuous. Stage, 11 ft. deep ; 2 dressing rooms. Prices, 4d. to 9d. Phone, Royal 3,509. Stations, Lime Street and Central, L.M.S.

KINGS PICTURE HOUSE (BTP), London Road.— Props., Kings Picture House (L'pool), Ltd , 1-3, Stanley Street. 950 seats. Continuous. Booked by Regent Enterprises, Ltd., 51, North John Street, Liverpool. Prices, 7d. to 1s. Phone, Royal 197. Station, Lime Street, L.M.S.

LYCEUM TALKIE THEATRE (RCA).—Prop., Empress Cinemas (Liverpool), Ltd. W. J. Grace, Man. Dir. 800 seats. Booked at Hall. Continuous, two shows Sat. Mats., Mon., Wed., Thurs. and Sat. Prices, 6d. to 1s. Proscenium width, 17 ft. Phone, Garston 527. Stations, Cressington or Garston, L.M.S.

LYTTON CINEMA (BTH), Lytton Street, Everton. —Prop., Exors. of T. C. Dolan. 600 seats. Booked at Hall. Continuous. Prices, 4d. to 6d. Phone, Anfield 445. Stage, 6 ft. deep ; one dressing-room. Stations, Lime Street and Central, L.M.S.

MAGNET CINEMA (BA), Wavertree.—Prop., Denman Picture Houses, Ltd. 1,100 seats. Continuous. Two changes weekly. Prices, 5d. to 1s. Phone, Wavertree 275. Station, Edge Hill, L.M.S.

MAJESTIC (WE), Daulby Street, London Road. —Prop., Liverpool Majestic, Ltd. 1,109 seats. Booked at Hall. Continuous. Prices, 6d. to 1s. 3d. Phone, Royal 2318.

MERE LANE SUPER CINEMA (WE), Mere Lane, Everton.—Prop., Mere Lane (Regent), Ltd. Booked at 51, North John Street, Liverpool. 984 seats. Continuous. Mat. daily. Two changes weekly. Prices, 6d. to 1s. Phone, Anfield 709. Station, Lime Street, L.M.S.

NEW ADELPHI CINEMA (BA), St. Anne Street.— Props., Byron Picture Houses, Ltd., 1, Stanley Street, Liverpool. Phone, Bank 9236. 1,134 seats. Booked at H.O. Twice nightly. Mat. daily. Prices, 3d. to 9d . Phone, North 574. Station, Lime Street, L.M.S.

NEW COLISEUM PICTURE HOUSE (RCA), Padding-ton.—Prop., Associated British Cinemas, Ltd., 30-31, Golden Square, London, W.1. Phone, Gerrard. 7887. 900 seats. Pictures and Variety. Continuous. Prices, 4d. to 1s. Two dressing rooms. Phone, Royal 3105.

NEW PREMIER PICTURE HOUSE (WE), Prescot Road, Old Swan.—Prop., New Premier P.H., Ltd. 858 seats. Booked by C.O. Davies. Continuous. Daily Mat. Pictures and Variety. Stage, 10 ft. deep ; two dressing rooms. Two changes weekly. Prices, 7d. and 1s. Phone, Old Swan 72.

OLYMPIA (WE), West Derby Road.—Prop., Associated British Cinemas, Ltd., 30-31, Golden Square, W.1. 2,911 seats. Booked at H.O. Continuous. Prices, 4d. to 2s. 6d. Phone, Anfield 1510. Station, Lime Street, L.M.S.

PALACE (BTH), Warbeck Moor, Aintree.— Prop., Aintree Picture Palace, Ltd. 900 seats. Booked at North Western Film Agency, 70, Lime Street, Liverpool. Continuous. Mon. to Fri. Two shows Sat. and Bank Holidays. Two changes weekly. Prices, 4d. to 1s. Phone, Walton 50. Station, Aintree, L.M.S.

PATHE GAZETTE—The Most Popular of News Reels !

PALAIS-DE-LUXE (BTH), Lime Street.—Prop., Liverpool Palais-de-Luxe, Ltd., 11-13, Victoria Street, Liverpool. 1,300 seats. Man. and Licensee, W. J. Ede. Continuous. Prices, 6d. to 2s. Phone, Royal 4911.

PALLADIUM (WE), West Derby Road.—Prop., Liverpool Palladium, Ltd. 905 seats. Continuous. Daily Mats. Two changes weekly. Phone, Anfield 90. Station, Tuebrook, L.M.S.

PARAMOUNT (WE), London Road.

COMPTON

ORGAN featured here.

PARK PALACE (WE), Mill Street.—Prop., Park Palace (Liverpool), Ltd. 961 seats. Booked at Hall. Two shows nightly and Mats. Prices, 4d. to 1s. Stage and four dressing-rooms. Phone, Royal 4288. Station, Liverpool termini.

PAVILION.—J. & H. Buxton Circuit, 4, Grange View, Leeds.

PICTUREDROME (BTH), KENSINGTON.—Prop., Liverpool Picturedrome, Ltd. 1,050 seats. Booked by North Western Film Booking Agency, 70, Lime Street, Liverpool. Continuous. Two changes weekly. Prices, 5d. to 1s. Phone, Anfield 863. All stations.

PLAZA (RCA), Gaumont-British Pictures Corpn., Ltd., New Gallery House, Regent Street, London, W. 1,400 seats. Continuous. Mats. daily. Café attached.

WURLITZER ORGAN
Installed in this Kinema

POPULAR PICTURE HOUSE (WE), Netherfield Road North.—Prop., Associated British Cinemas, Ltd., 30-31, Golden Square, London, W.1. Phone, Gerrard, 7887. 1,508 seats. Booked at H.O. Continuous. Prices, 5d. to 9d. Two dressing-rooms. Phone, Anfield 1163. Station, Lime Street, L.M.S.

PRINCE OF WALES PICTURE HOUSE (BTH), Clayton Square.—Props., News Theatre (Liverpool) Ltd., 1-3, Stanley Street, Liverpool. 700 seats. Booked at H.O. Continuous. Café attached. Prices, 1s. 3d. to 2s. 6d. Phone, Royal 5280. Stations, Lime Street, or Central.

PRINCES PICTURE HOUSE (RCA), Granby Street, —Props., Princes Picture House (Liverpool), Ltd. Booked at 51, North John Street, Liverpool, 600 seats. Booked at H.O. Continuous. Prices, 7d. to 1s. Phone, Royal 3424. Station, Liverpool, L.M.S.

PRINCESS CINEMA (WE), Selwyn Street, Kirkdale. —Props., Princess (Kirkdale), Liverpool, Ltd. 1,420 seats. Continuous. Prices, 6d. to 1s. 3d. Proscenium width, 28 ft. Phone, Bootle 1033. Station, Kirkdale, Liverpool.

QUEEN'S PICTURE HOUSE (WE), South Road, Waterloo.—Prop., Waterloo P.H., Ltd., 4, Harrington Street, Liverpool. 979 seats. Phone, Bank 3784. Booked by R. P. Rutherford at Queen's Picture House, Poulton Road, Seacombe. Continuous Daily. Mat. Prices, 6d. to 1s. 3d. Phone, Waterloo 189.

QUEEN'S PICTURE HOUSE (WE), Walton Road. —Prop., Walton Road Picture House, Ltd. 960 seats. Licensee and Manager, E. S. Jesse. Booked at Queen's Picture House, Poulton Road, Seacombe, Cheshire. Contin-

uous, two shows Sat. Prices, 4d. to 1s. Phone, North 1150. Station, Liverpool.

REGAL CINEMA (WE), Norris Green.—Prop., Associated British Cinemas, Ltd., 30-31, Golden Square, W.1. Phone, Gerrard 7887. 1,756 seats. Booked at H.O. Continuous. Prices, 6d to 1s. Proscenium width, 50 ft. Stage, 20 ft. deep; four dressing-rooms. Phone, Old Swan 1492. Station, Breck Road, L.M.S.

REGENT (WE), Knotty Ash, Liverpool.—Prop., Associated British Cinemas, Ltd., 30-31, Golden Square, London, W.1. Phone, Gerrard 7887. 1,140 seats. Continuous. Twice on Sat. Prices, 4d. to 1s. Phone, Old Swan 889. Station, Liverpool.

REO CINEMA (BTP), Longmoor Lane, Fazakerley. —Prop., Associated British Cinemas, Ltd., 30-31, Golden Square, London, W.1. 1,450 seats. Continuous. Proscenium width, 42 ft. Phone, Walton 133. Café attached. Station, Lime Street, Exchange and Central.

RIALTO THEATRE (WE), Upper Parliament Street.—Prop., General Theatres Corporation, Ltd., 123, Regent Street, London, W.1. 1,274 seats. Booked at H.O. Continuous. Prices, 6d. to 2s. Stage 18 ft. deep. Café and Ballroom attached. Phone, Royal 4576. Station, Liverpool, L.M.S.

Fitted "ARDENTE" Deaf Aids
See page 258

RITZ PICTURE HOUSE (BTH), Anfield.—Prop., Ritz Picture House (Liverpool), Ltd., 18, Hackins, Hey, 1,100 seats. Booked at Hall, Continuous. Two shows Sat. Daily Mat. Prices, 3d. to 1s. Phone, Anfield 1690. Stations, Lime Street and Central.

RIVOLI (BA), Aigburth.—Prop., Denman Picture Houses, Ltd., 123, Regent Street, London, W.1. 602 seats. Booked at H.O. Evenings Continuous. Mats. daily, two shows Sat. and holidays. Proscenium width, 23 ft. Stage, 12½ ft. deep; two dressing-rooms. Prices, 4d. to 1s. Phone, Lark Lane 127. All Liverpool stations.

ROSCOMMON PICTURE PALACE (BTP).—Prop., H. E. Radam, 152, Princes Road, Liverpool. Phone, Royal 5434. 800 seats. Booked at Hall. Prices, 3d. to 6d. Station, Lime Street, L.M.S.

ROYAL HIPPODROME (BA). Continuous. Prices, 5d. to 1s. 3d. Phone, Anfield 430.

ROYAL SUPER CINEMA (WE), Breck Road.— Booked at 51, North John Street, Liverpool. Phone, Bank 610. Continuous. Two changes weekly. Prices, 6d. to 1s. Phone, Anfield 358.

ST. JAMES' PICTUREDROME (BTH), St. James Street.—Prop., Palais Cinema Circuit, 70, Lime Street, Liverpool. Phone, Royal 4911. 935 seats. Res. Man. and Licensee, W. H. Lennon. Booked at H.O. Continuous. Mat. daily. Stage, 6¾ ft. deep. Prices, 3d. to 9d. Phone, Royal 2587.

SAVOY (BA), West Derby Road.—Prop., General Theatre Corporation, Ltd., 123, Regent Street, London, W.1. 681 seats. Booked at H.O. Continuous. Prices, 4d. to 9d. Phone, Anfield 676.

SCALA THEATRE (RCA), Lime Street.—Prop., Greater Scala (Liverpool), Ltd. Booked by Liverpool Cinema Feature Film Co., Ltd., 9, Ranelagh Street. Continuous. Prices, 1s. 3d. to 2s. Phone, Royal 1084. Station, Lime Street, L.M.S.

LIVERPOOL—Contd.

SEAFORTH PALLADIUM (WE), Seaforth Road.—
Prop., Seaforth Palladium Picture Palace,
Ltd. 905 seats. Continuous Mon. to Fri.
Twice nightly Sat. Prices, 6d. to 1s. Phone,
Waterloo 433. Station, Seaforth, L.M.S.

SMITHDOWN PICTURE PLAYHOUSE (BTH), Smith-
down Road.—Prop., Smithdown Picture
Playhouse, Ltd., 1 and 3, Stanley Street.
Liverpool. Phone, Bank 9236. 902 seats,
Booked by B. Allman at Tower Buildings,
Water Street, Liverpool. Continuous. Twice
on Sat. Daily Mat. Two changes weekly.
Prices 5d. to 1s. Phone, Wavertree 729,
Proscenium width, 27 ft. Station, Lime
Street, L.M.S.

STELLA PICTURE HOUSE (RCA), Seaforth.—
Prop., Stella Picture House Co. (1923). 1,200
seats. Booked at Hall. Continuous Phone,
Waterloo 234. Stations, Seaforth and Litherland, L.M S.

SWAN CINEMA (WE), Mill Lane, Old Swan.—
Prop., Oakhill Picture House, Ltd.
at 51, North John Street, Liverpool. 1,000
seats. Continuous. Prices, 6d. to 1s. Proscenium width 35 ft. Stage 8 ft. 6 in., two
dressing rooms. Phone, Old Swan 173.
Station, Lime Street, L.M.S.

TATLER NEWS THEATRE (RCA), 25, Church
Street.—Prop., Capital and Provincial News
Theatres, Ltd., 172, Buckingham Palace
Road, S.W.1. 600 seats. Booked at H.O.
Continuous. Prices, 6d. to 1s. Station, Lime
Street, L.M.S.

TIVOLI CINEMA (RCA) Roscommon Street.—
700 seats. Booked by E. Haigh and Son, 30,
Tarleton Street, Liverpool, 1. Twice daily
Daily Mat. Prices, 4d. and 6d. Phone, North
880. Station, Liverpool termini.

TROCADERO SUPER CINEMA (WE), Camden
Street.—Controlled by Provincial Cinemato-
graph Theatres, Ltd., 123, Regent Street,
London, W.1. 1,301 seats. Booked at H.O.
Continuous. Prices, 6d. to 2s. Phone, North
39. Station, Lime Street, L.M.S.

WURLITZER ORGAN
Installed in this Kinema

TUNNEL ROAD PICTUREDROME (WE).— Prop.,
Tunnel Road Picturedrome, Ltd. 811 seats.
Licensee, Robert E. Ratcliff. Booked at Hall.
Continuous. Mat. daily. Prices, 5d. to 1s.
Proscenium width, 54 ft. Phone, Royal
4042. Station, Edge Hill, L.M.S.

VICTORIA CINEMA (BTH), Cherry Lane, Walton.
—Prop., Victoria (Walton), Ltd., Booked by
Regent Enterprises, Ltd., 51, North John
Street, Liverpool. 1,100 seats. Continuous.
Prices, 5d. to 1s. Phone, Walton 124.
Station, Lime Street, L.M.S.

VICTORY PICTURE HOUSE (WE), Walton Road.—
Prop., Associated British Cinemas, Ltd., 30-31,
Golden Square, W.1. 1,131 seats. Con-
tinuous. Two shows Sat. and holidays. Prices,
6d. to 1s. Proscenium width, 30 ft. Phone,
Liverpool North 553. Station, Lime Street,
L.M.S.

WALTON VALE PICTURE HOUSE (WE), Walton
Vale.—Prop., Walton Vale Picture House
Co. (Liverpool), Ltd. Man. Dir., J. Leslie
Greene. 1,182 seats. Booked by him at 7,
Elliott Street, Liverpool. Phone, Royal 538.
Continuous. Daily Mat. Prices, 6d. to 1s.
Phone, Walton 234.

WARWICK CINEMA (Mihaly), 101, Windsor
Street.—Props., Mark Wilkinson, 26, Hanley
Avenue ,Higher Bebington, Birkenhead. 510
seats. Booked at Hall. Continuous. Twice
Sat. Prices, 3d. to 9d. Phone, Royal 4397.

WEST DERBY PICTURE HOUSE (BTH), Almonds
Green.—Prop., West Derby Picture House,
Co., Ltd., 18, Hackins Hey, Liverpool.
950 seats. Booked at Hall. Continuous.,
Mon. to Fri. Two shows Sat. and Bank
Holidays. Prices, 7d. and 1s. Phone, Old
Swan 1124. Stations, Lime Street, L.M.S. or
West Derby Village (Cheshire Lines).

WINTER GARDENS (BTP), Waterloo.—Prop.,
Winter Gardens, Waterloo (1933), Ltd. 300
seats. Booked at Hall. Continuous. Phone,
Waterloo 167. Station, Waterloo, L.M.S.

WOOLTON PICTURE HOUSE (BTH), Mason Street.
—Prop., Woolton Picture House Co., Ltd.
673 seats. Continuous. Booked at Hall.
Prices, 6d. to 1s. Station, Lime Street,
L.M.S.

LLANHILLETH (MON), **Pop. 10,950.**
PLAYHOUSE.
WORKMAN'S HALL (BA). 500 seats.

LOCKWOOD (YORKS), **Pop. 16,929**
EXCELDA PICTURE PALACE (WE). — Prop.,
Excelda Picture Palace Co., Ltd. 1,025 seats.
Booked at Hall. Continuous. Prices, 4d. to
1s. 3d. Phone, Lockwood 544. Station
Lockwood, L.N.E.R.

LOFTUS (YORKS), **Pop. 7,631.**
EMPIRE THEATRE (WE).—Prop., Thompson's
Enterprises, Ltd., 4, Palladium Bldgs., East-
bourne Road, Middlesboro'. Phone, Lin-
thorpe 88156. 622 seats. Booked at H.O.
Once nightly, Mon. to Fri. Three shows Sat,
Prices, 4d. to 1s. Phone, Loftus 13. Station.
Loftus, L.N.E.R., or Road Transport.

LONG BUCKBY (NORTHANTS), **Pop. 2,500.**
CO-OPERATIVE HALL (AWH), Church Street. —
Prop., Long Buckby Self Assistance Industrial
Society, Ltd. 270 seats. Once nightly. Two
shows Sat. Prices, 4d. to 1s. Booked at Hall.
Phone, Long Buckby 8. Station, Long
Buckby, L.M.S.

LONG EATON (DERBY), **Pop. 22,339.**
EMPIRE CINEMA (WE).—Prop., J. Langham
Brown. Booked at Hall by Prop. Con-
tinuous. Café. Ballroom and Car Park
attached. Prices, 6d. to 1s. 3d. Phone, Long
Eaton 209. Station, Long Eaton, L.M.S.
Films by Films Transport (Broxburne), Ltd.

PALACE THEATRE (WE), Market Place.—Prop.,
New Palace Theatre Co., Ltd. 687 seats.
Booked at Hall. Continuous. Prices, 4d. to
1s. Phone, Long Eaton 185.

SCALA (BTP).—Lessees, G. and D. Cinemas. 850
seats. Booked by S. Graham, Park House,
Friar Lane, Nottingham. Continuous. Occa-
sioual Variety. Prices, 6d. to 1s. Proscenium
width, 30 ft. Stage 20 ft. deep ; four dressing-
rooms. Phone, Long Eaton 110. Station,
Long Eaton, L.M.S. Films by Road Transport.

LONGRIDGE (LANCS), **Pop. 4,158.**
PALACE CINEMA (BTH), 28, Market Place.—
Props., James E. Fletcher and Mrs. N.
Fletcher. 450 seats. Booked at Manchester
and Liverpool. One show nightly. Twice
Sat. Prices 4d. to 1s. Stage 12 ft. deep,
three dressing-rooms. Proscenium width, 14ft.
Station, Longridge, L.M.S., and by Auto.

The BEST Is Cheapest; PATHE GAZETTE.

LONG SUTTON (Lincs), **Pop. 2,900.**
GEM CINEMA (Gyrotone).—Props., G. W. Gore. 300 seats. Continuous. Two shows Sat. Booked at Hall. Prices, 6d. to 1s. 6d. Proscenium width, 16 ft. Station, Long Sutton. Midland and Film Transport.

LONGTON (Staffs), **Pop. 37,479.**
ALEXANDRA PALACE (BTH), Edensor Road.— 850 seats. Continuous. Prices, 6d. to 1s. Phone, Longton 3223. Station, Longton, L.M.S.
ALHAMBRA PICTURE HOUSE (WE), Upper Normacot Road.—Prop., The Alhambra Picture House (Longton), Ltd. Gen. Man., L. Myatt. 926 seats. Booked at Hall. Continuous. Prices, 6d. to 1s. 3d. Stage and two dressing-rooms. Phone, Longton 3280. Station, Normacot, L.M.S.
CRITERION (AWH), Market Street.—Prop., F. C. Leatham. 600 seats. Booked at Hall. Continuous. Prices, 5d. to 1s. Proscenium width, 30 ft. Phone, Longton 3475. Station, Longton, I.M.S.
EMPIRE THEATRE (BTH), Commerce Street.— Props., Associated British Cinemas, Ltd., 30-31, Golden Square, W.1. Booked at H.O. 1,118 seats. Continuous. Prices, 3d. to 1s. Phone, Longton 3779. Station, Longton, L.M.S.
ROYAL PICTURE HOUSE (WE), Anchor Road.— Prop., Regal Cinema (Longton) Ltd. 1,002 seats. Continuous. Mats. twice weekly. Booked at Hall. Three changes weekly. Prices, 4d. to 1s. Proscenium width, 20 ft. Phone, Longton 3441. Station, Longton, L.M.S.

LONGTOWN (Cumb), **Pop. 1,600.**
PICTURE HALL.—Prop. and Res. Man., W. Benson. 350 seats. Booked at Hall. One show nightly. Prices, 6d. to 1s. Station, Longtown, L.N.E.R.

LOOE (Cornwall), **Pop. 2,878.**
CINEMA (BTH).—Prop. and Res. Man., L. Lennard. 150 seats. Booked at Hall. One show nightly. Prices, 6d. to 1s. 6d. Station, Looe, G.W.R.

LOUGHBOROUGH (Leicester), **Pop. 26,945.**
EMPIRE CINEMA (BTH), Market Place.—Prop., C. K. Deeming (Coalville) Circuit. 700 seats. Booked at H.O. Continuous. Mat. daily, except Wed. Prices, 6d. to 1s. 3d. Café attached. Phone, Loughborough 942. Station, Loughborough, L.M.S.
ODEON THEATRE (BTH).—Props., Odeon (Loughborough), Ltd., Bennett's Hill. Birmingham. Phone, Midland 2781. Booked at 49, Park Lane, N.1. Prices 6d. to 1s. 6d. Phone 2659.
THEATRE ROYAL CINEMA (BTH), Hill Street.— Prop., C. K. Deeming (Coalville) Circuit. 900 seats. Booked at H.O. Prices, 7d. to 1s. 4d. Station, Loughborough, L.M.S., and L.N.E.R.
VICTORY CINEMA (WE), Biggin Street.—Prop., C. K. Deeming (Coalville) Circuit. 1,023 seats. Booked at H.O. Twice nightly. Prices, 7d. to 1s. 3d. Phone, Loughborough 941. Station, Loughborough, L.M.S. and L.N.E.R.

LOUGHTON (Essex), **Pop. 7,390.**
LOUGHTON CINEMA (WE), High Road.—Props., Loughton Cinemas, Ltd., Controlled by Bernstein Theatres, Ltd., 36, Golden Square, W.1. Gerrard 3554. 700 seats. Booked at H.O. Continuous. Phone, Loughton 488.

LOUTH (Lincs), **Pop. 9,678.**
ELECTRIC PALACE (BTH), Eastgate.—Prop. and Man., E. E. Roberts. 700 seats. Booked at Hall. Twice nightly. Prices, 6d. to 1s. 3d. Proscenium width, 22 ft. Phone, Louth 176. Station, Louth, L.N.E.R.

PLAYHOUSE (WE), Cannon Street.—Prop., Louth Playhouse, Ltd. 700 seats. Pictures and Drama. Twice nightly Mon., Thurs., Sat.; once Tues., Wed., Fri. Prices, 6d. to 1s. 3d. Stage, 16 ft. deep; six dressing-rooms. Proscenium width, 30 ft. Phone, Louth 333. Station, Louth, L.N.E.R.

LOWESTOFT (Suffolk), **Pop. 41,768.**
GRAND CINEMA (WE), London Road South— Prop., Grand Cinema (Lowestoft), Ltd. 1,034 seats. Booked at Hall. Continuous. Prices, 6d. to 1s. 6d. Phone, Lowestoft 445. Station, Lowestoft, Central, L.N.E.R.

HIPPODROME (BTH), Battery Green Road.— Prop., Yarmouth and Lowestoft Cinemas, Ltd., 16, South Quay, Gt. Yarmouth. Phone, Gt. Yarmouth 40. 1,135 seats. Booked at H.O. Continuous nightly. Daily Mat. Prices, 6d. to 1s. 6d. Proscenium width, 27 ft. Stage, 25 ft; six dressing-rooms. Phone, Lowestoft 456. Station, Lowestoft Central, L.N.E.R., also by Motor.

MARINA (WE).—Prop., Associated British Cinemas, Ltd., 30-31, Golden Square, London, W.1. 962 seats. Booked at H.O. Continuous. Prices, 6d. to 2s. Proscenium width, 34 ft. Stage, 25 ft. deep; eight dressing-rooms. Phone, No. 186. Station, Lowestoft Central, and Road Transport.

ODEON THEATRE.—Prop., Odeon Theatres Ltd. Cornhill House, Bennett Hill, Birmingham. Phone, Midland 2781. Continuous. Booked at 49, Park Lane, W.1. Prices, 6d to 2s.

PALACE CINEMA (BTH), Royal Plain.—Prop., Yarmouth and Lowestoft Cinemas, Ltd., 16, South Quay, Gt. Yarmouth. 1,635 seats., Continuous. Booked at H.O. Prices, 6d. to 1s. 6d. Café and Dance Hall attached. Station, Lowestoft, L.N.E.R.

PLAYHOUSE. (BTP), London Road South.— Prop., Ludlow Picture House Co., Ltd. 631 seats. Booked at H.O. Continuous. Prices, 5d. to 1s. 6d. Proscenium width, 23 ft. Stage, 24 ft. deep; five dressing-rooms. Buffet. Phone, Lowestoft 265. Station, Lowestoft Central, L.N.E.R., and Motor Transport.

LOWTOWN (near Pudsey) (Yorks).
PALACE.—Prop., Greene's Pictures (Pudsey), Ltd. Continuous. Two changes weekly. Phone Stanningley 71453. Station, Lowton, L.N.E.R.

LUDLOW (Shropshire), **Pop. 5,642.**
PICTURE HOUSE (BA), Castle Square.—Prop., Leominster Entertainments, Ltd. 630 seats. Man. Dir., J. B. Binmore. Booked at Hall. Continuous. Prices, 7d. to 2s. Proscenium width, 24ft. Phone, Ludlow 13. Station, Ludlow, G.W.R.

LUTON (Beds), **Pop. 68,526.**
ALMA THEATRE (WE).—Controlled by Union Cinemas, Ltd., Union House, 15, Regent Street, London, S.W.1. Phone, Whitehall 8484. Booked at H.O. Continuous, films and variety.

Put Pep into Programmes With PATHE PICTORIAL.

LUTON—Contd.

Prices, 6d. to 2s. 4d. Stage, 23ft.; six dressing-rooms. Café and ballroom attached. Phone, Luton 1901. Station, Luton, L.M.S. Films by transport.

C O M P T O N
ORGAN featured here.

EMPIRE CINEMA (WE), Bury Park Road.—Controlled by Union Cinemas, Ltd., Union House, 15, Regent Street, London, S.W.1. Phone, Whitehall 8484. Booked at H.O. Continuous. Prices, 6d. to 2s. Proscenium width, 16 ft. Phone, Luton 1440. Station, Luton, L.M.S.

PALACE THEATRE (WE), Mill Street.—Prop., General Theatre Corporation, Ltd. Managed by Gaumont-British Picture Corporation, Ltd., 123, Regent Street, London, W.1. 1,160 seats. Booked at H.O. Continuous. Prices, 1s. to 2s. Stage, 17 ft. deep; five dressing-rooms. Phone, Luton 443. Station, Luton, L.M.S.
Fitted "ARDENTE" Deaf Aids
See page 258

PICTUREDROME (WE), Park Street.—Controlled by Union Cinemas, Ltd., Union House, 15, Regent Street, London, S.W.1. Phone, Whitehall 8484. Booked at H.O. Continuous. Prices, 5d. to 1s. 6d. Phone No. 121. Station, Luton, L.M.S.

PLAZA (AWH), Hightown.—Props., Plaza Cinema, Ltd., Union House, 15, Regent Street, London, S.W.1. Phone, Whitehall 8484. Booked at H.O. Continuous. Occasional variety. Prices, 3d. to 1s. 3d. Proscenium width, 22 ft. Phone, 728. Station, Luton, L.M.S., and Herts and Beds Transport.

RITZ.—Controlled by Union Cinemas, Ltd., Union House, 15, Regent Street, London, S.W.1. Phone, Whitehall 8484. Booked at H.O. Continuous. Station, Luton, L.M.S.

WELLINGTON CINEMA (BA).—Lessee and Man., H. W. Mead. 400 seats. Booked at Hall by Lessee. Continuous. Two changes weekly. Prices, 5d. to 1s. 3d. Phone, Luton 2241. Station, Luton, L.M.S.

LUTTERWORTH (LEICS.), **Pop. 2,100.**
CATHOLIC HALL (Morrison).—300 seats.
EMPIRE PICTURE THEATRE (Morrison).—Prop., C. J. Spencer, 12, Bank Street, Lutterworth. Booked at Hall. Once nightly. Three shows Sat.d Occasional Variety. Prices, 9d. to 1s. 3 .

LYDBROOK (GLOS.), **Pop. 2,388.**
ANCHOR HALL CINEMA.—(Closed.)
MEMORIAL HALL (BA).—Prop., The Trustees of Lydbrook Memorial Hall. Phone, 203. Thurs., Fri. and Sat. shows. Booked by Hon. Sec., Sydney Miles. Prices, 6d. to 1s. 3d. Movable stage and four dressing-rooms. Station, Upper Lydbrook, L.M.S. Films by Road Transport.

LYDD (KENT), **Pop. 2,778.**
LYDD CINEMA (Phillips).—Prop., W. McCormack, "Whitegates," Littlestone-on-Sea. 300 seats. Once nightly. Booked at "Whitegates." 300 seats. Prices, 6d. to 1s. 6d. Station, Lydd, S.R.

LYDNEY (GLOS.), **Pop. 3,776.**
PICTURE HOUSE (BA).—Prop., Albany Ward

Theatres, Ltd., New Gallery House, 123. Regent Street, London, W.1. 515 seats. Booked at H.O. Two shows, Mon. and Thurs. once Tues., Wed. and Fri.; three on Sat. Prices, 6d. to 1s. 6d. Phone, Lydney 20; Station, Lydney Junction, G.W.R.

LYE (WORC.), **Pop. 12,245.**
TEMPERANCE HALL (Gyrotone), Church Street.—Prop., I. H. Entwistle, 181, High Street, Lye. 500 seats. Booked at Hall. Continuous. Prices, 4d. to 9d. Proscenium width, 20 ft. Phone, Lye 108. Station, Lye, G.W.R.
VICTORIA CINEMA, High Street.—Prop., William Capewell. 650 seats. Res. and Bkg. Man., R. E. Hoare. Continuous. Prices, 3d. to 8d.

LYME REGIS (DORSET), **Pop. 2,620.**
CINEMA (Mihaly).—Prop., H. and M. Cinemas, Ltd. Booked at Hall. Once nightly. Mats., Wed., Thurs., Sat. Prices, 6d. to 2s. 4d. Proscenium width, 22 ft. Phone, Lyme Regis 53. Station, Lyme Regis, S.R.

LYMINGTON (HANTS), **Pop. 5,157.**
LYRIC THEATRE (Kalee), St. Thomas Street.—Prop., Lymington and New Forest Entertainments, Ltd. 775 seats. Booked at Hall. One show nightly. Two on Wed. and Sat. Three changes weekly. Prices, 9d. to 1s. 6d. Proscenium width, 28 ft. Phone, Lymington 336. Station, Lymington Town, S.R.

LYMM (CHESHIRE), **Pop. 5,642.**
CINEMA (BTH), Church Road.—Prop., R. W. Fox and H. Thomason. 700 seats. Booked at Hall. Once nightly. Twice Sat. Occasional variety. Stage, 20 ft. deep; four dressing-rooms. Prices, 6d. to 1s. Proscenium width, 22 ft. Cafe attached. Phone, Lymm 128. Station, Lymm, L.M.S.

LYNDHURST (HANTS), **Pop. 2,560.**
PLAZA (BTH), High Street.—Prop., Victor Corbin, Jessamine House, Lyndhurst. Phone, 190. 260 seats. Once Mon., Tues. and Thurs., twice Wed., Fri., Sat. Prices, 6d. to 1s. 6d. Proscenium width, 15 ft. 10 in. Phone, Lyndhurst 70. Station, Lyndhurst Road, S.R.

LYNTON (DEVON), **Pop. 2,012.**
B.B. CINEMA (Morrison), Queen Street.—Prop., J. H. Blackhurst, West Down, nr. Ilfracombe. Phone, Ilfracombe 7. 198 seats. Booked at Hall. Twice nightly. Prices, 9d. to 2s. Proscenium width, 18 ft. Station, Mortehoe, S.R. Films by Transport to Bickington.

LYTHAM (LANCS), **Pop. 25,760.**
PALACE (WE), Clifton Street.—Prop., Blackpool Tower Co., Ltd., Empress Bldgs., Blackpool. Phone, Blackpool 1. 1,300 seats. Booked at H.O. Three shows daily, one. Sun. evening. Prices, 9d. to 1s. 6d. Proscenium width, 32 ft. Phone, Lytham 6281. Cafe attached. Station, Lytham, L.M.S.
Fitted "ARDENTE" Deaf Aids
See page 258

MABLETHORPE AND SUTTON (LINCS), **Pop. 3,928.**
VICTORIA CINEMA (BTH), Victoria Road.—Prop., A. H. Moore, Hillvue, Sutton-on-Sea, Lincs. Phone, Sutton-on-Sea, 70. 750 seats. Booked at Hall. Continuous. Prices, 6d. to 1s. 6d. Proscenium width, 24 ft. Phone, Mablethorpe 66. Station, Mablethorpe, L.N.E.R.

MACCLESFIELD (CHESHIRE), **Pop. 34,902.**
MAJESTIC PICTURE HOUSE (WE), Mill Street.—
Prop., Macclesfield Majestic Picture House,
Ltd. 1,022 seats. Booked at Hall. Con-
tinuous. Mon. to Fri., two shows Sat. Mats,
Mon., Wed. and Sat. Occasional Variety.
Prices, 6d. to 1s. 4d. Cafe attached. Phone,
2412. Station, Macclesfield, L.M.S.
NEW CINEMA (BTH), Buxton Road.—900 seats.
Booked at Hall. Continuous. Two shows Sat.
Mat., Wed. Prices, 6d. to 1s. 3d. Phone,
Macclesfield 3265. Station, Hibel Road,
L.M.S. \
NEW REGAL (RCA), Duke Street.—Props.,
Regal Picture Theatre (Macclesfield), Ltd.
400 seats. Booked at Hall. Continuous.
Three on Sat. Prices, 4d. to 9d. Phone, 2449.
Station, Hibel Road, Macclesfield.
PICTUREDROME (WE), Chestergate.—Prop.,
Macclesfield Majestic Picture House, Ltd.,
Mill Street, Macclesfield. 820 seats. Phone,
Blackfriars 4078. Continuous. Twice nightly
on Sat. Prices, 5d. to 1s. 3d. Phone,
Macclesfield 2412. Stations, Hibel Road,
L.M.S., and Central, L.N.E.R.
PREMIER PICTURE HOUSE (BTP).— Prop.,
Premier Picture House (Macclesfield), Ltd.
800 seats. Continuous. Two shows Sat.
Prices, 4d., 6d. and 9d. Phone, Macclesfield
2367. Station, Hibel Road, L.M.S.
RITZ—Controlled by Union Cinemas, Ltd.,
Union House, 15, Regent Street, London,
S.W.1. Phone, Whitehall 8484. Booked at
R.O.

MADELEY (SALOP).
PARKHURST CINEMA (Gyrotone).

MAIDENHEAD (BERKS), **Pop. 17,520.**
PICTURE THEATRE, Bridge Street.—Controlled
by Union Cinema Co., Ltd., Union House, 15,
Lower Regent Street, London, S.W.1. Phone,
Gerrard 6363. Booked at H.O. Continuous.
Sundays, once nightly. Prices, 6d, to 1s. 3d.
Phone, 277. Station, Maidenhead, G.W.R.
Films by Road Transport.
PLAZA THEATRE (WE), Queen Street.—Con-
trolled by Union Cinemas, Ltd., Union
House, 15, Lower Regent Street, London,
S.W.1. Phone, Whitehall 8484. Booked at
H.O. Continuous. Sundays, once nightly.
Prices, 9d. to 2s. Phone, Maidenhead 277.
Station, Maidenhead, G.W.R.

WURLITZER ORGAN
Installed in this Kinema

RIALTO PICTURE THEATRE (WE), Bridge Street.
—Controlled by Union Cinemas, Ltd.,
Union House, 15, Lower Regent Street,
London, S.W.1. Phone, Whitehall 8484.
Continuous, Sundays, once nightly. Booked
at H.O. Prices, 6d. to 2s. Proscenium width,
33 ft. Café attached. Phone 1850.. Station,
Maidenhead, G.W.R. Films by Road Trans-
port.
RITZ—Controlled by Union Cinemas, Ltd.,
Union House, 15, Regent Street, London,
S.W.1. Phone, Whitehall 8484. Booked at
H.O. Prices, 9d. to 1s. 6d. Phone 1850.
Station, Maidenhead, G.W.R.

MAIDSTONE (KENT), **Pop. 42,259.**
CENTRAL PICTURE PLAYHOUSE (WE).—King
Street.—Controlled by Union Cinemas,
Ltd., Union House, 15, Regent Street,
London, S.W.1. Phone, Whitehall 8484.
Booked at H.O. Continuous. Prices, 7d. to

2s. Phone, Maidstone 3507. Café and dance
hall attached. All films by Kent Motor
Film Transport Co.
EMPIRE CINEMA (BTP), Earl Street.—Prop.,
A. C. Simmonds, "Oaklands," Sutton Road,
Maidstone. 400 seats. Booked at Hall.
Continuous. Mat., Wed. and Sat. Prices,
4d. to 1s. 3d. Proscenium width, 25 ft.
Station, Maidstone East, S.R.
GRANADA (WE).—Prop., Granada Theatres, Ltd.
Controlled by Bernstein Theatres, Ltd.,
36, Golden Square, London, W.1. Phone,
Gerrard 3554. 2,000 seats. Booked at H.O.
Continuous. Pictures and variety. Phone,
Maidstone 3838. Station, Maidstone.
PALACE THEATRE (WE), Gabriel's Hill.—Con-
trolled by Union Cinemas, Ltd., Union
House, 15, Regent Street, London, S.W.1.
Phone, Whitehall 8484. Booked at H.O.
Continuous. Prices, 6d. to 2s. Proscenium
width, 23 ft. Phone, Maidstone 3507.
RITZ (WE).—Controlled by Union Cinemas, Ltd.,
Union House, 15, Regent Street, London,
S.W.1. Phone, Whitehall 8484. Booked at
H.O. Prices, 6d. to 2s. Continuous. Pro-
scenium width, 50 ft. Phone, 3507. All Films
by Kent Motor Film Transport Co., Maidstone.

C O M P T O N
ORGAN featured here.

MALDON (ESSEX), **Pop. 6,559.**
EMBASSY (WE).— Prop., Shipman and King,
Shellmex House, Strand, W.C.2. Phone,
Temple Bar 5077. Booked at H.O. Continuous.
Mat. Wed., Thurs., Sat. Prices, 6d. to 2s.
HIPPODROME (WE).—Props., Shipman and King,
M.84, Shellmex House, Strand, London, W.C.2.
Phone. Temple Bar 5077. Booked at H.O.
Nightly. Mat., Wed. and Sat. Stage, 6 ft.
deep ; 3 dressing rooms. Prices, 3d. to 10d.
Proscenium width, 19 ft. Phone, Maldon 168.
Station, Maldon East, L.N.E.R.

WURLITZER ORGAN
Installed in this Kinema

MALMESBURY (WILTS.), **Pop. 2,334.**
ATHELSTAN CINEMA (BTP).—Prop., J. L. Mott,
10, Oxford Street, Malmesbury. 300 seats.
Phone, Malmesbury 152. Booked at H.O.
Twice nightly, Mon., Thurs., Sat., one show
Tues., Wed., Fri. Prices, 6d. to 1s. 6d. Pros-
cenium width, 30 ft. Station, Malmesbury,
G.W.R. and Film Transport.

MALTBY (YORKS), **Pop. 10,013.**
PICTURE HOUSE (Morrison), Muglet Lane.—
Prop., Maltby Picture House Co., Ltd., 35,
College Street, Rotherham. Phone, Rother-
ham 129. 980 seats. Booked at "Briar-
dene," Armthorpe Road, Doncaster. Twice
nightly, except Tues. and Wed. Prices, 5d.
to 1s. Proscenium width, 26 ft. Station,
Maltby, L.M.S. Films by Bradford and
Leeds Transport Co.

MALTON (YORKS), **Pop. 4,418.**
PALACE (WE).—Prop., C. S. Read, Broughton
Rise, Malton. 450 seats. Booked at Hall.
Continuous. Prices, 6d. to 1s. 3d. Phone,
Malton 173. Films by Road Transport.
MAJESTIC P.T. (WE).—Prop., C. S. Read. 800
seats. Continuous. Pictures and Variety.
Prices, 6d. to 1s. 3d. Phone, Malton 173.
Station, Malton, Yorks.; L.N.E.R., and Road
Transport.

PATHETONE WEEKLY, The Super Screen Magazine!

MALVERN (Worc.), **Pop. 15,632.**
PICTURE HOUSE (BA).—Lessee, Roy Limbert.
Direction, Ad-Visers, Ltd., Panton House, 25,
Haymarket, London, S.W.1. Phone, White-
hall 3332. 700 seats. Continuous. Prices, 6d.
to 1s. 6d. Phone, Malvern 777. Station, Gt.
Malvern, G.W.R.

MALVERN THEATRE (WE).—Lessee, Roy Limbert,
Ad-Visers, Ltd., Panton House, 25, Haymarket, London, S.W.1. Phone, Whitehall
3332. 918 seats. Films booked by R. W.
Limbert at Panton House, and Stage Shows
by Ad-Visers, Ltd. Continuous. Prices,
6d. to 3s. 6d. Stage 30 ft. deep; eight
dressing-rooms. Café attached. Phone, Malvern 777. Station, Gt. Malvern, G.W.R.

MALVERN LINK (Worc.), **Pop. 5,330.**
LINK PICTURE THEATRE (BA).—Lessee, Roy
Limbert, Direction, Ad-Visers, Ltd., Panton
House, 25, Haymarket, London, S.W.1.
Phone,.Whitehall 3332. 300 seats. Booked
at H.O. Continuous from 6 p.m. Prices, 7d.
to 1s. Phone, Malvern 999. Station, Malvern
Link, G.W.R.

MANCHESTER (Lancs.), **Pop. 766,333.**
ADELPHI CINEMA (BTP), Dean Lane, Moston.—
Prop., Victory Pictures, Manchester, Ltd.
700 seats. Man. Dir., H. D. Moorhouse.
Booked at Imperial Buildings, Oxford Road,
Manchester, by Man. Dir. Prices, 4d. to 9d.
Phone, Failsworth 1065. Station, Newton
Heath (Dean Lane).

ALHAMBRA THEATRE (BTP), Higher Openshaw.—
Prop., Alhambra (Manchester), Ltd. Phone,
Ardwick 2226. Man. Dir., H. D. Moorhouse.
2,000 seats. Continuous. Mat., Mon., Wed.,
Thurs. and Sat. Two changes weekly. Prices,
3d. to 1s. Phone, Droylsden 651. Station,
Gorton, L.N.E.R.

ALHAMBRA PAVILION, H. D. Moorhouse Circuit,
7, Oxford Road, Manchester. Phone, Ardwick 2226.

AMBASSADOR SUPER CINEMA (BTH), Langworthy
Road, Pendleton.—(PROP.), Ambassador Super
Cinema, Ltd., 13, St. Ann Street, Manchester.
Blackfriars 3731. 1,800 seats. Booked at
H.O. Continuous. Prices, 6d. to 1s. 6d.
Proscenium width, 40 ft. Stage, 16 ft.; six
dressing-rooms. Variety booked by A.
Pattman, Oxford Road, Manchester. Café
attached. Phone, Pendleton 1601. Station,
Pendleton, L.M.S.

ANCOATS PICTUREDROME (WE), Palmerston
Street.—800 seats. Booked at Hall. Twice
nightly. Three weekly. Prices, 2½d. to 6d.
Phone, Ardwick 2670.

ARCADIA (WE), Yew Tree Avenue, Levenshulme.
Prop., Northern Amusements Ltd., Prudential
Chambers, South Parade, Rochdale. Tel.
No. 2072. 989 seats. Booked at Hall.
Continuous nightly Mon. to Fri. Two shows
Sat. Two changes weekly. Prices, 4d. to 1s.
Proscenium width. 24 ft. Phone, Rusholme
4653. Station, Levenshulme, L.M.S.

ARDWICK PICTURE THEATRE (BTH), Ardwick
Green.—Prop., Associated British Cinemas,
Ltd., 30-31, Golden Square, W.1. 1,637
seats. Three shows daily. Prices, 3d. to
1s. Phone, Ardwick 3059. Station
London Road, L.M.S.

BLACKLEY EMPIRE (BA), Blackley.—Prop.,
Blackley Electric Theatre, Ltd., 2, Cathedral
House, Manchester. Booked by L. G. Bailey.
Two shows nightly. Two changes weekly.
Phone, Collyhurst 2024.

BUTLER ELECTRIC THEATRE (BTH), Butler
Street. 900 seats. Booked at Theatre. Two
shows nightly. Four Mats. weekly. Prices,
2d. to 6d.

CAPITOL (WE), Didsbury.—Controlled by Union
Cinemas, Ltd., 15, Regent Street, London,
S.W.1. Pictures and variety. Films booked
at H.O. Continuous. Mon. to Fri. Three
shows Sat. Prices, 6d. to 2s. Stage, 40 ft.
deep; eight dressing-rooms. Proscenium
width, 45 ft. Cafe attached. Phone, Didsbury
2464. Station, Didsbury, L.M.S.

CAPITOL TALKIE THEATRE (WE), Princess Road,
Moss Side, Manchester. 1,547 seats. Three
shows daily. Phone, Moss Side 1988. Station,
London Road, L.M.S.

CARLTON SUPER CINEMA (BTH), Aston New
Road, Clayton. Prop., Carlton Super Cinema,
Ltd., 13, St. Ann Street, Manchester. Phone,
Blackfriars 3731. 1,300 seats. Booked at
H.O. Pictures and Variety. Continuous.
Prices, 6d. to 1s. Stage, 14 ft. deep; six
dressing-rooms. Proscenium width, 35 ft.
Café attached. Phone, East 0257.

CASINO CINEMA (RCA), Wilmslow Road,
Rusholme.—Prop.,Associated British Cinemas,
30-31, Golden Square, London, W.1. 1,612
seats. Booked at H.O. Continuous evenings. Daily Mat. Café and Ballroom attached. , 4d. to 1s. Proscenium
width, 35 fices Phone, Rusholme 4465.
Stations, Central and London Road, L.M.S.

CEYLON PICTURE HOUSE (Picturetone), Ceylon
Street, Newton Heath.—Prop., Wilkinson,
Pickering & Co., Apsley House, Mossley,
nr. Manchester. Phone, Mossley 78. 550
seats. Booked at H.O. Continuous, Mon.
to Fri. Sat., twice nightly. Prices, 3d. to 6d.
Phone, Collyhurst 1006. Station, Newton
Heath, L.M.S.

CINEMA (BTP), Seedley.—H. D. Moorhouse
Circuit, 7, Oxford Road, Manchester. Phone,
Ardwick 2226.

CLAREMONT SUPER CINEMA (WE), Claremont
Road, Moss Side.—Prop., Associated British
Cinemas, Ltd., 30-31, Golden Square,
London, W.1. Phone, Gerrard 7887. 1,699
seats. Booked at H.O. Three shows daily.
Two changes weekly. Prices, 4d. to 1s.
Phone, Moss Side 2866.

COLISEUM (WE), Ardwick Green.—Prop.,
Coliseum (Manchester), Ltd., 20, Brazennose
Street, Manchester. 1,787 seats. Continuous.
Prices, 3d. to 6d. Phone, Ardwick 3150.
Station, London Road, L.M.S.

COLLEGE PICTUR HOUSE (BTP), Coupland
Street, Chorlton-on-Medlock.—Prop., Dorothy
Millar. Phone, Chorlton 1898. 1,000 seats.
Booked at Hall. Continuous. Prices, 4d. to
7d. Proscenium width, 26 ft. Phone, Ard-
wick 2006.

CORONA PICTURE THEATRE (BA), Birch Street,
West Gorton.—Prop., Gaumont British
Pictures Corpn., Ltd., 123, Regent Street,
London, W.1. Phone, Regent 8080. 1,100
seats. Booked at H.O. Continuous. Two
changes weekly. Prices, 4d. to 1s. Proscen-
ium width, 27ft. Phone, East 0369. Station,
London Road, L.N.E.R.

COSMO CINEMA (WE), Wellington Street, Gorton. Controlled by Union Cinemas, Ltd., 15, Regent Street, S.W.1. Phone, Whitehall 8484. Booked at H.O. Continuous. Prices, 4d. to 9d. Phone, East 0243. Station, London Road, Manchester.

CRESCENT CINEMA (Picturetone), Chapman Street, Hulme.—Prop., Picture Hall (Hulme), Ltd. 1,200 seats. Twice nightly. Two changes weekly. Booked at Hall. Prices, 4d. to 9d. Phone, Moss Side 2042. Station, Central.

CROMWELL PICTURE HOUSE (WE), Pendleton.— Prop., Cromwell Picture House, Ltd. 1,155 seats. Continuous. Prices, 3d. to 1s. Phone, Pendleton 1165. Station, Pendleton, L.M.S.

DEANSGATE PICTURE HOUSE (WE).—Prop. Deansgate Picturehouse (1936), Ltd. Seats 862. Booked at Hall. Continuous. Prices, 6d. to 2s. Cafe and ballroom attached. Phone, Deansgate 5252/3.

DEVONSHIRE CINEMA (WE), Boughton.— New Devonshire Theatre (Salford) Co., Ltd., 44, Corporation Street, Manchester. Phone, Blackfriars 3972. 1,300 seats.

DON CINEMA THEATRE (BTP), BESWICK.— Controlled by Union Cinemas, Ltd., 15, Regent Street, S.W.1. Phone, Whitehall 8484. Booked at H.O. Continuous. Prices, 4d. to 8d. Proscenium width, 28 ft. Phone, Ardwick 2926. Station, Victoria, Manchester, L.M.S.

ELLESMERE CINEMA.—East Lancashire Road, Worsley.

EMPIRE PICTURE THEATRE (WE), Higher Broughton.—Prop., Red Rose Cinemas, Ltd., Palace Picture House, Whitefield. Phone, Whitefield 37. 1,900 seats. Booked at H.O. Continuous. Twice nightly Sat. Prices, 6d. to 9d. Phone, Broughton 2652. Station, Manchester.

EMPRESS ELECTRIC THEATRE (PTA), Oldham Road.—Prop., C. and H. Talbot. 1,200 seats. Twice nightly. Two changes weekly. Prices, 3d. to 9d. Phone, Collyhurst 1490.

EMPRESS PICTURE PLACE (WE). 775 seats.

FORUM THEATRE (WE), Wythenshawe.—Props., Associated British Cinemas, Ltd., 30-31, Golden Square, W.1. 1,904 seats. Booked at H.O. Pictures and variety. Continuous evenings. Mats., Mons., Wed., Thurs., Sat. Twice nightly Sats. Booked at H.O. Prices, 6d. to 1s. 6d. Stage, 18 ft. 6 in. deep. Three dressing-rooms. Cafe and Ballroom attached. Phone, Wythenshawe 2408. Station, Northenden.

FREE TRADE HALL.—Prop., Manchester Corporation, Town Hall, Manchester. Occasional shows only.

GAIETY THEATRE (RCA), Peter Street.—Prop., Associated British Cinemas, Ltd., 30-31, Golden Square, London, W.1. Phone, Gerrard 7887. 1,434 seats. Booked at H.O. Continuously. Prices, 6d. to 2s. Phone, City 6215. Station, Manchester (Central), L.M.S.

GAUMONT (WE).—Prop., Gaumont British Picture Corpn., Ltd. 2,300 seats. Booked at H.O. Pictures and variety. Variety booked at H.O. Prices, 1s. 3d. to 3s. 6d. Continuous. Proscenium width, 50 ft. Stage, 23ft. deep. Nine dressing-rooms. Cafe and restaurant attached. Phone, Central 1323. Station, Manchester.

Fitted "ARDENTE" Deaf Aids
See page 258

WURLITZER ORGAN
Installed in this Kinema

GLOBE (BTP), Cornbrook Street, Old Trafford.— Prop., North-Western Entertainments, Ltd. Booked at Imperial Buildings, 7, Oxford Road, Manchester. 1,250 seats. Continuous. Two changes weekly. Prices, 3d. and 6d. Phone, Moss Side 2512. Stations, Manchester termini.

GLOBE (BTP), Thomas Street, Cheetham Hill.— Props., Globe Theatre Co. (Manchester), Ltd. Booked by H.D. Moorhouse Circuit. 750 seats. Continuous. Two changes weekly. Prices, 3d. to 6d. Phone, Cheetham Hill 2537. Station, Crumpsall, L.M.S.

GRAND JUNCTION THEATRE (BTP), Warwick Street, Hulme.—Props., J. & C. Lever, Hulme Hippodrome, Manchester. 1,120 seats. Pictures and Variety. Booked at H.O. Continuous Mon. to Fri. Twice nightly Sat. Prices, 3d. to 1s. Proscenium width, 30 ft. Phone, Moss Side 1351. Station, Manchester.

GRAND THEATRE (WE), Stockport Road, Levenshulme.—Props., Trevelyan Cinemas, Ltd. 687 seats. Booked at Hall. Continuous. Two changes weekly. Prices, 6d. to 1s. Phone, Rusholme 1108. Film Transport.

GREEN HILL CINEMA (BTP), Cheetham Hill Road. —Prop., Lessee E. J. Linsdell. 550 seats. Booked at Hall. Continuous Mon. to Fri. Twice nightly Sat. Two changes weekly. Prices, 3d. to 6d. Phone, Cheetham 1839. Station, Victoria.

GROSVENOR PICTURE PALACE (BTP), Oxford Road, All Saints.—Props., New Grosvenor (Manchester), Ltd., Imperial Buildings, Oxford Road, Manchester. Man. Dir., H. D. Moorhouse, J.P. 1,000 seats. Pictures. Booked at H.O. Twice nightly. Mat. daily. Prices, 6d. and 1s. Phone, Ardwick 3175. Stations, Victoria, London Road, Exchange, and Central.

HEATON PARK CINEMA (BTH), Bury Old Road. —Props., Heaton Park Cinema, Ltd., 13, St. Ann Street, Manchester. Phone, Blackfriars 3731. Pictures and Variety. Films booked at H.O., 13, St. Ann Street, Manchester, and Variety by A. Patman, General Variety Agency, Oxford Street, Manchester. Continuous Mon. to Fri. Two shows Sat. Mat., Mon., Wed. and Sat. Prices, 4d. to 1s. 2d. Stage, 6 ft. deep; two dressing-rooms. Cafe attached. Phone, Prestwich 1535. Station, Heaton Park, L.M.S.

PALACE CINEMA (BTP).—Props., Manchester Ice Rink, Ltd., Derby Street, Manchester. 2,000 seats. Booked at H.O. Prices, 2d. to 4d. Twice nightly. Phone, Blackfriars 9698. Station, Victoria, L.M.S.

IMPERIAL PICTURE THEATRE AND CAFE (WE), Chorlton Road, Brooks's Bar. Props., Cinemas (Manchester), Ltd., 20, Brazennose Street. Phone, Blackfriars 6965. 760 seats. Booked at H.O. Twice nightly. Mats., Mon., Wed., and Sat. Prices, 7d. to 1s. Phone, Moss Side 2735. Stage, 5 ft. deep; two dressing-rooms. Cafe attached. Phone 16. Station, Manchester Central.

PATHE PICTORIAL—Novel, Entertaining, Unique.

MANCHESTER—Contd.

JUNCTION THEATRE(BTP),Hulme.—Lessees, J. & C. Lever, Hippodrome, Hulme. Phone, Moss Side 1351. Booked at H.O. 1,200 seats. Continuous. Prices, 4d. to 9d. Proscenium width, 34 ft.

KING'S CINEMA (BTP), Longsight.—Props., Shaftesbury Cinemas Co., Ltd., Imperial Buildings, 7, Oxford Road, Manchester. Booked by H. D. Moorhouse Circuit. Continuous Mon. to Fri. Twice nightly Sat. Prices, 6d. to 1s. Proscenium width, 30 ft. Phone, Rusholme 4655. Station, Longsight.

KINGSWAY SUPER CINEMA (BTH), Levenshulme. —Controlled by Union Cinemas, Ltd., 15, Regent Street, London, S.W.1. Phone, Whitehall 8484. Pictures and Variety. Booked at H.O. Continuous. Prices, 6d. to 1s. 6d. Proscenium width, 42 ft. Stage, 16 ft. deep; six dressing-rooms. Cafe attached. Phone, Rusholme 2891. Station, Levenshulme.

LA SCALA (WE), Oxford Road.—Props., Associated British Cinemas, Ltd., Golden Square, W.1. 2,200 seats. Booked at H.O. Continuous. Pictures and Variety. Prices, 6d. to 1s. Proscenium width, 40 ft. Stage, 8 ft. deep. Phone, Ardwick 3559. Café attached. Stations, Manchester Termini.

LIDO SUPER CINEMA (WE), Didsbury.—Props., Anglo-Scottish Theatres, Ltd., 2, Cavendish Square, W.1. Pictures and Variety. Booked at " Pyramid," Sale. Prices, 6d. to 1s. 6d. Proscenium width, 36 ft. Stage, 15 ft. deep ; five dressing-rooms. Phone, Heaton Moor 2244. Café attached. Station, Manchester.

LYCEUM CINEMA (WE), City Road, Old Trafford. —Props., W. Stansfield & Co. 620 seats. Booked by H. D. Moorhouse. Continuous. Prices, 3d. to 9d. Phone, Trafford Park 1597. Station, Old Trafford, L.M.S.

MAYFAIR CINEMA.

MARKET STREET PICTURE HOUSE (WE).— Props., Oxford Street and Market Street (Manchester) Cinemas, Ltd. Phone, Deansgate 4771. 620 seats. Booked by J. F. Emery Circuit, Midland Bank House, Cross Street, Manchester. Phone, Blackfriars 0472. Continuous. Prices, 1s. to 2s. Café attached. Station, London Road.

MOSLEY PICTURE HOUSE (BTH), Stott Street, Beswick.—Props., Mrs. W. N. Watts, and J. U. Tune. 600 seats. Booked at Hall by Man. Two shows nightly. Prices, 3d. to 6d. Phone, East 0140. Stations, Manchester termini.

MOSTON IMPERIAL PALACE (WE), Hartley Street, —Props.,Moston Imperial Palace, Ltd. 1,400 seats. Booked at Hall. Continuous. Prices, 4d. to 9d. Proscenium width, 22 ft. Phone, Collyhurst 2160. Station, Victoria, L.M.S.

NEW CENTRAL (Picturedrome), Paley Street, Collyhurst.—Props., Emery and Wilkinson. 570 seats. Twice nightly. Two changes weekly. Prices, 2d. to 5d. Station, Manchester, L.M.S.

NEW MANCHESTER HIPPODROME (WE), Ardwick. —Stoll Circuit.

NEW OXFORD THEATRE (WE), Oxford Street.— Props., Oxford Street and Market Street (Manchester) Cinemas, Ltd. Phone, Central 3402. 1,150 seats. Booked by Emery's Circuit, Midland Bank House, Cross Street, Manchester. Continuous. Prices, 1s. to 2s. Phone, Blackfriars 7876.

NEW PALACE (BTP), Farmside Place, Stockpor Road, Levenshulme.—Props., Trustees o J. Harrison. 1,200 seats. Continuous. Two changes weekly. Prices, 6d. to 1s.

NEW POPULAR PICTURE HOUSE (Electrocord), Chapman Street, Hulme.—Props., A. L. Ward and A. C. Goulden, 6, Brown Street, Manchester. 400 seats. Booked at H.O. Twice nightly. Prices, 4d. to 6d. Phone, Moss Side 2158.

NEW ROYAL PICTURE THEATRE (RCA), Ashton New Road.—Props., Associated British Cinemas, Ltd., 30/31, Golden Square, London, W.1. Phone, Gerrard 7887. 1,244 seats. Booked at H.O. Continuous Mon. to Fri. Twice nightly Sat. Daily Mat. Prices, 5d. to 1s. Phone, East 0374. Stations, Manchester termini.

NEWS THEATRE.

OLYMPIA (WE), Hyde Road, Gorton.—Props. Gorton and District Cinemas, Ltd. 750 seats. Booked by Bert Abbott, at Regent, Fallowfield. Continuous. Three shows Sat. Stage, 12 ft. deep ; two dressing-rooms. Prices, 4d. to 11d. Phone, East 0436. Stations, Belle Vue and Hyde Road.

OSBORNE THEATRE (BTP), Oldham Road.— H. D. Moorhouse Circuit 7, Oxford Road, Manchester. Phone, Ardwick 2226. Booked at H.O. Continuous. Sat. twice nightly. Prices, 3d. to 9d. Phone, Collyhurst 1491. 1,571 seats.

PALACE CINEMA (WE), Collyhurst Street, Rochdale Road.—Props., Palace (Collyhurst), Ltd. 800 seats. Booked at Scala, Bury. Continuous. Mat., Mon. and Sat. Prices, 3d. to 6d. Phone, Collyhurst 2480. Station, Victoria, L.M.S.

PALACE, Levenshulme.—H. D. Moorhouse Circuit, 7, Oxford Road, Manchester. Phone, Ardwick 2226.

PALAIS DE LUXE (WE), Barlow Moor Road, Chorlton-cum-Hardy.—Props., Palais De Luxe (Chorlton), Ltd. Gen. and Bkg. Man., Sam Parkinson. 1,200 seats. Continuous. Three shows Sat. Two changes weekly. Prices, 6d. to 1s. 3d. Phone, Chorlton 635. Station, Chorlton-cum-Hardy.

PALATINE PICTURE HOUSE (BTP), Palatine Road, Withington.—Props., South Manchester Picture Co., Ltd. H. D. Moorhouse Circuit. Continuous Mon. to Fri. Twice on Sat. Mats., Mon., Thurs. and Sat. Two changes weekly. Prices, 6d. to 1s. Phone, Didsbury 3605.

PALLADIUM (WE), Rochdale Road. — Props., Blackley Palais De Danse, Ltd. 1,750 seats. Pictures and Variety. Films booked by F. E. Spring, 3, Parsonage, Manchester. Phone, Blackfriars 7905 ; and Variety by Percy Hall's Agency, Oxford Road, Manchester. Twice nightly ; Mats., Mon., Wed. and Sat. Prices, 5d. to 1s. 3d. Proscenium width, 40 ft. Stage, 12 ft. deep ; five dressing-rooms. Café and Dance Hall attached. Phone, Collyhurst 1058. Station, London Road, L.M.S.

PARAMOUNT THEATRE (WE), Oxford Street.— Props., Paramount (Manchester) Theatre, Ltd. 2,914 seats. Booked at Paramount Theatres, 104-8, Oxford Street, London, W.1. Continuous. Prices, 1s. 4d. to 3s. 6d. Phone, Manchester Central 3984/6. Café attached. All Manchester stations.

WURLITZER ORGAN
Installed in this Kinema

PAVILION (BTH), Church Street, Newton Heath.—Prop., Central Cinema Co. (Newton Heath), Ltd. 1,000 seats. Two shows nightly Mon. and Sat., continuous rest of week. Two changes weekly. Station, Dean Lane, L.M.S.

PICCADILLY THEATRE (WE).—Prop., Piccadilly Picture Theatre (Manchester), Ltd., 11, Piccadilly, Manchester. Phone, Deansgate 2516. 2,324 seats. Booked at H.O. Continuous. Prices, 1s. to 2s. 4d. Proscenium width, 38 ft. Café and Ballroom attached. Phone, Deansgate 2517. Stations, Manchester (all).

PLAYHOUSE (RCA), Oldham Road, Miles Platting.—Prop., Associated British Cinemas, Ltd., 30-31, Golden Square, London, W.1. Phone, Gerrard 7887. 1,847 seats. Booked at H.O. Continuous. Prices, 4d. to 9d. Phone, Collyhurst 2878. Station, Miles Platting, L.M.S.

PLAZA (BTP), West Gorton.—Prop., Amusall's, Ltd. 640 seats. Booked by F. Rigg, Parsonage, Manchester. Twice nightly. Prices, 3d. to 9d. Phone, East 0425. Station, Manchester.

PLAZA (PTA).—Prop., J. Sereno. 1,100 seats. Two shows nightly. Two changes weekly. Prices, 3d. to 9d. Station, Exchange.

POPULAR PICTURE PALACE (BTH), Wilson Street, Miles Platting.—Prop., Miles Platting I.L.P., 2A, Enoch Street, Miles Platting. Phone, Collyhurst 2601. 400 seats. Booked by E. J. Howarth. Two shows nightly, three mats. weekly. Prices, 3d. to 5d. Station, Miles Platting, L.M.S.

PREMIER CINEMA (WE), Cheetham Hill Road.—Prop., Associated British Cinemas, Ltd., 30-31, Golden Square, W.1. 1,887 seats. Booked at H.O. Continuous Mon. to Fri. Twice Sat. Prices, 4d. to 1s. 6d. Phone, Cheetham Hill 2076. Café attached. Station, Victoria, L.M.S.

PRINCE'S CINEMA (BTP), Grey Mare Lane.—Prop., Prince's Cinema (Openshaw), Ltd. Continuous Mon. to Fri. Twice Sat. Booked by H. D. Moorhouse Circuit. 1,557 seats. Proscenium width, 28 ft. Prices, 4d. to 9d. Phone, East 0641. Stations, Manchester termini.

PRINCESS CINEMA (BTP), Conran Street, Harpurhey.—Prop., Blackley Palais de Danse, Ltd., Rochdale Road, Harpurhey. 800 seats. Booked by F. Spring, 3, The Parsonage, Manchester. Twice nightly. Mats., Sat. Prices, 3d. to 9d. Phone, Collyhurst 2025.

PRINCESS PICTURE THEATRE (BTP), Raby Street, Moss Side.—Prop., G. S. Smith. 540 seats. Booked at Hall. Two shows nightly. Prices, 4d. to 9d. Phone, Moss Side 2724. Stations, London Road, Central and Victoria.

PUBLIC HALL, Alderley Edge.

QUEEN'S PICTURE HOUSE (WE), Ashton Old Road.—Prop., Associated British Cinemas, Ltd., 30-31, Golden Square, W.1. 1,205 seats. Booked at H.O. Three shows daily. Prices, 3d. to 9d. Phone, East 1040. Stations Mayfield or London Road, L.M.S.

QUEEN'S PICTURE THEATRE (WE), Stockport Road, Longsight. — Prop., Cinemas (Manchester), Ltd., 40, Brazennose Street, Manchester. Phone, Central 3620. Booked by Chas. Ogden, Palatine Buildings, Manchester. Twice nightly. Two changes weekly. Prices, 6d. to 1s. Phone, Rusholme

1004. Station, London Road, L.M.S. Films collected Manchester offices.

REGAL (BTP), Rochdale Road.—Prop., Mostyn Sereno. 600 seats. Continuous Sat, twice n ht . Mat., Mon. and Thurs. Prices, 3d. to 6dly

Fitted "ARDENTE" Deaf Aids
See page 258

REGENT SUPER CINEMA (BTH), Princes Road South.—Props., Gorton District Cinemas. Ltd. 1,200 seats. Pictures and Variety. Booked by Bert Abbott, Gen. Man. at Hall. Continuous. Prices, 6d. to 1s. 3d. Stage, 18 ft. deep; six dressing-rooms. Phone, Moss Side 1955. Station, Manchester (Welbraham Road Halt).

REX PICTURE HALL (BTH), Ashton Old Road.—Prop., Openshaw Picture Hall Co., Ltd. 600 seats. Booked at Imperial Buildings, 7, Oxford Road, Manchester. Continuous. Two changes weekly. Prices, 3d. to 6d. Phone East 0162. Station Manchester, L.M.S.

RIALTO (WE), Bury New Road, Higher Broughton. Prop., Associated British Cinemas, Ltd. 1,400 seats. Continuous. Prices, 6d. to 1s. Proscenium width, 40 ft. Stage, 13 ft. deep; seven dressing rooms. Phone, 1367. Café attached. Station, Victoria, L.M.S.

RIVIERA (WE), Cheetham Hill.—Prop., Anglo-Scottish Theatres, Ltd., 2, Cavendish Square, W.1. Pictures and Variety. 2,200 seats. Booked at Pyramid Sale. Variety booked by A. Pattman, Oxford Road, Manchester. Continuous. Prices, 6d. to 1s. Stage, 18 ft. deep; 4 dressing-rooms. Station, Manchester.

RIVOLI (RCA) Collyhurst. Prop., Ben Kanter. Booked at Hall. 1,194 seats. Continuous Mon. to Fri. Twice nightly. Prices, 4d. to 9d. Proscenium width, 45 ft. Phone, Collyhurst 1280. Station, London Road.

RIVOLI CINEMA, Denmark Road, Rusholme.—Prop., Rivoli Estates, Ltd., 44, Corporation Street, Manchester. 1,250 seats. Booked at Hall. Continuous. Prices, 4d. to 1s. Stage, 18 ft. deep; three dressing-rooms. Phone, Ardwick 1452. Station, Manchester Central.

RIVOLI (RCA) GORTON.—Prop., Ben Kanter. 1,512 seats. Booked at Manchester. Prices, 4d. to 1s. Continuous. Twice Sat. Phone, East 0404.

RIVOLI, Barlow Moor Road.—Prop., Ben Kanter. 1,520 seats.

ROYAL CINEMA (Picturetone), Buckley Street, Rochdale Road.—Prop., A. Wilkinson and J. Mooney. 600 seats. Two shows nightly. Two changes weekly. Prices, 2d. to 5d. Station, Victoria, L.M.S.

ROYAL PICTURE THEATRE, Pendleton. — Booked at 26, Cross Street, Manchester, by J. F. Emery. 780 seats.

ROY PICTUREDROME (Picturetone), Ashton Old Road, Ardwick.—Prop., G. Dewhurst. 600 seats.

SAVOY CINEMA (RCA), Manchester Road, Chorlton-cum-Hardy.—Prop., Associated British Cinemas, Ltd., 30-31, Golden Square, London, W.1. Phone, Gerrard 7887. 1,500 seats. Continuous. Mat., Mon., Wed. and Sat. Prices, 7d. to 1s. 3d. Phone, Chorlton 3708. Station, Chorlton, L.M.S.

SAVOY PICTURE PALACE (BTP), Renshaw Street, Hyde Road, West Gorton.—J. F. Emery Circuit, 26, Cross Street, Manchester. 500 seats. Twice nightly. Prices, 4d. to 6d. Phone, East 1004. Station, Manchester.

The Pick Of Variety And Radio Stars In PATHETONE WEEKLY.

MANCHESTER—Contd.

SCALA PALACE (WE), Wilmslow Road, Withington.—Prop., Withington Cinemas, Ltd., 44, John Dalton Street, Manchester, Phone, Blackfriars 2643. 675 seats. Booked at Hall. Continuous. Two shows Sat. Two changes weekly. Prices, 5d to 1s. Proscenium width, 18 ft. Phone, Didsbury 3301.

SHAFTESBURY CINEMA THEATRE (BTP), Stockport Road. — Prop., Shaftesbury Cinema Theatre Co. (Manchester), Ltd. 1,200 seats. Booked by H. D. Moorhouse at Imperial Bldgs., Oxford Road, Manchester. Two shows Sat. Continuous rest of week. Prices, 4d. to 9d. Phone, Rusholme 4103. Station, Longsight.

SHAKESPEARE PICTURE HALL (WE), Halliwell Lane, Cheetham Hill.—Prop., Swinton Entertainments, Ltd., Man. Dir., J. F. Emery, J.P., Midland Bank House, 26, Cross Street, Manchester. 900 seats. Booked at H.O. Three shows daily. Prices, 5d. to 1s. 3d. Phone, Cheetham Hill 2180. All Manchester Stations.

STAMFORD CINEMA (BA), Audenshaw.—Prop., L. Bailey, 22, Cathedral House, Manchester. 650 seats.

STAR PICTURE THEATRE (BTH), Gt. Ducie Street.—Prop., L. Burgess. 600 seats. Two shows nightly. Station, London Road, L.M.S.

TATLER THEATRE (RCA), Oxford Street.—Props., Times Theatres, Ltd., 3, Stanley Street, Liverpool 1. 300 seats. Booked at Hall. Continuous. Prices, 6d. and 1s. Proscenium width, 22 ft. Phone, Central 6015.

TEMPLE PICTORIUM (BTH), Cheetham Hill Road.—Prop., Temple Pictorium (Manchester) Ltd., Imperial Buildings, 7, Oxford Road, Manchester. 844 seats. Continuous, Mon. to Fri. Twice nightly, Sat. Two changes. Prices, 3d. to 9d. Stage, 14 ft. deep. Two dressing-rooms. Phone, Collyhurst 1939.

THEATRE ROYAL CINEMA (WE), Peter Street.—Prop., H. D. Moorhouse Circuit. Oxford Road Manchester. 1,935 seats. Continuous. Prices 1s. to 2s. Proscenium width, 33 ft. Cafe attached. Phone, Blackfriars 9366 and 5308. Station, Central, L.M.S.

COMPTON

ORGAN featured here.

TOWER CINEMA (BTP), Piercy Street, Ancoats.— Controlled by Union Cinemas, Ltd., 15, Regent Street, S.W.1. Phone, Whitehall 8484. Booked at H.O. Continuous. Proscenium width, 22 ft. Phone, Ardwick 2926. Station, Victoria, Manchester.

TOWER, Broughton.—H. D. Moorhouse Circuit, 7, Oxford Road, Manchester.

TRAFFORD PICTURE HOUSE (BTH), Talbot Road, Old Trafford.—Prop., Associated British Cinemas, Ltd., 30/31, Golden Square, W.1. 1,140 seats. Booked at H.O. Continuous. Four mats. weekly. Prices, 4d. to 1s. Proscenium width, 30 ft. Cafe attached. Phone, Trafford Park 0986. Station, Old Trafford.

TRIANGLE (Picturetone), Stretford Road, Hulme.—Props., A. Jacobs and A. Mitchell. 500 seats. Booked at Hall. Occasional Variety. Continuous. Prices, 2d. to 6d. Phone, Central 3487. Station, Manchester Central, L.M.S.

TROCADERO (BTP), Wilmslow Road, Rusholme.—Prop., Platt Picturedrome, Ltd. 850 seats.

Two shows daily. Two changes weekly. Prices, 5d. to 7d. Phone, Rusholme 4751.

TWIN REGAL KINEMAS (WE), Oxford Road.—Prop., Piccadilly Picture Theatre (Manchester), Ltd. 1,600 seats. Booked at 11, Piccadilly, Manchester. Phone, Central 3949. Continuous. Prices, 6d. to 1s. 6d. Stage, 6ft. deep.; four dressing-rooms. Phone, Central 2437. Cafe attached. Manchester Stations.

VERONA, Guide Bridge.

VICTORIA, Broughton.—H. D. Moorhouse Circuit, 7, Oxford Road, Manchester.

VICTORIA AVENUE CINEMA (WE), Higher Blackley.—Prop., S. Haling, 12, Moreton Street, Manchester. 1,400 seats. Continuous. Two shows nightly. Sats. Pictures and Variety. Booked at Hall. Prices, 6d. to 1s. Proscenium width, 42 ft. Stage, 50 ft.; six dressing-rooms. Phone : Cheetham Hill 1401. Film Transport.

VICTORIA HALL, Daniel Street, Butler Street, Ancoats.—Prop., Manchester and Salford Wesleyan Mission. Two shows, Sat. Price, 3d. Station, Central, C.L.C.

VICTORY, Middleton.—H. D. Moorhouse Circuit, 7, Oxford Road, Manchester.

VICTORY (BTP), Moston.

VICTORY CINEMA (BTP), Varley Street, Miles Platting.—450 seats. Booked at Hall. Twice nightly. Mats., Mon., Thurs. and Sat. Prices, 4d. to 7d. Phone, Prestwich 2615. Station, Miles Platting.

VICTORY PICTURE HOUSE (BTP), Blackley.—Prop., Victory Pictures (Manchester), Ltd. Man., H. D. Moorhouse. 900 seats. Booked at H.O. Continuous. Three changes weekly. Prices, 5d. to 1s. 3d. Phone, Cheetham Hill 495. Station, Victoria, L.M.S.

WEST END CINEMA (WE), Withington Road, Whalley Range.—Props., West End Cinema (Manchester), Ltd. 2,032 seats. Booked at Hall. Continuous, Mon. to Fri. Twice nightly, Sat. and holidays. Price, 6d. to 1s. 6d. Proscenium width, 46 ft. Phone, Moss Side 1668. Cafe attached. Stations, Manchester termini.

WHITEHALL CINEMA (BTH), Old Lane, Higher Openshaw.—Prop., Whitehall Cinema Co., Ltd. 800 seats. Booked at the Hall by H. Vost. Twice nightly. Prices, 4d. to 1s. Phone, Droylsden 1325. Stations, Victoria or Exchange.

YORK CINEMA (WE), York Street, Hulme.—Prop., Thomas and Norman Royle. 1,414 seats. Continuous. Booked at Hall. Twice nightly Sat. Prices, 5d. to 1s. Phone, Central 3823. Stations, Central, London Road, Victoria or Exchange.

(See also Salford.)

MANNINGTREE (ESSEX), **Pop. 2,500.**

PLAZA CINEMA (MPA), Station Road.—Prop., E. Owen Cooper. 400 seats. Booked at Palace, Hadleigh, Suffolk. Continuous. Prices, 6d. to 1s. 3d. Stage, 10 ft. deep ; two dressing-rooms. Proscenium width, 21½ ft. Station, Manningtree, L.N.E.R. Films by Road Transport.

MANSFIELD (NOTTS), **Pop. 46,075.**

EMPIRE SUPER CINEMA (BA), Stockwell Gate—Prop., Gaumont-British Picture Corpn., Ltd. 123, Regent Street, London, W.1. 931 seats. Booked at H.O. Continuous. Mat. daily. Prices, 6d. to 1s. 3d. Phone, Mansfield

297. Stage, 18 ft. deep. Station, Mansfield. London, W.1. Phone, Gerrard 7887. 1,179 **Fitted "ARDENTE" Deaf Aids See page 258**

GRAND THEATRE (WE).—Prop., Associated British Cinemas, Ltd., 30-31, Golden Square, London, W.1. Phone, Gerrard 7887. 1,179 seats. Booked at H.O. Continuous. Pictures and Variety. Prices, 6d. to 1s. 3d. Proscenium width, 33 ft. Stage, 40 ft. deep; 10 dressing-rooms. Phone, Mansfield 138. Stations, Mansfield, L.M.S. and L.N.E.R.

HIPPODROME (WE).—Prop., Granada Theatres, Ltd. Controlled by Bernstein Theatres, Ltd., 36, Golden Square, W.1. Phone, Gerrard 3554. Booked at H.O. Continuous. Prices, 6d. to 1s. Phone, Mansfield 926.

PALACE (BTH), Leeming Street.—Prop., Sherwood Palaces, Ltd. 800 seats. Booked at Hall. Continuous nightly. Two changes weekly. Prices, 5d. to 1s. Phone 882. Station, Mansfield, L.M.S.

PLAZA (WE), Westgate. — Prop., Granada Theatres, Ltd. Controlled by Bernstein Theatres, Ltd., 36, Golden Square, W.1. Phone, Gerrard 3554. Booked at H.O. Continuous. Phone, Mansfield 926. Café attached.

WURLITZER ORGAN Installed in this Kinema

ROCK PICTURE HOUSE (BA), Skerry Hill.—Prop., Denman Midlands Cinemas, Ltd. 760 seats. Booked at H.O. Continuous. Two changes weekly. Prices, 4d. to 1s. Phone, Mansfield 333. Station, Mansfield, L.M.S. and L.N.E.R.

MANSFIELD-WOODHOUSE (NOTTS), Pop. 13,707.

TIVOLI (Imperial), Station Street.—Prop., Tivoli Pictures (Mansfield-Woodhouse), Ltd., Station Street, Mansfield-Woodhouse. 322 seats. Booked by J. E. Barnes, The Pharmacy, Langwith, Mansfield. Continuous. Two shows and Mat. Sat. Prices, 6d. to 1s. Phone, Shirebrook 284. Station, Mansfield-Woodhouse, L.M.S.

MARCH (CAMB.), Pop. 11,276.

HIPPODROME (WE).—Prop., March Amusements, Ltd., Head Office, Darthill Road, March. 858 seats. Prices, 6d. to 1s. 6d. Proscenium width, 32 ft. Stage, 24 ft. deep. Five dressing-rooms. Phone, 78. Station, March, L.N.E.R.

REGENT (RCA).—Prop., March Amusements, Ltd. Pictures and Variety. 800 seats. Continuous. Prices, 6d. to 1s. 6d. Stage, 26 ft. deep. Five dressing-rooms. Proscenium width, 20 ft. Phone, March 3178. Station, March, L.N.E.R

MARGATE (KENT), Pop. 31,312.

ASTORIA (WE), Cliftonville.—Prop., Astoria (Cliftonville), Ltd. 1,505 seats. Continuous. Booked at H.O. Prices, 6d. to 1s. 6d. winter and 2s. summer. Proscenium width, 36 ft. Stage, 18 ft. Three dressing-rooms. Phone, Margate 1565. Café attached. Station, Margate.

CAMEO THEATRE (Morrison), Northdown Road. Prop., R. Senior, "Holly Mount," Foreland Avenue, Cliftonville. 475 seats. Continuous. Booked at Hall. Prices, 6d. to 2s. Phone, Margate 1207. Films by Motor Transport.

DREAMLAND SUPER CINEMA (WE).—Prop. Margate Estates Co., Ltd. 2,200 seats. Continuous. Prices, 6d. to 2s. Proscenium width, 40 ft. Phone, Margate 844. Café and dance hall attached.

COMPTON
ORGAN featured here.

HIPPODROME (RCA).—Prop., Associated Theatres (Margate), Ltd. Receiver, W. T. Thorn, 5, Cecil Square, Margate. 1,000 seats. Continuous. Prices, 6d. to 2s. Proscenium width, 30 ft. Stage, 20 ft. deep; six dressing-rooms. Phone, 1190. Station, Margate.

PARADE CINEMA (BA), The Parade.—Prop., W. J. Johns. 700 seats. Three shows daily. Prices, 7d. to 2s. 6d. Phone, Margate 299. Station, Margate West, S.R.

PLAZA (WE), High Street.—Props., Plaza Cinemas (Kent), Ltd. 450 seats. Booked at Hall by Jack Armstead. Twice nightly. Mat. daily. Prices, 7d. to 1s. 6d. Proscenium width, 22 ft. Phone, Margate 58. Station, Margate West, S.R.

REGAL (WE).—Prop., Regal (Margate), Ltd. 1,780 seats. Booked by County Cinemas, Ltd., Dean House, Dean Street, W.1.

WINTER GARDENS.

MARKET DEEPING (LINCS.).

EMPIRE CINEMA (BA).—Props., Bancroft Circuit. Booked at 56, Bridge Street, Peterborough. 500 seats. Continuous. Prices, 6d. to 1s. 6d. Phone, Deeping 336. Station, James Deeping and Tallington.

MARKET DRAYTON (SALOP), Pop. 4,749.

HIPPODROME (BTH).—Prop., T. E. Markhame, Ye Olde Wyche Theatre, Nantwich. Phone, Nantwich 5338. Booked at H.O. Once nightly, Mon. to Fri. Continuous, Sat. Mats., Wed. and Sat. Stage, 32 ft. deep. Four dressing-rooms. Prices, 6d. to 1s. 3d, Phone, Market Drayton 122. Station, Market Drayton, G.W.R.

TOWN HALL CINEMA.—Phone, Market Drayton 51.

MARKET HARBOROUGH (LEICESTER), Pop. 9,312.

COUNTY CINEMA (Gyrotone), 19, The Square.—Prop., Showfilms, Ltd., 55, St. Mary's Road, Market Harborough. Phone, Market Harborough 31. 600 seats. Booked at Oriental Cinema by R. Justice. Two shows Sat only. Prices, 5d. to 1s. 4d. Occasional Variety. Stage, 12 ft. deep; two dressing-rooms. Station, Market Harborough, L.M.S.

ORIENTAL CINEMA (WE), St. Mary's Road.—Prop., Showfilms, Ltd., 55, St. Mary's Road. 550 seats. Man. Dir., R. Justice. Booked at Hall. Twice nightly. Prices, 6d. to 1s. 6d. Phone, Market Harborough 31.

RITZ (WE).—Controlled by Union Cinemas, Ltd., 15, Regent Street, S.W.1. Phone, Whitehall 8484. Booked at H.O. Continuous. Prices, 3d. to 2s. Station, Market Harborough, L.M.S.

MARKET RASEN (Lincs.), **Pop. 2,048.**
Town Hall Cinema (Morrison).—Prop., J. F. Badley, The Terrace, Spilsby, Lincs. Phone, Spilsby 5. 350 seats. Booked at H.O. Once nightly. Continuous Sat. Prices, 4d. to 1s. 4d. Station, Market Rasen, also by Lincoln and District Film Transport Co., Boston.

MARKET WEIGHTON (Yorks.), **Pop. 1,717·**
Central Hall (awh).—Props., J. W. Garforth and ·Son. 300 seats. Booked by Props. Shows once nightly. Occasional Variety. Prices, 7d. to 1s. 6d. Proscenium width, 21 ft. Stage, 12 ft. Films by Transport.

MARLBOROUGH (Wilts.), **Pop. 3,492.**
Bouverie Hall, Pewsey.
Cinema (Mihaly), Upavon. 500 seats.
R.A.F. Cinema, Upavon.

MARLOW-ON-THAMES (Bucks.), **Pop. 5,087.**
County Cinema (we).—Prop., County Cinemas, Ltd., Dean House, Dean Street, London, W.1. Phone, Gerrard 4543. 328 seats. Booked at H.O. Twice nightly. Mat., Sat. Prices, 6d. to 2s. Phone, Marlow 227. Station, Marlow, G.W.R.

MARPLE (Cheshire), **Pop. 7,388.**
Regent Cinema (bth).—Prop., Marple Cinema Co., Ltd., 19, Howard Street, Sheffield. Phone, Sheffield 26002. 500 seats. Booked at H.O. and Hall. Twice nightly. Mat., Mon., Thurs. and Sat. Prices, 3d. to 1s. 3d. Occasional Variety. Proscenium width, 18 ft. Stage, 6 ft. deep ; two dressing-rooms. Phone, Marple 482. Station, Marple, L.M.S.

MARSDEN (Yorks.), **Pop. 5,720.**
Electric Theatre (rca).—Prop. and Man., T. Leyland. 550 seats. Once nightly. Two changes weekly. Station, Marsden, L.M.S.

MARTOCK (Som.), **Pop. 2,055.**
Electric Theatre (Mihaly).—Props., Walford Pictures, Chard, Somerset. Booked at H.O. Once nightly, Sat., Bank Holidays. Prices, 9d. to 1s. 6d. Proscenium width, 18 ft.
Liberal Hall.—Prop., Martock Liberal Hall Co., Ltd., Church Street. Sec., W. H. Tucker, East View, Stapleton, Martock. Hall to let for shows, etc. Rates on application to Secretary.

MARYPORT (Cumb.), **Pop. 10,182.**
Carlton Cinema (we), Senhouse Street.—Props., Graves Cinemas, Ltd., Athenæum Buildings, Maryport. 750 seats. Two shows nightly. Two changes weekly. Prices, 6d. to 1s. 3d. Phone, Maryport 43. Station, Maryport, L.M.S.
Empire Theatre (we), Senhouse Street.—Props., Graves Cinemas, Ltd., Athenæum Buildings, Maryport. 850 seats. Booked at H.O. Two shows nightly. Two changes weekly. Prices, 6d. to 1s. 3d. Phone, Maryport 7.
Palace Theatre, High Street.—450 seats, Booked at H.O. Two shows nightly. Two changes weekly. Phone, Maryport 16. Station, Maryport, L.M.S.

MASHAM (Yorks.), **Pop. 1,995.**
Town Hall Picturedrome.

MATLOCK (Derby), **Pop. 7,055.**
Cinema House (we), Causeway Lane.—Prop., Matlock Cinemas, Ltd. 940 seats. Booked at Hall. Continuous. Prices, 7d. to 1s. 6d. Pictures and Variety. Stage, 22 ft. deep.

Seven dressing-rooms. Café attached. Phone, Matlock 121. Station, Matlock, L.M.S.
Picture Palace (we), Dale Road.—Props., Matlock Cinemas, Ltd. 600 seats. Booked at Cinema House. Continuous. Prices, 4d. to 1s. Phone, Matlock 121. Station, Matlock, L.M.S.

MATLOCK BATH (Derby), **Pop. 1,750.**
Grand Pavilion (Morrison).—500 seats. Continuous nightly. Mat. Sat. Occasional Variety. Prices, 6d. to 1s. Proscenium width, 23 ft. Stage, 37 ft. deep. Five dressing-rooms. Phone, Matlock 257. Station, Matlock Bath, L.M.S. Films by Broxburn Transport.

MEADOWFIELD, BRANDON COLLIERY (Co. Durham).
Co-operative Kinema (we), Meadowfield.—Prop., Brandon and Byshottles Co-operative Society, Ltd. 608 seats. Mon. continuous. Tues. to Fri. once daily. Sat. two shows. Prices, 5d. to 9d. Proscenium width, 23 ft. Phone, Brandon Colliery 45. Station, Brandon Colliery, L.N.E.R.

MEASHAM (Leics.), **Pop. 2,500.**
Empire Cinema (Imperial).—Prop., Sankey Bros., " Red Tiles," Ashby Road, Woodville, Burton-on-Trent. 400 seats. Booked at H.O. Twice nightly, Mon., Fri., Sat. Once nightly, Tues., Wed. and Thurs. Prices, 6d. to 1s. Proscenium width, 40 ft. Phone, Measham 34. Station, Measham, L.M.S.

MELBOURNE (Derby), **Pop. 4,500.**
Empire (awh).—Prop., Sankey Bros., Beaumaris, Upper Midway. Burton-on-Trent. Phone, Swadlincote 7265. 250 seats. Booked at Beaumaris. Continuous. Prices, 6d. to 1s. 3d. Proscenium width, 30 ft. Phone, 78. Station, Melbourne, L.M.S.

MELKSHAM (Wilts.), **Pop. 3,881.**
Picture Hall (rca), Bank Street.—Prop., Melksham Pictures, Ltd., 6, Green Street, Bath. Phone, Bath 3939. 450 seats. Booked at H.O. One show nightly. Three on Sat. Prices, 6d. to 1s. 6d. Station, Melksham, G.W.R.

MELTHAM (Yorks.), **Pop. 5,051.**
Alhambra (Morrison).—Prop., Fred Haigh. 600 seats. Once nightly. Two changes weekly. Station, Meltham, L.N.E.R.

MELTON MOWBRAY (Leicester), **Pop. 9,312.**
Picture House (bth), King Street.—Prop. Melton Mowbray Picture House, Ltd., Allen House, Newmarket Street, Leicester. 855 seats. Booked by C. E. West at Evington Cinema, Leicester. Shows, Thurs. to Sat. Prices, 5d. to 1s. Phone, Melton Mowbray 251. Station, Melton Mowbray, L.M.S.
Regal (btp).—Props., Melton Mowbray Picture House, Ltd., Allen House, Newmarket Street, Leicester. 897 seats. Continuous. Mats. Tues. and Sat. Prices, 6d. to 1s. 6d.

MERE (Wilts).
Electric Palace.

MEXBORO' (Yorks,). **Pop. 15,856.**
Empire Picture Palace (we).—Prop., Mexboro' Theatres, Ltd. Man. Dir., J. J. Woffenden. 1,120 seats. Continuous. Two changes weekly. Phone, Mexboro' 108.
Hippodrome.

The BEST Is Cheapest; PATHE GAZETTE.

MAJESTIC (WE). Prop., Mexboro' Theatres, Ltd. Man. Dir., J. J. Woffenden. 884 seats Continuous. Two changes weekly. Station, Mexboro', L.N.E.R.

OXFORD PICTURE PALACE (BTH), Market Place. —Prop., Mexboro' Theatres, Ltd. Man. Dir., J. J. Woffenden. 500 seats. Two shows nightly. Two changes weekly. Station, Mexboro', L.N.E.R.

ROYAL CINEMA (BTH), Bank Street.—Prop. and Man., George Goodacre. 550 seats. Booked at Hall. Continuous. Twice nightly, Sat, Prices, 4d. to 1s. Phone, Mexboro' 112. Station, Mexboro', L.N.E.R.

MIDDLEHAM (YORKS.), Pop. 700.

PICTURE HOUSE (AWH).—Prop. and Man., W. C. Sykes, Yoreview, Middleham. 350 seats. Booked at Hall. Once nightly. Dance Hall attached. Prices, 6d. to 1s. 10d. Station, Leyburn, L.N.E.R.

MIDDLESBROUGH (YORKS), Pop. 138,489.

ELITE PICTURE THEATRE (WE), Linthorpe Road. Props., Elite Picture Theatre (Middlesbrough), Ltd. Controlled by Associated British Cinemas, Ltd., 30–31, Golden Square, W.1. 1,843 seats. Continuous. Daily Mat. Café attached. Prices, 6d. to 1s. 6d. Phone, Middlesbrough 3,400. Station, Middlesbrough, L.M.S.

Fitted "ARDENTE" Deaf Aids
See page 258

COMPTON
ORGAN featured here.

EMPIRE CINEMA.

GAUMONT PALACE (BA).—Props., Denman Picture Houses, Ltd. 1,600 seats. Booked at H.O. Continuous from 5.30 p.m. Station, Middlesbrough.

COMPTON
ORGAN featured here.

GEM PICTURE HOUSE (WE), High Street, North Ormesby.—Prop., The Palladium (Hartlepools) Ltd., Palladium Buildings, Eastbourne Road. Middlesbrough. Phone, Linthorpe 88156. 358 seats. Booked at H.O. Continuous nightly. Prices, 4d. to 1s. Phone, Middlesbrough 2893. Station, Cargo Fleet, L.N.E.R.

GLOBE (BTP).

GRAND ELECTRIC THEATRE (BTH), Newport Road.—Props., E. and M. R. Baker, Corporation Road (Phone, Middlesbrough 3833). 800 seats. Booked at Hall by T. Watson Smith. Continuous, Daily Mat. Prices, 5d. to 1s. 3d. Proscenium width, 20ft. Phone, Middlesbrough 2389. Station, Middlesbrough.

HIPPODROME (RCA), Wilson Street.—Prop., North of England Cinemas, Ltd. 1,400 seats. Booked at H.O. Continuous. Daily Mat. Two changes weekly. Prices, 4d. to 1s. Phone, Middlesbrough 341511. Station, Middlesbrough.

MARLBOROUGH CINEMA (BTP), Gilkes Street.— Prop., Marlborough (Middlesbrough), Ltd. 1,243 seats. Three shows daily. Two changes weekly. Prices, 4d. to 1s. Phone, Middlesbrough 2221. Station, Middlesbrough, L.N.E.R.

PALLADIUM (WE), Eastbourne Road, Linthorpe. —Prop., Palladium (Middlesbrough), Ltd., 4, Palladium Buildings, Middlesbrough. Phone, 88156. 783 seats. Booked at H.O. Twice nightly. Prices, 6d. to 1s. Proscenium width, 30 ft. Phone, Middlesbrough 8513. Station, Middlesbrough, L.N.E.R.

PAVILION (BA), Newport Road.—Prop., North of England Cinemas, Ltd., 797 seats. Booked at H.O. Two shows nightly. Prices, 1d. to 6d. Proscenium width, 22 ft. 4 in. Phone, Middlesbrough 397111. Station, Middlesbrough, L.N.E.R.

PAVILION (BTH), Gibson Street, North Ormesby. —Prop., North Ormesby Entertainment Co., Ltd. 900 seats. Booked at Hall. Continuous. Pictures and variety. Stage, 22 ft. deep. Prices, 3d. to 11d. Phone 311. Station, Cargo Fleet, L.N.E.R.

RITZ.—Controlled by Union Cinemas, Ltd., 15, Regent Street, London, S.W.1. Phone, Whitehall 8484.

ROYAL.—S.S. Blyth Kinemas, Ltd., Waterloo Chambers, Bath Lane, Newcastle-on-Tyne.

SCALA CINEMA (BA), Newport Road.—Prop., Associated British Cinemas, Ltd., 30–31, Golden Square, London, W.1. 1,100 seats. Continuous nightly. Two changes weekly. Prices, 5d. to 1s. 3d. Proscenium width, 21 ft. 6 in. Phone, Middlesbrough 3230.

THEATRE ROYAL (BTP), Sussex Street.—Prop.' Sol. Sheckman. 1,450 seats. Booked at H.O. Twice nightly. Prices, 3d. to 1s. 6d. Stage, 28 ft. deep and 7 dressing-rooms. Phone, Middlesbrough 3415. Station, Middlesbrough, L.N.E.R.

MIDDLETON (LANCS), Pop. 29,189.

EMPIRE THEATRE (BTP), Corporation Street.— Props., Victory Pictures (Manchester), Ltd. Booked at H.D. Moorhouse Circuit, Imperial Bldgs., Oxford Road, Manchester. Phone-Ardwick 2226. 900 seats. Continuous. Mon. to Fri., two shows Sats. Prices, 6d. to 1s. Stage, 26 ft. deep. Four dressing-rooms. Proscenium width, 21 ft. Phone, Middleton 2834. Station, Middleton, L.M.S.

PALACE (WE), Manchester Old Road.—Prop., Middleton Cinemas, Ltd. 966 seats. Two shows nightly. Mon. and Sat., one rest of week. Mat. Mon., Tues., Thurs. and Sat. Prices, 3d. to 9d. Phone, Middleton 252. Station, Middleton.

PICTURE HOUSE (BTH), Wood Street.—Prop., Victory Pictures (Manchester), Ltd. Booked at Imperial Buildings, 7, Oxford Road, Manchester. 650 seats. Continuous. Prices, 5d. and 9d. Phone, Middleton 2950. Station, Middleton, L.M.S.

TIVOLI (WE).—Prop., Goldstones (Cinemas), Ltd., 9, Wetherby Road, Leeds.

VICTORY.—Prop., H. D. Moorhouse Circuit, 7, Oxford Road, Manchester.

MIDDLETON-IN-TEESDALE (DURHAM), Pop. 1,976.

COSY CINEMA (AWH).—Prop., Teesdale Cinemas, Ltd., Hippodrome, Bishop Auckland. Phone, 121. 400 seats. Booked at H.O. Once nightly. Prices, 6d. to 1s. 3d. Station, L.N.E.R.

Put Pep into Programmes With PATHE PICTORIAL.

MIDDLEWICH (CHESHIRE), **Pop. 5,458.**
ALHAMBRA (WE).—Prop., Sandbach Cinemas, Ltd., Palace, Sandbach. Phone, Sandbach 103. Booked at H.O. Two shows nightly. Prices, 6d. to 1s. 3d. Phone, Middlewich 18. Station, Middlewich, L.M.S.
STAR CINEMA.—PROP., C. Whirehead. Head Office, Alhambra House, Middlewich. Prices, 4d. to 1s. Station, Middlewich, L.M.S.

MIDHURST (SUSSEX), **Pop. 1,896.**
CINEMA (AWH), North Street.—Prop., A. A. Scrase. 450 seats. Once nightly. Prices, 4d. to 1s. 9d. Proscenium width, 18 ft. Station, Midhurst, S.R.

MIDSOMER NORTON (SOMERSET). **Pop. 7,490.**
PALLADIUM (BTH).—W. Trueman-Dicken Circuit, " Majestic " Burnham-on-Sea. Continuous, Prices, 7d. to 1s. 6d. Phone 66. Station, Midsomer Norton, G.W.R. Films by Road Transport.

MILDENHALL (SUFFOLK).
COMET (BTF).—Props., Comet Cinema (Mildenhall), Ltd. 475 seats. Once nightly. Three shows Sat. Prices, 6d. to 2s. 4d. Phone, 2242. Station, Mildenhall.

MILLOM (CUMB) **Pop. 7,406.**
PALLADIUM (WE).—Prop., M.B.C. Cinemas,Ltd., Hippodrome, Workington. Phone, 194. 680 seats. Booked at H.O. by Morris Maud. Twice nightly. Prices 6d. to 1s. 3d. Stage 25 ft. deep; two dressing-rooms. Ballroom attached. Phone, Millom 53. Station, Millom, L.M.S.

MILNROW (LANCS), **Pop. 8,624.**
EMPIRE (WE).—Prop., Marks Circuit Cinemas, 6, St. Mary's Gate, Manchester. Phone, Blackfriars, 4078. 630 seats. Booked at H.O. Continuous evenings. Twice Sat. Pictures and Variety. Proscenium width, 19 ft. Stage, 4 ft. deep; two dressing rooms. Prices, 3d. to 9d. Phone, Milnrow 5308. Station, Milnrow, L.M.S. Films by Road Transport.

MILNSBRIDGE (YORKS), **Pop. 5,000.**
PICTURE PALACE (BTH), Savile Street.—Prop., Milnsbridge Picture Palace, Ltd. 650 seats. Booked at Leeds. Twice nightly. Prices, 4d. to 1s. Phone, 217. Station, Longwood, L.M.S.

MINEHEAD (SOMERSET), **Pop. 6,315.**
QUEEN'S HALL (WE), Sea Front. (Closed Winter). Props., Minehead Entertainments, Ltd., 62, Oxford Street, W.1. 750 seats. Booked at H.O. Occasional Plays. Prices, 9d. to 2s. Stage and six dressing-rooms. Phone, 211. Station, Minehead.
REGAL (WE), The Avenue.—Props., Minehead Entertainments, Ltd., 62, Oxford Street, W.1. Phone, Museum 5189. 1,250 seats. Booked at H.O. Occasional Variety. Prices, 1s. to 1s. 10d. Continuous, from 5.30. Summer, continuous 2.30 p.m. Stage, 27 ft. deep. Café and Ballroom attached. Phone, 439. Station, Minehead.

MIRFIELD (YORKS), **Pop. 12,099.**
REGENT (B.T.H.). — Lessee, G. Andsley. 539 Leeds Road Dewsbury. Continuous. Mon,, to Fri. Twice nightly Sat. Phone, Mirfield 210. Station, Mirfield, L.M.S.
TOWN HALL.—Props., J. & H. Buxton, 4, Grange View, Leeds.

MITCHAM (SURREY), **Pop. 56,860.**
MAJESTIC THEATRE (WE), Upper Green.—Prop., Associated British Cinemas, Ltd., 30-31 Golden Square, W.1. 1,511 seats. Booked at H.O. Continuous. Occasional Variety booked by Jackquello's Agency, 122, Charing Cross Road, W.C.2. Prices, 6d. to 1s. 6d. Proscenium width, 42 ft. Stage, 16 ft. deep; two dressing-rooms. Café attached. Phone, Mitcham 2719. Station, Mitcham, S.R.

Fitted "ARDENTE" Deaf Aids
See page 258

COMPTON
ORGAN featured here.

MONMOUTH (MON), **Pop. 4,731.**
PICTURE HOUSE (Cinephone).—Props., Provincial Cinematograph Theatres, Ltd., New Gallery House, 123, Regent Street, London, W.1. 600 seats. Booked at H.O. Once nightly, three times Sat. Prices, 6d. to 2s. 4d. Stage, 18 ft. deep. Five dressing-rooms. Phone, Monmouth 146. Station, Mayhill (Monmouth), G.W.R.
ROLLS HALL CINEMA.—Booked by J. Saunders 15, Middle Street, Yeovil. Nightly. Mat, Sat. Prices, 5d. to 1s. 6d. Station, Mayhill.

MORCHARD BISHOP (DEVON).
B. B. CINEMA (Morrison).—(Closed.)

MORDEN (SURREY), **Pop. 1,350.**
MORDEN CINEMA (WE), Aberconway Road.—Prop., Odeon Theatres, Ltd., Cornhill House, Bennett's Hill, Birmingham. Phone, Midland 2781. Booked at 49, Park Lane, W.1. Continuous. Prices, 9d. to 2s. Phone, Mitcham 2900.

Fitted "ARDENTE" Deaf Aids
Fitted "ARDENTE" Stage Amplification
See page 258

COMPTON
ORGAN featured here.

MORECAMBE (LANCS), **Pop. 24,586.**
ASTORIA SUPER CINEMA (BA), Promenade.—Props., Morecambe Amusements Co. 1,500 seats. Booked at Hall. Pictures and occasional Variety. Continuous. Stage, 30 ft. deep; 14 dressing rooms. Prices, 6d. to 3s. 6d. Proscenium width, 29 ft. Phone, Morecambe 248. Café attached. Station, Morecambe, L.M.S.
MORECAMBE TOWER (BA).—Prop., Denman Picture Houses, Ltd., New Gallery House, Regent Street,. London, W.F. 2,000 seats. Pictures, Musical Comedies and Variety. Booked at H.O. Open Sunday Evenings. Phone, Morecambe 116. Café and Dance Hall attached. Station, Morecambe (Euston Road), L.M.S.
NEW PLAZA CINEMA (WE), New Queen Street.—Lessee, W. Shaw, Senr., for Morecambe Amusements Co., Ltd., Astoria Cinema, Morecambe. 922 seats. Continuous in summer season. Oct. to June, once nightly. Mat. Wed. and Sat. Prices, 6d. to 1s. 3d. Proscenium width, 21 ft. Phone, Morecambe 408. Station, Morecambe, L.M.S.

PATHE GAZETTE: At All Events

ODEON THEATRE.—Prop., Odeon Theatres, Ltd., Cornhill House, Bennett's Hill, Birmingham. Booked at 49, Park Lane, W.I. (In course of construction.)

PALACE (WE).

PALLADIUM (BTH).—Prop., Palladium (Morecambe), Ltd. 1,000 seats. Booked at Hall. One show nightly in winter. Continuous in summer. Prices, 6d. to 1s. 3d. Phone, Morecambe 108. Station, Morecambe, L.M.S.

ROYALTY THEATRE.—1,000 seats.

WHITEHALL PICTURE HOUSE (BTH), Marine Road.—Prop., Morecambe Bay Cinemas, Ltd. 965 seats. Booked at Manchester and Liverpool. Continuous summer. Once nightly rest of year. Prices, 6d. to 1s. 6d. Proscenium width, 20 ft. Phone, Morecambe 224. Stations, Morecambe (Euston Road), L.M.S.

WINTER GARDENS (Pavilion Theatre) (PTA).— 2,960 seats. Once nightly. Pictures and Variety. Prices, 6d. to 2s. 6d. Phone, Morecambe 8. Stations, Euston Road and Promenade, L.M.S.

MORETON (CHESHIRE), Pop. 970.

PICTURE HOUSE (BTH).—Prop., Cheshire Picture Halls Co., Ltd., Park Road North, Birkenhead. 800 seats. Booked at H.O. by W. F. Williams. Continuous. Prices, 6d. to 1s. 3d. Phone, Upton 22. Station, Moreton, L.M.S.

MORETON-IN-MARSH (GLOS), Pop. 1,445.

PLAYHOUSE.—Prop., Playhouse (Moreton-in-Marsh) Ltd. Pictures and occasional Variety. Films booked at Plaza, Amesbury. Phone, Amesbury 354. Continuous nightly. Prices, 6d. to 1s. 6d. Stage, 12 ft. deep. Two dressing-rooms. Phone 73. Station, Moreton-in-Marsh, G.W.R.

MORLEY (YORKS), Pop. 23,397.

NEW PAVILION (WE).—Prop., Picture House (Morley) Ltd. 936 seats. Booked at Hall. Continuous. Picture and Variety. Prices, 7d. to 1s. Stage and 4 dressing-rooms. Phone, 281. Station, Morley, L.N.E.R.

PICTURE HOUSE (BTH), Queen Street.—Prop., Picture House (Morley), Ltd. 1,000 seats. Booked at Hall. Continuous. Prices, 7d. to 1s. Phone, Morley 232. Station, Morley, L.N.E.R.

MORPETH (NORTHUM.), Pop. 7,390.

CINEMA (AWH), Seahouses.—400 seats.

COLISEUM THEATRE (WE), North Road.—Prop., Stanley Rogers Cinemas, Ltd., 72, Grey Street, Newcastle. Phone, Newcastle 20317. 1,100 seats. Booked at H.O. Continuous. Prices, 3d. to 1s. 6d. Proscenium width, 26 ft. Occasional Variety. Stage, 23 ft. deep ; eight dressing-rooms. Café. Phone, Morpeth 192. Station, Morpeth.

JUBILEE HALL, Rothbury.

MINERS HALL (AWH), Pegswood.—Props., Pegswood Miners Welfare Committee. 350 seats. Proscenium width 20 ft. Prices, 6d. to 3s. Film Transport.

PLAYHOUSE (WE).—Booked at Wallaw Buildings, Ashington, Northumberland. Five changes weekly. Prices, 3d. to 1s. 2d. Phone, Morpeth 124. Station, Morpeth.

MOSSLEY (LANCS.), Pop. 12,041.

EMPIRE CINEMA (Picturetone), Apsley Gardens.—Lessees, C. A. Wilkinson and R. Plummer. 600 seats. Once nightly. Twice nightly Sat. Mat., Mon. and Sat. Booked at Manchester. Two changes weekly. Prices, 4d. to 10d. Phone, Mossley 78. Station, Mossley, L.M.S.

ROYAL PAVILION (Picturetone).—Lessees, C. A. Wilkinson and Downs, Apsley House, Mossley. 600 seats. Booked at Manchester. One show nightly. Mats., Tues. and Sat. Two changes weekly. Prices, 4d. to 10d. Station, Mossley.

MOTTRAM (CHESHIRE), Pop. 2,636.

SAVOY THEATRE (AWH).—Lessee and Man., F. A. Harrison. 500 seats. Booked at Hall. Once nightly. Twice Sat. Prices, 4d. to 1s. Station, Mottram.

MOUNTSORREL (LEICS.), Pop. 2,510.

ROCK CINEMA (Gyrotone), Leicester Road.— Props., G. G. Baum and J. Fisher. 290 seats. Booked at Hall. Once nightly, Mon., Tues., Thurs. and Sat. Prices, 5d. to 1s. Proscenium width, 19 ft. Phone, Rothley 164. Station, Sileby, L.M.S.

MUCH WENLOCK (SALOP), Pop. 1,400.

MEMORIAL HALL (Gyrotone).—Prop., E. Taylor, 19, The Square, Much Wenlock. 200 seats. Three performances two nights weekly. Booked at Hall. Prices, 4d. to 1s. 3d. Station, Much Wenlock, G.W.R.

MURTON COLLIERY (Co. DURHAM), Pop. 10,000.

EMPIRE (WE).—Prop., Murton Empire Picture Co., Ltd. 620 seats. Booked at Newcastle-on-Tyne. Two shows nightly. Prices, 6d. and 9d. Phone, Murton 11. Station, Murton Junction, L.N.E.R.

OLYMPIA (AWH).—Prop., Murton Empire Picture Co., Ltd. 400 seats. Booked at Newcastle-on-Tyne. Twice nightly, Mon. and Sat. Once nightly rest of week. Prices, 6d. and 9d. Phone, Murton 11. Station, Murton Junction, L.N.E.R.

NAILSWORTH (GLOS.), Pop. 3,129.

PUBLIC HALL CINEMA (Morrison).—Lessee, W. J. Beach. One show nightly. Two on Sat. Two changes weekly. Prices, 6d. to 1s. Phone, No. 69. Station, Nailsworth, L.M.S.

NANTWICH (CHESHIRE), Pop. 7,132.

COSY CINEMA.—(Closed.)

YE OLD WYCHE THEATRE (WE).—Prop., T. E. Markham. 1,300 seats. Booked at Hall. Continuous. Prices, 6d. to 1s. 6d. Proscenium width, 25 ft. Phone, Nantwich 5338. Café attached. Station, Nantwich, L.M.S.

NELSON (LANCS.), Pop. 33,306.

ALHAMBRA THEATRE, North Street.—Prop., Brown, Ltd. 600 seats. One show nightly. Three Sat. Two changes weekly. Prices, 4d. to 6d. Proscenium width, 20 ft. Stage, 14 ft. deep ; five dressing-rooms. Phone, No. 950. Station, Nelson.

GRAND THEATRE (WE), Market Street.—Prop., Hartley Cinema, Ltd., Palace Theatre, Leeds Road, Nelson. 1,502 seats. Booked at H.O. Once nightly. Twice nightly Sat. Daily Mat. Prices, 6d. to 1s. Proscenium width 30 ft. Phone, Nelson 566. Station, Nelson, L.M.S.

MAJESTIC THEATRE (WE), Scotland Road.— Prop., Victory Theatres, Ltd. Booked at H.O. Edgar Street, Accrington. Phone, Accrington 2,701. 1,100 seats. Three shows

NELSON—Contd.
daily. Prices, 6d. to 1s. 6d. Proscenium width 26 ft. Phone, Nelson 334. Station, Nelson, L.M.S.
PALACE (WE), Leeds Road.—Prop., A.V.O. Cinemas, Ltd. 460 seats. Booked at Hall. Twice nightly. Pictures and Variety. Prices, 6d. to 1s. Proscenium width, 35 ft. Stage, 25 ft. deep ; 12 dressing-rooms. Phone, Nelson 278· Station, Nelson, L.M.S.
QUEEN'S PICTURE THEATRE (WE), Broad Street.—Prop., Hartley Cinemas, Ltd., Palace Theatre, Leeds Road. 827 seats. Booked at H.O. Two shows nightly, three on Sat. Mats. daily. Two changes weekly. Prices, 7d. to 1s. 3d. Proscenium width 22 ft. Phone, Nelson 465. Café attached. Station, Nelson, L.M.S.
REGENT PICTUREDROME (WE), Leeds Road.— Prop., Regent Picturedrome Co., Ltd. 857 seats. Booked at Manchester. Once nightly, twice Sat. Two changes weekly. Prices, 4d. to 1s. 3d. Proscenium width, 25 ft. Phone, Nelson 7. Station, Nelson, L.M.S.
THEATRE DE LUXE (BTH), Railway Street.— Prop. and Man., R. C. Whitaker. 400 seats. Once nightly, twice Sat. Two changes weekly. Prices, 3d. to 6d. Station, Nelson, L.M.S.
TIVOLI (WE), Leeds Road.—Prop., Tivoli Theatre (Nelson), Ltd., 600 seats. Booked at Victory Theatres, Ltd., Accrington. Once nightly. Three shows Sat. Prices, 4d. to 9d. Phone, 515. Station, Nelson, L.M.S.

NESTON AND PARKGATE (CHESHIRE), Pop. 5,674.

NEW CINEMA (Cambriaglow), Chester Road.— Prop., J. F. Burns and Co., Prince of Wales Theatre, Holywell. Phone, Holywell 42. 470 seats. Booked at H.O. Once nightly, Tues. to Fri. Twice on Mon. and Sat. Prices, 6d. to 1s. 4d. Phone, Neston 190. Station, Neston, L.M.S., or Neston and Parkgate, L.N.E.R.

NETHERFIELDS (NOTTS), Pop. 6,386.
ALEXANDRA.—600 seats.
COSY CINEMA (BTH).—Prop., Joseph Wardle, Bentwall House, Arnold, Notts. 650 seats. Booked at H.O. Continuous. Prices, 7d. to 1s. Proscenium width, 17 ft. Station, Carlton, Notts, L.M.S.

NEWARK (NOTTS), Pop. 18,055.
NEWARK KINEMA (BTH).—Prop., Newark Cinemas, Ltd. 750 seats. Two shows nightly. Two changes weekly. Prices, 4d. to 9d. Phone, Newark 40. Station, Newark.
OLLERTON PICTURE HOUSE (BTH), New Ollerton. —Prop., Ollerton Pictures, Ltd. 630 seats. Booked at Hall. Twice nightly, Mon., Sat. Once nightly Tues., Wed., Thurs., Fri. Prices, 6d. to 1s. Phone, Edwinstowe 55x3. Station, Ollerton.
PALACE (WE), Appleton Gate.—Prop., Newark Cinemas, Ltd., National Provincial Bank Chambers, 11, York Street, Sheffield. Phone, Sheffield Central 27421. 1,100 seats. Booked at 37, Collegiate Terrace, Sheffield, by I. Graham. Twice nightly. Occasional Plays. Prices, 6d. to 1s. 6d. Proscenium width, 30 ft. Stage, 45 ft. ; 10 dressing-rooms. Café attached. Phone, Newark 199. Station, Newark, L.N.E.R. and L.M.S.

NEWBIGGIN-BY-THE-SEA (NORTHUMB.), Pop. 6,904.
WALLAW PICTURE HOUSE (BTH).—Prop., Lawson and Carter. 700 seats. One show nightly. Two changes weekly. Station, Newbiggin-by-the-Sea, L.N.E.R.

NEWBRIDGE (MONMOUTH).
GRAND (BA).—Prop., Attwood Theatres. 600 seats. Booked at Cardiff. Once nightly. Station, Newbridge, G.W.R.
MEMORIAL HALL (RCA).—Prop., Celynan Collieries Workmen. 1,000 seats. Booked at Cardiff. Occasional Revues. Once nightly, twice on Sat. Prices, 6d. to 1s. Large stage, four dressing-rooms. Dance Hall attached. Phone, Newbridge 32. Station, Newbridge, G.W.R.

NEW BRIGHTON (CHESHIRE), see Wallasey.

NEWBURN (NORTHUMB.), Pop. 19,539.
IMPERIAL ELECTRIC THEATRE (BTH).—Prop., Dunnan and Maughan. 550 seats. Booked at Hall by Man. Two shows, Mon. and Sat. One rest of week. Prices, 3d. to 8d. Phone, Newburn P.O. Station, Newburn-on-Tyne L.N.E.R.

NEWBURY (BERKS), Pop. 13,336.
CARLTON (WE), Cheap Street.—Controlled by Union Cinemas, Ltd., Union House, 15, Regent Street, London, S.W.1. Phone, Whitehall 8484. Booked at H.O. Continuous. Prices, 6d. to 1s. 6d. Phone, Newbury 91. Films by Roard Transport.
REGAL CINEMA (WE), Bartholomew Street.— Controlled by Union Cinemas, Ltd., Union House, 15, Regent Street, London, S.W.1. Phone, Whitehall 8484. Booked at H.O. Continuous. Prices, 6d. to 2s. 4d. Café attached. Phone, Newbury 410. Station, Newbury, G.W.R.

NEWCASTLE - ON - TYNE (NORTHUMB) Pop. 283,145.
ADELAIDE PICTURE HALL (WE), 385, Elswick Road.—Controlled by Union Cinemas, Ltd., Union House, 15, Regent Street, London, S.W.1. Phone, Whitehall 8484. Booked at H.O. Continuous. Prices, 5d. to 9d. Phone, Newcastle 33267. Station, Newcastle (Central), L.N.E.R.
APOLLO SUPER CINEMA (WE), Byker.—Prop., Tyne Picture House, Ltd., Central Buildings, Station Road, Wallsend-on-Tyne. Phone, Wallsend 63566. 1,634 seats. Booked at H.O. Twice nightly, daily Mat. Phone, Apollo 55830. Station, Heaton, L.N.E.R.
BAMBOROUGH ELECTRIC THEATRE (WE), Union Road, Byker.—Prop., Bamborough Pictures, Ltd. Booked at Hall. Two shows nightly. Prices, 5d. to 9d. Phone, 55619. Station, Newcastle-on-Tyne, L.N.E.R.
BRIGHTON ELECTRIC THEATRE (WE), Westgate Road.—Prop., Newcastle Entertainments, Ltd., Westgate Road. 1,040 seats. Continuous. Dance Hall attached. Prices, 6d. to 1s. Proscenium width, 24 ft. Phone, Central 34462. Station, Newcastle-on-Tyne.
BRINKBURN PICTURE THEATRE (BTP), Brinkburn Street, Byker.—Prop., Tyne Picture Houses, Ltd., Central Buildings, Station Road, Wallsend-on-Tyne. 850 seats. Booked at H.O. Two shows nightly. Phone, 56291. Station, Heaton, L.N.E.R.
CROWN ELECTRIC THEATRE (BTH), Scotswood Road, Elswick.—E. J. Hinge Circuit, 72, Grey Street, Newcastle-on-Tyne. 1,200 seats. Twice nightly, Mon., Fri. and Sat. Continuous, Tues., Wed. and Thurs. Two changes weekly. Prices, 4d. to 9d. Proscenium width, 26 ft. Phone, Dial 38891. Station, Newcastle, L.N.E.R.
ELECTRIC PALACE (WE), Heaton.—Prop., Heaton Assembly Hall Co., Ltd., 45, Heaton Road, Heaton, Newcastle-on-Tyne. Booked at Hall by F. Tabrah. Two shows nightly.

Two changes weekly. Prices, 5d. to 9d. Phone, Central 55400. Café, Dance Halls and Billiards Room attached. Station, Heaton, L.N.E.R.

GAIETY (BTP), Nelson Street.—E. J. Hinge Circuit, 72, Grey Street, Newcastle. 900 seats. Booked at H.O. Continuous. Prices, 4d. to 1s. Phone, Central 21131. Station, Newcastle Central.

GEM (BTH).— 500 seats.

GRAINGER PICTURE HOUSE (RCA), Grainger Street.—Prop., Associated British Cinemas, Ltd., 30-31, Golden Square, London, W.1. Phone, Gerrard 7887. 782 seats. Booked at H.O. Continuous. Prices, 6d. to 1s. 6d. Phone, 21758. Station, Newcastle, L.N.E.R.

GRAND CINEMA (BTP), Benwell.—E. J. Hinge Circuit, 72, Grey Street, Newcastle. Phone, 20317. 670 seats. Booked at H.O. Two shows nightly. Prices, 4d. to 9d. Proscenium width, 20 ft. Stage, 25 ft. deep ; three dressing-rooms. Phone, 33918. Station, Newcastle, L.N.E.R.

GRAND THEATRE (BTP), Byker.—Prop., Gaumont British Pictures Corporation, Ltd., 123, Regent Street, London, W.1. Phone, Regent 6641. 650 seats. Booked at H.O. Two shows nightly. Two Mats. Prices, 3d. to 9d. Phone, 55934. Stage, 36 ft. deep ; 10 dressing-rooms. Proscenium width, 30 ft. Station, Heaton, Newcastle, L.N.E.R.

HAYMARKET CINEMA (WE).—Prop., Associated British Cinemas, Ltd., 30-31, Golden Square, London, W.1. Phone, Gerrard 7887. 2,200 seats. Booked at H.O. Continuous. Prices 6d. to 2s. Café attached. Station, Central, L.N.E.R.

IMPERIAL PICTURE HALL (BTP), Byker.— Lessees, J. H. Dawe, Ltd., Gibb Chambers, Westgate Road, Newcastle-on-Tyne. 800 seats. Two shows nightly. Phone, Central 840. Station, Heaton.

JESMOND PICTURE HOUSE (WE), Lyndhurst. Avenue.—Prop., Jesmond Picture House Co. (1922), Ltd., 47, Pilgrim Street, Newcastle. Phone, 25791. 956 seats. Continuous Mon. to Fri. Twice nightly Sat., Two changes weekly. Prices, 9d. to 1s. Proscenium width, 26 ft. Phone, Jesmond 526. Station, West Jesmond, L.N.E.R.

LYRIC (WE), Heaton.—Prop., Tyne Picture Houses, Ltd., Central Buildings, Station Road, Wallsend. Phone, 63566. Booked at H.O. Continuous. 1,596 seats. Prices, 6d. to 1s. 3d. Proscenium width, 38 ft. Stage, 10 ft. deep. Café attached. Phone, 55463. Station, Heaton, L.N.E.R.

MAJESTIC (WE), Benwell.—Controlled by Union Cinemas, Ltd., Union House, 15, Regent Street, London, S.W.1. Prices, 9d. to 1s. Phone, Whitehall 8484. Booked at H.O. Continuous. Prices, 5d. to 9d. Phone, Newcastle 33202. Station, Newcastle (Cent.).

NEW WESTGATE PICTURE HOUSE (RCA), West-gate Road.— Prop., Denman Picture Houses, Ltd., Denman Stre et. W. 1,865 seats. Booked

at H.O. Continuous. One change weekly. Prices, 7d. to 1s. 6d. Proscenium width, 30 ft. Phone, 24981. Café. Station, Newcastle-on-Tyne, L.N.E.R.

Fitted "ARDENTE" Deaf Aids
See page 258

WURLITZER ORGAN
Installed in this Kinema

NEW THEATRE.—Prop., Dixon Scott, Haymarket House, Newcastle-on-Tyne.

OLYMPIA (WE), Northumberland Road.—Con-trolled by Union Cinemas, Ltd., Union House, 15, Regent Street, London, S.W.1. Phone, Whitehall 8484. Booked at H.O. Contin-nous. Mat. Sat. Two changes weekly. Prices, 4d. to 1s. Phone, 24223. Station, Central.

PALLADIUM (BTP), Groatmarket.—Prop., E. J. Hinge Circuit, 72, Grey Street, Newcastle. Phone 20384. 1,000 seats. Booked at H.O. Prices, 4d. to 1s. Continuous. Station Central.

PARAMOUNT (WE), Pilgrim Street.—Prop., Paramount Theatres, Ltd., 104, Oxford Street, London, W.1. Phone, Museum 4721. 2,602 seats. Booked at H.O. Continuous. Pictures and Variety. Prices, 1s. 4d. to 3s. 6d. Proscenium width, 54 ft. Stage, 21 ft. deep. 7 dressing rooms. Café. Phone, Newcastle 23248. Station, Newcastle Central.

WURLITZER ORGAN
Installed in this Kinema

PAVILION (RCA), Westgate Road.—Prop-Denman Picture Houses, Ltd., 123, Regen-Street, London, W.1. Booked at H.O. Con, tinuous. Prices, 5d. to 1s. 6d. Phone, New, castle 20376I. Station, Newcastle Central, L.N.E.R.

PICTUREDROME (BTH), Gibson Street.—Prop. and Res. Man., H. Millar. 375 seats. Two shows nightly. Two changes weekly. Prices, 3d. to 6d. Phone, 24739. Station, Newcastle-on-Tyne, L.N.E.R.

PICTURE HOUSE (BA).

PLAZA (BA), Westgate Road.—Prop., Plaza (Newcastle-on-Tyne), Ltd. 1,300 seats. Booked at 125, Westgate Road, Newcastle. Continuous. Two changes weekly. Prices, 6d. to 1s. Proscenium width, 30 ft. Phone, 33341. Stage, 18 ft. deep ; 6 dressing-rooms.

QUEEN'S HALL (WE), Northumberland Street. —Prop., General Theatre Corporation, Ltd., 123, Regent Street, London, W.1. 1,400 seats. Phone, Regent 6641. Booked at H.O. Con-tinuous. Prices, 1s. and 2s. Phone, 27888. Station, Newcastle (Central), L.N.E.R.

Fitted "ARDENTE" Deaf Aids
See page 258

RABY GRAND CINEMA (BTP), Commercial Road, Byker.—Prop., Castle Cinema Co., Ltd., 178, Westgate Road, Newcastle-on-Tyne. . 968 seats. Booked at H.O. by W. R. Marshall.

NEWCASTLE-ON-TYNE—Contd.

Two shows nightly. Mid-weekly change. Prices, 4d. to 6d. Phone, Central 55880. Station, Newcastle-on-Tyne.

REGAL (WE), Byker.—Prop., Black's Theatres, 115, Shaftesbury Avenue, London, W.C.2. Phone, Temple Bar 9324. 1,800 seats. Pictures and Variety. Booked at H.O. Variety by Richard and Marks, London. Prices, 6d. to 1s. 3d. Proscenium width, 40 ft. Stage, 30 ft. deep ; 4 dressing-rooms. Phone, Newcastle 55407. Station, Newcastle-on-Tyne Central.

C O M P T O N

ORGAN featured here.

REGAL (BTP), Church Street.—Prop., J. L. Davenport, 14, Rosewood Gardens, Sherrif Hill, Gateshead. 600 seats. Booked at Newcastle. Continuous. Prices, 4d. to 6d. Proscenium width, 22 ft. Phone, Wallsend 63428. Station, Walker.

REGAL CINEMA (BTP), Two Bell Lonnen, Fenham.—Prop., Suburban Cinemas (Newcastle), Ltd. E. J. Hinge Circuit, 72, Grey Street, Newcastle. Booked at H.O. Continuous. 1,300 seats. Prices, 6d. to 1s. Café. Phone, Newcastle-on-Tyne 20384. Station, Newcastle.

RIALTO, Benwell.—Prop. E. J. Hinge Circuit, 72, Grey Street, Newcastle-on-Tyne.

SAVOY CINEMA (BTP), Westmorland Road.— Prop., Savoy (Newcastle-on-Tyne) Plaza Theatre, Ltd., West Road, Newcastle. 700 seats. Booked at H.O. Twice nightly. Prices, 6d. to 1s.

SCALA (BA), Chillingham Road, Heaton.— Prop., General Theatre Corporation, Ltd., 123, Regent Street, London, W.1. Phone, Regent 6641. Booked at H.O. Continuous. Two shows Sat. Prices, 6d. to 1s. 3d. Phone, Newcastle-on-Tyne 554841. Station, Heaton-Newcastle-on-Tyne.

STOLL PICTURE THEATRE (WE), Westgate Road. —Lessee and Licensee, Sir Oswald Stoll, Coliseum Buildings, Charing Cross, London, W.C. Phone, Temple Bar 1500. 1,389 seats. Res. Man., A. C. Harris. Booked at H.O. Continuous. Café attached. Prices, 5d. to 3s. Proscenium width, 29 ft. Stage, 60 ft. 11 dressing-rooms. Phone, Newcastle 21551. Station, Central, L.N.E.R.

VAUDEVILLE (BTH), Walker.—Prop., C. L. and C. R. H. Baker, "Ingleside," Esplanade Avenue, Whitley Bay. Phone, Whitley Bay 192. 450 seats. Booked at Whitley Bay. Continuous. Two changes weekly. Prices, 4d. to 6d. Phone, Wallsend 63357. Station, Walker, L.N.E.R.

WELBECK CINEMA AND PLAYHOUSE (RCA), Scrogg Road, Walker.—Prop., Welbeck Cine and Playhouse Co., Ltd., 71, Howard Street, North Shields. 945 seats. Booked at Hall. Twice nightly. Two changes weekly. Prices, 5d. to 1s. Proscenium width, 29 ft. Stage, 30 ft. deep ; 6 dressing-rooms. Phone, Newcastle 55377. Station, Walker Gate, L.N.E.R.

WESTERHOPE PICTURE HOUSE (Electrocord).

NEWCASTLE-UNDER-LYME (STAFFS), Pop. 23,246.

PAVILION (WE), High Street.—Prop., R. Beresford, 49, High Street. 1,150 seats. Booked at Hall. Continuous. Prices, 4d. to 1s. 3d. Proscenium width, 25 ft. Phone, 67341. Station, Newcastle-under-Lyme, L.M.S.

PLAZA (Picturetone), Nelson Square.—Prop., Plaza (Newcastle-under-Lyme), Ltd. 650 seats. Booked at Pavilion. Continuous. Prices, 4d. to 1s. 3d. Proscenium width 18 ft. Phone, Newcastle-under-Lyme 6637. Station, Newcastle, Staffs, L.M.S.

REGAL (WE), High Street.—Prop., R. Beresford, 49, High Street. 1,044 seats. Continuous. Booked at Pavilion. Prices, 6d. to 1s. 3d. Phone, 67341. Station, Newcastle-under-Lyme, L.M.S.

SAVOY CINEMA (BTH).—Prop., Associated British Cinemas, Ltd., 30–31, Golden Square, W.1. 1,250 seats. Booked at H.O. Continuous. Prices, 4d. to 1s. Phone, 6565. Station, Newcastle, L.M.S.

NEW FERRY, near Birkenhead (CHESHIRE), Pop. 16,450.

LYCEUM (WE).—Prop., Lyceum Picture House, Ltd. Booked by Cheshire Picture Halls, Ltd., at Park Road, North Birkenhead. 1,176 seats. Two shows nightly. Twice weekly. Prices, 6d. to 1s. 6d. Station, Bebington and New Ferry, L.M.S.

NEWFIELD (CO. DURHAM), Pop. 7,000.

GRAND ELECTRIC THEATRE (BTH).—Prop., C. Buckton, South View, West Pelton. 600 seats. Booked at Hall. Two shows nightly. Two changes weekly. Prices, 3d. to 7d. Station, Pelton, L.N.E.R.

NEWHAVEN (SUSSEX), Pop. 6,790.

CINEMA DE LUXE (WE), High Street.—Prop. R. L. Cooke, Sussex Lodge, Newhaven. 494 seats. Two shows nightly. Mat., Sat. Two changes weekly. Prices, 6d. to 1s. 6d. Station, Newhaven, S.R.

KINEMA.—Lessee, C. Cooke, 12, Boughton Road, Newhaven. Booked at Hall. Continuous. Prices, 4d. to 9d.

NEW HERRINGTON (CO. DURHAM), Pop. 13,000.

TIVOLI (WE).—Prop., Fencehouses Palace, Ltd. Once nightly Sun. to Thurs. Twice nightly Fri. and Sat. Prices, 5d. to 9d. Proscenium width, 21 ft. Phone, Houghton 143. Station, Penshaw, L.N.E.R.

NEW MALDEN (SURREY), Pop. 12,650.

PLAZA (Cinephone), Malden Road.—Props., London and District Cinemas, Ltd. 62, Shaftesbury Avenue, W. 700 seats. Continuous. Booked at H.O. Two changes weekly. Prices, 7d. to 1s. 6d. Café. Phone, New Malden 0263. Station, New Malden, S.R.

NEWMARKET (CAMBS.), Pop. 9,753.

CINEMA, Exning.

KINGSWAY (BTP).—Prop., Kingsway (Newmarket), Ltd. 850 seats. Booked at Hall. Twice nightly. Prices, 7d. to 2s. 6d. Phone, Newmarket 406. Station, Newmarket, L.N.E.R. and Road Transport.

VICTORIA (Imperial), High Street.—Prop., Kingsway (Newmarket), Ltd. 550 seats. Pictures and occasional Variety. Booked at Hall. Two shows nightly. Two changes weekly. Prices, 7d. to 1s. 6d. Stage, 15½ ft. deep. Two dressing-rooms. Ballroom attached. Phone, Newmarket 229. Station, Newmarket, L.N.E.R.

NEW MILLS (near Stockport) (DERBYSHIRE), **Pop. 8,551.**
ART THEATRE (BTH), Jodrell Street.—Prop., New Mills Cinema (Sheffield), Ltd., 19, Howard Street, Sheffield. Phone, Sheffield 26002. 600 seats. Booked at H.O. Occasional variety Twice nightly. Prices, 4d. to 1s. 3d. Proscenium width, 22 ft. Stage, 22 ft. 5 dressing-rooms. Phone, New Mills 90. Station, New Mills, L.M.S.
CINEMA (WE), Union Road.—Prop., New Mills Cinema (Sheffield), Ltd., 19, Howard Street, Sheffield. Phone, Central 26002. 738 seats. Booked at H.O. Two shows Mon., Tues. and Thurs. Three rest of week. Prices, 6d. and 1s. Phone, New Mills 91. Station, New Mills, L.M.S.

NEW MILTON (HANTS), **Pop. 5,000.**
WAVERLEY (BTH).

NEWPORT (I. OF W.), **Pop. 11,313.**
GRAND THEATRE (BA), Lugley Street.—Prop., Isle of Wight Theatres, Ltd., Theatre Royal, Ryde. Phone, Ryde 237. 500 seats. Booked at The Queen's, Sandown. Twice nightly. Mat., Wed. and Sat. Prices, 6d. to 2s. 6d. Phone, Newport 300. Station, Newport (I.O.W.), S.R.
MEDINA CINEMA (WE), High Street.—Prop., Medina Cinema, Ltd., 36, Kingsway, W.C.2. 1,000 seats. Booked at Gem, Southall. Continuous. Mats. Wed. and Sat. Phone, Newport 291. Station, Newport (I.O.W.), S.R.
Fitted "ARDENTE" Deaf Aids See page 258
ODEON THEATRE.—Prop., Odeon Theatres, Ltd., Cornhill House, Bennett's Hill, Birmingham. Phone, Midland 2781. Booked at 49, Park Lane, W.1. Continuous. Prices, 9d. to 2s. Phone, Newport 515.

NEWPORT (MONMOUTH), **Pop. 89,198.**
CAPITOL (BA).— Dock Street. Prop., Western Theatres, Ltd. 1,000 seats. Continuous. Prices 6d. to 1s. 6d. Phone, Newport 3648. Station, Newport.
COLISEUM (RCA), Clarence Place.—Prop., Gaumont-British Picture Corpn., Ltd., 123, Regent Street, London, W.1. Phone, Regent 6641. 1,000 seats. Booked at H.O. Continuous. Two changes weekly. Prices, 6d. to 1s. 6d. Proscenium width, 26 ft. Phone, Newport 37761I. Station, Newport, G.W.R.
GEM CINEMA (KAMM).—Prop., H. Gill, "Carrigbawn," Maesglas. 300 seats. Booked at 23, Charles Street, Cardiff. Continuous. Prices, 3d. to 6d.
LYCEUM (WE).—Prop., Mr. and Mrs. S. Cooper. Lessees, Lyceum, Newport, Ltd. 1,100 seats. Booked at Hall. Continuous. Prices, 6d. to 1s. 6d. Proscenium width, 27 ft. Café. Phone, 2906. Station, Newport, G.W.R.
ODEON THEATRE.—Prop., Odeon Theatres, Ltd., Cornhill House, Bennett's Hill, Birmingham. (In course of construction).
OLYMPIA (WE).—Lessees, Associated British Cinemas, Ltd., 30-31, Golden Square, London, W.1. Phone, Gerrard 7887. 1,570 seats. Booked at H.O. Continuous. Prices 6d. to 1s. 6d. Proscenium width, 36 ft. Phone, Newport 2259. Station, Newport, Mon., G.W.R.
OLYMPIA (BA), Cwmbran.—500 seats.
RILL PALACE (BTH), 100, Commercial Road.—Prop., Mrs. Annie Averbuch, 21, Fields Road,

Newport. 350 seats. Booked at Hall. Continuous. Prices, 4d. to 9d. Proscenium width, 17 ft. Station, Newport, G.W.R.
RITZ (WE).—Controlled by Union Cinemas, Ltd., 15, Regent Street, S.W.1. Booked at H.O. Continuous. Station, Newport, G.W.R.
TREDEGAR HALL PICTURE HOUSE (WE), Stow Hill.—Prop., London and Southern Super Cinemas, Ltd., 32, Shaftesbury Avenue, London, W.1. Phone, Whitehall 0183. 1,019 seats. Booked at London. Continuous. Prices, 6d. to 1s. 6d. Proscenium width, 25 ft. Phone, Newport 2031.

NEWPORT (SALOP), **Pop. 3,439.**
PICTURE HOUSE, Town Hall.—Prop., Wright's Picture House (Newport), Ltd. 450 seats. Booked at Hall. Prices, 6d. to 1s. 3d. Proscenium width, 20 ft. Stage, 10 ft. Phone-Newport 58. Station, Newport, L.M.S.

NEWPORT PAGNELL (BUCKS), **Pop. 3,957.**
ELECTRA (BA), St. John Street.—Props., G. Salmons, L. Salmons and A. Bullard. 585 seats. One show nightly. Two shows Sat. One change weekly. Prices, 4d. to 1s. 3d. Phone, Newport Pagnell 29. Station, Newport Pagnell, L.M.S., or Film Transport Road Service.

NEWQUAY (CORNWALL), **Pop. 5,958.**
PAVILION (RGA).—Lessees, Sound and Movement Cinemas, Ltd., Oliver's Chambers, Frankfort Street, Plymouth. 750 seats. Booked at H.O. Three shows daily. Two changes weekly. Prices, 6d. to 1s. 6d. Proscenium width, 30 ft. Phone, Newquay 149. Station, Newquay, G.W.R.
VICTORIA THEATRE (BTH).—Prop., Sound and Movement Cinemas, Ltd., Oliver's Chambers, Frankfort Street, Plymouth. Phone, Plymouth 4981. 450 seats. Booked at H.O. Three shows daily. Phone, Newquay 341. Station, Newquay, G.W.R.

NEWSHAM (NORTHUMB.), **Pop. 6,985.**
KINO HALL (AWH).—Prop., M. Bice, 34, Barras Avenue, Plessey Road, Blyth. Phone, Blyth 281. 600 seats. Booked at Newcastle. One show nightly, two on Sat. Two changes weekly. Prices, 3d. to 1s. Proscenium width, 18 ft. Station, Newsham, L.N.E.R.
PLAZA.—Prop., Mrs. M. Brice, Blyth. Phone, Newcastle 25509.

NEW SILKSWORTH (CO. DURHAM).
HIPPODROME (BTP).—E. J. Hinge Circuit. Phone, Newcastle 20317. 638 seats. Booked at 72, Grey Street, Newcastle. Twice nightly. Occasional variety, booked by Hinge's Productions Ltd. Prices, 3d. to 6d. Phone, Ryhope 231. Station, Sunderland, L.N.E.R.

NEWTON ABBOT (DEVON). **Pop. 15,003.**
ALEXANDRA THEATRE (BTH).—550 seats.
IMPERIAL THEATRE (WE), Queen Street.— Newton Abbot Picture House, Ltd. 536 seats. Continuous evenings. Daily Mat. Booked by C. M. Myott, Lloyds Bank Chambers, Vaughan Parade, Torquay. Prices, 6d. to 1s. 6d. Proscenium width, 23 ft. Phone, 155. Station, Newton Abbot, G.W.R.
ODEON THEATRE (BTH). Wolborough Street.— Prop., Odeon (Newton Abbot), Ltd., Cornhill House, Bennett's Hill, Birmingham. Phone, Midland 2781. Booked at 49, Park Lane, W.1. Prices, 9d. to 2s. Phone, Newton Abbot 673.

PATHE PICTORIAL—Novel, Entertaining, Unique.

NEW WASHINGTON (Co. Durham), **Pop. 15,807.**

Alexandra (we).—Prop., Northern Victory Theatres, Ltd. 869 seats. One show nightly, two on Sat. Two changes weekly. Prices, 8d. to 1s. Station, Usworth, L.N.E.R.

Globe Theatre (bth).—670 seats.

NORMANTON (Yorks), **Pop. 15,684.**

Empire Theatre (we), Wakefield Road.—Booked by London and Southern Super Cinemas, Ltd., 32, Shaftesbury Avenue, London, W.1. 450 seats. Two shows nightly. Prices, 5d. to 1s. Phone, Normanton 120. Station, Normanton L.M.S.

Grand Picture House (bth), Castleford Road.—Props., J. & M. Segelman, 55, Cowper Street, Chapeltown. Phone, Leeds 41249. 525 seats. Twice nightly. Mats., Mondays, Thursdays, Saturdays. Prices, 4d. to 1s. Phone, Normanton 15. Proscenium width, 20 ft. Station, Normanton, L.M.S.

Majesty (we), High Street.—Prop., Star Cinemas (London), Ltd., 5, Manchester Avenue, E.C.1. 900 seats. Booked at Star Cinema, Castleford. Continuous. Prices, 4d. to 1s. Proscenium width, 28 ft. Phone, Normanton 103. Station, Normanton, L.M.S.

NORTHALLERTON (Yorks.), **Pop. 4,787.**

Central Picture House (bth).—Prop., Northallerton Cinema, Ltd. 500 seats. Booked at Hall by Man. Twice nightly. Prices, 5d. to 1s. 3d. Station, Northallerton, L.N.E.R.

Cinema de Luxe (bth).—Romanby Road.—Prop., Northallerton Cinema, Ltd. 370 seats. Booked at Hall by Man. Continuous. Prices. 3d. to 1s. Station, Northallerton, L.N.E.R.

NORTHAMPTON (Northants), **Pop. 92,314.**

Cinema de Luxe (we), Campbell Street.—Prop., Cinema de Luxe (Northampton), Ltd. 1,000 seats. Booked at Hall. Twice nightly. Daily Mat. Prices, 6d. to 1s. 3d. Stage, 12 ft. deep. Phone, Northampton 150. Station, Castle, Northampton, L.M.S.

Coliseum (Gyrophone), Kingsthorpe Hollow—Prop., Coliseum Cinema (Northampton), Ltd. Phone, Northampton 1350. 750 seats. Booked at Hall. Continuous. Prices, 6d. to 1s. 3d. Phone, Northampton 1350. Station, Castle, Northampton, L.M.S., and Road Transport.

Exchange Cinema (we), 4, The Parade.—Prop., Provincial Cinematograph Theatres, Ltd., New Gallery House, 123, Regent Street, London, W.1. Phone, Regent 8080. 2,212 seats. Booked at H.O. Two shows nightly. Mats. daily. Prices, 5d. to 1s. 6d. Café attached. Phone, Northampton 105. Station, Castle.

Fitted "ARDENTE" Deaf Aids
See page 258

WURLITZER ORGAN
Installed in this Kinema

Majestic Cinema (bth), Gold Street.—Prop., Associated British Cinemas, Ltd., 30–31, Golden Square, London. 778 seats. Booked at H.O. Twice nightly. Mats. daily ex. Fri. Two changes weekly. Prices, 3d. to 1s. Proscenium width, 19 ft. Phone, Northampton 170. Station, Northampton (Castle), L.M.S.

Picturedrome (we).—Prop., Picturedrome Syndicate. 700 seats. Booked at Cinema de Luxe, Northampton. Twice nightly. Prices. 6d. to 1s. 6d. Proscenium width, 18 ft, Phone, Northampton 628. Station, Castle, L.M.S.

Plaza (ba).—400 seats. Continuous. Mat. daily.

Regal Super Cinema (Morrison), Grove Road.—Prop., Mabel Norfolk. 1,000 seats. Continuous. Booked at Hall. Pictures and Variety. Prices, 7d. to 1s. 6d. Station, Castle, L.M.S.

Roxy.—Booked by S. Gasham, Park House, Friar Lane, Nottingham.

Savoy (we), Abington Square.—Props., Associated British Cinemas, Ltd., Golden Square, London, W.1. Booked at H.O. Phone, Northampton 3139. Station, Castle Street, L.M.S.

COMPTON
ORGAN featured here.

St. James Cinema (ba), West Bridge.—Prop., St. James Electric Cinema, Ltd. 1,000 seats. Continuous. Two changes weekly. Prices, 3d. to 1s. Phone, Northampton 1617. Station, Northampton (Castle), L.M.S.

Temperance Hall Cinema (Kamm), Newlands—Prop., Temperance Hall Cinema Co., Ltd. 750 seats. Booked at London and Birmingham. Continuous nightly. Mat. Fri. and Sat. Prices, 4d. to 1s. 3d. Proscenium width, 24 ft. Phone, Northampton 779. Station, Castle, L.M.S.

Tivoli (rca), Far Cotton.—Props., William Harris. 834 seats. Continuous. Prices, 6d. to 1s. 6d. Phone 2795. Station, Northampton.

NORTHENDEN (Cheshire), **Pop. 3,097.**

Forum (we).

WURLITZER ORGAN
Installed in this Kinema

Royal Electric Theatre (we), Longley Lane.—Prop. and Res. Man., Peter Leigh. 370 seats. Continuous Mon. to Fri. Three shows Sat. Booked at Hall. Two changes weekly. Prices 2d. to 8d. Proscenium width, 22 ft. Station, Northenden, Cheshire R.

NORTHFLEET (Kent), **Pop. 16,429.**

Northfleet Cinema.—Prop., Lion Cinematograph Co., Ltd., 43, Whitcomb Street, London. W.C.2. Station, Northfleet, S.R.

Strathcona (Kamm), High Street.—Props. Lion Cinematograph Co., Ltd., 43, Whitcomb Street, London, W.C.2. 800 seats. Booked at H.O. Continuous. Café and Dance Hall. Phone, Gravesend 1289. Station, Northfleet, S.R.

NORTH SHIELDS (Northumberland), **Pop. 56,000.**

Albion Cinema (rca), Albion Road.—Prop., Albion Cinema, Ltd. 1,066 seats. Booked at Hall. Two shows nightly. Prices, 6d. to 1s. Proscenium width, 38 ft. Stage, 21 ft. deep ; four dressing rooms. Phone, North Shields 498. Station, North Shields.

Borough Theatre (ba), Lower Rudyerd Street.—Prop., Denman Picture Houses, Ltd., 123, Regent Street, London. W.1. Phone, Regent 6641. 1,440 seats. Booked at H.O. Two shows nightly. Stage, 27½ ft. deep ; four dressing-rooms. Prices, 3d. to 1s. 3d. Phone, North Shields 323. Station, North Shields.

COMEDY (BTP).—Prop., David Hashman, 47, Preston Avenue, North Shields. 850 seats. Booked at Hall. Twice nightly. Mat. Mon. Prices, 4d. to 1s. Phone, North Shields 651.

GAIETY (Electrocord).—Prop. and Res. Man., J. Ritson, 9, Albany Park Road, Tynemouth. 500 seats. Booked at Newcastle-on-Tyne. Two shows nightly. Two changes weekly. Prices, 2d. to 6d. Proscenium width, 18 ft.

HOWARD HALL (BTP).—Prop., Shipcote Co., Ltd., Shipcote Hall, Gateshead. 1,160 seats. Booked at H.O. Continuous Mon. to Fri. Two shows Sat. Two changes weekly. Prices, 3d. to 6d. Proscenium width 30 ft. Phone, North Shields 450. Station, North Shields.

PRINCE'S THEATRE (WE), Russell Street.—Prop., Gaumont British Picture Corpn., Ltd. 1,790 seats. Continuous. Prices, 6d. to 1s. 6d. Phone, North Shields 999. Café attached. Station, North Shields, L.N.E.R.

TYNE PICTURE HALL (Filmophone).—Prop., Dixon Scott. Twice nightly. Two changes weekly. Prices, 3d. to 4d. Station, North Shields, L.N.E.R.

NORTH WALSHAM (NORFOLK), **Pop. 4,137**

REGAL (BTH), New Road.—Prop., V.E.H Cinemas, Ltd., The Lido, Aylsham Road Norwich. Phone, Norwich 894. 650 seats. Booked at H.O. Continuous. Twice on Sat. Prices, 7d. to 2s. Proscenium width, 30 ft. Phone, 115. Films by E. R. Ives, Ltd., Norwich.

NORTHWICH (CHESHIRE), **Pop. 18,728.**

NEW CENTRAL (RCA).—Prop., Cheshire County Cinemas, Ltd., The Empress, Runcorn. Phone, 199. 700 seats. Booked at H.O. Continuous. Prices, 5d. to 1s. Proscenium width, 22 ft. Phone, 188. Station, Northwich, L.M.S.

NEW THEATRE (Building).—Prop., Cheshire County Cinemas, Ltd. Empress Theatre, Runcorn.

PAVILION KINEMA (WE), Hayhurst Street.— Prop., Cheshire County Cinemas, Ltd. Phone, Northwich 199. Booked at Empress Kinema, Runcorn. 801 seats. Two shows nightly. Mats., Thurs. and Sat. Prices, 3d. to 1s. Phone, Northwich 256. Stage, 30 ft. deep ; five dressing rooms. Station, Northwich, L.M.S.

PLAZA KINEMA (WE).—Cheshire County Cinemas Ltd. Empress Kinema, Runcorn, Cheshire. Phone, 199. 1,182 seats. Booked at H.O. Twice nightly. Mats., Mon., Wed., Sat. Prices, 6d to 1s. 6d. Phone, Northwich 606. Café. Station, Northwich, L.M.S.

NORTHWOOD (MIDDLESEX), **Pop. 9,000.**

EMBASSY.—Prop., Shipman and King, A 84, Shell Mex House, Strand, W.C.2.

PLAYHOUSE (BTH).—Prop., Alfred Dove, 41, Lonsdale Road, Barnes, S.W.13. Phone, Riverside 1765. 250 seats. Continuous. Prices, 3d. to 1s. 6d. Phone, Northwood 132. Station, Northwood, Met. Rly. from Baker Street and L.N.E.R. and Film Transport Co.

NORTON (nr. Malton) (YORKS), **Pop. 3,934.**

MAJESTIC PICTURE THEATRE (WE).—Prop., C. S. Read. Booked at Malton. Pictures and Variety. Continuous. Prices, 6d. to 1s. 3d. Stage, 10 ft. deep ; two dressing-rooms. Phone, Norton 173. Station, Malton, L.N.E.R. Films by Road Transport.

NORTON-ON-TEES (CO. DURHAM), **Pop. 4,500.**

NORTON CINEMA (WE), Norton Avenue.—Prop., Superb Cinema Co., Ltd., 980 seats. Booked at hall. Continuous. Prices, 4d. to 1s. 3d. Proscenium width, 25 ft. Phone, Norton 117. Station, Stockton, L.N.E.R.

NORWICH (NORFOLK), **Pop. 126,207.**

CAPITOL (BTH), Aylsham Road.—Props., V.E.H Cinemas, Ltd., The Lido, Aylsham Road, Norwich. Phone, Norwich 894. 800 seats. Booked at H.O. Continuous. Prices, 7d. to 2s. Proscenium width, 35 ft. Phone, Norwich 2916. Road Transport.

CARLTON (WE), All Saint Green.—Prop., Norwich Cinemas, Ltd associated with County Cinemas, Ltd., Dean House, Dean Street, London, W.1. 1,920 seats. Booked at H.O. Continuous Mon. to Fri. Three shows Sat. Prices 6d. to 2s. Proscenium width 40 ft. Stage, 30 ft. ; six dressing-rooms. Café attached. Phone, Norwich 194. Station, Thorpe, L.N.E.R.

COMPTON
ORGAN featured here.

CINEMA PALACE (BTH), Magdalen Street.— Props., Chas. Thurston & Sons, 900 seats. Booked at Hall by Gen. Man., E. J. Protheroe. Continuous. Prices, 5d. to 1s. 4d. Proscenium width, 20 ft. Phone, Norwich 1169. Station, Thorpe, L.N.E.R.

EMPIRE PICTURE HOUSE (BTP), Oak Street.— Prop., Eastern Counties Cinemas, Ltd., Regent Theatre, Chelmsford. 550 seats. Booked at H.O. by R. Gerald Balls. Continuous. Children's Mat., Sat. Two changes weekly. Prices, 3d. to 9d. Phone, Norwich 1291. Station, Thorpe.

HAYMARKET PICTURE HOUSE (WE).—Prop., Denman Picture Houses, Ltd. Booked at H.O., 123, Regent Street, London, W.1. Continuous, Mon. to Fri. Three separate shows Sat. Three times daily. Prices, 6d. to 2s. 6d. Phone, Norwich 1047. Café attached. Station, Thorpe, L.N.E.R.

Fitted "ARDENTE" Deaf Aids
See page 258

COMPTON
ORGAN featured here.

HIPPODROME (WE).—Props., Associated British Cinemas, Ltd., 30-31, Golden Square, London, W.1. Phone, Gerrard 7887. 1,600 seats. Booked at H.O. Continuous. Mon to Fri. Three separate shows Sat. Prices, 6d. to 2s. Café attached. Station, Thorpe, Norwich, L.N.E.R.

LIDO (BTH), Aylsham Road.—Prop., V.E.H. Cinemas, Ltd. Booked at Hall. Prices, 7d. to 2s. Phone, Norwich 894. Films by Road Transport.

NORWICH ELECTRIC THEATRE (BTP), Prince of Wales Road.—Prop., Eastern Counties Cinemas, Ltd., Regent Theatre, Chelmsford. 1,000 seats. Booked at H.O. by R. Gerald Balls. Continuous. Prices, 7d. to 2s. 6d. Phone, Norwich 1388.

REGENT THEATRE (WE), Prince of Wales Road.— Prop., Alexandra Picture House and Theatre

The Pick Of Variety And Radio Stars In PATHETONE WEEKLY.

NORWICH—Cont.

Co., Ltd. Controlled by Associated British Cinemas, Ltd., 30-31, Golden Square, W.1. Phone, Gerrard 7887. 1,523 seats. Booked at H.O. Continuous, Mon. to Fri. Three shows Sat. Prices, 6d. to 2s. 4d. Proscenium width, 30 ft. Stage, 25 ft. deep; three dressing-rooms. Cafe and Ballroom attached. Phone, Norwich 331. Station, Norwich, Thorpe, L.N.E.R.

THEATRE-DE-LUXE (WE), St. Andrews Street.—Prop., Theatre-de-Luxe (Norwich), Ltd. 700 seats. Booked at Hall. Continuous. Phone, Norwich 1292. Station, Norwich, L.N.E.R., and Motor Transport.

NOTTINGHAM (NOTTS), Pop. 281,280.

ADELPHI.—Booked by S. Graham, Park House, Friar Lane, Nottingham.

ASPLEY PICTURE HOUSE (WE), Nuthall Road.—Prop., Aspley Picture House Co., Ltd. 1,294 seats. Pictures and Variety. Booked by E. M. Wright. Continuous. Prices, 6d. to 1s. Proscenium width, 56 ft. Stage, 25 ft. deep. Phone, Nottingham 76449. Station, Nottingham, L.M.S. and L.N.E.R.

BOULEVARD ELECTRIC THEATRE (WE), Radford Road.—Prop., State Electric Palaces, Ltd., 36, St. Mary's Gate, Derby. Phone, Derby 1673. 748 seats. Booked at Hall. Continuous. Three Mats. weekly. Two changes weekly. Prices, 6d. to 1s. Proscenium width, 20 ft. Phone, Nottingham 75381. Station, Midland.

CAPITOL. Booked by S. Graham, Park House, Friar Lane, Nottingham.

CURZON CINEMA (BTH), Mansfield Road.—Prop., Carrington Picture House Co. Booked by S. Graham, Park House, Friar Lane, Nottingham. Phone, Nottingham 65413. Station Nottingham, L.M.S.

DALE CINEMA (WE), Sneinton Dale. — Prop., Dale Cinemas, Ltd. 1,500 seats. Booked at Hall. Continuous, Mon., Thurs., Fri., Sat. Twice nightly Tues. and Wed. Prices, 7d. to 1s. 3d. Phone, Nottingham 43144. Station, Nottingham, L.M.S.

ELECTRA (BA), Alfreton Road.—Prop., Nottingham Cinemas, Ltd., Goldsmith Picture House. 800 seats. Booked at H.O. Continuous. Prices, 5d. to 1s. Phone, Nottingham 71061. Station, Nottingham, L.M.S.

ELITE PICTURE THEATRE (WE).—Prop., Elite Picture Theatre (Nottingham), Ltd., 1,500 seats. Continuous. Prices, 6d. to 2s. Restaurant, Ballroom & Tea Rooms attached. Phone, Nottingham 43640. Station, Nottingham, L.M.S., or Victoria, Nottingham, L.N.E.R.

Fitted "ARDENTE" Deaf Aids
See page 258

COMPTON

ORGAN featured here.

FORUM, Aspley.—Booked by Herbert Elton, Commerce Chambers, Elite Buildings, Nottingham.

GLOBE PICTURE HOUSE (WE), Trent Bridge.—Prop., Globe (Nottingham), Ltd. 709 seats. Booked by T. Wright, Goldsmith P.H., Nottingham. Continuous. Two changes weekly. Prices, 6d. to 1s. Proscenium width, 24 ft. Phone, Nottingham 84882. Station, Nottingham, L.M.S.

GOLDSMITH PICTURE HOUSE (WE).—Head office, Goldsmith Street. Prop., T. Wright, "St. Ives," Westdale Lane, Nottingham. Phone, Nottingham 65157. 700 seats. Booked at Hall. Continuous. Prices, 6d. to 1s. 4d. Stage, 25 ft. deep; three dressing-rooms. Proscenium width, 40 ft. Phone, Nottingham 44180. Station, Nottingham, L.M.S.

GRAND (BA), Hyson Green.—Prop., Provincial Cinematograph Theatres, Ltd., 123, Regent Street, London, W.1. Phone, Regent 6641. 800 seats. Booked at H.O. Phone, Nottingham 75300I.

HIGHBURY VALE CINEMA.

HIPPODROME (WE).—Prop., Provincial Cinematograph Theatres, Ltd., New Gallery House, 123, Regent Street, London, W.1. Phone, Regent 8080. 1,742 seats. Continuous. Booked at H.O. Prices, 7d. to 2s. 4d. Phone, Nottingham 44653. Stations, Nottingham, L.M.S., and Victoria, L.N.E.R.

Fitted "ARDENTE" Deaf Aids
See page 258

WURLITZER ORGAN
Installed in this Kinema

ILKESTON ROAD PICTURE HOUSE (BTH).—Prop., Radford Palace Co., Ltd. 920 seats. Booked by Mr. Wilcock, 8, Carlton Road, Nottingham. Continuous. Mat., Mon., Thurs., Sat. Prices 6d. to 1s. Phone, Nottingham 76113. Station, Nottingham, L.M.S.

IMPERIAL PICTURE HOUSE (WE), Wilford Road.—Prop., Meadows' Cinema (Notts), Ltd. 750 seats. Continuous. Two changes weekly. Booked by T. Wright at Goldsmith Street Picture House, Nottingham. Prices, 6d. to 1s. Phone, Nottingham 85533. Films by Road Transport.

KINEMA (BTH), Hayden Road, Sherwood.—Prop. and Res. Man., C. Woodward, 3, Osborne Ave., Sherwood. 860 seats. Continuous. Two changes weekly. Prices, 6d. to 1s. 3d. Phone, Nottingham 64854. Station, Nottingham.

LENO'S PICTUREDROME (WE), Radford Road.—Prop., Highbury Cinema, Ltd., Highbury Vale, Bulwell. 961 seats. Booked at H.O. Continuous. Mats., Mon., Thurs. and Sat. Prices, 7d. to 1s. Phone Nottingham 7354. Station, Nottingham, L.M.S.

LOUNGE PICTURE THEATRE (Marshall), Shakespeare Street.—Props., Notts and Derby Cinema Exchange, Ltd. 600 seats. Booked at Hall. Continuous. Prices, 6d. to 1s. Station, Victoria, L.N.E.R.

MAJESTIC (WE), Woodborough Road, Mapperley.—Prop., A. Severn & Son. 700 seats. Booked at Hall. Continuous. Prices, 6d. to 1s. 3d. net. Proscenium width, 24 ft. Phone, 64804. Station, Nottingham, L.M.S., and L.N.E.R.

MECHANICS' PICTURE HALL (BA), Milton Street.—Prop., Denman (Midland) Cinemas, Ltd., 123, Regent St., London, W.1. 1,200 seats Booked at H.O. Continuous. Prices, 4d to 1s. 6d. Phone, Nottingham 45403I. Station, Nottingham, L.M.S. and L.N.E.R.

NEW EMPRESS CINEMA (BTH), St. Ann's Well Road.—Props., Associated British Cinemas, Ltd., 30-31, Golden Square, London, W.1. 1,500 seats. Booked at H.O. Continuous. Prices, 5d. to 1s. 6d. Phone, Nottingham 42129. Stations, Victoria, L.N.E.R., or Midland, L.M.S.

NEWS HOUSE (BTP), Upper Parliament Street.—300 seats. Continuous. 6d. and 1s. Phone, Nottingham 3374. Station, Nottingham, L.M.S.

PALACE (WE), Trent Bridge.—1,000 seats.

PALACE THEATRE (Picturetone), Sneinton Road. —Props., EXORS. E. Widdowson, Bulwell. Phone, Bulwell 78438. 700 seats. Booked at H.O. Continuous. Prices, 4d. to 9d. Phone, Nottingham 45443. Station, Nottingham, L.M.S.

PICTURE HOUSE (WE), Berridge Road.—Props., Lenton Picture House, Ltd. 1,000 seats. Booked by T. Wright, Goldsmith Picture House, Nottingham. Continuous. Mats., Mon., Thurs. and Sat. Prices, 6d. to 1s. Proscenium width, 28 ft. Phone, Nottingham 75374. Stations, Nottingham, L.M.S. and L.N.E.R.

PLAZA CINEMA (WE), Trent Bridge.—Props., Plaza Entertainments, Ltd. 883 seats. Continuous. Prices, 7d. to 1s. 6d. Phone, Nottingham 85585. Station, Nottingham, L.M.S.

QUEENS (WE), Arkwright Street.—Props., the Queens Cinema Co., Ltd. 400 seats. Booked at Hall. Continuous. Prices, 6d. to 1s. Phone 84694. Station, L.M.S., Carrington Street.

REGENT HALL (WE), Mansfield Road. — Props., Peoples Cinema, Ltd. 800 seats. Booked at Hall. Continuous. Two changes weekly. Prices, 7d. to 1s. 4d. Proscenium width, 34 ft. Phone, 42159I. Stations, Nottingham, L.M.S. and L.N.E.R.

RITZ.—Booked by S. Graham, Park House, Friar Lane, Nottingham.

RITZ (WE), Angel Row.—Props., Ritz (Nottingham), Ltd., Dean House, Dean Street, London, W.1. Phone, Gerrard 4543. 2,500 seats. Booked at H.O. Continuous. Prices, 9d. to 3s. Phone, Nottingham 2244. Café and Ballroom.

ROXY.—Booked by S. Graham, Park House, Friar Lane, Nottingham.

SAVOY CINEMA (WE), Derby Road.—Props., Lenton Picture House, Ltd., Goldsmith Street, Nottingham. Phone, Goldsmith Street 44180. 1,300 seats. Booked at 6d to 1s. 6d. Booked at H.O.

SCALA THEATRE (WE), Market Street.—Props., Victory Cinemas, Ltd., 18, Low Pavement, Nottingham. Phone, Nottingham 41084. 900 seats. Booked at Hall. Continuous. Prices, 9d. to 1s. 6d. Phone, Nottingham 3633. Stations, Nottingham, L.M.S. and L.N.E.R.; and Transport.

TUDOR (WE), West Bridgford.—Props., Tudor Cinemas, Ltd. 1,391 seats. Booked by H. Stott, Tudor Cinema, West Bridgford, Nottingham. Phone, 85338. Station, Nottingham, L.M.S.

VERNON PICTURE HOUSE (WE), 320, Vernon Road, Basford.—Props., Vernon Picture House (Basford), Ltd. Booked at Hall. Continuous. Prices, 6d. to 1s. Phone, 7080. Station, Basford, L.M.S.

VICTORIA PICTURE HOUSE (BTH), Milton Street. —Props., Sherwood Picture House Co., Ltd. 700 seats. Booked at Hall. Continuous. Prices, 6d. to 1s. 3d. Phone, Nottingham 43771. Stations, Nottingham, Victoria, L.N.E.R., and Midland.

NUNEATON (WARWICKS), **Pop. 46,305.**

CINEMA, Arley.—Prop., Frank Voce. Booked at Hall. Continuous. Two changes weekly.

GRAND (RCA), Chapel End.—400 seats.

HIPPODROME (RCA), Bond Street. — Props., Associated British Cinemas, Ltd., 30-31, Golden Square, London, W.1. Phone, Gerrard 7887. 1,170 seats. Booked at H.O. Continuous. Mat. daily. Prices, 9d. to 1s. Proscenium width, 35 ft. Stage, 25 ft. deep ; five dressing-rooms. Phone, Nuneaton 58. Stations, Abbey Street and Trent Valley.

NEW PALACE (Film Industries). — Props., Smith and Clarke, 54, Queen's Road, Nuneaton. 990 seats. Booked at Hall. Continuous. Prices, 6d. to 1s. 3d. Proscenium width, 20 ft. Phone, Nuneaton 355. Dance Hall attached. Station, Nuneaton (Abbey Street and Trent Valley), L.M.S.

PRINCE'S (BTP), Market Place.—Prop., A. English, Higham Lane Road, Nuneaton. 413 seats. Booked at Leicester. Continuous nightly. Daily mat. Two changes weekly. Prices, 2d. to 1s. Phone, Nuneaton 225. Station, Nuneaton, L.M.S. (Abbey Street and Trent Valley); and Film Transport.

REGAL THEATRE (WE), Lister Street.—Props., Sheridan Film Service, Ltd., 179, Horninglow Street, Burton-on-Trent. Phone, 3324. Booked at H.O. Continuous nightly. Daily mat. Prices 6d. to 1s. 3d. Proscenium width, 30 ft. Phone, Nuneaton 576. Station, Nuneaton (Trent Valley).

RITZ (WE), Abbey Road.—Controlled by Union Cinemas, Ltd., 15, Regent Street, S.W.1. Phone, Whitehall 8484. Booked at H.O. Continuous. Station, Nuneaton (Abbey St. and Trent Valley), L.M.S.

ROYAL CINEMA (AWH), Stratford Street.—Prop., B. G. Hetherington, 134, Lutterworth Road, Nuneaton. Phone, 614. 260 seats. Continuous. Proscenium width, 22 ft. Prices, 6d. to 9d. Phone, Nuneaton 541. Station, Nuneaton, L.M.S.

SCALA (WE), Abbey Street.—Props., Scala (Midland Counties), Ltd. 900 seats. Continuous. Mat. daily except Fri. Prices, 6d. to 1s. 6d. Proscenium width, 28 ft. Phone, Nuneaton 196. Station, Nuneaton, L.M.S. (Trent Valley and Abbey Street).

OAKENGATES (SALOP), **Pop. 11,189.**

GROSVENOR CINEMA (WE).—Prop., H. M. Wright. Twice nightly. Prices, 6d., 9d. and 1s. Phone, Oakengates 48. Station, Oakengates.

OAKHAM (RUTLAND), **Pop. 3,191.**

PICTURE HOUSE (Imperial).—Prop., F. B. Salt, 5, Burley Road, Oakham. 250 seats. Booked at Hall. Continuous Thurs. and Sat. Once nightly rest of week. Prices, 3d. to 1s. 6d. Proscenium width, 16 ft. Stage, 17 ft. deep ; two dressing-rooms. Phone, Oakham 19. Station, Oakham, L.M.S.

REGAL (Morrison)—Prop., F. B. Salt, 5, Burley Road, Oakham. 480 seats. Booked at Hall. Continuous Mon., Thurs., Fri., Sat. Once nightly except Tues., Wed., Prices, 3d. to 1s. 6d. Phone, 19. Station, Oakham, L.M.S.

OKEHAMPTON (DEVON), **Pop. 3,352.**

CINEMA (BTH), Lodge Road. — Prop., S. Newcombe. 300 seats. Booked at Hall or 11, New Road, by C. Holmes. Twice nightly except Tues. ; three shows Sat. Prices, 9d. to 1s. 9d. Station, Okehampton, S.R.; and by Auto Transport.

For Snap And Sparkle PATHE PICTORIAL Cannot Be Beaten.

OLDBURY (WORCS), **Pop. 35,918.**
NEW PALACE OF VARIETIES (BTP), Freeth Street.—Prop., J. M. Dent, St. Romans, Somerville Road, Sutton Coldfield. Booked at Hall. Continuous. Pictures and Variety. Prices, 3d. to 1s. 3d. Proscenium width, 42 ft. Stage, 22 ft. deep : two dressing-rooms. Station, Oldbury, L.M.S.
PICTURE HOUSE (BTP), Birmingham Street.— Prop., T. Leach, " Ramleh," Charlemount Road, West Bromwich. 1000 seats. Booked at Queen's Picture House, West Bromwich. Continuous. Prices, 6d. to 1s. Phone, Broadwell 1069. Station, Oldbury, L.M.S.
REGENT (BA).

OLDHAM (LANCS), **Pop. 140,309.**
ALHAMBRA PICTURE HOUSE (Edibell), Horsedge Street.—Props., Shaws Amusements, Ltd. 450 seats. Booked at Hall. Evenings continuous. Holidays twice nightly. Mat. Sat. and holidays. Two changes weekly. Prices, 3d. to 6d. Station, Oldham (Mumps).
COSY CINEMA, Bridge Street.—Prop., Harry Shaw, 29, Briscoe Street, Oldham. 450 seats. Continuous nightly. Daily Mat. Twice nightly Sat. Prices, 3d. to 6d. Station, Oldham (Mumps).
ELECTRACEUM (BTP), King Street.—Props., Oldham District Land and Builders' Society. 820 seats. Booked at Hall. Continuous. Two changes weekly. Prices, 4d. to 8d. Proscenium width, 26 ft. Phone, Main 1216. Station, Oldham (Central).
EMPIRE (BTH), Waterloo Street.—Props., Pavilion Cinema (Oldham), Oxford Road, Manchester. Booked by H. O. Moorhouse Circuit. 2,000 seats. Continuous evenings. Twice nightly Sat. Mat. daily. Prices, 6d. to 1s. Phone, Oldham Main 4362. Station, Oldham (Mumps), L.M.S.
GEM PICTURE HOUSE (WE), Suffolk Street, Werneth.—Props., Gem Pictures (Oldham), Ltd. 1,167 seats. Booked at Hall. Continuous nightly Mon. to Fri. Twice nightly Sats. Mats. Mon., Thurs. and Sat. Prices, 4d. to 9d. Proscenium width, 20 ft. Phone, Oldham Main 920. Station, Oldham (Werneth), L.M.S.
GRAND THEATRE.—Props., Associated Provincial Picture Houses, Ltd., 123, Regent Street, London, W.1.
GROSVENOR SUPER CINEMA (WE), Union Street. —Props., Picture House (Oldham), 1927, Ltd. 1094 seats. Three shows daily. Booked by C. Ogden, 11, Piccadilly, Manchester. Prices, 6d. to 1s. 6d. Proscenium width, 26 ft. Phone, Main 4463. Station, Oldham (Central), L.M.S.
IMPERIAL (WE), Featherstall Road North.— Props., Palatine Cinema Co., Ltd. 801 seats. Booked at Hall. One show nightly. Two on Sat. Prices, 3d. to 8d. Phone, Oldham 1498. Station, Oldham (Werneth), L.M.S.
KING'S PICTURE HALL (BTH), Fairbottom St.— Props., Albion Picture Hall (Oldham), Ltd. 2,000 seats. Man. Dir., D. Cooper. Twice nightly. Mat. Sat. Prices, 4d. to 1s. 3d. Phone, Oldham 1403. Station, Oldham (Central), L.M.S.
ODEON THEATRE (BTH)—Props., Odeon(Oldham), Ltd., Cornhill House, Bennett Hill, Birmingham. Phone, Midland 2781. Booked at 49, Park Lane, W.1. Continuous. Prices,

6d. to 1s. 6d. Proscenium width, 32 ft. Phone, Main 1328.
PALLADIUM (WE), Union Street.—Props., Associated British Cinemas, Ltd., 30/31, Golden Square, W.1. Gerr. 7881. 2,000 seats. Booked at H.O. Continuous. Prices, 4d. to 1s. 3d. Phone, Oldham Main 1027. Station, Oldham (Central), L.M.S.
PAVILION PICTURE PALACE (Electrocord), High Street, Lees.—Prop., Harold Ward, 6, Brown Street, Manchester, 2. Phone, Deansgate 3542. 600 seats. Booked at H.O. Continuous. Prices, 4d. to 9d. Phone, Main 1768. Station, Lees, near Oldham.
RITZ.—Prop., L. Morris, 52, Shaftesbury Avenue, London, W.1. 2,000 seats.
SADDLEWORTH PICTURE PALACE.
SAVOY CINEMA (BTP), Huddersfield Road.— Prop., Savoy Entertainments (Oldham), Ltd. 750 seats. Booked at Hall. Continuous. Twice nightly Sat. Four Mats., weekly. Billiards room attached. Prices, 4d. to 9d. Phone, Main 2618. Station, Oldham (Mumps).
THEATRE ROYAL (WE).—Prop., F. E. Spring, 3, The Parsonage, Manchester. Phone, Bla. 7905. 1,000 seats. Booked at H.O. Prices, 4d. to 1s. 9d. Proscenium width, 30 ft. Stage, 40 ft. deep ; 12 dressing-rooms. Phone, Main 2549. Station, Oldham (Mumps), L.M.S.
VICTORY CINEMA (BTP), Union Street.—Prop., Pavilion Cinemas, Ltd. H. D. Moorhouse Circuit, 7, Oxford Street, Manchester. 1,021 seats. Continuous evenings. Twice nightly Sat. and holidays. Mat. daily. Prices, 4d. to 1s. Café attached. Phone, Oldham 1120.

OLD HILL (STAFFS), **Pop. 11,600.**
GRAND THEATRE (WE).—Prop., B. P. Priest. 890 seats. Booked at Hall. Continuous Tues., Wed., Thurs. and Fri. Twice nightly Mon. and Sat. Two changes weekly. Prices, 6d. to 1s. Phone, Cradley 6161. Station, Old Hill, G.W.R.

OLNEY (BUCKS), **Pop. 2,871.**
ELECTRIC CINEMA (Mihaly), 81, High Street.— Prop., J. E. Poyntz. 400 seats. Booked at Scala, Oxford. Once nightly. Three shows Sat. Prices, 6d. to 1s. 3d. Stage, 20 ft. deep ; two dressing-rooms. Station, Olney, L.M.S.

ONCHAN (I.O.M.), **Pop. 2,000.**
THE AVENUE (BTH).—Props., Oucham Cinemas, Ltd., c/o Gaiety Theatre, Douglas, I.O.M. Continuous Summer. Winter, Continuous. Mon., Thurs., Sat., once nightly Tues., Wed., Fri. 875 seats. Prices, 9d. to 1s. 6d. Proscenium width, 34 ft. Stage, 13 ft.; three dressing-rooms. Phone, Douglas 1331. Station, Douglas.

ORMSKIRK (LANCS.), **Pop. 17,121.**
PAVILION (WE).—Prop., F. S. Donaldson, Ormes Buildings, Parsonage, Manchester. 520 seats. Booked at H.O. Continuous evenings. Twice Sat. Prices, 6d. to 1s. Phone, Ormskirk 269. Station, Ormskirk, L.M.S.
REGAL.—Props., Regal (Ormskirk), Ltd., 10, Dale Street, Liverpool. Continuous nightly. Daily Mat. Prices, 6d. to 1s. 6d. Proscenium width, 34 ft. Phone, Ormskirk 444.

The BEST Is Cheapest; PATHE GAZETTE.

ORPINGTON (KENT), **Pop. 7,049.**
COMMODORE THEATRE (Kamm).—Prop., Commodore Cinema (Orpington), Ltd. 1,000 seats. Prices, 9d. to 2s. Café attached. Phone, Orpington 1000. Station, Orpington, S.R.
PALACE (disc.)—Prop. and Res. Man., A. Spencer May. 400 seats. Booked at 233, High Street, Orpington. Continuous. Two changes weekly. Prices, 6d. to 1s. 6d. Phone, Orpington 1000. Station, Orpington, S.R.

OSSETT (YORKS), **Pop. 14,838.**
PALLADIUM (WE), Town Hall Square.—Prop., Palladium (Ossett), Ltd. 846 seats. Booked by Mr. Friedman, 2, Bristol Street, Leeds. Twice nightly. Mat., Mon. and Sat. Prices, 6d. to 1s. Phone, Ossett 157. Station, Ossett, L.N.E.R.

OSWALDTWISTLE (LANCS.), **Pop. 14,221.**
EMPIRE PICTURE PALACE (BTP), Union Road.—Props., J. Whitaker and W. Reader, 500 seats. Two shows nightly. Mats., Mon., Wed. and Sat. Two changes weekly. Prices, 4d. to 8d.
PALACE CINEMA (BTP), Rhyddings Street.—Prop. and Res. Man., E. Wardle. 840 seats. One show nightly. Two changes weekly. Prices, 4d. to 9d. Phone, Accrington 2980.
PALLADIUM (WE), Union Road.—Prop., Associated British Cinemas, Ltd., 30-31, Golden Square, W.1. Phone, Gerrard 7887. 1027 seats. Continuous Mon. to Fri. Twice nightly Sat. Mat. Mon., Wed., Sat. Booked at H.O. Two changes weekly. Prices, 4d. to 9d. Proscenium width, 18 ft. Phone, Accrington 2825. Station, Church and Oswaldtwistle, L.M.S.

OSWESTRY (SHROPSHIRE), **Pop. 9,754.**
KING'S THEATRE (BTH).—Prop., Wm. C. Hill Black. 600 seats. Booked at Hall. Continuous. Prices 6d. to 1s. 6d. Phone, Oswestry 148. Station, Oswestry, G.W.R.
PLAYHOUSE (BTH) Oswald Road.—Prop., Wm. C. Hill Black, King's Theatre, Oswestry. 450 seats. Booked at Hall. Continuous. Prices, 4d. to 1s. Phone, 148. Station, Oswestry, G.W.R.
REGAL (WE).—Prop., Oswestry Regal Cinema Co., Ltd. Controlled by Bernstein Theatres, Ltd., 36, Golden Square, W.1. Gerrard 3554. 1,100 seats. Booked at H.O. Continuous. Phone, Oswestry 230.

OTLEY (near Leeds) (YORKS), **Pop. 11,020.**
WESTGATE CINEMA (AWH). 580 seats.

OTTERY ST. MARY (DEVON), **Pop. 3,715.**
SCALA PICTURE THEATRE (Morrison).—Honiton Cinema, Ltd., High Street, Honiton. 220 seats. Booked at H.O. Once nightly. Two changes weekly. Prices, 6d. to 1s. 6d. Proscenium width, 21 ft. Stage, 10 ft. deep. Phone 100. Station, Ottery St. Mary (S.R.). Films by Road Transport.

OUNDLE (NORTHANTS), **Pop. 2,000.**
VICTORIA.—Two shows Sat. only.

OUTWOOD (near Wakefield) (YORKS).
EMPIRE (Cinephone).—Prop., Rothwell Empire, Ltd. Phone, Rothwell 48. 750 seats. Booked at H.O. One show nightly. Prices, 4d. to 10d. Phone, Lofthouse Gate 7169. Station, Lofthouse for Outwood.

OVENDEN (YORKS), **Pop. 6,000.**
PIONEER PICTURE HOUSE (BTH), Wheatley Lane. Prop., Ovenden Pioneer Picture House Co.,

Ltd., Wheatley Lane, Lee Mount, Halifax. 700 seats. Booked at Hall by Man. Continuous. Prices, 4d. to 1s. Phone, Halifax 2004. Station, Ovenden (Parcel Office).

OXFORD (OX.), **Pop. 80,540.**
CINEMA, Wallington.
ELECTRA PALACE (WE), Queen Street.—Controlled by Union Cinemas, Ltd., Union House, 15, Regent Street, London, S.W.1. Phone, Whitehall 8484. Continuous. Booked at H.O. Prices, 9d. to 3s. Café attached. Phone, Oxford 2990. Station, Oxford, G.W.R. Films by Road Transport.
Fitted "ARDENTE." Deaf Aids See page 258
GEORGE STREET CINEMA (WE), 32, George Street. Controlled by Union Cinemas, Ltd., Union House, 15, Regent Street, London, S.W.1. Phone, Whitehall 8484. Booked at H.O. Continuous. Two changes weekly. Prices, 6d. to 1s. 10d. Phone, Oxford 2676. Station, Oxford, G.W.R. Films by Road Transport.
HEADINGTON CINEMA (F.I.)—E. James Hall, Clifton House, Headington. Phone 6812. 500 seats. Booked at Hall. Continuous. Prices, 6d. to 2s. Proscenium width, 24 ft. Phone, Headington 6718. Station, Oxford, G.W.R.
MAJESTIC (BTH).—Controlled by Union Cinemas, Ltd., 15, Regent Street, W.1. Phone, Whitehall 8484. Booked at H.O. Continuous. Prices, 5d. to 2s. 4d. Café and Dance Hall attached. Phone, Oxford 3727.
PALACE CINEMA (WE), Cowley Road.—Controlled by Union Cinemas, Ltd., Union House, 15, Regent Street, London, S.W.1. Phone, Whitehall 8484. Booked at H.O. Continuous. Prices, 6d. to 2s. Phone, Oxford 4022. Station, Oxford, G.W.R., or Road Transport.
PREMIER PICTURE PALACE, Middle Barton.
REGAL, Cowley.—Controlled by Union Cinemas, Ltd., Union House, 15, Regent Street, London, S.W.1. Phone, Whitehall 8484. Continuous. Booked at H.O.
RITZ, Cowley.—Controlled by Union Cinemas, Ltd., Union House, 15, Regent Street, London, S.W.1. Booked at H.O. Continuous. Films and Variety. Prices, 9d. to 3s. Phone, Oxford 4607. Café attached. Road Transport Station, Oxford, G.W.R. and L.M.S.

COMPTON

ORGAN featured here.

SCALA CINEMA (BTH), Walton Street.—Prop., J. E. Poyntz. 500 seats. Booked at Hall. Continuous. Prices, 6d. to 1s. 10d. Phone, Oxford 2967. Station, Oxford, G.W.R. Films by Road Transport.
SUPER CINEMA (WE), Magdalen Street.— Controlled by Union Cinemas, Ltd., Union House, 15, Regent Street, London, S.W.1. Phone, Whitehall 8484. Booked at H.O. Continuous. Two changes weekly. Prices, 9d. to 2s. 6d. Phone, Oxford 3067. Café attached. Station, Oxford, G.W.R. and L.M.S. Films by Motor Transport.

OXTED (SURREY), **Pop. 3,800.**
NEW CINEMA. 460 seats.
PLAZA (WE).—Prop., C. A. Lepine. Continuous nightly. Mat., Wed. and Sat. Prices, 7d. to 2s. 6d. Phone, Oxted 567. Films by Road Transport.

PADIHAM (LANCS.), **Pop. 11,632.**
GLOBE.—Prop., New Empire (Burnley), Ltd.
Empire Theatre, Burnley. Phone, Burnley
2453.
GRAND THEATRE (WE), Station Road.—Prop.,
New Empire (Burnley), Ltd. 1,232 seats. One
show nightly, two on Sat. Mat., Tues.,
Thurs. and Sat. Prices, 5d. to 1s. Stage,
30 ft. deep. Two dressing-rooms. Café
attached. Phone, Padiham 69. Station,
Padiham, L.M.S.

PADSTOW (CORNWALL), **Pop. 1,929.**
CINEDROME (Morrison).—Prop., E. J. and W.
E. Pope. 350 seats. Booked at Cinedrome,
Liskeard. Once nightly. Café attached.
Prices, 6d. to 2s. Proscenium width, 18 ft.
Phone, 44. Station, Padstow, S.R.

PAIGNTON (DEVON), **Pop. 18,405.**
ELECTRIC PALACE (Picturetone), Totnes Road.—
Prop., A. O. Ellis. Booked at H.O. Home-
side, Higher Warberry, Torquay. Phone,
Torquay 2895. 300 seats. Continuous.
Prices, 6d. to 1s. 3d. Proscenium width,
16 ft. Phone, Paignton 5353. Station,
Paignton, G.W.R.
PAIGNTON PICTURE HOUSE (WE), Torbay Road.
—Prop., Paignton Picture House, Ltd. 600
seats. Booked at Hall. Continuous. Phone,
Paignton 5544. Station, Paignton, G.W.R.
and Road Transport.
PALLADIUM (WE).—Prop., Paignton Palladium,
Ltd. 1,000 seats. Booked at Hall. Pictures
and Variety. Variety Booked at Hall. Prices,
6d. to 2s. Proscenium width, 34 ft. Stage,
12 ft. deep ; 3 dressing rooms. Cafe. Phone,
Paignton 82369. Station, Paignton, G.W.R.
**Fitted "ARDENTE" Deaf Aids
See page 258**
REGENT CINEMA (WE), Station Square.—Props..
Picture Playhouses, Ltd. Booked by W.
Farrant Gilley, 36, Torwood Street, Torquay.
1,500 seats. Continuous. Prices, 7d. to 2s,
Proscenium width, 27 ft. Phone 5017. Station
Paignton, G.W.R.

PARKSTONE (DORSET).
.REGAL CINEMA (WE), Ashley Road.—Prop.,
Regal (Parkstone), Ltd., Regent, Poole.
Booked at H.O. 1,200 seats. Continuous.
Prices, 9d. to 2s. Café. Station, Parkstone.
**Fitted "ARDENTE" Deaf Aids
See page 258**

PATELEY BRIDGE (YORKS), **Pop. 2,500.**
ODDFELLOWS HALL (Home Made). 400 seats.

PATRICROFT (near Manchester) (LANCS),
Pop. 17,923.
MAJESTIC (WE).—Prop., Lancashire Entertain-
ments, Ltd., Regent Cinema, Eccles.
Eccles 3843. 820 seats. Continuous nightly.
Mats., Mon., Thurs., Sat. Twice nightly Sat.
Two changes weekly. Prices, 6d. to 1s.
Proscenium width, 20 ft. Phone, Eccles 3109.
Station, Patricroft, L.M.S.
PALLADIUM (BTP).—Prop., Counties Cinema
(Patricroft), Ltd.—750 seats. Continuous,
Mon. to Fri. Two shows Sat. Booked at
Hall. Two changes weekly. Prices, 4d. to 8d.
Phone, Eccles 3524. Station, Patricroft
(Manchester), L.M.S.

PEACEHAVEN (SUSSEX), **Pop. 5,000.**
PAVILION (AWH).—Prop., P. H. Braithwaite,
South Coast Road, Telscombe Cliffs. 270

seats. Continuous. Prices, 6d. to 1s. Proscenium width, 20 ft. Films by Road Transport.

PEEL (I.O.M.).
PAVILION (AWH), Stanley Road.—Prop., Strand
Cinema Theatre Co. (1920), Ltd., 39, Strand
Street, Douglas, I.O.M. 400 seats. Phone,
Douglas 14. Booked by E. C. Clayton,
Bank Chambers, 70, The Moor, Sheffield,
Continuous Mon., Thurs. and Sat. Once
nightly Tues., Wed. and Fri. Prices, 6d. and
1s. Ballroom attached. Phone, Peel 224.
Station, Peel.

PELAW-ON-TYNE (CO. DURHAM), **Pop.
6,000.**
GRAND CINEMA (BTP), Joicey Street.—E. J
Hinge Circuit, 72, Grey Street, Newcastle.
700 seats. Booked at H.O. Twice nightly.
Prices, 3d. to 9d. Phone, Newcastle 82213.
Station, Pelaw Junction, L.N.E.R.

PELTON (CO. DURHAM), **Pop. 8,817.**
KING'S HALL. (BTP). 975 seats.

PEMBERTON (LANCS), **Pop. 23,642.**
CARLTON (BTP).—Prop., Eagle Picturedromes,
Ltd. Reg. Office, County Playhouse, King
Street, Wigan. Phone, Wigan 3476. Booked
by T. C. Robinson, Cromford House, Man-
chester. Twice nightly Mon. and Sat.,
one show other nights. Two changes weekly.
Prices, 5d. to 9d. Phone, 122. Station,
Pemberton, L.M.S.
QUEEN'S THEATRE (BTP), Ormskirk Road.—
Prop., Eagle Picturedromes Ltd., Reg.
Office, County Playhouse, King Street,
Wigan. Phone, Wigan 3476. Booked by
T. C. Robinson, Cromford House, Man-
chester. Two shows nightly. Prices, 5d.
to 9d. Phone, Pemberton 122. Station,
Pemberton, L.M.S.

PENDLEBURY (LANCS), **Pop. 9,966.**
PALACE (WE), Bolton Road.—Prop., Palace
de Luxe (East Lancashire), Ltd. 1,119 seats.
Booked at Hall. Continuous Mon. to Fri.
Twice nightly Sat. Occasional variety,
booked direct. Prices, 4d. to 9d. Proscenium
width, 30 ft. Stage, 7 ft. deep ; 2 dressing-
rooms. Phone, Swinton 1805. Station, Swinton, L.M.S.

PENGAM (MON). **Pop. 3,012.**
REGAL CINEMA (Kalee).—Prop., Palace Cinema
and Billiard Hall Co., Ltd., High Street.
500 seats. Pictures and Variety. Continuous
Mon. and Sat. from 6 p.m. Once nightly rest
of week. Films booked at Hall and Variety
by Selwyn's Agency, Newport. Prices, 4d.
to 1s. Stage, 21 ft. deep ; two dressing-rooms.
Proscenium width, 19½ ft. Dance and Billiard
Hall. Station, Pengam, G.W.R.
PALLADIUM.—Prop., Rowland Williams.

PENISTONE (YORKS), **Pop. 3,261.**
TOWN HALL PICTURE HOUSE (BTH).—Prop. and
Man., Joseph Jesson. 900 seats. Booked
at Hall. One show nightly. Mat. Sat.
Two changes weekly. Prices, 5d. to 1s.
Phone, Penistone 83. Station, Penistone,
L.M.S.

PENRITH (CUMB), **Pop. 9,065**
ALHAMBRA (BA).—Booking Man., A. V. Bran-
ford, H.O. Gaiety, Whitehaven. 800 seats.
REGENT (BTH), Old London Road.—Props.,
New Kinema (Penrith), Ltd., Golden Lion

Chas. Whitby. Phone 149. 713 seats. Booked at Waterloo Cinema, Whitby. Continuous evenings, Mon. to Fri. Three shows Sat. Mat., Tues. Prices, 6d. to 1s. 6d. Proscenium width, 45 ft. Café attached. Phone, 400. Station, Penrith.

PENZANCE (CORNWALL), **Pop. 11,342.**
CINEMA (BTP).—Prop., Penzance Cinema Ltd. 550 seats. Booked at H.O., Regent Hotel, Penzance. Phone, Penzance 146 and 330. Station, Penzance.

PAVILION THEATRE (BTP).—Prop., Penzance Cinema, Ltd. 600 seats. Booked at H.O., Regent Hotel, Penzance. Phone, Penzance 146 and 330. Station, Penzance, G.W.R.

REGAL (BTH).—Prop., Penzance Cinema, Ltd. 500 seats. Booked at H.O., Regent Hotel, Penzance. Phone, Penzance 146 and 330. Station, Penzance, G.W.R.

RITZ.—Controlled by Union Cinemas, Ltd., Union House, 15, Regent Street, London, S.W.1. Phone, Whitehall 8484. Booked at H.O. Continuous. Prices, 6d. to 2s. 4d. Proscenium width, 40 ft. Phone, 729. Station, Penzance, G.W.R.

C O M P T O N

ORGAN featured here.

WINTER GARDEN.—Prop., Penzance Winter Garden, Ltd. Phone, Penzance 146.

PERRANPORTH (CORNWALL), **Pop. 2,375.**
PALACE (Brown).—Prop., W. Dowling. 300 seats. Pictures and occasional Plays. Prices, 6d. to 1s. 6d. Proscenium width, 20 ft. Stage, 12 ft. deep; two dressing rooms. Station, Perranporth, G.W.R.

PERSHORE (WORCS), **Pop. 3,462.**
PLAZA (AWH).—325 seats. Booked at Plaza Bromyard. Continuous nightly. Mat., Sat. Prices, 6d. to 1s. 3d. Station, Pershore, G.W.R.

PETERBOROUGH. (NORTHANTS). **Pop. 43,558.**
BROADWAY KINEMA (RCA), Broadway.—Prop., Provincial Cinematograph Theatres, Ltd., 123, Regent Street, London, W.1. Phone, Regent 8080. 1,474 seats. Booked at H.O. Continuous. Prices, 6d. to 1s. 6d. Proscenium width, 30 ft. Phone, Peterborough 3125II. Station, Peterborough, L.N.E.R. and L.M.S.
Fitted "ARDENTE" Deaf Aids
See page 258

CITY CINEMA (RCA).—Prop., Peterborough Amusements, Ltd. 1,200 seats. Booked by H. Bancroft, Hippodrome, Wisbech, Cambs. Continuous. Cafe and Dance Hall attached. Prices, 6d. to 1s. 10d. Phone, Peterborough 2197. Stations, Peterborough, East or North.
Fitted "ARDENTE" Deaf Aids
See page 258

GEM CINEMA (Morrison), Palmerston Road, Woodston.—Prop., W. Harris. 550 seats. Continuous nightly. Mats. Mon., Thurs., and Sat. Prices, 7d. to 1s. 4d. Booked at Hall. Proscenium width, 20 ft. Stage, 8 ft. deep; two dressing rooms. Phone, Peterborough 2662. Station, Peterborough, L.N.E.R. and Film Transport.

NEW ENGLAND CINEMA (Morrison).—Prop. A. Alderman. 500 seats. Continuous. Two changes weekly. Prices, 6d. to 1s. 6d. Station, Peterborough.

ODEON THEATRE (BTH).—Prop., Odeon (Peterborough), Ltd., Cornhill House, Bennett's Hill, Birmingham. Phone, Midland 2781. Booked at 49, Park Lane, W.1.

PALACE (BA), Broadway.—Prop., R. Bancroft. 490 seats. Booked by H. Bancroft at Wisbech Hippodrome, Ltd. Continuous. Mat. Sat. Prices, 7d. to 1s. 10d. Phone, Peterborough 497.

PRINCESS THEATRE (WE), Lincoln Road.—Prop., Princess Theatre, Cornhill House, Bennett's Hill, Birmingham. Booked at H.O. Continuous. Mats. Mon., Wed., and Sat. Prices, 7d. to 1s. 6d. Phone, Peterborough 2821.

PETERSFIELD (HANTS), **Pop. 4,386.**
SAVOY (Edibell).—Prop., South Downs Cinemas, Ltd., 2, Rugby Road, Southsea. Phone, Portsmouth 3456. 850 seats. Booked at H.O. Continuous. Prices, 6d. to 2s. Phone, Petersfield 338. Station, Petersfield, S.R. Films by Marmion Motor Transport.

PETTS WOOD (KENT).
EMBASSY.—Prop., Shipman & King, Shell Mex House, W.C.2. Phone, Temple Bar 5077. Booked at H.O. Continuous. Prices, 6d. to 2s. Phone, Orpington 2943.
Fitted "ARDENTE" Deaf Aids
See page 258

PETWORTH (SUSSEX), **Pop. 3,050.**
PICTUREDROME (Imperial), Pound Street.—Prop., S. Collins, Grove House, Grove Street, Petworth. 160 seats. Booked at Hall. Once nightly. Continuous. Sat. Prices, 9d. to 1s. 9d. Station, Petworth, S.R., or Southdown Bus.

PEWSEY (WILTS), **Pop. 1,760.**
BOUVERIE HALL.

PICKERING (YORKS), **Pop. 3,668.**
CENTRAL CINEMA (BTH).—Prop., H. Boulton. 400 seats. Booked at Hall. Continuous. Mon. to Fri. Three shows Sat. Prices, 6d. to 1s. 3d. Proscenium width, 14 ft. Station, Pickering, L.N.E.R., also by Cleveland Film Transport Co., Leeds.

PILSLEY (DERBYSHIRE), **Pop. 2,820.**
RITZ.

PINNER (MIDDLESEX), **Pop. 9,402.**
IDEAL CINEMA (BTH), Field End Road, Eastcote.—Prop., W. A. Telling, Ltd., 62-64, Raymouth Road, Bermondsey. Phone, Bermondsey 1195. 448 seats. Booked at Hall. Continuous. Prices, 6d. to 1s. 6d. Proscenium width, 25 ft. Phone, Pinner 3178. Station, Ruislip and Ickenham, L.N.E.R.-G.W.R. Joint.

LANGHAM.—Props., Associated British Cinemas, Ltd., 30-31, Golden Square, London, W.1. Phone, Gerrard 7887.

NEW EMBASSY (RCA), Bridge Street.—Prop., Pinner Cinema Co., Ltd., 30-31, Golden Square, W.1. 1,500 seats. Booked at H.O. Prices, 6d. to 2s. Phone, Pinner 3242. Station, Pinner, Met. Rly.

PINXTON (NOTTS), **Pop. 5,105.**
PICTURE PALACE (Harley).—Prop., Ollerton Pictures, Ltd. 500 seats. Pictures and occasional Variety. Booked at Empire, Somercotes. Continuous. Two changes weekly. Prices, 6d. to 1s. Stage, 14 ft. deep; four dressing-rooms. Phone, No. 48. Station, Pinxton, L.M.S. and L.N.E.R.

PATHETONE WEEKLY, The Super Screen Magazine!

PITSEA (ESSEX), **Pop. 1,129.**
BROADWAY CINEMA.—Prop., Roger H. Howard, "Robeck," London Road, Pitsea. Phone, Vange 71· 600 seats. Booked at Hall. Continuous. Occasional Variety. Prices, 6d. to 1s. Phone, Vange 6. Café attached· Station, Pitsea.

PLATT BRIDGE (LANCS).
MINERS HALL (BA).—Props., Livesey and Forshaw. 420 seats. Booked at 48, Scholes, Wigan. Twice nightly. Two Mats. weekly. Prices, 4d. to 9d. Phone, 6198. Station, Platt Bridge, L.M.S.
PALACE PICTURE HOUSE (BTH).—Prop., Eagle Picturedromes, Ltd., Booked by T.C. Robinson, Cromford House, Manchester. Twice nightly. Two changes weekly. Prices, 4d. to 9d. Station, Platt Bridge, L.M.S.

PLYMOUTH (DEVON), **Pop. 208,166.**
BELGRAVE THEATRE (BA).—700 seats.
CINEDROME (WE), Ebrington Street.—Prop., Mrs. M. Hoyle. 900 seats. Booked at Hall. Continuous. Two changes weekly. Prices, 4d. to 1s. Phone, Plymouth 4810. Stations, Friary, S.R.; and North Road, G.W.R.
CRITERION KINEMA (BTH).—Prop., Frank Pearce. 600 seats. Continuous. Two changes weekly. Prices, 4d. to 1s. Station, Millbay, G.W.R.
ELECTRIC THEATRE (WE) Fore Street.—Prop., Electric Theatre (Devonport), Ltd. 2,300 seats. Booked at Hall. Continuous. Prices, 6d. to 1s. 6d. Stage and 6 dressing-rooms. Phone, Devonport 416. Station, Plymouth, North Road, G.W.R.
EMPIRE THEATRE (Picturetone), Union Street.— Prop., Empire (Plymouth), Ltd. 300 seats. Man., Dir., A. O. Ellis. Booked at "Homeside," Higher Warberry, Torquay. Phone, Torquay 2895. Continuous. Two changes weekly. Prices, 6d. to 9d. Phone, Plymouth 2640. Station, Millbay, G.W.R.
FORD PALLADIUM (RCA), St. Levan's Road, Devonport.—Prop., Henry B. Mather. 430 seats. Booked at Gaiety, Union Street. Continuous. Mats., Wed. and Sat. Prices, 7d. to 1s. Station, Plymouth (North Road); and Film Transport Services (Cardiff), Ltd.
GAIETY THEATRE (RCA). Union Street.—Prop., Henry B. Mather. 400 seats. Booked at Hall. Continuous. Prices, 6d. and 1s. Station, North Road, G.W.R.; or Film Transport Services (Cardiff), Ltd.
GAUMONT PALACE (BA).—Prop., Gaumont British P.C.T., 123, Regent Street, London. 2,025 seats. Booked at H.O. Continuous· Station, Millbay, G.W.R.

Fitted "ARDENTE" Deaf Aids
See page 258

COMPTON

ORGAN featured here.

GRAND (RCA), Union Street.—Prop., H. B· Mather Cinemas, Ltd. 1,400 seats. Booked at Hall. Continuous. Prices, 4d. to 1s. Phone, Plymouth 60139. Station, North Road, G.W.R.; or Film Transport Services.
HIPPODROME (RCA).—Prop., Associated Theatres (P. A & D.), Ltd. Controlled by County Cinemas, Ltd., Dean House, Dean Street, W.1. 2,000 seats. Booked at H.O. Con-

tinuous. Prices, 4d. to 2s. Proscenium width, 40 ft. Stage, 35 ft. deep; 11 dressing-rooms. Phone, Devonport 141-2 and 109. Station, North Road, G.W.R. or S.R.
PALLADIUM (WE), Ebrington Street.—Prop., Denman Picture Houses, Ltd., 123, Regent Street, London, W.1. 2,458 seats. Booked at H.O. Continuous. Prices, 6d. to 1s. 6d. Proscenium width, 32 ft. Phone, Plymouth 601141. Station, North Road, G.W.R.
PLAZA (RCA), Treville Street.—Prop., Associated British Cinemas, Ltd., 30–31, Golden Square, W.1. 1,000 seats. Booked at H.O. Prices, 6d. to 1s. 6d. Proscenium width, 30 ft. Phone, Plymouth 4450. Station, North End.
REGENT (RCA), Frankfort Street.—Prop., Associated Theatres (P. A. & D.), Ltd. Associated with County Cinemas, Ltd., Dean House, Dean Street, London,W.1. 3,300 seats. Continuous. Prices 6d. to 2s. Proscenium width 48 ft. Phone Plymouth 5392. Station, Plymouth, North Road, G.W.R.
ROYAL NAVAL BARRACKS CINEMA (BTH), Devonport.—Props., Canteen Committee, R.N. Barracks, Once nightly. Admission only to Naval Ratings. Phone, R.N. Barracks, 52, via Dockyard.
SAVOY PICTURE HOUSE (WE), Union Street.— Prop., Gaumont-British Picture Corpn., Ltd., 123, Regent Street, London, W.1. 1,400 seats. Book at H.O. Continuous. Prices, 4d. to 1s. 6d. Mats., 6d. and 1s. Phone, Plymouth 528. Station, North Road, G.W.R.
TIVOLI PICTURE HOUSE (BA), Fore Street. — Prop., Tivoli (Devonport), Ltd. 400 seats. Booked at Hall. Continuous. Two changes weekly. Prices, 4d. to 1s. Station, North Road, G.W.R.

POCKLINGTON (YORKS), **Pop. 2,640.**
CENTRAL HALL (AWH), Peter's Square.—Prop., Central Theatre Co., Ltd. 500 seats. Booked at Hall. Once nightly. Mon. to Fri. Two shows Sat. Prices, 4d. to 1s. Phone, Pocklington 46. Station, Pocklington, L.N.E.R.
MAJESTIC CINEMA (BA).—Prop., Majestic Cinema, (Pocklington), Ltd., Manor Buildings, The Mile, Pocklington. 550 seats. Booked at Leeds. Once nightly. Twice Sat. Prices, 4d. to 1s. 3d. Phone, Pocklington 37. Station, Pocklington, L.N.E.R.

POLESWORTH (WARWICKSHIRE), **Pop. 3,500.**
PALACE THEATRE (AWH).—Prop., G. Deeming, "The Limes," Polesworth. Phone, No. 87. 500 seats. Booked at Coalville Theatres, Ltd., near Leicester. One show nightly. Two changes weekly. Prices, 6d. to 1s. ·Phone, Polesworth 23. Station, Polesworth, L.N.E.R.

PONDERS END (MIDDLESEX), **Pop. 12,736.**
PLAZA (P & M), High Street.—Props., Plaza, Ponders End, Ltd. 500 seats. Booked at 23, Meard Street, W.1. Continuous. Mat. daily. Prices, 6d. to 1s. 3d. Phone, Enfield 0502. Road transport.

PONTEFRACT (YORKS), **Pop. 19,053.**
ALEXANDRA (RCA), Tanshelf.—Props., The Pontefract Cinema, Ltd. 860 seats. Booked at the Crescent. Prices, 6d. to 1s. 3d. Phone, No. 444. Stations, Monkhill and Tanshelf, L.M.S.

CINEMA FITZWILLIAM (BA), near Pontefract.—
Prop., Star Cinemas, Ltd., 5, Manchester
Avenue, London, E.C.1. 700 seats.

CRESCENT CINEMA (WE),. Ropergate.—Prop.,
Pontefract Cinema, Ltd. 1,190 seats. Booked
at Hall by Man. Once nightly. Mat., Mon.,
Thurs. and Sat. Dance Hall attached.
Prices, 6d. to 1s. 3d. Phone, Pontefract 188.
Stations, Monkhill and Tanshelf, L.M.S.

PLAYHOUSE CINEMA (WE).—Props., Playhouse
Cinema (Pontefract), Ltd. 853 seats. Booked
at Hall. Once nightly. Twice Sat. Mat.,
Mon., Thurs. and Sat. Phone, Pontefract 164.

PLAZA (WE), Fitzwilliam.—Prop., Star Cinemas,
Ltd., 5, Manchester Avenue, London, E.C.1.
Phone, Metropolitan 4292. Prices, 6d. to 1s.
Phone, Henworth 92.

PREMIER PICTURES (WE).—Prop., T. C. Holden
and Co. Booked at Hall. Once nightly.
Two shows Sat. Mat., Mon., Thurs. and Sat.
Prices, 6d. to 1s. Phone, 205. . Station,
Tanshelf, L.M.S.

STREETHOUSE PICTURE HOUSE (Cinephone), nr.
Pontefract.—Prop., West Yorkshire Cinemas,
Ltd., Aberford Road, Woodlesford, nr. Leeds.
450 seats. Once nightly. Twice on Sat.
Prices, 4d. to 1s. Station, Tharlston, L.M.S.
(L.Y. Sec.).

PONTNEWYNYDD (MON), **Pop. 9,000.**
SUPER PAVILION (Sound, Ltd.).—Prop., West
Pavilion, Ltd. Phone, Pontypool 77. Booked
at Cardiff. Continuous. Two changes weekly.
Prices, 7d. to 1s. 4d. Station, Pontnewynydd,
G.W.R.

WHITE ROSE CINEMA (Edibell).—400 seats.

PONTYPOOL (MON), **Pop. 6,788.**
PARK CINEMA (Sound, Ltd.).—Prop., The Ponty-
pool Cinema, Ltd. 1,050 seats. Booked at
Lyceum, Newport, Mon. Continuous. Phone,
Pontypool 120. Station, Crane Street, Ponty-
pool, G.W.R.

NEW ROYAL (BA), Osborne Road.—Prop.,
Pontypool Theatres, Ltd. 800 seats. Booked
at Pavilion, Abertillery. Continuous. Prices,
6d. to 1s. Proscenium width, 24 ft. Phone,
Pontypool 24. Station, Crane Street, Pontypool, G.W.R. ; and Road transport.

POOLE (DORSET), **Pop. 57,258.**
AMITY HALL (BTH), High Street.—Prop., South
Coast Theatres, Ltd. H.O., Regent Theatres,
High Street, Poole. Booked by J. Bravely,
Man. Dir. at H.O. Continuous. Mat. Sat.
Two changes weekly. Prices, 9d. to 1s. 4d.
Proscenium width, 24 ft. Phone, Poole 103.
Station, Poole, S.R.

REGENT (WE), High Street.—Props., South Coast
Theatres, Ltd. 1,000 seats. Booked at Hall.
Continuous. Prices, 9d. to 2s. Proscenium
width, 20 ft. Stage, 25 ft. deep. Seven
dressing-rooms. Phone, 3535. Station,
Poole, S.R.

Fitted "ARDENTE" Deaf Aids
See page 258

PORT ERIN (I.O.M.).
STRAND CINEMA.—Prop., Strand Cinema Theatre
Co. (1920), Ltd., 39, Strand Street, Douglas,
I.O.M.

PORTLAND (DORSET), **Pop. 12,020.**
REGAL (BTP).—Prop., J. H., J. W. and F. H.
Herbert. 562 seats. Continuous. Mats.,
Wed and Sat. Booked at Hall. Prices 6d.
to 1s. 6d. Proscenium width, 30 ft. Phone,
Portland 137. Station, Portland, G.W.R. and
S.R.

PORTSCATHO (CORNWALL), **Pop. 1,200.**
PUBLIC HALL.—Prop. and Man., A. E. Ham-
blin, 29A, St. Clement Street, Truro. Prices,
6d. and 1s. 2d.

PORTSLADE-BY-SEA (SUSSEX), **Pop. 9,521.**
PORTSLADE PICTUREDROME.—Prop. and Res.
Man., P. V. Reynolds, 298 seats. Booked in
London. Continuous. Two changes weekly.
Pictures and Variety. Prices, 6d. to 1s. 2d.
Phone, Portslade 282. Station, Portslade,
S.R., and Transport.

ROTHBURY CINEMA (BTH). Franklin Road.—
—Prop., Mrs. Merriman Langdon. 550 seats.
Continuous. Occasional variety. Booked at
Hall. Prices, 6d. to 1s. 6d. Proscenium width,
34 ft. Phone, Portslade 8752. Cafe and Dance
Hall attached. Station, West Hove and
Portslade.

PORTSMOUTH (HANTS), **Pop. 249,288.**
AMBASSADOR, Cosham.—Prop., London and
Southern Super Cinemas, Ltd., 32, Shaftesbury
Avenue, London, W.1.

C O M P T O N
ORGAN f e a t u r e d h e r e.

APOLLO (RCA), Albert Road, Southsea.—Prop.,
Apollo Kinematic Theatre (Southsea), Ltd.,
5, King's Terrace, Southsea. Phone, Ports-
mouth 5924. 1,455 seats. Booked at Theatre.
Continuous. Prices, 6d. to 1s. 6d. Phone,
Portsmouth 4995. Station, Portsmouth Town,
S.R. Films per London and Provincial
Films, Motor Transport.

Fitted "ARDENTE" Deaf Aids
See page 258

ARCADE CINEMA, The Arcade, Commercial
Road.—Prop., J. W. Mills, Bkg. Man., J. M.
Stedham, 8, Wilson Grove, Southsea. 500
seats. Continuous. Two changes weekly.
Prices, 5d. to 1s. Phone, Portsmouth 5834.

CARLTON (RCA), Cosham.—Props., Carlton
Cinema (Cosham), Ltd., 5, King's Terrace,
Southsea. Phone, Portsmouth 5924. 1,298
seats. Booked at Hall. Continuous. Prices,
6d. to 1s. 6d. Proscenium width, 40 ft. Phone,
Cosham 76635. Station, Cosham.

Fitted "ARDENTE" Deaf Aids
See page 258

CINENEWS (BTH).—Props., Capital and Pro-
vincial News Theatres, Ltd., 172, Buckingham
Palace Road, S.W.1. Phone, Sloane 2909.
426 seats. Booked at H.O. Continuous.
Prices, 6d. and 1s. Phone, Portsmouth 6014.
Stations, Portsmouth and Southsea.

COMMODORE THEATRE (WE), 137, Fawcett Road,
Southsea.—Prop., Associated British Cinemas,
Ltd., 30-31, Golden Square, W.1. 1,000 seats.
Continuous. Booked at H.O. Prices, 6d. to
1s. 6d. Phone, Portsmouth 5645. Station,
Fratton, S.R.

EMPIRE CINEMA (WE), Stamshaw Road.—
Props., A. and H. Levison, 19, Angerstein
Road, North End, Portsmouth. 574 seats.
Booked at Hall. Continuous. Prices, 6d. to
1s. 3d. Proscenium width, 22 ft. Phone,
Portsmouth 73967. Station, Portsmouth
Town, S.R.

GAIETY PICTURE HOUSE (WE), Albert Road,
Southsea.—Prop., Associated British Cinemas,
Ltd., 30-31, Golden Square, London, W.1.
1,382 seats. Booked at H.O. Continuous.
Prices, 7d. to 1s. 6d. Phone, Southsea 6350.
Stations, Portsmouth Town or Fratton, S.R.

PATHE PICTORIAL—Novel, Entertaining, Unique.

U

PORTSMOUTH—Contd.

GLOBE PICTURE HOUSE (wired), Fratton Road.
—Prop., John Smithson. 600 seats. Booked
at Hall. Continuous. Two changes weekly.
Prices, 6d. to 1s. 3d. Phone, Portsmouth
6428. Station, Portsmouth Town, S.R.

KING'S THEATRE (RCA).—Prop., Portsmouth
Theatres, Ltd., Theatre Royal, Portsmouth.
Phone, Portsmouth 2101.

MAJESTIC PICTURE THEATRE (WE), Kingston
Cross.—Prop., EXORS. of R. W. G. Stokes.
1,078 seats. Continuous. Prices, 6d. to 1s. 6d.
Phone, Portsmouth 6652. Station, Portsmouth Town, S.R.

NEW PRINCES (WE), Lake Road.—Prop., New
Princes (Portsmouth), Ltd. 1,500 seats.
Booked at Hall. Continuous. Prices, 7d. to
1s. 6d. Proscenium width, 28 ft. Phone,
2580. Station, Portsmouth, S.R., and Road
Transport.

NEW QUEEN'S CINEMA (BTH), Portsea.—Prop.,
J. Petters, 14, Queen Street, Portsmouth.
450 seats. Continuous. Mat., Sat. Prices,
5d. to 1s. 3d. Station, Portsmouth Town,
S.R.

ODEON THEATRE, Portsmouth.—Prop., Odeon
Theatres, Ltd., Cornhill House, Bennett's
Hill, Birmingham. Phone, Midland 2781.
Booked at 49, Park Lane, W.1. Continuous.
Prices, 6d. to 2s. Phone, Portsmouth 73175.

ODEON THEATRE (BTH), Testine Road, Southsea.—Prop., Odeon (Southsea), Ltd., Bennett's
Hill, Birmingham. Phone, Midland 2781.
Booked at 49, Park Lane, W.1. (In course of
construction.)

PALACE (WE), Commercial Road.—Props.,
Portsmouth Town Cinemas, Ltd. 626 seats.
Booked at Shaftesbury Cinema, Portsmouth.
Continuous. Phone, Portsmouth 5665. Station,
Portsmouth Town, S.R.

PLAZA (WE), Bradford Junction, Southsea.—
Prop., Associated Provincial Picture Houses,
Ltd., Regent Street, London, W.1. 1,700
seats. Booked at H.O. Continuous. Prices,
6d. to 2s. Phone, 718111. Station, Ports-
mouth Town, S.R.
Fitted "ARDENTE" Deaf Aids
See page 258

REGAL PICTURE HOUSE (WE), Eastney.—Prop.,
E. J. Baker and Son. 830 seats. Booked at
Hall. Continuous. Two changes weekly.
Prices, 7d. to 1s. 3d. Phone, Portsmouth
7191. Station, Fratton, S.R.

REGENT THEATRE (WE), 55, London Road.—
Prop., Associated Provincial Picture Houses,
Ltd., Regent Street, London, W.1. 1,972
seats. Continuous. Prices, 6d. to 2s. Stage,
40 ft. deep ; six dressing-rooms. Phone,
Portsmouth 725611. Station, Portsmouth
Town, S.R.
Fitted "ARDENTE" Deaf Aids
See page 258

RIALTO SUPER CINEMA (BTH), Arundel Street.—
Prop., Rialto (Portsmouth), Ltd., 12, Elm
Grove, Southsea. Phone, 5859. 1,250 seats.
Proscenium width, 27 ft. Three shows daily.
Prices, 6d. and 1s. 3d. Phone, Portsmouth
7107. Station, Portsmouth Town, S.R.

SCALA THEATRE (BTH), Elm Grove, Southsea.
Phone, Portsmouth 5859.—Prop., Rialto
(Portsmouth), Ltd., 12, Elm Grove, Southsea. 750 seats. Booked at Hall. Continuous. Two changes weekly. Prices, 6d.
to 2s. Station, Portmouth Town, S.R.

SHAFTESBURY CINEMA (WE), Kingston Road.—
Prop., Portsmouth Town Cinemas, Ltd
1,114 seats. Booked at Hall. Continuous
Prices, 7d. to 1s. 4d. Phone, Portsmouth
4976. Station, Portsmouth and Southsea
S.R., and Transport Service.

SOUTH PARADE PIER (BTH), Southsea.—Prop.
Portsmouth Corporation, 485 seats. Res
and Booking Man., F. G. Robson. Booked
at Hall. Twice daily. Prices, 6d. to 1s. 6d
Phone, Portsmouth 32251. Station, Fratton
S.R.

THEATRE ROYAL (Wired), Commercial Road.—
Prop., Portsmouth Theatres, Ltd. Phone
Portsmouth 2793. Station, Portsmouth
Town, S.R.

TIVOLI THEATRE (WE), Copnor Road.—Prop,
Tivoli (Portsmouth), Ltd. Buckingham
Place. Phone, 3842. 1,442 seats. Continuous.
Mats., daily. Booked at Hall. Prices, 9d. to
1s. 3d. Proscenium width, 35 ft. Stage, 25 ft.
deep ; 2 dressing-rooms. Phone, Portsmouth
6347. Station, Fratton, S.R.

VICTORIA HALL (WE), Commercial Road.—
Controlled by Union Cinemas, Ltd., Union
House, 15, Regent Street, London, S.W.1.
Phone, Whitehall 8484. Booked at H.O.
Continuous. Sundays once nightly. Two
changes weekly. Prices, 3d. to 1s. Pros-
cenium width, 28 ft. Phone, 2525. Station,
Portsmouth, Central, S.R. ; Films by Road
Transport.

WAVERLEY PICTURE THEATRE (RCA).—Prop.,
F. W. Olding. 545 seats. Continuous. Mats.,
Wed. and Sat. Prices, 6d. to 1s. Phone,
Portsmouth 76712. Station, Cosham, S.R.

POTTERS BAR (MIDDX.)

RITZ (WE), Darkes Lane.—1,170 seats. Continuous. Booked at Hall. Proscenium width,
39 ft. Stage, 20 ft. deep ; three dressing
rooms. Café and Dance Hall attached.
Phone, Potters Bar 718. Station, Potters
Bar, L.N.E.R. and Road Transport.

COMPTON
ORGAN featured here

POULTON (LANCS.), **Pop. 3,366.**

PICTURE HOUSE (BTH).—Prop., and Man., J. I.
Smith. Booked at Hall by Prop. Pictures,
Variety and Drama. One show nightly.
Mat., Sat. Prices, 6d. to 1s. 3d. Proscenium
width, 25 ft. Stage, 25 ft. deep ; 4 dressing-
rooms. Phone, Poulton 11. Station, Poulton,
L.M.S.

PRESCOT (LANCS.), **Pop. 9,396.**

LYME HOUSE CINEMA (WE), 22, Eccleston
Street.—Prop., Lyme House Cinemas, Ltd.,
980 seats. Booked by Eagle Picturedromes,
Wigan. Once nightly. Twice Sat. and Holidays.
Mat., Mon. Prices, 6d. to 1s. Proscenium
width, 22 ft. Phone, Prescot 6114. Station,
Prescot, L.M.S.

PALACE (BTH), Kemble Street.—Prop., Lyme
House Cinemas, Ltd. 700 seats. Once
nightly ; twice Sat. and Holidays. Prices,
5d. to 9d. Phone, Prescot 6430. Station
Prescot, L.M.S.

PRESTON (LANCS.), **Pop. 118,839.**

CARLTON (WE), Ribbleton, 975 seats. Phone,
Preston 84112.

COSY THEATRE (BTP), St. Peter's Street.—Prop.
and Res. Man., A. Wiles. 450 seats. Booked

at Hall. Two shows nightly. Daily Mat. Two changes weekly. Prices, 2d. and 3d. Proscenium width, 25 ft. Phone, Preston 875, Station, Central.

ELECTRIC THEATRE (Gramo-Radio), Craggs Row, —Prop., H. Bennett. 500 seats. Two shows nightly. Mat., Sat. Two changes weekly. Phone, Preston 490. Station, Preston, L.M.S.

EMPIRE (WE).—H. D. Moorhouse Circuit, Imperial Buildings, Oxford Road, Manchester. Phone, Preston 5033. 1,805 seats.

EMPRESS SUPER CINEMA (WE), Eldon Street.— Props., Empress Cinema (Preston), Ltd., 900 seats. Occasional Variety. Booked at Manchester and Liverpool. Continuous nightly. Daily Mat. Prices, 4d. to 1s. 2d. Proscenium width, 28 ft. Stage, 15 ft. deep; 2 dressing-rooms. Phone, Preston 2932. Station, Preston, L.M.S.

GUILD CINEMA (WE), Geoffrey Street.—Props., John Mather and Arthur Murray. 900 seats. Booked at Hall. Continuous. Two changes weekly. Prices, 4d. to 9d. Phone, Preston 4423. Station, Preston, L.M.S.

NEW VICTORIA (WE).—Prop., Provincial Cinematograph Theatres, Ltd., 123, Regent Street, London, W.1. Phone, Preston 28001I. 2,099 seats.

Fitted "ARDENTE" Deaf Aids
See page 258

WURLITZER ORGAN
Installed in this Kinema

PALACE THEATRE (PTA), Old Vicarage.—Prop.' Percy B. Broadhead. 2,340 seats.. Continuous. Two changes weekly. Prices, 4d. to 1s. Phone, Preston 3317. Station, Preston L.M.S.

PALLADIUM (WE), Church Street. — Prop., Preston Palladium, Ltd. 902 seats. Gen. Man., Ernest Angers. Continuous. Two shows Sat. Daily Mat. Prices, 4d. to 1s. 3d. Phone, Preston 3470. Station, Preston, L.M.S.

PICTUREDROME (BTH), Brackenbury Place. —Prop., Will Onda Two shows nightly. Mats., Mon., Thurs. and Sat. Two changes weekly. Prices, 3d. to 1s. Phone, Preston. 5465. Station, Preston, L.M.S.

PLAZA (WE)—Props., The Plaza (Preston), Ltd. 900 seats. Phone, Preston 2357.

PRINCE'S THEATRE (AWH)—Prop., Will Onda. 1,000 seats. Three shows daily, except Friday. Two changes weekly. Prices, 3d. to 1s. Phone, Preston 4165. Station, Preston, L.M.S.

PUBLIC HALL.—W. A. Davies, Borough Treasurer. Phone, Preston 1. Station, Preston, L.M.S.

QUEENS (AWH), Tarleton. 450 seats. Prop., High Park Picture Palace Co. (Southport). Twice weekly. Thurs. and Sat. Prices, 4d. to 1s. 3d.

QUEEN'S THEATRE (BTP).—Props., Bury Hippodrome, Ltd., 400 seats. Continuous. Three changes weekly. Prices, 3d. and 6d. Proscenium width, 11 ft. Phone, Preston 5004. Station, Preston, L.M.S.

REGAL CINEMA (BTP), Marsh Lane.—Prop., S. Kingston, 5, Woodlands Drive, Broughton, Preston. 640 seats. Booked at Hall. Continuous. Prices 2d. to 6d. Phone, 3598. Station, Preston, L.M.S.

RIALTO CINEMA (BTH), St. Paul's Road, Preston. —Prop., Rialto Cinema (Preston), Ltd. 700 seats. Booked at Hall. Twice nightly.

Prices, 5d. to 9d. Proscenium width, 18 ft. Phone, Preston 5598. Station, Preston, L.M.S.

SAVOY CINEMA (BTH), Ashton Street. —Prop., Savoy Cinema (Preston), Ltd. 800 seats. Booked at Hall. Continuous. Two changes w . Prices, 4d. to 6d. Phone, Preston 6weekly

STAR CINEMA (RCA), Corporation Street.— Prop., Arthur Hall. 857 seats. Booked at Hall. Continuous. Two shows Sat. Mat. daily. Occasional Variety. Prices; 3d. to 1s. Proscenium width, 30 ft. Stage, 10 ft. deep; two dressing rooms. Phone, Preston 3836.

THEATRE ROYAL (WE).—Prop., Associated British Cinemas, Ltd., 30-31, Golden Square, W.1. Phone, Gerrard 7887. 1,207 seats. Booked at H.O. Three shows daily. Phone, Preston 3694. Station, Preston, L.M.S.

PRESTWICH (LANCS), **Pop., 23,876.**

ASTORIA (WE).—Prop., Astoria (Prestwich) Ltd. 2,000 seats. Booked at H.O. Continuous. Twice nightly. Sat. Prices, 6d. to 1s. Proscenium width, 60 ft. Variety, booked direct. Stage, 26 ft. deep; six dressing rooms. Cafe and Dance Hall attached. Phone, Prestwich 2227.

PLAZA (BTH).—1,400 seats.

PRESTWICH PICTUREDROME.—Continuous. Two changes weekly. Phone, Broughton 23. Station, Prestwich, Manchester, L.M.S.

PRINCES RISBORO' (BUCKS), **Pop., 2,315.**

NEW PRINCES CINEMA (BTP).—Lessee, H. Wright. 450 seats. Booked at Hall by H. Wright. One show nightly. Two on Sat. Prices, 6d. to 1s. 6d. Station, Princes Risboro, G.W.R.

PRINCETOWN (DEVON).

B.B. CINEMA.—Prop., B.B. Cinema Circuit. Booked by Capt. J. H. Blackhurst at H.O. West Down, near Ilfracombe. Phone, Ilfracombe 7.

PRUDHOE-ON-TYNE (NORTHUMBERLAND), **Pop., 9,260.**

ELECTRIC THEATRE (BTP), Front Street.—Prop. Prudhoe Electric Theatre, Ltd., Haymarke House, Newcastle-on-Tyne. 791 seats. Booked at H.O. Continuous. Twice Sat. Two changes weekly. Prices, 6d. to 1s. Proscenium width, 22 ft. Phone, Prudhoe 29. Station, Prudhoe, L.N.E.R.

PUDSEY (YORKS), **Pop., 14,762.**

PALACE CINEMA (Electrocord). 700 seats. Once nightly. Mat., Mon., Thurs., and Sat. Two changes weekly. Prices 5d. to 1s.

PICTURE HOUSE (WE), Church Lane.—Prop., Picture House (Pudsey), Ltd. Booked at Hall. Continuous nightly. Mat., Mon., Thurs. and Sat. Two changes weekly. Prices, 6d. to 1s. 3d. Phone, Stanningley 71377. Station, Lowtown, Pudsey, L.N.E.R.

PULBOROUGH (SUSSEX), **Pop. 2,063.**
CINEMA.

PURLEY (SURREY). **Pop. 7,120.**

ASTORIA (WE) London Road.—Prop., E. E. Lyons, 62, Shaftesbury Avenue, London, W. Booked at Hall. Prices, 9d. to 2s. 6d. Proscenium width, 34 ft. Stage, 12 ft. deep; three dressing-rooms. Café. Station, Purley.

COMPTON
ORGAN featured here.

PURLEY—Contd.

REGAL (WE), Brighton Road.—Prop., Associated British Cinemas, Ltd., 30-31, Golden Square, London, W.1. Phone, Gerrard 7887. 1,606 seats. Continuous. Booked at H.O. Prices, 6d. to 1s. 3d. Proscenium width, 33 ft. Café. Phone, Uplands 2044.

QUEENBORO' (KENT), Pop. 2,941.

QUEEN'S CINEMA (AWH).—Prop., Queenboro' Cinema Co. 510 seats. Booked at Hall. Once nightly. Sat. continuous. Prices, 4d. to 1s. Proscenium width, 20 ft. Phone, Sheerness 255. Station, Queenborough, S.R.

QUEENSBURY (MIDX.)

PLAZA (Building).—Prop., General Cinema Theatres, Ltd., 19, Albermarle Street, London, W.1.

QUEENSBURY (YORKS), Pop. 5,763.

VICTORIA HALL (BA).—Prop., Greengates Cinema Co., Ltd., Bradford. Phone, Idle 249. 600 seats. Booked at Leeds. Once nightly. Mat. and two shows Sat. Prices. 4d. to 1s. Proscenium width, 26 ft. Phone, Thornton 24. Films by Carrier from Leeds.

RADCLIFFE (LANCS.), Pop. 24,674.

BRIDGE PICTURE HOUSE (BTP), Kenyon Street.— Props, New Empire (Burnley) Ltd. 500 seats. Booked at Manchester. Twice nightly. Mat. Sat. Prices, 4d. to 9d. Station, Radcliffe (New), L.M.S.

COLISEUM THEATRE (WE).—Props., New Empire (Burnley), Ltd. 846 seats. Twice nightly. Prices, 3d. to 9d. Stage, 38 ft. deep; 12 dressing-rooms. Phone, Radcliffe 2154. Station, Radcliffe (New), L.M.S.

ODEON THEATRE, Foundry Street.—Prop., Odeon Theatres, Ltd., Cornhill House. Bennett's Hill, Birmingham. (In course of construction). Booked at 49, Park Lane, W.1.

PICTUREDROME (WE), Water Street.—Prop., New Empire (Burnley) Ltd.. 750 seats. Booked at H.O. Two shows nightly. Mat., Thurs. and Sat. Prices, 4d. to 9d. Phone, Radcliffe 2086. Proscenium width, 26 ft. Station, Radcliffe (New).

RADCLIFFE-ON-TRENT (NOTTS.), Pop. 3,450.

NEW KINEMA—Continuous. 7d. to 1s.

RADLETT (HERTS).

CINEMA (BTH).—Prop., Radlett Cinema, Ltd., Watling Street, Radlett. Phone, Radlett 6779, 306 seats. Continuous. Prices, 9d. to 2s. Stage and three dressing rooms. Films by Road Transport.

RADSTOCK (SOM.), Pop. 3,620.

PALACE.—Prop., W. Trueman, Dicken Circuit, "Majestic," Burnham-on-Sea. Phone, Radstock 102.

RAINHAM (KENT), Pop. 5,000.

ROYAL CINEMA (AWH), London Road.—Prop., Mrs. Willis-Rust, Robin Hood House, Walderslade, near Chatham. Phone, Bluebell Hill 57. 374 seats. Booked at Hall. Twice nightly. Mat., Wed. and Sat. Prices, 4d. to 1s. 3d. Proscenium width, 25 ft. Station, Rainham, S.R.

RAINWORTH (nr. Mansfield) (NOTTS.), Pop. 3,500.

PALACE (BTP).—Prop., Rainworth Theatre, Ltd, 440 seats. Once nightly. Twice Sat. Prices, 4d. to 1s. Proscenium width, 24 ft. Phone.

Blidworth 58. Station, Mansfield, L.M.S., c.o. Parcels Office, or Broxburn Film Services, Ltd.

RAMSBOTTOM (LANCS.), Pop. 14,926.

EMPIRE (WE), Railway Street.—Prop., Blakeborough, Ltd. 650 seats. One show nightly. Two on Sat. Two changes weekly. Prices, 6d. to 1s. Proscenium width, 26 ft. Stage, 20 ft. deep; 2 dressing-rooms. Phone, Ramsbottom 70. Station, Ramsbottom, L.M.S.

ROYAL (WE).—Props., Blakeborough Ltd. Smithy Street, Ramsbottom. 700 seats. Once nightly. Twice Sat. Prices, 6d. to 1s. Proscenium width, 30 ft. Phone, Ramsbottom 70.

RAMSEY (HUNTS), Pop. 5,180.

GRAND (BTH).—Prop., Murkett Bros., Phone, Huntingdon 298. 800 seats. Twice nightly. Mat., Sat. Two changes weekly. Prices, 6d. to 1s. 6d. Station, Ramsey, L.N.E.R.

RAMSEY (I. OF M.), Pop. 5,328.

CINEMA HOUSE (BTH), Albert Road.—Props,. Ramsey Amusements, Ltd. 1,200 seats. Booked by R. E. Ratcliff, "Raheny," Roby, Lancs. Continuous including Sunday—Winter. Prices, 6d. and 1s. Phone, 87. Station, Ramsey.

PLAZA (BTH).—Prop., Ramsey Amusements, Ltd., Cinema House, Ramsey. Phone, 87. 950 seats. Booked by R. E. Ratcliff,"Raheny" Roby Lancs. Continuous. Occasional Variety. Prices, 6d. to 1s. Proscenium width, 32 ft. Stage, 14 ft. deep; 2 dressing-rooms. Phone, 224. Café attached. Station, Ramsey.

RAMSGATE (KENT), Pop. 33,597.

KING'S THEATRE (BTH).—Prop., Balexcro Theatres, Ltd., Broadmead House, 21, Panton Street, S.W.1. 1,200 seats. Booked in London. Continuous nightly. Mats. daily. Prices, 6d. and 1s. 6d. Phone, Ramsgate 209. Station Ramsgate and Film Transport.

ODEON THEATRE (BTH).—Prop., Odeon (Ramsgate), Ltd., Cornhill House, Bennett's Hill, Birmingham. Booked at 49, Park Lane, W.1. Continuous. Prices, 6d. to 2s. Phone, Ramsgate 1033.

PALACE THEATRE (WE), High Street.—Sole Lessee and Gen. Man., E. G. Casey. 1,482 seats. Booked at 13, Gerrard Street, W.1. Revue, Plays, Pictures, etc. Stage, 22½ ft. deep. Prices, 5d. to 2s. 4d. Phone, Ramsgate 31. Station, Ramsgate, S.R.

COMPTON

ORGAN featured here.

PICTURE HOUSE (WE).—Props., Balexcro Theatres, Ltd., Broadmead House, 21, Panton Street, S.W.1. 600 seats. Booked at London. Continuous evenings. Mats. daily. Phone, 124. Prices 6d. to 1s. 6d.

RAMSGATE PICTURE HOUSE (WE).—Props., H. Edward Bawn Cinemas,Pavilion,Ramsgate. Phone, 395. 580 seats. Booked at Pavilion. Continuous. Mats. daily. Prices, 6d. to 1s. 10d. Film Transport.

ROYAL VICTORIA PAVILION (RCA).—Prop., Balexcro Theatres, Ltd., Broadmead House, 21, Panton Street, S.W.1. 1,400 seats. Booked at H.O. Continuous. Prices, 6d. to

1s. 4d. Café attached. Phone, Ramsgate 395. Station, Ramsgate, S.R. Films by Kent Films Motor Transport, Ltd.

RAUNDS (NORTHANTS) **Pop. 3,683.**
PALACE (Ultramonic).—Prop., A. Hayward, The Cottage, Chelveston Road, Raunds. 360 seats. Booked at Hall. Once nightly, twice Sat. Mat., Sat. Pictures and Variety. Stage, 15 ft. deep ; two dressing-rooms. Prices, 6d. to 1s. 3d. Phone, Raunds 58 Station, Raunds, L.M.S.

RAWDON (near Leeds) (YORKS.), **Pop. 10,000.**
NEW EMPIRE CINEMA (Morrison), Leeds Road.— Booked at Hall. Continuous, Mon. to Fri. Pictures and Variety nightly. Three shows Sat. Prices, 4d. to 1s. Proscenium width, 24 ft. Phone, Rawdon 210. Films by Transport.

RAWMARSH (near Rotherham) (YORKS) **Pop. 18,570.**
PRINCESS PICTURE PALACE.—Prop. Princess Pictures, Ltd. 600 seats. Two shows nightly. Two changes weekly. Prices, 3d. to 8d. Station, Rawmarsh, L.N.E.R.
REGAL (WE).—Prop. Heeley and Amalgamated Cinemas, Ltd., 70, The Moor, Sheffield. 1,050 seats. Booked at Hall. Continuous. Prices, 5d. to 1s. Proscenium width, 32 ft. Phone, Rawmarsh 54. Stations, Parkgate and Rawmarsh, L.M.S.

RAWTENSTALL (LANCS), **Pop. 28,575.**
PALACE CINEMA (Imperial). Queen's Square.— Prop., Rossendale Pictures, Ltd. 600 seats. Once nightly. Booked at Manchester. Occasional Variety. -Prices, 4d. to 1s. Phone Rawtenstall, L.M.S.
PAVILION CINEMA (WE), Bury Road.—Prop., Rossendale Pictures, Ltd. 1,141 seats. Bkg. and Gen. Man., H. Cookson. One show nightly. Twice Sat. Three Mats.. Prices, 6d. to 1s. Phone, Rossendale 36. Station, Rawtenstall, L.M.S.
PICTURE HOUSE (WE), Bacup Road.—Props., Rossendale Pictures, Ltd. 1,309 seats. Once nightly. Booked at Manchester. Prices, 6d. to 1s. 3d. Phone, Rossendale 123. Station, Rawtenstall, L.M.S.

RAYLEIGH (ESSEX), **Pop. 6,256.**
COSY THEATRE (AWH), High Street.—Prop., Cosy Theatre (Rayleigh), Ltd.. 325 seats. Booked at Hall. Continuous. Prices, 6d. to 1s. 6d. Phone, Rayleigh 75. Station, Rayleigh, L.N.E.R., or Motor Transport.

RAYNES PARK (SURREY).
RIALTO CINEMA (WE), Pepys Road.—Prop., Courtwood Cinemas, Ltd., 361, City Road, E.C.1. Phone, Clerkenwell 5126. 708 seats Booked at H.O. Continuous. Two changes weekly. Prices, 6d. to 1s. 10. Phone, Wimbledon 2828. Station, Raynes Park, S.R.

READING (BERKS), **Pop. 97,153.**
CENTRAL PICTURE PLAYHOUSE (WE), Friar Street.—Prop., Associated British Cinemas, Ltd., 30–31, Golden Square, London, W.1. Phone, Gerrard 7837. 1,561 seats. Booked at H.O. Continuous. Prices, 6d. to 2s. Phone, Reading 3931. Station, Reading, G.W.R.
GRANBY (BTH).—Props., Granby Cinema (Reading), Ltd., London Road, Reading. Phone, 61465. 1,500 seats. Continuous. Prices, 6d. to 2s. Café. Transport.

ODEON THEATRE (BTH).—Prop., Odeon (Reading), Ltd., Cornhill House, Bennett's Hill, Birmingham. Phone, Midland 2781. Booked at 49, Park Lane, W.1.
PALACE.—1,200 seats. **Fitted "ARDENTE" Stage Amplification See page 258**
PAVILION (WE), Oxford Road.—Prop., Pavilion (Reading), Ltd. Associated with County Cinemas, Ltd., 1,380 seats. Continuous. Prices, 9d. to 2s. 6d. Phone, Reading 960. Station, Reading, G.W.R.

C O M P T O N
ORGAN featured here.

ROYAL COUNTY THEATRE (BTH).—Prop., R. J. Langley. 1,000 seats. Occasional Variety. Booked at Hall. Continuous. Prices, 6d. to 2s. Proscenium width, 35 ft. Stage, 40 ft. deep, nine dressing-rooms. Phone, Reading 4561. Station, Reading, G.W.R.
SAVOY (BTH), Basingstoke Road.—Props., Savoy (Reading), Ltd. Regency House, Warwick Street, W.1. Booked at H.O. 1,044 seats. Continuous. Prices, 6d. to 1s. 10d. Proscenium width, 35 ft. Stage, 7 ft. deep ; two dressing-rooms. Café. Phone, 81381. Station, G.W.R., Reading.
VAUDEVILLE THEATRE (WE), Broad Street.— Props., Pavilion (Reading), Ltd., associated with County Cinemas, Ltd., Dean House, Dean Street, London, W.1. Phone, Gerrard 4543. 1,457 seats. Booked at H.O. Continuous. Café. Prices, 9d. to 2s. 6d. Phone, Reading 97. Station, Reading, G.W.R.

REDCAR (YORKS) **Pop. 20,159.**
CENTRAL.—Prop., Thompson's Enterprises, Ltd. 4, Palladium Bldgs., Middlesbrough.
PALACE THEATRE (BTH), Esplanade.—Prop., Palace Theatre (Redcar), Ltd. 946 seats. Booked at Hall. Three shows daily. Prices. 4d. to 1s. 4d. Proscenium width, 20 ft. Café. Phone, Redcar 125. Station, Redcar. L.N.E.R.
PIER PAVILION.
REGENT (WE), High Street.—Prop., Thompson's Enterprises, Ltd., 4 Palladium Bldgs, Middlesborough. Phone, Linthorpe 88156. 852 seats. Booked at H.O. by Thos. Thompson. Two shows nightly. Mat. daily. Prices, 6d. to 1s. 6d. Phone, Redcar 28. Station, Redcar, L.N.E.R.

REDDISH (near Manchester) (LANCS), **Pop. 14,252.**
EMBASSY (WE), Gorton Road.—(Closed.) Phone, East 0920.
NEW BIJOU ELECTRIC THEATRE (Picturetone), Gorton Road.—Prop., Frank G. Donaldson, 14, The Parsonage, Manchester. Phone, Blackfriars 7242. 400 seats. Booked by Prop., at Manchester. Twice nightly. Prices, 4d. to 1s. Station, Reddish Central, L.M.S.
ROTA (WE).—Controlled by Union Cinemas, Ltd., 15, Regent Street, London, S.W.1. Phone, Whitehall 8484. Booked at H.O. Prices, 2d. to 1s. 3d. Phone, East 0640. Station, Denton, L.M.S.

REDDITCH (WORCS.) **Pop. 19,280.**
DANILO. (RCA). Prop., Danilo (Redditch) Ltd., 3, New St., Birmingham. Phone, Midland 0871. 1,400 seats. Occasional variety. Prices 6d. to 1/4. Proscenium width 35 ft. Phone, Redditch 572. Cafe attached.

Fitted "ARDENTE" Deaf Aids
See page 258

GAUMONT PALACE (BA), Church Road.—Prop., Gaumont British Picture Corpn., Ltd., 123, Regent Street, London, W.1. 1,400 seats. Booked at H.O. Matinees and continuous at evening shows. Prices, 3d. to 1s. 2d, Phone, Redditch 151.

PALACE THEATRE (WE), Alcester Street.— Props., Redditch Palace, Ltd. 600 seats. Booked at Birmingham. Continuous. Three shows Sat. Mat. daily. Prices, 4d. to 1s. 3d. Proscenium width 22 ft. Stage, 20 ft. deep. seven dressing-rooms. Phone, No. 48. Station, Redditch, L.M.S.

SELECT KINEMA (RCA), Alcester Street.—Props., F. W. Russel, Wayside, Astwood Bank. Phone, 48. 500 seats. Booked at Hall. Continuous. Twice Sat. Mat. daily. Two changes weekly. Occasional Variety. Prices, 6d. to 1s. 3d. Proscenium width, 20 ft. Stage, 15½ ft. deep. Two dressing-rooms. Phone, Redditch 285. Station, Redditch, L.M.S.

REDHILL (SURREY), **Pop. 17,998.**
ODEON THEATRE (BTH).—Props., Odeon (Redhill), Ltd., Cornhill House, Bennett's Hill, Birmingham. Phone, Midland 2781. (In course of construction).

PAVILION (WE), High Street.— Prop., A. & C. Theatres, Ltd., Station Road, Redhill. Phone, Redhill 104. 713 seats. Continuous. Booked at H.O. Prices, 6d. to 2s. Phone, Redhill 830. Station, Redhill, S.R.

PICTURE HOUSE (WE).—Station Road.—Prop., A. & C. Theatres, Ltd. 450 seats. Continuous. Booked at H.O. Prices, 6d. to 2s. Phone, Redhill 104. Station, Redhill, S.R.

REDRUTH (CORNWALL), **Pop. 9,904.**
GEM (BTH), Druid's Hall.—Prop., Sound and Movement Cinemas, Ltd., Olivers Chambers, Frankfort Street, Plymouth. Phone, 4,981. 450 seats. Booked at H.O. Continuous. Three on Sat. Two changes weekly. Prices, 6d. and 1s. 6d. Proscenium width, 23 ft. Phone, Redruth 33. Station, Redruth, G.W.R.

REGAL.

REIGATE (SURREY), **Pop. 30,830.**
HIPPODROME (RCA).—Prop., Reigate Theatres, Ltd., M 84, Shell Mex House, Strand, W.C.2. Phone, Temple Bar 5077. Booked at H.O. Continuous. Prices, 6d. to 1s. 10d. Phone, Reigate 2943. Station, Reigate, S.R.

MAJESTIC (WE).—Props., Reigate Theatres, Ltd., M 84, Shell Mex House, Strand, W.C.2. Phone, Temple Bar 5077. Booked at H.O. Continuous. Prices, 6d. to 2s. 6d. Phone, Reigate 2943. Café. Station, Reigate, S.R.

RETFORD (NOTTS), **Pop. 13,420.**
MAJESTIC (BTP).—Prop., C. Getliffe. 1,200 seats. Continuous. Mat., Wed. and Sat. Prices, 9d. to 1s° 6d. Station, Retford, L.N.E.R.

ROXY (WE).—Prop. and Man., C. Getliffe. 1,028 seats. Continuous. Two changes weekly.

Prices, 5d. to 1s. 3d. Station, Retford, L.N.E.R.

RITZ (BTP).—Prop., C. Getliffe. 665 seats. Continuous. Prices, 9d. to 1s. 3d.

TOWN HALL.—Occasional Pictures. Prices, 6d. to 1s. 3d.

RHYMNEY (MON.), **Pop. 10,505.**
VICTORIA HALL (BTH).—Lessee, Will Stone, New Hippodrome, Tonypandy. 600 seats. Booked at H.O. One show nightly. Two Sat. Two changes weekly. Proscenium width, 22 ft. Prices, 7d. to 1s. 4d. Phone, Tonypandy 54. Station, Rhymney, G.W.R.

RICHMOND (SURREY), **Pop. 37,791.**
ROYALTY KINEMA (WE), 5, Hill Street.—Prop., Joseph Mears Theatres, Ltd. 1,141 seats. Booked at H.O. Continuous. Café attached. Phone, Richmond 1760. Station, Richmond, S.R.

THE RICHMOND (WE), Hill Street.—Prop., Joseph Mears Theatres, Ltd. 1,533 seats. Booked by Frederick Clive at 5, Hill Street, Richmond. Continuous. Prices, 1s. to 2s. 5d. Phone, Richmond 1700. Station, Richmond, S.R.

COMPTON
ORGAN featured here.

RITZ (WE).—Controlled by Union Cinemas, Ltd., 15, Regent Street, S.W.1. Phone, Whitehall 8484 Booked at H.O. Continuous. Station, Richmond, S.R.

RICHMOND (YORKS), **Pop. 4,769.**
CAMP CINEMA (WE), Hipswell.—Man. Dir., F. L. Hastwell, c/o J. E. Latimer, Priestgate, Darlington. 701 seats. Prices, 6d. to 1s. 3d, CINEMA (WE), Queen's Road.—Prop., Frank L.. Hastwell, The Terrace, Richmond. 572 seats. Twice nightly. Prices, 6d. to 1s. 6d. Phone, Richmond 456. Station, Richmond (Yorks), L.N.E.R.

RICKMANSWORTH (HERTS), **Pop. 10,810.**
ODEON THEATRE (BTH).—Props., Odeon (Rickmansworth), Ltd., Cornhill House, Bennetts Hill, Birmingham. Phone, Midland 2781. Booked at 49, Park Lane, W.1. Continuous. Prices, 6d. to 2s. Phone, Rickmansworth 122.

RICKMANSWORTH PICTURE HOUSE (WE).— Prop., Messrs. W. Firth, D. G. Bliss, J. R. Poole. 697 seats. Booked at 90, Charing Cross Road, W.C.2. Continuous. Prices, 6d. to 2s. Dance Hall attached. Proscenium width, 32 ft. Phone, Rickmansworth 360. Film by Transport.

RIDDINGS (DERBYSHIRE), **Pop. 3,000.**
MARKET HALL.—(Closed).

REGENT (BTP).—Once nightly, two shows Sat. Prices, 4d. to 1s.

RINGWOOD (HANTS.), **Pop. 5,056.**
REGAL (AWH).— Prop., A. Austin Pilkington. 20, London Road, Salisbury. 700 seats. Booked at Hall. Continuous. Prices, 6d. to 1s. 6d. Phone, Ringwood 183. Station, Ringwood, S.R. Films by Southern Counties Transport Co.

RIPLEY (DERBY), **Pop. 13,415.**
EMPIRE (WE).—Prop., Midland Empire Theatres, Ltd., Commerce Chambers, Elite Bldgs., Nottingham. Phone, Nottingham 42364.

The BEST Is Cheapest; PATHE GAZETTE.

Booked at H.O. Continuous. Occasional Variety. Phone, Ripley 124. Station, Ripley, L.M.S.

HIPPODROME (BTH), High Street.—Prop., J. Marshall & Sons. 1,000 seats. Booked at Hall. Continuous. Two shows Sat. Two changes weekly. Prices, 6d. to 1s. 2d. Proscenium width, 30 ft. Dance Hall attached. Phone, Ripley 17. Station, Ripley, L.M.S. Films by Transport.

RIPON (YORKS.), Pop. 8,576.

OPERA HOUSE (WE), Low Shellgate.—Prop., Ripon Opera House, Ltd. 500 seats. Booked at Hall. Continuous. Mon. to Fri. Three shows Sat. Mat., Thurs. and Sat. Prices, 6d. to 1s. 3d. Phone, Ripon 306. Station, Ripon, L.N.E.R.

PALLADIUM (WE), Kirkgate.—Props., A. R. Wood and E. R. Wood, "Greta," Mallorie Park Drive, Ripon. Ripon 266. 910 seats. Booked at Leeds. Continuous. Twice nightly Sat. and Holidays. Mat., Thurs. and Sat. Prices, 6d. to 1s. 3d. Proscenium width 30 ft. Occasional Variety. Stage, 30 ft. deep. Three dressing-rooms. Café attached. Station, Ripon, L.N.E.R.

RITZ.—Controlled by Union Cinemas, Ltd., 15, Regent Street, London, S.W.1. Phone, Whitehall 8484.

RISCA (MON.), Pop. 16,605.

PALACE (BA).—Prop., Risca Cinemas, Ltd. 800 seats. Booked by S. Attwood Rosslyn, Glasllwch, Newport. Mon. Continuous. Two changes weekly. Prices 7d. to 1s. Proscenium width, 30 ft. Phone, Risca 7432. Station, Risca, G.W.R., and L.M.S

RISHTON (LANCS.), Pop. 6,631.

EMPIRE PICTURE PALACE (Gramo - Radio).— Prop., Ainsworth and Hudson. 600 seats. Booked at Hall. Once nightly, twice Sat. Two changes weekly. Prices, 4d. to 9d. Pho e, Gt. Harwood 27. Station, Rishton. L.M.S.

KING'S HALL.—Prop., Ainsworth and Hudson.

ROCHDALE (LANCS.), Pop. 110,000.

CEYLON CINEMA DE LUXE (RCA).—Prop., Jackson's Amusements, Ltd. 700 seats. Booked by P. H. Madigan, at Rialto, Rochdale. Two shows nightly. Mat., Sat. Two changes weekly. Prices, 4d. to 9d. Phone, Rochdale 2505. Station, Rochdale (Wardleworth), L.M.S.

COLISEUM (RCA), Oldham Road.—Prop., Jackson's Amusements, Ltd. 1,000 seats. Twice nightly. Two changes weekly. Prices, 3d. to 9d. Proscenium width, 22 ft. Phone, Rochdale 2334. Station, Rochdale, L.M.S.

EMPIRE DE LUXE (WE), Packer Street.—Prop., Jackson's Amusements, Ltd., Newgate Chambers, Rochdale. 941 seats. Booked at Rialto, Rochdale. Three shows daily except Friday, when two shows. Prices, 4d. to 1s. 4d. Proscenium width, 40 ft. Phone, Rochdale 4,000. Station, Rochdale, L.M.S.

HIPPODROME (RCA).—Prop., Jackson's Amusements, Ltd. 2,000 seats. Twice nightly. Mat. daily, except Friday. Phone, Rochdale 2161. Station, Rochdale, L.M.S.

KING'S CINEMA (WE).—Prop., Regal Cinema (Rochdale), Ltd. 835 seats. Continuous. Two changes weekly. Prices, 3d. to 9d. Phone, Rochdale 2341. Station, Rochdale, L.M.S.

PALACE TUDOR SUPER CINEMA (WE), Drake Street.—Prop., Northern Theatres Co., Ltd., 28, Clare Road, Halifax. Phone, Halifax 2512. 827 seats. Booked by Fred. A. Kay at H.O. Two shows nightly. Mat. Mon., Thurs. and Sat. Prices, 4d. to 1s. Phone, Rochdale 2740. Station, Rochdale.

PAVILION (BTP), St. Mary's Gate.—Prop., Pavilion (Rochdale), Ltd. H. D. Moorhouse Circuit, 7, Oxford Road, Manchester. Booked at Hall and Manchester. Continuous. Prices, 4d. to 1s. Phone, Rochdale 2818.

RIALTO (WE).—Props., Jackson's Amusements, Ltd., Newgate Chambers, Rochdale. Phone, 2161. 1848 seats. Daily mat. except Fri. Prices, 6d. to 1s. 6d. Proscenium width, 32 ft. Booked at Hall. Phone 3146.

RITZ.— Controlled by Union Cinemas, Ltd., 15, Regent Street, London, S.W.1. Phone, Whitehall 8484.

THEATRE ROYAL.—Prop., Northern Theatres Co., Ltd., Northcote House, Clare Road, Halifax. Phone, Halifax 2512. 1,000 seats.

VICTORY SUPER CINEMA (BTP), Imperial Bldgs., Oxford Road, Manchester. Phone, Ardwick 2226. 1,000 seats. Booked at Manchester. Continuous, Mon. to Fri. Twice nightly Sat, and holidays. Prices, 6d. to 1s. Phone. Rochdale 3602. Station, Rochdale, L.M.S.

ROCHESTER (KENT.), Pop. 31,200.

MAJESTIC (WE), High Street.—Prop., Majestic (Rochester), Ltd. 2,012 seats. Booked by Gaumont-British Corporation, New Gallery House, Regent Street, W.1. Continuous. Prices, 6d. to 2s. 6d. Proscenium width, 72 ft. Phone, Chatham 3272. Station, Rochester, Goods S.R.

**Fitted "ARDENTE" Deaf Aids
See page 258**

C O M P T O N

ORGAN featured here.

ROOK FERRY (CHESHIRE), Pop. 10,805.

ROCK FERRY ELECTRIC PALACE (BTH), New Chester Road.—Prop., Rock Ferry Electric Palace Co. 766 seats. Two shows nightly Sat., continuous rest of week. Mats., Mon., Thurs. and Sat. Two changes weekly. Phone, Rock Ferry 289. Station, Rock Ferry, L.M.S.

ROMFORD (ESSEX), Pop. 35,918.

HAVANNAH CINEMA.

C O M P T O N

ORGAN featured here.

LAURIE CINEMA (RCA), Market Place.—Prop., Romford Cinema, Ltd. 424 seats. Booked at H.O. by Arthur B. de Solla. Continuous. Prices, 6d. to 1s. 6d. Phone, Romford 113. Station, Romford, L.N.E.R., and Film Transport.

PLAZA SUPER CINEMA (WE), South Street.— Prop., New Victory Super Cinema (Romford), Ltd., 9, Western Road, Romford. 2,207 seats. Booked at Hall. Continuous. Prices, 9d. to 2s. Four dressing-rooms,

ROMFORD—Contd.
Phone, Romford 1,000. Station, Romford, L.N.E.R.
Fitted "ARDENTE" Deaf Aids
See page 258

COMPTON
ORGAN featured here

ROMSEY (HANTS), **Pop. 4,863.**
PLAZA (WE), Winchester Road.—Props., Humby's Cinemas, Ltd. 494 seats. Booked at Hall. Continuous. Prices, 6d. to 1s. 6d. Proscenium width, 25 ft. Phone 237. Station, Romsey, S.R.

ROSS-ON-WYE (HEREFORD), **Pop. 4,738.**
KYRLE PALACE THEATRE (Edibell), Gloucester Road.—Prop., Edwin Dekins. 400 seats. Booked by W. Reeves at Grantham House, Ross. Continuous. Mat., Sat. Prices, 6d. to 1s. 4d. Proscenium width, 18 ft. Station, Ross-on-Wye, G.W.R.
NEW THEATRE (BA), High Street.—400 seats, Booked at Hall. Continuous. Prices, 6d. to 1s. 4d. Stage, 18 ft. deep; two dressing-rooms. Proscenium width, 18 ft. Phone, 198. Station, Ross-on-Wye, G.W.R. Road Transport.

ROTHERHAM (YORKS), **Pop. 69,689.**
CINEMA HOUSE (BTH), Doncaster Gate.—Prop., Cinema (Rotherham) and Electra, Ltd., Regent Theatre, Howard Street, Rotherham. 900 seats. Continuous. Mats. daily except Fri. Two changes weekly. Phone, Rotherham 291. Station, Rotherham.
EMPIRE SUPER KINEMA (WE), High Street.—Lessees, Associated British Cinemas, Ltd., 30-31, Golden Square, London, W.1. Phone Gerrard 7887. 1,225 seats. Booked at H.O. Continuous nightly. Daily Mat. Three shows Sat. Prices, 6d. to 1s. Proscenium width, 32 ft. Phone, 402. Station, Rotherham, L.N.E.R.
HIPPODROME (BTH), Henry Street.— Prop., Rotherham Hippodrome, Ltd. 1,800 seats. Booked by W. C. Harte at Premier Picture Palace, Rotherham. Continuous. Prices, 3d. to 1s. Proscenium width, 30 ft. Phone, 399. Stations, Rotherham, L.M.S. and L.N.E.R.
PREMIER PICTURE PALACE (BTH), Kimberworth Road.—Prop., G. E. Smith. 700 seats. Booked at Hall. Continuous. Mat. Sat. Two changes weekly. Prices, 3d. to 1s. Proscenium width, 30 ft. Phone, Rotherham 263. Station, Masboro', L.M.S.
REGAL (WE).—Props., London and Southern Super Cinemas, Ltd., 32, Shaftesbury Avenue, London, W.1. Phone, Whitehall 0183.
REGENT (WE), Howard Street.—Props., Cinema (Rotherham) and Electra, Ltd. Booked at Hall. 1,000 seats. Continuous. Two changes weekly. Phone, 291. Station, Rotherham.
TIVOLI PICTURE HOUSE (WE), Masboro' Street. —Prop., Messrs. J. J. Woffenden, B. Barker and J. R. Whiteley. 910 seats. Booked at Hall. Continuous. Occasional Variety. Twice nightly Sat. Prices, 4d. to 1s. Proscenium width, 33 ft. Stage, 12 ft. deep, 4 dressing-rooms. Phone, Rotherham 135. Station, Masboro', L.M.S.
WHITEHALL THEATRE (WE), High Street.— Controlled by Union Cinemas, Ltd., 15, Regent Street, London, S.W.1. Phone,

Whitehall 8484. Booked at H.O. Continuous. Prices 3d. to 1s. Phone, Rotherham 122. Stations, Rotherham, Masboro' and Westgate, L.M.S., and Rotherham, L.N.E.R.

ROTHWELL (NORTHANTS), **Pop. 4,516.**
CINEMA ODDFELLOWS' HALL (Morrison).—Prop. and Man., Kilburn and Bailey. Two changes weekly. Station, Desborough, L M.S.

ROTHWELL (YORKS), **Pop. 15,639.**
PICTURE PALACE (BTH) Ingram Parade.— Props., Rothwell Public Service, Ltd. 1,000 seats. Booked at Hall. One show nightly. Two on Sat. and Holidays. Prices, 5d. to 9d. Phone, Rothwell 68. Station, Leeds, L.N.E.R. (c/o Parcels Office).

ROWLANDS GILL (CO. DURHAM).
PICTURE HOUSE (BTH).—Prop., Sidney H. Dawson, 31, Friarside Road, Fenham, Newcastle-on-Tyne. 450 seats. Booked at H.O. Stage, 7 ft. deep; Prices, 2d. to 9d. Station, Rowlands Gill, L.N.E.R.

ROYSTON (HERTS), **Pop. 3,831.**
PRIORY (Imperial), Priory Lane.—Prop., John R. Cox, 257, Chesterton Road, Cambridge. 600 seats. Booked at Hall. Continuous. Prices, 9d. to 2s. 4d. Proscenium width, 20 ft. Phone, Royston 133. Café and Bathing Pool. Station, Royston, L.N.E.R. Films by Road Transport.

ROYSTON (nr. Barnsley) (YORKS), **Pop. 7,156.**
PALACE (BTH).—Prop., Royston Theatres, Ltd 711 seats. Booked at Leeds. Once nightly. Twice Sat. Two changes weekly. Prices, 4d. to 9d. Phone, Royston 12. Station, Royston, L.M.S.

ROYTON (LANCS.) **Pop. 16,687.**
ELECTRA PALACE, Rochdale Road.—Prop., Palatine Cinema Co., Ltd. 400 seats. Booked at H.O. One show nightly. Two change, weekly. Prices, 3d. to 6d. Station, Royton, L.M.S.
IMPERIAL PICTURE PALACE.
ROYAL PAVILION (BTP).—Prop., Palatine Cinema Co., Ltd. 600 seats. Continuous. Two changes weekly. Prices, 3d. to 9d. Phone, Royton 2609.

RUGBY (WARWICK), **Pop. 23,824.**
HIPPODROME, Woodford Halse.
PLAZA (BTH), North Street.—Prop., Plaza Theatre (Rugby), Ltd., Crown House, Rugby. Phone, Rugby 2244. Controlled by Bernstein Theatres, Ltd., 36, Golden Square, W.1. Continuous. Prices, 9d. to 2s. Café attached. Car park. Phone, Rugby 2255. Station, Rugby, L.M.S.
REGAL (WE), Railway Terrace.—Props., Plaza Theatre (Rugby), Ltd., Crown House, Rugby. Controlled by Bernstein Theatres, Ltd., 36, Golden Square, W.1. Continuous. Twice Sat. Phone, Rugby 2425. Station, Rugby, L.M.S.
REGENT (BTH), Bank Street.—Props., Plaza Theatre (Rugby), Ltd., Crown House, Rugby. Phone, Rugby 2244. 1,200 seats. Booked at 36, Golden Square, W.1. Continuous. Prices, 6d. to 1s. 6d. Café attached. Phone, Rugby 2324. Station, Rugby, L.M.S.

SCALA (BTH), Henry Street.—Prop., Scala Cinema Syndicate, Cinema de Luxe, Northampton. 600 seats. Continuous. Mats., Mon., Wed. and Sat. Prices, 6d. to 1s. 3d. Phone, Rugby 3248.

RUGELEY (STAFFS), **Pop. 5,263.**
PICTURE HOUSE (WE), Horsefair.—Prop.,
Rugeley Picture House, Ltd. 600 seats,
Booked at Grand, Coalville. Continuous.
Prices, 4d. to 1s. 3d. Proscenium width,
40 ft. Stage, 24 ft. deep ; four dressing-rooms.
Phone, Rugeley 99. Station, Rugeley Town
or Trent Valley, L.M.S.

RUISLIP (MIDDLESEX), **Pop. 16,038.**
ASTORIA (WE), High Street.—Prop., Shipman
and King, M84, Shellmex House, Strand,
W.C.2. Phone, Temple Bar 5077. Contin-
ous. Booked at H.O. Prices, 6d. to 2s. 6d.
Proscenium width; 38 ft. Phone 2960.
Station, Ruislip, G. W. and G.C. Rlys.
RIVOLI (WE), Ickenham Road.—Prop., Shipman
and King, M84, Shellmex House, Strand,
W.C.2. Phone, Temple Bar 5077. Continuous.
Booked at H.O. Prices, 6d. to 1s. 10d.
Proscenium width, 36 ft. Phone, Ruislip
2960. Station, Ruislip, Met. R.

RUNCORN (CHESHIRE), **Pop. 18,158.**
EMPRESS KINEMA (WE), Lowlands Road.—
Prop., Cheshire County Cinemas, Ltd.
1,200 seats. Booked at Hall by R. H. Godfrey.
Two shows nightly. Three Mats. Prices, 6d.
to 1s. 3d. Phone, Runcorn 199.
KING'S KINEMA (WE).—Prop., Cheshire County
Cinemas, Ltd., Empress Kinemas, Runcorn.
700 seats. Phone 199. Booked at Empress
Kinema by R. H. Godfrey. Continuous. Two
shows Sat. Prices, 3d. to 1s. Proscenium
width, 25 ft. Phone, Runcorn 503. Station,
Runcorn, L.M.S.
SCALA (WE), High Street.—Prop., Cheshire
County Cinemas, Empress Theatre. Runcorn.
Booked at H.O. Continuous Mon. to Fri.
Twice nightly Sat. Prices, 3d. to 1s. Phone
140. Station, Runcorn.

RUSHDEN (NORTHANTS), **Pop. 14,247.**
PALACE (WE).—Prop., Palace Co. 722 seats.
Two shows nightly. Two changes weekly.
Prices, 4d. to 1s. 3d. Station, Rushden, L.M.S.
ROYAL THEATRE (BTH).—Prop., Rushden
Cinema Co., Ltd. 900 seats. Continuous.
Two changes weekly. Prices, 6d. to 1s. 4d.
Phone, Rushden 135. Station, Rushden.

RYDE (I. OF W.), **Pop. 10,519.**
COMMODORE.
ODEON (BTH).—Prop., Odeon (Ryde) Ltd.,
Cornhill House, Bennetts Hill, Birmingham.
(In course of construction.)
SCALA (BA), High Street.—Prop., Isle of Wight
Theatres, Ltd., Theatre Royal, Ryde. 555
seats. Booked at H.O. Two shows nightly.
Mat. Wed. Prices 6d. to 1s. 10d. Phone,
Ryde 2162. Station, Ryde Esplanade, S.R.
THEATRE ROYAL (BA), St. Thomas Square.—
Prop., Isle of Wight Theatres, Ltd. 650 seats.
Booked at Queen's, Sandown. Twice nightly.
Mat., Wed. and Sat. Prices, 6d. to 1s. 10d.
Phone, Ryde 237. Station, Esplanade, Ryde,
S.R.

RYE (SUSSEX), **Pop. 3,947.**
REGENT (WE).—Props., Shipman and King,
M84, Shellmex House, Strand, W.C.2. Booked
at H.O. Continuous, nightly. Mats., Tues.,
Thurs., Sat. Prices, 6d. to 2s. Phone 173.
Station, Rye, S.R.

RYHILL (YORKS), **Pop. 2,191.**
EMPIRE (Electrocord).—Prop., E. Silverwood.
553 seats. Booked at Hall by Prop. One
show nightly. Two on Sat., and Mat.

Prices, 3d. to 1s. Phone, Royston 31.
Station, Ryhill, L.N.E.R.

RYHOPE (CO. DURHAM).
GRAND THEATRE (WE).—Prop., Ryhope Palace,
Ltd. Gen. Man., I. T. Womphrey. 850 seats.
Booked at Hall. Twice nightly, Mon. and
Sat. Once nightly rest of week. Prices,
5d. to 1s. Phone, Ryhope 224. Station,
Ryhope, L.N.E.R.

SACRISTON (CO. DURHAM), **Pop. 8,000.**
CINEMA (BTH).
MINERS' MEMORIAL HALL (BTH).—1,450 seats.
THEATRE ROYAL (Echo).—Prop., John
Maddison, Church Street. Pictures, Variety
and Drama. Booked at Newcastle. Once
nightly, twice Sat. Prices, 6d. to 1s. Stage,
30 ft. deep. Station, Plawsworth, L.N.E.R.
VICTORIA THEATRE (BA).—Prop., Mrs. Mary
Tinsley, 14, South Parade, Sacriston. 700
seats. Booked at Hall. Once nightly (includ-
ing Sunday). Continuous, Mon. and Sat.
Prices, 4d. to 1s. Station, Plawsworth,
L.N.E.R.

SAFFRON WALDEN (ESSEX), **Pop. 5,930.**
THE WALDEN CINEMA (BTP), High Street.—
Prop., Tozer and Linsell, 55, Cambridge Street,
Pancras Road, N.W.1. 380 seats. Booked
at H.O. Continuous. Prices, 6d. to 1s. 6d.
Station, Saffron Walden, L.N.E.R.
PLAZA (BTH), Station Street.—Lessee, J. H.
Gotch, Regal Cinema, Soham, Cambs. Phone,
Soham 72. 450 seats. Booked at H.O.
Continuous. Three shows Sat. Prices, 6d. to
1s. 6d. Proscenium width, 19 ft. Phone,
Saffron Walden 217. Station, Saffron Walden,
L.N.E.R.

ST. AGNES (CORNWALL), **Pop. 3,350.**
REGAL (BTP).—Prop., Mrs. E. F. Knight,
Vicarage Road, St. Agnes. 240 seats. Once
nightly. Two shows Sat. Prices, 6d. to 1s. 3d.
Proscenium width, 14 ft. Station, St. Agnes.

ST. ALBANS (HERTS), **Pop. 28,625.**
CAPITOL (WE), London Road.—Props., Capitol
(St. Albans), Ltd., 225, Oxford Street, W.1.
1,728 seats. Booked at Cinema House, 225,
Oxford Street, London, W.1. Phone, Gerrard
4242. Continuous. Pictures. Prices, 9d. to 2s.
Proscenium width, 35 ft. Stage, 20 ft. deep ;
three dressing-rooms. Café. Phone 888.
Station, St. Albans, City, L.M.S.

COMPTON
ORGAN featured here.

CHEQUERS THEATRE (WE).—Prop., Capt. Fred
Webb. 1,000 seats. Occasional Variety.
Booked at Hall by Prop. Continuous.
Prices, 6d. to 1s. 6d. Phone, St. Albans 373.
Station, St. Albans.
GRAND PALACE THEATRE (WE), Stanhope Road.
—Prop., Hertfordshire Picture Theatres,
Ltd., Cinema House, 225, Oxford Street,
London, W.1. Phone, Gerrard 4242. 1,400
seats. Booked at H.O. Continuous. Prices,
9d. to 1s. 6d. Phone, St. Albans 700.
Station, St. Albans, City, L.M.S. Film
Transport.

ST. ANNES-ON-SEA (LANCS), **Pop. 15,401.**
EMPIRE (WE), St. George's Road.—Prop., Spring
Bros. and Crowther. 1,156 seats. One show
nightly. Mat., Wed. and Sat. Two changes

ST. ANNES-ON-SEA—Contd.

weekly. Booked at Manchester. Prices, 6d. to
1s. 6d. Stage, 12 ft. deep; four dressing-
rooms. Café. Phone, St. Annes-on-Sea 235.
Station, St. Annes-on-Sea.

PALACE CINEMA (WE), Garden Street.—Prop.,
Blackpool Tower Co., Ltd. Phone, Blackpool 1. 902 seats. Booked by B.T.C., Ltd.,
at Empress Chambers, Blackpool. Three
shows daily. Prices, 9d. to 1s. 6d. Proscenium
width, 28 ft. Café and Ballroom attached.
Phone, St. Annes 900. Station, St. Annes-on-
Sea, L.M.S.

**Fitted "ARDENTE" Deaf Aids
See page 258**

ST AUSTELL (CORNWALL), **Pop. 8,295.**

CAPITOL THEATRE (WE), 115 Alexandra Road.—
Prop., H. J. Watkins, Ltd. 680 seats. Booked
at Hall. Twice nightly. Prices, 9d. to 2s.
Ballroom, Café and Lounge attached. Pros-
cenium width, 25 ft. Phone, St. Austell 223.
Station, St. Austell, G.W.R.

ODEON THEATRE (BTH), Chandos Place.—Prop ,
Odeon (St. Austell) Ltd., Cornhill House,
Bennetts Hill, Birmingham. Phone, Midland
2781. Booked at 49, Park Lane, W.1. Continuous. Prices, 9d. to 2s.

SAVOY THEATRE (Film Industries), Truro Road.
—Prop., H. J. Watkins, Ltd., 115, Alexandra
Road. 365 seats. Booked at H.O. Nightly
at 7.30. Mat., Fri. and Sat. Prices, 6d. to
1s. 6d. Proscenium width, 25 ft. Phone, St.
Austell 435. Station, St. Austell, G.W.R.

ST. BLAZEY (CORNWALL), **Pop. 3,086.**

PALACE THEATRE (BA).—Prop., R. Hill, Palace
Theatre, Truro. 450 seats. Booked at H.O.
Once nightly. Mat. Sat. Prices, 6d. to
1s. 6d. Station, St. Blazey, G.W.R.

ST. COLUMB (CORNWALL), **Pop. 2,860.**

TOWN HALL CINEMA (BA).—Prop. and Man.,
P. E. G. Taylor, "Restormel," Mount Wise,
Newquay. Phone 404. 180 seats. Sat. evenings only. Prices 6d. to 1s. 6d. Non-inflammable films only shown. Proscenium width,
10 ft. Station, Newquay, G.W.R.

ST. DENNIS (CORNWALL), **Pop. 4,000.**

PLAZA THEATRE (BTH).—Lessee, Frank Chas.
Elgar. 400 seats. Booked at H.O. Once
nightly and one Mat. Prices, 3d. to 1s. 6d.
Proscenium width, 18 ft. Phone, Nanpean
1–8. Stations, St. Dennis and St. Austell,
G.W.R., and Road Motors.

ST. HELENS (LANCS), **Pop. 106,793.**

CAPITOL (WE), Capitol Corner.—Prop., Asso-
ciated British Cinemas, Ltd., 30–31, Golden
Square, London, W.1. Phone, Gerrard 7887.
1,600 seats. Booked at H.O. Twice nightly.
Daily Mat. Prices, 6d. to 1s. 6d. Phone, St.
Helens 3956. Station, St. Helens, L.M.S.

EMPIRE CINEMA (WE), Thatto Heath Road.—
Prop., Empire Picturedrome, Ltd. 600 seats.
Booked at Hall. Twice nightly. Daily Mat.
Prices, 5d. to 1s. Proscenium width, 15½ ft.
Phone, St. Helens 3493. Station, Thatto
Heath, L.M.S.

OXFORD PICTURE HOUSE (BTP), Duke Street.—
Prop., Oxford (St. Helens), Ltd., 1–3, Stanley
Street, Liverpool. 650 seats. Booked at Hall.
Three shows daily. Prices 4d. to 1s. Phone,
St. Helens 2485. Station, St. Helens, L.M.S.

PALLADIUM (BTH), Boundary Road.—Prop.,
Palladium (St. Helens), Ltd., 1–3, Stanley

Street, Liverpool. 550 seats. Booked, Imperial,
Liverpool. Continuous. Prices, 4d. to 1s.
Phone, St. Helens 3497. Station, St. Helens.

PAVILION (BTP), Jackson Street.—Prop., Picture
Theatres (St. Helens), Ltd. 700 seats. Booked
at Hall. Two shows nightly. Two changes
weekly. Prices, 4d. to 8d. Phone, St.
Helens 484. Station, St. Helens, L.M.S.

RIVOLI CINEMA (WE), Corporation Street.—
Prop., County Playhouses, Ltd., County
Playhouse, King Street, Wigan. Phone 3476.
1,000 seats. Booked by T. C. Robinson,
Cromford House, Manchester. Three shows
daily. Prices, 5d. to 1s. 4d. Phone, St.
Helens 4185.

SAVOY PICTURE HOUSE (BTP).—Prop., Asso-
ciated British Cinemas, Ltd., 30-31, Golden
Square, W.1. 1,513 seats.
Three shows daily. Two changes weekly.
Prices, 6d. to 1s. 6d. Proscenium width,
40 ft. Phone, St. Helens 3392. Café attached.
Station, St. Helens.

SCALA (BTP), Ormskirk Street.—Prop., Scala
(St. Helens), Ltd. 800 seats. Booked at
Hall by Man. Twice nightly; daily Mats.
Prices, 4d. to 1s. 2d. Phone, St. Helens 3654.

SUTTON EMPIRE (BTH), Junction Lane.—Prop.,
B. H. Franks. 700 seats. Booked at Empire,
Eccles. Twice nightly. Mats., Mon., Thurs,
and Sat. Prices, 4d. to 1s. Proscenium
width, 25 ft. Phone, St. Helens 3030. Station,
St. Helens Junction, L.M.S.

ST. IVES (CORNWALL), **Pop. 6,687.**

PALAIS CINEMA (Morrison).—Prop., St. Ives
Cinema (Cornwall) Ltd. Phone, St. Ives
143. 250 seats. Booked at Scala, St. Ives,
Twice nightly in season, and variety. Prices
6d. to 1s. 6d. Proscenium width, 18 ft. Stage,
14 ft. deep; two dressing-rooms. Dances also
held in hall.

ROYAL, Royal Square.—Prop., St. Ives
Cinema (Cornwall) Ltd. 666 seats. Booked
at Scala. Twice nightly. Prices, 6d. to 2s.
Proscenium width, 30 ft. Stage, 14 ft. deep.
Two dressing-rooms. Phone 143. Station,
St. Ives, G.W.R.

SCALA THEATRE (BTH).—Prop., St. Ives Cinemas
(Cornwall), Ltd. Phone, St. Ives 143. 450
seats. Booked at Hall. Twice nightly.
Prices, 6d. to 1s. 6d. Proscenium width,
17 ft. Stage, 15 ft. deep; three dressing-
rooms. Station, St. Ives (Cornwall), G.W.R.

ST. IVES (HUNTS), **Pop. 2,664.**

BROADWAY KINEMA (BTP).—Prop., Bury St.
Edmunds Cinemas, Ltd., 54, Chevalier Street,
Ipswich. Phone, 4036. 390 seats. Booked
by D. F. Bostock at H.O. Once nightly.
Three Sat. Two changes weekly. Prices, 3d.
to 1s. 6d. Proscenium width, 19 ft. Phone,
St. Ives 119. Station, St. Ives, L.N.E.R.
and Cambridge and District F. T.

ST. JUST (CORNWALL).

CINEMA (BTH). 330 seats.

ST. LEONARDS-ON-SEA (SUSSEX), **Pop .
12,339.**

ELITE PICTURE THEATRE (WE), Warrior Square.
Controlled by Union Cinemas, Ltd., Union
House, 15, Regent Street, London, S.W.1.
Phone, Whitehall 8484. Booked at H.O.
Continuous. Films and Variety. Prices,
6d. to 2s. Stage, 20 ft. deep; two dressing

rooms. Phone, Hastings, 282. Station, Warrior Square, St. Leonards-on-Sea, S.R.
KINEMA (WE), Norman Road.—Prop., Kinema Playhouses, Ltd. Man. Dir., Randolph E. Richards. 555 seats. Booked at Picturedrome, Eastbourne. Continuous. Phone, Hastings 184. Station, Warrior Square, S.R.
REGAL (WE), London Road.— Controlled by Union Cinemas, Ltd., Union House, 15, Regent Street, London, S.W.1. Phone, Whitehall 8484. Booked at H.O. Continuous. Films and Variety. Prices, 6d. to 2s. Proscenium width, 44 ft. Stage, 20 ft. deep ; three dressing-rooms. Café. Phone, Hastings 124. Station, Warrior Square.
Fitted "ARDENTE" Deaf Aids
See page 258

C O M P T O N

ORGAN featured here.

SILVERHILL PICTURE HOUSE (BTH).—Prop., Miss Daisy Meatyard. 450 seats. Booked at Hall. Continuous. Prices, 6d. to 1s. 3d. Phone, Hastings 1662. Station, Warrior Square, S.R.

ST. NEOTS (HUNTS), **Pop. 4,314.**
PAVILION (BA). 454 seats.

SALCOMBE (DEVON), **Pop. 2,383.**
TOWN HALL CINEMA (Mihaly).—Prop., Salcombe Town Hall Co., Ltd., 11, Fore Street, Booked at Hall. Prices, 4d. to 1s. 10d. Station, Kingsbridge, G.W.R.

SALE (CHESHIRE), **Pop. 28,063.**
PALACE (BTP).—Prop., Sale Public Hall, Ltd. Booked at Imperial Buildings, Oxford Road, Manchester. 1,000 seats. Three shows Sat. Continuous rest of week. Prices, 6d. to 1s. Phone, Sale 3524.
PYRAMID (WE).—Props., Anglo-Scottish Theatres Ltd., 2, Cavendish Square, London. Booked at Hall. Continuous. Pictures and Variety. Two shows Sat. Prices, 6d. to 2s. Proscenium width, 48 ft. Stage, 32 ft. deep ; six dressing-rooms. Café attached. Phone, 2247. Station Sale.
Fitted "ARDENTE" Stage Amplification
See page 258
SAVOY CINEMA (WE), Tatton Road.—Controlled by Union Cinemas, Ltd., 15, Regent Street, London, S.W.1. Phone, Whitehall 8484. Booked at H.O. Continuous. Prices, 6d. to 1s. Phone, Sale 1096. Station, Sale, M.S.J. and A.R.

SALFORD (LANCS), **Pop. 223,442.**
ALEXANDRA PICTURE HOUSE (BTP), Rumford Street.—Prop., A. and C. Ogden, 76, Victoria Street, Manchester. 850 seats. Booked at H.O. Twice nightly. Mats. Mon. and Thurs. Prices, 4d. to 9d. Phone, Pendleton 1235.
ARCADIA (Picturetone). Blackfriars Road.—Prop., B. Kanter. 700 seats. Booked at Hall. Twice nightly. Four changes weekly. Prices, 3d. to 6d.
BIJOU (BA), Pendleton.—Prop. and Man., J. T. Jones. 500 seats. Booked at Hall. Continuous, Mon. to Fri. Two shows Sat. Prices, 4d. to 7d. Proscenium width, 21 ft. Station, Pendleton, L.M.S.

BORO' CINEMA (BTP), Halliwell Street, Trafford Road.—H. D. Moorhouse Circuit, 7, Oxford Road, Manchester. Phone, Ardwick 2226. 850 seats.
DEVONSHIRE THEATRE (WE), Broughton.—Prop., New Devonshire (Salford), Ltd. 1,300 seats. Continuous. Prices, 6d. to 1s. Phone, Higher Broughton 2720. Stations, Exchange and Victoria, L.M.S.
DOMINION THEATRE (WE), Regent Bridge.—Prop., Salford Entertainments Co., Ltd. 1,394 seats. Pictures and Variety. Booked by J. F. Emery at Cross Street, Manchester. Continuous, Mon. to Fri. Three shows Sats. Prices, 6d. to 1s. 3d. Stage, 15 ft. deep. Five dressing-rooms. Proscenium width, 32 ft. Phone, Blackfriars 5936. Station, Central, L.M.S.
EMPIRE ELECTRIC THEATRE (WE), Trafford Road.—Prop., Abraham Ogden, 49 Trafford Road, Salford. 773 seats. Booked at H.O Three shows daily. Prices, 5d. to 9d. Proscenium width, 26 ft. Phone, Trafford Park 145.
EMPIRE THEATRE (WE), Gt. Cheetham Street.—Prop., Jefton Entertainments, Ltd., 26, Cross Street, Manchester. Phone, Blackfriars 0752. 950 seats. Booked at H.O. Continuous, Mon. to Fri. Twice on Sat. Mats. Mon. Wed. Thurs., Sat. Prices, 6d. to 1s. Proscenium width, 30 ft. Phone, Broughton 2652. Stations, Victoria, Manchester.
EMPRESS PICTURE PALACE (WE), Church Street, Pendleton.—Prop., J. F. Emery, Beech House, Bolton Road, Pendleton. 700 seats. Booked by J. F. Emery at Midland Bank Chambers, Cross Street, Manchester. Continuous. Two changes weekly. Café and Ballroom attached. Prices, 2d. to 6d. Phone, Pendleton 1703. Station, Pendleton, L.M.S.
FUTURIST CINEMA (BTH), Gt. Ducie Street.—Prop., L. Burgess, Combs, Chapel-en-le-Frith. Phone, Chapel 158. Booked at Hall. 600 seats. Continuous. Prices, 4d. to 9d. Proscenium width, 20 ft. Station, Exchange, Manchester, L.M.S.
KINGS PICTURE HALL (BA), Props., James-Caton. Phone, TRA/777. 540 seats. Prices, 3d. to 9d. Films collected.
LANGWORTHY PICTUREDROME (RCA), Langworthy Road.—Prop., Langworthy Picturedrome, Ltd., Newgate Chambers, Rochdale. Phone 3212. 755 seats. Booked at H.O. Twice nightly. Two changes weekly. Prices, 4d. to 1s. Phone, Pendleton 2419. Station, Seedley, L.M.S.
NEW CENTRAL HALL (WE), Gardner Street. Seats 580. Prices, 5d. and 6d. Proscenium width, 17 ft. Phone, Pen 1898. Station, Pendleton.
NEW MARLBOROUGH PICTURE HOUSE, St. James Road, Hightown.—Prop., A. Sereno, 404, Bury New Road, Salford. Phone, Broughton 1117. Booked at Hall. Two shows nightly. Prices, 5d. to 1s.
ORDSALL PICTURE HOUSE (WE), Ordsall Lane.—Prop., C. Ogden. 1082 seats.
PALACE CINEMA (BTP), Cross Lane.—Prop., Salford Palace, Ltd., Imperial Bldgs., Oxford Road, Manchester. Phone, Ardwick 2226. Booked by H. D. Moorhouse at H.O. Twice nightly. Mats. daily. Prices, 3d. to 9d. Phone, Pendleton 1657. Station, Cross Lane, L.M.S.

PATHE PICTORIAL—Novel, Entertaining, Unique.

ʃ ALFORD—Contd.

PALACE THEATRE (WE), Cross Lane.—Prop., Salford Palace, Ltd., Imperial Bldgs., Oxford Road, Manchester. Phone, Ardwick 2226. 1,600 seats. Booked at H.O. Continuous nightly. ˏMat. daily. Twice nightly Sat, Mat. daily except Sat. Prices, 4d. to 1s. Phone, Pendleton 1656. Station, Cross Lane, L.M.S.

PICTUREDROME (Picturetone), Broughton Lane. —Prop., Broughton Picturedrome Co., 450 seats. Twice nightly. Two changes weekly. Prices, 3d. to 6d. Station, Manchester, L.M.S.

PRINCES CINEMA (WE), Liverpool Street. Props., T. W. Berry. 600 seats. Booked at Hall. Continuous. Two shows Sat. Prices, 4d. to 6d. Phone, Pendleton 1120.

REX CINEMA (BA), Regent Road.—J. F. Emery Circuit, 26, Cross Street, Manchester. 500 seats. Booked at H.O. Two shows nightly. Two changes weekly. Prices, 3d. to 8d. Phone, Trafford Park 177. Station, Manchester termini.

ROYAL PICTURE THEATRE (WE), Fitzwarren Street, Pendleton.—Prop., Pendleton Picture Co., Ltd. Booked at Hall by R. Allen. Twice n ghtly. Prices, 4d. to 1s. Phone, Pendleton 166. Station, Manchester, L.M.S.

SALFORD CINEMA (BTH), Chapel Street.—Props., Williams and Pritchard. 750 seats. Booked at Hall by V. Tyldesley. Prices, 4d. and 6d. Stations, Manchester and Salford termini.

SCALA (WE), Ford Lane, Pendleton.—Prop., Pendleton Scala, Ltd. Gen. Man., Harold E · Buxton. 1,207 seats. Booked by J. F· Emery's Circuit, 26, Cross Street, Manchester· Continuous. Two shows, Sat. Pictures and Variety. Stage, 15 ft. deep. Two dressing-rooms. Prices, 3d. to 1s. Phone, Pendleton 2057 Station, Manchester, all stations.

SEEDLEY CINEMA (BTP), Langworthy Road.— Prop., Executrix, C. W. H. Bowmer. 650 seats. Two shows nightly. Prices, 3d. to 9d. Station, Manchester termini.

TOWER CINEMA (WE), Great Clowes Street, Broughton.—Prop., Tower (Broughton), Ltd. 1,280 seats. Booked at Imperial Buildings, Oxford Road, Manchester, by H. D. Moorhouse Circuit. Continuous, Mon. to Fri. Twice on Sat. Mat. Mon., Wed., Thurs. and Sat. Prices, 4d. to 9d. Phone, Broughton 2643. Stations, Victoria and Exchange.

VICTORIA THEATRE CINEMA (BTP), Great Clowes Street, Lower Broughton.—Prop., Broughton Cinema, Ltd., Imperial Bldgs., Oxford Road, Manchester. H. D. Moorhouse Circuit. Occasional Variety. Booked at H.O. Continuous. Prices, 3d. to 9d. Phone, Blackfriars 9847. Station, Manchester (London Road).

WEASTE CINEMA.—Prop., J. F. Emery's Circuit, 26, Cino Street, Manchester.

(See also Manchester).

SALISBURY (WILTS), Pop. 26,456.

GARRISON THEATRE (BTH), Bulford Camp. Prop., A. N. Kendal, Ltd. The Palace, Andover. Booked at H.O. 674 seats. Prices, 6d. to 1s. 3d. Films by Road Transport.

GARRISON CINEMA (BTH), Larkhill.—Prop., A. N. Kendal, Ltd., 73, North Wall, Winchester, 549 seats. Booked at H.O. Continuous, Prices, 6d. to 1s. 3d. Phone, Durrington Walls 227. Station, Amesbury, S.R.

GAUMONT PALACE (BA), Canal.—Prop., Albany Ward Theatres, Ltd. Booked at H.O., New Gallery House, 123, Regent Street, London,

W.1. Phone, Regent 8080. 1,675 seats. Continuous. Prices, 9d. to 2s. Phone, Salisbury 382. Station, Salisbury, S.R.

Fitted "ARDENTE" Deaf Aids See page 258

NEW.—Prop., Albany Ward Theatres, Ltd., 123, Regent Street, London, W.1.

PICTURE HOUSE (BA), Fisherton Street.—Prop., Gaumont-British Pictures Corpn. Booked at H.O. 514 seats. Three shows daily. Two changes weekly. Prices, 6d. to 1s. 10d. Proscenium width, 20 ft. Phone, Salisbury 294. Station, Salisbury, G.W.R. and S.R.

REGAL.—Prop., Associated British Cinemas, Ltd., 30-31, Golden Square, London, W.1.

SALTAIRE, SHIPLEY (YORKS).

SALTAIRE PICTURE HOUSE (BA), Bingley Road.— Prop., Gaumont-British Picture Corpn., Ltd., 123, Regent Street, London, W.1. Phone, Regent 6641. 1,140 seats. Continuous. Two shows Sat. Booked at H.O. Prices, 7d. to 1s. 3d. Phone, Shipley 594. Station, Saltaire, L.M.S.

SALTASH (CORNWALL), Pop. 3,603.

IMPERIAL PICTURE HOUSE (BTH).—Prop., Quick & Son. One show nightly. Proscenium width, 15 ft. Phone, Saltash 3129. Station, Saltash, Cornwall, G.W.R.

SALTBURN-BY-THE-SEA (YORKS), Pop. 3,911.

CINEMA (BTH), Milton Street.—Prop., Mrs. C. Miller, Beaumont, Saltburn. 340 seats. Booked at Hall. Continuous. Sat. twice nightly. Prices, 6d. to 1s. Proscenium width, 30 ft. Phone, Saltburn 134. Station, Saltburn, L.N.E.R.

SALTNEY (CHESHIRE).

PARK CINEMA (BTP).—Prop., Deeside Enterprise Cinemas, Ltd., Bridge House, Queens-ferry, Chester. Phone, Connah's Quay 49. 470 seats. Booked at h.O. Twice nightly. Mats., Wed. and Sat. Prices, 6d. to 1s. Proscenium width, 20 ft. Phone, Chester 1430. Station, Saltney, L.M.S.

SANDBACH (CHESHIRE), Pop. 6,411.

PALACE (WE), Congleton Road.—Prop., Sand bach Cinemas, Ltd. 550 seats. Booked at Hall. Twice nightly. Prices, 6d. to 1s. 3d. Phone, Sandbach 103. Station, Sandbach, L.M.S.

SANDGATE (KENT), Pop. 2,760.

PICTURE HOUSE (Morrison).—570 seats. Continuous. Prices, 6d. to 1s. 3d. Proscenium width, 30 ft. Stage, 9 ft. 6 in. deep. Two dressing-rooms. Station, Folkestone, Central

SANDOWN (ISLE OF WIGHT), Pop. 6167.

QUEEN'S CINEMA (BA), Albert Road.—Prop., Isle of Wight Theatres, Ltd., Theatre Royal, Ryde. 500 seats. Booked at Hall. Twice nightly. Mat. Sat. Prices, 6d. to 1s. 6d. Phone, Sandown 178. Films to Scala, Ryde. Station, Ryde Esplanade, S.R.

RIVOLI PICTURE HOUSE (BA), Station Avenue.— Props., Porters (Sandown), Ltd., 45, High Street, Sandown. Phone 14. Two shows nightly. Mats. Wed. and Sat. Two changes weekly. Prices, 6d. to 1s. 6d. Phone, Sandown 45. Station, Sandown, S.R.

SANDWICH (KENT), **Pop. 3,287.**
EMPIRE (Morrison), 15, Delf Street.—Prop. and Man., W.A. Campbell. 370 seats. Booked at Hall. One show nightly. Two on Thurs. and Sat. Prices, 4d. to 1s. 3d. Proscenium width, 30 ft. Station, Sandwich, S.R.

SANDY (BEDS), **Pop. 3,140.**
VICTORY CINEMA (AWH).—Prop., A. Hill and Sons, Empire, Biggleswade. Phone 97. 500 seats. Booked at H.Q. by E. A. Hill. Continuous Mon. to Fri.; twice Sat. Café attached. Prices, 6d. to 1s. 6d. Phone, Sandy 78. Station, Sandy, L.M.S. and L.N.E.R.

SAWBRIDGEWORTH (HERTS), **Pop. 2,604.**
CINEMA (BA).—Prop., Ernest E. Smith, Merlewood, Pine Grove Road, Bishop's Stortford. Phone, Bishop's Stortford 456. 297 seats. Booked at Regent, Bishop's Stortford. Continuous. Mat.. Sat. Two changes weekly. Prices, 6d. to 1s. 3d. Phone, Sawbridgeworth 67. Station, Sawbridgeworth, L.N.E.R. Films by Film Transport.

SAWSTON (CAMBS), **Pop. 1,550.**
NEW CINEMA.
SPICER'S THEATRE.

SAXMUNDHAM (SUFFOLK), **Pop. 1,260.**
MARKET HALL.

SCARBOROUGH (YORKS), **Pop. 41,791.**
ABERDEEN WALK PICTURE HOUSE (BA), Aberdeen Walk.—Prop., Aberdeen Walk (Scarborough), Picture House, Ltd., Westborough, Scarborough. Phone, 626. 915 seats. Booked at Leeds. Continuous. Two changes weekly. Prices 6d. to 2s. Proscenium width, 26 ft. Stage, 12 ft. deep. One dressing-room. Café attached. Phone 626. Station, Scarborou h, L.N.E.R.
CAPITOL CINEMA (WE), Albemarle Crescent.— Prop., Londesborough and Capitol (Scarborough), Ltd. Reg. Office, 26, Park Row, Leeds. Phone, Leeds 28775. 2,200 seats. Booked at H.O. Continuous. Prices, 6d. to 1s. 6d. Phone, Scarborough 1308. Station, Scarborough.
FUTURIST (WE).—Prop., Catlin's Scarborough Entertainments, Ltd. 2,393 seats. Summer, continuous, to 2s. Winter, twice daily, 6d. to 1s. 6d. Phone, 644, Station, Scarborough, L.N.E.R.
GRAND PICTURE HOUSE, Foreshore.—Props., H. A. Whitaker & Co. Phone, Scarborough 444. 1,800 seats. Booked at Leeds. Continuous. Prices, 6d. to 1s. 6d. Proscenium width, 24 ft. Phone, Scarborough 693. Station. Scarborough, L.N.E.R.
LONDESBOROUGH THEATRE (WE), Westborough. —Props., Londesborough and Capitol (Scarborough), Ltd. 1,268 seats. Continuous. Prices, 6d. to 1s. 6d. Phone 51. Station, Scarborough, L.N.E.R.
ODEON THEATRE (BTH).—Props., Odeon (Scarborough), Ltd., Cornhill House, Bennett's Hill, Birmingham. Phone, Midland 2781. Booked at 49, Park Lane, W.1. Continuous. Phone, Scarborough 1752.

SCOTSWOOD (NORTHUMBERLAND).
REGENT (BTP).—300 seats.

SCUNTHORPE and FRODINGHAM (LINCS), **Pop. 33,761.**
EMPIRE THEATRE.—(Closed.)
JUBILEE CINEMA DE LUXE (WE), Laneham Street.—Prop., Scunthorpe Co - operative Society, Ltd. 700 seats. Booked at Hall Three shows daily. Prices, 4d. to 1s. 3d. Phone, Scunthorpe 322. Café attached. Station, Scunthorpe, L.N.E.R.
MAJESTIC CINEMA (WE).—915 seats. Booked at Hall. Twice nightly. Prices, 4d. to 1s. 3d. Café. Phone, Scunthorpe 352. Station, Scunthorpe, L.N.E.R.
PALACE THEATRE (WE).—Prop., F. J. Butterworth. 1,500 seats. Booked at Hall. Continuous. Pictures and Variety. Prices, 6d. to 2s. Proscenium width, 35 ft. Stage, 45 ft. deep ; 12 dressing-rooms. Phone No. 88. Station, Scunthorpe, L.N.E.R.
PAVILION PICTURE HOUSE (BTP), Doncaster Road.—Prop., Arthur Watson, J.P., Fern Villa, Ashby, High Street, Scunthorpe. Phone, Scunthorpe 652. 1,650 seats. Booked at Hall. Continuous. Prices, 3d. to 1s. 3d. Proscenium width, 32 ft. Phone, Scunthorpe 39. Station, Scunthorpe and Frodingham, L.N.E.R.
RITZ (WE).—Controlled by Union Cinemas, Ltd., 15, Regent Street, S.W.1. Phone, Whitehall 8484. Booked at H.O. Continuous. Prices, 6d. to 1s. 6d. Station, Scunthorpe, L.N.E.R.
ROYAL CINEMA (BTH).—Prop., Royal Cinema Co. 900 seats. Booked at Hall. Continuous. Prices, 4d. to 1s. Proscenium width, 25 ft. Phone, Scunthorpe 340 and 18. Station, Scunthorpe, L.N.E.R.

SEACOMBE (CHESHIRE). **See Wallasey.**

SEAFORD (SUSSEX), **Pop. 6,570.**
EMPIRE CINEMA (BTH), Sutton Road.—Prop., Isobel Merriman-Langdon, Kingsway, Sutton Road, Seaford. 475 seats. Booked at Hall. Continuous. Two changes weekly. Prices, 6d. to 1s. 6d. Proscenium width, 25 ft. Phone, Seaford 355. Station, Seaford, S.R.
RITZ CINEMA (BTH), Dane Road.—Lessee, Isobel Merriman - Langdon, " Kingsway," Sutton Road, Seaford. Continuous nightly. Mats., Wed. and Sat. Booked at Hall. Prices, 9d. to 2s. Proscenium width, 45 ft. Phone, 355. Café, Dance Hall. Station, Seaford, S.R.

SEAFORTH (LANCS), **(See Liverpool).**

SEAHAM HARBOUR (Co. DURHAM), **Pop. 19,394.**
EMPIRE (WE), South Hackney.—Props., A. C. Harrison. 957 seats. Two shows nightly. Two changes weekly. Prices, 4d. to 1s. Phone, Seaham Harbour 45, Station, Seaham Harbour, L.N.E.R.
PRINCESS (WE).—Props., Princess Entertainments Co., Ltd., Melburn House, (Floor E.), Newcastle-on-Tyne. Phone No. 24944. Seats 1,000. Booked at Hall. Pictures and Occasional Variety. Twice nightly. Prices, 4d. to 9d. Stage, 20 ft. deep ; four dressing-rooms. Proscenium width, 35 ft. Phone 65. Station, Seaham Harbour, L.N.E.R.
THEATRE ROYAL (WE).—Prop., Executors of late A. C. Harrison. 1,005 seats. Booked at Newcastle. Twice nightly. Prices, 4d. to 9d. Stage 30 ft. deep ; 5 dressing-rooms. Proscenium width, 26 ft. Phone, Seaham 2263. Stations, Seaham and Seaham Harbour, L.N.E.R.

The Pick Of Variety And Radio Stars In **PATHETONE WEEKLY.**

SEATON (Devon), **Pop. 2,351.**
REGAL (BTH).—Props., Seaton Cinema Co., Ltd. 588 seats. Booked at Hall. Once nightly. Three Mats. Prices, 6d. to 1s. 8d. Café attached. Phone, Seaton 260. Station, Seaton, Devon.

SEATON BURN (near Dudley) (NORTHUMBERLAND).
QUEEN'S HALL (Knightfone). —Props., Exors. of W. Hutson (Decd.), and N. H. Chapman. 300 seats. Occasional Variety. Booked at Hall by Rd. Henderson. Once nightly ; two on Sat. Prices, 2d. to 8d. Station, Annitsford, L.N.E.R.

SEATON DELAVAL (NORTHUMBERLAND), **Pop. 7,377.**
QUEEN'S HALL (BTH).—Prop., Delaval Pictures, Ltd. 900 seats. Continuous, nightly. Two changes weekly. Phone, Station, Seaton, Delaval, L.N.E.R.

SEDBERGH (YORKS), **Pop. 2,586.**
CINEMA (Electrocord), 1, Long Lane.—Prop. W. D. Clark, Gimain Street, Sedbergh. 300 seats. Booked at Leeds. One show Thurs. Three on Sat. Prices, 7d. to 1s. 3d. Proscenium width 24 ft. Station, Sedbergh, L.M.S.

SELBY (YORKS), **Pop. 10,064.**
CENTRAL PICTURE HALL (BA), James Street.—Props., A. B. and J. Richardson. 565 seats. Booked at Hall. Two shows, Mon. and Sat. Once nightly Tues. to Fri. Prices, 6d. to 1s. 2d. Phone, Selby 97. Station, Selby, L.N.E.R.
HIPPODROME (WE).—Prop., European Theatres, Ltd. 54, Merrion Street, Leeds. Phone, Leeds 25008. 693 seats. Booked at H.O. Continuous. Twice Sat. Prices, 6d. to 1s. 3d. Proscenium width, 26 ft. Stage, 30 ft. deep ; eight dressing-rooms. Phone, Selby 107. Station Selby, L.N.E.R.

SELSEY (SUSSEX), **Pop. 3,000.**
PAVILION (Morrison).—Prop., A. Balfour Johnson. 260 seats. Pictures and Occasional Variety. Booked at Hall. Once nightly and Sundays. Prices, 6d. to 1s. 6d. Stage, 12 ft.; two dressing-rooms. Proscenium width, 20 ft. Station, Chichester, S.R.

SETTLE (YORKS), **Pop. 1,853.**
KIRKGATE KINEMA (Kinephone).—Prop., Settle Kinemas Ltd. 600 seats. Booked at Leeds. Once nightly. Prices, 5d. to 1s. 3d. Station, Settle L.M.S.

SEVEN KINGS (ESSEX), **Pop. 11,000.**
ASTORIA (RCA).—Prop. G. Westrich, 48, Lordship Park, N.16. Phone, Stamford Hill 5060. 1,450 seats. Booked by Prop. Continuous. Prices, 6d. to 2s. Proscenium width, 33 ft. Stage, 22 ft. deep ; three dressing-rooms. Phone, Seven Kings 1052. Station, Seven Kings, L.N.E.R.

SEVENOAKS (KENT), **Pop. 10,482.**
CARLTON (BA).—
CINEMA (WE), 152, High Street.—Prop., Sevenoaks Cinemas, Ltd. 1,200 seats. Booked at Hall. Continuous. Prices, 6d. to 2s. 4d. Café attached. Phone, Sevenoaks 838.

C O M P T O N
ORGAN featured here.

CINEMA (WE), Tub's Hill.—Prop., Sevenoaks Cinemas, Ltd., 152, High Street, Sevenoaks. 400 seats. Booked at H.O. Twice nightly. Mats., Wed. and Sat. Two changes weekly. Prices, 6d. to 2s. 4d. Phone, Sevenoaks 838. Station, Tub's Hill, S.R.
MAJESTIC (BA).—300 seats.

SHAFTESBURY (DORSET), **Pop. 2,366.**
SAVOY THEATRE (Bauer).—Prop., P. J. Carter. Booked at Palace, Blandford. Phone, Blandford 12. 380 seats. Once nightly. Prices, 6d. to 1s. 6d. Proscenium width, 24 ft. Stage, 20 ft. ; three dressing-rooms. Phone, Shaftesbury 101. Station, Semley, S.R., and Road Transport.

SHANKLIN (ISLE OF WIGHT), **Pop. 5,071.**
PLAYHOUSE (BTH), Palmerston Road.—500 seats. Two shows nightly. Prices, 6d. to 1s. 6d. Phone, Shanklin 201. Station, Shanklin, S.R.
REGAL (BTH).—Props., Playhouse (Shanklin), Ltd. Booked at Queen's, Sandown. Prices, 9d. to 1s. 10d. Proscenium width, 30 ft. Phone, No. 372. Station, Shanklin, S.R.

SHAW, nr. Oldham (LANCS.), **Pop. 5,065.**
ODDFELLOWS' INSTITUTE, Farrow Street.—Prop., T. Lucas.
PAVILION (WE), Beal Lane.—Prop., Shaw Picture-drome, Ltd., 16, Clegg Street, Oldham. Phone, Main 4357. 623 seats. Twice nightly. Mon. and Tues. Mat. Prices, 4d. to 9d. Proscenium width, 28 ft. Booked at Hall. Phone, Shaw 7112. Stations, Shaw and Crompton, L.M.S.
PRINCES CINEMA (BTH), Newtown.—Prop., Princes Cinema (Shaw), Ltd. 850 seats. Booked at Manchester. Twice nightly. Prices, 3d. to 9d. Phone, Shaw 7241. Stations, Shaw and Crompton, L.M.S.

SHEERNESS (KENT), **Pop. 16,721.**
ARGOSY (WE), The Broadway.—Prop., East Kent Cinemas, Ltd., East Street, Sittingbourne, Kent. Phone, Kent 333. Seats 1,000. Booked at 3, Hartsdown Mansions, Hartsdown Road, Margate. Continuous. Prices, 6d. to 1s. 6d. Occasional Variety. Proscenium width, 33 ft. Stage, 14 ft. deep ; two dressing-rooms. Café. Phone 333. Station, Sheerness.
HIPPODROME (WE), Broadway.—Prop., Cinema House, Ltd., 225, Oxford Street, London, W.1. Phone, Gerrard 3814. 918 seats. Booked at H.O. by Mr. Dyson. Continuous daily. Prices, 6d. to 1s. Phone, Sheerness 89. Station, Sheerness, S.R.
OXFORD CINEMA (BTH), Russel Street.—Booked at Cinema House, 225, Oxford Street, London, W.1. Continuous. Station, Sheerness, S.R.
REGAL.—Prop., L. Morris, 52, Shaftesbury Avenue, London, W.1. 1,400 seats.

SHEFFIELD (YORKS), **Pop. 511,742.**
ABBEYDALE PICTURE HOUSE (WE).—1,560 seats. Café, Ballroom, and Billiard room, attached. Phone, 50540. Station, Sheffield, L.M.S., and L.N.E.R.
ADELPHI PICTURE THEATRE (WE), Vicarage Road.—Prop., Adelphi (Sheffield), Ltd. 1,338 seats. Booked at Hall. Two shows nightly. Mats. Mon., Thurs. and Sat. Prices, 4d. to 9d. Phone, Attercliffe 41721.
ALBERT HALL (WE), Barker's Pool.—Prop., Gaumont British Picture Corporation, Ltd. 1,611 seats. Booked at H.O. Continuous.

Prices, 5d. to 2s. Proscenium width, 38 ft. Phone, 20563. Station, Sheffield, L.M. and L.N.E.R.

ATTERCLIFFE PALACE THEATRE (WE).—Prop., Palace Theatre, Attercliffe, Ltd. 1,000 seats. Booked at Hall. Continuous. Prices, 4d. to 9d. Stage, 21 ft. deep ; six dressing-rooms, Phone, Attercliffe 41433. Station, Sheffield. L.M.S. and L.N.E.R.

BALFOUR (WE) Staniforth Road.—Prop., Hallamshire Cinemas, Ltd., 3, Hartmead, Sheffield. Phone, Sheffield 20888. 966 seats. Booked at H.O. Continuous. Two changes weekly. Prices, 4d. to 9d. Proscenium width, 30 ft. Stage, 10 ft. deep ; two dressing-rooms. Phone, Sheffield 41712. Stations, Sheffield, L.M.S. ; Darnall, L.N.E.R.

CENTRAL PICTURE HOUSE (WE), The Moor.— Prop., Central Picture Houses (Sheffield), Ltd. 1,539 seats. Booked at Hall. Continuous. One change weekly. Prices, 6d. to 2s. Café attached. Phone, Sheffield Central 25022. Station, Sheffield, L.M.S. and L.N.E.R.

CHANTREY PICTURE HOUSE (BA), Chesterfield Road, Woodseats.—Prop., Chantrey Picture House, Ltd., 11, Figtree Lane, Sheffield. 1,400 seats. Booked at Hall. Continuous. Twice Sat. Prices, 4d. to 1s. Proscenium width, 26 ft. Billiards Room attached. Phone, Beauchieff 45333. Station, Heeley, L.M.S.

CINEMA (BTH). Thompson Hill.—Lessee, J. Gordon Viner, 311 seats. Booked at Hall. Once nightly. Prices, 6d. to 1s. Proscenium width, 24 ft. Phone, High Green 33. Station, Chapeltown, L.M.S.

CINEMA HOUSE (BTH), Fargate.—Prop., Sheffield and District Cinematograph Theatres, Ltd. Reg. Office, 3, Hartshead, Sheffield. Phone, Central 20888. 763 seats. Booked at H.O. Continuous. Café and Billiards Hall attached. Prices, 6d. to 1s. 6d. Phone, Central, 21522. Station, Sheffield, L.M.S. or L.N.E.R.

COLISEUM (WE), Spital Hill.—Prop., Coliseum (Sheffield), Ltd. 1,329 seats. Booked at Hall. Two shows nightly. Mats., Mon., Thurs. and Sat. Prices, 5d. to 9d. Proscenium width, 20 ft. Stage, 11 ft. deep ; two dressing-rooms. Phone, Central 21667. Stations, Sheffield, L.M.S. and L.N.E.R.

CROOKE'S PICTURE THEATRE (WE).—Prop., Hallamshire Cinemas, Ltd., 3, Hartshead, Sheffield. Phone, 20888. 692 seats. Booked at H.O. Twice nightly. Prices, 6d. and 9d. Phone, Broomhill 60568.

DARNALL CINEMA (SOF and disc).—Prop., W. C. Brindley, Glyngarth, South Anston, near Sheffield. 500 seats. Booked at Hall. Two shows nightly. Two changes weekly. Prices, 4d. to 8d. Phone, Attercliffe 41745. Station, Darnall, L.N.E.R.

DON PICTURE PALACE (Cinephone), West Bar.— Prop., Don Picture Palace Co., Ltd. 800 seats. Booked at Hartshead, Sheffield. Three shows daily, except Fri. and Sat. (two). Prices, 3d. to 9d. Phone, Sheffield 23434. Station, Sheffield, L.M.S. and L.N.E.R.

ELECTRA PALACE (WE), Fitzalan Square.— Prop., Sheffield and District Cinematograph Theatres, Ltd., 3, Hartshead, Sheffield. 587 seats. Booked at H.O. Continuous. Prices, 6d. to 1s. Phone, 25624. Station, L.M.S. and L.N.E.R., Sheffield.

GLOBE PICTURE HOUSE (BA), Attercliffe Common. —Props., Sheffield and District Cinematograph Theatres, Ltd., 3, Hartshead, Sheffield. Phone,

20888. 1,700 seats. Booked at H.O. Continuous nightly. Two Mats. weekly. Two changes weekly. Prices, 4d. to 9d. Phone, Attercliffe 41559. Stations, Sheffield, L.M.S. and L.N.E.R.

GREYSTONE'S PICTURE PALACE (BTH), Ecclesall Road.—Prop., Ecclesall and Endcliffe Picture Palace, Ltd. 800 seats. Booked at Hall by Directors. Two shows nightly. Prices, 4d. to 1s. Café and Dance Hall attached. Phone, 60709. Station, Sheffield, L.N.E.R. and L.M.S.

HEELEY COLISEUM (BA), London Road.—Prop., Heeley Coliseum, Ltd., 136, Derbyshire Lane, Sheffield. 900 seats. Continuous. Twice Sat. Phone, 51254. Station, Sheffield. L.M.S,

HEELEY GREEN THEATRE, Gleadless Road, Heeley.—Prop., Heeley Green Picture House, Ltd. 1,000 seats. Booked at Hall. Two shows nightly. Pictures, Variety and Revues. Stage, 21 ft. deep ; seven dressing-rooms. Prices, 6d. to 1s. Proscenium width, 32 ft. Phone, Sharrow 51272. Station, Heeley.

HEELEY PALACE (WE), London Road.—Prop., Heeley and Amalgamated Cinemas, Ltd. 1,100 seats. Booked by E. C. Clayton, Bank Chambers, 70, The Moor, Sheffield. Phone, Sheffield 24673. 1,100 seats. Continuous. Two shows Sat. Two changes weekly. Prices, 4d. to 9d. Phone, Sharrow 50253. Station, Heeley, L.M.S.

HILLSBOROUGH KINEMA HOUSE (WE), Proctor Place, Hillsboro'.—Prop., Grosvenor Hall and Estate Co., Ltd., 47, Bank Street, Sheffield. 1,202 seats. Booked at Hall. Two shows nightly. Mat. Mon., Thurs. and Sat. Two changes weekly. Prices, 4d. to 1s. Phone, Owlerton 43221. Station, Sheffield, L.M.S. and Bradford and Leeds Transport.

HIPPODROME (WE).—Controlled by Associated British Cinemas, Ltd., 30-31, Golden Square, W.1. 2,445 seats. Booked at H.O. Continuous. Station, Sheffield, L.M.S.

LANSDOWNE PICTURE HOUSE (WE), London Road.—Prop., Lansdowne Pictures, Ltd., 3, Hartshead, Sheffield. 965 seats. Booked at H.O. Twice nightly. Mats., Mon., Thurs. Prices, 4d. to 9d. Phone, Central 25823. Station, Sheffield, L.M.S.

LYRIC PICTURE HOUSE (BTH), Main Road, Darnall.—Prop., Lyric Picture House Co., Ltd., 11, Leopold Street, Sheffield. Phone, Sheffield 20289. 900 seats. Booked at Hall. Twice nightly. Two changes weekly. Prices, 5d. to 9d. Phone, Attercliffe 41710. Station, Darnall, L.N.E.R.

MANOR CINEMA (BA), Intake.—Prop., Manor P.H., Ltd. 1,570 seats. Booked at Hall. Continuous. Three shows Sat. Prices, 4d. to 9d. Proscenium width, 22 ft. Billiard Hall attached. Phone, Sheffield 20985. Station, Sheffield, L.M.S.

MONSEIGNEUR.—Prop., J. Davis Circuit, 147, Wardour Street, London, W.1.

NEW TIVOLI (WE), Norfolk Street.—Prop., Tivoli (Sheffield), Ltd. 500 seats. Man. Dir., Sydney Kirkham. Booked at Hall by Man. Dir. Continuous. Two changes weekly. Prices, 3d. to 1s. 6d. Proscenium width, 20 ft. Stage, 12 ft. deep ; two dressing-rooms. Phone, Central 21438. Station, Sheffield, L.M.S. and L.N.E.R.

NORFOLK PICTURE PALACE (WE), Duke Street.— Prop., Norfolk Picture Palace, Ltd. 1,000 seats. Booked at Hall by Man. and Sec.

For Snap And Sparkle PATHE PICTORIAL Cannot Be Beaten.

SHEFFIELD—Contd.
Two shows nightly. Mat. Sat. Two changes **weekly.** Prices, 3d. to 8d. Phone, Central 22867. Station, Sheffield, L.M.S. and L.N.E.R.

OXFORD PICTURE HOUSE (WE), Upperthorpe.— Prop., Heeley and Amalgamated Cinemas, Ltd., 70, The Moor, Sheffield. 658 seats. Booked at H.O. Two shows nightly. Two changes weekly. Prices, 4d. to 1s. Phone, 25,468. Billiard Hall attached. Station, Sheffield, L.M.S. and L.N.E.R.

PAGE HALL CINEMA (BTH), Idsworth Road, Pitsmoor.—Prop., Page Hall Cinema, Ltd. 1,400 seats. Man. Dir., E. Shepherd. Booked at Hall by E. Shepherd. Continuous, twice Sat. Mats., Mon. and Thurs. Café, Ballroom and Billiard Hall attached. Phone, Sheffield 41915. Stations, Sheffield, L.M.S. and L.N.E.R.

PALACE (WE), Wincobank.—Prop., Wincobank Picture Palace Co. 610 seats. Booked at Hall. Continuous. Two changes weekly. Prices, 3d. to 9d. Phone, Attercliffe 41714. Stations, Wincobank, L.M.S.

PALLADIUM (WE), Walkley.—Prop., Walkley Palladium, Ltd. 940 seats. Booked at Hall by A. R. Favell. Twice nightly. Two changes weekly. Prices, 4d. to 8d. Phone, Owlerton 43276. Station, Sheffield, L.M.S.

PARAGON CINEMA (RCA), Shiregreen.—Prop. Paragon Picture House (Sheffield), Ltd 1,300 seats. Booked at Hall. Twice nightly. Mat. Mon., Thurs. and Sat. Prices, 4d. to 10d Proscenium width, 40 ft. Café attached Phone, Sheffield 41642. Stations, Sheffield L.N.E.R. and L.M.S.

PARK PICTURE PALACE (BA), South Street, Park.—Prop., Sheffield Park Pictures, Ltd. Reg. Office, 13, Figtree Lane, Sheffield. 900 seats. Booked at Hall. Two shows nightly. Prices, 3d. to 9d. Phone, Central 26234. Station, Sheffield, L.M.S.

PAVILION (WE), Attercliffe Common.—Prop., Heeley and Amalgamated Cinemas, Ltd., 70, The Moor, Sheffield. Phone, 24673. 1,075 seats. Booked at H.O. Two shows nightly. Mat., Mon. and Thurs. Two changes weekly. Prices, 4d. to 1s. Phone, Attercliffe 41492.

PHŒNIX THEATRE (WE), Langsett Road, Hillsboro, Sheffield.—Prop., Phœnix Theatre (Sheffield), Ltd. 690 seats. Booked at Hall. Twice nightly. Prices, 4d. to 9d. Proscenium width, 30 ft. Stage, 8 ft. deep ; six dressing-rooms. Phone, Sheffield 43141. Stations, Sheffield, L.M.S. and L.N.E.R. ; and Film Tran_port.

REGAL.—Prop., J. F. Emery's Circuit, 26, Cross Street, Manchester.

REGAL (WE), Attercliffe.

REGENT (WE), Barker's Pool.—Prop., Provincial Cinematograph Theatres, Ltd., New Gallery House, 123, Regent Street, London, W.1. Phone, Regent 8080. 2,207 seats. Booked at H.O. Continuous. Prices, 9d. to 2s. Pictures and Variety. Stage, 25 ft. deep ; seven dressing-rooms. Café attached. Phone, Sheffield 21644. Stations, Sheffield, L.M.S. and L.N.E.R.

Fitted "ARDENTE" Deaf Aids
See page 258

WURLITZER ORGAN
Installed in this Kinema

ROSCOE PICTURE HOUSE (Symplaphone(Infirmary Road.—Prop., Sheffield Amusements Co., Ltd., 47, Bank Street, Sheffield. Phone, 25907. 900 seats. Booked at Hall. Two shows nightly. Prices, 4d. to 6d. Pros-

cenium width, 25 ft. Phone, 23728 Stations, Sheffield, L.M.S. and L.N.E.R., and Road Transport.

RUTLAND PICTURE HOUSE (BTH), Neepsend.— Prop., Rutland Picture House, Ltd. 900 seats. Booked at Hall. Two shows nightly. Prices, 3d. to 6d. Phone, Central 23866. Station, Sheffield, L.M.S. and L.N.E.R.

SCALA CINEMA (WE), Winter Street.—Prop., Scala Cinemas (Sheffield), Ltd., Winter Street. 1,020 seats. Booked at Hall. Continuous. Two shows on Sat. Prices, 6d. to 1s. Café and Dance Hall. Phone, Central 25406. Station, Sheffield, L.M.S.

SHEFFIELD PICTURE PALACE (WE), Union Street.—Prop., Sheffield Picture Palace, Ltd. 970 seats. Booked at Hall. Continuous. Prices, 3d. to 1s. 3d. Proscenium width, 24 ft. Café attached. Phone, Central 21608. Station, Sheffield, L.M.S.

STAR PICTURE HOUSE (WE), Ecclesall Road.— Prop., J. F. Emery, 26, Cross Street, Manchester. Phone, Blackfriars 0472. 1028 seats. Booked at H.O. Continuous evenings. Mat. daily. Twice Sat. Prices, 3d. to 1s. Proscenium width, 26 ft. Café and Billiard Hall attached. Phone, Central 25750. Station, Sheffield, L.M.S.

SUNBEAM PICTURE HOUSE (WE), Barnsley Road.—Props., Sunbeam Pictures, Ltd., 3, Hartshead, Sheffield. Phone, 20888. 1,156 seats. Booked at H.O. Continuous. Two shows Sat. Prices, 6d. to 1s. Phone, Attercliffe 36479. Station, Sheffield, L.M.S.

THEATRE ROYAL (BTP), Attercliffe.—(Closed). 1,000 seats.

TINSLEY PICTURE PALACE (WE).—Prop., Wincobank Picture Palace Co. 714 seats. Booked at H.O. Continuous. Two changes weekly. Prices, 4d. to 9d. Phone, Attercliffe 41713. Station, Tinsley, L.N.E.R. and L.M.S.

UNITY PICTURE PALACE (WE), Langsett Road.— Prop., Upperthorpe Picture Palace (Sheffield), Ltd. 900 seats. Booked at Hall. Continuous. Two shows Sat. Two changes weekly. Prices, 4d., 6d. and 9d. Phone, Sheffield 43714. Station, Sheffield, L.M.S.

VICTORY PICTURE PALACE (WE), Upwell Street, —Prop., J. Bickler, Roxholme; Harehill Lane, Leeds. Phone 41426. 900 seats. Booked at Leeds and Sheffield. Twice nightly. Prices, 3d. to 1s. Billiard room attached. Phone, 41485. Proscenium width, 20 ft. Stations, Sheffield, L.M.S. and L.N.E.R.

WESTON PICTURE PALACE (WE), 52, St. Phillips Road.—Prop., Hallamshire Cinemas, Ltd., 3, Hartshead, Sheffield. Phone, Central 20888. 700 seats. Booked at H.O. Two shows nightly. Prices, 4d. to 6d. Phone, Central 23785. Stations, Victoria, L.N.E.R. and Midland, L.M.S.

WICKER PICTURE HOUSE (BTH), The Wicker. Lessee, J. F. Emery. 1,022 seats. Continuous. Prices, 5d. to 1s. Phone, Central 20532. Station, Sheffield, e/o Parcels Office, L.M.S.

WOODSEATS PALACE (WE), Woodseats.—Prop., Heeley and Amalgamated Cinemas, Ltd., 70, The Moor, Sheffield. 640 seats. Continuous. Mon. to Fri. Twice nightly Sat. Prices, 3d. to 1s. Phone, 45535. Goods to Heeley ; Films to Sheffield.

SHEPSHED (LEICESTER), **Pop. 5,759.**

PALACE PICTURE HOUSE (BTH).—Prop., F. F. & S. E. Stafford, "Glengarry," Shady Lane, Evington, Leicester. Phone, Leicester 24881. 600 seats. Booked at H.O. Continuous. Prices, 6d. to 1s. Phone, Shepshed 18. Station, Shepshed, L.M.S.

SHEPTON MALLET (SOMERSET), **Pop. 4,108**.
REGAL (WE), Paul Street.—Prop., A. A. Pilkington, "Woodland," 20, London Road, Salisbury. 700 seats. Twice Mon. and Sat. Once rest of week. Booked at H.O. Prices, 7d. to 1s. 6d. Proscenium width, 30 ft. Phone, Shepton Mallet 107. Station, Shepton Mallet, G.W.R. or L.M.S.

Fitted "ARDENTE" Deaf Aids
See page 258

SHERBORNE (DORSET), **Pop. 6,542**.
CARLTON (BTH),—Prop., Carlton Theatre (Sherborne), Co., Palace, Blandford. Phone, Blandford 12. 500 seats. Booked at H.O. Twice nightly. Prices, 6d. to 2s. Proscenium width, 24 ft. Stage, 20 ft. deep ; five dressing-rooms. Station, Sherborne, S.R.

SHERBURN HILL (Co. DURHAM), **Pop. 2,918**.
CO-OPERATIVE PICTURES.—Prop., Co-operative Society. One show nightly, two on Sat. Prices, 4d. to 9d. Station, Sherburn Colliery, L.N.E.R.
UNITY CINEMA.—Lessees, W. W. Turnbull. 320 seats. Booked by W. W. Turnbull at Greenside, Coxhoe. Prices, 5d. and 6d. Station, Sherburn, L.N.E.R.

SHERBURN-IN-ELMET (YORKS), **Pop. 2,083**.
CINEMA (Electrophol).—South Milford. Lessee, H. Mills, Low Street. Four shows weekly on Mon., Tues., Fri., and Sat. Prices, 2d. to 1s. Stations, Sherburn-in-Elmet, or South Milford, L.N.E.R.

SHERINGHAM (NORFOLK), **Pop. 4,141**.
PICTURE HOUSE (Morrison), High Street.—Prop., J. H. Gotch, Regal, Soham, Ely. 300 seats. Booked at Regal, Soham. Once nightly, two shows Sat. Price, 6d. to 1s. 3d. Proscenium width, 21 ft. Stage, 15 ft. deep ; two dressing-rooms. Phone, Sheringham 39. Station, Sheringham, L.N.E.R.
REGENT HALL (BA), Cromer Road.—Prop., C. A. Sadler, trading as C. A. Sadler & Sons. 600 seats. Booked at The Office, Sheringham, by W. Sadler. One show nightly, two on Sat. Prices, 6d. to 2s. Phone 44. Station, Sheringham, L.N.E.R.

SHIFNAL (SALOP), **Pop. 3,300**.
BROADWAY CINEMA (Classitone).—Props., B. and B. Cinemas, Ltd., Central House, 75, New Street, Birmingham. Phone, Midland 5251. 330 seats. Continuous. Prices, 7d. to 1s. 4d. Station, Shifnal, G.W.R.

SHILDON (Co. DURHAM), **Pop. 12,690**.
HIPPODROME THEATRE (RCA).—Prop., Thompson's Enterprises, Ltd., 4, Palladium Buildings, Eastbourne Road, Middlesbrough, Yorks. 1,050 seats. Booked at H.O. Once nightly. Two shows Sat. Sunday opening. Stage, 35 ft. deep ; seven dressing-rooms. Variety booked by North Dramatic and Variety Agency, Sunderland. Prices, 4d. to 1s. Phone, Shildon 29. Station, Shildon, L.N.E.R.
MAGNET PICTURE HOUSE (AWH).—Prop., A. J. Goss. 450 seats.
PICTURE HOUSE (BTH), Station Street, Shildon. —Prop., E. MacDowell, "Oaklea," Byerley Road, Shildon. 500 seats. Booked at Newcastle. Twice nightly. Prices, 4d. to 1s. Phone, Shildon 18. Station, Shildon, L.N.E.R.

SHIPLEY (YORKS), **Pop. 30,243**.
GLENROYAL (WE), Briggate.—Props., Shipley Picture House Co., Ltd. 1,166 seats. Booked at Hall. Continuous nightly. Three shows Sat. Mat. Mon and Wed. Prices, 6d. to

1s. 3d. Proscenium width, 30 ft. Phone, 1. Station, Shipley, L.M.S.
PAVILION DE LUXE (BTH), Commercial Street.— Prop., Shipley Pavilion, Ltd. 700 seats. Booked at Hall. Continuous. Two changes weekly, Prices, 4d. to 9d. Phone, Shipley 315.
PICTURE HOUSE (WE), Briggate.—Prop., Shipley Picture House Co., Ltd. 1,550 seats. Twice nightly. Two changes weekly. Phone, Shipley 1. Station, Shipley, L.M.S.
PRINCE'S HALL (WE), Bradford Road.—Prop., Prince's Hall (Shipley), Ltd., 6, Park Row, Leeds. 1,100 seats. Booked at H.O. Continuous. Two changes weekly. Prices, 6d. to 1s. 3d. Phone, Shipley 429. Station, Shipley, L.M.S.

SHIPSTON-ON-STOUR (WORCS), **Pop. 1,500**.
PICTURE HOUSE (BA).—Prop., Mrs. E. Dicker. Booked at Hall. Once nightly. Mat., Sat. Continuous Sat. evening. Prices, 6d. to 1s. 6d. Proscenium width, 18 ft. Phone, Shipston-on-Stour 78. Films by Transport.

SHIREBROOK (DERBY), **Pop. 11,116**.
EMPIRE (WE).—Prop., T. Moorley. Booked by J. Pollard, Bentinck Chambers, Mansfield. 823 seats. One show nightly. Two on Sat. Two changes weekly. Prices, 6d. to 1s. Shirebrook 373. Stations, L.M.S. ; Shirebrook North, L.N.E.R.
TOWN HALL (BTH), Main Street.—Prop., T. Morley. Booked by J. Pollard, Bentinck Chambers, Mansfield. One show nightly ; two on Sat. Two changes weekly. Prices, 6d. to 1s. Phone, Shirebrook 205. Stations, Shirebrook, L.M.S. ; and Shirebrook North, L.N.E.R.

SHIREMOOR (NORTHUMBERLAND), **Pop. 5,000**.
PALACE (Filmophone).—Prop., R. and D. Hashman, 93, Park Crescent, North Shields. Phone, North Shields 651. 750 seats. Booked at Hall. One show nightly ; three on Sat. Pictures and Variety. Stage, 16 ft. deep. Prices, 3d. to 8d. Station, Backworth, L.N.E.R.

SHOEBURYNESS (ESSEX), **Pop. 5,930**.
PALACE THEATRE (BA).—Prop., W. R. Eve, 7, Connaught Gardens, Shoeburyness. Phone 105. 580 seats. Booked at Hall. Continuous. Prices, 6d. to 1s. 3d. Station, Shoeburyness, L.M.S.

SHOREHAM-BY-SEA (SUSSEX), **Pop. 8,757**.
COLISEUM (BTH).—Prop., F. J. Freeman. 750 seats. Booked at Hall. Continuous. Prices, 6d. to 1s. 6d. Proscenium width, 28 ft. Stage, 30 ft. deep ; eight dressing-rooms. Phone, Shoreham 90. Station, Shoreham-by-Sea, S.R.
NORFOLK CINEMA, Norfolk Bridge.—Prop., F. J. Freeman. 700 seats.

SHOTTON (CHES.).
EMPIRE.—E. J. Hinge Circuit, 72, Grey Street, Newcastle-on-Tyne.
RITZ CINEMA (BTP), Plymouth Street. Prop., C. Seager. 500 seats. Mon. to Fri. once nightly. Twice Sat. Mats., Mon., Thurs., Sat. Prices, 6d. to 1s.] 3d. Proscenium width, 20 ft. Phone, Connahs Quay 35. Station, Shotton, L.N.E.R.

SHOTTON COLLIERY (DUR.), **Pop. 8,800**.
THEATRE ROYAL (Kamm).—Lessee, A. Allom. 800 seats. Pictures and Variety. Once nightly, twice Mon. and Sat. Prices, 2d. to 6d. Stage, 31 ft. deep ; six dressing-rooms. Phone, Haswell 36. Station, Shotton Bridge, L.N.E.R.

SHREWSBURY (SHROPS.), **Pop. 32,370.**
EMPIRE (WE),—Props., Shrewsbury Empires, Ltd., Castle Gates, Shrewsbury. Phone, Shrewsbury 3026. Controlled by Bernstein Theatres, Ltd., at 36, Golden Square, London, W. Continuous. Café-Restaurant attached. Station, Shrewsbury, G.W. and L.M.S. Joint.
GRANADA (WE).—Prop., Shrewsbury Empires, Ltd., 6, Castle Gates, Shrewsbury. Controlled by Bernstein Theatres, Ltd., 36, Golden Square, W.I. Phone, Gerrard 3554. Continuous. Phone, Shrewsbury 3026/7. Café attached.
KING'S (WE), Wyle Cop.—Prop., Shrewsbury Empires, Ltd., Castle Gates, Shrewsbury. Phone, Shrewsbury 3026. Controlled by Bernstein Theatres, Ltd., at 36, Golden Square, London. Gerrard 3554. Continuous. Station, Shrewsbury, G.W. and L.M.S. Joint.
ROYAL COUNTY (FI).—Props., Shrewsbury Theatres, Ltd., Castle Gates, Shrewsbury. Phone, 3026. Controlled by Bernstein Theatres, Ltd., 36, Golden Square, W.I. Phone, Gerrard 3554. Continuous. Booked at H.O. Prices, 4d. to 1s. 6d. Proscenium width, 17 ft. 6 in. Station, Shrewsbury.

SIBLE & CASTLE HEDINGHAM (ESSEX) **Pop. 3,200.**
PLAZA (Philips).—Prop., G. J. Howell, 3, Short's Gardens, London, W.C.2. Booked at H.O. Phone, Hedingham 81. 400 seats. Once nightly Mon. to Fri., twice on Sat. Prices, 6d. to 1s. 3d. Station, Sible, L.N.E.R.

SIDCUP (KENT), **Pop. 12,360.**
DEON THEATRE (BTH).—Props., Odeon (Sidcup), Ltd., Cornhill House, Bennett's Hill, Birmingham. Phone, Midland 2781. Booked at 49, Park Lane, W.I. Prices, 9d. to 2s. Phone, Sidcup 1609. Station, Sidcup, S.R.
REGAL (WE), High Street.—Controlled by Union Cinemas Co., Ltd., 15, Regent Street London, S.W.I. Phone, Whitehall 8484. Continuous. Pictures and Variety. Prices, 6d. to 2s. Café attached. Phone, Sidcup 539. Station, Sidcup, S.R.

SIDMOUTH (DEVON), **Pop. 6,126.**
RAND (Cinephone).—Prop., Sidmouth Motor Co. and Dagworthy, Ltd. Phone, Sidmouth 318. 535 seats. Booked at Hall. Prices, 6d. to 2s. Phone, Sidmouth 279. Station, Sidmouth, S.R.
ADWAY THEATRE AND CINEMA (BTH).—Props., Sidmouth Motor Co. and Dagworthy, Ltd. Phone, Sidmouth 318. 750 seats. Booked at Hall. Prices, 6d. to 2s. Proscenium width, 27 ft. Stage, 20 ft. deep; four dressing-rooms. Phone, Sidmouth 85. Station, Sidmouth, S.R.

SILEBY (LEICS), **Pop. 3,500.**
FUTURIST CINEMA (Gyrotone), Swan Street.—Props., G. G. and E. Baum, Aysgarth, Leicester Road. 310 seats. Booked at Lock Cinema, Mountsorrel. Once nightly. Prices, 5d. to 1s. Proscenium width, 26 ft. Phone, Rothley 164. Station, Sileby, L.M.S.

SILLOTH-ON-SOLWAY (CUMB.).
PICTURE HOUSE (BA). 400 seats.

SILSDEN (YORKS), **Pop. 4,881.**
SILSDEN PICTURE PALACE (Gramo-Radio), Bradley Road.—Prop., Clifford Briggs. 550 seats. Booked by M. P. Cryer, Keighley. One show nightly. Two changes weekly. Prices, 3d. to 9d. Station, Steeton, L.M.S.

SILVERDALE (STAFFS), **Pop. 7,795.**
QUEEN'S PALACE (Imperial), High Street.— Props., Locker and Mason, 9, Park Avenue, Shelton, Stoke-on-Trent. 500 seats. Booked at Hall. Continuous. Two changes weekly. Prices, 5d. to 1s. Proscenium width, 20 ft. Station, Silverdale, L.M.S.

SITTINGBOURNE and MILTON (KENT). **Pop. 20,175.**
ODEON THEATRE (BTH), High Street.—Props., Odeon (Sittingbourne), Ltd., Cornhill House, Bennett's Hill, Birmingham. Phone, Midland 2781. Booked at 9, Park Lane, W.I. Continuous. Prices, 6d. to 1s. 6d.
PLAZA (WE), East Street.—Prop., East Kent Cinemas. 567 seats. Booked at Hall. Occasional Variety. Continuous. Mats. Mon., Wed., Thurs., Sat. Prices, 7d. to 1s. 4d. Proscenium width, 24 ft. Stage, 10 ft. deep; two dressing-rooms. Phone, Sittingbourne 182. Films by Kent Motor Transport.
QUEEN'S PICTURE THEATRE (AWH), High Street.—Prop., Sittingbourne Electric Theatre Co., Ltd. 750 seats. Booked at Hall. Continuous. Two changes weekly. Prices, 6d. to 1s. 6d. Phone, Sittingbourne 85. Station, Sittingbourne, S.R.

SKEGNESS (LINCS), **Pop. 9,121.**
CENTRAL CINEMA (BTP), Roman Bank.—Prop., Parade Cinemas (Skegness), Ltd., General Buildings, Bridlesmith Gate, Nottingham. 1,100 seats. Booked at H.O. Continuous nightly. Prices, 6d. to 1s. 10d. Proscenium width, 38 ft. Phone, Skegness 90. Station, Skegness, L.N.E.R.
GRAND PARADE (WE).—Prop., Parade Cinema (Skegness), Ltd., 3, Newcastle Chambers, Angel Row, Nottingham. 1,500 seats. Continuous. Booked at H.O. Prices, 7d. to 1s. 10d. Proscenium width, 40 ft. Phone, Skegness 525. Station, Skegness, L.N.E.R.
PARADE CINEMA (WE).—1,600 seats.
TOWER THEATRE (WE),—Prop., Skegness Entertainments, Ltd., General Bldgs, Bridlesmith Gate, Nottingham. 966 seats. Booked at H.O. Continuous. Prices, 6d. to 1s. 10d. Proscenium width, 30 ft. Phone, 102. Station, Skegness, L.N.E.R.

SKELMANTHORPE (YORKS), **Pop. 3,711.**
SAVOY (RCA).—980 seats. Once nightly. Two shows Sat. Prices, 6d. to 1s. Station, Skelmanthorpe, L.M.S.

SKELMERSDALE (LANCS), **Pop. 6,177.**
EMPIRE, Elson Road.—Prop., A. Shaw, 83, Barnsley Street, Wigan. 575 seats. Booked at Hall. Once nightly. Prices, 3d. to 9d. Station, Skelmersdale, L.M.S.
PALACE.—Prop., S. A. Shaw.

SKIPTON (YORKS), **Pop. 12,434.**
PLAZA (WE).
PREMIER PICTURE HOUSE (WE), Keighley Road. —Prop., Richard Dean. 566 seats. One show nightly, three on Sat. Two changes weekly. Prices, 6d. to 1s. 6d. Phone, Skipton 271. Station, Skipton, L.M.S.
REGAL (WE).—Props., Odeon (Skipton), Ltd., Cornhill House, Bennett's Hill, Birmingham. Booked at 49, Park Lane, W.I. Continuous. Prices, 6d. to 1s. 3d. Phone, 161. Station, Skipton, L.M.S.
TOWN HALL CINEMA (Electrocord), Grassington, nr. Skipton.—Prop., A. Graham, Jun., Settle, Yorks. 500 seats. Booked at Leeds. Prices, 4d. to 1s. Proscenium width, 20 ft. Station, Grassington.

SLAITHWAITE (Yorks), **Pop. 5,181.**
NEW THEATRE (BTP).—Prop., Hawthorne and King, Ltd. 558 seats. Sec. and Man., Geo. Taylor Smith. Booked at Cinema Exchange, Leeds. Once nightly. Two changes weekly. Stage, 10 ft. deep. Station, Slaithwaite, L.M.S.

SLEAFORD (Lincs), **Pop. 7,024.**
PICTUREDROME (BTH), Southgate.—Prop., Sleaford Picture Palace, Ltd. 975 seats. Once nightly. Continuous Sat. Prices, 6d. to 1s. 6d. Occasional Variety. Proscenium width, 24 ft. Stage, 26 ft. deep; six dressing-rooms. Café attached. Phone, Sleaford 87.

SLOUGH (Bucks), **Pop. 33,530.**
ADELPHI THEATRE (WE).—Controlled by Union Kinemas, Ltd., Union House, 15, Regent Street, London, S.W.1. Phone, Whitehall 8484. Booked at H.O. Continuous. Prices, 7d. to 2s. 6d. Phone, Slough 470. Café and Dance Hall attached. Station, Slough, G.W.R. Films by Road Transport.

COMPTON
ORGAN featured here.

AMBASSADOR (WE), Farnham Road.—Props., Farnham Royal Super Cinemas, Ltd., 32, Shaftesbury Avenue, London, W.1. Phone, Whitehall 0183. Booked at H.O. 1,319 seats. Continuous. Prices, 6d. to 1s. 6d. Prices, 6d. to 1s. 6d. Phone, Slough 1520. Station, Slough, G.W.R.

PALACE CINEMA (WE), High Street.—Prop.' the Slough Theatre Co., Ltd. 1,036 seats' Booked at Hall by Man. Continuous. Prices, 6d. to 1s. 6d. Phone, Slough 275.

SMALLTHORNE (Staffs), **Pop. 14,019.**
PICTURE PALACE (BTH).—Prop., Smallthorne Picture Palace Co., Ltd., South King Street. Continuous. Prices, 4d. and 6d. Phone, Hanley 7378. Station, Burslem, L.M.S.

SMETHWICK (Staffs), **Pop. 84,354.**
(See under Birmingham.)

SNODLAND (Kent), **Pop. 4,485.**
CINEMA (AWH).—Prop., Herbert W. Grose, Queens, Strood. 200 seats. Booked at Strood. Continuous. Prices, 6d. to 1s. 3d. Station, Snodland, S.R. Films by Road Transport.

SOHAM (Cambs), **Pop. 4,682.**
CENTRAL CINEMA (BTH).—Lessee, J. H. Gotch. 220 seats. Continuous nightly. Booked at Hall. Prices, 7d. to 1s. 6d. Proscenium width, 15 ft. 6 in. Occasional Variety. Stage, 15 ft. 6 in. deep. One dressing room. Station, Soham.

REGAL CINEMA (Ultramonic), Red Lion Square. —Prop., John H. Gotch. 400 seats. Booked at Hall. Once nightly. Mat. Sat. Prices, 6d. to 1s. 6d. Phone, 72. Station, Soham. Films by Cambridge Transport Co.

SOLIHULL (Warwickshire), **Pop. 21,000.**
(See Birmingham.)

SOMERCOTES (Derby), **Pop. 5,000.**
EMPIRE THEATRE (Morrison), Nottingham Road.—Prop., Ollerton Pictures, Ltd. Phone, Leabrooks 148. 500 seats. Booked at Hall. Continuous Mon. Once nightly Tues. to Fri. Three shows Sat. Occasional Variety. Prices, 6d. to 1s. 3d. Proscenium width, 20 ft. Stage, 20 ft. deep; three dressing-rooms. Station, Pye Bridge, L.M.S.

PREMIER ELECTRIC THEATRE (WE).—Prop. Geo. Beastall. 1,196 seats. Booked at Hall Two shows nightly, Mon. and Sat., one rest of week. Prices, 6d to 1s. 3d. Phone, Leabrooks 54. Station, Pye Bridge, L.M.S.

SOMERSHAM (Hunts), **Pop. 1,400.**
PARK HALL.—Prop. and Res. Man., M.Williams. Head Office, Picture Palace, Chatteris. Two changes weekly. Prices, 5d. to 1s. 6d. Station, Somersham, L.N.E.R.

SOUTHALL (Mddx.), **Pop. 38,932.**
DOMINION (WE), The Green.—Prop., Associated British Cinemas, Ltd., 30-31, Golden Square, W.1. Continuous. Booked at H.O. Prices, 6d. to 2s. Pictures and Variety. Stage, 22 ft. deep; six dressing-rooms. Proscenium width, 60 ft. Café and Ballroom attached. Phone, Southall 1681.

Fitted "ARDENTE" Stage Amplification See page 258

GEM CINEMA (WE), The Green.—Prop., Gem Cinema (Southall), Ltd. 800 seats. Booked at Hall. Continuous. Two changes weekly. Prices, 9d. to 1s. 6d. Phone, Southall 1325. Station, Southall, G.W.R.

KING'S HALL (BA), South Road.—Prop., Uxbridge and Southall, Wesleyan Mission. Superintendent Minister, Rev. Allen F. Parsons. Booked at Hall by Charles E. J. Abbott. Sats. only. Prices, 3d. to 6d. Children's Mat. Sat. Prices, 1d. and 2d. Phone, Southall 25. Station, Southall, G.W.R.

ODEON THEATRE (BTH).—Props., Odeon Theatre (Southall), Ltd., Cornhill House, Bennetts Hill, Birmingham. Booked at 49, Park Lane, W.1. Continuous. Prices, 9d. to 2s. Phone, Southall 1757.

PALACE CINEMA (BA), South Road.—Prop. United Picture Theatres, Ltd., 123, Regent Street, London, W.1. 2,000 seats. Booked at H.O. Continuous. Occasional Variety. Prices, 9d. to 1s. 6d. Stage, 15 ft. deep; four dressing rooms. Phone, Southall 0170. Station, Southall, G.W.R.

COMPTON
ORGAN featured here.

SOUTHAMPTON (Hants), **Pop. 176,025.**
ALEXANDRA (WE).—Controlled by Union Cinemas, Ltd., 15, Regent Street, London, S.W.1. Phone, Whitehall 8484.

ATHERLEY CINEMA (BTP), Shirley.—Prop., Associated British Cinemas, Ltd., 30-31, Golden Square, London, W.1. Phone, Gerrard 7887. Continuous. Mat., Wed. and Sat. Three changes weekly. Prices, 6d. to 1s. Phone, Southampton 71352.

BROADWAY CINEMA (WE).—Prop., Associated British Cinemas, Ltd., 30-31, Golden Square, W.1. 1,546 seats. Booked at H.O. Prices, 6d. to 1s. 3d. Continuous. Phone, Southampton 74329. Station, Southampton Central.

EMPIRE (WE), Commercial Road.—Props., Moss Empires, Ltd. Booked by Gaumont British Corporation. 2,358 seats. Continuous. Prices, 6d. to 2s. Proscenium width, 44 ft. Phone, Southampton 20011. Café. Station, Southampton Central.

Fitted "ARDENTE" Deaf Aids See page 258

FORUM (WE).—Props., Associated British Cinemas, Ltd., 30-31, Golden Square, London, W.1. Phone, Gerrard 7887. Booked at H.O. Con-

SOUTHAMPTON—Contd.
tinuous. 2,000 seats. Prices, 6d. to 1s. 6d.
Proscenium width, 48 ft. Stage, 17 ft. deep ;
four dressing-rooms. Phone, Southampton
5458. Café attached. Station, Central, S.R.

**Fitted "ARDENTE" Deaf Aids
See page 258**

C O M P T O N
ORGAN featured here.

GAIETY PICTURE HOUSE (WE), High Street.—
Prop., Gaiety Picture House (Southampton),
Ltd. 812 seats. Booked at Scala, Croydon.
Continuous. Prices, 6d. to 1s. Phone,
Southampton 2572. Stations, Southampton
Docks and Central, S.R. Films by Southern
Counties Road Transport.
GARRISON CINEMA, Netley.
HYTHE CINEMA (Mihaly), Hythe, Southampton
—287 seats. Booked at Hall. Prices, 6d. to
1s. 3d. Tel. No. 158. Station, Hythe, South-
ampton, S.R.
KING'S THEATRE (BTP); Kingsland Square.—
Prop., Chas. F. Wright. Continuous. 716
seats. Booked at Hall. Three shows daily.
Prices, 6d. to 1s. Phone, 2870. Station,
Southampton West, S.R.
LYRIC CINEMA (BA), St. Denys.—Prop.,
Palladium (Southampton), Ltd. 410 seats.
Booked at Hall. Twice nightly. Mat. Wed.
and Sat. Prices, 5d. to 1s. Phone, South-
ampton 75485. Station, Southampton West,
S.R.
NEW CENTRAL HALL, St. Mary's Street.—
Prop., Wesleyan Central Mission. Booked
at Hall. Kiddies' Kinema, etc. Prices, 3d.
to 1s. Phone, Southampton 4412. Station,
Southampton Docks, S.R.
PALLADIUM (WE), Portswood.—Prop., Palla-
dium (Southampton), Ltd. 628 seats. Booked
at Hall. Continuous. Two changes weekly.
Prices, 6d. to 1s. 3d. Phone, Southampton
74712. Station, St. Denys, S.R.

**Fitted "ARDENTE" Deaf Aids
See page 258**

PICTURE HOUSE (WE), Above Bar.—Prop.,
British Cinematograph Theatres, Ltd., 199,
Piccadilly. 1,541 seats. Booked at H.O.
Continuous. Prices, 6d. to 2s. Phone,
Southampton 2819. Station, Southampton
Central, S.R.
PLAZA CINEMA (WE), 201, Northam Road.—
Prop., Regal (Southampton), Ltd. 2,170
seats. Controlled by County Cinemas, Ltd.,
Dean House, Dean Street, London, W.1.
Daily, from 1.30. Phone, Southampton 3646.
Stations, Northam and Southampton West,
S.R.

**Fitted "ARDENTE" Deaf Aids
See page 258**

C O M P T O N
ORGAN featured here.

R.A.F. CINEMA (Mihaly), Calshot. Booked at
Cinema, Hythe. Prices, 6d. to 1s. 3d. 350
seats.
REGAL (WE), Above Bar.—Prop., Regal (South-
ampton), Ltd. 1,756 seats. Controlled by
County Cinemas, Ltd., Dean House, Dean
Street, London W.1.
REGENT CINEMA (WE), Park Street, Shirley.—
Prop., Palmer and Clement, "Shoreham,"

Luccombe Road, Southampton. 1,305 seats,
Booked at Hall by G. H. Clement. Continuous.
Prices, 6d. to 1s. 3d. Phone, 71555. Station,
Southampton Central.
RIALTO CINEMA (WE), Shirley Road.—Prop.,
Shirley Cinema Co. 956 seats. Booked at
Hall. Continuous. Prices, 6d. to 1s. Pro-
scenium width, 24 ft. Phone, Southampton
71273. Station, Southampton West, S.R.
STANDARD CINEMA (BTH), East Street.—Prop.,
J. W. Parker. 550 seats. Booked at Hall.
Continuous. Prices, 6d. to 1s. Proscenium
width, 18 ft. Stations, Southampton Docks
and Southampton West, S.R.
TOWN HALL

C O M P T O N
ORGAN featured here.

WOOLSTON PICTURE THEATRE (WE), Portsmouth
Road.—Prop., Union Cinemas, Ltd., 15,
Regent Street, London, S.W.1. Phone,
Whitehall 8484. Continuous, evenings. Mat.
daily. Prices, 6d. to 1s. Phone, Woolston
88323. Station, Woolston, S.R.
SOUTH BANK (YORKS), Pop. 15,000.
EMPIRE CINEMA (BTH).—Prop., Empire Cinema
(South Bank), Ltd. 1,100 seats. Booked at
Hall. Two shows nightly. Once on Sunday.
Occasional Variety. Prices, 4d. to 9d. Pro-
scenium width, 30 ft. Stage, 30 ft. deep ; four
dressing-rooms. Phone, South Bank 58337.
Station, South Bank, L.N.E.R.
HIPPODROME (BTH).—Prop., A. Campbell. 693
seats. Prices, 3d. to 7d.
MAJESTIC (WE).—Props., Majestic Cinemas
(South Bank), Ltd. 660 seats. Booked at
Middlesbrough by T. Watson Smith. Con-
tinuous. Daily Mat. Prices, 4d. to 1s.
Proscenium width, 20 ft. Phone, 58119.
Station, South Bank and Road Transport.
SOUTH CAVE, Nr. Hull (YORKS), Pop. 970.
THE INSTITUTE CINEMA (Marshall).—Prop.,
Moore and Alcock. 300 seats. Prices, 6d. to
1s. 3d. Phone, Brough 9 x 3. Station, South
Cave, L.N.E.R.
SOUTH ELMSALL (YORKS), Pop. 4,360.
EMPIRE (WE).—Prop., Walker, Issott & Co.,
Ltd. Man. Dir., A. Raynor. 972 seats.
Booked at Hall. Once nightly. Two on
Sat. Prices, 6d. to 1s. Proscenium width,
34 ft. Stage, 20 ft. deep ; seven dressing-
rooms. Phone, South Elmsall 71. Station,
South Elmsall, L.N.E.R.
PICTURE HOUSE (BTH).—Prop., South Elmsall
Picture Hall, Ltd. 897 seats. Prices, 6d. to
1s. Phone, South Elmsall 97.

SOUTHEND-ON-SEA (ESSEX), Pop. 131,000.
ASTORIA (WE), High Street.—Prop., Associated
Theatres (P.As.D.), Ltd. 2,745 seats. Booked
at Dean House, Dean Street, W.1. Continuous.
Pictures and Variety. Prices, 9d. to 2s.
Proscenium width, 56 ft. Stage, 40 ft. deep.
14 dressing-rooms. Café. Phone, Southend
4434/5. Station, Southend.

C O M P T O N
ORGAN featured here.

GARON'S IMPERIAL THEATRE (WE).—Broadway.
Prop., H. Garon, Ltd. 850 seats. Booked at
Hall. Continuous. Sundays at 8 p.m.
Phone, Southend 6201-7. Station, Southend,
L.M.S. and L.N.E.R., or Motor Transport.

GAUMONT PALACE (BA), Southchurch Road.—
Prop., General Theatres Corporation, Ltd.
1,589 seats. Booked at H.O. Station,
Southend, L.N.E.R. and L.M.S., or Motor
Transport.
**Fitted "ARDENTE" Deaf Aids
See page 258**
KURSAAL KINEMA (WE), Marine Parade.—Prop.,
Kursaal (Southend-on-Sea) Estates. Ltd.
720 seats. Booked at Hall. Continuous.
Prices, 6d. to 1s. Proscenium width, 25 ft.
Phone, Marine 6276-7. Stations, Southend
East, L.M.S. and L.N.E.R. Motor Transport
for films.
PLAZA CINEMA (RCA), Southchurch Road.—Prop.,
C. M. Cinemas, Ltd., 110, Cannon Street,
London, E.C. 1,225 seats. Booked at Hall.
Continuous. Prices, 6d. to 1s. Stage, 17 ft.
deep; two dressing-rooms. Phone, Marine
67628. Stations, Southend, L.N.E.R. and
Southend East, L.M.S., and Transport.
REGAL CINEMA (RCA), Tylor's Avenue.—600
seats. Continuous. Prices, 7d. to 1s. 6d.
Stage, 20 ft. deep. Four dressing-rooms.
Proscenium width, 38 ft. Phone, Marine
67053. Stations, Southend L.M.S. and
L.N.E.R., and Motor Transport.
RITZ.—Prop., Ritz (Southend), Ltd., Dean
House, Dean Street, London, W.1. Phone,
Gerrard 4543.
RIVOLI CINEMA (WE).—Controlled by Union
Cinemas, Ltd., Union House, 15, Regent
Street, London, S.W.1. Phone, Whitehall
8484. Booked at H.O. Continuous. Prices,
6d. to 3s. Phone, Southend 4580. Station,
Southend, or Motor Transport.
STRAND CINEMA (WE), High Street and Warrior
Square.—Prop., Warrior Square Picture
Theatre, Ltd. 1,650 seats. Booked at Hall.
by Frank Baker, Man. Dir. Continuous.
Sundays at 8 p.m. Prices, 6d. to 1s. 4d.
Proscenium width, 45 ft. Phone, Marine
67818. Billiard Saloon attached. Station,
Southend, or Motor Transport.
See also Westcliff-on-Sea and Leigh-on-Sea.

SOUTH KIRKBY (YORKS), Pop. 6,500.
NEW CINEMA (WE).—Prop., South Kirkby Cine-
mas (1924), Ltd. 350 seats. Booked at Hall.
Once nightly. Prices, 6d. to 1s. Station,
South Elmsall, L.M.S.
RITZ (WE).—Props., Star Cinemas, Ltd., 5,
Manchester Avenue, E.C.1. Phone, Metro-
politan 4,292. Booked at H.O. Prices, 6d.
to 1s. 3d. Phone, South Elmsall 28.

SOUTH MOLTON (DEVON).
SAVOY (BA).

SOUTH MOOR (CO. DURHAM).
ARCADIA (WE).—Prop., M.B.C. Cinemas, Ltd.,
Hippodrome, Workington. Seats 901. Phone,
Workington 194. Booked at H.O. Twice
nightly. Prices, 4d. to 9d. Phone, Stanley
123. Station, West Stanley.
TIVOLI (WE).—Prop., M.B.C. Cinemas, Ltd.,
Hippodrome, Workington. Phone, Working-
ton 194. Booked at H.O. Twice nightly.
Prices, 4d. and 6d. Station, West Stanley,
L.N.E.R.

SOUTH NORMANTON (DERBY), Pop. 7,000.
PALACE (Harlie).—Prop., Ollerton Pictures, Ltd.
500 seats. Booked at Empire, Somercotes.
Two shows nightly Sat., one rest of week.
Stage, 26 ft. deep. Prices, 6d. to 1s. Phone,
South Normanton 1. Station, Alfreton,
L.M.S.

SOUTH PETHERTON (SOM).
ELECTRIC THEATRE.—Prop., The Walford
Family, Chard, Somerset.

SOUTHPORT (LANCS), Pop. 78,927.
BEDFORD CINEMA (WE), Bedford Road, Birkdale.
—Prop., Bedford Park Cinema (Birkdale),
Ltd. 528 seats. Booked at Regent, Church-
town. Twice nightly. Mat. Sat. Prices,
7d. to 1s. 3d. Phone, Birkdale 6210. Station,
Birkdale, L.M.S.
COLISEUM (WE), Nevill Street.—Prop., Coliseum
Cinema (Southport), Ltd. 946 seats. Three
shows daily. Prices, 6d. to 1s. 6d. Phone,
Southport 3291.
FORUM (WE), Lord Street.—Prop., Southport
Picturedrome, Ltd., 3, Tulketh Street, South-
port. Phone, 3544. 532 seats. Booked at
Trocadero, Southport. Three shows daily.
Prices, 7d. to 1s. 6d. Proscenium width, 21 ft.
Phone, Southport 5019.
GARRICK.—Prop., Garrick Theatre (Southport),
Ltd.
PALACE (WE), Lord Street.—Prop., Coliseum
Cinema (Southport), Ltd. 1,121 seats.
Booked at Hall. Twice nightly and Mat.
Prices, 6d. to 2s. Phone, Southport 2736.
Station, Chapel Street, L.M.S.
PALLADIUM (BA).—Prop., General Theatre
Corporation, Ltd. 2,126 seats. Mat. Even-
ings, continuous. Two shows Sat. Prices,
6d. to 2s. Proscenium width, 65 ft. Stage,
30 ft. deep. Ten dressing-rooms. Phone,
3028II. Café. Station, Chapel Street,
Southport, L.M.S.
**Fitted "ARDENTE" Deaf Aids
See page 258**

COMPTON
ORGAN featured here

PLAZA (BTP), Liverpool Road, Ainsdale.—Prop.,
Coliseum Cinema (Southport), Ltd., 3, Tul-
keth Street. 624 seats. Continuous. Two
shows Sat. Prices, 6d. to 1s. Proscenium
width, 32 ft. Stage, 18 ft. deep. One dress-
ing-room. Café and Dance Hall attached.
Phone, Southport 78055. Station, Ainsdale.
L.M.S.
QUEEN'S CINEMA (AWH), Devonshire Road.—
Prop., High Park Picture Palace Co. (South-
port), Ltd. 300 seats. Two shows nightly.
Four changes weekly. Prices, 7d. to 1s.
Phone, Southport 8161. Station, Church-
town, L.M.S.
REGENT CINEMA (WE), Preston New Road,
Churchtown.—Prop., Birkdale Picture Palace,
Ltd., 413, Lord Street, Southport. 750 seats.
Booked at Hall. Twice nightly. One Mat.
weekly. Prices, 7d. to 1s. 3d. Proscenium
width, 30 ft. Phone, Southport 87326.
Station, Churchtown, L.M.S.
SCALA (WE), Kingsway.—Lessees, Coliseum
Cinema (Southport), Ltd., 3, Tulketh Street,
Southport. Phone, Southport 2426. 1,177
seats. Three shows daily. Station, Chapel
Street.
TROCADERO (WE), LORD STREET.—Prop., South-
port Amusements, Ltd. 1,357 seats. Booked
at Hall. Three shows daily. Phone, South-
port 3674.

COMPTON
ORGAN featured here.

SOUTHSEA (HANTS).
(SEE PORTSMOUTH.)

SOUTH SHIELDS (Co. Durham), Pop. 113,452.

PALACE THEATRE (WE), Frederick Street, High Shields.—Prop., High Shields Palace Theatre Ltd., 40, Westgate Road, Newcastle. 1,207 seats. Booked at H.O. Two shows nightly. Mat., Mon., Wed. and Sat. Prices, 4d. to 1s. Stage, 30 ft. deep. Phone. South Shields 267. Station, High Shields, L.N.E.R.

PALLADIUM (WE), Sunderland Road.—Prop., Palladium (S. Shields), Ltd. Man., Dir., Thomas Thompson. 995 seats. Booked at Thompson's Enterprises, Ltd., 4, Palladium Bldgs., Eastbourne Road, Middlesbrough. Continuous. Prices, 6d. and 1s. Phone, South Shields 284. Station, South Shields.

PAVILION (WE), Derby Street.—Prop., Wm. Arthur Shepherd. Phone, South Shields 688. 859 seats. Booked at Hall. Two shows nightly. Prices, 4d. to 1s. Phone, South Shields 688. Station, South Shields, L.N.E.R.

PICTURE HOUSE (BTH), Ocean Road.—Prop., Exors. of W. S. Shepherd. 622 seats. Booked at Pavilion Theatre, South Shields. Continuous. Prices, 3d. to 1s. Phone, South Shields 739. Station, South Shields.

QUEEN'S THEATRE (WE), Mile End Road. Prop., Essoldo (South Shields), Ltd., 11, Bath Lane, Newcastle-on-Tyne. 1,680 seats. Booked at Hall by Man. Three shows daily. Prices, 4d. to 1s. 6d. Proscenium width, 38 ft. Stage, 40 ft. deep ; six dressing-rooms. Phone, Newcastle 27864. Station, South Shields, L.N.E.R.

REGAL (WE), Props., Blacks (South Shields) Theatres, Ltd., 115, Shaftesbury Avenue, W.1. Phone, Temple Bar 9324.

COMPTON

ORGAN featured here.

REGENT (WE).—Thompson's Enterprises, Ltd., 4, Palladium Buildings, Eastbourne Road, Middlesbrough.

SCALA SUPER THEATRE (WE), Ocean Road.— Prop., General Theatres Corp., Ltd., New Gallery House, Regent Street, W.1. 1,500 seats. Booked at H.O. Continuous. Prices, 6d. to 1s. 6d. Proscenium width, 30 ft. Billiards Hall attached. Phone, South Shields 819. Station, South Shields, L.N.E.R.

WESTOE PICTURE HOUSE (WE), Chichester Road. —Props., Baldwin and Dawson. 750 seats. Booked at Newcastle. Continuous. Prices, 4d. to 9d. Proscenium width, 32 ft. Phone, South Shields 877. Station, South Shields, L.N.E.R.

SOUTHWELL (Notts), Pop., 2,989.

IDEAL (BA).—Prop., Ideal Cinema (Southwell), Ltd. Phone 29. 590 seats. Booked at Hall. Continuous. Proscenium width, 35 ft. Prices, 6d. to 1s. 6d. Station, Southwell, L.M.S.

SOUTHWICK (Sussex), Pop. 6,138.

NEW KINEMA (BTH). 65, The Crescent, Southwick. 461 seats. Continuous. Prices, 1d. to 1s. 6d. Booked at Hall. Phone, Southwick 9348. Station, Southwick.

PLAZA CINEMA.—Prop., P. V. Reynolds, Picturedrome, Portslade. Phone, Portslade 8492. 340 seats. Occasional Variety. Continuous. Booked in London. Prices, 4d. to 1s. Stage 10 ft. deep ; two dressing rooms. Phone, Southwick 9134. Station, Southwick, and Transport.

SOUTH WIGSTON (Leicester), Pop. 4,000.

PICTURE HOUSE (BTH), Blaby Road.—Prop. and Res. Man., George Smith, "Bangalore," 66, Saffron Road, South Wigston. 704 seats. Booked at Hall. Continuous. Two changes weekly. Prices, 6d. to 1s. 3d. Proscenium width, 18 ft. Phone, South Wigston 89285. Station, South Wigston, L.M.S.

SOUTHWOLD (Suffolk), Pop. 2,753.

THE CINEMA (WE).—Prop., Geo. Crick. Phone, 10. Seats 550. Booked by Prop. at Hall. Continuous. Prices, 5d. to 2s. Phone, Southwold 10. Station, Southwold, L.N.E.R., to Halesworth, thence by carrier. Films by Road Transport from Dansey Yard.

SOWERBY BRIDGE (Yorks), Pop. 14,679 ·

ELECTRIC THEATRE (BA), Wharfe Street.—Prop. National Electric Theatres, Ltd. Controlled by Gaumont-British Picture Corporation, Ltd., 123, Regent Street, London, W.1. Phone, Regent 8080. 812 seats. Booked at H.O. Continuous nightly. Two shows Sats. and Holidays. Mats., Wed. and Sat. Prices, 5d. to 1s. Proscenium width, 23 ft. Phone, Sowerby Bridge 81152. Station, Sowerby Bridge, L.M.S.

SPALDING (Lincs.), Pop. 12,592.

ODEON THEATRE (BTH), London Road.—Prop., Odeon Theatres, Ltd., Cornhill House, Bennett's Hill, Birmingham. (In course of construction.)

PRINCE'S CINEMA (BTH), Westlode Street.— Prop., Spalding Picture House, Ltd. 650 seats. Booked at New Theatre, Boston, by G. Aspland Howden. Prices, 6d. to 1s. 3d. Phone, Spalding 98. Station, Spalding. L.N.E.R.

REGENT THEATRE (WE), Sheep Market.—Prop. Spalding Picture House, Ltd. 398 seats. Booked at the New Theatre, Boston, by G, Aspland Howden. Twice Nightly. Cafe attached. Phone, Spalding 98. Prices, 7½d. to 1s. 3d.

SPENNYMOOR (Co. Durham), Pop. 16,361.

ARCADIA (WE).—Prop., M.B.C. Cinemas, Ltd., Hippodrome, Workington. 980 seats. Booked at H.O. Twice nightly. Prices, 4d. to 9d. Phone, Spennymoor 7. Station, Spennymoor, L.N.E.R.

CAMBRIDGE THEATRE (BTH). 650 seats.

TIVOLI, Cheapside.—Prop., Essolda, Ltd., 11, Bath Lane, Newcastle-on-Tyne. Phone, Newcastle 27864. 1,000 seats. Continuous. Prices, 4d. to 1s., ex. Sat. Prices attached.

TOWN HALL (BTH).—Prop., Sol. Speckman Theatres, Ltd., 11, Bath Lane, Newcastle. Phone, Newcastle 27864. 500 seats. Continuous.

SPILSBY (Lincs.), Pop. 1,400.

FRANKLIN CINEMA (Morrison).—Prop., J. F. Badley, The Terrace, Spilsby. 550 seats. Booked at Hall. Once nightly. Continuous Sat. Prices, 4d. to 1s. 4d. Phone 5. Station, Spilsby, L.N.E.R., and Lincoln and District Film Transport Co., Boston.

SPONDON (Derby), Pop. 3,140.

PICTURE HOUSE (BTP).—Prop., Spondon Cinema, Ltd. "Seven Stars," King Street, Derby. 500 seats. Booked at Hall. Once nightly, Mon. to Sat. Continuous from 6.30. Mat. Sat. Prices, 6d. to 1s. 3d. Station, Spondon, L.M.S.

STAFFORD (STAFFS.), **Pop. 29,485.**
ALBERT HALL (BTH).—Prop., Stafford Entertainments, Ltd. 480 seats. Booked at Picture House, Stafford. Once nightly. Mon. to Fri. Twice nightly Sat. Mats., Wed. and Sat. Prices, 6d. to 1s. Phone, 228. Station, Stafford, L.M.S.
ODEON THEATRE (BTH), Newport Road.—Props., Odeon (Stafford), Ltd., Cornhill House, Bennett's Hill, Birmingham. Phone, Midland 2781. Booked at 49, Park Lane, W.1. Continuous. Prices, 6d. to 1s. 6d. Phone, Stafford 877.
PICTURE HOUSE (BTH), Bridge Street.—Prop., Stafford Entertainments, Ltd. 900 seats. Booked at Hall. Twice nightly. Mats., Wed. and Sat. Prices, 9d. to 1s. 4d. Phone, Stafford 291. Station, Stafford, L.M.S.
**Fitted "ARDENTE" Deaf Aids
See page 258**
RITZ (WE).—Controlled by Union Cinemas, Ltd., 15, Regent Street, London, S.W.1. Phone, Whitehall 8484. Booked at H.O. Continuous. Prices, 6d. to 2s. Pictures and Variety. Station, Stafford, L.M.S.
SANDONIA (BTH), Sandon Road.—Prop., Stafford Entertainments, Ltd. 1,200 seats. Once nightly Mon. to Fri. Twice Sat. Mats., Wed and Sat. Booked at Picture House. Prices, 6d. to 1s. 4d. Phone, Stafford 328. Station, Stafford, L.M.S.

STAINCROSS (near **Barnsley**) (YORKS.), **Pop. 4,000.**
PICTURE HOUSE (BTH).—Prop., Staincross P.H., Ltd. 450 seats. Booked at Leeds by Sec. One show nightly. Two changes weekly, Prices, 3d. to 6d. Station, Staincross L.N.E.R.

STAINES (MDDX.), **Pop. 21,209.**
MAJESTIC THEATRE (WE).—High Street.—Controlled by County Cinemas, Ltd., Dean House, Dean Street, London. Phone, Gerrard 4543. 1,507 seats. Booked at H.O. Continuous. Prices, 6d. to 2s. Stage and seven dressing rooms. Café, Dance Hall attached. Phone, Staines 526. Station, Staines, S.R.

COMPTON
ORGAN featured here

NEW EMPIRE CINEMA (RCA), High Street.—Prop., Middlesex Cinemas, Ltd. 666 seats. Booked at Hall. Continuous. Prices, 6d. to 2s. Proscenium width, 25 ft. Phone, Staines 658. Station, Staines, S.R.

STAINFORTH (YOKS.), **Pop. 5,000.**
STAINFORTH CINEMA (BTH), Emmerson Avenue —Prop., Doncaster and District Cinema Co., King's Arcade, Doncaster. Phone, Doncaster 894. 650 seats. Booked at Hall. Continuous. Prices, 5d. to 1s. Phone, Stainforth 27. Stations, Stainforth and Hatfield, L.N.E.R.

STALYBRIDGE (CHESHIRE), **Pop. 24,823.**
GRAND (BTP).
HIPPODROME.—Booked by H D. Moorhouse at Imperial Buildings, Oxford Road, Manchester.
NEW PRINCES (BTH), Albert Square.—Prop,, New Princes Cinema (Stalybridge), Ltd. 700 seats. Booked by James Brearley, at 21. Bridge Street, Manchester. Continuous. Prices, 3d. to 1s. Phone, Stalybridge 485. Station, Stalybridge, L.M.S., and L.N.E.R.
PALACE (BTP), Market Street.—H. D. Moorhouse Circuit, 7, Oxford Road, Manchester,

850 seats. Continuous. Two shows Sat. Two changes weekly. Prices, 3d. to 1s. Phone, Ashington 136.

STAMFORD (LINCS.), **Pop. 9,946.**
CENTRAL CINEMA (WE), Broad Street.—Prop., Central Cinema (Stamford), Ltd. 565 seats. Booked at Hall. Continuous. Prices, 7d. to 1s. 10d. Phone, Stamford 179. Station, Stamford, L.M.S., and L.N.E.R.
PICTUREDROME (BA), Broad Street.—Prop., Picturedrome (Stamford), Ltd. 500 seats. Continuous. Booked at Central Cinema, Broad Street. Prices, 6d. to 1s. 10d. Phone, Stamford 179. Station, Stamford.

STANDON (HERTS.)
GEM (BA).—Prop., L. G. Attree, 12, Lindsay Terrace, Standon. 607 seats. Continuous. Prices, 6d. to 2s. Boxes, 10s. Proscenium width, 28 ft. Phone, Puckeridge 85. Café attached. Station, Standon, L.N.E.R.

STANDISH with LANGTREE (LANCS.), **Pop. 7,262.**
PALACE (Electrocord), High Street.—Prop., E. Bentham, Broomfield House, Standish. Phone 54. 500 seats. Booked at Manchester and Liverpool. Twice nightly except Tues., Wed. and Fri. Prices, 4d. to 10d. Station, Wigan, L.M.S.

STANFORD LE HOPE (ESSEX).
REGENT (WE).—Phone, Stanford le Hope 130.

STANHOPE (CO. DURHAM), **Pop. 1,746.**
TOWN HALL CINEMA (BTP).—500 seats.

STANLEY S.O. (CO. DURHAM), **Pop. 24,458.**
NEW VICTORIA (WE).
PAVILION CINEMA (WE) High Street.—Prop. T. Cass Craven. 1,100 seats. Booked at Hall. Continuous. Prices, 6d. to 1s. Proscenium width, 45 ft. Phone, Stanley 69. Café attached. Station, Stanley.

STANLEY (near **Wakefield**) (YORKS), **Pop. 14,570.**
PICTURE HOUSE (British Electric), Lake Lock. —Prop., Stanley Picture House Co., Ltd, 488 seats. Booked at Hall by Man. One show nightly. Two on Sat. Two changes weekly. Prices, 3d. to 9d. Phone, Lofthouse Gate 7178. Station, Stanley, L.N.E.R.

STANNINGLEY (YORKS), **Pop. 3,061.**
PAVILION (WE).—Prop., Associated Tower Cinemas, Ltd., The Tower, Briggate, Leeds. 685 seats. Booked at H.O. by C.H. Whincup. Phone, 71678. Station, Leeds.
ROYAL CINEMA (Electrocord), Bradford Road. —Prop., Films (Leeds), Ltd., 10, Mill Street, Leeds. Phone, 25524. 400 seats. Booked at H.O. Twice nightly. Prices, 3d. to 1s. Phone, Stanningley 71706. Station, Stanningley.

STANTON HILL (near **Mansfield**) (NOTTS).
STANTON HILL CINEMA (Marshall), near Mansfield.—Sec. and Man., Harry Moore. 600 seats. Continuous, 6 to 10.30. Twice Sat. Prices, 6d. to 1s. Phone, Mansfield 760. Station, Sutton-in-Ashfield,L.M.S.or L.N.E.R.

STAPLEFORD (NOTTS), **Pop. 11,516**
PALACE (Picturetone).—Prop., Exors. Edwin Widdowson. Booked at Bulwell by H. J. Widdowson, Secy. 650 seats. Continuous. Two shows Sat. Prices, 6d. to 1s. Station, Stapleford, L.M.S.

VICTORY CINEMA (BTP).—Prop., Midland Empire Theatres, Ltd., Commerce Chambers, Elite Bldgs., Nottingham. 800 seats. Booked at

STAPLEFORD—Contd.
H.O. by Herbert Elton. Phone, Nottingham 42364. Occasional Variety. Booked at H.O. Continuous. Two shows Sat. Phone, Sandiacre 120. Station, Stapleford, L.M.S.

STAVELEY (DERBY), **Pop. 12,018.**
EMPIRE (BTH), Chesterfield Road.—700 seats. Once nightly. Three shows Sat. Prices, 7d. to 1s.

STEVENAGE (HERTS), **Pop. 5,476.**
ASTORIA (Aerophone).—Prop., N. A. Ayres, Norton Ways, Letchworth. 750 seats. Continuous. Prices, 6d. to 1s. 6d. Phone, Stevenage 329. Herts. and Beds. Transport.
CINEMA (BA).—Prop. and Man., E. D. Hayward, Lawn View, London Road, Luton. 300 seats. Booked at Hall. Twice nightly. Two changes weekly. Prices, 4d. to 1s. 2d. Phone, Stevenage 143. Station, Srevenage, L.N.E.R.

STOCKINGFORD (WARWICK), **Pop. 14,000.**
PALACE (RCA), Short Street.—Prop., Sheridan Film Service, Ltd., 179, Horninglow Street, Burton-on-Trent. Phone, Burton-on-Trent 3324. 500 seats. Booked at H.O. Continuous. Prices, 4d. to 1s. Proscenium width, 16 ft. Phone, Nuneaton 547. Station, Stockingford, L.M.S.

STOCKPORT (CHESHIRE), **Pop. 125,505.**
ALEXANDRA CINEMA (WE), Castle Street, Edgeley.—Prop., Alexandra Cinema Co. (Edgeley), Ltd. 1,130 seats. Continuous evenings. Daily Mat. Booked at Hall. Two changes weekly. Prices, 6d. to 1s. 3d. Proscenium width, 25 ft. Phone, Stockport 2081. Station, Edgeley, L.M.S.
CINEMA (BTH), Bulkeley Road, Poynton.—Prop., R. Bailey, "The Chestnuts." Poynton Phone, Poynton 16. 360 seats. Booked at Hall. Once nightly, Tues. to Fri. Two shows Mon. and Sat. Prices, 6d. to 1s. 3d. Proscenium width, 18 ft. Phone, Poynton 16. Station, Poynton, L.M.S. and Films by Auto.
DON CINEMA (BTH), Bramhall Lane.—Prop. Rossendale Cinemas (1933), Ltd. 750 seats. Booked at Hall. Continuous. Two changes weekly. Prices, 6d. to 1s. 3d. Proscenium width, 30 ft. Phone, Stockport 2603. Station, Edgeley.
EDGELEY PICTURES (WE), Castle Street.—Prop., Elijah C. Aspden, The Patch, Bramhall Park Road, Bramhall, Cheshire. Phone, Bramhall 337. 669 seats. Booked at Star PictureTheatre. Continuous. Prices, 3d. to 1s. Phone, Stockport 2569.
GROVE CINEMA (WE), Commercial Road.—Props., P. & N. Hall. 441 seats. Continuous Mon. to Sat. Prices, 4d. to 1s. Proscenium width, 16 ft. Booked at Manchester. Phone, Great Moor 2732. Station (Hazel Grove), Stockport.
HIPPODROME (WE).—Props., Associated British Cinemas, Ltd., 149-151, Regent Street, London, W.1. Phone, Regent 6720. Booked at H.O. 899 seats. Continuous nightly. Daily mat. Prices, 6d. to 1s. Proscenium width, 28½ ft. Phone, Stockport 2412. Station, Edgeley.
KING'S CINEMA (RCA), Bentley Street.—Prop., King's Cinema (Stockport), Ltd. 700 seats. Man. Dir., Ernest Wardle. Booked at Hall. Continuous. Prices, 4d. to 7d. Phone, Stockport 3364. Station, Stockport, L.M.S.
NEW PICTORIUM (PTA).—Prop., G. Ray, 161, The Crescent, Arden Park, Woodley, Stockport. 480 seats. Booked at Hall. Continuous. Pictures and Variety. Prices, 5d. to 9d.

Proscenium width, 18 ft. Stage, 9 ft. deep ; one dressing-room. Phone, Stockport 2532. Stations, Edgeley or Teviot Dale, L.M.S.
PALACE (BTH), Bredbury.—Props., The Palace (Bredbury), Ltd. Once nightly. Twice Sat. Prices, 6d. to 1s. Proscenium width, 21 ft. Station, Bredbury.
PALLADIUM (WE), Princes Street.—Prop., Palladium (Stockport), Ltd. 1,000 seats. Booked at Hall. Continuous. Three performances Sat. Two changes weekly. Prices, 6d. to 1s. 3d. Proscenium width, 30 ft. Café attached. Phone, Stockport 2576. Station, Teviot Dale, L.M.S.
PICTUREDROME (BTH).—Props., Jackson and Newport (Stratford), Ltd.
PLAZA CINEMA (WE).—Props., Plaza Cinema (Stockport), Ltd., 13, St. Ann Street, Manchester. Blackfriars 3731. 1,800 seats. Booked at H.O. Continuous. Three shows Sat. Prices, 7d. to 2s. Café attached. Phone, No. 3818. Station, Stockport.

COMPTON
ORGAN featured here.

PRINCES PICTURE PALACE (WE), Princes Street. —Prop., Stockport Palace, Ltd. Phone, Stockport 2404. 516 seats. Booked at Super Cinema, Wellington Road South. Continuous. Prices, 3d. to 1s. 3d. Phone, Stockport 2404. Station, Edgeley, L.M.S. and Cheshire Lines.
QUEEN'S CINEMA (AWH), Portwood.—Prop., A. Jacobs, Triangle Cinema, Stretford Road, Manchester. Phone, Central 3487. 450 seats. Continuous. Two changes weekly. Prices, 3d. to 6d. Station, Teviot Dale, L.N.E.R.
RITZ (WE), Duke Street,—Controlled by Union Cinemas, Ltd., 15, Regent Street, S.W.1. Phone, Whitehall 8484. Continuous. Booked at H.O. Station, Stockport, L.M.S.
SAVOY (WE), Romiley.—Props., Savoy Cinema (Romiley), Ltd. Phone, Woodley 2131. 1,000 seats. Continuous. Twice Sat. Prices, 6d. to 1s. 6d. Proscenium width, 38 ft. Stage, 19 ft. deep ; three dressing-rooms. Café attached. Station, Romiley.
SAVOY CINEMA (WE), Heaton Moor Road.—Prop., Northern Amusements, Ltd., Prudential Chambers, South Parade, Rochdale. Phone, Rochdale 2072. 814 seats. Booked at Arcadia Cinema, Levenshulme, Manchester. Continuous nightly. Twice nightly Sat. Mats., Mon., Wed. and Sat. Prices, 6d. to 1s. 3d. Phone, Heaton Moor 2114. Station, Heaton Moor, L.M.S.
STAR PICTURE THEATRE (WE), Higher Hill Gate. —Prop., Elijah C. Aspden, The Patch, Bramhall Park Road, Bramhall, Cheshire. 746 seats. Phone, Bramhall 337. Booked at Hall. Continuous. Two changes weekly. Prices, 3d. to 1s. Proscenium width, 18 ft. Phone, 2542. Station, Edgeley, L.M.S.
SUPER CINEMA (WE), Wellington Road South.—Prop., Stockport Palace, Ltd., 1, Lord Street. Phone, Stockport 4050. 673 seats. Booked at Hall. Continuous. Prices, 2d. to 1s. 3d. Phone, Stockport 4455. Station, Edgeley, L.M.S
TUDOR, Bramhall.
VERNON PICTURE HOUSE (Picturetone), Carrington Road.—Prop., H. Lowe. 500 seats. Continuous. Two changes weekly. Prices, 4d. to 8d. Station, Teviot Dale.
WELLINGTON PICTURE HOUSE (RCA), Wellington Road South.—Prop., Wellington (Stockport) Picture House, Ltd., 7, Brazenose Street

Manchester. Blackfriars 5994. 1,002 seats. Booked at 76, Victoria Street, Manchester. Continuous Mon. to Fri. Two shows Sat. Mat. daily, except Fri. Prices, 4d. to 1s. Proscenium width, 28 ft. Phone, Stockport 2916. Stations, Edgeley, L.M.S., and Tiviot Dale, Cheshire Lines.

STOCKSBRIDGE (YORKS), Pop. 9,253.
PALACE (BTH).—Prop., Palace (Stocksbridge), Ltd. 1,000 seats. Booked at Hall. Once nightly. Twice Sat. Two changes weekly. Station, Deepcar, L.N.E.R.

STOCKSFIELD-ON-TYNE (NORTHUMB), Pop. 5,000.
COSY ELECTRIC PICTURE HALL (GB), Mickley.—Prop., R. S. & J. Stokoe, Rose Mount, Mickley, Nr. Stocksfield. 230 seats. Booked at Hall. One show nightly, two on Sat. Three changes weekly. Prices, 6d. to 9d. Proscenium width, 26 ft. Station, Prudhoe, L.N.E.R.

STOCKTON-ON-TEES (CO. DURHAM), Pop. 67,724.
CINEMA (WE).—Prop., Cinema (Stockton), Ltd. Man. Dir., F. C. Ewing. 1,475 seats. Booked at Hall by Man. Dir. Continuous. Prices, 6d. to 1s. 6d. Phone, Stockton 66239. Station, Stockton.
EMPIRE THEATRE (RCA), High Street.—Prop., Associated British Cinemas, Ltd., 30/31, Golden Square, W.1. 1,700 seats. Booked at H.O. Continuous. Prices, 4d. to 1s. 6d. Proscenium width, 32 ft. Stage and 10 dressing-rooms. Phone, Stockton-on-Tees 6426. Station, Stockton, L.N.E.R.
GLOBE PICTURE HOUSE (WE), High Street.—Stockton Palace, Ltd. 1,122 seats. Booked at Hall. Continuous. Two changes weekly. Prices, 7d. to 1s. 6d. Phone, Stockton-on-Tees 66646. Station, Stockton, L.N.E.R.
GRAND THEATRE (BTH).—770 seats.
HIPPODROME THEATRE (WE).—Props., North Eastern Entertainments, Ltd. Continuous. 1,700 seats. Prices, 6d. to 1s. 6d. Proscenium width, 40 ft. Stage, 30 ft. deep; 10 dressing-rooms. Phone, 66048. Station, Stockton-on-Tees.
PLAZA (BTH).—Prop., The Cinema (Stockton), Ltd. Continuous. Prices, 4d. to 9d. Phone, Stockton 66339.
REGAL (WE), High Street.

COMPTON
ORGAN featured here.

STOKE-ON-TRENT (STAFFS), Pop. 276,619.
HIPPODROME (RA), Kingsway.—Prop., Gaumont-British Picture Corpn., Ltd., 123, Regent Street, London, W.1. 1,550 seats. Booked at H.O. Continuous. Prices, 4d. to 1s. 5d. Phone, Hanley 48137. Station, Stoke-on-Trent; L.M.S.
KOSY KINEMA (BTH), Trent Vale.—Prop., Kosy Kinema Co., Ltd. 600 seats. Booked at Hall. Pictures and Variety. Once nightly. Mat., Sat. Prices, 4d. to 1s. Stage, 10 ft. deep; 3 dressing-rooms. Phone, Stoke-on-Trent 4595.
MAJESTIC CINEMA (WE), Campbell Place.—Prop., Associated British Cinemas, Ltd., 30-31, Golden Square, London, W.1. Phone, Gerrard 7887. 1,500 seats. Booked at H.O. Continuous. Prices, 4d. to 1s. 6d. Café attached. Phone, Hanley 4769. Station, Stoke-on-Trent, L.M.S.
MARSHLANDS PICTURE HALL (Morrison), High Street, Wolstanton.—Prop., Marshlands Pic-

tures, Ltd. 550 seats. Continuous. Two changes weekly. Station, Longport, L.M.S. (N.S. Section).
MILTON CINEMA (Imperial), Milton.—Prop., Locker and Mason. 350 seats. Booked at Queen's Palace, Silverdale. Continuous. Prices, 4d. to 9d. Proscenium width, 16 ft. Phone, 5424. Station, Milton, L.M.S., or Potteries Transport.
PRINCES CINEMA (Picturetone), Wharf Street. —Prop., Princes Hall Cinema Co., Ltd. 1,200 seats. Booked at Hall. Continuous. Mat., Sat. Two changes weekly. Prices, 4d. to 9d. Station, Stoke-on-Trent, L.M.S.
VICTORIA THEATRE (BTP), Hartshill.—Prop., Victoria Pictures (Hartshill), Ltd. 700 seats. Booked at Hall. Continuous. Two changes weekly. Prices, 4d. to 1s. Phone, Newcastle 6666. Station, Etruria.

STONE (STAFFS), Pop. 5,952.
PICTURE HOUSE (BTP), Town Hall.—Prop., Stone Cinema Co., Ltd. 430 seats. Booked at Hall. One show nightly, two on Sats. Two Mats. weekly. Two changes weekly. Prices, 6d. to 1s. 3d. Phone, Stone 42. Station, Stone, L.M.S.

STONEHOUSE (GLOS), Pop. 2,390.
REGAL (BTH).—Prop., A. F. Stratford. 300 seats. Continuous evenings. Prices, 6d. to 1s. 6d. Proscenium width, 16 ft. Stonehouse, L.M.S. and G.W.R.

STONY STRATFORD (BUCKS), Pop. 2,041.
SCALA (BTH).—Prop., Councillor G. H. Barber, Coronation House, Tunstall Park, Stoke-on-Trent. Phone, Hanley 253. 600 seats. Booked at Hall. Continuous. Prices, 7d. to 1s 4d.

STOURBRIDGE (WORCS), Pop. 19,903.
NTRAL THEATRE (WE), 65, High Street.—Prop., Stourbridge Central Theatre, Ltd. 1,500 seats. Booked at Hall. Continuous. Daily Mat. Prices, 6d. to 1s. 3d. Phone, Stourbridge 5030. Station, Stourbridge, G.W.R.

COMPTON
ORGAN featured here.

KINEMA, Kinver.
KING'S HALL (RCA).—Prop., Poole's Theatres, Ltd., Hippodrome, Gloucester. Phone, Gloucester 2127. 1,500 seats. Booked at H.O. Continuous. Prices, 4d. to 1s. Phone, Stourbridge 57148. Station, Stourbridge Junction, G.W.R.

Fitted "ARDENTE" Deaf Aids
See page 258

SCALA PICTURE PLAYHOUSE (WE), High Street, Lessee, G. Prickett. 1,135 seats. Booked at Hall. Continuous nightly. Mats., Mon. and Sat. Two changes weekly. Occasional Variety. Prices, 6d. to 1s. 3d. Phone, Stourbridge 26.

STOURPORT (WORCS), Pop. 5,949.
STOURPORT ELECTRIC THEATRE (Film Industries), Lickhill Road.—Prop., Stourport Electric Theatres, Ltd. 700 seats. Booked at Concordia, Stourport, by G. Jackson. Two shows nightly. Prices, 5d. to 1s. Phone, Stourport 28. Station, Stourport, G.W.R.

STOWMARKET (SUFFOLK), Pop. 4,296.
PALLADIUM (Wired).—Prop. and Man., John Eric Salter, Shelland, Woolpit, Bury St. Edmunds. 385 seats. Booked at Hall. Once

STOWMARKET—Contd.
nightly. Mat. and two shows Sat. Prices,
6d. to 1s. 3d. Station, Stowmarket, L.N.E.R.
REGAL.—Prop. V. E. H. Cinemas, Ltd.—The
Lido, Aylsham Road, Norwich.

STRATFORD-ON-AVON (WARWICK), **Pop.
11,616.**
PICTURE HOUSE (BA), Greenhill Street.—Prop.,
Stratford-on-Avon Picture House Co., Ltd,
1,064 seats. Booked by S. W. Clift, 5.
Union Street, Birmingham. Continuous.
Prices, 6d. to 2s. Proscenium width, 35 ft.
Stage, 30 ft. deep ; 10 dressing-rooms.
Stratford-on-Avon 2622. Station, Stratford-
on-Avon, G.W.R.

STREET (SOMERSET), **Pop. 4,458.**
PLAYHOUSE (BTH).—Prop., Mrs. H. Voake,
Leigh Cottage. 700 seats. Booked at Hall.
Once nightly. Three shows Sat. Pictures
and Variety. Prices, 6d. to 1s. 6d. Proscen-
ium width, 26 ft. Stage, 20 ft. deep ; 4 dress-
ing-rooms. Phone, Street 28. Stations,
Glastonbury and Street, S. and D.J.R.

STRETFORD (LANCS), **Pop. 56,795.**
CORONA SUPER CINEMA (WE), Moss Road.—
Prop., J. Maunders. 890 seats. Booked at
Manchester. Continuous Mon. to Fri. Twice
nightly Saturday. Stage, 6 ft. deep ; 2 dressing-
rooms. Prices, 6d. to 1s. Phone, Longford
1990. Stations, Manchester.
FUTURIST CINEMA (Gramo-Radio), Church Street.
—Props., L. Burgess, Combs, Chapel-en-le-
Frith, Stockport. 400 seats. Booked at Hall.
Two shows Sat. Continuous rest of week.
Prices, 5d. to 9d. Proscenium width, 17 ft.
Occasional Variety. Phone, Longford 1692.
Station, Stretford, L.M.S.
LONGFORD THEATRE (WE).—Props., Jackson and
Newport (Lancs)., Ltd. 2,009 seats. Con-
tinuous nightly. Twice nightly Sat. Mats.,
Mon., Wed., Thurs. Pictures and Variety.
Prices, 6d. to 2s. Phone, Longford 2233.
PICTUREDROME (WE), King Street.—Prop.,
Jackson and Newport (Stretford), Ltd. 800
seats. Continuous nightly. Sat., twice nightly.
Mats., Mon., Thurs. Prices, 6d. to 1s. Phone,
Longford 1429.

STROOD (KENT), **Pop. 16,279.**
INVICTA CINEMA (RCA), High Street.—Prop.,
Stanley H. Hinds, Berthons, Woodside
Park Avenue, Walthamstow, E.17. 500 seats.
Booked at Hall. Continuous. Two changes
weekly. Prices, 7d. to 1s. 6d. Phone, Chatham
7316. Station, Strood, S.R. Films by Kent
Films Motor Transport.
QUEENS (AWH), Station Road.—Prop., Herbert
W. Grose. 510 seats. Booked at Hall. Con-
tinuous. Prices, 4d. to 1s. Station, Strood,
S.R.

STROUD (GLOS), **Pop. 8,360.**
GAUMONT PALACE THEATRE (BA), Russell Street.
—Prop., Albany Ward Theatres, Ltd., New
Gallery House, Regent Street, W.1. 994 seats.
Booked at H.O. Continuous. Prices, 6d. to
2s. Phone, Stroud 409.
**Fitted "ARDENTE" Deaf Aids
See page 258**

STUDLEY (WARWICKSHIRE), **Pop. 2,000.**
IMPERIAL PICTURES (Gyrotone).—Prop. and
Man., J. F. Washbourne. Booked at Hall.
Twice nightly. Prices, 6d. to 1s. Proscenium
width, 14 ft. Phone, Studley 7 (Birming-
ham area). Station, Studley and Astwood
Bank, L.M.S.

SUDBURY (MIDDLESEX).
ODEON THEATRE (BTH).—Prop., Odeon (Sudbury), Ltd., Cornhill House, Bennett's Hill

Birmingham. Phone, Midland 2781. Booked
at 49, Park Lane, W.1. Prices, 6d. to 2s.
Phone, Wembley 1491.

SUDBURY (SUFFOLK), **Pop. 7,007.**
COUNTY CINEMA (WE).—Props., G. J. Howell,
53, Shorts Gardens, W.C.2. Booked at H.O.
687 seats. Continuous. Prices, 6d. to 2s.
Café Restaurant attached. Phone, Sudbury
165. Station, Sudbury, L.N.E.R.
GAINSBOROUGH THEATRE (WE).—Prop., Ager's
Cinema Circuit, Ltd. 10, Church Street, Colchester. 400 seats. Booked at H.O. Continuous. Prices, 7d. to 1s. 6d. Proscenium
width, 22 ft. Phone, Sudbury 176. Station,
Sudbury, L.N.E.R.

SUNDERLAND (CO. DURHAM), **Pop. 185,870.**
BLACK'S REGAL THEATRE (WE), Holmside.—
Props., Black's Theatres. Pictures and
Variety. 2,522 seats. Booked by A. Black
(Man. Dir.) at 115, Shaftesbury Avenue,
London, W. Temple Bar 9324. Continuous.
Prices, 6d. to 2s. Proscenium width, 57 ft.
Stage, 40 ft. deep ; 10 dressing-rooms.
Variety booked by Richards and Marks, 19,
Garrick Street, W. Café and Rink attached.
Phone, Sunderland 4881. Station, Sunder-
land, L.N.E.R.

COMPTON
ORGAN featured here.

BLACK'S ROYAL THEATRE.—Booked at 115,
Shaftesbury Avenue, London, W.C.2.
BROMARSH GRAND CINEMA (BTP). Bridge End.—
Prop., Bromarsh Grand Cinema Co. 700
seats. Two shows nightly. Mats., Wed. and
Sat. Two changes weekly. Prices 4d. to 7d.
Phone, Sunderland 4779. Station, Sunder-
land, L.N.E.R.
CORA PICTURE PALACE, Southwick Road.—
Props., Executors of the late J. H. Tindle.
Twice nightly. Two changes weekly. Prices,
4d. to 6d. Phone, Sunderland 4705. Station,
Sunderland, L.N.E.R.
GAIETY THEATRE, High Street (Magnatorque).
—700 seats. Twice nightly. Prices, 4d. to 6d.
Station, Sunderland, L.N.E.R.
HAVELOCK PICTURE HOUSE (WE), Fawcett
Street.—Prop., Provincial Cinematograph
Theatres, Ltd., New Gallery House, 123,
Regent Street, London, W.1. 1,504 seats.
Booked at H.O. Continuous. Prices, 7d. to
1s. 6d. Phone, Sunderland 500211. Station,
Sunderland, L.N.E.R.
**Fitted "ARDENTE" Deaf Aids
See page 258**

**WURLITZER ORGAN
Installed in this Kinema**

KING'S THEATRE (RCA), Crowtree Road.—Props.,
Denman Picture Houses, Ltd., 123, Regent
Street, London, W.1. 2,000 seats. Booked
at H.O. Continuous. Stage, 34 ft. deep ;
ample dressing-room accommodation. Café
attached. Prices, 3d. to 1s. 3d. Phone,
Sunderland 500811. Station, Sunderland
(Central), L.N.E.R.
MARINA (BTP), Sea Road, Fulwell.—Props.
Wearside Entertainments, Ltd., 72, Grey
Street, Newcastle-on-Tyne. Phone, 20317.
Twice nightly. 870 seats. Booked at H.O.
Proscenium width, 30 ft. Prices, 6d. to
1s. 3d. Phone, Sunderland 4943. Station,
Monkwearmouth.
MILLFIELD CINEMA (BTP), Hylton Road.—Prop.,
Millfield Cinema, Ltd., 72, Grey Street,
Newcastle-on-Tyne. Phone, 20317. Booked

at H.O. 900 seats. Twice nightly. Two changes weekly. Prices, 5d. to 9d. Station, Sunderland, L.N.E.R.

NEW RINK.—Prop., Black's Theatres, 115, Shaftesbury Avenue, London, W.C.2.

PALACE (RCA).—Prop., General Theatre Corpn., Ltd. Booked at H.O. Continuous. One change weekly. Prices, 3d. to 1s. 3d. Phone, Sunderland 34851. Station, Sunderland, L.N.E.R.

PICTURE HOUSE (WE), High Street West.—Prop., Consolidated Cinematograph Co., Ltd. 1,000 seats. Continuous. Prices, 4d. to 1s. 2d. Phone, Sunderland 4668. Station, Sunderland L.N.E.R.

PLAZA (WE), Pallion Road.—Props., Pallion (Sunderland) Cinema, Ltd., 40, Westgate Road, Newcastle-on-Tyne. Phone, 22401. Booked at F.O. Continuous. 1,100 seats. Prices, 6d. to 1s. Proscenium width, 37 ft. Phone, Sunderland 2261.

REGENT.— Props., Thompson's Enterprises, Ltd., 4, Palladium Bldgs., Middlesbrough.

ROKER THEATRE (BTH), Roker Avenue.—Props., Sunderland Amusements, Ltd., 34, King Street, South Shields. Phone, 3504. 1,047 seats. Booked at Hall. Two shows nightly. Prices, 4d. to 9d. Proscenium width, 30 ft. Stage, 30 ft. deep ; four dressing-rooms. Phone, Sunderland 1504. Station, Sunderland.

SAVOY ELECTRIC THEATRE (BTH), The Green, Southwick.—Prop. and Man., G. W. Oliver. 600 seats. Booked at Hall. Two shows nightly. Prices, 3d. to 8d. Phone, Sunderland 3471. Station, Sunderland, L.N.E.R.

VICTORY CINEMA (Perfectone).—Prop., B. Scott Elder. 700 seats. Two shows nightly. Prices, 4d. to 6d. Station, Central, L.N.E.R.

VILLIERS ELECTRIC THEATRE (BTH), Villiers Street.—Prop., Sunderland Amusements, Ltd. 37, King Street, South Shields. 900 seats. Booked at Newcastle. Two shows nightly. Prices, 4d. to 6d. Phone, Sunderland 3745. Station, Sunderland, L.N.E.R.

SUNNINGHILL (BERKS).

PICTURE HOUSE (Cinephone).—Prop., Sidney G. Prince. 320 seats. Twice nightly. Mat., Wed. and Sat. Prices, 6d. to 2s. 6d. Phone, Ascot 881. Station, Ascot, S.R. Films by Road Transport.

SURBITON (SURREY), **Pop. 29,396.**

CORONATION CINEMA (WE), St. Mark's Hill.— Prop., M. L. Syndicate, Ltd., 47, Essex Street, Strand, London, W.C.2. Phone, Central 6414. 894 seats. Booked at Hall. Continuous Prices, 6d. to 2s. Phone, Elmbridge 1266. Station, Surbiton, S.R.

ODEON THEATRE (BTH).—Prop., Odeon (Surbiton), Ltd. Cornhill House, Bennett's Hill, Birmingham. Phone, Midland 2781. Booked at 49, Park Lane, W.1. Prices, 6d. to 2s. Phone, Elmbridge 3884. Station, Surbiton, S.R.

SUTTON and CHEAM (SURREY), **Pop. 46,488.**

PICTURE THEATRE (WE), Cheam Road.—Prop., P. and S. Cinemas, Ltd. 600 seats. Booked at Hall. Continuous. Prices, 6d. to 1s. 10d. Phone, Sutton 855. Station, Sutton, S.R.

PLAZA (WE).—Prop., Plaza (Sutton), Ltd. 2,200 seats. Controlled by Bernstein Theatres Ltd., 36, Golden Square, W.1. Phone, Gerrard 3554. Booked at H.O. Continuous. Phone, Sutton 4440. Café attached.

COMPTON

ORGAN featured here.

SURREY COUNTY CINEMA (WE).—Prop., Associated Provincial Picture Houses, Ltd., 123 Regent Street, London, W.1. Phone, Regent 8080. 1,736 seats. Booked at H.O. Continuous. Prices 6d. to 2s. 6d. Proscenium width, 41 ft. Café. Phone, Sutton 1009. Station, Sutton, S.R.

Fitted "ARDENTE" Deaf Aids
See page 258

COMPTON

ORGAN featured here.

SUTTON BRIDGE (LINCS), **Pop. 2,835.**

CINEMA THEATRE (Mihaly).—Prop., A. Groves. Booked at Hall. Twice nightly. Prices, 6d. to 1s. 6d. Station, Sutton Bridge.

SUTTON COLDFIELD (WARWICK), **Pop. 29,924.**

EMPRESS CINEMA (WE).—Prop., G. Williams, 1,600 seats. Booked at Hall. Continuous. Two changes weekly. Prices, 6d. to 1s. 4d. Phone, Sutton Coldfield 2363. Station, Sutton Coldfield.

ODEON THEATRE (BTH), Lichfield Road.—Props., Odeon (Sutton Coldfield), Ltd., Cornhill House, Bennett's Hill, Birmingham. Phone, Midland 2781. Booked at 49, Park Lane, W.1. Prices, 6d. to 2s. Continuous. Phone, Sutton 2714.

SUTTON-IN-ASHFIELD (NOTTS), **Pop. 25,151.**

KING'S THEATRE (BTP).—Prop., Aleph Entertainments, Ltd., Westminster Bldgs., Theatre Square, Nottingham. Phone, Nottingham 42364. 1,300 seats. Booked at H.O. by Herbert Elton. Continuous. Two changes weekly. Price 6d. to 1s. Phone, Sutton 76. Station, Sutton-in-Ashfield, L.M.S.

PORTLAND.—Booked by Herbert Elton, Commerce Chambers, Elite Bldgs., Nottingham.

RIALTO.—Booked by H. Elton, Westminster Buildings, Theatre Square, Nottingham.

TIVOLI (WE), Outram Street.—Prop., Aleph Entertainments, Ltd., Westminster Buildings, Theatre Square, Nottingham. 782 seats. Booked at H.O. by Herbert Elton. Occasional Variety. Two shows nightly. Phone, Sutton 76. Station, Sutton-in-Ashfield, L.N.E.R.

SUTTON-ON-SEA (LINCS), **Pop. 1,190.**

SAVOY CINEMA (BA), High Street.—Props., Sutton-on-Sea, Cinemas, Ltd. 380 seats. Booked at Hall. Continuous nightly. Mat. Sat. Prices, 6d. to 1s. 6d. Station, Sutton-on-Sea, L.M.S.

SWADLINCOTE (DERBY), **Pop. 4,107.**

ALEXANDRA PICTURE HOUSE (Morrison).—Prop., Alexandra Picture House Co., Ltd. 750 seats. Booked at Hall. Continuous. Two changes weekly. Prices, 5d. to 1s. Station, Swadlincote, L.M.S.

MAJESTIC (WE).—Gen. Man., Percy McCann. 1,000 seats. Continuous, Mon. to Fri. Two shows Sat.

NEW EMPIRE (BTH).—Prop., Swadlincote Entertainment Co., Ltd. 450 seats. Gen. Man., Reg. A. Ball. Continuous, Mon. to Fri. Two shows Sat. Occasional Variety. Prices, 5d. to 1s. Proscenium width, 26 ft. Stage, 20 ft. deep ; four dressing-rooms. Station, Swadlincote, S. Transport.

SWAFFHAM (NORFOLK), **Pop. 2,783.**
REGAL CINEMA (BTP), Station Street.—Props., Bury St. Edmunds Cinemas, Ltd., 54, Chevallier Street, Ipswich. 508 seats.— Booked at H.O. Once nightly Mon. to Fri. Twice nightly and Mat. Sat. Prices, 6d. to 2s. Proscenium width, 24 ft. Phone, Swaffham 68. Station, Swaffham, L.N.E.R.

SWALLOWNEST (near Sheffield) (YORKS), **Pop. 5,000.**
PAVILION (BTH).—Lessees, Rotherham District Cinemas, Ltd., Empire, Killamarsh, nr. Sheffield. Phone, Rotherham 1013. 430 seats. Booked at Empire, Killamarsh, nr. Sheffield. Once nightly. Three shows Sat. Prices, 4d. to 1s. Stage, 12 ft. deep ; two dressing-rooms. Station, Woodhouse Mill, L.M.S. and Beighton, L.N.E.R.

SWANAGE (DORSET), **Pop. 6,276.**
GRAND THEATRE (WE), Station Road.—Props., Portsmouth Town Cinemas, Ltd., Shaftesbury Cinema, Kingston Road, Portsmouth. 500 seats. Continuous. Two changes weekly. Prices, 8d. to 2s.
SWANAGE CINEMA (WE). Station Road.—Props., Portsmouth Town Cinemas, Ltd., Shaftesbury Cinema, Kingston Road, Portsmouth. 595 seats. Continuous. Two changes weekly. Prices, 8d. to 2s. 4d. Phone, Swanage 74. Station, Swanage, S.R.

SWANSCOMBE (KENT).
JUBILEE (Kalee), Ames Road, Swanscombe.—Prop., G. A. Smedley. 420 seats. Booked at Hall. Prices, 6d. to 1s. 3d. Proscenium width, — ft. Variety. Stage, 14 ft. deep ; two dressing-rooms. Phone, Gravesend 1430. Station, Swanscombe Halt.

SWINDON (WILTS), **Pop. 62,407.**
ARCADIA (RCA), Regent Street.—Prop., Arcadia Palace Co. (Swindon), Ltd. 612 seats. Continuous nightly. Daily Mat. Booked at Vista Cinema, Westbury, Wilts. Phone, 75. Prices, 6d. to 1s. 6d. Phone, Swindon 497. Station, Swindon, G.W.R. Films by Road Transport.
EMPIRE (WE).—Prop., Swindon Entertainments, Ltd., 3, New Street, Birmingham. 1,470 seats. Booked at H.O. Continuous nightly. Daily Mat. Occasional Stage Companies. Prices, 6d. to 1s. 6d. Proscenium width, 40 ft. Stage, 40 ft. deep ; seven dressing-rooms. Phone, Swindon 96. Station, Swindon, G.W.R.
PALACE (BA), Gorse Hill.—Prop., Gaumont-British Pictures Corporation, New Gallery House, W.1. 900 seats. Booked at H.O. Continuous. Prices, 6d. to 1s. 6d. Proscenium width, 22 ft. Phone, Swindon 135. Station, Swindon, G.W.R.
PALLADIUM (RCA), Rodbourne Road.—Prop., Palladium Cinema Co., Ltd., Regent Circus. Swindon. 750 seats. Continuous. Mat. daily. Booked at Hall. Prices, 6d. to 1s. 4d. Phone Swindon 516.
PLAYHOUSE.—Late Mechanics' Hall.
REGENT (RCA).—Prop., Albany Ward Theatres, Ltd. Booked at 123, Regent Street, London, W.1. Continuous. Phone, Swindon 750.

Fitted "ARDENTE" Deaf Aids
See page 258

COMPTON
ORGAN featured here.

RINK CINEMA (RCA), Old Town.—Prop., Rink (Swindon), Ltd. 700 seats. Booked at Vista Cinema, Westbury, Wilts. Phone, 75. Continuous nightly. Mats., Mon., Wed. and Sat. Prices, 6d. to 1s. 6d. Phone, Swindon 222.
SAVOY.—Prop., Associated British Cinemas, Ltd., 30-31 Golden Square, London, W.1.

Fitted "ARDENTE" Deaf Aids
See page 258

SWINTON (LANCS), **Pop. 32,761.**
ELLESMERE SUPER CINEMA.—Props., Snape & Ward, 13, St. Ann Street, Manchester.
NEW ADELPHI (RCA), Market Place.—Prop., Swinton Entertainments, Ltd. 1,100 seats. Continuous. Booked by J. F. Emery at 26, Cross Street, Manchester. Prices, 6d. to 1s. 3d. Proscenium width, 28 ft. Phone, Swinton 1825. Station, Swinton, L.M.S.
PLAZA (WE).—Prop., Swinton Entertainments, Ltd., Adelphi Theatre, Market Place, Swinton. 753 seats. Booked by J. F. Emery at 26, Cross Street, Manchester. Continuous. Proscenium width, 24 ft. Phone, Swinton 1690. Dance Hall attached. Station, Swinton, L.M.S.

SWINTON (YORKS), **Pop. 13,820.**
PICTURE HOUSE (WE).—Prop., Mexborough Theatres, Ltd., Empire, Swinton Road, Mexborough. Phone, Mexborough 108. 904 seats. Two shows daily. Prices, 6d. to 1s. 3d. Phone, Mexborough 151. Station, Swinton, near Rotherham, L.M.S. or L.N.E.R

TADCASTER (YORKS), **Pop. 3,399.**
COSY PICTURE HOUSE (Eastern Electric).—400 seats.

TALKE (STAFFS), **Pop. 2,000.**
GRAND THEATRE (AWH), Butt Lane.—Lessee, Clarence Green. 500 seats. Pictures and Variety. Films booked at Globe Picture Playhouse, Burslem ; and Variety by Patterson, Manchester. Continuous. Mats., Mon. Thurs. and Sat. Prices, 4d. to 1s. Stage, 16 ft. deep ; three dressing-rooms. Proscenium width, 24 ft. Phone, Kidsgrove 111. Station, Harecastle, L.M.S.

TAMWORTH (STAFFS), **Pop. 7,510.**
GRAND (Imperial), George Street.—Prop., Palace Theatre (Tamworth), Ltd. 750 seats. Booked at Hall. Two shows nightly. Two changes weekly. Pictures and occasional Variety. Stage, 12 ft. deep. Café attached. Prices, 6d. to 1s. 3d. Phone, Tamworth 88. Station, Tamworth, L.M.S.
PALACE (WE).—Prop., Palace Theatre (Tamworth), Ltd. 1,400 seats. Booked at Hall. Continuous. Two changes weekly. Prices, 3d. to 1s. 6d. Phone, Tamworth 59. Station, Tamworth.
ROYAL CINEMA, Dordon.—(Closed).

TAUNTON (SOMERSET), **Pop. 25,177.**
GAIETY KINEMA (WE), Rowbarton.—Prop., George Vickery, Ltd. 672 seats. Continuous, 2.0 to 10.30. Mat. daily. Prices, 6d. to 1s. 6d. Station, Taunton, G.W.R.
GAUMONT PALACE (BA).—Prop., Gaumont British Picture Corporation, Ltd., 123, Regent Street, London, W.1. 1,486 seats. Booked at H.O. Continuous. Prices, 6d. to 2s. Stage, 21 ft. deep. Proscenium width, 50 ft. Café attached. Phone, Taunton 14. Station, G.W.R.

Fitted "ARDENTE" Deaf Aids
See page 258

ODEON THEATRE (WE).—Prop., Odeon (Taunton), Ltd., Cornhill House, Bennett's Hill, Birmingham. Phone, Midland 2781. Booked at 49, Park Lane, W.1. Prices, 6d. to 2s. Proscenium width, 28 ft. Phone, Taunton 2291.
VILLAGE HALL, Porlock.

TAVISTOCK (DEVON), **Pop. 3,790.**
CINEMA (Morrison).—Prop. and Man., C. J. Burow. 400 seats. Booked at Hall or Dreamland, Okehampton. One show nightly. Prices 6d. to 1s. 6d. Proscenium width, 30 ft. Stage. Station, Tavistock, G.W.R. and S.R.; and Road Transport.

TEDDINGTON (MIDDLESEX), **Pop. 23,369.**
SAVOY CINEMA (WE), High Street.—Prop., Associated British Cinemas, Ltd. 630 seats. Continuous and Mat. Two changes weekly. Prices, 6d. to 1s. 10d. Phone, Kingston 0910. Station, Teddington, S.R.

TEIGNMOUTH (DEVON), **Pop. 10,019.**
CARLTON CINEMA (BTH).—Prop., Arthur R. Phern. 500 seats. Booked at Hall. Prices, 9d. to 1s. 6d. Phone, Teignmouth 163. Station, Teignmouth, G.W.R.
LYCEUM PICTURE HOUSE (BTH).—Prop., A. R. Phern. 500 seats. Booked at Hall. Continuous. Prices, 7d. to 1s. 6d. Phone, Teignmouth 163. Station, Teignmouth, G.W.R.
RIVIERA CINEMA (WE).—Prop., A. W. Prince, Riviera Hotel, Teignmouth. 901 seats. Booked at Hall. Continuous. Prices, 9d. to 2s. Proscenium width, 45 ft. Café attached. Phone, Teignmouth 24. Station, Teignmouth.

TEMPLECOMBE (SOM.), **Pop. 720.**
ELECTRIC THEATRE.—Props., The Walford Family, Chard, Somerset.

TENBURY WELLS (WORCS.), **Pop. 2,000.**
PICTURE HOUSE (BA).—Prop., A. J. Smith, Oak House, Tenbury Wells. Booked at Oak House. One show nightly. Two on Sat. Prices, 7d. to 1s. 4d. Phone, Tenbury Wells 62. Station, Tenbury Wells, G.W.R.

TENTERDEN (KENT), **Pop. 3,473.**
ELECTRIC PALACE (WE).—Prop., Shipman and King, Shell Mex House, Strand, W.C.2. 310 seats. Booked at H.O. Continuous nightly. Mats., Wed. and Sat. Two changes weekly.
EMBASSY.—Prop., Shipman and King, M84, Shell Mex House, Strand, W.C.2.

TETBURY (GLOS.), **Pop. 2,237.**
PALACE CINEMA (Marshall).—Prop., G. Adams, White Hart Hotel, Tetbury. Booked at Cardiff. Prices, 6d. to 2s. Proscenium width, 16 ft. Dance Hall attached. Phone, Tetbury 39. Station, Tetbury, G.W.R.

TEWKESBURY (GLOS.), **Pop. 4,352.**
SABRINA (WE).—Prop., The Sabrina Cinema Co., Ltd., Tewkesbury. 650 seats. Continuous. Prices, 6d. to 1s. 6d. Phone, 143.

THAME (OXFORD), **Pop. 3,019.**
GRAND CINEMA (AWH), North Street. 400 seats. Booked at 98 Thame. Occasional Variety. One show nightly. Prices, 4d. to 1s. 6d. Films by Oxon. and Bucks. Transport Co. Station, Thame, G.W.R.

THETFORD (NORFOLK), **Pop. 4,097.**
PALACE (BTH), Guildhall Street.—Prop., B. C. Culey. 480 seats. Continuous. Booked in London. Prices, 6d. to 1s. 6d. Proscenium width, 30 ft. Phone, Thetford 79. Station, Thetford, L.N.E.R., and Road Transport.

THIRSK (YORKS), **Pop. 3,000.**
PICTURE HOUSE (WE), Westgate.—Prop., Mrs. Elizabeth Power, Belgrave Terrace, Thirsk. 450 seats. Booked at Hall. Twice nightly. Two changes weekly. Prices, 6d. to 1s. 3d. Phone, Thirsk 113. Station, Thirsk, L.N.E.R.
REGENT CINEMA (BTH).—Prop., W. Lund. 400 seats. Booked at Hall. Continuous. Mat., Sat. Prices, 6d. to 1s. 3d. Phone, Thirsk 141. Station, Thirsk, L.N.E.R., and Cleveland Film Transport Co.

THORNABY-ON-TEES (YORKS), **Pop. 21,233.**
CENTRAL HALL (BTH), Westbury Street.—Prop., and Man., S. W. Nightingale. 700 seats. Booked at Hall. Two shows nightly. Two changes weekly. Prices, 4d. to 9d. Phone, Stockton 66685.
QUEEN'S CINEMA (BTH), Mandale Road.—Prop. and Man., S. W. Nightingale (Phone, Stockton 66007). 700 seats. Booked at Central Hall. Twice nightly. Prices, 6d. to 9d. Station, Thornaby-on-Tees, L.N.E.R.

THORNBURY (GLOS.), **Pop. 2,646.**
PICTURE HOUSE (BTH).—Prop., Mrs. F. H. Grace, West Shen, Thornbury, Bristol. 350 seats. Booked at Hall. Continuous. Prices, 6d. to 1s. 6d. Proscenium width, 16½ ft. Phone, Thornbury 79. Station, Thornbury, L.M.S.

THORNE (YORKS), **Pop. 5,300.**
EMPIRE (WE).—Prop., Moorends Empire, Ltd. 1,045 seats. Booked at Sheffield and Leeds. Continuous. Prices, 5d. to 1s. Proscenium width, 30 ft. Phone No. 108. Station, Thorne, L.N.E.R. and G.C.R.
KENSINGTON PALACE (WE).—Prop., Carlton (Thorne), Ltd., 111, Boothferry Road, Goole. Phone, Goole 277. 887 seats. Booked at Carlton Picture House, Goole. Continuous. Prices, 4d. to 1s. Proscenium width, 20 ft. Phone, Thorne 66. Café attached.

THORNLEY (CO. DURHAM), **Pop. 3,380.**
HIPPODROME (BA).—Prop., Denman Picture Houses, Ltd., 123, Regent Street, London, W.1. 1,000 seats. Booked at H.O. Twice nightly. Once Sunday. Sat. Mat. Station, Thornley, L.N.E.R.

THORNTON HEATH (SURREY), **Pop. 10,819.**
PAVILION (BA), High Street.—Prop., W. A. Martin. 570 seats. Booked at Hall. Continuous. Two changes weekly. Prices, 6d. to 1s. 6d. Phone, Thornton Heath 1446. Station, Thornton Heath, S.R.
STATE (WE), London Road.—Props., Blue Halls, Ltd., 4, Lloyds Avenue, London, E.C.3. Royal 6159. 1,893 seats. Booked at H.O. Continuous Pictures and Variety. Prices, 9d. to 2s. Proscenium width, 44 ft. Stage, 20 ft. deep; five dressing-rooms. Variety booked by H. Sheldon's Agency, 26, Charing Cross Road, W.C. Café. Phone, Thornton Heath 2100. Station, Thornton Heath.

THRAPSTON (NORTHANTS), **Pop. 1660.**
PLAZA.—Once nightly, three shows Sat. Prices, 7d. to 1s. 6d.

THROCKLEY (NORTHUMBERLAND).
LYRIC CINEMA (BTP).—Prop., Lyric (Throckley), Ltd., 72, Grey Street, Newcastle. Phone, 20317. Booked at H.O. 860 seats. Prices, 4d. to 1s. Continuous. Twice nightly Sat. Café and Dance Hall attached. Phone, Leamington 173. Station, Newburn, L.N.E.R.

THURCROFT (nr. Rotherham), (YORKS), **Pop. 4,500.**
CINEMA HOUSE (Morrison).—535 seats. Continuous. Two changes weekly. Prices, 4d. to 9d. Station, Rotherham, L.M.S.

THURNSCOE (nr. Rotherham), (YORKS), Pop. 10,540.
CINEMA HOUSE (WE).—Prop., Thurnscoe Cinema Co., Ltd. 728 seats. Booked by Geo. Brocklesby, F.L.A.A., Holywell Lane, Conisborough nr. Rotherham. Phone, Conisborough 29. 780 seats. Continuous. Proscenium width, 18½ ft. Prices, 6d. to 1s. Stations, Hickelton, Thurnscoe (L.N.E.R.) or Darfield, L.M.S.

TIBSHELF (DERBY), Pop. 3,926.
PALACE CINEMA (Imperial).—Lessee, H. W. Hives, A.I.E.E. 400 seats. Picture and Variety. Booked at Hall. One show nightly. Twice Sat. Two changes weekly. Prices, 5d. to 1s. Stage, 17½ ft. deep ; two dressing-rooms. Proscenium width, 28 ft. Phone, Tibshelf 41. Stations, Tibshelf, L.M.S. and L.N.E.R.

TIDESWELL (nr. Buxton), (DERBYSHIRE).
PICTURE HOUSE.—Once nightly, Tues. and Thurs. Two shows Sat. Prices, 3d. to 1s. 3d.

TIDWORTH (HANTS), Pop. 4,840.
ELECTRIC THEATRE (BTH), Church of England Institute.—Prop., Church of England Board for Welfare of Imperial Forces, Bulford Camp, Salisbury. Phone, Bulford 71. Booked at Central Office, Bulford Camp, Salisbury, by R. J. Cooke. Continuous. Prices, 4d. to 1s. 2d. Phone, Tidworth 88. Café attached. Station, Tidworth.
GARRISON THEATRE (BTH).
HIPPODROME (WE).—Prop., A. N. Kendal, Ltd. 845 seats. Booked at 73, South Walls, Winchester. Continuous. Prices, 4d. to 1s. 6d. Café attached. Station, Tidworth, S.R.

TILBURY (ESSEX), Pop. 16,826.
PALACE CINEMA (Mihaly), Tilbury Dock.—400 seats. Booked at Hall. Continuous. Two Changes weekly. Prices, 5d. to 1s. 3d. Stage, 11 ft. deep ; two dressing-rooms. Station, Tilbury Dock, L.M.S., or Motor Transport.
TILBURY DOCK WORKING MEN'S CLUB AND INSTITUTE, Calcutta Road.—400 seats. Shows Mon. and Wed. Pictures and Variety (Sundays). Booked at Club. Price, 6d. Stage, 14 ft. deep ; two dressing-rooms. Dance Hall attached. Phone, Tilbury 102.

TIPTON (STAFFS), Pop. 35,792.
ALHAMBRA (RCA), Didley Rest.—Prop., The Sheridan Film Service, Ltd., 179, Horningbow Street, Burton-on-Trent. 850 seats. Continuous. Prices, 5d. to 1s. Proscenium width, 30 ft. Phone, Tipton 1400. Station, Dudley Port, L.M.S.
CINEMA (Gyrotone), High Street.—Prop., T. Hinkinson and C. Leatham. 380 seats. Booked at Hall. Continuous. Mat., Mon., Thurs. and Sat. Prices, 4d. to 9d. Proscenium width, 24 ft. Station, Tipton, L.M.S.
PICTURE HOUSE (BTH), Princes End.—Prop., Mrs. F. Jones. 500 seats. Booked at Hall. Continuous. Prices, 4d. to 8d. Phone, Tipton 1339. Station, Princes End (Staffs), G.W.R.
REGENT PICTURE HOUSE (WE), Owen Street.— Prop., Associated British Cinemas, Ltd., 30-31, Golden Square, London, W.1. 1,500 seats. Booked at H.O. Continuous. Prices, 4d. to 6d. Proscenium width, 30 ft. Phone, Tipton 1010. Station, Tipton, L.M.S.
VICTORIA CINEMA, Horseby Heath.

TIVERTON (DEVON), Pop. 9,611.
ELECTRIC THEATRE (Picturetone), Newport Street.—Prop., A. O. Ellis. Phone, Torquay

2895. 550 seats. Booked at H.O., "Homeside," Higher Warberry, Torquay. Continuous nightly. Mats., Thurs., and Sat. Phone, Tiverton 119. Station, Tiverton, G.W.R.
TIVOLI (BA).—Props., Eastmond and Hamlin, Ltd. 500 seats. Booked at Hall. Continuous prices, 6d. to 2s. Phone, Tiverton 157. Station, Tiverton, G.W.R.

TODMORDEN (YORKS), Pop. 22,223.
GEM PICTURE THEATRE (AWH), Harrison Street, Cornholme, nr. Todmorden.—Prop., B. Ormerod, 761, Town Hall Buildings, Cornholme. 476 seats. Booked at Hall. Once nightly ; three shows Sat. Prices, 6d. to 9d. Proscenium width, 16 ft. Phone, Cornholme 32. Station, Cornholme, L.M.S.
HIPPODROME (WE), Halifax Road.—Prop., Hartley Cinemas, Ltd. Booked at Manchester. Prices, 6d. to 1s. Phone, Todmorden, 210. Station, Todmorden, L.M.S.
NEW OLYMPIA (WE), Burnley Road.—Prop., H. Hartley. Booked at Manchester. Phone, No. 275. Station, Todmorden.

TOLWORTH (SURREY).
ODEON THEATRE (BTH).—Prop., Odeon (Tolworth), Ltd., Cornhill House, Bennett's Hill, Birmingham. Phone, Midland 2781. Booked at 49, Park Lane, W.1. Prices, 9d. to 2s. Phone, Elmbridge 3863. Station, Surbiton, S.R.

TONBRIDGE (KENT), Pop. 16,332.
CAPITOL (WE).—Prop., Tonbridge Cinemas, Ltd., 30, Gerrard Street, W.1. 641 seats. Booked at H.O. Continuous. Daily Mat. Prices, 7d. to 2s. 5d. Phone, Tonbridge 514. Station, Tonbridge, S.R.
NEW THEATRE (WE).—Prop., F. West. 550 seats. Continuous. Mat., Wed., Thurs. and Sat. Prices, 5d. to 1s. 10d. Station, Tonbridge.
PAVILION (WE), Avebury Avenue.—Prop., A. and C. Theatres, Ltd., Station Road, Redhill, Surrey. Phone, Redhill 104. 800 seats. Continuous. Booked at H.O. Prices, 6d. to 2s. 5d. Phone, Tonbridge 514. Station, Tonbridge, S.R.
RITZ (WE).—Controlled by Union Cinemas, Ltd., 15, Regent Street, W.1, Phone, Whitehall 8484. Booked at H.O. Continuous. Station, Tonbridge, S.R.
STAR CINEMA (WE).—Prop., Tonbridge Cinemas, Ltd., 30, Gerrard Street, W.1. 500 seats. Booked at H.O. Continuous. Prices, 6d. to 2s. Phone, No. 514. Station, Tonbridge, S.R.

TOPSHAM (DEVON) Pop. 3,000.
CINEMA (Morrison).—Prop., H. C. Gould. Booked at Cardiff and London. Prices, 6d. to 1s. 3d. Proscenium width, 25 ft. Stage, 16 ft. deep ; two dressing-rooms. Twice nightly. Dance hall attached. Phone, Topsham 8022. Station, Topsham, S.R.

TORPOINT (CORNWALL), Pop. 3,975.
GEM CINEMA (Imperial).—Prop., Mrs. Bertha E. Strutt. 500 seats. Booked at Hall. Shows, Wed. and Sat., 6 p.m. Mat. Sat. Prices, 7d. to 1s. Stage, 30 ft. deep ; two dressing-rooms. Station, Devonport.

TORQUAY (DEVON), Pop. 46,165.
BURLINGTON PICTURE HOUSE (WE), Union Street.—Prop., Associated British Cinemas, Ltd., 30-31, Golden Square, London, W.1. Phone, Gerrard 7887. 450 seats. Booked at H.O. Three shows daily. Prices, 6d. to 2s. Phone, Torquay 2567. Station, Torre, G.W.R.

CINEDROME (WE), Victoria Road.—Prop., Arthur Rowland. Booked . at Hall. Two shows nightly. Daily Mat. Two changes weekly. Prices, 9d. to 2s. 5d. Phone, Torquay 2585. Station, Torre, G.W.R.

ELECTRIC THEATRE (WE), Union Street.— Prop., Torquay Entertainments, Ltd. Lloyds Bank Chambers., 1, Vaughan Parade, Torquay. Phone, 4061. 1,060 seats. Booked by H.O. Continuous winter. Three shows daily summer season. Prices, 6d. to 2s. Café attached. Phone, Torquay 2146. Station Torre, G.W.R.

Fitted "ARDENTE" Deaf Aids
See page 258

EMPIRE (WE).—W. E. Willis Circuit, Globe Cinema, Albany Road, Penylan, Cardiff. Phone, Cardiff, 3072. 550 seats. Daily Mat. and two evening shows. Prices, 9d. to 2s. Phone, Torquay 2585.

PICTUREDROME (KAMM). 400 seats. (Closed).

REGAL CINEMA (WE).—Prop., Associated British Cinemas, Ltd., 30–31, Golden Square, London, W.1. Phone, Gerrard 7887. 1,600 seats. Booked at Hall. Continuous. Prices, 9d. to 2s. Proscenium width, 38.ft. Café.

COMPTON
ORGAN featured here.

ROYAL THEATRE (WE)—Props., Odeon (Torquay), Ltd., Cornhill House, Bennett's Hill. Birmingham. Phone, Midland 2781. Booked at 49, Park Lane, W.1. Continuous. Prices, 6d. to 2s. Proscenium width, 25 ft. Phone, Torquay 2324.

TUDOR THEATRE (Picturetone), Prop., Tudor Theatre (Torquay), Ltd. 500 seats. Man. Dir., A. O. Ellis. Booked at "Homeside," Higher Warberry, Torquay, Phone, Torquay 2895. Twice nightly. Mats., Wed. and Sat. Phone, Torquay 7704. Station, Torre, Torquay, G.W.R.

TORRINGTON (DEVON), Pop. 2,458.
THE CINEMA (BTH), Church Lane.—Prop., R. Long. Booked at Hall. Once nightly; twice Sat. Prices, 9d. to 1s. 6d, Proscenium width, 20 ft. Station, Torrington, S.R.

TOTNES (DEVON), Pop. 4,525.
CINEMA (BTH).—Prop., H. G. Tapley. 450 seats. Booked at Hall. Prices, 3d. to 2s. Phone, Totnes 158. Station, Totnes, G.W.R.

TOTTINGTON (LANCS), Pop. 6,532.
PALACE CINEMA (BA), Market Street.—Props., J. Harwood and Others. Phone, Bury 546. 480 seats. Booked at Hall. Twice nightly. Prices, 3d. to 9d. Proscenium width, 27 ft. Phone 110. Station, Tottington, L.M.S.

TOTTON (HANTS).
REGENT (BTH).—310 seats. Continuous. Prices, 6d. to 1s. 3d. Station, Totton, S.R., and Southern Counties Road Transport Co.

SAVOY (WE) Junction Road.—Props., Totton Developments Co., Ltd. 733 seats. Booked at Hall. Continuous. Prices, 6d. to 1s. 3d. Proscenium width, 28 ft. Phone, Totton 81116.

TOWCESTER (NORTHANTS), Pop. 2,148.
CINEMA.—Prop. and Man., Cyril A. Hall. Booked at Hall. Prices, 6d. to 1s. 3d. Phone, 76. Station, Towcester, L.M.S.

TOW LAW (CO DURHAM), Pop. 3,550.
PALACE (BTH).

TREDEGAR (MON.), Pop. 23,195.
OLYMPIA (WE). Morgan Street.—Prop., Olympia (Tredegar) Cinemas, Ltd., 5, Melbourne Chambers, Merthyr. Phone, 329. 1,400 seats. Booked at Hall. Continuous, Twice nightly. Prices, 6d. to 1s. Proscenium width 38 ft. Stage, 22 ft.; four dressing rooms. Phone, Tredegar 67.

WORKMEN'S HALL (BA).—Prop., Tredegar Workmen Institute Society. 700 seats. Booked at Cardiff. Continuous. Prices, 6d. to 1s. Proscenium width, 21 ft. Stage, 18 ft. deep; four dressing rooms. Road Transport

TRIMDON COLLIERY (CO. DURHAM).
IMPERIAL.—Lessees, C. J. T. Cinemas, Ltd. Gen. Man., Geo. M. Johnson.

TRIMDON GRANGE (CO. DURHAM). Pop. 5,259.
PICTUREDROME (BTH).—Lessees, C. J. T. Cinemas, Ltd. 450 seats. Gen. Man., Geo. M. Johnson. Booked at H.O. Once nightly; two shows Sat. Prices, 4d. to 8d. Station, Trimdon Grange, L.N.E.R.

VICTORY.—Lessees, C. J. T. Cinemas, Ltd. Gen. Man. Geo. M. Johnson.

TRING (HERTS), Pop. 4,364.
GAIETY CINEMA (AWH), Akeman Street.— Prop., A. C. Powell. 300 seats. Booked at Hall. Continuous. Mat. Sat. Prices, 6d. to 1s. 3d. Phone, Tring 68. Station, Tring, L.M.S.

TROWBRIDGE (WILTS), Pop. 12,011.
NEW CINEMA (BA).—458 seats. Booked at Hall. Prices, 6d. to 1s. 6d. Proscenium width, 28 ft. Phone No. 207. Station G.W.R. and Film Transport.

PALACE (BA), Fore Street.—Prop., Albany Ward Theatres, New Gallery House, 123, Regent Street, London, W.1. Phone, Regent 8080. 660 seats. Booked at H.O. Continuous. nightly, Mon. to Fri. Three shows Sat. Prices 6d. to 1s. 6d. Phone, Trowbridge 117. Station, Trowbridge, G.W.R.

TRURO (CORNWALL), Pop. 11,074.
REGENT (WE).—Prop., George Rees, Bristol 700 seats. Station, Truro, G.W.R.

PALACE THEATRE (WE).—Prop., R. Hill. 450 seats. Phone, Truro 167. Booked at Hall. Once nightly. Mats., Wed. and Sat. Two changes weekly. Prices, 6d. to 1s. 6d.

TUNBRIDGE WELLS (KENT), Pop. 35,367.
GREAT HALL (RCA).—Controlled by Union Cinemas, Ltd., Union House, 15, Regent Street, London, S.W.1. Phone, Whitehall 8484. Booked at H.O. Continuous. Prices, 6d. to 2s. Phone, Tunbridge, Wells 198. Station, Tunbridge Wells Central, S.R.

KOSMOS KINEMA (WE), Calverley Road.—Controlled by Union Cinemas, Ltd., Union House, 15, Regent Street, London, S.W.1. Phone, Whitehall 8484. Booked at H.O. Continuous. Two changes weekly. Prices, 6d. to 2s. Phone, Tunbridge Wells 1020. Station, Tunbridge Wells, S.R.

OPERA HOUSE (WE).—Controlled by Union Cinemas, Ltd., Union House, 15, Regent Street, London, S.W.1. Phone, Whitehall 8484. Booked at H.O. Continuous. Prices, 6d. to 2s. 5d. Films and Variety. Proscenium width, 27 ft. Café attached. Phone, 456. Station, Central.

RITZ (WE).—Controlled by Union Cinemas, Ltd., Union House, 15, Regent Street, London, S.W.1 Phone, Whitehall 8484. Booked at H.O. Continuous. Prices, 6d. to 2s. 5d. Films and

TUNBRIDGE WELLS—Contd.
Variety. Phone, Tunbridge Wells 270.
Restaurant and Ballroom attached. Station,
Tunbridge Wells Central, S.R.
**Fitted "ARDENTE" Stage Amplification
See page 258**

COMPTON
ORGAN featured here.

TUNSTALL (STAFFS), **Pop. 22,494.**
PALACE (BTP) Station Road.—Prop., Councillor
G. H. Barber. Phone, Hanley 253. 1,200
seats. Booked at H.O. Continuous. Mat.,
Sat. Two changes weekly. Prices, 4d. to
1s. 2d. Phone, Tunstall 253. Station, Tunstall, L.M.S.
REGENT (BTP) Hose Street.—Prop., Councillor
G. H. Barber, Palace, Tunstall. Phone,
Hanley 253. 700 seats. Booked at H.O.
Continuous. Two changes weekly. Prices,
4d. to 1s. 2d.
RITZ (WE).—1,612 seats.

TUTBURY (STAFFS), **Pop. 2,500.**
NEW PALLADIUM (RCA) Burton Street, Tutbury,
Burton-on-Trent.—Prop., Sheridan Film Service, Ltd., 179, Horninglow Street, Burton-on-
Trent. Phone, Burton-on-Trent 3324. 550
seats. Booked by S. A. Suffolk at H.O.
Continuous. Prices, 6d. to 1s. 3d. Stage,
13ft. deep. Proscenium width 20 ft. Phone,
Tutbury 6168. Station, Tutbury L.M.S.

TWICKENHAM (MIDDLESEX), **Pop. 39,906.**
LUXOR PICTURE THEATRE (WE) Cross Deep.—
Prop., Joseph Mears, 5, Hill Street, Richmond,
Surrey. Phone, Richmond 2,900. 1,573
seats. Pictures and Variety. Booked at
H.O. Continuous. Prices 9d. to 2s. 5d.
Stage, 17 ft. deep. Two dressing-rooms.
Café attached. Phone, Popesgrove 2835.
Station, Twickenham, S.R.

COMPTON
ORGAN featured here.

THE TWICKENHAM (WE), Richmond Road.—
Prop., Jos. Mears Theatres, Ltd., 5, Hill Street,
Richmond. 1,141 seats. Booked at H.O.
Continuous. Prices, 5d. to 1s. 10d. Café.
Phone Popesgrove 2575. Station, Twickenham, S.R.

COMPTON
ORGAN featured here

TYLDESLEY (LANCS), **Pop. 14,848.**
CARLTON CINEMA (RCA), Johnson Street.—Prop.,
Joseph Wood's Theatres, Ltd. 470 seats.
Booked at Hall. Two shows nightly. Two
changes weekly. Prices, 3d. to 9d. Phone
Atherton 244. Station, Tyldesley, L.M.S.
MAJESTIC CINEMA (WE). Castle Street.—Prop.,
Union Playhouses, Ltd., King Street, Wigan.
972 seats. Booked by T. C. Robinson, Cromford
House, Manchester. Once nightly. Prices,
5d. to 9d. Phone, Atherton 226.
THEATRE ROYAL (RCA), John Street.—Prop.,
Joseph Wood's Theatres, Ltd. 980 seats.
Booked at Carlton Cinema, Tyldesley. Two
shows, Mon. and Sat., one rest of week. Prices
4d. to 9d. Proscenium width, 24 ft. Stage,
40 ft. deep ; eight dressing-rooms. Phone,
Atherton 244. Station, Tyldesley, L.M.S.

TYNE DOCK (Co. DURHAM), **Pop. 20,000.**
CROWN ELECTRIC THEATRE (BTP), Hudson Street.
—Prop., Queen's Grand Cinema Co., 31, Westgate Road, Newcastle-on-Tyne. Phone, South
Shields 13. Two shows nightly. Mats., Wed.
and Sat. Two changes weekly. Prices, 3d.
to 6d. Station, Tyne Dock, L.N.E.R.
IMPERIAL PICTURE HOUSE (BTP).—Props.,
Stanhope (Newcastle-on-Tyne) Cinema Co.,
Ltd., 178, Westgate Road, Newcastle. Phone,
27451. 650 seats. Booked at H.O. Two
shows nightly. Prices, 4d. to 6d. Phone
South Shields 824. Station, Tyne Dock
L.N.E.R.

TYNEMOUTH (NORTHUMBERLAND), **Pop.
64,913.**
PLAZA (WE).—Prop., North Eastern Theatres
Ltd., 11, Bath Lane, Newc.-on-Tyne. 713 seats

UCKFIELD (SUSSEX), **Pop. 3,557.**
THE PICTURE HOUSE (Mihaly).—Prop., V. L.
& E. E. Duffield. 380 seats. Booked at Hall.
Continuous. Two changes weekly. Prices,
6d. to 1s. 6d. Phone, Uckfield 122. Station,
Uckfield, S.R.

ULVERSTON (LANCS), **Pop. 9,285.**
PALLADIUM CINEMA (BTP), Victoria Road.—
Prop., Palladium Cinema (Ulverston), Ltd.,
County Square, Ulverston. 815 seats. Booked
at Hall. Twice nightly, Mon. and Sat. One
show, other evenings. Prices, 4d. to 1s.
Phone, Ulverston 151. Station, Ulverston.

UPMINSTER (ESSEX), **Pop. 3,560.**
CAPITOL (WE).—Prop., Capitol (Upminster), Ltd.,
225, Oxford Street, London, W.1. Phone,
Gerrard 4242. 1,200 seats. Continuous.
Prices, 6d. to 1s. 6d. Café attached. Stage,
18 ft. deep ; four dressing-rooms. Phone,
Upminster 500. Station, Upminster, L.M.S

COMPTON
ORGAN featured here.

UPPERMILL (YORKS) **Pop. 2,000.**
PALACE CINEMA (Picturetone).—Prop. Mrs. A.
Wilkinson. 525 seats. Booked at Manchester.
Once nightly. Two changes weekly. Prices,
4d. to 10d. Station, Saddleworth, L.M.S.

UPPINGHAM (RUTLAND), **Pop. 2,452.**
COSY CINEMA (IMPERIAL).—Lessee, B. J. Wilson,
" Rose Lawn," Uppingham. 500 seats.
Booked at H.O. Continuous evenings.
Occasional Variety. Prices, 6d. to 2s.
Café. Phone, Uppingham 123. Station,
Uppingham, L.M.S.

UPTON-ON-SEVERN (WORCS), **Pop. 2,500.**
MEMORIAL THEATRE, Old Street.—Prop., G. B.
West, Kings Welcome, Battledown, Cheltenham. 300 seats. Occasional Variety. Booked at Birmingham. Continuous. Prices,
7d. to 1s. 3d. Proscenium width, 18 ft.
Stage, 20 ft.; two dressing-rooms. Station,
Upton-on-Severn, L.M.S.

URMSTON (LANCS), **Pop. 9,284.**
EMPRESS CINEMA (WE), Higher Road.—Controlled by Union Cinemas, Ltd., 15, Regent
Street, S.W.1. Phone, Whitehall 8484.
Booked at H.O. Continuous. Prices, 6d. to
1s. Proscenium width, 35 ft. Phone, Urmston 2070. Station, Urmston, L.M.S.

URMSTON PALACE (WE). Railway Road.—Prop., Warston Pictures, Ltd., 20, Brazennose Street, Manchester. Phone, Blackfriars 6965. 900 seats. Booked at 76, Victoria Street, Manchester by C. Ogden. Twice nightly. Prices 6d. to 1s. Proscenium width 35 ft. Stage 10 ft. deep ; two dressing-rooms. Phone, Urmston 2236. Station, Urmston, L.M.S.

USHAW MOOR (Co. DURHAM), Pop. 7,000.
CLUB HALL CINEMA (BTP).—Props., C. Skippen and J. H. Braves, 13, Fair View, Eshwinning. 500 seats. Once nightly. Twice Sat. Prices, 4d. to 6d. Station, Ushaw Moor, L.N.E.R.
EMPIRE (BTP).—Lessee and Gen. Man., J. Hateley. 650 seats. One show nightly. Two on Sat. Pictures and Variety. Stage, 25 ft. deep. Prices, 5d. to 9d. Station, Ushaw Moor, L.N.E.R.

USWORTH (Co. DURHAM), Pop. 7,980.
KING'S HALL (BTH), Station Road.—Prop., Ralph Brown, Southgate, Withington. 490 seats. Booked at Hall. Continuous. Prices, 5d. to 9d. Station, Usworth, L.N.E.R.

UTTOXETER (STAFFS), Pop. 5,907.
ELITE (BA).
QUEEN S CINEMA (Gyrotone).—600 seats. Booked by Prop., A. Thorley at 6, Picknalls, Uttoxeter. Booked at H.O. One show nightly. Twice Sat. and Mat. Prices, 5d. to 1s. 4d. Station, Uttoxeter, L.M.S.

UXBRIDGE (MIDDX.), Pop., 31,866.
LECTURE HALL CINEMA (AWH), R.A.F. Depot.— 700 seats. Two changes weekly. Phone, Uxbridge 1240. Station, Uxbridge, G.W.R.
ODEON THEATRE (BTH).—Prop., Odeon Theatres, Ltd., Cornhill House, Bennett's Hill, Birmingham.—(In course of construction).
REGAL (WE).—Controlled by Union Cinemas, Ltd., Union House, 15, Regent Street, London, S.W.1. Phone, Whitehall 8484. Booked at H.O. Continuous. Prices, 6d. to 2s. 6d. Phone, Uxbridge 909. Station, Uxbridge (Piccadilly Underground).

COMPTON
ORGAN featured here.

ROYAL.
SAVOY (BA), High Street.—Controlled by Union Cinemas, Ltd., 15, Regent Street, S.W.1. Phone, Whitehall 8484. Booked at Hall. Continuous. Prices 6d. to 2s. 4d. Phone, Uxbridge 81. Club attached. Station, Vine Street, G.W.R.

VENTNOR (I. OF W.), Pop. 5,112.
GAIETY (BA).—Prop., Isle of Wight Theatres. Ltd. Booked at Theatre Royal, Ryde. Twice nightly. Mats., Wed. and Sat. Prices, 6d. to 1s. 10d. Phone, Ventnor 263. Station, Ventnor, S.R. Theatre Royal, Ryde, I.O.W.

WADEBRIDGE (CORNWALL), Pop. 2,460.
CINEDROME (Parmeko).—Prop., E. J. & W. E. Pope. 700 seats. Booked at Cinedrome, Liskeard. Phone Liskeard 32. Once nightly. Mat., Sat. Prices, 6d. to 2s. Proscenium width, 30 ft. Phone, Wadebridge 91. Station, Wadebridge, S.R.

WAKEFIELD (YORKS), Pop. 59,115.
CARLTON PICTURE HOUSE (BA), Grove Road.— Prop., Gaumont-British Picture Corpn., Ltd., 123, Regent Street, London, W.1. Phone, Regent 6641. 1,010 seats. Booked at H.O.

Continuous. Two changes weekly. Phone, Wakefield 253511. Prices, 5d. and 6d. Station, Wakefield (Kirkgate), L.M.S.
EMPIRE (BA), Kirkgate.—Props., Gaumont-British Picture Corpn., Ltd., 123, Regent Street, London, W.1. Phone, Regent 6641. 977 seats. Booked at H.O. Continuous. Daily Mats. Prices, 6d. to 1s. Phone-Wakefield 2418. Station, Wakefield (Kirk, gate).
GRAND ELECTRIC THEATRE (Wired). West-gate.—Prop., Wakefield Picture House, Ltd. 800 seats. Continuous. Twice nightly, Saturdays and holidays. Two changes weekly. Prices, 4d. to 9d. Station, Wakefield (West-gate), L.N.E.R. and Kirkgate.
PALACE (Mihaly), Belle Vue, Wakefield.— Prop., Stephen Askew. 900 seats. Pictures. Once nightly. Booked at Leeds. Stage, 16 ft. deep ; three dressing-rooms. Prices, 5d. to 9d. Proscenium width, 24 ft. Station, Wakefield (Kirkgate), L.M.S.
PLAYHOUSE (WE), Westgate.—Props., Wakefield Picture House, Ltd. Gen. Man., Claude Shayler. 1,182 seats. Continuous. Mat. daily. Phone, Wakefield 2840. Prices, 9d. to 1s. 3d.
REGAL.—Props., Associated British Cinemas, Ltd., 30-31, Golden Square, London, W.1.
SAVOY (BTH), Middlestown. Prop., J. Jesson, Town Hall Pictures, Penistone. Phone, 83 350 seats. Prices, 4d. to 1s. Proscenium width, 18 ft. Dance Hall attached. Stations, Horbury and Ossett, L.N.E.R.
CINEMA, Sharlston.
STAR PICTURE HOUSE (BTH), Stanley Road, Eastmoor.—Prop., Star Cinemas (Yorks.),Ltd., 95, Roundhay Road, Leeds. 498 seats. Booked at H.O. Continuous. Prices, 3d. to 9d. Phone, Wakefield 3237. Stations, Wakefield, L.N.E.R. and L.M.S.

WALKDEN (LANCS), Pop. 4,958.
CRITERION PICTURE HOUSE (BTP), Bolton Road.—Lessees, Hyde Cinemas, Ltd. Booked by H. D. Moorhouse Circuit, Imperial Buildings, Oxford Road, Manchester. 700 seats. Booked at H.O. Continuous. Twice nightly Sat. Prices, 3d. to 9d. Phone, Walkden 2470. Proscenium width, 17 ft. Station, Walkden.
PALACE THEATRE (WE).—Props., Oxford Street and Market Street (Manchester) Cinemas. 950 seats. Films booked at 26, Cross Street, Manchester. Variety at Hall. Continuous. Prices, 3d. to 1s. Proscenium width, 30 ft. Stage, 6 ft. deep. Two dressing-rooms. Phone Walkden 2437. Station, Walkden, L.M.S.

WALLASEY (CHESHIRE), Pop. 97,465.
CAPITOL (BTH), Liscard Corner, Liscard.— Prop., Associated British Cinemas, Ltd., 30-31, Golden Square, London, W.1. 1,390 seats. Booked at H.O. Continuous Mon. to Fri. Separate shows Sat. Prices, 4d. to 1s. 3d. Phone, Wallasey 2917. Cafe and Dance Hall attached. All Liverpool Stations.
COLISEUM PICTURE HOUSE (BTH), Wallasey Village.—Prop., Coliseum (Wallasey), Ltd. 600 seats. Booked by G. Prince, Imperial Cinema, Bootle. Continuous. Stage, 40 ft. deep ; 8 dressing-rooms. Prices, 6d. to 1s. 3d. Phone, Wallasey 1079. Station, Wallasey (Grove Road).
COURT PICTURE HOUSE (BA), New Brighton.— Props., The Court Picture House (New Brighton), Ltd. 450 seats. Booked at Hall. Continuous. Mat. daily. Two changes weekly. Prices, 4d. to 1s. Phone, Wallasey 3687. Stations, Liverpool Termini and New Brighton.

WALLASEY—Contd.
GAUMONT PALACE (BA), King Street, Egremont. —Prop., Gaumont-British Picture Corpn. Ltd., 123, Regent Street, London, W.1. Phone, Regent 8080. 700 seats. Booked at H.O. Continuous. Daily Mat. Prices, 4d. to 1s. 3d. Proscenium width 44 ft. Phone, Wallasey 743.

Fitted "ARDENTE" Deaf Aids
See page 258

KING'S CINEMA (BTP), Liscard Road, Seacombe. —Prop., King's Cinema (Wallasey), Ltd. 400 seats. Booked at Liverpool. Continuous. Two changes weekly. Prices, 5d. to 1s. Proscenium width, 24 ft. Stage, 9 ft. deep. Phone, Wallasey 4054. Stations, Liverpool, Lime Street and Central.

LISCARD ELECTRIC PALACE (BTH).—Prop., Liscard Electric Palace, Ltd. Reg. Office, 11-13, Victoria Street, Liverpool. 966 seats. Continuous from 6.30. Mat. daily. Two changes weekly. Prices, 4d. to 1s. 3d. Phone, Wallasey 733. Stations, Lime Street or Central Liverpool.

MARINA CINEMA (BA), Brighton Street.—Prop., General Theatre Corporation, Ltd., 123, Regent Street, London, W.1. 950 seats. Booked at H.O. Continuous. Mat. daily. Two changes weekly. Prices, 4d. to 1s. Phone, Wallasey 756. Stations, Liverpool Termini.

MORETON PICTURE HOUSE (BTH).—Prop., Cheshire Picture Halls, Ltd., Avenue Cinema, Birkenhead. Phone, Birkenhead 3524. Booked at H.O. Continuous, Mat. daily. Prices 7d. to 1s. 3d. Phone, Upton 22. Station, Moreton, Wirral, L.M.S.

QUEEN'S PICTURE HOUSE (WE), Poulton Road, Wallasey.—Prop., Wirral Picturedromes Ltd. 712 seats. Booked at Hall by R. P. Rutherford. Continuous. Daily Mat. Two changes weekly. Prices, 6d. to 1s. Phone, Wallasey 877. Station, Liverpool termini.

ROYAL PICTURE HOUSE (BTP), King Street, Wallasey.—Prop., Wallasey Cinema, Ltd. Man. and Licensee, A. E. Brewer. 650 seats. Booked at Hall. Continuous. Daily Mat Prices, 5d. to 1s. Phone, Wallasey 1260. Stations, Liverpool terminus.

TIVOLI THEATRE (BA), New Brighton.—Prop., Associated Provincial Picture Houses, Ltd., 123, Regent Street, London, W.1. 636 seats.

TOWER THEATRE, New Brighton.—Prop., New Brighton Amusements, Ltd. Head Office, Tower Theatre, Wallasey. Pictures and Variety. Continuous. Booked at Hall. Stage and 12 dressing-rooms. Ballroom. Café and Tea-room attached. Phone, Wallasey 276. Station, New Brighton, L.M.S.

TROCADERO (BA), Victoria Road, New Brighton. —Prop., Gaumont-British Picture Corpn., Ltd., and Provincial Cinematograph Theatres. Ltd., 123, Regent Street, London, W.1. 1,000 seats. Booked at H.O. Continuous. Prices, 6d. to 1s. 3d. Phone, Wallasey 1560. Station, Lime Street, Liverpool, L.M.S.

WALLINGFORD (BERKS), **Pop. 2,840.**
REGAL (RCA).—Controlled by Union Cinemas, Ltd., 15, Regent Street, S.W.1 Phone, Whitehall 8484. Booked at H.O. Continuous. Prices, 6d. to 1s. 6d. Proscenium width, 28 ft. Phone, 1182. Station, Wallingford, G.W.R.

WALLINGTON (SURREY), **Pop. 8,502.**
ODEON THEATRE (BTH).—Prop., Odeon (Wallington), Ltd., Cornhill House, Bennett's Hill, Birmingham. Phone, Midland 2781. Booked

at 49, Park Lane, W.1. Continuous. Prices, 9d. to 2s. Phone, Wallington 1642, Station, Wallington, S.R.

WALLSEND (NORTHUMB.), **Pop. 44,582.**
BOROUGH THEATRE (BA), High Street East.— Lessees, Denman Picture Houses, Ltd. 1,100 seats. Booked at H.O. Prices, 3d. to 9d. Phone, Wallsend 634041. Station, Wallsend, L.N.E.R.

QUEEN'S HALL (BTP), Station Road.—Prop., Mid-Tyne Cinema Co., Ltd. 625 seats. Booked at H.O. Two shows nightly. Phone, Wallsend 254.

RITZ (WE).—Controlled by Union Cinemas, Ltd., 15, Regent Street, London, S.W.1. Phone, Whitehall 8484. Booked at H.O. Prices, 6d. to 1s. 6d. Station, Wallsend-on-Tyne, L.N.E.R.

ROYAL PICTURES (BRP).—Prop., Tyne Picture Houses, Ltd. 650 seats. Booked at H.O. Central Buildings, Station Road, Wallsend-on-Tyne. Two shows nightly. Prices, 4d. to 6d. Two changes weekly. Phone, Wallsend 63566. Station, Wallsend, L.N.E.R.

TYNE PICTURE THEATRE (BTP).—Prop., Tyne Picture Houses, Ltd. 825 seats. Booked at H.O., Central Buildings, Station Road Wallsend-on-Tyne. Two shows nightly. Two changes weekly. Phone, Wallsend 63566. Station, Wallsend, L.N.E.R.

WALMER (KENT), **Pop. 5,324.**
KING'S HALL KINEMA (BTH), North Barrack Road.—Prop., Deal and Walmer Amusements, Ltd., 4 and 5, Park Street, Deal. 350 seats. Bkg. Man., Chas. Collins. Royal Cinema, Deal. Continuous. Two Mats. weekly. Two changes weekly. Prices, 4d. to 1s. 4d. Phone, No. 620. Station, Deal.

WALSALL (STAFFS), **Pop. 102,102.**
CINEMA DE LUXE (WE), Stafford Street.—Prop., T. Birch. 844 seats. Booked at Hall. Continuous. Two changes weekly. Prices, 4d. to 1s. 2d. Phone, Walsall 2515. Station, Walsall, L.M.S.

EMPIRE (WE).—Prop., Thomas Jackson, "Woodlands," Richmond Hill Drive, Bournemouth. 980 seats. Booked at Hall. Continuous. Prices, 6d. to 1s. 3d. Phone, Walsall 4226. Dance Hall attached. Station, Walsall, L.M.S.

FORUM (BTH), Caldmore Green.—Prop., Sheridan Film Service, Ltd., 179, Horninglow Street; Burton-on-Trent. 728 seats. Booked at H.O. Continuous, Mon., Thurs. and Sat., from 2 ; and Tues., Wed. and Fri. from 6. Prices, 6d. to 1s. Phone, Walsall 2618. Station, Walsall (Parcels Office), L.M.S.

GRAND THEATRE (RCA), Park Street.—Prop., Associated British Cinemas, Ltd., 30-31, Golden Square, W.1. 630 seats. Booked at H.O. Continuous. Prices, 3d. and 6d. Phone, Walsall 4217. Station, Walsall, L.M.S.

HER MAJESTY'S THEATRE (WE), Town End Bank.—Prop., Associated British Cinemas, Ltd., 30-31, Golden Square, W.1. 1,050 seats. Continuous. Booked at H.O. Prices, 6d. to 1s. 3d. Proscenium width, 30 ft. Stage, 42 ft. deep ; nine dressing-rooms. Phone, Walsall 4217. Station, Walsall, L.M.S.

IMPERIAL PICTURE HOUSE (WE), Darwell Street. —Prop., Associated British Cinemas, Ltd., 30-31, Golden Square, W.1. 1,150 seats. Booked at H.O. Continuous. Prices, 6d. to 1s. Proscenium width, 30 ft. Phone, Walsall 4217. Station, Walsall (Parcels Office), L.M.S.

PALACE (BTH), The Square.—Prop., Associated British Cinemas, Ltd., 30-31, Golden Square, W.1. 1,600 seats. Continuous. Prices

4d. to 1s. Phone, Walsall 4217. Station, Walsall, L.M.S. (Parcels Office).
PICTURE HOUSE (WE), The Bridge.—Prop., Gaumont-British Picture Corporation, Ltd. 1,646 seats. Booked at H.O. Continuous. Prices, 6d. to 1s. 6d. Café attached. Phone, Walsall 275711. Station, Walsall, L.M.S.
Fitted "ARDENTE" Deaf Aids
See page 258
WURLITZER ORGAN
Installed in this Kinema
PICTURE PALACE, Walsall Wood.—Prop., Mr. Simpson. Two changes weekly. Phone, Brownhills 68. 1,100 seats.

WALTHAM CROSS (HERTS), Pop. 7,116.
EMBASSY.—Props., Shipman & King, M84, Shell Mex House, Strand, W.C.2. (Building.)
REGENT (WE).—Prop., Shipman & King, M84, Shell Mex House, Strand, London, W.C.2. Phone, Temple Bar 5077. Booked at H.O. Continuous. Prices, 6d. to 1s. 10d. Phone, Waltham Cross 144. Station, Waltham Cross, L.N.E.R.

WALTON-ON-NAZE (ESSEX), Pop. 3,066.
KINO CINEMA (BA), Shore Road.—Prop., V. E. H. Cinemas, Ltd., The Lido, Aylsham Road, Norwich. 450 seats. Booked at Hall. Continuous. Prices, 7d. to 1s. 6d. Phone. Walton-on-Naze 99. Station, Walton-on-Naze, L.N.E.R., and Transport.
REGAL (BTH), High Street.—Prop., V.E.H. Cinemas, Ltd., The Lido, Aylsham Road, Norwich. Phone, Norwich 194. 500 seats. Booked at H.O. Continuous. Prices, 7d. to 2s. Phone, Walton 74. Films by Road Transport.

WALTON-ON-THAMES (SURREY), Pop. 17,953.
REGENT CINEMA (Closed).—
THE CAPITOL (WE), High Street.—Prop., The Capitol (Walton-on-Thames), Ltd., 32, Shaftesbury Avenue, London, W.1. 1,100 seats, Booked at H.O. Pictures and Variety. Continuous. Prices, 9d. to 2s. Proscenium width, 40 ft. Stage, 15 ft. deep. Two dressing-rooms. Phone Walton-on-Thames, 870. Station, Walton-on-Thames, S.R.

WANTAGE (BERKS), Pop. 3,424.
WANTAGE CINEMA (AWH), Market Square.—Prop., Rosenthall and Bell. 250 seats. Continuous. Two changes weekly. Prices, 3d. to 1s. 3d. Station, Wantage Road, G.W.R.

WARBOYS (HUNTS), Pop. 1,700.
CINEMA (Gyrotone).—Prop., W. Peck, St. Ives, Hunts. Lessee, C. Symonds, Over, Cambs. Phone, Swavesey 26. Booked at H.O. Once weekly. Prices, 4d. to 1s. 3d. Station, St. Ives (Hunts), L.N.E.R.

WARE (HERTS), Pop. 6,171.
WARE CINEMA (BTH), Amwell End.—Prop., H. Reynolds. 400 seats. Booked at Hall Continuous. Mat. Sat. Station, Ware, L.N.E.R.

WAREHAM (DORSET), Pop. 1,994.
EMPIRE CINEMA (BA), West Street.—Prop., Cecil H. Elgar. 260 seats. Booked at Hall. Once nightly. Twice Sat. Prices, 6d. to 1s. 6d. Phone, Wareham 78. Station, Wareham, S.R.

WARMINSTER (WILTS.), Pop. 5,176.
PALACE THEATRE (AWH).—Lessee, C. Rowe. All communications to Vista Cinema, Westbury, Wilts. Phone, 75. 350 seats. Prices, 6d. to 1s. 6d. Phone, Warminster 169. Station, Warminster, G.W.R. Films by Road Transport.

REGAL (WE).—Props., Regal (Warminster) Ltd. Booked at Plaza, Amesbury, Wilts. Continuous evenings. 700 seats. Prices, 6d. to 1s. 6d. Phone, Warminster 112.

WARRINGTON (LANCS), Pop. 79,322.
EMPIRE (RCA), Buttermarket.—Prop., Warrington Picture House Co., Ltd. 1,400 seats. Booked at Hall. Continuous. Two changes weekly. Prices, 6d. to 1s. 6d. Phone, 532.

NEW GRAND SUPER CINEMA (WE), Bridge Foot.—Prop., Associated British Cinemas, Ltd. 1188 seats. Booked at H.O. Continuous. Mat daily. Prices, 7d. to 1s. 3d. Phone, Warrington 1045. Stations, Bank Quay, Warrington, L.M.S.; and Warrington Central (Cheshire Lines).

COMPTON

ORGAN featured here.

ODEON THEATRE (BTH), Buttermarket Street.—Prop., Odeon (Warrington), Ltd., Cornhill house, Bennett's Hill, Birmingham. Booked at 49, Park Lane, W.1. Continuous. Prices, 6d. to 1s. 6d.

PALACE (BTH), Friars Gate.—Props., Palace and Hippodrome (Warrington), Ltd. Nightly and four Mats. Booked by Macnaughton Vaudeville Circuit, Ltd., Angel Street, Sheffield. Prices, 6d. to 1s. 6d. Phone, 500. Station, Warrington, L.M.S.; and Road Transport.

PAVILION (BTH), Lovely Lane.—Prop., Merrill's Enterprises, Ltd. 500 seats. Continuous. Three Mats. weekly. Two changes weekly. Occasional Variety. Prices, 4d. to 9d. Proscenium width, 22 ft. Phone, Sankey Green 682. Station, Warrington, L.M.S.

PICTUREDROME (WE), Sankey Street.—Prop., Warston Pictures, Ltd., 20, Brazennose Street, Manchester. Phone, Blackfriars 6965. 473 seats. Booked by C. Ogden at 76, Victoria Street, Manchester. Continuous. Prices, 6d. to 1s. Phone, Warrington 3462. Stations, Warrington (Central) and Bank Quay, L.M.S. Films by Doyle Auto Service.

PICTURE HOUSE (WE).
PREMIER CINEMA (PTA), Powell Street, Latchford.—Prop., Latchford Premier Cinema, Ltd. 495 seats. Booked at Hall. Continuous. Two shows Sat. and holidays. Prices 4d. to 1s. Phone Warrington 345. Proscenium width 18 ft. Station Latchford L.M.S.

QUEEN'S PICTURE HOUSE (WE) Orford Lane.—Prop. Orford Lane (Warrington) Picture House Ltd. 2 & 4, Harrington Street, Liverpool. Phone, Bank 3784. 1,179 seats. Booked by R. P. Rutherford at Queen's P.H. Poulton Road, Seacombe. Continuous. Daily Mat. Two changes weekly. Prices, 4d. to 1s. Proscenium width, 33 ft. Phone, Warrington 483. Stations, Central, L.N.E.R.; and Bank Quay, L.M.S.

REGENT (WE), Scotland Road.—Prop., Regent (Warrington), Ltd. Booked at 51, North John Street, Liverpool. Phone, Bank 610. 600 seats. Continuous. Prices, 4d. to 1s. 3d. Phone, 1199. Station, Bank Quay, L.M.S.; and Central, L.N.E.R.

RITZ (WE).—Controlled by Union Cinemas, Ltd., 15, Regent Street, S.W.1. Phone, Whitehall 8484. Booked at H.O. Continuous. Station, Warrington, L.M.S.

STAR KINEMA (WE), Church Street.—Prop., Warston Pictures, Ltd., 20, Brazennose Street, Manchester. 627 seats. Booked by G Ogden, at 76, Victoria Street, Manchester.

X2

WARRINGTON—Contd.
Twice nightly. Mats. daily, except Wed. and Fri. Prices, 3d. to 9d. Stage, 6 ft. deep ; two dressing-rooms. Phone, Warrington 534. Station, Central, L.M.S.

WARSOP (NOTTS), Pop. 10,748.
PICTURE HOUSE (WE).—Prop., Warsop Theatre Co., Ltd., High Street, Warsop. Phone, 8. 769 seats. Booked at H.O. Twice nightly. Prices, 6d. to 1s. Proscenium width, 20 ft. Phone, Warsop 50. Station, Warsop, L.N.E.R.

WARWICK (WARWICK), Pop. 13,459.
COUNTY THEATRE (WE).—Prop., Associated British Cinemas, Ltd., 30-31, Golden Square, London, W.1. 699 seats. Pictures, Varieties and Plays. Continuous. Phone, Warwick 176. Station, Warwick, G.W.R. and L.M.S.
GRAND CINEMA (RCA), Chapel End.—Prop.. Sheridan Film Service, Ltd., 179, Horning-glow Street, Burton-on-Trent. Phone, 3324-450 seats. Continuous. Prices, 5d. to 9d. Booked at H.O. Station Nuneaton.

WASHINGTON (Co. DURHAM), Pop. 16,989.
ALEXANDRA THEATRE (Edibell).
GLEBE CINEMA (BTH), Derwent Terrace, Washington Station.—Prop., North Eastern Cinema de Luxe, Ltd. 657 seats. Booked at Newcastle Prices, 6d. to 1s. Proscenium width, 25 ft. Stage, 8 ft. deep ; two dressing-rooms. Phone, Washington 47. Station, Washington, L.N.E.R.
REGAL CINEMA.

WATCHET (SOMERSET), Pop. 1,936.
WATCHET PUBLIC HALL (Mihaly).—Prop., Watchet Public Hall Co. Secretary, F. Penny, Swain Street, Watchet. 300 seats. Once nightly. Occasional Variety. Prices, 6d. to 1s. 3d. Phone, Watchet 32. Station, Watchet, G.W.R.

WATERFOOT (LANCS), Pop. 3,145.
KING'S HALL (WE), Booth Street.—Prop., The Valley Entertainments (Waterfoot), Ltd. Reg. Office, Regal, Bacup. 752 seats. One show nightly ; three on Sat. Prices, 4d. to 1s. Stage, 18 ft. deep ; four dressing-rooms. Phone, Rosendale 487. Station, Waterfoot, L.M.S.

WATFORD (HERTS), Pop. 56,799.
CARLTON CINEMA (WE).—Prop., Watford Amusements, Ltd., 11, Berkeley Court, Baker Street, London, W.1. Phone, Welbeck 2301. 1,139 seats. Booked at H.O. Continuous. Prices, 6d. to 1s. 6d. Phone, Watford 4855. Station, Watford, L.M.S.
NEW COLISEUM (BTH), St. Alban's Road.—Props., Davies, Davies and Silverstone, 23, Meard Street, W.1. 960 seats. Booked at H.O. Continuous. Prices, 6d. to 2s. Phone, Watford 5112.
ODEON THEATRE (RCA), Parade, High Street.—Prop., Odeon (Watford), Ltd., Cornhill House, Bennett's Hill, Birmingham. Phone, Midland 2781. Continuous. Pictures and Variety. Prices, 6d. to 2s. 6d. Stage, 11 ft. deep ; four dressing-rooms. Café attached. Phone, Watford 2451. Stations, Watford, L.M.S., and Met.

COMPTON
ORGAN featured here.

NEW REGAL THEATRE (RCA), King Street.—Prop., Courtwood Cinemas, Ltd., 361, City Road, E.C.1. Phone, Clerkenwell 5126.

1,286 seats. Booked at H.O. Continuous. Prices, 6d. to 2s. Phone, Watford 3568. Station, Watford High Street, L.M.S.
Fitted "ARDENTE" Deaf Aids
See page 258

RITZ.—Prop., L. Morris, 52, Shaftesbury Avenue, London, W.1. 2,000 seats.
SUPER (BTP).
THE EMPIRE (WE), Market Street.—Prop., Watford Entertainments, Ltd. 800 seats. Booked at Hall. Continuous. Prices, 6d. to 1s. 10d. Phone, Watford 3093. Station, Watford Junction, L.M.S.

WATH-ON-DEARNE (YORKS), Pop. 13,653.
GRAND THEATRE (WE).—Prop., Mexborough Theatres, Ltd., Empire, Swinton Road, Mexborough. 698 seats. Pictures and Variety. Booked at H.O. Two shows nightly and Mats. Prices 4d. to 1s. Stage, 29 ft. deep ; eight dressing-rooms. Phone, Wath 18.
MAJESTIC CINEMA THEATRE (WE), High Street.—Prop., Wath Theatres, Ltd. 1,089 seats. Booked at Hall. Continuous. Pictures and Variety. Stage, 30 ft. deep. Prices, 6d. to 1s. 1d. Proscenium width, 28 ft. Stage, 30 ft. deep ; eight dressing-rooms. Phone, Wath 81. Station, Wath-on-Dearne, L.M.S. and L.N.E.R., and Road Transport.

WATTON (NORFOLK), Pop. 1,436.
REGAL.—Booked at 54, Chevallier Street, Ipswich.
WAYLAND HALL CINEMA (Morrison).—Prop., Mrs. G. Yeates. 200 seats. Booked at Cinema, Attleborough. Once nightly. Twice Sat. Prices, 6d. to 1s. 3d. Road Transport.

WEALDSTONE (MIDDX.), Pop. 27,001.
CORONET PICTURE THEATRE (Kamm), High Street.—Prop., Peerless Pictures, Ltd., 14-16, Regent Street, S.W.1. 300 seats. Booked at Hall. Continuous. Prices, 6d. to 1s. 6d. Phone, Harrow 1087. Stations, Harrow and Wealdstone, L.M.S.
ODEON THEATRE (BTH).—Props., Odeon (Wealdstone), Ltd., Cornhill House, Bennett's Hill, Birmingham. Phone, Midland 2781. Continuous. Booked at 49, Park Lane, W.1. Prices, 6d. to 2s. Proscenium width, 44 ft. Stage, 14 ft. deep ; two dressing-rooms. Café attached. Phone, Harrow 2981. Station, Wealdstone, L.M.S.

COMPTON
ORGAN featured here.

WEASTE (LANCS), Pop. 19,674.
WEASTE PICTURE HALL (WE), Eccles New Road, Pendleton.—Prop., Swinton Entertainments, Ltd., J. F. Emery, 26, Cross Street, Manchester. Phone, Blackfriars 7876. 896 seats. Booked at Manchester. Continuous evenings. Mats. Mon. and Thurs. Three shows Sat. Prices, 3d. to 1s. Station, Weaste, L.M.S.

WEDNESBURY (STAFFS), Pop. 31,534.
HIPPODROME.—800 seats.
IMPERIAL PICTURE PALACE (BTH), Upper High Street.—Prop., Wednesbury Picture Palace Co., Ltd. 500 seats. Booked at Palace Theatre, Bilston. Continuous. Three Mats. weekly. Two changes weekly. Prices, 4d. to 1s. Phone, Wednesbury 0220.

PICTURE HOUSE (RCA), Walsall Street.—Prop., Associated Provincial Picture Houses, Ltd. 851 seats. Booked at H.O. Continuous. Prices, 6d. to 1s. 3d. Phone, Wednesbury 0127. Station, Wednesbury, G.W.R.

RIALTO (BTH), Earp's Lane.—Prop., Associated British Cinemas, Ltd., 30-31, Golden Square, W.I. Phone, Gerrard 7887. Booked at H.O. Continuous. Mats., Mon., Thurs. and Sat. Prices, 3d. to 1s. Proscenium width, 40 ft. Phone, Wednesbury 0058. Station, Wednesbury, G.W.R. and L.M.S.

WEDNESFIELD (STAFFS), Pop. 9,333.

IDEAL THEATRE (Gyrotone).—Prop., John France, Ivy Villa, Trench, Wellington, Salop. Phone, Oakengates, 88. Booked at Trench Continuous. 400 seats. Prices, 5d. to 11d. Station, Wolverhampton.

REGAL (BTH), High Street.—Prop., Regal Cinema (Wednesfield), Ltd. 1,000 seats. Prices, 6d. to 1s. Station, Wolverhampton, L.M.S.

WELLING (KENT), Pop. 5,285.

ODEON THEATRE (BTH).—Props., Odeon (Welling), Ltd., Cornhill House, Bennett's Hill, Birmingham. Phone, Midland 2781. Booked at 49, Park Lane, W.I. Prices, 6d. to 1s. 6d. Phone, Bexleyheath 182. Station, Welling, S.R.

WELLINGBOROUGH (NORTHANTS), Pop. 21,221.

LYRIC.

COMPTON
ORGAN featured here.

PALACE (WE).—Prop., Palace Co. (Wellingborough), Ltd. Man. Dir., W. F. J. Hewitt. 974 seats. Pictures and Varieties. Booked at H.O. by W. F. J. Hewitt. Two shows nightly. Phone, Wellingborough 184.

REGAL (WE).—Prop., Palace Co. (Wellingborough), Ltd. Phone, Wellingborough 184. 700 seats. Man. Dir., W. F. J. Hewitt. Booked at H.O. Continuous. Twice nightly Sat. Mats. Mon. and Thurs. Two changes weekly. Prices, 6d. to 1s. 6d. Proscenium width 22 ft. Phone, Wellingborough 417.

SILVER CINEMA (BTH), Silver Street.—Prop., Wellingborough Cinema Co., Ltd., The Palace, Letchworth, Herts. Phone, Letchworth 721. Booked at H.O. Continuous. Twice nightly Sat. Two changes weekly. Prices, 6d. to 1s. 4d. Phone, Wellingborough 153.

WELLINGTON (SALOP), Pop. 8,185.

CINEMA (BA). 260 seats.
EMPIRE CINEMA, Stirchley.
GRAND THEATRE (WE). 966 seats.
PAVILION THEATRE.
TOWN HALL CINEMA (BTH).—Props., Miles, Evans and Stewart. 500 seats. Booked at Hall and Birmingham. Continuous. Prices, 4d. to 1s. 3d. Proscenium width, 20 ft. Station, Wellington, Salop, W.R.

WELLS (SOMERSET), Pop. 5,408.

PALACE THEATRE (Parmeco), Priory Road.— Props., E. S. L. and E. H. Collins, Little Burcott House, Wells. Phone, Wells 91. 450 seats. Booked at Hall. One show nightly Three on Sat. Prices, 6d. to 1s. 6d. Proscenium width, 21 ft. Stage, 20 ft. deep; eight dressing-rooms. Phone, Wells 127. Station, Wells, G.W.R., and S.R., and Road Transport.

REGAL (BTP).—600 seats. Booked at "Woodlands," London Road, Salisbury. 600 seats. Continuous each evening except Tues. and Fri. Prices, 6d. to 1s. 6d. Occasional Variety. Proscenium width, 28 ft. Stage, 45 ft. deep; four dressing-rooms. Phone, 195. Station, Wells, S.R. and S. & D.

WELLS-NEXT-THE-SEA (NORFOLK), Pop 2,505.

CENTRAL (AWH) Clubbs Lane.—Prop., Cyril A. Claxon, Holkham Road, Wells. 310 seats. Booked at Hall, Nightly at 7.30. Twice Sat. Dance Hall attached. Phone, 24. Station, Wells-next-the-Sea, L.N.E.R. and Transport.

WELWYN GARDEN CITY (HERTS), Pop. 8,585.

WELWYN THEATRE (BTH).—Prop., Shipman & King, M 8c, Shell Mex House, Strand, W.C.2. Phone, Temple Bar 5077. Booked at H.O. Continuous nightly. Mat., Mon. and Sat. Prices, 6d. to 1s. 10d. Phone, Welwyn Garden 456. Station, Welwyn Garden City.

WEM (SALOP), Pop. 2,157.

CINEMA (AWH) Town Hall.—Props., Cosy Cinemas, Dawley, Ltd. 480 seats. Separate performances. Prices, 3d. to 1s. 3d. Proscenium width, 18 ft. Dance Hall attached. Station, Wem, Salop.

WEMBLEY (MIDDX.), Pop. 48,546.

CAPITOL CINEMA (WE), Empire Way.— Prop., Associated Theatre (Wembley), Ltd., Controlled by County Cinemas, Ltd., Dean House, Dean Street, London, W.I. 1,637 seats. Booked at H.O. Continuous. Prices, 6d. to 2s. Café and Dance Hall attached. Phone, Wembley 3027. Station, Wembley Park.

COMPTON
ORGAN featured here.

MAJESTIC (WE), High Road.—Prop., Associated Theatre (Wembley), Ltd. Controlled by County Cinemas, Ltd., Dean House, Dean Street, London, W.I. 1,906 seats. Booked at H.O. Continuous. Prices, 6d. to 2s. Proscenium width, 48 ft. Café and Dance Hall attached. Phone, Wembley 3025. Station, Wembley, L.M.S.

COMPTON
ORGAN featured here.

REGAL.—Props., Associated British Cinemas, Ltd., 30-31, Golden Square, London, W.I. Phone, Gerrard 7887.
Fitted "ARDENTE" Deaf Aids
See page 258

WEMBLEY HALL CINEMA (RCA), High Road.— Prop., Nora Thomson. 1,050 seats. Booked at Hall. Continuous. Two changes weekly. Prices, 6d. to 1s. 6d. Phone, Wembley 4694. Station, Wembley Hill.

WENDOVER (BUCKS), Pop. 2,024.

R.A.F. CAMP THEATRE, (BTP) Halton Camp.— Prop., R.A.F. 1,000 seats. Booked at Hall. One show nightly. Three changes weekly. Prices, 6d. to 1s. 6d. Phone, Wendover 107. Station, Wendover, L.N.E.R.

WEOBLEY (HEREFORD), Pop. 900.

CINEMA.—Prop., F. Jones.—Booked at Birmingham. One show per week. Prices 6d. to 1s. 2d. Dance Hall attached.

WEST BROMWICH (STAFFS), Pop. 81,281.

HILL TOP PICTURE HOUSE (BTH).—Prop., Reel Academy, Ltd. 750 seats. Booked at Hall by J. Robbins. Continuous. Prices, 2d. to 8d. Phone, Wednesbury 0218. Stations, Wednesbury, L.M.S., and West Bromwich, G.W.R.

WEST BROMWICH—Contd.

IMPERIAL PICTURE HOUSE (WE), Spen Lane.—Prop., Picture House (West Bromwich), Ltd. 928 seats. Booked at Hall. Continuous. Two changes weekly. Prices, 6d. to, 1s. 3d. Phone, West Bromwich 0192. Station, West Bromwich.

PALACE (WE), High Street.—Prop., Palace Picture Co. 920 seats. Continuous. Prices, 6d. to 1s. 3d. Phone, West Bromwich 0358. Station, West Bromwich, G.W.R.

PLAZA SUPER CINEMA (RCA), Paradise Street.—Prop., Associated British Cinemas, Ltd., 30-31, Golden Square, W.1. Phone, Gerrard 7887. 1,100 seats. Booked at H.O. Continuous. Prices, 5d. to 1s. 3d. Stage, 30 ft. deep; six dressing-rooms. Phone, West Bromwich 0030. Station, West Bromwich, G.W.R.

QUEEN'S PICTURE HOUSE (BTP).—Prop., T. Leach. 1.400 seats. Booked at Hall. Continuous. Mat. daily. Phone, West Bromwich 0351. Station, West Bromwich, G.W.R.

ST. GEORGE'S PICTURE HOUSE (BTP), Paradise Street.—Prop., T. Leach. 700 seats. Booked at Queen's Picture House. Continuous. Mat. daily. Prices, 3d. to 1s.

TOWER.—Props., Associated British Cinemas, Ltd., 30-31, Golden Square, London, W.1.

COMPTON
ORGAN featured here.

WESTBURY (WILTS), Pop. 4,044.

VISTA CINEMA (AWH).—Prop. and Man., C Rowe. 440 seats. Booked at Hall. One show nightly. Three on Sat. Prices, 6d. to 1s. 6d. Phone, Westbury 75. Station, Westbury, G.W.R.

WESTBURY ON TRYM.

CARLTON CINEMA (BA). 850 seats.

WESTCLIFF-ON-SEA (ESSEX), Pop. 106,000.

KING'S CINEMA (BA), Hamlet Court Road.—Prop., Ashbys Grand Halls, Ltd. 800 seats, Booked at Hall. Continuous. Prices, 6d. to 1s. 6d. Phone, Southend 3263. Station, Westcliff-on-Sea, L.M.S., or Motor Transport.

MASCOT CINEMA (RCA), 511, London Road.—Prop., Mascot Cinemas. Ltd. 1,300 seats. Booked at Hall. Continuous, Sundays at 8 p.m. Prices 6d. to 1s. 6d. Phone, Southend 3600. Station, Westcliff-on-Sea, L.M.S., or Motor Transport.

See also Southend-on-Sea.

WEST CORNFORTH (CO. DURHAM), Pop. 6,400.

CLUB HALL CINEMA (BTH).—(Closed.)

WESTERHAM (KENT), Pop. 3,170.

SWAN PICTURE HALL (BA).—Prop. and Man., S. G. Outwin. 240 seats. Booked at Hall. Two shows Mon., Thurs. and Sat., once rest of week. Prices, 6d. to 1s. 9d. Phone, Westerham 109. Station, Westerham, S.R.

WESTGATE (CO. DURHAM).

TOWN HALL CINEMA, St. John's Chapel.

WESTGATE (KENT), Pop. 5,100.

CARLTON CINEMA (RCA).—Prop., Carlton Cinema (Westgate), Ltd. 490 seats. Booked at Hall. Continuous and 4 mats. weekly. Prices, 6d. to 1s. 6d Proscenium width, 30 ft. Phone, Westgate 322. Station, Westgate-on-Sea, S.R.

WEST HARTLEPOOL (CO. DURHAM), Pop. 68,134.

EMPIRE THEATRE (WE), Lynn St.—Prop., West Hartlepool Empire Palace Co., Ltd. 1,818 seats. Booked at Regal, Washington. Two shows nightly. Daily mat. Prices, 5d. to 1s. 3d. Phone, West Hartlepool 2116. Station, West Hartlepool, L.N.E.R.

GAIETY (WE), (late Palace Theatre).—Prop., North Eastern Entertainments, Ltd. 750 seats.

HIPPODROME (RCA), Lambton Street.—Prop., F. H. Pailor. 900 seats. Booked at Newcastle-on-Tyne. Twice nightly. Daily Mat. Prices, 5d. to 1s. 2d. Phone, West Hartlepool 2326.

MAJESTIC.—Props., Majestic Cinema (West Hartlepool), Ltd.

NORTHERN PICTURE HALL (BTH), York Rd.—Prop., Northern Pictures Ltd. 950 seats. Booked at Hall. Two shows nightly. Two changes weekly. Prices, 3d. to 1s. 3d. Phone, West Hartlepool 2714. Station, West Hartlepool.

PALLADIUM (WE), Northgate Street.—Prop., Palladium (Hartlepool), Ltd. 728 seats. Booked by Thompson's Enterprises, Ltd., 4, Palladium Bldgs., Eastbourne Road, Middlesbrough. Two shows daily. Prices, 3d. to 1s. Proscenium width, 20 ft. Phone, Hartlepool 6001. Station, East Hartlepool L.N.E.R,

PICTURE HOUSE (WE), Stockton Street.—Prop., North of. England Cinemas. ·2,055 seats. Booked at H.O. Continuous nightly. Daily Mat. Prices, 5d. to 1s. 6d. Café. Phone, West Hartlepool 203311.

QUEENS CINEMA (RCA).—Prop., Hartlepool Entertainments, Ltd. 900 seats. Twice nightly. Prices, 4d. to 1s. Phone, Hartlepool 6212.

RITZ, West Hartlepool.—Controlled by Union Cinemas, Ltd., Union House, 15, Regent Street, London, S.W.1. Phone, Whitehall 8484. Booked at H.O.

ROYAL ELECTRIC THEATRE (RCA), Whitby Street. —Lessee, Electric Theatre (W. Hartlepool), Ltd. 900 seats. Gen. Man., W. Reynolds. Three shows daily. Prices, 4d. to 1s. Phone, West Hartlepool 2049.

WEST END PICTURE HOUSE (BA), Collingwood Road.—Prop., West End Pictures, Ltd. 560 seats. Booked at Newcastle and Hall by Geo. B. Atkinson. Twice nightly. Mat., Sat. Prices, 4d. to 9d. Phone, West Hartlepool 2318. Station, West Hartlepool.

WESTHOUGHTON (LANCS.), Pop. 16,018.

EMPIRE (BTH), Market Street.—Prop., J. F. Emery, Cinema Circuit, Midland Bank House, 26, Cross Street, Manchester. Booked at H.O. 780 seats. Continuous nightly, two on Sat. Mats., Mon., ·Thurs. and Sat. Two changes weekly. Prices, 4d. to 1s. Phone, 174.

PALACE (WE), Church Street.—Prop., Marks. Circuit Cinemas, 6. St. Mary's Gate, Manchester. Phone, Blackfriars 4078. 800 seats. Continuous nightly. Booked at H.O. Two changes weekly. Prices, 4d. to 1s.. Billiard Hall attached. Phone 116. Station, Westhoughton, L.M.S.

WEST KIRBY (CHESHIRE), Pop. 6,511.

TUDOR (WE). Prop., K. & W. Cinemas Ltd. 1,000 seats. Continuous. Prices, 6d. to 1s. 3d. Phone, Hoylake 1192. Station, West Kirby, L.M.S.

WESTON-SUPER-MARE (SOMERSET), Pop. 28,555.

CENTRAL PICTURE HOUSE (RCA). 695 seats. Oxford Street. Booked at Hall. Continuous. Prices 6d. to 2s. Phone, Weston-super-Mare 474.

KNIGHTSTONE PAVILION (BTH).—Prop., Urban District Council. Lessee and Man., Gerald Alexander. 1,000 seats. Booked by G

Alexander at Pavilion. Occasional shows Prices, 6d. to 1s. 6d. Phone, Weston-super-Mare 75. Station, Weston-super-Mare, G.W.R.

ODEON THEATRE (BTH).—Props., Odeon (Weston-super-Mare), Ltd., Cornhill House, Bennett's Hill, Birmingham. Phone, Midland 2781. Booked at 49, Park Lane, W.1. Prices, 9d. to 2s. Stage, 15 ft. deep ; two dressing-rooms. Phone, Weston 1784. Station, Weston-super-Mare, G.W.R.

COMPTON

ORGAN featured here.

REGENT CINEMA (WE), Regent Street.—Prop., Gaumont-British Pictures Corpn., Ltd., 123, Regent Street, London, W.1. Phone, Regent 6641. 1,061 seats. Booked at H.O. Continuous. Café attached. Prices, 6d. to 1s. 6d. Phone, Weston-super-Mare 237.
Fitted "ARDENTE" Deaf Aids See page 258

TIVOLI (WE), Boulevard.—Prop., George Vickery, Ltd., Head Office, Taunton. 626 seats. Continuous. Prices, 9d. to 1s. 6d. Station, Weston-super-Mare, G.W.R.

WEST STANLEY (CO. DURHAM), Pop. 25,090.
ALBERT HALL (WE), Front Street.—Prop , Robert Reay, 11, Bath Lane, Newcastle-on-Tyne. Phone, Central 3703. 850 seats. Booked at H.O. by Prop. Two shows nightly. Prices, 4d. to 8d. Station, Shield Row, L.N.E.R.
NEW PAVILION.—Prop., T. C. Craven.
THEATRE ROYAL.—Prop., Robert Reay, 11, Bath Lane, Newcastle-on-Tyne. Booked at H.O. by Prop. Revue, Drama, Variety, Pictures. Twice nightly. Stage 28 ft. deep. Café attached. Prices, 3d. to 1s. 3d. Phone. Stanley 46. Station, Shield Row, L.N.E.R.

WEST WICKHAM (KENT), Pop. 6,230.
PLAZA (WE), General Cinema Theatres, Ltd., 19, Albemarle Street, W.1. 1,000 seats. Booked at H.O. Continuous. Prices, 9d. to 2s. 4d. Phone, Springpark 2059. Station, West Wickham, S.R.

WETHERBY (YORKS), Pop. 2,281.
PICTURE HOUSE (Eastern).—Prop., Wetherby Picture House Co. 500 seats. Booked at Leeds. Once nightly. Prices, 6d. to 1s. 6d. Phone, Wetherby 158. Station, Wetherby, L.M.S.

WEYBRIDGE (SURREY), Pop. 7,359.
COUNTY CINEMA (WE), Church Street.—Props., County Cinemas, Ltd., Dean House, Dean Street, London, W.1. Phone, Gerrard 4543. 461 seats. Booked at H.O. Continuous daily. Prices, 6d. to 2s. Café. Phone, Weybridge 556. Station, Weybridge, S.R. and Road Transport.
ODEON THEATRE (BTH).—Prop., Odeon (Weybridge) Ltd., Cornhill House, Bennett's Hill, Birmingham. Phone, Midland 2781. Booked at 49, Park Lane, W.1. Continuous. Prices, 6d. to 2s. 6d. Phone, Weybridge 1140. Station, Weybridge.

WEYMOUTH (DORSET), Pop. 21,982.
BELLE VUE CINEMA (BA).—Prop., Albany Ward Theatres Ltd. Continuous. Two changes weekly. Prices, 7d. to 1s. 6d. Phone, Weymouth 393. Station, Weymouth, G.W.R. and S.R.

ODEON THEATRE (BTH).—Prop., Odeon (Weymouth) Ltd., Cornhill House, Bennett's Hill, Birmingham. Phone, Midland 2781. Booked at 49, Park Lane, W.1. Prices, 9d. to 2s. Phone, Weymouth 847.
PAVILION (BTH).—900 seats.
REGENT THEATRE AND DANCE HALL (WE).—Prop., Provincial Cinematograph Theatres, Ltd., New Gallery House, 123, Regent Street, London, W. Phone, Regent 8080. 1,200 seats. Booked at H.O. Three shows daily. Prices, 9d. to 2s. 6d. Proscenium width, 38 ft. Stage, 30 ft. deep ; 8 dressing rooms. Café and Dance Hall attached. Phone, Weymouth 180.
Fitted "ARDENTE" Deaf Aids See page 258

WHALEY BRIDGE (CHESHIRE), Pop. 8,500.
PRINCES PALACE (Gramo-Radio).—Prop., W. E. Tyler. 475 seats. Two changes weekly. Station, Whaley Bridge.

WHEATLEY HILL (CO. DURHAM), Pop. 6,000.
MINERS' HALL (Wirephone and Echo).—Lessee, Mrs. M. G. Snaith, 2, Granville Terrace, Wheatley Hill. 650 seats. Booked at Newcastle-on-Tyne. Once nightly. Prices, 3d. to 8d. Station, Thornley, L.N.E.R.

PALACE THEATRE (RCA).—Props., J. Hateley, 9, Alexandra Terrace, Wheatley Hill. 850 seats. Booked at Hall. Once nightly, twice Mon. and Sat. Occasional variety. Prices, 3d. to 1s. Proscenium width, 22 ft. Stage, 24 ft. deep ; four dressing-rooms. Phone, Thornley 9. Station, Thornley.

WHITBY (YORKS), Pop. 11,441.
COLISEUM.—Twice nightly. Mat. if wet. Two changes weekly. Prices, 5d. to 1s.
EMPIRE (WE), Station Square.—Prop., Whitby Empire Electric Theatre, Ltd. 657 seats. Booked at Hall by Man. Continuous from 6.15. Mat. daily at 2.30. Prices: Summer, 9d. to 1s. 6d. Winter, 7d. to 1s. 3d. Phone, Whitby 94. Station, Whitby, L.N.E.R.
WATERLOO CINEMA (BTH).—500 seats. Twice nightly. Mat. Sat. Two changes weekly. Prices, 5d. to 1s.

WHITCHURCH (HANTS.).
PICTURE HOUSE (AWH), London Street.—Prop., David Smith and Partners. 450 seats. Booked at London. Once nightly ; three on Sat. Prices, 6d. to 1s. 6d. Proscenium width, 12½ ft. Phone, Whitchurch 43. Station, Whitchurch, S.R. and G.W.R.

WHITCHURCH (SALOP) Pop. 6,016.
GRAND CINEMA.—(Closed.)
PALLADIUM CINEMA (BTH).—Prop., T. E. Markham, Ye Olde Wyche Theatre, Nantwich. Phone, Nantwich 5338. 800 seats. Booked by Prop. at H.O. Continuous. Prices, 6d. to 1s. 6d. Phone, Whitchurch 132.
REGENT (WE).—450 seats.

WHITEFIELD (LANCS.), Pop. 9,107.
MAYFAIR (BA), Bury Old Road.—Props., Essrow Cinemas, Ltd. 1,500 seats. Continuous, Mon. to Fri. Twice Sat. Prices, 6d. to 1s. 3d. Proscenium width, 44 ft. Phone, No. 2201/2. Café.

PALACE PICTURE HOUSE (BA).—Prop., Red Rose Cinemas, Ltd. 800 seats. Pictures and Variety. Booked at Hall. Continuous, Mon. to Fri. Two shows Sat. Prices, 5d. to 1s. Phone, Whitefield 2437. Station, Besses-o'-th'-Barn, L.M.S.

WHITEHAVEN (Cumb.), **Pop. 21,142.** ·
EMPIRE THEATRE (WE).—Prop., Empire
(Whitehaven), Ltd., Hippodrome, Working-
ton. Phone, Workington 194. 927 seats.
Booked at H.O. by Morris Maud. Two shows
nightly. Prices, 3d. to 1s. Station, White-
haven, L.M.S.
GAIETY PICTURE HOUSE (WE).—Lessee, Alan V.
Branford. 1,400 seats. Booked at Hall.
Twice nightly. Prices, 3d. to 1s. Phone,
Whitehaven 312.
QUEEN'S CINEMA (BA).—Licensee, A.V. Branford,
1,100 seats. Two shows nightly. Phone,
Whitehaven 124.

WHITLEY BAY (Northumb.), **Pop. 11,436.**
EMPIRE CINEMA (BA), Esplanade.—Prop.,
North of England Cinemas, Ltd. (Gaumont-
British). 900 seats. Prices, 5d. to 1s. Phone,
Whitley Bay 496. Station, Whitley Bay,
L.N.E.R.
NEW COLISEUM (WE).—Prop., Associated
British Cinemas, Ltd., 30-31, Golden Square,
W.1. Phone, Gerrard 7887. 1,498 seats.
Booked at H.O. Continuous. Daily Mat.
Two changes weekly. Prices, 6d. to 1s. 3d.
Proscenium, 30 ft. Phone, Whitley 196,
Station, Whitley Bay, L.N.E.R.
PICTURE HOUSE (BTP), Promenade.—Stanley
Rogers Cinemas, Ltd. (E. J. Hinge Circuit),
72. Grey Street, Newcastle-on-Tyne. Phone,
Newcastle 20317. 600 seats. Booked at
H.O. Continuous. Prices, 6d. to 1s. Phone,
Whitley Bay 235.

WHITSTABLE (Kent), **Pop. 11,201.**
OXFORD CINEMA (BA), Oxford Street.—Prop.,
Whitstable Oxford Picture Hall, Co., Ltd.
825 seats. Continuous. Booked at Hall.
Two changes weekly. Prices, 6d. to 1s. 3d.
Phone, 736. Station, Whitstable Town, S.R.
PICTURE HOUSE (BTH), High Street.—(Closed).
TROCADERO (WE), Tankerton.—Prop., Associated
British Cinemas, Ltd., 30-31, Golden Square,
W.1. Gerrard 7887. 1,400 seats. Booked
at H.O. Continuous. Prices, 6d. to 1s. 4d.
Phone, Whitstable 20. Station, Whitstable.

WHITTLESEA (Cambs), **Pop. 8,299.**
CINEMA PALACE (BTH), Market Street.
Prop., C. S. Hart. 500 seats. Booked at Hall.
Continuous. Two changes weekly. Prices,
7d. and 1s. Station, Whittlesea, L.N.E.R.

WHITWELL (Derby), **Pop. 4,362.**
THE RITZ (BA), Station Road, Offices, 3. Wharf
Road, Mansfield. 360 seats. Once nightly.
Booked at Hall. Prices, 6d. to 1s. Pros-
cenium width, 19 ft. Phone, Mansfield 739.
Station, Whitwell, L.M.S.

WHITWORTH, nr. Rochdale (Lancs.)
Pop. 8,360.
PAVILION CINEMA (BA), Market Street.—Prop.,
J. Caton, Freda Villa, Offerton Lane,
Offerton, nr. Stockport. 700 seats. Pictures
and Variety. Booked at Manchester by Prop,
One show nightly. Two on Sat. Three changes
weekly. Prices, 4d. to 1s. Proscenium width,
21 ft. Stage, 12 ft. deep; two dressing-rooms.
Station, Whitworth, L.M.S.

WIDNES (Lancs), **Pop. 40,608.**
ALEXANDRA PICTURE HOUSE (WE).
BOZZADROME (BTP), Albert Road.—Prop.,
Arthur Bell, 27, Park Avenue, Widnes. 600
seats. Booked at Manchester and Liverpool.
Two shows nightly. Mat., Mon., Thurs. and
Sat. Prices, 4d. to 9d. Stage, 8 ft. deep; two
dressing-rooms. Proscenium width, 25 ft.
Phone, Widnes 832.

CENTURY PICTURE PALACE (BTP), West Street,
Prop., Century Pictures (Widnes), Ltd., West
Street. 504 seats. Booked at H.O. Twice
nightly. Mats., Tues., Thurs. and Sat. Prices,
4d. to 9d. Station, Widnes, L.M.S.
CO-OPERATIVE CINEMA DE LUXE (WE), Lugsdale.
Road.—Lessees ; Cheshire County Cinemas,
Ltd., Empress Theatre, Runcorn. Phone,
Runcorn 199. 700 seats. Booked at H.O.
Two shows nightly. Mats., Mon. and Thurs.
Proscenium width, 24 ft. Phone, Widnes
369. Station, Widnes, L.M.S. and Cheshire
Lines.
PICTUREDROME (BTP), Victoria Road.—Prop.
County Pictures (Widnes), Ltd., 3, Victoria
Road. 680 seats. Booked at H.O. Twice
nightly. Mat., Mon., Thurs. and Sat. Prices,
6d. to 1s. Phone, Widnes 109. Station,
Widnes (Central), L.M.S.
PREMIER PICTURE HOUSE (WE), Albert Road.—
Prop., Widnes Cinemas, Ltd., 4, Exchange
Bldgs., St. Mary's Gate, Manchester. 735 seats.
Booked at Hall. Twice nightly. Prices, 6d.
to 1s. Proscenium width, 35 ft. Stage, 10½ ft. ;
one dressing-room. Phone, Widnes 312.
REGAL (BTP).

WIGAN (Lancs), **Pop. 85,357.**
ALLIANCE CINEMA (BA).—Props., T. Kenyon and
S. Stephenson, 26, Guildford Avenue, Norbreck,
Blackpool. Phone, North Shore 51828. 750
seats. Booked at Hall. Twice nightly.
Prices, 3d. to 6d. Station, Wigan, L.M.S.

COUNTY PLAYHOUSE (WE), King Street.—
Prop., Eagle Picturedrome, Ltd. Phone,
Wigan 3476. Gen. Man. and Sec., T. C.
Robinson. 1,105 seats. Booked by T. C.
Robinson, Cromford House, Manchester.
Three shows daily. Prices, 5d. to 1s. 4d.
Phone, Wigan 2089. Station, Wigan, L.M.S.

**Fitted "ARDENTE" Deaf Aids
See page. 258**

COURT CINEMA (WE), King Street.—Prop.,
Wigan Entertainments Co., Ltd., 1, College
Avenue, Wigan. 1,295 seats. Booked at
H.O. Twice nightly. Daily Mat. Prices, 6d.
to 1s. 6d. Proscenium width, 38 ft. Phone,
Wigan 2394.

COMPTON
ORGAN featured here.

EMPIRE CINEMA (WE).—Prop., Empire Cinema
(Wigan), Ltd. 780 seats. Booked at 3, The
Parsonage, Manchester, by F. E. Spring.
Three shows daily. Prices, 4d. to 1s. Phone,
Wigan 2962. Station, Wigan, L.M.S.

EMPRESS CINEMA (Morrison), Billinge.—Prop.,
G. R. Allen, "Broadoak," Higher Lane,
Lymm, Nr. Warrington. 700 seats. Once
nightly. Prices, 4d. to 1s. Station, Orrell.

GIDLOW PICTURE HOUSE (BTH).—Prop., Eagle
Picturedromes, Ltd. 700 seats. Gen. Man. and
Sec., T. C. Robinson. Phone, Wigan 3476.
Booked by T. C. Robinson, Cromford House.
Manchester. Two shows nightly. Two
changes weekly. Phone, Wigan 3009
Prices, 5d. to 9d. Station, Wigan, L.M.S.

INCE PICTURE PALACE (PTA).—Prop. and Res
Man., C. W. Pennington. 325 seats. Booked
at Hall. Two shows nightly. Prices, 4d. and
6d. Station, Ince, near Wigan, L.M.S.

LABŌUR HALL (Ultramonic), Whalley.—Prop. and Man., W. Williams. 350 seats. Twice nightly. Station, Wigan.

PALACE PICTURE THEATRE (BTP), King Street.— Booked by H. D. Moorhouse Circuit, 7, Oxford Road, Manchester. Phone, Ardwick 2226. 700 seats. Continuous. Two shows Sat. Prices, 4d. to 1s. Phone, Wigan 2611.

PAVILION (WE), Library Street.—Prop., Wigan Entertainments Co., Ltd. 2,000 seats. Booked at H.O., 1, College Avenue. Twice nightly. Daily Mat. Prices, 3d. to 1s. Phone, Wigar, 3173. Station, Wigan, L.M.S.

PICTURE HOUSE (BTH), Scholes.—Prop., Thomas Atherton, Eskdale, Grunhill, Wigan. 700 seats. Booked at Manchester and Liverpool. Twice nightly. Mat. Mon. Wed. Thurs. and Sat. Prices, 3d. to 6d. Phone, Wigan 2957. Station, Wigan, L.M.S.

PRINĆES (RCA), Wallgate.—Prop., G. W. Bell. 1,200 seats. Booked at Theatre Royal, Hyde. Twice nightly ; daily Mat. Prices, 6d. to 1s. 3d. Proscenium width, 30 ft. Phone, Wigan 3858.

RITZ (WE).—Controlled by Union Cinemas, Ltd., 15, Regent Street, S.W.1. Booked at H.O. Continuous. Station, Wigan, L.M.S.

ROYAL CINEMA (BTH), Wallgate.—Prop., Merrill's Enterprises, Ltd., 17, North John Street, Liverpool. 479 seats. Booked by R. E. Ratcliff, Broadgreen Road, Roby, Liverpool. Booked at Hall. Twice nightly. Mats., Mon. Thurs. and Sat. Prices, 4d. to 6d. Station, Wigan, L.M.S.

WIGTON (CUMB.), Pop. 3,521.

PALACE (Mihaly), Meeting House Lane.—Prop., J. M. Cusack, "Elm Bank," Whitehaven Road, Workington. 264 seats. Booked by Branford, at Queen's, Whitehaven. Twice nightly. Two changes weekly. Prices, 3d. to 1s. Proscenium width, 15 ft. Station, Wigton, L.M.S.

WILLENHALL (STAFFS), Pop. 2,147.

DALE (WE).—Prop., Miss Norah Tyler. 1,150 seats. Booked at Hall. Continuous. Prices, 6d. to 1s. Phone, Willenhall 241. Station, Willenhall, L.M.S.

PICTURE HOUSE (RCA), Stafford Street.—Props., Associated Provincial Picture Houses, Ltd. Continuous. Two changes weekly. Prices, 4½d. to 1s. 3d. Phone, Willenhall 139.

WILLINGTON (CO. DURHAM), Pop. 8,960.

EMPIRE (BTH).—Props., Hateley & Co. 500 seats. One show nightly. Booked at Hall. Mat. and two shows Sat. Two changes weekly. Prices, 3d. to 9d. Proscenium width, 18 ft. Phone, Willington 9. Station, Willington, Co. Durham, L.N.E.R.

EMPRESS (BTH).—Props., Hateley & Co. 750 seats. Booked at Hall. Once nightly, twice on Sat. Stage, 24 ft. deep ; four dressing-rooms. Proscenium width, 24 ft. Prices, 6d. to 1s. Phone, Willington 9.

WILLINGTON QUAY - ON - TYNE (NORTHUMBERLAND), Pop. 4,350.

PEARL PICTURE PALACE (BTP).—650 seats. Twice nightly. Prices, 3d. to 6d. Phone, allsend 63674. Station, Willington Quay.

WILMSLOW (CHESHIRE), Pop. 9,760.

REX.

WILMSLOW PICTURE PALACE (BTP), Station Road.—Props., Wilmslow Picture Palace (1921), Ltd. 700 seats. Booked at Manchester. One show nightly. Two on Sat. Mat., Wed. and Sat. Café attached. Prices, 6d. to 1s. 6d. Phone, Wilmslow 181. Station, Wilmslow.

WIMBORNE (DORSET), Pop. 3,895.

CINEMA (Wired), The Square.—Prop., Sidney G. Prince. 350 seats. Booked at Hall. Continuous. Mat., Sat. Prices, 6d. to 1s. 6d. Phone, Wimborne 253. Station, Wimborne.

TIVOLI (WE), West Boro'.—Props., Tivoli (Wimborne), Ltd. 600 seats. Booked at Hall. Continuous. Mats., Wed. and Sat. Prices, 6d. to 1s. 6d. Proscenium width, 35 ft. Phone, Wimborne 326. Station, Wimborne.

VILLAGE HALL, Sturminster.

WINCANTON (SOM), Pop. 2,000.

PLAZA (Parmeko).—Props., Wincanton Pictures, Ltd., Palace, Blandford. Phone, Blandford 12. Booked at H.O. Once nightly. Prices, 6d. to 1s. 6d. Proscenium width, 24 ft. Station, Wincanton, S.R.

TOWN HALL.—Props., Walford's Talkies Head Office, Chard, Som.

WINCHESTER (HANTS), Pop. 22,969.

GUILDHALL.—Props., The Mayor and Corporation. 800 seats. Booked at Hall. Occasional shows. Non-flam films only. Proscenium width, 23 ft. Prices, 6d. to 3s. Phone, Winchester 1092. Applications to F.A. Grant, Supt. of Guildhall.

ODEON THEATRE (WE).—Props., Odeon (Winchester), Ltd., Bennett's Hill, Birmingham. Booked at 49, Park Lane, W.1. Prices, 6d. to 2s. Café attached. Phone, Winchester 592.

Fitted "ARDENTE" Deaf Aids
See page 258

COMPTON
ORGAN featured here.

NEW THEATRE CINEMA (AWH).—Prop., R. W. Sparrow, 400 seats. Booked at Hall. Continuous from 6 p.m. Prices, 5d. to 1s. 3d. Proscenium width, 18 ft. Phone, Winchester 1211. Station, Winchester, S.R.; and Film Transport.

PICTURE HOUSE (BTH).—(Closed).

ROYAL THEATRE (WE).—Props., County Cinemas, Ltd., Dean House, Dean Street, London. 557 seats. Booked at H.O. Continuous. Prices, 6d. to 2s. Phone, 437.

WINCHESTER PICTURE HOUSE (BTH), High Street.—Prop., A. N. Kendal, Ltd. 510 seats. Booked at the Regal, Winchester. Continuous. Prices, 6d. to 1s. 6d. Proscenium width, 20 ft. Phone, Winchester 193. Station, Winchester.

WINCHCOMBE (GLOS). Pop. 2,740.

OLD TANNERIES (BTH).—Prop., L. W. Barnard, 13, Imperial Square, Chelmsford. Phone, 3690. 450 seats. Continuous. Prices, 6d. and 1s. Proscenium width, 25 ft. Dance Hall attached. Phone, 2. Station, Winchcombe.

WINDERMERE (WESTMORLAND), **Pop. 5,701.**
CINEMA (BA), Beech Street.—Props., Windermere and Ambleside Cinemas, Ltd., H.O., 33, James Street, Liverpool. Phone, Bank 4000. 300 seats. Booked at 33, James' Street, Liverpool, by L. H. Clegg. Continuous. Prices, 4d. to 1s. 6d. Station, Windermere.

PUBLIC HALL (RCA).

ROYALTY THEATRE (RCA), Bowness-on-Windermere.—Props., Windermere and Ambleside Cinemas, Ltd., H.O., 33, James' Street, Liverpool. Phone, Bank 4000. 600 seats. Booked at 33, James' Street, Liverpool, by L. H. Clegg. Continuous. Prices, 5d. to 2s.

WINDSOR (BERKS.), **Pop. 20,284.**
EMPIRE CINEMA (WE), Peascod Street.—Prop. Enterprises (Windsor), Ltd. 636 seats. Booked at Hall. Continuous. Prices, 5d. to 1s. 3d. Proscenium width, 26 ft. Phone, Windsor 560.

PLAYHOUSE (WE).—Controlled by Union Cinemas, Ltd., Union House, 15, Regent Street, London, S.W.1. Phone, Whitehall 8484. Booked at H.O. Continuous. Prices, 6d. to 2s. 6d. Phone, Windsor 888. Café attached.

COMPTON
ORGAN featured here.

REGAL (WE), 113, Peascod Street.—Controlled by Union Cinemas, Ltd., Union House, 15, Regent Street, London, S.W.1. Phone, Whitehall 8484. Booked at H.O., Pictures and Variety. Continuous. Prices, 5d. to 2s. Proscenium width, 30 ft. Phone, Windsor 823.

ROYALTY CINEMA (WE).—Controlled by Union Cinemas, Ltd., Union House, 15, Regent Street, London, S.W.1. Phone, Whitehall 8484. Booked at H.O. Continuous. Prices, 6d. to 2s. Proscenium width, 28 ft. Phone, Windsor 107. Stations, Windsor, G.W.R.

WINGATE (Co. DURHAM), **Pop. 11,420.**
EMPIRE CINEMA (BTH), Front Street.—Prop., Beaumont, Murske Road, Saltburn. 495 seats. Booked at Newcastle-on-Tyne. Once nightly, Mon. to Fri. Twice Sat. Prices, 4d. to 9d. Proscenium width, 20 feet. Phone, Wingate 34.

PALACE THEATRE (WE).—Prop., H. Harrison, Oak Lea, Wingate. 820 seats. Booked at Newcastle-on-Tyne. Once nightly, twice on Sat. Prices, 4d. to 7½d. Stage, 18 ft. deep; two dressing-rooms. Proscenium width, 26 ft. Phone, Wingate 46. Stations, Wingate or Wellfield Junction.

WINSFORD (CHESHIRE), **Pop. 10,907.**
MAGNET (WE) Weaver Street.—Props., Sandbach Cinemas, Ltd., Palace, Sandbach. Phone, Sandbach 103. 682 seats. Booked at H.O. Twice nightly. Prices, 6d. to 1s. Phone, Winsford 2214. Stations, Over and Wharton.

PALACE (WE).—Props., Palace (Winsford), Ltd. 1,000 seats. Continuous. Booked at Picture House, Ludlow. Prices, 6d. to 1s. 3d. Phone, No. 2267. Films by Road Transport.

WIRKSWORTH (DERBY), **Pop. 3,911.**
WIRKSWORTH TOWN HALL (Metropolitan).—Props., J. Brown & Co. All correspondence to R. O. Brown, 228, Fullwood Road, Sheffield. Phone, Sheffield 61126. Once nightly. Prices, 4d. to 1s. Station, Wirksworth, L.M.S.

CINEMA (BTP)—Props., Warlton Entertainments, Ltd. 525 seats. Continuous. Prices, 6d. to 1s. 3d. Phone, Wirksworth 100.

WISBECH (CAMBS), **Pop. 12,005.**
EMPIRE (RCA).—Props., Wisbech Hippodrome, Ltd. Phone, Wisbech 532. 1,000 seats. Continuous. Prices, 6d. to 2s. 4d.

HIPPODROME (RCA).—Props., Wisbech Hippodromes, Ltd. Man. Dir., H. Bancroft. 1,100 seats. Booked at Theatre. Continuous. Two changes weekly. Prices, 4d. to 1s. 10d. Phone, Wisbech 116. Station, Wisbech.

REGENT (Kalee Univ.), Norfolk Street.—Props., Regent Theatre (Wisbech), Ltd. 433 seats. Booked at Hall. Continuous, Pictures and Variety. Prices, 6d. to 1s. 6d. Stage, 25 ft. deep; three dressing-rooms. Phone, Wisbech 440. Station, Wisbech, L.N.E.R.; and Cambs. and District Motor Transport Co.

WITHAM (ESSEX), **Pop. 4,367.**
WHITEHALL PICTURE HOUSE (WE)—Props., Mid-Essex Cinema Co., Whitehall, Witham. 576 seats. Booked at Hall. Continuous. Three shows Sat. Prices, 6d. to 2s. Phone, Witham 142. Station, Witham, L.N.E.R.

WITHERNSEA (near Hull) (YORKS), **Pop. 4,251.**
KINEMA (BA).—Props., Withernsea Kinema, Ltd. 666 seats. Booked at Hall. Once nightly. Prices, 4d. to 1s. Proscenium width, 16 ft. Phone, Withernsea 30. Station, Withernsea.

SAVOY (BTH), Queen Street.—Prop., B.S.F. Cinemas, Ltd., 58, Grange View, Leeds. Booked at H.O. 720 seats. Continuous. Prices, 4d. to 1s. Station, Withernsea.

WITNEY (OXFORD), **Pop. 3,409.**
PALACE CINEMA (BTH), Market Place.—750 seats. Prop., Witney Electric Theatre, Ltd. Booked at Hall. Continuous. Prices, 6d. to 1s. 6d. Proscenium width 22 ft. Phone, Witney 147. Station, Witney, G.W.R.

WITTON PARK (Co. DURHAM).
PARK KINEMA (AWH), Main Street.—Prop., Witton Park Kinema Co., Ltd. 300 seats. Booked at Hall. Once nightly. Prices, 4d. to 9d. Station, Etherley, L.N.E.R.

WOKING (SURREY), **Pop. 29,927.**
ASTORIA (WE), Duke Street.—Prop., London and Southern Super Cinemas, Ltd., 32, Shaftesbury Avenue, London, W.1. Phone, Whitehall 0183/4. 1,172 seats. Booked at H.O. Continuous. Prices, 9d. to 2s. 5d. Proscenium, 40 ft. wide. Phone, Woking 1275.

COMPTON

Cross Road, W.C. Phone, Whitehall 0183/4. 929 seats. Booked at H.O. Continuous. Prices, 9d. to 2s. 5d. Phone, Woking 1275.

RITZ (WE).—Controlled by Union Cinemas, Ltd.' 15, Regent Street, S.W.1. Phone, Whitehall 8484: Booked at H.O. Continuous.

WOKINGHAM (BERKS), **Pop. 7,294.**
RITZ (WE).—Controlled by Union Cinemas, Ltd., 15, Regent Street, S.W.1. Phone, Whitehall 8484. Booked at H.O. Continuous. Station, Wokingham S.R.

SAVOY THEATRE (AWH), 10, Broad Street.— Controlled by Union Cinemas, Ltd., 15, Regent Street, S.W.1. Phone, Whitehall 8484. Continuous. Booked at H.O. Prices, 6d. to 1s. 6d. Phone, Wokingham 415.

WOLSINGHAM (Co. DURHAM), **Pop. 3,414.**
PICTUREDROME.—Prop. and Res. Man., A. Todd, Prospect House, Wolsingham. Phone, Wolsingham 11. 190 seats. Booked at New-castle-on-Tyne. One show nightly; two on Sat. Two changes weekly. Prices, 5d. and 9d.

WOLVERHAMPTON (STAFFS), **Pop. 133,190.**
COLISEUM (WE), Dudley Road.—Prop., Madge Quigley. 880 seats. Continuous. Two changes weekly. Prices, 4d. to 1s. Phone, Wolverhampton 20876. Station, Wolverhampton.

DUNSTALL PICTURE HOUSE (WE).—Prop., Dunstall Picture House Co., Ltd. 1,400 seats. Booked at Hall. Continuous. Mat., Mon., Thurs. and Sat. Prices, 6d. to 1s. 3d. Proscenium width, 42 ft.

GAUMONT PALACE (WE), Snow Hill.—Prop., Associated Provincial Picture Houses, Ltd., 2,000 seats. Booked at H.O. Continuous. Prices, 9d. to 2s. Proscenium width, 40 ft. Stage, 23 ft. deep ; 8 dressing-rooms. Café attached. Phone, Wolverhampton 225341.
Fitted "ARDENTE" Deaf Aids See page 258

COMPTON
ORGAN featured here.

HIPPODROME.—Prop., General Theatre Corporation, Ltd. 1,500 seats.

GLOBE (BTH), Horseley Field.—Phone, Wolverhampton 21594.

ODEON THEATRE (BTH).—Prop., Odeon (Wolverhampton), Ltd., Bennetts Hill, Birmingham. Phone, Midland 2781. (In course of construction.)

OLYMPIA (WE), Thornley Street.—Prop., F. Appleby. 850 seats. Continuous. Two changes weekly. Prices, 3d. to 1s. Phone, Wolverhampton 21344.

QUEEN'S CINEMA.—Prop., Associated Provincial Picture Houses, Ltd., 123, Regent Street, London, W.1. Phone, Regent 8080. 1,012 seats. Booked at H.O.
Fitted "ARDENTE" Deaf Aids See page 258

SCALA (BA) Worcester Street.—Prop., Associated Provincial Picture Houses, Ltd., New Gallery House, 123, Regent Street, London, W.1. Phone, Regent 8080. Booked at H.O. Continuous. Mats. daily. Two changes weekly. Prices, 5d. to 1s. 3d. Phone, Wolverhampton 20121.

THEATRE ROYAL (WE).—Prop., Associated British Cinemas, Ltd., 30-31, Golden Square, London, W.1. Phone, Gerrard 7887. 1,073 seats. Booked at H.O. Continuous. Prices, 6d. to 1s. 3d. Stage, 45 ft. deep ; 12 dressing-rooms. Proscenium width, 28 ft.

WEST END CINEMA (BTH).—Prop., F. S. Sandover. 800 seats. Continuous. Mat. Mon., Thurs. and Sat. Booked at Hall. Prices, 6d. to 1s. Phone, Wolverhampton 20707.

WOLVERTON (BUCKS), **Pop. 12,870.**
EMPIRE (BTH).—Controlled by Union Cinemas, Ltd., Union House, 15, Regent St., London, S.W.1. Phone, Whitehall 8484. Booked at H.O. Prices, 6d. to 1s. 3d. Phone, Wolverton 91. Continuous.

PALACE (BTH).—Prop., Councillor G. H. Barber. Coronation House, Tunstall Park, Stoke-on-Trent. Phone, Hanley 7453. 650 seats. Booked at Hall. Continuous. Two changes weekly. Prices, 4d. to 1s. 2d. Station, Wolverton.

WOMBWELL (nr. Barnsley) (YORKS), **Pop 18,365.**
EMPIRE (WE), Park Street.—Prop., Mrs. B. Stewart. 975 seats. Booked at Hall. Two shows nightly. Two changes weekly. Prices, 4d. to 1s. 3d. Phone, Wombwell 19. Station, Wombwell, L.M.S.

PAVILION (WE).—Prop., Exors. E. Burns, Victoria Hotel, Hemsworth. Phone, Hemsworth 11. 980 seats. Booked at H.O. Two shows nightly. Pictures and Variety. Prices, 4d. to 1s. Proscenium width, 30 ft. Stage, 40 ft. deep ; 5 dressing-rooms. Phone, Wombwell 84.

WOODBRIDGE (SUFFOLK), **Pop. 4,734.**
WOODBRIDGE THEATRE (WE).—Booked by Ager Circuit, 10, Church Street, Colchester.

WOODHALL SPA (LINCS), **Pop. 1,372.**
THE KINEMA IN THE WOODS (Morrison).—Prop. and Man., Capt. C. C. Allport, " Sylvan-hay," Woodhall Spa. 320 seats. Booked at Hall. Single shows. Change Mon. and Thurs. Prices, 6d. to 1s. 6d. Proscenium width, 15 ft. Phone, Woodhall Spa 66. Station, Woodhall Spa, L.N.E.R.

WOODHOUSE (nr. Sheffield) (YORKS) **Pop. 5,308**
PICTURE PALACE (BTH), Market Street.—Prop., Scala Cinemas (Sheffield), Ltd., Winter Street, Sheffield. Phone, 25406. 800 seats. Booked at H.O. Continuous. Prices, 5d. to 9d. Proscenium width, 20 ft. Phone, Woodhouse 40532. Stations, Woodhouse, L.N.E.R., and Woodhouse Mill, L.M.S.

WOODLANDS (nr. Doncaster) (YORKS), **Pop. 8,000.**
PICTURE HOUSE (BTH).—Prop., Picture House (Woodlands), Ltd. Phone, Leeds 41249. 800 seats. Booked at Hall. Twice nightly. Two changes weekly. Prices, 3d. to 1s. Phone, Ardwick-le-Street 67. Station, Carcroft.

WOOL (DORSET), **Pop. 2,300.**
BOVINGTON CINEMA (Mihaly).—Prop., William Adams (Cinema) Co. Booked at Hall. Continuous. Prices, 5d. to 1s. Station, Wool, S.R

WOOLER (NORTHUMBERLAND).
DRILL HALL CINEMA (AWH).—Props., Redpath and Stoddart. 420 seats. Once nightly, twice Sat. and Mon. Prices, 3d. to 1s. 3d. Station, Wooler.

WOOTTON BASSETT (WILTS), **Pop. 1,991.**
PICTUREDROME (Imperial), High Street.— Prop., J. L. Mott, 10, Oxford Street, Malmesbury. Phone, Malmesbury 152. Booked at Malmesbury. Once nightly. Prices, 6d. to 1s. 3d. Station, Wootton Bassett, G.W.R.

WORCESTER (WORCS), **Pop. 50,497.**
GAUMONT (BA), Foregate Street.—Prop., Provincial Cinematograph Theatres, Ltd., Associated with G.-B.P. Corpn., Ltd., 123, Regent Street, W.1. 1,740 seats. Booked at H.O. Continuous. Prices, 6d. to 2s. Café. Phone, Wor. 1509. Station, Foregate Street and Shrubs Hill, L.M.S. and G.W.R.
Fitted "ARDENTE." Deaf Aids See page 258

COMPTON
ORGAN featured here.

ST. JOHN'S CINEMA (WE).—725 seats.
SCALA THEATRE (WE).—800 seats.
SILVER CINEMA (BTH), Foregate Street.— Prop., Odeon (Perry Bar), Ltd., Cornhill House, Bennetts Hill, Birmingham. Phone, Midland 2781. Booked at 49, Park Lane, W.1. Continuous. Prices, 6d. to 1s. 6d. Phone, Worcester 653.

WORCESTER PARK (SURREY).
ODEON THEATRE (BTH).—Prop., Odeon (Worcester Park), Ltd., Cornhill House, Bennett's Hill, Birmingham. Phone, Midland 2781. Booked at 49, Park Lane, W.1. Prices, 9d. to 2s. Derwent 2355.

WORDSLEY (STAFFS), **Pop. 6,000.**
OLYMPIA (Morrison).—Prop., F. C. Leatham. 600 seats. Booked at Hall. One show nightly. Continuous on Sat. Prices, 4d. to 1s. Proscenium width, 26 ft. Occasional Variety. Stage, 30 ft. deep ; 4 dressing-rooms. Station, Brettle Lane, Stourbridge, G.W.R.

WORKINGTON (CUMB.), **Pop. 24,691.**
HIPPODROME (WE), Falcon Place.—Prop., The Williams Cinemas, Ltd., Falcon Place, Workington. 950 seats. Booked at H.O. Twice nightly. Mat., Sat. Prices, 5d. to 9d. Proscenium width, 25 ft. Ballroom attached. Phone, Workington 194. Station, Workington, L.M.S.

OPERA HOUSE (WE).—Prop., Graves Cinemas, Ltd. 1,300 seats. Booked at H.O. Athenæum Buildings, Maryport. Twice nightly. Prices, 6d. to 1s. Phone, Workington 26.

OXFORD PICTURE HOUSE (WE).—Prop., Graves Cinemas, Ltd. Booked at H.O., Athenæum Buildings, Maryport. 1,100 seats. Twice nightly. Prices, 6d. to 1s. Phone, Workington 201. Station, Workington, L.M.S.

RITZ CINEMA.—Props., Graves Cinemas, Ltd., Athenæum Buildings, Maryport.—(In course of construction.

THEATRE ROYAL (WE).—Prop., Graves Cinemas, Ltd. Booked at H.O., Athenæum Buildings, Maryport. 450 seats. Two shows nightly. Prices, 6d. to 1s. Phone, Workington 201.

THE CARNEGIE (RCA).—Graves Cinemas, Ltd., Athenæum Buildings, Maryport, Cumberland. Phone, Maryport 16. 750 seats. Two shows nightly. Prices, 6d. to 1s. Phone, Workington 120.

WORKSOP (NOTTS), **Pop. 26,286.**
GAIETY THEATRE (WE), Bridge Street.—Prop., E. V. Pepper and G. W. Clark, 45, Bridge Street, Worksop. 600 seats. Continuous. Booked at Hall. Stage, 40 ft. deep ; 4 dressing-rooms. Prices, 3d. to 1s. 6d. Proscenium width, 18 ft. Phone, 299. Station, Worksop.

PICTURE HOUSE (BTH), Newcastle Avenue.— Prop., Picture House (Worksop), Ltd. 1,100 seats. Booked at Hall. Continuous. Prices, 5d. to 1s. 6d. Proscenium width, 20 ft. Phone, Worksop 189. Café attached.

REGAL CINEMA (WE).—Prop., Star Cinemas (London), Ltd., 5, Manchester Avenue, Aldersgate Street, E.C.1. Phone, Metropolitan 4292. 1,000 seats. Booked at H.O. Continuous nightly Mon. to Fri. Twice nightly Sat. Daily Mat. Prices, 6d. to 1s. 3d. Proscenium width, 33 ft. Occasional Variety. Stage, 17 ft. deep ; 5 dressing-rooms. Phone, Worksop 352. Café attached.

RITZ (WE).—Controlled by Union Cinemas, Ltd., 15, Regent Street, London, S.W.1. Phone, Whitehall 8484. Prices, 6d. to 1s. 6d. Station, Worksop, L.N.E.R.

VICTORIA PALACE (WE).—Prop., Hallamshire Cinemas, Ltd., 3, Hartshead, Sheffield. Phone, Sheffield 20888. 730 seats. Booked at H.O. Continuous. Prices, 2½d. to 9d. Proscenium width, 22 ft. Phone, Worksop 257. Station, Worksop, L.N.E.R.

WORTHING (SUSSEX), **Pop. 46,230.**
DOME CINEMA (WE), Marine Parade.—Prop. and Res. Man., C. A. Seebold. 875 seats. Booked at Hall. Continuous. Prices, 6d. to 2s. Phone, Worthing 461. Station, Worthing.

ODEON THEATRE (BTH).—Prop., Odeon (Worthing), Ltd., Cornhill House, Bennett's Hill, Birmingham. Midland 2781. Continuous. Booked at 49, Park Lane, W.1. Prices, 9d. to 2s. 6d. Proscenium width, 35 ft. Café attached. Phone, Worthing 2016.

COMPTON
ORGAN featured here.

PLAZA (WE), Rowlands Road.—Prop., Associated British Cinemas, Ltd., 30-31, Golden Square, London, W.1. 2,006 seats. Booked at H.O. Prices, 6d. to 2s. Proscenium width, 45 ft. Stage, 30 ft. deep. Café and Ball-room attached. Phone, Worthing 2392.

COMPTON
ORGAN featured here

RIVOLI CINEMA (WE), Chapel Road.—Prop., C. A. Seebold. 1,696 seats. Booked at Hall. Continuous. Prices, 9d. to 2s. 6d.

WOTTON-UNDER-EDGE (Glos.).

Picture House (SOF), Market Street.—Prop.'
W. T. Coe. 205 seats. Booked at Hall. Once
nightly. Prices, 6d. to 1s. 3d. Station,
Charfield, L.M.S.

WYMONDHAM (Norfolk), **Pop. 5,000.**

Picture Theatre (Morrison).—Prop., W. J.
Spalding, Hillside, Wymondham. 300 seats
Booked at Hall. Once nightly, twice Sat
Occasional Variety. Stage, 12 ft. deep; 2
dressing-rooms. Prices, 6d. to 1s. 6d. Pro-
scenium width 17½ ft. Station, Wymondham.

YEADON (nr. Leeds) (Yorks), **Pop. 7,671.**

Picture House (BTH), High Street.—Prop.,
Yeadon Picture Palace Co., Ltd., 2, Bristol
Street, Leeds. Phone, Leeds 22462. 850
seats. Booked at 2, Bristol Street, Leeds.
Once nightly. Mon. to Fri., two shows Sat.
Prices, 4d. to 1s. Phone, Rawdon 184. Films
collected from Leeds by Carrier.

Temperance Hall.—Prop., Gem Pictures.
800 seats. One show nightly; two Sat.
Two changes weekly. Prices, 4d. to 9d.
Station, Guiseley.

YEOVIL (Somerset), **Pop. 19,078.**

Central Cinema (WE), Church Street.—Prop.,
S. T. Thring. 540 seats. Booked at Hall.
Twice nightly. Mat. Sat. Prices, 6d. to 1s. 6d.
Phone, Yeovil 567.

Odeon Theatre (BTH).—Prop., Odeon (Yeovil),
Ltd., Bennett's Hill, Birmingham. Phone,
Midland 2781. Booked at 49, Park Lane,
W.1. Continuous.

Gaumont Palace (BA).—Prop., Gaumont
British Picture Corpn., Ltd.
Fitted "ARDENTE" Deaf Aids
See page 258

YIEWSLEY and WEST DRAYTON (Middx)
Pop. 13,057.

Marlborough Cinema (WE).—Controlled by
Union Cinemas, Ltd., Union House, 15,
Regent Street, London, S.W.1. Phone,
Whitehall 8484. Booked at H.O. Continu-
ous. Two changes weekly. Prices, 6d. to
1s. 10d. Phone, West Drayton 85. Stations,
West Drayton and Yiewsley, G.W.R.

YORK (Yorks), **Pop. 84,810.**

Electric Theatre (BA), Foss Gate.—Prop.,
National Electric Theatres, Ltd., 123, Regent
Street, London, W.1. Phone, Regent 6641.
Continuous. Phone, York 362411. Station,
York, L.N.E.R.

Grand Picture House (BTP) (Café and Ballroom), Clarence Street.—Prop., R. J. Pulleyn,
Clifton Croft, Clifton, York. 950 seats. Booked
by Prop. at Hall. Phone, York 3512.

Odeon Theatre (BTH).—Prop., Odeon (York),
Ltd., Bennett's Hill, Birmingham. Phone,
Midland 2781. Booked at 49, Park Lane,
W.1. Continuous. Prices, 6d. to 2s.

Picture House (BA), Coney Street.—Prop.,
Gaumont British Picture Corpn., Ltd.,
123, Regent Street, London, W.1. 920 seats.
Booked at H.O. by A. W. Jarratt. Con-
tinuous. Prices, 4d. to 1s. 6d. Café attached.
Phone, York 249311. Station, York, L.N.E.R.

Regent (RCA), Acomb.—Prop., Regent Cinema
(York), Ltd., 17, High Ousegate, York.
Phone 3643. 899 seats. Continuous. Prices,
9d. to 1s. 3d. Phone, 781381.

Rialto Cinema (BTP), Fishergate.—Prop.,
Winder and Prendergast. 1,800 seats.
Booked at Leeds. Continuous. Prices, 6d.
to 1s. 6d. Phone, York 2119.

COMPTON
ORGAN featured here.

St. George's Hall Cinema (WE), Castlegate.
—Prop., York Cinemas, Ltd., 123, Regent
Street, London, W.1. Phone, Regent 8080.
1,296 seats. Booked at H.O. Continuous.
Prices, 7d. to 1s. 6d. Stage and dressing-rooms.
Dance Hall and Café attached. Phone, 253811.

Tower Picture Theatre (WE), New Street—
Prop., Tower Picture Theatre (York), Ltd.
1,100 seats. Continuous. Two changes weekly
Prices, 6d. to 1s. 6d. Phone, York 2298.

TRAVELLING SHOWS.

Prop., Mr. W. J. Hocking.
Callington, Cornwall.—Mon. and Fri.
Millbrook, Cornwall.—Wed. and Sat.
Ivy Bridge, Devon.

Prop., Mr. Yardley.
Crowland, Lincolnshire.—Thurs.
Billingborough, Lincolnshire.—Fri.
Donington, Lincolnshire.—Sat.

Prop., D. J. Larner.
Holt.—
Cley.—Thurs.
Briston.—Fri. and Sat.

Prop., J. Cox.
Cranbrook.—Wed. and Sat.
Hawkhurst.—Tues.
Marden and Northiam.—Mon.
Robertsbridge.—Thurs.

Prop., H. Sullings.
Hollesley, Orford and Framlingham.—
Aylsham.—Sat.
Boxford.—Mon.
Coltishall.—Fri.

Props., S. and S. Cinemas (G. F. Bellamy).
Bruton.
Stalybridge.—S.n. Stalbridge.
Templecombe.
Wincanton.—Tues. and Thurs.
Warlock.

Prop., C. Hall
Towcester.—Sat.
Winslow.
Brackley.

WELSH KINEMAS.

The Sound system installed is shown after the name. (BTP) = British Talking Pictures, Ltd. ; (RCA) = RCA Photophone Inc. ; (WE) = Western Electric Co., Ltd., ; (BA) = British Acoustic ; (BTH) = British Thomson-Houston. Other systems are indicated by name.

ABERAMAN (GLAM), Pop. 16,100.
GRAND THEATRE (RCA).—Prop., Aberaman Cinema Co., Ltd., 10, Windsor Place, Cardiff. 1,200 seats. Phone, Cardiff 225. Booked at H.O. Continuous. Prices, 6d. to 1s. 3d. Proscenium width, 40 ft. Stage, 20 ft. deep ; four dressing-rooms. Phone : Aberaman 310. Station, Aberaman G.W.R.

ABERAYRON (CARDIGAN), Pop. 1,155.
MEMORIAL HALL (Morrison), Western Cinemas Circuit.—Prop., M. Jones and T. C. Price. Booked at 2, Penybryn Villas, Penydarren, Merthyr Tydfil. One show weekly.

ABERCWYMBOI (GLAM).
CINEMA.—Prop. and Res. Man., M. Freedman. One show nightly. Two changes weekly. Prices, 5d. to 1s. Station, Mountain Ash, G.W.R.

ABERCYNON (GLAM), Pop. 9,109.
EMPIRE CINEMA, Station Approach.—Prop., Principality Amusements, Ltd., Park Hall, Senghenydd, Glam. Booked at Palace. Pictures and Variety, twice nightly. Stage, 18 ft. deep ; 4 dressing-rooms. Prices, 6d. to 1s. Proscenium width, 22 ft. Café. Dance Hall. Station, Abercynon, G.W.R.
PALACE SUPER CINEMA (WE), Margaret Street.—Prop., Principality Amusements Ltd. 540 seats. Booked at Hall. Continuous. Prices, 5d. to 1s. 2d. Proscenium width, 20 ft. Station, Abercynon, G.W.R.
WORKMEN'S HALL (WE).—Prop., Abercynon Colliery Workmen. 1,203 seats. Two shows nightly. Two changes weekly. Prices' 4d. to 1s.

ABERDARE (GLAM), Pop. 48,751.
ABERDARE CINEMA (Picturetone).—Prop., Aberdare Cinemas (1923), Ltd. 800 seats. Booked at Hall. Continuous. Prices, 6d. to 1s. 3d. Phone, Aberdare 132. Station, Aberdare, G.W.R.
COSY KINEMA (WE), Market Street.—Prop., W. E. Willis, Globe Cinema, Penylan, Cardiff. 670 seats. Booked at Cardiff. Continuous. Mat., Sat. Prices, 6d. to 1s. 3d. Phone, Aberdare 89. Station, Aberdare.
EMPIRE AND PLAYHOUSE (BA).—Booked at Hall by Man. Occasional picture shows. Prices, 6d. to 1s. 6d. Station, Aberdare, G.W.R.
PALLADIUM (WE), Canon Street.—Prop., Hirwain Victoria Hall Co., Ltd. 870 seats. Booked at Hall. Three shows daily. Prices, 6d. to 1s. 3d. Proscenium width, 35 ft. Phone, Aberdare 135. Road Transport.
PARK CINEMA (Mihaly), Gadlys.—500 seats. Booked at Hall. Continuous. Pries, 4d. to 1s. 2d. Phone, Aberdare 77.
TOWN KINEMA (BTH).

ABERFAN (GLAM), Pop. 5,500.
LECTRIC THEATRE (BTH).—Prop., Aberfan Electric Theatres, Ltd., 5, Milbourne Chambers, Merthyr Tydfil. Phone, Merthyr Tydfil 329. 600 seats. Booked at Office by F. Taylor. Continuous. Two changes weekly. Prices, 4d. to 1s. Station, Aberfan, G.W.R.

ABERGELE AND PENSARN (DENBIGH) Pop. 2,651.
THE CINEMA (AWH), Market Street.—Prop., Abergele Entertainments, Ltd. 350 seats. Booked at Hall. Phone 42. One show nightly, twice Sat. Prices 3d. to 1s.

ABERGWYNFI (GLAM), Pop. 3,540.
WORKMEN'S HALL (Kamm).—Blaengwynfi. Prop., Abergwynfi Workmen. 460 seats. Booked at Cardiff. One show nightly. Two changes weekly. Prices, 1d. to 1s. Proscenium width, 16 ft. Station, Abergwynfi, G.W.R., via Bridgend.

ABERKENFIG (GLAM), Pop. 5,000.
CINEMA (RCA).—Prop., C. and S. Richards, 32, Coronation Street, Aberkenfig. 500 seats. Continuous. Booked at H.O. by Prop. Prices, 6d. to 1s. Proscenium width, 22 ft. Station, Tondu, G.W.R.

ABERTRIDWR (GLAM), Pop. 7,000.
WORKMEN'S HALL (WE).—Prop., Committee and Workmen of Windsor Collieries, The Square, Abertridwr. 750 seats. Phone, Senghenydd 22. Booked at Hall. Once nightly, twice Sat. Two changes weekly. Occasional Variety. Prices, 5d. to 9d. Station, Abertridwr, G.W.R.

ABERYSTWYTH (CARDIGAN), Pop. 9,474.
COLISEUM CINEMA (BA).—Prop., Mrs. O. M. Gale. 800 seats. Pictures and Variety. Continuous. Prices, 6d. to 1s. 3d. Proscenium width, 27 ft. Phone, Aberystwyth 226. Station, Aberystwyth, G.W.R.
FORUM (WE).—Prop., R. E. Gardiner. 750 seats. Booked at Liverpool and Cardiff. Continuous nightly. Occasional Variety. Prices, 6d. to 1s. 3d. Proscenium width, 22 ft. Stage, 9 ft. deep. Phone, Aberystwyth 421. Café and swimming bath. Station, Aberystwyth, G.W.R.
THE PIER CINEMA (AWH).—Prop., Aberystwyth Pier Co., Ltd. 1,000 seats. Booked at Hall. Continuous. Prices, 6d. to 1s. 6d. Café and Dance Hall. Proscenium width, 40 ft. Phone, Aberystwyth 620. Station, Aberyst. wyth, G.W.R.

AMLWCH (ANGLESEY), Pop. 2,561.
CINEMA (Marshall)—Prop., T. J. Jones, Llangefni, Anglesey. 600 seats. Booked at Hall. Continuous nightly. Mats., Sats. Prices, 9d. to 1s. 6d. Phone, Amlwch 24. Station, Amlwch, L.M.S.

AMMANFORD (CARMARTHEN), Pop. 7,160.
NEW CINEMA (ABTH).—Gwaun-Cae-Gurwen. 750 seats.
PALACE (WE).—Prop., South Wales Cinemas, Ltd., Albert Hall, De La Beche, Swansea. 895 seats. Booked at H.O. Prices, 6d. to 1s. 3d. Phone, Ammanford 59.

BANGOR (CARNARVON), Pop. 10,959.
COUNTY THEATRE (WE).—Prop. and Res. Man. James Hare. 1,000 seats. Booked at Hall. Continuous. Mat., Wed. and Sat. Prices,

9d. to 1s. 6d. Proscenium width, 30 ft· Stage, 40 f·. deep ; 6 dressing-rooms. Phone, Bangor 28i. Station, Bangor.

NEW CITY PICTURE HOUSE (RCA).—Prop., Saronies Enterprises, 12, Saxone Buildings, Church Street. Liverpool. Phone, Royal 2013. 900 seats. Booked at H.O. Continuous. Two changes weekly. Prices, 7d. to 1s. 6d.

PLAZA (RCA).—Prop., Saronies Enterprises, Saxone Buildings, Church Street, Liverpool. Booked at H.O. Continuous. Daily Mat. Prices, 1s. to 2s. Phone, 59, Station, Bangor.

BARGOED (GLAM), **Pop. 12,226.**

BARGOED PALACE (Sound Ltd.).—Prop., Alfred Withers, New Hall. 700 seats. Phone, Bargoed 72. Continuous. Booked at H.O Two changes weekly. Prices, 6d. to 1s. Phone, Bargoed 72. Station, Bargoed, G.W.R

NEW HALL CINEMA (Sound Ltd.).—Prop., Alfred Withers. 1,460 seats. Booked at Hall. Continuous. Prices, 6d. to 1s. Phone, Bargoed 72. Station, Bargoed.

BARMOUTH (MERIONETH), **Pop. 2,491.**

PAVILION (AWH).—Prop., Barmouth Pavilion, Ltd., Trinity Square, Llandudno. Phone, Llandudno 6271. 600 seats. Booked at Town Hall Chambers. Continuous (Winter only). Prices, 6d. to 1s. 6d. Proscenium width, 24 ft. Stage, 22 ft. deep ; two dressing rooms. Phone, Barmouth 44. Station, Barmouth, G.W.R.

WHITE CINEMA.—Prop., Davies Bros. 400 seats. Booked at Hall by Man. Continuous in summer, once nightly winter. Prices, 9d. to 1s. 6d. Phone, Barmouth 32. Station, Barmouth.

BARRY (GLAM), **Pop. 38,916.**

PALACE (BTP).—Prop., Barton Cinema Co., Ltd., 10, Windsor Place, Cardiff. Phone, Cardiff 225. 850 seats. Booked at H.O. Continuous. Prices, 6d. to 1s. 3d. Phone, Barry 475. Proscenium width, 30 ft. Station, Barry Dock, G.W.R.

ROMILLY CINEMA (RCA), Broad Street.— 1,250 seats. Continuous. Two changes Weekly. Prices, 1c to 1s. 6d. Proscenium width, 37 ft. Station, Barry G.W.R.

Fitted "ARDENTE" Deaf Aids
See page 258

ROYAL SUPER CINEMA (WE).—Prop., Barton Cinema Co., Ltd. 10, Windsor Place, Cardiff. 1,980 seats. Booked at Hall. Continuous. Stage, 25 ft. deep ; 12 dressing-rooms. Prices, 6d. to 2s. Proscenium width, 40 ft. Café. Phone, Barry 19. Station, Barry G.W.R.

BEAUMARIS (ANGLESEY), **Pop. 1,708.**

CINEMA (Marshall), Rating Row.—Prop., T. Clarke, 50, Castle Street, Beaumaris. 340 seats. Booked by Prop. Prices, 2d. to 1s. 3d. Station, Bangor, L.M.S.

BETHESDA (CARNARVON), **Pop. 4,476.**

PUBLIC HALL CINEMA (Uniquaphone).—Prop., E. H. James, 4, Cae Llan-Llanrwst. Booked at H.O. Once nightly. Two changes weekly. Price, 6d. Proscenium width, 25 ft. Station, Bethesda, L.M.S.

BLAENAU · FESTINIOG (MERIONETH), **Pop. 9,072.**

ASSEMBLY ROOMS (BTH).

EMPIRE PICTURE PALACE (BA).—Prop. and Res. Man., Capt. Lewis Davies, Shop, " Ycloch." 400 seats. Booked at H.O. Two changes, weekly. Prices, 6d. to 1s. Phone, Blaenau

Festiniog 27. Station, Blaenau Festiniog, L.M.S. and G.W.R.

FORUM (RCA).

PARK CINEMA (BA).—Prop., W. O. Thomas, Boston House, Blaenau Festiniog. 400 seats. Phone 47. Booked at Liverpool. Prices, 6d. to 1s. Proscenium width, 21 ft. Station, Blaenau Festiniog, L.M.S. and G.W.R.

BLAENGARW (GLAM.), **Pop. 10,000.**

CENTRAL CINEMA (BA), King Edward Street.— Prop., Blaengarw Cinemas, Ltd., 16, Courtland Terrace, Merthyr Tydfil, Phone, Merthyr 323. 650 seats. Continuous. Two changes weekly. Prices, 6d. to 1s. 3d. Proscenium width, 22 ft. Phone, Pontycymmer 4. Station, Blaengarw, G.W.R.

BLAEN-RHONDDA (GLAM.).

FERNHILL WORKMEN'S HALL (BTH).—Prop., Fernhill Workmen. 500 seats. Booked at Hall by Man. Continuous. Two changes weekly. Prices, 5d. to 1s. Phone, Treherbert 15. Station, Blaen-Rhondda, G.W.R.

BRECON (BRECKNOCK), **Pop. 5,334.**

NEW COLISEUM (WE), Wheat Street.—Props., Brecon Entertainments, Ltd. 650 seats. Booked at Cinema, Bridgend. Continuous. Two changes weekly. Stage, 25 ft. by 22 ft.; three dressing rooms. Prices, 7d. to 1s. 6d. Phone, Brecon 101. Station, Brecon, G.W.R.

BRIDGEND (GLAM.), **Pop. 10,033.**

CINEMA (WE).—Prop., Bridgend Cinemas, Ltd. 800 seats. Booked at H.O. Continuous. Prices, 6d. to 1s. 6d. Phone, Bridgend 101. Station, Bridgend, G.W.R.

PALACE (RCA).—Prop., Bridgend Cinemas, Ltd. 850 seats. Booked at H.O. Continuous. Prices, 6d. to 1s. 3d. Phone, Bridgend 101. Station, Bridgend, G.W.R.

PAVILION (Mihaly).—Props., Bridgend Cinemas, Ltd. 700 seats. Continuous, Evenings. Prices, 6d. to 1s. Phone, Bridgend 101. Station, Bridgend.

BRITON FERRY (GLAM.), **Pop. 9,176.**

PALACE KINEMA (RCA).—Prop., Palace Kinema Co. (Briton Ferry), Ltd. 650 seats. Booked at Hall. One show nightly, two on Sat. Two changes weekly. Prices, 3d. to 1s. Phone, Briton Ferry 45. Station, Briton Ferry, G.W.R., and R.T.

PICTUREDROME (RCA), Lowther Street.—Prop. and Man., O. J. Norman, Assembly Room Hotel. 475 seats. Booked at Hall. One show nightly, two on Sat. Prices, 6d. to 1s. Phone, 53. Station, Briton Ferry, G.W.R.

PUBLIC HALL CINEMA AND INSTITUTE.—(Closed).

BRYMBO (DENBIGH), **Pop. 4,906.**

CINEMA (Morrison).—Prop., A. Davies. Booked at Hall.

BRYNAMMAN (CARMARTHEN), **Pop. 7,500.**

PUBLIC HALL CINEMA (BA).—Props., West of England Cinemas, Ltd., 2, St. Andrews Place, Cardiff. Phone 1963. 994 seats. Booked at H.O. Prices, 6d. to 1s. 3d. Proscenium width, 38 ft. Stage, 20 ft. deep ; four dressing-rooms. Station, Brynamman. G.W.R

BRYNMAWR (BRECKNOCK), **Pop. 7,247.**

COSY CINEMA (Edibell).—Props., R. W. Phillips and Sons, 3, Greenland Road, Brynmawr. Phone, Brynmawr 39. 500 seats. Booked at Hall. Continuous. Prices, 4d. to 1s. Proscenium width, 25 ft. Station, Brynmawr, G.W.R.

BRYNMAWR—Contd.
Town Hall Cinema (Edibell).—Props., R. W. Phillips and Sons, 3, Greenland Road, Brynmawr. Phone, Brynmawr 39. 800 seats. Booked at Hall. Twice nightly. Stage, 30 ft. deep ; three dressing-rooms. Prices, 4d. to 1s. Proscenium width, 35 ft. Station, Brynmawr, L.M.S.

BUCKLEY (Flint), Pop. 6,900.
Palace (ba).—Prop., Cropper and Sons. 400 seats. Res. and Booking Man., T. N. Cropper. One show nightly, two on Sat. Two changes weekly. Prices, 5d. to 1s. Stations, Buckley Junction, L.N.E.R., and Padeswood and Buckley, L.M.S.
Tivoli Theatre (Filmophone). — Props., Buckley Picture House, Ltd. Phone 59. Booked at Hall. Pictures and Variety. Stage, 30 ft. deep ; six dressing-rooms. Prices, 3d. to 1s. 3d.

BUILTH WELLS (Brecknock), Pop. 1,663.
Kino Picture House (Kamm).—Props., Brecon Entertainments, Ltd. 500 seats. One show nightly. Prices, 5d. to 1s. 6d. Station, Builth Wells, G.W.R.

BURRY PORT (Carmarthen), Pop. 5,752.
Stepney Cinema, Snowden House.—Prop., Thomas Williams, 118, Penscoed Road. 350 seats. Continuous. Prices, 6d. and 9d. Phone, 58. Station, Burry Port.

CADOXTON (Barry) (Glam.), Pop. 5,844.
Palace (ba).—Props., Barton Cinema Co., Ltd., 10, Windsor Place, Cardiff. Phone, 225. 700 seats. Booked at H.O., Continuous. Two changes weekly. Prices, 4d. to 1s. Phone, Cardiff 477. Station, Cadoxton, Barry, G.W.R.
Plaza Cinema (rca).—Prop., Scott Selwyn Leek. 750 seats. Booked at Selwyn Variety Agency, Cardiff. Continuous. Prices, 4d. to 1s. Proscenium width, 45 ft. Stage, 12 ft. deep ; two dressing-rooms. Station, Cadoxton, G.W.R.

CAERAU (Glam.), Pop. 6,600.
Coliseum (we).—Prop., W. E. Jones, The Square, Caerau. 617 seats. Booked at Hall. Continuous. Two changes weekly. Prices, 3d. to 9d. Phone, Caerau 23. Station, Caerau, G.W.R.
Cosy Cinema (we).—Prop., W. G. Jones. 505 seats. Continuous. Booked at Hall. Occasional Variety. Stage, 16 ft. by 10 ft.; three dressing-rooms. Prices, 7d. and 1s. Proscenium width, 16 ft. Phone, Caerau 17. Station, Caerau, G.W.R.

CAERGWRLE (Denbigh), Pop. 1,520.
Derry Cinema (Cambria).—Props., E. and M. E. Rollason. One show nightly, two on Sat. Booked at Hall. Prices, 5d. to 1s. Proscenium width, 22 ft. Station, Caergwrle Castle, L.N.E.R.

CAERNARVON (Carnarvon), Pop. 8,469.
Empire Picture House (ba). Crown Street. Props., Caernarvon Cinema Co., Ltd., Bridge House, Queens Ferry, Nr. Chester. 512 seats. Booked at H.O. Continuous, Three shows on Sat. Prices, 6d. to 1s. 6d. Phone, Caernarvon 187. Station, Caernarvon, L.M.S.
Guild Hall (ba). 500 seats. /
Majestic (we)—Props., W. E. Pritchard and E. H. Jonathan. 1,050 seats. Booked at Hall. Continuous. Prices, 6d. to 1s. 6d. Proscenium width 26 ft. Phone, Caernarvon 16. Station, Caernarvon, L.M.S.
Plaza (we).—Prop., Capt. W. E. Pritchard, "Nant," Criccieth, North Wales. Phone, No. 36. 600 seats. Non-Continuous. Prices, 6d. to 1s. 6d. Phone, Caernarvon 11. Station, Penygroes, L.M.S.

CAERPHILLY (Glam.), Pop. 35,760.
Castle Cinema (we).—Prop., Castle Cinema (Caerphilly), Ltd., 7, St. Andrew's Crescent, Cardiff. Phone, Cardiff 7279. 800 seats. Continuous. Two changes weekly. Prices, 5d. to 1s. Station, Caerphilly, G.W.R.
Workmen's Hall (Picturetone).—Prop., Caerphilly Workmen's Hall and Institute Committee, 20, Castle Street. Phone, Caerphilly 168. 650 seats. Booked at Cardiff. Continuous. Prices, 5d. to 1s. Proscenium width, 18 ft. Road transport.

CARDIFF (Glam.), Pop. 223,648.
Canton Cinema (we), Cowbridge Road.—Prop., Splott (Cardiff) Cinema Co., Ltd., 14, St. Andrew's Crescent, Cardiff. Phone, Cardiff 2901. 1,000 seats. Booked at 15, Windsor Place, Cardiff. Continuous. Mats., Mon. and Sat. Prices, 6d. to 1s. 3d. Phone, Cardiff 4240. Station, Cardiff, G.W.R.
Capitol (we), Queen Street.—2,800 seats. Lessees, Paramount Film Service, Ltd. Booked at 104-108, Oxford Street, London. Museum 4721. Pictures and occasional Variety. Continuous. Prices, 9d. to 2s. Proscenium width, 45 ft. Stage, 10 ft. deep, five dressing-rooms. Café. Phone, Cardiff 6477-8. Station, Cardiff, G.W.R.
Central Cinema (we).—Prop., Castle and. Central Cinemas, Ltd. Phone, Cardiff 2982. 1,098 seats. Booked at Hall. Continuous. Prices, 4d. to 9d. Phone, Cardiff 2036. Station, Cardiff, G.W.R.
Coliseum (rca),139, Cowbridge Road, Canton. 900 seats. Prop., W. E. Willis, "Fairwell," Llandaff. Phone, 149 Llandaff. Continuous. Booked at Globe Cinema, Penylan, Cardiff. Prices, 7d. to 1s. Proscenium width, 25 ft. Phone, Cardiff 4434. Station, Cardiff, G.W.R.
Coronet (bth), Woodville Road.—Prop., New Coronet Cinema Co., Woodville Road, Cardiff, 600 seats. Booked at Hall. Continuous. Proscenium width, 16 ft. Prices, 6d. to 1s. Phone, Cardiff 2794. Station, Cardiff, G.W.R.

EMPIRE THEATRE (WE).—Props., Gaumont British Corporation, New Gallery House, Regent Street, W.1. 2,599 seats. **Fitted "ARDENTE" Deaf Aids See page 258**

C O M P T O N

ORGAN featured here.

GAIETY CINEMA (WE), City Road.—Prop., Splott (Cardiff) Cinema Co., Ltd., 14, St Andrew's Crescent, Cardiff. Phone, Cardiff 2901. 1518 seats. Booked at H.O. Continuous. Two changes weekly. Prices, 7d to 1s. 4d. Phone, Cardiff 3012. Station, Cardiff, G.W.R.

GLOBE (RCA).—Prop., W. E. Willis. 600 seats. Continuous evenings. Prices, 6d. to 1s. Phone, Cardiff 3072. Station, Cardiff.

NEW HIPPODROME (BA), Westgate Street.— Props., Matthews Cinemas, Ltd. Booked at Hall. Continuous. Prices, 5d. to 1s. Proscenium width, 40 ft. Phone, Cardiff 2393. Station, Central, G.W.R.

NINIAN PALACE (BTH). — Prop., Splott (Cardiff), Cinema Co., Ltd. 600 seats. Continuous. Two changes weekly. Prices, 7d. to 1s. 4d. Phone, Cardiff 3349. Station, Cardiff, G.W.R.

ODEON (BTH), Queen Street.—Props., Odeon (Cardiff), Ltd., Cornhill House, Bennett's Hill, Birmingham. Phone: Midland 2781. Booked at 49, Park Lane, London, W.1. Continuous. Prices, 9d. to 2s. Proscenium width, 50 ft. Phone : Cardiff 2358.

OLYMPIA (WE), Queen Street.—Props., Associated British Cinemas, Ltd., 30-31, Golden Square, London, W.1. Phone: Gerrard 7887. 1,850 seats. Continuous. Prices 6d. to 1s. 6d. Station, Cardiff, G.W.R.

PARK HALL CINEMA (WE) Park Place.—Prop., Park Hall and Hotel Co., Ltd., 3, Park Place, Cardiff. Phone, Cardiff 729. 1,850 seats, Booked at H.O. Continuous. One change weekly. Prices, 9d. to 2s. Phone, Cardiff 3687. Station, Cardiff, G.W.R.

PAVILION CINEMA (BTH), St. Mary Street.—Prop., Associated British Cinemas, Ltd., 30-31, Golden Square, W. Phone, Gerrard 7887. 1216 seats. Booked at H.O. Continuous. Prices 6d. to 1s 6d. Proscenium width, 27 ft. Café Dance Hall. Phone 670.

PLAZA CINEMA (WE), North Road.—Props., Gabalfa Cinema Co., Ltd., 14, St. Andrew's Crescent. Cardiff. Phone, Cardiff 2901. 1,500 seats. Continuous. Prices, 6d. to 1s. 4d. Booked at H.O. Phone, Cardiff 6232.

QUEEN'S CINEMA (WE), Queen Street. Prop., Associated British Cinemas, Ltd., 30-31, Golden Square, London, W. Phone, Gerrard 7887. 1,253 seats. Booked at H.O. Continuous. Prices, 7d. to 2s. Phone, Cardiff 3391. Station, Cardiff, G.W.R. **Fitted "ARDENTE" Deaf Aids See page 258**

REGENT (WE), Mill Road, Ely.—Props., Splott (Cardiff) Cinema Co., Ltd., 14, St. Andrew's Crescent, Cardiff. Phone, Cardiff 2901. 1591 seats.

RIALTO (WE).

SPLOTT CINEMA (WE), Agate Street.—Prop., Splott (Cardiff) Cinema Co., Ltd. 2,000 seats. Booked at 14, St. Andrews Crescent, Cardiff. Continuous. Mat. daily. Two changes weekly. Prices, 6d. to 1s. 4d. Phone Cardiff 4854. Station, Cardiff, G.W.R.

TIVOLI (WE), Station Road, Llandaff North.— Prop., Luxury Cinema Theatres, Ltd., 14, St. Andrew's Crescent, Cardiff. Phone, Whitchurch 850.

CARDIGAN (CARDIGAN), Pop. 3,309.
PAVILION (BTH).—Prop., Cardigan Cinema Co., Ltd. 800 seats. Once nightly. Twice on Sat. Two changes weekly ; three on holidays, Prices, 2d. to 1s. 6d. Phone 56.

CARMARTHEN (CARMARTHEN), Pop. 10,310.
CAPITOL (WE).—Props., Capitol (Carmarthen), Ltd. 828 seats. Pictures and occasional Variety.

EMPIRE, Blue Street.—Licensee, P. F. J. Bosisto. Pictures and Variety.

LYRIC THEATRE (WE), King's Parade.—Licensee., W. E. Morgan. 550 seats. Booked at Cardiff. Two shows nightly. Prices, 6d. to 1s. 6d. Proscenium width, 20 ft. Café. Phone, Carmarthen 207. Station, Carmarthen G.W.R.

CEFN (DENBIGH), Pop. 7,035.
GEORGE EDWARDS HALL (AWH).—Props., Parish Hall Committee, 600 seats. Twice nightly. Prices, 4d. to 1s. Phone, Cefn 97. Station Cefn, G.W.R.

PALACE CINEMA (BA).—Prop., J. Jones. 700 seats. Booked at Hall.

CHIRK (DENBIGH), Pop. 4,879.
PARISH HALL (Gyrotone), The Wharf.—Prop., Chirk Empire Cinema Co., Ltd. Regd. Office, Walnut Tree Cottage, Chirk. 450 seats. Continuous. Prices, 3d. to 1s. Stage and two dressing-rooms. Station, Chirk, G.W.R.

CLYDACH-ON-TAWE (GLAM.), Pop. 7,707.
GLOBE THEATRE (BTH).—Prop., J. Hopkin. 1,000 seats. Booked at Cardiff. One show nightly. Two shows Sat. Prices, 7d. to 1s. 3d. Proscenium width, 27 ft. Dance Hall attached. Phone, Clydach 46.

COLWYN BAY (DENBIGH), Pop. 20,885.
ARCADIA (WE).—Prop., Catlin's Arcadia Winter Gardens and Picture House. 1,000 seats, Booked at Hall. Continuous. Prices, 9d. to 2s. Proscenium width, 30 ft. Phone, Colwyn Bay 2765. Station, Colwyn Bay, L.M.S.

COSY CINEMA (BTH).—Prop., Cosy Cinema (Colwyn Bay), Ltd. 300 seats. Booked at Princess Theatre. Continuous. Prices, 6d. to 1s. 6d. Phone, Colwyn Bay 2105.

ODEON THEATRE (BTH), Cr. Conway Road and Marine Road.—Props., Odeon (Colwyn Bay), Ltd., Cornhill House, Bennett's Hill, Birmingham. Phone : Midland 2781. Booked at 49, Park Lane, London, W.1. Continuous. Prices, 9d. to 2s. Phone : Colwyn Bay 2827.

PRINCESS PICTURE THEATRE (BTH).—Props., M. A. Kenyon & Sons. 800 seats. Booked at Hall. Continuous nightly. Two changes weekly. Mats., daily. Prices, 9d. to 2s. Proscenium width 32 ft. Phone, Colwyn Bay, 2557.

RIALTO PICTURE HOUSE (WE).—Prop., Coast Cinemas, Ltd. Dirs., W. Whitehead and E. Pittingale. Continuous. Two changes weekly. Occasional Variety. Stage, 24 ft. deep ; 2 dressing-rooms. Café. Prices 8d. to 2s. Phone, Colwyn Bay 2054.

SUPREME CINEMA (WE), Old Colwyn.—Prop., Old Colwyn Picture Theatre, Ltd., Liverpool. 476 seats. Booked by L. H. Clegg, 33, James Street, Liverpool. Continuous. Prices, 6d. to 1s. 3d. Phone, Colwyn Bay 5549.

CONNAH'S QUAY (FLINT), Pop. 5,065.
ALHAMBRA (BA).

CONNAH'S QUAY—Contd.

HIPPODROME (BA), High Street, Connah's Quay.
—Prop., Deeside Enterprise Cinemas, Ltd., 1.
Hunter Street, Chester. Phone, Chester 530,
Booked at Bridge House, Queensferry. Once
nightly. Twice Sat. Prices, 6d. to 1s.
Phone, Connah's Quay 161. Station, Connah's
Quay, L.M.S.

CONWAY (CARNARVON), **Pop. 8,769.**

PALACE (WE). High Street.—Props., The Palace
Cinema, Conway. Continuous. Booked at
Hall. Prices, 9d. to 2s. Phone, 142. Station,
Conway, L.M.S.

TOWN HALL CINEMA (Kamm). 500 seats.—
Props., Conway Cinema Co., Ltd. Booked at
Hall. Continuous. Prices, 6d. to 1s. 6d.
Proscenium width, 24 ft. Stage, 18 ft. deep ;
two dressing-rooms. Station, Conway, L.M.S.

CRICCIETH (CARNARVON). **Pop. 1,449.**

MEMORIAL HALL CINEMA (BA).—Props., Criccieth
Memorial Hall Committee.

CRICKHOWELL (BRECKNOCK), **Pop. 2,000.**

CLARENCE HALL (BTH).

PICTURE HOUSE.—Prop., James Isaac. Booked
at Hall by Prop. Once nightly. Mat. Sat.
Prices, 4d. to 1s. 3d. Phone, Crickhowell 33.
Station, Abergavenny, G.W.R., thence by
motor.

CRYNANT (GLAM.).

MEMORIAL HALL CINEMA (BTF). 700 seats.

CWMAMAN (nr. Aberdare) (GLAM.), **Pop. 5,214.**

PALACE CINEMA (AWH).—Prop., W. E. Willis,
Fairwell, Llandaff.

CYMMER (GLAM.), **Pop. 2,521.**

COSY CINEMA (BA), Nr. Port Talbot.—Props.,
Thomas Davies, Glamorgan House, Cymmer.
380 seats. Phone No. 9. Booked at H.O.
Continuous. Prices, 6d. to 1s. Proscenium
width 24 ft. Station, Cymmer, via Bridgend,
G.W.R.

DENBIGH (DENBIGH), **Pop. 7,249.**

SCALA CINEMA (BA).—Props., Deeside Enterprise
Cinemas, Ltd., 1, Hunter Street, Chester.
Phone, Chester 530. 450 seats. Booked at
Bridge House, Queensferry, near Chester.
Once nightly. Prices, 6d. to 1s. 3d. Station,
Denbigh, L.M.S.

TOWN HALL CINEMA.—Prop., Deeside Enterprise
Cinemas, Ltd., 1, Hunter Street, Chester.
Phone, Chester 530. 900 seats. Booked at
Bridge House, Queensferry, near Chester.
Once nightly. Prices, 4d. to 8d.

DOWLAIS (GLAM.), **Pop. 18,112.**

ODDFELLOWS HALL (BTH), Union Street.—Prop.,
W. Stone, Hippodrome, Tonypandy. Phone,
Tonypandy 54. 500 seats. Booked at H.O.
Continuous. Stage, 27 ft. ; two dressing-
rooms. Prices, 4d. to 1s.

VICTORIA ELECTRIC THEATRE (RCA), High Street.
—Prop., Victoria Cinemas, Ltd. 500 seats.
Booked at 36, Union Street, Dowlais. Continuous. Prices, 5d. to 1s. Phone, Dowlais
39. Station, Merthyr Tydfil, G.W.R.

FERNDALE (GLAM.), **Pop. 18,144.**

TUDOR PALACEUM (WE).—Prop., F. Pellew. 710
seats. Continuous. Two changes weekly.

WORKMEN'S HALL (WE) 1,100 seats.—Props.,
Ferndale Workmen, 56/7, High Street,
Ferndale. 975 seats. Booked at Cardiff.
Two shows nightly. Prices, 6d. to 1s. Pro-
scenium width, 30 ft. Stage 25 ft. deep.
Six dressing rooms. Dance hall. Phone,
Ferndale 8. Station, Ferndale, G.W.R.

FISHGUARD (PEMBROKE), **Pop. 2,963.**

THE CINEMA (WE).—Props., Williams Bros.,
3, Main Street. Phone, Fishguard 223. 450
seats. Booked at H.O. One show nightly.
Two shows Wed. and Sat. Two changes
weekly. Prices, 5d. to 1s. 6d. Station,
Fishguard and Goodwick, G.W.R.

FLINT (FLINT), **Pop. 7,563.**

EMPIRE (AWH).—Prop. and Man., R. Davies.
700 seats. One show nightly. Three changes
weekly. Prices, 3d. to 8d. Phone, Flint 32.
Station, Flint, L.M.S.

GRAND KINEMA (AWH), Church Street.—Prop.
and Res. Man. R. Davies. 900 seats. Two
shows Mon. and Sat., one rest of week. Two
changes weekly. Pictures and Variety.
Stage, 26 ft. by 15 ft. ; 2 dressing-rooms.
Prices, 5d. to 1s. 3d. Phone, Flint 31.

GARNANT (CARMARTHENSHIRE).

WORKMEN'S HALL (WF).—Prop., Trustees
Workmen's Hall. 900 seats. Once nightly.
Twice Sat. Booked at hall. Prices, 5d. to
1s. 3d. Proscenium width, 26 ft. Station,
Garnant (G.W.R.).

GILFACH GOCH (GLAM.), **Pop. 9,000.**

GLOBE CINEMA (Morrison).— Prop., D. P.
Griffiths. 480 seats. One show nightly.
Two shows Sat. Two changes weekly. Prices,
4d. to 1s. Road Transport.

WORKMEN'S HALL (BTH), Glenavon Terrace
Prop., Workmen's Hall and Institute. 556
seats. Booked at Hall. Once nightly, two
shows Sat. Prices, 4d. to 1s. Phone, Gilfach
Goch 14. Station, Tonyrefail, G.W.R. Films
by Film Transport Service (Cardiff), Ltd.,
Newport Road, Cardiff.

GLANAMMAN (CARMARTHEN).

PALACE (RCA).—Props., Richards and Co. 400
seats. One show nightly. Two changes
weekly. Station, Glanamman, G.W.R.

GLYN-NEATH (GLAM.), **Pop. 4,000.**

NEW THEATRE (BTH).—Prop. Glyn-Neath
Picture and Variety Co., Ltd. 600 seats.
Booked at Hall. One show nightly. Prices,
6d. to 1s. 3d. Proscenium width, 22 ft.
Phone, Glyn-neath 13. Station, Glyn-neath
G.W.R.

GORSEINON (GLAM.), **Pop. 10,000.**

ELECTRA CINEMA (WE).— Prop., Gorseinon
Cinemas, Ltd. 784 seats. Booked at Hall.
Once nightly. Two changes weekly. Prices,
6d. to 1s. 6d. Proscenium width, 21 ft.
Phone, Gorseinon 14. Stations, Gorseinon,
L.M.S. and Gowerton, G.W.R.

LIDO (RCA), West End Square.—Lessees, Chris
and Jack Evans. 700 seats. Booked at
Capitol, Cross Hands. Continuous, 6.30 to 10.
Prices, 7d. to 1s. 6d. Proscenium width, 25 ft.
Stations, Gorseinon, L.M.S. and Gowerton,
G.W.R., and Cardiff transport by road.

GOWERTON (GLAM.), **Pop. 2,748.**

TIVOLI CINEMA (JTA).—Props., D. Thomas and
Son. 400 seats. Man. Dir., Frank H. Thomas.
Continuous Sats. Prices, 7d. to 1s. 3d.
Stations, Gowerton, L.M.S. and G.W.R.
Film Transport.

GWAEN-CAE-GARWEN (CARM.).
WELFARE HALL (BTH).—Props., The West of England Cinemas, Ltd., 2, St. Andrew's Place, Cardiff. Phone, Cardiff 1193. 966 seats. Continuous. Booked at H.O. Prices, 6d. to 1s. 3d. Proscenium width, 32 ft. Stage, 45 ft. deep ; nine dressing-rooms. Phone, 52. Film Transport.

HAVERFORDWEST (PEMBROKE), **Pop. 6,113.**
COUNTY THEATRE (WE).—Props., West of England Cinemas, Ltd., 2, St. Andrews Place, Haverfordwest, 235. 1,000 seats. Prices, 6d. to 2s. Continuous. Occasional Variety. Proscenium width, 35 ft. Stage 28 ft. deep ; 10 dressing rooms.
PALACE THEATRE (WE).—Prop., West of England Cinemas, Ltd., 2, St. Andrews Place, Cardiff. 800 seats, Booked at Hall. Continuous. Occasional Variety. Prices, 9d. to 1s. 6d. Proscenium width 33ft. Stage 35ft. deep ; six dressing-rooms. Phone, Haverfordwest 182. Station, Haverfordwest, G.W.R.

HIRWAIN (GLAM.), **Pop. 5,000.**
VICTORIA HALL (RCA).—Props, Hirwain Victoria Hall Co., Ltd. 500 seats. Res. and Booking Man., W. G. Brett, Aberdare. Two shows Mon. and Sat., one rest of the week. Two changes weekly. Prices, 5d. to 1s. Station, Hirwain. G.W.R.

HOLYHEAD (ANGLESEY), **Pop. 10,707.**
EMPIRE THEATRE (RCA), Stanley Street.—Props., Holyhead Empire Theatre Co., Ltd. 719 seats. Booked by D. D. Farquharson. Continuous. Mat., Sat. Prices, 6d. to 1s. 6d. Phone, Holyhead 44. Station, Holyhead, L.M.S.
HIPPODROME (BTP), Market Street.—Prop., Holyhead Hippodrome, Ltd. 488 seats. Booked at Hall. Continuous Prices, 6d. to 1s. 3d. Phone, Holyhead 222. Station, Holyhead.

HOLYWELL (FLINT), **Pop. 3,674.**
PRINCE OF WALES THEATRE AND CINEMA (Cambriaphone).—Prop., J. F. Burns and M. Clegg. Booked at H.O. Pictures and Variety. Continuous. Prices, 5d. to 1s. 3d. Phone, Holywell 42. Station, Holywell, L.M.S.

KENFIG HILL (GLAM.), **Pop. 3,700.**
THE CINEMA (RCA).—Prop., Kenfig Hill Cine Co., Ltd. 500 seats. Res. Man. Dir., G. F. Mullens. Phone, 36. Booked at 43, Pisgah Street, Kenfig Hill. One show nightly, two on Sat. Two changes weekly. Prices, 6d. to 1s. 3d. Station, Pyle, G.W.I., or Road Transport.
WELFARE HALL (BTH).—Props., Kenfig Hill and Pyle Welfare Association, 45, High Street, Cardiff. 434 seats. Booked at H.O. One show nightly, Sat. continuous. Prices 2d. to 1s. 3d. Café and Dance Hall attached. Film Transport.

KIDWELLY (CARMARTHEN). **Pop. 3,161.**
KIDWELLY CINEMA (BA).—Prop. and Res. Man. T. Foy. Booked at Hall. One show nightly, two on Sat. and Mat. Occasional Variety. Prices, 7d. to 1s. Proscenium width, 18 ft. Stage 7 ft. deep ; two dressing-rooms. Station, Kidwelly, G.W.R.

KNIGHTON (RADNOR), **Pop. 1,800.**
PICTURE HOUSE (Morrison).—Prop., D. J. Madigan, Hill Crest, Hay, Hereford. Phone,

Hay 4. 220 seats. Booked at Plaza, Hay. Prices, 6d. to 1s. 3d. Films by Road Transport to Hay.

LLANBERIS (CARNARVON), **Pop. 2,912.**
CONCERT HALL (Uniquaphone).—Props., E. H. James, 4. Cae Llan Llanrwst. Booked at H.O.
EMPIRE CINEMA (Electrocord).—Prop., and Man., C. S. Wakeham. Booked at Hall. One show nightly at 7 p.m. Two changes weekly. Prices, 6d. to 9d. Proscenium width, 18 ft. Station, Llanberis, L.M.S.

LLANBRADACH (GLAM.), **Pop. 3,000.**
WORKMEN'S HALL (BA), High Street.—Props., Llanbradach Colliery Workmen. 650 seats. One show nightly. Two changes weekly. Prices, 4d. to 9d. Phone, No. 26. Station, Llanbradach, G.W.R.
EMPIRE (Morrison).—Prop., W. R. Thomas, 21, Princes Avenue, Caerphilly. 550 seats. One show daily. Prices, 5d. to 1s. Phone No. 33.

LLANDILO (CARMARTHEN), **Pop. 1,886.**
CINEMA (BA).—Prop., H. W. Simonton, 26, New Road. 240 seats. Once nightly. Prices, 6d. to 1s. 4d. Proscenium width, 20 ft. Station, Llandilo.

LLANDOVERY (CARMARTHEN), **Pop. 1,980.**
KINEMA (Imperial), Victoria Crescent.—Prop., D. R. Williams. Phone, No. 37. 350 seats. Booked at Hall. Three days only in Summer. All week Winter. Prices, 6d. to 1s. 3d. Station, Llandovery, G.W.R. and L.M.S.

LLANDRINDOD WELLS (RADNOR), **Pop, 2,925.**
GRAND PAVILION CINEMA (BTH), Spa Road Recreation Ground.—Prop., Reg. F. Pickard Brynavon, Ithon Road, Llandrindod Wells. 1,000 seats. Continuous. Booked at Hall. Prices, 6d. to 1s. 6d. Proscenium width 35 ft. Occasional Variety. Stage 28 ft. ; twelve dressing-rooms. Cafe attached.
PLAZA SUPER CINEMA (AWH).—Lessee, D. J. Madigan, Hill Crest, Hay. Hereford. 400 seats. Continuous. Booked at Plaza, Hay. Prices, 3d. to 1s. 6d. Proscenium width 20 ft. Phone. 167. Station, Llandrindod Wells, L.M.S.

LLANDUDNO (CARNARVON), **Pop. 13,677.**
GRAND THEATRE (BA).—Prop., Art Entertainments, Ltd. Phone, 6,888. 1,000 seats.
NEW CINEMA (RCA). 900 seats.
NEW PRINCES THEATRE (WE).—Prop., Princes Kinema Co., Ltd. 773 seats. Continuous. Prices, 9d. to 2s. Phone, Llandudno 6371.
PALLADIUM (WE).—Prop., Llandudno Palladium, Ltd. 1,420. Booked at Hall. Continuous. Mat. daily. Prices, 9d. to 2s. Proscenium width, 31 ft. Stage, 30 ft. deep ; eight dressing-rooms. Cafe. Phone, Llandudno 6244.
PIER PAVILION 1,500 seats.
SAVOY (BTH), Mostyn Street.—Prop., Llandudno Cinema Co., Ltd., Palladium Theatre, Llandudno. Phone, Llandudno 6244 923 seats. Booked at H.O. Continuous. Mat. daily. Prices, 6d. to 1s. 6d. Café. Phone, Llandudno 6925.
WINTER GARDENS (BTH).—Props., Odeon (Llandudno), Ltd., Cornhill House, Bennett's Hill, Birmingham. Phone: Midland 2781. Booked at 49, Park Lane, London, W.1. Prices, 9d. to 2s. Proscenium width 40 ft., stage 30 ft. deep ; 14 dressing rooms. Cafe and Dance Hall attached. Phone : Llandudno 6666. Station, Llandudno, L.M.S.

LLANDYSSUL (CARDIGAN). **Pop. 902.**
TYSSUL HALL (Morrison).—Western Cinemas Circuit.—Props., M. Jones and T. C. Price, 2, Penybryn Villas,· Penydarren, Merthyr Tydfil. 500 seats. One show weekly. Prices, 1s. to 1s. 3d. Proscenium width 22 ft. Stage, 14 ft. deep ; two dressing-rooms. Station, Llandyssul, G.W.R.

LLANELLY (CARMARTHEN), **Pop. 38,393.**
ASTORIA CINEMA (WE).—Prop., West of England Cinemas, Ltd., 2, St. Andrews Place, Cardiff Phone, No. 1963. 842 seats. Continuous. Booked at H.O. Pictures and occasional Variety. Prices, 6d. to 1s. 3d. Proscenium width, 32'ft. Stage, 14 ft, deep ; six dressing rooms, Phone 252. Stations, Llanelly G.W.R.
CAPITOL (LEWIPHONE). Cross Hands, Nr. Llanelly.—Props., Chris & Jack Evans. 450 seats. Booked at Hall. Nightly. Occasional Variety. Two shows Sat. Prices, 6d. to 1s. 4d. Proscenium width, 22 ft. Stage, 22 ft. deep. Phone, Cross Hands 37. Road transport.
HIPPODROME (RCA).—Prop., Glandwr Cinemas, Ltd., 10 Windsor Place Cardiff. Phone, Cardiff 225. 1,009 seats. Booked at H.O. Continuous. Prices, 4d. to 1s. 4d. Phone, 383. Station, Llanelly, G.W.R.
LLANELLY CINEMA (WE), Stepney Street.—Prop., Llanelly Cinema, Ltd. 850 seats. Booked at Hall. Continuous. Prices, 5d. to 1s. 4d. Phone, Llanelly 41.
ODEON THEATRE (BTH).—Props., Odeon (Llanelly), Ltd., Cornhill House, Bennett's Hill, Birmingham. Phone : Midland 2781. In course of construction).
PALACE (WE), Market Street.—Prop., Palace (Llanelly), Ltd. 1,003 seats. Prices, 6d. to 1s. 4d. Continuous. Station, Llanelly.
PUBLIC HALL, Tumble.
REGAL (WE).—Prop., Fairbank Cinema Co., Ltd., 10. Windsor Place, Cardiff. 1,500 seats. Booked at H.O. Continuous. Prices, 5d. to 1s. 6d. Café. Phone, Llanelly 685.

LLANFAIRFECHAN (CARNARVON), **Pop. 3,162.**
TOWN HALL CINEMA (Uniquaphone).—Props., Llanrwst Cinema, Ltd.· Phone, Llanrwst 47 ; 354 seats. Booked by E. H. James, " Lyndhurst," 4, Cae-Llan, Llanrwst. Continuous. Mon. to Fri. Three shows Sat. Prices, 6d. to 1s. 3d. Proscenium width, 26 ft. Stage, 25 ft. deep. ; two dressing-rooms. Station, Llanfairfechan, L.M.S.

LLANGEFNI (ANGLESEY), **Pop. 1,782.**
ARCADIA CINEMA HALL (BA).—Prop., T. J. Jones. 400 seats. Booked at Hall. One show nightly. Prices, 9d. to 1s. 6d. Phone, Llangefni 24. Station, Llangefni, L.M.S.

LLANGOLLEN (DENBIGH), **Pop. 2,937.**
DOROTHY CINEMA (BA).—Props., R. A. Horspool. Phone No. 2398. 400 seats. Separate shows. Prices, 6d. to 1s. 3d. Café and Dance Hall. Station, Llangollen, G.W.R.
TOWN HALL CINEMA.—Prop., Llangollen Advertising Committee. Booked at Hall. Prices, 6d. to 1s. Stage, 20 ft. deep ; 2 dressing-rooms. Station, Llangollen, G.W.R.

LLANHARRAN (GLAM.), **Pop. 1,504.**
CINEMA (RCA).—Prop., P. Phillips. Booked at Cardiff. One show nightly. Two changes weekly. Prices, 4d. to 1s. Proscenium width, 25 ft. Phone, Llanharran 16. Station, Llanharran, G.W.R.

LLANIDLOES (MONTGOMERY), **Pop. 2,700.**
CINEMA (Morrison).—Prop., R. Jervis and E.

Jones. 250 seats. Booked at Gwalia Restaurant, Llanidloes. Prices, 3d. to 1s. 3d. Films by Road Transport.

LLANRWST (DENBIGH), **Pop. 2,360.**
ELECTRIC CINEMA (Uniquaphone).—Prop., Llanrwst Cinema, Ltd. 200 seats. Booked by E. H. James, 4, Cae Llan, Llanrwst. One show nightly, two on Mon., three on Sat. Prices, 5d. to 1s. 3d. Proscenium width, 20 ft. Phone, Llanrwst 47. Station, Llanrwst, L.M.S.

LLANTRISANT (GLAM.), **Pop. 15,048.**
CINEMA (RCA).—Prop., P. Phillips. 450 seats.

MACHYNLLETH (MONT.), **Pop. 1,890.**
POWYS CINEMA (Morrison).— Prop., William Williams, Powys House, Machynlleth. 260 seats. Twice nightly. Prices, 3d. to 1s. 3d. Phone, 84. Station, Machynlleth, G.W.R.

MAESTEG (GLAM.), **Pop. 25,552.**
COSY CINEMA (WE), Office Road.—Prop. and Res. Man., R. Dooner, 2, Office Road, Maesteg. Booked in Cardiff. Twice nightly. Prices, 6d. to 1s. 2d. Phone, Maesteg 73. Station, Port Talbot, G.W.R.
NEW THEATRE (WE), Commercial Street.— Props., Maesteg Cinemas, Ltd. 789 seats. Continuous. Prices, 6d. to 1s. 2d. Phone, Maesteg 60. Station, Maesteg, G.W.R.

MARDY (GLAM.), **Pop. 12,000.**
MARDY WORKMEN'S HALL (BA).—Prop., Workmen's Hall and Institute. 800 seats. Booked at Hall. One show nightly. Two changes weekly. Prices, 6d. and 9d. Phone, Mardy 12. Station, Mardy, G.W.R., and Road Transport.

MENAI BRIDGE (ANGLESEY), **Pop. 1,675.**
TOWN HALL CINEMA (Uniquaphone).—Prop., E. H. James, 4, Cae Llan, Llanrwst. Phone, 47. 262 seats. Once nightly. Three shows Sat. Booked at H.O. Prices, 3d. to 1s. Proscenium width, 30 ft. Station, Menai Bridge, L.M.S.

MERTHYR TYDFIL (GLAM.), **Pop. 71,099.**
CASTLE SUPER CINEMA (WE), High Street.— Props., Associated British Cinemas, Ltd., 30-31, Golden Square, W.1. 2,500 seats. Booked at H.O. Continuous. Prices, 4d. to 1s. 3d. Proscenium width, 22 ft. Stage 12 ft. deep ; two dressing-rooms. Café.
PALACE (WE). Pontmorlais Circus.—Prop., Mrs. O. M. Gale, Coliseum, Aberystwyth. 750 seats. Booked at Hall. Continuous. Two changes weekly. Prices, 4d. to 1s. 3d. Phone, Merthyr 362. Station, Merthyr, G.W.R.
TEMPERANCE HALL (RCA).—Prop. and Res. Man., Israel Price. 600 seats. Two shows nightly. Prices, 6d. to 2s. Phone, Merthyr 77.
THEATRE ROYAL (RCA), Pontmorlais.—Props., Associated British Cinemas, Ltd., 30-31, Golden Square, W.1. 1,217 seats. Booked at H.O. Twice nightly. Three Mats. Prices, 4d. to 9d. Stage 22 ft. deep ; six dressing rooms. Phone, Merthyr 2. Road Transport.

MILFORD HAVEN (PEMBROKE), **Pop. 10,116.**
ASTORIA (WE), Market Square.—Prop., Scard's Cinema, Ltd. Man. Dir., H. J. Scard, Jnr. 459 seats. Continuous. Occasional Variety. Prices, 7d. to 2s. Phone, Milford Haven 36. Station Milford Haven, G.W.R. Cross-overs must be from Main line.
EMPIRE (BTH).—Prop., H. E. Weight, 35, Plymouth Road, Penarth. 669 seats. Continuous. Pictures and Variety. Prices, 9d. to 1s. 6d. Proscenium width, 32 ft. Phone, 223.

PALACE (WE), Robert Street.—Prop., H. Scard Jnr. 275 seats. Continuous. Prices, 7d. to 1s. 6d. Phone, Milford Haven 36. Station, Milford Haven, G.W.R. Cross-overs must be from Main Line.

MOLD (FLINT), Pop. 5,133.
ASSEMBLY HALL AND PALAIS DE DANSE.— Lessee, John L. Schofield, Yorke House, Mold. Booked at Yorke House. One show daily. Prices, 6d. to 1s. Stage, 12 ft. deep. Phone, Mold 37. Station, Mold.
PICTURE PALACE.
SAVOY PICTURE PALACE (BA), Chester Street.— Prop., Mold Picture Palace, Ltd. Man. Dir., John L. Scholfield, J.P. 800 seats. Booked at Hall. Nightly. Three shows Sat. and Holidays. Prices, 3d. to 1s. 3d. Proscenium width, 30 ft. Stage, 18 ft. deep ; four dressing rooms. Phone, Mold 37. Station, Mold.

MORRISTON (nr. Swansea) (GLAM.), Pop. 10,814.
GEM CINEMA (BA), Clydach Road.—Prop., Merglen Cinema Co., Ltd., 10, Windsor Place, Cardiff. Phone, Cardiff 225. 300 seats. Booked at H.O. Once nightly. Mat. Sat. Prices, 4d. to 1s. 4d. Phone, Morriston 7425. Station, Morriston, G.W.R.
REGAL (RCA).—Prop., Swansea Cinemas, Ltd. 900 seats. One show nightly. Two changes weekly. Booked at Hall. Occasional Variety. Prices, 6d. to 1s. 4d. Phone, Morriston 7571. Station, Swansea, G.W.R., and Road Transport.
Fitted "ARDENTE" Deaf Aids
See page 258

MOUNTAIN ASH (GLAM.), Pop. 38,381.
EMPIRE CINEMA (RCA).—Props., Mountain Ash Cinema Co., Ltd. 750 seats. Booked at H.O. Continuous. Prices, 6d. to 1s. Proscenium width, 25 ft.
NEW THEATRE (BA).—Prop., Trustees Workmen's Institute. 1,000 seats. Booked at Hall. One show nightly. Two changes weekly. Prices, 6d. to 1s. Phone, Mountain Ash 16. Station, Mountain Ash, G.W.R., and Road Transport.
PALACE CINEMA (RCA).—Prop., Mrs. L. M. Richards. 700 seats. Booked at H.O. Continuous Pictures. Prices, 6d. to 1s. Proscenium width, 22 ft.

MUMBLES (nr. Swansea) (GLAM.) Pop. 10,000.
TIVOLI PICTURE THEATRE (WE).—Prop., T. E. Merrells, " Eastwood," Park Drive, Swansea. Phone, 2560. 639 seats. Booked at Hall. One show nightly. Prices, 6d. to 1s. 6d. Phone, 6188. Station, Oystermouth, Mumbles Rly., G.W.R.
REGENT CINEMA (WE).—Prop., Newton Road.—Prop., Mumbles Cinemas, Ltd. 800 seats. Booked at Hall. Once nightly. Prices, 6d. to 1s. 6d. Phone, Mumbles 6188. Station, Oystermouth, G.W.R.

NANTYMOEL (GLAM.), Pop. 10,000.
WORKMEN'S HALL (RCA).—Prop., Local Workmen. 800 seats. Continuous Prices, 7d. to 1s. Proscenium width, 18 ft. Phone, Nantymoel 7. Station, Nantymoel, G.W.R.

NARBERTH (PEMBROKE), Pop. 1,046.
GRAND CINEMA.—Lessee, Dennis Rowlands, Croft House, Narberth. One show nightly Thurs., Fri. and Sat. Booked at Croft House. Prices, 6d. to 1s. 6d. Station, Narberth, G.W.R.

VICTORIA CINEMA (Morrison), Western Cinemas Circuit.—Props., M. Jones and T. C. Price, Booked at 2, Penybryn Villas, Penydarren. Merthyr Tydfil. One show weekly.

NEATH (GLAM.), Pop. 33,322.
EMPIRE (WE), Rope Walk.—Lessees, Neath Empire Cinema and Variety Co., Ltd., 1,300 seats. Booked at Hall. Three shows daily. Prices, 6d. to 1s. 6d. Café and Dance Hall attached. Phone, Neath 437. Station, Neath G.W.R.
GNOLL HALL (WE).—South Wales Cinemas, Ltd., Albert Hall, De La Beche, Swansea. 763 seats. Booked at H.O. by W. J. Vaughan. Three shows daily. Two changes weekly. Phone, Neath 166. Station, Neath.
WINDSOR CINEMA (WE)—Prop., South Wales Cinemas, Ltd., Albert Hall, De La Beche, Swansea.

NELSON (GLAM.).
CINEMA (WE).—Props., Principality Amusements Ltd. 480 seats. Prices, 3d. to 9d. Continuous. Booked at Palace, Abercynon. Proscenium width 22 ft. Station Llancaich, G.W.R.
COSY (WE).—Props., Principality Amusements Ltd., Park Hall, Senghenydd, Glam. 620 seats. Prices, 6d. to 1s. Booked at Palace, Abercynon. Proscenium width, 26 ft. Phone, 18. Station, Nelson, G.W.R.

NEWCASTLE EMLYN (CARMARTHEN), Pop. 762.
CINEMA (Portable Talkies).—Lessee, J. R. Parkington, Market Square, Newcastle Emlyn. 450 seats. Booked at H.O. One show weekly. Prices, 6d. to 1s. 3d.

NEWPORT (PEMBROKE).
MEMORIAL HALL (Morrison).—Prop., Western Cinemas, 2, Penybryn Villas, Penydarren, Merthyr Tydfil. One show per week.

NEWTOWN (MONTGOMERY), Pop. 5,152.
SCALA CINEMA (Morrison).—Prop., B. C. Woods. 500 seats. Booked at Victoria Hall. Once nightly. Pictures and Variety. Stage, 18 ft. two dressing-rooms. Prices, 4d. to 1s. 2d.
VICTORIA HALL (Morrison).—Lessee, B. C. Woods. 450 seats. One show nightly. Prices, 4d. to 1s. 2d. Station, Newtown.

NEW TREDEGAR (GLAM.), Pop. 4,727.
EMPIRE CINEMA (Mihaly).—Prop., Attwood Theatres, Ltd. 1,000 seats. Booked at Hall. Continuous. Phone, New Tredegar 24. Station, New Tredegar.

OGMORE VALE and GARW (GLAM) Pop. 26,979.
OLYMPIA (WE), High Street.—Props., Maesteg Cinemas, Ltd. 800 seats. Continuous. Prices, 4d. to 1s. Phone, Ogmore Vale 17.
WORKMEN'S HALL (BTH).—Prop., Ogmore Vale Workmen. 800 seats. Sec., E. L. Howells. Phone, Ogmore Vale 28. Booked at Hall by Sec. Continuous. Prices, 6d. to 1s. Proscenium width, 25 ft. Stage, 18 ft. by 25 ft. ; two dressing-rooms. Dance Hall. Phone, Ogmore Vale 27. Station, Ogmore Vale, G.W.R.

PEMBROKE DOCK (PEMBROKE), Pop. 12,008.
GRAND CINEMA (WE), Meyrick Street.—Prop., Grand Cinema Co., Ltd. Man. Dir., H. Claypoole. 550 seats. Two shows nightly. Mat. Sat. Two changes weekly. Prices, 4d. to 1s. 6d. Phone, Pembroke Dock 25. Station, Pembroke Dock, G.W.R.

PEMBROKE TOWN (PEMBROKE), **Pop. 4,000.**
HAGGAR'S CINEMA (RCA).—Props., Grand Cinema Co., Ltd. Once nightly. Twice Sat. Prices, 7d. to 1s. 6d.

PENARTH (GLAM.), **Pop. 17,710.**
WINDSOR KINEMA (WE).—Prop., Willmore Bros., Ltd. Man. Dir., L. Willmore. 939 seats. Booked at Hall. Continuous. Two changes weekly. Prices, 6d. to 1s. 6d. Café. Phone, Penarth 72. Station, Penarth, G.W.R.

PENCLAWDD (GLAM.).
MEMORIAL HALL (BA).—Props., Public Trustees Memorial Hall. 400 seats. Booked at Cardiff. Once nightly, twice Sat. Prices, 3d. to 1s. Station Penclawdd, L.M.S.

PENMAENMAWR (CARNARVON), **Pop. 4,021.**
OXFORD PALACE (Kamm).—326 seats. Pictures and Variety. Continuous. Stage, 21 ft. deep; two dressing-rooms. Prices, 6d. to 1s. 6d. Café.

PENRHIWCEIBER (GLAM.), **Pop. 8,816.**
WORKMEN'S HALL (RCA).—Prop., Penrhiwceiber Colliery Workmen. 500 seats. Sec., John Peregrine. Booked at Hall by Committee. One show nightly. Prices, 4d. to 9d. Phone, Penrhiwceiber 19. Station, Penrhiwceiber, G.W.R. (Low Level).

PENTRE (RHONDDA) (GLAM).
GRAND THEATRE (WE).—Prop. and Res. Man., W. E. Willis. 420 seats. Continuous. Two changes weekly. Prices, 5d. to 1s. Station, Ystrad, G.W.R.
WORKMEN'S HALL.

PENYGROES (CARNARVONSHIRE).
PLAZA (WE).—Prop., W. E. Pritchard, Nant, Criccieth. 600 seats. Once nightly. Prices, 6d. to 1s. 6d. Phone, 36. Station, Penygroes, L.M.S.

PONTARDAWE (GLAM.), **Pop. 14,000.**
LYRIC (Phillips).—Prop., Mrs. V. Davies, 6, Holly Street, Pontardawe. 500 seats. Continuous Sats. only. Prices, 7d. to 1s. 3d. Proscenium width, 20 ft. Phone No. 119. Station, Pontardawe, L.M.S.
PUBLIC HALL (WE).—Prop., Mrs. V. Davies. 650 seats. Booked at Hall. Continuous. Pictures and Variety. Prices, 3d. to 1s. 1d. Phone No. 119.

PONTARDULAIS (GLAM.).
TIVOLI (WE).

PONTLOTTYN (GLAM.), **Pop. 4,891.**
COSY CINEMA (Morrison), School Street.—Prop., The Workmen's Institute, The Library. 600 seats. Booked at Hall and Variety by Scott Selwyn, Queen's Hill Crescent, Newport. Mon., one show nightly. Twice nightly Sat. Stage 21 ft. by 15 ft.; four dressing-rooms. Prices, 6d. to 1s. Proscenium width, 15 ft. Station, Pontlottyn, G.W.R.

PONTYBEREM (CARMARTHEN), **Pop. 3,021.**
PALACE (WE).—Prop., Pontyberem Cinematograph Co., Ltd. 500 seats. Booked at H.O., Osborne House, Pontyberem. Prices, 3d. to 1s. 3d. Station, Pontyberem, G.W.R.

PONTYCLUN, nr. Cardiff (GLAM.), **Pop. 1,800.**
PARK HALL (RCA).—Prop., Phillip Phillips. Booked at Cardiff. One show nightly.

Prices, 7d. to 1s. 3d. Proscenium width, 20 ft. Phone, Pontyclun 75. Station, Llantrisant, G.W.R.

PONTYCYMMER (GLAM.), **Pop. 6,302.**
PUBLIC HALL (Kamm.)—Prop., Will Stone, New Hippodrome, Tonypandy. Phone, Tonypandy 54. 650 seats. Booked at H.O. Pictures and Variety. One show nightly, Sat. and Holidays. Mat., Wed. and Sat. Two changes weekly. Prices, 5d. to 1s. 2d. Station, Pontycymmer, G.W.R. (via Bridgend) and R.T.

PONTYGWAITH (GLAM.), **Pop. 9,000.**
CINEMA (AWH).—Props., Rhondda Fach Cinema Co., Ltd. 700 seats. Booked at Hall. Continuous. Prices, 6d. to 1s. Proscenium width, 18 ft. Station, Pontygwaith, Tylorstown.

PONTYPRIDD (GLAM.), **Pop. 42,737.**
GAIETY THEATRE (BTP), Beddau.—Prop., Cwm and Llantwit Welfare Scheme Council. 420 seats. Booked at Hall. Continuous. Prices, 3d. to 1s. Station, Llantwit.

GREAT WESTERN WORKMEN'S HALL (BTP).—Props., Great Western Colliery Workmen. Phone, 431. 900 seats. Two shows nightly. Booked at Hall by Manager. Pictures and Variety. Prices, 5d. to 1s. Proscenium width, 28 ft. Stage, 17 ft. deep; two dressing-rooms. Station, Pontypridd Central, G.W.R.

NEW THEATRE (Edibell).—Prop., Trenchard and Jones. 800 seats. Booked at Hall by Man. Twice nightly. Prices, 3d. to 1s. 2d.

PALLADIUM (WE).—Prop., Pontypridd Cinemas, Ltd., 7, St. Andrew's Crescent, Cardiff. Phone, Cardiff 7279. 1.240 seats. Continuous Café attached. Phone, Pontypridd 252.

PARK CINEMA (BA), 450 seats.

OWN HALL (WE).

WHITE PALACE (BTH).—Prop., Pontypridd Cinemas, Ltd., 7, St, Andrew's Crescent, Cardiff. Phone, Cardiff 7279. Continuous.

PORTH (GLAM.), **Pop. 40,000.**
CENTRAL CINEMA (WE), Hannah Street.—Prop., Castle and Central Cinemas, Ltd., 3–7, The Hayes, Cardiff. Phone, Cardiff 2982. 896 seats. Booked at H.O. by A. Bowden. Continuous. Two changes weekly. Prices, 6d. to 1s. 3d. Proscenium width, 25 ft. Phone, Porth 35. Station, Porth, G.W.R.

EMPIRE (BTP).—Lessee and Res. Man., J. Walter Bynorth. 700 seats. Booked at Hall. Continuous. Prices, 6d. to 1s. Station, Porth.

PORTHCAWL (GLAM.), **Pop. 6,447.**
CASINO (WE).—Prop., G. Beynon & Sons. 740 seats. Continuous. Prices, 1s. 2d. to 2s. 4d. Occasional Variety. Café and Dance Hall. Phone 244.

COLISEUM (WE).—Prop., G. Beynon & Sons. 600 seats. Continuous. Occasional Variety. Café and Dance Hall. Prices, 1s. 2d. to 2s. 4d. Phone, 244.

COSY THEATRE.—Prop., Cosy Theatre Syndicate. 550 seats. Booked at Hall. Continuous. Prices, 9d. to 1s. 3d. Station, Porthcawl, G.W.R.

PORTMADOC (CARNARVON), **Pop. 3,986.**
COLISEUM (WE).—Prop., Capt. Pritchard. 630 seats. Twice nightly. Prices, 8d. to 2s.

PORT TALBOT (Glam.), **Pop. 40,672.**
Capitol (rca), Aberavon.—Props., Woodwards Theatres. Ltd. Booked at Grand. Continuous. Prices, 6d. to 1s. 3d.

Electric Theatre (rca).—Props., Woodwards Theatres, Ltd. 700 seats. Booked at Grand. Continuous. Prices, 6d. to 1s. 3d.

Grand Theatre (rca). Forge Road—Props. Woodwards Theatres, Ltd. 1,100 seats. Booked at Hall. Continuous. Two changes weekly. Prices, 6d. to 1s. 3d. Station, Port Talbot.

New Empire Theatre (Picturetone), Aberavon. Prop., H. J. Lewis. 700 seats. Booked at Hall. Twice nightly. Pictures and Variety. Stage, 32 ft. deep; six dressing-rooms. Prices, 6d. to 2s. Phone 91.

Odeon Theatre (bth), Bethany Square.— Props., Odeon Theatres, Ltd., Cornhill House, Bennett's Hill, Birmingham. Phone: Midland 2781. (In course of construction).

Olympic Cinema (bth), Cwmavon.—Prop., R. V. Ebley. 600 seats. Booked at "Hazeldene," Depot Road, Cwmavon. One show nightly. Two changes weekly. Prices, 6d. to 1s. 3d. Proscenium width, 27 ft. Phone, Port Talbot 21. Station, Cwmavon.

Palace Cinema, Water Street.

Picturedrome.—Prop. and Man., John Rees. 650 seats. Continuous. Two changes weekly. Prices, 6d. to 1s. 3d.

Picturedrome (rca), Taibach.—Prop. and Res. Man., C. Roberts, 21, Tan-y-groes Street, Port Talbot. 475 seats. Booked at Hall. One show nightly. Prices, 6d. to 1s. Proscenium width, 30 ft. Station, Port Talbot.

Workmen's Hall (btp), Glyncorrwg.—Props., Trustees, Workmen's Hall. 450 seats. Once nightly. Prices, 6d. to 1s. Proscenium width, 24 ft. Phone No. 4.

PRESTATYN (Flint), **Pop. 4,511.**
La Scala (rca).—Props., Saronies Enterprises. 7/8, Saxone Bldgs., Church Street, Liverpool. 550 seats. Phone : Prestatyn 365.

Palladium (bth), High Street.—Props., Prestatyn Picturedrome Co., Ltd. 853 seats. Continuous evenings. Two changes weekly. Prices, 6d. to 1s. 6d. Café. Dance Hall. Phone, Prestatyn 89. Station, Prestatyn, L.M.S.

PRESTEIGN (Radnor), **Pop. 1,102.**
Assembly Rooms (Morrison).—Lessee, D. J. Madigan; Hill Crest, Hay, Hereford. Phone, Hay 4. 200 seats. Booked at Plaza, Hay. Prices, 6d. to 1s. 3d. Films by Road Transport to Hay.

PWLLHELI (Carnarvon), **Pop. 3,599.**
Town Hall (bth).—Prop., Pwllheli Corporation. Res. and Bkg. Man., C. Lloyd Roberts. 800 seats. Booked at Hall. Once nightly. Twice Wed. and Sat. Prices, 6d. to 1s. 6d. Station, Pwllheli.

RESOLVEN (Glam.), **Pop. 3,831.**
New Pavilion (bth).—Prop., Resolven Picture Palace Co., Palladium, Aberdare. 500 seats. Phone, Aberdare 138. Booked at Palladium, Aberdare. One show nightly. Two on Sat. Two changes weekly. Prices, 6d. to 1s. Station, Resolven, G.W.R.

RHAYADER (Radnor), **Pop. 1,100.**
Castle Cinema (Morrison).—Prop., D. J.

Madigan, Hill Crest, Hay, Hereford. Phone, Hay 4. 300 seats. Booked at Plaza, Hay. Prices, 6d. to 1s. 3d. Films by Road Transport to Hay.

RHOSNEIGR (Anglesey).
Pavilion.—Prop. and Res. Man., T. R. Evans. Booked at Hall. One show nightly, summer season only. Prices, 3d. to 1s. 3d. Phone, Rhosneigr 6. Station, Rhosneigr, L.M.S.

RHOS-ON-SEA (nr. Colwyn Bay) (Denbigh), **Pop. 3,000.**
Playhouse (bth).—Prop., and Man., Sidney Frere. Continuous. Mat., Sat. Two changes weekly. Prices, 4d. to 2s. Phone, Colwyn Bay 4306. Station, Colwyn Bay.

RHYL (Flint), **Pop. 13,489.**
Cinema Royal (we), High Street.—Prop., Rhyl Entertainments, Ltd., Queens Hotel, Rhyl. 710 seats. Booked by R. Edwards. "Beechcroft," Brighton Road, Rhyl. Phone, 239. Continuous. Two changes weekly. Daily Mat. Prices, 9d. to 1s. 3d.

Odeon Theatre (bth), Brighton Road and High Street.—Prop., Odeon (Rhyl) Ltd., Cornhill House, Bennett's Hill, Birmingham. Phone, Midland 2781. (In course of construction).

Plaza (we), High Street.—Prop., Rhyl Entertainments, Ltd., Queen's Hotel, Rhyl. Phone, 174. 1,500 seats. Booked by R. Edwards, "Beechcroft," Brighton Road, Rhyl. Continuous. Daily Mat. Prices, 1s. to 1s. 6d. Proscenium width, 45 ft. Phone, Rhyl 442. Station, Rhyl, L.M.S.

Queen's Theatre (btp), Promenade.—Prop., Rhyl Entertainments, Ltd., Queen's Hotel, Rhyl. Phone 174. 1,270 seats. Booked at H.O. Continuous. Mat. daily. Two changes weekly. Prices, 9d. to 1s. 4d. Cafe attached. Proscenium width 18 ft. Phone, Rhyl 391.

RUABON (Denbigh), **Pop. 4,500.**
Parish Hall Cinema.—Props., Ruabon Parish Hall Committee. Booked at Hall.

RUTHIN (Denbigh), **Pop. 2,912.**
Cinema (rca).—Prop., Ruthin Cinema Co., Ltd. 375 seats. Once nightly. Three shows Sat. Prices, 3d. to 1s. 6d. Proscenium width, 18 ft. Stage, 20 ft. deep; one dressing-room. Phone, Ruthin 43. Station, Ruthin.

SENGHENYDD (Glam.), **Pop. 5,350.**
Park Hall Cinema (Cinetok).—Prop., Principality Amusements, Ltd. 475 seats. Booked by Harry S. Bowen at the Palace, Abercynon, Glam. Pictures and Variety. Seven shows weekly. Prices 5d. to 11d. Station, Senghenydd, G.W.R.

SEVEN SISTERS (Glam.), **Pop. 2,500.**
Welfare Hall (bth).—Prop., Seven Sisters Miners' Welfare Society. 620 seats. Booked at Cardiff. One show nightly. Two changes weekly. Prices, 6d. to 1s. Proscenium width. 20 ft. Stage, 14 ft. deep. Two dressing-rooms. Station, Seven Sisters, G.W.R.

SHOTTON (Flint)
Alhambra.—Prop., and Res. Man., John Jones. 1,200 seats. Booked at Hall. Once nightly. Two changes weekly. Prices, 5d. to 2s. Station, Shotton.

SKEWEN (GLAM.), **Pop. 9,584.**
NEW CINEMA (RCA).—Prop., New Cinema Co., Continuous. Two changes weekly. Prices, 6d. to 1s. Station, Skewen, G.W.R.

SWANSEA (GLAM.), **Pop. 164,825.**
ALBERT HALL (WE).—Prop., South Wales Cinemas, Ltd., Albert Hall. 2,000 seats. Booked at H.O. Continuous. Prices, 6d. to 2s. Phone, Swansea 4576.

CARLTON CINEMA (WE), Oxford Street.—Prop., South Wales Cinemas, Ltd., Albert Hall. Swansea. 971 seats. Booked at H.O. by W. J. Vaughan. Continuous. Prices, 6d. to 1s. 6d. Phone, Swansea 4596.

CASTLE CINEMA (WE), Worcester Place.—Prop., Castle and Central Cinemas, Ltd., The Hayes, Cardiff. Phone, Cardiff 2982. 1,135 seats. Booked at H.O. Continuous from 2.30 Prices, 6d. to 1s. 6d. Proscenium width, 32 ft. Phone, Swansea 3433.

ELYSIUM CINEMA (BTP), High Street,—Prop., Anima Co., Ltd., 900 seats. Continuous. Pictures and Variety. Two changes weekly. Prices, 6d. to 1s. 6d. Phone, Swansea 4330.

GRAND (WE).—Prop., W. E. Willis, Globe Cinema, Albany Road, Penylan, Cardiff. 1,200 seats.

LANDORE CINEMA (BA), Landore.—Prop., Swansea Cinemas, Ltd. 600 seats. Booked at Regal, Morriston. One show nightly. Prices, 4d. to 1s. 4d. Phone, Swansea 3412. Station, Landore, G.W.R. and Road Transport.

NEW PALACE CINEMA.—Booked by W. E. Willis, Globe Cinema, Albany Road, Penylan, Cardiff.

PICTURE HOUSE (WE).—Prop., South Wales Cinemas, Ltd., Albert Hall, Swansea. 750 seats. Booked at H.O. by W. J. Vaughan. Continuous. Prices, 6d. to 1s. 6d. Phone, Swansea 4598. Station, Swansea.

PLAZA CINAMA (WE).—Prop., Picton Cinema Co., Ltd., 10, Windsor Place, Cardiff. 3,020 seats. Booked at H.O. Continuous. Prices, 7d. to 2s. 4d. Proscenium width, 48 ft. Café.

RIALTO (WE), Wind Street.—Prop., Picton Cinema Co., Ltd., 10, Windsor Place, Cardiff. Phone No. 225. 1,040 seats. Continuous. Booked at H.O. Prices, 6d. to 1s. 6d. Proscenium width 25 ft. Stage ; six dressing-rooms. Phone, Swansea 4204. Stations, Swansea and Victoria. L.M.S. Film transport.

RITZ.—Controlled by Union Cinemas, Ltd., 15, Regent Street, London, S.W.1.

SCALA (BA), St. Thomas.—Prop., Walter Hyman' Regal, Morriston, Swansea. 450 seats. Once nightly. Booked at Morriston. Prices, 4d. to 1s. 4d. Proscenium width, 22 ft. Phone, Swansea 2756. Station, High Street.

TIVOLI (RCA).—(Closed).

UPLANDS CINEMA (RCA).—Prop., Uplands Cinema Co., Ltd. Phone, Swansea 2234. Booked at Hall. 414 seats. Once nightly. Booked in Cardiff. Prices 4d. to 1s. 4d. Station, Swansea, G.W.R., and Road Transport.

TENBY (PEMBROKE), **Pop. 4,108.**
NEW PAVILION (WE).—Prop., M. W. Shanly, 135, King Henry's Road, South Hampstead, N.W. 630 seats. Booked at H.O. Continuous. Prices, 6d. to 2s. Café and Dance Hall. Phone 135. Station Tenby, G.W.R.

ROYAL PLAYHOUSE (WE).—Prop., Miss H. A. Beard, Royal Gate House Hotel. 600 seats. Booked at Cardiff. Twice nightly. Prices, 4d. to 2s. 6d. Two dressing-rooms. Proscenium width, 35 ft. Phone 194.

SHANLEY'S SUPER CINEMA (WE).—Prop., M. W. Shanly. 135, King Henry's Road. South Hampstead. 493 seats. Booked at H.O. Continuous. Prices, 4d. to 2s.

TON PENTRE (GLAM.), **Pop. 6,000.**
MAINDY AND EASTERN WORKMEN'S HALL (RCA). —Props., Maindy and Eastern Colliery Workmen. 630 seats. Continuous. Mat. Sat. Two changes weekly. Prices, 4d. and 6d. Phone, Pentre 14. Station, Ystrad, G.W.R.

TONYPANDY (GLAM.), **Pop. 25,000.**
EMPIRE (WE).—Prop. and Man., W. E. Willis. 900 seats. Continuous. Two changes weekly. Prices, 3d. to 1s. 1d. Station, Tonypandy.

NEW HIPPODROME (Klang Film).—Lessee, Will Stone. Booked at Hall. Continous. Two changes weekly. Prices, 4d. to 1s. Phone, Tonypandy 54. Station, Tonypandy, G.W.R.

PICTUREDROME (AWH) Pandy Square, Pandyfield.—Prop., Pandyfield Picturedrome Co. 900 seats. Continuous. Two changes weekly. Prices, 6d. to 1s. Phone, Tonypandy 111.

ROYAL CINEMA, Dewinton Street.—Prop., Royal Cinema Co. (Welsh Hills Cinema Co., Ltd.), Danygraig House, Dinas. Phone, Tonypandy 182. 800 seats. Booked at H.O. by W. G. Hutt. Continuous. Prices 5d. to 1s. Phone, Tonypandy 191.

TONYREFAIL (GLAM.), **Pop. 10,000.**
NEW CINEMA (Mihaly).—Lessee, W. R. Thomas, Empire Theatre, Llanbradach. Phone, Llanbradach 33. 560 seats. Booked at Empire. Continuous. Prices 4d. to 1s. Proscenium width, 18 ft. Phone, Tonyrefail 50. Station, Tonyrefail, G.W.R.

TREFOREST (GLAM.), **Pop. 10,355.**
NEW CECIL CINEMA (BA).—Prop., Cyril T. Attwell, 79, Penhevall Street, Grange, Cardiff. Phone 5974. Booked at Hall. Continuous. Prices, 5d. to 1s. Phone, Pontypridd 102. Station, Treforest, G.W.R.

TREGARON (CARDIGAN.).
MEMORIAL HALL (Morrison).—Prop., Western Cinemas, 2, Penybryn Villas, Penydarren, Merthyr Tydfil. One show weekly.

TREHARRIS (GLAM.), **Pop. 8,818.**
PALACE THEATRE (Klang-Tobis), The Square.— Prop., Will Stone, Town Hall, Pontypridd. Phone, Pontypridd 2311. 750 seats. Once nightly, twice Sat. Booked at Cardiff. Prices, 6d. to 1s. 3d. Proscenium width, 28 ft. Stage 20 ft. deep ; three dressing-rooms. Phone, Treharris 30. Station, Treharris.

559 seats. Booked at Hall. Continuous. Stage, 15 ft. deep; one dressing-room. Prices, 4d. to 1s. Proscenium width, 26 ft. Phone. Treherbert 42. Station, Treherbert, G.W.R,

TREORCHY (GLAM.), **Pop. 3,000.**
ABERGORKY WORKMEN'S HALL (RCA), Treorchy. —W. E. Willis Circuit, Globe Cinema, Albany Road, Penylan, Cardiff. 600 seats. Continuous. Prices, 3d. to 1s. Phone, Treorchy 227. Station, Treorchy, G.W.R.

PARK AND DARE WORKMEN'S HALL (WE). 1,200 seats. Continuous. Two changes weekly. Prices, 3d. to 1s. 2d. Phone, Treorchy 12.

PAVILION (AWH), Station Road.—Props., F. Hughes and F. Hutt. 39, Victoria Avenue, Porthcawl. Phone, Porthcawl 380. 800 seats. Booked in Cardiff. Prices, 4d. to 1s. Proscenium width, 22 ft. Phone, Treorchy **231.**

TROEDYRHIW (GLAM.), **Pop 6,850.**
PICTURE PALACE (BTH), Bridge Street, Troedyrhiw.—Prop., Troedyrhiw Picture Palace Co, Ltd. 500 seats. Gen. Man., Henry Lucas. Booked at Hall. Once nightly. Two changes weekly. Prices, 4d. to 1s. 2d. Station, Troedyrhiw, G.W.R.

TYLORSTOWN (GLAM.), **Pop. 10,000.**
COLISEUM (BA).—Props., Tylorstown Coliseum. 9, Mill Lane, Cardiff. Phone, Cardiff 5561. 550 seats. Booked at Hall. Continuous. Prices, 6d. to 1s. Proscenium width 21 ft. Station, Tylorstown, G.W.R.

WELFARE HALL (WE).

WELSHPOOL (MONTGOMERY), **Pop. 5,637.**
CLIVE PICTURE HOUSE (BTH).—600 seats. Booked at Hall. One show nightly. Two changes weekly. Prices, 4d. to 1s. Phone, Welshpool 67. Station, Welshpool, L.M.S. and G.W.R.

WHITCHURCH (GLAM.)
RIALTO.—Prop., W. E. Willis, Oldchurch Road. Whitchurch. 450 seats. Booked at Hall, Continuous. Mat., Sat. Two changes weekly. Prices, 6d. to 1s. Station, Llandaff (North) or Whitchurch, G.W.R.

WREXHAM (DENBIGH), **Pop. 18,567.**
GLYNN CINEMA (BTH).—Prop., Glynn Cinema (Wrexham), Ltd., 1–3, Stanley Street, Liverpool. Phone, Bank 4371/2. 900 seats. Booked at Prince of Wales News Cinema, Liverpool. Continuous. Prices, 6d. to 1s. 1s. Phone, Wrexham 2095. Station, Wrexham, G.W.R.

HIPPODROME (BTP).—Props., Wrexham Entertainments, Ltd. 950 seats. H. D. Moorhouse Circuit, 7, Oxford Road, Manchester.

MAJESTIC (BTH), Regent Street.—Prop., Majestic Cinema (Wrexham), Ltd., Regent Street, Wrexham. 1,800 seats. Booked at North Western Film Booking Agency, 60, Lime Street, Liverpool. Continuous. Prices, 4d. to 1s. Phone, Wrexham 2025.

ODEON THEATRE (BTH), Brook Street. — Props., Odeon (Wrexham) Ltd., Cornhill House, Bennett's Hill, Brmingham. Phone, Midland 2781. Booked at 49, Park Lane London, W.1.

PAVILION (BTP), Rhos.—Prop., Pavilion (Rhos), Ltd., Bridge House, Queensferry, Chester. Phone, Connah's Quay 49. 900 seats. Booked at H.O. Twice nightly. Prices, 4d. to 9d. Proscenium width, 23 ft. Phone, 25. Station, Wrexham.

PUBLIC HALL PICTUREDROME, Rhos.—Prop. Hughes and Mills. Booked at Hall.

YNISHIR (GLAM.), **Pop. 11,141.**
WORKMEN'S HALL CINEMA (BTP).—Manager, Fred Terry, 57, Charles Street, Porth, Rhondda. 150 seats. Booked at Hall. Continuous. Two changes weekly. Stage; two dressing-rooms. Prices, 5d. and 8d. Station, Ynishir, Rhondda Fach, G.W.R.

YNYSYBWL (GLAM.), **Pop. 5,149.**
WORKMEN'S HALL (BA). —Props., Lady Windsor Colliery Workmen. 465 seats. Booked by Committee. Once nightly. Prices, 6d. to 9d. Proscenium width, 40 ft. Stage, 16 ft. deep. Phone, Ynysybwl 8. Station, Ynysybwl, G.W.R.

YSTALYFERA (GLAM.), **Pop. 7,185.**
CAPITOL CINEMA (BA).—Props., Ystalyfera Kinemas, Ltd., Swansea. Phone, Swansea 82344. 720 seats. Prices, 6d. to 1s. 4d. Continuous. Booked at Hall. Phone, Tstalyfera 52.

CENTRAL CINEMA.—Prop. and Res. Man., J. W. Edwards. Booked at Brynmair. One show nightly. Prices, 6d. and 1s.

COLISEUM (RCA).—Props., Tstalyfera Kinemas, Ltd., Swansea. Phone, Swansea 82344. 550 seats. Continuous. Booked at Capitol.

EMPIRE (BA).—500 seats. Props., Tstalyfera Kinemas, Ltd., Swansea. Phone, Swansea 82344. 450 seats. Booked at Capitol.

YSTRADGYNLAIS (GLAM.), **Pop. 10,471.**
ASTORIA (WE).—Prop., West of England Cinemas, Ltd., 2, St. Andrew's Place, Cardiff. Phone, Cardiff 1963. 675 seats. Occasional Variety. Booked at H.O. Continuous. Prices, 6d. to 1s. 4d. Phone, Ystradgynlais 38. Films by Road Transport.

CINEMA AND THEATRE.—Prop. and Res. Man., Harry Page. Booked at Hall. One show nightly. Prices, 6d. and 1s.

YSTRAD MYNACH (GLAM.), **Pop. 2,081.**
CINEMA (RCA), Blydwyn Road.—Prop., Ystrad Mynach Cinemas, Ltd. 600 seats. Continuous. Two changes weekly. Prices, 5d. to 1s. 3d. Station, Ystrad Mynach, G.W.R.

TRAVELLING SHOWS.
PROP., MR. BURROWS—
CINEMA, Llanidloes, Montgomery.

SCOTTISH KINEMAS.

The Sound system installed is shown after the name. (BTP) = British Talking Pictures, Ltd.; (RCA) = RCA Photophone Inc.; (WE) = Western Electric Co., Ltd.; (BA) = British Acoustic; (BTH) = British Thomson-Houston. Other systems are indicated by name.

ABERDEEN (ABERDEEN), Pop. 167,259.

ASTORIA CINEMA (RCA).—Props. Aberdeen Astoria Cinema Ltd. Controlled by J. F. McDonald (Abdn.) Ltd. 2,038 seats. Prices, 6d. to 1s. 6d. Proscenium width, 46 ft. Phone, Aberdeen 4900. Station, Aberdeen, L.M.S. and L.N.E.R.

COMPTON
ORGAN featured here.

BELMONT (BA), Belmont Street.—Props. Caledonian Theatre Ltd.,- 1, East Craibstone Street, Bon Accord, Square, Aberdeen. 777 seats. Continuous. Two changes weekly Prices, 5d. to 1s. Proscenium width, 20 ft. Stage, 10 ft. deep; two dressing-rooms. Phone 241. Joint Station, Aberdeen.

CAPITOL (WE), 431, Union Street. —Props., Aberdeen Picture Palaces, Ltd., 2, West Craibstone Street, Aberdeen. 2,100 seats. Continuous. Prices, 9d. to 2s. 6d. Proscenium width, 38 ft. Stage, 32 ft. deep; four dressing-rooms. Café. Phone, 379. Joint Station, Aberdeen, and road transport.
Fitted "ARDENTE" Deaf Aids
See page 258

COMPTON
ORGAN featured here.

CASINO (WE), Wales Street.—Prop., Mr. O. L. Kilgour, 15, Whitehall Terrace. Phone, Aberdeen 3618. Gen. Man. and Licensee, O. L. Kilgour. 871 seats. Booked at Hall. Stage, 11 ft. deep; three dressing-rooms. Prices, 5d. to 1s. Proscenium width, 27 ft. Phone, Aberdeen 1081. Station, Aberdeen, L.N.E.R. or L.M.S.

CINEMA (WE), Skene Terrace.—Prop., J. F. Donald. 673 seats. Continuous. Two changes weekly.

CITY (WE), George Street.—2,500 seats. Continuous. Prices, 4d. to 1s. Proscenium width, 45 ft. Phone, 5997. Station, Aberdeen.

GLOBE (WE), Nelson Street.—560 seats. Twice nightly. Two changes weekly. Prices, 4d. to 9d. Station, Aberdeen, L.M.S.

GRAND CENTRAL (WE), 286, George Street.— Prop., J. F. Donald (Aberdeen Cinemas), Ltd. Continuous. Prices, 6d. to 1s. 3d. Phone, 3716.

HIS MAJESTY'S (WE). —Props., J. F. McDonald (Aberdeen Cinemas) Ltd., 19, North Silver Street, Aberdeen. 2,180 seats. Booked at H.O. Prices, 6d. to 2s. Pictures and Variety. Variety booked by Max Fields, 17, Shaftesbury Avenue, London, W.1. Proscenium width, 30 ft.; six dressing-rooms. Phone, Aberdeen 493. Station, Aberdeen.

KING'S CINEMA (WE), 217, George Street.— 651 seats. Two shows nightly. Two changes weekly. Prices, 4d. to 6d. Phone, Aberdeen 3141. Station, Aberdeen.

MAJESTIC (WE).—Props., Caledonian Theatres Ltd., 1, East Craibstone Street, Aberdeen. 1,890 seats. Booked at hall. Continuous. Prices, 9d. to 2s. Occasional variety. Proscenium width, 30 ft. Café. Station, Aberdeen.
Fitted "ARDENTE" Deaf Aids
Fitted "ARDENTE" Stage Amplification
See page 258

PALACE THEATRE (RCA), Bridge Place.— Controlled by County Cinemas, Ltd., Dean House, Dean Street, London, W.1. 2,000 seats. Booked at H.O. Continuous. Prices, 6d. to 2s. Stage, 26 ft. deep; Proscenium width 43 ft. Phone, Aberdeen 1135. Station, Aberdeen Central, L.N.E.R.

PICTURE HOUSE (WE), Union Street.—Prop., Provincial Cinematograph Theatres, Ltd. 843 seats. Booked at H.O., 123, Regent Street, London. Continuous. Prices, 1s. to 2s. Phone, Central 2518. Station, Aberdeen, L.M.S. and L.N.E.R.
Fitted "ARDENTE" Deaf Aids
See page 258

PLAYHOUSE (WE), 477, Union Street.—Aberdeen Picture Palaces, Ltd., 2, West Craibstone Street, Aberdeen. Booked at H.O. 1,030 seats. Continuous. Prices, 6d. to 1s. 3d. Proscenium width, 25 ft. Phone No. 596. Café. Station, Aberdeen Joint. Groves Transport.
Fitted "ARDENTE" Deaf Aids
See page 258

QUEEN'S CINEMA (BA), Union Street.—Prop. J. F. Donald (Aberdeen Cinemas), Ltd., 19, North Silver Street. Aberdeen. Phone, 3716. 350 seats. Booked at H.O. Continuous. Two changes weekly.

REGENT CINEMA (RCA).—Controlled by County Cinemas, Ltd. Dean House, Dean Street, London, W.1. Booked at H.O. 2,000 seats. Continuous. Prices, 6d. to 2s. Phone, 3314. Station, Aberdeen.

STAR PICTURE PALACE (WE), Park Street.— Aberdeen Picture Palaces, Ltd. 780 seats. Two shows nightly. Mats., Tues., Thurs. and Sat. Two changes weekly. Prices, 5d. to 9d. Phone, Central 3066.

TOPICAL NEWS CINEMA (RCA).—Diamond Street.—Props., North of Scotland News Theatres (Abdn.) Ltd. 312 seats. Booked at Hall. Continuous. Prices, 6d. to 1s. Café and Dance Hall attached. Phone No. 6514. Station, Aberdeen, L.N.E.R. and L.M.S.
Fitted "ARDENTE" Deaf Aids
See page 258

TORRY PICTURE HOUSE.—Prop., Torry Cinemas, Ltd., 2, West Craibstone Street. Phone, Aberdeen 1173. 1,000 seats. Booked at Hall. Continuous. Mats., Weds. and Sats. Prices, 5d. to 1s. Stage 18 ft. deep; two dressing rooms. Proscenium width, 25 ft. Stations, Aberdeen, L.N.E.R., and L.M.S Road transport. Phone, Aberdeen 3767.

ABERFELDY (PERTH), **Pop. 1,505.**
CINEMA (TOWN HALL) (Mihaly).—Lessee, Mr.
Crerar (on Wednesday and Saturday). Booked
at Hall. Station, Aberfeldy.

AIRDRIE (LANARK), **Pop. 25,954.**
COLISEUM (Film Industries), 12, Hallcraig
Street.—Prop., Mrs. E. Porter. 780 seats.
Films booked at Glasgow. Occasional variety
booked by MacDonald Standard Variety
Agency, Glasgow. Prices, 6d. to 1s. Proscen-
ium width, 23 ft. Stage 24 ft. deep. Four
dressing rooms. Films by Glasgow and
Lanarkshire Transport. Phone, Airdrie 34.
NEW CINEMA (WE) Broomknoll Street.—Prop.
Airdrie Cinema, Ltd. Booked by A. B.
King, 167, Bath Street, Glasgow. 1,328 seats.
Continuous. Two changes weekly. Prices, 3d.
to 1s. 3d. Phone, Airdrie 2110. Station
Airdrie, L.N.E.R. and L.M.S.
PAVILION PICTURE HOUSE (WE), Graham Street.
—Prop., R.V. Singleton. 1,200 seats. Booked
by G. Singleton, at 39, Kirkpatrick Street,
Bridgeton, Glasgow. Phones, Bridgeton
1111-2, Continuous. Two changes weekly.
Prices, 4d. to 1s. 3d. Phone, Airdrie 383.
RIALTO PICTURE HOUSE (RCA).—Prop., Mrs. E.
B. MacKenzie. 540 seats. Continuous from
6.30. Three Mats. weekly. Booked at Hall.
Prices, 4d. to 1s. Proscenium width 26 ft.
five dressing rooms. Stage, 10 ft. deep;
Phone, Airdrie 185. Station Airdrie, L.M.S.

ALEXANDRIA (DUMBARTON), **Pop. 10,330.**
EMPIRE.—Prop., Premier Picture and Variety
Co., Public Hall. Station, Alexandria, L.M.S.
PUBLIC HALL (BA).—Prop., Premier Picture and
Variety Co. 900 seats. Booked at Hall.
Eight shows weekly. Prices, 6d. to 1s. 3d.
Station, Alexandria, L.N.E.R.
STRAND CINEMA (WE), Bank Street.—Prop.,
J. Wingate, Lossiebank, Dumbarton. Booked
by A. B. King, at 167, Bath Street, Glasgow.
1,054 seats. Continuous. Mat. on Sat. One
change weekly. Prices, 4d. to 1s. 3d. Phone,
135. Station, Alexandria, L.N.E.R.

ALLOA (CLACKMANNAN), **Pop. 18,244.**
CENTRAL PICTURE HOUSE (RCA), High Street.—
Prop., Leslie Lynn & Co., 44, High Street,
Alloa. 950 seats. Booked at Hall. Con-
tinuous. Twice Sat. Prices, 6d. to 1s. 3d.
Proscenium width, 30 ft. Phone, Alloa 347.
Station, Alloa, L.M.S. and L.N.E.R.
LA SCALA (BA), Mill Street.—Props., Gaumont
British Corporation and P.C.T. 900 seats.
Booked at H.O. Phone, Alloa 225. Continuous.
Mat. Tues., and Sat. Station, Alloa.
PAVILION (WE).—Prop., Alloa Theatre Co., Ltd.
Continuous. Booked at Hall. 900 seats.
Pictures and Variety. Stage, 20 ft., six
dressing-rooms. Variety booked at hall.
Prices, 6d. to 1s. 3d. Phone, 154. Station,
Alloa, L.N.E.R. and L.M.S.

ALVA (CLACKMANNAN), **Pop. 4,653.**
HILLFOOT PICTURE HOUSE(RCA).—Prop. and Res.
Man., Mr. Hudson. 800 seats. Continuous.
Station, Alva, L.N.E.R.   .

ALYTH (PERTH), **Pop. 2,629.**
TOWN HALL CINEMA (Wired).—Lessee, H.
Colligan, 45, Milnbank Road. Dundee.
500 seats. Booked at H.O. Continuous,
Tues., Thurs., Sat. Prices, 6d. to 1s. Phone,
Dundee 67424. Station, Alyth, L.M.S.

ANNAN (DUMFRIES), **Pop. 6,302.**
GRACIES BANKING KINEMA (Mihaly).—Prop.
Central Control Board. Lessee and Man.,
Victor Biddall. 350 seats. Booked at Hall

Continuous. Two to three nights weekly,
Prices, 3d. to 1s. Station, Annan, L.M.S.
PICTURE HOUSE (BA), Lady Street.—Prop.,
Annan Pictures, Ltd. 610 seats. Booked at
Hall by Man. Continuous. Prices, 6d. to 1s.
Phone, Annan 8. Station, Annan, L.M.S.

ANSTRUTHER (FIFE), **Pop. 1,275.**
EMPIRE PICTURE HOUSE (BTH).—Prop., Empire
Picture House (Anstruther), Ltd.
REGAL (Bauer), Crichton Street,—Props., S. and
C. M. Fuller, Station House, Anstruther. 800
seats. Booked in Glasgow. Continuous.
Two shows Sat. Prices, 6d. to 1s. 6d. Pro-
scenium width, 29 ft. Stage, 8 ft. deep ; one
dressing room. Phone, Anstruther 48. Sta-
tion, Anstruther.
TOWN HALL.—Lessee, F. Burrows.

ARBROATH (ANGUS), **Pop. 17,637.**
OLYMPIA THEATRE (RCA).—Prop., North of
Scotland Entertainments, Ltd. 900 seats.
Two shows nightly. Two changes weekly.
Prices, 6d. to 1s. Phone, Arbroath 197.
Station, Arbroath.
PALACE THEATRE (RCA), James Street.—Prop.,
Scottish Cinema and Variety Theatres, Ltd.,
105, St. Vincent Street, Glasgow. Phone.
Central 2830. 907 seats. Booked at Associ-
ated British Cinemas, Ltd., 30-31, Golden
Square, W.1. Continuous. Prices, 4d. to 1s.
Phone, Arbroath 212. Station, Arbroath
Joint.
PICTURE HOUSE (WE), High Street.—Prop.,
Arbroath Cinema Co., Ltd., South Street, St.
Andrews. Phone, St. Andrew, 69. Con-
tinuous. Booked at H.O. Prices, 6d. to
1s. 3d. Proscenium width, 40 ft. Phone
Arbroath 406. Station, Arbroath, L.M.S.
WEBSTER HALL.—Prop., Arbroath Town Council.
Occasional shows.

ARDROSSAN (AYR), **Pop. 13,736.**
LYRIC (BTH).—Props., Ardrossan Picture House
Co., Ltd. 630 seats. Booked at Hall.
Continuous. Prices, 6d. to 1s. Proscenium
width, 17 ft. Phone, 77. Station, Ardrossan,
L.M.S.

ARMADALE (WEST LOTHIAN), **Pop. 4,854.**
STAR THEATRE (BA).—Prop., Star Theatre,
(Armadale), Ltd. 780 seats. Booked by
I. R. Grove, Fairfield House, Broxburn.
Continuous. Two changes weekly. Prices,
6d. to 1s. Phone, Armadale 10. Station,
Armadale, L.N.E.R. Films by Film Trans-
port Services (Broxburn), Ltd.

AUCHINLECK (AYR), **Pop. 6,824.**
PICTURE HOUSE (BA), Main Street. 650 seats.
One show nightly, three on Sat. Three changes
weekly. Prices, 6d. to 1s. 6d. Station, Anchin-
leck, L.M.S.

AUCHTERARDER (PERTH), **Pop. 3,098.**
CINEMA (BTH), Townhead.—Prop., Auchterarder Cinema Co., Ltd., 450 seats. One
show nightly. Two on Sat. Two changes
weekly. Prices, 3d. to 1s. 9d. Proscenium
width, 22 ft. Phone, Townhead
141. Cafe attached. Station, Gleneagles,
L.M.S., and Road Transport.

AUCHTERMUCHTY (FIFE), **Pop. 1,748.**
VICTORIA HALL (Morrison).

AYR (AYRSHIRE), **Pop. 40,412.**
GAIETY THEATRE, Carrick Street.—Prop. and
Man., Ben Popplewell and Sons, Ltd. 1,000
seats. Variety and Theatrical. Twice nightly.
Phone, Ayr 2536. Station, Ayr, L.M.S.

AYR—Contd.

ORIENT CINEMA (WE), Main Street.—Prop., Crown Cinema Co., Ltd., 208, Bath Street, Glasgow. 1,604 seats. Booked by A. B. King, 167, Bath Street, Glasgow. Continuous. Prices, 6d. to 1s. 3d. Proscenium width, 40 ft. Stage, 25 ft. deep, three dressing rooms. Cafe. Phone, Ayr 3419. Station, Ayr.

PICTURE HOUSE (WE), High Street.—Prop., Ayrshire Cinematograph Theatres, Ltd 1,800 seats. Booked by Gaumont British Corporation, 123, Regent Street, London, W.1· Continuous. Prices, 6d. to 1s. 6d. Cafe. ·Phone. Ayr 275311.
Fitted "ARDENTE" Deaf Aids See page 258

PLAYHOUSE (WE), Boswell ¯Park.—Prop· George Green, Ltd., 182, Trongate, Glasgow Phone, Bell 1660. 3,060 seats. Booked at H.O. Continuous. Stage, 22 ft. deep; four dressing rooms. Prices, 6d. to 2s. Proscenium width, 52 ft. Cafe. Phone, Ayr 3702. Station, Ayr, L.M.S.

REGAL (BTH), Prestwick Road.—Prop., William Ross, 196, Prestwick Road, Ayr. 846 seats. Booked at Hall. Continuous from 6.30 p.m. Prices, 5d. to 1s. Phone Ayr 3914. Station Newton-on-Ayr.

RITZ (GB), New Road.—Prop., Newton-on-Ayr Picture House Ltd., 142, St. Vincent Square, Glasgow. 1,078 seats. Booked at hall. Continuous evenings. Prices, 6d. to 1s. 3d. Phone,.Ayr 2997. Station, Ayr.

BAILLESTON (LANARK), Pop. 3,400.

PAVILION (Klangfilm).—Lessee, W. Cargill. 560 seats.

BALLANTRAE (AYR), Pop. 1,076
PUBLIC HALL (Occasional shows).

BANFF (BANFF), Pop. 4,136.
PICTURE HOUSE (BA).—Prop., Banff Picture House, Ltd. 350 seats. Booked by A. G. Matthews. 8, Overwood Drive, Glasgow. Twice nightly. Prices, 6d. to 1s. 6d. Station, Banff Harbour, L.N.E.R.

BANNOCKBURN (STIRLING), Pop. 4,091.
NEW TOWN HALL (RCA).— Prop., Anderson & Sons.

REGENT PICTURE HOUSE (RCA). 550 seats.— Props. Charles Anderson & Co. Booked at Glasgow. Twice nightly. Prices 5d. to 1s. Proscenium width 28 ft. Phone, Bannockburn 5.

BARRHEAD (RENFREW), Pop. 12,308.
PAVILION (WE), Main Street.—Prop., Scott Theatres, Ltd. 1,000 seats. Booked by Thos. Roger at 18, Clyde Street, Motherwell. Phone, Motherwell 85. Pictures and Variety. Stage 22 ft. deep. Two changes weekly. Prices, 5d. to 1s. 2d. Station, Barrhead, L.M.S.

BATHGATE (WEST LOTHIAN), Pop. 18,064˙
CINEMA HOUSE (BA), Livery Street.—Prop.· Star Theatre (Bathgate), Ltd., Bloomfield House, Bathgate. Phone 48. 1,000 seats. Continuous. Mon. to Fri. Three shows Sat. Two changes weekly. Booked by I. R. Grove, Fairfield House, Broxburn. Phone, Broxburn 42. Prices, 4d. to 1s. 4d. Station, Bathgate, L.N.E.R. Films by Film Transport Services (Broxburn), Ltd. Phone, Bathgate. 36.

PAVILION (WE).—Prop., George Green, Ltd. Booked at H.O., 182, Trongate, Glasgow. Phone, Bell 1660. 1,377 seats. Two changes weekly. Prices, 4d. to 1s. 6d.

BEITH (AYR), Pop. 5,977.
NEW CINEMA (RCA). 700 seats.

PICTUREDROME (RCA).—Prop., The Picturedrome (Beith) Ltd. 700 seats. Booked at Hall. One show nightly, three on Sat. Three changes weekly. Prices, 7d. to 1s. Station, Beith, L.M.S. Motor Transport.

BELLSHILL (LANARKSHIRE), Pop. 3,500.
ALHAMBRA (WE).—Prop., Bellshill Alhambra Theatre, Ltd., Phone, 128. Man. Dir., Geo. Palmer. 998 seats. Booked at Hall. Continuous. Two changes weekly. Prices, 6d. to 1s.

PICTURE THEATRE (BA), Main Street.—Prop., Denman Picture Houses, Ltd., London. 750 seats. Booked at Head office. Twice nightly. Mat. Sat. Two changes weekly. Phone, Bellshill 53. Station, Bellshill.

BIGGAR (LANARK) CINEMA (BA), Town Hall.

BLACKBURN (WEST LOTHIAN). ·
PICTUREDROME.—(Closed.)

BLAIRGOWRIE (PERTH), Pop. 4,049.
THE PICTURE HOUSE (BA), Reform Street.— Props., The Picture House. 700 seats. Booked by Mr. Inverarity, 14, Allan Street, Blairgowrie. One show nightly, three on Sat. Two changes weekly. Prices, 3d. to 1s. 6d. Phone, Blairgowrie 105. Station, Blairgowrie, L.M.S.

BLANTYRE (LANARK), Pop. 17,015.
BLANTYRE PICTURE HOUSE (RCA).—Lessee, L.C.V. Circuit, 34, St. Enoch Square, Glasgow. Central 4465. Booked at H.O. 850 seats. Twice nightly. Prices, 4d. to 8d. Phone, Blantyre 29. Station, Blantyre, L.M.S.

BO'NESS (WEST LOTHIAN), Pop. 10,095.
HIPPODROME (BTH).—Prop., and Res. Man., L. D. Dickson. 1,004 seats. Booked at Hall. Continuous. Three on Sat. Stage, 22 ft.; four dressing rooms. Prices, 6d. to 1s. Phone, Bo'ness 73. Station, Bo'ness, L.N.E.R.

STAR THEATRE (BA).—Prop., Star· Theatre (Bo'ness) Ltd., Bloomfield House, Bathgate. Phone, No. 48. Booked by I. R. Grove, Fairfield House, Broxburn. 860 seats. Continuous. Three performances Sat. Two changes weekly. Prices, 3d. to 1s. 3d. Café attached: Phone, Bo'ness 156. Films by Film Transport Services (Broxburn) Ltd.·

BONNYBRIDGE (STIRLING), Pop. 5969.
PICTURE HOUSE (BTH).—Prop., Henry Harris. 600 seats. Twice weekly. Mon. and Sat. Prices, 2d. to 6d. Phone, Bonnybridge 1. Station, Bonnybridge Central, L.M.S.

BONNYRIGG (MIDLOTHIAN), Pop. (with LASSWADE), 4,483.
PICTURE HOUSE.—Prop., and Res. Man., Mrs. Readshaw, 69, High Street, Bonnyrigg. Booked at Glasgow. One show nightly, two on Saturday. Three changes weekly. Prices, 4d.· to 9d. Station, Bonnyrigg. L.N.E.R.

BRECHIN (ANGUS), Pop. 8,201.
KING'S CINEMA (RCA).—Prop., Brechin Cinemas, Ltd., Swan Street, Brechin. 775 Seats. Booked at Hall. Once nightly, three performances Sat. Prices, 5d. to 1s. 4d. Phone No. 184. Station, Brechin, L.M.S.

REGAL (BA), City Road.—Prop., and Man., J. D. McEwen. 650 seats. Once nightly, Mat. and two shows Sat. Prices, 5d. to 1s. 4d. Phone, Brechin, 40. Station, Brechin, L.M.S.

BRIDGE OF ALLAN (Stirling). **Pop. 2,897.**
Museum Hall.

BRORA (Sutherland), **Pop. 1,200.**
Drill Hall.

BROUGHTY FERRY (Angus). **Pop. 12,000,**
Regal Cinema (bth), Queen Street.—Props., J. Lyall and W. Bryce, Cinema House, Uphall, W. Lothian. Phone Broxburn 53. 721 seats. Continuous. Booked at H.O. Prices, 6d. to 1s. 6d. Proscenium width, 18 ft. Phone, Broughty Ferry 79058. Station, Broughty Ferry. L.M.S. and L.N.E.R.

BROXBURN (West Lothian), **Pop. 1,100.**
Central Picture House (G.B.), Main Street.—Prop., Broxburn Pictures, Ltd., 21, Blythswood Square, Glasgow, 1,150 seats. Pictures and occasional Variety. Booked by J. Hendry, 114, Union Street, Glasgow. Continuous. Two on Sat. Two changes weekly. Prices, 6d. to 1s. Proscenium width, 20 ft. Stage, 14 ft. deep ; two dressing rooms. Phone Broxburn 14. Station, Drumshoreland, L.N.E.R.

BUCKIE (Banff). **Pop. 8,688.**
Palace Cinema (we).—Prop., Elite Entertainments Syndicate. Phone No. 106. 1,005 seats.

BUCKHAVEN (Fife,) **Pop.** (with Methil) **17,643.**
Globe Theatre (ba). — Prop., Fifeshire Cinema Co., Ltd., Leven. 1,000 seats. Phone, Leven 147. Gen. Man., James Roden. Booked at H.O. Continuous. Prices, 5d. to 9d. Station, Buckhaven, L.N.E.R.

BURNBANK (Lanark), **Pop. 12,140.**
Plaza Picture House (we).—Prop., R. V. Singleton, 39, Kirkpatrick Street, Glasgow. Phone, Bridgeton 1111. 850 seats. Booked at H.O. Continuous. Three changes weekly. Prices, 4d. to 9d. Proscenium width, 24 ft. Station, Burnbank, L.N.E.R.

BURNTISLAND (Fife , **Pop. 5,809.**
Cinema House (bth).—Prop., Burntisland Cinema House, Ltd., Booked by T. Turnbull, Falkirk. Continuous. Three changes weekly. Prices, 6d. to 1s. 3d. Station, Burntisland, L.N.E.R.

Cambuslang (Lanark), **Pop. 27,128**
Ritz (we).—Prop., Scottish Cinema and Variety Theatres, Ltd., 105, St. Vincent Street, Glasgow. 1,595 seats. Booked at Associated British Cinemas, Ltd, 30, Golden Square, London, W.1. Continuous. Prices 6d. to 1s. Station, Cambuslang, L.M.S.
Savoy (we), Main Street, Cambuslang.— Props., Savoy (Cambuslang), Ltd., 135, Buchanan Street, Glasgow. Phone, Central 6394. 1,643 seats. Booked at Hall. Continuous. Prices, 6d. and 1s. Proscenium width, 36 ft. Stage, 12 ft. deep ; two dressing rooms. Phone, Cambuslang 558. Station, Cambuslang.

CAMPBELTOWN (Argyll), **Pop. 7,928.**
Picture House (bth), Hall Street. Props. The Picture House, Campbeltown, Ltd,. 566 seats. Booked at Hall. Twice nightly. Three changes weekly. Phone, No. 164, Station, Gourock, L.M.S.

CARDENDEN (Fife), **Pop. 9,000.**
Cinema (bth), Bowhill. 550 seats. Booked at Hall. One show nightly. Pictures and Variety. Prices, 3d. to 6d. Station, Cardenden, L.N.E.R.

Picturedrome (we), Bowhill.—Prop., Bowhill Public House Society, Ltd., Lessees, Commercial Cinematograph Co., Ltd., Bank Street, Lochgelly. Phone, No. 35. 998 seats. Booked at Cinema de Luxe, Lochgelly. One show nightly ; two on Sat. Three changes weekly. Prices, 3d. to 6d. Phone, Cardenden 59. Station and postal town, Cardenden. L.N.E.R.

CARLUKE (Lanark), **Pop. 10,507.**
Alhambra (bth).—Prop., M. Burns. 600 seats.
Town Hall, Stewart Street.—One show nightly, two on Sat. Three changes weekly. Station, Carlisle, L.M.S.

CARNOUSTIE (Angus), **Pop. 4,806.**
Pavilion (rca).—Prop., Carnoustie Public Hall Co. (Pavilion), Ltd. 560 seats. Res. and Booking Man., A. Webster, A.R.A.M. Continuous. Two changes weekly. Prices, 3d. to 1s. 3d. Phone, Carnoustie 159. Station, Carnoustie, D. & A. Jt. R.
Regal (bth). 900 seats.

CASTLE DOUGLAS (Kirkcudbright) **Pop. 3,008.**
Castle Douglas Cinema (Marshall), Queen Street.—Prop., William Slater, 39, King Street. 368 seats. Booked by Prop. at Hall . Twice nightly. Two changes weekly. Prices, 3d. to 1s. 3d. Proscenium width, 18 ft. Phone, No. 136. Station, Castle Douglas, L.M.S.
Palace (bth), St. Andrews Street, Castle Douglas.—Prop., Castle Douglas Theatres, Ltd., 63, King Street, Castle Douglas. Phone 141. 521 seats. Separate shows daily. Proscenium width, 24 ft. Prices 6d. to 1s. 6d. Booked at Hall. Station, Castle Douglas, L.M.S.

CATRINE (Ayr), **Pop. 2,274.**
Wilson Hall (bth), Bridge Street.—Lessee, F. Palmer, 500 seats. Booked at Lesmahagow by F. Palmer. Station, Catrine, L.M.S.

CLELAND (Lanark), **Pop. 3,591.**
Picture Palace (Occasional).

CLYDEBANK (Dumbarton), **Pop. 46,963.**
Bank Cinema (rca).—Prop., Scottish Cinema and Variety Theatres, Ltd., 105, St. Vincent Street, Glasgow. Phone, Central 2830. 1,071 seats. Booked in London. Continuous. Prices, 6d. to 1s. Phone, Clydebank 447.
Empire (we).—Prop., Scottish Cinema and Variety Theatres, Ltd. 1,217 seats. Two shows nightly. Two changes weekly.
Kinema (rca).—Prop., M. and I. B., 147, Bath Street, Glasgow. 640 seats. Continuous. Booked at Glasgow. Prices, 4d. to 6d. Film Transport.
Palace (btp). Kilbowie Road.—Prop., Scottish Cinema and Variety Theatres, Ltd. 800 seats. Continuous. Two changes weekly. Station, Singer, L.N.E.R.
Pavilion (we.) Kilbowie Road.—Prop., Clydebank Pavilion, Ltd. 1,400 seats. Booked at 18, Kilbowie Road, Clydebank. Continuous. Two changes weekly. Prices, 6d. to 9d. Phone, Clydebank 120. Films by Motor Transport.
Town Hall (ba).—Prop., Clydebank Town Council. Station, Singer, L.N.E.R.

COALBURN (Lanark), **Pop. 1,185.**
Picture House.—Prop., Jas. Shanks.

COALTOWN OF BALGONIE (Fife).
Cinema Balgonie (Morrison).—Prop., Dempsey Bros., The Garage, Coaltown of Balgonie.

COALTOWN OF BALGONIE—Contd.
350 seats. Booked at H.O. Prices, 6d. to
9d. Phone, Markinch 22. Station Markinch,
L.N.E.R.

COATBRIDGE (LANARK), **Pop. 43,056.**
B.B. PICTURE HOUSE (BA). Water Street.—
Prop., Gaumont British Picture Corporation
Ltd., 123, Regent Street, London, W.1. Phone
Regent 6641. 700 seats. Booked at H.O.
Continuous. Two changes weekly. Prices, 3d,
to 8d. Phone, Coatbridge 477.
CINEMA (WE), Bank Street.—Prop., Coatbridge
Cinemas, Ltd., Bank Street, Coatbridge.
1,150 seats. Booked by A. B. King. 167,
Bath Street, Glasgow. Continuous. Two
changes weekly. Prices, 4d. to 1s. Phone,
Coatbridge 293. Station, Coatbridge, L.M.S.
EMPIRE THEATRE (WE). — Props., United
Cinemas, Ltd., 144, Main Street, Glas-
gow. 1,150 seats. Booked by Mr. Singleton,
39, Kirkpatrick Street, Bridgeton, Glasgow.
Prices, 5d. to 1s. Proscenium width 24 ft.
Phone, No. 130. Station, Coatbridge, L.M.S.
GARDEN PICTURE HOUSE.—Whifflet.
REGAL (WE), Ellis Street.—Props., Garden
Cinema & Variety Theatres, Ltd., 105, St.
Vincent Street, Glasgow. Booked at A.B.C.
Offices, London. 2,000 seats. Prices, 6d. to
1s. 3d. Proscenium width, 34 ft. Café.
Phone No. 450. Station, Coatbridge Central,
L.M.S.
THEATRE ROYAL (WE), Main Street.—Prop.,
Coatbridge Varieties, Ltd. 1,000 seats.
Booked at 144, West Regent Street, Glasgow.
Twice nightly. Mats., Mon., Wed., Thurs.,
Sat. Prices 3d. to 9d. Phone, Coatbridge
129. Station, Coatbridge.
WHIFFLET PICTURE HOUSE (Mihaly, Newlands
Street, Coatbridge. Telephone C159.—Prop.,
and Man., Robert B. Peat. Continuous.
Booked at Hall. Proscenium width, 22 ft.
Prices 3d. to 9d. Mat. Sat. Two changes
weekly. Station, Whifflet, L.M.S.

COMRIE (PERTH), **Pop. 2,220.**
PUBLIC HALL.—Prop., Parish Council.

COUPAR ANGUS (PERTH), **Pop. 2,435.**
PICTURE PLAYHOUSE (Mihaly), Hay Street.—
Prop., Coupar and Prain. 350 seats. One
how nightly. Twice on Sat. Two changes
weekly. Prices, 4d. to 1s. 4d. Station,
Coupar Angus, L.M.S.

COWDENBEATH (FIFE), **Pop. 12,731.**
ARCADE ELECTRIC THEATRE (BTH).—Prop.
and Res. Man., John M. Slora. 950 seats.
Booked at Hall. Three nights twice nightly ;
three nights continuous. Two changes.
Phone, Cowdenbeath 60. Station, Cowden-
beath, L.N.E.R.
THE NEW PICTURE HOUSE (BTH).—Prop.,
Cowdenbeath Picture House Co., Ltd. 1,480
seats. Booked by A. B. King, Glasgow.
Continuous. Prices, 6d. to 1s. Phone, 37.
Station, Cowdenbeath. L.N.E.R.

CRAIGNEUK (LANARK), **Pop. 6,810.**
CRAIGNEUK PICTURE HOUSE (WE).—Lessee,
Miss Annie Burns. 800 seats. Continuous.
Three changes weekly. Prices, 3d. to 6d.
Station, Flemmington, L.M.S.

CRAIL (FIFE), **Pop. 1,596.**
CASTLE CINEMA. 350 seats.—(Closed).

CRIEFF (PERTH), **Pop. 6,058.**
CINEMA (BTH).—Prop., M. D. Souter. 650 seats.
Booked at Hall. One show nightly, three on
Sat. Two changes weekly. Prices, 3d. to
1s. 6d. Phone, Crieff 311. Station, Crieff,
L.M.S., and road transport.

CUMBERNAULD (DUMBARTON), **Pop. 4,829.**
THE CINEMA.—Prop., James Andrew.

CUPAR (FIFE), **Pop. 7,110.**
LA SCALA (RCA).—Prop., La Scala, Ltd. Booked
by Thos. Ormiston, 6, Brandon Street,
Motherwell.
REGAL (BA) South Union Street.—Prop., Q.M.C.
Craig. 649 seats. Booked at Hall. Con-
tinuous. Stage 24 ft. deep ; four dressing
rooms. Prices, 6d. to 1s. 3d. Proscenium
width, 24 ft. Phone, Cupar 3126. Station,
Cupar, L.N.E.R.

DALBEATTIE (KIRKCUDBRIGHT). **Pop.
3,011.**
PICTURE HOUSE (BTH).—Prop., and Res. Man,.
T. Maxwell, Milbrook, Dalbeattie. 600 seats.
Booked at Hall. Once nightly Mon. to Fri.
Three shows Sat. Two changes weekly.
Prices, 4d. to 1s. 6d. Station, Dalbeattie,
L.M.S.

DALKEITH (MIDLOTHIAN), **Pop. 7,854.**
PAVILION (BA).—Prop., and Man., Wm. H.
Albin. 1,025 seats. Booked at Hall. Two
changes weekly. Pictures and Variety.
Stage, 26 ft. by 15 ft. ; three dressing-rooms.
Prices, 6d to 1s. Phone, Dalkeith 109. Station,
Dalkeith, L.N.E.R.
Fitted "ARDENTE" Deaf Aids
See page 258

DALMELLINGTON (AYR), **Pop. 6,151.**
DOON CINEMA (BTH), High Main Street.—
Prop., Doon Cinema (Dalmellington), Ltd.
570 seats. Booked at New Carrick Cinema,
Maybole. Prices, 6d. to 1s. Station, Dal-
mellington, L.M.S.
PICTURE HOUSE (BA).—Lessees, W. G. Knotts
and E. R. Varley. Bridge Street, Girvan.
Phone, No. 93. 520 seats. Booked at Girvan.
Continuous. Prices, 6d. to 1s. Proscenium
width, 16 ft. Station, Dalmellington, L.M.S.

DALMUIR (DUMBARTON), **Pop. 11,490.**
REGAL (WE), Dumbarton Road.—Prop., Dal-
muir Cinema House, Ltd., 226, St. Vincent
Street, Glasgow. 1,140 seats. Booked at
Hall. Continuous. Two changes weekly.
Prices, 6d. and 9d. Proscenium width,
40 ft. Phone, Clydebank 131. Station,
Dalmuir, L.M.S.

DALRY (AYR), **Pop. 6,827.**
REGAL CINEMA (BTH), North Street.—Props.,
Dalry Picture House Co., Ltd., 50, High Street,
Maybole. Phone, Maybole 68. Booked at
Hall. Continuous. Prices, 6d. to 1s. Pro-
scenium width, 27 ft. Phone, Dalry 97.
Station, Dalry, L.M.S.
VICTORY CINEMA (Edibell), New Street.—Prop.,
Victory Cinema, Ltd. 600 seats. Booked at
Hall. Once nightly. Pictures and Variety.
Stage 10 ft. deep. Prices, 1d. to 1s. Pros-
cenium width, 30 ft. Road transport.

DARVEL (AYR), **Pop. 3,232.**
PICTURE HOUSE (BTH), West Main Street.—
Prop., Darvel Picture House, Ltd. 500 seats.
Booked at Glasgow. Once nightly. Twice
Sat. Prices, 6d. to 1s. Proscenium width,
17 ft., Phone No. 285. Station, c/o Par-
cels Office, Darvel, L.M.S.
TOWN HALL (Wired).—Prop., A. Claymore,
Forum Picture House, Kilmarnock. Phone,
Kilmarnock 776. 900 seats. Prices 4d. to 1s.

DENNY (STIRLING), **Pop. 9,488.**
PICTURE HOUSE (BA).—Prop., Commercial Cine-
matograph Co., Ltd. 400 seats. Station,
Denny, L.M.S. or L.N.E.R.

TOWN HALL (BA).—Lessees, Commercial Cinematograph Co.; Ltd. 650 seats. One show nightly, two Saturday.

DINGWALL (Ross and CROMARTY). **Pop. 2,763.**
THE PICTURE HOUSE (BTH).—Prop., Dingwall Picture House, Ltd., 68, High Street, Dingwall. Continuous. Prices, 6d. to 1s. 6d. Proscenium width, 24 ft. Phone, No. 63. Station, Dingwall.

DOUGLAS (LANARK), **Pop. 2,948.**
WATER MINERS' WELFARE CINEMA (RCA).—Prop., John Fraser, Secy., 22, MacAuclan Terrace, D.W. Booked by Mr. Jackson. 400 seats. Prices, 4d. to 9d. Station, Glasgow.

DUMBARTON (DUMBARTON), **Pop. 21,546.**
LA SCALA CINEMA HOUSE (RCA), Newtown.—Prop., La Scala (Dumbarton), Ltd., 95, Bath Street, Glasgow. 829 seats. Booked at H.O. Continuous. Two changes weekly. Prices, 4d. to 1s. Proscenium width, 21 ft. Phone, Dumbarton 215. Station, Dumbarton East. L.M.S.
PALACE.—Prop., Joseph Wingate, Lossiebank Dumbarton. 700 seats. Booked at Hall. Continuous from 6.30 to 10.30. Occasional Variety. Stage ; two dressing rooms. Prices, 4d. and 6d. Station, Dumbarton Central.
PICTURE HOUSE (RCA), High Street.—Prop., Dumbarton Picture House Co., Ltd., 1,100 seats. Continuous. Prices, 6d. to 1s. 3d. Café. Phone, Dumbarton 165. Station, Dumbarton.
RIALTO (RCA), College Street.—Prop., Scottish Cinema and Variety, Ltd., 105, St. Vincent Street, Glasgow. 1,245 seats. Continuous Mat., Wed., and Sat. Prices, 6d. to 1s. 3d. Phone, Dumbarton 43.

DUMFRIES (DUMFRIES), **Pop. 22,795.**
DUMFRIES ELECTRIC THEATRE (MARSHALL), Shakespeare Street.—Lessee, A. P. Bartlett, "Albany," Dumfries. Phone, No. 591. 600 seats. Booked at Hall by Man. Twice nightly. Prices, 4d. to 1s. 3d. Proscenium width, 21 ft. Phone, Dumfries 273. Station, Dumfries.
LYCEUM (BA), High Street.—Prop., Dumfries Theatre Co., Ltd., 75, Buccleugh Street. Phone, Dumfries 38. 2,000 seats. Booked by A. B. King, Glasgow. Continuous evenings. Two changes weekly. Prices, 6d. to 1s. 3d. Café. Phone, Dumfries, 262. Station, Dumfries, L.M.S.
PLAYHOUSE (BTH), Thornhill.—Props., Thornhill Cinema Co., Ltd., 1, West Morton Street, Thornhill. 320 seats. Booked at Glasgow.—Once nightly. Prices, 6d. to 1s. 6d. Station, Thornhill.
REGAL (WE).—Props., Scottish Cinema and Variety Theatres, Ltd., 105, St. Vincent Street, Glasgow. Licensee, John Darlisom. 1,699 seats. Booked at H.O. Continuous nightly, from 6.15. Mats. Thurs. Continuous Sat. Prices; 6d. to 1s. 3d. Proscenium width, 35 ft. Phone, 157. Station, Dumfries.

DUNBAR (EAST LOTHIAN), **Pop. 5,062.**
EMPIRE (Briton's Best).—Prop., Scott's Empires, Ltd. 900 seats. Three changes weekly. Station, Dunbar, L.N.E.R.

DUNBLANE (PERTH), **Pop,** (with LECROFT) **4,421.**
VICTORIA HALL (BA).—Props., Trustees. Secy.; John Stewart, Solicitor, Dunblane. Booked by A. Williamson, Public Hall Cinemas Newburgh. Twice weekly. Prices, 4d. to 1s. Phone, 17. Station, Dunblane, L.M.S., and Road transport.

DUNDEE (ANGUS), **Pop. 175,933.**
ALHAMBRA (Mihaly), Bellfield Street.—Prop., A. Henderson. 1,039 seats. Booked at Hall. Phone, Dundee 4985. Stations, Tay Bridge and Dundee West.
ASTORIA THEATRE (BA), Logie Street, Lochee.—Props., A. E. Binnall and Son. 900 seats. Booked at Hall. Continuous. Stage, 20 ft. deep : three dressing-rooms. Prices, 3d. to 1s. Phone, 67749. Station, Lochee, Dundee, L.N.E.R. :
BROUGHTY PICTURE HOUSE (BA), Gray Street, Broughty Ferry.—Props., J. Lyall and W. Bryce, Cinema House, Uphall. Phone. Broxburn 53. 1,100 seats. Continuous, Prices, 5d. to 1s. 3d. Phone, 7216. Station, Broughty Ferry, L.N.E.R.
CINERAMA (BTP), Tay Street.—Prop., John Pennycook Trustees. 98, Tullsdelph Road. Phone, 68021. 700 seats. Booked at Royal by W. C. Pennycook. Continuous. Prices, 3d. to 1s. Phone, 4934.
EMPIRE THEATRE (BA), Rosebank Street.—Props., United Cinemas, Ltd., 105, St. Vincent Street, Glasgow, C.2. 1,050 seats. Continuous. Booked by G. Singleton Circuit, 39, Kirkpatrick Street, Glasgow. Prices, 4d. to 1/-. Proscenium width, 24 ft. Phone, Dundee 6496. Station, Dundee, L.M.S. and L.N.E.R.
FOREST PARK CINEMA (BA), Forest Park Road.—Prop., C. R. W. Gray, 22, Muirfield Crescent, Dundee. Phone, 3229. 1,100 seats. Booked at Hall. Continuous. Prices, 4d. to 1s. Phone, 6223. Station, Dundee, L.N.E.R., and L.M.S.
GRAY'S PICTURE HOUSE (Film Industries) Shepherd's Loan.—Prop., C. R. W. Gray. Booked at Hall. Continuous. Prices, 4d. to 1s. Phone, 67631. Station, Dundee West, L.M.S.
KING'S (RCA), 27, Cowgate.—Props., Gaumont British Picture Corpn., Ltd., and Provincial Cinematograph Theatres, Ltd. 1,100 seats, Booked in London. Continuous. Café. Phone. 280411. Station, Dundee, L.M.S.

Fitted "ARDENTE" Deaf Aids See page 258

WURLITZER ORGAN
Installed in this Kinema

KINNAIRD PICTURE HOUSE (RCA), Bank Street. Prop., Kinnaird Picture House (Dundee), Ltd. 1,554 seats. Continuous. One change weekly. Prices, 6d. to 1s. 6d. Phone, Dundee 2862. Station, Dundee, L.N.E.R.
LA SCALA (WE), Murraygate.—Prop., Dundee Cinema Palace, Ltd., 187, Piccadilly. Booked at Hall. Continuous. Prices, 6d. to 2s. Phone, Dundee 3384. Station, Dundee West, L.M.S. and Tay Bridge, L.N.E.R.
MAJESTIC THEATRE (WE), Seagate.—Prop., Her Majesty's Theatre (Dundee), Ltd., 187, Piccadilly, W. Booked at La Scala, Murraygate. Continuous. Prices, 6d. to 2s. Phone, Dundee 5410. Café. Station, Dundee West, L.M.S., Tay Bridge, L.N.E.R.
NEW BRITANNIA (BTH), Small's Wynd.—Prop., J. B. Milne, 339, Clepington Road, Dundee. 1,100 seats. Booked at Victoria Hall. Prices, 3d. to 6d. Continuous evenings. Daily Matinee. Phone, Dundee 4793. Station, Dundee, L.M.S.
NEW GRAND (FI).—West King Street.—Prop., Robert Smith, 125, Dundee Road, Broughty Ferry. 850 seats. Booked at Hall. Continuous. Prices, 4d. to 1s. 3d. Phone, 7770. Station, Broughty Ferry, L.N.E.R.

DUNDEE—Contd.

NEW PALLADIUM (Wired), Alexander Street.—Prop., J. B. Milne, 339, Clepington Rd., Dundee. Phone, 5923. 900 seats. Booked at Victoria Theatre. Continuous nightly, daily matinee. Prices, 3d. to 6d. Proscenium width, 20 ft. Stage, 14 ft. deep ; five dressing-rooms. Phone 4793. Station, Dundee West, L.M.S.

PALACE (WE), Nethergate.—Scottish Cinema and Variety Theatres, Ltd., 105, St. Vincent Street, Glasgow. Central 2830. Booked by Associated British Cinemas, Ltd., 30/31, Golden Square, London. Continuous. Prices, 6d. to 1s. Phone, Dundee 5271. Station, Dundee, L.M.S., and L.N.E.R.

PLAYHOUSE (WE), Nethergate.—Props., George Green, Ltd. Circuit, 182, Trongate, Glasgow. 4,150 seats. Booked at H.O. Proscenium width 56 ft. Café. Phone, Dundee 5463.

PLAZA (WE), Hilltown.—Props., Scottish Cinema and Variety Theatres, Ltd., 105, St. Vincent Street, Glasgow. Phone, Central 2830. Continuous. Booked at London. Prices, 6d. to 1s. 3d. Proscenium width, 29 ft. Stage 31 ft. deep; seven dressing-rooms. Phone, 5808.

PRINCESS THEATRE (RCA), Hawkhill.—Props., Miss Minnie F. McIntosh. 900 seats. Booked at Hall. Continuous nightly. Prices, 4d. to 1s. Proscenium width, 26 ft. Stage, 14 ft deep; three dressing-rooms. Phone, Dundee 67210. Station, Tay Bridge, L.N.E.R., and Dundee West (L.M.S.).

REGENT (FI), Main Street.—Prop., Edward and Fraser. 1,000 seats. Booked at Tivoli, Bonnybank Road. Continuous. Prices, 4d. to 1s. Phone, 4258. Station, Dundee, L.M.S.

RIALTO (BA), High Street, Lochee.—Props., Binnall's Enterprises. Phone, 67749. 1,168 seats. Booked at Hall. Continuous. Prices 4d. to 1s. Station, Lochee, Dundee, L.N.E.R.,

ROYAL PICTURE HOUSE, Arthurstone Terrace. —Prop., Edward and Fraser. Two changes weekly. Prices, 4d. to 9d. Station, Dundee, L.N.E.R. and L.M.S.

ROYALTY KINEMA (WE), Baffin Street.—Prop., W. Pennycock, 155, Arbroath Road. Booked at Hall. Continuous nightly. Prices, 4d. to 1s. Phone 2910. Station, Dundee West, L.M.S. and L.N.E.R.

STOBSWELL CINEMA (Film Industries, Ltd.), Morgan Street.—Prop., Stobswell Cinema Theatre, Ltd. Man. Dir., S. Clive Gibbs. 850 seats. Continuous. Booked at Hall. Two changes weekly. Prices, 4d. to 1s. Phone, No. 6321. Station, Dundee.

TIVOLI (FI), Bonnybank Road.—Prop., W. S. Edward, 19, Adelaide Place. Phone, 4456. 1,000 seats. Booked at Hall. Continuous. Prices, 4d. to 9d. Phone, Dundee 4258. Station, Dundee, L.N.E.R.

VICTORIA THEATRE (BTH).—Prop., I. B. Milne, 339, Clepington Road, Dundee. 960 seats. Booked at Hall. Prices, 4d. to 1s. Proscenium width, 24 ft.; stage 20 ft. deep; six dressing-rooms. Phone, Dundee 479311. Station, Dundee West, L.M.S.

VOGUE, Strathmantine Road. Booked by George Singleton, 39, Kirkpatrick Street, Glasgow.

WELLINGTON.

DUNFERMLINE (FIFE), Pop. 40,918.

ALHAMBRA (BTH).—Prop., Alhambra (Dunfermline), Ltd., 9, East Port, Dunfermline. Phone, Dunfermline 105. 2,000 seats. Booked by A. B. King, 167, Bath Street, Glasgow. Continuous. Prices, 6d. to 1s. 6d. Phone, 498. Station, Dunfermline (Lower), L.N.E.R.

CINEMA HOUSE (BTH), East Port.—Prop., Dunfermline Cinema House, Ltd., Union Bank Chambers, High Street. Phone, Dunfermline 49. 1,200 seats. Booked at Hall. Continuous. Two changes weekly. Prices, 6d. and 1s. Phone, Dunfermline 466. Café. Station, Dunfermline, L.N.E.R.

PALACE KINEMA (WE), Pilmuir Street.—Prop., Palace Kinema (Dunfermline), Ltd., 24, Queen Anne Street. 1,300 seats. Booked at Hall. Continuous. Mats., Wed. and Sat. Prices, 6d. to 1s. Proscenium width, 31 ft. Phone, Dunfermline 466. Station, Dunfermline (Upper), L.N.E.R. and Film Transport.

REGAL PICTURE HOUSE (RCA).—Proprietor, Peter Crerar, High Street. Dunfermline. 2,000 seats. Booked at Rio Rutherglen. Continuous evenings. Daily Mat. Prices, 4d. to 1s. 3d. Proscenium width, 40 ft. Phone, No. 304. Café attached. Station, L.N.E.R., Lower Station.

DUNOON (ARGYLL), Pop. 8,780.

LA SCALA (WE).—Argyle Street.—Prop., Cowal Picture House Co., Ltd., 1,000 seats.

PICTURE HOUSE (WE).—Prop., Dunoon Picture House Co., Ltd., 227, St. Vincent Street, Glasgow. 1,100 seats. Booked by Geo. Taylor, 27, Merkland Street, Partick, Glasgow, W.2. Continuous. Two changes weekly, Phone, Dunoon, 110.

DUNS.

REGAL.

DYSART (FIFE), Pop. 4,202.

NORMAND MEMORIAL HALL. Prop., J. Roden. 600 seats. Booked at Regent, Leven. Continuous. Three changes weekly. Prices. 4d. to 6d. Phone, 59. Station, Dysart, L.N.E.R.

EAST KILBRIDE (LANARKSHIRE).
Pop. 5,290.

THE PICTURE HOUSE (BTH).—Lessee, F. Palmer, Booked at Lesmahagow.

EAST WEMYSS (FIFE).

EMPIRE.—Prop., Fifeshire Cinema Co., Ltd., Leven. Phone, Leven 147. Gen. Man., James Roden. Booked at H.O. Continuous. Prices, 3d. to 1s. Station, East Wemyss.

EDINBURGH (MIDLOTHIAN), Pop. 438,998

ASTORIA (WE), Manse Road, Corstorphine.— Prop., Corstorphine Picture House, Ltd. 1,369 seats. Booked at Hall. Continuous. Stage, 37 ft.; two dressing-rooms. Prices, 6d. to 1s. Phone, Corstorphine, 86357. Station, Waverley or Corstorphine, L.N.E.R.

BLUE HALL (WE).—Prop., Blue Halls (Edinburgh), Ltd., 30, St. Andrew's Square, Edinburgh. 1,771 seats. Continuous. Booked at Hall. Prices, 4d. to 9d. Phone, Edinburgh 27574. Stations, L.N.E.R. and L.M.S.

BUNGALOW (RCA), Bath Street, Portobello.— Prop., Portobello Pictures, Ltd., 92, Bath Street, Glasgow. Phone, Douglas 3073. 580 seats. Booked at Hall. Continuous. Prices, 3d. to 1s. Proscenium width, 16 ft. Station, Portobello, L.N.E.R. and Film Transport Services (Broxburn), Ltd.

CALEY PICTURE HOUSE (RCA), 31, Lothian Road.—Props., The Caley Picture House Co., Ltd., 7, North Andrew Street, Edinburgh. Phone No. 27361. 1,900 seats. Booked at Hall. Continuous. Prices, 9d. to 1s. 6d. Proscenium width, 50 ft. Phone, Central 26824. Station, Waverley or Princes Street, L.M.S., or L.N.E.R.

CARLTON (RCA), Piershill.

CENTRAL PICTURE HOUSE (BTH), High Street, Portobello.—Prop., Central Pictures (Portobello), Ltd. 900 seats. Booked at Playhouse, Edinburgh. Continuous. Two changes weekly. Prices, 4d. to 1s. Phone Portobello 81682. Station, Portobello, L.N.E.R.

GRAND (WE), St. Stephen Street.—Secy., C. Cochran, 55, West Regent Street, Glasgow. 1,650 seats. Booked by Mr. George Taylor, 27, Merkland Street, Glasgow. Continuous. Two changes weekly. Prices, 4d. to 9d. Phone, 24466. Station, Waverley, L.N.E.R.

HAYMARKET PICTURE HOUSE (WE), Dalry Road. —Prop., Haymarket Pictures, Ltd., 23, Walker Street. 669 seats. Booked in London. Continuous. Two changes weekly. Prices, 3d. to 9d. Proscenium width, 18 ft. Phone, 62644. Station, Waverley, L.N.E.R. Princes Street, L.M.S.

KING'S CINEMA (WE), Home Street.—Prop., Edinburgh and District Cinematograph Theatres, Ltd., 18, Walker Street, Edinburgh, 620 seats. Booked at Hall. Continuous. Prices, 6d. to 1s. Phone, Edin. 26822. Stations, Waverley, L.N.E.R., and Princes Street, L.M.S.

LA SCALA (Bauer), Nicholson Street.—Prop., La Scala, Ltd. 800 seats. Booked at Rio P.H., Rutherglen. Continuous. Two changes weekly. Prices, 5d. to 1s. Phone, 41839. Station, Waverley, L.N.E.R.

LYCEUM CINEMA (WE).—Props., Scottish Cinema and Variety Theatres, Ltd., 105, St. Vincent Street, Glasgow. 1,250 seats. Continuous. Prices, 9d. to 1s. 3d. Station, Waverley, L.N.E.R.

MONSEIGNEUR.—J. Davis Circuit, 147, Wardour Street, London, W.1. Phone, Gerrard 1416.

NEW COLISEUM (WE), West Fountainbridge.— Prop., The Palais de Danse and Cinemas (Edin., 1923), Ltd. 1,200 seats. Continuous, Two changes weekly. Prices, 4d. to 1s. Phone, 26915. Station, Waverley, L.N.E.R.

NEW PALACE PICTURE HOUSE (WE).—Lessee, J. Penn, 47, Minto Street, Edinburgh. Phone, No. 42617. 1,050 seats. Continuous. Booked at Hall. Prices, 4d. to 9d. Phone, No. 30400. Station, Waverley, L.N.E.R.

NEW PICTURE HOUSE (WE), Princes Street.— Prop., Provincial Cinematograph Theatres, Ltd., 123, Regent Street, London, W.1. 951 seats. Continuous. Prices, 1s. 3d. to 2s. Phone, Edinburgh 231711. Station, Waverley.

Fitted "ARDENTE" Deaf Aids
See page 258

WURLITZER ORGAN
Installed in this Kinema

NEW TIVOLI PICTURE HOUSE (BTH).—Gorgie Road. Prop., Mrs. E. Robertson, 25, Shandon Crescent, Edinburgh. 1,999 seats Booked at Hall. Continuous. Prices, 6d. and. 1s. Pictures and Variety. Variety. Booked by Cox, George Street, Glasgow. Stage, 25 ft.; six dressing rooms. Proscenium width, 38 ft. Phone, Edinburgh 61464. Station, Waverley.

Fitted "ARDENTE" Deaf Aids
See page 258

NEW VICTORIA (WE), Clerk Street.—Prop., Provincial Cinematograph Theatres, Ltd., 123, Regent Street, W.1. 2,006 seats, Booked at Head Office. Continuous. Prices.

9d. to 2s. 6d. Proscenium width 40 ft. Stage. 32 ft.; five dressing-rooms. Phone 438051. Cafe. Station, Waverley, L.N.E.R. .

WURLITZER ORGAN
Installed in this Kinema

OPERETTA HOUSE (BTH), Chambers Street.— Prop., J. H. and P. Sanders, Ltd. 800 seats. Booked at Hall. Continuous. Two changes weekly. Prices, 4d. to 8d. Proscenium width 20 ft. Phone, Central 26709. Station, Waverley, L.N.E.R.

PALACE (BTH), Princes Street.—Prop., Palace (Edinburgh), Ltd. Booked at Playhouse. Continuous. Six day bookings. Prices, 6d. to 2s. 6d. Phone, Edinburgh 23459. Cafe. Station, Waverley, L.N.E.R.

PALLADIUM (Edibell), East Fountainbridge.— Lessee, Fountains Theatre Co., Ltd. 900 seats. Proscenium width 26 ft. Phone, Edinburgh 31281. Station, Waverley, L.N.E.R.

PICTUREDROME (BTH), Easter Road.—Prop. and Res. Man., Alex. Black. 875 seats. Booked at Hall. Continuous. Two changes weekly. Prices, 4d. to 1s. Proscenium width, 30 ft. Phone, 75532. Station, Waverley, L.N.E.R.

PLAYHOUSE (WE).—Prop., Playhouse (Edinburgh), Ltd., 18/22, Greenside Place, Edinburgh. 3,000 seats. Continuous. Booked at Hall. Prices, 6d. to 2s. Cafe. Phone, 30377. Station, Waverley, L.N.E.R.

POOLE'S SYNOD HALL (RCA), Castle Terrace.— Prop., C. W. Poole's Entertainments, Hippodrome, Gloucester. 1,470 seats. Booked at Hall. Continuous. Prices, 6d. to 1s. 6d. Proscenium width, 40 ft. Phone, 21868. Stations, Waverley, L.N.E.R., and Princes Street, L.M.S.

PRINCES CINEMA (BTP), 131, Princes Street.— Prop. and Man., Philip S. L. Lucas, 47, Minto Street, Edinburgh. Phone, 42617. 670 seats. Booked at Hall. Continuous. Prices, 9d. to 1s. 4d. Cafe. Phone, 216681. Station, Princes Street, L.M.S.

REGENT (BA).—Props., General Theatre Corpn., Ltd. 142/150, Wardour Street, London, W.1. 1,800 seats. Pictures and Variety. Booked at H.O. Continuous, Prices, 4d. to 1s. Pictures and variety. Stage, 25 ft. deep; Two dressing rooms. Station, Waverley, L.N.E.R.

COMPTON

ORGAN featured here.

RIO (FIE), Wauchope Avenue, Craigmillar. Prop., M. E. Broadhurst, 38, Chalmers Street, Edinburgh. Phone, No. 30978. 1,235 seats. Booked at H.O. Prices, 4d. to 9d. Continuous.

RITZ (WE), Rodney Street.—Props, Scottish Cinema and Variety Theatres, Ltd., 105, St. Vincent Street, Glasgow. Phone, Central 2830. Booked by Associated British Cinemas, Ltd., 30-31, Golden Square, W.1. 1,925 seats. Continuous. Prices, 4d. to 1s. Proscenium width, 45 ft. Two dressing-rooms. Phone 23616. Station, Waverley, L.N.E.R.

RUTLAND CINEMA (WE). — Prop., General Theatres Corpn., Ltd. 2,187 seats. Booked at Head Office, London.

Fitted "ARDENTE" Deaf Aids
See page 258

ST. ANDREW SQUARE PICTURE HOUSE (WE).— Clyde Street.—Prop., Gaumont British Picture Corporation, Ltd., 123, Regent

EDINBURGH—Contd.
Street, W.1. 1,391 seats. Booked at H.O.,
Continuous. Prices, 9d. to 1s. 3d. Phone,
26758. Station, Waverley, L.N.E.R. Princes
Street, L.M.S.

SALISBURY PICTURE HOUSE (WE), South Clerk
Street. Prop., Salisbury Picture House
(Edinburgh) Ltd., Metropolitan Chambers,
118, Stockwell Street, Glasgow. Phone,
Bell 1975. 1,040 seats. Continuous. Booked
at H.O. Prices, 6d. to 1s. Phone, Edinburgh
41731. Station, Waverley, L.N.E.R.

SALON (BTH), 5, Baxter's Place. — Prop.,
Salon Picture House Co. 1,000 seats. Booked
at Hall. Continuous. Two changes weekly.
Prices, 4d. to 1s. 3d. Proscenium width,
26 ft. Stage, 6 ft. deep ; two dressing-rooms,
Phone, 25020. Station, Waverley, L.N.E.R.

SAVOY (RCA), St. Bernard's Row.—Props.,
Scottish Cinema and Variety Theatres, Ltd.,
105, St. Vincent Street, Glasgow. Phone,
Glasgow Central 2830. 1,000 seats. Continuous. Prices, 4d. and 6d. Phone, Edinburgh
25670. Stations, Waverley, L.N.E.R. ;
Princes Street, L.M.S.

SPRING VALLEY CINEMA, Morningside.—Prop.,
George M. Murray. 200 seats. Continuous.
Two changes weekly. Prices, 6d. to 1s. Sats.,
9d. to 1s. 3d. Station, Princes Street,
L.M.S.

STRAND. Stockbridge, Edinburgh. Booked by
G. Taylor, 27, Merkland Street, Partick,
Glasgow, W.1.

TOLLCROSS CINEMA (FI), Lauriston Place.—Props.
Scottish Trading Co., Ltd. 670 seats. Booked
at Hall. Continuous. Two changes weekly.
Prices, 4d. to 1s. 2d. Phone, Central 30978
Station, Princes Street, L.M.S.

ELGIN (MORAY), Pop. 10,192.

PICTURE HOUSE (BA), South Street.—Props.,
Caledonian Associated Cinemas, Ltd., Drummond Street, Inverness. 931 seats. Booked
by A. B. King, 167, Bath Street, Glasgow.
Continuous. Prices, 4d. to 1s. Proscenium
width, 24 ft. Phone, 680. Station, Elgin
L.M.S., or L.N.E.R.

PICTUREDROME (Mihaly).—Prop., John M.
Blyth. 350 seats. Booked at Hall. Continuous. Prices, 6d. and 1s. 3d. Stage, 9 ft.
deep ; one dressing-room. Station, Elgin.

PLAYHOUSE, (WE), High Street.—Props., Cale-
donian Associated Cinemas, Ltd., Drummond
Street, Inverness. Phone, 1. 1,208 seats.
Continuous. Booked by A. B. King, 167.
Bath Street, Glasgow. Prices 6d. to 2s.
Proscenium width, 40 ft. Cafe. Phone, 608.
Station, Elgin, L.M.S., and L.N.E.R.

ELIE (FIFE), Pop. 1,251.

TOWN HALL CINEMA (Morrison).—Prop., W.A.
Bromley, Bonnington House, Elie. 200 seats.
Booked by Prop. Sats. only. Two shows.
Prices, 6d. to 1s. 6d. Station, Elie, L.N.E.R.

EYEMOUTH (BERWICK), Pop. 2,321.

PICTURE HOUSE.—Prop., Border Cinema Co.,
One show nightly. Station, Eyemouth,
L.N.E.R.

FALKIRK (STIRLING), Pop. 45,443.

CASINO (Will Day), Bainsford.—Prop., Angus
B. Blair. 398 seats. Booked at Hall. Continuous. Prices, 3d. to 9d. Stations, Grahamston and Falkirk.

CINEMA (WE), Melville Street.—Prop., United
Cinemas, Ltd., 105, St. Vincent Street,
Glasgow, C.2. 600 seats. Booked by G.

Singleton, at 39, Kirkpatrick Street, Glas-
gow. Continuous. Two changes weekly.
Prices 6d. to 1s. Phone No. 167. Stations,
Grahamston, L.N.E.R., and Falkirk, L.M.S.

PAVILION (BA), Newmarket Street.—Prop.,
Gaumont British Corporation, 123, Regent
Street, London, W.1. 1,337 seats. Booked
at H.O. Continuous. Two changes weekly.
Prices, 5d. to 1s. 6d. Phone, Falkirk 85.

PICTURE HOUSE (RCA), Bank Street.—Prop.,
Associated British Cinemas, Ltd., 30-31,
Golden Square, W.1. 1,115 seats. Booked
at H.O. Continuous. Two changes weekly.
Prices, 4d. to 1s. Proscenium width, 26 ft
Phone, Falkirk 278. Station, Grahamston,
L.N.E.R.

REGAL (WE).—Prop., Scottish Cinema and
Variety Theatres, Ltd. 105, St. Vincent
Street. Glasgow. Phone, 2830. 2,000 seats.
Booked at Associated British Cinemas, Ltd.
30-31, Golden Square, W.1. Prices, 6d. to
1s. 6d. Proscenium width, 48 ft. Cafe attached. Phone, Falkirk 805. Station, Grahamston, L.N.E.R.

SALON PHOTO PLAYHOUSE (WE), Vicar Street.—
Prop., J. and A. Thomson. 760 seats.
Booked by Thomas Ormiston, Motherwell.
Continuous. Prices, 3d. to 1s. 3d. Proscen-
ium width, 24 ft. Cafe. Phone, Falkirk 21
Station, Grahamston, L.M.S.

FAULDHOUSE (WEST LOTHIAN), Pop. 4,890.

PALACE THEATRE (Mihaly).—Prop., Fauldhouse
Theatre, Ltd. 600 seats. Booked at Hall.
One show nightly. Prices, 5d. to 1s. Phone,
Fauldhouse 19. Station, Fauldhouse.

FOCHABERS (MORAY), Pop. 1,000.

PUBLIC INSTITUTE HALL.—Occasional shows.

FORFAR (ANGUS), Pop. 11,062.

PAVILION (WE), Prop., Fyfe & Fyfe, Ltd.,
55, Bath Street, Glasgow, Phone, Douglas
706. Booked at H.O. Once nightly. Twice
Sat. Two changes weekly. Prices, 6d. to
1s. 3d. Proscenium width, 25 ft. Stage,
25 ft. deep ; three dressing rooms. Phone,
No. 148 Station, Forfar, L.M.S.

REGAL (BTH), East High Street.—Props.,
Strathmore Picture Houses, Ltd., East High
Street, Kirriemuir. Phone, Kirriemuir 222.
900 seats. Booked at Hall, Nightly. Prices,
6d. to 1s. 6d. Phone, Forfar 222. Cafe
attached. Station, Forfar.

FORRES (MORAY), Pop. 4,698.

PICTURE HOUSE (BA).—Prop., Forres Picture
House, Ltd.; 103, High Street, Forres.
Phone No. 6. 550 seats. Booked by A. G.
Matthews, 8, Overwood Drive, Glasgow.
Continuous. Prices, 6d. to 1s. 6d. Proscenium
width, 21 ft. Phone No. 123. Station, Forres,
L.M.S.

FORTH (LANARK).

VICTORIA (BTH).—Prop., M. Burns.

FORT WILLIAM (INVERNESS), Pop. 2,527.

PLAYHOUSE (WE).—Props., Fort William Playhouse, Ltd., Royal Bank Buildings. Fort
William. Phone, 35. 700 seats. Separate
shows. Prices 6d. to 2s. Proscenium width,
38 ft. Booked by A. G. Matthews, 8, Overwood Drive, Glasgow. Phone 43. Station,
Fort William, L.N.E.R.

FOYERS (ARGYLL).

BUNGALOW.—Prop. and Man., F. A. MacRae,
Booked at Hall. Occasional shows. Prices,
6d. and 1s. Station, Inverness, thence per
steamer to Foyers Pier.

FRASERBURGH (ABERDEEN), **Pop. 10,203.**
EMPIRE (BTH).—Prop., Fraserburgh Picture House, Ltd. 900 seats. One show nightly.
PICTURE HOUSE (WE).—Prop., Fraserburgh Picture House, Ltd. 1,074 seats· Once nightly. Two Sat. Three changes weekly. Prices, 6d. to 1s. 3d.

GALASHIELS (SELKIRK), **Pop. 13,339.**
PAVILION THEATRE (WE).—Props., Fyfe and Fyfe, Ltd., 55, Bath Street, Glasgow. Phone, Douglas 706. Booked at H.O. 1,150 seats. Once nightly, daily matinee except Mon. Three shows Sat. Stage, 18 ft. deep; four dressing rooms. Prices, 6d. to 1s. 6d. Phone, Galashiels 270. Station, Galashiels, L.N.E.R.
PLAYHOUSE (WE).—Props., Scottish Cinema & Variety Theatres, Ltd., 105, St. Vincent Street, Glasgow. 1,032 seats. Booked by A.B.C., Ltd., London. One show nightly, two Sat. Mats. Tues. to Sat. Prices, 6d. to 1s. 9d. Phone, Galashiels 267.

GALSTON (AYR), **Pop. 6,345.**
THE PICTURE HOUSE (RCA), Wallace Street. Prop., Mrs. Margaret Gilroy, Manse Brae, Galston. Booked at Hall. Once nightly. Stage, 12 ft. deep; two dressing-rooms. Prices, 4d. to 1s Phone No. 27. Station Galston, L.M.S.

GIRVAN (AYR), **Pop. 6,056.**
PAVILION (BA). Bridge Street.—Prop., Pavilion (Girvan) Ltd. 800 seats. Booked at Hall. Continuous. Prices, 6d. to 1s. 6d. Proscenium width 24 ft. Phone, Girvan 111. Station, Girvan, L.M.S.
REGAL (WE), Dalrymple Street.—Prop., Regal Picture House (Girvan), Ltd. 1,056·seats. Booked at Glasgow. Continuous. Prices, 6d. to 1s. 6d. Proscenium width, 50 ft. Stage 16 ft. deep; two dressing-rooms. Phone, Girvan 1. Café attached. Station, Girvan, L.M.S.

GLASGOW (LANARK), **Pop. 1,088,417.**
ARCADIA PICTURE HOUSE (WE), 484 London Road, Bridgeton.— Props., Scottish Cinema and Variety Theatres Ltd. 1,409 seats. Booked at A.B.C., London, Continuous. Two changes weekly. Prices, 5d. and 6d. Phone, Bridgeton 28. Station, Bridgeton, Glasgow, L.M.S.
ARDGOWAN PICTURE HOUSE (WE), Tradeston. —Prop., Ardweir·Picture House, Ltd. 1,100 seats. Booked at Hall. Twice nightly. Prices, 4d. to 6d. Phone, South 1409.
ARGYLE PICTURE HOUSE (WE), Argyle Street. —Prop., B. Jacobs. 754 seats. Booked at Hall. Continuous. Prices, 4d. to 1s. Phone, Central 2131. Station, Glasgow termini. ·
ASTORIA CINEMA (WE), Possil Road.—Props., Astoria Cinema, Ltd., 208, Bath Street, Glasgow. 3,000 seats. Phone, Douglas 3718. Booked by A.B. King, 167, Bath Street,

Glasgow. Pictures and Variety. Continuous. Stage, 15 ft. deep; two dressing rooms. Prices, 2d. to 9d. Proscenium width, 40 ft. Phone, Douglas 3955. Station, Glasgow.
BEDFORD PICTURE HOUSE (RCA), S.S.—Prop. George Green, Ltd., 182, Trongate, Glasgow. Phone. Bell 1660. 1,800 seats.
BLACK CAT PICTURE HOUSE (BTH), Springfield Road, Parkhead.—Prop., Angus Pickard. 870 seats. Continuous. Two changes weekly. Phone, Bridgeton 480.
BLYTHESWOOD PICTURE HOUSE (RCA), 366, Maryhill Road.—Props., Blythswood Picture Hons:, Ltd., 344, Maryhill Road. Phone, Douglas 1240. Continuous. Prices, 5d. to 9d.
BOULEVARD PICTURE HOUSE (RCA), Knightswood.—Props., N.B. Theatres, Ltd. 1,100 seats. Booked at Picture House. Continuous. Prices, 6d. to 1s.. Phone, Scotstoun 2080.
BROADWAY (WE), Shettleston.—Prop., Shettleston Picture House, Ltd. 1,641 seats. Booked by G. Singleton, 39, Kirkpatrick Street, ·Glasgow, S.E. · Continuous. Prices, 5d. to 1s. 3d. Phone, Shettleston 487. Station, Shettleston.
CALDER PICTURE HOUSE, Calder Street, Govanhill.—Prop., Calder Picture House, Ltd., 144, West Regent Street, Glasgow. 1,250 seats. Booked at H.O.
CAMBRIDGE (WE), New City Road.—Prop., Grove Picture House Co., Ltd., 175, West George Street, Glasgow. Phone, Central 3411. 1,002 seats. Booked by A. B. King. Continuous, Two changes weekly. Prices, 3d. to 1s. Phone, Douglas 1262.
CAPITOL (WE), Ibrox.—Prop., Gaumont British Corporation, New Gallery House, Regent Street, W.1. 3,000 seats. Booked in London, Continuous. Prices, 7d. to 1s. 6d. Stage, 14 ft. deep. Phone, Ibrox 1261. Station, Glasgow.
CARLTON PICTURE HOUSE (WE), Castle Street.— Prop., J. Graham, 17, Blythswood Square, 1,619 seats.
CASINO (WE), Townhead.—Prop., Glasgow Casino, Ltd. 987 seats. Booked by A. B. King, 167, Bath Street, Glasgow. Continuous. Two changes weekly. Phone, Bell 2533. –
CATHCART PICTURE HOUSE (WE).
CINEMA (WE), Tollcross.—Prop., George Green, Ltd. Booked at 182, Trongate, Glasgow, by T. H. Reekie. Continuous.
COLISEUM (WE), Eglinton Street.—Prop., Associated British Cinemas, Ltd., 30-31, Golden Square, London. 3,000 seats. Booked at H.O. Continuous. Prices, 6d. to 2s. Phone, South 1500. Station, Glasgow Central.
COMMODORE. (WE), Dumbarton Road, Scotstoun, W.4.—Props., Scotstoun Picture House, Ltd., 105, St. Vincent Street, Glasgow. 2,000 seats. Continuous. Booked by G. Singleton, 39, Kirkpatrick Street, Glasgow. Prices, 6d. to 1s. 3d. Phone, Scotstoun 2115. Station, Scotstoun, L.M.S.

GLASGOW—Contd.

CRANSTON'S PICTURE HOUSE (RCA), Renfield Street.—Prop., Cranston's Picture House, Ltd., 180, St. Vincent Street, Glasgow. Phone, Central 1211. 750 seats. Continuous. Prices, 1s. to 2s. Phone, Central 3400. Tea Room, Station, Central.

CROSSHILL PICTURE HOUSE (Cosophone), Victoria Road—Props., Crosshill Pictures, Ltd. 500 seats. Booked at Hall by J. M. Drummond. Continuous.

CROWN CINEMA (BTH), Crown Street, S.S.—Prop., J. M. Drummond. 900 seats. Two changes weekly. Continuous. Prices, 3d. to 6d.

DALMARNOCK PICTURE HOUSE (BTP), Bridgeton.—Props., Dalmarnock Picture House, Ltd., 24, George Square, Glasgow. 1,175 seats. Booked at Hall by Mr. Anderson. Continuous.

DENNISTOUN PICTURE HOUSE (WE), Armadale Street.—Props, Scottish Cinema and Variety Theatres, Ltd., 105, St. Vincent Street, Glasgow. Phone, Central 2830. 1,429 seats. Booked in London. Prices, 4d. to 1s. Phone, Bridgeton 3149. Continuous. Station, Glasgow.

EGLINTON ELECTREUM (RCA), 25, Eglinton Street.—Prop., Eglinton Electreum, Ltd., 500 seats. Booked at H.O. Continuous. Prices, 3d. to 9d. Proscenium width, 24 ft. Stations, Central and St. Enoch, L.M.S.

ELDER PICTURE HOUSE (WE), Reid Street, Govan.—Prop., Caledon Pictures, Ltd., 21, Blythswood Square, Glasgow. Phone, Douglas 3908. 1,135 seats. Booked by A. B. King, 167, Bath Street, Glasgow. Phone, Douglas 1195. Continuous. Two changes weekly. Prices, 5d. to 9d. Proscenium width, 21 ft. Phone, Govan 370. Station, Govan, L.M.S.

ELEPHANT CINEMA (WE), Shawlands.—Prop., A. E. Pickard, 218, Maryhill Road, Glasgow. 1,734 seats. Booked at Hall. Continuous. Prices, 6d. to 5s. Proscenium width, 30 ft. Stage 7 ft. deep ; four dressing-rooms. Phone, Lang-side 2411-2.

EMBASSY (WE), Kilmarnock Road.—Prop., H. Wincour, 144, West Regent Street, Glasgow. 1,638 seats. Booked at H.O. Prices, 6d. to 1s. 3d. Proscenium width 41 ft. Phone, Langside 492. Road Transport.

FLORIDA (WE), King's Park.—Prop., Florida (Glasgow), Ltd., 166, Buchanan Street, Glasgow. Phone, Douglas 4251. 1,637 seats. Booked at Hall. Continuous. Prices, 6d. to 1s. Café. Phone, Langside 2267. Station, King's Park, L.M.S.

GAIETY THEATRE (WE), Anderston Cross.—Prop., Anderston Pictures and Varieties, Ltd. 1,403 seats. Booked by A. B. King, 167, Bath Street, Glasgow. Continuous. Two changes weekly. Prices, 3d. to 6d. Proscenium width, 34 ft. Phone, Central 4226. Station, Anderston Cross.

GEM PICTURE HOUSE (RCA), Gt. Western Road, Glasgow.—Props., Gem Cinema, Ltd. Phone, Douglas 271. 580 seats. Continuous. Mon. to Fri. from 6.30. Sat. from 2.30. Booked at Hall.

GOVAN CENTRAL CINEMA (RCA). — Prop., Scottish Cinema and Variety Theatres, Ltd.—105, St. Vincent Street, Glasgow. 1,209 seats. Booked by Associated British Cinemas, Ltd., 149, Regent Street, London. Continuous. Two shows Sat. Prices, 5d. to 9d. Phone, Govan 588. Transport.

GOVANHILL PICTURE HOUSE (WE).—Prop., Scottish Cinema and Variety Theatres, Ltd., 105, St. Vincent Street, Glasgow. 1,179 seats. Continuous. Prices, 4d. to 9d.

GRAFTON PICTURE HOUSE (BTH).—Prop., Albert Pictures, Ltd., 243, Parliamentary Road, Glasgow. Phone, Bell 115. 920 seats. Booked by S. A. Gratton, 9, Macfarlane Street, Glasgow. Continuous. Prices, 6d. to 9d. Proscenium width, 30 ft.

GRANADA CINEMA (WE), 1,321, Duke Street. Props., Bernard Frutin Picture House, Ltd., 118, Stockwell Street, Glasgow. Phone, Bell 1,975. 2,206 seats. Booked at H.O. Continuous. Prices, 4d. to 1s. Proscenium width 39 ft. Phone, Bridgeton 1404. Station, Parkhead, L.M.S.

GRAND CENTRAL PICTURE HOUSE (WE), Jamaica Street.—Prop., Grand Central Picture House, Ltd., 733 seats. Booked at Hall by Man. Continuous. Phone, Central 64. Station, Glasgow Central.

GROSVENOR (RCA), Byres Road, Hillhead.—Prop., Associated British Cinemas, Ltd. 30-31, Golden Square, W.1. 1,257 seats. Booked at H.O. Café. Continuous. Two changes weekly. Prices, 9d. to 1s. 6d. Phone, Western 4298. Station, Glasgow Termini.

HAMPDEN PICTURE HOUSE (BA), Westmoreland Street, Crosshill.—Prop., Hampden Picture House, Ltd. 1,040 seats. Booked by A. B. King, 167, Bath Street, Glasgow. Continuous. Prices, 5d. to 1s. Phone, Queen's Park 776. Local collection.

HILLHEAD SALON (RCA). Vinicombe Street, Hillhead.—Prop., Hillhead Picture House Co., (1922), Ltd., 127, St. Vincent Street, Glasgow. 600 seats. Booked at Hall. Continuous. Prices, 6d. to 1s. 6d.

IMPERIAL PICTURE HOUSE (WE), Paisley Road, Toll.—Prop., Glasgow Theatres, Ltd., 21, Blythswood Square, Glasgow. Phone, Douglas 3908. 1,100 seats. Booked by J. Meiklejohn, at 2, Jamaica Street. Continuous. Prices, 3d. to 1s. Phone, South 700.

KELVIN (WE), 1073, Argyle Street.—Prop., Kelvin Cinema, Ltd., 55, West Regent Street, Glasgow. Phone, Douglas 1840. 1,935 seats. Continuous. Prices, 4d. to 1s. Phone, Central 3734. Station, Central, L.M.S.

KING'S CINEMA (BTP), 520, Sauchiehall Street.—Prop., Scottish Cinema and Variety Theatres, Ltd., 105, St. Vincent Street. Booked by Associated British Cinemas, Ltd., 30-31, Golden Square, W.1. 622 seats. Continuous. Two changes weekly. Prices, 6d. to 1s. Café attached. Phone, Douglas 1298. Station, Glasgow, Central.

KING'S PICTURE THEATRE (BTH), St. James Street, Bridgeton.—Prop., King's Park Picture Theatre, Ltd. 1,300 seats. Three shows daily.

KINGSWAY (WE), Cathcart.—Prop., Kingsway Cinema, Ltd., 147, Bath Street, Glasgow. 1,432 seats. Booked at Hall.

LA SCALA (WE), 135, Sauchiehall Street.—Prop., Glasgow Photo Playhouse, Ltd., 180, Hope Street, Glasgow. Phone, Douglas 3438. 1,191 seats. Booked by A. B. King, 167, Bath Street, Glasgow. Continuous. Café. Prices, 1s. to 2s. Phone, Douglas 1228. Station, Queen Street, L.N.E.R.

LORNE CINEMA HOUSE (WE).—Prop., Caledon Pictures, Ltd., 21, Blythswood Square, Glasgow. Phone Douglas 3908. 1,265 seats. Booked by A. B. King, 167, Bath Street, Glasgow. Phone, Douglas 1195. Continuous. Prices, 5d. to 1s. Phone, Ibrox 324. Station, Glasgow termini.

LYCEUM THEATRE (WE), Govan Road, Govan.—
Prop., Caledon Pictures, Ltd., 21, Blythe-
wood Square. Phone, Douglas 3908. 2,050
seats. Continuous. Booked by A. B. King,
167, Bath Street, Glasgow. Prices, 5d. to 1s.
Proscenium width, 40 ft. Stage 12 ft. deep;
six dressing-rooms. Phone, Govan 199.

MAGNET CINEMA (Film Industries, Ltd.), Possil
Road.—Lessee, R. Pennycook. Booked at
Tonic Cinema, Glasgow. Continuous. Prices,
6d. to 9d. Station, Glasgow.

MAJESTIC THEATRE (BTH), Smith Street,
Govanhill.—Lessee, J. Anderson. 950 seats.
Booked at Hall. Continuous. Prices, 3d. to
7d. Proscenium width, 18 ft. Phone, Queen's
Park 572. Station, Govanhill.

MAYFAIR (WE), Battlefield.—Props., Scottish
Cinema and Variety Theatres, Ltd., 105,
St. Vincent Street, Glasgow. 1,340 seats.

MECCA (WE), Possilpark.—Prop., Mecca Cinema,
Ltd., 147, Bath Street, Glasgow. 1,632 seats.
Booked at Hall. Continuous. Prices, 6d. to
1s. Phone, Douglas 2830.

MOSSPARK PICTURE HOUSE (RCA).—Prop. and
Man., Duncan Campbell. 700 seats. Continu-
ous. Booked at Hall, Prices, 3d. to 1s. 4d.
Proscenium width, 16 ft.

NEW BEDFORD PICTURE HOUSE (RCA).—Booked
by A. B. King, 167, Bath Street, Glasgow.
Phone, Douglas 1195.

NEW CINERAMA (RCA), Victoria Road, Cross-
hill, S.S.—Prop., B.B. Pictures (1920), Ltd.,
6, Brandon Street, Motherwell. Booked at
New Gallery House, Regent Street, W.1.
Continuous. Prices, 6d. to 1s. 6d. Station,
Queen's Park 1151 Station, Central, L.M.S.

NEW GRAND THEATRE (WE), Cowcaddens Street.
—Prop., The Grove Picture House, Ltd.,
175, West George Street, Glasgow. Contin-
uous. Booked by A. B. King, 167, Bath
Street, Glasgow. Prices, 3d. to 1s. Phone,
Douglas 4187. Station, Central, L.M.S.

NEW KINEMA (WE), Springburn.—Prop., New
Kinemas (Springburn), Ltd. 855 seats.
Booked at Hall. Continuous. Pictures and
Variety. Stage, 30 ft. by 40 ft.; two dressing-
rooms. Prices, 4d. to 1s.

NEW SAVOY THEATRE (BA), Hope Street.—
Prop., Gaumont British Corporation, Ltd.
2,000 seats. Booked at H.O. Continuous.
Prices, 5d. to 2s. 6d. Tea Rooms. Phone,
Douglas 3997.

NEW STAR CINEMA (WE), Maryhill.—Prop.,
Maryhill Star Palace, Ltd. 1,744 seats.
Booked by G. Taylor, 27, Merkland Street,
Glasgow. Continuous. Prices, 3d. to 9d.
Phone, Maryhill 341.

NORWOOD (Cinema), St. George's Road, Glasgow.

OLYMPIA (WE), Bridgeton.—Prop., Glasgow
Olympia Theatre of Varieties, Ltd., 116,
Hope Street, Glasgow. Phone, Central
4905. 1,739 seats. Booked at Palace
Theatre, Glasgow, by Stuart Forbes. Twice
nightly. Prices, 3d. to 8d. Phone, Bridgeton
354.

ORIENT KINEMA (WE).—Geo. Taylor Circuit,
27, Merkland Street, Partick, Glasgow. 2,529
seats. Booked at H.O. Phone, Bridgeton
229.

OXFORD CINEMA (RCA), 45, Keppochhill Road.—
Prop., B. Frutin, 118, Stockwell Street,
Glasgow. Phone, Bell 1975. 1,400 seats.
Booked at Hall. Stage 14 ft. deep; four
dressing rooms. Prices, 4d. to 1s. Continu-
ous. Proscenium width, 40 ft. Phone,
Bell 602. Station, Springburn.

PALACE THEATRE (WE), Gorbals.—Prop., Harry

McKelvie. 1,821 seats. Continuous evenings.
Two changes weekly. Prices, 3d. to 1s.
Phone, South 270.

PALACEUM (WE), Edvour Street, Shettleston.—
Prop., Scott Theatres, Ltd., Brandon Street,
Motherwell. 900 seats. Booked at Hall.
Stage, 30 ft.; three dressing-rooms. Three
shows daily. Pictures and Variety. Prices,
4d. to 1s. Phone, Shettleston 413. Station,
Carntyne, L.N.E.R.

PALLADIUM (BTP), Pollokshaws.—Prop., James
Graham, 17, Blythswood Square, Glasgow.
Phone, Western 2305.

PANOPTICÓN (AWH), 115, Trongate.—Prop.,
Peter Pickard. 700 seats. Continuous. Pic-
tures and Variety. Both booked at Hall.
Prices, 3d. to 6d. Proscenium width, 20 ft.
Stage, 10 ft. deep; three dressing rooms.
Phone, Bell 2181. Station, Glasgow Central.

PARADE CINEMA (BA), Meadowpark Street.
—Props., Denman Picture Houses, Ltd.,
New Galley House, Regent Street, London,
W.1. 1,500 seats. Booked at H.O. Continu-
ous. Prices, 5d. to 1s. Phone, Bridgeton
2699. Station, Central, L.M.S.

PARAGON PICTURE HOUSE (BA), 403, Cumber-
land Street.—Prop., United Cinemas, Ltd.,
105, St. Vincent Street, Glasgow. Phone,
Central 8791. 1,380 seats. Booked by G.
Singleton, 39, Kirkpatrick Street, Bridgeton,
Glasgow. Continuous. Prices, 4d. and 6d.
Proscenium width, 35 ft. Phone, South 297.

PARAMOUNT (WE).

COMPTON
ORGAN featured here.

PARK CINEMA (RCA), Marne Street, Dennistoun.
—Prop., Eastern Picture House Co., Ltd.,
203, Hope Street, Glasgow. Phone, Douglas
3431. 1,100 seats. Booked at H.O. Continuous Prices, 5d. to 1s. Phone, Bridgeton
2827. Station, L.M.S. Central.

PARKHEAD PICTURE PALACE (BTH), 49, Tollcross Road.—Prop., Scottish Cinema &
Variety Theatres, Ltd., 105, Vincent Street,
Glasgow. Phone, Central 2830. 1,250 seats.
Booked at 30-31, Golden Square, W.1. Continuous. Prices, 5d. to 9d. Proscenium
width, 30 ft. Station, Parkhead, L.M.S.

PARTICK PICTURE HOUSE (WE), Vine Street,
Partick.—Prop., Partick Picture House, Ltd.
1774 seats. Continuous. Two changes weekly. Prices, 4d. to 1s. Phone, Western 2766.
Station, Partick.

PHOENIX (BTP), Sawfield Place.—Props., The
Scottish Cinema and Variety Theatres, Ltd.,
105, St. Vincent Street, Glasgow. 980 seats.
Continuous. Booked by Associated British
Cinemas, Ltd., London. Prices, 3d. and 4d.
Proscenium width, 22 ft. Station, Central.

PICTUREDROME (WE), Gorbals Cross.—Prop,
George Green, Ltd. 970 seats. Booked at
182, Trongate, Glasgow, by T. H. Reekie.
Continuous. Two changes weekly. Prices,
6d. to 1s. Proscenium width, 2 ft. Phone,
South 129. Station, Glasgow, Central.

PICTURE HOUSE (WE), Saracen Street, Possilpark.—Prop., J. Graham. 1,282 seats. Booked
at H.O., 17, Blythswood Square, Glasgow.
Continuous. Phone, Douglas 2477.

PICTURE HOUSE, Sinclair Drive.

PICTURE HOUSE (WE), Wellfield Street, Springburn.—Prop., J. Graham, 17, Blythswood
Square, Glasgow. Phone, Central 6629.
1,535 seats. Continuous. Three changes
weekly. Pictures and Variety. Variety

GLASGOW--Contd.

booked by Standard Agency, Renfrew Street, Glasgow. Stage, 8 ft. deep ; 2 dressing-rooms. Prices, 3d. to 6d. Station, Central, L.M.S.
**Fitted "ARDENTE" Deaf Aids
See page 258**

PLAYHOUSE (WE), Renfield Street.— Props. George Green, Ltd., 182, Trongate, Glasgow. 4,200 seats. Booked at H.O. Continuous. Café and Dance Hall. Stage, 16 ft. deep. Prices, 7d. to 3s. Phone, Bell 1661.

PREMIER PICTURE HOUSE (RCA), Bridgeton.— Prop., R. V. Singleton. 800 seats. Booked by G. Singleton, at 39, Kirkpatrick Street, Glasgow. Twice nightly. Phone, Bridgeton 1111.

PREMIER THEATRE (Electrocord), Shettleston Road, Shettleston.—Prop., Scott's Theatres, Ltd., 18, Clyde Street, Motherwell. 432 seats. Continuous. Two changes weekly. Prices, 3d. and 4d. Station, Carntyne, L.N.E.R.

PRINCE'S PICTURE HOUSE (RCA), Gourlay Street, Springburn.—Prop., Scottish Cinema and Variety Theatres, Ltd. 950 seats. Continuous. Two shows nightly. Two changes. Prices, 4d. and 6d.

PUBLIC HALL (BTP), Nitshill.

RED CINEMA (RCA).

REGAL CINEMA (RCA), Sauchiehall Street.— Prop., Scottish Cinema and Variety Theatres, Ltd., 105, Vincent Street, Glasgow. 2359 seats. Booked by Associated British Cinemas Ltd., London. Prices, 1s. to 1s. 6d. Continuous. Phone, Douglas 2700. Café attached

COMPTON
ORGAN featured here.

REGENT PICTURE HOUSE (WE), Renfield Street —Prop., Glasgow Picture House Co., Ltd 1,199 seats. Booked by A. B. King, 167 Bath Street. Continuous. Prices, 1s. to 2s Phone, Douglas 3303.

REX PICTURE HOUSE (WE), Riddrie.—Prop., Scottish Cinema and Variety Theatres, Ltd., 105, St. Vincent Street, Glasgow. Phone, Central 2830. 2,237 seats.

RHUL PICTURE HOUSE (WE), Burnside.—Prop., Burnside Picture House Co., Ltd. 1,264 seats. Booked at Hall by W. Shaw. Continuous. Phone, Rutherglen 484.

RIALTO (WE), 15, Castle Road, Cathcart.— Prop., Scottish Cinema and Variety Theatres Ltd., 105, St. Vincent Street, Glasgow. 1,311 seats. Booked in London. Prices, 7d, to 1s. Phone, Merrylee 2122. Station, Cathcart, L.M.S.

RIO (RCA), Cannesburn Toll, Bearsden.—Prop., Peter Crerar, Innesmohr, Crieff. 1,120 seats. Continuous nightly, Sat. from 2.30. Prices, 6d. to 1s. 3d. Proscenium width, 60 ft. Phone, Bearsden 112. Films by Carrier. Café attached.

RITZ (WE), Oatlands.—Props., Scottish Cinema and Variety Theatres, Ltd., 105, St. Vincent Street, Glasgow. Phone, Central 2830. 1,555 seats. Booked at A.B.C., London. Continuous. Prices, 4d. to 6d. Phone, South 1197.

ROSEVALE CINEMA (WE), 467, Dumbarton Road, Partick.—Prop., Rosevale Cinema, Ltd. Booked by A. B. King, 167, Bath Street, Glasgow. Phone, Douglas 1195. 1,800 seats. Continuous. Two changes weekly. Prices, 6d. to 1s. Proscenium width, 30 ft. Phone, Western 1245. Station, Partick.

ROXY (WE), 1397, Maryhill Road.—Prop., James Graham. 2,270 seats. Booked at 17, Blythswood Square, Glasgow. Continuous. Pictures and Variety. Stage, 20 ft.; four dressing-rooms. Prices, 3d. to 1s. 3d. Phone, Maryhill 246.

ROYAL PICTURE PALACE (WE). Main Street, Bridgeton. Prop., Shawfields Picture House, Ltd., 144, St. Vincent Street, Glasgow. 504 seats. Booked at H.O. Two shows nightly. Three changes weekly. Prices, 2d. to 4d. Station, Bridgeton Cross, L.M.S.

ST. ENOCH PICTURE THEATRE (BTH), Argyle Street.—(Closed).

ST. GEORGE'S CROSS PICTURE HOUSE (BTH), New City Road. Continuous. Two changes weekly. Phone, Charing Cross 1087. Station, Glasgow termini.

ST. JAMES' PICTURE HOUSE (BTH), Stirling Road, Townhead.—Prop., James Hamilton, Ardgowan Picture House, Glasgow. 502 seats. Booked at H.O. Two shows nightly. Prices, 3d. and 5d. Phone, Bell 1853. Station, Glasgow termini.

SCENIC PICTURE HOUSE (Mihaly), Paisley Road, Toll.—Prop., Wm. Hamilton, 355, Wellshot Road, Tollcross, Glasgow. Phone, Shettleston 371. 800 seats. Booked at Hall. Continuous. Prices, from 3d. Phone, South 2017. Station Glasgow termini.

SCOTIA PICTURE HOUSE (WE).—Props., Douglas Picture House Co., Ltd. 1,256 seats. Phone, Bridgeton 1877. Continuous.

SEAMORE PICTURE HOUSE (WE), Maryhill Road. —Prop., N. B. Cinemas, Ltd. Phone, Douglas 3883.

STANDARD PICTURE HOUSE (WE), Dumbarton Road, Partick.—Prop., James Graham. Continuous. Prices, 3d. to 4d. Station, Central, L.M.S.

STRATHCLYDE CINEMA (WE).—Summerfield Street, Dalmarnock Road.—Prop., Strathclyde Cinema, Ltd., Man. Dir., John McAlister. 1,910 seats.

THE PICTURE HOUSE (WE), Sauchiehall Street. —Prop., Provincial Cinematograph Theatres, Ltd., 123, Regent Street, London, 1,572 seats. Continuous. Booked at H.O. Prices, 6d. to 1s. Café. Station, Central, L.M.S.
**WURLITZER ORGAN
Installed in this Kinema**

TIVOLI (WE), 53, Crow Road.—Props., Glasgow Tivoli, Ltd., 1,918 seats. Continuous. Prices, 4d. to 2s. Stage, 15 ft. deep; four dressing rooms. Phone, Western 3488. Partick, L.N.E.R.
**Fitted "ARDENTE" Deaf Aids
See page 258**

TOLEDO (RCA), Clarkston Road.—Prop., Scottish Cinemas and Variety Theatres, Ltd. 1,600 seats. Continuous. Station, Muirend.

VICTORIA THEATRE (RCA), Whiteinch.—Prop., Alpha Theatres (Glasgow), Ltd., 20, West Campbell Street, Glasgow. Phone, Central 8878. 736 seats. Variety, twice nightly. Booked by Standard Variety Agency, 14, Renfrew Street, Glasgow. Proscenium width, 26 ft. Stage, 15 ft. deep ; two dressing rooms. Prices, 6d. to 1s. Phone, West 5490. Station, James Street, Whiteinch.

WAVERLEY PICTURE HOUSE (WE), Shawlands Cross.—Prop., Scottish Cinema and Variety Theatres, Ltd., 105, St. Vincent Street, Glasgow. 1,320 seats. Tea Room. Continuous. Two changes weekly. Prices, 6d. to 1s. 3d. Phone, Langside 1119.

WELLINGTON PALACE (RCA), Commercial Road. —Prop., Wellington Palace. 1,600 seats.

Booked at Picture House, Wishaw. Continuous. Two changes weekly. Prices, 4d. to 6d. Phone, South 574. Station, Glasgow.

WESTERN CINEMA (RCA), 177, Dumbarton Road, Partick.—Prop., Western Cinema Company, Ltd. Booked at 175, West George Street, Glasgow. Continuous. Two changes weekly. Prices, 6d. to 1s.—Phone, Western 3725. Station, Partick, L.M.S.

WESTWAY (WE), Cardonald.

GLENBOIG (LANARKSHIRE).
CINEMA.

GLENCRAIG (FIFESHIRE).
PEOPLES PICTURE PALACE (Edibell).

GOUROCK (RENFREW), Pop. 8,844.
PICTURE HOUSE (New Era), Kempock Place.—Prop., Gourock Picture House, Ltd. 650 seats. Booked by Thomas Ormiston, Sec., 6, Brandon Street, Motherwell. Phone, Motherwell 381-2. Continuous. Three changes weekly. Prices, 4d. to 9d. Phone, Gourock 121. Station, Gourock, L.M.S.

GRANGEMOUTH (STIRLING), Pop. 11,000
LA SCALA (BA).—Prop., A. H. Faulkner. 700 seats. Continuous. Phone, Grangemouth 103. Station, Grangemouth, L.M.S.

GRANTOWN-ON-SPEY (MORAY), Pop. 1,577.
PICTURE HOUSE (Morrison Electric).—Prop., J. G. Anderson, The Square, Grantown-on-Spey. Phone, No. 60. 450 seats. Booked at Hall. Twice nightly. Prices, 6d. to 1s. 6d. Café attached. Station, L.M.S.

GREENOCK (RENFREW), Pop 77,928.
B.B. CINEMA (WE), Argyle Street.—Prop., Greenock B.B. Cinema, Ltd., 33, Cathcart Street, Greenock. 1,311 seats. Booked by A. B. King, 167, Bath Street, Glasgow. Continuous. Two changes weekly. Prices, 4d. to 1s. 3d. Phone, Greenock 91. Station, Central, L.M.S.

CENTRAL PICTURE HOUSE (BTH), West Blackhall Street.—Prop., The Central Picture House, (Greenock), Ltd. 750 seats. Continuous. Two changes weekly. Prices, 4d. to 1s. Phone. No. 539. Station, Princes Pier, L.M.S.

KING'S SUPER KINEMA (WE), West Blackhall Street.—Prop., King's Theatre (Greenock), Ltd. 1,500 seats. Continuous. Booked by Sydney Friedman, 950, Finchley Road, London. Prices, 3d. to 2s. 5d. Pictures and Variety. Variety booked by Collins Variety Agency. 115, Renfield Street, Glasgow. Stage, 30 ft. deep. Phone, 614. Station, Central, Greenock.

LA SCALA (BTH) Inverkip Street, Greenock West. —Props., W. G. McAulay, Sen., G. B. McAulay, 3-5, Captain Street. Phone, Greenock 425. 1,186 seats. Booked at 48, Inverkip Street, Greenock. Prices, 4d. to 1s. Phone, Greenock 425. Station, Greenock West, L.M.S.

PAVILION (RCA), 42, Rue End Street.—Prop., Pavilion Picture House (Greenock), Ltd., 3, Captain Street, Greenock. 1,100 seats. Sec., Geo. B. McAulay. Booked at Hall. Continuous. Three changes weekly. Prices, 4d. to 1s. Proscenium width, 23 ft. Phone, 425.

PICTURE PALACE (RCA), Brougham Street.—Prop., Greenock Picture Palace Co., Ltd., 95 Bath Street, Glasgow. Phone, Douglas 2769. 1,710 seats. Booked at H.O. Continuous. Two changes weekly. Prices, 5d. to 1s. 3d. Phone, Greenock 893.

REGAL (WE), West Blackhall Street.—Props., The Scottish Cinema & Variety Theatres, Ltd., 105, St. Vincent Street, Glasgow. Phone, Central 2830. 1,700 seats. Booked at London. Continuous. Prices, 4d. to 1s. Proscenium width, 24 ft. Phone No. 287. Station, Greenock, L.M.S.

HADDINGTON (EAST LOTHIAN), Pop. 5,682.
NEW COUNTY CINEMA (WE).—Props., Scot and Paulo. 998 seats. Booked at Hall. Continuous. Prices, 6d. to 1s. 3d. Phone, Haddington 125. Station, Haddington.

HAMILTON (LANARK), Pop. 44,224.
HIPPODROME (RCA).—Prop., E. H. Bostock & Sons, Ltd., 69, Dalhousie Street, Glasgow. Phone, Douglas 498. Booked at 34, St. Enoch Square, Glasgow. Twice nightly. Prices, 4d. to 1s. Phone No. 131. Station, Hamilton, L.M.S., L.N.E.R.

LA SCALA (RCA).—Prop., Denman Picture Houses, Ltd., London. 1,500 seats. Booked at H.O. Continuous. Phone, Hamilton 300.

PLAYHOUSE, Quarry Street.—Prop., E. H. Bostock & Sons, 69, Dalhousie Street, Glasgow. 600 seats. Booked by Mrs. H. Urquhart, 34, St. Enoch Square, Glasgow. Phone, Douglas 1857. Continuous. Prices 2d. to 6d. Phone, Hamilton 131.

REGAL (WE), Townhead Street.—Prop., Scottish Cinema and Variety Theatres, Ltd., 105, St. Vincent Street, Glasgow. Phone, Central 2830. 2023 seats. Booked in London. Daily Mat. Continuous evenings. Prices, 4d. to 1/-. Phone, Hamilton 339. Station, Hamilton Central.

ROXY PICTURE HOUSE (RCA).—Prop., H. Martles, 65, W. Regent Street, Glasgow. Phone, Douglas 3933. 700 seats. Booked at H.O. Continuous. Prices, 4d. to 1s. Phone, Hamilton 142. Station, Hamilton Central, L.M.S.

HARTHILL (LANARK), Pop. 4,000.
CINEMA (RCA).—Sec., Jas. H. Laird, 11, Polkemmet Road, Harthill. Booked at Hall. One show nightly. Prices, 4d. to 8d. Station, Westcraigs, L.M.S.

HAWICK (ROXBURGH), Pop. 18,214.
KING'S CINEMA (BA).—Prop., United Cinemas, Ltd., 105, St. Vincent Street, Glasgow, C.2. 1,292 seats. Booked by G. Singleton, 39, Kirkpatrick Street, Glasgow, Once nightly. Three shows Sat. Prices, 5d. to 1s. 3d. Dance Hall. Phone, Hawick 245. Station, Hawick, L.N.E.R.

PAVILION THEATRE (WE), High Street.—Prop., Scott's Theatres, Ltd., 56, Brandon Street, Motherwell. Phone, Motherwell 601. 1,110 seats. Booked at H.O. Continuous. Three on Sat. Stage, 25 ft. deep; three dressing-rooms. Two changes weekly. Prices, 5d. to 1s. 3d. Proscenium width, 30 ft. Phone, Hawick 245. Station, Hawick, L.N.E.R., and Road Transport.

THE THEATRE (ELECTROCORD), Croft Road.—Prop., Scott's Theatres, Ltd., 56, Brandon Street, Motherwell. Phone, Motherwell 601. 572 seats. Booked at H.O. Continuous. Three shows Sat. Two changes weekly. Prices, 4d. to 1s. Proscenium width, 22 ft. Station, Hawick.

HELENSBURGH (DUMBARTON), Pop. 8,893.
LA SCALA (WE), James Street.—Prop., Helensburgh Picture House, Ltd., 190, West George Street, Glasgow. 692 seats, Booked by A. B.

HELENSBURGH—Contd.
King, 167, Bath Street, Glasgow. Continuous. Two changes weekly. Prices 6d. to 1s. 6d. Phone, 615. Station, Helensburgh.
TOWER PICTURE HOUSE (WE), Colquhoun Square.—Props., Scottish Cinema and Variety Theatres, Ltd., 105, St. Vincent Street, Glasgow. 812 seats. Continuous. Pictures and variety. Prices, 6d. to 1s. 3d. Proscenium width, 40 ft. Stage, 14 ft. deep; two dressing-rooms. Phone, No. 564. Station, Helensburgh.

HOLYTOWN (LANARK), Pop. 8,850.
NEW STEVENSON PICTURE HOUSE (RCA).—700 seats.

HUNTLY (ABERDEEN), Pop. 4,579.
PALACE CINEMA (RCA).—Prop., Elite Entertainments Syndicate. 545 seats. One show nightly. Two changes weekly. Prices, 6d. to 1s. 6d. Proscenium width, 27 ft. Station, Huntly, L.N.E.R., and Road Transport.

INNERLEITHEN (PEEBLESSHIRE),Pop.3,740.
CINEMA (BTH).—600 seats.

INVERGORDON (ROSS AND CROMARTY).
PLAYHOUSE (BA).—Props., Invergordon Picture House Co., Royal Bank Buildings, Inverness. 500 seats. Prices, 6d. to 1s. Occasional Variety. Booked by A. B. King, 167, Bath Street, Glasgow. Proscenium width 27 ft. Stage 14 ft. deep; three dressing rooms. Phone No. 48. Station, Invergordon, L.M.S.

INVERKEITHING (FIFE), Pop. 4,968.
MAJESTIC THEATRE (BTH).—Props., Fife Talking Pictures, Ltd. 705 seats. Booked at Hall. Continuous evenings. Prices, 3d. and 1s. Proscenium width, 30 ft. Station, Inverkeithing, L.N.E.R.

INVERNESS (INVERNESS), Pop. 22,582.
EMPIRE (BA), Academy Street. — Prop., Caledonian Associated Cinemas, Ltd., Royal Bank Bldgs., Inverness. Phone No. 1. 1,001 seats. Booked by A. B. King, 167, Bath Street, Glasgow. Continuous. Two changes weekly. Pictures and Variety. Prices, 6d. to 1s. 6d. Variety booked by W. R. Galt, 13, Sauchiehall Street. Proscenium width, 28 ft. Stage, 26 ft. deep; seven dressing-rooms. Phone, Inverness 999. Station, Inverness, L.M.S.
LA SCALA PICTURE HOUSE, LUNCHEON AND TEA ROOMS (BA), Academy Street.—Prop., Caledonian Associated Cinemas, Ltd., Royal Bank Buildings. Phone No. 1. 1,200 seats. Booked by A. B. King, 167, Bath Street, Glasgow. Continuous. Two changes weekly. Prices, 6d. to 2s. Proscenium width, 28 ft. Restaurant attached. Phone, Inverness 302. Station, Inverness, L.M.S.
PLAYHOUSE (WE), Academy Street.—Prop., Caledonian Associated Cinemas, Ltd., Royal Bank Bldgs., Inverness. 1,469 seats. Phone N. 1. Continuous. Booked by A. B. King, 167, Bath Street, Glasgow. Prices, 6d. to 2s. 4d. Café. Phone, Inverness 30. Station, Inverness, L.M.S.
SCALA (RCA).

INVERBERVIE (KINCARDINE), Pop. 1,032.
INVERBERVIE CINEMA.—Prop., Bervie Cinema Syndicate. Booked by Mr. Lyon at King Street, Inverbervie. Two shows weekly. Prices, 3d. to 9d. Phone, Inverbervie 9. Station, Inverbervie, L.N.E.R.

INVERURIE (ABERDEEN), Pop. 4,415.
TOWN HALL (WE).
VICTORIA CINEMA (BA).—Props., Inverurie Picture House, Ltd. 500 seats. Continuous evenings. Prices, 6d. to 1s. 6d. Proscenium width, 29 ft. Phone 36. Station, Inverurie, L.N.E.R. (G.N.S.R. Branch).

IRVINE (AYR), Pop. 12,032.
GREEN'S PICTUREDROME (WE), Bank Street.— Prop., George Green, Ltd., 182, Trongate, Glasgow. Phone, Bell 1660. 770 seats. Booked at H.O. Continuous. Two changes weekly. Prices, 6d. to 1s. Proscenium width, 30 ft. Phone, 217. Station, Irvine, L.M.S.
PALACE PICTURE HOUSE (RCA).—Prop., A. S. Blair. 450 seats. Booked by Prop. at Hillhead Salon, Glasgow. Continuous. Prices, 4d. to 9d. Station, Irvine, L.M.S.
REGAL (WE).—Prop., H. Martles, 65, W. Regent Street, Glasgow. 475 seats. Booked at H.O. Continuous. Prices, 6d. to 1s. Phone No. 15.

JEDBURGH (ROXBURGH), Pop. 4,110.
THE CINEMA (Parmeko).—Lessee, A. C. Pinder. 500 seats. Booked at Playhouse, Kelso. Once nightly. Three shows Sat. Prices, 3d. to 1s. 3d. Phone No. 29. Station, Jedburgh, L.M.S.

JOHNSTONE (RENFREW), Pop. 12,837.
GEORGE PICTURE HOUSE.—Prop., George Street (Johnstone) Picture House Co., Ltd. Continuous. Booked at Hall.
PAVILION THEATRE (WE).—Prop., George Green, Ltd., 182, Trongate, Glasgow, C.1. Phone, Bell 1660. 1,109 seats. Booked at H.O. Continuous. Stage, 36 ft.; three dressing-rooms. Prices, 4d. to 1s. Phone, 140. Station, Johnstone, L.M.S.

KEITH (BANFF), Pop. 6,082.
PALACE (RCA).—Prop., Elite Entertainments Syndicate, 21A, East Church Street, Buckie. 298 seats. Booked at H.O. One show nightly. Two changes weekly. Prices, 6d. to 1s. 3d. Station, Keith, L.N.E.R.
PLAYHOUSE (WE).—Prop., Caledonian Associated Cinemas, Ltd. Royal Bank Buildings, Inverness. Phone, Inverness 1. 650 seats. Booked by A. B. King, Glasgow. Continuous. Prices, 6d. to 2s. Proscenium, 32 ft. Phone, Keith 123. Station, Keith.

KELSO (ROXBURGH), Pop. 4,279.
ROXY (BTH).—Prop., W. G. Gilchrist, 28, The Square. Phone No. 206. 400 seats. Once nightly. Twice Sat. Booked at Hall. Prices, 3d. to 1s. 6d. Proscenium width, 36 ft. Phone No. 209. Station, Kelso, L.N.E.R.
THE PLAYHOUSE (D.A.), Havannah Court.— Lessee, A. C. Pinder. 600 seats. Booked at Hall. Once nightly. Three Shows Sat. Prices, 3d. to 1s. 6d. Proscenium width, 30 ft. Stage, 18 ft. deep. Two dressing rooms. Phone, Kelso 52. Station, Kelso, L.M.S.

KELTY (FIFE), Pop. 8,736.
GOTHENBURG PICTURE HOUSE (BA).—Prop., Kelty Public House Society, Ltd. 1,140 seats. Booked at Hall by Man. Once nightly, three on Sat. Prices, 3d. to 6d. Proscenium width, 40 ft. Stage, 17 ft. deep. Phone, 15. Station, Cowdenbeath, L.N.E.R.

KILBIRNIE (AYR), Pop. 8,193.
PICTURE HOUSE (Film Industries).—Prop. Kilbirnie Picture House, Ltd. 820 seats

Continuous. Booked by Thos. Ormiston, Sec., at 6, Brandon Street, Motherwell, Phone. Motherwell 381. Three changes weekly. Prices, 6d. to 1s. Phone, 69 Beith. Station, Kilbirnie.

KILMARNOCK (Ayr), Pop. 38,099.

ELECTRIC THEATRE (Morrison), Regent Street. —Prop., Arthur Talboys. 500 seats. Continuous. Two changes weekly. Prices, 4d. to 9d. Proscenium width, 16 ft. Station, Kilmarnock, L.M.S.

EMPIRE PICTURE HOUSE (BA), Titchfield Street. —Prop. Empire Picture House, Kilmarnock, Ltd., 154, St. Vincent Street, Glasgow. Central 5674. 900 seats. Booked at 167, Bath Street. Continuous. Two changes weekly. Prices, 6d. to 1s. 3d. Station, Kilmarnock, L.M.S.

FORUM PICTURE HOUSE (RCA), Titchfield Street —Prop. and Man., A. Claymore. 700 seats Continuous. Prices, 6d. to 1s. Phone, 776 Station, L.M.S.

GEORGE PICTURE HOUSE (WE), West George, Street.—Prop., Scottish Cinema and Variety. Theatres, Ltd., 105, St. Vincent Street, Glasgow. Phone, Central 2830. 1,126 seats. Booked in Glasgow. Continuous. Prices, 6d. to 1s. Phone, 536. Films by Road Transport.

IMPERIAL PICTURE HOUSE (BTH), Union Street, —Prop., McLean and Pollin. Booked by Wm. B. Pollin, 3, Macfarlane Street, Paisley. Phone, Paisley 2026. 700 seats. Theatre Phone, Kilmarnock 126. Continuous. Prices, 4d. to 9d.

KING'S THEATRE (WE), Titchfield Street.— Prop., Scottish Cinema and Variety Theatres, Ltd. Phone, Kilmarnock 234. 1,268 seats.

PALACE (BA), Green Street.—Prop., H. Martles, 65, West Regent Street, Glasgow. Phone, Douglas 3933. 620 seats. Booked in Glasgow. Continuous. Two changes weekly. Stage, 25 ft.; 5 dressing-rooms. Prices, 6d. to 1s. 3d. Phone, Kilmarnock 551. Station, Kilmarnock, L.M.S.

REGAL.

KILSYTH (Stirling), Pop. 10,047.

KING'S CINEMA (RCA).—Prop. and Res. Man., M. Stark. 500 seats. Twice nightly. Three changes weekly. Prices, 4d. to 9d. Proscenium width, 30 ft. Phone, Kilsyth 38. Station, Kilsyth, L.N.E.R.

PAVILION (RCA).—1,168 seats. Booked by S. A. Grattan, 9, McFarlane Street, Glasgow.

KILWINNING (Ayr), Pop. 8,531.

KINGSWAY (RCA), Almwell Road.—Prop., Helen W. Urquhart, 34, St. Enoch Square, Glasgow. 500 seats. Booked at H.O. Continuous. Prices, 5d. to 1s. Proscenium width, 21 ft. Stage, 18 ft. deep ; four dressing rooms. Phone, Douglas 1857. Station, L.M.S.

KINGHORN (Fife), Pop. 2,016.

REGAL (BTH). — Pettycur Road. — Props., Luciani Bros., 22, High Street, Kinghorn. 600 seats. Pictures and Variety. Booked at Glasgow. Once nightly. Continuous Sat. Prices, 7d. to 1s. Proscenium width, 27 ft. Stage 12½ ft. deep ; two dressing-rooms. Phone, Kinghorn 34. Café attached. Station, Kinghorn, L.N.E.R.

KINGUSSIE (Inverness-shire), Pop. 2,360.

VICTORIA HALL (BA).—Props., Kingussie Picture House Co., Ltd., Royal Bank Buildings, Drummond Street, Inverness. 309 seats. Booked by A. B. King, 167, Bath Street, Glasgow. Continuous. Prices, 6d. to 1s. 6d. Proscenium width, 20 ft.

KINLOCHLEVEN (Argyll), Pop. 1,700.

PUBLIC HALL (BTH).—Prop., Kinlochleven Village Improvement Society, Ltd. 380 seats. Booked in Glasgow. Three times weekly in winter. Twice weekly in summer. Prices, -6d. and 1s. Phone, Kinlochleven 243. Station, Ballachulish.

KINROSS (Kinross), Pop. 3,137.

KINROSS CINEMA (BTH).—Prop., h. Coleman. 370 seats. Booked at Hall. One show nightly. Prices 6d. to 1s. Station, Kinross Junction, Kinross.

KIRKCALDY (Fife), Pop. 43.874,

OPERA HOUSE (WE).—Prop., Scottish Cinema and Variety Theatres, Ltd. 1,311 seats. Booked at London. Continuous

PALACE (RCA).—Prop., Scottish Cinema and Variety Theatres, Ltd., 105, St. Vincent Street, Glasgow. 1,000 seats. Booked at 30-31, Golden Square, London. Continuous. Daily matinee. Station, Kirkcaldy, L.N.E.R.

PALLADIUM (BTH), Rosslyn Street, Gallatown.— Prop., T. Leishman. 450 seats. Booked at Hall. Continuous. Three changes weekly, Prices, 3d. to 9d. Station, Kirkcaldy, L.N.E.R.

PATHHEAD PICTURE HOUSE (BTH).—Lessee, F. W. Carlow,"Woodlea," Viceroy Street, Kirkcaldy. 600 seats. Continuous. Three shows Sat. Booked at Hall. Prices, 6d. to 9d. Proscenium width, 20 ft. Phone No. 2802. Station, Sinclairtown, L.N.E.R.

PICTURE HOUSE (WE), Port Brae.—Prop., Kirkcaldy. Entertainments, Ltd. 616 seats. Continuous. Booked at H.O. Prices, 3d. to 9d.

RIALTO (BA), 204, High Street.—Prop., Denman Picture Houses, Ltd., 123, Regent Street, London, W.1. 1,212 seats. Booked at H.O. Continuous. Prices, 6d. to 1s. 6d. Phone, 2587. Station, Kirkcaldy, L.N.E.R.

**Fitted "ARDENTE" Deaf Aids
See page 258**

KIRKCONNEL (Dumfries), Pop. 3,962.

CINEMA (BTH).—Prop. and Res. Man., Harry Bradley. Once nightly. Three shows Sat, Prices, 7d. to 1s. 3d. Station, Kirkconnel. L.M.S.

KIRKCUDBRIGHT (Kirkcudbright), Pop. 3,188.

PICTURE HOUSE (BTH).—Prop., E. Macalister and B. T. and R. A. Austin, 27, St. Mary's Drive, Kirkcudbright. 500 seats. Booked at Hall. One show nightly. Prices, 5d. to 1s. 6d. Phone, Kirkcudbright 11. Station, Kirkcudbright.

KIRKINTILLOCH (Dumbarton), Pop. 17,308.

BLACK BULL CINEMA (Mihaly).—Prop., Black Bull Cinema (Kirkintilloch), Ltd., 58, West Regent Street, Glasgow. Phone, Douglas 594. 1,020 seats. Continuous. Twice Sat. Prices, 4d. to 9d. Phone, Kirkintilloch 242. Station, Kirkintilloch.

PAVILION (BA), Oxford Street.—Prop., Denman Picture House, Ltd., London. 1,000 seats. Booked at Head Office. Continuous. Twice Sat. Three changes weekly. Prices, 3d. to 1s. Phone, Kirkintilloch 47.

KIRKMUIRHILL (Lanark).

CINEMA (Morrison).—275 seats.

KIRKWALL (Orkney), Pop. 3,517.

ALBERT KINEMA (BA), Albert Street.—Props., D. B. Peace and E. M. Shearer. One show nightly. Two changes weekly. Prices, 6d. to 1s. 9d. Station, Thurso, Scotland, L.M.S.

KIRRIEMUIR (ANGUS), **Pop. 4,755.**
REGAL (BTH), High Street.—Prop., Strathmore Picture Houses, Ltd.; Regal, East High Street, Forfar. 450 seats. Booked at H.O. One show nightly, three on Sat. Two changes weekly. Prices, 4d. to 1s. 6d. Station, Kirriemuir, L.M.S.

LANARK (LANARK), **Pop. 9,133.**
ELECTRIC THEATRE (BTH).—Props., McAndrew & Co. 600 seats. Once nightly, twice Sat.
PICTURE HOUSE (BTH), Castlegate.—Lessees, McAndrew & Co. 800 seats. Booked at Alhambra, Carluke. Two changes weekly. Prices, 4d. to 1s. Phone, Lanark 146. Station, Lanark, L.M.S.
REGAL (WE).—Props., Regal Pictures (Lanark), Ltd., 156, St. Vincent Street, Glasgow. Phone, Central 449. 1,300 seats. Booked by A. B. King, 167, Bath Street, Glasgow. Prices 6d. to 1s. 6d. Proscenium width, 30 ft. Phone, Lanark 333.

LANGHOLM (DUMFRIES), **Pop. 2,770.**
BUCCLEUCH HALL CINEMA.—Props., T. and F. Milligan, Buccleuch Square, Langholm. 900 seats. Booked at Hall. Once nightly. Pictures and Variety. Prices, 6d. to 1s. Proscenium width, 20 ft. Stage 14 ft. deep; two dressing rooms. Station, Langholm, L.N.E.R.

LARBERT (STIRLING), **Pop. 13,029.**
PICTURE PALACE (BA).—Prop., A. H. Faulkner, "The Point," Stenhousemuir. Phone No. 125. 700 seats.

LARGS (AYR), **Pop. 8,470.**
LARGS PICTURE HOUSE (BA).—Prop., Largs Picture House Co., Ltd., 1, Sandringham Terrace, Largs. 700 seats. Booked at Hall. Pictures and Variety. Continuous evenings; Mats., Wed. and Sat. Prices, 6d. to 1s. Stage, 46 ft. deep; three dressing-rooms. Café and Dance Hall. Phone, Largs 200. Station, Largs, L.M.S.
PICTURE PAVILION (F.I.).—Prop., Largs Electric Picture Pavilion, Ltd. 400 seats. Booked by S. Forbes, Palace Theatre, Glasgow, S.S. Continuous. Two changes weekly. Prices, 5d. to 1s.

LARKHALL (LANARK), **Pop. 14,980.**
EMPIRE (WE), 4, King Street.—Props., Scott Theatres, Ltd., 56, Brandon Street, Motherwell. Phone, Motherwell 601. 868 seats. Booked at H.O. Stage, 18 ft. deep; Continuous. Two changes weekly. Prices, 4d. to 6d. Phone, Larkhall 116. Station, Larkhall Central.
PICTURE HOUSE (BTH), Public Hall.—Lessee, M. Burns. 500 seats. Continuous, Two changes weekly. Prices, 5d. to 1s. Station, Larkhall Central, L.M.S.
REGAL (RCA).—Prop., Mr. Train. 900 seats. Booked at Hall. Continuous. Prices, 4d. to 8d. Proscenium width 24 ft. Stage, 20 ft. deep; three dressing rooms.

LAURENCEKIRK (KINCARDINE), **Pop. 1,713.**
CINEMA.—Booked by A. Ross, at Stonehaven. Shows, Wed. and Sat.

LEITH (MIDLOTHIAN), **Pop. 81,654.**
ALHAMBRA (WE).—Prop., Harry Lees and Robert Saunders. 1,423 seats. Booked at Hall. Continuous. Prices, 3d. to 1s. Proscenium width 26 ft. Stage, 22 ft. deep; eight dressing rooms. Station, Waverley, Edinburgh.

CAPITOL (WE).—Prop., Gaumont British Corporation, New Gallery House, Regent Street, W.1. 2,390 seats. Booked at H.O. Continuous. Prices, 7d. to 1s. Phone, Leith 1417.
CENTRAL KINEMA, 12, Hope Street.—(Closed).
GAIETY THEATRE (WE), Kirkgate.—Prop., Leith Entertainers, Ltd., 21, Blythswood Square, Glasgow. Phone, Douglas 3908/9. 1,400 seats. Booked by A. B. King, at 167, Bath Street, Glasgow. Phone, Douglas 1195. Continuous evenings. Mats. Wed. and Sat. Prices, 4d. to 1s. Proscenium width 30 ft. Stage, 35 ft. deep; 11 dressing rooms, Phone, Leith 35915. Station, Leith Central.
PALACE (BTH), Duke Street.—Prop., Leith Public Hall and Property Co., Ltd. 1,600 seats. Continuous. Mat., Sat. Two changes weekly. Booked at Hall. Prices, 6d. to 1s. Phone, Leith 36033. Station, Leith Central, L.N.E.R.
PICTURE HOUSE (BA), Laurie Street.—Prop. Joseph Penn, 151, Dalkeith Road, Edinburgh. Phone No. 43536. 375 seats. Booked at Hall Continuous. Two changes weekly. Prices, 3d. to 6d. Phone, Leith 36163.

LERWICK (SHETLAND), **Pop. 5,948.**
NORTH STAR CINEMA (BTH).—Prop., North Star Cinema Co., Ltd., 9, Golden Square, Aberdeen. Phone, Aberdeen 271. 576 seats. One show nightly. Two changes weekly. Prices, 3d. to 1s. 9d. Proscenium width, 19 ft. Station, Aberdeen (Joint).

LESLIE (FIFE), **Pop. 3,983.**
TOWN HALL CINEMA (Wired).—Props., A. & W. Shaw. Booked at. 9, Bank Place, Leslie. Two shows weekly. Prices, 2d. to 1s. Station, Leslie, L.N.E.R.

LESMAHAGOW (LANARK), **Pop. 11,661.**
PICTURE HOUSE (BTH).—Prop. and Man., A Palmer. 400 seats.

LEVEN (FIFE), **Pop. 7,411.**
REGENT (BTH).—Prop., Fifeshire Cinema Co., Ltd. Phone, Leven 147. Booked at Hall. 1,000 seats. Continuous. Prices, 3d. to 1s. Proscenium width, 30 ft. Station, Leven.
TROXY (Bauer), North Street.—Prop., Alexander Stevenson, "Braemar," Largo Road, Leven. Phone No. 190. 1,036 seats. Prices, 4d. to 1s. 3d. Continuous evenings. Phone No. 319. Station, Leven, L.N.E.R.

LINLITHGOW (WEST LOTHIAN), **Pop. 7,157.**
EMPIRE CINEMA (Britain's Best).—Lessees: Scott's Empires, Ltd. 1,000 seats.

LOANHEAD (MIDLOTHIAN), **Pop. 3,940.**
THE PICTURE HOUSE (BA).—Prop. and Res. Man., Arthur Brodie. 700 seats. Booked at Hall. Once nightly. Continuous Saturday. Prices, 4d. to 1s. Proscenium width, 18 ft.

LOCHGELLY (FIFE), **Pop. 9,297.**
CINEMA DE LUXE (WE), Bank Street.—Prop., Commercial Cinematograph Co., Ltd., Man. Dir., Tom Timmons. 979 seats. Two shows nightly. Three changes weekly. Prices, 3d. to 1s., Phone, Lochgelly 35. Station, Lochgelly.
OPERA HOUSE (BTH), Main Street.—Prop., Lochgelly Picture House, Co., Ltd., East Port, Dunfermline. 1,120 seats. Booked by A. B. King, 167, Bath Street, Glasgow. Phone, Douglas 1195. Continuous. Two changes weekly. Prices, 4d. to 9d. Phone, Lochgelly 20. Station, Lochgelly, L.N.E.R.

LOCHORE (FIFE), **Pop. 3,000:**
STAR THEATRE (BA).—Props., Star Theatre (Lochore), Ltd., Bloomfield House, Bathgate. Booked by I. R. Grove, Fairfield House, Broxburn. Twice nightly. Phone, Lochgelly 90. Film Transport Services (Broxburn), Ltd.

LOCHWINNOCH (RENFREW), **Pop. 3,868·**
PICTURE HOUSE (BTH).—Prop., J. Manders.

LOCKERBIE (DUMFRIES), **Pop. 2,574.**
REX (WE), Prop., Lockerbie Cinema Co., Ltd., Bank of Scotland Chambers, Lockerbie. 816 seats. Continuous. Booked by G. Green, Ltd., 182, Trongate, Glasgow. Prices, 6d. to 1s. 6d. Proscenium width, 31 ft. Station, Lockerbie L.M.S.

LONGRIGGEND (LANARK).
MINERS' WELFARE INSTITUTE.

LOSSIEMOUTH (MORAYSHIRE), **Pop. 3,912.**
TOWN HALL CINEMA (BTH), High Street.—350 seats. Booked at Hall. Once nightly. Continuous Sat. Prices 6d. to 1s. Station, Lossiemouth, L.M.S.

LUMPHANAN (ABERDEEN), **Pop. 830.**
PARISH HALL.—Prop., Deeside District Council. Booked by Secretary, Public Assistance Office.

LUNDIN LINKS (FIFE).
LA SCALA PICTURE HOUSE (Morrison).—Prop., Mrs. J. Clayton. Booked at Hall. Prices, 6d. to 1s. Proscenium width, 24 ft. Dance Hall. Station, Lundin Links, L.N.E.R.

MACDUFF (BANFF), **Pop. 3,276.**
THE CINEMA (Morrison).—Prop., T. MacNab, Skene Street, Macduff. Phone No. 16. Pictures and occasional Variety. Stage 12 ft. deep; two dressing rooms. Prices, 6d. to 1s. 6d. Proscenium width, 24 ft. Stage, 12 ft. deep; two dressing rooms. Station, Macduff.

MAUCHLINE (AYR), **Pop. 2,484.**
PICTURE HOUSE (BTH), The Loan.—Prop., J. Lawrence, 18, Earl Grey Street, Mauchline. 450 seats. Four shows weekly. Prices, 3d. to 1s. Phone, 19. Station, Mauchline.

MAYBOLE (AYR), **Pop. 4,200.**
NEW CARRICK (BTH) Welltiees Street.—Prop., Carrick Cinema (Maybole), Ltd., 142, St. Vincent Street, Glasgow. Phone, Central 1,400. 650 seats. Booked at Hall. Continuous. Occasional Variety. Stage, 7 ft. deep, two dressing rooms. Prices, 4d. to 1s. Proscenium width, 20 ft. Station, Maybole, L.M.S.

METHIL (FIFE), **Pop. 2,558.**
IMPERIAL CINEMA (BA), (New Hall).—Props., Stevenson and Gray. 820 seats. Continuous. Two changes weekly. Prices, 5d. to 1s. 3d. Proscenium width, 22 ft. Phone, Leven 235.
PALACE (BTH), High Street.—Prop., Cowdenbeath Picture House Corpn., Ltd., 9, East Port, Dunfermline. 1,100 seats. Booked by A. B. King, 167, Bath Street, Glasgow. Phone, Douglas 1195. Continuous. Three changes weekly. Prices, 5d. to 1s. 3d.
WESTERN THEATRE (WE).—Prop., Stage Productions, Ltd., Redburn Chambers, Phone, Kirkcaldy, 2477. 650 seats. Booked at H.O. Continuous Prices, Mon. to Fri. 4d. to 1s.; Sats. 6d. to 1s: 3d. Two dressing rooms. Proscenium width, 35 ft. Phone, Buckhaven 78. Station, Methil (L.N.E.R.).

MID-CALDER (MIDLOTHIAN), **Pop. 2,793.**
MID-CALDER INSTITUTE, known as THE STAR CINEMA.—Booked at Daisy Cottage, East Calder, by Man. One show weekly. Prices, 4d. to 6d. Station, Mid-Calder.

MILLPORT (BUTE) **Pop. 2,083.**
MILLPORT PICTURE HOUSE (Mihaly), Town Hall —Prop., Millport Picture House, Ltd. Once nightly. Booked by L. C. V. Circuit, 34, St. Enoch Square, Glasgow. Prices, 5d. to 1s. 3d. Station, Millport Pier, L.M.S.

MILNGAVIE (DUMBARTON), **Pop. 5,056.**
DOUGLAS PICTURE HOUSE (RCA).—Prop., Mrs. Breckenridge, " Reevoch," Milngavie. Phone, Milngavie 271. 550 seats. Booked at H.O. Continuous. Prices, 4d. to 1s. Phone No. 271. Station, Milngavie, L.N.E.R.

MOFFAT (DUMFRIES), **Pop. 2,522.**
BATH HALLS.—500 seats.
MOFFAT CINEMA (Morrison).—Prop., W. R. Cameron, Ashgrove Terrace, Lockerbie. Four shows weekly. Prices, 4d. to 1s. 6d. Station, Moffat.

MONIFIETH (ANGUS), **Pop. 3,921.**
ALHAMBRA CINEMA (BTH), High Street.—Props., Alhambra (Monifieth), Ltd. 515 seats. Booked at Regal, Carnoustie. Continuous. Prices, 6d. to 1s. 3d. Proscenium width, 24 ft. Phone, Monifieth 13. Station, Monifieth, L.M.S. and L.N.E.R.

MONTROSE (ANGUS), **Pop. 11,889.**
KING'S (RCA), Hulme Street.—Prop., Scottish Cinema and Variety Theatres, Ltd., 105, St. Vincent Street, Glasgow. Phone, Central 2830. 1,000 seats. Booked by Associated British Cinemas, Ltd., London, W.1. Continuous. Two changes weekly. Prices, 6d. to 1s.
PLAYHOUSE (WE).—Prop., Caledonian Associated Cinemas, Ltd. 1,037 seats. Booked by A. B. King, 167, Bath Street, Glasgow. Prices, 6d. to 1s. 6d. Phone, Montrose 202.

MOSSEND (LANARK), **Pop. 10,000.**
REGAL (WE).—Props., George Palmer. 841 seats. Booked at Hall. Continuous. Stage, 30 ft. deep; five dressing-rooms. Proscenium width, 25 ft. Station, Mossend, L.M.S.

MOTHERWELL (LANARK), **Pop.** (with WISHAW), **64,708.**
LA SCALA (WE), Brandon Street.—Prop., Scottish Cinema and Variety Theatres, Ltd. 888 seats. Booked at London. Continuous. Two changes weekly. Prices, 3d. to 1s. Phone, Motherwell 326.
NEW CINEMA(Brown:,Barrie Street.—Prop.,C.A. Guberman. 1,148 seats. Booked by A. G. Matthews at 93, Hope Street, Glasgow. Continuous. Two changes weekly. Prices, 4d. to 9d. Phone Motherwell 433. Station, Motherwell, L.M.S.
PAVILION (BA), Brandon Street.—Prop., The Gaumont-British Pictures Corpn., Ltd. 1,200 seats. Continuous. Two changes weekly. Prices, 4d. to 1s. Phone, Motherwell 214.
REX, Windmill Street.—Prop., Scottish Cinema & Variety Theatres, Ltd., 105, St. Vincent Street, Glasgow.

MUIRKIRK (AYR), **Pop. 4,358.**
PICTURE HOUSE (BTH).—Prop., William Coutts Weir, Mason's Arms Hotel, Muirkirk. 500 seats. Continuous. Booked in Glasgow. Pictures and Variety. Variety booked by J. A. Cox, George Street, Glasgow. Prices, 4d. to 1s. Stage 15 ft. deep; two dressing rooms. Dance Hall. Station, Muirkirk. Films by carrier.

MUSSELBURGH (MIDLOTHIAN), **Pop. 16,996**
CENTRAL PICTURE HOUSE (BTH).—The Mall.—
Prop., Central Pictures (Musselburgh), Ltd.
1,200 seats. Booked at Playhouse, Edinburgh.
Stage, 12 ft. deep ; 2 dressing rooms. Con-
tinuous. Two changes weekly. Prices, 5d.
to 1s. 3d. Phone, Musselburgh 133. Station,
Musselburgh, L.N.E.R.
HAY WEIGHTS CINEMA (BTH), Bridge Street.—
Prop., D. Di Rollo, 800 seats. Booked at
Hall. Continuous. Prices, 3d. to 9d. Phone,
204. Station, Musselburgh, L.N.E.R.
PAVILION (WE).—Props., John Macmillan.
600 seats. Booked at Hall. Continuous.
Prices, 6d. to 1s. Phone, No. 313.

NAIRN (NAIRNSHIRE), **Pop. 5,282.**
PALACE CINEMA (RCA), Church Street.—Prop.,
J. Archibald, 21, East Church, Buckie.
500 seats. Booked at H.O. One show nightly, '
Three on Saturday. Prices, 6d. to 1s. 4d.
Proscenium width, 18 ft. Station, Nairn,
L.M.S.

NEWBURGH (FIFE), **Pop. 2,019.**
PUBLIC HALL CINEMA (Morrison), High Street.—
Prop., Public Hall Cinema Co. Booked by A.
Williamson, at 217, High Street, Newburgh.
Saturday and Wednesday periodically. Prices,
4d. to 1s. Station, Newburgh, L.N.E.R.

NEW CUMNOCK (AYR), **Pop. 6,419.**
PICTURE HOUSE (Mihaly),. The Castle.—Prop.,
New Cumnock Picture House, Ltd. 500
seats. Once nightly, twice Sat. Prices, 3d.
to 1s. Station; New Cumnock, L.M.S.

NEWMILLS (FIFE), **Pop. 2,200.**
THE PICTURE HOUSE.—Continuous. Booked
at Hall. Station, Torryburn.

NEWMILNS (AYR), **Pop. (with GREENHOLM)**
3,979.
PICTURE HOUSE (BTH), Main Street.—Prop.,
Mrs. E. Young, 32, Brackenbrae Avenue.
Bishopbrigg, Glasgow. Booked at Hall. 514
seats. Once nightly. Two shows Sat.
Booked at H.O. Prices, 4d. to 1s. Station,
Newmilns, L.M.S.

NEW STEVENSTON (LANARK).
THE PICTURE HOUSE (RCA).—Prop., J. Shilliday.
Booked at Hall.

NEWTON GRANGE (MIDLOTHIAN), **Pop.**
4,468.
NEWTON GRANGE PALACE (BTH).—Prop., Burnt-
island Picture Palace Company, Manse
Place, Falkirk. Phone, Falkirk 327. 740
seats. Booked at Hall. Once nightly.
Twice Sat. and Mon. Prices, 6d. to 1s.
Phone, Gosebridge 63. Station, Newton
Grange, L.N.E.R.

NEWTON-ON-AYR (AYR), **Pop. 9,755.**
RITZ (GB), New Road.—Props., Newton-on-Ayr
Picture House, Ltd., 142, St. Vincent Street,
Glasgow. Booked at Hall. Continuous.
Prices, 6d. to 1s. 3d. Proscenium width,
26 ft. Phone, Central 1400. Station, New-
ton-on-Ayr.

NEWTON-STEWART (WIGTOWN), **Pop.**
1,914.
PICTURE HOUSE (Mihaly), 12, Victoria Street.—
Prop., G. H. Gouldson. 500 seats. Booked
at Hall. Once nightly. Twice Saturday.
Prices, 6d. to 1s. 3d. Phone, 58. Station,
Newton-Stewart, L.M.S., and Road Trans-
port.

NORTH BERWICK (EAST LOTHIAN), **Pop.**
4,083.
EMPIRE CINEMA (Britain's Best).—Prop., Scott's
Empires, Ltd., Empire Cinema, Dunbar.
600 seats.

OBAN (ARGYIL), **Pop. 5,759.**
CINEMA HOUSE (BTH), George Street.—Prop.,
Oban Cinema House, Ltd., 26, Alexandra
Street. 600 seats. Booked at Hall. Con-
tinuous. Two changes weekly. Prices, 6d.
to 1s. 3d. Phone, Oban 75. Station, Oban,
L.M.S., and R.T.
PLAYHOUSE (WE), Argyll Square.—Prop.,
Oban Playhouse, Ltd. 1,114 seats. Booked
at Hall. Continuous. Prices, 6d. to 1s. 6d.
Proscenium width, 30 ft. Phone, Oban 244.
Tea Room and café attached.

OLD CUMNOCK (AYR), **Pop. 5,637.**
PICTURE HOUSE (BA).—Prop., Cumnock Picture
House Co., Ltd. 750 seats. Booked at Hall.
Continuous. Prices, 7d. to 1s. Proscenium
width, 24 ft. Station, Old Cumnock, L.M.S.

ORMISTON (EAST LOTHIAN), **Pop. 2,200.**
KINETONE KINEMA (Kinetone).—Prop., Mrs.
M. Renouf, 52, Monktonhall Terrace, Musselburgh. 496 seats. Booked at Hall. Once
nightly. Three changes weekly. Prices,
9d. to 1s. Phone, Pencaitland 46, Station,
Ormiston, L.N.E.R.

PAISLEY (RENFREW), **Pop. 120,268.**
ALEXANDRIA CINEMA (WE), 25, Neilston Road.—
Prop., Caledon Entertainers, Ltd., 227, St.
Vincent Street, Glasgow. Phone, Central
1046. 1,509 seats. Booked by George Taylor,
Partick Picture House, Glasgow. Continuous.
Two changes weekly. Prices, 5d. to 9d.
Phone, Paisley 3446.
ASTORIA (WE), Lawn Street.—Props., H. and
C. Wincour, 108, West Regent Street, Glasgow.
Phone, Douglas 5215. Booked at H.O.
Continuous. Prices, 5d. to 9d. Proscenium
width, 23 ft. Phone, No. 3490.
KELBURNE CINEMA (WE), Glasgow Road.—
Prop., Caledonian Associated Cinemas, Ltd.,
Inverness. Phone, Inverness 1. 1,731 seats.
Booked by A. B. King, 167, Bath Street,
Glasgow. Continuous. Prices, 6d. to 1s. 3d.
Proscenium width, 35 ft. Tea Rooms.
LA SCALA PICTURE THEATRE (WE), The Cross,
Paisley.—Prop., Paisley La Scala, Ltd., 21,
Blythswood Square, Glasgow. Phone, Doug-
las 3908. Booked by A. B. King, 167, Bath
Street, Glasgow. Phone, Douglas 1195.
Continuous. Two changes weekly. Stage,
30 ft. deep ; four dressing rooms. Prices,
6d. to 1s. 6d. Proscenium width, 30 ft.
Café attached. Phone, 2442.
PAISLEY PALLADIUM (WE), New Street.—Prop.,
Palladium (Paisley), Ltd. 946 seats. Con-
tinuous. Two changes weekly. Prices, 4d.
to 1s. Phone 2310. Station, Paisley (Gil-
mour Street).
PICTURE HOUSE (WE), High Street.—Prop.,
Paisley Entertainments, Ltd., 144, West
Regent Street, Glasgow. 2,281 seats. Booked
at H.O. Continuous. Two changes weekly.
Stage, 18 ft. deep ; four dressing rooms.
Prices, 6d. to 1s. 6d. Proscenium width,
42 ft. Phone, Paisley 2466. Restaurant and
Dance Room. Station, Gilmour Street,
Paisley.

REGAL (WE).—Props., Scottish Cinema & Variety Theatres, Ltd., 105, St. Vincent Street, Glasgow, C.2. Phone, Central 2380. 2,054 seats. Booked by Associated British Cinemas, London. Continuous. Prices, 6d. to 1s. 6d. Proscenium width, 45 ft. Phone, Paisley 4240. Station, Paisley, Gilmour Street, L.M.S.

COMPTON

ORGAN featured here.

WEST END CINEMA (WE), Broomlands.—Props., The Star Cinema (Paisley), Ltd., 55, West Regent Street, Glasgow. Continuous. Booked by G. Taylor, 27, Merkland Street, Partick, Glasgow, W.2. Western 2766. Prices, 4d. to 1s. 3d. Phone, 2473.

PEEBLES (PEEBLES), Pop. 5,853.
BURGH CINEMA.—Prop., Scott's Empires Ltd. Cinema, Dunbar.
EMPIRE (WE).—Props., Scott's Empires, Ltd. 700 seats. Twice nightly. Three changes weekly. Booked at Hestival House, Dunbar. Station, Peebles.
**Fitted "ARDENTE" Deaf Aids
See page 258**

PLAYHOUSE (WE), High Street.—Prop., Caledonian Associated Cinemas, Ltd., Drummond Street, Inverness. Phone, Inverness 1. 802 seats. Booked by A. B. King, Bath Street, Glasgow. Continuous evenings and on Sat. from 2.30. Prices, 6d. to 1s. 6d. Proscenium width, 42 ft. Stage, 8 ft. deep. Phone, No. 100. Station, Peebles, L.N.E.R. and L.M.S.
ROYAL BURGH CINEMA (Britain's Best), Chambers, Town Hall.—Props., Scott's Empires, Ltd., 35, Northgate, Peebles. Booked at Hestival House, Dunbar. Prices, 7d. to 1s. 3d. Station, Peebles, L.N.E.R., and Film Transport.

PENICUIK (MIDLOTHIAN), Pop. 5,198.
EMPIRE CINEMA (Britain's Best).—Props., Scott's Empires, Ltd., Empire Cinema, Dunbar.

PERTH (PERTH), Pop. 34,807.
ALHAMBRA (BA).—Prop., Denman Picture Houses, Ltd., London. 1,500 seats. Phone, 265. Booked at Head Office.
**Fitted "ARDENTE" Deaf Aids
See page 258**

B.B. CINERAMA (BA), Victoria Street.—Prop., Denman Picture Houses, Ltd., London. 1,195 seats. Booked at H.O. Continuous. Prices, 6d. to 1s. 3d. Proscenium width, 30 ft. Phone, No. 1195. Station, Perth, L.M.S.
CITY HALL (RCA).—Lessee, Town Council. 2,000 seats. Occasional pictures. Proscenium width, 20 ft. Prices, 4d. to 9d. Phone, No. 683.
KING'S CINEMA (WE), 55, S. Methuen Street.—Props., Perth Picture House Co., Ltd., 174, West George Street, Glasgow. Phone, Douglas 350. 1,032 seats. Booked by J. Wallace, 32, Lannock Drive, Bearsden, Dumbartonshire. Continuous. Prices, 6d. to 1s. 3d. Proscenium width, 27 ft. Phone. Perth 598.
PLAYHOUSE (RCA) Murray Street.—Prop., Caledonian Associated Cinemas, Ltd., Drummond Street, Inverness. Phone, Inverness 1. 1,700 seats. Continuous. Booked by A. B. King, 167, Bath Street, Glasgow. Prices, 6d. to 1s. 6d. Phone, Perth 1226. Café. Station, Perth.

PETERHEAD (ABERDEEN), Pop. 15,285.
PICTURE HOUSE (WE).—Prop., Peterhead Public Hall Co., Ltd. 751 seats. Booked by A. G. Matthews, 8, Overwood Drive, Glasgow. Continuous. Two changes weekly. Prices, 6d. to 1s. Proscenium width, 31 ft. Dance Hall. Station, Peterhead, L.N.E.R.
PLAYHOUSE (WE), Queen Street.—Prop., Caledonian Associated Cinemas, Ltd., Royal Bank Buildings, Inverness. 1,260 seats. Continuous. Booked by A. B. King, Glasgow. Prices, 6d. to 1s. 6d. Proscenium width, 40 ft. Café. Phone, No. 94. Station, Peterhead.

PITLOCHRY (PERTH), Pop. 2,240.
REGAL (Parmeko).—Props., The Picture House, Pitlochry, Ltd., Union Bank Buildings, Pitlochry. Phone, No. 31. 420 seats. Prices, 3d. to 1s. 6d. Booked at H.O. Phone, No. 60. Station, Pitlochry, L.M.S.

PITTENWEEM (FIFE), Pop. 1,644.
PICTURE HOUSE (Morrison), Backgate.—Prop., Dempsey Bros., Coaltown of Balgonie Markinch. Phone, Markinch 22. One show Mon. and Thurs. Two on Sat. Booked at H.O. Prices, 3d. to 1s. Station, Pittenweem, L.N.E.R.

POLMONT (STIRLING), Pop. 7,619.
PICTURE HOUSE (Mihaly).—Prop., W. and T. Duncan. 500 seats. Continuous. Booked Glasgow. Three changes weekly. Prices, 4d to 1s. Phone, Polmont 64. Station, Polmont, L.N.E.R.

PORT GLASGOW (RENFREW), Pop. 19,616.
ECLIPSE PICTURES (Electricord).—Prop., Eclipse Pictures Co., Ltd. 800 seats. Continuous. Two changes weekly. Booked by A. B King, 167, Bath Street, Glasgow. Prices, 4d. to 1s. Phone, Port Glasgow 60.

PRESTONPANS (EAST LOTHIAN), Pop. 5,986.
BIDDALLS PICTURE HOUSE (BA).—Prop., Albert Biddall. 380 seats. Booked at Hall. Once nightly. Prices, 6d. to 1s. Station, Prestonpans, L.N.E.R.

PRESTWICK (AYR), Pop. 8,538.
BROADWAY (WE).—Props., Prestwick Cinema Co., Ltd. 1,060 seats. Booked at Hall. Continuous. Prices, 6d. to 1s. 6d. Proscenium width, 34 ft. Phone, Prestwick 7272. Station, Prestwick, L.M.S.
PICTURE HOUSE (BTH).—Props., Prestwick Picture House, Ltd., 1, George Street, Burnbank, Hamilton. Phone, Prestwick 152. 800 seats. Booked by H.O. Prices, 4d. to 1s. Continuous. Station, Prestwick.

RENFREW (RENFREW), Pop. 40,816.
PICTURE HOUSE (BTH), Moorpark. Prop. and Res. Man., J. W. Cruikshank. 550 seats. One show nightly, two on Sat. Two changes weekly.
REGAL (RCA), Ferry Road.—Props., Renfrew Pictures, Ltd. 1,100 seats. Booked by J. Hendry, 114, Union Street, Glasgow. Continuous. Prices, 4d. to 1s. Phone, 39. Station, Renfrew.

RENTON (DUMBARTON), Pop. 5,011.
ROXY (BTH).—Prop., R. J. Pennycook, "Londee," Cardross Road, Helensburgh. 510 seats. Once nightly. Booked at Hall. Prices, 4d. to 9d. Proscenium width, 18 ft. Stage, 12 ft. deep. Station, Renton, L.M.S.

ROSYTH (FIFE), **Pop. 3,000.**

NAVAL CINEMA.—300 seats.

PALACE (WE), Queensferry Road.—Prop., Palace (Rosyth), Ltd. 848 seats. Continuous. Prices, 4d. to 1s. Proscenium width 29 ft. Phone, Inverkeithing 78.

ROTHESAY (BUTE), **Pop. 9,346.**

PALACE CINEMA (BA).—Prop., Palace Cinema, Ltd. 882 seats. Booked at Hall. Continuous. Booked by A. B. King, Glasgow. Prices, 6d. to 1s. 6d. Phone, Rothesay 133. Dance Hall and Café attached.

THEATRE DE LUXE (BTH).—Prop., F. R. Burnette, 22, Hamilton Drive, Glasgow. Phone, Western 775. 500 seats. Booked at H.O. Continuous. Two changes weekly. Prices, 6d. to 1s. 4d. Proscenium width, 30 ft. Phone, 120. Station, Rothesay. Pier.

RUTHERGLEN (LANARK), **Pop. 34,223.**

CINEMA (WE).—Prop., Geo. Green, Ltd. Booked at 182, Trongate, Glasgow. Continuous. Prices, 6d. to 1s.

GRAND CENTRAL (WE), Main Street.—Prop., Scott Theatres, Ltd., 11, Clyde Street, Motherwell. Booked by T. Rogers, Motherwell. Continuous. Two changes weekly. Prices, 4d. to 1s. Phone, Rutherglen 450.

RIO (RCA).—Prop., P. Crerar. 2,017 seats. Booked at Hall. Continuous. Prices, 6d. to 1s. Proscenium width, 60 ft. Phone, Rutherglen 1244. Station, Rutherglen.

VOGUE (——)

SALTCOATS (AYR), **Pop. 10,173.**

COUNTESS PICTURE HOUSE (WE).—Lessee Mrs. M. Thomson. 740 seats. Booked by A. B. King, Glasgow. Continuous.

LA SCALA (WE), Hamilton Street.—Prop., H. Kemp. 1,000 seats. Booked at H.O. Continuous. Two changes weekly. Stage, 20 ft. deep ; three dressing-rooms. Prices, 6d. to 1s. 3d. Phone No. 345. Station, Saltcoats.

REGAL (WE).—Prop., H. Kemp. 1,090 seats. Booked at Hall. Continuous. Twice on Sat. Prices, 6d. to 1s. 6d. Stage 20 ft. deep; five dressing-rooms. Proscenium width, 40 ft. Phone, Saltcoats 345.

SANQUHAR (DUMFRIES), **Pop. 3,346.**

SANQUHAR PICTURE HOUSE, High Street.— Prop., and Res. Man., T. Hughes. One show nightly.

SELKIRK (Selkirk), **Pop. 7,075.**

ETTRICK PICTURE HOUSE (WE).—Prop., Selkirk Picture Hall Co. One show nightly. Two on Sat. Three changes weekly.

PICTURE HOUSE (WE).—Props., Selkirk Picture Hall Co. 850 seats. Prices, 6d. to 1s. 3d. Phone 163. Station, Selkirk, L.N.E.R.

SHOTTS (LANARK), **Pop. 20,537.**

EMPIRE THEATRE (BA), Station Road.—Prop., Shotts Empire Theatre, Ltd. 950 seats. Booked by Thos. Ormiston, Sec., Motherwell.

SOUTH QUEENSFERRY (WEST LOTHIAN) **Pop. 1,798.**

DAYBELLS CINEMA (Scottish Prods.).—Res.

and Booking Man., R. Edmondson. 500 seats. Booked at Bridge House, South Queensferry. Proscenium width, 40 ft. Two shows Sat. and Mon. Prices, 4d. to 9d. Dance hall attached. Occasional variety. Station, Dalmeny.

ST. ANDREWS (FIFE), **Pop.** (with ST. LEONARDS) **9,987.**

CINEMA HOUSE (WE).—Prop., St. Andrew's Cinema House Co., Ltd., 115, South Street, St. Andrews. Phone, 69. 861 seats. Booked by A. B. King, 167, Bath Street, Glasgow. Continuous nightly. Daily Mat. Two changes weekly. Prices, 6d. to 1s. 6d. Phone, 164. Station, St. Andrews, L.N.E.R.

NEW PICTURE HOUSE (WE).—Prop., New Picture House (St. Andrews), Ltd., 936 seats. Continuous from 6.15 p.m. Daily Mat. Prices, 6d. to 2s. Proscenium width, 35 ft. Stage 18 ft. deep ; six dressing-rooms. Café. Phone, No. 509.

STEVENSTON (AYR), **Pop. 11,572.**

DE LUXE CINEMA (RCA). New Street.—Prop., Stevenston Picture House, Ltd., 7, Hamilton Street, Saltcoats. Phone, Saltcoats 45. 700 seats. Booked at H.O. by Harry Kemp. Twice nightly. Two changes weekly. Pictures and Variety. Stage, 20 ft. deep ; three dressing-rooms. Prices, 6d. to 1s. 6d. Proscenium width, 28 ft.

STEWARTON (AYRSHIRE), **Pop. 3,701.**

STEWARTON PICTURE HOUSE (BTH).—Prop., Stewarton Picture House, Ltd., 115, St. Vincent Street, Glasgow. 600 seats. Booked at Pavilion, Girvan. Prices, 6d. to 1s. Phone. Stewarton 4. Station, Stewarton, L.M.S.

STIRLING (STIRLING), **Pop. 22,897.**

ALHAMBRA (BTH).

KINEMA, Orchard Place.—Prop., Menzies. Bros. 800 seats. Continuous. Two changes weekly. Prices, 4d. to 9d. Phone, Stirling 837. Station, Stirling, L.N.E.R.

MINERS' INSTITUTE (RCA).—302 seats.

PICTURE HOUSE (WE).—Prop., Stirling Cinemas and Variety Theatres, Ltd., Orchard Place, Stirling. 1,003 seats. Booked at H.O. Twice nightly. Prices, 6d. to 1s. 3d. Phone, Stirling 837.

QUEEN'S KINEMA (WE).—Prop., Stirling Cinema, and Variety Theatres, Ltd., Orchard Place, Stirling. 1,000 seats. Booked at H.O. Continuous. Prices, 6d. to 1s. Phone, 837.

RANDOLPH.

REGAL (WE).—Prop., Scottish Cinema & Variety Theatres, Ltd., 105, St. Vincent Street, Glasgow. 2,226 seats. Continuous. Booked at H. O., Associated British Cinemas, London. Prices, 6d. to 1s 6d. Proscenium width, 40 ft. Stage, 15 ft. deep ; Café. Phone 766. Station, Stirling, L.N.E.R. and L.M.S.

STONEHAVEN (KINCARDINE), **Pop. 4,185.**

PICTURE HOUSE (WE), Allardice Street.—Prop., J. F. McDonald (Aberdeen Cinemas), Ltd., 19, North Silver Street, Aberdeen. 1,000 Seats. Booked at H.O. Prices, 6d. to 1s. 6d. Proscenium width 34 ft. Phone, Stonehaven 196. Station, Stonehaven, L.M.S., L.N.E.R.

STONEYBURN (West Lothian), Pop. 1,500.
Picture Palace (bth). 500 seats.—Closed.
Welfare Hall Cinema.—Three shows weekly.

STORNOWAY (Ross and Cromarty), Pop. 3,771.
Lewis Picture House (we), Keith Street. One show nightly. Three changes weekly, Pictures and Variety. Stage, 10 ft. deep Prices, 6d. to 1s. 10d. Proscenium width, 17 ft. Station, Kyle of Lochalsh.
Playhouse (we).—A. G. Matthews Circuit, 8, Overwood Drive, Glasgow.

STRANRAER (Wigtown), Pop. 6,490.
Kinema (bth), St. Andrew's Street.—Prop., Eric R. Varley. The Pavilion, Girvan. Phone, Girvan 111. 1,000 seats. Booked at Girvan. Continuous nightly. Mat. Sat. Two changes weekly. Prices, 6d. to 1s. 6d. Phone, 108. Station, Stranraer, L.M.S.
Regal (we), Dalrymple Street.—Prop., The Stranraer Picture House, Ltd., 21, Blythswood Square, Glasgow. Phone, Douglas 3908. 1,100 seats. Continuous. Booked at H.O. Prices, 6d. to 2s. Proscenium width, 44 ft. Phone, No. 242. Station, Stranraer, L.M.S.

STRATHAVEN (Lanark), Pop. 4,210.
Avondale Cinema (ba).—Prop., J. Stewart. 550 seats. Continuous. Booked at Hall. Prices, 3d. to 1s. Station, Strathaven. L.M.S.

STROMNESS (Orkney), Pop. 2,116.
Town Hall, North End.—Prop., J. Anderson and J. M. Linklater. Booked at Hall. Two shows weekly. Prices, 4d. to 1s. 3d.

STRONSAY (Orkney), Pop. 974.
Cinema.—Prop., H. Maxwell, Honsbay, Stronsay. Booked at Hall. Three times weekly. Pictures and Variety. Booked in Glasgow. Stage, 20 ft. deep ; 2 dressing-rooms. Prices, 6d. to 1s.

TAIN (Ross and Cromarty). Pop. 2,176.
Picture Palace (ba).—Props., Tain Picture House, Ltd., Royal Bank Buildings, Inverness. Continuous, four nights weekly. 380 seats. Booked by A. B. King, 167, Bath Street, Glasgow. Prices, 6d. to 1s. 6d. Station, Tain, L.M.S.
Town Hall (ba). 385 seats.

TARBERT (Argyll), Pop. 1,933.
Picture House (bth).—Prop., J. McArthur. Booked at 14, Belhaven Terrace, Glasgow

TAYPORT (Fife), Pop. 3,164.
Picture House (bth), Prop., J. B. Milne, 339, Clepington Road, Dundee. Booked at Victoria Theatre, Dundee. Phone, Dundee 5923. 560 seats. Once nightly. Continuous Sat. Prices, 6d. to 1s. 3d. Proscenium width, 20 ft. Phone, No. 87. Station, Tayport, and Film Transport.

THORNTON (Fife), Pop., 2,408.
Cinema (Morrison).—Prop., Dempsey Bros. Booked at The Garage, Coaltown of Balgonie, Markinch. One show Mon. and Thurs. Two shows Sat. Stage and 2 dressing rooms. Prices, 7d. to 9d. Station, Thornton, L.N.E.R.

THURSO (Caithness), Pop. 4,095.
Picture House (bth).—Prop., Thurso Picture House Co., Ltd. 500 seats. Booked by A. G. Matthews, Glasgow. Twice nightly. Prices, 7d. to 1s. 9d. Proscenium width, 29 ft. Station, Thurso, L.M.S.

TILLICOULTRY (Clackmannan), Pop. 4,461.
Town Hall Cinema (bth).—Prop. W. Hunter Byars. 510 seats. Continuous. Two shows Sat. Prices, 4d. to 1s. 3d. Proscenium width, 19 ft. Phone 28, Station, Tillicoultry, L.M.S. and L.N.E.R.

TRANENT (East Lothian), Pop. 9,002. .
Picture House (bth).—Prop., Mrs. R. Codona. 596 seats. . Once nightly. Booked at Hall. Prices, 6d. and 1s. Proscenium width, 28 ft. Station, Prestonpans, L.N.E.R.

TROON (Ayr), Pop. 8,544.
Pavilion (ba), 15, Templehill.—Prop., Pavilion (Troon), Ltd., 15, Templehill, Troon. 800 seats. Booked at Hall. Continuous. Prices, 6d. to 1s. 6d. Phone, Troon 345.
Picture House (ba), Portland Street.—Prop., Troon Picture House, Ltd. 850 seats Booked by H. McCall, Pavilion P.H., Troon. Continuous. Two changes weekly. Stage, 15 ft. deep ; two dressing-rooms. Prices 7d. to 1s. 4d. Proscenium width, 22 ft.

TURRIFF (Aberdeen), Pop. 3,944.
Town Hall.—Prop., Turriff Town Hall Cinema Co. Two shows weekly. Prices 6d. to 1s. 6d. Station, Turriff.

UDDINGSTON (Lanark), Pop. 8,420.
New Picture House (fi).—Prop., Horton and Pettigrew. 700 seats. Booked at Hall. Continuous.
Pavilion (bth).—Prop., Uddingston Picture House Co., Ltd., 550 seats. Continuous. Two changes weekly. Booked at Hall. Prices, 4d. to 9d. Station, Uddingston, L.N.E.R.
Town Hall (btp).

UPHALL (West Lothian), Pop. 11,119.
Cinema House (Will Day).—Prop., Wm. Bryce and J. Lyall. 600 seats. Continuous. Booked at Glasgow. Prices, 5d. to 1s. Proscenium width 30 ft. Phone, Broxburn 53. Station, Uphall, L.N.E.R.

WALKERBURN (Peebles), Pop. 1,170.
Cinema.—Prop., Walkerburn Cinema Co. Booked at Hall.

WEST CALDER (Midlothian), Pop. 6,817.
People's Palace Theatre (Mihaly).—Lessee West Calder Properties, Ltd. Clough Brae, West Calder, 600 seats. Continuous. Two shows Sat. Four changes weekly. Prices 6d. to 9d. Proscenium width, 21 ft. Phone West Calder 7.

WEST KILBRIDE (Ayr), Pop. 3,946.
Picture House (Mihaly).—Prop., The Picture House (West Kilbride), Ltd. 600 seats. Booked at Hall. Shows nightly. Prices, 3d. to 1s. 3d. Station, West Kilbride, L.M.S.

WHITBURN (West Lothian), Pop. 12,619.
The Picture House (bth).—Prop., G. Wright. Harthill. 500 seats. Booked at Glasgow. One house nightly. Continuous Fri. and

WHITBURN—Contd.

Sat. Prices, 3d. to 9d. Proscenium width, 40 ft. Films by Carrier.

MINER'S WELFARE HALL (BTH).—Props., Miners' Welfare Committee. 720 seats. Booked at Glasgow. Continuous Mon., Fri. and Sat. and once nightly. Prices, 3d. to 9d. Stage 18 ft. deep ; three dressing rooms. Phone, Whitburn 32. Films by Motor Transport.

WHITHORN (WIGTOWN), **Pop 1,796.**

STAR ELECTRIC CINEMA.—Prop., W. McLean Booked at Hall. Station, Whithorn (Port Patrick and Wigtown joint sections), L.M.S

WICK (CAITHNESS), **Pop. 10,383.**

BREADALBANE HALL.—Booked by A. B. King, 167, Bath Street, Glasgow.

PAVILION (BA).—Prop., Caledonian Associated Cinemas, Ltd., Royal Bank Bldgs., Drummond Street, Inverness. 626 seats. Booked by A.B. King, 167, Bath Street, Glasgow. Continuous. Prices, 6d to 1s. 6d. Proscenium width, 28 ft. Phone, Wick 35. Station, Wick, L.M.S.

WINDYGATES (FIFE), **Pop. 2,629.**

CINEMA, Station Road.—Res. and Booking Man., Jas. P. Lister. Two houses Wed. and Sat. Prices, 3d. to 8d. Phone, Leven 118. Station, Cameron Bridge, L.N.E.R.

WISHAW (LANARK), **Pop. 25,263.**

PICTURE HOUSE (RCA), Main Street.— Prop., Wishaw Picture Palace, Ltd. 1,000 seats. Booked at Hall. Continuous. Prices, 4d. to 1s. Phone, Wishaw 4, Station, Wishaw, L.M.S.

PLAZA (RCA).—Prop., Scottish Cinema and Variety Theatres, Ltd. 1,090 seats. Booked

by Associated British Cinemas, Ltd., London. Continuous. Prices, 4d. to 9d. Station, Wishaw, L.M.S.

WISHAW CINEMA (BA), Kirk Road.— Prop., Denman Picture Houses, Ltd., London. 1,100 seats. Booked at Head Office. Continuous. Two changes weekly. Prices, 4d. to 1s. Phone, Wishaw 117.

WIGTOWN (WIGTOWNSHIRE).

PICTURE HOUSE (BTH).

TRAVELLING SHOWS.

CINEMA, Gatehouse-on-Fleet, Kirkcudbright.

CINEMA, Creetown, Kirkcudbright.—Saturdays only.

CINEMA, Port William, Wigtownshire.

CINEMA, Port Patrick, Wigtownshire.

CINEMA, Ardrishaig, Argyllshire.

CINEMA, Lochgilphead, Argyllshire.

CINEMA, Inveraray, Argyllshire. Closed.

CINEMA, Strachur, Argyllshire.

CINEMA (BA), Callander, Perthshire.

CINEMA (BA), Dollar, Clackmannan.

CINEMA (BA), Doune, Perthshire.

CINEMA (BA), Strathmiglo, Fifeshire.

NORTHERN CINEMAS.—Prop., Cay, Laurencekirk Tarland, Turiff, Torphins, Aboyne, Braemar.

Prop., H. C. Stewart.—Cullen, Nethybridge, Newtonmore, Boat of Garten, Fort George, Aviemore, Dufftown (Fochabers), Carr Bridge.

Prop., J. Crerar.—Aberfeldy, Killin.—Pitlochry, —Closed.

Prop., D. Dempsey.—Thornton, Pittenweem (Coaltown of Balgonie).—Closed on Wednesday.

IRELAND

IRISH FREE STATE KINEMAS.

The Sound system installed is shown after the name. (BTP) = British Talking Pictures, Ltd. ; (RCA) = RCA Photophone Inc. ; (WE) = Western Electric Co., Ltd. ; (BA) = British Acoustic ; (BTH) = British Thomson-Houston. Other systems are indicated by name.

In view of the difference in Customs and other duties between Northern Ireland and the Irish Free State, the Irish kinemas are given in two sections. There are no Customs barriers between Northern Ireland and Great Britain, but there are duties on films, etc., sent to the Irish Free State from Great Britain and Northern Ireland. The Free State kinemas are given first.

ARDEE (COUNTY LOUTH)

BOHEMIAN KINEMA (ER).—H. C. Thorne & S. Markey. 300 seats. Once nightly. Booked at H.O. Prices, 4d., 1s., and 1s. 6d.

ARKLOW (Co. WICKLOW), **Pop. 4,500.**
ELECTRIC CINEMA.—A. McGowan.
GAIETY CINEMA (Zisis).—P. Sweeney. 500 seats. Nightly except Sat. Prices, 4d. to 1s. 6d. Nearest station, Arklow.

ATHBOY (Co. MEATH), **Pop. 510.**
ST. JAMES' HALL (Electra).—Prop., James Garry, Athboy. 280 seats. Once nightly. Prices, 8d. to 1s. 4d. Station, Athboy, G.S.R.

ATHLONE (Co. WESTMEATH), **Pop. 6,620.**
GARDEN VALE KINEMA (RCA).—Mr. Shercliffe. 500 seats. Booked at Hall. One show nightly. Mat. Sun. Prices, 4d. to 1s. 6d. Station, Athlone, G.S.R.

ATHY (Co. KILDARE), **Pop. 4,500.**
ATHY PICTURE PALACE (BA).—Prop., Athy P.P. Ltd. 600 seats. Dir. and Man., Captain H. J. Hosie. Booked at Hall. Once nightly. Mat. Sun. Prices, 4d. to 1s. 3d. Station, Athy

BAGENALSTOWN (Co. CARLOW), **Pop. 2,160.**
PALACE CINEMA (Sound on Film).—Prop. H. Godfrey Brown. Booked in Dublin Twice daily on four days in the week. Prices, 4d. to 1s. 6d. Stage, 8 ft. deep ; two dressing rooms. Proscenium width, 14 ft. Station, Bagenalstown.

BALLINA (Co. MAYO), **Pop. 5,000.**
ARCADIA (RCA). 500 seats.
ESTORIA (RCA).—Prop., Estoria Cinema Co. 715 seats. Once nightly. Mat. Sun. Booked at Hall and at Dublin. Prices, 4d. to 1s. 6d. Proscenium width, 20 ft. Phone, Ballina 5. Station, Ballina.

BALLINASLOE (Co. GALWAY), **Pop. 4,970.**
PLAZA CINEMA (RCA), Society Street.—Prop., M. P. McGing, Society Street. 500 seats. Five nights weekly. Mat. Sun. Prices, 9d. and 1s. 4d. Booked at Dublin. Proscenium width, 27 ft. Station, Ballinasloe.

BALLINROBE (Co MAYO), **Pop. 1,600.**
ROBE CINEMA (RCA), Main Street.—300 seats Prop., Miss Elizabeth Cooney. Booked at Hall. Four shows weekly. Prices, 1s. and 2s.

Proscenium width, 20 ft. Station, Ballinrobe G.S.R.
POPULAR CINEMA.—380 seats.

BALLYSHANNON (Co. DONEGAL).—**Pop. 222.**
ROCK CINEMA (Electra).—Prop., W. McMenanim, Stranolar, co. Donegal. Booked in Dublin. 400 seats. Once nightly. Prices, 4d. to 1s. 4d. Proscenium width, 14 ft. Station, Ballyshannon.

BANDON (Co. CORK), **Pop. 3,500.,**
CINEMA HALL, Bandon (RCA).—Prop., C. A. Powell, Knockbrogan. Park, Bandon. 450 seats. Booked at Hall. One show nightly for six days. Mats., Sat. and Sun. Prices, 4d. to 1s. 6d. Station, Bandon.

BANTRY (Co. CORK), **Pop. 3,000.**
CINEMA, Bere Island.
STELLA CINEMA (WE).—Prop., W. McSweeney, Central Hotel, Bantry. 398 seats. Booked at Tralee: Pictures and Variety. One show nightly. One dressing room. Phone, Bantry 5. Station, Bantry.

BIRR (OFFALY), **Pop. 4,500.**
RIALTO CINEMA.—Mr. Murphy. 500 seats. Nightly on Sun., Mon., Wed. and Thurs. Mat. Sun. Prices, 4d. to 1s. 9d.

BOYLE (ROSCOMMON), **Pop. 2,500.**
BOYLE PICTURE THEATRE (RCA), Bridge Street.—Prop., John Lowe, Bridge Street, Carrick-on-Shannon. Phone No. 8. 320 seats. Booked at H.O. Nightly on Sun., Mon., Thurs. and Fri. Mat. Sun. Prices, 10d. to 2s. Proscenium width, 15 ft. Stage, 12 ft. deep ; two dressing-rooms. Phone, Boyle 18.

BRAY (WICKLOW), **Pop. 8,000.**
PICTURE HOUSE (RCA), Quinsboro' Road.—Prop. and Res. Man., J. E. MacDermott. 550 seats. Continuous. Three changes weekly. Mat. Sun. Prices, 4d. to 1s. 3d. Station, Bray, D. & S.E. Rly.
STAR.—450 seats. Nightly. Prices, 4d. to 1s. 3d.

BRUFF (LIMERICK), **Pop. 1,760.**
PICTURE HOUSE.—Prop. and Res. Man., Wm. O'Donovan. Two changes weekly. Available for Dramatic, Revue and Variety companies. Station, Kilmallock, G.S. & W.R.

BUNCRANA (Co. DONEGAL).
PAROCHIAL CINEMA (WE).—Prop., Rev. Peter Tracy, Railway Road. 400 seats. Prices, 6d., 9d., and 1s. Proscenium width, 22 :t. Station, Buncrana.

BUNDORAN (DONEGAL).
ST. PATRICK'S HALL.—Nightly. Mats. Mon. Wed., Fri. and Sun. Prices, 4d. to 2s.

CAHIR (TIPPERARY).
CINEMA.—Occasional evening shows.

CAHIRCIVEEN (KERRY), **Pop. 2,013.**
KINGDOM CINEMA (Napier Equipment).—
Prop., Chas. Troy, Main Street, Cahirciveen.
400 seats. Once nightly. Prices, 1s. 6d.,
9d. and 4d. Booked at Dublin. Variety Acts.
Proscenium width, 24 ft. Stage, 18 ft. deep ;
three dressing-rooms. Station, Cahirciveen.

CALLAN (KILKENNY), **Pop. 1,520.**
GREEN VIEW CINEMA (BTH).—Prop., W. F.
Egan. 400 seats. Three shows weekly.
Prices, 6d. to 1s. 6d. Station, Kilkenny.
G.S. & W. Rly.

CARLOW (CARLOW), **Pop. 7,200.**
CINEMA (WE).—Prop., F. Slater. One show
nightly including Sun. Four changes weekly.
Prices, 3d. to 1s. 6d. Proscenium width,
30 ft. Station, Carlow, G.S. & W.R.

CARNDONAGH (CO. DONEGAL).
PAROCHIAL HALL (RCA).

CARRICK-ON-SHANNON (CO. LEITRIM),
Pop. 1,100.
ARCADIA CINEMA (BTH).—Mr. McManus. 200
seats.
GAIETY (RCA), Bridge Street.—Prop., John J.
Flood, 61, Main Street, Carrick-ou-Shannon.
500 seats. Booked at Hall. Once nightly.
Occasional Variety. Prices, 4d. to 2s. Stage,
18 ft. deep ; three dressing-rooms. Pros-
cenium width, 22 ft. Phone, Carrick-on-
Shannon 12. Café and Dance Hall attached.
Station, Carrick-on-Shannon.

CARRICK-ON-SUIR (TIPPERARY), **Pop.
6,025.**
PARK VIEW CINEMA.—Prop. and Man., Mr.
Daly. 300 seats Six shows weekly. Pictures
and Variety. Station, Carrick-on-Suir.

CASHEL (TIPPERARY), **Pop. 3,020.**
ROCK (BTH).—500 seats. Nightly Sun., Mon.,
Tues. and Wed. Mat. Sun. Prices, 4d. to
1s. 6d. Station, Cashel, G.S. & W. Rly.

CASTLEBAR (MAYO), **Pop. 4,400.**
CONCERT HALL, Town Hall.—Prop., Very Rev.
Archdeacon Fallon, The Presbytery. Res.
and Booking Man., J. Corcoran. Occasional
shows. Prices, 6d. to 3s. Station, Castlebar.
ELLISON CINEMA.—Props., Bourke Bros.,
400 seats. Nightly except Sat. Prices, 4d. to
1s. 6d.

CASTLECOMER (KILKENNY).
THE HALL CINEMA (AWH).—Props., Quinn &
McKenna. 350 seats. Nightly, Thurs. and
Mon. only. Booked at Hall. Prices, 4d. to
1s. 4d. Proscenium width, 16 ft. Station,
G.S. Rly. Road van for film delivery.

CASTLE ISLAND (KERRY).
CARNEGIE HALL.—400 seats.
CINEMA (Napier).—300 seats. Nightly Sun.,
Tues. and Thurs.

CAVAN (CAVAN), **Pop. 3,550.**
CINEMA (Kamm), Town Hall—Mr. Verdon.
600 seats. Occasional shows. Prices, 4d.
to 1s. 4d.
MAGNET (RCA), Farnham Street.—Props., Cavan
Cinema Co., Ltd., Cavan. Phone, Cavan 53.
650 seats. Once nightly. Sat. Mat. Prices,
4d. to 2s. Proscenium width, 30 ft. Station,
Cavan.

CHARLEVILLE (CO. CORK), **Pop. 2,000.**
THE PAVILION (RCA), Main Street, Charleville.—
Prop., T. J. Hurley. 500 Seats. Nightly
Sun. to Fri. Booked at Dublin. Pictures and
Variety. Prices, 4d. to 1s. 6d. Stage, 30 ft.

deep ; two dressing rooms. Proscenium
width, 30 ft. Dance Hall attached. Phone,
Charleville 17. Station, Charleville.

CLARA (OFFALY).
CINEMA.

CLAREMORRIS (MAYO),
TOWN HALL CINEMA (BTH).—300 seats. Nightly,
Sun. and Mon. only.

CLONAKILTY (CO. CORK), **Pop. 2,600.**
THE CINEMA (Napier), Strand Road, Clonakilty.
Phone 26.—Prop., T. Lowney & Co., Strand
Road. 350 seats. One show nightly. Booked
at Hall. Prices, 4d., 9d. and 1s. 4d. Pro-
scenium width, 22 ft. Stage, 14 ft. deep ; two
dressing-rooms. Phone, Clonakilty 26.
Station, Clonakilty, Co. Cork.

CLONES (CO. MONAGHAN), **Pop. 2,220.**
ST. JOSEPH'S TEMPERANCE HALL.—Props.,
Clones Catholic Club. Every Tuesday only
in winter. Prices, 4d. to 1s. 3d. Booked in
Dublin. Station, Clones, G.N.R.

CLONMEL (TIPPERARY), **Pop. 12,000.**
CLONMEL THEATRE (WE).—Prop., W. O'Keefe.
Gen. Man., W. Symes. 950 seats. Booked at
Hall. One show nightly. Mat., Mon., Thurs.
and Sat. Prices, 9d. to 2s. Station, Clonmel,
G.S. & W. Rly.

COBH (CO. CORK). **Pop. 9,500.**
ARCH CINEMA (AAH).—Prop., J. J. Frenett. 450
seats. Films booked, Dublin. Twice nightly.
Prices, 4d. to 1s. 6d.
COLISEUM (Electra).—Props., Queenstown Picture
House, Ltd. 480 seats. Two shows nightly.
Phone 36. Prices, 4d. to 1s. 6d. Station,
Queenstown.

CORK (CO. CORK), **Pop. 72,000.**
ASSEMBLY ROOMS PICTUREDROME (WE). Phone
No. 52.—Prop., Reid & Goodwin. 730 seats.
Daily 3, 7 and 9 o'clock. Mat. Sun. Prices,
3d. to 1s. 3d. Proscenium width, 16 ft.
Stage, 18 ft. deep ; two dressing-rooms.
Booked at Hall. Station, G.S. & W.
COLISEUM (Phillips), McCurtain Street.—Props.,
Southern Coliseum, Ltd., 3, Grafton Street,
Dublin. Phone, Dublin 44034. 701 seats.
Booked at H.O. Continuous. Daily Mat.
Prices, 4d. to 1s. Phone, Cork 893. Station,
Cork, G.S.R.
IMPERIAL CINEMA (Morrison), Oliver Plunkett
Street.—Lessee, Stephen Whelan. 350 seats.
Booked at Dublin. Three shows daily, 3, 7,
and 9 o'clock. One show on Sunday, 8.15.
Two changes weekly. Prices, 4d. to 1s. 4d.
LEE CINEMA (WE), Winthrop Street.—Prop.,
Lee Cinema, Ltd. 452 seats. Continuous.
Booked at Cork. Prices, 4d. to 1s. 8d. Phone,
Cork 1138. Station, Glanmire, G.S.R.
LIDO (RCA)—Twice nightly, once Sun. Mat.
Sat. Prices, 1½d. to 1s.
PALACE (WE), MacCurtain Street, Cork.
Phone 614.—Prop., The Palace Theatre
(Cork), Ltd. Talking Pictures and occasional
Variety, at 3, 6.50 and 9 daily. Sun. at 8.30.
Prices, 9d. and 1s. 4d. Sundays, 1s. and 2s.
Seating, 1,100. Station, Cork, G.S. Rly.
PAVILION (WE), Patrick Street.—Prop., Jas.
Tallon, Clontarf, Dublin. Phone, Clontarf 210.
775 seats. Continuous. Once nightly on
Sun. Prices, 1s. to 1s. 10d. Booked at
Dublin. Proscenium width, 26 ft. Café.
Phone, Cork 891. Station, Cork, G.S. Rly.
ST. MARY'S HALL (Napier), St. Mary's Road.—
Prop., Parochial Hall. 400 seats. Two shows
nightly. Once Sun. Three changes weekly.
Prices, 4d. to 8d.

SAVOY CINEMA AND RESTAURANT (WE), Patrick Street.—Prop., Irish Cinemas, Ltd., 32, Shaftesbury Avenue, London, W.1. Man. Dir., J. E. Pearce. Phone, Gerrard 3306. 2285 seats. Continuous. Once on Sun. Prices, 9d. to 2s.

COMPTON

ORGAN featured here.

WASHINGTON CINEMA (RCA), Washington Street, —Props., Washington Cinema, Ltd. Man. Dir., J T. Carpenter. 600 seats. Booked at Hall. Three shows daily. Once Sun. Mats. daily. Prices, 4d. to 1s. 3d. Station, Cork, G.S. & W.E.

CURRAGH CAMP (Co. KILDARE).
PICTURE HOUSE (BTP).—Mr. Silvester. 600 seats. Nightly. Mat. Sat. Prices, 4d. to 1s. 6d.
SANDES CINEMA (BA).—Miss Magill. 400 seat Nightly.

DINGLE (KERRY), Pop. 2,020.
CINEMA (G. R. Sound).—Nightly, Sun. only.

DROGHEDA (LOUTH), Pop. 13,000
BOYNE CINEMA (BTP).—Props., Boyne Cinemas. 330 seats. Continuous. Mat. Sat. Prices, 4d. to 1s. 4d. Phone, Drogheda 70. Station, Drogheda, G.N.R.
CINEMA HOUSE.—Twice nightly. Mat. Sat. Prices, 4d. to 1s. 3d.
WHITWORTH HALL (RCA).—Prop., Dundealgan Electric Theatres, Ltd., St. Helena, Dundalk. Phone, Dundalk 116. 380 seats. Twice nightly. Prices, 4d. to 1s. 3d. Phone, 59. Variety. Stage, 16 ft. deep ; two dressing rooms. Station, Drogheda, G.N.R.

DUBLIN (DUBLIN), Pop. 400,000.
SUN DRIVE CINEMA (RCA).—680 seats.
BOHEMIAN PICTURE THEATRE (WE), Phibsborough Road. —Prop., Bohemian Picture Theatre (1931), Ltd., 154-155, Phibsborough Road, Dublin. Phone, Dublin 52529. 805 seats. Continuous. Booked at Local Renters' Offices. Prices, daily, 1s. and 1s. 4d.; Sun. Evg., 1s. 4d. and 2s. Mat., Sat. and Sun., 9d. and 4d. Pictures and Variety. Stage, 10 ft. by 22 ft. ; two dressing rooms. Proscenium width, 26 ft. Station, Dublin.
BROADWAY CINEMA (RCA), Manor Street.—Prop., Associated Picture Houses, Ltd. 650 seats. Continuous.
CAPITOL THEATRE (WE), Princes Street.—Lessees, Capitol Theatre, L'td. 2057 seats. Continuous. Prices, 1s. 4d. to 3s. 9d. Phone, Dublin 44490.
CORINTHIAN PICTURE THEATRE (WE), Eden Quay.—Prop., Dublin Kinematograph Theatres, Ltd. Phone, 44611. 830 seats. One change weekly. Prices, 1s. to 2s.

ELECTRIC THEATRE (RCA), 45, Talbot Street.—Prop., E. L. Coghlan. 550 seats. Continuous. Three changes weekly. Prices, 4d. to 1s. Phone, Dublin 44493. Station, Kingsbridge.
FAIRVIEW GRAND CINEMA. (BTH), Fairview Avenue, Dublin. 1,400 seats. Continuous. Three changes weekly. Booked by L. E. Ging, Manager and Director. Prices, 4d. to 1s. 8d. Proscenium width, 30 ft. Phone, Drumcondra 442.
FOUNTAIN PICTURE HOUSE (BA), James' Street. Res. and Booking Man., C. Marston. 550 seats. Continuous. Three changes weekly. Prices, 5d. to 1s. Phone, Dublin 51950.
GRAFTON PICTURE HOUSE.—Props., Grafton Picture House Co., Ltd., 72, Grafton Street, Dublin.
GRAND CENTRAL CINEMA (RCA).—Seats 800. Props., Irish Kinematograph Co. (1920), Ltd., 6-7, Lr. O'Connell Street, Dublin. Booked at Hall. Phone, 43877. Continuous. Proscenium width, 40 ft. Café. Station, Dublin. Prices, 1s. and 2s. Phone, 43877.
GRAND CINEMA (RCA).—Prop., Drumcondra Grand Cinema, Ltd. 1,200 seats. Booked at Fairview Cinema, Dublin, by L. E. Ging. Man. Dir. Continuous. Prices, 4d. to 1s. 8d. Proscenium width, 31 ft. Phone, Drumcondra 218.
INCHICORE CINEMA (WE), Inchicore.—Prop. R. G. Rinkham, Belmont Ave., Donnybrook, Dublin. Phone, 52020. 723 seats. Continuous. Booked at Dublin. Two changes weekly. Prices, 4d. to 1s. 4d.
LYCEUM PICTURE THEATRE (NaPier), Mary Street.—Prop., G. H. Porter, 202, Contary Road, Dublin. 600 seats. Continuous. Prices, 4d. to 9d. Station, Amiens Street, G.N.R.
MARY STREET CINEMA (RCA), 12-13, Mary Street, Dublin. Phone, 22813.—Prop., Irish Kinematograph Co. (1920), Ltd., 6-7, Lr. O'Connell Street, Dublin. 1,119 seats. Continuous. Prices, 4d. to 7d. and 10d. Booked locally. Station, Dublin.
MASTERPIECE PICTURE HOUSE (RCA), 99, Talbot Street. 400 seats.
METROPOLE CINEMA (WE), O'Connell Street.—Props., Metropole & Allied Cinemas. Ltd. Phone, 22231. 1,008 seats. Continuous. One change weekly. Prices, 1s. 4d. to 2s. Proscenium width, 30 ft. Café, Restaurant and Ballroom. Station, Westland Row, Dublin.
OLYMPIA THEATRE (Napier).—1,750 seats.
PALACE CINEMA (BA), 42, Pearse Street.—Props., Simon Eppel and Mendel Weiner. 600 seats. Continuous. Occasional Variety. Prices, 4d. 7d. and 10d. Phone, Dublin 44687.
PAVILION CINEMA.
PHIBSBORO PICTURE HOUSE (RCA), Blacquier, Phibsboro.—Prop., Phibsboro Picture House Co., Ltd. 500 seats. Continuous. Three changes weekly. Prices, 4d. to 1s. 6d. Phone, Dublin 51837. Station, Dublin.

DUBLIN—Contd,

PHOENIX PICTURE HOUSE (BTH), Ellis's Quay. Prop., Phoenix Picture Palace, Ltd. Lessee, R. J. G. Aherne. 750 seats. Continuous. Three changes weekly. Pictures and Variety. Variety booked by Star Variety Agency, Dublin. Stage, 12 ft.; two dressing rooms. Prices, 4d. to 1s. Phone, Dublin 22937.

PILLAR PICTURE HOUSE (RCA), Upper O'Connell Street.—Props., Irish Kinematograph Co., Ltd. 400 seats. Continuous. Two changes weekly.

PLAZA (RCA).—1,200 seats.

PRINCESS CINEMA (WE), Rathmines Road.— Props., Rathmines Amusements Co., Ltd. 800 seats. Continuous. Three changes weekly. Prices, 8d. to 1s. 6d. Station, Westland Row. Phone, Rathmines, 140.

QUEEN'S THEATRE (WE), Pearse Street. Phone, 44455.—Props., Dublin Kine. Theatres, Ltd., Queen's Theatre, Pearse Street. 1,200 seats. Cine-Variety. Continuous. Proscenium width, 28 ft. Prices, 4d. to 3s. Booked all renters. Variety Acts booked through Elliman & Edwards, 83a, Bold Street, Liverpool. Stage. Legitimate theatre. Fully equipped; 12 dressing-rooms.

REGAL CINEMA (BTH), Ringsend, Dublin.— Prop., Percy W. Whittle. Phone, Ballsbridge 728. 900 seats. Continuous from 6.45 to 11 p.m. weekdays. Mat. Sats., Sundays, 3 o'clock and 8.30. Proscenium width, 22 ft. Prices, weekdays, 4d., 7d. and 9d.; Sundays, 4d., 9d. and 1s. 3d. Booked at Hall. Films collected from Renters' offices.

ROTUNDA CINEMA (RCA), Cavendish Row.— Props., Exors. of William Kay. 1,200 seats. Booked at Hall. Continuous. Three changes weekly. Prices, 4d. to 10d. Phone, 1627.

SACKVILLE PICTURE HOUSE (ELECTRO REPROD.), Lr. Sackville Street.—Props., Sackville Picture House Co. Man. Dir., R. Morrison. 300 seats. Continuous. Two changes weekly. Prices, Afternoon, 4d., 6d. and 9d.; Evenings, 9d. and 1s. 4d. Phone, Dublin 45300. Station, Amiens Street, G.N.R.

SANDFORD CINEMA (WE), Sandford Road, Ranelagh, Dublin.—Prop., Suburbia Cinemas, Ltd. 634 seats. Continuous. Prices, 9d. to 1s. 6d. Phone, Rathmines 192.

SAVOY CINEMA (RCA), 19, Upper O'Connell Street, Dublin.—Prop., Irish Cinemas, Ltd. Man. Dir., J. E. Pearce, 19, Upper O'Connell Street, Dublin. London Office: 32, Shaftesbury Avenue. Phone, Gerrard 3306. 3,000 seats. Continuous. Sundays, two performances. Proscenium, 1s. to 2s. 6d. Booked at Theatre. Phone, Dublin 44788/90 Restaurant attached. Station, Dublin.

COMPTON

ORGAN featured here.

STELLA CINEMA (WE) Rathmines.—Prop., Stella Picture Theatre, Ltd. Rathmines, Continuous. Prices, 9d. to 1s. 10d. Phone, 91281.

STEPHEN'S GREEN CINEMA (WE).—Prop, Stephen's Green Cinema Co., Ltd. 1,600 seats. Continuous. Prices, 1s. 3d. to 2s. 6d. Proscenium width, 26 ft. Cafe attached.

SUNDRIVE CINEMA (WE), Sundrive Road, Kimmage.—Props., Sundrive Cinema, Ltd., 30, Lower Ormond Quay, Dublin. Phone, Dublin 44417. 700 seats. Continuous. Prices, 4d. to 9d. Proscenium width, 30 ft. Phone, Dublin 91151. Station, Dublin.

THEATRE DE LUXE (WE), 84 & 86, Lr. Camden Street.—Prop., Metropole and Allied Cinemas, Ltd., O'Connell Street, Dublin. Phone, Dublin 22231 (private exchange). 1,400 seats. Pictures booked at Hall and Variety by Edward & Elliman, 83a, Bold Street, Liverpool. Continuous. Prices, 9d. to 2s. Stage, 32 ft. deep; four dressing-rooms. Proscenium width, 30 ft. Phone, Dublin 51840. Station, Dublin.

THEATRE ROYAL (WE).—Props., Dublin Theatre Co., Ltd. 3,850 seats. Continuous Cine. Variety. Prices, 1s. to 2s. 6d. Variety booked by Foster's Agency, Piccadilly House, London, W.1. Stage, 40 ft. deep; 14 dressing-rooms. Café attached. Phone, 44441. Station, Westland Row.

COMPTON

ORGAN featured here.

DUNDALK (LOUTH), Pop. 16,000.

ORIEL CINEMA (BTH).—Prop., Boyne Cinemas. 300 seats. Booked at Boyne Cinema, Drogheda. Phone, Drogheda 70. Twice nightly. Mat. Sat. Prices, 4d. to 1s. 4d. Station, Dundalk, G.N.R.

PARK STREET CINEMA (BTP), Park Street, Dundalk. Phone 35.—Props., Irish Empire Palaces, Ltd., 3, Grafton Street, Dublin. Phone, 44034. 450 seats. Twice nightly. Mat. Sat. Prices, 1s. 3d. 9d. and 4d. Booked at Dublin. Station, G.W.R.

TOWN HALL CINEMA (RCA).—Prop., W. C. Robinson, 43, Castle Road, Dundalk. 900 seats. Twice nightly. Mat. Sat. Prices, 4d. to 1s. 3d. Station, Dundalk, G.N.R.

DUNGARVAN (WATERFORD), Pop. 4,500.

CINEMA (BTH).—Props., Daniel Crotty & Sons. 400 seats. Booked at Hall. Continuous. Mat. Mon. and Thurs. Pictures and Variety. Stage, 23 ft. deep; three dressing-rooms. Prices, 4d. to 1s. 9d. Proscenium width, 30 ft. Dance Hall. Phone, Dungarvan 8. Telegrams, Crotty Cinema, Dungarvan. Station, Dungarvan, G.S. & W.R.

DUN LAOGHAIRE (Co. DUBLIN), Pop. 20,000.

KINGSTOWN PICTURE HOUSE (BTH), George's Street.—Prop., Associated Picture Houses, Ltd., 49, Up. O'Connell Street, Dublin. Phone, Dublin 44413. 500 seats. Booked at Dublin. Continuous. Sun., Mat., and evening show. Proscenium width, approx. 20 ft. Prices, 7d., 1s. and 1s. 4d. Station, Dun Laoghaire, G.S.R.

PAVILION GARDENS (WE)—Marine Road. Props. Pavilion Gardens (Kingstown), Ltd. 820 seats. Booked at Hall. Continuous. Sunday Mat. and evening show. Three changes weekly. Prices, 4d. to 1s. 6d. Café. Phone, 61 Dun Laoghaire. Station, Dun Laoghaire.

DUNMANWAY (Co. CORK), Pop. 1,200.

BROADWAY CINEMA (ERP).—Props., Barnabas Deane, Dunmanway. 400 seats. Sun. only. Prices, 10½d., 7d. and 4d.

CINEMA.—Mr. Houssett.

EDENDERRY (OFFALY), Pop. 1,200.

FATHER PAUL MURPHY HALL.—Lessee, Wm. Higgins, Barrow View, Portarlington. Napier Electro-Reprod. Nightly, Sun. and Thurs. Mat. Sun. Prices, 9d., 1s. 3d. and 1s. 6d. Station, Portarlington.

ENNISCORTHY (Co. WEXFORD) **Pop. 6,000.**
GRAND CENTRAL CINEMA (BTH).—Prop., K.
G. Gould. Nightly. Booked at Hall. Prices,
4d. to 1s. 3d. Station, Enniscorthy, G.S.R.

FERMOY (CORK), **Pop. 3,300.**
PALACE THEATRE AND HALL (ERF).—Prop.,
M. A. O'Brien, The Manor, Fermoy. 500 seats.
Nightly, Sun., Mon., Tues., Wed. and Thurs.
Mat. Sun. Prices, 7d., 1s. 2d. and 1s. 8d.
Variety occasionally. 4 dressing-rooms.
Dance Hall. Phone 42. Station, Fermoy.

GALWAY (GALWAY), **Pop. 15,000.**
CORRIB (RCA).—Prop., Walter A. McNally,
900 seats. Booked at Hall. Once nightly.
Mat. Sun. Prices, 4d. to 1s. 4d. Phone,
Galway 28. Station, Galway.
NEW CINEMA.—(In course of construction.)
SAVOY (RCA).—1,300 seats.
TOWN HALL CINEMA (BTH).—Mr. Hardiman.
450 seats. Nightly. Mat. Sun. Prices, 4d.
to 1s. 3d.

GOREY (WEXFORD), **Pop. 2,500.**
TOWN HALL (BTH).—Prop., Chas. O'Brien,
49, Lower Newtown, Waterford. 200 seats.
Nightly except Sat. Winter only. Prices, 7d.
to 1s. 6d. Variety Acts ; two dressing-rooms.
Station, G.S. and Western Rly.

GREYSTONES (WICKLOW).
PICTURE HOUSE (Electra)—210 seats. Nightly
Sun., Mon., Wed. and Thurs. Prices, 4d. to
1s. 3d.

KANTURK (Co. CORK), **Pop. 1,860.**
COSY (BA).—Props., J. O'Sullivan and M. J.
Bowman. 300 seats. Nightly Sun. and Mon.
Mat. Sun. Booked at Hall. Prices, 4d. to
1s. 6d. Proscenium width, 24 ft. Station,
Kanturk.

KELLS (Co. MEATH), **Pop. 2,400.**
ST. VINCENT HALL (Napier).—Props., Trustees,
Parochial Committee. 500 seats. Booked at
Ludlow Street, Navan. Two shows weekly,
Tues. and Fri. Prices, 7d. to 1s. 6d. Pro-
scenium width, 15 ft. Station, Kells.

KILDARE (Co. KILDARE), **Pop. 2,600.**
TOWER CINEMA (BTH).—Prop., Breslin & Whelan,
204, Pearse Street, Dublin. Phone 44829.
500 seats. Once nightly. Proscenium width,
20 ft. Prices, 6d., 1s. and 1s. 6d. Booked at
Dublin. Variety Acts booked by Manager.
Depth of stage, 16 ft. ; two dressing-rooms.
Station, Kildare, G.S.R.

KILKEE (Co. CLARE), **Pop. 2,500.**
TOWN HALL CINEMA (Cintok).—Prop., Carron
Cinema Co. Res. and Booking Man., J.
G. Carron. 400 seats. Booked at Hall. One
show nightly. Prices, 9d. and 1s. 6d. Dance
Hall. Station, Kilkee, G.S. & W. Rly.

KILKENNY (Co. KILKENNY), **Pop. 10,000.**
CINEMA (WE), Kilkenny.—Prop., The Kilkenny
Cinema Co., Ltd., Kilkenny. 700 seats.
Once nightly. Occasional Mat. Sun. Prices,
4d. to 1s. 2d. Booked at Theatre. Station,
Kilkenny, G.S.R.

KILLARNEY (KERRY), **Pop. 6,000.**
CASINO (BTH), Mr. Cooper. Once nightly.
Occasional Mat. Prices, 4d. to 1s. 3d.
KILLARNEY PICTUREDROME (BTH), East Avenue
Hall.—Prop., Private Co. 750 seats. One

show nightly. Sun., Mon., Thurs. and Fri.
Three changes weekly. Prices, 8d. to 1s. 10d,
Station, Killarney, G.S. & W.R.

KILLORGLIN (KERRY), **Pop. 1,600.**
CARNEGIE PICTURE HALL.—Props., Carnegie
Trust Committee. Booked at Hall by Man-
ager. One show on Sunday only on occasions,
Prices, 6d. to 1s. Station, Killorglin,
G.S.W.R.

KILMALLOCK (Co. LIMERICK) **Pop. 1,100.**
PEOPLE'S HALL (BTH).—Props., Kilmallock
Co-operative Friendly Society, Ltd., Kilmal-
lock, Co. Limerick. 600 seats. Periodical
shows. Width of Proscenium opening, 5 ft.
Prices variable. Variety Acts booked through
Manager. Stage, 20 ft. ; two dressing-rooms.
Dance Hall attached. Station, Kilmallock.

KILRUSH (Co. CLARE), **Pop. 4,000.**
PALACE CINEMA (Napier).—Prop., P. Tubridy.
350 seats. Booked at Hall. One show nightly.
Prices, 7d. to 1s. 4d. Station, Kilrush.

LETTERKENNY (DONEGAL), **Pop. 3,000.**
CINEMA (Sound).—Props., Letterkenny Cinema
Co. 250 seats. Booked in Dublin. Prices, 4d.
to 1s. 3d. Station, Letterkenny.
LA SCALA.—A. C. Cinemas, Ltd., City Pictures,
Ltd. 250 seats.

LIMERICK (LIMERICK), **Pop. 38,000.**
ATHENÆUM (WE).—Lessee, P. J. Cronin. 450
seats. Two shows nightly. Daily Mat. Prices,
4d. to 1s. 6d. Station, Limerick, G.S.
COLISEUM (WE).—Props., Helena and Thos.
Gough. Booked by T. Gough. 600 seats. Two
shows nightly. Mat. Thurs. and Sat. Two
changes weekly. Prices, 7d. to 1s. 3d. Phone,
Limerick 259. Station, Limerick, G.S.
GRAND CENTRAL (RCA), Bedford Row.—Props.,
A. E. Goodwin. 650 seats. Continuous.
Prices, 7d. and 1s. 4d. Phone, Limerick 361.
Station, Limerick, G.S.
LYRIC (WE).—Mr. Ashleigh. 900 seats. Twice
daily. Mat. Thurs. and Sat. Prices, 4d. to
1s. 6d.
SAVOY THEATRE.

COMPTON
ORGAN featured here.

THOMOND.
TIVOLI (RCA), The Mall.—Props., Paul and May
Bernard. 350 seats. Two shows nightly. Three
changes weekly. Daily Mat. Prices, 2d.
to 9d.

LISMORE (WATERFORD), **Pop. 2,000.**
THE CINEMA, Lismore.

LISTOWEL (KERRY), **Pop. 4,000.**
THE CINEMA.—P. Coffey. Nightly Sun. and
Mon. Mat. Sun. Occasional shows other
days.

LONGFORD (LONGFORD), **Pop. 3,400.**
PALACE CINEMA (Electro Reproductions).—
Prop., M. J. Lyons. 600 seats. Booked at Hall.
Nightly. Mat. Thurs. and Sun. Prices, 4d.
to 2s. Station, Longford, G.S.R.

STAFFORD'S CINEMA (RCA).—Prop., and Res.
Man., K. Stafford, 1, Main Street, Longford.
325 seats. Booked in Dublin. One show
nightly. Mat. Thurs. and Sun. Prices, 4d.
to 2s. Phone, Longford 20. Station, Longford, G.S.R.

LOUGHREA (Co. GALWAY), **Pop. 2,570.**
TOWN HALL (RCA).—Prop., Loughrea Town Hall,

LOUGHREA—Contd.

Ltd. 380 seats. Four or five shows weekly. Prices, 4d. to 1s. 4d. Proscenium width 10 ft. Phone, Loughrea 4. Dance Hall attached. Station Loughrea.

Macroom (Co. Cork).

Castle Cinema.—Nightly. Four times weekly. Mat. Sun. Prices, 4d. to 1s. 3d.

MALLOW (Co. Cork), Pop. 4,800.

Capitol.—Robinson and Ward. 300 seats. Nightly except Sat. Mat. Sun. Prices, 7d. to 1s. 6d.

Central Hall (rca), Main Street.—Prop. and Res. Man., C. M. Donovan. 300 seats. Booked at Hall. Once nightly except Sat. Mat. Sat. and Sun. Prices, 7d. to 1s. 6d. Pictures and Variety. Telegrams, Donovan, Central Hall. Station, Mallow, G.S. & W.R.

MARYBOROUGH (Leix), Pop. 3,382.

Electric Cinema (awh).—Prop., P. Delany. 400 seats. Booked at 20, Main Street, Maryborough. One show nightly. Sat. excepted. Mat. Sunday. Prices, 4d. to 1s. 4d. Proscenium width, 18 ft. Station, Maryborough, G.S.R.

MIDDLETON (Co. Cork), Pop. 2,500.

Star Cinema (Napier).—Prop., Southern Star Cinema Co., Ltd. 500 seats. Booked at Dublin. Once nightly. Sun. Mat. Prices, 9d. and 1s. 3d. Proscenium width, 15 ft. Station, Middleton.

MITCHELSTOWN (Co. Cork), Pop. 2,000.

Savoy Cinema (bth).—A. E. Russell. 400 seats. Nightly five days a week. Mat. Sun. Prices, 4d. to 1s. 6d.

Star Cinema (Morrison).—Prop., G. H. Sharp. 400 seats. Booked at Hall. Once nightly except Sat. Mat. Sun. Prices, 4d. to 1s. 4d. Station, Mitchelstown.

MONAGHAN (Co. Monaghan), Pop. 2,926.

Town Hall Cinema (rca).—Lessee and Manager. Martin Rennie. 450 seats.

MOUNTMELLICK (Leix), Pop. 2,000.

C.Y.M.S. Cinema (Electro Reproductions).— Props., C.Y.M.S. Society. 350 seats. Booked at Dublin. Nightly Sun., Mon., Thurs. and Fri. Mat. Sun. Prices, 4d. to 1s. 3d. Station, Mountmellick, G.S.R.

MULLINGAR (Co. Westmeath). Pop. 7,000.

Coliseum Cinema (Napier).—Props., Healy Bros. 450 seats. Booked at Dublin. Nightly except Sat. Mat. Sun. Prices, 4d., 9d. and 1s. 6d. Station, Mullingar.

County Hall (we), J. R. Downe. 700 seats. Booked at Hall. Prices 4d. to 1s. 6d. Station, Mullingar.

Naas (Co. Kildare), Pop. 4,000.

Cinema (btp).—Prop., C. S. Silvester, Curragh Picture House. 300 seats. Booked at Dublin. Once nightly. Prices, 9d. to 1s. Station, Naas.

Town Hall (btp). Nightly except Sat. at Sun. Prices, 4d. to 1s. 6d.

NAVAN (Meath). Pop. 3,654.

Navan Picture Palace (Electric Reproduction), Ludlow Street.—Prop., Navan Picture Palace Co., Ltd. 360 seats. Booked at Office, Ludlow Street. One show daily. Mat. Sun. Prices, 4d. to 1s. 4d. Proscenium width, 14 ft. Station, Navan.

NENAGH (Tipperary), Pop. 4000.

Ormond Cinema (awh).—Prop., Willie F. Maloney, Summerhill, Nenagh. 250 seats. Nightly five days a week. Mat. Sun. Prices, 4d. to 1s. 3d. Station, Nenagh, G.S.R.

Town Hall Cinema (Electra).—Prop., E. O'Kennedy. 420 seats. Booked at Hall. Nightly. Four days a week. Mat. Sun. Prices, 4d. to 1s. 4d. Station, Nenagh.

NEWBRIDGE (Co. Kildare).

Newbridge Picture Palace.—Lessees, Foy & McGovern. 500 seats. Booked at Hall. Occasional Variety, four nights weekly, Sun., Mon., Wed. and Thurs. Prices, 4d., 9d. and 1s. 3d. Stage and two dressing-rooms.

NEWCASTLE WEST (Limerick), Pop. 3,000.

Latchford's Cinema.—Mr. Latchford. 250 seats. Nightly Tues. and Fri.

NEWPORT (Co. Mayo), Pop. 1,000.

New Cinema (rca).—Booked at Dublin. Priors, 8d. to 1s. 8d. Café and Dance Hall. Station, Westport.

NEW ROSS (Wexford), Pop. 5,000.

Town Hall Cinema (rca).—Prop., New Ross Cinema Co. 800 seats. One show nightly. Mat., Sat. and Sun. Prices, 4d. to 1s. 6d. Station, New Ross, G.S. and W.R.

Portarlington (Leix), Pop. 2,500.

Electric Cinema.—W. Higgins. 500 seats. Nightly, Sun. and Wed. Mat. Sun. occasionally.

PORTUMNA (Co. Galway), Pop. 1,000.

Town Hall.

Roscrea (Tipperary), Pop. 3,000.

New Hall.—Mr. Moynihan. 200 seats. Nightly. Sun. and Mon. Prices, 4d. to 1s. 6d.

Temperance Hall (bth).—Joseph Bailey Secretary.

Skerries (Dublin), Pop. 2,000.

Pavilion and Cinema (Napiers, Sound Production), Skerries, Co. Dublin.—Prop., Wm. H. Flanagan, New Street, Skerries. 400 seats. Proscenium width, 16 ft. Prices, 8d., 1s. 3d. and 1s. 6d. Booked at Dublin. Station, G.N. Rly.

SKIBBEREEN (Cork), Pop. 3,750.

Coliseum.—Prop., M. S. D. Driscoll, 53, Bridge Street. 300 seats. Nightly, Sun. and Mon. Prices, 9d. to 1s. 3d. Station, Skibbereen.

SLIGO (Co. Sligo), Pop. 10,000

Gaiety (we), Wine Street.—Props., The Gaiety (Sligo), Ltd. Phone, Sligo 151. 1,000 seats. Once nightly, Mon. to Fri. Mats. Sun. and Wed. Continuous Sat. Prices, 4d. to 1s. 9d. Booked at Hall. Station, Sligo, S.S.R.

Pavilion (rca)—Props., Kingannon & Sons, Ltd. 500 seats. Twice nightly. Mat. Sun. Prices, 4d. to 1s. 3d. Phone 78. Station, Sligo, S.S.

Savoy Cinema (rca), Market Street.—Prop., Savoy Cinema Co. (Sligo), Ltd. 1,000 seats. Pictures. Booked at Hall. Once nightly. Mats., Wed., Sat. and Sun., 4 p.m. Proscenium width, 22 ft. Prices, 4d., 9d., 1s. 4d. and 1s. 9d. Stage, 11 ft. to 12 ft. deep. Phone, Sligo 130. Station, Sligo, G.S.R.

Sligo Picture Theatre (rca).—Prop., Kingannon & Sons. 500 seats. Phone 78. Once nightly. Mat. Wed. and Sat. Three changes weekly. Prices, 4d. to 1s. Station, Sligo, G.S.

TEMPLEMORE (TIPPERARY), Pop. 2,300.

ABBEY CINEMA (Electro Reprod.), Templemore, Co. Tipperary.—Prop., James Guidera, Abbey Cinema, Templemore. 450 seats. Booked at Dublin. Nightly, Sun., Mon. and Tues. Proscenium width, 20 ft. by 22 ft. Prices, 8d. to 1s. 4d. Dance Hall. Station, Templemore.

THURLES (TIPPERARY), Pop. 4,420.

NATIONAL THEATRE (Electro Reprod.).—Lessee, Patrick McGrath. 500 seats. Once nightly. Mat., Sun. Prices, 4d., 9d. and 1s. 4d. Films booked Dublin. Variety occasionally. Two dressing-rooms. Station, Thurles, G.S. and W.R.

NEW THEATRE (BTP), Mr. Delabunty. 600 seats. Nightly, four days a week. Prices, 8d. to 1s. 6d.

TIPPERARY (TIPPERARY), Pop. 6,000.

PICTUREDROME (Marshall), James St.—Props., W. G. Evans & Son. 430 seats. One show nightly. Two Mats. weekly. Three changes weekly. Prices, 4d. to 2s. Café. Phones Tipperary 4. Station, Tipperary.

TIVOLI (RCA), Henry Street.—Prop., B. O'Donnell, Hill View, Tipperary. Phone 11. 500 seats. Booked at Hall. Once nightly except Sat. Mat. Wed. and Sun. Prices, 4d. to 1s. 6d. Dance Hall. Station, Tipperary, G.S.R.

TOWN HALL.—Once nightly. Mat. Wed., Sat. and Sun. Prices, 4d. to 1s. 6d.

TRALEE (KERRY), Pop. 11,000.

ASHE MEMORIAL HALL (WE).—Prop., A. McSweeney. 900 seats. Twice nightly. Two shows Sun. Prices, 4d. to 1s. 8d. Occasional Variety. Phone, 95. Station, Tralee, G.S.R.

PICTUREDROME (WE).—Prop., P. Coffey. Twice nightly. Two shows Sun. Prices, 4d. to 1s. 6d. Station, Tralee, G.S.R.

TRAMORE (WATERFORD), Pop. 2,000.

STRAND CINEMA.—Prop., Mrs. E. Piper. Res. and Booking Man., J. J. O'Shaughnessy. Booked at Hall. Continuous. Prices, 7d. to 1s. 6d. Station, Tramore, G.S. & W.R.

TRIM (Co. MEATH), Pop. 1,560.

CINEMA (Echo).

TUAM (GALWAY), Pop. 3,000.

MALL CINEMA (RCA).—Prop., Jos. McHugh, High Street, Tuam. 450 seats. One show daily. Prices, 9d. to 2s. Booked at Mrs. J. O'Connor, St. Tarlath's Terrace, Bishop Street, Tuam. Phone, Tuam 11. Station Tuam, G.S.R.

TULLAMORE (OFFALY), Pop. 5,000.

C.Y.M.S. CINEMA (BA).—Prop., Catholic Young Men's Society. 400 seats. Booked at Hall One show nightly except Sat. Mat. Sun. Prices, 4d. to 1s. 3d. Phone, 10. Station, Tullamore, G.S.R.

GRAND CENTRAL CINEMA (Napier), Tullamore.—Props., Mahon and Cloonan, Tullamore. Phone, 13 Tullamore. 400 seats. Booked at Dublin. Once nightly. Mat. Sun. Prices, 4d. to 1s. 6d. Proscenium width, 12 ft. Variety. Stage, 21 ft.; two dressing-rooms. Dance Hall. Station, Tullamore.

TULLOW (CARLOW), Pop. 2,000.

CINEMA.—Prop. and Man., R. J. Lawson. Nightly four days a week. Mat. Sunday. Prices 4d. to 1s. 6d.

WATERFORD (WATERFORD), Pop. 28,000.

CINEMA (RCA), Broad Street.—Prop., Waterford Cinemas, Ltd., 205, Pearse Street, Dublin. Phone, Dublin 44965. 800 seats. Booked at Dublin. Three changes weekly, three mats. per week. One show nightly. Prices, 9d. to 1s. 10d. Station, Waterford. G.S. and W.R.

COLISEUM (RCA), Adelphi Quay. 700 seats, Booked at Hall. One show nightly. Mats., Thurs. and Sat. Three changes weekly. Prices, 4d. to 1s. 6d. Station, Waterford.

SAVOY.—Once nightly. Daily Mat. Prices, 4d. to 1s. 6d.

THEATRE ROYAL (RCA).—Prop., Martin S. Breen, Bridge Hotel, Waterford. Phone, Waterford 291. 900 seats. Pictures and all Stage Shows. Booked at Dublin. Once nightly. Daily Mat. Prices, 4d. to 1s. 8d. Stage, 26 ft. deep; eight dressing-rooms. Proscenium width, 18½ ft. Phone, Waterford 356. Station, Waterford.

WESTPORT (Co. MAYO).

NEW CINEMA THEATRE (RCA).—Props., Stanton, Ruddy, Kenny & Joyce. 430 seats. One nightly except Sat. Mat. Sun. Prices, 7d. to 1s. 4d. Proscenium width, 23 ft.

WEXFORD (Co. WEXFORD), Pop. 11,000.

CAPITOL CINEMA (WE).—Prop., Capitol Cinema (Wexford), Ltd. Phone, 43 Wexford. 750 seats. Booked at Hall. Continuous. Prices, 4d. to 1s. 8d. Proscenium width, 24 ft. Station, Wexford, G.S.R.

CINEMA PALACE (RCA), Harper's Lane.—Prop., Wexford Cinema Palace, Ltd. 600 seats. Res. and Booking Man., R. W. Latimer. Twice nightly. Once Sun. Prices, 4d. to 1s. 4d. Phone, Wexford 50. Station, Wexford, G.S.R.

WICKLOW (Co. WICKLOW), Pop. 3,500.

EXCELSIOR CINEMA —350 seats. Nightly four days a week. Mat. Sun. Prices, 4d. to 1s. 6d.

YOUGHAL (CORK), Pop. 5,300.

HORGAN'S PICTURE THEATRE (Kamm).—Prop., T. Horgan. 600 seats. Booked in Dublin. Nightly except Fri. Mat. Sun. Prices, 3d. to 1s. 3d. Proscenium width, 12 ft. Station, Youghal.

HURST'S PICTURE PALACE (Morrison).—Prop., R. Hurst, Friar Street, Youghal. 425 seats. Booked at Dublin. Daily shows. Mat. Wed. and Sun. Prices, 4d. to 1s. Proscenium width, 16 ft. Station, Youghal, G.S. & W.

TRAVELLING SHOWS.

STAR COMPANY. Operating generally in Midlands, but no regular schedule. Portable equipment.

CANNONS CINEMA. Operates in Co. Donegal:—Ballyshannon every Wednesday; Ballybofey every Tuesday; Donegal every Sunday and Monday.

DANIELS TALKIES. Operating generally in South, but has no regular time-table. Portable equipment.

PROVINCIAL CINEMAS.

SWANLINBAR.
DRUMSHANBO.
CARRIGALLEN.
BELTURBET.
BALLYJAMESDUFF.
BAILLIEBOROUGH.

IRELAND
NORTHERN IRELAND KINEMAS.

The Sound system installed is shown after the name. (BTP)=British Talking Pictures, Ltd. ; (RCA) = RCA Photophone Inc. ; (WE) = Western Electric Co., Ltd ; (BA)=British Acoustic ; (BTH) = British Thomson-Houston. Other systems are indicated by name.

ANTRIM (ANTRIM), **Pop. 1,825.**
THE CINEMA (RCA).—430 seats. Once nightly on Mon., Tues., Thurs., Fri. and Sat. Prices, 6d. and 1s. Proscenium width, 20 ft. Phone, Antrim 26. Station, Antrim, L.M.S. Films by N.I. Road Transport.

ARMAGH (ARMAGH), **Pop. 6,600.**
CITY CINEMA (WE).—Prop., City Cinema (Armagh), Ltd. 500 seats. Booked at Hall. Continuous. and Sunday at 8 p.m. Prices, 6d. and 1s. Phone 117. Armagh and B.O.C.
PICTURE HOUSE (BTP), Russell Street.—Prop., Irish Empire Palaces, Ltd. 400 seats. Continuous. Occasional Variety. Mat. Sat. Prices, 4d. to 1s. Proscenium width, 20 ft. Phone, Armagh 165. Station, Armagh, G.N.R
RITZ (WE)—Controlled by Union Cinemas, Ltd., 15, Regent Street, London, S.W.1. Phone, Whitehall 8484. Continuous. Booked at H.O. Prices, 6d. to 1s. 6d. Station, Armagh, G.N.R.

BALLYCASTLE (ANTRIM), **Pop. 2,000.**
NEW CINEMA.—Props., A. C. Cinemas, Ltd. Continuous. 450 seats. Booked at 29, Donegall Street, Belfast. Prices, 6d. to 1s. 3d. Phone, Ballycastle 218.

BALLYCLARE (ANTRIM), **Pop. 4,000.**
CINEMA (RCA).—Prop., Mr. Logan, 35, Royal Avenue, Belfast, Phone, Belfast 1996. 350 seats. Booked at Belfast. Continuous. Mat. Sat. Prices, 6d. to 1s. Station, Ballyclare, L.M.S.

BALLYKINLAR (DOWN).
SANDES CINEMA.—Two shows weekly. 250 seats. Station, Tullymurry, Co. Down.

BALLYMENA (ANTRIM), **Pop. 11,000.**
LYRIC CINEMA (BTH).—Props., Logan and Walsh, 35, Royal Avenue, Belfast. Phone, Belfast 1996. 700 seats. Continuous. Mat. Sat. Prices, 6d. to 1s. 3d. Proscenium width, 30 ft. Phone, Ballymena 306. Station, Ballymena, L.M.S.
PICTURE HOUSE (BA).—Prop., Sam Eagleson, Ballymena Picture Palace Co., Ltd. 550 seats. Continuous. Mat. Sat. Prices, 3d. to 1s. 3d. Phone, Ballymena 20. Station, Ballymena, L.M.S. (N.C.C.).
RITZ (WE).—Controlled-by Union Cinemas, Ltd., 15, Regent Street, London, S.W.1. Phone, Whitehall 8484. Booked at H.O. Continuous. Station, Ballymena, L.M.S.

BALLYMONEY (ANTRIM), **Pop. 3,000.**
CINEMA (BTH).—300 seats. Twice nightly. Mat. Sat. Prices, 6d. and 1s. 3d. Station, Ballymoney.

BALLYNAHINCH (DOWN), **Pop. 1,600.**
THE PICTURE HOUSE (BTH).—B. H. Bloomfield, Scotch Street. Downpatrick. Phone 43, 375 seats. Not continuous. Mon., Tues., Thurs. and Sat. Prices, 3d. to 1s. Station, Ballynahinch, Co. Down.

BALLYWALTER (DOWN).
MID ARDS CINEMA.

BANBRIDGE (DOWN), **Pop. 5,000.**
PICTURE HOUSE (Parmeko).—Prop., J. U. Finney, Belmont, Banbridge. 703 seats. Booked at Irish Pictures, Ltd., 79, Donegall Street, Belfast: Twice nightly, Mon., Thurs., Sat. Once Tues., Wed., Fri. Mat. Sat. Prices, 6d. and 1s. Proscenium width, 16 ft. Phone, Bambridge 10. Station, Bambridge.

BANGOR (DOWN), **Pop. 12,500.**
ADELPHI (BTP), Main Street.—Prop., Bertie Walsh. 500 seats. Booked at Hall. Continuous. Prices, 4d. to 1s. 6d. Station, Bangor, C.D.R.
PICTURE PALACE (BTH).—Prop., Irish Electric Palaces, Ltd., 79, Donegall Street, Belfast. Phone, Belfast 5800. 600 seats. Booked at Head Office. Continuous. Two changes weekly. Prices, 4d. to 1s. 6d Phone, Bangor 187,
THE TONIC (WE).—Props., John H. O'Neill, Hamilton Road, Bangor. 2,000 seats. Booked at Hall. Continuous. Prices, 6d. to 1s. 6d. Proscenium width, 49 ft. Stage, 25 ft.; two dressing rooms. Café. Phone, Bangor 830. Station, Bangor, B. & C.D.R.

COMPTON
ORGAN featured here.

BELFAST (ANTRIM), **Pop. 450,000.**
ALHAMBRA THEATRE (BTH), North Street.—Prop., Alhambra Theatre, Ltd. 800 seats. Three shows daily. Prices, 4d., 6d. and 1s. Proscenium width, 25 ft. Phone, Belfast 20380. Steamship service.
APOLLO CINEMA (BTH), Ormeau Road, Belfast.—Prop., J. H. McVea. 1,000 seats. Booked at Hall. Continuous. Daily Mat. Prices, 6d. and 1s. Proscenium width, 45 ft. Phone, Belfast 27049. Steamship service.
ARCADIAN (BTH), Albert Street.—Props., James Boyle and John O'Neill. 600 seats. Booked at Hall. Twice nightly. Prices, 3d. and 6d. Proscenium width, 25 ft. Stage 24 ft. deep; two dressing rooms. Phone 6900. Station, Belfast, G.N.R. and L.M.S.
ASTORIA (RCA), Upper Newtownards Road.—Props., M. Curran and Sons, Ltd., 403, Antrim Road, Belfast. Phone, Belfast 44096. 1,240 seats. Booked at H.O. Continuous. Prices, 6d. to 1s. 6d. Proscenium width, 30 ft. Phone, 53733. Café attached. Station, Belfast.

CAPITOL (WE), Antrim Road.—Props., M. Curran & Sons, Ltd., 403, Antrim Road.—1,000 seats. Booked at Antrim Road office. Continuous from 1.45 p.m. Prices, 1s. to 1s. 6d. Cafe attached.

CASTLE CINEMA (RCA) Castlereagh Road.—Props., Jas. M. Crawford. 900 seats. Booked at Hall. Prices, 6d. to 1s.

CASTLEREAGH CINEMA.—Prop., D. D. Young. Building.

CENTRAL PICTURE THEATRE (Majestone), Smithfield.—Prop., Central Belfast Picture Theatre Co., Ltd. 500 seats. Booked at Hall. Continuous. Two changes weekly. Prices, 3d. to 6d. Phone, 20739.

CLASSIC CINEMA (WE), Castle Lane.—Prop., Classic Cinemas, Ltd., Castle Lane, Belfast. 1,730 seats. Booked by A. W. Jarratt at New Gallery House, 123, Regent Street, London, W.1, and Gaumont-British. Continuous. Prices, 6d. to 1s. 6d. (Mat.), 1s. to 2s. 4d. (Even.) Phone, Belfast 24987. Cafe and Dance Hall attached. All Belfast Stations and Donegall Quay.

Fitted "ARDENTE" Deaf Aids
See page 258

WURLITZER ORGAN
Installed in this Kinema

CLONARD PICTURE HOUSE (WE), Falls Road.—Prop., Clonard Hall Co., Ltd. 1,000 seats. Two shows nightly. Two changes weekly. Booked at Hall. Prices, 4d. to 1s. Proscenium width, 32 ft. Phone, Belfast 1958.

COLISEUM (BTH) Grosvenor Road.—Prop., Belfast Coliseum, Ltd. 79, Donegall Street. Phone 25800. 1,000 seats. Three shows daily. Prices, 4d. to 1s. Proscenium width, 27 ft. Stage, 30 ft. deep; four dressing rooms. Phone, Belfast 25692. Steamship Service.

CRUMLIN PICTURE HOUSE (RCA), Crumlin Road, —Prop., Crumlin Picture House, Ltd. 973 seats. Continuous. Four mats. weekly. Two changes weekly. Prices, 3d. to 6d. Phone 44135. Station, Belfast.

DIAMOND PICTURE HOUSE (BTH).—600 seats. Prices, 5d. and 8d. Phone 5200.

DUNCAIRN PICTURE THEATRE (BTH), 12, Duncairn Gardens.—Prop., Duncairn Picture Theatre Co., Ltd. 950 seats. Gen. and Booking Man., Will White. Continuous. Prices, 6d. to 1s. Proscenium width, 20 ft. Phone, Belfast 43532. Stations, Belfast, M. or G.N.

GAIETY, North Street.—Prop., The Belfast Gaiety Picture Theatre Co., Ltd. 800 seats. Res. and Booking Man., J. Quin. Twice nightly, 6.45 and 9. Phone 22746. Prices, 3d., 5d. and 6d. All Belfast Stations and Cross-channel boats.

HIPPODROME (WE), Gt. Victoria Street.—Props., Hippodrome Belfast, Ltd. Lessees, Assoc.

British Cinemas, Ltd., 30-31, Golden Square, London, W.1. Phone, Gerrard 7887. 1,800 seats. Continuous. Booked at Head Office, 30/31, Golden Square, London, W.1. Prices, 3d. to 1s. 6d. Stage 36 ft. deep; ten dressing rooms. Proscenium width, 36 ft. Phone, Belfast 22981. N.C.C. and L.M.S. and G.N. Railways and Steamers. B.S.S.Coy. and Heysham S.S. Co.

IMPERIAL PICTURE HOUSE (BAUER), Cornmarket.—Prop., Ulster Cinematograph Theatres, Ltd. Man. Dir., B. N. McDowell. 1,000 seats. Booked at Hall. Continuous from 1 to 10.30. Prices 6d. to 1s. 3d. Cafe. Phones, 21160 and 24980. Telegrams. Paramount, Belfast. Station, Donegall Quay, M.R. and G.N.R.

KELVIN PICTURE HOUSE (RCA).—College Square East.—Prop., Kelvin Picture Palace Co., Ltd. 500 seats. Continuous. Two changes weekly. Prices, 6d. to 1s. Phone, Belfast 21191.

LYCEUM CINEMA (WE), Antrim Road.—Prop., M. Curran. 950 seats. Phone, 1191.

LYRIC (RCA), High Street.—Props., Lyric Cinema Co. 750 seats. Continuous. Booked at Hall. Prices, 6d. to 1s. Phone 3434. Stations, all Belfast Stations and boats.

MAJESTIC (RCA), Lisburn Road.—Controlled by Union Cinemas, Ltd., Union House, 15, Regent Street, London, S.W.1. Phone, Whitehall 8484. Booked at H.O. Continuous. Prices, 3d. to 1s. 6d. Phone, Belfast 65390. Station Cross Channel Steamers from Liverpool, Heysham and Stranraer and Glasgow.

MIDLAND PICTURE HOUSE (BTH), Canning Street.—Prop., McKibbin Estate, Ltd., 7-9, Canning Street. 600 seats. Three shows daily. Two changes weekly. Booked at Hall. Prices, 3d. to 6d. Stage, 8 ft. deep; two dressing-rooms. Phone, 43694.

NEW PRINCESS PALACE (BTH).—Prop., City and Suburban Cinemas, Ltd. 650 seats. Booked at Hall. Twice nightly. Prices, 4d. to 6d. Proscenium width, 30 ft. Stage, 20 ft. deep, two dressing rooms. Phone, Belfast 3451. Station, Belfast.

PICTUREDROME (BTH), Mount Pottinger.—Prop., Mount Pottinger Cinemas, Ltd., 79, Donegall Street. 1,000 seats. Booked at Hall. Twice nightly. Prices, 4d. to 1s. Phone, 3063. Station, Belfast, G.N.R.

PICTURE HOUSE (WE), Royal Avenue.—Prop., Northern Theatres, Ltd. 850 seats. Continuous. Booked at Hall. Prices, 6d. to 2s. Proscenium width, 29 ft. For L.M.S. Rly. Theatre Phone, Belfast 27058. Café Phone, Belfast 2513.

POPULAR PICTURE THEATRE (Majestone), Newtownards Road. 700 seats.

QUEEN'S PICTURE THEATRE (Majestone), 250, York Street.—Prop., Belfast Gaiety Theatre Co., Ltd., Upper North Street, Belfast. Phone, 43038. 500 seats. Twice nightly, 6.15 and 9. Prices, 3d. and 5d.

BELFAST—Contd.

REGAL (WE), Lisburn Road.—Props., M. Curran & Sons, Ltd., 403, Antrim Road. Phone, 44096. 1,270 seats. Booked at Antrim Road office. Continuous from 2 p.m. Prices, 6d. to 1s. 6d. Café attached. Phone, 66730.

RITZ (RCA).—Controlled by Union Cinemas Ltd., Union House, 15, Regent Strect, London, S.W.1. Phone, Whitehall 8484. Continuous. Booked at H.O. Prices, 6d. to 3s. 6d. Phone, Belfast 22484. Dance Hall and Cafe attached. Station, York Street L.M.S. Docks, Donegall Quay.

C O M P T O N
ORGAN featured here.

ROYAL CINEMA (WE).—Prop., Warden, Ltd. 698 seats. Booked at Hall. Continuous. Prices, before 4.30 p.m. (Sats. and Holidays excepted), 6d. and 1s. ; after 4.30 p.m., 1s. and 1s 6d. Café. Phone, Belfast 20480. Station, Belfast L.M.S. (N.C.C.). Boats from Liverpool and Heysham.

SANDRO CINEMA (RCA), 67a, Sandy Row.—Prop., Sandro Cinema, Ltd. Phone, 24368. Four seats. Twice nightly. Booked at Hall. Prices, 3d., 5d. and 6d. Mat. prices, 2d. and 3d. Proscenium width, 22 ft. Stations, G.N.R. (I) and L.M.S

SAVOY (RCA), Crumlin Road.—Props., Savoy Picture House, Ltd. 1,088 seats. Booked at Hall. Twice nightly. Prices, 4d. to 1s. Proscenium width 25 ft.

SHANKILL PICTUREDROME (BTH), 148, Shankill Road.—500 seats. Three shows daily. Two changes weekly. Prices, 3d. and 6d. Phone, Belfast 21715. Station, Belfast, G.N.

STRAND (RCA).—Controlled by Union Cinemas, Ltd., Union House, 15, Regent Street, London, S.W.1. Phone, Whitehall 8484. Continuous. Booked at H.O. Prices, 3d. to 1s. 6d. Phone, Belfast 53760. Station, Steamship Service.

TROXY (RCA), Shore Road. Props., Strand Cinema Co., Ltd. 1,300 seats.

WEST END PICTURE HOUSE (BTH), 108, Shankill Road. Phone 4422.—Props. Mrs. Craig Mrs. Newel and H. A. Newel. 800 seats. Three shows daily. Prices, 1d., 3d. and 6d.

WILLOWFIELD PICTURE HOUSE (BTH), Woodstock Road.—Prop., Willowfield Unionist Club. 1,000 seats. Booked at Hall. Twice nightly. Two changes weekly. Prices, 4d. to 6d. Phone, 3741. G.N.R.

CARRICKFERGUS (ANTRIM), Pop. 4,310.

IDEAL CINEMA (BA).—350 seats. Once nightly. Twice nightly Sat. Mat. Sat. Prices, 6d. to 1s. 3d.

COALISLAND (TYRONE), Pop. 2,000.

THE PICTURE PALACE (BTH). Coalisland—Prop., Coalisland Picture Palace Co. 300 seats. One House nightly, Sundays excepted. Proscenium width 18 ft. Prices, 3d. 6d., 1s. and 1s 3d. Station, Coalisland, C. & M. and L.M.S. Booked at Hall.

COLERAINE (LONDONDERRY), Pop. 8,000.

PALLADIUM (RCA). —P one 248. — Prop., J. Mcnary, 37, North Parade, Belfast, Phone,

41664. Continuous. Booked at H.O. 950 seats. Prices, 4d. to 1s. 3d. Café.

THE PICTURE HOUSE (RCA), Railway Road.— Props., Coleraine Picture Palace Co., Ltd. 500 seats. Continuous nightly. Mat. Wed. and Sat. Prices, 6d. to 1s. 3d. Station, Coleraine, L.M.S. (N.C.C.).

RITZ (WE).—Controlled by Union Cinemas, Ltd., 15, Regent Street, London, S.W.1. Phone, Whitehall 8484. Booked at H.O. Continuous. Station, Coleraine, L.M.S.

COMBER (CO. DOWN).

PICTURE HOUSE (Marshall), Castle Street, Comber.—Props., Comber Picture House, Ltd. Phone, Knock 1251. 330 seats. Once nightly, two shows Sat. Mat. Sat. Films booked at 22/26, Academy Street, Belfast. Proscenium width, 18 ft. Prices, 6d. and 1s. Phone, W. Liscabbey 126.

COOKSTOWN (TYRONE), Pop. 3,400.

COOKSTOWN PICTURE HOUSE (BTP).—Prop., C. H. Donaghy, Glenearne, Campsie, Omagh. Phone No. 98. 450 seats. Booked at H.O. Nightly, Mat. Sat. Prices, 3d. to 1s. 3d. Proscenium width, 18 ft. Stage 12 ft. deep ; two dressing rooms. Phone, Cookstown 74. Station, Cookstown, per L.M.S. and G.N.R.

DONAGHADEE (DOWN), Pop. 2,800.

REGAL CINEMA (Picturetone), Manor Street.— Props., Solar Cinemas, Ltd., 44-46, Corporation Street, Belfast. Phone, Belfast 23838. 300 seats. Booked at H.O. Once nightly. Sat. Mat. and two shows nightly. Prices, 6d. and 1s. Proscenium width, 20 ft. Phone, Donaghadee 144.

DOWNPATRICK (DOWN), Pop. 2,000.

GRAND CINEMA (RCA), Market Street.—Prop. and Man., Thos. Breen. 560 seats. Prices, 6d. to 1s. 6d., including Sun. Once nightly. Continuous Sat. Phone, Downpatrick 39. Station, Downpatrick.

REGAL (RCA).

DROMORE (DOWN), Pop. 2,000.

DROMORE CINEMA (Morrison).—Props., J. and R. W. Dale, Church Street. 280 seats. Nightly Fri. and two shows Sat. Sometimes Mon. and Tues. Prices, 3d. to 1s. Station, Dromore, G.N.R.

DUNGANNON (CO. TYRONE), Pop. 3,800.

CASTLE (BTH).

CINEMA (BTH), Market Square.—Props., L. and W. Cinemas, Ltd., 35, Royal Avenue, Belfast. Phone, Belfast 1996. 500 seats. Booked at H.O. Twice nightly. Phone, Dungannon 88. Prices, 6d. to 1s. 6d. Station, Dungannon, G.N.R.

WEST END PICTURE PALACE (RCA).—300 seats. Twice nightly. Once on Sun. Mat. Sat. Prices, 4d. to 1s.

ENNISKILLEN (FERMANAGH), Pop. 5,430.

REGAL.

TOWN HALL (RCA).—Prop., Dundealgan Elec. Theatres, Ltd. 500 seats. Twice nightly. Mat. Sat. Prices, 3d. to 1s. 3d. Occasional variety. Station, Enniskillen, G.N.R.

HOLYWOOD (Down), Pop. 4,500.

MAYPOLE CINEMA (WE).—Props., M. W. Kennedy and Co., 22/28, Academy Street, Belfast. Phone, Belfast 453. 450 seats. Booked at H.O. Continuous. Mat. Sat. Prices, 3d. to 1s. Phone, Holywood, 285. Station, Holywood, B. and C.D.

NEW CINEMA (BTH).—Prop., Mrs. R. B. Noble. 500 seats. Phone, Knock 501. Continuous. Prices, 3d. to 1s. 3d.

KILKEEL (Co. Down), Pop. 1,400.

ROYAL CINEMA.—Prop., John Rooney. 250 seats. Once nightly. Mat. Mon. and Thurs. Prices 6d. to 1s. 6d.

KILLYLEAGH (Co. Down). Pop. 1,300.

CINEMA.—Prop., H. S. McMurray. 300 seats. Booked at High Street. Nightly, Mon., Tues., Fri. and Sat. Mat. Sat. Prices, 6d. and 1s. N.I.T.B. Rail Comber.

LARNE (Antrim), Pop. 8,000.

PICTURE HOUSE (BTH), Main Street. Phone, Larne 60.—Prop., Irish Electric Palaces, 79, Donegal Street, Belfast. Phone, 25800. 650 seats. Booked at H.O. Two shows nightly. Mat. Tues., Thurs., and Sat. Prices, 4d. to 1s. Station, Larne, L.M.S.

RITZ (WE).—Controlled by Union Cinemas, Ltd., 15, Regent Street, London, S.W.1. Phone, Whitehall 8484. Booked at H.O. Prices, 3d. to 1s. 6d. Station, Larne, L.M.S.

LIMAVADY (Londonderry), Pop. 3,000.

THE PICTURE HOUSE (RCA), Town Hall.—Prop., Frank J. Coghlan Limavady. 500 seats. Booked at H.O. Continuous. Mat. Sat. Prices, 4d. to 1s. 3d. Proscenium width 12-13 ft. Station, Limavady, L.M.S.

LISBURN (Antrim), Pop., 6,000.

THE PICTURE HOUSE (BTH), Market Square.—Prop., Lisburn Electric Palace, Ltd., The Picture House, Market Sq. Lisburn. 650 seats. Twice nightly. Mats., Mon., Thurs., and Sat. Proscenium opening 23 ft. Prices, 3d. to 1s. Phone, Lisburn 231. Station, G.N. Rly. Lisburn.

RITZ (WE).—Controlled by Union Cinemas, Ltd., 15, Regent Street, London, S.W.1. Phone, Whitehall 8484. Continuous. Booked at H.O. Station, Lisburn, G.N.Rly.

LONDONDERRY (Londonderry), Pop. 40,000.

CITY CINEMA (WE), William Street. Seats 1,000. —Props., City Pictures, Ltd. Booked at Hall, Continuous. Mat. Wed. and Sat. Prices 4d. to 1s. 3d. Phone, Londonderry 807. Station, Londonderry, L.M.S. and G.N.

MIDLAND (WE).—Lessees, M. Curran & Sons, Ltd. Booked at H.O., Capitol, Belfast. 850 seats. Continuous. Prices, 3d. to 9d. Station, Londonderry, L.M.S. and G.N.R.

OPERA HOUSE (WE).—Prop., City Pictures, Ltd. 1,200 seats. Booked at Hall. Twice nightly. Daily Mat. Prices, 4d. to 1s. 3d.

Proscenium width, 24 ft. Stage 20 ft. deep ; seven dressing rooms. Phone, 567, Pte. Exchange. Station, Londonderry, G.N.R.

PALACE (RCA), Shipquay Street, Londonderry. Phone, 567 Pte. Exchange.—Lessees, Rialto Theatres, Ltd., Market Street, Londonderry. 800 seats. Twice nightly. Mat. Mon., Thurs., and Sat. Proscenium width 25 ft. Prices, 6d. to 1s. 3d. Bookings, J. Boughton. London, Occasional Variety. Stage, 7 ft. deep ; two dressing-rooms. Rly., G. W. Rly., L.M.S., also Catherwood's Bus Service.

RIALTO THEATRE (RCA), Market Street. Phone 567, Pte. Exchange.—Prop., Rialto Theatres, Ltd., Market Street, Londonderry. 800 seats. Continuous. Proscenium width 22 ft. Prices, 6d. and 1s. 3d. Station, G.N. Rly. and L.M.S. also Catherwood's Bus Service. Stage 17 ft. deep ; four dressing rooms.

RITZ (WE).—Controlled by Union Cinemas, Ltd., 15, Regent Street, London, S.W.1. Phone, Whitehall 8484. Booked at H.O. Continuous. Prices, 6d. to 2s. Station, Londonderry L.M.S. and G.N.Rly.

ST. COLUMB'S HALL (WE), Orchard Street—Prop., St. Columb's Hall Committee. 1,100 seats. Sec., J. Bonner. Continuous. Occasional Variety. Mat. Sat. Booked at Hall. Two changes weekly. Prices, 4d. to 1s. Station, G.N.R.

STRAND (WE). Strand Road, Londonderry.—Props., M. E. Curran & Sons, Antrim Road, Belfast. 1,050 seats. Prices, 6d. to 1s. 6d. Bookings at H.O., Antrim Road, Belfast. Café attached.

LURGAN (Armagh), Pop. 12,135.

FOSTER'S PICTURE HOUSE (BTH).—Prop., J, Foster. 450 seats. Twice nightly. Mat. Mon., Wed., Fri., and Sat. Prices, 3d. to 1s. 6d.

LYRIC CINEMA (BTH)—Prop., J. M'Murray. 500 seats. Twice nightly. Mat. Mon., Wed., Fri. and Sat. Prices, 3d. to 1s. 6d. Station, Lurgan.

RITZ (WE).—Controlled by Union Cinemas, Ltd., 15, Regent Street, London, S.W.1. Booked at H.O. Continuous. Prices, 3d. to 1s. 6d. Station, Lurgan.

MAGHERA (Co. Londonderry). Pop. 1,000.

THE CINEMA (RCA), Main Street.—Props. Supreme Cinemas, Ltd., 35, Royal Avenue Belfast. Phone, Belfast 21996. 300 seats. Booked at H.O. Once nightly. Twice on Sun. Mat. Sat. Prices, 6d. and 1s. Proscenium width, 18 ft. Phone, Maghera 30. Station, Maghera, L.M.S.

NEWCASTLE (Down), Pop. 1,600.

PALACE PICTURE HOUSE (BTH).—Prop., B. Cusack. 300 seats. Booked at hall. One show nightly. Mat. Sat. Prices, 6d. to 1s. 3d. Station, Newcastle.

NEWRY (Down), Pop. 12,000.

FRONTIER (WE), Irish National Forresters Benefit Society, John Mitchell Place, Newry. Phone 206. 800 seats. Films booked at office. Twice nightly. Once Sun. Mat., Tues., Thurs. and Sat. Prices, 6d. and 1s. Station, G.N.R.

NEWRY—Contd

IMPERIAL (RCA).—Prop., Frank Murtagh. 320 seats. Twice nightly. Once Sun. Prices, 6d. and 1s.

SAVOY CINEMA (BTH).—Prop., Derek Finney and J. U. Finney. 750 seats. Twice nightly. Mat. Tues., Thurs. and Sat. Prices, 6d. and 1s.

NEWTOWNARDS (DOWN), Pop. 5,000.

PALACE (BA).—350 seats. Booked at Hall. One show nightly. Two on Fri. and Sat. Prices, 6d. to 1s. Phone, 41. Station, Newtownards, Belfast and Co. Down Rly.

RITZ (WE).—Controlled by Union Cinemas, Ltd., 15, Regent Street, London, S.W.1. Phone, Whitehall 8484. Booked at H.O. Continuous. Prices, 6d. to 1s. 6d. Station, Newtownards, Belfast and Co. Down Rly.

OMAGH (TYRONE), Pop. 5,124.

PICTURE HOUSE (BTP), High Street.—Prop., C. H. Donaghy, Glenearne, Campsie, Omagh. Phone 98. 750 seats. Once nightly. Booked at Hall. Prices, 4d. 6d., 1s. and 1s. 3d. Phone No. 121. Station, Omagh, G.N.R.

STAR KINEMA (BTH), Sedan Avenue.—Prop., Chas. H. Donaghy, Glenearne, Campsie, Omagh. Phone, 98. 450 seats. Once nightly. Booked at Hall. Proscenium width, 15 ft. Prices, 4d. to 1s. 3d. Phone, Omagh 121, Station, Omagh, G.N.R.

PORTADOWN (ARMAGH) Pop., 13,000.

PICTURE HOUSE (BTP). Phone 98.—Prop., Irish Empire Palaces, Ltd., 3, Grafton Street, Dublin. Phone, Dublin 44034. 750 seats. Booked at Hall. Continuous. Mat. Sat. Proscenium width, 18 ft. Prices 1s. 6d. and 4d. Station, Portadown, G.N.R. (Ireland).

REGAL CINEMA (WE), Bridge Street.—Prop., Regal Theatres, Ltd., 9, Garfield Chambers, Royal Avenue, Belfast. 900 seats. Continuous. Prices, 6d. and 1s. 3d. Phone, Portadown 261. Station, Portadown, G.N.R.

SAVOY CINEMA (BTH).—Props., Robert Spence. Booked at Hall. Continuous. Prices, 4d. to 1s. Station, Portadown.

PORTAFERRY (DOWN), Pop. 1,500.

THE CINEMA (Morrison).—Prop., J. K. Hinds, High Street, Portaferry. 350 seats. Four nights weekly. Mat. Sat. Prices, 6d. to 1s. 3d. Stage 25 ft. deep. Three dressing rooms. Proscenium width, 15 ft. Phone, Portaferry 15. Northern Ireland Road Transport Co., Belfast. Films booked, Liverpool, Glasgow and Belfast.

PORTRUSH (ANTRIM), Pop. 3,000.

THE PICTURE HOUSE (BTH).—Prop., The Portrush Estate Co., Ltd., Main Street, Portrush. 650 seats. Booked at Hall. Continuous. Mat. Sats. 3 p.m. Summer season, Mats. Daily, 3 p.m. Proscenium width, 24 ft. Prices, 2s., 1s. 3d., and 6d. Café attached Phone, Portrush 34. Station, Portrush. L.M. & S.

PORTSTEWART (LONDONDERRY), Pop. 3,000.

PALLADIUM CINEMA (BTH), Portstewart, Co. Derry.—Prop., J. Menary, 37, North Parade, Belfast. Phone, Belfast 41664. Booked at H.O. 700 seats. Continuous. Mat. when wet. Prices, 6d. and 1s. 3d. Booked at 37, North Parade, Belfast. Phone, Portstewart 58. Station, Portstewart, L.M.S., N.C.C. Regal Dance Hall attached.

STRABANE (TYRONE). Pop. 5,000.

COMMODORE CINEMA.—Props., Wilton and Barry. 600 seats.

THE PALLADROME (RCA).—(Closed). 500 seats.

TANDRAGEE (CO. ARMAGH).

NEW CINEMA.—Props., Robert Spence. Booked at Hall. Prices, 6d. to 1s. 320 seats.

WARRENPOINT (DOWN), Pop. 2,800.

GARDEN CINEMA (RCA).—Props., Cinemas & General Finance Corporation, Ltd., 29, Donegall Street, Belfast. 300 seats. Films booked, 29, Donegall Street, Belfast. Twice nightly, once Sun. Prices, 6d. and 1s. 3d. Phone, Warrenpoint 79. Station, Warrenpoint, G.N.R.

MEMORANDA

MEMORANDA

MEMORANDA

Index to Advertisements.

JESSIE MATTHEWS IN "IT'S LOVE AGAIN"   *Photograph by courtesy of Gaumont-British*

"It's love **again**" ...

Filmgoers everywhere unanimously agreed that "It's
Love Again" is one of the outstanding films of the year.
And fine photography helped to make it! As with every
other film, it was projected on to the majority of Cinema
screens by Taylor-Hobson lenses.

No other projection lenses can compare with those made
by Taylor-Hobson for sharp definition and fidelity to
detail. Always ask for these famous lenses by name.

... but it's
TAYLOR - HOBSON
L E N S E S
always !

TAYLOR, TAYLOR & HOBSON LTD., LEICESTER & LONDON